Short Story Criticism

Guide to Gale Literary Criticism Series

For criticism on	Consult these Gale series
Authors now living or who died after December 31, 1999	*CONTEMPORARY LITERARY CRITICISM (CLC)*
Authors who died between 1900 and 1999	*TWENTIETH-CENTURY LITERARY CRITICISM (TCLC)*
Authors who died between 1800 and 1899	*NINETEENTH-CENTURY LITERATURE CRITICISM (NCLC)*
Authors who died between 1400 and 1799	*LITERATURE CRITICISM FROM 1400 TO 1800 (LC)* *SHAKESPEAREAN CRITICISM (SC)*
Authors who died before 1400	*CLASSICAL AND MEDIEVAL LITERATURE CRITICISM (CMLC)*
Authors of books for children and young adults	*CHILDREN'S LITERATURE REVIEW (CLR)*
Dramatists	*DRAMA CRITICISM (DC)*
Poets	*POETRY CRITICISM (PC)*
Short story writers	*SHORT STORY CRITICISM (SSC)*
Black writers of the past two hundred years	*BLACK LITERATURE CRITICISM (BLC)* *BLACK LITERATURE CRITICISM SUPPLEMENT (BLCS)*
Hispanic writers of the late nineteenth and twentieth centuries	*HISPANIC LITERATURE CRITICISM (HLC)* *HISPANIC LITERATURE CRITICISM SUPPLEMENT (HLCS)*
Native North American writers and orators of the eighteenth, nineteenth, and twentieth centuries	*NATIVE NORTH AMERICAN LITERATURE (NNAL)*
Major authors from the Renaissance to the present	*WORLD LITERATURE CRITICISM, 1500 TO THE PRESENT (WLC)* *WORLD LITERATURE CRITICISM SUPPLEMENT (WLCS)*

ISSN 0895-9439

Volume 41

Short Story Criticism

Criticism of the
Works of Short Fiction Writers

Jenny Cromie
Editor

GALE GROUP

Detroit
New York
San Francisco
London
Boston
Woodbridge, CT

STAFF

Lynn M. Spampinato, Janet Witalec, *Managing Editors, Literature Product*
Kathy D. Darrow, *Product Liaison*
Jenny Cromie, *Editor*
Mark W. Scott, *Publisher, Literature Product*

Anja Barnard, *Editor*
Linda Pavlovski, *Associate Editor*
Vince Cousino, *Assistant Editor*
Mary Ruby, Patti A. Tippett, *Technical Training Specialists*
Deborah J. Morad, Kathleen Lopez Nolan, *Managing Editors*
Susan M. Trosky, *Director, Literature Content*

Maria L. Franklin, *Permissions Manager*
Sarah Tomasek, *Permissions Associate*

Victoria B. Cariappa, *Research Manager*
Tracie A. Richardson, *Project Coordinator*
Tamara C. Nott, *Research Associate*
Sarah Genik, Timothy Lehnerer, Ron Morelli, *Research Assistants*

Dorothy Maki, *Manufacturing Manager*
Stacy L. Melson, *Buyer*

Mary Beth Trimper, *Manager, Composition and Electronic Prepress*
Carolyn Roney, *Composition Specialist*

Michael Logusz, *Graphic Artist*
Randy Bassett, *Imaging Supervisor*
Robert Duncan, Dan Newell, *Imaging Specialists*
Pamela A. Reed, *Imaging Coordinator*
Kelly A. Quin, *Editor, Image and Multimedia Content*

Library of Congress Catalog Card Number 88-641014
ISBN 0-7876-4701-2
ISSN 0895-9439
Printed in the United States of America

10 9 8 7 6 5 4 3 2 1

Contents

Preface vii

Acknowledgments xi

Marcel Aymé 1902-1967 1
*French short story writer, novelist, dramatist, children's fiction writer,
and essayist*

Jorge Luis Borges 1899-1986 36
*Argentinian short story writer, poet, essayist, critic, translator,
biographer, and screenwriter*

Anton Chekhov 1860-1904 188
*Russian short story writer, novelist, and playwright; single-work entry
on "The Duel"*

Dazai Osamu 1909-1948 225
Japanese novelist, short story writer, and essayist

Susan Glaspell 1876-1948 277
*American playwright, novelist, short story writer, and biographer;
single-work entry on "A Jury of Her Peers"*

Evelyn Waugh 1903-1966 308
*English novelist, short story writer, travel writer, essayist, critic,
biographer, journalist, and poet*

Literary Criticism Series Cumulative Author Index 369

SSC Cumulative Nationality Index 443

SSC Cumulative Title Index 445

Preface

*S*hort Story Criticism (*SSC*) presents significant criticism of the world's greatest short story writers and provides supplementary biographical and bibliographical materials to guide the interested reader to a greater understanding of the authors of short fiction. This series was developed in response to suggestions from librarians serving high school, college, and public library patrons, who had noted a considerable number of requests for critical material on short story writers. Although major short story writers are covered in such Gale series as *Contemporary Literary Criticism (CLC)*, *Twentieth-Century Literary Criticism (TCLC)*, *Nineteenth-Century Literature Criticism (NCLC)*, and *Literature Criticism from 1400 to 1800 (LC)*, librarians perceived the need for a series devoted solely to writers of the short story genre.

Scope of the Series

SSC is designed to serve as an introduction to major short story writers of all eras and nationalities. Since these authors have inspired a great deal of relevant critical material, *SSC* is necessarily selective, and the editors have chosen the most important published criticism to aid readers and students in their research.

Approximately eight to ten authors are included in each volume, and each entry presents a historical survey of the critical response to that author's work. The length of an entry is intended to reflect the amount of critical attention the author has received from critics writing in English and from foreign critics in translation. Every attempt has been made to identify and include the most significant essays on each author's work. In order to provide these important critical pieces, the editors sometimes reprint essays that have appeared elsewhere in Gale's Literary Criticism Series. Such duplication, however, never exceeds twenty percent of an *SSC* volume.

Organization of the Book

An *SSC* entry consists of the following elements:

- The **Author Heading** cites the name under which the author most commonly wrote, followed by birth and death dates. Also located here are any name variations under which an author wrote, including transliterated forms for authors whose native languages use nonroman alphabets. If the author wrote consistently under a pseudonym, the pseudonym will be listed in the author heading and the author's actual name given in parentheses on the first line of the biographical and critical introduction. Uncertain birth or death dates are indicated by question marks. Single-work entries are preceded by the title of the work and its date of publication.

- The **Introduction** contains background information that introduces the reader to the author and the critical debates surrounding his or her work.

- A **Portrait of the Author** is included when available.

- The list of **Principal Works** is ordered chronologically by date of first publication and lists the most important works by the author. The first section comprises short story collections, novellas, and novella collections. The second section gives information on other major works by the author. For foreign authors, the editors have provided original foreign-language publication information and have selected what are considered the best and most complete English-language editions of their works.

- Reprinted **Criticism** is arranged chronologically in each entry to provide a useful perspective on changes in critical evaluation over time. All short story, novella, and collection titles by the author featured in the entry are printed in boldface type. The critic's name and the date of composition or publication of the critical work are given at the beginning of each piece of criticism. Unsigned criticism is preceded by the title of the source in which it appeared. Footnotes are reprinted at the end of each essay or excerpt. In the case of excerpted criticism, only those footnotes that pertain to the excerpted texts are included.

- Critical essays are prefaced by brief **Annotations** explicating each piece.

- A complete **Bibliographical Citation** of the original essay or book precedes each piece of criticism.

- An annotated bibliography of **Further Reading** appears at the end of each entry and suggests resources for additional study. In some cases, significant essays for which the editors could not obtain reprint rights are included here. Boxed material following the further reading list provides references to other biographical and critical sources on the author in series published by Gale.

Cumulative Indexes

A **Cumulative Author Index** lists all of the authors that appear in a wide variety of reference sources published by the Gale Group, including *SSC*. A complete list of these sources is found facing the first page of the Author Index. The index also includes birth and death dates and cross references between pseudonyms and actual names.

A **Cumulative Nationality Index** lists all authors featured in *SSC* by nationality, followed by the number of the *SSC* volume in which their entry appears.

A **Cumulative Title Index** lists in alphabetical order all short story, novella, and collection titles contained in the *SSC* series. Titles of short story collections, separately published novellas, and novella collections are printed in italics, while titles of individual short stories are printed in roman type with quotation marks. Each title is followed by the author's last name and corresponding volume and page numbers where commentary on the work is located. English-language translations of original foreign-language titles are cross-referenced to the foreign titles so that all references to discussion of a work are combined in one listing.

Citing *Short Story Criticism*

When writing papers, students who quote directly from any volume in the Literature Criticism Series may use the following general format to footnote reprinted criticism. The first example pertains to material drawn from periodicals, the second to material reprinted from books.

Henry James, Jr., "Honoré de Balzac," *The Galaxy* 20 (December 1875), 814-36; reprinted in *Short Story Criticism*, vol. 5, ed. Thomas Votteler (Detroit: The Gale Group), 8-11.

Linda W. Wagner, "The Years of the Locust," *Ellen Glasgow: Beyond Convention* (University of Texas Press, 1982), 50-70; reprinted and excerpted in *Short Story Criticism*, vol. 34, ed. Anna Nesbitt Sheets (Farmington Hills, Mich.: The Gale Group), 80-82.

Suggestions are Welcome

Readers who wish to suggest new features, topics, or authors to appear in future volumes, or who have other suggestions or comments are cordially invited to call, write, or fax the Managing Editor:

Managing Editor, Literary Criticism Series
The Gale Group
27500 Drake Road
Farmington Hills, MI 48331-3535
1-800-347-4253 (GALE)
Fax: 248-699-8054

Acknowledgments

The editors wish to thank the copyright holders of the excerpted criticism included in this volume and the permissions managers of many book and magazine publishing companies for assisting us in securing reproduction rights. We are also grateful to the staffs of the Detroit Public Library, the Library of Congress, the University of Detroit Mercy Library, Wayne State University Purdy/Kresge Library Complex, and the University of Michigan Libraries for making their resources available to us. Following is a list of the copyright holders who have granted us permission to reproduce material in this volume of *SSC*. Every effort has been made to trace copyright, but if omissions have been made, please let us know.

COPYRIGHTED EXCERPTS IN *SSC*, VOLUME 41, WERE REPRODUCED FROM THE FOLLOWING PERIODICALS:

The British Journal of Aesthetics, v. 30, July, 1990, for "Literature, Philosophy, Nonsense" by B. R. Tilghman. Copyright © 1990 by The British Journal of Aesthetics. Reproduced by permission of the publisher and the author.—*Bulletin of Hispanic Studies,* v. LXXV, April, 1998. Copyright © 1998 Liverpool University Press. Reproduced by permission.—*Chasqui,* v. XXV, May, 1996. Reproduced by permission.—*CLA Journal,* v. XLII, September, 1998. Copyright, 1998 by The College Language Association. Used by permission of The College Language Association.—*Commonweal,* December, 1998. Copyright © 1998 Commonweal Publishing Co., Inc. Reproduced by permission of Commonweal Foundation.—*Comparative Literature Studies,* v. 24, 1987. Copyright 1987 by The Pennsylvania State University. Reproduced by permission of The Pennsylvania State University Press.—*Economist,* v. 350, January, 1999. Copyright © 1999 The Economist Newspaper Group, Inc. Reproduced with permission. Further reproduction prohibited. http://www.economist.com—*The Explicator,* v. 52, Spring, 1994. Copyright © 1994 Helen Dwight Reid Educational Foundation. Reproduced with permission of the Helen Dwight Reid Educational Foundation, published by Heldref Publications, 1319 18th Street, NW, Washington, DC 20036-1802.—*Extrapolation,* v. 37, Winter, 1996. Copyright © 1996 by The Kent State University Press. Reproduced by permission.—*Hispanofila,* v. 125, January, 1999. Reproduced by permission.—*The Modern Language Review,* v. 83, January, 1988. Reproduced by permission.—*Narrative,* v. 7, October, 1999. Copyright © 1999 by Ohio State University Press. All rights reserved. Reproduced by permission.—*New Literary History,* v. 24, Spring, 1993. Copyright © 1993 by The Johns Hopkins University Press. Reproduced by permission.—*The New York Review of Books,* October 22, 1998. Copyright © 1988 Nyrev, Inc. Reproduced with permission from The New York Review of Books.—*The New York Times,* November 22, 1982. Copyright © 1982 by The New York Times Company. Reproduced by permission./ November 14, 1982 for "Old Young Waugh" by Frances Donaldson. Copyright © 1982 by The New York Times Company. Reproduced by permission of PFD on behalf of the Estate of Lady Frances Donaldson.—*New York Times Book Review,* v. 1, February 20, 1949. Copyright © 1949 by The New York Times Company. Reproduced by permission.—*Notes On Contemporary Literature,* v. XXIX, September, 1999. Copyright © by William S. Doxey. Reproduced by permission.—*Philosophy and Literature,* v. 17, October, 1993. Copyright © 1993 by The Johns Hopkins University Press. Reproduced by permission.—*Poetics Today,* v. 13, Fall, 1992. Copyright © 1992 by Porter Institute for Poetics and Semiotics. Reproduced by permission of Duke University Press.—*Representations,* no. 56, Fall, 1996, for "The Library of Forking Paths" by Robert L. Chibka. Copyright © 1996 by The Regents of the University of California. Reproduced by permission of the publisher and the author.—*Romance Notes,* v. XXXIII, Spring, 1993. Reproduced by permission.—*Romanic Review,* v. 86, January, 1995. Reproduced by permission.—*Russian Literature,* v. XXXV, February, 1994. Reproduced by permission.—*Studies in Short Ficiton,* v. 15, Winter, 1978; v. 21, Winter, 1984; v. 26, Fall, 1989; v. 33, Summer, 1996. Copyright © 1978, 1984, 1989, 1996 by Newberry College. All reproduced by permission.—*Studies in Twentieth Century Literature,* v. 22, Summer, 1998. Copyright © 1998 by Studies in Twentieth Century Literature. Reproduced by permission.—*Symposium,* v. 53, Fall, 1999. Copyright © 1999 Helen Dwight Reid Educational Foundation. Reproduced with permission of the Helen Dwight Reid Educational Foundation, published by Heldref Publications, 1319 18th Street, NW, Washington, DC 20036-1802.—*The Times Literary Supplement,* June, 1988; No. 4572, Month 11, 1990; January, 1999. Copyright © 1988, 1990, 1999 by The Times Literary Supplement. All reproduced by permission.—*Twentieth Century Literature,* v. 31, Winter, 1985. Copyright 1985, Hofstra University Press. Reproduced by permission.—*World Literature Today,* v. 64, Summer, 1990. Copyright 1990 by the University of Oklahoma Press. Reprinted by permission of the publisher.

COPYRIGHTED EXCERPTS IN *SSC*, VOLUME 41, WERE REPRODUCED FROM THE FOLLOWING BOOKS:

Aarons, Victoria. From *Portraits of Marriage in Literature.* Western Illinois University, 1984. Copyright © 1984 by Western Illinois University. Reproduced by permission.—Alazaraki, Jaime. From "Structure as Meaning in 'The South'," in

Marcel Aymé
1902–1967

(Also wrote under the pseudonym Claquebue) French short story writer, novelist, dramatist, children's fiction writer, and essayist.

INTRODUCTION

A prolific writer in various genres, Marcel Aymé is today widely admired for his short stories, most of which incorporate elements of the *fantastique*. Although many of Aymé's stories can be read as children's tales, critics have found them to have a more complex level of social and political allegory, and he is considered a moralist and philosopher comparable to Rabelais and Voltaire.

BIOGRAPHICAL INFORMATION

Aymé was born in Joigny, France, in 1902, the youngest of six children. His father, Joseph, was a blacksmith; his mother, Emma Monany, died when Aymé was two years old. Joseph Aymé sent his youngest son to live with Emma's parents in the village of Villers-Robert, where he remained for eight years. Aymé then went to live with an aunt in Dôle, a small city in the Franche-Comté region. He completed his studies there and served as a soldier in the French army. After leaving the military Aymé worked in a variety of trades, including journalism. Aymé eventually settled on a career as a fiction writer and published his first novel, *Brûlebois,* in 1926. In 1932 Aymé married Marie-Antoinette Arnaud. Two years later he experienced international success with the publication of his novel *La Jument verte (The Green Mare),* which some consider a masterpiece of Rabelaisian farce. The couple moved to the Montmartre section of Paris, where Aymé became a recognized member of the literary scene. During the German occupation of France during World War II and the widespread search for and prosecution of collaborators after liberation, Aymé continued to publish his works even though several other writers were prosecuted. Associated with the Right, Aymé wrote for collaborationist newspapers during the war, and was disgusted by what he considered the erosion of morals beginning with the occupation. In his later writings, however, Aymé was nonpartisan in skewering all politics. In 1950 Aymé gained success in the theater with *Clérambard,* although the play scandalized many audience members and critics. Many of his other plays were equally provocative. Also in 1950 Aymé was invited by *Collier's* magazine to visit the United States and contribute articles. His reaction to the country was one of discomfort, particularly with the political and business

atmosphere. In the early 1960s Aymé grew more disillusioned with and troubled by the age of technology, as evidenced by his plays of the time. The rest of Aymé's life was spent quietly, writing short stories and plays.

MAJOR WORKS OF SHORT FICTION

Aymé's numerous short stories are generally better known than his longer works and, most critics agree, contain some of his best and most imaginative writing. Settings and characters in Aymé's works fall into two categories; the rural French countryside with its resident farmers, and the urban proletariat of Montmartre in Paris. Most of his short fiction involves elements of the fantastic, which sometimes takes the form of science fiction and sometimes of fantasy or fairy tales. While Aymé did feel affection for the country people about whom he wrote, and with whom he lived as a child, his stories sometimes evidence a caustic criticism that cuts across lines of geography, political partisanship, and social status. This is particularly true of his stories set in realistic environments but containing elements of science fiction, such as "La Traversée de Paris" ("Across Paris"), which takes place during the occupation of Paris, and "La Carte" ("The Life-Ration"), in which war-time shortages and rationing lead to the distribution of cards representing the number of days each citizen is allowed to live each month according to his or her "usefulness." Other stories can be classified in the tradition of the French fabulists, featuring mythological figures and talking animals and usually ending in a moral lesson that may include a miracle. The stories in several of Aymé's most popular books, *Les Contes du Chat perché* (1934), *Autres Contes du Chat perché* (1950), and *Derniers Contes du Chat perché* (1958), concerning the adventures of two little farm girls and their interactions with a variety of talking barnyard animals, best illustrate Aymé's fabulist literature.

CRITICAL RECEPTION

Despite his role as a celebrated literary figure prior to World War II, Aymé's reputation suffered after the liberation of France, largely because of his outspoken criticism of what he considered the hypocrisy of left-wing France after the war, but also because of his work on collaborationist newspapers. Accordingly, he was blacklisted, along with many other writers, and his work was ignored for years. Today some critics consider Aymé's stories to be among the best twentieth-century French short fiction, and ironically, many argue that his stories are best understood and interpreted in French. Locating Aymé's place within French literature, Dorothy Brodin wrote: "Aymé was a fundamentally French writer who might at times seem desperately cynical, or, on the contrary, too conservative, unless one realizes that his roots run deep in the French skeptical and humanistic tradition, the tradition of Rabelais, La Fontaine, Molière, and the eighteenth-century philosophers."

PRINCIPAL WORKS

Short Fiction

Le puits aux images 1932
Les Contes du Chat perché 1934
Le Nain 1934
Derrière chez Martin 1938
Le Passe Muraille [*The Walker-through-Walls and Other Stories*] 1943
Le Vin de Paris [*Across Paris and Other Stories*] 1947
Autres Contes du Chat perché 1950
En arrière 1950
The Wonderful Farm 1951
The Magic Pictures: More about the Wonderful Farm 1954

Return to the Wonderful Farm 1954
Derniers Contes du Chat perché 1958
Soties de la ville et des champs 1958
The Proverb and Other Stories 1961
Enjambées 1967
La Fille du shérif [edited by Michel Lecureur] 1987

Other Major Works

Brûlebois (novel) 1926
Aller retour (novel) 1927
Les Jumeaux du diable (novel) 1928
La Table aux crevés [*The Hollow Field*] (novel) 1929
La Rue sans nom (novel) 1930
Le Vaurien (novel) 1931
La Jument verte [*The Green Mare*] (novel) 1934
Maison basse [*The House of Men*] (novel) 1935
Silhouette du scandale (essays) 1938
Travelingue [*The Miraculous Barber*] (novel) 1941
Vogue la galère (drama) 1944
Le Trou de las serrure (essays) 1946
Lucienne et le boucher (drama) 1947
Uranus [*The Barkeep of Blémont;* republished as *Fanfare in Blémont*] (novel) 1948
Le Confort intellectuel (essays) 1949
La Tête des autres (drama) 1952
La Mouche bleue (drama) 1957
Les Tiroirs de l'inconnu [*The Conscience of Love*] (novel) 1960
Les Maxibules (drama) 1962

CRITICISM

Claude Vigée (essay date 1959)

SOURCE: "The Turbulent Spring of Experience," in *The Saturday Review,* Vol. XLII, No. 4, January 24, 1959, pp. 18, 31.

[*In the following essay, Vigée reviews* Across Paris and Other Stories, *praising Aymé's characteristic "duality," which, Vigée notes, requires readers to approach his writing with both "childlike innocence" and "ferocious irony."*]

For more than thirty years Marcel Aymé has captured the fancy of French readers of fiction, both young and old. By now he has become something of an ageless classic, the heir of the anonymous medieval *fabliaux* writers. Yet, in spite of an abundant literary production, ranging from comedy or satirical essay to the novel and the children's tale, he remains a puzzle to orderly critics. They would like to label him and find themselves lost in contradictions as they compare him simultaneously to Rabelais, Voltaire, Franz Kafka, and Alphonse Daudet! There is, in this clearest of all authors, something unpredictable—like the Spanish *duende*—a power of renewal and invention not far removed from sorcery. His quality of imagination cannot be ascribed solely to his gift for unbridled fantasy; he has a sharp eye for the bleak realities of life on many levels of society, from crude peasants to Parisian artists or black-marketeers. His work owes its brilliance and freshness to an original blend of truth and daydream.

Dichtung und Wahrheit at best achieve an unstable combination. But it is from this effervescent mixture that genuine human experience springs. Marcel Aymé's writings depend upon a strange, uneasy tension of opposites. The souls of his shabby characters are crushed by acceptance of frustration, ennui, the endless flow of empty years, and lifted by the wildest leaps toward freedom, bliss, paradise. Their moods vary from resigned indifference to things to outbursts of maniacal passion. The drabness of daily living on archaic farms or in modern cities merges with the universe of wish-fulfilment through magic, crime, and madness. The bureaucrat's office hours and his escapes into the realm of the supernatural are both seen as commonplace events. As a consequence, the reader passes without transition through worlds which, in his own adult experience, usually remain far apart. He becomes, like Aymé's hero, M. Dutilleul, a "Walker-through-Walls." It is not the least among our writer's achievements that his semifantastic, seminaturalistic tales almost inadvertently turn into parables of the readers' secret life and longings.

The short stories collected in this handsome volume [*Across Paris and Other Stories*] all bear witness to the duality of Aymé's outlook, a conflict which can be overcome only by childlike innocence or a ferocious irony. Aymé applies both remedies to the old wound. He constantly shuttles back and forth between a humor which, as in **"The Picture-Well,"** screens off the pit of despair and misery, and a sense of wonder through which everything dreadful becomes simple again, plain as the miracle of daylight. Sometimes—and here we find Aymé at his best—this *merveilleux quotidien* functions like a deluding prism through which the stark light of frustrations and hatreds is broken into the beautiful hues of consoling dreams. Underlying the delightful fairy tale created and actually carried out by the innocent dreamer in real life, is a frightening human story of unsatisfied lusts, compulsive aggression, and breakdown into insanity. Thus the two distant spheres of Desire and Action sometimes do coincide, at the expense of the hero who did not know how to keep them separate.

Duvilé, in **"The Wine of Paris,"** has to pay the price for his pent-up anger and for exacting a vicarious revenge against the world. After years of rationing caused by the war this humiliated little man is possessed by an overwhelming thirst for red wine, which looks so much like fresh blood. This wish suddenly causes him to see all human shapes going down the street in the likeness of "dozens and dozens of bottles of every vintage." Frustrated in pride and drink, as he has been all these years of war and married life, is it surprising that Etienne Duvilé, armed with a heavy poker, should try to take the neck off many such miraculous bottles, "just level with the shoulders, neat as anything"? He naturally started with his nagging, bald-headed father-in-law, "for he was particularly fond of Burgundy." But, the narrator hopefully concludes, the doctors soon release Duvilé from the insane asylum to send him to the wine-growing Arbois country, where the abundance of real red wine will soon cure him of all his wartime and matrimonial frustrations: thus a natural reconciliation is humorously held out by Aymé as a possible solution to man's existential conflicts and metaphysical duality.

"The State of Grace" is written in the same charitable Christian spirit. The saintly M. Duperrier from Montmartre certainly did his utmost in the way of the Seven Deadly Sins in order to get rid of the embarassing halo Divine Grace had bestowed upon him. This heavenly gift was incompatible with his earthly life: his wife complained that "the light of the halo, bathing the pillows, made it impossible for her to sleep at night." But all his exertions in the direction of sin were of no avail. Aymé coyly describes him ending his career as a pimp on the Boulevard de Clichy, where he supervises the labors of Marie-Jeannick of Landivisiau, an ex-maid-of-all-work from Brittany. He can be seen by everyone, "waiting at the hotel door to count her takings by the light of the halo." Yet, from the depths of his heroic degradation and inverted martyrdom, there sometimes rises to his lips "a prayer of thanksgiving for the absolute gratuity of the gifts of God." Above the pitiful contingencies of mundane existence floats a never-never land where all conflicts are blissfully transcended.

It is, of course, a little distressing to discover that the two kingdoms should be related only through incongruities: dreams, madness, sins, or miracles. Even after he finally gets caught within the stone wall he dared so often to walk through, Aymé's wretched hero still feels "the restless hankering which was in some sort the call of the other side of the wall." When cruel life has denied him the levity of his dreams, his faithful artist-friend "comes to console the unhappy prisoner with a song, and the notes, flying from the benumbed fingers, pierce to the heart of the stone like drops of moonlight." Thus, through the medium of art and poetry, illusion keeps feeding on human nostalgia at the very core of disillusionment.

Poor Jouque had a sadistic drunkard of a husband, who used to put her down his well, standing in the bucket, while everyone in the village kept silent "because the simplicity of the fields is by nature indulgent to brutes." Welled-in Jouque stared at the image of the two Hollywood-style lovers she fancied she saw reflected on the dark surface of the subterranean waters: "Jouque saw their lips were about to touch. She signed to them to wait for her, and plunged in." One wonders why the translator suppressed the last sentence of this edifying drama: "The pagan gods were celebrating that day in Pignol's well." It gives the story a joyful, melancholy, skeptical resonance, which is in keeping with Marcel Aymé's outlook on things. But, in general, the translation is both accurate and alive. It restores to the English reader something of the unique flavor of Aymé's style, where clever understatement of the main motives and emphatic treatment of apparently irrelevant detail constantly clash and mingle.

The choice of stories is excellent and covers a long period of the author's life. However, one regrets not finding any of the exquisite **Contes du Chat Perché** included in this volume. As it is, **Across Paris** constitutes but an introduction to the rich universe of Marcel Aymé. To do him full justice the reader must turn to novels like *The Green Mare*, *La Vouivre*, and *Uranus*, where the short storyteller's wit, talent, sense of fantasy are woven into a broad tapestry depicting in quasi-Rabelaisian tone the lives and times of quaint French petty bourgeois, or peasants.

William Dunlea (essay date 1959)

SOURCE: "Adult Fables," in *Commonweal,* Vol. LXIX, No. 21, February 20, 1959, pp. 550–51.

[*In the following essay, Dunlea praises* Across Paris and Other Stories *for Aymé's ability to defy twentieth-century scientific and psychological analysis with his magical fables.*]

The novels of Marcel Aymé are all things to all readers, and the same may be said of his stories; they are adult fables, fantasies, fairytales, and seldom short. Superficially they are intellectual gags, the quintessence of his farcical expertise; but this is more than expertise playing at art, and like the most authentic art it is finally irreducible. In fact, such is the ease of Aymé's legerdemain, he nourishes the suspicion that perfection can be a gift.

Aymé is as capable of unadulterated charivari as of sheer sorcery. A sentimental mocker who lets the moral take care of itself, he is sly but he never really pinks. He evokes masterfully life's spontaneous disorders, yet he couldn't be more serious than when he leads off with "Once upon a time. . . ."

The opening lines of most of these stories are like charms: "In his thirty-fifth year the dwarf belonging to the Cirque Barnaboum suddenly grew."

> The best Christian in the Rue Gabrielle was a certain Monsieur Duperrier, a man of such piety that God, without awaiting his death and while he was still in the prime of life, crowned his head with a halo which never left it by day or by night.

> [Dermuche] had murdered a family of three in order to get possession of a gramophone record he had coveted for several years.

> Noel Tournebise had so many marriageable daughters and so little memory that he could not recall their names and had to keep a list.

> There lived in Montmartre on the third floor of No. 75, Rue d'Orchampt, an excellent man named Dutilleul who possessed the singular gift of being able to walk through walls without experiencing any discomfort.

Barring one such supernatural aberration apiece, these individuals go on, or rather try to go on, functioning normally; they have no choice, for the irony of Aymé's fantasy is that it calls no general moratorium on physical law. Along with the stories where the afflatus is gay and altogether earthy, there are ones, like **"Rue de l'Evangile," "The Seven League Boots," "The Picture-Well,"** that leave not only a tingle but an almost tragi-comic twinge as well. A prime example of Aymé's versatility—indeed his talent is more protean than original—is **"Across Paris,"** which is the longest story here and the only one narrated from an angle of intensely realistic insight. Nevertheless, this now-famous tale (it was filmed as *Four Bags Full*) of wartime black-marketeers on a safari through the blacked-out City of Light, has an atmosphere fully charged with mystery.

In the ribald vein Aymé is sub-acid and very sure; when he ventures to lure the sanctity-afflicted into his range he becomes conspiratorial and arch, and the muse is stifled. He is grated by an abstract Tartuffe in whom he finds no genuine comic leverage: he has neglected to offer a humanly concrete projection of his attitude toward formal religion. This failure lays bare the vital dimensions Aymé lacks as a satirist. The great risk faced by the writer who sets out to deflate the illusions of human vanity is that in its own extravagance his laughter will cease to be tonic and will merely belittle, even contort.

To call even the most piquant of these drolleries "Rabelaisian" is forcing the pace, even though this has become the frozen epithet for Aymé. It implies an artificial context in which he appears least refreshing, and in this respect these stories cast some light on his novels. Life is relished in these novels without being affirmed; theirs is a wondrous world but wanting. Its creator is a fabulous realist but equally an epicurean, and the epicurean, in his passivity, leaves a certain taste of deception.

But Marcel Aymé is delightfully out of step with the age of analysis. He can turn reality upside down without any evident temptation to turn man inside out. He is not sounding the soul's desolate spaces; he holds his analysis to reason's absurd reductions. Yet all the while it is reality's own magic he is conjuring with.

The Atlantic Monthly (essay date 1961)

SOURCE: "A French Satirist," in *Atlantic Monthly,* Vol. CCVII, January-June, 1961, pp. 102–03.

[*In the following essay, the anonymous critic reviews* The Proverb and Other Stories, *finding that it affirms that Aymé is "a born storyteller."*]

Marcel Aymé, currently represented by ***The Proverb and Other Stories,*** has been highly praised by American reviewers, and I find it a bit puzzling that he should have so limited an audience. He is, to be sure, an oddity among contemporary French writers, but his oddity is such as might be expected to recommend him to American readers. Aymé has never become involved in literary and ideological cults; he is an old-fashioned individualist, more interested in people than in ideas. He is, moreover, a born storyteller, one of the best practicing in any language, and even in translation his prose is elegant and extremely readable. What possibly disconcerts some Anglo-Saxons is that Aymé's satire and farce grow out of a profound and tolerant cynicism. He distrusts or finds ridiculous high-minded idealists, revolutionary middle-class intellectuals—in fact, people of all kinds who want to remake the human animal or bowdlerize the truth about his nature. For Aymé, hypocrisy is more vicious than the natural vices of man, and one senses in his work a strong affection for life as it is. Within this framework, his range is wide. In addition to being consistently amusing, he can be gay, tender, cruel, horrifying, or sardonic.

A couple of stories in the present collection are memorable examples of Aymé's distinctive combination of fantasy and down-to-earth realism. **"The Life-Ration"** describes, through the diary of a novelist, the consequences of a wartime law which rations people to so many days of existence a month according to their usefulness. **"La Bonne Peinture,"** which seems to me a masterpiece, begins with the discovery that the canvases of a minor painter are as physically nourishing as *la grande cuisine* and ends with the satiric vision of a French utopia: all of the arts have become "effective," and France is fed by painting and heated by poems and novels, its people are made beautiful by looking at sculpture, and its machines are driven by music. **"The Bogus Policeman"** is a grisly parody of the idealistic orgies of "purification" which swept France after the Liberation. And **"Backwards"** parodies the French climate of opinion, which makes it prudent and fashionable for the very rich to represent themselves as socialists and champions of the masses.

There are twelve stories in the book, and more than half of them are outstanding. Among the readers who have so far missed Aymé's work, there must be a good many who would find this volume an entertaining introduction to the fictional world of a first-rate writer.

Mark J. Temmer (essay date 1962)

SOURCE: "Marcel Aymé, Fabulist and Moralist," in *The French Review,* Vol. XXXV, No. 5, April, 1962, pp. 453–62.

[*In the following essay, Temmer examines Aymé's fables and classifies the writer as a traditional French fabulist.*]

Fables should have a moral that pleases the reader's mind as well as his heart, and there is no doubt that Aymé's tales meet this first condition. He appeals to the intellect, and, as for matters of conscience, he follows the tradition of French fabulists who are not intent upon improving the world but prefer to analyze it in a manner that is both lucid and humorous. His ***Contes du Chat Perché*** is a lively commentary on French life, and his wit spares neither beast nor man. The viewpoint is more fantastic than poetic, the language more natural than formal, and it is precisely this smooth juxtaposition of the fantastic and the natural which characterizes not only his fables but also his many short stories. Aymé's works exhibit *le bon sens français* that shuns poetic exaggeration and seeks what he has defined as *le confort intellectuel,* namely "ce qui assure la santé de l'esprit, son bien-être, ses joies et ses aises dans la sécurité."[1] Fortunately, Aymé is a better writer than philosopher, and the interest of his stories, it will be seen, resides less in their moral than in their dramatic action, which differs in every tale.

These fables, however, do share common traits in terms of their setting, style, formal development and characters. The human protagonists, as opposed to their animal counterparts, are few: a nameless Father and Mother and their children, Delphine and Marinette. Occasionally sentimental, rarely loving and never poetic, the parents are forever badgering their little girl with threats and admonitions. Typical French farmers, they tend to be thrifty and unimaginative—the black rooster is to them but a *coq-au-vin.* Furthermore, they seem cruel—are they not willing to sell their children after they have assumed the shape of a donkey and a horse? In contrast to *les parents,* who reflect the author's disenchantment, Delphine and Marinette are delightful heroines. Invested with a goodness and mischievousness abstracted from real life, these little girls have no personal history and yet they live, representative of girlhood in particular and mankind in general. Knowingly, the fabulist appeals to adult nostalgia for lost innocence and purifies this yearning of sadness. There is a breath of fresh air in these stories which relate the girl's adventures with fox and hens in the timeless setting of a French farm. Our fantasy is freed, and our belief and trust in the pleasures of childhood are once more justified.

It is likewise possible to isolate certain constants in the structure of the intrigues. Hostile intrusions or misdeeds with unforeseeable consequences disrupt the daily life of play and study. The girls consult their animal friends who offer advice and intervene to prevent disaster. The gods, however, are neither called upon nor even mentioned. The *dénouement* contains elements of surprise that are often imaginative or fantastic in nature. Frequently the logical order of life breaks down. Causes are no longer efficient; effects no longer predictable. Yet, despite this seeming reversal of the actual order, the essential facts of life are never disregarded, for Aymé's fantasy does not invoke supernatural powers. As in *Alice in Wonderland,* the result of fancy is truth, and madness but disguise.

Outlines, however, are of little use in describing Aymé's extraordinary imagination whose capriciousness defies any reduction to schemas. The tale entitled **"Les Bœufs"** illustrates the very vanity of such pedantry and of knowledge in general. Reminiscent of *Bouvard et Pécuchet,* the story begins with a speech by a sous-préfet belaboring a group of children on the advantages of a good education: "Mes chers enfants, dit-il, l'instruction est une bonne chose et ceux qui n'en ont pas sont bien à plaindre."[2] Intoxicated by his harangue, the girls exhort their oxen to become students of higher things. The red ox resists, but the white one begins to "orner son esprit." He reads extensively, investigates problems in physics and takes pleasure in quoting Victor Hugo: "J'admire, assis sous un portail. . . ." Gradually, our scholar turns into a bore who scorns his friends and neglects his duty which is to pull the plow. About to be sold to the butcher, he refuses to abandon his *idée fixe* and replies to the entreaties of his companion: "Oui, Monsieur, j'ai méprisé vos conseils, comme je les méprise aujourd'hui. Sachez que je ne regrette rien, et quant à vouloir oublier quoi que ce soit, je refuse. Mon seul désir, ma seule ambition, c'est d'apprendre encore et toujours. Plutôt mourir que d'y renoncer" (p. 42).

Although the implications of Aymé's stories are sometimes sad, the *genre* and forms of the apologue are, by their very nature, gay and sprightly and thus mitigate any satire the apologue may contain. Aymé stops short of exaggeration and eschews the now fashionable gloom of expressionistic allegorists such as Kafka and Beckett. Quite circumspect in his use of the principle of the *reductio ad absurdum,* he criticizes what is, without, however, questioning ideals of loyalty, camaraderie and compassion. To the insulting speech of the white ox, the red one replies: "Si tu venais à mourir, j'aurais du chagrin, tu sais." But the intellectual has become corrupted and doubts his companion's love: "Oui, oui, on dit ça, et puis dans le fond. . . ." Finally, the white ox joins a circus and out of friendship his mate follows him. The moral of the story is "qu'à moins de trouver place dans un cirque, les bœufs ne gagnent rien à s'instruire, et que les meilleures lectures leur attirent les pires ennuis" (p. 50).

The fable entitled **"Le Chien"** is a study in selfishness and altruism. Delphine and Marinette meet a blind dog whom they befriend and who tells them his sad tale. He had been a seeing-eye dog of a blind beggar and out of pity, had assumed his master's affliction: "Chien, veux-tu prendre mon mal et devenir aveugle à ma place?" (pp. 79, 80). Abandoned by the thankless wretch, he ingratiates himself with the girls and parents and quickly succeeds in making the cat feel guilty who in turn assumes his blindness and revels in his new found goodness: "Ronron . . . je suis bon . . . ronron . . . je suis bon." He, too, is neglected, and perchance, catching a mouse, does not waste any time in forcing the rodent to accept his blindness. His friend's reactions are revealing: "Quand le chien arriva à son tour,

il fut si heureux de la guérison de son ami, qu'il ne put cacher sa joie devant la souris. Le chat a été très bon, dit-il, et voyez ce qui arrive: il en est récompensé aujourd'hui! C'est vrai, disaient les petites, il a été bon. . . . C'est vrai murmurait le chat j'ai été bon. . . . Hum! faisait la souris, hum! hum!" (p. 90) The dog interprets the miracle as a divine act of Providence which recompenses the just and the girls agree whereas the cat, traditionally realistic, mutters with a mixture of regret and relief: "j'ai été bon." The mouse's "hum" speaks louder than words. The beggar, unwilling to work and unaware of the subsequent transmissions of his blindness, returns and beseeches first the dog, and then the cat to give him the affliction in exchange for helping him find his way. They refer him to the mouse who gladly consents to the bargain. As he stumbles off, led by his fragile guide, the dog can no longer contain himself and rushes back to his former master not daring to look back at the girls and the cat who are in tears. The moral is left to the discretion of the readers. Should we infer that we are neither exclusively compassionate nor selfish, or should we conclude that it is impossible to draw a moral about mice and men and that there is but one certainty, namely, that a dog is man's best friend?

In any case, Aymé's fables demonstrate a basic truth, that life triumphs over those who are victims of preconceived ideas about their destiny and instincts. Fate and instinct, however, are not always in accord. Such is the moral of **"Le Cerf et le chien."** A stag arrives in the courtyard pursued by hounds. The girls hide him and the lead dog, Pataud, taking pity on him, leads the pack astray: "Après tout le cerf ne m'a rien fait. D'un autre côté, bien sûr, le gibier est le gibier et je devrais faire mon métier. Mais, pour une autre fois. . . ."[3] The noble stag remains on the farm to assume an oxen's yoke. But after being beaten and brutalized by the parents, he returns to the life of the forest. Pataud, unable to prevent his death, and sickened by his trade, becomes a watch-dog: "Je ne veux plus entendre parler de la chasse. C'est fini." His remorse, so simple and evident, is far more telling than wordy self-accusations and confessions. Although one's guilt be only circumstantial, it should be redeemed by self-awareness if not by change. Passions must be curbed, for, as the pig declares: ". . . s'il ne fallait écouter que son appétit, on aurait bientôt dévoré ses meilleurs amis."[4]

The tale of the **"Le Mauvais Jars"** is a variation on the same theme. Its protagonists are the Bad Gander and the Clever Jack-ass. The former is a remarkable portrait of a bully, a kill-joy and vexatious husband. His choleric outbursts are borne patiently by Mother Goose whose conjugal reply, "Mais voyons, mon ami!," never varies. The Jack-ass, a tragic-comic character, endures the gander's mockery and, like a true clown, joins in the merriment. When the gander confiscates the girls' ball, he consoles them by allowing, nay, by urging them to stroke his long ears. Compulsive about exhibiting the objects of his ridicule, he invites injurious comments. The girls oblige him. It is in vain that he bemoans the injustice of his fate; Delphine and Marinette are not convinced, for his *bêtise* is proverbial and they cannot believe that things might be otherwise. Here is the turning point of the fable: "Il comprit qu'il ne réussirait pas à les convaincre de l'injustice dont il était victime. Elles ne le croiraient jamais sans preuves."[5] The remainder of the fable tells the donkey's vengeance. The gander is punished and our author concludes his tale in a spirit of ironic justice: "Aussi n'est-il plus question, depuis ce jour-là, de la bêtise de l'âne; et l'on dit, au contraire, d'un homme à qui on veut faire compliment de son intelligence qu'il est fin comme un âne" (p. 140).

It is of paramount importance that everyone, men and beasts, act according to the prescribed rules of society. To transgress openly their limits is to court disaster: witness *le petit coq noir* who lives on the assumption that to be eaten by one's master is a "règle sans exception." Seduced by Reynard's call to live freely and encouraged by the children to become the leader of his race, he is soon killed by the fox and eaten by the parents. Worst of all, the girls are scolded for meddling, and they now realize that "le mensonge et la désobéissance sont d'affreux péchés."[6] Thus, Aymé derides empty precepts by contrasting them with a reality that operates under its own laws. There is a lag between the logic of life and the logic of justice. Indeed, the punishment does not always fit the crime, and sometimes, one is chastized regardless of what one has done. Cognizant of this fact, the girls soon learn to defend themselves by assuming a rôle, and the resulting contrast between pretense and reality creates comic effects. As the wolf stares at them through the window, Marinette laughs at his pointed ears. But Delphine knows better. Clasping her sister's hand she declares: "C'est le loup. Le loup? dit Marinette, alors on a peur? Bien sûr, on a peur."[7]

Despite these oscillations between sincerity and irony, Aymé takes great care to inform the reader of the true feelings of any given character at any given time. Even the wolf enjoys feelings of tenderness and contrition until the confession of his evil deeds turns into torment when he is overcome by "le souvenir d'une gamine potelée et fondant sous la dent" (p. 14). The insertion of colloquial expressions in the dialogue furthers the dramatic development of his character. Thus, the girls propose to *jouer au loup* and as he participates in the game of being himself he quite *naturally* becomes himself and devours them. However, in contrast to Thurber, whose fables and morals are often derived from a commonplace (e.g., "Early to rise and early to bed makes a male healthy and wealthy and dead.") Aymé rarely subordinates his intrigue to the dramatic possibilities offered by a reinterpretation of a proverbial saying. Puns and jests have their place, but action is prior to style.

In order to be fabulistic, this action must be both human and animal, that is to say, the successful fabulist should understand man and beast, capture the essences of each and then invest the animal with those human qualities that best stress its respective folkloristic character. At the same time, he should grant the human protagonists a clear in-

sight into animal psychology. Aymé is a master at creating a natural interplay between the children and the denizens of the barnyard and surrounding fields. Their conversations are spontaneous, their dialogues dramatic. Narration alternates pleasingly with direct discourse which enlivens the intrigue and serves as a convenient vehicle for parodying braggarts and pedants. In this respect, he belongs to a distinguished tradition of French writers that begins with the anonymous authors of *Le Roman de Renart* and has as its most illustrious member the immortal La Fontaine. Surely his *Fables* must have been Aymé's *livre de chevet,* for **Les Contes du chat perché** are pervaded by a similar spirit of classical restraint and mediaeval realism. And above all, Aymé, like La Fontaine, is an acute observer of the human and animal kingdoms. The story entitled **"La Patte du chat"** is excellent proof of his talent to distill the quintessence of cat. The intrigue is simple: Alphonse, the feline, tries to save the girls from being punished for having broken an old and valued piece of china. They are to pay a call to Aunt Mélina, a fearsome hag, and in order to stave off the dreadful visit, he causes rain by washing his face. The angry parents put him into a weighted sack and are about to drown the self-sacrificial cat, who insists on perishing for the sake of his friends. Heartbroken, Delphine and Marinette seek counsel from the duck: "C'était un canard avisé et qui avait beaucoup de sérieux. Pour mieux réfléchir, il cacha sa tête sous son aile. J'ai beau me creuser la cervelle, dit-il enfin, je ne vois pas le moyen de décider Alphonse de sortir de son sac."[8] The melodrama ends with a delightful scene in which the cat assumes the thaumaturgic rôle of a pagan rainmaker: "Le soir même de ce même jour—le plus chaud qu'on eût jamais vu—Delphine et Marinette, les parents et toutes les bêtes de la ferme formerent un grand cercle dans la cour. Au milieu du cercle, Alphonse était assis sur un tabouret. Sans se presser, il fit d'abord sa toilette et, le moment venu, passa plus de cinquante fois sa patte derrière l'oreille. Le lendemain matin, après vingt-cinq jours de sécheresse, il tombait une bonne pluie, rafraîchissant bêtes et gens" (p. 40).

It would be unjust to Aymé as well as to poetry, to classify him as a poetic prose-writer. His *Confort intellectuel* is a traditional bourgeois attack against Baudelaire in particular, and, in general, against all forms of symbolist prose and poetry, "celle qui consiste à dire des choses fausses ou à ne rien dire."[9] Whether or not this refusal or incomprehension is the negative side of his talent is debatable. Yet poetic he is, at times, not in terms of metaphor, concept or rhythm, but in terms of his dramatic situations. They should not be simply subsumed under the heading of "realistic fantasy" and any difficulty we may encounter in defining this poetic feeling should not deny its residual presence. His poetry is an integral part of his composition; perhaps it is the fabular spirit itself. Despite his prejudices against those who do not write "clearly," Aymé may well be more closely allied to the surrealists than is good for his own *confort.* His revolt against, and transcendence of, the sociological norms of perception and behavior, suggest surrealistic influences. Above all, Aymé the fabulist rejects utilitarianism and in this respect Jules Monnerot's definition of poetry is à propos: "Il y a poésie quand l'affectivité charge une manifestation humaine d'un sens qui ne se laisse pas ramener sans résidu à la notion vulgaire de l'utile. L'efficace poétique est autre que l'efficience d'une modification du monde préméditée et exécutée selon le principe de réalité, les normes de l'entendement."[10] The fable of **"Le Paon"** furnishes a splendid illustration of this principle. The girls undergo a *crise de vanité* which affects everyone, especially the pig. Envious of the peacock, he wants to lose weight and, above all, acquire a tuft and feathers to make a wheel. All succumb to discouragement except the dandy whose perseverance elicits ridicule and much headwagging. Yet, at the end, when hope seems gone, a rainbow converges on the pig's tail who mistakes it for plumage. Desire for beauty, a forgivable folly, is rewarded, and dreams turn to reality: "Derrière lui, l'arc-en-ciel fondit tout d'un coup et se déposa sur sa peau en couleurs si tendres, et si vives aussi, que les plumes du paon, à côté, eussent été comme une grisaille."[11] The tale of **"La Buse et le cochon"** has a similar ending. Through the intervention of his friends, the pig escapes the butcher's knife by flying away with the wings of the buzzard who has been stripped of his pinions (*buse* signifying also blockhead). Gracefully, he cruises above the yard, shouting to the astonished parents: 'J'aime mieux quitter la maison que d'y finir au saloir. Adieu, et apprenez à être moins cruels."[12] This, too, is poetry.

The fables entitled **"Le Problème, Les Boîtes de peinture,"** and **"Les Eléphants"** have metaphysical implications. The first one illustrates pragmatism. The girls, unable to do their homework, seek help from their friends to solve their problem: "Les bois de la commune ont une étendue de seize hectares. Sachant qu'un are est planté de trois chênes, de deux hêtres et d'un bouleau, combien les bois de la commune contiennent-ils d'arbres de chaque espèce?"[13] "La petite poule blanche" resolves the question by proposing that they count the number of beeches, oaks, etc. within the territorial limits of the village. In so doing, the group meets a wild boar who cannot bear the sight of the pig. It is worthwhile to quote him: "Que cet animal est donc laid. Je n'arrive pas à m'y habituer. Cette peau rose est d'un effet vraiment écœurant. Mais n'en parlons plus. Je vous disais donc qu'à vivre la nuit je suis resté ignorant de bien des choses. Qu'est-ce qu'une maîtresse d'école par exemple. Et qu'est-ce qu'un problème?" (p. 46) In the ensuing discussion, scholarly endeavors are divested of meaning and assume an air of absurdity when confronted with the pleasures of *l'école buissonière.* In the final scene the school mistress tries to explain to the animals that the assigned problem does not correspond to anything real. Angrily they retort that the terms of a problem must be related to reality if the problem is to have any value.

Common sense, however, should not impair the powers of fancy and imagination. When the children paint a donkey and grant him but two legs, he actually turns into a biped. Art becomes constitutive of reality. At times, Aymé favors philosophical idealism and questions the realness of the exterior world. Such is the conclusion of the whimsical tales **"Les Eléphants."** Wanting to play "Noah's Ark," the girls herd their friends into the kitchen, where the cow stares at a pitcher of milk and slice of cheese, murmuring all the while to herself: "Je comprends, maintenant, je comprends."[14] "La petite poule blanche" wants to join the expedition, but is *de trop* unless she changes into an elephant. The hen concentrates and *ipso facto* assumes the shape of a stately pachyderm. After the conclusion of the game, she refuses to become her former self. The parents arrive and, puzzled by the shaking walls, finally open the door to the kitchen which, lo and behold, is empty save for a small white chicken. There is no explanation and Delphine and Marinette themselves begin to doubt the reality of the metamorphosis. Is it a fiction of childish fancy, or could it be that games and fables need neither proof nor justification?

In only one fable, **"Les Cygnes,"** do the parents enter the domain of the fabulous and *le merveilleux,* and it is characteristic of Aymé that this adult vision should be clouded with tears. Marinette and Delphine stray from the beaten path and join other creatures in search of the "rendez-vous des enfants perdus." The meeting is held under the auspices of swans who refuse to let the children return home. But an old swan intercedes in their favor and leads them back to the farm. At that moment the parents appear and witness the following scene:

> Le vieux cygne s'écarta de la haie, puis, rassemblant ses dernières forces, s'élança en courant vers le milieu des champs. . . . Alors, il se mit à chanter, comme font les cygnes quand ils vont mourir. Et son chant était si beau qu'à l'entendre, les larmes venaient dans les yeux. Sur la route, les parents s'étaient donné la main et, sans prendre garde qu'il tournaient le dos à la maison, s'en allaient à travers les champs à la recontre de la voix. Longtemps après que le cygne eut cessé de chanter, ils marchaient encore dans la rosée et ne pensaient pas à rentrer.

> Dans la cuisine, Delphine et Marinette cousaient sous la lampe. Le couvert était mis et le feu allumé. En entrant, les parents dirent bonjour d'une petite voix qu'elles ne reconnaissaient pas. Ils avaient les yeux humides et, ce qui ne leur était jamais arrivé, n'en finissaient pas de regarder au plafond.

> —Quel dommage, dirent-ils aux petites. Quel dommage que vous n'ayez pas traversé la route tout à l'heure. Un cygne a chanté sur les prés.[15]

The moral of this tale is sad. The tragedy, Aymé tells us in a matter-of-fact tone, is not that we must die, but that we are like the parents, often heartless, yet unable to maintain our composure and indifference when we hear the song of a dying swan. The tears they shed are tears of remorse for not having lived the life of poetry and friendship. Unwilling to tell their children the truth, they conceal it behind an impersonal statement: "Un cygne a chanté sur les prés." Only once are the parents freed from their own guilt and pomposity, and this against their will when *la panthère aux yeux d'or* forces them to become playful: "Depuis qu'elle s'était installée au foyer, la vie avait changé et personne ne s'en plaignait. Sans parler du vieux cheval qui ne s'était jamais vu à pareille fête, chacun se sentait plus heureux. Les bêtes vivaient en sécurité et les gens ne traînaient plus comme autrefois le remords de les manger. Les parents avaient perdu l'habitude de crier et de menacer, et le travail était devenu pour tout le monde un plaisir."[16] Fleetingly, Aymé suggests the age of innocence, the golden age so dear to Supervielle. But whereas the latter's wit and humour are purely poetic and mythological, our fabulist's realistic evocations are forever threatened by his own laughter and disbelief. Salvation depends on a complete and improbable reversal of rôles: "C'est à peine si Delphine et Marinette trouvaient le temps d'apprendre leurs leçons et de faire leurs devoirs. Venez jouer, disaient les parents. Vous ferez vos devoirs une autre fois" (p. 173).

It is regrettable that Aymé's style does not always match the excellence of his fantasy and imagination. His prose, dry and functional, is not marred by any specific flaw or "little rift within the flute," but rather by a dull absence of ornament, design and metaphor. Admittedly, Aymé's ideal is simplicity, and he has bitterly attacked misuse of language: "Quand les mots se mettent à enfler, quand leur sens devient ambigu, incertain, et que le vocabulaire se charge de flou, d'obscurité et néant péremptoire, il n'y a plus de recours pour l'esprit." Yet, as we have suggested, this refusal of pretentiousness may well mask his weakness. Wanting to be natural, he tends to be *artless,* and his discourse lacks the diction, tension and luster of great prose. In art, nature is fashioned of art. Had he been as exacting towards himself as towards others, his fables might already be a part of France's literary patrimony. To be sure, Aymé, the fabulist, holds a very respectable position among the representatives of the *genre mineur,* of the fabular spirit which refuses to die, but the question of whether or not he has succeeded in immortalizing Delphine and Marinette remains the subject of much doubt.

Notes

1. Marcel Aymé, *Le Confort intellectuel* (Paris, 1949), p. 12.

2. Marcel Aymé, *Les Contes du chat perché* (Paris, 1939), p. 29.

3. Marcel Aymé, *Derniers Contes du chat perché* (Paris, 1958), p. 80.

4. *Les Contes du chat perché,* "La Buse et le cochon," p. 156.

5. *Ibid.,* "Le Mauvais Jars," p. 132.

6. *Ibid.,* "Le Petit Coq noir," p. 13.

7. *Ibid.,* "Le Loup," p. 10.

8. *Autres Contes du chat perché* (Paris, 1950), p. 29.

9. *Le Confort intellectuel,* p. 14.

10. Jules Monnerot, *La Poésie moderne et le sacré* (Paris, 1945), pp. 15, 16.

11. *Les Contes du chat perché,* "Le Paon," p. 201.

12. *Ibid.,* "La Buse et le cochon," p. 160.

13. *Derniers Contes du chat perché,* "Le Problème," p. 40.

14. *Les contes du chat perché,* "L'Eléphant," p. 105.

15. *Autres Contes du chat perché,* "Les Cygnes," pp. 55–6.

16. *Les Contes du chat perché,* "Le Canard et la Panthère," p. 172.

Graham Lord (essay date 1980)

SOURCE: "Faerie and Fantastic Phenomena and Motifs," in *The Short Stories of Marcel Aymé,* University of Western Australia Press, 1980, pp. 11–17, 20–56.

[*In the following essay, Lord examines Aymé's stories that fall into the traditions of fairy tales and tales of the fantastic.*]

> *Les fées sont agréables à fréquenter. Les hommes aussi.*
>
> —Marcel Aymé

It is the physical fantasies that are most commonly accepted as Aymé's trade-mark. All three pastiches of his work stress this kind of story. Commentators trying to analyse Aymé's extremely varied use of the physically unreal have had recourse to a multitude of terms to qualify it: *fantaisie, merveilleux, surréel, fantastique, fabuleux, absurde, non-sens, miraculeux, féerique, science-fiction.* This list makes the analysis of Aymé's unreal stories seem a particularly daunting project, but in fact many of these terms are wrongly or too vaguely applied. Aymé's unreal has little connection with the vogue of Surrealism, the 'littérature of the Absurd' or the rather anglophone trend towards verbal nonsense, and the theoreticians of the unreal tend to condemn the terms *merveilleux* and *fantaisie* as being too general, along with the once precise but now vague use of *miraculeux* and *fabuleux.*

Part of Aymé's originality is that he dabbles in several different currents of fantasy. Apart from a thin vein of science fiction, Aymé's imagination can be divided between the two widely accepted currents of *féerique* and *fantastique.* It is important to make a clear distinction between these two because Aymé tends to disregard literary convention by mingling them and adapting them to his own purposes. The *féerique* implies a world apart, like C. S. Lewis's Narnia or J. R. R. Tolkien's Middle Earth, a world inhabited by fairies, unicorns and sorcerers. Its normal phenomena are spells, magic lamps and moonlight. Describing the faerie world of Perrault, Marcel Schneider writes of 'un monde où tout vit, où tout parle, où tout agit. Ce monde a un sens.' It is also a moral world where man's causality is absent even though his attributes may be reflected in humanized animals; Isabelle Jan underlines the tradition of 'L'Ours-valeureux', 'le Cochon-tyran', 'le Renard-fripon' and 'le Chat-brigand'. Man's presence is not obligatory but Aymé obviously finds that faerie is much more relevant and interesting if man participates. Yet this participation will usually be temporary; man will return to the security of his own world at the end.

The literature of the fantastic tends to be taken more seriously than faerie because it talks of our world, our own time and space coordinates. Humans provide most of its protagonists even if they have some frightening new power, and where there are monsters—vampires and werewolves—they often reflect man in their creation. Several common themes recur: metamorphoses, time manipulation, invisibility, voyages to a 'beyond', statues that come to life, pacts with occult powers, monstrous psychological reflections of human feelings or experiences. The essence of the fantastic is the intrusion of something strange and frightening into our secure world. The fear is stressed because our security is threatened; man himself is closely involved and usually helpless before the fantastic. He could kill a fire-breathing dragon but the spectres that he encounters now are often part of himself, the *fantastique intérieur* that is so important in the work of Hoffmann and Poe.

There are elements of both faerie and the fantastic in the stories of Marcel Aymé. He admits appreciation of the work of Andersen and Perrault and has written prefaces to the stories of both. In his comments on his own childhood Aymé refers to the influence of fairy stories as well as to his penchant for Jules Verne and the comtesse de Ségur. All of these influences are to be seen in borrowings of material, but what is more interesting is the way Aymé adapts, distorts and often parodies that material.

. . . . .

Aymé's most recognizable borrowings are from faerie literature. He does not exploit faerie very often, perhaps because the inventive and nonconformist *conteur* felt constrained by the particularly strong rules of a tradition which 'n'admet pas d'acte vraiment créateur ou vraiment libre'. What is more, Aymé is essentially a humanist and faerie is too far removed from man. He has exploited only a few truly faerie characters: a water-sprite, a wicked ogre and a centaur; but several stories are infected in a more general way by the faerie spirit.

Aymé's break with tradition starts very early. The water-fairy Udine in **'Au clair de la lune'**, after nine hundred years at the bottom of her river, enters man's time and space scale. She is quite a conventional fairy: long blonde hair 'comme elles ont toutes', magic wand, crystal and jade chariot drawn by white rabbits. One of Aymé's recurrent themes is the clash between reality and fantasy. This is accentuated here by bringing Udine out of her traditionally closed context into our world. Udine is quickly threatened with a fine for driving on the highway without lights. An evil fairy, smiles Aymé, would have turned the gendarme into a merino ram or a coffee-grinder, but Udine is a kind fairy: she adapts to his world by telling him she is 'la femme du préfet'. The clash of real and fantasy contin-

ues as Udine tries to help young Jacot win the hand of his Valentine. Reality threatens to turn her *conte rose* into a *conte gris*: she sees her rabbits beaten by Jacot's sports car and then she is so disturbed that she muddles up her magic spells. Aymé's sad smile persists at the end: Udine does manage to bring the lovers together but must go on her way discouraged by a world where man's law requires head-lights even though 'la lune éclate au firmament étoilé comme la rose livide dans un parterre de jasmins' (*PI* 171) and where Jacot cannot go and 'chanter la romance éternelle sous les fenêtres de Valentine (. . .) dans ces jardins tout parfumés de blanche aubépine et de tendre péché' (*PI* 179) because Valentine's father has set traps in the flower-beds!

Aymé's ogre in **'Conte du milieu'** suffers even more than Udine in his confrontation with man's world. This ogre no longer inhabits a cave in Fairyland but runs a café near the Porte St. Martin. His particular vice is to touch young ladies on the cheek with his magic ring and mutter the incantation 'Calvados, Cognac, Fine Champagne' to shrink them and store them in his salad bowl until he wants to take his pleasure or eat them. After bringing this faerie out of its context into the reality of Paris Aymé almost parodies a conventional fairy-story plot. The young hero's mistress is spirited away and Janot sets out to rescue her, turns the ogre's own weapon against him, rescues Riri la Blonde and they live happily ever after as proprietors of a brothel. We do not need Pierre Berger's ribald etchings in the separate edition of this tale to realize that it is pure entertainment.

Aymé enlivens several of his more serious short stories by borrowing faerie accessories and effects from their traditional context and applying them in a very real frame. At the end of a rather lengthy account of an unmarried mother's sacrifices to give her young son enough to eat, Aymé introduces magic into **'Les Bottes de sept lieues'** to provide a happily-ever-after ending that he shows to be sadly impossible if we remain tied to reality. The boots enable young Antoine to escape his life of poverty and bring back poignantly simple treasures to his mother in their cold attic:

> En dix minutes, il fut à l'autre bout de la terre et s'arrêta dans un grand pré pour y cueillir une brassée des premiers rayons du soleil qu'il noua d'un fil de la Vierge.
>
> Antoine retrouva facilement la mansarde où il se glissa sans bruit. Sur le petit lit de sa mère, il posa sa brassée brillante dont la lueur éclaira le visage endormi et il trouva qu'elle était moins fatiguée.
>
> (*PM* 230)

Magic tears, gestures and incantations are used in *Les Contes du chat perché* as well as the eerie sound-effects that accompany the metamorphosis in **'L'Ane et le cheval'**: rattling chains, a music box and the howling of a non-existent storm. Aymé further mixes his genres by applying moonlight effects to the fantastic time jump in **'La**

Fabrique' and the strange storm motif accompanies the time movement and metamorphosis in **Le Décret**, which by its structure and theme belongs well and truly in the fantastic vein.

The novels *La Table aux crevés*, *Gustalin* and *La Vouivre* are coloured by elements of Aymé's native Jurassian mythology that should clearly be classed as faerie. Yet, despite its influence on his childhood, this pagan faerie with its mysterious trees and rocks, its enchanted ponds and snake-charming nymphs, touches only one short story, **'Les mauvaises fièvres'**, and there as hardly more than an accessory. Aymé more often exploits the faerie of classical mythology. **'Fiançailles'** is the story of a young centaur called Aristide who has the torso and face of a charming adolescent but the body of a stallion. Here, too, the intrusion of fantasy into reality and man's own reaction are underlined. Aristide has been born to the marquise de Valoraine and then hidden away to avoid social scandal. The story describes his discovery of the outside world, his sexual coming of age and his choice between the two sides of his nature. He becomes excited by the budding young god-daughter of the local bishop and thinks that it must be his 'âme' that he feels stirring at the sight of her rounded 'croupe'. His spontaneity, candour and evident lack of social conditioning provide some rather amusing situations, the best of which is the proposed marriage of real and fantasy. The bishop is at first shocked by the proposition, seeing nothing but 'péché' and 'animalité' in the uneducated Aristide, but soon jumps at the opportunity to marry off his ward.

Aymé turns this story into a light-hearted dig at the religious and social constraints that the untutored centaur cannot comprehend. Aristide relives Udine's experience with the representative of society's law and order: the gendarme in this case regards Aristide's very existence as an affront to authority and threatens to arrest him for 'attentat à la pudeur publique'. Aristide is confused and instinctively decides that his animal half must be the better one. He rather symbolically breaks out of the park and runs off into the forest with the first real mare he meets, leaving poor Ernestine to have her stirrings repressed by the nuns of the école Sainte-Thérèse de l'Enfant-Jésus.

Just as recognizable as Aristide or the seven-league boots are several images which are biblical or at least religio-moral in origin while being *féerique* in spirit. Aymé's preface to the stories of Andersen shows that he regarded this as a legitimate extension of faerie material. Whether his irreverent story is to be based on Samson's magic hair, a comic-strip God astride a cloud, the Devil riding up to the pearly gates on a broomstick to parley with St. Peter, or St. Francis of Assisi appearing to a sadist to ask him to read his *Vita* (Editions du Ciel, of course), Aymé's parodic exploitation of the image is similar to his use of more conventional material.

'La Fosse aux péchés' exploits the biblical parable tradition with a story of allegorical monsters acting out the battle between good and evil. Aymé uses a dream to frame a ribald pastiche of the whole tradition. This is one of several stories where the ironic Aymé subjects a pure character to temptation. The hero this time is Martin, a 'professeur de pureté' who gives in to temptation in a very familiar pattern: he sells his soul to the Devil for a golden calf but the Devil snaps him up on his way to spend it. The following scene in hell, where an English pastor does battle with the Devil's seven deadly henchmen, allows Aymé to indulge his Rabelaisian streak of verbal amusement. The pastor vanquishes one by one the grotesque sins which take the form that the sinner imagines them to have. Here is Aymé's vision of pride:

> Son corps avait la forme d'une commode Louis XV. (. . .) Il avait le derrière empanaché d'un flot de tentacules multicolores où dominaient l'or et la pourpre. Ses jambes de pierre étaient d'un blanc laiteux, ses pieds et ses cuisses couleur merde d'oie. Il portait en sautoir, imprimé sur la peau, un grand cordon violet fileté de blanc et, sur son torse Louis XV, deux rangées de décorations qui étaient ses excroissances naturelles aux coloris des plus chatoyants. Ses cornes étaient dorées, ses oreilles de veau d'un rouge éclatant.
>
> (*VP* 138–9)

At the end of the epic struggle hell vomits its prey, but this ending is deceptive. Aymé's target is once again the constraints placed on man by a religio-social educative process, so he arranges a reversal of the standard moral ending: the Devil's pleasure-creed 'Le péché est la substance essentielle de la vie' wins the day. Once back among his disciples, Professor Martin tells them:

> —Déchirez mon traité de prophylaxie de l'âme. (. . .) Si vous voulez vous garder des mauvaises tentations, ne haïssez pas le péché, mais familiarisez-vous avec le péril. Ne soyez pas bêtement modestes, ne méprisez pas les bonnes nourritures, ne fuyez pas les femmes, etc.
>
> (*VP* 150)

Hypocritical conceptions of virtue are ridiculed more bitterly when Aymé uses the décor of heaven and an imaginary country for his **'Légende poldève'**. The exaggerated virtue of the old maid Mlle Borboïe is Aymé's target. Her virtue is constrained, ritual and above all egoistic. All her actions are directed towards her own entry into paradise. Aymé's satire of her self-righteousness continues right up to the gates of a heaven that is disturbingly like an administrative office. She pleads her 'dossier' with St. Peter as with any other public servant and tries to get him to take a personal interest in her case:

> —. . . Prière du matin, action de grâces, puis messe de six heures par tous les temps. Après la messe, invocation spéciale à saint Joseph et remerciement à la Vierge. Chapelet à dix heures, suivi de la lecture d'un chapitre des Evangiles. *Benedicite* à midi . . . (. . .)
>
> —Ecoutez, dit ce bon archange, votre cas me paraît intéressant. Je veux tenter quelque chose pour vous.
>
> (*PM* 156–7)

Aymé subjects the hypocritical old maid to a final test: to attain paradise she must pretend to be whore to a regiment of hussars! In **'Légende poldève'** Aymé is very close to Voltaire in his blend of ironic humorist and bitter moralist. This is visible not only in his imitation of the style of *Candide* and his satire of the spinster and her heaven, but also when he describes the comic-strip war fought for national honour:

> Un petit garçon de Molletonie pissa délibérément par-dessus la frontière et arrosa le territoire poldève avec un sourire sardonique. C'en était trop pour l'honneur du peuple poldève dont la conscience se révolta, et la mobilisation fut aussitôt décrétée.

> (*PM* 151–52)

Wartime God-on-our-side sentiments and the idea that wholesale slaughter becomes moral when backed by a 'noble' cause are mocked as Aymé reveals the ignoble side of militarism: the swaggering local soldiery assault, rape and plunder the very civilians they are supposed to be protecting. And of course all combatants (and only combatants), automatically 'morts pour la patrie' and also 'pour le bon droit' even if they are the enemy, are admitted to heaven with no questions asked.

True to Voltairian tradition, Aymé works through irony rather than direct statement. Certainly he is exploiting the faerie mode to satirize reality, but faerie is only a ruse. Aymé's main weapon is his language itself. His attitude is conveyed by tone rather than by the actual events that are narrated. A good example of this is his treatment of the contrast between Marichella Borboïé and her nephew Bobislas. The nephew is a thorough scoundrel: we follow his career through lechery and drunkenness to theft, rape and pillage. Aymé appears to have created an obvious candidate for the fires of hell and yet the joyous, flowing narrative contradicts these appearances: it provokes a smile which lures the reader into feeling a certain sympathy for the ribald Bobislas:

> Un chapelet d'abominables jurements l'annonçait du bout de la rue où demeurait la vieille demoiselle. Titubant, son grand sabre cognant et s'embarrassant à tous les meubles, sans autre bonjour qu'un blasphème, il lui signifiait, éructant et braillant, qu'elle eût à sortir son argent et à se hâter. Plusieurs fois même, comme elle tardait à s'exécuter, il avait à moitié dégainé son bancal et menacé la sainte fille de la partager en deux dans le sens de la longueur

> (*PM* 153)

while the dry irony of the sentences devoted to the 'virtuous' but stupid old spinster and her misguided faith leaves no doubt as to Aymé's opinion of her:

> Pendant cinq ans, Mlle Borboïé voulut croire qu'il s'amenderait un jour et lui prodigua inlassablement les bons conseils et les pieuses exhortations avec tout l'argent qu'il fallait pour les faire fructifier.

> (*PM* 151)

The theme, the reversal structure and above all the rather *féerique* accessories of **'Légende poldève'** recur in the very similar **'L'Huissier'**. The comic potential of the heavenly décor is more fully realized here; it is brought into more profitable contrast with reality. Aymé opens the story with another light-hearted parody of a Last Judgement trial scene. The magistrate is St. Peter with his book of records, the defendant is an over-zealous, cynical and self-righteous bailiff called Malicorne, the evidence is a large vat full of the tears of the widows and children he has evicted, and the appeals judge is God, who enters on his cloud to the accompaniment of a roll of thunder. Malicorne's refusal to be cowed by the situation provides some rather splendid dialogue. Undeterred by St. Peter's opening remark that there are hardly any bailiffs in paradise, he suavely assures the guardian of the gates that he does not really insist on being with his colleagues. . . . Asked about his 'bonnes oeuvres', he searches back fifteen years in his memory and cites the occasion when he gave ten *centimes* to a beggar. The objection that the coin was counterfeit leaves him unperturbed too; the beggar would have passed it on quite easily. Naturally there is also a dark side to this humour. Malicorne's cynical defence is that he was only doing his job to the best of his ability ('Dieu merci, mes affaires marchaient bien et je n'ai pas chômé', *PM* 232), but he was obviously rather too zealous a bailiff. St. Peter is all for stoking up the fires of hell and washing down Malicorne's burns with the salt water from the vat, but Malicorne appeals against this judgement. The appeal is heard, because 'La procédure est la procédure', even in heaven. God deems that St. Peter was rather too hasty in his condemnation: it is not the bailiff (over-zealous or not) who is at fault, but the human laws whose agent he is. Yet they can hardly allow a bailiff into heaven because 'Ce serait un scandale'.

Malicorne is sent back to earth to redeem himself. He tries to buy his way back into heaven by performing good deeds and he records these for St. Peter in a little notebook drawn up with debit and credit columns:

> 'J'ai, spontanément, augmenté de cinquante francs par mois mon clerc Bourrichon qui ne le méritait pourtant pas.'

> (*PM* 236)

At the end of his first day of reprieve Malicorne has performed twelve of these empty 'bonnes oeuvres' at a noted cost of 600 francs. It seems that the only good deeds he can think of involve money. Aymé is not only using his faerie borrowings, complete with suggestive dream frame, to scourge those hypocrites who would purchase salvation with their 'charité intéressée'; he has also treated us to a neat ironic reversal. We have before us a miser who is now determined to part with his fortune. It is almost as if Aymé had started a new story by suggesting that 'Il y avait, à Paris, un méchant huissier qui, un jour, décida de devenir bon.' This is a particularly fruitful premise because Aymé has chosen a rather excessive bailiff to start with:

Il y avait, dans une petite ville de France, un huissier qui s'appelait Malicorne et il était si scrupuleux dans l'accomplissement de son triste ministère qu'il n'eût pas hésité à saisir ses propres meubles.

(*PM* 231)

Obviously there is great potential for humour in this reversal. Imagine the bewilderment of the bailiff's staff when their tyrannical master suddenly doubles their salary! Malicorne sets his target of good deeds at twelve a day, but increases this whenever an ache or pain makes him afraid his end might be near. At the end of a year he has filled six exercise-books, and Aymé indulges in a superb parody of the classic Scrooge image: Malicorne gloating as he weighs his tally-books and leafs delightedly through their pages (*PM* 241).

Here, too, there is a dark side to the humour, a sombre dramatic irony in the bailiff's first post-metamorphosis encounter with his client, the landlord Gorgerin, who does not know that Malicorne is now working against his interests. There is even more bitter irony in the comparison between the two men's ambitions: Malicorne is trying to be known as 'bon' while Gorgerin is desperately trying to avoid it. Money is the only tool Malicorne knows. As the bailiff does his rounds dispensing alms to the poor, Aymé builds a case against Malicorne's former clients, the heartless slum landlords like Gorgerin who exploit the poor in their defenceless misery. Malicorne is received in heaven at the end but it has nothing to do with his false generosity. He is finally moved by the poverty of a tawdry seventh-floor garret and, in his first truly spontaneous gesture, turns on Gorgerin shouting 'A bas les propriétaires'. He is shot dead for his treason and of course goes straight to Aymé's anti-serious heaven that is reserved, like his sympathies, for the meek and the down-trodden:

Dieu, émerveillé, commanda aux anges de jouer, en l'honneur de Malicorne, du luth, de la viole, du hautbois et du flageolet. Ensuite, il fit ouvrir les portes du ciel à deux battants, comme cela se fait pour les déshérités, les clochards, les claque-dents et les condamnés à mort. Et l'huissier, porté par un air de musique, entra au Paradis avec un rond de lumière sur la tête.

(*PM* 245–46)

This unexpected reversal motif, already visible in '**La Fosse aux péchés**' and '**Légende poldève**', is a favourite one with Aymé. He uses another faerie image to pursue it in '**Conte de Noël**', where 'l'enfant Noël' distributes joy to the ladies of a brothel instead of to spoilt little rich children, and again in '**Dermuche**' where 'le petit Jésus' comes down to die instead of a morally innocent criminal. '**La Grâce**' explores the same thematic area with a hero who is so virtuous that he is awarded a halo. He has to wear it around the streets of Montmartre. Here Aymé is again combining two genres; the halo is essentially a faerie accessory but the situation—a mortal has a strange gift conferred upon him within his own context—is clearly fantastic. Duperrier is quite embarrassed by his distinction.

At first he replaces his bowler hat with a wide-brimmed one to hide the halo, but finally tries to get rid of it. This is where the common notion of virtue comes under fire. It seems reasonable to the victim that he should simply sin to get rid of it. This neat paradox—a saint trying desperately to sin—provides Aymé with some very comic situations. Duperrier is innocent of lust, for example, and has to consult 'un livre révoltant où se trouvait exposé, sous forme d'un enseignement clair et direct, l'essentiel de la luxure' (*VP* 95). He tries pride, anger, greed, envy, laziness and avarice as well as lust but all to no avail. He finally becomes a pimp on the boulevard de Clichy, counting the night's takings by the light of his halo. Aymé's notion of sin and virtue is no ordinary one. His spokesman is perhaps the Devil in *Les Jumeaux du diable* when he says to St. Peter:

—Vraiment le monde est trop vertueux. C'est un scandale. Tu ne recevrais pas dix âmes par an, si le monde allait raisonnablement.

(*JD* 10)

In '**Samson**', Aymé pastiches the biblical story line while adapting it to his own ends. His hero has magic hair and a lucid knowledge of his destiny, but Aymé adds to the psychological interest of the theme by describing a superman who is 'désespérément seul', who aspires to mediocrity and anonymity and whose submission to Dalila is quite conscious. '**Samson**' is a rather heavy tale and not as typical of Aymé's style as the lighter hearted and much freer adaptation of the same motif in '**Le faux policier**', where Martin's mistress Dalila insists he shave off his moustache, thus changing his appearance and bringing catastrophe.

The entertainer in Aymé is very fond of parody. This comes out again in '**Le Mendiant**', which adapts the biblical Nativity theme to a modern American setting. Aymé's intermediary is the *pauvre type* (American style) Theo Bradley who is pitied by all his friends because he has to drive a car that is several years old. One night Bradley is visited by an angel who takes him to a ramshackle Detroit garage where a young couple are just putting the finishing touches to a car that has taken them nine months' effort. We witness the ecstatic moment of completion ('il est né!') and the arrival of three worshippers from afar bearing petrol, oil and water. From what seems to be a dream, Bradley wakes with a sense of purpose: he will be the prophet of 'Le Grand Moteur' and will found 'La Grande Eglise Motorisée'. The tale grows bitter now as Aymé satirizes the commercialization of the new religion and acidly underlines the American worship of the motor car. He sketches the repressed, hypocritically puritan, racist matriarchy that preoccupied him in the plays *Louisiane* and *La Mouche bleue*. Aymé was criticizing the United States from first-hand experience. In 1949 he had been invited to the United States by *Collier's* magazine, which planned to publish his impressions in article form. '**Le Mendiant**' was part of his offering. It was politely declined.

Aymé's rather liberal attitude towards literary convention is visible again in the special case of *Les Contes du chat perché.* This collection is one of Aymé's best-known works. It won him the Prix Chanteclair and has been consistently re-edited ever since its first publication. In 1979 several of the tales were even adapted for the theatre by a young Parisian troupe, the Compagnie de la Licorne. Outwardly, these stories seem to have been written for children. Aymé intimated quite early that they were part of 'l'art d'être grand-père' and that they were written for his granddaughter Françoise, but he later confessed: 'Mes contes pour enfants, je les ai écrits pour moi-même. Je ne crois pas à la littérature enfantine.' His second *prière d'insérer* to these tales was probably more honest: like so many so-called children's books, **Les Contes du chat perché** were 'écrits pour les enfants âgés de quatre à soixante-quinze ans'. For Marcel Aymé there was certainly an element of personal nostalgia in them too: they harked back to his games of 'chat' in the Cours St Maurice at Dôle and to the happy days of his early childhood in Villers-Robert and his adventures with his cousins in his uncle's mill.

These tales are special in two ways: firstly, because Aymé makes a faerie world apart out of a very real setting, and, secondly, because some of the unreal within that world is distinctly fantastic in character. The seventeen stories are set in a special farmyard and centred on the farmer's two young daughters, Delphine ('l'aînée') and Marinette ('la plus blonde') and their animal friends. This is an ideal frame for faerie. Aymé encourages the feeling of this being a world apart not only by setting the action in the farmyard and its surrounds but also because the stories feature an esoteric child's point of view. The farm is a children's world like so many that have been exploited in literature, an

> univers enfantin séparé, replié sur lui-même et où peuvent faire irruption l'improbable, l'étrange et même l'impossible.

We are much closer here to the Wonderland of Peter Pan or Alice than to a Fairyland of giants and magic spells. Alice and Wendy are surely related to Delphine and Marinette and a long line of young girls whose imagination and sensitivity have been exploited to link fantasy and reality.

The magic of the farm mainly surrounds the animals. It is not the simple magic proposition of Aymé's earlier novel *La Jument verte,* where he proposed a storytelling horse with a highly refined sensuality; here it is much more episodic. The animals can talk and play humanized roles and to a certain extent they can use their reason.

Aymé is clearly conscious of the tradition which produced the 'Cochon-tyran' and the 'Renard-fripon' but he varies his characterization. His fox is the traditional wily creature but his pig is usually stupid, vain and rather nasty, his duck very clever and helpful, his cat rather passive and his rooster proud, arrogant and even treacherous. Yet any stability from story to story depends on Aymé's whim and on the girls' imagination. The pig turns out smart enough to play the detective in **'Les Vaches'** and the ass, normally stupid and obstinate of course, appears as sensitive and intelligent in **'Le mauvais jars'**.

Most of the action depends on contact between the girls and their animal friends. There is complicity and understanding only between them. The girls try to educate an ox; the animals help the girls with their homework and troop into the classroom to see the results. As well as occasionally adopting human roles, the beasts change roles among themselves: a deer swaps with an ox, a panther comes to live on the farm, a wolf wants to play 'chat perché' with the girls and a duck turns world-traveller. Animals talking and thinking is not an end to the magic. Aymé waves his wand once more and we see blindness transferred by telepathy, a hen that changes into an elephant, two white cows that disappear and a horse that shrinks to the size of a rooster. The fantastic even touches Delphine and Marinette to change them into an ass and a horse. This potentially frightening situation is eased somewhat by the fact that it occurs within a frame where such events seem almost acceptable.

The magic often starts with mischief; one of the girls' pranks backfires on them or one of the animals does something unnatural. A frequent story pattern starts with the parents going to town for the day and warning their daughters against doing one particular thing in their absence. Of course Delphine and Marinette disobey and promptly get into a fix. Their situation worsens as they try to repair the damage and the ominous moment when their parents will return approaches. This tension is usually eased by a convenient last-minute solution. It is the girls' curious predicaments and the inventive solutions that provide much of the charm of these tales.

Delphine and Marinette's pranks are caused by their very innocence. Aymé is presenting the world through unconditioned eyes. He has created a frame where the girls can question the constraints, the conventions and the routines of the adult world and find them lacking. There is fantasy not only in the metamorphoses but also in the girls' minds: perhaps the wolf would make a nice playmate after all; perhaps the donkey is really quite clever despite what people say; and why should a panther not live on the farm? It is their fecund and strangely logical imagination that often provokes the magic. In **'Les Boîtes de peinture'** Delphine and Marinette try to draw the two white cows, but it is not possible to draw them on white paper, say the girls, or at least they would not be visible: 'C'est comme si vous n'existiez pas.' So the offended animals promptly disappear. The animals apply the same innocent process to the girls' homework. The problem is to calculate how many trees there are in a hypothetical forest, so the animals simply set out to count the trees in their own real forest. And when the girls want it to rain so they will not have to go and visit their nasty old aunt, what more natural solution than to ask Alphonse the cat, transposed from the Aymé apartment on the rue Paul-Féval, to wash his whiskers?

Naturally the parents cannot participate in this innocence. They are depersonalized, being referred to and even addressed as 'les parents'. In fact the other adults suffer the same fate, becoming 'la maîtresse', 'l'inspecteur' and 'l'aveugle'. Even aunt Mélina and uncle Alfred tend to be stereotyped figures. When they are active, the parents are always enemy figures. They seem hard-hearted, suspicious and miserly. What little dialogue they are accorded is unsympathetic: they spend their time scolding the girls or else rather optimistically warning them to 'soyez sages . . .', and they whisper ominously to each other as they watch the pig or the chicken growing plumper each day. There is a communication barrier represented by different attitudes to the animals. For the practical parents they are beasts of burden and work and candidates for the cooking pot, while for the girls they are playmates. The parents' main function in this faerie is obviously to represent the parallel, real world, the world of farm chores, homework and the threatened 'pain sec', a world to which the girls usually return after each episodic tale.

Strange things may occur and the girls will get into all sorts of scrapes, but in the end all will be put right. The animals will be restored to their proper forms and proportions, Delphine and Marinette will cease to be a horse and an ass and the blind man will retrieve his blindness. The kidnapped hens are brought back, the lost cows are found and the little black rooster can employ all the guile he can muster but will end up *au vin* in the pot all the same.

Often a return to reality includes a moral ending. Good deeds are rewarded and pride, hard-heartedness, arrogance and treachery are suitably punished whether in the pig, the rooster, the drunken soldier or the parents. Yet these moral punishments almost never involve Delphine and Marinette. Grandfather Aymé is clearly trying to teach the girls a lesson without actually punishing them. The threatened punishments for disobedience are miraculously waived (an exception: their 'affreux péchés' of falsehood and disobedience in '**Le petit coq noir**'). Sometimes this is simply because Aymé finds the parents too malicious: the girls fool their parents and allow Alphonse the cat to escape his drowning in '**La Patte du chat**' because the parents were being quite unjust. Sometimes it is because the girls have had a fright and already learned their lesson: they are temporarily eaten by the wolf in '**Le Loup**', harshly whipped as animals in '**L'Ane et le cheval**' and made to feel thoroughly ashamed in '**Les Boîtes de peinture**'. But more often it is simply that the girls have got into a fix through their own innocence or generosity: they are led into mischief in '**Le Loup**' and '**Le petit coq noir**'. Good intentions and the saviour figure of uncle Alfred retrieve the situation in '**Le Mouton**'. The girls seem to deserve punishment in '**Les Cygnes**' because they have again disobeyed their parents, but their pure hearts and good intentions save them once more.

Delphine and Marinette are not wilfully disobedient; it is just that girls will be girls. . . . This same reasoning is even applied to the animals. The pig's raving vanity should perhaps be punished in '**La Buse et le cochon**' but he is let off because Nature made him the ugliest of all; and

when the wolf eats the girls he is only being his natural self. So when he is painfully cut open to free them he is sewn up again instead of being left to die. And in any case, he seems to have learned a lesson so why punish him? It is he, rather than the scolding parents or a moralizing Aymé who rounds off the tale: 'Je vous jure qu'à l'avenir on ne me prendra plus à être aussi gourmand. Et d'abord, quand je verrai des enfants je commencerai par me sauver' (*CP* 182).

The reprieve in '**Les Cygnes**' gives the entertainer in Aymé a chance to show off his talents in a superb ending. The girls have crossed the road in spite of their parents' admonitions and are being held prisoner by some swans who turn out to be harsh disciplinarians. They are finally liberated by a wise old swan and returned to the farmhouse just in time to welcome their parents. But the effort costs their liberator his life: it is his swansong that will enchant the parents just long enough to let the girls scurry home. The final irony lies in the parents' comment: 'Quel dommage que vous n'ayez pas traversé la route tout à l'heure. Un cygne a chanté sur les prés' (*CP* 325).

Les Contes du chat perché is the work of a storyteller much more than of a moralist. This is clear above all in his endings. When the animals cause an uproar in the classroom trying to help the girls with their arithmetic homework, the teacher gives them 'zéro de conduite'. But the inspector, fortuitously present that day, saves the story by giving them the 'croix d'honneur' for their originality! This is the Aymé who, having allowed an ass a certain measure of cunning to teach the nasty gander a lesson, rounds off his tale with:

> Aussi n'est-il plus question, depuis ce jour-là, de la bêtise de l'âne; et l'on dit, au contraire, d'un homme à qui l'on veut faire compliment de son intelligence qu'il est fin comme un âne.
>
> (*CP* 264)

Aymé has often been called a fabulist more than a moralist. Indeed there is something of the simple world of La Fontaine or the medieval *fabliaux* in stories like '**Le petit coq noir**', '**Le Paon**' or '**Le mauvais jars**', where the animals interact among themselves. The moral character of this world cannot be denied. It has been stressed by almost all those who have written on Aymé. Yet for him the purity lies not so much in the moral character as in the lack of artificial adult preoccupations. In his first *prière d'insérer* Aymé wrote:

> Je les écrivais pour reposer mes lecteurs éventuels de leurs tristes aventures où l'amour et l'argent sont si bien entremêlés qu'on les prend à chaque instant l'un pour l'autre, ce qui est forcément fatigant. Mes histoires sont donc des histoires simples, sans amour et sans argent.

The fact that we are adventuring in a moral world should not necessarily provoke a search for an individual lesson at the end of each story. This has been a common failing among commentators, who have felt obliged to label as many stories as possible. The formulae 'A chacun sa fonction dans la vie', 'la sottise des gens qui vont à l'encontre de leurs talents naturels' or the more complicated 'la dangereuse séduction dont jouissent les révolutionnaires dans les milieux intellectuels' may not be actually wrong, but to sum up Aymé's tales like this is absolutely to miss the essence of his talent. This kind of formulation (and thus limitation) quite destroys the *conteur*'s nostalgic, whimsical, grandfatherly charm. Such activity is as futile as the criticism of André Rousseaux, who missed the point entirely when he accused Aymé of 'lèse-réalisme', asserting that 'Si les bêtes parlaient, elles tiendraient un tout autre langage.' Aymé's ironic reply is contained in his second *prière d'insérer*:

> Il avait bien raison. Rien n'interdit de croire en effet que si les bêtes parlaient, elles parleraient de politique ou de l'avenir de la science dans les îles Aléoutiennes. Peut-être même qu'elles feraient de la critique littéraire avec distinction.

. . . . .

Jules Verne and the comtesse de Ségur are two of Aymé's most often avowed sources of inspiration. Ségur's influence is easily seen in the *Contes du chat perché*, but it is only when we move towards Aymé's fantastic vein that we encounter a thin vein of science fiction which might be a product of Aymé's penchant for Verne. For Aymé, science fiction seems to be an extension of the fantastic. He avoids the traditional thematic material—interstellar invasions, space stations and one-eyed Martians:

> Habituellement, je n'éprouve pas de sentiment bien vif pour le genre science-fiction. Dans la réalité, les exploits des spoutniks ne m'ont jamais fait battre le coeur.

Aymé's science fiction is more humanized, like his faerie and like the more traditional fantastic. He often uses future man to focus attention on present man.

Aymé's most significant contribution to the science fiction genre is a long and serious *nouvelle* called *Pastorale*. He launches into the futurism of a seventeenth Republic where a series of skyscraper villages shelter the whole of France. On the surface this is pure fantasy but on closer examination it is an Orwellian world closely based on reality, reflecting present problems like over-population, centralization and government control of all aspects of life. Aymé describes a society where the social authorities exercise total control over the individual, the kind of society that Aymé foresees and criticizes not only in stories like 'La Carte' and the play *La Convention Belzébir* but also in several polemic articles devoted to civil liberties. It is a society where nothing is left to chance. The number and sex of all children are regulated, dreams are monitored, excess population is exterminated, all desires find immediate satisfaction and poets are re-educated in mathematics and the physical sciences in case they upset society's logic. The ugly buildings and lifeless inhabitants of *Pastorale* al-

low Aymé to exercise his acid wit against many of our social and political customs and institutions.

Futuristic imagination sparkles even more darkly in a story called 'La Fille du shérif' and subtitled 'Le roman que je n'écrirai jamais'. This is an undeveloped sketch for a longer story, rather clumsily blending Aymé's black humour and his post-Liberation political views. Several of his magazine and newspaper articles of the period strongly criticize the government's attempts to tie France's defence to America and N.A.T.O. Written in 1951 and supposedly set in 1953, 'La Fille du shérif' tells of an atomic war between Russia and America using France as the battleground. France is obliterated and then abolished by the U.N. Most of the French have been killed and the rest are enslaved by the United States. Aymé once again takes the opportunity to scourge de Gaulle: during the atomic war a government of 'la France libre' is set up in Missouri and their radio broadcasts tell the French to give their lives willingly for France. Their post-war *épuration* executes 100,000 and imprisons twice that number.

The fantastic genre seems to be less governed by literary convention than Fairyland or Flash Gordon and more widely accepted as a tool of 'legitimate' literature. Aymé takes full advantage of this freedom. In Fairyland, Aymé's man has worn seven-league boots, made love to a dryad and defeated a magic ogre, but here his Everyman, so often called Martin, will be more personally and more disturbingly involved. Yet Aymé still anchors his fantastic creations in reality. Reality is his source material even more visibly than it was with his faerie. One of the rules accepted by most writers of the unreal is that one must not get too far from the recognizably real:

> Pour arriver à créer une oeuvre viable, en quelque domaine que ce soit, il est nécessaire de s'éloigner assez du réel pour le dominer, tout en restant assez près de lui pour ne pas le perdre de vue.

Like most creative minds, Aymé starts with known elements and rearranges them rather than indulging in total creation. He can suggest that two minds may inhabit the same body or that one being can have multiple bodies, but they will be real bodies. They will never have three arms or two heads. Aymé never goes as far as the grotesque. Man may be given a halo or a changed face, but not green horns or a tail. Aymé's fantastic images are usually either extensions or reversals of reality. An extension is proposed in *Le Décret*, where instead of the government advancing the clock one hour in summer, the move proposed is seventeen years in order to reach the end of an interminable war. 'La Liste' is an extension of a different kind: a poor farmer has so many daughters that he has to have a list to remember their names. When one name is accidentally torn off the list, he forgets the particular daughter and the poor girl disappears. A reversal of reality is the basis of 'La Grâce', where Duperrier wears his halo despite what is normally regarded as a life of sin. Mostly Aymé tries to reverse or extend the more certain elements of man's existence—death, space, time, identity—so that our shock is all the greater.

Spectres, vampires and werewolves, the traditional fantastic creatures, do not interest Aymé much more than 'les exploits des spoutniks'. The closest he comes to this tradition is in *Les Jumeaux du diable* with its supernatural twins. It is man and his society that concern Aymé. Much of his fantastic is concerned with giving new capacities to man and then exploring the consequences. Just as the faerie of **'L'Huissier'**, **'La Fosse aux péchés'** or **'Légende poldève'** and the science fiction of *Pastorale* were used to mask social criticism, so Aymé's fantastic is put to this use. In **'Dermuche'** capital punishment and the cruelty of prison authorities chained by impersonal regulations come under strong attack. The simpleton Dermuche is condemned for a triple murder but he has no comprehension of a crime he committed simply because he liked the tinkling of a music box. He is morally innocent, having 'une petite âme claire comme une eau de source' (*VP* 122). Dermuche has long talks with the prison chaplain about 'le petit Jésus' and on the eve of his execution he writes to heaven to be allowed to have his little music box when he reaches paradise. That night Dermuche's soul dominates his body to the extent of transforming him into a new-born baby complete with the same tattoos. It seems that the soft-hearted Aymé has granted Dermuche a reprieve, and this would be a typical Aymé ending, but this time he is not in the mood for reprieves. The chief warder is stubbornly unmoved: 'je ne veux pas d'histoires'. The rules are the rules even in the face of a miracle. We are treated to several pages of Aymé's blackest irony as the guards coldly verify Dermuche's birthmark and fingerprints and carry the child up to the guillotine regardless. As with *Pastorale* and **'La Fille du shérif'**, Aymé is using the unreal mode to complement the real mode; he criticized the judicial system and capital punishment in several polemic articles and in his notorious play *La Tête des autres*.

Aymé's satire is not quite as bitter when he underlines the commercial exploitation of creative artistry in *La bonne peinture*. The fantastic premise of this *nouvelle* is a concretization of the intellectual satisfaction derived from the contemplation of a work of art. Lafleur's canvases have very special qualities:

> sa peinture était devenue si riche, si sensible, si fraîche, si solide, qu'elle constituait une véritable nourriture et non pas seulement pour l'esprit, mais bien aussi pour le corps. (. . .) Le menu variait selon le sujet du tableau, sa composition et son coloris, mais il était toujours très soigné, très abondant et il n'y manquait même pas la boisson.
>
> (*VP* 171)

Like **'Avenue Junot'**, *La bonne peinture* is a rambling frolic through Aymé's familiar Montmartre with his artist friends, but here there is more direction to the tale. The basic situation is familiar: the poor but happy artist whose lifestyle is threatened by fame and fortune and the grasping parasites—critics, gallery-owners and journalists—who are attracted by his success. Aymé exploits his premise for its comic potential by satirizing the American scientists who try to analyse Lafleur's gift and the art critics who

are nonplussed by the tangible qualities of his work. In another comic scene the dealer Hermèce gets indigestion from feasting his eyes.

Of course there is a darker side to this humour. Hermèce and his fellow parasites think of nothing but profit. The dealer doesn't even want to tell Lafleur about his talent, and buys up the paintings as fast as he can. The state soon puts a stop to this by nationalizing Lafleur, and Aymé's cynical wit now describes the artist as one of France's 'instruments de production' with a factory and the associated bureaucracy. Art has become 'efficace', a political tool and a means to material rather than intellectual comfort.

Aymé obviously found the *conte fantastique* well suited to social criticism. More than with his faerie, the entertainer now often takes second place to a more serious side of Aymé. Many of his ridiculous situations are used to present parallel realities through which Aymé can snipe at the corresponding real situations. This process is used particularly well in **'La Carte'**. Yet in general, Aymé's fantastic is still much more personal than his faerie; it is above all the more individual human failings that he underlines. The social or political criticism is often accessory to his story's primary effect.

The little ironic twists introduced into reality often provide Aymé or his protagonist with a rather special position, a privileged point of view from which to reassess reality. The short story seldom allows room to discuss this advantage and it is the novel *La Jument verte* that provides Aymé's most explicit comments. When the painter Murdoire endows a canvas of a green mare with the gift of observation so that she can spy on the Haudouin family from her wall, the mare offers her remarks directly to the reader:

> Je m'appliquai à observer mes hôtes, à réfléchir sur le spectacle qu'ils me livraient de leur vie intime. (. . .) Tandis que l'observateur ambulant ne peut s'attacher à découvrir dans le monde que les harmonies des grands nombres et le secret des séries, l'observateur immobile a cet avantage de surprendre les habitudes de la vie.
>
> (*JV* 21)

A much more personal advantage is gained for Cérusier by his change of face in *La belle image*. Since his friends no longer recognize him, he can overhear what they say about him behind his back. But what he hears is not always to his liking:

> Tiens, dit Joubert le sculpteur, voilà la bonne de Cérusier. A propos, qu'est-ce qu'il devient, ce pauvre Cérusier?
>
> —Pauvre, protesta Garnier. Il n'est pas à plaindre.
>
> —Je ne dis pas qu'il soit à plaindre, mais c'est quand même un pauvre type.
>
> Quoiqu'il en eût dit, le ton de ses paroles exprimait une commisération à mon égard.
>
> (*BI* 43)

Cérusier, too, has time to reflect on this new ability to see beneath his own façade, 'examiner sa vie avec un lucide regard d'outre-tombe et pénétrer en étranger dans ses propres secrets' (*BI* 85).

The novel *La belle image* deserves in many ways to be treated as a short story. It starts with the same absurd premise and proceeds to explore the consequences and the protagonist's reactions. It is almost as if an ideal short story situation has been stretched and padded artificially to fill a novel. In fact this kind of situation is much better suited to the pace and concision of a short story. Much the same could be said of the play *Les Oiseaux de lune* except that there Aymé stretches his situation with much more subtlety and variety.

An almost identical advantage is engineered in **'Le Nain'**, where the dwarf Valentin suddenly grows up and is not recognized any more. The truths he overhears are more flattering than Cérusier's but equally revealing. Delphine and Marinette are given an unpleasant insight into what it is like to be an animal on their parents' farm in **'L'Ane et le cheval'**, and a spoilt young *bourgeoise* in **'La Fabrique'** is given a much more instructive appreciation of her own existence by means of a jump in time. Valérie is told that if she does not stop biting her fingernails by Christmas there will be no presents this year. We see her wake on Christmas Eve to discover that she has indeed bitten them again:

> Elle eut un mouvement de retraite comme pour échapper à la triste réalité, et croyant s'enfoncer sous les couvertures, elle s'enfonça dans la nuit des temps et de cent vingt ans en arrière, en sorte qu'elle se retrouva en 1845.
>
> (*EJ* 121–22)

This trip is a lesson in humility. Valérie is put in the position of invisible observer of a day in the life of an underprivileged family. This new reality chills her to the bone. The youngest son is dying of consumption but he is still sent to work in the freezing factory because the family needs the pittance he will earn and above all because if he is left at home his retarded brother will probably assault him. Hippolyte knows he is going to die, just as many of his young colleagues have that winter, but he has heard of the visits that 'l'enfant Noël' pays to little rich children and wants to see a Christmas tree before he dies. At the end of his terrible day's work, the speechless Valérie follows him home. On the way, he hears hammering: 'C'est Papa qui cloue mon arbre de Noël', but in fact his father is making a little coffin. Valérie can bear it no more: taking him by the hand she succeeds in translating them both back to her century. On Christmas morning she gives him her tree and her presents and is just about to tell her parents she has a little brother for Christmas when his exhaustion and happiness finally kill him and he disappears. **'La Fabrique'** is a rarity in Aymé's work, a story completely devoid of humour. It was the last short story Aymé ever wrote and was published after his death. One of the most moving of Aymé's tales, **'La Fabrique'** was very successfully adapted for television by Pascal Thomas and shown on Christmas Eve 1979.

Cérusier's 'coup d'oeil oblique' is also reflected throughout the **Contes du chat perché** in the innocent, unconditioned eyes through which Delphine and Marinette interpret the world, but a richer exploitation of it is found in **Le Décret**, with its voyage seventeen years into the future and abrupt return. The anti-serious Aymé uses this premise to provoke several comic situations. The narrator tries to return a cycle he hired during his stay in the future and discovers that the shop still sells umbrellas! The owner, who has the same name as the cycle seller, finds rather ridiculous the idea that one day he might sell 'bécanes'. Seriousness returns as the narrator continues:

> Tandis qu'il parlait ainsi, je comparais à ce jeune visage frais et rieur, un autre visage de dix-sept ans plus âgé, dont un lupus déformait tout un côté.
>
> (*PM* 116)

It is this ability to see through present appearances to a future reality that is the most disquieting aspect of the narrator's position and the most fruitful for Aymé's social commentary too. Here he meets a friend in the *métro*:

> Il est très déprimé et me confie qu'il est dans une situation extrêmement difficile. Je regarde avec curiosité cet être minable qui, dans une dizaine d'années, se trouvera à la tête d'une fortune colossale, malhonnêtement gagnée à de scandaleux trafics. Tandis qu'il me parle de sa misère présente, je le revois dans sa future opulence. (. . .) je suis partagé entre la compassion et le dégoût que m'inspire sa brillante carrière.
>
> (*PM* 123–24)

The splitting effect of this privileged position is the main theme of this long humanist *nouvelle*. The victim can see things that are invisible to others. He does not always like what he sees; he quickly rejects his privilege, effectively 'forgetting' the future. Like Samson, he wants to be nothing more than an ordinary man.

Aymé's physical unrealities also serve him particularly well by providing a tangible image for an abstract process, sentiment or quality. This often borders on the traditional role of the *fantastique intérieur* with its physical representations of psychological activity. Aymé is not so much a moralist here as a very serious humanist. **Le Décret** gives a physical dimension to the feeling of *déjà vu* and, as young Valentin changes more and more of his friends into birds in *Les Oiseaux de lune,* we are afforded a bleak look at the effects of absolute power on man's soul. Both of these show a particularly serious Aymé. His lighter tone returns in the use of Duperrier's halo to represent his inner virtue in **'La Grâce'**, or in the concretization of inner satisfactions in **La bonne peinture**. **'Le Romancier Martin'** is perhaps the most fruitful example of the mental becoming physical. Here Aymé uses the fantastic to give a concrete dimension to the experience of artistic creation. He adopts the Pygmalion gift of life motif (akin to what the French theoreticians call the *statue vivante*) in portraying a novelist who creates his characters so thoroughly that they come to life and manage to exist on the same plane as their author. They have a will of their own and try to change the course of their novel. Finally some of them even escape from Martin's control. The powerless novelist confesses: 'J'abandonne mes personnages, mais leur vie continue.'

The special experience of childhood is to some extent made concrete in *Les Contes du chat perché* and Aymé proposes a tangible image for the next stage of the human cycle in **'Le Nain'**. Valentin's body becomes adult but he still has the innocence of a child. Like the narrator in *Le Décret* and the centaur in **'Fiançailles'**, he is torn between what he was and what he is becoming. His metamorphosis also reflects Aristide's potentially traumatic discovery of sex through the eyes of someone who knows nothing of social convention and constraint. His clumsy but spontaneous advances to Germina are rejected. The ex-dwarf tries frantically to learn another circus trick so that he can stay in the circus and win back the love that Germina bore him. But that love was innocent and can never be the same. He reluctantly leaves the artificial, protected, childhood life of the circus where he no longer belongs and goes to face the adult responsibilities of earning a living and forming mature relationships. M. Barnaboum finally announces: 'Le nain est mort.'

The physical image in **'Le Couple'** intensifies the next stages in the human cycle: marriage and divorce. Antoine and Valérie love each other so much that their bodies fuse together into one. Society's sexism is reflected in the choice of Antoine's body to express the union. Valérie lacks physical presence and effectively loses her identity in this marriage. She finds no fulfilment wearing her husband's body so the union disintegrates after a few weeks. The experience of death is explored somewhat less seriously in **'La Carte'** and **'Le Temps mort'**, which propose a sort of relative death through the total disappearance of a victim for a short period. But Aymé is more interested in the manipulation of time in these stories and, apart from touching on man's egoistic resentment that the world will keep on turning when he is gone, hardly explores the notion of death any further.

Man's solitude, a strong element in the modern literary conception of man, is often Aymé's primary target in these fantastic intensifications. Newly unrecognizable characters are placed in a situation where their isolation from others is increased by their fantastic affliction. After his face change, Cérusier feels that 'Cette solitude soudaine dans un monde qui ne vous connaît plus, c'est une chose épouvantable' (*BI* 90) and the dwarf Valentin feels cut off in the same way when his metamorphosis removes him from his friends:

> Valentin regardait Mlle Germina galoper sur la piste.
> Debout sur son cheval, et le bras tendu vers la foule,

> l'écuyère répondait par des sourires aux applaudissements, et Valentin songeait qu'aucun de ces sourires n'était pour lui. Il se sentait las et honteux de sa solitude.
>
> (*NA* 27)

Valentin is not spared Aymé's irony: his happiness lay in his deformity itself.

The most striking intensification of man's solitude is probably the image of the superman Samson who feels cut off from other men because of his magic hair and wants to return to the ranks of ordinary mortals to discover 'la sensation d'équilibre que procure une force musculaire à la mesure de l'homme'. Despite its rather faerie character, Samson's magic hair serves as a fantastic intensification of the absurdity of his condition and provides a physical metaphor for his frustration when faced with the forces of a destiny he cannot control. This is another reason why he tries to have his magic hair cut off: his superhuman strength is too strong for his merely human will. He is not in control of himself:

> Ma force m'apparaissait comme une personne surajoutée à la mienne, un maître qui se servait de mes membres, de mes mains, de mon corps et disposait sans discussion de ma volonté. Ecrasé sous la pression de ce géant et emporté par son élan imbécile, je n'étais qu'une créature dérisoire, reléguée dans un coin de mon être et moins libre que ne peut l'être un paralytique.

Samson has a split image of himself as man and superman, 'assis entre deux sièges'. He is very conscious of his destiny as national liberator but he wants to be just human. The impossibility of this is brought out by his symbolic attempt at suicide: he goes to Gaza looking for a girl who will sell him to the Philistines. Shaved, blinded and chained to a mill-stone, he seems to have escaped the 'présence étrangère' and found his human self. But his hair is beginning to grow again . . .

Aymé had already tried to give a physical dimension to grace and free will by describing man's life as predestined and controlled by a guiding master in *Les Jumeaux du diable*, but the novel's length and heavy style negate the potential advantage of Aymé's graphic image. *Les Jumeaux du diable*, like *La belle image*, is easier to appreciate if it is considered more as a short story mistakenly stretched to novel length. The opening of the novel reflects the tongue-in-cheek tone and the easy style that were to become the trade-marks of the *conteur*:

> A travers les infinis où les dimensions se reposent, Satan chevauchait un manche à balai qui est le véhicule ordinaire aux créatures infernales d'occident. Il avait hâte, murmurant à chaque instant: Keibal, Ikal, formule incomparable pour presser l'allure des manches à balai
>
> (*JD* 9)

and Aymé follows up the image with the sort of proposition that was to become the backbone of his short stories:

—Céphas, j'ai rêvé un jeu amusant. J'imaginais deux hommes de la Terre, deux hommes tout pareils, d'âme et d'apparence, (. . .) Je n'ai pas imaginé plus avant, Céphas. Seulement, je m'interrogeais s'ils étaient promis au Ciel ou à l'Enfer.

Le Diable sourit.

—même, je me suis demandé s'il se pouvait que l'un fût damné et l'autre élu de Dieu.

(*JD* 10–11)

But what follows is an over-long and rather unimaginative exploitation of the early momentum of the story and is totally lacking in the charm of Aymé's later developments of this kind of proposition. The novel is a clumsy mixture of the mysterious and the banal. Aymé clearly sensed the failure of this, his first venture into the unreal: he always refused to have the novel reprinted, calling it 'un très mauvais roman'.

'Le Romancier Martin' shows what *Les Jumeaux du diable* might have become had it been written ten years later. Aymé explores a similar thematic area through the image of a god-author who cannot refrain from ending his novels with a massacre:

Il y avait un romancier, son nom était Martin, qui ne pouvait pas s'empêcher de faire mourir les principaux personnages de ses livres, et même les personnages de moindre importance. Tous ces pauvres gens, pleins de vigueur et d'espoir au premier chapitre, mouraient comme d'épidémie dans les vingt ou trente dernières pages, et bien souvent dans la force de l'âge.

(*DM* 9)

Siné's humorous sketch on the cover of the Livre de Poche edition shows bodies sandwiched between pages of manuscript while Martin eyes off the fleeing remnants of his characters, wondering whom to impale next with his giant pen. The main action of this story is a revolt by Armandine Soubiron, who comes to plead with her creator and 'maître' in a prayer situation. She is upset by her 'fatalité' and Martin's excessive use of arbitrary power over his characters' destinies. Martin protests that he is not really in control and Armandine comes to realize that she is free as long as she doesn't regard herself as a prisoner of destiny. She finally escapes completely from Martin's novel.

The frantic running out of time as man rushes towards his absurd death is given a physical dimension in 'Le Temps mort', where another Martin simply ceases to exist every second day. Aymé has also given a solid dimension to the relativity of time. For Martin, time actually does pass twice as fast as for everyone else. His solitude is intensified by the difficulty of communication with those around him. His mistress is used to bring out the way two people develop at different rates:

Son amour, qui durait depuis deux années pleines, n'avait ni la fraîcheur, ni l'élan que gardait celui de Martin, âgé d'une année seulement.

(*DM* 107)

Aymé exploits Martin's predicament, drawing brief glimmers of comedy from his pathetic ruses to make time go more slowly and from the situations he finds himself in when he suddenly comes back to life.

The fantastic time rationing of 'La Carte' is probably Aymé's most striking attempt to give a concrete dimension to the abstract. Here, too, the relativity of time is intensified. He describes the inhuman logic of a governmental decree that institutes time rationing, a situation reminiscent of the authoritarian excesses of *Pastorale*. Those citizens whose work is regarded as socially productive will live full time while all unproductive consumers will be rationed by time cards and 'tickets de vie'. The relativity of time is well underlined by Aymé's marvellous stretching month. A humble painter may experience a month of only fifteen days while the necessary butcher lives the full thirty-one and a corrupt official or a wily black-marketeer may stretch the month even further! This relativity leads to interesting problems of communication. How can the painter and the butcher share their experiences, since for one of them time goes twice as fast as for the other and a month only contains half as much experience? How can Flegmon arrange a rendezvous with his mistress when the day in question will have a different date for each of them?

This kind of intriguing invention allows Aymé to touch on potentially complicated concepts of time and then move on quickly before the story is slowed down by intellectualism. Aymé's story of fluid time is also a pretext for him to explore the humorous consequences of his premise: Monsieur Dumont arranges to have his fifteen days of existence in the second half of the month so as to avoid his shrewish wife, while the Roquenton couple come back to life in their bed separated by Lucette's lover. The guilty pair pretend not to know each other but the outraged husband finds their story 'bien invraisemblable'. But Aymé is a realist as well as a humorist; there will always be serious consequences too. The government's draconian decree only remains valid for as long as it takes the resourceful few to profit by it or find a way around it. One of Flegmon's rivals takes advantage of his temporary annihilation to manoeuvre against his candidature for the Académie Française. All efforts to change to a useful job are soon declared illegal, and very few citizens succeed in their attempts to obtain additional time tickets. So we soon see more sinister solutions. Flegmon and many others take to living at twice the pace, eating twice as much to make up for the days when they will not exist. To his credit, Flegmon also tries to work at twice the pace. Trading in time tickets begins, soon to blossom into a flourishing and well-organized black-market. The rich and the wily exploit their weaker fellows and amass large numbers of tickets, and they find themselves able to lengthen a month beyond its normal thirty-one days. Finally the decree has to be repealed because the expected economy of food has not been realized, but not before Aymé has used the consequences of his premise to highlight man's inhumanity, his lack of courage and moral fibre and his blatant egoism, all illustrated by the intellectual Flegmon.

Of course Marcel Aymé is using his fantastic time rationing to comment on reality. '**La Carte**' is not one of Aymé's frivolous fairy tales; it is a very dense story and contains some of his most serious socio-political commentary. And far more than just being a pseudo-philosophical glance at the relativity of time, Aymé's tale is an indictment of events in the France of 1943. The time being taken away by decree in '**La Carte**' is a metaphor for the human life that was being so callously disposed of during the Deportation. Of course the time rationing in '**La Carte**' is a reflection of food rationing, but is not food a source of life? Aymé's pattern of trading, hoarding and black-marketeering closely follows the real patterns induced by wartime food rationing. But Aymé's story of relative death (so it is christened by the trendy set at their death soirées) is really an indictment of French acquiescence in deportation and extermination. The arbitrary but rationalized nature of the time decree:

> Afin de parer à la disette et d'assurer un meilleur rendement de l'élément laborieux de la population, il serait procédé à la mise à mort des consommateurs improductifs

(*PM* 71)

could not fail to suggest Hitlerian policies to the Frenchman of 1943. The economic reasons given reflect some of the lame justifications advanced by the Nazis for their persecution of the Jews in the 1930s. Aymé's choice of victims for the fantastic rationing reflects the Nazis' deportation priorities too: among them are artists, prostitutes, intellectuals and of course Jews. The latter are allowed only half a day's existence per month.

It is above all people's reactions to this crisis that interest Marcel Aymé. Frenchmen who peeped from behind curtains (or worse, who stood and stared in the market-places) as their Jewish countrymen were trucked to the Vélodrome d'Hiver must have felt a little guilty on reading Aymé's fantasy: in '**La Carte**' no one who is untouched by the decree pleads for the victims, no one protests, all are silently thankful that they are not on the list. Not even the Church, in the person of its bishop (a stand-in for Pope Pius XII, who was criticized for not denouncing Hitler's policies forcefully enough) is prepared to condemn the measures. Indeed, many people stand to gain from their colleagues' temporary deaths, just as neighbours and competitors must have often benefited from the Jewish deportations. To the sinister reactionary Maleffroi, society as a whole has benefited from the decree:

> On se rend compte alors à quel point les riches, les chômeurs, les intellectuels et les catins peuvent être dangereux dans une société où ils n'introduisent que le trouble, l'agitation vaine, le dérèglement et la nostalgie de l'impossible.

(*PM* 83–4)

Nor are the victims of the decree totally blameless. None of them seem revolted by the ghastly inhumanity, the absurdity, the arrogance of the decree; they are all too busy trying to gain some personal advantage. Collective resistance is undermined by individual egoism. In Flegmon's diary entry for 18 February Aymé reiterates the often-voiced suggestion that Europe's Jews went into the Vélodrome d'Hiver, the cattle trucks and even the gas chambers without putting up much resistance. That day's entry describes a queue of victims waiting to register for their card. It is very like a *rafle,* complete with French police doing the dirty work and the victims' faces seeming to say, 'Je ne veux pas mourir encore.' But no one really resists. Flegmon tells us of his own 'cri de révolte', but adds that it was bellowed 'mentalement'. This suggestion of the victims' resignation to their fate blends into a brief, pessimistic comment on the speed with which man can adapt to and passively accept this kind of measure, his perception of injustice dulled by the fact that the decree is official and perhaps by the knowledge that many of his fellows are similarly afflicted. Flegmon gets used to his fate with rather unhealthy rapidity: just before his first disappearance he is 'angoissé' but the very next time he expresses 'Aucune appréhension'. Roquenton's second experience of death is even greeted with 'bonne humeur'.

Aymé's experiments with time also lead him to indulge in conventional time travel. He matches Valérie's trip backwards in time in '**La Fabrique**' with a double time movement in *Le Décret*. Cathelin stresses the *conte philosophique* aspect of both '**La Carte**' and *Le Décret* and Dumont devotes a whole chapter to Aymé's time manipulation, referring to the theories of Lavelle, Bergson and Bridoux, but in fact Aymé's stories are much more human, more personal than these critics suggest. Just as Aymé avoids Jules Verne or H. G. Wells time machines, so he avoids getting out of his depth with philosophical complications. The first half of *Le Décret* is Aymé's only failing in this respect. The story starts very slowly because Aymé spends several pages telling of man's growing awareness of compressible, relative, physiological and subjective time and his efforts to control it (including a reference to the previous tale, '**La Carte**'). It is only after eight pages that Aymé's victim starts to tell of the trip to the Jura and the inexplicable (and for him gratuitously mysterious) reversion to 1942, and it takes him several more pages to ascertain that he is in fact the only person who has retained a memory of the future.

At this point the orientation and quality of Aymé's story changes. It is almost as if the learned arguments about time, the narrator's difficulties in adapting to 1959, his trip to Dôle with its mysterious forest and strange fall back through time were nothing more than a pretext. Aymé's *conte philosophique* is really about man's loss of control in his attempts to master time, and his subsequent confusion. Psychological chaos results for a narrator split between time zones and not really knowing where he belongs. As he says, belonging is not just a matter of changing the clock:

> 'Etre d'une époque, pensai-je, c'est sentir l'univers et soimême d'une certaine manière qui appartient à cette époque.'

(*PM* 112)

The discussion of time in the first half of this long *nouvelle* leads to a much more human discussion in the second half. More explicitly than in **'L'Huissier'**, Aymé seems to start a new story: 'Il y avait, à Montmartre, en 1942, un homme qui connaissait l'avenir.' Once again, Aymé sets out to discover the human consequences of the special gift. The same loss of control is visible in **Rechute** when time is reversed by a similar governmental decree. The Assemblée Nationale institutes a 'projet de loi visant à instituer l'année de 24 mois'. This seems reasonable enough except that in Aymé's world it means that everyone's age in years is thereby halved! The result is the kind of split already seen in stories like **'Fiançailles'**, **'Samson'**, **'Le Nain'** and *Le Décret*: Josette now has the body of a child but the experience of an eighteen-year-old. For her it is not only disconcerting but humiliating:

> 'Si mon bébé pleure, j'appelle le grand loup méchant', disait maman. Et papa: 'Comme tu dois être contente! C'est si charmant d'être une vraie petite fille!' Leur enjouement m'était odieux, j'enrageais d'entendre leurs sottises. J'aurais voulu les écarter, les chasser d'auprès de mon lit, mais, en face de ces grandes personnes, je n'étais qu'une fillette de neuf ans que ses larmes ne protégeaient pas.
>
> (*EA* 51)

Youth stages armed revolt against the egoism of their elders' abuse of power and the law is abrogated.

Rechute is a longer, more complicated *nouvelle* than many. The rather high-handed and egoistic actions of the adults, and above all their official hypocrisy and lies, are certainly criticized here. Yet a more pertinent theme in 1950, when the story was published, was young Bernard's collaboration. Aymé describes Bernard's situation and justification very fairly. The young man's metamorphosis leaves him with naturally divided loyalties: while Josette and Pierre revert fully to physical childhood despite their emotional advance, Bernard was just old enough to keep his 'réalités physiologiques' as well as the memory of what they were for. So, although partly a child, he is tempted to side with the adults. When he is accused of collaboration and threatened with the *comité d'épuration* (a practice that Aymé's polemic articles describe as being hardly better than the excesses of the Occupation forces), his defence is that of so many Frenchmen who simply tried to pick the winning side and lost:

> —Je nai pas collaboré! proteste-t-il. Comme tant d'autres, j'ai eu tout d'un coup treize ans, j'ai dû m'accommoder d'une situation moralement très pénible et, matériellement, des plus menaçantes. Bien sûr, l'idée ne m'est pas venue qu'un coup de force pouvait rétablir l'ordre légitime, mais je ne suis pas le seul à n'y avoir pas pensé.
>
> (*EA* 90)

Josette forgives him but only because he is part of the sexuality that she is just rediscovering.

The confusion provoked by these manipulations of time is also a feature of several stories where Aymé explores the multiplicity of man's personality. The duality of someone who is placed in the position of having to choose between two sides of himself recurs in **'Le Passe-muraille'**. Dutilleul is an unassuming *pauvre type* whose monotonous existence is divided between his job as civil servant (third class) and his leisure hours reading the paper and sorting his stamp collection. Aymé has created a particularly ordinary character in order to use him as a vehicle for the clash between reality and fantasy. One day, Dutilleul discovers that he has the ability to walk through walls without encountering the slightest resistance. At first he has no idea what to do with this 'étrange faculté qui semblait ne répondre à aucune de ses aspirations' (*PM* 8). His early, hesitant steps in the world of fantasy provide Aymé with some rather hilarious moments. First of all Dutilleul scares his tyrannical superior Lécuyer by appearing head and shoulders on the wall of his office like a hunting trophy. Having whetted his appetite, Dutilleul takes his crusade to extremes: he terrorizes Lécuyer to such an extent that within a day the poor fellow has lost a pound in weight. Within a week he is fading away, having taken to eating his soup with a fork, and he is spirited off by men in white coats. This light-hearted vein in **'Le Passe-muraille'** is the one chosen by Jean Boyer to exploit in his film version of Aymé's story, made in 1950. Unfortunately, the adaptation made by Boyer and Michel Audiard takes some quite unjustified liberties with Aymé's plot and characters. It fails completely to reproduce Aymé's symbiosis of solid reality and outrageous fantasy, leaning towards the tradition of boulevard comedy instead. It is worth seeing only for Bourvil's performance as Dutilleul.

Aymé's **'Le Passe-muraille'** does not rely much on comedy. Dutilleul's next step is to become a burglar—an ideal profession for someone with his particular talents. By day he continues as the modest Dutilleul but by night he becomes the romantic Garou-Garou who grandly autographs each crime in red chalk. This second self is of course the antithesis of the meek civil servant from which it sprang. Dutilleul soon has the police baffled, and provokes the resignation of the Minister for the Interior, since he can escape at will through the challenging walls of the Santé prison. Dutilleul's adventure is of course a revolt against mediocrity and anonymity. He longs to be someone. When the mysterious Garou-Garou starts to become famous, Dutilleul cannot resist confessing to his colleagues at the ministry, 'Vous savez, Garou-Garou, c'est moi.' Mortified by their scornful laughter, he allows himself to be arrested and is vindicated by the appearance of his photograph on the front page of the paper. His colleagues start growing little goatees like Dutilleul's in homage and admiration; Dutilleul has acceded to full existence. Soon he abandons his dual life, preferring that of Garou-Garou. He buys different clothes, shaves off his beard and takes a new apartment. His metamorphosis seems complete. In reality, of course, Dutilleul is still there beneath the mask.

The duality light-heartedly sketched in **'Le Passe-muraille'** is made tangible in a different way in **'Le Cocu nombreux'**. A vagabond traveller arrives in a village where the relationships between the people he meets begin to seem rather complicated. Slowly he realizes that each person has two complementary bodies. Here is Aymé's description of one of the women he meets:

> C'était pour un quart, une petite femme sèche, à la voix pointue, et pour les trois autres quarts, une gaillarde ventrue et fessue, aux bras énormes, à la voix de tonnerre.
>
> (*DM* 131)

Always on the lookout for the most outrageous side effects of his inventions, Aymé describes a husband who has been cuckolded by another of his own bodies! The traveller tries to question them about their multiplicity but they cannot communicate because they have not the same 'notion de personne'. But there is a still more troubling aspect of the side effects. Aymé underlines society's conditioning towards 'normality' and the repression of the individual: the only person to live by the one body-one mind ratio has a black cross painted on his house and is known as 'le fou'.

'Héloïse' provides an excellent image of fluidity with its Martin who changes into a woman (Héloïse) every night and then back again every morning. 'Les Sabines' intensifies the same fluidity of identity and gives Aymé the opportunity to pursue the consequences of his initial situation much further through the metamorphosis motif. Variety of experience is given a physical dimension by Sabine's ability to multiply her body at will. She starts by creating a twin 'pour la commodité d'examiner son visage, son corps et ses attitudes' (*PM* 23) but soon tastes the joys of a varied existence, wanting ever more variety. Here, again, the humorist gives free rein to his penchant for Rabelaisian enumeration: Sabine is

> dans le même instant, lady Burbury, assise à une table de bridge en face du comte de Leicester; la bégum de Gorisapour, étendue dans son palanquin porté à dos d'éléphant; Mrs Smithson, occupée dans l'Etat de Pennsylvanie à faire les honneurs de son château Renaissance synthétique; Barbe Cazzarini dans une loge de l'Opéra de Vienne où ténorisait son illustrissime; Rosalie Valdez y Samaniego, couchée sous la moustiquaire, dans une hutte d'un village de Papouasie, . . .
>
> (*PM* 41–2)

'Les Sabines' is perhaps rather long, given the premise Aymé is working from, but he succeeds in rescuing his tale to some extent by bringing it back towards a more easily manageable duality. He does this by describing a moral struggle taking place within Sabine: she is tempted by her infinite, luxurious variety but deep down she feels she should belong to one man. Aymé develops the struggle between 'la Providence' and 'le Péché'. Some Sabines turn to charity and repentance to make up for their sinful sisters. Dark realism contrasts with fantasy when Louise Megnin, one of the repentant ones, goes on a mission of charity and self-sacrifice to the *zone* St. Ouen, 'ce dernier cercle de l'enfer terrestre' (*PM* 59) where she is abused, raped and finally murdered to atone for the excesses of her other embodiments.

In these exploitations of the fantastic to underline certain aspects of reality there are clearly some very serious themes involved, yet the anti-serious ironist is always hovering nearby and the result is often an irritating refusal to pursue them. The essence of Aymé's *conte* is still the invention of a disturbing situation and a brief exploration of its most interesting consequences. Social commentary and pseudo-philosophical discussion take second place to this. The confusion in stories like *Le Décret*, 'Le Cocu nombreux' or 'Les Sabines' is the final stage; Aymé proposes no solutions, offers no intellectual discussion. His primary goal is to find an image that will intrigue us, disturb us, increase our awareness and amuse us.

It seems inevitable that with this questioning of what is often regarded as stable and absolute—one of Aymé's greatest short story successes—he should venture further than confusion of time and identity. Indeed, the stability of reality and existence themselves suffers half mocking, half serious distortion too. In 'La Clé sous le paillasson' Aymé exploits a less exaggerated image of fluidity than in 'Les Sabines' but moves the reader further towards a fluid reality. The basic movement of the story is a gentleman burglar's search for his lost family and his true identity among all the aliases that he has been using:

> 'J'ai eu tant d'états-civils, depuis que je cours l'aventure, et tant de faux parents respectables que je ne suis pas fichu de m'y retrouver. Aussi bien, je me demande quel est mon nom véritable?'
>
> Il porta la main à son front et cita rapidement une cinquantaine de noms.
>
> (*NA* 251)

To add to the confusion, Rodolphe is initially proposed as a character who has escaped from between the pages of a detective novel to arrive in a real country town! His search involves a constant mingling of two levels of reality.

Aymé pursues this transfer between two levels of reality much further in 'Le Romancier Martin'. Not only do the novelist's creations now leave their fictional frame to attain the same level of reality as their author, but Martin has the power to remove people from real life and imprison them in a purely literary reality. A thorough mingling results: Martin's editor falls in love with one of his characters and another friend wants the novelist to translate his mistress Jiji into a 'personnage de troisième plan' so that he can be rid of her. It is rather surprising that an author so interested in images of mingled identity and fluid reality should have missed the ideal figure of a spy; maintaining two or three identities at once and living in an unstable world of changing loyalties and disintegrating façades, the spy could have combined Cérusier, Rodolphe and the bewildered time traveller in *Le Décret* to become Aymé's greatest creation.

Most of Aymé's short stories question reality to some extent. He often seems to create absurdities in order to have them accepted as realities, whether by the victim, who hardly has any choice, or by the reader, who is equally bound if he wants to read on. Cérusier is at first bewildered by his face change and goes through a period of confusion when he concludes that 'le monde feint d'exister' (*BI* 85). Finally he accepts Roland Colbert, his new self, as a 'nouvelle réalité'. In *Le Décret* Aymé does not just aim at confusion of time for his victim but goes as far as the brief suggestion of a parallel existence:

> J'arrivais à cette conclusion baroque qu'il existait simultanément deux villes de Dôle, l'une vivant en 1942, l'autre en 1959.

> (*PM* 114)

Aymé suggests very strongly that this other reality is perhaps only ever mental; the deeper reality is in the eye of the beholder. **'Oscar et Erick'** deals directly with this important theme. Oscar has for a long time been painting only imaginary things, but the people of the northern kingdom of Ooklan where he lives hardly appreciate his inventiveness and (shades of the villagers of **'Le Cocu nombreux'**) call him 'Oscar le fou'. One day his Viking brother comes home from the sea bearing real objects that appear to be the exact models for Oscar's fantasy canvases. The unreal has become real, or what is unreal in Ooklan exists as reality elsewhere.

It is this fantastic vein that is most often regarded as typical of Aymé's short stories. The three successful pastiches of his stories all stress this vein of the unreal. Yet anthologists of the fantastic have tended to ignore Aymé, probably because his fantastic is so often anti-serious and contains so little of the deep-rooted fear that is so essential in Poe, Hoffmann and even marginal writers like Lovecraft. There are occasional thematic similarities but Aymé's attitude to his material and his adaptation of it to accentuate reality is different. Because of Aymé's disarming, anti-serious, anti-intellectual stand it would also be wrong to align him too closely with the Surrealists who were often among his friends and who used similar processes in arriving at their strange images, or with the dramatists of the Absurd whose phenomena and situations so often resemble his own. Aymé has created his own distinctive blend of faerie, fantastic and reality. The accumulation of unreal imagery in his fictional world gives the impression that it is a special world apart where any absurdity is allowed. Exploring story after story, the reader feels that the fantastic is really quite banal and, what is worse, even expected. Masson's pastiche best captures this atmosphere when it describes a world where

> Le merveilleux est partout. Seulement il se cache. Et le plus souvent, vous mourrez avant de vous être aperçu du don que les fées vous ont donné au berceau.

So we see his hero Mouton (read Martin) wondering what his next gift will be—transmutation of cobblestones into gold or the power to stop a bus with nothing more than telepathic commands. Sadly enough, Masson was right: after reading a lot of Aymé we are tempted to expect phenomena whose charm should really be in their unexpectedness.

Robin Buss (essay date 1988)

SOURCE: "Poor Little Martin," in *The Times Literary Supplement*, No. 4,445, June 10–16, 1988, p. 642.

[*In the following essay, Buss praises the stories collected in* La Fille du shérif *for their nostalgic insight into the French lower classes.*]

These twenty-five stories [in **La Fille du Shérif**] have been gleaned from Marcel Aymé's papers and provided with a minimal critical apparatus by Michel Lecureur, some of whose notes ("unidentified review, probably in Morocco in the 1960s") intrigue more than they inform. But apart from such puzzles, and one previously unpublished story for which Lecureur does not hazard a date, most of the pieces are traced to periodicals of the early 1930s and early 1950s, when the French social and political scene provided Aymé with ready targets for satire.

Comparisons across the period (1929 to 1962) covered by the stories reveal the consistency of Aymé's method and the continuity of his themes. **"Le Monument"**, for example, exposes a snobbery and narrow-mindedness typical of small-town politics in the Third Republic; in fact, it was published during the Fourth. After the war, he directed his attention to left-wing rather than conservative targets and renounced the crudeness of **"Premier prix de comédie"**, directly parodying 1930s politicians, for a more oblique approach and for his characteristic brand of fantasy. This starts from an absurd situation (the man, for example, who changes sex regularly twice a day), explores the logical, and therefore still more absurd, consequences (he falls in love with herself and vice versa), some further implications (their love is doomed, since they can never meet) and developments (they get pregnant), while gently poking fun at conventional responses to this incongruity (the real wife's "what will my parents say?").

This does not provide the basis for hard social criticism or for very profound imaginative writing, and it runs the danger of whimsy which Aymé usually avoids by the vigour of his writing and the wry detachment of a narrator who has to record improbable or impossible events. There is a hint of coldness in his treatment of human beings and their relationships, and one suspects that if he appears most feeble when attempting direct political satire, it is because he did not care deeply enough about politics to be more than mildly unpleasant to politicians.

In any case, politics is about power, while Aymé's sympathies are with the little man. His characters, often with the generic name "Martin", act against their better natures under the pressure of events: the dutiful chemist's assistant

becomes a blackmailer, the sensitive doctor a mass murderer. The Martins remain what they always were, it is
fate that is cruel. He turns from Martin to the biblical
Samson to show that strength is a dubious blessing ("si tu
faisais le compte de tout ce qu'il a brisé depuis qu'il est
au monde, tu serais moins fier de sa force", Samson's
uncle complains): in Aymé's version of the story, Samson
is a leader on whom God has imposed an unwanted burden. He plans his haircut as a return to normality and a re-
discoverery of himself.

Aymé still enjoys a faithful readership twenty years after
his death, as do other writers, such as Pierre MacOrlan,
who celebrated the clerks and artisans of the lower middle-
class, and their homes in small provincial towns or the
"village" of Montmartre. The settings and the type may
have lingered beyond the war, but both have since changed
beyond recognition. Aymé explores what is now, increasingly, their nostalgic charm, and he occasionally reveals
more than that: a perceptiveness about sexual relationships, a sardonic humour. All are represented in this collection.

B. R. Tilghman (essay date 1990)

SOURCE: "Literature, Philosophy, Nonsense," in *The British Journal of Aesthetics,* Vol. 30, No. 3, July 1990, pp.
256–65.

*[In the following essay, Tilghman examines the philosophi-
cal significance of nonsense in Aymé's tales of the marvelous.]*

In this [essay] I want to suggest a thesis about the relation
between philosophy and literature and I will do this by an
examination of the role of nonsense in some of the short
stories of the French author Marcel Aymé.

Nonsense became a philosophical category only in the
early twentieth century and was first introduced by, I believe, Bertrand Russell with the theory of types. It was the
syntactical restrictions enjoined by the theory of types that
allowed Russell to charge that many of the assertions of
earlier philosophers were not simply false, but in fact
made no sense. Nonsense was given a deeper dimension
by Wittgenstein in the *Tractatus* with the distinction between the sayable and the unsayable: nonsense results
from the attempt to say the unsayable but, ironically, it
was everything of importance in life that he believe to be
comprehended under the latter. That aspect of the *Tractatus* was totally missed by logical positivism which sought
to use the verification theory of meaning to distinguish the
meaningful statements of empirical science from the nonsensical pseudo-statements of metaphysics. Wittgenstein
went on to provide a still richer exploration of nonsense in
the *Philosophical Investigations* where he locates a craving for nonsense in certain deep aspects of our language
and our life. It is this craving that he believes is respon-

sible for much of traditional philosophy which, on his
view, turns out to be grounded in conceptual confusion
and therefore a kind of nonsense.

Given the fact that a good case can be made that the notion of meaning and all it implies for the distinction between sense and nonsense has been the primary concern of
twentieth-century philosophy, at least Anglo-American
philosophy, it is surprising that in their aesthetic studies
the role that nonsense has played in literature has gone almost unnoticed by philosophers. Lewis Carroll's *Alice*
books are, of course, the obvious exception to this, but the
attention they have drawn has usually been directed towards picking out the philosophical theses and jokes rather
than towards the larger possibilities of nonsense as a literary device.

It may not be so surprising that literary critics and commentators have not seen those same possibilities or have
not even been aware of the existence of the kind of nonsense I want to call attention to. To be sure, literature has
always recognized a garden variety of nonsense that exploits made-up words, silly situations, and unlikely juxtapositions exemplified by *Jabberwocky,* the 'nonsense' verse
of Edward Lear, and that American folk classic 'I Was
Born About Ten Thousand Years Ago'.[1] What I have in
mind, however, is rather different from that and can be illustrated by some of the short stories of Marcel Aymé.

Marcel Aymé (1902–1967) has not been widely read in the
English-speaking world and very few of his seventeen
novels, twelve plays, and eighty-three short stories have
been translated into English. Aymé is generally considered
to be a writer of what the French call *contes des
merveilleux,* tales of the marvellous. What can be categorized generically as the marvellous has long been a staple
of French literature. Since at least the twelfth century the
literature of France has been populated by sorcerers, giants, ogres, fairies, and strange events. Literary historians
have devised a number of ways of sorting out and classi-
fying the various themes of these *contes des merveilleux.*
Marcel Schneider, for one, distinguishes between fairy
tales, horror tales, and fantasy literature.[2] In slicing up the
domain of the marvellous it has not been recognized that
one of its sub-divisions belongs to a brand of nonsense. I
want to direct attention to the literary and philosophical
importance of that brand of nonsense and at the same time
to call attention to an interesting author who has unfortunately been neglected by English-speaking readers.

Many of Aymé's stories clearly are *contes des merveilleux.*
One of his best known is **"Le passe muraille,"**[3] 'the man
who could walk through walls'. A clerk of modest and
regular habits suddenly discovers that he has the ability to
walk through walls unhindered. Worried by this derange-
ment in his daily life, he went to the doctor who readily
diagnosed his problem and prescribed two powders together with a regimen of overwork that would surely put
him to rights again. He took one of the powders but put
the other aside and forgot about it. Meanwhile he began to

learn that his new talent had certain advantages. He thrust his head through the wall of the office of his tyrannical boss and shouted imprecations at him. After a few repetitions of this the unfortunate man had to be taken to the mad house. He discovered that he could walk in and out of bank vaults and serve himself as he pleased. The headlines soon spoke of little else than the phantom bandit. He entered into an affair with a married woman and found it most convenient to walk directly through the wall into her bedroom. One day he suffered from a headache and so took some headache powders before going off to visit his lady love. Alas, however, it was not only a headache powder that he took, but the forgotten prescription as well. The additional dosage took effect just as he entered the wall and before he emerged on the other side. And he is still there lamenting the untimely end of his career.

And then there is **"Fiançailles,"**[4] **"The Betrothal"**. It seems that a woman had read so much Greek mythology that when her son was born he turned out to be a centaur. The father kept this shame hidden away from public view on his large estate and had him privately educated. One day when luncheon guests were strolling about the grounds they accidentally encountered the young centaur. The guests had a daughter—the first human female he had seen apart from his mother—and he was immediately smitten with her and she with him. An engagement was arranged on the spot and to celebrate the girl hoisted her skirts, climbed on the back of the centaur, and went for a trot around the estate. Both, needless to say, found the experience rather erotic. He seized the occasion to venture for the first time beyond the walls of the estate. Once beyond the grounds he had his first encounter with the realities of life when a passing policeman gave him a summons for indecent exposure. It was then that he spied a young mare in the pasture across the way. She was the first of her kind that he had ever seen and something deep was stirred in the other half of his nature. He threw his betrothed into the ditch and galloped off with the mare. Neither has been seen since.

Delightful as they are, it is not these stories that I want to talk about, but three others that treat, in a fast and loose manner, of the subject of time. These three are **"La carte,"** **"Le décret,"** and **"Rechute."**[5] **"La carte"** is set in Paris during the German occupation. Shortages of nearly everything make life increasingly difficult and it is decided that in the interest of efficiency time, like all else, should be rationed. Ration cards are issued. Strong and productive workers and those in necessary occupations are, naturally, given more days to exist per month than old people and those in less vital capacities. Prostitutes are allotted only seven days per month and Jews, regardless of age, sex, or occupation, are permitted to exist only a half day each month.

There are, of course, inconveniences in the new order brought about by the decree. An old man married to a young wife is in bed when his time period runs out. He returns to existence in the same place as before only to find himself between his wife and her more virile lover. In no time at all a black market in time cards has sprung up. Poor workers sell their cards to feed their families; the wealthy are buying them up and living more than their share. Some are able to amass enough tickets to live forty, fifty, even sixty days a month. Fortunately, however, another administrative decision soon cancels the programme.

The story entitled **"Le décret"** also begins in wartime Paris. It has long been a custom each summer to set the clock ahead an hour or two to take advantage of the extra daylight but now the authorities decide on a far bolder step. The war has become a terrible burden for all sides and so the warring powers agree—and it is a universal agreement—to set the clock ahead seventeen years in hopes that the war will have been over by that time. Once the decree takes effect it is found that the war is indeed over and fortunately another has not broken out.

The narrator must take a trip to a small rural town to visit an old friend who is ill. When he arrives in the town he is surprised to encounter German soldiers and upon enquiring for his friend is startled to learn that he is still a prisoner of war in East Prussia. He wonders whether the decree has somehow never been announced in this remote corner of the country but then the truth begins to sink in and he realizes that he really is back in 1942. He returns to Paris to find it in the throes of the German occupation; he returns to an apartment house that hasn't been built yet and he must find his old place; and he returns to children that are still small and two of whom haven't been born yet. He sees people in the streets whose acquaintance he won't make for years. He remembers all the things that are going to happen. Little by little, however, these memories of the future begin to grow dim and before long all is as it was.

"Rechute," unlike the other two, is not a story of the occupation. The Chamber of Deputies has just passed the 'twenty-four' law making the year twenty-four months long. As soon as the law took effect everyone found himself exactly half of his previous age. Grandmother who was in her late sixties is now ready to go out on the town. The girl who is the principal character in the tale was eighteen and just engaged to be married; she wakes up to find herself nine years old and her fiancé thirteen. The army is suddenly composed of ten and eleven year olds whose adult uniforms swallow them and who can scarcely carry their automatic weapons. All, however, retain the experiences and habits of mind of their former ages.

The girl's fiancé now scorns the child of nine for, as he says, between nine and thirteen there is an abyss and he reminds her that they are divided by certain physiological realities. Later on, with the aid of her brother, she forces him to reveal those physiological realities which turn out, alas for him, to be in proportion to his scrawny thirteen year old frame. As we should expect, the class of newly created children is restive, there is disorder in the streets, the army of children—let's not say 'infantry'—cannot be relied upon, and eventually the twenty-four law is repealed and all is returned to where it was before.

Unlike the other stories, these three exploit a kind of conceptual nonsense and do not simply trade in fantasy and whimsy. It is the kind of nonsense that results from misusing the word 'time' and its friends and relations by assimilating its grammar to that of some other concept. Thus time is spoken of in the way that we speak of commodities that can be bought and sold, rationed and hoarded, and so on. Or the notion of moving the clock up for summer time is assimilated to rescheduling an event or changing its venue. Or time is treated as if its dimensions were subject to legislation as the dimensions of the football pitch can be changed by action of the rules committee. What Aymé has given us in each of these tales is a *picture* of time, i.e., the word 'time' is incorporated into a series of descriptions that are appropriate only for another notion.

What is perhaps the most familiar picture of time that we often make use of is that of a river upon which our life and the world is carried from past to future. As a poetic conceit this is certainly harmless and sometimes may even be apt. Gripped by this picture, nevertheless, we may be led to push the figure into doing duty for which it was not intended and begin to ask questions about it that we would ask about real rivers: how fast does time flow and might its rate change? Is there some high ground or vantage point from which we might see what is around the next bend in the future? Might we not turn the barque of our lives around and paddle back upstream? While these are exactly the questions we want to ask about rivers, they have no application to time; no sense has been given to them. An innocent trope can lead us to ask 'What then is time?' and we find ourselves in nonsensical metaphysical speculation.

It is this very idea of a picture that is the basis of Wittgenstein's criticism of traditional philosophy in the *Philosophical Investigations*. Philosophical problems are said to arise when language *goes on holiday* [§38] and thus is not doing its usual job, that is, when the use of certain expressions is mistakenly assimilated to that of others so that these expressions turn out to have no use, no role to play in either language or life. Thus are born those misleading analogies that are the stuff of philosophical theories, those pictures that hold us captive [§109] and prevent us from seeing the world aright. In the stories I have just mentioned Marcel Aymé is exploiting—deliberately—exactly the kind of nonsense that Wittgenstein believes is the very stuff of philosophical theory.

The illusion of sense surrounds many of these events. We may think we can imagine a sudden transformation in which everyone has a body just like the one he had at half his age, or people vanishing for so many days each month and then reappearing. It is tempting to comprehend all this under the traditional category of fantasy and to think it is one with what the wicked witch does in changing the prince into a frog. We hide all the difficulties by whispering 'Magic!' and think no more about it.

Whatever the intelligibility of any of that, the nonsense at work in the stories that I want to consider enters with the description of the goings on as alterations in *time* brought about by legislative enactment. It is as if these descriptions are offered as explanations of the strange events: 'Why is Josette in **"Rechute"** suddenly a little girl again?' we ask and are told that it is because they passed that law doubling the length of the year. It is important to focus our question on the right target. It is one thing to note that a piece of legislation cannot bring about a physical change, no act of Congress by itself can increase the length of the Mississippi River; that is an empirical truth. In addition to the legislative enactment it would require digging new channels and raising new levees. We can describe clearly what it is that the act of Congress cannot by itself bring about. Can a law nevertheless change the year? Our inclination is to say no. We can always divide the year into twenty four rather than twelve months or decide to count two revolutions of the earth about the sun as one year instead of two, but that changes only how we count birthdays—recall the unfortunate chap in *The Pirates of Penzance* who was born on February 29 of a leap year—but that is not at issue and in any event temporal processes continue the same. (What would it be like if they didn't?) Since no other sense has been given to the expression 'changing the year' we cannot say what it is that the piece of legislation is supposed not to be able to do.

That these stories of Aymé's are built around a piece of nonsense has not been recognized by his commentators. Jean-Louis Dumont, for example, says that 'Aymé has found in the concept of time the possibility of a notion contrary to the one men have of it'[6] and again, 'his intentions are neither to horrify nor terrify his reader; he simply wants to make him laugh by upsetting the natural order of things'.[7] This is surely wrong. He has not presented us with another possibility at all nor has he upset the natural order which he would have to do by suggesting some alternative order. If he is talking nonsense, then he has removed all place for a new possibility or revised order of things. What we laugh at is the nonsense wrapped up in a picture that radiates the illusion of sense. Each of these stories is an extended conceptual joke.

Equally off the mark is Graham Lord's comment that **"La carte"** is in part 'a pseudo-philosophical glance at the relativity of time'.[8] The relativity of time belongs to the esoteric reaches of physical theory and has nothing to do with Aymé's playing fast and loose with our ordinary ways of talking. To be sure, **"Le décret"** mentions several theories of time, including relativity, but that itself is all part of the joke.

Although it is not specifically about Marcel Aymé, the following remark of Marcel Schneider's is revealing:

> It is science itself which restores fantasy to the universe rationalized by the encyclopedists and from which the scientism of the 19th century had pretended to extort its secrets, not only in inventing prodigious machines and means of destruction which disorient

thought, but also in rendering precarious, vacillating, and illusory all the certainties on which scientists had built their edifice and which serve as religious dogmas for modern man.[9]

Schneider is obviously referring to the replacement of Newtonian concepts of absolute space and time by Einstein's relativized ones, to Heisenberg's uncertainty principle and quantum theory with its particles that aren't anywhere or are two places at once, to Gödel's theorem, and the like. In other words, twentieth-century science is supposed to have done a great many of the very things that the fiction of fantasy has done. It is in this spirit that Graham Lord mentions, apropos of Aymé, 'this questioning of what is often regarded as stable and absolute'. Jean Cathelin, for another, sees him as writing a kind of science fiction, only doing it better than the likes of Arthur C. Clark and Isaac Asimov.[10]

In the next paragraph after these reflections on modern science Schneider suggests that the French may have something to learn from Lewis Carroll whom they had hitherto dismissed as merely a children's writer. The juxtaposition of these topics implies that Lewis Carroll may be one of those who have put the conceptual certitudes of our world in doubt. This has to be a misreading of the adventures of Alice. We recognize Carroll's nonsense as nonsense precisely because we see it against a background of sense. Carroll's point in playing with nonsense is not to put anything in doubt or to entertain any new conceptual possibilities, but is to remind us where sense is to be found.[11] And so it is, I think, with Marcel Aymé. His play with the nonsense about time is intended to remind us of what the conceptual restraints on our lives really are.

Everyone is agreed that something more, quite a bit more, is going on in these stories in addition to the time fantasy. By and large the critics are right about the nature of this something more—at any rate, it is not necessary to dispute any of the details of it with them. Of **"La carte"** Cathelin says:

> the satire here is at once social, philosophical and political; the fantasy here serves only to highlight more intensely character traits in a time of penury, of an inhuman and ferocious bureaucratism which believes that in order to find a solution to no matter what problem it is enough to regulate something.[12]

It is worth pausing to add that one of the explicit themes of **"La carte"** is the resentment of the narrator, a writer, at being included in the decree along with these other 'useless' ones. Writers are characterized as among the 'consumers whose maintenance is not compensated for by any real return'. The narrator admits that he would have expected the decree to apply to painters and musicians. Aymé's playful but not quite unobtrusive proposition is that writing (and reading) are in danger of being understood as uncompensated, or improperly compensated, consumptions of time. We might reasonably take this story as making an issue, however playfully, about the importance

of writing and about whether, in particular, it is worth the time that it takes.[13]

It is much the same with **"Le décret."** The nonsense about remembering the future directs attention to something important about life and human relations. Think how our relation to another is altered when we know what is going to happen to him; that the company has, for example, already decided to fire him and you are bound not to tell him. The narrator's reflection that 'youth which has nothing to learn is not youth' is a reminder that our concept of youth is not simply a chronological one, a matter of from these years to those, but is in addition the concept of a moral, that is, a human condition, a stage on life's way, if you would. This very same reminder is what makes **"Rechute"** such a wonderful commentary on the nature of childhood and the logical conditions that make the relation of parent to child what it is. The authority of the parent over the child is not merely a matter of discrepancies in size and physical competence, but is in part a function of the moral incompleteness of the child who must be guided and led and pushed and prodded not only into the paths of righteousness, but also into satisfying the daily necessities of life. This is brought home to us by representing the moral competence of the adult clothed in the body of a child. The unfortunate composite being is forced to submit to the direction and correction appropriate to a child and the result can only appear as degradation to the adult in child's clothing.

Aymé's stories must not be understood as offering speculative theses about the nature of time, theses which careful examination show to be nonsense. The stories do not advance theories that could demand examination independently on their own merits. Aymé is using nonsense deliberately to say something about the human condition. What is going on in his stories must be distinguished from the inadvertent introduction of nonsense into literature where the aim is to present a piece of philosophy. Sartre's *La Nausée* is a case in point. There is little doubt that Sartre meant *La Nausée* to present metaphysical theses about the nature of the world, that everything in the world is contingent and therefore human practices have no justification, and so on. As philosophy this is elementary confusion and scarcely worth the effort of straightening out. In using his novel to state philosophical theses Sartre falls victim to all the snares and delusions of that kind of philosophy. Fortunately for his readers it is possible to take the novel as offering something other than metaphysics. When we read it carefully in order to follow the fortunes of its hero we sense that Roquentin's worries about necessity and contingency, being and becoming, may be better understood as the manifestation of his dissatisfaction with the lack of direction in his own life and his repugnance at the bourgeois culture of Bouville. What is presented as philosophy becomes instead the vehicle for the expression of what in the most general terms can be described as a mood or frame of mind and is thus not really philosophy at all.

What I have been saying about philosophical theses in literature is in direct opposition to a view of the relation between the two held by Peter Jones. In *Philosophy and the Novel* Jones says, 'I do not examine the literary embodiment of the philosophical views I abstract from the text, . . . I do not consider the particular contexts within the novel which occasion the philosophical utterances. . . .'[14] When we look closely at the context in which those supposedly philosophical remarks occur we do not find them conveying philosophical theses at all, but instead expressing or describing some observation about the course of the world or human relations. It is only when they are taken out of context that they can appear to be *theses*.

It will be instructive to end with a comparison of Aymé's way with nonsense and the way of a philosopher who had learned much from Wittgenstein about how to expose nonsense by telling stories. I am referring to O. K. Bouwsma who raised to an art form the technique of teasing and tickling us with nonsense by telling stories intended to produce philosophical insight, a technique that others practice at their peril. Aymé never explains to us that his nonsense is nonsense. He lays out a situation with a perfectly straight face and proceeds to talk about things just as if they did make sense and were the most ordinary in the world. It must dawn on us that it is all nonsense. To get the point we must already have a nose for it, a quickened sense of the queer, as it were. Aymé, after all, is teaching us about people and not about nonsense. He is teaching us about people through the medium of the nonsense of conceptual jokes.

Aymé's literary practice is thus rather different from Bouwsma's philosophical practice, the fact notwithstanding that Bouwsma's practice is also very much a literary one. We can see this in his article 'Descartes' Evil Genius'[15] where the Evil Genius undertakes to deceive the innocent and unsuspecting Tom. His first evil essay in that direction is to make everything out of paper. For a time Tom is deceived into thinking that the flowers, his beloved Millie, and even his own body are real, but before long he is undeceived by suspicious crinklings and tearings. Bouwsma makes it explicit that this story trades on our ordinary understanding and familiar use of words such as 'deception', 'illusion', 'real', and the like; in this part of the story we find whimsy, but not nonsense.

Having failed in his first attempt the Evil Genius tries again and this time succeeds, but only too well. All conceivable tests for flowers and Millie turn out positive. The Evil Genius suggests to Tom that nevertheless he is being fooled about all those things, but Tom naturally fails to understand his evil insinuations. The criterion of reality and, consequently, of deception being invoked by the Evil Genius now proves to reside in a sense possessed only by Tom's Adversary. In other words, he does not mean what we mean when we speak of real things and deceptions and their ilk and, furthermore, by the terms of the story we can never know what he means. Now the nonsense has entered and Bouwsma can point out to us how Descartes' talk of the possibility of total illusion is the result of the misuse of language—our language—and that it is really without

sense. Bouwsma has used these stories to instruct us in the nature of nonsense, how it can get started and the mischief it can work.

Bouwsma, following Wittgenstein, sees the task of the philosopher as one of turning disguised nonsense into patent nonsense [PI, §464]. The point of this exercise is not merely to remove impediments to theorizing or to permit the beauty of clarity to shine through, but is to remove impediments to seeing the world aright, to seeing other people and ourselves aright and this kind of understanding has much to do with how we are to live our lives. And, I would add, with how we are to allow literature to enter our lives.

In his stories Marcel Aymé exploits patent nonsense, but it is nonsense that passes for neither philosophical theory nor philosophical therapy. Anyone who has developed a philosopher's nose for the use and misuse of language is in a position to distinguish what Aymé is doing in these tales from fantasy and the marvellous and to note its conceptual nature as well as its kinship with the confusions of traditional philosophical theory. And especially are we now in a position to appreciate how this species of nonsense can be a vehicle for conveying important insights about human beings and their lives and problems.

There may not be enough literary examples of the kind of conceptual nonsense I have been talking about to justify identifying it as a distinct genre, nevertheless there is a significant role for it to play in literature. If this recognition of this role has no other result, it should at least lead us to rethink the spectrum of possible relations between literature and philosophy.

Notes

1. I was born about ten thousand years ago, And there's nothing in this world that I don't know.
   I saw Peter, Paul, and Moses
   Playing ring around the roses;
   I can whip the guy who says it isn't so. (And so on.)

2. Marcel Schneider, *La littérature fantastique en France* (Paris: Libraries Arthème Fayard, 1964). Schneider's book is a useful survey of the marvellous in French literature.

3. In *Le passe muraille* (Paris: Gallimard, 1943).

4. In *En arrière* (Paris: Gallimard, 1950).

5. *La carte* and *Le décret* are both published in *Le passe muraille*; *Rechute* is in *En arrière*.

6. Jean-Louis Dumont, *Marcel Aymé et le merveilleux* (Paris: Debresse, 1967), p. 122. (All translations from the French are mine.)

7. Dumont, p. 177.

8. Graham Lord, *The Short Stories of Marcel Aymé* (Nedlands: University of Western Australia Press, 1980), p. 48.

9. Schneider, p. 391.

10. Jean Cathelin, *Marcel Aymé* (Paris: Debresse, 1958), p. 145.

11. Or perhaps he should be understood sometimes as pointing out the mischief that can be occasioned by inattention to sense and conceptual restraint. The White Queen, for example, favours a system of justice in which the punishment, i.e., imprisonment, comes first, followed by the trial, with the crime coming last. And it is all the better if the crime is not committed at all. This, of course, is to make nonsense of the notion of punishment, not to mention the notion of justice, since the concept of punishment is logically linked to that of wrong doing. We can, nevertheless, imagine imprisonment for crimes not committed—actual examples unfortunately abound. This bears a suspicious resemblance to the idea of 'preventive detention' advocated by some upholders of the law in the name of justice.

12. Cathelin, p. 146.

13. I owe this understanding of the story to Timothy Gould.

14. *Philosophy and the Novel* (Oxford: Clarendon Press, 1975), p. 148.

15. In *Philosophical Essays* (Lincoln: University of Nebraska Press, 1965).

Christopher Lloyd (essay date 1996)

SOURCE: "Myths and Ironies of the Occupation: Marcel Aymé's 'Traversee de Paris,'" in *Myth and Its Legacy in European Literature*, edited by Neil Thomas and Francoise Le Saux, University of Durham, 1996, pp. 49–61.

[*In the following essay, Lloyd analyzes Aymé's story "Traversée de Paris" for its insight into the German occupation of Paris during World War II.*]

L'homme n'est qu'un animal mythologique.

—Michel Tournier[1]

Myth, says Michel Tournier, is 'une histoire fondamentale', and humanity is defined by its capacity to mythologise, its receptivity 'au bruissement d'histoires, au kaléidoscope d'images' which it perceives from cradle to grave. Myth unites story, history and the urge to express some basic truth about humanity. Like Tournier, Marcel Aymé (1902–1967) was a compelling storyteller, whose fictions pleasingly combine the fabulist's art with moral and historical reflexion on his age. With their richly atmospheric evocation of period and place, their grimly humorous depiction of the attempt to hold on to values and identity in a world where the collapse of order and annihilation have become the norm, the works which Aymé wrote about the Second World War illustrate his creative talents at their best. In

addition, novels like *Le Chemin des écoliers* (1946), *Uranus* (1948) and the story **'Traversée de Paris'** (1946) have a documentary interest and a strong narrative line which have drawn film-makers as much as readers. Cinematic adaptations of these texts by, respectively, Michel Boisrond (1959), Claude Berri (1990) and Claude Autant-Lara (1956), not only continue to gain Aymé a wider popular audience but also help sustain the never-ending process of interpretation of the Occupation, which is itself a significant phenomenon of post-war French culture. In this respect, one need only recall the latest controversy about President Mitterrand's wartime record as a decorated Vichy turncoat, or the conviction of Paul Touvier earlier in 1994 for crimes against humanity, in a trial that had effectively been drawn out for half a century. For the purposes of this brief discussion of Aymé's literary contribution to the debate, I shall concentrate on the 20,000-word story **'Traversée de Paris'**, together with Autant-Lara's film version, retitled *La Traversée de Paris* or *Pig Across Paris* in some English versions.[2]

K. K. Ruthven suggests that myths contain 'para-history', that is what people believe or hope happened in the past. Moreover, 'to be preoccupied with myth reveals a yearning for order in the midst of upheavals and fragmentariness'.[3] While myths as cosmological allegories, esoteric philosophy, eschatological systems, or the devious attempts of the bourgeoisie (as anatomised by Barthes) to maintain cultural hegemony by making ideology into nature, need not concern us here, more useful is the notion of the foundation myth outlined by Henry Tudor, which seeks to (re)explain past events in order to justify and reinforce the authority of those holding power or influence in the present. Myths in this sense may be garbled history, but the shaping of their narrative serves an eminently practical purpose, of effecting or upholding social and political cohesion. Thus, as Tudor observes, there is nothing primitive, rudimentary, or merely literary about myth.[4] Consequently, it is as legitimate and fruitful to talk about myth in the context of modern historical events like the Second World War as it is regarding ancient theogonies, medieval legend, or the metamorphoses wrought by the artistic imagination.

Myths are not untruths (except in popular parlance), but rather attempts to locate truths in convenient fictions. Insofar as irony depends on a perceived gap between semblance and reality, along with a position of sceptical detachment on the part of the ironist (and those who share his perspective), one could argue that myth is fundamentally ironic, at least in the historiographical sense which is attached to it in this discussion. To talk, for instance, of the myths of the Occupation and Liberation of France in 1940–44, is to acknowledge that one has seen through them, while perhaps recognising their necessity. The excessively naive or cynical belief that history is either absolute truth or complete bunk can be replaced by a more ironic awareness that historical meaning is constantly constructed and reconstructed, as much by the observer as by the events he records. Ironic detachment can of course easily degenerate into smug condescension. *The Times* published a leading article on 27 August 1994, entitled 'La Libération: Paris has been reliving a healing national myth'. The quaint use of the Gallic term and the personification of Paris show the anonymous editorialist lapsing into the clichéd evocation of mythic forces, of which he (or she) was perhaps unaware. The writer goes on to argue that the Parisians 'Dancing until dawn yesterday on the Place de la Concorde' were possessed with the mythic spirit summoned up fifty years before by General de Gaulle's famous celebration of 'la France éternelle' in the act of self-liberation. That the liberation of Paris was actually due to Allied military dominance and to the restraint of General von Choltitz, rather than to heroic French freedom fighters, was conveniently omitted in the attempt to restore national unity. (A glance at Angus Calder's skilful anatomisation of *The Myth of the Blitz* (London: Jonathan Cape, 1991) serves as a salutory reminder that the British have no reason to be complacently superior in this domain.)

The novelist who takes his material from historical and social reality can hardly avoid presenting the official version of history in an ironic light in his fiction. For Marcel Aymé's characters, patriotism and honesty are dangerously outmoded values, at least as conventionally accepted. **'Traversée de Paris'** recounts the attempt by two small-time black-marketeers to smuggle the carcass of a pig across occupied Paris, on foot, in the winter of 1942–43. Central issues in the story are how identity and social responsibility are defined. The reversals and moral ambiguities of Aymé's plot constantly rehearse and ironise some of the key myths of Occupation existence. The film is more overtly comic, attenuating the characters' existential rage in favour of more entertaining, farcical business, and widening out the story's account of period detail. Apart from its conclusion, however, the film remains faithful to Aymé in spirit and tone, matching his verbal shafts in the excellent script of Aurenche and Bost and the memorable central performances by Bourvil and Jean Gabin. In this respect, it is unique among the cinematic adaptations of Aymé's works, which are mostly undistinguished dilutions of his stories.

An early biographer of Aymé, Jean Cathelin, observed that the writer set out in his pre-war essay *Silhouette du scandale* (1938), stimulated by the repercussions of the Stavisky affair, to 'décrypter les mythes de la société contemporaine'. At the same time, myth decoded may mean myth reenacted in a new form; hence perhaps the 'renouveau de littérature mythique et symbolique' in the decade after 1940.[5] Before pursuing this analysis, it would be helpful to recall some of the central myths of Occupation. Unsurprisingly, the founding myth is not that of the débâcle of 1940 or of Pétain the saviour, but that of Resistance, often referred to as 'résistancilisme'. Obvious literary examples which help elaborate such a myth are Vercors's *Le Silence de la mer,* Vailland's *Drôle de jeu,* and, in more allegorical mode, Sartre's *Les Mouches* and Camus's *La Peste.* Michel Tournier, to quote him again, ex-

emplifies a common post-1968 urge to demystify the notion of 'résistancialisme', when he asserts that 'En vérité Résistance n'est devenue un phénomène d'ampleur nationale qu'après le départ des Allemands. [. . .] Les authentiques résistants furent souvent noyés, submergés, écœures par l'explosion du mythe de la Résistance après la Libération'.[6] According to Tournier, Marcel Ophuls's celebrated documentary film *Le Chagrin et la pitié,* shown in French cinemas in 1971, helped re-establish a more truthful view of the Occupation. The historian Henry Rousso, author of *Le Syndrome de Vichy,* a fascinating historiographical study of post-war representations of the Occupation, which he sees as reflecting a national, collective neurosis, reiterates Tournier's critique, albeit more subtly.[7] The film certainly enraged the official guardians of memory, whether of left or right, by its insistence on collaboration or compliance with the enemy as the norm, rather than Resistance, but its own partiality runs the risk of replacing the myth of 'résistancialisme' with a new one of universal cowardice and abjection.

Rousso sees Autant-Lara's film of **'La Traversée de Paris'** as an anticipatory gesture of iconoclastic defiance: 'A sa manière, le film est une première pierre lancée dans le jardin des mythes naissants'.[8] In fact, Aymé and Autant-Lara subvert the myth of Resistance, not by frontal assault, but by omission. The heroic resister (a central figure in a novel like Kessel's *L'Armée des ombres* (1943) and the Melville film which followed the book a generation later in 1969) is replaced by his mercenary counterpart, the profiteer. In one scene in the film (not found in Aymé's story), a young woman shelters Gabin and Bourvil from a German patrol in the hallway of her tenement, on the ingenuous assumption that they are Resistance members on the run. While the sardonic Grandgil plays her along, the hapless Martin soon betrays their real profession. But the idea of fresh pork proves as seductive to the girl as that of 'parachutage'; while Gabin is as ever willing to offer her 'une petite côtelette' as a reward, Bourvil with his petty crook's code of honour refuses to share booty which doesn't belong to him. The message, then, is that even if the French are not united in Resistance, they share the same greed and urge for gain; the virtuous pose of the girl and Martin is undercut by the reality of their behaviour and by Grandgil's more knowing opportunism.

Aymé and Autant-Lara may seem simply to have replaced 'résistancialisme' with an early version of the more heretical outlook typical of the so-called 'mode rétro' of the 1970s and 1980s. Alan Morris characterises 'résistancialisme' as depending on four propositions:[9] that there were few real collaborators; that the vast majority of the population were patriotic; that the real interests of France were pursued by an élite of freedom fighters; that de Gaulle led and personified the Resistance. What is significant about the 'mode rétro', on the other hand, is not merely that it blurs these categories (implicitly rehabilitating collaboration, say, by equating it with Resistance as an option dictated by chance rather than choice: the theme of Louis Malle's well-known-film, *Lacombe Lucien*), but also that it makes heresy fashionable; an equivocal nostalgia for period detail and mores replaces condemnation. It is certainly true that Aymé's writings about the Occupation reject the Gaullist legend. While he marginalises Resistance, and dismisses de Gaulle as a dictator, 'venu de l'autre rive de la Manche se faire le geôlier de la nation',[10] he portrays most French people as self-interested opportunists, reserving his strongest scorn for those who hypocritically adopt ideological allegiances in order to dominate and exploit the uncommitted. Nevertheless, there is nothing nostalgic about the novels and stories written during and just after the war; the world they depict is a bleak one, of deprivation, fear and imminent catastrophe. At the same time, Aymé's fictional universe is sharply delineated and his ironies, however subversive of the official line, point to clear-cut moral options. He is remote from the obsessive cataloguing of period bric-à-brac and oneiric interaction of fact and fancy which one founds in the novels of Patrick Modiano, who is usually held to be the best current practitioner of the 'mode rétro'.

Jean Dutourd writes in his novel *Au bon beurre, ou dix ans de la vie d'un crémier* (1952) that 'Au-dessus de la politique, il y avait les affaires'.[11] Aymé shares this perception. In '**Traversée de Paris**', survival has become a matter of business. Martin trades in black-market meat, Grandgil in paintings, while in the film version the Germans are shown trading off the lives of hostages to pay for Resistance incursions. In any case, politics is only another form of business. In *Uranus,* the double-dealing of the Communist Party includes the protection of the gross profiteer Monglat, at the expense of lesser fry like the café-owner Léopold or the collaborator Loin. In *Le Chemin des écoliers,* the protagonist Michaud eventually learns to reject his outmoded humane values and becomes a successful black-marketeer, having followed in the footsteps of his sixteen-year-old son Antoine. More is at stake here than cynical adaptation to changed social conditions. As Dutourd observes in a later passage of his novel, all substance has become illusory under the Occupation, as the ersatz replaces the real:

> Les lames de rasoir ne coupaient pas, le savon était une pierre ou du sable, le dentifrice du plâtre, le café de l'orge, le cuir du papier, la toile de la fibre de bois. On était entouré d'apparences, on se mouvait dans des mirages, la vie réelle n'était pas plus véridique que des accessoires de théâtre: poulets de carton, bouteilles d'eau teintée, sabres en fer-blanc.[12]

Instead of giving the illusion of reality, the novel chronicles the reality of illusion.

Dutourd's characters tend to remain odious stereotypes; when Marshal Pétain appears, he is no longer a saviour but a sort of grotesque doll. Aymé is more successful at taking us beyond caricature and engaging us with the inner world of his central characters The public or political arena is held at a distance, at least in '**Traversée de Paris**'. Is there however a mythologisation or metaphysic of daily living? Like Dutourd's observer, Aymé's Martin (the name

of the common man, which is given to many of the protagonists of the author's stories) is aware at times of the flimsiness of his surroundings. Entering a café, its sordid appearance makes him think of 'un décor de théâtre d'un réalisme indiscret' (*VP*, 51). This *mise en abyme* teasingly reverses the customary referential gesture towards an extratextual reality: here the world of theatrical illusion again invades the everyday. That the other principal character, Grandgil, is a painter adds of course to the possibilities of such ironic manipulations.

Novelists and film-makers may in practice be better equipped than historians to track down and convey the determinants of ordinary life, which leave few official traces. In this context, the ambiguities of *attentisme* and the black economy fall into that area between fact and fiction which readily invites the elaboration of new myths.[13] Are such marginal figures as the profiteer and wide boy despicable exploiters of others' needs or rather lovable rogues untrammelled by hypocritical convention? When, as the historian Roderick Kedward observes, up to half the food supply was channelled through the black market, it is actually misleading to call them marginal. In *Le Chemin des écoliers,* the black-marketeering school-boy Antoine controls his circumstances far more effectively than the supposedly dominant adults who surround him. The control of the food supply determines the survival of social bonds as much as that of individuals; as Aymé observes in the allegorical story, '**La Bonne Peinture**', 'c'est par le ventre qu'on commence à se sentir avec les autres' (*VP*, 188). In an extensive study of *Trafics et crimes sous l'Occupation,* Jacques Delarue argues that the black market, far from reflecting the spirit of French enterprise or rebelliousness, was in fact largely controlled by the Germans.[14] Goods in short supply were often channelled through *bureaux d'achat* offering higher prices than official ones; these 'officines allemandes' were nominally run by French middlemen, who were often convicted felons and Gestapo agents. He cites the extraordinary success of such notorious profiteers as the Russian Szkolnikoff (murdered in June 1945) and the Romanian Joinovici (who was finally incarcerated in 1947).

In effect, a clandestine secondary economy was set up, which outstripped the official one in some sectors such as the leather trade. At the same time, those outside the system suffered increasing hardship. In 1943, the official daily food ration was 1,500 calories—1,000 below the basic requirement; infantile mortality rose by 50 per cent and deaths from tuberculosis by nearly 100 per cent during the Occupation. One of the great merits of Aymé's storytelling is to reveal the practical consequences of such bare facts; he prefers concrete detail and caustic humour to false pity or overblown rhetoric. Most of the characters in '**Traversée de Paris**' are at the very bottom of the economic ladder, and remote from the large-scale profiteers found in real life or Aymé's other works. The chain of supply and demand portrayed in the story excludes the Germans (unlike Autant-Lara's adaptation, as will be seen). Aymé is less interested in the morality of the black market than in its effect on the behaviour of his characters. Both Grandgil and Martin are offered a sort of freedom in their clandestine venture, which ultimately neither is willing or able to accept. Violence is finally perpetrated by the enraged Martin when he resolves the enigma of Grandgil's identity and kills him; after this cathartic act, he is content to be taken off to prison, having refused the temptations offered by his mysterious partner. In the film, on the other hand, the final act is determined from without by the intrusion of the Germans.

The action of **'Traversée de Paris'** is motivated partly by the topography of the characters' nocturnal odyssey, and partly by the clash of their antagonistic personalities. Reversal of fortunes and characters is a constant device, reflecting both the upheaval of Occupation and the author's fondness for surprising his readers. In the opening sentence, we read: 'La victime, déjà dépecée, gisait dans un coin de la cave sous des torchons de grosse toile' (*VP*, 27). The false drama of butchery carried out by the quaking grocer Jamblier and the arrival of Martin who resembles 'un inspecteur de police' (28), might lead us to assume the existence of a crime worthy of Dr Petiot (the infamous mass murderer of the Occupation) or his acolytes, the 'faux policiers' of the rue Lauriston, particularly if we recall the atrocious murders and scenes of cannibalism which Aymé laconically recounts in *Le Chemin des écoliers*. The victim of course is a pig, whose 100-kilo carcass is to be transported eight kilometres from the rue Poliveau (near the Jardin des Plantes, in the 5ème) to the rue Caulaincourt in Montmartre. These addresses locate the story in a real Paris, whose streets and monuments are carefully indicated to mark the stages of the journey. But the travellers, weighed down by their heavy suitcases, also move across a landscape as equivocal as their business. (Autant-Lara's film was shot entirely on studio sets, without location work, and presents a Paris both realistic and stylised in its obvious markers of Occupation life.)

In the café on the Boulevard de la Bastille where they first meet, Martin and Grandgil contemplate the sunset over the canal. The narrator notes that 'la lumière du soir durcissait les lignes et les plans', whereas for Martin, 'cette agonie lucide du crépuscule' is a gloomy and chilling symbol of life's shortcomings (32–33); he assumes erroneously that Grandgil shares this perspective. Only towards the end of the story are we shown the urban landscape painting in Grandgil's studio which recalls the opening sunset scene (68). The correspondence which Grandgil finds thus differs radically from Martin's; the painter attempts to possess and dominate the landscape, just as he comes to dominate Martin and finally draws his portrait after he has fallen asleep in exhaustion. Yet Grandgil is not particularly successful in his ventures as a highbrow artist, which he signs with his real name Gilouin. Martin is more impressed by the lurid, erotic drawings which Grandgil exchanges for commodities in the neighbourhood ('Avant-hier, pour une femme à poil, j'ai eu un jambon', 67). While Grandgil's commercial art is thus equated with their commerce of the pig (and Grandgil himself is constantly described as hav-

ing 'de petits yeux de porc' and resembling a 'bélier'), his true vocation leaves him more vulnerable, for in it he surrenders 'cette ironie un peu distante où le peintre semblait trouver son équilibre le plus sûr' (69). Overhearing Grandgil boasting contemptuously on the telephone about his black-market exploits ('Ce sont les mous qui font les durs', 71), the humiliated and envious Martin attacks Grandgil's 'proper' paintings and kills him in the ensuing struggle. After delivering the pig, however, Martin is arrested by the police who have discovered his portrait, incriminatingly signed with the date, in the artist's studio.

Three perspectives run parallel in the story and create its ironic manner: the small-minded survival skills of Martin, the born loser whose judgement invariably falls short of the facts; the ironic pose of Grandgil, who admits to being a painter but proves to be as effective as a petty gangster, and whose insouciance is matched by considerable practical skill; and the judgements of the reader, for whom **'Traversée de Paris'** is an evocation of occupied Paris as well as a clash of conflicting protagonists. While Martin constantly betrays his flaws and weaknesses in words and deeds to his companion (for instance, his common-law wife Mariette has just left him; Grandgil tells him patronisingly that given her advanced years she'll soon be back), Grandgil witholds his true identity behind his taciturn detachment, while also proving far more effective as a man of action. Typically, Martin assumes that Grandgil is a down-at-heel housepainter. The reader, noting the 'insolente ironie' of Grandgil's gaze (31), is unlikely to share this hasty supposition. Consequently, as Grandgil increasingly dominates the situation, both Martin and reader are driven to reinterpret his character, and to question Martin's own ethic, which clings on to a dubious notion of honesty even in flagrantly illegal dealings.

Until the final revelation of Grandgil's true identity, his actions constantly speak louder than Martin's words, despite the latter's naive belief in his own adroitness and experience. When a customer in the first café aggressively denounces the pair as 'poulets', policemen or agents provocateurs, Martin protests ineffectually while Grandgil pushes the belligerent man out of the way. On discovering the treasure trove of foodstuffs which Jamblier is hoarding in his cellar, Grandgil extorts 5,000 francs from the grocer instead of the 450 which Martin was content with. The carcass itself is worth 15,000 francs, but Martin refuses Grandgil's suggestion that they dispose of it themselves. Both Jamblier and Martin affect indignation at Grandgil's 'duplicité monstrueuse' (42), although the narrator points out the paradox of their convenient expectation of honesty in criminal dealings. Martin attempts to explain Grandgil's extorsion on his own moral terms, as a legitimate desire to receive a better reward for the risks they are taking (whereas it is more probably gratuitous bravado). Nonetheless, 'Martin, lui, ne voyait rien d'immoral ni de scandaleux dans le trafic clandestin et ses bénéfices réputés exorbitants. Le vol et l'illégalité étaient à ses yeux choses distinctes' (*VP*, 45). Grandgil himself imagines that he has captured 'le personnage moral de Martin' in his sketch of him, and revealed 'ce qu'est l'honnêteté d'un homme: un sentiment de fidélité à soi-même, commandé par l'estime qu'il a de sa propre image, telle que la lui renovie le miroir de la vie sociale' (70).

Grandgil considers himself above this 'moyenne honorable' (70); the artist shapes his own image by playing at the role of gangster or contemptor of humanity, while also recording an image of others and their world in his paintings. When they enter another café half-way through their journey, Grandgil intimidates the surly owner and his repulsive wife (who are illegally employing a Jewish girl), with a denunciatory (and anti-Semitic) tirade. He also insults the covetous clients who are measuring up the suitcases with their 'yeux de demi-affamés' (51): 'Foutez-moi le camp, salauds de pauvres [. . .] Allez aboyer contre le marché noir' (53). The 'salauds de pauvres', which the film made famous, and the gold teeth which his disdainful laugh reveals, evidently confirm his status as an antipathetic character, yet also demonstrate a rejection of the myth of solidarity. The weak are in effect shown as envious, contemptible and deserving of being crushed; their complaints rarely lead to action. That both Aymé and Autant-Lara were men of right-wing views, whose nonalignment with Resistance virtues got them into trouble at the Liberation, doubtless helps explain the venom of **'Traversée de Paris'** in this area.

Nevertheless, the dandyish Grandgil is eventually disposed of by his partner, and a more conventional moral order thereby restored. The opening sunset is further replicated by the blood spreading over his defaced painting of the Boulevard de la Bastille: both the artist and his demonstration of aesthetic superiority have been eradicated. Although art is in a sense avenged when the portrait betrays Martin as the likely killer, Martin in any case is content to surrender to the law since he cannot tolerate the thought of others perceiving him as a murderer. His final act is to drop the envelope containing Grandgil's 5,000 francs in the street, in the hope that a passer-by will post it back to Jamblier. The story concludes: 'Jamais il n'avait eu une foi aussi entière en la vertu de ses semblables' (79). There are, it seems, no winners. Both Grandgil and Martin have failed to survive their enterprise, either practically or morally. As a result, the reader is likely once again to regard Martin's faith as entirely misplaced and to draw a more radically pessimistic conclusion.

The ending of **'Traversée de Paris'** is not altogether satisfactory. The conclusion of Autant-Lara's film is quite different. Aymé nihilistically rejects the morality of the detached artist as much as that of the common man; both are defeated by their own weaknesses rather than circumstance. The film, on the other hand, relies on circumstance (that is, the intrusion of the Germans, whom Aymé largely excludes from his story other than as passing figures). Whereas Aymé's story is more powerful and coherent in relying on ethic rather than event, as far as plot and character are concerned the violent outcome still seems rather contrived. Martin's capacity to kill has been established by

recollections of his stabbing a Turkish soldier in the Dardanelles during the First War. Nevertheless, when he attempts to attack Grandgil earlier in the evening, his more powerful companion repels him effortlessly, just as he floors an inquisitive policeman with one blow.

It is the betrayal of Grandgil's double identity, the last of several betrayals of their odyssey, which enrages Martin and which also removes the artist's shield of protective irony. The demands of symbolism over-ride those of verisimilitude, in other words. One could in fact argue that Grandgil has a triple identity, as apprentice gangster, commercial painter, and the budding highbrow artist Gilouin. It is the last who is sacrificed. Similarly, there are three conclusions offered, if one fuses Aymé's story with Autant-Lara's film. This is because the director's wishes were eventually overruled by his producer, who demanded that a supposedly happy ending be grafted on to his existing dénouement.[15] In effect, the murder of the pig replaces that of Grandgil; in Aurenche and Bost's script, Martin (now teasingly christened Marcel, though he is called Eugène in the story) plays the accordion in the opening sequence to conceal the fracas caused as Jamblier (played by Louis de Funès) and his family chase the luckless swine round the cellar before finally succeeding in slaughtering it. Aymé's ironies of identity are to a large extent replaced by such farcical albeit macabre interludes. In a later scene, Gabin and Bourvil are joined by a retinue of famished dogs which, like the howling wolves in the Jardin des Plantes, are drawn by the smell of the meat and only dissuaded when bribed with a sample from the suitcase.

Finally, Gabin and Bourvil are arrested as they attempt to deliver the suitcases. A German officer recognises Grandgil and has him released, while the less fortunate Martin is driven off with a lorryload of French hostages. What follows this grim reversal was described by Claude Mauriac as 'Une fin postiche, anodine et qui sonne faux'. Brief shots of the Liberation, victory parades and the playing of the Marseillaise denote the end of the war (sarcastically echoing the opening shots of German triumph). We move to the post-war Gare de Lyon and discover a wealthy Grandgil boarding a train, assisted by a railway porter, who turns out to be Martin, a survivor after all but still the eternal 'porteur de valises'. Yet survival hardly betokens optimism. Other reviewers noted that whereas Aymé chose to chastise Grandgil's amoralism, Autant-Lara's production shows him to be a 'gentil collaborateur'. Claude Mauriac observed that 'Il fallait aux auteurs le visage humain et sympathique de Gabin pour faire passer l'odieux de certaines de ses paroles et de quelques-uns de ses actes'.[16] (Jean Gabin in fact often played the sort of virtuous gangster whose morality Aymé mocked in his story; in addition, he was one of the few major showbusiness figures of the period not to have been compromised under the Occupation.)

Be that as it may, it is hard to avoid concluding that the ironic configurations of both story and film produce a grimly bleak representation of the Occupation. Pierre

Ajame asserts that the film is 'un chef-d'œuvre de méchanceté'; not only do Aymé and Autant-Lara deride the patriotic myths of Resistance and national solidarity, but they demonstrate that 'L'amitié est une blague, la culture un élément de troc, le dévouement une bêtise, l'héroïsme une foutaise, l'amour une escroquerie'.[17] Yet are **'Traversée de Paris'** and *La Traversée de Paris* really such destructive, nihilistic exercises in derisive debunking? Their very popularity tends to indicate that this is an overstatement. Both writer and director achieve a comic complicity with their audience, as they subvert the false heroism of official propaganda and the cynical anti-heroism of the black-marketeer. The truth may be unpalatable or intangible, yet the reader and spectator are enabled to observe one possible version of it from an ironic perspective, where recognition and detachment become fully compatible.

Notes

1. M. Tournier, *Le Vent Paraclet* (Paris: Gallimard, Folio, 1977), pp. 188, 191.

2. References to 'Traversée de Paris' in my text are taken from *Le Vin de Paris* (Paris: Gallimard 1947) and abbreviated as VP. For the script of the film, see *L'Avant-scène cinéma*, 66 (January 1967).

3. K. K. Ruthven, *Myth* (London: Methuen, 1976), p. 82.

4. H. Tudor, *Political Myth* (London: Pall Mall Press, 1972).

5. J. Cathelin, *Marcel Aymé, ou le paysan de Paris* (Paris: Nouvelles Editions Debresse, 1958), p. 170, 211.

6. Tournier, pp. 79–80.

7. See H. Rousso, *Le Syndrome de Vichy de 1944 à nos jours* (Paris: Seuil, 1990), pp. 127ff. See also G. Kantin and G. Manceron, eds, *Les Echos de la mémoire: tabous et enseignement de la Seconde Guerre Mondiale* (Paris: Le Monde-Editions, 1991), and E. Conan and H. Rousso, *Vichy: un passé qui ne passe pas* (Paris: Fayard, 1994).

8. Rousso, p. 262.

9. A. Morris, *Collaboration and Resistance Reviewed: Writers and the Mode Rétro in Post-Gaullist France* (New York: Berg, 1992).

10. M. Aymé, *Vagabondages*, ed. M. Lecureur (Besançon: La Manufacture, 1992), p. 315. For a fuller discussion, see C. Lloyd, *Marcel Aymé: 'Uranus' and 'La Tête des autres'* (Glasgow: University of Glasgow French and German Publications, 1994).

11. J. Dutourd, *Au bon beurre* (Paris: Le Livre de poche, 1958), p. 179.

12. Dutourd, p. 214.

13. H. R. Kedward writes: 'there can be no simple conclusion about the French day-to-day existence under the Occupation, and no single answer to the question of whether or not the severity of the Nazi presence was directly reflected in daily behaviour'. *Occupied France: Collaboration and Resistance 1940–1944* (London: Blackwell, 1985), p.14. See also J. Tosh, *The Pursuit of History,* 2nd ed. (London: Longman, 1991).

14. J. Delarue, *Trafics et crimes sous l'Occupation* (Paris: Fayard, 1968).

15. See M. Lecureur, 'Claude Autant-Lara nous a parlé de Marcel Aymé', *Cahiers Marcel Aymé,* 1 (1982), pp.134–35.

16. Quoted in *L'Avant-scène cinéma*, p. 47.

17. *L'Avant-scène cinéma*, p. 47.

FURTHER READING

Criticism

Brodin, Dorothy. *Marcel Aymé.* New York and London: Columbia University Press, 1968, 48 p.
   Critical study of Aymé's life and works.

Grigson, Geoffrey. "Out of the Fashion." *Spectator* 206, No. 6931 (28 April 1961): 618.
   Highly recommends Aymé's *The Proverb and Other Stories,* finding the book reminiscent of stories by Maupassant and Turgenev.

Loy, J. Robert. "The Reality of Marcel Aymé's World." *French Review* XXVIII, No. 2 (December 1954): 115–27.
   Analyzes realistic elements in Aymé's fantasy literature.

Jorge Luis Borges
1899–1986

(Also wrote under the pseudonym F. Bustos, and with Adolfo Bioy Casares under the joint pseudonyms Honorio Bustos Domecq, B. Lynch Davis, and B. Suarez Lynch) Argentinian short story writer, poet, essayist, critic, translator, biographer, and screenwriter. For additional criticism on Borges's short fiction, see *SSC*, Volume 4.

INTRODUCTION

During his lifetime, Borges was highly regarded as a writer of labyrinthine short fictions, often written in the form of metaphysical detective stories. Characteristically, they blur the distinction between reality and the perception of reality, between the possible and the fantastic, between matter and spirit, between past, present, and future, and between the self and the other. They are usually situated in the nebulous confines of allegorical locations, whether identified as bizarre dimensions of the universe, Arabian cities, English gardens, the Argentine pampa, amazing libraries, or the neighborhoods of Buenos Aires. Since his death, Borges has attained the status of one of the major literary figures of the twentieth century, a master poet and essayist, as well as an architect of the short story. His work has not only influenced the way writers write but also the way readers read. Using science fiction and fantasy literature, western adventures, detective stories, self-reflective raconteurs as narrators, philosophical perplexities, and phenomenological uncertainty, Borges created a body of fiction concerned with ideas, archetypes, environments, and paradoxes rather than with character, psychology, or interpersonal and social interactions.

BIOGRAPHICAL INFORMATION

Borges was born into an old, Argentinian family of soldiers, patriots, and scholars in Buenos Aires, where he spent most of his childhood. His father was an intellectual, a university professor of psychology and modern languages, a lawyer, and a writer. Borges, whose paternal grandmother was English, was raised to be bilingual and learned to read English before Spanish. When Borges was seven, his Spanish translation of Oscar Wilde's *The Happy Prince* appeared in an Uruguayan newspaper. A visit to Switzerland in 1914 became an extended stay when the outbreak of the World War I made it impossible for the family to return to Argentina. Borges enrolled in the College de Geneve, and studied Latin, French, and German.

He also studied European philosophers, particularly Schopenhauer and Bishop Berkley, whose dark pessimist and anti-materialist influences can be perceived in the worldview of his literary work. After earning his degree in 1918, Borges traveled to Spain. There he joined with the avant-garde Ultraistas, who combined elements of Dadaism, Imagism, and German Expressionism, and published reviews, essays, and poetry. Borges returned to Buenos Aires in 1921 and was recognized as a leading literary figure in Argentina with the publication of his first books of poetry, *Fervor de Buenos Aires* (1923), *Luna de enfrente* (1925), and *Cuaderno San Martin* (1929) During these years, Borges also helped establish several literary journals, and published essays on metaphysics and language, which were collected in *Inquisiciones* (1925) and *El tamaño de mi esperanza* (1926). In 1938, the same year his father died, Borges developed a form of blood poisoning called septicemia. Fearful that his ability to write might have been impaired by his illness, Borges began writing short fiction rather than poetry, intending to attribute possible failure to inexperience in the genre rather than diminished literary skill. The result was "Pierre Menard, autor del Quijote," a story highly acclaimed both as a fiction and as a precursor to deconstructionist textual analysis.

Though he spoke of his disdain for politics, Borges was always politically outspoken. He opposed European fascism and anti-Semitism and the dictatorship of Juan Peron in Argentina. After Peron's overthrow in 1955, Borges was named as director of the National Library of Argentina, where he worked as an assistant before Peron removed him in 1946 for opposing his regime. In 1957 he was appointed professor of English literature at the University of Buenos Aires. In 1961, he was a corecipient—along with Samuel Beckett—of the Prix Formentor, the prestigious International Publishers Prize, which gave him international fame. Borges did not oppose the Argentinian military coup or the terrorism of the Videla junta in the seventies until 1980, when, apologizing, he signed a plea for those whom the regime had caused to "disappear." Similarly he supported the Pinochet dictatorship in Chile, calling the general a "gentleman," and commending his imposition of "order" in the face of communism. Many believe that these incidents prevented Borges from winning the Nobel Prize. Nevertheless, the list of his awards and honors is long and distinguished. Borges spent his last years a literary celebrity, traveling and lecturing. Even though he was blind in his later years, Borges continued to write by dictation to his mother and to his student and companion, Maria Kodama, whom he married shortly before his death.

MAJOR WORKS OF SHORT FICTION

Borges's *Historia universal de la infamia* (1935; *A Universal History of Infamy*) features stories that capture local color and the lowdown argot of gangsters. Written with the erudition of an intellectual posing as a roughneck, they show posturing toughs engaged in macho assertion through gratuitous and egotistical violence. In his second collection, *Ficciones* (1944; *Fictions*), Borges invented a form for the short story that combines elements of detective fiction, metaphysical fantasy, philosophical discourse, and scholarly monographs complete with footnotes, references, and commentary. Thematically the stories are about the conflict between the integrity of the "I" and the overwhelming power of the other—whether the other is a person, a force, a book, a dream, a dagger, or a labyrinth. In the late 1950s, Borges began to write simplified short stories, parables, and fables of a less baroque structure and diction than the masterpieces of his middle period. The stories, however, are paradoxical and philosophically complex mythic narratives. In the afterward to his collection *El libro de arena* (1975;*The Book of Sand,*), Borges called these stories "dreams," which he hoped would "continue to ramify within the hospitable imaginations" of his readers.

CRITICAL RECEPTION

A highly literate and intellectual author, Borges's works are enjoyed both by general readers and intellectuals. Although a celebrated author in Argentina and Latin America since the 1920s, Borges's first story in English appeared in 1948 in *Ellery Queen's Mystery Magazine*. It was not until 1962, after he had already produced a significant body of literature that Borges became known to the English-speaking reader when two English translations of his short stories were published. Other stories, such as "The Circular Ruins," "The Babylonian Lottery," "The Library of Babel," and "The Aleph" were printed in *Encounter*. Borges was immediately acclaimed by other writers and by readers as a master, and his influence on other writers has been profound. During the last years of his life, Borges was showered with honors, awards, and lectureships. Critical commentary on Borges's work has been as various and as copious as the work itself. It extends from popular reportage on his lifestyle and work habits to literary, philosophical, and psychological investigations of his works.

PRINCIPAL WORKS

Short Fiction

Historia universal de la infamia [*A Universal History of Infamy*] 1935

El jardin de senderos que se bifurcan 1942

Ficciones, 1935–1944 [*Fictions*] 1944

El Aleph [*The Aleph and Other Stories, 1933–1969*] 1949

El hacedor [*Dreamtigers*] (prose and poetry) 1960

Labyrinths: Selected Stories and Other Writings (short stories and essays) 1962

Elogio de la sombra [*In Praise of Darkness*] (prose and poetry) 1969

El informe de Brodie [*Dr. Brodie's Report*] 1970

El congreso [*The Congress*] 1971

El libro de arena [*The Book of Sand*] 1975

Obras Completas (short stories, essays, and poetry) 1977

Collected Fictions: Jorges Luis Borges 1999

Other Major Works

Fervor de Buenos Aires (poetry) 1923

Inquisiciones (essays) 1925

Luna de enfrente (poetry) 1925

El tamaño de mi esperanza (essays) 1926

El idioma de los argentinos (essays and lectures) 1928

Cuaderno San Martín (poetry) 1929

Evaristo Carriego (essays) 1930

Discusión (essays and criticism) 1932

Historia de la eternidad (essays) 1936

Poemas 1923–1943 (poetry) 1943

Otras inquisiciones 1937–1952 [*Other Inquisitions 1937–1952*] (essays and lectures) 1952

Para las seis cuerdas (poetry) 1965

Obra poética, 1923–1967 [*Selected Poems,* 1923–1967] (poetry) 1967

El otro, el mismo (poetry) 1969

El oro de los tigres (poetry) 1972

La rosa profundo (poetry) 1975

La moneda de hierro (poetry) 1976

Historia de la noche (poetry) 1977

La cifra (poetry) 1981

Nueve ensayos dantescos (essays) 1982

Los conjurados (poetry) 1985

Selected Nonfiction: Jorge Luis Borges (nonfiction) 1999

Selected Poems: Jorge Luis Borges (poetry) 1999

CRITICISM

Daniel Balderston (essay date 1988)

SOURCE: "The Mark of the Knife: Scars as Signs in Borges," in *The Modern Language Review,* Vol. 83, No. 1, January, 1988, pp. 67–75.

[*In the following essay, Balderston discusses the significance of scars in Borges's work.*]

> . . . ese paciente laberinto de líneas traza la imagen de su cara.
>
> (Borges)[1]

> . . . if one wants to call this inscription in naked flesh 'writing', then it must be said that speech in fact presupposes writing, and that it is this cruel system of inscribed signs that renders man capable of language, and gives him a memory of the spoken word.
>
> (Deleuze and Guattari)[2]

At the close of a long conversation with Borges about his favourite Victorian and Edwardian writers—Stevenson, Kipling, Chesterton, Wells, and others—the doorbell rang and the next visitor, a young Paraguayan writer, was shown in. Borges, hearing the nationality of the newcomer, asked me: 'Do you remember the dictator of Paraguay?' Not sure which one he was referring to, I ventured: 'Stroessner? Doctor Francia?' 'No, no', said Borges; 'the one with the scar'. Obviously he was not speaking of a historical figure, but was still discussing literature. The Paraguayan dictator he was referring to was John Vandeleur in Stevenson's *New Arabian Nights,* an Englishman who is described in *The Rajah's Diamond* as 'the biggest adventure, the best judge of precious stones, and one of the most acute diplomatists in Europe', known for his 'exploits and atrocities when he was Dictator of Paraguay'. Stevenson describes him thus:

> Old John Vandeleur was of remarkable force of body. . . . His features were bold and aquiline; his expres-

sion arrogant and predatory; his whole appearance that of a swift, violent, unscrupulous man of action; and his copious white hair and the deep sabre-cut that traversed his nose and temple added a note of savagery to a head already remarkable and menacing in itself.[3]

This description corroborates another character's assertion in Stevenson's novella that Vandeleur has prodigious claims to both fame and infamy.[4]

Borges had been blind for many years at the time of this conversation and lived in a world of books he remembered with eerie precision. His question about the Paraguayan dictator was disconcerting because he failed to make clear that he was thinking of a fictional rather than a historical dictator. It reveals how fascinated Borges, perhaps the most bookish writer who ever lived, felt by the world of arms and violence. In retrospect, however, the most revealing aspect of the question is the detail that Borges found so striking and so unmistakable about this particular dictator of Paraguay: the scar that crossed his nose and temple. Stevenson never tells the story of Vandeleur's scar, but it is the ultimate proof of his violent and adventurous past, and serves to caution both characters and readers to be suspicious of the former dictator. It is not surprising that Borges, blind reader and rereader of a world of literature that lived in his memory, should have had a special place for Vandeleur in his gallery of scoundrels.

Vandeleur's scar is both repulsive and fascinating, as scars often are in literature and the visual arts (and, for that matter, in real life). As a visual image, his aquiline face, marked by a long lateral sabre cut, is striking; as the initial image of a character in a story, the description is notable for its economy, since the scar acts for the reader as sign of past and future violence. The scar is also, at least initially, an ambiguous sign: it suggests violence but does not clarify whether Vandeleur acquired it when acting in a heroic or in a treacherous manner: whether, in a word, it needs to be read as a sign of fame or infamy. Indeed, since Stevenson never tells its story, it can be considered a sort of floating signifier throughout the novella.

Vandeleur's scar, then, is a sign of unpredictable violence which constantly threatens to erupt again, to envelop the whole of the story. The scar-sign derives further power in the story from its alliance with a linguistic sign which—for Stevenson's original readers as for us—cannot but signify violent conflict: Paraguay. The former dictator, the missing link in a history which runs from Gaspar Rodríguez de Francia to Alfredo Stroessner, though once the authoritative user of a language of power, is now consigned by the instability of that power to the oblivion of history. His scar is a sign of his passage through history, indeed the only sign of that passage. Instead of putting his mark on the history of Paraguay, he has been marked by it. The permanence and emblematic character of that mark, though, do not serve to clarify the meaning of Vandeleur's past: the scar's unspecified origin suggests the ambiguous and unstable nature of his participation in a more public story.

Scars have a rich and far-reaching iconographic history, from ancient times through Dante and Hawthorne to Stevenson, Borges, and beyond. Even though a complete catalogue of scars in literature is impossible, it is important to note that facial scars (significant because they are visible) have functioned as signs with various meanings. In addition to the physical scar indicative of past heroism or villainy, scars have also been imposed by divine mandate, as in the mark of Cain, which protects him from the violence of others at the same time as it serves to remind them of his crime, or, symbolically, in the seven *P*s on Dante's brow in the *Purgatorio,* signifying the seven deadly sins. Societies have marked or mutilated transgressors as a punishment and as a means to assure their identity. Cervantes refers to this practice of branding the faces of slaves in one of his exemplary novels.[5] Scars (especially those on the body, usually hidden from view) are important as literary devices in dramatic texts as guarantors of identity, particularly in cases where a character comes back after a long time, transformed in other external respects, such as the case of Oedipus discussed by Aristotle in the *Poetics.* But scars may have a further virtue in narrative fiction: they evoke an enigma in the character's past which can be resolved only by the telling of a story, usually a violent one, in which the scar constitutes the inscription of that story on the character's body and on the body of the text.

A key to Borges's use of the scar as literary image is found in one of his essays on description in narrative. In this essay he ridicules those writers who catalogue the assorted parts of a body and articles of clothing and expect their readers to be able to construct a unified whole from these diverse parts. He says that the patching of lips of a particular kind to cheeks and nose is an impossible operation for the mind to perform.[6] It is better, he suggests, to introduce only such elements as are necessary for the reader to visualize the character in action, or details which by their anomalous nature force the reader to invent circumstances to justify their presence.

Borges's ideas on narrative description are closely related to Stevenson's theory of narrative.[7] In an early essay on verisimilitude, 'La postulación de la realidad' (1929), Borges gives interesting examples of what he calls 'circumstantial details', termed 'circumstantial' because they evoke images not only of themselves but of contexts extraneous to the images themselves. He gives several examples of such details which suggest stories not told in the text. For instance, in an Argentine historical novel, Enrique Larreta's *La gloria de don Ramiro,* Borges points to an image of covers for soup pots secured with locks (*OC,* p. 220). The locks that protect the soup from the hungry servants not only serve to describe the pots but also tell us a great deal about wealth and poverty in the society.

Borges labels the 'circumstantial details' as 'de larga proyección' (*OC,* p. 221), an idea derived from Stevenson's essay 'A Gossip on Romance', his most important discussion of the theory of narrative. Stevenson uses as an example a sea story in which the discovery of some coins comes to him as reader 'like a surprise I had expected; whole vistas of secondary stories, besides the one in hand, radiated forth from that discovery, as they radiate from a striking particular in life'.[8] These 'secondary stories' are, of course, imagined by the reader, being only subtly implied in the text, but the invention of them is part of an open, playful reading, one which fixes especially on the stories not told in the one that is. For Stevenson, then, the coins in the sea story were 'of long projection', as they sent his imagination travelling off after the implied stories, just as the 'circumstantial details' of the soup pots for Borges suggested stories of hunger and need.[9]

The first of Borges's stories to hinge on a scar[10] is **'El incivil Maestro de Ceremonias Kotsuké no Suké,'** in *Historia universal de la infamia,* a series of biographies of scoundrels retold from various sources, published in book form in 1935. The story of Kotsuké no Suké and the forty-seven Ronins is retold from A. B. F. Mitford's *Tales of Old Japan.* In Mitford's version Kotsuké no Suké insulted his visitor, Takumi no Kami, who became so enraged that he drew his short sword and 'aimed a blow at his head; but [since] Kotsuké no Suké [was] protected by the Court cap which he wore, the wound was but a scratch, so he ran away'.[11] For this breach of courtly rules Takumi no Kami is arrested and obliged to commit hara-kiri. Years later, his forty-seven retainers discover Kotsuké no Suké in the palace and pursue him until they find him cowering in a closet: 'Oishoi Kuranosuké, bringing a lantern, scanned the old man's features, and it was indeed Kotsuké no Suké; and if further proof were wanting, he still bore a scar on his forehead where their master, Asano Takumi no Kami, had wounded him during the affray in the castle' (Mitford, p. 16). When their prisoner refuses to commit hara-kiri they kill him, then kill themselves for having committed murder.

Borges's version subtly stresses the scar, making the story hinge on this mark of Kotsuké no Suké's cowardice and treachery. Takumi no Kami, the Lord of the Tower of Ako, wounds Kotsuké no Suké on the forehead: 'El otro huyó, apenas rubricada la frente por un hilo tenue de sangre' (*OC,* p. 321). The word *rubricado*—signed or initialed with someone's rubric or signature—is highly charged here as elsewhere in Borges's work, since it serves to link the realms of arms and letters, making clear the relation Borges perceived between the knife and the pen.[12] In the recognition scene, separately entitled 'La cicatriz', Kotsuké no Suké is found hiding not in a closet but behind a bronze mirror: 'Una espada temblorosa estaba en su diestra. Cuando bajaron, el hombre se entregó sin pelear. Le rayaba la frente una cicatriz: viejo dibujo del acero de Takumi no Kami' (*OC,* p. 322).

In the conclusion of the story Borges projects the meaning of the scar onto future generations and onto his readers. Mitford's tale ends with a bloody sequel: in 1868 an indigent warrior committed hara-kiri on the grave of the forty-seven Ronins, 'at about two hundred yards from my house, and when I saw the spot an hour or two later, the ground was all bespattered with blood, and disturbed by the death-struggles of the man' (p. 24). Borges ends the story with the idea that the sequel is the retelling of the story itself: 'Este es el final de la historia de los cuarenta y siete hombres leales—salvo que no tiene final, porque los otros hombres, que no somos leales tal vez, pero que nunca perderemos de todo la esperanza de serlo, seguiremos honrándolos con palabras' (*OC,* p. 323). Borges's open-ended conclusion, which consists of the telling and retelling of a story of infamy, derives its power in large measure from our recognition that we share in the events told: that we too are marked by the story much as Kotsuké no Suké was.

In a story central to the present argument, **'La forma de la espada'** (1942), the scar provides the title, the first sentence, the leitmotiv, and the enigma of the story, and is essential for the final recognition and reversal. In this story, the so-called 'Inglés de La Colorada', whom the narrator (named Borges in the story) visits at his ranch in Uruguay, has a grisly scar reaching from his temple to his mouth in a half-moon shape, as we are informed in the first sentence: 'Le cruzaba la cara una cicatriz rencorosa: un arco ceniciento y casi perfecto que de un lado ajaba la sien y del otro el pómulo' (*OC,* p. 491). The story the scarred man tells of his youth in Ireland revolves around a traitor to the Irish cause, John Vincent Moon, and the events in a house full of scimitars shaped like half-moons. The so-called Englishman's story ends as he takes one of the scimitars and wounds the traitor on the cheek (with Borges again employing the verb *rubricar*): 'Con esa media luna de acero le rubriqué en la cara, para siempre, una media luna de sangre' (pp. 494–95). A moment later he reveals what the reader already suspects: that he is himself the traitor John Vincent Moon, as shown by the 'cicatriz que me afrenta' (p. 494), a neat play on words which refers both to the locus of the scar, the 'frente' or forehead, and to the scar as sign of his infamy. The story ends with Moon's words: '¿No ve que llevo escrita en la cara la marca de mi infamia? Le he narrado la historia de este modo para que usted la oyera hasta el fin. Yo he denunciado al hombre que me amparó: yo soy Vincent Moon. Ahora desprécieme' (p. 495).

Mary Louise Pratt has studied this story as an example of a narrative that violates one of the basic conventions of discourse: that narrators are truthful about their identities. She states that the Irishman, in order to tell his story,

> feels he must place it in jeopardy by misleading the listener. . . . Both the violation and the flouting [of the convention that the narrator does not lie] are perceptible only because we have the contextual information that the Irishman has a scar, and we get this information only because we get the story secondhand. On its own, the Irishman's story is a perfectly felicitous narrative of personal experience and bears no sign of the lie.[13]

The story of the scar is told as a story of heroism and treachery by one who assumes the position of the hero,

but is set within a story, narrated by Borges as narrator, in which the treachery changes sign, and in which the scar, the 'mark of my infamy', serves not only to prove Moon's identity but also to reverse the identity he assumed when telling his story. The scar is overdetermined in the whole of the story: it is the shape of a half-moon, which is also the shape of the sword that carved it in the face of a character who is named Moon. Even so, it remains ambiguous. The most we can say as we read is that the scar is a sign of past violence, but the specifics of that act of violence become clear only as the story comes to its close.

Moon says at the end that he had to tell the story from the hero's point of view for it to be heard. The story is audible or legible only when told by one who can be assumed to tell the truth, which a traitor cannot be. Yet the reader may not be persuaded of the complete reversal, since there is a greater ambiguity than is immediately apparent. Such an ambiguity is found in the Borges story **'Tema del traidor y del héroe'**, in which Kilpatrick, to purge his treachery and serve the Irish cause, is condemned to die a hero's death. Paradoxically, then, he is both hero and traitor. Similarly, the end of another story, **'Los teólogos'**, reveals that 'para la insondable divinidad, [Aureliano] y Juan de Panonia (el ortodoxo y el hereje, el aborrecedor y el aborrecido, el acusador y la víctima) formaban una sola persona' (*OC,* p. 556).

For Borges, to tell a story is to assume a persona: thus, when Zaid impersonates his cousin Abenjacán he *was* Abenjacán (*OC,* p. 606), and Pierre Menard finds it easier (and therefore less interesting) to rewrite *Don Quixote* by becoming Cervantes than it is when he remains himself (*OC,* p. 447). Along the same lines, the John Vincent Moon who impersonates the friend he betrayed when he tells his story is that heroic figure for the duration of the story, and the final reversal cannot be complete. Moon closes his tale by telling Borges that he betrayed his friend and protector, and asks to be repudiated by his listener. Yet most readers are likely to feel admiration for Moon's ingenuity in telling the story as well perhaps as embarrassment for having been taken in. Moon has earlier committed an act of moral chicanery, telling the story of his scar to persuade the original owner of 'La Colorada' to sell the ranch to him (*OC,* p. 491).[14] Stories of heroism and treachery are sobering precisely because of the moral ambiguity they reveal not only in the characters but in us as readers.[15]

'La forma de la espada' is made up of a very few elements: two characters, a weapon, two countries, friendship and treachery. In the frame tale, Borges (an Argentine) is forced by adverse weather to stop at the Irishman's house in Uruguay. His host's hospitality is compromised when the visitor asks to be told the story of the scar, which the Irishman will tell only on condition that he be allowed to tell it in a way that will leave its horror complete. In the frame tale, then, there is a conflict between hospitality and truthfulness. Friendliness is possible only when the relation between Borges and Moon is superficial, and when underlying enigmas are left undisturbed. Borges's demand for truthfulness, however, leads to the revelation of Moon's past treachery, and forces a new act of treachery: namely, Moon's lie about his own identity. Similarly, Moon's tale reveals that the superficial friendship between the two members of the Irish revolutionary group masked one of the most terrible of human crimes: betrayal of a friend and companion. The Irish story has left a mark on the narrator's face; in the frame tale the same mark becomes the sign of infamy and treachery, not only at the level of the events narrated but also at that of the narration itself.

The Irish story acquires a new meaning from the place and the circumstances in which it is retold. In British literature (I have instanced Stevenson) the scar is a literary device. In the culture of the River Plate countries, however, it is a cultural mark of great importance.[16] In his appropriation of the Irish story, Borges endows it with a more specific and historically-grounded reading of Moon's scar.

In *Facundo,* the 1845 work which analyses Argentine society through the character of the gaucho, Domingo Faustino Sarmiento notes that when a gaucho challenges a rival to a knife-fight, he seeks not to kill but mark his opponent:

> El gaucho, a la par de jinete, hace alarde de valiente, y el cuchillo brilla a cada momento, describiendo círculos en el aire, a la menor provocación, sin provocación alguna, sin otro interés que medirse con un desconocido, juega a las puñaladas como jugaría a los dados. . . . El hombre de la plebe de los demás países toma el cuchillo para matar, y mata; el gaucho argentino lo desenvaina para pelear, y hiere solamente. Es preciso que esté muy borracho, es preciso que tenga instintos verdaderamente malos o rencores muy profundos, para que atente contra la vida de su adversario. Su objeto es sólo *marcarlo,* darle una tajada en la cara, dejarle una señal indeleble. Así se ve a estos gauchos llenos de cicatrices, que rara vez son profundas.[17]

To kill is a misfortune ('desgracia'), to mark is a triumph. Sarmiento also declares: 'Si sucede alguna *desgracia,* las simpatías están por el que se *desgració*' (p. 69). The killer suffers the misfortune and is the tragic hero.

Thirty years later, in José Hernández's *Martín Fierro* (1872), the hero kills a black man early in the poem. Because of the fame of this incident, he becomes known as a knife fighter. In the poem's second part (1879), only with some difficulty does he avoid fighting the man's younger brother, who challenges him to a song contest and, implicitly, to a fight. Although he has never been wounded in a fight, Fierro (whose very name refers to the iron of the knife) is very much a marked man, marked, in effect, by the success of the poem itself.

Evaristo Carriego, a poet of the then modest Buenos Aires neighbourhood of Palermo in the early years of this century (who later became the subject of a book-length essay by Borges, published in 1930), has a poem about the figure of the neighbourhood thug, 'El guapo'. Carriego writes:

> Le cruzan el rostro, de estigmas violentos,
> hondas cicatrices, y quizás le halaga
> llevar imborrables adornos sangrientos:
> caprichos de hembra que tuvo la daga.
>
> La esquina o el patio, de alegres reuniones,
> le oye contar *hechos* que nadie le niega:
> ¡con una guitarra de altivas canciones
> él es Juan Moreira, y él es Santos Vega![18]

The scars are again a sign that the thug or *compadrito* has lived the violent life he tells of, but Carriego ironically keeps silent about whether the thug actually committed the deeds he relates.[19] No one denies his stories to his face: to do so would be to provoke him to a fight, and perhaps be marked in turn.

Borges has written numerous poems about knife fights, poems which seem to summon up the violence of the vanished *compadritos* and *cuchilleros* who inhabited the Buenos Aires of his boyhood. In one poem about Juan Muraña, another well-known knife fighter from turn-of-the-century Palermo, Borges reduces the identity and memory of Muraña to that of his knife:

> El cuchillo. La cara se ha borrado
> Y de aquel mercenario cuyo austero
> Oficio era el coraje, no ha quedado
> Más que una sombra y un fulgor de acero.
> Que el tiempo, que los mármoles empaña,
> Salve este firme nombre, Juan Muraña.
>
> (*OC,* p. 827)[20]

And the poem 'El tango' (1958), an evocation of the rough Buenos Aires underworld from which the dance emerged, ends:

> . . . El tango crea un turbio
> Pasado irreal que de algún modo es cierto,
> El recuerdo imposible de haber muerto
> Peleando, en una esquina de suburbio.
>
> (*OC,* p. 889)

The ending of this poem recalls that of the story **'El Sur'** (1953), in which the character Dahlmann dies in a knife fight or dreams on the operating table that he is dying in a knife fight, the death he in any case would have chosen:

> Sintió, al atravesar el umbral, que morir en una pelea a cuchillo, a cielo abierto y acometiendo, hubiera sido una liberación para él, una felicidad y una fiesta, en la primera noche del sanatorio, cuando le clavaron la aguja. Sintió que si él, entonces, hubiera podido elegir o soñar su muerte, ésta es la muerte que hubiera elegido o soñado.
>
> (*OC,* p. 530)

In **'El Sur'** the character prefers to die in a knife fight, and would even have the mark on his forehead (actually the mark of life in a modern city, since he wounded himself climbing a staircase) be remembered as the mark of the wad of paper thrown at him by the gaucho who provoked him to fight. Similarly, in 'El tango' Borges states that the music and violent lyrics of the tango create an imaginary past in which he, sedentary writer turned man of action, died as knife fighter. The violence of the Argentine past leaves its mark on his imagination and on his text. Writing himself and his readers into the place of the victim, he reverses the *topos* inherited from Sarmiento, for whom the killer is the tragic hero, assured of sympathy in his 'misfortune', a view also expressed in *Martín Fierro.* For Borges, on the other hand, to tell—or to hear—one of these violent tales is to be marked by it.

The scar on Moon's face demands to be explained, but those who succumb to impertinent curiosity are duly rewarded, as they too find themselves marked by his infamy. The previous owner of the ranch, 'La Colorada', sold it and fled the scene after hearing Moon's story.[21] Borges cast himself as a character in his narrative to suggest that each retelling will produce another fearful recognition. In their powerful brevity Borges's stories embody the paralysing violence which is so often their subject. Borges suggests in his essay 'Magias parciales del *Quijote*' that the technique of fictions within fictions, like the play within the play in *Hamlet,* owes its efficacy to the fact that we, too, as readers or spectators, are ensnared in the conflicts we intend to observe at a distance (*OC,* p. 669). In **'La forma de la espada'** the fiction within the fiction is the thing that catches at our conscience, that makes us aware of our complicity.

Far from being an empty or conventional literary sign, facial scars in Borges (as well as in his admired Stevenson) take on an added meaning of treachery and intrigue. Starting from broad principles of the literary function of details, Borges comes to develop the meaning of the sign of the facial scar within the specific context of an Argentine literary tradition, in which being marked signifies loss or defeat. The scar, representing a fundamental ambiguity in fiction, becomes in Borges a mark on writer and reader of fantasized violence. Scars, the marks left by the past, are signs that constitute a coded language that evokes untold stories of violence and betrayal, and at the same time inscribes those stories within the ethos of the Argentine knife fighter.

Notes

1. Jorge Luis Borges, *Obras completas* (Buenos Aires, 1974), p. 854. Except where otherwise noted, all parenthetical references to Borges in the text are to this edition (hereafter *OC*).

2. Gilles Deleuze and Félix Guattari, *Anti-Oedipus: Capitalism and Schizophrenia,* translated by Robert Hurley, Mark Seem, and Helen R. Lane (Minneapolis, 1983), p. 145.

3. Robert Louis Stevenson, *Works,* edited by Charles Curtis Bigelow and Temple Scott, 10 vols. (New York, 1906), 1, 115.

4. Stevenson, 1, 114.

5. See Miguel de Cervantes, *Novelas ejemplares,* edited by Francisco Rodríguez Marín, 2 vols.

(Madrid, 1917), 1, 98. In a long note, Rodríguez Marín clarifies that it was Spanish custom to brand the faces of slaves, and refers even to the example of rebus writing on the face of a slave who had an *S* written on one cheek and a picture of a nail ('clavo') on the other, spelling out the word which described his condition, 'esclavo'.

6. 'Sobre la descripción literaria,' *Sur,* 97 (1942), 100–02 (p. 101).

7. On the relation between Borges and Stevenson, see Sylvia Molloy, *Las letras de Borges* (Buenos Aires, 1979), pp. 120–25, and my *El precursor velado: R. L. Stevenson en la obra de Borges* (Buenos Aires, 1985).

8. Stevenson, VI, 128. For a further discussion, see Balderston, pp. 31–35.

9. An example of the use of a scar as a circumstantial detail occurs in the opening description of Billy Bones in Stevenson's *Treasure Island,* one of Borges's favourite books: 'the brown old seaman, with the sabre cut', 'a tall, strong, heavy, nut-brown man; his tarry pigtail falling over the shoulder of his soiled blue coat; his hands ragged and scarred, with black broken nails; and the sabre cut across one cheek, a dirty, livid white' (II, I). The power of this description derives not only from its vividness but also from its ability to spur our imagination to invent a world of violence and adventure in which to insert him, very different from the tranquil domain of squires and doctors and innkeepers. The entire description is included in the parenthesis of the double reference to the sabre cut: an external mark which is significant because it allows the reader to infer a great deal about the past history and character of the man. As with Vandeleur's scar in *The Rajah's Diamond,* the story of Billy Bones's scar is never told; Stevenson feels that some 'circumstantial details' are more powerful if left unexplained. The scar as attribute of Billy Bones is the first in a series of details which mark all the pirates in the story, and evoke the violent world of the buccaneer: Black Dog has two fingers missing, Pew is blind, and Long John Silver has lost his left leg.

10. Scars function as central motifs in the two stories discussed here, 'El incivil Maestro de Ceremonias' and 'La forma de la espada'. A scar is also important in the portrait of Richard Burton in an essay on the translators of the *Arabian Nights,* which opens with the sentence: 'En Trieste, en 1872, en un palacio con estatuas húmedas y obras de salubridad deficientes, un caballero con la cara historiada por una cicatriz africana—el capitán Richard Francis Burton, cónsul inglés—emprendió una famosa traducción . . .' (*OC,* p. 397).

11. A. B. F. Mitford, *Tales of Old Japan* (London, 1906), p. 8.

12. For further comments on the use of *rubricar,* see Molloy, *Las letras de Borges,* p. 70.

13. *Towards a Speech Act Theory of Literary Discourse* (Bloomington, Indiana, 1977), p. 193.

14. Similarly, in 'Abenjacán el Bojarí', Zaid buys Rector Allaby's silence by telling him his story (*OC,* p. 601).

15. John Sturrock, in *Paper Tigers: The Ideal Fiction of Jorge Luis Borges* (Oxford, 1977), reads the story more as one of a disjunction between heroism and treachery. He writes: 'Moon, the provisional source of light, is ultimately exposed as a sham. He is also a man in a state of civil war, a man divided. He is both agent and patient. As agent he inflicts on his patient half the mark—a half-moon—which symbolizes his divided state. But that division lasts only as long as his narration lasts, it is a division forced on him by the necessary disjunction of narrative itself. Once the "solitary game" is over, Moon can revert to being a full moon again, instead of two warring halves' (p. 179). I think that the disjunction is nowhere near as absolute as Sturrock asserts. Moon's is perhaps a reflected glory, but we need not deny him his share of it. It would certainly not seem to be Borges's intention here—any more than in 'Tema del traidor y del héroe' or 'Deutsches Requiem'—to write a fiction which would be ultimately unambiguous. His fictive incursions into twentieth-century history are meant to be disquieting.

16. On the importance of the knife fight in Borges, see R. K. Britton, 'History, Myth, and Archetype in Borges's View of Argentina', *MLR,* 74 (1979), 607–16 (pp. 613–15), and Eduardo Tijeras, 'La sugestión del arrabal porteño y el duelo malevo en Borges', *Cuadernos Hispanoamericanos,* 319 (1977), 143–47. On the motif of betrayal in Borges, see Jean Franco, 'The Utopia of a Tired Man: Jorge Luis Borges,' *Social Text,* 4 (1982), 58–63, 72–75.

17. Domingo Faustino Sarmiento, *Facundo* (Madrid, 1970), pp. 68–69.

18. Evaristo Carriego, *Poesías completas* (Buenos Aires, 1968), pp. 66–67.

19. The *compadrito*'s heroes are derived from an already literary past: Juan Moreira was the subject of a popular novel by Eduardo Gutiérrez (later adapted for the stage), and Santos Vega, an Argentine Faustlike figure, was the subject of several gauchesque poems and of numerous ballads.

20. Another poem about Juan Muraña is the 'Milonga de Juan Muraña' in *La Cifra* (Buenos Aires, 1974), pp. 55–56. Muraña is also the subject of a story in *El informe de Brodie* (*OC,* pp. 1044–47). I have discussed Muraña in 'Evocation and Provocation in the Poetry of Borges: The Figure of Juan Muraña,' in *Borges the Poet,* edited by Carlos Cortínez (Fayetteville, Arkansas, 1986), pp. 325–32.

21. The name of the ranch, 'La Colorada,' suggests the colour of blood; more specifically, since it is located in Uruguay, it evokes the long civil conflict between the two main parties in that country, the Blancos and the Colorados.

Jaime Alazraki (essay date 1988)

SOURCE: "Structure as Meaning in 'The South,'" in *Borges and the Kabbalah,* Cambridge University Press, 1988, pp. 65–76.

[*In the following essay, Alazraki argues that the structure of Borges's story, "The South," is instrumental in creating a complexity in the text that allows two contradictory value systems to be represented as coexisting.*]

> Quand j'ai écrit **"Le Sud,"** je venais de lire Henry James et de découvrir qu'on peut raconter deux ou trois histoires en même temps. Ma nouvelle est donc ambiguë. On peut la lire au premier degré. Mais aussi considérer qu'il s'agit d'un rêve, celui d'un homme qui meurt à l'hôpital et aurait préféré mourir sur le pavé, l'arme à la main. Ou celui de Borges qui préférerait mourir comme son grandpère le général, à cheval, plutôt que dans son lit—ou encore que l'homme est tué par son rêve, cette idée du Sud, de la Pampa, qui l'avait conduit là.
>
> —Borges, *L'Express,* May 1977

Is there a structuring principle underlying Borges' short fiction? How are his stories made, and to what degree is it possible to derive from them a narrative code? How do his narratives *signify*? In other words, how are the literary signs organized and what meanings or functions do they propose, beyond their explicit content? Borges' work has repeatedly and perhaps excessively been examined at the level of its content, as a denotative language no different from that of the press. If, as Hjelmslev says, literature is a semiotic system whose means of expression is another semiotic system—language—it must be concluded that in a literary text there is, first, a linguistic function, a vehicle common to language and to literature that explains that "all the words with which a Garcilaso sonnet is written, appear *verbatim* in any dictionary of the Spanish language," as Cortazar has remarked. But it must also be recognized that in the literary discourse the linguistic sign becomes a signifier with functions or signifieds absent in the system of signs of language. The literary sign absorbs the linguistic sign in order to convert it into a new signifier whose signified transcends the orbit of language. The "*fiction* of literary language seeks not to clear up the meaning of a word but to reconstruct the rules and norms of elaboration of that meaning."[1] The literary text "unfolds in some way in order to add to its own explicit or literal signification, or denotation, a supplementary power of connotation that enriches it with one or several secondary meanings."[2] Literature is "a domain of a translinguistic or metalinguistic nature that comprises techniques of signification situated not next to language, but above or inside it."³ Gerard Genette explains this effect of oversignification in literature with an example from classical rhetoric:

> In the synecdoche *sail-ship* there is a signifier, *sail,* and there is an object (or concept) signified, *the ship*: that's the denotation. But since the word *sail* has substituted the noun *ship,* the relationship (signification) that unifies the signifier with the signified constitutes a figure. This figure, in turn, designates clearly, within the rhetorical code, a poetic state of the discourse. The figure functions, then, as the signifier of a new signified—poetry—over a second semantic plane, that of the rhetorical connotation. The inherent quality of connotation is, in fact, its capacity to establish itself above (or underneath) the first signification, but in an unconnected fashion, using the first meaning as a means of designating a second concept.⁴

This second concept, inserted in the first, would then be the object of literary studies or at least of one type of study, since a text becomes literature when it produces poetic functions which organize themselves in a coherent system of signs, when it transforms natural language into a second language, when it abandons the denotation of the linguistic code and gives way to connotation to create with it its own expressive code. This transformation constitutes an operation by means of which the writer interrogates the world. The function of the critic would then be to examine this operation, since if for a writer literature is "a first language or language-object, criticism is a discourse about a discourse, a second language or metalanguage."⁵

Being a reader as well as a critic of his own work, Borges was the first to suggest that his story **"The South"** "could be read as a direct narration of fictional facts and also as something else" (*F,* 105). Asked about this second way, he answered:

> Everything that happens after Dahlmann leaves the hospital could be interpreted as his own hallucination when he is about to die of septicemia, as a fantastic vision of how he would have chosen to die. Hence the slight correspondences between the two halves of the story; the volume of *One Thousand and One Nights,* that appears in both parts; the horse-carriage that first takes him to the hospital and then to the railroad station; the resemblance between the tavern's owner and a hospital worker; the touch Dahlmann feels on his forehead when wounded and the touch of the bread-crumb thrown by the "compadrito" to provoke him.⁶

This interpretation suggested by Borges himself escapes the denotative or literal level. At that level, Borges wrote a linear story in which Dahlmann recovers in the hospital and travels to his ranch to convalesce. It is in the make-up of the story that a second meaning is implied. The text has been organized in such a way that the first signifier is forced to fold over onto itself and generate a second signifier capable of new poetic functions. This organization consists of an introduction and two parts. In the first part, the protagonist is introduced and the conflict is presented: in the clash between his two lines of descent, we are told,

Juan Dahlmann chose the line of his romantic ancestor, the one with a romantic death. It should be noticed that the Argentina of the 1930s is not the romantic country of Francisco Flores, and that Juan Dahlmann, librarian, reader of *Martín Fierro* and of the *One Thousand and One Nights,* leads a life closer to that of his Germanic ancestor than to that of his *criollo* grandfather. His circumstances are Argentine, but his name is the same as that of the evangelical minister, and so is his faith in culture. This element of the conflict appears in the introduction. Juan Dahlmann is a symbol of his country's fate: the conflict between his two lineages is an expression of Sarmiento's formula "civilization and barbarism." Dahlmann chooses the first of these alternatives, but the country will force him to face the second. The first link of the story is thus a compendium of the story as a whole.

The autobiographical character of this story is obvious. Juan Dahlmann is a mask of Borges, of a Borges who chooses, like his ancestor Laprida, books, but who knows that the deep reality of his other lineage is pierced by violence—a violence he abhors and whose futility he has repeatedly underlined, but which he recognizes as "an apocryphal past, at the same time stoic and orgiastic, in which any Argentine has defied and fought to finally fall silently in an obscure knife-fight."⁷ There is a second factor of a psychological nature. Grandchild and great-grandchild of colonels, offspring of heroes of the wars of independence, Borges has expressed in several poems his admiration for those military ancestors who shaped Argentine history. Secluded in a humble library, Borges has given in, more than once, to a nostalgic fascination for that past he views as epic. In his "Autobiographical Essay" he has said: "On both sides of my family I have military forebears; this may count for my yearning after that epic destiny which my gods denied me, no doubt wisely."⁸ Borges returns to that epic universe of his ancestors seeking neither a futile violence that he condemns nor an empty bravery that he insistently calls "useless," but a virtue that our time, predominantly individualistic, has forgotten. It is no accident that Bernard Shaw was one of his favorite writers. In him, Borges finds an alternative of liberation to the anxiety of modern man, and through Shaw he defines the meaning of that virtue he admires in his ancestors:

> Bernard Shaw is an author to whom I keep returning. . . . He has epic significance, and is the only writer of our time who has imagined and presented heroes to his readers. On the whole, modern writers tend to reveal men's weaknesses, and seem to delight in their unhappiness; in Shaw's case, however, we have characters like Major Barbara or Caesar, who are heroic and whom one can admire. Contemporary literature since Dostoievski—and even earlier, since Byron—seems to delight in man's guilt and weaknesses. In Shaw's work the greatest human virtues are extolled. For example, that a man can forget his own fate, that a man may not value his own happiness, that he may say like our Almafuerte: "I am not interested in my own life," because he is interested in something beyond personal circumstances.⁹

In his heroic forefathers, Borges seeks to rescue that virtue: an epic sense of life, values that transcend the narrow limits of our individual selves and propose a stoic dimension that liberates life from its existential bounds. To the values of the novel—centered in the destiny of the self—Borges opposes the axiology of the epic: acts of courage that prove that people are capable of transcending their own egos in defense of humanistic ideals and elevated tasks. Violence is thus understood as a cathartic agent. The destruction of a life is not a gratuitous act, nor a macho's boastful display of guts. A hero—reasons Borges—defends a cause (a virtue, a destiny, a duty) whose value far exceeds that of his own life. In the duel between Juan Dahlmann and the boisterous *compadrito* who forces him to fight, Dahlmann succumbs as victim of a violence he has not chosen and of which he does not feel part, but in the final analysis the decision to fight is Dahlmann's. When Dahlmann bends over to pick up the knife thrown to him by "the old ecstatic gaucho in whom *he* saw a cipher of the South," he understands that he will be able to defend his injured dignity with the only language his provoker knows: the knife. The *compadrito* fights motivated by laws of honor which Borges has unequivocally condemned as a form of barbarism. Dahlmann's motivation is quite different. Dahlmann defends a moral value—his injured dignity—with his life. From this act one must conclude that for Dahlmann—for that Dahlmann who is dreaming his death in an innocuous hospital bed where he indeed is dying of "physical miseries"—dignity is dearer than the life that holds it. Viewed from this set of values, it is understandable that Dahlmann chose to pick up the knife that "would justify his killing." Between his death and the loss of his honor, Dahlmann chooses death.

But this choice is framed within a dream. When he is about to die of septicemia, prostrate in a hospital bed, Dahlmann confesses to himself that "if he had been able to choose, *then*, or to dream his death, this would have been the death he would have chosen or dreamt."[10] The adverb (*then*) is important on two accounts. First, because it points to the circumstances under which that violent death was chosen. Second, because it refers to a literary dream that restores an Argentine myth: "a lowly knife fight dreamed by Hernández in the 1860's."[11] Dahlmann's dream represents, in a way, the dream of all Argentines. It is just an avatar of that fight in which "a gaucho lifts a black off his feet with his knife, throws him down like a sack of bones, sees him agonize and die, crouches down to clean his blade, unties his horse, and mounts slowly so he will not be thought to be running away."[12] Hernández's dream—Borges adds—"returns infinitely." The whole of Argentine history is ciphered in that dream that time has turned into a "part of the memory of all." Before dying, Dahlmann returns to that dream he knows he is part of. He chooses the dream of his *criollo* lineage, but only when nearing death. Dahlmann's life, devoted to books, has been an effort to correct the violence of that lineage. But as an Argentine vulnerable to the "imperatives of courage and honor," Dahlmann is forced to return to that "dream" of one man which is part of the memory of all, he is compelled to go back to that myth that defines the essence of his violent condition.

Borges' story presents with deliberate ambiguity the futility of that dream, and at the same time its paradoxical inevitability. There is not a single and logical meaning, and yet Borges has articulated his story with impeccable logic. The laws of that logic go beyond syllogism. Its coherence stems from the text itself and from a very Borgesian world-view, but this world-view is contained as a whole in the narrative. The text, in its etymological sense of texture, tissue, structure, contains the answers to its seeming incongruities: How does one explain the fact that Dahlmann, who has devoted his life to books, would agree to a "useless" fight that amounts to his own destruction? Borges' answer is formulated through the organization of the narrative. By dividing the story into two halves—the accident and the trip to the South—and by suggesting that the second half, connected to the first by subtle symmetries, is a dream that the protagonist dreams before dying in the hospital, Borges faces the question of the credibility of the knife fight by turning it into a dream. By doing this, he gives the fight a precise meaning: this fight—Borges seems to imply—exists only as a dream, and that dream is no different from the one dreamed by Hernández in *Martín Fierro*. Because it is "part of the memory of all," we return to this dream infinitely as to a collective unconscious which intrinsically defines Argentines, as to a mirror that, more than reflecting a façade, gives back the image of *the other*, a violent face waiting to tear the surface with a knife. For the image of *the other* to appear, Borges takes his character to the South—the last stronghold of courage, the last sanctuary of that religion of gauchos and compadres—and to dispel all doubt about his condition of dream, or, what amounts to the same thing, of expression of an intimate collective unconscious, Borges structures the story like a mirror in which the second half is a symmetrical reflection of the first. This structure suggests that the second half is a dream and that in this dream, Dahlmann would fulfill the duties of courage. He will carry them out as any Argentine for whom Hernández's fight is the cipher of his own destiny would, and for whom the purpose of the tango is "to give Argentines the conviction of having been brave, of having complied with the requisites of courage and honor."[13]

In the poem "Junín," Borges, the poetic speaker, searches for *the other* in the battle of his forebears. Like Juan Dahlmann, he also seeks to rescue that mythical being which defines him in his most essential condition:

> I am myself but I am also *the other*
> The man who died, the man whose blood and name
> Are mine: a stranger here, yet with a fame
> He won keeping Indian spears at bay,
> I come back to this Junín I have never seen,
> To your Junín, grandfather Borges.[14]

The poem shows a greater degree of explicitness than the story. In this imaginary return to the "epic Junín," Borges recreates in more abstract terms the trip of Juan Dahlmann to the South. It could be argued that the historical battle is not a knife fight in a humble country tavern, and that while the first is an indisputable epic event, the knife fight is merely an expression of showy courage. But for Borges, there is a common denominator between the battle and the duel: in both acts there prevails a cult of courage that turns the duel into an epic act, and the battle into an expression of personal bravado. Speaking about the civil war that followed Argentina's war of independence, Borges has said of the *caudillos*: "Fighting a war was not for them the coherent execution of a plan but a game of manliness."[15] And referring, in *Evaristo Carriego,* to the knife fight between Wenceslao and the *Santafesino,* he alludes to this duel as "the epic of Wenceslao," adding that the episode has "a clearly epic and even knightly character,"[16] which is not to say that the wars of independence and the duels of the knife fighters have for him the same value. If there is any doubt regarding Borges' aversion towards this type of vain violence, it will suffice to refer to his more recent short story **"Rosendo Juarez"** to dispel it. At the same time, this kind of aversion does not exclude his admiration for the violent side of a knife fight. Otherwise, his preference and pleasure for knife-fight stories could not be understood. Nor could it be understood that in order to explain the etymology of the word *virtue* he wrote: "*Virtus,* which in Latin means courage derives from *vir,* which means man."[17] Or that, in order to demonstrate that the tango and the milonga seek to express "the conviction that fighting can be a feast,"[18] he resorted in his book, *Evaristo Carriego,* to the major epic poems of European literature (the *Iliad,* the *Beowulf,* the *Chanson de Roland* and *Orlando*). If we add that courage, which could also be an epic trait found in a knife fight, is the virtue most worshipped by Argentines as an act or as a dream, Borges' evocation of Junín and Dahlmann's dream assume an unequivocal meaning.

As a linear story, **"The South"** leaves the impression of an arbitrary act and a gratuitous gesture. But if Borges had said in the text that Dahlmann's trip to the South *was a dream* of the patient who was dying in a hospital, the fight would have lost much of its effectiveness, and the text itself would not have had the tension and the precision that it has. "Since everything could happen in dreams—we would have reasoned—the fight impresses us as any other arbitrary act." Borges' solution lies in preserving the linear narrative at the level of the denotation and in correcting it at the level of connotation through the structure of his text. This double solution is a technical achievement, but it also represents the counterpart—at the level of the signifier—of the duality of meanings that, like a double-edged weapon, the trip to the South suggests. Through the linear reading of the story, Borges condemns the fight as an act of vanity—vanity in the *compadrito*'s provocation, vanity in Dahlmann's acceptance, vanity in a blind act that subscribes to and celebrates barbarism. From this point of view, Dahlmann does not choose his death: he fatalistically succumbs to the law of the knife. Through the reading suggested by the structure of the story, on the other hand, the fight reorganizes itself as a dream. Before dying

in his hospital bed, Dahlmann dreams a death in consonance with that of his forebears. This dream is an encounter with *the other,* with the blood of his grandfather killed by the Indians of Catriel; it is an encounter with the epic sense of a fight in which one chooses to die to prove a virtue more important than life. Dahlmann's dream is also an encounter with his past, it is a last journey to that history that exhausts itself in "a lowly knife fight," a last effort to enter into that "dream of one man that is part of the memory of all," the fight narrated in *Martín Fierro.*

It could be argued that the two meanings are contradictory; that violence cannot be reproved and, at the same time, celebrated; that a knife fight cannot be an epic act and, at the same time, empty bravado. But, like most of Borges' work, **"The South"** plays with contradictory meanings that resolve themselves in ambiguous paradoxes. Like the tango and the milonga that are reminiscent of "a stoic and orgiastic past," the fight that Dahlmann dreams is an excess and a deprivation, a destruction and a form of fulfillment, a negation and an act of affirmation. Borges' answers are not causal: they assimilate, like an oxymoron, two terms that seemingly contradict and reject each other. In a way, **"The South"** is a story that holds two stories, and each of them suggests a contradictory version of the meaning of Dahlmann's fight. But in order to suggest a second meaning, it was necessary to interpolate in the story a second signifier incorporated into the first one. The narrative presents difficulties that the poem ignores. In "Junín," the first line says straightforwardly: "I am myself but I am also the other, the man who died." To convey a similar idea in the story, Borges constructs a mirror structure: the second half of the story reflects the image of *the other* that Juan Dahlmann seeks to be, and in order to preserve the verisimilitude of the story—a librarian suddenly turned into a knife fighter—that *other* surfaces, as if in a dream, from the agonies of a dying librarian.

Borges has warned that "the verbs *to live* and *to dream,* according to the Idealist doctrine, are strictly synonyms."[19] He has also said that "literature is a controlled dream."[20] Through literature, through literature's dream, Borges "returns to Junín where he had never been"; he is "a vague person and also the man who stopped the spears in the desert." Dahlmann also will rescue his *other* through a dream and, like Pedro Damian in **"The Other Death,"** he will die two deaths. Most of Borges' stories offer this double level, a false bottom of sorts; the second of these levels, like a mirror, returns the image of the first, but inverted. Like Borges, who recognized himself as a divided personality in the short prose piece **"Borges and I,"** Juan Dahlmann is that frail librarian fascinated by the marvels of books, and that violent *other* whose final fulfillment happens in a knife-fight dream.

In many ways, **"The South"** is the inverted version of a poem from *San Martin Copybook* (1929), entitled "Isidoro Acevedo." Borges' maternal grandfather, Acevedo, was not a military man, but "he fought in the battles at Cepeda and Pavón." In the poem, Borges sets out "to rescue his last day," or, more accurately, "an essential dream" of the last day of his life: "For in the same way that other men write verse / my grandfather elaborated a dream." In this young Borges, the formula "literature = dreams" already appears as an equation of interchangeable terms. Here, as in Dahlmann's last dream in the poem, Borges will fulfill the epic destiny of his grandfather in an apocryphal dream. This fictitious dream of a heroic death, when Acevedo is actually dying of a pulmonary disease in his bedroom, will be, however, his true death, "the death that he [like Dahlmann] would have chosen or dreamed, if he had been able to choose or to dream his death." The story and the poem are motivated by the same effort: to force destiny to correct itself, to make it comply with the requisites of courage, to be part of that memory in which, consciously or unconsciously, all Argentines recognize themselves. This is the dream that Borges makes his grandfather dream.

> While a lung ailment ate away at him
> And hallucinatory fevers distorted the face of the day,
> He assembled the burning documents of his memory
> For the forging of his dream.
>
> His dream was of two armies
> Entering the shadow of battle;
> He enumerated the commands, the colors, the units,
> "Now the officers are reviewing their battle plans,"
> He said in a voice you could hear,
> And in order to see them he tried sitting up.
>
> He made a final levy,
> Rallying the thousands of faces that a man knows without
> Really knowing at the end of his years:
> Bearded faces now growing dim in daguerreotypes;
> Faces that lived and died next to his own at the battles
> Of Puente Alsina and Cepeda.
>
> In the visionary defense of his country that his faith
> Hungered for (and not that his fever imposed),
> He plundered his days
> And rounded up an army of Buenos Aires ghosts
> So as to get himself killed in the fighting.
>
> That was how, in a bedroom that looked onto the garden,
> He died out of devotion for his city.[21]

In this dream that Borges weaves, like a mask of his grandfather, death gives expression to an intimate will, to a strong necessity to exalt that epic side that Borges admires in Shaw's characters. Man's epic sense of life finds in death its ultimate challenge. Acevedo, killed by a pulmonary disease, and Dahlmann, killed by septicemia, refute that heroic side of life in which they believed. Such an innocuous death negates that stoic past of their heroic ancestors, an epic past to which Borges relentlessly returns and with which he identifies. It also negates the substance that makes up the gaucho or the *compadre* or any Argentine for whom courage is still the highest virtue. In order to correct those fortuitous deaths unworthy of his heroic sense of life, and in order to comply with the requisites of courage, Borges resorts to dreams or to their homologue,

literature. Freud thought of dreams as the blurred fulfillment of desires and needs intimately repressed (or postponed), and Jung's contribution to the theory of dreams was his idea of a collective unconscious and its reverberations in archetypal dreams, in myths that express not the individual but the species. Borges' intent is to rescue that collective dream that is part of the memory of all. He compels Juan Dahlmann, Isidoro Acevedo, Pedro Damián and even Martín Fierro himself, in his story **"The End,"** to dream it.

In **"The South,"** as in **"The Other Death," "The End,"** and in the poem "Isidoro Acevedo," there are two deaths, and those two deaths embody two different signifieds expressed also through two different signifiers. The first signifier finds its expression linearly; the second is coined through the structure, through those two symmetrical halves of the story that induce us to read the second part as a dream. The story leaves a perplexing aftertaste because the two signifieds proposed by those two signifiers are contradictory. On the one hand, courage is presented as a useless virtue that forces Dahlmann to a death no less useless; on the other, courage is presented as Dahlmann's last attempt to return to a stoic past. His death makes possible the fulfillment of a dream in which Dahlmann meets the epic past of his grandfather who died a romantic death.

These two opposite sides of courage are intertwined in the story as an oxymoron through which Borges expresses his two-fold and contradictory view of courage. For Borges as an individual and a book lover, courage is useless, a token of barbarism, a primitive state fitting a nation of shepherds and riders who do not understand urban civilization. For Borges as a member of a national group that sees in bravery the most precious of virtues, and as a descendant of heroes who wove a good stretch of the history of his country, courage is a yearning, an intimate epic necessity, a romantic death-wish that expresses itself in an apocryphal dream, a dream that is part of the memory of all. As a conscious reflection, as an act of lucidity, Borges rejects and condemns courage; voicing the dictates of a collective unconscious that glorifies bravery, Borges sees courage as a myth he knows himself to be part of, as a myth that fulfills the dark depths of his blood. Borges' literary accomplishment in **"The South"** lies in having given expression to that ambivalent vision, in having turned the first signifier (the linear narrative) into another signifier (the second narrative suggested through the structure), and finally in having chosen the plane of the linear or causal narration to express his lucid version of courage, while at the same time permitting his mythical or unconscious version of courage to be expressed, as it were, underneath the text, through the structure of the story or, what amounts to the same thing, through an implied dream.

Notes

1. Roland Barthes, *Essais critiques* (Paris: Seuil, 1964), p. 306.

2. Gerard Genette, *Figures* (Paris: Seuil, 1966), p. 213.

3. *Ibid.*

4. *Ibid.,* p. 215.

5. Roland Barthes, *op.cit.,* p. 304.

6. J. Irby, N. Murat and C. Peralta, *Encuentro con Borges* (Buenos Aires: Galerna, 1968), p. 34. Borges' interpretation of his own story has prompted a rather long and fertile controversy. Allen W. Phillips was the first to deal with this aspect of "The South" in his article "'El Sur' de Borges" (*Revista Hispánica Moderna,* vol. XXIX, no. 2, April 1963, pp. 140–147). I discussed his interpretation and suggested a different reading of the story in *La prosa narrativa de J. L. Borges* (Madrid: Gredos, 2nd ed. 1984), chapter IX (pp. 122–137). Subsequent articles by Z. Gertel ("'El Sur' de Borges: búsqueda de identidad en el laberinto," *Nueva Narrativa Hispanoamericana,* I, 2, Sept. 1971, pp. 35–55), Robert M. Scari ("Aspectos realista-tradicionales del arte narrativo de Borges," *Hispania,* LVII, 4, Dec. 1974, pp. 899–907), and particularly John B. Hall ("Borges' 'El Sur': A Garden of Forking Paths?" *Iberoromania,* Göttingen, no. 3, neue folge, 1975, pp. 71–77) have contributed new views and enriched the discussion of this story.

7. Jorge Luis Borges, *Evaristo Carriego* (Buenos Aires: Emecé, 1955), p. 149.

8. J. L. Borges, "An Autobiographical Essay," in *The Aleph and Other Stories 1933–1969* (New York, Dutton, 1970), p. 208.

9. Rita Guibert, *Seven Voices* (New York: Vintage, 1973), pp. 97–98.

10. Jorge Luis Borges, *Ficciones* (New York: Grove, 1962), p. 174.

11. J. L. Borges, "Martín Fierro," in *Dreamtigers* (University of Texas, 1964), p. 40.

12. *Ibid.*

13. J. L. Borges, *Evaristo Carriego,* p. 149.

14. J. L. Borges, *Selected Poems 1923–1967* (Delacorte Press/Seymour Lawrence, 1972), p. 211.

15. J. L. Borges, *Evaristo Carriego,* p. 124.

16. *Ibid.,* p. 154.

17. *Ibid.,* p. 146.

18. *Ibid.,* p. 147.

19. J. L. Borges, *El Aleph,* p. 113.

20. J. L. Borges, *Other Inquisitions,* p. 72.

21. J. L. Borges, *Selected Poems 1923–1967,* pp. 53–56.

Floyd Merrell (essay date 1991)

SOURCE: "According to the Eye of the Beholder," in *Unthinking Thinking: Jorge Luis Borges, Mathematics, and the New Physics,* Purdue University Press, 1991, pp. 32–42.

[*In the following excerpt, Merrell explores Borges's use of paradox.*]

> I don't like writers who are making sweeping statements all the time. Of course, you might argue that what I'm saying is a sweeping statement, no?
>
> —*Jorge Luis Borges*

1.

It has been said that paradox is truth standing on its head to attract attention, and that truth is paradox crying out to be transcended. The word comes from the Greek *para doxos,* meaning *beyond belief,* which is actually not befitting, for many paradoxes are the source of deep-seated convictions, if not "truth." More appropriately, then, we might say that paradoxes are trains of thought condensed into a point of time and space. Contemplating a paradox has been compared to meditating on a Zen Koan, gazing at a mandala, entering momentarily into the realm of the infinite. A world free of paradox is the stuff only dreams are made of, yet rationalism, even logic itself, in the final analysis "teaches us to expect some dreaminess in the world, and even contradictions" (Peirce 1960; 4:79). According to Kierkegaard, reason ultimately leads to paradox, and faith is needed to remedy it. But a paradox is not resolved by faith alone, nor can it logically be disposed of in many cases. It remains coiled at the very heart of our reasoning process.

Guillermo Sucre (1970, 469) correctly remarks that Borges's writing is a "fusion of contradictions." What he fails to note is that such fusion is inescapable, for the knowledge paradox inheres in all viable thinking, whether one be a nominalist, realist, idealist, Vaihingerian "fictionalist," Meinongian, or whatever. That is, the fusion of one's knowledge (what one believes one knows) with one's "meta-knowledge" (one's knowledge *about* one's knowledge) breeds paradox, for, like the "preface paradox" that marked the beginning of this book, at the second level one ultimately knows one does not, and cannot, be in possession of absolute "truth"; some of one's knowledge is, unfortunately, always either inconsistent or incomplete, yet at the first level one tends to persist in believing it may well be absolute. Rather than "truth" standing on its head, then, the knowledge paradox is "truth" as an asymmetric object looking at itself in a mirror. It sees its own inverse, its right side becomes its left side: its mirror image is its own falsity, and it can do no more than oscillate between the two poles of the contradiction ad infinitum.

Richard Burgin (1968, 115) observes that Escher's work in visual terms compares favorably with some of Borges's cherished themes. Indeed, some of Borges's stories elicit what Douglas Hofstadter (1979, 94–95; 688–89) calls the "authorship triangle." There are three authors, A, B, and C. A exists in a novel by B, B in a novel by C, and, strangely, C is to be found in A's novel. This tangled triad is analogous, Hofstadter tells us, to Escher's well-known print of a hand drawing a second hand which is in turn drawing the first hand. How are such puzzles explained? Authors A, B, and C, necessarily unaware of their predicament, will, we must presume, happily tred through life believing they are real people. But another author, say, D, from a "meta-perspective," knows that they are mere imaginary beings. So assume D writes his own novel about those three unfortunate souls who think they are real people. Fine. But how is he to know that he is not a character in another novel by author E? We can gaze at Escher's hands drawing themselves and with confidence remark on the anomaly from our "superior" vantage point. We know that behind this print lurks Escher's invisible hand drawing the two appendages. But the problem is not resolved thus, for, like the knowledge paradox, from a "meta-perspective" there is still no guarantee that what we know is not false (or fictitious). There is no recourse but to oscillate between the two horns of the dilemma.

On speaking of such dilemmas, we are introduced to one of Borges's finest stories, **"The Circular Ruins"** (*L*, 45–50), which I will treat in some detail here in order that its paradoxical force may be effectively highlighted. In an exotic setting, a magician-priest arrives at the charred ruins of an ancient circular temple. The purpose which guided him "was not impossible, though it was supernatural" (*L*, 46). He wanted to dream a human being and insert him into reality. After failing in his initial attempt to dream a multitude of young boys and select from them the most promising candidate, he embarked on a second effort: to dream an individual, starting with the heart, and creating outward to the skeleton and finally to each of the innumerable hairs. After gradually accustoming this arduously dreamt boy to reality, the magician sent him downstream to the north "to be born." His son was now, for practical purposes, a part of "reality": in fact, "all creatures except Fire itself and the dreamer would believe him to be a man of flesh and blood" (*L*, 48). One night the magician was awakened by two boatmen who told him of another magician to the north who could walk on fire without being burned. As any good father, the dreamer feared for the emotional well-being of his son, for if he meditated on his rare privilege and discovered that he was a mere image it would be humiliating. However, his thoughts were cut short, for a jungle blaze threatened from the south. The old man, cognizant of his imminent death, walked boldly into the "concentric" blaze only to realize "with relief, with humiliation, with terror," that the flames could not consume him, for "he too was a mere appearance, dreamt by another" (*L*, 50).

"The Circular Ruins" reveals one of Borges's strategies for creating contradictions, paradoxes, and infinite regresses, which will have a bearing on later sections of this inquiry. The first step entails a set of apparent oppositions. The magician came from the south, where he had dwelled in "one of the infinite villages upstream." On the other hand, after sufficiently preparing his "unreal" son for integration into "reality," the magician sent him downstream to the north, where there lay the ruins of "another propitious temple, whose gods were also burned and dead" (*L*,

47). The conditions of the son's environment are reciprocally identical to those of the magician. Only the infinitely repetitive trees of the jungle separate one temple from another. Hence, the spatial trajectories of father and son compose two symmetrical oppositions, up(stream)/down(south) and down(stream)/up(north), which structurally produce a "cancellation effect." As a result, the action of the story terminates simultaneously everywhere and nowhere: at the center of the charred ruins of a circular temple where the magician created his dream image. This symmetry of space reveals the fallacy of what Alfred North Whitehead (1925, ch. 4) calls "simple location." The story alludes not to precise geographic points but to vague notions of circular surfaces, which become almost as haptic as they are visual.

In contrast to these spatial indices, at the outset it appears that time is linear, and it accumulates with increasing torpidity. The magician required fourteen days to perfect the heart of his subject, one year to create the skeleton, a little less than two additional years to complete his project, and two more long years to prepare his son for "birth." The son's development, then, is first decelerated and finally halted altogether when the magician interpolates him into the world. However, this effort to annihilate the past is ultimately futile. Temporal recurrence is foretold by the magician's impression that "all this had happened before" (*L*, 45). If the obliteration of "simple location" of space coupled with vague images of spatial circularity implies a denial of linear movement, concomitantly, the attempt to annihilate the past and establish an eternal "now" stems from an implicit attempt to deny temporal irreversibility.

The "invincible purpose" that drives the magician can be explicated on two levels: concrete and abstract. On a concrete level, the magician strives to coordinate his activities with those of his son. He daily prostrates himself at dawn and at twilight "before the stone figure, imagining perhaps that his unreal child was practicing the same rites, in other circular ruins" (*L*, 49). By means of these ritualistic acts, he gradually becomes "as all men," and his absent son is nurtured with the progressive diminution of his maker's own soul. When the magician's purpose in life is finally completed, he assumes that his son's immortality is now projected into the physical world, an event that at once symbolically represents the concretion of the "unreal" (dream) and the eternal coexistence of the "real" (physical) world. On an abstract level, the coexistence of "real" father with "unreal" son coheres with the symbolic coexistence of space and time. Spatial and temporal synchronicity portrayed in Borges's story is a condition quite unlike the linear temporal existence of the physical world. In this sense, physical existence, which presupposes human finitude, is opposed to the dream world of spaceless and timeless coexistence. In the material sphere of existence, the contradiction between life and death is presumably irreconcilable. On the other hand, in the nonmaterial order, governed by spatio-temporal synchronicity, this contradiction is nonexistent.

Consider the possibility that in **"The Circular Ruins"** a projection of spatio-temporal synchronicity into linear existence entails a symbolic abolition of the life/death dichotomy. This assumes an implicit attempt to overcome temporal existence wherein spatial hierarchy and temporal linearity predominate. In more concrete terms, the magician's "purpose" stems from a desire to make his "unreal" son part of tangible "reality" and vicariously to transcend mortality himself, for even though all fathers "are interested in the children they have procreated," this interest is at the same time self-interest. Therefore, the constraint in the text subjected to potential restructuring is the life/death duality, perhaps the most intransigent of all. For obvious reasons, the protagonist is a "magician" and the story reads like a "myth."

The relation between father and son ("reality" and dream) can be illustrated by an abstract scheme, in which the sequential and parallel planes intersect where there is potential movement in the narrative toward a more complex level of organization. The desired goal entails actualization of relations of similitude between father-son and "reality"-dream. By inserting dream image into "reality," the son can become a "man" and the magician can vicariously transcend the finitude of his physical existence. In order to accomplish this goal, the magician must activate a fusion of opposites wherein the son's *timelessness* predominates over the father's *temporality* and the father's *essence* over the son's *materialessness*. However, the "logical" end prevails: the magician realizes he is an integral part of dream existence, which discounts the son's supposed entry into "reality," and the "unreal" enjoys synonymity with the "real." . . .

According to the reading I have proposed, this impossible intersection of the "unreal" and the "real" becomes manifest at the end of the story. The magician assumes that his monumental task is completed, but when the parallel and sequential axes converge, the paradox underlying his project potentially becomes apparent. His status as the object of yet another dream is obviously a proposition embedded in his mind, since his own maker had instilled in him, as he in his son, complete oblivion of his apprenticeship. Hence, from the very beginning, it may be conjectured, the magician's grand design is doomed to failure. In the first place, he strives to force the dreamt image into his own supposedly tangible form of existence in order to concretize the sequential chain of mental events (dream "reality") that are the product of unlimited semiotic activity and to establish lines of similarity where ordinarily there would exist only lines of opposition. In other words, he tries to make dream "reality" denote something other than what it would ordinarily denote. In the second place, realization of the magician's desire would be equivalent to a desiring subject's becoming part of the imagined world he has created and at the same time a prisoner of/in his own desires. The fusion cannot be actualized, however, and what the magician presumed to accomplish at one level backfires at another level.

To determine more precisely the nature of the magician's dilemma, let us return to the implicit purpose guiding his action. After the magician's preliminary effort to create a "real" son fails, he realizes that his project will be much more arduous than "weaving a rope of sand or coining the faceless wind" (*L,* 47). This passage reveals two metaphorical (oxymoronic) images, which on a local level represent the impossible conjunction of distinct classes of things: rope (fibered) out of sand (nonfibered) or coin (malleable-solid) out of wind (nonmalleable-nonsolid). The magician now attempts to construct a solitary dreamt image by means of another approach. The problem is that to integrate the attributes of this image into his own world logically implies a simultaneous rupture of boundaries. In other words, two distinct classes, *A* and *B,* are governed by different logical orders, and they cannot be integrated while maintaining intact the logical order of either *A* or *B,* but both, on becoming members of the same class, must be subjected to a different order. Hence, the magician cannot conjoin two distinct spheres of existence into his own without altering both. If, on the other hand, the magician had conceived of his dream world as does primitive man, as merely another facet of the same "reality," his project would nonetheless have been equally futile. For to make a dream coexist with "reality" would be nonsensical, given the fact that in the primitive's animistic conception of things, the two entities could not represent an intractable dualism in the first place.

Fire might have been construed as a potential mediator between the "reality" of the magician and the "nonreality" of the boy, since fire symbolically "converts" essence to nonessence (matter to energy). Following this metaphorical line of reasoning, the magician would be attempting to reverse the process and convert his "unreal" son (nonessence) to "reality" (essence). Moreover, only fire would be able to discern the created being's lack of essence, since it cannot consume that which is the final product of its consummatory process. In fact, fire appears as an earthly god in one of the magician's dreams and offers to give life to his inert dream image. However, the fire deity is helpless against that over which it presumably exercises dominion: its very sanctuary, as in centuries past, is destroyed by fire. This destruction recapitulates the paradox inherent in the magician's project. That is, the god of fire is the "symbolic," or "archetypal," expression of fire, and as such it rests at a distinct level of organization. The symbol can be representative of fire but cannot coexist on the same logical level as fire; it cannot be fire itself. When the magician assumes he possesses the ability to annihilate the boundaries between logical categories, all distinctions between symbol and referent, dreamer and dreamt, become nonexistent, and he loses his capacity, as *Homo symbolicus,* to create an ideal world that rests in contradiction to "real" reference.

"The Circular Ruins" is merely one exemplary instantiation of Borgesian paradoxes. Like the Aleph itself, most of these paradoxes entail an untenable collaboration of the infinite and the finite, time and timelessness, continuity and discontinuity, the One and the Many. These are "hyperfictions" in the extreme; that is, they imply oxymoronic collusion at the deepest level. Weaving a rope of sand or coining the faceless wind serve as microcosmic embellishments of the larger tragedy being played out, which is equally oxymoronic, but, in addition to its poetic qualities, it is also metaphysical—cosmic metaphors, which place Borges's fictions in the same orb with the range of Vaihingerian fictions and scientific models-fictions.

Regarding further the nature of Borges's paradoxes, Bruce Lorich (1973, 53)—and he is certainly not alone here—disparagingly proclaims that most of Borges's fictions are "heretical texts for solipsists." The Argentine writer, he declares, "has created a complex, labyrinthine puzzle of paradoxes in which pedantic psyche-twisters, related only to themselves and to a philosophical stance, appear more regularly than do ingenious truly fictional artifices. Most of his so-called fictions are intellectual games."[1] Lorich, I believe, is correct on one point: Borges's fictions are intellectual games. But they are far from trivial. The fact is that all paradoxes potentially bear on "truth," but in a negative manner, for negation (i.e., Nietzsche's "lie") is one of the prerequisites for their existence. For example, a variation of the Liar paradox, "This sentence is false," entails negation, since it says of itself that it is *not* true. It also entails two other conditions necessary for paradox: self-reference and infinite regress. The sentence self-referentially speaks of its own lack of truthfulness, and hence if it is true, then it is false, and if so, then it is true, and so on, ad infinitum.

These three conditions—negation, self-reference, and infinite regress—should reveal many pseudoparadoxes being passed off as logical paradoxes in Borges criticism and elsewhere. As a case in point, the injunction places the reader in a quandary, but it is not logically paradoxical, since, rather than reflect upon itself, it includes the reader; it constitutes merely a "pragmatic" paradox. That is to say, the reader, having already read the sign, cannot ignore it so as to obey the injunction, hence there is no infinite regress. Nor can self-reference alone create paradox, in spite of the overenthusiastic claims of certain contemporary literary critics of poststructuralist ilk. It might simply create an absurd situation comparable to Lewis Carroll's mythical island whose inhabitants earn a living by taking in each other's washing. With respect to Borges's work, for example, critics have often commented on the "paradox" inherent in *History of Eternity,* since eternity is atemporal and hence incompatible with the notion of historicity. However contradictory this title may be, it is not paradoxical, for there is no infinite regress.

The essence of Borges's genius lies in his recognition of false dichotomies and his uncanny ability to dramatize paradox within an ethereal, timeless framework. Borges seems to suggest that if the universe operates consistently at all, it operates consistently on paradox, and insofar as it does so, the universe may be rational instead of absurd, a rationalism, nonetheless, edified upon inconsistent premises. Paradox, like infinity, is contingent upon simultaneity. "This sentence is false" must, logically speaking, be construed at once as both true and false. However, the mnemonic function of the brain is linear. It entails sequential expression and analysis, which contradicts the simultaneity essential for Borges's and other paradoxes to emerge. Properly perceiving paradox, then, involves the perceiver's oscillating between the *either* and the *or,* an oscillation in time, but, since it goes nowhere so to speak, it is timeless. It has no tenses of past and future, for the oscillations in their composite are static.

Paradox viewed from two perspectives, the temporal and the timeless, can be illustrated by what is called the "prisoner paradox." It is Sunday. A group of prisoners is told by the warden that they will be executed on one day of that week, but they will not be informed which day it will be until the arrival of that very day, hence it will be a surprise. These prisoners happen to have found a quite astute lawyer. He reasons, after some deliberation, that assuming the warden to have told them the truth, they cannot be executed, for if the fatal day is to be Saturday, then it cannot be a surprise, since it will be the only day remaining. By this mode of reasoning neither can it be Friday, for Saturday now having been eliminated, Friday is no longer a candidate. The same can be said of Thursday, and so on down to Sunday. Therefore they cannot legitimately be executed. Now, there seems to be a flaw somewhere, and there is, but it has nothing to do with logic. The problem is that the lawyer's reasoning is strictly by logical means; he can certainly afford to be logical, for his life is not at stake. In contrast, the prisoners' very existence is in jeopardy. They are rightly concerned over how much time remains of their life, and time is precisely the issue here. The lawyer's logic is timeless, and within this framework the paradox springs forth in full force. But the prisoners, their emotions having understandably taken precedence over their reasoning faculties, exist in time, hence try as their lawyer may to convince them otherwise, they cannot reason away their expectations of an unexpected moment announcing their death. Trapped inside their particular mind-set, they are condemned to temporality.

Existentially the human organism cannot help but project into the future and carry within itself conglomerate memories of the past, for without such memories, there is no future anticipation. Such would be a rudimentary form of animal consciousness, which, as Borges often reiterates in his works, is situated outside time. We humans, in contrast, are caught within a temporality that, for better or for worse, generates quandaries necessary to our very existence. For example, the narrator's obsession with the twenty-centavo coin in **"The Zahir"** exhibits our unwillingness to let go of the past: he simply cannot forget the coin, yet at times he feels so confident he can forget it that he "deliberately recalled it to mind" (*L,* 160–61). Here Borges reveals the subtle "forgetfulness paradox." The narrator gives himself the injunction "Don't think about the Zahir" or "Forget the Zahir." But if he does not think about it, then he runs the risk of forgetting what it is he is supposed to forget and he might think about it; therefore he must maintain mindfulness of it so as not to forget he must forget it. This pragmatic paradox depends as much on memory as does the "prisoner paradox" on anticipation. And both are existential rather than purely logical, time-bound rather than atemporal.

Interestingly, in Borges's **"The Secret Miracle"** (*L,* 88–94) we have another variation on the prisoner paradox. Jaromir Hladik is condemned to die before a firing squad at dawn, the twenty-ninth of March, 1943. He "infinitely anticipated the process of his dying, from the sleepless dawn to the mysterious volley" (*L,* 89). He imagined himself dying hundreds of deaths "in courtyards whose forms and angles strained geometrical probabilities, machine-gunned by variable soldiers in changing numbers, who at times killed him from a distance, at others from close by" (*L,* 89). One day he reflects that

> reality does not usually coincide with our anticipation of it; with a logic of his own he inferred that to foresee a circumstantial detail is to prevent its happening. Trusting in this weak magic, he invented, *so that they would not happen,* the most gruesome details. Finally, as was natural, he came to fear that they were prophetic. Miserable in the night, he endeavored to find some way to hold fast to the fleeting substance of time. He knew that it was rushing headlong toward the dawn of the twenty ninth. He remembered aloud: "I am now in the night of the twenty second; while this night lasts (and for six nights more), I am invulnerable, immortal."
>
> (*L,* 89–90)

Hladik is a writer who has never been satisfied with the fruits of his craft. Perhaps his most successful book was the one entitled, significantly, *Vindication of Eternity.* The first volume "gave a history of man's various concepts of eternity, from the immutable being of Parmenides to the modifiable past of Hinton" (*L,* 90).[2] The second denied that "all the events of the universe make up a temporal series, arguing that the number of man's possible experiences is not infinite, and that a single 'repetition' suffices to prove that time is a fallacy. . . . Unfortunately, the arguments that demonstrate this fallacy are equally fallacious" (ibid.).[3] Indeed, with such remarkable precedents, how could Hladik possibly be overtaken by time?

To "redeem himself" of his past failures, Hladik has been writing a play in verse entitled *The Enemies,* which remains unfinished. He petitions God that he be granted an extra year to finish it before his execution. It is granted. Then, on the twenty-ninth, before the firing squad and at the moment the command is given to execute him, the "physical universe comes to a halt": Hladik's "weak magic" had triumphed. For the duration of one year, motionlessly, secretly, he then "wrought in time his lofty, invisible labyrinth. . . . nothing hurried him. He omitted, he condensed, he amplified. . . . He concluded his drama" (*L,* 94). Then he was shot at dawn, on the twenty-ninth.

For the prisoners, existence took precedence over logic. For Hladik, like the prisoners' lawyer, logic took prece-

dence over existence. The lawyer's reasoning was helpless in the face of "reality," since the prisoners were sure to die on the designated day. Hladik's reasoning powers, in contrast, *became* "reality" in much the sense of scientific theories, which, purely imaginary mental constructs in the beginning, can subsequently become in the minds of their believers synonymous with the "real" (i.e., the Newtonian-Cartesian machine model of the universe and other such models and metaphors).

Notes

1. It bears mentioning that Lorich does attribute excellence to Borges's "The South" (*F,* 167–74), since, like Julio Cortázar's short story, "Axolotl," it does not merely "depend upon convoluted abstractions."

2. Borges's interest in and allusion to C. Howard Hinton is most appropriate. Hinton held some strange ideas, among them the notion that the ultimate components of our nervous system are of a higher dimension, thus affording us the capacity to imagine four-dimensional space. The fourth dimension will be discussed in conjunction with relativity theory in the second section of Chapter Four.

3. This quote is relevant to Borges's "New Refutation of Time."

Works Cited

Burgin, Richard. 1968. *Conversations with Jorge Luis Borges.* New York: Holt, Rinehart & Winston.

Hofstadter, Douglas R. 1979. *Goedel, Escher, Bach: An Eternal Golden Braid.* New York: Basic Books.

Lorich, Bruce. 1973. "Borges's Puzzle of Paradoxes." *Southwest Review* 58: 53–65.

Peirce, Charles Sanders. 1960. *Collected Papers.* Ed. C. Hartshorne and P. Weiss. Cambridge, Mass.: Harvard University Press, Belknap Press.

Sucre, Guillermo. 1970. "La biografia del infinito." *Eco,* No. 125: 466–502.

Whitehead, Alfred North. 1925. *Science and the Modern World.* New York: Macmillan

Martin S. Stabb (essay date 1991)

SOURCE: "The Canonical Texts," in *Borges Revisited,* edited by David W. Foster, Twayne Publishers, 1991, pp. 37–68.

[*In the following discussion of Borges's fiction, Stabb analyzes the elements that define the pieces as characteristically Borgesian.*]

Borges's present fame rests on a relatively small number of short narratives. While his complete works fill many volumes, and although his essays, poems, and literary musings complement his central achievement, it is this corpus of quintessentially Borgesian texts that have established him as a major voice among Western postmodernists. The bulk of these pieces appear in *Ficciones* (*Ficciones,* 1944) and *El Aleph* (*The Aleph,* 1949, 1952): in terms of their date of composition they represent his work of the mid-thirties through the early fifties. These texts, perhaps only twelve or fifteen in number, have been frequently reedited, widely anthologized, intensively studied, and extensively translated. It is possible that a few of the narratives written in his later years, that is, from the publication of *El hacedor* (*Dreamtigers,* 1960) till his death, will come to be included among this canonical group; but their significance will, I think, always be viewed in relation to his earlier work.

Although he is often considered to be a *cuentista,* a writer of short stories, it is with some trepidation that critics apply this term to Borges. He himself preferred to use the terms *narratives, fictions,* even *artifices* to describe many of these texts, perhaps he sensed that they did not conform to the generally held notion of a short story. Indeed, if one looks for a well-structured plot line complete with some development and a climax, many of Borges's *ficciones* (perhaps the most commonly used descriptive term) will be found lacking. Yet other pieces among the canonical texts are characterized by plots so highly structured that early critics attacked them for being too "geometrical." In short, it is difficult to generalize about Borges's prose fiction, especially if a traditional definition of the genre is used. A number of these pieces could almost be considered fictionalized essays, given the dominance of an idea, a philosophic notion, or a literary concept over narration. Thus in my earlier study of Borges, I used the somewhat awkward term *essayistic fiction* to describe a group of these texts. Finally, the very fact that Borges violated traditional generic boundaries—an acknowledged characteristic of postmodern letters—has contributed to his significance as a major figure the century.

There are many ways in which Borges's canonical texts might be classified: by date of publication, by theme, or by dominant structural features. A novel scheme might be based on his choice of setting, that is, stories of the mysterious East, Argentine tales, English-Irish pieces, and so forth. The matter of taxonomy is of course quite arbitrary, as Borges himself has wittily pointed out. My own classification of these well-known texts is admittedly idiosyncratic, though I trust not as strange as the zoological taxonomy found in a certain Chinese encyclopedia that Borges once described.

THE RELUCTANT NARRATOR: "STREETCORNER MAN" AND "THE APPROACH TO AL-MU'TASIM"

The two prefaces that Borges wrote to his *Historia universal de la infamia* (*A Universal History of Infamy,* 1935) are very revealing. In the first, preceding the original edition, he refers to the book as a collection of "exercises in narrative prose." He modestly goes on to note that "they overly exploit certain tricks: random enumerations, sudden shifts of continuity, and the paring down of a man's whole life into two or three scenes. . . . They are not, they do not try to be, psychological."[1] In the preface to the second edition (1954), he refers to these pieces as "the irresponsible game of a shy young man who dared not write stories and so amused himself by falsifying and distorting (without any aesthetic justification whatever) the tales of others" (*UHI,* 12). The reference to "tales of others" is not without foundation. In a display of literary candor he appends a list of specific sources for the collection: several books on American history, the *Encyclopaedia Britannica,* Mark Twain, etc. Only one text, **"El hombre de la esquina rosada"** (**"Streetcorner Man"**), could be considered a genuine and original short story. It is of some significance that Borges first published it under the pseudonym "F. Bustos" in the literary supplement to the Buenos Aires newspaper *Crítica.* Another crucial text for tracing the emergence of Borges's fiction has already been mentioned briefly, **"The Approach to al-Mu'tasim,"** which despite its narrative elements lay buried among the essays of *Historia de la eternidad.*

Critics have offered a number of explanations regarding Borges's early reluctance to write fiction: most of these derive from personal or political factors. Clearly the decade of the thirties was a difficult time for Argentines, especially the country's intellectuals. The first three decades of the century had seen considerable progress toward democracy and material well-being, but with the fall of civilian government in 1930 and the onset of military rule and of what Argentine historians have called "the absurd decade," the mood of the nation became ugly. A reflection of this pessimistic, disruptive atmosphere may be seen in Borges's work, as the critic Emir Rodríguez Monegal has pointed out.[2] It could be argued that the times produced a general insecurity that was hardly propitious for expanding one's horizons or doing new things; and, for Borges, fiction would be a new venture. His essential reserve, his shyness and timidity may well have played a role here: stated simply, he had achieved a modest success as a poet and essayist and was reluctant to strike out into unfamiliar literary territory. Other factors may also lie behind his reluctance to write fiction. We have seen in his literary essays that he had considerable reservations regarding the kind of narratives most appreciated since the nineteenth century—namely the "draggy novel of character," the psychological novel, and similar forms. It is even conceivable that the popularity of this kind of fiction encouraged him to seek innovative forms for his own fictional experiments. In short, during the thirties Borges seemed interested in turning toward fiction but was not quite sure of the path he should follow. Why he finally decided, as the decade closed, to move decisively in this direction is a question that will be answered shortly.

Historia universal de la infamia (*A Universal History of Infamy,* 1935) is a miscellany consisting of eight short sketches or vignettes dealing with famous and not-so-famous ne'er-do-wells; one short story, **"Streetcorner Man"**; and five very brief glosses of various literary texts. Borges tells us at the outset that "the word 'infamy' in the title is thunderous, but behind the sound and fury there is nothing" (*UHI*, 12). And indeed there is not a great deal here except the charming, and often very funny, manner in which Borges retells the bizarre histories of his antiheroes: Lazarus Morrell, the "atrocious redeemer of slaves," who earned a tidy living by encouraging Negroes to flee their masters and then resold the escapees to other slaveholders; Tom Castro, a subequatorial confidence man who for many years deceived a comfortable widow by claiming to be her long-lost son; the Widow Ching, a completely incongruous cymbal-clashing pirate queen of the China Seas; Monk Eastman, a New York mobster of the turn of the century who, after ten years in Sing Sing Prison and a military career, dies at the hands of an unknown assassin; the cold-blooded Bill Harrigan—alias Billy the Kid—whose real and mythical exploits are well known to American readers; one Kotsuké No Suké, a samurai of ancient Japan, whose unforgettable person gives Borges the opportunity to explicate certain details of ancient Nippon's honor code; and finally Ha'kim de Merv, the mysterious and resplendent Veiled Prophet of Islamic lore who is ultimately revealed as a hideously deformed leper. Borges deliberately informs the reader of his factual sources for most of the items—a further indication of his timidity, his desire to appear as a commentator, as a reteller of tales rather than as an original writer. But he was not content simply to recast in his own words what others had written. Rather, Borges changed, modified, and reworked the original materials, expanding a small detail of a source text, omitting or alternating an important event, adding a character here or eliminating a character there. In short, he had begun to write fiction.

"Streetcorner Man" was a rather different text and one that did not depend on other sources unless one counts two very sketchy versions of the story that Borges had written some eight years before. The setting is one that figures in some of his early poetry and one that would haunt him till his death—the picturesque, violent, almost mythic world of Buenos Aires' lower-class neighborhoods of yesteryear. The tale's plot is fairly simple: a *compadre,* or local tough, is challenged by a rival from another district; the first man appears to be a coward and backs off; the rival takes off with his opponent's woman (a sensual beauty, the pride of the local dance hall in which the action takes place); and the narrator, a member of the coward's gang, apparently goes after the rival intruder. The reader is not told exactly what happens, but after a brief absence the narrator returns and a bit later the girl, followed by the dying and bloody abductor, appears. After the latter dies, the unnamed narrator examines his knife and remarks "I turned the blade over, slowly. It was as good as new, innocent-looking, and there wasn't the slightest trace of blood on it" (*UHI*, 98). This frequently anthologized story has enjoyed considerable popularity and was even adapted for the cinema, though in interviews Borges often belittled it.

For students of Borges, **"Streetcorner Man"** is extremely interesting. The thematic elements—knife fights, the fine line dividing cowardice from valor, the world of the tango, and the general flavor of Buenos Aires street culture—have come to be regarded as hallmarks of Borges's *criollista* modality. Certain narrative techniques typical of his later work also appear in this piece: these include the use of a second-level narrator (the story is told to "Borges" by an anonymonous first-person narrator who is one of the chief actors in the plot); the creation of an ambiguous denouement; and the interjection of one or more clues as to what actually happened. Yet other aspects of the story are quite atypical. The language, for example, is at times almost indecipherable to those unfamiliar with *lunfardo,* the street slang of Buenos Aires. Moreover, the coarseness of the language and the direct references to sexual activity at one point in the text seem entirely out of keeping with the voice and tone of Borges's later work. As critics have suggested, the use of a pseudonym and the device of presenting the story as another's tale may stem from Borges's desire to save his proper middle-class family the embarrassment of acknowledging such an audacious author as one of their own.

"The Approach to al-Mu'tasim" is of approximately the same vintage as the *Infamy* vignettes and has some superficial resemblances to them. It too was inspired by other texts, namely, the critical remarks of Phillip Guedalla and Cecil Roberts regarding a book recently published in Bombay by one Mir Bahadur Alí. In his own comments, Borges supplies a fairly detailed plot résumé of the Indian's book and gives considerable information on its publication history, noting that the well-known writer of detective fiction Dorothy Sayers did a prologue for its English edition. At the end of the piece, we are also given, in a long footnote, some erudite material on the author's sources. The unique aspect of this "review," and what makes it different from the *Infamy* pieces, is that it is not a modification of other texts but a cleverly presented hoax: whereas Guedella, Roberts, and Sayers were real people, Mir Bahadur Alí and his fascinating novel never existed. However, the calculated mention of familiar publishers, genuine literary reviews, and real critics give the entire text an air of convincing authenticity. The hoax succeeded so well that Borges later recalled friends who had tried to order copies of **"The Approach"** from London booksellers. The résumé of the nonexistent novel's plot does, nonetheless, give Borges an opportunity to create his own narrative. Thematically, the tale is of interest because it reveals Borges's early fascination with Middle Eastern culture and letters. Structurally, it is necessarily schematic as it purportedly recounts an entire novel in some five pages. **"The Approach"** is especially important in that it provided a model for the kind of ventures in literary gamesmanship that would in future charm many a reader while repelling others.

That the thirties were difficult years for the nation and for Borges has already been noted. The close of the decade especially saw some major changes in his personal life that had a considerable bearing on his literary career. His father's declining health and death in 1938 created a situation that led Borges to take a post in a rather drab municipal library. Up to that date young "Georgie," as his Anglophile mother was wont to call him, had not really worked at any remunerative occupation. His activities as a writer and his editorial work for various periodicals absorbed his time but produced very little income. Considering his erudition, it is ironic that he did not have any university training and thus could not lay claim to a truly professional position. This same period also saw a marked deterioration in his vision (a genetic problem that eventually led to almost total blindness), as well as frequent bouts with insomnia. To these problems may be added the fact that he apparently had some unhappy love affairs at the time.[3] Not surprisingly, these years are marked by relatively little creative output: his bibliography for 1937 and 1938 lists only a few very short journalistic essays, a few film reviews, and his one-page book reviews in the popular "family" magazine *El Hogar*.[4] Finally, late in 1938—on Christmas Eve to be exact—he suffered an accident that may have had a profound influence on his literary career. Returning to his apartment late one evening, he slipped on a poorly lit staircase and in falling struck himself sharply on the head.[5] For two weeks he remained hospitalized and in a serious condition. During this period he was plagued by insomnia, fever, and nightmares. While convalescing the fear that his mental powers and writing ability had suffered as a result of the accident constantly disturbed him. Because he had written only a few narratives and thus had no reputation as a creator of fiction, he chose to write some stories just to see if his fears were justified: "I thought I would try my hand at writing an article or poem. But I thought: 'I have written hundreds of articles and poems. If I can't do it, then I'll know at once that I am done for.' . . . So I thought I'd try my hand at something I hadn't done: if I couldn't do it, there would be nothing strange about it."[6]

The immediate result of this experiment was the story **"Pierre Menard, autor del Quijote,"** which appeared in the spring of 1939 in *Sur*. About a year later, **"Tlön, Uqbar, Orbis Tertius"** appeared, to be followed by the steady stream of "fictions" that brought Borges fame.

There are several slightly different versions of these events, but perhaps not too much importance should be attached to the affair. In retrospect it is difficult to accept the idea that this accident marked a genuine shift in his literary trajectory; after all, with the *Universal History of Infamy,* **"Streetcorner Man,"** and the **"Approach to al-Mu'tasim,"** Borges had already taken, albeit hesitantly, the first steps that would lead to international fame as a writer of fiction.

DREAMFICTIONS: "THE SOUTH," "THE CIRCULAR RUINS," AND "THE SECRET MIRACLE"

That life is or may be a dream is a notion that has found expression in the work of many writers, and in Borges's poems, essays, and fiction, sleep, dreams, and the possibility of dreams occupy an important place. Upon finishing **"El Sur"** (**"The South"**), for example, many readers would conclude that the entire text is the recounting of a dream, if not a nightmare. Yet the earlier pages of the text have a rather realistic quality, and the most fascinating aspect of the narrative is that the dream—if there actually is one—seems to consume reality. Thus the reader wonders at just what point the narrator's awake state ends and his dream begins. **"The South"** is doubly interesting for those intrigued by the appearance, in thinly disguised form, of autobiographical material: many commentators have pointed out the remarkable parallels between the tale's plot line and the details of Borges's 1938 Christmas accident.

The story itself is deceptively simple. A third-person narrator describes the background of one Johannes Dahlman, a "profoundly" Argentine citizen of German-*criollo* ancestry, who identifies more with the "romantic" heroes of his Argentine forebears than with his staid German ancestors. Though a quiet soul (who incidentally works in a municipal library), he cherishes the old sword of his grandfather, a military hero of the Indian wars on the pampas. Other details, too, reflect the author's own life, not the least of which is that one evening "late in February 1939" (note the minor alteration of the date) he hurts his head by striking something while climbing a dark staircase. As a result of the wound and the septicemia that ensues he is hospitalized for an indefinite period. He is finally released to convalesce at the family ranch somewhere off in the South. Borges describes his protagonist's ride through the city to the railroad terminal, the long train trip into the country, his getting off at a small rural station (an alternate one, not the usual one), and his slight uneasiness on seeing the half-familiar town itself. While waiting for a horse and buggy to be prepared for the final part of the journey, Dahlman decides to eat something in the local general store. It is here that the story builds to its climax. Some rough country types, evidently half drunk, pick a fight with him: one of the group, an especially tough customer, is toying with a knife and eventually challenges Dahlman to a duel. It is at this point, the narrator tells us, that something "unforeseeable" occurs. A mysterious old gaucho, whom Dahlman had noticed earlier, throws a naked dagger at his feet. It may be noted in passing that this is one of many examples in Borges's work of how weapons, especially knives, appear suddenly and are infused with almost magical, autonomous powers. "It was as if the South had resolved that Dahlman should accept the duel. Dahlman bent over to pick up the dagger, and felt two things. The first, that this almost instinctive act bound him to fight. The second, that the weapon, in his torpid hand, was no defense at all, but would merely serve to justify his murder. . . . *They would not have allowed such things to happen to me in the sanatarium,* he thought."[7] Though he is unskilled in knife fighting and feels certain he will die, at the every end of the story Dahlman accepts his destiny with the thought that when on that distant night in the sanatarium they stuck him with a needle, "that to die in a knife fight, under the open sky . . . would have been a liberation, a joy, and a festive occasion. . . . He felt that if he had been able to choose, then, or to dream his death, this would have been the death, he would have chosen or dreamt" (*PA,* 23).

This ambivalent conclusion suggests, but does not clearly establish, that the bulk of the tale has been simply a dream. The possibility that virtually everything since "a masked man" injected Dahlman in the hospital has existed only in the sick man's delirious imagination is very strong. A number of other details in the text point toward this interpretation: the fact that Dahlman thinks that the owner of the general store looks like one of the hospital staff; the thought that events like these "would not have been allowed . . . in the sanitarium." Yet the brief mention earlier in the story that Dahlman dozes on and off during the train trip and especially the narrator's description of the protagonist's reflections while traveling invite us to conjecture that the dream begins on the train: "Tomorrow I'll wake up at the ranch, he thought, and it was as if he were two men at a time: the man who traveled through the autumn day and across the geography of the fatherland, and the other one, locked up in a sanitarium" (*PA,* 19). An even earlier starting point for the "dreamt" portion of the text is obliquely suggested by Borges's underscoring the significance of Dahlman's crossing Rivadavia Street on his way to the railroad station: "Every Argentine knows that the South begins on the other side of Rivadavia . . . that whoever crosses this street enters a more ancient and sterner world" (*PA,* 18). In other words, he crosses over from the real world to a mythic—or dreamlike—realm. These speculations inevitably lead back to the question of deciding whether or not the tale, or a portion of it, is in fact a dream. But why should we concern ourselves with this problem? After all, are not all fictions by definition simply creations of the imagination which may thus be considered a kind of literary dream? And if this is so, a "dream" inserted into any fictional piece becomes nothing more than a dream within a dream.

"Las ruinas circulares" ("The Circular Ruins"), a tale that is structured around a very Borgesian extension of the dream concept, is deservedly one of the most anthologized pieces in *Ficciones.* Unlike several of the other texts in the collection, it is a genuine story complete with an element of suspense and a kind of surprise ending. The opening lines set a mood of mystery well calculated to capture the reader's attention: "No one saw him disembark in the unanimous night, no one saw the bamboo canoe sinking into the sacred mud, but within a few days no one was unaware that the silent man came from the South and that his home was one of the infinite villages upstream on the violent side of the mountain, where the Zend tongue is not contaminated with Greek."[8] The mysterious traveler, described as "the gray man," kisses the mud, ascends the river bank, without pushing aside the brambles that "dilacerated" his flesh, and lies exhausted and asleep. A significant detail that Borges notes parenthetically is that he "probably did not feel" the thorns as he passed through them.

The spot where the stranger lies asleep is a "Circular enclosure crowned by a stone horse or tiger, which once was the color of fire and now was that of ashes. This circle was a temple, long ago devoured by fire" (*L,* 45). Upon awakening, Borges tells us, the man knows that this is the precise place required to carry out his "purpose," the exact nature of which is clarified shortly: "The purpose which guided him was not impossible, though it was supernatural. He wanted to dream a man: he wanted to dream him with minute integrity and insert him into reality" (*L,* 46). What follows is the detailed description of how the protagonist goes about his task.

At first he attempts to dream a "class" of disciples—a large group from whom he might select, or "redeem," a single individual to "insert" into reality. After a number of unsuccessful efforts he decides that he must concentrate intensely on just one of the group. But his attempt fails; he suffers insomnia; he becomes infuriated and frustrated. Finally he comes to the conclusion that he must abandon his original method completely, He spends a month recuperating his powers before again undertaking his arduous task. He gives up trying to dream and, as a result, he finds he sleeps more easily and that once again he is able to dream. Ready to begin his project anew, "he purified himself in the waters of the river, worshiped the planetary gods, uttered the permitted syllables of a powerful name and slept" (*L,* 47). At this point he dreams of a beating heart. He now understands how he can accomplish his objective. As a sculptor carefully chisels a masterpiece, the "gray man" slowly fashions his creation. Starting with the internal organs he painstakingly dreams the arteries, the skeleton, and the eyelids. "The innumerable hair was perhaps the most difficult task," he tells us. After a year, the dream child is physically complete. Finally, "In the dreamer's dream, the dreamed one awoke" (*L,* 48).

The protagonist devotes some two years to instructing his child in the mysteries of the universe and in the enigmatic details of the "fire cult." The son is now ready to leave: his father kisses him and sends him off to another temple far downstream where, presumably, he would fulfill his duties as a priest of his cult. However, before he departs, his father instills in him the "complete oblivion of his years of apprenticeship" (*L,* 49). His purpose in doing this, as Borges notes parenthetically, is to make him think that he is a man, not a phantom. At any rate, the son leaves, and the parent, saddened by his departure, is left to meditate. His thoughts continue to be troubled by the fear that his son might in some way learn that his existence was merely illusory, and he muses, "Not to be a man, to be the projection of another man's dream, what a feeling of humiliation, of vertigo!" (*L,* 50).

At this point in the story, smoke appears in the distance, then the flight of animals. Finally the "gray man" realizes that a ring of fire is closing in on him. At first he thinks of trying to escape into the river; but he is old and tired, and he knows that inevitable death is coming to "absolve him of his labors." The flames come closer and begin to engulf him. But he feels neither heat nor combustion. The last two lines of the tale reveal what the astute reader has perhaps already guessed: "With relief, with humiliation, with terror, he understood that he too was a mere appearance, dreamt by another" (*L*, 50).

A wealth of Borgesian ideas underlies the story: the Berkeleyan notion of existence as a function of perception, carried to the extreme of "dreaming" objects into the real world, is blended with Gnostic cosmology and the idea of a creator-behind-the-creator. The suggestion of an infinite regression also is evident: the "gray man" dreams a son who quite naturally will dream another son, and so on. Yet these ideas lie just below the surface. Except for a brief mention of the Gnostics and the ancient cult of fire, the story flows smoothly along in the best tradition of genuine fantastic fiction. And, as in detective stories, the most minute details become significant once we know the story's final outcome. For example, the color *gray*, which Borges first uses to describe his protagonist, clearly suggests his shadowy existence; the early mention of *another* distant temple may well be a reference to the protagonist's own origins; and his careful plan to erase all memory of his son's creation may be viewed as an echo of what had been done to him. To sum up, the balancing of all these elements—the underlying philosophic concepts, the mood and language of genuine fantasy, and the structure of a detective story—have produced one of Borges's most impressive compositions. Moreover, for the student of narratology the story raises an interesting question. Note again the very first lines, "no one" sees the protagonist embark: in other words, we have what may be called an "impossible narrator," unless one imagines a divinely omniscient god-narrator, a thought that perhaps adds to the tale's total impact.

Borges's ever-present obsession with time is closely related to his interest in dreams. We know from our own experience and from what psychologists tell us that the duration of dreams bears little relationship to the time perceived by the dreamer. Another aspect of the question arises from the folkloric tradition of considering dreams as capable of carrying us forward in time, as being prophetic. Finally, the imagination, the creative process may be viewed as a kind of dreaming in a special state. These three notions come together very effectively in **"El milagro secreto"** (**"The Secret Miracle"**), our last example of what I have called dreamfictions. The story is set in Prague during World War II. Jaromir Hladík, a scholar and author of works dealing with Jewish philosophy, dreams of a long chess game in which the players were entire families and the stakes "enormous." Hladík's confused dream is abruptly ended at dawn, as he hears the rumble of German armor entering the city. He soon gets into difficulties with the Nazis; Hladík is eventually arrested and sentenced to death, though his crimes are nothing more than his Jewish blood and the signing of a protest against the German occupation. Having presented these basic facts, Borges describes in some detail Hladík's literary interests; not only is he a writer of scholarly works, but he is a poet and dramatist as well. His current project, a drama in verse that he had hoped would be his masterpiece, was, at the time of his arrest, only partially completed, though its main features were all sketched out in his mind.

While awaiting execution he fearfully imagines the circumstances of his forthcoming death: "Before the day set . . . he died hundreds of deaths in courtyards whose forms and angles strained geometrical possibilities. . . . He faced these imaginary executions with real terror (perhaps with real bravery); each simulacrum lasted only a few seconds" (*L*, 89). To escape from these thoughts he desperately seeks surcease in sleep. As 29 March, the day of execution, approaches, he reasons, "I am now in the night of the twenty-second; while this night lasts . . . I am invulnerable, immortal" (*L*, 90). He also becomes increasingly concerned about his yet uncompleted drama, *The Enemies*. Borges sets forth the main lines of this mysterious tragicomedy, the most interesting feature of which is its circularity: in Hladík's rough plot sketch the drama begins in the evening as the clock strikes seven, ends as the same hour is struck, and concludes with an actor repeating the same lines that he had spoken at the play's beginning. But while Hladík had formulated this plot he had only completed the first act. The very night before he is to face the firing squad, just a few minutes before dropping off to sleep, Hladík asks God to grant him a year to complete the entire drama. He falls into a deep sleep but as dawn approaches, Borges tells us, Hladík has yet another confused dream in which he searches for God—in a library—and is finally rewarded by hearing a voice tell him, "The time of your labor has been granted" (*L*, 92). He wakes and at precisely 8:44 he is taken out to the barracks wall. His execution is scheduled for nine o'clock sharp.

Borges etches the scene in fine detail: "Someone pointed out that the wall was going to be stained with blood; the victim was ordered to step forward a few paces. Incongruously, this reminded Hladík of the fumbling preparations of photographers" (*L*, 93). Note this last detail: a very ordinary comparison—one within the experience of any reader—drives home the horror of the scene with chilling fidelity. The guns converge on Hladík, and the sergeant raises his arm to signal the squad to fire, but at this instant Hladík sees the world before him "freeze." The wind stops; the soldiers are motionless; a bee in the courtyard casts "an unchanging shadow." Hladík himself is paralyzed: only his mind is active. He feels no fatigue and even falls asleep. Upon awakening, the scene before him remains frozen exactly as it was. After a while he realizes that God has granted his request. Overcome with gratitude, he begins his year's work—the composition of the remaining portions of his drama. Using only his memory, he lovingly and meticulously revises and reworks the last two acts of his masterpiece. Finally, "He had only the problem of a single phrase. He found it . . . He opened his mouth in a maddened cry, moved his face, dropped under the quadruple blast" (*L*, 94). In the last sentence Borges notes that "Jaromir Hladík died on March 29, at 9:02 a.m."

"The Secret Miracle" is, like **"The South"** and **"The Circular Ruins,"** a well-structured tale in which the line between explicable reality and the unreal is deliberately indeterminate, or "blurred."⁹ Though quite different in each story, a device that produces this blurred quality or ambiguity is some form of dream or mental activity akin to dreaming.

THE AMBIVALENT HERO: "THE SHAPE OF THE SWORD," "THE GARDEN OF THE FORKING PATHS," AND "THE LIFE OF TADEO ISIDORO CRUZ"

In a substantial number of Borges's stories the protagonist has what may facetiously be called a serious identity problem. In these pieces the central character may have a double existence, he may be defined entirely by his relationship to a counterpart character, or he may be hidden behind the narrator's voice. We have already seen some heroes of this type: Dahlman is both a convalescing librarian and a knife fighter facing death on the pampa; the "gray man" of the **"Circular Ruins"** is the product of another's dream; and even Hladík, although he is a real person and has no double, has a somewhat ambiguous personality as seen when he is described as facing the firing squad "with real terror" *or* "perhaps with real bravery." The mystical idea that all men are one, and its corollary that under certain circumstances the villain may be a hero, or vice versa, appears frequently in Borges's work. Even his interest in the Gnostic inversion of good and evil—the Judas figure, for example—may be related to his conviction that only the finest of lines divides the world's saints and heroes from its most despised villains. Borges's fascination with the notion of ambivalence in personality may well be a reflection of his own psyche. Though the temptation to psychoanalyze is great, it should be resisted: suffice it to say that despite his retiring manner, Borges had always been intrigued by bandits—*compadritos*—and by men of action and violence. But aside from the theme's psychological or philosophical ramifications, it certainly provides the basis for a good story.

"A spiteful scar crossed his face: an ash-colored and nearly perfect arc that creased his temple at one tip and his cheek at the other. His real name is of no importance" (*L,* 67). With this vigorous description Borges introduces the protagonist of **"La forma de la espada"** (**"The Shape of the Sword"**). We learn that "the Englishman," as his Latin American neighbors call him, is in fact a hard-drinking, cruel, taciturn Irishman who has immigrated to the border country of southern Brazil and northern Argentina. How he earns his living is uncertain: some say he's a smuggler, others a sugar grower. One evening, a sudden rise in a river forces the narrator, who incidentally is revealed as 'Borges' at the tale's end, to spend an evening with this colorful expatriate. The two strike up an after-dinner conversation in the course of which "the Englishman" relates his adventures as a rebel in the Irish independence movement.

The central figure in his tale is John Vincent Moon, another young rebel whom he describes as "slender and flac-

cid at the same time; he gave the impression of being invertebrate." As the tale develops, it becomes clear that Moon was, in sharp contrast to the narrator, a coward. Moon flees the thick of battle, makes much of a superficial wound, and is given to nervous sobbing when the going gets rough. The fortunes of the revolution meanwhile take a turn for the worse, and the city the Irish rebels are trying to hold falls to the British. One afternoon, the narrator discovers Moon talking on the telephone—obviously to the enemy, and obviously informing on the Irish. Infuriated, he pursues the traitor, seizes him, and then, using an old curved cutlass from the wall of the house in which they are staying, carves into Moon's face "a half-moon of blood." As "the Englishman" relates these events his hands begin shaking. When the narrator inquires as to the ultimate fate of the traitor, he is told that "He collected his Judas money and fled to Brazil" (*L,* 71). At this point the "Englishman" cannot continue; when urged to go on, he blurts out the truth: "Don't you see that I carry written on my face the mark of my infamy? I have told you the story thus so that you would hear me to the end. . . . I am Vincent Moon. Now despise me" (*L,* 71).

Both the framing device and the "switch" at the end are old techniques in the art of fiction. Certainly they are familiar to readers of detective tales and other popular genres. As in the best examples of this kind of work, there is a certain pleasure in reexamining the story to find the thinly veiled clues that hint at the final outcome. Such clues abound in Borges's tale. The very first line mentions the "*spiteful* scar" on the "Englishman's" face; before the narrator begins his story he tells Borges that he's not English but Irish, at which point he is described as "stopping short, as if he had revealed a secret" (*L,* 68), and at the start of his narration, he mentions that many of his comrades were by now dead, including "the most worthy, who died in the courtyard of a barracks" (*L,* 68). Like the other clues, this last one is obviously a reference to the rebel leader whom Moon denounced to the British; but like all good clues, they only become obvious after the cat is let out of the bag. As the "Englishman" reveals more of his story, the clues become more frequent and perhaps more obvious: the fact that Moon, though young and new to the group, was constantly inquiring into the plans of the rebel unit is a case in point. And just before the denouement the "Englishman" comes very close to revealing his true identity when he describes Moon: "This frightened man mortified me, as if I were the coward, not Vincent Moon" (*L,* 70). His philosophic musings following this statement shed further light on some of Borges's own notions regarding individuality: "Whatever one man does, it is as if all men did it. For that reason it is not unfair that one disobedience in a garden should contaminate all humanity; for that reason it is not unjust that the crucifixion of a single Jew should be sufficient to save it. Perhaps Schopenhauer was right: I am all other men; any man is all men, Shakespeare is in some manner the miserable John Vincent Moon" (*L,* 70).

A number of other well-known *ficciones* are structured in a somewhat similar manner. **"El tema del traidor y el** héroe" ("**Theme of the Traitor and the Hero**") is one, as is the complex and very bookish "**El inmortal**" ("**The Immortal**"). Unfortunately, space does not permit a discussion of these tales here.[10]

On first reading, many would consider "**El jardín de senderos que se bifurcan**" ("**The Garden of the Forking Paths**") to be simply a spy or detective story, albeit with an unusual twist at the end. Indeed, Borges himself characterizes it as such in the charmingly innocent prologue to the collection in which it first appeared. Yet this deceptively straightforward tale has intrigued many a critic and provides a wealth of material illustrative of Borges's narrative techniques, not the least of which is his creation of ambivalent characters.

The story itself is related in the form of a dictated statement by a Dr. Yu Tsun whom we learn, as the tale unfolds, is in England and is awaiting execution as a condemned agent for the Germans during World War I. The plot, leaving aside the considerable rich internal detail, is quite simple. Yu Tsun is a Chinese professor of English who had taught at a German school in Tsing Tao. For motives that are not entirely clear, though pride in his race seems to be one, he becomes an agent for the Germans. His specific objective in this story is to communicate to Berlin the exact name of the town in which the British were massing their artillery preparatory to a major offensive. However, the protagonist's immediate superior, one Viktor Runeberg,[11] has been captured, and hence Yu knows that his normal lines of communication to Berlin no longer exist, that the British agents are surely aware of his own identity as a spy, and that even now they are hot on his trail. Convinced that escape is impossible, he is nonetheless determined to communicate his information to Berlin. In the space of ten minutes he devises a plan, the nature of which is only revealed at the story's end. He studies the telephone directory in his room and enigmatically observes that it "listed the name of the only person capable of transmitting the message; he lived in the suburb of Fenton, less than a half hour's ride away" (*L,* 47). Yu quickly takes the train for the suburb, and even as it leaves the station he sees the British agent Madden running desperately down the platform after him. Arriving in the country, he hurries to the home of a Mr. Stephen Albert, who, by a strange coincidence, happens to be a former missionary to China and an ardent sinologist. Albert, who apparently mistakes his visitor for an acquaintance in the Chinese consular service, invites Yu in. The two soon become engaged in a discussion of the work of one Ts'ui Pên, an ancient Chinese astrologer and writer who was, coincidentally, an ancestor of the protagonist. Because Yu calculates that it will be an hour before his pursuers can overtake him, he chats amiably with Albert about the ancient sage and the literary labyrinth he had composed—an unusual book, entitled *The Garden of the Forking Paths* (*El jardín de senderos que se bifurcan*). But Yu's brief hour hurries by, and finally he is forced to perform the act that had brought him to this particular place. When his host's back is turned, Yu Tsun carefully withdraws his revolver and

kills Stephen Albert. At this moment the British agent Madden breaks in and arrests Yu. In the last paragraph of the story we learn that the newspaper reports of the murder of one Stephen Albert by a certain Yu Tsun reach Berlin, and that from them the chief German intelligence officer easily extracts a vital bit of information, namely, that the British were massing artillery, preparatory to an offensive, at the French town of Albert. At the tale's conclusion Yu Tsun explains: "The chief had deciphered this mystery. He knew my problem was to indicate (through the uproar of the war) the city called Albert, and that I had found no other means to do so than to kill a man of that name. He does not know (no one can know) my innumerable contribution and weariness" (*L,* 29).

As noted, critics have found in this text a variety of effective Borgesian narrative techniques: the prefiguring of the outcome by carefully embedded details, the tale-within-a-tale device, as seen in Albert's literary detective work to determine the nature of the original "**Garden of the Forking Paths**," and the insertion (deliberate?) of "loose ends," or unresolved details that in a sense "open" the text to the possibility of additional untold stories.[12] But "**The Garden**" is especially interesting as an example of Borges's penchant for developing ambivalent protagonists. In the first place, Yu Tsun gains Albert's confidence through his host's apparently mistaking him for someone else, namely, "Hsi P'eng," a Chinese consul in Britain. Yu Tsun never corrects his host's misconception; thus one may assume that the entire plot from this point on is driven by mistaken identity. Even if we overlook this detail, it can be argued that the almost mathematically balanced characterizations of Yu Tsun and Stephen Albert produce a situation of inverted doubles in which the two are in effect "identical and opposite."[13] But this analogous relationship is only part of Borges's threat to what one critic has called "the absolute autonomy of the self":

> The very repetition of the act of variation, involving a chain of quotations, makes the story a perfect example of what Jakobson calls "speech within speech" and divorces the various characters from their own discourse. In addition to the real author's speech to the real reader, crystallized in that of the implied author to the implied reader, the whole story is the speech of an extradiegetic-heterodiegetic narrator who, in a footnote, calls himself "editor". . . . First as the editor quotes T'sun, so T'sun, an extradiegetic-homodiegetic narrator, quotes Albert who in turn quotes T'sui Pên. . . . Quotation, then, is a dominant narrative mode in this story, and quotation is the appropriation by one person of the speech of another. Since a person is to a large extent constituted by his discourse, such an appropriation implies, at least partly, an interpenetration of personalities. Thus both repetition through analogy and repetition through quotation threaten the absolute autonomy of the self.[14]

A different sort of loss of autonomy shapes the central character of "**Biografía de Tadeo Isidoro Cruz**" ("**The Life of Tadeo Isidoro Cruz**"). In this case the ambivalent nature of the hero depends to a great extent on the reader's familiarity with the background material on which the story is based. The innocent reader, who would almost have to be a non-Argentine, finds the text to be an apparently historical account of one Tadeo Isidoro Cruz, an obscure gaucho born out of wedlock during Argentina's civil wars of the early nineteenth century. Borges tells us how he grew up in total ignorance of civilization, how he got into a knife fight, killed a man, was thrown into the army as a punishment, and was wounded in combat with the Indians. The author makes no claims to completeness or accuracy in his recounting of Cruz's life; however, he does carefully inform us that "Of the many days and nights that make up his life, only a single night concerns me; as to the rest, I shall tell only what is necessary to that night's full understanding."[15] He also notes, in a hint that Argentines and students of its literature might pick up, that "The episode belongs to a famous poem—that is to say, to a poem which has come to mean 'all things to all men'" (*AOS,* 82). At any rate, Borges completes "the dim and hardy story" of his protagonist's life to that decisive point "during the last days of the month of June 1870" when Cruz, now a sergeant, is sent out with a squad of men to capture a notorious outlaw and deserter from the army.

On the night of 12 July, we are told, he finds his quarry, who refuses to surrender, forcing Cruz and his men to fight. Borges slyly observes, "An obvious reason keeps me from describing the fight that followed. Let me simply point out that the deserter badly wounded or killed several of Cruz's men" (*AOS,* 84). He goes on to analyze his protagonist's transformation at this point in the tale: "He understood that one destiny is no better than another, but that every man must obey what is within him. . . . He understood that his real destiny was a lone wolf, not a gregarious dog. He understood that the other man was himself. . . . Cruz threw down his kepi, called out that he would not be a party to the crime of killing a brave man, and began fighting against his own soldiers, shoulder to shoulder with Martín Fierro, the deserter" (*AOS,* 85).

There are a number of reasons why the foregoing well illustrates the Borgesian penchant for ambiguity and for undermining the identity of his characters. In the first place, the piece—for those familiar with its historical and literary allusions—presents a strange situation indeed: the "intersection" of a completely fictional creation from a literary work ("Sargento Cruz" appears in José Hernández's 1871 epic poem of the gaucho, *Martín Fierro*) with another seemingly historical person to whom Borges gives a first name and enough biographical detail to make him quite believable. Second, the specific incident in the *Martín Fierro* that Borges focuses on itself provides an excellent example of ambivalence and change of identity. Sergeant Cruz (as his very name implies) "crosses over" from the world of law and order to join Fierro the outlaw; moreover, his life and to an extent his attitudes form a set of doubles and counterparts to those of Fierro so that "the other man was himself," to use Borges's exact words. Even the motivation for Cruz's decision is fraught with ambiguity: since his men were being decimated by Fierro, there is a real question as to why he made his dramatic

move. Was Cruz a genuine hero who could not witness the sight of the outnumbered Fierro fighting off the soldiers, or was he a cowardly opportunist who, sensing that the tide of battle was going against him, decided to save his skin by joining the outlaw? Of course these questions are not dealt with in Borges's text, but for the knowledgeable reader they are inherent in the story. Thus, by a masterful stroke of intertextual appropriation, Borges takes full advantage of the underlying ambivalence in another text, namely, Hernández's celebrated epic poem of the nineteenth century.

GAMES OF THE MIND: "FUNES THE MEMORIOUS," "THE LIBRARY OF BABEL," "THE LOTTERY IN BABYLON," AND "TLÖN, UQBAR, ORBIS TERTIUS"

The texts to be examined next belong to a group of almost unclassifiable pieces that derive from mathematical notions or philosophical ideas. Although they have definite narrative elements, they have a stronger expository thrust and thus can almost be thought of as "essayistic fiction." They are highly imaginative, very cerebral, and often spiced with details dear to bibliophiles.

A few words will suffice to describe one of the least complex of these texts, **"Funes el memorioso" ("Funes the Memorious")**, a piece that recalls Borges's long-standing interest in problems of language and in the nature of memory. The central character, Ireneo Funes, is a lad of the Uruguayan pampas who, after a serious accident, becomes aware of the fact that he has a complete and photographic memory. Bits and pieces of his strange existence are described: how he calmly and effortlessly memorized the entire Latin text of Pliny's *Natural History*; how the complete causal train of events that stand behind any perceived object was known to him; how he attempted to organize and codify the vast storehouse of his memory; and how he suffered insomnia as a result of the myriads of precise impressions that crowded his mind. Borges uses the piece to digress on such arcane themes as the possibility of establishing an "infinite vocabulary" corresponding to the natural series of numbers, and Locke's project of devising "an impossible language in which each individual thing, each stone, each bird, and each branch, would have its own name" (*L,* 65). These themes are closely related to Borges' interest in nominalism and to his ideas on language, as expressed in such essays as "Indagación de la palabra" (Inquiry into words) and "The Analytical language of John Wilkins. Though there is a note of horror in Funes's unusual gift—or curse—Borges emphasizes the intellectual content of the piece rather than the protagonist's personal destiny. Thus, a single line describes the end of Funes's shadowy existence: "Ireneo Funes died in 1889, of congestion of the lungs" (*L,* 66). Of greater importance, perhaps, is Borges's comment on the relationship of memory and forgetting to the nature of understanding: "With no effort he had learned English, French, Portuguese and Latin. I suspect, however, that he was not very capable of thought. To think is to forget differences, generalize, make abstractions. In the teeming world of Funes, there were only details, almost immediate in their presence" (*L,* 66).

From his earliest years as a writer Borges was fascinated by logical paradoxes, by numerology, and (though he seldom used the technical terms) by such concepts as subsets, probability, permutations, and combinations. In two well-known texts, **"La biblioteca de Babel"** (**"The Library of Babel"**) and **"La lotería in Babilonia"** (**"The Lottery in Babylon"**), mathematical notions figure prominently. These two pieces also illustrate Borges's cultivation of a single object or institution—a book, a sphere, a library, or even a text—that provides the key to the universe: the "emblem" or "open sesame" revealing a hidden order or secret plan of the cosmos.

"The universe (which others call the Library) is composed of an indefinite and perhaps infinite number of hexagonal galleries" (*L*, 51), Borges tells us in the opening lines of **"The Library of Babel."** The parenthesis immediately informs us that the particular symbol or emblem of reality to be employed in the piece is the Book, or, to be more accurate, a collection of books, the Library. The various ways in which the narrator attempts to render the physical aspect of the Library echoes a number of other Borgesian pieces: its form is geometric, an indefinite number of hexagonal galleries placed one atop the other with a central shaft or air space throughout, but its extent is infinite. Like a great circular book, "The Library is a sphere whose exact center is any one of its hexagons and whose circumference is inaccessible" (*L*, 52).

In the main portion of the piece the nameless narrator explains the principal "axioms" on which the Library is organized. First of all, the Library exists eternally; second, there are twenty-five orthographical symbols on which all the Library's books are based (twenty-two letters, comma, period, and space). He explains that each book consists of 410 pages; each page of forty lines; and each line of approximately eighty letters. In brief, the Library is the product of all the possible permutations and combinations of the twenty-five symbols arranged within the format just described. While the number of different volumes would necessarily be incredibly huge, given these specific limitations, it would not be infinite. Yet the structure of the Library itself, as we just saw, is described in terms clearly suggesting infinitude. Borges's final resolution of the problem posed by the situation—a finite number of items filling an infinite space—is perfectly logical: *The Library is unlimited and cyclical.* If an eternal traveler were to cross it in any direction, after centuries he would see that the same volumes were repeated in the same disorder (which, thus repeated, would be an order: the Order)" (*L*, 58). If we recall that the Library is equated with the universe, we can see a number of typically Borgesian ideas reflected in this symbolism. If the "books" are thought of as people or events, notions of cyclical historicism and the idea that there is nothing really new under the sun immediately come to mind.

But **"The Library of Babel"** is more than an intellectual exercise in permutation and combination. The "Men of the Library," mysterious and tragic figures who roam the endless galleries in search of general truth or specific answers to troublesome questions, are seldom rewarded for their labors. More often than not they find only hopelessly garbled volumes that often contain only one line of tantalizingly clear language. All possible languages, and combinations of language, are found in the *almost* infinite number of volumes. For example, one "chief of an upper hexagon" discovers, after much study, that a certain volume is written in "a Samoyedic Lithuanian dialect of Guarani, with classical Arabian inflections" (*L*, 54). There are virtually no conceivable orthographic combinations not found in the Library. The narrator tells how, in his own hexagon, may be found such intriguing titles as *The Combed Thunderclap*, *The Plaster Cramp*, or, even better, *Axaxaxas mlö*.[16] Borges notes that "these phrases at first glance incoherent, can no doubt be justified in a cryptographical or allegorical manner" (*L*, 57). Even more dizzying is the thought that somewhere in the Library the *key* to such cryptic works must exist! Some of the lonely librarians (their number, we are told, seems to be steadily diminishing) search for books of prophecy; others for "vindications," that is, books that "justify" the existence of a particular individual; still others seek among endless galleries of "false" catalogues the "catalogue of catalogues."

Lurking just below the surface of all this description is a rich and provocative Borgesian allegory of universal history, of man's search for truth, of his ephemeral moments of triumph, of the folly of his sectarian conflicts, and most of all, of the futility of his attempts to solve riddles of an eternal or absolute nature. Borges's description of the "official searchers" as they return from their labors brings out this mood very effectively: "they always arrive extremely tired from their journeys; they speak of a broken stairway which almost killed them . . . sometimes they pick up the nearest volume and leaf through it, looking for infamous words. Obviously, no one expects to discover anything" (*L*, 55). Although **"The Library of Babel"** has no plotted story, the dramatic allegorical rendering of man's quest sets it apart from Borges's essays and his essayistic fiction.

"The Lottery in Babylon" bears some resemblance to the tale just discussed. "Babylon," like the word "library," is an emblem or rubric that stands for the universe. In this story, however, Borges emphasizes a slightly different aspect of man's puny efforts to make sense out of an essentially unfathomable world. The broad metaphor of "the lottery," as Borges develops it, deals with the notion that there is a clearly distinguishable difference between chance happenings and ordered events. People quite naturally believe—at least before they read **"La lotería en Babilonia"**—that this is so. After all, theologies have been constructed about the crucial concepts of free will versus determinism, and philosophical systems have used the notions of contingency and necessity as basic building blocks. The nameless narrator of **"The Lottery,"** however, comes from a place where these important distinctions are blurred, a "dizzy land where the lottery is the basis of reality" (*L*, 30).

The story of how the lottery developed from an elementary pastime to become the dominant feature of the world provides the basic material for this piece. The narrator explains how at first the lower classes of Babylon would buy "chances" for a few pennies in the hopes of winning a small prize; barbers were the traditional lottery vendors, and drawings were uncomplicated affairs held in the open. Gradually, to encourage interest, a new element was added. Some of those who held "unlucky" numbers not only lost their original investment but also had to pay small fines. If these unfortunate players refused to pay these trifling amounts, the "Company" (for the lottery was now institutionalized and controlled by a mysterious organization) might sue them and even put them in jail. After a while, the losers were not fined at all, but simply incarcerated for a fixed number of days. In this manner the lottery's original monetary basis was altered so that soon both winners and losers received their prizes or punishments in non-monetary form. In time the "Company" succeeded in making the operation of the lottery secret, free, and obligatory for all. Further refinements were soon added: a loser's ultimate fate might be altered by a "bifurcation," or lottery-within-the-lottery. The moment before his execution he might be forced to draw nine numbers, one of which could mitigate this extreme penalty, another of which might grant him a full pardon, while yet another might entitle him to a great prize. In like manner, a winner might find a treasure snatched from his grasp at the last moment: "In reality the *number of drawings is infinite*. No decision is final, all branch into others" (*L,* 34). In characteristic Borgesian fashion, the central idea of the all-pervading lottery is unrelentingly carried to its logical conclusion. "Babylon" becomes so thoroughly infused with chance that the very meaning of the word is lost. Behind all these happenings is the enigmatic "Company" whose orders, incidentally, *may* not be genuine, but rather the work of "impostors." In such a world who can distinguish what is counterfeit from what is genuine? In the last paragraph of the piece the narrator concludes, "The Company's silent operations, comparable to God's, give rise to all sorts of conjectures . . . that the Company has not existed for centuries and that the sacred disorder of our lives is purely hereditary, traditional . . . that the Company is omnipotent, but that it only has influence in tiny things. . . . Another, in the words of masked heresiarch, *that it has never existed and will not exist*. Another, no less vile, reasons that it is indifferent to affirm or deny the reality of the shadowy corporation, because Babylon is nothing else than an infinite game of chance" (*L,* 35).

Like a number of other Borgesian texts, **"The Lottery"** is developed from the relentless and vertiginous expansion of a relatively simple idea into nightmarish proportions. Certain formal features of the piece also contribute to this effect. For example, recent critics, sensitive to the subtleties of narrative art, have noted that lurking behind Borges's text we have a very human and very harried narrator, whose only personal remark in the midst of the account, "I don't have much time left; they tell us the ship is about to weigh anchor" (*L,* 33), opens up the text to the possibility of another, untold, but very intriguing tale.

From its enigmatic title to the pathos of its final paragraphs, few texts of Borges have elicited more critical attention or have confounded more readers than **"Tlön, Uqbar, Orbis Tertius."** As one of his longer pieces, it provides ample opportunity for Borges to explore and interrelate several favorite themes: Berkeleyian idealism, "the book" or collection of books as an emblem of the universe, and the arbitrary nature of language. Moreover, **"Tlön,"** as James Irby has astutely observed, "perhaps more fully than any other of his fictions . . . declares their basic principles, characteristically making of that declaration a fictionalized essay, a creation which studies itself."[17] Its essayistic or philosophical content notwithstanding, **"Tlön"** has considerable narrative structure, a genuine plot that only becomes obvious when the final section is read. The text is further enriched by Borges's oblique comments regarding the contemporary world, the perils of the future, and his own retreat into the protective cover of literary activity.

The piece consists of three main divisions: the "discovery" and description of Uqbar, an apocryphal land vaguely suggestive of somewhere in the Middle East; the essay on the strange planet of Tlön, where idealism and psychological association dominate; and finally, the crucial "1947 Postscript," which despite its apparent date was an integral part of the original 1940 text. Borges, as the identified narrator, begins the first section in a chatty, familiar tone by telling how one evening his very real friend Bioy Casares happened to make a casual reference to a religious writer of Uqbar. When Borges confessed that he was unfamiliar with both the writer and the land of Uqbar, Bioy replied that his information came from the *Anglo-American Cyclopedia,* a set of which just happens to be in the house Borges had recently rented. However, on examining the encyclopedia (a "delinquent pirating" of the tenth edition of the *Britannica,* Borges notes parenthetically), they find no article on Uqbar. Dismayed and confused, they agree that it must exist somewhere in either the Near or Middle East. The next day Bioy calls Borges to inform him that he has located a copy of the encyclopedia, which does indeed contain the piece on Uqbar. On careful examination of the particular volume they find that Borges's copy contains only 917 pages, whereas Bioy's had 921, the four extra pages being those describing Uqbar. The article itself, characterized by "rigorous prose" beneath which was "a fundamental vagueness," gave no concrete statement regarding Uqbar's exact location. Further checking, in such standard works as Perthe's atlas and Ritter's geography, reveals nothing whatever about this mysterious land.

The riddle of Uqbar is left unsolved, and the events described in the second section take place two years later. At this point Borges relates, in detail too complicated to be discussed here, how he came into possession of an even more mysterious work, a single volume of *A First Encyclopedia of Tlön* (Vol. XI, Hlaer to Jangr). Though only one tome of the *Encyclopedia of Tlön* could be located—even after such worthies as Alfonso Reyes, Ezequiel Martín Estrada, and Nestor Ibarra[18] are enlisted in the search for companion volumes—Borges finds enough material in the book to sketch out certain basic features of Tlönian culture. After explaining the "congenital idealism" of the planet, Borges discusses Tlön's languages in some detail. Because the Tlönian's basic worldview denies the existence of objects in space, there are no nouns in their languages; instead "there are impersonal verbs, modified by monosyllabic suffixes (or prefixes) with an adverbial value" (*L,* 8). Thus, Borges explains, they have no substantive for "moon," but rather a verb "to moon" ("lunar") or "to moonate" ("lunecer"); hence the sentence, "The moon rose above the river" is "hlör u fang axaxaxas mlö," or literally "upward behind the onstreaming it mooned" (*L,* 8). Tlönian science—what there is of it—is dominated by the planet's "classical" discipline, psychology. Because Tlönians have no conception of objects in space persisting in time, our notion of causality is nonexistent: "The perception of a cloud of smoke on the horizon and then of a burning field and then of the half-extinguished cigarette that produced the blaze is considered an example of the association of ideas" (*L,* 9). Moreover, Borges tells us, on Tlön every mental state is "irreducible"; hence the idea of classification suggests falsification and as a result "there are no sciences on Tlön, not even reasoning" (*L,* 10). Yet in a sense, there are sciences on Tlön, but such an infinitude of scientific systems exists that they are better thought of as individual "dialectical games." Neither Tlön's "scientists" nor its metaphysicians seek truth as we understand the term. Instead they seek "astounding" theories; as Borges puts it, the Tlönians have "an abundance of incredible systems of pleasing design or sensational type" (*L,* 10). A few misguided individuals insist on materialism and on systems that rest upon our usual notions of cause and effect. In a series of amusingly inverted paradoxes, Borges shows how Tlön's more sober minds have refuted these heresies.

Borges's analysis of Tlönian literary theories and practices is rich in self-caricature. We are informed that on Tlön books are not usually signed, for the idea "that all works are the creation of one author, who is atemporal and anonymous," seems to dominate literary attitudes. Plagiarism is, of course, a meaningless concept. "The critics often invent authors: they select two dissimilar works—the *Tao Te Ching* and the *Thousand and One Nights,* say—attribute them to the same writer and then determine most scrupulously the psychology of this interesting *homme de lettres*" (*L,* 13). Borges also notes that a favorite device in Tlönian fiction is the use of a single plot, but arranged in all its possible permutations.

Perhaps the most curious Tlönian phenomenon is the appearance of *hrönir,* that is, objects that are produced by various kinds of mental activity. As Borges blandly notes, "Centuries and centuries of idealism have not failed to influence reality" (*L,* 13). At first merely "accidental products" of distraction and forgetfulness, the *hrönir* were later deliberately produced. Thus Tlönian archaeologists who wish to prove a point simply *think* the necessary artifacts into existence.

The so-called postscript is devoted to a lengthy explanation of events and discoveries that supposedly take place between 1941 and 1944 and that shed light on the true authors of the *Encyclopedia of Tlön.* It seems that a seventeenth-century secret society dedicated to hermetic studies and the Cabala decided to "invent" a country. Although the original members of the group failed to carry out this objective, the society and their plan persisted. After a few centuries it sprang up again in the antebellum South of the United States. One Ezra Buckley, an eccentric millionaire of Memphis, Tennessee, whom Borges slyly describes in a footnote as a "freethinker, a fatalist, and a defender of slavery," becomes the patron of the resuscitated society. Buckley, who could easily have stepped out of the pages of *A Universal History of Infamy,* was apparently given to Gnostic heresies: he agrees to subvent the society's preparation of a forty-volume encyclopedia of the fictional planet provided "The work will make no pact with the imposter Jesus Christ" (*L,* 17). Evidently these terms were accepted, for many years after Buckley's demise (we are told, with no further explanation, that he was poisoned in 1828) the secret printing of the *Encyclopedia* was distributed to the society's members. Finally, Borges reports, in 1944 a complete forty-volume edition is discovered in the Memphis, Tennessee public library! The discovery of the *Encyclopedia*'s origins would seem to resolve all the questions that surrounded the apocryphal world of Tlön. But while Borges drops this veil of mystery he raises another. Inexplicable objects—a strangely heavy metal cone, a compass marked with the symbols of Tlön's alphabet—begin to appear. In short, a fantastic world intrudes on our world of reality.

If **"Tlön"** were to end at this point, which it does not, the reader would be confronted by a narrative structure rather typical of fantasy fiction, for beneath the philosophizing and games of the mind, a simple plot has unfolded. A person tells of a fantastic land whose puzzling existence is inexplicable; finally, its origins and true nature (a hoax perpetrated by a secret society) are revealed; and we breathe a sigh of relief only to discover that "real" objects from the nonplace have entered our own world. The pattern is similar to tales in which a narrator describes a crime of violence, then informs his reader that "it was just a dream," only to discover on awakening that a bloody dagger lies on the floor next to his bed.

But Borges steps back from this kind of conclusion to consider other possibilities. In a rather serious vein he notes that the world, on learning of Tlön and upon receiving the "corroborating" evidence of the strange objects noted above, seemed all too willing to "yield" reality to the attractive symmetry of this well-ordered planet. "The truth is that it longed to yield. Ten years ago any symmetry with a semblance of order—dialectical materialism, anti-Semitism, Nazism—was sufficient to entrance the minds of men.[19] How could one do other than submit to Tlön, to the minute and vast evidence of an orderly planet? (*L,* 17) At the tale's conclusion Borges finds the world as he has known it slipping away: history is being rewritten, language is being transformed by the "conjectural, primitive" idiom of Tlön, and all fields of learning will soon be profoundly altered. In short, "The world will be Tlön." Despite the uncertainties of what is about to take place, Borges writes, "I pay no attention to all this and go on revising . . . an uncertain Quevedian translation (which I do not intend to publish) of Browne's *Urn Burial*" (*L,* 18).

"**Tlön,**" then, may be approached in a number of different ways. On one level it is a sophisticated essay expounding certain favorite Borgesian themes; on another it is an almost classical tale of fantasy, featuring a kind of twist at the end that subverts the "explanation"; finally, it provides Borges with an opportunity to express some serious reactions to what has been happening in the real world of this century. Yet all these facets of the text are successfully unified by the central element: the discovery, the "explanation," and the final destiny of Tlön.

THE LAST LAUGH: "DEATH AND THE COMPASS," "THE ALEPH," AND "PIERRE MENARD, AUTHOR OF THE QUIXOTE"

Although Borges may be taken very seriously, he remains a superb humorist. In fact he might well have been the greatest writer of humor to have appeared in Hispanic America before the "boom" of the 1950s. This may explain why early commentators often ignored or disliked his work, since until recently Spanish Americans have demanded an essential seriousness and propriety from their writers. At any rate, Borges's humor was evident in his earliest narrative work—*The Universal History of Infamy,* for example—and is present in a great many of the canonical texts. At times it takes the form of a single sly epithet in a serious context, at others it may appear as a quietly outrageous oxymoron, while in some pieces the better part of an entire text is revealed as a cosmic joke. Most important, while his is usually a gentle humor, it has an undermining, subversive quality. To borrow a phrase from J. D. Crosson, one of the few critics to have examined this essential facet of Borges's literary persona, it constitutes "a raid on the articulate."[20]

Cast as a detective story—one of Borges's favorite genres since his early readings of Chesterton—"**La muerte y la brújula**" ("**Death and the Compass**") is not especially unusual in its plotting. Reduced to essentials, it involves three apparent murders which occur at intervals of exactly one month apart and at locations which, when traced on a map, form an equilateral triangle. The supersleuth Erik Lönnrot is clever but not quite clever enough. He concludes that a fourth murder is to occur and that its time and place would be defined by forming a diamond-shaped figure on the base of the equilateral triangle. He traces the point on a map of the city and goes there exactly one month after the third murder. Lönnrot, hoping to forestall

the crime and capture the killer, reaches the precise point indicated by his calculations, whereupon he is seized by two men, disarmed, informed in excruciating detail of how he has been lured to the spot, and then of course killed by his enemy the archcriminal Red Scharlach, alias "The Dandy."

The charm of the piece resides in its fundamental irony, in the interplay of Borgesian ideas, and in the tale's frequent sly bits of humor. The scene of the story is itself delightfully unlikely: a Talmudic congress at an unnamed French city that is, as Borges himself points out in one of his prologues, nothing more than a thinly veiled double of Buenos Aires. The characters in the tale are an equally unlikely group: the first victim, the scholarly rabbi of Podolsk, and student of Cabala, Dr. Marcel Yarmolinsky; the protagonist, the supersleuth Erik Lönnrot, a man of "reckless discernment"; Red Scharlach, author of the "fiendish series" of killings; the enigmatic third victim, one Ginsburg, also known as "Gryphius"; the innkeeper, Black Finnegan; various thugs, harlequins (the periods covered by the crimes includes Carnival); and a "myopic, shy atheist" who is the editor of the *Yidische Zaitung*. The two principal characters have names that tempt readers and critics into interesting speculations: why, for example, should the detective's name be Lönn*rot* (i.e., Lönn-*red*) and the criminal's name be *Red Scharlach* (Scharlach = Scarlet)?[21]

The device by which Lönnrot is duped could not be more Borgesian. The four points indicating the four "murders" (actually only three, since we learn at the tale's end that the third was a hoax) correspond to the mystic figure of the tetragrammaton, a Cabalistic emblem of the four Hebrew letters, JHVH, that make up the name of God. Scharlach, who is an old enemy of Lönnrot and who has sworn to kill him (this ridiculously obvious hint is given in the tale's first paragraph!) carefully designs the crimes knowing full well that his enemy will follow all the deliberately placed clues and thus fall into his trap. With infinite sangfroid, Scharlach tells his victim, just before he shoots him, the details of the complex plan: "I . . . interspersed repeated signs that would allow you, Erik Lönnrot, the reasoner, to understand that the series was quadruple. A portent in the north, others in the east and west, demand a fourth portent in the south. . . . I sent the equilateral triangle to (Inspector) Treviranus. I foresaw that you would add the missing point . . . the point which fixes in advance where a punctual death awaits you. I have premeditated everything" (*L,* 86).

The ironies that underlie "**Death and the Compass**" should be obvious to those who know Borges well. Note that Scharlach addresses Lönnrot as "you, the reasoner." The detective is just that. Like most men who have faith in reason, he attempts to find some scheme, some plan to his little universe; but in trying to be clever he finds only defeat and death. As in "**The Library of Babel,**" as in "**The Circular Ruins,**" or as in any number of other pieces, Borges is again underscoring the theme of human vanity and futility. Perhaps the ultimate irony of **"Death and the Compass"** lies in the fact that the very first "crime" was merely a mistake—Yarmolinsky was killed by a drunken thug who was supposed to be robbing the room across the hall. In this manner a *chance* happening provides the opportunity for Scharlach to build his entire plot. Thus, even in the designs of the gods—for Scharlach in his almost omnipotent manipulation of the situation seems to have godlike powers—chance may well play an important role.

Despite these serious overtones, just as Scharlach has the last laugh on Lönnrot, Borges seems to enjoy playing games with the reader. For example, his use of triple motifs as opposed to quadruple elements, as when he names the inspector *Tre*viranus or has the same character dismiss complicated solutions to the crimes as "looking for a three-legged cat," is typical of his playful intercalation of hints and clues that become all too obvious in retrospect.

The title story of Borges's 1949 collection *El Aleph* (*The Aleph*) is another text that is often interpreted very seriously, if not solemnly, and yet is extremely funny. The basic philosophical notion underlying it—the mystical identity of the macrocosm and the microcosm is one that Borges had explored in other pieces such as in his essay "The Fearful Sphere of Pascal" and in one of the retold tales of the *Universal Infamy* collection, **"The Mirror of Ink."**

Actually **"The Aleph"** is a curious hybrid. Although the last few pages take up the question of the single small object that magically encompasses the universe, more than half the text consists of a delightfully humorous caricature or vignette of a certain Carlos Argentino Daneri, a contemporary *porteño* (native of Buenos Aires), full of literary pretensions, verbose, and a complete bore, whose mental activity, writes Borges, "was continuous, deeply felt, far-ranging, and all in all, insignificant" (*AOS,* 17). For several pages Daneri annoys Borges by showing him selections of his verse—dreadful bits of doggerel from his epic description of the planet, modestly titled "La tierra." After each example of verse Borges is forced to listen to a long-winded justification of the particular selection: "I saw, however, that Daneri's real work lay not in the poetry, but in his invention of reasons, by which it should be admired" (*AOS,* 19). In view of Borges's verbal sensitivity, the fact that this half-baked literary buffoon should be named Carlos *Argentino* Daneri cannot be attributed to chance. Clearly Carlos is a caricature of some of the rather stupid, but nonetheless influential, members of Argentina's literary establishment. Even though **"The Aleph"** was written in 1945, it is quite possible that when Borges created Carlos Argentino he had in mind some of the jury that had denied him recognition in 1942. Support for this interpretation is found in the "postscript" to the story. Dated March 1943, this addendum explains how Carlos's magnificent literary efforts were crowned with the second National Prize for Literature whereas Borges's own **"Los naipes del Tahur"** (**"The Gambler's Deck"**)—a nonexistent work, of course—did not even figure in the voting!

The apparently serious part of the story begins when Borges receives a frantic telephone call from Daneri. It seems that the venerable house of his parents and grandparents is about to be demolished and, with it, a priceless treasure. Argentino explains that in the basement of the house there is "an Aleph," without which he could not possibly write his monumental epic poem. Argentino further explains that "an Aleph is one of the points in space that contains all other points" (*AOS,* 23). Borges still doesn't quite understand, and so Argentino tells how he found it as a child, how it belongs to him, and how everything in the world is contained within it. Borges, his confusion compounded, decides to visit the house with Carlos to see for himself just what an "Aleph" might be. With Argentino as his guide, Borges descends the basement stairs, meticulously arranges himself and various objects according to the instructions of Argentino (whom he now fears may be a homicidal maniac), closes his eyes and then opens them.

At this point he sees the Aleph. Yet he complains, "here begins my desperation as a writer . . . how can I translate into words the limitless Aleph, which my floundering mind can hardly encompass?" (*AOS,* 26). He recalls that one ancient sage described this mystic point which is all points as "a sphere whose center is everywhere and whose circumference is nowhere," while other writers used different images. At any rate, despite the problems involved, Borges attempts a direct—and perhaps tongue-in-cheek—description of the Aleph and what he experienced by virtue of it: "On the back part of the stairway, toward the right, I saw a small iridescent sphere of almost unbearable brilliance. At first I thought it was revolving; then I realized that this movement was an illusion. . . . The diameter of the Aleph was probably little more than an inch, but, all space was there, actual and undiminished" (*AOS,* 26). Borges then devotes almost two pages to a fantastic enumeration of all that he saw in the Aleph. Among the infinitude of times are included "all the mirrors of the world and all without my reflection"; "a silvery spiderweb in the center of a dark pyramid"; "all the ants in the world"; "a beach along the Caspian Sea";[22] bison, tigers, obscene letters, and so on. In short, Borges remarks, he saw "the unimaginable universe" and felt "infinite wonder, infinite pity" (*AOS,* 28). At this dramatic moment he hears "a jovial and hateful voice": friend Argentino, calling from the top of cellar stairs, is inquiring if "Che Borges" enjoyed the spectacle and if he saw everything in color!

The contrast between the mystery and wonder of the Aleph's revelations and Argentino's banal comment is perhaps the most effective part of the story. More important, it serves to define the piece as an essentially humorous subversion of a philosophical notion. Borges often complained that he was taken too seriously: when writers criticize a story such as **"El Aleph"** on the ground that the fantastic elements in the piece are presented in an awkward or inept manner, they are doing precisely what Borges objects to. Taken as a serious example of fantastic fiction or as a solemn exposition of the mystical notion of the identity between the macrocosm and microcosm, the piece falls flat. Taken as a half-philosophical, basically playful composition—generously sprinkled with Borgesian irony and satire—**"El Aleph"** comes off rather well.[23]

Our examination of the canonical texts will close with the very first of the *ficciones,* the frequently cited **"Pierre Menard, autor del Quijote"** (**"Pierre Menard, Author of the Quixote"**). Its early date of composition (1939) notwithstanding, for many reasons **"Menard"** is a wonderful example of Borges's last laugh. The unnamed narrator, though he is often ignored by commentators, provides a masterful parody of the critical establishment; the central character (Menard can hardly be considered a protagonist) is one of the most cleverly conceived apocryphal figures in Borges's fiction; and finally the narrator's comment on Menard's principal achievement occupies that tenuous middle ground between high-powered critical intelligence and rampant sophisticated lunacy.

The overall framing device of the text, as perceptive readers soon discover, is a literary article appearing in a decidedly snobbish French journal. The first-person narrator affects the tone of a pretentious academic hack: his first task is to rectify certain unpardonable omissions "perpetrated" by another—and obviously less competent—student of Menard's work. After a paragraph of charmingly pompous name-dropping, the author presents a two-page bibliography of Menard's publications. Though completely apocryphal, the works listed show much internal consistency, bookish humor, and gentle irony. To appreciate fully Menard's far-ranging interests (chess, seventeenth- and eighteenth-century philosophy, French symbolism, and Paul Valéry), one must be a bit of an expert on these subjects, and on Borges as well. Not only does the author give us an enumeration of Menard's publications, but he even includes dates, footnotes, and the names of real journals in which he supposedly wrote. But all this is a mere preliminary. The main part of the piece describes Menard's writing of the *Quijote*—not just "another *Quijote* . . . but the *Quijote* itself!" Menard's expression of this modest desire, as Borges reports it, is "My intent is no more than astonishing" (*L,* 39).

To prepare for this task, Menard first thinks of immersing himself in the world of Cervantes, of learning Spanish, of fighting the Moors, of recovering his lost Catholic faith, and of forgetting all the post-Cervantine history he had ever learned. Realizing the impossibility of this approach, he concludes that he would go on being simply Pierre Menard and would attempt, in some manner, to reach the *Quijote* through his own experiences.

At any rate, Menard writes his *Quijote* and Borges undertakes a close textual comparison of Cervantes' work with that of the Frenchman. The two texts, we are told, "are verbally identical, but the second is almost infinitely richer" (*L,* 42). Borges, half tongue in cheek, also points out that Menard's *Quijote* is more subtle and more ambitious than Cervantes' effort. After all, wasn't Menard a

contemporary of William James and Bertrand Russell? And isn't Nietzschean influence clearly evident in his work? In the last few pages Menard's hazy existence is almost completely obscured by the provocative essayistic digressions Borges introduces. He concludes the piece with the thought that "Menard (perhaps without wanting to) has enriched, by means of a new technique, the halting and rudimentary art of reading: this new technique is that of the deliberate anachronism and the erroneous attribution" (*L,* 44). Finally, he suggests some possible applications of the technique: for example, why not attribute the *Imitation of Christ* to James Joyce, or why not consider the *Odyssey* as coming after the *Aeneid*? **"Pierre Menard, Author of the Quixote"** will strike those who are well grounded in literature, literary criticism, and Borges as clever, sophisticated, and quite funny. Others may find it dull, obscurely bookish, and quite pointless. The first group of readers will enjoy Borges's feigned pomposity, the inside jokes, the caricature of the literary world's petty feuds. They may also see a not-too-implausible reflection of Borges himself in Pierre Menard. Certainly the underlying ideas regarding the flow of time, authorship, plagiarism, and the philosophic interest in the contingent versus the necessary are Borges's as well as Menard's. Occasionally, an offhand remark describing Menard's personal quirks has a remarkably introspective ring. For example, Borges points out Menard's "resigned or ironical habit of propagating ideas which were the strict reverse of those he preferred" (*L,* 42). We are even more likely to make this association when Borges writes that Menard "decided to anticipate the vanity awaiting all man's efforts; he set himself to an undertaking which was exceedingly complex and from the very beginning, futile" (*L,* 43–44).

Anyone who has the temerity to write about Borges's **"Pierre Menard"** (or the work of any great author, for that matter) will, of course, run the risk of doing just what the story's pompous, self-important narrator attempted, namely, to seek fame and recognition vicariously through association with "the great man." Thus the text's main thrust may well be the subversion of the critical act itself. Details such as Menard's unwitting creation of a new technique of literary analysis, the bizarre and pretentious "deliberate anachronism and erroneous attribution," support this view. In sum, if this is his message to critics and scholars Borges has indeed had the last laugh.

Notes

1. Jorge Luis Borges, *A Universal History of Infamy,* trans. Norman Thomas di Giovanni (New York: Dutton, 1972), 13. Succeeding references are noted parenthetically in the text as *UHI.*

2. Emir Rodríguez Monegal, *Jorge Luis Borges: A Literary Biography* (New York: Dutton, 1978), 244.

3. Note, as indicative of his mood, the "Two English Poems" discussed in the previous chapter.

4. Regarding these items, see chapter 1, note 24.

5. There are a number of versions of the accident. Cf. Rodríguez Monegal, *Borges: A Literary Biography,*

320–22; Jurado, *Genio y figura,* 42; and Borges's own "An Autobiographical Essay" appended to *The Aleph and Other Stories,* trans. Norman Thomas di Giovanni (New York: Dutton, 1978), 242–43.

6. Cited by Ronald Christ in "The Art of Fiction: Jorge Luis Borges," *Paris Review* 40 (1967):124.

7. Jorge Luis Borges, *A Personal Anthology,* ed. with a foreword by Anthony Kerrigan (New York: Grove, 1967), 23. Succeeding references are noted parenthetically in the text as *PA.*

8. Jorge Luis Borges, *Labyrinths: Selected Stories and Other Writings,* ed. Donald A. Yates and James E. Irby (New York: New Directions, 1962), 45. Although other translations of these texts are, in some cases, available, I have chosen to use those appearing in *Labyrinths* because they have had very wide circulation and, for English readers, have become "canonical" translations. Succeeding references to works appearing in this collection are noted parenthetically in the text as *L.*

9. On this technique, see the perceptive discussion in Silvia Molloy's *Las letras de Borges* (Buenos Aires: Sudamericana, 1979), 234.

10. For an analysis of these texts, see my *Jorge Luis Borges* (New York: Twayne, 1970), 118–19 and 129–32.

11. Borges's penchant for creating an interlocking system of apocryphal names is well illustrated here. Another text of this collection, "Three Versions of Judas," centers about the life and works of a fictitious scholar named Nils Runeberg. With two Runebergs in the same collection, the reader begins to assume their reality. Note also the meaning of "rune," and old Scandinavian word denoting "a secret, a mystery," and by extension, a letter of the alphabet or a cipher.

12. For an interesting discussion of this and related techniques, see Molloy, *Letras,* 119–20, 166, 175–76.

13. On this point, see Roslyn M. Frank and Nancy Vosburg, "Textos y Contra-Textos en 'El jardín de senderos que se bifurcan,'" *Revista Iberoamericana* 100–101 (1977): 326.

14. Shilomith Rimmon-Kenan, "Doubles and Counterparts: 'The Garden of the Forking Paths,'" in *Modern Critical Views: Jorge Luis Borges,* ed. with an introduction by Harold Bloom (New York: Chelsea House, 1986), 191.

15. Jorge Luis Borges, *The Aleph and Other Stories 1933–1969,* ed. and trans. Norman Thomas di Giovanni (New York: Dutton, 1970), 81. Succeeding references are noted parenthetically in the text as *AOS.*

16. A curious slip here—perhaps intentional—in that Borges uses the dieresis over the *o.* This would naturally increase the total number of possibilities in

the Library, as Borges specifically states that only the comma, period, space, and the regular alphabet constitute its orthographic elements. See *Labyrinths,* 53n.

17. James E. Irby, "Borges and the Idea of Utopia," in Bloom, *Critical Views: Borges,* 93–94. This essay also appears in *The Cardinal Points of Borges* edited by Lowell Dunham and Ivan Ivask (Norman: University of Oklahoma Press, 1970).

18. The three writers were, of course, very real, well-known figures. Alfonso Reyes was a highly regarded Mexican essayist and humanist, Ezéquiel Martínez Estrada, an Argentine poet and essayist, and Nestor Ibarra, a Franco-Argentine critic.

19. Though hardly an activist, Borges did take strong political positions. Regarding some of these, see Rodríguez Mongeal, *Borges: A Literary Biography,* 296–305, 344–46, 391–93. For a general view of the political situation of Argentine writers during these years, see my "Argentine Letters and the Peronato: An Overview," *Journal of Inter-American Studies and World Affairs* 3–4 (1971): 434–55.

20. John Dominic Crossan, *Raid on the Articulate: Comic Eschatology in Jesus and Borges* (New York: Harper & Row, 1976). This work's title is from the book's epigraph: "And so each venture is a new beginning, a raid on the articulate" (from T. S. Eliot's *East Coker*).

21. Many critics have noted Borges's penchant for the color red and have commented on its obvious—and at times less obvious—symbolism. A particularly rich discussion of this point appears in Carter Wheelock's *The Mythmaker: A Study of Motif and Symbol in the Short Stories of Jorge Luis Borges* (Austin: University of Texas Press, 1969).

22. Jorge Luis Borges, *El Aleph* (Buenos Aires: Losada, 1949), 140–41. In this case, I use my own translation because the di Giovanni version (see note 15) departs substantially from the original Spanish of this passage.

23. The point is confirmed by María Esther Vázquez, a close friend and collaborator of Borges. In an interview with him she reports Borges as saying that he wrote the story "riéndome porque me causaba mucha gracia." See her "Entrevista" appended to Borges's *Veinticino agosto 1983 y otros cuentos* (Madrid: Siruela, 1983), 72.

Leo Corry (essay date 1992)

SOURCE: "Jorge Borges, Author of *The Name of the Rose,*" in *Poetics Today,* Vol. 13, No. 3, Fall, 1992, pp. 425–45.

[*In the following essay, Corry shows the influence of Borges's fictions on Umberto Eco's novel* The Name of the Rose.]

Few books have been as quickly and unanimously acclaimed throughout the world as Umberto Eco's *Name of the Rose* (1983 [1980]). Its most obvious reading—as a detective story—is probably also its most exciting one; throughout the development of the plot, the reader's effort is concentrated on answering one question: *Whodunit*? But besides the book's value as a fine mystery novel, *The Name of the Rose* has fostered a brisk commentary industry from the very first day of its appearance on the shelves.[1] It quickly became a commonplace that the secret of the book's somewhat surprising success derives from the multitude of layers underlying its plot; this multilayered structure renders the book attractive to an astonishingly wide spectrum of readers.[2] The present essay is yet another contribution to the interpretation industry generated by *The Name of the Rose,* which is intended to shed new light on some of the book's central features.

While it is rather typical for artists with a fruitful career behind them to take a pause in their creative work in order to reflect on the nature of their art and thereby produce some kind of theoretical book, Eco is a unique example of a theoretician with a fruitful career behind him who takes a pause in his critical work in order to confront his theoretical ideas about art by way of artistic creation. Hence, when Eco the theoretician becomes Eco the novelist, his own interpretation of the novel has been, in a sense, written beforehand. Because of this, we must approach Eco's novel with prejudice.

The least we might expect from Eco is his having built a text in accordance with a foreseen audience and, consequently, his having anticipated the most likely interpretations. Yet, to claim that this foresight is part of the generative process of the book would still be, according to Eco, no more than a generality. What is necessary is "to represent an 'ideal' text as a system of nodes or joints and to establish at which of them the cooperation of the Model Reader is expected and elicited" (Eco 1979: 33).

I do not intend to uncover here all the "nodes" which require the "cooperation" of a "model reader" of *The Name of the Rose*; this would be far beyond the scope of a single article and far beyond my own competence. I will, however, attempt to uncover the "nodes" that call for the "cooperation" of a particular type of reader, and I will claim that these "nodes" play a central role in the semiotic strategy of the book. I am thinking, namely, of the "nodes" which elicit the "cooperation" of readers well versed in the writings of Jorge Luis Borges. A detailed study of the intertextual interplay between Eco's novel and Borges's works presents a twofold interest. On the one hand, it brings to the fore many hidden aspects of the novel and helps to actualize its literary potential. On the other hand, it leads to some theoretical insights into the nature of literary allusion as a specific device of intertextuality. In what follows, therefore, I will first explore the intertextual aspects of Eco's novel and Borges's writings, emphasizing the role of allusion therein, and, in my final section, I will discuss the relevance of this remarkable example to elucidating the general mechanism of literary allusion.

JORGE DE BURGOS—JORGE LUIS BORGES

The strong Borgesian flavor of Eco's novel and the transparent similarity between Eco's character Jorge de Burgos and Jorge Luis Borges were readily noted by many commentators on *The Name of the Rose*. Eco has since explained that this name resulted from a desire to pay his debts to Borges (Eco 1985: 27–28). What kinds of debts is Eco talking about? It would be enough to glance briefly at some of Borges's writings in order to grasp the degree to which Borgesian ideas pervade the conceptual world of Eco, especially concerning the active role of the reader in the literary experience. For example, in his article on George Bernard Shaw, Borges addressed himself to the problem of the possibility of creating art through mechanical devices. After mentioning some of the thinkers who had contributed to that debate, either by enthusiastically encouraging such a possibility or by sadly accepting it with resignation, Borges expressed his own opinion on the issue by succinctly stating his belief in the active role of the reader, as follows:

> A book is more than a verbal structure, or a series of verbal structures; it is the dialogue in which it engages with the reader. . . . The book is not an isolated entity: it is a relationship, it is an axis of innumerable relationships. One literary tradition differs from those previous or subsequent, less in the text itself than in the fashion in which it is read.

(Borges 1974i [1952]: 747 [translation mine])

We could, then, follow the path leading from Borges's ideas to Eco's theories and from Eco's theories to *The Name of the Rose*. This path would indicate the nature of Eco's debts to Borges and would show how they are repaid in the novel. But Borges's ideas are much more central to *The Name of the Rose* than this path would suggest. The presence of Borges in the novel is a constitutive feature and not a superfluous detail imposed upon the writer by the initial setting of the plot, as Eco's claims in *Reflections* would have us believe. The intertextual relationship between the novel and Borges's writings is not simply one of borrowed ideas and motifs, but is a much subtler and more intricate one.

Certainly, from the outset of the story, we are confronted with classical Borgesian motifs: labyrinths, mirrors, libraries, and books about books. A considerable number of the issues discussed in the novel, either as part of the intricate plot or through the philosophical debates implicitly or explicitly conducted in it, are typical of Borges. But, as a matter of fact, Borges's presence is felt even before the plot begins to unfold.

In his introduction to *The Name of the Rose,* Eco describes his sources in a typical Borgesian fashion: we are told that we are dealing with a French, neo-gothic version of the seventeenth-century Latin edition of an original manuscript from the end of the fourteenth century, which was written in Latin by a German monk. This introduction brings to mind the opening paragraphs of many short stories by Borges: a painstaking description of characters, dates, recondite historical facts, erudite philosophical debates, and detailed bibliographical references, each of which serves to blur the border between reality and imagination.[3] Certainly, this literary resource is neither Borges's invention nor his monopoly; however, hardly anything else could be considered more characteristic of his writing than that blurring of reality and imagination which perplexes the uninitiated reader and causes him to read and reread in order to solve the mystery. This blurring effect is created in Borges's works, in the first place, by the recurrent use of introductions like the one presented here by Eco. Eco himself has elsewhere explained the centrality of the introduction to determining the character of a fictional text, since, by means of the introduction, "the reader is invited not to wonder whether the reported facts are true" (Eco 1979: 12–13).

The profusion of characters, the scholarly quotations, and the endless references to books and writers which appear throughout *The Name of the Rose* reinforce our feeling of definitely being in Borgesian surroundings. But the interesting point is that neither Borges's name nor his books are explicitly mentioned; they are, instead, *alluded to.* Literary allusion has been persistently cited as the essential characteristic of Borges's style: "His stories are allusions to other stories, his characters are allusions to other characters and their lives are allusions to other lives" (Christ 1969. 38). Borges developed the aesthetic strategy of allusion throughout his writings, which, in turn, are liberally alluded to in *The Name of the Rose.* In fact, Eco alludes to several different levels of Borges's work: to Borges's favorite themes, to Borges's plots, to Borges's own allusive techniques, etc. It is this variety of connections which makes the study of the intertextual relationship between Borges and Eco worth pursuing and, especially, which sheds new light on the theoretical aspects of literary allusion as a particular device of intertextuality.

In **"The Library of Babel"** Borges (1974c [1942]) describes a library representing the universe, and through an analysis of the structure of the library and its contents, he discusses the possibility of knowing the world. Borges, a staunch skeptic, denies such a possibility. A similar analysis is carried out as part of the detective's investigation in *The Name of the Rose*: the detective succeeds in deciphering the secret interior layout of the library only through examination of its exterior and with the help of mathematics. The very possibility of discovering the design of the library is properly founded on epistemological grounds akin to the detective's general philosophical approach.

> Here is the point: we must find, from the outside, a way of describing the Aedificium as it is inside. . . . We will use the mathematical sciences. Only in the mathematical sciences, as Averroës says, are things known to us identified with those known absolutely. . . . Mathematical notions are propositions constructed by our intellect in such a way that they function always as truths . . . and the library was built by a human mind that thought in a mathematical fashion, because

without mathematics you cannot build labyrinths. And therefore we must compare our mathematical propositions with the propositions of the builder, and from this comparison science can be produced, because it is a science of terms upon terms.

> (Eco 1983 [1980]: 215)

Eco's and Borges's libraries are similar in some ways and different in others. Both libraries are mazes representing the labyrinth of the universe. The plot in both stories concerns the search for a book found on the shelves of the library—a book containing the sum of all the books in the library, in the case of Borges, and the second book of Aristotle's *Poetics,* in the case of Eco. Borges suggests searching for the desired book by examining the contents of the library's other books, but this entails an infinite regression and, hence, is impractical. Eco's detective succeeds in finding his book with the help of other books in the library, but his success is only fleeting and the book soon disappears before the detective's astonished eyes.

An interesting difference between the two libraries lies in their physical design, a fact that seems to underline, as it were, their essential identity. In Borges's library, we find an infinite number of hexagonal rooms; in Eco's, there are fifty-six rooms: four are heptagonal and the rest, "more or less square." The building is composed of four towers with five rooms each, one of them being heptagonal and the others having four walls. An octagonal fossa forms the center of the building. With this design, which seems to avoid by any and all means the number six, the library builders achieved the "maximum of confusion" through "the maximum of order" (ibid.: 217). Borges's library also attains total chaos by means of its compulsive order since, for Borges, absolute order and absolute chaos are nothing but two sides of the same coin.

EPISTEMOLOGICAL METAPHORS

Up to this point, we have considered some aspects of the Borgesian atmosphere in which the plot of *The Name of the Rose* unfolds: the introduction, the intermingling of reality and imagination, Borges's obsessive images, and so forth. However, as Eco himself has emphasized, "what matters is not the various issues in themselves but the maze-like structure of the text" (Eco 1979: 9). The next step, then, is to see if the plot itself is Borgesian; as a matter of fact, Eco takes an actual Borges plot and introduces some variations to it in order to present an epistemological picture that differs from Borges's. The plot in question is that of Borges's detective story **"Death and the Compass"** (Borges 1974e [1942]).

In **"Death and the Compass"** we meet a detective investigating a series of murders. He believes that he has discovered the series to have been designed in accordance with a plan taken from written sources: in this case, all of the clues are derived from works of Jewish mysticism. Eco's detective, Brother William, discovers a similar plan, but all of his clues are, naturally, derived from works of Catholic mysticism. Detective stories provide an appropriate framework for the formulation of conjectures; both Eco and Borges are deeply interested in the philosophical issues entailed by such formulation of conjectures.

An underlying meta-conjecture of most inquisitive activities based on conjecture formulation is "that all the events have a logic, the logic that the guilty party has imposed on them" (Eco 1985: 54). However, as we shall see, this meta-conjecture is considered by Eco and by Borges in different terms. We shall next proceed, then, to explain the ways in which Eco's and Borges's detectives elaborate their conjectures and how these conjectures are related to reality. We thus return for now to Eco the theoretician.

Eco coined the term "epistemologic metaphor" to describe the manner in which a literary work can illuminate unrecognized aspects of scientific theories or philosophical systems, either by developing the tenets of such theories to their most extreme consequences or by turning their central images into literary ones. In this way, we can sometimes consider artistic productions as mediating agents which link the abstract categories of science to everyday life, while pointing out hitherto unknown aspects of the world and of the theories as well (Eco 1965: 120). This is one of Eco's key tools in his work as a literary critic; it is also very well suited to defining Borges's literary work[4] and, as we shall see, Eco's own novel as well.

Borges has stressed the centrality of metaphor as the foremost rhetorical device. In fact, his mature writing has sometimes been characterized as an effort to develop an entire story as one big metaphor. But Borges does not limit the centrality of metaphor to its place in literature. He goes further and considers all philosophical and scientific writings as no more than metaphors; according to Borges, the whole intellectual history of humanity is nothing more than the history of a small number of metaphors. Borges is an extreme relativist who believes that all theories about the universe must fail because they presuppose the existence of a "cosmos," or a given order. To Borges, the universe is, on the contrary, in a state of chaos, or, at best, it is a maze in which we can never find the right path. Hence, claims Borges, we should refrain from judging theories according to their truth-value—since all of them are equally wrong—and instead judge them only according to their aesthetic value. Epistemological metaphors, such as those written by Borges, may indeed help us to assess the aesthetic value of the philosophical theories behind them.

In the epistemologic metaphor, **"Death and the Compass,"** Borges contrasts his own view of the universe with the implicit view in the traditional detective story. He challenges the traditional presupposition of a "cosmos." Eco's novel represents, as well, a further epistemologic metaphor concerning chaos and cosmos.

The classic detective in literature is usually interested only in finding out the truth; neither justice nor law enforcement is his business. The process of discovering the truth is based on the assumption that the detective's universe of inquiry—including the world of human thoughts and drives—is a cosmos which behaves according to an already established scheme as well as according to the principles of logic and to simple, fixed laws. The aim of the detective is to decipher that scheme and those laws, which will lead him directly to the murderer. It is precisely this assumption which is challenged by Borges in **"Death and the Compass."**

Eric Lönnrot, the detective of **"Death and the Compass,"** is precisely the classical type. His insatiable intellectual curiosity enables him to become absorbed in the study of any subject—however abstruse and complicated—whenever it may help him in his pursuit of the truth. However, Lönnrot is willing to acknowledge from the start what most of his colleagues and literary analysts would be ashamed to admit: that his aim as a detective is just to produce conjectures. The only requirement imposed upon these conjectures is that they be interesting. Even less, however, is required of reality—reality can afford to be uninteresting. Lönnrot rejects any conjecture in which randomness plays a significant role, even when it is plausible, only because it is uninteresting.

The first victim in the series of murders investigated by Lönnrot is a Talmudic scholar named Marcelo Yarmolinsky. The following unfinished sentence was found on the piece of paper left in his typewriter: *The first letter of the name has already been pronounced.* Since the case deals with the murder of a rabbi, and the only clue is a rabbinical one, Lönnrot begins an intensive study of Jewish mystical tradition in order to produce an interesting conjecture stated in purely rabbinical terms, in open contradiction to the police inspector, who suggests an easy (although uninteresting) solution. Lönnrot's sudden interest in Jewish philosophy is reported by the newspapers. Next to the second victim in the series, Lönnrot finds written on the wall: *The second letter of the name has already been pronounced.* He can then easily guess what text will be found near the third victim in the series.

At this stage, the basic rabbinical presuppositions held by Lönnrot have been fairly well corroborated, and he sets about deciphering the meaning of the series in order to discover the murderer. Assisted by several clues and a liberal dose of geometry, Lönnrot is able to predict the time and place of the next murder, which is to be the last in the series. According to the plan discovered by Lönnrot, it is absolutely clear that there will be exactly four murders in the series, as there are four letters in the Jewish name of God. Lönnrot arrives at the location of the expected crime (a maze-like country house), where he meets the murderer, who is waiting for him; indeed, Lönnrot himself is to be the fourth victim, but he has not anticipated this particular detail. A brief exchange between detective and murderer is enough to clarify the "whole truth." Red Scharlach (the murderer) has been planning Lönnrot's murder for several years, after the latter had sent the former's brother to prison. An unexpected opportunity presented itself when

Lönnrot was commissioned to investigate a murder in which Scharlach had been involved. Hearing of Lönnrot's sudden interest in Jewish philosophy, Scharlach decided to support Lönnrot's conjecture by creating corroborative evidence. Lönnrot convinced himself of the truth of his conjectures, as Scharlach had planned, and Scharlach's scheme led Lönnrot—driven now by a slight arrogance due to the success of his discoveries—directly into the hands of the murderer, who, before shooting him, explains to his victim all the details of the crimes as they really happened.

That is the plot of the story. What then is its epistemologic moral? Borges here clearly rejects the basic assumption that the universe is a cosmos whose code the detective (as well as the scientist and the philosopher) is trying to decipher. Lönnrot builds theories upon details collected from reality, and with the help of mathematics he tries to predict the next murder in the series. But in the end he is deceived: there is nothing in common between his conjecture and reality. Any attempt at knowing the universe is hopeless, claims Borges, and every theory is arbitrary and no more than a conjecture. We do not even understand the concept of universe, and we do not know whether that concept refers to something real. Even so, Borges insists, "the impossibility of penetrating the universe's divine scheme cannot deter us from planning human schemes, even when these are merely provisional" (Borges 1974a: 708 [translation mine]). The formal similarity between *The Name of the Rose* and **"Death and the Compass"** should be evident to the reader at this stage. However, before we proceed to analyze this similarity in detail, let us return once more to Eco the theoretician.

In 1983 Eco edited (with Thomas Sebeok) a book devoted entirely to the analysis of detective stories in terms of the philosophy of C. S. Peirce (Eco and Sebeok 1983). The short time that elapsed between the publication of the novel (Eco 1980) and of the theoretical work suggests that it would be worthwhile to digress and briefly comment on the latter. One of the articles collected there (Truzzi 1983) explicitly deals with Sherlock Holmes's method. The author had discovered a fact which Holmes scholars typically overlook (but which Borges had clearly seen back in 1942): that is, despite Holmes's avowed empiricism, a close inspection of his methods shows that Holmes resorts to hypothesis more often than not; more specifically,

> although Holmes often speaks of his *deductions,* these are actually rarely displayed in the canon. Nor are Holmes's most common inferences technically *inductions.* More exactly, Holmes consistently displays what C. S. Peirce has called *abductions.* . . . Peirce sometimes called abductions *hypotheses* . . . and in the modern sense, that is what the conclusion in the abduction represents: a conjecture about reality which needs to be validated through testing.[5]
>
> (Ibid.: 69–70 [Truzzi's emphases])

Eco's own article in this volume deals with the conjectural character common to both the scientist's and the detec-

tive's work. Usually, claims Eco, our conjectures are produced within conceptual frameworks which are themselves taken for granted. Johannes Kepler's theory of elliptic orbits, for instance, is a bold conjecture grounded on a very stable framework, namely, that planets move in regular orbits. However, it may also happen that particular conjectures lead us into questioning the very paradigm in which we are working and a further conjecture must be added, namely, that the "possible universe outlined by our first-level abductions is the same as the universe of our experience" (Eco 1983: 207). Eco calls this last kind of conjecturing "meta-abduction," and he remarks on the importance of considering these two levels of conjecturing separately. As a matter of fact, it is by means of the meta-abduction that Eco classifies diverse types of conjectural thinking. For example, rationalistic thinking in general is characterized by the very passage from simple abduction to meta-abduction that presupposes a perfect correspondence between the conjecturer's mind and the outside world. Holmes's simplistic meta-abductions provide the basis for his certainty in the soundness of his own abductions.

As Eco remarks, Karl Popper and Peirce both knew, in contradistinction to Holmes, that science does not enjoy this certainty regarding its meta-abductions. Borges asserted, as long ago as 1942, the conjectural character of any inquiry (detectivesque, scientific, or metaphysical) and refused to endow it with any kind of certainty at any level. Eco's detective too, conducting his fourteenth-century investigation, was able to acknowledge the conjectural character of science within a strictly scholastic conceptual world. Some of the views expressed by William of Baskerville had already been clearly stated in Eco's 1983 article, while the plot of the novel seems to follow rather closely, although not identically, that of Borges's skeptical detective story.

William of Baskerville is depicted by Eco as a classic British detective. In language heavily flavored with Scholastic terminology, William claims that his interest is only in the truth, disavowing any concern with questions of justice or ethics. Despite such claims, however, we find many instances in the plot where William seems to be more troubled by problems of morality and the administration of justice than his modern colleagues in detective fiction are. Moreover, as Adso—William's apprentice—points out, William seems to be amusing himself by "imagining how many possibilities were possible" (i.e., formulating conjectures), rather than pursuing the truth (Eco 1983 [1980]: 306).

The first display of William's abilities takes place at the moment of his arrival at the outskirts of the monastery, when he correctly guesses that the abbot's horse has run away from the stables, thereby impressing Adso and the other monks with his analytic abilities. This episode is taken, almost word for word, from a fragment of Voltaire's *Zadig* which Eco quotes in full in his article on Holmes, where he explains his own ideas on abduction and meta-abduction. This self-allusion by Eco to a quotation from one of his own works, a typical Borges device, is rather significant in the present context and may indeed throw some light on the meta-story of *The Name of the Rose*. As Eco explains,

> Whereas in criminal stories an omnipotent God verifies the hypotheses forever, in "real" scientific inquiries (as well as in real criminal, medical, or philological detection) meta-abductions are a frightening matter. *Zadig* is not a detection story but a philosophical tale because its deep subject is exactly the vertigo of meta-abduction.
>
> (Eco 1983: 219)

Borges tacitly declared his own meta-abductional position very clearly through the philosophical tale **"Death and the Compass"**: any meta-abduction bestowing the status of reality upon a conjecture is nonsense because all conjectures about the universe are equally false and can *never* reflect its true structure. By now it should be clear that **"Death and the Compass"** is "not a detection story but a philosophical tale," and that the same holds true for *The Name of the Rose*.

William starts his inquiry into the series of murders and soon conjectures that the series is part of a preconceived plan, with the circumstances of all the cases fitting the description of the seven trumpets of the Apocalypse. The first murder takes place during a day of hailstorms, the second victim is drowned in a barrel full of blood, and so forth. Based on this assumption, William's investigation does lead him to the murderer's hiding place. This scenario, in which the victim waits patiently (very often in the center of a maze, as is the case in *The Name of the Rose*) for the one who must come to execute him, is also typical of Borges. Usually, in these cases, a transmutation takes place, with victim and executioner exchanging roles, and it is hard to decide finally who is who. In **"The House of Asterión"** (Borges 1974f [1947]), for example, the Minotaur waits in the center of the maze for Theseus's arrival; in **"Abenjacán the Buckharian, Dead in His Labyrinth"** (Borges 1974h [1951]), Zaid waits for Abenjacán, who must come to execute him. Likewise, Scharlach waits for Lönnrot in a maze-like country house. There are many other examples of this kind. In *The Name of the Rose*, William discovers the real identity of the murderer and succeeds in getting to his hiding place. When William finally meets the murderer, a very erudite conversation takes place between them, and William learns that the first two murders in the series occurred in circumstances which were not originally related to any plan; rather, it was only chance that united them into an assumed series. Despite the crimes' coinciding with William's assumptions, to have considered them as part of a preconceived series was misleading.

But the interesting point (and here the plot begins to differ slightly, but meaningfully, from that of Borges) is that, somehow, the murderer had heard of William's conjecture and had himself become convinced that his crimes were, in fact, part of a divine plan forced upon him by the will of God and that it was his duty to carry out that plan. The murderer, accordingly, consummated the plan by committing the crimes it entailed, as though those first two murders had indeed been part of a scheme imposed on the murderer against his will.

The whole process can be summed up as follows: in the course of his inquiry, William conjectured a correspondence between the series of murders and the book of the Apocalypse; consequently, the entire course of his investigation was biased in that direction. Although William came across a great deal of data contradicting his theory, he decided to stick to it while simultaneously elaborating possible alternative conjectures. Toward the end, sunk in a deep despair because his original conjecture had failed to lead him to the right person, William almost rejected that theory, but decided to give it one last shot in deciphering the sixth murder. Then, almost by chance (and, incidentally, with the help of a dream which, in the style of Borges, intermingled with reality), an improvement in the conjecture led him to the murderer's hiding place. In solving the mystery, William exploited the most important tools that fourteenth-century knowledge had to offer: Aristotelian logic, Scholastic theology, and the philosophy of nature of Roger Bacon, his teacher and friend.

When he finally does meet the murderer, William finds that his quarry has been waiting for him with the same feeling of self-confidence, tinged with excitement, with which Scharlach had awaited Lönnrot's arrival in Borges's story. William's fate, however, is different from Lönnrot's; he is not shot to death and he even manages to escape, while the murderer dies in the burning monastery. Eco's murderer character behaves like many executioners in Borges's stories: he expresses his sincere belief that his deeds did not proceed from coarse human drives, such as love, hate, or greed—"I have killed no one. Each died according to his destiny because of his sins. I was only an instrument" (Eco 1983 [1980]: 471).[6]

Eco not only tells us his philosophical tale, but he also analyzes some of its epistemological implications through the discussion that William and Adso hold at the end of the novel. William expresses his doubts about the possibility of ever knowing the truth. Adso, who has slowly mastered his mentor's methods of analysis and inference, disagrees with this conclusion: at various points along the investigation, he claims, William did succeed in correctly interpreting many clues leading to the discovery of hitherto unknown facts. Indeed, replies William, it is possible for us to learn from signs about *individual* facts, but we should refrain from formulating conjectures which attempt to explain the universe. Any connection between our theories and reality is only accidental, and, even though those theories may be useful, we should always be aware of their fictitious character. William's epistemological formulations display a rather modern spirit, and he even "quotes" Wittgenstein in ancient German:

> The order that our mind imagines is like a net, or like a ladder, built to attain something. But afterward you

must throw the ladder away, because you discover that, even if it is useful, it was meaningless. Er muoz gelîchesame die leiter abewerfen, sô er an ir ufgestigen [*sic*].

(Ibid.: 492)

William's exhaustive inquiry has led him to the same pessimistic conclusion that Borges had reached before him: it is beyond our capabilities to decipher the mystery of the universe. To assume, to guess—perhaps; to apprehend God's plan of the universe—never. However, William should in fact listen more carefully to Adso, his metainductive consciousness, and accordingly, his conclusion should be slightly more optimistic than Borges's. After William had conjectured the existence of a preconceived guiding plan for all of the crimes, the murderer actually began to act in accordance with William's theory, and this fact did enable the detective to predict the murderer's behavior. Both Lönnrot's and William's investigations were guided by the presupposition that the crimes were part of a pattern whose essence might be elucidated. But while Lönnrot was led astray by an artificial plan designed by Scharlach deliberately to deceive him, William's conjecture did have the power to constrain the murderer's deeds and, finally, to enable his predictions to be fulfilled. Both detectives discovered at the end of the story that the logic of events was no more than "the logic that the guilty party had imposed on them"; but the logic imposed by Borges's murderer character was an arbitrary one, while that imposed by Eco's character was a logic constrained by the investigator's own conjecture.

As we have seen, Borges asserts the conjectural character of any scientific or metaphysical theory. No theory, in his view, may be considered true. Nevertheless, as it happens, when a single conjecture must be chosen from among the various possible ones, it must be evaluated according to some kind of criteria. In making his choice, Borges relies on aesthetic criteria. Thus, Lönnrot chose a "purely rabbinical" conjecture when analyzing Yarmolinsky's murder. Borges's epistemological metaphors address the abductive and the meta-abductive simultaneously: since all theories are equally conjectural, they are all equally false, and, therefore, there can be no connection between them and the universe out of which they are formulated. Eco recognizes the conjectural character of science as well, but he also recognizes a historical fact which Borges reluctantly ignores, namely, the predictive power of science. These diverging positions are reflected in the different metaphors that inform the works of Eco and of Borges. For a better understanding of this divergence, let us return once more to Eco's theoretical views on the issue, views which, in fact, constitute an elaboration of Peirce's epistemology.

Peirce has been widely praised for having been able, back in the nineteenth century and before the Einsteinian revolution, to formulate and develop ideas that later became so central to contemporary philosophy of science concerning the fallible character of the scientific enterprise. Peirce's views on the issue are, in some senses, similar to those found in Popper's philosophy of science, but there are important differences between the two.

According to Popper, the way in which hypotheses are attained is of no interest to philosophy of science. Science begins from ideas and leads to further ideas, while facts enter the scientific process only in order to refute hypotheses. Although Popper firmly believes in the objectivity of science and in its constant advance toward truth, he has no means of explaining how, among the infinite number of possible conjectures, scientists happen to choose highly improbable ones, including those which are hard to refute and, hence, quite close to the truth. Likewise, Popper does not say how the elimination of a finite number of refuted hypotheses from among the infinite number of possible ones moves us any closer to truth. Peirce seems to have posed, beforehand, questions which address these particular aspects of Popper's philosophy.

A man must be downright crazy to deny that science has made many true discoveries. But every single item of scientific theory which stands established today has been due to abduction.

But how is it that all this truth has ever been lit up by a process in which there is no compulsiveness nor tendency towards compulsiveness? Is it by chance? . . . Think of what trillions of trillions of hypotheses might be made of which one only is true; and yet after two or three or at the very most a dozen guesses, the physicist hits pretty nearly on the correct hypothesis.

(Peirce 1965: 106)

Peirce's theory of abduction proposes an answer to the questions elided by Popper, as Peirce attempts to explain the act of reasoning which starts from data and moves toward hypothesis formulation, namely, abduction. Plain trial-and-error methods, claims Peirce, cannot account for the historically rapid development of science. Man must be naturally predisposed to penetrate the secrets of nature, and studying the logical process of abduction should enable us to elucidate the essence of such a predisposition. We are not concerned here, of course, with assessing Peirce's theory of abduction vis-à-vis Popper's philosophy of science, but only with describing the background of Eco's epistemological metaphor. In his above-mentioned article on detectivesque inquiry, Eco (1983) elaborates further on some of Peirce's ideas about abduction which are more central to the present analysis.

At least in terms of face value, we could consider two different kinds of abduction. First, as in the case of scientific discoveries, there are abductions in which a series of surprising facts leads to the formulation of a general law. Second, as in the case of crime detection, a series of particular facts may lead to the identification of another particular fact as what has generated all of the relevant facts in the case. These two kinds of abductions, one proceeding from facts to laws and the other, from facts to facts, are suggested in Peirce's texts. Eco refers to them as abductions dealing with *universes* and with *texts*, respectively, denoting by the word "text" any sequence of "propositions linked together by a common topic or theme." Thus, a sequence of events investigated by a detective can be considered a text in such a sense (and, significantly enough, William finds the key to the series of crimes precisely in a text—in the literal sense of the word). The interesting point is that Eco does not consider these two kinds of abduction as essentially different.

> I think that the general mechanism of abduction can be made clear only if we assume that we deal with universes as if they were texts and with texts as if they were universes. . . . [In] scientific discovery one figures out laws through the mediating discovery of many further facts; and in text interpretation one identifies new relevant facts by presupposing certain general (intertextual) laws.

(Ibid.: 205)

This description is quite interesting in the context of an intertextual reading of Eco and Borges. Eco starts with Peirce's epistemological claims, discusses them in the light of some central Borgesian metaphors (the universe as a text, the text as an open universe, detectivesque inquiry as text deciphering, text deciphering through intertextual reading, etc.), and develops his own general theory of abduction. Like Borges, Eco recognizes the epistemological value of considering all conjectural thinking from the same point of view. Like Peirce, but unlike Borges, he believes that, sooner or later, abduction will lead him to truth. In the framework of this discussion, then, he is led to distinguish two levels in the process of inquiry: abduction and meta-abduction. Eco agrees with Borges at the abductive level, but disagrees with him at the meta-abductive one.

Now we come to a very subtle point in Eco's theory, as well as in his metaphor. Eco began by postulating a single process of abduction: conjecture formulation is the same whether one is speaking of "scientific" (from facts to laws) or "detectivesque" (from facts to facts) inquiry. Here the terms "scientific" and "detectivesque," let us note once more, denote the kind of conjecture formulated and not the professional training of the researcher. However, the unitary approach disappears when one reaches the meta-abductive level, where, Eco believes, the attitudes of scientists and detectives are significantly different: the latter, according to him, demonstrate a greater meta-abductional flexibility than the former.

One of the central features of scientific activity, in Popper's opinion, is the critical attitude of the scientist toward his own conjectures. Eco remarks that this critical attitude pertains to the meta-abductive level. Unlike the scientist, a detective can afford a more relaxed meta-abductional attitude. Not only can he afford it, but he is, in fact, *socially conditioned* to adopt that attitude.

> This is why "real life" detectives commit more frequent (or more frequently visible) errors than scientists. Detectives are rewarded by society for their impudence in betting by meta-abduction, whereas scientists are so-

cially rewarded for their patience in testing their abductions. . . . Their difference from detectives stands in their refusal to impose their beliefs as a dogma, in their firmness not to repudiate their motivated conjectures.

(Ibid.: 220)

Obviously, the terms "scientist" and "detective" each denote here a professional group and not, as above, a typical strategy of conjecture formulation. Eco's epistemological views may now be summed up as follows: All intellectual activity based on conjecture formulation proceeds according to a single process, namely, abduction. Particular activities based on conjecture formulation differ at the meta-abductional level, and this difference may be *socially conditioned*.

This summary corresponds, to be sure, to a very small portion of Eco's article, but I emphasize it here since it underlines a significant difference between Eco and Borges. His distinction between two levels of abduction enables Eco to introduce sociological considerations into his epistemology. Naturally, such factors are absolutely alien to Borges's worldview, in which only disembodied ideas count. Here lies also the difference between the fates of Eco's and Borges's detectives.

Eco follows Peirce in his belief in science's faculty for eventually attaining truth, and William is indeed led to the hiding place of the murderer. Lönnrot's uncritical approach to his own abductive reasoning leads him directly to death, at the hands of Scharlach. William, in his double role of detective and scientist, meta-abduced ambiguously—sometimes carefully and sometimes less carefully. And, indeed, this ambiguity came close to misleading him in his inquiry. Fortunately for him, Jorge de Burgos, by failing (like Jorge Luis Borges) to distinguish between the two levels of abduction, believed himself compelled to act according to William's conjecture and, finally, burned himself to death amidst his beloved books. However, as William's last statement quoted above shows, he did learn his epistemological lesson and did finally understand the need for a more critical attitude toward any tentative interpretation of signs.

Adso and William escape from the burning monastery. This marks the end of the plot but not of the book. As Borges does for many of his stories, Eco adds a final chapter intended to undermine, once more, our belief in the manuscript's authenticity. To be more precise, in the final section of his story **"The Immortal,"** Borges not only suggests the possibility that the whole manuscript on which his story is based might be apocryphal, but he also closes with a sentence which Eco seems to have paraphrased in concluding his own novel: "Words, words displaced and mutilated words, words of others, were the poor pittance left him by the hours and the centuries" (Borges 1964: 149 [Spanish original]; 1974g [1947]: 544). As one of his critics has put it, "Borges demands that we make a distinction between the labyrinth *in* the story and the labyrinth *of* the story" (Christ 1969: 172). William of Baskerville disen-

74

tangled for us the labyrinth *in* Eco's story; in the discussion above, I have tried to shed some light on the labyrinth *of* that story. We can now turn to some theoretical lessons that we might draw from Eco's allusions to Borges.

SOME THEORETICAL IMPLICATIONS

Allusion, as I said above, constitutes Borges's most prominent literary device. Borges's use of allusion does not merely reflect his aesthetic inclinations but, rather, is deeply rooted in his metaphysical convictions and in his idea of literature, both of which are tightly interwoven. A study of the theoretical implications of Borges's art of allusion would certainly be rewarding.[7] Unfortunately, such a study is far beyond the scope of the present article, and I shall postpone it for another occasion. I shall undertake here a much more modest task: building upon my analysis of Eco's allusions to Borges, I shall discuss some theoretical aspects of literary allusion in general.

An illuminating study of literary allusion as a peculiar mode of intertextuality has been done by Ziva Ben-Porat, who defines literary allusion as "a device for the simultaneous activation of two texts" (Ben-Porat 1976: 107). According to Ben-Porat, this simultaneous activation is triggered by a special sign within the alluding text, which she calls a "marker" in order to distinguish it from the literary device itself. Furthermore, she claims, the marker points to a larger "referent," which "is always an independent text" (ibid.).

The crucial difference between literary allusion and allusion in general (in the intuitive sense of "indirect reference" or "hint"), in Ben-Porat's theory, lies in their divergent processes of actualization. The actualization of a general allusion is rather straightforward and yields an expected interpretation which remains strictly within the context of the alluding text. Literary allusion, on the contrary, has much more complicated interpretative consequences (minutely described by Ben-Porat), which result in "the formation of intertextual patterns whose nature cannot be predetermined" (ibid.: 108).

Eco's allusion to Borges's work, described above, is certainly a good example of the complex intertextual relations provided by literary allusion, but at the same time it seems to suggest the need for further clarification of the "marker" and the "referent," as described by Ben-Porat. It is clear that Ben-Porat's concept of "marker" is meant to be as comprehensive as possible. However, what is implicit in her formulation is that she has in mind only clearly delimited word combinations: a single word, a phrase, maybe a whole paragraph. *The Name of the Rose* points to Borges's work through an entire system of markers of a more elusive nature.

The question thus becomes: *Which* marker is *the* marker of Eco's allusion to Borges? Chronologically speaking, *the* marker is the introduction to the book. My analysis above shows that a reader acquainted with Borges's works will recognize this marker immediately (I, for one, had this experience when I read the book). However, even if the reader is unfamiliar with Borges's writings, he might still identify the marker provided either by Jorge de Burgos's name or by some of the character's features (e.g., a blind librarian). Moreover, even if all of these markers are not identified, the Borgesian elements comprising the plot (e.g., mirrors, libraries, etc.) might still trigger recognition of the allusion. Finally, it is possible that, none of the above having done the trick, the reader could directly identify the homology between the plots of the novel and of **"Death and the Compass."** Clearly, then, whatever functions as a "marker" here appears to be a reader-dependent property.

As a matter of fact, Ben-Porat's theory contemplates the possibility that the simultaneous activation of two texts will be triggered by "many different elements dispersed throughout" the alluding text (ibid.: 126). That is the case when two texts are initially so closely connected that it becomes possible to interpret the alluding text only inasmuch as all of its literary relations with the text to which it alludes are actualized.[8] Yet the case under consideration here is quite different. For one thing, the interpretive contribution of Borges's work to *The Name of the Rose*, however extensive, is neither exclusive (since the novel is intertextually related to many other works) nor conclusive (since the novel may be interpreted without actualizing this particular intertextual aspect). Secondly, and this is my main point here, the nature of Eco's "markers" and "referent" is essentially different from those contemplated (at least explicitly) by Ben-Porat. Let me consider this point in greater detail.

The four possible markers I mentioned above (and there are perhaps many more) are rather different in nature from one another. The introduction to the novel reminds us of some similar instances occurring throughout Borges's writings. However, we cannot pinpoint any particular word, or combination of words, as the one that triggers recognition of the allusion. Rather, it is the introduction in its entirety that brings to mind similar constructions in Borges. The same may be said of the novel's plot as a marker pointing to Borges's **"Death and the Compass."** We might call these kinds of markers "structural markers," although it must be noted that there are important differences between the two examples. While, in the first case, a section of the alluding text points to similar sections appearing in various works by Borges, in the second case, the general structure of the novel's plot points to the general structure of a specific short story by Borges.

The remaining two kinds of markers certainly consist of specific combinations of words, yet they are worth some attention in their own right. "Jorge de Burgos" is an obviously direct hint to Borges, but the hint could work equally well had the character been differently named. The character and the writer share enough traits to make the identification easy. Again, in such a case, the allusion-triggering would be accomplished by some means other than a delimited, particular wording. Finally, the Borgesian elements dispersed throughout the novel (e.g., mirrors) are diverse enough to render problematic any attempt to pinpoint and explicate all of them.

The device of allusion is activated in Eco's novel, then, through a wide variety of markers which cannot be instantiated by a single word or a particular combination of words. Furthermore, the discussion above has already brought to light some peculiarities of the referent in Eco's allusion. In the novel's allusions to Borges's **"Death and the Compass"** and **"The Library of Babel,"** the referents are "independent texts," as stipulated by Ben-Porat. However, if we consider all the markers mentioned above, we can identify other kinds of referents as well. In the first place, we have the reference to Borges the man. This is, of course, an indirect way of addressing his writings, but it is by no means an "independent text." Clearly, the real referent of Eco's allusion is Borges's corpus as a whole. For specific purposes, individual works from this corpus are activated as interpretive devices, but it is only after we have understood the necessity of taking the real referent—that is, the whole corpus—into account that the full power of the allusion is activated. Ben-Porat's description of the structure and the process of activating literary allusion is essentially valid in the case of *The Name of the Rose,* but the novel clearly shows that the nature of the elements involved in this process is more variable than initially believed.

Finally, I would venture to say that Eco's mode of alluding to Borges's writings overall is a meta-allusion to Borges's own style of allusion. It should be noted that, while many other books and authors are intertextually linked to his novel, Eco takes special pains over actualizing his many relations to Borges exclusively through the Borgesian device of allusion. By considering meta-allusion as a further manifestation of literary allusion, we can extend, in a completely new and unexpected direction, the list of possible markers and referents in literary allusion. Moreover, such a move brings us back, full circle, to where my discussion began: We have returned, as it were, to Eco the theoretician, who becomes involved in a theoretical discussion of literary allusion. By alluding to the peculiar traits of Borgesian allusion, Eco seems to be pointing to hitherto unnoticed aspects of this literary device.

Notes

1. A score of such interpretive articles, which appeared in literary supplements of newspapers throughout the world, were collected (in Italian translations) by Renato Giovanolli (1985). For other collections, see Hans-Jürgen Bachorski (1985) and Theresa Coletti (1988), as well as an issue of *SubStance* (Rubino 1985) which included articles from a colloquium held at the University of Texas at Austin in the fall of 1984 and an issue of *Hebrew University Studies in Literature and the Arts* (17:1 [1989]) which included articles from a symposium held at the Hebrew University in Jerusalem, on April 18, 1988.

In the latter collection, Myrna Solotorevsky (1989) deals with issues closely connected to those that I consider here, and our two articles interestingly complement each other in approach as well as in the details analyzed.

2. Obviously, not only literary considerations, but also to a great extent pure marketing factors account for the book's commercial success. An interesting analysis of this issue has been done by Gerd Kruse (1985).

3. Of the innumerable instances of such a technique in Borges's writings, the best known is perhaps found in Borges (1974b [1940]). For other examples, see Borges (1974d [1942]) and (1974j [1970]). In particular, the introduction to Borges (1974g [1947]) strongly resembles Eco's.

4. This has been shown by Jaime Alazraki (1983: esp. 275–301).

5. A detailed exposition of Peirce's theory of inference and abduction, and of its connection to the Sherlock Holmes stories, can be found in Thomas Sebeok and Jean Umiker-Sebeok (1983).

6. A long, although not exhaustive, list of executioners in Borges's stories who act in a similar way has been compiled by Alicia Jurado (1980: 107–8).

7. As stated in his title, Ronald Christ (1969) does deal with *Borges' Art of Allusion.* However, he only analyzes certain traits of Borges's style and does not address the issue from the wider perspective of literary allusion in general.

8. Ben-Porat analyzes the example of the 1966 poem "Dantès, No" by the Israeli poet Nathan Zach. She shows that the poem can be sensibly interpreted only by fully actualizing its allusion (and its multilayered links) to Alexandre Dumas's *Le Comte de Monte Cristo* (Ben-Porat 1976: 122–26).

Works Cited

Alazraki, Jaime. 1983. *La Prosa Narrative de Jorge Luis Borges* (Madrid: Gredos).

Bachorski, Hans-Jürgen, ed., 1985. *Aufsätze zu Umberto Ecos "Der Name der Rose"* (Göppingen: Kummerle Verlag).

Ben-Porat, Ziva. 1976. "The Poetics of Literary Allusion," *PTL* 1: 105–28.

Borges, Jorge Luis. 1964. *Labyrinths: Selected Stories and Other Writings,* edited and translated by D. A. Yates and James E. Irby (Harmondsworth: Penguin Books).

———. 1974a. *Obras Completas, 1923–1972* (Buenos Aires: Emecé).

———. 1974b [1940]. "Tlön, Uqbar, Orbis Tertius," in Borges 1974a: 431–43.

———. 1974c [1942]. "La Biblioteca de Babel," in Borges 1974a: 465–71.

―――. 1974d [1942]. "El jardín de los senderos que se bifurcan," in Borges 1974a: 472–80.

―――. 1974e [1942]. "La Muerte y la brújula," in Borges 1974a: 499–507.

―――. 1974f [1947]. "La Casa de Asterión," in Borges 1974a: 568–70.

―――. 1974g [1947]. "El inmortal," in Borges 1974a: 533–44.

―――. 1974h [1951]. "Abenjacán el Bojarí, muerto en su laberinto," in Borges 1974a: 600–606.

―――. 1974i [1952]. "Nota sobre (hacia) Bernard Shaw," in Borges 1974a: 747–49.

―――. 1974j [1970]. "El informe de Brodie," in Borges 1974a: 1073–78.

Christ, Ronald. 1969. *The Narrow Act: Borges' Art of Allusion* (New York: New York University Press).

Coletti, Theresa, ed. 1988. *Naming the Rose: Eco, Medieval Signs, and Modern Theory* (Ithaca and London: Cornell University Press).

Eco, Umberto. 1965. *L'Oeuvre ouverte* (Paris: Editions du Seuil).

―――. 1979 *The Role of the Reader* (Bloomington: Indiana University Press).

―――. 1980. *Il Nome della rosa* (Milan: Bompiani).

―――. 1983. "Horns, Hooves, Insteps: Some Hypotheses on Three Types of Abduction," in Eco and Sebeok 1983: 198–220.

―――. 1983 [1980]. *The Name of the Rose*, translated by William Weaver (New York: Harcourt Brace Jovanovich).

―――. 1985. *Reflections on The Name of the Rose*, translated from the Italian by William Weaver (London: Secker and Warburg).

Eco, Umberto, and Thomas Sebeok, eds. 1983. *The Sign of Three: Dupin, Holmes, Peirce* (Bloomington: Indiana University Press).

Giovanolli, Renato. 1985. *Saggi su "Il Nome della Rosa"* (Milan: Bompiani).

Jurado, Alicia. 1980. *Genio y Figura de Jorge Luis Borges* (Buenos Aires: Eudeba).

Kruse, Gerd. 1985. "Der geplante Erfolg eines Überraschungs-Bestsellers," in Bachorski 1985: 272–319.

Peirce, C. S. 1965. *The Collected Papers of Charles Sanders Peirce*. Vol. 5, *Pragmatism and Pragmaticism*, edited by Charles Hartshorne and Paul Weiss (Cambridge, MA: Belknap Press, Harvard University Press).

Rubino, Carl, ed. 1985. "In Search of Eco's Roses." Special issue of *SubStance* (47).

Sebeok, Thomas, and Jean Umiker-Sebeok. 1983. "'You Know My Method': A Juxtaposition of Charles S. Peirce and Sherlock Holmes," in *Eco and Sebeok* 1983: 11–54.

Solotorevsky, Myrna. 1989. "The Borgesian Intertext as an Object of Parody in Eco's *The Name of the Rose*," *Hebrew University Studies in Literature and the Arts* 17(1): 82–97.

Truzzi, Marcello. 1983. "Sherlock Holmes: Applied Social Psychologist," in *Eco and Sebeok* 1983: 55–80.

Theodore G. Ammon (essay date 1993)

SOURCE: "A Note on a Note in 'The Library at Babel,'" in *Romance Notes*, Vol. XXXIII, No. 3, Spring, 1993, pp. 265–69.

[*In the following essay, Ammon interprets Borges's "The Library of Babel" as a commentary on the philosopher Ludwig Wittegenstein's* Tractatus.]

In Borges' story **"The Library of Babel"** there occurs the following curious footnote:

> I repeat: it suffices that a book be possible for it to exist. Only the impossible is excluded. For example: no book can be a ladder, although no doubt there are books which discuss and negate and demonstrate this possibility and others whose structure corresponds to that of a ladder.

> (*Labyrinths* 57)

In recent history the most important book in the West that purports to be a ladder is arguably Wittgenstein's *Tractatus*. In proposition #6.54 Wittgenstein writes:

> My propositions serve as elucidations in the following way: anyone who understands me eventually recognizes them as nonsensical, when he had used them—as steps, to climb up beyond them. (He must, so to speak, throw away the ladder after he has climbed up it.)

> He must transcend these propositions, and then he will see the world aright.

What exactly Wittgenstein means has of course been the subject of scholarly dispute, but I believe that his meaning can be made clear enough to show that Borges must be alluding to the *Tractatus* in his footnote in **"The Library of Babel."** If so, then it is important in understanding **"The Library of Babel"** to understand why Borges would deny the possibility of a ladder-book such as the *Tractatus*.

First, what does Wittgenstein mean that we should use the *Tractatus* as a ladder which can then be dispensed with? And second, how can we come "to see the world aright" by the use of propositions which themselves turn out to be nonsensical? These two questions are really two different ways of asking the same thing, for the answer to one implies an answer to the other.

The short answer to the question of why the *Tractatus* must be used, according to Wittgenstein, as a disposable ladder is found in his conception of philosophy:

> 4.112 Philosophy aims at the clarification of thoughts.
> Philosophy is not a body of doctrine but an activity.
> A Philosophical work consists essentially of elucidations.
> Philosophy does not result in 'philosophical propositions,' but rather in the clarification of propositions.
> Without Philosophy thoughts are, as it were, cloudy and indistinct: its task is to make them clear and to give them sharp boundaries.
> 4.113 Philosophy sets limits to the much disputed sphere of natural science.
> 4.114 It must set limits to what can be thought; and, in doing so, to what cannot be thought.
> It must set limits to what cannot be thought by working outwards through what can be thought.
> 4.115 It will signify what cannot be said, by presenting clearly what can be said.

Wittgenstein distinguishes what can be said from what can be *shown,* but not said. There *are* things that can only be shown, and these things cannot be put into words: they are what is transcendental and therefore mystical:

> 6.522 There are, indeed, things that cannot be put into words. They make themselves manifest. They are what is mystical.

That which is mystical, and hence that which cannot be stated, consists of the existence of the simple objects in the world (why there is something rather than nothing), the sense of the world, ethics, the logical form of representation of propositions. For example, a proposition is a "picture" of a fact, but the proposition cannot picture this logical form; it is rather on the basis of this form that the picturing of facts takes place. Wittgenstein therefore claims that "Logic is transcendental" (6,13). Why exactly the above issues belong to the mystical according to Wittgenstein would require a full explication of the *Tractatus.* Suffice it to say that there are such matters and they are in principle beyond the possibility of language to describe. However, what is mystical nevertheless makes possible what can be said and thought even though the mystical itself cannot be said or thought. What is mystical makes itself manifest in the thinking and saying that philosophy clarifies. The problem with the *Tractatus* is that it goes far beyond merely clarifying the propositions of natural science, the primary enterprise of philosophy according to Wittgenstein. The *Tractatus* is a metaphysical work, and in it Wittgenstein attempts to say what he himself argues cannot be said. And further, the *Tractatus* is a set of philosophical propositions which attempts to say what the limits of thought are. In the penultimate proposition of the work (6.54 quoted above) Wittgenstein tells us that he has violated his own criteria of what philosophy is by the attempt to "speak" of such limitations.

And what sort of perspective on language, thought and reality is one supposed to be able to gain from this nonsensical text?:

> 6.45 To view the world sub specie aeterni is to view it as a whole—a limited whole. Feeling the world as a limited whole—it is this that is mystical.

But how can Wittgenstein "say" that the world is a limited whole? The propositions that he writes seem to require precisely the sort of perspective that he denies we can have. We think from within language, from the inside out, as it were. We cannot get out of language in order to achieve a non-linguistic vantage-point from which we can then consider the limitations imposed by language upon thought. If we could think both sides of the limit, or even know one side of the limit *as a limit,* then the limitation would disappear. Therefore, in trying to give us a perspective on the limitations of language, philosophy and thought, the *Tractatus* fails, it seems Wittgenstein would have us believe, except to the extent that we can use it as a peculiar sort of metaphysical heuristic device. If we climb the *Tractatus* and come closer to feeling the world as a limited whole, then we can kick the *Tractatus* away once we see the world aright.

But, protests Borges, no book can be a ladder. Borges holds Wittgenstein to the terms of the *Tractatus.* If philosophy cannot generate philosophical propositions and if philosophy cannot even sketch the horizon of what must be passed over in silence then the *Tractatus* fails to provide the sort of ladder Wittgenstein suggests it can. And thus we cannot, with the *Tractatus* or any other book, gain a mystical perspective which would allow us to feel the world as a limited whole.

To feel the world as a limited whole is to have some sense, a mystical intuition, of how language determines the limits of cognition. Whatever can be thought can be thought clearly and can be put into words; according to Wittgenstein:

> 5.6 *The limits of my language* mean the limits of my world.
> 5.61 . . . We cannot think what we cannot think; so what we cannot think we cannot *say* either.
> 5.62 . . . The world is *my* world: this is manifest in the fact that the limits of *language* (of that language which alone I understand) mean the limits of *my* world.

That which is beyond language, and hence beyond thought, determines that there is a world, but what can be known about our world is determined by the language we understand. If, according to Borges, there is no special vantage-point on the language from which we could gain an insight or mystical feeling about the limits of language, then, to put it bluntly, we are stuck in language.

"The Library of Babel" is a story about being stuck in language. If the entire universe is a library then there is nothing until there is a text, no reality until a text is selected and read. And our fate is that of being a visitor to the library; all the texts have been written, in spite of our creative pretensions. Writing a new text is analogous to selecting one from the shelf of the universal library. The texts are determined by language; we are merely the occasion of one or more pieces of language being selected. And there is no exploration of reality in **"The Library of Babel"** that yields propositions that are not already on the shelf. We may select this or that book in the Library of Babel but we do not write them. Perhaps we engage in speculation, formulate ideas like that of the "Man of the Book." The Man of the Book is the person who has stumbled across and read the book that is "the formula and perfect compendium of all the rest" (56). Of such a book Borges writes: "It does not seem unlikely to me that there is a total book on some shelf of the universe; I pray to the unknown gods that a man—just one, even though it were thousands of years ago!—may have examined and read it" (56–7). (This last sentence, by the way, is the one to which is attached the note that engendered this note of mine.) The "total book" is possible but not the ladderbook. How do the two differ? The total book is only a compendium and formula for the rest. That is to say, it would provide a synopsis of the contents of all other books and perhaps a formula for the arrangement of the orthographic symbols in them. The conception of such a book does not violate what Borges objects to in the *Tractatus*. The total book as described by Borges is purely descriptive of some of what one could discover on one's own during an eternal perusal of the library. The *Tractatus* in theory allows us to climb out of the library entirely and look back upon it. But there is no more a ladder out of the library than there is an eternal perusal of its holdings. We are of course free to entertain ourselves with both fictions.

Works Cited

Borges, Jorge Luis. *Labyrinths: Selected Stories and Other Writings*. Ed. Donald A. Yates and James E. Irby. New York: New Directions, 1964.

Wittgenstein, Ludwig. *Tractatus Logico-Philosophicus*. Trans. D. F. Pears and B. F. McGuinness. London: Routledge and Kegan Paul, 1971.

John T. Irwin (essay date 1993)

SOURCE: "The False Artaxerxes: Borges and the Dream of Chess," in *New Literary History,* edited by Ralph Cohen, Vol. 24, No. 2, Spring, 1993, pp. 425–45.

[In the following essay, Irwin uses psychoanalytic methodology to postulate the symbolic significance of chess for Borges.]

In Borges's first collection of pure fictions, *The Garden of Forking Paths* (1941), the game of chess is mentioned in four of the volume's eight stories and alluded to in the epigraph to a fifth. Let me recall briefly three of these references. In the volume's final tale (the detective story that gives the collection its title), Stephen Albert, the murder victim, asks the killer Dr. Yu Tsun, "In a guessing game to

which the answer is chess, which word is the only one prohibited?" To which Yu Tsun replies, "The word is *chess*."[1] In the volume's sixth story, **"An Examination of the Work of Herbert Quain,"** the narrator, summarizing Quain's literary career, outlines the plot of his detective novel *The God of the Labyrinth*: "An indecipherable assassination takes place in the initial pages; a leisurely discussion takes place toward the middle; a solution appears in the end. Once the enigma is cleared up, there is a long and retrospective paragraph which contains the following phrase: 'Everyone thought that the encounter of the two chess players was accidental.' This phrase allows one to understand that the solution is erroneous. The unquiet reader rereads the pertinent chapters and discovers *another* solution, the true one. The reader of this book is thus forcibly more discerning than the detective."[2] The third example is from the volume's opening story, **"Tlön, Uqbar, Orbis Tertius."** In the tale Borges recalls a figure from his childhood named Herbert Ashe, an English engineer and friend of his father, who, Borges later realizes, was part of a group involved in the creation of the idealist world of Tlön and in the secret project of insinuating that fictive world into the real one. Borges remembers that when he was a boy the childless widower Ashe and Borges's father "would beat one another at chess, without saying a word," sharing one of those English friendships "which begin by avoiding intimacies and eventually eliminate speech altogether."[3]

One would assume that if an image occurs in half the stories in a collection, it reflects some central concern of the volume as a whole, and part of the rationale for listing these three examples in the reverse order of their appearance in the book is to move backward toward the origin of that concern. In the first instance cited, chess is evoked as the answer to a riddle, the solution to a mystery; in the second, it is linked to the structure of a detective story; and in the third, it is associated with Borges's father and with the invention of a world of "extreme idealism" (**"T"** 24), a world created, as Borges says, by "the discipline of chess players" (**"T"** 34).

Chess has, of course, a long-standing connection with the detective genre. In the first Dupin story, "The Murders in the Rue Morgue" (1841), the narrator cites it as an example, along with draughts and whist, to illustrate the workings of the analytic power; and in the third Dupin story, "The Purloined Letter," Poe presents us with a scenario strongly reminiscent of a chess game—there is a king and queen, and a battle between two knights (Dupin is a Chevalier, and we must assume that his double the Minister D——is at least of equal rank), a battle for possession of a letter that concerns the queen's honor and that in the minister's hands could reduce the queen to being a pawn. Moreover, a chess game is one of the most frequently used images for the battle of wits between detective and criminal in the tradition of the genre, an image of the detective's attempt to double the thought processes of his opponent in order to end up one move ahead of him. This doubling of an opponent's thoughts, in which one plays out possible variations against an antithetical mirror image of one's own mind, is reflected in the physical structure of the game itself, for the opposing chess pieces at the start of the game face each other in a mirror-image relationship. Borges's association of the detective story with chess is, then, fairly easy to explain. But this still leaves the question of the game's link with Borges's father and with idealist philosophy. In making these associations in his first book of pure fictions, Borges seems simply to have transposed into art connections already present in real life. Borges's father was a chess player; he taught his son the game; and, as Borges tells us in "An Autobiographical Essay," he used the chessboard to begin his son's philosophical education: "When I was still quite young, he showed me, with the aid of a chessboard, the paradoxes of Zeno—Achilles and the tortoise, the unmoving flight of the arrow, the impossibility of motion. Later, without mentioning Berkeley's name, he did his best to teach me the rudiments of idealism."[4]

During Borges's visit to Hopkins in 1983, I asked him about the way his father had demonstrated Zeno's paradoxes at the chessboard. He said that he had used the pieces aligned on the first rank, showing him that before he could travel the distance between the king's rook and the queen's rook he had first to go half that distance (that is, from the king's rook to the king), but that before he could go from the king's rook to the king he had first to go half *that* distance (that is, from the king's rook to the king's knight), and so on. To the extent that the paradoxes of Zeno reveal "the impossibility of motion," they are in effect tropes of helplessness, of impotence. Their moral is that nothing can really be accomplished in this world. A person cannot even move from point A to point B, since between the two points yawns an abyss of infinite regression. And if motion is impossible, then our physical world in which motion seems constantly to occur must be an illusion. This world does not have a real, independent (that is, material) existence; its existence is wholly apparential, a function of mental states. From the paradoxes of Zeno, then, it is a short step, as the passage from "An Autobiographical Essay" implies, to the "rudiments of idealism" and the philosophy of George Berkeley. But if the paradoxes of Zeno are, as we have suggested, tropes of impotence, then a father's decision to teach them to his young son might seem at best ill considered and at worst faintly hostile. Indeed, if there is an element of veiled hostility in this act—a sense on the father's part that he has accomplished little of what he set out to do, not because he failed, but because nothing could really be achieved in a world where motion is an illusion; and a warning to the son not to show his father up, not to defeat him, by trying to accomplish something on his own—then certainly the chessboard is the right place for the father to convey that message, since virtually every psychoanalytic reading of the game's structure and symbolism sees it as a ritual sublimation of father murder.

The game's goal is, of course, the checkmate of the opponent's king. One seeks to place the king under a direct at-

tack from which he is powerless to escape, so that on the next move he can be captured and removed from the board. (Indeed, the word *checkmate* derives from the Persian *Shah mat,* "the king is dead.") But this capture and removal (the killing of the king) never actually takes place, for the game always ends one move before this with the king's immobilization in check. Which is simply to say that in the game's sublimation of aggression, the murder of the father even in a symbolic form is repressed. According to the psychoanalyst and chess master Reuben Fine, since "genetically, chess is more often than not taught to the boy by his father, or by a father substitute," it naturally "becomes a means of working out the father-son rivalry."[5] In this ritual mime of the conflicts surrounding the family romance, the mother plays a major role. In his essay on the American chess champion Paul Morphy, Ernest Jones points out that "in attacking the father the most potent assistance is afforded by the mother (Queen)" (23), the strongest piece on the board. As one chess critic has noted, "chess is a matter of both father murder and attempts to prevent it. This mirror function of chess is of extreme importance; obviously the player appears both in a monstrous and a virtuous capacity—planning parricide, at the same time warding it off; recreating Oedipal fantasy, yet trying to disrupt it. Yet the stronger urge is the monstrous one; the player wants to win, to kill the father rather than defend him, although one could clearly speculate on the problems of players who habitually lose at last" (100–101). Fine argues that the king not only represents the father but, as a hand manipulated, carved figure, "stands for the boy's penis in the phallic stage, and hence rearouses the castration anxiety characteristic of that period. . . . It is the father pulled down to the boy's size. Unconsciously it gives the boy a chance to say to the father: 'To the outside world you are big and strong, but when we get right down to it, you're just as weak as I am'" (42).

That Borges understood this Oedipal component of chess is clear from a passage in the last book he published before his death, *Atlas* (1984), a collection of short essays devoted for the most part to geographic locales associated with the psychic terrain of his past. The essay on Athens begins:

> On the first morning, my first day in Athens, I was proffered the following dream. In front of me stood a row of books filling a long shelf. They formed a set of the *Encyclopaedia Britannica,* one of my lost paradises. I took down a volume at random. I looked up Coleridge: the article had an end but no beginning. I looked up Crete: it concluded but did not begin. I looked up the entry on Chess. At that point the dream shifted. On an elevated stage in an amphitheater filled to capacity with an attentive audience, I was playing chess with my father, who was also the False Artaxerxes. (His ears having been cut off, Artaxerxes was found sleeping by one of his many wives; she ran her hand over his skull very gently so as not to awaken him; presently he was killed.) I moved a piece; my antagonist did not move anything but, by an act of magic, he erased one of my pieces. This procedure was repeated various times.

I awoke and told myself: *I am in Greece, where everything began, assuming that things, as opposed to articles in the dream's encyclopedia, have a beginning.*[6]

It seems only fitting that this dream, with its images of castration and father murder, should have been "proferred" to Borges in Athens, the city where the blind parricide Oedipus ultimately sought shelter and where he was welcomed by Theseus, who, according to Plutarch, cannot himself "escape the charge of parricide" because of his "neglect of the command about the sail" that caused his father's death.[7] (Recall that when Theseus left for Crete to slay the Minotaur, his father Aegeus, the ruler of Athens, told him to have his crew hoist a white sail upon returning if Theseus was alive and a black sail if he was dead. Theseus forgot his father's command, and when his ship returned flying a black sail, Aegeus, in despair at his son's supposed death, leapt from a cliff.)

Borges's dream in Athens begins as a search for origins, an attempt to recover or return to a "lost paradise" represented in the dream by a set of the *Encyclopaedia Britannica*. In terms of an individual's biological origin, that lost paradise is the maternal womb, and the fact that Borges's attempt to penetrate the "lost paradise" of the encyclopedia (by delving into one of its volumes) leads almost immediately to an image of conflict with the father and the threat of castration suggests that the *Britannica* functions here as a figure of the mother's body. In the dream Borges takes a volume of the *Britannica* from the shelf (the volume for the womblike letter C, to judge from its entries) and finds that in the first two articles he reads (on Coleridge and Crete) the attempt to return to origin is frustrated: each article has an end "but no beginning." The reference to Crete seems to be a fairly straightforward allusion to the island's legendary labyrinth, that underground enclosure of winding passageways that Freud interprets as an image of the matrix, an enclosure which the hero Theseus enters and from which he is reborn, with the help of the umbilical thread, after having slain the monster, who symbolizes the fear of castration or death that the son must face when he tries to rival the father by entering the mother's body.

In contrast, the dream reference to Coleridge seems less clear at first glance, but a passage from Borges's essay on nightmares in the 1980 volume *Seven Nights* gives us a clue. According to Borges, Coleridge maintains that

> it doesn't matter what we dream, that the dream searches for explanations. He gives an example: a lion suddenly appears in this room and we are all afraid; the fear has been caused by the image of the lion. But in dreams the reverse can occur. We feel oppressed, and then search for an explanation. I, absurdly but vividly, dream that a sphinx has lain down next to me. The sphinx is not the cause of my fear, it is an explanation of my feeling of oppression. Coleridge adds that people who have been frightened by imaginary ghosts have gone mad. On the other hand, a person who dreams a ghost can wake up and, within a few seconds, regain his composure.

I have had—and I still have—many nightmares. The most terrible, the one that struck me as the most terrible, I used in a sonnet. It went like this: I was in my room; it was dawn (possibly that was the time of the dream). At the foot of my bed was a king, a very ancient king, and I knew in the dream that he was the King of the North, of Norway. He did not look at me; his blind stare was fixed on the ceiling. I felt the terror of his presence. I saw the king, I saw his sword, I saw his dog. Then I woke. But I continued to see the king for a while, because he had made such a strong impression on me. Retold, my dream is nothing; dreamt, it was terrible.[8]

The progression of images in this passage forms an instructive gloss on the associative logic of Borges's dream at Athens. Starting with the name of Coleridge and the dictum that "the dream searches for explanations" by creating images which correspond with, and thus account for, emotions we feel, the passage introduces the example of a lion as a symbolic expression of fear; to which Borges adds the example of his own dream that a sphinx has lain down beside him, the image of the sphinx serving as "an explanation of my feeling of oppression." The associative link between the images of lion and sphinx seems plain: the multiform sphinx is traditionally depicted with a lion's body. But the sphinx is, of course, the monster associated with Oedipus. She threatens the hero with death if he doesn't solve her riddle; her name (*strangler*, from the Greek *sphingein*, origin of the English *sphincter*) evokes the dangerous, constricting passageway out of and into the mother's womb; and her form, with one shape issuing from another, suggests the child's body emerging from the mother's at birth, according to Otto Rank.

The passage's imagery now shifts from the figure of a sphinx to that of a ghost, with the dictum that people frightened by an imaginary ghost in waking life have gone mad but that those who dream a ghost can wake up and regain their composure. The connection between sphinx and ghost is unclear at first, until we recall that in Borges's third detective story, **"Ibn Hakkan al-Bokhari, Dead in His Labyrinth,"** the three faceless corpses found in the labyrinth are those of a king, a slave, and a lion and that the explanation for the crime contrived by the killer is that the three have been murdered by the ghost of the king's vizier. The murderer is in fact this same king's vizier Zaid, who, along with his black slave and lion, had come to the small Cornish village of Pentreath masquerading as the king Ibn Hakkan, built the labyrinth, lured the real king into it, killed him and then obliterated his face (along with that of the slave and lion) to cover the previous imposture and effect his escape. Given the associative link between sphinx and lion in Borges's discussion of nightmares and that between king, ghost, and lion in **"Ibn Hakkan al-Bokhari,"** the progression of images in the nightmare passage becomes easier to follow: The image of the lion (the king of the beasts) serves as a middle term connecting the image of the sphinx (with its lion's body) to that of the king. But this linking of sphinx and king also implicitly connects the images of sphinx and ghost, for the king in

Borges's nightmare is clearly coded as a spectral apparition. Thus the associative chain underlying the passage from the nightmare essay runs: lion (king of the beasts) / sphinx (creature with a lion's body who tests King Oedipus) / king / ghost (of a king). But in the passage Borges reverses the order of the last two links in the chain by moving directly from the dream image of the sphinx to a discussion of ghosts in waking life versus ghosts in dreams, and only then going on to describe his "most terrible" nightmare about "a very ancient king." Since it is dawn and the king is at the foot of Borges's bed, one assumes that in the dreamed scene Borges is just awakening from a night's sleep and that the uncertainty as to whether he is, within the dream, awake or dreaming, whether the figure of the king is an imaginary ghost or a ghost in a dream, forms part of the dream image's terror, a frightening sense of ambiguity that is confirmed when Borges actually awakens and yet continues "to see the king for a while" because the image has "made such a strong impression."

That the figure of the "ancient king" is coded as a ghost seems obvious from the way in which the account of Borges's nightmare grows out of his comment about the difference between thinking we see and dreaming we see a ghost. Moreover, I would suggest that this "King of the North" is a very specific ghost indeed. Borges identifies him as the king of Norway, but that is undoubtedly a displacement within the dream. He is the king of Denmark, the ghost of Hamlet's father returned to confront his son with the Oedipal task of avenging the father's murder and with the epistemological dilemma of whether this demanding appearance is a real ghost, a dream, or a hallucination. (Recall that at the start of Shakespeare's play we are told that Hamlet had killed Fortinbras, the King of Norway, in combat, thus causing young Fortinbras to seek revenge for his father's death.) In the dream the king's "blind stare" is "fixed on the ceiling," at once a reminder of the punishment which Oedipus inflicted on himself for incest and parricide, for usurping the true king's place, and an evocation of Borges's own father who went blind from a hereditary eye ailment, an ailment which he in turn passed onto *his* son who also went blind.

Indeed, the imagery of the dream suggests the extent to which Borges may have experienced his blindness on some unconscious level as an Oedipal transmission. In the dream, Borges sees the king, his sword, and his dog. The sword would seem to be both a phallic symbol of the father's authority and a metonym for the punishment (castration) meted out to those who would usurp that authority; while the king's dog probably bears something of the same relationship to the dreamer that the Sphinx does to Oedipus and the Minotaur does to Theseus—a symbol of the animal (that is, sexual) realm, who confronts the aspirant (son) with a life-threatening test by which the real king (or his lawful successor) is distinguished from usurpers or impostors. At the end of **"Ibn Hakkan al-Bokhari,"** one of the characters describes the cowardly murderer of the king as "a good-for-nothing who, before becoming a

nobody in death, wanted one day to look back on having been a king or having been taken for a king."[9] The message seems plain enough: though the usurper might be able to murder a king, he could not take the king's place; not every son who can kill his father can become a father.

Now if we are correct in thinking that the image of the encyclopedia entry on Coleridge in Borges's dream at Athens represents the dreamwork's condensation of the chain of associations grouped around Coleridge's name in the essay on nightmares, then it seems clear that the progression of images in the Athens dream is essentially the same as that in the nightmare essay, with two revealing substitutions in the signifying chain. Starting with the name of Coleridge, the passage in the essay from *Seven Nights* moves first to the image of a lion, and then to that of a sphinx, a lion-bodied animal whose name evokes the figure of Oedipus. From the sphinx, the passage shifts to the image of ghosts (either hallucinated or dreamed) and then ends with the nightmare figure of an ancient, blind king holding a sword, the reference to ghosts serving to associate the dream's image of the king of Norway (that is, Denmark) with the opening of *Hamlet* and thus code the blind king as the ghost of a murdered father appearing to his son. In a similar manner the chain of associations in Borges's dream at Athens begins by invoking the name of Coleridge but then instead of moving on to the image of the sphinx (that is, to a direct allusion to Oedipus), the dream obliquely calls up a screen-figure of Oedipus (Theseus) through the reference to the encyclopedia entry on Crete (that is, the Cretan labyrinth, the Minotaur, and the Minotaur's slayer). In place of Oedipus, who kills his father and marries his mother, stands Theseus, the man who penetrates the symbolic womb of the labyrinth and accidentally causes the death of his father through an act of forgetfulness. From the reference to Crete, the dream then shifts to the encyclopedia entry on Chess, the veiled allusion to the womblike, Cretan labyrinth giving way to the image of the labyrinthine network of a chessboard on which one symbolically kills the father. And this image in turn suddenly shifts to that of a real chess game and brings us to the second major substitution in the signifying chain. For instead of culminating, as the passage from Borges's essay on nightmares did, with the terrifying image of a blind king holding a sword, the Athens dream ends with an image of Borges's own father (who went blind) as a false king mutilated by a sword. And with this final figuration the reason for the substitutions in the associative chain becomes obvious.

In the passage from the essay on nightmares, Borges can directly allude to Oedipus through the mention of the sphinx precisely because the blind king is *not* explicitly identified as Borges's father. But in the Athens dream the figure whom Borges confronts in a chess game (a ritual sublimation of father murder) *is* so identified; and consequently, the direct Oedipal allusion which followed the mention of Coleridge's name in the nightmare essay is repressed by Borges in favor of a veiled reference to the Oedipal screen-figure Theseus, the man who welcomed the aged, blind Oedipus to Athens (remember that the aged, blind Borges is dreaming this dream in Athens) and who became Oedipus's spiritual son.

Perhaps the most striking detail in the Athens dream is the description of Borges's father as "the False Artaxerxes," whose ears had been cropped. It seems only fitting that since the dream begins with the image of the *Encyclopaedia Britannica,* we should turn to that work for an explanation of this figure. The eleventh edition of the *Britannica* identifies the false Artaxerxes as one "Bessus, satrap of Bactria and Sogdiana under Darius III": "When Alexander pursued the Persian king [Darius III] on his flight to the East (summer 330), Bessus with some of the other conspirators deposed Darius and shortly after killed him. He then tried to organize a national resistance against the Macedonian conqueror in the eastern provinces, proclaimed himself king and adopted the name Artaxerxes." Taken prisoner by treachery, Bessus was sent by Alexander to Ecbatana where he was condemned to death: "Before his execution his nose and ears were cut off, according to the Persian custom; we learn from the Behistun inscription that Darius I punished the usurpers in the same way."[10] Bessus, the false Artaxerxes, was then a usurper, someone able to kill a king but unable to take the king's place, an impostor like Zaid, the murderer in **"Ibn Hakkan."** In Borges's dream the cutting off of the usurper's ears is an obvious image of castration, reminiscent of the destruction of Oedipus's eyeballs with the pin of Jocasta's brooch; and the suggestion of maternal complicity in the attack on the father is present as well: "His ears having been cut off, Artaxerxes was found sleeping by one of his many wives; she ran her hand over his skull very gently so as not to awaken him; presently he was killed."

While the image of paternal mutilation and death in Borges's dream would seem to be simply an expression of the son's desire to inflict on the father the same violence with which he feels threatened, the nature of the paternal threat to the son's power, as figured in the moves of the chess game, is more complex than that reading suggests. For the image of the father in Borges's dream is not that of a true king, an absolute ruler with complete power to inflict whatever injury he chooses on the son, but that of a false king, a usurper, who is castrated and put to death. Which is to say that the father in Borges's dream threatens the son's potency by presenting himself as a castrated son trapped within a generational line and doomed to death, threatens him by showing that the father is not an absolute source but merely the son's immediate predecessor who has been rendered helpless, made unoriginal, by his own predecessor. Describing the moves of the chess game, Borges says, "I moved a piece; my antagonist did not move anything but, by an act of magic, he erased one of my pieces. This procedure was repeated various times." One cannot help but recall that Borges's father had used the chessboard not only to teach his son the game but to acquaint him with the paradoxes of Zeno, tropes of impotence figuring, as Borges says, "the impossibility of motion." The logic of the scene is plain: To play a game of chess, one must move pieces from one square to another until finally one places the king in a check from which he cannot escape. But if checkmating the king is a symbolic murder of the father, then the father who teaches this game to his son might well try to protect himself from the Oedipal combat for paternal power by convincing his son that no such power exists for them to fight over. Thus in the dreamed chess game, Borges moves a piece, but his father does not move anything (motion is impossible). Instead, "by an act of magic" (the paradoxes of Zeno which reveal the magical, that is, illusory, nature of action), he erases one of his son's pieces; he makes it vanish like the dream it is. In erasing his son's chess piece with these magical paradoxes, the father castrates him not physically by exercising superior strength, but psychologically by showing him that in this illusory world nothing can be done, that everyone is helpless, father and son alike. (Recall in this regard that Borges's poem "Chess" [1960] concludes by questioning the traditional scholastic explanation of the origin of motion which traces movement, through a series of intermediate causes, back to an unmoved first mover, the All-Father: "God moves the player, he, in turn, the piece. / But what god beyond God begins the round / of dust and time and dream and agonies?"[11]) No wonder, then, that when Borges awakens from this dream in Athens of unreachable origins and illusory grounds, this dream in which he discovers, during the course of a chess game, the person who conceived him depicted as a sleeping king (that is, when Borges discovers himself [the dreamer of the Athens dream] as a figure in the dream of the Other), no wonder that the force of the dream persists into waking consciousness as a doubt about whether origins and original power exist in real life, a persistence of the dream state that seems to blur the distinction between reality and illusion (as when Borges awakened from his nightmare of the blind King of the North yet "continued to see the king for a while"): "I awoke and told myself: *I am in Greece, where everything began, assuming that things, as opposed to articles in the dream's encyclopedia, have a beginning.*"

When one sees the psychological point of Borges's association of his father with the game of chess, then "the encounter of the two chess players" (the elder Borges and Herbert Ashe) in the story **"Tlön, Uqbar, Orbis Tertius"** seems far from "accidental" indeed, to use Herbert Quain's words from his detective novel *The God of the Labyrinth.* And the encounter takes on still greater significance when we consider that "the faded English engineer Herbert Ashe" is, according to Borges's friend José Bianco, simply "a portrait" of Borges's father.[12] That Borges should imagine a chess game in which his father competes against "a portrait" of himself is not surprising, given his use of the game's mirror-image structure to evoke the mental duel between antithetical doubles in the detective story. But this encrypted image of a specular chess game played by the father against himself becomes even more interesting when we recall that, at the beginning of **"Tlön, Uqbar, Orbis Tertius,"** fatherhood and mirroring are invoked as analogous forms of duplicating human beings. Borges says that he owed the discovery of the idealist worlds of the story's title to "the conjunction of a mirror and an encyclopedia." He and his friend Bioy Casares had dined one evening and talked late into the night. During their conversation, Borges noticed that "from the far end of the corridor, the mirror was watching us; and we discovered, with the inevitability of discoveries made late at night, that mirrors have something grotesque about them. Then Bioy Casares recalled that one of the heresiarchs of Uqbar had stated that mirrors and copulation are abominable, since they both multiply the numbers of man" ("**T**" 17). Asking for the source of this "memorable sentence," Borges is told that it comes from the article on Uqbar in the *Anglo-American Cyclopaedia*. As it happens, the villa where they are staying has a copy of the reference work, but try as they might, they cannot find the article on Uqbar. The next day Bioy telephones to say that he has found in another copy of the work the article in question and that the passage he had paraphrased the night before reads: "For one of those gnostics, the visible universe was an illusion or, more precisely, a sophism. Mirrors and fatherhood are abominable because they multiply it and extend it" ("**T**" 18). Borges and Bioy compare the two versions of the encyclopedia and find that the sole difference between them is the additional four pages of the article on Uqbar, a discovery that ultimately reveals the existence of a secret project pursued by a band of intellectuals over the years to introduce the idealist world of Tlön into this world and thereby alter the shape of reality.

The opening image of "**Tlön, Uqbar, Orbis Tertius**" ("the conjunction of a mirror and an encyclopedia") is almost certainly an allusion to the fact that in the Middle Ages a work of encyclopedic knowledge was commonly referred to in Latin as a *speculum,* a mirror (for example, the thirteenth-century *Speculum majus* of Vincent of Beauvais), a name that figures the encyclopedia as a written mirror of the universe. Given the sexual overtones of "conjunction," the opening image also sets the stage for the subsequent association of a mirror, first with copulation, and then with fatherhood. And if, in this conjunction of a mirror and an encyclopedia, the mirror is equated with the male principle, then the encyclopedia would obviously be equated with the female (the matrix)—the same association found in Borges's dream at Athens where the *Encyclopaedia Britannica* is described as a "lost paradise" and then immediately linked to the image of the womb-like labyrinth through the reference to Crete. (Significantly enough, the *Anglo-American Cyclopaedia* in "**Tlön, Uqbar, Orbis Tertius**" is "a literal if inadequate reprint of the 1902 *Encyclopaedia Britannica*" ["**T**" 17].)

If for Borges mirror and encyclopedia are gender coded as male and female respectively, then the description Borges gives in *Seven Nights* of two of his recurring nightmares, two dreams that frequently blend into one, seems like a gloss on that conjunction of a mirror and an encyclopedia that begins "**Tlön, Uqbar, Orbis Tertius**":

> I have two nightmares which often become confused with one another. I have the nightmare of the labyrinth, which comes, in part, from a steel engraving I saw in a French book when I was a child. In this engraving were the Seven Wonders of the World, among them the labyrinth of Crete. The labyrinth was a great amphitheater, a very high amphitheater. . . . In this closed structure—ominously closed—there were cracks. I believed when I was a child (or I now believe I believed) that if one had a magnifying glass powerful enough, one could look through the cracks and see the Minotaur in the terrible center of the labyrinth.
>
> My other nightmare is that of the mirror. The two are not distinct, as it only takes two facing mirrors to construct a labyrinth. . . .
>
> I always dream of labyrinths or of mirrors. In the dream of the mirror another vision appears, another terror of my nights, and that is the idea of the mask. Masks have always scared me. No doubt I felt in my childhood that someone who was wearing a mask was hiding something horrible. These are my most terrible nightmares: I see myself reflected in a mirror, but the reflection is wearing a mask. I am afraid to pull the mask off, afraid to see my real face, which I imagine to be hideous. There may be leprosy or evil or something more terrible than anything I am capable of imagining.
>
> (SN 32–33)

As the dream at Athens begins with the image of a book (the *Britannica*) and immediately moves (via the reference to Crete) to the image of the labyrinth, so this passage from the nightmare essay begins with the image of the labyrinth and moves immediately to the image of a book—a French book in which Borges saw a steel engraving of the labyrinth when he was a child. Though Borges does not say what kind of book it was, the mention of a "steel engraving" recalls a remark from his "Autobiographical Essay" about the books he enjoyed most as a child in his father's library: "I have forgotten most of the faces of that time . . . and yet I vividly remember so many of the steel engravings in *Chambers's Encyclopaedia* and in the *Britannica*" (A 209).

In the engraving in the French book the labyrinth is shown as "a closed structure," a "very high amphitheater," a description that gives added meaning to the setting for the chess game in the Athens dream: "On an elevated stage in an amphitheater filled to capacity with an attentive audience, I was playing chess with my father, who was also the False Artaxerxes." That Borges imagines the labyrinth as an enclosed amphitheater suggests yet again that the amphitheater which serves as the site of the chess game with his father, a game of kings and queens played out on a labyrinthine network of squares, represents the maternal space of origin for whose possession they are competing. And the fact that the labyrinth as symbol of the matrix, as the scene of the contest with the father, is closely associated in these passages with another womb symbol (the image of a book as a "lost paradise") suggests that the real-life arena into which the Oedipal struggle between Borges and his father had been displaced was not the game of chess but the realm of literature in which the virgin space of the page, inseminated by ink from the phallic pen, can produce an offspring longer-lived than any child, an off-spring almost immortal if the author only be original enough. Borges's father in addition to being a lawyer had, of course, been a minor poet and fiction writer before he went blind, and, as Borges recalls in his "Autobiographical Essay," "From the time I was a boy, when blindness came to him, it was tacitly understood that I had to fulfill the literary destiny that circumstances had denied my father. . . . I was expected to be a writer" (*A* 211). An oddly contradictory legacy: that the son fulfill the literary destiny denied to the father by becoming the successful writer his parent had never been, in effect surpassing, defeating, the father in an implicit literary competition.

If the images that dominate Borges's two recurring nightmares (the mirror and the labyrinth) are associated respectively with fatherhood and motherhood, then Borges's assertion that "the two are not distinct" suggests a union of male and female principles reminiscent of "the conjunction of a mirror and an encyclopedia" at the beginning of **"Tlön, Uqbar, Orbis Tertius."** This blending of mirror and labyrinth in Borges's dreams, like the conjunction of mirror and encyclopedia in the tale, seems to be the symbolic figuration of a primal scene, an evocation of the dreamer's parents in the act of engendering the dreamer. And to judge from the imagery that follows from this blending of mirror and labyrinth in Borges's account, the product of that union is experienced as something monstrous—a masked figure whose mask conceals "something more terrible than anything" the dreamer is "capable of imagining."

According to the associative logic of the passage, two of Borges's nightmare images, in becoming "confused with one another," are in effect equated with one another—the labyrinth and the mirror. As the labyrinth contains a monstrous figure (the Minotaur with a man's body and a bull's head), so the mirror contains an equally monstrous figure (a masked man with a human body and a concealed face). In one case the bull's head, in the other the masked face, makes the figure terrifying. But what is that frightening content at once concealed and evoked by the masked face and animal head? Recall that in his entry on the Minotaur in *The Book of Imaginary Beings* (1967), Borges says that the Cretan labyrinth was built "to confine and keep hidden" Queen Pasiphae's "monstrous son,"[13] the product of an unnatural union of animal and human. And if the bull's head is the visible trace of a monstrous copulation, then are we to assume, given the equation of the bull-headed monster of the labyrinth and the masked figure in the mirror, that the masked face also evokes the image of a monstrous copulation, or more precisely, evokes the image of copulation as something monstrous? Noting the "revulsion for the act of fatherhood . . . or copulation" found in **"Tlön, Uqbar, Orbis Tertius,"** Borges's biographer Rodriguez Monegal wonders how much this feeling "has to do with the discovery of the primal scene through the complicity of a mirror" when Borges was a child. He points out as evidence for this possibility a passage from Borges's poem "The Mirror":

Infinite I see them, elementary
executors of an old pact,
to multiply the world as the generative
act, sleepless and fatal.

(*JLB* 33)

Monegal notes that in the tale **"The Sect of the Phoenix"** (1952) Borges imagines a pagan cult bound together by a shared secret that assures its members immortality, a secret hinted at in the tale but never named—the act of copulation. In the story Borges says that though the secret "is transmitted from generation to generation . . . usage does not favor mothers teaching it to their sons." He continues, "Initiation into the mystery is the task of individuals of the lowest order. . . . The Secret is sacred, but it is also somewhat ridiculous. The practice of the mystery is furtive and even clandestine and its adepts do not speak about it. There are no respectable words to describe it, but it is understood that all words refer to it, or better, that they inevitably allude to it. . . . A kind of sacred horror prevents some of the faithful from practicing the extremely simple ritual; the others despise them for it, but they despise themselves even more." To many members of the sect, the secret seemed "paltry, distressing, vulgar and (what is even stranger) incredible. They could not reconcile themselves to the fact that their ancestors had lowered themselves to such conduct."[14] When asked by the critic Ronald Christ about the secret shared by the sect of the Phoenix, Borges replied, "The act is what Whitman says 'the divine husband knows, from the work of fatherhood.'—When I first heard about this act, when I was a boy, I was shocked, shocked to think that my mother, my father had performed it. It is an amazing discovery, no? But then too it is an act of immortality, a rite of immortality, isn't it?"[15]

If, as we have suggested, the masked figure in the mirror evokes for Borges the bull-headed monster of the labyrinth ("it only takes two facing mirrors to construct a labyrinth"), that is, evokes the monstrous offspring of an unnatural copulation, and if that bull-headed figure symbolically represents in turn the act of copulation as something monstrous, as the assault of a male animal on the mother (Freud notes that in the fantasy of the primal scene the child frequently misinterprets parental intercourse as an act of sadomasochistic violence by the father against the mother), then the terror that Borges feels at the nightmare image of seeing his masked reflection, a terror both of the mask and of pulling off the mask to see the real face beneath, seems to be compounded of two related emotions. First, there is probably, in Monegal's words, a "revulsion for the act of fatherhood . . . or copulation" (*JLB* 33), a sense (left over from childhood or adolescence) of the reproductive act as terrifying or humiliating, as an act unworthy of those godlike beings one's parents, and as an origin unworthy of oneself, unworthy of that spiritual entity which finds itself imprisoned in the earthy cave of the body (with its physical constraints and sexual drives) as surely as the Minotaur (a symbol of the sun during its daily descent into the underworld) is imprisoned in the subterranean labyrinth. And what is particularly terrifying in this regard about the dream image is that while the mirror, a traditional figure of reflective self-consciousness, appears to contain, to restrain within its verge, the frightening visage that evokes the animal body, we know that the reflective self which the mirror symbolizes is equally contained within, and subject to the instinctual imperatives of, that body.

The second emotion the dream image seems to express is the son's feeling of helplessness, his feeling of being trapped in the cycle of generation, doomed to repeat and transmit this cycle by doing the thing his father did. Indeed, for Borges, part of the peculiar terror of the masked figure in the mirror seems to be that it not only evokes the primal scene as the bestial copulation of a male animal with the mother, it also suggests that the face hidden beneath the mask worn by the son's mirror-image is not his own but his father's, suggests that, in this reversal of the master/slave relationship between self and mirror-image, the son is simply a reflection of the father helplessly repeating his physical gestures, trapped within a corporeal body and a material world only because he has been physically engendered.

All of which brings us back to the image of Borges's father teaching him the paradoxes of Zeno and idealist philosophy at the chessboard and to the question of what it was that Borges learned from that teaching. For to judge from the number of stories in which the theme recurs, the lesson would seem to be that the most powerful defense the self can muster against external threats to its own integrity, against sexual conflict and the threat of checkmate, is a massive reinterpretation of the surrounding world that substitutes mind for body, the intellectual for the sexual—a substitution whose autobiographical dimension is almost always present in the Borgesian text. In **"Tlön, Uqbar, Orbis Tertius,"** for example, this sublimation of the bodily is carried to an extreme in the image of a world (Tlön) where mental states are the only reality: "The men of that planet conceive of the universe as a series of mental processes, whose unfolding is to be understood only as a time sequence" (**"T"** 24). Since "the nations of that planet are congenitally idealist" (**"T"** 23), there is "only one discipline, that of psychology" (**"T"** 24). Consequently, "among the doctrines of Tlön, none has occasioned greater scandal than the doctrine of materialism. . . . To clarify the general understanding of this unlikely thesis, one eleventh century heresiarch offered the parable of nine copper coins, which enjoyed in Tlön the same noisy reputation as did the Eleatic paradoxes of Zeno in their day" (**"T"** 26).

The irony, of course, is that in an idealist world like Tlön a parable of materialism seems as paradoxical as the anti-materialist parables of Zeno seem in ours. But this mention of the paradoxes of Zeno also suggests the autobiographical link between the imaginary world of Tlön and the detail of Herbert Ashe's chess games with Borges's father. For if the fictive chess games between the elder Borges and Ashe (a veiled portrait of Borges's father) are based on those real games during which the elder Borges

taught his son the paradoxes of Zeno, and if, as Borges suggests in "An Autobiographical Essay," it was a natural transition from these paradoxes to his father's instructing him in "the rudiments of idealism" without ever "mentioning Berkeley's name" (**"T"** 207), then that trajectory in Borges's personal life—from paradoxes at the chessboard demonstrating "the impossibility of motion" to a philosophical system that treats the material world as an illusion—is evoked in the story by having the same person who plays chess with Borges's father be one of the secret inventors of an imaginary idealist world, a world created through the writing of its fictive encyclopedia, through fiction writing.

In effect, Tlön is a world of perfect sublimation, and its significance for Borges is a function of the way in which his knowledge of Berkeley's idealism originated from a scene of sublimated conflict with his father at the chessboard, a scene which suggested idealist philosophy as an effective means of extending to life as a whole chess's sublimation of (sexual) violence, its transformation of physical conflict into a mental duel where opponents match wits but remain ultimately untouchable because physical motion is an impossibility. No wonder, then, that the world of Tlön is described as exhibiting "the discipline of chess players" (**"T"** 34) or that one of the members of that "benevolent secret society" which "came together" in the seventeenth century "to invent a country" (the society which counted Herbert Ashe among its latterday members) was "George Berkeley" (**"T"** 31).

The imaginary world of Tlön represents for Borges, then, the substitution of a mental life for a physical one, of inventing stories for living them. Recalling his boyhood in "An Autobiographical Essay," Borges says, "I was always very nearsighted and wore glasses, and I was rather frail. As most of my people had been soldiers . . . and I knew I would never be, I felt ashamed, quite early, to be a bookish kind of person and not a man of action" (A 208). In one of the essays in *Other Inquisitions,* Borges speaks of his as "a lifetime dedicated less to living than to reading," and he recalls that "Plotinus was said to be ashamed to dwell in a body"[16] so devoted was he to the life of the mind, a remark that Borges applied to himself and to his own lifetime devotion to the imagination in a conversation we had during his visit to Hopkins in 1983.

Given that Borges's predilection for idealist philosophy is to some degree a function of this philosophy's valorization of mind at the expense of body (a valorization that precisely suited the temperament of a bookish child who knew that he was not destined to be a man of action), and given further that Borges's acquaintance with the principles of idealist philosophy began as a child within the context of a combative game that favored mental acuity rather than physical strength, a game of sublimated father-murder taught him by his own father, it is certainly not surprising that in those stories of Borges's concerned with idealist philosophy there is usually present some form of veiled father/son competition, a competition in which the son not infrequently tries to effect a wholly mental procreation, tries to occupy the place of the father by imagining or dreaming into existence a son of his own. Thus in **"The Circular Ruins"** the magician sets out "to dream a man" into existence, "to dream him in minute entirety and impose him on reality."[17] But the relationship of dreamer and dreamed soon becomes in the story that of father and son: "When he closed his eyes, he thought: *Now I will be with my son.* Or, more rarely: *The son I have engendered is waiting for me and will not exist if I do not go to him*" (61). In order to keep his son from ever knowing that he is merely a mental apparition, the magician wipes out "all memory of his years of apprenticeship":

> Of all the creatures that people the earth, Fire was the only one who knew his son to be a phantom. This memory, which at first calmed him, ended by tormenting him. He feared lest his son should meditate on this abnormal privilege and by some means find out he was a mere simulacrum. Not to be a man, to be a projection of another man's dreams—what an incomparable humiliation, what madness! Any father is interested in the sons he has procreated (or permitted) out of the mere confusion of happiness; it was natural that the wizard should fear for the future of that son whom he had thought out entrail by entrail, feature by feature, in a thousand and one secret nights.
>
> (62)

But what the magician finally discovers is that father and son share the same substance, that he (the magician) can dream a phantom man into existence only because he is himself a phantom dreamed by another—a realization that comes to the magician when the ruined temple in which he dwells is engulfed by a forest fire, a fire that, as its flames caress him "without heat or combustion," claims him as its own.

As I said at the start, the game of chess is mentioned in four out of the eight stories in *The Garden of Forking Paths* and alluded to in the epigraph to a fifth. That fifth is **"The Circular Ruins,"** and its epigraph, taken from chapter four of Lewis Carroll's *Through the Looking Glass*, runs "And if he left off dreaming about you. . . ." The line occurs in the scene where Alice, in the company of the mirror-image twins Tweedledum and Tweedledee, comes upon the sleeping Red King. As you recall, at the start of the book Alice falls asleep in the drawing room and dreams that she climbs through the mirror above the mantelpiece into the drawing room of Looking-glass House. When she steps outside the house, Alice finds that the garden is laid out like a chessboard, and her subsequent movements become part of a bizarre chess game. Gazing at the sleeping Red King, Tweedledee asks Alice what she thinks he's dreaming about. When she says that nobody can guess that, Tweedledee replies,

> "Why, about *you*! . . . And if he left off dreaming about you, where do you suppose you'd be?"
>
> "Where I am now, of course," said Alice.
>
> "Not you!" Tweedledee retorted contemptuously. "You'd be nowhere. Why, you're only a sort of thing in his dream!"

> "If that there King was to wake," added Tweedledum, "you'd go out—bang!—just like a candle!"[18]

In the kind of Aleph-like oscillation of container and contained that obsessed Borges, Alice dreams the Red King, who dreams Alice, who dreams the Red King, and so on in an endless progression/regression. And just as Alice's mental existence as "a sort of thing" in the Red King's dream is evoked in an image of fire (if he awakens, she will go out like the flame of a candle—the traditional figuration of mind as light), so in **"The Circular Ruins"** fire is also invoked as a figure of a purely mental existence ("Of all the creatures that people the earth, Fire was the only one who knew his son to be a phantom").

What the epigraph to **"The Circular Ruins"** does in effect is to assimilate the relationship between the magician and his son, each of whom is an image in the dream of another, to that between Alice and the Red King, who dream one another, thus associating the context of the latter scene (a chess game) with the phantasmatic father-son relationship of the former. (Recall that when Alice comes upon the Red King, she is playing the role of a white pawn in the chess game, so that there is a mutually threatening quality to their encounter: if the King awakens, Alice goes out of existence, say the mirror-image twins; but on the other hand, when Alice, as a white pawn, finally reaches the eight rank and is promoted to a queen, she checkmates the Red King, which is to say that at the end of the game it is she who awakens from her dream and the Red King who goes out of existence.) **"The Circular Ruins"** and its epigraph bring together, then, in one spot those themes of fatherhood, mirroring, chess, dreams, and idealist philosophy that haunt Borges's work, images whose conjunction was established for Borges in a childhood scene of instruction in which a father faced, across the mirror-image alignment of pieces on a chessboard, his son (a diminutive image of himself) and, in demonstrating the paradoxes of Zeno and Berkeleyan idealism, showed him the dreamlike status of reality. In thinking back on that scene, perhaps Borges was reminded of Alice's words near the end of *Through the Looking Glass*: "So I wasn't dreaming, after all . . . unless—unless we're all part of the same dream. Only I do hope it's *my* dream, and not the Red King's! I don't like belonging to another person's dream" (293).

Notes

1. Jorge Luis Borges, "The Garden of Forking Paths," in his *Ficciones,* ed. Anthony Kerrigan (New York, 1962), p. 99.

2. Jorge Luis Borges, "An Examination of the Work of Herbert Quain," in *Ficciones,* p. 74.

3. Jorge Luis Borges, "Tlön, Uqbar, Orbis Tertius," in *Ficciones,* p. 20; hereafter cited in text as "T."

4. Jorge Luis Borges, "An Autobiographical Essay," in his *The Aleph and Other Stories 1933–1969* (New York, 1978), p. 207; hereafter cited in text as Λ.

5. Reuben Fine, quoted in Alexander Cockburn, *Idle Passion: Chess and the Dance of Death* (New York, 1974), p. 42; hereafter cited in text.

6. Jorge Luis Borges, *Atlas,* tr. Anthony Kerrigan (New York, 1985), p. 37.

7. Plutarch, "Theseus and Romulus," *Lives,* tr. Bernadotte Perrin (Cambridge, Mass., 1914), I, 197.

8. Jorge Luis Borges, *Seven Nights* (New York, 1984), p. 36; hereafter cited in text as *SN.*

9. Jorge Luis Borges, "Ibn Hakkan al-Bokhari, Dead in His Labyrinth," in *The Aleph and Other Stories,* p. 125.

10. *Encyclopaedia Britannica,* 11th ed. (New York, 1910–11), III, 824.

11. Jorge Luis Borges, "Chess," in *Borges: A Reader, A Selection from the Writings of Jorge Luis Borges,* ed. Emir Rodriguez Monegal and Alastair Reid (New York, 1981), p. 281.

12. Emir Rodriguez Monegal, *Jorge Luis Borges: A Literary Biography* (New York, 1978), p. 285; hereafter cited in text as *JLB.*

13. Jorge Luis Borges, *The Book of Imaginary Beings* (New York, 1970), p. 158.

14. Jorge Luis Borges, "The Sect of the Phoenix," in *Ficciones,* pp. 165–66.

15. Ronald Christ, *The Narrow Act: Borges' Art of Allusion* (New York, 1969), p. 190, n. 19.

16. Jorge Luis Borges, *Other Inquisitions 1937–1952* (New York, 1965), p. 60.

17. Jorge Luis Borges, "The Circular Ruins," in *Ficciones,* p. 58; hereafter cited in text.

18. Lewis Carroll, *The Annotated Alice* (Cleveland, 1963), p. 238; hereafter cited in text.

Jon Stewart (essay date 1993)

SOURCE: "Borges on Immortality," in *Philosophy and Literature,* Vol. 17, No. 2, October, 1993, pp. 295–301.

[*In the following essay, Stewart explicates Borges's concept of immortality.*]

The various conceptions of immortality in most every culture evince at once the basic human fear of death and at the same time the equally basic hope for a more congenial future beyond mundane existence. The Greek and Christian views of immortality, which have been so influential in Western philosophy and theology, represent two different, yet generally quite positive, visions of eternal life. Although for the Greeks immortality in Hades was not, as Achilles' lament indicates, a thing to be eagerly anticipated, nevertheless the Olympian gods with their immense power and influence represented a positive picture of perennial existence. The Christian account presents another perhaps even more optimistic view of immortality since it teaches that eternal existence is possible for humans who live righteous lives and hold correct beliefs. The Christian

promise of an everlasting life in heaven in the state of perfect bliss has long been held up by theologians as representing the apex of human happiness and fulfillment.

"The Immortal,"[1] by Jorge Luis Borges, hints at something fundamentally wrong about the very concept of immortality. Most philosophical criticisms of this concept concentrate on attacking the notion of a separable soul which survives the death of the human body, thus approaching the question of immortality essentially as a mind-body problem. Borges's story, on the other hand, focuses on the concept of immortality itself and on what we might call its internal consistency. Reflecting on **"The Immortal,"** Borges says that the story shows us "the effect that immortality would have on men," and he explains that the story offers "a sketch of an ethic for immortals."[2] **"The Immortal"** can be seen as a thought experiment: Borges proposes that we imagine that we are immortal,[3] and he then calls on us to examine our conception of that imagined existence to see if it can be thought consistently. We shall see that in the end our traditional views of immortality are contradictory and that the consistent conception represents something quite different from our preconceptions and—surprisingly—something far from desirable. Although the most obvious target of criticism in Borges's story is the Greek conception of immortality, on closer inspection he is, I would like to argue, also concerned to criticize the Christian view. This reading has, in my opinion, been neglected by many commentators,[4] the majority of whom would see in this work an affirmation of the power of literature over death and finitude.[5]

According to Augustine and Aquinas, the immortality of the blessed souls in the supernal state consists essentially in participating in the *visio beatifica.* To behold God in this vision is to take part in eternal life. Aquinas claims that only by viewing God can one obtain "perfect bliss"[6] and immortality. In an argument largely appropriated from Aristotle's *Nicomachean Ethics,* Aquinas contends that man, who naturally desires to know, is never perfectly satisfied provided that there remains something unexplained. In his terrestrial condition, always seeking and desiring, man is in a tragic situation since he can never unravel the ultimate causes and thus attain perfect beatitude. In heaven, however, man obtains ultimate bliss since in beholding God, who is the first cause of all things, man thus sees and understands the workings of all things. With the comprehension of the first cause, all the other causes become apparent as well. Aquinas also argues that when we behold the workings of the entire universe in the *visio beatifica,* in fact, we are merely beholding God himself or more exactly the omnipresent *divina substantia.* Augustine describes the vision as follows: "Similarly, in the future life, wherever we turn the spiritual eyes . . . we shall discern . . . the incorporeal God directing the whole universe."[7] Observing how God governs the universe, our intellect gains ultimate satisfaction, and there remains nothing more to be known. But yet God does not exist in time as do finite things. This means that our vision of God is not a temporal one but rather an eternal one. Likewise, since the universe is nothing other than the divine substance which is God, we behold the entire workings of the universe simultaneously as if in one moment, just as we behold God in one eternal moment. Therefore, in the participation in the *visio beatifica* one entirely loses the mundane temporal perspective. Insofar as one participates in this vision, one is immortal since the *visio* is extratemporal. The *visio* is the pivotal concept of the Christian theory of immortality since it is through the atemporal nature of the *visio* that eternal life is established.

One natural corollary of the Christian view of immortality with complete knowledge of God is that in heaven there will be nothing that resembles human activity as we know it on earth. Augustine characterizes this state as one of perfect rest: "But now restored by him and perfected by his greater grace we shall be still and at leisure for eternity, seeing that he is God. . . . this we shall then know perfectly, when we are perfectly at rest and in stillness see that he is God" (pp. 1090–91). Since there will no longer be anything to see or to desire, for we will know everything there is to know in beholding God and the workings of the universe, there will be no difficulties or mysteries remaining. We can thus rest contented in this state of perfect leisure for all eternity.

The point of Borges's story is to demonstrate the internal contradictions in this Christian picture of immortality and to provide us with a view which, if not attractive, is at least internally consistent. On Borges's vision of immortality we are presented with a picture of neither gods nor saints but rather a loathsome and placid barbarian tribe called troglodytes, who lie in the sand consuming lizards. The Roman military tribune Marcus Flaminius Rufus, both narrator and protagonist of the story, determines to set out in search of the River of Immortality and the City of the Immortals. After several trying adventures, he arrives tired and ailing at the labyrinthine City of the Immortals and displays great repugnance toward the abject and quiescent creatures who are the inhabitants there. At first sight, the troglodytes seem entirely to lack the benefits of reason and culture. They have no speech and possess no visible means of communication. Moreover, although they do not seem to sleep, the troglodytes are entirely docile and listless creatures who neither farm, nor hunt, nor provide themselves with shelter. They appear almost comatose, entirely oblivious to their surroundings, neither helping the feverish tribune nor heeding him when he speaks. As the tribune surprisingly discovers on one rainy morning, this miserable assemblage of troglodytes, which he so condescendingly regards, is the remnant of the Olympian gods, and their pathetic condition is the logical and inevitable result of their immortality. The infinity of time, he learns, has stultified them and rendered them reticent and base creatures. The astonishment of this discovery simultaneously moves both the reader and the tribune who had imagined immortality quite differently, and herein lies the irony of the work.[8]

Through the passage of the centuries the lives of the immortals had degenerated into an apathetic condition in which they did nothing. The infinity of time involved in the life of immortality had deprived the lives of the gods of meaning, and thus they had fallen into their wretched condition. Borges's tribune observes, death "makes men precious and pathetic. . . . every act they execute may be their last. . . . Everything among the mortals has the value of the irretrievable and the perilous" (p. 146). In contrast, for the immortals, "every act (and every thought) is the echo of others that preceded it in the past, with no visible beginning, or the faithful presage of others that in the future will repeat it to a vertiginous degree" (p. 146). Borges's point is the fundamental existentialist claim that it is only in the finitude of human existence that actions and life have their meaning. Only because we know that our lifespans are limited are we concerned and motivated to accomplish our projects. There are, of course, other motivations both noble and base, but these lose their value when a finite existence is expanded to an infinite one. In an eternity our lives become tedious and banal. Our individuality and personal identity are lost in an infinity of time since in an eternity we would have the opportunity to play the roles of all human beings and to accomplish all things. Since one can do all things, one could not define one's life by the continuity of the specific deeds done or the projects accomplished. Thus, the main characters of Borges's story, the antiquary Cartaphilus and the Roman tribune Marcus Flaminius Rufus, are not two different individuals but rather one universal person who spans the ages.[9]

For the immortals there is no challenge or difficulty great enough which cannot be accomplished in an eternity. The construction of the city of labyrinths was the ultimate desperate project undertaken by the immortals before they drifted off into the grey eternity of indifference: "This establishment was the last symbol to which the Immortals condescended; it marks a stage at which, judging that all undertakings are in vain, they determined to live in thought, in pure speculation" (p. 144). The creation of the labyrinth represents a pointless task whose accomplishment is more of a fatuous game than a meaningful project. The gods erected the labyrinthine city in a manner modeled after their own absurd and meaningless lives. The architectural irregularities and asymmetries that form the city represent a world of chaos lacking meaning and order.[10] While lost in the labyrinth prior to discovering the truth of the troglodytes, the tribune concludes, "The gods who built it were mad" (p. 140). Although at the time he could not know, the tribune's ironic words captured the truth of the immortals' dilemma since their lives, busied only with Sisyphean projects and having become wholly indifferent to the usual tasks of life, indeed represent a kind of madness.

Borges makes the comparison of such a life of immortality with that of animals or subhuman creatures: "To be immortal is commonplace; except for man, all creatures are immortal, for they are ignorant of death; what is divine, terrible, incomprehensible, is to know that one is immortal" (p. 144). Animals, lacking the faculty of reflection and thus not knowing of their inevitable deaths, live, like the troglodytes, everyday like every other day. Their lives cannot be said to be meaningful in the way human lives are. Only humans have history, culture, and language, all of which would gradually disappear, as they did for the immortals, were we to live forever. Borges constantly uses the pejorative simile of a dog to describe the troglodytes (pp. 139, 141). The tribune disdainfully names one of them "Argos" after Odysseus' faithful old hound in the *Odyssey*. This deprecatory appellation, which seems to us so unbecoming of immortals, gives evidence for the interpretation that Borges issues here a criticism of the notion of immortality itself. The tribune says in his ignorance that the troglodytes, i.e., the gods, "did not inspire fear but rather repulsion" (p. 139). The juxtaposition of the words "fear" and "repulsion" is the key here. We would expect to feel terror before the gods, but instead our sensation is one of disgust. The repulsion that we feel towards the troglodytes indicates that there is something repellent about our notion of immortality if it were carried to its logical conclusion. This kind of life strikes us as an insult to the integrity of human existence.

The conclusion of **"The Immortal"** confirms the criticism of the very notion of immortality. The immortals reason that if there is a river whose waters grant immortality, there must also be a river that renders one mortal once again. They thus decide to set out in search of the river that will cure them of their immortal condition. We see here an ironical mirror image of the story of the Fall in which mankind was exiled from his happy immortal state to one of pain and death. The immortals embark on a quest for the river of death which will liberate them from the onus of immortality and which will again invest their lives with meaning by rendering them finite. When at last the former tribune drinks from the waters that efface immortality and for the first time in almost two thousand years becomes finite and vulnerable, he receives the first wound and feels the first tinge of pain after so many centuries. Borges uses the peculiar adjective "precious" (p. 147) to describe the formation of the drop of blood from the wound. This word is used throughout the story to indicate the meaning bound up with a finite life; something which can be infinitely repeated cannot *ipso facto* be precious. Only in a life threatened by death are individual events meaningful. Despite all that he has seen and done through so many years, the protagonist, the former tribune, is happy only by regaining death and finitude.

Although Borges's story seems at face value to be a criticism solely of the Greeks' conception of immortality, since after all it is the Olympian gods that the tribune finds in such a base state, nevertheless Borges clearly intends for this criticism also to be valid for the Christian view. He refers directly to the Christian doctrine once (p. 144), but in addition to this direct reference, there are other subtler bits of evidence that single out specifically the Christian doctrine of immortality.[11] The state of the immortals is described as one of "pure speculation" (p. 144), which is precisely the description of the *visio beatifica* given by

Augustine and Aquinas, in which one contemplates God and the workings of the universe for all eternity. The immortals are described as being so lost in the realm of thought that they gradually lose touch with the mundane: "Absorbed in thought, they hardly perceived the physical world" (p. 144). This accords with Aquinas's analysis that in the *visio beatifica* we behold only *divina substantia*. The blessed perceive the universe only in terms of divine substance and thus do not see the physical world or mundane substance *per se*. The blessed state of the immortals is also alluded to when the tribune observes that "the Immortals were capable of perfect quietude" (p. 145). This then echoes the claim of Aquinas that in the *visio beatifica* we will enjoy perfect bliss as well as Augustine's claim that we will be perfectly at leisure. The tribune, having become immortal, explains how the greatest pleasure was pure thought: "There is no pleasure more complex than that of thought and we surrendered ourselves to it" (p. 145). Here we see the claim of Augustine and Aquinas that pure speculation in the *visio beatifica* is the greatest bliss that man can experience.

The problem that **"The Immortal"** presents is how to reconcile the optimistic account of immortality that Christianity offers with the fact, which Borges so poignantly illustrates, that such a life of immortality would be meaningless, bovine, and undesirable. Not accidently the *visio beatifica* reduces the life of immortality to a troglodyte condition insofar as it precludes meaningful activity by removing obstacles and by introducing an infinite time frame. The sort of difficulties and challenges that render our mundane existence meaningful are precisely what makes heaven appear at first glance attractive. If, indeed, it is true that at the termination of our mundane existence, we will become immortal, then as Borges shows, we will not become holy saints living blissfully in heaven beholding God and the universe for an eternity but rather base and indifferent troglodytes eating lizards and tracing inchoate figures in the sands of unknown deserts.

Notes

1. "The Immortal" is quoted from Jorge Luis Borges, *Labyrinths, Selected Stories and Other Writings,* ed. Donald A. Yates and James E. Irby (New York: Penguin, 1981).

2. Jorge Luis Borges, *Obras Completas* (Barcelona: Emercé Editores S.A., 1989), p. 629, my translation.

3. See Gene H. Bell-Villada, *Borges and His Fiction* (Chapel Hill: University of North Carolina Press, 1981), p. 230.

4. See L. A. Murillo, *The Cyclical Night: Irony in James Joyce and Jorge L. Borges* (Cambridge: Harvard University Press, 1968), p. 215.

5. E.g., Ronald Christ, *The Narrow Act: Borges' Art of Allusion* (New York: New York University Press, 1969), p. 211.

6. St. Thomas Aquinas, *Summa Theologica,* vol. 16, trans. Thomas Gilby, (New York: McGraw-Hill, 1969), p. 83.

7. Augustine, *City of God* (New York: Penguin, 1976), pp. 1086–87.

8. See Jacques Réda, "Commentaire de 'L'Immortal' de J. L. Borges," *Cahiers du Sud* 49 (1962–63): 439.

9. See Gene H. Bell-Villada, p. 230; Jaime Alazraki, *La Prosa narrativa de Borges* (Madrid: Biblioteca Románica Hispánica, 1968), p. 71.

10. See L. A. Murillo, p. 226.

11. It seems to me that the commentators on "The Immortal" have fully missed this point. See, for example, Estela Cédola, *Borges o la coincidencía de los opuestos* (Buenos Aires: Eudeba, 1987), p. 144. Adelheid Schaefer, *Phantastische Elemente und ästhetische Konzepte im Erzählwerk von J. L. Borges* (Frankfurt am Main: Humanitas Verlag, 1973), pp. 64ff.

Daniel Balderston (essay date 1993)

SOURCE: "On the Threshold of Otherness: British India in 'El hombre en el umbral,'" in *Out of Context: Historical Reference and Representation of Reality in Borges*, Duke University Press, 1993, pp. 98–114.

[*In the following essay, Balderston examines Borges's use of colonial India in his fiction, and his attitude toward colonialism, contrasting Borges's story "The Man on the Threshold" with Rudyard Kipling's "On the City Wall."*]

I have never found one among them [the Orientalists] who could deny that a single shelf of a good European library was worth the whole native literature of India and Arabia.[1]

—Macaulay, qtd. in Majumdar 10:83

"Mr. Gandhi, what do you think of Western civilization?"

"It would be a good idea."[2]

"El hombre en el umbral" brings into sharp focus the issues of colonialism and foreign domination that are present in a less obvious way in such other Borges stories as **"El jardín de senderos que se bifurcan"** and **"El milagro secreto."** The choice of venue this time is British India,[3] a choice that is interesting because India was one of the most thorough of the Western experiments in colonialism in the Third World[4] and because its struggle opened the way for the movement to dismantle the British, French, Dutch, and Portuguese empires in Africa and Asia. The story was first published in *La Nación* in 1952, five years after the independence (and partition) of India. Written under the tutelage of Kipling, the story's politics are far removed from the politics of Kipling's narratives of India.[5] In this story Borges and Bioy are situated in some relation to the memory and narrative of colonial rule; the exact nature of that relation is what will be unraveled here.[6]

The story consists of two parts, the second much more extensive than the first. The first is a brief paragraph describing a conversation in Buenos Aires between the narrator,[7] Adolfo Bioy Casares, and Christopher Dewey of the British Council. The second is Dewey's account of his search for a kidnapped British official he calls David Alexander Glencairn, which is divided into three parts: the story of his mission, then the story told him by an old man sitting in a doorway, and a brief final paragraph describing Dewey's encounter with the mad judge and with the body of "Glencairn." I shall discuss the old man's story first, then return to consider the frame narratives situating Dewey, Borges, and Bioy.

The old man in the threshold says: "El hecho aconteció cuando yo era niño. No sé de fechas, pero no había muerto aún Nikal Seyn (Nicholson) ante la muralla de Delhi" (614) [The event occurred when I was a child. I do not know about dates, but Nikal Seyn (Nicholson) had not yet died before the walls of Delhi]. As is usual with Borges, the historical reference is precise. John Nicholson was one of the leading officials in the British colonial administration during the Dalhousie and Canning administrations, known to his fellow officers (because of his cruelty to the native population) as "the autocrat of all the Russias" (Majumdar 10: 348). Hibbert describes him thus:

Nicholson had arrived in India in July 1839 and had served as a young infantry officer in the Afghan War. Since then, however, most of his time had been spent in civil appointments, principally in the Punjab where he stamped out lawlessness in the districts under his control with the utmost severity, pursuing criminals personally and displaying their severed heads upon his desk. His strange and forceful personality so impressed the natives that numbers of them worshipped him as their spiritual guide and deity, falling down at his feet in reverent submission.[8]

(292–93)

Nicholson was active particularly in the Punjab around Amritsar (mentioned in the story) and Ferozpur. Called to Delhi to aid in the crushing of the mutiny of the Indian units of the colonial army in 1857, he died in an attack on the sepoys by the Delhi city wall on 14 September (Dodwell, *Indian Empire* 6: 195)[9] and was later termed "the Hero of the mutiny" (Majumdar 9: 600).

Nicholson was also the proponent of a bill legislating torture in cases of rebellion and had this to say about such remedies:

As regards torturing the murderers of the women and children: If it be right otherwise, I do not think we should refrain from it, because it is a Native custom. We are told in the Bible that stripes shall be meted out according to faults, and if hanging is sufficient punishment for such wretches, it is also severe for ordinary mutineers [*sic*]. If I had them in my power to-day, and knew that I were to die tomorrow, I would inflict the most excruciating tortures I could think of on them with a perfectly easy conscience.[10]

(Majumdar 9: 600)

Yet the anonymous *Encyclopaedia Britannica* article on Nicholson describes him both as a "severe ruler" and as "eminently just," quotes Lord Roberts as saying that he was "the *beau idéal* of a soldier and a gentleman," and reports that "the natives worshipped him as a god under the title of Nikalsain." One of his officers is quoted at length as saying:

> He was a man cast in a giant mould, with massive chest and powerful limbs, and an expression ardent and commanding, with a dash of roughness; features of stern beauty, a long black beard, and a deep sonorous voice. There was something of immense strength, talent and resolution in his whole frame and manner, and a power of ruling men on high occasions which no one could escape noticing. His imperial air, which never left him, and which would have been thought arrogant in one of less imposing mien, sometimes gave offence to the more unbending of his countrymen, but made him almost worshipped by the pliant Asiatics.[11]
>
> (19: 657)

In Kipling's *Kim,* the Ressaldar, who was loyal to the Crown during the Mutiny in 1857 and fought against his own people, sings the "song of Nikal Seyn before Delhi—the old song" (93): "Wail by long-drawn wail he unfolded the story of Nikal Seyn (Nicholson)—the song that men sing in the Punjab to this day. . . . *'Ahi! Nikal Seyn is dead—he died before Delhi! Lances of North take vengeance for Nikal Seyn'*" (93).[12]

The reference to Nicholson in the Borges story is more than a casual one, since the picture of the domineering British official painted by the old man in the threshold closely resembles that of the cruel sadist, his desk decorated with the severed heads of his victims, reported in some of the accounts. The physical description of "Glencairn" in the story reads:

> Una sola vez lo vieron mis ojos, pero no olvidaré el cabello muy negro, los pómulos salientes, la ávida nariz y la boca, los anchos hombros, la fuerte osatura de viking.
>
> (612)

> Only once did my eyes see him, but I will never forget his raven black hair, prominent cheekbones, avid nose and mouth, broad shoulders, strong Viking bone structure.

This closely matches the description given of Nicholson in the encyclopedia article, as does the story of the "peace" established by the stern ruler:

> El mero anuncio de su advenimiento bastó para apaciguar la ciudad. Ello no impidió que decretara diversas medidas enérgicas. Unos años pasaron. La ciudad y el distrito estaban en paz; *sikhs* y musulmanes habían depuesto las antiguas discordias y de pronto Glencairn desapareció.

> The mere announcement of his coming sufficed to pacify the city. This fact did not prevent him from decreeing various decisive measures. Some years passed.

The city and the district were at peace; Sikhs and Moslems had laid down their ancient discords and all of a sudden Glencairn disappeared.

> On the annexation of Punjab he [Nicholson] was appointed deputy commissioner of Bannu. There he became a kind of legendary hero, and many tales are told of his stern justice, his tireless activity and his commanding personality. In the course of five years he reduced the most turbulent district on the frontier to such a state of quietude that no crime was committed or even attempted during his last year of office, a condition of things never known before or since.
>
> (*Encyclopaedia Britannica* 19: 657)

Even the question of the "pliant Asiatics" worshipping Nicholson as a god is somewhat more equivocal in the old man's story of the judge whom Dewey calls "Glencairn":

> Cuando se pregonó que la reina iba a mandar un hombre que ejecutaría en este país la ley de Inglaterra, los menos malos se alegraron, porque sintieron que la ley es mejor que el desorden. Llegó el cristiano y no tardó en prevaricar y oprimir. . . . No lo culpamos, al principio; la justicia que administraba no era conocida de nadie y los aparentes atropellos del nuevo juez correspondían acaso a válidas y arcanas razones. *Todo tendrá justificación en su libro,* queríamos pensar, pero su afinidad con todos los malos jueces del mundo era demasiado notoria, y al fin hubimos de admitir que era simplemente un malvado. Llegó a ser un tirano y la pobre gente (para vengarse de la errónea esperanza que alguna vez pusieron en él) dio en jugar con la idea de secuestrarlo y someterlo a juicio.
>
> (614)

When it was announced that the queen was going to send a man who would carry out the law of England in this land, the least recalcitrant were happy because they felt that law is better than disorder. The Christian arrived and was not long in acting corruptly and oppressively. . . . We did not blame him at first; the justice he administered was not familiar to any of us, and the apparent excesses of the new judge were perhaps due to valid (if arcane) reasons. *Everything must be justified in his book,* we wanted to believe, but his affinity with all the evil judges in the world was too obvious, and we finally had to admit that he was simply a scoundrel. He turned into a tyrant, and the poor people (to avenge the mistaken hope they had once deposited in him) began playing with the idea of kidnapping him and bringing him to justice.

Thus the devotion that Nicholson inspired in the "pliant Asiatics"—according to the British sources—is revealed in the old man's story as the vain hope that the subject people feel until they meet their man.

Furthermore, Nicholson's main area of activity was focused on the city of Amritsar, and according to Dewey the story of Glencairn took place in the Punjab (616), though he initially equivocates and says condescendingly: "La exacta geografía de los hechos que voy a referir importa muy poco. Además, ¿qué precisión guardan en Buenos

Aires los nombres de Amritsar o de Udh?" (612) [The exact geography of the events I am going to tell matters very little. Besides, what exactitude can the names of Amritsar or Oudh have in Buenos Aires?]. Of course the difference between Amritsar in the Punjab and the native state of Oudh or Avadh (now Uttar Pradesh) matters a great deal, not least in the fact that there is repeated reference in the story to the unpeaceful coexistence in the city of Sikhs, Moslems, and Hindus, which would be true of Amritsar but not, say, of Lucknow in Oudh.[13]

The "A or B" structure is used again a bit later in the story when Dewey doubts whether the old man can be a reliable informant about something that happened only recently (in the period between the world wars): *"Nuevas de la Rebelión o de Akbar podría dar este hombre* (pensé) *pero no de Glencairn. Lo que me dijo confirmó esta sospecha"* (613) [*This man could give news of the Mutiny or of Akbar* (I thought) *but not of Glencairn. What he said confirmed this suspicion*]. The old man of course could have lived through the events of the 1857 Mutiny (and the cruel repression that followed), but the second possibility is offered as a red herring: the old man could hardly offer testimony about Akbar, the great Mogul ruler of India from 1556 to 1605.[14] (Unless, however, the old man is "ageless," as implied in the stereotypical description: "Los muchos años lo habían reducido y pulido como las aguas a una piedra o las generaciones de los hombres a una sentencia" [613] [The many years had reduced and polished him like the waters a stone or the human generations a saying]).[15] This time, though, the "A or B" structure, in which B is an obvious red herring, shows Dewey the dupe of his own stereotype: the event that the old man narrates happened not in his childhood during the Mutiny, nor in the distant past; it is happening right here, right now, and everyone knows it but Dewey.[16]

"Amritsar" is one clue to the contemporaneity of the story. Though the city played an important role in the history of the Mutiny of 1857, it was equally important in the history of the twentieth-century movement toward independence, a movement unexpectedly reinvigorated with the passage of the Rowlatt Acts of March 1919. It was at Amritsar, on 13 April 1919, that British troops massacred a peaceful Indian crowd in a square called Jallianwalla Bagh, an event that Sir Valentine Chirol called "that black day in the annals of British India" (qtd. in Fischer 179). Louis Fischer remarks: "For Gandhi it was a turning point. Indians never forgot it" (179),[17] and even Philip Mason, usually an apologist for British rule, acknowledges: "After Amritsar, the whole situation was changed. Government had been carried out with the consent of the governed. That consent was now changed to mistrust" (288). Though the dates of Dewey's residence in India are not given in the story except in general terms ("entre las dos guerras" [612] [between the two wars]), even that lack of precision indicates that he visited Amritsar after the massacre at Jallianwalla Bagh. If he reads "Amritsar" in the book of history as referring exclusively to the events of the Mutiny (or to Nicholson), he is indeed a poor observer (or reader) of the history of his own time.[18]

Dewey is also distracted as an observer by his assumption that India is a land of the spirit where politics has no place. Thus, he observes after coming to the house where "Glencairn" is being tried that "en el último patio se celebraba no sé qué fiesta musulmana" (613) [in the last patio I know not what Moslem festival was being celebrated]; the "no sé qué" is interesting, since it acknowledges his ignorance of Moslem religious customs yet also reveals his mistaken idea that the "fiesta" taking place inside is a religious one. In fact, he interrupts his telling of the old man's story several times to inform his listeners of the comings and goings in the house: first, "unas mujeres . . . entraban en la casa" (614) [some women . . . were entering the house], then "unas personas . . . se iban de la fiesta" (615) [some people . . . were leaving the festival], and then finally, and most tellingly, after the old man has finished his story:

> Una turba hecha de hombres y mujeres de todas las naciones del Punjab se desbordó, rezando y cantando, sobre nosotros y casi nos barrió.
>
> (616)

> A crowd composed of men and women of all the nations of the Punjab overflowed, praying and singing, pushing against and almost trampling us.

The old man has already said that people of all the faiths of the region were involved in the trial:

> Alcoranistas, doctores de la ley, *sikhs* que llevan el nombre de leones y que adoran a un Dios, hindúes que adoran muchedumbres de dioses, monjes de Mahavira que enseñan que la forma del universo es la de un hombre con las piernas abiertas, adoradores del fuego y judíos negros, integraron el tribunal, pero el último fallo fue encomendado al arbitrio de un loco.
>
> (614–15)

> Scholars of the Koran, doctors of law, Sikhs who bear the name of lions and who worship a single God, Hindus who worship a multitude of gods, monks of Mahavira who teach that the universe has the form of a man with his legs crossed, fire-worshippers and black Jews made up the tribunal, but the final judgment was left to the determination of a madman.

Dewey, then, is duped by his own certainties of the roles played by the colonizers and the colonized; he cannot tell a religious festival of whatever creed from a trial and execution. He is a victim of what Francis Hutchins has called the "ideology of permanence": "The certainty of a permanent Empire in these years, however, seemed to increase in proportion to its fragility, and to serve for many people as a defense and retreat from reason long after the course of events had proved its impossibility" (xii).

In *El género gauchesco: Un tratado sobre la patria* [*The Gauchesque Genre: A Treatise on the Fatherland*], Josefina Ludmer has discussed the conflict in the gauchesque works in Argentine literature between two laws: the written law of the nation-state and the oral law of the gaucho community (227–36). A similar conflict is set up in this story, between the "justice" of the British Raj (which is presented as unjust, arbitrary, and cruel) and the "justice" of the people's court.[19] What is interesting in the latter instance is the recourse to a judge who is literally insane. The subterfuge depends on a knowledge of the British system of justice, which will not punish an insane man for casting judgment (or for carrying out the death sentence, since the madman serves both as judge and as executioner). Yet it also plays in an astute way with the colonizers' stereotypes of the Indian people as childlike, irrational, and more than a little bit mad.

The notion of a law so universal and so transparent that it would be obvious even to a madman implies also that the community shares notions of right and wrong and can communicate them (even to an inquiring British official). First, then, the colonized community must find unity, even if it is the temporary unity of the oppressed against the colonial power; thus, even Dewey sees representatives of "todas las naciones del Punjab" at what he first took to be a Moslem religious festival.[20] Second, the old man must discover a "pedagogy of the oppressed," a way of communicating this universal sense of right and wrong to his obtuse British interlocutor. The narrative strategy he adopts has almost a fairy tale structure at first: "El hecho aconteció cuando yo era niño. No sé de fechas. . . . El tiempo que se fue queda en la memoria; sin duda soy capaz de recuperar lo que entonces pasó" (614) [The event took place when I was a child. I know nothing about dates. . . . The time that has gone remains in memory; no doubt I am capable of recovering what happened then]. Later, though, he makes clear that his story, though archetypal in structure, has gone from generals to particulars: "En esta ciudad lo juzgaron: en una casa como todas, como ésta. Una casa no puede diferir de otra: lo que importa es saber si está edificada en el infierno o en el cielo" (615) [In this city they judged him, in a house like all the others, like this one. One house cannot differ from another; what matters is knowing whether it is built in hell or in heaven]. Moral absolutes thus reestablished (on a universal level, and therefore no longer as the property of the colonial power), he ends his story and the body is revealed. Thus the story closes with a mute writ of habeas corpus: "You shall have the body," he seems to be telling Dewey, "but take the story with it."

Of course the narrative devices employed in the story are familiar to readers of the *Arabian Nights*. Thus, the nesting of narratives through what Todorov calls "hommes-récits" [story-men] and the spinning out of the story until some action can be accomplished behind the scenes (in this case, the execution of "Glencairn") are typical "Oriental" stratagems. Even more important, though, is the British stereotype of Indian "guile," a stereotype that played an important role in the misunderstandings between the two peoples (Nandy 77, 110, 112, and passim). This "guile," which Nandy prefers to call "a fluid open self-definition" (112), was part of a literary stereotype used in characterizations of Indians by Stevenson (in *The Master of Ballantrae*, in which the Indian servant does not let on

for most of the novel that he speaks English), Kipling,[21] and many others. Interestingly, the same concept was often used to characterize Gandhi, whom Nandy finds often compared to Charlie Chaplin (104),[22] though Nandy prefers to point to what he calls Gandhi's "political and psychological shrewdness" (49). (Orwell asserts much the same thing when he says of Gandhi that "inside the saint, or near-saint, there was a very shrewd, able person" [463].)

An old man clad in traditional garb sitting in a doorway, who possesses sufficient guile to delay and educate his British listener with a story (or with a reinterpretation of history), and whose story tells of a subject people's discovery of the evil of the foreign invaders and of the stratagems employed to reassert traditional judicial and ethical authority: the description closely matches that given by exasperated British officials who dealt with Gandhi. Winston Churchill's comment is the most famous, on "the nauseating and humiliating spectacle of this one-time Inner Temple lawyer, now seditious fakir, striding half-naked up the steps of the Viceroy's palace, there to negotiate and to parley on equal terms with the representative of the King-Emperor" (qtd. in Fischer 277). That Gandhi would never have condoned the execution of a British official, however corrupt, or have entrusted the case to the judgment of a madman, does not prevent defenders of the British Raj from seeing his nonviolence as a subterfuge or something worse. Thus Percival Griffiths writes:

> We are not concerned with the history of that sterile [noncooperation] movement, nor with the terrorist activity which naturally grew out of it. It is doubtful if noncooperation or its successor, civil disobedience, advanced self-government by a single day. On the other hand, it engendered a racial bitterness, which has fortunately disappeared since the transfer of power, and a disregard of law and order which has left an enduring mark on the youth of India.
>
> (83; see also 73)

Thus, the "man in the threshold," despite his obvious differences from Gandhi, functions in the story as the projection of British paranoid self-doubt (Nandy 100) in the face of the self-rule movement, a condition born of what we could call (after Hutchins) the "disillusion with permanence."

One of the tasks that British education set itself in India was the implantation of a Western idea of a linear progression in history. Chatterjee has studied the impact of this model on the thought of Bankimchandra Chattopadhyay (1838–1894), an important Bengali man of letters. Bankimchandra's task, according to Chatterjee, was to separate myth from history (59), to foster the "knowledge of its own history" that for him was national consciousness (58), to create pride through historical writing (82; see also Nandy 23).[23] Chatterjee sees Gandhi's critique of modern civilization as extending to this progressive ideology and its obsession with history (86, 93–94, 97), while Nandy asserts that Gandhi "rejected history and affirmed the primacy of myths over historical chronicles" (55). Nandy sees a conflict between two different models for thinking about the relation between past and present: "If for the West the present was a special case of an unfolding history, for Gandhi as a representative of traditional India history was a special case of an all-embracing permanent present, waiting to be interpreted and reinterpreted" (57). Of course the extent to which Gandhi was a "representative of traditional India" is open to debate, but what is significant for **"El hombre en el umbral"** is the willingness of militants for self-rule to use the "all-embracing permanent present" of Mother India[24] to mobilize the subject people and to frustrate and ultimately drive out the occupying power.[25]

To return to Dewey's first description of the old man:

> A mis pies, inmóvil como una cosa, se acurrucaba en el umbral un hombre muy viejo. Diré como era, porque es parte esencial de la historia. Los muchos años lo habían reducido y pulido como las aguas a una piedra o las generaciones de los hombres a una sentencia.[26]
>
> (613)

> At my feet, motionless as an object, a very old man was curled up in the threshold. I will describe what he looked like because it is an essential part of the story [historia]. The many years had reduced and polished him like the waters a stone or the human generations a saying.

Dewey's problem here is a conflict of paradigms. His Western concept of history (and this description is, he says, "parte esencial de la historia," with all the resonances of that last word) cannot cope with this figure from the "all-embracing perpetual present" except as someone who is outside of human history as it is taught in the British schools. So Dewey sees the old man as a figure from the world of myth, as a representative of "traditional" (ageless, eternal, ahistorical) India. But because he needs to have it one way or the other, he is not prepared for the truth, which is that the old man has something to tell him about "Glencairn," his own mission, himself, and the present time.[27]

Now to return to the first paragraph of the story, which serves as a sort of narrative frame. It reads:

> Bioy Casares trajo de Londres un curioso puñal de hoja triangular y empuñadura en forma de H; nuestro amigo Christopher Dewey, del Consejo Británico, dijo que tales armas eran de uso común en el Indostán. Ese dictamen lo alentó a mencionar que había trabajado en aquel país, entre las dos guerras. (*Ultra Auroram et Gangen,* recuerdo que dijo en latín, equivocando un verso de Juvenal.) De las historias que esa noche contó, me atrevo a reconstruir la que sigue. Mi texto será fiel: líbreme Alá de la tentación de añadir breves rasgos circunstanciales o de agravar, con interpolaciones de Kipling, el cariz exótico del relato. Este, por lo demás, tiene un antiguo y simple sabor que sería una lástima perder, acaso el de las Mil y una noches.
>
> (612)

Bioy Casares came back from London with a strange dagger with a triangular blade and a handle in the shape of an H; our friend Christopher Dewey of the British Council said that arms like that were common in Hindustan. This declaration encouraged him to mention that he had worked in that country in the period between the wars. (*Ultra Auroram et Gangen* [Beyond the Dawn and the Ganges] I remember he said in Latin, misquoting a line from Juvenal.) Of the stories he told that night, I will venture to reconstruct the one that follows. My text will be faithful: may Allah save me from the temptation to add brief circumstantial details or to exaggerate the exotic character of the tale with interpolations from Kipling. The tale, besides, had an ancient and simple flavor that it would be a shame to lose, perhaps that of the *Arabian Nights.*

Dewey's error in quotation of a line from Juvenal's tenth satire is most interesting. In the initial reported conversation with Borges and Bioy, the sight of the dagger leads him to memories of Hindustan and then to Juvenal. By an association of ideas here, Dewey's ability to identify the dagger authorizes his memories, among them the quotation, yet the error in the quotation threatens to unravel his authority, as the narrator quietly notes. The original passage in Juvenal reads:

> Omnibus in terris, quae sunt a Gadibus usque Auroram et Gangen, pauci dinoscere possunt vera bona atque illis multum diversa, remota erroris nebula. quid enim ratione timemus aut cupimus? quid tam dextro pede concipis, ut te conatus non paeniteat votique peracti?
>
> (10.1–5)

> In every land, from furthest west (Cádiz) to furthest east (the Ganges), few only can discern true blessings from their counterfeits, clear from all mist of error. For what do we with reason fear, covet with reason? What do you undertake with foot so right, with a start so lucky, but you rue your attempt and the success of your desire? (Mayor trans. 2:65)

Dewey remembers the verse as referring to travel beyond [ultra] the bounds of the known world, whereas Juvenal refers instead to the known world within marked limits (Cádiz in the west, the Ganges or the place of dawn in the east). "Usque" here means "as far as" or "up to" those thresholds. Within the world as he knew it, Juvenal sees the realm of error and self-deception; the whole of this satire is concerned with those who err when they overreach, whether as warriors, as rulers, as scholars, or in hopes of good health or good fortune. As one example of such an overreacher Juvenal cites Alexander, who, though he did not reach the Ganges, reached the Indus, but in the process lost all:

> Unus Pellaeo iuveni non sufficit orbis, aestuat infelix angusto limite mundi, ut Gyari clusus scopulis parvaque Seripho; cum tamen a figulis munitam intraverit urbem, sarcophago contentus erit. mors sola fatetur, quantula sint hominum corpuscula.
>
> (10.168–73)

For Pella's youth one globe is all too small; he chafes, poor soul, in the narrow bounds of the universe, as though pent in Gyara and tiny Seriphus; yet, let him once set foot in Babylon that city of brick, and a stone coffin will satisfy his every want: death and death alone betrays the nothingness of men's puny frames, what dwarfs our bodies are.

(Mayor trans. 2: 118)

Alexander's example is recalled in the story in association with David *Alexander* Glencairn. Dewey comments: "Los dos nombres convienen; porque fueron de reyes que gobernaron con un cetro de hierro" (612) [The two names are appropriate because they were those of kings who ruled with scepters of iron]. Going beyond the narrow limits of one's world is rash and dangerous, then, as the new empire-builders discover in the story. The "manifest destiny" that Juvenal speaks of is of being content with one's own lot, with one's own world:

'Nil ergo optabunt homines?' si consilium vis, permittes ipsis expender numinibus, quid conveniat nobis rebusque sit utile nostris.

(10.346–48)

Is nothing then to be sought by our vows? If you wish my counsel, leave the gods themselves to decide what is meet for us, what can promote our welfare.

(Mayor trans. 2: 172)

Dewey's lapsus, then, is linked with his having overreached himself and with the excessive and rash nature of the British adventure in India.

Where does that leave Dewey's interlocutors? Bioy is present here simply as intermediary, as traveler and collector, and of course in light of the theme of the story it is interesting that he should have just returned not from India but from London, that great emporium of objects from the colonies.[28] Borges is there only to correct Dewey's Latin and to record one of his many stories in written form, or so he says. In fact, though, he turns the tables on Dewey, since he reveals himself as the superior Latinist, despite the fact that he was largely self-educated and did not have access to the British tradition of the classical education.[29] Similarly, his pledge not to change Dewey's story by adding "circumstantial details"[30] or cribbing from Kipling gives away his conviction that Dewey is guilty of both offenses.[31]

Dewey tells Borges and Bioy a tale cribbed from Kipling. He was not really ever there (in the sense that his perceptions were so clouded by his preconceptions that he could not see around him), as Borges slyly points out when he corrects the quotation from Juvenal. But even subtler is the implication of the story, which though cribbed from Kipling is most unlike that author's work in its politics.[32] For the story that Dewey relates—or that "Dewey" is used as a mouthpiece to relate—is one that tells of the end of British colonialism in India, as surely as that colonialism ended in the Gandhian campaigns of the 1920s and particularly during the Salt March (see Fischer 274 and Nandy 62–63 on Gandhi's breaking out of the colonial mind).

And though the tale is told through stereotypes ("circumstantial details")—the dutiful British soldier, the sly old Muslim, the tyrannical British officer—the old man's "guile" is not contemptible as so often in Kipling; it is not the justification for colonial rule but the means of undoing that rule. "Quit India," it says in all clarity. The old man may look to Dewey like that "naked fakir" that Churchill saw in Gandhi, but he is the one who is controlling the narrative.

Yet, oddly enough, this move too was anticipated by Kipling. In "On the City Wall," the British narrator addresses his audience after he has been duped by his beloved, the prostitute Lalun, and her friends into rescuing the disguised political prisoner Khem Singh: "Of course you can guess what happened? I was not so clever. When the news went abroad that Khem Singh had escaped from the Fort, I did not, since I was then living this story, not writing it, connect myself, or Lalun, or the fat gentleman of the gold *pince-nez,* with his disappearance" (329). Dewey is less than nothing, though: he neither lives the story nor writes it. He is a witness too dim to see what is happening before his very eyes, too steeped in prejudice to see things for what they are. Yet years later in Buenos Aires he still has an air of superiority about him ("¿qué precisión guardan en Buenos Aires los nombres de Amritsar o de Udh?"), an air quite undeserved as it turns out. For once again, speaking to Borges (who knows quite well the distance from Amritsar to Oudh), he does not know to whom, or about what, he is speaking.

In "On the City Wall," Kipling argues that Indians will never be capable of self-rule (4: 305) and makes fun of British sympathizers with the self-rule movement: "Overmuch tenderness of this kind has bred a strong belief among many natives that the native is capable of administering the country, and many devout Englishmen believe this also, because the theory is stated in beautiful English with all the latest political color" (4: 306). Here the rewriting of the political message in Borges's version is clearest.[33] The stereotypes that Dewey uses to process his experience in India—or his reading of India, if, as I suspect, he was never really there—include notions of Indian spirituality, detachment, and timelessness, and these lead him to accept the authority of the old man in the threshold, at the same time that he convinces himself that the old man is telling him a tale of long ago, of the Mutiny or of the Mogul invasion. That is to say, the old man knows how to use British stereotypes of India against Britain, and at the same time to educate the earnest young British official in the iniquities of British rule. What Josefina Ludmer has called "las tretas del débil" [the snares of the weak] in her essay on Sor Juana Inés de la Cruz describes the process that is happening here.[34]

Of course that same process marks the frame tale. Borges, by correcting Dewey's Latin, does not merely establish himself as the better Latinist. He discredits Dewey as a narrator and more subtly shows that Dewey's "experience" of India is in every way derivative: Dewey was no more in India than Borges or Bioy were, and his Argentine friends at least have the advantage of postcolonial detachment from the British Raj (and perhaps identification up to a certain point with the colonized subjects). The conversation in Buenos Aires restates the one in the uncertain Indian city, and once again Dewey is denied all authority.

One other element of the story that becomes clearer when it is compared with "On the City Wall" is the extent to which Borges has suppressed domesticity. The encounter between the British soldier and the representative of the self-rule movement in the Kipling story is mediated through the prostitute Lalun, her servant Nasiban, and several other characters; indeed the story is cast initially as a love intrigue. In the Borges story all mediation (and in this particular rewriting that means particularly all female mediation) is excluded from the face-to-face encounter between Dewey and the old man. Dewey is distracted by what he assumes is a religious festival going on inside the final patio, just as the narrator of "On the City Wall" is distracted by the love intrigue, but Dewey's distraction is still the stuff of public history, given the extraordinary degree of fusion between the religious and the political in the most dramatic years of what Chatterjee calls "the Gandhian intervention in the politics of the nation" (155).[35]

The contrast with Borges's earlier story/essay of India, **"El acercamiento a Almotásim"** (1936) [**"The Approach to Al-Mutasim"**], is instructive. **"Almotásim"** is assembled out of the same materials as **"El hombre en el umbral"**: readings of Kipling and Burton, of Eastern religious texts (especially here of Farīd od-Dīn 'Attār's *Conference of the Birds*), and of the British press. Yet **"Almotásim"** is a story wholly concerned with Eastern mysticism, whereas **"El hombre en el umbral"** uses the religious elements to make way for the political revelation. One sentence is particularly interesting in **"Almotásim"**:

> Algún inquisidor ha enumerado ciertas analogías de la primera escena de la novela con el relato de Kipling *On the City Wall*; Bahadur las admite, pero alega que sería muy anormal que dos pinturas de la décima noche de muharram no coincidieran.
>
> (418)

> Some inquisitor has enumerated certain analogies between the first scene of the novel and Kipling's story "On the City Wall"; Bahadur recognizes them but alleges that it would be very strange if two portraits of the tenth night of Muharram did not coincide.

"On the City Wall" has a much closer relation to **"El hombre en el umbral"** than to **"Almotásim,"** precisely because of the political intrigue, and indeed **"El hombre en el umbral"** is fashioned as a sort of reply to the Kipling story, a reply in which the subaltern is given voice.

In one sense, though, Borges is already up to the same tricks in 1936 that he uses to greater effect in 1952. He calls attention to the origin of Almotásim's name, which is that of one of the Abbasid caliphs (417), a maneuver that

has the effect of calling attention to Bahadur's own name: Bahadur Shah II ruled Delhi at the time of the Mutiny, while "the Company Bahadur" was the first name used for British "paramountcy" or colonial rule in India (Spear 203–14). Similarly, the reference to the tenth day of Muharram may refer tangentially to the battle of Arcot, fought on that day in 1751, a battle in which the British established themselves over the French as the prime colonial power in India (Mason 27). But the historical references in **"Almotásim,"**, if that is what they are, do not connect with each other in a rich thematic web. Between 1936 and 1952 much happened, both in the development of Borges's ideas about the representation of reality and in that world outside of his fiction: India and Pakistan were independent, Gandhi was dead at the hand of an assassin, and those facts, too, were "parte esencial de la historia."

In "On the City Wall," the Westernized Indian Wali Dad says to the narrator: "India has gossiped for centuries—always standing in the bazars until the soldiers go by. Therefore—you are here today instead of starving in your own country, and I am not a Muhammadan—I am a Product—a Demnition Product. That also I owe to you and yours: that I cannot make an end to my sentence without quoting from your authors" (4: 310–11).[36] Thus, quotation—or interpolation, as Borges calls it in the first paragraph of **"El hombre en el umbral"**—is the mark of colonial language par excellence,[37] and yet consciousness of this vicious habit may be a first step toward breaking out of the colonized mind.

Significantly, Wali Dad, Kipling's Westernized colonial who becomes "converted" back to Islam by the religious and political excitement associated with the particular feast of Muharram when Khem Singh escapes from prison, is described for the last time near the end of the story: "On returning to Lalun's door I stumbled over a man at the threshold. He was sobbing hysterically, and his arms flapped like the wings of a goose. It was Wali Dad, Agnostic and Unbeliever, shoeless, turbanless, and frothing at the mouth, the flesh on his chest bruised and bleeding from the vehemence with which he had smitten himself. A broken torch-handle lay by his side, and his quivering lips murmured, '*Ya Hasan! Ya Hussain*' as I stooped over him" (4: 336). A moment later the narrator sees "a man . . . bending over a corpse" in the square by the mosque (4: 336). When Borges rewrites this story in **"Hombre en el umbral,"** the "man at the threshold"[38] recovers his dignity, and the corpse in the patio is British. He might have said with Wali Dad, "I cannot make an end to my sentence without quoting from your authors,"[39] but the quotation in this case marks the distance from the world of the original.

Notes

1. Cf. Bertrand Russell in 1916: "We in England boast of the *Pax Britannica* which we have imposed, in this way, upon the warring races and religions in India. If we are right in boasting of this, if we have in fact conferred a benefit upon India by enforced

peace, the Germans would be right in boasting if they could impose a *Pax Germannica* upon Europe. Before the war, men might have said that India and Europe are not analogous, because India is less civilized than Europe; but now, I hope, no one would have the effrontery to maintain anything so preposterous" (*Why Men Fight,* 104).

2. I cannot find a published source for this famous quip. Even if it may be apocryphal, Gandhi's attitude toward Western civilization was indeed that it would be a good idea; see Chatterjee's analysis of Gandhi's *Hind Swaraj* (1909), in which Gandhi says that modern civilization is "a civilization only in name" (85ff.). Similarly, in 1920 Gandhi wrote: "By Western civilization I mean the ideals which people in the West have embraced in modern times and the pursuits based on these ideals. The supremacy of brute force, worshipping money as God, spending most of one's time in seeking worldly happiness, breath-taking risks in pursuit of worldly enjoyments of all kinds, the expenditure of limitless mental energy on efforts to multiply the power of machinery, the expenditure of crores on the invention of means of destruction, the moral righteousness which looks down upon people outside Europe,—this civilization, in my view, deserves to be altogether rejected" (Martin Green 5), and in 1924 he wrote: "There is no such thing as Western or European civilization, but there is a modern civilization, which is purely material" (Iyer 293).

3. The eleventh edition of the *Encyclopaedia Britannica,* the one that Borges knew so well, opens with the following dedication: "Dedicated by Permission to His Majesty George the Fifth King of Great Britain and Ireland and of the British Dominions beyond the Seas Emperor of India and to William Howard Taft President of the United States of America" (1: v). The possession of India is here one of the principal attributes of the British king, indeed it is because of India that "king" becomes "emperor," that "kingdom" becomes "empire."

4. Of the many works I consulted on British India, the best account of the British attempts to shape the colonized people is Francis Hutchins's *Illusion of Permanence.*

5. There are many studies of Kipling's representation of India; I have found particularly helpful those by Rao, Moore-Gilbert, and Paffard.

6. Berveiller has already suggested some sort of relation between Kipling's struggle for an English identity and Borges's own situation when, after commenting on Conrad's internationalism, he says that Borges associates his own case with that of "the Eurasian Rudyard Kipling, for Kipling, having being born an Anglo-Indian in Bombay, therefore wanted to be all the more English [and] was devoted to Englishness. Did not [Borges's] own Argentineness

proceed from comparable circumstances?" (271). The problem of Borges's relation to British culture is, however, strangely out of focus in Berveiller's discussion.

7. The narrator is unnamed but seems to be Borges by virtue of his friendship with Bioy and his interest in Kipling and in things British.

8. Another account that makes Nicholson sound almost like a model for Kurtz in *Heart of Darkness* is given by Michael Edwardes in *Red Year.* In addition to further details about the native "worship" of the god "Nikalseyn" (especially 49–50), he gives the text of a song on Nicholson's death (179–80) and a theory on Nicholson's latent homosexuality (see especially 237, note on the "sexuality of imperialism").

9. Collier (246–64) gives quite a full account of Nicholson's last weeks, presenting Nicholson as a larger-than-life hero. See especially his account of Nicholson's charge on the Lahore Gate of Delhi: "All his life he had subdued both mind and body to his iron will; now it was inconceivable he could not spur other men on the path to glory. His mighty frame fought through the press, until he towered at their head. Eyes blazing, he turned to face them" (261). Hibbert is much more critical of Nicholson's actions at Delhi, which he presents as rash and irresponsible (301–9). A heroic painting of the storming of Delhi by W. S. Morgan shows Nicholson urging his men on with sword upraised (Edwardes 45).

10. For examples of the excruciating tortures that were actually applied, see Majumdar 9: 591–602.

11. Nicholson is shown without the beard in Edwardes, *Red Year* 48. A more heroic image (with beard) is given in Edwardes, *Battles of the Indian Mutiny* 21.

12. The spelling of Nicholson's nickname in the Borges story matches Kipling's (Nikal Seyn) and not the encyclopedia's (Nikalsain), thus suggesting that Kipling is the more important source here. However, Kipling gives little of Nicholson's story and indeed was reproached by his contemporaries for not writing directly on the Mutiny (Rao 16). His passing reference to Nicholson in *Kim* depends on his readers (including Borges) knowing much more about Nicholson, and about the Mutiny of 1857, than is told.

13. The reference to Oudh in the story is fully as interesting as that to Amritsar, though I pursue the latter in greater detail here. At the time of the Mutiny, Oudh (or Avadh) was as important a center of unrest as the Punjab, and there were great battles between the insurgent and colonial armies for possession of Lucknow (see Edwardes, *Battles of the Indian Mutiny* 57–149; Hibbert 216–66, 347–66; and Majumdar 9: 536–48, 636–37). During the twentieth-century struggle for independence, Oudh

did not take as central a role as it had during the Mutiny, partly due to the cozy relationship between the British and the Nizam of Oudh; see, however, Shahid Amin on Gandhi's activities in the Gorakhpur district of eastern Uttar Pradesh in 1921–22. If Borges's intention, then, is to find a city or region that played an important role in both the Mutiny and the struggle for independence, Amritsar is a much more appropriate choice than Oudh.

14. See Sylvia Molloy's comments on another of these narrative disjunctions, the information in the story that the literature of Uqbar "never referred to reality, but instead to the two imaginary regions of Mlejnas or Tlön" (432): "The story is guided by a description of *one* of the two imaginary regions, brought out of a literature in which they serve, in turn, as referents. Mlejnas is cast aside, already without force in the text" (*Letras* 170). The same technique is used at the opening of "Tema del traidor y del héroe" ["Theme of the Traitor and of the Hero"]: "La acción transcurre en un país oprimido y tenaz: Polonia, Irlanda, la república de Venecia, algún estado sudamericano o balcánico. . . . Digamos (para comodidad narrativa) Irlanda; digamos 1824" (496) [The action takes place in a stubborn, oppressed country: Poland, Ireland, the republic of Venice, some South American or Balkan state. . . . Let's say (for narrative convenience) Ireland; let's say 1824].

15. Cf. Suleri: "An astonishing development in the narratives of Anglo-India is the rapidity with which the British understanding of the dynamics of Indian civilization atrophied into a static and mistrustful interpretation of India as a locus of all things ancient, a backdrop against which the colonizing presence could not but be startled by its own novelty" (33).

16. On the importance of stereotypes to colonialist discourse, see Bhabha, "The Other Question." Bhabha considers such stereotypes in light of Freudian ideas on fetishism.

17. For further details, see Fischer 179–84 and Dodwell, *Indian Empire* 765–70. One odd note: though Fischer says that the Amritsar massacre was a "turning point" in Gandhi's political development, Gandhi's own writings in 1919 mention it only tangentially, since Gandhi was preoccupied at the time with lapses from the discipline of nonviolence by demonstrators in Ahmedabad. One of Gandhi's few references at the time to the massacre at Amritsar is in a letter to J. L. Massey, dated 14 April 1919: "Though the events at Amritsar are, so far as I can see, unconnected with satyagraha and my arrest, I feel sure that had I been able to proceed to these places [Delhi, Amritsar, and Lahore], the awful occurrences could have been avoided" (219).

18. Amritsar is also mentioned in Kipling's "Miss Youghal's Sais" (in a volume of stories often mentioned by Borges, *Plain Tales from the Hills*) as the site of one of the first adventures of Detective Strickland: "His crowning achievement was spending eleven days as a *faquir* or priest in the gardens of Baba Atal at Amritsar, and there picking up the threads of the great Nasiban Murder Case" (32).

19. This notion of a law distinct from and more powerful than British colonial law seems to derive here, oddly enough, from Kipling, particularly from the *Jungle Books*. See Noel Annan's essay, "Kipling's Place in the History of Ideas," in Rutherford, *Kipling's Mind and Art,* for a discussion of Kipling's concept of law (especially 109).

20. Note that the Punjab was partitioned between India and Pakistan when self-rule came, and that its place in postcolonial India is still a contested one, as witnessed by the frequent clashes over the issue of Sikh independence or autonomy. The "unity" the story speaks of is purely a matter of historical conjuncture, of opposition to the British Raj when it manifested itself in particularly cruel ways.

21. Cf. Suleri on the lama in *Kim:* "The sale of information and the economy of colonial knowledge . . . is by no means beyond the ken of the 'otherworldly' lama. He not only understands the structure of oppression, but furthermore has an intuitive knowledge of the price that very literally accompanies such a reality" (122).

22. Interestingly enough, Borges's single reference to Gandhi in the *Obras completas* places Gandhi and Chaplin in close proximity: "¿Quién iba a atreverse a ignorar que Charlie Chaplin es uno de los dioses más seguros de la mitología de nuestro tiempo, un colega de las inmóviles pesadillas de Chirico, de las fervientes ametralladoras de Scarface Al, del universo finito aunque ilimitado, de las espaldas cenitales de Greta Garbo, de los tapiados ojos de Gandhi?" (222) [Who dares ignore that Charlie Chaplin is one of the most secure gods in the mythology of our time, a colleague of the motionless nightmares of Chirico, of the fervent machine guns of Scarface Al, of the finite but limitless universe of the zenithal back of Greta Garbo, of Gandhi's covered eyes?]. Louis Fischer's biography includes a photograph of a meeting between Gandhi and Chaplin (276).

23. Nandy studies the same "newly created sense of linear history in Hinduism" (26) in the thought of Swami Dayanand Saraswati and Swami Vivekananda (both active in the late nineteenth century).

24. Chatterjee gives a wonderful account of Nehru's problems in getting used to these mythic formulations (146–57).

25. Besides the review of Chaplin's *City Lights,* there are a few other passing references to Gandhi's life

and thought in Borges's works (see Balderston, *Literary Universe,* 58), none of them very profound. However, it would have been impossible for Borges and Bioy to be altogether immune to Gandhian influences, because Victoria Ocampo considered herself a Gandhian, published articles in *Sur* and elsewhere on India, and sponsored visits to Buenos Aires by Rabindranath Tagore, Lanza del Vasto, and others associated with the Gandhian movement (see King 34, 60, 103, 138, 179, 197). Borges gives his own impression of Tagore in a funny note in *El Hogar,* which opens: "Hace trece años tuve el honor un poco terrible de conversar con el venerado y melifluo Rabindranath Tagore" (*Textos cautivos,* 139–40) [Thirteen years ago I had the rather terrible honor of conversing with the venerated and mellifluous Rabindranath Tagore].

26. In chapter 1 I mentioned that the same phrase is used to describe the old gaucho in "El Sur." Thus, in the broader outlines of Borges's work, the question posed by "El hombre en el umbral" is not only the conflict between East and West but one between traditional (eternal, ageless) cultures and historical ones, and he sees Argentina as also caught up in this conflict. But, as noted before, the same sentence, when inscribed in a different context, can mean quite different things, a lesson we learned from Pierre Menard.

27. Once again, here is Chatterjee: "To Gandhi, then, truth did not lie in history, nor did science have any privileged access to it. Truth was moral: unified, unchanging and transcendental. It was not an object of critical inquiry or philosophical speculation. It could only be found in the experience of one's life, by the unflinching practice of moral living" (97).

28. There is perhaps a hint of envy on the narrator's part for Bioy, who had the means in the 1940s and 1950s to travel, which Borges did not, and perhaps also a note of condescension for Bioy, who has gone all the way to London to bring back that most *criollo* and most *borgeano* of objects, a dagger! Bioy insisted, by the way, in a conversation in July 1991 that he never bought a dagger in London or anywhere else and says that the whole story, and Christopher Dewey himself, were invented by Borges. I have not been able to confirm Dewey's existence or career by other means; the British Council in London could not grant access to personnel records in April 1991, and later in the same year the British Council in Buenos Aires was still putting its records in order after the renewal of relations between Britain and Argentina.

29. Borges began studying Latin at the Collège Calvin in Geneva ("Autobiographical Essay," 214) and later continued with a priest in Majorca (Jurado, 33).

30. For a full discussion of this technique, see Balderston, *El precursor velado* 29–41.

31. Kushigian fails to note the irony of this statement, calling the use of details and local color "two unforgivable offences, personally odious to Borges" (36). Molloy's comments are more to the point: "It should be clarified that the story he reconstructs does not disdain either the brief circumstantial detail or interpolation. The paradoxical invocation names two techniques frequently employed by Borges: perhaps those that provide him—as writer or as reader—the greatest pleasure" (*Letras,* 171).

32. There is a large and important body of criticism that explores the subtleties and contradictions of Kipling's attitudes toward the empire, including essays by Edmund Wilson and George Orwell in Rutherford, *Kipling's Mind and Art,* and Rao, *Rudyard Kipling's India.* I do not wish to oversimplify the issues involved in the debates here, but clearly Kipling, even in his more critical moments, was still an apologist for the empire.

33. Note Borges's reservations about Kipling's ethical stance even in this comment on *Kim:* "Kipling inventa un Amiguito del Mundo Entero, el libérrimo Kim: a los pocos capítulos, urgido por no sé qué patriótica perversión, le da el horrible oficio de espía. (En su autobiografía literaria, redactada treinta y cinco años después, Kipling se muestra impenitente y aun inconsciente.)" (733) [Kipling invents a little Friend of All the World, the free spirit Kim; a few chapters later, spurred on by I know not what patriotic perversion, he gives him the horrid profession of spy. (In his literary autobiography, written thirty-five years later, Kipling reveals himself to be unrepentant and even unconscious)]. But compare with this later remark from the *Introducción a la literatura inglesa:* "Cuentista, novelista y poeta, Rudyard Kipling (1865–1936) se impuso la tarea de revelar a sus distraídos compatriotas la existencia del dilatado Imperio Británico. Esta misión tiene la culpa de que muchos lo juzgaron, y aún lo juzgan, por sus opiniones políticas, no por su genial labor literaria" (*Obras completas en colaboración* 846) [Short-story writer, novelist, and poet, Rudyard Kipling (1865–1936) set himself the task of revealing to his distracted compatriots the existence of the vast British Empire. This mission has the drawback that many people judged him, and judge him even today, for his political opinions, not for his brilliant literary work]. Note that in the earlier comment, Borges does not rigidly separate aesthetic from political judgments. For Kipling's unrepentant backward view, see *Something of Myself* (e.g., 45, 212).

34. Ludmer is perhaps overly optimistic about the possibilities of communication by the oppressed in a colonial society, and it should be remembered that in the last years of her life Sor Juana sold her library and stopped writing. On a similar limit-situation, see Gayatri Chakravorty Spivak, "Can the Subaltern Speak?" (on widow-sacrifice). Another useful reflection on these issues is R. Radhakrishnan's "Negotiating Subject Positions in

an Uneven World." My debt to Radhakrishnan is considerable, since the argument of this chapter came to me during the presentation of his 1989 Modern Language Association paper on Gandhi and Nehru (now published as "Nationalism, Gender, and the Narrative of Identity").

35. Cf. Nehru: "I used to be troubled sometimes at the growth of this religious element in our politics. . . . I did not like it at all" (qtd. in Chatterjee 151).

36. Sandra Kemp says of Wali Dad that he "speaks and writes in the English tradition but cannot 'live' in it" (22). The phrase that Wali Dad is marking as a quotation from an English author, "Demnition Product," is not actually an exact quotation but a new phrase invented on the abundant models provided by Dickens in *Nicholas Nickleby* for use of the American slang term "demnition" for "damned," "damn," and "damnation." In the Dickens novel, the character Mr. Mantalini, who had changed his surname from the original Muntle in an attempt to make a successful name for himself as a London dressmaker (106–7), uses the words "demd" and "demnition" at least once in almost every sentence he speaks. See, for instance, his use of "demnition miserable" (176), "demnition discount" (365), "the demnition gold and silver" (365), "the same little engrossing demnition captivater" (368), and "demnition sweetness!" (494). In his final appearance in the novel, having "gone to the dogs," he says of himself: "It is all up with its handsome friend! He has gone to the demnition bow-wows" (703). What is interesting in Wali Dad's use of the term is his creative application of Mantalini's word to himself as the Product of a colonial establishment, thus emphasizing the links between a dependent economy and a psychocultural condition.

37. Borges's own contribution to the notion of "postcolonial discourse" is most notable in his 1950 speech "El escritor argentino y la tradición" [The Argentine Writer and Tradition], included in later editions of *Discusión*. For a discussion of the uncanny parallels between this Borges essay and an essay from the 1870s by Machado de Assis, "Instinto de nacionalidade" ["The Instinct of Nationality"], see Davi Arrigucci. At a conference on Borges at Pennsylvania State University in April 1991, Edna Aizenberg gave a fascinating paper on the appropriation of certain ideas and techniques from Borges in various African and Middle Eastern postcolonial writers; her study of this topic is forthcoming.

38. Another sense of this phrase is given by Kipling's sister, in her memoir of being left with her brother as boarders in England: they felt, she says, "almost as much as on a doorstep" (qtd. in Nandy 66). This phrase reminds us of another context in which people find themselves on thresholds: as foundlings. Note the various displacements suffered in the notion of being "on a threshold" or "in a doorstep."

Freud significantly called this sense of estrangement a "liminal state"; see Homi Bhabha, "DissemiNation," for a discussion of how "discursive liminality" is characteristic of modern notions of "writing the nation" (295–97).

39. Compare Borges to Irby (and many other similar declarations in other interviews): "Todo lo que yo he hecho está en Poe, Stevenson, Wells, Chesterton y algún otros" (*Encuentro con Borges*, 37–38) [Everything I have done is already in Poe, Stevenson, Wells, Chesterton, and some others]. Chatterjee notes the same concern with imitation in the early Bengali nationalist Bankimchandra Chattopadhyay, who wrote: "One cannot learn except by imitation. Just as children learn to speak by imitating the speech of adults, to act by imitating the actions of adults, so do uncivilised and uneducated people learn by imitating the ways of the civilised and the educated. Thus it is reasonable and rational that Bengalis should imitate the English" (qtd. in Chatterjee 65). Gandhi also acknowledges the impact of the West, but his analysis does not stop where Chattopadhyay's does: "Everyone of the Indians who has achieved anything worth mentioning in any direction is the fruit, directly or indirectly, of western education. At the same time, whatever reaction for the better he may have had upon the people at large was due to the extent of his eastern culture" (qtd. in Nandy, 75).

Works Cited

Chatterjee, Partha. *Nationalist Thought and the Colonial World: A Derivative Discourse?* London: Zed Press, 1986.

Dodwell, H. H., ed. *The Indian Empire, 1858–1918, with Additional Chapters, 1919–1969. The Cambridge History of India*, vol. 6. Delhi: S. Chand 1969.

Fischer, Louis. *The Life of Mahatma Gandhi.* New York: Harper and Brothers, 1950.

Griffiths, Percival. *Modern India.* 4th ed. New York: F. A. Praeger, 1965.

Hutchins, Francis G. *The Illusion of Permanence: British Imperialism in India.* Princeton: Princeton University Press, 1967.

Kipling, Rudyard. *Kim: The Writings in Prose and Verse of Rudyard Kipling,* vol. 4, New York: Charles Scribner's Sons, 1920.

———. "On the City Wall." *In Black and White. The writing in Prose and Verse of Rudyard Kipling,* vol. 4. New York: Charles Scribner's Sons, 1920. 302–39.

Ludmer, Josefina. *El genero gauchesco: Un tratado sobre la patria.* Buenos Aires: Editorial Sudamericana, 1988.

Majumdar, R. C., ed. *British Paramountcy and Indian Renaissance. The History and Culture of the Indian People,* vols. 9–10. Bombay: Bharatiya Vidhya Bhavan, 1963–65.

Mason, Philip. *The Men Who Ruled India.* New York: W.W. Norton, 1985.

Nandy, Ashis. *The Intimate Enemy: Loss and Recovery of Self Under Colonialism.* Delhi: Oxford University Press, 1983.

Orwell, George. "Reflections on Gandhi." *In Front of Your Nose, 1945–1950. The Collected Essays, Journalism, and Letters of George Orwell,* vol. 4. Ed. Sonia Orwell and Ian Angus. New York: Harcourt, Brace and World, 1968. 463–70.

Spear, Percival. *India: A Modern History.* Ann Arbor: University of Michigan Press, 1972.

Jose Eduardo Gonzalez (essay date 1994)

SOURCE: "Borges 'The Draped Mirrors,'" in *The Explicator,* Vol. 52, No. 3, Spring, 1994, pp. 175–76.

[*In the following note on "The Draped Mirrors," Gonzalez describes how Borges uses the concept of narcissism.*]

Critics have associated Borges's use of mirrors in his short stories with ideas of representation and repetition.[1] Although the problematic relationship between mimesis and literature is a central element of Borges's aesthetics, the symbol of the mirror can also be given a different interpretation, one that is too often ignored: In some borgesian texts, mirrors can also be said to symbolize narcissism. In **"The Draped Mirrors,"**[2] for example, Borges uses the Narcissus myth as a subtext for his story. But Borges does not merely rewrite the Greek story using contemporary characters, he also distorts the original story and transforms it into an entirely different one. The final result, as we will see, is a new interpretation of narcissism.

In Ovid's classical rendition of the myth,[3] Echo, a nymph, falls in love with Narcissus, only to be treated with indifference by him. She dies and disappears, and all that remains of her is her voice. Finally, Narcissus looks at himself in the waters of a pool and falls in love with his own image. Borges realizes a double inversion of the myth: the actions of the main characters in his story are similar to those of Echo and Narcissus, but the results are completely different. More important, the whole structure of the story has been reversed. Thus, at the beginning of **"The Draped Mirrors,"** Borges (Narcissus) looks into a mirror, but instead of falling in love with himself, he is afraid of his own image.[4] In what is obviously an inversion of Echo's story, Julia is introduced "as a nameless, faceless voice," and later on she, or her body, "appears."[5] This time the two protagonists are at first indifferent to each other ("There was no love between us, or even pretense of love" [27]); at the end, instead of love for Borges/Narcissus, Julia feels hatred. In Borges's version of the myth, it is not Narcissus who becomes insane but Echo, and her insanity is also related to mirrors: "Now, I have just learned that she has lost her mind and that the mirrors in her room are

draped because she sees in them my reflection, usurping her own. . . . This odious fate reserved for my features must perforce make me odious too, but I no longer care" (27–8). Here Borges's idea of narcissism is even more destructive than the traditional one: even though in the story "Borges" does not love his own image, he steals other people's images and substitutes his for theirs.[6]

In many other stories, Borges repudiates mirrors simply because of their ability to reproduce reality. But in **"The Draped Mirrors,"** the dislike of mirrors is also explained as a precondition for narcissism, for once the narrator has recognized that his image is repulsive, he can only be narcissistic if he is no longer able to look at himself in a mirror.

Notes

1. See, for example, Jaime Alazraki, *Versiones, Inversiones, Reversiones: el espejo como modelo estructural del relato de Borges* (Madrid: Gredos, 1977) and Paul de Man, "A Modern Master," *Critical Essays on Jorge Luis Borges,* ed. Jaime Alazraki (Boston: G. K. Hall, 1987) 55–62.

2. Jorge Luis Borges, *Dreamtigers* (Austin: U of Texas P, 1964) 27–28.

3. Ovid, *The Metamorphoses* (Baltimore: Penguin, 1986) 83–87.

4. According to Rodríguez Monegal, Borges's fear of mirrors can be traced to his childhood. In his biography of Borges, Rodríguez Monegal also presents a psychoanalytical interpretation of the symbol of the mirror in Borges's texts. See Emir Rodríguez Monegal, *Jorge Luis Borges. A Literary Biography* (New York: Paragon, 1978) 30–33.

5. Borges seems to be alluding to Ovid's narration of the Echo myth, which begins with the sentence, "She still had a body then, she was not just a voice" (Ovid 83, note 3 above).

6. The critic Juan Manuel Marcos has linked this idea of narcissim to Borges's modernist will-to-style. He argues that Borges's "stylistic narcissism" is so powerful that the only voice that we hear in Borges's short stories is his voice. Borges does not provide his characters with individual voices. It does not matter whether it is an old poor man in India or an illiterate gaucho in Argentina, they all speak like Borges; in other words, they have been deprived of their image. See Juan Manuel Marcos, rev. of *Critical Essays on Jorge Luis Borges,* ed. Jaime Alazraki, *Revista Iberoamericana.* 140 (1987): 707.

Michael Wreen (essay date 1995)

SOURCE: "Don Quixote Rides Again!" in *Romanic Review,* Vol. 86, No. 1, January, 1995, pp. 141–63.

[*In the following essay, Wreen presents a philosophical argument for reading Borges's story "Pierre Menard, Author of the Quixote" as a version of* Don Quixote.]

In a recent article, "Once Is Not Enough?", I argued that a book word-for-word identical with Cervantes' *Quixote* wouldn't be a new *Quixote,* numerically distinct from Cervantes', if it were produced in the manner described in Borges' short story **"Pierre Menard, Author of the Quixote."** Menard's novel would simply be Cervantes', I tried to show, although admittedly produced in a very odd way. But philosophical issues (such as the individuation of works of art) are one thing, literary interpretation quite another. In this paper I'll be offering a comprehensive interpretation of Borges' story and arguing, against a number of critics,[1] that **"Pierre Menard"** is philosophically correct, i.e., that the correct interpretation of Borges' story doesn't have Menard as the author of a new *Quixote.* Even more importantly, I'll be arguing that the story is an extremely penetrating one, with philosophical depths as yet unexplored, although its main interest, metaphysical and otherwise, lies in a direction other than the individuation of works of art. These being my main theses, let me also issue an advance warning that my approach is itself more than a little philosophical.

I

Given my purely philosophical examination of the duplicate *Quixote* case, the most direct way to approach Borges' story would be to ask, Why on earth would anyone ever reproduce Cervantes' novel in the way that Menard does? But the more indirect route, and the one I'll be traveling here, is to marshal evidence bit by textual bit, all the while proceeding with the aim of constructing a unified and comprehensive interpretation. That methodology begs no critical questions, as the first one evidently does.

Structurally, **"Pierre Menard"** has three parts. In the first, the setting, dramatic voice, and mode of narration are established; the main character, Pierre Menard, is introduced; the prevailing tone is set; and a number of themes are broached. The story is cast in the form of an elaborate literary obituary and memoir written by an unnamed friend and admirer of Menard. Supposedly, it's an official, formal assessment and appreciation of the great man, an intellectual and a figure of stupendous, even revolutionary, but unfortunately unknown, literary achievement. Superficially, the piece resembles the sort of literary honorarium found not so much in professional journals as in the self-appointed flagships of high art, i.e., in literary magazines with pretensions to high culture. We soon discover, however, that the narrator's assessment may be somewhat biased and skewed — that he may be, in other words, an unreliable narrator. His first few sentences show him to be patronizing and bullying, and within two paragraphs his political conservatism, hauteur, and condescending attitude toward any and all who don't share his convictions are made evident. After first taking an altogether gratuitous snipe at Protestants and Masons, he proceeds to name-drop a title or two, in order, he says, to establish his authority to write an assessment of Menard and his oeuvre, but actually to call attention to himself and his aristocratic connections. Moreover, his prose style is pretentious, bom-

bastic, and affected, and smacks more than a little of the fourth-rate symbolist:

> One might say that only yesterday we gathered before his [Menard's] final monument, amidst the lugubrious cypresses, and already Error tries to tarnish his Memory. . . . Decidedly, a brief rectification is unavoidable.
>
> (Borges 36)

Clearly, this is not an assessment to be trusted. But even more clearly, and even more importantly, this is fiction, not nonfiction, despite the obituary/literary-memoir format. No piece of nonfiction would ever be as blatantly prejudiced, arrogant, or inflated as **"Pierre Menard."** Moreover, given only what has been said so far, it's quite probably a parody of a certain kind of *littérateur* and literary document, and quite probably a story whose prevailing tone is ironic. If that is so, what we should be on the lookout for is exactly the opposite of what we see glittering brightly on the surface. In fact if that's the case, if we don't look any farther than the surface, we're liable to miss what the story is really all about. Taking the story to be an argument for the numerical distinctness of Menard's *Quixote* would be to be blind to the story's pervasive irony, in particular that regarding Menard's creative activity.

II

Part one of the story concludes with a slightly annotated list of Menard's "visible" work. From the list we learn that Menard is a very minor symbolist poet and an intellectual with a number of disparate, narrow, and highly idiosyncratic interests. Menard has published a sonnet and written a sonnet cycle "for the Baroness de Bacourt," and has done extensive work in literary theory and criticism. In addition to writing "an invective against Paul Valéry," an invective which expresses "the exact opposite of his true opinion of Valéry," he has

> written a monograph on the possibility of constructing a poetic vocabulary of concepts which would not be synonyms or periphrases of those which make up our everyday language, "but rather ideal objects created according to convention and essentially designed to satisfy poetic needs."
>
> (37)

He's also examined the "essential metric laws of French prose," as well as replied to "Luc Durtain (who denied the existence of such laws), [using] examples [culled] from Luc Durtain['s own work]." His other achievements include having fashioned a "determined analysis of the 'syntactical customs' of Toulet," having translated Quevedo's *Aguja de navegar cultos* and Ruy Lopez's book on chess, *Libro de la invención liberal y arte del juego del axedrez,* and having transposed the maligned Valéry's *Le Cimetire marin* into alexandrines. But various obscure corners of philosophy were also peeking places for Menard. He composed work sheets for a monograph on George Boole's symbolic logic, and wrote "a monograph on 'certain connections or affinities' between the thought of Descartes, Leibniz and John Wilkins," a monograph on Leibniz's *Characteristica universalis,* a monograph on Raymond Lully's *Ars magna generis,* and a book, *Les problémes d'un probléme,* on the different solutions to the problem of Achilles and the tortoise. Rounding out the list of Menard's "visible" achievements are a number of other odd items: "a technical article on the possibility of improving the game of chess [by] eliminating one of the rook's pawns," an article in which Menard "proposes, recommends, discusses, and finally rejects the innovation"; "a preface to the Catalogue of an exposition of lithographs by Carolus Hourcade"; "a 'definition' of the Countess de Bagnoregio, in the "'victorious volume' . . . published annually by this lady to rectify the inevitable falsifications of journalists'"; and "a manuscript list of verses which owe their efficacy to their punctuation" (37–38).

The picture drawn here is both consistent and complete: Menard is a *précieux,* a turn-of-the-century decadent, a symbolist, and a snobbish cultivator of social connections. So far, then, he's a man rather like the narrator. But he's a decadent and symbolist of a rather more complex sort than the narrator, since he's also a poet and a very peculiar and desiccated academic as well. Moreover, while academics and poets are known for their eccentricities and narrow and peculiar interests, Menard's quantitative differences from other poets and academics in these respects make for a qualitative difference. For the list is little more than an extended catalogue of arrant academic twaddle, of intellectual pettiness without a point. It thus shows that Menard, unlike other poets and academics, has completely lost sight of what is truly important and interesting about poetry and intellectual matters, and thus lost contact with the real world, the world that gives poetry and academic matters their value in the first place. His, instead, is an autotelic universe, a universe circumscribed and defined by interests fabricated by his own exhausted intellect. His vitality, as a real man and a thinker, has diminished to the point that his studies are well-nigh useless, and he himself simply a curious life form, culturally speaking. No wonder Borges said that the list is "a diagram of [Menard's] mental history"[2] and thus that "il y a chez lui [Menard] un sens de l'inutilité de la littérature."[3] The theme that Barrenechea finds in so many of Borges' works, that of the writer as noncreative (46), is present in **"Pierre Menard"** from the start, in both the narrator's introduction and the catalogue of Menard's "achievements."

III

The second part of the story is a description and explanation of what the narrator regards as far and away Menard's greatest accomplishment, invisible though it may be. "I turn now," he says, "to [Menard's] other work: the subterranean, the interminably heroic, the peerless. And—such are the capacities of man!—the unfinished" (38). Yes, such are the capacities of man that men don't finish their work. But small ironies such as this aside, what is perhaps the "most significant [work] of our time," the narrator tells us,

"consists of the ninth and thirty-eighth chapters of the first part of *Don Quixote* and a fragment of chapter twenty-two" (39). Menard has written a *Quixote,* or at least part of a *Quixote,* that is word-for-word identical with Cervantes' but not identical with Cervantes'. To say as much is to affirm an absurdity, the narrator admits, but Menard is capable of the absurd, capable of achieving the impossible.

Here, for the first time, another major theme is introduced, that of literary creation as necessarily an impossible task, a theme consistent with but stronger than the uselessness of literature. In addition, one of the themes hinted at earlier, the logical inseparability of the man of letters—whether reader or writer—from the literary work—whether fictional or nonfictional—is explicitly drawn out and underscored. For since Menard symbolizes the man of letters, literature and *littérateur* fuse in Borges' story: the man, Menard, has no more reality than the performance of the literary task. Indeed, he lives within the task, Borges tells us, since he lives within books alone. The written word eventually makes those who live by it part of it, Borges seems to say—probably not a little a propos of himself. As I'll try to show below in section XII, even this strong thesis will eventually need strengthening.

Menard was inspired by two very different sources to undertake his "impossible" task: a "philological fragment by Novalis [whoever he might be, if anyone at all] . . . which outlines the theme of total identification with a given author, [and] . . . one of those parasitic books which situate Christ on a boulevard, Hamlet on La Canebire or Don Quixote on Wall Street" (39). Literature draws upon literature, both in Novalis and in the parasitic book, and thus the theme of the autotelic nature of literature and the literary life, here again represented by Menard, is reinforced. Menard's life—literature's life—is not only essentially parasitic upon the extraliterary world; at its worst, in the terminal stages of its inevitable decline, it is parasitic upon itself, unable to draw inspiration from anything other than itself. The result is an anemic and decadent literature, both uninspired and uninspiring. In the case of Menard, in fact, the disease has spread even further: he was "inspired" by two pieces of literature, one a fragment of an essay, one probably a novel, which are themselves already parasitic pieces of literature, dependent for their existence on the prior existence of literature in general (the essay fragment) and specific literary works (the novel). Menard's undertaking, to replicate—"duplicate" would be more accurate—an already existent literary work, the *Quixote,* was itself inspired by two pieces of literature already parasitic on literature. Hence once again, but at a new level, the theme of the autotelic nature of literature—or, what is the same thing, Menard's autotelic world and the autotelic nature of his mind. But hence also a new thesis: this is a world in which, in the long run, the distinction between author and fictional character is only a nominal distinction, only a distinction of words—which, of course, is the only kind of distinction there *could* be in such a world.

IV

Following a statement of Menard's intended project, the narrator lets Menard speak for himself, quoting a letter he supposedly wrote him. "'My intent is no more than astonishing,'" Menard wrote, "'The final term in a theological or metaphysical demonstration—the objective world, God, causality, the forms of the universe—is no less previous and common than my famed novel. The only difference is that the philosophers publish their intermediary stages of their labor in pleasant volumes and I have resolved to do away with those stages.' In truth," as the narrator says, continuing the story where Menard left off, "not one worksheet remains to bear witness to his years of effort" (39).

This is parody once again, only this time concerning the inflated self-images of *artistes* and assorted defenders of the intellectual realm. It's also a send-up of the sort of Manifesto of Grand Artistic Purpose that self-righteous guardians of high culture are usually only too glad to issue. "Manifesto of Grand Delusion" would be more accurate in most cases, though, but especially apt in this one, because the parody and irony here are particularly pointed: whether he knows it or not, Menard's "famed novel" is famed for no other reason than that it *is* Cervantes'. I say this because (1) to intend to produce a novel word-for-word identical with one that already exists; (2) to use word-for-word identity with it as the standard for completion of your task; and (3) to rely, as Menard evidently did, on his memory of that novel in producing his text—for not only had he read Cervantes' book (admittedly, many years past), he had to look at Cervantes' text in order to make sure that his 'rough drafts' were indeed rough drafts (that is, not word-for-word identical with the relevant parts of Cervantes') and thus undoubtedly re-approached his job with some memory of Cervantes' text in mind—to do all of that is just to reproduce Cervantes' text in a very roundabout, strange way. Given the context, then, the irony is more pointed than a mere parody of the sort of person or document in question would otherwise be. Menard is a ridiculous figure not only because of his inflated self-image, self-congratulatory and self-satisfied manner, and pompous prose posing, but because his studious seriousness is put in the service of a *logically* impossible task. Again, this is the theme of literary creation as an impossible task, but again there is an enrichment: here the task really is literally impossible.

That, of course, didn't deter Menard. Various plans to accomplish his objective occurred to him. Rejected as too easy was to "know Spanish well, recover the Catholic faith, fight against the Moors or the Turk, forget the history of Europe between the years 1602 and 1918, *be* Miguel de Cervantes" (40). But since doing that is logically impossible, Menard's proposed *modus operandi* is, with an irony that is perhaps too heavy, hardly too easy: being numerically distinct people is logically impossible, just as squaring the circle, or writing a *Quixote* numerically distinct from Cervantes' while exactly duplicating

the book, intending to so duplicate it, and checking your production for accuracy against it is. This, however, the unnamed narrator readily admits: "[But being Cervantes is] impossible! my reader will say. Granted, but the undertaking was impossible from the very beginning and of all the impossible ways of carrying it out, this was the least interesting" (40). That the method and task itself are impossible is conceded by the narrator, but being the spiritual kin of Menard, he rejects the plan because it's not interesting, not because it's not possible. *That* is the sort of solipsistic and autotelic universe that the narrator and Menard inhabit.

V

The plan that Menard decided upon was "to go on being Pierre Menard and to reach the *Quixote* through the experiences of Pierre Menard." "'My undertaking is not difficult, essentially,'" Menard wrote to the narrator. "'I should only have to be immortal to carry it out'" (40). But this self-absorbed posturing conceals yet another contradiction. Since it's impossible—physically, not logically this time—to be immortal, the "undertaking" is just the opposite of "essentially easy," and Menard, like the narrator, is anything but rational for brushing aside the contradiction as of little moment. Besides, it's not at all clear that immortality would guarantee completion of the task. If the task is logically impossible (given Menard's methods), then eternity guarantees only never-ending frustration.

The narrator is not essentially different from Menard. He shares his delusions of literary grandeur, and prefers specious but personally satisfying rationalization to common sense. Again like Menard, he prefers a world of pleasant literary fantasies to one of cold literary—and literal—facts. "Some nights past," he says,

> while leafing through chapter XXVI [of the *Quixote*]—never essayed by him—I recognized our friend's style and something of his voice in this exceptional phrase: "the river nymphs and the dolorous and humid Echo." This happy conjunction of a spiritual and a physical adjective brought to my mind a verse by Shakespeare which we discussed one afternoon: "Where a malignant and turbaned Turk . . ."
>
> (40)

But to interpret passages not written by someone as if they were and to delight in the thoughts and emotions thereby evoked is to abandon hard, cold reality—including the hard, cold reality of literary interpretation—for a dream world of delicious delusions, and to do so, in this case, in an especially bizarre and fatuous fashion. For what the narrator is implicitly doing here is attributing a style to Menard and then reading Cervantes against the backdrop of that style. He is, in other words, reading Cervantes as a logically posterior writer and stylist. Philosophically speaking, this is worse than interpretation turned inside out. There is no logically independent style of Menard that can act as a backdrop, because no logically independent work of his exists. The only work there is is Cervantes'. Hence it is logically impossible to read Cervantes the way the narrator does, much less to savor, as he evidently does, that reading. Cervantes is not the logically posterior writer because there isn't, and couldn't be, any logically anterior one.

Icing for the cake here, adding to the perversity of the narrator's delight, is his aesthetic insensitivity. To quote Shakespeare's line "Where a malignant and turbaned Turk . . ." with approval is to love The Bard not wisely but too well. The line is undoubtedly one of the thousand that Jonson would have blotted, for the conjunction of the adjectives is anything but delicate or aesthetically subtle. Rather, it's ludicrous and unintentionally humorous, the literary kin, aesthetically speaking, of Dickens' famous line about leaving the room in a flood of tears and a sedan chair. Drawing attention to Menard's—really, Cervantes'—"exceptional phrase" regarding "dolorous and humid Echo" by comparing it with Shakespeare's blunder is to draw attention to its obvious defects, two of which, in addition to the one already hinted at in regard to the line from Shakespeare, are its decadent languidness and vapidity. Unlike Othello, the narrator is easily wrought, both logically and aesthetically; but like Othello, being wrought, he's perplexed in the extreme.

VI

Recovering from the listless digression regarding Menard and Shakespeare he's fallen into, the narrator asks, Why did Menard choose to re-create the *Quixote*? Why the *Quixote* rather than some other book? Menard himself provided the answer, the narrator tells us, in a letter he wrote him. The *Quixote* is "'not . . . inevitable,'" he said there; it's "'a contingent book; the *Quixote* is unnecessary. I can premeditate writing it, I can write it, without falling into a tautology'" (41).

This is simply philosophical confusion. Strictly speaking, as I've already argued, Menard can't write the *Quixote* at all—not without falling into a (logical) contradiction. In that sense, of course, he can certainly avoid "falling into a tautology," contradictions being just the opposite of tautologies. But writing the *Quixote*—or anything else—and actually falling into a tautology? What would it be like to do that? What, in other words, does Menard mean by "tautology"? The context here is replete with philosophical terms, "contingent," "unnecessary," and "inevitable" among them, and that fact, in conjunction with Menard's documented philosophic interests and background, would make it seem that the term is also being used in a philosophical sense. Philosophically speaking, tautologies are logically compound statements which are truth—functionally true, that is, true under all assignments of truth values to their component parts. Tautologies in this sense are necessarily true, and therefore true in every possible or imaginable universe. They're not contingently true, not true in this but not every possible or imaginable universe. Menard's dichotomy of tautologies, necessity, and the inevitable on the one hand, and contingencies and what he can

imagine the universe not containing—such as the *Quixote*—on the other, thus seems secure and well founded.

But it isn't, not really. Remember, in this sense a tautology is a statement, and no statement of the form "X wrote Y" or "Y exists," where X is a person and Y a book, is truth—functionally true, or even analytically true (true solely in virtue of the meanings of the terms found in it). Every statement of either form couldn't be anything but non-tautologous, and thus contingently true, if true at all. There's simply nothing on the other side of Menard's implied contrast, then, no statement concerning the existence of a book or authorship that's tautologous. Consequently, the statements "The *Quixote* exists" and "Cervantes is the author of the *Quixote*" are non-tautologous, just as Menard has them. That's hardly enlightening or surprising, however, and the truth of Menard's claim, given the similar non-tautologous nature of all statements of the same form, thus provides no reason for choosing the *Quixote* over any other book.

But maybe this way of reading Menard, a technical and highly philosophical one, isn't the right way to read him. Menard does say that he can't imagine the universe without Poe's line, "Ah, bear in mind this garden was enchanted!" or without the *Bateau Ivre* or the *Ancient Mariner,* and the statement "The *Quixote* exists" is supposed to contrast with them. But how? "Poe wrote the line 'Ah, bear . . . ,'" "The *Bateau Ivre* exists," and "The *Ancient Mariner* exists" are one and all non-tautologous and contingent. But once again, so is "The *Quixote* exists." And though it's easy to imagine the universe without the statement about the *Quixote* being true, it's equally easy to imagine the universe without the others being true as well, contrary to what Menard says. Besides, soon after making his remarks about the *Quixote*'s being contingent and contrasting Cervantes' work with other "inevitable" ones, Menard goes on to say that "to compose the *Quixote* at the beginning of the seventeenth century was a reasonable undertaking, necessary and perhaps even unavoidable," thus flatly contradicting himself (41). No master of logic he, Menard.

Perhaps, though, despite the philosophical context he himself has established, and despite his own philosophical interests and background, Menard doesn't intend "tautology" in a philosophical sense at all; perhaps he means it simply in its everyday sense, as a needless repetition of something, whether a statement, a question, a command, or whatever. Menard's main idea, then, would be that he wouldn't be *needlessly* repeating Cervantes in undertaking a new *Quixote,* though repeating him he would certainly be. Now, however, the notion of inevitability can come into play—and can come to Menard's rescue, even. "Inevitable" similarly doesn't mean *necessary* in any logical or causal sense, or any other sense common to philosophical discourse, Menard could say; rather, it means *aesthetically necessary.* Menard's claim would then be that he wouldn't be repeating Cervantes needlessly, in that he wouldn't be repeating him in an aesthetically unnecessary way. There's room, aesthetically speaking, for a new *Quixote*, Menard thinks, and that's why Cervantes' work is contingent—and that, in fact, is what he, Menard, *means* by "contingent": *aesthetic possibility.* According to him, Cervantes' *Quixote* has made new aesthetic possibilities possible, including the possibility of a work word-for-word identical with it but numerically and aesthetically distinct from it. By way of contrast, the aesthetic possibilities of romantic literature have been exhausted, the death knell having been sounded by the decadents. That's why Menard mentions Poe's line, the *Ancient Mariner,* and the *Bateau Ivre* all in the same breath. No new aesthetic possibilities remain for romantic literature, for its successor has exhausted them all. Hence, for his crowning literary achievement the *Quixote* is perfect, while romantic literature not even possible.

While this generous interpretation of Menard is consistent with his remarks and, moreover, is in keeping with what we know of the man—I think in particular of the aesthetic sensibilities revealed in the catalogue of his "visible achievements"—it's as problematic as the others. The central difficulty is not so much the obviously vague and unexplained concept of aesthetic possibility as the claim that it's possible for Menard to create an aesthetically distinct *Quixote* but not an aesthetically distinct *Ancient Mariner.* Numerical distinctness may ensure aesthetic distinctness, but aesthetic distinctness—itself bound up with the concept of aesthetic possibility, it would seem—is predicated on the logically prior notion of numerical distinctness, and not vice versa. Thus aesthetic distinctness presupposes numerical distinctness, and so even on this interpretation of Menard's remarks, it must be possible for him to create a numerically distinct *Quixote* but not a numerically distinct *Mariner.* Even waiving the objection that creating the former isn't really possible in this case, why isn't the latter possible if the former is? *If* it's possible to create a new *Quixote* in the way Menard envisages, why not a new *Mariner?* He supplies no reason for distinguishing the cases as far as the individuation of works of art is concerned, and logically and ontologically they certainly seem on a par. That's a very good reason for thinking that they can't be distinguished. As far as the main issue is concerned, then, the conclusion that should be drawn is that if there is a reason for Menard's choosing the *Quixote* over every other book—and I think there is, and will be discussing it in due course—it has nothing to do with the argument Menard himself supplies, regardless of how generously it's interpreted. Instead, the passage about his choice of the *Quixote* should be read in light of what we already know about Menard himself. So read, it doesn't function philosophically, since its purpose isn't to provide us with insights on the nature of the aesthetic; rather, it functions literarily, so to speak, since its purpose is to deepen our understanding of the *précieuse* and provide yet another ironic fix on the pathetic, illogical, solipsistic, and academic, in the worst sense of the word, character that he is.

VII

The third major section of the story is partly a critical evaluation of Menard's *Quixote,* partly a panegyric of the man, and partly a theoretical reflection on the aesthetic lessons taught us by him. Panegyric and theoretical reflection are inextricably bound up with each other, however, and thus will be considered together below. Also, the third section is far and away the richest of the three, from a philosophical point of view, and so a fair amount of space will need to be devoted to it in order to do it justice. First, then, the narrator's critical assessment of Menard's magnum opus.

Having detailed how difficult it was to pull off the trick of writing a new *Quixote* at all, the narrator proceeds to argue that the new *Quixote* is aesthetically superior to the original. Menard's book is "more subtle" than Cervantes', for instance, because Menard doesn't

> oppose . . . to the fictions of chivalry the tawdry provincial reality of his country; Menard selects as his 'reality' the land of Carmen during the century of Lepanto and Lope de Vega. . . . He neglects altogether local color. This disdain points to a new conception of the historical novel [and] condemns *Salammbô,* with no possibility of appeal.
>
> (42)

But even if Menard's were a new *Quixote* I doubt that it would be quite so easy to "condemn" Flaubert's novel. *Salammbô*'s place in the historical record is a little too secure to be dislodged by any single event in the literary world, even the mysterious appearance of the *Quixote* (or a new *Quixote*). But the narrator's remark here is probably just critical hyperbole, not intended to be taken literally. He may just mean that Menard's achievement casts a new light on Flaubert's work, locating it in the historical development of the novel in an altogether new and unexpected fashion. To which the proper reply is, true enough—but only if Menard's book is indeed a new one. If it's not and the reader is intended to know as much, the narrator's remark will need to be reinterpreted in the context of the story as a whole. Independent evidence I've already marshalled in fact suggests all three: (1) that the novel wouldn't be a new one; (2) that the reader is intended to know as much; and thus (3) that the narrator's critical remarks should be understood ironically. We have a fairly complete mental history of Menard and a slightly annotated bibliography of his published work to draw upon in interpreting just what his literary capacities are, and we have something similar, first hand, in the case of the narrator, namely the evidence provided by his own prose in the story. All such evidence, from the first paragraph of the story onwards, suggests an ironic reading of the argument for Menard's greater subtlety.

So does the passage itself. For at least two reasons, to argue for Menard's greater subtlety on the basis of his having selected the land of Carmen during the century of

Lepanto and Lope de Vega as his "reality" is just the sort of nonsense that is an strong indication of irony. First, since Menard's overarching intention was simply to produce a text word-for-word identical with Cervantes', he didn't select, in the sense the narrator seems to have in mind, namely *intend to write about,* the land of Carmen. . . . Even if, as is very likely, Menard knew that the country and century depicted in Cervantes was the land of Carmen . . . , that doesn't entail that he intended to write about the land of Carmen. . . . (When I walk home from school, I know that my shoes will wear down a little bit, but that doesn't mean that I intend that they wear down a little bit.) On the contrary, the odds are very high that, wrapped up in his imitative task as he was, concentrating on reproducing Cervantes' text word-for-word, thoughts, much less intentions, respecting the land of Carmen . . . never crossed his mind. The narrator's saying that Menard selected the land of Carmen . . . , in the sense of *intending to write about,* is merely another instance of his abandoning a person in reality for a pleasant projection in a dream world.

Second, contrary to the narrator's suggestion, the "A selects B" construction is what contemporary philosophers would call referentially transparent. Roughly speaking, a sentence is referentially transparent if and only if co-designative terms can be substituted for each another in it *salva veritate,* that is, without change of truth value. If "Menard selected the land of Carmen" is true, and the land of Carmen . . . is Spain in the 17th century, then "Menard selected Spain in the 17th century" is true. So if Spain in the 17th century is the land and time that Cervantes selected and wrote about—which it certainly is—then Menard and Cervantes selected and wrote about the same land in the same century—they selected and wrote about the same thing, in other words. Thus philosophical analysis upholds the commonsense conviction that, despite the narrator's evident delectation, Menard can't be distinguished from Cervantes on the basis of what he selected to write about. The argument for Menard's greater subtlety is a sham, then, and the narrator merely spinning wheels in a fantasy land of his—and Menard's—own creation. The literary effect of this, given the immediacy of its impact and given the narrator's stilted and overly cultured means of expression, is pitched but merry irony. But the acme of irony is yet to come.

VIII

Before it does, though, an ironic flourish of a different sort is cleverly drawn. "It is well known," says our bombastic narrator,

> that Don Quixote . . . decided the debate [on arms and letters] against letters and in favor of arms. Cervantes was a former soldier: his verdict is understandable. But that Pierre Menard's Don Quixote—a contemporary of *La Trahison des clercs* and Bertrand Russell—should fall prey to such nebulous sophistries!.
>
> (42)

But the nebulous sophistries are in the passage itself, not the *Quixote*—or even *any Quixote,* including, *arguendo,*

the one written by Menard. If Don Quixote decided the debate in favor of arms, it certainly doesn't follow that Cervantes did, though the narrator asserts as much without argument. Considered *per se,* inferences from what a fictional character says to what the author of the fiction believes, are notoriously shaky and unreliable. More importantly, the inference the narrator makes here is facilitated by the fact that he *identifies* Cervantes and Quixote, and thus blurs the distinction between reality and fiction, a distinction he and Menard have been attacking, consciously or not, since the advent of their literary careers. As I'll try to show below, in the long run Borges himself is attacking the same distinction, though not unwittingly, and with deliberate literary and philosophical purpose in mind. Recognition of Borges' intentions in this regard is essential to understanding his overarching purpose in the story.

For the present, however, we need only note that the narrator's attempted removal of the barrier between fact and fiction, implicit in his identification of Cervantes and Don Quixote, is continued in his remark about "Menard's Don Quixote." Even granting for the sake of argument that Menard's is not Cervantes' Quixote, the claim that his Quixote is a contemporary of Bertrand Russell is still, on many philosophers' views, simply a category mistake:[4] the former is a fictional character, and thus in one logical category; the latter is a real man, and thus in quite another. That being the case, it's nonsense, strictly speaking, these philosophers would maintain, to regard the two as existing within the same time frame, and thus nonsense to regard them as contemporaries. Again, the narrator assimilates fact to fiction—or vice versa; it makes no difference within the bounds of the story itself. The concept of a category mistake being a much disputed one, however, the charge of nonsense probably shouldn't be pressed. Still, the narrator is far from off the logical hook. For even if comparing fictional characters and real people is sometimes possible, in this case the comparison remains logically egregious. Menard's Quixote is obviously not a contemporary of Russell: Russell was born in 1872; Don Quixote, even, by the narrator's admission, in Menard's "new" story, lived in the late 16th and early 17th centuries. Rather, Menard's Quixote is a contemporary of Cervantes' Quixote. Since Menard, from what we can infer from the story, was born in approximately 1870, he and not his Quixote is the true contemporary of Russell. Once again—and irrespective of the contestable charge of a category mistake—there is a logical, indeed a metaphysical, confusion of the fictional and the factual, of character and author. The narrator identifies Menard with the fictional character he created, just as he previously identified Cervantes with the fictional character he created.

But the confusion is compounded and thus enriched here, in the second case, for Menard's Quixote is not only said to be a contemporary of Russell but of a book, *La Trahison des clercs.* The notion of a category mistake thus begs to be granted admission for the third time, but even if the request is again denied, the idea of people and books being contemporaries is an inherently odd one—until, that is, the idea is coupled with an understanding of the narrator's and Menard's persistent inability to distinguish fact from fiction. Given an open door between the two realms, the most natural comparison is with the door itself, namely a book. The supreme irony topping the whole thing off, of course, is that the conflation of the distinction between the real and fictional exists only within a piece of fiction itself, Borges' story.

But to return to the main issue: since the narrator's argument for an evaluatively important difference between the "two" *Quixotes*—a difference concerning the aesthetic quality of the passages favoring arms over letters—rests on a number of logical and metaphysical confusions, there is no good reason for thinking the two different in that respect. There is thus no difference that needs to be explained—and what the narrator does next is tender an explanation—and thus also no basis for thinking that the conclusion that he immediately draws from his "finding" concerning arms versus letters, the conclusion that Menard's text is "infinitely richer" than Cervantes', is anything but wishful thinking. Indeed, even if the narrator had made a good case for his claim respecting arms versus letters, the argument would still be poor a one, the inductive leap from a single piece of evidence to an outrageously strong conclusion respecting infinite richness being one of several light years.

IX

But the narrator has other arguments to offer. Compare, he says, the following passage from Cervantes:

> . . . truth, whose mother is history, rival of time, depository of deeds, witness of the past, exemplar and adviser to the present, and the future's counselor . . .

with this one from Menard:

> . . . truth, whose mother is history, rival of time, depository of deeds, witness of the past, exemplar and adviser to the present, and the future's counselor. . . .
>
> (43)

Since Cervantes wrote in the 17th century, his passage is "mere rhetorical praise of history." The passage from Menard, on the other hand, originating in the 20th century as it did, is "astounding." Menard takes history to be the mother of truth, not "an inquiry into [truth's] origin. Historical truth, for him, is not what has happened; it is what we judge to have happened. The final phrases—*exemplar and advisor to the present, and the future's counselor*—are brazenly pragmatic" (43). Vast differences of an evaluative nature exist between the two books, then.

But it's hard to shake the feeling that the argument here is itself more sophistical than any of the "nebulous sophistries" found in the *Quixote*. The narrator telling us that two passages of very distinctive prose, passages which are word-for-word identical, differ radically in their aesthetic properties—that beggars comparison with Ionesco's psy-

chotic professor telling his pupil that instead of saying "The roses of my grandmother are as yellow as my grandfather who was Asiatic" she is saying "The roses of my grandmother are as yellow as my grandfather who was Asiatic" (Ionesco 67). There *has* to *be* something wrong with the argument.

And there is. The imputed differences between the passages doesn't really depend so much on their being products of different time periods—though, admittedly, their being such could warrant interpreting them differently, even differently in aesthetically important ways—as on an equivocation in the narrator's reading of them. The crucial terms in both his glosses are "history" and, though only implicit in his reading of Cervantes, "truth." Depending on why the narrator thinks that the passage from Cervantes is mere rhetorical praise of history—he doesn't tell us—the first and possibly the second of these terms are equivocated on.

One way to understand his claim about Cervantes is with "history" taken to denote those actual, concrete, (in the main) non-linguistic events and facts that occur or exist out there in the world. With "truth" being taken in its usual sense to denote a property of propositions, namely their correspondence with (again, in the main) extra-linguistic event or fact, history is the mother of truth in that events and facts are logically prior to, and the metaphysical determinates of, the correspondence relation. Events and facts make, metaphysically, true propositions true. The other way to understand his claim about Cervantes is with "truth" taken in its common and colloquial sense of *knowledge*: "truth" is *what we know to be true,* in the first sense of the term. "History," then, understood in the sense just mentioned, would be the mother of truth in that our knowledge of what is the case would be logically and ontologically dependent upon the existence of those actual concrete events and facts out there in the world. "History" could even be taken in a second sense, in the sense of an oral or written record of history in the first sense of the term, and slightly weaker remarks of a similar nature would still hold good. Our knowledge of events and facts is dependent, as a matter of contingent fact, on "history" in the sense of an oral or written record. Any of these readings of Cervantes makes sense, but none will help the narrator escape the charge of equivocation.

The reason is that his reading of Menard takes "history" and/or "truth" in an altogether different sense (or senses). In claiming that Menard defines history as the origin of reality, and then going on to say that for Menard, historical truth—that is, history, in the first of the senses just identified[5]—is what we judge to have happened, the narrator gives evidence for his claim that Menard's remark is astounding, no mere rhetorical praise of history. Why is it astounding? Because Menard's passage is budding pragmatism: what we judge to have happened determines, ontologically, what did happen. That's what the claim that history is the mother of truth amounts to. But notice that "history" here has to be understood in terms of what we judge to be the case—basically, the written or oral record—and not extra-linguistic, out-there, concrete reality. "History," then, is not to be understood in the sense that it probably should be in the passage from Cervantes, for there it had to do with extra-linguistic fact. Even on the reading of Cervantes on which "history" is taken as the written or oral record, an equivocation remains, since in his reading of Cervantes, "truth" has to be understood in the sense of knowledge, and the claim that history is the mother of truth read as a contingent claim which basically states that our knowledge of extra-linguistic events and facts is dependent, as a matter of contingent, causal fact, on the oral and written record. Obviously, the narrator means something much more philosophically significant than that in his reading of Menard, since he reads him as propounding a central tenet of pragmatism, that what is the case is determined by what we judge to be the case.[6] An equivocation of some sort thus remains, no matter how the narrator's remarks are read, and no matter what argument is imputed him respecting his claim about Cervantes; and the most natural way to read him is with an equivocation on "history."

"What of that, though?" someone might object. "What is pejoratively identified as an equivocation might be simply reading one passage one way and another another, that's all. Even if the two passages are verbally identical, that doesn't necessarily mean that the narrator misinterpreted anything. Said on one occasion, 'I went to the bank' might mean that I took a trip to the financial institution; said on another, that I headed for the local fishing hole. No equivocation there, just correct interpretation. Why isn't the narrator doing just the same thing? After all, Cervantes lived way back when, Menard at the turn of this century, and that seems to be the basis for his different interpretations. So what's really wrong with reading the passages as he does?"

In principle, this is a good objection—indeed, I've already agreed that two passages could be verbally identical yet differ markedly in meaning and aesthetic significance. I don't think that it'll do here, however. Without doing anything more than dipping my big toe into the murky waters of the theory of interpretation, I can at least say that the burden of proof lies on those who would give different readings to verbally identical texts. True, my critic and the narrator make some effort to shoulder that burden, since both mention the life-dates of our authors, and the narrator the pragmatism of William James. Mere passage of time doesn't ensure difference of meaning, however (else language would be extremely unstable, probably impossible), and even assuming that Menard's *Quixote* isn't Cervantes', the putative reference to James remains just that, putative, unless the passage in question can be tied to James in some way. If an allusion isn't clear from a passage, the usual way to establish its presence is to consult the surrounding verbal environment. Since Menard's prose is from first to last orthographically identical with Cervantes', though, no help from that quarter can be expected here. For the same reason, the passage from Menard actually

has to understood in exactly the same way as the corresponding passage from Cervantes, a fact reinforced if the circumstances surrounding the production of Menard's work are considered. The equivocation charge, then, is not out of place. The narrator once again willfully interprets as he chooses, never bothering with such matters as consistency if it doesn't suit him.

A more important objection, at least to my way of thinking, concerns not the "whether" of my analysis, but the "why." "Why make such heavy weather about it? Isn't it obvious that something's wrong, that his remarks are ludicrous? Why go on to explain the joke—for that is what it is—when it's obvious? That's just to kill it, and taking it in without detailed analysis is essential to appreciating it, and also essential to the story."

Yes and no, on that last point. Many times jokes, like stories in general, have to be read with a pair of glasses, and not a microscope, when first encountered in order for the reader to be properly affected. Future readings and complete understanding, however, often require a painstaking analysis of elements whose nature and interactions aren't at all obvious, even if their effects are. Here, my aim is not only to explain what underlies our sense of the ludicrous in reading the narrator's remarks, but also to provide evidence for my more global thesis that the story is misunderstood unless read as ironic through and through. That last point is hardly obvious.

X

The narrator's last point respecting his critical assessment of Menard can be more briefly considered. According to him, there is a vast difference in style between Cervantes' and Menard's works. This time the advantage is Cervantes', however.

> The archiac style of Menard—quite foreign, after all [since Menard is French]—suffers from a certain affectation. Not so that of his forerunner, who handles with ease the current Spanish of his time.
>
> (43)

But this is absurd. Menard steeped himself in the Spanish of Cervantes' time, and may well have written 17th century Spanish with ease—one suspects that he did, given his determination and seriousness. The fact that he didn't live in 17th-century Spain certainly doesn't entail, in and of itself, that his style is affected, any more than Cervantes' living in 17th century Spain entails that his isn't. In fact, even if Menard did write in the 20th century, and even if he, in contrast to Cervantes, didn't handle 17th-century Spanish with ease, that doesn't entail that his style was affected, and Cervantes' not. Psmith, a character in a number of P. G. Wodehouse's novels, handles the particular brand of English he speaks with ease, but his speech is affected nonetheless. And even if Psmith didn't handle it with ease but with great and grave difficulty, his speech would still be affected. People who have trouble expressing themselves don't *ipso facto* speak in an affected manner. The prominent factors that go into making speech affected include vocabulary, syntax, paragraph construction, and so on, such factors perhaps being relativized to (usually unstated) vocabulary, syntax, paragraph construction, and so on, that are taken as normative, i.e., taken as natural, not affected. Ease or difficulty of production and historical placement *per se* have nothing to do with it. A denizen of the 25th-century France who wrote the sort of English found in this paper wouldn't be writing in an affected manner.[7] The narrator's argument concerning style is thus as shoddy as all his other arguments, and his delight in difference once again nothing more than demonstration of duncery. It is thus, in the context of the story's studied tone, further demonstration of Borges' superb irony, as well as his uncanny ability to parody prose that is itself affected. In this case, the result of the latter is an additional layer of irony, since because affectation here turns on itself, mocks and parodies itself, the narrator's apotheosis of Menard's "achievement"—duplicating another's exact words and claiming not just (numerical) difference but superiority—is itself a similar duplicative and dubious achievement: the prose of praise exemplifies the very affectation it denigrates. The narrator once again shows himself the spiritual kin of Menard.

XI

Praise of a man is a natural concomitant of praise of his achievement, and so Menard's alter ego proceeds to heap effusive praise on him. Beginning with the world-weary and intellectually dispiriting, if not condescending, remark that "there is no exercise of the intellect which is not, in the final analysis, useless," and illustrating his dolorous thesis with a comment to the effect that the eventual fate of entire philosophies is to pass into mere paragraphs or names in a history of philosophy, the narrator thus eases into his true topic: Menard, the man who transcended such *fin de siecle* truths, the artist who truly did create *ex nihilo*—or almost, anyway. His praise of the man, however, is as odd and unintentionally condemnatory as his claims respecting his achievement. Menard

> derived from these nihilistic verifications [a] singular . . . determination. He decided to anticipate the vanity awaiting all man's efforts; he set himself to an undertaking which was exceedingly complex and, from the beginning, futile. He dedicated his scruples and his sleepless nights to repeating an already extant book in an alien tongue. He multiplied draft upon draft, revised tenaciously and tore up thousands of manuscript pages. He did not let anyone examine these drafts and took care [that] they should not survive him. In vain have I tried to reconstruct them.

> (43–44)

Taken seriously, this is praise that unwittingly damns both its object and itself. If all is for nought and Menard is deliberately imitating the universe, then he is deliberately pursuing nothing, and must be judged accordingly. Similarly, if the book he plans to write already exists and his aim is to repeat it, his task is indeed futile, as the narrator

says, but not for any grand metaphysical reason having to do with the transient nature of all things. A much more mundane reason concerning actions which merely duplicate part of our intellectual history will do in this case. Sleepless nights, copious drafts, and efforts to cover one's artistic tracks are, in the light of the duplicative nature of Menard's task, its evident futility, and the lack of any artistic value of its end product, no grounds on which to praise the "artistic genius" behind them. Rather, they're good reasons to think that the so-called genius is mad, and that he prefers personally gratifying ego-projections to decidedly less gratifying encounters with reality. Ironically, the only fictional world Menard succeeds in creating is not one he himself would recognize, since it's the one he lives in, and mistakes for reality. The same goes for the narrator, of course. Thus the narrator's further remarks on Menard's creative efforts—

> [the] "final" *Quixote* [is, or can be seen as] a kind of palimpsest, through which the traces—tenuous but not indecipherable—of our friend's "previous" writing should be translucently visible . . . unfortunately, only a second Pierre Menard, inverting the other's work, would be able to exhume and revive those lost Troys.

—reinforce previous themes (44). Ironically, even on the narrator's and Menard's own principles, nothing, neither the final *Quixote* nor the discarded drafts nor anything else, could be counted as a "Troy," Nihilism doesn't allow that, and our two principals are, by their own admission (43), nihilists. In fact, of course, their entire philosophy of literature, whether of its creation (as with Menard) or its criticism (as with the narrator), is founded on a self-contradiction. Nihilism can be used neither as a theoretical support for artistic creation—there would be nothing to aspire to—nor as a theoretical underpinning for value judgments—all such judgments would contradict their philosophical foundation. The narrator's praise of Menard's work, and so also of Menard, thus undermines itself.

Last and probably funniest of all, however, is praise of Menard because he "enriched . . . the halting and rudimentary art of reading" by adding a new "technique" to the usual repertoire,

> that of . . . deliberate anachronism and . . . erroneous attribution. This technique, whose applications are infinite, prompts us to go through the *Odyssey* as if it were posterior to the *Aeneid* and the book *Le Jardin du Centaure* of Madame Henri Bachelier as if it were by Madame Henri Bachelier. This technique fills the most placid works with adventure.

> (44)

Menard not only created a masterpiece; he taught us something new about the nature of artistic creation, namely that it's futile, but that one can nonetheless accomplish great things by repeating extant works. The fact that the lesson is self-contradictory is of no moment, apparently. And Menard, we now learn, not only added to literature and to the fundamentals of the theory of artistic creation; he also taught us something about the theory of reading and added to the fundaments of the philosophy of interpretation. Now when we read we can attribute what we like to whom we like, and proceed accordingly. "Deliberate anachronism" and "erroneous attribution"—this is such stuff as the new reading (proto-deconstruction?) is made on. But it is also such stuff as illusions are made on. Since the applications of this new technique are, as the narrator rightly says, "infinite," what has really been issued is a crypto-invitation to make all interpretations equally valid, because all equally well founded. The fact that the theory thus undermines itself, because it allows itself to be read anachronistically, and with anyone as its author, ironically escapes the narrator's notice. It, too, like his theory of value, is built on a self-destructive premise. Thus nihilism in the evaluative realm meets its theoretical counterpart, anarchy, in the interpretive. The result is further immersion in the dream world of Borges' ironic tale.

XII

If the above is even roughly correct, Borges' story is a multi-leveled parody, thoroughly ironic in tone, and from first to last deadly serious in the way that only a sophisticated piece of humor can be. The very claim registered in its title, **"Pierre Menard, Author of the Quixote,"** is a focal point for the pervasive irony found throughout. But there is another level of enveloping irony not yet explored. Three routes lead to it, one from the *Quixote* itself, one from an essay of Borges on the *Quixote,* and one from elements within the story itself.

Consider first the *Quixote*. The story of the *Quixote* is basically quite simple. Don Quixote, an otherwise sane man, has had his wits scrambled by an inordinate devotion to literature, in particular, romances of chivalry. He imagines himself to be called upon to roam the world in search of adventures, ill-fitted though he undoubtedly is for trying encounters of any kind. Initially luring Sancho Panza, his loyal and credulous sidekick, with the prospect of governorship of an island, Quixote proceeds to wander the countryside and seek adventures befitting a grand knight. In his distorted mind everyday objects are transformed into things threatening, romantic, or noble, and he is thus plunged into absurd misadventure after absurd misadventure, always with unfortunate consequences for himself. He is finally "rescued" when one of his old friends disguises himself as a knight, overthrows him, and requires him to refrain from chivalrous exploits for a year. Soon after returning to his village, however, Don Quixote falls ill and dies.

My thesis is that the story of *Don Quixote* is, *mutatis mutandis,* the story of **"Pierre Menard."** Menard is the new Quixote, not the new Cervantes.

Consider now Borges' piece on the *Quixote,* "Partial Magic in the *Quixote*." "The form of the *Quixote*," Borges writes there, "made [Cervantes] counterpose a real prosaic world to an imaginary poetic world. . . . For Cervantes the real

and the poetic were antinomies" (193). The same real and prosaic world is counterposed to an imaginary and poetic world in **"Pierre Menard,"** although in that world letters has won over arms, and the chief battleground is thus the page, not the plain. Just as, in Borges' words, "the plan of [Cervantes'] book precluded the marvelous [that is, the magical and the physically and logically impossible], [although] the latter had to figure in the novel, at least indirectly, as crimes and mystery [have to figure] in a parody of a detective story," so, too, the marvelous, the physically or logically impossible, has to figure in a parody of artistic creation, literary criticism, and creative genius. Like Cervantes, Borges could not "resort to talismans or enchantments, but [rather had to] insinuate . . . the supernatural in a subtle—and therefore more effective—manner" (194). In his "intimate being," Borges tells us, "Cervantes loved the supernatural." So did he, Borges. He showed his love by eventually resolving the antinomy between the poetic and the prosaic, and doing so without contradiction. The resolution can be found, in fact, in **"Pierre Menard"** and other of his fictional works.

If "Cervantes takes pleasure in confusing the objective and subjective, the world of the reader and the world of the book," so, once again, does Borges. But so, too, do Menard and the narrator! There are crucial differences between the cases, however. Menard and his Sancho Panza have no initial fix on the difference between reality and illusion, and act, like Quixote and his Sancho Panza but unlike Cervantes and Borges, in dead but parodic earnest. The one fictional pair mistake barbers' basins for helmets, the other minuscule and useless academic studies for intellectual achievements. Our authors, on the other hand, are fully cognizant of the difference between reality and illusion, but delight in deliberately blurring the boundaries between them. They do so in order to achieve a number of artistic effects and, always in the case of Borges, sometimes in the case of Cervantes, to explore certain logical and metaphysical problems. To cite one important instance: Cervantes explicitly introduces himself into the *Quixote* as a character, introduces the *Quixote* into the *Quixote* as a book, and, in one chapter, slyly, playfully, and ironically advances the idea that he is not the author of the *Quixote*. Parallels with paradoxes of self-reference, for instance, Bertrand Russell's concerning the class of all classes not members of themselves, immediately suggest themselves. Borges introduces himself into his *Quixote* more subtly. On my reading, **"Pierre Menard"** is a scaled-down mock heroic parable set in the 20th century, with Menard as the 20th century equivalent of Don Quixote. Borges occupies—at least initially—Cervantes' position in relation to the story. But that changes; he like Cervantes, enters into his own story as a character. How he does this is complex, so I hope that the explanation which follows does justice to its complexity.

Menard is a 20th century knight-errant, that is, an academic. He's thus a 20th century figure in a profession held in high esteem but also frequently the object of ridicule, the latter because of the well-known tendency of academics to foist their own particular brand of high falutin' and pretentious nonsense on other academics and unsuspecting members of the general public. Menard tilts at the windmills of erudition with learned-sounding but effectively pointless monographs and articles until he succumbs to his final and grandest delusion, that of writing a new book word-for-word identical with one he knows already exists, the *Quixote*. Here is the point at which Borges enters into the explanation. Borges is himself an academic *par excellence* and more than a little given to such fanciful, if not high falutin', nonsense as the denial of the existence of material objects. He's also and more than a little given to writing in a style that borders on the pretentious—as he himself well knows. Simply in rewriting, in a very transformed fashion, the *Quixote* as **"Pierre Menard,"** Borges undertakes a task parallel to that—artistically identical with that—of his protagonist. He introduces himself into the story, in other words, as his own failed author, Menard, in his attempt to create a new a story which is identical with one that already exists, one found in the *Quixote*. Unlike Cervantes, he identifies with his own very confused protagonist, all the while knowing that he's not him and doesn't suffer his delusions or mania. Yet, like Menard, he continues his efforts at creation, thinking all the while that all he's doing is repeating the work of another man. And, in a sense, he is. The laughable incidents, the grandiose scheme, the self-delusion, the misdirected attempts for the highest value that man can attain, the loyal companion, above all the parody and ironic tone—all are there in both Cervantes and Borges. Borges doesn't succumb to his Menard's delusion, of course, in trying to write a book word-for-word identical with Cervantes, but he comes as close as possible while managing to avoid stepping over the psychotic edge. Thus we see that Menard is Quixote, suitably modernized and intellectualized, and Menard is also Borges, suitably fictionalized and exaggerated. But since Borges himself is Cervantes, suitably modernized and intellectualized, Cervantes is Borges is Menard is Quixote. The antinomy between the prosaic and the poetic, the real and the magical, fact and fiction, is ultimately resolved by Borges, then, in thoroughly blurring the distinction between them: in essence, at the metaphysical depths, there is no difference between them, or at least none that is discernible by us. That is one of Borges' philosophical insights, an insight that is ontological in nature. A second is actually metaphilosophical and methodological. It's that one important way to write metaphysics is to write metaphysical fiction, and that one way to write metaphysical fiction is to write metafictional fiction. In this case, that involves writing fiction (**"Pierre Menard"**) about fiction (*Don Quixote*) that *is,* in the sense of the "is" of identity, the fiction written about. But if these are Borges' philosophical insights, he's also left us with at least three residual paradoxes to ponder and delight in. As might be expected, all are paradoxes of self-reference.

The first is that Borges pokes fun at himself—and all other creative artists, too, of course, Cervantes and Menard included—and yet understanding the folly of the creative endeavor requires simultaneously understanding that it is se-

rious business, hardly folly, and anything but laughable. To get Borges' point we have to take him and his story seriously; but to get his point we also have to see that he and his story, and so by implication all authors and stories, are not to be taken seriously. Authors are self-deluded fools, and writing a worthwhile story an impossible task. But to understand that, we have to interpret the author as anything but a self-deluded fool and his story as anything but worthless.

The second paradox concerns the fact that proper interpretation of Borges' story requires us to realize that Menard's *Quixote* won't be numerically distinct from Cervantes'. Menard's *Quixote* simply is Cervantes', even though it's thought by him to be a new and important work. Much of the story's irony, and so worth, depends on the fact that Menard failed and had to: reproducing another's work while knowing it and using it as a standard for the creation of your own necessarily means that nothing new has been achieved, no new object of worth has come into existence. Yet if Borges created **"Pierre Menard"** by intentionally reproducing another's work, all the while knowing it and using it as a standard for the creation of his own, then on the grounds just mentioned, grounds implicit in Borges' story itself, Borges himself failed to produce anything new and valuable. In other words, if Borges' story is good, that is at least in part because Menard didn't create a new and valuable work; but on the same grounds that condemn Menard, neither did Borges create a new and valuable work. The novelty—numerical distinctness—and value of the story depend, internally, on grounds that, applied externally, condemn the story itself.

The third paradox is akin to the second but fully external. It's that **"Pierre Menard"** is an essentially parasitic work, well-nigh a reproduction of the essential features of Cervantes' *Quixote*. As such, it would seem to be the *Quixote,* or at least share its fate and have no value apart from it, no value not shared with it. But that's just not so. **"Pierre Menard"**'s existence is its own, and its value, as I hope to have shown, likewise its own. The paradox, quite simply, is how, contrary to the seemingly impeccable argument that duplication means identity, duplication can sometimes make for difference; or, equivalently, how Don Quixote can ride again, even though his spurs have long been on the rack.[8]

Notes

1. For instance, André Maurois, in his "Preface" to Jorge Luis Borges, *Labyrinths,* p. xi. Maurois doesn't get the descriptive details of the story right, either.

2. Georges Charbonnier, *El escritor y su obra* (Veintiuno Editores, Mexico: 1967), p. 75; as reported by Gene H. Bell-Villada, p. 122.

3. George Charbonnier, *Entretiens avec Jorge Luis Borges* (Paris: 1967), p. 161; as reported by D. L. Shaw, p. 23.

4. The notion of a category mistake is explained in the first chapter of Gilbert Ryle's *The Concept of Mind.*

5. The term "historical truth" has to be read in the way indicated, or the narrator's claim respecting Menard's pragmatism would be baseless.

6. Since it might not be evident why such a doctrine is central to a philosophy known as "pragmatism," I should add that on pragmatism, one of the central, and justifiable, determinants of what we believe is cognitive convenience. In addition, the pragmatist holds that in the long run it's impossible to draw a distinction between what we justifiably believe to be the case and what is the case. This doesn't mean that for a pragmatist anything goes, i.e., that we can judge anything we like to be the case and it thereby will be so. Experience sets relatively strict constraints on what we can justifiably believe, as do other factors, such as consistency and coherence. For the pragmatist, though, justifiable belief is underdetermined by all such factors, and that necessitates the use of an additional criterion. According to him, that criterion is cognitive convenience.

7. I hope.

8. My thanks to Walter L. Weber for his comments, dogmatic though even he admits they were, on an earlier draft of this paper.

Works Cited

Barrenechea, Ana Maria. *Borges: The Labyrinth Maker.* Trans. Robert Lima. New York: New York University Press, 1965.

Bell-Villada, Gene H. *Borges and His Fiction.* Chapel-Hill: The University of North Carolina Press, 1981.

Borges, Jorge Luis. *Labyrinths.* Trans. James E. Irby. New York: New Directions Books, 1962.

Ionesco, Eugene. *Four Plays.* Trans. Donald M. Allen. New York: Grove Press, Inc., 1958.

Ryle, Gilbert. *The Concept of Mind.* London: Hutchinson and Company, Ltd., 1949.

Shaw, D. L. *Borges: Ficciones.* London: Grant and Cutler, Ltd., 1976.

Wreen, Michael, "Once Is Not Enough?". *British Journal of Aesthetics,* vol. 30, no. 2 (1990):149–58.

Herbert J. Brant (essay date 1995)

SOURCE: "The Queer Use of Women in Borges' 'El Muerto' and 'La Intrusa,'" in *Hispanofila*, Vol. 125, January, 1999, pp. 37–50.

[*In the following essay originally published in 1995, Brant argues that the relationship between male characters in two of Borges's stories is defined by a repressed homoeroticism.*]

Sex and women are two very problematic components in the fiction of Jorge Luis Borges: the absence of these two elements, which seems so casual and unremarkable, really highlights the strangeness of their exclusion. For example, scenes of sexual acts are almost totally lacking in Borgesian writing (Emma Zunz's sexual encounter with an anonymous sailor is the most notable exception) and even the most veiled suggestion of erotic activities is limited to only a very few stories. Similarly scarce, too, are female characters who figure prominently in the narration and who seem to possess an independent personhood. The fictional world created by Borges is a place where women, if they appear at all, seem to exist mainly as debased objects for the purpose of providing men with an opportunity for sex and where such sexual activities, by means of a female body. Sex and women are used primarily as bargaining chips in the relationship between men, never for the traditional purposes of either procreation or pleasure. Sex in Borges' fiction, by means of an objectified female body, is nothing more than a maneuver that gives definition and dynamism to the interaction between men.

In opposition to the traditional critical standpoint that male-male interaction in Borgesian fiction is merely homosocial and, therefore, purely nonsexual, a closer inspection of Borges' work reveals the clear but playfully veiled presence of homoerotic desire. My purpose here is to analyze two stories, **"El muerto"** and **"La intrusa,"** to expose the way in which the homosocial element of Borges' fictional world slides across the continuum towards the homosexual side when men in each story make use of a communal woman for the purpose of connecting physically and emotionally with another man. In these two stories, the erotic desire of the two men is plainly not directed towards a female, but rather towards each other, with the female as the intermediary focal point at/in which the two men may coincide. This type of sexual activity has the dual objective of fulfilling the societal mandate of "compulsory heterosexuality" when the males use the requisite female body for sexual purposes, while at the same time circumventing the proscription of male homosexual contact. In other words, Borges has substituted an intervening female body between the men as a way to permit the men to connect physically without transgressing heteropatriarchal prohibitions. In this manner, Borges is able to give expression to a relationship between men that simultaneously attracted him and repulsed him.

In this study I explore the similarities, differences, and significance in the use of the shared woman in **"El muerto"** and **"La intrusa"** and I propose that, far from the traditional critical appraisal, voiced by Robert Lima, that "Borges has concerned himself with heterosexual relations to the exclusion of other types" (417), sexual acts in Borges' fiction are not only homosocial, but also, in most cases, homosexual. Despite some rather substantial similarities between the two stories, **"El muerto"** and **"La intrusa"** provide two very different portrayals of the union of two men through the body of a woman. The setting for both stories, for example, is located outside urban society, that is, on the plains of the Río de la Plata basin. The time period for both stories is the 1890s. The male characters in both stories are known to be violent, severe, and willing to kill for their honor in stereotypical macho fashion. But aside from these parallels, the two stories have markedly different outcomes and purposes. In **"El muerto,"** one man desires to coincide with another and through the use of a communal woman, the two men are connected in a way that creates a shift in authority, leading the second man to seek revenge on the first for his transgression of the male power dynamic. In **"La intrusa,"** two brothers, through the use of a communal woman, suddenly come to understand how much they desire each other and once their passion is recognized, they preserve and reinforce it by disposing of the barrier between them, the woman who brought them together.

"El muerto," originally published in 1946 and later collected in the first edition of ***El Aleph*** (1949), is the story of a handsome young *compadrito* from Buenos Aires, Benjamín Otálora, who has killed a man and must leave the country. He heads for Uruguay with a letter of introduction for Azevedo Bandeira, a local *caudillo*. While searching for this Bandeira, he participates in a knife-fight and blocks a lethal blow intended for the man he discovers later to be Bandeira himself. Having earned Bandeira's trust and gratitude, Otálora joins his band of gaucho smugglers. Little by little, Otálora becomes more greedy and ambitious, taking more risks, making more decisions, and befriending Bandeira's body guard, Ulpiano Suárez, to whom he reveals his secret plan to take Bandeira's place as leader of the group. The plan is the result of his desire to possess Bandeira's most important symbols of power: his horse, his saddle, and his woman with the bright red hair. One day, after a skirmish with a rival band of Brazilians, Otálora is wounded and on that day, he rides Bandeira's horse back to the ranch, spills blood on the saddle, and sleeps with the woman. The end of the story occurs on New Year's Eve in 1894 when, after a day of feasting and drinking, at the stroke of midnight, Bandeira summons his mistress and brutally forces her to kiss Otálora in front of all the men. As Suárez aims his pistol, Otálora realizes before he dies that he had been set up from the very beginning and that he had been permitted the pleasure of power and triumph because in the end, to Bandeira, he never was anything more than a soon-to-be dead man.

The usual critical stance regarding this story emphasizes the time-honored view that in this tale, as in similar stories such as **"La muerte y la brújula,"** Borges is showing the reader the inherent foolishness of the human presumption that we are in control of our own destinies. Jaime Alazraki, for example, states that **"El muerto"** demonstrates a "tragic contrast between a man who believes himself to be the master and the maker of his fate and a text or divine plan in which his fortune has already been written" and that this contrast "parallels the problem of man with respect to the universe: The world is impenetrable, but the human mind never ceases to propose schemes" (19). George R. McMurray makes the case that the story sym-

bolizes "the absurd condition of all men who strive for success without suspecting that fate—often a fate of their own making—is all the while plotting their destruction" (21). Gene H. Bell-Villada notes that the tale "is a thriller with parable overtones; it has the ring of those old moral fables in which the harshly sealed fate of one overly presumptuous individual seems to stand as a cautionary tale to us all" (182). E. D. Carter, too, indicates that the ending of the story is a clear illustration of the "punishment" that awaits the man who tries to create his own destiny by challenging a force greater than himself (14). Despite the striking consensus among most critics that Otálora is struck down because of his ambition and greed, the element that seems to go almost unperceived and uncommented is his desire to possess not only Bandeira's power and prestige, but also his person; Otálora wants to be Bandeira, to be in him and to see as he sees, to feel as he feels, to possess what he possesses. The desire for one man to be inside another man, to coincide with him, to possess him, is undeniably homoerotic.

The two central characters of the story are, as McMurray has noted, "antithetical doubles" (20): Otálora is a strapping young lad ("mocetón") of Basque descent with light coloring, while the older Bandeira "da, aunque fornido, la injustificable impresión de ser contrahecho" and whose mixed ancestry of Portuguese Jew, African, and Native American underscores his darkly colored patchwork appearance (*Aleph* 42). Common between the two, however, a link that unites them, is the remarkably significant Borgesian facial scar. As I have shown elsewhere, the visible scar in Borges has the value of marking a man for all the world to see as one who is brave and manly on the outside, but whose macho exterior is merely a mask disguising a deceitful and, therefore, feminine interior. In other words, a man whose homosocial character has transgressed the line of homosexual desire (a "man's man" who has become "interested in men"), is permanently branded by an object (a knife or sword) that symbolizes what he most desires (the phallus). Western cultural norms dictate that those men who violate heteropatriarchal traditions by loving other men must be of inferior moral status and this condition is given tangible form: as Cirlot explains, "[i]mperfecciones morales, sufrimientos (? son lo mismo?) son, pues, simbolizados por heridas y por *cicatrices de hierro* y fuego" (127; emphasis added).

Otálora's desire for Bandeira is signaled from the very beginning of their association by the young man's intense need for visual contact; he yearns to see the man he desires and to be seen and recognized by him. For example, shortly after becoming a part of Bandeira's group, during his gaucho apprenticeship, the narrator mentions that Otálora is only able to see Bandeira once, but that "lo tiene muy presente." To add to the older man's desireability, Otálora is reminded by the others that Bandeira is the master and model ("ante cualquier hombrada, los gauchos dicen que Bandeira lo hace mejor") and Bandeira becomes, for Otálora, an absent but urgently coveted object of desire. Otálora, in an attempt to get Bandeira to take special notice of him, to make Bandeira see him, wounds one of his gaucho *compañeros* in a fight and takes his place on a smuggling mission so that his cunning and daring will be noted by Bandeira. Otálora hopes that Bandeira will suddenly realize that *"yo valgo más que todos sus orientales juntos"* (*Aleph* 45; original emphasis). Once he returns to the Big House, the narrator again notes that "pasan los días y Otálora no ha visto a Bandeira" (*Aleph* 45). Otálora's desire for contact with Bandeira through a male-male gaze is an early indication of his longing to connect with the man he wishes to replace.

As Otálora's hunger for Bandeira grows, he begins to crave Bandeira's many different possessions so that he can satisfy his desire through a metonymic ownership of things contiguous to Bandeira. When Otálora first sees Bandeira's bedroom, the first objects that he notices are highly symbolic: "hay una larga mesa con un resplandeciente desorden de taleros, de arreadores, de cintos, de armas de fuego y de armas blancas" (*Aleph* 46). These objects are traditionally linked to both masculine sexuality and the dominance/domination and violent power of masculine gender. Otálora's interest in and appetite for these specifically masculine attributes of Bandeira is highlighted when the narrator describes the objects on the table with the adjective "resplandeciente" while in contrast, when another of Bandeira's "objects," his mistress, enters the room barefoot and bare-breasted, Otálora observes her indirectly (as a reflection in a mirror) with only "fría curiosidad" (*Aleph* 46).

Otálora's desire for Bandeira's prized possessions is a clear example of René Girard's conceptualization of "triangular desire." Sharon Magnarelli, in her study of women in Borges' fiction, summarizes Girard's thesis, stating that "desire is dependent upon a triangular relationship: the object of desire (O) is desirable to one individual (A) to the extent that it is desired by another (B)." She notes, further, that "the object of desire (O) is an empty receptacle needing to be filled with what is projected upon it by the subjects of that desire (A and/or B)" (143). Applying this model of triangular desire to the fiction of Borges, Magnarelli finds that his female characters often serve the function of desired objects in a triangle and it is through these objects that sexual intercourse becomes "the gesture which links all men . . ." (143).

Magnarelli indicates that the result of this triangular relationship, so abundant in Borges' fiction, is what has usually been called simply "rivalry." But this rivalry in Borges is never the consequence of a powerful tie between a man and a woman, but rather between two men. Sedgwick, in applying Girard's theory to English literature, extends Girard's theory and finds that the rivalry between two men that is expressed through desire for the same woman is a bond "as intense and potent as the bond that links either of the rivals to the beloved." In fact, "the bond between rivals in an erotic triangle [is] even stronger, more heavily determinant of actions and choices, than anything in the bond between either of the lovers and the beloved" (21).

In Borges, as we will see, the action that is determined in response to the rivalry of triangular desire is always violent.

In **"El muerto,"** Otálora fervently desires to take possession of several different prized objects belonging to Bandeira: his horse with its saddle and blanket, and the red-headed woman. Otálora wants them with so much intensity precisely because Bandeira has invested so much desire in them, or as Magnarelli puts it, "the objects are coveted because the prestige of Bandeira has been projected on them; they have no intrinsic value" (144). Indeed, Otálora does not desire the horse for its equine qualities, nor does he desire the mistress for her feminine qualities. And although they may not possess an intrinsic value, they do have a functional one. Unlike other objects that symbolize Bandeira's power, the saddle on the horse and the woman are two things on/in which the two men can physically connect: when Otálora mounts first the horse, and then later mounts the woman, he is, in effect, mounting Bandeira himself.

Once he achieves his objective and comes into possession of all of Bandeira's most valued objects, Otálora enjoys his triumph at a New Year's Eve celebration. Otálora has fulfilled his desire to coincide with Bandeira, to connect with him indirectly through the body of the red-headed woman and although he does not know it yet, he must now die. Otálora's death is required, not simply because he was too ambitious and too greedy and tried to take command of things that he had no right to control, but because he has dared to place himself in the position of power in the "unimaginable contact" that would turn Bandeira into the so-called "passive" partner in male-male sexual intercourse. As Borges himself made clear in his 1931 essay "Nuestras imposibilidades," among the Buenos Aires gangsters and hoodlums there is no shame for the "active" partner in "sodomy," "porque lo embromó al compañero" (*Discusión* 16–17) while it is only the "passive" partner who suffers dishonor and condemnation. The affront that Bandeira must avenge is his "getting screwed" by Otálora, the fact that he finds himself in the shameful and *feminized* position of receptor in the contact between them.

Bandeira's revenge takes place precisely when Otálora's pleasure and excitement are at its peak. In fact, the narrator's description gives the clear impression that Otálora has a metaphorical erection, symbolizing his active, inserter role: "Otálora, borracho, *erige* exultación sobre exultación, júbilo sobre júbilo; esa *torre* de vértigo es un símbolo de su irresistible destino" (*Aleph* 49; emphasis added). As long as Otálora is alive, wielding his power as macho inserter, Bandeira cannot recover his role as the regional strongman. The narrator is careful to note that when Bandeira speaks at the end of the story, he speaks "con una voz que *se afemina* y se arrastra" (*Aleph* 50; emphasis added). Weakened by the feminized position in which Otálora has put him, Bandeira himself cannot wreak his vengeance on Otálora; that job is left to Suárez who symbolically and violently penetrates Otálora with a gunshot and consequently destroys the rival that had appropriated Bandeira's phallic power.

The story, **"La intrusa,"** offers quite a different outcome from that of **"El muerto."** In this story, rather than the death of a man who dares to usurp male sexual power from another man by means of a communal woman, in **"La intrusa"** it is the communal woman who must die in order to cement the bonds of desire between two men. **"La intrusa"** was first printed in the third edition of *El Aleph* (1966) and was later included in the collection, *El informe de Brodie* (1970). It is the story told of two brothers, Cristián and Eduardo Nilsen, who were infamous for both their rough and brutal ways as well as their unusual closeness. According to the legend, the incidents occur in the 1890s when the elder brother, Cristián, brings home a prostitute named Juliana Burgos. When Eduardo "falls in love" with her, too, rather than starting a terrible fight, Cristián tells him to "use" her if he likes. Soon, their joint use of Juliana gives rise to an emotional tension between the two brothers and in order to resolve the conflict, Cristián decides to sell Juliana to a brothel outside of town and share the money with his brother. Unfortunately, their need to share her continues as they both make trips to see her at the bordello. Cristián decides to buy Juliana back and take her home again. But the jealousy between the two brothers becomes worse. Finally, on a Sunday, Cristián tells Eduardo that they must take a trip to sell some "skins." When they arrive at a deserted field, Cristián confesses that he has killed Juliana and put an end to their disharmony. The brothers embrace, almost crying, linked even more closely by this "sacrifice."

This story, unlike the majority of Borges' tales, has occasioned quite widely divergent views among critics with respect to its content and artistry. Some critics have found the story's content to be quite troubling, even alarming, and that the narration seems to signal a clear break with Borges' earlier, that is, more accomplished style. For example, Bell-Villada, with particularly forceful condemnation, finds that "[i]t seems almost inconceivable that the same man who created **'Emma Zunz'** could also have written **'The Intruder,'** a disturbing yarn of jealousy and frontier violence that implicitly celebrates a male companionship strengthened by misogyny" (188). Bell-Villada continues to berate the work, concluding that despite its "polished prose," the story is shallow and sketchy and that "[i]t goes without saying that the story's gratuitous violence against a female can only strike negative chords at this moment in history" (189). Martin Stabb also remarks that "[a] superficial reading of this piece might suggest that it was the work of another writer, certainly not the Borges of *Ficciones* and *The Aleph*. [. . .] . . . the story itself—revolving around crudeness, sex, and prostitution—was hardly reminiscent of the Borges of earlier years" (86). Stabb, however, does go on to link this story with Borges' "canonical" texts, especially through thematic content. Gary Keller and Karen Van Hooft, too, argue that there is a continuity between Borges' earlier and later pro-

duction but that this story incorporates significant innovations in Borgesian narrative, particularly the development of plot as depending less on "the familiar devices of magic, the exotic, or game-playing" and more "on a psychologically authentic succession of grave actions and enhanced self- and other-awareness" (300).

But most critics do seem to agree on one thing: the theme of friendship/fraternity as an ultimate goal over heterosexual love/sex. McMurray (143) views this theme as a result of Borges' fascination for the cult of "machismo" and this idea is echoed by Bell-Villada who states that "[t]he tie stressed here, of course, is of a rather archaic sort, the macho bonds between men in the wilderness, a relationship of the kind one might encounter at all male clubs, on athletic teams, or in men's-magazine stories about deer hunting" (189). Lima (and repeated in Carter), however, makes the case that Borges' personal fear and loathing of sex and sexuality are the basis of the theme. Lima concludes that in killing the woman, Cristián "has confronted the erotic 'demon' in himself and executed it. He has opted for the fraternal rather than for the sexual bond" and this is due to "Borges' view that coition, because of its appeal to man's lower nature, can function only as a means to an end. In this instance, that end is the reaffirmation and strengthening of fraternal ties" (415).

The question in this story of fraternal love that has crossed over on the homosocial-homosexual continuum to the homosexual side has been an issue since the story first appeared. For some critics, the homosexual implications of the Nilsen brothers' relationship can be neutralized by Borges' use of a female intermediary, while for others, she is the catalyst to a more physical bonding between the brothers. Lima's conclusion above, however, indicates that there are those that cannot conceive of the possibility that fraternal bonds and sexual bonds can coincide, that brothers can also be lovers. And it is important to note that among those who cannot imagine brothers as sexual partners is the author himself. In fact, according to Emir Rodríguez Monegal and Alastair Reid, the tale is based on a real incident that Borges found necessary to modify: the "chief alteration was to make the protagonists brothers instead of close friends, to avoid any homosexual connotations. (Perhaps unwillingly, he added incest)" (361). Canto, too, states that when she discussed the story with Borges, "[l]e dije que el cuento me parecía básicamente homosexual. Creí que esto—él se alarmaba bastante de cualquier alusión en este sentido—iba a impresionarle. [. . .] Para él no había ninguna situación homosexual en el cuento. Continuó hablándome de la relación entre los dos hermanos, de la bravura de este tipo de hombres, etc." (230).

In spite of Borges' objections and his attempts simultaneously to expose and disguise the nature of the relationship between the brothers, I have no doubt that there is a clear homosexual content in the story. For example, the opening epigraph, indicated only by the chapter and verse designation "2 Reyes, I, 26," seems to announce the theme of fraternal love. But, as Balderston points out, this is one of Borges' clever deceptions to express and, at the same time, suppress the homosexual context he would establish for the story. The biblical reference that Borges gives is, as Woscoboinik has mentioned, a "picardía" that bashfully disguises its own content (129). Balderston explains that "[t]he first chapter of the second book of *Kings* does not have a twenty-sixth verse, but the second book of *Samuel,* sometimes also known as the second book of *Kings,* contains the most famous of all declarations of homosexual love: 'I am distressed for thee, my brother, Jonathan: very pleasant hast thou been unto me; thy love to me was wonderful, passing the love of women'" (35). Once the reader has deciphered the reference and found the actual passage, it becomes clear that the epigraph sets up the story as one that will convey the power of a man's passion for another man, a love that will surpass the love of a woman.

Several details indicate that the Nilsen brothers are not like the other men of the region. First of all, their peculiar nature makes them unusually removed and antisocial: no one dares intrude on their privacy and they never let people into their house because the brothers "defendían su soledad" (***Brodie*** 18). Furthermore, they are of an uncertain ethnic lineage which makes them appear physically different: "[s]é que eran altos, de melena rojiza. Dinamarca o Irlanda, de las que nunca oirían hablar, andaban por la sangre de esos dos criollos" (***Brodie*** 18); "[f]ísicamente diferían del compadraje que dio su apodo forajido a la Costa Brava" (***Brodie*** 19). The narrator concludes that it is this physical difference, as well as "*lo que ignoramos,* ayuda a comprender lo unidos que fueron. Malquistarse con uno era contar con dos enemigos" (***Brodie*** 19; emphasis added). What makes them distant, what makes them so odd, but above all, what makes them so *close,* is due to something we do not and cannot know. Given the context of the rest of the story, however, the narrator's feigned ignorance appears to be a clear case of not being able to name explicitly the "peccatum illud horribile, inter christianos non nominandum," that is, homosexuality, the love/sin that dare not speak its name.

It is significant that immediately following the acknowledgment that the narrator is unaware of what causes the two men to be so attached to each other, he mentions their sexual customs: it is known that their "episodios amorosos" have only ever been sexual encounters with prostitutes. It is clear that the brothers have never courted a woman with whom they could consider maintaining a long-term relationship or with whom they could satisfy the heteropatriarchal distate of marriage. So when Cristián brings the prostitute Juliana Burgos home to live with them, his intention is not to form a heterosexual bond, but rather to acquire a live-in maid ("[e]s verdad que ganaba así una sirvienta"), and more importantly, to be able to show her off as his companion when he goes out in public ("la lucía en las fiestas") (***Brodie*** 19). This second use of Juliana as a visible heterosexual partner—a "beard"—is quite necessary to deflect the already circulating accusations of homoerotic desire between the brothers as the nar-

rator suggests with a modest coded phrase, "la *rivalidad latente* de los hermanos" (***Brodie*** 20; my emphasis).

The most valuable use of Juliana, however, is her position as a sexual intermediary between the brothers. She is the third point of the love triangle and as such, "[s]he . . . has no intrinsic value, her value is the result of [the mediator's, the other's prestige. Cristián desires her because Eduardo does and viceversa" (Magnarelli 144). So as the brothers share her, connecting man-to-man through her body, Juliana loses any identity as a human being and becomes a mere sexual apparatus that permits the two men to have intimate physical relations with each other without actually engaging in male-male sexual intercourse. The understanding of the true nature of their relationship emerges when, as Keller and Van Hooft demonstrate, "Juliana comes to serve as a catalyst and a foil for a more profound intrusion—the emergence of a conscious awareness of fraternal love, an awareness which is intolerable to the brothers" (305). This frightening knowledge, as Balderston points out, is "what Sedgwick and others have called 'homosexual panic'" (35), the startling realization that a man's relationship to another man could be construed as homoerotic and must, therefore, reveal (unconscious) homosexual desire.

Their mutual desire ("aquel *monstruoso* amor" ***Brodie*** 22; my emphasis), however, becomes so overwhelming that the brothers must find a release from the tension it causes. After a long discussion, the two men decide to sell Juliana to a brothel and in that way they may succeed in eliminating the instrument that makes their physical love possible and in calming their own homophobic feelings of guilt. This response does not solve the problem. Their need to connect through her grows more powerful than their fear of acknowledging their homosexual passion for each other. As a result, the brothers are forced to buy her back after they visit her repeatedly in an attempt to recreate the erotic structure that once united them. From an initial state of homophobic panic, the two brothers come to accept their desire for each other and their need to bond in a more complete manner. The true union of the two brothers, however, will require the elimination of Juliana.

Despite the seeming inevitability of the conclusion of the story, the tragic murder of Juliana Burgos poses serious difficulties in the interpretation of the meaning of the relationship between the brothers and to the communal woman that brings them together. For me, the death of Juliana at the hands of the Nilsen brothers is not a Christ-like sacrifice "to atone for their 'sin' of love," as McMurray would have it (144), nor is it a sacrifice of their despised homosexuality and the destruction of their inner femininity, as Magnarelli concludes (148). These and other interpretations fail to take into account the strength of the passion between the two brothers, which, as the epigraph reminds us, "passes the love of women." Cristián kills Juliana, not because he hates this woman or women in general, but rather because as long as Juliana exists as an intermediary, an impediment that keeps the brothers from realizing fully their homoerotic desire, the two men will never be able to connect to each other directly. The two need to move beyond a relationship with a communal woman as surrogate to a relationship with their true object of desire. In order to accomplish this, they remove the obstacle that keeps them apart and through this "sacrifice," they are joined permanently in a more intimate way.

Borges' fictional world is an essentially and unquestionably homosocial space. In the vast majority of his stories, where there is a total absence of female characters or where they are merely decorative, the homosociality in the texts only hints at a possible queer sexuality between the male characters. But as the two stories **"El muerto"** and **"La intrusa"** show, the presence of a female deployed as a structural element of the plot has the paradoxical effect of highlighting and underscoring the sexual nature of the relationships among males. Were it not for the inclusion of the red-headed woman in **"El muerto,"** Otálora's scheme to unite with Bandeira and rob him of his male sexual power could never have taken place. Unlike the other cherished objects such as the horse and saddle which merely suggest an undercurrent of sexuality, Bandeira's woman provides a site at which the sexual aspect of Otálora's desire can be given more complete expression. Likewise, the presence of Juliana Burgos in **"La intrusa"** furnishes the Nilsen brothers with a physical link through which they can fulfill their heretofore unacknowledged and growing passion for each other. Their fame in the community for being both strange and unusually intimate implies from the very beginning that all they need is a catalyst to change their homosocial relationship into a homosexual one. It is Juliana, in her role as communal sexual body, that provides the transformative element. In the end, the use of communal women in these stories serves to provide only the appearance of fulfilling the mandates of "compulsory heterosexuality," while underneath this façade of sex between men and women it becomes quite plain that something very queer is going on.

Works Cited

Agheana, Ion T. *Reasoned Thematic Dictionary of the Prose of Jorge Luis Borges.* Hanover [NH]: Ediciones del Norte, 1990.

Altamiranda, Daniel. "Borges, Jorge Luis (Argentina; 1899–1986)." *Latin American Writers on Gay and Lesbian Themes: A Bio-Critical Sourcebook.* Ed. David William Foster. Westport: Greenwood Press, 1994. 72–83.

Balderston, Daniel. "The Fecal Dialectic: Homosexual Panic and the Origin of Writing in Borges." *[[questiondown]]Entiendes? Queer Readings, Hispanic Writings.* Eds. Emilie L. Bergmann and Paul Julian Smith. Durham: Duke University Press, 1995. 29–45.

Bell-Villada, Gene H. *Borges and His Fiction. A Guide to His Mind and Art.* Chapel Hill: U of North Carolina Press, 1981.

Borges, Jorge Luis. *El Aleph.* Buenos Aires: Emecé, 1989.

———. *Discusión.* 1st ed. Buenos Aires: M. Gleizer, 1932.

———. *El informe de Brodie.* Madrid: Alianza, 1970.

Brandes, Stanley. "Like Wounded Stags: Male Sexual Ideology in an Andalusian Town." *Sexual Meanings: The Cultural Construction of Gender and Sexuality.* Eds. Sherry B. Ortner and Harriet Whitehead. Cambridge: Cambridge University Press, 1981. 216–239.

Brant, Herbert J. "The Mark of the Phallus: Homoerotic Desire in Borges' 'La forma de la espada.'" *Chasqui* (in press).

Canto, Estela. *Borges a contraluz.* Madrid: Espasa-Calpe, 1989.

Carter, E. D., Jr. "Women in the Short Stories of Jorge Luis Borges." *Pacific Coast Philology* 14 (1979): 13–19.

Cirlot, Juan-Eduardo. *Diccionario de símbolos.* 3rd edition. Barcelona: Editorial Labor, 1979.

Dorfman, Ariel. "Borges and American Violence." *Some Write to the Future: Essays on Contemporary Latin American Fiction.* Trans. George Shivers with the Author. Durham: Duke University Press, Hughes, Psiche. "Love in the Abstract: The Role of Women in Borges' Literary World." *Chasqui* 8.3 (May 1979): 34–43.

Keller, Gary D. and Karen S. Van Hooft. "Jorge Luis Borges' 'La intrusa:' The Awakening of Love and Consciousness/The Sacrifice of Love and Consciousness." *The Analysis of Hispanic Texts: Current Trends in Methodology.* Eds. Lisa E. Davis and Isabel C. Tarán. New York: Bilingual P, 1976. 300–319.

Lima, Robert. "Coitus Interruptus: Sexual Transubstantiation in the Works of Jorge Luis Borges." *Modern Fiction Studies* 19 (1973): 407–417.

Magnarelli, Sharon. "Literature and Desire: Women in the Fiction of Jorge Luis Borges." *Revista/Review Interamericana* 13.1–4 (1983): 138–149.

McMurray, George R. *Jorge Luis Borges.* New York: Frederick Ungar, 1980.

Molloy, Sylvia. *Signs of Borges.* Trans. Oscar Montero. Durham: Duke University Press, 1994.

Rivero, María Cristina. "Interpretación y análisis de 'El muerto.'" *Universidad* [Santa Fe] 77 (1969): 165–193.

Rodríguez Monegal, Emir. *Jorge Luis Borges: A Literary Biography.* New York: Paragon House, 1988.

———. and Alastair Reid, eds. *Borges: A Reader. A Selection from the Writings of Jorge Luis Borges.* New York: E. P. Dutton, 1981.

Sedgwick, Eve Kosofsky. *Between Men: English Literature and Male Homosocial Desire.* New York: Columbia University Press, 1985.

Silvestri, Laura. "Borges y la pragmática de lo fantástico." *Jorge Luis Borges: Variaciones interpretativas sobre sus procedimientos literarios y bases epistemológicas.* Eds. Karl Alfred Blüher and Alfonso de Toro. Frankfurt am Main: Vervuert Verlag, 1992. 49–66.

Stabb, Martin S. *Borges Revisited.* Boston: Twayne, 1991.

Woscoboinik, Julio. *El secreto de Borges. Indagación psicoanalítica de su obra.* Buenos Aires: Editorial Trieb, 1988.

C. J. Buchanan (essay date 1996)

SOURCE: "J. L. Borges's Lovecraftian Tale: 'There Are More Things' in the Dream Than We Know," in *Extrapolation,* Vol. 37, No. 4, Winter, 1996, pp. 357–63.

[*In the following essay on Borges's debt to the writer H. P. Lovecraft, Buchanan discusses the nature of the minotaur in the Borgesian labyrinth.*]

This tale of Jorge Luis Borges, **"There Are More Things,"** is almost unremarked in Barton Levi St. Armand's wide-ranging, incisive essay "Synchronistic Worlds: Lovecraft and Borges." We do find a slight reference to it, however, in this best collection of articles yet published in the field of the weird tale. St. Armand quotes Borges speaking in a 1978 interview with Paul Theroux: "I like Lovecraft's horror stories. His plots are very good, but his style is atrocious. I once dedicated a story to him" (300).

That story is, of course, the one presently under discussion. In other remarks, however, Borges indicates what amounts to a disdain for Lovecraft (St. Armand 289–91). St. Armand details this ambivalence of Borges toward his predecessor and offers a theory to account for it which is the thrust of his essay. It seems to him that Lovecraft anticipated many of Borges's ideas (St. Armand might object that I have simplified his thesis). He finds many similar conceptions in Lovecraft's works and in those of Borges, and since Lovecraft died fifty years before the latter, I fail to see why a critic must drag in "synchronicity" to explain what seems as obvious as Samuel Clemens's influence on Hemingway, acknowledged by Papa near the beginning of *Green Hills of Africa.* However, I will not dispute St. Armand's thesis further. My main point lies in quite a different area: that through his imitation of Lovecraft's work in **"There Are More Things,"** Borges revealed an intuitive understanding of how thoroughly efficacious the Lovecraftian fiction is, irrespective of his comments on the style. Perhaps in the end, I have no substantial disagreement with the author of "Synchronistic Worlds."

To begin my analysis of Borges's story with what seems a minor observation, we find, in the eighth paragraph (54) the names "Edwin" and "Muir" appearing separately but in close proximity. The tale thus contains an homage-within-of the house at the story's end, escaping the monster. This we may surmise anyway, since he is telling the tale we have before us.

The second additional meaning of the phrase is the twist of reality that multiplies possible meanings of the story to a labyrinthine degree of perplexity. The phrase of the dream may be interpreted as if spoken by the *other* dreamer—that is, by the dreamed Minotaur in its dream since "to be is to be perceived." We then understand that he/it finally sees the true shape of the man in his dream, that he understands the puzzle from his alien point of view, which is perhaps identical to our own: man looking at beast-man looking at man-beast in a wilderness of mirrors (T. S. Eliot's phrase). We may surmise that it is the Minotaur, also, who will make it out of the house, the gnarled dwelling, that the Minotaur's dream is also, perhaps, a wish-fulfillment.

Whose wish-fulfillment is the dream-phrase of escape finally pointing to? It is the narrator's ultimately (within the fictional confines), since the dream process is his own. Then how does he make his escape? In what sense?

He escapes by viewing the Minotaur at the story's end, having sufficiently tracked him down and thoroughly identifying, empathizing, with the beast by accepting the dual nature of his own self. His escape (and here is the Lovecraftian essence) is into his own past and through it, as Lovecraft's Outsider and Randolph Carter and others made their escapes. Arnett manages, through the tangles of his adult search, to relive his fondly remembered boyhood: he "toys with" unearthly angles and the mysteries of the Ideal that are symbolized by the "complicated exercises with multicolored cubes" and references to Berkeley et al in the story's opening paragraph when he is reminiscing about the idyllic childhood visits to the uncle whose death is the incident that instigates the plot.

The story, like Arnett's dream, is nearly static, although, as I've indicated, I think a psychological escape takes place after the tale's end. It is a bit like a chess game, its actions centered on the house-as-labyrinth. The "move" referred to (56) is a chess move from the games of the initial paragraph. Chess, of course, is a labyrinth two minds conspire at entering and solving together: they make their escape from the maze of the board in unison; they raise their human heads and gaze upon each other, but how different their feelings *are* at the end, those who have shared every move and postulation! (Although in the story the narrator and his mirror self, the Minotaur, are the players of this "chess game" [like the two theoried Minotaurs mentioned above], by his dedication and many other indications Borges subtly informs us that this game is between himself and Lovecraft.)

Precisely when the narrator is "bullied" (!) and "even debased" by the passage of time, the summer, he becomes lost in a storm wherein he "wandered about looking for a tree" (57). He thus partakes of the taurian or bull aspect of the Minotaur in three ways, after which "in the sudden glare of a lightning flash [of insight] I found myself a few steps from the fence" (57). "I found myself" indeed. He is about to face himself, as in writing this homage to Lovecraft, Borges faces a particularly dark side of himself.

The stone ramp he next ascends, inside the house itself, is purely Lovecraftian, from "The Shadow Out of Time" and other such locales. At this point, the reader wonders just how alien, how out of space and time the beast man, in the end, appears and how inconceivable it may be. Perhaps it's something of a cone-based, *sliding* animal; there may be a marked deformity of locomotion.

Anticipating the final revelation, Arnett says, "Let me explain myself. To see a thing one has to comprehend it" (58). He makes clear this phenomenology of perception through examples warning the reader that a physical description will be inadequate to convey the monster in the maze-house. As with any sacred mystery, horror is in the eye of the beholder, and words are inadequate as they always are to Lovecraft's narrators attempting to relate the ineffable. Yet the entire story is pointed toward exactly that unrevealable revelation!

(Allow me to interpolate here that criticism on this story beyond a mere summary of the plot is hard to locate, but this sample is typical: "The episode, which comes during the final two pages, is truly spine-chilling, but unfortunately Borges takes up eight pages of complicated subplots before getting there and spoils a basically sound idea" [Bell-Villada 256]. Yes, that is what passes for interpretation of this tale.)

Borges has imitated Lovecraft's method and style to tell his Lovecraftian homage. Lovecraft's proliferate adjectives, for example, are indispensable to underline for us what Borges accents with *his own* repetition of incident and symbol: notably, Arnett's encounters-through-questing with other characters in the story, which Bell-Villada found so objectionable. As in the Outsider's case, description may only gnaw at the edges of the thing's mind blasting Form, as unreal in our world as a Platonic Form. That perfect passage from Lovecraft's original tale is worthy of study:

> I cannot even hint what it was like, for it was a compound of all that is unclean, uncanny, unwelcome, abnormal, and detestable. It was the ghoulish shade of decay, antiquity, and dissolution; the putrid dripping eidolon of unwholesome revelation, the awful baring of that which the merciful earth should always hide. God knows it was not of this world—yet to my horror I saw in its eaten-away and bone-revealing outlines a leering, abhorrent travesty on the human shape; and in its mouldy, disintegrating apparel an unspeakable quality that chilled me even more.
>
> (51)

That "unspeakable quality" is what Lovecraft quested after in all his work, as does his Argentine follower in this tale. Borges's hints of the creature's "true" nature are wondrous and cosmic, as is the best of Lovecraft's vision. Both are focused on the unknowable nature of man as he looks in the mirror of his mental labyrinth.

Borges mentions, near his finale in thunder, "a V of mirrors that became lost in the upper darkness" (59). Surely this is the *V* outlined by the shape of a constellation's horns in the night sky, the shape of Taurus the Bull faced by the Hunter, Orion, with his upraised club. Orion can never finally encounter the Bull, nor can the symbolism of the Minotaur be finally unraveled: there is no Ariadne anhomage to that celebrated cotranslator (with his wife) of Kafka; Edwin Muir also wrote many remarkable poems, often about myths and mazes.[1]

These labyrinths are the reason for Muir's "appearance" in the story. Borges alerts us in this subtle fashion to his own central concern: a certain ambiguity within a labyrinth in the narrator's dream. (We shall see that Borges's way of resolving this ambiguity requires the Lovecraftian method; it is just because Borges is writing a Lovecraftian story that he finds himself forced to use the same tool as Lovecraft for presenting his material.)

According to Borges (*Imaginary Beings* 158), the traditional monster within King Minos's labyrinth, the Minotaur, is a man with a beast's head. Borges notes, however, that Dante "imagined the minotaur with a man's head and a bull's body" (159). This creature is the offspring of Queen Pasiphaë's unholy lust for a bull that her husband, the king, has imprisoned in a network of walls, the original labyrinth. (Minos had been obligated to sacrifice that splendidly beautiful bull to Poseidon but had failed to do so; hence, Poseidon made Minos's wife fall in lust with the beast.) Most painters of this traditional mythological subject have depicted it traditionally, not as the Dantean beast.

Borges adds immediately that he suspects *labrys,* a Greek two-headed ax, to be the root of labyrinth, although I've found that sources are uncertain about any root underlying *labyrinthos* itself. Borges concludes his brief commentary: "Most likely the Greek fable of the Minotaur is a late and clumsy version of far older myths, the shadow of other dreams still more full of horror" (159). My hypothesis is that Borges is, unconsciously, fascinated by the dual nature of an Ur-Minotaur, as I call it. Dante's conception seems as abhorrent to the imagination as the mermaid whose fish and human halves are reversed (see the nontraditional painting by Magritte). Which conception of the Minotaur is the original conception, and which, if the question is not unanswerable, is the true one?

Perhaps the traditional monster, a man with a bull's head, symbolized the bestial mind of man (King Minos) trapped in the lovely human form, the proper and just result of Minos's greed to keep the perfect bull and of his queen's bestial lust. That conception of the Minotaur emphasizes man's closeness to the beast, whereas the bull with a man's head would emphasize the power of lofty human reason dominant over the animal. Consider the centaur, for instance, a type of noble creature, except during those occasions when wine or lust overcame his "humanity." One of these centaurs, the famous Chiron, was the tutor of, among others, Aesculapius, the first great physician, a minor god.

Did the first Greeks, or those from whom their ur-myths derived, think of man as closer to the beasts than later thinkers? Did Dante? There seem to be alternations, contradictions, about our conception of ourselves, symbolized by the dual nature of the Minotaur. It is with this essential question about the nature of man that Borges is concerned, as so often was Lovecraft (in "The Outsider," for example).

It is not quite the traditional Minotaur that nephew Arnett, Borges's story's narrator, sees in his dawn dream of a labyrinth.

> That night I did not sleep. Around dawn, I dreamed about an engraving that I had never seen before or that I had seen and forgotten; it was in the style of Piranesi, and it had a labyrinth in it. It was a stone amphitheater ringed by cypresses, above whose tops it reached. There were neither doors nor windows; rather, it displayed an endless row of narrow vertical slits. With a magnifying glass, I tried to see the Minotaur inside. At last, I made it out. It was a monster of a monster, more bison than bull, and its human body stretched out on the ground, it seemed to be asleep and dreaming. Dreaming of what or of whom?
>
> (55)

The tall cypresses and stone amphitheater as well as the magnifying glass through which he views them in his dream hint that this Piranesi-like engraving is a disguised dream of Arnold Böcklin's painting *The Isle of the Dead,* especially when we recall that we read in Dante of Judge Minos, just the other side of the River Styx, directing men into the various suites of Hell.

Let us look as closely as we can at the dream sequence, the heart of this tale. The narrow vertical slits through which Arnett peers are an echo of the house built by architect Muir, which a mysterious Praetorius has had altered; they "no longer opened, but chinks of light could be made out in the dark" (53). The bison seen through the chinks of the dream's labyrinth may be distinguished from a bull primarily by its hairiness, I suggest, as a mammoth differs from an elephant in being shaggier, less defined. The narrator calls it "a monster of a monster, more bison than bull"; although it is described as possessed of a human body, the duality is hinted at by the "bisonic" characterization.[2] If we accept Joseph Campbell's interpretation of the Minotaur as representing the essential "dark and terrible night aspect" (248) that one seeks to hide in a maze of denial, perhaps part of the myth's point and part of the dream's message is that we cannot, finally, know what we are. "Account for *me,*" cries the horsegod in Peter Shaffer's *Equus* through the vehicle of a psychologist seeking to understand the nature of searching and healing the human psyche. In the end, there is no explaining why or what we are.

In Arnett's dream, the bison-man is dreaming. "Dreaming of what or of whom?" he asks, and we must conclude that it is dreaming of him dreaming of it, and we are back to the butterfly-man dilemma.[3] (A certain Chinese philosopher relates that he dreamed he was a butterfly, and, upon waking, could not decide whether he was a man who had dreamed so, or a butterfly now dreaming that he was a man.[4])

Arnett's efforts to glimpse the creature have afforded the "action" of this dream. "At last, I made it out," he says, commenting on his own dream, meaning that he has "made out" the shape of the thing.

If we now attach this sentence to the end of the entire story's situation, it functions with two additional meanings. The first is that Arnett "makes it out" to aid this Theseus, man questing for the solution to his essential, unspeakable duality.

And does the Minotaur looking at himself perceive a like duality? I suspect not.[5]

Notes

1. Here is an excerpt pertinent to the spirit of Borges's story and this essay, from Edwin Muir's "The Labyrinth":

   Since I emerged that day from the labyrinth,
   Dazed with the tall and echoing passages,
   The swift recoils, so many I almost feared
   I'd meet myself returning . . .
   . . .—since I came out that day,
   There have been times when I have heard my footsteps
   Still echoing in the maze, and all the roads
   That run through the noisy world, deceiving streets
   That meet and part and meet, and rooms that open
   Into each other—and never a final room—
   Stairways and corridors and antechambers
   That vacantly wait for some great audience,
   The smooth sea-tracks that open and close again,
   Tracks undiscoverable, indecipherable,
   Paths on the earth and tunnels underground,
   And bird-tracks in the air—all seemed a part
   Of the great labyrinth. And then I'd stumble
   In sudden blindness, hasten, almost run,
   As is the maze itself were after me
   And soon must catch me up . . .
   Oh these deceits are strong almost as life.
   Last night I dreamt I was in the labyrinth,
   And woke far on. I did not know the place.

   Neither do I know that place, no matter how long I trace the lines of this maze.

2. Elsewhere Borges speaks of the "prehistoric pathways of the bison" (from the poem "Last Evening" in *The Paris Review* 125 [n.d.]: 229). This animal has extraordinary connotations for him.

3. Interestingly, and perhaps not coincidentally, Riane Eisler, in a description of the ancient Minoan civilization, tells us that the double-bladed ax or labrys "shaped like the hoe axes used to clear land for the planting of crops . . . was also a stylization of the butterfly, one of the Goddess's symbols of transformation and rebirth." (36) The butterfly's dual nature as a wormlike writhing creature and a lovely insect that is a symbol of beauty (and often of the human soul) makes me intuit a parallelism between

larva-butterfly and bull-man. The way that certain moths are used by Poe in "The Gold-Bug" and by Thomas G. Harris in *The Silence of the Lambs* reinforces my idea.

4. ". . . por toda la vida es sueno, y los suenos, suenos son." Calderón.

5. I surmise that he sees himself as a unique entity, perhaps godlike, perhaps maimed. He may see an inevitability in his condition that justifies it. Here I contradict an earlier assertion of this paper, perhaps. But if he dreams of himself as a man, he might infer an incompleteness to such a thing.

Works Cited

Bell-Villada, Gene H. *Borges and His Fiction: A Guide to His Mind and Art.* Chapel Hill: U of South Carolina P, 1981.

Borges, Jorge Luis. *The Book of Imaginary Beings.* New York: Dutton, 1970.

————. "There Are More Things." *The Book of Sand.* Trans. Norman Thomas di Giovanni. New York: Dutton, 1977. 51–59.

Campbell, Joseph. *The Hero with a Thousand Faces.* Princeton: Princeton UP, 1968.

Eisler, Riane. *The Chalice and the Blade.* San Francisco: Harper, 1988.

Hamilton, Edith. *Mythology.* Boston: Little, Brown, 1942.

Lovecraft, H. P. "The Outsider." In *The Dunwich Horror and Others.* Sauk City, WI: Arkham House, 1963. 46–52.

Muir, Edwin. "The Labyrinth." *Chief Modern Poets of Britain and America.* Vol. I. Ed. M. L. Rosenthal et al. New York: Macmillan, 1970.

St. Armand, Barton Levi. "Synchronistic Worlds: Lovecraft and Borges." In *An Epicure in the Terrible.* Ed. David E. Schultz and S. T. Joshi. Cranbury, N.J: Associated UP, 1991. 298–323.

Herbert J. Brant (essay date 1996)

SOURCE: "The Mark of the Phallus: Homoerotic Desire in Borges' 'La forma de la espada,'" in *Chasqui*, Vol. XXV, No. 1, May, 1996, pp. 25–38.

[*In the following explication of Borges's short story "The Shape of the Sword," Brant suggests a homosexual subtext motivates the story's manifest content.*]

> Envidia.
> Envidia siente el cobarde . . .
> Envidia.
> Envidia amarga y traidora,
> Envidia que grita y llora.

> La que causa más dolor
> es la envidia por amor.

>　　　　　(José González Castillo, "Envidia")

The fiction of Jorge Luis Borges is intriguing and yet, unsettling. These qualities seem to originate in what I consider two principal characteristics of Borges' work: confounding ambivalence and a clever use of paradox. His work is paradoxical insofar as it is macrocosmic, and yet microcosmic; central, and yet peripheral; collective—it seems to speak with many voices—and yet it is deeply personal and evokes the strongest emotional responses, especially in lyrical passages that reveal the unmistakable presence of Borges himself. It is precise, concise, and straightforward in its expression, and yet there is something ambiguous, nebulous, and absent in its style. These and other contradictory qualities amplify the richness and suggestivity of Borges' stories and may help explain the extraordinary quantity of criticism devoted to them.

Paradox in Borges' work is frequently indicated by a mask used to disguise a false identity. As critics such as Emir Rodríguez Monegal (29–32) and Sylvia Molloy (18–25) have noted, Borges' fascination (and discomfort) for masks, a life-long obsession with paradoxical dualities in which truth is concealed by false appearance, becomes a central organizing principle in Borges' writings. The craft of fiction for Borges, then, is the unmasking of the reality lying below the surface of the false façade. And this process of revelation is accompanied by the simultaneous sensations of pleasure and uneasiness. In this essay, I will examine how Borges cleverly uses a visible mark as a mask, concealing as well as displaying the truth regarding the main character in the story, **"La forma de la espada."** The reality that the Borgesian mask both disguises (closets) and reveals (outs) is homoerotic desire.

There is no doubt, in my opinion, that there is something fundamentally queer[1] about Borges' writing. The literary universe that Borges has projected is an essentially homo*social* space, populated almost exclusively by men who love each other, hate each other, betray each other,[2] sacrifice for each other; it is a world where no man successfully relates either socially or sexually to any woman; it is also a place where men interact passionately with other men through art and culture, intellectual games, battles and duels. It is, in other words, an imagined location in which men form deep, intimate bonds and relationships with other men in the almost total absence of women. The extent of the homosocial nature of Borges' world becomes immediately apparent when the reader discovers that there are central female characters in only nine stories by Borges (Agheana 381) and that most of them are closely related to themes of "death, violence and often sacrifice" (Magnarelli 142).

A close look at Borges' fictional world reveals relationships between men indicating more than a bond of friendship or a meeting of minds, more than a fusion of identities. In story after story, Borges has made a practice of replacing the traditional image of the union of opposites represented in *sexual* terms (female and male) by substituting the *gender* opposites (feminine and masculine) existing within each individual man. Borges does not follow the social and literary custom of men seeking delight and fulfillment in the "opposite sex." Instead, men in the Borgesian universe must join with other *men* to find wholeness, peace and symmetry. As a result, in Borges' stories the act of union or fusion of two men, physically, spiritually and emotionally manifests graphically the now infamous Borgesian obsession with completeness, totality, and harmony as a release or escape from the tyranny of chaos and fragmentation.

For some critics, it may be a bold or even a shocking project to link the work of such an important canonical writer as Jorge Luis Borges with a gay theme. In their insightful studies on Borges, both Daniel Altamiranda and Daniel Balderston ("Fecal") note that Borges himself found the topic of homosexuality extremely troubling and made strongly negative public statements about it. One frightful example can be found in Borges' 1931 essay called "Nuestras imposibilidades," from the first edition of his collection, *Discusión*. This essay, removed from later editions, criticizes what Borges believes to be certain unpleasant traits among the citizens of Buenos Aires and includes this condemnation of the cynical admiration for the "active" partner in sodomy among certain *porteños*: "En todos los países de la tierra, una indivisible reprobación recae sobre los dos ejecutores del inimaginable contacto. [. . .] No así entre el malevaje de Buenos Aires, que reclama una especia de veneración para el agente activo—porque lo embromó al compañero" (*Discusión* 16–17). There can be no doubt that Borges was openly homophobic when confronting the topic directly, but as is usually the case with his writing, things are more complicated than the surface might indicate. As this essay will demonstrate, despite the fact that Borges codifies the same-sex desire of a specific fictional character in unambiguously dreadful terms, it is my contention that that condemnation may be a clever way to mask his own unconscious identification with the character.

Part of the difficulty in locating a queer theme in Borges' writing is that there is nothing *explicitly* homosexual in any of Borges' stories. In societies which have vilified and demonized non-traditional sexualities—and within the Latin American context Argentina is particularly notable for its homophobic traditions, as Acevedo (220–239) and Jáuregui (157–93) demonstrate, the open, clear, explicit expression of homosexual desire is quite rare before the middle of the twentieth century. Before that time, only the most audacious and courageous writers dared to speak of the "unspeakable" or mention the "unmentionable." It is important to remember, as Lee Edelman illustrates, that the expression of same-sex desire has been classified throughout the centuries as the "love that dare not speak its name" or the "peccatum illud horribile, inter christianos non nominandum." In the Western tradition, then, homosexual desire has been considered so heinous, so infamous,

so offensive that the mere *mention* of it can have damaging and noxious effects on society as a whole (5). In light of the Judeo-Christian history of virulent opposition to the simple designation of homosexuality, as well as of Borges' infamous aversion to sexuality itself (his characters almost without exception speak of sex as a "cosa horrible" as in **"Emma Zunz"** and in **"La secta del fénix,"** sex is labeled ridiculous, vulgar, incredible, trivial, distressing and despicable), it certainly would be surprising to find an unveiled representation of homosexual themes or behavior in any of his fictions. In fact, in several stories Borges displays a veritable disgust with regard to sexual activity itself.

Unfortunately, there are those who demand "concrete evidence" of a homosexual element in a work of literature before anyone can even suggest that a character might be codified as gay. Such protestations demonstrate on the one hand, a naive ignorance of the Western cultural prohibitions on nontraditional sexualities, and, on the other, a limited view of the ways fictional art functions. Until very recently, both in life and in literature, heterosexuality could automatically be assumed, without evidence, as the orientation of all living beings. But as so much research has shown, that assumption has never been valid. Consequently, calls for explicit and concrete, yet strictly forbidden images of same-sex desire in certain works of literature suggest what Eve Kosofsky Sedgwick calls an "arrogant intent of maintaining ignorance" (51).

Given Borges' open hostility to homosexuality (or any sexuality, for that matter), how can we say that there is anything gay in any of his texts? Despite the social injunction against the outright naming of homosexuality, same-sex desire has been insinuated for centuries by codification and camouflage. The code effectively conceals and obscures the homosexuality within the work, making it merely appear invisible or nonexistent. One cannot, however, equate the *appearance* of nonexistence with nonexistence itself; the masking or coding of homosexuality does not translate into its absence. How, then, can a critic, as Edelman puts it, "see or recognize 'the homosexual' in order to bring 'homosexuality' into theoretical view? How, that is, can 'homosexuality' find its place in the discourse of contemporary criticism so that it will no longer be unmarked or invisible or perceptible only when tricked out in the most blatant thematic or referential drag?" (3–4). The answer must reside in the de-coding, the un-masking of the veiled expressions of same-sex desire and the subsequent revelation of hitherto unsuspected sexual variation in literary works, especially those works as loaded with masks, camouflages, and disguises as Borges' **"La forma de la espada."**

"La forma de la espada" is rare among Borges' stories: it has received decidedly mixed reviews and is, consequently, one of the texts least studied by critics. Of the negative appraisals of the story, probably the most unfavorable is Gene Bell-Villada's in which he calls **"La forma de la espada"** a "rather slight little tale" and goes so far as to say that it is "marred by its peevish and heavy-handed political judgments" (73). He points out that even Borges himself considered it a mere "trick story" (Burgin 145). But in contrast to these facile dismissals, most critics agree that it is a well written mystery story and that its surprise ending is playfully suggestive in its implications about the nature of human identity and the relationship between self and other.

The story's theme, according to most critics, is perfectly congruent with the traditional list of Borgesian themes established by scholars over the past thirty years: obsession with circularity, pantheism and the double. Donald McGrady, for example, analyzes the circularity inherent in the numerous clues with regard to the identity of the narrator. Helene Weldt, applying Barthes' principles of the five codes as explored in *S/Z,* also explores the textual circularity of the story and concludes that

> la técnica que Borges emplea en [**"La forma de la espada"**] . . . va más allá de un mero esparcimiento de "pistas". Su creación literaria se construye principalmente a través de esta red de alusiones e interconexiones sutiles que le obligan al lector a que abandone una sola lectura lineal, tradicional, a favor de las múltiples lecturas circulares.
>
> (225–26)

Jaime Alazraki examines the question of identity and concludes that in this story, circularity and the "pantheistic notion that one man is all men implies the negation of individual identity, or more exactly, the reduction of all individuals to a general and supreme identity which contains all and at the same time makes all contained in each one. In the stories **'The Shape of the Sword'** and **'Abenjacán the Bojarí, Dead in His Labyrinth,'** this notion functions as a narrative technique" (24). Like McGrady, George McMurray notes that the "most striking element" of the story is its surprise ending and then concurs with Alazraki that the "apparent fusion of opposites also serves to suggest the pantheistic theme that any man can be all men" (94) and that the "compression of time, which parallels the fusion of antithetical identities, reinforces the story's theme of pantheistic unity" (95).

Circularity, interconnectedness, fusion of opposite identities—all within a society of men. Circularity of men, interconnectedness of men, fusion of men. The critics all seem to agree on the basic abstract implications of the story, and once they place the story into the standard Borgesian categories, they stop. They stop before they get to the point where they would have to investigate what all this fusion of men might *really* suggest.

In the story **"La forma de la espada,"** the main character, John Vincent Moon, acquires a coded sign that *marks* him, literally and figuratively, as queer. In the frame of the story, a man identified as "Borges" (**"Forma"** 139) must stay at the ranch of a man called "El Inglés de La Colorada" whose face bears a scar in the shape of a crescent moon beginning at the temple of one side of his head and

extending to the cheek of the other side. Borges asks the man to tell how he got the scar. The man reveals his "secret": he explains that he is really Irish, not English, and that the story begins in Ireland during the wars of independence. "El Inglés" states that during one of the conflicts, he saves the life of a particularly cowardly revolutionary, John Vincent Moon. Moon's terror makes him utterly useless for street fighting, and once superficially wounded, he stays in an old house which was "desmedrado y opaco y abundaba en perplejos corredores y en vanas antecámaras" (**"Forma"** 136–37). The two men remain in the house for nine days—"Esos nueve días, en mi recuerdo, forman un solo día, salvo el penúltimo" (**"Forma"** 138)—during which Moon spends the day studying the plans and papers of the revolutionary group while he recuperates. Returning to the house early one day, the narrator discovers Moon in telephone contact with the English, betraying his protector and friend. The narrator of the tale chases Moon through the labyrinthine corridors and passageways of the house and finally corners him. He delivers a slash with a scimitar across Moon's face, leaving a scar that will mark him forever as someone who is cowardly and treacherous—someone duplicitous. Moon collects his "dineros de Judas" and sets off for Brazil. The narrator finishes his story by declaring outright what the reader might already suspect: he himself is the betrayer, John Vincent Moon.

Some of the details of this story do not seem to make sense; there are a number of unexplained elements that, at first glance, are troubling. For example, although the courageous and experienced revolutionary saves Moon from certain death in the streets by taking his arm and pulling him to safety, Moon is only superficially wounded as a direct consequence of his own weakness and cowardice. Considering that the wound is not life-threatening, why do the two men hide out in an empty house rather than rejoining their comrades? Why does the courageous young revolutionary not only nurse the wound, but also insist on tending personally to Moon and keeping him there alone with him? Why do the two men remain together, side by side, night after night for nine days, in a strange old house, secluded and isolated from their companions? Could one or both of the men have engineered their seclusion in response to intense homoerotic desires?

I find that the answer to these questions lies in the highly codified figure of John Vincent Moon. He is described from the very beginning as a very queer sort of fellow—he seems to be many different things all at once. "El Inglés" states that Moon "era flaco y fofo a la vez, daba la incómoda impresión de ser invertebrado" (**"Forma"** 135). As McGrady indicates, the "contradictory condition of being at the same time "flaco y fofo" suggests not a neutral Janus-like duality of temperament, but—because of the negative connotations of the two adjectives—"devious duplicity" (143). These gender-charged words used to describe Moon as skinny and soft, weak and spineless ("invertebrate") all indicate that Moon is not at all the brave and masculine warrior who courageously battles for the honor, either personal or national, that every "real" man is traditionally obliged to defend. Rather, the description of Moon specifically paints him as unmanly, effeminate and vulnerable. The image of Moon described here typifies the "misplaced femininity" with its resultant duplicity that heteropatriarchal societies attribute to any man who does not display typically "macho" qualities.

In addition to the physically feminine elements that characterize John Vincent Moon, a very important character trait plainly defines him as unmanly: his paralyzing fear and cowardice in the face of danger: "la pasión del miedo lo invalidaba." Not only is Moon rendered useless in the skirmish, but he also whimpers and cries: after he was wounded, "[él] prorrumpió en un débil sollozo" (**"Forma"** 136). Moon's humilliating inability to confront the hazards of fighting becomes even more apparent when the man who saved him suggests that they leave the house and join their comrades. After getting his gun he finds Moon "tendido en el sofá, con los ojos cerrados. Conjeturó que tenía fiebre; invocó un doloroso espasmo en el hombro" (**"Forma"** 137). Moon's need to pretend that he is too hurt to leave the house focuses attention on the fact that Moon is terrified by what is traditionally perceived of as an archetypally masculine activity, combat. This image of Moon, lying on his back in a traditionally passive, feminine posture, connects the characterization of Moon as both uncourageous *as well as* feminine, creating a link in the reader's mind between his unwillingness to fight and his weak, passive, unmanliness. Cowards are made "effeminate" and effeminate men are made cowardly because cultural norms have defined bravery as a masculine and heterosexual trait, while cowardice is fixed as feminine and homosexual.

It would be difficult to overstress the powerful resonance in the context of Argentine society of this portrait of Moon as an effeminate man who is frightened of combat. Such men are not only a danger to society because they might betray their own nation, but also because they have already betrayed their own gender: they are queers. In strongly heteropatriarchal cultures, behaviors that are considered nonconformist in terms of gender are equated instantaneously and automatically with sexual nonconformity: effeminate men are categorized as homosexuals by virtue of the lack of those macho features specifically prescribed by the culture. In fact, as David Buchbinder and Barbara Milech affirm, "[e]ffeminacy in the male becomes for the normative heterosexual culture, the sign of homosexuality itself, of deviance from the masculine, heterosexual norm, of ab-'normality'" (71). In Hispanic cultures, too, as Lillian Manzor-Coats states, the designation of a man as "homosexual" is determined primarily by his gender identity:

> The category homosexual is not necessarily occupied by the one who is inolved in same-sex erotic practices, but by the one who deviates from the gender constructs. In other words, in most societies in Latin America a man who engages in homosexual activity with other men is considered to be queer, *maricón,* only if and when he does not play his role as macho—that is, when

he assumes the sexual and social role of the passive, the open, the weak; when he assumes the position and plays the role of woman. As long as he plays his active role as macho properly, the gender of his sexual partner is inconsequential, and he remains indistinguishable from the rest of the male population.

(xxi)

The distinctly Hispanic construction of homosexual identity helps provide a culturally specific context for assessing the implications of Borges' characterization of Moon. In the text, Moon's queerness resides primarily in his gender nonconformity which metonymically proclaims his sexual "deviation."

The issue of cowardice also has specifically Argentine reverberations. Zelmar Acevedo, in his study on homosexuality, for example, discusses the intimate link between Argentina's traditional glorification of military values and its crushing heterosexism. The numerous military dictatorships throughout Argentina's history could be considered both an underlying cause as well as an effect of socially reinforced homophobia and almost without exception, every military government in Argentina since the turn of the twentieth century has launched a carefully orchestrated and public crack-down on homosexuals. This homophobic project is exemplified by an article, "Acabar con los homosexuales," which appeared in the early 1970s in a right-wing magazine called *El Caudillo*. As Acevedo notes, the magazine's director was José López Rega, M. Estela Martínez de Perón's minister of Social Welfare. The article affirms that

> . . . los maricones deben ser erradicados de nuestra sociedad. / Deben prohibirse las exhibiciones de cine, televisión o teatro que difundan esa perversión al pueblo. El enemigo quiere y busca un país vencido. / A los que ya son proponemos que se los interne en campos de reeducación y trabajo, para que de esa manera cumplan con dos objetivos: estar lejos de la ciudad y compensar a la Nación—trabajando—la pérdida de un hombre útil. / Hay que acabar con los homosexuales. / Tenemos que crear Brigadas Callejeras que salgan a recorrer los barrios de las ciudades para que den caza a estos sujetos vestidos como mujeres, hablando como mujeres, pensando como mujeres.

(216)

These opinions express with great clarity the fascist cultural beliefs that 1) homosexual men are dangerous because they weaken a nation, making it vulnerable to its enemies, 2) homosexual men are useless and represent the loss or waste of a "real man," and 3) the femininity of homosexual men makes them not only appear womanly, but even causes them to *think* like women. It is this feminine thinking that is so perverse and menacing.

In Argentine culture, as in the work of Borges, the overtly expressed admiration and even veneration of the concept of masculine power is manifested through military authority.[3] As a result, Borges, in this story, makes the link between a threat to masculine gender and the threat to military strength by collapsing the perceived menace in the figure of an effeminate traitor who betrays the masculine fighter. As a soldier in the fight for Irish independence, Moon actually becomes more dangerous than the English enemy because he represents the "subversive" element that threatens other soldiers from within their own camp.

Moon is incapable of any type of direct action that characterizes his brave protector and it is precisely this passivity that is accentuated by a description of his thoroughly intellectual and abstract approach to war: "[m]i compañero me esperaba en el primer piso: la herida no le permitía descender a la planta baja. Lo rememoro con algún libro de estrategia en la mano . . ." (**"Forma"** 138). The contrast between the two men is made explicit: the admirable, honorable, manly aspects of the hero find their opposition in the despicable, disgraceful, and feminine elements of the traitor. As a result, there can be no mistake about the description of Moon: he appears to be the very picture of the stereotypical weak, soft, and passive "sissy." The result of such unmistakable feminine characteristics present in a male are not only disturbing ("incómoda impresión"), but also, as the ending reveals, dangerous.

To reinforce and emphasize Moon's femininity and passivity as well as his inconsistency, Borges has selected a curiously symbolic surname. As Juan-Eduardo Cirlot indicates, the relationship between the moon, feminine sexuality and changeability is ancient and runs across a variety of cultures: "[e]l hombre percibió, de antiguo, la relación existente entre la luna y las mareas; la conexión más extraña aún entre el ciclo lunar y el ciclo fisiológico de la mujer" (283); "[p]or su carácter pasivo, al recibir la luz solar, es asimilada al principio del dos y de la pasividad o lo femenino" (284). As a scholar on symbolism and metaphor in both the Eastern and Western traditions, and as an author who was playful in his use of symbolic names, it is probable that Borges chose the name "Moon" for its specific symbolic connotations. Certainly Borges was fully aware of the link between the feminine and the lunar. Julio Woscoboinik, for example, correctly indicates that "[n]o podemos dejar de mencionar que Luna es una metáfora muy frecuente en Borges para decir acerca de la mujer" (154).

In addition to the feminine qualities of the moon, Cirlot indicates another very important symbolic quality of moon: it constantly varies and transforms itself, yet it remains a single entity. "[P]or encima de todo, es el ser que no permanece siempre idéntico a sí mismo, sino que experimenta modificaciones 'dolorosas' en forma de círculo clara y continuamente observable" (283). The phases of the moon from new to crescent to full, all characterize the ever-changing identity of John Vincent Moon. The fact that Moon appears to embody a multiplicity of seemingly opposing attributes is underscored, again, by his name. He may appear to be many different things, but he is, despite all the disguises, one person. Woscoboinik perceptively points out that ". . . Borges hace referencia a la palabra

LUNA y la compara con MOON, su designación en inglés. Le place MOON "porque obliga la voz a demorarse'. Palabras sugerentes: a Borges no le pasó inadvertido, que luna tiene involucrada una y que moon, fonéticamente (mun), también encierra *un*" (154). John Vincent Moon is the physical embodiment of the unification of opposites, the conjunction of paradoxical dualities: feminine and masculine; unity and duality; love and betrayal.

The emphasis placed on Moon's feminine inconstancy serves to make Moon's treachery appear more understandable and consistent with his character. But this linking of femininity within the confines of a male body with the heinous crime of betrayal also serves to reinforce and strengthen the stereotypes that Western heteropatriarchal societies have utilized in order to demonize homosexuals. As a result, Borges' characterization of John Vincent Moon amplifies the infamy of gay men by conjoining same-sex desire with deceitfulness. Since "El Inglés" never explains the reasons underlying Moon's decision to betray his comrade, the reader is left with the impression that the action was unmotivated, and therefore, simply to be expected in a man like Moon: Moon exposes his inherently treacherous nature when he repays his protector and savior with disloyalty for what seems like no good reason. As will be shown later in this study, money alone does not and cannot account for the betrayal: there are no textual indications that would suggest that Moon was in desperate need of money, or was particularly greedy. In fact, the references to Moon's Marxist political affiliation effectively negate the love of money as a motivating force in his actions.

The narrator's depiction of Moon (i.e. himself) in homophobic terms taps into the commonly held belief that homosexuals are condemned to commit ignoble actions: "[g]ays are viewed first and foremost simply as morally lesser beings, like animals, children, or dirt, *not* as failed full moral agents. . . . Such acts as gays are thought to perform—whether sexual, gestural, or social—are viewed socially as the expected or even necessary efflorescence of gays' lesser moral state, of their status as lesser beings . . ." (Mohr 245–46).

John Vincent Moon lacks the nobility of character embodied in the masculine hero figure: courage and bravery, physical strength, constant devotion to the ideal. Although Moon's betrayal of the young republican may be understood as the vile, but inevitable, action directly resulting from his status as a spiritually degenerate pervert, the critical motivation underlying his action becomes clear at the moment when he is explicitly connected to the archetype of the treacherous and envious traitor: Judas. Moon arranges the betrayal of his companion by informing the British soldiers that they can arrest him as he crosses through a garden, and then, after the horrible deed is done, Moon "[c]obró los dineros de Judas y huyó al Brasil" (**"Forma"** 139). The Judas archetype is a very powerful one and its potency lies in the fact that, as Carl Jung puts it, ". . . envy does not let mankind sleep in peace" (31).

Envy is one of the central and defining features of Moon's character: a weak and feminine man feels an unbridled envy for the attractive, desirable qualities of a friend and this envy leads to murder. In the process, the murderer is permanently marked. The homosexual, a freakish woman imprisoned in a male body, must possess the worst imaginable "feminine" impulses. At this point, it might help to recall that since Borges' father was a professor of psychology, it is therefore possible, if not very likely, that Borges, due to his remarkably wide reading interests, language abilities, and access to his father's exceptional library, had come across the work of Karl Heinrich Ulrichs and his formulation of sexual "inversion" as a "woman's soul trapped in a man's body" ("anima muliebris virili corpore inclusa") and that it was this and other Victorian concepts that formed his understanding of same-sex desire. In his study of the Argentine theorization of homosexuality at the turn of the century, Daniel Bao notes that the traditional negative stereotypes of women were, in fact, transferred over to "inverts" because of their supposed female "essence." Bao quotes a particularly revealing text from 1908 by the lawyer and criminologist, Eusebio Gómez, which states that

> [a]l rasgo que acabamos de indicar en los invertidos, la venalidad, ó más bien dicho, el parasitismo, únese su *carácter caprichoso,* sus *envidias,* la ruindad de todos sus procederes, su *deseo de venganza,* y sus *rencores ilimitados.* Tarnowski dice que reunen en sí todos los defectos de las mujeres sin tener ninguna de sus cualidades, careciendo, además de las condiciones que *hacen amable el carácter viril.*

> (198–99)

Gómez further notes that inverts "[s]on *celosos* y esta pasión los lleva hasta el crimen. Un sensacional proceso recientemente debatido ante la justicia militar, acaba de dar la prueba al respecto" (199; emphasis added). It is fascinating to find that a scandal within the Argentine military at the turn of the century caused debate on the question of "inverts" among the soldiers. Fascinating, too, is the fact that in 1942, only two years before Borges' story appeared, the Argentine military again suffered another devastating scandal involving cadets from the Colegio Militar. As Acevedo remarks, the events stunned a military so proud of its martial heritage: "[p]recisamente en momentos en que las FF.AA. daban forma a sus ambiciones totalitarias y una perorata de conceptos como virilidad y honor llenaban todas las bocas, la relación entre cadetes y homosexuales, en la que no participaba ninguna violencia, los desnudaba en sus límites y en sus contradicciones; y si es verdad que este affaire los tomó por sorpresa, de ahí en más combatirían la 'inmoralidad' adelantándose a los hechos" (229). This prevailing cultural conceptualization of homosexuality may elucidate Borges' attitude that homosexuals can't be trusted; you can't turn your back on them; they are, by nature, treacherous and their fiendish kisses mark the victims of their betrayal.

But Borges goes even further. Invoking two Biblical models, one from the Old Testament and the other from the New, Borges combines the envy of Cain and his killing of Abel (Gen. 4:3–8) with the envy of Judas that leads him to mark Jesus for death with a kiss (Matt. 27:18, Mark 15:10) and concentrates their attributes in the person of John Vincent Moon. In this way, Moon becomes a contemporary incarnation of a long series of deadly betrayers. Moon's heritage, then, is that of the primordial fratricide as well as the assassin of God.

By linking the image of Cain/Judas with the image of a cowardly, envious, feminized man, Borges makes the case that homosexuals pose a danger and a threat to the security and safety of us all. In order to protect us from their envy, jealousy, duplicity, disloyalty, and deceitfulness, homosexuals need to be identified and labeled as quickly and easily as possible. So Borges returns to the symbolism of Cain and, like the Old Testament God, he marks his character with a sign. This marking of Moon follows a Western tradition of attempting to find a visible, physical difference in homosexuals so that their particularly frightening menace would become obvious to all and could then be neutralized. As a consequence of the need to locate and label homosexuals, scientists in the nineteenth century came to theorize that gays were indeed physically different in appearance—their bodies bore a mark, a sign, a stigma that could be recognized instantly. Indeed, Michel Foucault asserts that it is this marking that, in effect, provides homosexuals with a distinct identity and selfhood:

> The nineteenth-century homosexual became a personage, a past, a case history, and a childhood, in addition to being a type of life, a life form, and a morphology, with an *indiscreet anatomy* and possibly a *mysterious physiology.* Nothing that went into his total composition was unaffected by his sexuality. It was everywhere present in him: at the root of all his actions because it was their insidious and indefinitely active principle; *written immodestly on his face and body* because it was a secret that always gave itself away. It was consubstantial with him, less a habitual sin than as a singular nature.

> (43; emphasis added)

Edelman further stresses the "textuality" and "readability" of the queer body insofar as "homosexuals themselves have been seen as producing—and, by some medical 'experts,' as being produced by—bodies that bore a distinct, and therefore legible, anatomical code. . . . Homosexuals, in other words, were not only conceptualized in terms of a radically potent, if negatively charged, relation to signifying practices, but also subjected to a cultural imperative that viewed them as inherently textual—as bodies that might well bear a 'hallmark' that could, and must, be read" (5–6). Given this social context, it becomes clear why the young hero, once he discovers Moon's act of betrayal, does not use his gun and simply shoot Moon dead, but rather chases him through a dark and somewhat unfamiliar house with, of all things, a scimitar: Moon's desires for men and his betrayal of them must be made visible to society in such a way that he is instantly identifiable. John Vincent Moon, with the crescent moon-shaped scar running across his face, forever bears the mark of the man who has desired and deceived another man and, lest he escape imperceptibly to love and betray again, he is permanently branded by an object (a sword) that symbolizes what he most desires (the phallus). The proscribed desire of one man for another that comes from a presumed inferior moral status is given tangible form: "[i]mperfecciones morales, sufrimientos (¿son lo mismo?) son, pues, simbolizados por heridas y por *cicatrices de hierro* y fuego" (Cirlot 127; emphasis added).

As Balderston has noted ("Mark"), this is not, of course, the only instance in which a man marked with a facial scar appears in Borges' work. One of the most unusual and perhaps unfamiliar is a line drawing made by Borges himself which, as Woscoboinik indicates, was published in the magazine *Valoraciones de La Plata* in August of 1926. The drawing is called "Compadrito de la edad de oro" and in it there is a figure of one of the young toughs that so fascinated and disgusted Borges. Woscoboinik interprets the drawing in this way:

> Mientras el rostro aindiado muestra una expresión dura, desafiante, prepotente, de mirada atenta y provocativa, bigotes marcados y una clara cicatriz, el cuerpo insinúa elementos de inseguridad y ambigüedad sexual. cortada la figura por encima de las rodillas, las caderas son de formas redondeadas, femeninas . . . Pero lo más llamativo, es la cicatriz en el rostro. Este trazo de dos líneas cruzadas, se repite en el cuello, más claramente en axilas, hombro derecho, en lo que serían los bolsillos del saco del pantalón y en la zona genital.
>
> (120)

In this drawing Borges clearly demonstrates that although a man may appear to be tough, courageous and manly on the outside, there seems to be a subtle femininity that belies the outward appearance. The outward image projected by the "compadrito" would appear to be the ultimate in courage, honor and masculinity, but on closer inspection the figure is marked with several obvious feminine characteristics and with a scar on the face to inform the world that he is not what he appears to be. The danger of the "compadrito," like the danger of John Vincent Moon (in his "El Inglés" persona), is precisely the fact that a man can appear to be manly on the outside, but he can be womanly on the inside and that for Borges, the unreliable nature of this "complexio oppositorum" is monstrous indeed: it combines attractive virile qualities such as activity, bravery, and heroism with such despicable feminine qualities as passivity, cowardice, and treachery.

The ending of the story, the result of Moon's betrayal, is curious. Following the biblical allusions, Borges can select from two choices: Moon can either give back the money and hang himself out of shame and guilt like Judas (Matt. 27:3–5) or he can become a fugitive like Cain (Gen. 4:12–14) and leave his homeland. In an odd move, Borges chooses a combination of the two: Moon flees Ireland, runs off to South America, and buys a ranch with the "Judas money" he got from the English. But because of the permanent scar on his face to inform others of his nature, he is forced into making a spectacular decision: he can either continue to live as the cowardly and "feminine" John Vincent Moon, wearing the mark of shame and being the object of derision, or he can convert himself into what was his most fervent desire. With the death of his comrade, the man he adored but had to betray, he is able to come into possession of him by literally becoming him. The copula of the two men is complete when Moon's desire for the young hero becomes so intense and so powerful that the desire is transformed ultimately into identity. The soft and spineless John Vincent Moon disappears; the coward actually converts himself into the courageous and manly hero. Moon, in effect, acquires the identity of his comrade and now wears the mask of a hero. In this way, the soft, youthful sissy-boy, despite being marked with the stigma of his desire, continues to fool people, continues to keep his queerness a secret by putting on the drag of the hypermasculine rancher and living within the exclusively male environment of a ranch.

The treacherous, timid and feminine John Vincent Moon, in a remarkable reversal of imagery, becomes respected and feared: "[d]icen que era severo hasta la crueldad, pero escrupulosamente justo" (**"Forma"** 133). By betraying his friend, Moon (as "El Inglés") ultimately earns the respect of others; by acting fearfully, Moon is eventually feared by others. But those who respect and fear him do not know the ugly secret of "El Inglés": he is a mere imitation, a simulacrum, a fake. What we find in Borges, then, is a conflict between the truly courageous hero and those who, out of a desire to be (like) them, possess them, have them, usurp their position of honor by putting on the mask of masculinity and imitating them. In Borges, the portrayal of the hero can be quite contradictory. Lanin Gyurko has noted: "[t]he cult of the *Macho,* of the man who affirms his virility through a violent public display of courage and prowess, is viewed ambivalently by Borges in his short stories. [. . .] The caricaturing of the [machismo] cult and the debunking of the hero are seen in many of Borges' stories, which depict persons who are publicly accepted as champions but who are really braggarts, incompetents, cowards and liars" (128). Perhaps part of Borges' contempt for certain macho heroes comes from his suspicion that in addition to being cowards and liars, beneath the mask of the tough guy there may also be hiding a cowardly queer. In a 1977 interview with Milton Fornaro, for example, Borges draws a very clear distinction between the brave fighter, worthy of admiration, and the sexually questionable cowards and "rufianes":

> Del cuchillero, lo que yo admiro es la idea de un individuo que, como decía Carriego, es cultor del coraje, que tiene el culto del coraje. [. . .] El cuchillero es un hombre desinteresado. El cuchillero despreciaba al rufián. El rufián era una persona muy despreciada entre el malevaje, y el cobarde también. El rufián sí, porque el rufián es una persona que vive de las mujeres, era casi peor que ser maricón. No se le veía como nada admirable.
>
> (113)

Like his creation, Moon, Borges admires the courageous macho man. In fact, Moon and Borges have a great deal in common. Considering the relentlessly negative characterization of Moon, it is odd that Borges would make the character so much like himself. For example, the desire for the virile qualities that led Moon to adopt the identity of his dead companion represents the very same yearning that Borges expressed so often with respect to his own heroic ancestors. Borges spoke frequently and passionately about the esteem and regard he held for his noble and courageous forefathers, while in contrast to them, he speaks of himself in these terms:

> I felt *ashamed,* quite early, to be a bookish kind of person and *not a man of action.* Throughout my boyhood, I thought that to be loved would have amounted to an injustice. I did not feel I deserved any particular love, and I remember my birthdays filled me with *shame,* because everyone heaped gifts on me when I thought that I had done nothing to deserve them—that *I was a kind of fake.*
>
> ("Autobiographical Essay" 208–209; emphasis added)

The self-deprecating phrases he uses for himself, the fact that he did not feel worthy of love because of his lack of manly activity, and his believing himself to be a "fake" are all elements suggesting a close affinity between Moon and Borges. Although by nature neither Moon nor Borges participate in virile pursuits, they both admire and delight in them and feel ashamed for that lack of "masculinity" in themselves. It is clear that Borges, like Moon, is *envious* of those men who embody masculine virtues. Furthermore, both of them share a pronounced intellectual bent. As "El Inglés" says of Moon, "[p]ara mostrar que le era indiferente ser un cobarde físico, magnificaba su soberbia mental" (**"Forma"** 138). In the end, it appears that the figure of John Vincent Moon represents those characteristics of Borges that he most despised in himself: the cowardice, the passivity, the envy—all those despicable *feminine* attributes that may have caused Borges to question his own sexuality.

Given the cultural context in which Borges grew up, it is unfortunate, although not surprising, that he would link same-sex desire with fear and loathing. So just when Moon might have gotten away with his monstrous secret, he is confronted by the character Borges on his ranch and, on the specific condition that Borges "no mitigar ningún oprobio, ninguna circunstancia de infamia" (**"Forma"** 134–35), Moon both explains the origin and cause of the scar, and in the process "outs" himself to the reader by revealing his true identity as a coward, a betrayer, and a homosexual. Moon's confession of his "secreto" reinforces the misconception that homoerotic desire cannot have positive results and that it ultimately leads to tragedy and death. He is living proof that gays must be immediately identifiable. The mark or brand will serve to keep society safe from the dangers that queers present if they are permitted to roam freely, to "pass" undetected among us. John Vincent Moon, the Judas who kisses and then betrays the men he most admires and desires, disfigured forever, serves as the example of what horrors same-sex desires bring. Moon's final words to Borges, the final words of the story, summarize the lesson that society has been pounding into homosexuals' heads for centuries: now that you know who and what I am, "[a]hora desprécieme" (**"Forma"** 140). [Now despise me.]

Notes

1. The use of the word "queer" remains quite controversial. For some, the original meaning of "strange" or "abnormal" used in a harmful and aggressive way against homosexuals still retains the painful stigma of an insult. For others, including myself, the appropriation of the word by those who had been harmed by it has neutralized its offensive value and has provided a convenient way of expressing a wide array of non-heterosexual sexualities as well as a critical stance that opposes assumptions of monolithic sexual identity.

2. Jean Franco, in her excellent 1981 study, points out that many of Borges' stories are based on his obsession with the themes of betrayal and cowardice and that "[t]reachery is thus the rule of human interaction and entropy is the most powerful law of Borges's world; solidarity, on the other hand, becomes an absurd and idealist illusion" (74).

3. Borges' conservative political ideology and esteem for Argentine military heritage are well known. See Benedetti and Orgambide for rather negative assessments of Borges' position. It must be said, however, that at the end of his life, when confronted with the horrors of the "Dirty War" conducted by the Argentine military, Borges repudiated his earlier views.

Works Cited

Acevedo, Zelmar. *Homosexualidad: Hacia la destrucción de los mitos.* Buenos Aires: Del Ser, 1985.

Agheana, Ion T. *Reasoned Thematic Dictionary of the Prose of Jorge Luis Borges.* Hanover, N.H.: Ediciones del Norte, 1990.

Alazraki, Jaime. *Jorge Luis Borges.* New York: Columbia U P, 1971. Columbia Essays on Modern Writers 57.

Altamiranda, Daniel. "Jorge Luis Borges (Argentina; 1899–1986)." *Latin American Writers on Gay and Lesbian Themes: A Bio-Critical Sourcebook.* Ed. David William Foster. Westport: Greenwood P, 1994. 72–83.

Balderston, Daniel. "The Fecal Dialectic: Homosexual Panic and the Origin of Writing in Borges." *¿Entiendes? Queer Readings, Hispanic Writings.* Eds. Emilie L. Bergmann and Paul Julian Smith. Durham: Duke UP, 1995. 29–45.

———. "The Mark of the Knife: Scars as Sign in Borges." *The Modern Language Review* 83.1 (1988): 67–75.

Bao, Daniel. "Invertidos Sexuales, Tortilleras, and Maricas Machos: The Construction of Homosexuality in Buenos Aires, Argentina, 1900–1950." *Journal of Homosexuality* 24.3–4 (1993): 183–219.

Bell-Villada, Gene H. *Borges and His Fiction: A Guide to His Mind and Art.* Chapel Hill: U of North Carolina P, 1981.

Benedetti, Mario. "Borges o el fascismo ingenioso." In his *El recurso del supremo patriarca.* México, D. F.: Nueva Imagen, 1979. 93–99.

Borges, Jorge Luis. "An Autobiographical Essay." In *The Aleph and Other Stories 1933–1969.* New York: E. P. Dutton, 1970. 201–260.

———. *Discusión.* 1st ed. Buenos Aires: M. Gleizer, 1932.

———. *Ficciones.* Madrid: Alianza, 1982.

Buchbinder, David and Barbara H. Milech. "Construction Site: The Male Homosexual Subject in Narrative." *Works and Days: Essays in the Socio-Historical Dimension of Literature and the Arts* 9.18 (Fall 1991): 67–87.

Burgin, Richard. *Conversations with Jorge Luis Borges.* New York: Avon Books, 1970.

Cirlot, Juan-Eduardo. *Diccionario de simbolos.* 3rd edition. Barcelona: Editorial Labor, 1979.

Edelman, Lee. *Homographesis: Essays in Gay Literary and Cultural Theory.* New York: Routledge, 1994.

Fornaro, Milton. "El otro, el mismo Borges." *Texto Crítico* 3.8 (1977): 108–16.

Foucault, Michel. *The History of Sexuality. Volume 1: An Introduction.* Trans. Robert Hurley. New York: Vintage, 1980.

Franco, Jean. "The Utopia of a Tired Man: Jorge Luis Borges." *Social Text* 4 (Fall 1981): 52–78.

Gyurko, Lanin A. "Borges and the *Machismo* Cult." *Revista Hispánica Moderna* 36.3 (1970–71): 128–45.

Jáuregui, Carlos Luis. *La homosexualidad en la Argentina.* Buenos Aires: Ediciones Tarso, 1978.

Jung, C. G. *Symbols of Transformation: An Analysis of the Prelude to a Case of Schizophrenia.* Vol. 5 of *The Collected Works of C. G. Jung.* Trans. R. F. C. Hull. 2nd ed. Bollingen Series XX. Princeton: Princeton UP, 1967.

Lancaster, Roger N. "Subject Honor and Object Shame: The Construction of Male Homosexuality and Stigma in Nicaragua." *Ethnology* 27.2 (1987): 111–125.

Magnarelli, Sharon. "Literature and Desire: Women in the Fiction of Jorge Luis Borges." *Revista/Review Interamericana* 13.1–4 (1983): 138–149.

Manzor-Coats, Lillian. "Introduction." *Latin American Writers on Gay and Lesbian Themes: A Bio-Critical Sourcebook.* Ed. David William Foster. Westport: Greenwood P, 1994. xv–xxxvi.

McGrady, Donald. "Prefiguration, Narrative Transgression and Eternal Return in Borges' 'La forma de la espada.'" *Revista Canadiense de Estudios Hispánicos* 12.1 (1987): 141–49.

McMurray, George R. *Jorge Luis Borges.* New York: Frederick Ungar, 1980.

Mohr, Richard D. *Gay Ideas: Outing and Other Controversies.* Boston: Beacon P, 1992.

Molloy, Silvia. *Signs of Borges.* Trans. Oscar Montero. Durham: Duke UP, 1994.

Orgambide, Pedro. *Borges y su pensamiento político.* México: Comité de Solidaridad con el Pueblo Argentino, 1978.

Rodríguez Monegal, Emir. *Jorge Luis Borges: A Literary Biography.* New York: Paragon House, 1988.

Salessi, Jorge. "The Argentine Dissemination of Homosexuality, 1890–1914." *Journal of the History of Sexuality* 4.3 (1994): 337–368.

Sedgwick, Eve Kosofsky. *Epistemology of the Closet.* Berkeley: U of California P, 1990.

Weldt, Helene. "La forma del relato borgiano: Las lecturas circulares de 'La forma de la espada.'" *Symposium* 45.3 (1991): 218–227.

Woscoboinik, Julio. *El secreto de Borges. Indagación psicoanalítica de su obra.* Buenos Aires: Editorial Trieb, 1988.

Alice E. H. Petersen (essay date 1996)

SOURCE: "Borges's 'Ulrike'—Signature of a Literary Life," in *Studies in Short Fiction*, Vol. 33, No. 3, Summer, 1996, pp. 325–31.

[*In the following essay, Petersen defends Borges's later fiction against criticism that it is inferior to his earlier work.*]

When readers of Borges reach for his later works, they are often a little disappointed by what they find. Collections like ***The Book of Sand*** (which contains the short story **"Ulrike"**) and ***Doctor Brodie's Report,*** which both appeared in the 1970s, are often passed over because they lack the obvious touches of "Borges" associated with metaphysical whimsy and the yellow tigers that stalked the works of an earlier age. Many critics resort to paraphrase instead of analysis, as if there is no more to be done with Borges but reiterate his own tales. Writing about ***The Book of Sand,*** Gene Bell-Villada complains that there are "no over-arching concerns, thematic or otherwise. . . . Although certain subjects do recur, they do not add up to any systematic set of preoccupations" (Bell-Villada 255).

I suggest that the line of Borges's narrative development precludes the explicit statement of "over-arching concerns." Over the years, the concerns of Borges have become so familiar to both author and reader that the barest hint of a personal preoccupation in the text suffices to recall a vast expanse of meaning. The preoccupations remain the same, but the manner of revoicing them has changed. In "The Fearful Sphere of Pascal," Borges comments: "it may be that history is the history of the different intonation given a handful of metaphors" (*Labyrinths* 227). It would not be untrue to suggest that the history Borges speaks of is not just literary history but also the personal history of a literary career. It may be that Borges's last works are not his greatest, but they are nonetheless the signature of a lifetime of significant literary activity.

Borges's consciousness of the past involved not just an awareness of literary tradition but also a sense of his own career as it developed within that tradition. He saw that he was not unaltered by his creative life, writing, "I think a writer is being changed all the time by his output. So that perhaps at first what he writes is not relevant to him. And if he goes on writing, he'll find that those things are ringing bells all the time" (Barnstone 92–93). Thus, he continued, everything was to be found in one way or another in that first book of poetry, *Fervor de Buenos Aires* (1923).

Borges was never one to be weighted down by the anxieties of influence. Rather, he reveled in the possibility of being indebted to the past. His method of freeing himself from the ancestral writer was to rewrite that ancestral figure, in effect, to recreate the past. He writes in "Kafka and His Precursors," "the writer creates his own precursors. His work modifies our conception of the past, as it will modify the future" (*Labyrinths* 236).

A footnote referring the reader to a collection of T. S. Eliot's essays, *Points of View,* indicates the source of the model of artistic invention which Borges appropriated in "Kafka and His Precursors." In "Tradition and the Individual Talent," contained in this collection, Eliot describes all existing works of art as forming an ideal order, changed by the introduction of new works:

> What happens when a new work of art is created is some thing that happens simultaneously to all the works of art which preceded it. The existing monuments form an ideal order among themselves, which is modified by the introduction of the new (the really new) work of art among them. . . . Whoever has approved this idea of order, of the form of European, of English literature will not find it preposterous that the past should be altered by the present as much as the present is directed by the past.
>
> (*Points of View* 25–26)[1]

For Borges, the theory of Platonic archetypes is the means by which the individual, through the act of literary creation, becomes part of the timeless; it also became the means by which he realized his unique position as a writer as well as his own necessary subjugation to tradition.

Borges recognized that rewriting a tale brings fresh life to both ancestral and contemporary texts. The unique intonation of each writer ensures that what goes on within the text remains a movement forward, a dynamic pulse toward the next reincarnation of the archetype. The word within the text is charged with a sense of imminence, of becoming. Borges writes concerning this:

> Music, states of happiness, mythology, faces molded by time, certain twilights and certain places—all these are trying to tell us something, or have told us something we should not have missed, or are about to tell us something; that imminence of a revelation that is not yet produced is, perhaps, the aesthetic reality.
>
> (*Labyrinths* 223)

As the author becomes older, and his sense of tradition stronger, the fragility of the contemporary text becomes more pronounced; the voice that reiterates is both humbled by its forbears, but at the same time borne up by their example. To return to a dominant theme in Borges's work—there are very few metaphors, and these few are merely renewed by successive generations after the manner that most pleases them. However, the manner of renewing the metaphor must be in keeping with the simplicity of the ideal archetype, and this is the responsibility and the prerogative of the individual voice. One of the strengths of Borges's late works lies in his espousal of the simplicity required by the basic forms of tradition. At the age of 80, he verbally renounced the willful obscurity and baroque style of earlier days: "now I am daring and I write in a straightforward way and use no word to send a reader to the dictionary, and avoid violent metaphors" (Barnstone 123).

"Ulrike" demonstrates both the simplicity that characterizes the later narratives of Borges and the strength that these tales draw from the concept of a Platonic tradition of literary forms. It is a new emanation of a very old tale, and as such, it is driven by its precursor, demonstrating the Platonic push forward toward the next revelation of the text. At the same time, however, it is infused with Borges's particular intonation and his language of personal symbols.

In the tale, Borges rewrites a section of William Morris's translation of the *Saga of the Volsungs* using a contemporary English setting. In the Morris work, the warrior-maid Brynhild has vowed to wed Siguard the dragon-slayer, the only man with enough courage to brave the wall of flames surrounding her castle. However, before the marriage can take place, Sigurd is beguiled into marrying Queen Gudrun. The Queen's brother Gunnar becomes enamored of Brynhild but lacks the courage to pass through the flames surrounding her castle. Sigurd, to aid Gunnar's cause, changes forms with Gunnar, so that Sigurd's spirit of courage within Gunnar's body plunges through the fire. Gunnar, having proved his "courage" betroths himself to Brynhild, and lies with her, although Sigurd's sword Gram physically separates them. Eventually Brynhild discovers the deception. She is distraught, but steadfast in her decision to remain true to her oath to Gunnar or die. Brynhild refuses Sigurd's rather belated offer to install her as Queen in place of Gudrun, and instead she organizes his death.

Borges identifies the section of the tale that he is choosing to revoice in the epigraph to **"Ulrike"**: "He took the sword Gram and laid it naked between them" (*The Saga of the Volsungs* 29; **The Book of Sand** 11).[2] At this point Brynhild is being deceived by Sigurd, who has taken on the semblance of Gunnar.

In the course of **"Ulrike,"** the time between Morris's and Borges's versions of the tale is negated as the main protagonist Ulrike becomes Brynhild seeking to resolve the anguish of her eternal separation from her would-be lover Sigurd. Brynhild and Ulrike share a common search for resolution, and they are brought together by the cyclical nature of that search and of time. However, Borges also extends the meaning of the original text by bringing to it his own preoccupations. The reconciliation of Sigurd and Brynhild is ostensibly impossible—it never happened—yet in **"Ulrike,"** this resolution appears to take place in a fantastic merge of time and identity.

In the character of Ulrike, Borges has worked to mask his originating tale in contemporary garb. Ulrike is a Brynhild of the 1970s, and Ulrike's attributes are Brynhild's—but adapted to a contemporary context. Brynhild is a female hero with sword, helmet and mailcoat. She yearns for bloody weapons and the call of battle, and turns her back on all that would constrain her. Ulrike too refuses to be stereotyped. When offered a drink, she refuses it saying, "I am a feminist . . . I am not out to ape men. I dislike their tobacco and their alcohol" (**The Book of Sand** 11). Ulrike is like a modern derivation of Brynhild. She denies the masculine attributes that Brynhild appropriates, but her defiant stance presents the same message.

Ulrike echoes Brynhild in other ways too. She shares Brynhild's gift for divining the future:

> "Listen. A bird is about to sing."
> A moment or two later we heard the song.
> "In these lands," I said, "it's thought that a person about to die sees into the future."
> "And I am about to die" she said.
>
> (**The Book of Sand** 13)

Ulrike's impending "death" is related to her identity as the living Brynhild, and the sexual act that she is about to commit. Brynhild has sworn to wed only the man who braved the conflagration about her castle, or die. Each time Ulrike/Brynhild breaks her oath in her search for Sigurd, she "dies." For a time however, Ulrike prohibits her lover from touching her: "I'll be yours in the Inn at Thorgate. Until then, I ask you not to touch me. It is better that way" (**The Book of Sand** 13). The request prompts this response from her companion: "Brynhild, you're walking as if you wished a sword lay between us in bed" (**The Book of Sand** 14).

As the moment of physical consummation approaches, the temporal convergence of the ancient and contemporary tales escalates. Specific details of setting link the two texts, telescoping the distance between them. The cry of the wolf is heard again, a sound from outside the timeframe of the contemporary narrative: "From the top of the stairs Ulrike called down to me, 'Did you hear the wolf? There are no longer any wolves in England. Hurry'" (**The Book of Sand** 14).

The pair climb to an upstairs room papered after the style of William Morris. It is not often that the bedroom wallpaper has a bearing upon a romantic union. However, given the knowledge that William Morris was both a designer of interiors and an unwearying rewriter of Icelandic sagas, the wallpaper becomes a crucial factor, binding the text to its precursor and emphasizing the unification of contemporary Ulrike with the Brynhild of the past. The wallpaper is one of those points at which the contemporary text articulates with Morris's text and its antecedents. The characters are inside a William Morris room: the reader is inside the originating text.

"Ulrike" is one of the few tales in which Borges links the physical aspects of love to some emotional feeling. In fact, the consummation of the relationship between Javier and Ulrike constitutes a rare moment of unalloyed sentiment from the author of such a tale as **"The Sect of the Phoenix"** in which the sexual act is reduced to an obscure clandestine code. When Javier comes together with Ulrike, he feels complete—in a dimension beyond time. The sword Gram, signifying the obstacle to the unification of Sigurd and Brynhild, is removed:

> The awaited bed was duplicated in a dim mirror, and the polished mahogany reminded me of the looking glass of the scriptures. Ulrike had already undressed. She called me by my real name—Javier. I felt that the snow was falling faster. Now there were no longer any mirrors or furniture. There was no sword between us. Time passed like the sands. In the darkness, centuries old, love flowed, and for the first and last time I possessed Ulrike's image.
>
> (**The Book of Sand** 14)

The bed is "awaited," a word suggestive not only of the anticipation of the protagonists but also of the inevitability of the chosen moment. For the narrator, the moment is one of heightened apprehension: "She called me by my real name—Javier"—a name which Ulrike had found too difficult to pronounce but a moment before. No longer acting under the semblance of being Sigurd and Brynhild, Javier is now *truly* known—a point emphasized by the reference to the "looking glass of the scriptures" found in 1 Corinthians 13: 12: "For now we see in a mirror, darkly; but then face to face: now I know in part; but then I shall know even as also I have been known."

The moment of true knowledge recalls another instance of insight found in Borges's tale **"The Aleph"** that tells of a corner of the world in which all sight lines and angles converge, and in which one can glimpse the universe. A character regards it with terror and amazement:

> in the Aleph I saw the earth; I saw my own face and my own bowels; I saw your face; and I felt dizzy and wept, for my eyes had seen that secret and conjectural object whose name is common to all men but which no man has looked upon—the unimaginable universe.

> **(*The Aleph and Other Stories* 28)**

Certainly, the moment of revelation produced for the male protagonist by the unification of Sigurd/Javier and Brynhild/Ulrike is touched by that quality of infinite expansion followed by withdrawal and the recollection of mortality so characteristic of Borges. In the poem "Things," Borges has listed those objects *that can not be.* These are the things that only Berkeley's God sees: "The indecipherable dust, once Shakespeare," "The volume with its pages still unslit," "the triangular disc" (***The Book of Sand*** 109–11). The mysterious heroine of **"Ulrike"** might also be included in the recitation. No longer needing to express openly the impossibility of attaining the states of being, or obtaining the things known only to Berkeley's God, Borges sums them up in a single name—Ulrike/All-ríkr. The common Norwegian name becomes the abbreviated form of a vast symbol, All-ríkr (in Old Icelandic, the All-powerful) that lies beneath the text. The duality of the name suggests two of Borges's most obsessive preoccupations, namely the encompassing of the entire universe within a single entity, and the human tendency to long for those things that can not be. The name becomes an archetype, set into an individual text, but invoking an entire corpus.

When Javier possesses the image of Ulrike the woman, he also possesses the image of All-ríkr the "all-powerful." Yet the image of the "all-powerful" *is* just that thing that can not be possessed or comprehended; it is the unimaginable fulfillment of the promise of imminence. Indeed, because the promise of imminence can not be fulfilled, Borges builds a typical skeptical proviso into the framework of the story, inevitably suggesting that the events of the tale are a figment of the narrator's imagination, and that the revelation and the denial of that revelation are subject to the same control:

> "All this is like a dream, and I never dream," I said. "Like the King who never dreamed until a wizard made him sleep in a pigsty," Ulrike replied.

> **(*The Book of Sand* 13)**

Ulrike's sharp response reminds us of Borges's characteristic intonation. Having proffered a vista of infinite expansion, he quietly withdraws from the scene through a small private door.

A tale like **"Ulrike"** affirms that the voice of Borges with its own particular intonation lived on in later life, despite

the movement away from the glitzy metaphysical speculations of *Other Inquisitions* and the acute eye for absurdity and historical aptness displayed in the essays. The late works are those of a mature writer—one who has nothing new to tell the reader or himself. In these works speaks the voice of one who recognizes that he merely reiterates a set of personal symbols that describe his own experience within life quietly, and modestly, without the need to be explicit.

Gene Bell-Villada has claimed that Borges's later stories are "an unfortunate instance of a genius no longer animated by a grander conception of life and no longer holding a vital link with common experience" (Bell-Villada 261). Perhaps Bell-Villada fails to recognize that these last works are those of a man who has sought out the symbols that underlie his own conception of common experience and has refined and internalized them to the point at which even single words become active in promoting the hidden inner life.

Notes

1. Eliot's essay was originally published in *The Sacred Wood* (1919), but Borges makes reference to the later edition.

2. The quotation in fact comes from Chapter 26, for Chapter 29 deals with Brynhild's grief at having been made to break her oath to Sigurd. This may be a deliberate misnumbering on Borges's part to reward the attention of the curious, but is more probably a scribal error. The numbering is the same in other editions.

Works Cited

Barnstone, Willis, ed. *Borges at Eighty: Conversations.* Bloomington: Indiana UP, 1982.

Bell-Villada, Gene H. *Borges and His Fiction: A Guide to His Mind and Art.* Chapel Hill: U of North Carolina P, 1981.

Borges, Jorge Luis, *Labyrinths: Selected Stories and Other Writings.* Ed. Donald A. Yates and James E. Irby. London: Penguin, 1964.

———. *The Aleph and Other Stories 1933–1969.* Trans. and ed. Norman Thomas di Giovanni. New York: Dutton, 1970.

———. *The Book of Sand.* Trans. Norman Thomas di Giovanni. London: Allen Lane, 1979. [Also contains *The Gold of the Tigers.* Trans. Alastair Reid.]

Eliot, T. S., *Points of View.* Ed. John Hayward. London: Faber, 1941.

Morris, William, *The Story of Sigurd the Volsung and the Fall of the Niblungs.* London: Longmans Green, 1911. Vol. 12 of *The Collected Works of William Morris.* 24 vols. 1905–15.

Robert L. Chibka (essay date 1996)

SOURCE: "The Library of Forking Paths," in *Representations,* No. 56, Fall, 1996, pp. 106–22.

[*In the following essay on the proliferation of versions of a manuscript in Borges's story "The Garden of Forking Paths," Chibka examines the significance of the proliferation of alternative, apparently trivial, details in several editions of the Spanish and English texts of that story.*]

PROLOGUE

Alors je rentrai dans la maison, et j'écrivis, Il est minuit. La pluie fouette les vitres. Il n'était pas minuit. Il ne pleuvait pas.

    —Samuel Beckett, *Molloy*[1]

I begin this essay about Jorge Luis Borges's **"The Garden of Forking Paths,"** appropriately enough, with a small confession. I am here engaged in a practice of which I generally disapprove: writing professionally on a text in whose language of composition I am illiterate. That a trivial discrepancy between two English translations of **"El jardín de senderos que se bifurcan"** started me down this path is a paltry excuse.[2] Yu Tsun, whose sworn confession constitutes all but the first paragraph of **"The Garden of Forking Paths,"** has this advice for the "soldiers and bandits" he sees inheriting the world: *"Whosoever would undertake some atrocious enterprise should act as if it were already accomplished, should impose upon himself a future as irrevocable as the past"* (*F,* 92–93). Typically, Yu places his emphasis squarely on the individual will (in this case, will masquerading as destiny), as if we deliberately chose both our atrocious enterprises and the means of pursuing them. I, on the contrary, seem to have been led by the world's most brilliant (and devious) librarian through certain half-lit stacks without regard to (if not precisely against) my will. I have watched this enterprise gradually come to appear less atrocious and less revocable. Like spying for foreign powers, the scholarly mission can take on a compulsive tinge.

I have something of a bibliographical detective story to tell, one that disrupts common assumptions about the nature of texts and their relations to the world they both constitute a part of and purport to document. The burden of my story is that, in reading **"The Garden of Forking Paths,"** we can become characters in another story that is incited and "scripted," if not precisely written, by Borges. Reading this tale (and reading around it), we are encouraged simultaneously, disconcertingly, to replicate and to question Borges's story, the stories of spy narrator-murderer Yu Tsun and Sinologist-metaphysician-corpse Stephen Albert, and the story we inhabit and habitually, blithely, call "history." As readers, we seek the source of a crime; as critic, I have sought the source of a citation.

Generically, **"The Garden of Forking Paths"** is multiply suggestive.[3] As a spy thriller, it depends on the forward momentum toward a mysterious but univocal climax that such stories generally exploit; Yu Tsun's narrative emphasizes linear time pressure—a conscious deadline, a short headstart, the maddeningly implacable Richard Madden hot on the trail—with dozens of temporal markers. Borges, in his prologue to **Ficciones,** called it "a detective story; its readers," he continued, "will assist at the execution, and all the preliminaries, of a crime, a crime whose purpose will not be unknown to them, but which they will not understand—it seems to me—until the last paragraph" (*F,* 15). This story partakes of the subsubgenre sometimes referred to as "metaphysical" or "analytic" detective stories. Readers of detective fiction, from metaphysical to pulp, may always be in some sense accomplices (to mystery, at least, if not to mayhem), but this story is unusual in its inversions of typical mystery form: the murder occurs at the end, we seek not perpetrator but rationale, and we "solve" the crime a couple of sentences after it takes place. Further, the reader-as-accomplice has a conflict of interest, since, as Stephen Rudy notes, the reader is also "the real 'detective' in the story."[4] Ironically, the character who "plays detective" (deciphering past actions and motives, solving the mystery of Yu's great-grandfather Ts'ui Pên's apparently unaccountable literary behavior) is the victim, Stephen Albert. But **"The Garden of Forking Paths"** bears in its opening paragraph the trappings of another genre that interprets, or "solves," the past in a different way: it presents itself as a footnote to a history book, purporting to document a causal chain of specific, knowable, more or less explicable events. This is where my detective story will begin, in the bibliographical and pseudohistorical opening paragraph of Borges's story; or, more precisely, of two English translations thereof.

I

In still another, I utter these same words, but I am a mistake, a ghost.

    —Jorge Luis Borges, **"The Garden of Forking Paths,"** *Labyrinths*[5]

In yet another, I say these very same words, but am an error, a phantom.

    —Jorge Luis Borges, **"The Garden of Forking Paths"** (*F,* 100)

Reading a memorable text in two translations can occasion a touch of the uncanny, like meeting a friend's close relatives. The conjunction of near congruence with nonidentity allows an unnerving intuition: *déjà-lu.* Even without verbatim recall, one senses that memory has shifted—broken into pieces and recombined—while one was looking the other way. Phrases, images, tonalities, narrative gestures, all stored in the same organ as recollections of childhood, can induce a dreamlike feeling of revisiting a familiar house whose furniture has been rearranged in some imponderable way, a feeling perhaps not unlike Yu Tsun's when he revisits his ancestor's "shapeless mass of contradictory rough drafts," "translated" by Stephen Albert not only into English but into a work of philosophical genius (*F,* 96,100).

Reading a memorable text in two translations, one can also feel betrayed, not only by an unexamined faith in the efficacy or transparency of translation, but also by personal memory, private lectorial history. Even when translations appear compatible, their differences explicable, one can feel betrayed, as I do by that **"Garden of Forking Paths"** whose final sentence proclaims Yu's "innumerable contrition and weariness" (*L,* 29) rather than his "infinite penitence and sickness of the heart" (*F,* 101). The idea of enumerating contrition or weariness is certainly (in English) gauche, but offends me more than it ought to because it vies with a preferred phrase.[6] The reader-in-translation is at the mercy of both authorial representations and an intermediary's interpretive *re*presentation. If translations differ not only in matters of taste ("contrition" versus "penitence"), but in the simplest, least disputable facts, one feels obliged to take sides, to get to the bottom of a presumably not bottomless mystery.

My Grove Evergreen edition of *Ficciones* contains a story called **"The Garden of Forking Paths"** (translated by Helen Temple and Ruthven Todd) that begins:

> In his *A History of the World War* (page 212), Captain Liddell Hart reports that a planned offensive by thirteen British divisions, supported by fourteen hundred artillery pieces, against the German line at Serre-Montauban, scheduled for July 24, 1916, had to be postponed until the morning of the 29th. He comments that torrential rain caused this delay—which lacked any special significance.

> (*F,* 89)

My New Directions edition of *Labyrinths* contains a similar story, also called **"The Garden of Forking Paths"** (translated by Donald A. Yates), that begins:

> On page 22 of Liddell Hart's *History of World War I* you will read that an attack against the Serre-Montauban line by thirteen British divisions (supported by 1,400 artillery pieces), planned for the 24th of July, 1916, had to be postponed until the morning of the 29th. The torrential rains, Captain Liddell Hart comments, caused this delay, an insignificant one, to be sure.

> (*L,* 19)

The text that follows, both translations agree, will cast "unsuspected light" on this delay.

We note first, in both passages, the typically Borgesian urge to pin down a new explanation for something whose insignificance all versions of the story wryly stipulate. We may suppose the difference in titles (*A History of the World War* versus *History of World War I*) to be a function of Borges's translation of an English title into Spanish and its subsequent retranslation into the language where it started. The discrepancy in page references (212 versus 22) looks like a simple typographical error in one edition or the other. So far, so good; we scholars are all too familiar with the everyday perils of transcription and typesetting.[7]

We are also notorious, though, for being easily upset by details—however significant or trivial—that refuse to co-

here, such as the asymmetry of these numeric palindromes. Were it not for this discrepancy, I might have shared John Sturrock's aggressively breezy attitude toward Borges's reference to Liddell Hart: "I have not checked this quotation because it does not matter in the least whether it is accurate."[8] Personally, I might positively favor *in*accuracy; Borges, after all, has the uncanny ability (even in translation) to create the illusion that he invented not only Franz Kafka and Pierre Menard, but the very idea of the encyclopedia, or of the tiger. I would prefer, for instance, to be allowed the conviction that Borges invented "Liddell Hart" in homage to Lewis Carroll. Instead, knowing that actuality provided this name before Borges could conjure it up, I am forced to view this nominal bit of history as something like a "found poem," a delicious morsel of linguistic nature that Borges dressed to advantage. Likewise, in a text concerned with the supposition that we inhabit not a universe but a multiverse, a polyverse, I feel obliged to seek a rationale for the appearance of two incompatible page numbers. Borges, most fantastical of writers, often chastens his readers' predilection for fantasy.

Dialing up mainframes or riffling through obsolete paper card catalogs to determine which translation got title and page reference right (and, by the by, since we know Borges was a tricky devil, what the historian "historically" wrote), we learn that Captain Basil Henry Liddell Hart produced no fewer than two histories of that World War generally designated, without fear of inaccuracy (without fear, that is, of discovering multiple, proliferating First World Wars), "I." His titles, by emphasizing unitary, bedrock actuality, tend to belie their own multiplicity: *The Real War, 1914–1918* appeared in 1930; *A History of the World War, 1914–1918,* a revised, expanded edition of *The Real* (the surreal, the ultrareal?), in 1934. We find in *The Real War* a paragraph on the insignificant delay of an attack against the Serre-Montauban line: "The bombardment began on June 24; the attack was intended for June 29, but was later postponed until July 1, owing to a momentary break in the weather . . . the assaulting troops, . . . after being keyed up for the effort, had to remain another forty-eight hours in cramped trenches under the exhausting noise of their own gunfire and the enemy's retaliation—conditions made worse by torrential rain which flooded the trenches." This paragraph appears not on page 22, not on page 212, but on pages 233–34. *A History of the World War* includes an identical paragraph, postponed some eighty pages to 314–15.[9]

Critics who notice such discrepancies usually dismiss them as simple irony—"La référence est, en effet, très précise mais, en fait, inexacte"[10]—or typical Borgesian playfulness. But vigorous play can evoke serious vertigo, and those critics who attend to the Liddell Hart citation tend to show symptoms of the disorientation that labyrinths traditionally produce. Mary Lusky Friedman, who notes that the tale is presented "as a sort of corrective footnote to Liddell Hart's standard history," requires a corrective footnote of her own. "The narrator of the story's first paragraph," she writes, "recalls Germany's bombardment of a

British artillery park during World War I and promises that what we are about to read will shed light on events surrounding the surprise attack."[11] The narrator of the various first paragraphs I have read recalls no such thing; Friedman conflates the Allied offensive with the German attack that, according to Yu Tsun, postponed it. Gene Bell-Villada contends that "the report of a postponed British attack on Serre-Montauban . . . is mostly 'Borgesian' invention. Hart does allude to a battle in 1916 near Montauban, in which the same number of British divisions (thirteen) were involved, but there is no mention of a postponement; and the heavy rains took place in November, not July, as Borges indicates."[12] Does the corresponding paragraph in Bell-Villada's copy of Liddell Hart mention the battle, then, but omit the two-day delay and the torrential rains?

Stephen Rudy's more meticulous reading remarks several discrepancies: that "the action on the Somme took place a month earlier than Borges quotes Liddell Hart, falsely, as having stated"; that "Borges refers in various places to Liddell Hart's book under [three different] titles"; that Liddell Hart published two versions of what Friedman calls the "standard history." Finally, he notes that "the page references to Liddell Hart given in the two English translations differ: p. 22 according to *Ficciones*; p. 212 according to *Labyrinths*. Neither has anything to do with the Battle of the Somme," he concludes, and leaves it at that (a later note, however, mentions "p. 315 of *A History*," making it clear that Rudy tracked down the appropriate reference to the Somme).[13] Thus, in the footnotes to his illuminating analysis of plot elements, Rudy points to virtually all the incongruities I have mentioned so far—without seeming to notice that they make **"The Garden of Forking Paths"** (taken as the sum of its printed versions) enact something similar to what Albert's theory of repetitive divergence describes. As if Borges's labyrinth allows no one safe passage, Rudy rechristens the London publisher "Faber and Facer,"[14] though this error, like the delay of the British offensive, is "an insignificant one, to be sure."

I would be surprised to learn that I have emerged unscathed, have not gotten some big or little thing wrong; part of Borges's game consists in misleading and confounding readers; with reference to the sometimes atrocious enterprise of criticism, he seems to have played this game with remarkable success. Professional readers, in this regard, are ironically more vulnerable than amateurs; like martial artists who exploit opponents' weight and momentum, Borges's story lets our own aggressive impulses toward textual mastery throw us off balance. The gremlins that afflict translators do not spare critics, and discussing **"The Garden of Forking Paths,"** like hooking a Persian rug, seems to require a flaw.

The page of a particular volume on which a particular sequence of words appears ought not to mean a thing. Excepting a couple of Laurence Sterne's typographical quips, pagination is an accident of layout and leading, formatting and font. To seek numerological patterns in, say, *The Faerie Queene,* one examines verbal echoes, poetic subdivi-sions—stanzas, cantos, books—not edition-specific ordinals. The latter are dead twigs on the tree of causality, with no purpose more intriguing than idiotically predictable sequencing. If we found the word *armadillo* on all pages divisible by seventeen, but on no other pages, of some contemporary novel, we might think it worthy of cocktail chat, but not of *Notes and Queries*. In fact, we would never discern that pattern, because we would not be looking for it, or anything like it. We cast pariah page references out of syntax, marking them as untext with the stigmata of parentheses. Because they are as dumb and devoid of significance as they are necessary and useful, they are the last place we should expect to find any intimation of a cosmic labyrinth. By incorporating the inconsequential sequentiality that all books display—the very emblem of linear textuality—as a problematic feature of his story, Borges points obliquely to Liddell Hart's question about the weather, Yu Tsun's question at the instant of pulling the trigger, the question the best fiction always poses more complicatedly than it can answer: What weighs, what matters, what signifies?

II

No book is ever published without some variant in each copy. Scribes take a secret oath to omit, interpolate, vary.

—Jorge Luis Borges, **"The Babylon Lottery"** (*F*, 71)

Ignoring the discrepancy in dates (which echoes and reinforces the page-number puzzle but would entail a distracting bifurcation), we sally into musty stacks to determine which page of which work Borges's narrator actually cited.[15] Our willingness to ignore certain "facts" (the dates) makes us resemble Yu after the commission of his crime: "What remains [that is, his arrest and condemnation to death—not to mention the upshot of a World War] is unreal and unimportant" (*F*, 101). Our obsession with precision, our library research, our conviction that one page in one book will give us what we need, make us more closely resemble Yu planning his crime, searching the telephone directory for "the name of the one person capable of passing on the information" (*F*, 91). Both American editions claim (*F*, 4; *L*, iv) to translate the same Spanish *Ficciones*—published in 1956 as volume 5 of Emecé's ten-volume *Obras completas* (1953–71)—in which **"El jardín de senderos que se bifurcan"** begins: "En la página 22 de la *Historia de la Guerra Europea* de Liddell Hart" (thus also Emecé's 1956 two-volume *Obras completas*).[16] This might have been the end of the story: no mystery at all, but a garden-variety mistranscription by a compound culprit, the suggestively named translating team of Temple and Todd.

Borges rarely affords such easy egress. Nor, in this case, do his publishers, who counterintuitively managed eighteen years later to condense the still-growing "Complete Works" into one volume. Perhaps Emecé took to heart the suggestion in the brilliant final footnote of **"The Library of Babel"**: "Strictly speaking, *one single volume* should suffice: a single volume of ordinary format, printed in nine or ten type body, and consisting of an infinite number of infinitely thin pages" (*F,* 88; Anthony Kerrigan's translation). In any case, one needn't have Spanish to see that the narrator of **"El jardín"** in *Obras completas, 1923–1972* (1974) turns over a new leaf to keep our story interesting: "En la página 242 de la *Historia de la Guerra Europea* de Liddell Hart" (thus also a 1980 Barcelona compilation of Borges's *Prosa completa*).[17]

Another country heard from, and mystery reinstated. Clearly, the **Obras** were no more *completas* in 1974 than in 1956, and not only because Borges would live another dozen years; a truly complete edition (even ignoring translations)—an *Obras completas completa,* if you will—would apparently include at least two (trivially different) **"El jardín"**'s. This new and thoroughly Argentine discrepancy shows, at least, that translation is not the source of the problem, but merely one of several sites where citations can proliferate. Compilation may be another; if so, we need to consult the *in*complete works. In the original story, then—the one *Borges* wrote, the one we might wish, following Liddell Hart, to call the *real* story—what page is cited? This desire to know what something really was or first was—this fetishizing of the origin—is the futile wish for "history" *an sich,* the "actual" offensive, the "actual" delay, of which Liddell Hart's reports are, as it were, only later editions. Clever postmodern theories of representation notwithstanding, however, we seem to have a right to ask, in so simply numerical a case, what the blind librarian himself cited.

Working backward toward an elusive origin, I recall Borges's analysis in "Kafka and His Precursors" of the way that a prior past can be irreversibly redefined by subsequent developments in a more recent past. He is quite convincing on the slippery, intuitive issue of literary "influence"; but such an argument ought not to apply to something so finite and (unmeta)physical as a page number. Because no matter how much we enjoy playing Borgesian games, no one finally believes that the planet we live on follows their rules. No idealist's "proof" of immateriality makes anyone (even the idealist) sit less heavily, chew less thoroughly, or feel less rotten about being trapped in a cramped trench flooded by torrential rains. And so we can't stop short of first editions: lovers of fiction, we seek fact; like historians, we desire the original, crave the truth.

The truth: the first edition of *El jardín de senderos que se bifurcan* (1942) and the first edition of *Ficciones* (1944) both cite page 252.[18]

This (historically) first page number is the sixth one on my list. Through what combination of errata, corrections, hypermetropia, and/or disinformation were these bifurcating, trifurcating, hexafurcating variants introduced? Is there in our libraries a book to reconcile or, at least, explain them? Perhaps a Spanish translation of Liddell Hart (of *which* Liddell Hart, we wonder in passing): the book Borges's narrator refers to, entitled *Historia de la Guerra Europea.*

This *History of the European* (not the *World,* not the *Real*) *War* may provide the clue we bibliographical detectives crave. Such a volume could contain a paragraph describing an insignificant delay on page 212, 22, 233, 314, 242, or 252. More likely, it would add a seventh number to my list. And an eighth, a ninth: revised, expanded editions of this work might in their turn present incompatible paginations. But this path seems to be, as some forks must be, a cul-de-sac; I have tried, and failed, to ascertain evidence that Liddell Hart's work ever found a Spanish translator.[19]

There may be a relatively sensible explanation—of the sort that Captain Liddell Hart would favor—for this history of proliferative, hence indeterminate, citations, this bibliotechnical version of the Stephen Albert/Ts'ui Pên phenomenon, whereby simple facts become trembling constellations of possibilities. If so, life has only accidentally imitated art, giving our Boolean searches a suspiciously Borgesian plot. Whether accidentally or conspiratorially, though, what happens, in short, is this: **"The Garden of Forking Paths"** breaks the binding of any book that seeks to contain it, sending us through stacks that begin eerily to resemble the Library of Babel, full of possibly insignificant variants on indeterminately significant texts. Recalling the volume of *The Anglo-American Cyclopaedia* described in Borges's **"Tlön, Uqbar, Orbis Tertius"**—the single copy that differs from others in a single crucial detail—we may begin to wonder whether each volume we consult accurately represents the edition of which it is an example. I located one of my Spanish "originals," for instance, in the collection of Wellesley College and received a photocopy of the other from Middlebury College; if I happened to live in Chicago and had examined midwestern copies instead, might this essay now be headed in a different direction?

Generally impervious to the charms of mysticism, I find the direction it *has* taken quite disconcerting. **"The Garden of Forking Paths"** makes me ask strange questions whose answers generate stranger ones. The story (taken, again, as the sum of its versions) presents not the familiar musical format of theme and variations but variants with a theme. Differences one would otherwise deem quite "insignificant" (in **"El jardín de senderos que se bifurcan,"** in **"The Garden of Forking Paths,"** and in the histories to which they ostensibly refer) become thematically charged when one of the story's explicit themes is, precisely, that of proliferant variations.

Given Liddell Hart's oddly redundant publishing history and Borges's oddly nonredundant citations, we may view Stephen Albert's theory of forking time in a new light. Our libraries become themselves gardens of forking paths—in space, not time—labyrinths that problematize the unitary status of Liddell Hart, of Borges, and (of course) of the story itself. Like the fragment of a letter that affords Albert the clue he needs to decipher Ts'ui Pên's life, like Yu Tsun's fragmentary deposition that constitutes nearly all of this story, all texts and explanatory impulses begin to appear incomplete, elusive, teasing.[20] We rely implicitly on the idea that any text—Yu's deposition, Albert's scrap of a letter, Ts'ui Pên's chaotically fragmentary "novel," Liddell Hart's history, our own scholarly article—has the capacity to cast light ("unsuspected" or otherwise) on its subject; here, in contrast, we find arresting intimations that texts offer only shadowy glimpses of mutating, more or less irrelevant, necessarily indefinitive possibilities ("a shapeless mass of contradictory rough drafts," as Yu calls Ts'ui's manuscript). Between these opposing ideas an insoluble tension arises. It recreates in readers' experience the tension in the story's structure between the illusion of precise, linear, forward momentum in Yu's singleminded plot and the illusion of infinitely branching, looping movements (both experiential and narrative) in Albert's reading of Ts'ui Pên's theory of the universe. The unlikely publishing histories of a British military historian ("external to" this story) and an Argentine librarian (its creator) combine to reinforce a British Sinologist's notion of radical contingency.

But Borges's characteristically metaphysical undercutting of metaphysics ought to remind us that Albert's, like all other "theories of the universe," is far more theoretical than universal. "The universe, the sum of all things," Borges wrote in "A New Refutation of Time," "is a collection no less ideal than that of all the horses Shakespeare dreamt of—one, many, none?—between 1592 and 1594. I add: if time is a mental process, how can thousands of men—or even two different men—share it?" (*L*, 223; James E. Irby's translation). He made the same point more bluntly in "The Analytic Language of John Wilkins": "There is no classification of the universe that is not arbitrary and conjectural. The reason is very simple: we do not know what the universe is."[21] Such idealist sentiments may place an extravagant theory like Albert's on the same plane as our everyday understandings, but only by throwing common sense into crisis, not by giving the extravagant theory a leg to stand on. Truly radical uncertainty leaves no stone undoubted, and its theorists may find themselves hobbling on toes stubbed against the actual.

Albert, whose name makes him a useful corpse in the same "accidental" way that Liddell Hart's name recalls the imponderable conundra of Carroll's Alice books, ironically facilitates his own death by proposing a theory in which personal responsibility is muted (even mooted) by multiple realities. Yu's pulling of the trigger is made easier, more likely, by the idea that this encounter has alternative, indeed innumerable, upshots. Yu's method for convincing himself of his own courage—*impos[ing] upon himself a future as irrevocable as the past*" (*F*, 93)—suggests the linear inevitability of traditional notions of fate. But Albert's precisely opposite idea of a temporal labyrinth serves Yu's purpose even better by reducing every future, if not to revocability, then at least to inconsequentiality, to the status of one among many.

Yu never considers the mind-boggling ramifications of Albert's theory of ramification (I cite just one: that in "other branches of time," Ts'ui Pên did no such thing as what Al-

bert, in his unequivocally explanatory reading of a labyrinthine manuscript, claims he did). Nevertheless, Yu allows this theory to mitigate the horror of what he is about: the irrevocable murder of a man who is singular in two senses. Since the telephone directory contains but one Albert, this *one* must be killed in order to transmit a municipal name to Yu's hateful German Chief (some people will do anything for the sake of a pun). But of all human beings, Albert is precisely the *one* Yu is least inclined to kill: "An Englishman—a modest man—who, for me, is as great as Goethe" (*F*, 91). The entire story, in terms of plot, is built on this tension between Yu's goal-oriented mission and the notion of infinitely meandering possibilities. In terms of character, it is built on the tension between Yu's unequivocal adoption of his mission and the equivocations inevitably introduced by Albert's theory—which, by redeeming the honor of Yu's ancestor, makes Albert both a latterday version of Ts'ui and a personal hero for Yu. Whatever vacillations he feels, however, Yu relates to the wavering, multiplying "pullulation" (*F*, 100) he senses at the brink of the atrocious act, the "swarming sensation" (*L*, 28) that seems to confirm Albert's theory, and thus, paradoxically, to minimize moral equivocation.

Yu, who calls himself "a timorous man" (*F*, 91), must welcome a theory that can mitigate his inexcusable act; but he sees in the image of "Albert and myself, secretive, busy, and multiform in other dimensions of time" (*F*, 100–101) a "tenuous nightmare" (*L*, 28), and this vision of multiplicity quickly yields to one indivisible fact: "In the black and yellow garden there was only a single man" (*F*, 101). The deposition returns at the story's climactic moment to the figure with which it began: the implacable Madden who takes Yu as his singular target, just as Yu has taken Albert. Of course, Yu's mission is more complex than Madden's. If, by killing Albert, he proves to his hated Chief "that a yellow man could [temporarily] save his armies" (*F*, 91), he also (permanently) destroys the source of his rehabilitated family honor. Albert stands in for Ts'ui by translating his humiliating work into an instance of familial, if not racial, pride; insofar as Albert regenerates and "embodies" Ts'ui, he not only makes a long-deceased ancestor killable, but authorizes, with a stroke of Ts'ui's own pen as it were, Yu's annihilation of his own great-grandfather.

Albert thus participates in a highly personal, hyper-Oedipal drama whereby Yu proves his "manhood" (and, he fancies, redeems his race) by eliminating his most formidable male ancestor.[22] Borges's story does not entail, as Stephen Rudy asserts, a consistent "negation of the concept of 'individuality,'" in "characters [who] act as 'functions' (much as they do in the folk tale)," by a thorough "suppression of the psychological element"[23]; such a claim locates only one of the opposing forces that structure the story. The other is suggested by Bell-Villada: "Yu's narrative is held together by an underlying unity of tone and sentiment—a combination of fear, sadness, and guilt. Yu Tsun is neither the hard-boiled nor the coldly rational operative. Indeed, for a spy he is oddly sensitive and conscience-ridden."[24] Yu's conscience is visible not only in the way he ends his confession, with an implied wish for absolution, but in his touching, if hopeless, attempt to mitigate his report of the crime: "I swear his death was instantaneous, as if he had been struck by lightning" (*F*, 101). To the extent that "instantaneous" suggests removal from the temporal realm of cause, effect, and personal responsibility, this sentence states a wish, not a fact; Albert is struck not by lightning, but by a bullet Yu inscribed with his name and "fired with the utmost care" into his back (*F*, 101). The astonishing detachment of Yu's act works its finest effect only in concert with our full belief in his "infinite penitence and sickness of the heart" (*F*, 101).

Borges's genially bewildering narrative experiments often lead critics to emphasize their more surprising, metaphysical extremes and understate the counterpoint of their more conventional, almost "realist," aspects.[25] Thus, for instance, Rudy claims that "history, chronological time, has no place in Borges's universe," that Borges "correct[s] Liddell Hart (ostensibly in the interests of historical truth), outdoing the very concept of cause and effect to the point that it turns on itself, and all notions of history, causal time, and truth are overthrown by the 'unfathomable.'" Rudy's reading of "two parallel yet incompatible plots, one of a detective, the other of a metaphysical, nature" is both sensitive and insightful, but **"The Garden of Forking Paths"** presents only a single, relentlessly chronological plot, in the course of which one character propounds a *theory* of plot that, while perhaps problematizing the story we read, does not govern it.[26] Rudy's "metaphysical plot" exists only by implication, and then only if we (temporarily) accept Albert's theory as accurately describing not only Ts'ui Pên's fictional *Garden of Forking Paths* but also our world. Albert writes up a one-way ticket to a startling and seductive destination, but the story in which he appears sends us on a round trip. For the momentary sake of argument, we may entertain Albert's entertaining theory; but even before we emerge from the story to resume our extra-Borgesian lives, Yu Tsun's contrite coda restores something like our "usual" understandings of causality, psychology, and history. Only against the always implicit ground of such understandings, in fact, would the contrary theory appear so seductive. Even the once-crimson slip of paper that gives Albert his crucial clue to the meaning of Ts'ui Pên's work is "faded with the passage of time" (*F*, 97).

No single version of **"The Garden of Forking Paths"** bears any structural similarities whatsoever to Ts'ui's *Garden of Forking Paths*. Borges's plot does not pretend to enact infinity; it contains within it a discussion of infinity, but its shape relentlessly enforces temporal finitude. Even Ts'ui Pên's work makes only the most transparent pretence of enacting infinity, merely alluding indirectly to the idea—just as a couple of (re)quoted sentences can deftly establish the idea of Pierre Menard's (re)writing of the *Quixote* by gesturing toward it, not (re)presenting it. Albert claims that each character in *The Garden of Forking Paths* "chooses—simultaneously—all" imaginable alternatives, that "in the work of Ts'ui Pên, all possible outcomes occur" (*L*, 26). This is not true by a long, an infinite, shot. All the alternatives Albert cites from Ts'ui's work are perfectly conventional, drawn from a stagnant pool of plot components collected from epic, tragic, and detective traditions. They embrace armies marching into battle and murderers knocking at doors, but no broken shoelaces or mediocre stir-fries, no ingrown hairs or wrong numbers, nary a subepic inconsequentiality. In the "two versions of the same epic chapter" (*F*, 98) Albert reads to Yu, "all possible outcomes" comprise, with trenchant irony, winning a battle and winning it again. To judge from Albert's samples, this version of infinity is poor indeed, its complexity and novelty entirely conceptual, its notion of cause-and-effect far closer to Liddell Hart's than to Borges's.

Albert's speculations about the ways in which a book might approach infinity include mental gymnastics familiar from other Borges stories—circularity, infinite regress—but conclude with the idea of "a Platonic hereditary work, passed on from father to son, to which each individual would add a new chapter or correct, with pious care, the work of his elders" (*F*, 97). This concept of infinity-as-lineage is not even remotely labyrinthine; on the contrary, it is as unidirectional as Borges's plot (or Liddell Hart's, for that matter) and scarcely distinguishable from what the vernacular calls "family history."[27]

The broad counterpoint between singular and plural (or, if you will, between plot and theory) is echoed, on smaller scales, in many internal reflections duly noted by critics. But if Borges, like Ts'ui, struggles (or chafes, at least) against the linear and the finite, he does so in a medium that is incontrovertibly finite and unremittingly linear, both temporally and spatially. Only in such a medium can he work his particular brand of narrative magic (as, for instance, only an audience that implicitly owns the notion of a unified self is fit to hear the lovely, disconcerting ironies of the prose poem, "Borges and I"). In the case of **"The Garden of Forking Paths,"** however, Borges manages to break the mold of his medium and press into service the world outside the story. Albert's theory could be safely contained—as a fine and ephemeral fancy—within the very finite limits of Yu's deposition, if only our libraries did not teem with wrong page numbers, intimating an invasive, mutating Albert-virus that infects readers with Yu's "swarming sensation." Liddell Hart's works, like his name, function in the manner of "found poems"; their iterativity plants a germ of the uncanny in the most unlikely spot.[28] The pullulating variants of the Borgesian text spread the contagion, so that we find *outside the bounds of the story* what we expect to have left between the closed covers of a single volume. Like "the victim within" a "strong labyrinth" in one critic's description, we "experience a bending of apparently straight lines, a perplexing of space, even while [we], in playing back, [attempt] to straighten them";[29] and this perplexity is visited upon us in libraries, our bastions of order and precision, if not necessarily or exclusively of truth.

III

It seems probable that if we were never bewildered there would never be a story to tell about us; we should partake of the superior nature of the all-knowing immortals whose annals are dreadfully dull so long as flurried humans are not, for the positive relief of bored Olympians, mixed up with them.

—Henry James, preface to *The Princess Casamassima*[30]

Finally, we in our libraries, like Yu in his prison cell, occupy an impossible, an untenable position. Regardless of theories of the universe, we live the lives we live, consult the volumes we have at our disposal, variants, discrepancies, fragmentarity and all; like Yu, faced with odd echoes and unexpected twists, we do what little we can. Yu has a thought, early in his journey to Ashgrove, that reverberates later as a counterweight to the Ts'ui Pên/Albert theory: "Then I reflected that all things happen, happen to one, precisely *now.* Century follows century, and things happen only in the present. There are countless men in the air, on land and at sea, and all that really happens happens to me" (*F.* 90). That Yu negates, even as he alludes to, the "countless men" suffering and dying in a war more real than anything Liddell Hart ever wrote is, I hope, chilling to us. What disturbs him at story's end is something quite different, however: his *"now"* in which "all things happen" comprises more than time; the "me" to whom "all that really happens happens" is constructed and defined by a horribly singular past, the story's ending insists. "What remains"—the attestable, publishable account of an event— "is unreal and unimportant" to Yu not in an absolute sense but by contrast to the *subjective* aftermath of an irrevocable action. His "infinite penitence and sickness of the heart," which the Chief "does not know, for no one can" (*F.* 101), announce a different kind of infinity: selfsame, unvarying through time, "innumerable" because it represents the final victory of singular over plural. Liddell Hart's delay is "insignificant" not to a soldier trapped in a flooded trench but to the scholar whose magisterial view cannot afford to accommodate either the emotional bewilderment that comes to Yu as "sickness of the heart" or the intellectual bewilderment that can affect a critic like a fever of the brain. With the (unwitting, I presume) assistance of publishers and translators, Borges reinstates such bewilderment as the most genuine response to the nightmare of history.

The excruciatingly coincidental encounter of Yu Tsun and Stephen Albert underscores singularity in both senses. It emerges from an infinity of possible stories as the one worth telling, the one told; at the same time, this singular coincidence constitutes a merging of people and ideas, the opposite of a forking path. The story counterbalances the striking "theory" of bifurcation with the even more striking (and, for Yu, heartbreaking) "fact" of convergence. Let us stipulate, though no one believes it for a second, that time "actually" resembles the labyrinth Albert finds in Ts'ui's work; even so, for any given mortal, situated instantaneously at a given spot on a given branch, no labyrinth will exist. Borges said of his own "A New Refutation of Time": "I believe in the argument logically, and I think that if you accept the premises, the argument may stand— though at the same time, alas, time also stands."[31] Language may win a battle, but time wins the war. In a fight to the death between time and a theory, it would be simply foolish to put one's money on the theory.[32]

Within **"The Garden of Forking Paths,"** Yu stands in for time, killing the beautiful theory (or, at least, the theorist); in doing so, he collaborates with narrative's linear form. If Albert, Liddell Hart, farsighted copy editors, errant translators, and who knows what printer's devils have conspired to provide an intimation of the labyrinth, narrative form nevertheless enforces the irrevocable, heartbreakingly finite nature of life "as we know it." We are left with the effect Borges described in reviewing Liddell Hart's meditation on war psychology and the dangers of military gigantism, *Europe in Arms,* for the 30 April 1937 issue of *El hogar*: "Goce desengañado, goce lúcido, goce pesimista."[33] Disillusioned pleasure, lucid pleasure, pessimistic pleasure. One imagines this is exactly the sort of pleasure the historical Borges must have derived from concocting—in the midst of a war that would retroactively transform the Great War, the Real War, the war to end them all, into the first of a series—a story of repetition, divergence, and wishful escape from the inescapably vectored movement of time. Albert's hope that he might retreat from worldly (and World War) concerns into placid scholarly contemplation—as Ts'ui did in another place and time by retiring to the Pavilion of the Limpid Solitude—is unequivocally dashed: "The reality of the war conquers. It's sad, but it must be so."[34] The "unsuspected light" Yu's narrative casts on history is dark indeed.

Notes

1. Samuel Beckett, *Molloy* (Paris, 1951), 239; "Then I went back into the house and wrote, It is midnight. The rain is beating on the windows. It was not midnight. It was not raining" (Samuel Beckett, *Molloy,* trans. Patrick Bowles [New York, 1955], 241).

2. That a "former teacher of English at the Tsingtao *Hochschule*" would presumably have "dictated" a deposition to his British captors *in English* affords neither excuse nor solace; Jorge Luis Borges, *Ficciones,* ed. Anthony Kerrigan, various translators (New York, 1961), 89. This volume will be cited in the text as *F.*

3. Here is a skeletal version of Borges's plot: Yu Tsun, a Chinese spy for the Germans in England during World War I, has been found out. Before he is captured or killed, he must somehow transmit to his chief in Berlin the secret location of a new British artillery park: the city of Albert. He will do so by murdering a stranger named Stephen Albert; his chief, poring over newspapers for word of his minions' activities, will find the name Yu Tsun linked with the name Albert and solve the riddle.

Before he can kill Albert, Yu discovers that the latter, once a missionary in China, has devoted his energies to solving another riddle: that of Yu's great-grandfather, Ts'ui Pên, who "gave up temporal power to write a novel . . . and to create a maze in which all men would lose themselves. . . . His novel had no sense to it and nobody ever found his labyrinth" (*F,* 93). Albert has concluded that book and maze are one and the same, that Ts'ui's novel, *The Garden of Forking Paths,* portrays a temporal labyrinth: "Your ancestor," Albert tells Yu, "did not think of time as absolute and uniform. He believed in an infinite series of times, in a dizzily growing, ever spreading network of diverging, converging and parallel times. This web of time—the strands of which approach one another, bifurcate, intersect or ignore each other through the centuries—embraces *every* possibility" (*F,* 100). The former missionary is now proselytizing to redeem the metaphysical theory and reputation of Yu's ancestor, who died in disgrace under suspicion of lunacy; Albert proclaims Ts'ui's *Garden of Forking Paths* not a senseless jumble but a work of genius. Yu murders Albert anyway, is arrested, and dictates, under a sentence of death, the deposition that we read.

4. Stephen Rudy, "The Garden *of* and *in* Borges' 'Garden of Forking Paths,'" in Andrej Kodjak, Michael J. Connolly, and Krystyna Pomorska, eds., *The Structural Analysis of Narrative Texts: Conference Papers* (Columbus, Ohio, 1980), 142 n. 15. Rudy goes on to differ with Borges about the story's secret, saying that the reader-detective "should be able to anticipate the 'solution' offered in the last paragraph" (142 n. 15). Borges, I think, gauges the prescience of his typical reader more accurately.

5. Jorge Luis Borges, *Labyrinths: Selected Stories and Other Writings,* ed. Donald A. Yates and James E. Irby, various translators (New York, 1964), 28. This volume will be cited in the text as *L.*

6. Borges's word is "innumerable," quite rightly linked to the "innumerables futuros" Albert sees in Ts'ui Pên's work by Donald L. Shaw, *Borges: Ficciones* (London, 1976), 44.

7. In a 1971 seminar at Columbia University, Norman di Giovanni, who collaborated with Borges on numerous translations, quoted two versions of the sentence about torrential rain as his "whole textbook on translation." He severely critiqued Yates's version in *Labyrinths:* "It should be obvious that the elements of the . . . sentence are put together all wrong" (Norman Thomas di Giovanni, Daniel Halpern, and Frank MacShane, eds., *Borges on Writing* [New York, 1973], 134, 135). Borges, who was at his elbow, did not disagree. The alternative Giovanni praised, however, was not Temple and Todd's; in any case, his critique concerned effective English syntax rather than accuracy.

8. John Sturrock, *Paper Tigers: The Ideal Fictions of Jorge Luis Borges* (Oxford, 1977), 191.

9. B. H. Liddell Hart, *The Real War, 1914–1918* (Boston, 1930), 233–34; B. H. Liddell Hart, *A History of the World War, 1914–1918* (London, 1934), 314–15.

10. Michel Berveiller, *Le cosmopolitisme de Jorge Luis Borges* (Paris, 1973), 281 n. 113; "The reference is, in effect, very precise but, in fact, inexact" (my translation).

11. Mary Lusky Friedman, *The Emperor's Kites: A Morphology of Borges' Tales* (Durham, N.C., 1987), 17.

12. Gene H. Bell-Villada, *Borges and His Fiction: A Guide to His Mind and Art* (Chapel Hill, N.C., 1981), 93.

13. Rudy, "The Garden," 133, 141 n. 6, 141 n. 8.

14. *Ibid.,* 141 n. 6.

15. For a discussion of the story's historicity that makes much of the discrepancy in dates between Borges and Liddell Hart, see Daniel Balderston, *Out of Context: Historical Reference and the Representation of Reality in Borges* (Durham, N.C., 1993), 39–55.

16. Jorge Luis Borges, *Ficciones,* vol. 5 of *Obras completas* (1953–71), 10 vols. (Buenos Aires, 1956), 97; Jorge Luis Borges, *Obras completas,* 2 vols. (Buenos Aires, 1956), 2:97.

17. Jorge Luis Borges, *Obras completas, 1923–1972* (Buenos Aires, 1974), 472; Jorge Luis Borges, *Prosa completa* (Barcelona, 1980), 1:396.

18. Jorge Luis Borges, *El jardín de senderos que se bifurcan* (Buenos Aires, 1942), 107; Jorge Luis Borges, *Ficciones* (Buenos Aires, 1944), 109. Balderston reveals that the first British edition of *The Real War* (as opposed to the first American edition cited in my note 9) contains the passage in question on page 252; *Out of Context,* 151 n. 5. It appears, then, that once upon a prelapsarian time, page numbers in "El jardín" and in one version of *The Real War* corresponded neatly. But seeds of discrepancy, already sown in Liddell Hart's multiple editions of history, eventually sprouted to full-blown inconsistency in various versions of Borges's "Garden."

19. "Borges: . . . I've done most of my reading in English" (Giovanni et al., *Borges on Writing,* 137). But see James Irby's footnote to a similar statement: "Bien que Borges soit systématiquement anglophile et surtout saxophile il énoncerait un jugement très différent selon la nationalité de son interlocuteur: à un Italien il parlerait de Dante; à un Français de Hugo, Baudelaire ou Toulet. C'est là un trait essentiel de son comportement social" [Although Borges is systematically an Anglophile and above all a Saxophile, he would pronounce a very different

judgment depending on the nationality of his interlocutor: to an Italian he would speak of Dante; to a Frenchman of Hugo, Baudelaire or Toulet. That is an essential trait of his social deportment]; James E. Irby, "Entretiens avec James E. Irby," in Dominique de Roux and Jean de Milleret, eds., *Jorge Luis Borges*, L'Herne, no. 4 (1964; reprint, Paris, 1981), 388–403, at 401 (my translation).

20. Friedman, *Emperor's Kites*, notes that "the compromising letter Yu pulls from his pocket, a letter whose contents the reader never learns, has a double in the exquisitely penned fragment of a letter, key to interpreting Ts'ui Pên's chaotic novel, that Albert will later take from a lacquered drawer" (19). Yu's never-explained letter, "which I decided to destroy at once (and which I did not destroy)" (*F*, 91), is unusual among the texts in this story in not being described explicitly as a fragment; but it is the ultimate fragment in the sense that one can make absolutely nothing of it.

21. Jorge Luis Borges, "The Analytic Language of John Wilkins," in *Other Inquisitions, 1937–1952*, trans. Ruth L. C. Simms (Austin, Texas, 1964), 104.

22. Borges, who would undoubtedly dislike my Freudian lingo, nevertheless saw Albert as a parent-figure for Yu: "Il est plus pathétique que Yu Tsun tue un homme ayant su comprendre l'énigme de son propre ancêtre, un homme devenant ainsi presque son parent" [It is more moving that Yu Tsun kill a man who has solved the riddle of his own ancestor, a man who thus becomes almost his parent]; Irby, "Entretiens," 394 (my translation).

23. Rudy, "The Garden," 137, 138.

24. Bell-Villada, *Borges and His Fiction*, 96.

25. Balderston, who believes that Borges's historical references push this story "much closer to the realistic than to the fantastic variety of narrative," expresses surprise at "how often Stephen Albert's theory of parallel universes has been taken as an explanation of the text"; "critics [who] speak of games with time," he argues, "repeat . . . Stephen Albert's position in the story, deprived of its dialectical punch"; *Out of Context*, 51, 6, 40.

26. Rudy, "The Garden," 133, 134, 135.

27. This progressive work, ever subject to revision and expansion but infinite only in the very limited sense of remaining unfinished, is not only more commonplace but infinitely more practicable than the others that Borges and Albert enjoy daydreaming about. The single all-encompassing volume posited at the conclusion of "The Library of Babel" would simplify reference protocols but, by the same token, render citation useless; the distress of a scholar attempting to verify a quotation from "p. ∞" could properly be characterized as boundless.

28. Borges listed Liddell Hart's work (at least) twice among the most reread and annotated books in his library; his transmigrational phrasing adumbrates a problematic of uncanny repetition and incompatible variation by now familiar to my reader. His review of Liddell Hart's *Europe in Arms* begins: "Revisando mi biblioteca, veo con admiración que las obras que más he releído y abrumado de notas manuscritas son el *Diccionario de la Filosofía* de Mauthner, *El mundo como voluntad y representación* de Schopenhauer, y la *Historia de la guerra mundial* de B. H. Liddell Hart"; Jorge Luis Borges, *Textos cautivos: Ensayos y reseñas en "El hogar,"* ed. Enrique Sacerio-Garí and Emir Rodríguez Monegal (Barcelona, 1986), 125. His review of Edward Kasner and James Newman's *Mathematics and the Imagination* begins: "Revisando la biblioteca, veo con admiración que las obras que más he releído y abrumado de notas manuscritas son el *Diccionario de la Filosofía* de Mauthner, la *Historia biográfica de la filosofía* de Lewes, la *Historia de la guerra de 1914–1918* de Liddell Hart, la *Vida de Samuel Johnson* de Boswell y la psicología de Gustav Spiller: *The Mind of Man, 1902*"; Borges, *Obras completas, 1923–1972*, 276. The former review appeared in *El hogar* (30 April 1937); the latter first appeared in *Sur* (October 1940) and was collected with other "Notas" in a 1957 revision of the 1932 *Discusión*; see Roux and Milleret, *Jorge Luis Borges*, 448; Horacio Jorge Becco, *Jorge Luis Borges: Bibliografía total, 1923–1973* (Buenos Aires, 1973), 49. Both reviews foresee the addition of the volume under review to their respective lists.

29. Robert Rawdon Wilson, "Godgames and Labyrinths: The Logic of Entrapment," *Mosaic* 15, no. 4 (December 1982): 18.

30. Henry James, *The Princess Casamassima* (New York, 1991), xxxi.

31. Giovanni et al., *Borges on Writing*, 63. Shlomith Rimmon-Kenan, arguing that "the same phenomenon of repetition which disintegrates the autonomy of the individual also defines it," quotes, from the text of "A New Refutation of Time," a longer and more beautiful but tonally similar passage, which concludes, with piercing resignation: "The world, unfortunately, is real; I, unfortunately, am Borges"; "Doubles and Counterparts: 'The Garden of Forking Paths,'" in Harold Bloom, ed., *Jorge Luis Borges* (New York, 1986), 192.

32. The romantic dichotomy between concrete human constructions (gilded monuments, hard copy) and their intellectual or aesthetic counterparts (powerful rhymes, theories of the universe) is deconstructed by the recognition that the latter are transmissible only by concrete means: mortal tongues (like Albert's, forever silenced), physical texts (like Yu's, its opening pages irretrievably lost), diskettes and drives (like mine, subject to surges and crashes). The nature of language as continually mediating between abstraction and concretion collapses the

pretty notion that writing (a sonnet, a military history, a short story, an e-mail flame) is less susceptible to sluttish time's besmearments, less inherently finite, than any material medium (a stone tablet, a bound volume, a snippet of paper faded from crimson to sickly pink, a fiber-optic cable). These days, when information seems to depend less on dimensionality (what would Borges have made of the Internet and World Wide Web?), access relies more than ever on hardware. I may have more memory than I'll ever use, but I can no longer work in the absence of a grounded outlet. All the world's knowledge in CD-ROM format becomes a mere source of frustration when the system goes down. Our only route to the "virtual" is by way of the actual: the material and temporal. (Even thoughts we keep to ourselves depend for processing, storage, and retrieval on hard-wired nervous systems.)

33. Borges, *Textos cautivos,* 125.

34. This is my translation of the final two sentences of Borges's response when asked why, after discovering in Albert a soulmate ("frère spirituel"), Yu pursues his murderous plan anyway [La réalité de la guerre vaine. C'est triste, mais cela doit être ainsi]; Borges quoted in Irby, "Entretiens," 394, 395. Donald L. Shaw quotes the answer to this question in Spanish; the sentences I have quoted read: "La realidad de la guerra vence. Es triste, pero tiene que ser así"; *Jorge Luis Borges: Ficciones* (Barcelona, 1986), 116. The entire Spanish interview may be found in James E. Irby, Napoléon Murat, and Carlos Peralta, *Encuentro con Borges* (Buenos Aires, 1968). Borges seems to have meant that "cela doit être ainsi" for aesthetic reasons: "Pour que l'effet soit bouleversant, pathétique"; Irby, "Entretiens," 394. I would say that his decision to show Albert and Yu both destroyed by the brutal reality of war makes the story not only more surprising and moving, but also truer.

Ian Almond (essay date 1998)

SOURCE: "Tlön, Pilgrimages, and Postmodern Banality," in *Bulletin of Hispanic Studies,* Vol. LXXV, No. 2, April, 1998, pp. 229–35.

[*In the following essay, referring to Borges's story "Tlön, Uqbar, Orbis Tertius," Almond considers Borges's relation to postmodernism.*]

When Heidegger was asked in an interview whether he could provide a single maxim for his readers to keep in their heads as they worked their way through his difficult, at times elusive writings, he replied (and the fact that he gave a reply at all is surprising): 'Possibility is higher than actuality'.[1] It is a maxim which—to use a very un-Heideggerian verb—sums up many of the philosopher's own preoccupations concerning *Dasein* and the world: the

refutation of substance (*ousia*) and doing (*praxis*) as being ontologically superior to thought and thinking (*theoria*), along with the dismissal of a single objective reality 'out there' in which one must 'realize' one's plans and projects. It is also, however, a maxim which might have been uttered by one of the metaphysicians of Tlön.

How much Borges knew of Heidegger (or even cared) is anyone's guess—in his entire *Obras Completas* he refers to *Sein und Zeit* twice, implying at least a nodding familiarity with the German's precocious foray into the very problems of time and reality which, ten years later, Borges himself would be writing about on the sixth floor of his Buenos Aires library. Whether Borges was ever able to appreciate the word 'postmodern' (he died in 1986) is also difficult to ascertain—in at least one discussion, he publicly declared 'Deconstructionism' to be 'a mistake, a really pedantic mistake',[2] although Borges' responses to any kind of criticism or theory in these discussions are often disparaging and dismissive, the poet's stereotypical response to the academic. The intention, however, is not to try and find out exactly what the historical personage Borges was thinking while he wrote **'Tlön, Uqbar, Orbis Tertius'**, but whether such a text can correspond in any way to the kinds of things which have been going on in discourse since Nietzsche. Borges has already told us, in his various praises of ambiguity, that we are not to ask the writer questions: 'God must not engage in theology: the writer must not destroy by human reasonings the faith that art requires of us'.[3] Again, whether Borges wanted to write something analogous to what Derrida calls the 'event' or 'rupture' in the history of thinking—that historic moment when 'language invaded the universal problematic' and everything 'became discourse'[4]—is not the question. What the story itself has to say in the presence of such texts as (for example) 'Structure, Sign and Play', *Letter on Humanism* and *A Genealogy of Morals*—this is the object of our attention.

Borges' story is uncanny, in the most German sense of the word (*unheimlich,* lit. 'unhomely'). It acquaints us with something which is not of this world. Its account of a fictitious encyclopedia suddenly appearing in the narrator's own 'reality', bringing with it an imaginary universe with laws and worldviews diametrically opposed to our own ideas of 'common-sense', has a definite, unnerving quality about it. The peculiar, resigned tone of the narrator; the strange, inexplicable deaths; the nebulous, quasi-Masonic society of Orbis Tertius and its secret, calculating deliberations; the mysterious objects or *hrönir* which begin to appear everywhere; the blending of 'fictitious' names (some of them made up from lists of Borges' family tree and close friends) with 'factual' ones (De Quincey, Berkeley, Lucerne, Memphis); all these contribute to give the text an otherworldly feel, as if it, too, were a product of Tlön.

This would not be too hard to believe. Borges' story is a story about books, a story full of literary cross-references and philosophical quotations, a story where one always refers to an encyclopedia in order to justify a truth-claim, never to reality. It is a story about a snippet from an encyclopedia which ultimately leads to the discovery of another encyclopedia, which in turn promises to deliver yet another ('de aquí a cien años alguien descubrirá los cien tomos de la Segunda Enciclopedia de Tlön').[5] Texts upon texts upon texts, spiralling endlessly into infinity.

The question, then, which Borges' story raises for the contemporary reader, reared on Heidegger, Nietzsche and Derrida, is so obvious that to cite it seems banal: is Borges' Tlön the postmodern vocabulary, creeping surreptitiously into our dictionaries of common-sense, infecting everything with its distrust of materialism, instilling into everything we do its indifference to truth? And if so, what idea are we meant to have of Tlön, the 'reality' to which we 'have longed to yield'? Menacing, ominous, inevitable? Does Borges' carefully-crafted text constitute a warning or an endorsement of a new age? Are we to laugh or cry?[6] This all rather depends on how much the world of Tlön resembles what we construe to be the Postmodern. At first glance, nothing might seem farther from the truth: 'Las naciones de ese planeta son congénitamente—idealistas' (21). Tlön is a cosmos subject to intimate laws, to a 'rigour' which smacks of rigid, closed totalities, an 'uncountable number' of doctrines, not that different in structure from the rationalist systems of Hegel, Descartes or Aquinas. Even the controversies seem similar to our own— the 'escándalo' which 'el materialismo' arouses is not unlike the sort of criticism Darwin, Freud or the Dadaists had to undergo. The heresiarch's daring analogy, proffered to sustain the 'scandalous' thesis that objects exist independently of their being observed, might have been taken straight out of St. Anselm or Boethius. However, as we soon learn, it is not the belief-systems themselves but the attitude cultivated towards them that distinguishes Tlön from our own all-too-empirical reality:

> El hecho de que toda filosofía sea de antemano un juego dialéctico, *una Phillosophie des Als Ob*, ha contribuido a multiplicarlas. Abundan los sistemas increíbles, pero de arquitectura agradable o de tipo sensacional.
>
> (23)

Despite the mention of 'dialectical games', suggesting a Hegelian progress towards a certain goal, we do find ourselves uncannily close to Wittgenstein's 'language games', autonomous value-systems which always generate their meaning *internally*, without trying to correspond or refer to a reality or truth 'outside' in order to justify their existence. The narrator continues:

> Los metafísicos de Tlön no buscan la verdad ni siquiera la verosimilitud: buscan el asombro. Juzgan que la metafísica es una rama de la literatura fantástica.
>
> (24)

It is a metaphysics which would certainly fit Lyotard's definition of the postmodern as 'incredulity towards metanarratives'. Tlön is a world where nothing has to be taken seriously. Its various doctrines, proposed by all manner of *Weltanschauungen*, are judged purely on their pragmatic and/or aesthetic bases (i.e. if they 'astound'). Whether they coincide with a truth or 'reality' out there is considered irrelevant. This does, admittedly, create something of a difficulty in the story—if there is no 'reasoning' on Tlön, only an 'uncountable number' of doctrines, then why does materialism encounter such a 'scandalous reception' amongst those whom Borges mischievously calls 'los defensores del sentido común' (25)? If there are no dialectical games which actively seek the truth, then why are people so angry about the particular reality suggested by materialism? The answer, presumably, might be that materialism contests the fundamental tenet of Tlön's innumerable doctrines: that Thinking is Being. Materialism insists on the unalterable existence of substance even when it is no longer perceived. As we already know, no-one on Tlön believes 'en la realidad de los sustantivos' (22). The world is 'sucesivo, temporal, no espacial' (21). The 'real' is whatever we perceive or imagine—once we perceive it no longer, it ceases to be. Materialism would be the exact contrary of this—in the heresiarch's analogy, the nine lost copper coins still exist, even when they are out of sight.

In one sense, the difference in Borges' story between Tlön and the narrator's world does teach us something about what postmodernism means in a world still rife with passionate ideologies. Postmodernism is not so much an '-ism' in itself as a means of looking at other '-isms'. It does not expect the Islamic fundamentalist or the Southern Baptist or the Neo-nazi to change their *beliefs*, but simply the way they talk about them. It does not ask totalities to dismantle themselves and dissolve into a nihilistic pool of non-belief; it simply wants them to 'lighten up' a little, to stop talking (as Tlön's innumerable doctrines did long ago) about words like Truth and Reality with such competitive seriousness, as if they were the only things that mattered. Like Tlön, Postmodernism wants the world's totalizers to acknowledge, once and for all, that one cannot arrive at any kind of 'truthful knowledge about the ways of the world'.[7] Bereft of this ancient *raison d'être,* most totalities find themselves scratching their heads in a postmodern age, wondering why they should bother to exist at all. Tlön already had the answer long ago; truth-claims aren't supposed to *convince,* they were made to delight. Why bother chasing after boring old Truths and Realities? Astonishment and uncertainty, as both Tlön and Derrida might have said, are so much more fun.

AN ATROCIOUS AND BANAL REALITY

So in Tlön we have, like the Postmodern, 'no longer a world of eternal verities but a series of constructions'.[8] A world of mystery, perhaps, but also a world of truthlessness and 'endless play,' one which will seep into our own and colour everything we do with its own inimitable, ironic hue. Reading **'Tlön, Uqbar, Orbis Tertius'** a second time does give it the feel of a horror story—the slow succumbing of our familiar 'homely' reality to an alien order unsettles and disturbs. The curiosity of Borges' story lies in the fact that even after we learn of Tlön's earthly, calculated origins, the uncanniness of the tale remains untouched. In the Twenties and Thirties the American popular novelist H. P. Lovecraft wrote a series of horror novels called the Cthulu series, in which a secret and malevolent hierarchy of demigods, hidden from the world, wreak their evil designs and chaotic whims upon an unsuspecting reality. Towards the end of these novels the main characters invariably lose their minds, as the more one learns of this ancient evil, the more deranged one becomes, until madness finally ensues. The most powerful god of them all, significantly, is a blind, cackling idiot.

Borges' story begins with a conversation after dinner. It is a relaxed, easy beginning to a tale and we quickly forget, as we move on with the story, the subject of that fateful conversation which was to provoke Bioy Casares' quotation and ultimately lead the narrator to Tlön (or Tlön to the narrator):

> . . . nos demoró una vasta polémica sobre la ejecución de una novela en primera persona, cuyo narrador omitiera o desfigurara los hechos e incurriera en diversas contradicciones, que permitieran a unos pocos lectores—a muy pocos lectores—la adivinación de una realidad atroz o banal.
>
> (13)

Is Borges taking us for a ride? The disfiguring and invention of 'facts' is a regular feature throughout the story (Borges' wonderful, sadly fictitious German title *Lesbare und lesenswerthe Bemerkungen ueber das Land Ukkbar in Klein-Asien,* for example). And yet the suggestion, so early in the story, seems almost too obviously placed to be taken seriously: is **'Tlön, Uqbar, Orbis Tertius'** itself the first-person novel? Can we trust the narrator who is speaking to us—how do we know what details he is omitting, what facts he is disfiguring? Is he telling us the 'truth' even at this very moment? And what exactly would be the 'realidad atroz o banal' mentioned, with such teasing vagueness, at the end of the passage?

However unreliable the narrator may be, his own attitude towards Tlön changes quite dramatically from the beginning of the story to the end. The initial reaction—one of baffled, then consuming curiosity—eventually transforms itself into 'un vertigo asombrado y ligero' as he stumbles across the eleventh volume of the first edition:

> Ahora tenia en las manos un vasto fragmento metódico de la historia total de un planeta desconocido, con sus arquitecturas y sus barajas, con el pavor de sus mitologías y el rumor de sus lenguas, con sus emperadores y sus mares . . . , con su controversia teológica y metafísica.
>
> (19)

The narrator is in rapturous delight as the incommensurable richness of an *unfamiliar* planet lies before him (possibility, remember, always being higher than actuality). We could speak about the allure of the non-present here,

the Proustian sweetness of the sign which is never quite signified, the world which is never quite realized, the necessary incompleteness which Tlön is at that moment. Perhaps this explains the startlingly different tone of the narrator towards the end of the story, as he speaks about the invasion of Tlön in increasingly negative and fearful terms:

> El contacto y el hábito de Tlön han desintegrado este mundo. Encantada por su rigor, la humanidad olvida y torna a olvidar que es un rigor de ajedrecistas, no de ángeles. Ya ha penetrado en las escuelas el (conjetural) 'idioma primitivo' de Tlön; ya la enseñanza de su historia armoniosa (y llena de episodios conmovedores) ha obliterado a la que presidió mi niñez . . .
>
> (35)

And of the sciences:

> Han sido reformadas la numismática, la farmacología y la arqueología. Entiendo que la biología y las matemáticas aguardan también su avatar . . . Una dispersa dinastía de solitarios ha cambiado la faz del mundo.
>
> (36)

Hardly the advent of a glorious New Age. The various sciences and dogmas fall, one by one, in a way uncannily similar to the intellectual erosion which science's credibility has suffered in the advent of postmodernism: science, once the vanquisher of myths, has become for many people a myth in its own right, finding itself relegated now to the status of just another informed opinion, just one more language game amongst many. Again, a host of possibilities presents itself on reading these passages. Tlön might be the sweeping promise of the Third Reich or the Great Leap Forward, attractive and alluring at the outset, ultimately destructive and disenchanting as soon as it is badly translated into 'reality'. Or Tlön might represent the inevitable fate of every Idealism which seeks to realize its values in the world of matter—the Platonic idea, descending into the world of forms, quite loses its charm. Is Tlön a false prophet, promising fantasy and astonishment but bringing only disarray, chaos and subjection? Or does Tlön's fate show what happens when no-one believes any more in the 'realidad de los sustantivos'?

To recap: in Borges' story, the narrator's world encounters a different language game, one which it immediately falls in love with. It yields to Tlön and slowly, move by move, begins to learn a new set of rules—the refutation of reality, the abandonment of epistemological certainties, not to mention the denial of the persistence of substance beyond perception—and soon 'el mundo será Tlön'. The story ends ominously and unclearly: the narrator is visibly reluctant to participate in the general enthusiasm aroused by the 'la Obra Mayor de los Hombres', without explaining why. The only real clue we have to the nature of the narrator's fears lies in his references to the 'rigor' of Tlön, a rigour 'de ajedrecistas, no de ángeles', hinting perhaps at an unspoken resentment of man-made religions. The mysteries of Tlön are artificial, not transcendental—'artificial' in the sense that they have been fabricated by a 'una dispersa dinastía de solitarios' and financed by an atheist and free-thinker. We already know from the story that Buckley's own personal involvement in the Tlön project does seem something akin to the Tower of Babel in its aims and goals—the desire to prove to this 'Dios no existente' that man can be His equal, that he is just as capable of creating miraculous works as the Creator Himself. In a surprising number of Borges' most important stories this idea reappears, where human beings take on the role and responsibilities of an absent God, trying (and not always in vain) to perform a deictic role in the affairs of society. In **'La Lotería en Babilonia'** a secret organization determines the various fates of an entire city through a non-monetary lottery whose rewards and punishments involve favours, murders, promotions, marriages and are always delivered in secret, so that it is impossible to know whether a piece of good fortune has been determined by the lottery or by chance. In **'Tema del traidor y del héroe'** an Irish politician, found by his fellows to be guilty of treachery, agrees to his own public assassination through the re-enactment of the play *Julius Caesar*, thus displaying a Christ-like foreknowledge of a death he knows he must endure. In **'Tlön, Uqbar, Orbis Tertius'** the Orbis Tertius society takes over God's role as the Maker of Mysteries—creating a mystery which comes to entrance the minds of men and to enslave them. Slowly, through scattered *hrönir*, chance quotations, solitary volumes stumbled across in dead men's libraries, the artificial mysteries of Tlön contaminate the narrator's world and make it its own, a situation about which the narrator clearly expresses no joy. Unlike Tlön's sea of newfound converts, the narrator sees it for what it is: not a religion but an elaborate game, devised by earthly 'chessmasters' and set loose upon a world yearning for novelty and 'astonishment'.

Derrida puts before us two different ways of considering the 'status of discourse'. There is the nostalgic way, the one that seeks the 'truth'—that is, reassurance, origins, the end of play. It is the path one would take who seeks to know ultimate answers and explanations. Derrida calls this the 'sad' and 'guilty' choice—in contrast to

> . . . the Nietzschean affirmation, that is the joyous affirmation of the play of the world and of the innocence of becoming, the affirmation of a world of signs without fault, without truth and without origin, which is offered to an active interpretation.[9]

It reaffirms a widely-held credo in postmodern thinking, namely that the Truth-less world of the Postmodern is an exciting, lively, uncertain one, as opposed to the 'ruined', closed world of the transcendentalizing totalities where 'play' is of minimal significance or even nonexistent. Which path do we want to take? Derrida seems to be asking. Rousseauistic boredom, guilt and sadness? Or Nietzschean joy, chance and un-sureness? Do we want to carry on, trying to 'decipher' the Grand Truth we feel to be somewhere out there, or should we simply abandon it altogether? For Derrida—as for Nietzsche—there really is no doubt as to which would be the more 'interesting' choice.

Exactly how interesting it is to live in a world with no ultimate truth, no truth-seekers, no facts outside language or sense of the mystical (what Wittgenstein defined in the *Logico-Tractatus* as the 'sense of the world as a limited whole') still remains, at least for the narrator of **'Tlön, Uqbar, Orbis Tertius'**, undecided. We have already seen how Tlön's affinities with the world of the Postmodern amount to three—a deliberate indifference towards Truth, an awareness of the limited, distorting and radically unique nature of our own perspectiveness ('el hombre que se desplaza modifica las formas que lo circundan' [27]), the belief that one doesn't refer to reality, one makes it, and the related idea that this kind of reality which thought or language produces is by no means ontologically inferior to the reality scientists or materialists talk about ('thought', Borges writes, being 'a perfect synonym for the cosmos'). The disparaging attitude of postmodernism towards truth-seeking—that is, in Rortyian terms, the futile attempt to overcome one's own finite cultural contingency by arriving at a 'final vocabulary' which would explain all the other ones which have led up to it—is best summed up by Nabokov:

> . . . The unfortunate image of a 'road' to which the human mind has become accustomed (life as a kind of journey) is a stupid illusion. We are not going anywhere, we are sitting at home. The other world surrounds us always and is not at all at the end of some pilgrimage.[10]

The idea that there is something at the end of the pilgrimage that we must seek, something which would somehow justify all our toils, is illusory for the postmodernist and rooted in the belief that there is something 'outside' the world (i.e. outside language) which has to be discovered and described (*mimesis*), not invented or unveiled (*aletheia*). Borges takes this one step further in Tlön, where language and thought literally create matter. Tlön is a world awash with private languages and dialectical games, none of them with the slightest interest in seeking the truth. In a postmodern world, the whole idea of pilgrimage is rendered vain by the fact that there is nothing 'extra-discursive' or 'extra-linguistic' at the end of it—no matter how many leaps of faith he takes, the pilgrim can never really leave his language game or transcend his perspectiveness, he will always be 'sitting at home'. Perhaps this is the banal, atrocious reality which will one day 'disintegrate' our world; perhaps, echoing Nabokov, what we see is all there is. No hidden Truths or gods, no ultimate Realities, no mystical 'beyonds', just an endless number of games, played by an endless number of (seated) chessmasters.

Notes

1. Thomas Sheehan, 'Reading a Life: Heidegger and Hard Times', in the *Cambridge Companion to Heidegger* (Cambridge: Cambridge U.P., 1993), 93.

2. Carlos Cortínez, ed., *Borges the Poet* (Fayetteville: Univ. of Arkansas Press, 1986), 83.

3. André Malraux's Introduction to Jorge Luis Borges, *Labyrinths* (London: Penguin, 1964), 10.

4. Jacques Derrida, 'Structure, Sign and Play in the Human Sciences', in *Writing and Difference,* trans. Alan Bass (London: Routledge and Kegan, 1995), 280.

5. Jorge Luis Borges, *Ficciones* (Madrid: Alianza, 1982), 36. All references are to this edition.

6. A question posed by Elizabeth Ermarth in *Sequel To History* (Princeton: Univ. of Princeton Press, 1992), 153.

7. T. Docherty, *Postmodernism: A Reader* (London: Harvester Wheatsheaf, 1993), 36.

8. Patricia Waugh, *Metafiction* (London: Routledge, 1988), 27.

9. Derrida, *op. cit.,* 292.

10. Quoted in Ermarth, *op. cit.,* at the beginning of the book.

Armado F. Zubizarreta (essay date 1998)

SOURCE: "'Borges and I,' A Narrative Sleight of Hand," in *Studies in Twentieth Century Literature,* Vol. 22, No. 2, Summer, 1998, pp. 371–81.

[*In the following essay, Zubizarreta advances interpretive strategies for reading "Borges and I" as a short story.*]

AN AUTOBIOGRAPHICAL PAGE?

Due to its autobiographical appearance, **"Borges and I,"** a brief work published in *El Hacedor* (1960), seems to present, under the pattern of a dual personality, what a writer actually feels, or imagines he may feel, in confronting his social persona.[1] Because this text, usually understood as a confession, offers some aesthetic insights and succinct information about thematic changes, quotations have frequently been taken from it to corroborate conclusions about the author and his work. Criticism, nonetheless, has paid little attention to its narrative quality.

Can **"Borges and I"** be considered a narrative text, a short story whose writing shows the author's original technique?[2] In her analysis of Borges's *Evaristo Carriego,* Sylvia Molloy states that this biography is where "the future maker of fictions, undertakes the possibility of re-creating and inscribing a character" to add that "it is also a place where he [Borges] inaugurates the possibility of erasing the very character he has inscribed" (13–14). In her view, Borges had already anticipated the basic characteristic that he assigns to the short story in his conception and exercise of biography. Thus, observing that most of the characters of Borges's narrative are "narrative functions," Molloy goes on to conclude that "the dissolution of a forseeable character *is* the situation in his stories" (40–41). Once this primacy of situation over character has been accepted, it isn't surprising that he who would deny the personality's entity as such shows it at the beginning

of **"Borges and I"** as split into two entities or contrary characters whose conflicting relation is described.

Yet it is neither enough to describe characters—the *writer I* (the intellectual) and the *vital I* (the existential)—nor only to describe the conflictive relation in which they are involved to create the narrative fiction. At first glance, it seems impossible to deny that nothing happens while we are reading the text and that, although it abundantly provides information about events that usually happen—by using the present tense—and about some events that have happened in the past, no actual present action takes place in the text.

It is true that Borges—an author who has accustomed us to seeing him in the ludic exercise of erasing the limits not only between imagination and experienced realities but also between opposing concepts—finally blurs the distinction between the characters, the writer Borges and the vital I, in the concluding sentence of the text. This one sentence that follows the text's body, an almost page-long paragraph, has an ambiguity that, in this case, seems perfectly suited to the presentation of a psychological phenomenon in which those characters are the poles of a divided personality. But the fact that the text belongs to Borges's infinite and reversible universe is not enough to justify viewing it as a narrative piece. Nor is it sufficient to argue that some of the author's other short stories present two opposite characters temporarily superimposed through narrative impersonation (**"The Shape of the Sword"**), or two ethically opposed qualifications competing to define a character in order to determine what he really is (**"Theme of the Traitor and the Hero"**) or a negative characteristic that shifts from one opposite individual personality to another (**"The Theologians"**).[3]

THE DIALECTIC OF VICTIM AND VICTIMIZER

In **"Borges and I"** the vital I declares that both he and the writer I share preferences: hourglasses, maps, seventeenth-century typography, the taste of coffee, and Stevenson's prose. At the same time it is made clear that the vital I is subject to exploitation by the writer I, who takes over his experiences of the surroundings to create literature: "Yo vivo, yo me dejo vivir, para que Borges pueda tramar su literatura" 'I live, let myself go on living, so that Borges can contrive his literature' (*Lab* 246).[4] Nonetheless, it can be observed too that the vital I accepts this exploitation, conceiving it as an exchange, when he confesses "esa literatura me justifica" 'this literature justifies me' (*Lab* 246), that is to say, that he admits that this literature gives some meaning—meaning pursued, we think, by every human being—to his life.

Yet while the writer I achieves his goal of creating his literature, the vital I doubts the extent to which he himself, his actual self, may truly be saved in these literary creations. He points out that even the writer's "válidas" 'valid' pages cannot save him, "quizá porque lo bueno ya no es de nadie, ni siquiera del otro, sino del lenguaje o de la tradición" 'perhaps because what is good belongs to no one, not even to him, but rather to the language and to tradition' (*Lab* 246), and also declares that he doesn't recognize himself—his individuality—in the author's books. It is true that, in the midst of his confidences, he asserts that "sólo algún instante de mí podrá sobrevivir en el otro" 'only some instant of myself can survive in him' (*Lab* 246). Yet he concludes the description of the relationship and his sense of despoilment by declaring his stoic pessimism: "así mi vida es una fuga y todo lo pierdo y todo es del olvido, o del otro" 'Thus my life is a flight and I lose everything and everything belongs to oblivion, or to him' (*Lab* 247).

It is evident that each of the two characters has clearly defined his specific, positive attributes, as well as his negative ones. To speak of a double, the parallelism of the two characters has its origin in a complement of desire by which one covets what the other possesses.[5] Molloy points out that in the double rivalry of Borges's narrative, "Once desire is sated, those fragments [of a character] revert to the same 'nothingness of personality,' to the same zero degree of desire" (47). The case is, however, that while the writer I comfortably benefits by despoiling the vital I's capacity to experience, the vital I feels disappointed with the exchange of life for literature and aspires to have his part in the work of art socially recognized—perhaps to reveal himself as its actual source—a goal that, to some extent, he has begun pursuing in so far as he is exercising the function of an "historian" I.

Within the dialectic of the I and the Other, the text which, to our understanding, had begun in a disparaging tone in the first sentence—"Al otro, a Borges, es a quien le ocurren las cosas" 'The other one, the one called Borges, is the one things happen to' (*Lab* 246)—has ended by asserting that the other is the one who abusively takes over everything. To prove this, the vital I enumerates the topics of his interest—"las mitologías del arrabal" 'the mythologies of the suburbs' (*Lab* 246) and "los juegos con el tiempo y con lo infinito" 'the games with time and infinity' (*Lab* 246–47)—which throughout his life and the writer I's production have been the objects of despoilment.

Such detailed information indicates that the vital I is, to some degree, a victim of the writer I. Yet we may be somewhat disoriented, but not convinced of the contrary, when the vital I declares: "sería exagerado afirmar que nuestra relación es hostil" 'It would an exaggeration to say that ours is a hostile relationship' (*Lab* 246). But the victim's hostility cannot be hidden, despite his cautious dissimulation in trying to deny how serious the conflict is, because it appears clearly revealed by the kind of terms used to characterize the writer I's behavior: he shares preferences "de un modo vanidoso que las convierte en atributos de un actor" 'in a vain way that turns them into the attributes of an actor' (*Lab* 246), he has a "perversa costumbre de falsear y magnificar" 'perverse custom of falsifying and magnifying things' (*Lab* 246). Because of this, we can suspect that the relationship described, a symbiotic one

within which convenient dissimulations like those mentioned take place, deserves to be considered a sort of sadomasochistic relationship. It isn't too audacious, therefore, that we begin to doubt the verbal behavior of the vital I, a masochist who has a part in the conflictive relationship in which the masochistic and the sadistic roles are reversed along the lines of a painful and cruel game.

From a philosophical point of view, **"Borges and I"** may also be considered a precise revelation, one example among many of the lack of the subject's unity, as well as of the metaphysical enigma of personal identity, a topic that, without any doubt, points to the influence of Schopenhauer.[6] Mourey has pointed out that "Borges's narration puts on stage by means of the complexity of his narrative devices the absence of an origin—I and the gap of the Real" (18), and has specifically asserted that Borges is aware of "the impossibility of a univocal and non-problematic constitution of them [the characters Borges used by the author] as subjects of/in the writing" (33).

In our opinion, the split of the personality in **"Borges and I"** is a necessary literary pattern so that the writer may set on the narrative's fictional stage the idea of the subject's illusory reality. Yet we think that in order to understand the extent of the interplay of Borges's philosophical ideas and his literary creations, Borges's final statement in "A New Refutation of Time," an essay in *Other Inquisitions,* has to be carefully taken into consideration:

> Negar la sucesión temporal, negar el yo, negar el universo astronómico, son desesperaciones aparentes y consuelos secretos. . . . El tiempo es la sustancia de que estoy hecho. . . . El mundo, desgraciadamente, es real; yo, desgraciadamente, soy Borges.

> Denying temporal succession, denying the self, denying the astronomical universe, are apparent desperations and secret consolations. . . . Time is the substance I am made of. . . . The world, unfortunately, is real; I, unfortunately, am Borges.

> (*OC* 771; *Lab* 233–34)

A SLANDEROUS PLOT?

Although the ambiguity of the conflict shown above is not unusual in an autobiographical document and by itself cannot bestow narrative quality on the text, readers would have let themselves be taken in by the obvious if they hadn't found it extremely odd that the description ends with a brief yet tantalizing sentence set apart from the long paragraph, a sentence that comes back from the past to the present—in the Spanish original neither 'escribió' nor 'ha escrito'—to tell us, despite the fact that it belongs to the informing voice: "No sé cuál de los dos escribe esta página" 'I do not know which one of us has written this page' (*Lab* 247).[7]

The last statement of **"Borges and I"** cannot be accepted without a good reason to justify it; it obviously doesn't make sense.[8] Yet Mourey takes it literally and points out that, within the logical matrix offered by the short story's title and its final statement, the text may be interpreted as either I or Borges, or as neither I nor Borges, this last a double negation which leads to an infinite polemic (39 n. 89). Thus, he concludes: "Structural failure of the enunciation's subject in the subject of what is enunciated, a failure that the text, in its process, puts on stage, re-presents" (39). Our main objection to Mourey is that, by extracting a logical text, which only partially takes into account Borges's text, he loses sight of the complex short story's narrative action.

If we well know that the vital I describes the relation in this autobiographical confession as a first-hand witness, and if we know also without the slightest doubt that the writer I is the one who, according to his precise characterization, writes, it seems apparent that the writer I is the one who has just written this page and that the vital I ought to know it. Therefore, the vital I's final statement may not be a dissimulation but, instead, a flagrant lie. If that is the case, there would be good ground to suspect that the entire text is a falsehood, the product of a compulsive intent to falsify.

From this perspective, the text's nature changes radically: it becomes a "story" (a "lie") by which we see the vital I (the narrating character) in the very act of deceiving the reader (narrative action), a deception which he was about to achieve if he hadn't betrayed himself in the last statement, which allows the readers—participating, active readers—to escape the deception into which they might otherwise have fallen. Such an interpretation is attractive: we might assert that we have the short story of a lie, of the deceiving process, whose deception is unveiled. Yet to assert that would be, perhaps, to let ourselves be led too easily into an error by Borges's ludic magic.

THE SHORT STORY'S RITE OF PASSAGE

If we attributed short story quality to such a narrative simply because it is well written and is signed by a well known writer, we would be obliged to acknowledge that we have a short story that is only a topical one which uses a quite simple technique. But because simplicity isn't one of Borges's sins, we may dare venture the hypothesis that in this short story we are in the presence of a much more subtle narrative architecture which masterfully offers a much more substantial action than what we have seen so far.

A more careful examination of the text requires that we not believe in the vital I's candor. We already know that he isn't trustworthy, not only because of his first-person narrator's role, but also because of his dubious statements. We must conceive of him as a person who is or feels himself a victim, or who wants us to believe he is, who may be able to use better strategies to achieve his goal of defending himself or of deceiving us.

It shouldn't be forgotten that the vital I has given us two examples of a repeatable pattern of thievery. Guided by

that pattern, we observe that, in flight from Borges, after having first abandoned to him the mythologies of the enclaves at the city outskirts and, second, the games with time and infinity, now, on the page we are reading, the vital I has deliberately focused on his own psychological anguish to implement a sweet vengeance. We may suspect then that, because he wants to reveal to the readers his condition of victim in his relation to the writer I, the vital I sets himself to create a trap. We then become aware that he knows that, attracted by this new and interesting vital experience, the writer I will repeat once more his compulsive stealing pattern to take it over by virtue of his writing, thus falling into that mousetrap.

Given the fact that the vital I has issued an accusation against the writer I, it is the unsuspecting Borges I, who, by his own hand, turns it into a literary page, a text that becomes a written self-indictment handed to the reader. To avoid Borges's guessing the danger and escaping from the temptation as well as to alert the reader who will witness the accusation, the vital I completes the implementation of his strategic design by "dictating" the ironical last sentence, underscoring it through its separation from the long paragraph. With such a statement about not knowing which of the two writes the page (which is ambiguous only on the surface) the completion of the vital I's vengeance has been secured. Certainly such a vengeance, aimed at discrediting the writer I, is a signal of how the victim and victimizer roles have been inverted.

The delivery process of the vital I's vengeance has been the narrative action which, impelled by the revenge motif, has taken place in the short story while we were reading it, an action within which the vital I and the writer I played their roles as protagonist and antagonist, true characters of the plot. These basic narrative elements escape a superficial reading because the literary discourse conceals them by a well calculated maneuver that almost annihilated them only to reserve a dazzling final surprise for the reader. Doubtless, Jorge Luis Borges is always Jorge Luis Borges: he actually invites the reader to participate, not only as recipient of the victim's message, but also as witness, in a true initiation rite into the narrative's thaumaturgy.[9]

It is necessary now to show a meaningful intertextual game that takes place in this short story in order to gain access to the ultimate meaning of Borges's art. Mentioning the phrase that affirms that "todas las cosas quieren perseverar en su ser" 'all things long to persist in their being' (*Lab* 246) is to accept—without saying so—the daring exegesis by don Miguel de Unamuno of the man "of flesh and bone," Spinoza. Unamuno claimed that this statement of the sixth proposition of the third part of the *Ethics* is proof of an unyielding desire for immortality which goes beyond the metaphysical system of the pantheist philosopher.[10] Given Borges's special use of philosophy, it appears clear that avoiding a reference to Unamuno allowed the author to stay out of the Spanish thinker's philosophical and religious context and to create his literature freely. But it is also true that the insertion of that statement underlines the powerful desire felt by the hurt vital I—whether it be useless or not—to survive into the fate—whatever it might be—of the literary text.

Readers often feel that the verbal, literary construction of Borges's infinite and reversible universe seems to be a flight from personal existence and from the human anguish in trying to find life's meaning. However, alerted by the quotation from Spinoza with which the protagonist of **"Borges and I"** supports his most deep-seated aspiration, we may try to have a clearer glimpse of the dramatic point of departure of Borges's literary creation. A poem entices us to pursue in that endeavor. In the poem "El espejo" ("The mirror") Jorge Luis Borges reveals the awe with which a mirror filled him in his childhood: "Yo, de niño, temía que el espejo / Me mostrara otra cara o una ciega / Máscara impersonal que ocultaría / Algo sin duda atroz" 'Being a child, I used to fear that the mirror / Would show to me another face or a blind / Impersonal mask which would hide / Something doubtlessly atrocious'; and that still he felt it as a mature man: "Yo temo ahora que el espejo encierre / El verdadero rostro de mi alma, / Lastimada de sombras y de culpas, / El que Dios ve y acaso ven los hombres" 'Now I fear that the mirror keeps / The true face of my soul, / hurt by shadows and by misdeeds / The one God sees and maybe men see' (**Historia** 107; my translation). Taking into consideration that even the most nihilistic literary text originates in the writer's impossible task of escaping from a dreadful human experience (see Blanchot 4–20), one can conjecture that Borges's dread was tamed thanks to scientific formulas and philosophical systems that, taken as great metaphors, served his literary purposes as a stoic neo-fantastic writer.

No critic denies that interpreting Borges's literary works is an extremely difficult task and that in trying to provide the readers with an adequate access to Borges's art we run the risk of oversimplifying. As Mourey describes it, Borges's ludic magic is "a play with truth and with the reader's belief, specular and labyrinthic spaces exhibition, evocation of a marvelous Sign which might include, destroy or create its Referent" (6). Without trusting standard patterns of analysis, and without risking getting lost in the gallery of mirrors or in the labyrinths of interpretation, we wanted to share our reading of **"Borges and I,"** to invite the reader to enjoy such a succinct and, at the same time, complex narrative text, so apparently transparent on the surface that it almost eludes us, a short story in which the tenacious search for an individual's "instant" that perhaps could be saved is revealed and narrated. Thanks to that fictional creation of a split author's alter ego, a tour de force in which life and creative will are meshed, Borges's reader may gain access to the dreadful vision not only of the process from which the literary work of art emerges but also of the author's intent—between Orpheus's longing and Sisyphus's resignation—of creating himself as a subject.[11]

Notes

1. This and other prose works by the author are quoted from his *Obras Completas*, hereafter referred to as

OC. In that edition the entire text is on page 808. English quotations of Borges's prose texts are from *Labyrinths,* hereafter referred to as *Lab.* Translations of the quotations taken from criticism are mine.

2. Jean-Pierre Mourey, whose work shows a rigorous use of contemporary literary analysis, recognizes the narrative nature of "Borges and I" (38–39). See also Aguadé (171–75) and McGuirk (43–49).

3. Alazraki states that the two theologians in conflict are one individual and offers a text by Schopenhauer to justify his interpretation (*La prosa* 64–65).

4. In my opinion, *me dejo vivir* isn't fully rendered by the usual translations "[I] let myself go on living" or "I allow myself to live." The symbiotic relationship context, Spanish parallel constructions like *dejarse querer,* and the term "vividor" lead me to think that the meaning in the Spanish original is 'to be used' by the other.

5. For Borges's autobiographical convention and the double, see Mourey (33–45). The double, a specular metaphor, at odds with a realistic conception of literature as a mirror of life, is the aesthetic axis of Borges's neo-fantastic literature, which allows him to avoid the recourse to terror used in the preceding fantastic literature. For the neo-fantastic, see Alazraki, "Neofantástico."

6. On Schopenhauer's influence, see Paoli 121–91.

7. Yates informs us that Borges had deleted "ha escrito" in the original manuscript (318). The definitive Spanish text reads "escribe," which is better rendered by the present progressive "is writing."

8. About the final statement of the text, McGuirk opens up a pertinent question: "Coda or supplement? Trace of I in the 'other'?" (47).

9. Hutcheon thinks that, because what she considers a mimesis of the product is insufficient to understand postmodernist creation, a mimesis of the "process" is necessary (39). That seems quite justified by this text by Borges, which implicates the reader to such a degree.

10. See Unamuno 132–33. In this particular case it isn't possible to say, as Molloy does, that "it hardly matters whether Borges refers directly to works he has read or to commentators of those works" (105). For an overview of the Unamuno-Borges relation, see Kerrigan and Koch.

11. By staging a conflict among the selves, the text illuminates the drama of the individual self, but at the same time shows a poetic self-identifying intent in which a postulated subject aspires to overcome heterogeneity by indicting the masks born from the experience of the social context.

Works Cited

Aguadé, Jorge. "Reflejos en el espejo." *Escritura* 11.27 (1989): 171–80.

Alazraki, Jaime. *La prosa narrativa de Jorge Luis Borges.* Madrid: Gredos, 1968.

———. "¿Qué es lo neofantástico?" *Mester* 19.2 (1990): 21–33.

Blanchot, Maurice. *The Gaze of Orpheus.* Trans. Lydia Davis. New York: Station Hill, 1981.

Borges, Jorge Luis. *El Hacedor.* Buenos Aires: Emecé, 1960.

———. *Historia de la noche.* Buenos Aires: Emecé, 1977.

———. *Labyrinths.* Ed. Donald A. Yates and James E. Irby. New York: New Directions, 1964.

———. *Obras Completas (1923–1972).* Buenos Aires: Emecé, 1974.

Christ, Ronald. "Borges Justified: Notes and Texts toward Stations of a Theme." *TriQuarterly* 25 (1972): 52–87.

Hutcheon, Linda. *Narcissistic Narrative: The Metafictional Paradox.* Waterloo: Wilfrid Laurier UP, 1980.

Kerrigan, Anthony. "Borges/Unamuno." *TriQuarterly* 25 (1972): 294–311.

Koch, Dolores M. "Borges y Unamuno: Convergencias y divergencias." *Cuadernos Hispanoamericanos* 408 (1984): 113–22.

McGuirk, Bernard. "'Borges and I': Jorge Luis Borges and the 'Discerned' Subject." *Romance Studies* 16 (1990): 43–49.

Molloy, Sylvia. *Signs of Borges*: Durham: Duke UP, 1994.

Mourey, Jean-Pierre. *Jorge Luis Borges: Vérité et univers fictionnels.* Liège-Bruxelles: Pierre Mardaga, 1989.

Paoli, Roberto. *Tre saggi su Borges.* Roma: Bulzoni, 1992.

Unamuno, Miguel de. *Del sentimiento trágico de la vida. Obras completas* 16. Madrid: Afrodisio Aguado, 1964.

Yates, Donald A. "Behind 'Borges and I.'" *Modern Fiction Studies* 19 (1973): 317–24.

Eric Pennington (essay date 1998)

SOURCE: "Vestiges of Empire: Toward a Contrapuntal Reading of Borges," in *CLA Journal*, Vol. XLII, No. 1, September, 1998, pp. 103–17.

[*In the following essay, Pennington relies on the historical and social contexts surrounding Borges's "The Ethnographer" to elucidate the text.*]

This essay takes as a point of departure the Borges short story titled **"El etnógrafo,"** found in *Elogio de la sombra*

(1969) and classified in the general category of Borges's later prose. In addition to commenting on its literary structure, I will examine its application to the world outside the text: the milieu from which the structure sprang. That is, rather than a strictly literary interpretation centering on the important narratorial silences and the denial of the text, this discussion will include observations on cultural and historical referents in the text. It is hoped that, in the end, the literary and the socio-historical will be seen as equally significant in the analysis of this story and that we may envision a closer relationship between the two spheres.

Approaching the text to investigate its extratextual messages follows a pattern that teachers of literature have been pursuing more and more these days. This revivified interest in background, history, and context stems from the realization that we live in a time when we may no longer have the luxury of studying texts as autonomous artifacts, divorced in time and context from the author and the environment that produced them. And though many texts resist any application to cultural or historical relevance, it is also true that we have not seen such connections because we have been trained not to look for them, or we deem them secondary to purely literary analyses.

The works of Borges have universally fallen into this category of self-contained worlds of autonomous discourses. You will rarely find a story, essay, or poem of his that has a readily apparent reference to reality or a passage that requires an extratextual explanation. His great short stories such as **"La muerte y la brújula," "La biblioteca de Babel," "El sur," "Las ruínas circulares,"** and so many others from the 1930s and 1940s are simply masterpieces within their own confines. For example, though **"La muerte y la brújula"** is situated in Paris, it could just as well be set in any other city in the world and not lose its power. Questions about its location, temporality, and even its references to Jewish culture have not been seen as significant in analyzing the text. However, in contrast to these classic works, Borges's later (much shorter) stories do seem to contain more decipherable contexts. When the author swore off all his "mirrors, labyrinths, tigers, towers [and] knives" in favor of a more skeletal prose in the late 1960s,[1] he generally disappointed his critics with the "lighter" stories that followed.[2] But if we look carefully, we may find a promising trade-off: Borges left behind the baroque artifice, erudition, footnotes, obliqueness, and convoluted clauses of his earlier prose. What he substituted is a more poetic structure with themes and plots that yield much more in the area of cultural commentary. I would like to look at **"El etnógrafo"** as a case of synecdoche and see if this small textual part could be representative of the whole of the Borgesian oeuvre, as regards the question as to whether the author's texts are as autonomous and divorced from referentiality as we have thought, or whether they may indeed have roots in history and culture that we have ignored.

The short story in question is very brief and accessible; it has been included in at least one undergraduate anthology,

Aproximaciones a la literatura hispánica. The plot is straightforward enough: Fred Murdoch, an American graduate student, open to all ideas and inclinations, is advised to go to an Indian reservation in the Southwest of the United States and learn the secret rites of one of the tribes there. When he comes back he can publish his research as his thesis. Fred goes, stays two years, learns the secret, and then abruptly leaves the Indians. When he returns, he refuses to publish his discoveries, not because he is bound by language, but because (it is implied) he does not want to trivialize his experience. The story suddenly ends, almost in a comical fashion, reporting, "Fred se casó, se divorció y es ahora uno de los bibliotecarios de Yale."[3]

In classroom discussions, students have almost always been puzzled by the abruptness of the ending. On one occasion a young man framed this memorable question, in light of the story's truncated conclusion: "Did Borges have some kind of deadline to meet?" Given that the ending of the story elicits such reactions, the direction of the analysis often turns at the outset toward Poststructuralist theories of reader reception, as students and teachers verbalize expectations as to what more Borges should have written, what is left out, what we (as authors) would have added, and why we feel the text needs something more. After exploring such themes, one could turn the discussion to what appears to be Borges's intention of withholding the traditional text by denying us the expected falling action and dénouement (see Wheelock). An instructor would feel obliged to stress how, with this abrupt ending, the author subtly makes the point of showing us how tradition-bound we are, to what degree he refuses to play that game, and how literature can still be rewarding without structural or thematic conventions.

A typical analysis of this tale might also resort to New Critical approaches, searching for literary symbols and interpreting them. The story, brief though it is, provides sufficient material for such an analysis. Readers home-in on one point in the plot where Murdoch is revealed the desired secret in his dreams. He dreams of "bisontes" (56). (The Borges-authorized translation of "mustangs" is inexplicable, except in light of how Borges typically throws the reader false clues, as with his penchant for bogus footnotes from his earlier stories.) Students have taken the reference to bison and consulted their dictionaries of myths to find, in one case, that for the Navajo Indians of the American Southwest, the bison mentioned in the story symbolized the importance and preservation of knowledge. We can link this observation with the fact that Fred eventually ended up as a Yale librarian, recall that that institution has a justifiably famous Rare Book Library, and thus conclude—in a New Critical leap of faith—that our protagonist lived up to the promise or admonition of his mysterious dreams on the prairie.

This story also provides the opportunity to open the discussion to the questions of narratology and self-consciousness in writing. It can quickly be shown how the narrator is totally unreliable. He or she states that the story was relayed by someone else, and that it did not even occur in the state where he or she heard it: "El caso me lo refirieron en Texas, perio habia acontecido en otro estado." The storyteller is also uncertain as to the protagonist's name ("Se llamaba, creo, Fred Murdock"). Despite this unfamiliarity, the narrator can amazingly speak to Murdock's thoughts (how he foresaw the difficulties before him, how he later longed to be back on the prairies), yet he or she cannot tell exactly what the young man's thesis director said in reply to his refusal to reveal the secret. The narrator wraps up the climactic conversation between Fred and his advisor by saying, "Tal fue, en esencia, el dialogo." We also note that Fred is described as a person who "no descreia de los libros," and wonder if the narrator is implying that we are equally as naive in trusting what the present text says. Then when we learn that Fred tore up his notes from which his story is supposedly taken, we sense a reference to the artifice of fiction and conclude that this is a narration we cannot trust. Faced with so much narratorial sputtering and feigning, the novice critic then starts to feel uncomfortable with the formalist analysis of symbols and meaning. If the narrator cannot get it straight, how can we even trust that the reference to the bison is correct? How can we analyze what is now dubious? At this point we come full circle to our earlier remarks about reader expectations. The student expects a reliable narration with which he or she can comfortably suspend disbelief and slip into the world of fiction. But when the framer of that fiction reminds us six times in the space of two pages of the fictionality of the story presented, the traditional reader will abandon all hope, or at least all confidence, realizing that we have an overtly self-conscious text celebrating its structure more than any referentiality found through symbols.

But despite the metafictional tendencies of the text, one should also take the opportunity to analyze Fred's quest and relate it to Borge's other fiction where the search for mystic secrets and disks is pervasive. Such investigations yield parallels with the quest archetype, the innocence and initial lack of sophistication of the hero, the trials of the hero (two years on the prairie—changing his mode of dress, eating, and thinking), the descent into the underworld (figuratively, in Fred's dreams), the acquiring of light and understanding (through the shaman's revelation), and our modern-day displacements of the same archetypes. Much has been written on "Borges and the Esoteric,"[4] and this brief text shows that, though Borges may have turned from mirrors and labyrinths, his later prose still reveals his enduring interest in ancient secrets and mysteries. In brief, there is always substance for an archetypal approach to Borges, if one is so inclined.[5]

These discussions of textual expectations, symbols, archetypes, and the style of narration unquestionably have their place in the investigation of Borges's text. But after New Critical and Poststructuralist analyses of the text, we might want to continue the examinations by asking how some passages in the text connect with a very real world outside. Poststructuralism, particularly Deconstruction, closed the boundaries of the text even more than Formalism. But unlike Formalism, which at least acknowledged an exterior world, Derridean philosophy asserted that that world was a construct also, built by language and concepts without foundation. All foundations are soft, built only on former conceptions. There is no original Truth. For the literary critic, this meant that even if one tried to make a reference to the historical world of, say, Cervantes, there was now the belief that anything we think we know about Cervantes and his epoch is just another discourse, shaped and biased like any other fiction. So readers of literature who had been taught to abhor the intentional fallacy and affective fallacy were now told, in essence, that all reference is fallacy. By the late 1970s, the New Historicist impulse had arisen and began to take Deconstructionists to task, making the general point that we have better things to do than happily tease out warring forces and hunt for *aporias*. Feminist critics and Cultural Materialists also urged our fields toward more social relevancy in the 1980s. Today, literary analysis as a field has become uncomfortable with the idea of separating text from context, and many would argue that we err in an ethical sense by doing so: we relegate too many voices to silence if we ignore referents, and this silencing has led in a very real and tangible way to the suppression of people and cultures. Though dyed-in-the-wool Deconstructionists would never countenance the concept of a valid referential reality, the Poststructuralist movement does indeed contribute significantly to the burgeoning interest in new historico-cultural studies. For, above all else, the Deconstructionist impulse taught critics to read, analyze, question, decenter, and reconstitute everything. This style of a closer reading has not been abandoned by contemporary critics, whether their purposes are textual or contextual. One could argue that a deconstructively close reading of marginalia is essential to bringing to the center what has historically been ignored and shoved to the periphery.

An approach of combining a decentering reading with a desire to comment on and exhort social and cultural change can best be seen in the works of Edward W. Said. In 1978 he published *Orientalism,* which has since become a classic, must-read opus.[6] Through impressive readings and scholarship, Said shows how many great works of English literature promoted beliefs and assumptions regarding other geographic regions and other ethnic groups that created "the cultural preconditions for and no doubt enabled the work of empires."[7] He successfully argues that our concepts of the Middle East and all of the Orient are built upon groundless foundations, just as Derrida has characterized our Western metaphysics. When we peel away the layers to get to our perceptual foundations, we see they are not based on reality, but on some voyager's, visitor's, or writer's interpretation about the cultures of the Orient. His point is readily apparent. What we superficially know about India is often derived from *Kim, A Passage to India, The Jungle Book* and the movie *Gandhi,* or even remarks by Shakespeare's Caliban or Brontë's Mrs. Rochester. Subsequently, everything we hear about that subcontinent

is filtered through those very finite points of reference. Further refining such theories, Said in 1994 published an arguably more important book, *Culture and Imperialism.* He speaks in the latter study of how virtually all cultures of the world have been touched and changed by the great empires of the past. For example, by 1914, Europe held a grand total of roughly 85 percent of the earth as colonies, protectorates, dependencies, dominions, and commonwealths.[8] This later tome analyzes how literature, as representative of culture—buttresses, nourishes, and countenances the ideology of empire. Through multiple examples of reading marginal references to the Other—the repressed and exploited races and ethnic groups in canonical texts—Said makes the almost undeniable point of how literature is complicit with the furthering of empire and the subjugation of minorities. It is doubtful that any professor of literature could read this book and not reevaluate what he or she is doing by teaching foreign literatures and cultures. We are leaving out remarks on the transgenerational imprints of imperialism.

In *Culture Imperialism,* Said is not so much interested in the physical phenomenon of empire, or direct colonialism, which largely ended at the conclusion of the second World War. He argues that imperialism lingers where it has always been, in a kind of general cultural sphere as well as in the specific, economic, and social practices. He investigates the impressive ideological formations that allowed the idea of empires and colonies to exist and grow. He is particularly intrigued at how these concepts continue in ideological terms today, long after the empires themselves have been dismantled. His book is a call for all scholars to include the voices of the colonized and the subjugated in any discussion of literature, because "scarcely any attention has been paid to the privileged role of culture in the modern imperial experience" (5). Throughout his treatise he tries to show that literature itself makes constant references to itself as somehow participating in imperial expansion and therefore creates "structures of feeling" that support, elaborate, and consolidate the practice of empire (14). Though his readings are subversive, he is not calling for a rejection of the canon or attacking literature we cherish. Indeed, with his references to British, Russian, and French novels it is clear that he values those texts also. He compares his way of rereading the literature of empire as "contrapuntal" (51), but he does not simply mean to define his perceptions as counterpoints to traditional commentaries. His adjective is taken from the metaphor of the baroque fugue or invention, where two, three, or four lines move in harmony and balance, but contrapuntally to the tonic theme. Take one of the voices away, and the fugue is no longer a fugue. This is to say, without the contrapuntal reading of the role of empire in culture, we have incomplete interpretations and limited perspectives of literature.

I have taken this sidetrack from **"El etnógrafo"** by way of introducing my preferred way of interpreting and teaching this story. It seems to me that the most salient issue in the text is its "structure of feeling" that allows, condones, and embraces Murdock's adventure among the Native Americans. In a classroom discussion, I would ask my students to review why Fred felt linked to these Indians. An "inverse symmetry" is created as we realize that one of his ancestors had been killed in the Indian wars.[9] I would then inquire as to what my students know about the conquest of the West and Manifest Destiny. The discussion would turn to the United States as an often merciless empire of expansion, subjugation, and enslavement in the nineteenth century. As much as we might try to sanitize our history in the West, there is just no way in which the past can be quarantined from the present. Past and present inform each other, each implies the other and, in the totally ideal sense intended by Elliot, each co-exists with the other. Therefore, the past, containing the massacre of the Indian tribes, co-exists with the present of Murdock's quest. Borges, being the master he is, has subtly imbedded it in this seemingly trivial story. But as important as the facts of history are, it is more imperative to recognize how fundamentally similar the present actions of Fred and his university advisors are when compared to the American colonizers of the West. This young anthropologist is the new and improved imperialist. He does not go with firearms, but he possesses essentially the same purpose: to impose his will on a minority race and take what he needs, just as his forebears did. His action reaffirms the Indians' subjacent position and incorporation into the empire. Murdock is not unlike Marlow, as he repeats and confirms Kurtz's action in *Heart of Darkness*. Marlowe figuratively restored Africa to European hegemony by historizing and narrating its strangeness. The natives, the wilderness, their peculiarities and their secrets all reaccentuate Marlow's need to place the colonies on the imperial map and the "overarching temporality of narratable history" (*Culture* 164).

Is Murdock, in his attempts to learn, record, and publish his deceptively gained knowledge any different? When we further examine the tale, we see that Fred has been commissioned to bring back the most secret, private, and special aspect of the Indians' culture. He is on a mission of intellectual rape and exploitation, to be published and recorded in the archives of an institution of higher learning, watered down, and later to be placed on the optional reading list of some graduate seminar, no doubt. What kind of an ideology could include such notions that territories and peoples require and beseech domination, exploration, and investigation? The culture of empire and, even more repugnant, the culture of the benevolent empire that believes it has the endowed right to take from minorities their land, rights, lives, and most cherished secrets and rites. The irony is that while many readers can condemn the expansionism of the nineteenth century, they can see no connection between those actions and the contiguous adventures of Fred Murdock. But they only differ in degree, not in kind. They are about plundering for the gain of the dominant culture. There is in this text an insuperable contradiction between the politico-historical actuality based on force (the defeat of the Indians), and the scientific and humane desire (on Fred's part) to understand the Other hermeneutically and in modes *not* influenced by force (a doctoral dissertation). But there is just no way of apprehending the

Indian experience without also grasping the imperial contest itself. The ethnographic enterprise in general is epistemologically and ethically corrupt from its inception to its most subtle and sympathetic modes. Though Fred's activities in **"El etnógrafo"** would be classified as sympathetic, we should not be misled. Such expeditions are attempts to do what the original, physical empires could not accomplish. No longer able to suppress or transcribe alterity, the West has lapsed into contemplative irony by trying to "study" the unfamiliar by means of its anthropologists. As Catherine Martin states, "The inevitable result of this hypocritical discourse is not to elucidate but to silence its Other(s), primitive or at least, non-Western society. Because in anthropology, especially, the imperial setting after all is pervasive and unavoidable."[10] The concept—the structure of feeling—of the benevolent empire with its anthropologists reclaiming and preserving important truths is what sanctions our culture to continue to exploit. In other words, anthropologists are not cultural saviors recovering and preserving important races from extinction and oblivion. They are minions of a postcolonial enterprise, out to dominate and subjugate by discovering, explaining, implicitly relegating inferior positions to the subjects of their studies, and thus dominating the lesser peoples in a way the former empires could not.

Seen in this light, Fred's refusal to publish his findings is significant. Borges at this point is signaling a distinction between Murdock's actions and the interests of the colonizers, as embodied in the desires of his thesis advisors. Fred, it would appear, has sensed on some level what the game is all about. He now values the knowledge he has obtained and understands that to turn it over to scholars would be to vulgarize and derogate the experience. He rejects the attempt to include this knowledge of the Indians into the hegemony that the educational establishment would prefer. As opposed to what an initial reading might reveal, Murdock is not just a student who "went native" for two years and came back and lost interest in scholarly pursuits. He is figuratively saying "no" to the modernist, thinly disguised imperialist culture that continues today.

Sadly, the reasons behind Fred's refusal are often discounted as secondary to the desire to know what it is that Fred discovered. Virtually all readers want to focus on what the secret is that he never reveals. But can we not see this is indicative of the power and influence empire has in shaping our interests and presumptions? Why shouldn't we be allowed to know this? Our explorers regularly bring us knowledge that delights and entertains. We don't like it when a secret is withheld. What, indeed, is wrong with this graduate student? These questions consciously or subconsciously are being asked by the readers of the story. This is why we feel that the ending of the story is so incomplete. The expectations of postcolonial readers have been denied. And to show how thoroughly immersed we are in the culture of empire, we want to rewrite the story or resort to dictionaries of symbols to discover what this secret is that Fred denies us.

But it is not ours. The secret is not ours to have, learn, exploit, categorize, trivialize, enjoy or demean. The presumption that it is our right is reflective of our own arrogance. Fred is possessor of the knowledge because he is now, in effect, a member of the Indian culture. He makes it clear that the secret is available to anyone, if he or she wants to go through what he experienced: "Esos caminos hay que andarlos" (57). But citizens of an empire do not want to do that. They expect those mystic secrets, that special knowledge, those trinkets, those magic disks, that coffee, and that cotton to be delivered by someone else. They are dominant, dependent on their subjects for what they enjoy. The academics awaiting Fred's return (the plundering, intellectual colonizers in this story), have no more interest in "traveling those paths" than the protagonists of Jane Austen's *Mansfield Park* had in going to the Caribbean to see how their own sugar was produced.

I trust we can see that this short, short story contains important references to the past and even more substantive comments for the present. It is to be hoped that a fuller discussion would evolve to include a sober examination of our continuing subjugation of Native Americans and the quasi-genocidal Federal and cultural attitudes toward these tribes. I am also optimistic that as we read more about cultures and imperialism we will become increasingly adept at recognizing texts (and passages in texts) where we might continue our global self-examination. As an example, we could turn to other Borges stories and look very closely at what his kings, soldiers, and especially his gauchos are doing and saying. Someone else could turn to the *Quijote* and review the references to the far-flung Golden Age empire. As we study Pablo Neruda's "La United Fruit Co.," we should go beyond the parody in the poem to the root causes of the misery and humiliation depicted. If we examine Rosario Ferré's "La muñeca menor," we must not dodge the question as to what is the base of the older Puerto Rican family's wealth and privileged position (the sugar plantations). The contemporary short stories, "Father's Day," "Míster Taylor," and "And We Sold the Rain," demand similar attention.

We can find vestiges of empire in many textual nooks and crannies if our consciousness is sufficiently heightened. Why should we care what texts say about imperialism and their legacies? Said has responded well:

> More important than the past itself is its bearing upon cultural attitudes in the present. For reasons that are partly imbedded in the imperial experience, the old divisions between colonizer and colonized have re-emerged in what is often referred to as the North-South relationship, which has entailed defensiveness, various kinds of rhetorical and ideological combat, and the simmering hostility that is quite likely to trigger devastating wars—in some cases it already has. Are there ways we can reconcile the imperial experience in other than compartmentalized terms, so as to transform our understanding of both the past and the present and our attitude toward the future? . . . A more interesting type of secular interpretation can emerge, altogether more rewarding than the denunciations of the past, the ex-

pressions of regret for its having ended, or—even more wasteful because it is violent and far too easy and attractive—the hostility between Western and non-Western cultures that leads to crises. The world is too small and interdependent to let these passively happen.

(Culture 19)

In conclusion, I am sure that it is not lost on us that in Borges's story the most obvious representatives of the dominant, presumptuous culture are Fred's fictional members of the academy. These characters are so bent on research and publication that they miss the larger point of how they are pawns in a subjugating enterprise. It is incumbent on us, the actual representatives of higher education, to recognize and resist any complicity we have with the projects of imperialism in all its manifestations. We can start in our classrooms, by examining our choice of texts, and, more importantly, by reviewing how we read and present the *contexts* we have historically been taught to relegate to an inferior status.

Notes

1. Carter Wheelock, "Borges' New Prose," in *Jorge Luis Borges,* ed. Harold Bloom (New York: Chelsea, 1986) 106. Hereafter cited parenthetically in the text.

2. James Woodall, *The Man in the Mirror of the Book: A Life of Jorge Luis Borges* (London: Hodder & Stoughton, 1996) 251.

3. Jorge Luis Borges, "El etnógrafo," in *Elogio de la sombra* (Buenos Aires: EMECÉ, 1969) 5–7. All quotations from the primary source text come from pages 56–57. Given the brevity of the text and the proximity of all such quotes, I will subsequently dispense with documenting the location of each quotation cited from the story.

4. See Robert Lima, "Introduction: Borges and the Esoteric," *Crítica Hispánica* 15.2 (1993). (All essays in this volume correspond to the topic, "Borges and the Esoteric.")

5. George R. McMurray, "Borges and the Absurd Human Condition," in *Jorge Luis Borges* (New York: Frederick Ungar, 1980) 3.

6. See Edward W. Said, *Orientalism* (New York: Random, 1978).

7. Julie Rivkin and Michael Ryan, eds., *Literary Theory: An Anthology* (Malden, MA: Blackwell, 1998) 853.

8. Edward W. Said, *Culture and Imperialism* (New York: Random, 1994) 8. Hereafter cited parenthetically in the text.

9. Naomi Lindstrom, *Jorge Luis Borges: A Study of Short Fiction* (Boston: Twayne, 1990) 94.

10. Catherine Gimelli Martin, "Orientalism and the Ethnographer: Said, Herodotus, and the Discourse of Alterity," *Criticism* 32.4 (1990): 511.

J. M. Coetzee (review date 1998)

SOURCE: "Borges's Dark Mirror," in *New York Review of Books,* Vol. 45, No. 16, October 22, 1998, pp. 80–82

[*In the following review of* Collected Fictions, *a new translation of Borges's short fiction, Coetzee traces the development of Borges's stories, evaluates the new translation, and discusses the peculiar problems that arise when the author has translated some of his own work.*]

1.

In 1961 the directors of six leading Western publishing houses (Gallimard, Einaudi, Rowohlt, Seix Barral, Grove, Weidenfeld and Nicolson) met on the Mediterranean island of Formentera to establish a literary prize that was meant to single out writers who were actively transforming the world literary landscape, and to rival the Nobel Prize in prestige. The first International Publishers' Prize (also known as the Prix Formentor) was split between Samuel Beckett and Jorge Luis Borges. That same year the Nobel Prize was awarded to the Yugoslav Ivo Andri'c, a great novelist but no innovator. (Beckett won the prize in 1969; Borges never won it—his advocates claimed that he was scuppered by his political utterances.)

The publicity surrounding the Prix Formentor catapulted Borges onto the world stage. In the United States, Grove Press brought out seventeen stories under the title *Ficciones.* New Directions followed with *Labyrinths,* twenty-three stories—some overlapping the *Ficciones,* but in alternative translations—as well as essays and parables. Translation into other languages proceeded apace.

Besides his native Argentina, there was one country in which the name Borges was already well known. The French critic and editor Roger Caillois had spent the years 1939–1945 in exile in Buenos Aires. After the war, Caillois promoted Borges in France, bringing out *Ficciones* in 1951 and *Labyrinths* in 1953 (the latter substantially different from the New Directions *Labyrinths*—the Borges bibliography is a labyrinth of its own). In the 1950s Borges was more highly regarded, and perhaps more widely read, in France than in Argentina. In this respect his career curiously parallels that of his forerunner in speculative fiction, Edgar Allan Poe, championed by Baudelaire and enthusiastically taken up by the French public.

The Borges of 1961 was already in his sixties. The stories that had made him famous had been written in the 1930s and 1940s. He had lost his creative drive, and had furthermore become suspicious of these earlier, "baroque" pieces. Though he lived until 1986, he would only fitfully reproduce their intellectual daring and intensity.

In Argentina Borges had by 1960 been recognized, along with Ernesto Sábato and Julio Cortázar, as a leading light of his literary generation. During the first regime of Juan Perón (1946–1955) he had been somewhat of a whipping boy of the press, denounced as *extranjerizante* (foreign-loving), a lackey of the landowning elite and of international capital. Soon after Perón's inauguration he was ostentatiously dismissed from his job in the city library and "promoted" to be inspector of poultry and rabbits at the municipal market. After the fall of Perón he became fashionable again; but his support for unpopular causes (the Bay of Pigs invasion of Cuba, for instance) made him vulnerable to denunciation from the left as well as by nationalists and populists.

His influence on Latin American letters—where writers have traditionally turned to Europe for their models—has been extensive. He more than anyone renovated the language of fiction and thus opened the way to a remarkable generation of Spanish-American novelists. Gabriel García Márquez, Carlos Fuentes, José Donoso, and Mario Vargas Llosa have all acknowledged a debt to him. García Márquez—poles apart from Borges in his politics—spoke as follows in 1969: "The only thing I bought [in Buenos Aires] was Borges' *Complete Works.* I carry them in my suitcase; I am going to read them every day, and he is a writer I detest. . . . On the other hand, I am fascinated by the violin he uses to express his things."

For a decade after Borges's death in 1986, his literary estate remained in a state of confusion as various parties contested the terms of his will. Happily that confusion has now been resolved, and the first fruits we have in English are a *Collected Fictions,* newly translated by Andrew Hurley of the University of Puerto Rico. This volume brings together Borges's early stories from *A Universal History of Iniquity,* (1935), the *Fictions* of 1944 (which includes the stories of *The Garden of Forking Paths,* 1941), *The Aleph* (1949), the prose pieces of *The Maker* (1960), five short prose pieces from *In Praise of Darkness* (1969), *Brodie's Report* (1970), *The Book of Sand* (1975), and four late stories, collected here under the title *Shakespeare's Memory* (1983).

Of the hundred-odd pieces in the volume, ranging in length from a single paragraph to a dozen pages, only the last four have not hitherto been available in English. The notes appended by Hurley, while valuable in themselves, are limited in scope, "intended only to supply information that a Latin American (and especially Argentine or Uruguayan) reader would have and that would color or determine his or her reading of the stories." For the rest, the reader in difficulties with this learned and allusive writer is directed to *A Dictionary of Borges* by Evelyn Fishburn and Psiche Hughes, a commendable work of reference which, however, fails to rise to the challenge of providing an entry for J.L. Borges, a character—fictional? real?—who appears in the story **"Borges and I"** and numerous other pieces.

The *Collected Fictions*—the first of three Borges volumes planned by Viking—is based on the Spanish *Obras completas* of 1989. As an edition without scholarly apparatus, it does not aspire to rival the French *Oeuvres complètes,* scrupulously edited for Gallimard's Bibliothèque de la Pléiade by Jean-Pierre Bernès, which not only attempts to collect the totality of Borges's writings (including journalism, reviews, and other ephemeral writings) but, more importantly, goes a long way toward tracking the revisions which Borges—himself a fussy editor—carried out on successive printings of his own texts ("[Borges's] habit of changing texts from edition to edition, of suppressing, or excising, sometimes reintroducing in modified form, words, phrases, lines . . . has landed any potential bibliographer with a lifetime's toil," remarks Borges's biographer James Woodall).

2.

Jorge Luis Borges was born in 1899 into a prosperous middle-class family, in a Buenos Aires where Spanish—to say nothing of Italian—descent was not deemed a social asset. One of his grandmothers was from England; the family chose to stress their English affiliations and to bring up the children speaking English as well as Spanish. Borges remained a lifelong Anglophile. Curiously for a writer with an avant-grade reputation, his own reading seemed to stop around 1920. His taste in English-language fiction was for Stevenson, Chesterton, Kipling, Wells; he often referred to himself as *"un ser victoriano,"* a Victorian person.

Englishness was one part of Borges's self-fashioning, Jewishness another. He invoked a rather hypothetical Sephardic strain on his mother's side to explain his interest in the Kabbalah, and, more interestingly, to present himself as an outsider to Western culture, with an outsider's freedom to criticize and innovate. (Indeed, one might add, to pillage whole libraries for citations.)

In 1914 the whole Borges family traveled to Switzerland in search of a cure for Borges senior's eye condition (detached retinas—a condition inherited by his son). Trapped in Europe by the war, the children received a French-language education. The young Borges also taught himself German and read Schopenhauer, who exerted a lasting influence on his thought. German also led him to the new Expressionist poets, painters, and filmmakers, and thus to forays into mysticism, thought transmission, double personalities, the fourth dimension, and so forth.

After a spell in Spain, Borges returned to Argentina in 1921 a proponent of Ultraismo, a Spanish version of Imagism. Yet even in his rather conventional youthful radicalism there are flashes of originality—for instance, in his proposal for a language in which one word will stand simultaneously for sunset and the sound of cattle bells.

In 1931 the wealthy patroness of the arts Victoria Ocampo launched the magazine *Sur* and threw open its pages to Borges. Ocampo's inclinations were European and internationalist; in his years as chief contributor to *Sur* Borges worked his way beyond the rather tired issues of Argentine literary debate (naturalism versus modernism, Europeanism versus nativism). The stories that make up *The Garden of Forking Paths*—the stories that mark the beginning of his major period—appeared in *Sur* in a burst between 1939 and 1941.

"Pierre Menard," the earliest of the group, is, as fiction, the least satisfactory: a cross between spoof scholarly essay and *conte philosophique*. Borges excluded it from his *Personal Anthology* of 1968. Nevertheless, its intellectual daring is remarkable. Pierre Menard, minor contemporary of Paul Valéry, absorbs himself totally in the world of Cervantes so as to be able to write (*not* rewrite) *Don Quixote* word for word.

The ideas on which **"Pierre Menard"** is built can be found in David Hume (the past, including the age of Cervantes, has no existence except as a succession of present mental states). What Borges achieves is to invent a vehicle (imperfect in this case, but rapidly perfected in the stories that follow) in which the paradoxes of philosophical skepticism can be elegantly staged and followed to their vertiginous conclusions.

The finest of the stories of *The Garden of Forking Paths* are **"Tlön, Uqbar, Orbis Tertius"** and **"The Library of Babel"**—finest in the sense that the philosophical argument folds discreetly into the narrative, and the fiction takes its course with the certainty of a game of chess in which the reader is always a move behind the author. The technical innovation on which these fictions rest, and which allows them their swift pace—the reader is outflanked and overwhelmed before he knows where he is—is that they use as model the anatomy or critical essay, rather than the tale: with narrative exposition reduced to a bare minimum, the action can be condensed to an exploration of the implications of a hypothetical situation (an infinite library, for instance).

In interviews given in the 1960s, Borges suggested that, besides exploring the intellectual possibilities of inventing a world by writing a total description of it, **"Tlön"** explores the "dismay" of a narrator "who feels that his everyday world . . . , his past . . . [and] the past of his forefathers . . . [are] slipping away from him." Thus the hidden subject of the story is "a man who is being drowned in a new and overwhelming world that he cannot make out."

Like all authors' readings of their own work, this reading has its own interest. But as an account of **"Tlön"** it misses something important: the excitement, even creative triumph, however somber its shading, with which the narrator records the stages in which an ideal universe takes over a real one, a takeover capped, in a turn of the screw of paradox characteristic of Borges, by the realization that the universe of which we are part is more than likely already a simulacrum, perhaps a simulacrum of simulacra that go on to infinity. Revisiting his 1940 story a quarter of a century later, Borges finds in it an emotional coloring that belongs to his older, more pessimistic self.

Yet to conclude that Borges misreads his story is to miss the Borgesian (or Menardian) point. There is no Tlön, just as there is no 1940, outside the conceptions of Tlön and 1940 that mankind collectively holds in the present. Just as the all-comprehending encyclopedia of Orbis Tertius takes over the universe, our fictions of the fictions of the past take over these fictions. (Gnostic cosmology, in which Borges was deeply read, suggests that the universe in which we believe we live is the work of a minor creator nested within a universe which is the handiwork of a slightly less minor creator who is nested within another creation, and so on 365 times.)

Of the *Fictions* of 1944, **"Funes, His Memory"** is the most astonishing. Ireneo Funes, an untutored country boy, is possessed of an infinite memory. Nothing escapes him; all of his sensory experience, past and present, persists in his mind; drowned in particulars, unable even to forget the changing formation of all the clouds he has seen, he cannot form general ideas, and therefore—paradoxically, for a creature who is almost pure mind—cannot "think."

"Funes" follows the by now familiar Borgesian pattern of pressing a *donnée* to its dizzying conclusions. What is new in the story is a confidence with which Borges embeds his Funes in a recognizable Argentine social reality, as well as a touch of human pity for the afflicted boy, "the solitary, lucid spectator of a multiform, momentaneous, and almost unbearably precise world."

It is not hard to see why daringly idealistic fictions about worlds created by language or characters enclosed in texts should have found resonance in a generation of French intellectuals who had just discovered the structural linguistics of Ferdinand de Saussure, to whom language is a self-regulating field within which the human subject functions without power, more spoken by language than speaking it, and the past ("diachrony") is reducible to a series of superposed present ("synchronic") states. What Borges's French readers found startling—or perhaps just piquant—was that he had found his way to *textualité* along routes of his own devising. (In fact there is reason to believe that Borges found his way there via Schopenhauer and, particularly, the German philosopher Fritz Mauthner (1849–1923). Mauthner is little read nowadays; there is no entry for him in Fishburn and Hughes's *Dictionary of Borges,* despite the fact that Borges alludes to him several times.)

The three collections that comprise Borges's middle and major period—*The Garden of Forking Paths*, *Fictions*, and *The Aleph*—were followed in 1952 by *Other Inquisitions*, a mosaic of pieces culled from Borges's critical writing. The fact that many of these pieces, with their vast erudition in a range of languages, first appeared in newspapers says much for the upper reaches of the Buenos Aires press. Many of the ideas explored in the fiction can be found half-grown here, not yet ready to show their teeth.

Reading the essays side-by-side with the fictions prompts what is perhaps the central question about Borges: What do the operations of fiction offer this scholar-writer that

enable him to take ideas into reaches where the discursive essay, as a mode of writing, fails him?

Borges's own answer, following Coleridge, is that the poetic imagination enables the writer to join himself to the universal creative principle; following Schopenhauer, he would add that this principle has the nature of Will rather than (as Plato would say) of Reason. "In the course of a lifetime dedicated less to living than to reading, I have been able to verify repeatedly that aims and literary theories are nothing but stimuli; the finished work frequently ignores and even contradicts them."

Yet it would be obtuse not to hear, in pronouncements like this one, tones of parody and self-parody. The voices that speak the *Other Inquisitions* are much like the voices of the narrators of the fictions; behind the essays is a persona whom Borges had already begun to call "Borges." Which Borges is real, which is the other in the mirror, remains dark. The essays allow the one Borges to dramatize the other. Put in other terms, the distinction between fiction and nonfiction used by Viking is open to question (Viking plans to follow the *Collected Fictions* with a collection of poems and a selection from the nonfiction).

El hacedor (1960) is a compendium of prose and verse, from which the Viking *Collected Fictions* drops the verse. The title alludes—rather cryptically, for a Spanish-speaking audience—to the archaic English "maker," or poet, which is the word that Hurley takes over; Mildred Boyer and Harold Morland, in their 1964 translation, retitle the book *Dreamtigers*. Borges called it "my most personal work, and to my taste, maybe the best." There is a touch of defiance in this pronouncement, since nothing in the collection measures up to the best of the fictions of the period 1939–1949. But by 1960 Borges had already begun to put a distance between himself and what he would later, disparagingly, call "labyrinths and mirrors and tigers and all that."

The truth was that the Prix Formentor of 1961 caught Borges in the middle of a long creative slump. His newfound fame brought invitations to lecture, which he was happy to accept. Accompanied by his mother, he traveled widely. From the North American lecture circuit he began to enjoy a steady income. Rarely did he refuse an interview; he became, in fact, garrulous. He searched actively for a wife, found one, and for three years, in his late sixties, suffered an unhappy marriage.

In 1967 Borges met the American translator Norman Thomas di Giovanni. An association developed: not only did di Giovanni translate, or collaborate with Borges to translate, a number of works and help with his business affairs, but he coaxed Borges back into writing fiction. The fruits can be seen in the eleven stories of *Brodie's Report* (1970). The mirrors and labyrinths are gone. The settings are the Argentine pampas or the outskirts of Buenos Aires; the language is simpler, the plots are more conventional (in his foreword Borges points to Kipling as a model). Borges was proudest of **"The Interloper,"** but **"The Gos-**

pel according to St. Mark," in which a student, having introduced the Christian gospel to a backlands gaucho family, is accepted as their savior and solemnly crucified, is as good. With its concentration on jealousy, physical bravery, and laconically treated violence, *Brodie's Report* is the most ostentatiously masculine of Borges's collections.

The Book of Sand (1975) and *Shakespeare's Memory* (1983) recycle old themes (the Doppelgänger, possession, the interpenetration of universes) as well as exploring Borges's enthusiasm for Germanic mythology. There is much tired writing in them; they add nothing to his stature.

3.

Borges's gnosticism—his sense that the ultimate God is beyond good and evil, and infinitely remote from creation—is deeply felt. But the sense of dread that informs his work is metaphysical rather than religious in nature: at its base are vertiginous glimpses of the collapse of all structures of understanding including language itself, flashing intimations that the very self that speaks has no real existence.

In the fiction that responds to this dread, the ethical and the aesthetic are tightly wound together: the light but remorseless tread of the logic of his parables, the lapidary concision of the language, the gradual tightening of paradox are stylistic traces of an ironic self-control that stares back into the abysses of thought without the Gothic hysteria of a Poe.

> Under the step, toward the right, I saw a small iridescent sphere of almost unbearable brightness. At first I thought it was spinning; then I realized that the movement was an illusion produced by the dizzying spectacles inside it. The Aleph was probably two or three centimeters in diameter, but universal space was contained inside it. . . . I saw the populous sea, saw dawn and dusk, saw the multitudes of the Americas, saw a silvery spiderweb at the center of a black pyramid, saw a broken labyrinth (it was London) . . . saw the circulation of my dark blood, saw the coils and springs of love and the alterations of death, saw the Aleph from everywhere at once, saw the earth in the Aleph, and the Aleph once more in the earth and the earth in the Aleph, saw my face and my viscera, saw your face, and I felt dizzy, and I wept, because my eyes had seen that secret, hypothetical object whose name has been usurped by men but which no man has ever truly looked upon: the inconceivable universe. . . .
>
> Out in the street . . . all the faces seemed familiar. I feared there was nothing that had the power to surprise or astonish me anymore, I feared that I would never again be without a sense of *déjà vu*. Fortunately, after a few unsleeping nights, forgetfulness began to work in me again.

("The Aleph")

Borges has been criticized for falling back on the aesthetic for salvation. Harold Bloom, for instance, suggests that

Borges would have been a greater writer if he had exercised a less iron control over his creative impulse—a control whose purpose Bloom sees as self-protective. "What Borges lacks, despite the illusive cunning of his labyrinths, is precisely the extravagance of the romancer. . . . [He] has never been reckless enough to lose himself in a story, to our loss, if not to his."

I am not sure that these strictures take into account those stories of Borges's that focus on the confrontation with death. **"The South"**—which ends with the hero accepting the challenge of a knife duel he is sure to lose—is the most haunting of these; but there are numerous other more realistic tales of gaucho or hoodlum life in which characters, following an unarticulated stoic ethic, choose death rather than loss of honor, recovering themselves from disgrace and discovering their truth in the same moment.

These stories, laconic in expression and sometimes brutal in content, reveal the attractions of a life of action for their bookish and rather timid author. They also show Borges trying to situate himself more forthrightly in an Argentine literary tradition and to do his bit toward Argentine national mythmaking.

The word "camel," observes Borges in a lecture entitled "The Argentine Writer and Tradition" (1953), does not occur in the Koran. The lesson? That "we can believe in the possibility of being Argentine without abounding in local color."

But his own later stories—particularly those collected in *Brodie's Report*—do in fact abound in local color. They represent a tenacious return to the task that Borges, on his return to Buenos Aires in the 1920s, saw before him: to hold on to the density of culture that was part of his generations-old *criollo* heritage, yet to get beyond mere regionalism and localism. "There are no legends in this land," he wrote in 1926. "That is our disgrace. Our lived reality is grandiose yet the life of our imagination is paltry. . . . We must find the poetry, the music, the painting, the religion and the metaphysics appropriate to [the] greatness [of Buenos Aires]."

Set in the seedier Buenos Aires suburbs of the turn of the century, or even further back in time on the Argentine pampas, the *Brodie's Report* stories can hardly be claimed to confront the reality of modern Argentina. They embrace a romantic, nativistic streak in Argentine nationalism, turning their back both on the enlightened liberalism of the class into which Borges was born and on the new mass culture and mass politics—represented in his lifetime by Perónism—which he held in abhorrence.

4.

Borges's prose is controlled, precise, and economical to a degree uncommon in Spanish America. It eschews (as Borges notes with some pride) "Hispanicisms, Argentinisms, archaisms, and neologisms; [it uses] everyday words rather than shocking ones." In his work up to and including **The Aleph,** the clear surface is disturbed now and again by unusual, even disturbing verbal collocations. In his late phase such moments are rare.

Although any translator will be challenged to match the simultaneous concision and force of Borges's Spanish, and to find renderings for his sometimes riddling metaphors, his language presents no irresolvable problems, except on those occasions when it is colored—deliberately, one is sure—by English verbal patterns (such patterns, as soon as they are reproduced in English translation, of course sink into invisibility).

There is a set of difficulties of a more practical nature, however, created by the fact that Borges, late in life, acted as his own (co)translator (of **The Aleph** and **Brodie's Report,** as well as of much poetry), and in the process of translating availed himself of the opportunity to do some revising.

These revisions can be quite sweeping in scale: half a page of rather dated satire is cut from "**The Aleph,**" for instance. Borges also felt free to work into his English texts information that the protocols of the craft would constrain an ordinary translator to relegate to footnotes: a cryptic mention of *la revolución de Aparício,* for instance, is expanded to "a civil war . . . between the Colorados, or Reds, who were in power, and Aparício's Blancos, or Whites."

But Borges's revisions have a subsidiary purpose as well: to tone down his own Spanish. Resounding trademark adjectives of the middle phase, like *abominable, enigmático, implacable, interminable, notorio, perverso, pérfido, vertiginoso, violento*—are softened: the "violent [*violento*] flank of the mountain" becomes its "steep slope," a woman's "violent [*violenta*] hair" becomes her "tangled hair."

The justification offered by Borges and di Giovanni for this toning down, and for the general smoothness of their English versions, is that Spanish and English embody "two quite different ways of looking at the world." They have tried less to transpose the original Spanish into English, they say, than "to rethink every sentence in English words," aiming for prose that "[reads] as though . . . written in English."

Hurley—correctly, to my mind—ignores the example Borges sets. However, that cannot be the end of the story. The changes that Borges (as the creative partner in the collaboration) introduces in the process of translating himself can be regarded as authorial revisions capable, at least in theory, of being reintroduced into the Spanish text; or, at the very least, as revisions authorially approved for the stories in their English guise.

Hurley does not, in his brief "Note on the Translation," address this problem. What he might have said—if one may be allowed to put words in his mouth—is that there are times when editors and translators have a duty to protect Borges from himself. *Pace* the author, the versions of Borges that we want to read are not necessarily those that sound as if English were their native tongue: if there is indeed a degree of grandiloquence in the originals, the reader may prefer to hear that grandiloquence and detect for himself what is authentically Borgesian in it, what native to the Spanish, rather than have the language uniformly muted on his behalf.

There is one respect, however, in which it would be rash not to take Borges's lead, namely, when he offers privileged access to his own intentions. Borges writes that a character goes home to his *rancho.* Hurley quite reasonably translates the word as "ranch." But Borges—going back, one presumes, to the picture he had in his mind's eye when he wrote the story—uses the less obvious "shack." *Un alfajor* can be any of a variety of regional sweetmeats. Which did Borges have in mind? A sugared cake, his translation reveals. Hurley pretends not to know this and calls it, vaguely, a "sweet offering." If one puts one's ear against a certain stone column in Cairo, says Borges, one can hear the *rumor* of the Aleph inside it. "Rumour," says Hurley, where Borges could have helped with "hum."

A quick check against Borges-di Giovanni could even have prevented plain errors. The desert nomads need foreigners to do their "carpentry," says Hurley. The word is *albanileria,* masonry.

Borges has had distinguished translators in the past, among them Anthony Kerrigan, Donald A. Yates, and James E. Irby, to say nothing of the di Giovanni collaborations. Nevertheless, there is much to be said for an integral retranslation of the whole of Borges such as Viking has set in motion. Hurley's versions are generally excellent, marked by accuracy of word choice and a confident sense of narrative style.

If there is one weakness to them, it is that Hurley's feel for the level of formality of English words is not always reliable. Words like "leery," "rambunctious," "hornswoggle," phrases like "a little ways from," give rise to colloquial effects for which there is no parallel in the original.

Hurley also performs a rather disturbing revision of his own. In "**The Circular Ruins,**" a story about male generative power and male birth, Borges writes: "*A todo padre le interesan los hijos que ha procreado,*" "Every father feels concern for the sons he has procreated." Hurley translates this: "Every parent feels concern for the children he has procreated."

Gene Bell-Villada (review date 1998)

SOURCE: "Now in English Revision of Collected Fictions," in *Commonweal,* Vol. 125, No. 22, December 18, 1998.

[*In the following review, Bell-Villada praises* Collected Fictions.]

From the midsixties through the early eighties, Argentine writer Jorge Luis Borges—the man and his thoughts both—seemed well-nigh ubiquitous. There were the appearances on TV, the standing-room-only lectures at college campuses, the bylines in the weeklies, even an interview in *Commonweal* (October 25, 1968). A shy, reclusive man, renowned for his complex, difficult art, Borges somehow burgeoned forth as everyone's favorite foreign author, the international man of letters for that era.

Following his death in Geneva in 1986, Borges's best works have settled into the rarefied ranks of the world's classics, while his most striking ideas have remained reliable currency, a part of our fin-de-siecle literary exchange. Fantastical realms invading ours; an effete French poet setting out to write *Don Quixote*; a cosmic library that houses every possible volume; a point in space containing all other points—these are some of the wilder notions that have made the term "Borgesian" almost as recognizable in its implications as are the familiar adjectives "Orwellian" or "Kafkaesque."

Ironically, by the time the elder Borges's face and voice had become ordinary fixtures within the broader cultural milieu, the artist's greatest work was well behind him. Those three-dozen short stories, penned between 1938 and the mid-fifties, started drawing admiration from overseas literati in the post-war years, and got a major boost in 1961 when Borges shared with Samuel Beckett the International Publishers' Prize. By then the sixtyish Argentinean was almost completely blind, and could write only via a hired amanuensis.

He also felt dried up as a fiction writer; the ideas just weren't coming like they used to. Enter his translator and secretary from 1967, Norman Thomas di Giovanni, who piqued Borges's muse and urged him to write stories once again. The results, alas, were disappointing. The pieces gathered in *Brodie's Report* (1970) and *The Book of Sand* (1975) were but a dim reflection of the grand, luminous visions that had shined forth in *Ficciones* (1944) and *El Aleph* (1949). The once-fresh intuitions had hardened into sententious tics, the cosmic insights narrowed into formulaic mannerisms. Intrinsically, Borges's later texts weren't all that bad; from a lesser writer, they'd be deemed worthy, "promising." But they are ever in the shadow of the playfully brooding, quietly dazzling, thoroughly inspired works of the genius at mid-century. They're like Shakespeare's *Cymbeline* or Faulkner's *The Town*; the Bard and the Mississippian, we know, did better than that.

Englishings of Borges are a history unto themselves. In 1962, two American volumes of his prose chanced to come out from avant-garde houses: the *Ficciones* (Grove, edited by Anthony Kerrigan) and an anthology, *Labyrinths* (New Directions, edited by James Irby and Donald Yates). The latter collection in particular achieved standard-item status,

with sales somewhere in the six figures. Later, in the 1970s, di Giovanni did his own renderings of select works for E. P. Dutton, in which the Argentine's high style was "Americanized" somewhat, and both author and translator revised a bit here, deleted a tad there. Meanwhile, Anglophone readers have lacked a single, authoritative translation of all the stories, from apprenticeship to final statements.

Now comes the *Collected Fictions,* translated by Andrew Hurley, a professor of English at the University of Puerto Rico. An expert hand, Hurley has previously rendered a half-dozen Hispanic authors, some of them forbiddingly colloquial in style and hence a challenge to the most seasoned translator. The Borges project, a labor of love, has been years in the making. The results are almost consistently first-rate, with supple rhythms that roll trippingly on the tongue, and a liberal use of contractions, even in descriptive passages. Fashioning a uniformly smooth voice for all 110 pieces, Hurley distills them into a "universal" kind of English, largely unspecific to any time or place and thus not subject to fast fading. (Still, he isn't averse to translating the obscenity pendejo—in **"Man on Pink Corner"**—as "asshole," an improvement over di Giovanni's "kid.")

Some choices for titles exemplify his skill. For the early collection, *Historia universal de la infamia,* the concluding word is changed to "iniquity," which scans better, almost rhymes. The unforgettable classic story, **"Funes el memorioso,"** often previously rendered as **"Funes the Memorious,"** now achieves extra clarity as **"Funes, His Memory."** For **"La intrusa,"** concerning a love-triangle, **"The Interloper"** seems more layered and evocative than di Giovanni's "The Intruder." Similarly, the succinctness of **"The Wait"** (for **"La espera"**) has a visual impact, absent from **"The Waiting"** in *Labyrinths.*

At times Hurley's search for natural rhythms leads to a loss, at least for those of us who know earlier versions. Take the ending of **"Emma Zunz,"** which Yates in *Labyrinths* renders thus: "True was Emma Zunz's tone, true was her shame, true her hate. True also was the outrage she had suffered. Only the circumstances were false. . . ." Hurley, by contrast, remakes it, "Emma Zunz's tone was real, her shame was real, her hatred was real. The outrage that had been done to her was real. All that was false were the circumstances. . . ." While Hurley's prose sounds more idiomatic, like everyday speech, Yates's, with its inversions that mirror the original yet also strike us with their strangeness, seems appropriate to the odd mental conceit being argued here.

Every reviewer has quibbles; I shall air mine. "Imbecilic" (page 505) sounds stilted; I would say "idiotic." In English we don't "consecrate" (page 381) but rather "dedicate" an essay to a topic. "Notorious" (page 143) is a false cognate for *notorio*, which actually signifies "well-known" or "obvious." One jarring adaptation is Hurley's use of "working class" (page 302), a sociopolitical construct about which

Borges was simply clueless; "slum dwellers" better captures the spirit of the original. (On the other hand I liked Hurley's coining the term "trivia police," page 347.)

Such lapses are few; the **Collected Fictions** stands as a noble, indeed monumental endeavor. In addition, Hurley includes forty pages of detailed endnotes that elucidate obscure references, particularly those regarding matters South American. Still, I doubt that this volume will supplant earlier efforts, notably **Labyrinths,** which gathers both fiction and essays, is selective and manageable, and exists as a publishing event in its own right. But Hurley's Borges—like Robert Fitzgerald's Greeks, or those Penguin Russians many of us were nourished on—is here to stay.

Ilan Stavans (essay date 1999)

SOURCE: "The English Borges," in the *Times Literary Supplement,* January 29, 1999, p. 24.

[*In the following review, Stavans evaluates the Andrew Hurley translation of Borges's* Collected Fictions, *and offers comparisons with other translations.*]

Jorge Luis Borges is no longer a writer but a tradition. His descendants are vital in a myriad of tongues: Danilo Kiš and Salman Rushdie, Umberto Eco and Julio Cortázar. For decades, his work in English—the language he loved most, in which he first read *Don Quixote*—was less a unity than a multiplicity; it was fragmented and anarchically dispersed in anthologies, translated by too many hands, the most distinguished among them Norman Thomas di Giovanni, Donald A. Yates, Alastair Reid, W. S. Merwin, Richard Wilbur, Mark Strand, John Hollander and James E. Irby. Borges himself encouraged this abundance by allowing different people to work on the same text at once. The most prominent translator is di Giovanni, an Italian-American who worked with him first in Cambridge, Massachusetts, and then in Buenos Aires from 1967 to 1972, and with whom Borges produced a total of ten books. To this day, these volumes remain controversial because they are what I call reverse translation; it appears that more than once di Giovanni suggested emendations to the original for the English version and then persuaded Borges to implement them in future Spanish reprints.

A translation, Nabokov once suggested, should read as such; it should not avoid reminding the reader of its artificiality, its counterfeit nature. Borges's Spanish syntax has an Englishness to it. In his youth, he dared to compose several brief poems in Shakespeare's tongue (much as T. S. Eliot did in French); he must have felt at least some sympathy towards these attempts, for he didn't exile them from his **Obras Completas,** which he compiled for Emecé Editores in Buenos Aires at the end of his life. This in part explains why most available translations are more than satisfactory; to translate Borges into English is to bring him home. Furthermore, since many of these translations

were instrumental in his global rise in the 1960s, after he was awarded the Prix Formentor along with Samuel Beckett, they are to be considered his ticket to the canon—or better, they themselves are the canon. The fact that they are scattered but not unreachable is a Borgesian device in itself; his library, like Pascal's sphere, has its centre everywhere and its circumference nowhere.

The Borges tradition has sparked a veritable industry; more biographies, photograph albums, bibliographies and scholarly studies are published annually about him than about any other Hispanic literary luminary, Cervantes, Sor Juana Inés de la Cruz and Gabriel García Márquez included. Too many pockets are making a buck. María Kodama, Borges's widow, now wants order. She has done everything to centralize power: instituting a Borges Foundation in Buenos Aires with an ever-expanding data base; bringing out early collections which the author himself did not wish ever to be reprinted (*Inquisiciones* and *El tamaño de mi esperanza*); reissuing old titles in Spanish in an improved format; and, perhaps most flagrantly, hiring the literary agent Andrew Wylie to orchestrate a centenary (Borges was born in 1899), by bringing together his vastly influential oeuvre in English under the imprimatur of a single publishing house and in new translations. Viking, already one of Borges's English-language publishers, is the beneficiary of this re-accommodation. It has responded with an ambitious multi-volume campaign. **Collected Fictions,** a volume of short stories translated by Andrew Hurley, is its first instalment; it is to be followed by a selection of Borges's poems edited by Alexander Coleman, which will mix existing translations by Merwin, Reid and others with fresh ones; then there is to be a selection by Eliot Weinberger of retranslated essays; and, finally, the project is to be crowned by a major biography (one of several in progress) by Edwin Williamson.

Such compartmentalization seems wrong. After all, this most cosmopolitan of Argentinians, whose personal life was as ordinary as his mind was extraordinary, spent his career advancing the promiscuity of literary genres: **"Pierre Menard, author of the Quixote"** is modelled as an *éloge*; **"The Approach to Al-Mu'tasim"**, which first appeared as a book-review of a work which Borges claimed had just been reprinted in London with a foreword by Dorothy L. Sayers, so inspired its readers that more than one requested the book from its publisher Victor Gollancz; and many parts of **The Maker** (1960) read more like poetry than prose. The overall order of the Viking project seems to be an idiosyncratic gesture of the Anglo-Saxon mind. Bookshops in the Hispanic hemisphere do not separate their literature sections into fiction, nonfiction and poetry; they simply organize titles alphabetically. The authoritative three-volume **Obras Completas,** on which Andrew Hurley's translation is based, is structured chronologically, not generically. This, I am convinced, is the approach to Borges that does him justice. He himself was instrumental in shaping the Spanish edition.

How authoritative that Spanish edition really is is another issue. Time has cleansed errors and other infelicities from

it, but it still has no overseeing editor's mind, no explanation of its rationale and no footnotes. There is a particular
danger in producing a scholarly version of Borges. Should
an author who delighted in quoting obscure, tangential
sources, one engaged in selecting his own audience by
alienating those uninitiated in the labyrinths of metaphysics, be clarified, and therefore made more accessible than
he ever wanted to be? The excellent two-volume Pléiade
edition—the second one still in preparation—edited by
Jean-Pierre Bernès, is by far the most intelligent edition
available, including as it does a sharp introduction, well-
informed notes and variants. Without being intrusive, it is
the closest readers have to a scholarly edition. (It includes
the translations done by Roger Caillois, which were responsible for Borges's early reputation in France and much
of Europe.)

One criticism of the Emecé Spanish volumes, which are
ordered sequentially, can also be applied to the projected
Viking edition. Borges loved Emerson, Oscar Wilde, Hawthorne, Melville and Stevenson. The frequency with which
he quotes Shakespeare outdoes that of any other individual
author with the exception of God. Shouldn't the English
reader have a better thought-out, better-informed edition?
Shouldn't the language as a whole pay him a more suitable tribute? This is not to say that Hurley's efforts at re-
translating Borges are not anything but heroic. His versions are concise, elegant, crystalline, if also self-
conscious. The mere thought of producing a version that
will compete with Donald Yates's **"Emma Zunz"** and
"Death and the Compass" is daunting.

Hurley succeeds quite well in capturing the stiffness of the
original. Minor lapses do occur, but the overall style is admirable. The fear of sounding too much like his predecessors makes him take unwonted routes sometimes, but his
command of the language is enrapturing. He is, however,
expansive and sometimes needlessly verbose. Compare the
following portions of **"Borges and I"**. First Irby's translation:

> The other one, the one called Borges, is the one things
> happen to. I walk through the streets of Buenos Aires
> and stop for a moment, perhaps mechanically now, to
> look at the arch of an entrance hall and the grillwork
> on the gate; I know of Borges from the mail and see
> his name on a list of professors or in a biographical
> dictionary. I like hourglasses, maps, eighteenth-century
> typography, the taste of coffee and the prose of Steven-
> son; he shares these preferences, but in a vain way that
> turns them into the attributes of an actor. It would be
> an exaggeration to say that ours is a hostile relation-
> ship; I live, let myself go on living, so that Borges may
> contrive his literature, and this literature justifies me. It
> is no effort for me to confess that he has achieved some
> valid pages, but those cannot save me, perhaps because
> what is good belongs not to one, not even to him, but
> rather to the language and tradition. . . . Years ago I
> tried to free myself from him and went from the my-
> thologies of the suburbs to the games with time and in-
> finity, but those games belong to Borges now and I
> shall have to imagine other things. Thus my life is a

> flight and I lose everything and everything belongs to
> oblivion, or to him.

> I do not know which of us has written this page.

Now Hurley's:

> It's Borges, the other one, that things happen to. I walk
> through Buenos Aires and I pause—mechanically now,
> perhaps—to gaze at the arch of an entryway and its in-
> ner door; news of Borges reaches me by mail, or I see
> his name on a list of academics or in some biographi-
> cal dictionary. My taste runs to hourglasses, maps,
> seventeenth-century typefaces, etymologies, the taste of
> coffee, and the prose of Robert Louis Stevenson;
> Borges shares those preferences, but in a vain sort of
> way that turns them into the accoutrements of an actor.
> It would be an exaggeration to say that our relationship
> is hostile—I live, I allow myself to live, so that Borges
> can spin out his literature, and that literature is my jus-
> tification. I willingly admit that he has written a num-
> ber of sound pages, but those pages will not save *me*,
> perhaps because the good in them no longer belongs to
> any individual, not even to that other man, but rather to
> language itself, or to tradition. . . . Years ago I tried to
> free myself from him, and I moved on from the my-
> thologies of the slums and outskirts of the city to games
> with time and infinity, but those games belong to
> Borges now, and I shall have to think up other things.
> So my life is a point-counterpoint, a kind of fugue, and
> a falling away—and everything winds up being lost to
> me, and everything falls into oblivion, or into the hands
> of the other man.

> I am not sure which of us it is that's writing this page.

Hurley uses twenty-six words more than Irby; he mistakes
siglo dieciocho for the seventeenth century; has a preference for ambiguous synonyms remote from the original
("accoutrements," "point-counterpoint," "fugue"); itali-
cizes where the meaning is already clear; and editorializes
too much. But the result is a worthy one; he does not at-
tenuate but emphasizes the affectation of the whole translating enterprise and, as a result, makes Borges more baroque. Hurley's English readers can appreciate the
Argentinian writer from behind a thicker mantilla, thus allowing for a better appreciation of his convex meanings
and bright colours.

A few of his title choices make me uncomfortable: **"Monk
Eastman, Purveyor of Iniquities"**, **"Funes, His
Memory"**, **"The Interloper"**. There are, on the other
hand, lucid clarifications in his version, such as the title of
Jaromir Hladík's book in **"The Secret Miracle"**. Harriet
de Onís, its previous translator, believed he had written a
single book, when actually the title and subtitle refer to
two different works, *The Enemies* and *Vindication of Eternity*. And some of Hurley's renderings are simply superior,
as in **"The Aleph"** which for the most part is given cleaner
treatment. Here is the opening sentence:

> The same sweltering morning that Beatriz Viterrbo
> died, after an imperious confrontation with her illness
> in which she had never for an instant stooped to either

sentimentality or fear, I noticed that a new advertisement for some cigarettes or other (*blondes,* I believe they were) had been posted on the iron billboards of the Plaza Constitución; the fact deeply grieved me, for I realized that the vast, unceasing universe was already growing away from her, and that this change was but the first in an infinite series.

The translation of the Aleph itself is a *tour de force*:

> [I] saw the Aleph from everywhere at once, saw the earth in the Aleph, and the Aleph once more in the earth and the earth in the Aleph, saw my face and my viscera, saw your face, and I felt dizzy, and I wept, because my eyes had seen that secret, hypothetical object whose name has been usurped by men but which no man has ever truly looked upon: the inconceivable universe.

A fine translator is not only as close as we get to the perfect reader but also the author's unremitting attorney. Perhaps the most instructive example of Hurley's re-elucidation is his approach to **"Pierre Menard, author of the Quixote"**, a pseudo-essay in which a translator appears as protagonist:

> It is a revelation to compare *Don Quixote* of Pierre Menard with that of Miguel de Cervantes. Cervantes, for example, wrote the following:
>
> (Part 1, Chapter IX)
>
> . . . truth, whose mother is history, rival of time, depository of deeds, witness of the past, exemplar and advisor to the present, and the future's counsellor.

This catalogue of attributes, written in the seventeenth century, and written by the "ingenious layman" Miguel de Cervantes, is mere rhetorical praise of history. Menard on the other hand writes:

> . . . truth, whose mother is history, rival of time, depository of deeds, witness of the past, exemplar and advisor to the present, and the future's counsellor.

History the *mother* of truth!—the idea is staggering. Menard, a contemporary of William James, defines history not as *delving into* reality but as the very *fount* of reality. Historical truth for Menard is not "what happened"; it is what we *believe* happened.

The same paragraph in James E. Irby's translation reads:

> History, the *mother* of truth: the idea is astonishing. Menard, a contemporary of William James, does not define history as an inquiry into reality but as its origin. Historical truth, for him, is not what happened; it is what we judge to have happened.

Again Hurley needs more words to deliver the job. His explanation of Menard's triumph is none the less unequivocal: "delving into reality" is more cryptic than "an inquiry into reality"; "a fount of reality" darkens the easier "origin". Hurley's view of reality is as a deep reservoir, whereas Irby sees it as a reflecting surface.

Aside from the translation, Hurley has been trusted by Viking with an editorial job he only half-heartedly endorses. He acknowledges his intention to be the production of a "reader's edition", neither an annotated nor a scholarly one, but he fills the last forty pages with a stream of dispensable notes. "These notes", he writes, "are intended only to supply information that a Latin American (and especially Argentinian or Uruguayan) reader would have and that would color his or her reading of the stories." But for the most part, they are inadequate and unbalanced, lengthy explanations of a character's name, partial listings of secondary studies on Borges.

All in all, this refurbishing of Borges, while the result of an ill-thought-out marketing exercise, is quite attractive and can be recommended. Its full triumph will only come, however, if Viking allows its other translations—at least the volume **Labyrinths,** first published in Penguin Twentieth-Century Classics in 1970 and reprinted two dozen times since then—to remain available, for Borges in perfect order is Borges distorted. But even if they aren't, even if order gives the appearance of triumph, I am not worried; an intelligent reader learns to discriminate.

Thus, the Borges tradition marches on. I have heard its source depicted, bizarrely, and I'm afraid without a nod to Pablo Neruda and Octavio Paz, as the most esteemed export from Latin America since *cacao*—esteemed first and foremost abroad, where it has been masterfully repackaged as an invaluable parable of the whole of Western civilization, and then sold back to the Americas at a much higher price. This reversal angers some, but it has no real consequence, for quality cannot be copyrighted. Besides, didn't this most un-Argentinian of Argentinians once suggest that originals have a way of being unfaithful to their translations? And yet, only in translation is Borges truly appreciated.

The Economist (essay date 1999)

SOURCE: "Jorge Luis Borges Big Man, Much to Say," in *The Economist,* Vol. 350, No. 8104, January 30, 1999, p. 80

[*In the following review of the* Collected Fictions, *the writer sees Borges as a "master of intellectual subtleties."*]

A single substantial book of short stories may seem a relatively modest output for a lifetime. But Jorge Luis Borges, the blind Argentine librarian who was probably the greatest 20th-century author never to win the Nobel prize for literature, was one of fiction's most playfully paradoxical spirits, and he would surely have disagreed. For Borges, an immensely erudite man whose whole life was consumed by a passion for books and the idea of bookishness, was a miniaturist who found no virtue in length for its own wearisome sake. He had no desire to write novels, for example. Much better to embed the summary of the plot of a novel within the framework of a paradoxical short story, and thus distil its essence.

Collected Fictions gathers together all the short stories in a single volume, in English, for the first time; later in the year there will be a collection of his poetry, and, finally, a compilation of nonfiction. The last will include essays, and a selection of his considerable output of journalism on the cinema—he wrote extensively about Charlie Chaplin, for example.

Borges's first collection of stories, *A Universal History of Iniquity* was published in Spanish in 1935, but he did not make it into print in the English language until 1948—in *Ellery Queen's Mystery Magazine,* it was not until 1960, by which time he had written the best of his fiction, that a full selection of his stories was published in the English-speaking world—and immediately acclaimed by the likes of John Updike and John Barth.

The talent of this man was immediately recognised to be odd, brilliant, inimitable, as distinctively different in its own way from almost anything that had gone before as Franz Kafka's had been.

What exactly is Borges's way of writing? It is an intellectually beguiling mixture of fantasy and erudite detective fiction, all spiced up with games-playing, wit and paradox. Every word, each small detail, counts. Stories come tricked out with erudite references to literary matters. But these are never presented in order to dazzle us with recondite knowledge alone. In fact, they are often fake references, clues only within an elaborate game.

One of the curiosities of Borges is that his stories often read as though they had been written in English in the first place. Why does this syntax seem to resemble our own so closely, we ask ourselves, somewhat bemused?

This is not wholly surprising. Borges was raised by an English nanny and an English grandmother, and he had a life-long passion for English literature. Robert Louis Stevenson and G. K. Chesterton were among his favourites.

Generally speaking, his best stories were written between 1940 and the mid-1950s—such models of laconic precision and scrupulous economy as **"The Lottery in Babylon"**, **"The Library of Babel"**, and **"Pierre Menard, Author of the Quixote"**. The first two take place within fantastically absurd, hermetically sealed worlds of the imagination. The rules of the Babylonian lottery are like no other, and include the unusual notion of a "negative draw"—which means imprisonment or death for the unlucky winner. In **"Pierre Menard"**, the story's central character sets himself the heroic task of writing—not rewriting—a great epic word for word. In this case, it is Cervantes's *Don Quixote*.

These stories reveal Borges at his most characteristic, using the most rigorous logic in the service of the most bizarre and illogical propositions. His self-conscious artfulness as a writer, his relentless examination through writing of the very idea of fictionality, has influenced Nabokov, Malraux, Foucault and many others.

The very last story in this book, among his best and translated into English for the first time, is about a man who is offered the gift of the memory of William Shakespeare and, believing it to be the greatest gift that a literary man could ever be vouchsafed, accepts with eagerness. The consequence is less good than he had imagined. There was a profound difference, he discovers, between Shakespeare the man and Shakespeare the writer. He had been offered the memory of the man. The great writer surpassed his mere manhood in his writing. A lovely, subtle point, and one so typical of this great and enduring master of intellectual subtleties.

Eric Pennington (essay date 1999)

SOURCE: "Death and Denial in Borges's Later Prose," in *Notes On Contemporary Literature,* Vol. XXIX, No. 4, September, 1999, pp. 2–4.

[*In the following essay, Pennington interprets one of Borges's later stories, "El disco," as a criticism of his critics.*]

The prose works of Jorge Luis Borges from 1969 are not considered by some critics to be as significant as his earlier stories (James Woodall, *The Man in the Mirror of the Book: A Life of Jorge Luis Borges* [London: Hodder and Stoughton, 1996], p. 251). The great tales of the 1940s, such a **"Death and the Compass," "The Library of Babel,"** and **"The Circular Ruins"** are dense, clinical, cosmic, and baroque, not lending themselves to easy readings or interpretations. But in 1967, Borges announced that he was tired of labyrinths, mirrors, and tigers, and stated that his prose would now take a different, purer form.

In attempting to answer why Borges's fiction took what, on the surface, seems a radical turn, critics have generally ignored the fact that by the 1960's the author had become completely blind. He no longer possessed the abilities to read longer fiction, proof it, and rewrite it. He dictated virtually everything he produced from that time forward. His love of poetry is often not considered either. Borges's first acclaim as an ultraista came through his poetry, and he continued to compose poems throughout his literary life (Linda S. Maier, *Borges and the European Avant Garde* [NY: Peter Lang, 1996], pp. 21–38). Borges considered himself a good poet, and it is noteworthy that at this point in his life, when the sea change from sight to blindness fully concluded, he chose poetry to express his feelings about this loss, as evident in the title of his collection of poems [and stories] from this period, *In Praise of Darkness* (1969). We also note that his inclusion of two short stories in this collection of poetry adumbrates the years to come when his prose would resemble poetry to great degree, both in economy and style.

Perhaps critics find Borges's later short stories lacking because they are not as heavily endowed as the more famous tales he wrote decades before. All are briefer and, most noticeably, practically devoid of narrative complexity (Naomi Lindstrom, *Jorge Luis Borges: A Study of the Short Fiction* [Boston: Twayne, 1990], p. 131). The plots are straightforward and bare-boned. The scarcity of metaphors is glaring, but we should keep in mind what Jaime Alazraki observed about Borges's preferred use of metonymy some time ago (*Borges and the Kabbalah* [Cambridge: Cambridge UP, 1988], pp. 238–71).

It is really to Carter Wheelock we should turn for the most important clue for reading these stories. In an article written in 1972, he put forth the thesis that the recent fiction of Borges seemed to revolve around a central theme of the death of the text ("Borges New Prose," in *Prose for Borges* [Northwestern UP, 1972]; reprinted in Harold Bloom, ed., *Jorge Luis Borges. Modern Critical Views* [NY: Chelsea House, 1986), pp. 120–21). That is to say, there have been many observations on Borges and the aesthetic response, the theses being that Borges's fiction has as its goal such a response in the reader, that there are no exterior referents and nothing outside the parameters of the text; all is creation and fiction. If the story is enjoyed, it is only for aesthetic reasons, not because there is a message, a connection, identification, or an interpretation that we can internalize or extrapolate. Carter's argument is that the stories are not about aesthetic pleasure per se, but rather the expectation of, the anticipation of, or the moment immediately before, the aesthetic sensation. For Borges, the aesthetic event is the "imminence of a revelation, which never comes" (107).

These stories, then, are fictions of denial, lacking epiphanies, recognition, and logical patterns and, as such, against interpretation. In contrast with his earlier works, these are anti-stories. It is as if Borges has gone to war with the Other in **"Borges and I."** Not unlike Hemingway, who (once he was critically acclaimed) had to wrestle with the powerful conceptions of what "Hemingway literature" should be, the author battles with the old Borges that the critical world now expects. He finds himself like Cervantes, after learning that Avellaneda has composed the spurious second part of the Quixote, recognizing that there are assumptions and preferences about which directions his texts should take. But in the same way that Cervantes refused to send Don Quixote to Barcelona in his subsequent authentic Part Two, Borges denies his readers and critics the fulfillment of their expectations and the pleasure of the text from this point forward.

Borges refuses to give the interpreters what they want. In his skeletal stories he consistently denies closure and textual unity, in the traditional sense. Wheelock has shown how the stories of ***Dr. Brodie's Report*** (1970) symbolize

the death and destruction of the text (and hence, any aesthetic response). The refusal to rise to critics' expectations continues in Borges's collection, ***The Book of Sand*** (1975), a story of which, **"El disco,"** is virtually left without critical comment, though it might be taken as an example of synecdoche applying to all of the author's later fiction. The tale involves a woodsman in Medieval England (not "somewhere in Scandinavia," as Lindstrom reports [104]), who is visited by an aged Norseman, who declares that he is of royal lineage, showing as proof a one sided shining disk he holds in his hand. When the opportunity presents itself, the covetous woodsman murders him. The disk falls free from his hand, and the woodsman-narrator, reports that he has been searching for the disk all his days.

One attuned to the theme of the death of the text, or the denial of the aesthetic response should discern that this tale is an allegory on reading especially on reading Borges. The woodsman is the reader/interpreter whose will is dominant and unopposed. The old man, a worshipper of Odin, represents a tradition that predates the era of the woodsman and his beliefs (Christianity). Symbolically, the former is the traditional, long-standing text, with its secrets and riches represented by the disk. The reader destroys the text in search of its inherent riches, only to find them denied him. But the unshakable belief that there must be value in that which was lost keeps the woodsman searching (closure, meaning, aesthetic pleasure) for the rest of his life. He will not let it go, though he will never find it. Following the logic of this narrative, the one- sided nature of the disk meant that it only had existence or a 'side' when held in the hand of the old man while embedded in the text. The reader has destroyed the text, and any meaning, separated from the text, remains forever imperceptible.

In a final note, it is worth underlining that the woodsman is described as dim-witted as well as primitive, a departure from Borges's penchant for providing duelists/antagonists of roughly equivalent capacity. If the woodsman is to symbolize the reader/critic, then Borges has made a transparent comment on the nature, power, and motivation (and intelligence) of those who review his texts and seek his disks. Little wonder he got tired of labyrinths, even less of a wonder why he concretely diminishes his later texts and metaphorically destroys them. If we take **"El disco"** as the part standing for the whole of his later fiction, we have our answer as to why many critics find the stories less satisfying.

Eynel Wardi (essay date 1999)

SOURCE: "The Stories of Emma Zunz," in *Narrative*, Vol. 7, No. 3, October, 1999, pp. 335–56.

[*In the following essay, Wardi applies psychoanalytic techniques to the interpretation of Borges's story "Emma Zunz."*]

In a talk given at the Freudian School of Psychoanalysis in Buenos Aires, Borges confessed: "My father warned me against Freud. He was a psychology teacher. He had tried to read Freud and failed, and it may well be that I inherited this incapacity."[1] But as his professional hosts obviously thought and the reporter of this quotation emphatically notes, this is a case of inappropriate self-effacement. It is true that Borges does not generally show much interest in the psychic life of his characters, whom he tends to subject to the requirements of his plots and his philosophical thematizations, but **"Emma Zunz"** is a different story. It is an exception that confirms the sense of inappropriate, if not false, modesty in his "confession" to the psychoanalysts. Recording and reflecting on the pathological adventures of its protagonist, Emma Zunz, on the basis of a presumed intimate confession by her, this story invites a reading of it as a psychoanalytical case history. It does so by suggesting the unconscious motivations and mechanisms underlying Emma's conspiracy to avenge her dead father with such compelling subtlety of psychological insight and narrative manipulation that testify to both Borges's interest in Freudian psychoanalysis and consummate skill in shaping a narrative that reflects the cunning of the Freudian unconscious. Moving elegantly between Emma's manifest actions, thoughts, feelings and psychosomatic symptoms, and the deepest recesses of her mind, the narrative intimates to us that the manifest story of a daughter's revenge is, essentially, a classical Oedipal story:[2] Emma's carefully plotted murder of Loewenthal and the alibi she prepares to cover for it—namely, her prostitution with a foreign sailor—turn out to be the compulsive, displaced enactments of ambivalent Oedipal wishes, which are cathected by the traumatic event of her father's death. Emma's manifest story of willed revenge thus masks another Freudian story, one that is motivated by trauma and compulsion, by repression and wish-fulfillment.[3]

The latent story of Emma's motives for the murder and of its place in her psychic economy shares, as I will show, a great number of narrative elements with Freud's own case histories. But Borges's virtuosity here does not lend itself to be taken at face value. Rather, the very narrative techniques that ingeniously evoke the classically constructed Freudian case history also challenge its ultimate validity. Ambiguities in the narrative position, tone, and perspective provide leading hints for the story's psychoanalytical reading, but at the same time introduce a measure of subversive self-irony that puts into question both the suggested psychoanalytical reading and its theoretical premises. In **"Emma Zunz"** Borges, the master ironist, succeeds in embedding a seemingly airtight Freudian narrative within a story that has the earmarks of radically different modes: of the flatly naturalistic story—with its tale of revenge and of meaningless suffering and squalor—and of the detective story of the "perfect crime" (Chrzanowski 100). In mounting these narrative modes on each other, Borges subordinates the Freudian interest to his own: Emma's case and its criminal and psychological aspects are subjected to Borges's chief concern, which I take to be, here as always, with *stories*. Here Borges seems to be

playing with psychoanalysis out of a recognizable interest in the logic of narratives and of representations in general. He does this through the superimposition of a variety of stories representing different narrative perspectives on the same sequence of events, and by experimenting with the possible—but by no means necessary—symbolic relations between them.[4]

In what follows I will first extricate the Freudian narrative from the manifest crime story that is **"Emma Zunz,"** and then briefly ponder the grounds of Borges's interest in such a narrative. I will suggest that the appeal for him of the Freudian construct can be understood in terms of similarities between some of Freud's master plots and his own—as well as in terms of metanarrative elements that his stories share with Freud's constructions of the life of the psyche.

THE NARRATIVE LOGIC OF "EMMA ZUNZ"

"Emma Zunz" generates a first reading of the text as a kind of an inverted detective story, in which the initial givens are the identity of the murderess and her motivations, and the mystery is the crime. The inquest moves forward in synchronicity with the plotting in anticipation for something which is not even known to be its criminal object: the reader follows Emma's plotting and preparations, the purpose of which s/he understands only after Emma finally murders Loewenthal and calls the police. However, as soon as the mystery is resolved, a reversal takes place which introduces a new mystery and a new hermeneutic code, which is to be deciphered, by way of a properly retroactive inquest this time, in a second reading of the text. A step or two backwards in the story line will clarify this shift.

After having murdered Loewenthal according to her plan to constitute "the justice of God" by avenging her father, having then disarranged the divan and unbuttoned the dead man's jacket, Emma calls the police and tells the story of her alibi: *"Something incredible has happened . . . Mr. Loewenthal had me come over on the pretext of the strike . . . He abused me . . . I killed him. . . ."* (*Labyrinths* 168, 169 emphasis original; unless otherwise noted all citations from Borges are from this text). At this point, the inverted detective inquest ends, with the exposure of the function of Emma's "prostitution" with a sailor earlier the same evening. Its purpose turns out to be an alibi for justifying Loewenthal's murder as a reaction to an act of sexual violation. In reference to these last words, the narrator of **"Emma Zunz"** resumes his story with a rather curious remark: "Actually, the story *was* incredible, but it impressed everyone because substantially it was true. True was Emma Zunz's tone, true was her shame, true was her hate. True also was the outrage she had suffered: only the circumstances were false, the time and one or two proper names" (169).

This perplexing remark casts a certain doubt on the credibility of the narrative which it concludes. The affirmation of the truth of a story which has been clearly introduced as a lie raises the possibility that, although the narrator has the tone of a reliable heterodiegetic narrator, we need to consider whether he is unreliable, and if so, whether we must look to him or past him for his author's purpose in making him so. My sense is that at this point, at least, the text encourages us to assume that the voice which confuses us is that of an ironic, manipulative narrator, who invites us to follow his lead into a revealing second reading of the text. This sense is reinforced by the narrator's implicit thematization of the problem of truth and credibility raised in view of Emma's discourse and its reception, which reflects back on his own, self-conscious discourse as well as on the metanarrative concerns which, as a fellow storyteller, he shares with his author.

The amazement provoked by the narrator's final statement may be formulated in two questions. First, how come? How is it possible that the alibi is true, given that the events are altogether incongruous with those which take place in the narrator's story, to say nothing of the ultimate emotional motivation for the murder, and the fact that Emma herself regards it as a deliberate lie? The second question is a metanarrative one, the answer to which constitutes the clue for the interpretation of the story: what, according to the narrator's view, is the 'substantial truth' of a story? This second question, as a key question, specifies the first: do Emma's alibi-story and the narrator's story of **"Emma Zunz,"** the latter of which we have so far considered to be the true story, share a substantial truth by which they can be reconciled (and if so, how)? And if not, what is the meaning of the narrator's story, which is implied in this case to be false, and what, ultimately, is the unreliable narrator's game?

As to the second question, the narrator's remark clarifies that what determines the substance of a story are *not* the circumstances of the action, the time and the identity of the characters ("*only* the circumstances were false, the time and one or two proper names"), but rather the way in which they are, or seem to be, or to have been, experienced: the emotions which they evoke and their impact or intensity ('the shame,' 'the hate,' 'the outrage'). An additional determining factor pertains to an aspect of narration: "True was Emma Zunz's *tone*" (my emphases) when she relates the news of Loewenthal's murder to the police. As the authenticity of Emma's tone manifests itself in the *explanation* she gives for the murder of Loewenthal, we may infer that the emotions which determine the substantial truth of a story are such that they function as the *psychological* motivations which constitute its causal logic. The shift in the hermeneutic code is obvious: the elements that are most pertinent to a detective inquest are dismissed as irrelevant to the 'substance' of the story, and so we pass on to a psychological inquest.

As regards the first question, that of the absurd credibility of Emma's alibi, there does seem to be a 'substantial' common denominator between the alibi story and the narrator's, which is manifested in Emma's feelings as she faces her victim. The shame and the hate are there in both stories, and both seem to *stem*, at least in part, from an "outrage" suffered by Emma as the effect of an atrocious sexual experience: in the alibi story there is rape, inflicted upon her by Loewenthal, and in the narrator's story there is the intercourse with the sailor with whom she chooses to prostitute herself. Moreover, in both stories, the feelings of shame and hate constitute, in a way, the cause for Loewenthal's murder: when Emma finally reaches the critical stage in the execution of her righteous stratagem of revenge, "things did not happen as Emma Zunz had anticipated" (168) when she planned down to its minutest detail the emotional process she was to undergo in order "to permit the justice of God to triumph over human justice" (168). Revising her plan on the afternoon before its realization, "she thought that the final stage [the murder] would be less horrible than the first [prostitution with the sailor] and that it would undoubtedly afford her the taste of victory and justice" (166), which would enable her to force a confession from Loewenthal and declare his death as a verdict for causing her father's death. But things did not happen that way. "In Aaron Loewenthal's presence, more than the urgency of avenging her father, Emma felt the urgency of inflicting punishment for the outrage *she* had suffered. She was unable not to kill him after that thorough dishonour" (168 my emphasis).

But can we really consider the local causality introduced by this deviation from Emma's plan as the causality which determines the substance of the story as a whole? Hardly, it seems, as this deviation is no more than an accidental by-product of the larger scheme to which it is ultimately subordinated. Emma planned the murder with the intention of avenging her father for the mortal outrage which he had suffered—to implement divine justice—and the outrage which she had suffered was something she brought upon herself deliberately in order to escape, by way of an alibi, the consequent decree of human justice. She was no passive object of victimization, but the active subject in her 'dishonouring,' which was a contrived pretext for the murder. Therefore, even if we accept the narrator's notion of the insignificance of the circumstances, the time and the identity of the characters, and take the emotional causality as the determining factor of a story's substantial truth, there still remains a substantial incongruity between the two stories, consisting in the inversion of their causal logic. And if this is indeed the case, and we accept the narrator's authority with respect to his final remark, that is, that Emma's alibi story is true, then we are left with the perplexing conclusion that the narrator's story is false. Perplexing indeed, because the narrator's unreliability challenges the authority of his final remark as well, which brings us to a dead end.

The way out of there that is not a way back, that is, the disentanglement of the "liar's paradox," is to be sought in the narrative technique of focalization employed in the text. In narrating the story of **"Emma Zunz,"** the narrator does tell a false story, yet this story is not his, but Emma's story. Emma's revenge story seems to be narrated from her point of view; one gets the impression that the narrator relies on some confession by Emma as the source of information for his story, as he clearly suggests, for example, in "How can one make credible an action which . . . today the memory of Emma Zunz repudiates and confuses?" (166). Whatever he attempts to reconstruct himself that is not explicit in her memory is carefully restricted to the status of hesitant speculation: "Perhaps on the infamous Paseo de Julio she saw herself multiplied in mirrors . . . but it is more reasonable to suppose that she wandered, unnoticed, through the indifferent portico" (166). However, it is precisely in these hesitant remarks and in the ambiguities which they create that the hints to another, fuller story lie. That second, more plausible story is the narrator's psychoanalytical interpretation of Emma's story, which points to its hidden (Freudian) plot by filling in the meaningful gaps "which today the memory of Emma Zunz repudiates [or] confuses" (166). Thus, the narrative of **"Emma Zunz"** unfolds two simultaneous stories: Emma's manifest story, with its distortive gaps of consciousness and repressive rationalizations, and the narrator's latent interpretative story. The latter, psychoanalytic narrative corresponds, as I shall try to show in the course of the analysis, to Emma's "true" alibi story, which lends light to its reconstruction. This stereophonic narrative structure, which constitutes **"Emma Zunz"** as a detective story, makes the reader an active participant in the psychoanalytic process which it dramatizes—a compliant accomplice of an omniscient analyst.

A single deviation from the narrator's careful restriction of perspective to Emma's text occurs towards the end of the story, when Emma finally enters her victim's residence. Here, there is a local shift of focalization to Loewenthal's point of view. But this shift, one might argue, does not seem to convey any information which Emma would not know herself, and which lies, therefore, within the scope of the narrator's verisimilar speculations. It may even be read as the unmediated dramatization of Emma's consciousness as she approaches her cheated victim, trying to imagine what goes on in his mind. Moreover, the deviation in the technique of perspective is backgrounded by the effect of the gap of information between the plotting Emma and the reader, which creates the illusion of her being the ultimate authority of her story and, by absorbing the reader's attention in the expectation of finding out what she is up to, distracts it from whatever might challenge Emma's apparent authoritative status. Only once that gap is closed, the reader is free to adhere to the narrator's whispered asides. That gap closes, as I said, by the narrator's final, enigmatic remark, which invites us to reconstruct the "real" story—the fantasy of an authoritative analyst of whose authority we set out to partake. Compelled by the narrator (or perhaps by our own unconscious?) to repeat, let us, then, play our little game of mastery.

THE PLOTTING OF EMMA ZUNZ AND THE PLOT OF "EMMA ZUNZ"

Let me first summarize the manifest story, and then proceed to reconstruct the latent one, while pointing out the subordination of the first to the second.

Emma's story: In 1916, Loewenthal stole the money from the cash box of the factory of which he was the manager, and consequently the cashier, Emanuel Zunz, was unjustly convicted for the crime, evicted of his property and exiled—or compelled to escape—to Brazil (it is perhaps more likely that he escaped, by the fact that he changed his name from Zunz to Maier). His life in exile, without an identity and away from his home and from his daughter, became unbearable for him and drove him, within six years (1922), to commit suicide. Upon receiving the news of his death, his daughter Emma, who is the only person to whom he had revealed the truth of his innocence, resolves to avenge him—to restore divine justice where human justice has failed—by killing Loewenthal, who had in effect caused her father's death. In order to save herself from punishment (which would be yet another unjust triumph of human justice), she plans to justify the murder to the police by telling them that Loewenthal abused her. To ensure the credibility of this pretext in an expected gynecological examination, she contrives an alibi by prostitution with a sailor whose ship is bound to leave on the same night. Her project is executed as planned, except for the performance of the little trial she has planned to effect just before killing Loewenthal, which does not take place.

The latent story of Emma Zunz is the story of an outrage she had indeed suffered, as the narrator confirms in his final remark, but the identity of the violator is neither the one she incriminates in the alibi story, *nor* the one she chooses to be violated by as an alibi for her criminal reaction to the violation. This is insinuated by yet another enigmatic detail in the narrator's remark: among the false elements of Emma's alibi story which are qualified as irrelevant to its substantial truth are "one or *two* proper names" (my emphasis). The substitution of the sailor by Loewenthal is not, then, the only instance of displacement in her account to the police, and so the reader is directed to trace the identity of a third (which is actually the first) displaced violator-figure. Since no such figure reveals itself in what she takes to be her true story, the reader must go beyond it, that is, beyond Emma's alibi to herself. Thus, the narrator's insinuation of a *double displacement* leads us to transcend the manifest level of the text to its latent one, in which the absent third figure plays a central role (Chrzanowski 103).

In 1916 Emma's father stole the money out of the cashbox of the factory where he worked as cashier, was justly convicted and expelled—or escaped—to Brazil. On the night before his departure he swore to his daughter confidentially that the real thief was Loewenthal, and not himself, probably out of an understandable wish to save her respect for him (Ludmer 477) and not lose her as a daughter, and to reduce her agony at the change that was about to take place in her life. It was probably for the very same reasons that his daughter believed him. The falseness of this secret information and the reason for Emma's believing it are hinted at by the narrator's ironically hesitant speculation as to Emma's motivation for keeping her father's acquitting secret to herself: "Perhaps she was shunning profane incredulity" (165)—and quite justifiably so, for if she was the only one who knew the secret which her father had not even bothered to reveal to the police, there was no reason why anyone should have believed her. A second (and not contradictory) possibility is that "she believed that the secret was a link between herself and the absent parent" (165), which indeed it was, for that secret enabled Emma to suppress the criminal truth of which she had most likely been very well aware at the time, as well as the consequent loss of her father. It also enabled her to repress her affective response to that loss—namely, her pain and her hatred and criminal impulse towards the real thief—and, thanks to that repression, to act upon them by killing his fantasized surrogate with a clean conscience.

The events of 1916 and 1922 have a traumatic impact on Emma's life, in that they activate an oedipal conflict in her. Trauma, according to Freud, involves *at least two* events, the first of which is manifested in an unconscious content, including primal and repressed fantasies. The second event, which occurs at a later stage, charges the first with "pathogenic force" retroactively, by dint of an associative relation to it. Although traumas are essentially sexual, the second event need not necessarily be of a sexual nature. In Emma's case there are at least three events, the first (chronologically) being the fantasmic enactment of her primal oedipal ambivalence, which, the text suggests, is cathected by the two real events of her father's loss—first his betrayal and exile and then his death. The trauma of the event of 1916, which took place in the crucial time of her early adolescence (she was nineteen in 1922), accounts for her "pathological fear" of men (165). This pathological fear reflects not only the effect of the outrage and the violation of trust which she had suffered as her *father's* victim, but, possibly, also her unconscious sense of guilt for her repressed aggressive reaction towards him, as well as for the oedipal desire which binds her to him. Her "pathology" reflects, in short, her fantasmic organization of her traumatic experience as one of sexual violation for which she must avenge herself. Her guilty aggressive wish also suggests itself in her well known and apparently counter-reactive objection to "all violence" (165), which will be the ironic source of *her* victim's fatal trust in the informer who comes to his office "on [the] pretext of the strike" (169). The violence she nonetheless plots to commit will be balanced, for innocence's sake, by her sacrificial subjection to a self-inflicted violation by the ugly sailor.

The news of her father's death in 1922 reactivate in Emma the trauma of 1916 to the effect of recharging its underlying oedipal fantasies with fresh, compulsive pathogenic force, while offering her the opportunity to give vent to her repetition compulsion. To undo what has been done to her, she must, as it were, repeat her father's loss and violence actively through prostitution and murder, whereby she can also realize her oedipal wishes. It is no coincidence, therefore, that it is at this point that Emma becomes "the person she would be" (164) and which she has in fact always been. Her father's death reawakens in her conflicting feelings towards him with such force that they must be enacted and reconciled, while constituting the pretext and the occasion for their expression. Nor is it a coincidence, therefore, that the text's "first narrative," in Genette's terms, begins precisely here, when Emma is born into her new identity, while the presentation of whatever preceded this "second birth" in Emma's history takes place in the form of flashbacks.

A close reading of Emma's reaction to the letter announcing her father's death may elucidate the psychological dynamics which bring about the acting out of her repressed drives under the sublimatory guise of a moral alibi. The text evokes a mental process of perception, denial, failure of the denial, and consequent flash of recognition that is immediately translated into rationalized assertive reaction. It is possible to distinguish, in this process, between spontaneous, irrational reactions, which touch more directly on the contents of Emma's unconscious, and defensive reactions of both a rational and an irrational nature. This distinction is textually effected by the respective occurrences of the narrative techniques of foregrounding and distancing—notably manipulations of point of view and duration (Genette)—which disclose the narrator's perspective with regard to Emma's real motives by creating an effect of irony.

There are four references in the text to Emma's reception of the news of her father's death. The first is a short *summary* of the dry facts of the event, narrated from a distant, detached and objective perspective: "Emma Zunz discovered . . . a letter . . . which informed her that her father had died" (164). The second reference moves closer, to evoke the perceptive process, the details of which can each also be read as symbolic of the psychological process of Emma's reaction. Thus, "[t]he stamp and the envelope deceived her at first" (164) suggests an initial reaction of instantaneous denial: Emma probably mistakes the letter to be from her father in Brazil, which implies that he is still alive, that is, a symbolic denial of his death; "then the unfamiliar handwriting made her uneasy" (164)—unsettling failure of the denial; then, "[n]ine or ten lines tried to fill up the page" (164)—impending recognition, "trying" to fill up the space of Emma's consciousness (in the Spanish original the lines are qualified as "borroneadas," designating "blurred" or "doodled": the information is not yet clearly grasped); and finally, the recognition: "Emma read that Mr. Maier had taken by mistake a large dose of veronal and had died in the third of the month in the hospital" (164). However, the recognition is countered by an immediate, second denial: "Emma dropped the paper" (164).

In the following reference the description shifts from the perceptual to the emotional realm. Here, too, there is an alternation of recognition and its repression, which culminates in the triumph of recognition in a dramatic instance of self-awareness. After the "Freudian slip" of the letter from Emma's hands, "[h]er first impression was of a weak feeling in her stomach and in her knees; then of *blind guilt,* of *unreality,* of coldness, of *fear*" (164 my emphases). Emma's unconscious threatens to overcome repression: the repressed reverberates in a feeling of guilt at the face of the unexpected realization of her wish for her father's death, which arouses in her a fear of punishment. Her anxiety is also the "uncanny" effect of the "return of the repressed" which, subjected to her attempt to deny its contents, manifests itself in the sense of "unreality." The uncanny feeling which seizes Emma is associated with a sense of repetition, whose compulsive occurrence she conceives to be the fateful design of some mysterious, irrational powers which dominate her life. This is given expression in a following instance of undesirable insight on Emma's part, which she first tries to fend off in wishing "that it were already the next day" (164). "Immediately afterwards," however, "she realized that that wish was futile because *the death of her father was the only thing that happened in the world, and it would go on happening endlessly*" (164 my emphasis). The revelatory value of this insight is underscored by the use of "transparent speech" ("the realization that"), whereby the narrative perspective as it were zooms-in to create a close-up effect: the narrator lends his voice to the manifestation of Emma's inner truth. This realization foregrounds to Emma's consciousness—even if she does not comprehend it in these terms—of the notion of the psychological determinism to which she is subjected. The death of her father is the obsessive wishful image which dominates Emma's mind, delineating the horizon of her memory and of her vision of the future. It happened in the past—as a recurrent fantastic wish-fulfillment—ever since Emanuel Zunz's death to his daughter in 1916 (that is, *by* his daughter); and it will happen again in the future, as Emma preconceives in intuiting "the ulterior facts," which "she had already begun to suspect . . . perhaps" (164), the narrator speculates.

The death of Emma's father must happen again because it is not satisfying; the fulfillment of Emma's wish by her father's actual death cannot free her from the obsessive power of that wish and thereby break the spell, as it were, of the psychological determinism in which she is caught, because a dispelling mastery of its originating trauma requires an *active* reaction on Emma's part. In this respect, the letter introduces a certain obstacle in the path to wish-fulfillment, for its content implies the impossibility of Emma's killing her father with her own hands. This obstacle is symbolically removed by Emma's "furtively" hiding the letter "in a drawer" (164), as if to deny the facts that it discloses so as to make possible their recurrence in the ulterior facts (the voluntary concealment of the letter, contrasted by its former Freudian slip, illustrates Emma's active, controlling role in the ulterior facts).

The fourth reference to Emma's confrontation of the news occurs in the paragraph describing the events of the night which ends with the completion of her plan. "In the growing darkness, Emma wept . . . for the suicide of Manuel Maier," thus motivating his death for her own purposes. Her inference of her father's suicide from the letter informing her that "Mr. Maier had taken *by mistake* a large dose of veronal" (164 my emphasis) is, it seems, a misinterpretation that is consistent with her secret misconception of her father's role in the earlier traumatic event, and which provides, moreover, a just cause for avenging him. It might be argued here that by qualifying Mr. Maier's death as a mistake the informer meant to soften the harsh reality of his suicide, but he had no particular reason to do so if, as the narrator cares to point out, he had "no way of knowing that he was addressing the deceased's daughter" (164). Emma needs her father's death to be suicide in order to establish a direct connection between the would-be wrong that was done to him and his as-if consequent tragic death of despair. This distortive manipulation is met by the distancing effect of the narrator's ironic play, once again, with "one or two . . . names." In a conspicuous contrast with the first reference, where the event of the father's death is reported as "*her father* died," here, as "suicide," it is attributed to the bearer of the false name "*Manuel Maier,*" which marks Emma's dissociation from her true feelings towards the object of her mourning (my emphases). This dissociation, and the original dissociation from her father brought about by the trauma and his consequent wishfully fantasized death, are symbolically evoked by the reference to the change of the father's family name from Zunz to Maier, and of his first name from *Ema*nuel to Manuel ("Emma wept . . . for the suicide of Manuel Maier, who in the happy old days was Emmanuel Zunz" [164]). Emma's mourning, then, is ironically the lamentation of a *stranger's* suicide, which serves, at least to some extent, as an emotional alibi for killing her *father.*

Emma's moral alibi, namely her religious mission to restore divine justice, is related in more than one way to her epiphanous revelation of the obsessive idea that her father's death "was the only thing that happened in the world, and it would go on happening endlessly" (164). In his essay on "Obsessive Actions and Religious Practices," Freud explains (away?) the nature of religions and religious ideas as compulsive-obsessive symptoms in a way that is pertinent to Emma's case: "Vengeance is mine, saith the Lord" (1907, 41), he quotes to illustrate the ulterior function of deities, which he views as projected agencies to which prohibited instinctual pleasures are sacrificed, as it were, to the effect of both relieving the guilt associated with them and legitimizing their satisfaction as sacrificial acts. Emma's piety enables her to satisfy her forbidden desires in the most direct forms of actual sex and murder, both of which are regarded by her as self-sacrificial acts. With God on her side (the Hebrew Emanu-el [[òî ååì denotes "God is on our side," and nothing is too farfetched with Borges as far as "one or two names" are concerned), she may conscientiously set out to kill Emanuel, and free herself once and for all of her obsession: "the handing over to [the Deity] of bad and so-cially harmful instincts," says Freud in reference to the origins of religion, "was the means by which man *freed himself of their domination*" (41 my emphasis). The conventionalized irrationality of religion legitimizes Emma's irrational intention and contributes to its successful imposition on reality by exempting it from some of the requirements of reality-testing. This exemption is further facilitated by the secrecy which secures the pretext for the revenge: Emma keeps the improbable secret which her father told her on the night of his departure because "perhaps she was shunning *profane incredulity*" (165, my emphasis).

The origins of Emma's "new" identity as an emissary of divine justice are further elucidated at this point in the narrative by a few glimpses into her previous incarnation through textual flashbacks. These flashbacks consist of certain reminiscences on Emma's part which belong to the time prior to the fixation of the trauma of 1916, as well as some details of her life afterwards which illustrate, by way of negation, the exclusive predominance of the perpetual wishful image of the father's death. The significance of the scenes from her past which come to Emma's mind on the night she mourns her father's death is suggested by the selective quality of her recollection, and, once again, by the narrative manipulation of techniques of distancing and foregrounding.

Emma's reminiscences vary according to the degree of their accessibility, their coherence and their intensity. There are the things which Emma simply "*remembered*," such as "the summer vacations . . . the little house at Lanús . . . the yellow lozenges of a window," which pertain to the "prehistoric" time before 1916, and such which pertain to the traumatic event of that year—"the warrant for arrest, the ignominy . . . the poison-pen letters with the newspaper's account of 'the cashier's embezzlement'" (164–65 my emphasis). As distinct from these, there is what she "*tried to remember*," namely, her mother, and what she "*never forgot*," namely, "that her father . . . had sworn to her that the thief was Loewenthal" (164–65), which marks the beginning of her pathological history in repression. The emergence of the first series of reminiscences takes place in the "return of repressed" scene which is stimulated by the shocking effect of the letter. The intensity of these reminiscences as such is reflected in their fragmentary emergence as isolated images, represented by a series of nouns suggesting a form of pictorial reminiscing that is not mediated by any kind of interpretative or "secondary" organization. The static nature of such recollected images endows them with a sense of atemporality and immanence that liberates them from their context in the past, and thereby intensifies their presence in the moment of reminiscing. The series of images evoking the events of 1916 is particularly intense, as they reverberate strong scenes of action, which is linguistically illustrated by the condensation of a sequence of action into verbal nouns ("the warrant for arrest" [164–65], "the cashier's embezzlement" [165], etc.). By contrast, the actions in the reminiscence of

what Emma "never forgot" are represented by verbs within a coherently organized phrase ("her father . . . *had sworn* to her"; "the thief *was* Loewenthal" [my emphasis]) and are temporally contextualized by a time adverbial ("on the last night" [165]), which indicates the indirect and hence less intense quality of their recollection as a kind of "secondary revision." The reduced intensity of this recollection is also evoked by the indirect representation of its content within a subordinate clause: Emma "remembered . . . *that* (Spanish: "que") her father . . . had sworn to her *that* the thief was Loewenthal" (in contrast with the direct form of "she remembered the"). The second-hand information disclosed in this secondarily-revised scene is the clearest and most accessible event in Emma's memory, as it was "guarded" by her "since 1916" as a kind of screen that was designed to ward off all memories of previous times. Its repressive function is to conceal the affective significance of scenes from the lost "happy days" and from the actual circumstances of the loss, i.e., the "open account" with the cause of that loss, which is thereby fixated to delineate Emma's memory as "the only thing that had happened in the world" (164).

As for what Emma "tried to remember"—where, actually, is Emma's mother? Well, if the least accessible memory is really the most significant, then we can trust her to return from the dead at some later point in the analysis.

The period between 1916 and 1922 is marked by a complete ellipsis in Emma's life as far as significant action is concerned. References to this period are iterative evocations of passive habits which have originated as the effects of the events of 1916 (165): the guarding of the secret, Emma's declaring herself "as usual" against all violence, her pathological fear of men, etc. The description of the routine of the day before the crime, which Emma "tried to make . . . like any other" (165) and which indeed elapses, like any other day in her life, "laborious and trivial" (165), also bears an iterative implication, which corresponds to the fact that nothing really happened in Emma's life ever since it was taken over by the one and only event of her father's wishful death.

THE STAGE-SETTING AND ENACTMENT OF EMMA'S PLOT AND THE RETURN OF EMMA'S MOTHER

Before going to the waterfront Emma tears up the letter announcing her father's death and sets out to kill him with her own hands. Apart from the practical significance of destroying incriminating evidence, the act of tearing up the letter has a symbolic meaning as well: in order to kill the father it is required that he should be alive, and therefore the evidence of his death must be destroyed.

In order that the repetition of the trauma be properly traumatic, Emma picks the short and coarse sailor in place of a younger one whom she feels "might inspire some tenderness in her," thus making sure "that the purity of the horror might not be mitigated" (166). The masochistic element (Chrzanowski 103) in this choice may also be understood as a means of an *a priori* self-punishment which the sufferer of a "pathological fear of men" inflicts upon herself in order to relieve herself of the guilt associated with the subsequent murder—a relief that is indeed manifested in the spontaneity with which she kills Loewenthal "for the outrage she had suffered" (169). A third possibility is that she is simply afraid of enjoying the sexual act, for otherwise why should she fear feeling tenderness towards the younger sailor? The suggestion of this possibility throws a suspicious light on Emma's pathological attitude towards men, which might be, at least in part, a reaction formation of her guilty fondness of them. A close reading of her experience as a prostitute supports this hypothesis.

Among the "disconnected and atrocious sensations" (166) which mark Emma's unmastered "hellish experience" are two free associations which correspond to her former experience of the "return of the repressed." The window she sees in the vestibule has lozenges that are "identical to those in the house at Lanús" (166)—an association of the home of the happy days, which eventually leads to the emergence of its inhabitant which Emma has formerly tried to remember: during the intercourse with the sailor, "she thought (she was unable *not* to think [this time]) that her father had done to her mother the hideous thing that was done to her now" (167, my emphasis). The significance of this association is foregrounded by the narrator, who this time raises explicitly the question of Emma's real motives by asking: "did Emma Zunz think *once* about the dead man who motivated the sacrifice?" (167, emphasis original). The answer to this ironic question is introduced as a speculation on the part of the narrator: "It is my belief that she did think once" (167) he conjectures, thus motivating the reader to ask what leads him to this "belief," which he then proceeds to convey so authoritatively.

Emma's spontaneous comparison between the "hideous thing" that was being done to her and what her father had done to her mother calls for the obvious combination of her father doing it to her—a "seduction scene" behind the screen of the "hideous" "primal scene." Emma's action and thought here are an effective "compromise formation" which at once represses and manifests her positive oedipal wish, thus accounting for the liquidation of Emma's mother from the scene of her memory: instead of remembering her, Emma reenacts her figure, with whom she identifies as her father's sexual partner to the point of literal incorporation.

Emma's prostitution with the sailor is not, then, merely an alibi to the police or to herself, but also the fulfillment of a primal wish, even as Loewenthal's "just" murder fulfills the negative counterpart of that oedipal wish. Her plot thus enables her to reconcile the conflicting, positive and negative aspects of the Oedipus complex through their full enactment under the cover of effective repressive strategies. She manages to reconcile the aspects of her oedipal ambivalence by splitting up its object into two figures of displacement, which enables her to realize her unconscious wishes to *both* have sex with her father *and then* kill him.

The organization of the ambivalence within a cohering narrative and plot sequence (Emma's interpretation of the reality of her father's tragic fate and her plan of reaction to it) facilitates its reconciliatory enactment both practically and psychologically, as do the reversals of the roles of victims and aggressors in the two parts of her story. Moreover, the realization of the positive Oedipus within the framework of a *mere* alibi contrived to cover up a deliberate lie to the police is designed to maintain Emma's dissociation from its unconscious motivation, and to camouflage its true relation to the realization of the negative Oedipus by placing it on a different level of intention.

The insinuation of the double displacement by the word "two" in the story's closing sentence ("one or two proper names") beckons the reader to transcend this defensive split and trace its unified origin, the alternative "one." Supporting this manipulation is a suggestion of a symbolic equivalence between Loewenthal and the sailor as representatives of a split oedipal father figure, which is implied, ironically enough, by Emma herself in her *truer* alibi story. Emma's report to the police, *"He abused me, I killed him"* (169), is true, psychologically, because it reunites the figure of her real object—the "seducer" and the object of her death wish. The fact that the roles of seducer and seduced are inverted here (it was Emma who seduced Loewenthal) does not detract from the psychological truth of the statement, in view of the Freudian notion of primal fantasies. Primal fantasies are "characterized by the absence of subjectification" ("Fantasy and the Origins of Sexuality" 13–14), and are therefore *transitive*. Thus, according to Laplanche and Pontalis, in "a father seduces a daughter," "nothing shows whether the subject will be immediately located as daughter; it can as well be fixed as *father* or even in the term *seduces*" (13–14).

The truth of Emma's statement is further betrayed by its syntax, that is, by the absence of subordination between the two verbal phrases in *"he abused me, I killed him."* In her excitement, Emma omits the causal link between the two actions which is the basis for her alibi not only to the police, but also to herself (as well as for the unconscious, secondary organization of the conflict of ambivalence activated by the events of 1916: Mr. Maier's crime and departure are conceived by Emma as an act of textual abuse which at once represents a sexual wish and justifies the father's killing). The sexual abuse is no longer the cause or the pretext for the murder (nor is, for that matter, Loewenthal's abuse of Emma's father); the ambivalent oedipal wishes are represented as if disconnected, as they would be in their primary representation in the unconscious, prior to any secondary, conscious or unconscious, narrative organization.

The actual realization of Emma's primal fantasies also escapes aspects of their secondary organization. In the enactment of some of the details of Emma's plot there is *no time* for its stage-setting: the events of Emma's adventure with the sailor occur in a time that is outside time, which is experienced in that way "because the parts which form these events do not seem to be consecutive" (166–67). These events seem to resist the narrative relations that are imposed on them by way of their sequential organization in time, drawing their meaning from their direct, or "truthful" relation to the atemporal scenes of Emma's wishful unconscious. The directness of this minimally compromised wish fulfillment is indeed quite an achievement in terms of the imposition of fantasy on reality—an imposition that avails a taste of the real thing, almost. Almost, and at the risk of the "return of the repressed," which endangers the whole project, and accounts for Emma's experience of the apparent discontinuity of the events as "chaos" (166). This chaos is no more than a defense against the clarification of the meaning of the events, which magnetize their unconscious signifieds into consciousness. The reverberation of the repressed oedipal fantasy in the returning primal scene suspends, for a brief moment, Emma's safe movement from one of its temporal displacements to another, by rendering "the immediate past" of the event that stimulates it "as if disconnected from the future" (167)—or its teleological function. The analogical thought concerning "the hideous thing" "endanger[s] her desperate undertaking" (167) because it threatens to refute her conscious fantasy by exposing its compulsive cause, and as Emma escapes back to the "chaos", she "took refuge, quickly, in vertigo" (167), and then sealed the matter with a rationalization: "He was a tool for Emma, as she was for him, but she served him for pleasure whereas he served her for justice" (167).

After the event Emma tears up the money that the man has left her "as before she had torn the letter" (167). This analogy symbolizes her refusal, in both cases, to be compensated for the "outrage she had suffered" (168) as remaining uncompensated will give her the emotional and the moral strength to avenge herself and, as has already been noted, the "undoing of what has been done" requires an active (and perpetual) compensation.

"You, Hypocrite Lecteur, Mon Semblable, Mon Frere" or: "Read My Lips"

When Emma finally reaches the stage of realizing her righteous intention, her righteousness fails her, as has been noted earlier in reference to the unexpected deviation from her plan. In complicity with this ironic deviation and the exposure of a portion of Emma's hypocrisy, the narrator deviates from his technique of focalization in order to convey a different perspective on Emma's revenge ordeal. A description of Loewenthal which gradually zooms into his mind enables the narrator to distance himself from his heroine, and to express his alienation from her by way of an analogy between her and her victim. The description of Loewenthal evokes the most repulsive type of religious hypocrite, who "believed he had a secret pact with God which exempted him from doing good in exchange for prayers and piety" (168). The obvious analogy to Emma's secret pact with God is ironically reinforced by Loewenthal's projection of his own pious pragmatism onto Emma as she enters the gate: "He saw . . . Emma's lips

were moving rapidly, like those of someone praying in a low voice" (168) whereas in fact they were reciting the sentence he was to hear before his death. He never did, though, because Emma had no "time for theatrics" (168).

Emma is given no time for theatrics so that her "true" story may come out directly, spontaneously: "she was unable not to kill him after that thorough dishonour" (168). Kill whom? Symbolically, perhaps, she shoots Loewenthal three times: one for each of her abusers, who are all one to her. Given the outrage she had suffered, what are one or two missed shots? "She squeezed the trigger twice" (169) and then once again, to silence the "obscene lips" that "swore at her in Spanish and in Yiddish" (169) as if in response to the verdict which Loewenthal failed to read on her own, pious-looking lips.

Emma's muted theatrics, like her next justificatory gesture, is at once deceptive and revealing. Like her voiced alibi with its authenticating tone, Emma's lip-pantomime betrays the substantial truth of her story through the tone of its articulation—by the *narrator,* this time. The rhetorical, distancing shift of focalization which facilitates the staging of the "pantomime" disrupts the "rhetoric of intimacy" (Brodzki 338) so far established by the empathic "psychoanalytical" narrator, which now gives way to an emphatic expression of disapproval: as though refusing to hear Emma's perverse self-righteous speech, the narrator mutes it, leaving it to her equally perverse *double* to read and interpret. Meanwhile he proceeds to blur the identities of the victim and the aggressor and their respective roles in a hyperbolic gesture that is extended to include all three main protagonists in Emma's story. Emanuel Zunz, whose name suggests his own secret pact with God, is also implicated in that gesture, which begins in the preceding introduction of Loewenthal. Loewenthal's demonstrative mourning of the unexpected death of his rich wife who was less loved than her money not only illustrates the hypocrisy he shares with Emma, but also suggests the greediness of the other suspected embezzler, whose wife, too, has mysteriously disappeared from the story's scene. The narrator's sweeping gesture suggests his abandoning of the psychoanalytical strategy he has been manipulating us to reconstruct: it effaces the psychological identity of his "analysand," while parodying the interchangeability of "one or two proper names" which contributed to its construction. Indeed, it can be read as an ironic remark on such interchangeability in practical psychoanalysis, with its suspension of reality and value judgments and, of course, as an ironization of the narrator's own final remark, with its implications about the substantial truth of stories.[5]

Does the indignant narrator seek to unravel, by this second turn of the screw, the psychoanalytical code he has manipulated us to follow, in order to make a moral statement about self-righteousness, and thus to restore, perhaps, the detective story's legal code of *human* justice? Possibly, but not without a simultaneous ironic subversion of his move, which turns the screw further still. For the narrator's generalized indignation is based on common anti-

Semitic stereotypes, in the light of which Zunz, Loewenthal, Maier & Co. are interchangeable, representing the same combination of avarice and piousness accompanied by curses "in Spanish and in Yiddish" (Ludmer 475) (uttered by the bald, fat, bearded Loewenthal as he realizes that he has only an impotent *dog* on his side). This conflation of stereotypes cannot be anything but ironic, reflecting a self-righteousness that is no less grotesque than that of the characters which it serves to condemn, and the dehumanizing lack of discrimination which it betrays displaces the Freudian unconscious by a no more ethical, collective one, which the narrator now comes to represent.[6] Whether or not he is conscious of it, the irony of the "mirror-scene" points beyond the naturalistic positivism and the solemnities of the narrative voice to what might well be the substantial truth of Borges's story. Emma's providential author points to the truth of the tale she figures in by means of a graceful and grace-conferring gesture of relenting: that is, in his failure to give her time for theatrics at what she meant to be the climactic moment of her melodrama. His motive, it may be imagined, is solidarity between authors, and this despite a certain competition between them.

Indeed, beyond all other attitudes to Emma, the text projects a certain sympathy for her need to generate fiction—to be the author of the story of her life—and an undisguised respect for her initiative and skill in filling her uneventful life with drama. As J. B. Hall suggests, Emma can be seen as "a kind of a Quixote-figure, reacting against the tedium of her prosaic life characterized by her work in the factory, insipid meals . . . and an absence of excitement and romance"—for which she compensates a little in her spare time by pursuing "her interest in the *cinema*" (Hall 263, my emphasis). We know that she goes to the cinema with her girlfriends on Sunday afternoons, and that the only man in her conscious life is "the silent film-hero Milton Sills," whose picture "she keeps in her bedroom chest of drawers." The death of her father may be imagined to have given Emma the opportunity to change this reality and "to become the person she would be" (164), that is, a star in her own movie, of which she is both scriptwriter and director. Once she realizes that "the death of her father was the only thing that had happened in the world [. . . and which] would go on happening endlessly" she rebels and sets out to spin her own, wishful tale—to weave her own destiny *out* of her fated lot as a worker in the *textile factory,* or in Spanish: "*fábrica* de tejidos" (1989, 564). The success of her fabrications is remarkable: she manages to perform a variety of exciting roles—prostitute, martyr, informer, killer—in a drama which she bases on a wishful interpretation of reality, and which she adapts to that reality so well that she can get away with its performance, including the bloody murder that is its climax. She imposes her fantasy on reality so effectively that it becomes, in a way, the truth, and this is why everyone believes her when she repeats her alibi. The relevant question, of course, is whether she herself believes in her own fantasy when it comes to the test of its realization. For at that crucial moment, "[t]hings did not happen as Emma

Zunz had anticipated": she does *not* experience the feeling of triumph and justice she has expected to feel, and the trial she intended to conduct while pointing the victim's pistol at him does not take place. At this point of her story, she loses control to Fate (or is it the divine justice, which refuses to be misarticulated?). "Ever since the morning before, she had imagined herself wielding the firm revolver, forcing the wretched creature to confess his wretched guilt" (168). Fate, however, does not allow the realization of this fantasy, fortunately for her: for if it did, she might have had to face the possible truth of Loewenthal's denial of his guilt and the painful explosion of her fantasy. This is Fate's, or Borges's, gift of Grace to Emma: they save her story for her, with its substantial truth intact, and hence her power to manipulate her own, private fate.

FATE, BORGES, AND FREUD

It should be more than clear by now that it is Borges's fascination with the play of fictions in narrative and in "reality" that governs the inner life of the *story* **"Emma Zunz,"** and of its representation and of the presumed inner life of Emma herself. Its embedded Freudian narrative, however, merits further consideration, especially in view of Borges's emphatic lack of interest in human subjectivity and its determinations.

In pondering Borges's manifestly non-psychological interest in Freud, I have come to think that the appeal for him of the Freudian narrative must have lain in the structural similarity between some of Freud's master plots and his own. "Fate loves repetitions, versions, symmetries" (1972, 11) Borges writes in accounting for the narrative motivation of the plot of one of his stories, **"The Plot."** In that little story, the death of the *gaucho* at the hands of some other *gauchos,* among whom he suddenly spots his godson, occurs for no other reason than the satisfaction of fate's capricious taste for playing a variation on Julius Caesar's "pathetic" address to his young favorite: "You, too, my son?" (1972, 11). Both the arbitrariness and the horror of this fatality are curiously consonant with the concept of the *repetition compulsion* in Freud, with the morbid arbitrariness of its inner determinism and of its ultimate mythological agent, the death instinct. A notion of fatal repetition akin to Freud's governs the latent story of **"Emma Zunz,"** where the action emerges as the compulsive reenactment of traumatic events and the unconscious fantasies which they trigger and cathect.

The crossing of two discrepant plot-logics in a single event which might be the result of either or both at the same time figures, of course, in **"Emma Zunz,"** but is not unique to it or to its psychoanalytic underpinnings. The intersection and forking of paths is a characteristic Borgesian landmark, configuring the writer's perpetual preoccupation with the roles of causality and hazard, synchronicity and coincidence in generating chains of events. This is the case, for example, in **"The Encounter"** ("El encuentro" 1989, II: 417–21), which is a story about the development of a silly argument between two drunken guests at a party into a tragically unintended mortal duel, in which one of them is killed. The tragic meaninglessness of the event is in a way redeemed by a parallel plot line which motivates blind fate's mischief: the accident turns out to be the possibly inevitable result of the settling of old accounts between the two daggers involved, who have been waiting eagerly for the opportunity to pursue their unfinished business. A similar motivation marks the morbid mechanism of Freud's "repetition compulsion." In "Beyond the Pleasure Principle," Freud associates compulsive repetition with a need to control the unconscious impact of a traumatic event—to "undo what has been done" to one—through its active initiation and/or reenactment. This, of course, is the logic that governs Emma's suggested compulsive behavior after the event of her father's death. The father's death triggers in her a delayed traumatic reaction to the earlier violent event of separation from him, whose emotional impact she seeks to control by reenacting its fantasmatic oedipal configurations. Thus, converging with Emma's plot of vengeance is another scheme of reckoning, leading to the same consequent actions.

Freud's fatal principle of repetition is more or less redeemed from its morbidity, in Borges's fiction, by being aesthetically motivated (by Fate's *love* of repetitions, symmetries, etc.), thus reconciling the pleasure principle with the fatal drive lying as it were "beyond" it. Morbid compulsion and pleasure also combine to motivate Emma's plot of traumatic reenactment, and this, once again, in line with the Freudian theory of the drives. Predominant in Freud's mechanism of trauma is the pressure of unconscious drives and their fantasmatic representations to reach consciousness in one way or another. Hence the retroactive cathexis of primal, oedipal fantasies, which pertain to the imaginary domain of the pleasure principle, in the case of Emma's response to her father's death.

The repressed events which Emma reenacts are fictive ones; they are fantasies which embody her oedipal ambivalence in scenes of incest and patricide—or is it the narrator's fantasy, or perhaps our own, conscious or unconscious Freudian fantasies? The identity of the subject of the psychoanalytical narratives, and especially of the unconscious fantasies attributed to the analysand, is of necessity indeterminate. This indeterminacy, which is opened by the text of **"Emma Zunz,"** is part of the larger problematics of the hermeneutic as well as causal relations between fiction and reality in psychoanalytical narratives, which Borges formulates elsewhere in reference to his own interests.

In "the beginning of all literature is the myth, and in the end as well," Borges states in his "Parable of Cervantes and the Quixote" (278). This no doubt holds true for the Freudian literature, which locates the history of the subject between originary mythological fantasies and retroactive fantasies of origins. Underlying all psychic life, according to Freud, are the endogenic primal fantasies of origins which represent the mythological structure of the Oedipus. These fantasies, which include the scenes of castration, se-

duction, and the primal scene (and the fantasy of the return to the womb), are bound to, and represent, the unconscious oedipal wishes from which all our conscious and unconscious fantasy life derives. Indeed, "[e]ven aspects of human behavior that are far removed from imaginative activity, and which appear at first glance to be governed solely by the demands of reality, emerge as emanations, as "derivatives" of unconscious fantasy. In the light of this evidence, it is the subject's life as a whole which might be called "a fantasmatic" ("une fantasmatique") (Laplanche and Pontalis 1968, 317). The derivative origin of that fantasmatic and its instances lies, however, not only in their underlying unconscious fantasies, but also in their interpretation in the light of the psychoanalytic fantasmatic. The ambiguous origins of the components of that fantasmatic is brought to bare on by the narrative ambiguities in **"Emma Zunz,"** which thus challenges its own narrative authority and interpretative code. The story relativizes the very status of the psychoanalytic myth (or fantasy) in the light of which it manipulates us to read it, to the effect of drawing our attention to its main, self-reflexive narrative concerns.

The ironic mirror scene as it projects itself in the second (psychoanalytic) reading of the story is the site of a narrative crisis which leads us through the looking glass, so to speak, and into what might as well be the story's "substantial truth." The shift in the technique of focalization in that scene does not only question the ethical aspect of the psychoanalytic approach, with which the unreliable ironic narrator has been pretending to identify, but it also puts in question the actual validity of that approach, which the "psychoanalytic" narrator's so far accepted authority made us take for granted. His authority was established despite, but even more so *because,* of the narrator's repeated conscientious acknowledgments of the speculative nature of many of the details of his story (the "perhapses," etc.), which lent credibility to his character and hence to his account. The speculative aspect of the "omniscient analyst's" story, however, is thrown into relief by that heterodiegetic narrator's rhetorical transgression of his boundaries in the mirror scene—a deviation which generates the effect of defamiliarization. His unexpected hyperbolic gesture towards narrative omniscience, coupled with the abrupt change in his moral perspective, makes us wonder about the authority of the narrator's earlier speculations and about the grounds of probability which supposedly validated them. A close analysis of the following speculation, which is, perhaps, the strongest lead into the psychoanalytic story of Emma Zunz, lays bare the story's underlying myth and the way in which it is established as such. "During that time outside time, in that perplexing disorder of disconnected and atrocious sensations, did Emma Zunz think *once* about the dead man who motivated the sacrifice? It is my belief that she did think once. . . . She thought (she was unable not to think) that her father had done to her mother the same thing that was being done to her now. She thought of it with weak amazement." (167). The narrator's belief here is grounded in the as-if axiomatic necessity of the Freudian myth (the extra-temporal oedipal thought which Emma was *"unable not to think"*), and it is further confirmed by the subsequent specification of *how* Emma experienced the thought, which turns the thought into an established fact: "She [positively] *thought,"* and the "weak amazement" with which she did so makes the strange thought all the more real, because of the involuntary way in which it dawns upon its passive subject. Thus, the narrator's imaginative zooming-in into Emma's consciousness (which is not more imaginative than when applied to Loewenthal) emerges as a technique of *familiarization,* which the shift in focalization undoes so as to reveal the primal scene underlying the psychoanalytical story of **"Emma Zunz"** and of its Freudian protagonist.

Borges's ironic strategy is not so radical or systematic as to unravel the psychoanalytic tale which the narrative so effectively spins, nor does it seem to serve an attempt to invalidate its Freudian premises. Its purpose, it seems, is rather to confuse the status of the first and to relativize the truth of the second, in the service of what turns out to be the story's central metanarrative preoccupation with stories and their substantial truths, and with the relation of that truth to credibility and to narrative manipulations towards producing its effect. *Within* that context of interest, the Freudian "story" emerges as a very good story indeed—a story whose narrative potentialities Borges explores with manifest delight and respect, but without commitment. **"Emma Zunz"** can indeed be read as a tribute to psychoanalysis even as it subordinates it to its self-reflexive interests; a tribute which hails the Freudian story with its foundational myths and constructs (notably the unconscious), with its interpretative apparatus and its impressive explanatory power. The latter, it should be noted, figures in Borges's story as *one* form of the *truth-making* power of stories; another is, of course, the sort that manifests itself in the tone and pitch of Emma's voice when she tells her alibi to the police, and another is the "magic function" of the kind that sustains Emma's righteous rage and her and Loewenthal's pious pacts with God, another still is verisimilitude, etc.

The narrator shares his author's interests as a storyteller, which is what he is, primarily, beyond his tentative personae of psychoanalyst (or lay psychoanalyst) and anti-Semitic Porteño. He is the one who introduces the theoretical question of the substantial truth of stories at the end, as well as practical ones concerning manipulative strategies to the effect of its representation: "How to relate with some reality. . . . How could one make credible an action?" These questions suggest, of course, a certain ambiguity regarding the challenge of "truthful" representation—or fabrication?—of the events of the narrator's story, which, as an effective interpretation (of Borges's story), must be both true to fact and rhetorically convincing. The limitation of knowledge that differentiates the narrator from his author serves to blur the distinction between these two requirements for truth, by equating the status of story and interpretation as narratives both. For the heterodiegetic narrator, the story of **"Emma Zunz"** is both a challenge, as it is for the police, of reconstructing a story

from the sole testimony of its protagonist, and a source of practical and theoretical reflection on the challenges of truth and credibility in writing and in reading alike, that is, in narrative as interpretation and vice versa.

The ironic technique employed in the service of this reflection (that of juxtaposing various narratives and trying out some of them on the duped reader) leads, then, to the serial laying bare of their truth-conferring premises and devices, and so to the relativization of the notion of the substantial truth of stories. We thus have the inverted detective story, which shifts the essence of stories from facts to their conscious motivations, and then, with the turn to the psychoanalytic story—to their unconscious motivations. The latter move involves a shift of focus from an ethical perspective on, and of a moral consciousness to that of the as-if amoral psychology of the unconscious. This shift is inverted, however, in view of the gap, laid bare by the psychoanalytical inquest itself, between Emma's conscious and her unconscious motivations: this gap, which foregrounds Emma's self-righteousness, brings back the ethical question and directs an ironic criticism at the psychoanalytic approach which, in focusing so intently on the substantial truth of the subject's emotional reality, ends up overlooking the reality of the moral distortions which it uncovers. The same turns out to apply, however, to the narrative perspective which exposes that blindness, which betrays collective racist beliefs while mocking the beliefs of its stereotyped objects.

The question of whether the narrator is conscious of the irony here remains indeterminate, thus making ambiguous his status as Borges's full ironic accomplice. His ironic awareness is strongly suggested, however, by his reference to his own view of the events as "my belief" (167), which resonates too strongly with the recurrent references to Emma and Loewenthal's "pious . . . beliefs" (167–68) to escape the storyteller who is so keenly involved in exploring the very issue of belief, creed, credibility, and making credible. But in a final analysis, the resolution of the ambiguity does not really matter in terms of the story's substantial truth as I see it. What matters is the generalized effect of this and the many other ambiguities and indeterminacies in the story (sometimes regardless even of their terms), namely, the spirit of tentativeness which enables Borges to play with a variety of beliefs and their common and respective roles in the making of the truths of, and about, stories.

The manipulative power of stories is, perhaps, the highlight issue in **"Emma Zunz,"** and it is also the focus of Borges's tribute to psychoanalysis, which extols the genial construct of the unconscious as a wonderful story-making machine. We see this on the levels of plot and of narration alike: while Borges's ironic narrator wonders "how to make credible" the stories which he lures us in and out of, his colleague Emma, an equally gifted storyteller, demonstrates the ingenuity of a joint intertextual effort whose authors are herself, Borges and Freud. The point of the story, let me specify, is the wonderful way in which Emma manages to impose her Freudian fantasies and fantastic stories on reality, subjecting it to her own needs by way of mastery and wish-fulfillment. Hers is a story of "the perfect crime": a plotted murder covered up by an effective alibi which enables her to act out her forbidden oedipal wishes and come out clean. Through cunning manipulation of both the external and her own, internal reality, she succeeds, like Fate, Borges's authorial alter-ego, in subjecting the reality principle to the pleasure principle and to that which lies "beyond" it, while rationalizing it effectively to herself as well as to others. Her remarkable imposition of her stories on reality impresses Borges's narrator, who comments on the absurd credibility of her alibi story to the police which "impressed everyone" (169; the literal meaning of the original Spanish: "se impuso a todos" [1989, 568] is "*imposed itself* on everyone"). However, this ironic *finale* is but a retrospective reference to the ironic structure of the story as a whole as a story which deals not only with the ultimate credibility of the lies one tells others, but also with the incredibility of the apparent truths—or fantasies—which one tells oneself. This "compromise formation"—a sophisticated manipulation of the genial Freudian construct—embodies not only the happy possibility of fulfilling one's criminal wishes away from the eyes of consciousness as well as the police, but also the subtle wish of realizing one's secret desires without even knowing it.

Notes

1. Eduardo Muller, a review of "Conferencias inéditas de Borges: a review of *Borges en la Escuela Freudiana de Buenos Aires*" in *La nación* (Buenos Aires), 15.8.1993 (my translation).

2. I wish to give credit to Joseph Chrzanowski for his pioneer Freudian interpretation of the story, "Psychological Motivations in Borges' 'Emma Zunz.'" (1978).

3. Grinor Rojo associates "the dilemma of the feminine Oedipus" in the revenge tale of "Emma Zunz" with the Electra complex, drawing on Kristeva's psychoanalysis of Sophocles' *Electra* as a case of a sublimation of incestuous sexuality achieved through the avenging daughter's appropriation of the "Name of the Father" (Kristeva 1974, 36). He points out the suggestion of such paternal identification in the similarities between Emma's name and her father's two names, Emanuel Zunz and Manuel Maier (with its double m) (103).

4. Clearly, I agree with Bella Brodzki that "Borges would take issue with any effort to 'unearth' a text's sedimented symbolic meaning towards the end of solving its mystery by using psychoanalytic methods." He nonetheless "reinforces the reader's desire to do so," Brodzki claims, as part of his strategy of "[undermining] the concepts of authoritarian fictions," which consists in "guiding the reader by constantly posing alternatives, leaving their traces, and offering new, alternative strategies for these alternatives (337n, 345, 343).

5. Rojo's essay suggests that the validity of the narrator's psychological "story" is relativized by its analogy to Emma's story, which is also an interpretation of an ambiguous "pre-text" (and "pretext"!), the ambiguously "blurred" lines of which are signed by one Fein *or* Fain (Rojo 97). This line of suspicion based on analogy can be taken even further if we follow once again the text's hermeneutic clue of double displacement, which might lead us beyond Fein and Fain, to "feign" (an association which also occurred to Hall [261]). Could it be that someone *feigned* the letter announcing the death of Emma's father, because she would *fain* have it true? Extended to the psychoanalytical narrative which suggests it, this interpretation falls in line with the general association of letters with feigning ("fiction, inauthenticity and deception" [261]) in Borges's story, on which Hall, Rojo and others center their interpretations.

6. I am grateful to Ruth Fine for pointing out to me this ironic displacement of one unconscious by another, and for referring me to Borges's following, somewhat perplexing account, in an interview, of his use of anti-Semitic stereotypes in "Emma Zunz." In answer to a comment about the infernal aspect of Emma's adventures, Borges said: "The whole atmosphere about this story is atrocious. A mediocre atmosphere. Even the name, isn't it? *Emma Zunz.* I deliberately chose an ugly name. I put in a Jewish name so that the reader would accept this story, which is a little strange. So that the reader might think: 'Well, these things can happen among Jews'. Had I put in López, the reader would not have accepted the story. He would accept *Emma Zunz,* though, which seems a little far away" (Carrizo 234 my translation).

Works Cited

Borges, Jorge Luis. *Labyrinths.* Translated by D. A. Yates. Edited by D. A. Yates, and James Irby. Harmondsworth: Penguin, 1978.

———. *Obras Completas.* Buenos Aires: Emecé, 1989.

———. *A Personal Anthology.* London: Pan Books, 1972.

Brodzki, Bella. "'She was unable not to think': Borges' 'Emma Zunz' and the Female Subject." *MLN* 100:2 (March 1985): 330–47.

Carrizo, Antonio. *Borges—El Memorismo* (conversaciones de Jorge Luis Borges con Antonio Carizzo). México: Fondo de Cultura Económica (Colección Tierra Firme), 1982.

Chrzanowski, Joseph. "Psychological Motivations in Borges' 'Emma Zunz.'" *Literature and Psychology* 28 (1878), 100–104.

Freud, Sigmund. "Beyond the Pleasure Principle" (1920). In *The Pelican Freud Library,* translated and edited by James Strachey. Harmondsworth, Penguin, 1985, vol 11.

———. "Obsessive Actions and Religious Practices" (1907). In *The Pelican Freud Library,* 1986. vol 13.

Hall, J. B. "Deception or Self-Deception? The Essential Ambiguity of Borges' 'Emma Zunz.'" *Forum for Modern Language Studies* 18:3 (1982), 258–65.

Kristeva, Julia. *Des Chinoises.* Paris: Editions des Femmes, 1974.

Laplanche, J. and Pontalis, J. B. *The Language of Psychoanalysis.* London: The Hogarth Press and The Institute of Psychoanalysis, 1983.

———. "Fantasy and the Origins of Sexuality." *International Journal of Psychoanalysis* 49 (1968).

Ludmer, Josefina. "Las justicias de Emma." *Cuadernos hispanoamericanos* 505–507 (1992) 473–80.

Rojo, Grinor. "Sobre Emma Zunz." *Revista Chilena de Literatura* 45 (Nov. 1994) 87–106.

David Laraway (essay date 1999)

SOURCE: "Facciones: Fictional Identity and the Face in Borges's 'La Forma de la Espada,'" in *Symposium,* Vol. 53, No. 3, Fall, 1999, pp. 151–163.

[*In the following essay, Laraway considers the implications of Borges's strategy of moving between first-and third-person narration in "The Mark of the Sword."*]

A scar, as Homer knew long ago, is more than a distinguishing mark that permits one to be identified: it is the promise of a story to be told. Upon Odysseus's return to Ithaca, his old nurse Eurykleia, without yet recognizing her master, prepares to bathe his feet. Richmond Lattimore's translation renders the ensuing scene in these words: "Now Odysseus / was sitting close to the fire, but suddenly turned to the dark side; / for presently he thought in his heart that, as she handled him, / she might be aware of his scar, and all his story might come out" (*Odyssey* 19.388–91). Not only does Odysseus's scar elicit the story of his own identity; it will later give rise to Erich Auerbach's ambitious telling of the story of mimesis in the Western literary tradition (3–3). Of course a scar may also be a mark of fame or infamy, a sign of pains inflicted, pains suffered, or both. As Daniel Balderston has observed, the scar is an inherently ambiguous sign (68).

The primary function of the scar in Homer is the facilitation of a moment of *anagnorisis,* or recognition, in which the identity of the hero is disclosed. But such recognition scenes need not appeal to any corporeal criteria of identity to acquire their force. Indeed, Aristotle considered revelations of identity based on external tokens such as scars ultimately inferior to discoveries that emerge naturally in the unfolding of a narrative's internal logic. In his view, the *anagnorisis* of Oedipus provides the example par excellence of how recognitions should be effected in a well-

executed literary work (*De Poetica* 1454b19–455a21). Material signs, Aristotle claims, are incapable of expressing the same logical necessity as that displayed by a carefully crafted narrative. They are paralogistic, encouraging an interpreter to engage in fallacious reasoning in order to make the identification in question.[1] Whatever the virtues of Homer's famous homecoming scene, Aristotle would nevertheless detect a blemish in the weaving of the fiction itself, the introduction of a *deus ex machina* to advance the plot by external means when a more suitable internal mechanism is unavailable (1455a16–1).

Of course when Aristotle maintains that external criteria of identification are not constitutive of narrative necessity and offer but a poor substitute for it, he is concerned with identification as a literary phenomenon and not a metaphysical one.[2] For him, physical marks of identification ultimately threaten to cancel the mimetic effect that a literary work should produce. Borges, an able defender of Aristotelian literary theory in many respects, arrives at a similar conclusion but regards scars and other such tokens as invitations for a deeper interrogation of the pretensions of literary mimesis than anything Aristotle had envisioned. Borges's tacit critique of mimesis in his fiction raises the possibility that literary and philosophical modes of identification may not be sharply delineated, as it might at first appear, and that external tokens of identification such as the scar are structurally analogous with fictional discourse in general.

Though it by no means occupies a unique position among Borges's works, **"La forma de la espada"** provides a telling study of the complex relation between material signs of identity and the workings of internal narrative necessity, and thereby provides a suitable point of depature for the questions at hand.[3] From the opening line, the story announces the pivotal role the scar is to play as a distinguishing facial feature. "Le cruzaba la cara una cicatriz rencorosa," the narrator reports, "un arco ceniciento y casi perfecto que de un lado ajaba la sien y del otro el pómulo" (*Obras* 1: 491). If, as Donald McGrady has suggested, the story belongs to the detective genre because "its object is to discover who committed a certain crime" (149), here we would seem to have a first clue. But as a hint for identifying a key player in the drama—and at this early stage it is unclear whether the scar belongs to the perpetrator of a crime or a victim—it is a curious one, because the narrator shows little interest in identifying its possessor by name: "Su nombre verdadero no importa" (491).[4] At any rate, it is clear from the outset that the question of its bearer's identity is to be broached only by means of the scar. The distinguishing mark is not an accidental feature of its bearer, as it was in Odysseus's case. Indeed, it would be more appropriate to say that the bearer is to be identified solely in reference to the scar: **"La forma de la espada"** is, in an important respect, as much the story of the scar as the story of the protagonist ostensibly identified by it.

The tale on one level admits of a relatively straightforward telling. The primary first-person narrator, known simply as

"Borges," finds himself obliged by inclement weather to spend the night at La Colorada ranch, and in the course of his conversation with *el Inglés,* the ranch's owner, he happens to mention his host's distinctive scar. After some initial hesitation, *el Inglés* agrees to tell the tale under one condition: "la de no mitigar ningún oprobio, ninguna circunstancia de infamia," a caveat whose importance only later becomes clear (491–92).

The warning is significant, for the tale that follows examines not only the theme of betrayal, but also an intimate relationship between treachery and the elaboration of fictions in general. According to *el Inglés*'s telling of the story, a zealous young Communist named John Vincent Moon had taken up the cause of Irish nationalism and associated himself with the narrator and his comrades in the fight for independence. Suffering from "una cobardía irreparable" (493) and mortified by the prospect of hand-to-hand combat alongside his comrades, Moon remains in an unoccupied house, idly strategizing while exaggerating the effects of a minor wound. On one occasion, however, the narrator unexpectedly returns and overhears Moon making arrangements for his colleague's capture while securing guarantees of his own safety. Pursuing the traitor throughout the house, the narrator manages to slash Moon's face with a sword before being apprehended by the British soldiers that had been summoned.

At this point the embedded narrative breaks off, prompting "Borges" to inquire as to Moon's eventual fate. *El Inglés,* in turn, makes his own identity explicit with regard to the tale:

> —¿Usted no me cree?—balbuceó—. ¿No ve que llevo escrita en la cara la marca de mi infamia? Le he narrado la historia de este modo para que usted lo oyera hasta el fin. Yo he denunciado al hombre que me amparó: yo soy Vincent Moon. Ahora desprécieme.
>
> (495)

This reversal of identities—with the attendant ethical questions it raises—is by any account striking, and it is fitting that the morally ambivalent status of the protagonist/narrator has long received the attention of critics.[5] A divided soul, Moon's narrative appears on the one hand to exonerate him through the performative aspects of confession while on the other to indict him anew for the crime; indeed, his guilt may even be compounded by the deception he has practiced on his audience, the readers of **"La forma de la espada"** as well as "Borges." As a result, the reader is confronted with a question as apparently unanswerable as it is unavoidable. As John Sturrock puts it, "should we admire [the narrator] or despise him all the more for the expertise of his deception?" (179).

Any possible response to the inquiry must hinge in part on the narrative stance Moon adopts as he begins to tell his story. The most obvious indication of this transition in the text is, of course, verbal: the first-person voice that had previously belonged to "Borges" is now assumed by Moon.

But Moon's narrative is not framed solely by the shift from the grammatical first person to the third. The attention of his audience is initially directed toward the countenance of the speaker at the outset of the embedded narrative.

The bodily nature of this parenthesis becomes evident as Moon's tale is introduced. "Borges's" reference to the scar serves not only as a tacit invitation for his host to take up the role of storyteller; it also brings about a visible transformation in his interlocutor. Upon mention of the distinguishing mark, *el Inglés*'s face immediately takes on a nearly indecipherable expression: "La cara del Inglés se demudó; durante unos segundos pensé que me iba a expulsar de la casa," the narrator reports (491). Only gradually does the tempest of emotion in his countenance subside, and, as if finally consenting to let the truth be told, *el Inglés* assumes, in effect, a straight face—his "voz habitual"—preparatory to the telling of his story (491).

The conclusion is similarly marked. Hearing his interlocutor's request to elaborate on its obscure ending, the protagonist's reaction is no less physically expressive in its closing of the narrative frame: "Entonces un gemido lo atravesó; entonces me mostró con débil dulzura la corva cicatriz blanquecina" (494).

It would certainly be curious if the inclusion of these details were but an empty rhetorical device, a gesture toward realism from a writer who was swift to criticize excesses in mimetic representation. Instead, the description of Moon's passionate response to the burden of his tale might better be regarded as a sublimation of the tension between the voluntary and the involuntary, an indication of an agonic relationship between the speaker's intentions and his physical presence, as embodied in his countenance and the timbre of his voice. The contrast between the transformation of Moon's visage and the ordinary tone of voice that he assumes in narrating his story is the contrast between competing impulses toward truthfulness and dissemblance.

The philosophical itinerary of this idea in Borges's works may be traced back at least as far as the essay "El truco," published in *El idioma de los argentinos* (1928). In his analysis of the traditional Argentine card game, Borges draws important connections between fiction, the voice, and the face:[6]

> La habitualidad del truco es mentir. La manera de su engaño no es la del poker: mera desanimación o desabrimiento de no fluctuar, y de poner a riesgo un alto de fichas tantas jugadas; es acción de voz mentirosa, de rostro que se juzga *semblanteado* y que se defiende, de tramposa y desatinada palabrería.
>
> (28)

The game's appeal is thoroughly corporeal: by controlling the tone of the voice or making the expression of the face resistant to analysis, successful players are able to exploit their opponents' natural tendency to conjecture about their intentions based on bodily cues. In short, they are led to engage in the sort of paralogistic reasoning that Aristotle would criticize. Talented players are endowed with observational skills more powerful than their opponents' ability to master their own bodies and voices. By positing a gap between voluntary and involuntary bodily movements, astute players are able to "read" their competitors physically. Bodies and intentions are locked in a struggle for control: to play *truco* well is to exploit this opposition. In the case of **"La forma de la espada,"** to posit a gap between intentions on the one hand and their outward tokens on the other is at the same time to raise the possibility of exploiting that gap. Everything hinges on whether Moon's interlocutor is able to detect the tension between Moon's designs and his presumably involuntary facial expressions.

It may not at first be clear why Moon affirms that the narrative strategy he has adopted is necessary if "Borges"—and, by extension, the reader of **"La forma de la espada"**—is to hear the tale through to the end. The story is shocking enough—all the more so when we realize that the narrator is himself the villain—but surely squeamishness on the part of his audience cannot explain why Moon feels obliged to adopt a third-person perspective in its telling.[7] In light of his confession, we must take up a set of intertwined questions regarding the nature of the narrator's explicit self-identification as the story's protagonist as well as the relationship between self-identification in general and the narrative stances adopted in the telling of the story.[8]

The scar is the sign that transacts the passage from the primary to the embedded narrative and back again. The defining feature of the protagonist's physiognomy as well as of the story's plot appear to be the ultimate guarantor of its bearer's identity. Much as Odysseus's scar served as a uniquely identifying physical trait for his nurse Eurykleia, Moon's scar is an external token by means of which his identity is disclosed to "Borges" and the reader alike. But if Odysseus's scar could become an occasion for a learned excursus on mimesis—opening up a world, in Auerbach's words, of "externalized, uniformly illuminated phenomena" (11)—Moon's scar conceals as much as it reveals. **"La forma de la espada"** therefore weaves together these points: the face is the site where identity is disclosed, and its ostensibly pre-discursive character opens the possibility of deception or fraud, even as it appears to underwrite credible discourse.

One of the primary problems the story addresses is how the scar may be regarded both as an identifying mark of a particular fictional character and as a mark of what might be called an absence of character, provided this latter term is understood in all its moral and literary valences. Here is where the lines between self-disclosure and the duplicitous nature of narrative are most tightly drawn. Mary Louise Pratt's brief but insightful discussion of **"La forma de la espada"** brings these threads together in light of speech-act theory. In her view, the story's primary interest lies in its violation of the communicative maxim to avoid speaking falsely precisely in order to speak the truth: a know-

ingly deceptive speech act is embedded within a truthful one (192–193). The efficacy of Moon's confession is predicated upon the persuasiveness of the internal narrative.

In retrospect, it seems possible that an astute reader may have identified Moon with *el Inglés* well before the moment of his full disclosure.[9] Nevertheless, as McGrady has noted, "if we are sincere with ourselves, each of us will probably be forced to admit that the ending [. . .] did indeed come as a surprise the first time we read the story" (146). As an empirical claim, this may well be true. But it does not go far enough in capturing what John Irwin, in a different context, has referred to as "the sense of the mysterious" that we may discern in the story, especially given that the tale, insofar as it partakes of the conventions of the analytic detective genre, should logically exhaust its meaning in its resolution (2).[10] The real issue is not whether the readers of Vincent Moon's story are sufficiently adept at picking up clues to guess the secret relationship between narrator and protagonist before the story's end (and, correspondingly, whether Moon's self-explicit identification is superfluous). More to the point is Borges's framing of the problem of discerning between truthfulness and dissemblance. Unlike the mark that identifies the epic hero, in **"La forma de la espada"** the scar is not a self-interpreting sign, for not until the story's conclusion is the identity of the narrator fully disclosed, and then it is only done by Moon himself.

Critics who have faulted the text for saying too much, particularly at the moment when Moon reveals his own identity, have failed to appreciate one of the most salient lessons of the story.[11] The physical tokens presented as evidence of Moon's identity cannot be self-interpreting: their meaning must be narrated explicitly. The very nature of his infamy and its disclosure is such that he alone is able to do so. This, in part, must be the significance of the claim that his story could not have been told otherwise than it has been (*Obras* 1: 495). The nature of his offense both necessitates and undermines confession. To communicate fully a story of betrayal, one must be capable of betrayal in kind. The suggestion is unmistakable, if still obscure in the details: the continual threat of deception is somehow endemic to faces and fictions alike. How can the relationship between the two be clarified?

The problem may be brought into sharper relief by considering the aspirations of the pseudoscience of physiognomy in the later eighteenth and early nineteenth centuries.[12] Hegel devotes a number of pages of his *Phenomenology of Spirit* to the discipline's theoretical underpinnings, and even though its institutional prestige was short-lived, the issues physiognomy raised endure even now in other guises.[13] In his discussion of the various stages of the history of self-consciousness as reason, Hegel examines the claims of physiognomy in its attempt to discover law-like correlations between the observable characteristics of a human face and a given set of otherwise unobservable psychological states. In its attempt to correlate the occult essence of an individual human being—including one's intentions and desires—with its tangible manifestations, reason, Hegel maintains, is led to posit a distinction between the inner and the outer. Physiognomy attempts to codify scientifically the relation between the two:

> Physiognomy [. . .] considers specific individuality in the *necessary* antithesis of an inner and an outer, of character as a conscious disposition, and this again as an existent shape, and the way it relates these factors to each other is the way they are related by their Notion; hence these factors must constitute the content of a law.

> (188)

Hegel does not deny that we frequently bring to bear details of a person's appearance—including their visage—in judging their intentions, desires, and so forth. He is interested rather in historicizing and thus criticizing the tendency to seek causal connections between psychological states and facial expressions. As one might expect, he takes a dim view of the project. He observes that physiognomy misconceives facial characteristics and other external phenomena as signs referring to corresponding internal entities. The problem is not that such a relationship could yield nothing better than contingent or arbitrary associations; it would be mistaken in positing a crude metaphysical dualism in the first place. As Hyppolite puts it in his commentary on the *Phenomenology,* this formulation of the problem is already fatally flawed in that it presupposes "a pure exterior and a pure interior each distinct in its own right" (268).

The Hegelian criticism of physiognomy suggests a pair of related difficulties that Borges thematizes in **"La forma de la espada."** First, if we abandon traditional dualisms with their division of labor between pure interiorities and pure exteriorities, we must be prepared to provide other criteria by which persons may be individuated. That is, if the connections between intentions and external means of communicative expression—faces, voices, bodies, words—are neither causal nor arbitrary, their relationship must be accounted for in other terms. Furthermore, one must account for the frequent failure of intentions to be directly expressed by means of outward appearances or signs. It would appear that, as Michael Emerson observes, "speech and action fail as outer expressions of the inner because they express the inner and internal both too little and too much," and it is not immediately clear with what the traditional accounts are to be replaced (139).[14]

Hegel's solution to the problem is to deny that either supposed interiorities or external signifying mechanisms can be properly considered in isolation. Individuals, rather, are distinguished through their deeds, which are not so much combinations of discrete, observable physical phenomena as they are actions already essentially invested with meaning in a determinate historical context. Moreover, words typically inform and shape those deeds, supplementing them with, in effect, a contemporaneous self-narrative. Hegel puts it this way: "This is the speaking presence of the individual who, in expressing himself in action, at the same time exhibits himself as inwardly reflecting and contemplating himself, an expression which is itself a movement" (195). In this same spirit, he approvingly cites the following dictum of Lichtenberg, intended to undercut physiognomy's explanatory pretenses: "'Suppose the physiognomist ever did take the measure of a man, it would only require a courageous resolve on the part of the man to make himself incomprehensible again for a thousand years'" (191). In its broadest outlines, Hegel's account is not at all out of harmony with contemporary work being done on these and related problems: we are much more likely today to affirm that the meaning of human expression is located neither in any *a priori* interior realm, nor in a world of indifferent physical phenomena, but is rather constituted through complex webs of actions and narratives.[15]

Consistent with the contours of Hegel's thought, Borges dramatizes in **"La forma de la espada"** the failure of the inner/outer model with respect to physiognomy and fiction alike, but he undercuts the primacy Hegel would accord to deeds in individuating the self. Hegel believed that a proper account of human action demonstrates that the "outward" expressions of "inward" psychological states are always realized in concrete historical circumstances, and this fact suffices to individuate persons without resorting to either a purely physical or a purely psychological set of concepts. Borges, for his part, idealizes and then brings up short the capacity of individuating deeds to remedy the failure of the dualistic model, suggesting instead a profound skepticism with regard to the integrity of the self in its first-person character. Where Hegel would reduce skepticism to a transitory moment in the history of self-consciousness, Borges regards it as a defining characteristic of fictional narrative itself.

In Borges's stories, the primacy of action—including its narrative component—in individuating the self typically takes the shape of a privileging of courageousness, often in view of a character's already determined destiny. Whereas **"La forma de la espada"** may not be so forthright in dramatizing its protagonist's resolve as several of Borges's other texts,[16] it is nevertheless clear that Moon's telling of his story is meant in part to own up to his treachery, initially with reluctance and finally with an almost overbearing insistence. Returning again to the insights of speech-act theory laid out by Pratt, we are prepared now to recognize the import of Moon's confession. It is an illocutionary act, welding deed to narrative and dramatizing the protagonist's courage in its telling. It is not difficult to see what significance Moon would wish to associate with his disclosure. An act of confession would, by its very nature, be undertaken with a view to achieving some measure of redemption, no matter how small or fleeting. The tangible mark of Moon's infamy, forever engraven upon his countenance, would become, if not a quasi-religious stigma, at least a complex sign: a token of contrition as well as deceit.

But this exculpation of the first-person narrator is precisely what **"La forma de la espada"** will not allow. If the story

Moon tells in proffering his confession would be an individualizing deed—a speech-act not only presupposing the agency of its utterer but in a sense guaranteeing it—the narrative itself collapses the first-person voice of the confessor into an impersonal, third-person voice of uncertain ownership. For Hegel a courageous deed might individuate persons by inscribing their "genuine being" (Hegel 194) into observable behavior—thereby making their "inner" qualities legible—in a way that the pseudoscience of physiognomy was incapable of grasping. In Moon's case, however, his confession effectively dis-individuates him, condemning him to a kind of metaphysical anonymity.

Given the complexity of the questions I have touched on, it is not surprising that many critical discussions have turned on the ontological significance of the story's mode of narration. Gérard Genette, for instance, regards **"La forma de la espada"** as a paradigmatic case of narrative transgression, finding the concealment of the first-person narrator in the third-person narrative a move toward a more general disintegration of character typical of modern literature. I mentioned earlier his conclusion, which he states with panache: "The Borgesian fantastic, in this respect emblematic of a whole modern literature, does *not accept person*" (Genette 246–47).[17] Genette may well be indulging here in a bit of hyperbole—the question of personhood in Borges's work is considerably more nuanced than he seems prepared to acknowledge—but his declaration draws support from a crucial passage in the text. Recalling his revulsion at discovering Moon's cowardice, the narrator goes on to explain:

> Me abochornaba ese hombre con miedo, como si yo fuera el cobarde, no Vincent Moon. Lo que hace un hombre es como si lo hicieran todos los hombres. Por eso no es injusto que una desobediencia en un jardín contamine al género humano; por eso no es injusto que la crucifixión de un solo judío basta para salvarlo. Acaso Schopenhauer tiene razón: yo soy los otros, cualquier hombre es todos los hombres, Shakespeare es de algún modo el miserable John Vincent Moon.
>
> (***Obras*** 1: 493)

If Moon's confession is initially offered as a means for clarifying his identity with respect to the scar that marks him, it can only be done if the grammatical first person is effaced by the third. The consequence is a literary embodiment of an avatar of philosophical skepticism, not in its most familiar form in which the subject is taken to be self-grounding while the existence of the world or other minds is held to be dubious, but rather the contrary: the uniqueness of the first-person perspective is itself called into question. By adopting the third-person narrative stance in place of the first-person voice, Moon effectively voids the distinction between the two, and as a result it becomes obscure how, if at all, that distinction is to be regained.[18]

The consequences of collapsing the first person into the third in **"La forma de la espada"** are profound. It initially appeared that the scar that marked the face of *el Inglés* was an identifying feature, a tangible sign of his unique identity. But the telling of the story of the scar

could only be undertaken in such a way as to occlude that same person to whom it was thought to refer. The consequence is that the form of the tale itself embodies the same critique of the inner and the outer provided by Hegel but in such a way as to imperil any attempt to secure Moon's identity by virtue of his confession. For Borges, as for the narrator of Conrad's *Heart of Darkness,* "the meaning of an episode was not inside like a kernel, but outside, enveloping the tale which brought it out only as a glow brings out a haze" (Conrad 30).

The tendency of modern narrative to collapse the inner/outer model and to dissolve character into anonymity may be brought into sharper focus by Schopenhauer's very different appreciation of physiognomy's claims.[19] To be sure, his treatment of the pseudoscience is far less rigorous than is Hegel's and (perhaps consequently) far more generous in its appraisal of physiognomy's merits. According to Schopenhauer, our ordinary tendency to seek a correlation between intentions and the defining characteristics of the human face contains the germ of a profound insight: that the studied consideration and application of the tools of physiognomy can in theory insulate us from certain kinds of deception. He writes:

> Moreover, as everyone is anxious to gain for himself esteem or friendship, so will the man to be observed at once apply all the different arts of dissimulation already familiar to him. With his airs he will play the hypocrite, flatter us, and thereby corrupt us that soon we shall no longer see what the first glance had clearly shown us.
>
> (637)

Much as dissimulation is a characteristic strategy employed by the players of *truco*—without it the game would be unimaginable—the interpretation of the human face implies an unavoidable element of risk on the part of the interpreter. To make sense of a face, to attempt to read off from it a set of unobservable motives and desires, one must expose oneself to the possibility of misinterpretation. Furthermore, if we are sometimes liable to be mistaken in judging talent and character, we have no one to blame but ourselves: "For a man's face states exactly what he is, and if it deceives us, the fault is ours, not his" (637).

Though the essay does no great credit to Schopenhauer's analytical skills—especially set alongside Hegel's more nuanced discussion—it does suggest a provocative way of thinking about the relationship between ordinary, off-the-cuff appeals to physiognomic observation and more rigorously philosophical treatments of the issue. "All tacitly start from the principle that everyone *is* what he *looks like*," Schopenhauer notes in that same essay (635). As a bit of folk psychology, the claim is hardly noteworthy, but regarded as a hermeneutic principle, it offers an intriguing perspective on the relationship between faces and fictional discourse. Though naively positing a distinction between the inner and the outer may ultimately prove unacceptable for some of the reasons elucidated by Hegel, it does not follow that one's tendency to seek such a starting point may be obviated simply by being historicized. Following Borges, we might better regard it as a provisional posit, necessary for getting the project of interpretation off the ground, even if it is ultimately forsaken or found untenable.

In this regard, the shared qualities of faces and fictions explored in **"La forma de la espada"** are not fortuitous. As David Cockburn has argued, the face holds a place of the greatest importance for us as human beings, especially with regard to understanding other persons. We take one's countenance primarily to reflect genuine attitudes, held involuntarily, and only secondarily is it understood to aid in bringing off ulterior purposes, including deceptive ones (484–485). Not coincidentally, it is precisely this interpretive presupposition that raises the specter of skepticism that I mentioned earlier. If there are no distinguishing characteristics of truth or identity—no fail-safe way of marking the first person, for example—we would seem to be obliged to accept a thoroughgoing skepticism with respect to the question of personal identity, especially as regarded from the first-person point of view. The dilemma is forcefully articulated in lines well known to every reader of Borges: "Así mi vida es una fuga y todo lo pierdo y todo es del olvido, o del otro. No sé cuál de los dos escribe esta página" (*Obras* 2: 186).

It is a corollary of this form of skepticism that, as **"La forma de la espada"** suggests, if the visage is the site where one's inner being seems to receive its most definitive and most visible articulation, it may nevertheless be sufficiently vague as to preclude any substantial identity claim from being predicated upon it.[20] A consequence of this profound ambivalence—the face as the site where identity is both consolidated and dissipated—is that readers must remain open to the possibility that they themselves are reflected in the text; in a word, that the visage with which the text is concerned is in some respect their own, as the narrator of **"La forma de la espada"** comes to recognize. In this same spirit we may appreciate Balderston's suggestion that the investigation of the theme of treachery in **"La forma de la espada"** transgresses an essential boundary between fictional characters and the story's readers (72).

More than any other aspect of a person's bodily presence, the face is the site where one's identity is made apparent. But not only does the face, like fictional narrative itself, play upon an interpreter's deep-seated propensity to seek meanings hidden beneath the surface; in a number of Borges's texts it also becomes the emblem of a further possibility: an epiphanic moment in which one's own true countenance is glimpsed and recognized, and one finally discovers, as it were, one's own place. In this moment of *anagnorisis* the trajectories of skepticism and self-identification cross. It must fall to a future study to explicate more fully Borges's examination of this possibility.[21]

Notes

1. Terence Cave notes evidence to the effect that in the scholia "Aristotle was said to have criticized [. . .]

the scene where Eurycleia recognizes Odysseus on the grounds that 'according to the poet, by this reckoning everyone who has a scar is Odysseus'" (42).

2. Aristotle's account of personal identity is complex and I shall not attempt to summarize it here. For a discussion of this and related issues, see Terence Irwin 279–302.

3. The scar figures prominently in a number of Borges's texts, beginning with "El incivil maestro de ceremonias Kotsuké no Suké" in *Historia universal de la infamia* (*Obras* 1: 320–323) and culminating in "La forma de la espada" from *Ficciones* (491–495). While in Odysseus's case the scar is found on the hero's thigh, in Borges's stories the scar is typically a feature of the protagonist's face, thematizing an intimate connection between physiognomy and fictional narrative. In addition to the central or defining roles played by facial scars in the texts already mentioned, they also figure in more incidental descriptions of characters from stories such as "El proveedor de iniquidades Monk Eastman" (312) and "El muerto" (545).

4. The narrator's lack of curiosity about the protagonist's real name finds a parallel in the community's lack of interest in identifying with any precision his place of origin: "Todos en Tacuarembó le decían el Inglés de la Colorada" (*Obras* 1: 491). This ambivalence will become symptomatic of identificational difficulties of a different order: first, because the possibility of making a definitive identification by naming the protagonist is dramatically brought up short, even as he finally names himself; second, because his placelessness—an Irishman, taken for an Englishman, having come to Uruguay via Brazil—comes to assume metaphysical proportions.

5. Representative discussions of this aspect of the text may be found in Stabb 49–50 and Shaw 50.

6. It would be difficult to overstate the importance that Borges attributed to the conceit in his formative works. Not only does a poem from *Fervor de Buenos Aires* bear the same title and share a number of expressions with the essay, but the essay was later reprinted, unmodified, along with other miscellany in *Evaristo Carriego* (*Obras* 1: 145–147).

7. Moon's case in this regard bears comparison with that of Otto Dietrich zur Linde, the protagonist of "Deutsches Requiem." Linde nevertheless adheres to his first-person mode of confession in recounting his licensing of the death of David Jerusalem. And, as with Moon, the face is once again regarded as the site of self-identification: "Miro mi cara en el espejo para saber quién soy, para saber cómo me portaré dentro de unas horas, cuando me enfrente con el fin. Mi carne puede tener miedo; yo, no" (*Obras* 1: 581).

8. Balderston rightly notes that the question of Moon's trustworthiness helps to explain why he initially portrays himself as the hero (71); my purpose here is to address the broader question of why this must be so.

9. For a discussion of details that appear sufficient to guide the reader to infer el Inglés's identity with Moon, see McGrady 142–146.

10. Irwin's study of several issues closely related to the ones I address here is impressive, but he omits "La forma de la espada" from his discussion.

11. Shaw, for one, has questioned whether the final lines of the story are necessary at all, suggesting that Moon's explicit self-identification is provided simply "for the benefit of less attentive readers" (50). McGrady likewise wonders if Borges does not deprive "the careful reader of the pleasure of unraveling that problem [i.e., the mystery of the narrator's identity] for himself" (146–147).

12. For a brief sketch of the career and reception of physiognomy, as well as its role in the modern novel, see Tytler.

13. Alasdair MacIntyre, for one, finds successors to physiognomy and its companion, phrenology, in various strands of contemporary philosophical materialism (224–225).

14. Emerson elaborates on the difficulty: "The inner is expressed too much in speech and action because there remains no distinction within them between the inner intention and its outward expression [. . .] But they also express too little of the interiority of the inner because in speech and action the inner motives, reasons, and intentions of the individual are turned into actualities of the world which are different and distinct from the inner. Both speech and action may fail to express and truly represent what is internal to the individual if a particular phrase or action, for example, leads observing reason to ascribe the wrong intention and meaning to the individual" (139).

15. Whether acknowledged or not, many of the insights won by Hegel have since helped to frame contemporary discussions of similar problems. Emerson, for instance, mentions some similarities to Wittgenstein's work in this regard (141–143). For a few general words regarding Hegel's continuing importance for contemporary thought, see Taylor 166–169.

16. This is an issue in Borges that still awaits its scholarly treatment. For a brief orientation, see Wheelock.

17. Others have followed the leads of narratology and structuralism in their interpretations of the text. McGrady's study, for instance, is informed by Genette's work; for a reading informed by Lévi-Strauss, see Weldt.

18. For an engaging study of the philosophical problems of reconciling these perspectives, see Nagel.

19. Though I am aware of no hard evidence that Borges consciously drew from his mentor in this regard, it should be noted that the source of Schopenhauer's essay "On Physiognomy" is *Parerga und Paralipomena,* a text that Borges has explicitly and emphatically acknowledged as a source of inspiration (cf. *Obras* 1: 279).

20. One might bear in mind here the oxymoronic characterization of Arthur Orton's facial features as "rasgos de una infinita vaguedad" (*Obras* 1: 302) or the description of Joseph Cartaphilus in "El inmortal": "Era [. . .] de ojos grises y barba gris, de rasgos singularmente vagos" (*Obras* 1: 533).

21. I owe a special thanks to John Kronik, Debra Castillo, and Joan Ramón Resina for their comments on an earlier draft of this article.

Works Cited

Aristotle. *De Poetica.* Trans. Ingram Bywater. *Basic Works of Aristotle.* Ed. Richard McKeon. New York: Random House, 1941. 7–37.

Auerbach, Erich. *Mimesis: The Representation of Reality in Western Literature.* Trans. Willard R. Trask. Princeton: Princeton UP, 1973.

Balderston, Daniel. "The Mark of the Knife: Scars as Signs in Borges." *Modern Language Review* 83.1 (1988): 67–75.

Borges, Jorge Luis. *El idioma de los argentinos.* Barcelona: Seix Barral, 1994.

———. *Obras completas.* 4 vols. Buenos Aires: Emecé, 1989.

Cave, Terence. *Recognitions: A Study in Poetics.* Oxford: Clarendon P, 1988.

Cockburn, David. "The Mind, the Brain and the Face." *Philosophy* 60 (1985): 477–493.

Conrad, Joseph. *Heart of Darkness.* Ed. Paul O'Prey. Middlesex: Penguin, 1986.

Emerson, Michael. "Hegel on the Inner and the Outer." *Idealistic Studies* 17.1 (1987): 133–147.

Genette, Gérard. *Narrative Discourse: An Essay in Method.* Trans. Jane E. Lewin. Ithaca: Cornell UP, 1980.

Hegel, G. W. F. *Phenomenology of Spirit.* Trans. A. V. Miller. Oxford: Oxford UP, 1977.

Homer. *The Odyssey.* Trans. Richmond Lattimore. New York: Harper Perennial, 1991.

Hyppolite, Jean. *Genesis and Structure of Hegel's Phenomenology of Spirit.* Trans. Samuel Cherniak and John Heckman. Evanston: Northwestern UP, 1974.

Irwin, John. *The Mystery to a Solution: Poe, Borges, and the Analytic Detective Story.* Baltimore: The Johns Hopkins UP, 1994.

Irwin, Terence. *Aristotle's First Principles*. Oxford: Clarendon P, 1990.

MacIntyre, Alasdair. "Hegel on Faces and Skulls." *Hegel: A Collection of Critical Essays*. Ed. Alasdair MacIntyre. Garden City, NY: Doubleday, 1972. 219–236.

McGrady, Donald. "Prefiguration, Narrative Transgression and Eternal Return in Borges's 'La forma de la espada.'" *Revista Canadiense de Estudios Hispánicos* 12 (1987): 141–149.

Nagel, Thomas. *The View From Nowhere*. New York: Oxford UP, 1986.

Pratt, Mary Louise. *Toward a Speech Act Theory of Literary Discourse*. Bloomington: Indiana UP, 1977.

Schopenhauer, Arthur. "On Physiognomy." *Parerga and Paralipomena*. Trans. E. F. J. Payne. Vol. 2. Oxford: Clarendon P, 1974. 634–641.

Shaw, Donald L. Borges: *Ficciones*. London: Tamesis, 1976.

Stabb, Martin S. *Borges Revisited*. Boston: Twayne, 1991.

Sturrock, John. *Paper Tigers: The Ideal Fictions of Jorge Luis Borges*. Oxford: Clarendon P, 1977.

Taylor, Charles. *Hegel and Modern Society*. Cambridge: Cambridge UP, 1978.

Tyler, Graeme. *Physiognomy in the European Novel: Faces and Fortunes*. Princeton: Princeton UP, 1982.

Weldt, Helene. "La forma del relato borgiano: las lecturas circulares de 'La forma de la espada.'" *Symposium* 45 (1991): 218–227.

Wheelock, Carter. "Borges, Courage and Will." *International Fiction Review* 2 (1975): 101–105.

FURTHER READING

Bibliographies

Foster, David William. *Jorge Luis Borges: An Annotated Primary and Secondary Bibliography*. New York: Garland, 1984, 328 p.
    Scholarly in its depth and comprehensive in its range.

Loewenstein, C. Jared. *A Descriptive Catalogue of the Jorge Luis Borges Collection at the University of Virginia Library*. Charlottesville and London: University Press of Virginia, 1993, 254 p.
    Provides "reliable information about the origins and development" of Borges's texts.

Biography

Woodall, James. *Borges: A Life*. New York: Basic Books, 1997, 333 p.
    Contains comprehensive information about Borges's life and works.

Criticism

Balderston, Daniel. "Borges, Averroes, Aristotle: The Poetics of Poetics." *Hispania*, Vol. 79, No. 2 (May 1996): 201–07.
    Explores Borges's postulation of the absolute dependency of language on context for meaning.

Bell-Villada, Gene H. *Borges and his Fiction: A Guide to His Mind and Art*. Austin: University of Texas Press, 1999, 325 p.
    A handbook useful for understanding Borges's place in literature.

Friedman, Mary Lusky. *The Emperor's Kites*. Durham: Duke University Press, 1987, 219 p.
    Argues that there is a narrative paradigm or plot beneath the surface of Borges's fictions.

Molloy, Sylvia. *Signs of Borges* Translated and adapted by Oscar Montero. Durham: Duke University Press, 1994, 142 p.
    Drawing on his short stories, analyzes Borges's vision of the relationship between what is personal and what is real.

"The Duel"

Anton Chekhov

The following entry presents criticism of Chekhov's short story "The Duel," first published in 1891. For a discussion of Chekhov's short story "Gooseberries" (1898), see *SSC*, Volume 28. For an overview of Chekhov's short fiction, see *SSC*, Volume 2.

INTRODUCTION

Chekhov is considered the most significant Russian author of the literary generation to succeed Leo Tolstoy and Fedor Dostoevski. Preeminent for his stylistic innovations in both fictional and dramatic forms, he is revered for his depth of insight into the human condition. While Chekhov's most characteristic writings began in extremely personal feelings and observations, their ultimate form was one of supreme emotional balance and stylistic control. It is precisely this detached, rational artfulness that distinguishes his work from the confessional abandons of Dostoevski or the psychological fantasies of Nikolai Gogol. This artistic control makes Chekhov one of the masters of what has come to be a well-defined modern style of story-writing, and his works have been widely influential, especially among English and American writers. Representative of his mature work in the genre of short fiction, his story "The Duel" offers a skeptical view of Tolstoy's ideas and displays a highly effective and innovative approach to short-story structure and technique as it recounts the life of a "superfluous man" living in a Black Sea port in the late nineteenth century.

PLOT AND MAJOR CHARACTERS

"The Duel" takes place in a seaside town of the Caucasus and opens with the discussion of two friends, Ivan Andreitch Laevsky, an idle 28-year-old, and Alexandr Daviditch Samoylenko, an army doctor. Laevsky explains his troubles with his mistress, Nadyezha Fyodorovna, a married woman who has been living with him for the past two years. Recently, Laevsky received a letter informing him that Nadyezha's husband had died. Now, faced with the possibility of marrying her, he has determined that he is no longer in love and wishes to run away to Petersburg. That evening Samoylenko dines with Dr. Nikolay Vassilitch Von Koren, a willful zoologist studying marine fauna in the region, and Pobyedov, a young deacon. During their conversation Von Koren expresses his dislike for Laevsky, viewing him as depraved and corrupt. A few days later Laevsky, Samoylenko, Von Koren, Nadyezha, and several

others attend a picnic in the mountains. Some tensions are aroused at the gathering, but Nadyezha passes the day in a light-hearted mood. Afterward, Von Koren remarks to Samoylenko that Laevsky's mistress should be returned to her husband and observes that society would be bettered if Laevsky himself were destroyed. Meanwhile, Laevsky reveals to Nadyezha the news of her husband's death. The following day Laevsky asks Samoylenko for several hundred rubles, in order that he might pay his debts and depart for Petersburg. The doctor agrees but explains that he will have to borrow some of the money himself. He approaches Von Koren for the rubles, but the zoologist flatly refuses upon learning that the money will go to Laevsky. Von Koren later changes his mind, on the condition that Laevsky be urged to take Nadyezha with him. On a subsequent visit to Samoylenko, Laevsky encounters Von Koren in his friend's drawing room. The two argue and Von Koren proposes a duel to settle their differences. An enraged Laevsky accepts. As the day of the duel arrives, an ashen-faced and fearful Laevsky appears. He offers an apology, which Von Koren denies. Von Koren aims his pistol at Laevsky's forehead, but does not kill him. Three months pass. Von Koren is now leaving the region, but before he goes he pauses to see Laevsky, who is now married to Nadyezha. The two men shake hands, and Von Koren makes his way to a departing ship.

MAJOR THEMES

Critics of "The Duel" generally see the work as Chekhov's dramatization of the superfluous man in nineteenth-century Russian society. An idle, neurasthenic drinker and card-player, Laevsky is viewed as a socially degenerate figure, and an inauthentic hero who rejects the world, seeking to flee from his problems. Nevertheless, most commentators see Laevsky as an individual who is reformed by the close of the story, having found his salvation in the realization of his love for Nadyezha. He is contrasted with Von Koren, a hard-headed, rational, moralistic, and unsympathetic scientist. The duel itself is perceived as the culmination of the ideological tensions personified by these two characters, particularly between a Spencerian notion of "survival of the fittest" represented by Von Koren, and a Christian view of redemption through suffering at work in the figure of Laevsky.

CRITICAL RECEPTION

Scholars have noted that Laevsky and Von Koren both have ideological precursors in Chekhov's 1887 drama *Ivanov*. Despite certain similarities to earlier figures, however, many critics have praised the psychological depth and complexity of Chekhov's characterization in "The Duel," as well as the work's atmospheric and symbolic depiction of an enclosed, almost claustrophobic Black Sea port. Also of principal interest to critics, the juxtaposition of religious and scientific modes of thought in "The Duel" has been studied in light of nineteenth-century theories of evolutionary degeneration. Such theories have been applied to Laevsky as a representative of the Russian upper-class, whose degenerate qualities are thought to be countered by his moral reform at the close of the story. Other critics of "The Duel" have noted that the work represents a reaction to the views of love, marriage, and aristocratic life expressed in the fiction of Leo Tolstoy, particularly in his "Kreutzer Sonata." Still other commentators have further emphasized the highly allusive nature of "The Duel" and have noted influences from Tolstoy's works, the Bible, and from the writings of Herbert Spencer, Charles Darwin, Mikhail Lermontov, Aleksandr Pushkin, and others in the story.

PRINCIPAL WORKS

Short Fiction

Pestrye rasskazy 1866
Nevinnye rechi 1887
Rasskazy 1889
The Black Monk, and Other Stories 1903
The Kiss, and Other Stories 1908
The Darling, and Other Stories 1916
The Duel, and Other Stories 1916
The Lady with the Dog, and Other Stories 1917
The Party, and Other Stories 1917
The Wife, and Other Stories 1918
The Witch, and Other Stories 1918
The Bishop, and Other Stories 1919
The Chorus Girl, and Other Stories 1920
The Horse-Stealers, and Other Stories 1921
The Schoolmaster, and Other Stories 1921
The Cook's Wedding, and Other Stories 1922
Love, and Other Stories 1922

Other Major Works

Ivanov [*Ivanoff*] (drama) 1887
V sumerkakh (novel) 1887
Leshii [*The Wood Demon*] (drama) 1889
Chaika [*The Seagull*] (drama) 1896
Diadia Vania [*Uncle Vanya*] (drama) 1899
Tri sestry [*The Three Sisters*] (drama) 1901
Vishnevyi sad [*The Cherry Orchard*] (drama) 1904
Plays (dramas) 1912
Neizdannaia p'esa [*That Worthless Fellow Platonov*] (drama) 1923

CRITICISM

Beverly Hahn (essay date 1977)

SOURCE: "The Duel," in *Chekhov: A Study of the Major Stories and Plays*, Cambridge University Press, 1977, pp. 178–205.

[*In the following excerpt, Hahn describes "The Duel" as "novelistic" in form and method, explores its theme, and compares the work to the fiction of Tolstoy.*]

> But life is never a material, a substance to be moulded. If you want to know, life is the principle of self-renewal, it is constantly renewing and remaking and changing and transfiguring itself, it is infinitely beyond your or my inept theories about it.
>
> (Boris Pasternak, *Doctor Zhivago*, Chapter 10 (London: Collins, 1958), p. 373).

The second great work to emerge from Chekhov's highly complex reaction to Tolstoy is **"The Duel"** (1891). In his letters Chekhov calls it a 'novel', and it is indeed one of the most novelistic of his works. To begin with, it has [. . .] an unusually wide range of fully developed characters. Apart from Von Koren and Laevsky, there are three other characters—Nadyezhda, the deacon and Samoylenko—who are created in some psychological depth, and there are a number of minor figures as well. The interaction of these characters is also unusually volatile: their temperaments and their particular situations interact to cause decisive changes in one another's lives, although at all times throughout the story we are made to feel the unpredictability of the result. Finally, the very motion of the narrative in **"The Duel"** might be described as novelistic, since its situations develop in a fluid way, not returning upon themselves as they tend to do in the more static settings of the early stories, including even **"Easter Eve"** and **"Lights"**. Chekhov now seems to be letting his understanding move through a range of situations and characters with a sense of confidence that an order in his art will spontaneously emerge. I do not mean that the development is not (in one way) planned: the basic conception of the duel itself ensures that Chekhov will have a firm line of conflict to develop and resolve, between Von Koren and Laevsky. But as if in reaction to that highly programmed quality increasingly evident in Tolstoy's work, whereby both "The Death of Ivan Ilych" and "The Kreutzer Sonata" begin with an outcome and move backward through a rigid line of causes, Chekhov seems more and more impelled to immerse himself in his materials and to direct them gently from point to point to test where they might go. In **"The Duel"** he has developed a special milieu for the narrative events: the highly sensuous and yet also lethargic environment of a Black Sea port, with its leisurely sense of time, which itself seems to encourage an unusual fluidity in human relationships and events. But the unusual spirit of the story derives less from these effects of its setting than from the new sense of freedom and confidence, and a cautious optimism about life, which have now entered Chekhov's work. Of course, the conditions in the story are special, and no general deductions can be made from them; but in tracing the process of Laevsky's salvation from its unlikely beginning through to the point where he adopts his 'new life' at the end, Chekhov has affirmed his faith in a crucial human possibility. He has let his art do what he envisages life as having done in Laevsky's case: put itself at the service of just a chance—almost, it seems, of a miracle—and then gently nurtured that chance until it slowly assumes a life and probability amid circumstances which seemed initially hostile to it. Moreover, in affirming this possibility of life conspiring, as it were, on its own behalf, Chekhov traces the events in Laevsky's life with such ease that the reader is readily convinced that, at least within the story's special circumstances, events could just as easily take this benevolent direction as not.

Behind at least some elements of **"The Duel"** is Chekhov's reaction to Tolstoy's "The Kreutzer Sonata". Chekhov's letter . . . says that he found "The Kreutzer Sonata" stimulating while obviously marred by prejudice.[1] Pozdnyshev is Tolstoy's conception of a reformed man; Laevsky is Chekhov's. Pozdnyshev's reformation seems to have come about through some cathartic effect of his violence

in killing his unfaithful wife. Laevsky is saved (such is Chekhov's basic faith in life) by his suddenly renewed love for Nadyezhda when he discovers her infidelity and sees in it the reflection of his own ruin, and by the experience of facing the violence of the duel from which he is rescued by the deacon's impetuous shout. Tolstoy's case seems to have interested Chekhov sufficiently for him to wish to take up similar interests in his own art, an art which inevitably modified or even transformed them. I think, for example, that the disproportionate space devoted to Nadyezhda's thoughts and feelings in **"The Duel"** comes from Chekhov's concern for what was omitted from Tolstoy's account of Pozdnyshev's wife: the account of her state of mind when she reaches out from an apparently barren and even hostile relationship to some new form of romantic love. Tolstoy, at this stage, was beyond a sympathetic appreciation of individual psychologies: in "The Death of Ivan Ilych" and "The Kreutzer Sonata" his moral purpose is such that his characters' fates, and even their supposedly private thoughts and feelings, are ultimately less personal than exemplary. Perhaps understandably, then, Chekhov's reaction seems to have been to determine to understand his characters more warmly and individually, and to do so at least partly for understanding's sake. Nadyezhda is actually less directly instrumental in bringing about Laevsky's salvation than Von Koren or the deacon or Samoylenko—though what brings about his salvation is larger than any of them. Nadyezhda's essential passivity in the major events means that she does not earn the amount of interest Chekhov shows in her; but in the context of Chekhov's reaction to "The Kreutzer Sonata", the careful and sustained realism with which he accounts for her reactions is explicable and probably even called for.

More generally, Nadyzhda's presence in the story and the account of her response to the 'soft waves' and the warm air show Chekhov's valuing of sensual experience, which is again in contrast to Tolstoy's withering asceticism in his artistic old age. **"The Duel"** sets out, first of all, to capture the particular atmosphere of a Black Sea port in the Caucasus, with its sultry heat and anaemic palms and its changing sensual stimuli at different times of day. As evocation of a hot climate it surely equals—if it does not actually surpass—Conrad's much-praised descriptions of Sulaco in *Nostromo*. And as in *Nostromo* the portrayal of the landscape is inseparable from the definition of the author's major preoccupations, as in this description of Nadyezhda's state of feeling:

> The long, insufferably hot, wearisome days, beautiful languorous evenings and stifling nights, and the whole manner of living, when from morning to night one is at a loss to fill up the useless hours, and the persistent thought that she was the prettiest young woman in the town, and that her youth was passing and being wasted, and Laevsky himself, though honest and idealistic, always the same, always lounging about in his slippers, biting his nails, and wearying her with his caprices, led by degrees to her becoming possessed by desire, and as though she were mad, she thought of nothing else day and night. Breathing, looking, walking, she felt nothing

but desire. The sound of the sea told her she must love; the darkness of evening—the same; the mountains—the same . . . And when Kirilin began paying her attentions, she had neither the power nor the wish to resist, and surrendered to him . . .

Now the foreign steamers and the men in white reminded her for some reason of a huge hall; together with the shouts of French she heard the strains of a waltz, and her bosom heaved with unaccountable delight. She longed to dance and talk French.

(II. 42–3)

The warm, close nights and the murmur of the sea make the setting potently romantic, well suited to Chekhov's interest here in portraying sexual desire and a desire for romantic love. Similarly, the sultriness, and the pace of life so different from that in Petersburg, are associated with listlessness and possible boredom, thus intensifying the essential inertia of Laevsky's and Nadyezhda's life, which Chekhov portrays as typifying the situation of certain intellectuals in his day and of certain members of the privileged class. The long, fluid first sentence of the quotation—'The long, insufferably hot, wearisome days, beautiful languorous evenings . . .'—with its leisurely syntax, is simultaneously defining a quality of the climate and the quality of Nadyezhda's life; and her desire is so intimately bound up with the special atmosphere of the landscape, the foreign steamers and the shouts of French which suggest the freedom and adventure of faraway places, that it is impossible to say which is putting a particular interpretation on which. The warm air and soft waves ensure that bodily sensations have an unusual force, but it is the psychology of her general relationship with Laevsky which directs her desire towards Kirilin and the imagined men at the ball. So although the story as a whole is critical of such a romantic conception of love—we remember Samoylenko's speech to Laevsky about the great thing in marriage being patience and duty, and the quite unromantic final image of Laevsky's and Nadyezhda's renewed love—this definition of Nadyezhda's state of mind has a certain warmth of understanding.

This drawing-out of qualities inherent in the characters' personal lives by setting them in an environment which intensifies them is an essential part of the story's method—except that with Laevsky himself the understanding is initially much less willing. In his case, the atmosphere of the resort intensifies our sense of his idleness and lack of energy or purpose, but it does not explain his disposition even to the extent that the romantic elements of the landscape explain Nadyezhda's. He has left Petersburg in the hope of a better life in the South, and now he wishes to leave the South for a better life in Petersburg. In fact, he is suffering from an acute form of that spiritual malaise, so common in the characters of the later drama, which expresses itself as alienation from one's immediate environment. In that sense there is little real interaction between Laevsky's feelings and the created setting, except that his physical reaction to the heat gives some credibility to Chekhov's physical portrait of him, which otherwise might

seem too contrived. His perspiring face and the signs of his insomnia of course help to define his psychological state:

Laevsky grew pensive. Looking at his stooping figure, at his eyes fixed dreamily on one spot, at his pale, perspiring face and sunken temples, at his bitten nails, at the slipper which had dropped off his heel, displaying a badly darned sock, Samoylenko was moved to pity.

(II. 11)

As the images somewhat single-mindedly suggest, Laevsky is caught in a self-perpetuating lethargy, the physical and mental conditions of which are at most reinforced by the sultriness of the environment. Frequently, in fact, the climate, with the sticky closeness of the heat, acts simply as a correlative for his debilitating self-absorption: never does it actually elicit an imaginative response from him. His relation to it is entirely negative, while against it his imagination asserts a counter-image of the cold North:

Hurrah for freedom! One station after another would flash by, the air would keep growing colder and keener, then the birches and the fir-trees, then Kursk, Moscow . . . In the restaurants cabbage soup, mutton with kasha, sturgeon, beer, no more Asiaticism, but Russia, real Russia. The passengers in the train would talk about trade, new singers, the Franco-Russian *entente*; on all sides there would be the feeling of keen, cultured, intellectual, eager life . . . Hasten on, on! At last Nevsky Prospect, and Great Morskaya Street, and then Kovensky Place, where he used to live at one time when he was a student, the dear grey sky, the drizzling rain, the drenched cabmen . . .

(II. 17–18)

But while Chekhov himself obviously has a feeling for the North and a patriotic love of the emblems of the national life, the implication here is directly critical, in a way that the description of Nadyezhda's response to the waves, the warm air and the snatches of French from the men in white on the foreign steamer is not. Here the environment is obviously idealized and (despite the particularity of some of the detail) has something of the quality of an intellectual construct, rather than of an actual place. Furthermore, if the lives in this story are to have a positive outcome (the story progressively makes us feel), the attraction of that landscape in Laevsky's mind must be gradually negated by positive forces—forces he initially resists and resents—which are unique to his particular environment in the South.

"The Duel", then, anticipates *Three Sisters* in imaging Laevsky's escapism in geographical terms—first his flight to the South and then his wanting nothing but to return to the pure life in Petersburg. Laevsky himself is also a type of the 'superfluous man' whom Chekhov had portrayed in *Ivanov* and whom many writers see as the dominant type, though in more subtle form, in the late plays. It is true that in this story one can feel, in embryo, some of the basic conceptual elements of those plays. But, as I have said, the development of character in **"The Duel"** is essentially novelistic; and, in contrast to the situations of the characters in *Ivanov* or the later *Three Sisters,* the closing-in of the immediate environment around Laevsky is in fact what saves him. Laevsky, like Ivanov, is conceived quite deliberately as a 'type'. He might even be a stereotype, were it not for the fact that he *knows* that the part he is acting is stereotyped and uses even that knowledge to rationalize and confirm what he is and does. He does not merely evade but continuously rationalizes his evasion of the difficulties and responsibilities of living a different kind of life. For example:

> 'I know very well you cant help me,' he said. 'But I tell you, because unsuccessful and superfluous people like me find their salvation in talking. I have to generalize about everything I do. Im bound to look for an explanation and justification of my absurd existence in somebody else's theories, in literary types—in the idea that we, upper-class Russians, are degenerating, for instance, and so on. Last night, for example, I comforted myself by thinking all the time: "Ah, how true Tolstoy is, how mercilessly true!" And that did me good. Yes, really, brother, he is a great writer, say what you like!'
>
> (II. 6)

The supposed self-analysis here simply lets us know the characteristics of the type we are dealing with, confirming them in the act of enumerating them. Laevsky's explanation of why he is talking quite shamelessly of his private life to Samoylenko is an excuse for going on doing so; and just as he reaches the telling near-sarcasm of his recounted reaction to Tolstoy—where the analysis might really begin to take effect—he instinctively retreats into direct praise of Tolstoy, presumably for so 'mercilessly' capturing his type. Such literature 'justifies' his existence by making him feel that such types as he are fated to be, that his symptoms are those of the age, and therefore that there is no point in trying to rectify them.

It is clear, then, that Laevsky can be of no real help to himself. His efforts at self-analysis ('knowing himself') come to nothing until the night before the duel, because until then he analyses only what he can afford to analyse—past, not present, self-deceptions:

> 'My God!' sighed Laevsky; 'how distorted we all are by civilization! I fell in love with a married woman and she with me . . . To begin with, we had kisses, and calm evenings, and vows, and Spencer, and ideals, and interests in common . . . What a deception! We really ran away from her husband, but we lied to ourselves and made out that we ran away from the emptiness of the life of the educated class . . . Alien people, an alien country, a wretched form of civilization—all that is not so easy, brother, as walking on the Nevsky Prospect in one's fur coat, arm-in-arm with Nadyezhda Fyodorovna, dreaming of the sunny South. What is needed here is a life and death struggle, and Im not a fighting man. A wretched neurasthenic, an idle gentleman . . . From the first day I knew that my dreams of a life of labour and of a vineyard were worthless.'
>
> (II. 7–8)

Apart from the obvious point that Laevsky is now really running away from Nadyezhda and not from the collapse of his ideal, there is the self-deception and futility of his running anywhere if he cannot escape himself. And escaping himself would mean escaping that facile and debilitating conception of himself as 'a wretched neurasthenic, an idle gentleman' which allows him to remain so purposeless and irresponsible and thus gradually to slip into a mire of laziness and deceit. For there are signs that Laevsky actually could be better than he is, that unconsciously his indolence and irresponsibility are a strain even to him. Not only is he self-critical within limits (though the limits, as we have seen, are severe), but his nerves seem to be continually frayed—and not, as he thinks, from the frustration of his attempts to get away, but actually from inner self-dissatisfaction and half-recognized feelings of guilt. This exacerbation of Laevsky's nervous state culminates in his fit of hysterics and then, more overtly, in his fit of temper at Samoylenko's, which leads to the challenge and the duel. In both scenes it is the shame of feeling his moral shabbiness exposed that motivates the nervous reaction, rather than any simple feeling that he is physically trapped into remaining with Nadyezhda. In any case, his dissatisfaction with Nadyezhda is really also dissatisfaction with himself—which is one of the reasons why she can do nothing to bring about the needed change in him. Now and then in the relationship between Nadyezhda and Laevsky Chekhov makes us feel parallels with Anna and Karenin; he cannot resist such Tolstoyan effects as Laevsky's irritation at the carefully arranged curls on the back of Nadyezhda's neck and at the angle of her head when she reads. But the emotional situation which Chekhov develops between them is actually a further and possibly even stronger development out of that intense Tolstoyan realism. For one of the important insights of the story concerns the way Chekhov has Laevsky's developing self-hatred express itself as an aversion to the woman who shares his mode of life. Disliking himself, Laevsky feels irrationally annoyed that Nadyezhda continues to accept him, and his aggression is thus directed against what is specifically sexual about her—that is, specifically feminine things like her curl-papers, her powders and medicines, and the fevers she suffers because of her 'female complaint'. The effect is to make us newly aware of the irrational (but, in retrospect, fairly common?) process by which personal dissatisfaction and self-dislike may express themselves as aversion to one who is sexually close, and aversion specifically to the small indicators of his or her different sex.

How, then, is such a man as Laevsky to be redeemed? In considering this, **"The Duel"** becomes directly involved with differing theories of morality—particularly the Christian as against the Darwinian conceptions of the appropriate relationship between strong and weak. So as well as the basic temperamental opposition between Laevsky and Von Koren, the puritanical zoologist (an opposition which can at times seem over-schematic), there is a wider philosophical dispute embodied in the story, between the Christian and scientific theories. Significantly, the theories are not in pure form: they are shown as particular characters hold them and are therefore complicated by factors of temperament. Chekhov is not arbitrating between the two views but testing their viability in terms of the kinds of temperaments they attract and the kinds of behaviour to which they may give rise. This is so even during the open argument between Von Koren and the deacon in Part 16:

> 'The moral law, let us suppose, demands that you love your neighbour. Well? Love ought to show itself in the removal of everything which in one way or another is injurious to men and threatens them with danger in the present or in the future. Our knowledge and the evidence tells us that the morally and physically abnormal are a menace to humanity. If so you must struggle against the abnormal; if you are not able to raise them to the normal standard, you must have strength and ability to render them harmless—that is, to destroy them.'
>
> 'So love consists in the strong overcoming the weak.'
>
> 'Undoubtedly.'
>
> 'But you know the strong crucified our Lord Jesus Christ,' said the deacon hotly.

(II. 123)

The deacon obviously is not strong in argument and expresses his convictions only by the emotional way he reacts. Intellectually, he relinquishes the argument to the more intelligent Von Koren by uncritically accepting Von Koren's basic terms and definitions, and his persuasiveness as a theoretician is not enhanced by his infantile sense of humour which can suddenly distract him at almost any point. Moments later Von Koren (and Chekhov too, fleetingly) will react with a sense of comic delight to the deacon's refusal to attend the duel because he is in a 'state of grace'—he who so delights in calling Laevsky and Nadyezhda the 'Japanese monkeys' and whose laughter explodes in the hall after seeing the scene of the challenge to the duel. Von Koren, on the other hand, speaks consistently with a callous deliberation which makes nonsense of his supposed 'love' of the race. His acceptance of the notion of some innate moral law, according to which some species must be systematically destroyed, also runs directly counter to the true Darwinian conception of natural selection. In effect, he has incorporated into Darwinian theory elements from Spencer and Nietzsche which accord with his arrogant, puritanical and somewhat sinister temperament and with what seems to be a natural bent for destruction. His argument thus depends on the fallacies that physical and moral strength are synonymous and that the process by which natural and unconscious organisms are physically perfected is analogous to that by which human beings might attain moral perfection. The story, in its entire development leading up to Laevsky's reformation, exposes these fallacies; but the deacon is not sharp enough to perceive them, and at the theoretical level the argument for the destruction of Laevsky seems to carry the day.

Considering what Chekhov valued in "The Kreutzer Sonata," he too seems to want his work to be a stimulus to thought. The fact that the theories are complicated or even altered in presentation by aspects of character does not hinder the reader's intellectual excitement in engaging with them, especially in the urgency of the story's created circumstances. In any case, they give a theoretical framework to our understanding of why some things in the narrative are as they are—for example, why Samoylenko is, apart from being delightful, of such importance. It is the novelist in Chekhov who has created Samoylenko so lovingly and in such detail as a good-natured, self-satisfied man with an inoffensive love of ceremony:

> When, bulky and majestic, with a stern expression on his face, he walked along the boulevard in his snow-white tunic and superbly polished boots, squaring his chest, decorated with the Vladimir cross on a ribbon, he was very much pleased with himself, and it seemed as though the whole world were looking at him with pleasure. Without turning his head, he looked to each side and thought that the boulevard was extremely well laid out; that the young cypress-trees, the eucalyptuses, and the ugly, anaemic palm-trees were very handsome and would in time give abundant shade, that the Circassians were an honest and hospitable people.
>
> 'Its strange that Laevsky does not like the Caucasus,' he thought, 'very strange.'

(II. 14)

Without entering into the depths of Samoylenko's personality, Chekhov immediately creates a warmly affectionate sense of him—enhanced, if anything, by the faint touch of the ridiculous in his self-consciously dignified bearing. His self-satisfaction so generously expands into a basic good will towards the world at large that he makes a very positive contribution to the general morale of those around him and in a way to that of the reader, who finds in him a source of hope and a centre of well-being in what initially seems to be a somewhat blighted context. He also compares more than favourably with those much-celebrated, genial, middle-aged figures in Conrad. But through him Chekhov is also investigating the efficacy of practical and instinctive Christian good will in helping to redeem Laevsky, and in this respect Samoylenko is finally found wanting. His love for his neighbour is too simplistic to cope with the psychological complexities of Laevsky's situation, and he is too intimidated by Laevsky's intellectual pretensions to be appropriately stringent with him. He vastly overrates Laevsky to begin with because he cannot quite separate his sense of people's morality from his sense of their intelligence. And the reason why he cannot really *help* Laevsky is that his love is of a passive and serving kind, which has not sufficient force to combat the kind of psychological deterioration from which Laevsky is suffering.

It might seem at first a very negative thing that the most powerful force immediately evident in the story is Von Koren's hatred and unremitting self-will. In every respect Von Koren emerges as anti-sensuous and anti-life. For example, look at what happens even to the big flowers on his shirt in the opening description of him:

Von Koren was usually the first to appear. He sat down in the drawing-room in silence, and taking an album from the table, began attentively scrutinizing the faded photographs of unknown men in full trousers and top-hats, and ladies in crinolines and caps. Samoylenko only remembered a few of them by name, and of those whom he had forgotten he said with a sigh: 'A very fine fellow, remarkably intelligent!' When he had finished with the album, Von Koren took a pistol from the whatnot, and screwing up his left eye, took deliberate aim at the portrait of Prince Vorontsov, or stood still at the looking-glass and gazed a long time at his swarthy face, his big forehead, and his black hair, which curled like a negro's, and his shirt of dull-coloured cotton with big flowers on it like a Persian rug, and the broad leather belt he wore instead of a waistcoat. The contemplation of his own image seemed to afford him almost more satisfaction than looking at photographs or playing with the pistols. He was very well satisfied with his face, and his becomingly clipped beard, and the broad shoulders, which were unmistakable evidence of his excellent health and physical strength. He was satisfied, too, with his stylish get-up, from the cravat, which matched the colour of his shirt, down to his brown boots.

(II. 23–4)

The dull-coloured shirt with big flowers 'like a Persian rug' gives the effect of something blatant and self-assertive, yet without sensuous appeal and unassociated with liveliness or spontaneity. Moreover, the scrupulously matching cravat, broad leather belt and brown boots give his appearance a Prussian harshness which makes even his physical strength seem slightly sinister. Beyond that, the attitudes in which he is cast are highly stylized, having both the force and the partial crudity of similar kinds of stylization in the conception of Solyony in *Three Sisters*: the strange self-absorption in his contemplation of his own image, the fascinated playing with the pistols and the masterly effect of his silent scrutiny of the old photographs. Such stances are the means by which Chekhov anticipates the cruelty of both characters, in both of whom potentially gregarious energies are tensely indrawn and thus perverted, so that their natures seem to be turned in on themselves, poised for some future explosion of aggression. But Von Koren is potentially even more dangerous than Solyony, because unlike Solyony he is convinced of his infallibility. Part of what is disturbing in his looking at the old photographs is the feeling that he is scrutinizing blemishes, somehow judging with the evolution of the race in mind. And the linearity of his posture and the deliberateness of his aim provide assurance—necessary for the remarkable tension of the later duel scene—that he is not an amateur with his pistols. Even his scientific research is done, Laevsky tells us, in this spirit of defiant self-will and personal arrogance:

'What does he want here?'

'He is studying the marine fauna.'

'No, no, brother, no!' Laevsky sighed. 'A scientific man who was on the steamer told me the Black Sea

was poor in animal life, and that in its depths, thanks to the abundance of sulphuric hydrogen, organic life was impossible. All the serious zoologists work at the biological station at Naples or Villefranche. But Von Koren is independent and obstinate: he works on the Black Sea because nobody else is working there; he is at loggerheads with the university, does not care to know his comrades and other scientific men because he is first of all a despot and only secondly a zoologist.'

(II. 72)

This information comes effectively from Chekhov himself, and we believe it easily because we have already watched Von Koren emphasizing discipline to the deacon, subordinating people to grandiose abstractions in the course of argument, and holding his opinions with a dangerous self-certainty and fixity.

It is important to stress, then, that it is not Von Koren's hatred that reforms Laevsky, either—that his hatred would actually have killed Laevsky had the deacon not distracted him with his horrified cry. Chekhov gives the credit of physically saving this now-valuable life to the Christian ethic of brotherly love represented nominally—and at last actually—by the deacon. Von Koren's hatred is a catalyst to Laevsky's reformation—but his reformation itself is something in which every one of his acquaintances, each event, and even the physical nature of the village where he lives, all mysteriously play a co-operative part. This is where the great originality of **"The Duel"** lies. For we have been used to Chekhov's realism revealing the frustration of people's lives, the cruelty of chance in operating against their hopes, the misunderstandings which rob them of one another's comfort, and so on. His portrayal of these circumstances and reactions as people pursue their separate and conflicting ends may indeed make us feel that realism and pessimism are much the same thing. But it is Chekhov's consistency to his own principles that makes him recognize in **"The Duel"**, and to some extent in the later **"The Lady with the Dog"**, that the same element of chance, the same intersection of people's conflicting personalities and needs, might work the other way around—that is, actually to give fulfilment where one would not expect it. So the unexpectedly optimistic outcome of **"The Duel"** is not the result of Chekhov's suddenly abandoning his usual realism but a natural corollary of it and of his highly developed sense of life's unpredictability. **"The Duel"** offers no guarantee that life will work this way even once in a thousand times; but it could do so, and to acknowledge that possibility matters quite as much as defining a general sense that life habitually does resolve itself less happily. Given all the prerequisites for a pessimistic tale—Laevsky's discontent with his mistress, her infidelity to him, and Von Koren's hatred of them both—Chekhov places his psychological perception and capacity for constructing organically inter-connected events at the service of that occasional benevolence in life itself which somehow survives through, and despite, the more general tragedy of the human condition. Life is seen acting on its own behalf, at least this once, to replenish and in a sense to perfect itself.

The first element in this psychologically significant combination of circumstances and events by which Laevsky is reformed is the very isolation and sense of claustrophobia of the village from which he wishes to escape. The town is not named in the story, and Laevsky says it is not even on the map: there is, therefore, a certain likeness to the constricting self-enclosure of the provincial estates in the plays (one remembers especially the ludicrous irrelevance of Vanya's map of Africa in his study, in *Uncle Vanya*). But though this constriction is unpleasant for Laevsky, particularly since it means that he comes inexorably up against Von Koren's hatred wherever he goes, it does force him eventually to face himself and thus has a positive effect on his life. Laevsky must have none of the comforts of a big city: he cannot simply choose whom to avoid, nor seek the companionship solely of his own kind. He must feel himself to be alone; he must meet Von Koren on nearly every social occasion he attends, must share the same acquaintance and must even depend on him, indirectly, for the money he needs to get away. Only in such uncomfortable—but, as it turns out, propitious—circumstances will Von Koren's hatred, working together with Samoylenko's innocent betrayal of confidences and Nadyezhda's unfaithfulness, act as a catalyst in the reformation of Laevsky's life. The fullness with which the atmosphere of the seaport is evoked and the sense of greater Russia stretching beyond the Caucasus ensure that the environment feels convincingly real. But it is important for the optimistic outcome of the story that life in the town be virtually self contained. Samoylenko simply must go to Von Koren to get money for Laevsky: had he anyone else to go to he might help Laevsky leave his obligations behind and so fail him in a deeper sense. Von Koren is able to taunt Laevsky at the party, to make him shame himself by his fit of hysterics and thus indirectly to prepare for the challenge to the duel, because he has special information from Samoylenko. Likewise, Laevsky is made to see the extent of his own ruin by having it objectified in the sight of Nadyezhda lying beside Kirilin, because Atchmianov knows both men and is jealous of Nadyezhda himself. All the lines of people's lives in this self-enclosed society converge unconsciously towards Laevsky's being brought to recognize, and come to terms with, his life and himself.

I have said that **"The Duel"** is one of the most novelistic of Chekhov's stories. At the same time it anticipates the major drama in many respects. Chekhov's dramatic skills maximize tension through conversations that otherwise proceed with a novelistic sense of leisure and novelistic length:

> Von Koren opened a box and took out a hundred-rouble note.
>
> 'The mole has a powerful thorax, just like the bat,' he went on, shutting the box; 'the bones and muscles are tremendously developed, the mouth is extraordinarily powerfully furnished. If it had the proportions of an elephant, it would be an all-destructive, invincible animal. It is interesting when two moles meet underground; they begin at once as though by agreement digging a little platform; they need the platform in or-

der to have a battle more conveniently. When they have made it they enter upon a ferocious struggle and fight till the weaker one falls. Take the hundred roubles,' said Von Koren, dropping his voice, 'but only on condition that youre not borrowing it for Laevsky.'

(II. 87–8)

The concentration of feeling in the lower voice and terse utterance at the end, the significant and tense postponement of action, and the oblique (but in this case somewhat crude) reference of the monologue to the later duel, are clearly preparatory to recurrent effects in the dramatic work. But, even more importantly, the psychological sequence by which the mental duel between Von Koren and Laevsky becomes a physical one and the tightening of tension which accompanies it clearly anticipate the development (say) between Acts I and III of *Uncle Vanya* or, less directly, the subtle and completely plausible sequence of events in *Three Sisters* by which Natasha eventually takes control of the house.

After the first five parts, in which we meet each character more or less on his or her own terms, all the people in **"The Duel"** are collected together at the mountain picnic. The scene of the picnic will later be the scene of the duel; and, as in the late plays, the change in the dramatic and psychological situation from one occasion to the other is felt through the changed appearance of the scene. However, in this case Chekhov seems over-interested in the directly symbolic properties of this essentially static locale. So apart from conveying a quite legitimate sense of geographical claustrophobia, as the mountains close around the people and the night closes around both, the picnic scenery reveals Chekhov trying to combine literal details and an opportunistic symbolism:

> When in the rapidly falling darkness the trees began to melt into the mountains and the horses into the carriages, and a light gleamed in the windows of the *du-han*, she climbed up the mountain by the little path which zigzagged between stones and thorn-bushes and sat on a stone. Down below, the camp-fire was burning. Near the fire, with his sleeves tucked up, the deacon was moving to and fro, and his long black shadow kept describing a circle round it; he put on wood, and with a spoon tied to a long stick he stirred the cauldron. Samoylenko, with a copper-red face, was fussing round the fire just as though he were in his own kitchen, shouting furiously:
>
> 'Where's the salt, gentlemen? I bet youve forgotten it. Why are you all sitting about like lords while I do all the work?' . . .
>
> On the further bank some unknown persons made their appearance near the drying-shed. The flickering light and the smoke from the camp-fire puffing in that direction made it impossible to get a full view of them all at once, but glimpses were caught now of a shaggy hat and a grey beard, now of a blue shirt, now of a figure, ragged from shoulder to knee, with a dagger across the body, then a swarthy young face with black eyebrows, as thick and bold as though they had been drawn in charcoal.

(II. 56–7)

Such writing is powerfully 'atmospheric'. One feels the characters doubly displaced—from Russia, and then from their village in the Caucasus—as they are drawn into the uncannily enclosed atmosphere of the ravine, amid natural forms made partly menacing by the darkness and among people whom the firelight reveals only as flickering shapes. The familiarity preserved with those we do know—the superb management of Samoylenko's outburst, for instance—almost allows Chekhov to get away with his superfluous 'atmosphere'. But there is a problem of exactly what to make of the surreal effects of the figures on the other bank—the dagger across the body, the thick charcoal eyebrows—and indeed of the heathen overtones of the deacon's ritual round the cauldron. The effects are conspicuous as such, while their meanings are vague. From the fact that there is some incongruous joke lingering around the deacon making fish soup for the multitude, and that his dream of the time when he will be a bishop involves a hierarchically organized religious procession quite opposite from the disorder of the present scene, it can be deduced that this occasion epitomizes something more violent and elemental. On the way to the picnic the carriages have passed the junction of the Black River with the Yellow River, where 'the water black as ink stains the yellow and struggles with it' (II. 52); and we will later be given that image of Laevsky feeling the heat of the campfire on his back and the heat of Von Koren's hatred beating on his breast. The occasion both epitomizes and intensifies the animosity between the two men, preparing the way for their later violence. But the meeting of the Black and Yellow rivers also ambiguously suggests reconciliation, as does the Tartar *duhan* flying the Russian flag; and in that sense the imagery seems to look forward to an end to conflict and thus implicitly to some resolution of the developing confrontation between Laevsky and Von Koren. Furthermore, Chekhov is attending equally to all who are present at the scene, and for all those—like Marya Konstantinovna, Nikodim Alexandritch, Katya, Kostya, the deacon and Samoylenko—who have peace of mind, much of this suggestive 'atmosphere' feels and is irrelevant. As a whole it is an impressive episode, particularly in the definition it gives to Von Koren's aggression and Laevsky's discomfort and developing self-hatred; but its imagery is too strained and ambitious for it to rival the more specific dramatic realism of the later episode at Kostya's birthday party.

From the picnic to Kostya's party where Laevsky has his fit of hysterics to the scene at Samoylenko's house when Laevsky first abuses Samoylenko and then challenges Von Koren to the duel, Chekhov is accumulating tension both within Laevsky himself and between Laevsky and others. The outright challenge comes as a relief both to Laevsky and in the story as a whole; and the storm which follows, that night, seems both to underline that partial sense of release and to anticipate the greater release of aggression and anxiety in the duel the next day. Chekhov makes the storm brilliantly ambiguous in significance: it objectifies the turbulence in men's minds, yet it diminishes our sense of the importance of such emotional storms by its own su-

perior display of might. It forces people apart, as they seek the refuge of their own homes; but in that it seems godlike, directing each to face himself and the implications of what is to happen at dawn:

> Behind them on the sea, there was a flash of lightning, which for an instant lighted up the roofs of the houses and the mountains. The friends parted near the boulevard. When the doctor disappeared in the darkness and his steps had died away, Von Koren shouted to him:
>
> 'I only hope the weather won't interfere with us tomorrow!'
>
> 'Very likely it will! Please God it may!'
>
> 'Good-night!'
>
> 'What about the night? What do you say?'
>
> In the roar of the wind and the sea and the crashes of thunder, it was difficult to hear.
>
> 'It's nothing,' shouted the zoologist, and hurried home.
>
> (II. 129–30)

The roar of the wind interposes itself in the spaces between people, but though the storm feels mighty it does not feel malevolent. To Laevsky, alone in his study after the shock of having Nadyezhda's infidelity revealed to him, it brings a sudden new sense of life as an active agency larger than himself, and a sudden impulse to worship—'Dear storm!' Under its impetus he undertakes that exhaustive Tolstoyan examination of his life which I have already discussed (p. 144). The existence of the storm, with its impersonal drive to cleanse the world by its release of energy, and Laevsky's self-cleansing release of all the suppressed areas of his guilt, in a way both communicate hope. They feel too momentous simply to go to waste in Laevsky's death at the duel—and yet we cannot be sure. By the time the rain has stopped Laevsky has faced fully the consequences of the life he has led, but there is no sign of triumph either in himself or in the world outside:

> Laevsky put on his overcoat and cap, put some cigarettes in his pocket, and stood still hesitating. He felt as though there was something else he must do. In the street the seconds talked in low voices and the horses snorted, and this sound in the damp, early morning, when everybody was asleep and light was hardly dawning in the sky, filled Laevsky's soul with a disconsolate feeling which was like a presentiment of evil.
>
> (II. 135–6)

One feels here the advantages for Chekhov of a mode of directly interpretative commentary learnt, at least partially, from Tolstoy. Laevsky's feelings are expounded for us and not simply left implicit between the lines, as are Tusenbach's feelings in similar circumstances in *Three Sisters*. Tusenbach's speech about the dead tree swaying in the wind is a profoundly moving moment of poetic expansion in the play and is certainly very impressive in combining a strong apprehension of human mortality with an impulse for worship. But the dramatic form of the episode, being restricted to dialogue and external gesture, does not allow a full entering into Tusenbach's state of mind, leaving us to speculate *quite* what that state is and so, in a way, allowing us to have a more accepting sense that he is fated to die. In **"The Duel"**, where we have interpretative access to Laevsky's state of mind, his consciousness seems so full—of dread anticipation, guilt, memories of the past and of his childhood—that it seems, as it seems with Petya Rostov in *War and Peace,* that such fullness could not suddenly die: hence the shock when Petya's consciousness does suddenly cease. The death of Tusenbach does not carry quite that kind of shock, because we do not know him so well. Although there is, then, obviously a danger for an author in attempting to give interpretative definition to such highly complex and untypical states of mind as those before the two duels, it does seem to me that the interpretative narrative in **"The Duel"** is potentially capable of projecting a more genuine, more unbearable pathos in the circumstances than the dramatic scene in *Three Sisters* can manage through speech and gesture alone.

In comparing these two scenes, which have in common the situation of an impending duel, with the seeming certainty of his imminent death weighing on each man's mind, we will also be aware once again of the importance Chekhov ascribes to love as giving value and meaning to life. For whereas Laevsky's despair of finding comfort from any source inside or outside himself is suddenly relieved by his impulsive love for Nadyezhda, and Laevsky lives, Tusenbach pleads unsuccessfully for one word of love from Irena and dies. I think it highly probable, in fact, that Chekhov is far more critical of Irena in that scene in *Three Sisters* than most commentators make out. But the upsurge of love which Laevsky feels and the self-knowledge he has achieved do not, of course, guarantee that he will live. His immediate feeling is still that there is no alternative but death, and he is, at least consciously, resigned to being shot.

Yet in the greyness of this first light Chekhov begins, at first tentatively and then more boldly, to sound a new note of hope for Laevsky's life. It begins with Laevsky's hesitation—his feeling that there is something left to do before he must die. He has not quite taken leave of life, because he has not yet taken leave of Nadyezhda; and in going to take leave of her he actually has his hold on life intensified, first by his pity for the wretched figure as she lies hunched up on the bed, and then by his sudden renewal of love as she speaks of her shame. Something is working mysteriously to preserve and redeem Laevsky, through these perfectly plausible new reactions in new circumstances. So later, when (after we have followed the deacon making his way in secret up the river) Von Koren arrives exclaiming about the sudden peculiar beauty of the dawn light, that too seems obliquely reassuring:

> 'It's the first time in my life I've seen it! How glorious!' said Von Koren, pointing to the glade and stretching out his hands to the east. 'Look: green rays!'

> In the east behind the mountains rose two green streaks of light, and it really was beautiful. The sun was rising.

> (II. 143)

After the turbulence of the night of storm there is the calm of renewal and regeneration in the natural world which seems to prophesy a similar outcome in the human events. Yet this is far from being a facile optimism expressed through the hackneyed dawn symbolism that is part of the stock-in-trade of any writer. The strangely beautiful and sudden apparition of the shafts of light does feel like an impersonal event in nature, with the unexpectedness of such an event: it has not been anticipated by what has gone before, though it seems so in retrospect. It is characteristic of the story as a whole that the pre-conditions for this moment have been carefully laid to make it completely plausible, but there is no sense (as in Tolstoy) of effects being mapped out in the process of preparation. The direction of events always feels fluid, and only on looking back does one see the organic connection between one event and another which makes it almost inevitable that things should happen as they have done. Even the apparition of the light assumes a sure significance only after the duel has been fought without mishap, and it has to wait for its full significance until Chekhov gives us images of a reformed Laevsky at the very end of the story. At the time, Von Koren's response to the rays seems ostentatious, a way of covering nervousness and an indirect manifestation of aggression in the calm he wishes to display before Laevsky. Also, the strangely beautiful colour of the light is ambiguous in suggestion, connected somehow with a sense of imminent catharsis but removed in significance from the blinding white light of revelation. And the spectacle of the light, in Laevsky's immediate response to it, produces only an odd apathy:

> Laevsky felt the exhaustion and awkwardness of a man who is soon perhaps to die, and is for that reason an object of general attention. He wanted to be killed as soon as possible or taken home. He saw the sunrise now for the first time in his life; the early morning, the green rays of light, the dampness, and the men in wet boots, seemed to him to have nothing to do with his life, to be superfluous and embarrassing. All this had no connection with the night he had been through, with his thoughts and his feeling of guilt, and so he would have gladly gone away without waiting for the duel.

> (II. 143–4)

Laevsky's perception of the brightness of the natural world for the first time just when he thinks he has lost it is in essence a Tolstoyan effect, albeit one Chekhov manages again triumphantly with Tusenbach in *Three Sisters*. But Laevsky's feeling that nature's vividness is 'superfluous and embarrassing' is something quite different from what we would find in Tolstoy, an aspect of Chekhov's bleaker psychological realism. It is also impossible that Tolstoy in his late phase could have imagined a light dawning which, at least as the character himself feels it, 'had no connection with the night he had been through, with his thoughts and his feeling of guilt'.

The duel itself is the objective expression of a psychological duel which has reached a point of absolute crisis. It is the occasion of total release of aggression, tension and frustration which have had preliminary release in Laevsky's humiliating fit of hysterics at Kostya's party; and it takes place on the same site as that of the picnic, with most of the same characters assembled. There is no escaping a comparison with the construction of the late plays—where, as Chekhov himself said, his dramatic tensions still seem to want to resolve themselves in a pistol-shot. But the anticlimax of the characters' returning to their carriages, after Laevsky has deliberately missed Von Koren and the deacon has distracted Von Koren from his aim, is accompanied by a sudden relief and expansion in the writing, with the comedy of the deacon's breakfast with the Tartar Kerbalay. The trial of seeing whether a vision that is both realistic and optimistic will work is over. From the whole nature of this new episode it is clear that Chekhov knows that that possibility has been successfully realized in his art; and the sense of triumph communicates itself through the good-humoured exuberance of this comic interlude within the more generally serious framework of the story. Just temporarily, the main concerns of the achievement of human understanding and the reconciliation of differences are translated into the lighter vein of the deacon's misjudged idiom to a man who speaks perfect Russian ('Come to the *duhan,* drink tea . . . Me wants to eat') and their subsequent muddled discussion of their different conceptions of God. The interlude also tactfully provides a space before we turn to Laevsky again.

The images of the redeemed state itself are deliberately few. They are sufficient to make us feel that Laevsky is indeed a reformed man and to suggest the rather bleak mode of life that that reformation actually adds up to. Certainly they make nonsense of the view that Chekhov is a faint-hearted writer who could not go beyond commiseration with doomed, 'superfluous' men: Laevsky is lifted right out of that syndrome by which Chekhov is said to have been so fascinated. But it is a sign of Chekhov's primary interest in the strange *process* of Laevsky's reformation, rather than in the polemics of what constitutes a 'good life', that he does not linger too long with Laevsky and Nadyezhda in their new mode of life. After the picnic, when Laevsky is suffering from a sense of claustrophobia about Von Koren's hatred of him (and, though he does not realize it, from his own self-contempt), he passes on the way to Samoylenko's a lighted passenger ship in the harbour, with the red light of the little Customs boat going out to it. As we read of it, it seems a completely natural and unobtrusive part of the scene, and Laevsky merely envies the passengers their apparent peace of mind. But again, in retrospect, the timing of the ship's coming in is just right (this is the point at which most of the preconditions for the duel have been set); and it gives significance to the ship's departure, carrying Von Koren away, at the end, where there is an explicit symbolism attaching to the little boat heading out to join the steamer through the rough waves:

The boat turned briskly out of the harbour into the open sea. It vanished in the waves, but at once from a deep hollow glided up on to a high breaker, so that they could distinguish the men and even the oars. The boat moved three yards forward and was sucked two yards back.

'Write!' shouted Samoylenko; 'it's devilish weather for you to go in.'

'Yes, no one knows the real truth . . .' thought Laevsky, looking wearily at the dark, restless sea.

'It flings the boat back,' he thought; 'she makes two steps forward and one step back; but the boatmen are stubborn, they work the oars unceasingly, and are not afraid of the high waves. The boat goes on and on. Now she is out of sight, but in half an hour the boatmen will see the steamer lights distinctly, and within an hour they will be by the steamer ladder. So it is in life . . . In the search for truth man makes two steps forward and one step back. Suffering, mistakes, and weariness of life thrust them back, but the thirst for truth and stubborn will drive them on and on. And who knows? Perhaps they will reach the real truth at last.'

'Go-o-od-by-e,' shouted Samoylenko.

'There's no sight or sound of them,' said the deacon. 'Good luck on the journey!'

It began to spot with rain.

(II. 161)

This is more open symbolism than most English writers would risk, a more open exposition of Laevsky's feelings which here seem to bear the burden of Chekhov's feelings also. The story as a whole has worked to ensure that the imagery of the boat's struggle does not feel trite, that the journey metaphor has appropriate weight, and that the cautiously tendered optimism about the boat's reaching the steamer has been dramatically substantiated in the events of Laevsky's life. What exactly it is within the events of **"The Duel"** and the accumulation of tension between Laevsky and Von Koren that is redemptive is never actually said; and the partial mystery of such processes, and the sense that redemption itself is not so much a state as a continuing process, lie behind Laevsky's repetition of the words 'no one knows the real truth'. But by the very nature of its organization the story is optimistic in implying that life can in some cases be self-redeeming—even if the redemption is never quite final—and that it will be so regardless of the various theories of perfectibility advanced by both religion and science.

Note

1. Letter to A. N. Pleshcheyev (Moscow, 15 February 1890), in Friedland (ed.), *Letters by Anton Chekhov,* p. 205.

John Tulloch (essay date 1980)

SOURCE: "The Epic Vision: Nature and the World," in *Chekhov: A Structuralist Study,* Macmillan Press Ltd., 1980, pp. 114–31.

[In the following excerpt, Tulloch interprets "The Duel" in light of evolutionary degeneration theory, and views the conflict between an "ambivalence of false choice" and the story's "epic vision of hope and suffering."]

The inauthentic hero is related to science in a number of stories, but perhaps most powerfully in **"Dreary Story"** and **"The Duel."** I shall concentrate my attention here on **"The Duel,"**[1] prefacing my remarks with the point demonstrated earlier: that for Chekhov medical science was not separable from human science (though science *was* separable, in its methods, from the materialist philosophies of ideologues and reformers).

In **"Dreary Story"** Chekhov showed the dangers inherent in separating the scientific method from its proper concern with the whole man; in **"The Duel"** he demonstrated that the evolutionary vision itself was subject to perversion. Russia, we have seen, was relatively immune to the 'tooth and claw' philosophy of Social Darwinism, but less so to another outgrowth of evolutionary thinking, degeneration theory, which crops up quite frequently in Chekhov's literature.

Degeneration . . . according to the founder of the hypothesis, Morel, was caused by the upsetting of man's natural adaptation to the environment by sudden changes in the external situation. Extending the theory, Max Nordau pointed out that hysteria and degeneration always existed, but only sporadically, and normally had no importance in the life of a whole community. It was the sudden impact of the 'era of discoveries and innovations' which overfatigued the organism and 'created favourable conditions under which these maladies could gain ground enormously and become a danger to civilisation'.[2]

So for Nordau degeneration in its 'epidemic' form was the product of modernisation, and, crucially, it was thought to be transmissable by heredity. The effect of the various disturbances which set degeneration into motion was to produce a nervous disposition, which in the next generation would become neurosis, in the next psychotic breakdown, and finally idiocy and sterility. The theory was therefore both individually fatalistic and socially hopeful. The degenerate breed would die out and society would be purged.

> Degenerates must succumb therefore. They can neither adapt themselves to the conditions of Nature and civilisation nor maintain themselves in the struggle for existence against the healthy. But the latter will rapidly and easily adapt themselves to the conditions which the new inventions have created for humanity.[3]

The influence of Nietzsche is apparent in Nordau's men of will, as it is in the portrayal of Van Koren in **"The Duel."** But much more important from Chekhov's point of view was the systematisation of these ideas within the inner sanctum of *evolutionary* theory, and thence its widespread social acceptance. Degeneracy theory dominated psychiatry for decades, and was extended to the study of genius and criminality by Lombroso, to great artists and thinkers

(including Nietzsche himself) and even to entire races by Nordau. In Russia . . . acceptance of the theory did not include its fatalism. Chekhov was taught to be more concerned with healing possibilities for the individual organism predisposed to degeneration, and with its specific (and mutual) relationship with its milieu, than is evident in Nordau.

Significantly, whenever Chekhov makes a character, particularly if he is a man of science, speak on behalf of the fatalistic variant of degeneration theory, he makes him one-sided, fixed in his opinions, a partial, inhuman man unable to serve others or love wholly. The doctor in **"Nervous Breakdown,"** for example, has forgotten how to feel. He is simply 'polite and frigidly dignified', and able to smile only on one side of his face. Chekhov was probably consciously ironic in this detail, since Lombroso mentioned facial asymmetry and motor anomalies on one side as characteristic of degeneracy: in which case the doctor himself becomes the degenerate! Similarly, in **"Black Monk,"** Chekhov describes his hero's addiction to the ideas of Nordau and Nietzsche as a case of 'mania grandiosa', one of the later stages of mental degeneration, and was careful to detail the familiar *social* pressures which may have caused it.

In contrast to Chekhov, the doctor in **"Nervous Breakdown,"** like the hero's student friends, 'objectively' dislikes prostitution, which means in fact that they all ignore it, its context and its victims. When asked whether prostitution is an evil, the doctor agrees and, fatalistically, ignores the issue. He and the other students speak about the women in 'frigid and indifferent' tones, and to the hero suffering neurotically from his experience, the doctor merely offers therapy—bromide and morphia—to ease a sickness that requires social prophylactics. As a proponent of degeneration theory, he simply pacifies his patients with drugs, and leaves things to fate.

Chekhov's opposition to Nordau was thus not over the theory itself, but over the latter's fatalistic and anti-individualistic reading of it. Nordau, ignoring the possibilities of environmental modification, put all his emphasis on the strong will of the healthy and the certain destruction of the weak. In his book *Paradoxes,* which Chekhov mentions reading, Nordau speaks of the man of genius who will counteract the evils of degeneracy. He will be a man of great will and judgment, rather than feeling or artistic sense. 'He is in no way of the sentimental turn. He gives one on that account the impression of being hard and cold. These words, however, indicate nothing else except that he is purely cognitional and not emotional.'[4]

In **"The Duel,"** Van Koren is, by his own estimation, precisely this man. He is the brutal man of will, totally unsentimental about the harshness of natural selection. He is a ruthless exponent of degeneration theory who bases his feelings in the mind, not in the heart:

> Don't you be hypocritical about that force. Don't defy it secretly. . . . Instead, look it straight in the eye, and submit to its reason and necessity.

'Our love for our fellow men should not be from our hearts, nor from the base of our stomachs. . . . It must be from here!' Van Koren tapped his forehead.

Opposing Van Koren in **"The Duel"** is the neurasthenic Layevskii, who fulfils in every particular Nordau's catalogue of the symptoms of degeneracy: great emotionalism; excessive excitability; feebleness of perception, of will, memory and judgment; inattention and instability. For Nordau the task of the man of intellect and will is to help the healthy in ruthlessly crushing the degenerate breed who endanger civilisation by their example. In *Paradoxes* he speaks of the need to rid society of 'the miserable weakling, whose imbecile brain has not the power to oppose any resistance to his emotions of love',[5] and extends the theory to whole degenerate races which, inexorably, must succumb to the will of Nature in a merciless struggle for existence.[6]

Apart from the racialist extension, every main feature of this philosophy of fatalistic natural selection is evident in Van Koren. Where Nordau speaks of degenerates as 'antisocial vermin',[7] Van Koren talks of a 'diseased, degenerate and feeble breed'. Where Nordau asserts the need to mercilessly crush the degenerate and pitilessly beat to death the 'lusting beast of prey'[8] to protect civilisation, Van Koren affirms the need to remove the lusting erotic maniacs from society:

> Science and our own common sense inform us that mankind is threatened by those who are morally and physically subnormal. In which case we have to fight these freaks. If it's impossible to lift them to the norm, then we've got the ability and power to render them inactive. Frankly, exterminate them.

Where Nordau predicts the extirpation 'root and branch' of weak by strong, and extols killing as the moral right hand of superior peoples marching inevitably to perfection, Van Koren proclaims the moral validity of killing in accordance with the laws of natural selection, a force superior to man and working for his greater humanity:

> There's no more chance of preventing it than of stopping that cloud drifting in from the sea.

Like Nordau, he would agree that 'The prospect here disclosed is a gloomy one, but it cannot terrify the man who has become reconciled to the severity of the universal law of life'.[9]

The point is that in Chekhov's judgment the evolutionist Van Koren is not a genuine scientist at all, but an inauthentic one. Layevskii remarks that Van Koren ignores the significant areas of marine biological research in order to make a name for himself. He rejects the thriving scientific centres on the Mediterranean (which Chekhov himself was very interested in) for the Black Sea, an area extremely poor in marine fauna, simply because he prefers to be 'the leader of a village rather than one of the pack in the city'. Chekhov makes Layevskii's criticism precise to demon-

strate that Van Koren lacks the true scientist's humility: he is 'a despot first of all, and only after that a zoologist'.

Checkov also underwrites Layevskii's description with details of character. We notice that Van Koren is not in the least objective in his treatment of people: like Professor Stepanovich in **"Dreary Story,"** he never analyses their inner feelings. He does not consider the mental and environmental influences which have made Layevskii and Nadezhda what they are, and prefers to regard them as unchangeable objects, condemned to extinction—and the sooner the better. Even when they reform, he does not relinquish his brutal, necessitarian philosophy: it is simply, he feels, that he has chosen the wrong objects for its exposition. Lacking a genuine objectivity and a concern for the individual organism, Van Koren resorts to grand generalisations and talks, in Chekhov's view, as an ideologue would. As Layevskii points out, all his ideals and actions 'are done, not through love of his neighbour, but on behalf of abstractions such as Man, future societies, or an ideal breed of men. He sees it as his task to improve our breed. And in that respect he sees us as mere serfs—cannon fodder or beasts of burden'. Unable to love one other individual being because of his fatalism and his ideological abstractions, Van Koren succumbs to hatred. When he prepares to kill Layevskii his whole figure, for all his commitment to reason against the passions, is 'entirely bound up with hatred and scorn'. Like Kovrin in **"Black Monk,"** Van Koren himself suffers from the 'mania grandiosa' of according to himself the task of purifying the human race—and it has made of him a blind beast of Nature.

In a letter to Suvorin, Chekhov wrote:

> I am sick and tired of all this philosophising, and I read fools like Max Nordau with considerable distaste.[10]

In the place of abstract theorising, Chekhov emphasises in his letter his belief in natural science and the materialistic movement. This is what finally distinguishes his evolutionary vision from that of Nordau, who ignored Mechnikov's warning that science must not sanction the law of might in natural selection but should strive to balance its 'cruel or harmful effects'.

The inhumane man of science made his appearance in Chekhov's work before **"The Duel,"** of course. Critics have often remarked on the continuity of *Ivanov* and **"The Duel,"** since the play's opposition of the ruthless Dr. Lvov and the apathetic neurasthenic Ivanov is reformulated as the central drama of the novella, culminating in an external collision between Van Koren and Layevskii. Deeper continuities than those of characterisation and theme, however, are suggested by the incorporation of Chekhov's 'son of a serf' statement within the text itself in the later work. The years which had passed since the writing of the play seem to have contained an intensification of Chekhov's crisis of literary identity[11]—prefigured in the public reception of *Ivanov* (to which the original 'son of a serf' statement was intimately related), clear in his letters and in his

"Dreary Story" (where he contrasted the inauthentic worlds of science and art), and culminating in his journey to Sakhalin. Chekhov was preparing his book on Sakhalin at the same time that he was struggling with **"The Duel,"** and there is no doubt that he regarded the scientific thesis as more important than the novella. We should remember when analysing **"The Duel"** that *Sakhalin Island* sought to demonstrate that degeneration of human beings—not simply convicts but intellectuals as well—was the result of appalling social and natural conditions. Now, in **"The Duel,"** by choosing a locale which he regarded as especially beautiful and favourable to natural life, Chekhov was emphasising the primacy of bad *social* conditions in causing degeneration. The rather emphatic 'scientific' thesis of **"The Duel"** is certainly connected with Chekhov's personal concerns at this time; and the idle luxury of cards, vodka and women with which Layevskii degrades the beauty of the Caucasus brings to mind another visit which Chekhov made between the Sakhalin expedition and writing **"The Duel"**—his journey to Monte Carlo where 'the roulette luxuriance reminds one of an opulent water-closet. The atmosphere of this place blights one's feelings for decency and somehow makes the scenery, the sounds from the sea and the moon seem vulgar.'[12]

Out of the social and natural inhospitability of Sakhalin and the purely social decay of the Mediterranean gambling town, Chekhov distilled the Caucasus of **"The Duel,"** a place of wondrous beauty to the author, but barren and fearful to the effete Layevskii. And since Layevskii yearned instead for the Russian capitals, Chekhov was concerned to show that life in Moscow and Petersburg was essentially the same. Layevskii's trail of false choices and ruined women began there, his personal and social determinants—aristocratic idleness and brutality—were there; and in bringing Nadezhda to the Caucasus, Layevskii unites local values with those of the capitals. Only the locale and the class of Nadezhda's lovers is different.

The social pattern is the same, and this is also clear in the portrayal of the minor characters; the kind but rank-conscious Samoilenko, the ritual-minded Deacon, the piously moral Mar'ya Konstantinova who likes to abstract men and women into inferiors and superiors, the idle bureaucrats steeped in dishonesty, cards and vodka, the brutal police chief Kirilin. Each demonstrates in his turn the all-pervasive value system and power relations of the ascriptive society.

Sakhalin was probably responsible for a difference of characterisation between the novella and *Ivanov*, where Chekhov had taken the case of a man who was initially far from weak to demonstrate the problem of the intelligentsia in the eighties. In *Sakhalin Island* the underlying implication was that even the most degraded could be saved from degeneration by means of the correct social and natural milieu. This was also the main point of his contention with Wagner at the time he wrote **"The Duel."** So it can hardly be a coincidence that in Layevskii he chose to portray an extremely weak degenerate who finally, in a beautiful location and with the love of a fundamentally good woman, achieves a new liberation.

The fact that Chekhov chose to portray the collision between Van Koren and Layevskii in terms of false responses to science and art suggests that the dynamic of the story was something much more personal,[13] and ambivalent, than the cool portrayal of a degraded world built out of the minor characters. Both these concerns—with false science and with false art—were very much in his mind at the time, as is clear from his two major articles of 1891; one, 'in Moscow', implied the bankruptcy of Russian literary criticism via a character very similar to Layevskii; the other, 'Conjurors', criticised the fraudulently unscientific zoological station of Professor Bogdanov. There are further biographical pointers in Van Koren himself. Like Chekhov he believes that art and the human sciences 'will prove intellectually suitable when they finally become one with the exact sciences'; but unlike his author he rejects the present and the potential of history for fatalistic dogma, believing that 'The entire world will be covered over with a sheet of ice before that comes to pass'. In fact, Chekhov, after Sakhalin, has little sympathy for Van Koren. By rejecting living people in the present, isolating human thought from the herd and, equally, separating human action from evolutionary hope, Van Koren divides the inner man from his environment, and his mind from Nature. For Chekhov, Van Koren is a false scientist, a systematiser.

The central problem of **"The Duel"** is the ambivalence of false choice which in its extreme possibilities embraces both destruction—as typified by the duel itself—and the epic vision of hope and suffering which is evident in Layevskii's final conversion. The impossibility of a third stance—of any mediating or stabilising of this opposition—is suggested by Van Koren when he says:

> Only men who are honest and men who are cheats are able to find solutions in each situation. Anyone who wishes to be both honest and a cheat at the same time will find no solution.

He applies this critique of ambivalence to Layevskii, but essentially it applies to the position of all inauthentic heroes.

Layevskii, too, typifies the fatalism of degeneration theory. Whereas Van Koren stands for the inhuman solutions of a Nordau, and therefore for false science, Layevskii represents the social and psychological *functions*—the hopeless, enervating pessimism—of the theory itself, and its utility in perpetuating a degraded world. Deprived of the will to formulate any coherent identity, Layevskii looks for authenticity via the mediation of some general theory, the search for 'tendencies' which Chekhov rejected:

> I find it necessary to generalise about all my actions. I need to discover the explanation and vindication of my absurd existence in another person's theories, in literary types, in the idea, for example, that we men of the nobility are degenerating.

Like all of Chekhov's inauthentic heroes he rejects the 'banal vulgarity of this life', and seeks to replace it with a succession of quests for something better. Incapable of making life an objective and free enterprise, these characters attach themselves to an adjacent cliché which will quickly pre-empt the need for thought—like Layevskii's model of the superfluous man and his convenient adherence to degeneracy theory. Each one of his 'solutions'—whether involved with saving prostitutes, with art, with the Tolstoyan ideal of labour, or with the 'higher culture' of the capitals—has also been concerned with the division of women between high ideal and base pleasure. So, like Van Koren, Layevskii divides human beings; and each one of his solutions has in fact been a reunion with the traditional Russia he rejects.

His habits incorporate the impedimenta of that society, the 'poshlost' that Chekhov presents through his works. In his drinking, his card playing, idleness, sense of rank, brutality, vulgarity and dirty habits Layevskii himself is part of the 'totality of objects' of a debased society which, through his search, he extends to the Caucasus. The man of intellect but not knowledge sanctions and extends traditional customs, for all his superficial rejection of them; and in the seduction of Nadezhda, in turn, by the intellectual, the brutal official and the merchant the pattern of social evolution is clear. Each inauthentic solution of a false journey carries, as at Sakhalin, the degenerative evolution a stage further.

Near the end, failure itself becomes the source of ideals for Layevskii. As with Masha in **"My Life,"** the act of journeying itself is the ultimate truth:

> He would jump on a train and leave, and so solve the predicament of his existence. Beyond that he didn't think.

It was, after all, the inevitable decree of his fate. Van Koren classifies the dishonesty of this stance:

> 'he smiles bitterly in answer to all my questions and says "I'm a failure, a superfluous man", or, "What can you hope from us, dear chap, the fag-ends of a serf-owning class?" Or, "We're degenerating . . ." . . . The reason for his excessive lust and shamelessness is likewise not to be found in himself, but elsewhere, in a vacuum, outside. By this brilliant trick it is not *this* man by himself who is dissolute, neurotic and base, but *we* . . . "We men of the eighties", "We idle and nervous children of serf-owners, we who have been crippled by civilisation! . . ." In fact we are to understand that a man of Layevskii's quality is supreme even in defeat, that his vice, ignorance and slovenliness constitute a law of evolution, purified by inevitability; that the reasons are universal, natural, and that we should burn a candle to Layevskii as destiny's sacrifice, a victim of his era, a product of his heredity, and so on.'

Van Koren is of course being inconsistent in rejecting Layevskii's appeal to fatalistic laws of evolution and he-

redity while himself rigidly adhering to them in demanding his extermination (and in fact he immediately resorts to degeneration theory after the speech by using Nordau's 'erotomania' concept to categorise Layevskii's preoccupation with women). Layevskii is likewise inconsistent in using the evidence of science, in which he professes not to believe, to clarify the falseness of Van Koren's position. In fact, the 'underground lucidity' of both these men is that of their author. Chekhov makes both of them appeal for identity to the solutions of a false science, and in the light cast by their shrewd perception of each other he presents the audience with an inverted image of something better. The space encapsulated by their dialogue and their duel is that transient point between a human and inhuman evolution.

Like Van Koren, Layevskii contains the potential to destroy. Nordau's metaphor of 'lusting beast of prey' is appropriately applied, since, as Layevskii himself admits, his relationships with people and with nature have always been destructive:

> surrounded by living things . . . he had done nothing but destroy, ruin, lie and lie . . .

In his cruelty to Nadezhda, particularly in his use of a letter containing news of her husband's death, he is as guilty of ignoring her inner feelings as Van Koren. Both condemn her in their way. Neither, until Layevskii's final conversion, show much awareness of the *social* causes of her fall. For both of them she is a weak—and therefore ordained—victim for exploitation and destruction.

So both men are beasts of prey, and Samoilenko's question to the scientist in fact relates each one to the cruel and humanly unmediated process of natural selection which they proclaim:

> He ruins and kills every other creature that gets in his way . . . crawls into other's burrows, destroys ant hills, breaks open snails . . . Tell me, what is the use of this creature? For what purpose was it created?

Van Koren attributes the creation of this blind beast to the cruel but beneficial process of natural selection, thereby, in effect, justifying the position of both himself and Layevskii, each of whom has crawled into others' burrows: Van Koren with the intent to destroy Layevskii, and Layevskii with the effect of destroying Nadezhda's husband. Van Koren goes on to speak of the merciless struggle when two such blind beasts meet, and the theme of the duel is given its real perspective, untouched by humanity or the human mind:

> It is an interesting fact that when two moles meet each other underground they both start creating a platform, as though by common agreement. The platform is necessary for their fight, and when they have completed it, they begin a terrible struggle, which continues until the weaker of the two falls.

The duel of cruel predators is one extreme of the inauthentic search.

But the duel to destruction is only one of the potential resolutions. As Layevskii and Van Koren mark out the ground of that extreme, the principles of humanity and knowledge through suffering are kept alive by Samoilenko and the Deacon, characters who are themselves too trivial and too bound up with the rank and ideology of an ascriptive society to present dramatic alternatives themselves. Their function is, first of all, to comment on the inhumanity of the forces which drive the action on, and second, to confine them so that the ultimate polarisation (and final choice) may occur: Samoilenko ensures that Layevskii does not escape, the Deacon that he does not die. As he prepares to see them fight, as fascinated by their violence as Mar'ya Konstantinova is by Nadezhda's immorality, the Deacon contrasts the easy and elegant childhood the combattants have had with the harshness, poverty and vulgarity of his own, compares their ensuing ignorance of urgent social problems and tendency to intellectual clichés with his own ant's-eye view of them:

> If they had experienced the poverty which had been his lot since childhood. . . . How then they would have reached out to each other, how quickly they would have forgiven each other's failings, how they would have valued the good things in each other! After all, the number of people in the world who were even superficially decent was few enough . . . Rather than being led by apathy or misunderstandings of various kinds, into seeking out degeneracy, heredity, extinction and other incomprehensible things in each other, wouldn't it be far better to look closer to the ground and focus their bitter anger on the places where whole districts are crushed beneath gross ignorance, covetousness, vice, foul language and cries of pain.

The speech is both a challenge to the inhuman fatalism of Van Koren and Layevskii and a clue to their failure. The life of intellect derived from a luxurious upbringing has deprived them of the social contact which Chekhov knew as a zemstvo worker. Hence the popular focus for progress and change is outside their scope. Yet without their intellectual background nothing is possible either, as the trivialised potential of the Deacon testifies.

Chekhov's own mobility synthesised this contradiction: thesis and antithesis are presented with sympathy, but within a structured perspective which is the author's own. If Van Koren accurately points to the stagnation of lowly people like the Deacon who 'see everything through a fog', the latter clarifies in turn the falsity of the zoologist's life, where great expeditions and a powerful mind are betrayed into submission to Nature through lack of faith in men. So 'everything stays as it was': Van Koren's stagnation is merely at a higher level.

But between the scientific brutality of Van Koren and the befogged and helpless cry for humanity of the Deacon a new perspective opens. Layevskii walks from the duel a new man, open to human love and for the first time appreciative of the world and natural beauty. Layevskii's conversion was as logical and necessary for Chekhov as it has

seemed weak and unmotivated to most of his critics. He was anxious to show that even the weakest degenerate could be saved, and having postulated the extreme possibilities of destruction and social concern, he makes Layevskii choose correctly for the first time. The drama is not in the external action of the duel, which Chekhov deliberately makes into an absurd non-event, but in the confrontation of two worlds demarcating the ambivalence of inauthentic choice; or, to put it another way, in the stripping away of false mediators between the only real alternatives of a degenerate or a human evolution.

The problems critics have with Layevskii's conversion tend to be of two kinds: one to do with motivation and the other with verisimilitude. An example of the first kind is presented by Kramer when he complains that the conversion is weak because of the employment of 'exaggeration without any intensity of feeling'. He quotes Eric Bentley's opinion that in drama, 'Intensity of feeling justifies formal exaggeration in art, just as intensity of feeling creates the "exaggerated" forms of childhood fantasies and adult dreams'.[14] It should be noted, in fact, that Layevskii's moment of recognition comes, not at the duel, but after the trauma of finding Nadezhda in bed with Kirilin. His conversion is not the result of a pistol shot, but in the awakening of love and an inner understanding for a woman he has previously treated as a sexual object—a process few critics seem to have found exaggerated in **"Lady with a Little Dog."**[15] This is a moment of enclosure (between discovery of Nadezhda's faithlessness and imminent death in the duel, and between the claustrophobia of his study and the storm outside) when Layevskii summons up, recognises and rejects *his* childhood fantasies and adult dreams.

> There had never been any need for truth. He hadn't even looked for it. His conscience, dazzled by evil and lies, had stayed asleep or kept quiet. Like an alien being, someone from another world, he had kept himself apart from the daily life of men, had been cold to their sufferings, ideas, religious beliefs, knowledge, aspirations and struggles. He had never offered a kind word to anybody, nor had he written anything that was not trivial and banal. He had done absolutely nothing for others, but he had been prepared to eat their food, drink their wine, take their wives, live on their ideas. And to vindicate this parasitic existence to himself and to others, he had always adopted a superior air, as though he was above them. Lies, lies, lies . . .

Separated from men by his own choice, above the world, and lacking any values of his own, Layevskii can find nothing when his search is forced to stop. He recalls the past, and considers the intense innocence of his childhood. But the image of his mother is frightening. He remembers the cruel parent of a brutal son: seemingly an inevitable evolution in his world. If there is no escape in the past there is none in space either; the false intellectual who looks for salvation in Petersburg 'will never find it. The entire world will be the same for him'.

Finally, he recognises that salvation lies in no external place of escape, but in the inner man, in the search for truth with which the quotation above begins, in rejecting the suppression of knowledge with which it ends, in his relations with Nature as he plants trees, and in his relations of love with other human beings. He recognises that there is no future in Samoilenko's naivety, none in the Deacon's inane laughter, none in Van Koren's hatred.

> We have to find salvation in ourselves. If we can't find it there, there's no point in wasting time further. One might as well kill oneself.

The seconds now come to carry him off to the meaningless and inevitable death which his own and Van Koren's fatalism have predicted. But there is another possibility. As he prepares to go, 'he felt that there was somehow something still to be done'; something, of course, of a social nature that he has never done before. He goes to Nadezhda, finds her wrapped helplessly in a rug and looking like an embalmed object—which in effect is what he has made of her. He recognises that 'this wretched, sinful woman was the one person close to him, the one person whom no-one could replace'; and he loves her without mediation for the first time in his life. Women are no longer objects to idealise or degrade: Nadezhda lives at last outside *other* peoples' ideas. Life with Nadezhda now, the text makes clear, will be one of suffering, of hard work and of grinding poverty at the grass roots which the Deacon describes but Layevskii has not known. The suffering, however, is permeated with a new hope, a new will, a 'certain freshness of expression in his face and even in his walk'.

The blind beasts have fought, and as Layevskii watches the scientist leaving on his great expedition, battling through the waves, it is the other potential that he considers:

> That boat is hurled back. It makes two steps forward, and then one back. Yet the oarsmen endure, they row on tirelessly, and are not frightened by the enormous waves. The boat drives on and on . . . In seeking the truth men make two steps forward and then one back. Miscalculations, suffering, and the tedium of life throw them back, but the thirst for truth and a stubborn will drive them on and on. And who knows? Maybe one day they will arrive at the real truth . . .

The perepeteia at the end of **"The Duel"** is by no means arbitrary. What one could call the subtextual sequence which always underlies Chekhov's dominant associative motif 'inauthentic hero rejects the world and is crushed' (the characterisation of Layevskii before conversion) is here made overt: hero, with a vision of knowledge and suffering, will endure. The final physical and mental divergence of Layevskii and Van Koren replaces the blind duel of natural selection with the *individual* man in search of truth. This sequence, of the epic vision, is of course only the opposite of the first by *convention*—or in other words within Chekhov's *own* construction of reality. Which is also an answer to the verisimilitude debate. The conversion is potentially 'lifelike' within Chekhov's *perceived* concept of reality: he had, after all, his whole medical training to tell him it was so.

Notes

1. For an analysis of *Dreary Story*, see J. Tulloch 'Conventions of Dying: Structural Contrasts in Chekhov and Bergman'.
2. See Max Nordau, *Degeneration.* (London: Heinemann, 1895) p. 537.
3. *Ibid.*, p. 541.
4. M. Nordau, *Paradoxes* (London: Heinemann, 1896) p. 176.
5. *Ibid.*, p. 237.
6. *Ibid.*, p. 329.
7. Nordau, *Degeneration,* p. 557.
8. *Ibid.*, p. 557.
9. Nordau, *Paradoxes,* p. 331.
10. Chekhov to Suvorin, 27 Mar. 1894.
11. See Tulloch, *Anton Chekhov,* ch. 6.
12. Chekhov to Mikhail Chekhov, Apr. 1891.
13. For a development of this point, see Tulloch, *Anton Chekhov,* ch. 6, and Tulloch, 'Sociology of Knowledge and the Sociology of Literature.'
14. Karl Kramer, *The Chameleon and the Dream: The Image of Reality in Cexov's Stories* (The Hague: Mouton, 1970) p. 124.
15. As for 'intensity of feeling', perhaps it is wise to recall Chekhov's own struggle with 'childhood fantasies and adult dreams' (and his connection with the despair and suicide of writers like Garshin whose saving 'red flower' had itself been a fantasy) before considering Layevskii's despair. (see Tulloch, *Anton Chekhov,* ch. 6.)

Irina Kirk (essay date 1981)

SOURCE: Irina Kirk, "Search for a Philosophy of Life," in *Anton Chekhov,* Twayne Publishers, 1981, pp. 56–92.

[*In the following excerpt, Kirk discusses plot, character, and theme in "The Duel."*]

"The Duel" was serialized in the periodical *Novoe vremya* in 1891. While Chekhov was writing the story he often met and talked with the zoologist Nikolai Wagner about the survival of the fittest, heredity, degeneration, and other topics which were in vogue at that time. Chekhov's position in these conversations was that the human spirit is capable of conquering the weaknesses of heredity and of overcoming certain character deficiencies. Of course, Chekhov was not speaking in a religious sense when he mentioned the "human spirit," but rather in the existential frame of reference that Albert Camus had in mind in *The Plague* when he wrote, "to state quite simply what we learn in time of pestilence: there are more things to admire in men than to despise." However, this particular story does not portray a great victory of the human spirit. Rather it deals with the kind of modest, unromantic self-knowledge in which man is capable of coming to terms with his own mediocrity, and accepting it.

The editor of *Novoe vremya* proposed that the title of this novelette should be changed from **"The Duel"** to "The Lie." However, Chekhov declined this suggestion replying:

> For my story your title, "The Lie," is not a fitting one. It would have been fitting in a place where the lie is conscious. The unconscious lie is not a lie but an error.

Indeed, Chekhov's story places a much greater emphasis on unconscious self-deception and role playing than on the deliberate lying of his protagonist. Chekhov's intention in this story is to unmask those characters who are evading reality behind the cloak of ideology and whim, and he chooses the central incident of the duel to accomplish this.

The personality conflict between Von Koren and Laevsky is developed from the third chapter of the novelette, and culminates in the nineteenth chapter with the actual duel between the two men. The epiphany which follows the duel and its effects on the characters are dealt with in the last two chapters. It is interesting to note that each of these characters has an ideological predecessor in Chekhov's play *Ivanov* (1889): Laevsky is modeled after the ineffectual "superfluous man" Ivanov, and Von Koren, after the dogmatic, self-righteous Dr. Lvov.

The prosaic opening lines of **"The Duel"** create an atmosphere immediately:

> It was eight in the morning—the time when the officers, local officials, and the visitors usually took their morning dip in the sea after the hot, stifling night, and then went to the pavilion to drink tea or coffee.
>
> (VII, 99)

Chekhov purposely does not begin the first chapter with a description of the majestic mountains or the beautiful sea, but rather he chooses this viewpoint because it accords with his character Laevsky's perception of the scene. Romanticism is further undercut in the next few paragraphs. Laevsky and Dr. Samoilenko are bathing in the sea, discussing Laevsky's hypothetical statement concerning the termination of a love affair, when a wave breaks over both of them.

After dressing and seating themselves in the pavilion, Laevsky and Samoilenko resume their conversation. Laevsky is established almost immediately as either a romantic or a pseudo-romantic by his statement: "We are crippled by civilization" (VII, 101). This cry was first uttered by Rousseau, and was later repeated by the leading art figures of the nineteenth century, including Tolstoi, who wore a medallion with Rousseau's portrait on it from the time he was fifteen years old.

Yet Laevsky proceeds to tell Samoilenko that the dreams he cherished of fleeing from civilization, and the new meaningful life he had envisaged in the Caucasus were all "self-deception." He had dreamed of this romantic ideal with Nadezhda Fedorovna, a married woman with whom he fled to the south, but now after two years he confesses that he has no intention of ever beginning a "life of labor and a vineyard." Moreover, Nadezhda's advanced education and feminine charms no longer have any appeal for Laevsky:

> As for love, I ought to tell you that living with a woman who has read Spencer and has followed you to the ends of the earth is no more interesting than living with any Anfisa or Akulina. There's the same smell of ironing, powder and of medicines, the same curl-papers every morning, the same self-deception.
>
> (VII, 101–102)

To this the doctor replies, "You can't get along without an iron in a household." Obviously Samoilenko has totally failed to understand the disillusioned romanticism that Laevsky is trying to communicate to him, and he responds with advice that is consistent with his own values:

> Love cannot last long. You have lived two years in love, and now evidently your married life has reached the point when, in order to preserve equilibrium, so to speak, you ought to exercise patience.
>
> (VII, 102)

The doctor's philosophy is rather simple: the best approach to an ethico-philosophical problem is to avoid it, to elevate patience above all, and to adopt a role that will not disturb the surface of the established routine.

The placid, prosaic character of the doctor is also conveyed with several other details in the subtext, which portray him much more vividly than the opening descriptive paragraphs. It is mentioned that Samoilenko has never read Tolstoi, and his mundane nature is further underlined by his sensual enjoyment of coffee, cognac, and ice water as he gazes out at the sea, after which he comments, "Remarkably splendid view" (VII, 100).

Nadezhda Feydorovna is first introduced through Laevsky's impression of her in chapter 3. When he returns to their apartment, Laevsky finds his mistress dressed, drinking coffee, and reading a thick magazine. His immediate reaction is that she is deliberately posing before him, and he is enraged by her pretensions. He looks at her neck with aversion, and recalls how in Tolstoi's novel Anna Karenina felt a similar disgust at her husband's ears. Laevsky's identification with Anna is ironical in this instance. It would seem that Nadezhda, who left her husband for Laevsky and very likely might be destroyed by him, would feel a much closer parallel to Anna's position. But there is another, more pervasive irony which runs throughout this chapter. It is only later that the reader learns that Nadezhda Fedorovna herself has become bored with Laevsky, and has already had an affair with the police captain, Kirilin.

In addition to Laevsky's extreme irritation with Nadezhda, chapter 2 also focuses on his desire to escape to St. Petersburg. Laevsky feels that all of his problems would immediately be solved if only he could somehow return to that city: an illusion which will later be echoed in Chekhov's *Three Sisters* called, "To Moscow, to Moscow." The word *bezhat* (to run away) is nostalgically spoken eight times by Laevsky in this chapter, and it repeatedly draws attention to his inability to face reality.

Laevsky is understandably guilt-ridden at the thought of abandoning his mistress, and chides himself that there is no "guiding principle" in his life. He forces himself to be saccharinely polite to Nadezhda, calling her "golubka" (darling) rather than expressing his true feelings. He concludes that his psychological conflicts and indecision are very similar to those suffered by Hamlet. Yet this literary allusion also is not without irony. In chapter 1 Laevsky is described with a sufficient number of mundane details to make a comparison between himself and the lofty, regal Hamlet comic. Laevsky gnaws at his fingernails, shuffles his feet, and wears loose slippers over badly darned socks!

In chapters 3 and 4 Laevsky's ideological antagonist, the zoologist Von Koren is introduced. Von Koren's aggressive personality and his vanity are conveyed in the opening description of him as habitually admiring his swarthy good looks in the mirror, and aiming his pistol at a prince's portrait in Samoilenko's parlor. The latter detail foreshadows Von Koren's role as an instigator in the forthcoming duel.

The dynamics of the conflict between Laevsky and Von Koren are developed in this chapter with the psychological portrait the scientist draws of Laevsky and his brutal reaction to it. Hatred has indeed sharpened Von Koren's appreciation of his opponent's faults, and he is convinced that "To drown him [Laevsky] would be a service." However, Von Koren is careful to justify his personal criticism of Laevsky with that man's negative sociological and genetic influences on other people:

> I should have passed him by if he were not so noxious and dangerous. His noxiousness lies first of all in the fact that he has great success with women and so threatens to leave descendants—that is, to present the world with a dozen Laevskys as feeble and depraved as himself. Secondly, he is in the highest degree contaminating. I have spoken to you already of vint and beer. In another year or two he will dominate the whole Caucasian coast . . . In the interests of humanity and in their own interests, such people ought to be destroyed.
>
> (VII, 115–116)

In chapters 6 and 7 all the characters congregate at an evening picnic where relationships between them are further defined. Von Koren disagrees with and insults Laevsky at every opportunity, and the latter is afraid and embarrassed by this. Nadezhda Fedorovna is in a flirtatious, lighthearted mood, and throughout the chapter there are descriptions of her feelings of flight:

> She wanted to skip and jump, to laugh, to shout, to tease, to flirt . . . She seemed to herself little, simple, light, ethereal as a butterfly.
>
> (VII, 128)

Nadezhda's flighty mood makes her impervious to the threats of her jilted lover Kirilin, whose warning advice to her is: "I venture to assure you I am a gentleman, and I don't allow anyone to doubt it. Adieu!" (VII, 130) She is much more involved in her new interest in Achmianov, the shopkeeper's young and handsome son:

> If she, for instance, were to turn the head of this handsome young fool! How amusing, absurd, wild it would be really! And she suddenly felt a longing to make him love her, plunder him, throw him over, and then to see what would come of it.
>
> (VII, 130)

Nadezhda's mood shifts rapidly when she is upbraided by Laevsky for being a coquette, and she immediately feels "heavy, stout, coarse, and drunk" (VII, 132). This depression deepens when later at home Nadezhda is presented with a letter bearing the news of her husband's death, and she sobs like a child to Laevsky, "What a sin, what a sin! Save me, Vanya, save me . . . I have been mad . . . I am lost" (VII, 134).

However, Laevsky is thinking only of escape, and in his desperation crawls out of a window to seek asylum at Samoilenko's house. He begs his friend for a loan to return to St. Petersburg, and in a shaking voice which recalls Nadezhda's plea to him a short while before he begs: "Save me! I beseech you, I implore you" (VII, 134). Samoilenko agrees to help Laevsky, who, as in the first chapter, reminds him of a "weak, defenseless child."

In the ensuing conversation with Samoilenko, Laevsky weaves between lies and truth, which in his jubilant mood he doesn't distinguish. He declares joyfully that he will send for Nadezhda after he has reached St. Petersburg, although he has no intention of doing this. There follows a very astute judgment of Von Koren's despotic character, and a confession which is not totally sincere:

> I am a foolish, worthless, depraved man. The air I breathe, this wine, love, life in fact—for all that, I have given nothing in exchange so far but lying, idleness, cowardice, till now I have deceived myself and other people . . . I'm glad I see my faults clearly and am conscious of them. That will help me become a different man. My dear fellow, if you only knew how passionately, with what anguish, I long for such a change.
>
> (VII, 137)

Later, when upon Von Koren's insistence, Samoilenko stipulates that Laevsky must send Nadezhda on to St. Petersburg before him, Laevsky is terrified to think that perhaps the doctor has detected his deception:

> He began to understand that he would need deception not only in the remote future, but today, and tomorrow,

and in a month's time, and perhaps up to the very end of his life . . . He would have to lie to Nadezhda Fedorovna, to his creditors, and to his superiors in the service . . . he would have to resort to a regular series of deceptions, little and big, in order to get free of her . . . Deception and nothing more.

(VII, 151)

Laevsky is not the only character who is snared in the mesh of deception. Three days after the picnic a neighborhood gossip with "a bittersweet expression" comes to "console" Nadezhda Fedorovna on the death of her husband, and to recommend strongly that she marry Laevsky. Nadezhda is not so anxious to be saved as she was a few nights before, and besides she doesn't want to marry Laevsky in view of her relations with Kirilin and Achmianov. Her neighbor responds with a series of harsh truths about Nadezhda's immoral, "unclear" behavior. Nadezhda finds the deprecating remarks about her clothes the most shocking revelation, as "she had always had the highest opinion of her costumes" (VII, 141). However, she is also visibly moved by her neighbor's criticism of her unwifely, coquettish behavior. She feels thoroughly chastened and decides that her only recourse is to escape to Russia where she will "do a translation . . . . or open a library" (VII, 142).

Nadezhda says nothing of her plans to Laevsky, and their mutual deceit further develops the irony introduced in chapter two. Later that night at the very same party where Laevsky is unmasked by the doctor's stipulation to his loan, Nadezhda is brutally awakened from her reveries of moral regeneration. She is musing how she "would live in some far remote place . . . and send Laevsky 'anonymously' money, embroidered shirts and tobacco, and would return to him only in his old age or if he were dangerously ill and needed a nurse" (VII, 152), when she receives a note from Kirilin: "If you don't give me an interview today, I shall take measures" (VII, 152).

The dramatic pace of the novelette accelerates from this point as Laevsky and Nadezhda are confronted with both their own and other people's deceptions. The police chief, Kirilin, is furious that Nadezhda has wearied of him after only two rendezvous, and feels that his honor has been impugned. He demands to meet with her that night and the next, or else he threatens to create a scandal. Nedezhda complies, forgetting her previous engagement for that evening with Achmianov, who thinks, "It's deceit, deceit . . ." (VII, 157).

The following morning Laevsky heads toward Samoilenko's, having already decided that he will lie "not all at once, but piecemeal" (VII, 157). However, Laevsky is met with a rude shock when he finds Von Koren there, and he becomes increasingly irritated by that man's hostile remarks. When Von Koren mentions that he is well aware of Laevsky's present position and considers it "hopeless," Laevsky can no longer control himself. He vents his anger on Samoilenko, who has just entered, and is ignorant of the preceding conversation.

At this point Laevsky self-righteously considers that he has been deceived by the doctor, whom he accuses of gossiping about his private affairs. Samoilenko is offended, an argument ensues, but Von Koren resolves it with the statement,

> Now we understand . . . Mr. Laevsky wants to amuse himself with a duel before he goes away. I can give him that pleasure. Mr. Laevsky, I accept your challenge.

(VII, 160)

The night before the duel is painful and terrifying for Laevsky. The surge of confidence he had felt earlier that afternoon vanishes as the sun goes down:

> It was dread at the thought of something unknown. He knew that the night would be long and sleepless, and that he would have to think not only of Von Koren and his hatred, but also of the mountain of lies which he had to get through, and which he had not the ability to dispense with.

(VII, 162)

The first lie which Laevsky is confronted with is not his own, but rather that of his mistress, Nadezhda. Motivated by jealous revenge, the "deceived" Achmianov leads Laevsky to the hotel where Kirilin and Nadezhda are meeting for their second night together.

The knowledge of Nadezhda's deceit jars Laevsky from his mood of terrified anxiety to a painful acceptance of his situation. In the night that follows, Laevsky admits all his former deceits, including the illusion that escaping to St. Petersburg would redeem him: "He must look for salvation in himself alone, and if there were no finding it, why waste time? He must kill himself, that was all" (VII, 171).

Significantly, a storm arises during this night of revelation with violent gusts of wind and flashes of lightning that parallel the spiritual crisis Laevsky is passing through. As it begins to get light, the storm subsides and the carriage that will take Laevsky to the duel arrives. Before he leaves, however, Laevsky embraces the repentant Nadezhda, who he realizes is "the one creature near and dear to him, whom no one could replace" (VII, 172). Laevsky has finally understood the meaning and beauty in reality as it is, and "when he went out of the house and got into the carriage he wanted to return home alive" (VII, 172).

Von Koren arrives late at the designated spot for the duel, and comments upon the beauty of the rising sun:

> "It's the first time in my life I've seen it! How glorious!" said Von Koren, pointing to the glade and stretching out his hands to the east. "Look, green rays."

(VII, 175)

His lines recall Pechorin's speech in Mikhail Lermontov's *A Hero of Our Time* before the duel with Grushnitsky:

I do not remember a bluer and fresher morning. The sun had just appeared from behind the green summits, and the merging of the first warmth of its rays with the waning coolness of the night pervaded all one's senses with a kind of delicious languor.[1]

It would seem that the parallel between these passages was created intentionally by Chekhov, especially in view of Pechorin's description of his feelings before the duel:

Out of life's storm I carried only a few ideas—and not one feeling. For a long time now I have been living not with the heart, but with the head.[2]

This similarity between Von Koren and Pechorin is ironical in that they differ radically in their personal philosophies. However, their conceit and their cold aloofness unite them at a very essential point. Von Koren's identification with Pechorin also gives an indication that he will have the upper hand in the forthcoming duel, which will indeed be the case.

In contrast to Von Koren's bold excitement, Laevsky is in a state of exhaustion and nervous agitation before the duel. His estrangement is reflected in his stiff, awkward walk, which causes the deacon to compare him with an old man, and in his desire "to be killed as soon as possible or taken home" (VII, 176).

The duel itself parodies famous descriptions of such confrontations in Russian literature. No one present has ever witnessed a duel, and there is an initial doubt as to procedure. Von Koren laughs and says, "Gentlemen, who remembers the description in Lermontov? In Turgenev, too, Bazarov had a duel with someone . . ." (VII, 178) Laevsky magnanimously fires into the air, and Von Koren prepares to kill his hated opponent as Pechorin did in *A Hero of Our Time,* when the deacon shouts, "He'll kill him!" The shot intended for Laevsky just grazes his neck, and the entire event ends on a comic note.

His ridiculous duel is the turning point of the story. After it, Laevsky returns home to be reconciled with Nadezhda Fedorovna and to begin a new life with her. He permanently abandons his romantic illusions, and accepts a mediocre life of constant work and frugality.

Von Koren and Laevsky are also reconciled. The last chapter describes Von Koren's departure from the town in uncertain, stormy weather. Chekhov purposely uses this description to underline Von Koren's increased awareness of the uncertainties in life, which even scientific knowledge cannot always predict. Von Koren bids farewell to Laevsky and admits:

I was mistaken in regard to you, but it's easy to make a false step even on a smooth road, and in fact, it's the natural human lot: if one is not mistaken in the main, one is mistaken in the details.

(VII, 183)

At the end of **"The Duel"** both Laevsky and Von Koren have met the impact of reality and adjusted their philosophy to its demands. Both realize that neither science nor the human imagination is the ruling force of the universe, and there is a resemblance between their last words that unites the two men, as well as expressing the theme of the story. "There is no such thing as truth . . ." says Laevsky, reaffirming Von Koren's comment that "it's easy to make a false step even on a smooth road," and eloquently stating both his own and the general human condition (VII, 185).

Notes

1. Mikhail Lermontov, *A Hero of Our Times,* trans. Nabokov (New York, 1958), p. 161.

2. *Ibid.*, p. 162.

V. S. Pritchett (essay date 1988)

SOURCE: *Chekhov: A Spirit Set Free,* Hodder & Stoughton, 1988, pp. 97–111.

[*In the following excerpt, Pritchett analyzes "The Duel," focusing on character and the work's "playlike architecture."*]

In **"The Duel"** we see the conflict between Tolstoy's Christian ethic and Darwinism and a reply to the accusation that Chekhov had evaded the crucial Russian demand for a statement of his "convictions." In this letter he calls **"The Duel"** a novel. It is not episodic and haphazard like the discarded *Stories of the Lives of My Friends,* but a long, carefully designed piece of work held together by a central conflict of ideas sustained to the end and rooted in the interplay of the characters and the influences of the scene. It is one of his most sustained yet various and discreetly ordered fictions. It seems to have been provoked by a meeting with a German zoologist, a strong Darwinian and a dogmatic believer in the survival of the fittest. In the story Chekhov describes a zoologist, Von Koren, who happens to be staying briefly at a Caucasian seaside resort before setting out on a scientific expedition to the Bering Strait. In the resort he passes the time with an idle hospitable doctor, studies the guests and decides that one of them, Layevsky, is a decadent and irresponsible Petersburg type whom Nature will reject as unfit to survive. If the Layevskys of this world are not disposed of they will corrupt and destroy civilization. They are vain, they are loose in their morals, they corrupt women, they are irresponsible and idle. The mere sight of Layevsky wandering about the town in his slippers, playing cards all night and talking about himself and his ideals, condemns him in Von Koren's eyes.

And indeed, in one of the most original ironical opening scenes Chekhov ever wrote, we see Layevsky at his most lamentable. He and the amiable doctor—one of Chekhov's skeptics who are ashamed of their good nature—have gone to the beach to take a morning dip and are up to their shoulders in water. The secretive Layevsky has chosen this moment to ask the doctor's advice: "Suppose you had loved a woman and had been living with her for two or three years, and then left off caring for her, as one does, and began to feel that you had nothing in common with her. How would you behave in that case?" Just tell her to go where she pleases, says the doctor. But suppose, says Layevsky, she has no friends to go to, no money, no work. Five hundred rubles down or an allowance of twenty-five a month, the doctor says. Nothing more simple. But, Layevsky says, even supposing you have five hundred rubles and the woman is educated and proud, *how* would you do it?

> Samoylenko was going to answer, but at that moment a big wave covered them both, then broke on the beach and rolled back noisily over the shingle. The friends got out and began dressing. "Of course, it is difficult to live with a woman if you don't love her," said Samoylenko, shaking the sand out of his boots. "But one must look at the thing humanely, Vanya. If it were my case, I would never show a sign that I did not love her, and I should go on living with her till I died." He was at once ashamed of his own words; he pulled himself up and said: "But for aught I care, there might be no females at all. Let them all go to the devil."

Layevsky nags away shamelessly. He is one of those "superfluous men of the sixties"—we have seen the type in *On the Road* and in *Ivanov*. "I have to generalize about everything I do," Layevsky continues. "Last night, for example, I comforted myself by thinking all the time: Ah, how true Tolstoy is, how mercilessly true!" He had run away with a married woman to live an idyll, the simple life in the Caucasus, but now they are quarreling. The house smells of ironing, powder, medicine. The same curling irons are lying about every morning. The doctor says: "You can't get on in the house without an iron," and blushes at Layevsky speaking "so openly of a lady he knew."

There is no hotel in the little resort. The doctor, who loves his food, runs a little table d'hôte where he entertains his friends, who include a silly young deacon who is Von Koren's butt because he will talk of nothing but religion. The deacon's only resource is liability to accident, a matter of importance to the story later on.

We now see Nadezhda Fyodorovna at home. She has no idea that Layevsky is plotting to leave her. She is absorbed in her restlessness. She has been unable to resist going to bed with a vulgar police officer in the town and is also being tempted by the son of a shopkeeper to whom she owes money for her gaudy dresses. She knows she cannot control her sexuality. **"The Duel"** is one of the rare Chekhov stories in which the sexual subject is explicit. Her state is activated by an intimate illness.

> She was glad that of late Layevsky had been cold to her, reserved and polite, and at times even harsh and rude; in the past she had met all his outbursts, all his

contemptuous, cold or strange incomprehensible glances, with tears, reproaches, and threats to leave him or starve herself to death; now she only blushed, looked guiltily at him, and was glad he was not affectionate to her. If he had abused her, or threatened her, it would have been better and pleasanter, since she felt hopelessly guilty towards him.

In her kitchen she flushes "crimson" when she looks at her cook, as though fearing the cook might hear her thoughts.

In another beach scene we see her sharing a bathing hut with a deeply respectable married woman. Later, after Nadezhda's husband has died, this woman will tell her that it is her duty to society to marry Layevsky at once, and will refer to the state of Nadezhda's underclothes—emblems of sin—which she has seen at the beach. She cannot allow her children to come near her. Nadezhda is naïvely incredulous. While she lies in bed all day, Layevsky, who has a minor and neglected job in the Civil Service, is out all day and night on secretive journeys, intriguing to get the doctor to lend him money or to raise it from his friends, so that he can leave his mistress and go to Moscow.

We notice that Chekhov has the art of building his stories out of small journeys that lead to longer and more decisive journeys, in which his people gather together and then redistribute themselves and unknowingly create the stages of their fate. In **"The Duel"** the picnic scene is one of the most impressive examples of this art. His people drive in coaches to a gorge in the wild mountains where all will have the sensation that Nature has shut them in. As if a chorus, silent peasants, perhaps alien Tatars, will creep out and watch the picnic as polite Samoylenko lights a fire and fusses over cooking a meal. The tourists wander about and Layevsky provokes an argument with Von Koren. Later, Von Koren talks of Layevsky and Nadezhda as a pair of immoral brainless Japanese monkeys. She is wandering gaily off, followed by her ex-lover, the coarse police captain, whom she is ashamed of, and now snubs. He works himself up into a stage speech: "And so it seems our love has withered before it has blossomed, so to speak," and sulks off. She is now approached by a beach acquaintance, the dandyish son of a rich shopkeeper, and is surprised to find herself thinking that she could easily get her large debt to him wiped out if she agreed to go to bed with him. It would be fun to do that and then send him packing.

The peasants, sitting apart in the darkness, start quietly singing, and this stirs the naïve deacon and sends his mind traveling in the dream that in ten years' time he will be a holy archimandrite, leading beautiful religious processions in his uncle's church. At midnight the party will return quarreling, each frantic to pursue a secret dream. Nadezhda will be forced to give in to the police captain once more; his rival, the shopkeeper's son, will take his revenge and in a very dramatic night scene will take Layevsky to the low house of rendezvous, where he will be convinced of his mistress's guilt. Layevsky will have an attack of hysteria and accuse the doctor and Von Koren of "spying" on him and will fling at them a challenge to a duel. Firmly the challenge is accepted by Von Koren; he has been itching for it.

Chekhov is dramatic, but never melodramatic. Once more the rippling details of the journeys of the mind disperse melodrama. He has an instinct for the musical interweaving of changing moods. It is perfect that the duel is at dawn, at the remote, innocent scene of the picnic, where the morning landscape is changed after a stormy night. We see the foolish deacon, frightened and yet unable to resist the deplorable sight of a duel. In his way the deacon is a comic, calming, diversionary character, born to lose the thread of his ideas, but he is delightful in his naïve curiosity, which saves him from his doubts: though duelists are heathens and an ecclesiastical person "should keep clear of their company," was it just to shun them?

"They are sure to be saved," he says aloud, lighting a cigarette. "Human life," he reflects, "is so artlessly constructed. . . ." He compromises, when he arrives at the scene, by hiding in a field to watch.

How does Chekhov evoke the first sign of daylight? By a simple, strange detail: the deacon knows that daylight has come because he can at last see the white stick he is carrying.

The duel itself is amateurish. Von Koren has brought two young officers as seconds; they have never been present at a duel and bicker comically about the formalities. Is this the moment to propose a reconciliation? There is a doctor, who is careful to demand his fee. Layevsky is certain, as he stares at Von Koren, that the man intends to kill him. A second before Von Koren fires the deacon jumps up in the maize field and shouts and the shot faintly grazes Layevsky's neck.

To later critics the final act of the story is spoiled by its moral ending in the Tolstoyan fashion, for the lovers forgive each other. This is, however, very convincing. Layevsky has had a fright and gets down seriously to work in order to pay his debts. He and his mistress move into a humbler house. We hear no more of the minor characters, who have played their part in the indispensable chorus. On second thoughts we see the end is open, even after the reconciliation, which embarrasses the two enemies. Layevsky eagerly goes to see his enemy off at the harbor. Von Koren is rowed out to the steamer that will take him on his expedition. The sea is very rough. Born to dramatize and moralize about his situation, Layevsky watches the boat driven back by the waves yet, in the end, strongly making progress. He thinks:

> So it is in life . . . in the search for truth man makes two steps forward and one step back . . . And who knows? Perhaps they will reach the real truth at last.

Chekhov took great trouble with the last lines of his stories. Here he is dryly dismissive:

> It began to spot with rain.

The strength of **"The Duel"** lies in the ingenuity of its playlike architecture, in which the major characters make speeches and the minor characters act as a chorus. They are not a passive moralizing chorus—they incite the action. The Tatar onlookers watch almost in silence. To them the imbroglio is alien. If, as everyone has noticed, Tolstoy's influence is still marked, Chekhov is more forgiving of Nadezhda's sexual misdemeanor than Tolstoy is of the wife in "The Kreutzer Sonata." Reserve rather than abstinence, pity rather than condemnation, are more characteristic of Chekhov.

Andrew R. Durkin (essay date 1993)

SOURCE: "Allusion and Dialogue in 'The Duel,'" in *Reading Chekhov's Text*, edited by Robert Louis Jackson, Northwestern University Press, 1993, pp. 169–78.

[*In the following essay, Durkin investigates allusions to the writing of N. S. Laskov in "The Duel," and examines the opposition between science and the humanities in the story.*]

The central characters in **"The Duel"** (**"Duel"**, 1891), the "humanist" Laevsky and the "scientist" von Koren, exist in an atmosphere thick with literary and cultural allusion, from Shakespeare through Pushkin, Lermontov, and Turgenev to Darwin, Herbert Spencer, and Tolstoy's "Kreutzer Sonata." Indeed the conflict that arises between Laevsky and von Koren can be read in part as a struggle over which of them truly deserves the designation of hero, the figure who defines the world of the literary work. The resultant cacophony of egos in large part derives from the fact that Laevsky and von Koren, for all their apparent difference, in fact can be seen as two phases of a dominant literary and cultural figure of the nineteenth century, the romantic hero, characterized by L. Zvonnikova as successively a follower of "the Romantic model of behavior" and "the realistic movement" (in Lidya Ginzburg's terminology).[1] Each advances a claim to the authority of his own position. Laevsky by appeal to literary tradition, von Koren by scientific argument. In fact, **"The Duel"** discredits both claims to authority, in part by juxtaposing to them an alternative literary tradition that by implication may contain more of value for the modern, postromantic man. The young deacon Pobedov is connected with a literary mode and with values that serve as a counterpoint to the tradition of which both Laevsky and von Koren are products. This alternative mode of literature derives from Leskov and posits both a hero and a literary form that differ sharply from those of the "high" novel.

Although Chekhov's name has not often been linked with that of Leskov, there is biographical evidence indicating Chekhov's esteem for Leskov's works as well as Chekhov's interest in some of Leskov's works at the time of composition of **"The Duel."** We know from Chekhov's letters that he met Leskov in 1883, during a visit by

Leskov to Moscow with Nikolai Leykin, the editor of *Oskolki,* to which both Leskov and Chekhov were contributors at the time. Chekhov describes his first meeting with Leskov in a letter from late October 1883 to his brother Aleksandr and relates how Leskov anointed Chekhov as a writer as Samuel anointed David.

> Along with Leykin there came my favorite writer [*pisaka,* a familiar term for a writer that could be translated as "scribbler"], the famous N. S. Leskov. The latter visited us, went with me to the Salon [*des variétés*] and to the Sobolev puppet booths [the houses of prostitution in Sobolev Alley]. He gave me his works with an autograph. Once I am riding with him at night. He turns to me half drunk and asks: "Do you know who I am?"[2] "I know." "No, you don't know . . . I am a mystic . . ." "I know that too . . ." He goggles his old eyes at me and prophesies: "You will die before your brother." "Could be." "I shall anoint thee with balm, as Samuel anointed David . . . Write." This fellow resembles an elegant Frenchman and at the same time a defrocked village priest. Quite a person, worth attention. When I'm in Petersburg, I'll visit him. We parted as friends.[3]

The semihumorous anointing was, apparently, the first time that Chekhov's talent was recognized by a representative of the previous generation of writers. Later, in February 1891, Chekhov sent copies of several works of Leskov's (along with many other books) to Sakhalin for use in the primary schools there. In the summer of the same year, when Chekhov was working on **"The Duel,"** he ordered several works by Leskov (as well as works of other authors) from Posrednik, the publishing firm established by Tolstoy to provide inexpensive editions of serious literature for mass readership. Upon receiving the books, Chekhov wrote to the manager of the press, Gorbunov-Posadov, on September 4 (after the completion of **"The Duel"**): "I'm very grateful to you. The vast majority of the books are being read with interest. The things by Tolstoy and Leskov are particularly good. Epictetus is presented very well. The vignettes are good, particularly on "Conscience-stricken Daniel" and on the Pushkin fairy tale. In general, in outward appearance, and in inner content, and in spirit, the shipment produced the most joyful impression in me."[4]

What were possible reasons that Chekhov referred to Leskov as his "favorite writer" (*liubimyi pisaka*) and, more important, employed one of his works as a crucial subtext in **"The Duel"**? Apart from Leskov's linguistic inventiveness and humor, he had been a pioneer in moving away both from the novel as the hierarchically dominant genre and from the central figures typical of the Russian novel, namely members of the educated, Europeanized gentry or *intelligentsia.* Leskov developed (or returned to) forms in which clearly defined novelistic structure was replaced by episodic or open narratives. In addition, the typical Leskov character of the 1870s (as well as of his shorter works of the 1860s) is an exemplar of the "truly" Russian—a member of the clergy, an Old Believer, a peasant, or a craftsman. Even longer works of the 1870s, such as *Cathedral*

Folk (Soboriane, 1872) or *The Enchanted Wanderer* (Ocharovannyi strannik, 1873) are conceived as chronicle or picaresque rather than novel. Not only does Leskov break the mold of the novel with its coherent plot and tidy closure, but his characters speak in highly idiosyncratic, often substandard language, an indication of their own autonomous existence as well as of the social heterogeneity of Russia and by implication of all society. They are also often comic or ludicrous characters, such as Flyagin in *The Enchanted Wanderer,* or at least they seem so from the perspective of the Europeanized elite and its preferred literary forms and heroes. In fact, they offer a way out of the dead end of the novel, in Leskov's view a European form incapable of expressing the essence of Russian life.

In the 1880s Leskov undertook an even more radical experiment in a direction away from the novel; instead of depicting the Russian people in all their linguistic and social diversity, he adopted (and adapted) a preferred literary form of the people themselves, the parable. Drawing on the Prolog, a collection of early Christian and Russian parables and saints' lives arranged for daily reading, he composed a series of stylizations in this mode. They include "The Tale of the God-favored Wood-cutter" (Povest' o bogougodnom drovokole, 1886), "The Tale of Theodore the Christian and His Friend Abraham the Hebrew" (Povest' of Fedore-khristianine i o druge ego Abramezhidovine, 1886), "The Beautous Aza" (Prekrasnaia Aza, 1888), and "The Legend of Conscience-stricken Daniel" (Legenda o sovestnom Danile, 1888), of which the last is the most important with regard to **"The Duel."**[5]

In keeping with his increasing sympathy with Tolstoyan views, one of Leskov's principal points in his selection and adaptation of these texts was to demonstrate the power of simple Christian faith and charity, outside the structures of the official Church that claims to act on the authority of the precepts of Christ. This point is made particularly forcefully in "The Legend of Conscience-stricken Daniel," which first appeared in *Novoe vremia* in 1888 and was included in the 1889 Suvorin edition of Leskov's works. In the late 1880s Chekhov was both a contributor to and a regular reader of *Novoe vremia*; he also owned a copy of the Suvorin edition of Leskov's works, which he later donated to the public library in Taganrog.

"The Duel" contains clear indications that what may be termed a popular, nonheroic element, linked primarily with Leskov, plays an essential role in the story. We know that in March 1891, when the composition of the story was under way, Chekhov wrote to his family during his first trip to Europe, requesting that they buy him a copy of a Russian folk print (*lubok*) with a depiction of a miracle of St. Varlaam, showing, according to Chekhov, St. Vaarlam "riding on a sleigh; in the distance on a balcony stands the bishop, and below, beneath the picture, is the [text of] the life of St. Varlaam. Buy it and put it on my desk for me" (March 20, 1891). Chekhov had in mind a depiction of a miracle attributed to St. Vaarlam of Khutynsk, who prayed for a brief frost in June to control worms that were destroying the crops; in anticipation of snow, the saint rode to the bishop in a sleigh, and on the appointed day, waist-deep snow fell. This exemplum of the mixture of unquestioning faith and seemingly ludicrous behavior posited on it is replaced in the final text of **"The Duel"** by the deacon's story about his uncle, a priest who takes his umbrella and leather coat with him when he goes out in the fields to pray for rain. This version also recalls Leskov's "Tale of the God-favored Woodcutter," in which the prayers of a humble woodcutter bring rain. In all three stories, the logical absurdity of faith, as well as its power, is emphasized.

The deacon is thus linked with popular faith by an anecdote that points to a legend about a Russian saint and to a tale from the Prolog as reworked by Leskov. The deacon's clerical background of course also suggests connections with Leskov's fictional world, as do his origins in the central Russian territory that is one of Leskov's favored locales. (Leskov himself was from this region, being a native of Orel.) In addition, the deacon displays a Leskovian absurdity, spending his time fishing (although fishing was the profession of Peter before he was called to be "a fisher of men"), playing a guitar and singing a seminarians' drinking song in mock-Church Slavonic, wholeheartedly enjoying children's party games while others are using them for cover for more sinister messages, and viewing everything in a comic light. Particularly in conversation with the hyperrational von Koren, the deacon often seems to be illogical or naive in the style of one of "God's fools."

Unlike Laevsky or von Koren, who are clearly conscious of the literary models that dictate their behavior, the deacon lacks the awareness of his literary antecedents that leads von Koren and Laevsky (as well as Nadezhda Fedorovna) to cast themselves and others in predetermined roles or to draw frames around experience. In keeping with his Leskovian absurdity, the deacon's most frequent reaction to the behavior or statements of those around him is laughter. The deacon is surrounded by an aura of laughter; in the first paragraph to give any hint of his character, words based on the root *smekh*, "laughter," occur six times:

> The deacon was very prone to laughter [*smeshliv*] and laughed [*smeialsia*] at every trifle to the point of getting a pain in his side or collapsing. It seemed that he liked to be among people only because they have their comic [*smeshnye*] sides and because one can give them funny [*smeshnye*] nicknames. He called Samoilenko a tarantula, his orderly a drake, and was in rapture when von Koren once called Laevsky and Nadezhda Fedorovna macaques. He would look intently at people's faces, listen without blinking, and one could see how his eyes would fill with laughter [*smekhom*] and his face would become tense waiting for the moment he could let himself go and roll with laughter [*smekhom*].[6]

At first glance, the deacon would seem to be the ally of von Koren in the latter's denigration of Laevsky and Nadezhda Fedorovna, and von Koren himself doubtless feels that the deacon is a totally malleable disciple (von Koren

attempts to recruit the deacon for his expedition, uses him as a secretary, and lectures to him, particularly in chapter 16). Certain aspects of the deacon's attitude toward others, however, distinguish it from von Koren's censorious mockery. Although the deacon also employs animal metaphors and finds von Koren's use of them amusing, there is an essential difference in the principle on which the deacon's metaphors are based. As his comparisons of the portly, close-cropped Samoilenko to a tarantula and of his tenor-voiced orderly to a drake suggest, the deacon's animal metaphors rely on visual, external resemblance and do not involve moral judgment. Even the metaphor the deacon appropriates from von Koren, Laevsky and Nadezhda Fedorovna as macaques, undergoes a translation. For von Koren, the metaphor is a condemnation, combining the traditional use of monkeys as an emblem of sexual license with pseudo-Darwinist prejudice concerning the evolutionary hierarchy of primates. For the deacon, however, an alternative association of monkeys as morally innocent, and hence as amusing imitators of human activity, may be operative; von Koren's comparisons of Laevsky to invertebrates, microbes, or mad dogs elicit no response from the deacon, for these comparisons lack potential for anything but a negative moral judgment. Finally, the deacon's most significant use of an animal metaphor similarly borrows from von Koren while simultaneously revaluing the comparison. In chapter 11, von Koren cites moles' underground fights to the death over territory as part of his argument concerning the universality and teleological necessity of the struggle for existence and the survival of the fittest; earlier, he also praised the weasel's apparently excessive and indiscriminate killing on the same grounds, turning Samoilenko's argument around. Von Koren has already asserted his willingness to apply the same principle to human conflicts. On the morning of the duel, as the deacon watches the preliminaries from his place of concealment, the word *moles* (*kroty*) flashes through his mind. To von Koren's emphasis on the strength and courage (or instinct) of moles in their combats, the deacon doubtless adds a more usually noted characteristic of the animals in question: their blindness.

In addition, there is a peculiarity about the deacon's laughter itself. During lunch at Samoilenko's, for example, the deacon twice starts to guffaw at von Koren's characterizations of Laevsky, and the true object and possible motivation of the deacon's laughter are often left unspecified and ambiguous. Von Koren takes the deacon's laughter as agreement but at the same time feels that such a reaction lacks appropriate seriousness of concern. In fact, it could be that the deacon's laughter is in part evoked by the very vehemence with which von Koren argues his case against Laevsky. In Bakhtinian terms, the deacon's laughter could be taken as an indication of the acceptance of von Koren's position as authoritative (the result von Koren himself of course desires and assumes), or it could be taken as a true reply, a dialogic response that treats von Koren's discourse as one among many and therefore relativized and without absolute authority. This is not to say that the deacon's perception of the comic aspects of people who take themselves very seriously is therefore the fully valid perspective. The deacon's reaction to the argument that leads to the challenge to the duel is laughter at Samoilenko's red face and agitated manner, and his expectations in going to watch the duel surreptitiously are of an amusing and bloodless spectacle that will serve as the subject of jokes and stories:

> The deacon began to consider this question [whether good people such as von Koren and Laevsky can be saved even if they are not believers], but he recalled what a funny [*smeshnaia*] figure Samoilenko had cut today, and this interrupted the course of his thoughts. He imagined how he would sit down under a bush and watch, and when tomorrow at lunch von Koren would start to boast, he, the deacon, would start to relate to him, laughing [*so smekhom*], all the details of the duel. . . .
>
> It would be so good to describe the duel in a comic light [*v smeshnom vide*]. His father-in-law would read it and laugh [*smeiat'sia*]; don't give his father-in-law anything to eat, just tell him or write to him something funny [*smeshnoe*].

The deacon's expectations of the duel as a purely comic event are of course shattered, although it is his intervention that changes the duel's potentially tragic outcome to an essentially comic one. Nevertheless, his perspective suggests the underlying foolishness of the entire episode.

The question of authority in discourse is directly raised, with explicit links to Leskov, in chapter 17, the discussion concerning science and the humanities, in which von Koren's rhetorical unassailability and authority over the plot are at their apparent peak. Von Koren bases his decision to eliminate Laevsky and his purportedly baneful influence on the principle of natural selection, arguing that when it

> "wishes to annihilate a sickly, scrofulous, degenerate tribe, then don't hinder it with your pills and quotations from a poorly understood Gospel. In Leskov there is a conscientious Daniel, who finds a leper outside town and feeds him and keeps him warm in the name of charity and Christ. If that Daniel really loved people, then he would have dragged the leper farther from town and thrown him in a ravine and gone himself to serve the healthy. Christ, I hope, preached to us a love that was rational, sensible, and useful."
>
> "What sort of person are you!" laughed the deacon. "If you don't believe in Christ, why do you mention him so often?"

Von Koren of course misses, or refuses to accept, the point of the emblematic incident in Leskov, itself a variant of the parable of the Good Samaritan, namely that true love of one's neighbor is the highest value in human existence, outweighing the instinct for self-preservation (Laevsky is coming to this conclusion by a different path at approximately the same time). It is important, however, that von Koren cites his source precisely; it is in fact one of the few occasions, if not the only one, in **"The Duel"** in which a character cites a work that is not clearly part of the *intel-*

ligentsia's "required reading." In addition, von Koren refers to a precise incident in detail; characters in **"The Duel"** more usually recall a single motif (e.g., Karenin's ears) or make vague references (to the duels in *Hero of Our Times* and *Fathers and Sons*).

Von Koren's precision of citation, however, masks a more important omission or misreading with regard to Leskov's story. (Von Koren's failure or deliberate distortions as reader also raise the question of the accuracy of his "reading" of Laevsky, to this point seemingly authoritative.) Von Koren focuses on a relatively minor episode and overlooks the applicability to himself of the thematics of the main part of Leskov's story. The incident with the leper appears only in the final paragraphs of the story and has a clearly "added-on" character, occupying less than two pages out of a total of eighteen. In the longer, first part of the story, the Egyptian hermit Daniel inadvertently kills a pagan in self-defense while escaping captivity. Beset by his conscience, he seeks advice from various patriarchs, the pope, and a prince, but they all, despite or because of their doctrinal quarrels with one another, agree that Daniel has not only not committed a sin but has even performed a service for the Church and the state by killing one of their enemies. As the patriarch of Alexandria explains to Daniel.

> "Why do you weary yourself and without reason disturb our serenity with trifles? You were in captivity by force, and you bear no sin for having killed an unbaptized barbarian."
>
> "But my conscience tortures me—I recall the commandment by which it is not permitted to kill anyone."
>
> "The killing of a barbarian is not included. That is not the same as the killing of a person, but equal to the killing of a beast."

The patriarch's comment to Daniel recalls von Koren's constant reduction of human behavior, and particularly that of his opponent Laevsky, to the level of animals and his willingness to rid the world of these harmful nonhumans. On the basis of science (or of pseudo science), von Koren is able to interpret as he sees fit Christ's command to love one's neighbor and justifies the same sort of murderous act the patriarch condones on religious grounds. In both cases the moral error arises from the desire to give one's own discourse full authoritativeness, ripping it out of the dialogic world of human languages and giving it the absolute power reserved for divine utterance. In Daniel's further searchings, Leskov points directly at the tendency of the limited discourse of an individual to take on the authority of absolute, divinely revealed truth:

> Daniel related everything to the prince and added how he had visited all the patriarchs and the pope, and what they had answered him.
>
> "Well then. Could it be that this did not relieve you?" inquired the prince.
>
> "No, things became even more difficult."
>
> "Why?"

"Because, o prince, I began to think: May the words of men not hide from our eyes the Word of Christ, for then justice [*spravedlivost'*, "fairness"] will depart from men and the law of Christian love will be to them as if unknown. I fear temptation and do not seek further instruction from the consecrated but have come before you and beg punishment for the death of a human being."

This contradiction between the falsely authoritative language of the individual and the real authority of moral (and natural) truth is dramatized in **"The Duel"** at the moment of greatest tension, the duel itself. The complexity of intersecting lines at this moment requires that the passage (the end of chapter 19 and the beginning of chapter 20) be cited at length:

"Hurry up and shoot!" thought Laevsky, and he felt that his pale, trembling [a mark of crisis in Chekhov] face must be arousing even greater hatred in von Koren.

"Now I'll kill him," thought von Koren, taking aim at Laevsky's forehead and already fingering the trigger. "Yes, of course, I'll kill . . ."

"He'll kill him!"—a desperate shout was heard somewhere very close by.

Just then the shot rang out. Seeing that Laevsky was still standing in his place and had not fallen, everyone looked in the direction from which the shout had come and saw the deacon. Pale, with damp hair that had stuck to his forehead and cheeks, all wet and dirty, he was standing on the opposite bank [of the stream] in the corn and was smiling oddly and waving his wet hat. Sheshkovsky started laughing from joy, then burst into tears and walked off to one side . . .

A short while later von Koren and the deacon met near the footbridge. The deacon was upset and breathing heavily and avoided looking von Koren in the eyes. He was ashamed of being afraid and of his dirty, wet clothes.

"It seemed to me as though you wanted to kill him . . ." he muttered. "How contrary that is to human nature! How unnatural that is! [*Do kakoi stepeni eto protivoestestvenno*!]

This is the first time that von Koren's thoughts are directly reported, but at this moment of his complete certainty in the correctness of his own action and in the inevitability of a plot development that will confirm him as the unquestioned hero, his position is suddenly revealed as erroneous and limited. His own inner monologue is appropriated and made public by the deacon, and this recontextualization and "publication" function as a serious parody, in which von Koren's false authoritativeness is replaced by the full weight of moral truth.

The fact that the deacon's words are not attributed to any speaker ("a desperate shout") further enhances their suprapersonal, absolute authoritativeness. The participants in the duel, as well as the reader, are surprised by a disembodied voice that calls things by their right names. When

the speaker is finally identified, he presents a strange mixture of the prophetic man of God in his clerical garb and the man of nature, rising wet and muddy from his hiding place. Chekhov has of course held the deacon "in reserve" until this moment; the deacon has played no direct role in the complex relations among the other characters that constitute the intrigue of **"The Duel,"** a plot in which even a minor character such as Acmianov has played a pivotal part. Now, however, the deacon, seemingly naive and unable to counter adequately von Koren's weighty arguments in favor of the philanthropy of murder, has delivered the simple truth that confounds the fictive logic of von Koren's rationalizations. The deacon himself has of course had a deeper look into human nature; what he had expected to be a comedy has been something quite different in which he has been morally obligated to participate. His early direct look at the faces of others is replaced by a reluctance to look von Koren in the eyes. All that remains of his habitual laughter is a weak smile, and his laughter is shifted to Sheshkovsky, who both laughs and cries at the release of tension, suggesting the ambiguous nature of the tragicomedy in which they have all participated.

That religious and moral doctrine on the one hand and true science and logic on the other concur in the condemnation of murder is suggested by the deacon's comments to von Koren: "How contrary [or "repellent," *protivno*] that is to human nature! How unnatural that is!" The first statement recalls the arguments of natural law ethics, while the second (*protivoestestvenno*) suggests something contrary to man's biological nature itself. Von Koren's sophistic opposition of religion and science, in favor of the latter, dissolves in the face of a single, stubborn truth: the deliberate killing of another human being is murder.

Notes

1. Zvonnikova, "Skvernaia bolezn' (K nravstvenno-filosofskoi problematike 'Dueli')," *Voprosy literatury,* no. 3 (1985):160. The term *cacophony of egos* is also Zvonnikova's.

2. Chekhov quotes Leskov as using the second-person singular form, *ty,* indicating either closeness or, in this context, a certain mock solemnity. Chekhov himself does not use a second-person form to Leskov. I have retained Chekhov's shift to historical present, which renders action more vividly and is common in standard literary Russian.

3. A. P. Chekhov, *Polnoe sobranie sochinenii i pisem,* 30 vols. (Moscow, 1974–83), *Pis'ma* 1:88. All translations are my own.

4. *Ibid.*, 4:269.

5. N. S. Leskov, "Legenda o sovestnom Danile," in N. S. Leskov, *Polnoe sobranie sochinenii,* vol. 30 (St. Petersburg, 1903), 3–19. All translations are my own.

6. "The Duel" appears in Chekhov, *Sochineniia* 7. All translations are my own.

Willa Chamberlain Axelrod (essay date 1994)

SOURCE: "The Biblical and Theological Context of Moral Reform in 'The Duel,'" in *Russian Literature,* Vol. XXXV, February 15, 1994, pp. 129–52.

[*In the following essay, Axelrod sees "the need for salvation and moral reform" as central to "The Duel," and traces biblical references underlying this theme in the work.*]

In **"The Duel"** (**"Duel"** 1891), one of A. P. Čechov's longest stories, there are numerous allusions to the Old and New Testaments and to the teachings of the Russian Orthodox Church. Without understanding the biblical and theological references, one cannot respect the genius and artistry of this masterpiece, which has been neglected because of its allegedly "artificial" and "absurd" ending.[1] Critics from Čechov's time and the present perceive the outcome of **"The Duel"**, that is Ivan Andreič Laevskij's reformed life, as unconvincing and unanticipated. A. M. Skulbiševskij, for example, believes Laevskij's sudden change is impossible, and K. Medvedskij does not perceive any reason or impetus for his moral metamorphosis and thinks the story would be more convincing had he committed suicide.[2] Carolina de Maegd-Soëp claims that "the portrayal of both Laevsky and Nadezhda at the end of the novel seems rather artificial and even melodramatic".[3] Ronald Hingley considers the ending "perhaps the worst writing to be found in any of Chekhov's mature work".[4] Such common and unjust interpretations of **"The Duel"** illustrate that one cannot understand and appreciate the story while being ignorant of the extensive biblical allusions in **"The Duel."**

The central issue of the story is the need for salvation and moral reform. Moral reform is discussed on two levels:

1) on an individual one, as it concerns the main protagonist, Ivan Andreič Laevskij, and, to a lesser extent, the zoologist Nikolaj Vasil'ič fon Koren; and,

2) on a general level, as it concerns a greater Russian population. Laevskij experiences a major change of heart and succeeds in reforming his life. His search for renewal and his eventual reform represent the need for salvation of the Russian population.

Čechov draws mainly from Psalm 79, the Books of Isaiah and Jeremiah, and from the Gospels, to develop the theme of moral reform or salvation. Psalm 79 is a supplicatory prayer for the salvation or restoration of the Kingdoms of Israel and Judah, allegedly written during the Babylonian exile. The vine, a central metaphor in Psalm 79, which represents the Israelites, is a constant image associated with salvation throughout the Bible, and is a leitmotif in **"The Duel"**.

In the Books of Isaiah and Jeremiah, the prophets foretell of a new age to follow the Babylonian exile: eventually

God will restore Israel and Judah and initiate a new, eternal covenant. This messianic promise of salvation and of a new covenant is an underlying biblical motif in **"The Duel"**. This new covenant, which the Christian Church interprets as inaugurated and fulfilled by Christ, will still require obedience to the Law, but three additional terms will be added:

1) spontaneous forgiveness of sins;

2) individual retribution for sins rather than collective punishment; and

3) interiorization of religion, that is, the Law will not only guide external behavior, but it will inspire the heart.

These three terms of the new covenant are associated with Laevskij's reform.

Fundamental signs from the Gospels, such as the eucharistic meal, the breath of the Holy Spirit, and the image of Christ as sacrifice in exchange for salvation, are central to Laevskij's conversion. The three virtues of Christianity, Faith, Hope, and Love, are focal to Laevskij's reform.

The central event in **"The Duel"** is Laevskij's drastic change from a superfluous ne'er-do-well and philanderer, who spends his days in slippers, drinking and playing vint, to a humble and devoted husband who works hard to pay off his debts. For most of the story's twenty-one chapters, Laevskij speaks of "saving" his life, of "renewal" and "rebirth", and for most of the story, he seeks salvation to no avail in material things and in man. Towards the end, in Chapter XVII, however, he experiences a spiritual rebirth initiated by himself and others around him but ultimately realized through divine grace. This sudden change occurs on the eve of the duel. The duel, which has extensive religious implications, occurs the morning after Laevskij's moral reform and thus emphasizes his rebirth in that it saves him physically.

The main characters, the army doctor Aleksandr Davidyč Samojlenko, the young deacon Pobedov, and fon Koren, are astounded by Laevskij's reformed life. The Darwinist fon Koren, who despises Laevskij, the "superfluous man", is especially surprised. He considers Laevskij's immoral behavior, that is, his excessive drinking, mindless cardplaying, cohabitation with Nadežda Fedorovna, a married woman, and lack of respect for his administrative career, a menace to "the perfection of mankind". He is so morally sick, according to fon Koren, that reform is impossible. Thus, the zoologist thinks that to destroy this immoral and spineless person is a service to humanity (VII: 394).[5] In Chapter XV, when Laevskij, in a fit of anger, impulsively threatens Samojlenko and fon Koren with a fight, fon Koren eagerly takes this as a challenge to a duel and schedules one for the following morning.

Although the night before the duel the zoologist concludes that killing Laevskij is not worth three years in prison, during the duel he is so overcome by disgust for him, that he decides to kill Laevskij. The deacon, however, causes fon Koren to miss his aim, thus Laevskij is saved. Subsequently, a new man, he begins his humble life of virtue. The story closes with fon Koren, who himself is somewhat humbled by Laevskij's conversion, paying the hard working Laevskij a farewell visit. The two men shake hands and fon Koren departs on a journey.

1. THE PICNIC, PSALM 79, AND THE IMAGE OF THE VINE

In Chapter VI, a Sunday, the principal and secondary characters are seen together for the first time as they leave for a picnic dinner (Chapters VI-IX). This is the first event of the story and is thematically crucial in that it intensifies the need for renewal for Laevskij as well as for all the characters.

The picnic dinner unites the characters under the image of the biblical vine and is an allegory of the eucharistic meal. The picnic as eucharistic ritual is suggested by the food consumed, the location of the picnic, and, most importantly, the deacon's vision of himself as Bishop, blessing his congregation or "vine". The picnic dinner is consumed on Sunday evening with "religious solemnity" (VII: 391). The only food and drink mentioned are fish (in the form of fish soup), salt, bread, and wine, all biblical symbols of the eucharist or the new covenant initiated through Christ. Fish, a traditional symbol of Christ,[6] is associated in **"The Duel"** with the deacon Pobedov, hence underlining its religious value. On the way to the picnic spot, the deacon sits next to the basket of fish, and he picks up the fish after it is cleaned for the soup. "Deacon, where's the fish?" asks Samojlenko (VII: 389). Moreover, the deacon spends his days catching bullheads (VII: 389).

Along with wine and fish soup, salt is also associated with the picnic. "Where is the salt?" Samojlenko asks (VII: 388). Salt, a biblical synonym for essential life-giving forces, seasons all sacrifices in the Old Testament (Lev. 2: 13; Ezek. 43: 24) and it symbolizes the making of a covenant (The Book of Numbers, 18: 19). In the Russian Liturgy, salt seasons the bread of the eucharist. Bread and wine represent the body and blood of Christ and call to mind his sacrifice and salvation.

Shortly before the picnic meal begins, the deacon imagines himself serving the Liturgy in a cathedral. Indeed the glorious natural setting for the picnic evokes the grandeur of a cathedral. The dark mountains, "piled together by nature out of huge rocks" (VII: 385), like walls of a basilica, emit "dampness and mystery". The many gorges or recesses in the cliffs are the alcoves which line the nave. Distant mountains are pink, lilac, smokey, or flooded with light, colors which suggest incense and sunlight pouring through stained glass. A melody drifts over from the other shore of the river. It sounds like a Lenten hymn. The deacon envisions himself dressed in a golden miter, carrying the "panagija", or bread honoring the Virgin.[7] In preparation for the Epistle reading, he blesses the congregation, holding two- and three-branched candelabra ('dikerion' and 'trikerion') and pronouncing.

> Look down from heaven, O God, behold and visit this vine which your right hand has planted.[8]
>
> (VII: 389)

This fifteenth verse of Psalm 79 is recited only by a bishop when a bishop participates in serving the Liturgy. While the deacon envisions himself blessing the congregation and reciting the above-mentioned verse, he hears the choir sing the Trisagion (Trisvjatoe or Svjatyj Bože). This prayer, asking for God's mercy, reads:

> O Holy God, Holy Mighty, Holy Immortal
> One, have mercy upon us [three times].
> Glory be to the Father, and to the Son,
> and to the Holy Spirit, now and forever,
> and unto the ages of ages. Amen.

The vine mentioned in Pobedov's blessing, implicitly implies all present at the picnic. The picnickers are the vine to be visited by God and tended by the deacon. This association of the story's characters with the vine is also evoked in the final chapter. In response to Laevskij's reformed life and fon Koren's farewell visit to his former enemy, Pobedov paraphrases verse fifteen of Psalm 79, exclaiming.

> My God, what people! It's true the
> right hand of God has planted this vine!
> Lord! Lord!
>
> (VII: 453)

The vine, a common metaphor for Israel in the Old Testament prophets, is a central image in Psalm 79. God initially bestows favor on his people: "You [God] brought a vine out of Egypt, you drove out the nations and planted it. You cleared the ground for it, and it took root and filled the land," sings Asaph, the putative author of Psalm 79.[9] After the vine flourishes, it is disloyal to God and thus God abandons it. The vine is sacked by Israel's enemies: "Boars from the forest ravage it, and the creatures from the field feed on it."[10] Asaph beseeches God to tend his vine once again and to save his people. Thrice he sings: "God Almighty, renew us; let your face shine upon us that we may be saved."[11] For church-going Russian Orthodox, this refrain comes to mind when Pobedov recites verse fifteen. The refrain epitomizes the theme of salvation in **"The Duel"**.

In the Old Testament, a flourishing vine or vineyard is thus a sign of divine blessing. The verse "everyone under his vine and his fig tree" (1 Kings 4: 25; Micaiah 4: 4) is a metaphor for prosperity and divine blessing. A sacked vineyard or the absence of one, represents devastation (Jeremiah 35: 7) and the need for restoration. In Isaiah, God's punishment of the wicked is likened to the treading of a winepress (Isaiah 63: 1-3).

In the New Testament, Christ adapts the image of the vine to describe his relationship with his disciples and his future Church. Christ is "the true vine" and his people are its branches (John 15: 1). Russian Orthodox priests commonly sign letters to each other with "May God bless you in your work in the vineyard of Christ". "The fruit of the vine" is the symbol of salvation or the new covenant, which is celebrated in the eucharistic sacrament. In **"The Duel"**, Čechov draws from the Old Testament image of the vine as a people in need of salvation and from the New Testament image of "the fruit of the vine" as a sign of salvation through sacrifice.

The main characters and all the 'Laevskijs', or superfluous people embodied by Ivan Andreič, are likened to the biblical image of the Israelites in need of salvation, by the fact that 1) they are an uprooted people living away from their homeland, and 2) they are associated with the image of the vine either through specific reference to a vineyard or to wine.

The theme of exile is subtly introduced in Chapter I: the setting is a small resort town on the Black Sea, inhabited by a transitory and non-native population. At the end of the first chapter, the simple mentioning of a Jew points to the theme of exile. Samojlenko orders a drink of soda water from an elderly Jewish woman ("evrejka") who gives herself out to be a Georgian. In Chapter II, Laevskij speaks of his life on the Black Sea as "cursed slavery" ("prokljataja nevolja"; VII: 364). The picnic site is carefully described as a spot where two rivers flow into each other. This geographical detail skillfully hints at the city of Babylon, a place of Jewish exile, situated where the Euphrates River most closely approaches the Tigris. Samojlenko, who has not been to Russia in eighteen years, and forgets what the homeland looks like (VII: 359), is the son of "David" (Aleksandr Davidyč), an uncommon name among non-Jewish Russians. Fon Koren's physical appearance is semitic. He has a swarthy complexion and curly hair, and he wears a flowered shirt which looks like a "Persian carpet" (VII: 367). In the nineteenth century, ancient Semites were thought to have populated the area from Persia to Africa. Laevskij, using the pejorative Russian word "žid", denigratingly refers to fon Koren, who has an obviously German name, as one of those "Germans, Jewish by birth" (VII: 426).

All of the main characters are associated with the image of the vine. In Chapter I, the vineyard is mentioned by Laevskij three times. He tells how he and Nadežda came to the Caucasus two years before to escape the "pošlost' and emptiness of life" in the capital and to work by the sweat of their brow on their own plot of land, where they would plant a vineyard (VII: 355). While the desire for physical toil and a plot of land evoke Tolstoyan and Voltairian ethics, Laevskij's dream of his own vineyard especially signifies the Old Testament ideal of peace, prosperity, and divine blessing. Laevskij soon realizes, however, that his dream of "physical work and a vineyard are for the devil" (VII: 356). But he admits that someone like Samojlenko or

fon Koren could, no doubt, leave their heirs "a rich vineyard and three thousand acres of corn" (VII: 356). Laevskij's failure to procure a vineyard, especially in the fertile land of Black Sea Georgia where viticulture flourishes, symbolizes the devastation of his existence and his need for salvation.

To illustrate Laevskij's perverted outlook on life, fon Koren claims that the former is not able to perceive the beauty in "a bunch of grapes", for he thinks only of their ugliness once they are chewed and digested. This image of chewed grapes, and also Laevskij's fantasy of trampling on his archenemy the zoologist (VII: 427), evoke the treading of grapes in the winepress, an image of divine disfavor. Thus Čechov suggests, once again, the ruined state of the metaphorical vine.

Late Sunday night, after returning from the picnic, Laevskij visits Samojlenko and twice begs him to save him. ("Save me, Vanja, save me [. . .] Aleksandr Davidyč, save me!"; VII: 396) The doctor offers Laevskij wine from his own vineyard. But his wine has a bitter taste. Nevertheless, according to Laevskij, the doctor's fruit of the vine has life-giving qualities. Over three bottles, Laevskij twice thanks Samojlenko for "rejuvenating" him ("Ja ožil." "Ty oživil menja"; VII: 396, 399). This delusive rejuvenation prefigures his genuine rebirth. The bitterness of the wine suggests that Samojlenko's wine is not of the "true vine". Church regulations warn priests to take special care that the eucharistic wine is not bitter.[12] As we shall see shortly, bitter grapes and a bunch of grapes are specific references to the Books of Jeremiah and Isaiah respectively. Both Nikodim Aleksandryč Bitjugov and Egor Alekseič Kirilin, minor characters, speak of "their own" wine, implying that, like Samojlenko, they too have vineyards. At the picnic, there is an abundance of wine: thirty bottles for nine adults and two children, who even drink a little. Given the eucharistic suggestions of the picnic, these thirty bottles of wine evoke 1) the passion of Christ; the thirty bottles hint at the thirty silver pieces Judas receives for betraying Jesus; and 2) the blood of Christ, or "the cup of salvation", which the new covenant promises the Israelites.

2. LAEVSKIJ'S SEARCH FOR MORAL REFORM IN THE MATERIAL WORLD

From the beginning of the story, Laevskij is obsessed with the need "to save" or "renew" his life, and continually speaks of "salvation", of "saving" his life from "lies and deception" and from his "absurd" existence with a woman he does not love. In the third year of his relationship with Nadežda Fedorovna, he wants to abandon her and the Caucasus, and return to St. Petersburg to start a new life.

He perceives himself as "an empty, destroyed, fallen person" (VII: 399). Along with the rest of the Russian gentry, he is degenerating (VII: 355, 370) and therefore professes "to thirst for renewal" and hopes to be "resurrected and become a different person" (VII: 399). He confides in Samojlenko his disrespect for himself:

The air I breathe, this wine, love, life in fact, for all that, I have given nothing in exchange so far but lying, idleness, and cowardice . . . I bow my back humbly before fon Koren's hatred because at times I hate and despise myself.

(VII: 399)

Laevskij is a weak man, but he perceives his own weaknesses and wants help.

For most of the story, his search for new life is unsuccessful. He seeks, or thinks he seeks, salvation in a new locale, money, and, most significantly, in literature and ideas. That is, he seeks salvation in material things and in solely secular terms. To "renew" his life, he must have 300 rubles to run away to St. Petersburg, convinced he will die if he remains in the Caucasus with Nadežda. In Chapter IX, late Sunday night after the picnic, Laevskij asks Samojlenko for a 300 ruble loan. Like an addicted gambler, he is haunted by this sum which, allegedly, will save his life. On Wednesday of the same week, "with excitement", he asks the doctor if he has the money yet. His face expresses "fear, extreme uneasiness, and hope" (VII: 405). On Thursday, at Kostja Bitjugov's birthday party, Samojlenko promises Laevskij that he will have the money by Friday. But neither the 300 rubles nor his escape to the capital will save his life. Material and geographical change do not guarantee moral change.

Laevskij also believes salvation is found in literature and ideas. Before his reform, it is implied that he has no God. He admits this himself (VII: 436), and the deacon Pobedov refers to him as a non-believer. Laevskij turns to literature, not theology, to find a reason for living. He sees justification for his life and actions in the literary and social idea that the aristocracy is degenerating. This is an excuse for the weak Laevskij not to take action and reform his ways. In Chapter I, he admits to Samojlenko that

[. . .] all salvation is in talking. I have to generalize each one of my actions; I have to find an explanation and justification for my absurd existence in someone else's theories, in literary types, in that we, the landowning class are degenerating . . .

(VII: 355)

Literary figures define Laevskij's moral standards and guide his thoughts. Always in slippers, like Oblomov, Laevskij lives in the shadow of past literary figures. He considers his behavior to be organically dependent on the natures of his "fathers of flesh and spirit", "Onegin, Pečorin, Byron's Cain, and Bazarov". He takes himself for Faust, and a "second Tolstoj" (VII: 374), and he ironically refers to himself as Wilhelm Tell (VII: 427). Through the epigraph of Chapter XVII, Laevskij is associated with Puškin's poetic persona who laments his past ('Vospominanie', 1828).

Laevskij thinks of his own existence in terms of Tolstoj's presentation of life. "How true is Tolstoj!" ("Kak prav Tolstoj!"; VII: 355), he thinks when reflecting on his own ex-

istence. He places personal experience in the context of literature. When he feels repulsed by Nadežda's white neck, for example, he thinks of Anna Karenina's hatred for Karenin expressed by her aversion for his ears. "How true it is, how true it is," exclaims Laevskij ("Kak èto verno, kak verno!"; VII: 362). In his indecision, Laevskij reminds himself of Hamlet: "How truly Shakespeare describes it! Ach, how truly!" (VII: 366). Laevskij's faith is in man and his literary creation. For Laevskij, man is truth, not God.

This emphasis on truth is starkly juxtaposed to Laevskij's frequent mention of lies and deception. The contrast of truth and falsehood is a significant theme running through the story, climaxing in the final scene when the reformed Laevskij states "No one knows the real truth" (VII: 453). Before his conversion, however, Laevskij believes Tolstoj knows the truth. Tolstoj is the truth. Shakespeare is the truth. Truth for Laevskij before his reform is only man and his ideas. In the Bible, only God, not man, is Truth. According to the Russian Catechism, the image of God is defined by "righteousness and the holiness of truth" ("pravda i prepodobie istiny").[13]

In addition, while man is truth for Laevskij, man is also his source of hope. This is suggested in Chapter IX, when he declares to Samojlenko "all hope is in you", as preface to his request for 300 rubles. The Russian Catechism states that hope in man ("čelovekonadejanie") is one of the thirteen sins which defile the First Commandment, "I am your God, you shall not have any other god beside me".[14]

3. LAEVSKIJ'S MORAL REFORM

The material stimuli for Laevskij's conversion in Chapter XVII are many: the zoologist's hatred for him and the prospect of the duel, the doctor's suspicion of his plan to leave Nadežda behind in the Caucasus, and Nadežda's betrayal. In addition, Laevskij is by nature an introspective person. This is established already in Chapter I, when he remarks that his thoughts keep him awake at night. But introspection, acknowledgment of one's weaknesses, and outside material stimuli, are not enough to save him. It does, however, set the stage for the insight or wisdom which he receives through grace at the beginning of Chapter XVII.

When it grows dark on Friday, the same day Laevskij and fon Koren agree to duel on Saturday, Laevskij suddenly loses interest in card-playing and the people he always plays with. As if he "suddenly fell ill", he has the urge to go home, "lie motionless in bed, and prepare his thoughts for the coming night" (VII: 427). He is frightened by the idea that something unprecedented in his life will occur the next morning. And he is frightened by the approaching night. The desire to lie motionless and make ready his mind is an unconscious preparation for the divine grace he receives in the following scene:

At home in his study (beginning of Chapter XVII), his thoughts focus on Nadežda and himself. He has just witnessed Nadežda secretly meeting with the police officer Kirilin at Mjuridov's place, and he is stunned by the sight. He perceives himself and Nadežda as "dead" (VII: 435). Nothing matters, including the outcome of the duel. Death is on his mind. Then suddenly the window blows open.

> Suddenly the window opened with a bang. A violent wind burst into the room, and the papers fluttered from the table. Laevskij closed the windows and bent down to pick up the papers. He was aware of something new in his body, a sort of awkwardness he had not felt before, and his movements were strange to him. He moved timidly, jerking with his elbows and shrugging his shoulders; [. . .] His body had lost its suppleness.[15]

This strong wind clearly implies the Holy Spirit, as when, in The Acts of the Apostles (2: 2), that Spirit descends in the room of the disciples like a strong wind: "Suddenly a sound like the blowing of a violent wind came from the heaven and filled the whole house . . ."[16] This descent makes a loud noise, translated in **"The Duel"** by the slamming of the window. The suddenness of the wind's descent in the biblical account is repeated in **"The Duel"** and in both instances it is a "violent wind" ("sil'nyj veter"). The Holy Spirit, in the Old and New Testaments, bestows inspiration, power, and wisdom on all the prophets, Jesus, and the disciples. In **"The Duel"**, Laevskij is suddenly graced with wisdom. His physical change, that is, jerky, awkward movements and loss of suppleness, is a sudden onslaught of old age, or a metaphor for the mental maturity or wisdom received through the Holy Spirit. This wisdom is the "something new in his body". This wisdom is the essence of his reform or new life. His sudden maturation is noticed the following morning by the deacon: 'Strange,' thought the deacon, not recognizing Laevskij's walk. 'It's as if he's an old man'" (VII: 443). Nadežda also comments on Laevskij's "strange walk" (VII: 450). Literally overnight, Laevskij changes from a "defenseless child", as Samojlenko describes him in Chapter I, to "an old man", as the deacon perceives him in Chapter XVIII. Grace, according to Russian Orthodoxy, however, does not infringe upon man's free will. One must be willing to receive God's grace. This is an important point, for it implies that Laevskij the superfluous man is not all bad nor his situation hopeless, as fon Koren contends. From the start, there is the will in him to be virtuous, and he does recognize his weaknesses, feel pity for Nadežda, and, most importantly, he desires to amend his life. But he is weak. He becomes spiritually strong, however, through the third term of the new covenant foretold by the prophets: through the interiorization of religion, or God's grace, which gives spiritual knowledge or truth, thus strengthening one's faith.

The insight Laevskij receives through grace enables him to realize that he cannot renew his life through a new locale, through money, literature, or people. He comes to the conclusion that he must find salvation within himself, and if he does not find it there, then he must die (VII: 438).

> One must seek salvation only within one's self, and if one does not find it, why waste time? One must kill oneself, and that is all . . .
>
> (VII: 438)

Orthodox theology places great emphasis on the doctrine of the image of God, which, based on Genesis 1: 26, asserts that the image and likeness of God is in every man and woman. "The best icon of God is man," states the priest during the Russian Orthodox Liturgy.[17] Thus, to find God, one must look within oneself. The Orthodox hero, St. Anthony of Egypt states: "Know yourself . . . He who knows himself knows God."[18] Another authority, St. Isaac the Syrian declares: "If you are pure, heaven is within you; within yourself you will see the angels and the Lord of the angels."[19] St. Luke states: "The Kingdom of God is within you" (17: 21). Thus, Laevskij's resolution at the end of his spiritual catharsis is that if he cannot find goodness, implicitly the divine image, hidden under the "pile of lies" which characterize his past life, then there is no reason to live. More vividly, at the end of Chapter XVII, Laevskij deduces that "if there is no God", then Nadežda may as well die, because then she "has no reason to live" either (VII: 439). Laevskij's insight acquired through grace enables him to understand the extent and meaning of Nadežda's suffering and, therefore, to love her, and it enables him to pray and ask forgiveness. Because of this grace, Laevskij's hatred changes to love, his pride to humility. His understanding of love and hope is no longer secular but approaches the Christian ideal of these virtues. It is also suggested that his faith is no longer in man but beginning to turn to God. During this stormy Friday night, Laevskij feels anguish, despair and loathing towards himself for having only "destroyed, ruined, and lied . . ." throughout his life. He realizes he has destroyed Nadežda, causing her great suffering, epitomized by her unwilling submission to Kirilin. He understands that Kirilin and the shopkeeper's son, Ačmianov, have learned their ignoble philandering from him: they take advantage of Nadežda as Laevskij took advantage of her when he stripped her of her husband, friends, and native city (VII: 437). Nadežda can only reflect "like a mirror, his idleness, viciousness, and lies—and that was all she had to fill her weak, listless, pitiable life" (VII: 437). Laevskij realizes that Nadežda is his "victim" or "sacrifice" ("žertva"), and that he, in effect, has caused her "death". Under the old law of Moses, sacrifices or offerings are the most prominent aspect of worship. Animal sacrifices are offered to God for atonement and thanksgiving. All sacrifices are sprinkled with salt. In the New Testament, Jesus Christ is the sacrificial offering who dies on the Cross for the atonement of humanity's sins. In **"The Duel"**, Nadežda is the sacrifice offered for the atonement of Laevskij's sins. She is referred to as a sacrifice: "but she was his sacrifice" ("no ona byla ego žertvoj"; VII: 438) and, at the end of the picnic, she is subtly associated with salt: "Ona ponjala čto peresolila, vela sebja sliškom razvjazno" (VII: 392). As sacrifice, Nadežda metaphorically dies for Laevskij. He "fears her as if she were dead" (VII: 438), and when departing for the duel, Laevskij approaches Nadežda, who is wrapped in a blanket, lying motionless like "an Egyptian mummy" (VII: 439). As sacrifice and expiation for Laevskij's past life of vice, it is not surprising, therefore, that Nadežda is called "Hope". The Russian Catechism defines Hope as the trust in salvation as promised by God.[20] Thus, Nadežda is Laevskij's hope in new life.

On Friday night, Laevskij has the urge to pray and ask forgiveness. He wishes he could replace "lies with truth, idleness with hard work, boredom with happiness, and he would return chastity to those from whom he took it, and would find God and justice" (VII: 438). His desire to pray is first suggested by his urge to write to his mother. He jots down "Matuška!" and later calls out "Matuška!". This invocation suggests the calling out to the Mother of God, the Divine Intercessor and Mother of Humanity. But he keeps thinking only of his literal, unsympathetic mother, and therefore his thoughts move on to the storm, his childhood, and back to Nadežda. As Laevskij calls out to his mother, so does he call out to the storm. "'The storm,' whispered Laevskij; he had a longing to pray to someone or to something, if only the lightning or storm clouds. 'Dear storm!'" (VII: 436). This invocation parallels "Matuška!" at the head of his letter. And although praying to lightning or the storm appears like pagan worship, in, especially, Exodus, Psalms, and the Gospels, God is often associated with such forces of nature.

Laevskij's desire to pray is an expression of his hope in new life. The Russian Catechism states that "the means for attaining saving hope" are "first prayer; secondly the true doctrine of blessedness and its applications".[21] Not only does Laevskij pray for the first time in Chapter XVII, but as of Friday night he begins to live by the majority of the nine beatitudes or doctrines of blessedness. The first four beatitudes are:

> 1) Blessed are the poor in spirit, for theirs is the Kingdom of Heaven.
>
> 2) Blessed are those who mourn, for they will be comforted.
>
> 3) Blessed are the meek, for they will inherit the earth.
>
> 4) Blessed are those who thirst and hunger for truth, for they will be satisfied.[22]

The first beatitude blesses spiritual poverty or humility. Through recognition of his shortcomings, his pleas for forgiveness, and his effort to pray, Laevskij shows humility. During the duel, Laevskij demonstrates humility by offering fon Koren his forgiveness. Thus, Laevskij is also a peacemaker, the person blessed in the seventh beatitude: "Blessed are the peacemakers, for they will be called children of God." On the eve of the duel, Laevskij manifests sorrow and contrition of heart, a virtue blessed in the second beatitude. After his reform, he adopts "a quiet disposition of spirit", a requirement for the third beatitude which blesses meekness. His new humble disposition is especially obvious in Chapter XXI, which takes place three months after the duel. He speaks little and meekly invites fon Koren, Samojlenko, and the deacon into his home: "I humbly beseech you . . ." he says ("Pokornejše prošu"; VII: 452). He bows to fon Koren when the latter takes leave. At the end of Chapter XXI, Laevskij speaks of "the

thirst for truth" ("žažda pravdy") and strongly implies that he himself searches for truth. Thus he embodies also the fourth beatitude, "Blessed are they who hunger and thirst for truth, they shall be fulfilled." "Who are they who hunger and search for truth?" asks the Catechism.

> They who love to do good, but do not count themselves righteous, nor rest on their own good works, but acknowledge themselves sinners and guilty before God; and who, by the wish and prayer of faith, hunger and thirst after the justification of grace through Jesus Christ as after spiritual meat and drink.[23]

After his reform, Laevskij also manifests a new understanding of the third theological virtue, love. The last third of the Russian Catechism, the section on the virtue of love, discusses the Ten Commandments, the obligations required to fulfill them, and the sins which defile them. Love is manifested through "good works", which are distinguished from "bad works" by the Ten Commandments. The Commandments are divided into two kinds of love: 1) love for God, treated in the first four commandments, and 2) love for neighbor, treated in the last six. St. Paul says that the inclusive commandment is to love your neighbor, for this subsumes love for God. ("For the entire law is summed up in one command: 'Love your neighbor as yourself'"; Galatians 5: 14). The emphasis on neighborly love strongly distinguishes the old covenant from the new. Love for one's neighbor is a significant theme in **"The Duel"**, the meaning of which is debated in Chapters III, IV, and XVI, by the zoologist, doctor, and deacon. The last six commandments require love and honor for one's neighbor:

> 5) Honor your father and mother.
>
> 6) You shall not kill.
>
> 7) You shall not commit adultery.
>
> 8) You shall not steal.
>
> 9) You shall not bear false witness against your neighbor.
>
> 10) You shall not covet your neighbor's possessions.[24]

The Catechism paraphrases these laws: One is not to hurt one's neighbor's life, nor the purity of his morals, nor his property; one is not to hurt him by word, or to wish to hurt him. Before his reform, Laevskij shows little if any love for his neighbor. He commits adultery, thus contaminating the purity of Nadežda's morals, who was satisfied in her married life. He hurts his neighbor's life, in particular the lives of Nadežda and her husband. The latter grows sick and dies after Laevskij steals his wife. Laevskij even feels responsible for his death. In a rage, he slanders his neighbor, calling Samojlenko "a snooper" ("syščik"; VII: 425), which strongly offends him, and disparagingly refers to fon Koren as one of those "Germans born of Jews" ("nemeckie vychodcy iz židov"; VII: 425). He wishes to hurt his neighbor: he imagines trampling fon Koren underfoot. The sin of "eating the bread of idleness", of which Laevskij is obviously guilty before his reform, is one of the eight sins forbidden by the eighth commandment, "You shall not steal".

The love Laevskij acquires after his reform is similar to the ideal of Judeo-Christian love. He shows respect and honor for his neighbor, bears no malice towards his one-time archenemy fon Koren, who attempts to kill him. He lives in peaceful matrimony with Nadežda, and no longer "eats the bread of idleness". In addition, his love for Nadežda is associated with fear for her. This fear suggests a spiritual love. Although he wants to "fall at her feet and kiss her hands and feet", "he feared her as if she were dead" (VII: 438). One of the obligations in fulfilling the first commandment, "I am the Lord your God, you shall not have any other Gods", is "to fear God or stand in awe of him".[25]

At the end of Chapter XXI, it is also suggested that Laevskij's faith is redirected from man to God. Concerning scientific theories, fon Koren tells Laevskij: "No one knows the real truth." ("Nikto ne znaet nastojaščej pravdy"; VII: 453). Agreeing with the zoologist, Laevskij responds: "Yes, no one knows the real truth." He repeats this to himself later on as he sadly looks at the rough, dark sea (VII: 455). Laevskij's ambiguous statement for the first time shows lack of faith in man's knowledge. While before his reform he has faith in man's knowledge ("How true is Tolstoj!", "How truly Shakespeare noticed things!"), at the end of the story he shows a lack of faith in this knowledge. In addition, "No one knows the real truth" may be understood in a spiritual sense, referring to God. The Catechism states that the image of God consists of "righteousness and holiness of truth" ("pravda i prepodobie istiny"); thus, "pravda" and "istina". In the Old and New Testaments, God is both moral truth (pravda) and intellectual truth (istina). In **"The Duel"**, 'pravda' suggests both kinds of truth. While fon Koren's use of 'pravda' refers to man's acquired knowledge, Laevskij seems to pick up on this specified use of 'pravda' and attribute a more comprehensive, abstract, and spiritual meaning to 'truth'. Thus, to say "No one knows the truth", is to state a theological commonplace: one does not know or understand God.

Russian Orthodoxy, however, emphasizes the doctrine of 'deification' or the potential to be assimilated with God through virtue. The life of the Russian Orthodox Christian is to be a search for God. Through contemplation, prayer, and good deeds, one will "find God" and potentially unite with him, while remaining distinct. The full deification of the body will occur at the Last Judgment.[26] Laevskij's final words reveal faith as well as hope in the potential to find truth or God. He responds to his own statement "No one knows the real truth" with "Who knows? Maybe they [people] will find real truth . . ." ("I kto znaet? Byt' možet, doplyvut do nastojaščej pravdy . . ."; VII: 455).

In ecclesiastical writings, as in **"The Duel"**, the search for God or truth by man or woman is often represented as a boat sailing on a rough sea. Once one finds God, as the

Church Father St. John Chrysostom writes, the waters become calm.[27] In the final scene of **"The Duel"**, as Laevskij, Samojlenko, and Pobedov accompany fon Koren to the boat, Laevskij compares mankind's life, which he perceives as a search for truth, to a boat on a rough sea. As a boat sails forward and backwards on restless water, so

> People, in search for truth take two steps forward and one step backwards, but the thirst for truth and a strong will chase one forward and forward. And who knows? Maybe they will sail to the real truth.
>
> (VII: 455)

The storm at the end of the story, like the earlier wind in Chapter XVII, thus serves a major thematic and theological purpose.

4. FAITH VERSUS KNOWLEDGE

Laevskij's reformed attitude towards Faith, Hope, and Love, is prefaced by a discussion between the zoologist and the priest on the relationship between love and faith and the distinction between faith and knowledge (Chapter XVI). The discussion occurs unexpectedly, on the eve of the duel, and rather unrealistically, thus implying a strong thematic purpose. Love is discussed in terms of love for neighbor, which subsumes love for God, as Saint Paul states (Galatians 5: 14). According to fon Koren, love is ultimately guided by reason, by "knowledge and evidence". The "moral law", organically inherent to all humanity, instinctively dictates love for neighbor. Common sense and rationality define love for neighbor as preservation of the strong by destruction of the weak. "The exact sciences", or "evidence and the logic of facts", distinguish the weak from the strong. The zoologist believes that this love reflects Christ's teaching, for he assumes that "Christ taught a love that is rational, intelligent, and practical" (VII: 432). That is, a love derived from reason and acquired knowledge, love born of the mind, not of the heart.

Obviously, this sharply opposes Orthodox teachings. The Catechism states that Love, i.e. good deeds shown to one's neighbor, is derived from Faith. Without Faith, there is no Love. "Faith without deeds is dead," states the deacon, quoting the Catechism and James 2: 20, 26, "but works without faith is still worse, mere waste of time and nothing more," he concludes (VII: 433). The deacon implies that fon Koren practices "works without faith". "Faith moves mountains," the deacon says, echoing Matthew 21: 21. And if fon Koren had faith, his work as zoologist would produce results (VII: 433). In other words, faith, not knowledge, makes things happen:

> Yes . . . here you are teaching all the time, fathoming the depths of the ocean, dividing the weak and the strong, writing books and challenging to duels, and everything remains as it is; but look, some feeble old man will mutter just one word through the holy spirit, or a new Mahomet, with a sword will gallop from Arabia, and everything will be topsy turvy, and in Europe not one stone will be left standing on another.
>
> (VII: 433)

This last phrase, "not one stone will be left standing on another", is another use of Matthew (24: 2), in which Jesus speaks of the Second Coming when nothing will remain the same. Once again, faith is what makes things happen, not knowledge. The distinction between faith and knowledge is also discussed in the Catechism. God, "invisible and incomprehensible", cannot be understood by knowledge but only through faith. "Faith is the substance of things hoped for, the evidence of things not seen," states the Catechism, citing Hebrews 11: 1.[28]

This theological discussion in Chapter XVI serves two purposes. First, it reveals fon Koren's lack of faith, and second, strategically placed before Laevskij's conversion, it alerts the reader to the faith Laevskij acquires as a result of his spiritual rebirth. The discussion of love and faith, read with the Russian Catechism in mind, a tract which Russian Orthodox children of the nineteenth century learned by heart, implies that if one manifests love and hope, then, it goes without saying that one has faith: love is dependent on faith and faith is "the substance of things hoped for". And if one has faith, anything can happen: a superfluous Laevskij can even become a useful citizen overnight.

5. The Duel as Religious Rite

If Laevskij is spiritually resurrected on the stormy Friday night, he is bodily saved on Saturday morning during the duel. The priest saves his life by causing the zoologist to miss his aim. Therefore, after the duel, Laevskij is able to say that he feels as if he were returning from a funeral, "where they buried a wearisome, insufferable person" (VII: 450). Yes, he returns from his own funeral, but alive, in body and soul. He is bodily resurrected during the duel. Before the duel begins, "for the first time in his life he sees the sunrise" (VII: 443). This sunrise symbolizes his renewed life. His natural and domestic surroundings, which previously generated scorn and frustration, now provoke "lively, child-like happiness" (VII: 450). Though his mind has acquired the wisdom of old age, his heart expresses child-like happiness and innocence. To be of such a spirit fulfills a Christian ideal. The New Testament teaches the wisdom of a child-like nature, Jesus says: "I tell you the truth, unless you change and become like little children, you will never enter the kingdom of heaven" (Matthew 18: 3).

The spiritual nature of the duel, that is the duel as a religious rite, is implied by its association with the picnic. Both take place in the same spot: in the cathedral of nature. If the picnic is an allegory of the eucharistic meal, the duel is also a memorial of the passion and redemption. Laevskij leaves the duel alive, but there are intimations of his death. When he arrives on the scene, he feels the exhaustion and weariness of a person who may soon die (VII: 443), and when he realizes fon Koren is aiming at him with the intention to kill, Laevskij thinks it's all over (VII: 447). An important but subtle detail are the 30 rubles which are to be paid to Dr. Ustimovič for the victim's

dead body, that is for the sacrifice (VII: 444) of the duel. In the Gospels, Judas is paid 30 silver pieces for identifying Jesus, that is, 30 silver pieces for the body of Christ. In addition, these thirty rubles echo the thirty bottles of wine at the picnic and the 300 ruble loan. The duel, hence, is an allegorical celebration of the death and resurrection, as is the sacrament of the eucharist.

6. Fon Koren's Change of Heart

Although fon Koren does not practice love for neighbor in the Christian sense, and values knowledge over faith, it is implied in the final chapter, that he has a spiritual change of heart, catalyzed by Laevskij's reform.

Although physically Laevskij and fon Koren are opposites: Laevskij is blond and frail, the zoologist dark and strong, they do have similar natures to the extent that both are in need of salvation. The deacon states this need when, as he walks to the site of the duel early Saturday morning, he assures himself that his "non-believing" friends, Laevskij and fon Koren, "will be saved" ("They are non-believers, but they are good people and will be saved . . . certainly they will be saved!"; VII: 440). The non-believers are also united through their association with evolutionism, a science which contradicts the beliefs of the Russian Church, as cited in a nineteenth century treatise on "teachings opposed to Christianity and Russian Orthodoxy".[29]

Fon Koren's views on the weak and strong of society, his definition of love, defined by destruction of the weak in order to protect society's strong, obviously affiliates him with Darwinism and distances him from the Church. Laevskij is united with fon Koren through his association with Spencerian philosophy. The Russian Church refutes Spencer's theory, derived from Darwinism, that morality also is a product of evolution, that one's moral nature is dependent on that of previous generations. This philosophical claim is opposed to Orthodoxy because it denies the likelihood of sudden moral change, inspired, for example, by divine grace.[30] Laevskij is initially attracted to Nadežda because she reads Spencer, and he brags of this detail. More significantly, however, his apathetic and hopeless attitude towards his own immoral and lazy character implies faith in the evolutionary theory of morality. According to fon Koren, Laevskij presents his own character as organically dependent on those of his "fathers of flesh and spirit", "Onegin, Pečorin, Byron's Cain, and Bazarov" (VII: 370). Fon Koren explains:

> We are to understand that . . . his [Laevskij's] dissoluteness, his lack of culture and moral purity, is a phenomenon of natural history, sanctified by inevitability, that the causes of it are worldwide, elemental.
>
> (VII: 370, 371)

Fon Koren inadvertently groups himself with Laevskij and those whom he represents, thus accentuating that he too, in biblical terms, is of the same vine in need of restoration, as is his weak neighbor. Paraphrasing Laevskij, he mocks, "it is not the [Laevskij] who is dissolute, false, disgusting, but we. . . 'we men of the eighties', 'we the spiritless, nervous offspring of the serf-owning class'" (VII: 370). And indeed, in Chapter XVIII the deacon points out that the two have similar upbringings: "if they had not been spoiled from childhood by the pleasant surroundings and the select circle of friends they lived in, [. . .]" they would not hate each other so strongly (VII: 442). They both are "of the serf-owning class". In addition, the deacon associates Laevskij with fon Koren by likening them to moles. As he surreptitiously watches the two prepare for the duel, the priest whispers "moles" ("kroty"; VII: 447), recalling how fon Koren in Chapter XI explains that when two moles meet underground, they instinctively fight each other until the weakest dies. In one of Isaiah's visions concerning everlasting peace for Jerusalem, the mole represents decadence and idolatry (Isaiah 2: 20). Isaiah groups the mole with the bat: two animals who live in darkness, a common metaphor for spiritual emptiness. Curiously enough, the zoologist also mentions the bat when speaking about the mole's great physical strength (VII: 407). Fon Koren is like the bat and mole: physically strong but spiritually weak, living in darkness.

Fon Koren's reform is suggested in Chapter XXI, mainly by his show of unprecedented humility, which is praised by the deacon. But first, fon Koren's reform is hinted at through the expedition which he plans to take in three years from the setting of the story. This expedition, significantly in the third year (as Laevskij's crisis occurs in the third year of his relationship with Nadežda), and mentioned at various points throughout the story, is first introduced during the picnic. After the picnic, Laevskij speaks to Samojlenko about this expedition, not as a trip to the Arctic, but as a trek across the desert. Laevskij calls fon Koren "the despot and czar of the desert" (VII: 397). In biblical terms, the desert, as in Exodus, is a symbol of conversion.

Fon Koren manifests considerable humility in his farewell visit to Laevskij before leaving the Black Sea resort-town. He is still too proud to admit that his theories of the strong and weak may be wrong, and he tells Laevskij that he does not stop by to excuse himself. Nevertheless, he admits that concerning Laevskij's allegedly "hopeless situation" he was wrong. His humility is further revealed by the subtle implication that he seeks Laevskij's forgiveness. The Russian verb 'proščat'sja/prostit'sja', 'to say good-bye', repeated four times in the context of fon Koren's farewell visit to Laevskij, is distinguished from the verb 'to forgive' only by the reflexive particle 'sja': 'proščat'/prostit''. As fon Koren rows off on the stormy sea, his last word is "Proščaj!" or "Good-bye". 'Proščaj', however, is also the imperfective command of the verb 'to forgive' ('proščat''). As Laevskij previously receives instantaneous forgiveness from Nadežda, so fon Koren obtains forgiveness from Laevskij, as symbolized in Laevskij's humble welcome and in the farewell handshakes of the two (VII: 453, 454). This forgiveness of sins evokes the first term of the new covenant foretold by the Old Testament prophets: God's spontaneous forgiveness of sins.

The deacon praises the zoologist for overcoming man's greatest vice, pride: "You conquered man's greatest enemy—pride" (VII: 453). Prior to this statement, the deacon paraphrases verse 14 of Psalm 79, exclaiming "My God, what people! It's true the right hand of God has planted this vine! Lord! Lord", and adds a verse from First Kings 18: 7 (1 Samuel 18: 7): "One man vanquishes thousands and another tens of thousands." In First Kings, these two vanquishers are Saul and David respectively. In "The Duel", the two conquerors are fon Koren and Laevskij. While Laevskij has "conquered tens of thousands", that is vanquished many vices through his moral reform, fon Koren too has done great things by "conquering thousands", that is "pride". While Laevskij has accomplished more, fon Koren is also to be praised.

The ultimate victor, however, is neither of these two individuals, but Christian morality and the terms of the new covenant as presented by the Church; and the deacon embodies the teachings of the Church. The deacon's name, Pobedov, is derived from the word 'conquest' or 'pobeda'. The fisher-of-men, Pobedov, who spends his days catching bullheads, is the ultimate victor of souls.

One may infer still more from the reference to First Kings. Through this allusion, Laevskij is very loosely paralleled with King David. In Christian doctrine, David is a prefiguration of Christ, which insinuates a parallel between Laevskij and Christ. As Christ is the sacrifice for humanity, so Laevskij is the sacrifice for "the men of the eighties", "the serf-owning class", the progeny of "Onegin, Pečorin, Byron's Cain, and Bazarov", and for all the 'Laevskijs' whom Ivan Andreič represents. Laevskij dies and is reborn for their sake. In Chapter XVII and during the duel, there are numerous intimations of death and rebirth. Laevskij as sacrifice is subtly suggested by the facts that he is referred to as "the sacrifice of the times" ("žertva vremeni"; VII: 374), and prior to his reform, Nadežda looks at Laevskij "as she would look at an icon" (VII: 415). But most importantly, his moral reform occurs on Friday night. This day, and the anguish and torment which Laevskij endures, evoke the Passion of Christ.

It is crucial to note, however, that in this story carefully chronicled by the days of the week, the duel takes place on Saturday, not Sunday, the day of the Resurrection. This detracts from the parallel between Christ and Laevskij. Thus, similar to David, Laevskij is a foreshadowing of Christ. His spiritual and physical rebirth is more reminiscent of the release of those in Hell on Holy Saturday, or the raising from the dead of Lazarus, celebrated on the Saturday before Holy Week. The Harrowing of Hell and Lazarus Saturday are signs of things to come. So is Laevskij's rebirth. It is a sign of the times. A sign of the times in Russia. The agitated sea in the last scene also suggests times yet to come. The time of the new covenant, initiated by the Resurrection, has not yet arrived; for as St. John Chrysostom writes, with Christ there is "peaceful sailing" on the sea of life. The sea is restless in the centuries before Christ as it is restless at the end of **"The Duel"**. As the prophets at the close of the sixth century B.C. foretell of ruin and new life to come, so Čechov, at the end of the nineteenth century, prophesies future times in Russia of passion and redemption, when "not one stone will be left on another".

Notes

1. Thomas Winner, *Chekhov and his Prose.* New York 1966, 103.

2. A. M. Skabičevskij, 'Duèl'-Žena'. *Novosti i Birževaja gazeta,* 41, Febr. 13, 1892.

   K. Medvedskij, 'Žertva bezvremen'ja'. *Russkij vestnik,* 7, 1896, 242.

3. Carolina de Maegd-Soëp, *Chekhov and Women.* Columbus, Ohio 1987, 307.

4. Ronald Hingley, *A New Life of Anton Chekhov.* New York 1976, 152.

5. All citations refer to Vol. VII of A. P. Čechov, *Polnoe sobranie sočinenij i pisem v tridcati tomach.* Moskva 1974–1982.

6. This symbolism is derived in part from the Greek word for fish, 'ichthys', which is the acronym of Jesus (i) Christ (ch), God's (th), Son (y), Savior (s).

7. The 'panagija' is the second of five loaves consecrated during the first part of the Liturgy ('Proskomidija'). It is blessed after the first loaf or lamb ('agnec'), which represents Christ. Reference to the bread honoring Mary foreshadows the eucharist or the covenant of salvation.

8. Psalom 79: 15–16.

9. Psalom 79: 9, 10.

10. Psalom 79: 14. Russian: "Lesnoj vepr' podryvaet ee, i polevoj zver' ob"edaet ee." Church Slavonic: "Uzoba i vepr u dubravy, i uedinenyj divyj poede i."

11. Psalom 79: 4, 8, 20. Russian: "Bože sil! Vosstanovi nas; da vossijaet lice Tvoe, i spasemsja!" Church Slavonic: "Bože sil naverni nas i pokaži lice tvoe, i budemo spaseni."

12. Konstantin Nikol'skij, *Ustav bogosluženija pravoslavnoj cerkvi.* Sankt-Peterburg 1900, 378.

13. Filaret, Metropolitan of Moscow, *Prostrannyj christianskij katichizis.* Moskva 1909, 23.

14. *Katichizis, ibid.,* 87.

15. [Russian translation deleted.]

16. [Russian translation deleted.]

17. Paul Evdokimov, *L'Orthodoxie.* Paris 1959, 218.

18. Timothy Ware, *The Orthodox Church.* New York 1986, 226.

19. Evdokimov, *ibid.,* 88.

20. *Katichizis, ibid.,* 67.

21. *Katichizis, ibid.,* 67.

22. [Russian translation deleted.]

23. *Katichizis, ibid.,* 77.

24. [Russian translation deleted.]

25. *Katichizis, ibid.,* 86.

26. Ware, *ibid.,* 236, 237.

27. Ioann Zlatoust, *Polnoe sobranie tvorenij svjatogo otca Ioanna Zlatoustogo,* IV. Sankt-Peterburg 1898, 903–905.

28. *Katichizis, ibid.,* 3.

29. [Russian translation deleted.]

30. Bulgakov, *ibid.,* 211.

FURTHER READING

Criticism

Johnson, Ronald L. "The Short Fiction." In *Anton Chekhov: A Study of the Short Fiction,* pp. 50–75. New York: Twayne Publishers, 1993.

   Briefly summarizes the thematic arc of "The Duel" as a conflict of ideologies: "The struggle between the superfluous man and the man of science."

Additional coverage of Chekhov's life and career is contained in the following sources published by the Gale Group: *Contemporary Authors,* **Vols. 104, 124;** *DISCovering Authors;* *DISCovering Authors: British;* *DISCovering Authors: Canadian;* *DISCovering Authors Modules: Dramatists, Most-Studied Authors;* *Drama Criticism,* **Vol. 9;** *Something About the Author,* **Vol. 90;** *Twentieth-Century Literary Criticism,* **Vols. 3, 10, 31, 55, 96; and** *World Literature Criticism.*

Dazai Osamu
1909–1948

(Born Tsushima Shuji) Japanese short story writer, novelist, and essayist.

INTRODUCTION

Dazai Osamu is considered one of the most important storytellers of postwar Japan. While known primarily as a novelist, Dazai also earned recognition for his numerous short stories, including "Omoide" ("Memories"), "Sarugashima" ("Monkey Island"), and "Ha" ("Leaves"), which were published in *Bannen*, his first collection of short stories. Like most of his longer fiction, Dazai's short stories are autobiographical and reflect a troubled life marred by alcoholism, drug addiction, and several suicide attempts. Nevertheless, Dazai's fiction showcases his artistic imagination and unique confessional narrative technique.

BIOGRAPHICAL INFORMATION

Dazai was born the youngest of ten children in Kanagi, a small town in northern Japan, to one of the wealthiest families in the region. While Dazai's later years were turbulent, he grew up a sensitive child in comfortable surroundings. Later in his life, however, his wealthy background led to self-consciousness, contributing to a nagging sense of isolation that is an undercurrent throughout his fiction. Dazai underwent his apprenticeship in writing during the 1920s while attending secondary schools in Aomori and Hirosaki and published many of his early stories in magazines founded and run by aspiring young authors. By the time he attended Hirosaki Higher School, however, Dazai began to live the unconventional lifestyle that brought him much fame. Despite his widely recognized talent, however, alcoholism, drug addiction, affairs with geishas, suicide attempts, and frequent psychological traumas plagued him the rest of his life. In 1930, Dazai enrolled in the Department of French Literature at Tokyo University, but by the end of his first year, he ceased attending classes. Instead, Dazai became involved with left-wing politics, caroused, and renewed his relationship with a geisha he met while attending Hirosaki Higher School. His family disapproved of this relationship, leading to one of Dazai's suicide attempts. He attempted to take his own life on at least three other occasions and finally succeeded in a double suicide with a young war widow in 1948. This episode, among several instances of double suicide in Dazai's fiction, is retold in his widely acclaimed novel, *No Longer Human*.

MAJOR WORKS OF SHORT FICTION

Dazai's highly autobiographical fiction first garnered popular and critical attention after the publication of his first collection, *Bannen* (*The Final Years*). The first and most significant of these stories is "Omoide"("Memories"). With its highly personal tone, "Memories" reveals a common narrative technique in Dazai's writing. Revealing his childhood and adolescent traumas, as well as his need for companionship and love, Dazai's first-person narrative attracts the reader's sympathy while raising doubts about the authenticity of the narration because of exaggerated rhetoric. "Gangu" ("Toys"), another tale in *Bannen*, illustrates Dazai's playfulness. In this tale, the narrator—after briefly relating his financial troubles—details his plans to concoct a tale recounting the memories of an infant. While these and other early pieces exemplify the personal tone of much of Dazai's work, another group of tales shows his talent for imaginative storytelling. Two tales—"Gyofukuki," translated as "Metamorphosis," and "Sarugashima," translated as "Monkey Island"—provide good examples of this. In place of the Dazai-like protagonist present throughout most of his other short fiction, "Metamorphosis" is about a peasant girl who, on the verge of puberty, takes on the appearance and identity of a fish. "Monkey Island" presents two humanoid monkeys as its protagonists. In astonishment, one of the monkeys soon realizes they are the objects of attention, rather than the spectators, of the humans walking through the zoo. In his final years, he composed a series of stories that evince his interest in domestic issues, as titles such as "Villon's Wife," "Father," and "Family Happiness"—suggest. As critics have remarked, the stories of these collections are among the few works of artistic value produced by a Japanese author under the strict government censorship during World War II.

CRITICAL RECEPTION

While famous in Japan and avidly read—especially by the younger generation—Dazai has not achieved the international stature of Japanese writers such as Natsume Sseki, Kawabata Yasunari, Mishima Yukio, and End Shusaku. This is partly due to problems with translating Dazai's highly personal style. Yet Dazai has earned himself a position in modern Japanese letters more or less comparable to that of an F. Scott Fitzgerald, as opposed to a William Faulkner, in modern American literature. Donald Keene, Dazai's principal English translator, has described him as a Japanese writer "who emerged at the end of World War II as the literary voice of his time." While Dazai's body of work is sometimes criticized for its narrow scope, many critics maintain that his fiction contains some of the most beautiful prose in modern Japanese literature.

PRINCIPAL WORKS

Short Fiction

Bannen [*The Final Years*] 1937
"Hashire merosu" 1940
"Kakekomi uttae" ["I Accuse"] 1941
"Kojiki gakusei" 1941
Otogi zōshi 1945
Shinshaku shokoku banashi 1945
"Buiyon no tsuma" ["Villon's Wife"] 1947
"Cherries" 1953
"Of Women" 1953
"Osan" 1958
Dazai Osamu zenshu (short stories, novels, and essays) 1962
"Leaves" 1968
"Metamorphosis" 1970
"Monkey Island" 1971
Crackling Mountain, and Other Stories 1989

Other Major Works

Dōke no hana (novel) 1937
Shin Hamuretto (novel) 1941
Tsugaru [*Return to Tsugaru*] (nonfiction) 1944
Shayō [*The Setting Sun*] (novel) 1947
Ningen shikkaku [*No Longer Human*] (novel) 1948

CRITICISM

James A. O'Brien (essay date 1975)

SOURCE: "The War Years (1941–1945)," in *Japan,* edited by Roy E. Teele, Twayne Publishers, 1975, pp. 91–118, 166–69.

[*In the following essay, O'Brien discusses Dazai's writings during the war years (1941–1945), focusing on his retelling of both fairy tales and the writings of Ihara Saikakau.*]

A RETELLING OF THE TALES FROM THE PROVINCES

Although the title of this work is based on Ihara Saikaku's *Tales from the Provinces,* a collection of thirty-five stories published in 1685, only one of Dazai's twelve tales, **"Stubborn in Poverty,"** is based on this particular Saikaku collection. The remainder are scattered throughout such other works by Saikaku as *The Eternal Storehouse of Japan* and *Tales of Warriors and Duty.*

The stories in *A Retelling of the Tales from the Provinces* were initially published in various magazines from January to November, 1944. The following January the entire collection was brought out under its present title by the Seikatsusha Publishing Company. In a short preface Dazai claimed that his works were not translations of Saikaku into modern Japanese—something he called a "meaningless exercise." Nevertheless, the adaptations from Saikaku are closer to the originals than the *Collection of Fairy Tales* he was to retell shortly. Okuno Tateo has conjectured that Dazai, who calls Saikaku in his preface the "world's greatest writer," was probably constrained by his great respect for Saikaku.

This relative fidelity on Dazai's part results in a preservation of much of Saikaku's quality. Dazai successfully incorporates the social background and value clashes of the earlier stories, and even manages to capture something of Saikaku's quick wit and deft character typing.

"STUBBORN IN POVERTY"

The range of Dazai's selection suggests a wide acquaintance with Saikaku's work. His stated purpose in writing raises the question of why he chose these particular twelve stories out of such a great number—one story, for example, out of a total of thirty-five from Saikaku's *Tales from the Provinces.* **"Stubborn in Poverty,"** the one selection from *Tales from the Provinces,* affords ample material for a comparative study between Dazai and his source. After giving a comparative analysis of these two tales, it will be well to briefly describe each tale, concentrating especially on those features of the narrative that might have prompted Dazai to choose it.

"Stubborn in Poverty," the first story in Dazai's collection, centers on a New Year's party given for his friends by a poor *ronin,* or masterless samurai, named Harada Naisuke. His samurai guests, as poor as he, have been invited to celebrate Harada's good fortune in receiving a gift of ten *ryo* from his brother-in-law, a doctor living near the Kanda Myojin shrine. At first Naisuke's seven guests are downcast. One of them confesses that he has gone so long without sake that he has forgotten how to drink; the others confess that they have forgotten how to get drunk. Nonetheless, once the guests understand that Naisuke has come into a windfall and will not charge them for the sake, they set about drinking with gusto. Once the party has livened up, Naisuke passes around the ten coins he has received. When they come back Naisuke finds one missing, but he is too timid to issue a challenge. After he finally reveals that one coin is missing, everyone, with a single exception, disrobes to prove that he has not stolen the coin. Eventually two coins turn up; the men discover one by the lamp stand, and Harada's wife finds another in the kitchen, stuck to the lid of a bowl from which the guests have been served. Naisuke is furious at this unexpected turn of events—he will not, despite his poverty, accept charity from his friends nor will he be made a fool of. When no one will admit to planting the extra coin, Naisuke works out a scheme whereby the owner may pick up his coin at the front door unseen.

Saikaku's original story, entitled "A New Year's Reckoning That Didn't Figure," is less elaborate than Dazai's retelling. Harada's brother-in-law, a doctor, sends a witty prescription in hopes of curing a case of poverty. Finding himself the recipient of ten *ryo,* a "marvelous medicine" for curing countless ills, Harada invites seven of his samurai cronies to celebrate the windfall. After they arrive Harada passes the coins around, and finds one missing when they are returned to him. Two of the guests remove their sashes to show they have no money, but a third balks at putting himself to the test. Having just sold some goods he happens to have one *ryo* and some change on his person. He is on the verge of disemboweling himself when the missing coin is suddenly discovered in the shadow of the lamp stand. The appearance of the wife announcing the discovery of a second coin and Harada's stratagem for allowing the anonymous donor to get his *ryo* back without revealing his identity are basically the same in Saikaku's original as in Dazai's retelling.

Saikaku spins his yarn with characteristic brevity. He gives only an occasional glimpse of the characters he is portraying. The four or five opening lines of the tale suffice to tell

the reader the basic facts of Harada Naisuke's existence: his lack of the necessities of life, his disheveled appearance, his threatening look as he makes an appeal to a rice-shop clerk. Harada the *ronin* has had to borrow a sword from the clerk, and he asks why he cannot keep it past the New Year into spring.

Saikaku packs his narrative tightly with brief details and shifts the focus of his tale from Harada to the brother-in-law to the seven friends and back to Harada with his customary speed and dexterity. Dazai, by contrast, is more concerned than Saikaku that the reader develop a definite conception of Naisuke. Dazai takes the poverty of Saikaku's Harada as an invitation to portray situations and responses recalling aspects of his own life. Describing the gift by the brother-in-law, he borrows Saikaku's witty pun, but—no doubt mindful of his own benefactors—he adds a touch of hauteur to the relatively benign figure of the brother-in-law in Saikaku. With Harada feigning insanity at the approach of New Year's Eve with its obligation to pay off all debts, his wife appeals to her doctor brother. The doctor's prescription, a "dose" of money, seems in the Dazai version a rather poor joke. Dazai implies that penurious souls like Harada (and himself) can readily be made fools of by their affluent relatives.

Harada, though, is not simply portrayed as the victim of his poverty. Departing radically from his source story, Dazai describes Harada refusing at first to accept charity. And, once he does accept, Harada feels an obligation to share his bounty with friends. No doubt Saikaku's Harada Naisuke is moved by similar feelings. Dazai, however, takes pains to make this feeling of obligation very explicit in his narrative.

Saikaku, after briefly describing Harada's character, sets the plot moving and proceeds to the end without any delaying commentary. Dazai, on the contrary, is constantly tampering with Harada. As usual, Dazai is interested in the tale for its moral. Harada stands forth as the victim required by circumstances to accept charity, and as the plucky underdog who, within the limits possible to him, insists on his honor and dignity.

Despite the serious note, **"Stubborn in Poverty"** is very much a comic story. To read it in conjunction with Saikaku's tale provides insights into certain of Dazai's comic techniques. The economy of Saikaku's narrative style afforded Dazai a number of opportunities to rewrite or expand the original. In several instances Dazai, more conscious than Saikaku of the possibilities and demands of realism, creates in his characters a range of response wider than did Saikaku. Once the extra coin is discovered, the guests in Dazai's version bring forth the very plausible suggestion that Harada's brother-in-law might have added the extra coin just for fun. In Saikaku, on the other hand, the guests are silent on this question.

Again Dazai spells out meanings that are only implicit in the Saikaku narrative. In Saikaku, once it becomes clear that the owner of the extra coin will not reveal himself, Harada simply says that he will place a measuring box with the coin inside on the garden wash basin. The guests are to leave one by one; thus, the owner of the coin will be able to pick it up in private.

In his closing scene, Dazai is very explicit about making it difficult for the other six guests to gather any hints in leaving as to who the owner of the coin might be. Dazai's Harada says: "If we put the coin at the edge of the step in the darkest place, no one will be able to see whether or not it's there. The owner of the coin alone is to feel around with his hand, then go out as if nothing were amiss."

The interesting aspect of this is not the idle question of which version is more effective or foolproof. Rather, the reader should simply be aware of the double irony involved in Dazai's reordering of Saikaku. For Saikaku himself had taken similar liberties as an author, writing parodies of earlier Japanese literature with such titles as *Nise Monogatari* and *The "Gay" Tale of the Heike*. Saikaku even tampered with the best of classical Japanese fiction. The fifty-four chapters of *The Man Who Spent His Life in Love* parallel the fifty-four chapters of *The Tale of Genji*; the multiple sordid adventures of Saikaku's hero Yonosuke parody the Genji tradition of high romance.

Dazai's intentions, then, in writing **"Stubborn in Poverty"** involve certain aspects of his own life and the possibilities he saw in the Saikaku original for the application of comic techniques of style. That he wrote about the *ronin* so soon after describing Minamoto Sanetomo in his historical novel, *Sanetomo, Minister of the Right,* reveals Dazai's continued interest in the relation of the samurai ethic to life.

Dazai could also have been drawn to the original tale by the ambiguity inherent in Saikaku's narrative method. Readers of the several excellent English translations of Saikaku's *koshokubon,* or erotic works, will realize the difficulty of determining the author's attitude toward events and characters he describes. In *Five Women Who Loved Love,* for example, Saikaku's characters often fall in love in ways that violate social law and custom only to meet "justice" ultimately on the execution ground. In these cases, Saikaku appears to sanction the harsh penalties of the Tokugawa code; at the same time, he describes the illicit love affair with such gusto that no reader can believe he is absolutely condemning his lovers.

A similar ambiguity exists in Saikaku's "New Year's Reckoning That Didn't Figure." The subject of Saikaku's work is listed as *giri,* or obligation. But the reader, having finished the tale, is less than certain of Saikaku's feelings. "In the quick wit of the host, the behavior of his familiar guests, indeed in many ways the relations among the samurai are different [i.e., from those of the townsmen]," Saikaku declares, ending his tale. But, as so often happens in Saikaku, the final moral comment can hardly obliterate the import of the narrative. One feels with Saikaku that

the samurai are rather foolish in their insistence on dignity. Why should the mere sum of one *ryo* create such havoc? Why should a man under suspicion by his friends for a petty crime ready his sword to take his life? Surely the merchants and townsmen who read Saikaku found such behavior strange.

Shortly before he began his **Retelling of the Tales from the Provinces,** Dazai had expressed his admiration for the samurai virtues in *Sanetomo Minister of the Right.* In **"Stubborn in Poverty"** he examines the lives of *ronin* at the very bottom of the samurai class. If the *shogun* Sanetomo represents an ideal, the *ronin* in **"Stubborn in Poverty"** perhaps represent what is amiss with the ethic of the warrior. Or, rather, they represent attitudes and behavior of noble samurai diminished (perhaps to the point of absurdity) by the poverty in which these men now find themselves. As usual, the reader of Dazai finds it difficult to pin down his elusive, ironic author. Surely Dazai saw something noble in the samurai virtues; perhaps he felt that these were the sole virtues that could survive the war. Regardless of whether he looked foolish or pompous, a man ought to cling to such a heritage.

"GREAT STRENGTH"

The second tale, a thin piece entitled **"Great Strength"** and taken from Saikaku's *Twenty-four Instances of Unfilial Conduct in Our Country,* details the feats of a sumo wrestler, Saibei. An uncouth youth given to beating up other people, Saibei is urged by his father to try his hand at other sports, football, for example, or even flower arrangement. His mother, hoping to plant in him the seeds of compassion, persuades him to take a bride. Unfortunately, as Saibei reveals to his wife on their wedding night, he has taken a vow to the god Marishiten never to touch a woman. The story ends abruptly when Waniguchi, Saibei's old wrestling tutor, defeats his ex-pupil in a wrestling match by a clever stratagem. Dazai was prompted to retell the story, one might imagine, to capitalize on the opportunities for wit and humor it afforded at a number of points.

"THE MONKEY'S GRAVE"

The third tale, **"The Monkey's Grave,"** is drawn from *The Inkstone of Nostalgia* and is clearly Dazai's kind of story. As in the case of **"Great Strength,"** Dazai was doubtless intrigued by the comic potential of **"The Monkey's Grave."** Jiroemon dispatches a friend to talk to the father of his beloved Oran about arranging a marriage. The father is anxious that Oran, brought up in the Nichiren Buddhist sect, marry a fellow believer, and he immediately traps the hapless go-between into admitting ignorance of Jiroemon's religion. Then, to make matters worse, the go-between blurts out that this makes no difference; Jiroemon, regardless of his present beliefs, can always convert to Nichiren. Condemning this opportunism, Oran's father reveals that he has already betrothed her to another, a firm Nichiren believer.

Oran and Jiroemon, taking matters into their own hands, decide to elope. At this point in the story enters Dazai's favorite animal, a monkey.

This monkey, named Kichibei, was so attached to Oran it hobbled off in pursuit the night she ran away with a strange man. When Jiroemon and Oran had covered about three miles, the girl noticed her pet. Though she scolded and pelted him with stones, the monkey limped along after her. Finally, Jiroemon took pity. "He's followed you this far. Let him join us."

"Here boy," Oran beckoned and the monkey came bounding. As she hugged him the monkey looked mournfully at his two companions and blinked his eyes.

After Oran and Jiroemon settle in a humble cottage, Kichibei helps about the house. With the birth of a son, Kikunosuke, the monkey becomes a baby-sitter.

The story comes to a tragic end, though, just as Oran and Jiroemon are laying plans to return to society to give Kikunosuke the advantages of a respectable upbringing. They leave Kichibei to tend the baby while they go off to discuss a business deal with a neighboring farmer.

> In a little while Kichibei recalled it was time for the infant's bath. So he lit a fire under the stove to boil some water—precisely, he recalled, as Oran always did.
>
> When bubbles started to rise Kichibei poured the steaming water into a basin to the very rim. Without bothering to test the water he stripped the child naked, lifted him, and—peering into his face in imitation of Oran—gently dipped the child two or three times in the basin.
>
> "Waa!" The parents, hearing the shrill cry of the scalded baby, glanced at each other and came running back to the house. The stunned Kichibei stood transfixed as the baby floated about the basin. Oran, lifting the corpse, could scarcely bear the sight of this "broiled lobster."

The hysterical Oran tries to kill Kichibei, but Jiroemon intervenes to save the monkey.

One hundred days after the infant's death, Kichibei, standing on the new grave, takes his own life in atonement. Oran and Jiroemon bury him sadly; they have forgiven him the crime he committed in his animal innocence and have come to realize that, after the baby's death, Kichibei is the only thing they have.

Kichibei, then, is one of a considerable group of symbolic monkeys in Dazai's works. Kichibei represents a Dazai ideal: unselfish service to the interest of another. At the same time, his innocence causes him to blunder in such a way that his ideals, like the author's, bring destruction and sorrow.

"MERMAID SEA"

The following tale, taken from Saikaku's *A Record of Traditions of the Warrior's Way,* is entitled **"Mermaid Sea."** Like *Sanetomo, Minister of the Right,* **"Mermaid Sea"** is an expression of certain samurai virtues.

A boat encounters a freak storm on the ocean. Everyone aboard gradually loses consciousness, with the exception of the virtuous samurai Chudo Konnai. When a mermaid appears in the waves, he shoots her with an arrow. She sinks, the storm subsides, and Chudo's companions regain consciousness.

When a report of this feat is made to the regional lord, one of the samurai in attendance expresses disbelief. Aozaki, the samurai in question, is described by Dazai as a good-for-nothing who holds a high official position only by virtue of the exploits of his father. But so forcefully does Aozaki express his contempt toward wondrous events that the other samurai present at the occasion become utterly bewildered. Chudo, in true samurai fashion, will not rest with his word called into question. He organizes a search of the area of the sea where the slaying occurred. Yet, when a thorough search uncovers no evidence of his feat, he begins himself to doubt the event.

At this point, the narrative switches to Chudo's house, where his daughter and her attendant are growing restless and concerned over his safety. Finally, they set out in search, only to find his corpse on the beach wrapped in seaweed. A samurai follower of Chudo's arrives on horseback. He dismisses the entire question of the truth or falsity of Chudo's account and charges the daughter to avenge her father by killing Aozaki. The latter is guilty of slandering and sending him to his death. The daughter kills Aozaki and marries a young samuari, who takes the name Chudo in order to carry on the dead man's family name. Finally, for good measure, the skeleton of a mermaid, with Chudo's arrowhead embedded in the shoulder blade, is washed ashore.

"BANKRUPTCY"

In paying deference to Saikaku in his preface to *A Retelling of the Tales from the Provinces,* Dazai added the caveat that, for him, Saikaku's series of erotic stories were not to his taste. But, of course, this was Saikaku's métier, and most Japanese readers today, as well as Westerners who have read him in translation, associate Saikaku with this series of works.

The next two stories, **"Bankruptcy"** and **"Naked in the River,"** deal with another important concern of Saikaku—money. **"Bankruptcy"** comes from the collection treating the crafty practices of the Osaka merchant, *The Eternal Storehouse of Japan.* **"River of the Naked,"** along with the next tale, **"Obligation,"** is taken from *Tales of the Knightly Code of Honor.*

"Bankruptcy" slyly narrates the downfall of the prosperous house of Yorozuya. The owner of the family business is a self-made man of nearly fanatical thrift. Fearing for the future of the business, he disinherits his effeminate son and adopts in his stead a young man whose thrifty habits appear to guarantee continued prosperity for the house. With admirable foresight the adopted son recommends that a jealous woman be found for him to marry. The hard opposition of a shrew will protect him from the temptation so common among the merchants of Tokugawa Japan of squandering the family fortune in the pleasure quarter.

Unfortunately the wife proves to be such a killjoy that her husband is soon looking for relief. When his foster parents die, he leaves for Kyoto and squanders his fortune in a year. Returning home he sets to work rebuilding the family business in hopes of returning to Kyoto for another round of fun. Concealing his actual penury, he operates a thriving brokerage simply on the appearance of wealth. Before he can recoup his fortune, an accident upsets his well-laid plans. One New Year's Eve, the night for clearing all debts, a poor *ronin* enters his office demanding change to pay off a trifling debt. The broker does not have the money to make the transaction, and so small is the amount that he cannot plead that he is short of ready cash. The poor *ronin*'s cry of surprise informs the neighbors that the apparently prosperous business is in fact bankrupt.

"River of the Naked"

The opening scene of **"River of the Naked"** shows an official of the Kamakura Bakufu named Aotosaemon transporting government funds across a river. Opening the money pouch, he accidentally drops eleven coins into the river. Although the loss represents a small sum, Aotosaemon hires at considerable expense to himself a group of peasants who search the river for the missing coins.

One of the searchers, a scoundrel named Asada, has hired on simply to share in the reward. Bored with the search and aware that the subsidy from Aotosaemon greatly exceeds the value of the lost coins, Asada decides to conclude matters by pretending to find the coins. Deceiving his companions, he pretends to probe the river bottom with his foot as he surreptitiously slips the requisite coins from his own sash.

While the peasants celebrate the find with a banquet, Aotosaemon returns home and happily reports to his family the details of the incident. Suddenly he is taken aback by a remark of his daughter. She reminds him that he was carrying two coins fewer than usual, and thus his original calculation that eleven coins had fallen into the river must be revised.

Enraged, Aotosaemon returns to the river and compels Asada to search alone for the money, insisting that he stay in the river until every missing coin is recovered. Asada emerges on the ninety-seventh day, having turned up, in addition to the coins, numerous articles people have lost or discarded in the river over the years. His task finished, Asada unabashedly demands from Aotosaemon the eleven "counterfeit" coins.

"Obligation"

In his next selection from Saikaku, [**"Obligation"**], Dazai again portrays a man willing to carry out unhesitatingly an action imposed on him by the dictates of a feudal society.

In this instance Dazai's protagonist is a samurai compelled by obligation to sacrifice his innocent son.

The villains and heroes are clearly marked in this work. Muramaro, the son of an important lord of the province of Settsu, decides on a whim to make a journey to the distant northern island of Hokkaido. To accompany his son, the lord chooses a varied group of men from among his followers. A trusted samurai named Kamizaki Shikibu is to oversee the journey; Kamizaki's son Katsutaro, along with a youth named Tanzaburo, are designated to make the trip as companions to the son of the lord. Like his father Shikibu, Katsutaro is a model samurai; Tanzaburo, the son of an official associated with Shikibu, is lazy and pleasure loving.

As the group heads north, progress is delayed by the carousing habits of Tanzaburo and the young lord. Each night, at a different inn, the two youths stay up late feasting and reveling with the serving-maids. Mornings they remain slugabed, while the members of the retinue idly await their pleasure.

Eventually the travelers reach the Oi River, which empties into the Pacific midway between Kyoto and Tokyo. Kamizaki Shikibu, responsible for the general welfare, counsels that the group pass the night at a nearby inn and attempt the difficult crossing the following morning. But the young lord, impetuous by nature, urges an immediate crossing; spurred on by the thoughtless Tanzaburo, the young lord fords the treacherous stream on horseback. Tanzaburo begins to regret his role in calling for an immediate crossing the moment his own turn arrives. Although Shikibu and Katsutaro try to guide their charge carefully, Tanzaburo falls from his saddle and disappears in the current.

As soon as Kamizaki Shikibu reaches the shore, he orders his son Katsutaro to drown himself in the river. Prior to the journey, Kamizaki had guaranteed to Tanzaburo's father the safety of the son. Once the pledge is broken, Kamizaki, in true samurai fashion, demands of himself the same loss inflicted on the father of Tanzaburo.

When the entourage finally returns to Settsu, Kamizaki and his wife exile themselves from society to pray for the salvation of Katsutaro. Hearing of Shikibu's sacrifice, the father of Tanzaburo is impelled to leave society with his family and likewise pray for the salvation of the unfortunate Katsutaro.

"Female Bandits"

Most of the works in Dazai's *A Retelling of the Tales from the Provinces* have a rural setting. Occasionally a story has both a rural and an urban setting. **"Female Bandits"** is one of these latter tales; it is also the only story in the collection to explicitly contrast urban and rural values.

A prosperous bandit from the northern region of Sendai arrives at the capital of Kyoto to amuse himself. Though uncouth, he gains a considerable reputation throughout the town as a liberal spender. One day he catches sight of an attractive girl and falls immediately in love. Overwhelming the girl's greedy father with munificent gifts, the bandit wins the girl as his bride and takes her off to Sendai.

At first the girl is appalled at the barbarism of life in the north; she is also shocked to discover the source of her husband's prosperity. Within a short time, however, she becomes accustomed to her new life. After giving birth to two girls, she sees to it that both are brought up wise in the methods of brigandage.

When the daughters reach late adolescence, their father is crushed to death in an avalanche of snow. At first, there is some argument as to whether the two daughters, with help from their mother, can continue their dangerous and demanding way of life.

Eventually a strange turn of events brings their operation to a halt. Having divided a stolen fabric, each sister concocts a secret scheme to kill the other. Disillusioned with the uncouth ways of Sendai, each sister has begun yearning for a feminine mode of life. Each sister wants the other's fabric to make herself a lined kimono.

Before anything drastic can occur, the younger sister breaks into tears and begs forgiveness. Having caught sight of smoke rising from a nearby crematorium, she has suddenly come to realize the vanity and evanescence of human life. The elder sister, needless to say, makes a similar confession and asks forgiveness. Thereupon the two sisters, in the company of their mother, renounce the world and take up a life of prayer in expiation for the misdeeds of their past.

"The Great Red Drum"

[In **"The Great Red Drum,"**] Tokubei, a weaver in the Nishijin area of Kyoto, has always been an industrious worker and upright person. Despite his good qualities, he seems destined to live out his life in poverty. While the other weaving establishments carry on a thriving business, Tokubei's remains close to bankruptcy.

When it becomes known throughout Nishijin that Tokubei will be hard pressed to meet his debts at year's end, ten of his peers agree to donate ten *ryo* apiece in hopes of giving the worthy man the start he needs. They deliver the money to Tokubei's house and celebrate the occasion with a boisterous party. After the guests depart, Tokubei and his wife discover that the money is also gone. Despondent over the loss, the couple decide to put an end to their misfortunes.

> Tokubei's wife adorned herself in the white kimono she had managed to keep despite their poverty. Then, facing the mirror to comb down the black hair people had praised from her childhood, she mourned her nineteen years of conjugal intimacy suddenly reduced to a mere predawn dream.
>
> She composed herself and gently woke her two children. The older child, a girl, mumbled drowsily: "Is it

New Year's, Mommy?" The younger, a boy, asked whether she would buy him a top today.

> Blinded by tears Tokubei and his wife set the children without a word before the alter. Holding aloft the vigil lamps with their quivering flames, each member of the family joined his hand in prayer to the ancestral spirits.

In the nick of time a nursemaid rushes in to put a stop to the proceedings. When word of the theft spreads in the neighborhood, the famous Judge Itakura is called in to solve the crime.

His solution is ingenious. After narrowing the number of suspects to a group of ten men, he decrees that each suspect, with the assistance of his nearest female relative, must carry a large red drum from his office to the Hachiman shrine and back. Ten days later, when each couple has carried the drum once, Itakura assembles the suspects:

> Now among this group there is one woman who, upon entering the cedar forest with the great drum, raised such an insane racket she seemed to be possessed by a devil. One by one she brought up her husband's past blunders, while he tried in vain to calm her. So nettled did the husband grow at the increasing clamor that, as they emerged from the forest into the field, he counseled her in a hushed voice: "Calm down please. If we can persevere in this nasty chore, the one hundred *ryo* will be ours. When we return home take a look in the chest of drawers."
>
> Surely the speaker remembers his own strange words. The gods didn't inform on him. But the young acolyte I ordered to hide inside the drum heard all and reported back to me. Now you know why that red drum was so heavy.

"The Refined Man"

Dazai wrote several stories between the end of World War II and his death in 1948 that seem to reflect his awareness that he was not fulfilling his role as a husband and father. Typically these stories depict a man squandering his income while his wife remains at home trying to meet her household responsibilities as best she can. The present story, **"The Refined Man,"** might well be considered the first in this thematic series of tales.

It is the last day of the year, that favored day in Saikaku's writings when all debts must be cleared. Dazai's **"Refined Man"** departs early from home, leaving his wife with only a few inadequate coins to meet the crowd of anticipated creditors. Arriving at one of the few teahouses where he is unknown, the protagonist presents himself as a wealthy patron looking for a place to pass the time. He tells the teahouse matron that his wife is expected to bear a child this very day, and that the people attending her have chased him from home.

The matron, wise in the ways of the world, sees through this tale, but goes along with his pretension. She serves up a boiled egg and a plate of herring roe, along with several cups of sake. With the help of an aging geisha, the matron soon relieves the "Refined Man" of his paltry fortune.

Unable to maintain the pretense of wealth any longer, the man dismisses the geisha and stretches out on the floor of the teahouse parlor to sleep through the rest of the day. Presently two henchmen burst in to admonish him for wasting the money he owes his creditors. They strip him of his jacket, kimono, and sword. Left with only his underwear, the "Refined Man" fabricates an outlandish explanation for the intrusion and insists on remaining in the teahouse until evening in order to leave unseen.

"ADMONITION"

"Admonition" describes an adventure of three young dandies from Kyoto. Bored with the pleasures of their own city, the dandies journey in search of new amusements to Edo, the city that developed into modern Tokyo. At first they find Edo little different from Kyoto. Eventually, however, their attention is drawn to a store where goldfish are sold for considerable sums. Awestruck, the three friends do not recognize in the seedy fellow selling mosquito larvae for goldfish food their bosom friend of earlier days, Tsukiyo no Risa. The latter, who has recognized his old cronies, tries to slip away unnoticed, but, before he can escape, the three dandies catch up with him and begin railing at his aloofness.

Tsukiyo no Risa invites his old friends to a wretched tavern and treats them to drinks with the money he has just earned selling larvae. Eventually the four companions wend their way to Tsukiyo no Risa's house, where the three Kyoto blades renew another old acquaintanceship. Once an attractive Kyoto geisha, Tsukiyo no Risa's wife Kichishu is now a careworn housewife with four "monkey-faced" boys to look after. Appalled by the squalor of Tsukiyo no Risa's life, the three friends surreptitiously leave behind some money as they depart from the house. Their friend stubbornly refuses such charity and leaves shortly thereafter for the countryside with his family. The three dandies return home, vowing to amend their lives. The sight of an old friend fallen into misfortune has served as a reproach to their own carefree, luxurious mode of life.

"MOUNT YOSHINO"

[In **"Mount Yoshino"**] ayoung man, for reasons never precisely disclosed, has rejected society and exiled himself deep in the Yoshino Hills of Nara Prefecture. Confessing that his action was rash and regrettable, the hermit writes an old friend lamenting his exile and imploring certain favors.

The harsh demands of a solitary life in the wild have obliterated the vague romantic notions that seem to have prompted the move into exile. Mentioning an aristocratic poem which "elegantly confuses" snow on a bush with the eagerly awaited spring flowers, the writer bitterly complains that, for him, snow is simply snow. He reserves even harsher criticism for the peasants and farmers in the

vicinity. By the hermit's reckoning, these scoundrels are out to gouge him for the simple necessities he must buy just to survive.

In the course of the letter, he confesses his desire to return to society. But several considerations prevent such a move, particularly the thought of his fearsome grandmother who might have already discovered that he has stolen her cache of money. After asking his correspondent to carry out several transactions, the hermit brings his letter to a close on an uncertain note. Unable to return to society, he expresses the hope that his acquaintances will see their way to paying him a visit in the spring.

A RETELLING OF THE TALES FROM THE PROVINCES IN RETROSPECT

The hermit in **"Mount Yoshino"** is the closest figure in the collection to what might be termed a Dazai surrogate. In general, the stories depict outgoing people active within their respective societies. The brooding, withdrawn figure so common in Dazai's earlier works is almost nonexistent in the world of Saikaku.

This is not to imply that Dazai, in choosing to re-create Saikaku, misjudged the nature of his own talent. Quite the contrary, for some of the finest passages in *A Retelling of the Tales from the Provinces*—the drinking scene in **"Stubborn in Poverty"** with its gruff camaraderie, for example—represent social activities. And Dazai, it must be added, was not simply borrowing Saikaku's deft skill at colloquial, idiomatic dialogue. In his next important work, *Tsugaru,* Dazai utilized his own talent for dialogue to vividly re-create scenes of nostalgic camaraderie he experienced himself on a trip through the region of his birth. Indeed, in reading *Tsugaru,* one almost feels that Saikaku has taught Dazai to relax and enjoy himself in the company of others. The priggish Dazai of **"Beggar-Student"** is nowhere in evidence in *Tsugaru.*

On another plane Dazai conceivably sought in Saikaku some kind of religious or ethical guidance. Readers familiar with Saikaku's superficial treatment of certain moral and religious problems of early Tokugawa Japan may well question such a suggestion. It is nonetheless remarkable how often religion plays a momentary but crucial role in *A Retelling of the Tales from the Provinces.* Consider, for example, Waniguchi's monkish guise in **"Great Strength,"** the religious obstacle to the marriage proposed in **"The Monkey's Grave,"** the Buddhistic sense of life's emptiness in the final scene of **"Female Bandits,"** the moral lesson of a friend's decline in **"Admonition,"** the sense of futility at leading the purest kind of religious life in **"Mount Yoshino."** And a careful search will begin to uncover here and there in the collection Dazai's own moral notions presented as a natural expression of character or plot. One recalls Naisuke in **"Stubborn in Poverty,"** ready to claim a right precisely when it goes against his self-interest, or the monkey Kichibei in **"The Monkey's Grave,"** unselfishly carrying out a service which becomes a disaster for those he would serve. The brooding Dazai surrogate may be missing, but the style and the "ideas in disguise" reveal the author behind these tales.

Above all, Dazai possibly saw many of the characters of *A Retelling of the Tales from the Provinces* as examples of simplicity in the face of complex urbanity, and frugality in the face of extravagance. Such themes are especially evident in **"Bankruptcy," "River of the Naked,"** and **"Obligation,"** where the simple demands and prompt, virtuous actions of samurai figures contrast with the deceptive and selfish behavior of the commoners, the merchants, and the pampered higher nobility. A sophisticated contemporary reader might criticize Dazai for seeking anything other than the entertainment values of good narrative in the world of Saikaku; but it seems likely that Dazai saw in such virtues as frugality and simplicity a bulwark against the self-destructive conduct of his youth. In this sense *A Retelling of the Tales from the Provinces* reaffirms the resolution that Dazai voiced on the occasion of his marriage to Ishihara Michiko to develop his talents in pursuit of a useful life.

A COLLECTION OF FAIRY TALES: "TAKING THE WEN"

The first of Dazai's four tales is entitled **"Taking the Wen."** In his introductory comments to this tale, Dazai records his belief that the earliest extant text is that contained in the thirteenth-century collection *Tales from Uji*. Evidently Dazai read to his daughter during the war from one of the children's editions of fairy tales, editions which generally rework the original story in a simple, colloquial style.

The *Uji* text of **"Taking the Wen"** is vague about the domestic situation of the main character, an old firewood gatherer. The first paragraph, after mentioning the wen on the man's right cheek, moves quickly to a description of a storm that detains the wood gatherer in the forest one day. Hiding in the hollow of a tree, the old man notices a swarm of hideous demons gathering nearby. The demons drink themselves into a merry state, and presently each is in turn performing his favorite dance. So entranced by their spirit is the old man that he ventures forth to perform the most exciting dance of all.

The demons ask the old man to return another day to dance; to guarantee his return, they take the wen from his cheek as a kind of security. Thereupon the wood gatherer returns home and reveals the adventure to his wife and neighbor. The neighbor, an old man with a wen on his left cheek, decides to have his wen removed in the same way. But he dances so poorly that the demons decide to attach the first man's wen to the right cheek of the second. A moral, appended at the end of the tale, cautions against envy.

Dazai expands the tale considerably. As in his adaptation of Saikaku's "Stubborn in Poverty," he makes the action of **"Taking the Wen"** more diverse and the characters more complex. He describes at length the old wood gatherer, a mediocre man with a cold, efficient wife and a virtuous prig of a son. The old man seems impelled to drink as a cure for loneliness; with no friends whatever, he is reduced to regarding the wen on his cheek as the focus of his affections.

In Dazai's version the wood gatherer goes forth to dance in front of the demons, emboldened by an evening of solitary drinking. The demons are again so pleased by the dance that they take the wen to assure the old man's return. Upon his arrival at home, only the neighbor with the wen on his left cheek seems interested in the old man's adventure. As in the original, the neighbor enters the woods in hopes of having his wen removed, only to end up with a wen on both cheeks.

Dazai's alterations of the original tale tend to underline the theme of camaraderie. The wood gatherer is not depicted as lonely in the original tale, and his wen is simply a physical deformity. Dazai's wood gatherer, quite tipsy at the time, seems drawn to the demons mainly by their revelry. The demons, in turn, are greatly impressed by the utter spontaneity with which the old man performs his simple folk dance.

Dazai implies that self-dignity and formality are obstacles to friendship and camaraderie. The son of the old man takes his meals in decorous silence and responds in absurdly formal language to the naïve questions of his father. The neighbor exasperates the demons with his self-consciously formal attempt to perform a dance as he declaims a strange poetic passage derived from such diverse sources as No drama and Shimazaki Toson. Finally, in a long, emphatic (and totally irrelevant) passage, Dazai intrudes to contemptuously dismiss the reverence accorded by the Japanese to certain paragons of contemporary culture.

The two earlier works already treated in this chapter, *A Retelling of the Tales from the Provinces* and *Tsugaru*, help to illuminate the motives behind Dazai's decision to turn the old man in **"Taking the Wen"** into a figure of pathos. In the two earlier works, scenes of warm friendship most commonly occur when men gather together for drinking. In **"Taking the Wen"** the old man forgets his habitual loneliness and grows ecstatic just once: when he realizes that the creatures before him, although hideous demons, are nonetheless drinkers like himself.

Still, his trust in the demons proves to be misplaced. For, in accordance with the traditional tale, the demons deprive the old man of his sole consolation, the wen he has come to regard as an affectionate grandchild. In the end, a reader might conclude that the demons simply show their true colors. Dazai, however, nullifies such an interpretation with his parting remark. He declares everyone blameless—including the supposedly "envious" neighbor who, by Dazai's correct reading of the original, is guilty only of being overly tense about performing in front of the demons. The tale becomes a comedy of errors demonstrating, in Dazai's terms, the "tragicomedy" of human character. Dazai has returned to the world of **"The Monkey's Grave,"** where the innocent and well-intentioned being becomes victimized by his own actions.

"THE TALE OF URASHIMA"

In **"The Tale of Urashima,"** on the other hand, he quotes only a snatch or two from a traditional version near the end of his retelling. Indeed, reading Dazai's work, one sometimes has the impression that the author is more intent on elaborating certain of his pet ideas than in rendering a modern version of a traditional tale.

The original Urashima is often referred to as the Japanese Rip Van Winkle. Urashima, a young man from a fishing village, rescues a sea turtle from some mischievous children and sets the animal free on the beach. Later the turtle returns to thank Urashima and to take the young man on his back to the underwater realm of Ryugu. Urashima visits the princess of Ryugu and passes a number of carefree days in her realm before deciding to return home. Upon his departure the princess gives Urashima a small box with instructions never to open it.

When he reaches the beach near his village, Urashima fails to recognize the scenes and people he knew before. Disappointed, he opens the box, in spite of the princess's warning. Thereupon, a puff of white smoke comes forth from the box and Urashima instantly turns into an old man in tatters.

Dazai, assuming a knowledge of the traditional tale in his reader, spends his early paragraphs developing a portrait of Urashima. Dazai's Urashima is an eldest son, with certain pretensions that draw criticism from his younger brother and sister. Proud of his aesthetic and cultural sense, he longs for a world where people are not subjected to the harsh criticisms of others. In this wish, he conceivably represents his creator, Dazai. In most of his attitudes, Urashima resembles the typical eldest son of a propertied family of the times, a conservative in line to inherit the wealth and status that assure a life of comfort.

Thus, his reluctance at first to accept the turtle's offer of a ride is quite understandable. A true aesthete by nature, Urashima believes that such mythical places as Ryugu exist only in the minds of poets. Only after the turtle affirms that criticism and cavil do not exist in the underworld realm and that Urashima's reluctance to make the trip reveals a lack of trust in the turtle does the young man consent to the ride.

When Urashima arrives at the underwater realm, he finds practiced certain ideals he would like to see in human society. For example, the princess who welcomes Urashima possesses a self-reliant composure; she neither criticizes others nor covets their praise for herself. She plays the *koto* or Japanese harp beautifully, with no concern whether others hear her music.

Yet, Urashima soon discovers the negative side of his ideals. After meeting the lovely princess, Urashima follows her toward what he assumes will be her palace. But the human courtesies, along with the bickering, do not exist under the sea. The princess, the turtle explains to Urashima, has already forgotten her guest, as she goes in pursuit of whatever pleases her fancy at the moment.

The underwater world, then, is peaceful (an intimation, perhaps, of Dazai's suicide by drowning); but it is not very interesting. There is no anxiety and, thus, in Dazai's terms, there can be no literature. Urashima spends his days eating, drinking cherry wine, and, eventually, frolicking in the princess's chamber. But, as he finally admits, he "is a human and belongs on land." Again, unlike the turtle ("Is this amphibious creature a fish of the sea or a reptile of the land?" Urashima ponders), he is all of a piece and cannot divide his time between two fundamentally different spheres. Ultimately, Urashima turns missionary. Unwilling to simply renounce the peace of the underwater world for the interest of the human, he decides to teach this latter world the ideals he has learned.

Dazai's narrative from the departure of Urashima for home to the end is much closer to the traditional tale than the early part of his work. Within the narration of events, only one crucial difference occurs: the princess in Dazai's version says nothing in giving the box to Urashima.

The traditional tale, brief and cryptic, does not venture a statement as to the moral of the events. Dazai, however, seems bent on wrenching some significance from these strange happenings. He spends several paragraphs examining the differences between the outcome of the Greek story of "Pandora's Box" and the Urashima legend. Since the gods were taking revenge on man and the box still contained "hope" after all the evils were let loose, the Greek tale seems more acceptable to "human" understanding than the Japanese. Nevertheless, Dazai regards **"The Tale of Urashima"** as representative of the "profound compassion" discernible in the Japanese fairy tale. "The passing of time is man's salvation; forgetfulness is man's salvation," the author recites in almost the final lines of his work. The nostalgia Urashima might feel for the past is swiftly foreclosed as he moves three hundred years into the future. And, Dazai adds with no warrant from the traditional tale, he "lived ten years thereafter as a happy old man."

"THE CRACKLING MOUNTAIN"

More clearly than the other three works of this collection, **"The Crackling Mountain"** reveals Dazai's method of abstracting a "moral" or "truth" from the original tale, then clarifying his discovery by alterations and additions in the retelling. In Dazai's version of **"The Crackling Mountain,"** the traditionally virtuous hare is revealed as a scheming vixen while the traditionally villainous badger becomes a pathetic victim of cruelty.

In the traditional tale an old man and his wife have a pet hare. One day a badger gobbles up the food intended for the hare. Seizing the badger, the old man ties him to a tree and threatens to kill him. When the man goes off to cut wood, the desperate badger cajoles the wife into setting him free. Then, avenging himself on the old man, the badger kills the wife and makes a broth with her remains. When the old man returns, the badger transforms himself into the form of the wife and serves the dish. After the meal the badger assumes his true form and tells the man he has just relished the remains, not of a badger, but of his wife.

Having learned of the tragedy, the hare determines to wreak vengeance on the badger. First, the hare sets fire to the faggots the badger carries on his back. (The title of the story derives from a remark during this episode; when the badger detects a strange "crackling" sound at his back, the hare explains away the phenomenon as a regular occurrence on "Crackling Mountain.") Later, feigning concern, the hare applies a poultice of cayenne pepper to the badger's back. The climax occurs as the hare tricks the badger into making a journey to the moon in a clay boat. The hare ventures forth on a river in his wood boat, followed by the badger in his boat of clay. Only when the badger's boat begins to sink does the hare show his true feelings. In the vivid language of Mitford's translation:

> . . . then the hare, seizing his paddle and brandishing it in the air, struck savagely at the badger's boat until he had smashed it to pieces, and killed his enemy.
>
> When the old man heard that his wife's death had been avenged, he was glad in his heart, and more than ever petted the hare, whose brave deeds had caused him to welcome the returning spring.

From the opening paragraph of his retelling, Dazai evinces a concern for the fate of the badger. Apparently the children's version Dazai read to his daughter had the badger wound rather than kill the old woman. His daughter, reacting to the violence of the conclusion, remarked about the "poor badger," and Dazai seems to have sympathized with her response. Upset in particular with what he regarded as the unjust treatment of the badger, Dazai decided to give both animals in the tale entirely new representational roles.

The hare becomes an attractive girl of sixteen, with a dawning realization of her power over infatuated males. The badger becomes a thirty-seven-year-old man, a lecher and glutton with an extremely dark complexion. It should be added that Dazai does not portray these two figures as a girl and a man; he merely says that, in fact, the badger is such a man and the hare such a girl. Focusing intently on these two figures, Dazai, except for brief references, eliminates the old man and woman from his account.

As with the two previous tales, Dazai adds "personalities" to the cardboard figures of the traditional badger and hare. The badger, anxious to present himself in the best possible light to the hare, lies about his age and shows himself willing to go along with the merest whim of the hare. But so lazy and lecherous is the badger that he cannot conceal these weaknesses and thus becomes an easy prey for the watchful hare.

To a degree Dazai describes the badger in terms suggestive of himself. The dark complexion of the animal recalls an adolescent concern of the author; the actual age of the badger is perilously close to Dazai's at the time he wrote the tale. When the badger drools in sexual anticipation, packs a lunch in a box the size of an "oil can," or fails to see that the hare selling him medicine is the vengeful hare, the reader is sorely tempted to conclude that Dazai's penchant for self-satire is again at work. And then, one reads in the commentary by Okuno Tateo that Dazai in fact is poking fun at a friend, Tanaka Eiko. With that piece of knowledge, there dawns a new realization concerning Dazai's art: he has developed methods of comedy and satire so firmly in his earlier works of self-denigration that the attempt to satirize another runs the risk of emerging as self-satire. Dazai had saddled himself with a method, and he remained in large measure subject to the limitations of that method until the final work of his career, a brief fragment entitled "Good-bye."

"The Split-Tongue Sparrow"

Like two other stories in the volume, **"The Split-Tongue Sparrow"** describes an adventure involving an elderly married couple. As in the case of **"Taking the Wen,"** the couple in **"The Split-Tongue Sparrow"** are at odds with one another.

The old man has a pet sparrow which he nurtures with great care. One day the sparrow pecks away at his wife's starch paste, whereupon the enraged woman cuts out the sparrow's tongue. When the old man returns and hears that the unfortunate sparrow has fled, he decides to search out the bird.

Presently the old man finds himself at the sparrow's home in the woods. After a hospitable reception and visit with the sparrow's family, the old man is offered the choice of a parting gift. Two wicker baskets, one heavy and one light, are put before him. Explaining that he is too decrepit to carry a heavy burden, the old man chooses the lighter basket and sets out for home. When he opens the basket at home, he discovers a treasure of gold, silver, and other valuables.

His wife, unable to control her greed, asks the way to the sparrow's home and immediately sets out in hopes of securing a second treasure. She manages to find the house and persuade the sparrow to offer her a gift. Once again, two wicker baskets are brought forth, and the woman unhesitatingly chooses the heavier one. On the way home she opens her booty—only to release a host of goblins who torment and frighten her to death. The old man adopts a son and lives a prosperous life thenceforth.

In his recreation of **"The Split-Tongue Sparrow,"** Dazai again acts more as commentator than storyteller. He explains that he initially intended to include among his stories the celebrated tale of "Peach-Boy." However, Peach-Boy is simply too perfect a hero for Dazai's taste. A weak person like himself, Dazai apologizes, simply cannot identify with such a hero.

Of course, self-abasement is a theme common to much of Dazai's writing. But, as Edward Seidensticker has pointed out, Dazai's self-abasement alternates with sudden manifestations of pride. In his version of **"The Split-Tongue Sparrow"** there is no such explicit manifestation by the author. Yet, in remarking that the old man is not quite forty years old, Dazai hints that the man is a surrogate for himself and thus nudges the reader to identify the old man's psychology as his own.

The old man makes an interesting study. A subdued, gentle creature almost overwhelmed by a shrewish wife, the old man can scarcely articulate his ideas and reactions. He feels most comfortable bent over a book or scattering seeds for his pet sparrow. Only in conversing with the sparrow does the old man show himself verbally adept. Late in Dazai's story, when he finds the sparrow mute because of her split tongue, the old man is perfectly content, as the sparrow also seems to be, to sit and enjoy the quiet.

Such a man can hardly endure the assaults of criticism. When his wife claims she overheard him talking in their house to a girl with a charming voice and demands an explanation, the old man meekly acknowledges his conversation with the sparrow. Imagine a callous wife accepting a tale like that! And, even when the sparrow criticizes him for inactivity, the old man can only claim that he is hopefully awaiting the arrival of a task he alone can perform.

How seriously should the reader take this old man? Dazai's ending, though slightly different from the traditional version, has the old man surviving his greedy wife to live in prosperity. The old man in Dazai's tale attains a high official position, and refers sardonically to the role his wife's "efforts" have played in his rise to prominence.

Dazai does not explicitly show any sympathy for the pathetic wife. Yet, recalling his sympathetic treatment of the traditionally evil badger of **"The Crackling Mountain"** and the envious old neighbor of **"Taking the Wen,"** one wonders whether the author didn't harbor like sympathy for the woman. Shrewish and greedy she is. But she does hear her husband speaking to someone with a charming, feminine voice; and she is unable to communicate with him, not because he is genuinely timid, but simply because pride keeps him from dealing with people in a normal, human way. Perhaps the old man is correct in claiming that people simply lie to one another and, therefore, it is best to remain silent. But the reader of Dazai suspects that his author was capable of regarding such an attitude as a mere pretension of superiority, as he hinted in **"Mount Yoshino."** Again, in portraying the sparrow as a puppet two feet high, Dazai, according to Okuno Tateo, intimates that the old man's interest in his pet is erotic in nature. There is little in the man's reactions to the sparrow to confirm such a judgment, but one is always left with the unsolved question of why Dazai changed the neutral, color-

less sparrow of the traditional work into a young female with an enchanting voice.

Makoto Ueda (essay date 1976)

SOURCE: "Dazai Osamu," in *Modern Japanese Writers and the Nature of Literature,* Stanford University Press, 1976, pp. 145–72.

[*In the following essay, Ueda maintains that Dazai, while saying little about his own works, used the autobiographical tone of his stories and novels to present his thoughts and ideas on the novel and the role and responsibilities of the writer and artist.*]

It may at first seem strange that Dazai Osamu (1909–48), noted for his garrulity, said little about literature or about his own works in his essays and letters. One should recall, however, that he was basically a very shy person who could not bear talking much about himself in an open manner. Writing about his own works seemed to him like bragging about his looks. "A writer should be ashamed of himself," he once said, "to give even one word of explanation or apology regarding his own work." Such being the case, Dazai's idea of the novel has to be sought mainly in his works of fiction. Fortunately, he was an autobiographical novelist, and a writer or an artist often appears in his fiction as a thinly disguised spokesman for the author. Dazai's attitude toward literature is therefore everywhere visible. In this respect he was very much like Shiga, a writer he intensely disliked in his later years.

DROWNING OF A SHIPWRECKED MAN

Of all Dazai's works, the one that most directly reveals his ideas on the art of writing is a relatively unknown novel called *A Women's Duel.* It is based on a short story of the same name, "Ein Frauenzweikampf" by Herbert Eulenberg (1876–1949). Dazai read this German work in Japanese translation, and was so dissatisfied with it that he was moved to rewrite it in his own way. [This information is given by the narrator of the story. Since his name is Dazai, the assumption is that Dazai himself is speaking.] By examining why he was dissatisfied and how he went about rewriting it, we can learn much about Dazai's attitude toward literary realism, as well as toward the relationship between art and objective external reality.

"Ein Frauenzweikampf" is a story only a few pages long. Its main character is a Russian woman named Constance, who has just discovered her husband's infidelity. She wants to dissolve the love triangle by a duel between herself and her husband's young mistress, a medical student. They duel in a field at the edge of town, and Constance, who has never handled a revolver before, somehow manages to shoot her opponent to death. Immediately, she gives herself up to the authorities and enters a jail, where, before anyone notices, she starves herself to death. In a letter left behind she testifies that she is killing herself as a martyr of love; she lost all purpose in living, she says, when she discovered that her victory at the duel saved her honor, but not her love.

Why was Dazai dissatisfied with the story? Because, he said, the author was too realistic in describing the incidents. After quoting the first couple of pages from the original story, Dazai addressed his readers:

> How about that? If you are a seasoned reader of fiction, I must have quoted enough for you to notice something strange about the writing. In a word, there is a certain *coldness* about it; there is *indifference*—so much so that it is almost insulting. If you ask what is being insulted, I would answer it is the facts themselves. Too accurate a description of an actual fact has a disquieting effect on the reader. Newspapers, in reporting a murder or some even more repugnant crime, sometimes carry a sketch of the scene of the crime, outlining, among other things, the body of the slain woman sprawled like a doll in her bedroom. You surely know the kind of thing I mean. I can't stand that sketch. I feel like yelling "Take it away!" This story has the same sort of nakedness. Don't you begin to feel that way as you read it?

Elsewhere, Dazai compares Eulenberg to a camera; in his judgment, Eulenberg's story is just a police photograph of the scene of a crime. From all this he concludes that "when a story describes a scene with outrageous frankness, the reader, though impressed, will come to hold serious misgivings."

Dazai had a theory to explain why the author wrote the story in a way so realistic as to make the reader sick. According to him, Eulenberg had been physically exhausted at the time of writing.

> When a tired man writes a story, he tends to write in a hostile tone—even, at times, a reproachful one. On such occasions, he is capable of revealing the bitterest, cruelest aspects of reality with the utmost nonchalance. Perhaps man is cold and heartless in his innermost nature. With his body exhausted and will power diminished, he is capable of attacking someone off guard and unceremoniously cutting him down. Sad, isn't it?

Dazai imagined that Eulenberg had been a tired man when he wrote "Ein Frauenzweikampf." In fact, he must have been so tired that he allowed himself to "take an unkind attitude toward human life, toward the humble way in which man lives day by day." Such was Dazai's verdict on realism.

If a novelist should not portray reality as it is, how should he portray it? Dazai's answer is revealed in the way in which he rewrote Eulenberg's story. The greatest difference between Eulenberg's original and Dazai's adaptation is that the latter tells us far more about what is going on in the minds of the story's three main characters. The German writer says almost nothing about the medical student's feelings when she received Constance's challenge to a duel. Dazai, on the other hand, delves deep into her

mind and makes clear the psychic process through which she reaches the decision to accept the challenge. As he tells us, she has already become disillusioned with her lover, whom she finds ugly, weak-willed, and snobbish. Constance's challenge to a duel deeply chagrins her, because she has just awakened to her role as a marriage wrecker; she has even begun to feel sympathy toward the married woman, who, she thinks, has also been victimized by the same hypocrite. Her sympathy, however, quickly evaporates from her mind on the day of the duel, when she meets Constance for the first time and recognizes dogged determination in her. At once she resolves to accept the challenge.

The difference between the original story and its adaptation is even more noticeable in the treatment of Constance's husband, for, whereas he makes no appearance in the former, he plays a major role in the latter. As might be expected, in Dazai's version he is Eulenberg himself. According to Dazai, the husband was an indecisive intellectual who had two vices characteristic of the artist: amorousness and curiosity. He remained indecisive even when he knew that his wife and his mistress were to fight a duel on account of him; not knowing what to do, he timidly watched the duel from behind a tree. When he saw his mistress shot to death, he hurried back home and sank back in his sofa. At the police interrogation he answered that he knew nothing about the duel, that he wished both women were alive. He was deeply moved, however, when he learned of his wife's suicide and her motive for it as revealed in her letter. He was touched by the "violent seriousness" with which human life could be lived—so touched that he even thought of killing himself to join his wife. Real life, however, was not so romantic, and he did not commit suicide. Instead, he became a writer of popular fiction and lived a long, comfortable life. He never married again.

The portraits of the medical student and her lover, thus drastically modified by Dazai, change the entire story and affect the image of its heroine, Constance, too. In the Eulenberg story she is depicted with a detachment that prompted Dazai to imagine that the author had harbored personal hostility toward her. In contrast, Dazai's adaptation presents her as an intense, pure-hearted woman who thinks life is not worth living if it is bereft of love. The proud, almost arrogant woman who feared neither God nor man in the original story turns into a young idealist who lives for love and dies for love. Although Dazai does not delve into her psychology, he contrasts her both with the medical student and with the artist-husband. Out of the contrast she emerges as a person of heartfelt sincerity.

The reason why Dazai was tempted to change the story and its three main characters is now clear: he wanted to make every one of the characters a person worthy of the reader's sympathy. Constance, her husband, and his mistress, being human, are all potentially "cold and heartless"—as Eulenberg seemed to imply in his original story. Dazai did not deny this, but he also felt that they were redeemed from complete egotism by a degree of insight into their own emotions. The medical student found herself sympathizing with her rival in love, the wife who shot the student felt obliged to commit suicide, and the husband who learned of the suicide gave up his ambition to be a respectable writer. The situation was an ugly one, but the characters in the story were painfully aware of this. To depict them as if they were not aware of it, or as if no one ever had a decent thought or feeling, was to distort reality, not copy it.

> As people live their daily lives, all sorts of beautiful and ugly thoughts cross their minds from one moment to the next. Nevertheless, some people conclude that ugly thoughts alone are true, forgetting that people are capable of beautiful thoughts, too. This is wrong. The images that keep passing through the mind may exist as "fact," but it is a mistake to regard them as "truth."

The same idea is suggested elsewhere in Dazai's writings. *A Women's Duel* was not the only story by another author that he reworked. In every case, he made his characters more sympathetic figures than they had been in the original. By and large, these characters were well aware of their own depravity. In *The New Hamlet* Claudius, Gertrude, and Polonius are far more sympathetic characters than in Shakespeare's play, because they are more aware of their own weaknesses. Similar traits can be found in the stories collected as **Nursery Tales**. The Bad Old Man in **"The Old Man with a Wen"** is pitiably obsessed with a large wen on his cheek. The Bad Badger in **"The Rabbit's Revenge"** is a clumsy, ugly-looking animal who is hopelessly in love with the Good Rabbit and is cruelly victimized by her. The Bad Old Woman in **"The Tongue-Cut Sparrow"** is a former maid who for many years looked after her frail, impractical husband, the Good Old Man in the original tale. In *Sanetomo the Minister of the Right,* the assassin Kugyō is described as a nobleman who, "despite his care-free appearance, had something timid and subservient in his smile, the kind of smile one would expect to see in someone whose life since childhood had been wracked with care." In **"Appeal to the Authorities,"** the "bad" man is no less than Judas Iscariot. He emerges as a sympathetic character who is trying to protect the charismatic but naïve Jesus from the pressures of the practical world. In order to keep his master pure amid the impurities of daily life, Judas himself sinks deeper into the mire. His struggle is threefold, for he has to fight with the ill will of the Pharisees, with the whims of his unpredictable master Jesus, and with his own introspective, and hence indecisive, mind. All those characters, as they appear in the stories rewritten by Dazai, have personalities that appear weak rather than evil. Indeed, it is because of their weakness that they have won Dazai's sympathy and are held up by him for the reader's sympathy as well.

For Dazai, then, weakness is a sign of goodness, not of evil. In his view, an evil person is a man who has no understanding of, and therefore no sympathy for, human weakness. He is like the Rabbit in **"The Rabbit's Revenge,"** a beautiful maiden who tortures the ugly Badger

to death, or like Hōjō Yoshitoki in *Sanetomo the Minister of the Right,* a master politician who takes advantage of the weak, impractical lord named in the title. Horiki, in *No Longer Human,* and Hirata, in **"The Courtesy Call,"** are also of this type. So is Shiga Naoya, the only contemporary Japanese author to whom Dazai awarded this dubious honor. In "Thus Have I Heard," one of his last essays, Dazai savagely attacked Shiga, chiefly for having no understanding of human weakness; the beauty of weakness, Dazai argued, had passed Shiga by. [. . .] Shiga thought that the basis of human nature was an instinctive animal wisdom, which he urged all men to follow with confidence. To Dazai, this belief of Shiga's seemed far too optimistic, far too self-indulgent, and far too inconsistent with man's sinful nature. "He does not understand the beauty of weakness," Dazai once wrote of Shiga. "He despises human weakness," he wrote elsewhere. In Dazai's opinion, the hero of *Voyage Through the Dark Night,* who struggles to reach a state of mind in which he can forgive his grandfather's incest and his wife's infidelity, is an intolerably arrogant person because he never stops to ask whether he really has the right to "forgive" either person, or whether indeed he himself is not as weak and sinful as they.

The same point is made in a short story by Dazai entitled **"Seagulls."** It includes a scene in which the hero, whose name is Dazai, is asked what he thinks is most important in literature. Is it love, humanism, beauty, social justice, or something else? His answer is instantaneous: he says it is regret. "A literary work devoid of regret is nothing," he says. "Modern literature—the very spirit of the modern age—was born of regrets, confessions, reflections, and things like that." He goes on to explain that all these self-incriminating thoughts are derived from one's "awareness that one is a dirty fellow." Dazai was nothing if not faithful to this principle. His very first work of creative writing, entitled **"Recollections,"** resulted from his wish to "bare a record of my sins since childhood." In his last complete novel, *No Longer Human,* the hero's opening words are those of regret: "My past life is filled with shame." Other works by Dazai show the same characteristic. In **"Villon's Wife,"** both husband and wife are aware that all men are criminals; the difference between them is that he always thinks of suicide, whereas she wants to live on even as a criminal. Naoji, a leading character in *The Setting Sun,* who eventually commits suicide, also suffers from the painful knowledge that there could be no man who is not depraved, while his sister Kazuko, who shares this belief, decides she can live with it. The reason why the heroes choose death over life and the heroines do the reverse (though both suffer equally from the knowledge of man's basic depravity) is related to Dazai's belief that women are more capable of withstanding the world's evil. Young, innocent women are an exception, however. In **"Metamorphosis,"** for instance, the young daughter of a woodcutter flings herself over a waterfall when she is raped by her drunken father. Constance, in *A Women's Duel,* wants to die when she discovers her husband's infidelity; failing to die in a duel, she starves herself to death.

Dazai's ideas concerning the relationship between life and art can be summed up as follows. In his view, human reality was ultimately filthy and ugly, and human nature inherently depraved. He maintained, however, that literature should not concern itself wholly with that fact. The reason he gave was that it might be fact, but it was not truth. Truth, according to Dazai, lay with the "weak" people who were painfully aware that human reality is ugly and human nature foul. Their sufferings, their regrets, their remorseful reflections, their desperate attempts to ward off the ugliness and filth of life—all these were beautiful. The prime concern of literature was to depict that beauty.

Dazai expressed these views eloquently in a parable, which will serve as a fitting conclusion to this section:

> The man was shipwrecked. Turbulent waves swallowed him up. Flung against the shore, he found himself desperately clinging to a window frame. It was the lighthouse keeper's cottage! Joyfully he peered into the room, intent on crying for help. The lighthouse keeper, his wife, and their little daughter were sitting happily at a modest dinner. "Oh, no!" he said to himself. "As soon as they hear my cry for help, the peace of their happy home will be shattered." For a moment he hesitated, suppressing his urge to yell out. The next instant, this timid-hearted man was attacked by a colossal wave and carried far out to sea. He was lost forever.
>
> Now this man's behavior was admirable. But who was watching him? No one was. The lighthouse keeper's family, unaware of what had happened outside, went on with their happy dinner. Meanwhile, the shipwrecked man met a lonely death amid the angry waves. I rather fancy it was snowing; at any rate, neither moon nor stars witnessed the incident. And yet this man's admirable behavior is a fact that cannot be denied.
>
> How do I know all this? I had a vision of it one night. But that doesn't mean I made it all up. The fact actually exists; somehow, it is now part of this world of ours. The wonder of the novelist's fantasy lies in precisely that. People say that fact is stranger than fiction. Yet there are facts to which there are no witnesses. And in many instances, such facts are all the more precious, shining like jewels in the dark. It is to present such facts that a novelist writes a story. [Dazai liked the episode well enough to write it twice, once in an essay called "A Promise," and again in the novel *Parting*. A similar incident is also described in *No Longer Human*. The shipwrecked man in the episode is to be interpreted figuratively—a man shipwrecked on the voyage of life.]

FRIEND OF THE WEAK

If the function of a novel is to depict a man painfully aware of his innate depravity, a novelist's prime qualification is to have a thorough and sympathetic understanding of basic human weakness. Dazai repeatedly emphasized this. On one occasion he remarked: "Artists have always been friends of the weak," and on another: "To be a friend of the weak—that is the artist's point of departure as well as his ultimate goal." He pleaded with Shiga, who he

thought was too "strong": "Become a little weaker. Be weak, if you are a man of letters. Be more flexible. Try to understand people who are different from you; try to understand their agonies." He wanted a novelist to understand the weakness of Constance, of Gertrude, of the Bad Badger. He criticized Shiga for not understanding Akutagawa's mental anguish. Just as strongly, he approved of Akutagawa as an artist well acquainted with the dark side of human nature.

All through his writings Dazai can be seen elaborating on this concept of human weakness. "Agony of a fugitive. Weakness. The Bible. Fear of life. Prayer of a loser." Such are the associations that it had for him. "A fugitive"—the word occurs frequently in Dazai's writings—is defined as "a wretched loser, a delinquent," in *No Longer Human*. The term evidently refers to a person like Oba Yōzō, who, because of his awareness of "a lump of evil" lying deep within him, cannot be aggressive, and therefore cannot win a victory in the struggle for survival that is life. "Fear of life" is another favorite term of Dazai's; it denotes the fear of a man who lives a fugitive's life. For instance, the poet Ōtani in **"Villon's Wife"** says he is "always fighting with fear"; he is afraid of God, who has seen through the "lump of evil" within him and who might punish him for it at any time. Dazai's reference to the Bible should be taken in the same context. In Christian terminology, all men are guilty of original sin; they are all depraved. The "prayer of a loser" is a prayer to Jesus, who was crucified to redeem humanity from original sin. Kazuko in *The Setting Sun* when she realizes that becoming a sinner is the condition of being alive in this world, says: "Labeled a delinquent. That's the only kind of label I want to be crucified under." In **"Appeal to the Authorities,"** Judas cannot convince himself of his absolute innocence, and he suffers painfully from it. "A leading characteristic of geniuses," says one of the letter-writers in **"Letters in the Wind,"** "is that they are one and all convinced of their own sinfulness." In Dazai's opinion, this applies with peculiar force to geniuses who write novels.

But if a novelist is firmly convinced of his own depravity, will he not become a kind of holy man, and turn from literature to seek God and redemption? Dazai's answer is in the negative, unless "holy man" is interpreted in the broadest sense. Indeed, Yōzō in *No Longer Human* is "a good boy, like an angel"; Uehara in *The Setting Sun* is "a noble martyr"; and Ōtani in **"Villon's Wife"** is a poet who lives in fear of God. Yet they are all far from being saints or sages of any religion, Eastern or Western. In fact, they resemble Judas Iscariot more than the rest of the apostles. Dazai was too conscious of his own shortcomings to create a character in search of redemption. He was so sensitive on this score that it was difficult for him not to see a touch of pride (and hypocrisy) in the image projected by any religious leader. Convinced of basic human depravity, and moved by the nobility of men suffering from their awareness of it, he was too introverted, too self-conscious, and too timid to take any positive action. "A road leading to construction is a false road," he once wrote in a letter. "For today's young men, the only right road is the road to despair."

When Dazai said the novelist was a friend of the weak, he did not mean that he actually offered a helping hand to them. What he meant was that the novelist understood the weak and spoke on their behalf—bashfully, to be sure. Dazai once drew a portrait of the artist in an essay called "For Fifteen Years":

> I am sure you all know about Böcklin, an artist who was fond of painting sea monsters. His paintings have an immature quality and may not be considered first-rate, but I cannot forget a work of his called "The Artist." It shows a huge tree covered with thick green leaves standing on a small island in the ocean, and in the tree's shade there is an ugly-looking, awkward creature with a little flute in his mouth. Hiding his hideous figure behind the tree, he is playing the flute. Lovely mermaids have gathered on the shore and are listening to the tune with ecstasy. No doubt they would faint with shock if only they could see the flute player. Knowing that, the latter has done his best to hide himself; he reveals nothing of himself but the sound of his flute. This is the wretched, lonely fate of the artist in a nutshell—and the true beauty and nobility of art. This doesn't quite say what I mean, but art is pretty much like that, I can tell you. A true artist is an ugly man.

The artist, then, is bashful, because he knows how ugly he is. He never preaches at a lectern; he never lectures from a dais. He conceals himself behind a tree and lets others hear his music. That is all.

Similar implications can be deduced from Dazai's better-known comparison of the artist with a pig. It appears in a dialogue that is part of a brief note called "A Faint Voice":

> "What is art?"
>
> "A violet."
>
> "Is that all?"
>
> "What is an artist?"
>
> "A pig's snout."
>
> "I protest!"
>
> "That snout can smell a violet."

Needless to say, the violet represents the beauty of human weakness, the beauty of those who, because they understand human nature, are harsh toward themselves and gentle toward others. Of these, some understand human weakness through conscious effort and others by instinct. Dazai was more attracted to the latter. He poured out his affection on those who were instinctively gentle and forgiving, those who could fully sympathize even with villains, criminals, and outcasts. In Dazai's stories they are mostly women; in his view, women were instinctively more gentle and forgiving. Sometimes, however, they fell prey to villains who took advantage of their innocence and

gentleness. This happened to Yoshiko in *No Longer Human,* and to Mrs. Ōtani in **"Villon's Wife."** They were like violets trampled underfoot by callous men.

Most of Dazai's leading characters can be roughly classified as either "pigs" or "violets." In the former category are the two Japanese monkeys in **"The Monkey Island,"** Tarō the Lazy, Jirōbei the Fighter, and Saburō the Liar in **"Romanesque,"** the mental patient in **"The Lost,"** Judas in **"Appeal to the Authorities,"** the suicidal husband in **"Osan,"** Tsuruta Keisuke in **"The Criminal,"** Ōtani in **"Villon's Wife,"** Naoji in *The Setting Sun,* Yōzō in **"Recollections"** and *No Longer Human,* and Dazai in **"The Cherries"** and many other stories. Among the violets are little Suwa in **"Metamorphosis,"** the mother and daughter in **"One Hundred Views of Mount Fuji,"** Meros and his friend in **"Run, Melos!",** the heroine in **"Mrs. Hospitality,"** Shūji in **"The Courtesy Call,"** [Shūji was the given name of Dazai in real life. The English translation by Ivan Morris has changed it to Osamu, his pen name.] and Kazuko's mother and Mrs. Uehara in *The Setting Sun,* in addition to Yoshiko in *No Longer Human.* Mrs. Ōtani in **"Villon's Wife"** and Kazuko in *The Setting Sun* are violets at the outset, but they end up as pigs. Their stories are structured around their progress (or degradation, depending on how one looks at it) from the former to the latter.

From Dazai's point of view, then, all novelists must be pigs; those who are not are hypocrites, liars, or fakes. Dazai in his last years seemed to attack Shiga from this viewpoint. He charged that Shiga was self-indulgent in making himself to be a "good boy" in everything he wrote. "An athlete with his face made up," Dazai jeeringly called him. "A bully. An egotist. It looks as if he has muscles. I saw a photograph of him as an old man; he looked exactly like the decrepit foreman of a plant nursery." Shiga's works, Dazai pointed out, never descend into hell; all one sees is a storm in a teacup, like someone catching the flu. Dazai's attack on Shiga is often emotional and sometimes unfair, but there can be no doubt that Shiga was not a pig in Dazai's sense of the term; in fact, he tried hard to escape becoming a pig, and eventually succeeded. Dazai could not forgive him this.

If the novelist is a pig, it follows that the first principle in writing a novel is for the author to depict himself as a pig, that is, as an outcast and criminal and born loser. A Dazai-like narrator in **"Spring Bandit"** says:

> Even in the *ich-Roman,* most writers depict themselves as "good boys." Has there ever been an autobiographical novel in which the hero is not a "good boy"? Akutagawa, as I recall, has said something to that effect somewhere in his writings. I was bothered by this question, and I therefore tried to describe my hero, "I," as a most ill-natured and monstrous person.

To Dazai's way of thinking, the heroes of autobiographical novels must be self-appointed pseudo-villains. They must be thieves, libertines, prodigals, and scoundrels who have consciously become what they are. They must refuse to become happy, because it is wrong to want happiness in this world of men who, they know, are all depraved.

There is some question, however, as to whether Dazai's own heroes are cast exactly in this mold. The protagonists of **"Villon's Wife,"** *The Setting Sun,* and *No Longer Human*—perhaps his three best works—are still "good boys" in some respects, and not without the author's knowledge. *No Longer Human* ends with the comment that its alcoholic hero, Yōzō, was "a good boy, like an angel." Uehara, in *The Setting Sun,* is a "noble martyr." Otani, in **"Villon's Wife,"** is compared to the famous French poet. Dazai has often been criticized for being too indulgent toward his heroes, despite his promise to make them "most ill-natured and monstrous." His critics have a point. It should be remembered, however, that the characters Dazai attempted to create were pseudo-villains, not just plain villains. His heroes were ill-natured and monstrous, but they knew it—and suffered. If Dazai was overlenient toward them, it was because of his own good nature.

TENDERNESS, SORROW, HUMOR AND A TOUCH OF NOBILITY

Dazai's views on how a literary work should affect the reader have already been touched on. In a word, he liked the beauty of weakness. To him, this was the beauty that emerges from a confession by a sensitive person who knows the sinful nature of man, is pained by the knowledge, and refuses to be happy. The episode of the shipwrecked man is characteristic of Dazai's approach to literature. The episode in itself is too naïve: a good work of literature would be more complex, as life is complex. "What else does it [a novel] need," wrote Dazai in his comment on **The Declining Years.** "if it is tender, sorrowful, humorous, and noble?" The qualities imparted by a successful work of literature are tenderness, sorrow, humor, and nobility.

Of these four, sorrow is the one most closely connected with human weakness. The reader feels sorrow when he reads a novel describing human weakness, or when he reads about a man who suffers from his knowledge of the weakness that is in him. As an example of such sorrow, one can do no better than quote Dazai himself:

> This happened five years ago, when I was living in Funabashi. One day I left home feeling depressed and somehow found myself in Ichikawa. There I sold some books I had brought with me, and used the money to see a movie. It was *Brother and Sister.* Watching it, I wept unabashedly. Mon's tearful protests made me unbearably sad. I kept crying aloud, until I could no longer stand it and took refuge in the washroom. It really was a powerful movie.

Brother and Sister is in fact a starkly realistic film that depicts a working-class family in rural Japan. [The original story by Murō Saisei (1889–1962) is available in English translation. See Ivan Morris, ed., *Modern Japanese Stories.*] Mon, the sister in the title, is a young girl who falls

in love with a college student; she is soon jilted by him and subsequently goes to the bad. One day the student, somewhat regretful of what he has done to her, visits her home and is beaten up by her rough, quick-tempered brother. Mon, who had been away at the time, hears about the beating upon her return and furiously remonstrates with her brother. Dazai was particularly touched by this scene; he found the girl's continuing love for the student "unbearably sad." Dazai's essay containing this episode is entitled "Food for the Weak." A movie becomes "food for the weak" when it conveys a forgiving attitude toward human nature rather than an indignant one. Goodness is weak, and is therefore always defeated. The fact that it nevertheless remains goodness is the source of Dazai's sorrow.

Dazai's own stories tend to lack the obvious emotional impact of *Brother and Sister,* but they are clearly in the same vein. His main characters may be weaklings in the conventional sense, but they are drawn in such a way as to inspire the reader's deepest sympathy. Here, for instance, is Uehara talking to Kazuko in *The Setting Sun:*

> I don't care if I do drink myself to death. Life's too sad—I can't stand it. It's worse than just feeling lonely or depressed. I'm sad, I tell you. How can you be happy when the very walls are sighing all around you? How would you feel if you discovered there was no way you could find happiness or fame during your lifetime? Work harder? Hungry beasts will eat it up, that's all. There are too many wretched people. Is that a snobbish thing to say?

Kazuko, herself a child of misfortune, allows him to make love to her. Uehara, as Kazuko has just realized, is dying of tuberculosis. And yet he apologizes for being too snobbish, and indulges in a great deal of amusing intellectual banter. With touches like these, Dazai evokes real sympathy not only for his characters but for all people caught in a situation they cannot control. This, he seems to say, is the fate of all of us, and we should pardon each other's weaknesses.

Hence the "tenderness" that Dazai spoke of as another important literary effect. Dazai defined it as "sensitivity to the loneliness, melancholy, and misery of others."

> The ideogram *yū* makes me think. It is read as *sugureru* (to excel) and is used in such compounds as *yūshū* (championship) or *yū ryō ka* (excellent, good, fair). But there is another reading for it: *yasashii* (to be tender). If you take a close look at the ideogram, you will recognize its two components: "man" on the left and "to grieve" on the right. To grieve over men, to be sensitive to the loneliness, melancholy, and misery of others—this is "to be tender," to excel as a human being. [The Japanese often amuse themselves by analyzing an ideogram in some fanciful way. Dazai's analysis of *yū* here is done in the same lighthearted mood and may or may not be correct in a scholarly sense.]

A number of characters in Dazai's stories display this quality of tenderness. The hero of **"Osan"** is a married

DAZAI

SHORT STORY CRITICISM, Vol. 41

man who dies in a suicide pact with his mistress. Yet his widow remembers him as "a tender husband" and counts herself a happy woman to have loved such a man. The poet in **"Villon's Wife"** is a thief, drunkard, and libertine, yet his poor wife comes to conclude, toward the end of the story, that he is "more tenderhearted than most men around." A short story called **"Mrs. Hospitality"** describes a woman who, because of her innate "tenderness," cannot help offering the warmest hospitality to all and sundry, even though some of her visitors deliberately take advantage of her good nature. Her male counterpart is the narrator-hero of **"The Courtesy Call,"** who finds himself unable to refrain from offering all his precious whiskey to a boorish guest whom he intensely dislikes; the story could be retitled "Mr. Hospitality." The adjective "tenderhearted" recurs many times in *The Setting Sun,* in most cases applied to Kazuko's mother. The epithet is not idly bestowed, as can be seen from this dialogue with her son Naoji, who is a drug addict. The pathos is heightened by the fact that it is Naoji who records this in his diary.

"Scold me, mother."

"How, Naoji?"

"Say I'm a weakling."

"You are a weakling. Are you satisfied now?"

Mother's goodness is unparalleled. When I think of her I feel like crying. I'm going to die in apology to her.

And Naoji does indeed commit suicide later in the book. He is not so much a depraved character as a weak one. Indeed, his weakness evokes so much sympathy that his depravity appears in a new light. "I wonder if depravity does not mean tenderness," says his sister Kazuko. By "depravity" she means one's own awareness that one is a "weakling," that is, a person who is too tenderhearted to take advantage of weakness in others. As Kazuko and her mother are kind to Naoji because he is a weakling, so are the female characters in *No Longer Human* kind to the unhappy Yōzō. Instinctively, they sense the goodness of heart that underlies his dissipated appearance. "My tender heart," Yōzō himself reflects, not without irony, "was so tender that it enchanted even myself." Of course, it also enchants the novel's readers, as Dazai intended.

We can see now why Dazai disapproved so much of "Ein Frauenzweikampf": its author was entirely lacking in tenderness toward its three main characters. Dazai criticized Shiga on the same account, saying, "He does not even understand what tenderness is." Specifically assailed in this respect were two short stories by Shiga, "A Gray Moon" and "The Patron Saint." The former is a postwar story about a starving young workman being made fun of in a train by the other passengers; Dazai charged that nowhere in the story was any sympathy expressed toward the young workman. The latter story is about a wealthy man who, having by accident witnessed the wretched plight of a low-paid apprentice at a store, treats him to a feast at an expensive restaurant without revealing his identity. Dazai,

referring to this story, wonders if the author "realizes how cruelly he is treating the poor." This may seem a little unfair of Dazai, but there can be no doubt that Shiga's realism, at least, is really an unconscious double standard that judges the poor far more severely than the rich.

"Nobility," the third of Dazai's array of desirable literary effects, is also related to tenderness. To be sympathetic and kind toward others presupposes a capacity for self-sacrifice, a capacity to keep selfish thoughts in check. An egotist can never be noble, because he is not sensitive to the suffering of others. A work of art, Dazai thought, should create an impression of nobility by describing sensitive, tenderhearted people. He implied as much when he made Naoji fall in love with the gentle wife of "a certain oil painter" and say: "If that painter's works breathe the noble fragrance of true art, it is because his wife has touched them with her tenderness." Elsewhere he declared: "Literature is always a *Tale of the Heike.*" This rather eccentric definition of literature makes sense when *The Tale of the Heike* is understood as an epic eulogizing the fall of good but weak people, cultured to a fault, nobly meeting a tragic fate at the hands of their inferiors.

Many of Dazai's own works can be considered tales of this sort. The most obvious example, of course, is *The Setting Sun,* which may be considered an elegy mourning the death of the nobility in twentieth-century Japan. Kazuko's mother, with her extreme refinement and gentleness, best represents that nobility; she is "the last noblewoman in Japan." But Naoji also prides himself on his noble birth and concludes his suicide note by saying "I am a nobleman." The word "noble," in these instances, has at once social and moral implications, suggesting that a member of the nobility is likely to have a noble character, too. The commoners, on the other hand, are physically energetic, mentally robust, and aesthetically crude. They are the rough warriors who destroy the refined, gentle-hearted courtiers. The sad inevitability of this outcome is narrated in a tone of Buddhist resignation in *The Tale of the Heike,* but Dazai preferred to see it in the context of a Marxist view of history. He seems to have thought that the people of noble birth, including himself, would have no place in the utopian society that would emerge after the forthcoming proletarian revolution. His pessimism is shared by Naoji, Yōzō, Ōtani, and other Dazai heroes, many of whom are of aristocratic birth. They are of "the perishing class," as Dazai called them. "They get beaten, they perish, and their mutterings become our literature," he explained; and elsewhere: "Despair begets elegance." Presumably this "elegance" in literary form is what Dazai meant by nobility.

There are occasions, however, when despair begets humor rather than elegance. It is, of course, humor with a difference, a kind of gallows humor. No doubt it is to humor of this kind that Ōtani, in **"Villon's Wife,"** is referring when he writes of "a great big laugh at the end of the world." His wife uses these words to describe the unexpected laughter that grips her when she learns that her husband is not only a thief but hopelessly in debt. Her laughter is directed at herself and her husband, who have long found life without meaning but have nevertheless gone on living it. When Dazai speaks of humor, then, it is of this kind of existentialist laughter. In the very last line of *The Setting Sun,* Kazuko calls Uehara "My Comedian." Kazuko herself, who was an elegant lady of the nobility at the story's beginning, ends up as a comic rather than a tragic figure, since she outlives both her mother and brother and is determined to make some sort of life for herself and her illegitimate child. The main character of *No Longer Human* is a conscious comedian: Yōzō has always tried hard to make other people laugh. When he is small his audience is his parents, brothers, and sisters; when at school, his teachers and classmates; as a grown-up, his friends and acquaintances. Appropriately, he becomes a professional cartoonist.

Despair can be overcome by laughter. As Dazai observed: "Pain, when there is too much of it, seems to transcend itself and turn into humor." Ōtani's wife, who turns her plight into a transcendental joke, and Kazuko, who willingly makes a fool of herself, both overcome pain and decide to live on. Yōzō becomes a mental patient, but he is not the "I" of the novel; there is a distance between him and the writer. In a postscript to his stories Dazai observed that he had written some of them out of pain and indignation, but that as he read them again he felt humor instead. That humor had arisen from the distance between Dazai the writer and Dazai the reader: the latter could look at the former with detachment and laugh at him. The haiku poet Bashō had a similar notion of humor; in order to distinguish it from the ordinary kind, he called it "lightness" (*karumi*). Apparently Dazai shared Bashō's view. In *Pandora's Box,* he wrote:

> The spirit of the new age is certainly here with us. It is as light as a robe of feathers, as clean as the water of a shallow brook flowing over white sand. Mr. Fukuda, one of my middle-school teachers, once told me that Bashō in his last years advocated what he termed "lightness," placing it far above *wabi, sabi,* and *shiori.* [*Wabi, sabi,* and *shiori* are aesthetic-moral concepts Bashō advocated in his later years. Traditionally, they have been considered to represent his highest poetic ideals. *Wabi* and *sabi* imply the beauty of a simple life, while *shiori* refers to a capacity for empathy.] We can hardly contain our pride when we think that our age, simply by following the natural course of events, has now soared to spiritual heights so sublime that even a great genius like Bashō could not conceive of, far less attain them until his last years. "Lightness" does not mean levity. No one will understand that frame of mind until he reaches a point at which he is able to see his desires, his life itself, as nothing. It is a gentle breeze that comes after long hours of hard, agonizing labor. It is a light bird with transparent wings that was born of tense air amid the great chaos of the world. Those who do not understand it will be left behind the times, forever standing outside the current of history. Everything grows old with time. There can't be any argument about it. The peace and calm of a person who has lost everything: that is "lightness."

Pandora's Box was the first novel Dazai wrote after the Second World War. "The new age," therefore, refers to the chaotic period immediately following the war, when many Japanese felt as if they had lost everything that was dear to them. In Dazai's view, it was this sense of utter loss that led to the lightness of which he spoke. Lightness, then, comes very close to what he elsewhere called humor.

Dazai, however, was perhaps a bit too exuberant in *Pandora's Box.* His own works in the postwar period do not really express this "spirit of the new age." There is far more to *The Setting Sun* than lightness: it also has tenderness, sorrow, and nobility. The same can be said of *No Longer Human,* except, perhaps, that there is more sorrow and less nobility. If Dazai had come close to achieving lightness in his last years, this would surely be evident in his last novel, *Good-bye.* Indeed, this unfinished work, to judge from what there is of it, has more humor than any of Dazai's other desired effects. Its prose style is also more even than that of most other Dazai stories. Unfortunately, the novel is unfinished because Dazai killed himself. The reader is left wondering whether its hero, Tajima, will be able to say good-bye to the "tense air amid the great chaos of the world." But Dazai's suicide was probably his answer to that question. In the end he found himself unable to transcend the world's chaos. He chose to hurl himself into the muddy turbulence of the Tama River rather than to patiently seek out a shallow brook flowing over white sand.

THOUGHTS AFTER THOUGHTS AFTER THOUGHTS

In general, the formal elements of a literary work do not seem to have occupied Dazai overmuch. He was so deeply concerned with the novelist's moral attitudes that questions of plot and style appeared to him rather trivial in comparison. Consequently, he seldom discussed structural or stylistic questions in his writings. On the rare occasions when he did, he tended to minimize their importance.

Once, on one of those rare occasions, Dazai hinted at his ideas on the subject of plot. This was in a letter in which he revealed his feelings about his own story **"Metamorphosis."** The story describes the sad destiny of Suwa, a young girl who, after being raped by her own father, flings herself into a waterfall and becomes a carp. Recalling his frame of mind when he wrote the tale, Dazai said:

> Even before I began writing the story, I had the concluding sentence in mind. It was, "Three days later Suwa's poor corpse was found under a bridge near the village." However, I cut it out after I finished the story. It was because I realized, to my despair, that my talent fell far short of elevating the story to the level of truth implied in that concluding sentence. I cleverly took an easy way out. I followed the dictum: "Aim at a sparrow on the eaves rather than at a hawk deep in the woods." When I discovered that I would have a well-constructed story but for the concluding sentence, I decided to remove the obstacle before anyone knew about it, even though I was aware that by doing so I would diminish the scale of the story. Now I know I did the wrong thing. The writer should voice his intent in his story until his voice becomes hoarse and his strength

expires. He should do so even if he knows that, as a result, he will wreck his novel's structure and thereby expose himself to the attacks of the so-called critics. I am deeply regretful of what I did at that time.

At the opposite extreme, Dazai spared no pains in writing **"Flowers of a Clown."** This early work of his was initially an autobiographical story entitled **"The Sea"**; it described the aftermath of an attempted double suicide by its hero, Yōzō, and a barmaid he knew. Narrated from Yōzō's point of view, it told how he felt about the tragedy, and how he tried to rebuild his personal life after it happened. In Dazai's opinion, the story had a simple, straightforward, almost classical beauty. A few months after writing it, however, he came to dislike it so much that he drastically revised it, transposing it into the first person (with suitable monologues here and there) and cutting the original story apart, although Yōzō, not the author, is still the protagonist. **"Flowers of a Clown"** was the title of this new version. Clearly Dazai had been unable to put all he wanted to say or think into the character of Yōzō in the original story, and therefore had to add a part for himself. The result is that the new story is more complex—perhaps overly complex—since the events described are viewed by both Yōzō and the author-narrator. The flow of the narrative is interrupted whenever "I" appears and makes comments on the writing of the story. The author himself is aware of this. "This story is confusing in many places," he writes. "I see myself tottering along. I don't quite know what to do with Yōzō or Hida. They are irritated at my clumsy pen and want to go their own way."

A typical Dazai novel is more like **"Flowers of a Clown"** than **"Metamorphosis"** or **"The Sea."** Rarely does it have a plot that unravels by a single thread; rather, the flow of the story is interrupted here and there, sometimes for a disproportionate length of time. The reason for the interruption is usually for the sake of making the author's intention crystal-clear; the author has sacrificed a well-knit plot in his eagerness to clarify his theme. The interruption is usually caused by one of two factors: a multiple viewpoint or a long monologue. Conspicuous intrusion of the authorial "I" occurs in *A Women's Duel*, **"Spring Bandit," "Revolving Lantern of Romance,"** and *Nursery Tales,* not to mention **"Flowers of a Clown."** In such works as **"Schoolgirl," "On Clothes,"** and **"On Keeping a Dog,"** "I" cannot be said to intrude into the story because he is the protagonist. Nevertheless, he gives the impression of figuring a bit too prominently for the purpose of the story. "I" is not quite so obtrusive in *No Longer Human,* but one still wonders whether the epilogue, which is written in the first person, could not have been shortened or even cut out altogether. Instances of a long monologue clogging up the flow of the story are seen in **"Das Gemeine,"** *The New Hamlet, Parting,* and **"Villon's Wife."** In *The Setting Sun,* the narrative is interrupted by a lengthy quotation from Naoji's diary as well as by his suicide note. Whereas these constitute an integral part of the story, a writer more plot-conscious than Dazai would have made Naoji participate more in the action of the story instead of recording his confessions in the form of diaries and notes.

Even though he paid relatively little attention to plot construction, Dazai was exceptionally careful about one element of plot, the beginning. He seemed to believe that a good story must begin in an interesting way. "The fact that the story has an interesting beginning implies the writer's kindness," he wrote. The novelist, a humble outcast of society, should be kind to the reader, entertaining him as a clown does. To this end, a novel should begin with a sentence by which the reader will feel irresistibly drawn.

To show what he meant by "an interesting beginning," Dazai cited the opening lines of eight German short stories that he considered exemplary in this respect. Here are three of them: [These passages have been retranslated from the Japanese in order to approximate the way Dazai read them. The original stories were "Sara Malcolm" by Jacob Wassermann; "The Death of a Bachelor" by Arthur Schnitzler; and "The Earthquake in Chile" by Heinrich von Kleist.]

> It was toward the end of 1732. England was under the reign of George II. A London nightwatchman was making his round one night, when he came upon a young maiden lying collapsed on a road near Temple Bar.

> Someone knocked at the door. Very gently.

> It was when the great earthquake of 1647 was about to strike Santiago, the capital of Chile. A young boy was standing against a prison pillar. This native of Spain, named Jeronimo Rugera, had given up all hope in this world and was about to hang himself.

An interesting beginning, as conceived by Dazai, is a suspenseful beginning, one that whets the reader's appetite for more. "How about those?" Dazai asked his readers. "Aren't they well written? They make you want to read more, don't they? If I were to write a story, I'd certainly like to open it with sentences like these."

Although all storytellers wish to seize their readers' attention from the outset, Dazai's wish seems more fervent than most. In **"Flowers of a Clown,"** for example, the author-narrator stresses the importance of its opening line ("A City of Sorrow beyond this point . . .") and says he would not erase it even if its presence ruined the entire story. The hero of **"Monkey-Faced Youngster"** is a novelist who believes that "the opening line determines the fate of the entire novel, no matter how lengthy it may turn out to be." As for Dazai himself, the works that are generally considered his best have the following beginnings: [These passages are from **"Metamorphosis," "Appeal to the Authorities," "Villon's Wife,"** *The Setting Sun,* and *No Longer Human,* in that order.]

> The mountain range at the northernmost edge of the main island of Japan is called Bonju. It is not shown on an ordinary map, because it is just a stretch of low hills less than one thousand feet long.

> Please let me speak to you, sir. Please. He is an awful man. Awful! Yes, sir, he is a disgusting fellow. A rascal. I can't stand him. I just can't let him live on.

With a loud clatter the front door sprang open. The noise woke me up. But I remained in bed without saying a word, because I knew it was only my husband, arriving home dead drunk in the middle of the night.

"Oh!"

Mother uttered a faint cry as she sipped a spoonful of soup at breakfast in our dining room.

I have seen three photographs of him.

One was a portrait of him in what seemed to be his childhood, for he looked about ten years old. Surrounded by many women (presumably his sisters and cousins), the child stood at the edge of a garden pond dressed in a broadly striped garment and showing an unpleasant smile on his face, his head slanted about thirty degrees to the left.

There is no doubt that these beginnings show more ingenuity than is found in the corresponding passages of most Japanese novels. The same quality is seen more clearly in some of Dazai's less famous stories. The first few paragraphs of **"The Monkey Island"** are tantalizingly ambiguous, paving the way for the big shock that is to follow a little later. The first couple of pages in **"One Hundred Views of Mount Fuji"** are devoted to discussion of Mount Fuji's vertical angles as depicted by great artists of the past, and the reader is left wondering what the story is all about. **"The Criminal"** tells of an attempted murder and suicide in the manner of a detective story; it certainly invites Shiga's criticism that a story should not deliberately keep the reader in suspense, that the reader should be given the same information the author has.

Dazai's concept of structure, then, must be said to be a peculiarly calculated one. In his opinion, a novel should begin with a very intriguing passage, involving the reader in the world of fiction as soon as he reads it. Once the reader is hooked, the writer can pay less attention to him and move on to what he wants to say. He need not weave an interesting plot; he may even break up the story to insert a long monologue here and there. The reader will stay with him to the end of the novel as long as he has something important to say, whether the plot is interesting or not. A good novel will grip the reader at the very beginning and never let him go until he has heard everything the novelist has to say.

Dazai's idea that the novel should above all express the author's intent is also reflected in his concept of style. He once said that "a good piece of prose is one in which 'words, charged with emotion, pour forth singing out what truly lies within the heart.'" [The quotation is from the writings of Ueda Bin (1874–1916), a scholar famous for his translations of Western symbolist poetry into Japanese.] Dazai, in other words, favored a style that was more expansive than deliberate. More than anything else, he wanted to say what he wanted to say; he did not particularly care about how it was said. He thought that the right words would naturally come pouring out of one's mouth if one's heart was brimming with intense emotion.

Dazai's prose style, then, can be characterized as expansive, emotional, and spontaneous. These adjectives are, of course, relative terms; no style can be completely devoid of intellectual restraint. But Dazai's style is far more spontaneous than that of any other modern Japanese writer of the first rank. Even compared with the style of Tanizaki, who termed his own style a "flowing" one, Dazai's style seems less strained, more artless. In a description of his own working habits, Dazai showed why this was so.

> Hateful, hateful. Thoughts after thoughts after thoughts after thoughts. They spring up in an endless succession, filling the space all around me, till I wonder where to begin. My method in the past was to let this flood of mushy liquid congeal around my desk, cut it up into various sizes, and then patch the parts together into a piece of composition. But today I have decided to scoop up this overflowing liquid and put it down on paper just as it is, in all its shapelessness. I'm sure this will work.

Dazai is being disingenuous here: the truth is that to "scoop up this overflowing liquid" was his usual method of composition. And many of his works create the impression that this liquid had not congealed. This is particularly true of such works as **"Appeal to the Authorities,"** **"Schoolgirl,"** and **"The Lost."** It is also true of such famous passages as the restaurateur's long complaint in **"Villon's Wife,"** Naoji's notes and Kazuko's letters in *The Setting Sun*, and Yōzō's second and third notebooks in *No Longer Human*. It is less true elsewhere in his writings, but it is always true to some extent. His sentences tend to be extra long or extra short, their subjects changing capriciously from clause to clause. The narrative logic shows unexpected leaps from time to time. His syntax is often whimsical, his grammar strained. His tempo is quick, his rhythm uneven, his tone informal if not colloquial. His paragraphs vary a great deal in length; some of the long ones last for several pages, while short ones consisting of only one word are not uncommon. Altogether the style approaches the "stream-of-consciousness" technique, giving the impression that the writer wrote down whatever thoughts and impressions came into his mind just as they were, without paying much attention to the formal elements of prose style.

It is, of course, doubtful that Dazai's style really stemmed from artlessness. Many "stream-of-consciousness" writers have been self-conscious artists, and Dazai had plenty of models to choose from. Yet it is true that Dazai's style, more than that of any other Japanese writer, gives the impression of being spontaneous, of being spoken directly by the author. The reader can almost hear him breathing. The effect is particularly marked in his adaptations of other stories. Eulenberg, Hamlet, the Bad Badger—all speak in the Dazai fashion, once his pen has taken them over. The leading characters in his novels—Naoji, Yōzō, and many others—are as uninhibited, emotional, and moody as Dazai himself. If one likes Dazai and what he has to say, one will find his style most engaging because it is so intensely personal. If not, then reading Dazai can seem like being buttonholed by a lunatic.

FOOD FOR LOSERS

Dazai's ideas on the function of literature are most clearly suggested in **"An Owl's Letter,"** a largely factual account of his lecture tour to Niigata in November 1940. Toward the end of the story the hero, a novelist named Dazai, goes to a local restaurant for dinner with a group of high school students. As dinner proceeds, the students' questions become faster and more direct:

> "Do you feel guilty at all, sir, for having succeeded in becoming a novelist and living your life as such? I'm sure there are lots of people who aspire to be writers but can't be, for various reasons, and have to keep wasting their talents on other pursuits."
>
> "You've got it the wrong way round. I became a writer precisely because I had failed at everything else."
>
> "There's hope for me, then. I've failed at everything."
>
> "You haven't done anything yet, young man. You can't say you've failed until you've actually tried, until you've fallen flat and hurt yourself. You say you've failed even before you try. That's laziness."
>
> The dinner was over, and I said good-bye to the students.
>
> "When you're in college and have personal problems, look me up," I said. "A writer can be a bum and still be able to help a bit in such cases."

In Dazai's view, then, literature is basically of little practical use and the novelist is a good-for-nothing. And yet it may be helpful to people with serious problems. But it is clear that the circumstances under which it is helpful are always exceptional ones. Dazai repeatedly stressed the uselessness of both art and artist in the practical domain. When he compared art to a violet he implied, at least in part, that art was beautiful but impractical. Similar metaphors abound in Dazai's writings: art is "an airplane that does not fly," "a steed that does not gallop," "an exploding firework," "a small box made of colored paper," etc. In *A Women's Duel,* Dazai has the medical student (that is, a practical person) jeer at her artist boyfriend as "a big idiot" and as "a dummy who has stopped growing." In a postscript to **The Declining Years** he warns his readers: "Reading my stories would not help you earn your living, nor would it help you rise in the world. It wouldn't help you in anything. Therefore, I can't much recommend these stories to you."

The reason why art and artist seemed useless is self-evident. For him, the artist was a criminal who was aware of his guilt, and a work of art was the song of a criminal on his way to the guillotine. The artist, because of his awareness of guilt, is passive toward others; he can never be aggressive. He is a social outcast because he chooses to be. He is too tenderhearted and sympathetic toward others to be a successful businessman. He would rather be Mr. Hospitality; he cannot stand to have other people pay for his drink—or even for their own drinks, when he is present. The artist is a nobleman. The rough seas of ordinary living are too much for him; he is always in danger of drowning. Even when he is fortunate enough to drift to a lighthouse, he is so timid that he cannot cry for help.

Why, then, did Dazai advise the students to come and see him if they had personal problems? Because the artist was a friend of the weak and suffering. Literature was a kind of food for losers. When a person who had failed at everything in life read a novel, he would find in it a character who exactly resembled him. He would then know that he had a friend, that, in fact, all of nature's noblemen and noblewomen were losers like him.

This being the case, the help that literature supplies is by way of understanding, sympathy, and consolation. But it is not a positive kind of help; it is not of the kind that actively stirs up the reader's courage and gives him renewed hope for life. Literature can never offer that kind of help as long as it rests on the premise that life is evil, that man is born to sin. On the contrary, it is possible that literature may cause the reader to wish for death, rather than for a new life. The reader, convinced that to live is to suffer, may choose to follow in the footsteps of Suwa, Constance, Tsuruta, and Naoji, all of whom killed themselves. So did Dazai, and the woman who died with him was someone who had come to consult him about her personal problems. The same thing might have happened to any of the students in Niigata, if they had turned to Dazai for help as he suggested. Some of his characters, of course, like Kazuko and Ōtani's wife, choose to live on. But they do so after losing all hope in life, and thereby arriving at some kind of existentialist affirmation of it. Can a literary work provide consolation to a despairing mind when its implications are nihilistic, or, at best, existentialist? For some it can, and for others it cannot; it all depends on the reader's age, temperament, and philosophy of life (Dazai would have wanted to add sex, too). For that reason, Dazai's works are balm for some and poison for others. All literature is like that to a certain extent; Dazai's case is an extreme.

Phyllis I. Lyons (essay date 1985)

SOURCE: "Fatal Success," in *The Saga of Dazai Osamu: A Critical Study with Translations,* Stanford University Press, 1985, pp. 149–77.

[*In the following essay, Lyons explores parallels between Dazai's work and life.*]

> I returned to Tokyo [from Tsugaru] feeling something akin to confidence in the pure Tsugaru character that flowed in my blood. In other words, it was rejuvenating to discover that in Tsugaru there was no such thing as "culture," and accordingly, I, a Tsugaru man, was not in the slightest a "man of culture." My work after that seemed to change somewhat. . . . I thought to myself that even if I died at that point, I could be said to have left good enough work as a Japanese writer.
>
> —Dazai Osamu, **"Fifteen Years"**[1]

As far as the Osamu Saga was concerned, *Tsugaru* had been preceded and now was followed by relative silence. Dazai was obviously busy, but his major writings at the end of the war were, except for *Tsugaru,* not part of the saga, and a number of them were removed from the twentieth century or even from ordinary reality. This was at least partly in defense against the strict censorship of which Dazai had already had experience. *New Tales of the Provinces* was a retelling of seventeenth-century tales; *Regretful Parting* had been commissioned by the government; *Fairy Tales* was a collection of classic folk tales retold by Dazai.

For a writer engaged in so many large projects, the year between the trip to Tsugaru and Japan's unconditional surrender sped by quickly. The dislocations of fleeing from American aerial bombing compressed time even more. Almost before he realized it, Dazai was back in Tsugaru, a refugee with his family augmented by one. The husband and wife and two children lived in the annex that had been the domain of Shūji's grandmother so many years earlier. Dazai was fortunate, he supposed, that if the war were to pursue and catch them this far away, still he would be dying at home.

The silence of the end of the war was reflected in the relative silence of the writer. *Regretful Parting* and *Fairy Tales* came out in September and October respectively, but they had been completed months earlier, before Dazai had left the Tokyo area. Nothing came from Tsugaru to Tokyo publishers for months, until the flow of stories started again with **"Niwa,"** (**"The Garden"**) published in January 1946. By the time he left Tsugaru in November 1946 to pick up his life in Tokyo, Dazai had written some fourteen stories and two plays; and *Pandora's Box* (the misfortune-plagued *Voice of the Lark,* from 1943) had appeared serially in a newspaper in Sendai. The tone of the early 1946 stories is quiet and reflective, as might well be appropriate to a man, and a nation, stunned by the end of an era. By the later part of the same year, Dazai's tone had darkened significantly; the impending return to Tokyo clearly presaged an ominous future. Now that the public war was over, Dazai was girding himself for his own private fight to the finish.

CULTIVATING ONE'S OWN GARDEN

Three stories from 1946 are of particular interest, as they bring the Osamu Saga into present time. **"The Garden"** shows the author evacuated from Tokyo and living parasitically (he feels) off his brother's largess in Tsugaru. It is an after-ripple of *Tsugaru.* **"An Almanac of Pain"** and **"Fifteen Years,"** on the other hand, take long, overreaching looks at the past, in the manner of **"Recollections"** and **"Eight Views of Tokyo,"** and are the final autobiographical summaries of the author's life. Once these stories were completed, the experiences could be organized and fictionalized into *No Longer Human.*

The five-page **"The Garden"** is a vignette, a conversation between Bunji and Shūji as they work to clean up the garden that had gone half to ruin while family attention was turned to the war effort. Now that the war is over, Bunji is returning to private order. The author's tone is ironic as he describes the prudent reserve of the younger brother, a "barbarian" with little interest in the historical tradition behind the style of garden landscape that the Tsushima garden represents, who nevertheless listens politely as befits a guest, a "parasite" living off his brother; and the condescending, complacent, unimaginative elder brother. Their central topic of conversation is a disguised debate on their own interaction: the relationship between the sixteenth-century tea master, landscape designer, and general cultural arbiter Sen no Rikyū and his employer the general Toyotomi Hideyoshi, called the "Taikō." Bunji wants to know why Shūji doesn't write about Rikyū, an interesting man. Shūji is ambiguously uncommunicative, his explanation being (to his reading audience) that "the parasite younger brother, too, when conversation turned to the novel, demonstrated quite a bit of the fastidiousness of the specialist." (8: 137). This Shūji is prudent, not intimidated.

Bunji ignores Shūji's reticence, and goes on happily with his lecture. He interprets Shūji's reserve as a sign that he doesn't know anything about Rikyū, and twits him for being an "unscholarly *sensei."* Shūji's only response to his brother's mockery is that he doesn't like Rikyū very much. That's because Rikyū is a complex man, Bunji retorts smugly. Shūji takes him up on that: "Right! There are a lot of cloudy issues. At the same time that he seemed to have contempt for the Taikō, he couldn't bring himself to break away from him. . . ." (8: 138.) Bunji's understanding of what Shūji means is shallow. He finds the answer simple: Rikyū was drawn by Hideyoshi's charismatic character. Bunji deals only with external, basically static contrasts: Hideyoshi starting out poor, ugly, and unlettered, giving rise to the extravagant, brilliant Momoyama style that he made famous; Rikyū wellborn, educated, handsome, opposing the ostentation of Hideyoshi's *nouvel arrivé* taste with the restrained elegance of aesthetic rusticity that the Japanese call *wabi.*

Shūji ponders to himself what *he* means by the ambiguity in the Rikyū-Hideyoshi relationship. He is interested in the psychological clash between the two, lord and retainer. The outcome of the contest was set from the start by their relative positions, he feels. If Rikyū was such a truly superior, elegant man, why did he not just let Hideyoshi have his fun? Why did he always have to prove he was right? If Rikyū was so sick of ostentation, why did he not just leave it all and travel, like Bashō? No, Shūji decides, there was something about Rikyū that made him need to hang around the seat of power. It was Hideyoshi's *power,* and not his personality, that was charismatic.

Bunji finishes his monologue and looks at his brother with light disgust. He exclaims in irritation, "It doesn't seem you're going to write about him. You should go and study the adult world more. Ah, you are an ignorant *sensei*!" (8: 139.) The thirty-seven-year-old kid Shūji does not rise to the bait. He observes to his readers: "I bow out from the

Rikyū [contest]. I don't want to beat out my brother, [especially] while I'm living off him. This business of competition is shameful. Even if I weren't living off him—I have never once tried to compete with my brother. From birth, the outcome was set." (8: 139–40.) Clearly, Dazai is using the Rikyū-Hideyoshi clash to serve several purposes. First is the identification of Rikyū with the establishment, meaning such people as Bunji, Shiga, and Kawabata, and of Hideyoshi with Dazai. By refusing to compete with his brother, Shūji shows himself to be superior to Rikyū. Yet, since the same phrase, "the outcome was set," is used to describe both Rikyū's and Shūji's contests, their fates must be linked. In the end, Hideyoshi won by ordering Rikyū to commit suicide. Of course, Rikyū's aesthetic contribution survived his death, and so (perhaps Dazai is saying) history has adjudged him to be the winner. By implication, he links together, in himself, the ugly, unlettered Hideyoshi and the smug, aesthetically elegant Rikyū, thus making himself the aesthetician of weakness and roughness. It is the discoveries of *Tsugaru,* that he is his own man and yet is inevitably an extension of his family, that enable Dazai to continue quietly to assert his moral superiority while acknowledging the precariousness of his physical security in its dependence on his brother. The Japanese writers Bunji approves of are Nagai Kafū and Tanizaki Jun'ichirō, and he also reads Chinese essayists. The next day he is expecting a Chinese writer to visit; Shūji, sitting at the fire nursing a cold, thinks of his brother out weeding the garden. He consoles himself with the thought that the Chinese visitor, like himself, might also have rather appreciated a dilapidated garden with clumps of grasses here and there. Shūji is a connoisseur of true rustic style.

"The Garden" is a nice little piece. It bridges the time from *Tsugaru* through the end of the war to the present with great economy, and presents a vivid but relaxed portrait of personality conflict. **"An Almanac of Pain"** is considerably tenser and more argumentative. With the Occupation well established and national political life picking up again (there is mention in **"The Garden"** of the possibility of Bunji's running for representative to the Diet, or for governor), "isms" are in the air. Dazai decides to write the history of his "isms": democracy, "philanthropism," humanitarianism, communism, terrorism, militarism, conservatism—these are the kinds of "thought" his experiences have brought through his life, from the would-be democracy of his childhood to the self-congratulatory liberalism of the 1946 present.

"An Almanac of Pain" has been mentioned so often already, and it is so short (only nine pages), that all that is necessary at this point are some comments on its place in the saga. In form, it is fragmentary. Short passages, separated by asterisks, contain references to an idea, or an aside on some issue, or an explanation of a position. Some relate personal experiences, some are commentaries on the events of the day. After a general explanation of his ideas on the place of "thought" in history (none) and the evolution of his own "thought" ("I don't have any such thing . . . Only likes and dislikes"), Dazai places himself in

time and space (family background, with peasants present and "thinkers" conspicuously absent), and launches into an impressionistic and often ambiguous account of his life. Only the reader who has followed Dazai's work so far will know, for example, the story underlying a passage, inserted between an account of a scandal contemporaneous with the attempted military coup of February 26, 1936, and a description of spreading international hostilities: "What next? I had already tried suicide unsuccessfully four times by then. And naturally, I thought of death several times a week." (8: 210.) This is the period between the split with Hatsuyo and the marriage to Michiko. But no names or references we have come to recognize appear: no Hatsuyo, no Michiko, no *sempai,* no hospitals. The names are public, the incidents newsworthy: Salvation Army, proletarian literature, the Osada Incident, strikes, the Manchurian Incident, Tōjō, the Emperor. An embittered Osamu floats from ideas of "proletarian dictatorship," to guarded resignation to the tides of militarism, to contempt for present critics of the Emperor. What has prompted this review seems to be a nightmarish feeling that, through all these years, nothing essentially has changed. Stupidity, terror, ignorance, cruelty—all remain. Osamu has been through so much—is he at the beginning again? His understated, devout prayer for the future sums up his life: "At ten, a democrat; at twenty, a communist; at thirty, a pure aesthete; at forty, a conservative. And then does history repeat itself after all? I hope it does not." (8: 212.)

"An Almanac of Pain" is pump priming of a most elementary sort. After the emotional respite occasioned by *Tsugaru,* and the physical recuperation made possible by the orderly life provided at his brother's home, Dazai was starting to shift gears in order to take up his own life again. Reacting to the agitation of the day, felt only distantly in Tsugaru through newspapers and letters from friends, Dazai here answers the unasked question, "What do you think of the present schools of thought?" by dredging through the past in a form not attempted since **"Eight Views of Tokyo."** Actually, the antecedents of **"An Almanac of Pain"** go back farther; although not chaotic as the earlier stories were, the work is in intention and, to some extent, tone quite similar to **"Human Lost"** or **"Leaves."**

Dazai's autobiographical impulse was now strongly in motion again. **"Fifteen Years"** is less elliptical than **"An Almanac of Pain,"** organized as a postscript to **"Eight Views of Tokyo."** This time, instead of the places in which he has lived, or the "isms" he has experienced, Dazai will use the books he has written to organize the story of his life as a writer—his "fifteen years."[2] It begins almost identically to **"The Garden,"** with the account of why he happens to be in Tsugaru, and how he got there. But there is one important addition: not only has he had great difficulty getting his children to safety—they are the reason he is in Tsugaru. If it had been just himself (and his wife, presumably), he would have stuck it out in Tokyo; but it was necessary to get them to a place of shelter. Parenthood was an extraordinary burden to Dazai and to all his narrators male and female. Here, the sense of responsibility (which elsewhere is transformed into willful irresponsibility) seems a response to guilty resentment that children demand and need so much care, and that by their dependence they get attention he himself wanted. Osamu had at least been charmed by his daughter in **"Hometown"** and concerned about her in *Tsugaru*, but the guilt and resentment appear increasingly from **"Fifteen Years"** on, in such stories as **"Hakumei" ("Faint Light"), "Chichi" ("The Father"), "Osan" ("Osan"),** and **"Ōtō"** (**"Cherries"**) with its ironic repeating refrain: "The parent is more important than the child." (9: 354.) In **"Fifteen Years"** there is little resentment, for with the children as an excuse, Dazai was able to attain something that might otherwise have been beyond his reach: the chance to live in his brother's home. The price he pays is that "parasitic" self-consciousness that he is living off his brother and has to be careful of what he says and does.

He supposes that "most people know that for a long time, relations had not been good between me and my family. To put it crudely, I had been disowned because of the dissipation of my twenties." (8: 213.) Almost as if he had not written *Tsugaru*, he observes how strange it is to be back in the country, to find it so little changed, and himself so peasant-like, stolid, and rough. **"Fifteen Years"** will be an attempt to discover how this "man with the blood of Tsugaru dirt farmers" had managed to live in Tokyo all that time without picking up any city refinement. He wants to establish his "countrified basic nature." Actually, **"Fifteen Years"** is an affirmation of his city life, a self-reassurance that there *is*, after all, a novelist named Dazai Osamu, although at the moment, in this rustic setting that seems to deny any time has passed since his childhood here, it is hard to believe in another whole existence.

Dazai quotes lengthy passages from three of his stories, **"Eight Views of Tokyo," "The Firebird,"** and *Pandora's Box*, and he synopsizes a letter to "a *sempai*." In keeping with his intention of looking at his life from a professional viewpoint, he is very restrained and sparing with personal details. The same narrative is there, but approached more abstractly. Even in describing the emotional upheaval of leaving his beloved house in Funabashi to go into a mental hospital, he gives no indication of why he was leaving or who was making him go. A passage from **"Eight Views of Tokyo"** is there simply to explain how he came to write the stories in *The Final Years*. Instead, his analytical faculties (displayed in emotional bursts of reaction) are turned to sorting out what it is about the world "out there" that has so appalled his Tsugaru soul that it has curled into itself, refusing to form contact with so-called refined circles. Dazai's covering metaphor for the hypocrisy, self-seeking, backbiting, kowtowing, stupidity, and cruelty he has seen and experienced in his contacts with the literary establishment is *saron no geijutsu* ("salon art"). "An elegant salon is the most frightful of human decadence," he posits, and he uses the concept to cover wide ground. Subsumed under it is his fear of the responsibilities of orderly home life. "If I were to have an elegant, salon-like home life,

that would clearly mean that I had betrayed someone," he feels. (8: 221.) What he calls "the selfishness of the home circle" is the source of strength for the smug Shiga Naoyas of the world, he says in "Thus Have I Heard." "The happiness of the home," he concludes in the 1948 essay of that title, "is the source of all evils." (9: 353.) The essay examines his feelings that acts of terrible cruelty can be committed by people piously dedicated to upholding this "happiness." Such is the thrust of his struggle against the hypocrisy of conventional morality.

Contrasted to the healthy, handsome supporters of home, with their sturdy children, is Dazai, whose homes, without his willing it, seem spontaneously to crumble and fall apart over and over again. Twenty-five moves in fifteen years, twenty-five times when he has, as he puts it, "gone bankrupt," losing everything and having to start over from scratch. It is like the history of Tsugaru's crop failures. Sickly children. No home. Ill health. All the things Shiga Naoya has, Dazai has not. It is his desperate response to the unfairness of the situation that gives him his clear vision of the truth. If he had been able to partake of the others' comfortable success and easy words, he might have been as dull and imperceptive as they. His is the clarity of starvation, which sounds like feverish hallucination to the well fed. Dazai's refuge is in the story of the Ugly Duckling. Artists cannot be beautiful, he implies, for they would use up the beauty in themselves and have none left for their art. He uses a painting by Böcklin to symbolize the plight of the true artist: a lush tropical island, an ugly little creature hidden in the wild green trees, playing a flute; beautiful mermaids gathered on the shore margin, listening captivated to his piping. The artist's sad, solitary fate is that he must hide himself, revealing only his voice. If he were to show his true form, in all its ugliness, his audience would flee in terror. Likewise, the fledgling swan does not have the appeal of the fluffy little ducklings: "it has none of the cuteness suitable for the salon." As for the salon itself, he professes difficulty in finding words bad enough to describe it. "House of prostitution for intelligence" is too complimentary, because even whorehouses have the occasional decent inmate. "Thieves' market for intelligence" won't do either; sometimes a real gold ring turns up in one. Finally, he has it: the salon is "a wartime-Japan newspaper for intelligence." What he means by this, he explains, is that during the war, there was not a page in the newspaper that reported the truth; all that appeared were "painful evasions." The only part people could believe was one small corner of one page each day: the obituary column. That told the truth. (8: 217–18.)

As a footnote here, Dazai talks about the attitude of the public, himself included, to what they knew were lies in the newspapers: "(But we willed ourselves to believe, we were prepared to die. When a parent has gone bankrupt, and his back is to the wall, and he tells transparent lies, does the child expose them? No—he realizes his fate is set, and silently goes down with him.)" (8: 218.) The passage from **"The Firebird"** quoted in **"Fifteen Years"** later expands upon this: a mother tells the story of her son's giving up the schooling and career he was beginning in Tokyo to return to the country out of filial duty to take care of his father who has lost both his money and his mind through gambling. **"The Firebird"** was written in 1936, years before the Pacific War, and was intended to exorcise some of the aftershocks of the Enoshima suicide attempt; Dazai must himself have been impressed at how apt a metaphor he had produced here.

The war had been the main event between **"Eight Views of Tokyo"** and the present, and references to attitudes toward it are an important theme in **"Fifteen Years."** Long before war began with the United States and England, "it was truly perilous to wave your own flag on problems of love, or belief, or art"; both **"An Almanac of Pain"** and **"Fifteen Years"** attest that Japan had been at war for years before the bombing of Pearl Harbor. Dazai persisted as best he could in hewing to his own line, but not out of any logical principles:

> It was peasant stubbornness. However, I am not saying here, like some people, "I never did want war. I was an enemy of the Japanese militarists. I am a liberal"— these new-style opportunists who, once the war was over, immediately began attacking Tōjō and making a big racket over war guilt and the like. Now even socialism is being debased by "salon thought." . . .

> During the war, I was disgusted at Tōjō, and I felt contempt for Hitler; and I went around telling everyone. But at the same time, I was trying my best to be a supporter of Japan. I realized that it would probably not help one bit if someone like myself were an advocate, but I did my best for Japan. I would like to be clear on this point: right from the start, there was no hope, but Japan went on and did it.

[8: 224.]

During the war, Dazai's determination to stand by his "parent" had been sorely tried. First, if Japan won with conditions of oppression at home as they were, "it would not be the Land of the Gods—it would be the Devil's Country." But more personally crucial, his loose talking and reputation for loose living had given him an image of unreliability:

> The rumor went out that I was under suspicion by the Office of Information, and requests from publishers for manuscripts disappeared. This may sound stingy, but with the cost of living going up and up, and my children growing, with hardly any income, I was in a terrible state. . . . Since everyone, except for war profiteers, was having a hard time, I felt I could not talk about just my living difficulties, as if I were the only one, so I did my best to feign lightheartedness; but nevertheless, I was so up against it that I sent a letter to a certain *sempai*. . . .

[8: 227.]

In the letter, he discussed suicide. What held him back, he said, was not just concern for his wife and children.[3] Rather, he said (perhaps a bit grandiosely), it was concern for the propaganda effect news of his death might have in

giving aid and comfort to the enemy, and its demoralizing effect on his young friends at the front. In **"Fifteen Years"** Dazai asserts that the chief concern should be not for the survivors, but for the actor. The sources of pain in all human beings do not change; only the degree of tolerance does. Some men can bear the pain, some cannot. To Dazai, home and family were the least of the considerations in an act of such magnitude as self-destruction.

It was at this point that *Tsugaru* entered the picture—to give him a source of income and a new lease on life, he says in **"Fifteen Years"**. With the attention of the entire nation focused to the south, on the Pacific, he went north. He found health in Tsugaru's clumsiness, its inelegance, its incompetence, its confusion in the face of what city people called culture. But he saw in its "great incompletion" the possibility of a new culture, a new expression of love. Tragically, he would find the wellsprings of renewal dry in himself, for his task was not to begin new business, it was to complete old.

Now the war is over. Japanese culture is in an even worse state. All the leaders of culture are shouting this "ism" and that, and it all smacks of "salon thought." If he could swallow it, he feels, he too could be a success, but it sticks in his countrified throat. He cannot lie about his own perceptions. Far from becoming cultured, he is growing more and more peasant-like. "Salon thought" is getting farther and farther away. **"Fifteen Years"** ends with a passage from *Pandora's Box,* Dazai's novel about a young tuberculosis patient striving to recover in a sanatorium (a rather obvious metaphor for postwar Japan). Three of his nicknamed fellow patients, Kappore Dancer, Echigo Lion, and Hard Bread, are discussing "liberal thought." Echigo Lion concludes that Christ is the original freethinker, and that the roots of Japan's defeat in the war lie in its having taken the external manifestations of Western culture blindly, without understanding the ramifications that are there to be studied in the Bible. Christ, in contrast to today's self-proclaimed liberals who are only floating with the tide, shows that the liberal *has* to be in conflict with the status quo. And as for today's freethinker:

> At this late date in Japan, to attack the militarists of yesterday is not liberal thinking. . . . To be a true courageous liberal, there is something you have to cry, no matter what else: To the Emperor—Banzai! Until yesterday, that was old-fashioned—or worse, a fraud. But today it is the newest of liberal thinking. This is where the liberalism of ten years ago differs from today's. This is not mysticism. It is true natural human love. I have heard that America is the land of freedom. Then surely they will recognize this cry of true freedom from Japan.

[8: 236.]

This ending sounds vaguely hopeful, but it is clearly visionary and more than a little silly. Japan is not liberal, he knows; he is not liberal. Nor are they free, any of them.

In *Tsugaru* and the other books following it, he felt he had produced work of a quality to assure the continuance of his name "even if I died at that point" through accident of war. But now, in the peace, it was time for him to turn his full confidence in the power of his craft to the accomplishment of his task, the telling of the story of "what kind of a terrible child I had been."

PREPARING THE FINAL MAP

When *The Setting Sun* began to appear in June 1947, it signaled a new fictionality in the Osamu Saga. It was not the striking story line that marked a change in the author but his attitude toward his characters and the way he transformed fact into fiction. Up until 1947, while Dazai had embroidered upon the facts he used to tell the story of his life, while he had been less or more candid, he still had not tampered significantly with the sequence of real events as he transferred them to his stories. Perhaps he had never revealed what he and his brother discussed in the summer of 1932. He may have claimed that he and the woman in his second suicide attempt tried to drown themselves, when actually they took sleeping pills on the shore. But the events, in the saga's accounts of them, come where they came in his life, and they happen to characters named Osamu and Shūji. And Dazai found each attempt at telling the story inadequate to his vision of what needed to be said. Now with *The Setting Sun*, seemingly, he had stumbled on the clue for which he had searched so long: truth is better stalked through indirection than through confrontation.

Women show the way. Women became his vehicle as he rapidly worked out his method. For a time, the saga stories (such as **"Chance"** in 1946, and **"Morning"** and **"The Father"** in 1947) come to occupy a secondary position, and a new set of female-centered stories show what is happening to the writer's art. Although Dazai had often in the past used a female narrator, and although women had often appeared as prominent characters, there were now additions: a new kind of character, the embittered and disillusioned woman determined to survive her tribulations; and a new theme, the rape of innocents or what is shown as the near crime of unloving copulation between non-innocents. It was as if, having been disarmed by the love he found in *Tsugaru*, which he articulated in relation to women and through childlike, dependent emotions, Dazai had to abuse women in his stories in order to gain the strength to finish his story of Osamu. Japan's defeat in the war must also have played a part in producing both the rage and the paralysis exhibited by the male characters in these stories.

What is different about, for example, **"Villon's Wife,"** *The Setting Sun,* and *No Longer Human* is that the characters have independent existences of their own. Kazuko in *The Setting Sun* is, of course, modeled on Ōta Shizuko, and her rhetoric sounds Dazaiesque; Ōba Yōzō in *No Longer Human* is undeniably modeled on Dazai himself. But Kazuko's ambiguities, her shallowness and her deep anguish, are completely her own. "Villon's wife," Mrs. Ōtani, is not simply a stick figure intended to backlight her repro-

bate husband; she is a live woman, deeply wronged and quietly, unemotionally, liberated through pain. Yōzō is one of the most bizarre and emotionally touching characters in Japanese fiction.

Three "woman stories" show the direction of Dazai's change in course, as he works out the complexities of the need for and failures in love, security, and fidelity in human relationships. Dazai had been puzzling out these problems for years with the Osamu persona; now he does so through a series of strong female characters, who survive against great odds, and of weak male figures, who are defeated by life despite their struggles. In this way he hints at the conclusion of the Osamu Saga. *Fireworks in Winter* is a play that appeared in June 1946; the short story **"Villon's Wife"** came in March 1947, and the novel *The Setting Sun* in June.

Fireworks in Winter is talky and melodramatic, more a series of overwrought monologues than an integrated drama. Its central characters are Kazue, aged twenty-nine, her stepmother Asa, and three men, two not present: Kazue's six-year-old daughter's father, missing in action; her secret lover in Tokyo; and a village suitor, Seizō. The time is a year after the end of the war, the place Kazue's home village in Tsugaru, whence she had evacuated toward the end of the war. The play is about love, guilt, and despair. In a letter to a friend a couple of months after the play was published in the journal *Tembō*, Dazai tied its theme to a quotation from the Bible, "To whom little is forgiven, the same loveth little." (Luke 7: 47.) Only one who bears a deep sense of sin within can love deeply, Dazai continued; hence the passionate sins of the women, Kazue's clear from the start, Asa's hidden until near the end. As a playwright, however, Dazai proves unequal to controlling the emotions of the theme, and the play remains confused and inconclusive, demonstrating in Kazue more a sense of anger at betrayal than love and compassion. These women, Kazue and her mother, cannot forgive themselves, so they feel their only choice of response is death or revolution. "Revolution" as Dazai uses it in the woman stories is an amorphous word only loosely connected with politics. Kazue in *Fireworks in Winter* and Kazuko in *The Setting Sun* speak of some sort of moral revolution that gives them the impetus to overturn conventional standards; the husband in **"Osan"** mouths inarticulate riddles about revolution that seem political until his wife discovers he is involved with another woman. Yet both women and men who use that battle cry are aiming at the same sort of freedom that, in Dazai's life and writings alike, is represented by suicide. Especially for men, in Dazai's view, death is immanent in revolution.

In outline, the plot of *Fireworks in Winter* sounds fairly silly. After a ten-year absence, Kazue had returned to her country home in Tsugaru to escape wartime bombing. During the years in Tokyo, she had become involved with a novelist, had possibly married him, and had borne him a daughter, Mutsuko. How she had supported herself and the child after the writer was drafted and reported missing in action, Kazue's father has suspicions, which he airs at the opening of the play. He accuses her of selfishness, willfulness, and leading a dissolute life. Dembei had watched his wife lavish attention on Kazue through the years—more than she gave her own son, Eiichi, Kazue's half-brother, who is also missing in the war—but the selfish girl has never acknowledged it. The parents have surmised that Kazue has a lover in Tokyo, and now the father asks, on Asa's behalf, that Kazue leave little Mutsuko with them; the girl will only be a hindrance to Kazue's "free" life, he says bitterly. He and Kazue insult and verbally abuse each other. That night, Kazue has a secret and uninvited caller, Seizō, who claims he has waited the ten long years for Kazue to come back from Tokyo (where she had insisted on going to school) and marry him. He will kill her with his little dagger if she will not be his. Asa, listening in the hall, now enters at Kazue's appeal, seizes the knife, and tries to stab Seizō, who escapes.

Ten days later, Kazue is attending Asa, who has been confined to bed ever since she collapsed following the events of that night. Asa speaks weakly of wanting to die. Kazue, in an ecstasy of self-abnegation, assures Asa that she must not die; Kazue loves her and needs her so, she will give up her Tokyo lover and spend the rest of her life as a farmer here in the country, caring for Asa. Asa is good, the best and purest woman in the world, she cries hysterically. Asa then reveals her deep secret: six years earlier, she had been seduced by Seizō. The other night she had not been protecting Kazue—she had tried to kill Seizō for her own sake. Faced with the perfidy of the world, Kazue cackles wildly and determines to return to Tokyo immediately, "to fall as far as one can fall."

The issues with which Dazai was grappling could have made a better story, but the method and direction were too unfamiliar to him. Extended dialogue had never been his forte; his strength was the brief, telling comment embedded in a framework of exposition. The amount of exposition in the speeches of Kazue's father and Seizō is tiresome, as are Kazue's tirades. As a play, *Fireworks in Winter* fails so completely that no further discussion of its plot is necessary. It is important for other reasons. The play shows Dazai's attempt to truly get within the skin of a woman. Kazue is an independent voice, as the female narrators of earlier stories had not been. But her kinship to Dazai is at the same time inescapable, as will be Kazuko's in *The Setting Sun*. If he had been a woman, and had still been the person he was, this would have been his salvation, Dazai seems to be saying. In **"Hometown"** and *Tsugaru*, Dazai had betrayed his intuition that women live a life that is truer to the emotions, one not open to men with their social abstractions. In effect, Kazue's defiant determination to return to her younger lover and "fall as far as one can fall," and Kazuko's dedication to a "moral revolution," are little different from young Shūji's throwing himself into the leftist cause in the late 1920's and early 1930's. At the same time, there is something vital and palpable in the women's revolt (symbolized by the child Kazuko carries in her womb, and by Kazue's

daughter) that was lacking in the man's. Death was the only outcome for male abstraction; the women might experience degradation and hardship, but Dazai saw in them something that was darkly if melodramatically triumphant. Most of the women in the late stories are mothers already or desperate to bear a child. The woman's child in these stories is not an abstract "hostage to fate"; it is an ally, a talisman that ensures the woman's survival. The women in a number of the late stories see themselves as victims, and yet victors; but when in **"Osan,"** for instance, the husband tries, in a suicide letter to his wife, to strike a similarly martyred pose, the wife reacts with contempt: "A letter full of nonsense. I wonder: does a man have to tell lies and strike poses to the end? Does he have to cling to his solemn purposes? . . . to die shouting about revolutions! I saw how worthless he had been. . . . I was less angry and sad than appalled at the utter nonsense." (9: 258–59; tr. Seidensticker 1960, 49–50.) Her disgust, aimed at a husband who claimed he loved his wife to the end, even though he was dying with the mistress he had gotten pregnant, is at the emotional waste caused by men's dishonesty:

> Men are wrong when they think it their duty to be remembering their wives. Do they tell themselves it is right, do they salve their consciences, do they find it manly, to go on remembering their wives after they have found other women? A man begins to love another woman, and he heaves dark sighs in front of his wife, he exhibits his moral anguish. Presently the contagion is passed on to the wife, who must also sigh. If the husband would be brisk and airy about it all, the wife might be spared this hell.

> [9: 255; tr. Seidensticker 1960, 47.]

Having had it both ways, suffering as a man in physical life, and as a woman through his heroines in the last stories, Dazai came to the conclusion that there was truly no way out of his dilemma as a man.

The real conflict in *Fireworks in Winter* is not what Dazai thought it was. The failure of love and the absence of forgiveness more properly describe the world of *No Longer Human*. The significance of the tie between Kazue and Asa lies in a throwaway line from act 1, "Don't they say, 'The one who brought you up, rather than the one who bore you'?" (8: 344.) This is a folk saying about the person to whom one owes filial piety. The reverberations of Dazai's conclusions about his mother and Take in *Tsugaru* are still strong. *Fireworks in Winter* is the story of the price that must be paid for Asa's utter, almost pathological trust and selflessness, so like Yoshiko's in *No Longer Human*; but Asa's perfection, and the powerful effect that her fall from grace has on Kazue, depends on her being Kazue's stepmother—not the one who bore her but the one who brought her up. In *The Setting Sun*, Dazai will strip the plot of such artificial complications to underline more clearly the ambiguity of Kazuko's relations with her mother; but here he is still working out the ramifications of emotional ties between people for whom the commitment must be conscious instead of customary. Thus the basis of Dembei's resentment is that he has watched Asa for years stinting herself to provide for an ungrateful wretch who is of his flesh, not hers. His seems to be the anger of impotence, for he has felt himself incapable of intervening. Kazue's attack, when she accuses Asa of loving Eiichi more than her, is all the more unreasonable, in his eyes; Eiichi is, after all, Asa's own child. But reasonableness is not the point. The father does not see that the issue is that Kazue needs to be shown proof in order to feel secure, which she does not. She is conscious of the extent of Asa's sacrifices for her, but that is not enough. She has felt so much love for Asa it sometimes had seemed to her that they must be lovers (Kazue says "lesbian love"). But the moment of Kazue's total capitulation to Asa's goodness comes when she sees Asa attacking Seizō with the dagger, like a lioness coming to the aid of her cub. The betrayal of Kazue's suddenly absolute trust comes when she discovers Asa's "selfishness" in trying to avenge her own honor. Any sign of ego in a love object thrusts Kazue again out into the cold. In *No Longer Human* this idea will be carried to its extreme, when the blameless Yoshiko is raped as a result of too much trust, and Yōzō is cast into outer darkness because he is made aware that he cannot control all aspects of his world. Take remained the object of Dazai's love only because she had no real part in his life. In *Tsugaru*, one visit in thirty years rekindles the smouldering flame. Kazue exemplifies Dazai's recognition that such an infantile demand for absolute attention cannot survive the test of everyday life.

The importance of *Fireworks in Winter*, then, is that it shows the development of the Kazuko character. In a dozen details, it also shows itself to be a major step in Dazai's working out of the action of *The Setting Sun*. Ōta Shizuko's life and diary went into the making of the novel, as did Dazai's thoughts about Chekhov and *The Cherry Orchard*, and about the downfall of his family and Japanese society. But *The Setting Sun* did not appear fullblown, with no preparation. *Fireworks in Winter* might be called its rough draft. The resemblance between the two heroines' names is the first and most obvious connection. Kazue, like Kazuko, is twenty-nine. In both stories, the father is there for reasons of plot, not of characterization. The mother is an essential part of the story. Kazue's relationship with her wavers between violent love and as violent resentment. She accuses the mother of loving her brother more. The brother is missing in action. The novelist father of Mutsuko, and the lover in Tokyo, are in reputation like Uehara in *The Setting Sun*. Kazue's "secret man" in Tokyo prefigures Kazuko's "secret." Asa's helping Kazue surreptitiously is elaborated into Kazuko's helping Naoji. There are no more "Rising Sun" flags, so numerous during the war, in the toy shops of the defeated nation, so the only toys for Mutsuko are the unseasonal "fireworks in winter" of the title; this symbol fairly shouts out the image of "the setting sun." The mother is sick and wants to die, while the daughter nurses her, grimly determined to have her live. Like Kazuko, Kazue makes up her mind to become a farmer. She is firmly anti-intellectual, to the point of planning to urge her lover to give up painting in Tokyo and

come make a paradise with her in the country; in the same way, Kazuko, for all her reading and arguing, is calling for a revolution of feeling, not ideology, and she gives evidence of her own lack of intellectuality. Kazue's lover is a painter; Naoji disguises Uehara as a painter in his suicide note. Asa might as well be speaking of Kazuko when she says to Kazue near the end of the play: "Women all have secrets. It's just that you haven't hidden yours." (8: 370.)

In such ways, Dazai developed his plan for *The Setting Sun*. But another story, **"Villon's Wife,"** also had an important contribution to make, in the area of character development. More of the flotsam and jetsam of Dazai's immediate life and surroundings float up in this story; it is both more realistic and more focused than *Fireworks in Winter*. Ōtani, the narrator's common-law husband, is the younger son of country aristocracy, a brilliant poet according to popular opinion, slowly going downhill with drink and women. He spends little time at home, leaving his wife and four-year-old son, possibly retarded, to struggle along in abject poverty.[4] When the story opens, he has just stolen money from a bar he has been patronizing regularly for several years. Mrs. Ōtani promises the proprietor that she will pay him back, to keep the man from calling the police, although she has no idea where she will find the money. The next day she starts working at the shop as a barmaid, hoping for some miracle. That evening one occurs, in a sense, when Ōtani comes into the bar with an older woman who pays back the stolen money. With that immediate worry off her mind, Mrs. Ōtani now asks if her husband has a balance on his account there. She determines to pay it back by continuing to work at the bar. Suddenly her life starts looking up: she is popular with the customers, and no longer has to sit alone in misery, her only companion the child whose very appearance makes her weep. Why hadn't she thought of this before? She is amazed to discover what her stupidity has cost her in suffering. A quiet revolution has begun to make her independent.

Several weeks pass; she is happy in her work, and is taking a new interest in clothes and cosmetics. Ōtani stops by often to drink, letting her pay the bill and frequently going home with her. Then late one night she is raped by a customer who gains her confidence by professing interest in Ōtani's poetry. The next morning Ōtani is at the bar, reading a newspaper, when she arrives. She tells him nothing, acting with complete nonchalance. She announces simply that she is giving up their squalid house and from now on will probably live at the shop. He supposes that is a good idea.

Mrs. Ōtani is perhaps Dazai's fullest female portrait, for all that **"Villon's Wife,"** is only one-fifth the length of *The Setting Sun*. She starts out thoroughly submissive, like Uehara's wife, anxious not to cause her husband any trouble, swallowing his insults, and silently taking on all the responsibilities he shirks. Gradually, through his delinquencies, her world expands; without shrillness or hysteria, she learns independence while still loving Ōtani and happy to see him. A terrible experience then snaps the bond that holds her to Ōtani, so that she no longer needs the drain of Ōtani's selfishness. In this she is like Kazuko, who will discard Uehara when she is finished with him. Unlike Kazuko, however, Mrs. Ōtani has no such defensive ego that makes her shout her independence defiantly. She is simply, quietly determined to stay alive.

The male figure is still not well delineated. Ōtani seems at heart a good person, and that is why his wife had stayed loyal to him. The proprietor of the bar liked him, and felt he behaved badly because he was "sick." In fact, he feels that "if only he had paid the bill he would have been a good customer." Mrs. Ōtani recognizes the external manifestations of his mental anguish:

> I don't know where he goes or what he does. When he comes back he is always drunk; and he sits there, deathly pale, breathing heavily and staring at my face. Sometimes he cries and the tears stream down his face, or without warning he crawls into my bed and holds me tightly. "Oh, it can't go on. I'm afraid. I'm afraid. Help me!"
>
> Sometimes he trembles all over, and even after he falls asleep he talks deliriously and moans. The next morning he is absent-minded, like a man with the soul taken out of him.

[9: 29; tr. Keene 1960, 406–7.]

Despite this, Ōtani comes across simply as selfish and childish. Dazai, still working out his method for showing emotional relationships between the characters in his stories, fills out only one portrait at a time. This is Mrs. Ōtani's story. Later, in Ōba Yōzō's story, Dazai will describe the rape more vividly, since here his purpose is to show its effect on Yōzō; in **"Villon's Wife,"** where it is Ōtani's desertion, leaving her vulnerable, and not the act itself that is significant to Mrs. Ōtani, she describes it neutrally: "The next morning at dawn without ceremony he took me." Ōtani's sins are ones of omission, and he is so weak that she cannot feel anger or even reproach. The light just goes out.

Ōtani is not Dazai, although he resembles the portrait of himself that Dazai was drawing at the time in several other stories, and that probably accounts in part for the sketchiness. Ōtani's torment even sounds gratuitous, for he seems too insignificant to suffer—a whipped puppy. When, in *The Setting Sun*, Dazai divides Ōtani into two Osamu-like figures, Uehara and Naoji, paradoxically he succeeds in creating somewhat more rounded characters.

FINAL DESTINATION IN SIGHT

The Setting Sun is, compared with *Fireworks in Winter* and **"Villon's Wife,"** a tightly integrated and subtle story. It still contains some weaknesses of structure and time sequence—weaknesses that will disappear in *No Longer Human*—but the vibrant will of its heroine to survive remains echoing long after the reader has closed the book.

"Ruin. No, not only we. Everyone in Japan, and especially everyone in Tokyo, drained of life, moving about sluggishly as if just to move were a great effort." (9: 245; tr. Seidensticker 1960, 39.) This, from **"Osan,"** describes the world of *The Setting Sun*. The novel describes the complex emotional intertwinings of a mother and her two adult children. Mother, Kazuko, and Naoji are sadly adrift in the aftermath of the war. Mother is slowly dying, spiritually as well as physically, as postwar bankruptcy forces her to give up the family home in Tokyo and move to the seashore. She is both the dependent of her children and a catalyst for not-so-hidden rivalry between them for her love. Kazuko, through her own fault, has been divorced by her husband after the stillbirth of her baby. Her brother Naoji (one of the two Osamu-like characters in the novel) has been released from the hell of war and drug addiction, but is in a self-destructive frenzy of drink and dissipation. By the end of the novel, he is dead, a suicide. Uehara, Naoji's novelist "teacher" and the other Osamu figure, becomes Kazuko's lover as she pursues him with a fierce desire to have a baby by him, even though he is married. He too is dying from within. Everywhere is financial ruin, social and moral bankruptcy. This is the nightmare from which they all seek release, in their different ways.

In the midst of the chaos, trapped between the sensitive ones who have lost the will to live and the smug and prudent ones (exemplified by Kazuko's Uncle Wada) who walk the tightrope of solvency by cutting their losses, Kazuko refuses to give up—and, in the process, discovers the steely strength of her own will. If she seems to be turning hard and disillusioned, well, the times demand it. Do I nourish a serpent in my breast? wondered the protagonist of **"Osan,"** quoting the eighteenth-century playwright Chikamatsu Monzaemon who created the original character.[5] Kazuko knows she does, one that in the course of the novel battens on her mother and swells as that mother fades to a pale shadow. It is the twin of the "rainbow" Kazuko also carries in her breast (for that is what she calls her love for Uehara). The image of the snake that crawls through the novel is appropriate to the sexual aggression Kazuko equates with love. "Outbreak of hostilities" is how she describes the final stage of her pursuit of Uehara.

It is as easy to be harsh on Kazuko as it is to admire her vitality or pity her the emptiness of a life that makes her frantic struggle so imperative. Kazuko's deepest fault, and her most sympathetic quality, is the honesty with which she pursues her dreams, which are wildly romantic. She wants life to be bigger and riper and more vibrant than it can ever be. Kazuko, in other words, is an instinctive artist, but one with no form to contain her visions. Like the woman in **"Suisen"** (**"Narcissus"**), who left her husband and plunged into the bohemian life of Tokyo in order to develop her talent as a painter and "fall as far as one can fall" (the same phrase Kazue utters in *Fireworks in Winter*), Kazuko is determined to do whatever is necessary to live within her definition of beauty. Six years before the present, Kazuko had destroyed her marriage through ill-advised ecstasy over the work of a certain painter. Now she is feverish about a novelist. Her approach is intellectu-alized but not rational: she was "wild" about Hosoda's paintings and pored over Uehara's novels, just as she de-voured Rosa Luxemburg's theoretical writings. But it is not Rosa Luxemburg's economic theories that galvanize her to action; it is "the sheer courage the author demon-strated in tearing apart without any hesitation all manner of conventional ideas." As Luxemburg "gave tragically her undivided love to Marxism," so Kazuko thinks she will destroy the bankrupt order of the present in order to per-fect anew. She even recognizes that the new dream of per-fection may never come, but she is committed to destroy, "in the passion of love." (9: 191; tr. Keene 1956, 112.) In this, Kazuko betrays her ancestry: she is one with those wild, unbridled heroines of Tokugawa popular literature, based on real figures like Oshichi, who attempted to burn down Edo in order to be reunited with the boy she loved.[6] Kazuko is not new; her passion is one of the vital myths of a repressed society in which opportunity scarcely exists.

One might think that, through his portrait of Kazuko, Dazai is patronizing women as mindless masses of emotion and selfishness. The men *do* things: they paint the paintings, write the novels, discuss the philosophy. All Kazuko has is her silly, passionate soul and her demanding body. In fact, she remembers from her school days, she once returned unread a book of Lenin's writings, which she had not read because "I hated the color of the jacket." Now spouting theories of life and art, she still seems to merit her friend's comparison of her to the "spineless" women of centuries earlier. But *The Setting Sun* makes it clear, if we did not know it already, that Dazai does not give Kazuko passion as a consolation prize. It is, in his eyes, the *only* real thing. The husband in **"Osan"** weeps weakly as, lost in thoughts of the sadness and beauty of destruction, he thinks of the French Revolution. He dies on "the cross of revolution," and his words seem empty. In *The Setting Sun*, Naoji and Uehara's death is foretold. But Kazuko lives, and the child within her lives. In a final letter to Uehara, she exults in her pregnancy: "I cannot possibly think of it in terms of a hideous mistake or anything of the sort. Recently I have come to understand why such things as war, peace, unions, trade, politics exist in the world. I don't suppose you know. That's why you will always be unhappy. I'll tell you why—it is so that women will give birth to healthy ba-bies." (9: 239; tr. Keene 1956, 172.)

While motherhood is a crucial status in these powerful late stories, Kazuko's passion to bear Uehara's child has less to do with her love for him than it does with the force of life within her. Her relationship with her mother is like-wise a central issue in *The Setting Sun*. Her ambivalence toward her mother is a combination of infantile need (which she calls "love") and resentment at that mother-hood as a silent reproach to her own childlessness. In the snake, Dazai found a vivid image to objectify and focus these emotions. It is used both symbolically and concretely, for a many-layered effect. As the snake Kazuko imagines in her breast, which she accuses of having devoured her unborn baby, and which grows stronger as Mother grows

weaker, it has the elemental association with sex. It is a force that stands in opposition to social values, one that cannot be controlled or denied. Dazai had described its power years earlier in that same image in **"The Stylish Child."** Again, in *The Setting Sun*, Dazai uses Kazuko's preoccupation with a mother snake in the garden of their new seaside home to expose the feelings about her mother that she herself cannot express. Kazuko finds a clutch of snake eggs and—to the delight of the neighborhood chil-dren—burns them in a bonfire. She is quite casual about it, even burying the scorched eggs in a mock ceremony; but her mother reproaches her, calling it cruelty. Kazuko then remembers that Mother has had a "mortal dread" of snakes ever since seeing some under mysterious circumstances the day Kazuko's father had died. Kazuko remembers clearly the ominous snake-related incidents accompanying her father's death (she was, after all, nineteen at the time). Now she is tormented by the thought that she may unwit-tingly have laid a curse on her mother. But obviously, she could not have been entirely unconscious of the signifi-cance of now attacking a mother snake in her most vulner-able spot. Kazuko uses the excuse of protection (she was "afraid" they might be viper eggs, instead of the ordinary snake's they turned out to be), and the response of re-morse, to cover the real antagonism in her actions.

For mother snake and Mother are not so separate in Kazu-ko's mind. In fact, Kazuko's description of the delicate, graceful, sad beauty of the snake crawling slowly and wearily around the garden, as if searching for and mourn-ing her babies, echoes the fragile sadness of Mother, ex-hausted by worry over her children. The snake lifting its head elegantly and flicking its "flame-like" tongue calls to mind Kazuko's description of Mother's "charming" and "strangely erotic" way of eating soup:

> Mother . . . lightly rests the fingers of her left hand on the edge of the table and sits perfectly erect, with her head held high and scarcely so much as a glance at the plate. She darts the spoon into the soup and like a swal-low—so gracefully and cleanly one can really use the simile—brings the spoon to her mouth at a right angle, and pours the soup between her lips from the point. Then, with innocent glances around her, she flutters the spoon exactly like a little wing, never spilling a drop of soup or making the least sound or clinking the plate.

> [9: 99; tr. Keene 1956, 4–5.]

Kazuko uses the simile of a bird, but there is something snakelike about her description. She calls it "appealing" and "really genuine" as her mother sits there "serenely erect," instead of eating as etiquette demands; but if there is something erotic in Mother's innocent coquetry, there is also something unpleasant in Kazuko's description, some-thing that calls to mind the feelings usually associated with a snake. What, according to Kazuko, is genuine and truly aristocratic actually comes across tinged with deca-dence. And Kazuko is aware of what she is doing: "It oc-curred to me then that Mother's face rather resembled that of the unfortunate snake we had just seen, and I had the feeling, for whatever reason, that the ugly snake dwelling in my breast might one day end by devouring this beautiful, grief-stricken mother snake." [9: 109; tr. Keene 1956, 16.]

Mother must not be thought of as an innocent victim of Kazuko's emotions, however. For Mother's delicacy and charm are her children's downfall. Mother is and, one has the impression, has been for a long time, the one who demands to be taken care of. A mere accident of time, one might think; after all, it was not her fault that the war left them penniless so that they had to sell the house that had been her emotional support through the years. Kazuko is strong and young, Mother is aging, so it should seem natural that Kazuko take over care of her physical needs when they move to the country. But it is Mother, Kazuko recognizes, who is playing her and Naoji off against each other, keeping Naoji dependent and yet seeming to demand that he be the man of the family, while keeping Kazuko in a state of disorder by leaning on her, petting her, and yet turning to Naoji the moment he returns. The times have little to do with the involutions of the relationships in this family. Their complications antedate the war. The events surrounding Naoji's drug addiction six years earlier, events that had contributed to the breakup of Kazuko's marriage, showed two children trying to keep the secret from their mother, not because it would have hurt her, but because she was too ethereal, they thought, to deal with it. By contrast, their own mundaneness comes to seem to them dirty and undesirable, thereby interfering with their ability to deal with reality. Even Kazuko's most direct and nearly neutral description of the children's dilemma hints at depths: "My brother Naoji says that we are no match for Mother, and I have at times felt something akin to despair at the difficulty of imitating her." (9: 109; tr. Keene 1956, 16.)

In this portrait of the way passivity can have as much destructive power as action, Dazai is dealing forever with his feelings about "the one who bore you." Kazuko and Naoji, in their feverish clinging to a mother who keeps them tied to her by pulling emotional strings, seemingly without guile yet also without giving them emotional sustenance, act out Dazai's feelings about all the women—Tane, Kiye, Take, Hatsuyo—who failed him in that most crucial area, emotional trust. Accordingly, once Mother is dead in *The Setting Sun*, Naoji sinks, and Kazuko floats away to fulfill her own destiny now that she has won the battle. She is the inheritor, the new Mother. When, in *No Longer Human*, Dazai returns again to Osamu's story, there is no need for a mother. Dazai has killed her off in *The Setting Sun*.

The Setting Sun does not, however, show a world without love. There is more than enough—Kazuko's for Uehara, Naoji's for Uehara's wife, Kazuko's and Naoji's for Mother, Mother's for her children—but it is all twisted and off target, and incapable of helping either lover or loved. In one of the most poetic passages he ever wrote, Dazai epitomizes the absolute confused hopelessness of such love in search of an object. The thoughts are Kazu-

ko's as she watches Uehara sleep after she has finally yielded to him:

> When the room became faintly light, I stared at the face of the man sleeping beside me. It was the face of a man soon to die. It was an exhausted face.
>
> The face of a victim. A precious victim.
>
> My man. My rainbow. My Child. Hateful man. Unprincipled man.
>
> It seemed to me then a face of a beauty unmatched in the whole world. My breast throbbed with the sensation of resuscitated love. I kissed him as I stroked his hair.
>
> The said, sad accomplishment of love.
>
> [9:225; tr. Keene 1956, 151.]

Dazai was now prepared to finish the story of Osamu. He wrote about a dozen stories and a number of essays in the year between *The Setting Sun* and *No Longer Human*, among them the excellent **"Osan"** and **"Cherries."** When he turned to *No Longer Human*, it was with a technical mastery that matched the sureness of story conception.

THE END OF THE ROAD

No Longer Human is a writer's story. It is in a sense a rewriting of **"Recollections"** and **"Eight Views of Tokyo."** The main part of the novel, narrated by Ōba Yōzō, is the story of Yōzō's life from childhood to a kind of living death at the age of twenty-seven; but it is framed by the comments of a carefully anonymous writer who has just "happened" upon Yōzō's notebooks and some photographs of him. (Dazai had tried out the technique of telling an **"Eight Views of Tokyo"** by describing photographs, in the 1942 **"Chiisai arubamu"** [**"A Little Album"**].) Therefore, one thing to keep in mind, for all the seeming passion and terror of Yōzō's narrative, is that this is a very calm and calculated story. Yōzō-Osamu "dies" at an early date, when he is "disqualified as a human being" in a mental institution; Dazai remained behind briefly to tell the story, in the last chapter of the Osamu Saga. The writer had known for more than eight years that he would have to write this novel:

> Today is November 13. Four years ago on this day, I was permitted to leave a certain unlucky hospital. That day was not as cold as today. It was a clear, crisp autumn day, and in the hospital garden some flowers were still blooming. When another five or six years have passed, and I can be more composed, I intend to try writing slowly and carefully about that period. I intend to call it *No Longer Human*.
>
> [3: 75.]

In fact, it took Dazai longer than he had expected to become "more composed," and his composure turned out to be a calm preceding death.

"The First Notebook" covers roughly the period of part I of **"Recollections,"** but with a world of difference. **"Rec-**

ollections" showed a very human little Osamu, sad, lonely, but also closely a part of a peopled world, with games, childish terrors, comforts, guilt, and pleasures all mixed together. Yōzō's world is empty and echoing. He is, by his own description, a bizarre little fellow. By some accident of fate, he has been placed in a world whose first principles he cannot even discern. What it means to be human is a puzzle to him. They are many and he is one, so he must adapt to survive; but like a little creature from outer space plunked down on an alien planet, he can only change his surface coloration and pray that his truly different metabolism will not be discovered. Of course, Yōzō's weirdness is only a kind of metaphor. As with Akutagawa's water sprite in his Swiftian story "Kappa," the warped perceptions of Dazai's Yōzō expose the author's perceptions of truths about human ugliness—and beauty. If Yōzō stands appalled at human hypocrisy, stupidity, and mindless cruelty, he also is sadly unable to respond to the warmth, love, and trust that also exist in the human world. He is the alien yardstick of both human depravity and greatness.

One change from the earlier story of Osamu's childhood is immediately noticeable: there are no personified women in Yōzō's first notebook. Mothers, sisters, women servants are there, but they are shadowy and merge into a generalized mass, "women." Women are to be important to Yōzō, but never will he be able to receive or truly understand a woman's warmth. They are, if anything, the enemy:

> Women led me on only to throw me aside; they mocked and tortured me when others were around, only to embrace me with passion as soon as everyone had left. Women sleep so soundly they seem to be dead. Who knows? Women may live in order to sleep. These and various other generalizations were products of an observation of women since boyhood days, but my conclusion was that though women appear to belong to the same species as man, they are actually quite different creatures. . . . I have often felt that I would find it more complicated, troublesome and unpleasant to ascertain the feelings by which a woman lives than to plumb the innermost thoughts of an earthworm.

[9: 383, 385; tr. Keene 1958, 48–49, 51–52.]

Father is, however, a strongly personified and continuing negative force in Yōzō's life. In the context of Dazai's perception of the power of life in women and the emptiness of abstraction in men, this difference between the facts of the author's life and their symbolic transformation into Yōzō's is crucial. In the pedestrian truth of semiautobiography, Osamu's father died in "Recollections" while Osamu was still a child. The death of Dazai's mother, which came much later in his life, had, until *No Longer Human*, far more emotional impact on his writing. Now, having fictionalized the story to a much greater extent, he was free to work out an alternate reality to help him deal with the father he had so far largely neglected. That father, whose sexuality so troubled the youthful Dazai that he doubted his parentage, and in "Bottomless Hell" made the father of the protagonist such a monster of corruption that

he tears away from one mistress the baby he has fathered on her and gives it to another mistress; the father who haunted Dazai the adult to such a degree that he went to Kizukuri during his Tsugaru trip in an attempt to find a clue to understanding him; this is the father who is a strong background presence in *No Longer Human*. In the novel, Yōzō's mother is a negligible quantity, and his father lives until after Yōzō's confinement in a mental institution at the age of twenty-four. In spirit, Yōzō and his father die together.[7] Yōzō will respond to his father's death as if he himself had died: "The news of my father's death eviscerated me. He was dead, that familiar, frightening presence who had never left my heart for a split second. I felt as though the vessel of my suffering had become empty, as if nothing could interest me now. I had lost even the ability to suffer." (9: 470; tr. Keene 1958, 168.) When the bar madam at the end says, "It's his father's fault," that is Dazai's judgment on his life. If his father had not abandoned him, in life or in death, when he was in high school, his life would have been different. We can remonstrate that the outcome would have been the same, but the child in Dazai only repeats, "It was his fault."

"The Second Notebook" spans part II of "Recollections" and the early part of "Eight Views of Tokyo," but again with crucial additions and deletions. The ocean side school by the cherry-blossomed park is there from before, but Takeichi is a new addition. In "Recollections," a sympathetic friend warns Osamu that his behavior at school will cause him trouble; in *No Longer Human*, Takeichi sees through Yōzō's deliberate attempts to be clumsy in physical education class, and by telling Yōzō that he knows he did it on purpose, makes Yōzō feel "as if I had seen the world before me burst in an instant into the raging flames of hell." (9: 465-66; tr. Keene 1958, 168.) Again, what was in "Recollections" a touching, amusing scene of Osamu's younger brother helping him paint acne medicine on his face, is transformed in *No Longer Human* into a horror scene of Yōzō swabbing out Takeichi's pus-filled ears to keep him, so he hopes, from revealing the truth behind Yōzō's self-protective clowning. Yōzō's pathological "fear of human beings" has evolved from all the ordinary, human kinds of insecurity, self-consciousness, and fears that Dazai has depicted in Osamu's world so far. Takeichi, this strange and ugly potential betrayer of Yōzō's "secret identity," turns out unexpectedly to be almost a friend. It is he, and not such self-communion as gave Osamu the inspiration to aspire to be a writer, who teaches Yōzō that his salvation could have been in art. Their discussion of what Takeichi called "ghost paintings"—their special, aberrant interpretation of some paintings by Modigliani and Van Gogh that Yōzō showed him—finally makes clear what were the "unfathomable shudders" Osamu had felt in "Recollections" at the point he prayed to become a writer. Other artists had these same terrible visions of truth:

> There are some people whose dread of human beings is so morbid that they reach a point where they yearn to see with their own eyes monsters of ever more horrible shapes. And the more nervous they are—the quicker to take fright—the more violent they pray that every storm

will be. . . . Painters who have had this mentality, after repeated wounds and intimidations at the hands of the apparitions called human beings, have often come to believe in phantasms—they plainly saw monsters in broad daylight, in the midst of nature. And they did not fob people off with clowning; they did their best to depict these monsters just as they had appeared. Takeichi was right: they had dared to paint pictures of devils. I was so excited I could have wept. . . . Takeichi's words made me aware that my mental attitude towards painting had been completely mistaken. What superficiality—and what stupidity—there is in trying to depict in a pretty manner things which one has thought pretty. The masters through their subjective perceptions created beauty out of trivialities. They did not hide their interest even in things which were nauseatingly ugly, but soaked themselves in the pleasure of depicting them. In other words, they seemed not to rely in the least on the misconceptions of others. Now that I had been initiated by Takeichi into these root secrets of the art of painting, I began to do a few self-portraits, taking care that they not be seen by my female visitors.

The pictures I drew were so heartrending as to stupefy even myself. Here was the true self I had so desperately hidden. I had smiled cheerfully; I had made others laugh; but this was the harrowing reality.

[9: 387–88; tr. Keene 1958, 53–54, 55.]

As Yōzō's relationship with Takeichi is only a parody of intimacy, so too his means of communication with the world has to remain clowning. His life is empty and deformed, and so he does not in fact become a fierce protector of his art. Instead, he debases his talent, becoming a cheap cartoonist whose only subject increasingly is pornographic. Osamu fought, throughout **"Eight Views of Tokyo,"** to preserve his private vision of artistic integrity, and that persistence became the strength in Dazai that made his career. Above all, Dazai's world was filled with love—failed though it mostly was—while Yōzō's is devoid of it; and that is the difference.

There is no Miyo in Yōzō's story, and most strikingly, no Hatsuyo.[8] The transition between high school in the North to university in Tokyo is handled simply: Father has Yōzō enter college to become a bureaucrat, even though the youth wants secretly to go to art school, and Yōzō, tired of high school, acquiesces and begins living at his father's Tokyo house. To tighten the storyline, Dazai brings in the devil-figure Horiki. In real life, the causes of Dazai's plunge from potential solid citizen to a life of chaos were to him complicated, the threads torn and knotted—*gidayū* lessons, Akutagawa's death, the class struggle, Hatsuyo, family, guilt, resentment, fear—no wonder Dazai could not get the story right. In *No Longer Human,* the control afforded by pure fiction makes it neater.

Osamu in **"Eight Views of Tokyo"** has already encountered serious troubles in his life by the time he comes to Tokyo, and his brother's death soon afterward does not help matters. Yōzō, to the contrary, lives quietly and comfortably in Tokyo at first, pursuing his own interests. People frighten him, and classes at university are "te-

dious," so he takes private art lessons. If he is not doing as his father had planned, at least his days seem constructive. It is Horiki, a fellow art student, who draws him out into the world, initiating him into the mysteries of "drink, cigarettes, prostitutes, pawnshops and leftwing thought."

Yōzō and Horiki are a natural combination, Yōzō terrified by the "realities of life" but financially comfortable, Horiki brash and confident, at ease in the worlds of pleasure, and a past master at spending other people's money to maximum mutual benefit. Yōzō blooms under Horiki's tutelage; chameleon-like, he adapts to his new circumstances so readily that before long even Horiki begins to call him a "ladykiller," a fate Takeichi had prophesied. His most kindred spirits are the prostitutes he frequents:

> I never could think of prostitutes as human beings or even as women. They seemed more like imbeciles or lunatics. But in their arms I felt absolute security. I could sleep soundly. It was pathetic how utterly devoid of greed they really were. And perhaps because they felt for me something like an affinity for their kind, these prostitutes always showed me a natural friendliness which never became oppressive. Friendliness with no ulterior motive, friendliness stripped of high pressure salesmanship, for someone who might never come again. Some nights I saw these imbecile, lunatic prostitutes with the halo of Mary.

[9: 393; tr. Keene 1958, 63.]

Thanks to Horiki, he begins to prostitute himself to the communist movement. But here he maintains private intellectual reservations; he finds it "uproariously amusing" to see his "comrades" solemnly discussing "theories so elementary they were on the order of 'one and one makes two.'" Then disaster strikes. Yōzō's financial base is cut out from under him when his father sells the Tokyo house, so that he has to live solely on his allowance. Without the cushion that had held reality off, life quickly becomes intolerable. And Tsuneko enters to play her part.

She has not become dehumanized like Yōzō. Her tale of misery is all too human. It is a misery that overcomes Yōzō's dread of people and brings him close to her. A "feeling of comradeship for this fellow sufferer from poverty," an emotion of pity, are to Yōzō the first intimations he has had of that feeling humans call "love." Yōzō and Tsuneko consummate their love with a decision to die together. She mentions the subject first, and he acquiesces: "She too seemed to be weary beyond endurance of the task of being a human being; and when I reflected on my dread of the world and its bothersomeness, on money, the movement, women, my studies, it seemed impossible that I could go on living. I consented easily to her proposal." (9: 409; tr. Keene 1958, 86.) Tsuneko dies, Yōzō lives to enter a new phase. "The Third Notebook" covers a period of time that in Osamu's life in **"Eight Views of Tokyo"** was bracketed between the Enoshima suicide attempt and institutionalization for drug addiction—in essence, the years with *H.* Again, the events are all transformed negatively.

In that portion of **"Eight Views of Tokyo,"** Osamu shows how he tried to write a suicide note and started instead to become a writer, although at the time he could not see the progress for the hell of daily life. But Yōzō's life in *No Longer Human* after the suicide attempt is filled with great silences. For some three or four months he lives blankly at Flatfish's house, under a kind of house arrest. Mean, stingy, ugly, unctuous Flatfish, with his clandestine "business," becomes Yōzō's guardian, and never for a moment does he allow Yōzō to forget that he considers the youth an extraordinary bother and probably mentally incompetent to boot. Yōzō passively allows Flatfish to violate his soul, just as he had and would allow others—the household servants when he was a child, his communist "comrade" in his party days, the old servant who takes care of him at the end of the book—to violate his body. In a traditional image he discovers soon after crawling away from Flatfish's house ("running" is too assertive a verb), when he sees a kite caught in telephone wires, he is a captive kite, at the mercy of anyone who tugs his string. Yōzō would like to think of the kite, battered and buffeted about, as struggling in some kind of affirmation, like Osamu; but clearly, it is a prisoner.

Shizuko is the next holder of his string—an inversion of the "red string" in **"Recollections."** She combines the best and worst of a woman. she cares for Yōzō, she loves him, she keeps him safe from the world, she attempts to help him develop a career; and at the same time, by her very control of all aspects of his life, she emasculates him. Yōzō remains emotionally insulated from every prospect she offers, but for a year, he continues as her kept man. It is only the sight of Shizuko and her five-year-old daughter Shigeko, unaware he is watching them secretly, playing happily together one day, that brings home to him that he has no part in that happiness. The realization drives him to his next keeper, the bar madam who, at the end of the novel, is the guardian of his notebooks.

Yet another year passes with Yōzō adapted to the society of the night, the patrons of the bar. And then Yōzō discovers seventeen-year-old Yoshiko, who works in a nearby tobacco shop. He does not fall in love with her. It is something more solemn, fragile, and absolute he feels: he trusts her, and he trusts in her innocence. With the bar madam's assistance, he marries her. Then, while he and Horiki are engaged in a drunken conversation, she is raped by a shopkeeper for whom Yōzō draws cartoons. Yoshiko is not to blame, except for being too trusting, but Yōzō feels that his faith in her has been betrayed. Why does he feel a "bottomless horror" surpassing anything he has known so far?

The answer lies in the nature of Yōzō's character, not Yoshiko's. Yōzō's emotional metabolism is totally different from that of the people surrounding him. To him, they are like another race of beings; he finds their emotions wholly mysterious and impenetrable. Just once, with the trustful Yoshiko, an instant came when it seemed that he had a meeting point with these beings. Her absolute trust in him elicited an extreme response in him. He took what was for him a terrible risk, and placed his soul in her

keeping. The violation of Yoshiko is the violation of her "immaculate trustfulness"—the one virtue, Yōzō confesses to himself, that he had depended on.

Yōzō's extreme reaction, then, makes sense in terms of his extreme personality, which Dazai draws with masterly strokes. But from its effect on Yōzō, we can tell that the rape of Yoshiko is also a metaphor for Hatsuyo's unfaithfulness. And that in turn explains the relationship of *No Longer Human* to the rest of the Osamu Saga. The Osamu of **"Recollections"** was already stricken with a fatal disease. One cannot live without hope; trust is the foundation of hope; but all the mainstays of Osamu's life were untrustworthy—the child had learned that love could disappear in the blinking of an eye. *H* in **"Eight Views of Tokyo"** only dealt the final blow. Dazai, the teller of the tale, was under a self-imposed sentence of death from **"Recollections"** on, and that is why Yōzō is twenty-four (Dazai's age when he wrote **"Recollections"**) when he enters the hospital. When Dazai was twenty-seven, Yōzō's age at the end of *No Longer Human,* he himself became the "human lost" through his hospital stay, which was the occasion for Hatsuyo's final betrayal. Dazai does seem truly to have loved Hatsuyo. Like Yōzō's "miserable Tsuneko," she "really was the only one" he loved, the only one he had chosen of himself. And so she is transfigured into the crushingly innocent Yoshiko, her casual sexuality and consenting adultery dehumanized into the rape of solemn, pure Yoshiko. The effect is the same: the death of the possibility of love. *No Longer Human* is both an apology to Hatsuyo and an expression of helplessness from Dazai.

Yōzō's fatal flaw is, like that of Camus's "outsider," his pathological incapacity for the self-assertion that means life. Midway through the novel, he sits paralyzed in a cabaret, knowing that Tsuneko is "going to be kissed in another few minutes" by Horiki (the verb in the passive to emphasize her victim-like status); but he feels himself not qualified to *do* anything to affect the course of action. Later he watches, suffocating, while Yoshiko is violated; all he can do is flee, pursued by an overpowering "ancestral" fear, as if of a god. If Dazai had read Kierkegaard, he might have found the vocabulary for the existential dread that characterizes Yōzō's life. For him, even to feel guilty at his failure to act is too great an assertion of will. Yōzō's heart is filled with negatives—emptiness, nonaction, self-abdication, omitted action—and it is this that disqualifies him from a humanity defined by desire and striving, murky and petty though its aspirations generally are.

This negative apotheosis of Osamu after all his striving was, finally, the literary image Dazai had been seeking. Emotion and art had met, joining seeming contradictions: with passion, with pity and love, Dazai had depicted a cold, echoing world. Yōzō has no emotion other than fear, no desire but to escape observation. He never connects with any character in the novel, not even Yoshiko. He deals with the fear—of life, of love, of trust, of commitment—by passively letting events flow around him without touching him. Here is finally the perfect metaphor for

Osamu's experiences of failed love: a world where love is defined out of existence in the empty silence of Yōzō's soul. In this silence is the sad conclusion of the saga.

Yōzō is both crazy (one commonsense explanation for his lifelong feeling of alienation) and infinitely pitiable, for being so in need of love and so blocked from it. He sets humanity's weaknesses into harsh relief, just as Dazai himself railed against the deceit, insensitivity, and arrogance he saw around him; he is thus disqualified from participating in humanity's warmth, as Dazai was unable ultimately to draw sustenance from the supports of family and friends. Through Yōzō, the story was finally told of how the "dirty child" had lived—and how he had failed. Dazai, "disqualified as a human being," was released from his self-imposed task. Osamu was not necessarily finished, for he resiliently surfaces again, like Till Eulenspiegel, in *Good-bye*; but his creator was. It is here that the split between Osamu and Dazai at last is clear.

Notes

1. *Zenshū* 8:229–30.

2. Because in "Fifteen Years" the narrator of the Osamu Saga is speaking of Dazai's professional life, he merges with the writer and is here called "Dazai."

3. This is Dazai's prescient answer to Shiga Naoya. In 1948, after Dazai's death, Shiga wrote an essay absolving himself of any responsibility for Dazai's death. With magnificent insensitivity, Shiga dismisses criticism that he had been insensitive to such famous "vulnerable" writers as Akutagawa Ryūnosuke, Oda Sakunosuke, and Dazai, and had accordingly contributed to their deaths. With the "selfishness of the home circle," he sympathizes with the suicide's poor wife and children and friends—but there is not a word of sympathy for the poor suicide. He sees the act as a kind of self-imposed euthanasia (about which he had recently read in *Reader's Digest*); but nowhere does he express curiosity or concern about the "disease" from which the sufferer was seeking release. In his zeal to prevent any legends about his condescension toward Dazai and other young writers, Shiga if anything added fuel with his own hands. See his "Dazai Osamu no shi" [The Death of Dazai Osamu], *Shiga Naoya Zenshū* (Tokyo: Iwanami Shoten, 1955–56), vol. 9, 229–35.

4. Dazai often expressed concern and despair in his stories over his own son's health. The child is described as weak and frail, with retarded muscular and mental development, in (for instance) "Villon's Wife," "I'm Looking for Someone," and "Cherries."

5. Osan is the abused heroine of the eighteenth-century puppet play *Shinjū ten no Amijima*, whose husband commits suicide with a courtesan. See Donald Keene, trans., *Love Suicides at Amijima*, in *Major Plays of Chikamatsu* (New York: Columbia University Press, 1961), 387–425.

6. The story of Oshichi the greengrocer's daughter is contained in *Kōshoku gonin onna,* a collection of stories about real women who cast aside morality and social responsibility for passion, by the seventeenth-century writer Ihara Saikaku. See William Theodore de Bary's translation, *Five Women Who Loved Love* (Rutland, Vt., and Tokyo: Charles E. Tuttle Co., 1956), 159–94.

7. This can be seen as an inversion of Kazue's and Asa's (spiritual) double suicide in *Fireworks in Winter.*

8. Curiously, though, Horiki fills in *No Longer Human* the same place in time as *H* in "Eight Views of Tokyo."

James M. Vardaman, Jr. (essay date 1987)

SOURCE: "Dazai Osamu's 'Run, Moerus!' and Friedrich Schiller's 'Die Burgschaft,'" in *Comparative Literature Studies*, Vol. 24, No. 3, 1987, pp. 243–50.

[*In the following essay, Vardaman compares Dazai's short story "Run, Melos!" with Friedrich Schiller's ballad "Die Bürgschaft."*]

Dazai Osamu (1909–48) is perhaps best known for his novels *Shayō* (*The Setting Sun*) and *Ningen Shikaku* (*No Longer Human*). As a result, he is usually viewed as a writer of gloom and decadence. However, there is a lighter, more optimistic side of Dazai which is visible in lesser-known works such as *Otogi Zōshi* (*A Collection of Fairy Tales*) and a reworking of tales modelled on stories by Saikaku. An obvious example of Dazai's "brighter" side is the short story **"Hashire Merosu"** (1940, **"Run, Melos!"**),[1] widely read in Japan as a story of fidelity and endurance in the face of adversity. Though most Japanese have read, or at least know of, the story, perhaps few are aware that Dazai borrowed the essential elements from Johann Christoph Friedrich von Schiller's "Die Bürgschaft" ("The Hostage"). A close reading of Schiller's ballad reveals the source of almost every major development in Dazai's prose story.

Ono Masafumi has previously examined when and how Dazai first discovered the Schiller ballad and has speculated upon Dazai's motives for taking up the subject in a short story so many years thereafter.[2] In this article I compare Dazai's retelling with Schiller's poem in order to show both the elements they share and the additions and alterations which Dazai made in making the tale significantly different from Schiller's.

As Ono has convincingly shown, Schiller himself "borrowed" the story of faithful friendship from an earlier writer. Cicero records the story of two fourth-century B.C. citizens of the Roman state of Syracuse, named Damon and Phintias (Pythias), who were followers of the philosopher Pythagoras and known for their friendship with each other. But Schiller's source, and hence Dazai's, is more probably the Latin poet Hyginus, in whose account the two friends are named Moerus and Selinuntius. The original story is simple. Moerus is implicated in a plot against Dionysius, the tyrant of Syracuse, and condemned to death. He begs a brief reprieve in order to take care of his affairs (one version says he wanted to say farewell to his mother). He leaves his close friend as a hostage in guarantee for his return. The tyrant Dionysius tells him that if he does not return by the appointed time his friend will be executed in his place. Moerus is detained after taking care of his affairs and a crowd gathers as Selinuntius is brought out to the execution ground. The appointed hour arrives, but Selinuntius remains confident that his friend will come. At the last moment Moerus returns and Selinuntius is released unharmed. Dionysius is so moved by this display of friendship, in which life itself is at stake, that he releases both men.

In Hyginus' tale Moerus is delayed only by a swollen stream, but Schiller adds a band of robbers and a blazing sun to the obstacles which Moerus faces. In a major departure from Hyginus, Schiller has love and faith win over the tyrant's heart, and Dionysius not only releases the two men, but also entreats them to allow him to become a third party in their devoted friendship. Critics from Goethe on have found fault with Schiller's expansion of Moerus' trials. How, Goethe points out, could Moerus be so thirsty after running in the rain, swimming across the torrent, and continuing on his way in wet clothes? And would a man who is so single-mindedly racing to save his friend's life be bothered by mere physical fatigue? Our concern here is not to evaluate Schiller's additions, which Dazai subsequently adopts almost in their entirety, but rather to discover how he too adapted the story to his own taste. Throughout the following discussion I shall note the significant points of departure between the modern writers' versions.

The first major decision between Schiller's version and that of Dazai is that from Schiller's very first stanza Moerus is already in the city of Syracuse and intent on eliminating the tyrant. We learn nothing of Moerus except that in quick succession he is captured, questioned, and sentenced to death. We learn nothing about the king except that he is a tyrant. In Dazai's version, by contrast, we learn that Moerus is a kind, simple village herdsman who has travelled the twenty-five miles to Syracuse to buy clothes and food for the coming wedding of his sixteen-year-old sister. After accomplishing his purpose in the city, he walks toward the house of his friend from childhood, Selinuntius. The streets are deserted and he senses that the fall of darkness is not the cause of the eerie silence that has replaced the cheery evening atmosphere he remembers from previous visits.

Moerus stops several passersby in order to find out why the city has lost its formerly lively character and why everyone has closed their doors to the outside world. An old man is finally coerced by Moerus into answering his questions. The people, he explains, now live in fear of their lives. The paranoid king suspects any subject who displays signs of conviviality or extravagance of plotting to usurp his power. Because of this deep mistrust of those around him, the king has already had executed his sister's husband, his own heir, his sister, the sister's child, the queen, and the trusted courtier Alexis.

> Moerus was outraged at what he had heard. "The king is disgusting. He cannot be allowed to live."

> Moerus was an uncomplicated man. With his purchases on his back, he plodded off toward the palace. Immediately a guard stopped him and searched him. When his dagger was discovered, the disturbance grew louder and Moerus was brought before the king.

All of the preceding events take place in Dazai's version, whereas Schiller's version begins immediately with some man whose name is Moerus going into the palace with the sole intent of assassinating the tyrant.

As in Schiller's ballad, Dazai's Moerus calmly accuses the king of the disgraceful crime of doubting the loyalty and integrity of other people. Where Schiller's king is completely villainous, however, Dazai allows his villain a direct appeal for sympathy and understanding. Dazai's king claims that he, too, wants peace and wants to trust others, but that observing the behavior of those around him he has concluded that everyone thinks only of his own self. People may talk about love, truth, and friendship, but when they have to make a sacrifice for these supposed ideals, self-interest always wins. The king then opens his heart in a brief moment of weakness. "Poor soul," says the king, "you could never understand my loneliness." This brief confession makes Dazai's king more human than Schiller's pure tyrant, and thereby makes the conclusion somewhat more believable. If the king is so purely cruel and cynical, could be realistically shed his doubts about human nature even at their demonstration of willing self-sacrifice?

Moerus pleads for a three-day stay of execution so that he can marry off his sister. The king laughs at the idea of letting him go and expecting him to return. Dazai's Moerus seems to feel that his word is his bond, but the king tells him that a bird which escapes from the cage will not willingly return. The king does, however, accept the idea of a hostage. If Moerus does not return within the stipulated period, the hostage will die in his place. Moerus has his close friend Selinuntius summoned. He explains the situation, Selinuntius silently nods acceptance, and Moerus is off to return to his village.

Moerus races home, eventually persuades the groom to agree to an early ceremony, prepares the wedding feast and sees his sister safely married. Before his departure for Syracuse to fulfill his destiny, Dazai's Moerus delivers a short sermon to his sister:

> Just remember that your brother hates doubting other people and telling lies, so you must harbor no secrets

from your husband. That's all I have to say. Your brother may prove to be a courageous man, so be proud that you are his sister.

Having overtly committed himself to these ideals in front of his only relative, he is assured of censure from the only family member that he has left should he renege on Selinuntius. There is no such scene in Schiller's ballad, which dismisses the village and marriage scene in four lines. It seems as if Schiller's Moerus is almost unconscious of his own fate, as if he hastens to keep his pledge to return by a definite time. On the contrary, Dazai's hero is acutely conscious of the fate that awaits him. His race is less against time than against the possibility that his friend may die and that the king's evil insinuation that Moerus plans to escape death altogether may be realized, whether he intends it or not.

It is typical of Schiller to glorify the friendship between the two men. The tension that grows in Schiller's ballad has nothing to do with the relationship itself, for it never enters his protagonist's mind to betray his friend. Rather the tension hinges on the confrontation of fate and ideal. Everything is done to show how a person who has already lost his own life, as Moerus in essence has, will, because of honor and friendship, endure any tribulation in order to save the life of a friend. Even when the steward Philostratos tells Moerus that he is too late, he does not give up and go home.

In Schiller, the friendship has no psychological or ethical motivation; it is pure ideal. One expects a tragic ending because of the parable-like nature of the story. But Moerus succeeds in the struggle against time and fate. That friendship in this pure ideal form also averts the tragedy and converts the tyrant is anticlimactic.

The friends of Dazai's story, by contrast, are not men of steely trust. Although Moerus succeeds in crossing the "surging, swirling, sucking stream" and striking down the bandits who accost him in the mountain pass (and who Moerus feels have been sent by the evil king to delay him), the effort takes its toll. He collapses under the heat of the sun which appears after the morning rain. Moerus bemoans his weakness.

> 'Because your friend Selinuntius trusted in you, he will soon be killed. You are a rare unreliable man and you will prove the tyrant's suspicions correct.' But his whole body was heavy with fatigue and he could not raise himself from the ground. When the body is tired, so is the spirit. Thoughts unworthy of a brave man crept into his mind and he was almost beyond caring.

He tells himself that he has done everything that anyone could do to fulfill his promise, but that fate would have it otherwise. He is sure that Selinuntius still patiently waits his return and is grateful for his friend's trust, "the greatest treasure in the world." But he surrenders to exhaustion and accepts the reputation of being a betrayer which doubtlessly awaits him. He collapses and falls asleep spread-eagled on the ground.

Dazai adds another twist to the story at this point. Moerus is awakened by the sound of running water, drinks from the spring that has mysteriously appeared at his feet, and significantly recuperates from his exhaustion. Hope springs forth in his heart and he has renewed confidence that he cannot only uphold his side of the friendship, as in Schiller, but also perform his "duty" and maintain his honor. His moment of darkness is over.

> I gave my word. That's the only thing that matters. Run, Moerus! I am believed in and trusted in. The whispering that I heard in my heart was an evil voice in a dream. When the body is tired, it is tempted to believe such evil. . . . Thanks to the gods I will be able to die a righteous man.

Moerus arises and races on toward Syracuse and his fate.

Schiller and Dazai both submit the protagonist to one further temptation by having him encounter Philostratos, a servant in the house of Selinuntius. "He is about to be put to death," Philostratos informs Moerus In the Dazai version, Philostratos continues as follows.

> Stop, please! Stop running! It is important to save your own life now. He believed in you even when they took him out to the place of execution. Even when the king mocked him, he showed his strong faith in you and kept saying, "Moerus is sure to come."

Assuaging Moerus' fear that Selinuntius may have doubted his trustworthiness, Philostratos encourages him to avoid becoming the second victim of the cruel king. Both writers have Moerus demur. Late though he may be, he will show the tyrant the strength of their bond. He is, he says in Dazai's version, "running for something larger." "It makes no difference whether I am late or whether I can save his life." Dazai's Moerus has taken the nature of his individual effort to the level of principle.

When Moerus finally bursts upon the scene where the crowd stands awaiting the execution, in the Schiller ballad he is immediately recognized, but in the Dazai version he still has to fight his way through the throng and then convince the executioner that he is the one who should rightfully be executed. More importantly, Schiller straightway delivers the two friends into one another's arms, but Dazai's friends first share a moment of confession. Moerus confesses to his friend that he listened to the voice of temptation along the road. He feels he has betrayed his friend in his heart and therefore must ask his friend's forgiveness before anything else. "Slap me in the face," he says, "or I have no right to embrace you." Though the reader has only followed the actions of one half of the pair, we learn at this point that the doubts were not only on one side.

> Selinuntius nodded as if he were able to read Moerus' mind completely. He struck his friend's right cheek so hard that the crack resounded through the execution place. Then he smiled gently and said, "Now strike me, friend Moerus, as I just did. My faith in you faltered

during these three days for the very first time. Unless you strike me, I have no right to embrace you either."

Having made their confessions and forgiven each other, they embrace in joy.

Although Schiller and Dazai both focus not upon the hostage and his thoughts during the three days, but upon "the one waited upon," Dazai possibly found Schiller's character too perfect to be believable and decided that they would be more realistic if they had had lapses in conscience and if they had suffered from temptation. Regardless of the reasons, Dazai's characters seem far less fable-like. The reader feels more sympathy for the character who struggles with his conscience as well as struggling to overcome physical obstacles in order to save his friend's life by sacrificing his own.

Ono Masamfumi sees in the Dazai version a reflection of Dazai's own emotional world. That Dazai was supported through university by his family and that he was unable to graduate from Tokyo Imperial University, despite several extensions of financial support, may have weighed upon his conscience. Or perhaps it had something to do with many other ways in which he was unable to meet his family's expectations. Ono suggests that Dazai's own inability to live up to certain expectations led Dazai to choose to write a story in which a character who is not superhuman, as Schiller's Moerus sometimes seems, is nevertheless able to do what he says he will do. In Dazai's story, if not in his life, we see good intentions and a happy ending. Truth, friendship, and trust win the day.

Both writers follow Hyginus in their respective conclusions. The friends are reunited and Moerus prepares to die at the hand of the executioner. The king, however, is miraculously moved by the example of their commitment to one another. He frees Moerus and Selinuntius and even asks that they include him in their number. This anticlimax is a bit weak in Schiller's ballad because the tyrant has never been shown to have human sentiments. It is far more tolerable in Dazai's story because we have had a brief glimpse into the sad and lonely heart of the king.

As has been shown, Dazai Osamu has taken a story of occidental origin and reworked it as a part of his own repertoire. Though his short story appears to be merely a translation and expansion in Japanese, it is actually quite different from both the Hyginus version and that of Schiller. The reader may find Dazai's story too moralistic or too falsely occidental, but it should at least be clear that Dazai's repertoire includes a work which is optimistic and which concludes that man *can* be virtuous, even at the cost of his own life. Dazai's reputation as a writer of gloom and decadence deserves some reconsideration.

Notes

1. James M. Vardaman, Jr., "'Run, Melos!': A Translation of Dazai Osamu's *Hashire Merosu*," *Tohoku Gakuin University Review* 74 (November

1983): 1–15. I have used the name Moerus throughout this paper to prevent confusion.

2. Ono Masafumi, *"Hashire Merosu no Sozai ni tsuite"* ("Concerning the Materials of 'Run, Moerus!'") in Sekii Mitsuo, ed., *Dazai Osamu no Sekai* (Tokyo: Tōjusha, 1977) 128–48.

Frank Tuohy (essay date 1990)

SOURCE: "At the Edge of Existence," in *The Times Literary Supplement,* November 16, 1990, p. 1233.

[*In the following essay, Tuohy praises Dazai's earlier works but looks less favorably upon the collection* Crackling Mountain and Other Stories.]

Osamu Dazai was one of the most prominent Japanese novelists to be introduced to Western readers in the postwar period. His career had culminated in 1948: an obsession with suicide, not rare among his compatriots, had ended in a love-pact with one of his mistresses, according to the traditional pattern: pairs of shoes placed together, the bodies tied with a red cord.

Dazai's best-known novels, *The Setting Sun* and *No Longer Human,* were translated in the 1950s by Donald Keene, who later commented on the very different ways in which they were received abroad and in Japan. Western critics praised the novelist for his accessibility, his freedom from "cherry blossom reveries and oriental character motivations" and they compared him with Camus, Kafka and Dostoevsky. His countrymen, on the other hand, viewed him as belonging to the tradition of autobiographical fiction which has persisted throughout Japanese literature. The Japanese reader, Keene tells us, might feel betrayed if it was discovered that the "I" of a Dazai novel was unlike the author: it would be like discovering that a man has lied in his diary. An Anglo-Saxon might react rather differently in this case, feeling the author's prowess somehow diminished.

In the event, Dazai's technique often involved seeing himself, or someone very like himself, a creature whom his addictions had brought to the edge of existence, through the eyes of other characters—Kazuko the sister in *The Setting Sun* the protagonist's wife in the brilliant story called **"Villon's Wife."** This technique is shown in one of the stories in the present collection, **"The Sound of Hammering."** **"Memories"** is a vivid if desultory account of a childhood and adolescence very like the author's. Otherwise *Crackling Mountain* is something of a ragbag, concentrating on an earlier stage in Dazai's career, before he embarked on the work for which he became famous.

"Heed my Plea" and **"Melos, Run"** are two curiosities, the first a view of Christ through the eyes of Judas Iscariot, the second—popular in Japanese schools, we are told—a Greek tale of endurance and loyalty rewarded.

Both give an odd impression of the sort one gets from old woodblock prints representing Westerners. Much more rewarding are the two recensions of stories by Ihara Saikaku, adding irony and psychological depth to a seventeenth-century writer whose fictions sometimes seem monotonously matter of fact. **"A Poor Man's Got his Pride"** portrays a group of *samurai* on their uppers, and perhaps reflects Dazai's own situation as a dispossessed member of the former upper class.

The three retellings of medieval tales, though obviously of interest, are not helped by a singularly clumsy translation. The title story, **"Crackling Mountain"**, which deals with a conflict between a rabbit and a badger, obviously cries out for a lighter touch than it receives here: such unfortunate phrases as "And was he ever weary" and "Am I ever hungry" appear on the same page. Elsewhere a young girl is referred to as a "teen".

It will be concluded that the present selection has no great appeal to anyone embarking on Dazai as a new writer. The good news in fact appears on the dust-jacket: the same publisher has kept in print both *No Longer Human* and *The Setting Sun* in the Keene translations. New readers should begin there.

Alan Wolfe (essay date 1990)

SOURCE: "Dying Twice: Allegories of Impossibility," in *Suicidal Narrative in Modern Japan: The Case of Dazai Osamu*, Princeton University Press, 1990, pp. 121–43, 237–39.

[*In the following essay, Wolfe examines suicidal narratives, focusing on Dazai's "Metamorphosis" and "Reminiscences."*]

> Allegories are always allegories of metaphor and, as such, they are always allegories of the impossibility of reading.
>
> —Paul de Man, *Allegories of Reading*

> [W]hen the imagination of death fails you on some primary level, its commonplace or stereotypical representations need to be repeated, worked through, and exhausted by a narrative which, having taken you through death unsuccessfully a first time, can now recuperate this failure by bringing the reading mind up short against the unpremeditated shock of a *second* dying.
>
> —Fredric Jameson, *Fables of Aggression*

Writers and critics both seem caught in a bind. Their writing calls for control, mastery, concentration of thought, coordination of mind and hand—all aspects of our notion of a unified, coherent self. And yet their efforts to focus on and create narratives of similarly coherent subjects are subverted by a flashing awareness that those subjects exist only so long as the mind sees them as such. Critics such

as Lang, Beaujour, and Hutcheon in a sense seek to meet the contradiction head on by legitimizing a writing that is skeptical of itself, and by locating acts of textual resistance to the prevalence for hypostasizing unmediated subjectivity and meaning.

That suicidal narratives should provide an instance of such resistance is not strange. Suicide is a challenge both to the individual and to the collectivity, for it threatens the extinction of all life and human consciousness. But there is a significant difference between suicide as a theme within a narrative and suicide as the structural component of narrative meaning. In the present [essay], we will consider a short story of Dazai's in which suicide functions to thwart meaning. This early work, **"Metamorphosis"** (**"Gyofukuki,"** 1933), involves the transformation of presumed subjects into nonhuman forms, suggestive in Kafkaesque terms of escape from the oppressiveness of society and self. But above all it features a curious second suicide, leading to an insistence on the metaphoricity of self, death, and meaning.

Dazai wrote a number of other "fictional" stories in addition to **"Metamorphosis."** But at the same time, he began writing what was to become a lifelong narrative of first-person accounts of events of his life as well as reflections on private and public matters. These writings highlight suicidal intention as a generator of Dazai's texts. From his earliest texts, suicide becomes a goalpost toward which the writer aims. And as the narrative grows by both displacing (postponing) and surviving attempts at self-destruction, it becomes clear that suicide is a metaphor for resistance to narrative closure.

THE DROWNING FISH

The story **"Metamorphosis"** is particularly suitable for demonstrating the allegorical nature of Dazai's life narrative in that double sense of (a) a process of establishing an extratextual meaning (negativity), and (b) an attempt to subvert that process even as it unfolds. We shall first see how this brief but concentrated piece of writing can be shown not only to prefigure Dazai's future work and life but also to contain an awareness of the futility of literature as allegory as well as of the fundamental metaphorical nature of language itself.[1] To the extent that the language of allegory is itself a metaphor for another "truth," a truth that remains forever at one remove, allegory, as Paul de Man suggests, can at best stand not for that truth but for the impossibility of reaching it. Thus, we shall argue, Dazai's image of the suicidal fish, a fish that appears to realize the metaphor of negative meaning by drowning (!) into nonbeing, seeks to subvert the process of allegorization even as it develops.

Three contextual categories are relevant for our analysis. First, there is the historical context of Japan in the 1930s, including the effective suppression of the entire political left by 1932, and the forced (under police duress) apostasy or recantation (*tenkō*) of numerous writers and other public figures, both of these set against a background of increasing domestic instability and expanding Japanese imperialism in Asia. Second, in a more biographical vein, there are the student and underground left associations of the author Dazai; his confusion and guilt toward his provincial landlord class background; his traumatic involvement in an abortive double-suicide in which his companion, a bar hostess, drowned while he was absolved of all suspicion as the son of a "good" family; his stormy relationship with a geisha from his home in the north of Japan and tensions with his family as a result of this; and his almost simultaneous breakup with her and official abnegation of the left-wing. And third, mention must be made of that "bracketed" post-textual context of Dazai's subsequent success and notoriety as a decadent, nihilistic writer from the late 1930s until his premature death in 1948.

Written in 1933, when Dazai was twenty-four, **"Metamorphosis"** is based on an earlier tale titled "The Carp That Came to My Dream" by the eighteenth-century author Ueda Akinari (1734–1809).[2] In Ueda's tale a dying priest, Kogi, who has been duly observant of the Buddhist dictum to respect all forms of life and who is very skillful at painting fish, is granted his desire to be transformed into the object of his art, a beautiful golden carp. He swims leisurely about Lake Biwa but is caught and sold to a restaurant. He is just about to be carved into filets when he awakens to find he has been dreaming. Ueda leaves the question of dream and reality open, however, by maintaining that Kōgi was indeed dead during those three days and that the fish had in fact been caught and prepared for dinner.

In Dazai's story, the hero is no longer a priest but an adolescent girl, Suwa, the daughter of a gruff, taciturn charcoal maker in a remote and isolated region of northern Japan. During the summer months Suwa runs a small concession where she sells lemonade to tourists who come to visit the waterfall. Minor details and incidents, including the accidental death of a botany student who slips into the waterfall while looking for plants, heighten the atmosphere of gloom and premonition. Suwa herself, through a process of observation and reflection, mostly of the waterfall, seems to change from a lighthearted girl to a moody, rebellious young woman. She expresses this change at one point by confronting her father, whose life rotates between making charcoal and getting drunk after selling it in town, with the suggestion that he leads a meaningless life. He is infuriated and almost strikes her. Shortly thereafter on a wintry, snowy, ghostly night, he returns from town drunk and rapes her. She runs out in a state of shock, heads instinctively for the waterfall, and plunges into the basin.

It is here that Dazai incorporates the earlier tale, but with a peculiar twist. Suwa is transformed into a carp and swims leisurely about, apparently enjoying her newfound freedom. Suddenly, the fish comes to a halt, pauses as if in meditation, and then swims directly toward the whirlpool beneath the fall where its body is "sucked up like a dead leaf" (288).

In this brief tale, Dazai draws on all the history, myth, and lore of his native northern region: the legend-filled mountains of the charcoal-makers, the woodcutters, the aborigines, and the demons. He combines just enough precise geographical information to give a sense of immediacy and reality with an aura of remote antiquity extending back to prehistoric mysteries to allow for the possibility of the unreal. Early mention of the geological fact that this entire region was once a lake establishes a link between geo-historical supposition and narrative legend and lore, as well as suggesting the possibility of the evolutionary transformation and physical separation by water that activate the story.

Narrative resistance to a cohesive voice is already apparent in the narrator's self-intrusion into the description of the story's setting. In the midst of an otherwise "objective" account of the landscape, the voice assertively affirms its own idiosyncratic view in place of the local folklore. Though popular tradition has named the mountain in question "Horse Hill" for its resemblance to a galloping horse, the narrator says: "In fact . . . it resembles the profile of a decrepit old man" (285). Although the insertion serves to heighten the ominous tone of the piece, it also has the effect of interposing, and indeed calling attention to, the presence of a subjective mind between the reader and the story.

"Metamorphosis" takes as its time a few crucial days in a year of a girl's life. We know that Suwa's life is not always as intense as the sparse description in the story makes it. Yet we also sense that the boredom, futility, revolt, and violence are not unreal. This effect is achieved through a simultaneous reduction and suspension of time. The setting is presented as an impermanent creation of nature, subject to the whims of geology (glacier, erosion) and history (mention is made of Japan's most beloved hero, Yoshitsune). Even rocks and mountains, as we have seen above with Horse Hill, are subject to interpretation, depending on how one looks at them. Japan is after all an island, surrounded on all sides by water. Against this backdrop are glimpsed the lives of two small people, lives whose duration is further reduced to less than a year's time, then to a few days, and hours, and minutes. Set as they are against the ever-recurring seasons of nature, however, the moments of passion, as of boredom, become suspended in the vast expanse of geological and historical time. Suwa's moments of perception—the accidental fall into water, the sudden pain of sexual violence, and her own deliberate leap into water—as small as the human imagination can make them in literature, become large beyond belief, out of perspective, as they do in human life itself.

Against this backdrop of geological time, the action of **"Metamorphosis"** is in dramatic correspondence with the changing seasons and the immediate scenery. Each of the first three parts of the story cinematically zooms in from a panorama to a clearly focused scene, defining the time successively as a day in late summer, a day in early autumn, and a day in late autumn. With each shift of scene and time, the surrounding nature imagery shifts to accommodate the season and the dramatic mood. Certain traditional images, leaves and water, become specifically symbolic of change, impermanence, and the maturation process. Significantly, the final image of the story, "sucked up like a fallen leaf," identifies the return to nothingness that Suwa is trying to engineer.

Water is a structurally unifying element in **"Metamorphosis."** Physically and spiritually it is the medium that moves the action, advancing Suwa's evolution. The watery death at the beginning is a prelude to the watery transformation at the end, connected by the story of Hachirō's watery transformation into a serpent in the middle,[3] as well as by Suwa's constant intimacy with the waterfall. The story of Hachirō and Saburō, recalled while watching the waterfall, unites all the elements of Suwa's past, present, and future experience (286–287). It connects her observation of death with the idea of change and transformation inspired by her contemplation of the waterfall. And beyond adding the element of transformation, which will soon affect her own physical body, it adds another one: separation. Suwa recalls that when she heard the story from her father as a small child, she found the plight of the two brothers sad. Her spontaneous baby gesture was to place her father's finger in her mouth. Since Suwa's mother has apparently never existed for her, the suggestion here is also "separation" from the force that gave her life. At the same time, and in view of the succeeding events in the story, and the proclivities of two isolated human beings, the sexual implications begin to emerge.

Both bluntness and brevity of dialogue accentuate the antisocial character one would expect of isolated people and draw attention to the unusual importance of every remark. In this mountain area, no resources are wasted: the coal, the mushrooms, the scenery, and of course human energy, which, as we gather from the story, seems to include not only human language but even human thought and affection. The implication seems to be that human capacities are indeed valuable, but not to the same degree as material resources. One wonders if there is not implicit a criticism of Dazai's own family, especially in the light of such works as **"Reminiscences,"** which highlights the author-narrator's impression of having been a neglected child, and of his high school works, which castigate family and father in particular. In reacting against this sense of affective deprivation as a child, Dazai was also, from his alienated vantage point as a "younger son," calling attention to the ranking of children in the order of future economic and social importance.

The scarcity and bluntness of dialogue in the case of Suwa and her father is not, as is sometimes the case, to suggest intuitive understanding and affection; its effect is rather to underline a process of progressive estrangement. The use of a single word in dialect often has a very telling effect: the term used by Suwa to refer to her father, "Odo," is uttered dramatically at the last moment, just as Suwa is

about to plunge into the water. It is said softly, in contrast to the "'Dumb ass!'" (*ahō*) that Suwa had previously screamed at her father, suggesting that she has now reconciled herself to her fate. Perhaps on the verge of death, she loses some of her hostility to her father and is ready to consider him human again (unlike wishing him dead before). Or perhaps the word signals a nostalgic reference to him in memory of her early childhood, when he acted more like a daddy, more like her "Odo."

"Metamorphosis" may be seen as an attempt to strip reality to its bare essentials in the form of allegory and symbol. In the attempt to find a suitable narrative voice, however, Dazai finds himself shifting uneasily from the point of view of the objective storyteller to the subjective mind of Suwa or of himself as author-narrator unable to remain aloof. From the accidental death at the waterfall to Suwa's newly discovered freedom as a fish, the text moves us in and out of the heroine's mind. At a critical juncture, however, the narrator describes what Suwa is thinking in an encapsulated, metaphorical, and unemotional way, giving a synthetic and purposeful account of her development. Contemplating the seemingly never-ending quantity of water that falls from the mountain, and the apparently unchanging shape of the cascade, Suwa goes through an elaborate series of observations and deductions, noting that there is a definite physical change from one substance to another, evidenced by changing in color and texture. The elaborate rendering of this thought process through the use of a sequence of verbs of perception and logic (discovered, realized, understood, supposed, considered) suggests the maturation process of an adolescent in terms of her "subjective" existence.

Suwa has already experienced excitement and curiosity about the waterfall with three of her senses: sight (the drowning); touch (swimming nude in the pool); and hearing (the story of the two brothers, Hachirō and Saburō, which she recalls from her childhood). She has lived in implicit immersion in either the substance or the sight and sound of the water. It is only natural that at the time her body awakens as a woman her mind should also awaken, and that the object of her attention should be that substance which has embraced and consoled her on occasion. There is here the poetic suggestion that Suwa, in realizing that water *does* change form, also realizes that she herself *can* change form (from girl to woman, from slave to free person, but also from human to animal, from being to nothingness).

The process of thought itself as described in this passage further reinforces Suwa's capacity to think for herself and to distinguish forms. Her appreciation, moreover, that natural forms (including human beings and their creations) are all in a process of perpetual change suggests a Buddhist appreciation of impermanence. The ambiguity of form (water or cloud) recalls the initial confusion over the shape of Horse Hill, but what is strikingly present in the girl and apparently lacking in the narrator is a readiness to accept change. It would seem that the latter is in struggle with his own story and with his own heroine. He insists on his own version of the mountain, resisting the implications of the geological history of the area that change is inevitable. With Suwa, on the other hand, the insight begins to emerge, though it remains elusive, that death, in the broad context of time, is not a final enslaving process but a part of a process of transformation that means renewal, liberation, and freedom.

It is the conclusion of **"Metamorphosis"** that crystallizes the textual dilemma. There is an ambivalence here that is not just a lapse of consciousness. First there is a leap from a heavy realism to legend-inspired fantasy. Prior to part 4 (Suwa's metamorphosis), in spite of allusions to and intimations of the fantastic, the story has been overpoweringly realistic, even surrealistic, in terms of the bold contours that Suwa and her father carve out of the clear, stark setting of the north. The transition to part 4 is narrated simply and dryly. "Gray darkness surrounded her when she came to her senses. . . . Cold permeated her flesh" (288). There is no suggestion that this is a dream. The ambiguity intensifies as the point of view seems to shift suddenly once again in the middle of part 4. From the subjective mind of the fish-Suwa, the reader is reintroduced to the original omniscient narrator who describes *a* fish. It is never established that the fish described from here to the final whirlpool is actually Suwa. This is of course the expectation of the reader, and the fish's subsequent actions tend to confirm our identification of the fish as Suwa. It is also possible, however, that it is the drowning Suwa who is observing this fish, or that it is she transformed into a fish observing a second fish. In the final analysis, it is not really clear whether death or transformation or both have taken place. A fish has been sucked into the whirlpool. The story ends there.

SUICIDE AND SECOND DEATH

"Metamorphosis" projects a world that may be described as surreal. The interweaving of two psychological "real" human beings interacting with a traditional ghostly setting makes their harsh compressed existence stand out in dramatic relief. Postwar readers, invariably familiar with the details of Dazai's life (from his fear of an authoritarian father to numerous incidents of revolt against family, school, and society) have little trouble in identifying Suwa with Dazai as a victim of oppression (adjusting of course for the transfer to a female victim), pushed to the point of revolt and desperate escape through suicide or self-delusion. Most attractive to the critic in this connection are the two traumatic incidents previously mentioned that occurred prior to the writing of **"Metamorphosis"**: Dazai's attempted love suicide with a barmaid in which she drowned and he survived (November 1930), and his defecting from the communist movement by "giving himself up" to the police in the summer of 1932. The circumstances surrounding both events are obscure, yet it is not hard to see how the rebellion and suicide of **"Metamorphosis"** can be interpreted in terms of the author's real life experience. Indeed, Dazai was to refer on several occasions to the death

of the barmaid as the "black spot" spreading out and "staining" his writing and his life.[4]

It is Suwa's suicide and transformation that raise the issue of escape and freedom from oppression. The world beneath the water is, in traditional Japanese folklore, simultaneously a place of death and of utopian freedom.[5] Suwa's metamorphosis, like Kōgi's in "The Carp That Came to My Dream," is an imagined realization of pure freedom entailing a fundamental separation from the conditions of her oppression. Involving a shift to a new medium (from land to water) and a new form (from human to fish), it is no less an escape from time itself, from the present, or, in evolutionary terms, from an advanced to a lower and less complex state of existence. It is hence a liberation not just from the bonds of human society but from the essence of humanity itself, which, as Suwa's reflections on the protean nature of water suggest, is intuitively connected with the process of "thinking," of consciousness.

It is Suwa's "second suicide," however, in her metamorphosed fish form, that suggests that liberation as escape is somehow inadequate. As Dazai put it, a bird must have air resistance in order to fly. Thus, in a vacuum, in total isolation, and no less in the idealist reaches of past time, there is no oppressor and therefore no oppressed. But by the same token, there is no responsibility, no history, no society, and no need for freedom. There is only oblivion, nothingness. And so, it may be argued, Dazai has his fish swim toward the whirlpool in search of an absolute, final death. Freedom is impossible, so why bother? With this coherent interpretation, we have the prefiguration of Dazai's later despair, suicide attempts, and generally self-destructive, decadent nature.

There are, however, a number of loose ends. There is, first of all, the paradox of the drowned fish (how does a fish drown?). There is the ambiguity of the final disappearance—the fish is not destroyed but merely drawn into what may very well be an even lower state of evolution, one suggested by the final plant image, a leaf. There is the extratextual evidence of Dazai's own comments, in which his preoccupation with his self-esteem would appear to preclude any interest in revitalizing Ueda's Buddhist metaphor for the dream-like nature of life: "I read the tale during a very trying period of my life. . . . I fantasized about becoming a fish myself in order to get the last laugh on those who had humiliated and oppressed me. This scheme of mine seems to have failed. Maybe it wasn't such a great idea after all."[6] Finally, there is his letter to a friend, in which he revealed that his original impulse had been to end the story with an additional sentence: "Three days later Suwa's unsightly corpse washed up against the village bridge."[7] In the same letter, Dazai wrote that he later regretted having removed this sentence. Presumably this other ending would have given the impression of actual death and of narrative closure, which the final version avoided. It would have accounted for the possibility that Suwa did not actually turn into a fish but only had hallucinations as she drowned. The fish in the whirlpool might not have been Suwa at all but an imagistic dream equivalent of her drowning. The final version, however, reinforced by a shift in narrative perspective, suggests a desire for an open-ended narrative that links this work with Dazai's ongoing string of narratives of death and suicide, of repeated and endless displacements of death.

In this connection, it may be helpful to consider the implications of "second death" raised by Fredric Jameson in the last chapter, titled "How to Die Twice," of his study of Wyndham Lewis,[8] and then to examine how Dazai's suicidal narrative is displaced toward his experiment with autobiographical fiction, in his **"Reminiscences,"** written at the same time as **"Metamorphosis."** Jameson borrows the notion of "second death" from Jacques Lacan's interpretation of it as it appears in the Marquis de Sade's *Histoire de Juliette.* Lacan's project is to explain why Sade and his libertine protagonist Saint-Fond find it necessary to subvert their own libertinism and posit a belief in an afterlife, in which their victims' suffering may be extended. Jameson argues that both Lacan's and Freud's notion of desire (including Freud's death wish), as an instinctual drive that cannot ultimately be satisfied, has significant implications for narrative. Desire invariably becomes a representation of some sort, even within the subject's imagination, thus acknowledging the existence of a "structure gap between the text of desire and its reenactment" (165). What Sade's "higher level" pornography does, according to Lacan, is to demonstrate the impossibility of an actual and gratifying realization of desire, and instead to substitute for it a symbolic reduplication of physical death.

> "Second death" is thus here taken as an index of the way in which desire, exasperated by the unsatisfying immediacy of its nominal fulfillment in the here-and-now, seeks perpetually to transcend itself, and to project the mirage and the "beyond" of a fuller imaginary satisfaction upon the horizon and beyond the "reality" of its sheerly physical enactment.
>
> (167)

Even more suggestive for our analysis of **"Metamorphosis"** is the link Jameson makes with the death wish, defined by Freud as "an urge inherent in organic life to restore an earlier state of things":

> It must be an *old* state of things, an initial state from which the living entity has at one time or other departed and to which it is striving to return by the circuitous paths along which its development leads. If . . . everything living dies for *internal* reasons—becomes inorganic again—then we shall be compelled to say that *"the aim of all life is death"* and, looking backwards, that *"inanimate things existed before living ones"*. . . . For a long time, perhaps, living substance was thus being constantly created afresh and easily dying, till decisive external influences altered in such a way as to oblige the still living substance to diverge ever more widely from its original course of life and to make ever more complicated *detours* before reaching its aim of death.[9]

Jameson here shifts the emphasis from death to sex, seeing the ultimate aim of the death wish Thanatos not so much as physical death as the "radical extinction of sexual desire itself" (169). Thus, in **"Metamorphosis"** too, the strong urge to escape the "trials and tribulations" of sexuality, including rape and incest, leads first to a physical death by drowning and subsequently to an imagined second death involving the return to an "old state of things," in which the living being (Suwa-fish) aims toward inanimateness and an inorganic state ("a dead leaf").

In Jameson's discussion of Lewis and Sade, desire appears as an unrepentant negative, its object unrestrained sex, violence, or death. Yet **"Metamorphosis"** suggests that the same analysis could apply to that other goal of desire—love, affection, and communication with the Other. Here, too, the impossibility of realizing a satisfying communion is rendered by imaginary displacements. Unlike Sade, who projects sexual violence as pure metaphysical desire, in **"Metamorphosis"** the incestuous rape occurs after an incipient rebellion on the part of the daughter-victim. That rebellion itself, however, was an expression of desire for a fuller communion, for a living human connection. As with Jameson's reading of Freud, in this instance too, the aim of extinguishing (satisfying) that desire ends up as "the extinction of the subject itself" (169). This dynamic leads in turn, as in the watery world of **"Metamorphosis,"** to the "projection of another, and radically different, space in which the implacable demand of the death wish for some total and ultimate satisfaction, manifestly unavailable in the everyday 'real' world of Eros, may finally be met" (169). Moreover, the dissatisfaction of the author—in Jameson's case, Sade—with his own textual representation leads to his fictional character Saint-Fond, in *L'Histoire de Juliette,* "reproducing Sade's dissatisfaction within his own reality (now Sade's representation)" and "open[ing] up a text beyond the text itself, a textual 'beyond' or afterlife in which ultimate, transcendent satisfaction is to be imagined" (170).

To be sure, Dazai's story appears too simple to lend itself to such convoluted renderings of representation, and yet these reflections on Saint-Fond's "second death," which "marks Sade's episode as autoreferential" by "reproducing within the representation itself Sade's own relationship to it" (170), suggest a new way of understanding this otherwise perplexing episode of "second suicide" in **"Metamorphosis."** Where Saint-Fond seeks to prolong his victim's suffering and physical death "beyond the very limits of eternity" (166), however, Dazai's drowning fish projects a "transcendent realm beyond its own material remains, in order there the more surely to die a second time" (171). What interests us here is the open-ended textuality that must result from the author's attempts to represent death. As almost an epigraph to Dazai's subsequent life of narrative endeavor, we may quote Jameson's description of the operative dynamic of such texts: "[T]he figure you kill is already imaginary so that for this first-level representation a second must be substituted—an imaginary of the Imaginary itself—and for that second one, yet another, and so forth, in a regression which has no end" (170).

SUICIDAL SIGNIFIERS

Not a few critics have called attention to the subversive nature of allegory, whether focusing on overtly socio-political, psychological, or more elusive rhetorical categories. Probably few have done so, however, as radically as has Paul de Man in his *Allegories of Reading* or in essays such as "Shelley Disfigured," in which he asserts with "rigor" and "lucidity" that only an open-ended allegorical process of the kind he perceives in Shelley's unfinished poem *The Triumph of Life* can avoid the critical pitfalls of "the recuperative and nihilistic allegories of historicism."[10]

Much like the case of the poet Shelley, whose accidental drowning could not be dissociated from the intertextual fabric of his unfinished "fragmented" poem, *The Triumph of Life,* Dazai's dramatic death by drowning in yet another (his fifth) suspicious suicide attempt at the peak of his flamboyant career also led to his corpse being critically "transformed into [a] historical and aesthetic object." And as with Shelley's and "all the other dead bodies that appear in romantic literature," so might Paul de Man's words apply to the corpse and literary corpus of Dazai and other Japanese romantics: "What we have done [is] to bury them in their own texts made into epitaphs and monumental graves. They have been made into statues for the benefit of future archeologists 'digging in the ground for the new foundations' of their own monuments."[11] In the case of Dazai's death at a critical juncture of the postwar period, we have a prime example of critical efforts toward "the recuperative and nihilistic allegories of historicism," for Dazai's negativity was almost immediately enshrined (via the collaborative dynamic of the mass media and the Japanese literary establishment) as a naturalized component of the postwar literary scene under the American Occupation.

One may also, as we do here, read Dazai's texts as seeking to subvert attempts to impose coherent meaning. Many of the apparent paradoxes of his texts, whether conflicting accounts of supposedly autobiographical truths, or the problematic ending of **"Metamorphosis"** involving the apparent "second suicide," may be seen as efforts to resist a sense of imminent closure. The second death of the metamorphosed girl-fish Suwa, after disillusionment with her "utopian" escape from a repressive human existence, amounts moreover to a rejection not only of a personal allegory (the writer's life) and a political allegory (repression/freedom), but also of a utopian interpretation of the kind that would allow integration into a unified and intelligible scheme of reading. Dazai's rejection of the alternative ending allows him to maintain the negativity intact, to disallow any facile naturalization of his text as a modern retelling of Ueda's Buddhist parable and its postulation of a more conventional allegorical theme.

The "antiallegorical" stance of Dazai's text suggests rather the type of open-endedness that de Man sees in Shelley's text as a result of its unintended fragmentation. It is in this sense that **"Metamorphosis"** reveals the paradoxical aspect of allegory as a revelation of the impossibility of

meaning. The "failure" of Dazai's "scheme" refers to more than a transparent allegory of an "impossible freedom." As the fish seeking to drown in water, it posits the undermining of the very medium of its own existence, which is the language of literature. But, as the fish metaphor also suggests, even the freedom to escape, to "laugh at one's oppressors" from a "safe haven," is an illusion because the conditions of oppression are the medium itself. Fish and water, language and meaning—there is no getting outside their totality. There is no escaping the prison of language.

Dazai's strategy, then, is to call attention to the suicidal nature of the signifier, that metaphor which sacrifices itself in order to give life to the signified, whose own essence turns out to be no less metaphorical than its signifier's and hence as inevitably suicidal. Suwa's oppression (resulting as much from lack of communication as from verbal and physical abuse) makes her, via the story of Hachirō and Saburō, aspire to read herself as less than human, or nonhuman. Thus does she become another form of meaning, a fish, and aspire to yet another form of existence, which is ultimately that nonexistence itself metaphorically represented as the space, gap, or aporia between the signifier and the signified. But that space, represented by water here, is both separation and connection, and as such (sub)merges and sustains (buoys up) the distinction. The paradoxical nature of desire/meaning is here conveyed as requiring that distance, gap, aporia in order to exist in the first place. Complete absorption, identity, indifference would negate desire and the quest for meaning.

It is with this perception that Dazai will also incorporate into his autobiographical writing an aporetic quality, a distance between narrator and subject that persistently calls attention to the tenuous and metaphorical nature of his enterprise. And as his persona takes on, through criticism and journalism, its own allegorical hue, his work demonstrates the impossibility of reading him (both his writing and his life) as a predetermined signified.

Allegory for Dazai thus involved an intimate questioning not only of his life and goals, his involvement with society, politics, and women, but also of the role and function of literature. Up until this period of 1933, he had written a series of works in the socialist realist vein, texts designed to further the abstract idealized notion of class struggle with which he romantically identified as a disaffected, alienated member of Japan's ruling class. Dazai's personal dilemma, internalized as an ironic melancholy over his incapacity to change his class role (whereby he rationalized his suicide attempts as his contribution to the "perishing of the ruling class"), merged with his romantic nostalgia for a bohemian literary lifestyle. Yet his turn to a literature of negativity and decadence was at the same time a recognition of the abstract and intellectual nature of the Japanese left, one of the reasons for its easy dismantlement. The ending to **"Metamorphosis"** presages the type of narrative strategy that became characteristic of Dazai's later works. It suggests a tentative rejection of utopian solutions of the type he associated with Japanese Marxists as well as of the romantic idealizations of his early period. Embracing allegory as a metaphor of resistance was to recognize the impossibility of meaning not in absolute terms but in a Japan unable to liberate itself from the oppression of political rhetoric. Utopian schemes might have their place in a future world, when art might realize a revolutionary function. But for the time being, art was but the fragrance of a flower and the artist but the "snout of a pig" able to sniff at it.[12]

SEAMY SUICIDE: THREADING THE "I"

As de Man's analogy between archeologist and critic suggests, the critic seeks to dig up and resurrect the body (corpus) of the author. Writing is thus a process of "disinterring" from the crypt of the text and "revitalizing" those signs of meaning. But it is particularly apt in the case of Dazai, whose text, narrative structure, and language continuously call attention to the process of burial or repression inherent in writing and textuality itself. For Dazai, writing about death and suicide becomes a lifelong "undertaking" in which writing and death are inextricably merged while the very conditions giving rise to writing/ dying are themselves submerged in the text. The opening fragment of Dazai's early work **"Leaves"** encapsulates this process:

> I planned to die. In January I received a New Year's gift of a gray-striped robe. It was clearly a summer kimono. I thought I might as well go on living until summer.[13]

The casual tone here, or what Miyoshi calls "insouciance,"[14] belies the process of "suicidal narration" that is Dazai's project. The above statement is in fact a narrative sandwiched within a narrative, with no apparent or organic connection between the two. The decision to die is displaced by the decision not to die, with as little causal or logical sequence as that between a trivial gift and a life-and-death decision. Yet it is the gap, the space, the *absence* of logic that is the issue here. It is that which is not and cannot be expressed that structures the experience of textuality. It is not the "voice" of Dazai so much as it is the impossibility of determining voice, intention, and meaning.

This brief, evocative passage, also written in 1933, may be seen in retrospect to announce Dazai's subsequent career as a writer. The idea, the act, the story of suicide, punctuates his life and writing up until that summer some fifteen years later when his own ambiguous death, labeled "suicide," marks an end as arbitrary and incon*sequential* as this initial narrative *sequence*. Dazai's professional writing career thus begins with a brief narrative, the opening fragment of **"Leaves,"** in which the intention to die is displaced and deferred by a seemingly insignificant and irrelevant reflection on a piece of woven cloth. His life and writing are subsequently shaped by a series of suicide attempts, culminating in his double suicide death with Yamazaki Tomie in 1948. These "textualizations" of suicide and death come to constitute, as it were, the warp and

woof of Dazai's autobiographical and literary corpus.[15] Dazai's string of failed suicides raises suspicions about his intentions, suspicions that serve, however, to call attention to the process of writing itself in Dazai's literature. The notion of "seam," enhanced by several morphological and harmonic affiliations (seamy, seem, seme), will provide us with a suggestive framework for considering suicidal narrativity.

The association of weaving with seeding, along with that of semen and semantics, is well developed in Derrida's *Dissemination.*[16] The Anglo-Saxon word "seam," however, fits well with Dazai's interweaving of life and writing. For the seam would appear, like various examples of Derrida's nonbinary logic—those "undecidable" terms, the pharmakon, the supplement, the hymen—to signal a "neither/nor, that is, *simultaneously* either/or."[17] The analogy here in Dazai's **"Leaves"** is between writing and weaving: the product, both text and kimono, may be realized only through a process of writing/sewing that achieves a semblance of coherence or meaning by stitching together fragments of meaning/fabric into an apparent (seeming) whole. That this coherent whole is no more than a fabric-ation or a fiction is apparent from its "seams," those points of suture or juncture where a text, like a piece of clothing, may also, conversely, most easily be undone, or risk "coming apart at the seams." There is here, then, a triple anagrammatic play, for what *seems* to constitute a *seme* (meaning) does so, provisionally, by virtue of its *seams.* The same seam that joins and constitutes meaning is simultaneously the means of undoing the whole. Thus the verb seam, which initially means to join, by sewing together, two pieces of material, comes in a secondary instance to refer to the *mark* of that joining: the fold line, groove, ridge, interstice. And, in a third instance, it comes to mean the making of a seam where none previously existed: to line, cut, scar, wrinkle, furrow, or to become fissured or ridgy, to crack open. The ultimate extension of "seam" would be purling, where stitches are inverted to create the impression of a seam, to give a material a ribbed appearance for decorative effect. This spectrum of meanings emphasizes the impossibility of deciding whether the seam is that which holds material together or that which allows it to come apart, whether it is that which hides the provisional nature of joining or that which reveals it. The derivative adjective "seamy," in its literal sense referring to the rough seams of the underside of a garment, takes on the figurative sense of the "underside" of social life, that which is judged, from the confines of respectability, to be unpleasant, disreputable, or unpresentable.

In thematic terms, Dazai may be, and has been, reduced to a writer who pits an individual, alienated, and weak self against a strong, cold, and brutal society. Yet it is insufficient to see a mere static opposition between self and society here, for Dazai's writing, both overtly and implicitly, calls attention repeatedly to a process of slipping and sliding that belies any such transparent reduction. One of the ways in which this self-referentiality occurs is in the recognition of a necessity for opposition, antithesis, oppression, and friction in order for there to be resistance, revolt, and movement. Another is in the often discordant and abrupt intrusions of narrative or authorial voice that rupture (or suture) the text. This seaming of the authorial "I" looking at its autobiographical self suggests a convoluted self-referentiality rendered all the more intricate by its ironic twist, or inversion, of the private and public spheres. As a reading of **"Reminiscences"** demonstrates, the ethics of society are no more than decorative seams to conceal a vast apparatus of oppression.

The Japanese word for "seam," which we have not yet mentioned, is no less appropriate to Dazai's text: *nuime* from *nuu* (sew, stitch) and *me*, literally "eye" and, in a series of extended meanings, mesh, stitch, weave, texture, as well as the eye of a needle. The fabric of Dazai's text is constituted by a series of poorly sewn stitches or "eyes" (inserting the presence of the first-person "I" of the narrator-author) focused on the uneven, unseemly seams of the narrator's past. The rough or coarse (*me no arai*) texture of the discourse, however, is there to call attention to itself. Masao Miyoshi has argued, "If Dazai's art were no more than a cloak of rags to be torn away to disclose the truth, his work would prove quite tedious at the end, being merely the redundant self-analysis of a seedy self-indulgent individual."[18] Indeed, however, Dazai's text seeks to show itself as a cloak of rags and *no more*, and to portray a seedy, self-indulgent individual and *no more*. It is the idea of a different, or a single, ultimate truth, of a more presentable individual, a more authentic author that would jeopardize Dazai's writing.

Thus Dazai's project is avowedly to reveal the "seamy" side of his own "self." **"Reminiscences,"** the longest piece in his first published collection ***Declining Years,*** has as its stated intent to "lay bare my evil," to "confess the existence of this wicked child." The contingent and relative nature of this evil, as of his childhood and later life, however, has the effect of revealing the undecidable nature of the seam. As intimated in **"Leaves,"** his project is to integrate his life, that striped cloth of past, present, and future, into a text that will be of no use as soon as it is completed. The provisionality of the writing is identified here with Dazai's decision to await the summer "because" his kimono is intended (by social convention) for summer wear. Once summer comes, there will no longer be any reason to wait: both writing and kimono, as pretext and pre-text, to paraphrase Derrida's opening to his *Hors Livre,* "will (therefore) not have been."[19]

The collection ***Declining Years,*** which contains both **"Metamorphosis"** and **"Reminiscences,"** begins, then, with this intonation of intention to die, already rendered suspect by the medium of its message. Its title, ***Bannen,*** also rendered "twilight years" or "later years," invokes a premature old age as an ironic ground to the melodic theme of failed suicides. The string of suicides stitched together from ***Declining Years*** (1936) through *No Longer Human* (1948) form a seam whose undecidability is both the *sine qua non* of Dazai as monument of negativity and the means whereby Dazai's writing effects a radical undermining of the Japanese autobiographical fiction tradition.

Declining Years begins the process of turning the autobiographical I-novel, with its assumption of a hidden but true self, inside out. It is not just, as Usui Yoshimi suggests, that Dazai combines the third person "he" (*kare*) of the objective novel (*kyakkan shōsetsu*) with the "I" (*watakushi*) of the I-novel in an effort to merge the undesirable extremes of majestic omniscience in the former and distorting banality in the latter.[20] It is rather a textual effect of the desire to become a "living dead." It is not so much a matter, as Ōmori Morikazu puts it, of transforming a "loss of humanity" (*ningen shikkaku*) into a "human divinity" (*ningen shinkaku*), but rather a distancing of self from life through a textuality of death.[21] In Dazai's words, "I am now not a person, but that strange creature known as an artist. I should like to introduce you to this great author who has dragged his corpse behind him for sixty years. Not that there is any point in trying to penetrate the mysteries of this cadaver's sentences."[22] The point is not, in other words, to substitute a transcendental truth—be it private and personal or public and national (via the emperor as god)—for an immanent one in an attempt to compensate for the instability of the latter. Rather, it is an attempt to undo the oppositional logic itself by radically questioning the assumptions on which it is based. Thus it is that Dazai's writing is filled with monsters, ghosts, but above all human paradoxes, created by a self-referential language conveyed through a disembodied narrative voice. Thus it is that the reader is cajoled into seeing the "no longer human" ghostly persona of Dazai as "all too human."

SOLITARY SUMO: DAZAI'S "REMINISCENCES"

"Reminiscences" constitutes Dazai's earliest attempt to "thread the 'I'" of his narrative needle. The self-referential quality of this early work of autobiographical fiction is colorfully conveyed by Kamei Katsuichirō's description of it as "solitary sumo" (*hitorizumō*).[23] A Japanese equivalent of "quixotic" or "fighting windmills," the term is used by Kamei in reference to the narrator's one-sided love fantasy with Miyo, a young servant girl. But the concern of the text with writing, autobiography, and lineage makes it a suggestive description of the self-referentiality of the narrative itself.

"Reminiscences," taken as a unitary text, would appear to be a paradigmatic example of romantic autobiography depicting an "authentic self in constant danger of alienation."[24] Consider, for instance, Okuno Takeo's depiction of it as "an unusual way of writing about one's adolescence":

> Along with innocence growing up, there is the direct expression of a perhaps dulled and chaotic passivity, lapsing neither into sentimentality nor into self-degradation. . . . The important elements of Dazai's literature are here: secret feelings of inferiority, the elite awareness of having to be better than the masses, a feeling of alienation from family and friends, desperate buffoonery, weakness, compassion for the oppressed, formation of a private world, and a sense of destiny.[25]

It is only in the perspective of Dazai's collective text of ***Declining Years*** and later works up to and including *No*

Longer Human that the deconstructive nature of his project becomes apparent, as does the death tapestry Dazai has woven around, or seamed into, **"Reminiscences"** by preceding it with **"Leaves."** Ultimately, and throughout his writing, Dazai returns to a preoccupation with birth and death as "the only true facts," and hence "not susceptible to human interpretation." Beneath the anti-transcendental urgency of this deceptively transparent statement lies an appeal to conceive of a state in which interpretation does not function. This state is located at the borders of human existence, prior to birth and posterior to death, with the nonconsciousness imputed to it marked by those flags of birth and death. The "truth" of these facts, then, is not due to a superior interpretation or capacity to interpret; rather, it is due to their very immanence and the impossibility, for the individual at those instants prior and posterior to, of giving meaning to them.

Between and against these "facts" lies the terrain of life and consciously perceived reality. Unlike the "facts" of nonconscious nonbeing, which can only be hinted at and never described, the content of life "between the facts" is associated with a physical body and self-aware consciousness. As such, it cannot escape the burden of interpretation, which in turn entails an endless succession of signifiers, all pointing to an ultimate signified. Interpretation cannot be avoided, but it can be undone or shown to be untenable. Dazai's autobiographical writing points to this disjunction of signifier and signified by constituting a "life" whose coherence depends on a series of "deaths." It is through the seams of this life that the abyss of nonconscious truth, where signifier and signified are both one and nothing, is glimpsed. Suicide in Dazai's texts will come to function as the ultimate sliding signifier, whose instability reveals the absence of any signified.

In **"Reminiscences,"** which was to have been a "posthumous letter," suicide is only extratextually invoked. Having engineered his own alienation from humanity ("I was of no use to anyone . . . even my one and only Hatsuyo"), he was resolved to die: "Once again I planned to die. . . . I had absolutely nothing to go on living for." But still he needed a justification, and the chose his perennial "role" as a member of the "doomed" class: "I would faithfully play the tragic, cowardly role assigned me by fate."[26] If suicide is not prominent in **"Reminiscences,"** however, death is tangentially invoked through an account of the narrator's father's death:

> That spring, while the snow still covered the ground, my father died of a hemorrhage at a Tokyo hospital. The local newspapers put out a special edition announcing his death. I was excited more by the publicity than by the fact of his death. My name also appeared in the papers together with the names of nobility. Father's body came home by sled in a big coffin. I went out to the neighboring village to meet it along with a large group of people. . . . When I saw it emerging from the woods I thought it was beautiful. The next day, the family gathered in the room where the coffin had been laid. When the lid was raised, everyone began crying. Father looked like he was asleep. . . . Hearing everyone cry, I began to cry too.[27]

One is reminded here of Albert Camus's *The Stranger* (*L'Etranger*), in which the narrator-protagonist Meursault's opening lines recounting his mother's death ("Mother died today. Or, maybe yesterday; I can't be sure.") appear to be as significant in condemning him for murder as the act itself.[28] As Camus himself suggests, Meursault is condemned because he refuses to play by the rules of the game.[29] What we have here with the narrator of **"Reminiscences"** is, to the contrary, a brutally honest admission of how a child can play the rules of the game without sincerity, without "truth."

It is also of course possible to read the child's (and Meursault's) "alienation" in terms of that more familiar assumption that "'real' death is for all of us rigorously unimaginable."[30] In this perspective, the matter of death becomes in essence a problem of "personality," for which there are narrative questions and answers, with the qualification: "[I]t being understood that the question is in fact unanswerable and that the narrative 'answer' is in reality a kind of sleight of hand."[31] Thus, for example, in the case of Meursault, the unrelated events of his life occurring between his mother's death and the murder are presented at his trial "in a logically organized whole as the basis of an interpretation of Meursault's personality."[32]

And with Dazai, this instance of brutal honesty becomes possible through the "memory" of childhood naiveté and its collaboration in the fabrication of emotion. Crying is the accepted way of masking the "unanswerable," which the child learns to do. In terms of Dazai's narrative development, it provides a decided contrast—as a hypothetical closure, replete with death and burial, coffin and mourning—to Dazai's string of ambiguous narrative deaths and suicides.

But Dazai is also an accomplice in the construction of a particular personality. For all his insistence on revealing his own "evil" side, his account here, as throughout his autobiographical narratives, develops the portrait of a helpless child buffeted by the cruel world of adults. Critics like Okuno read **"Reminiscences"** literally as a "confession," seeing Dazai's narrative as an ethical act, an attempt to turn his "example" into a warning to others. Dazai portrayed it as the verification of the presence of evil within himself, after which (self-)execution would be legitimate. Yet in the process, his attribution of evil to his individual self seemed to be contested by a notion of social and institutional evil.

Thus does **"Reminiscences"** begin with several recollections by Dazai of himself at an early age in the company of his aunt, followed by the less than innocent observation: "I have several recollections of my aunt but unfortunately not a single memory of my mother and father at that time." To be sure, the narrative then, in accordance with his stated intent of "laying bare my evil life," begins to suggest perversity in the nature of this child. Even with his doting aunt, he deliberately feigns ignorance to make himself amusing, and in another instance causes her distress and humiliation as she trips over herself running to see what he is crying about during their visit to a waterfall. Another recollection involves a dream that he had while living with his aunt, evoking a child abandoned by his parents and living in nightmarish fear of rejection by the only person he sees as a source of affection—an image hardly likely to evoke a reader's antipathies.

> One night I dreamed that my aunt was leaving the house, abandoning me. Her chest blocked the entire doorway. Beads of sweat trickled down her large, swollen red breasts. She spat at me: "I've had enough of you." I pushed my face between her breasts, sobbing and pleading with her not to leave me. When I awoke from my dream, shaken awake by my aunt, I found myself on my bed in tears, with my face against her bosom. Even after I was completely awake, I remained sad and cried quietly for a long while.[33]

The year preceding elementary school had also seen Dazai's separation from his aunt Kie, who, benefiting from the marriage of her daughter to a successful dentist, moved away with her family to set up house. Dazai originally went off with them, a move that had resulted in further insecurity for him about his true status in the family.

> It was during the winter. I was crouched in a corner of the sled with my aunt. Just as the sled was about to depart, my brother called me an "adopted son" and poked me in the rear through the sled's awning. I clenched my teeth and suffered the insult. I was convinced I had been adopted by my aunt, but when it came time to enter school, I was sent back home.
>
> (15)

It is from this school period that further revelations of "evil" are disclosed. "Once I began school, I was no longer a child." Developing an adult personality meant learning to lie. "The fact is that whenever I wrote the truth in a composition something bad always happened" (16). One instance of "truth"—writing in a composition that he did not love his father—led to his being called to account by the school authorities. The child who desired passionately to be considered a good student, "to be acclaimed by everybody," found he had to cheat and lie not only to show that he was bright and worthy, but to prove his "legitimacy" in his own family. At the same time, however, he felt a need to "delegitimize" his family, by insisting to his teachers that his father was "not human like everyone else."

> My father was an extremely busy man, and was not at home very often. Even when he was at home, he didn't spend much time with his children. I was afraid of this father of mine. . . . Once when my younger brother and I were playing in the storeroom among the stacks of rice-sacks, my father appeared in the doorway and yelled at us to get out. Even now I feel uneasy recalling my fright before his huge coal-black silhouette against the sunlight at his back.
>
> (17)

As for his mother, "I was not close to [her] either. I was weaned by a wet-nurse and grew up in the care of my aunt, so that until my third year of school I didn't even recognize [my own mother]" (17). All in all, there is material here to construct the prototypical romantic figure, the neglected child and anguished artist, and **"Reminiscences"** is very much a text in that genre. Given that Dazai took to heart his mentor Ibuse Masuji's advice to read such writers as Pushkin, Chekhov, and Proust, it is not surprising that he then earned Ibuse's praise ("first-rate in execution")[34] for the Chekhov-inspired **"Reminiscences,"** which featured such passages as the following:

> I was a flower petal being blown about, quivering at the slightest gust of wind. I agonized over the most trivial insult, to the point of wanting to die. . . . I saw myself surely headed for fame and greatness; but if I was unable to ignore adult contempt for the sake of my honor, how would I be able to avoid the fatal effects of disgracefully flunking out. . . . I felt the presence of a hundred invisible enemies and remained extremely cautious.
>
> (25)

As Jameson suggests for Wyndham Lewis, the fact that representations of death turn out to be narrative displacements of a complex and symbolic nature is related to the problem of personality wherein Lewis as satirist seeks to absolve himself of responsibility for his fictional victims' deaths. The paradox ensues from Lewis's ideological belief in the value of personality and the consequent need for death to be "real," as only in this way can the "strong personality" be said to exist. To create fictional characters whose lives are unreal allows for deaths that are equally unreal, and hence do not count. What we see in Dazai, from his very beginnings as a writer, is an effort to create not necessarily a "strong" personality but a "real" personality, and to do so by means of revealing the often inconsistent and contradictory nature of narrative construction of the personality. **"Metamorphosis"** reveals the uncertainty, the striving in the direction of a strong personality, but it succumbs to a sense of disbelief in the possibility of that personality's extinction. At this level, it is an attempt to absolve the narrator of responsibility for the death of both his creation and his victim.

The actual incident involving Dazai and the drowning death of a barmaid, which serves as partial context for **"Metamorphosis,"** becomes a fascinating source of narrative manipulation, evoking again Dazai's paradox of self-condemnation and desire to be free of guilt. Donald Keene points out how Dazai's multiple and repeated versions of this incident differ from each other in significant detail and observes that Dazai "seems to have been unable, ever since he was a child, to tell the unadorned truth."[35] If, however, one reads Dazai's series of dialogues with his "victim[s]" and the contradictory accounts of death as an acknowledgment of the impossibility of narrating the truth in the first place, they become paradoxically an affirmation of the reality of both the incident and the personality of the narrator. Similarly, it may be argued, the way in which a writer and a subject establish their own reality (and hence the possibility of their own real death) is not by constructing a coherent "strong" personality, but rather by projecting a fragmented, contradictory subject.

In this way, there is an important link beween Dazai's imaginary and autobiographical fiction. The latter is ostensibly an attempt to reconstitute the past through memory, although what makes Dazai's efforts so different from those of the Japanese I-novelist is precisely this conception of memory as itself a fabrication. Thus it is helpful to see Dazai's **"Reminiscences"** in conjunction with **"Metamorphosis."** Each is in its own way a complex displacement of representations of death, incorporating the textual construction of a personality and initiating an open-ended narrative of repeated displacements of death. In the stitching of Dazai's autobiographical fiction, these meditations on death and suicide recur in the fabric and in the seams. Let us briefly consider several instances of **"Reminiscences"** involving the establishment of personality in conjunction with the reality of death.

The narrative of **"Reminiscences"** relies predominantly on a series of self-referential devices to question its signifier status. These include the undecidability of birth, love, ideology, and writing, as reflected in the narrator's doubts about his being the son of his parents, about the response of Miyo to his silent "love," about the servants' inability to grasp and practice "democracy," and about the status of literature as a resolution to one's psychological and social dilemmas. In each instance, the narrator manipulates the signifier in question to conform to a paradigmatic figure, that of the alienated, outcast poet, suggesting that **"Reminiscences"** is as much a portrait of the author's "present" consciousness as it is a story of his "past." The ultimate discovery of "infidelity" on the part of Miyo and the narrator's "disillusionment" are paralleled in the author-Dazai's actual relationship with Hatsuyo.

Let us consider several of these textual nodes in **"Reminiscences"** in order to see how the metaphor of "second death" generates a series of displacements for romantic and sexual insecurity in tandem with political uncertainties in Japan of the 1930s. In the next chapter we will explore the notion of survival (resistance to death) in Dazai's personal life in its political representation as defection (*tenkō*), which in turn acts as a metaphor for literary suicide or *littératuricide*.

First we may note, with Dazai's snide smile in the background, that his story of unrequited love for a servant girl Miyo is not as innocent as it appears. It is the narrator, after all, who makes clear his own strong sense of class consciousness here, imposing itself on his romantic fantasies. Then a literary experience, of a distinctively European cast, revives his waning passion. He reads Pushkin's *Eugene Onegin*.

> It was based on the true experience of a woman prisoner whose mistake had been allowing herself to be seduced by a university student, the aristocratic nephew of her husband. Oblivious to the larger meaning of the novel, I inserted a dead leaf as a marker in the page where the two lovers exchanged their first kiss under the scattering lilac petals. I was incapable of reading an absorbing novel without getting involved, and in this

> case I was painfully aware of the resemblance between these two lovers and Miyo and myself. If I could just be a little bit bolder, I should be like this aristocrat. The mere thought was enough to remind me of my cowardice. . . . I felt I wanted to become a brilliant sufferer in life.
>
> (34)

After reading Pushkin, Dazai reveals to his brother that his secret love is Miyo. His brother startles him by asking whether he intends to marry her. Marriage? The thought had never occurred to him. When his brother suggests that it probably will not be possible because of family opposition, he peevishly draws his brother into a fight, but they soon laugh and make up. Dazai's friends are more accommodating, quick to bolster his imagination with schemes and machinations for conquering Miyo's heart. During summer vacation, Dazai pressures two friends into accompanying him home, ostensibly to study for high school entrance exams, but "also with the idea of showing Miyo" to them. The situation prompts a certain uneasiness on his part about questions of class status.

> I prayed that my friends would not seem disreputable to my family. My elder brothers' friends were all young men from noted, if provincial, families. They didn't wear coats with just two brass buttons like my friends did.
>
> (35)

> I was troubled by the notion of mediocrity. Since the business with Miyo had begun, wasn't I acting like a fool? Anyone can be in love with a woman, but my love is different. It isn't so simple; my situation is not low-class.
>
> (38)

Dazai arrives home for his last vacation before graduation from middle school only to find that Miyo has been seduced by a male servant and sent away. Thus Miyo's pure image has been thoroughly tarnished and the narrator's sense of betrayal by women and servants reinforced. Implicit here already is the theory of *ressentiment* (whereby working-class anger becomes the "explanation" for revolt), for Miyo is described by brother Eiji as having been "really headstrong" and having "had a fight with grandmother." The bourgeoisie here imputes to the rebellious attitude of the servant class a motivation of resentment. We shall see how this theory operates in Dazai's postwar writing in Chapter Eight, but here we note Dazai's admixture of romantic fantasy and its denouement. The matter is, however, even more explicit in an earlier section in which the precocious protagonist instructs the servants in "democratic ideas."

> Around my fourth or fifth year of elementary school I had learned from my brother (Keiji) about the idea of "democracy." I also heard my mother complaining to some visitors that it was because of democracy that taxes were going up so much, that almost all the rice production was being stolen by taxes. I was pretty confused and unsure of its meaning. Later on that summer

I decided to help the servants with the grass-cutting in the garden, and in the winter I gave them a hand removing the snow from the roof, and while doing all this, I instructed them in democratic ideas. After a while I realized that the servants weren't all that happy with my help. Apparently they had to redo the sections I had done.

(27–28)

The portrait of the young aristocrat seeking to "declass" himself by contributing to the democratic movement of history, although a vignette here, was in fact an obsession for Dazai while he was writing **"Reminiscences."** [. . .]

Notes

1. Donald Keene suggests how much of a craftsman Dazai was and how much anxiety he suffered over his art in "The Artistry of Dazai Osamu," *East-West Review* 1 (Winter 1965): 241–253. Dazai's letter of March 1, 1933, to Kiyama Kempei, which makes mention of "Metamorphosis," is indicative of his concern about the writer's craft. "A writer should have the overall conception well laid out and the conclusion well in mind before beginning to write . . . it could turn out quite badly if he veers even a bit from the course leading to the conclusion" [in *Zenshū* (1972 ed.), 11: 15–16].

2. "Gyofukuki" in [*Zenshū*, 1: 61–70] was originally published in March 1933 in the inaugural issue of *Azarashi* (Seal). The English version, "Metamorphosis," translated by Thomas Harper, appeared in *Japan Quarterly* 17 (1970): 285–288. Ueda Akinari's story of 1768, "The Carp That Came to My Dream" (*Muō no rigyō*), is translated and annotated by Leon M. Zolbrod in *Ugetsu Monogatari: Tales of Moonlight and Rain* (Toronto: George Allen and Unwin Ltd., 1974), 132–138. Dazai's title derives from the original Chinese tale upon which Ueda's story is based and literally means "a tale of fish clothing." Subsequent page references in the text are to Harper's translation.

3. Suwa's recollections include being told this folk tale by her father while being held in his arms. The story involves two woodcutter brothers, Saburō and Hachirō, who are separated from each other when Hachirō turns into a scaly river serpent.

4. "Eight Views of Tokyo," in *Nihon no bungaku*, 65: 147.

5. See Moriyasu Masafumi's discussion of Dazai's morbid fascination with water and its archetypal ramifications in his article titled "Gyofukuki," in his *Dazai Osamu no kenkyū* (Shinseisha, 1968), 201–218.

6. "'Gyofukuki' ni tsuite," in *Zenshū* (1972 ed.), vol. 12. The constraints of the master-disciple relationship may also be a factor here, as the following suggests: "This story was the beginning of my life as a writer, although when it aroused an unexpected public response, Ibuse [Dazai's mentor] was surprised. Up until then he had been discreetly correcting my crude provincialisms, but now he looked troubled and said to me, 'It really should not have done so well. I wouldn't let it go to your head. It might be some kind of mistake'" ["For Fifteen Years" (1946), in *Zenshū*, 8: 216].

7. Letter to Kiyama Kempei, *Zenshū* (1972 ed.), 11: 15.

8. Fredric Jameson, *Fables of Aggression: Wyndham Lewis, the Modernist as Fascist* (Berkeley: University of California Press, 1979), 160–177. Subsequent page references appear in the text in parentheses.

9. Sigmund Freud, *Beyond the Pleasure Principle*, vol. 18 (London: Hogarth Press, 1955), 38–39, cited in Jameson, ibid., 168.

10. Paul de Man, *Allegories of Reading: Figural Language in Rousseau, Nietzsche, Rilke, and Proust* (New Haven, Conn.: Yale University Press, 1979), and "Shelley Disfigured," in *Deconstruction and Criticism* by Harold Bloom et al. (New York: Seabury Press, 1979), 67.

11. de Man, "Shelley Disfigured," 67.

12. "A Faint Voice" (*Kasuka na koe*), quoted in Makoto Ueda, *Modern Japanese Writers*, 155.

13. "Leaves," in *Zenshū*, 1: 5.

14. Miyoshi, *Accomplices of Silence*, 127.

15. The association of writing with kimono cloth evokes a linguistically unrelated play on the Latin-derived "text" (weave) metaphor. Dazai, through his narrative of the summer kimono in "Leaves," equated the weaving with the telling, thus making both contextual to his decision not to die.

16. The English translator, Barbara Johnson, in discussing the difficulty of translating Derrida, finds in this instance a felicitous "sympathy." "One might almost believe . . . that . . . *Dissemination* had been waiting all along for the English homonymy between 'sow' and 'sew' to surface" (*Dissemination*, "Translator's Introduction," xix).

17. Derrida, *Positions*, trans. Alan Bass (Chicago, Ill.: University of Chicago Press, 1981), 42–43. Cited by Johnson in Derrida's *Dissemination*, xvii.

18. Miyoshi, *Accomplices of Silence*, 127.

19. "This (therefore) will not have been a book" (Derrida, *Dissemination*, 3).

20. Usui Yoshimi, "Dazai Osamu ron," in *Dazai Osamu kenkyū*, vol. 1, ed. Okuno Takeo (Chikuma Shobō, 1978).

21. Ōmori Morikazu, *Bannen*, in *Dazai Osamu no kenkyū*, ed. Moriyasu, 122.

22. "Sea Gull" (*Kamome*), in *Zenshū*, 3: 79.

23. Kamei, ed., *Kindai bungaku kanshō kōza 19: Dazai Osamu*, 61.

24. See Chapter Four for a discussion of the Romantic foundations of autobiography as elaborated by Lang in her "Autobiography in the Aftermath of Romanticism."

25. Okuno, *Dazai Osamu ron,* 136.

26. "Eight Views of Tokyo," in *Nihon no bungaku,* 65: 149.

27. "Reminiscences" (*Omoide*), in *Nihon no bungaku,* 65: 23–24.

28. Conor Cruise O'Brien, *Camus* (London: Fontana, 1970), 14.

29. Albert Camus, "Avant-Propos," *L'Étranger* (New York: Appleton-Century-Crofts, 1955), vii.

30. Jameson, *Fables of Aggression,* 160.

31. *Ibid.,* 161.

32. Germaine Brée, *Camus* (New York: Harcourt, Brace, and World, 1964), 113.

33. "Reminiscences," 13. Subsequent page references appear in the text in parentheses.

34. Cited in Keene, *Dawn to the West,* 1: 1038–1039.

35. *Ibid.,* 1027–1028.

Sanroku Yoshida (review date 1990)

SOURCE: "Japan," in *World Literature Today*, Vol. 64, No. 3, Summer, 1990, p. 530.

[*In the following review, Yoshida praises the faithful translation of* Crackling Mountain and Other Stories, *which includes ten of Dazai's eleven major representative works written before 1945.*]

One of the misconceptions about Osamu Dazai (1909–48) is that he is a postwar writer. This probably resulted from his sudden visibility in the early postwar period, notably through his tremendously successful novel *Shayō* (1947; Eng. *The Setting Sun,* 1956). Most of his fifteen-year literary career, however, spanned the prewar and war period. The bulk of his writing in those years dealt with literary themes that would become more applicable to the concerns of postwar society, such as the "loss of identity" and "disorientation and alienation." Thus the very nature of Dazai's writing made him an important figure right after the war.

The significance of *Crackling Mountain and Other Stories* is that it includes ten of Dazai's eleven major representative works written before 1945, stories that give the reader a more complete picture of this tragic genius's work than did *Shayō.* (He committed suicide at the age of thirty-nine.) The collection shows an extremely wide range of literary talent, leading the reader to the revelation that, in addition to being a writer of the confessional I-novel, for which he is usually known, Dazai was also a master craftsman of storytelling. **"A Poor Man's Got His Pride"** and **"The Monkey's Mound,"** for example, remind the reader of the short fiction of Maupassant and O. Henry. **"Taking the Wen Away"** and **"Crackling Mountain"** retell medieval tales from ***Otogi Zoshi,*** their new interpretations giving a totally modern outlook to fairy tales popular with Japanese children of all times. In the confessional style, **"Memories,"** Dazai's first published story (he was twenty-four), vividly describes the alienated life of the young author as the son of a large wealthy family in early twentieth-century Japan. **"On the Question of Apparel"** is an anecdotal reminiscence. Unexpectedly for Dazai, ambiguity and the use of symbolism are illustrated by his seemingly simplistic and modernistic **"Undine." "The Sound of Hammering"** concerns the psychic problem of a desperate young man in a land ruined by the war. **"Melos, Run!"** is surprising for its didacticism. In whatever category, Dazai's stories share one common quality: an unmistakable tone of immediacy, desperation, and humor.

James O'Brien, the stories' translator, is the author of the Twayne series monograph on Dazai (1975; see *BA* 50:1, p. 240). Most of the selections in the present volume were previously published in the Cornell East Asia Papers Series. O'Brien has revised them for the Tuttle edition. His prefatory note to each piece explains the circumstances in which Dazai wrote the story and gives a summary and evaluation of Japanese criticism on it, plus his own analysis. The translation is a linguistic tour de force, is faithful to the original, and reads extremely well. Japanese idiomatic phrases, often considered untranslatable, are deftly rendered into English. The only area yet to be explored is Japanese onomatopoeia, although the question of precisely how to deal with it in English seems altogether an impossible one.

Osamu Dazai is currently a popular subject for American scholars of Japanese literature. *Crackling Mountain and Other Stories* will undoubtedly enhance his standing.

Additional coverage of Dazai's life and career is contained in the following sources published by the Gale Group: *Contemporary Authors*, Vol. 164; *Dictionary of Literary Biography*, Vol. 182; and *Twentieth-Century Literary Criticism*, Vol. 11.

"A Jury of Her Peers"

Susan Glaspell

The following entry presents criticism on Glaspell's short story "A Jury of Her Peers" (1917).

INTRODUCTION

Known primarily as a playwright, Glaspell's short fiction went largely unnoticed until 1973 when her short story, "A Jury of Her Peers" was rediscovered. Though the author of forty-three short stories, Glaspell's "A Jury of Her Peers" is her most widely anthologized piece of short fiction and is based on an actual court case Glaspell covered as a reporter for the *Des Moines Daily*. The story, which she adapted from her one-act play *Trifles* in 1917, has attracted the attention of feminist scholars for its treatment of gender-related themes. On its surface, "A Jury of Her Peers" appears a simple detective story, but through extensive dialogue between two women, Glaspell slowly reveals the story's true underlying conflict: the struggle of women in a male-dominated society.

PLOT AND MAJOR CHARACTERS

"A Jury of Her Peers" opens with controversy surrounding Minnie Foster Wright, who is in jail on suspicion that she murdered her husband by strangling him. Mrs. Wright's story is told indirectly through a conversation between Martha Hale—whose husband discovered the body of John Wright—and Mrs. Peters, the wife of the local sheriff. The sheriff asks Mrs. Hale to accompany them to the Wright's house so she can keep his wife company while the men investigate the murder scene. Thrown together by circumstance, the women form an immediate bond as they begin gathering some of Minnie's belongings to bring to her in her jail cell. Concluding that there is nothing in the kitchen except for "kitchen things," the men begin their investigation in the upstairs of the house and in an outside barn. Left alone in Minnie's kitchen, however, the two women begin discovering their own clues about Minnie's possible motive for killing her husband. Gradually, Mrs. Hale and Mrs. Peters begin noticing details about Minnie's life that escape the notice of their husbands. They notice Minnie's desolate, isolated existence, her broken furniture, the run-down kitchen where she had to cook, and the ragged clothing she was forced to wear because of her husband's miserly insensitivity. Eventually the two women stumble across two clues that piece Minnie's case together. They

spot the crooked stitching on one of the quilts Minnie was working on, speculating that she must have been upset while trying to complete the project. The two women also find Minnie's cherished canary strangled and carefully tucked away in a box inside her sewing basket. After discovering these clues, the two women begin talking about how Minnie, once sociable and cheerful, evolved into an introverted, lonely woman after marrying her silent, cold husband. Both women also notice the broken hinge on the bird cage, speculating that John Wright might have strangled Minnie's canary, much the way he killed his wife's spirit with his overbearing manner. After the discovery of Minnie's strangled canary, the two women conjecture that Minnie strangled her husband just as he had strangled her canary. Empathizing with Minnie, the women decide not to tell their husbands about the results of their own investigation. Instead, they repair the erratic stitching on Minnie's quilt and concoct a story about the canary's disappearance, blaming a runaway cat. In silent collusion,

Mrs. Hale and Mrs. Peters cover up the clues that reveal Minnie's motive, quietly acquitting Minnie from wrongdoing without their husbands' knowledge.

MAJOR THEMES

Now considered a feminist classic, "A Jury of Her Peers" examines the predicaments of women in a male-dominated society. Critics believe that Glaspell, who based this story on a real murder trial in which women were not allowed to serve as jurors, created a jury of those female peers in her story to mete out their own form of justice. A detective story on the surface, "A Jury of Her Peers" is more of a commentary about female oppression, justice, the confining nature of rigid stereotypes, and the differences in perspective between men and women. Throughout "A Jury of Her Peers," the men in the story never acknowledge Minnie Wright's oppression and how it led her to a desperate act. The men in the story also view their wives as the weaker sex, only valuable as overseers of the domestic arena—an area the men consider insignificant. Bound by rigid stereotypes and the inability to step into Minnie's shoes to solve the crime, the men who are supposed to be the primary investigators in the case, miss all of the clues and are unknowingly outwitted by their wives. After the two women solve the case, they silently decide to protect one of their own, ultimately becoming the true investigators, the judge, and the jury on Minnie's case.

CRITICAL RECEPTION

A winner of the Pulitzer Prize for her drama *Alison's House*, Glaspell attained much critical acclaim as a playwright and as an important contributor to the development of modern American drama. Her short fiction, however, was often considered regional, sentimental, and full of formulaic plots. Most of her forty-three short stories fell into the genre of local color writing, the staple of many magazines at the turn of the twentieth century. Many of Glaspell's stories were published in magazines such as *Good Housekeeping* and the *Woman's Home Companion*. Of all her short fictional works, however, critics have hailed "A Jury of Her Peers" as a feminist classic, noting the story's significance-laden details and its insight into motivations of men and women. In 1912, a reviewer for the *Boston Evening Transcript* praised Glaspell, saying: "Rarely do we meet with a writer who lifts the masks of life, who shows us the naked souls of men, their dreams, their sufferings, their hopes."

PRINCIPAL WORKS

Short Fiction

Lifted Masks 1912
"A Jury of Her Peers" 1917

Other Major Works

The Glory of the Conquered (novel) 1909
The Visioning (novel) 1911
Fidelity (novel) 1915
Suppressed Desires [with George Cram Cook] (drama) 1915
Trifles (drama) 1916
Close the Book (drama) 1917
The Outside (drama) 1917
The People (drama) 1917
Tickless Time [with George Cram Cook] (drama) 1918
Woman's Honor (drama) 1918
Bernice (drama) 1919
Inheritors (drama) 1921
The Verge (drama) 1921
Chains of Dew (drama) 1922
The Road to the Temple (biography) 1926
Brook Evans (novel) 1928
The Comic Artist [with Norman Matson] (drama) 1928
Fugitive's Return (novel) 1929
Alison's House (drama) 1930
Ambrose Holt and Family (novel) 1931
Cherished and Shared of Old (juvenilia) 1940
The Morning Is Near Us (novel) 1940
Norma Ashe (novel) 1942
Judd Rankin's Daughter (novel) 1945

CRITICISM

Karen Alkalay-Gut (essay date 1984)

SOURCE: "Jury Of Her Peers: The Importance of Trifles," in *Studies in Short Fiction*, Vol. 21, No. 1, Winter, 1984, pp. 1–9.

[*In the following excerpt, Alkalay-Gut analyzes details of "A Jury of Her Peers."*]

The continuing popularity of Susan Glaspell's story, **"Jury of Her Peers,"** and the play *Trifles* from which it emerged, can not really be explained by an examination of the plot. Two housewives, Mrs. Hale and Mrs. Peters, accompanying their husbands who are investigating the murder of a man by his wife, discover in the kitchen the clues which indicate the motive of the murderess, and silently agree to withhold this evidence from their husbands. Despite the increasing contemporary interest in women in literature, it is difficult to perceive from the simple progress of events a complexity of thought warranting the current fascination with this work.

Critics tend to agree on the basic theme indicated by the sequence of events: Loyalty to and sympathy for the murderess, Minnie Foster (Mrs. Wright), determine the women's decision to conceal the truth from their husbands and the law. The following statement of Karen Stein in her commendable article on *Trifles* [in *Women in American Theatre*] is typical of the general approach:

> The women here realize, through their involvement in the murder investigation, that only by joining together can they, isolated and insignificant in their society, obtain for themselves and extend to others the support and sympathy that will help them endure the loneliness and unceasing labor required of them.

Underlying this attitude is the assumption that the women's lives are individually trivial, and their only strength and/or success can come from banding together. Triviality is not a value, but it can be overcome by large numbers, by the community of women.

The limitation of the present critical approach lies precisely in this assumption of the negative value of trivia, since it is through the trivial that the greatness of the story can be revealed. The most productive approach to this story is one that acknowledges and imitates the pattern of these women's lives, since it is specifically the connective, the accumulative details of experience, that provide the structural key for the comprehension of the story. More than this, it portrays an entire approach to experience, while the lives of their men together with their conceptions of reality and factuality, provide precisely the inappropriate approach based on abstractions that may mislead the devoted reader of this story.

To comprehend the story one may follow the technique of the housewives, who in making their comprehensive patchwork quilt, sort and sift through trivia and discarded material, match small scraps together, and then sew piece after piece into ever enlarging squares. The "log cabin" patchwork the women discover in Minnie Foster's sewing basket is made exactly in this fashion: Rectangular scraps are sewn around the original square or rectangle, followed by a series of longer scraps which are measured to the increasing size of the quilt. The colors are coordinated and contrasted for balance and relationship, but the general pattern is one that emerges with the quilt.

In the same way one may attempt to comprehend the story by beginning, not with the general presumption of valid motive later to be substantiated through factual evidence, but with the scraps of specific places, relationships, and methods of operation. The organization of these details into patterns of oppositions and interrelations reveals larger concepts of criminality and justice that place the murder and the significance of the story in a different context. By beginning with the detailed polarization of specific relationships, places, and methods of operation, concepts of criminality and justice that form the basis for the story can more clearly be determined.

Like the patches in Mrs. Wright's basket, these details are cut to fit a pattern, and the pattern is one of ironic revela-

tion. As Mrs. Hale and Mrs. Peters approach an understanding of the murder and Minnie Foster's motivation for the murder, they become further alienated from the men who are unified with the society and its definitions. There are three basic polarizations which work together: 1) The opposition between the world outside, where important events occur and murder and truths are revealed, and the kitchen, where menial and mechanical work is accomplished. 2) The opposition between the mentality and humanity of men and women, associated with the spacial polarizations. 3) The distinctions between the law, which comes to be defined as the imposition of abstractions on individual circumstances, and justice, which is characterized by the extrapolation of judgment from individual circumstances.

We may begin, as does Mrs. Hale, in the kitchen, a world immediately associated with the ordinary and contrasted to the "farther from ordinary . . . thing that had ever happened in Dickson country." It is a world of simple imperatives: cleanliness, order, productivity, fruitfulness. The interruption of the order of these imperatives causes a disturbance in Mrs. Hale that immediately suggests a warped sense of values. She keeps the investigators of the murder waiting out in the sled while she considers completing the task of sifting flour. She is shocked at herself for considering this at such a time. But almost half way through the story she recalls this impulse, and the thought of her unfinished sifting helps her to comprehend the significance of her hierarchy of values as she associates Minnie's interruption with her own.

✳ Mrs. Hale's association with Minnie Foster increases when the order of Minnie's kitchen is criticized by the men. "Dirty towels!" exclaims the county attorney, and extrapolates from this detail a serious character flaw: "Not much of a housekeeper, would you say, Ladies!" Later Mrs. Hale realizes that the towel is dirty because the deputy wiped his hands on it when he made the fire, but her defence of Minnie is initially based on the hard life she knows a farm woman must lead, and the impossibility of perfection when the laws of the kitchen are created and violated by men. Both Mrs. Hale and the attorney know here that if a women is an indifferent housewife, as Minnie appears to be, she is suspect as a woman, and this anti-feminine behavior would indicate potential homicidal tendencies inconceivable in a good wife. The broken jars of preserves— also the fault of the men who neglected to keep her kitchen stove going when they imprisoned her—is another false indication of unfeminine character, or, when Mrs. Hale affirms Minnie's concern over her preserves, a trivial ridiculous one. These are double bind exhibits of evidence that will be used against the defendant no matter how they are interpreted by the jury because the men cannot fundamentally comprehend the lives of the women. In fact, the half wiped table, the half poured sugar, and the dirty pans, point to something quite different: the sudden change in the woman managing the kitchen indicates an important discovery that forced Minnie Foster out of the pattern of her chores.

As Mrs. Hale discovers more and more about Minnie Foster's kitchen, she begins to understand the situation of the woman working in it, and her comprehension of the distance between the laws of the kitchen and the outside world increases. "The law is the law," she admits, "and a bad stove is a bad stove." The fact that Mrs. Wright has been forced to maintain housewifely standards with equipment that could only be faulty due to the avarice of her husband indicates that the mutual responsibility of husband and wife has been violated. This consideration in turn modifies Mrs. Wright's responsibility to her husband. Although she can have no recourse to the law, her life has been made miserable by an individual who has complete control of her. The laws of the world can not apply here, and yet it is from these individual considerations, these trifles, that the entire situation arises. The laws of the kitchen are those of individual considerations which modify judgment and can comprehend these seeming details.

The men comprehend the distinction between kitchen and world, but their manner of distinguishing the two areas is to trivialize the laws of the kitchen. "'Nothing here but kitchen things,'" the sheriff says, "with a little laugh for the insignificance of kitchen things." Then the county attorney mocks Minnie's concern for her preserves: "I guess before we're through with her she may have something more serious than preserves to worry about." And Mr. Hale, who has previously exhibited comprehension of Mrs. Wright's dilemma, joins in with the men against the feminine concerns: "'Oh well,' says Mrs. Hale's husband with good natured superiority, 'Women are used to worrying over trifles.'" He is defined here as Mrs. Hale's husband and not Mr. Hale because he has, for the first time, betrayed his wife's sex. Influenced by the attitudes of his peers, he identifies himself as a man by aligning himself against the women. Certainly the nature of the crime demands this alignment. The murder of a husband by a wife casts doubt on the justice of the accepted code of women's submission to a responsible, chivalrous man and forces Mr. Hale to identify himself with the husbands.

While the standard polarization of human beings in a crime story is normally determined by dividing law abiding citizens from the criminal, the characters here are soon divided on the basis of sex differences. The Hales, a close couple, separate as the story develops because of the social pressures which enforce a division between men and women. The women are in the kitchen and the kitchen work is trivial, while the men study the "layout" of the house and the barn, gathering what they consider to be significant information. The mentality of the men and women are gradually seen as appropriate to these two different realms. One may characterize the distinctions as follows:

MAN'S WORLD	WOMAN'S WORLD
World	Kitchen
Significant	Trivial
Community of men: achievement of goals (solving murder, putting in telephone)	Community of women: community, rather than goal oriented (quilting, protection)
Knowledge of facts which lead to general truths and legal definitions	Knowledge of people which make facts useful for understanding people & situations

The distinctions develop as the story progresses and can most clearly be seen in Mr. Hale's alteration in the story. At first sympathetic to Minnie, condemning her husband's tyranny and her probable reaction, he becomes less and less concerned. During the interrogation, Hale exhibits a desire to explain Minnie's motivation and her unique and painful circumstances, but is cut off by the condescending attorney. His next and final speech reveals that he has consciously taken on the role suggested to him by the others:

> Mr. Hale rubbed his face after the fashion of a showman getting ready for pleasantry. "But would the women know a clue if they did come upon it?" he said, and having delivered himself of this, he followed the others through the stair door.

After this final bit of wisdom, Mr. Hale falls silent for the rest of the story, the other men speaking for him, reflecting his attitudes and values in their search for the relevant truth.

Mrs. Hale, on the other hand, joins a community of women. Gradually, with no motivation other than understanding, she begins to associate herself with two other women who appear to be opposites, the accused woman and the sheriff/accuser's wife. Her guilt at her alienation from Minnie Foster, which makes her initial entry into the Wright house difficult, is transformed by her identification with her old friend, and her pejorative evaluation of Mrs. Peters who "didn't look like a sheriff's wife," becomes an identification with her as well, precisely because she is not like a sheriff's wife.

Arthur Waterman [in *Susan Glaspell*] correctly evaluates Mrs. Hale's initial position when he notes: "She had heard of Wright's abuse of his wife and pitied her, but she had never the courage to befriend her." However, the guilt that this attitude engenders in Mrs. Hale alters as events reveal their association. Clearly it is guilt that initially motivates Mrs. Hale's reiterated wish that nothing be revealed to worsen Mrs. Wright's position. Her memory of Minnie is of a "real sweet and pretty, but kind of timid and fluttery (girl)" and her desire to protect this innocent creature from the condemning eyes of strangers.

But the similarity in the lives and habits of the three women, made salient by the supercilious sneers of the men, leads to an empathy that transcends the pity. Aware of the amount of work involved in canning fruit, Mrs. Hale reacts differently from the County Attorney who upon discovering the exploded jars exclaims, "Here is a nice mess." Her association with the fruit is of the process: "I remember the afternoon I put up my cherries last summer." Yet despite this growing identification, she cannot bring herself to sit in Minnie's rocking chair, cannot put herself in her friend's place. The shabbiness of Minnie's clothes and the logical explanation of Wright's stinginess diminishes the alienation, and the threat of mockery from the men brings her even closer. However, it is the sudden comprehension of the significance of the unfinished work in the kitchen that brings Mrs. Hale to Minnie's side. Minnie left her work because something sudden and important happened, just as Mrs. Hale was forced to leave her own work half finished.

The most significant detail, of course, is the strangled bird, not only because it provides the motive for the murder and the method of murder, but also because it provides a clue to the entire relationship of Mr. and Mrs. Wright. The fact that Minnie strangled her husband because he strangled the bird indicates to Mrs. Hale that Minnie understood her husband's action as a symbolic strangling of herself, his wife. It is not just because he killed the bird, but because Minnie herself was a caged bird (like the girl of the popular song of the time) and he strangled her by preventing her from communicating with others. This comprehension makes the murder totally understandable.

Minnie's existence and her behavior are determined by her man who makes the rules she lives by. In this respect all three women are the same. Their behaviour varies only because different men motivate different behaviour. Mrs. Hale, blessed with a generally understanding husband, could have committed the same crime as Minnie had she been married to Mr. Wright. Mrs. Peters knows this well: "Married to the law," she is granted a measure of trust and responsibility otherwise forbidden to women. Married to Wright, she would be the target for Mr. Peters' investigation. Mrs. Hale's understanding of Peters' selective behaviour to different people "particularly genial with the law-abiding, as if to make it plain that he knew the difference between criminals and non-criminals" reveals that his distinction is an artificial one when it comes to women, since it is their partner that determines their behaviour.

Despite her attempts to maintain her husband's values when she affirms "The law is the law," Mrs. Peters responds to Mrs. Hale's criticism of the broken stove and the financial neglect of the kitchen with "A person gets discouraged—and loses heart." As she emerges as an individual, distinct from her role of sheriff's wife, her identification with Minnie is rapid and becomes complete. She relates two events from her own life which enable her to comprehend the motivation and the justification of the murder—her reaction to the murder of her kitten, and her feeling of emptiness when her child died. These are uniquely female experiences, and they link Mrs. Peters to the murderess as they separate her from the men.

They link Mrs. Peters to Mrs. Hale as well, and the women come to be so close that they talk in suggestions rather than statements, aware that the implications of their oblique and symbolic sentences will be understood. Their final decision to cooperate in concealing the evidence they have uncovered comes after a long debate that seems a series of non sequiturs. "I know what stillness is," says Mrs. Peters, and then adds, "The law has got to punish crime." "I wish you'd seen Minnie Foster," Mrs. Hale replies, and then proceeds to blame herself for not visiting Minnie. "If I was you I wouldn't tell her her fruit is gone! Tell her it ain't." Underlying these apparently isolated statements is the question of their responsibility to their newly discovered values and to their innocent peer.

Suddenly faced with proof of the murder, as well as the deep significance of Minnie's act, Mrs. Peters retreats once more to the role of insignificant woman. In so doing, she both uses and underlines the men's incapacity to comprehend the motivation: "'My!' she began, in a high, false voice, 'It's a good thing the men can't hear us! Getting all stirred up over a little thing like a—dead canary.' She hurried over that. "As if that could have anything to do with—with—My, wouldn't they LAUGH!'"

The two worlds are complete, the masculine world that would mock the apparent trivia of woman, and the secret trifle-language of women in which lie momentous truths of their existence, like the strangled bird in the childish box. Moreover, this polarization becomes associated with the third division that has emerged in the course of the plot—the opposition of law and justice. "The law is the law—and a bad stove is a bad stove," says Mrs. Hale early in her discoveries. And when she has discovered the necessity of communication and the pain of alienation, she cries out:

> "I might 'a' known she needed help! I tell you, it's queer, Mrs. Peters. We live close together, and we live far apart. We all go through the same things—it's all just a different kind of the same thing. If it weren't— why do you and I UNDERSTAND? Why do we KNOW—what we know this minute?"

Associating the understanding to which the women have come about the murder with the obligation she had ignored, suffered, and now acknowledges, she shifts the very nature of criminality to an enforced alienation from society.

It is not that Minnie should be absolved of her crime because "of her sex," as Waterman notes . . . , but because sex and the understanding of the communal nature of identity and interrelationship of the individual alter their very conception of crime. "Oh, I wish I'd come over here once in a while!" Mrs. Hale exclaims, "That was a crime! That was a crime! Who's going to punish that!" The greater crime, as Mrs. Hale has learned, is to cut oneself off from understanding and communicating with others, and in this context John Wright is the greater criminal and his wife the helpless executioner. The other men, including Mr.

Hale, are to a lesser extent guilty as well, as their constant callous banter underlines. Unlike the women, they have not learned the lesson of Minnie Foster, and are therefore excluded from full knowledge at the end. Mrs. Hale's protection of Minnie shrives her from her previous crime of unneighborly behavior, and Mrs. Peters is absolved of her obsequiousness and denial of her own sensitivity. But the men have not been able to recognize their failings and are therefore in no position to judge the nature of the crime.

The central image for this conclusion of communality is the quilt. Not only is quilting a simple communal task in which the trivial becomes integrated vitally into a larger framework, but there are hidden patterns and significances in the work. To quilt a blanket is to sew the joined patches to the lining all the way around the borders of the patch. It is to make a thin, flat quilt, in which all the thicknesses are equal. To knot a quilt is to sew the fabric together, generally through a thicker lining, only at the corners of each patch. Quilting equalizes the thickness of the blanket, knotting emphasizes the distinctions. When the women inform the men at the conclusion of the story that Minnie was planning to knot the quilt, although they had not discussed this matter between them, they have determined to differentiate between the legal definition of the crime, in which all considerations external to the act itself are meaningless and equal, and their moral definition of the crime, in which nothing is even and flat. Distinctions must be made and they have made them.

Patchworking is conceived as a collective activity, for although it is the individual woman who determines the pattern, collects, cuts the scraps, and pieces them together, quilting work on an entire blanket is too arduous for one person. Minnie's patchwork would have been knotted and not quilted because knotting is easier and can be worked alone. Clearly this significance enters into the considerations of the guilty-hearted Mrs. Hale.

With her hand against the pocket of her coat where the bird is hidden, Mrs. Hale emphasizes the additional meanings of the term "knot it," meanings she is sure her investigators will not comprehend. "Knot it" conveys the sense of knotting the rope around the husband's neck: they have discovered the murderess. And they will "knot" tell. Mrs. Hale speaks a language that Mrs. Peters can now understand, but from which those who are merely concerned with universally interchangeable facts will be excluded.

The decision of the women is motivated, then, not by sexism, but by the realization that the gap between the sexes extends to a concept of law which negates the possibility of a "fair trial" for Minnie Foster. The title of the story almost certainly echoes Lucy Stone's plea for a fair trial for Lizzie Borden by a "jury of her peers." Stone argued that Borden's motivations and actions could only be comprehended by women, and it is clear that this concept is relevant here. Minnie may be let off, as were Lizzie Borden and many husband and father murderers of the nineteenth century, because "you know juries when it comes to

women," but she will not be understood, for woman's concept of justice involves not only social but individual influences, together with the details that shaped the specific act. The prevailing law is general, and therefore finally inapplicable to the specific case. Minnie Foster can only be judged by a jury of her peers.

In the beginning of **"Jury of her Peers"** Mrs. Hale is brought along because Mrs. Peters needs the company of a woman. The women are indeed united only by fear. By the concluding lines a network of women is created on the basis of mutual understanding and a secret knowledge of truth, not only of the murder but also of the significance of the small, accumulative details of existence. The women are not afraid and conspiratory, but clearly secure in their justice. The secretive manner is one of superiority, and a sense that their men need protection from the truly painful facts of life.

Susan Glaspell is often criticized as a mere local colorist, whose stories and plays, banal and insignificant, are now being rescued from oblivion because the paucity of good literature by women necessitates the reincarnation of second rate works. It is essential to any further research on this author to emphasize the philosophy that is revealed in her most popular work: Trifles are the essential material of life that create a world of women essentially different from the world of men.

Victoria Aarons (essay date 1984)

SOURCE: "A Community of Women: Surviving Marriage in the Wilderness," in *Portraits of Marriage in Literature,* Western Illinois University, 1984, pp. 141–49.

[*In the excerpt below, Aarons stresses that American pioneer women needed the support of a larger female community in order to withstand the isolation of pioneer life.*]

American fiction written by women during the years surrounding the turn of the century illustrates the mounting tension between the rigid social structures of patriarchal conventions and the women who stood as pioneers in the often oppressive wilderness. The women protagonists in this corpus of fiction characteristically are portrayed as immigrants who find themselves isolated on the prairies, the plains, the remote countrysides, in a constant struggle with loneliness and hardship. More often than not, these protagonists are married, a convention only broken by the stigma of spinsterhood or the death of a spouse. And the kinds of matrimonial conventions illustrated in the fiction of the American wilderness compound the protagonists' struggle. Such conventions create an externally imposed conflict between husband and wife, a conflict derived from the disparity between social decorum and psychological needs.

Lee Edwards and Arlyn Diamond, in *American Voices, American Women,* describe this conflict that emerges from marriage as "a tension between social duty and psychological integrity." For the most part, women struggle with this tension more than their husbands because they are placed in a societal framework in which their psychological needs are continually denied. This denial tends to result in a battle of wills, a battle in which the ante is high, and from which the women emerge as victors, as survivors.

Two classical American short stories published twenty-six years apart reflect these tensions within marriage, and the difficulties experienced by the women protagonists in adjusting their private lives to conventional dictates. Both "The Revolt of Mother," by Mary Wilkins Freeman, and **"A Jury of Her Peers,"** by Susan Glaspell define this condition as a fundamental difference in vision between male and female perceptions of individual roles and the need for community. With their characteristic flavor of regional color and realism, both Glaspell and Freeman dramatize the struggle of their heroines to assert their sense of self against the backdrop of the wilderness and the demands of social expectations and male dominance.

This connection between the two stories, one written directly before and one following the turn of the century, has been suggested previously although, curiously enough, little criticism on either story exists. In *American Voices, American Women* we find the following description: "Freeman's . . . New England Village women and Glaspell's prairie matrons, bound by poverty and limited experience, fight heroic battles on tiny battlefields. Even the most barren lives, we learn from these heroines, can reveal an unsuspected strength of will and capacity for imaginative action." Such commentary, however, is sparse, unfortunate because both stories demonstrate, with a vivid urgency that transcends literary and historical periods, the consequences—both tragic and uplifting—of dramatic actions born from the struggle to survive.

In "The Revolt of Mother" (published 1891), Mary Wilkins Freeman recreates the tranquil springtime New England countryside against which a domestic drama unfolds. Freeman portrays a couple, married forty years, who have arrived at a seemingly irreconcilable stand-off. Adoniram Penn is well underway in his construction of a new barn which stands in the place of the promised house for his wife and two children. Sarah Penn, who has spent her life "making do," saving money so her husband could build a respectable and comfortable home, breaks from her deferential role. In an act of defiance and determination she moves her family into the new barn and prepares to take possession of it. Sarah's "revolt" can only be viewed as a major undertaking, one that violates conventional standards of decorum:

> During the next few hours a feat was performed by this simple, pious New England mother which was equal in its way to Wolfe's storming of the Heights of Abraham. It took no more genius and audacity of bravery for Wolfe to cheer his wondering soldiers up those steep precipices, under the sleeping eyes of the enemy,

than for Sarah Penn, at the head of her children, to move all their little household goods into the new barn while her husband was away.

Yet, as the description implies, Sarah's feat is only significant because she perceives it as an act of extreme moment. And her dawning recognition of the power she has held all along becomes the focus of the story.

Sarah Penn's evolution controls the structural tension of the story. The reader sees, long before Sarah does, the contradictions in the way she carries herself and the underlying strength of her character. The initial depiction of Sarah portrays her as a woman who is used to waiting, an attitude underlined by her submissive posture:

> She was a small woman, short and straight-waisted like a child in her brown cotton gown. Her forehead was mild and benevolent between the smooth curves of gray hair; there were meek downward lines about her nose and mouth. . . .

While Sarah's physical description would seem to diminish her capabilities, it only cloaks a forcefulness of which both she and her husband are unaware. The conflict with her husband over building the new barn is the catalyst which finally uncovers her inner strength: ". . . her eyes, fixed upon the old man, looked as if the meekness had been the result of her own will, never of the will of another. . . . She looked as immovable to him as one of the rocks in his pasture-land, bound to the earth with generations of blackberry vines."

Sarah's submissive posture, her forty-year long deference to Adoniram, stems from her willingness to bend to the conventions of a society structured by the stubbornness of a tradition in which decisions are determined on the basis of gender.

Adoniram, as the masculine head of his household, exerts his will over his wife not because of a firm belief in the moral righteousness of his actions, but because of his firm sense of place. His unrelenting determination is born of his notion of how he should act in accordance with conventional standards befitting his role as husband and provider.

The entire patriarchal structure of the society in which they live bolsters Adoniram's position. When Sarah moves her household into the barn during her husband's precipitous absence, the entire community is awe-struck: "Men assembled in the store and talked it over, women with shawls over their heads scuttled into each other's houses before their work was done. Any deviation from the ordinary course of life in this quiet town was enough to stop all progress in it."

While the town's response provides a comic portraiture of provincialism, Sarah's independent action is anything but comic; it accentuates her nobility and strength of character. And why she should choose at this juncture of her marriage, after a lifetime of submission and compliance, to show her rebellious spirit is pivotal to an understanding of the outward change in her nature and to the argument in the text.

The nature of her relationship with Adoniram during the entire course of their marriage has been determined by strict social codes, firmly cemented by generations of tradition which place Sarah in the domestic realm and Adoniram in the position of decision-maker and breadwinner. Adherence to these roles has led both husband and wife to view the world from vastly different perspectives. Sarah Penn's awakened spirit is beyond the imagination of the small New England village. Sarah's confrontation with the minister, who has come to reason with her, mirrors Adoniram's own inadequacies:

> He could expound the intricacies of every character study in the Scriptures, he was competent to grasp the Pilgrim Fathers and all historical innovators, but Sarah Penn was beyond him.

It is finally a matter of vision: Adoniram views his wife's domestic position as trivial, insignificant in light of his place in the community. Freeman, however, views her protagonist's domestic role as a source of achievement and richness: "She was a masterly keeper of her box of a house. . . . She was like an artist so perfect that he has apparently no art." Adoniram views himself as a man of great abilities, who has built "a fine edifice for this little village," a barn to house his most prized possessions. He measures his success in terms of numbers of cows and fine horses, carries himself "with a rasped dignity," and responds silently with injured pride to his wife's lack of admiration for the new barn.

It is Adoniram's silence that suggests his weakness and highlights his tenuous power. For the battle between husband and wife is a linguistic power struggle as well as a battle of wills. When Sarah verbally confronts Adoniram he refuses to speak. He is in silent collusion with tradition and doesn't need to support his position with argument. His silence is testimony to that tradition: "'I wish you'd go into the house, mother, an' 'tend to your own affairs,' the old man said then. He ran his words together, and his speech was almost as inarticulate as a growl." Adoniram's dogged silence—"I tell ye I ain't got nothin' to say about it, mother; an' I ain't goin' to say nothin'"—is his only response to his wife's inappropriate meddling in the affairs of men.

While Adoniram only responds to Sarah with inarticulate resignation, her argument is eloquent. She, unlike her husband, knows her rights; her argument is based on principle. She perceives her place in the world in a way her husband cannot, as she tells her daughter: "You hadn't ought to judge father, though. He can't help it, 'cause he don't look at things jest the way we do."

The forcefulness of Sarah's position comes from her connection with her daughter, both women who share the same vision of things. What gives Sarah the courage to "revolt" is her close bonding with her daughter. In fact, what we find in this story is discovery of the importance of community to women which Marjorie Pryse, in the introduction of *Selected Stories of Mary E. Wilkins Freeman*, describes as a common symbol in the stories: "Freeman depicts two women or women in small groups . . . facing life together. Such sisterhood threatens the patriarchal structure of American society. . . ."

This sense of community between mother and daughter gives Sarah Penn the strength to terminate her subordination to her husband. She recognizes her daughter's need to remain close to her mother. Without a larger house Sarah tells her husband,

> Nanny she can't live with us after she's married. She'll have to go somewheres else to live away from us, an' it don't seem as if I could have it so, noways, father. She wa'n't ever strong. She's got considerable color, but there wa'n't never any backbone to her. I've always took the heft of everything off her, an' she ain't fit to keep house an' do everything herself. She'll be all worn out inside of a year.

Her daughter's need gives Sarah a kind of divine sanction for her revolt. It is this communal bonding that finalizes Sarah's resolve to take control of her life and share in the direction of her family's future.

Sarah's newly practiced control deflates Adoniram. He was "like a fortress whose walls had no active resistance." From Adoniram's posture tradition emerges as a precarious bastion of antiquated conventions. As Sarah moves into the foreground, "overcome by her own triumph," leaving Adoniram weeping, a resolution has taken place. Sarah Penn has discovered her strength by recognizing the essential difference in male and female visions of the world. She discovers that actions function where words cannot. Her act gives her husband a new vision while reinforcing her own. For Freeman, in this process of discovery the very conventions that for centuries have bolstered male-dominated institutions—marriage, religion, familial and societal hierarchies—become undermined, overshadowed by the strength of a community of women, a communal spirit.

Despite differences in locale, in time, and in tone, both "The Revolt of Mother" and **"A Jury of Her Peers"** relate to one another in their common sense of what it means to be a woman in a male-dominated society. Both stories reflect the struggle that arises between men and women from their disparate visions of the world; both stories focus on women in the process of discovering these differences, a discovery made clearer by the contrast of social conventions and private demands; and finally, both stories demonstrate that through the spirit of a community of women the protagonists emerge as victors, as survivors whose very survival depends upon making independent choices. In Susan Glaspell's **"A Jury of Her Peers,"** however, the consequences of independent actions are not

nearly as benign and regenerative as they are in "The Revolt of Mother." Rather, **"A Jury of Her Peers"** is distinguished from Freeman's story by a tragic resolution in
which desperate actions result from isolation and from the
death of human spirit.

"A Jury of Her Peers" (published 1917) tells the story of
Minnie Foster Wright who, when the story begins, is being
held for suspicion of murdering her husband, discovered
dead with a rope around his neck. Minnie Wright's story
is told indirectly by her "peers." Two other women, Martha Hale, the wife of the man who discovered John
Wright's body, and Mrs. Peters, the wife of the sheriff,
have accompanied their husbands to the Wright's home
where the men intend to find evidence, to find a motive by
which Minnie Wright can be found guilty of murder.

An immediate bond is established between the two women,
a kind of intimacy that is not built from long-term acquaintance. Instead it is a bond created of necessity in the
face of life on the prairies where farmhouses are at a great
distance from one another, and human contact rare. This is
why both women find themselves at the "scene of the
crime": . . . the sheriff came running in to say his wife
wished Mrs. Hale would come too—adding, with a grin,
that he guessed she was getting scary and wanted another
woman along. So she had dropped everything right where
it was." This solidarity between the two women connects
them in an unspoken alliance which holds them together
throughout the story, both in terms of their emotional responses and their physical placement.

Together the women remain in the kitchen gathering some
of Minnie's belongings to bring to her in jail while the
men roam the house searching for clues. It is the women,
however, who unearth the evidence, evidence damaging to
Minnie Wright, evidence the women withhold from their
husbands. They withhold it because the picture created of
Minnie Wright's tragic life on the isolated prairie acquits
her in the eyes of her "peers."

Through a skillful and gradual building of tension, the author depicts Minnie Wright as a woman who dies a spiritual and psychological death, abandoned on the prairie
without human contact. Once an attractive, lively young
woman, she marries a man who lacks warmth or the desire
for communication. They lived in poverty, not out of necessity but because of John Wright's miserly insensitivity
to the needs of his wife. The broken furniture, barren
rooms, Minnie Wright's ragged clothing all serve to create
an atmosphere of abject desolation. Childless, living with
a husband who asserts his will by maintaining a silence so
severe that they are removed from all human contact, Minnie Wright purchases a bird. Mrs. Hale, wondering aloud
after the discovery of a birdcage in the kitchen, speculates
about their neighbors, the Wrights:

> "But he was a hard man, Mrs. Peters. Just to pass the
> time of day with him—." She stopped, shivered a little.
> "Like a raw wind that gets to the bone." Her eye fell

upon the cage on the table before her, and she added,
almost bitterly: "I should think she would've wanted a
bird!"

But the birdcage is empty and broken and both women
come to feel a sense of violence and despair that perme-
ates the house.

The evidence continues to mount until the women discover the bird, tucked away in a box, its neck broken,
wrung like the neck of John Wright. A dawning horror
grows upon the two women, foreshadowed all along by
the gathered pieces of information that testify to the accumulated wreckage of Minnie Wright's life:

> "No, Wright wouldn't like the bird, . . . a thing that
> sang. She used to sing. He killed that too."

Although both women recognize the evidence, the motive
that would lead Mrs. Wright to kill her husband, they are
reluctant to admit to the atrocity of the situation. Mrs.
Hale finally articulates what is now plain to both women
and to the reader: "If there had been years and years of—
nothing, then a bird to sing to you, it would be awful—
still—after the bird was still."

The two women recognize much more than the blatant
fact that Minnie Wright killed her husband. They realize,
without articulating it aloud, that she had no choice but to
kill him. The clues they find—the erratic stitching on the
quilt, for example—call attention to Minnie Wright's desperate attempts to channel her emotions, to quiet her anger. But it is clear that she could not. The domestic conventions that kept her in check for so long, that required a
kind of stoic resignation to the ways of her husband, fail
to withstand the emotion, finally unleashed, after the only
thing she loved was killed. In fact, the very description of
Minnie Wright, when Mr. Hale found her in the kitchen
with the dead body of her husband in the room above,
shows her as stunned, paralysed. She tells Mrs. Hale, "I
didn't wake up," when questioned about her husband's
murder.

The other women understand Minnie Wright's violent response. It was "as if the distracted thoughts of the woman
. . . were communicating themselves. . . ." They are
bound to one another by a common sense of the meaning
of stillness, of isolation. As both women recount their
losses—the death of a child and that of a pet—we discover an arrested undercurrent of violence, a conscious attempt to meet the demands of convention. Mrs. Peters, in
describing the boy who killed her cat, reveals, "'If they
hadn't held me back I would have'—she caught herself,
looked upstairs where footsteps were heard, and finished
weakly—'hurt him.'" It is clear that Minnie Wright was
forced to kill her husband; her very survival depended on
it.

The stillness, the isolation, and the social exclusion that
Minnie Wright must have endured, bound to a marriage
ill-suited to her, yet an institution that permitted her no es-

cape, drove her to such an extreme act of violence. Both Mrs. Hale and Mrs. Peters respond to this knowledge with a shared experience, a common bond. The reader finds the two women positioning themselves in silent collusion against their husbands, on the side of the exiled Mrs. Wright, their sense of justice having been fulfilled.

At the same time, both women perceive themselves as intruders in the home of the absent woman:

> Even after she had her foot on the doorstep, her hand on the knob, Martha Hale had a moment of feeling she could not cross that threshold. And the reason it seemed she couldn't cross it now was simply because she hadn't crossed it before. Time and time again it had been in her mind, "I ought to go over and see Minnie Foster"—she still thought of her as Minnie Foster, though for twenty years she has been Mrs. Wright. And then there was always something to do and Minnie Foster would go from her mind.

As the women recognize the kind of existence Minnie Wright must have endured they feel an enormous amount of guilt. They identify with her in a way the men cannot. They see what their husbands fail to see, and so are shamed by their neglect of the lonely, stoic woman. They, too, are to blame. In a very moving dialogue, Mrs. Hale underscores the feelings of both women:

> "But I tell you what I *do* wish, Mrs. Peters. I wish I had come over sometimes when she was here. I wish—I had. . . . I stayed away because it weren't cheerful—and that's why I ought to have come. I"—she looked around—"I've never liked this place. Maybe because it's down in a hollow and you don't see the road. I don't know what it is, but it's a lonesome place, and always was. I wish I had come over to see Minnie Foster sometimes. I can see now—" She did not put it into words.

The women's growing awareness of their role in Minnie Wright's exile, their vision of the kind of life she led, cause them to create a protective shield around her, a community bond in which they draw together, silently acquit her, and vow to conceal the telling evidence:

> There was a moment when they held each other in a steady, burning look in which there was no evasion nor flinching. Then Martha Hale's eyes pointed the way to the basket in which was hidden the thing that would make certain the conviction of the other woman—that woman who was not there and yet who had been there with them all through that hour.

Unlike Adoniram in "The Revolt of Mother," the men in **"A Jury of Her Peers"** are deprived of an awakened sensitivity. They remain short-sighted and never come to understand the hidden force behind Minnie Wright's oppressed position. Throughout the story the men view their wives as weak, as keepers of a domestic arena which is insignificant. Surveying the kitchen, in which unbeknownst to them all, lies the most telling evidence of Minnie Wright's guilt, the sheriff agrees that nothing of signifi-

cance could be hidden there: "'Nothing here but kitchen things,' he said, with a little laugh for the insignificance of kitchen things."

But the women's shared vision of domestic affairs—of cooking, sewing, and cleaning—as a source of power and accomplishment, alienates them from their husbands. It is a poignant reminder of the differing perspectives held by men and women. As in "The Revolt of Mother," the women's attention to domestic affairs is a way of constructing order, of finding the only place possible given the societal restrictions placed on women. It is here that they can excel, make sense of experience and give their lives meaning. This is why the first real clue for the women in **"A Jury of Her Peers"** is Minnie Wright's disorganized kitchen. They sense immediately that something is amiss. Their husbands, however, cannot see this because they don't recognize the value of domestic concerns. Moreover, they view themselves and their place in society as superior to that of their wives.

The men are portrayed as trapped in a social convention that requires their blind maintenance of superiority over women, an arrogance that provides much of the tragic irony of the story. This stance allows Mr. Hale to ask with great patronage: "'But would the women know a clue if they did come upon it?' he said; and, having delivered himself of this, he followed the others through the stair doors." Glaspell undermines this stance by contrasting it to the way in which the women regard their husbands. When, for instance, Mr. Hale begins to relate his version of finding the body, "Mrs. Hale, still leaning against the door, had that sinking feeling of the mother whose child is about to speak a piece. Lewis often wandered along and got things mixed up in a story." Glaspell's women consciously choose not to act on their own superiority, on their recognition of the power and strength that comes from years of endurance and of watching.

The conflict between husbands and wives created by their different perspectives of their places in the world results in a positioning of the women against their husbands. Minnie Wright, isolated for the duration of her marriage from the needed community of women within which she could have met the challenges of the wilderness, is driven to an act of tragic violence. She survives, protected finally by those who share her vision, but only at a great cost. The communal bond built by Mrs. Hale and Mrs. Peters insures Minnie Wright's survival. Her "jurors" arrive at their own sense of justice; John Wright has been justly punished for causing the spiritual death of his wife.

Both **"A Jury of Her Peers"** and "The Revolt of Mother" address the struggle to survive and to reassert one's self-worth and place in the world. The larger implications of these stories is really three-fold. We can draw inferences concerning feminist fiction, the American pioneer experience in literature, and fiction in general as a genre of social history.

Freeman and Glaspell can be viewed as forerunners of modern feminist fiction, as part of the tradition which raises issues of women's experience. Both stories reveal the woman's spirit exiled from her outward role as wife and homemaker. A common vision of experience is reflected in the fiction. Still, the woman's experience is varied, is rich in its diverse levels of meaning, and in its response and reaction to one's place in society.

As paradigms of the American "pioneer" literature both stories address the real meaning of survival, of a spiritual or psychological response to the wilderness. The kind of alienation and isolation perceived by the female protagonists gives new meaning to the immigrant experience. These works portray women as immigrants in their own homeland, as noble figures trying to secure a place for themselves, creating their own communities. Grace Paley [in "Mom," *Esquire*] describes these women in terms of their "powerful pioneer dispositions." The strength and power of the pioneer woman comes from her struggle to balance her nature with the rigors of her environment.

Within an even larger context, the stories dramatize human conflict. Both writers view marriage as a social institution that restricts women's mobility and freedom to find a comfortable position within male-dominated traditions. This literature, then, reflects a kind of social history where marriage is placed within the context of society at large. Marriage emerges as an institution which serves to uphold the differences between men and women. Finally, these two stories express the human experience as a process of coming to understand the limitations and strengths of human beings struggling against rigid social structures. These structures ultimately bend when confronted by the human spirit and the will to survive.

Judith Fetterley (essay date 1986)

SOURCE: "Reading About Reading: 'A Jury of Her Peers,' 'The Murders in the Rue Morgue,' and 'The Yellow Wallpaper,'" in *Gender and Reading: Essays on Readers, Texts, and Contexts*, edited by Elizabeth A. Flynn and Patrocinio P. Schweickart, The John Hopkins University Press, 1986, pp. 147–64.

[*In this excerpt from a larger treatment of gender-based reading, Fetterley discusses how Glaspell attempted in "A Jury of Her Peers" to teach male readers how to "read" female narratives.*]

As a student of American literature, I have long been struck by the degree to which American texts are self-reflexive. Our "classics" are filled with scenes of readers and readings. In *The Scarlet Letter,* for example, a climactic moment occurs when Chillingworth rips open Dimmesdale's shirt and finally reads the text he has for so long been trying to locate. What he sees we never learn, but for him his "reading" is complete and satisfying. Or, to take another example, in "Daisy Miller," Winterbourne's misreading of Daisy provides the central drama of the text.

Indeed, for James, reading is the dominant metaphor for life, and his art is designed to teach us how to read well so that we may live somewhere other than Geneva. Yet even a writer as different from James as Mark Twain must learn to read his river if he wants to become a master pilot. And, of course, in *Moby Dick,* Melville gives us a brilliant instance of reader-response theory in action in the doubloon scene.

When I first read Susan Glaspell's **"A Jury of Her Peers"** in Mary Anne Ferguson's *Images of Women in Literature,* I found it very American, for it, too, is a story about reading. The story interested me particularly, however, because the theory of reading proposed in it is explicitly linked to the issue of gender. **"A Jury of Her Peers"** tells of a woman who has killed her husband; the men on the case can not solve the mystery of the murder; the women who accompany them can. The reason for this striking display of masculine incompetence in an arena where men are assumed to be competent derives from the fact that the men in question can not imagine the story behind the case. They enter the situation bound by a set of powerful assumptions. Prime among these is the equation of textuality with masculine subject and masculine point of view. Thus, it is not simply that the men can not read the text that is placed before them. Rather, they literally can not recognize it as a text because they can not imagine that women have stories. This preconception is so powerful that, even though, in effect, they know Minnie Wright has killed her husband, they spend their time trying to discover their own story, the story they are familiar with, can recognize as a text, and know how to read. They go out to the barn; they check for evidence of violent entry from the outside; they think about guns. In their story, men, not women, are violent, and men use guns: "There was a gun in the house. He says that's what he can't understand." Though Mrs. Hale thinks the men are "kind of *sneaking . . .* coming out here to get her own house to turn against her," in fact she needn't worry, for these men wouldn't know a clue if they came upon it. Minnie Foster Wright's kitchen is not a text to them, and so they can not read it.

It is no doubt in part to escape the charge of "sneaking" that the men have brought the women with them in the first place, the presence of women legitimating male entry and clearing it of any hint of violence or violation. But Mrs. Hale recognizes the element of violence in the situation from the outset. In Sheriff Peters, she sees the law made flesh. "A heavy man with a big voice" who delights in distinguishing between criminals and noncriminals, his casual misogyny—"not much of a housekeeper"—indicates his predisposition to find women guilty. Mrs. Hale rejects the sheriff's invitation to join him in his definition and interpretation of Minnie Wright, to become in effect a male reader, and asserts instead her intention to read as a woman. Fortunately, perhaps, for Minnie, the idea of the woman reader as anything other than an adjunct validator of male texts and male interpretations ("a sheriff's wife is married to the law") is as incomprehensible to these men as is the idea of a woman's story. With a parting shot at the incompetence of women as readers—"But would the women know a clue if they did come upon it?"—the men leave the women alone with their "trifles."

Martha Hale has no trouble recognizing that she is faced with a text written by the woman whose presence she feels, despite her physical absence. She has no trouble recognizing Minnie Wright as an author whose work she is competent to read. Significantly enough, identification determines her competence. Capable of imagining herself as a writer who can produce a significant text, she is also capable of interpreting what she finds in Minnie Wright's kitchen. As she leaves her own house, Martha Hale makes "a scandalized sweep of her kitchen," and "what her eye took in was that her kitchen was in no shape for leaving." When she arrives at Minnie Wright's house and finds her kitchen in a similar state, she is prepared to look for something out of the ordinary to explain it—that is, she is in a position to discover the motive and the clue which the men miss. Identification also provides the key element in determining how Mrs. Peters reads. From the start, Martha Hale has been sizing up Mrs. Peters. Working from her perception that Mrs. Peters "didn't seem like a sheriff's wife," Martha subtly encourages her to read as a woman. But Mrs. Peters, more timid than Mrs. Hale and indeed married to the law, wavers in her allegiance: "'But Mrs. Hale,' said the sheriff's wife, 'the law is the law.'" In a comment that ought to be as deeply embedded in our national folklore as are its masculinist counterparts—for example, "a woman is only a woman but a good cigar is a smoke"—Mrs. Hale draws on Mrs. Peters's potential for identification with Minnie Wright: "The law is the law—and a bad stove is a bad stove. How'd you like to cook on this?" At the crucial moment, when both motive and clue for the murder have been discovered and the fate of Minnie Wright rests in her hands, Mrs. Peters remembers her own potential for violence, its cause and its justification: "'When I was a girl,' said Mrs. Peters, under her breath, 'my kitten—there was a boy took a hatchet, and before my eyes—before I could get there—' She covered her face an instant. 'If they hadn't held me back I would have'— she caught herself, looked upstairs where footsteps were heard, and finished weakly—'hurt him.'"

At the end of the story, Martha Hale articulates the theory of reading behind **"A Jury of Her Peers"**: "We all go through the same things—it's all just a different kind of the same thing! If it weren't—why do you and I *understand*? Why do we *know*—what we know this minute?" Women can read women's texts because they live women's lives; men can not read women's texts because they don't lead women's lives. Yet, of course, the issues are more complicated than this formulation, however true it may be. A clue to our interpretation of Glaspell's text occurs in a passage dealing with Mrs. Peters's struggle to determine how she will read: "It was as if something within her not herself had spoken, and it found in Mrs. Peters something she did not know as herself. 'I know what stillness is,' she said, in a queer, monotonous voice." Obviously, nothing less than Mrs. Peters's concept of self is

at stake in her decision. The self she does not recognize as "herself" is the self who knows what she knows because of the life she has lived. As she reads this life in the story of another woman, she contacts that self from which she has been systematically alienated by virtue of being married to the law and subsequently required to read as a man.

When I was in high school and first introduced to literature as a separate subject of study, I was told that one of the primary reasons people read, and, thus, one of the primary justifications for learning how to read, is to enlarge their frame of reference through encountering experiences that are foreign to them which are not likely to happen in their own lives and, thus, to enrich and complicate their perspective. Since as a young woman reader I was given to read primarily texts about young men, I had no reason to question the validity of this proposition. It was not until I got to college and graduate school and encountered an overwhelmingly male faculty intent on teaching me how to recognize great literature that I began to wonder about the homogeneity of the texts that got defined as "classic." But of course it took feminism to enable me finally to see and understand the extraordinary gap between theory and practice in the teaching of literature as I experienced it. If a white male middle-class literary establishment consistently chooses to identify as great and thus worth reading those texts that present as central the lives of white male middle-class characters, then obviously recognition and reiteration, not difference and expansion, provide the motivation for reading. Regardless of the theory offered in justification, as it is currently practiced within the academy, reading functions primarily to reinforce the identity and perspective which the male teacher/reader brings to the text. Presumably this function is itself a function of the sense of power derived from the experience of perceiving one's self as central, as subject, as literally because literarily the point of view from which the rest of the world is seen. Thus men, controlling the study of literature, define as great those texts that empower themselves and define reading as an activity that serves male interests, for regardless of how many actual readers may be women, within the academy the presumed reader is male.

Outside the academy, of course, women, operating perhaps instinctively on the same understanding of the potential of reading, have tended to find their way to women's texts. One of the most striking experiences of my own teaching career occurred recently, when I taught a graduate course designed to introduce students to the work of nineteenth-century American women writers. Though I had been working on these writers for three years and was engaged at the time in writing about them, I nevertheless arrived in the classroom full of anxiety, for I was still sufficiently a product of the system that had trained me to worry that my students might resent being asked to read literature that was not "classic." I was, however, completely mistaken in my apprehension, for in fact my women students (and the class was almost entirely women) loved the literature of nineteenth-century American women, and at the end of the course they indicated in a variety of ways their intention to keep on reading it. Many of them spoke movingly about the ratification and legitimization of self, indeed the sense of power, they derived from reading these texts and the relief they felt at finding within the academy an opportunity to read something other than texts by and about men. At one class session, however, an interesting phenomenon emerged. My students began describing the various methods they had developed for hiding from husbands, lovers, male professors, employers, and other male graduate students the nature of the texts they were reading. As we began to explore the reasons behind this behavior, we came to understand most immediately how politicized the act of reading is in a sexist culture. For it is not simply the case that men, in determining what is read, wish to provide a certain experience for themselves; it is equally the case that they do not want women to have this experience. Nothing else can explain the intensity and the persistence of male resistance to the inclusion of women writers on reading lists, examination lists, bibliographies, and so forth, where the concept of inclusion is almost always token and at best is an equal sharing of time and space. My students, in playing with the title of E.D.E.N. Southworth's popular novel of 1859 and describing themselves as reading with "a hidden hand," hit on the fact that women's reading of women's novels is not a culturally validated activity. Indeed, to the degree that such reading, by giving women the experience of seeing themselves as central, subject, and point of view, empowers the woman reader, and to the degree that such empowerment contravenes the design of patriarchal culture, women's reading of women's texts is literally treason against the state and of necessity must be a covert and hidden affair.

Our discussion led us to feel closer to nineteenth-century women readers as well as to women writers, for we began to think that we might understand in some essential way why nineteenth-century American women read with such passion, even avidly, the work of their contemporaries, despite the steady stream of warnings delivered to them on the abuses of novel reading. And, playing still further with the implications of "the hidden hand," we began to speculate on the degree to which the reading of women's texts by women might have been and might still be eroticized. For what else might one have to do with a hidden hand besides read? And might not the gratifications of masturbation and the gratifications of reading women's texts be similar for women? In a sexist culture, which has as one of its primary components institutionalized and enforced heterosexuality designed to serve the sexual interests of men, masturbation for women carries with it the potential of putting women in touch with their own bodies, of giving us a knowledge of our flesh which permissible sexual activity does not necessarily provide. Similarly, the reading of women's texts has the potential for giving women a knowledge of the self, for putting us in contact with our real selves, which the reading of male texts can not provide. Which, of course, brings us back to Mrs. Peters and **"A Jury of Her Peers"** and to a final question that the story raises.

Just as the women in the story have the capacity to read as men or as women, having learned of necessity how to recognize and interpret male texts, so are the men in the story presumably educable. Though initially they might not recognize a clue if they saw it, they could be taught its significance, they could be taught to recognize women's texts and to read as women. If this were not the case, the women in the story could leave the text as they find it; but they don't. Instead, they erase the text as they read it. Martha Hale undoes the threads of the quilt that, like the weaving of Philomel, tells the story of Minnie Wright's violation and thus provides the clue to her revenge; Mrs. Peters instinctively creates an alternate story to explain the missing bird and then further fabricates to explain the absent cat; and Mrs. Hale, with the approval of Mrs. Peters, finally hides the dead bird. Thus, we must revise somewhat our initial formulation of the story's point about reading: it is not simply the case that men can not recognize or read women's texts; it is, rather, that they will not. At the end of the story, the county attorney summarizes the situation "incisively": "It's all perfectly clear, except the reason for doing it. But you know juries when it comes to women. If there was some definite thing—something to show. Something to make a story about. A thing that would connect up with this clumsy way of doing it." But why, if it is all so perfectly clear to them, have the men made so little intelligent effort to find that "something" that would convince and convict? Why, in fact, has this same county attorney consistently deflected attention from those details that would provide the necessary clues: "Let's talk about that a little later, Mr. Hale"; "I'd like to talk to you about that a little later, Mrs. Hale." This is the question that **"A Jury of Her Peers"** propounds to its readers, making us ask in turn why it is more important for the men in this story to let one woman get away with murder than to learn to recognize and to read her story?

Part of the answer to this question has already been suggested in the previous discussion. The refusal to recognize women as having stories denies women the experience it ensures for men—namely, reading as a validation of one's reality and reinforcement of one's identity. But there is still more at issue here. Let us return for a moment to that gap between theory and practice which I mentioned in connection with my own introduction to reading. Certainly in theory there is nothing wrong with the idea that one might read to experience a reality different from one's own, to encounter the point of view of another who is other, and thus to broaden one's own perspective and understanding. Indeed, there is much to be said for it, for as Patsy Schweickart has cogently argued in her commentary on an earlier draft of this paper, the extreme anxiety raised by the issue of solipsism in masculine Western thought derives from that pattern of habitually effacing the other, of which the control of textuality is but one manifestation. However, it may well be the case that the gap between theory and practice at issue here has less to do with a need to effect the other than with a need to protect a certain concept of the self. In a sexist culture the interests of men and women are by definition oppositional—what is good for men is bad for women, and vice versa, given the nature of men's definition of their "good" in a sexist context. Inevitably, then, texts produced in a sexist culture will reflect this fact. Thus, texts written by men in such a context will frequently be inimical to women; and, while I would argue that there is no equivalent in the literature of women for the palpable misogyny of much of male literature, nevertheless, as the analysis of **"A Jury of Her Peers"** demonstrates, women's texts frequently present a radical challenge to the premises of men's texts, premises that men rely on to maintain the fictions of their own identity. Thus, when men ask women to read men's texts under the guise of enlarging their experience and perspective, they are in fact asking women to undergo an experience that is potentially inimical to them; and when men insist that men's texts are the only ones worth reading, they are in fact protecting themselves against just such an experience. If we examine **"A Jury of Her Peers"** with this hypothesis in mind, we may find in the story an answer to the question that it propounds. For what is the content of the text that Minnie Wright has written and that the men are so unwilling to read? It is nothing less than the story of men's systematic, institutionalized, and culturally approved violence toward women, and of women's potential for retaliatory violence against men. For the men to find the clue that would convict Minnie Foster Wright, they would have to confront the figure of John Wright. And if they were to confront this figure, they would have to confront as well the limitations of their definition of a "good man," a phrase that encompasses a man's relation to drink, debt, and keeping his word with other men but leaves untouched his treatment of women. And if a man's treatment of women were to figure into the determination of his goodness, then most men would be found not good. Thus, for the men in the story to confront John Wright would mean confronting themselves. In addition, were they to read Minnie Wright's story, they would have to confront the fact that a woman married to a man is not necessarily married to his law, might not in fact see things "just that way," might indeed see things quite differently and even act on those perceptions. They might have to confront the fact that the women of whom they are so casually contemptuous are capable of turning on them. For, of course, in refusing to recognize the story of Minnie Wright, the men also avoid confrontation with the story of Mrs. Hale and Mrs. Peters—they never know what their wives have done alone in that kitchen.

Male violence against women and women's retaliatory violence against men constitute a story that a sexist culture is bent on repressing, for, of course, the refusal to tell this story is one of the major mechanisms for enabling the violence to continue. Within **"A Jury of Her Peers,"** this story is once again suppressed. Mrs. Hale and Mrs. Peters save Minnie Foster Wright's life, but in the process they undo her story, ensuring that it will never have a public hearing. The men succeed in their refusal to recognize the woman's story because the women are willing to let the principle stand in order to protect the particular woman. Thus, if the men are willing to let one woman get away

with murder in order to protect their control of textuality, the women are willing to let the men continue to control textuality in order to save the individual. The consequence of both decisions is the same: Minnie Wright is denied her story and hence her reality (What will her life be like if she does get off ?), and the men are allowed to continue to assume that they are the only ones with stories. So haven't the men finally won?

Glaspell, of course, chooses differently from her characters, for **"A Jury of Her Peers"** does not suppress, but, rather, tells the woman's story. Thus, Glaspell's fiction is didactic in the sense that it is designed to educate the male reader in the recognition and interpretation of women's texts, while at the same time it provides the woman reader with the gratification of discovering, recovering, and validating her own experience. For **"A Jury of Her Peers,"** I would argue, from my own experience in teaching the text and from my discussion with others who have taught it, is neither unintelligible to male readers nor susceptible to a masculinist interpretation. If you can get men to read it, they will recognize its point, for Glaspell chooses to make an issue of precisely the principle that her characters are willing to forgo. But, of course, it is not that easy to get men to read this story. It is surely no accident that **"A Jury of Her Peers"** did not make its way into the college classroom until the advent of academic feminism.

Leonard Mustazza (essay date 1989)

SOURCE: "Generic Translation and Thematic Shift in Susan Glaspell's 'Trifles' and 'A Jury of Her Peers,'" in *Studies in Short Fiction*, Vol. 26, No. 4, Fall, 1989, pp. 489–96.

[*In the following essay, Mustazza maintains that when Glaspell adapted the play* Trifles *into the short story, "A Jury of Her Peers," she changed the focus from the so-called trivial details of women's lives to women's powerlessness in the American legal system.*]

Commentators on Susan Glaspell's classic feminist short story, **"A Jury of Her Peers"** (1917), and the one-act play from which it derives, *Trifles* (1916), have tended to regard the two works as essentially alike. And even those few who have noticed the changes that Glaspell made in the process of generic translation have done so only in passing. In his monograph on Glaspell, Arthur Waterman, who seems to have a higher regard for the story than for the play, suggests that story is a "moving fictional experience" because of the progressive honing of the author's skills, the story's vivid realism owing to her work as a local-color writer for the *Des Moines Daily News,* and its unified plot due to its dramatic origin. More specifically, Elaine Hedges appropriately notes the significance of Glaspell's change in titles from *Trifles,* which emphasizes the supposedly trivial household items with which the women "acquit" their accused peer, to **"A Jury of Her**

Peers," which emphasizes the question of legality. In 1917, Hedges observes, women were engaged in the final years of their fight for the vote, and Glaspell's change in titles thus "emphasizes the story's contemporaneity, by calling attention to its references to the issue of women's legal place in American society." Apart from these and a few other passing remarks, however, critics have chosen to focus on one work or the other. Indeed, thematic criticisms of the respective pieces are virtually indistinguishable, most of these commentaries focusing on the question of assumed "roles" in the works.

On one level, there is good reason for this lack of differentiation. Not only is the overall narrative movement of the works similar, but Glaspell incorporated in the short story virtually every single line of the dialogue from *Trifles.* By the same token, though, she also added much to the short story, which is about twice as long as the play. The nature of these additions is twofold, the first and most obvious being her descriptions of locales, modes of utterance, characters, props, and so on—the kinds of descriptions that the prose writer's form will allow but the dramatist's will not. The other type of alteration is more subtle, and it involves the revisions, embellishments, and redirections that occur when an existent story is retold. When, for instance, a novel is turned into a film or a play, the best that can be said about the generic translation is that it is "faithful," but never is it identical. So it is with **"Jury."** It is certainly faithful to the play, but it is also different in a variety of ways, and it is these differences, which took place in the act of generic translation, that I would like to consider here.

In her article on *Trifles,* Beverly Smith makes an interesting observation. Noting that the women in the play, Mrs. Hale and Mrs. Peters, function as defense counsel for and jury of their accused peer, Minnie Foster-Wright, she goes on to suggest that the men's role, their official capacities notwithstanding, are comparable to that of a Greek Chorus, "the voice of the community's conscience," entering at various points to reiterate their major themes—Minnie's guilt and the triviality of the women's occupations, avocations, and preoccupations. This equation is, I think, quite useful, for the periodic entries, commentaries, and exits of the male characters in both Glaspell works do in fact mark the progressive stages of the narrative, which primarily concerns the women, including the absent Minnie Foster. Though not on stage for the entire drama, as is the Greek Chorus, the men nevertheless function in much the same way, providing commentary and separating the major movements of the narrative. What is more, if we regard the men's exits from the stage as marking these movements, we will recognize the first principal difference between the play and the story—namely, that the latter contains twice as many movements as the former and is therefore necessarily a more developed and complex work.

Trifles opens with Mr. Hale's account of what he found when he arrived at the Wright farm the day before. Of the women themselves, we know almost nothing beyond their general appearances as described in the opening stage directions—that Mrs. Peters, the sheriff's wife, is "a slight wiry woman [with] a thin nervous face"; and that Mrs. Hale, the witness's wife, is larger than Mrs. Peters and "comfortable looking," though now appearing fearful and disturbed as she enters the scene of the crime. Standing close together as they enter the Wrights' home, the women remain almost completely undifferentiated until, some time later, they begin to speak. Thus, Glaspell underscores here the male/female polarities that she will explore in the course of the play.

Her entire narrative technique is different in the prose version. That story begins in Mrs. Hale's disordered kitchen, which will later serve as a point of comparison with the major scene of the story, Mrs. Wright's kitchen. Annoyed at being called away from her housework, she nevertheless agrees to Sheriff Peters' request that she come along to accompany Mrs. Peters, who is there to fetch some personal effects for the jailed woman. Quite unlike the play's opening, which emphasizes the physical closeness of and the attitudinal similarities between the women, **"Jury,"** taking us as it does into Mrs. Hale's thoughts, emphasizes the women's apartness:

> She had met Mrs. Peters the year before at the county fair, and the thing she remembered about her was that *she didn't seem to like the sheriff's wife.* She was small and thin and didn't have a strong voice. Mrs. Gorman, the sheriff's wife before Gorman went out and Peters came in, had a voice that somehow seemed to be backing up the law with every word. But if Mrs. Peters didn't look like a sheriff's wife, Peters made up for it in looking like a sheriff . . . a heavy man with a big voice, who was particularly genial with the law-abiding, as if to make it plain that he knew the difference between criminals and non-criminals. (emphasis added)

Interestingly, for all the added material here, Glaspell omits mention of what the women look like. In fact, we will get no explicit statements on their appearance.

On the other hand, what we do get in this revised opening is much that sharply differentiates the story from the play. In the latter, we are provided with no indication of Mrs. Hale's bad feelings about the sheriff's wife, and, if anything, their close physical proximity leads us to conclude the opposite. Although the women in the story will later assume this same protective stance when they enter the accused's kitchen and then again when the county attorney criticizes Mrs. Wright's kitchen, the movement together there is little more than reflexive. Elaine Hedges has argued that the latter movement together there is little more than reflexive. Elaine Hedges has argued that the latter movement together begins the process of establishing "their common bonds with each other and with Minnie." This may be so of their physical proximity in the play, where no distance is established between the women at the outset, but the story presents a different situation altogether, for any emotional closeness we might infer from their act is undercut by our knowledge of Mrs. Hale's lack of respect for Mrs. Peters, particularly by comparison with her predecessor, Mrs. Gorman.

Ironically, however despite her seeming mismatch with her husband, her lack of corporal "presence," Mrs. Peters turns out to be more suited to her assumed public role than Mrs. Hale had suspected—all too suited, in fact, since she perfectly assumes her male-approved role. "Of course Mrs. Peters is one of us," the county attorney asserts prior to getting on with his investigation of the house, and that statement turns out to be laden with meaning in the story. In *Trifles,* when the men leave to go about their investigative business, the women, we are told, "listen to the men's steps, then look about the kitchen." In **"Jury,"** however, we get much more. Again here, the women stand motionless, listening to the men's footsteps, but this momentary stasis is followed by a significant gesture: "Then, *as if releasing herself from something strange,* Mrs. Hale began to arrange the dirty pans under the sink, which the county attorney's disdainful push of the foot had deranged" (emphasis added). One is prompted here to ask: what is this "something strange" from which she releases herself? Though the actions described in the play and the story are the same, why does Glaspell not include in the stage directions to the play an indication of Mrs. Hale's facial expression?

The answer, I think, lies again in the expanded and altered context of **"Jury,"** where the author continually stresses the distance between the women. If Mrs. Peters is, as the county attorney has suggested, one of "them," Mrs. Hale certainly is not, and she distances herself from her male-approved peer in word and deed. The something strange from which she releases herself is, in this context, her reflexive movement towards Mrs. Peters. Mrs. Hale is, in fact, both extricating herself from the male strictures placed upon all of the women and asserting her intellectual independence. Karen Alkalay-Gut has correctly observed that, to the men, the disorder of Mrs. Wright's kitchen implies her "potential homicidal tendencies, inconceivable in a good wife." For her part, Mrs. Hale is rejecting the men's specious reasoning, complaining about the lawyer's disdainful treatment of the kitchen things and asserting, "I'd hate to have men comin' into my kitchen, snoopin' round and criticizin'," obviously recalling the disorder in her kitchen and resenting the conclusions about her that could be drawn. Lacking that opening scene, the play simply does not resonate so profoundly.

Even more telling is a subtle but important change that Glaspell made following Mrs. Hale's testy assertion. In both the play and the story, Mrs. Peters offers the meek defense, "Of course it's no more than their duty," and then the two works diverge. In *Trifles* Mrs. Peters manages to change the subject. Noticing some dough that Mrs. Wright had been preparing the day before, she says flatly, "she had set bread," and that statement directs Mrs. Hale's attention to the half-done and ruined kitchen chores. In effect, the flow of conversation is mutually directed in the play, and the distance between the women is thus mini-

mized. When she wrote the story, however, Glaspell omitted mention of the bread and instead took us into Mrs. Hale's thoughts, as she does at the beginning of the story:

> She thought of the flour in her kitchen at home—half sifted, half not sifted. She had been interrupted, and had left things half done. What had interrupted Minnie Foster? Why had that work been left half done? She made a move as if to finish it,—unfinished things always bothered her,—and then she glanced around and saw that Mrs. Peters was watching her—and she didn't want Mrs. Peters to get that feeling she got of work begun and then—for some reason—not finished.
>
> "It's a shame about her fruit," she said . . .

Although mention of the ruined fruit preserves is included in the play as well, two significant additions are made in the above passage. First, there is the continual comparison between Mrs. Hale's life and Mrs. Wright's. Second, and more important, we get the clear sense here of Mrs. Hale's suspicion of Mrs. Peters, her not wanting to call attention to the unfinished job for fear that the sheriff's wife will get the wrong idea—or, in this case, the right idea, for the evidence of disturbance, however circumstantial, is something the men may be able to use against Mrs. Wright. In other words, unlike the play, the story posits a different set of polarities, with Mrs. Peters presumably occupying a place within the official party and Mrs. Hale taking the side of the accused against all of them.

We come at this point to a crossroads in the story. Mrs. Hale can leave things as they are and keep information to herself, or she can recruit Mrs. Peters as a fellow "juror" in the case, moving the sheriff's wife away from her sympathy for her husband's position and towards identification with the accused women. Mrs. Hale chooses the latter course and sets about persuading Mrs. Peters to emerge, in Alkalay-Gut's words, "as an individual distinct from her role as sheriff's wife." Once that happens, "her identification with Minnie is rapid and becomes complete."

The persuasive process begins easily but effectively, with Mrs. Hale reflecting upon the change in Minnie Foster Wright over the thirty or so years she has known her—the change, to use the metaphor that Glaspell will develop, from singing bird to muted caged bird. She follows this reminiscence with a direct question to Mrs. Peters about whether the latter thinks that Minnie killed her husband. "Oh, I don't know," is the frightened response in both works, but, as always, the story provides more insight and tension than does the drama. Still emphasizing in her revision the distance between the women, Glaspell has Mrs. Hale believe that her talk of the youthful Minnie has fallen on deaf ears: "Much difference it makes to her whether Minnie Foster had pretty clothes when she was a girl." This sense of the other woman's indifference to such irrelevant trivialities is occasioned not only by Mrs. Hale's persistent belief in the other woman's official role but also by an odd look that crosses Mrs. Peters' face. At second glance, however, Mrs. Hale notices something else that melts her annoyance and undercuts her suspicions about the sheriff's wife: "Then she looked again, and she wasn't so sure; in fact, she hadn't at any time been perfectly sure about Mrs. Peters. She had that shrinking manner, and yet her eyes looked as if they could see a long way into things." Whereas the play shows the women meandering towards concurrence, the short story is here seen to evolve—and part of that evolution, we must conclude, is due to Mrs. Hale's ability to persuade her peer to regard the case from her perspective. The look that she sees in Mrs. Peters' eyes suggests to her that she might be able to persuade her, that the potential for identification is there. Hence, when she asks whether Mrs. Peters thinks Minnie is guilty, the question resonates here in ways the play does not.

Accordingly, Mrs. Hale will become much more aggressive in her arguments hereafter, taking on something of the persuader's hopeful hostility, which, in the case of the story, stands in marked contrast to the hostility she felt for Mrs. Peters' official role earlier. Thus, when Mrs. Peters tries to retreat into a male argument, weakly asserting that "the law is the law," the Mrs. Hale of the short story does not let the remark pass, as the one in Trifles does: "the law is the law—and a bad stove is a bad stove. How'd you like to cook on this?" Even she, however, is startled by Mrs. Peters' immediate response to her homey analogy and *ad hominem* attack: "A person gets discouraged—and loses heart," Mrs. Peters says—"That look of seeing . . . through a thing to something else" back on her face.

As far as I am concerned, the addition of this passage is the most important change that Glaspell made in her generic translation. Having used this direct personal attack and having noted the ambivalence that Mrs. Peters feels for her role as sheriff's wife, Mrs. Hale will now proceed to effect closure of the gap between them—again, a gap that is never this widely opened in *Trifles*. Now Mrs. Hale will change her entire mode of attack, pushing the limits, doing things she hesitated doing earlier, assailing Mrs. Peters whenever she lapses into her easy conventional attitudes. For instance, when Mrs. Peters objects to Mrs. Hale's repair of a badly knitted quilt block—in effect, tampering with circumstantial evidence of Minnie's mental disturbance the day before—Mrs. Hale proceeds to do it anyway. As a measure of how much she has changed, we have only to compare this act with her earlier hesitation to finish another chore for fear of what Mrs. Peters might think. She has no reason to be distrustful of Mrs. Peters any longer, for the process of identification is now well underway.

That identification becomes quite evident by the time the women find the most compelling piece of circumstantial evidence against Mrs. Wright—the broken bird cage and the dead bird, its neck wrung and its body placed in a pretty box in Mrs. Wright's sewing basket. When the men notice the cage and Mrs. Hale misleadingly speculates that a cat may have been at it, it is Mrs. Peters who confirms the matter. Asked by the county attorney whether a cat was on the premises, Mrs. Peters—fully aware that there

is no cat and never has been—quickly and evasively replies, "Well, not *now*. . . . They're superstitious, you know; they leave." Not only is Mrs. Peters deliberately lying here, but, more important, she is assuming quite another role from the one she played earlier. Uttering a banality, she plays at being the shallow woman who believes in superstitions, thus consciously playing one of the roles the men expect her to assume and concealing her keen intellect from them, her ability to extrapolate facts from small details.

From this point forward, the play and the short story are essentially the same. Mrs. Hale will continue her persuasive assault, and Mrs. Peters will continue to struggle inwardly. The culmination of this struggle occurs when, late in the story, the county attorney says that "a sheriff's wife is married to the law," and she responds, "Not—just that way." In **"Jury,"** however, this protest carries much greater force than it does in Trifles for the simple reason that it is a measure of how far Mrs. Peters has come in the course of the short story.

Appropriately enough, too, Mrs. Hale has the final word in both narratives. Asked derisively by the county attorney what stitch Mrs. Wright had been using to make her quilt, Mrs. Hale responds with false sincerity, "We call it—knot it, Mr. Henderson." Most critics have read this line as an ironic reference to the women's solidarity at this point. That is quite true, but, as I have been suggesting here, the progress towards this solidarity varies subtly but unmistakably in the two narratives. Whereas *Trifles*, opening as it does with the women's close physical proximity, reveals the dichotomy between male and female concepts of justice and social roles, **"A Jury of Her Peers"** is much more concerned with the separateness of the women themselves and their self-injurious acquiescence in male-defined roles. Hence, in her reworking of the narrative, Glaspell did much more than translate the material from one genre to another. Rather, she subtly changed its theme, and, in so doing, she wrote a story that is much more interesting, resonant, and disturbing than the slighter drama from which it derives.

Sherri Hallgren (essay date 1995)

SOURCE: "'The Law is the Law—and a Bad Stove is a Bad Stove': Subversive Justice and Layers of Collusion in 'A Jury of Her Peers,'" in *Violence, Silence, and Anger: Women's Writings as Transgression*, edited by Deirdre Lashgari, University Press of Virginia, 1995, pp. 203–18.

[*In the following essay, Hallgren demonstrates how readers of "A Jury of Her Peers" are meant to collude with Glaspell-as-narrator in the same ways the female characters band together to mete out justice.*]

Susan Glaspell's 1917 short story **"A Jury of Her Peers"** has been quietly stunning women readers since its reappearance in a feminist anthology nearly twenty years ago. A novelist and playwright who won a Pulitzer Prize in 1931 for her novel *Alison's House,* Glaspell had been all but forgotten until her story was reprinted in Lee R. Edwards and Arlyn Diamond's *American Voices, American Women.* On the surface a detective story about two Iowa women who unintentionally solve a crime right under the noses of their officious husbands, who cannot see the very clues they're searching for, the plot of **"A Jury of Her Peers"** is an in-joke among women, who recognize the narrative's clues.

When the story opens, a farm woman, Martha Hale, is being called from her bread baking to accompany her husband, John, along with the sheriff and his wife and the county attorney, on a trip to the neighboring farmhouse where Minnie Foster Wright has been arrested for the murder of her husband. When John Hale had gone to see Wright the day before, Minnie had said her husband could not speak to him "'cause he's dead," and explained further that "he died of a rope around his neck."[1] Today the small party that has come to Minnie's house to investigate the crime consists of three men and two women: Sheriff Peters, Mr. Henderson the county attorney, and John Hale, along with Mrs. Peters, who has come to get some things for Minnie, who is being held in the county jail, and Mrs. Hale, who has come to keep Mrs. Peters company. The men are looking for the crucial piece of evidence: "the motive—the thing that shows anger or sudden feeling."

While the men search the barn and the upstairs bedroom where Wright was found hanging, the women are left to themselves in the kitchen and the parlor. Nervously waiting, they discover their own bits of evidence to solve the crime that has taken place. Essentially, Minnie Foster Wright has killed her husband because he has strangled her canary. At the end of the story the women hide the dead bird—the piece of evidence that would certainly convict Minnie Wright—from their husbands, the law. These are the "facts" of the story. In one sense, then, the story functions as a "who done it" battle between the sexes, and its initial delight comes from seeing the "little women" outsmart—out-intuit—the sheriff and their husbands.

Critics have noted the qualities of feminist mystery writing obvious in the text. Sandra Gilbert and Susan Gubar place this story in a tradition continued by Agatha Christie's Miss Jane Marple, in that the women "understand the crime even while they implicitly vindicate the woman who committed it."[2] Annette Kolodny suggests that "the intended emphasis [in **"Jury"**] is the inaccessibility of female meaning to male interpretation," pointing out that the men in the story lack the "proper interpretive strategies" to unravel the motive.[3] She terms this blindness to a set of details "sex-coding," and suggests that "lacking familiarity with the women's imaginative universe, that universe within which their acts are signs, the men in these stories can neither read nor comprehend the meaning of the women closest to them—and this in spite of a common language."[4]

It's Lucy and Ethel triumphing over Ricky and Fred, and their solving the murder and then not telling is wickedly satisfying.[5] Kolodny calls it a happy ending. But it's not a secret shopping spree that is at stake here; a woman has murdered her husband and will get away with it. This initial imbalance—that the life of a man, a woman's husband, even, could be equal to that of a pet bird—increases what should be the social outrage at the crime they cover up. At its core, this story is radically subversive in all it implies about the different experiences, modes of interpretation, and potential for power in men and women. As the title suggests, what Glaspell explores in **"A Jury of Her Peers"** is a parallel system of justice, one in which women can be judged according to context and truly by their peers. It is in this way an exploration into female ethics. Even more subversive, though, it reveals a vigilante form of justice, one enacted in secret, in unspoken collusion between members of a group who speak the same language in a way that eschews language. But it is not simply the plot that makes this story compelling. Its subversive power comes, even more importantly, from what Glaspell does with the narrative, which enacts between the narrator-Glaspell and her readers the same collusion she depicts between her characters.

The first scene in the Wrights' home sets up the differing perspectives of the women and the men in the story. The three men who represent the prosecuting forces of law—Sheriff Peters, who arrested Minnie and will conduct this investigation; Mr. Henderson, the county attorney who will prosecute; and John Hale, the testifying witness—investigate the scene of the crime. Glaspell sets these men up as figures of authority and expertise—Sheriff Peters "made it plain he knew the difference between criminals and non-criminals"—only to undermine them. They don't see, don't understand, don't know. They come into the story only briefly at the beginning, at the end, and once in the middle, to stroll through the kitchen chitchatting pieces of legality and patronizing the women, saying there's "nothing here but kitchen things," and giving "a little laugh for the insignificance of kitchen things." That they are looking specifically for female anger, the clue to the motive for murder, and are completely unable to see it, is the story's biggest and most resonant joke.

The county attorney, more derisive than dismissive, complains, "Dirty towels! not much of a housekeeper, would you say, ladies?" and, with a disdainful and aggressive gesture that will contrast with the women's treatment of the objects in Minnie's house, he kicks some pans under the sink. In the same way that the man of law assumes he has an infallible sense of who is and isn't a criminal, this prosecutor presumes to judge Minnie, acting as an arbiter of excellence in the realm that is appropriately hers. (Elaine Hedges's research on the circumstances of female farm life and work, documenting the hours of labor required of a farmwife to produce among other items in the week's laundry, one clean towel, makes even clearer to modern readers what the impact of this identification would have been for the farmwives, pointing out the enor-

mity of the over-sight, as well as of the insult and ignorance, of the sheriff's comment.)[6] His remark invites the
other two housewives to collude with him in his estimate,
but they remain silent.

When Mrs. Hale remembers that Minnie had worried the
evening before about her fruit, Mr. Hale, the expert witness exclaims, "Well, can you beat the woman! Held for
murder and worrying about her preserves!" With "good-
natured superiority," he says, "women are used to worrying over trifles." Whether arrogant, hostile, or patronizing,
the men clearly feel they are in control and that the wom-
en's presence on this mission is superfluous.

As they leave the kitchen, Henderson says it will be all
right to leave the women unattended because "of course
Mrs. Peters is one of us"; he cautions her to keep her "eye
out . . . for anything that might be of use. No telling; you
women might come upon a clue to the motive—and that's
the thing we need." As he leaves, Mr. Hale musingly says,
"but would the women know a clue if they did come upon
it?".

The women, as it turns out, do keep their eyes open and it
is with their eyes that they conduct their own investigation
and carry out a sentence; the result, however, will be a
collaboration with rather than a condemnation of Minnie's
revolt, as they too betray their husbands. When the men
leave, the narrator stays with Martha Hale and Mrs. Peters,
in the territory that is Minnie's: the kitchen and the parlor.
Without meaning to, and only because they unavoidably
find themselves literally in Minnie Foster's place, the two
women come to understand the crime, find the clues, including the dead canary, the all-important piece of evidence that supplies the motive for the killing, and come to
their own verdict, reading the details of Minnie's life that
tell her story.

In the same way that the house is its own separate world
from the world of the barn, the system of those who live
in the house is different from that of the world of the men.
The sheriff and his men are interlopers in this territory,
and their methods do not help them understand what happened and why. Because they cannot "see" the significance of the women's lives, they do not look for clues in
Mrs. Wright's life, and therefore they literally cannot see
the clues to the motive for the killing—the one crucial detail needed for a murder conviction in their legal system.
The women's method is intuitive and empathetic. Martha
Hale's first comment after the men have left is, "I'd hate
to have men comin' into my kitchen . . . snoopin' round
and criticizin'." She recognizes the signs of "things half
done," in a sugar bucket with its lid off and a half-filled
bag beside it, and thinks of her own kitchen, her own task
interrupted. What the men interpret as inept housekeeping
Mrs. Hale is able to discern as a process interrupted, as
her own process of bread baking has been interrupted to
come on this mission. Her identification with (as opposed
to Henderson's judgment of) Minnie's activity tells her
something.

Later she finds an erratically stitched quilt block and feels
"queer, as if the distracted thoughts of the woman who
had perhaps turned to it to try to quiet herself were communicating themselves to her." This is passive investigation, possible only by someone who not only can understand sewing but also can get into the mind of the woman
who sews. This whole scene is filled with examples of the
two women's indulging in the pathetic fallacy as they read
Minnie's life. The dingy red rocker "didn't look in the
least like Minnie Foster"; the house itself looks "lonesome
this cold March morning . . . and the poplar trees around
it were lonesome-looking trees." Mrs. Hale remembers
Minnie Foster, "kind of like a bird herself," "singing in
the choir."

Unlike Mrs. Hale, Mrs. Peters is not moved by memories
of Minnie Foster, nor is she disturbed by the physical disorder of the house. What ties her to Minnie is similar experience, thinking of the work gone to waste when the
preserve jars break. Mrs. Peters decides to take quilt blocks
for Minnie to work on in jail, and it is this gesture of
kindness to the other woman, and not the legal investigation with the intent to convict, that turns up the telling evidence of motive, for in the sewing box they find a dead
bird, its neck broken, lovingly wrapped in silk and placed
in a pretty box. Mrs. Peters, horrified, remembers "When I
was a girl . . . my kitten—there was a boy took a hatchet,
and before my eyes—before I could get there . . . If they
hadn't held me back I would have . . . hurt him," conjuring both the specter of violence in even a small boy and
her own potential for violent retribution.

All along, Mrs. Peters, wife of the sheriff, has reminded
Mrs. Hale that "the law is the law." It is not until she identifies with Minnie that she has the resolve to join with
Mrs. Hale in covering up the crime. When Mrs. Hale suggests how still it would have been "if there had been years
and years of—nothing, then a bird to sing to you, it would
be awful—still—after the bird was still," Glaspell notes
that "it was as if something within her not herself had spoken, and it found in Mrs. Peters something she did not
know as herself." That something in women that finds itself in other women is making the case, without saying it
outright, that Minnie's crime is justifiable.

Mrs. Peters responds with a memory of her isolation on a
homestead in Dakota, when her baby died. Although she
falters at this point in her reverie, saying, "The law has
got to punish crime, Mrs. Hale," what has been building
for her as well as for Martha Hale is a sense of unity with
Minnie. In identifying with Minnie Foster, they break the
principle of objectivity in crime detection. They are slowly
allowing their values of what constitutes life to enter into
their judgment. At one point Mrs. Hale says, "It seems
kind of sneaking: locking her up in town and coming out
here to get her own house to turn against her!" again per-
sonifying a housewife's house; and Mrs. Peters counters,
"But Mrs. Hale, the law is the law." The subtext to the entire conversation is a debate about the ethics of murder, a
question that in this case is not abstract; they are verging
on being accomplices.

Caught in a moment of trying to work Minnie's stove (the meaning here is probably heightened if we think of March in Iowa before central heating), Mrs. Hale responds, "The law is the law—and a bad stove is a bad stove." Again without saying so explicitly, she proposes an equality of values and perspectives: the patriarchal, abstract system of justice that the men in the room above them represent, and the system into which the women themselves are slowly, literally feeling their way.

At this point, they put on trial John Wright and the life-draining barrenness of living with him. When Mrs. Peters observes that the townfolk considered Wright a "good man," Mrs. Hale grimly concedes that "he didn't drink, and kept his word as well as most . . . and paid his debts. But he was a hard man . . . like a raw wind that gets to the bone." For these wives, a husband is indeed the climate in which they must live. She notes that he wouldn't have liked the bird, "a thing that sang. She used to sing. He killed that too." At this moment, when Mrs. Hale superimposes the image of Minnie onto that of the strangled bird, she names what Wright, in his enforced silence and poverty, has done to Minnie—"killed"—thus indicting not her crime but his. Seen in this way, Minnie's act is not only retribution for the twisted neck of her bird but also revenge for the loss of the one thing that brought contact to her life.

Essentially, **"A Jury of Her Peers"** asks us to understand and to condone the murder of a man for the murder of a canary; or at least these are the "facts" as the sheriff and county attorney would see them. These are certainly what the facts would be in a court of law, and, as Mrs. Peters has remembered her husband saying, things don't look good for Minnie Foster Wright. More specifically, we are to see how these two deaths are equivalent—that of a husband and that of a pet.

While the official police investigation has been going on in the upstairs bedroom and out in the barn, literally and figuratively both above and beyond the scope of the women's concerns, the narrative point of view has stayed with the women in the shabby and cold farmhouse kitchen, as alienated as these farmwives from the men who have appeared only once to joke about the quilt blocks, asking if they thought Minnie had intended to "knot it or quilt it." Because the narrative voice has kept the reader in the same room with these women, moving as close as possible to their unspoken thoughts, the reader has done the same sympathetic exploration of Minnie's wretched, lonely life. The legal case the story makes is the same as the women's, and it is presented seductively rather than ironically, persuading us to become part of the sympathetic jury of Minnie Foster Wright's peers.

And yet, in real legal terms, the truth is that a woman has killed her husband and may not be prosecuted. In contemplating their cover-up, Mrs. Hale and Mrs. Peters are about to overturn the system not simply of justice but of conventional values, instituting a female system of ethics for that of the patriarchy.

Carol Gilligan's work on women's morality suggests that women handle the inevitable aggression in the world very differently from the system of laws and regulations our patriarchal society has created. Gilligan proposes that "if aggression is tied, as women perceive, to the fracture of human connection, then the activities of care . . . are the activities that make the social world safe, by avoiding isolation and preventing aggression rather than by seeking rules to limit its extent." "In this light," she argues, "aggression appears no longer as an unruly impulse that must be contained but rather as a signal of a fracture of connection, the sign of a failure of relationship."[7]

Mrs. Peters and Mrs. Hale, then, in their empathy and their desire to help Minnie Wright—their "activities of care"—are doing more to "make the social world safe" than are the sheriff and attorney who seek to see Minnie punished. Also, if fracture of connection is the dangerous activity, then Wright's "crime" in this female version of an ordered and safe world is, first, his isolation and emotional abandonment of his wife, and, finally, his destruction of what did constitute her connection with something that would communicate with her—her canary. When Wright kills "the singing" in Minnie, he has fractured connection, which, according to Gilligan, is what makes life meaningful and safe for women; in this system of values, then, this is indeed a heinous crime: Wright is clearly wrong.

Gilligan also studies the ways in which women judge others. In describing the reactions and justifications of one participant in her study as she makes a moral choice, Gilligan says, "She ties morality to the understanding that arises from the experience of relationship, since she considers the capacity to 'understand what someone else is experiencing' as the prerequisite for moral response." In generalizing about women's ability to judge, she cites studies indicating that "the moral judgments of women differ from those of men in the greater extent to which women's judgments are tied to feelings of empathy and compassion and are concerned with the resolution of real as opposed to hypothetical dilemmas." For Mrs. Hale, the law may be the law, but in Minnie Foster Wright's case, that rocker and that bad stove, not to mention her bird, are the real facts of the case and the details that guide her judgment.

Mrs. Hale and Mrs. Peters don't stop in their indictment of Minnie's husband; they judge themselves as well. Gilligan explains that "although independent assertion in judgment and action is considered to be the hallmark of adulthood, it is rather in their care and concern for others that women have both judged themselves and been judges." Each time Mrs. Hale uncovers another aspect of Minnie's dismal life she is pained by the thought that she had not come to visit her more often; perhaps if Minnie had been less lonely she might also have been less desperate. Her guilt overcomes her when she invokes the young Minnie Foster, "when she wore a white dress with blue ribbons, and stood up there in the choir and sang." Glaspell continues the narrative to explain: "The picture of that girl, the fact that she had lived neighbor to that girl for twenty years, and had let her die for lack of life, was suddenly more than she could bear. "Oh, I *wish* I'd come over here once in a while!" she cried. "That was a crime! That was a crime! Who's going to punish that?"

Again Martha Hale uses the term "death" to describe what Minnie's life has become, and she blames herself for having let Minnie "die." Her understanding of the crime is that Minnie has died and that physically and emotionally harsh living can indeed kill someone. In these terms, Minnie was already dead before she murdered her husband.

Martha Hale concludes, "I might 'a' *known* she needed help! I tell you, it's *queer*, Mrs. Peters. We live close together, and we live far apart. We all go through the same things—it's all just a different kind of the same thing! If it weren't—why do you and I *understand*? Why do we *know*—what we know this minute?" The "we" in this passage can only be female, for it is evident in this story that the men are not "going through the same things" that their wives are. It is because women "all go through the same things—just a different kind of the same thing" that they understand what they do about Minnie Foster Wright. The sheriff and the county attorney and even farmer Lewis Hale do not understand the life of this house, and so they do not "know" and "understand" what Mrs. Peters and Mrs. Hale do. At this moment, Martha Hale understands the bonds that tie her to Minnie and to Mrs. Peters; what she understands as well is that their knowledge cannot be spoken aloud.

Their entire investigation—their coming to figure out how Minnie had been interrupted in filling her sugar bucket probably when Wright killed her bird; that then in anger she had killed him in a way that matched his strangulation of the canary (and his metaphoric "strangling" of her singing, or the "life" in her); then had tried to calm herself by stitching on her log cabin quilt, producing the uneven stitches—has come about not through direct conversation and statement but rather through allusion and insinuation. Susan Lanser cites **"A Jury of Her Peers"** as an example of a text that demonstrates women's ability to speak in a "double voice," two women protecting a third "from a conviction for murder by communicating in 'women's language' under the watchful but unseeing eyes of the Law."[8]

In the following passage, Glaspell enacts her characters' "double voice" when Mrs. Peters points out to Martha Hale the badly stitched quilt block:

> "The sewing," said Mrs. Peters, in a troubled way. "All the rest of them have been so nice and even—but—this one. Why it looks as if she didn't know what she was about."
>
> Their eyes met—something flashed to life, passed between them; then as if with an effort, they seemed to pull away from each other. A moment Mrs. Hale sat there, her hands folded over that sewing which was so

unlike all the rest of the sewing. Then she had pulled a knot and drawn the threads.

> "Oh, what are you doing, Mrs. Hale?" asked the sheriff's wife, startled.
>
> "Just pulling out a stitch or two that's not sewed very good," said Mrs. Hale mildly.
>
> "I don't think we ought to touch things," Mrs. Peters said, a little helplessly.
>
> "I'll just finish up this end," answered Mrs. Hale, still in that matter-of-fact fashion.

The way they are acting and what they are saying are in direct opposition to the understanding they achieve when their eyes meet. Mrs. Hale is "mild" and "matter-of-fact" and just casually fixing a few stitches. What they both know is that she is destroying evidence and that she shouldn't be. Mrs. Peters, though not physically assisting, nevertheless colludes with this action, as her protestation is "a little helpless." Even the narrative voice averts its eyes, pretending not to see the action itself, when Mrs. Hale "had pulled" a knot and drawn the threads, the verb tense shifting from past tense to past perfect.

After they have found the bird the women have another of their coded talks:

> "I wonder how it would seem," Mrs. Hale at last began, as if feeling her way over strange ground—"never to have had any children around?" Her eyes made a slow sweep of the kitchen, as if seeing what that kitchen had meant through all the years. "No, Wright wouldn't like the bird," she said after that—"a thing that sang. She used to sing. He killed that too." Her voice tightened.
>
> Mrs. Peters moved uneasily.
>
> "Of course we don't know who killed the bird."
>
> "I knew John Wright," was Mrs. Hale's answer.
>
> "It was an awful thing was done in this house that night, Mrs. Hale," said the sheriff's wife. "Killing a man while he slept—slipping a thing round his neck that choked the life out of him."
>
> Mrs. Hale's hand went out to the bird-cage.
>
> "His neck. Choked the life out of him."
>
> "We don't *know* who killed him," whispered Mrs. Peters wildly. We don't *know*."

When Mrs. Peters, here called "the sheriff's wife," protests that they don't "know" who killed the bird or who killed Wright, she is speaking in terms of the legal system. Of course, they have not actually witnessed either event and so they do not technically, legally "know" for sure. But they have witnessed the life in the house; Martha Hale's response that she "knows" John Wright asserts her own intuitive interpretation of justice as well as interposing her own sense of what it is to "know" something, as when she asks, "Why is it we know what we know?" Mrs. Peters is "wild," of course, because she uses "know" in both senses, the double identification utterly upsetting her; what is at stake is the possibility that Minnie's murder is justified.

In the same way that their investigation has proceeded by allusion, their verdict is passed without words. What is interesting here is that neither woman has ever stated the case directly: "Wright had been awful to live with alone for twenty years, Minnie killed him, and the dead bird is the evidence that would supply a motive and convict her for the crime. We don't want her caught, therefore we will help her. What we are doing is of course, illegal. Nevertheless, we are women, we understand this, we too are guilty of letting life go untended. We will never tell what we know." The most direct they have been with language is to ask: *"Why do we know what we know?"*

Mrs. Hale and Mrs. Peters, married to the men they're married to, and in the house for the purpose that they are—to gather evidence to convict Minnie Foster Wright of murder—cannot speak what they know, for to speak would move them into the discourse of a system of rules they are by their silence and actions breaking. If they never say it aloud, then indeed, it is not public fact that they know who killed John Wright. For them to state explicitly what they know and what they could do would place them in the realm of spoken, public discourse, the world of convention, the patriarchal, male world. Further, they also do not dare to speak the truth about the crime because to speak it would disqualify the alternative set of values they are using to judge the situation and decide upon the appropriate action. Speaking the truth would bring their intuitive and feminine understanding out into the world that is structured according to the male perspective and explained in the language that is used to maintain that structure. There is no room in the legal system, or in the patriarchal system of the world that has created that system, for justifying a woman's murder of her husband on the grounds of pet-ricide and neglect.

And yet the women, who have felt Minnie's life through identification and through what they know of their own lives, understand and exonerate her and take action to protect her by hiding the evidence. Their reading of this situation and their intended action make sense according to their shared values but fly in the face of conventional, patriarchal morals. To speak what they know would bring them face to face with the subversive nature of their withholding of evidence. They have been struggling with their consciences all along, and it is only when they recognize and acknowledge that their "we" knows and understands something that is at odds with the system of their husbands that they decide to take an action that unites them with each other and against the legal system. As long as they remain "silent" they remain in the female realm and are not bound by the justice system in the patriarchal land. Thus they use language indirectly, to imply and suggest; the real communication between them happens with their eyes, or through their bodies.

When Mrs. Hale and Mrs. Peters, relative strangers, are in the kitchen listening to Mr. Hale's descriptions of the day

before and he excuses their concern for Minnie's frozen jam jars by saying, "Oh, well . . . women are used to worrying over trifles," Glaspell notes that "the two women moved a little closer together. Neither of them spoke." This unconscious gesture physically allies the two women and prefigures the bond that will build between them as the story progresses.

Told to "look for clues" by the unseeing eyes of the law, the women always use their eyes to read the details of the situation. Martha Hale's "eye was caught" by a dishtowel on the table, and it is as if "her mind tripped on something; her "eye was held" by the half-filled sugar bucket; and Minnie's life becomes clear to her when "her eyes made a slow sweep of the kitchen" and it is as if she could "see what that kitchen had meant" through the years.

Mrs. Hale reads Mrs. Peters' reactions with her eyes as well. She notes that Mrs. Peters' eyes "looked as if they could see a long way into things," and later, when they hear the men's footsteps above them, Martha Hale notes that "that look of seeing into things, of seeing through a thing to something else, was in the eyes of the sheriff's wife now." These two women use their eyes to understand what has happened, and they also use them to communicate what they are really thinking. They use verbal discourse to "tell it slant" or to disguise the truth they relay through their glances.

When they notice the irregular stitching on the quilt block, Glaspell notes that "their eyes met—something flashed to life, passed between them; then, as if with an effort, they seemed to pull away from each other." When they find the mangled birdcage, "again their eyes met—startled, questioning, apprehensive. For a moment neither spoke nor stirred." And when they come to realize that Wright killed Minnie's canary, Glaspell says, "again the eyes of the two women met—this time clung together in a look of dawning comprehension, of growing horror."

In the same way that the two women move physically closer to each other in response to the men's derision early in the story, they move together through their gazes psychically and emotionally as they uncover Minnie's story. The language Glaspell uses to describe this collusion is nearly erotic. When their eyes meet, "something flashes to life between them" and it is "with an effort" that they "seem to pull away." Later, when their eyes meet they "cling together," and, when the men enter the room, the women's eyes "found one another." The bonding that takes place between them goes beyond the battle-of-the-sexes taking of sides that initially delights us in this story. This is a profound re-identification process. Both these women cast their allegiance with another woman and with each other, implicitly breaking the bonds of loyalty they have had with their husbands.

In fact, it is at the end of the story when the county attorney (who had at the beginning called Mrs. Peters "one of us") suggests that she is "married to the law" that Mrs. Peters takes action to align herself with the other women, in effect divorcing the law. In prose that is rather more elegant than the rest of this farm-simple story, suggesting that the voice and point of view are Glaspell's rather than those of her characters, Glaspell describes their final decision:

> Again—for one final moment—the two women were alone in that kitchen.
>
> Martha Hale sprang up, her hands tight together, looking at that other woman, with whom it [their decision] rested. At first she could not see her eyes, for the sheriff's wife had not turned back since she turned away at that suggestion of being married to the law. But now Mrs. Hale made her turn back. Her eyes made her turn back. Slowly, unwillingly, Mrs. Peters turned her head until her eyes met the eyes of the other woman. There was a moment when they held each other in a steady, burning look in which there was no evasion or flinching. Then Martha Hale's eyes pointed the way to the basket in which was hidden the thing that would make certain the conviction of the other woman—that woman who was there with them all through that hour.

There has been no discussion about this between them, only this slow, tentative identification and bonding, signified by their gazes. The images of physical positioning and of eyes as emblematic of the female perspective come together in this final visioning of the truth. Mrs. Hale's eyes "make" Mrs. Peters turn to her, and in this moment "they held each other in a steady, burning look in which there was no evasion or flinching"; this is a depiction of rare honesty and truth and it certainly transcends the sense of "knowing" the women have with their husbands. If female connection is, as Gilligan suggests, the crucial element of women's psychology, then Minnie, the woman who was not there and yet who had been "there with them through that hour" becomes a third party to this intimate bonding.

It is then that Mrs. Peters decides to "do it"; she rushes forward and tries to put the box holding the dead bird into her handbag. When she discovers it won't fit, Mrs. Hale snatches the box from her as the men enter the room and places it safely in her coat pocket. At the story's end, the evidence showing motive has been hidden or destroyed, and presumably Minnie Foster Wright will go free. Nobody but them is any wiser. At the story's end, there are three men who are even more ignorant than they were at the beginning of the story, and there are three women who know everything. And one of them will go free—the woman who murdered her husband.

Overall, this seems a moment of triumph for the women. Some critics, however, disagree, casting it as a Pyrrhic victory, if any. Carolyn Heilbrun has commented that students reading this story in a class on women's narratives "saw the absence of any narrative that could take the women past their moment of revelation and support their bid for freedom from the assigned script."[9] Judith Fetterley also expresses the frustration that "the women are willing to let the men continue to control textuality in order to

save the individual. . . . Minnie Wright is denied her story and hence her reality (What will her life be like if she does get off ?), and the men are allowed to continue to assume that they are the only ones with stories. So haven't the men finally won?"[10]

Perhaps we should concede that in this case, male superiority and the presumptions of the patriarchy go unchallenged in any overt sense; the women keep silent about what they know. But that is within the level of the story of the text, and even there a murderess is going free. In the world outside the text, however, the story seems even more subversive because of this intact silence. The women in the story have not had to discuss their decisions, their reasoning, their rationale. They uncovered evidence, weighed it, and passed a sentence that exonerates Minnie, indicts the men's tradition of justice, and asserts the validity of their own assessments of their power. The women use the men's assumptions, their language, against them, to free one of their own, breaking marriage bonds and social convention.

The point of the story is not what the women know, but how they know it. It is not that the women knew to look in the kitchen and were able to find that misstitched quilt block, the canary with its broken neck, the half-mixed flour, nor is it merely that they can make the logical leap that a half-finished job indicates disruption, that faulty sewing indicates nervousness, and that the dead bird gives a reason for anger and retaliation. What they know is the thing they are referring to when they say "Why do we know—what we know?" Mrs. Hale has exclaimed, "We all go through the same things—it's all just a different kind of the same thing! If it weren't—why do you and I *understand*?"

They have brought to bear an identification based on similar experiences with Minnie Foster; the witness they bear is personal, experiential, culturally female. And further, they know that for all the not always exactly good-natured joking the men do about women's place, women's difference, they really don't know the half of it. The men in the story truly believe that a woman is married to the law, that *Mrs.* Hale and *Mrs.* Peters are essentially bonded to their husbands, and, through their husbands, will owe allegiance to the patriarchal structure of the world. All this is what the women have quietly turned upside down.

Fetterley has pointed out that Glaspell does not keep silent as her characters do, saying that **"A Jury of Her Peers"** does not suppress, but, rather, tells the woman's story" and suggesting that it "is didactic in the sense that it is designed to educate the male reader in the recognition and interpretation of women's texts." And it does, to the extent that all readers know what the men in the story do not: that official representatives of patriarchal justice in this text missed the evidence, the criminal, and the cover-up. The men in the story do not know, as the reader does, that there is a secret between the women. Given that the story stops there, though, the point is also that none of us knows where the women will go from here—what they will now do, knowing this secret, and knowing that they know it. At this moment Glaspell's female characters have a kind of power that is perhaps more subversive because it is circumscribed by the silence of women's shared knowledge. Nothing any of them has said is actionable. Nor, significantly, is anything the narrator has said.

The truly subversive nature of this text is not that it records the acts of the women, nor that it reveals their manner of acting without once uttering an incriminating word, but that Glaspell has used language to create the same collusive bond between her narrative and her readers; to the end, Glaspell's narrator has never admitted anything that the characters have not. In merely recording the enactment of this alternative form of justice, she shows a female shared experience that is not articulated, perhaps not articulable. What it is is the full resonance of their question: why do we know what we know?—which is of course in the text most immediately a question about knowing why Minnie has killed her husband. But as the story itself shows, there is a shared female experience of life that goes beyond the facts of spending more time in the kitchen than in the barn and knowing multiple methods of quilting. The shared experience is of living in a culture where those in power "laugh at the insignificance of kitchen things" and the question, "would women know a clue if they saw one?" brings a laugh.

Women reading the story, if they identify with the circumstances of the women's lives in the text, will share as well the insights of the characters about the bonds between women and their lariatlike facility with language and subtext. The story ends with a pun on the words "knot-it," which is the women's response to the attorney when he says "facetiously, 'at least we found out that she was not going to quilt it. She was going to—what is it you call it, ladies?'"

The women intentionally call up the knot of Minnie's noose, which brings unnervingly to mind the image of all those farm women knotting hundreds of knots daily in the fabric of their lives (how many necks could those knots noose?) and is also a pun on "not-it." To the patronizing of the male legal authorities, to the daily strangulations of husbands, these women's actions shout, as do today's teenagers, "Not!" With this repudiation, they are restitching the faulty fabric of life, as Mrs. Hale explains, "replacing bad sewing with good."

Notes

1. Susan Glaspell, "A Jury of Her Peers," in *American Voices, American Women*, ed. Lee R. Edwards and Arlyn Diamond, 363. All further references to this source will be cited parenthetically in the text.

2. Sandra M. Gilbert and Susan Gubar, *No Man's Land*, 1:91.

3. Annette Kolodny, "A Map for Rereading," 464.

4. *Ibid.*, 463.

5. Lucy, Ethel, Ricky, and Fred were characters in "I Love Lucy," a television situation comedy popular in the United States from the early 1950s.

6. See Elaine Hedges, "Small Things Reconsidered."

7. Carol Gilligan, *In a Different Voice*, 43.

8. Susan S. Lanser, "Toward a Feminist Narratology," 618.

9. Carolyn G. Heilbrun, *Writing a Woman's Life*, 42.

10. Judith Fetterley, "Reading about Reading," 154.

Elaine Hedges (essay date 1995)

SOURCE: "Small Things Reconsidered: 'A Jury of Her Peers,'" in *Susan Glaspell: Essays on Her Theater and Fiction*, edited by Linda Ben-Zvi, The University of Michigan Press, 1995, pp. 49–67.

[*In the excerpt below, first published in 1986, Hedges reconstructs women's social history of the nineteenth-century American West to explain the symbolism of Glaspell's story "A Jury of Her Peers."*]

Susan Glaspell's **"A Jury of Her Peers"** is by now a small feminist classic. Published in 1917, rediscovered in the early 1970s, and increasingly reprinted since then in anthologies and textbooks, it has become for both readers and critics a familiar and frequently revisited landmark on our "map of rereading." For Lee Edwards and Arlyn Diamond in 1973 it introduced us to the work of one of the important but forgotten women writers who were then being rediscovered, and its characters, "prairie matrons, bound by poverty and limited experience [who] fight heroic battles on tiny battlefields," provided examples of those ordinary or anonymous women whose voices were also being sought and reclaimed. For Mary Anne Ferguson, also in 1973, Glaspell's story was significant for its challenge to prevailing images or stereotypes of women—women as "fuzzy minded" and concerned only with "trifles," for example—and for its celebration of female sorority, of the power of sisterhood. More recently, in 1980, Annette Kolodny has read the story as exemplary of a female realm of meaning and symbolic signification, a realm ignored by mainstream critics and one, as she urges, that feminist critics must interpret and make available. Rediscovering lost women writers, reclaiming the experience of anonymous women, reexamining the image of women in literature, and rereading texts in order to discern and appreciate female symbol systems—many of the major approaches that have characterized feminist literacy criticism in the past decade have thus found generous validation in the text of **"A Jury of Her Peers."** The story has become a paradigmatic one for feminist criticism.

Whatever their different emphases, all of these approaches, when applied to Glaspell's story, have in common their central reliance, for argument and evidence, on that set of small details describing women's daily, domestic lives that constitutes the story's core. These details—the "clues" through which in the story the two farm women, Mrs. Hale and Mrs. Peters, solve the mystery of the murder of John Wright—include such minutiae as a soiled roller towel, a broken stove, a cracked jar of preserves, and an erratically stitched quilt block. So central are these details not only to the story's plot but to its larger symbolic meanings that Glaspell gave them precedence in the title of the dramatic version she originally wrote, the one-act play *Trifles,* which she produced for the Provincetown Players in 1916. It is by decoding these "trifles," which the men ignore, that the two women not only solve the murder mystery but also develop their sense of identity as women with Minnie Wright and demonstrate their sisterhood with her by acting to protect her from male law and judgment. It is, therefore, essentially through these trifles that Glaspell creates in her story that female world of meaning and symbol that, as Kolodny says, feminist critics must recover and make accessible.

My interest here is in extending the story's accessibility, making it more possible for contemporary readers to enter into and respond to the symbolic meanings of the details on which it is so crucially based. Any symbol system, as Jean Kennard for one has shown in her discussion of literary conventions, is a shorthand, a script to which the reader must bring a great deal of knowledge not contained in the text. Critical exegeses of the symbolic worlds of male writers—the forest, the river, the whaling ship—may by now have enabled us imaginatively to enter those worlds. But the same is not yet true for women writers. What is needed, as Kolodny says, is an understanding of the "unique and informing contexts" that underlie the symbol systems of women's writing. Only after these contexts are made accessible are we likely to be able to enjoy that "fund of shared recognitions" upon which, as Kolodny also notes, any viable symbol system depends.

In Glaspell's story Mrs. Hale and Mrs. Peters constitute an ideal (if small) community of readers precisely because they are able to bring to the "trivia" of Minnie Wright's life just such a "unique and informing context." That context is their own experience as Midwestern rural women. As a result, they can read Minnie's kitchen trifles with full "recognition and acceptance of . . . their significance." For contemporary readers, however, who are historically removed from the way of life on which Glaspell's story depends, such a reading is not so readily available. Superficially, we can of course comprehend the story's details, since women's work of cooking, cleaning, and sewing is scarcely strange, or unfamiliar, either to female or to male readers. But to appreciate the full resonance of those details requires by now an act of historical reconstruction. Glaspell's details work so effectively as a symbol system because they are carefully chosen reflectors of crucial realities in the lives of nineteenth-and early-twentieth-century Midwestern and western women. The themes, the broader meanings of **"A Jury of Her Peers,"** which are what encourage us to rediscover and reread it today, of course extend beyond its regional and historical origins.

Women's role, or "place," in society, their confinement and isolation, the psychic violence wrought against them, their power or powerlessness vis-à-vis men, are not concerns restricted to Glaspell's time and place. But these concerns achieve their imaginative force and conviction in her story by being firmly rooted in, and organically emerging from, the carefully observed, small details of a localized way of life.

I would therefore like to reenter Glaspell's text by returning it to that localized, past way of life. Such reentry is possible by now, given the recent work of social historians in western women's history. The past six to seven years, especially, have seen the publication of works on the lives of western women by such historians as John Faragher, Julie Jeffrey, Norton Juster, Sandra Myres, Glenda Riley, and Christine Stansell. And the same years have seen a resurgence of interest in women's writings in nontraditional forms—the diaries, letters, journals, and autobiographies of nineteenth- and early-twentieth-century pioneer and farm women, women less silenced than Minnie Wright in Glaspell's story—on which, indeed, much of the published social history depends. It is this body of material, as well as my own researches into the autobiographical writings of nineteenth-century women, on which I shall draw in order to recreate, however imperfectly, some of the historical reality that informs the responses of Mrs. Hale and Mrs. Peters to Minnie Wright's life. Again and again in **"A Jury of Her Peers"** Mrs. Hale and Mrs. Peters perform acts of perception in which a literal object opens out for them into a larger world of meaning. At one point in the story Glaspell describes these acts as a way of "seeing into things, of seeing through a thing to something else." To uncover that "something else"—the dense, hidden background reality of rural women's lives—may enable us to participate more fully in those acts of perception and thus to appreciate Glaspell's achievement, the way in which, by concentrating on a small, carefully selected set of literal details, she communicates, in one very brief short story, an extraordinarily rich, multilayered sense of women's sociocultural place in late-nineteenth- and early-twentieth-century American society.

By the time she published **"A Jury of Her Peers,"** in 1917, Susan Glaspell had been living in the east for several years, both in Greenwich Village and in Provincetown, Massachusetts. But she had been born and raised in Iowa, and her earliest fiction had dealt with the people of her native Midwest, and especially with the confined lives, whether on the isolated farm or in the Midwestern small town or village, of women. In writing her play *Trifles,* and then her story, therefore, she was returning to her Midwestern origins and to the lives of women of her mother's and grandmother's generations.

"A Jury of Her Peers" is set in the prairie and plains region of the United States. The story itself contains a reference to the county attorney's having just returned from Omaha, which would literally locate the action in Nebraska. And a further reference to "Dickson County," as the place where the characters live, might suggest Dixon County, an actual county in the northeastern corner of Nebraska where it borders on Iowa. In the narrowest sense, then, given Glaspell's own Iowa origins, the story can be said to refer to the prairie and plains country that stretches across Iowa into Nebraska—a country of open, level or rolling land, and few trees, which generations of pioneers encountered during successive waves of settlement throughout the nineteenth century. More broadly, the story reflects the lives of women across the entire span of prairie and plains country, and some of the circumstances of Minnie Wright's life were shared by women further west as well. While emphasizing Iowa and Nebraska, therefore, this essay will draw for evidence on the autobiographical writings by women from various western states.

Glaspell's references to the outdoor setting are few. As the story opens, she emphasizes the cold wintry day and the emptiness of the terrain through which the characters travel on their way to the Wright homestead, where they are going to investigate the murder. But the very sparseness of her detail serves to suggest the spare, empty lives of her characters, and especially of Minnie Wright's. What Mrs. Hale notes as the group approaches the Wright farm is the "loneliness" both of the farmhouse and its surroundings. Three times in as many sentences she uses the words *lonely* or *lonesome* to describe the locale. (The road is lonely, and the farm, "down in a hollow," is surrounded by "lonesome looking poplar trees.") Kolodny has suggested that this sensitivity to place distinguishes the women in the story from the men, who confine their talk to the crime that was committed the day before. Whether or not one can generalize from this difference (as Kolodny does) to conclusions about gender-linked perceptions, it does seem to be the case that nineteenth-century pioneer women were more strongly affected than men by a sense of the loneliness of the landscape they encountered in the west.

In spring, when the wildflowers were in bloom, the western prairie might seem "a perfect garden of Eden," as it did to an Iowa woman in 1851. But frequently the women's voices that we hear from that pioneer past express dismay at what they saw when they arrived. A prairie burned by the autumn fires that regularly ravaged the land might understandably seem "black and dismal," as the Illinois prairie did to Christiana Tillson in 1822. Other women, however, even when viewing a less seared and searing landscape, found the prairie unsettling, especially as they moved farther west. "What solitude!" exclaimed the Swedish visitor Fredrika Bremer, arriving in Wisconsin in the 1850s. "I saw no habitation, except the little house at which I was staying; no human beings, no animals; nothing except heaven and the flower-strewn earth." And Mrs. Cecil Hall, visiting the northern territories in 1882, wrote: "O the prairie! I cannot describe to you our first impression. Its vastness, dreariness, and loneliness is [*sic*] appalling."

When a male pioneer registered his sense of the land's emptiness it was often to recognize that the emptiness

bore more heavily upon women. Seth K. Humphrey wrote of his father's and his own experiences, in the Minnesota territory in the 1850s and in the Middle Northwest in the 1870s, and he remembered that "the prairie has a solitude way beyond the mere absence of human beings." With no trees, no objects to engage or interrupt the glance, the eyes "stare, stare—and sometimes the prairie gets to staring back." Women, he observed, especially suffered. They "fled in terror" or "stayed until the prairie broke them." Women themselves reported that it was not unusual to spend five months in a log cabin without seeing another woman, as did a Marshall County, Iowa, woman in 1842, or to spend one and a half years after arriving before being able to take a trip to town, as did Luna Kellie in Nebraska in the 1870s. The absence both of human contact and of any ameliorating features in the landscape exacerbated the loneliness felt by women, who had often only reluctantly uprooted themselves from eastern homes and families in order to follow their husbands westward.

Minnie Wright is not, of course, living in circumstances of such extreme geographical isolation. By the time of Glaspell's story established villages and towns have replaced the first scattered settlements, and networks of transportation and communication link people previously isolated from one another. But John Wright's farm, as we learn, is an isolated, outlying farm, separated from the town of which it is formally a part. Furthermore, he refuses to have a telephone, and, as we also learn, he has denied his wife access to even the minimal contacts that town life might afford women at that time, such as the church choir, in which Minnie had sung before her marriage. Minnie Wright's emotional and spiritual loneliness, the result of her isolation, is, in the final analysis, the reason for her murder of her husband. Through her brief opening description of the landscape Glaspell establishes the physical context for the loneliness and isolation, an isolation Minnie inherited from and shared with generations of pioneer and farm women before her.

The full import of Minnie's isolation emerges only incrementally in Glaspell's story. Meanwhile, after the characters arrive at the Wright farm, the story confines itself to the narrow space of Minnie's kitchen—the limited and limiting space of her female sphere. Within that small space are revealed all the dimensions of the loneliness that is her mute message. And that message is, of course, conveyed through those "kitchen things," as the sheriff dismissingly calls them, to which Mrs. Hale and Mrs. Peters respond with increasing comprehension and sympathy.

One of the first "kitchen things," or "trifles," to which Glaspell introduces us is the roller towel, on which the attorney condescendingly comments. Not considering, as the women do, that his own assistant, called in earlier that morning to make up a fire in Minnie's absence, had probably dirtied the towel, he decides that the soiled towel shows that Minnie lacked "the homemaking instinct." The recent researches of historians into the lives of nineteenth-century women allow us today to appreciate the full ironic force of Mrs. Hale's quietly understated reply: "There's a great deal of work to be done on a farm." One of the most important contributions of the new social history is its documentation of the amount of work that pioneer and farm women did. The work is, as one historian has said, "almost endless" and, over the course of a lifetime, usually consisted of tasks "more arduous and demanding than those performed by men." Indoors and out, the division of labor "favored men" and "exploited women." Sarah Brewer-Bonebright, recalling her life in Newcastle, Iowa in 1848, described the "routine" work of the "women-folk" as including "water carrying, cooking, churning, sausage making, berry picking, vegetable drying, sugar and soap boiling, hominy hulling, medicine brewing, washing, nursing, weaving, sewing, straw platting, wool picking, spinning, quilting, knitting, gardening and various other tasks." Workdays that began at 4:30 A.M. and didn't end until 11:30 P.M. were not unheard of. Jessamyn West's description of her Indiana grandmother—"She died saying, 'Hurry, hurry, hurry,' not to a nurse, not to anyone at her bedside, but to herself"—captures an essential reality of the lives of many nineteenth- and early-twentieth-century rural women.

The work involved for Minnie Wright in preparing the clean towel that the attorney takes for granted is a case in point. Of all the tasks that nineteenth- and early-twentieth century women commented on in their diaries, laundry was consistently described as the most onerous.

> Friday May 27 This is the dreaded washing day
>
> Friday June 23 To day Oh! horrors how shall I express it; is the dreaded washing day.

This entry from an 1853 diary is typical of what are often litanies of pain, ritualistically repeated in the records that nineteenth-century women have left us of their lives. In her recent study of housework, *Never Done*, Susan Strasser agrees that laundry was woman's "most hated task." Before the introduction of piped water it took staggering amounts of time and labor: "One wash, one boiling, and one rinse used about fifty gallons of water—or four hundred pounds—which had to be moved from pump or well or faucet to stove and tub, in buckets and wash boilers that might weigh as much as forty or fifty pounds." Then came rubbing, wringing, and lifting the wet clothing and linens and carrying them in heavy tubs and baskets outside to hang. It is when Mrs. Peters looks from Minnie's inadequate stove, with its cracked lining, to the "pail of water carried in from outside" that she makes the crucial observation about "seeing into things . . . seeing through a thing to something else." What the women see, beyond the pail and the stove, are the hours of work it took Minnie to produce that one clean towel. To call Minnie's work "instinctual," as the attorney does (using a rationalization prevalent today as in the past) is to evade a whole world of domestic reality, a world of which Mrs. Hale and Mrs. Peters are acutely aware.

So too with the jars of preserves that the women find cracked and spoiled from the cold that has penetrated the

house during the night. It is the preserves, about which Minnie has been worrying in jail, that lead Mr. Hale to make the comment Glaspell used for the title of the dramatic version of her work. "Held for murder, and worrying over her preserves . . . worrying over trifles." But here again, as they express their sympathy with Minnie's concern, the women are seeing through a thing to something else: in this case, to "all [Minnie's] work in the hot weather," as Mrs. Peters exclaims. Mrs. Hale and Mrs. Peters understand the physical labor involved in boiling fruit in Iowa heat that one historian has described as "oppressive and inescapable." By the same token they can appreciate the seriousness of the loss when that work is destroyed by the winter cold.

The winter cold is, as has been said, one of the few references to outdoor setting that Glaspell includes in her story. When at the beginning of the story Mrs. Hale closes her storm door behind her to accompany the others to the Wright farm, it is a "cold March morning," with a north wind blowing. Later we are told that the temperature had fallen below zero the night before. Historians have described the prairie and plains winters, their interminable length, the ceaseless winds that whipped across the treeless spaces, the "infamous" blizzards peculiar to the region—storms not of snow but of ice particles that penetrated clothes and froze the eyes shut. Eliza Farnham, traveling through the prairie in 1846, described the cold in the uninsulated log cabins and frame houses: "The cups freeze to the saucers while [the family] are at table." And Mary Abell, living in Kansas in 1875, related how "my eyelids froze together so I picked off the ice, the tops of the sheets and quilts and all our beds were frozen stiff with the breath. The cold was so intense we could not breathe the air without pain." Such weather demanded heroic maintenance efforts to keep a family warm and fed. Engaged as they were in just such maintenance efforts (at the beginning of the story Mrs. Hale is reluctant to leave her kitchen because her own work is unfinished) the women can appreciate the meaning of the loss of Minnie's laboriously prepared food.

Hard as the work was, that it went unacknowledged was often harder for women to bear. The first annual report of the Department of Agriculture in 1862 included a study of the situation of farm women, which concluded that they worked harder than men but were neither treated with respect as a result nor given full authority within their domestic sphere. And Norton Juster's study of farm women between 1865 and 1895 leads him to assert that women's work was seen merely as "the anonymous background for someone else's meaningful activity," never attaining "a recognition or dignity of its own." Indeed, he concludes, women's work was not only ignored; it was ridiculed, "often the object of derision." Mr. Hale's remark about the preserves, that "women are used to worrying over trifles," is a mild example of this ridicule, as is the attorney's comment, intended to deflect that ridicule but itself patronizing: "Yet what would we do without the ladies." It is this ridicule to which Mrs. Hale and Mrs. Peters especially react. When Mr. Hale belittles women's work we are told that "the two women moved a little closer together," and when the attorney makes his seemingly conciliatory remark the women, we are further told, "did not speak, did not unbend." Mrs. Hale and Mrs. Peters, who at the beginning of the story are comparative strangers, here begin to establish their common bonds with each other and with Minnie. Their slight physical movement toward each other visually embodies that psychological and emotional separation from men that was encouraged by the nineteenth-century doctrine of separate spheres, a separation underscored throughout the story by the women's confinement to the kitchen, while the men range freely, upstairs and outside, bedroom to barn, in search of the "real" clues to the crime.

Women's confinement to the kitchen or to the private space of the home was a major source of their isolation. Men didn't appreciate how "their own toil is sweetened to them by the fact that it is out of doors," said one farm woman, and Juster has concluded that the lives of farm women in the second half of the nineteenth century were lives "tied to house and children, lacking opportunity for outside contacts, stimulation, or variety of experience." In Glaspell's story Mrs. Hale moves only from one kitchen to another. That she hasn't visited Minnie, whom she has known since girlhood, in over a year she guiltily attributes to her antipathy to the cheerlessness of the Wright farm. But there is truth in Mrs. Peters's attempt to assuage that guilt: "But of course you were awful busy . . . your house—and your children."

"A walking visit to neighbors was not a casual affair but could take an entire morning or afternoon," says Faragher in describing the settlement on separate farmsteads, often far distant from each other, and, like Juster, he concludes that "the single most important distinction between the social and cultural worlds of men and women was the isolation and immobility of wives compared to husbands." "Grandma Brown," whose one-hundred-year life span from 1827 to 1927 is recorded in her autobiography, lived on an Iowa farm for fourteen years, from 1856 to 1870. They were, she said, "the hardest years of my life. The drudgery was unending. The isolation was worse." Both during the frontier stage and in later periods of village settlement men routinely enjoyed more opportunities for social life than women. They traveled to town with their farm produce, to have their grain and corn milled, to trade surpluses, to have wool carded or skins tanned. In **"A Jury of Her Peers"** John Wright's murder is discovered because Mr. Hale and his son stop at the Wright farm while traveling to town with their potato crop. Once in town men had places to congregate—the market, the country store, the blacksmith shop, the saloon. That "women really did little more than pass through the masculine haunts of the village," as Faragher concludes, was a reality to which at least one nineteenth-century male writer was sensitive. "The saloon-keepers, the politicians, and the grocers make it pleasant for the man," Hamlin Garland has a character comment in his story of Midwestern rural life, "A Day's

Pleasure"; "But the wife is left without a word." Garland wrote "A Day's Pleasure" to dramatize the plight of the farm wife, isolated at home, and desperate for diversion. Mrs. Markham has been six months without leaving the family farm. But when, over her husband's objections and by dint of sacrificed sleep and extra work to provide for her children while she is gone, she manages to get into town, she finds scant welcome and little to do. After overstaying her leave at the country store, she walks the streets for hours, in the "forlorn, aimless, pathetic wandering" that, Garland has the town grocer observe, is "a daily occurrence for the farm women he sees and one which had never possessed any special meaning to him."

John Wright's insensitivity to his wife's needs parallels that of the men of Garland's story. Lacking decent clothes, Minnie doesn't travel into town. What she turns to in her isolation is a bird, a canary bought from a traveling peddler. It is after her husband strangles that surrogate voice that, in one of those "intermittent flare-ups of bizarre behavior," as one historian has described them, which afflicted rural women, she strangles him.

Here again Glaspell's story reflects a larger truth about the lives of rural women. Their isolation induced madness in many. The rate of insanity in rural areas, especially for women, was a much-discussed subject in the second half of the nineteenth century. As early as 1868 Sarah Josepha Hale, editor of the influential *Godey's Lady's Book,* expressed her concern that the farm population supplied the largest proportion of inmates for the nation's insane asylums. By the 1880s and 1890s this concern was widespread. An article in 1882 noted that farmers' wives comprised the largest percentage of those in lunatic asylums. And a decade later the *Atlantic Monthly* was reporting "the alarming rate of insanity . . . in the new prairie States among farmers and their wives." Abigail McCarthy recalled in her autobiography stories she had heard as a girl in the 1930s about the first homesteaders in North Dakota, two generations earlier. Women could be heard, she wrote, "screaming all night long in the jail after the first spring thaw. Their husbands had brought them into town in wagons from the sod huts where they had spent the terrible Dakota winter; they were on their way to the insane asylum in Jamestown."

That the loss of her music, in the shape of a bird, should have triggered murderous behavior in Minnie Wright is therefore neither gratuitous nor melodramatic, as is sometimes charged against Glaspell's story. In the monotonous expanses of the prairie and the plains the presence of one small spot of color, or a bit of music, might spell the difference between sanity and madness. Mari Sandoz, chronicler of the lives of Nebraska pioneers, describes in her short story "The Vine" a woman so desperate for some color in the brown, treeless expanse of the prairie that she uses precious water—scarce during a drought—to keep alive a trumpet vine outside the door of her sod house. When her husband, enraged at her wastefulness, uproots and kills the vine, she goes mad. In *Old Jules,* her account of the life of her homesteading father, Sandoz relates the true story of a farm wife who suddenly one afternoon killed herself and her three children. At her funeral a woman neighbor comments, "If she would a had even a geranium—but in that cold shell of a shack—." Again and again in their recollections of their lives on the prairie and plains women described the importance of a bit of color or music. The music might come, as it did for Minnie Wright, from a canary in a cage. Late-nineteenth-century photographs of families outside their Dakota and Nebraska sod huts routinely show the birdcage hung to one side of the front door. Indoors it was likely to be one of the deep windows carved into the thick sod walls that provided the "spot of beauty" so necessary to psychological survival. As late as 1957, the *Nebraska Farmer* published interviews it had secured with women who had experienced the conditions of pioneer settlement. The comment of Mrs. Orval Lookhart is typical of many the journal received. She remembered the special window in the prairie sod house that was invariably reserved for "flowers and plants . . . a place where the wife and mother could have one spot of beauty that the wind the cold or the dry weather couldn't [sic] touch." There is no spot of beauty in Glaspell's description of Minnie's kitchen, which is presented as a drab and dreary space, dominated by the broken stove, and a rocking chair of "a dingy red, with wooden rungs up the back, and the middle rung was gone, and the chair sagged to one side." When the women collect some of Minnie's clothes to take to her in prison, the sight of "a shabby black skirt" painfully reminds Mrs. Hale by contrast of the "pretty clothes" that Minnie wore as a young girl before her marriage.

Unable to sing in the church choir, deprived of her surrogate voice in the bird, denied access to other people, and with no visible beauty in her surroundings, Minnie, almost inevitably one can say, turned in her loneliness to that final resource available to nineteenth- and early-twentieth-century women—quilting. Minnie's quilt blocks are the penultimate trifle in Glaspell's story. The discovery later of the strangled bird and broken bird cage explain the immediate provocation for Minnie's crime. But it is with the discovery of the quilt blocks, to which the women react more strongly than they have to any of the previously introduced "kitchen things," that a pivotal point in the story is reached.

The meaning of quilts in the lives of American women is complex, and Glaspell's story is a valuable contribution to the full account that remains to be written. Quilts were utilitarian in origin, three-layered bed coverings intended to protect against the cold weather. But they became in the course of the nineteenth century probably the major creative outlet for women—one patriarchically tolerated, and even "approved," for their use, but which women were able to transform to their own ends. Through quilting, through their stitches as well as through pattern and color, and through the institutions, such as the "bee," that grew up around it, women who were otherwise without expressive outlet were able to communicate their thoughts and feelings.

In *Trifles* Glaspell included a reference she omitted from **"A Jury of Her Peers"** but which is worth retrieving. In the play Mrs. Hale laments that, given her husband's parsimony, Minnie could never join the Ladies Aid. The Ladies Aid would have been a female society associated with the local church, in which women would have spent their time sewing, braiding carpets, and quilting, in order to raise money for foreign missionaries, for new flooring or carpets, chairs or curtains for the church or parish house, or to add to the minister's salary. Such societies, as Glenda Riley has observed, provided women with "a relief from the routine and monotony" of farm life. They also provided women with a public role, or place. And through the female friendships they fostered they helped women, as Julie Jeffrey has noted, to develop "feelings of control over their environment," mitigating that sense of powerlessness that domestic isolation could induce.

Denied such associations, Minnie Wright worked on her quilt blocks alone, and it is the effect of that solitude that the women read in her blocks and that so profoundly moves them. It is, specifically, the stitches in Minnie's blocks that speak to them and, particularly, the "queer" stitches in one block, so unlike the "fine, even sewing," "dainty [and] accurate," that they observe in the others. Nineteenth-century women learned in childhood to take stitches so small that in the words of one woman, it "required a microscope to detect them." Mothers were advised to teach their daughters to make small, exact stitches, not only for durability but as a way of instilling habits of patience, neatness, and diligence. But such stitches also became a badge of one's needlework skill, a source of self-esteem and of status, through the recognition and admiration of other women. Minnie's "crazy" or crooked stitches are a clear signal to the two women that something, for her, was very seriously wrong.

Mrs. Hale's reaction is immediate. Tampering with what is in fact evidence—for the badly stitched block is just such a clue as the men are seeking: "Something to show anger—or sudden feeling"—she replaces Minnie's crooked stitches with her own straight ones. The almost automatic act, so protective of Minnie, is both concealing and healing. To "replace bad sewing with good" is Mrs. Hale's symbolic gesture of affiliation with the damaged woman. It is also the story's first intimation of the more radical tampering with the evidence that the two women will later undertake.

In so quickly grasping the significance of Minnie's quilt stitches, Mrs. Hale is performing yet another of those acts of perception, of seeing through a detail or trifle to its larger meaning, on which Glaspell's dramatic effects depend throughout her story. As she holds the badly stitched block in her hand, Mrs. Hale, we are told, "feels queer, as if the distracted thoughts of the woman who had perhaps turned to it to try and quiet herself were communicating themselves to her." Resorting to needlework in order to "quiet oneself," to relieve distress or alleviate loneliness, was openly recognized and even encouraged throughout the nineteenth century, especially in the advice books that proliferated for women. One of the earliest and most popular of these was John Gregory's *A Father's Advice to His Daughters,* published in 1774 in England and widely read both there and in the United States well into the nineteenth century. Gregory recommended needlework to his female readers "to enable you to fill up, in a tolerably agreeable way, some of the many solitary hours you must necessarily pass at home." By 1831, as advice manuals began to be produced in this country, Lydia Child in *The Mother's Book* urged mothers to teach their daughters needlework, such as knitting, as a way of dealing with the "depression of spirits" they would inevitably experience in later life. "Women," Child wrote, "in all situations in life, have so many lonely hours, that they cannot provide themselves with too many resources." And as late as 1885 popular writer Jane Croly introduced a book of needlework instructions with a parable in which an angel, foreseeing the "abuse" that woman would suffer from men, urged God not to create her. God refused. Out of pity, however, woman was given "two compensating gifts." These were "tears, and the love of needlework." Although one woman who read Croly's book tartly rejoined, in a letter to *The Housekeeper,* a magazine for women, that she would prefer to keep the tears and give men the needlework, for numbers of others needlework served, in Croly's words, as "that solace in sorrow—that helper in misfortune." That it might have so served Minnie Wright, Mrs. Hale can immediately appreciate.

Minnie's stitches speak with equal directness to Mrs. Peters. It is she who first discovers the badly stitched block, and, as she holds it out to Mrs. Hale, we are told that "the women's eyes met—something flashed to life, passed between them." In contrast to the often outspoken Mrs. Hale, Mrs. Peters has been timid, self-effacing, and "indecisive," torn between sympathy for Minnie and resigned submission to the authority of the law, which her husband, the sheriff, represents. She has evaded Mrs. Hale's effort to get her more openly to choose sides. The flash of recognition between the two women, a moment of communication the more intense for being wordless, is, as one critic has said, "the metamorphizing spark of the story." It presages Mrs. Peter's eventual revolt against male authority. That revolt occurs when she snatches the box containing the dead bird—the evidence that could condemn Minnie—in order to conceal it from the men. Her defiant act is, of course, the result of the effect on her of the accumulated weight of meaning of all of the so-called trifles she has perceived and interpreted throughout the story. But it is here, when she reads Minnie's stitches, that she is first released from her hesitancy into what will later become full conspiratorial complicity with Mrs. Hale.

In examining Minnie's quilt blocks, Mrs. Hale observes that she was making them in the "log cabin pattern." The log cabin pattern was one of the most popular in the second half of the nineteenth century, frequently chosen for its capacity to utilize in its construction small scraps of leftover fabric. For Minnie in her poverty it would have

been a practical pattern choice. But there accrued to the pattern a rich symbolism that would not have escaped a farm woman like Mrs. Hale and that adds yet another rich layer of meaning to Glaspell's exploration of women's place. The log cabin quilt is constructed of repetitions of a basic block, which is built up of narrow overlapping strips of fabric, all emanating from a central square. That square, traditionally done in red cloth, came to represent the hearth fire within the cabin, with the strips surrounding it becoming the "logs" of which the cabin was built. As a replication of that most emotionally evocative of American dwelling types, the log cabin quilt came to symbolize both the hardships and the heroisms of pioneer life. More specifically, it became a celebration of women's civilizing role in the pioneering process: in the words of one researcher, "women's dogged determination to build a home, to replace a wilderness with a community."

The nineteenth-century ideology of domesticity defined woman's sphere as that of the home, but within that home it gave her, in theory, a queenly role, as guardian and purveyor of the essential moral and cultural values of the society. That role was frequently symbolized, especially in the popular domestic fiction of the nineteenth century, by the hearth fire, over which the woman presided, ministering, in the light of its warm glow, to the physical and emotional needs of her family. Julie Jeffrey has demonstrated the willingness and even determination with which women resumed this domestic role upon their arrival in the trans-Mississippi west after the dislocations induced by the overland journey, their sense of themselves as the culture bearers and civilizers. And in her recent *The Land before Her: Fantasy and Experience of the American Frontiers, 1630–1860* Annette Kolodny shows that on the earlier Mississippi Valley frontier (and in Texas as well) women's dreams were above all domestic: to create a home as a paradise.

That Minnie is making a log cabin quilt—and the women find a roll of red cloth in her sewing basket—is, both in this historical context and in the context of her own life, both poignant and bitterly ironic. The center of her kitchen is not a hearth with an inviting open fire but, instead, that stove with its broken lining, the sight of which, earlier in the story, had "swept [Mrs. Hale] into her own thoughts, thinking of what it would mean, year after year, to have that stove to wrestle with." In Glaspell's story the cult of domesticity has become a trap; Minnie's home has become her prison. Minnie has asked Mrs. Peters to bring her an apron to wear in jail, a request the sheriff's wife at first finds "strange." But when Mrs. Peters decides that wearing the apron will perhaps make Minnie feel "more natural," we can only agree, since in moving from house to jail she has but exchanged one form of imprisonment for another.

In 1917, when Glaspell rewrote and retitled *Trifles,* feminists were engaged in their final years of effort to free women from at least one of the "imprisonments" to which they had been historically subject—the lack of the vote.

Her change of title emphasized the story's contemporaneity, by calling attention to its references to the issue of woman's legal place in U.S. society. The denouement depends on that issue. It is immediately after the county attorney, patronizing as always, expresses his confidence that, in carrying things to Minnie in jail, Mrs. Peters will take nothing suspicious because she is "married to the law," that she proceeds to divorce herself from that law by abetting Mrs. Hale in concealing the dead bird. With that act the two women radically subvert the male legal system within which they have no viable place. Throughout much of the nineteenth century married women were defined under the law as "civilly dead," their legal existence subsumed within their husbands, their rights to their own property, wages, and children either nonexistent or severely circumscribed. Nor did they participate in the making and administering of the law. In 1873 Susan B. Anthony had challenged that legal situation, in a defense that was widely reprinted and that would have been available to Glaspell at the time of the final agitation for the vote. Arrested for having herself tried to vote, and judged guilty of having thereby committed a crime, Anthony had argued that the all-male jury that judged her did not constitute, as the Constitution guaranteed to each citizen, a "jury of her peers." So long, she argued, as women lacked the vote and other legal rights, men were not their peers but their superiors. So, in Glaspell's story, Mrs. Hale and Mrs. Peters decide that they, and not the men, are Minnie's true peers. They take the law into their own hands, appoint themselves prosecuting and defense attorneys, judge and jury, and pass their merciful sentence.

In committing her "crime," Mrs. Peters resorts not to any constitutional justification but to a bit of sophistry cunningly based on the trivia that are the heart of Glaspell's story. Why reveal the dead bird to the men, she reasons, when they consider all of women's concerns insignificant? If the men could hear us, she suggests to Mrs. Hale, "getting all stirred up over a little thing like a—dead canary. . . . My, wouldn't they *laugh*?" But it is the women who have the last laugh (in a story in which potential tragedy has been transformed into comedy), and that laugh hinges upon a very "little thing" indeed. Glaspell gives literally the last word to one of the story's seemingly least significant details. As the characters prepare to leave the Wright farm, the county attorney facetiously asks the women whether Minnie was going to "quilt" or "knot" her blocks. In having Mrs. Hale suggest that she was probably going to knot them (that is, join the quilt layers via short lengths of yarn drawn through from the back and tied or knotted at wide intervals across the top surface, rather than stitch

through the layers at closer intervals with needle and thread), Glaspell is using a technical term from the world of women's work in a way that provides a final triumphant vindication of her method throughout the story. If, like Mrs. Hale and Mrs. Peters, the reader can by now engage in those acts of perception whereby one sees "into things, [and] through a thing to something else," the humble task of knotting a quilt becomes resonant with meaning. Minnie has knotted a rope around her husband's neck, and Mrs. Hale and Mrs. Peters have "tied the men in knots." All three women have thus said "not," or "no," to male authority, and in so doing they have knotted or bonded themselves together. Knots can entangle and they can unite, and at the end of Glaspell's story both men and women are knotted, in separate and different ways, with the women having discovered through their interpretation of the trifles that constitute Minnie's world their ties to one another. One nineteenth-century woman described quilts as women's "hieroglyphics"—textile documents on which, with needle, thread, and bits of colored cloth, women inscribed a record of their lives. All of the trifles in Glaspell's story together create such a set of hieroglyphics, but it is a language we should by now begin to be able to read.

FURTHER READING

Bibliography

Papke, Mary E. *Susan Glaspell: A Research and Production Sourcebook.* Westport, Conn.: Greenwood Press, 1993, 299 p.

    This complete bibliography of Glaspell's works includes archival material, plot summaries, production histories, and review summaries of her plays, as well as an annotated bibliography of secondary sources.

Criticism

Kolodny, Annette. "A Map for Rereading; or, Gender and the Interpretation of Literary Texts." In *The Mother Tongue: Essays in Feminist Psychoanalytic Interpretation,* pp. 241–59. Edited by Shirley Nelson Garner, Claire Kahane, and Madelon Sprengnether. Ithaca, New York: Cornell University Press, 1985.

    Discussion of gender-related variations in reading texts, including Glaspell's "A Jury of Her Peers."

Additional coverage of Glaspell's life and career is contained in the following sources published by the Gale Group: *Dictionary of Literary Biography,* **Vols. 7, 9, 78;** *Drama Criticism,* **Vol. 10;** *Twentieth-Century Literary Criticism,* **Vol. 55; and** *Yesterday's Authors of Books for Children,* **Vol. 2.**

Evelyn Waugh
1903–1966

(Full name Evelyn Arthur St. John Waugh) English novelist, short story writer, travel writer, essayist, poet, critic, biographer, and journalist.

INTRODUCTION

Evelyn Waugh is considered by many scholars to be one of the most talented and significant British writers of the twentieth century. Waugh is primarily known for his novels such as *Brideshead Revisited* and *The Loved One,* but also earned acclaim for his short stories. Waugh's novella, *Decline and Fall,* is his best-known work of short fiction.

BIOGRAPHICAL INFORMATION

Waugh was born in 1903 in Hampstead, London, to a literary family. His father, Arthur, was an editor and publisher; his older brother, Alec, also became a novelist. Waugh began attending Oxford in 1921 and started writing stories for literary magazines. The author, however, was forced to leave Oxford in 1924 without earning a degree. Following his departure from Oxford, Waugh taught briefly in private schools and also worked for awhile as a journalist for the *Daily Express.* In 1928, Waugh married Evelyn Gardener. During the same year, he also published a biography of the painter and poet Dante Gabriel Rosetti, as well as his novella, *Decline and Fall,* which marked the beginning of his career as a writer. In 1930 Waugh divorced his wife, traveled to Africa, and published his novel *Vile Bodies,* which earned critical acclaim. Waugh's extensive travels are reflected in some of his novels, including *Black Mischief, A Handful of Dust,* and *Scoop.* In 1936 Waugh received the Hawthornden Prize for his biography of the Elizabethan Jesuit martyr, *Edmund Campion.* By the early 1940s, Waugh had earned the reputation as one of the most respected satirists of his age. Shortly after the start of World War II, Waugh enlisted in the Royal Marines. Waugh continued writing during and after the war, but his works grew increasingly somber and reflected his increasing sense of despair about the decay of the modern world. Waugh's most famous and controversial work, *Brideshead Revisited,* which is about the decadence of a wealthy Catholic family during the 1920s, was published in 1945 and earned great critical acclaim. While on a voyage to Ceylon in 1954 he suffered a mental breakdown, which is detailed in his semi-autobiographical novel, *The Ordeal of Gilbert Pinfold.* Waugh died in 1966 following a sudden heart attack at the age of 63.

MAJOR WORKS OF SHORT FICTION

Waugh's first collection of stories, *Mr. Loveday's Little Outing and Other Sad Stories,* was published in 1936. The title story—a witty tale with elements of the grotesque—is about an elderly asylum inmate who is released by a social reformer. Throughout the story, Waugh uses satire and black humor to mock pretensions of social scientists and experimenters. Waugh's satirical touch also is reflected throughout other stories in the volume. The stories include "Bella Fleace Gave a Party," which is about an elderly aristocrat who throws an elaborate Christmas party that no one attends, and "Winner Takes All," which deals with the misfortunes of a young man who is always overlooked due to favoritism shown to his elder brother. Waugh's next volume of short stories, *Work Suspended, and Other Stories Written Before the Second World War,* was most likely published for financial rather than artistic reasons. The collection includes seven stories that appeared in *Mr. Loveday,* "An Englishman's Home," as well as the title story—a fragment of an unfinished novel. Many of these stories reappeared again in *Tactical Exercise* and in the 1982 collection *Charles Ryder's Schooldays, and Other Stories.* In 1998 all of Waugh's thirty-nine stories were issued in one volume.

In addition to short stories, Waugh also penned three novellas, *Decline and Fall: An Illustrated Novelette, Scott-King's Modern Europe,* and *Love Among the Ruins. Decline and Fall,* the story of a young innocent dismissed from Oxford, contains a similar brand of satire used in his early stories. *Scott-King's Modern Europe* is a satirical fable about a middle-aged classics master who clings to forgotten values in the postwar world of Neutralia. *Love Among the Ruins,* which details disappointments in the life of Miles Plastic, is a harsh attack against state interference in people's personal lives in the postwar world.

CRITICAL RECEPTION

During his lifetime Waugh's short stories enjoyed a measure of commercial and critical success. Contemporary reviewers admired the style and wit of his stories, but many considered his short works to be minor efforts from the pen of a great novelist. Some later critics dismissed the stories as insignificant. Waugh's biographer, Christopher Sykes, for example, considered them an unimportant literary feature in the author's life. Others consider the stories insightful because they anticipate themes and ideas developed in his longer fiction. Waugh's stories continue to be praised by readers for their cleverness, stylistic elegance, and ability to entertain. Waugh's novellas, however, have enjoyed more sustained critical attention. *Decline and Fall* is considered Waugh's first serious literary work. The work continues to elicit interest from scholars for the insight it provides into Waugh's development as an artist and for its literary merit. Some reviewers criticized Waugh's postwar novellas for their sharp satire. Novelist George Orwell, for example, found *Scott-King's Modern Europe* "lacking the touch of affection that political satire ought to have." These late novellas are not considered Waugh's best works, but are noted for their dystopian quality and biting criticism of the corruption, decay, and moral and intellectual sterility of postwar Europe.

PRINCIPAL WORKS

Short Fiction

Decline and Fall: An Illustrated Novelette 1928
Mr. Loveday's Little Outing and Other Sad Stories 1936
Scott-King's Modern Europe (novella) 1947
Love Among the Ruins (novella) 1953
Tactical Exercise 1954
Charles Ryder's Schooldays, and Other Stories 1982
The Complete Stories of Evelyn Waugh 1998

Other Major Works

The World to Come (poetry) 1916
Rossetti: His Life and Works (biography/criticism) 1928
Vile Bodies (novel) 1930
Black Mischief (novel) 1932
A Handful of Dust (novel) 1934
Ninety-Two Days: An Account of a Tropical Journey Through British Guiana and Part of Brazil 1934
Edmund Campion (biography) 1935
Waugh in Abyssinia (travel essay) 1936
Scoop (novel) 1938
Put Out More Flags (novel) 1942
Brideshead Revisited: The Sacred and Profane Memories of Captain Charles Ryder (novel) 1945
The Loved One (novel) 1948
Helena (novel) 1950
Men at Arms (novel) 1952
Officers and Gentlemen (novel) 1955
The Ordeal of Gilbert Pinfold (novel) 1957
The Life of the Right Reverend Ronald Knox (nonfiction) 1959
A Tourist in Africa (travel essay) 1960
Unconditional Surrender (novel) 1961
Basil Seal Rides Again; or, The Rake's Regress (novel) 1963
A Little Learning (autobiography) 1964
Sword of Honour (trilogy of novels) 1965
A Little Order: A Selection from His Journalism [edited by Donat Gallagher] 1977
The Letters of Evelyn Waugh [edited by Mark Amory] 1980

CRITICISM

George Orwell (review date 1949)

SOURCE: "Review of 'Scott-King's Modern Europe,'" in *New York Times Book Review,* Vol. 1, No. 25, February 20, 1949, pp. 1, 25.

[*In the following review of* Scott-King's Modern Europe, *Orwell argues that Waugh's work is conservative in outlook and lacks necessary elements of political satire.*]

Mr. Evelyn Waugh's recent book, *The Loved One,* was an attack, and by no means a good-natured attack, on American civilization, but in **Scott-King's Modern Europe** he shows himself willing to handle his native Continent with at least equal rudeness. America worships corpses but Europe mass-produces them, is what he seems to be saying. The two books are indeed in some sense complementary to one another, though **Scott-King's Modern Europe** is less obviously brilliant than the other.

The book has a general resemblance to *Candide,* and is perhaps even intended to be a modern counterpart of *Candide,* with the significant difference that the hero is middle-aged at the start. Nowadays, it is implied, only the middle-aged have scruples or ideals; the young are born hard-boiled. Scott-King, age about 43, 'slightly bald and slightly corpulent,' is senior classics master at Granchester, a respectable but not fashionable public school. A dusty, unhonored figure, a praiser of the past, a lover of exact scholarship, he fights a steadily losing battle against what he regards as the debasement of modern education.

'Dim,' we are told, is the epithet that describes him. His hobby is the study of a poet even dimmer than himself, a certain Bellorius, who flourished in the seventeenth century in what was then a province of the Habsburg Empire and is now the independent republic of Neutralia.

In an evil hour Scott-King receives an invitation to visit Neutralia, which is celebrating the tercentenary of the death of Bellorius. It is the wet summer of 1946—a summer of austerity—and Scott-King envisions garlicky meals and flasks of red wine. He succumbs to the invitation, although half aware that it is probably a swindle of some kind.

At this point any experienced reader of Waugh's works would predict unpleasant adventures for Scott-King and he would be right. Neutralia, a compound of Yugoslavia and Greece, is ruled over by a 'Marshal,' and there is the usual police espionage, banditry, ceremonial banquets and speeches about Youth and Progress. The commemoration of Bellorius is in fact an imposture. Its object is to trap the visitors into endorsing the Marshal's regime. They fall for the trap and later learn that this stamps them everywhere as 'Fascist Beasts.' Thereafter Neutralia's hospitality ends abruptly.

Some of the visitors are killed and the others stranded, unable to get out of the country. Airplanes are reserved for VIP's, and to leave Neutralia any other way entails weeks and months of besieging embassies and consulates. After adventures which Mr. Waugh suppresses because they are too painful for a work of light fiction, Scott-King ends up stark naked in a camp for illegal Jewish immigrants in Palestine.

Back at Granchester, amid the notched desks and the draughty corridors, the headmaster informs him sadly that the number of classical scholars is falling off and suggests that he shall combine his teaching of the classics with something a little more up-to-date:

> 'Parents are not interested in producing the "complete man" any more. They want to qualify their boys for jobs in the modern world. You can hardly blame them, can you?'

> 'Oh, yes,' said Scott-King, 'I can and do.'

> Later he adds: 'I think it would be very wicked indeed to do anything to fit a boy for the modern world.' And

when the headmaster objects that this is a short-sighted view, Scott-King retorts, 'I think it the most long-sighted view it is possible to take.'

This last statement, it should be noted, is intended seriously. The book is very short, hardly longer than a short story, and it is written with the utmost lightness, but it has a definite political meaning. The modern world, we are meant to infer, is so unmistakably crazy, so certain to smash itself to pieces in the near future, that to attempt to understand it or come to terms with it is simply a purposeless self-corruption. In the chaos that is shortly coming, a few moral principles that one can cling to, and perhaps even a few half-remembered odes of Horace or choruses from Euripides, will be more useful than what is now called 'enlightenment.'

There is something to be said for this point of view, and yet one must always regard with suspicion the claim that ignorance is, or can be, an advantage. In the Europe of the last fifty years the diehard, know-nothing attitude symbolized by Scott-King, has helped to bring about the very conditions that Mr. Waugh is satirizing. Revolutions happen in authoritarian countries, not in liberal ones, and Mr. Waugh's failure to see the implications of this fact not only narrows his political vision but also robs his story of part of its point.

His standpoint, or Scott-King's, is that of a Conservative—that is to say, a person who disbelieves in progress and refuses to differentiate between one version of progress and another—and his lack of interest in his opponents induces, unavoidably, a certain perfunctoriness. It was a mistake, for instance, to present Neutralia as a dictatorship of the Right while giving it most of the stigmata of a dictatorship of the Left. 'There is nothing to choose between communism and fascism,' Mr. Waugh seems to be saying; but these two creeds, though they have much in common, are not the same, and can only be made to appear the same by leaving out a good deal. Again, Mr. Waugh's portraits of scheming Neutralian officials would have been more telling if he were not too contemptuous of the kind of state that calls itself a 'people's democracy' to find out in detail how it works.

This is an extremely readable book, but it lacks the touch of affection that political satire ought to have. One can accept Scott-King's estimate of the modern world, and perhaps even agree with him that a classical education is the best prophylactic against insanity, and yet still feel that he could fight the modern world more effectively if he would occasionally turn aside to read a sixpenny pamphlet on Marxism.

Munro Beattie (review date 1955)

SOURCE: Review of *Tactical Exercise,* in *The Canadian Forum,* Vol. XXXV, No. 42, May, 1955, p. 44.

[*In the following review of* Tactical Exercise, *Beattie calls the volume "minor Waugh," arguing that many of the stories have gimmicky surprise endings. Nevertheless, Beattie concedes the tales are witty and entertaining.*]

This collection of stories and sketches is chronologically arranged. The first story Evelyn Waugh wrote when he was aged 7 years 1 month. It need never have been published; the Daisy Ashford aspect of Waugh we might at least have been spared. The other stories, which appeared originally between 1932 and 1953, are all amusing in diverse ways and to various degrees. The 1932 story **"Cruise"** comprises letters and postcards written by a middle-class ingenue on a Mediterranean cruise: rather dim wit, an occasional chuckle. **"Bella Fleace Gave a Party"** (1932) is richer in details of décor and temperament. It is the first of several stories in the book which are structurally alike, each leading the reader, more or less unexpectedly, to a surprise ending—a "gimmick" I believe it is called in other areas of the entertainment world—which sorts ill with the superb sophistication of the kind of story telling we used to associate with the name of Waugh. Of these anecdotes by the Mayfair O. Henry the most interesting is the title story, **"Tactical Exercise,"** which must have proved a bit of a blow to many readers of *Good Housekeeping*, where it first appeared. **"Mr. Loveday's Little Outing"** (1935), a bland blend of the gruesome and the hilarious, comes closer to the authentic Waugh than any of the other stories.

The best of these pieces, however, is the longest: **"Work Suspended"** (1941), about 100 pages of a novel which was never finished. This is a charming fragment, abounding in wit and invention. But one agrees with the author: it was getting nowhere; the drift is delectable but unprofitable. The worst of the pieces is the most recently written, a would-be-macabre study of Welfare Britain in the next generation. **"Love Among the Ruins,"** published as a separate book in 1953, relates the romance of an incendiary orphan, reared at the expense and according to the wisdom of the State, and a ballet-girl with a golden beard. The blurb suggests that it is similar in tone to *The Loved One*. In tone, perhaps, but assuredly not in artistry. *The Loved One*, repulsive little creation though it is, is a deft narrative stylishly written. **"Love Among the Ruins"** is only nasty and proves conclusively what many of us have been suspecting about Waugh's work for some time: that satire generated by disdain is rarely first-rate.

This book, then, is minor Waugh. Nevertheless, it is more elegant and entertaining than the best that most other storytellers of the day can manage. Those who here meet Waugh for the first time will derive from *Tactical Exercise* an evening's diversion though they may not understand what all the shouting has been about. Those of us who used to do the shouting and who began—exultantly—buying Waughs in the vintage years of *Decline and Fall* and *Vile Bodies* will be pleased, at all events, to round out our collections.

Frederick J. Stopp (essay date 1958)

SOURCE: "Four More Entertainments, 1942–1953," in *Evelyn Waugh: Portrait of an Artist,* Chapman & Hall LTD, 1958, pp. 136–42, 152–57.

[*In the following excerpt, Stopp discusses* Scott-King's Modern Europe *and* Love Among the Ruins, *which he finds to be sad but humorous, and lacking in brutality or sentimentalism.*]

Scott-King's Modern Europe is a sad little story, finely wrought and economical in its effects, but sad. Superficially it owed its origin to a visit to Spain, where Mr Waugh joined in the celebrations in the summer of 1945 for the tercentenary of Vittoria, at Salamanca, and had his first experience of the machinery of official hospitality in the post-war world. But it contains his first reflections on the wider scene of mid-twentieth century Europe. Even without the footnote that 'The Republic of Neutralia is imaginary and composite and represents no existing state', we should recognize overtones of Jugoslavia and the Dalmatian coast, and the wider echoes of decay in European historical values everywhere. Combined with this is the radical uncertainty whether anything positive can ultimately have been achieved by a war which, appearing first through the medium of common-room wirelesses under a heroic and chivalrous disguise, became later 'a sweaty tug-of-war between teams of indistinguishable louts'. Uncertainty of the achievement, certainty of the losses incurred, these are the sad strains of the music which is here played.

The musician selected to perform is himself the reverse of distinguished. After failing to achieve a College Fellowship Scott-King has been classical master at Granchester for twenty-one years; Paul Pennyfeather, if he had stayed at Llanabba, would have been his contemporary. He has become a school institution, lamenting in a slightly nasal voice over modern decadence, and rejoicing in his reduced station through the defection of classical specialists to the Modern Side, fascinated by obscurity and failure, his own first and foremost. And his strange adventures during that summer of 1946 strike a note of dimness all along the line. Neutralia, through remaining out of the second World War physically, as did Scott-King spiritually, 'became remote, unconsidered, dim'. Dim also was Whitemaid, his sole English academic counterpart at the celebrations at Bellacita. Care and the fear of failure dogged and finally overcame Arturo Fe, Doctor of Bellacita University and official in the Ministry of Rest and Culture, Bogdan Antonic, the International Secretary, 'whose face was lined with settled distress and weariness', and Garcia the Engineer. Even with Lockwood, a former prize pupil and Scott-King's rescuer from No. 64 Jewish Illegal Immigrants Camp, the same mournful note is struck. 'Sad case, he was a sitter for the Balliol scholarship. Then he had to go into the army.'

But all these scattered notes of failure, of promise run to seed, of high hopes dashed, are gathered together in the name of Bellorius, 'The Last Latinist', the poet whose 1,500 lines of tedious Latin hexameters gained for him from an ungrateful Hapsburg nothing more than the cancellation of his court pension. Bellorius died poor and in some discredit in 1646; he is the patron-saint of dimness in this work, and it is this 'blood-brotherhood in dimness' which first drew Scott-King to study his work. The new-old and degenerate state of Neutralia could not have made a better choice when it put its first International Secretary on to searching the records for some suitable anniversary to commemorate, some occasion out of which to make political capital. And what irony in the subject to which this unknown early Neutralian humanist chose to devote his Latinity: 'a visit to an imaginary island of the New World where in primitive simplicity, untainted by tyranny or dogma, there subsisted a virtuous, chaste and reasonable community.' Such was the humanist dream which held Scott-King enthralled for fifteen years. The temptation represented by the engraved and embossed card on his breakfast table fell on fruitful soil in a man who for years had been secretly wedded to the warm Southern seas—'all that travel agent ever sought to put in a folder, fumed in Scott-King's mind that drab morning'—and he went. The awakening could hardly have been ruder.

It was a world of unreason into which he thus stepped, with the one fundamental nightmare characteristic of unreason: nothing is as it seems, all is facade, covering an ugly reality. The air stewardess seems an amalgam of midwife, governess, and shopwalker; Miss Bombaum might be an actress or harlot or lady-novelist, but is in fact a topliner in modern journalism; Arturo Fe might be a slightly ageing film-actor, but is scholar, lawyer, and civil servant. The Hotel 22nd March, known through its political past under a score of aliases, but always referred to as the Ritz; the National Memorial at Simona, which turns out to commemorate a piece of political thuggery; Bellorius himself, confused by Miss Bombaum with the totally different Byzantine General Belisaurus, and finally commemorated by an appalling statue commissioned years before by a fraudulent commercial magnate, representing no one, show that even institutions have but an uncertain hold on reality and stability. It is perhaps but a belated recognition of the power of the genius loci when Scott-King departs by the 'underground railway' as an Ursuline nun, and arrives in Palestine as an illegal Jewish immigrant. All appearances are deceptive in this modern masquerade—a stage-set indeed, but an ominous one.

Appearances are deceptive since in this constant process of scene-shifting which calls itself modern European history the features of the new dispensation are constantly becoming apparent beneath the fading outlines of the old; and in this general dissolution the new is ugly and brash and the dispossessed old is tired and uncomprehending: too wise to be chagrined, too cultured to protest. Those few remaining Neutralian aristocrats, descendants of the Crusaders and Knights of Malta, who haunt the Ritz like lingering shades, gazing with 'inky, simian eyes' at that portent of the new Europe, the statuesque Miss Sveningen,

are blood-brothers of the Arabs of East Africa whom Mr. Waugh met in the clubs of the seaboard towns; dispossessed by protectorates in Somalia, Aden, Tanganyika, and Zanzibar (*Black Mischief*, *Remote People*), and by more ruthless methods of penetration in Harar (*Waugh in Abyssinia*).

It is to this aristocracy of the dispossessed that Scott-King finally and defiantly commits himself in his last words to the headmaster: '"I think it would be very wicked indeed to do anything to fit a boy for the modern world. . . . I think it is the most long-sighted view that it is possible to take."' Long-sighted, since Scott-King has finally seen the fallacy of moving with the times: taking up economic history because of the decrease in classical specialists. For change, like revolution, has the saturnine propensity of eating its own children. The more international politics become, the more men reach across the barriers of communities to link up with their ideological brethren, the more of their fellow-men find themselves displaced, dispossessed, outcast. '"It is extraordinary how many people without the requisite facilities seem anxious to cross frontiers today."' Thus the Neutralian Major of Police, who significantly doubles his official functions with running the underground escaping organization. '"That is where my position in the police is a help. . . . I also have a valued connexion with the Neutralian government. Troublesome fellows whom they want to disappear pass through my hands in large numbers."' The machinery of the modern state is Janus-headed, facing both ways, creating both tyranny and graft, 'supporting a vast ill-paid bureaucracy whose work is tempered and humanized by corruption'. Miss Bombaum was more right than she knew when, quoting from one of her recent articles, she described the underground as 'an alternative map of Europe . . . the new world taking shape beneath the surface of the old . . . the new ultra-national citizenship'. And the new world is the caricature of the old. The 'Republic' of Neutralia is itself a travesty of that more ancient form of state which reaches back to the Greek polis. The Underground, the symbol of the new fraternity of the displaced person, as it takes shape below the surface of old citizenships, is appropriately enough expressed in the symbols of the French Revolution. At the little seaport of Santa Maria, itself a palimpsest of Mediterranean history, from Athenian colony to Napoleonic conquest, there lies on the cobbled water-front a large warehouse, now Underground dispersal centre, a birthplace of the new ultra-national citizenship. Here, ensconced in a bed by the door, whose coverlet was littered with food, weapons, and tobacco, lay the female guardian, sometimes making lace like a tricoteuse of the Terror, while her husband, as supervising officer, made a brief appearance at the door in the hour before dawn, and called the roll of those who were to be 'despatched' on that day.

This was Scott-King's last visual impression of modern Europe when he embarked on the final stage of his adventure—that sea-journey in the battened-down hold of a ship over whose horrors the narrator draws a veil, and from which he emerges, first fully conscious, 'sitting stark naked while a man in khaki drill taps his knee with a ruler'. And at this point a memory from an earlier work of Waugh comes back, a parallel to this total loss of personality insistently demands entry to the mind. Is not the spiritual odyssey of Scott-King which takes him from Granchester to Granchester via Bellacita, the Underground and a Palestinian camp, this escape from the innocence of academic life into the seaminess of modern existence, and a return incognito across the waters—is not this all strangely reminiscent of the progress of Paul Pennyfeather from Scone to Scone via Lanabba, King's Thursday, the Latin-American Entertainment Co. Ltd (another underground railway), and Blackstone Gaol? And if this is so, has nothing been achieved in the twenty-one years in which Scott-King has dreamed his dream of the Mediterranean? Paul, when restored to Scone and reflecting how right the Church had been to put down early Christian heresy, has at least laid the ghost of religious doubt. What ghost has been laid by Scott-King's excursion into the world of unreason? Can it be Bellorius? In the staff-room on his return to Granchester he admits:

> "To tell you the truth I feel a little *désoeuvré*. I must look for a new subject."
>
> "You've come to the end of old Bellorius at last?"
>
> "Quite to the end."

But why, we may ask, must Bellorius go? Or rather why, in the years which lie ahead of Scott-King, may we be certain that no other Bellorius will absorb his devoted powers? Had there been still some mark of imperfection, one small blemish on the otherwise perfectly dim mental outlook of Scott-King? Even this suggestion seems strange in a man so abstracted from the realities of the moment as Scott-King, who finished the work of translating Bellorius's Latin hexameters into Spenserian stanzas 'at the time of the Normandy landings', and who composed his threnody on 'The Last Latinist' at the time of the peace celebrations; or for a man who 'positively rejoiced in his reduced station'. Far from harbouring a baffled sense of having missed all the compensations of life, he was definitely blasé; and a passage of concealed quotation from Pater's famous description of La Gioconda gives him, in this freedom of the mind, the mysterious agelessness of one who was 'jaded with accumulated experience of his imagination'. And his description of himself as 'an adult, an intellectual, a classical scholar, almost a poet', becomes his leitmotif in the undignified situations into which he is plunged.

And yet, when the story opens, Scott-King is still one small, one minute stage removed from genuine detachment: though superficially content with, nay fascinated by his reduced station, he compensates with the life of the dreamer. After years of labour on his translation, his opus, his 'monument to dimness', the shade of Bellorius still stood at his elbow demanding placation—that shade which was perhaps the temptation to glory in the distinction of being 'The Last Latinist', to create a mental Utopia in the

form of an imaginary island governed by reason and free from tyranny and dogma, the temptation to escape and to dramatize the conditions of escape, to invert the pattern of one's own dimness by erecting a model to dimness elsewhere. So, to discharge his last obligation to Bellorius, Scott-King distilled his learning, wrote his last little essay and thereby gave a hostage to the outside world of noisy Neutralians—and the embossed and engraved invitation on the breakfast-table was the sign that the challenge had been accepted. There he was to learn the total irrelevance of the mental landscape of his mind to the modern age, to be finally disabused of the expectation of ever finding a 'virtuous, chaste and reasonable community', be these qualities never so diluted.

More than that, the man who has raised one monument to Bellorius is brought to make a speech before another monument, and, having done so, and the cord having released the enveloping cloth, is confronted with a likeness, in the eyes of the world, of his hero: 'It was not Bellorius . . . ; it was not even unambiguously male; it was scarcely human.' That unveiling was the last lesson which Scott-King has to learn, to be reconciled finally to his own dimness, and to the dimness, seen in the light of the world, of the subject and outlook which he represents. In the state of mind in which he returns, even the erection of monuments to a forgotten world is a senseless gesture, even the consciousness of being 'an adult, an intellectual' is excessive, even to be blasé is hybris. The only thing is to accept one's own obscurity, to be content to administer a wasting patrimony, without even the consolation of being a martyr, an outpost, a forlorn cause. The intellectual and classical scholar was, in the academic life, as was Bellorius at the court of the Hapsburgs, a pensioner of such figures of the new order as Griggs, the civics master, dilating on the sufferings of the Tolpuddle Martyrs. Now even the pension has been cancelled, and no voice will be raised to extol the humanist and regret his passing. A sad story—delicately wrought, but still sad.

In a lecture given in 1953, Professor Romano Guardini commented on the loss by modern man of the primeval images of human existence: the road, the spring of water, the flame of fire. The road was no longer a thing to be walked, stumbled, toiled along, an image of man's earthly way, but the geometrically shortest route between map reference A and B; flowing water was no longer a reminder of time, an occasion of reflection on the whence and the whither of human life, but a jet of liquid from a tap; fire was no longer both comfort and retribution, the living, leaping flame of inspiration, but a tamed demon in a lighter, flicked on, flicked off, to accompany the inevitable cigarette.

In the last sentence of ***Love Among the Ruins,*** written during work on the Crouchback novels to provide an hour's amusement for the still civilized, Mr Waugh strikes just this same note: 'Miles felt ill at ease during the ceremony and fidgeted with something small and hard which he found in his pocket. It proved to be his cigarette-lighter, a most uncertain apparatus. He pressed the catch and instantly, surprisingly, there burst out a tiny flame—gemlike, hymeneal, auspicious.'

Hymeneal, auspicious? An augury for the success of his nuptials with the State-provided Miss Flower? Or a comforting reminder that there was always a way out? Did he feel that 'something small and hard' with the comfort of a groom fingering the ring in his waistcoat pocket, or of a cornered criminal fingering his knuckle-duster? Probably the latter. Faced with the hideous mess the State had made of his lover's, Clara's face, he had walked out at random and anguished, and arrived at Mountjoy Castle, the scene of his imperfect rehabilitation by a beneficent if not beneficial State policy. 'He knew what he wanted. He carried in his pocket a cigarette lighter which often worked. It worked for him now. . . .' After the great holocaust, his mind was calm and empty. 'The scorched earth policy had succeeded. He had made a desert in his imagination which he might call peace . . . the enchantments that surrounded Clara were one with the splendours of Mountjoy.' All the paraphernalia of the State, the Ministers of Rest, Culture and Welfare, the Mountjoys Old and New, the Dome of Security, and Service of Euthanasia, the Method of Reform, Remedial Repose and Rehabilitation, even the Result, Miles Plastic, as shown to the world, are one and all no more than stage properties of this Grand Guignol of the future. The genuine symbol, the touch of mania in the whole scene, that rich glint of lunacy in the eye which distinguished Aimée from her fellow receptionists, the note of a primeval urge distorted and diverted from its proper channel, is seen in that small and hard object which enables man to burn his past without however being able to rise, Phoenix-like, from the ashes. No liberating action, this, as when Dennis Barlow burnt his immediate past in the furnaces of the pet's cemetery, no sloughing off of a young heart before returning enriched to the roots of one's culture. Miles, the Modern Man, is the conditioned personality who recognizes his own image when confronted with a simple, rough packing case, model of the new Mountjoy Castle to rise on the ruins of the old. For him, there is no ticket back home; the gutted prison and the rehabilitated prisoner means no more than the destruction of a richer past for the benefit of a poorer future; the Revolution, as in *Scott-King,* eats its own children. The Common Man is an inverted myth, a counter-Prometheus, not one who steals fire from the Gods, but one who fondles a small hard presence in his pocket as a guarantee of the power of unlimited destruction.

The story is a 'romance' of the not so distant future. Mr Waugh is pleased to imagine, for our entertainment, the condition of a State-made desert in which the boredom of prison is the general condition of society, and a certain tranquil melancholy, conducive to some degree of culture and individuality, is only to be found in prison. Social life in the Welfare State is a fate worse than death, the Euthanasia Centre—a kind of Whispering Glades in reverse—the most popular service. Short of Euthanasia, residence in places like Mountjoy Castle under a new Penology, whose fundamental principle is that 'no man could be held responsible for the consequences of his own acts', is the most desirable thing.

Here lies a rich quarry of material for flashes of paradoxical humour: the law-court, which all but acquits Miles for incendiarism, and all but commits the bystanders, bereaved relatives of the airmen he has incinerated, for contempt of court; the Euthanasia Service, slack when a strike or anything of human interest is afoot, but normally so popular that foreigners with one-way tickets are turned back at Channel ports; the infinite advantages of being an Orphan rather than the product of a Full Family Life; and the minor diverting possibilities of the State newspeak—*State be with you, State help me.* The new Penology descends ultimately from Sir Wilfred Lucas-Dockery, Governor of Blackstone Gaol, as the old lags of Mountjoy, Sweat and Soapy, with their melancholy regret that 'there's no security in crime these days', echo the sturdy individualism of the aged burglar at Egdon Heath, who urged Paul to stand up for his rights when given caviar for cold bacon.

The planned dilapidation of Satellite City and of its main permanent State building, the Dome of Security, is the contemporary note: an ironic comment on communal lack of enterprise by one who saw only too keenly the shadow side of the *panem et circenses* provided by the 1951 Festival buildings, and by their most prominent feature, the Dome of Discovery. The Dome of Security itself is an epitome of the whole self-defeating nature of social security schemes in this story: 'The eponymous dome had looked well enough in the architect's model'—say, for instance, the Beveridge Report—'shallow certainly but amply making up in girth what it lacked in height. . . . But to the surprise of all, when the building arose and was seen from the ground, the dome blandly vanished'. Security for all is planned, but blandly evades the planners, just as 'great sheets of glass planned to "trap" the sun, admitted a few gleams from scratches in their coat of tar'. A prime urge of the human race vanishes into thin air at the touch of a blueprint; the sun cannot be trapped, and fire is reduced to the incendiary possibilities of a cigarette-lighter.

The pointlessness of the plan at large is paralleled by the desultory progress of Miles Plastic's last, melancholy attempt to achieve love among the ruins; his affair with Clara, on whom two State-enforced operations end by foisting a facial mask as unnatural and obscene as the smirking travesty of a face given to Frank Hinsley at Whispering Glades; and his final resort to the last ecstasy of wholesale conflagration. And it is in a desultory and whimsical manner that Mr. Waugh has chosen to point his reflections on the decline of our culture by the allusive employment of fragments from three artists of a banished age: Tennyson, Browning, and the neo-classical sculptor Canova. Tennyson's 'Now sleeps the crimson petal, now the white', and 'Come into the garden, Maud', provide the setting and the concealed quotations for that 'rich, old-fashioned Tennysonian night' at Mountjoy Castle, which is Miles's last night in Arcadia before an inscrutable State decrees his rehabilitation and thrusts him out into the world for which he has been conditioned. Browning's poem 'Love among the Ruins' takes over the setting: 'the site once of a city great and gay', treeless slopes where once

> . . . the domed and daring palace shot its spires
> Up like fires . . .

Here there remains of past glory but a single turret, but the poet knows

> That a girl with eager eyes and yellow hair
> Waits me there . . .

as Clara waits for Miles in her cubicle in a Nissen hut, filled with the bric-a-brac of a vanished civilization. And Henry Moses's reproductions of Canova's marbles—so reminiscent, in its 1876 binding, of the Victorian drawing-room with perhaps a Venus de Milo in the corner—provides the starting point for the illustrations. By means of a homely paste book technique which must have given Mr. Waugh much innocent amusement, he constructed the figures for the ironic juxtapositions of life in the Greek Polis and in Satellite City: the drawings 'Exiles from Welfare', 'Experimental Surgery', and others, bearing such inscriptions as 'Canova fee., Moses delin., Waugh perfec.'

To Tennyson's mysterious Maud and to Browning's girl with the yellow hair, to Canova's groups of Cupid and Psyche and of the Three Graces, Mr. Waugh has added one further, delightful fancy, that 'long, silken, corn-gold beard', which was the only feature that broke the canon of pure beauty in Clara's face when Miles first beheld it, complemented as it was by the voice, with its 'deep, sweet tone, all unlike the flat, conventional accent of the age'. But for Miles, this crowning feature, whether seen in the clear light of Satellite day, or 'silvered like a patriarch's in the midnight radiance' of another Tennysonian night, *is* the canon of beauty. '"On such a night as this," said Miles, supine, gazing into the face of the moon'—and echoing all unknowingly the *Merchant of Venice*—'"on such a night as this I burnt an Air Force station and half its occupants."' That was the only moment of ecstasy he had then known. The beard brought, for Miles, the dawning of the proscribed emotion of love, 'a word seldom used by politicians and by them only in moments of pure fatuity', which singles out two persons from the herd and gives them an indelible, rubber-stamp obliterating impress. But what State has given, as an unexpected result of the Jungmann operation, State may take away. The removal of the beard by experimental surgery, and its replacement by a synthetic rubber skin, 'a tight, slippery mask, salmon pink', is the end. Miles retches unobtrusively, walks off and burns down Mountjoy; revolt is exorcized in a moment of ecstasy. '. . . his brief adult life lay in ashes; the enchantments that surrounded Clara were one with the splendours of Mountjoy; her great golden beard, one with the tongues of flame that had leaped and expired among the stars. . . .'

The theme of the lovers brought together, and parted, the one disfigured by act of State, is common to this work and

to George Orwell's *1984*. But here we must at least say, *thank State for the beard*; for it is that which discharges harmlessly, like a lightning conductor, the more sultry implications of this sad little love story. Orwell develops the theme with the full attendant resources of brutality which seem now inevitable in any sombre view of the future. Mr. Waugh's short story never loses its astringent humour and freedom from sentiment. Both qualities are guaranteed, not only by his own style and outlook, but also, in this particular case, by the beard.

James F. Carens (essay date 1966)

SOURCE: "Africa, Europe, and the Dreary Future," in *The Satiric Art of Evelyn Waugh,* University of Washington Press, 1966, pp. 148–56.

[*In the following excerpt, Carens examines the postwar novellas* Scott-King's Modern Europe *and* Love Among the Ruins, *noting their bleak pessimism and defeatist sentiments.*]

Two grim, short political satires with none of *Scoop's* ebullience or consolation—*Scott-King's Modern Europe* and *Love Among the Ruins*—followed the Second World War. The first of these recounts the visit of Scott-King, Classical Master at Granchester for twenty-one years, to a mythical totalitarian state called Neutralia. The second satire was in the tradition of *Brave New World* and *1984*; Waugh's inverted Utopia depicted a fully socialized England of the near future. Both works are bleakly pessimistic in outlook.

The form of *Scott-King's Modern Europe* resembles that of *Scoop*; the opening and conclusion of the novel, which place Scott-King at Granchester, frame the confusions and distractions of his journey to the tercentenary of Bellorius, Neutralia's late Latin poet, in the same way that the Boot Magna sections of *Scoop* frame the terrors of William Boot's journey to Ishmaelia. Waugh himself has made the most penetrating analysis of *Scott-King's Modern Europe.* Explaining to an interviewer that he was sure "there's a good thing hidden away in" the satire "somewhere" but that he had not "done it," Waugh said that if he were to do the book over he would try to suggest "more of the real horror" of such a journey. Burdened with "too much insignificant detail"[1] for so short a piece, as Waugh admitted, *Scott-King's Modern Europe* does not convey any of the real terrors of the contemporary totalitarian state. Waugh's subject is not, to be sure, Nazi Germany or Soviet Russia. A small "republic" which has managed to remain on the sidelines during the Second World War, Neutralia is, nevertheless, "a typical modern state, governed by a single party, acclaiming a dominant Marshal, supporting a vast ill-paid bureaucracy."

Waugh directs his satire at the absurd pretensions of Neutralia, which contrast with its seedy reality, and at the clumsy propagandistic motive of the bogus tercentenary. His Neutralia, reminiscent of Anthony Powell's Venusberg, is a mélange of baroque memorials and shabby, unfinished modern buildings. The Neutralian officials—Dr. Arturo Fe, who is in charge of the program, and Bogadin Antonic, a minor bureaucrat—are engaged in a desperate struggle for survival against inflation, low wages, and rivals. At the banquet honoring the visiting dignitaries, the servants stuff their pockets with food for their families. The real purpose of the celebration soon becomes obvious. Scott-King and his fellow guests are duped into attending a luncheon at party headquarters and visiting the memorial of a particularly vicious massacre; photographs of the compromised delegates are distributed to the press. The delegates fall out among themselves when they discover that they are being used for Neutralian propaganda; and only Scott-King, who has been accused of being a "Fascist beast," attends the unveiling of a memorial to his ideal, Bellorius, composer of a poem that had celebrated a rational Utopia in Latin hexameters. The statue, like the tercentenary celebration, is a travesty:

> The figure now so frankly brought to view had lain long years in a mason's yard. It had been commissioned in an age of free enterprise for the tomb of a commercial magnate whose estate, on his death, had proved to be illusory. It was not Bellorius; it was not even the fraudulent merchant prince; it was not even unambiguously male; it was scarcely human; it represented perhaps one of the virtues.

If Waugh was entitled to emphasize only the shabbiness, phoniness, and poverty of such totalitarian regimes as those of Spain and Yugoslavia (the countries that provided him with models for Neutralia) and to ignore their more vicious aspects, he ought, at the same time, to have softened the ending of *Scott-King's Modern Europe.* Nothing in the middle of the satire prepares for the ironic pessimism of the conclusion. To be sure, Scott-King has had to escape from Neutralia by the underground—not because he was in danger from the regime, but because his own consulate would not help him—and has consequently turned up stark naked in a camp for illicit immigrants in Palestine. But such satire is directed primarily at the difficulties of travel in modern Europe in the period following the Second World War and only secondarily at the evils of totalitarianism. Consequently, Scott-King's abandonment of the rationalist idealism of Bellorius and his refusal, on returning to Granchester, to do anything "to fit a boy for the modern world" seem excessive reactions to his actual experiences. The defeatist tone of the conclusion of *Scott-King's Modern Europe* typifies Waugh's postwar satires. William Boot, at least, had been able to find security at Boot Magna Hall; Scott-King returns to Granchester to discover that there are fifteen fewer classical specialists for the coming term. And he is fully convinced, as the headmaster warns, that the time may come when there will be no more classical boys at all.

There are no classical boys in the England of *Love Among the Ruins.* Miles Plastic, the antihero of this satire, lives at a period perhaps two decades or so in the future; a product of a state orphanage, he has been scientifically reared to adjust to the modern world. The anti-Utopia in which Miles lives has definitely been influenced by other contemporary works in the genre. Waugh's "State be with you" echoes prayers and oaths in the name of Ford in Huxley's *Brave New World*; the golden beard of Waugh's heroine, consequence of an unsuccessful sterilization, suggests both the condition of the "freemartins" of *Brave New World* and the deformity of the heroine of *Ape and Essence.* Allusion to the prevalence of sexual promiscuity also associates Waugh's satire with Huxley's.

In its drabness, however, Waugh's totalitarian future resembles Orwell's *1984.* Scarcity, disorder, and grubbiness, rather than the glistening, antiseptic orderliness which Huxley described, characterize the England of the future as Waugh, following Orwell, has imagined it. As in Huxley's book and in Orwell's, the state is hostile to love, but it encourages promiscuity and frequent divorce. Certain details of *Love Among the Ruins* are similar to elements in the satirical poem "The Unknown Citizen" by W. H. Auden. The poem satirizes the tendency of the modern bureaucratic state to reduce human personality to a series of numbers and notations on file cards. The terms "Citizen" and "Modern Man," used to describe the subject of Auden's poem, are both applied to Miles Plastic, whose identity has also been reduced to a social psychologist's report. "In less than a minute," says the Deputy-Chief of the Ministry of Welfare, when Miles is released from corrective treatment, "you become a Citizen. This little pile of papers is *You.* When I stamp them, Miles the Problem ceases to exist and Mr. Plastic the Citizen is born."

These similarities to other satirical protests against the authoritarianism, dehumanization, and mechanization of life in the modern world are not defects in Waugh's novel. His short book is a much slighter anti-Utopia than Huxley's or Orwell's. *Love Among the Ruins* does not reveal such inventive fantasy as *Brave New World,* or the intellectual grasp of the nature of totalitarianism, accumulative power of sordid detail, and sense of evil of *1984.* Nevertheless, within its own limits, it is an effective variation on what has now become a traditional theme.

Little can be gained from judging such satires as *Brave New World, 1984,* or *Love Among the Ruins* as prophecies of the condition of life in the future. The real point of these novels is that the brave new world is *now*; 1984 is 1944, 1954, or 1964; the ruins described in Waugh's short novel surround us. The satirical force of these works derives from the fact that the authors have carried to certain extremes of exaggeration tendencies which already undeniably exist. Huxley's soma, his feelies, his Malthusian drill are pointless if regarded as predictions; pertinent if regarded as parody of the abandoned materialism, mindless popular entertainments, and sexual indulgences of the present. Orwell's analysis of Newspeak, doublethink, and crimestop is, in fact, an analysis of the slave-mentality which sometimes dominates the modern world; the systematic destruction of the past which he describes is really, according to both Orwell and Waugh, what the newspapers have been doing for years, and the sport of heresy hunters throughout the world for many decades. Waugh's "ruins" are not in the remote future. The Dome of Security, whose eponymous dome, which had looked so well in the blueprints, failed even to show when the building was completed, is a travesty of the Dome of Discovery, a building in the best contemporary style erected for the 1951 Festival of Britain.[2] And Waugh's Department of Euthanasia is an exaggeration of the British public's interest in mercy killing.

Once again, the satirist launches an assault on a favorite subject: modern penology and that kind of social psychology which assumes that no man can "be held responsible for his own acts." The central attack in **Love Among the Ruins** is leveled at this denial of freedom of the will, a position which shocks Waugh as conservative and as Catholic. Mr. Sweat, an aged criminal who is receiving "corrective treatment" with Miles at the luxurious country seat, Mountjoy Castle, assails the modern attitude toward the criminal: "There's no understanding of crime these days like what there was. I remember when I was a nipper, the first time I came up before the beak, he spoke up straight: 'My lad,' he says, 'you are embarking upon a course of life that can only lead to disaster and degradation in this world and everlasting damnation in the next.' Now that's talking." But, alas, Mr. Sweat has fallen upon evil days; he has become, with Miles, an "antisocial phenomenon."

To achieve his satirical effect, as he sets out after the warped sentimentalism he regards as a feature of the welfare state, Waugh inverts all the traditional values. In the most painfully funny episode of the satire, Miles is brought before the court for having burned up an air force station and its occupants. "Arson, Wilful Damage, Manslaughter, Prejudicial Conduct, and Treason" have all been struck from the indictment, which has been reduced to the single charge of antisocial activity. The trial proceeds with the same illogical logic. "Widows, mothers, and orphans of the incinerated airmen" may resent the fact, but the hearing develops into "a concerted eulogy of the accused." The prosecution's old-fashioned attempt to emphasize the damages caused by the arson is futile; the judge insists that the jury expunge from its memory the sentimental details:

> "May be a detail to you," said a voice from the gallery. "He was a good husband to me."
>
> "Arrest that woman," said the judge.

When the jurymen bring in a verdict of guilty and recommend "mercy toward the various bereaved persons who from time to time in the course of the hearing had been committed for contempt," the judge reprimands them for impertinence and sends Miles off to the pleasures of Mountjoy Castle.

Sad epilogues to the history of Utopian literature, *Brave New World, 1984, Ape and Essence,* and **Love Among the**

Ruins also make a striking commentary on contemporary history's impact on writers. When Aldous Huxley wrote *Brave New World* in 1932, he did offer some positive alternative to a mechanized and increasingly totalitarian world. Though his satire ended with the death of John the Savage, it indicated that something in human nature was impervious to total regimentation. Even after the Second World War, when Huxley wrote *Ape and Essence,* an infinitely depressing vision of life after the devastation of atomic warfare, he offered, as an alternative to the desolate, guilt-ridden, devil-worshiping society he described, the religious-communal society to which his hero and heroine escape. Orwell's *1984,* appearing a year later than *Ape and Essence,* suggested no alternative at all. Its antihero, Winston Smith, experiences a few elusive moments of happiness in his love affair with Julia; but the depressing conclusion of *1984* gives us a pair of lovers who, subjected to the diabolical torture of the Ministry of Love, have lost the one thing they believed could not be destroyed: their love for one another.

Waugh is no easier on us in *Love Among the Ruins.* As in *1984,* sexual love and some fragments of the past seem to grant his central characters a release from the drabness and tedium of society. When Miles meets Clara, the golden-bearded former ballet dancer, "hope" has appeared. In the cubicle of a Nissen hut, where Miles finds that Clara has preserved two eighteenth-century French paintings, a gilt clock, and a mirror framed in porcelain flowers, these two find a refuge from the hideous present. As in Orwell's work, however, the "state" will not countenance love. Because Clara is found to be with child, a more accomplished state surgeon than the first successfully completes the "Klugmann" that failed. He also manages to remove the skin of Clara's lower face and to substitute a synthetic rubber that takes greasepaint perfectly. Miles stares at the tight, slippery mask of salmon pink. He retches unobtrusively. Even Clara's unorthodoxy, her devotion to her art, for which she is willing to surrender everything, is corruptible by the state.

Miles has, to be sure, one other alternative—the pleasure of arson, which twice permits him to escape from being the "Modern Man." When the short satire ends, Miles is preparing to tour the country as the ministry's sole example of a successful corrective treatment—all others having died in the fire Miles set to destroy Mountjoy. In expectation of an early divorce, he is being married, as the Minister wishes, to Miss Flower, a "gruesome" young woman. Miles seems to have submitted completely to the scheme of things. But as his hand fidgets in his pocket during the ceremony at the Registry, it encounters his cigarette lighter. When Miles presses the catch, a flame rises, "gemlike, hymeneal, auspicious," and boding no good to Miss Flower.

This conclusion, mingling violence and the comic, is another example of Waugh's favorite shock effect. Its meaning, as a conclusion to the satire, is grim enough. Carried any further, the dehumanizing tendencies that the satirist observes in contemporary England may create a civilization in which rebellion itself can be only futile and destructive. The full irony of the title of the work is borne home. In Browning's "Love Among the Ruins," the speaker, who surveys the ruins of a great city of the past, disdains the mortal glory which has passed away and turns to the love of the blonde girl who waits for him in the ruins; in Waugh's satire, no girl waits, and, as in *1984,* only the ruins remain.

Notes

1. Harvey Breit, "Evelyn Waugh," *The Writer Observed* (Cleveland, Ohio, 1956), pp. 43–4.

2. Stopp, *Evelyn Waugh,* p. 46.

Christopher Hollis (essay date 1966)

SOURCE: In an introduction to *Decline and Fall,* by Evelyn Waugh, Heinemann Educational Books LTD, 1966, pp. ix–xx.

[*In the following introduction to* Decline and Fall, *Hollis places the novella in the context of Waugh's life and writings.*]

The younger generation came in his last years to think of Evelyn Waugh as the very symbol of reaction. He appeared to them as a champion of a vanishing order, of whose survival he despaired. He wrote about peers and county families. He jeered at the crudities of Hoopers of lowly birth or of transatlantic adventurers like Rex Mottram who had invaded and annexed for themselves the privileges of British life. All foreigners were to him merely comic. In art he condemned the formlessness of modern painters. In literature he despised the poverty of vocabulary, the inattention to grammar, to coherence and to the structure of the sentence of the younger novelists. He was without hesitation in proclaiming that he had lived on into an age of total decay, in which he made a pose of being a man old beyond his years. To those who had known him for a life-time it was amusing to remember that it was as a leader of the so-called Bright Young Things—of those who were in revolt against the starchiness of their age— that he first made his name in the world. He was then hailed as the first spokesman of the rising generation, which was being criticized by its elders and professed betters as anarchical and irresponsible, as an underminer of the fabric of society.

Decline and Fall, published in 1928, was Evelyn Waugh's first novel, his first public bid for leadership of the rising generation. One says 'public bid', because he had won for himself a considerable reputation a few years before at Oxford. The reputation was not one of which tutors and college authorities approved. Although he had gone up to Hertford College as a scholar he had not distinguished himself in his Schools, any more indeed than had the friends with whom he associated. He had not won any

post of distinction even in Societies that were not narrowly academic. But he had won for himself a formidable reputation as one of the leading figures in an Oxford society, which, if not quite so bizarre as the Bollinger Club and the first chapters of *Decline and Fall,* was not far different from the Oxford in which Charles Ryder lived at the opening of *Brideshead Revisited.*

He started with advantages in the literary world, if connections with well-known names are indeed an advantage. His father, Arthur Waugh, was the Chairman of Chapman and Hall, the publishers. His brother, Alec, had a few years before sprung suddenly into fame and, in the eyes of some traditionalists, into obloquy by his *Loom of Youth,* in which the alleged crudities of his public school, Sherborne, were depicted. Evelyn Waugh had himself before *Decline and Fall* already published a book on Rossetti. His knowledge of painting was considerable. Indeed at Oxford his friends would, I think, have been uncertain whether his future would be that of an artist or a writer. He not only wrote but also illustrated—very competently—the first edition of *Decline and Fall.* But the public for a book on Rossetti was not that, which, as the spokesman of a whole generation, he was to reach with his early novels.

Decline and Fall is the story of a young theological student who at the opening of the book is an undergraduate at Scone College, Oxford. He is of middle class origin. He has been at a minor public school. An orphan, he is being brought up by a guardian. (It is a curiosity that none of Waugh's comic characters have a regular family background.) He is debagged one night in the Scone quad by the hearty aristocrats of the Bollinger Club, inebriated after their annual dinner, and is most unjustly sent down by the college authorities for indecent exposure. He obtains a post as schoolmaster at an absurd school in North Wales, where he becomes involved with a rich parent, Margot Beste-Chetwynde. She pretends that she is going to marry him, but in fact involves him in taking the responsibility for the white slave traffic activities in which she is involved. As a result he goes to prison, from which he is finally released through the exercise of her influence in Government circles. A forged certificate makes it appear that he has died under an operation for appendicitis and after a period of retirement in her villa on Corfu he returns, passing himself off as his own distant cousin, to his theological studies at Scone.

Waugh's apparent passage from rebellion in youth to reaction in old age is in a measure merely another example of the familiar story of *Milestones.* It happens with every generation that the young are irreverent iconoclasts who jeer at the traditions which they are invited to inherit, and the old become reluctant to change and hostile to their juniors who are threatening to rob them of all that has made life comfortable for them. Such a process has repeated itself throughout all the generations of history, and there have of course been special reasons why the young of Waugh's youth and the young of his old age—the young of today—should be critical of traditions. Both lived in the aftermath of a World War, in a threatened and crumbling society, and were at least tempted to believe, whether fairly or not, that it was their parents' excessive adherence to old ways which led them into their catastrophe. But, is there therefore an exact parallel between Waugh's rebellious youth and the rebellion of the youth whom he later criticized? Is there nothing between them except the span of forty years?

I do not think that that would be quite true. If a rebel is a man who thinks that some bad cause is on the throne and some good cause ought to supplant it, then neither in *Decline and Fall* nor elsewhere was Waugh ever exactly a rebel. Neither there nor elsewhere, it is hardly necessary to say, did he ever write of the Kitchen Sink. It was not so much that he attacked it or that he defended it. He was not interested in it. It can hardly be said—though very careless critics have said it—that *Decline and Fall* is a snobbish book in the sense that Waugh presents in it any glamourized picture of the upper classes. Both the aristocrats and the plutocratic adventurers in *Decline and Fall* are people singularly—and, if we are to consider them as in any way portraits of real people—almost inhumanly without principle or even the beginnings of an understanding of moral worth. It is a work of labefaction. The society of *Decline and Fall* is a society in which certainly the rich are able to see to it that it is always the humble and meek who pay. It is the wealthy members of the Bollinger Club who after their dinner roll home and make the College quad hideous. It is Paul Pennyfeather who suffers. But there is no suggestion that because they are rich they are therefore admirable. On the contrary they are portrayed as exceptionally unattractive young men. Their predecessors had three years before brought a fox in a cage into College and stoned it to death with champagne bottles. They attacked and debagged the wholly unoffending Pennyfeather and allowed him to be sent down for their offence. It was only afterwards that Alastair Digby-Vane-Trumpington had a certain twinge of conscience, which he assuaged by the insolent device of giving Pennyfeather twenty pounds. Margot Beste-Chetwynde is enormously beautiful and enormously rich but, again, she is as unattractive as possible—not merely incontinent but callous and brutal in her unhesitating readiness to make Pennyfeather pay the penalty for her sins. Waugh, it is true, is not concerned to deliver an overt Osbornean attack on the misdemeanours of these rich people, but he is only not so prepared because he finds an irredeemable futility in all mankind—so much so that it would indeed be a waste of trouble to depose one governing class in order to put in its place another equally worthless and equally absurd—to put down Lady Circumference and Sir Alastair Digby-Vane-Trumpington in order to put up Grimes and Philbrick. A straight-laced Conservative might have criticized—indeed many straight-laced Conservatives did criticize—the book on the ground that the effect of its picture of universal labefaction would be inevitably subversive, but no one could pretend that its purpose was to subvert. It was not the book of a radical. Its purpose was, as Waugh claims without qualification, to amuse.

'Please bear in mind throughout that IT IS MEANT TO BE FUNNY', he wrote in his Author's Note.

The author of *Decline and Fall* was indeed even at that stage of his life not a radical but a conservative—not indeed a conservative of principle (one who believes that a special order of society is divinely founded)—but a conservative of the school of David Hume, who believes that since power so inevitably corrupts whoever wields it, it is a waste of energy to trouble with the exchange of one set of masters for another. *Decline and Fall* gives the impression that it is the work of a young man who thinks that the world is a cruel and pitiless place and quite frankly derives amusement from contemplating its lack of pity. The characters are, it is true, so two-dimensional and unreal that, as has been said, serious compassion at their misfortune is hardly possible. The death of the young Lord Tangent from Mr Prendergast's starting gun at the Llanabba sports cannot tempt the reader to the sympathy which he must feel, in spite of its surrounding absurdities, at the death of young John Last in *A Handful of Dust*.

In spite of its general cynicism about human nature however, its picture of a society where no one—the Dons at Scone, the masters at Llanabba, the prison officials—does properly the work which he pretends to do and for which he receives his renumeration, *Decline and Fall* does not show human beings as at all influenced by standards in their conduct. There are no virtuous characters in the book—no characters indeed in the least influenced by virtue. But he had then, as fully as he has kept it through life, an artistic standard. He had an intense regard for the writing of good prose. In this *Decline and Fall* is a very different sort of book from, say, *Lucky Jim* and it is this difference which accounts for Waugh's distaste for Kingsley Amis's work. The sentences of *Decline and Fall* are shorter and more allusive than in his later novels in which he is concerned with what one might call three-dimensional characters—characters that have about them some aura of probability. Sometimes, as in Grime's assertion that Paul was in love, there was a trace, I fancy, of the influence of P. G. Wodehouse, whose style Waugh so greatly admired.

'Old boy,' said Grimes, 'you're in love.'

'Nonsense.'

'Smitten?' said Grimes.

'No, no.'

'The tender passion?'

'No.'

'Cupid's jolly little darts?'

'No.'

'Spring fancies, love's young dream.'

'Nonsense.'

'Not even a quickening of the pulse?'

'No.'

'A sweet despair?'

'Certainly not.'

'A trembling hope?'

'No.'

'A *frisson? a Je ne sais quoi?*'

'Nothing of the sort.'

'Liar,' said Grimes.

There was a long pause.

This is the unmistakable Wooster touch, and in general *Decline and Fall,* like all Waugh's works, and unlike the works of so many contemporary novelists, is the work of a man who is intensely concerned with the problem of style—who, before putting pen to paper, has most carefully thought out what he wants to say, how he can say it with the greatest economy, and is most exact in saying it.

Astonishingly mature as the work is, considering that Waugh was at the time only twenty-five, Waugh does of course here and there fall from the style that he has set himself as he would not have done in a later book. Thus when in the middle of the book Grimes, before the awful threat of his second marriage, bursts out into reflections of serious remorse we cannot but feel that Waugh had for the moment slipped from the style that he had set himself. Such a character as Grimes should not be allowed to mar himself by a relapse, however transient, into the language of decency. But such lapses are rare.

Always careful of language, Waugh has also been careful of language in another sense. It would not be possible to deduce from *Decline and Fall* any evidence that Waugh at that time was particularly oppressed by the problems of sexual conduct. His characters, from Margot Beste-Chetwynde at the one extreme to Grimes at the other, are cheerfully immoral in sexual as in other affairs. There is no attempt to disguise the fact that they are so—or to conceal their acts. White slaving is discussed light-heartedly as though it were more a matter for amusement than anything else. Yet Waugh does not here—or indeed anywhere else—think it necessary in modern fashion to sprinkle his prose with four-letter words. He would have thought that to do so was an evidence of literary insufficiency rather than of moral indecency.

It is again true enough to say that there is indeed a great contrast between the Waugh who wrote *Decline and Fall* and the other early two-dimensional novels, such as *Vile Bodies, Scoop* and *A Handful of Dust,* and the later author, say, of *Edmund Campion* and *Helena.* It would be clearly impossible to find such a character as the older Crouchback (of the Second World War trilogy) in *Decline and Fall.* It would be grotesque to imagine him there and indeed Waugh would certainly have denied it with contempt if some too careful expositor had pretended to find in *Decline and Fall* incipient evidence of the religious or political opinions to which he was subsequently to come. Cer-

tainly at the time when Waugh wrote the book he was a young man who, along with most of his companions, merely took it for granted that the Christian religion was untrue and irrelevant and had no passing suspicion that he would ever come to think it otherwise. Yet he had had a religious upbringing. His father was a practising High Churchman. He was sent to Lancing—a Woodard school. In his middle years there, he was, as he tells us in *A Little Learning,* for a time a pious communicant. He had a large number of Anglican clerical relations. His upbringing was very different from that of those moderns who have been raised in families quite uninvaded by any whisper of the possibility of religious practice or belief. It is not as easy as is sometimes thought wholly to slough off early religious influences, even when one wants to. The clouds of glory have a way of treading their path into shades of the prison house—even if sometimes in somewhat oddly filtered forms. No one—at any rate no one who goes back to it after reading Waugh's later books—can fail to be struck, considering its utterly worldly tone, with the extraordinarily large number of references to religion in *Decline and Fall.* It would be hard to think of any other writer who would have introduced so many into such a work. These references are not, it is true, in the least complimentary to religion. Without exception they hold it up to ridicule. Prendergast had been a clergyman who had abandoned his Orders because of 'Doubts' and then returned to them on the discovery that 'there is a species of person called a Modern Churchman who draws the full salary of a beneficed clergyman and need not commit himself to any religious belief.' He became a prison chaplain, where he was murdered by a religious maniac, filled with the belief that he was the Avenging Sword of the Lord. Philbrick is reported in a passing phrase to have been 'a Roman Catholic.' The other prison chaplain—at Egdon Heath—and the chaplain at Scone College are introduced and held up to mild ridicule. Margot Beste-Chetwynde's negro protégé, Chokey, makes absurd religious protestations. Paul Pennyfeather himself is a theological student at Scone at the beginning of the book and again a theological student there at the end, destined for Holy Orders. The contrast with Waugh's later properly religious books is so obvious as not to be worth drawing, but even without going forward to them, there is no suggestion in *Decline and Fall* of any character of the strength of Father Rothschild in *Vile Bodies,* who speaks with deeper understanding than the empty men and women around him. Yet throughout the book religion, if a subject for ridicule, is nevertheless always strangely present.

Waugh, the superior of his rivals in wit, is not unique in writing of characters who are unrelieved by virtue. If one knew nothing of him but these early novels, the temptation, to which so many critics fell, would be to dismiss him as a nihilist—a man who did not believe that life had a purpose or that there existed such things as values. One would only hesitate in such a verdict—only distinguish him from so many other modern authors—by noting that, though he did not appear to see much value in men, he saw much value in words. His devotion was to good prose, and this is a faith the more striking because, standing by itself, it is so evidently unreasonable. The art for art's sake of the nineties is not much now in fashion, but the belief in the value of words for words' sake still has its devotees. Cyril Connolly has told us that nothing is ultimately worth doing except the writing of a masterpiece. 'Words alone are certain good,' said Yeats. Sartre has confessed how in his youth he saw writing as 'the dedicated career.' Yet, if men are valueless, it is hard to see how writing exactly about them can be very valuable. Why should it matter what one says, if it does not matter what happens? So, whatever may be the enthusiasms of youth, it is only reasonable either to go forward from such a half-way house or to slip back from it. Sartre slipped back. He came, as he said, to think of this dedication as what he called 'squalid nonsense', to jeer at words as 'the little swift black mercenaries', to take refuge in confessed unreason. 'I have renounced my vocation', he writes, 'but I have not unfrocked myself. I still write. What else can I do?' Samuel Butler said the same. 'In that I write I am damned.' Waugh took the opposite road—did not abandon belief but logically moved forward from believing a little into believing more. It would be a false affectation to pretend that one could deduce such a development from *Decline and Fall*. Nobody did in fact draw any such deduction at the time. Waugh himself did not dream of drawing it. It was only with Father Rothschild and *Vile Bodies* that some bold spirits began timidly to hint at the sort of development that might be before the nation's then most talked-of young novelist. But, in retrospect at any rate, it is possible to see that even in unbelief he could not keep himself from continually adverting to the eccentricities of belief or wholly abandon values.

At the time of his writing of the book Waugh had of course been at Oxford, and, as readers of *A Little Learning* will remember, had taught at a school in North Wales, which was at least sufficiently bad and sufficiently bizarre to serve as an inspiration for Llanabba. No one will pretend that either Dons or school authorities, ridiculous as they often are, are quite as ridiculous as Waugh makes the Dons of Scone or the authorities of Llanabba, but comic satire need not apologize for exaggeration, if it is exaggeration *à propos*. Even if it be granted that Waugh was using the satirist's privilege to exaggerate, yet there were then, and indeed still, are private schools so bad that their absurdities are almost beyond exaggeration, and, since he had no other more solid advantages to offer, Dr Fagan, the headmaster of Llanabba, would doubtless have boasted as much as he could about his own superior breeding and that of his pupils. But, while he would have done all that he could to attract the rich and the aristocratic to his school and certainly would, as such schoolmasters do, have pretended that the boys were a great deal more highly born than they really were, it is by no means clear why he should in fact have had any success in attracting them— why Lady Circumference should have sent there her son, Viscount Tangent, or why Margot Beste-Chetwynde, a lady, as we are so often told, both of enormous wealth and possessed of vast powers of influence, should not have used those powers and that influence to get her son into some school of better standing.

But beyond that Waugh, though he had been to school and university, had never been to prison. He had taken the trouble to examine those who had had that experience and was careful when he exaggerated the details of prison life—of the harshness of the regime, the absurdities of reforming governors—to be sure that he was at least exaggerating reality. But the necessities of his story set him a problem which it was not easy to solve and which it cannot be pretended that he solved quite successfully. The needs of his story required him to show that life was, as the absurd charlatan Professor Otto Silenus described it, like 'the big wheel at Luna Park'. Some found their seats near the centre of the wheel and moved very little. Others were on the circumference, rose high and sank very low, but in the end all ended up very much where they began. Thus it was necessary by the end of the story to bring Paul Pennyfeather back as a theological student to Scone College where he had been in residence when the novel began. To get him there Waugh had to get him out of prison. Waugh had perhaps a little strained probability in his description of Pennyfeather's condemnation and of the ease with which Mrs Beste-Chetwynde was able to keep her part in the white slave traffic out of the case. But we are asked to take it on trust that because Maltravers, a Cabinet Minister, was infatuated with her, she had an almost overwhelming influence over official action, and this we must accept. That she should have had the power to see to it that Paul received in prison titbits that were forbidden by the prison regulations is not beyond belief. But the possibility of a bogus death certificate and Pennyfeather's reappearance under the same name and as the cousin of his former self, changed only by the addition of a moustache and his acceptance in that form by the authorities of Scone, a little defies credibility even in such a work of fun and high spirits as this.

It is a temptation to a young writer, anxious for paradox, to write as if the pleasures of life were exactly the opposite to those which are generally pretended—as if a life, for instance, of solitary confinement in prison was a life preferable to that of the world's social round. It is amusing to write,

> The next four weeks of solitary confinement were among the happiest of Paul's life. The physical comforts were certainly meagre, but at the Ritz Paul had learnt to appreciate the inadequacy of purely physical comfort. It was so exhilarating, he found, never to have to make any decision on any subject, to be wholly relieved from the smallest consideration of time, meals or clothes, to have no anxiety ever about what kind of impression he was making; in fact, to be free.

but Waugh had not himself been in prison—still less in solitary confinement. The life that he was choosing for himself and living at that time was much more nearly the life of King's Thursday—Margot's luxurious home—than the life of prison, and the sentences do not ring true. In general throughout the book Waugh is describing what is happening to people. The amusement of the story comes precisely from those deadpan objective statements—from the fact that he does not linger to consider what he characters thought about the adventures that came their way. The essay in interpretation which he contributes here for Paul Pennyfeather is not in character—is evidence perhaps that he was here a little beyond his depth, in describing an experience which he has not in fact encountered instead of, as in the scenes at Scone and at Llanabba, amusing himself by exaggerating experiences with which in essence he was familiar. He did not really know how a prison worked and how prisoners reacted to it.

These are but passing points. The total achievement for a man of twenty-five was an achievement of remarkable maturity and at once won for Waugh the deserved reputation which he has since held. We still turn to *Decline and Fall* for sheer amusement, but we turn also to see the shadow of coming events. It has been said with some truth that every history is always in truth a history of its own times, and in the same way every biography, real or fictional, is in a measure always an autobiography. A man cannot escape from his own character, and, even when he is least conscious that he is doing so, he is in fact always revealing it. Certainly with Waugh in *Decline and Fall,* little though he guessed his own future, the child was there the father of the man.

Christopher Sykes (essay date 1975)

SOURCE: In *Evelyn Waugh: A Biography,* Little, Brown and Company, 1975, pp. 78–82, 162–64.

[*In the following excerpt from his biography of Waugh, Sykes discusses Waugh's short stories as well as* Mr. Loveday's Outing and Other Sad Stories, *which Sykes believes is "not an important feature in Evelyn's literary life."*]

[Waugh's] earliest work had not only shown little promise but no firm indication of what sort of writer, if a writer at all, he was likely to become. The greatest literary critic imaginable would be unable to identify from the text alone the authorship of *Anthony Who Sought The Things That Were Lost* as that of Evelyn Waugh. The only characteristic of his later work to be found in that essay in preciosity is a certain boldness of approach, but this boldness is vitiated and almost cancelled by the evident vagueness of intention.

The most interesting of his early writings is **'The Balance,'** subtitled 'A Yarn of the Good Old Days of Broad Trousers and High Necked Jumpers.' Though it cannot be described as good, a literary detective might possibly discern its authorship from internal evidence. It contains dialogue, and though the most important single dialogue in the book is inept, some of it has a glimmer of Evelyn's later sparkle. It is difficult to say what the story is about as the narrative

line is self-consciously complicated in the endeavour to be as modern as possible. It does emerge that there is a young man named Adam Dour, an art student, who is unhappily in love with a fashionable girl called Imogen Quest; that his frustrated suit drives him to attempt suicide by poison; that the attempt fails as he cannot prevent himself vomiting (closely described) thus expelling the lethal dose; that he then writes a farewell letter to Imogen and is about to drown himself but is dissuaded in the course of a conversation which he holds on a bridge, with his reflection in the water, and in which the two discuss 'the balance' between life and death. What makes the story especially difficult to follow is that most of it, following the 'inspiration' at Aston Clinton, takes the form of a film scenario which is represented as being watched by a large audience, some of whose comments are given. The people in the film spill over into the 'real life' story. It is easy to imagine James Joyce using a device of this kind. There are a few Joycean touches in the writing and it is possible that Evelyn had recently plunged into *Ulysses.* Joyce may have begotten this weak and misshapen child but he was not to be an influence on Evelyn. This was very fortunate. Like that of Wagner in the nineteenth century the influence of Joyce on his contemporaries in the twentieth was usually destructive and often fatal.

The failure of the story was inevitable from the fact that, as is apparent throughout, the author was attempting a picture of modern life without sufficient experience. The subject, almost against the writer's wish, so one may feel, gravitates back to Oxford. It begins as a parody of the debased drama of the cinema, but the story told by the fictitious film is concerned with the rakish life of Evelyn's undergraduate days, a subject wholly untypical of the cinema of the time. (Harold Lloyd's immortal *College Days* provides no exception.) As a result, the element of parody is entirely misdirected: it makes mock of a kind of film which no one had made or was likely to make. (*A Yank at Oxford* again provides no exception.) The climax of the story, the conversation between the hero and his reflection, is an abysmal mixture of sophistry and sentimentalism. In favour of **'The Balance,'** apart from some bright dialogue, can be claimed convincing descriptions of the squalor of debauchery. Evelyn wisely never had it reprinted, and I never heard him mention it. I was unaware of its existence until after his death. . . .

In the middle of June [1936] Chapman and Hall published *Mr. Loveday's Little Outing and Other Sad Stories.* The . . . book is not an important feature of Evelyn's literary life, so it need not detain the reader beyond a couple of paragraphs.

The excellence of the eponymous story is in no doubt. It may have been based on the report of some atrocity of the kind in the newspapers; it was widely remembered some twenty years later when an almost identical disaster occurred as a result of misguided progressivism in the treatment of criminal lunatics, a grim subject which Evelyn had already effectively guyed in *Decline and Fall.* Under the title 'By Special Request', the mild ending to *A Handful of Dust* contrived for the American serialization was reprinted. It has been discussed already. The third piece, **'Cruise'**, was an excursion into a style of glossy-magazine gossip-writing story which has happily disappeared. In **'Cruise'** Evelyn fell, probably unawares, under the influence of A. P. Herbert's once much lauded *The Trials of Topsy*. The story which followed it, **'Period Piece'**, was a skilful variation on the theme of *Plus ça change plus c'est la même chose* and was as fully worthy of Evelyn as **'On Guard'** . . . was not.

'Incident in Azania' should have become better known than it did. The scene of the story was life in an outpost of the British Empire and was set in the Protectorate regime of Azania following the events related in *Black Mischief*. The kind of incident and the kind of life depicted had been both more thoroughly dealt with by Somerset Maugham, but the 'truth to nature' of Evelyn's picture of that now vanished world will strike any witness of it as authentic. By 1936 Somerset Maugham had made the subject over-familiar, a fact which may account for the neglect of **'Incident in Azania'**. The stories which followed it showed Evelyn indulging his taste for fantasy conjoined with realism. **'Out of Depth'** is a not wholly successful little outing on the Time-Machine; the debt to H. G. Wells (against whom Evelyn was unashamedly prejudiced) is too obvious. The succeeding story, **'Excursion in Reality'**, is one of Evelyn's few ventures into the obscene unreality of the film-world. Here a reader may strongly feel that, for all its many excellencies, the story is a display of raw material for a fine piece of fiction rather than the thing itself. **'Love in the Slump'** is based on the over-worked material of his early novels; it reads like a parody of his writing. (Strange that no other writer has parodied his intensely idiosyncratic style.) The last two stories are both flawed. **'Bella Fleace Gave a Party'** is supposed to be based on an incident which did actually happen: an ambitious hostess, it was related, gave a party but the invitations were not posted. The legend or fact was very well known in those days and by 1936 had grown 'something musty'. Many readers must have known the end of the story from the beginning. The same fatal weakness was in the last story, **'Winner Takes All'**. It is designed to have a surprise ending, but, as Raymond Mortimer noticed in a review, the title gave the show away early on.

The book enjoyed success in England and later on in the United States where it was published in October. It kept Evelyn's reputation in the public eye, but, except possibly for the title-story, added little to the reputation. Even his most fervent admirers could not but notice that the quality of the stories was very uneven. . . .

Alain Blayac (essay date 1978)

SOURCE: "'Bella Fleace Gave a Party' or, The Archetypal Image of Waugh's Sense of Decay," in *Studies in Short Fiction*, Vol. 15, No. 1, Winter, 1978, pp. 69–73.

[*In the following essay, Blayac argues that as a metaphor for changing social conditions "Bella Fleace Gave a Party" ranks among Waugh's best works of short fiction.*]

In his somewhat controversial biography of Evelyn Waugh, Christopher Sykes tentatively discards some of the writer's early novels as uneven and immature;[1] he is even more censorious of the short stories which, except for **"Mr. Loveday's Little Outing"** and **"Period Piece,"** he repeatedly finds fault with.[2] They are, he suggests, repetitive, impersonal, and occasionally marred by too close an imitation of well-known stories or writers. As a case in point, Mr. Sykes writes that **"Bella Fleace Gave a Party"**[3] "is supposed to be based on an incident which did actually happen: an ambitious hostess, it was related, gave a party but the invitations were not posted. The legend or fact was very well known in those days and by 1936 had grown 'something musty.' Many readers must have known the end of the story from the beginning."[4] Mr. Sykes' summary, focussing on the trivial and the superficial, will hardly do justice to a short story whose essential meaning he fails to grasp. For us, Waugh used the largely drawn upon anecdote[5] as a mere platform for the voicing of a serious and thoroughly consistent outlook on life. He wove it into a grim, ironic, archetypal satire not so much of Ireland and the Irish in themselves as of a modern world which has forsaken the glory and grandeur of its past. As such the short story assumes a new significance, for which Waugh's art certainly comes off the better, and **"Bella Fleace"** in the process comes to rank among the writer's most meaningful short works.

The simplicity of the structure underlines Waugh's intentions. Through an apparently objective description—reminiscent of the Blue Guide Style used in *A Handful of Dust* to introduce Hetton Abbey[6]—the reader is successively acquainted with Ballingar, "a typical Irish town," Fleacetown, Bella's manor in "typical Irish country," and the Fleaces themselves seen through historical perspective. This introduction provides the story with a coherent background of reference, arouses the reader's attention by gradually travelling towards a close-up on[7] the house and family, and keeps his interest awake with a number of outside elements used as counterpoints to the main theme. In fact it strikes the "change and decay" note.

Ballingar, the typical Irish town, proves to be the very image of poverty and dereliction; Fleacetown, although "unusually habitable," will barely "survive its owner;" the eponymous heroine is revealed to be the last descendant of a once-thriving family. Waugh evokes a favorite theme, Decadence and Death; in this respect the flashback on the Fleace story (providing the anecdote with a temporal background) is a clever stroke which exemplifies, both technically and ideologically, the ineluctable waning of house and family. This is traced from the heroic times when the Fleaces were a strong, warlike tribe living in a "stockaded fort" to the eighteenth-century splendor of an already "enervated" though "still wealthy and influential" family, and eventually the steady decline which, through "no heroic debauchery,"[8] ended in the generation of eccentrics culminating—or tapering off—in Bella herself. The very mutilation of the latter's name from Miss Annabel Rochfort-Doyle-Fleace to plain Bella Fleace, and even Bella is one more token of the overwhelming corruption that submerges the world. Annabel—etymologically grace and beauty—is now Bella, an old woman over 80, lame in one leg—a witch in appearance.

At this stage, one must remark that Waugh is too much of an artist to state his theme in an overly simple manner. The degradation of property, family and last representative is made more dramatic by a number of variations and counterpoints which obliquely state the author's point of view: the mere juxtaposition of declining ancient values with rising modern fashions endows the episode with almost universal significance. The anecdote becomes the central archetype of Waugh's earlier fiction—that of the decline and fall of Man in these, our modern times.

Concurrently to the decadence of Fleacetown, other neighboring houses undergo resurrection of a sort. Electric light, central heating and a lift have been installed in "the rival Gordontown," which, together with Mock House, Newhill, together with Castle Mockstock, is provided with "neatly raked gravel, bathrooms and dynamos." Although these advantages are not to be dismissed lightly, the houses are now "the wonder and ridicule of the country."[9] The very names Waugh assigns them betoken his dissatisfaction with them. Newhill is probably the new fad of some gross upstart, Mock House and Castle Mockstock deride their very origins by the acceptance of modern conveniences. Thriving as they look, such edifices appear to repudiate tradition and the past from which they were issued; they have ceased to be Irish altogether, nay, have lost both function and identity. Mock House and Newhill, now leased to sporting Englishmen, are deserted most of the year; Castle Mockstock has been defiled by Lord Mockstock's marrying beneath him; Gordontown, bought by the American Lady Gordon, heralds the invasion of the island by the barbarians from the New Continent. Waugh, viewing architecture as the emblem and the touchstone of civilization, gloomily broods on the rise of change and modernism.

This overture points at Waugh as a committed writer. It proposes a riddle which the anecdote will solve, and announces a revelation. The arrival of Bella's only relative, a distant London cousin named Archie Banks,[10] sets the plot going. The interest the young man manifests in the library rare books induces Bella to sell them. Rather than be "fleeced," she chooses to spend the money from the sale on a Christmas party which is momentarily to restore the splendor of yore. She will muster the families of ancient, reliable lineage and reject the snobbish, uncultured social climbers. Unwonted activity stirs the house for a while, then, once the last details are completed, D-day comes. At 8 o'clock Bella limps downstairs to welcome her guests; at half past twelve nobody has come when Lady Mockstock, the draper's daughter, and Lady Gordon, the Ameri-

can, attempt gate crashing and are duly repelled. Bella, unable to bear the double shock, dies the next day. Later, Archie Banks arrives at Fleacetown to organize the funeral and set the house in order: ". . . sorting out her effects . . . [he finds] in her escritoire, stamped, addressed, but unposted, the invitations to the ball."[11]

This bare outline is inadequate to suggest the moral of a story which casts a crude light on the shortcomings of the age. Our times are devoid of humanity. The world of tradition and order is upside down as upstart hordes storm in while truly noble families pass out to be ironically taken over by "Banks." Taste, good fellowship, candor are superseded by vulgarity, envy and dissimulation. Burke's *Peerage* is no longer to be trusted as American Gordons now pullulate. A strange world, and a sadly insane one!

It would be misleading, however, to think that Waugh extols the virtues of Bella while disparaging the modern barbarians. At no time in the short story is Bella presented as a civilizing influence, even less as a potential counterweight to the growing importance of those who mock lineage and style. On the contrary, far from being invested with the sacred role of Defender of the Past, Bella stands up as a caricature of nobleness and nobility—in the same way as Fleacetown never represents anything better than the more modern houses do. Indeed, the writer is most careful to "describe her [the heroine's] appearance closely . . . , because it [seems] in contradiction to much of her character. She was over eighty, very untidy and very red; steaky grey hair was twisted behind her head into a horsy bun, wisps hung around her cheeks; her nose was prominent and blue veined; her eyes pale blue, blank and mad. . . ."[12] Later he lays definite emphasis on her decrepitude: ". . . Bella herself was increasingly occupied with the prospect of death. In the winter before the one we are talking of, she had been extremely ill. She emerged in April, rosy cheeked as ever, but slower in her movements and mind."[13]

Although it seems "in contradiction to much of her character," Bella's appearance reflects her real nature. An old woman, with mad eyes and a slow mind, she never grasps the issues she should be fighting for. Here a comparison with Aldous Huxley's *Antic Hay* may help understand the inadequacies of Bella and of her house.

Contrarily to the model of St. Paul's cathedral which, with its grace and proportion, becomes an ideal that Huxley's misfits should strive to attain, Fleacetown can by no means be held as symbolic of civilized enlightenment. The humor of the description cannot blind the reader to the reality of its decrepitude. At best Fleacetown can be seen as the sorely degraded, half-ruined image of the homely, comfortable hall of the eighteenth century.

In contrast to Gumbril Sr. who keeps in touch with mankind and has reached wisdom and insight, Bella remains isolated, foolish and blind to reality. Most of her contemporaries have already departed this world, or are about to do so.[14] Bella's fight, if considered as a crusade against the infidels, can at best be a singlehanded, rearguard skirmish which stands little chance of stemming the tidal wave of barbarism. After her, nothing will remain of the past.

Besides, Bella is never made to display—let alone embody—any redemptive quality. Whereas Gumbril Sr. consistently demonstrates his liberal humanism, Bella always bases her action on egotistic misconceptions. In order to thwart her cousin Archie Banks' so-called schemes, she does away with the treasures of the Hall Library. She barters books for money, squanders it on a meaningless party, and demeans herself to lower levels than the moderns she combats. The reader realizes that the taint of modernism has touched her to such an extent that she chooses the least meaningful ceremony to revive the past. Or rather, ironically, she selects the right ceremony for the wrong motive, thus depriving it of its essentially positive value. In the party Bella only sees the garish and the tawdry. She warps its meaning for she never senses the humanism that used to pervade such gatherings in Fielding and Addison's times. Her re-decoration of Fleacetown is patchy and of little durable worth; the party is essentially intended as a bolstering up of her sick, reeling mind. In the same way that she dissipates the heritage of the past by selling the books, she misunderstands it by organizing a party to debase her hated neighbors. No doubt that, by doing so, she believes she emulates Sir Roger de Coverley, Squire Allworthy and their likes, when in fact she betrays their philosophy. Then the squire would entertain the village community at the Hall, giving everybody from top to bottom of the social ladder a feeling of community. The reunions, the merrymaking tightened the ties, uniting an already close-knit social group.

Bella utterly misunderstands the inner significance of such functions. She even distorts it to such a point as to endow it with the opposite meaning. Far from trying to unite the county community, she endeavors to disrupt it. Bella cuts, carves, destroys; therefore, the conclusion definitely introduces an idea of retributive justice into the anecdote. Bella is chastised for having sinned against the Spirit of the Past. What's more, by appointing Christmas as the time of revenge, she proves as sacrilegious as Adam and Nina were in *Vile Bodies* two years before. Bella's death comes as a timely, justified punishment. The notion of fate, so important in Waugh's early works—and already suggested here by the ironic demise of Bella's brother—is made again to intervene in order to show that tampering with morals and tradition is a crime that the gods severely punish.

For all these reasons, **"Bella Fleace Gave a Party,"** far from being the simple imitation of a well-known story, is a terse but forcible statement of Evelyn Waugh's personal philosophy. It illustrates the writer's obsessive fear that all sanity and values have been suppressed from our world. The Roman Catholic novelist warns his readers that, in the Waste Land, nothing can save Man from his Fall. The choice is not between Bella and the others, but outside

them all, indeed perhaps in isolation, confinement and the self. Whatever one may think of the shortcomings of such a philosophy, **"Bella Fleace Gave a Party"** expresses it perfectly. The short story, seen in this light, remains not only an essential link between *Vile Bodies* and *A Handful of Dust*, but also an archetypal illustration of Evelyn Waugh's embittered human and religious stances.

Notes

1. Christopher Sykes, *Evelyn Waugh*: a Biography (New York: Little, Brown & Co., 1975).

2. Evelyn Waugh, *Mr. Loveday's Little Outing and Other Sad Stories* (Boston: Little, Brown & Co., 1936).

3. Ibid., pp. 185–204.

4. Sykes, p. 164.

5. Oscar Wilde's "Aunt Jane" plays on the same theme.

6. Evelyn Waugh, *A Handful of Dust* (London: Chapman and Hall, 1934), p. 27. "Bella Fleace Gave a Party" is the first instance of this style, which Waugh was to use so often in his later fiction.

7. Such technical terms remind us that Waugh, although often disgusted with the "7th Art," was always attracted by it; he even was a cinema critic for *The Isis* in his student days at Oxford.

8. p. 190.

9. p. 189.

10. Etymologically, "Noble Banks" or "Rule of the Banks."

11. p. 203.

12. p. 191.

13. p. 192.

14. Ibid., pp. 197–98. "Many of those whose names were transcribed were dead or bedridden; some whom she just remembered seeing as small children were reaching retiring age in remote corners of the globe; many of the houses she wrote down were blackened shells, burnt during the troubles and never rebuilt."

Robert Murray Davis (essay date 1981)

SOURCE: In *Evelyn Waugh, Writer*, Pilgrim Books, Inc., 1981, pp. 32–9, 70–2.

[*In the following excerpt, Davis compares and contrasts Waugh's early short fiction, exploring his techniques and influences.*]

Waugh's undergraduate fiction, except for **"Anthony: Who Sought Things That Were Lost,"** was written in first person and consisted largely of parochial anecdotes.

"The Balance," sub-titled "A Yarn of the Good Old Days of Broad Trousers and High Necked Jumpers," shows him working toward but not entirely trusting a technique by which he could present as objectively as possible his own subjective reactions and thus transmute autobiography into fiction. From the devices of the film he adapted techniques by which he was able, sporadically, to achieve authorial distance from the characters and to present selected glimpses of physical action economically and vividly.

The plot of **"The Balance"**[1] is not particularly remarkable: Adam Doure, an art student recently down from Oxford, has his romance with Imogen Quest broken off as a result of her mother's objection. In rather self-conscious despair he resolves to commit suicide, sells his books to raise money, and goes to Oxford with the object of saying a dignified, Petronian farewell to his friends. However, only Ernest Vaughan, talented but thoroughly debauched, is able to accompany him, and the farewell dinner degenerates into a series of drunken misadventures culminating in the wreck of an impulsively commandeered automobile. Alone in his hotel room, Adam drinks poison—only to vomit profusely and fall asleep. Wandering into the fields near the river on the following morning, he sleeps again; then, looking into the water, he engages his reflection in a rather sophomoric dialogue about the meaning of life. Finally he comes to an understanding of the balance between life and death: the appetite, which is governed by circumstances, determines whether man wishes to live or die.

Of much greater interest than the story is the variety of techniques that Waugh employed to tell it. Each of the four sections is told in a different narrative mode: "Introduction," which shows the attitudes of the Bright Young People toward Adam, is almost wholly in dialogue; "Circumstances," which is by far the longest section, ends with Adam taking poison and uses the conventions of the silent film that Waugh had learned from reviewing and from *The Scarlet Woman*; "Conclusion," which concludes with Adam's decision to accept the verdict of chance and live, is developed partly by formal exposition of Adam's mental state and partly by his dialogue with himself; and "Continuation," which returns to the gay and thoughtless world of Adam's contemporaries, uses a third-person observer to reflect on the lightly malicious gossip. It is not surprising that Conrad Aiken, while praising the story for its "astonishingly rich portrait of a mind" and predicting that Waugh might "do something very remarkable," made the reservation "if he is not too clever."[2]

Waugh did not get beyond his depth in the first and last sections, where the dialogue clearly presages that of the novels, or in the structure, which like that of **Decline and Fall** shows the central character being separated from an unsuitable world through a counterfeit death. In his most ambitious section. "Circumstances," however, he obviously found that the techniques of the film scenario were inadequate for his purpose, and he added several elements. First, to expand the speaking parts beyond the limits of the

caption, he introduced additional lines of dialogue, which, he says in a note, "are deduced by the experienced picture-goers from the gestures of the actors; only those parts which appear in capitals are actual 'captions'". Next, to provide some kind of framework for his script and to point up the contrast between his story and stereotyped movie plots, he selected three members of the audience to present the conventional filmgoers' views, recording their comments in italic type. First introduced are Ada and Gladys, two servants, who make obvious comments on the action and try vainly to place the plot in a familiar category: comedy, "society," "murder," or romance. The third spectator, selected for his contrasting views, is a young Cambridge man who desires that the characters talk like ladies and gentlemen, labels without difficulty as "expressionismus" the film's technique, and understands the significance of the action little better than Ada and Gladys.

This machinery is ponderously established, intrusive, and uneconomical, but Waugh did even greater violence to the film convention. Strictly speaking, the characters' internal reactions could not be shown in a film, but Waugh further strained his device to include them—and even added background information in the neutral voice of the detached author.

When Waugh is dealing with dialogue, his devices are fairly successful, though a bit cluttered, as in the luncheon conversation between Adam and Imogen:

> She sits down at the table.
>
> "You haven't got to rush back to your school, have you? Because I'm never going to see you again. The most awful thing has happened—you order lunch, Adam. I'm very hungry, I want to eat a *steak-tartare* and I don't want to drink anything." [This dialogue is to be inferred by the filmgoer.]
>
> Adam orders lunch.
>
> LADY R. SAYS I'M SEEING TOO MUCH OF YOU. ISN'T IT TOO AWFUL?
>
> *Gladys is at last quite at home. The film has been classified. Young love is being thwarted by purse-proud parents.*

When the story has to deal with a setting, however, the scenario fails to translate into verbal description the swiftness of the film's visual impact, and in fact Waugh sometimes abandons physical detail for generalized evaluation. A good example is the description of Lady Rosemary Quest's house:

> An interior is revealed in which the producers have at last made some attempt to satisfy the social expectations of Gladys and Ada. It is true that there is very little marble and no footmen in powder and breeches, but there is nevertheless an undoubted air of grandeur about the high rooms and Louis Seize furniture, and there is a footman. The young man from Cambridge estimates the household at six thousand a year, and though somewhat overgenerous, it is a reasonable

guess. Lady Rosemary's collection of Limoges can be seen in the background.

When Waugh is faithful to the limits of his convention, the description is sometimes awkwardly obtrusive. In attempting to give something of the atmosphere of a bookstore, where a minor bit of action takes place, he is forced by his cinematic method to use a great deal of space for description, for analysis, and for a short scene with a wholly irrelevant character.

Waugh's attempt to reproduce the effect of the movie amply justifies itself, however, when he uses its characteristic qualities: the ability to translate ideas and attitudes into visual terms, to control the physical distance of the audience from the action, to select only the relevant details, to shift rapidly from scene to scene without formal transition, and to control the speed of the action. Particularly noteworthy in **"The Balance"** is Waugh's use of Adam's visions of death: first, a realistic view of the effect his suicide will have on his family, "scenes of unspeakable vulgarity involving tears, hysteria, the telephone, the police"; next, "a native village in Africa" from which "a man naked and sick to death . . . draws himself into the jungle to die alone"; and, finally, a "hall, as if in some fevered imagining of Alma Tadema, . . . built of marble, richly illuminated by burning Christians," where in an atmosphere violent and decadent a Roman patrician leisurely takes his life. Like a film shot, the second vision is spliced into later action to reveal Adam's growing sense of isolation as he vainly seeks someone with whom to share a last feast and as he lies down to die after drinking the poison.[3] While the physical details of the third vision are not repeated, the whole series of squalid episodes of Adam's drunken wanderings through Oxford is implicitly contrasted with the decadent splendor of the Roman's death.

As significant as the visual rendering of thought is the effect of the cinematic device on the narrative style, for Waugh is able to give the sense of drunken confusion without using the character's mind as the center of observation. As a result, he can avoid subjective analysis and speed the pace and rapidity of transition, as in this sequence:

> A public-house in the slums. Adam leans against the settee and pays for innumerable pints of beer for armies of ragged men. Ernest is engrossed in a heated altercation about birth control with a beggar whom he has just defeated at "darts."
>
> Another public-house: Ernest, beset by two panders, is loudly proclaiming the abnormality of his tastes. Adam finds a bottle of gin in his pocket and attempts to give it to a man; his wife interposes; eventually the bottle falls to the floor and is broken.
>
> Adam and Ernest in a taxi; they drive from college to college, being refused admission. Fade out.

At least as effective is the series of scenes in which Adam tries to find a dinner companion, for they portray economically a wide variety of Oxford types.

That the story is on the whole a failure can be attributed partly to Waugh's choice of too complicated a variety of narrative methods and partly to his attitude toward the material. Like the circumstances of almost all of Waugh's other central characters, Adam's closely parallel, though they do not reproduce, those of his creator. Like Evelyn Waugh in 1924 and 1925, Adam has left at Oxford a circle of friends whom he misses and from whom he feels estranged; like Waugh, he attends a scrubby art school, where he learns very little; like Waugh, he is without means, is separated from the girl with whom he thinks himself in love, seeks to renew Oxford friendships, and fails, in an ignominious anticlimax, to commit suicide. When he wrote **"The Balance,"** he was too close to the emotions of Adam Doure to treat them, especially in "Conclusion," in other than solemn fashion. Moreover, it is difficult to discern any reason besides the claims of autobiography for the art-school scenes. This failure in economy is only one effect of Waugh's incomplete detachment of himself from Adam; the other was the need to justify Adam's difference from his contemporaries and in general to gain sympathy for him. This necessity accounts for the three sections of the story that are outside the film convention (by itself a means of gaining objectivity); for the movie audience, whose incomprehension is intended to deepen the reader's awareness; and for the authorial analysis of Adam's feelings.

"The Tutor's Tale"[4] resembles Waugh's later short stories in being thin and formulaic, but it does represent a different kind of objectivity from that of **"The Balance."** To narrate the brief emergence from captivity of the supposedly retarded but in fact ingenuous George, Marquess of Stayle and heir to the Duke of Vanbrugh, Waugh resurrected from **"The Balance"** the character Ernest Vaughan, drunken companion of and foil to Adam Doure and object of Imogen Quest's interest on the story's final page. As tutor to the young man and narrator he is used to set off by his cynicism and experience the dottiness of George's relatives and keepers and George's "fresh and acute critical faculty and a natural fastidiousness which shone through the country bumpkin". As Ernest notes, sometimes "nature, like a lazy author, will round off abruptly into a short story what she obviously intended to be the opening of a novel"; George's relatives change their minds about sending him abroad and recall him to imprisonment on the family estate. The story is a great deal lighter in tone than **"The Balance"**; George looks forward to certain release, and Ernest's calm objectivity keeps the audience from empathizing with wronged innocence.

Perhaps as important as his experiments with point of view is that Waugh had begun to people the imaginative world upon which his early novels would draw. Ernest never recurs, but the names Vanburgh (or Vanbrugh), Philbrick, and others in the comedy-of-manners convention do, and a hint of the characters of the Bright Young People has begun to appear. The clearest indication of Waugh's progress from self-pitying autobiography is the shift in his use of Imogen Quest. In the undergraduate effort—a term chosen advisedly—**"Fragments: They Dine with the**

Past," the character Imogen never appears, but she pervades the dinner party at which her name is not spoken: ". . . the thought of her was about and between us all; with such shy courtesy did we treat her, who had been Queen, for all who had loved her were gathered there and none dared even speak her name."[5] The character is so vague that she does not have a surname. In **"The Balance,"** despite her portentous name and "rather a lovely head, shingled and superbly poised on its neck", Imogen is an ordinary girl, speaking in the argot of the Bright Young People who appear briefly in *Decline and Fall* and prominently in *Vile Bodies*. In the latter novel the name is again used of an idealized character, but this time in a conscious travesty of literary creation and considered mockery of the social scene: Adam Fenwick-Symes invents her in his gossip column as "the most lovely and popular of the young married set" who becomes "a byword for social inaccessibility—the final goal for all climbers" who envy her set's "uncontrolled dignity of life."[6] In Imogen's first appearance she is a vague figure created to allow young men the indulgence of self-pitying, nostalgic stoicism. In her final appearance she is used to parody the aspiration of her admirers.

Of course, Waugh had always had, as his diaries reveal, a sharp eye for the inherent absurdities of people and institutions. Social snobbery and self-protection were as central to **"Edward of Unique Achievement"** as they were to the opening pages of *Decline and Fall*. In the undergraduate story Edward murders his dim tutor, Mr. Curtis, and escape detection when Lord Poxe, who has drunkenly collapsed next to the body, is the obvious suspect. Poxe, however, is let off with a fine of thirteen shillings because of a fifteenth-century precedent and because the Warden's wife, thinking her husband has killed her lover, confesses her misdeeds, whereupon the Warden hastens to conceal the crime. The chief difference between the story and the novel is not subject but point of view. **"Edward"** is narrated by a first-person observer, uninvolved except with the Warden's wife, and the cynicism is overt.[7] *Decline and Fall* is narrated by an omniscient author so assured that he can descend from mandarin to slang usage and rise again without apology or self-consciousness. . . .

Even before Waugh completed Chapter 3 of *Black Mischief,* in which he used England to frame the action in Azania, he was making it the center of a smaller picture. **"The Patriotic Honeymoon,"** retitled **"Love in the Slump"** for *Mr. Loveday's Little Outing,* deals with the marriage of Tom Watch and Angela Trench-Troubridge as "completely typical of all that was most unremarkable in modern social conditions."[8] The two marry out of a sense of desperation on her side and bewildered acquiescence to "one of the few bright fragments remaining from his glamorous [undergraduate] past" on his. They are separated by accident; Tom discovers hunting on his host's new mare and Angela satisfactory sex with the same Etonian-Oxonian friend of Tom's who gives them a cottage near his estate in Devon, which "would be such a good place for her to go sometimes when she wanted a change". As

students of *A Handful of Dust* will realize, the story is almost a negative image of the novel: Tom, the Beaverish Londoner with neither qualities nor prospects, is cuckolded by a lively country squire, a counter-Tony, in a cottage, as opposed to a flat in London, both "very suitable for base love."

The themes of the faithless wife and of the mild man whose betrayal he cannot even recognize are repeated in a story commissioned for the *John Bull* series on "The Seven Deadly Sins of Today." Waugh chose the one sin to which he can never have felt the slightest temptation: tolerance. In the introduction to the series Waugh asserted, "It is better to be narrowminded than to have no mind, to hold limited and rigid principles than none at all." The danger, he continued, was "to put up with what is wasteful and harmful with the excuse that there is 'good in everything'—which in most cases means the inability to distinguish between good and bad."[9] Set in Africa, where everyone else has pronounced opinions on every subject, the story presents the monologue of "a jaunty, tragic little figure, cheated out of his patrimony by his partner, battened on by an obviously worthless son, deserted by his wife, an irrepressible, bewildered figure striding off under his topee, cheerfully butting his way into a whole continent of rapacious and ruthless jolly good fellows." Reacting against Victorian ideas of marriage, he lets his wife pursue her own interests and activities and is mildly surprised because "after she'd been going out with this fellow for some time she suddenly fell in love with him and went off with him."[10]

"Bella Fleace Gave a Party," completed before Waugh left for British Guiana, deals with the decay of a once lively country house and the failure, through senile oversight, of Bella to maintain her sense of superiority. In contrast, **"Period Piece,"** dated 1934 in *Tactical Exercise* shows the betrayed husband losing his wife to his parasitical heir but acquiescing in her return and rejoicing when she bears him a son. Both in his actions and in the tone of Lady Amelia, the story's narrator, one hears "the organ voice of England, the hunting-cry of the *ancien régime*."[11] Privilege is asserted, the outsiders kept outside.[12] Though **"Period Piece"** was almost certainly written after **"The Man Who Liked Dickens"** and perhaps after *A Handful of Dust,* its resolution in the birth of a new heir mirrors the ending to the serial version, **"A Flat in London,"** in which Brenda, subdued and carrying the heir of Hetton, is regarded as unlikely to escape it again.

Ordinarily Waugh did not seem to take his short fiction very seriously, but he was enthusiastic about **"The Man Who Liked Dickens"** from the time it was written, telling Peters that it was "first-rate" and should command a large fee on the American market.[13] Technically it is superior to his other short pieces. The middle, a flashback that recounts the origin and dissolution of the Anderson expedition, is weakened by rather obvious attempts at humor, but in the scenes at the house of Mr. McMaster (Todd in the novel) that enclose the flashback the major themes are implied through dialogue and setting rather than overtly stated, as they had been in **"Love in the Slump,"** by a knowing, superior narrator. The story shares with its predecessors the theme of the casually faithless wife. In this case, like Virginia Crouchback in *Sword of Honour,* whose conversational style she anticipates, Mrs. Henty falls in love with a captain of the Coldstream Guards. Henty is less dim than the central male figures of the other short stories; his impotence is the result more of circumstance than of character. The theme of confinement runs through several stories from this period: the dim wife of **"Period Piece"** has the walled "Garden of Her Thoughts" where nothing grows; the flirt of **"On Guard"** is rendered a harmless and lonely spinster when her dog bites off her adorable nose; the central character in **"Out of Depth"** is thrust forward in time to a shattered London whose denizens have degenerated into barbarism.

This story is especially important in the gestation of *A Handful of Dust* because it introduces the major theme of that novel, which Waugh described as "a study of other sorts of savage at home and the civilized man's helpless plight among them."[14] The central figure, Rip Van Winkle, lives in an "orderly succession of characterless, steam-heated apartments, . . . cabin trunks and promenade decks, . . . casinos and bars and supper restaurants."[15] Displaced, he is submerged in delirium, more fully rendered than Henty's in **"The Man Who Liked Dickens,"** from which he emerges only after perceiving "a shape in chaos" at a Roman Catholic mass. This overtly religious theme is at most implied in *A Handful of Dust,* but the story presents London as a waste inhabited by "other sorts of savage" and moves a step further toward the portrait of contemporary London as essentially sordid and dull present in Waugh's fiction from *Black Mischief.*

Notes

1. Evelyn Waugh, "The Balance," *Georgian Stories, 1926* (London: Chapman and Hall, 1926), pp. 253–91; (New York: G. P. Putnam's Sons, 1926), pp. 279–323. I cite the latter text parenthetically.

2. Conrad Aiken, *Literary Review* 23 (April 9, 1927): 4.

3. Although I do not use the same terminology, I am indebted for the concepts to Joseph and Harry Feldman, *Dynamics of the Film* (New York: McLeod, 1952); and to Edward Fischer, *The Screen Arts: A Guide to Film and Television Appreciation* (New York: Sheed and Ward, 1960).

4. Evelyn Waugh, "The Tutor's Tale: A House of Gentlefolks," *The New Decameron: The Fifth Day* (Oxford: Basil Blackwell, 1927), pp. 101–16.

5. Evelyn Waugh, "Fragments: They Dine with the Past," *Cherwell,* September 5, 1923, p. 42; signed "Scaramel."

6. Evelyn Waugh, *Vile Bodies* (London: Chapman and Hall, 1965), pp. 114–15. This is the last edition supervised by Waugh.

7. Evelyn Waugh, "Edward of Unique Achievement," *Cherwell,* August 1, 1923, pp. 14–18.

8. Evelyn Waugh, "Love in the Slump," *Mr. Loveday's Little Outing and Other Sad Stories* (London: Chapman and Hall, 1936), p. 167. Subsequently this story, "Incident in Azania," and "Out of Depth" disappeared from the canon in Waugh's later collections, *Work Suspended and Other Stories Written Before the Second World War* (London: Chapman and Hall, 1949), and *Tactical Exercise* (Boston: Little, Brown and Co., 1954).

9. *John Bull,* April 2, 1932, p. 7.

10. Evelyn Waugh, "Too Much Tolerance," *John Bull,* May 21, 1932, p. 24.

11. Evelyn Waugh, *Vile Bodies* (London: Chapman and Hall, 1965), p. 101.

12. The same social truth is enunciated in "Winner Takes All," written in July, 1935, in which the elder son consistently receives the benefit of the younger's efforts. Waugh obviously remembered his father's label of Alec as "the heir of Underhill." See Alec Waugh, *My Brother Evelyn and Other Portraits* (New York: Farrar, Straus & Giroux, 1967), p. 164.

13. Letter to A. D. Peters, February 15, 1933.

14. Waugh, "Fan-Fare," p. 58.

15. *Mr. Loveday's Little Outing,* p. 136.

Frances Donaldson (review date 1982)

SOURCE: "Old Young Waugh," in *The New York Times,* November 14, 1982, p. 25.

[*In the following review of* Charles Ryder's School Days and Other Stories, *Donaldson states that while the collection is of mixed quality, "Mr. Loveday's Little Outing," and "Bella Fleace Gives a Party" deserve praise.*]

There is a story told by Max Beerbohm of how, on his way to his club to find a review that contained a new story by Henry James, he ran into the great man himself. James asked him to accompany him to some art exhibition and instinctively Beerbohm refused. Trying to decide afterwards why he had done so, he came to the conclusion that even for the company of the Master, he could not bear to delay the anticipated pleasure of reading his story.

When asked to review **Charles Ryder's Schooldays,** a volume including a manuscript by Evelyn Waugh found in his agent's office a couple of years ago and 11 short stories, including an alternative ending to *A Handful of Dust,* I accepted in something of the spirit of Beerbohm. In spite of a pile of manuscripts overdue for delivery lying on my own desk, I could not wait to lay hands on this splendid trophy. And when I received the book and found that the

11 stories had been published in England many years ago in the collections **Mr. Loveday's Little Outing** and **Work Suspended,** I still felt rather as someone might who was called upon to review *Pride and Prejudice* or, if that pushes it too far, the "Just So Stories."

For in England we have accepted the notion that Evelyn Waugh has passed the tests, whatever they are, that ensure posterity. Nine out of ten Englishmen, asked which of our mid-20th-century authors will survive, are likely to reply, "Well, Evelyn Waugh . . . Graham Greene . . . ," and only offer differing opinions with the third choice.

All these stories were written, when Waugh was young and belong to the mood that produced **Decline and Fall** and *Vile Bodies.* Some are mere idle fancies, such as **"Cruise"** the letters of a very 1920-ish girl on a sea voyage—and **"On Guard"**—the tale of Millicent Blake, who possessed a nose that, although not one to appeal to painters, was one "to take the thoughts of English manhood back to its schooldays, to the doughy-faced urchins on whom it had squandered its first affections, to memories of changing room and chapel and battered straw hats." But at least two, **"Mr. Loveday's Little Outing"** and **"Bella Fleace Gave a Party,"** are the stuff of which anthologies are made.

The first is the story of the inmate of a mental hospital who, after many years of sane, even saintly, behavior, is allowed to leave. It is told with the gently satirical interest in aristocratic society and in mental hospitals that Waugh retained all his life, but there liews in ambush one of the most shocking denouements in English literature. The second, **"Bella Fleace,"** is said to have been taken from a real-life incident and is a perfect vehicle for the writer's power of observation, for his ability to draw character in one or two lines of dialogue and for a melancholy humor as well as wit.

I would not have it thought that the stories themselves are any the worse for being reprints. Indeed, if, as the publishers tell us, they appeared before in America only in a limited edition in 1936, it is a great service to make them freely available. And so we come to the title fragment. It is not in any sense a sequel to *Brideshead Revisited,* which would be a resumption or continuation of the story; this is an account of an earlier period in the life of the narrator, Charles Ryder. What seems to have happened is that the pages were originally written as part of *Brideshead* but cut as inappropriate to that book. Then, after the enormous success of the novel in America, Waugh took it up again with a view to continuing it differently. It is not difficult to understand why he finally abandoned the task, because it seems to offer no scope for development. The hero makes no close relationships, and nothing is disclosed about him that seems intended to lead one on.

What remains is simply a glimpse of a few days in the life of and English public school, and, I am told by someone with experience of one, an absolutely authentic view. Un-

disguisedly set at Lancing, Waugh's own school, it gives, with the minimum of direct description but by narration and the use of dialogue, a picture of the terrible heartlessness of young boys in gangs. By the smallest touches we are told much about the individual characteristics of several of them, as well as of one of the masters and of Charles Ryder. Of the last, it can be said that his hobbies are much like Waugh's own and that there is a coldness, a separateness, in his relationships with other people that exceeds the normal qualities of youth. That is all, but it is enough, and for those who know Waugh's work well, the new edition can be recommended for the Charles Ryder fragment alone.

Anatole Broyard (review date 1982)

SOURCE: "Books of the Times," in *The New York Times,* November 22, 1982, p. 16.

[*In the following review of* Charles Ryder's Schooldays and Other Stories, *Broyard finds the work completely without merit.*]

With the exception of *Put Out More Flags,* I think I've liked all of Evelyn Waugh's fiction, and so it saddens me to report that **Charles Ryder's School Days and Other Stories,** most of which were published in a limited edition in 1936, is not very good.

Perhaps the most conspicuous example of the difference between Waugh at his best and worst is the piece called **"By Special Request,"** which is an alternative ending to *A Handful of Dust.* At the end of that novel, Tony Last was disillusioned by the affair of his wife, Brenda, with a man named Beaver, and he went off on a trip to South America, where he was held prisoner in the jungle by an illiterate old man who forced him to read Dickens aloud, over and over again, presumably to the end of his life.

For reasons he doesn't give, Mr. Waugh chose to tamper with that unimprovable ending. In **"By Special Request,"** Tony merely goes on an idle cruise to places like Haiti and returns home to find that Brenda has been abandoned by Beaver and wishes to give up her flat in London and to live again with Tony in the country. She insists on his canceling the lease on the flat, but unknown to her, Tony decides to keep it. The implicit assumption is that the once-serious and austere Tony is planning to have affairs there himself—unless he means to throw Brenda out or to keep it for her next affair.

The tone of **"By Special Request"** reminds me of Joan Didion's *Play It as It Lays.* Tony and Brenda are confined to half-thoughts expressed in self-consciously flat, simple declarative sentences. If the ending is pregnant, it's not a very promising pregnancy, for in each of the possible uses of the flat, both Tony and Brenda lose interest as characters. The available ironies are not significant enough to animate the flatness of the passages between Tony and Brenda.

"Charles Ryder's School Days" is, according to the book jacket, "a recently discovered sketch about the early life and family background of Charles Ryder, the nostalgic hero of *Brideshead Revisited*." What this piece comes down to, though, is an incomprehensible fuss about who is elected to the Settle, some sort of honorific club in the university; who is head of the dormitory; who is keen on whom, and why a character named Apthorpe is moved from the lower anteroom to the upper anteroom.

The first story in the book, which gave the earlier edition its title, *Mr. Loveday's Little Outing and Other Sad Stories,* is an absolutely predictable piece about a mild-mannered man, who, after having strangled a young woman in his youth, has passed 35 years in a mental hospital, where he has become so sane, useful and well loved that he is generally taken for an exceptional guard rather than a patient. When someone secures his release, it takes no great effort to imagine the first thing he does.

"Cruise" is a series of semiliterate letters written by a debutante traveling with her parents. It must have been a very dark day in Evelyn Waugh's life when he wrote it. **"Period Piece,"** an elderly woman's account of an ancient and humorless quarrel between two now-dead men seems gratuitous at best. **"On Guard"** is an excruciatingly cute story about a dog and a young woman. [. . .]

"Winner Takes All" is one of those infernal older-brother versus-younger-brother stories peculiar to the English. In this one, a scheming mother steals all the younger brother's accomplishments for the older one. Waugh's irony here seems to be suffering from something like mental fatigue. Believe it or not, there's also a story about a mad and reclusive old woman who spends her last penny on a magnificent ball and forgets to mail the invitations.

So we have the melancholy spectacle of one of the century's best authors writing badly. Reading *Charles Ryder's School Days* is like visiting an old friend who's out of sorts. In Evelyn Waugh's work, such occasions are very rare.

Robert Murray Davis (essay date 1984)

SOURCE: "Waugh Reshapes 'Period Piece,'" in *Studies in Short Fiction,* Vol. 21, No. 1, Winter, 1984, pp. 65–8.

[*In the following essay, Davis argues that a comparison of the original typescript and the final version of Waugh's frame story "Period Piece" reveals that his revisions, extended the story and added depth and resonance to it.*]

Evelyn Waugh's story **"Period Piece"** is one of his most complex in narrative method—it uses a frame tale, a narratee, and a literary and social context in which the most cynical narrative and social monstrosities are accepted as the norm—and one of his most interesting thematically, for it anticipates by a quarter of a century the resolution of

the dynastic plot of *Sword of Honour.* Furthermore, it is the only Waugh short story for which a manuscript or typescript has been discovered, and a comparison of carbon typescript and printed versions shows how carefully Waugh reconsidered questions of style, character, and narrative strategy.

In the frame tale, Miss Myers reads to her employer, Lady Amelia, a work of "strong" modern fiction. Lady Amelia finds the novel anemic, "painfully reticent," and unduly concerned with vulgar probability, and she offers in contrast an anecdote from her experience that comprises the central section of **"Period Piece."** In that story, Billy Cornphillip, wealthy and dull, marries the would-be artistic Etty, to the distress of Ralph Bland, his nearest relative, presumptive heir, and attractive sponger on women. Billy and Etty produce no heir, but after an escalating series of quarrels between the two men, Ralph elopes with Etty, impregnates and abandons her, and leaves her to return to her husband, who accepts the situation and the child who is legally if not genetically his heir, dispossessing Ralph and his legitimate son.

The twelve pages of carbon typescript—titled **"The Case of Lord Cornphillip"** and provided, as the stamp shows, by the long-suffering "ALEX McLACHLAN, Literary Typecopying Specialist," whom Waugh used from the early 1930's until McLachlan's death in 1946—vary from the text in *Mr. Loveday's Little Outing and Other Sad Stories*[1] in a number of significant ways. Judging from Waugh's letter to his agents about October 3, 1936, the story had not yet been published even though it is elsewhere dated 1934.[2] As was often the case, Waugh obviously sought between typescript and publication greater precision and economy in language; he rearranged the order in which events were narrated to make it more logical; he deleted extraneous material; and he added details to strengthen the narrator's link to events and to emphasize her casual, aristocratic brutality.

Waugh's stylistic revisions are best exemplified in his treatment of the quarrel between Lord Billy Cornphillip and his cousin and heir Ralph (in typescript Harry) Bland:

Typescript

Coming as it did towards the end of a large and gloomy Christmas party this remark could not be disregarded or forgotten. It made the first serious breach between the two cousins. . . . There is no limit to the extremes to which they [relatives] will go.

"Period Piece"

It was towards the end of a large and rather old-fashioned Christmas party, so no one was in a forgiving mood. There was a final breach between the two cousins. . . . There is no limit to the savagery to which they will resort.

(61)

"Savagery" and "resort" are more precise and emphatic than the words replaced, and the ironic assumption that "old-fashioned" means disastrous strengthens the more obvious contrast between Christmas and implacable resentment.

Revisions of structure are a bit more complex. Because Lady Amelia's narrative is reminiscent and expository rather than dramatic, Waugh was not forced to rely on chronology as a structural principle, and in typescript he made several false steps. Thus in a passage corresponding to pp. 57–58 of **"Period Piece,"** he originally introduced Bland before he had finished explaining the circumstances which led to Billy's marriage and his wife Etty's reaction to his dullness. In revision, Waugh first established the context of the marriage and then described the intruder Bland. And after Bland has failed to secure a seat in Parliament, the typescript turned to Etty's growing dissatisfaction with Billy before describing Bland's paranoia which leads him to elope with her in revenge. **"Period Piece"** puts the mania first, then Etty's dissatisfaction, then the elopement. Since Ralph initiates the action, this order is more logical.

Waugh also recognized the blunting of emphasis by unnecessary detail in the typescript. In the final paragraphs of the story, Lady Amelia mentions the occasion on which the present Lord Cornphillip learned that he is Bland's, not Billy's son. Both in typescript and printed text, her nephew Simon reveals the information, but the typescript gives his motive, a quarrel about capital punishment. Waugh clearly saw that the topic was irrelevant to the theme, and the final text merely mentions the revelation.

More important, on two other occasions Waugh deleted material about the fate of Bland. The typescript introduced him with Lady Amelia's memory of her last sight of him playing for minimum stakes at Monte Carlo. In **"Period Piece,"** she does not "know *what* became of him" (58). Having dropped from polite society, the revision implies, he no longer exists for people of her circle. Later, in presenting Bland's parliamentary campaign, Billy's "accusation against Ralph of corrupt practices," and Bland's loss of his seat, both typescript and printed text establish that the campaign is more expensive than Bland's means allow. The typescript summarizes the aftermath, including Harry's bankruptcy and the Queen's displeasure at Billy's behavior; **"Period Piece"** moves directly from Ralph's losing his seat to his developing paranoia.

However, Waugh augmented where he saw the opportunity. The typescript states that the campaign was "more in fact than Harry could well afford" and ends the sentence there. **"Period Piece"** continues: "but in those days Members of Parliament had many opportunities for improving their position, so we all thought it a very wise course of Ralph's—the first really sensible thing we had known him to do" (61–62). In the printed story, therefore, Billy has not merely cost Ralph money but ruined his prospects of gaining more, additional motive for Ralph's sense of grievance.

Other additions after typescript seem to be intended to establish Lady Amelia's narrative authority, especially those about Etty's wedding announcement and Lady Amelia's serving as a bridesmaid (57, 58). Others emphasize the callousness with which she accepts the events she narrates and her aristocratic brutality towards her companion, Miss Myers. Near the beginning of the story, after Miss Myers has commented that the author of the novel she is reading aloud "must have come from a terrible home," the typescript makes the transition to Lady Amelia's reminiscence about her own circle by her characterizing them as "people who come from the most unexceptionable homes," delivering the judgment "with a sharp glance at her companion." The printed text picks up Miss Myers' unfortunate phrase and adds a simile which underlines, especially by the use of "ivory," the rebuke at her unconscious presumption in criticizing her betters, who are "'people who come from anything but terrible homes,' she added with a glance at her companion; a glance sharp and smart as a rap on the knuckles with an ivory ruler" (55).

More subtle is the revision of Lady Amelia's bullying of her companion at the end of her narrative, signalled both in typescript and printed text by the arrival of the tea-tray:

Typescript

You will have plenty of time for your tea, Miss Myers. The library does not close until six o'clock.

"Period Piece"

. . . I see that Mrs. Samson has made more of those little scones which you always seem to enjoy so much. I am sure, dear Miss Myers, you would suffer much less from your *migraine* if you avoided them. But you take so little care of yourself, dear Miss Myers . . . Give one to Manchu.

(66)

The typescript sought to impose symmetry by returning at the end to the subject of the beginning: Lady Amelia's taste for novels. The revision assumes her moral rather than her social superiority to Miss Myers, and with its subtle parallel of her diet with the self-indulgence of Ralph Bland, makes both the authors of their own misfortunes and emphasizes the polite rapaciousness which Billy and Lady Amelia share beneath the façade of manners. The fact that Manchu is a dog and casually given that which Miss Myers should deny herself is an added fillip.

Waugh's revisions added to, if they did not entirely create, what depth and resonance the story has, and they show that his sense of craftsmanship extended to a story that by comparison with his novels he considered minor. Obviously his repeated advice to Nancy Mitford was the result of long practice: "No more complaints about headaches. Revision is just as important as any other part of writing and must be done con amore."[3]

Notes

1. *Mr. Loveday's Little Outing and Other Sad Stories* (London: Chapman and Hall, 1936), p. 55. This edition cited parenthetically hereafter.

2. For the letter and a physical description of the typescript, see my *A Catalogue of the Evelyn Waugh Collection at the Humanities Research Center, The University of Texas at Austin* (Troy, NY: Whitston Publishing Company, 1981), items E296, A13. The story is dated 1934 in *Tactical Exercise* (Boston: Little, Brown, 1954). No periodical publication has been discovered.

3. *The Letters of Evelyn Waugh,* ed. Mark Amory (New Haven and New York: Ticknor and Fields, 1980), p. 347.

Jerome Meckier (essay date 1985)

SOURCE: "Evelyn Waugh's 'Ryder by Gaslight': A Post-mortem," in *Twentieth Century Literature,* Vol. 31, No. 4, Winter, 1985, pp. 399 409.

[*In the following essay, Meckier posits that, although "Ryder by Gaslight" is well-written, Waugh was correct not to publish it.*]

Truly posthumous writings, by the author himself, raise different questions than writings *about* him issued after his death.[1] One could ask, for example, which, if any, of the strictly posthumous materials—letters, diaries, and a chapter of *Charles Ryder's Schooldays*—did Waugh wish succeeding generations to see? "Ryder by Gaslight" poses subtler problems than the diaries or letters: namely, does one help or hinder a novelist's growing posthumous reputation by printing a story he seems to have considered a misfire?

Michael Sissons, who gave "Ryder by Gaslight" to the *Times Literary Supplement,* conjectures that Waugh never went on with the story because "the time wasn't ripe" or else A. D. Peters, his literary agent, talked him out of proceeding.[3] Be that as it may, Waugh, by not printing the piece, was consigning it to oblivion with a deliberateness impossible for him to exert upon his diaries and letters. Taking up the matter of posthumous writings, therefore, means behaving as Waugh's literary executor.

In the case of the only chapter about Ryder's schooldays that Waugh finished, one can hardly tell where executory mandate ends and exhumation begins. *Time* magazine clearly had strong reservations about the story when it first appeared in print, thirty-seven years after Waugh abandoned it. The title of its notice—"A Stillborn Son of *Brideshead*"—put the blame on Waugh's errant midwifery. Instead, one should fault the resurrection men of the Peters Agency. Sissons, its managing director, describes how Chapter One "dropped" out of an office file on Waugh. As in the *Time* review, there is the suggestion of a birth. Better to say the opening segment has been forcibly recalled to a posthumous life Waugh never intended it to lead.

As an unpublished fragment, "Ryder by Gaslight" testifies not so much to Waugh's talent as to his sound judg-ment. His decision to suspend work on the novel and bury the only completed chapter probably ought not to have been reversed. The question to ask concerning *Charles Ryder's Schooldays* is not whether Waugh wished posterity to have any part of it, but why he clearly hoped it would not.

Even the popularity of *Brideshead Revisited,* Waugh must quickly have realized, could not carry *Charles Ryder's Schooldays* to glory. On the contrary, it would have worked against it, the inevitable comparison unveiling the latter's deficiencies. Branding the only existing episode a "twit's guide" to British schoolboy slang, as *Time*'s reviewer went on to do, is surely unfair, but not entirely. The fragment dwells on what Ryder himself calls "the trivial round of House politics." Who should be on the Settle? Do library privileges need to be extended? What are the niceties of a public school hierarchy in late September 1919? These were not subjects to enthrall a general audience, especially not the American readers of *Brideshead Revisited,* who had just made the author an international best seller.

The most that can be said for "Ryder by Gaslight" is that the chapter is remarkably compact and well written. It covers events from September 24, 1919, through the 27th, four days at the beginning of term for a third-year boy in the Classical Upper Fifth at Spierpoint, a school much like Waugh's Lancing. Waugh blends dramatized events, which move forward almost entirely in dialogue, with Charles's reflections on them as they are happening and then, in retrospect, in his diary. An effective flashback to Charles's second term relates his reception of the news of his mother's death. One also savors a vignette of Ryder's father: he stops reading family prayers in August of 1914 on grounds that "there was nothing left to pray for."

Despite the high quality of flashback and vignette, however, Waugh had reason to feel uncomfortable, in 1945, about preemptions of his work. In *Eyeless in Gaza* (1936), Aldous Huxley lingered over the death of Anthony Beavis' mother. He also skillfully satirized John Beavis, the boy's absurdly pedantic father. Much of Huxley's novel relies upon chapter-length excerpts from Beavis' diary, a device the novelist exploits again in the final segment of *Time Must Have a Stop* (1945), when Sebastian Barnack reviews his notes for a book that will presumably be similar to *The Perennial Philosophy.*

Four in number, the hero's main experiences in "Ryder by Gaslight" seem intended to prove formative. Charles helps Graves, the new Head, to assemble a small hand printing press, an exercise that excites his artist's sensibility. He disowns his own illumination, by hand, of Ralph Hodgson's "The Bells of Heaven," indicating thereby a capacity for self-criticism. Defiance of "Dirty Desmond," who is on the Settle in place of more qualified aspirants, gets Ryder and his accomplices caned. Most important, Charles lends his prestige by signing Curtis-Dunne's petition for more liberal library privileges, even though this request comes from a younger boy whose eccentricities have made him unpopular. In all four instances, Ryder must reach decisions—ethical, aesthetic, or both—about where to bestow approval and support, just as he will be called upon to do several times in *Brideshead Revisited*. In disobeying Desmond O'Malley, a prototype for Hooper, Charles achieves a moral victory over upstarts, unsuited for authority. He also rejects the liberal attitude of the new Head, who believes power will improve O'Malley's weak character.

Unfortunately, Ryder's experience of injustice scarcely matches Stephen Dedalus' first taste of it when struck across the palms by Father Dolan's pandybat. Joyce overwrites the crisis in Chapter One of *A Portrait of the Artist as a Young Man*. He suggests both the hero's genuine dismay and his own realization, upon looking back at his younger self, that the punishment, despite being undeserved and eye-opening about the world, was not the catastrophe it seemed at the time. Having Ryder report on recent events in his diary seems less inventive than Joyce's double perspective. Ryder is older at Spierpoint than Dedalus at Clongowes Wood College, but his aesthetic sense and potential for heroism do not burgeon as impressively. If Waugh's point is that Charles's English schooldays are more realistic than Stephen's in Dublin, the latter still make the better story.

One passage in **"Ryder by Gaslight"** has frequently been singled out for praise by reviewers. Unfortunately, Ryder's crucial declaration of independence seems mishandled. Charles signs Curtis-Dunne's petition because

> today and all this term he was aware of a new voice in his inner counsels, a detached, critical Hyde who intruded his presence more and more often on the conventional, intolerant, subhuman, wholly respectable Dr. Jekyll; a voice, as it were, from a more civilized age, as from the chimney corner in mid-Victorian times there used to break sometimes the sardonic laughter of grandmama, relic of Regency, a clear, outrageous, entirely self-assured disturber among the high and muddled thoughts of her whiskered descendants.

This "new voice" is clearly as important to Ryder as "the voice" of rocks, woods, and mountain torrents that a "gentle shock of mild surprise" carries into the heart of the boy of Winander. But that boy is obviously the Wordsworth who will write "Tintern Abbey," whereas Waugh, not Ryder, becomes a major satirist; he, not the Ryder of *Brideshead Revisited,* speaks out as the "self-assured disturber," a "voice . . . from a more civilized age."

Waugh depicts the "disturber," who is actually civilization's ultimate defense, as a second or secret self and then as a "sardonic" old lady. Individually, the images seem unattractive, only marginally appropriate. Nor do they complement each other very well. The "relic of Regency" can still puncture Victorian pretense but has been pushed to one side unceremoniously. Ryder, by contrast, is just starting out. It will not do to liken the fledgling satirist to an old crone.

Jekyll's split personality makes a dubious model for a model schoolboy, even one beginning to realize that he harbors a rebel within. Hyde is vile and violent rather than "detached" or "critical." Alluding to Stevenson's "Strange Case" is less efficacious than having an "old artificer" stand for soaring creativity. When Dedalus rebels, he identifies with Lucifer, who was splendid and majestic, at least until the moment of disobedience. When Stephen sees himself as Satan, Joyce preserves the note of mock-heroic self-inflation first sounded in the martyrdom scene with Father Dolan. Waugh accepts Ryder's view of himself as Hyde uncritically. As the debased half of Jekyll's dual nature, Hyde is simian, dwarfish, and seemingly deformed. He, not Jekyll, is "subhuman." Since Hyde proves increasingly difficult for the doctor to repress, he cannot emblematize an inner voice whose volume Waugh thinks Ryder would be wise to raise.

Waugh had already chronicled Ryder's more important schooldays in the Oxford episodes of "Et in Arcadia Ego."[4] Many consider these the best part of *Brideshead Revisited.* Waugh's reluctance to continue **Charles Ryder's Schooldays** can be attributed to its having been precluded not only by other modern novelists but by the author himself.

Brideshead Revisited was already a bildungsroman. In Ryder's case, however, the child does not prove father to the man. Waugh challenges the premise upon which traditional novels of growth and development generally rest. Instead, the profane is prelude to the sacred. Sebastian serves as Charles's conductor to Julia and she, in turn, conducts him to God. The novel's thesis about providential signs and forerunners, a combination of typology and teleology, reverses the process of secularization Waugh maintained had ruined the Western world. It also shows Ryder to be superior as a sign-reader to Dedalus. In *Ulysses,* the latter contends that artists like himself are born to read the "Signatures" in all things.[5] As Waugh's picture of an artist who converts to Catholicism, Ryder parodies the alleged progress of Joyce's famous aesthete. This made it unnecessary, if not impossible, for **"Ryder by Gaslight"** to compete effectively with *Portrait of the Artist*.

Having encountered the wading girl in Joyce's climactic fourth chapter, Dedalus forsakes his family's faith and the possibility of priesthood. He dedicates himself to the celebration in art of profane, earthly beauty, which the apparition of the girl, virtually a replay of the Annunciation, providentially symbolizes. Thanks to Julia, Ryder's journey takes him from art to the faith Dedalus resigned. A "rider" means, among other things, an amendment. Waugh tries to amend what he considered Joyce's unfounded jubilation over Dedalus' moment of purely secular self-realization. His declaration of faith in the worthwhileness of an exclusively temporal order, Waugh objects, cannot turn out to be genuinely salvific.

After completing **"The Man Who Liked Dickens,"** Waugh says that he "wanted to discover how the prisoner" at Chez Todd "got there."[6] He wrote his fourth novel as a way of finding out, using the already published story as Chapter Six. It became the conclusion to *A Handful of Dust,* the finest of the early novels. Inquiring how Ryder reached Oxford, how he schooled himself for the all-important contacts that would lead him from the profane to the sacred or, better, from the first to a perception of the second at work in it, would have been unoriginal. Waugh would have produced a positive yet less compelling variation on his earlier success.

For Waugh to ask how Ryder passed from Spierpoint to Oxford and Brideshead was the wrong interrogative. It was right to be curious about prior events in the case of a man like Tony Last. His plight constitutes a dead end and was designed for a novel that underscores precisely that point about secular humanism. Ryder's future, not his past, demanded further examination. What would become of the thesis about life illustrated by someone like Ryder, not how had his life gone before it describes the circle that brings him back to Brideshead—that was the real question. In 1951, as Waugh began writing *Men at Arms,* he was undertaking the first of three novels that form the true sequel to *Brideshead Revisited.*

Waugh never resumed the Ryder project because, having fretted for six years since setting it aside,[7] he finally had a better idea. Subsequent events confirmed his decision. In 1951 Anthony Powell published *A Question of Upbringing,* volume one in the first of four sequential trilogies. Opening scenes at Eton outdo those at Spierpoint as thoroughly as Widmerpool eclipses "Dirty Desmond." Powell's obnoxious upstart precludes whatever uses Waugh might have had for O'Malley as a threat to traditional standards for determining excellence and advancement. If Waugh did not feel preempted by Huxley and Joyce, he would definitely have been upstaged by Powell. On the other hand, by pushing ahead with *Men at Arms,* Waugh staked out ground Powell would not reach until *The Valley of Bones* (volume seven) in 1964.

Charles Ryder's Schooldays was not discarded because Waugh shrank from in-depth self-presentation. Admittedly, he preferred deflection to what Holden Caulfield calls "all that David Copperfield kind of crap."[8] But *Sword of Honour* indicates that he was not averse to the sort of intellectual autobiography Dickens practiced in *Great Expectations* or Voltaire in *Candide.* Satirists generally choose indirection when it comes to autobiography: stories that trace growth or change in their philosophical outlook. Indirection serves as a means of securing objectivity, hence of maintaining a uniformly satirical tone.

Candide is hardly Voltaire any more than Pip is Dickens. Yet in each case the young man's intellectual odyssey from a ridiculous optimism to a saner retrenchment of it clearly resembles the author's. **"Ryder by Gaslight"** is the *David Copperfield* Waugh decided not to write. Like *Great Expectations, Sword of Honour* records substantial revisions of its author's previous attitudes. These are found to have been too romantic and must be heavily revised if they are to be salvaged.

Guy Crouchback is the idea behind Ryder extended, reconsidered, and then, even though one hates to use the word, partially deconstructed. His story is Waugh's sober-minded reappraisal of the thesis Ryder encounters in the real world: that one can still "trace the workings of the divine purpose in a pagan world."[9] Crouchback wonders if one can cooperate with it heroically and, going further, presumes to direct it. As Guy's surname suggests from the start, however, the hypothesis controlling *Brideshead Revisited* has to be modified, especially in light of England's acceptance of Stalinist Russia as an ally against Germany. This development caused Waugh much personal disappointment. Pressure from turns being taken by World War II was breaking in upon Waugh's confidence about determining divine workings even as he wrote to express it. That may help to explain the surfeit of nostalgia in *Brideshead Revisited.*

Like other modern satirical novelists, Waugh ends his career probing the validity of his own solution to the state of affairs his earlier work spent most of its energy deploring. *Sword of Honour* tests the realism of *Brideshead Revisited* in ways no account of Ryder's schooldays could have. It reinvestigates the credibility of a providential supervision for temporal concerns as a solution to the human situation. It does so as sharply as Waugh once tested the persuasiveness of Dickens' Victorian humanism against Tony Last's misadventures throughout *A Handful of Dust.*[10]

Despite the epical dimensions of *Sword of Honour,* Waugh has great difficulty explaining God's ways to Guy. Dickens and Wilkie Collins experienced fewer problems in tracing providential designs for the benefit of their protagonists. Box-Bender resentfully notes that Guy's happiness with Domenica Plessington and Trimmer's son "turned out very conveniently" for him.[11] He ought to have said the outcome was providential without being spectacularly so. Waugh manages to preserve for modern fiction a sense of extraterrestrial superintendence, but only by curtailing expectations Victorian novelists had of benefits to be derived from it. *Sword of Honour* makes clearer than *Brideshead Revisited* had that recognizing God's hand in men's affairs can be a humbling experience.

God's providence, Waugh wants to emphasize, is both more demanding and less glamorous than Joyce's secularization of it. This involves a concession that Waugh's own treatment in *Brideshead Revisited* was too melodramatic. Waugh sent Ryder such signs as Sebastian and Julia in succession. He also allowed him to witness the twitch on the thread that pulls a dying Lord Marchmain back into the fold. Waugh put providential care in a context it was often taxing for recipients of its attentions to accept joyously. Marchmain's deathbed repentance, for example, costs Julia her scheduled marriage to Ryder. But Waugh was still not sufficiently removed from the misconception of providence as gratification of an individual's desires. This is the sort of kindness that supplied the wading girl for a Dedalus who had been anxious, since his schooldays, "to meet in the real world the unsubstantial image which his soul so constantly beheld.""[12] As a bildungsroman, **Charles Ryder's Schooldays** would have been obliged to build toward ego-fulfillment for its protagonist. Waugh would have found this inconvenient at a time when, having shown Marchmain and Julia giving in to God, he may have felt obliged to scrutinize further the merits of submission, not of self-assertion.

Dedalus elects to serve earthly beauty in his art as a means of saying "*non serviam*" to Church and State alike. Guy's insistence that the war with Germany become a modern crusade sounds commendable but is actually his way of refusing to serve God. Crouchback wants his will to be done, his view of things to prevail, not God's. Guy's military career can be called a form of apostasy; it is not just a belated example of the delusion, common in the politically oriented Thirties, that one attains a kind of salvation through immersion in larger causes.

Carlyle never ceased to regard events such as the French Revolution as divine punishments that descend on unjust nations for their crimes. This idea of providence also pervades Victorian masterpieces of melodramatic realism, particularly *Bleak House* and *The Woman in White*. Guy eventually rebukes himself for trying to convert war against Germany into a campaign against godlessness in the modern world. Such a framework, Waugh concedes, fails to apply, not because it is now a "pagan world" but because such heretical overviews are an attempt to explain God's ways to God Himself. Tracing divine purposes, Guy realizes, often means detecting the wisdom in whatever God sends.

Crouchback's role becomes virtually a parody of the more heroic mission he would like to have performed. Instead of rescuing Mme Kanyi and her people, he will, to quote Waugh's words, "rescue Trimmer's son from a disastrous upbringing."[13] In place of Guy's grandiose, overlying pattern for international events and Ryder's belief in twitches from God for even the most recalcitrant, Waugh draws back to offer a lesser thesis: "that God creates no man without a special purpose,"[14] provided he schools himself to see and accept it.

Crouchback's story is not just a failed attempt to enhance the thesis illustrated by Ryder's; one could argue that it tones down *Helena* as well. Resolving to obtain proofs of the historicity of the Crucifixion seems no less ambitious than wanting to orchestrate the defeat of godlessness in the modern age. Helena experiences miraculous confirmation that the pilgrimage she undertakes is indeed God's errand. Without vital directions from the Wandering Jew, who addresses her in a dream, Helena would not find her relics. The Jew makes an odd but effective equivalent for the wading girl, the providential messenger or living signpost provided for Dedalus. But *Sword of Honour* is the real continuation of *Brideshead Revisited*. In *Helena*, Waugh casts back into classical antiquity for a semi-historical, mostly legendary example of the sort of providential direction for human endeavor he would like to write about in the modern world. Difficulties Waugh had in finishing *Helena*—it took him five years—must have filled him with foreboding.

Waugh's recension of *Sword of Honour* in 1966 from a trilogy to a novel as long as *Pickwick Papers* or *Bleak House* is a revision of a revision of *Brideshead Revisited*. First, Guy's role was cut back to saving Trimmer's son instead of the world. In the recension, Waugh retrenches further by deleting two boys Guy fathered by Domenica. Crouchback tastes victory only in the form of ignominious defeat for a mistaken ideal, his and Waugh's own overestimate of the divine purpose's operations. The pattern was set when the Messiah, executed as a common criminal, accomplished the rescue of each man's soul but not, as many had foolishly hoped, of the Jewish Empire from the Romans.

The recension puts the "workings of the divine purpose" in a more modest perspective. Waugh decides that countless "workings" go on constantly in the profane world. He finds no single "purpose" to redeem the world itself, however, no master plan for national salvation, in Guy's sense of the term, and no clearly pinpointed moments of intercession to bolster the individual's faith, as happens in Ryder's case and Helena's. Instead, Guy must toil past a series of false signs or messengers, bogus forerunners, some of whom are parodies of him and his inapplicable ideals: Apthorpe, Ritchie-Hook, Trimmer, Ivor Claire, and Ludovic. Guy finally discovers a legitimate messenger and model in the last place that Dedalus, in search of Bloom, would ever have looked. He falls back upon his own saintly, unobtrusive father.[15] Absence of a master plan for saving the world by means of World War II is part of the elder Crouchback's meaning when he discounts "Quantitative judgements."[16]

In *Sword of Honour,* the secular arena is once again an object of unrelenting derision, and the errant hope of proving that it can be resanctified becomes still another target. Writing in the 1960s, Waugh finds modern secular society just as purposeless, just as circular, as it appeared in **Decline and Fall** and *Vile Bodies*. The crucial difference is that it is also a place in which, through a multitude of different ways and less ostentatiously than Ryder or Helena imagine, some individuals work out their salvation. Often they do so by learning, as does Guy, not to engage the world beyond a certain point.

Ensconced in the agent's house at Broome, Guy, with his second wife and Trimmer's son, establishes a pocket of sanity. Superficially, it is not unlike Mr. Pickwick's withdrawal to Dulwich after emerging, sadly disillusioned, from the Fleet. But Waugh's is clearly the more religious resolution. Dickens' secular Edens, surrogates or facsimiles of the real thing, invariably serve as final resting places; they become ends in themselves. Waugh's never take seriously the idea of the City of God as a temporal phenomenon. As did Huxley, who collapses Pala in *Island*, Waugh contends that a religious solution to the human situation has to be personal, never society-wide or national.

The protagonist of **"Ryder by Gaslight"** is at a much earlier stage in the struggle between participation in the world and recusancy; he is only beginning to contemplate what forms of service to render and which to withhold or refuse. Waugh apparently found this stage interesting to recall in 1945, but he must have realized it would have been a step backward for him as a thinking novelist, indeed an escape from responsibility. No matter how long Ryder's schooldays lasted, his emerging image of himself as a rebel ("detached," "outrageous") would have been insurmountable. It would have prevented him from learning to appreciate beauty and heroic humility in the necessity of Guy's surrendering unconditionally to God's will.[17]

Waugh's career as a satirical novelist need not have been over in 1966 with the revision of *Sword of Honour* into a single novel. Although resignation appears to have replaced indignation (the "self-assured disturber"), death makes it impossible to say what might otherwise have happened. Waugh took nearly a decade to round off the trilogy, six of those years between volumes two and three. This suggests he had great difficulty scaling down his former conception of the "divine purpose." It was harder to do than fashioning Helena as a trial version of a person who discerns remarkable coincidence between the task she elects and the "special purpose" for which she was created. The two form a painful discrepancy for Crouchback. One thing seems certain: Waugh could never have resumed **Charles Ryder's Schooldays** once he finished *The End of the Battle*. To do so would have been to return to 1919 as though nothing had happened in the meantime. This would have been more duplicitous than Pennyfeather's return to Scone as his own cousin.

In at least two ways, **"Ryder by Gaslight,"** more so than diaries or letters, confirms the growing estimate of Waugh as one of the century's foremost satirical novelists. Not the lesser of these ways is by its evident inferiority to the incomparable novels Waugh chose to pursue to their close. On several of these, to mention the second way, a postmortem shows that **"Ryder by Gaslight"** can shed light.[18]

Notes

1. Bruce Stovel, on the other hand, defines "posthumous material" broadly enough to encompass reprintings of Waugh's journalism, checklists of holdings at the Humanities Research Center, and studies of additions and deletions Waugh made to his novels in manuscript. See "Waugh at Play," *Ariel,* 14 (July 1983), 60–81.

2. The editor of Waugh's letters exonerates himself for collecting them but impugns Mark Davies, who published the diaries. Waugh allegedly "foresaw" his letters being issued. See Mark Amory, ed., *The Letters of Evelyn Waugh* (London: Weidenfeld and Nicolson, 1981), p. vii.

3. See the *Times Literary Supplement* for 5 March 1982, pp. 255–58. Waugh apparently worked on the story in September-October of 1945.

4. When Thomas Hughes followed Tom Brown's scholastic career, he began with the hero's public school life, then moved on to Oxford.

5. James Joyce, *Ulysses* (New York: Random House, 1946), p. 38.

6. See "Fan-Fare" in *Life* (8 April 1946), p. 58.

7. *Scott-King's Modern Europe, The Loved One,* and *Helena*—all of which were written between *Brideshead Revisited* and *Men at Arms*—cannot be dismissed as dereliction of duty. Nevertheless, they are, among other things, postponements of it. Waugh worked on "Ryder by Gaslight" and *Helena* simultaneously, putting the former aside first, then delaying to complete the latter until 1950.

8. J. D. Salinger, *The Catcher in the Rye* (New York: Signet Books, 1959), p. 5.

9. Waugh's declaration of theme appeared on the inside flap of the dust jacket for *Brideshead Revisited.* It is reprinted in Martin Stannard, ed., *Evelyn Waugh: The Critical Heritage* (London: Routledge & Kegan Paul, 1984), p. 236.

10. See Jerome Meckier, "Why the Man Who Liked Dickens Reads Dickens Instead of Conrad: Waugh's *A Handful of Dust,*" *Novel,* 13 (Winter 1980), 171–87.

11. Evelyn Waugh, *Sword of Honour* (Boston: Little, Brown, 1966), p. 796.

12. James Joyce, *A Portrait of the Artist as a Young Man* (New York: Viking, 1958), p. 65.

13. Waugh provides this statement as part of a succinct summary of the controlling ideas at work in the war trilogy. The summary appears on a card addressed to W. J. Igoe for 4 August 1961. See *Letters,* p. 571.

14. *Ibid.*

15. Waugh's most pointed remarks about Joyce follow closely upon completion of the war trilogy. Waugh told Julian Jebb (April 1962) that Joyce "started off writing very well, then you can watch him going mad with vanity. He ends up a lunatic." See "Evelyn Waugh" in *Writers at Work* (London: Secker and Warburg, 1968), pp. 110–11. It is not clear how much direction Waugh gave Frederick J. Stopp for *Evelyn Waugh: Portrait of an Artist* (1958), but he must have relished the title. Rather than alluding to Joyce, it suggests Waugh is the archetypal artist.

16. Waugh, *Sword of Honour,* p. 699.

17. *Unconditional Surrender* was the title of the third and final volume in the trilogy now known as *Sword of Honour,* where it gives its name to Chapter Eleven.

18. A version of this essay was presented at the special Waugh session on his posthumous writings during the 1984 meeting of the Modern Language Association in Washington, D.C.

Martin Stannard (essay date 1986)

SOURCE: In *Evelyn Waugh: The Early Years 1903–1939*, W. W. Norton & Company, 1986, pp. 114–19, 296–99, 344–49.

[*In the following excerpt, Stannard discusses some of the short stories as they relate to Waugh's development as a writer and his career as a novelist.*]

The 'novel' which had begun as a 'cinema film' was knocked into shape as a long, *avant-garde* short story. 'I have finished my story', [Waugh] noted on 26th August, 'which I have called **"The Balance"** and took it to be typed. It is odd but, I think, quite good.'[1] Christopher Sykes states that it was, in fact, rather bad. That is unfair. The tale, of course, lacks the accomplished touch of Waugh's later stories and he himself thought it second-rate. It has never been reprinted. But, at the lowest estimate, it is an arresting piece of experimental writing and was recognised as such when it appeared. From a biographical viewpoint it is even more intriguing. As his first sustained attempt at fiction, written during a protracted period of misfortune, completed less than two months after the aborted suicide, it represents an effort (as earlier with 'Anthony') to rationalise his disordered life through artistic expression.

'The Balance' draws heavily on personal experience. It is the only piece of Waugh's fiction which included the Oxford book auction, the Art School setting or the attempted suicide. Other details—the carelessness of the heroine for the hero's love, the failure as an artist, the pretentious valedictory Latin note and the apparent indifference of his Oxford cronies—can leave us in no doubt. Waugh was summing up his life here.

The 'balance' concerned is 'the balance between appetite and reason'. A bold experiment in narrative technique, the story is for the most part written as a scenario for a silent film about the characters involved. Large captions indicating place, time, and occasionally, dialogue, break up the page and shift the scenes. The characters speak a great deal but this is, presumably, not heard by the audience. Gladys and Ada (a cook and a parlourmaid) and someone 'with a Cambridge accent' sit in the stalls offering bemused or arrogantly 'arty' comments: 'These Bo'emians don't 'alf carry on, eh, Gladys?' or 'It is curious the way that they can never make their heroes and heroines talk like ladies and gentlemen—particularly in moments of emotion.' The film, the second of four sections, ends with Adam Doure's (the hero's) death by suicide in an Oxford hotel bedroom and the audience leaves uttering banalities. But there follows a 'Conclusion' in lucid analytical prose, in which Adam revives from his coma and remembers vomiting ingloriously over the balcony during the night, despite all efforts to hold down his poison.

He takes stock of the situation and recalls an incident when, as a child, he had fallen from a chair balanced precariously at a great height:

Later he learned to regard these periods between his fall and the dismayed advent of help from below, as the first promptings towards that struggle for detachment in which he had not, without almost frantic endeavour, finally acknowledged defeat in the bedroom of the Oxford hotel.

The first phase of detachment had passed and had been succeeded by one of methodical investigation. Almost simultaneously with his acceptance of continued existence had come the conception of pain—vaguely at first as of a melody played by another to which his senses were only fitfully attentive, but gradually taking shape as the tangible objects about him gained in reality, until at length it appeared as a concrete thing, external but intimately attached to himself. Like the pursuit of quicksilver with a spoon, Adam was able to chase it about the walls of his consciousness until at length he drove it into a corner in which he could examine it at his leisure. Still lying perfectly still, with his limbs half embracing the wooden legs of the chair, Adam was able, by concentrating his attention on each part of his body in turn, to exclude the disordered sensations to which his fall had given rise and trace the several constituents of the bulk of pain down their vibrating channels to their sources in his various physical injuries.[2]

The metaphorical parallel between Waugh's and Adam's new position of detachment is self-explanatory. As Adam walks along the 'towing path away from Oxford' he thinks abstractedly of his fellow guests in the hotel that morning:

All around him a macabre dance of shadows had reeled and flickered, and in and out of it Adam had picked his way, conscious only of one insistent need, percolating through to him from the world outside, of immediate escape from the scene upon which this bodiless harlequinade was played, into a third dimension beyond it.[3]

It is a dangerous and largely futile business attempting to correlate an author's life with incidents in his fiction. Waugh suffered greatly in later years from misguided critics searching for models of his fictional characters. He always insisted, quite rightly, that the good writer created and transformed, never transcribed. But **'The Balance'** is, perhaps, the most significant exception to this rule in his *opus*. Indeed, it alluded to autobiographical secrets (such as the attempted suicide) not revealed until the publication of *A Little Learning* (1964). Quite apart from any aesthetic consideration of the story's technical merit, one of the reasons for his refusal to reprint it must have been the embarrassing intimacy of its subject-matter. It gave too much of himself away. There is a great deal of the young Waugh in Adam Doure and the author's friends must have recognised the correspondence. All the evidence points to the fact that his hero's vision of the world as a 'bodiless harlequinade' and his resulting 'struggle for detachment' were Waugh's own.

The third section, 'Conclusion', ends with a dialogue between Adam and his reflection as he leans over a bridge after the destruction of the suicide note. He has found no secret, it appears, only 'bodily strength' in the discovery of the true nature of 'the balance', that necessary state of mental equilibrium in a phantasmagoric and unreliable world. Unlike the Romantic and Victorian dilemmas, this is not seen as a balance between 'life and death', but between 'appetite and reason' in which 'the reason remains constant' (but largely ineffectual) and 'the appetite varies'. The implicit difficulty in this realisation is that appetite has no absolute value as a directing principle; its object achieved, it either ceases to exist or is re-directed and re-defined. Even the appetite for death 'is appeased by sleep and the passing of time'. There is no 'reason', no 'honour to be observed to friends', no 'interpenetration, so that you cannot depart without bearing away with you something that is part of another'. Even Adam's art is only 'the appetite to live—to preserve in the shapes of things the personality whose dissolution you foresee inevitably'. And in the end 'circumstance decides', not the individual. The paradox suggested by this vision is of man simultaneously isolated ('no interpenetration') and left without individual identity.

For the artist seeking to depict this dilemma the problem of his own subjectivity generates further complications; he must somehow detach himself from the life he describes while at the same time suggesting that detachment in all but the most superficial respects is impossible. This led to Waugh's use of the film scenario here and largely governed the more subtle stylistic detachment, the apparent comic indifference, of his early novels. They are not flippant, as so many reviewers presumed; quite the reverse.

He became a serious writer as much interested in stylistic innovation as Joyce or Gertrude Stein. He was even concerned with the identical aesthetic problem of developing a new form of literary expression which banished the author's intrusive voice. But there is an essential difference between Waugh and the 'serious' *avant-garde*. Behind all their experiments lies the assumption that there exists a reality, disjointed and cacophonous, but a reality waiting to be described in all its complexity. In **'The Balance,'** indeed in all Waugh's later work, this assumption is challenged. Circumstance decides but, however accurately observed, these constituent events are not 'truth', merely an accurate description of falsehood. Neither man's actions, nor his words, can embody an empirical truth. Circumstance alone decides and, at this stage (1925–6), circumstance is seen as the inadvertent product of collective action.

The last section is entitled 'Continuation', the implication being that no conclusion is possible, that the individual, swept along by circumstance, can exert little influence over his condition. The scene is the elegant luncheon table of a country house. The hostess, mother of one of Adam's Oxford friends, has invited all the bright young people of her son's set. They sit about gossiping. Adam has not been invited. He flickers briefly in the conversation and then is extinguished. They pass on to the next trivial issue. Imogen Quest, the heroine, wants desperately to meet a man who is 'short and dirty with masses of hair'. Throughout

the brief interlude there are constant references to the guests smoking at table—something Waugh, with his fastidious manners, found repulsive. The hostess thinks the scene charming and '*chic*'. Waugh offers no authorial comment but the implication is clear enough. He is mocking them. There is a scarcely suppressed rage at their treatment of Adam, a bitter resentment that his 'reality', his complex psychological and moral 'being', is no more to them than a shadow in a piece of amusing tattle.

At the root of many of Evelyn's complex emotional difficulties, surely, there lay this obsessive fear of enforced anonymity. What happened to Adam must never happen to him. He would *not* be absorbed into the crowd. In the *Diaries* of the period we see: 'This morning a letter from Richard [Greene] telling me that the Greene family are quarrelling with me. I just don't mind. This sort of thing has happened before so often that it has ceased to shock me. I shall have to regard all my friendships as things of three to six months. It makes everything easier.'[4] . . .

While at work on [*Black Mischief*] in March 1932, Waugh wrote his story for the *John Bull* series, eventually entitled **'The Seven Deadly Sins of Today'**. His short advertisement for the tale appeared in April:

> Twenty-five years ago it was the fashion for those who considered themselves enlightened and progressive to cry out against intolerance as the one damning sin of their time.
>
> The agitation was well-founded and it resulted in the elimination from our social system of many elements that are crude and unjust. But in the general revolution of opinion that has followed, has not more been lost than gained?
>
> It is better to be narrow-minded than to have no mind, to hold limited and rigid principles than none at all.
>
> That is the danger which faces so many people today—to have no considered opinions on any subject, to put up with what is wasteful and harmful with the excuse that there is 'good in everything'—which in most cases means inability to distinguish between good and bad.
>
> There are still things which are worth fighting *against*.[5]

Waugh's approach is fundamentally aggressive. This 'preface' precisely describes his distaste for his father's benevolent optimism. The story which followed was entitled **'Too Much Tolerance'**.

The tale (never re-published) was printed under the heading 'Real Life Stories' and is told in the first person. It describes his meeting (probably in Djibouti) with a whimsical, middle-aged liberal humanist who (like Arthur) has reacted against the strictures of a repressive Victorian childhood. He sees no fault in anyone but, as confidence grows between narrator and subject, a life of betrayal and humiliation is revealed. 'As I watched', it concludes, 'he finished his business and strode off towards the town—a jaunty, tragic little figure, cheated out of his patrimony by his partner, battened on by an obviously worthless son, deserted by his wife, an irrepressible, bewildered figure striding off under his bobbing topee, cheerfully battering his way into a whole continent of rapacious and ruthless jolly fellows.'[6] 'Jolly fellows', of course, is heavily ironical. The anti-hero of the story had been quite unable to discriminate between the various races and their internecine factions: '"Can't understand what all the trouble's about. They're all jolly chaps when you get to know them."' 'British officials, traders, Arabs, natives, Indian settlers—they were all to my new friend jolly good chaps.'[7]

To Waugh there were fundamental racial distinctions to be made, particularly between the Arabs and the Indians. Africa was an analogue for the world at large. Rather than adopting his father's gently tolerant belief in the essential goodness of man, Waugh saw the world as largely populated by a rabble of potential or actual savages, 'rapacious', vigilant for the first signs of weakness to move in for the kill. This savagery was all the more dangerous when disguised beneath the trappings of civilization.

Waugh wrote several other short stories during or immediately after the composition of *Black Mischief* and all can be related to this theme, just as the theme itself becomes a structural *leit-motif* of the novel. **'The Patriotic Honeymoon'**, **'Bella Fleace Gave a Party'**, **'Cruise'** and **'Incident in Azania'** are light pieces written hastily for a quick cash return. But Waugh wrote nothing badly and all touch on serious themes: infidelity, death, the dereliction of the English language and the consequent, implicit inability of the characters to comprehend their own active cruelty. In Waugh's phrase, they 'have no mind'; beneath their complacent, dull surfaces, they are mad, bad and dangerous to know, insane with the vanity of benevolence, driven by malice, or simply effete. Violence and betrayal characterise their world. . . .

[Mid-1933] It was a period of considerable anxiety and one in which he appears to have associated himself with the recurrent figure of the lost man. Both **'The Man Who Liked Dickens'** and **'Out of Depth'** centre on this image. The first effectively represents the scenes of Tony Last's imprisonment by Mr Todd (only the names and other minor details being altered) and will be best dealt with later in the context of *A Handful of Dust*. **'Out of Depth'** . . . merits close examination here as a of his mood. It is a substantial piece, subtitled 'An Experiment Begun in Shaftesbury Avenue and Ended in Time'.[8]

He wrote it in July 1933, immediately after finishing the *Passing Show* series, 'I Step Off the Map' (a running title which possibly had more than literal significance). The story concerns a forty-three-year-old American, Rip Van Winkle. Born a Catholic he has become a fashionable, cosmopolitan agnostic. Like Waugh, he had 'reached the age when he disliked meeting new people'. Unlike Waugh, though, he has lived immune from questions about 'time and matter and spirit'. Taking dinner at Margot Metroland's he meets a Mr Jagger ('Kakophilos' in the revised

1936 text) who speaks in 'a thin Cockney voice'. The man is introduced as a magician and appears to be fraudulent (his accent slips from sonorous, 'poetic' intonation to shrill East End vocables).

Jagger is cold, rude and threatening. Later in the evening when Alastair Trumpington and Rip return to the man's flat, he parades in a 'crimson robe embroidered with gold symbols and a comical crimson hat', garments which provoke unrestrained hilarity in the two drunken *boulevardiers*. Jagger asks them which period of history they would choose to visit were it possible for them to become time-travellers. Alastair randomly selects the age of Ethelred the Unready and Rip, with equal facetiousness, states that, being an American, he 'would sooner go forward—say five hundred years'. Leaving the man's house in search of more drink, they turn a corner and drive broadside into a mail van 'thundering down Shaftesbury Avenue at forty-five miles an hour'.

Rip awakens in the same place but in the twenty-fifth century. All signs of 'civilisation' have disappeared. The tube station is a flooded hole in the ground. Symbolically, Eros (the Greek god of Love) is missing from its pedestal in what was Piccadilly Circus. No buildings exist other than fifty or so huts on stilts to raise them above the tidal floods and mud flats of the Thames. The night is characterised by a penetrating silence. Darkness and chaos rule. The people of this 'Lunnon' are savages, shy and ignorant, their aesthetic sensibility and language decayed: 'They spoke slowly in the sing-song tones of an unlettered race who depend on an oral tradition for the preservation of their lore'. In his incongruous evening suit, Rip appears first as an object of mystery.

Silently the savages surround him and begin 'to finger his outlandish garments, tapping his crumpled shirt with their horny nails and plucking at his studs and buttons'. Their curiosity is soon supplanted by suspicion: gently they place him under guard, feeding him as the days pass on 'fish, coarse bread and heavy, viscous beer', squatting on their haunches to discuss him in unintelligible patois. Rip closes his eyes and says to himself, '"I am in London, in nineteen-thirty-three, staying at the Ritz Hotel. I drank too much at Margot's. Have to go carefully in future. Nothing really wrong. I am in the Ritz in nineteen-thirty-three."' Forcing his 'will towards sanity', he is at last convinced of the truth of his proposition. But when he opens his eyes again he sees '. . . early morning on the river, a cluster of wattle huts, a circle of barbarous faces'.

'Lunnon', the surrounding villages, and by implication the world, are ruled by negroes, some of whom arrive in a launch to barter goods. The Londoners spend their time raking the debris of their civilisation in a form of crude archaeology. In return for 'pieces of machinery and ornament, china and glass and carved stonework' the black overlords (dressed smartly in vaguely fascist uniforms of leather and fur) provide 'bales of thick cloth, cooking utensils, fish hooks, knife-blades and axe-heads'. Once discovered, Rip is taken by the leader on a 'phantasmagoric' journey down river. "'This is not a dream,"' he says to himself. "'It is simply that I have gone mad." Then more blackness and wilderness.' Something, however, saves his sanity:

> And then later—how much later he could not tell—something that was new and yet ageless. The word 'Mission' painted on a board: a black man dressed as a Dominican friar . . . and a growing clearness. Rip knew that out of strangeness, there had come into being something familiar; a shape in chaos. . . . Something was being done that Rip knew; something that twenty five centuries had not altered; of his own childhood which had survived the age of the world. In a log-built church at the coast town he was squatting among a native congregation . . . ; all round him dishevelled white men were staring ahead with vague, uncomprehending eyes, to the end of the room where two candles burned. The priest turned towards them his bland, black face.
>
> 'Ite, missa est.'[9]

The tale ends with Rip, back in the twentieth century, coming round in hospital. Talking to the priest at his bedside, he asks the cleric how he (the priest) came to be there. Sir Alastair apparently had asked for him. Alastair wasn't a Catholic but he had suffered a disturbing dream about the Middle Ages and had felt the need for a priest. Learning that Rip was in the same establishment, the priest had come along to see how he was. "'Father,"' Rip replies in the last line, "'I want to make a confession . . . I have experimented in black art.'"

In some ways it is a simple fable, dexterously told. Waugh himself presumably considered it slight as he refused to have it reprinted. In one sense it is a Christmas story reaffirming the continuity and lucidity of Catholic teaching. Rip's return to the Church from the apathetic sleep of agnosticism signals his unconscious recognition of the link between civilisation and faith. The horror he experiences, though, is not unlike that of Conrad's Marlow in *Heart of Darkness*: 'And this, also [London], has been one of the dark places of the earth.'[10] As has been said, there is no evidence of Waugh's having read this work. Unlike Graham Greene, Waugh found Conrad an unsympathetic writer. But the comparison remains useful both for the similarities and differences it throws up.

The second half of Waugh's tale is strongly reminiscent of Marlow's voyage on the Congo, even to the 'phantasmagoric journey downstream' and Rip having his head measured with callipers. Both works suggest the temporary nature of civilisation. 'The dreams of men, the seed of commonwealths, the germs of empires'[11] are powerful emblems of man's attempts to impose idealisms upon chaos. To both Waugh and Conrad, this materialist idealism is delusory. Both refute nineteenth-century concepts of progress and question the validity of seeing history as a linear sequence of cause and effect. Yet there is an obvious point at which they part company. Where Conrad suggests that chaos and darkness must inevitably reclaim all attempts at control, Waugh remains a stolid, fundamentalist theologian. The artefacts and culture of a civilisation may decay but the Faith, that island of sanity in a raving world, will survive.

The story is of particular interest from a biographical point of view in that it represents Waugh's first overtly apologetic work of fiction. From this, one inevitably looks forward to *Brideshead Revisited* (1945) and what renders this tale even more peculiar is that there was a twelve-year gap before Waugh's defence of his faith finds its way back into his fiction. His 'Open Letter' had stressed the idea that he was not, as a writer who was a Catholic, required to produced overtly propagandist art. Suddenly, only two months later, he did precisely that.

Notes

1. *Ibid.,* 26 August, 1925, p. 218.
2. Evelyn Waugh, 'The Balance. A Yarn of the Good Old Days of Broad Trousers and High-Necked Jumpers,' *Georgian Stories 1926,* ed. Alec Waugh (Chapman & Hall, 1926), p. 286.
3. *Ibid.,* p. 287.
4. *Diaries,* 18 May, 1925, p. 212.
5. *JB,* 2 April, 1932, 7.
6. 'Too Much Tolerance,' *JB,* 21 May, 1932, 21, 24.
7. *Ibid.,* p. 21.
8. 'Out of Depth' was reprinted with substantial revisions in Waugh's collection, *Mr Loveday's Little Outing and Other Sad Stories* (Chapman and Hall, 1936), pp. 121–38, and in Charles A. Brady (ed.), *A Catholic Reader* (Buffalo, NY, Desmond and Stapleton, 1947) with a commentary by Brady, pp. 78–9. Waugh did not include it in Penguin Books' *Work Suspended and Other Stories* (Harmondsworth, 1943), nor has it appeared in subsequent Penguin editions with this title. Quotations are from the *Mr Loveday* text unless otherwise stated.
9. 'Out of Depth,' *Mr Loveday's* . . . , pp. 136–7.
10. Joseph Conrad, *Heart of Darkness* (first published 1902; reprinted Harmondsworth, Penguin Books, 1973 and 1976), p. 7.
11. *Ibid.,* p. 7.

Katharyn W. Crabbe (essay date 1988)

SOURCE: "Decline and Fall," in *Evelyn Waugh, Continuum,* 1988, pp. 25–36.

[*In the following excerpt, Crabbe praises* Decline and Fall *as hysterically funny and very appealing, while exploring the depth and complexity of Waugh's plot and structure.*]

Decline and Fall, Waugh's first novel, is for those who love farce, one of the funniest of English novels. The constant appearance, disappearance, and reappearance in another identity of the characters puts one immediately in mind of the opening and closing doors and the circular structures of plot that characterize farce. Although Waugh's approach is often oblique and ironic rather than straightforward and broadly humorous, it is stunningly effective. Even now, more than fifty years after its original publication, *Decline and Fall* is readily available in bookstores and libraries, and each succeeding generation learns to laugh at the Candide-like existence of Paul Pennyfeather.

Although Waugh had hoped *Decline and Fall* would be a real money maker, it was not. It was, however, very well received by the reviewers, and it brought his name before a much larger audience than his biographical study, *Rossetti,* could ever have done. The *Observer* found it "richly and roaringly funny,"[1] and J. B. Priestley noted that "Mr. Waugh has done something very difficult to do, he has created a really comic character."[2]

The title of the novel cannot but remind the reader of the other great *Decline and Fall,* Gibbon's history of the Roman Empire. In alluding to Gibbon, Waugh suggests to the reader that his book, too, will trace the crimes, follies, and misfortunes of mankind. A second choice for the title, which would have struck the same note but which would have been a little less accessible to the general reader was "Untoward Incidents." Waugh suggested the title to his editor at Duckworth's (where the novel was eventually rejected) and explained, "The phrase, you remember, was used by the Duke of Wellington in commenting on the destruction of the Turkish Fleet in time of peace at Navarino. It seems to set the right tone of mildly censorious detachment."[3] As a description of the authorial tone of *Decline and Fall,* "censorious detachment" is hard to beat.

As the novel opens, Paul Pennyfeather is a student in Scone College of Oxford University and is innocently unaware of the chaotic forces underlying modern society. When he runs the length of the quad in his underwear after his trousers are forcibly removed by the drunken members of the Bollinger Club, Paul is dismissed from his college for "indecent behavior." He leaves Oxford with the words of the college porter in his ears: "I expect you'll be becoming a schoolmaster, sir. That's what most of the gentlemen does, sir, that gets sent down for indecent behavior." Turned out of the house by his greedy guardian who sees a chance to appropriate Paul's inheritance for his own daughter, Paul indeed becomes a schoolmaster at Llanabba Castle, a minor public school in Wales. His fellow masters are Grimes, a pederast who, ironically, comes to represent the forces of life in the novel, and Prendergast, the representative of organized religion, who, again ironically, becomes a symbol of death.

Paul's favorite student at Llanabba is Peter Beste-Chetwynde whose mother, Margot, is an international white slaver. Paul falls in love with Margot and is about to be married to her when she sends him to France to help clear the way for her latest group of South American-bound prostitutes. He succeeds and returns to London only to be arrested on the way to the altar through the efforts of his college chum, Potts (now in the employ of the League of Nations). Convicted of procuring, Paul is sentenced to prison. Margot arranges to have him removed from the prison to a private hospital, ostensibly for an appendectomy. When the proprietor reports to the authorities that he has died on the operating table, Paul escapes to Margot's retreat on Corfu to consider his future. Eventually, he turns to Scone, sporting a new mustache as a disguise and posing as his own cousin.

One of the great appeals of Waugh's fiction is likewise one of the great appeals of those adolescent adventure stories that were the backbone of the nineteenth-century boy's books—the hero is almost always a young man on his own. In Waugh's vision in the early novels, however, the hero has had independence thrust upon him, that is, he is an exile from a society of which he would love to be a part. This is especially true in the first two novels, *Decline and Fall* and *Vile Bodies.*

Paul Pennyfeather, for example, is an orphan. His parents died when he was at public school. His guardian, who has control of Paul's money until Paul is twenty-one, has no compunctions about confiscating the money and throwing Paul out. His teachers are similarly exploitative, more interested in the founder's port than in justice. His employer, Dr. Fagan, and his fiance, Margot, are equally predatory.

Paul's essential feature is his *outsideness* or his status as an exile. Indeed, exile is one of the few consistent aspects of his life. His parents, the narrator reveals, "had died in India at the time when he won the essay prize at his preparatory school." Having survived the first exile (public school) of the English gentleman, Paul is, in short order, exiled from his college and from his home, the house of the prosperous solicitor in Onslow Square. As the novel progresses, Paul finds himself even further estranged from the world he *thought* he knew and the code he *thought* it followed: "For generations the British bourgeoisie have spoken of themselves as gentlemen, and by that they have meant, among other things, a self-respecting scorn of irregular perquisites," he reminds himself. This code, which may work for the British bourgeoisie who can remain safely within the social framework they understand, is woefully inadequate in the chaotic modern world in which the very walls and towers of the old order are being taken down and replaced by vast constructs of chromium and glass. Paul's code, the code of the gentleman, is perfectly admirable, and his ingenuous character is a reflection of that charming construct, but the code cannot, and does not, prepare him to meet the new world that has evolved around him.

Note, for example, that in his first interview with Dr. Fagan, Paul resolves to tell the truth about his past: "I was sent down, sir, for indecent behavior." Dr. Fagan's response, "I have been in the scholastic profession long enough to know that nobody enters it unless he has some very good reason which he is anxious to conceal," simply and wittily illustrates that the world outside Scone College is playing a different game by a set of rules that Paul has not yet even begun to understand.

Similarly, Paul's failure to understand the nature of Margot's business, Latin-American Entertainments, Ltd., and his innocent observation that the League of Nations "seem to make it harder to get about instead of easier," suggest his inability to understand the world or to understand that anyone of his class could be less than honorable. Introducing the first of a long line of doubles in his fiction, Waugh has the narrator observe that Paul Pennyfeather has mysteriously disappeared and will be replaced by a shadow whose only interest "arises from the unusual series of events of which his shadow was witness." In doing so, he suggests that there is something in the air of England at the time that is eliminating the British gentleman and replacing him with an empty facade.

> Back in his familiar habitat with Potts, Paul becomes again what he had once been: . . . an intelligent, well-educated, well-conducted young man, a man who could be trusted to use his vote at a general election with discretion and proper detachment, whose opinion on a *ballet* or a critical essay was rather better than most people's, who could order dinner without embarrassment and in a creditable French accent, who could be trusted to see to luggage at foreign railway stations, and might be expected to acquit himself with decision and decorum in all the emergencies of civilized life.

The difficulty, of course, is that the life Waugh surveys in *Decline and Fall* is not what one would call civilized. Thus, as soon as Paul leaves the restaurant and the discussion of Otto Silenus and re-enters the modern world as it is reflected in the new King's Thursday, the man he was educated to be disappears and the shadow he has become appears in his stead.

Paul Pennyfeather is a fine young man with no vices when he is at Scone studying for the church. Despite his virtue, Paul is not very well treated by the authorities at his college. The moral failure of the faculty and administration is clear in the master's deciding to dismiss Paul from the college because he would probably not be able to pay a heavy fine. The Junior Dean and the Domestic Bursar are interested only in the amount of money collected in fines and what that implies for the quality of the after-dinner port. Even the chaplain, who might be expected to demonstrate more charity than the others, fails to acknowledge that Paul has been treated unfairly and that his life has been ruined. The chaplain's concern is solely for himself and for the return of a book he had lent Paul: "Oh, Pennyfeather, before you go, surely you have my copy of Dean Stanley's *Eastern Church?*

Having left Scone, Paul has a series of experiences that are equally hard on the church and churchmen. He first meets Mr. Prendergast, a defrocked clergyman who "lost his faith" because he could not understand, metaphorically, the first thing about his own religion: "You see, it wasn't the ordinary sort of Doubt about Cain's wife or the Old Testament miracles or the consecration of Archbishop Parker. I'd been taught how to explain all that while I was at college. No, it was something deeper than all that. *I couldn't understand why God had made the world at all.*"

Prendy, the reader learns, resigned his ministry for the same reason Paul decided to refuse Digby-Vaine-Trumpington's twenty pounds—it seemed the only honorable thing to do. That certainly sounds like a positive value. The sad condition of religion in the modern world, however, is revealed when Prendy discovers the "Modern Churchman," defined as "a species of person . . . who draws the full salary of a beneficed clergyman and need not commit himself to any religious belief." For strong religious feeling, the only representative in *Decline and Fall* is the lunatic murderer of Prendergast, who has visions of a wonderfully bloody apocalypse and who regards himself as the "sword of Israel" and "the Lion of the Lord's Elect."

Finally, when Paul returns to Scone to read once more for the church, his education seems to focus not on doctrinal development but on heresies: "There was a bishop in Bithynia, Paul learned, who had denied the Divinity of Christ, the immortality of the soul, the existence of good, the legality of marriage and the validity of the Sacrament of Extreme Unction. How right they had been to condemn him." And in the "Epilogue," "So the ascetic Ebionites used to turn towards Jerusalem when they prayed . . . Quite right to suppress them." Only at a remove of several centuries is it possible for Paul (or modern man, whom he represents) to be certain of anything.

Not only are the public institutions of education and religion ineffectual against the disintegration of modern society, the family as an institution seems helpless as well. Paul's guardian cheats Paul out of his inheritance; Lady Circumference regards her son as "a dunderhead" who "wants beatin' and hittin' and knockin' about generally, and then he'll be no good." Indeed, the very names of Lady Circumference and Lord Tangent suggest that the connection between them is slight at best. The Llanabba bandmaster pimps for his sister-in-law; Grimes regards marriage simply as a hole card to be played only when he is in more trouble than he can manage; and Margot's ill-developed sense of family is so slight as to allow her to demolish the family seat, King's Thursday, and to feel that the primary importance of the family title is that "it may be nice for Peter to have [it] when he grows up."

One can continue to enumerate institutions that fail in *Decline and Fall.* Medicine does not save Tangent, whose heel was merely "grazed" by Prendergast's bullet. At the end of the novel, Paul is taken to Fagan's sanatorium not be cured but to have his death faked so that he can escape from prison. Similarly, the criminal-justice system, which regards Paul as the corrupter of Margot and is itself presented as corrupt (in the behavior of the prison guards) and lunatic (in the behavior of the warden) clearly provides no protection for the innocent abroad in the land.

If every social organization—educational, religious, political—is so obviously unable to hold off the forces of chaos in the novel, how, then, does Waugh manage to bring Paul Pennyfeather to a happy ending of sorts? It is here that the circular structure of the novel, which brings Paul back to the position he occupied at the beginning, and the central powerful symbol of the wheel at Luna Park are particularly helpful.

In the "Prelude" of the novel, Paul Pennyfeather is in "his third year of uneventful residence at Scone"; that is, he is nearly at the end of his conventional education. He has spent the evening at a meeting of "the League of Nations Union" and has heard" a most interesting paper about plebiscites in Poland." His idea of relaxation is to read a little of the *Forsyte Saga,* an Edwardian rendition of the instinct to possess and the shattering of social values following World War I. He knows nothing of the behavior or even of the existence of the Bollinger Club, a group representing all that is degenerate, ignorant, prejudiced, and destructive.

The "Epilogue" recapitulates the "Prelude." From the opening sentence, "It was Paul's third year of uneventful residence at Scone" and Stubbs' observation, "That was an interesting paper tonight about the Polish plebiscites," there is every indication that Waugh intends the reader to hear what he has heard before. But I think we must differ with James F. Carens's assessment that "[Paul] dies, he reappears, but he is not reborn. Nothing that has happened has had any effect upon him,"[4] for Paul's responses are vastly different the second time around. This time, he is finishing his real education.

The second time around, Paul knows about the Bollinger Club and has sense enough not to attract their attention. In his dialogue with Peter Pastmaster, Paul's responses to the boy's drunken questions are a series of assertions, "I remember." And it is remembering that helps to keep him safe. Something less prosaic and more threatening, however, has also happened to Paul, and, it seems to be argued, is helping to keep him safe. Paul has replaced the worldly vision of *The Forsyte Saga* with the history of the church. His view of the "ascetic Ebionites [who] used to turn towards Jerusalem when they prayed" is the view of a detached scholar rather than that of a participant in life. It is true that his detachment will protect him from the wasteland of Llanabba Castle and Blackstone Gaol, but it will also separate him from the voluptuous richness and excess of Margot Metroland and those other "dynamic" characters of whom Professor Silenus, that Dionysian spirit, once spoke. The modern world has cast him out just as he would cast out the "ascetic Ebionites" and the notorious Bishop of Bithynia.

Waugh also uses the descriptions of Paul's three celebratory meals to call attention to the circularity of the world

he is describing. The first is with Grimes and Prendy at Llanabba Castle; the second is with Alastair Digby-Vaine-Trumpington and Peter Beste-Chetwynde at the Ritz, and the third is with Dr. Fagan and Alastair at Fagan's sanatorium where Paul's death has just been falsely reported. The parallels are instructive.

At the first dinner, which takes place in part one, Paul, Prendy and Grimes celebrate Paul's "recent good fortune" (on the face of it the twenty pounds he has from Alastair Digby-Vaine-Trumpington, but in reality his liberation from the closed existence he has had at Scone College) and Grimes's impending marriage. The irony is lavish here, since what is depicted is Paul's first compromise with his image of himself as a gentleman. His earlier toast, "To the durability of ideals," is a wonderful illustration of the way Waugh makes meaning change by changing context. When Paul first uses the phrase, "the durability of ideals," he is really talking with himself about who he is and about the nature of the English gentleman. He explains at some length that in refusing Digby-Vaine-Trumpington's money he is satisfying "a test case of the durability of my ideals." When, however, Grimes reveals that he has saved Paul from himself by accepting Trumpington's money for him, Paul feels ". . . a great wave of satisfaction surge up within him." When he repeats the toast, "To the durability of ideals," he, like the reader, is conscious of the irony involved.

The meal motif is picked up in the scene depicting Paul's wedding luncheon at the Ritz, where a new toast is introduced. "To Fortune—a much maligned lady" is the utterance of a contented man who has once again closed his eyes to all of the ungentlemanly activities of the world around him. Alastair's ingenuous observation "No one could have guessed that when I had the Boller blind in my rooms it was going to end like this" seems to signal a happy ending; in fact, it only signals another complication as Inspector Bruce of Scotland Yard arrests Paul as an international white slaver and closes another episode in his eventful life.

The third celebratory meal takes place in part three after Paul is freed from prison through a scheme in which he is falsely declared to have died in a hospital. Dr. Fagan, once the head of Llanabba school and now the proprietor of a private hospital, articulates the importance of Paul's "death," by noting that "it is the beginning of a new phase of life." When Dr. Fagan proposes the toast "To Fortune—a much maligned lady," he is toasting the end of Paul's life as a convict and his rebirth as a student of theology.

The final version of the toast occurs in the closing scene when Peter Beste-Chetwynde (now Peter Pastmaster) appears in Paul's rooms in college. In the "Epilogue" as in the "Prelude," the "annual gathering of the Bollinger" coincides with Paul's "third year of uneventful residence at Scone." At Scone, as at the Ritz years earlier, Peter is a little drunk. In fact, he is so drunk that, having reiterated

Paul's toast, "To Fortune—a much maligned lady," he immediately finds himself unable to recall how it goes.

Paul's values and those of Otto Silenus form an interesting and informative contrast. Silenus, who in mythology was a forest spirit, the oldest of the satyrs, and the foster father and teacher of Dionysus, finds an ironic namesake in the young architect whose instincts are fundamentally antisocial (his artistic credo is "the elimination of the human element from the consideration of form") and whose counsel is to avoid participation in life and to seek stasis. To make his point, he compares life to a ride on the great wheel at Luna Park. The great wheel is a rotating disk and the challenge is to stay aboard it once it begins to spin. Professor Silenus explains,

> People don't see that when they say "life" they mean two different things. They can mean simply existence, with its physiological implications of growth and organic change. They can't escape that—even by death, but because that's inevitable they think the other side of life is too—the scrambling and excitement and bumps and the effort to get to the middle. And when we do get to the middle, it's just as if we never started.

Paul, on the other hand, is of a type open to much human experience but with the perspective of the old, the traditional, the poetic, the nonmechanistic about him. His love for Margot is born of a response to her physical beauty, a beauty which seems at first immortal but which he comes to fear is all too transitory. His imaginative vision of King's Thursday is pure nineteenth century romanticism:

> "English spring," thought Paul. "In the dreaming ancestral beauty of the English country." Surely, he thought, these great chestnuts in the morning sun stood for something enduring and serene in a world that had lost its reason and would so stand when the chaos and confusion were forgotten.

For Otto Silenus, however, Margot's beauty is not poetic at all. For him, "in all her essential functions—her digestion for example—she conforms to type." His strictly mechanistic view is also reflected in his first question to Paul: "What do you take to make you sleep?" Paul, by contrast, takes nothing to make him sleep and rests easily throughout the novel—in Scone College, in King's Thursday, and back in Scone.

Withdrawal from life may be advisable, but it is not a very positive solution to the problem. If this is a world in which people are rewarded strictly according to the laws of chance rather than according to the laws of merit, then there is nothing a person like Paul can do except refuse to live, for he does not seem to be blessed with traditional luck. If, on the other hand, Paul's bad treatment at the hands of the world is appropriate, what has he done to deserve it? His only error is innocence—ignorance of the ways of the world. Seen in that light, the structure of the novel is not comic but ironic, for it is a structure in which a fundamentally blameless fellow is treated much more badly than he deserves. On the other hand, Paul is not

real, he has no feelings or motives and, in the way farce works, he isn't damaged by anything that happens to him. He simply comes back, good as new, after his pratfalls.

Thus *Decline and Fall* tells a very funny story with a very discomfiting implication. True to the conventions of farce, characters in *Decline and Fall* disappear through one door to reappear, in a different form, through another. Paul's "great friend," Potts, reappears as the League of Nations representative whose work leads to Paul's arrest and conviction. Dr. Fagan, the headmaster of Llanabba Castle, reappears as the proprietor of the private hospital where Paul "dies" and as the author of a book on Welsh culture called *Mother Wales*. Grimes, the pederastic master at Llanabba, is first transformed into the "manager" of one of Margot's South American enterprises and then into a convict. Prendergast, the other master, becomes a modern churchman, and Philbrick the butler, that master of intrigue and disguise, finally appears in Oxford in an open motor car, looking very like one of the idle rich.

Thematically, the fact that nearly all the characters in *Decline and Fall* play multiple roles is significant. First, it suggests that reality is not very stable in this world, and that one might well be exceptionally careful in making judgments, because things are almost never what they seem to be. In addition, it is significant in determining the ways one can think about the characters in the novel. If Paul Pennyfeather is sometimes a nice young man studying for the ministry, sometimes a social celebrity, and sometimes a convict, how is one to think about him as a real person with real emotions, real motives and believable responses to events? The short answer is that one cannot. One cannot talk sensibly about how this character might reasonably be expected to act because one has no real sense of who he is. He is a type, and the type is the innocent. But he is never flesh and blood.

In *Decline and Fall,* as in his next two novels, Waugh restricted his characters to these comic types in order to avoid engaging his readers' emotions. Instead, he encourages his readers to a distanced, intellectual enjoyment of his indictment of a world where chance reigns supreme, ideals are superfluous if not outright dangerous, and the laws of cause and effect have been suspended.

Notes

1. Gerald Gould, review of *Decline and Fall* in Stannard, p. 81.

2. J. B. Priestley, review of *Decline and Fall* in Stannard, p. 84.

3. Waugh, *Letters,* p. 27.

4. James F. Carens, *The Satiric Art of Evelyn Waugh* (Seattle: University of Washington Press, 1966), p. 11.

Robert Murray Davis (essay date 1989)

SOURCE: "The Failure of Imagination: Waugh's School Stories," in *Evelyn Waugh and the Forms of His Time*, edited by Virgil Nemoianu, The Catholic University of American Press, 1989, pp. 178–88.

[*In the following excerpt, Davis examines an untitled early fragment of a story and "Charles Ryder's Schooldays" in an attempt to discern the autobiographical nature of Waugh's stories.*]

The publication of Evelyn Waugh's biography, diaries, letters, and collected journalism over the past ten years had confirmed without much altering the suspicion of earlier readers that there is in his novels a very clear and at the same time uneasy relationship between what he lived and what he imagined. His heroes, all the way from Pennyfeather to Pinfold, obviously share some of their creator's experiences, and just as obviously Waugh isolated and inflated some of his own fears and fantasies into such diverse types as Adam Fenwick-Symes, Basil Seal, and Guy Crouchback. The conversion of fact into fiction or, more recently, the embodiment of psychic patterns in the fiction has furnished material for a kind of high-level gossip (which Waugh would by no means have deplored) or even for studies of the way in which his imagination worked. However, Waugh's efforts to escape into realism, into a more or less direct presentation of the persona of the everyday, discursive-prosewriting self, throw considerable light on his mind and method precisely because he failed to do so.

Two obvious occasions in which he flirted with self-revelation in fiction are *Work Suspended* and *The Ordeal of Gilbert Pinfold,* but in both he used techniques of displacement, first into invented circumstances, next into a split between conscious and unconscious mind, resolved only by suppression of the unconscious which Pinfold and his creator regard as victory. Less well known, but more interesting as attempts at self-presentation, are two fragments, written twenty-five years apart, in which Waugh tried and failed to make realistic fiction from biographical fact. The first is a fragmentary novel, written at the end of 1920 while he was still a schoolboy;[1] the second is **"Charles Ryder's Schooldays,"** written about the time of his forty-second birthday in 1945.[2]

The untitled fragment—actually a fragment of a fragment, since the manuscript at the Humanities Research Center ends in mid-sentence—is a highly self-conscious attempt to enter "the family trade of literature." The work is dedicated "To Myself," and the dedicatory letter speaks of the difficulties faced by an author whose "surroundings . . . have been entirely literary." Willing to accept responses like "Another of these precocious Waughs . . . one more nursery novel," he concludes that he has "not been crushed in the mill of professionalism." As evidence from the diaries and from the fragment itself indicate, Evelyn aspired to authorship in order to compete with his brother Alec, the elder by five years. In 1920, Alec was clearly dominant. His first novel, *The Loom of Youth,* portrayed school life so realistically that Evelyn could not attend his brother's—and father's—school, and Alec's war service was

enviable but not emulable. On the other hand, Evelyn had a low opinion of Alec's friends and on occasion an even lower opinion of his style. During Evelyn's Lancing years, Alec's appearances frequently inspired Evelyn to turn from schoolwork to writing. In fact, his first note about the novel—assuming that the manuscript at HRC and the one mentioned in the *Diaries* are the same—calls it "the study of a man with two characters, by his brother" (*Diaries,* 107) and came about a week after Alec and his first wife—commemorated in *A Little Learning* as Evelyn's guide and playfellow—rescued him from a boring day at Lancing.

The story opens with Peter Audley's waking to a bleak March day in 1918 and follows him to his pit, or study; to breakfast; to a boring history lesson; and to preparations for Physical Training. A telegram summons him home for the visit of his brother Ralf, on leave after three years in the trenches. Greeted by Ralf and by Moira Gage, the vicar's daughter, he is just beginning to analyze his brother when the manuscript breaks off.

As one might expect in a schoolboy's novel, the autobiographical elements are obvious. Selchurch is recognizably Lancing; Peter Audley and Ralf are, like the Waughs, five years apart; Moira Gage, as far as the story goes attached to neither brother, is modeled on Barbara Jacobs, though Moira is made Peter's contemporary rather than two or more years his senior. Waugh does relocate the family home from Hampstead to "the Hall" at Bulfrey Combe, a small rural village, and he makes Peter and Ralf three years older than the Waugh brothers.

Some Waugh critics would no doubt attribute the last two modifications of fact to Evelyn's desire to present his alter ego as more mature and more highly placed socially, but the fragment is remarkable because it is far less self-aggrandizing than exploratory. There is not much evidence from which to infer Waugh's attitude toward the setting because very little of the surviving manuscript is set in Bulfrey and the characters never reach Bulfrey Combe. Judging from the contrast between Bulfrey Combe, which "still kept most of the appearance of a country village," and Bulfrey, "a small town with two or three streets of cheap shops, a bank, and a small glass factory which formed the nucleus of a large area of slum which was gradually spreading its grimy tentacles along the roads," he was establishing the village as a refuge, already threatened, from the changes accelerated by the war. As the vicar's daughter, Moira was given a more stable background than Barbara Jacobs, whose parents battled over progressive versus traditional education as well as many other topics.

Waugh's motive for altering the ages of the chief characters was based more on social history than on personal aggrandizement. In March 1918, Evelyn was fourteen and a half; Peter is seventeen and a half for two reasons: first, to allow Waugh to place him at Selchurch in the summer term of 1914, so that he can contrast the opulence, ease, and intellectual distinction of that period with the privation, academic slackness, and war mania of 1918; second, so that Peter is faced with the immediate prospect of leaving school for the battlefront, and he knows and resents the fact that the Officer Training Corps (OTC) has not prepared him to function in that world. (One might compare Peter's reflections on the OTC exercise with Alastair Trumpington's and Cedric Lyne's experiences of maneuvers and battle in *Put Out More Flags* and Guy Crouchback's in *Sword of Honour.*) Furthermore, he is not at all sure that he can measure up to his brother's attitudes and accomplishments because "Ralf saw everything so abstractedly with such imperturbable cynicism. Peter flattered himself that he would not be able to stand it; Ralf had won the D.S.O. some months ago."

Although Peter has begun to judge Ralf's witty utterances as calculated for effect, the fragment ends before Peter can assert himself as rival in war, love (note the effect of making Peter and Moira contemporaries), or words. What does emerge is a portrait of Lancing and by extension of English society which accords very closely with much of Waugh's editorial journalism in the *Lancing College Magazine*; in "The War and the Younger Generation" in 1928; by implication in *Vile Bodies*; and finally in *A Little Learning*: his generation had been denied the pleasures promised for their youth and frustrated in the possibility of testing themselves in battle. As Peter says, in an argument over discontinuing sports prizes to divert energy and attention to the war, "Everything has been done . . . to make school life excessively unpleasant. . . . What little of the old life does remain, is what keeps it just tolerable." More seriously, Waugh, Peter, and their contemporaries, cast into a world where old values had been destroyed or corroded, were left to find their own. At no time in his life did Waugh have much confidence in the individual's ability to do so. In 1920, portraying a class of history students given no stimulation and anticipating no rewards, Waugh asserted that "Youth[,] far from being the time of burning quests and wild, gloriously vain ideals beloved of the minor poets, is essentially one of languor and repose." The language is very similar to the passage in *Brideshead Revisited* which celebrates "The Languor of Youth," "the relaxation of yet unwearied sinews, the mind sequestered and self-regarding, the sun standing still in the heavens and the earth throbbing to our own pulse."[3] However, the judgment is very different: in 1919 the languor is the result of slackness rather than the condition for spiritual fermentation. It was much easier to look back at 1922 than forward to it.

In 1920, Waugh could objectify in the war his fears of the adult world, his resentment of the system that was preparing him for it so badly, and his early, grudging respect and resentment of the elder brother who seemed to be winning the prizes—manhood, marriage, literary success—to which Evelyn aspired by means that he could not yet clearly imagine. Perhaps this is the real reason that the novel was never completed. However, Evelyn provided himself with more obvious means of escape from authorship. His first diary entries marvel at the amount of work involved—

"each chapter will have to be about two sections of College bumph." When he took home the manuscript for Christmas vacation, he found

> Alec apprehensive of a rival, Mother of my ruin through becoming a public figure too soon. Father likes it. Meanwhile I plot on and on at it, trying to make it take some form or shape. At present it seems a mere succession of indifferently interesting conversations. However, I believe it is fairly good and I am pretty sure to be able to get it published. It's a bloody sweat, however.
>
> (*Diaries*, 108)

Even the prospect of fame soon vanished because of "my family's disapproval and my own innate sloth," and by 10 January 1921 he had abandoned the effort. It is also possible that he could not imagine what was to happen—to him as much as to his characters—and that, having outlined his social themes but finding himself unwilling to face even an imaginative rivalry with Alec, he welcomed the return to schoolboy status.

Twenty-five years later, Waugh found a more difficult if less complex transition to a very different kind of postwar world. Although, judging from his diaries and letters, he was not dissatisfied with the kind of man he had become, he exhibited considerable doubts about the kind of writer he was to be in the future. Early in the process of writing *Brideshead* (his hero was still named Peter at this stage) he speculated that it might be the first of his novels—by which he apparently meant the novel in the English realistic tradition—rather than his last. Two years later, he promised his readers that future work would be concerned with style and with the presence of God in the world of the novel. In 1945, while he was letting his war experiences settle into usable form and was perhaps unwilling to test his ability to deal with the postwar world, he began research for *Helena*. But the success of *Brideshead* made it unnecessary, even unwise, for him to work very hard, and four months after he first mentioned Helena he turned to his own past, reading "my Lancing diaries through with unmixed shame" and for the next month working on "a novel of school life in 1919—as untopical a theme as could be found" (*Diaries*, 636) After the diary entry made on his forty-second birthday, we hear no more of the story **"Charles Ryder's Schooldays"** until my *Catalogue* of the University of Texas materials in 1981 and the independent discovery of a carbon typescript at his agent's office later in the same year.

"Charles Ryder's Schooldays" begins the day after the first entry in Waugh's Lancing diaries; like them, it deals with resentment at the new appointments by and the very existence of a new house tutor. Unlike the diaries, the story presents the tutor's appeal to Ryder for cooperation and compassion and ends with Ryder's scorning apologies and offer of compensation from the man—with very much the same words Waugh recorded in *A Little Learning*. There is little consecutive action; there is a good deal of detail about the customs by which the boys stratify themselves.

There are at least three obvious and not always discrete ways of looking at the story: in the context of *Brideshead,* to which it forms a prequel; in the context of the *Diaries,* though I am more interested in style than in content; and in the context of the earlier school story as another attempt at self-creation. In the first context, Waugh's epigraph to *Brideshead,* "I am not I" and so on, clearly does not apply to the Charles Ryder of the story or, as B. W. Handford shows,[4] to anyone else in it. First, Charles' experiences are drawn more directly from those of the youthful Waugh than at any other place in Waugh's fiction; second, because in the story there *is* no "I" because Waugh tells the story in third rather than first person. The two are very closely related, I think: Waugh wanted to use the mass of material, no doubt rediscovered as he was rearranging his life and his effects at Piers Court after a six-year absence, but he also wanted to distance himself as author and person not only from his abhorred earlier self but from the character of Ryder. As he must have come to recognize, along with a number of subsequent critics, the chief problem with *Brideshead* is that many perceptive and otherwise sympathetic readers regard Ryder as a very unpleasant character. However, it is not at all clear how far the author shares this view or is even aware of the possibility that someone might conceive it. This was a problem that no amount of revision of the text of the novel could resolve. By using third person, Waugh was able to set Ryder in a physical and social context rather than let him create and dominate it. In fact, Waugh uses setting in a much different way than he had in the 1920 fragment. There all was subordinated to Peter's viewpoint. Discomforts are imposed from without by the system. In **"Charles Ryder's Schooldays,"** the characters are dwarfed and dominated by the scene, the system is internalized, the boys oppressing each other and themselves by accepting and elaborating on a social code designed to regulate attitudes as well as behavior.

Besides third person, Waugh uses two other techniques to place and judge Ryder: in conversations among the boys, he does not include identifying tags, so that individual personality is shown to be submerged in schoolboy argot; and in diary entries by Ryder he shows the boy's immature habit of simplifying character and event into adolescent commonplaces. Compare, for example, the episode of the master—Gordon at Lancing, Graves at Spierpoint—and the printing press. In the *Diaries,* Waugh wrote:

> In the afternoon, as it was raining, Fremlin and I returned early from our walk and helped Gordon to mend his printing press. It would be priceless to have one but they are rather costly. He invited us to tea and we sat round his fire talking scandal and eating toast till chapel. Perhaps he isn't really so bad after all.
>
> (*Diaries,* 28)

In **"Charles Ryder's Schooldays,"** the press is at first merely mentioned and provides Charles—more wistful internally and more callous externally than the Waugh of the diaries—with daydreams of "the tall folios, the wide mar-

gins, the deckle-edged mould-made paper, the engraved initials, the rubrics and colophons of his private press" (296–297). Later the master enlists Ryder and Tamplin (clearly based on Fremlin) to help him assemble it. Tamplin escapes, but Charles remains to finish the job and Graves confides in him about O'Malley's need for Ryder's support as head of the dormitory. In Charles Ryder's diary for 28 September this is reuced to

> After luncheon Tamplin and I were going for a walk when Graves called us in and made us help put up his printing press. Tamplin escaped. Graves tried to get things out of me about ragging Dirty Desmond but without success.

Charles cannot admit, in writing, in his official schoolboy self, his desire for a press, and he wilfully misunderstands the tutor's motives, as Waugh did not entirely do. Elsewhere, similar incidents are treated by Ryder as diarist in a more curt and simple fashion than in Waugh's diaries, where the level of vocabulary is far higher and the complexity of sentence structure far greater than in Ryder's diary:

> I don't think we shall be able to rag Woodard long, but meanwhile we are making hay. He is trying to make us use the new pronunciation in Latin, and it is an endless source for supposed misunderstanding. We have also some splendid attempts such as SOOBYOONGTEE-WAY for the pronunciation of Subjunctive. He got quite bored when, on his using the new pronunciation in Greek, his pronunciation was greeted with a longdrawn wail of oooh! He threatened to send us all to our Housemasters, and I believe he will carry out the threat.
>
> (*Diaries,* 20–21)

> Peacock deigned to turn up for Double Greek. We mocked him somewhat. He is trying to make us use the new pronunciation; when he said oú there was a wail of "ooh" and Tamplin pronounced subjunctive soobyoongteeway—very witty. Peacock got bored and said he'd report him to Graves but relented.
>
> [Ryder's entry, 25 September 1919]

And throughout the story, the contrast between Ryder's style and that of the omniscient narrator is even greater.

Of course, the diaries do not have a plot—though, to use E. M. Forster's distinction, they do have a story—and while the story did not progress far enough for a line of action to emerge, we can discern threads which would probably have been woven into a design that was in part dictated by events already mentioned in *Brideshead.* Chief among these is the death of Ryder's mother (here and in the manuscript of *Brideshead* killed by a German shell in Bosnia; in pre-1960 *Brideshead* dying of an unspecified cause; and in 1960 dying of exhaustion, perhaps to show her self-sacrifice in a way that death as a result of combat would not). Waugh must have recognized that Charles' response, or rather his lack of response, to his mother's death in *Brideshead* was inadequate, not merely in terms of Ryder's psychology but in novelistic terms, and by emphasizing in the story Charles' memory of the news and associating it with the Spierpoint setting, he may have been preparing to link her death with Charles' rejection of Spierpoint values, his outward callousness, and his inward refusal—unlike the youthful Waugh—to analyze himself or others. A second major theme is adumbrated in the series of models for young Ryder, especially the masculine and intellectual A. A. Carmichael, contrasted with the almost maternal and emotional Frank Bates as "that one the ineffable dweller on cloud-capped Olympus, this the homely clay image, the intimate of hearth and household, the patron of threshing-floor and olive-press." Charles' worship of these deities, like the atheism or agnosticism of the Sixth Form, embodied most brilliantly in Symonds, who reads the Greek Anthology in chapel, is obviously intended to anticipate Charles' account of his irreligious background in *Brideshead*. Set between the two masters is Graves, who attempts to draw Ryder out of his contemptuous rejection of human responses. Even in the fragment he emerges not simply to illustrate a point but to stand as a complex character to set off rather than complement Charles' attitudinizing.

However, the complexity of character, especially in the conception and treatment of Charles, created what proved to be insuperable problems. For one thing, the Charles of *Brideshead* was much more reserved and sophisticated than the Waugh revealed in *A Little Learning* and other memoirs. The Ryder of the fragment, on the other hand, is far less sophisticated in style and general response and far less active intellectually and academically than the Waugh of the diaries—though, like the Ryder of *Brideshead*, he is a restaurant snob. Moreover, it does not seem possible that the rather cold and priggish Ryder of Spierpoint—however much he was beginning to reject conventional reactions—could have become the Oxonian "in search of love" who went to Sebastian's luncheon party "full of curiosity and the faint, unrecognized apprehension that here, at last, I should find that low door in the wall . . . which opened on an enclosed and enchanted garden, which was somewhere, not overlooked by any window, in the heart of that grey city" (*Brideshead*, 31). By attempting to use the harsh fact of what Waugh repeatedly felt to be caddishness, Waugh had blocked the way towards the nostalgia that is the older Ryder's most endearing quality. The "I" of Charles Ryder was not, and finally could never be, the "I" of Evelyn Waugh.

Alec Waugh believed that life could, in fact *should*, be lived in watertight compartments, and this dictum so impressed Evelyn that he used it in his diary, in both school stories, and at least by implication in *A Little Learning*. In fact, as I argued in Chapter 4, Waugh's acceptance of this belief found embodiment in the technique of his first five novels, where he used fragmentation, caricature, and discontinuity as major principles of selection and organization and distancing as a feature of characterization. If the method of the realist novel is, as various critics have argued, linked to liberal, humane values, and if Forster's "only connect" is a formal as well as a thematic principle,

then Waugh was never in serious danger of becoming a realist, and the unwitting fragmentation of Charles Ryder in the story is evidence that he could not breach and perhaps not even formally recognize the gap. Various recent critics, including Ian Littlewood, have shown that he objectified conflicts rather than analyzing them.[5]

Perhaps, as is clearly the case in **"Charles Ryder's Schooldays,"** Waugh could not bring himself to deal directly with the causes of his own coldness and misanthropy. It is certain that he did not complete any serious attempt to portray anything like his own character, either in the schoolboy fragment *Work Suspended* or in **"Charles Ryder's Schooldays."** Had he been able to do so, as J. B. Priestley argued in his review of *The Ordeal of Gilbert Pinfold*,[6] he might have been able to cure himself. At least he might have been able, as he never was in art or, as far as one can tell, in life, to imagine himself in a realistic mode. We cannot know, and probably he would have doubted, whether this was a Good Thing. If so, he would not have sought the methods of displacement and deflection that make him one of the most original novelists and master stylists of his generation. But then art is art, not therapy, and the fragments and failures are much less important, and finally less vital, than the completed fictions created by an incomplete man.

Notes

1. The text of the story, titled "Fragment of a Novel," is printed in *Evelyn Waugh, Apprentice,* ed. Robert Murray Davis (Norman: Pilgrim Books, 1985).

2. *Work Suspended and Other Stories, Including Charles Ryder's Schooldays* (Harmondsworth: Penguin, 1982). "Charles Ryder's Schooldays" has an introduction by Michael Sissons.

3. *Brideshead Revisited* (Boston: Little, Brown, 1946), p. 79.

4. *Times Literary Supplement,* 9 April 1982, p. 412.

5. Ian Littlewood, *The Writings of Evelyn Waugh* (Totowa, N. J.: Barnes & Noble, 1982). Though in no sense a work of scholarship, this book contains isolated insights about Waugh's style.

6. J. B. Priestley, "What Was Wrong with Pinfold," *New Statesman,* 54 (31 August 1957), 244.

Robert R. Garrett (essay date 1990)

SOURCE: "Decline and Fall: 'Grimes, You Wretch!'" in *From Grimes to Brideshead: The Early Novels of Evelyn Waugh,* Bucknell University Press, 1990, pp. 37–57.

[*In the following excerpt, Garrett explores the nature of the humor in* Decline and Fall, *praising Waugh's use of language and narrative structure.*]

In September 1927, staying with his parents at Underhill and still working on *Rossetti*, Waugh observed in his diary: "How I detest this house and how ill I feel in it. The whole place volleys and thunders with traffic. I can't sleep or work. I . . . have begun on a comic novel."[1] Sometime later he read the first ten thousand words to Anthony Powell, and at some point he read the early chapters to Dudley Carew as well:

What he read to me that night, sitting in the chair where Arthur was wont to proclaim that beautiful Evelyn Hope was dead, were the first fifty or so pages of *Decline and Fall.* A happiness, a hilarity, sustained him that night, and I was back giving him my unstinted admiration as I did at Lancing. It was marvellously funny and he knew that it was. As was his habit in those old, innocent days, he roared with laughter at his own comic invention.[2]

According to Powell, the novel was originally called *Picaresque: or the Making of an Englishman.* But, Powell recalled, "Some months after the reading aloud of these chapters—probably a moment towards the end of the same year—I asked Waugh how the novel was progressing. He replied: 'I've burnt it.'"[3] He had not, in fact, but by November the manuscript seems to have been set aside and then ignored until after Christmas.

The later chapters advanced slowly. Early in the new year he wrote to Harold Acton: "The novel does not get on. I should so much value your opinion on whether I am to finish it."[4] Once again, as with **"The Temple at Thatch,"** he seems to have been ready to defer to Acton's critical judgment. In this case, however, Acton claims to have been enthusiastic about the manuscript. A draft of the novel was complete in April, but, worried about its length, Waugh wrote to Powell, who was working at Duckworth:

I hope the novel will be finished in a week. I will send it to you as soon as it is typed & then want to revise it very thoroughly and enlarge it a bit. I think at present it shows signs of being too short. How do these novelists make their books so long. I'm sure one could write any novel in the world on two post cards.[5]

In May he submitted the manuscript to Duckworth, where it was rejected on "the odd grounds of its indelicacy" (Waugh later wrote), with demands for alterations he declined to make.[6] Chapman and Hall soon accepted the novel but also stipulated some bowdlerizing changes. This time Waugh acceded, and *Decline and Fall* was published in September 1928, subtitled *An Illustrated Novelette.*

The facetious subtitle announced the novel's modest pretensions. As far as Waugh was concerned, it was a potboiler; weightier literary work might come later, but at the moment he needed money to get married. It also was something in the nature of an inside joke designed to amuse friends, for whom he inserted private allusions ranging from the Christian names of his two closest friends, Alastair and Olivia, to the surname of his detested Hertford tutor, Cruttwell. The names of two derisory minor characters so closely resembled those of two young men of Waugh's acquaintance that in the second printing new names were prudently substituted. The names of other friends and acquaintances had already been edited out in manuscript. The ideal reader was a recent Oxonian with Waugh's own aristocratic predilections and schoolmastering experience—someone like John Betjeman, for example. Perhaps swayed by the dedication to himself, even Harold Acton signified his approval; Waugh replied in acknowledgment: "I am glad to think it amused you a little. Anyway I enjoyed writing it which is more than I can say about Rossetti."[7] Fearing, however, that it might be damaging for a serious man of letters, or art critic, or whatever he might become, to have a comic novel in his canon, Waugh considered publishing it (Alec Waugh recalled) under a pen name.

Yet *Decline and Fall*'s comic accomplishment owed much to its lack of artistic ambition. Aside from urgent practical motives, Waugh's chief stimulus was playfulness, for in writing the novel he was burlesquing his own recent experience. He did not write it carelessly or in a spirit of holiday levity; he was serious about the novel, but he knew the novel itself was not a serious thing.

The challenge Waugh set himself was to exploit the comic potential of his material, "that the texture of life should be made to yield a comic response." Unlike life, which could be and in Waugh's case often was refractory and disheartening, language was something he could control and manipulate with confidence and élan; living was a skill he had not mastered, but writing was a game he could play well and one that yielded satisfying consolation when played successfully. Much of the "meaning" of *Decline and Fall* lies simply in its deployment of language to achieve comic effect. In this first novel, Waugh achieved a concentration of comic style that he never really surpassed; *Decline and Fall* had no broad artistic ambitions or thematic motives to divert him from comic play or to persuade him to defer immediate effects for larger purposes. The page in hand was everything; the next page would take care of itself. His ambition was straightforward; as he insisted at the very beginning, "IT IS MEANT TO BE FUNNY."

Comic density and intensity were the goal; consistency was not a dominating concern. Waugh readily sacrificed consistency in tone, point of view, satire, or rhetoric if immediate comic impact could be gained by doing so. At one point, grandiloquent parody might serve the purpose, while in the next paragraph it might be severe understatement and, in the next paragraph yet, flagrant hyperbole; or he might at one point adopt the perspective of one of his characters, then a few sentences later suddenly step back from the same character with bland indifference. Behind all such variations, however, is a principle of understatement and precision, and *Decline and Fall*'s comic tone is based on a continual tension between the skillfully controlled language of the narration—selective, concise, lucid, exact, reticent (usually)—and the freewheeling, idiosyncratic energy of the novel's characters.

Playing with language meant, for Waugh, not primarily wit (he seldom played with words in the sense of puns or *double entendres,* for example) or elaboration, but sharpness and compression: packing the most significance into the fewest words. One of his gifts was finding the strikingly apt word or phrase; he preferred a single, well-aimed shot to a fusillade. But this effort of precise and accurate diction was part of a larger goal. Whether understating with clipped brevity or launching into mock grandiloquence, his object was to assert control over his material, and by extension over life, with skillfully deployed comic rhetoric. Near the beginning of *Decline and Fall,* for example, there occurs an often cited passage describing the annual Bollinger Club dinner:

> . . . from all over Europe old members had rallied for the occasion. For two days they had been pouring into Oxford: epileptic royalty from their villas of exile; uncouth peers from crumbling country seats; smooth young men of uncertain tastes from embassies and legations; illiterate lairds from wet granite hovels in the Highlands; ambitious young barristers and Conservative candidates torn from the London season and the indelicate advances of debutantes; all that was most sonorous of name and title was there for the beano.
>
> (13–14)

The passage is an adjectival extravagance, but scarcely an uncontrolled one: the rhetorical force of the description springs from the strong vocabulary and the carefully measured, rhythmically orotund sequence of balanced parallel phrases, alliterated almost like Old English prosody, building to the slangy anticlimax, "beano."[8] Though a long sentence, it has the effect of compression. Its comic force derives not simply from the jocular rhetorical deflation at the end, but even more from the mismatch between the promiscuous diversity of the Bollinger membership and the nicely calculated order and diction of their description.

Constantly crowded against this precise, controlled narrative voice is the spontaneous, quirky energy of the novel's characters. The narrator does not describe them; the characters describe themselves by their speech. We meet Lady Circumference, for example, talking to Paul Pennyfeather and Doctor Fagan about her son Lord Tangent:

> The boy's a dunderhead. If he wasn't he wouldn't be here. He wants beatin' and hittin' and knockin' about generally, and then he'll be no good. That grass is shockin' bad on the terrace, Doctor; you ought to sand it down and resow it, but you'll have to take that cedar down if you ever want it to grow properly at the side. I hate cuttin' down a tree—like losin' a tooth—but you have to choose, tree or grass; you can't keep 'em both. What d'you pay your head man?
>
> (81)

It is not psychological depth or complexity or even plausibility that Waugh was interested in extracting from the figure of Lady Circumference, but her "comic texture"—idiosyncratic character expressed in uninhibited, slangy speech. Though the vitality of the character is likely to attract a reader's sympathy (and Waugh's as well, I think), the narrative voice itself remains formally uncommitted

and unappreciative.[9] Another passage, chosen more or less at random, will show some of the main features of *Decline and Fall*'s comic grammar:

> Ten men of revolting appearance were approaching from the drive. They were low of brow, crafty of eye and crooked of limb. They advanced huddled together with the loping tread of wolves, peering about them furtively as they came, as though in constant terror of ambush; they slavered at their mouths, which hung loosely over their receding chins, while each clutched under his ape-like arm a burden of curious and unaccountable shape. On seeing the Doctor they halted and edged back, those behind squinting and mouthing over their companions' shoulders.
>
> "Crikey!" said Philbrick. "Loonies! This is where I shoot."
>
> "I refuse to believe the evidence of my eyes," said the Doctor. "These creatures simply do not exist."
>
> (78)

Here the narrative voice initially seems to share the perspective of Doctor Fagan and Philbrick as they view with alarm the advancing musicians (as they turn out to be). Satire on the Welsh is a recurrent amusement in the early chapters of *Decline and Fall*; the particular tactic here is an extended metaphor crowding together vivid zoo and madhouse images in a series of rhythmic and balanced phrases and sentences. Scarcely a word fails to contribute to the joke, the smooth urbane mastery of language by itself creating an ironic contrast to the Welsh provincials.

But with the switch from description to dialogue, the narrative voice at once recedes from the perspective of Doctor Fagan and Philbrick to a more remote vantage point, which surveys the musicians, Fagan, and Philbrick from roughly the same ironic distance. From this perspective, the latter are no longer privileged observers but comic objects themselves, with Philbrick's emphatic vernacular and dramatic, crudely violent impulse posed against the suave ironic incredulity of Doctor Fagan. Their responses reveal their humors, and the juxtaposition of their clashing humors is the comic point. This single short passage thus contains several characteristic . . . of *Decline and Fall*'s comic grammar: the concentration and marshalling of vivid language; the willingness, even eagerness, to shift point of view if the shift will augment the immediate comic effect; dialogue recorded without comment to display quirks of individual character and their comic confrontation.

Another passage shows some of the same methods. The subject is Margot Beste-Chetwynde's and Paul Pennyfeather's projected wedding:

> Society was less certain in its approval, and Lady Circumference, for one, sighed for the early nineties, when Edward Prince of Wales, at the head of *ton,* might have given authoritative condemnation to this ostentatious second marriage.
>
> "It's maddenin' Tangent having died just at this time," she said "People may think that that's my reason for refusin'. I can't imagine that *anyone* will go."

"I hear your nephew Alastair Trumpington is the best man," said Lady Vanbrugh.

"You seem to be as well informed as my chiropodist," said Lady Circumference with unusual felicity, and all Lowndes Square shook at her departure.

(176)

This passage is often cited for its shockingly casual disclosure of little Tangent's death, but its comic grammar is more complex. The first paragraph, with its mock deference to the notion of Society, Lady Circumference's nostalgia for Victorian decorum, the French "ton," and the polysyllabic formality, momentarily establishes an elevated style of discourse and manners, in order to prepare for the sharp contrast of Lady Circumference's blunt style and savage insensitivity. Her rejoinder to Lady Vanbrugh's feline comment further compresses several comic elements: the countess gossiping with a chiropodist; the unusual and ambiguous authorial comment—"with unusual felicity"; the mock-heroic cliché "shook at her departure," applied absurdly to the aristocratically fashionable Lowndes Square. What ties all the techniques and jokes together is the play with language to achieve immediate and striking comic effect.[10]

Waugh was also playing with recent personal history.

The book Waugh had in mind when he began writing was a burlesque of his schoolmastering experience, especially his initiation into schoolmastering at Arnold House in North Wales. **"The Balance,"** too, had sprung from his misery in Wales, but having escaped Wales, freed himself from schoolmastering, and reconciled himself to Olivia Greene's romantic indifference by the time he began writing *Decline and Fall,* he could look back on his griefs at Arnold House with greater emotional detachment and with a greater appreciation of their comic aspect. As Paul Pennyfeather, sitting comfortably in a London restaurant with his equally conventional Oxford friend Potts, reflects on his experience at Llanabba, it all seems a phantasmagoric aberration: "Llanabba Castle, with its sham castellations and preposterous inhabitants, had sunk into the oblivion that waits upon even the most lurid of nightmares" (145). In 1927, Waugh's own perspective on Arnold House was comparable, and *Decline and Fall* exaggerates the bad-dream metaphor into *Alice in Wonderland* dislocation, combining his departure from Oxford and his exile in Wales to create a myth of unheroic descent into a bizarre scholastic underworld, a purely comic Dotheboy's Hall. Beneath all the exaggerations and inventions of the novel, Paul's history follows a pattern similar to Waugh's: banishment from the agreeably sheltered life of an Oxford undergraduate, followed by a plunge into a strange and unsettling new world. Waugh's descent from Oxford to Arnold House provided the original comic impetus of *Decline and Fall.*

Although *Decline and Fall* parodies Waugh's experience, Paul Pennyfeather is not a close self-portrait of Waugh himself. A studious, mild-mannered undergraduate leading a blamelessly dull life, Paul is entirely unacquainted with Waugh's bohemian, pleasure-loving Oxford; he has certainly never visited the Hypocrites, and the circumstances of his expulsion from the University scarcely resemble Waugh's routinely unsuccessful departure. But Paul's middle-class background deliberately echoes Waugh's. Paul arrived at the University "after a creditable career at a small public school of ecclesiastical temper on the South Downs, where he had edited the magazine, been President of the Debating Society, and had, as his report said, 'exercised a wholesome influence for good' in the House of which he was head boy" (15–16)—very much like Waugh at Lancing. The difference between Paul and Waugh is that Paul seems hardly to have changed at Oxford; he seems, in fact, modeled on Waugh not as he departed from Oxford in 1924, but as he arrived from Lancing two and a half years earlier: spending his early months at Hertford quietly, reading and daydreaming, eating in hall, taking walks by himself in the country, making few friends; on Waugh as he might have remained but for the Hypocrites and Harold Acton. In ridiculing Paul's quiet sobriety, Waugh was mocking one possible version of himself. Not long before writing *Decline and Fall,* he had interviewed to become an Anglican clergyman; was there in Waugh the stuff of a placid suburban vicar?

Paul's relation to Waugh is thus ambiguous, partly autobiographical, partly antithetical. Although sometimes derisively conventional and dull-witted, polite to a fault, Paul is at other times a sympathetic figure—decent, ingenuous, abused, but uncomplaining. In this latter aspect he caricatures the unassuming, unlucky hero of Waugh's diaries, a semifictional character Waugh had been developing across the years for his own consolation and diversion. Paul Pennyfeather is such a diffident and unassertive hero that it is easy to overlook his importance to *Decline and Fall* and to Waugh's subsequent fiction. The buffeted, baffled, unworldly hero, of which Paul was the prototype, enabled Waugh to maintain an ironically detached perspective on his own experience and even on himself; self-caricature prevented self-absorption and self-pity. Paul Pennyfeather might take himself seriously, but Waugh can laugh at him; and in thus comically distancing himself from his protagonist, Waugh opened up to himself all the comic possibilities of his own experience, painful as it may have been at the time. The virtue of the reticent Pennyfeatheresque hero is amply demonstrated by his absence in *Work Suspended* and *Brideshead Revisited,* in which discursive first-person narration involved Waugh in unprecedented difficulties.

Waugh had a rough plot idea when he began writing—to follow Paul Pennyfeather's descent from Oxford to Llanabba—but *Decline and Fall* soon became improvisational, especially as the action began to move away from its autobiographical origins. Even in the novel's early chapters, when he was still drawing material from his schoolmastering experience, Waugh seems to have let the plot develop as his daily inspiration directed, picking up and incorporating stray and unconnected bits of material as he wrote. The figure of Lady Circumference, for example, was closely modeled on Alastair Graham's mother, with whom Waugh was already well acquainted. But as he wrote some of the novel's early chapters he happened to be staying at her Warwickshire house, and the erratic hospitality he enjoyed there gave him immediate material and perhaps motive for sketching Lady Circumference's character. For example, as a friend of Alastair's who had often visited Barford before, Waugh was considered not so much a guest as a member of the household, and Mrs. Graham expected him to pull his own weight:

> This morning there was great trouble with a large truculent under-gardener who is under notice to go and will not allow his successor to use his cottage. Mrs. G.: "Here am I left without a *man* in the house"—looking hard at me—"if Hugh were alive he'd have *kicked* him out."[11]

This incident must have been fresh in Waugh's mind when he introduced this exchange into the novel:

> ". . . Greta, Mr Pennyfoot knows Alastair."
>
> "Does he? Well, that boy's doing no good for himself. Got fined twenty pounds the other day, his mother told me. Seemed proud of it. If my brother had been alive he'd have licked all that out of the young cub. It takes a man to bring up a man."
>
> "Yes," said Lord Circumference meekly.
>
> (83)

While this sort of extemporaneous borrowing helped to fill in the novel's first half, it became the governing method of the later chapters, when the novel wandered far beyond its original field of action.

By about the middle of *Decline and Fall* as it now stands, Waugh seems to have exhausted his schoolmastering experience, and from that point the novel grows remote from his personal history. As he resorted to other sources for material, his inventions became more exotic. His personal experience was limited in range, but he gathered scraps of material from here and there, piecing together current newspaper topics, gossip, sightseeing snapshots, and various of his own private interests. Margot Beste-Chetwynde's and Grimes's involvement in prostitution, for example, as well as Potts's sleuthing, was prompted by the well-publicized release in December 1927 of a League of Nations report on international white slave traffic. He set Margot's villa on Corfu because he had been impressed by the amenity of the island during a very brief stop there the year before, returning from a visit to Alastair Graham in Greece. Because its sources were eclectic, the second half of *Decline and Fall* grew more diffuse, topical, episodic, and peripatetic than the first half, and threatened to veer off into random satiric adventures.

Fortunately, however, by the time the autobiographical inspiration flagged, a new and accidental influence—Captain Grimes—had already begun to channel the novel's energies in a new direction. Grimes was modelled on one of Waugh's colleagues at Arnold House. "Young, the new usher, is monotonously pederastic and talks only of the beauty of sleeping boys," he noted in his diary a few weeks into his second term.[12] Young nonetheless proved a convenient drinking companion, and one evening as they drank together, he divulged some highlights of his personal history:

> . . . Young and I went out and made ourselves drunk and he confessed all his previous career. He was expelled from Wellington, sent down from Oxford, and forced to resign his commission in the army. He has left four schools precipitately, three in the middle of the term through his being taken in sodomy and one through his being drunk six nights in succession. And yet he goes on getting better and better jobs without difficulty.[13]

Waugh was greatly impressed by the narrative, "all very like Bruce and the spider." Several years later, with military rank and a wooden leg, Young became Grimes; and then, without, it seems, any clear intention on Waugh's part, Captain Grimes grew into the hero of *Decline and Fall,* the embodiment of the novel's sympathy with impulsiveness and anarchy.

On his first entrance Grimes appears an unlikely hero: "The door opened, and a very short man of about thirty came into the Common Room. He had made a great deal of noise in coming because he had an artificial leg. He had a short red moustache, and was slightly bald" (30). But when he discloses his history to Paul, his distinction emerges; he has a genius for falling "in the soup" and landing on his feet. Grimes is an emblem of spontaneity and irrepressibility; he is the weed poking up through the crack in the sidewalk. While his past more or less duplicates Young's, Grimes's powers of survival grow mythic. He cannot be extinguished. "I can stand most sorts of misfortune, old boy, but I can't stand repression," he remarks to Paul in prison, shortly before escaping (230). He glides undaunted through embarrassment and disaster. Mr. Prendergast, diffident and timid, a foil to Grimes's insouciant recklessness, is tormented by "Doubts," but as Grimes himself explains:

> When you've been in the soup as often as I have, it gives you a sort of feeling that everything's for the best, really. You know, God's in His heaven; all's right with the world. I can't quite explain it, but I don't believe one can ever be unhappy for long provided one does just exactly what one wants to and when one wants to. The last chap who put me on my feet said I was "singularly in harmony with the primitive promptings of humanity". I've remembered that phrase because somehow it seemed to fit me.
>
> (45)

Grimes's revival in the second half of the novel, after apparently drowning, and his later escape from prison confirm his superhuman vitality. He becomes "one of the immortals," "a life force":

> Sentenced to death in Flanders, he popped up in Wales; drowned in Wales, he emerged in South America; en-

gulfed in the dark mystery of Egdon Mire, he would rise again somewhere at some time, shaking from his limbs the musty integuments of the tomb.

(232)

After this panegyric, Grimes's reappearance would be anticlimactic; and his role in the novel, though not his spirit, here comes to an end.

If the figure of Paul Pennyfeather suggests the pre-Oxford Waugh, Paul's encounter with Grimes is analogous to Waugh's experience with the Hypocrites. Unexpectedly, the reprobate Grimes has a wholly salutary influence on Paul. Sober, studious, unadventurous, Paul has led a wastefully narrow life at Oxford:

> For two years he had lived within his allowance, aided by two valuable scholarships. He smoked three ounces of tobacco a week—John Cotton, Medium—and drank a pint and a half of beer a day, the half at luncheon and the pint at dinner, a meal he invariably ate in Hall. He had four friends, three of whom had been at school with him.

(16)

Paul's idea of nightlife is attending a meeting of the League of Nations Union to hear a paper on Polish plebiscites ("You talk as though all that were quite real to you," Waugh once remarked, incredulously, to a friend discussing central European politics).[14] After an evening of plebiscites, Paul retires to his rooms to read *The Forsyte Saga,* presumably Waugh's notion of respectable, dull reading, and smoke a pipe in solitude before bed. Imaginatively straitened by conventional ideas and personal inhibitions, Paul very much needs an infusion of Grimes's zest. "Paul had no particular objection to drunkenness—he had read rather a daring paper to the Thomas More Society on the subject—but he was consumedly shy of drunkards" (16). He is shy of life, in fact, academically cloistered and very unfamiliar with the exuberant variety and unpredictability of the world beyond Oxford, or even beyond his own small circle at Oxford, for he has never even heard of the aristocratic Bollinger Club, with its boisterous revelries.

After this bland closeted life at Oxford, Paul is astounded by Llanabba, whose inmates (except for Prendergast) are unreservedly eccentric. From a circle in which it is considered the height of daring to challenge a conventional opinion, even in an essay, Paul is dropped into a happy society of criminals and charlatans: Dr. Fagan with his absurd elegance, his fraudulent school, and his two horrible daughters; Philbrick the protean imposter; Grimes himself; and, superadded to the ordinary inhabitants, the Sports-day visitors, including the ill-matched pair of Lady Circumference, an earthy aristocrat in the Squire Western tradition, and Margot Beste-Chetwynde, the cosmopolitan adventuress, with her unexpected consort, the excitable Chokey. When all these characters assemble at the Sports, the conversation becomes a chaos of dissonant voices, representing in small scale the world of random and diverse human energies beyond Paul's straitened experience:

> "I had such a curious conversation just now," Lord Circumference was saying to Paul, "with your bandmaster over there. He asked me whether I should like to meet his sister; and when I said, 'Yes, I should be delighted to,' he said that it would cost a pound normally, but that he'd let me have special terms. What *can* he have meant, Mr Pennyfoot?"
>
> "'Pon my soul," Colonel Sidebotham was saying to the Vicar, "I don't like the look of that nigger. I saw enough of Fuzzy-Wuzzy in the Soudan—devilish good enemy and devilish bad friend. I'm going across to talk to Mrs Clutterbuck. Between ourselves, I think Lady C. went a bit far. I didn't see the race myself, but there are limits. . . ."
>
> "Rain ain't doin' the turnip crop any good," Lady Circumference was saying.
>
> "No, indeed," said Mrs Beste-Chetwynde. "Are you in England for long?"
>
> "Why, I live in England, of course," said Lady Circumference.
>
> "My dear, how divine!"

(94–95)

Even Prendergast gets drunk at the Sports and contributes with unwonted spirit, chatting volubly and shooting little Tangent in the foot. Though reticent and bemused, Paul is not unaffected. Llanabba's cheerful defiance of middle-class convention begins to erode the drab values he has brought with him from Onslow Square, school, and Oxford, and what begins as an awful ordeal turns into a liberating experience.

While Grimes best represents the spirit of Llanabba, another spirit beckons to Paul from Oxford: the ghost of his own past, embodied in the person of Arthur Potts, one of Paul's four friends. A monitory figure, Potts is what Paul was at Oxford, and what he might become. Potts, like Grimes, resembles one of Waugh's fellow ushers, in this case a certain Attwell whom Waugh knew briefly at Aston Clinton:

> He was educated at King's School, Worcester, and retains a slight accent, and at Christ Church, Oxford, where he seems to have led the dullest life imaginable. He is very keen on education and I have only just begun to cure him of talking to me seriously about it. . . . He took a second in English Literature and is not wholly uneducated, but he has a mean and ill-digested mind with a sort of part rationalism and part idealism.[15]

Even down to the keenness on education, this describes Potts almost perfectly. Potts, for example, writes to Paul at Llanabba:

> There is a most interesting article in the *Educational Review* on the new methods that are being tried at the Innesborough High School to induce co-ordination of the senses. They put small objects into the children's mouths and make them draw the shapes in red chalk. Have you tried this with your boys?

(57)

The absurdity of such rarefied theory in the context of Llanabba reveals the great gap between Paul's arid Oxford education and the more fruitful lessons of Llanabba. While Potts combines rationalistic theories with a horrible complacency ("Are your colleagues enlightened?"), Paul has encountered actual life—irrational, intractable, disruptive, immensely vigorous.

Like good and bad angels in a morality play, Potts and Grimes compete for Paul's soul. The lines of battle emerge from Alastair Trumpington's offer to compensate Paul for his expulsion from Oxford. Recognizing the offer as "a test-case of the durability of my ideals," Paul deliberates conscientiously about whether to accept the money. The spirit of Grimes and Llanabba urges Paul to cast off his scruples. Even Prendergast counsels common sense: "My dear boy, it would be a sin to refuse" (55). On the other hand, the spirit of Potts whispers in Paul's ear, priggishly:

> If I refuse, I shall be sure of having done right. I shall look back upon my self-denial with exquisite self-approval. By refusing I can convince myself that, in spite of the unbelievable things that have been happening to me during the last ten days, I am still the same Paul Pennyfeather I have respected so long.
>
> (55)

The alternatives are clear—and Paul not surprisingly chooses Potts, explaining to Grimes: "I'm afraid you'll find my attitude rather difficult to understand. . . . It's largely a matter of upbringing" (55). But the significance of the incident lies not in Paul's characteristic decision nor even, really, in Grimes's equally characteristic intervention—wiring Potts in Paul's name to send the twenty pounds—but in Paul's unexpected reaction when Grimes confesses that he has done so. Against all his upbringing and education, Paul is delighted: "'Grimes, you wretch!' said Paul, but, in spite of himself, he felt a great wave of satisfaction surge up within him. 'We must have another drink on that'" (56). Potts, "something of a stinker," as Grimes astutely infers, writes in response: "I cannot pretend to understand your attitude in this matter" (56–57); but Paul has been liberated from the puritan self-righteousness of Potts and initiated into the more tolerant ethos of Llanabba:

> "To the durability of ideals," said Paul as he got his pint.
>
> "My word, what a mouthful!" said Grimes; "I can't say that. Cheerioh!"
>
> (56)

Free-spirited and impulsive, Grimes has defeated Potts—at least for the moment.

Paul's Llanabba has become the equivalent of Waugh's Oxford—not the insipid Oxford of Potts, but the sparkling Oxford of Harold Acton and the Hypocrites.

The Grimesian spirit governs *Decline and Fall,* but not without a murmur of dissent here and there, and particularly in the somewhat digressive chapter on the background of King's Thursday, which Waugh added in revision to help fill out the book.

This chapter focuses on Margot Beste-Chetwynde's Hampshire country house, the modernistic creation of one Otto Silenus, whose name recalls the book about Silenus ("a Falstaff forever babbling o' green fields") that Waugh had projected in 1925. The Silenus of *Decline and Fall,* however—mechanistic and indeed scarcely human—has little to do with Falstaff or green fields. A satiric allusion to the functionalist, factory-inspired "international style" creeping into England in the 1920s from Germany, Silenus combines the "significant form" aesthetics of Clive Bell and Roger Fry with the technocrat's passion for efficiency:

> The problem of architecture as I see it . . . is the problem of all art—the elimination of the human element from the consideration of form. The only perfect building must be the factory, because that is built to house machines, not men. I do not think it is possible for domestic architecture to be beautiful, but I am doing my best. All ill comes from man. . . . Man is never beautiful; he is never happy except when he becomes the channel for the distribution of mechanical forces.
>
> (142)

The unruly inefficiency of human energy saddens him:

> "I suppose there ought to be a staircase," he said gloomily. "Why can't the creatures stay in one place? Up and down, in and out, round and round! Why can't they sit still and work? Do dynamos require staircases? Do monkeys require houses?"
>
> (144)

And Silenus himself hums with turbo-electric energy, recharging as he lies sleepless at night, ". . . his brain turning and turning regularly all the night through, drawing in more and more power, storing it away like honey in its intricate cells and galleries, till the atmosphere about it became exhausted and vitiated and only the brain remained turning and turning in the darkness" (152). Rationalist and utilitarian, puritanically unornamented, the international style asserted values profoundly inimical to *Decline and Fall*'s celebration of spontaneity, diversity, and quirkiness—the Grimesian virtues. Gropius's leading academic champion, Nikolaus Pevsner, several years later summarized the ideological implications of the new architecture:

> The profound affinity of this modern enthusiasm for *planning* (architectural as well as political) with the style of Gropius's Fagus factory is evident. The forms of the building reveal the mind of an artist but also of a concentrated thinker. . . . The warm and direct feelings of the great men of the past have gone; but then the artist who is representative of this century of ours must needs be cold, as he stands for a century cold as steel and glass, a century the precision of which leaves less space for self-expression than did any period before.

However, the great creative brain will find its own way even in times of overpowering collective energy, even with the medium of the new style of the twentieth century which, because it is a genuine style as opposed to a passing fashion, is totalitarian.[16]

A manifesto not greatly unlike Waugh's parody, but Pevsner wrote in earnest admiration, and the terms of his praise unmistakably suggest that there will be no place for someone like Grimes in the brave new world of the international style.

The new King's Thursday's chilly modernity contrasts sharply with the exaggerated backwardness of the old house, and it is in sketching the background of the original King's Thursday that Waugh's reservations about Grimesian anarchy emerge.

As part of his field researches for *Rossetti,* Waugh visited Kelmscott, William Morris's country house west of Oxford, shortly after he began writing **Decline and Fall.** A gabled Elizabethan manor house of Cotswold stone, sitting snugly within a small enclosed garden, Kelmscott stands, still relatively isolated, among meadows flanking the upper Thames. Surprised by Kelmscott's compactness, Waugh wondered how it could have accommodated Morris's large household: "The rooms are very low and dark and the whole effect rather cramped and constricted. We could not conceive how so many people lived there."[17] The diminutive scale was a characteristic disappointment—"I had imagined it all so spacious"—for someone who preferred the grand scale of Brideshead. But during his study of Rossetti Waugh had developed a sympathetic appreciation of Morris's values and the little estate where Morris "found sacramentally embodied all that he held of high account of beauty and sweetness and dignity," as Waugh observed in *Rossetti.* "Here, in small compass, lay everything for which his art and his work was striving—peace, fellowship, love, childhood, beauty, simplicity, abundance" (183–84), Waugh wrote; then he quoted a character in Morris's utopian fantasy *News From Nowhere,* which concludes with a journey up the Thames to a house based on Kelmscott: "O me! O me! How I love the earth and the seasons and weather, and all things that deal with them, and all that grows out of them—as this has done" (184).

As Waugh thought about the sort of chic house suitable for Margot Beste-Chetwynde, Kelmscott seems to have come to mind as the exact antithesis to her turbulent modern spirit. Paul Pennyfeather first arrives at King's Thursday on a pleasant spring day:

> The temperate April sunlight fell through the budding chestnuts and revealed between their trunks green glimpses of parkland and the distant radiance of a lake. "English spring," thought Paul. "In the dreaming ancestral beauty of the English country." Surely, he thought, these great chestnuts in the morning sun stood for something enduring and serene in a world that had lost its reason and would so stand when the chaos and confusion were forgotten? And surely it was the spirit of William Morris that whispered to him in Margot Beste-Chetwynde's motor-car about seed-time and harvest, the superb succession of the seasons, the harmoni-

ous interdependence of rich and poor, of dignity, innocence and tradition?

(148)

But such sentiments prove inept when the house itself bulks into view, for the venerable old King's Thursday, "enduring and serene," has been demolished and replaced by the creation of Otto Silenus.

The old King's Thursday was absurdly backward, but for all its absurdity it preserved certain William Morris values to which Waugh responded sympathetically:

> The estate-carpenter, an office hereditary in the family of the original joiner who had panelled the halls and carved the great staircase, did such restorations as became necessary from time to time for the maintenance of the fabric, working with the same tools and with the traditional methods, so that in a few years his work became indistinguishable from that of his grandsires.

(137–38)

Waugh's reading of Morris and his admiration for a well-cut dovetail here converged, products respectively of *Rossetti* and of his own recent carpentry lessons.

But such calm and stability do not prosper in the modern world as it is imagined in **Decline and Fall.** Governed by random, violent energy, that world resents the quiet enjoyment of life wherever such tranquillity might be lurking. When the slow-moving Pastmasters abandon King's Thursday, Margot Beste-Chetwynde quickly razes it, capriciously and perversely considering the rare old house common: "I can't think of anything more bourgeois and awful than timbered Tudor architecture" (140) ("I find that I am beginning to detest Elizabethan architecture owing to the vulgarities of Stratford-on-Avon," Waugh had written in his diary).[18] The image of Margot knocking down the old King's Thursday suggests Waugh's conflicting impulses: he was sympathetic with both the reckless impulsiveness of Margot and the quieter values enshrined in the old house, but in 1928 he was much more deeply enchanted with Margot.

A decade later, Waugh was mourning the demolition of many of London's old houses, but **Decline and Fall** is scarcely touched by such tender sentiments. The half-hearted attempt of Jack Spire, editor of the *London Hercules,* to save King's Thursday is derisive:

> Mr Jack Spire was busily saving St Sepulchre's, Egg Street (where Dr Johnson is said once to have attended Matins), when Margot Beste-Chetwynde's decision to rebuild King's Thursday became public. He said, very seriously: "Well, we did what we could," and thought no more about it.

(141)

Spire is a transparent allusion to J. C. Squire, who (Waugh thought) represented the folklore image of a merry-old, cricket-playing England that Waugh considered as spurious as modern timbered architecture. The Waugh of *Decline and Fall* scorned, or affected to scorn, sentimental wistfulness for preindustrial life, or at least for the quaint trappings of agrarian England. A year later he compiled a catalogue of what he considered antiquarian offenses:

> . . . arts and crafts, and the preservation of rural England, and the preservation of ancient monuments, and the transplantation of Tudor cottages, and the collection of pewter and old oak, and the reformed public house, and the Ye Olde Inne and the Kynde Dragone and Ye Cheshire Cheese, Broadway, Stratford-on-Avon, folk dancing . . .
>
> (*Labels,* 55–56)

and so on at great length. Under the guise of historical preservation, entrepreneurs traded on nostalgic sentimentality to spawn middle-class tourist "attractions." Writing in 1929 in praise of the slums of Naples, he asserted: "In England, the craze for cottages and all that goes with them only began as soon as they had ceased to represent a significant part of English life. In Naples no such craze exists because the streets are still in perfect harmony with their inhabitants" (*Labels,* 56). The old King's Thursday harmonized with the indolent Pastmasters, who had never themselves arrived in the twentieth century, but the antiquarianism of people like Jack Spire or the Pastmasters' neighbors was self-indulgent, soft-boiled, dilettante:

> "I thought we might go over to tea at the Pastmasters'," hostesses would say after luncheon on Sundays. "You really must see their house. Quite unspoilt, my dear. Professor Franks, who was here last week, said it was recognized as the finest piece of domestic Tudor in England."
>
> (138)

After calling on the Pastmasters, "they would drive away in their big motor-cars to their modernized manors" and sit "in their hot baths" (138). Perhaps this sort of weekend nostalgia was close enough to Waugh's own wistfulness to make him feel a little uncomfortable; perhaps Margot's wrecking ball was an oblique attack on his father's theatrical Victorian sentimentality. In any event, *Decline and Fall* does not go easy on nostalgia.

For all its confusion of grim factory style and splashy Art Deco—bottle-green glass floors and black glass pillars, malachite bath and kaleidoscopic drawing-room—Silenus's King's Thursday nonetheless represents the vital energy of the era. A "new-born monster to whose birth ageless and forgotten cultures had been in travail," it is an architectural image of 1920s England. In 1928 Waugh was twenty-four years old, his appetite for experience was keen, and the "new-born monster," despite its aesthetic horrors, represented the world as it lay before him. Despite his fond backward glance at the old King's Thursday of the Pastmasters, he confronted the contemporary world with high relish for its "vitality and actuality." *Decline and Fall*'s strongest sympathies are with the impulsive, anarchic energy of Grimes and Margot; and *their* impulse is to knock down old houses when the fancy strikes them.

From architecture *Decline and Fall* turns to other adventures: Margot's recruitment of prostitutes; Paul's trip to Marseilles; his arrest, trial, and conviction for abetting Margot's business; prisons; Paul's "death" at Dr. Fagan's bogus nursing home; his revival at Margot's villa at Corfu. Grimes turns up now and then in the later chapters, but Paul's continuing education is largely taken over by Margot. Wealthy, worldly, exquisitely elegant and fashionable, "the first breath of spring in the Champs-Elysées" (89), she is superficially very unlike the peg-legged, hand-to-mouth Grimes, but like Grimes she is spiritually anarchic, wholly amoral, beyond conventional standards of judgment. Although her restless energy leaves a wake of destruction, with Paul one of her victims, he easily forgives her; just as Grimes is one of the immortals, Margot too is a goddess. Neither can be confined by stone walls. Margot combines and burlesques two extremes, the criminal underworld and the high opulent style, spanning the novel's range of sympathies.

As Margot drives the action forward, Paul is pulled along behind. Though often baffling, his schooling in life continues, confirming and supplementing the lessons of Llanabba. Beyond the cramped circle of conventional respectability and neat academic theory to which he was previously limited, a multifarious and chaotic world flourishes. It can be ignored or condemned, but it refuses to be suppressed. The most spectacular collision between Grimes's and Potts's worlds is provoked by Sir Wilfrid Lucas-Dockery, the professorial prison warden whose enlightened reforms at Blackstone Prison, as irrelevant to actual prison conditions as Potts's educational ideas were to Llanabba, are dramatically refuted by the bloodthirsty visionary who decapitates Prendergast: a sad end for Prendergast, but a happy example of anarchy triumphant. Paul's passage through the underworld gives him the liberal education he was not getting at Oxford.

But Paul is not Grimes, nor was meant to be. At Llanabba, at King's Thursday, and in prison, he learns the limitations of his own background; but he can never quite escape it. His narrow, conventional self keeps surfacing. When Philbrick, for example, narrates one of his criminal fantasies, Paul responds indignantly: "'But, good gracious,' said Paul, 'why have you told me this monstrous story? I shall certainly inform the police. I never heard of such a thing'" (70)—exactly what Potts would have said and done. Hopelessly naive about Margot Beste-Chetwynde's South American brothels, Paul travels to Marseilles, only to shrink from the crowded street life of the slums: "He turned and fled for the broad streets and the tram lines where, he knew at heart, was his spiritual home" (181). As he moves through the implausible events of the novel's latter half, he grows less censorious about the irregularities he encounters, but he can never really become a free spirit himself.

And in the end he returns to Oxford and to all appearances resumes the life he had led before his expulsion, reading divinity at Scone and bicycling to talks on Polish plebiscites, while a dull character named Stubbs replaces the dull Potts as his friend. After Paul's liberation from Potts at Llanabba, he seems to have fallen straight back into Potts's dreary milieu, a flagrant case of recidivism. But he actually belongs neither to Potts's nor to Grimes's world now, and instead stands aloof from both. Although his Oxford life is superficially unchanged, it has become a charade:

> On one occasion he and Stubbs and some other friends went to the prison to visit the criminals there and sing part-songs to them.
>
> "It opens the mind," said Stubbs, "to see all sides of life. How those unfortunate men appreciated our singing!"
>
> (247)

Paul doesn't answer; the gap between his varied experience of the world and Stubbs's complacent insularity is too wide to bridge. Though back in his old Oxford routine, Paul is no more at home at Oxford now than he had been at Llanabba. Outwardly occupied with his bland, studious routine and his circle of tedious acquaintances, Paul is nonetheless wiser and rather tougher now, aware of how much life pullulates beyond the smooth and tidy quadrangles of Scone. With this knowledge, there can be no genuine return to Potts.

Aware that Stubbs and Potts and their kind are *his* kind, however, and represent his future, he acts a deliberately chosen role, resigning himself to essay societies and cocoa, subduing his uneasy knowledge of his own futility, living at second hand in the passions of dusty theological controversies:

> There was a bishop in Bithynia, Paul learned, who had denied the Divinity of Christ, the immortality of the soul, the existence of good, the legality of marriage, and the validity of the sacrament of Extreme Unction! How right they had been to condemn him!
>
> (248)

Timid scholarly ferocity substitutes for any real engagement with life. The world boils with heterodox energy, with eccentrics and criminals, heretics and lunatics, with irrepressible weedlike vigor, but all that is outside and Paul has shut the door on it. Just beyond his rooms, in fact, the Bollinger Club is again partying noisily. Until the very last night of his first undergraduate career, Paul had never heard of the Bollinger, and if he had known of them he would have disapproved. Now, very much aware of them, he is neither sympathetic nor disapproving; but he does not want to get involved again, does not even want to be reminded of his earlier involvement with the Bollinger and all its consequences.

Peter Beste-Chetwynde, stumbling into his rooms, is a further reminder of the past, and Paul resents the intrusion. Peter is "dynamic" and Paul is "static"; Paul acknowledges this truth and disciplines himself to be content with his lot. When Peter leaves, Paul goes to bed—to sleep his life away, as it were, while others live theirs, awake.

Peter and Paul, in fact, both originate in Waugh himself. Peter is very drunk, but evidently more as a consequence of boredom than of celebration: "Oh, damn, what else is there to do?" he complains (252). Waugh too was sometimes a Bollinger in spirit, riotous and reckless; but he derived little solid comfort from his excesses, and, like Paul, he sometimes wanted to retreat, to close the door against the noisy outer world. Though bubbling throughout with comic effervescence, *Decline and Fall* ends on a subdued note of withdrawal.

The fruitless circularity of Paul Pennyfeather's experience, the uncertain mood of the ending, a series of playful religious and ecclesiastical allusions, and a knowledge of Waugh's later career—all these elements of the novel have, in some combination, led more than one critic to detect a deliberate and profound moral argument in *Decline and Fall.* Jerome Meckier, for example, finds the novel's meaning concealed in "symbolic shorthand"; in fact, "Symbols are always the key to Waugh's art." With this in mind, Paul's circular experience can be seen as a modern parody of the fruitful cycle of the seasons and the sacred cycle of the Christian calendar, models that expose the futility of the contemporary secular world. Paul, then, is "a parodic Christ"; Philbrick the butler is a "bogus Messiah" whose fantastic autobiographical inventions are a parody of the Transfiguration; Prendergast is a "parodic martyr"; and so on.[19]

This is one way to read *Decline and Fall,* of course—anyone who puts out money for the book owns his own copy—but it seems a particularly pedantic and humorless reading, and one that certainly would have astounded Waugh himself; the furthest thing from his mind was an allegorical parody of secular society or a history of the moral decline of Christian civilization. *Decline and Fall* is a mythic transformation of intensely private experience into broad comedy: an amorphous lump of his own life moulded into aesthetically satisfying shape. It had very little to do with his politico-religio-moral ideology, whatever it may have been at the time. The wistful and despairing tone of the ending suggests the novel's roots in Waugh's unsettled feelings, the comic possibilities of life competing with, and consoling him for, painful experience.

But the governing spirit of the novel is not at all ambiguous. *Decline and Fall* belongs to Grimes and Margot and their fellows, the characters who live most dangerously and most fully:

> Let us roll all our strength, and all
> Our sweetness, up into one ball;
> And tear our pleasures with rough strife
> Thorough the iron gates of life.

Decline and Fall is vernal and youthful, eager for experience, in love with the living and the actual. It is the novel of a young man on the outside, familiar with disappointment but unscarred, inclined to wistfulness but brimming with inventiveness and anarchic zest. Waugh's comic genius never flourished more happily.

Notes

1. *Diaries,* 3 September 1927.

2. Dudley Carew, *A Fragment of Friendship* (London: Everest Books, 1974), pp. 81–82.

3. Anthony Powell, *Messengers of Day,* Vol. 2 of *The Memoirs of Anthony Powell* (New York: Holt, Rinehart and Winston, 1978), p. 22.

4. To Harold Acton, undated (early 1928) (*Letters,* p. 25).

5. To Anthony Powell, 7 April 1928 (*Letters,* p. 27).

6. Preface to *Decline and Fall,* revised ed. (London: Chapman and Hall, 1962), p. 11.

7. To Harold Acton, undated (September/October 1928) (*Letters,* p. 28).

8. The comic rhetoric of this passage is discussed in detail in Walter Nash, *The Language of Humour* (London: Longman, 1985), pp. 22–25.

9. Jeffrey Heath, *Picturesque Prison,* warns against being seduced into liking Waugh's bad characters: "The discrepancy between the levels of action and parable creates an ambivalent tone of condemnation and compassion; as a result of this deceptive tone Waugh is able to ambush readers who mistakenly sympathize with characters whom he in fact deplores" (122). I think that this comment confuses fiction with life. Characters like Lady Circumference—based on the mother of Waugh's friend Alastair Graham—might be boring and awful as houseguests or neighbors and might even be morally deplorable, but they may be fascinating and even sympathetic characters in fiction, where they are aesthetic objects to which we respond with different standards. Replying, years after *Decline and Fall,* to an interviewer who mentioned fictional characters like Pistol and Moll Flanders, Waugh remarked: "Ah, the criminal classes. . . . They have always had a certain fascination." To assert that the dramatic interest of Falstaff (to take another example) is that he demonstrates Shakespeare's disapprobation of robbery, cowardice, lying, lechery, and drunkenness not only would be banal, but would altogether mistake Shakespeare's, and our, attitude to Falstaff.

10. Good discussions of Waugh's comic style may be found in William J. Cook, Jr., *Masks, Modes, and Morals: The Art of Evelyn Waugh* (Rutherford, N.J.: Fairleigh Dickinson University Press, 1971); and in Littlewood, *Writings of Waugh,* pp. 36–65.

11. *Diaries,* 2 October 1927.

12. *Ibid.,* 14 May 1925.

13. *Ibid.,* 3 July 1925.

14. Claud Cockburn, "Evelyn Waugh's Lost Rabbit," *The Atlantic,* December 1973, p. 54.

15. *Diaries,* 8 February 1927.

16. Nikolaus Pevsner, *Pioneers of the Modern Movement: From William Morris to Walter Gropius* (New York: Frederick A. Stokes, 1937), pp. 205–6.

17. *Diaries,* 6 October 1927.

18. *Ibid.,* 11 September 1925.

19. Jerome Meckier, "Circle, Symbol and Parody in Evelyn Waugh's *Decline and Fall,*" *Contemporary Literature* 20 (1979): 51–75.

Frederick L. Beaty (essay date 1992)

SOURCE: "Decline and Fall," in *The Ironic World of Evelyn Waugh: A Study of Eight Novels,* Northern Illinois University Press, 1992, pp. 32–51.

[*In the following essay, Beaty analyzes the ironic tone of* Decline and Fall.]

For **Decline and Fall,** in manuscript subtitled "The Making of an Englishman," Waugh invents a complex of shocking disparities through which to demonstrate the reeducation of his central character, Paul Pennyfeather, whose initial beliefs about the world are shattered by his experiential discoveries of its actual nature. The series of riotous picaresque adventures that strip away Paul's illusions about honor, love, society, education, the church, the law, the prison system, and even human nature detail his fall from blissful naiveté to a painful awareness of evil. Although exposure to the chaos of modern life forces him to question the behavioral codes of his stable, upper middle-class background—precepts which he confidently assumed to be adequate and appropriate for coping with any difficulties—the conflict between idealism and disillusionment is never wholly resolved. Ultimately he comes to realize that since neither approach offers the complete truth about life each must, as in Hegelian dialectics, be used to temper the other. The novel as a whole may therefore be viewed as an ironic parody of the Bildungsroman—one which, neither debasing the genre nor treating it seriously, merely plays with it in unexpected ways.[1]

Contributing much to the success of irony in **Decline and Fall** is the positioning of a detached narrator between author and central character. The novel's apparent cynicism toward suffering and death is therefore not necessarily the sentiment of the author, who has distanced himself from the work, but rather of an indifferent storyteller who represents the usual callousness of humanity. The disinterested pose of the narrator serves negatively, however, to stimulate the increased emotional involvement of the reader, who might consider obtrusive condemnation of evil as preachy or, especially in this fallen world, where innocence is often equated with stupidity, might regard overt sympathy with the victim as sentimental.

The narrator's disengagement also permits him, in the Belgravia interlude, to add an unusual dimension as he steps back from his story to comment interpretively on his own art, temporarily breaking the artistic illusion in a way typical of romantic irony.[2] This brief digression, strategically placed midway in the novel to show how incomplete Paul's education still is, allows the narrator to play ironically with both the central character and the reader about the nature of reality.[3] For a few hours Paul emerges from the disjointed world into which ill circumstances have thrust him to reenter a civilized milieu where he believes a gentleman can feel at home, although the betrayals he has suffered in Oxford and West End London would seem to belie his trust in such an environment. His conviction that he is once again a solid person in a solid world is also contrasted ironically with his fading memory of recent misadventures amid the "sham" of Llanabba as if they were only "nightmares." But the narrator, while confirming the dichotomy of Paul's two worlds, offers no clear resolution of which is reality and which is illusion. He merely explains that he is obliged to return Paul to the shadowy subworld, where the extraordinary adventures which are "the only interest about him" will be resumed.[4] Implying that a passive character like Paul is incapable of the heroism expected by readers of 1920s thrillers, the narrator comments that the "book is really an account of the mysterious disappearance of Paul Pennyfeather, so that readers must not complain if the shadow which took his name does not amply fill the important part of hero for which he was originally cast" (163).

In presenting the circumstances that lead eventually to Paul's "disappearance," the narrator, whose customary stance is almost complete objectivity, can indicate the confusion in Paul's life merely by detailing the physical objects in a certain environment as clues to the actions and characters associated with it. In such cases, metonymy functions ironically by indirectly conveying ideas about people and places without ever stating them. Although Waugh had toyed with this technique in **"The Balance"** by hinting information about Adam's friends through the contents of their rooms, he developed it fully for the first time in **Decline and Fall.** The particulars of Silenus's Bauhaus renovations at King's Thursday suggest the architect's own sterile, mechanically oriented mind. The description of Margot's "Sports Room" in her London home proclaims the kind of jobs being offered to the "young ladies" whom she interviews there: the lights are in testicular glass balls; the furniture is "ingeniously" constructed of phallic bats, polo sticks, and golf clubs; and a wall is decorated with the painting of a prize ram, presumably a symbol of male potency. The masters' common room at Llanabba, which Paul surveys apprehensively upon first encounter, provides him as well as the reader, through its material jumble, with a foretaste of the school's zany teaching staff. Scattered about in defiance of order are pipes, academic gowns, "golf clubs, a walking stick, an umbrella and two miniature rifles . . . a typewriter . . . a bicycle pump, two armchairs, a straight chair, half a bottle of invalid port, a boxing glove, a bowler hat, yesterday's *Daily News,* and a packet of pipe cleaners" (19–20).

Lack of cohesion also exists in social relations. Paul, an orphan, has no real family, and his uncaring guardian exploits him and his inheritance whenever possible. In the Fagan and Trumpington families the generations show little understanding of each other, and the elder Circumferences seem to have no genuine love for their son. Marriage becomes just another contractual business to Margot Beste-Chetwynde, Maltravers, Silenus, and Grimes, while the many instances of casual sex provide no lasting connection. The relations between instructors and students, at both Llanabba and Oxford, are a burlesque of the ideal, for each group takes advantage of the other. Paul's best friend, Potts, betrays their friendship, and Philbrick's tales suggest that there can be no trust between any men. Members of the upper class—the Circumferences, Peter Pastmaster, and the parvenu Maltravers—ignore their traditional obligations of leadership in favor of self-interest. Members of the Bollinger Club, in their destruction of items symbolizing music, art, and poetry, prove themselves not just indifferent but hostile to culture. From the perspective of the ironic narrator, all this indicates a civilization that has lost its bearing—one in which traditional bonds no longer hold it together. Hence Silenus's analogy of a turning carnival wheel is an apt symbol of frenzied circular motion with only centrifugal force and no advancement. As Yeats put it, "Things fall apart; the center cannot hold; / Mere anarchy is loosed upon the world."[5]

Even Scone College—that Oxonian Eden from which Paul is banished and to which he returns only in reincarnation—is itself part of the fallen world. Yet until its evil is thrust upon him, he is as oblivious as was the youthful Waugh, who reminisced in his autobiography about an Oxford that seemed "a Kingdom of Cokayne," where he "was reborn in full youth" after a cocoonlike development in a public school.[6] Blind to the perils that surround him, Paul is rudely shaken out of his chrysalis existence and then borne along on a stream of events that, at every turn, frustrate his hopes and desires. Naively assuming that external appearances are the indications of ultimate validity, he discovers to his repeated sorrow that people are not what they seem. Inexperienced and highly vulnerable, he becomes the victim of many schemes and situations in a world ruled not by justice or reason but by capricious fortune.

Paul's true education begins with the opening episode at Scone. This fast-moving sequence of events, seen from several perspectives, serves as catalyst for all subsequent action and, as a particularly successful display of ironic artistry, merits detailed analysis. Even the names of the characters seem unsuitable. "Pennyfeather" symbolizes an insignificance at odds with the main character's central position. "Sniggs" and "Postlethwaite," by their ludicrously undignified sounds, hint at the fraudulent nature of these college dons, while the uncommonly pretentious names of Bollinger members (Alastair Digby-Vaine-Trumpington and Lumsden of Strathdrummond) imply a boastfulness not in keeping with true aristocrats. Other touches of irony intrude through inappropriate words, phrases, or tones. "Lovely" is the narrator's term to describe both the depredations of the Bollinger Club and the subsequent meeting of college officials to assess punishment. The hyperbolic "What an evening that had been!" (1) characterizes destruction during the Club's previous reunion. When the drunken Lumsden encounters Paul, the laird's primitive instincts are implied in an analogy likening him to "a druidical rocking stone" (5). Another irony pivots upon the mention of "*outrage*," which the college dons fear may occur if they interfere with the Bollinger attack on Paul, whereas an outrage of a different sort does occur because they do nothing. When Paul is described as one who "does the College no good" (7), the ostensible reference to academic reputation cloaks an actual allusion to financial gain. The chaplain's enigmatic suggestion that the "ideals" Paul has "learned at Scone" may be of use in the business world is subject to several interpretations. It may insinuate that someone like Paul, whose values seem to be less than ideal, should do well in a profession not noted for idealism. It may imply that what Paul has recently learned in college about human behavior is contrary to what a university ought to teach. Or it may indicate the naïveté of a chaplain mouthing his usual, but in this case highly inappropriate, platitudes to a departing student.

The action of the Scone episode also abounds in contradiction, some of which cuts in more than one direction. The willful and extensive damage to several college rooms during the Bollinger Club's rampage, for which its members are assessed relatively low fines, contrasts with the damage noticed in Paul's room—two slight, certainly unintentional, cigarette burns, for which the bursar assesses comparatively high charges. These minor burns, in turn, contrast with the colossal injury done to Paul himself by that same bursar, who witnessed yet did not interfere with Paul's debagging; and the moderate fining of the Bollinger members, compared with Paul's expulsion for something of which he was completely innocent, represents a further miscarriage of justice. In the realm of cause and effect, substantial losses to the unpopular students—china, a piano, a Matisse painting, and a manuscript—result in only minimal benefit to the dons of some Founder's port. Conversely, the seemingly insignificant mistaking of Paul's tie, the stripes of which differed only by a quarter of an inch in width from those of the Boller tie, sets off a chain of disastrous occurrences that result in the complete obliteration of Paul's identity.

Underlying and controlling these sharply contrasting events at Scone are broader incongruities of perspective; and the hilarity of the episode derives largely from the clash between the distinctive attitudes of Paul Pennyfeather, the college authorities, and the Bollinger members about Paul's inadvertent fall from innocence. The wielders of academic power—the bursar, the junior dean, the master, and the chaplain—think and behave, in view of their obligations, contrary to what the reader and Paul would expect. Even the porter, by assuming Paul's guilt, echoes their demoralizing point of view. The dons who gleefully watch the Bollinger mayhem from a darkened window, without any intention of halting it, dwell upon their own potential benefit from the anticipated fines—the more horrendous the destruction, the greater the gain. Hence Sniggs can utter, according to his own logic, the illogical prayer, "Oh, please God, make them attack the Chapel" (3). A hypocritical conscience besets them momentarily when they think a titled student has run afoul of the Bollinger members but evaporates when they realize that the victim is only Pennyfeather, "some one of no importance" (6). The same double standard is exhibited by the master, who decides to expel Paul ostensibly for running through the quad "*without his trousers*" but actually because he is not wealthy enough to profit the college through substantial fines. In a burlesque of sweetness and sympathy, the chaplain bids Paul look on the bright side of his disgrace—that he has discovered so early his "unfitness for the priesthood" (8). But the porter's juxtaposed observation—that most students who are "sent down for indecent behaviour" (8) become schoolmasters—implies Paul's suitability for a profession usually thought to abide by principles as high as those of the clergy.

Members of the Bollinger Club, far from living up to their aristocratic titles, prove themselves to be barbarians. Their overweening sense of self-importance is skillfully undermined in the opening passages describing the gathering of old members for the annual "beano." Through repeated wrenching of tone involving overstatement deflated by pejorative adjectives or demeaning nouns, the narrator alerts the reader to the discrepancy between their social status and their true character: "Epileptic royalty from their villas of exile; uncouth peers from crumbling country seats; . . . illiterate lairds from wet granite hovels in the Highlands" (1-2). Their behavior at reunions suggests their belief that they are above the gentlemanly code, just as Lady Circumference's defiance of grammar implies her assumption that she is not bound by conventional rules. Liberated by alcohol, the Bollinger members give vent to their atavistic hunting instincts, perpetuated, long after being essential for survival, in the ritualistic sport of county families. Their quarry may be a caged fox, which they pelt to death with champagne bottles, or unpopular students, whose prized possessions they destroy. To indicate the bestiality of their reversion to habits of primitive ancestors, the narrator employs animal analogies—"confused roaring" (1) and "baying for broken glass" (2). The absurdity of their pretensions is further exposed when the oafish Lumsden, whose dubious distinction stems from wild chieftain forebears, becomes incensed at Paul for wearing what appears to be a Boller tie. In Lumsden's way of thinking, such presumption in a middle-class Englishman merits public disgrace.

Paul's acquaintance with Dionysian forces has been more theoretical than actual, and his confident unawareness of the evil around him has reduced his ability to cope with it. So oblivious has he been to the very existence of the Bollinger Club that he cannot conceive of having done anything to incur the wrath of its members. What transpires in his mind while he is being debagged or what his response is to the college authorities when they expel him is never recorded. The detached narrator so rarely delves into characters' innermost thoughts that the reader is often held in a state of uncertainty that heightens the irony of this crucial situation. Although it is possible to deduce from external evidence that neither the guilty Bollinger members nor the witnessing dons, who presumably offer only partial and therefore misleading evidence to the master, have the slightest interest in justice, the bitter reaction of their abused, maligned victim is revealed only when Paul utters his valedictory curse on all the malefactors.

The world into which Paul is thrust also evaluates according to outward manifestations rather than true worth. Every phase of his life as a schoolmaster is fraught with discrepancies. He is initially forced to seek employment because his guardian views expulsion from Oxford as sufficient reason to abrogate Paul's inheritance; the employment agency, though euphemistically recording "indecent behaviour" as "education discontinued for personal reasons" (12), uses Paul's disgrace to refer him to a school of the lowest category; and his employer finds it an excuse to hire him at reduced pay. Even the appearance of the Llanabba school building, misnamed a castle, accentuates the discrepancy between the genuine and the sham, for what had originally been a Georgian country home (and remains so from the back) has had a pretentious medieval fortress superimposed upon its front. Compounding the incongruity of the structure is the irony of Paul's inability to notice it because he arrives at night in a closed taxi.

The instructional system itself is a jumble of contradictions, for Llanabba is dedicated not to teaching and learning but to the semblance of education for wealthy boys who cannot gain admission to a reputable public school. The disparate assessments of young Lord Tangent, first by the unctuous headmaster, Dr. Fagan, and later by Tangent's brutally candid mother, stem from the conflict between rosy façade and harsh reality. Fagan, explaining that "many of the boys come from the very best families," characterizes "little Lord Tangent . . . , the Earl of Circumference's son," as "such a nice little chap, erratic, of course, like all his family, but he has *tone*" (16). Lady Circumference cuts through the veneer with "The boy's a dunderhead. If he wasn't he wouldn't be here" (85). Although Fagan may equivocate about the quality of his pupils, his less guarded statements and actions expose his fraudulence. While spouting the positive philosophy of educationists, paying lip service to "professional tone," "vision," and the "ideal of service and fellowship" (15–16), he encourages his masters to practice something quite different. Under his tutelage, Paul learns to "temper discretion with deceit" (24)—passing himself off as an expert in athletics or organ playing even when he has no competence whatever. On advice from another master, Paul forgets about teaching the boys anything and concentrates upon merely keeping them quiet with busywork. While he struggles with the down-to-earth problems of his situation, the high-flown educational theories offered by his pompous friend Potts further emphasize the discrepancy between educational philosophy and its misapplication at Llanabba.

That Fagan's choice of masters is dictated not by pedagogical considerations but solely by the impressions they make on his patrons is clear from his comments on unsatisfactory employees. Fagan tells of one master "who swore terribly in front of every one" (76) when bitten by a parent's dog; of another he states, "He is *not* out of the top drawer, and boys notice these things"; of a third, "He used to borrow money from the boys . . . and the parents objected" (16). Fagan's primary concern is to perpetuate the scholastic charade, which is staged to gain financial support from the school's affluent patrons. The masters, therefore, as part of "the act," must be favorably received on the superficial level; and their real characters do not matter. When Fagan declines to inquire into the details of Paul's "indecent behaviour," he lays bare his cynicism and contempt for ideals in his most self-betraying remark: "I have been in the scholastic profession long enough to know that nobody enters it unless he has some very good reason which he is anxious to conceal" (15).

Against this background, the incident of the £20 offered Paul by Alastair Trumpington to compensate for the ruination of his Oxford career is presented through a delightful series of ironies undermining the inviolable honor code of English gentlemen. Paul's moral dilemma occurs when Potts's incensed refusal of the money is countermanded by less idealistic colleagues at Llanabba. In fact, when Paul admits with double entendre that the £20 represents "a temptation," the Rev. Prendergast, following through in the religious vein with advice unexpected of a clergyman, replies that "it would be a sin to refuse" (52). Paul's subsequent struggle with his conscience, in which temptation is overcome by the need to keep his self-respect and to prove "the durability of . . . ideals" (53) bred into him as a gentleman, appears incompatible with his facile accommodation to Fagan's dishonest ways. Since Paul seems to feel no guilt for having compromised educational values, his belief that it would be dishonorable to accept compensation for personal damages becomes particularly absurd. New dimensions in the irony are introduced when the unscrupulous Grimes resolves the problem quite simply. Having forged an acceptance in Paul's name, Grimes explains: "I'm a gentleman too . . . and I was afraid you might feel like that, so I . . . saved you from yourself" (54). Paul's delighted response, "in spite of himself," with a toast "to the durability of ideals" (54) explodes the original meaning of these words. In this altered context a tribute to the undeviating code that Grimes ignores signifies (whether or not Paul realizes it) a more pragmatic orientation toward ideals. Waugh's narrator makes a final comic pass at this episode during the later sports event, when Lady Circumference tells Paul that, according to her sister's account, her nephew Trumpington has recently been fined £20. Only Paul and the reader can deduce the unstated—that Trumpington, to allay his conscience for a previous wrongdoing, has committed another by getting the money under false pretenses.

Though Waugh's account of the Llanabba sports event provides verbal pleasures and unexpected occurrences of small dimension, the main ironic thrust in this section is on a much grander scale. The conflict between assumed appearance and underlying reality is, in fact, presented on two levels—the chaotic sports themselves serving as a microcosm for the competitive tensions of society at large. While Fagan virtually ignores matters necessary for the actual sports (a defined racing course, proper equipment, and rules for judging), he lavishes attention on unessential trivia (flags, fireworks, gilded programs, and champagne cup) designed to curry favor with influential parents. But his elaborate preparations have an uncanny way of backfiring by inducing consequences opposite to what he intends. His desire to effect style by using a real pistol for starting the races brings about the accidental wounding of Lord Tangent. His hope of lending dignity with a band results in unbearably monotonous music and the bandmaster's attempts to pimp for his sister-in-law. The predetermination of athletic winners from among boys of prominent families, which obliges Grimes to declare Clutterbuck a winner despite his cheating, precipitates the embarrassing scene in which Lady Circumference refuses to award the prize. Thus Fagan's misguided hopes of gaining favor turn the gala into a fiasco, and the fraudulence with which the sports are staged totally destroys the sportsmanship supposedly generated by healthy competition.

The visiting parents also lack any sense of fair play in their social competitiveness, as the unresolved tensions among three class-conscious groups illustrate. The Clutterbucks, with a brewing fortune but as yet no seat in Parliament, are defensive about their nouveau-riche status. The obtuse Earl of Circumference and his horsey, outspoken countess exude the smug self-confidence of landed aristocrats. Margot Beste-Chetwynde, fortified by beauty, extraordinary wealth, social standing in Mayfair, and a son who is heir apparent to an earldom, feels so secure that she dares to challenge conventional standards of propriety. She defiantly flaunts her black American lover, whose unconvincing claims to culture further add to the incongruous situation in which everyone seems to be jockeying for position. Amidst expressions of racial prejudice, social antagonism, and political bias, the parental gathering is wrecked by the very people Fagan expected to beguile.

The other principal characters whom Paul meets at Llanabba are also at variance with their outward aspects. The two masters, Grimes and Prendergast, each of whom possesses a serious defect that periodically upsets his equilibrium, are to some extent ironic inversions of one another. Prendergast is well-bred and well-meaning, but his basic inclination to do good is thwarted by lack of strong belief in anything, including himself. Consequently he

cannot carry through his intentions or deal with simple problems such as sharing the bath. Unable to resolve theological doubts, he has given up his vocation as parish priest. Yet he fares no better at Llanabba, where his self-pitying, defeatist attitude makes it impossible for him to keep order among the students, win their respect, or associate easily with the other masters. In contrast, Grimes, though vulgar by nature and confirmedly hedonistic, has the self-assurance to be outgoing with his colleagues and to discipline the boys, who respect him partly because his artificial leg has led them to conclude, erroneously, that he was wounded in the war. Most crucial, he has no "doubts." He is as confident of his "old boy" connections with Harrow as Browning's Pippa is of providential care and knows they will repeatedly get him out of "the soup." Hence a distinguished public school, the traditional breeding ground of English gentlemen, serves paradoxically as a perpetual safety net for one who is clearly no gentleman.

If the Rev. Prendergast is a burlesque of the questing Anglican clergyman and Capt. Grimes of the immoral schoolmaster, the butler Philbrick is a caricature of the criminal on his way to success. He seems to have no fixed identity but delights in playing different roles in a kaleidoscopic monodrama. The various autobiographical tales he offers to create a protean, polymorphous self are so imaginative as to indicate a superb con artist. All one can be sure of is that a butler with diamonds, pistol, and police on his trail is no ordinary servant. Although Prendergast's overdeveloped conscience is instrumental in his undoing, an ironic detachment from conventional morality enables Philbrick, like Grimes, to flourish, at least for the time being, in a mad world.

Grimes's eventual downfall provides an excellent example of what Muecke labels an irony of events in which the very act designed to prevent an unwanted result becomes the instrument for producing it.[7] Just as Fagan's efforts to impress his patrons at the sports event have the opposite effect, so Grimes's marriage to his employer's daughter Flossie turns into agony. Having become engaged to her as a means of protecting his job the next time his homosexual indiscretions are discovered, he weds her when in danger of being fired, not knowing that his consequent unhappiness would destroy his ability to stay in the job. He realizes with horror that, despite his lack of sexual interest in women, his primrose path of dalliance has led him directly, in another irony of events, to revolting domesticity; and his fears are reinforced by the vicar's nuptial sermon on "Home and Conjugal Love," which becomes farcical when viewed against the cynicism that brought the couple together.

Grimes's changed status generates further ironies. Especially with his father-in-law constantly belittling him, he suffers a marked alteration in personality. Just as Prendergast, under the influence of drink, had once become self-confident enough to cane twenty-three boys, so Grimes, under the impact of marriage, becomes despondent, self-pitying, and paranoid. While he at first sees a painful irony in the fact that the elder Clutterbuck's letter about an attractive job in the brewery arrives too late to prevent the marital fiasco, the reader sees an even more poignant irony in Grimes's subsequent misinterpretation of this genuine offer as only a cruel hoax perpetrated against him—one to which any response would be useless. Flossie's attitude toward the unsatisfactory relationship with Grimes is divulged ironically when she refuses to wear mourning after his ostensible suicide. Her cryptic explanation—"I don't think my husband would have expected it of me" (148)—sidesteps her real reason. A hidden irony, of which neither Flossie nor the reader could be aware at this point, arises from the fact that Grimes is still alive.

Whereas the first book begins by focusing on the fall of an innocent, the second book begins by developing King's Thursday, Margot's country home, as an ironic symbol of progress. The Bauhaus monstrosity that Paul finds at the end of an avenue of great chestnuts presents modernity at its worst. Not only is this combination of concrete, steel, and glass quite unappealing in itself, but it is further diminished by comparison with the fine example of Tudor architecture that had until recently stood on the same spot. Although Waugh implies amusing inconsistencies about the earlier mansion—that its original character had been "preserved" by the inaction of indifferent, impecunious earls, and that its crumbling beauty had been most admired by modern preservationists who did not have to cope with its discomforts—the main thrust of the irony is directed toward the new building and the bad taste of its rich new owner. Margot, contrary to the assumptions of neighbors and antiquarians that her wealth would surely restore the ancient structure, demolishes what she considers "bourgeois and awful" to replace it with "something clean and square" (155–56).

Just as illogical is her choice of an architect whose chief qualifications are a rejected factory design and the decor for a film without any human characters. Prof. Silenus's preference for the machine over man, shown in his parody of Hamlet's praise of humanity, has caused him to reduce architecture—domestic as well as industrial—to a problem of accommodating machines rather than people. Since he considers human beings to be only inferior machines, he tells Paul that in ten more years Margot "will be almost worn out" (169). Believing that the machine is the perfection to which humanity should aspire, he makes himself ridiculous by imitating its actions as he tries to eat a biscuit. His fixed expression and the regular motion of his hand and jaws illustrate the assertion of Henri Bergson, one of Waugh's favorite philosophers at the time, that "the attitudes, gestures and movements of the human body are laughable in exact proportion as that body reminds us of a mere machine."[8]

The mystery surrounding Margot's wealth is presented as an evolving irony, with both Paul and the reader initially in the dark. Gradually through a series of clues the reader is enlightened, whereas Paul, dazzled by Margot's beauty and glamorous world, remains blind to all indications that she is engaged in international prostitution. Grimes's explanation that he got a job with her syndicate because he had no problem controlling himself around women should have suggested to Paul the sexual nature of her enterprise. Her incisive manner in questioning prospective employees could have alerted him to the type of women she is dealing with, while her preference for inexperienced girls, who do not even need to know Spanish to work in Latin America, might have aroused more than mild curiosity or puzzlement. Certainly Philbrick's warning that the League of Nations Committee will soon be after Margot, to which Paul ingenuously replies, "I haven't the least idea what you mean" (196), should have raised serious suspicions. But Paul interprets everything according to his erroneous perception that Margot can do no wrong. When sent to Marseilles, where some of the girls are having emigration difficulties, he naively assumes, upon finding them in a red-light district, that Margot is showing her usual concern for the welfare of employees "unwittingly exposed to such perils" (203); and the officials' oblique allusions to the League of Nations and its efforts to stop white slave traffic are totally lost on him. Comprehending neither the girls' situation nor the winks and innuendos of the authorities, he concludes his negotiations with the perfectly innocent remark, which they take to be ironic humor, that the League of Nations seems "to make it harder to get about instead of easier" (207).

The involvement of Arthur Potts in the exposé of Margot's syndicate is another ironic thread running through this section of the novel. Having once been Paul's best friend, he becomes his nemesis. Had Paul been shrewder, he might have attached some significance to Potts's recurring appearances as a League of Nations representative just when Margot is transacting business—at King's Thursday with Grimes, in London with the interviewees, and in Marseilles through Paul's assistance. But not having learned enough about either Margot's profession or Potts's work, Paul sees no relationship and cannot fit the pieces of the puzzle into one another. Indeed it seems unlikely to him that, as Potts apparently thinks, his journey to France could interfere with his forthcoming wedding. Yet it is Potts's evidence at the trial that convicts Paul and does prevent the ceremony from taking place. Paul's expectations of a bright future, indicated by his toast to Fortune as "a much-maligned lady," are shattered by his arrest and prison sentence while the guilty Margot, whom the judge calls "a lady of . . . stainless reputation" (216), goes scot-free.

Much of the irony in Paul's prison experience is satiric, for Waugh attacks avant-garde theories of penology that seem to lack practical value. He appropriately names the first house of correction to which Paul is sent Blackstone Gaol, after one of Britain's most famous legal theoreticians, Sir William Blackstone; and for his prime target he creates the character of Sir Wilfred Lucas-Dockery, a former sociology professor turned prison governor. Sir Wilfred, who dabbles in psychoanalysis for the rehabilitation of prisoners, is one of Waugh's fatuous do-gooders whose theories crumble upon contact with reality and who therefore do more harm than good. Disapproving of Paul's request for continuation of the solitary confinement to which he had happily adjusted, the governor, believing that Paul has become misanthropic as the result of inferiority feelings, devises a complicated scheme "to break down his social inhibitions" (234). In trying to apply another of his favorite ideas—that inmates should continue the professional interests of their former life—Sir Wilfred is completely frustrated because Paul's alleged profession, white slave trafficking, cannot be carried on in prison. Even so, the self-deceived governor assumes that, in addition to bringing about a revolution in sociological statistics, he can improve Paul's self-image by removing prostitutional crime from its customary "sexual" classification and placing it in the less reprehensible "acquisitive" category (226).

One of Sir Wilfred's hypotheses—"that almost all crime is due to the repressed desire for aesthetic expression" (226)—has most unexpected results throughout the prison. There are several attempted suicides in the arts and crafts school because of easy access to sharp tools, and the men in the bookbinding shop eat the library paste because it tastes better than their porridge. Finally there is a murder—of Prendergast, now prison chaplain, who has reappeared as a "Modern Churchman" with no need to "commit himself to any religious belief" (188). That he should be done in by a bloodthirsty religious fanatic who considers him "no Christian" is certainly ironic, though possibly not inappropriate, justice. But that the saw with which the former carpenter cuts off Prendergast's head should have been supplied by prison authorities is the climactic example of Sir Wilfred's theories gone awry. Although the saw may have provided the carpenter a means of self-expression, the result is the opposite of what the governor intended.

While Paul is in prison, his comprehension of both human nature and moral complexity is enhanced to the point that he ceases to be a naif. Since his reflections about Margot during many weeks of solitary confinement lead him to conflicting conclusions, he is forced to step back from his infatuation with her and take a more realistic view. Though sure that by shielding her from prosecution he has done what the code of an English gentleman demands, he also realizes that, despite her gifts of books, flowers, sherry, and exotic food, she has not done right by him. Moreover, he suspects that there is "something radically inapplicable" about the gentlemanly code when the woman he has protected is so obviously guilty and therefore unworthy of his sacrifice (252). But in trying to imagine Margot adapting to prison life—"dressed in prison uniform, hustled down corridors by wardresses, . . . set to work in the laundry washing the other prisoners' clothes" (253)—he is convinced that such circumstances would be inconceivable. Interpreting the troublesome contradiction in terms of "one law for her and another for himself" (253), he is able for the first time to approach a problem ironically, acknowledging that there is no absolute right or wrong in either of the radically disparate perspectives.

Even so, Paul is still not sophisticated enough to perceive the deviousness of Margot's thinking, which she never elucidates. Waugh's superb use of irony, however, makes it possible for the reader to surmise what transpires in her mind without ever requiring the narrator to explain. While one cannot be certain which choice Margot expects Paul to make—being released immediately if she marries Home Secretary Maltravers or waiting until he has served his sentence to marry her himself—Paul's decision to wait is apparently not what she wants. Although the reader is never told why she finally goes to see him in prison, one can deduce that she wishes to conclude their relationship in an amicable fashion. Yet her method is so oblique—she herself admits "how difficult it is to say anything" (263)—that Paul fails to comprehend. The clues to Margot's underlying thoughts are two seemingly unrelated, though juxtaposed, statements—that Lady Circumference has snubbed her and that "poor little Alastair" is falling in love with her (260)—first expressed in her letter to Paul and later reiterated in their prison conversation. But Paul sees no connection between these assertions or any significance beyond their literal meaning, nor can he follow her subsequent reasoning. Since his replies reveal his own very different train of thought, the conversation takes place on two planes that never intersect.

His inquiry about Alastair leads Margot to lament that she is being cut socially by people who no longer regard her as "a respectable woman" (261); but this response then prompts Paul to ask about her "business," to which he would logically attribute society's rejection. Although in answering his direct question Margot asserts that she is selling out because "a Swiss firm" has created difficulties, she insists that the ostracism must be caused by her age. When Paul again fails to grasp the connection she is trying to convey—that high society thinks her too old to be carrying on with young men such as Alastair—she abandons indirection and simply announces her decision to marry Maltravers. Since she never explains why such a marriage would be the best solution to her multifarious problems, all that Paul learns from their meeting is that, to his astonishment, he is pained not by the breaking off of their engagement but by his own failure to care. The reader, on the other hand, is able to conclude, from what is already known about Margot and Maltravers, that Margot needs married respectability and political influence to protect her prostitution syndicate from the law and that Maltravers would also be the sort of husband to ignore her nymphomania if she shared her income with him. Clearly, what is never explicitly stated in the conversation is far more important than what is said. This disparity between thought and spoken word, in combination with the characters' divergent ways of interpreting the same ideas and with the basic discrepancy between pretense and reality, creates an unusually ingenious way of presenting the episode.

But if resignation is the key to Paul's survival, such is not the case with Grimes, whose free spirit cannot bear restraint. His marriage to Flossie, which was expected to save him and his career from homosexual disgrace, has instead landed him, through conviction for bigamy, in a prison from which no inmate has successfully escaped. In a burlesque of adventure-story flights from incarceration, the narrator offers a mock-heroic account of Grimes's disappearance that is bolstered by the author's sketch of Grimes riding a white charger into the heavens and bearing a pennant inscribed "Excelsior." Although circumstantial evidence points to the likelihood that the prisoner perished in the bog, Paul confidently believes that Grimes is immortal—an elemental life force, indeed the sex drive itself. In a parodic imitation of Pater's imaginative criticism of La Gioconda, Paul employs wildly extravagant allusions to convince himself that a man who "had followed in the Bacchic train of distant Arcady, . . . taught the childish satyrs the art of love," and withstood divine wrath "while the Citadels of the Plain fell to ruin about his ears" (269) will follow his usual pattern of turning up alive elsewhere. While Pater's ecstatic eulogy of the Mona Lisa as the embodiment of eternal life and the summation of all human experience is appropriate for da Vinci's masterpiece, Paul's hyperbolic reveries about Grimes as undying sexuality become ludicrous when placed in the same framework. Furthermore, in the light of Paul's belief in the immortality of Grimes, whose fate is never determined, the chaplain's self-reproach for not having prevented Grimes's death adds another ironic twist to the episode entitled "The Passing of a Public-School Man."

Paul's escape from prison is a carefully orchestrated charade of death, about which he knows nothing in advance. A number of inexplicable occurrences lead Paul, as well as the reader, to suspect that he may be headed for execution on the operating table. His scheduled appendectomy seems ridiculous since he no longer has an appendix; he is asked to sign a previously witnessed last will and testament leaving his worldly goods to Margot; the warder who escorts him to the nursing home makes ambiguous winks and sly innuendos about the possibility of death; and the drunken surgeon utters maudlin lamentations. Since Prendergast and Grimes have been finally disposed of in the two preceding episodes, the reader has even more reason to think that the hero will be finished off in the chapter entitled "The Passing of Paul Pennyfeather." But all aspects of the "death," arranged by Home Secretary Maltraves and Alastair Trumpington in the service of Margot, turn out to be fraudulent: the nursing home is run by Dr. Fagan (now M.D. rather than Ph.D.), no operation is performed, and the surgeon signs a fake death certificate. In this manner, some of the very people who contributed to Paul's downfall and imprisonment achieve his liberation; by staging his "death," they give him a new existence.

Imbedded in the account of Paul's demise are numerous ironic comparisons, both parallel and inverse, with his aborted wedding. At the luncheon preceding the nuptial ceremony, he is "the centre of interest of the whole room" (209); but while Fagan, Alastair, and the surgeon deal with the legal documents, "no one [pays] much attention" to him (275). Each occasion results in a dramatic change in Paul's status, but while the first one, about which he has

great expectations, plunges him from fame into disgrace, the second, about which he suffers considerable apprehension, turns his imprisonment into freedom. Fagan's toast to "Fortune, a much-maligned lady," recalls Paul's previous tribute to that fickle goddess just before his arrest. This time Margot assumes the role of Fortune and, instead of bringing bad luck, aids Paul with all her resources, while Alastair, in managing details of the "death" and in accompanying Paul to Margot's waiting yacht, plays a role analogous to his earlier function as best man. In another ironic comparison, Paul's transition into apparent death is cleverly set up as a parallel to Tennyson's account of the passing of Arthur. The farewell on the seashore, in which Sir Alastair is recast as Sir Bedivere watching the dying King Arthur embark for Avalon, places Paul's unromantic escape from imprisonment in the context of hallowed legend. Just as Arthur is spirited away to an island paradise to be healed of his wound and possibly to return, so Paul is carried off to Corfu to be resurrected with a new identity. But the mock-heroic manner of his departure and the inappropriateness of the allusions serve to emphasize the unheroic nature of the old Paul Pennyfeather.

After Paul's legal extinction, it is incongruous that one of the most profound judgments on his past life should be uttered by the pompous fool Silenus. Despite having failed in all his undertakings (including a belated decision to marry Margot), this self-deceived, self-styled "professor" pontificates with characteristic lack of humility on how Paul went wrong. According to his mechanistic theory, life is like a giant carnival wheel surrounded by a seated audience, and humanity is divided into two species—the dynamic, who scramble onto the revolving wheel, and the static, who merely watch. The majority of those on the wheel are repeatedly thrown off by centrifugal force; the successfully hedonistic, like Margot, cling tenaciously to the rapidly moving outer rim for maximum thrills, while those whom Silenus enigmatically labels "the professional men" make their way with determination toward the hub, where it is easier to stay on. In Silenus's opinion, Paul's error was to have climbed onto the wheel at all; his place should logically have been among the spectators. The most obvious error, however, is Silenus's own assessment of himself. Unable to distinguish between the stability of the wheel's fixed center and the immobility of the stationary audience, he thinks he has arrived very near the center when he is most certainly on the sidelines.

However Paul's mistake may be interpreted, he does not repeat it. The subtle montage of the last section, whereby his altered responses are superimposed on recollections of his earlier Oxford existence, shows that Paul has profited from the intervening experiences without becoming radically different. Oxford itself is unchanged: the chaplain and Paul's scout continue to judge his "distant cousin," the "degenerate" Pennyfeather, solely on erroneous hearsay. Paul, again the ordinand but this time heavily mustachioed, gravitates toward a friend who, like Potts, is also interested in the League of Nations Union, penal alleviation, and theology. Yet Paul's attitude toward all this has matured from what it was in his previous incarnation. Though he continues to be concerned with social and religious causes, he has become more cautiously conservative toward life and religion.

That Paul deliberately severs detrimental links to his past is clear. By placing Fagan's book *Mother Wales* beside Stanley's *Eastern Church,* an account of religious schism, he tacitly implies rejection of both. By not responding to the now opulent Philbrick's invitation and by falsely identifying him as Arnold Bennett (in an ironic allusion to another con artist who had parlayed questionable talents into wealth), Paul denigrates that connection as well. In dealing with Peter Pastmaster, now the embodiment of the Bollinger, he concedes his own folly in having become involved with Margot and her "dynamic" breed; but, with the observation that Peter has already drunk too much, he brushes aside the proposal of a toast to "Fortune, a much-maligned lady." Having previously allowed himself to be buffeted by fortune, Paul is determined to wrest control of his own destiny whenever possible. Ironic detachment, even if it means withdrawal from the whirligig of life, can serve as a practical defense against the world's corruption. Experience has taught him something about where to engage and where, in the interest of survival, to disengage himself. True sophistication, he has discovered, depends on knowing which strategy to employ.

Notes

1. Jerome Meckier considers the novel to be an attack on the Bildungsroman. See his "Cycle, Symbol, and Parody in Evelyn Waugh's *Decline and Fall,*" *Contemporary Literature,* 20 (1979): 51–75.

2. Muecke identifies romantic irony primarily with the contradictions of art and relates it to general irony—awareness of the ineluctable contradictions of life. See *Compass of Irony,* 159–215. The breaking and remaking of artistic illusion is especially associated with the German writers Ludwig Tieck and Jean Paul Richter, as well as the English poets Coleridge and Byron.

3. Philosophical discussion about reality versus illusion or appearance, stimulated by the writings of F. H.

Bradley, continued to be in vogue at the time *Decline and Fall* was composed.

4. Waugh, *Decline and Fall* (1928; reprint, Boston: Little, 1977), 164. Subsequent quotations from this edition of the novel are cited parenthetically in the text.

5. W. B. Yeats, "The Second Coming," lines 3–4.

6. Waugh, *Little Learning,* 169, 171.

7. Muecke, *Compass of Irony,* 102.

8. Henri Bergson, *Laughter,* trans. Cloudesley Brereton and Fred Rothwell (New York: Macmillan, 1914), 29. Waugh's *Letters* (3) and *Diaries* (215, 218) establish his reading of Bergson, which he began at Lancing. Stannard (*Evelyn Waugh: Early Years*) and McCartney (*Confused Roaring*) have discussed Bergsonian philosophy in Waugh's writing but have not mentioned the essay *Laughter.*

FURTHER READING

Biography

Hastings, Selina. *Evelyn Waugh.* London: Sinclair-Stevenson, 1994, 723 p.
    Regarded as one of the most reliable and factually accurate biographies about Waugh.

Criticism

McCartney, George. *Confused Roaring: Evelyn Waugh and the Modernist Tradition.* Bloomington: Indiana University Press, 1987. 191 p.
    Consideration of Waugh's interest in modernism, along with discussions about Waugh's novellas and short stories.

Stannard, Martin. *Evelyn Waugh: The Early Years (1903–1939).* New York: Norton, 1986. 330 p.
    Includes discussions of *Decline and Fall* and Waugh's early stories.

How to Use This Index

The main references

list all author entries in the following Gale Literary Criticism series:

BLC = *Black Literature Criticism*
CLC = *Contemporary Literary Criticism*
CLR = *Children's Literature Review*
CMLC = *Classical and Medieval Literature Criticism*
DA = *DISCovering Authors*
DAB = *DISCovering Authors: British*
DAC = *DISCovering Authors: Canadian*
DAM = *DISCovering Authors: Modules*
        DRAM: *Dramatists Module;* **MST:** *Most-Studied Authors Module;*
        MULT: *Multicultural Authors Module;* **NOV:** *Novelists Module;*
        POET: *Poets Module;* **POP:** *Popular Fiction and Genre Authors Module*
DC = *Drama Criticism*
HLC = *Hispanic Literature Criticism*
LC = *Literature Criticism from 1400 to 1800*
NCLC = *Nineteenth-Century Literature Criticism*
NNAL = *Native North American Literature*
PC = *Poetry Criticism*
SSC = *Short Story Criticism*
TCLC = *Twentieth-Century Literary Criticism*
WLC = *World Literature Criticism, 1500 to the Present*

The cross-references

list all author entries in the following Gale biographical and literary sources:

AAYA = *Authors & Artists for Young Adults*
AITN = *Authors in the News*
BEST = *Bestsellers*
BW = *Black Writers*
CA = *Contemporary Authors*
CAAS = *Contemporary Authors Autobiography Series*
CABS = *Contemporary Authors Bibliographical Series*
CANR = *Contemporary Authors New Revision Series*
CAP = *Contemporary Authors Permanent Series*
CDALB = *Concise Dictionary of American Literary Biography*
CDBLB = *Concise Dictionary of British Literary Biography*
DLB = *Dictionary of Literary Biography*
DLBD = *Dictionary of Literary Biography Documentary Series*
DLBY = *Dictionary of Literary Biography Yearbook*
HW = *Hispanic Writers*
JRDA = *Junior DISCovering Authors*
MAICYA = *Major Authors and Illustrators for Children and Young Adults*
MTCW = *Major 20th-Century Writers*
SAAS = *Something about the Author Autobiography Series*
SATA = *Something about the Author*
YABC = *Yesterday's Authors of Books for Children*

Literary Criticism Series
Cumulative Author Index

20/1631
See Upward, Allen

A/C Cross
See Lawrence, T(homas) E(dward)

Abasiyanik, Sait Faik 1906-1954
See Sait Faik
See also CA 123

Abbey, Edward 1927-1989 .... CLC 36, 59
See also CA 45-48; 128; CANR 2, 41; DA3;
MTCW 2

Abbott, Lee K(ittredge) 1947- .... CLC 48
See also CA 124; CANR 51; DLB 130

Abe, Kobo 1924-1993 ...... CLC 8, 22, 53, 81;
DAM NOV
See also CA 65-68; 140; CANR 24, 60;
DLB 182; MTCW 1, 2

Abelard, Peter c. 1079-c. 1142 ...... CMLC 11
See also DLB 115, 208

Abell, Kjeld 1901-1961 .... CLC 15
See also CA 111

Abish, Walter 1931- .... CLC 22
See also CA 101; CANR 37; DLB 130, 227

Abrahams, Peter (Henry) 1919- .... CLC 4
See also BW 1; CA 57-60; CANR 26; DLB
117, 225; MTCW 1, 2

Abrams, M(eyer) H(oward) 1912- ... CLC 24
See also CA 57-60; CANR 13, 33; DLB 67

Abse, Dannie 1923- .... CLC 7, 29; DAB;
DAM POET
See also CA 53-56; CAAS 1; CANR 4, 46,
74; DLB 27; MTCW 1

Achebe, (Albert) Chinua(lumogu)
1930- ...... CLC 1, 3, 5, 7, 11, 26, 51, 75,
127; BLC 1; DA; DAB; DAC; DAM
MST, MULT, NOV; WLC
See also AAYA 15; BW 2, 3; CA 1-4R;
CANR 6, 26, 47; CLR 20; DA3; DLB
117; MAICYA; MTCW 1, 2; SATA 38,
40; SATA-Brief 38

Acker, Kathy 1948-1997 .... CLC 45, 111
See also CA 117; 122; 162; CANR 55

Ackroyd, Peter 1949- .... CLC 34, 52
See also CA 123; 127; CANR 51, 74; DLB
155; INT 127; MTCW 1

Acorn, Milton 1923- .... CLC 15; DAC
See also CA 103; DLB 53; INT 103

Adamov, Arthur 1908-1970 .... CLC 4, 25;
DAM DRAM
See also CA 17-18; 25-28R; CAP 2; MTCW
1

Adams, Alice (Boyd) 1926-1999 .. CLC 6, 13,
46; SSC 24
See also CA 81-84; 179; CANR 26, 53, 75,
88; DLBY 86; INT CANR-26; MTCW 1,
2

Adams, Andy 1859-1935 .... TCLC 56
See also YABC 1

Adams, Brooks 1848-1927 .... TCLC 80
See also CA 123; DLB 47

Adams, Douglas (Noel) 1952- .... CLC 27, 60;
DAM POP
See also AAYA 4, 33; BEST 89:3; CA 106;
CANR 34, 64; DA3; DLBY 83; JRDA;
MTCW 1; SATA 116

Adams, Francis 1862-1893 .... NCLC 33

Adams, Henry (Brooks)
1838-1918 .... TCLC 4, 52; DA; DAB;
DAC; DAM MST
See also CA 104; 133; CANR 77; DLB 12,
47, 189; MTCW 1

Adams, Richard (George) 1920- ... CLC 4, 5,
18; DAM NOV
See also AAYA 16; AITN 1, 2; CA 49-52;
CANR 3, 35; CLR 20; JRDA; MAICYA;
MTCW 1, 2; SATA 7, 69

Adamson, Joy(-Friederike Victoria)
1910-1980 .... CLC 17
See also CA 69-72; 93-96; CANR 22;
MTCW 1; SATA 11; SATA-Obit 22

Adcock, Fleur 1934- .... CLC 41
See also CA 25-28R, 182; CAAE 182;
CAAS 23; CANR 11, 34, 69; DLB 40

Addams, Charles (Samuel)
1912-1988 .... CLC 30
See also CA 61-64; 126; CANR 12, 79

Addams, Jane 1860-1945 .... TCLC 76

Addison, Joseph 1672-1719 .... LC 18
See also CDBLB 1660-1789; DLB 101

Adler, Alfred (F.) 1870-1937 .... TCLC 61
See also CA 119; 159

Adler, C(arole) S(chwerdtfeger)
1932- .... CLC 35
See also AAYA 4; CA 89-92; CANR 19,
40; JRDA; MAICYA; SAAS 15; SATA
26, 63, 102

Adler, Renata 1938- .... CLC 8, 31
See also CA 49-52; CANR 5, 22, 52;
MTCW 1

Ady, Endre 1877-1919 .... TCLC 11
See also CA 107

A.E. 1867-1935 .... TCLC 3, 10
See also Russell, George William

Aeschylus 525B.C.-456B.C. .. CMLC 11; DA;
DAB; DAC; DAM DRAM, MST; DC
8; WLCS
See also DLB 176

Aesop 620(?)B.C.-(?)B.C. .... CMLC 24
See also CLR 14; MAICYA; SATA 64

Affable Hawk
See MacCarthy, Sir(Charles Otto) Desmond

Africa, Ben
See Bosman, Herman Charles

Afton, Effie
See Harper, Frances Ellen Watkins

Agapida, Fray Antonio
See Irving, Washington

Agee, James (Rufus) 1909-1955 ...... TCLC 1,
19; DAM NOV
See also AITN 1; CA 108; 148; CDALB
1941-1968; DLB 2, 26, 152; MTCW 1

Aghill, Gordon
See Silverberg, Robert

Agnon, S(hmuel) Y(osef Halevi)
1888-1970 .... CLC 4, 8, 14; SSC 30
See also CA 17-18; 25-28R; CANR 60;
CAP 2; MTCW 1, 2

Agrippa von Nettesheim, Henry Cornelius
1486-1535 .... LC 27

Aguilera Malta, Demetrio 1909-1981
See also CA 111; 124; CANR 87; DAM
MULT, NOV; DLB 145; HLCS 1; HW 1

Agustini, Delmira 1886-1914
See also CA 166; HLCS 1; HW 1, 2

Aherne, Owen
See Cassill, R(onald) V(erlin)

Ai 1947- .... CLC 4, 14, 69
See also CA 85-88; CAAS 13; CANR 70;
DLB 120

Aickman, Robert (Fordyce)
1914-1981 .... CLC 57
See also CA 5-8R; CANR 3, 72

Aiken, Conrad (Potter) 1889-1973 .... CLC 1,
3, 5, 10, 52; DAM NOV, POET; PC 26;
SSC 9
See also CA 5-8R; 45-48; CANR 4, 60;
CDALB 1929-1941; DLB 9, 45, 102;
MTCW 1, 2; SATA 3, 30

Aiken, Joan (Delano) 1924- .... CLC 35
See also AAYA 1, 25; CA 9-12R, 182;
CAAE 182; CANR 4, 23, 34, 64; CLR 1,
19; DLB 161; JRDA; MAICYA; MTCW
1; SAAS 1; SATA 2, 30, 73; SATA-Essay
109

Ainsworth, William Harrison
1805-1882 .... NCLC 13
See also DLB 21; SATA 24

Aitmatov, Chingiz (Torekulovich)
1928- .... CLC 71
See also CA 103; CANR 38; MTCW 1;
SATA 56

Akers, Floyd
See Baum, L(yman) Frank

Akhmadulina, Bella Akhatovna
1937- .... CLC 53; DAM POET
See also CA 65-68

Akhmatova, Anna 1888-1966 ..... CLC 11, 25,
64, 126; DAM POET; PC 2
See also CA 19-20; 25-28R; CANR 35;
CAP 1; DA3; MTCW 1, 2

Aksakov, Sergei Timofeyvich
1791-1859 .... NCLC 2
See also DLB 198

Aksenov, Vassily
See Aksyonov, Vassily (Pavlovich)

Akst, Daniel 1956- .... **CLC 109**
See also CA 161

Aksyonov, Vassily (Pavlovich)
1932- .... **CLC 22, 37, 101**
See also CA 53-56; CANR 12, 48, 77

Akutagawa, Ryunosuke
1892-1927 .... **TCLC 16**
See also CA 117; 154

Alain 1868-1951 .... **TCLC 41**
See also CA 163

Alain-Fournier .... **TCLC 6**
See also Fournier, Henri Alban
See also DLB 65

Alarcon, Pedro Antonio de
1833-1891 .... **NCLC 1**

Alas (y Urena), Leopoldo (Enrique Garcia)
1852-1901 .... **TCLC 29**
See also CA 113; 131; HW 1

Albee, Edward (Franklin III) 1928- . **CLC 1,
2, 3, 5, 9, 11, 13, 25, 53, 86, 113; DA;
DAB; DAC; DAM DRAM, MST; DC
11; WLC**
See also AITN 1; CA 5-8R; CABS 3;
CANR 8, 54, 74; CDALB 1941-1968;
DA3; DLB 7; INT CANR-8; MTCW 1, 2

Alberti, Rafael 1902-1999 .... **CLC 7**
See also CA 85-88; 185; CANR 81; DLB
108; HW 2

Albert the Great 1200(?)-1280 ...... **CMLC 16**
See also DLB 115

Alcala-Galiano, Juan Valera y
See Valera y Alcala-Galiano, Juan

Alcott, Amos Bronson 1799-1888 .... **NCLC 1**
See also DLB 1, 223

Alcott, Louisa May 1832-1888 . **NCLC 6, 58,
83; DA; DAB; DAC; DAM MST, NOV;
SSC 27; WLC**
See also AAYA 20; CDALB 1865-1917;
CLR 1, 38; DA3; DLB 1, 42, 79, 223;
DLBD 14; JRDA; MAICYA; SATA 100;
YABC 1

Aldanov, M. A.
See Aldanov, Mark (Alexandrovich)

Aldanov, Mark (Alexandrovich)
1886(?)-1957 .... **TCLC 23**
See also CA 118; 181

Aldington, Richard 1892-1962 .... **CLC 49**
See also CA 85-88; CANR 45; DLB 20, 36,
100, 149

Aldiss, Brian W(ilson) 1925- . **CLC 5, 14, 40;
DAM NOV; SSC 36**
See also CA 5-8R; CAAS 2; CANR 5, 28,
64; DLB 14; MTCW 1, 2; SATA 34

Alegria, Claribel 1924- .... **CLC 75; DAM
MULT; HLCS 1; PC 26**
See also CA 131; CAAS 15; CANR 66;
DLB 145; HW 1; MTCW 1

Alegria, Fernando 1918- .... **CLC 57**
See also CA 9-12R; CANR 5, 32, 72; HW
1, 2

Aleichem, Sholom .... **TCLC 1, 35; SSC 33**
See also Rabinovitch, Sholem

Aleixandre, Vicente 1898-1984
See also CANR 81; HLCS 1; HW 2

Alepoudelis, Odysseus
See Elytis, Odysseus

Aleshkovsky, Joseph 1929-
See Aleshkovsky, Yuz
See also CA 121; 128

Aleshkovsky, Yuz .... **CLC 44**
See also Aleshkovsky, Joseph

Alexander, Lloyd (Chudley) 1924- ... **CLC 35**
See also AAYA 1, 27; CA 1-4R; CANR 1,
24, 38, 55; CLR 1, 5, 48; DLB 52; JRDA;
MAICYA; MTCW 1; SAAS 19; SATA 3,
49, 81

Alexander, Meena 1951- .... **CLC 121**
See also CA 115; CANR 38, 70

Alexander, Samuel 1859-1938 .... **TCLC 77**

Alexie, Sherman (Joseph, Jr.)
1966- .... **CLC 96; DAM MULT**
See also AAYA 28; CA 138; CANR 65;
DA3; DLB 175, 206; MTCW 1; NNAL

Alfau, Felipe 1902- .... **CLC 66**
See also CA 137

Alfred, Jean Gaston
See Ponge, Francis

Alger, Horatio Jr., Jr. 1832-1899 .... **NCLC 8,
83**
See also DLB 42; SATA 16

Algren, Nelson 1909-1981 ..... **CLC 4, 10, 33;
SSC 33**
See also CA 13-16R; 103; CANR 20, 61;
CDALB 1941-1968; DLB 9; DLBY 81,
82; MTCW 1, 2

Ali, Ahmed 1910- .... **CLC 69**
See also CA 25-28R; CANR 15, 34

Alighieri, Dante
See Dante

Allan, John B.
See Westlake, Donald E(dwin)

Allan, Sidney
See Hartmann, Sadakichi

Allan, Sydney
See Hartmann, Sadakichi

Allen, Edward 1948- .... **CLC 59**

Allen, Fred 1894-1956 .... **TCLC 87**

Allen, Paula Gunn 1939- .... **CLC 84; DAM
MULT**
See also CA 112; 143; CANR 63; DA3;
DLB 175; MTCW 1; NNAL

Allen, Roland
See Ayckbourn, Alan

Allen, Sarah A.
See Hopkins, Pauline Elizabeth

Allen, Sidney H.
See Hartmann, Sadakichi

Allen, Woody 1935- .... **CLC 16, 52; DAM
POP**
See also AAYA 10; CA 33-36R; CANR 27,
38, 63; DLB 44; MTCW 1

Allende, Isabel 1942- . **CLC 39, 57, 97; DAM
MULT, NOV; HLC 1; WLCS**
See also AAYA 18; CA 125; 130; CANR
51, 74; DA3; DLB 145; HW 1, 2; INT
130; MTCW 1, 2

Alleyn, Ellen
See Rossetti, Christina (Georgina)

Allingham, Margery (Louise)
1904-1966 .... **CLC 19**
See also CA 5-8R; 25-28R; CANR 4, 58;
DLB 77; MTCW 1, 2

Allingham, William 1824-1889 ...... **NCLC 25**
See also DLB 35

Allison, Dorothy E. 1949- .... **CLC 78**
See also CA 140; CANR 66; DA3; MTCW
1

Allston, Washington 1779-1843 .... **NCLC 2**
See also DLB 1

Almedingen, E. M. .... **CLC 12**
See also Almedingen, Martha Edith von
See also SATA 3

Almedingen, Martha Edith von 1898-1971
See Almedingen, E. M.
See also CA 1-4R; CANR 1

Almodovar, Pedro 1949(?)- .... **CLC 114;
HLCS 1**
See also CA 133; CANR 72; HW 2

Almqvist, Carl Jonas Love
1793-1866 .... **NCLC 42**

Alonso, Damaso 1898-1990 .... **CLC 14**
See also CA 110; 131; 130; CANR 72; DLB
108; HW 1, 2

Alov
See Gogol, Nikolai (Vasilyevich)

Alta 1942- .... **CLC 19**
See also CA 57-60

Alter, Robert B(ernard) 1935- .... **CLC 34**
See also CA 49-52; CANR 1, 47

Alther, Lisa 1944- .... **CLC 7, 41**
See also CA 65-68; CAAS 30; CANR 12,
30, 51; MTCW 1

Althusser, L.
See Althusser, Louis

Althusser, Louis 1918-1990 .... **CLC 106**
See also CA 131; 132

Altman, Robert 1925- .... **CLC 16, 116**
See also CA 73-76; CANR 43

Alurista 1949-
See Urista, Alberto H.
See also DLB 82; HLCS 1

Alvarez, A(lfred) 1929- .... **CLC 5, 13**
See also CA 1-4R; CANR 3, 33, 63; DLB
14, 40

Alvarez, Alejandro Rodriguez 1903-1965
See Casona, Alejandro
See also CA 131; 93-96; HW 1

Alvarez, Julia 1950- .... **CLC 93; HLCS 1**
See also AAYA 25; CA 147; CANR 69;
DA3; MTCW 1

Alvaro, Corrado 1896-1956 .... **TCLC 60**
See also CA 163

Amado, Jorge 1912- .... **CLC 13, 40, 106;
DAM MULT, NOV; HLC 1**
See also CA 77-80; CANR 35, 74; DLB
113; HW 2; MTCW 1, 2

Ambler, Eric 1909-1998 .... **CLC 4, 6, 9**
See also CA 9-12R; 171; CANR 7, 38, 74;
DLB 77; MTCW 1, 2

Amichai, Yehuda 1924- ... **CLC 9, 22, 57, 116**
See also CA 85-88; CANR 46, 60; MTCW
1

Amichai, Yehudah
See Amichai, Yehuda

Amiel, Henri Frederic 1821-1881 .... **NCLC 4**

Amis, Kingsley (William)
1922-1995 ...... **CLC 1, 2, 3, 5, 8, 13, 40,
44, 129; DA; DAB; DAC; DAM MST,
NOV**
See also AITN 2; CA 9-12R; 150; CANR 8,
28, 54; CDBLB 1945-1960; DA3; DLB
15, 27, 100, 139; DLBY 96; INT
CANR-8; MTCW 1, 2

Amis, Martin (Louis) 1949- .... **CLC 4, 9, 38,
62, 101**
See also BEST 90:3; CA 65-68; CANR 8,
27, 54, 73; DA3; DLB 14, 194; INT
CANR-27; MTCW 1

Ammons, A(rchie) R(andolph)
1926- ...... **CLC 2, 3, 5, 8, 9, 25, 57, 108;
DAM POET; PC 16**
See also AITN 1; CA 9-12R; CANR 6, 36,
51, 73; DLB 5, 165; MTCW 1, 2

Amo, Tauraatua i
See Adams, Henry (Brooks)

Amory, Thomas 1691(?)-1788 .... **LC 48**

Anand, Mulk Raj 1905- .. **CLC 23, 93; DAM
NOV**
See also CA 65-68; CANR 32, 64; MTCW
1, 2

Anatol
See Schnitzler, Arthur

Anaximander c. 610B.C.-c.
546B.C. .... **CMLC 22**

Anaya, Rudolfo A(lfonso) 1937- ...... **CLC 23;
DAM MULT, NOV; HLC 1**
See also AAYA 20; CA 45-48; CAAS 4;
CANR 1, 32, 51; DLB 82, 206; HW 1;
MTCW 1, 2

Andersen, Hans Christian
1805-1875 .... **NCLC 7, 79; DA; DAB; DAC; DAM MST, POP; SSC 6; WLC**
See also CLR 6; DA3; MAICYA; SATA 100; YABC 1

Anderson, C. Farley
See Mencken, H(enry) L(ouis); Nathan, George Jean

Anderson, Jessica (Margaret) Queale
1916- .... **CLC 37**
See also CA 9-12R; CANR 4, 62

Anderson, Jon (Victor) 1940- . **CLC 9; DAM POET**
See also CA 25-28R; CANR 20

Anderson, Lindsay (Gordon)
1923-1994 .... **CLC 20**
See also CA 125; 128; 146; CANR 77

Anderson, Maxwell 1888-1959 .... **TCLC 2; DAM DRAM**
See also CA 105; 152; DLB 7, 228; MTCW 2

Anderson, Poul (William) 1926- .... **CLC 15**
See also AAYA 5, 34; CA 1-4R, 181; CAAE 181; CAAS 2; CANR 2, 15, 34, 64; CLR 58; DLB 8; INT CANR-15; MTCW 1, 2; SATA 90; SATA-Brief 39; SATA-Essay 106

Anderson, Robert (Woodruff)
1917- .... **CLC 23; DAM DRAM**
See also AITN 1; CA 21-24R; CANR 32; DLB 7

Anderson, Sherwood 1876-1941 ..... **TCLC 1, 10, 24; DA; DAB; DAC; DAM MST, NOV; SSC 1; WLC**
See also AAYA 30; CA 104; 121; CANR 61; CDALB 1917-1929; DA3; DLB 4, 9, 86; DLBD 1; MTCW 1, 2

Andier, Pierre
See Desnos, Robert

Andouard
See Giraudoux, (Hippolyte) Jean

Andrade, Carlos Drummond de CLC 18
See also Drummond de Andrade, Carlos

Andrade, Mario de 1893-1945 .... **TCLC 43**

Andreae, Johann V(alentin)
1586-1654 .... **LC 32**
See also DLB 164

Andreas-Salome, Lou 1861-1937 ... **TCLC 56**
See also CA 178; DLB 66

Andress, Lesley
See Sanders, Lawrence

Andrewes, Lancelot 1555-1626 .... **LC 5**
See also DLB 151, 172

Andrews, Cicily Fairfield
See West, Rebecca

Andrews, Elton V.
See Pohl, Frederik

Andreyev, Leonid (Nikolaevich)
1871-1919 .... **TCLC 3**
See also CA 104; 185

Andric, Ivo 1892-1975 .... **CLC 8; SSC 36**
See also CA 81-84; 57-60; CANR 43, 60; DLB 147; MTCW 1

Androvar
See Prado (Calvo), Pedro

Angelique, Pierre
See Bataille, Georges

Angell, Roger 1920- .... **CLC 26**
See also CA 57-60; CANR 13, 44, 70; DLB 171, 185

Angelou, Maya 1928- .... **CLC 12, 35, 64, 77; BLC 1; DA; DAB; DAC; DAM MST, MULT, POET, POP; WLCS**
See also AAYA 7, 20; BW 2, 3; CA 65-68; CANR 19, 42, 65; CDALBS; CLR 53; DA3; DLB 38; MTCW 1, 2; SATA 49

Anna Comnena 1083-1153 .... **CMLC 25**

Annensky, Innokenty (Fyodorovich)
1856-1909 .... **TCLC 14**
See also CA 110; 155

Annunzio, Gabriele d'
See D'Annunzio, Gabriele

Anodos
See Coleridge, Mary E(lizabeth)

Anon, Charles Robert
See Pessoa, Fernando (Antonio Nogueira)

Anouilh, Jean (Marie Lucien Pierre)
1910-1987 .... **CLC 1, 3, 8, 13, 40, 50; DAM DRAM; DC 8**
See also CA 17-20R; 123; CANR 32; MTCW 1, 2

Anthony, Florence
See Ai

Anthony, John
See Ciardi, John (Anthony)

Anthony, Peter
See Shaffer, Anthony (Joshua); Shaffer, Peter (Levin)

Anthony, Piers 1934- .... **CLC 35; DAM POP**
See also AAYA 11; CA 21-24R; CANR 28, 56, 73; DLB 8; MTCW 1, 2; SAAS 22; SATA 84

Anthony, Susan B(rownell)
1916-1991 .... **TCLC 84**
See also CA 89-92; 134

Antoine, Marc
See Proust, (Valentin-Louis-George-Eugene-) Marcel

Antoninus, Brother
See Everson, William (Oliver)

Antonioni, Michelangelo 1912- .... **CLC 20**
See also CA 73-76; CANR 45, 77

Antschel, Paul 1920-1970
See Celan, Paul
See also CA 85-88; CANR 33, 61; MTCW 1

Anwar, Chairil 1922-1949 .... **TCLC 22**
See also CA 121

Anzaldua, Gloria 1942-
See also CA 175; DLB 122; HLCS 1

Apess, William 1798-1839(?) .... **NCLC 73; DAM MULT**
See also DLB 175; NNAL

Apollinaire, Guillaume 1880-1918 .. **TCLC 3, 8, 51; DAM POET; PC 7**
See also Kostrowitzki, Wilhelm Apollinaris de
See also CA 152; MTCW 1

Appelfeld, Aharon 1932- .... **CLC 23, 47**
See also CA 112; 133; CANR 86

Apple, Max (Isaac) 1941- .... **CLC 9, 33**
See also CA 81-84; CANR 19, 54; DLB 130

Appleman, Philip (Dean) 1926- .... **CLC 51**
See also CA 13-16R; CAAS 18; CANR 6, 29, 56

Appleton, Lawrence
See Lovecraft, H(oward) P(hillips)

Apteryx
See Eliot, T(homas) S(tearns)

Apuleius, (Lucius Madaurensis)
125(?)-175(?) .... **CMLC 1**
See also DLB 211

Aquin, Hubert 1929-1977 .... **CLC 15**
See also CA 105; DLB 53

Aquinas, Thomas 1224(?)-1274 ..... **CMLC 33**
See also DLB 115

Aragon, Louis 1897-1982 .. **CLC 3, 22; DAM NOV, POET**
See also CA 69-72; 108; CANR 28, 71; DLB 72; MTCW 1, 2

Arany, Janos 1817-1882 .... **NCLC 34**

Aranyos, Kakay
See Mikszath, Kalman

Arbuthnot, John 1667-1735 .... **LC 1**
See also DLB 101

Archer, Herbert Winslow
See Mencken, H(enry) L(ouis)

Archer, Jeffrey (Howard) 1940- ...... **CLC 28; DAM POP**
See also AAYA 16; BEST 89:3; CA 77-80; CANR 22, 52; DA3; INT CANR-22

Archer, Jules 1915- .... **CLC 12**
See also CA 9-12R; CANR 6, 69; SAAS 5; SATA 4, 85

Archer, Lee
See Ellison, Harlan (Jay)

Arden, John 1930- .... **CLC 6, 13, 15; DAM DRAM**
See also CA 13-16R; CAAS 4; CANR 31, 65, 67; DLB 13; MTCW 1

Arenas, Reinaldo 1943-1990 . **CLC 41; DAM MULT; HLC 1**
See also CA 124; 128; 133; CANR 73; DLB 145; HW 1; MTCW 1

Arendt, Hannah 1906-1975 .... **CLC 66, 98**
See also CA 17-20R; 61-64; CANR 26, 60; MTCW 1, 2

Aretino, Pietro 1492-1556 .... **LC 12**

Arghezi, Tudor 1880-1967 .... **CLC 80**
See also Theodorescu, Ion N.
See also CA 167

Arguedas, Jose Maria 1911-1969 .... **CLC 10, 18; HLCS 1**
See also CA 89-92; CANR 73; DLB 113; HW 1

Argueta, Manlio 1936- .... **CLC 31**
See also CA 131; CANR 73; DLB 145; HW 1

Arias, Ron(ald Francis) 1941-
See also CA 131; CANR 81; DAM MULT; DLB 82; HLC 1; HW 1, 2; MTCW 2

Ariosto, Ludovico 1474-1533 .... **LC 6**

Aristides
See Epstein, Joseph

Aristophanes 450B.C.-385B.C. .... **CMLC 4; DA; DAB; DAC; DAM DRAM, MST; DC 2; WLCS**
See also DA3; DLB 176

Aristotle 384B.C.-322B.C. .... **CMLC 31; DA; DAB; DAC; DAM MST; WLCS**
See also DA3; DLB 176

Arlt, Roberto (Godofredo Christophersen)
1900-1942 .... **TCLC 29; DAM MULT; HLC 1**
See also CA 123; 131; CANR 67; HW 1, 2

Armah, Ayi Kwei 1939- . **CLC 5, 33; BLC 1; DAM MULT, POET**
See also BW 1; CA 61-64; CANR 21, 64; DLB 117; MTCW 1

Armatrading, Joan 1950- .... **CLC 17**
See also CA 114; 186

Arnette, Robert
See Silverberg, Robert

Arnim, Achim von (Ludwig Joachim von Arnim) 1781-1831 ..... **NCLC 5; SSC 29**
See also DLB 90

Arnim, Bettina von 1785-1859 .... **NCLC 38**
See also DLB 90

Arnold, Matthew 1822-1888 ..... **NCLC 6, 29, 89; DA; DAB; DAC; DAM MST, POET; PC 5; WLC**
See also CDBLB 1832-1890; DLB 32, 57

Arnold, Thomas 1795-1842 .... **NCLC 18**
See also DLB 55

Arnow, Harriette (Louisa) Simpson
1908-1986 .... **CLC 2, 7, 18**
See also CA 9-12R; 118; CANR 14; DLB 6; MTCW 1, 2; SATA 42; SATA-Obit 47

Arouet, Francois-Marie
See Voltaire

Arp, Hans
See Arp, Jean

Arp, Jean 1887-1966 .... **CLC 5**
   See also CA 81-84; 25-28R; CANR 42, 77
Arrabal
   See Arrabal, Fernando
Arrabal, Fernando 1932- ... **CLC 2, 9, 18, 58**
   See also CA 9-12R; CANR 15
Arreola, Juan Jose 1918- .... **SSC 38; DAM**
   MULT; HLC 1
   See also CA 113; 131; CANR 81; DLB 113;
   HW 1, 2
Arrick, Fran CLC 30
   See also Gaberman, Judie Angell
Artaud, Antonin (Marie Joseph)
   1896-1948 .. **TCLC 3, 36; DAM DRAM**
   See also CA 104; 149; DA3; MTCW 1
Arthur, Ruth M(abel) 1905-1979 ..... **CLC 12**
   See also CA 9-12R; 85-88; CANR 4; SATA
   7, 26
Artsybashev, Mikhail (Petrovich)
   1878-1927 .... **TCLC 31**
   See also CA 170
Arundel, Honor (Morfydd)
   1919-1973 .... **CLC 17**
   See also CA 21-22; 41-44R; CAP 2; CLR
   35; SATA 4; SATA-Obit 24
Arzner, Dorothy 1897-1979 .... **CLC 98**
Asch, Sholem 1880-1957 .... **TCLC 3**
   See also CA 105
Ash, Shalom
   See Asch, Sholem
Ashbery, John (Lawrence) 1927- .. **CLC 2, 3,**
   4, 6, 9, 13, 15, 25, 41, 77, 125; DAM
   POET; PC 26
   See also CA 5-8R; CANR 9, 37, 66; DA3;
   DLB 5, 165; DLBY 81; INT CANR-9;
   MTCW 1, 2
Ashdown, Clifford
   See Freeman, R(ichard) Austin
Ashe, Gordon
   See Creasey, John
Ashton-Warner, Sylvia (Constance)
   1908-1984 .... **CLC 19**
   See also CA 69-72; 112; CANR 29; MTCW
   1, 2
Asimov, Isaac 1920-1992 ..... **CLC 1, 3, 9, 19,**
   26, 76, 92; DAM POP
   See also AAYA 13; BEST 90:2; CA 1-4R;
   137; CANR 2, 19, 36, 60; CLR 12; DA3;
   DLB 8; DLBY 92; INT CANR-19; JRDA;
   MAICYA; MTCW 1, 2; SATA 1, 26, 74
Assis, Joaquim Maria Machado de
   See Machado de Assis, Joaquim Maria
Astley, Thea (Beatrice May) 1925- .. **CLC 41**
   See also CA 65-68; CANR 11, 43, 78
Aston, James
   See White, T(erence) H(anbury)
Asturias, Miguel Angel 1899-1974 .... **CLC 3,**
   8, 13; DAM MULT, NOV; HLC 1
   See also CA 25-28; 49-52; CANR 32; CAP
   2; DA3; DLB 113; HW 1; MTCW 1, 2
Atares, Carlos Saura
   See Saura (Atares), Carlos
Atheling, William
   See Pound, Ezra (Weston Loomis)
Atheling, William, Jr.
   See Blish, James (Benjamin)
Atherton, Gertrude (Franklin Horn)
   1857-1948 .... **TCLC 2**
   See also CA 104; 155; DLB 9, 78, 186
Atherton, Lucius
   See Masters, Edgar Lee
Atkins, Jack
   See Harris, Mark
Atkinson, Kate CLC 99
   See also CA 166

Attaway, William (Alexander)
   1911-1986 .... **CLC 92; BLC 1; DAM**
   MULT
   See also BW 2, 3; CA 143; CANR 82; DLB
   76
Atticus
   See Fleming, Ian (Lancaster); Wilson,
   (Thomas) Woodrow
Atwood, Margaret (Eleanor) 1939- ... **CLC 2,**
   3, 4, 8, 13, 15, 25, 44, 84; DA; DAB;
   DAC; DAM MST, NOV, POET; PC 8;
   SSC 2; WLC
   See also AAYA 12; BEST 89:2; CA 49-52;
   CANR 3, 24, 33, 59; DA3; DLB 53; INT
   CANR-24; MTCW 1, 2; SATA 50
Aubigny, Pierre d'
   See Mencken, H(enry) L(ouis)
Aubin, Penelope 1685-1731(?) .... **LC 9**
   See also DLB 39
Auchincloss, Louis (Stanton) 1917- .. **CLC 4,**
   6, 9, 18, 45; DAM NOV; SSC 22
   See also CA 1-4R; CANR 6, 29, 55, 87;
   DLB 2; DLBY 80; INT CANR-29;
   MTCW 1
Auden, W(ystan) H(ugh) 1907-1973 . **CLC 1,**
   2, 3, 4, 6, 9, 11, 14, 43; DA; DAB;
   DAC; DAM DRAM, MST, POET; PC
   1; WLC
   See also AAYA 18; CA 9-12R; 45-48;
   CANR 5, 61; CDBLB 1914-1945; DA3;
   DLB 10, 20; MTCW 1, 2
Audiberti, Jacques 1900-1965 .... **CLC 38;**
   DAM DRAM
   See also CA 25-28R
Audubon, John James 1785-1851 . **NCLC 47**
Auel, Jean M(arie) 1936- .... **CLC 31, 107;**
   DAM POP
   See also AAYA 7; BEST 90:4; CA 103;
   CANR 21, 64; DA3; INT CANR-21;
   SATA 91
Auerbach, Erich 1892-1957 .... **TCLC 43**
   See also CA 118; 155
Augier, Emile 1820-1889 .... **NCLC 31**
   See also DLB 192
August, John
   See De Voto, Bernard (Augustine)
Augustine 354-430 .... **CMLC 6; DA; DAB;**
   DAC; DAM MST; WLCS
   See also DA3; DLB 115
Aurelius
   See Bourne, Randolph S(illiman)
Aurobindo, Sri
   See Ghose, Aurabinda
Austen, Jane 1775-1817 ...... **NCLC 1, 13, 19,**
   33, 51, 81; DA; DAB; DAC; DAM
   MST, NOV; WLC
   See also AAYA 19; CDBLB 1789-1832;
   DA3; DLB 116
Auster, Paul 1947- .... **CLC 47, 131**
   See also CA 69-72; CANR 23, 52, 75; DA3;
   DLB 227; MTCW 1
Austin, Frank
   See Faust, Frederick (Schiller)
Austin, Mary (Hunter) 1868-1934 . **TCLC 25**
   See also CA 109; 178; DLB 9, 78, 206, 221
Averroes 1126-1198 .... **CMLC 7**
   See also DLB 115
Avicenna 980-1037 .... **CMLC 16**
   See also DLB 115
Avison, Margaret 1918- .... **CLC 2, 4, 97;**
   DAC; DAM POET
   See also CA 17-20R; DLB 53; MTCW 1
Axton, David
   See Koontz, Dean R(ay)
Ayckbourn, Alan 1939- ...... **CLC 5, 8, 18, 33,**
   74; DAB; DAM DRAM; DC 13
   See also CA 21-24R; CANR 31, 59; DLB
   13; MTCW 1, 2

Aydy, Catherine
   See Tennant, Emma (Christina)
Ayme, Marcel (Andre) 1902-1967 ... **CLC 11;**
   SSC 41
   See also CA 89-92; CANR 67; CLR 25;
   DLB 72; SATA 91
Ayrton, Michael 1921-1975 .... **CLC 7**
   See also CA 5-8R; 61-64; CANR 9, 21
Azorin CLC 11
   See also Martinez Ruiz, Jose
Azuela, Mariano 1873-1952 . **TCLC 3; DAM**
   MULT; HLC 1
   See also CA 104; 131; CANR 81; HW 1, 2;
   MTCW 1, 2
Baastad, Babbis Friis
   See Friis-Baastad, Babbis Ellinor
Bab
   See Gilbert, W(illiam) S(chwenck)
Babbis, Eleanor
   See Friis-Baastad, Babbis Ellinor
Babel, Isaac
   See Babel, Isaak (Emmanuilovich)
Babel, Isaak (Emmanuilovich)
   1894-1941(?) .... **TCLC 2, 13; SSC 16**
   See also CA 104; 155; MTCW 1
Babits, Mihaly 1883-1941 .... **TCLC 14**
   See also CA 114
Babur 1483-1530 .... **LC 18**
Baca, Jimmy Santiago 1952-
   See also CA 131; CANR 81, 90; DAM
   MULT; DLB 122; HLC 1; HW 1, 2
Bacchelli, Riccardo 1891-1985 .... **CLC 19**
   See also CA 29-32R; 117
Bach, Richard (David) 1936- .... **CLC 14;**
   DAM NOV, POP
   See also AITN 1; BEST 89:2; CA 9-12R;
   CANR 18; MTCW 1; SATA 13
Bachman, Richard
   See King, Stephen (Edwin)
Bachmann, Ingeborg 1926-1973 .... **CLC 69**
   See also CA 93-96; 45-48; CANR 69; DLB
   85
Bacon, Francis 1561-1626 .... **LC 18, 32**
   See also CDBLB Before 1660; DLB 151
Bacon, Roger 1214(?)-1292 .... **CMLC 14**
   See also DLB 115
Bacovia, George TCLC 24
   See also Vasiliu, Gheorghe
   See also DLB 220
Badanes, Jerome 1937- .... **CLC 59**
Bagehot, Walter 1826-1877 .... **NCLC 10**
   See also DLB 55
Bagnold, Enid 1889-1981 ...... **CLC 25; DAM**
   DRAM
   See also CA 5-8R; 103; CANR 5, 40; DLB
   13, 160, 191; MAICYA; SATA 1, 25
Bagritsky, Eduard 1895-1934 .... **TCLC 60**
Bagrjana, Elisaveta
   See Belcheva, Elisaveta
Bagryana, Elisaveta 1893-1991 .... **CLC 10**
   See also Belcheva, Elisaveta
   See also CA 178; DLB 147
Bailey, Paul 1937- .... **CLC 45**
   See also CA 21-24R; CANR 16, 62; DLB
   14
Baillie, Joanna 1762-1851 .... **NCLC 71**
   See also DLB 93
Bainbridge, Beryl (Margaret) 1934- . **CLC 4,**
   5, 8, 10, 14, 18, 22, 62, 130; DAM NOV
   See also CA 21-24R; CANR 24, 55, 75, 88;
   DLB 14; MTCW 1, 2
Baker, Elliott 1922- .... **CLC 8**
   See also CA 45-48; CANR 2, 63
Baker, Jean H. TCLC 3, 10
   See also Russell, George William

Baker, Nicholson 1957- .... CLC 61; DAM POP
    See also CA 135; CANR 63; DA3; DLB 227
Baker, Ray Stannard 1870-1946 .... TCLC 47
    See also CA 118
Baker, Russell (Wayne) 1925- .... CLC 31
    See also BEST 89:4; CA 57-60; CANR 11, 41, 59; MTCW 1, 2
Bakhtin, M.
    See Bakhtin, Mikhail Mikhailovich
Bakhtin, M. M.
    See Bakhtin, Mikhail Mikhailovich
Bakhtin, Mikhail
    See Bakhtin, Mikhail Mikhailovich
Bakhtin, Mikhail Mikhailovich
    1895-1975 .... CLC 83
    See also CA 128; 113
Bakshi, Ralph 1938(?)- .... CLC 26
    See also CA 112; 138
Bakunin, Mikhail (Alexandrovich)
    1814-1876 .... NCLC 25, 58
Baldwin, James (Arthur) 1924-1987 . CLC 1, 2, 3, 4, 5, 8, 13, 15, 17, 42, 50, 67, 90, 127; BLC 1; DA; DAB; DAC; DAM MST, MULT, NOV, POP; DC 1; SSC 10, 33; WLC
    See also AAYA 4, 34; BW 1; CA 1-4R; 124; CABS 1; CANR 3, 24; CDALB 1941-1968; DA3; DLB 2, 7, 33; DLBY 87; MTCW 1, 2; SATA 9; SATA Obit 54
Ballard, J(ames) G(raham) 1930- . CLC 3, 6, 14, 36; DAM NOV, POP; SSC 1
    See also AAYA 3; CA 5-8R; CANR 15, 39, 65; DA3; DLB 14, 207; MTCW 1, 2; SATA 93
Balmont, Konstantin (Dmitriyevich)
    1867-1943 .... TCLC 11
    See also CA 109; 155
Baltausis, Vincas
    See Mikszath, Kalman
Balzac, Honore de 1799-1850 ... NCLC 5, 35, 53; DA; DAB; DAC; DAM MST, NOV; SSC 5; WLC
    See also DA3; DLB 119
Bambara, Toni Cade 1939-1995 ...... CLC 19, 88; BLC 1; DA; DAC; DAM MST, MULT; SSC 35; WLCS
    See also AAYA 5; BW 2, 3; CA 29-32R; 150; CANR 24, 49, 81; CDALBS; DA3; DLB 38; MTCW 1, 2; SATA 112
Bamdad, A.
    See Shamlu, Ahmad
Banat, D. R.
    See Bradbury, Ray (Douglas)
Bancroft, Laura
    See Baum, L(yman) Frank
Banim, John 1798-1842 .... NCLC 13
    See also DLB 116, 158, 159
Banim, Michael 1796-1874 .... NCLC 13
    See also DLB 158, 159
Banjo, The
    See Paterson, A(ndrew) B(arton)
Banks, Iain
    See Banks, Iain M(enzies)
Banks, Iain M(enzies) 1954- .... CLC 34
    See also CA 123; 128; CANR 61; DLB 194; INT 128
Banks, Lynne·Reid CLC 23
    See also Reid Banks, Lynne
    See also AAYA 6
Banks, Russell 1940- .... CLC 37, 72
    See also CA 65-68; CAAS 15; CANR 19, 52, 73; DLB 130
Banville, John 1945- .... CLC 46, 118
    See also CA 117; 128; DLB 14; INT 128

Banville, Theodore (Faullain) de
    1832-1891 .... NCLC 9
Baraka, Amiri 1934- . CLC 1, 2, 3, 5, 10, 14, 33, 115; BLC 1; DA; DAC; DAM MST, MULT, POET, POP; DC 6; PC 4; WLCS
    See also Jones, LeRoi
    See also BW 2, 3; CA 21-24R; CABS 3; CANR 27, 38, 61; CDALB 1941-1968; DA3; DLB 5, 7, 16, 38; DLBD 8; MTCW 1, 2
Barbauld, Anna Laetitia
    1743-1825 .... NCLC 50
    See also DLB 107, 109, 142, 158
Barbellion, W. N. P. TCLC 24
    See also Cummings, Bruce F(rederick)
Barbera, Jack (Vincent) 1945- .... CLC 44
    See also CA 110; CANR 45
Barbey d'Aurevilly, Jules Amedee
    1808-1889 .... NCLC 1; SSC 17
    See also DLB 119
Barbour, John c. 1316-1395 .... CMLC 33
    See also DLB 146
Barbusse, Henri 1873-1935 ... TCLC 5
    See also CA 105; 154; DLB 65
Barclay, Bill
    See Moorcock, Michael (John)
Barclay, William Ewert
    See Moorcock, Michael (John)
Barea, Arturo 1897-1957 .... TCLC 14
    See also CA 111
Barfoot, Joan 1946- .... CLC 18
    See also CA 105
Barham, Richard Harris
    1788-1845 .... NCLC 77
    See also DLB 159
Baring, Maurice 1874-1945 .... TCLC 8
    See also CA 105; 168; DLB 34
Baring-Gould, Sabine 1834-1924 ... TCLC 88
    See also DLB 156, 190
Barker, Clive 1952- ...... CLC 52; DAM POP
    See also AAYA 10; BEST 90:3; CA 121; 129; CANR 71; DA3; INT 129; MTCW 1, 2
Barker, George Granville
    1913-1991 .... CLC 8, 48; DAM POET
    See also CA 9-12R; 135; CANR 7, 38; DLB 20; MTCW 1
Barker, Harley Granville
    See Granville-Barker, Harley
    See also DLB 10
Barker, Howard 1946- .... CLC 37
    See also CA 102; DLB 13
Barker, Jane 1652-1732 .... LC 42
Barker, Pat(ricia) 1943- .... CLC 32, 94
    See also CA 117; 122; CANR 50; INT 122
Barlach, Ernst (Heinrich)
    1870-1938 .... TCLC 84
    See also CA 178; DLB 56, 118
Barlow, Joel 1754-1812 .... NCLC 23
    See also DLB 37
Barnard, Mary (Ethel) 1909- .... CLC 48
    See also CA 21-22; CAP 2
Barnes, Djuna 1892-1982 .... CLC 3, 4, 8, 11, 29, 127; SSC 3
    See also CA 9-12R; 107; CANR 16, 55; DLB 4, 9, 45; MTCW 1, 2
Barnes, Julian (Patrick) 1946- .... CLC 42; DAB
    See also CA 102; CANR 19, 54; DLB 194; DLBY 93; MTCW 1
Barnes, Peter 1931- .... CLC 5, 56
    See also CA 65-68; CAAS 12; CANR 33, 34, 64; DLB 13; MTCW 1
Barnes, William 1801-1886 .... NCLC 75
    See also DLB 32
Baroja (y Nessi), Pio 1872-1956 ..... TCLC 8; HLC 1
    See also CA 104

Baron, David
    See Pinter, Harold
Baron Corvo
    See Rolfe, Frederick (William Serafino Austin Lewis Mary)
Barondess, Sue K(aufman)
    1926-1977 .... CLC 8
    See also Kaufman, Sue
    See also CA 1-4R; 69-72; CANR 1
Baron de Teive
    See Pessoa, Fernando (Antonio Nogueira)
Baroness Von S.
    See Zangwill, Israel
Barres, (Auguste-) Maurice
    1862-1923 .... TCLC 47
    See also CA 164; DLB 123
Barreto, Afonso Henrique de Lima
    See Lima Barreto, Afonso Henrique de
Barrett, (Roger) Syd 1946- .... CLC 35
Barrett, William (Christopher)
    1913-1992 .... CLC 27
    See also CA 13-16R; 139; CANR 11, 67; INT CANR-11
Barrie, J(ames) M(atthew)
    1860-1937 .... TCLC 2; DAB; DAM DRAM
    See also CA 104; 136; CANR 77; CDBLB 1890-1914; CLR 16; DA3; DLB 10, 141, 156; MAICYA; MTCW 1; SATA 100; YABC 1
Barrington, Michael
    See Moorcock, Michael (John)
Barrol, Grady
    See Bograd, Larry
Barry, Mike
    See Malzberg, Barry N(athaniel)
Barry, Philip 1896-1949 .... TCLC 11
    See also CA 109; DLB 7, 228
Bart, Andre Schwarz
    See Schwarz-Bart, Andre
Barth, John (Simmons) 1930- ... CLC 1, 2, 3, 5, 7, 9, 10, 14, 27, 51, 89; DAM NOV; SSC 10
    See also AITN 1, 2; CA 1-4R; CABS 1; CANR 5, 23, 49, 64; DLB 2, 227; MTCW 1
Barthelme, Donald 1931-1989 ... CLC 1, 2, 3, 5, 6, 8, 13, 23, 46, 59, 115; DAM NOV; SSC 2
    See also CA 21-24R; 129; CANR 20, 58; DA3; DLB 2; DLBY 80, 89; MTCW 1, 2; SATA 7; SATA-Obit 62
Barthelme, Frederick 1943- ...... CLC 36, 117
    See also CA 114; 122; CANR 77; DLBY 85; INT 122
Barthes, Roland (Gerard)
    1915-1980 .... CLC 24, 83
    See also CA 130; 97-100; CANR 66; MTCW 1, 2
Barzun, Jacques (Martin) 1907- ...... CLC 51
    See also CA 61-64; CANR 22
Bashevis, Isaac
    See Singer, Isaac Bashevis
Bashkirtseff, Marie 1859-1884 .... NCLC 27
Basho
    See Matsuo Basho
Basil of Caesaria c. 330-379 .... CMLC 35
Bass, Kingsley B., Jr.
    See Bullins, Ed
Bass, Rick 1958- .... CLC 79
    See also CA 126; CANR 53; DLB 212
Bassani, Giorgio 1916- .... CLC 9
    See also CA 65-68; CANR 33; DLB 128, 177; MTCW 1
Bastos, Augusto (Antonio) Roa
    See Roa Bastos, Augusto (Antonio)
Bataille, Georges 1897-1962 .... CLC 29
    See also CA 101; 89-92

Bates, H(erbert) E(rnest)
1905-1974 . **CLC 46; DAB; DAM POP; SSC 10**
See also CA 93-96; 45-48; CANR 34; DA3; DLB 162, 191; MTCW 1, 2

Bauchart
See Camus, Albert

Baudelaire, Charles 1821-1867 . **NCLC 6, 29, 55; DA; DAB; DAC; DAM MST, POET; PC 1; SSC 18; WLC**
See also DA3

Baudrillard, Jean 1929- .... **CLC 60**

Baum, L(yman) Frank 1856-1919 ... **TCLC 7**
See also CA 108; 133; CLR 15; DLB 22; JRDA; MAICYA; MTCW 1, 2; SATA 18, 100

Baum, Louis F.
See Baum, L(yman) Frank

Baumbach, Jonathan 1933- .... **CLC 6, 23**
See also CA 13-16R; CAAS 5; CANR 12, 66; DLBY 80; INT CANR-12; MTCW 1

Bausch, Richard (Carl) 1945- .... **CLC 51**
See also CA 101; CAAS 14; CANR 43, 61, 87; DLB 130

Baxter, Charles (Morley) 1947- .... **CLC 45, 78; DAM POP**
See also CA 57-60; CANR 40, 64; DLB 130; MTCW 2

Baxter, George Owen
See Faust, Frederick (Schiller)

Baxter, James K(eir) 1926-1972 .... **CLC 14**
See also CA 77-80

Baxter, John
See Hunt, E(verette) Howard, (Jr.)

Bayer, Sylvia
See Glassco, John

Baynton, Barbara 1857-1929 .... **TCLC 57**

Beagle, Peter S(oyer) 1939- .... **CLC 7, 104**
See also CA 9-12R; CANR 4, 51, 73; DA3; DLBY 80; INT CANR-4; MTCW 1; SATA 60

Bean, Normal
See Burroughs, Edgar Rice

Beard, Charles A(ustin)
1874-1948 .... **TCLC 15**
See also CA 115; DLB 17; SATA 18

Beardsley, Aubrey 1872-1898 .... **NCLC 6**

Beattie, Ann 1947- ..... **CLC 8, 13, 18, 40, 63; DAM NOV, POP; SSC 11**
See also BEST 90:2; CA 81-84; CANR 53, 73; DA3; DLBY 82; MTCW 1, 2

Beattie, James 1735-1803 .... **NCLC 25**
See also DLB 109

Beauchamp, Kathleen Mansfield 1888-1923
See Mansfield, Katherine
See also CA 104; 134; DA; DAC; DAM MST; DA3; MTCW 2

Beaumarchais, Pierre-Augustin Caron de
1732-1799 .... **DC 4**
See also DAM DRAM

Beaumont, Francis 1584(?)-1616 .... **LC 33; DC 6**
See also CDBLB Before 1660; DLB 58, 121

Beauvoir, Simone (Lucie Ernestine Marie Bertrand) de 1908-1986 .... **CLC 1, 2, 4, 8, 14, 31, 44, 50, 71, 124; DA; DAB; DAC; DAM MST, NOV; SSC 35; WLC**
See also CA 9-12R; 118; CANR 28, 61; DA3; DLB 72; DLBY 86; MTCW 1, 2

Becker, Carl (Lotus) 1873-1945 ..... **TCLC 63**
See also CA 157; DLB 17

Becker, Jurek 1937-1997 .... **CLC 7, 19**
See also CA 85-88; 157; CANR 60; DLB 75

Becker, Walter 1950- .... **CLC 26**

Beckett, Samuel (Barclay)
1906-1989 .. **CLC 1, 2, 3, 4, 6, 9, 10, 11, 14, 18, 29, 57, 59, 83; DA; DAB; DAC; DAM DRAM, MST, NOV; SSC 16; WLC**
See also CA 5-8R; 130; CANR 33, 61; CD-BLB 1945-1960; DA3; DLB 13, 15; DLBY 90; MTCW 1, 2

Beckford, William 1760-1844 .... **NCLC 16**
See also DLB 39

Beckman, Gunnel 1910- .... **CLC 26**
See also CA 33-36R; CANR 15; CLR 25; MAICYA; SAAS 9; SATA 6

Becque, Henri 1837-1899 .... **NCLC 3**
See also DLB 192

Becquer, Gustavo Adolfo 1836-1870
See also DAM MULT; HLCS 1

Beddoes, Thomas Lovell
1803-1849 .... **NCLC 3**
See also DLB 96

Bede c. 673-735 .... **CMLC 20**
See also DLB 146

Bedford, Donald F.
See Fearing, Kenneth (Flexner)

Beecher, Catharine Esther
1800-1878 .... **NCLC 30**
See also DLB 1

Beecher, John 1904-1980 .... **CLC 6**
See also AITN 1; CA 5-8R; 105; CANR 8

Beer, Johann 1655-1700 .... **LC 5**
See also DLB 168

Beer, Patricia 1924-1999 .... **CLC 58**
See also CA 61-64; 183; CANR 13, 46; DLB 40

Beerbohm, Max
See Beerbohm, (Henry) Max(imilian)

Beerbohm, (Henry) Max(imilian)
1872-1956 .... **TCLC 1, 24**
See also CA 104; 154; CANR 79; DLB 34, 100

Beer-Hofmann, Richard
1866-1945 .... **TCLC 60**
See also CA 160; DLB 81

Begiebing, Robert J(ohn) 1946- .... **CLC 70**
See also CA 122; CANR 40, 88

Behan, Brendan 1923-1964 ...... **CLC 1, 8, 11, 15, 79; DAM DRAM**
See also CA 73-76; CANR 33; CDBLB 1945-1960; DLB 13; MTCW 1, 2

Behn, Aphra 1640(?)-1689 .... **LC 1, 30, 42; DA; DAB; DAC; DAM DRAM, MST, NOV, POET; DC 4; PC 13; WLC**
See also DA3; DLB 39, 80, 131

Behrman, S(amuel) N(athaniel)
1893-1973 .... **CLC 40**
See also CA 13-16; 45-48; CAP 1; DLB 7, 44

Belasco, David 1853-1931 .... **TCLC 3**
See also CA 104; 168; DLB 7

Belcheva, Elisaveta 1893- .... **CLC 10**
See also Bagryana, Elisaveta

Beldone, Phil ''Cheech''
See Ellison, Harlan (Jay)

Beleno
See Azuela, Mariano

Belinski, Vissarion Grigoryevich
1811-1848 .... **NCLC 5**
See also DLB 198

Belitt, Ben 1911- .... **CLC 22**
See also CA 13-16R; CAAS 4; CANR 7, 77; DLB 5

Bell, Gertrude (Margaret Lowthian)
1868-1926 .... **TCLC 67**
See also CA 167; DLB 174

Bell, J. Freeman
See Zangwill, Israel

Bell, James Madison 1826-1902 ... **TCLC 43; BLC 1; DAM MULT**
See also BW 1; CA 122; 124; DLB 50

Bell, Madison Smartt 1957- ...... **CLC 41, 102**
See also CA 111, 183; CAAE 183; CANR 28, 54, 73; MTCW 1

Bell, Marvin (Hartley) 1937- ...... **CLC 8, 31; DAM POET**
See also CA 21-24R; CAAS 14; CANR 59; DLB 5; MTCW 1

Bell, W. L. D.
See Mencken, H(enry) L(ouis)

Bellamy, Atwood C.
See Mencken, H(enry) L(ouis)

Bellamy, Edward 1850-1898 ...... **NCLC 4, 86**
See also DLB 12

Belli, Gioconda 1949-
See also CA 152; HLCS 1

Bellin, Edward J.
See Kuttner, Henry

Belloc, (Joseph) Hilaire (Pierre Sebastien Rene Swanton) 1870- .... **TCLC 7, 18; DAM POET; PC 24**
See also CA 106; 152; DLB 19, 100, 141, 174; MTCW 1; SATA 112; YABC 1

Belloc, Joseph Peter Rene Hilaire
See Belloc, (Joseph) Hilaire (Pierre Sebastien Rene Swanton)

Belloc, Joseph Pierre Hilaire
See Belloc, (Joseph) Hilaire (Pierre Sebastien Rene Swanton)

Belloc, M. A.
See Lowndes, Marie Adelaide (Belloc)

Bellow, Saul 1915- . **CLC 1, 2, 3, 6, 8, 10, 13, 15, 25, 33, 34, 63, 79; DA; DAB; DAC; DAM MST, NOV, POP; SSC 14; WLC**
See also AITN 2; BEST 89:3; CA 5-8R; CABS 1; CANR 29, 53; CDALB 1941-1968; DA3; DLB 2, 28; DLBD 3; DLBY 82; MTCW 1, 2

Belser, Reimond Karel Maria de 1929-
See Ruyslinck, Ward
See also CA 152

Bely, Andrey TCLC 7; PC 11
See also Bugayev, Boris Nikolayevich
See also MTCW 1

Belyi, Andrei
See Bugayev, Boris Nikolayevich

Benary, Margot
See Benary-Isbert, Margot

Benary-Isbert, Margot 1889-1979 .... **CLC 12**
See also CA 5-8R; 89-92; CANR 4, 72; CLR 12; MAICYA; SATA 2; SATA-Obit 21

Benavente (y Martinez), Jacinto
1866-1954 .... **TCLC 3; DAM DRAM, MULT; HLCS 1**
See also CA 106; 131; CANR 81; HW 1, 2; MTCW 1, 2

Benchley, Peter (Bradford) 1940- . **CLC 4, 8; DAM NOV, POP**
See also AAYA 14; AITN 2; CA 17-20R; CANR 12, 35, 66; MTCW 1, 2; SATA 3, 89

Benchley, Robert (Charles)
1889-1945 .... **TCLC 1, 55**
See also CA 105; 153; DLB 11

Benda, Julien 1867-1956 .... **TCLC 60**
See also CA 120; 154

Benedict, Ruth (Fulton)
1887-1948 .... **TCLC 60**
See also CA 158

Benedict, Saint c. 480-c. 547 .... **CMLC 29**

Benedikt, Michael 1935- .... **CLC 4, 14**
See also CA 13-16R; CANR 7; DLB 5

Benet, Juan 1927- .... **CLC 28**
See also CA 143**

Benet, Stephen Vincent 1898-1943 . **TCLC 7; DAM POET; SSC 10**
See also CA 104; 152; DA3; DLB 4, 48, 102; DLBY 97; MTCW 1; YABC 1

Benet, William Rose 1886-1950 .... **TCLC 28; DAM POET**
See also CA 118; 152; DLB 45

Benford, Gregory (Albert) 1941- ..... **CLC 52**
See also CA 69-72, 175; CAAE 175; CAAS 27; CANR 12, 24, 49; DLBY 82

Bengtsson, Frans (Gunnar)
1894-1954 .... **TCLC 48**
See also CA 170

Benjamin, David
See Slavitt, David R(ytman)

Benjamin, Lois
See Gould, Lois

Benjamin, Walter 1892-1940 .... **TCLC 39**
See also CA 164

Benn, Gottfried 1886-1956 .... **TCLC 3**
See also CA 106; 153; DLB 56

Bennett, Alan 1934- .... **CLC 45, 77; DAB; DAM MST**
See also CA 103; CANR 35, 55; MTCW 1, 2

Bennett, (Enoch) Arnold
1867-1931 .... **TCLC 5, 20**
See also CA 106; 155; CDBLB 1890-1914; DLB 10, 34, 98, 135; MTCW 2

Bennett, Elizabeth
See Mitchell, Margaret (Munnerlyn)

Bennett, George Harold 1930-
See Bennett, Hal
See also BW 1; CA 97-100; CANR 87

Bennett, Hal CLC 5
See also Bennett, George Harold
See also DLB 33

Bennett, Jay 1912- .... **CLC 35**
See also AAYA 10; CA 69-72; CANR 11, 42, 79; JRDA; SAAS 4; SATA 41, 87; SATA-Brief 27

Bennett, Louise (Simone) 1919- ...... **CLC 28; BLC 1; DAM MULT**
See also BW 2, 3; CA 151; DLB 117

Benson, E(dward) F(rederic)
1867-1940 .... **TCLC 27**
See also CA 114; 157; DLB 135, 153

Benson, Jackson J. 1930- .... **CLC 34**
See also CA 25-28R; DLB 111

Benson, Sally 1900-1972 .... **CLC 17**
See also CA 19-20; 37-40R; CAP 1; SATA 1, 35; SATA-Obit 27

Benson, Stella 1892-1933 .... **TCLC 17**
See also CA 117; 155; DLB 36, 162

Bentham, Jeremy 1748-1832 .... **NCLC 38**
See also DLB 107, 158

Bentley, E(dmund) C(lerihew)
1875-1956 .... **TCLC 12**
See also CA 108; DLB 70

Bentley, Eric (Russell) 1916- .... **CLC 24**
See also CA 5-8R; CANR 6, 67; INT CANR-6

Beranger, Pierre Jean de
1780-1857 .... **NCLC 34**

Berdyaev, Nicolas
See Berdyaev, Nikolai (Aleksandrovich)

Berdyaev, Nikolai (Aleksandrovich)
1874-1948 .... **TCLC 67**
See also CA 120; 157

Berdyayev, Nikolai (Aleksandrovich)
See Berdyaev, Nikolai (Aleksandrovich)

Berendt, John (Lawrence) 1939- ...... **CLC 86**
See also CA 146; CANR 75; DA3; MTCW 1

Beresford, J(ohn) D(avys)
1873-1947 .... **TCLC 81**
See also CA 112; 155; DLB 162, 178, 197

Bergelson, David 1884-1952 .... **TCLC 81**

Berger, Colonel
See Malraux, (Georges-)Andre

Berger, John (Peter) 1926- .... **CLC 2, 19**
See also CA 81-84; CANR 51, 78; DLB 14, 207

Berger, Melvin H. 1927- .... **CLC 12**
See also CA 5-8R; CANR 4; CLR 32; SAAS 2; SATA 5, 88

Berger, Thomas (Louis) 1924- .. **CLC 3, 5, 8, 11, 18, 38; DAM NOV**
See also CA 1-4R; CANR 5, 28, 51; DLB 2; DLBY 80; INT CANR-28; MTCW 1, 2

Bergman, (Ernst) Ingmar 1918- ...... **CLC 16, 72**
See also CA 81-84; CANR 33, 70; MTCW 2

Bergson, Henri(-Louis) 1859-1941 . **TCLC 32**
See also CA 164

Bergstein, Eleanor 1938- .... **CLC 4**
See also CA 53-56; CANR 5

Berkoff, Steven 1937- .... **CLC 56**
See also CA 104; CANR 72

Bermant, Chaim (Icyk) 1929- .... **CLC 40**
See also CA 57-60; CANR 6, 31, 57

Bern, Victoria
See Fisher, M(ary) F(rances) K(ennedy)

Bernanos, (Paul Louis) Georges
1888-1948 .... **TCLC 3**
See also CA 104; 130; DLB 72

Bernard, April 1956- .... **CLC 59**
See also CA 131

Berne, Victoria
See Fisher, M(ary) F(rances) K(ennedy)

Bernhard, Thomas 1931-1989 ..... **CLC 3, 32, 61**
See also CA 85-88; 127; CANR 32, 57; DLB 85, 124; MTCW 1

Bernhardt, Sarah (Henriette Rosine)
1844-1923 .... **TCLC 75**
See also CA 157

Berriault, Gina 1926-1999 .... **CLC 54, 109; SSC 30**
See also CA 116; 129; 185; CANR 66; DLB 130

Berrigan, Daniel 1921- .... **CLC 4**
See also CA 33-36R; CAAS 1; CANR 11, 43, 78; DLB 5

Berrigan, Edmund Joseph Michael, Jr.
1934-1983
See Berrigan, Ted
See also CA 61-64; 110; CANR 14

Berrigan, Ted CLC 37
See also Berrigan, Edmund Joseph Michael, Jr.
See also DLB 5, 169

Berry, Charles Edward Anderson 1931-
See Berry, Chuck
See also CA 115

Berry, Chuck CLC 17
See also Berry, Charles Edward Anderson

Berry, Jonas
See Ashbery, John (Lawrence)

Berry, Wendell (Erdman) 1934- ... **CLC 4, 6, 8, 27, 46; DAM POET; PC 28**
See also AITN 1; CA 73-76; CANR 50, 73; DLB 5, 6; MTCW 1

Berryman, John 1914-1972 ... **CLC 1, 2, 3, 4, 6, 8, 10, 13, 25, 62; DAM POET**
See also CA 13-16; 33-36R; CABS 2; CANR 35; CAP 1; CDALB 1941-1968; DLB 48; MTCW 1, 2

Bertolucci, Bernardo 1940- .... **CLC 16**
See also CA 106

Berton, Pierre (Francis Demarigny)
1920- .... **CLC 104**
See also CA 1-4R; CANR 2, 56; DLB 68; SATA 99

Bertrand, Aloysius 1807-1841 .... **NCLC 31**

Bertran de Born c. 1140-1215 .... **CMLC 5**

Besant, Annie (Wood) 1847-1933 ..... **TCLC 9**
See also CA 105; 185

Bessie, Alvah 1904-1985 .... **CLC 23**
See also CA 5-8R; 116; CANR 2, 80; DLB 26

Bethlen, T. D.
See Silverberg, Robert

Beti, Mongo CLC 27; BLC 1; DAM MULT
See also Biyidi, Alexandre
See also CANR 79

Betjeman, John 1906-1984 ...... **CLC 2, 6, 10, 34, 43; DAB; DAM MST, POET**
See also CA 9-12R; 112; CANR 33, 56; CDBLB 1945-1960; DA3; DLB 20; DLBY 84; MTCW 1, 2

Bettelheim, Bruno 1903-1990 .... **CLC 79**
See also CA 81-84; 131; CANR 23, 61; DA3; MTCW 1, 2

Betti, Ugo 1892-1953 .... **TCLC 5**
See also CA 104; 155

Betts, Doris (Waugh) 1932- ...... **CLC 3, 6, 28**
See also CA 13-16R; CANR 9, 66, 77; DLBY 82; INT CANR-9

Bevan, Alistair
See Roberts, Keith (John Kingston)

Bey, Pilaff
See Douglas, (George) Norman

Bialik, Chaim Nachman
1873-1934 .... **TCLC 25**
See also CA 170

Bickerstaff, Isaac
See Swift, Jonathan

Bidart, Frank 1939- .... **CLC 33**
See also CA 140

Bienek, Horst 1930- .... **CLC 7, 11**
See also CA 73-76; DLB 75

Bierce, Ambrose (Gwinett)
1842-1914(?) .... **TCLC 1, 7, 44; DA; DAC; DAM MST; SSC 9; WLC**
See also CA 104; 139; CANR 78; CDALB 1865-1917; DA3; DLB 11, 12, 23, 71, 74, 186

Biggers, Earl Derr 1884-1933 .... **TCLC 65**
See also CA 108; 153

Billings, Josh
See Shaw, Henry Wheeler

Billington, (Lady) Rachel (Mary)
1942- .... **CLC 43**
See also AITN 2; CA 33-36R; CANR 44

Binyon, T(imothy) J(ohn) 1936- .... **CLC 34**
See also CA 111; CANR 28

Bion 335B.C.-245B.C. .... **CMLC 39**

Bioy Casares, Adolfo 1914-1999 ... **CLC 4, 8, 13, 88; DAM MULT; HLC 1; SSC 17**
See also CA 29-32R; 177; CANR 19, 43, 66; DLB 113; HW 1, 2; MTCW 1, 2

Bird, Cordwainer
See Ellison, Harlan (Jay)

Bird, Robert Montgomery
1806-1854 .... **NCLC 1**
See also DLB 202

Birkerts, Sven 1951- .... **CLC 116**
See also CA 128; 133; 176; CAAE 176; CAAS 29; INT 133

Birney, (Alfred) Earle 1904-1995 .. **CLC 1, 4, 6, 11; DAC; DAM MST, POET**
See also CA 1-4R; CANR 5, 20; DLB 88; MTCW 1

Biruni, al 973-1048(?) .... **CMLC 28**

Bishop, Elizabeth 1911-1979 ..... **CLC 1, 4, 9, 13, 15, 32; DA; DAC; DAM MST, POET; PC 3**
See also CA 5-8R; 89-92; CABS 2; CANR 26, 61; CDALB 1968-1988; DA3; DLB 5, 169; MTCW 1, 2; SATA-Obit 24

Bishop, John 1935- .... **CLC 10**
See also CA 105
Bissett, Bill 1939- .... **CLC 18; PC 14**
See also CA 69-72; CAAS 19; CANR 15;
DLB 53; MTCW 1
Bissoondath, Neil (Devindra)
1955- .... **CLC 120; DAC**
See also CA 136
Bitov, Andrei (Georgievich) 1937- ... **CLC 57**
See also CA 142
Biyidi, Alexandre 1932-
See Beti, Mongo
See also BW 1, 3; CA 114; 124; CANR 81;
DA3; MTCW 1, 2
Bjarme, Brynjolf
See Ibsen, Henrik (Johan)
Bjoernson, Bjoernstjerne (Martinius)
1832-1910 .... **TCLC 7, 37**
See also CA 104
Black, Robert
See Holdstock, Robert P.
Blackburn, Paul 1926-1971 .... **CLC 9, 43**
See also CA 81-84; 33-36R; CANR 34;
DLB 16; DLBY 81
Black Elk 1863-1950 .... **TCLC 33; DAM MULT**
See also CA 144; MTCW 1; NNAL
Black Hobart
See Sanders, (James) Ed(ward)
Blacklin, Malcolm
See Chambers, Aidan
Blackmore, R(ichard) D(oddridge)
1825-1900 .... **TCLC 27**
See also CA 120; DLB 18
Blackmur, R(ichard) P(almer)
1904-1965 .... **CLC 2, 24**
See also CA 11-12; 25-28R; CANR 71;
CAP 1; DLB 63
Black Tarantula
See Acker, Kathy
Blackwood, Algernon (Henry)
1869-1951 .... **TCLC 5**
See also CA 105; 150; DLB 153, 156, 178
Blackwood, Caroline 1931-1996 .... **CLC 6, 9, 100**
See also CA 85-88; 151; CANR 32, 61, 65;
DLB 14, 207; MTCW 1
Blade, Alexander
See Hamilton, Edmond; Silverberg, Robert
Blaga, Lucian 1895-1961 .... **CLC 75**
See also CA 157; DLB 220
Blair, Eric (Arthur) 1903-1950
See Orwell, George
See also CA 104; 132; DA; DAB; DAC;
DAM MST, NOV; DA3; MTCW 1, 2;
SATA 29
Blair, Hugh 1718-1800 .... **NCLC 75**
Blais, Marie-Claire 1939- .... **CLC 2, 4, 6, 13, 22; DAC; DAM MST**
See also CA 21-24R; CAAS 4; CANR 38,
75; DLB 53; MTCW 1, 2
Blaise, Clark 1940- .... **CLC 29**
See also AITN 2; CA 53-56; CAAS 3;
CANR 5, 66; DLB 53
Blake, Fairley
See De Voto, Bernard (Augustine)
Blake, Nicholas
See Day Lewis, C(ecil)
See also DLB 77
Blake, William 1757-1827 .... **NCLC 13, 37, 57; DA; DAB; DAC; DAM MST, POET; PC 12; WLC**
See also CDBLB 1789-1832; CLR 52;
DA3; DLB 93, 163; MAICYA; SATA 30
Blasco Ibanez, Vicente
1867-1928 .... **TCLC 12; DAM NOV**
See also CA 110; 131; CANR 81; DA3; HW
1, 2; MTCW 1

Blatty, William Peter 1928- .... **CLC 2; DAM POP**
See also CA 5-8R; CANR 9
Bleeck, Oliver
See Thomas, Ross (Elmore)
Blessing, Lee 1949- .... **CLC 54**
Blight, Rose
See Greer, Germaine
Blish, James (Benjamin) 1921-1975 . **CLC 14**
See also CA 1-4R; 57-60; CANR 3; DLB
8; MTCW 1; SATA 66
Bliss, Reginald
See Wells, H(erbert) G(eorge)
Blixen, Karen (Christentze Dinesen)
1885-1962
See Dinesen, Isak
See also CA 25-28; CANR 22, 50; CAP 2;
DA3; MTCW 1, 2; SATA 44
Bloch, Robert (Albert) 1917-1994 .... **CLC 33**
See also AAYA 29; CA 5-8R, 179; 146;
CAAE 179; CAAS 20; CANR 5, 78;
DA3; DLB 44; INT CANR-5; MTCW 1;
SATA 12; SATA-Obit 82
Blok, Alexander (Alexandrovich)
1880-1921 .... **TCLC 5; PC 21**
See also CA 104; 183
Blom, Jan
See Breytenbach, Breyten
Bloom, Harold 1930- .... **CLC 24, 103**
See also CA 13-16R; CANR 39, 75; DLB
67; MTCW 1
Bloomfield, Aurelius
See Bourne, Randolph S(illiman)
Blount, Roy (Alton), Jr. 1941- .... **CLC 38**
See also CA 53-56; CANR 10, 28, 61; INT
CANR-28; MTCW 1, 2
Bloy, Leon 1846-1917 .... **TCLC 22**
See also CA 121; 183; DLB 123
Blume, Judy (Sussman) 1938- .. **CLC 12, 30; DAM NOV, POP**
See also AAYA 3, 26; CA 29-32R; CANR
13, 37, 66; CLR 2, 15; DA3; DLB 52;
JRDA; MAICYA; MTCW 1, 2; SATA 2,
31, 79
Blunden, Edmund (Charles)
1896-1974 .... **CLC 2, 56**
See also CA 17-18; 45-48; CANR 54; CAP
2; DLB 20, 100, 155; MTCW 1
Bly, Robert (Elwood) 1926- .... **CLC 1, 2, 5, 10, 15, 38, 128; DAM POET**
See also CA 5-8R; CANR 41, 73; DA3;
DLB 5; MTCW 1, 2
Boas, Franz 1858-1942 .... **TCLC 56**
See also CA 115; 181
Bobette
See Simenon, Georges (Jacques Christian)
Boccaccio, Giovanni 1313-1375 ... **CMLC 13; SSC 10**
Bochco, Steven 1943- .... **CLC 35**
See also AAYA 11; CA 124; 138
Bodel, Jean 1167(?)-1210 .... **CMLC 28**
Bodenheim, Maxwell 1892-1954 .... **TCLC 44**
See also CA 110; DLB 9, 45
Bodker, Cecil 1927- .... **CLC 21**
See also CA 73-76; CANR 13, 44; CLR 23;
MAICYA; SATA 14
Boell, Heinrich (Theodor)
1917-1985 ..... **CLC 2, 3, 6, 9, 11, 15, 27, 32, 72; DA; DAB; DAC; DAM MST, NOV; SSC 23; WLC**
See also CA 21-24R; 116; CANR 24; DA3;
DLB 69; DLBY 85; MTCW 1, 2
Boerne, Alfred
See Doeblin, Alfred
Boethius 480(?)-524(?) .... **CMLC 15**
See also DLB 115
Boff, Leonardo (Genezio Darci) 1938-
See also CA 150; DAM MULT; HLC 1;
HW 2

Bogan, Louise 1897-1970 .... **CLC 4, 39, 46, 93; DAM POET; PC 12**
See also CA 73-76; 25-28R; CANR 33, 82;
DLB 45, 169; MTCW 1, 2
Bogarde, Dirk 1921-1999
See Van Den Bogarde, Derek Jules Gaspard
Ulric Niven
Bogosian, Eric 1953- .... **CLC 45**
See also CA 138
Bograd, Larry 1953- .... **CLC 35**
See also CA 93-96; CANR 57; SAAS 21;
SATA 33, 89
Boiardo, Matteo Maria 1441-1494 .... **LC 6**
Boileau-Despreaux, Nicolas 1636-1711 . **LC 3**
Bojer, Johan 1872-1959 .... **TCLC 64**
Boland, Eavan (Aisling) 1944- .. **CLC 40, 67, 113; DAM POET**
See also CA 143; CANR 61; DLB 40;
MTCW 2
Boll, Heinrich
See Boell, Heinrich (Theodor)
Bolt, Lee
See Faust, Frederick (Schiller)
Bolt, Robert (Oxton) 1924-1995 ...... **CLC 14; DAM DRAM**
See also CA 17-20R; 147; CANR 35, 67;
DLB 13; MTCW 1
Bombal, Maria Luisa 1910-1980 ...... **SSC 37; HLCS 1**
See also CA 127; CANR 72; HW 1
Bombet, Louis-Alexandre-Cesar
See Stendhal
Bomkauf
See Kaufman, Bob (Garnell)
Bonaventura **NCLC 35**
See also DLB 90
Bond, Edward 1934- .... **CLC 4, 6, 13, 23; DAM DRAM**
See also CA 25-28R; CANR 38, 67; DLB
13; MTCW 1
Bonham, Frank 1914-1989 .... **CLC 12**
See also AAYA 1; CA 9-12R; CANR 4, 36;
JRDA; MAICYA; SAAS 3; SATA 1, 49;
SATA-Obit 62
Bonnefoy, Yves 1923- .. **CLC 9, 15, 58; DAM MST, POET**
See also CA 85-88; CANR 33, 75; MTCW
1, 2
Bontemps, Arna(ud Wendell)
1902-1973 ..... **CLC 1, 18; BLC 1; DAM MULT, NOV, POET**
See also BW 1; CA 1-4R; 41-44R; CANR
4, 35; CLR 6; DA3; DLB 48, 51; JRDA;
MAICYA; MTCW 1, 2; SATA 2, 44;
SATA-Obit 24
Booth, Martin 1944- .... **CLC 13**
See also CA 93-96; CAAS 2
Booth, Philip 1925- .... **CLC 23**
See also CA 5-8R; CANR 5, 88; DLBY 82
Booth, Wayne C(layson) 1921- .... **CLC 24**
See also CA 1-4R; CAAS 5; CANR 3, 43;
DLB 67
Borchert, Wolfgang 1921-1947 .... **TCLC 5**
See also CA 104; DLB 69, 124
Borel, Petrus 1809-1859 .... **NCLC 41**
Borges, Jorge Luis 1899-1986 ... **CLC 1, 2, 3, 4, 6, 8, 9, 10, 13, 19, 44, 48, 83; DA; DAB; DAC; DAM MST, MULT; HLC 1; PC 22; SSC 4, 41; WLC**
See also AAYA 26; CA 21-24R; CANR 19,
33, 75; DA3; DLB 113; DLBY 86; HW 1,
2; MTCW 1, 2
Borowski, Tadeusz 1922-1951 .... **TCLC 9**
See also CA 106; 154
Borrow, George (Henry)
1803-1881 .... **NCLC 9**
See also DLB 21, 55, 166

Bosch (Gavino), Juan 1909-
See also CA 151; DAM MST, MULT; DLB 145; HLCS 1; HW 1, 2
Bosman, Herman Charles
1905-1951 .... **TCLC 49**
See also Malan, Herman
See also CA 160; DLB 225
Bosschere, Jean de 1878(?)-1953 ... **TCLC 19**
See also CA 115; 186
Boswell, James 1740-1795 ...... **LC 4, 50; DA; DAB; DAC; DAM MST; WLC**
See also CDBLB 1660-1789; DLB 104, 142
Bottoms, David 1949- .... **CLC 53**
See also CA 105; CANR 22; DLB 120; DLBY 83
Boucicault, Dion 1820-1890 .... **NCLC 41**
Bourget, Paul (Charles Joseph)
1852-1935 .... **TCLC 12**
See also CA 107; DLB 123
Bourjaily, Vance (Nye) 1922- .... **CLC 8, 62**
See also CA 1-4R; CAAS 1; CANR 2, 72; DLB 2, 143
Bourne, Randolph S(illiman)
1886-1918 .... **TCLC 16**
See also CA 117; 155; DLB 63
Bova, Ben(jamin William) 1932- ...... **CLC 45**
See also AAYA 16; CA 5-8R; CAAS 18; CANR 11, 56; CLR 3; DLBY 81; INT CANR 11; MAICYA; MTCW 1; SATA 6, 68
Bowen, Elizabeth (Dorothea Cole)
1899-1973 . **CLC 1, 3, 6, 11, 15, 22, 118; DAM NOV; SSC 3, 28**
See also CA 17-18; 41-44R, CANR 35; CAP 2; CDBLB 1945-1960; DA3; DLB 15, 162; MTCW 1, 2
Bowering, George 1935- .... **CLC 15, 47**
See also CA 21-24R; CAAS 16; CANR 10; DLB 53
Bowering, Marilyn R(uthe) 1949- ..., **CLC 32**
See also CA 101; CANR 49
Bowers, Edgar 1924- .... **CLC 9**
See also CA 5-8R; CANR 24; DLB 5
Bowie, David **CLC 17**
See also Jones, David Robert
Bowles, Jane (Sydney) 1917-1973 ..... **CLC 3, 68**
See also CA 19-20; 41-44R; CAP 2
Bowles, Paul (Frederick) 1910-1999 . **CLC 1, 2, 19, 53; SSC 3**
See also CA 1-4R; 186; CAAS 1; CANR 1, 19, 50, 75; DA3; DLB 5, 6; MTCW 1, 2
Box, Edgar
See Vidal, Gore
Boyd, Nancy
See Millay, Edna St. Vincent
Boyd, William 1952- .... **CLC 28, 53, 70**
See also CA 114; 120; CANR 51, 71
Boyle, Kay 1902-1992 .... **CLC 1, 5, 19, 58, 121; SSC 5**
See also CA 13-16R; 140; CAAS 1; CANR 29, 61; DLB 4, 9, 48, 86; DLBY 93; MTCW 1, 2
Boyle, Mark
See Kienzle, William X(avier)
Boyle, Patrick 1905-1982 .... **CLC 19**
See also CA 127
Boyle, T. C. 1948-
See Boyle, T(homas) Coraghessan
Boyle, T(homas) Coraghessan
1948- .... **CLC 36, 55, 90; DAM POP; SSC 16**
See also BEST 90:4; CA 120; CANR 44, 76, 89; DA3; DLBY 86; MTCW 2
Boz
See Dickens, Charles (John Huffam)
Brackenridge, Hugh Henry
1748-1816 .... **NCLC 7**
See also DLB 11, 37

Bradbury, Edward P.
See Moorcock, Michael (John)
See also MTCW 2
Bradbury, Malcolm (Stanley)
1932- .... **CLC 32, 61; DAM NOV**
See also CA 1-4R; CANR 1, 33, 91; DA3; DLB 14, 207; MTCW 1, 2
Bradbury, Ray (Douglas) 1920- .... **CLC 1, 3, 10, 15, 42, 98; DA; DAB; DAC; DAM MST, NOV, POP; SSC 29; WLC**
See also AAYA 15; AITN 1, 2; CA 1-4R; CANR 2, 30, 75; CDALB 1968-1988; DA3; DLB 2, 8; MTCW 1, 2; SATA 11, 64
Bradford, Gamaliel 1863-1932 .... **TCLC 36**
See also CA 160; DLB 17
Bradley, David (Henry), Jr. 1950- ... **CLC 23, 118; BLC 1; DAM MULT**
See also BW 1, 3; CA 104; CANR 26, 81; DLB 33
Bradley, John Ed(mund, Jr.) 1958- . **CLC 55**
See also CA 139
Bradley, Marion Zimmer
1930-1999 .... **CLC 30; DAM POP**
See also AAYA 9; CA 57-60; 185; CAAS 10; CANR 7, 31, 51, 75; DA3; DLB 8; MTCW 1, 2; SATA 90; SATA-Obit 116
Bradstreet, Anne 1612(?)-1672 ...... **LC 4, 30; DA; DAC; DAM MST, POET; PC 10**
See also CDALB 1640-1865; DA3; DLB 24
Brady, Joan 1939- .... **CLC 86**
See also CA 141
Bragg, Melvyn 1939- .... **CLC 10**
See also BEST 89:3; CA 57-60; CANR 10, 48, 89; DLB 14
Brahe, Tycho 1546-1601 .... **LC 45**
Braine, John (Gerard) 1922-1986 . **CLC 1, 3, 41**
See also CA 1-4R; 120; CANR 1, 33; CD-BLB 1945-1960; DLB 15; DLBY 86; MTCW 1
Bramah, Ernest 1868-1942 .... **TCLC 72**
See also CA 156; DLB 70
Brammer, William 1930(?)-1978 ...... **CLC 31**
See also CA 77-80
Brancati, Vitaliano 1907-1954 .... **TCLC 12**
See also CA 109
Brancato, Robin F(idler) 1936- .... **CLC 35**
See also AAYA 9; CA 69-72; CANR 11, 45; CLR 32; JRDA; SAAS 9; SATA 97
Brand, Max
See Faust, Frederick (Schiller)
Brand, Millen 1906-1980 .... **CLC 7**
See also CA 21-24R; 97-100; CANR 72
Branden, Barbara **CLC 44**
See also CA 148
Brandes, Georg (Morris Cohen)
1842-1927 .... **TCLC 10**
See also CA 105
Brandys, Kazimierz 1916- .... **CLC 62**
Branley, Franklyn M(ansfield)
1915- .... **CLC 21**
See also CA 33-36R; CANR 14, 39; CLR 13; MAICYA; SAAS 16; SATA 4, 68
Brathwaite, Edward (Kamau)
1930- ...... **CLC 11; BLCS; DAM POET**
See also BW 2, 3; CA 25-28R; CANR 11, 26, 47; DLB 125
Brautigan, Richard (Gary)
1935-1984 .... **CLC 1, 3, 5, 9, 12, 34, 42; DAM NOV**
See also CA 53-56; 113; CANR 34; DA3; DLB 2, 5, 206; DLBY 80, 84; MTCW 1; SATA 56
Brave Bird, Mary 1953-
See Crow Dog, Mary (Ellen)
See also NNAL

Braverman, Kate 1950- .... **CLC 67**
See also CA 89-92
Brecht, (Eugen) Bertolt (Friedrich)
1898-1956 .... **TCLC 1, 6, 13, 35; DA; DAB; DAC; DAM DRAM, MST; DC 3; WLC**
See also CA 104; 133; CANR 62; DA3; DLB 56, 124; MTCW 1, 2
Brecht, Eugen Berthold Friedrich
See Brecht, (Eugen) Bertolt (Friedrich)
Bremer, Fredrika 1801-1865 .... **NCLC 11**
Brennan, Christopher John
1870-1932 .... **TCLC 17**
See also CA 117
Brennan, Maeve 1917-1993 .... **CLC 5**
See also CA 81-84; CANR 72
Brent, Linda
See Jacobs, Harriet A(nn)
Brentano, Clemens (Maria)
1778-1842 .... **NCLC 1**
See also DLB 90
Brent of Bin Bin
See Franklin, (Stella Maria Sarah) Miles (Lampe)
Brenton, Howard 1942- .... **CLC 31**
See also CA 69-72; CANR 33, 67; DLB 13; MTCW 1
Breslin, James 1930-1996
See Breslin, Jimmy
See also CA 73-76; CANR 31, 75; DAM NOV; MTCW 1, 2
Breslin, Jimmy **CLC 4, 43**
See also Breslin, James
See also AITN 1; DLB 185; MTCW 2
Bresson, Robert 1901- .... **CLC 16**
See also CA 110; CANR 49
Breton, Andre 1896-1966 .. **CLC 2, 9, 15, 54; PC 15**
See also CA 19-20; 25-28R; CANR 40, 60; CAP 2; DLB 65; MTCW 1, 2
Breytenbach, Breyten 1939(?)- .. **CLC 23, 37, 126; DAM POET**
See also CA 113; 129; CANR 61; DLB 225
Bridgers, Sue Ellen 1942- .... **CLC 26**
See also AAYA 8; CA 65-68; CANR 11, 36; CLR 18; DLB 52; JRDA; MAICYA; SAAS 1; SATA 22, 90; SATA-Essay 109
Bridges, Robert (Seymour)
1844-1930 ... **TCLC 1; DAM POET; PC 28**
See also CA 104; 152; CDBLB 1890-1914; DLB 19, 98
Bridie, James **TCLC 3**
See also Mavor, Osborne Henry
See also DLB 10
Brin, David 1950- .... **CLC 34**
See also AAYA 21; CA 102; CANR 24, 70; INT CANR-24; SATA 65
Brink, Andre (Philippus) 1935- . **CLC 18, 36, 106**
See also CA 104; CANR 39, 62; DLB 225; INT 103; MTCW 1, 2
Brinsmead, H(esba) F(ay) 1922- ...... **CLC 21**
See also CA 21-24R; CANR 10; CLR 47; MAICYA; SAAS 5; SATA 18, 78
Brittain, Vera (Mary) 1893(?)-1970 . **CLC 23**
See also CA 13-16; 25-28R; CANR 58; CAP 1; DLB 191; MTCW 1, 2
Broch, Hermann 1886-1951 .... **TCLC 20**
See also CA 117; DLB 85, 124
Brock, Rose
See Hansen, Joseph
Brodkey, Harold (Roy) 1930-1996 ... **CLC 56**
See also CA 111; 151; CANR 71; DLB 130
Brodskii, Iosif
See Brodsky, Joseph

Brodsky, Iosif Alexandrovich 1940-1996
See Brodsky, Joseph
See also AITN 1; CA 41-44R; 151; CANR
37; DAM POET; DA3; MTCW 1, 2

Brodsky, Joseph 1940-1996 ..... CLC 4, 6, 13,
36, 100; PC 9
See also Brodskii, Iosif; Brodsky, Iosif Alexandrovich
See also MTCW 1

Brodsky, Michael (Mark) 1948- .... CLC 19
See also CA 102; CANR 18, 41, 58

Bromell, Henry 1947- .... CLC 5
See also CA 53-56; CANR 9

Bromfield, Louis (Brucker)
1896-1956 .... TCLC 11
See also CA 107; 155; DLB 4, 9, 86

Broner, E(sther) M(asserman)
1930- .... CLC 19
See also CA 17-20R; CANR 8, 25, 72; DLB
28

Bronk, William (M.) 1918-1999 .... CLC 10
See also CA 89-92; 177; CANR 23; DLB
165

Bronstein, Lev Davidovich
See Trotsky, Leon

Bronte, Anne 1820-1849 .... NCLC 4, 71
See also DA3; DLB 21, 199

Bronte, Charlotte 1816-1855 ...... NCLC 3, 8,
33, 58; DA; DAB; DAC; DAM MST,
NOV; WLC
See also AAYA 17; CDBLB 1832-1890;
DA3; DLB 21, 159, 199

Bronte, Emily (Jane) 1818-1848 ... NCLC 16,
35; DA; DAB; DAC; DAM MST, NOV,
POET; PC 8; WLC
See also AAYA 17; CDBLB 1832-1890;
DA3; DLB 21, 32, 199

Brooke, Frances 1724-1789 .... LC 6, 48
See also DLB 39, 99

Brooke, Henry 1703(?)-1783 .... LC 1
See also DLB 39

Brooke, Rupert (Chawner)
1887-1915 .... TCLC 2, 7; DA; DAB;
DAC; DAM MST, POET; PC 24; WLC
See also CA 104; 132; CANR 61; CDBLB
1914-1945; DLB 19; MTCW 1, 2

Brooke-Haven, P.
See Wodehouse, P(elham) G(renville)

Brooke-Rose, Christine 1926(?)- ...... CLC 40
See also CA 13-16R; CANR 58; DLB 14

Brookner, Anita 1928- .... CLC 32, 34, 51;
DAB; DAM POP
See also CA 114; 120; CANR 37, 56, 87;
DA3; DLB 194; DLBY 87; MTCW 1, 2

Brooks, Cleanth 1906-1994 . CLC 24, 86, 110
See also CA 17-20R; 145; CANR 33, 35;
DLB 63; DLBY 94; INT CANR-35;
MTCW 1, 2

Brooks, George
See Baum, L(yman) Frank

Brooks, Gwendolyn 1917- ..... CLC 1, 2, 4, 5,
15, 49, 125; BLC 1; DA; DAC; DAM
MST, MULT, POET; PC 7; WLC
See also AAYA 20; AITN 1; BW 2, 3; CA
1-4R; CANR 1, 27, 52, 75; CDALB 1941-
1968; CLR 27; DA3; DLB 5, 76, 165;
MTCW 1, 2; SATA 6

Brooks, Mel CLC 12
See also Kaminsky, Melvin
See also AAYA 13; DLB 26

Brooks, Peter 1938- .... CLC 34
See also CA 45-48; CANR 1

Brooks, Van Wyck 1886-1963 .... CLC 29
See also CA 1-4R; CANR 6; DLB 45, 63,
103

Brophy, Brigid (Antonia)
1929-1995 .... CLC 6, 11, 29, 105
See also CA 5-8R; 149; CAAS 4; CANR
25, 53; DA3; DLB 14; MTCW 1, 2

Brosman, Catharine Savage 1934- ..... CLC 9
See also CA 61-64; CANR 21, 46

Brossard, Nicole 1943- .... CLC 115
See also CA 122; CAAS 16; DLB 53

Brother Antoninus
See Everson, William (Oliver)

The Brothers Quay
See Quay, Stephen; Quay, Timothy

Broughton, T(homas) Alan 1936- ..... CLC 19
See also CA 45-48; CANR 2, 23, 48

Broumas, Olga 1949- .... CLC 10, 73
See also CA 85-88; CANR 20, 69

Brown, Alan 1950- .... CLC 99
See also CA 156

Brown, Charles Brockden
1771-1810 .... NCLC 22, 74
See also CDALB 1640-1865; DLB 37, 59,
73

Brown, Christy 1932-1981 .... CLC 63
See also CA 105; 104; CANR 72; DLB 14

Brown, Claude 1937- .... CLC 30; BLC 1;
DAM MULT
See also AAYA 7; BW 1, 3; CA 73-76;
CANR 81

Brown, Dee (Alexander) 1908- . CLC 18, 47;
DAM POP
See also AAYA 30; CA 13-16R; CAAS 6;
CANR 11, 45, 60; DA3; DLBY 80;
MTCW 1, 2; SATA 5, 110

Brown, George
See Wertmueller, Lina

Brown, George Douglas
1869-1902 .... TCLC 28
See also CA 162

Brown, George Mackay 1921-1996 ... CLC 5,
48, 100
See also CA 21-24R; 151; CAAS 6; CANR
12, 37, 67; DLB 14, 27, 139; MTCW 1;
SATA 35

Brown, (William) Larry 1951- .... CLC 73
See also CA 130; 134; INT 133

Brown, Moses
See Barrett, William (Christopher)

Brown, Rita Mae 1944- .... CLC 18, 43, 79;
DAM NOV, POP
See also CA 45-48; CANR 2, 11, 35, 62;
DA3; INT CANR-11; MTCW 1, 2

Brown, Roderick (Langmere) Haig-
See Haig-Brown, Roderick (Langmere)

Brown, Rosellen 1939- .... CLC 32
See also CA 77-80; CAAS 10; CANR 14,
44

Brown, Sterling Allen 1901-1989 ...... CLC 1,
23, 59; BLC 1; DAM MULT, POET
See also BW 1, 3; CA 85-88; 127; CANR
26; DA3; DLB 48, 51, 63; MTCW 1, 2

Brown, Will
See Ainsworth, William Harrison

Brown, William Wells 1813-1884 ... NCLC 2,
89; BLC 1; DAM MULT; DC 1
See also DLB 3, 50

Browne, (Clyde) Jackson 1948(?)- ... CLC 21
See also CA 120

Browning, Elizabeth Barrett
1806-1861 ...... NCLC 1, 16, 61, 66; DA;
DAB; DAC; DAM MST, POET; PC 6;
WLC
See also CDBLB 1832-1890; DA3; DLB
32, 199

Browning, Robert 1812-1889 . NCLC 19, 79;
DA; DAB; DAC; DAM MST, POET;
PC 2; WLCS
See also CDBLB 1832-1890; DA3; DLB
32, 163; YABC 1

Browning, Tod 1882-1962 .... CLC 16
See also CA 141; 117

Brownson, Orestes Augustus
1803-1876 .... NCLC 50
See also DLB 1, 59, 73

Bruccoli, Matthew J(oseph) 1931- ... CLC 34
See also CA 9-12R; CANR 7, 87; DLB 103

Bruce, Lenny CLC 21
See also Schneider, Leonard Alfred

Bruin, John
See Brutus, Dennis

Brulard, Henri
See Stendhal

Brulls, Christian
See Simenon, Georges (Jacques Christian)

Brunner, John (Kilian Houston)
1934-1995 .... CLC 8, 10; DAM POP
See also CA 1-4R; 149; CAAS 8; CANR 2,
37; MTCW 1, 2

Bruno, Giordano 1548-1600 .... LC 27

Brutus, Dennis 1924- .... CLC 43; BLC 1;
DAM MULT, POET; PC 24
See also BW 2, 3; CA 49-52; CAAS 14;
CANR 2, 27, 42, 81; DLB 117, 225

Bryan, C(ourtlandt) D(ixon) B(arnes)
1936- .... CLC 29
See also CA 73-76; CANR 13, 68; DLB
185; INT CANR-13

Bryan, Michael
See Moore, Brian

Bryant, William Cullen 1794-1878 . NCLC 6,
46; DA; DAB; DAC; DAM MST,
POET; PC 20
See also CDALB 1640-1865; DLB 3, 43,
59, 189

Bryusov, Valery Yakovlevich
1873-1924 .... TCLC 10
See also CA 107; 155

Buchan, John 1875-1940 .... TCLC 41; DAB;
DAM POP
See also CA 108; 145; DLB 34, 70, 156;
MTCW 1; YABC 2

Buchanan, George 1506-1582 .... LC 4
See also DLB 152

Buchheim, Lothar-Guenther 1918- .... CLC 6
See also CA 85-88

Buchner, (Karl) Georg 1813-1837 . NCLC 26

Buchwald, Art(hur) 1925- .... CLC 33
See also AITN 1; CA 5-8R; CANR 21, 67;
MTCW 1, 2; SATA 10

Buck, Pearl S(ydenstricker)
1892-1973 .... CLC 7, 11, 18, 127; DA;
DAB; DAC; DAM MST, NOV
See also AITN 1; CA 1-4R; 41-44R; CANR
1, 34; CDALBS; DA3; DLB 9, 102;
MTCW 1, 2; SATA 1, 25

Buckler, Ernest 1908-1984 .... CLC 13; DAC;
DAM MST
See also CA 11-12; 114; CAP 1; DLB 68;
SATA 47

Buckley, Vincent (Thomas)
1925-1988 .... CLC 57
See also CA 101

Buckley, William F(rank), Jr. 1925- . CLC 7,
18, 37; DAM POP
See also AITN 1; CA 1-4R; CANR 1, 24,
53; DA3; DLB 137; DLBY 80; INT
CANR-24; MTCW 1, 2

Buechner, (Carl) Frederick 1926- . CLC 2, 4,
6, 9; DAM NOV
See also CA 13-16R; CANR 11, 39, 64;
DLBY 80; INT CANR-11; MTCW 1, 2

Buell, John (Edward) 1927- .... CLC 10
See also CA 1-4R; CANR 71; DLB 53

Buero Vallejo, Antonio 1916- ..... CLC 15, 46
See also CA 106; CANR 24, 49, 75; HW 1;
MTCW 1, 2

Bufalino, Gesualdo 1920(?)- .... CLC 74
See also DLB 196

Bugayev, Boris Nikolayevich
1880-1934 .... TCLC 7; PC 11
See also Bely, Andrey
See also CA 104; 165; MTCW 1

Bukowski, Charles 1920-1994 ... **CLC 2, 5, 9, 41, 82, 108; DAM NOV, POET; PC 18**
See also CA 17-20R; 144; CANR 40, 62; DA3; DLB 5, 130, 169; MTCW 1, 2

Bulgakov, Mikhail (Afanas'evich) 1891-1940 . **TCLC 2, 16; DAM DRAM, NOV; SSC 18**
See also CA 105; 152

Bulgya, Alexander Alexandrovich 1901-1956 .... **TCLC 53**
See also Fadeyev, Alexander
See also CA 117; 181

Bullins, Ed 1935- .... **CLC 1, 5, 7; BLC 1; DAM DRAM, MULT; DC 6**
See also BW 2, 3; CA 49-52; CAAS 16; CANR 24, 46, 73; DLB 7, 38; MTCW 1, 2

Bulwer-Lytton, Edward (George Earle Lytton) 1803-1873 .... **NCLC 1, 45**
See also DLB 21

Bunin, Ivan Alexeyevich 1870-1953 .... **TCLC 6; SSC 5**
See also CA 104

Bunting, Basil 1900-1985 ..... **CLC 10, 39, 47; DAM POET**
See also CA 53-56; 115; CANR 7; DLB 20

Bunuel, Luis 1900-1983 .. **CLC 16, 80; DAM MULT; HLC 1**
See also CA 101; 110; CANR 32, 77; HW 1

Bunyan, John 1628-1688 ... **LC 4; DA; DAB; DAC; DAM MST; WLC**
See also CDBLB 1660-1789; DLB 39

Burckhardt, Jacob (Christoph) 1818-1897 .... **NCLC 49**

Burford, Eleanor
See Hibbert, Eleanor Alice Burford

Burgess, Anthony **CLC 1, 2, 4, 5, 8, 10, 13, 15, 22, 40, 62, 81, 94; DAB**
See also Wilson, John (Anthony) Burgess
See also AAYA 25; AITN 1; CDBLB 1960 to Present; DLB 14, 194; DLBY 98; MTCW 1

Burke, Edmund 1729(?)-1797 .... **LC 7, 36; DA; DAB; DAC; DAM MST; WLC**
See also DA3; DLB 104

Burke, Kenneth (Duva) 1897-1993 ... **CLC 2, 24**
See also CA 5-8R; 143; CANR 39, 74; DLB 45, 63; MTCW 1, 2

Burke, Leda
See Garnett, David

Burke, Ralph
See Silverberg, Robert

Burke, Thomas 1886-1945 .... **TCLC 63**
See also CA 113; 155; DLB 197

Burney, Fanny 1752-1840 .. **NCLC 12, 54, 81**
See also DLB 39

Burns, Robert 1759-1796 . **LC 3, 29, 40; DA; DAB; DAC; DAM MST, POET; PC 6; WLC**
See also CDBLB 1789-1832; DA3; DLB 109

Burns, Tex
See L'Amour, Louis (Dearborn)

Burnshaw, Stanley 1906- .... **CLC 3, 13, 44**
See also CA 9-12R; DLB 48; DLBY 97

Burr, Anne 1937- .... **CLC 6**
See also CA 25-28R

Burroughs, Edgar Rice 1875-1950 . **TCLC 2, 32; DAM NOV**
See also AAYA 11; CA 104; 132; DA3; DLB 8; MTCW 1, 2; SATA 41

Burroughs, William S(eward) 1914-1997 .. **CLC 1, 2, 5, 15, 22, 42, 75, 109; DA; DAB; DAC; DAM MST, NOV, POP; WLC**
See also AITN 2; CA 9-12R; 160; CANR 20, 52; DA3; DLB 2, 8, 16, 152; DLBY 81, 97; MTCW 1, 2

Burton, SirRichard F(rancis) 1821-1890 .... **NCLC 42**
See also DLB 55, 166, 184

Busch, Frederick 1941- .... **CLC 7, 10, 18, 47**
See also CA 33-36R; CAAS 1; CANR 45, 73; DLB 6

Bush, Ronald 1946- .... **CLC 34**
See also CA 136

Bustos, F(rancisco)
See Borges, Jorge Luis

Bustos Domecq, H(onorio)
See Bioy Casares, Adolfo; Borges, Jorge Luis

Butler, Octavia E(stelle) 1947- .... **CLC 38, 121; BLCS; DAM MULT, POP**
See also AAYA 18; BW 2, 3; CA 73-76; CANR 12, 24, 38, 73; CLR 65; DA3; DLB 33; MTCW 1, 2; SATA 84

Butler, Robert Olen (Jr.) 1945- .... **CLC 81; DAM POP**
See also CA 112; CANR 66; DLB 173; INT 112; MTCW 1

Butler, Samuel 1612-1680 .... **LC 16, 43**
See also DLB 101, 126

Butler, Samuel 1835-1902 . **TCLC 1, 33; DA; DAB; DAC; DAM MST, NOV; WLC**
See also CA 143; CDBLB 1890-1914; DA3; DLB 18, 57, 174

Butler, Walter C.
See Faust, Frederick (Schiller)

Butor, Michel (Marie Francois) 1926- .... **CLC 1, 3, 8, 11, 15**
See also CA 9-12R; CANR 33, 66; DLB 83; MTCW 1, 2

Butts, Mary 1892(?)-1937 .... **TCLC 77**
See also CA 148

Buzo, Alexander (John) 1944- .... **CLC 61**
See also CA 97-100; CANR 17, 39, 69

Buzzati, Dino 1906-1972 .... **CLC 36**
See also CA 160; 33-36R; DLB 177

Byars, Betsy (Cromer) 1928- .... **CLC 35**
See also AAYA 19; CA 33-36R, 183; CAAE 183; CANR 18, 36, 57; CLR 1, 16; DLB 52; INT CANR-18; JRDA; MAICYA; MTCW 1; SAAS 1; SATA 4, 46, 80; SATA-Essay 108

Byatt, A(ntonia) S(usan Drabble) 1936- ..... **CLC 19, 65; DAM NOV, POP**
See also CA 13-16R; CANR 13, 33, 50, 75; DA3; DLB 14, 194; MTCW 1, 2

Byrne, David 1952- .... **CLC 26**
See also CA 127

Byrne, John Keyes 1926-
See Leonard, Hugh
See also CA 102; CANR 78; INT 102

Byron, George Gordon (Noel) 1788-1824 .... **NCLC 2, 12; DA; DAB; DAC; DAM MST, POET; PC 16; WLC**
See also CDBLB 1789-1832; DA3; DLB 96, 110

Byron, Robert 1905-1941 .... **TCLC 67**
See also CA 160; DLB 195

C. 3. 3.
See Wilde, Oscar (Fingal O'Flahertie Wills)

Caballero, Fernan 1796-1877 .... **NCLC 10**

Cabell, Branch
See Cabell, James Branch

Cabell, James Branch 1879-1958 .... **TCLC 6**
See also CA 105; 152; DLB 9, 78; MTCW 1

Cable, George Washington 1844-1925 .... **TCLC 4; SSC 4**
See also CA 104; 155; DLB 12, 74; DLBD 13

Cabral de Melo Neto, Joao 1920- ... **CLC 76; DAM MULT**
See also CA 151

Cabrera Infante, G(uillermo) 1929- . **CLC 5, 25, 45, 120; DAM MULT; HLC 1; SSC 39**
See also CA 85-88; CANR 29, 65; DA3; DLB 113; HW 1, 2; MTCW 1, 2

Cade, Toni
See Bambara, Toni Cade

Cadmus and Harmonia
See Buchan, John

Caedmon fl. 658-680 .... **CMLC 7**
See also DLB 146

Caeiro, Alberto
See Pessoa, Fernando (Antonio Nogueira)

Cage, John (Milton, Jr.) 1912-1992 . **CLC 41**
See also CA 13-16R; 169; CANR 9, 78; DLB 193; INT CANR-9

Cahan, Abraham 1860-1951 .... **TCLC 71**
See also CA 108; 154; DLB 9, 25, 28

Cain, G.
See Cabrera Infante, G(uillermo)

Cain, Guillermo
See Cabrera Infante, G(uillermo)

Cain, James M(allahan) 1892-1977 .. **CLC 3, 11, 28**
See also AITN 1; CA 17-20R; 73-76; CANR 8, 34, 61; DLB 226; MTCW 1

Caine, Hall 1853-1931 .... **TCLC 97**

Caine, Mark
See Raphael, Frederic (Michael)

Calasso, Roberto 1941- .... **CLC 81**
See also CA 143; CANR 89

Calderon de la Barca, Pedro 1600-1681 .... **LC 23; DC 3; HLCS 1**

Caldwell, Erskine (Preston) 1903-1987 .. **CLC 1, 8, 14, 50, 60; DAM NOV; SSC 19**
See also AITN 1; CA 1-4R; 121; CAAS 1; CANR 2, 33; DA3; DLB 9, 86; MTCW 1, 2

Caldwell, (Janet Miriam) Taylor (Holland) 1900-1985 .. **CLC 2, 28, 39; DAM NOV, POP**
See also CA 5-8R; 116; CANR 5; DA3; DLBD 17

Calhoun, John Caldwell 1782-1850 .... **NCLC 15**
See also DLB 3

Calisher, Hortense 1911- ..... **CLC 2, 4, 8, 38; DAM NOV; SSC 15**
See also CA 1-4R; CANR 1, 22, 67; DA3; DLB 2; INT CANR-22; MTCW 1, 2

Callaghan, Morley Edward 1903-1990 ...... **CLC 3, 14, 41, 65; DAC; DAM MST**
See also CA 9-12R; 132; CANR 33, 73; DLB 68; MTCW 1, 2

Callimachus c. 305B.C.-c. 240B.C. .... **CMLC 18**
See also DLB 176

Calvin, John 1509-1564 .... **LC 37**

Calvino, Italo 1923-1985 .... **CLC 5, 8, 11, 22, 33, 39, 73; DAM NOV; SSC 3**
See also CA 85-88; 116; CANR 23, 61; DLB 196; MTCW 1, 2

Cameron, Carey 1952- .... **CLC 59**
See also CA 135

Cameron, Peter 1959- .... **CLC 44**
See also CA 125; CANR 50

Camoens, Luis Vaz de 1524(?)-1580
See also HLCS 1

Camoes, Luis de 1524(?)-1580
See also HLCS 1

Campana, Dino 1885-1932 .... **TCLC 20**
See also CA 117; DLB 114

Campanella, Tommaso 1568-1639 .... **LC 32**

Campbell, John W(ood, Jr.) 1910-1971 .... **CLC 32**
See also CA 21-22; 29-32R; CANR 34; CAP 2; DLB 8; MTCW 1

Campbell, Joseph 1904-1987 .... **CLC 69**
See also AAYA 3; BEST 89:2; CA 1-4R; 124; CANR 3, 28, 61; DA3; MTCW 1, 2

Campbell, Maria 1940- .... **CLC 85; DAC**
See also CA 102; CANR 54; NNAL

Campbell, (John) Ramsey 1946- ..... **CLC 42; SSC 19**
See also CA 57-60; CANR 7; INT CANR-7

Campbell, (Ignatius) Roy (Dunnachie) 1901-1957 .... **TCLC 5**
See also CA 104; 155; DLB 20, 225; MTCW 2

Campbell, Thomas 1777-1844 .... **NCLC 19**
See also DLB 93; 144

Campbell, Wilfred TCLC 9
See also Campbell, William

Campbell, William 1858(?)-1918
See Campbell, Wilfred
See also CA 106; DLB 92

Campion, Jane CLC 95
See also AAYA 33; CA 138; CANR 87

Camus, Albert 1913-1960 ...... **CLC 1, 2, 4, 9, 11, 14, 32, 63, 69, 124; DA; DAB; DAC; DAM DRAM, MST, NOV; DC 2; SSC 9; WLC**
See also CA 89-92; DA3; DLB 72; MTCW 1, 2

Canby, Vincent 1924- .... **CLC 13**
See also CA 81-84

Cancale
See Desnos, Robert

Canetti, Elias 1905-1994 .. **CLC 3, 14, 25, 75, 86**
See also CA 21-24R; 146; CANR 23, 61; 79; DA3; DLB 85, 124; MTCW 1, 2

Canfield, Dorothea F.
See Fisher, Dorothy (Frances) Canfield

Canfield, Dorothea Frances
See Fisher, Dorothy (Frances) Canfield

Canfield, Dorothy
See Fisher, Dorothy (Frances) Canfield

Canin, Ethan 1960- .... **CLC 55**
See also CA 131; 135

Cannon, Curt
See Hunter, Evan

Cao, Lan 1961- .... **CLC 109**
See also CA 165

Cape, Judith
See Page, P(atricia) K(athleen)

Capek, Karel 1890-1938 ... **TCLC 6, 37; DA; DAB; DAC; DAM DRAM, MST, NOV; DC 1; SSC 36; WLC**
See also CA 104; 140; DA3; MTCW 1

Capote, Truman 1924-1984 . **CLC 1, 3, 8, 13, 19, 34, 38, 58; DA; DAB; DAC; DAM MST, NOV, POP; SSC 2; WLC**
See also CA 5-8R; 113; CANR 18, 62; CDALB 1941-1968; DA3; DLB 2, 185, 227; DLBY 80, 84; MTCW 1, 2; SATA 91

Capra, Frank 1897-1991 .... **CLC 16**
See also CA 61-64; 135

Caputo, Philip 1941- .... **CLC 32**
See also CA 73-76; CANR 40

Caragiale, Ion Luca 1852-1912 ...... **TCLC 76**
See also CA 157

Card, Orson Scott 1951- ..... **CLC 44, 47, 50; DAM POP**
See also AAYA 11; CA 102; CANR 27, 47, 73; DA3; INT CANR-27; MTCW 1, 2; SATA 83

Cardenal, Ernesto 1925- .... **CLC 31; DAM MULT, POET; HLC 1; PC 22**
See also CA 49-52; CANR 2, 32, 66; HW 1, 2; MTCW 1, 2

Cardozo, Benjamin N(athan) 1870-1938 .... **TCLC 65**
See also CA 117; 164

Carducci, Giosue (Alessandro Giuseppe) 1835-1907 .... **TCLC 32**
See also CA 163

Carew, Thomas 1595(?)-1640 . **LC 13; PC 29**
See also DLB 126

Carey, Ernestine Gilbreth 1908- ...... **CLC 17**
See also CA 5-8R; CANR 71; SATA 2

Carey, Peter 1943- .... **CLC 40, 55, 96**
See also CA 123; 127; CANR 53, 76; INT 127; MTCW 1, 2; SATA 94

Carleton, William 1794-1869 .... **NCLC 3**
See also DLB 159

Carlisle, Henry (Coffin) 1926- .... **CLC 33**
See also CA 13-16R; CANR 15, 85

Carlsen, Chris
See Holdstock, Robert P.

Carlson, Ron(ald F.) 1947- .... **CLC 54**
See also CA 105; CANR 27

Carlyle, Thomas 1795-1881 .. **NCLC 70; DA; DAB; DAC; DAM MST**
See also CDBLB 1789-1832; DLB 55; 144

Carman, (William) Bliss 1861-1929 .... **TCLC 7; DAC**
See also CA 104; 152; DLB 92

Carnegie, Dale 1888-1955 .... **TCLC 53**

Carossa, Hans 1878-1956 .... **TCLC 48**
See also CA 170; DLB 66

Carpenter, Don(ald Richard) 1931-1995 .... **CLC 41**
See also CA 45-48; 149; CANR 1, 71

Carpenter, Edward 1844-1929 .... **TCLC 88**
See also CA 163

Carpentier (y Valmont), Alejo 1904-1980 ..... **CLC 8, 11, 38, 110; DAM MULT; HLC 1; SSC 35**
See also CA 65-68; 97-100; CANR 11, 70; DLB 113; HW 1, 2

Carr, Caleb 1955(?)- .... **CLC 86**
See also CA 147; CANR 73; DA3

Carr, Emily 1871-1945 .... **TCLC 32**
See also CA 159; DLB 68

Carr, John Dickson 1906-1977 .... **CLC 3**
See also Fairbairn, Roger
See also CA 49-52; 69-72; CANR 3, 33, 60; MTCW 1, 2

Carr, Philippa
See Hibbert, Eleanor Alice Burford

Carr, Virginia Spencer 1929- .... **CLC 34**
See also CA 61-64; DLB 111

Carrere, Emmanuel 1957- .... **CLC 89**

Carrier, Roch 1937- .... **CLC 13, 78; DAC; DAM MST**
See also CA 130; CANR 61; DLB 53; SATA 105

Carroll, James P. 1943(?)- .... **CLC 38**
See also CA 81-84; CANR 73; MTCW 1

Carroll, Jim 1951- .... **CLC 35**
See also AAYA 17; CA 45-48; CANR 42

Carroll, Lewis NCLC 2, 53; PC 18; WLC
See also Dodgson, Charles Lutwidge
See also CDBLB 1832-1890; CLR 2, 18; DLB 18, 163, 178; DLBY 98; JRDA

Carroll, Paul Vincent 1900-1968 ...... **CLC 10**
See also CA 9-12R; 25-28R; DLB 10

Carruth, Hayden 1921- ..... **CLC 4, 7, 10, 18, 84; PC 10**
See also CA 9-12R; CANR 4, 38, 59; DLB 5, 165; INT CANR-4; MTCW 1, 2; SATA 47

Carson, Rachel Louise 1907-1964 ... **CLC 71; DAM POP**
See also CA 77-80; CANR 35; DA3; MTCW 1, 2; SATA 23

Carter, Angela (Olive) 1940-1992 ...... **CLC 5, 41, 76; SSC 13**
See also CA 53-56; 136; CANR 12, 36, 61; DA3; DLB 14, 207; MTCW 1, 2; SATA 66; SATA-Obit 70

Carter, Nick
See Smith, Martin Cruz

Carver, Raymond 1938-1988 ..... **CLC 22, 36, 53, 55, 126; DAM NOV; SSC 8**
See also CA 33-36R; 126; CANR 17, 34, 61; DA3; DLB 130; DLBY 84, 88; MTCW 1, 2

Cary, Elizabeth, Lady Falkland 1585-1639 .... **LC 30**

Cary, (Arthur) Joyce (Lunel) 1888-1957 .... **TCLC 1, 29**
See also CA 104; 164; CDBLB 1914-1945; DLB 15, 100; MTCW 2

Casanova de Seingalt, Giovanni Jacopo 1725-1798 .... **LC 13**

Casares, Adolfo Bioy
See Bioy Casares, Adolfo

Casely-Hayford, J(oseph) E(phraim) 1866-1930 ...... **TCLC 24; BLC 1; DAM MULT**
See also BW 2; CA 123; 152

Casey, John (Dudley) 1939- .... **CLC 59**
See also BEST 90:2; CA 69-72; CANR 23

Casey, Michael 1947- .... **CLC 2**
See also CA 65-68; DLB 5

Casey, Patrick
See Thurman, Wallace (Henry)

Casey, Warren (Peter) 1935-1988 .... **CLC 12**
See also CA 101; 127; INT 101

Casona, Alejandro CLC 49
See also Alvarez, Alejandro Rodriguez

Cassavetes, John 1929-1989 .... **CLC 20**
See also CA 85-88; 127; CANR 82

Cassian, Nina 1924- .... **PC 17**

Cassill, R(onald) V(erlin) 1919- ... **CLC 4, 23**
See also CA 9-12R; CAAS 1; CANR 7, 45; DLB 6

Cassirer, Ernst 1874-1945 .... **TCLC 61**
See also CA 157

Cassity, (Allen) Turner 1929- .... **CLC 6, 42**
See also CA 17-20R; CAAS 8; CANR 11; DLB 105

Castaneda, Carlos (Cesar Aranha) 1931(?)-1998 .... **CLC 12, 119**
See also CA 25-28R; CANR 32, 66; HW 1; MTCW 1

Castedo, Elena 1937- .... **CLC 65**
See also CA 132

Castedo-Ellerman, Elena
See Castedo, Elena

Castellanos, Rosario 1925-1974 .... **CLC 66; DAM MULT; HLC 1; SSC 39**
See also CA 131; 53-56; CANR 58; DLB 113; HW 1; MTCW 1

Castelvetro, Lodovico 1505-1571 .... **LC 12**

Castiglione, Baldassare 1478-1529 ...... **LC 12**

Castle, Robert
See Hamilton, Edmond

Castro (Ruz), Fidel 1926(?)-
See also CA 110; 129; CANR 81; DAM MULT; HLC 1; HW 2

Castro, Guillen de 1569-1631 .... **LC 19**

Castro, Rosalia de 1837-1885 ... **NCLC 3, 78; DAM MULT**

Cather, Willa
See Cather, Willa Sibert

Cather, Willa Sibert 1873-1947 ...... **TCLC 1, 11, 31; DA; DAB; DAC; DAM MST, NOV; SSC 2; WLC**
See also Cather, Willa
See also AAYA 24; CA 104; 128; CDALB 1865-1917; DA3; DLB 9, 54, 78; DLBD 1; MTCW 1, 2; SATA 30

Catherine, Saint 1347-1380 .... **CMLC 27**

Cato, Marcus Porcius 234B.C.-149B.C. .... **CMLC 21**
See also DLB 211

Catton, (Charles) Bruce 1899-1978 . **CLC 35**
See also AITN 1; CA 5-8R; 81-84; CANR 7, 74; DLB 17; SATA 2; SATA-Obit 24
Catullus c. 84B.C.-c. 54B.C. .... **CMLC 18**
See also DLB 211
Cauldwell, Frank
See King, Francis (Henry)
Caunitz, William J. 1933-1996 .... **CLC 34**
See also BEST 89:3; CA 125; 130; 152; CANR 73; INT 130
Causley, Charles (Stanley) 1917- .... **CLC 7**
See also CA 9-12R; CANR 5, 35; CLR 30; DLB 27; MTCW 1; SATA 3, 66
Caute, (John) David 1936- .... **CLC 29; DAM NOV**
See also CA 1-4R; CAAS 4; CANR 1, 33, 64; DLB 14
Cavafy, C(onstantine) P(eter)
1863-1933 ...... **TCLC 2, 7; DAM POET**
See also Kavafis, Konstantinos Petrou
See also CA 148; DA3; MTCW 1
Cavallo, Evelyn
See Spark, Muriel (Sarah)
Cavanna, Betty CLC 12
See also Harrison, Elizabeth Cavanna
See also JRDA; MAICYA; SAAS 4; SATA 1, 30
Cavendish, Margaret Lucas
1623-1673 .... **LC 30**
See also DLB 131
Caxton, William 1421(?)-1491(?) .... **LC 17**
See also DLB 170
Cayer, D. M.
See Duffy, Maureen
Cayrol, Jean 1911- .... **CLC 11**
See also CA 89-92; DLB 83
Cela, Camilo Jose 1916- .... **CLC 4, 13, 59, 122; DAM MULT; HLC 1**
See also BEST 90:2; CA 21-24R; CAAS 10; CANR 21, 32, 76; DLBY 89; HW 1; MTCW 1, 2
Celan, Paul CLC 10, 19, 53, 82; PC 10
See also Antschel, Paul
See also DLB 69
Celine, Louis-Ferdinand CLC 1, 3, 4, 7, 9, 15, 47, 124
See also Destouches, Louis-Ferdinand
See also DLB 72
Cellini, Benvenuto 1500-1571 .... **LC 7**
Cendrars, Blaise 1887-1961 ...... **CLC 18, 106**
See also Sauser-Hall, Frederic
Cernuda (y Bidon), Luis
1902-1963 .... **CLC 54; DAM POET**
See also CA 131; 89-92; DLB 134; HW 1
Cervantes, Lorna Dee 1954-
See also CA 131; CANR 80; DLB 82; HLCS 1; HW 1
Cervantes (Saavedra), Miguel de
1547-1616 .. **LC 6, 23; DA; DAB; DAC; DAM MST, NOV; SSC 12; WLC**
Cesaire, Aime (Fernand) 1913- . **CLC 19, 32, 112; BLC 1; DAM MULT, POET; PC 25**
See also BW 2, 3; CA 65-68; CANR 24, 43, 81; DA3; MTCW 1, 2
Chabon, Michael 1963- .... **CLC 55**
See also CA 139; CANR 57
Chabrol, Claude 1930- .... **CLC 16**
See also CA 110
Challans, Mary 1905-1983
See Renault, Mary
See also CA 81-84; 111; CANR 74; DA3; MTCW 2; SATA 23; SATA-Obit 36
Challis, George
See Faust, Frederick (Schiller)
Chambers, Aidan 1934- .... **CLC 35**
See also AAYA 27; CA 25-28R; CANR 12, 31, 58; JRDA; MAICYA; SAAS 12; SATA 1, 69, 108

Chambers, James 1948-
See Cliff, Jimmy
See also CA 124
Chambers, Jessie
See Lawrence, D(avid) H(erbert Richards)
Chambers, Robert W(illiam)
1865-1933 .... **TCLC 41**
See also CA 165; DLB 202; SATA 107
Chamisso, Adelbert von
1781-1838 .... **NCLC 82**
See also DLB 90
Chandler, Raymond (Thornton)
1888-1959 .... **TCLC 1, 7; SSC 23**
See also AAYA 25; CA 104; 129; CANR 60; CDALB 1929-1941; DA3; DLB 226; DLBD 6; MTCW 1, 2
Chang, Eileen 1920-1995 .... **SSC 28**
See also CA 166
Chang, Jung 1952- .... **CLC 71**
See also CA 142
Chang Ai-Ling
See Chang, Eileen
Channing, William Ellery
1780-1842 .... **NCLC 17**
See also DLB 1, 59
Chao, Patricia 1955- .... **CLC 119**
See also CA 163
Chaplin, Charles Spencer
1889-1977 .... **CLC 16**
See also Chaplin, Charlie
See also CA 81-84; 73-76
Chaplin, Charlie
See Chaplin, Charles Spencer
See also DLB 44
Chapman, George 1559(?)-1634 .... **LC 22; DAM DRAM**
See also DLB 62, 121
Chapman, Graham 1941-1989 .... **CLC 21**
See also Monty Python
See also CA 116; 129; CANR 35
Chapman, John Jay 1862-1933 .... **TCLC 7**
See also CA 104
Chapman, Lee
See Bradley, Marion Zimmer
Chapman, Walker
See Silverberg, Robert
Chappell, Fred (Davis) 1936- ..... **CLC 40, 78**
See also CA 5-8R; CAAS 4; CANR 8, 33, 67; DLB 6, 105
Char, Rene(-Emile) 1907-1988 .... **CLC 9, 11, 14, 55; DAM POET**
See also CA 13-16R; 124; CANR 32; MTCW 1, 2
Charby, Jay
See Ellison, Harlan (Jay)
Chardin, Pierre Teilhard de
See Teilhard de Chardin, (Marie Joseph) Pierre
Charlemagne 742-814 .... **CMLC 37**
Charles I 1600-1649 .... **LC 13**
Charriere, Isabelle de 1740-1805 .. **NCLC 66**
Charyn, Jerome 1937- .... **CLC 5, 8, 18**
See also CA 5-8R; CAAS 1; CANR 7, 61; DLBY 83; MTCW 1
Chase, Mary (Coyle) 1907-1981 .... **DC 1**
See also CA 77-80; 105; DLB 228; SATA 17; SATA-Obit 29
Chase, Mary Ellen 1887-1973 .... **CLC 2**
See also CA 13-16; 41-44R; CAP 1; SATA 10
Chase, Nicholas
See Hyde, Anthony
Chateaubriand, Francois Rene de
1768-1848 .... **NCLC 3**
See also DLB 119
Chatterje, Sarat Chandra 1876-1936(?)
See Chatterji, Saratchandra
See also CA 109

Chatterji, Bankim Chandra
1838-1894 .... **NCLC 19**
Chatterji, Saratchandra -1938 .... **TCLC 13**
See also Chatterje, Sarat Chandra
See also CA 186
Chatterton, Thomas 1752-1770 ..... **LC 3, 54; DAM POET**
See also DLB 109
Chatwin, (Charles) Bruce
1940-1989 . **CLC 28, 57, 59; DAM POP**
See also AAYA 4; BEST 90:1; CA 85-88; 127; DLB 194, 204
Chaucer, Daniel
See Ford, Ford Madox
Chaucer, Geoffrey 1340(?)-1400 .. **LC 17, 56; DA; DAB; DAC; DAM MST, POET; PC 19; WLCS**
See also CDBLB Before 1660; DA3; DLB 146
Chavez, Denise (Elia) 1948-
See also CA 131; CANR 56, 81; DAM MULT; DLB 122; HLC 1; HW 1, 2; MTCW 2
Chaviaras, Strates 1935-
See Haviaras, Stratis
See also CA 105
Chayefsky, Paddy CLC 23
See also Chayefsky, Sidney
See also DLB 7, 44; DLBY 81
Chayefsky, Sidney 1923-1981
See Chayefsky, Paddy
See also CA 9-12R; 104; CANR 18; DAM DRAM
Chedid, Andree 1920- .... **CLC 47**
See also CA 145
Cheever, John 1912-1982 ..... **CLC 3, 7, 8, 11, 15, 25, 64; DA; DAB; DAC; DAM MST, NOV, POP; SSC 1, 38; WLC**
See also CA 5-8R; 106; CABS 1; CANR 5, 27, 76; CDALB 1941-1968; DA3; DLB 2, 102, 227; DLBY 80, 82; INT CANR-5; MTCW 1, 2
Cheever, Susan 1943- .... **CLC 18, 48**
See also CA 103; CANR 27, 51; DLBY 82; INT CANR 27
Chekhonte, Antosha
See Chekhov, Anton (Pavlovich)
Chekhov, Anton (Pavlovich)
1860-1904 .... **TCLC 3, 10, 31, 55, 96; DA; DAB; DAC; DAM DRAM, MST; DC 9; SSC 2, 28, 41; WLC**
See also CA 104; 124; DA3; SATA 90
Chernyshevsky, Nikolay Gavrilovich
1828-1889 .... **NCLC 1**
Cherry, Carolyn Janice 1942-
See Cherryh, C. J.
See also CA 65-68; CANR 10
Cherryh, C. J. CLC 35
See also Cherry, Carolyn Janice
See also AAYA 24; DLBY 80; SATA 93
Chesnutt, Charles W(addell)
1858-1932 .. **TCLC 5, 39; BLC 1; DAM MULT; SSC 7**
See also BW 1, 3; CA 106; 125; CANR 76; DLB 12, 50, 78; MTCW 1, 2
Chester, Alfred 1929(?)-1971 .... **CLC 49**
See also CA 33-36R; DLB 130
Chesterton, G(ilbert) K(eith)
1874-1936 . **TCLC 1, 6, 64; DAM NOV, POET; PC 28; SSC 1**
See also CA 104; 132; CANR 73; CDBLB 1914-1945; DLB 10, 19, 34, 70, 98, 149, 178; MTCW 1, 2; SATA 27
Chiang, Pin-chin 1904-1986
See Ding Ling
See also CA 118
Ch'ien Chung-shu 1910- .... **CLC 22**
See also CA 130; CANR 73; MTCW 1, 2

Child, L. Maria
  See Child, Lydia Maria
Child, Lydia Maria 1802-1880 .. **NCLC 6, 73**
  See also DLB 1, 74; SATA 67
Child, Mrs.
  See Child, Lydia Maria
Child, Philip 1898-1978 .... **CLC 19, 68**
  See also CA 13-14; CAP 1; SATA 47
Childers, (Robert) Erskine
  1870-1922 .... **TCLC 65**
  See also CA 113; 153; DLB 70
Childress, Alice 1920-1994 .. **CLC 12, 15, 86, 96; BLC 1; DAM DRAM, MULT, NOV; DC 4**
  See also AAYA 8; BW 2, 3; CA 45-48; 146; CANR 3, 27, 50, 74; CLR 14; DA3; DLB 7, 38; JRDA; MAICYA; MTCW 1, 2; SATA 7, 48, 81
Chin, Frank (Chew, Jr.) 1940- .... **DC 7**
  See also CA 33-36R; CANR 71; DAM MULT; DLB 206
Chislett, (Margaret) Anne 1943- ...... **CLC 34**
  See also CA 151
Chitty, Thomas Willes 1926- .... **CLC 11**
  See also Hinde, Thomas
  See also CA 5-8R
Chivers, Thomas Holley
  1809-1858 .... **NCLC 49**
  See also DLB 3
Choi, Susan CLC 119
Chomette, Rene Lucien 1898-1981
  See Clair, Rene
  See also CA 103
Chomsky, (Avram) Noam 1928- ..... **CLC 132**
  See also CA 17-20R; CANR 28, 62; DA3; MTCW 1, 2
Chopin, Kate TCLC 5, 14; DA; DAB; SSC 8; WLCS
  See also Chopin, Katherine
  See also AAYA 33; CDALB 1865-1917; DLB 12, 78
Chopin, Katherine 1851-1904
  See Chopin, Kate
  See also CA 104; 122; DAC; DAM MST, NOV; DA3
Chretien de Troyes c. 12th cent. - . **CMLC 10**
  See also DLB 208
Christie
  See Ichikawa, Kon
Christie, Agatha (Mary Clarissa)
  1890-1976 .... **CLC 1, 6, 8, 12, 39, 48, 110; DAB; DAC; DAM NOV**
  See also AAYA 9; AITN 1, 2; CA 17-20R; 61-64; CANR 10, 37; CDBLB 1914-1945; DA3; DLB 13, 77; MTCW 1, 2; SATA 36
Christie, (Ann) Philippa
  See Pearce, Philippa
  See also CA 5-8R; CANR 4
Christine de Pizan 1365(?)-1431(?) .... **LC 9**
  See also DLB 208
Chubb, Elmer
  See Masters, Edgar Lee
Chulkov, Mikhail Dmitrievich
  1743-1792 .... **LC 2**
  See also DLB 150
Churchill, Caryl 1938- .... **CLC 31, 55; DC 5**
  See also CA 102; CANR 22, 46; DLB 13; MTCW 1
Churchill, Charles 1731-1764 .... **LC 3**
  See also DLB 109
Chute, Carolyn 1947- .... **CLC 39**
  See also CA 123
Ciardi, John (Anthony) 1916-1986 . **CLC 10, 40, 44, 129; DAM POET**
  See also CA 5-8R; 118; CAAS 2; CANR 5, 33; CLR 19; DLB 5; DLBY 86; INT CANR-5; MAICYA; MTCW 1, 2; SAAS 26; SATA 1, 65; SATA-Obit 46

Cicero, Marcus Tullius
  106B.C.-43B.C. .... **CMLC 3**
  See also DLB 211
Cimino, Michael 1943- .... **CLC 16**
  See also CA 105
Cioran, E(mil) M. 1911-1995 .... **CLC 64**
  See also CA 25-28R; 149; CANR 91; DLB 220
Cisneros, Sandra 1954- . **CLC 69, 118; DAM MULT; HLC 1; SSC 32**
  See also AAYA 9; CA 131; CANR 64; DA3; DLB 122, 152; HW 1, 2; MTCW 2
Cixous, Helene 1937- .... **CLC 92**
  See also CA 126; CANR 55; DLB 83; MTCW 1, 2
Clair, Rene CLC 20
  See also Chomette, Rene Lucien
Clampitt, Amy 1920-1994 .... **CLC 32; PC 19**
  See also CA 110; 146; CANR 29, 79; DLB 105
Clancy, Thomas L., Jr. 1947-
  See Clancy, Tom
  See also CA 125; 131; CANR 62; DA3; DLB 227; INT 131; MTCW 1, 2
Clancy, Tom CLC 45, 112; DAM NOV, POP
  See also Clancy, Thomas L., Jr.
  See also AAYA 9; BEST 89:1, 90:1; MTCW 2
Clare, John 1793-1864 ... **NCLC 9, 86; DAB; DAM POET; PC 23**
  See also DLB 55, 96
Clarin
  See Alas (y Urena), Leopoldo (Enrique Garcia)
Clark, Al C.
  See Goines, Donald
Clark, (Robert) Brian 1932- .... **CLC 29**
  See also CA 41-44R; CANR 67
Clark, Curt
  See Westlake, Donald E(dwin)
Clark, Eleanor 1913-1996 .... **CLC 5, 19**
  See also CA 9-12R; 151; CANR 41; DLB 6
Clark, J. P.
  See Clark Bekedermo, J(ohnson) P(epper)
  See also DLB 117
Clark, John Pepper
  See Clark Bekedermo, J(ohnson) P(epper)
Clark, M. R.
  See Clark, Mavis Thorpe
Clark, Mavis Thorpe 1909- .... **CLC 12**
  See also CA 57-60; CANR 8, 37; CLR 30; MAICYA; SAAS 5; SATA 8, 74
Clark, Walter Van Tilburg
  1909-1971 .... **CLC 28**
  See also CA 9-12R; 33-36R; CANR 63; DLB 9, 206; SATA 8
Clark Bekedermo, J(ohnson) P(epper)
  1935- .. **CLC 38; BLC 1; DAM DRAM, MULT; DC 5**
  See also Clark, J. P.
  See also BW 1; CA 65-68; CANR 16, 72; MTCW 1
Clarke, Arthur C(harles) 1917- .... **CLC 1, 4, 13, 18, 35; DAM POP; SSC 3**
  See also AAYA 4, 33; CA 1-4R; CANR 2, 28, 55, 74; DA3; JRDA; MAICYA; MTCW 1, 2; SATA 13, 70, 115
Clarke, Austin 1896-1974 ... **CLC 6, 9; DAM POET**
  See also CA 29-32; 49-52; CAP 2; DLB 10, 20
Clarke, Austin C(hesterfield) 1934- .. **CLC 8, 53; BLC 1; DAC; DAM MULT**
  See also BW 1; CA 25-28R; CAAS 16; CANR 14, 32, 68; DLB 53, 125
Clarke, Gillian 1937- .... **CLC 61**
  See also CA 106; DLB 40

Clarke, Marcus (Andrew Hislop)
  1846-1881 .... **NCLC 19**
Clarke, Shirley 1925- .... **CLC 16**
Clash, The
  See Headon, (Nicky) Topper; Jones, Mick; Simonon, Paul; Strummer, Joe
Claudel, Paul (Louis Charles Marie)
  1868-1955 .... **TCLC 2, 10**
  See also CA 104; 165; DLB 192
Claudius, Matthias 1740-1815 .... **NCLC 75**
  See also DLB 97
Clavell, James (duMaresq)
  1925-1994 .. **CLC 6, 25, 87; DAM NOV, POP**
  See also CA 25-28R; 146; CANR 26, 48; DA3; MTCW 1, 2
Cleaver, (Leroy) Eldridge
  1935-1998 . **CLC 30, 119; BLC 1; DAM MULT**
  See also BW 1, 3; CA 21-24R; 167; CANR 16, 75; DA3; MTCW 2
Cleese, John (Marwood) 1939- .... **CLC 21**
  See also Monty Python
  See also CA 112; 116; CANR 35; MTCW 1
Cleishbotham, Jebediah
  See Scott, Walter
Cleland, John 1710-1789 .... **LC 2, 48**
  See also DLB 39
Clemens, Samuel Langhorne 1835-1910
  See Twain, Mark
  See also CA 104; 135; CDALB 1865-1917; DA; DAB; DAC; DAM MST, NOV; DA3; DLB 11, 12, 23, 64, 74, 186, 189; JRDA; MAICYA; SATA 100; YABC 2
Cleophil
  See Congreve, William
Clerihew, E.
  See Bentley, E(dmund) C(lerihew)
Clerk, N. W.
  See Lewis, C(live) S(taples)
Cliff, Jimmy CLC 21
  See also Chambers, James
Cliff, Michelle 1946- .... **CLC 120; BLCS**
  See also BW 2; CA 116; CANR 39, 72; DLB 157
Clifton, (Thelma) Lucille 1936- .... **CLC 19, 66; BLC 1; DAM MULT, POET; PC 17**
  See also BW 2, 3; CA 49-52; CANR 2, 24, 42, 76; CLR 5; DA3; DLB 5, 41; MAICYA; MTCW 1, 2; SATA 20, 69
Clinton, Dirk
  See Silverberg, Robert
Clough, Arthur Hugh 1819-1861 ... **NCLC 27**
  See also DLB 32
Clutha, Janet Paterson Frame 1924-
  See Frame, Janet
  See also CA 1-4R; CANR 2, 36, 76; MTCW 1, 2
Clyne, Terence
  See Blatty, William Peter
Cobalt, Martin
  See Mayne, William (James Carter)
Cobb, Irvin S(hrewsbury)
  1876-1944 .... **TCLC 77**
  See also CA 175; DLB 11, 25, 86
Cobbett, William 1763-1835 .... **NCLC 49**
  See also DLB 43, 107, 158
Coburn, D(onald) L(ee) 1938- .... **CLC 10**
  See also CA 89-92
Cocteau, Jean (Maurice Eugene Clement)
  1889-1963 .... **CLC 1, 8, 15, 16, 43; DA; DAB; DAC; DAM DRAM, MST, NOV; WLC**
  See also CA 25-28; CANR 40; CAP 2; DA3; DLB 65; MTCW 1, 2

Codrescu, Andrei 1946- .... **CLC 46, 121;
DAM POET**
  See also CA 33-36R; CAAS 19; CANR 13,
  34, 53, 76; DA3; MTCW 2
Coe, Max
  See Bourne, Randolph S(illiman)
Coe, Tucker
  See Westlake, Donald E(dwin)
Coen, Ethan 1958- .... **CLC 108**
  See also CA 126; CANR 85
Coen, Joel 1955- .... **CLC 108**
  See also CA 126
The Coen Brothers
  See Coen, Ethan; Coen, Joel
Coetzee, J(ohn) M(ichael) 1940- ...... **CLC 23,
33, 66, 117; DAM NOV**
  See also CA 77-80; CANR 41, 54, 74; DA3;
  DLB 225; MTCW 1, 2
Coffey, Brian
  See Koontz, Dean R(ay)
Coffin, Robert P(eter) Tristram
  1892-1955 .... **TCLC 95**
  See also CA 123; 169; DLB 45
Cohan, George M(ichael)
  1878-1942 .... **TCLC 60**
  See also CA 157
Cohen, Arthur A(llen) 1928-1986 ...... **CLC 7,
31**
  See also CA 1-4R; 120; CANR 1, 17, 42;
  DLB 28
Cohen, Leonard (Norman) 1934- ...... **CLC 3,
38; DAC; DAM MST**
  See also CA 21-24R; CANR 14, 69; DLB
  53, MTCW 1
Cohen, Matt 1942- .... **CLC 19; DAC**
  See also CA 61-64; CAAS 18; CANR 40,
  DLB 53
Cohen-Solal, Annie 19(?)- .... **CLC 50**
Colegate, Isabel 1931- .... **CLC 36**
  See also CA 17-20R; CANR 8, 22, 74; DLB
  14; INT CANR-22; MTCW 1
Coleman, Emmett
  See Reed, Ishmael
Coleridge, M. E.
  See Coleridge, Mary E(lizabeth)
Coleridge, Mary E(lizabeth)
  1861-1907 .... **TCLC 73**
  See also CA 116; 166; DLB 19, 98
Coleridge, Samuel Taylor
  1772-1834 .... **NCLC 9, 54; DA; DAB;
DAC; DAM MST, POET; PC 11; WLC**
  See also CDBLB 1789-1832; DA3; DLB
  93, 107
Coleridge, Sara 1802-1852 .... **NCLC 31**
  See also DLB 199
Coles, Don 1928- .... **CLC 46**
  See also CA 115; CANR 38
Coles, Robert (Martin) 1929- .... **CLC 108**
  See also CA 45-48; CANR 3, 32, 66, 70;
  INT CANR-32; SATA 23
Colette, (Sidonie-Gabrielle)
  1873-1954 . **TCLC 1, 5, 16; DAM NOV;
SSC 10**
  See also CA 104; 131; DA3; DLB 65;
  MTCW 1, 2
Collett, (Jacobine) Camilla (Wergeland)
  1813-1895 .... **NCLC 22**
Collier, Christopher 1930- .... **CLC 30**
  See also AAYA 13; CA 33-36R; CANR 13,
  33; JRDA; MAICYA; SATA 16, 70
Collier, James L(incoln) 1928- .... **CLC 30;
DAM POP**
  See also AAYA 13; CA 9-12R; CANR 4,
  33, 60; CLR 3; JRDA; MAICYA; SAAS
  21; SATA 8, 70
Collier, Jeremy 1650-1726 .... **LC 6**
Collier, John 1901-1980 .... **SSC 19**
  See also CA 65-68; 97-100; CANR 10;
  DLB 77

Collingwood, R(obin) G(eorge)
  1889(?)-1943 .... **TCLC 67**
  See also CA 117; 155
Collins, Hunt
  See Hunter, Evan
Collins, Linda 1931- .... **CLC 44**
  See also CA 125
Collins, (William) Wilkie
  1824-1889 .... **NCLC 1, 18**
  See also CDBLB 1832-1890; DLB 18, 70,
  159
Collins, William 1721-1759 . **LC 4, 40; DAM
POET**
  See also DLB 109
Collodi, Carlo 1826-1890 .... **NCLC 54**
  See also Lorenzini, Carlo
  See also CLR 5
Colman, George 1732-1794
  See Glassco, John
Colt, Winchester Remington
  See Hubbard, L(afayette) Ron(ald)
Colter, Cyrus 1910- .... **CLC 58**
  See also BW 1; CA 65-68; CANR 10, 66;
  DLB 33
Colton, James
  See Hansen, Joseph
Colum, Padraic 1881-1972 .... **CLC 28**
  See also CA 73-76; 33-36R; CANR 35;
  CLR 36; MAICYA; MTCW 1; SATA 15
Colvin, James
  See Moorcock, Michael (John)
Colwin, Laurie (E.) 1944-1992 .... **CLC 5, 13,
23, 84**
  See also CA 89-92; 139; CANR 20, 46;
  DLBY 80; MTCW 1
Comfort, Alex(ander) 1920-2000 .... **CLC 7;
DAM POP**
  See also CA 1-4R; CANR 1, 45; MTCW 1
Comfort, Montgomery
  See Campbell, (John) Ramsey
Compton-Burnett, I(vy)
  1884(?)-1969 .... **CLC 1, 3, 10, 15, 34;
DAM NOV**
  See also CA 1-4R; 25-28R; CANR 4; DLB
  36; MTCW 1
Comstock, Anthony 1844-1915 ...... **TCLC 13**
  See also CA 110; 169
Comte, Auguste 1798-1857 .... **NCLC 54**
Conan Doyle, Arthur
  See Doyle, Arthur Conan
Conde (Abellan), Carmen 1901-
  See also CA 177; DLB 108; HLCS 1; HW
  2
Conde, Maryse 1937- .... **CLC 52, 92; BLCS;
DAM MULT**
  See also BW 2, 3; CA 110; CANR 30, 53,
  76; MTCW 1
Condillac, Etienne Bonnot de
  1714-1780 .... **LC 26**
Condon, Richard (Thomas)
  1915-1996 ...... **CLC 4, 6, 8, 10, 45, 100;
DAM NOV**
  See also BEST 90:3; CA 1-4R; 151; CAAS
  1; CANR 2, 23; INT CANR-23; MTCW
  1, 2
Confucius 551B.C.-479B.C. .. **CMLC 19; DA;
DAB; DAC; DAM MST; WLCS**
  See also DA3
Congreve, William 1670-1729 .... **LC 5, 21;
DA; DAB; DAC; DAM DRAM, MST,
POET; DC 2; WLC**
  See also CDBLB 1660-1789; DLB 39, 84
Connell, Evan S(helby), Jr. 1924- . **CLC 4, 6,
45; DAM NOV**
  See also AAYA 7; CA 1-4R; CAAS 2;
  CANR 2, 39, 76; DLB 2; DLBY 81;
  MTCW 1, 2

Connelly, Marc(us Cook) 1890-1980 . **CLC 7**
  See also CA 85-88; 102; CANR 30; DLB
  7; DLBY 80; SATA-Obit 25
Connor, Ralph TCLC 31
  See also Gordon, Charles William
  See also DLB 92
Conrad, Joseph 1857-1924 .... **TCLC 1, 6, 13,
25, 43, 57; DA; DAB; DAC; DAM
MST, NOV; SSC 9; WLC**
  See also AAYA 26; CA 104; 131; CANR
  60; CDBLB 1890-1914; DA3; DLB 10,
  34, 98, 156; MTCW 1, 2; SATA 27
Conrad, Robert Arnold
  See Hart, Moss
Conroy, Pat
  See Conroy, (Donald) Pat(rick)
  See also MTCW 2
Conroy, (Donald) Pat(rick) 1945- ... **CLC 30,
74; DAM NOV, POP**
  See also Conroy, Pat
  See also AAYA 8; AITN 1; CA 85-88;
  CANR 24, 53; DA3; DLB 6; MTCW 1
Constant (de Rebecque), (Henri) Benjamin
  1767-1830 .... **NCLC 6**
  See also DLB 119
Conybeare, Charles Augustus
  See Eliot, T(homas) S(tearns)
Cook, Michael 1933- .... **CLC 58**
  See also CA 93-96; CANR 68; DLB 53
Cook, Robin 1940- .... **CLC 14; DAM POP**
  See also AAYA 32; BEST 90:2; CA 108;
  111; CANR 41, 90; DA3; INT 111
Cook, Roy
  See Silverberg, Robert
Cooke, Elizabeth 1948- .... **CLC 55**
  See also CA 129
Cooke, John Esten 1830-1886 .... **NCLC 5**
  See also DLB 3
Cooke, John Estes
  See Baum, L(yman) Frank
Cooke, M. E.
  See Creasey, John
Cooke, Margaret
  See Creasey, John
Cook-Lynn, Elizabeth 1930- . **CLC 93; DAM
MULT**
  See also CA 133; DLB 175; NNAL
Cooney, Ray CLC 62
Cooper, Douglas 1960- .... **CLC 86**
Cooper, Henry St. John
  See Creasey, John
Cooper, J(oan) California (?)- .... **CLC 56;
DAM MULT**
  See also AAYA 12; BW 1; CA 125; CANR
  55; DLB 212
Cooper, James Fenimore
  1789-1851 .... **NCLC 1, 27, 54**
  See also AAYA 22; CDALB 1640-1865;
  DA3; DLB 3; SATA 19
Coover, Robert (Lowell) 1932- ...... **CLC 3, 7,
15, 32, 46, 87; DAM NOV; SSC 15**
  See also CA 45-48; CANR 3, 37, 58; DLB
  2, 227; DLBY 81; MTCW 1, 2
Copeland, Stewart (Armstrong)
  1952- .... **CLC 26**
Copernicus, Nicolaus 1473-1543 .... **LC 45**
Coppard, A(lfred) E(dgar)
  1878-1957 .... **TCLC 5; SSC 21**
  See also CA 114; 167; DLB 162; YABC 1
Coppee, Francois 1842-1908 .... **TCLC 25**
  See also CA 170
Coppola, Francis Ford 1939- ... **CLC 16, 126**
  See also CA 77-80; CANR 40, 78; DLB 44
Corbiere, Tristan 1845-1875 .... **NCLC 43**
Corcoran, Barbara 1911- .... **CLC 17**
  See also AAYA 14; CA 21-24R; CAAS 2;
  CANR 11, 28, 48; CLR 50; DLB 52;
  JRDA; SAAS 20; SATA 3, 77

Cordelier, Maurice
See Giraudoux, (Hippolyte) Jean
Corelli, Marie 1855-1924 .... TCLC 51
See also Mackey, Mary
See also DLB 34, 156
Corman, Cid 1924- .... CLC 9
See also Corman, Sidney
See also CAAS 2; DLB 5, 193
Corman, Sidney 1924-
See Corman, Cid
See also CA 85-88; CANR 44; DAM POET
Cormier, Robert (Edmund) 1925- ... CLC 12, 30; DA; DAB; DAC; DAM MST, NOV
See also AAYA 3, 19; CA 1-4R; CANR 5, 23, 76; CDALB 1968-1988; CLR 12, 55; DLB 52; INT CANR-23; JRDA; MAICYA; MTCW 1, 2; SATA 10, 45, 83
Corn, Alfred (DeWitt III) 1943- .... CLC 33
See also CA 179; CAAE 179; CAAS 25; CANR 44; DLB 120; DLBY 80
Corneille, Pierre 1606-1684 ..... LC 28; DAB; DAM MST
Cornwell, David (John Moore)
1931- .... CLC 9, 15; DAM POP
See also le Carre, John
See also CA 5-8R; CANR 13, 33, 59; DA3; MTCW 1, 2
Corso, (Nunzio) Gregory 1930- .... CLC 1, 11
See also CA 5-8R; CANR 41, 76; DA3; DLB 5, 16; MTCW 1, 2
Cortazar, Julio 1914-1984 ... CLC 2, 3, 5, 10, 13, 15, 33, 34, 92; DAM MULT, NOV; HLC 1; SSC 7
See also CA 21-24R; CANR 12, 32, 81; DA3; DLB 113; HW 1, 2; MTCW 1, 2
Cortes, Hernan 1484-1547 .... LC 31
Corvinus, Jakob
See Raabe, Wilhelm (Karl)
Corwin, Cecil
See Kornbluth, C(yril) M.
Cosic, Dobrica 1921- .... CLC 14
See also CA 122; 138; DLB 181
Costain, Thomas B(ertram)
1885-1965 .... CLC 30
See also CA 5-8R; 25-28R; DLB 9
Costantini, Humberto 1924(?)-1987 . CLC 49
See also CA 131; 122; HW 1
Costello, Elvis 1955- .... CLC 21
Costenoble, Philostene
See Ghelderode, Michel de
Cotes, Cecil V.
See Duncan, Sara Jeannette
Cotter, Joseph Seamon Sr.
1861-1949 ...... TCLC 28; BLC 1; DAM MULT
See also BW 1; CA 124; DLB 50
Couch, Arthur Thomas Quiller
See Quiller-Couch, SirArthur (Thomas)
Coulton, James
See Hansen, Joseph
Couperus, Louis (Marie Anne)
1863-1923 .... TCLC 15
See also CA 115
Coupland, Douglas 1961- .... CLC 85, 133; DAC; DAM POP
See also AAYA 34; CA 142; CANR 57, 90
Court, Wesli
See Turco, Lewis (Putnam)
Courtenay, Bryce 1933- .... CLC 59
See also CA 138
Courtney, Robert
See Ellison, Harlan (Jay)
Cousteau, Jacques-Yves 1910-1997 .. CLC 30
See also CA 65-68; 159; CANR 15, 67; MTCW 1; SATA 38, 98
Coventry, Francis 1725-1754 .... LC 46
Cowan, Peter (Walkinshaw) 1914- .... SSC 28
See also CA 21-24R; CANR 9, 25, 50, 83

Coward, Noel (Peirce) 1899-1973 . CLC 1, 9, 29, 51; DAM DRAM
See also AITN 1; CA 17-18; 41-44R; CANR 35; CAP 2; CDBLB 1914-1945; DA3; DLB 10; MTCW 1, 2
Cowley, Abraham 1618-1667 .... LC 43
See also DLB 131, 151
Cowley, Malcolm 1898-1989 .... CLC 39
See also CA 5-8R; 128; CANR 3, 55; DLB 4, 48; DLBY 81, 89; MTCW 1, 2
Cowper, William 1731-1800 . NCLC 8; DAM POET
See also DA3; DLB 104, 109
Cox, William Trevor 1928- ... CLC 9, 14, 71; DAM NOV
See also Trevor, William
See also CA 9-12R; CANR 4, 37, 55, 76; DLB 14; INT CANR-37; MTCW 1, 2
Coyne, P. J.
See Masters, Hilary
Cozzens, James Gould 1903-1978 . CLC 1, 4, 11, 92
See also CA 9-12R; 81-84; CANR 19; CDALB 1941-1968; DLB 9; DLBD 2; DLBY 84, 97; MTCW 1, 2
Crabbe, George 1754-1832 .... NCLC 26
See also DLB 93
Craddock, Charles Egbert
See Murfree, Mary Noailles
Craig, A. A.
See Anderson, Poul (William)
Craik, Dinah Maria (Mulock)
1826-1887 .... NCLC 38
See also DLB 35, 163; MAICYA; SATA 34
Cram, Ralph Adams 1863-1942 ..... TCLC 45
See also CA 160
Crane, (Harold) Hart 1899-1932 .... TCLC 2, 5, 80; DA; DAB; DAC; DAM MST, POET; PC 3; WLC
See also CA 104; 127; CDALB 1917-1929; DA3; DLB 4, 48; MTCW 1, 2
Crane, R(onald) S(almon)
1886-1967 .... CLC 27
See also CA 85-88; DLB 63
Crane, Stephen (Townley)
1871-1900 .... TCLC 11, 17, 32; DA; DAB; DAC; DAM MST, NOV, POET; SSC 7; WLC
See also AAYA 21; CA 109; 140; CANR 84; CDALB 1865-1917; DA3; DLB 12, 54, 78; YABC 2
Cranshaw, Stanley
See Fisher, Dorothy (Frances) Canfield
Crase, Douglas 1944- .... CLC 58
See also CA 106
Crashaw, Richard 1612(?)-1649 .... LC 24
See also DLB 126
Craven, Margaret 1901-1980 .... CLC 17; DAC
See also CA 103
Crawford, F(rancis) Marion
1854-1909 .... TCLC 10
See also CA 107; 168; DLB 71
Crawford, Isabella Valancy
1850-1887 .... NCLC 12
See also DLB 92
Crayon, Geoffrey
See Irving, Washington
Creasey, John 1908-1973 .... CLC 11
See also CA 5-8R; 41-44R; CANR 8, 59; DLB 77; MTCW 1
Crebillon, Claude Prosper Jolyot de (fils)
1707-1777 .... LC 1, 28
Credo
See Creasey, John
Credo, Alvaro J. de
See Prado (Calvo), Pedro

Creeley, Robert (White) 1926- .. CLC 1, 2, 4, 8, 11, 15, 36, 78; DAM POET
See also CA 1-4R; CAAS 10; CANR 23, 43, 89; DA3; DLB 5, 16, 169; DLBD 17; MTCW 1, 2
Crews, Harry (Eugene) 1935- ..... CLC 6, 23, 49
See also AITN 1; CA 25-28R; CANR 20, 57; DA3; DLB 6, 143, 185; MTCW 1, 2
Crichton, (John) Michael 1942- .... CLC 2, 6, 54, 90; DAM NOV, POP
See also AAYA 10; AITN 2; CA 25-28R; CANR 13, 40, 54, 76; DA3; DLBY 81; INT CANR-13; JRDA; MTCW 1, 2; SATA 9, 88
Crispin, Edmund CLC 22
See also Montgomery, (Robert) Bruce
See also DLB 87
Cristofer, Michael 1945(?)- ... CLC 28; DAM DRAM
See also CA 110; 152; DLB 7
Croce, Benedetto 1866-1952 .... TCLC 37
See also CA 120; 155
Crockett, David 1786-1836 .... NCLC 8
See also DLB 3, 11
Crockett, Davy
See Crockett, David
Crofts, Freeman Wills 1879-1957 .. TCLC 55
See also CA 115; DLB 77
Croker, John Wilson 1780-1857 .... NCLC 10
See also DLB 110
Crommelynck, Fernand 1885-1970 .. CLC 75
See also CA 89-92
Cromwell, Oliver 1599-1658 .... LC 43
Cronin, A(rchibald) J(oseph)
1896-1981 .... CLC 32
See also CA 1-4R; 102; CANR 5; DLB 191; SATA 47; SATA-Obit 25
Cross, Amanda
See Heilbrun, Carolyn G(old)
Crothers, Rachel 1878(?)-1958 .... TCLC 19
See also CA 113; DLB 7
Croves, Hal
See Traven, B.
Crow Dog, Mary (Ellen) (?)- .... CLC 93
See also Brave Bird, Mary
See also CA 154
Crowfield, Christopher
See Stowe, Harriet (Elizabeth) Beecher
Crowley, Aleister TCLC 7
See also Crowley, Edward Alexander
Crowley, Edward Alexander 1875-1947
See Crowley, Aleister
See also CA 104
Crowley, John 1942- .... CLC 57
See also CA 61-64; CANR 43; DLBY 82; SATA 65
Crud
See Crumb, R(obert)
Crumarums
See Crumb, R(obert)
Crumb, R(obert) 1943- .... CLC 17
See also CA 106
Crumbum
See Crumb, R(obert)
Crumski
See Crumb, R(obert)
Crum the Bum
See Crumb, R(obert)
Crunk
See Crumb, R(obert)
Crustt
See Crumb, R(obert)
Cruz, Victor Hernandez 1949-
See also BW 2; CA 65-68; CAAS 17; CANR 14, 32, 74; DAM MULT, POET; DLB 41; HLC 1; HW 1, 2; MTCW 1

Cryer, Gretchen (Kiger) 1935- .... **CLC 21**
See also CA 114; 123

Csath, Geza 1887-1919 .... **TCLC 13**
See also CA 111

Cudlip, David R(ockwell) 1933- .... **CLC 34**
See also CA 177

Cullen, Countee 1903-1946 .... **TCLC 4, 37;
BLC 1; DA; DAC; DAM MST, MULT,
POET; PC 20; WLCS**
See also BW 1; CA 108; 124; CDALB
1917-1929; DA3; DLB 4, 48, 51; MTCW
1, 2; SATA 18

Cum, R.
See Crumb, R(obert)

Cummings, Bruce F(rederick) 1889-1919
See Barbellion, W. N. P.
See also CA 123

Cummings, E(dward) E(stlin)
1894-1962 .... **CLC 1, 3, 8, 12, 15, 68;
DA; DAB; DAC; DAM MST, POET;
PC 5; WLC**
See also CA 73-76; CANR 31; CDALB
1929-1941; DA3; DLB 4, 48; MTCW 1,
2

Cunha, Euclides (Rodrigues Pimenta) da
1866-1909 .... **TCLC 24**
See also CA 123

Cunningham, E. V.
See Fast, Howard (Melvin)

Cunningham, J(ames) V(incent)
1911-1985 .... **CLC 3, 31**
See also CA 1-4R; 115; CANR 1, 72; DLB
5

Cunningham, Julia (Woolfolk)
1916- .... **CLC 12**
See also CA 9-12R; CANR 4, 19, 36;
JRDA; MAICYA; SAAS 2; SATA 1, 26

Cunningham, Michael 1952- .... **CLC 34**
See also CA 136

Cunninghame Graham, R. B.
See Cunninghame Graham, Robert
(Gallnigad) Bontine

Cunninghame Graham, Robert (Gallnigad)
Bontine 1852-1936 .... **TCLC 19**
See also Graham, R(obert) B(ontine) Cun-
ninghame
See also CA 119; 184; DLB 98

Currie, Ellen 19(?)- .... **CLC 44**

Curtin, Philip
See Lowndes, Marie Adelaide (Belloc)

Curtis, Price
See Ellison, Harlan (Jay)

Cutrate, Joe
See Spiegelman, Art

Cynewulf c. 770-c. 840 .... **CMLC 23**

Czaczkes, Shmuel Yosef
See Agnon, S(hmuel) Y(osef Halevi)

Dabrowska, Maria (Szumska)
1889-1965 .... **CLC 15**
See also CA 106

Dabydeen, David 1955- .... **CLC 34**
See also BW 1; CA 125; CANR 56

Dacey, Philip 1939- .... **CLC 51**
See also CA 37-40R; CAAS 17; CANR 14,
32, 64; DLB 105

Dagerman, Stig (Halvard)
1923-1954 .... **TCLC 17**
See also CA 117; 155

Dahl, Roald 1916-1990 ...... **CLC 1, 6, 18, 79;
DAB; DAC; DAM MST, NOV, POP**
See also AAYA 15; CA 1-4R; 133; CANR
6, 32, 37, 62; CLR 1, 7, 41; DA3; DLB
139; JRDA; MAICYA; MTCW 1, 2;
SATA 1, 26, 73; SATA-Obit 65

Dahlberg, Edward 1900-1977 .. **CLC 1, 7, 14**
See also CA 9-12R; 69-72; CANR 31, 62;
DLB 48; MTCW 1

Daitch, Susan 1954- .... **CLC 103**
See also CA 161

Dale, Colin **TCLC 18**
See also Lawrence, T(homas) E(dward)

Dale, George E.
See Asimov, Isaac

Dalton, Roque 1935-1975
See also HLCS 1; HW 2

Daly, Elizabeth 1878-1967 .... **CLC 52**
See also CA 23-24; 25-28R; CANR 60;
CAP 2

Daly, Maureen 1921- .... **CLC 17**
See also AAYA 5; CANR 37, 83; JRDA;
MAICYA; SAAS 1; SATA 2

Damas, Leon-Gontran 1912-1978 .... **CLC 84**
See also BW 1; CA 125; 73-76

Dana, Richard Henry Sr.
1787-1879 .... **NCLC 53**

Daniel, Samuel 1562(?)-1619 .... **LC 24**
See also DLB 62

Daniels, Brett
See Adler, Renata

Dannay, Frederic 1905-1982 . **CLC 11; DAM
POP**
See also Queen, Ellery
See also CA 1-4R; 107; CANR 1, 39; DLB
137; MTCW 1

D'Annunzio, Gabriele 1863-1938 ... **TCLC 6,
40**
See also CA 104; 155

Danois, N. le
See Gourmont, Remy (Marie Charles) de

Dante 1265-1321 .... **CMLC 3, 18, 39; DA;
DAB; DAC; DAM MST, POET; PC
21; WLCS**
See also Alighieri, Dante
See also DA3

d'Antibes, Germain
See Simenon, Georges (Jacques Christian)

Danticat, Edwidge 1969- .... **CLC 94**
See also AAYA 29; CA 152; CANR 73;
MTCW 1

Danvers, Dennis 1947- .... **CLC 70**

Danziger, Paula 1944- .... **CLC 21**
See also AAYA 4; CA 112; 115; CANR 37;
CLR 20; JRDA; MAICYA; SATA 36, 63,
102; SATA-Brief 30

Da Ponte, Lorenzo 1749-1838 .... **NCLC 50**

Dario, Ruben 1867-1916 .... **TCLC 4; DAM
MULT; HLC 1; PC 15**
See also CA 131; CANR 81; HW 1, 2;
MTCW 1, 2

Darley, George 1795-1846 .... **NCLC 2**
See also DLB 96

Darrow, Clarence (Seward)
1857-1938 .... **TCLC 81**
See also CA 164

Darwin, Charles 1809-1882 .... **NCLC 57**
See also DLB 57, 166

Daryush, Elizabeth 1887-1977 ...... **CLC 6, 19**
See also CA 49-52; CANR 3, 81; DLB 20

Dasgupta, Surendranath
1887-1952 .... **TCLC 81**
See also CA 157

Dashwood, Edmee Elizabeth Monica de la
Pasture 1890-1943
See Delafield, E. M.
See also CA 119; 154

Daudet, (Louis Marie) Alphonse
1840-1897 .... **NCLC 1**
See also DLB 123

Daumal, Rene 1908-1944 .... **TCLC 14**
See also CA 114

Davenant, William 1606-1668 .... **LC 13**
See also DLB 58, 126

Davenport, Guy (Mattison, Jr.)
1927- .... **CLC 6, 14, 38; SSC 16**
See also CA 33-36R; CANR 23, 73; DLB
130

Davidson, Avram (James) 1923-1993
See Queen, Ellery
See also CA 101; 171; CANR 26; DLB 8

Davidson, Donald (Grady)
1893-1968 .... **CLC 2, 13, 19**
See also CA 5-8R; 25-28R; CANR 4, 84;
DLB 45

Davidson, Hugh
See Hamilton, Edmond

Davidson, John 1857-1909 .... **TCLC 24**
See also CA 118; DLB 19

Davidson, Sara 1943- .... **CLC 9**
See also CA 81-84; CANR 44, 68; DLB
185

Davie, Donald (Alfred) 1922-1995 .... **CLC 5,
8, 10, 31; PC 29**
See also CA 1-4R; 149; CAAS 3; CANR 1,
44; DLB 27; MTCW 1

Davies, Ray(mond Douglas) 1944- ... **CLC 21**
See also CA 116; 146

Davies, Rhys 1901-1978 .... **CLC 23**
See also CA 9-12R; 81-84; CANR 4; DLB
139, 191

Davies, (William) Robertson
1913-1995 .... **CLC 2, 7, 13, 25, 42, 75,
91; DA; DAB; DAC; DAM MST, NOV,
POP; WLC**
See also BEST 89:2; CA 33-36R; 150;
CANR 17, 42; DA3; DLB 68; INT
CANR-17; MTCW 1, 2

Davies, Walter C.
See Kornbluth, C(yril) M.

Davies, William Henry 1871-1940 ... **TCLC 5**
See also CA 104; 179; DLB 19, 174

Da Vinci, Leonardo 1452-1519 ...... **LC 12, 57**

Davis, Angela (Yvonne) 1944- .... **CLC 77;
DAM MULT**
See also BW 2, 3; CA 57-60; CANR 10,
81; DA3

Davis, B. Lynch
See Bioy Casares, Adolfo; Borges, Jorge
Luis

Davis, B. Lynch
See Bioy Casares, Adolfo

Davis, H(arold) L(enoir) 1894-1960 . **CLC 49**
See also CA 178; 89-92; DLB 9, 206; SATA
114

Davis, Rebecca (Blaine) Harding
1831-1910 .... **TCLC 6; SSC 38**
See also CA 104; 179; DLB 74

Davis, Richard Harding
1864-1916 .... **TCLC 24**
See also CA 114; 179; DLB 12, 23, 78, 79,
189; DLBD 13

Davison, Frank Dalby 1893-1970 ..... **CLC 15**
See also CA 116

Davison, Lawrence H.
See Lawrence, D(avid) H(erbert Richards)

Davison, Peter (Hubert) 1928- .... **CLC 28**
See also CA 9-12R; CAAS 4; CANR 3, 43,
84; DLB 5

Davys, Mary 1674-1732 .... **LC 1, 46**
See also DLB 39

Dawson, Fielding 1930- .... **CLC 6**
See also CA 85-88; DLB 130

Dawson, Peter
See Faust, Frederick (Schiller)

Day, Clarence (Shepard, Jr.)
1874-1935 .... **TCLC 25**
See also CA 108; DLB 11

Day, Thomas 1748-1789 .... **LC 1**
See also DLB 39; YABC 1

Day Lewis, C(ecil) 1904-1972 . CLC 1, 6, 10;
   DAM POET; PC 11
   See also Blake, Nicholas
   See also CA 13-16; 33-36R; CANR 34;
   CAP 1; DLB 15, 20; MTCW 1, 2
Dazai Osamu 1909-1948 .. TCLC 11; SSC 41
   See also Tsushima, Shuji
   See also CA 164; DLB 182
de Andrade, Carlos Drummond 1892-1945
   See Drummond de Andrade, Carlos
Deane, Norman
   See Creasey, John
Deane, Seamus (Francis) 1940- ...... CLC 122
   See also CA 118; CANR 42
de Beauvoir, Simone (Lucie Ernestine Marie
      Bertrand)
   See Beauvoir, Simone (Lucie Ernestine
   Marie Bertrand) de
de Beer, P.
   See Bosman, Herman Charles
de Brissac, Malcolm
   See Dickinson, Peter (Malcolm)
de Campos, Alvaro
   See Pessoa, Fernando (Antonio Nogueira)
de Chardin, Pierre Teilhard
   See Teilhard de Chardin, (Marie Joseph)
   Pierre
Dee, John 1527-1608 .... LC 20
Deer, Sandra 1940- .... CLC 45
   See also CA 186
De Ferrari, Gabriella 1941- .... CLC 65
   See also CA 146
Defoe, Daniel 1660(?)-1731 .... LC 1, 42; DA;
   DAB; DAC; DAM MST, NOV; WLC
   See also AAYA 27; CDBLB 1660-1789;
   CLR 61; DA3; DLB 39, 95, 101; JRDA;
   MAICYA; SATA 22
de Gourmont, Remy(-Marie-Charles)
   See Gourmont, Remy (-Marie-Charles) de
de Hartog, Jan 1914- .... CLC 19
   See also CA 1-4R; CANR 1
de Hostos, E. M.
   See Hostos (y Bonilla), Eugenio Maria de
de Hostos, Eugenio M.
   See Hostos (y Bonilla), Eugenio Maria de
Deighton, Len CLC 4, 7, 22, 46
   See also Deighton, Leonard Cyril
   See also AAYA 6; BEST 89:2; CDBLB
   1960 to Present; DLB 87
Deighton, Leonard Cyril 1929-
   See Deighton, Len
   See also CA 9-12R; CANR 19, 33, 68;
   DAM NOV, POP; DA3; MTCW 1, 2
Dekker, Thomas 1572(?)-1632 . LC 22; DAM
   DRAM; DC 12
   See also CDBLB Before 1660; DLB 62, 172
Delafield, E. M. 1890-1943 .... TCLC 61
   See also Dashwood, Edmee Elizabeth
   Monica de la Pasture
   See also DLB 34
de la Mare, Walter (John)
   1873-1956 ..... TCLC 4, 53; DAB; DAC;
   DAM MST, POET; SSC 14; WLC
   See also CA 163; CDBLB 1914-1945; CLR
   23; DA3; DLB 162; MTCW 1; SATA 16
Delaney, Franey
   See O'Hara, John (Henry)
Delaney, Shelagh 1939- .... CLC 29; DAM
   DRAM
   See also CA 17-20R; CANR 30, 67; CD-
   BLB 1960 to Present; DLB 13; MTCW 1
Delany, Mary (Granville Pendarves)
   1700-1788 .... LC 12
Delany, Samuel R(ay, Jr.) 1942- .. CLC 8, 14,
   38; BLC 1; DAM MULT
   See also AAYA 24; BW 2, 3; CA 81-84;
   CANR 27, 43; DLB 8, 33; MTCW 1, 2

De La Ramee, (Marie) Louise 1839-1908
   See Ouida
   See also SATA 20
de la Roche, Mazo 1879-1961 .... CLC 14
   See also CA 85-88; CANR 30; DLB 68;
   SATA 64
De La Salle, Innocent
   See Hartmann, Sadakichi
Delbanco, Nicholas (Franklin)
   1942- .... CLC 6, 13
   See also CA 17-20R; CAAS 2; CANR 29,
   55; DLB 6
del Castillo, Michel 1933- .... CLC 38
   See also CA 109; CANR 77
Deledda, Grazia (Cosima)
   1875(?)-1936 .... TCLC 23
   See also CA 123
Delgado, Abelardo (Lalo) B(arrientos) 1930-
   See also CA 131; CAAS 15; CANR 90;
   DAM MST, MULT; DLB 82; HLC 1; HW
   1, 2
Delibes, Miguel CLC 8, 18
   See also Delibes Setien, Miguel
Delibes Setien, Miguel 1920-
   See Delibes, Miguel
   See also CA 45-48; CANR 1, 32; HW 1;
   MTCW 1
DeLillo, Don 1936- ..... CLC 8, 10, 13, 27, 39,
   54, 76; DAM NOV, POP
   See also BEST 89:1; CA 81-84; CANR 21,
   76; DA3; DLB 6, 173; MTCW 1, 2
de Lisser, H. G.
   See De Lisser, H(erbert) G(eorge)
   See also DLB 117
De Lisser, H(erbert) G(eorge)
   1878-1944 .... TCLC 12
   See also de Lisser, H. G.
   See also BW 2; CA 109; 152
Deloney, Thomas 1560(?)-1600 .... LC 41
   See also DLB 167
Deloria, Vine (Victor), Jr. 1933- ...... CLC 21,
   122; DAM MULT
   See also CA 53-56; CANR 5, 20, 48; DLB
   175; MTCW 1; NNAL; SATA 21
Del Vecchio, John M(ichael) 1947- .. CLC 29
   See also CA 110; DLBD 9
de Man, Paul (Adolph Michel)
   1919-1983 .... CLC 55
   See also CA 128; 111; CANR 61; DLB 67;
   MTCW 1, 2
DeMarinis, Rick 1934- .... CLC 54
   See also CA 57-60, 184; CAAE 184; CAAS
   24; CANR 9, 25, 50
Dembry, R. Emmet
   See Murfree, Mary Noailles
Demby, William 1922- .... CLC 53; BLC 1;
   DAM MULT
   See also BW 1, 3; CA 81-84; CANR 81;
   DLB 33
de Menton, Francisco
   See Chin, Frank (Chew, Jr.)
Demetrius of Phalerum c.
   307B.C.- .... CMLC 34
Demijohn, Thom
   See Disch, Thomas M(ichael)
de Molina, Tirso 1584(?)-1648 .... DC 13
   See also HLCS 2
de Montherlant, Henry (Milon)
   See Montherlant, Henry (Milon) de
Demosthenes 384B.C.-322B.C. ...... CMLC 13
   See also DLB 176
de Natale, Francine
   See Malzberg, Barry N(athaniel)
Denby, Edwin (Orr) 1903-1983 .... CLC 48
   See also CA 138; 110
Denis, Julio
   See Cortazar, Julio
Denmark, Harrison
   See Zelazny, Roger (Joseph)

Dennis, John 1658-1734 .... LC 11
   See also DLB 101
Dennis, Nigel (Forbes) 1912-1989 ...... CLC 8
   See also CA 25-28R; 129; DLB 13, 15;
   MTCW 1
Dent, Lester 1904(?)-1959 .... TCLC 72
   See also CA 112; 161
De Palma, Brian (Russell) 1940- ...... CLC 20
   See also CA 109
De Quincey, Thomas 1785-1859 ..... NCLC 4,
   87
   See also CDBLB 1789-1832; DLB 110; 144
Deren, Eleanora 1908(?)-1961
   See Deren, Maya
   See also CA 111
Deren, Maya 1917-1961 .... CLC 16, 102
   See also Deren, Eleanora
Derleth, August (William)
   1909-1971 .... CLC 31
   See also CA 1-4R; 29-32R; CANR 4; DLB
   9; DLBD 17; SATA 5
Der Nister 1884-1950 .... TCLC 56
de Routisie, Albert
   See Aragon, Louis
Derrida, Jacques 1930- .... CLC 24, 87
   See also CA 124; 127; CANR 76; MTCW 1
Derry Down Derry
   See Lear, Edward
Dersonnes, Jacques
   See Simenon, Georges (Jacques Christian)
Desai, Anita 1937- ..... CLC 19, 37, 97; DAB;
   DAM NOV
   See also CA 81-84; CANR 33, 53; DA3;
   MTCW 1, 2; SATA 63
Desai, Kiran 1971- .... CLC 119
   See also CA 171
de Saint-Luc, Jean
   See Glassco, John
de Saint Roman, Arnaud
   See Aragon, Louis
Descartes, Rene 1596-1650 .... LC 20, 35
De Sica, Vittorio 1901(?)-1974 .... CLC 20
   See also CA 117
Desnos, Robert 1900-1945 .... TCLC 22
   See also CA 121; 151
Destouches, Louis-Ferdinand
   1894-1961 .... CLC 9, 15
   See also Celine, Louis-Ferdinand
   See also CA 85-88; CANR 28; MTCW 1
de Tolignac, Gaston
   See Griffith, D(avid Lewelyn) W(ark)
Deutsch, Babette 1895-1982 .... CLC 18
   See also CA 1-4R; 108; CANR 4, 79; DLB
   45; SATA 1; SATA-Obit 33
Devenant, William 1606-1649 .... LC 13
Devkota, Laxmiprasad 1909-1959 . TCLC 23
   See also CA 123
De Voto, Bernard (Augustine)
   1897-1955 .... TCLC 29
   See also CA 113; 160; DLB 9
De Vries, Peter 1910-1993 ..... CLC 1, 2, 3, 7,
   10, 28, 46; DAM NOV
   See also CA 17-20R; 142; CANR 41; DLB
   6; DLBY 82; MTCW 1, 2
Dewey, John 1859-1952 .... TCLC 95
   See also CA 114; 170
Dexter, John
   See Bradley, Marion Zimmer
Dexter, Martin
   See Faust, Frederick (Schiller)
Dexter, Pete 1943- .. CLC 34, 55; DAM POP
   See also BEST 89:2; CA 127; 131; INT 131;
   MTCW 1
Diamano, Silmang
   See Senghor, Leopold Sedar
Diamond, Neil 1941- .... CLC 30
   See also CA 108

Diaz del Castillo, Bernal 1496-1584 .. **LC 31;
  HLCS 1**
di Bassetto, Corno
  See Shaw, George Bernard
Dick, Philip K(indred) 1928-1982 ... **CLC 10,
  30, 72; DAM NOV, POP**
  See also AAYA 24; CA 49-52; 106; CANR
  2, 16; DA3; DLB 8; MTCW 1, 2
Dickens, Charles (John Huffam)
  1812-1870 .... **NCLC 3, 8, 18, 26, 37, 50,
  86; DA; DAB; DAC; DAM MST, NOV;
  SSC 17; WLC**
  See also AAYA 23; CDBLB 1832-1890;
  DA3; DLB 21, 55, 70, 159, 166; JRDA;
  MAICYA; SATA 15
Dickey, James (Lafayette)
  1923-1997 .... **CLC 1, 2, 4, 7, 10, 15, 47,
  109; DAM NOV, POET, POP**
  See also AITN 1, 2; CA 9-12R; 156; CABS
  2; CANR 10, 48, 61; CDALB 1968-1988;
  DA3; DLB 5, 193; DLBD 7; DLBY 82,
  93, 96, 97, 98; INT CANR-10; MTCW 1,
  2
Dickey, William 1928-1994 .... **CLC 3, 28**
  See also CA 9-12R; 145; CANR 24, 79;
  DLB 5
Dickinson, Charles 1951- .... **CLC 49**
  See also CA 128
Dickinson, Emily (Elizabeth)
  1830-1886 ..... **NCLC 21, 77; DA; DAB;
  DAC; DAM MST, POET; PC 1; WLC**
  See also AAYA 22; CDALB 1865-1917;
  DA3; DLB 1; SATA 29
Dickinson, Peter (Malcolm) 1927- .. **CLC 12,
  35**
  See also AAYA 9; CA 41-44R; CANR 31,
  58, 88; CLR 29; DLB 87, 161; JRDA;
  MAICYA; SATA 5, 62, 95
Dickson, Carr
  See Carr, John Dickson
Dickson, Carter
  See Carr, John Dickson
Diderot, Denis 1713-1784 .... **LC 26**
Didion, Joan 1934- .... **CLC 1, 3, 8, 14, 32,
  129; DAM NOV**
  See also AITN 1; CA 5-8R; CANR 14, 52,
  76; CDALB 1968-1988; DA3; DLB 2,
  173, 185; DLBY 81, 86; MTCW 1, 2
Dietrich, Robert
  See Hunt, E(verette) Howard, (Jr.)
Difusa, Pati
  See Almodovar, Pedro
Dillard, Annie 1945- .. **CLC 9, 60, 115; DAM
  NOV**
  See also AAYA 6; CA 49-52; CANR 3, 43,
  62, 90; DA3; DLBY 80; MTCW 1, 2;
  SATA 10
Dillard, R(ichard) H(enry) W(ilde)
  1937- .... **CLC 5**
  See also CA 21-24R; CAAS 7; CANR 10;
  DLB 5
Dillon, Eilis 1920-1994 .... **CLC 17**
  See also CA 9-12R; 182; 147; CAAE 182;
  CAAS 3; CANR 4, 38, 78; CLR 26; MAI-
  CYA; SATA 2, 74; SATA-Essay 105;
  SATA-Obit 83
Dimont, Penelope
  See Mortimer, Penelope (Ruth)
Dinesen, Isak **CLC 10, 29, 95; SSC 7**
  See also Blixen, Karen (Christentze
  Dinesen)
  See also MTCW 1
Ding Ling **CLC 68**
  See also Chiang, Pin-chin
Diphusa, Patty
  See Almodovar, Pedro

Disch, Thomas M(ichael) 1940- ... **CLC 7, 36**
  See also AAYA 17; CA 21-24R; CAAS 4;
  CANR 17, 36, 54, 89; CLR 18; DA3;
  DLB 8; MAICYA; MTCW 1, 2; SAAS
  15; SATA 92
Disch, Tom
  See Disch, Thomas M(ichael)
d'Isly, Georges
  See Simenon, Georges (Jacques Christian)
Disraeli, Benjamin 1804-1881 ... **NCLC 2, 39,
  79**
  See also DLB 21, 55
Ditcum, Steve
  See Crumb, R(obert)
Dixon, Paige
  See Corcoran, Barbara
Dixon, Stephen 1936- .... **CLC 52; SSC 16**
  See also CA 89-92; CANR 17, 40, 54, 91;
  DLB 130
Doak, Annie
  See Dillard, Annie
Dobell, Sydney Thompson
  1824-1874 .... **NCLC 43**
  See also DLB 32
Doblin, Alfred **TCLC 13**
  See also Doeblin, Alfred
Dobrolyubov, Nikolai Alexandrovich
  1836-1861 .... **NCLC 5**
Dobson, Austin 1840-1921 .... **TCLC 79**
  See also DLB 35; 144
Dobyns, Stephen 1941 .... **CLC 37**
  See also CA 45-48; CANR 2, 18
Doctorow, E(dgar) L(aurence)
  1931- .... **CLC 6, 11, 15, 18, 37, 44, 65,
  113; DAM NOV, POP**
  See also AAYA 22; AITN 2; BEST 89:3;
  CA 45-48; CANR 2, 33, 51, 76; CDALB
  1968-1988; DA3; DLB 2, 28, 173; DLBY
  80; MTCW 1, 2
Dodgson, Charles Lutwidge 1832-1898
  See Carroll, Lewis
  See also CLR 2; DA; DAB; DAC; DAM
  MST, NOV, POET; DA3; MAICYA;
  SATA 100; YABC 2
Dodson, Owen (Vincent)
  1914-1983 .... **CLC 79; BLC 1; DAM
  MULT**
  See also BW 1; CA 65-68; 110; CANR 24;
  DLB 76
Doeblin, Alfred 1878-1957 .... **TCLC 13**
  See also Doblin, Alfred
  See also CA 110; 141; DLB 66
Doerr, Harriet 1910- .... **CLC 34**
  See also CA 117; 122; CANR 47; INT 122
Domecq, H(onorio Bustos)
  See Bioy Casares, Adolfo
Domecq, H(onorio) Bustos
  See Bioy Casares, Adolfo; Borges, Jorge
  Luis
Domini, Rey
  See Lorde, Audre (Geraldine)
Dominique
  See Proust, (Valentin-Louis-George-
  Eugene-) Marcel
Don, A
  See Stephen, SirLeslie
Donaldson, Stephen R. 1947- .... **CLC 46;
  DAM POP**
  See also CA 89-92; CANR 13, 55; INT
  CANR-13
Donleavy, J(ames) P(atrick) 1926- .... **CLC 1,
  4, 6, 10, 45**
  See also AITN 2; CA 9-12R; CANR 24, 49,
  62, 80; DLB 6, 173; INT CANR-24;
  MTCW 1, 2

Donne, John 1572-1631 .... **LC 10, 24; DA;
  DAB; DAC; DAM MST, POET; PC 1;
  WLC**
  See also CDBLB Before 1660; DLB 121,
  151
Donnell, David 1939(?)- .... **CLC 34**
Donoghue, P. S.
  See Hunt, E(verette) Howard, (Jr.)
Donoso (Yanez), Jose 1924-1996 ... **CLC 4, 8,
  11, 32, 99; DAM MULT; HLC 1; SSC
  34**
  See also CA 81-84; 155; CANR 32, 73;
  DLB 113; HW 1, 2; MTCW 1, 2
Donovan, John 1928-1992 .... **CLC 35**
  See also AAYA 20; CA 97-100; 137; CLR
  3; MAICYA; SATA 72; SATA-Brief 29
Don Roberto
  See Cunninghame Graham, Robert
  (Gallnigad) Bontine
Doolittle, Hilda 1886-1961 . **CLC 3, 8, 14, 31,
  34, 73; DA; DAC; DAM MST, POET;
  PC 5; WLC**
  See also H. D.
  See also CA 97-100; CANR 35; DLB 4, 45;
  MTCW 1, 2
Dorfman, Ariel 1942- ...... **CLC 48, 77; DAM
  MULT; HLC 1**
  See also CA 124; 130; CANR 67, 70; HW
  1, 2; INT 130
Dorn, Edward (Merton) 1929- ,,, **CLC 10, 18**
  See also CA 93-96; CANR 42, 79; DLB 5;
  INT 93-96
Dorris, Michael (Anthony)
  1945-1997 .... **CLC 109; DAM MULT,
  NOV**
  See also AAYA 20; BEST 90:1; CA 102;
  157; CANR 19, 46, 75; CLR 58; DA3;
  DLB 175; MTCW 2; NNAL; SATA 75;
  SATA-Obit 94
Dorris, Michael A.
  See Dorris, Michael (Anthony)
Dorsan, Luc
  See Simenon, Georges (Jacques Christian)
Dorsange, Jean
  See Simenon, Georges (Jacques Christian)
Dos Passos, John (Roderigo)
  1896-1970 ... **CLC 1, 4, 8, 11, 15, 25, 34,
  82; DA; DAB; DAC; DAM MST, NOV;
  WLC**
  See also CA 1-4R; 29-32R; CANR 3;
  CDALB 1929-1941; DA3; DLB 4, 9;
  DLBD 1, 15; DLBY 96; MTCW 1, 2
Dossage, Jean
  See Simenon, Georges (Jacques Christian)
Dostoevsky, Fedor Mikhailovich
  1821-1881 . **NCLC 2, 7, 21, 33, 43; DA;
  DAB; DAC; DAM MST, NOV; SSC 2,
  33; WLC**
  See also DA3
Doughty, Charles M(ontagu)
  1843-1926 .... **TCLC 27**
  See also CA 115; 178; DLB 19, 57, 174
Douglas, Ellen **CLC 73**
  See also Haxton, Josephine Ayres; William-
  son, Ellen Douglas
Douglas, Gavin 1475(?)-1522 .... **LC 20**
  See also DLB 132
Douglas, George
  See Brown, George Douglas
Douglas, Keith (Castellain)
  1920-1944 .... **TCLC 40**
  See also CA 160; DLB 27
Douglas, Leonard
  See Bradbury, Ray (Douglas)
Douglas, Michael
  See Crichton, (John) Michael
Douglas, (George) Norman
  1868-1952 .... **TCLC 68**
  See also CA 119; 157; DLB 34, 195

Douglas, William
See Brown, George Douglas
Douglass, Frederick 1817(?)-1895 .. NCLC 7, 55; BLC 1; DA; DAC; DAM MST, MULT; WLC
See also CDALB 1640-1865; DA3; DLB 1, 43, 50, 79; SATA 29
Dourado, (Waldomiro Freitas) Autran 1926- .... CLC 23, 60
See also CA 25-28R, 179; CANR 34, 81; DLB 145; HW 2
Dourado, Waldomiro Autran 1926-
See Dourado, (Waldomiro Freitas) Autran
See also CA 179
Dove, Rita (Frances) 1952- .... CLC 50, 81; BLCS; DAM MULT, POET; PC 6
See also BW 2; CA 109; CAAS 19; CANR 27, 42, 68, 76; CDALBS; DA3; DLB 120; MTCW 1
Doveglion
See Villa, Jose Garcia
Dowell, Coleman 1925-1985 .... CLC 60
See also CA 25-28R; 117; CANR 10; DLB 130
Dowson, Ernest (Christopher) 1867-1900 .... TCLC 4
See also CA 105; 150; DLB 19, 135
Doyle, A. Conan
See Doyle, Arthur Conan
Doyle, Arthur Conan 1859-1930 .... TCLC 7; DA; DAB; DAC; DAM MST, NOV; SSC 12; WLC
See also AAYA 14; CA 104; 122; CDBLB 1890-1914; DA3; DLB 18, 70, 156, 178; MTCW 1, 2; SATA 24
Doyle, Conan
See Doyle, Arthur Conan
Doyle, John
See Graves, Robert (von Ranke)
Doyle, Roddy 1958(?)- .... CLC 81
See also AAYA 14; CA 143; CANR 73; DA3; DLB 194
Doyle, Sir A. Conan
See Doyle, Arthur Conan
Doyle, Sir Arthur Conan
See Doyle, Arthur Conan
Dr. A
See Asimov, Isaac; Silverstein, Alvin
Drabble, Margaret 1939- ...... CLC 2, 3, 5, 8, 10, 22, 53, 129; DAB; DAC; DAM MST, NOV, POP
See also CA 13-16R; CANR 18, 35, 63; CDBLB 1960 to Present; DA3; DLB 14, 155; MTCW 1, 2; SATA 48
Drapier, M. B.
See Swift, Jonathan
Drayham, James
See Mencken, H(enry) L(ouis)
Drayton, Michael 1563-1631 ..... LC 8; DAM POET
See also DLB 121
Dreadstone, Carl
See Campbell, (John) Ramsey
Dreiser, Theodore (Herman Albert) 1871-1945 .... TCLC 10, 18, 35, 83; DA; DAC; DAM MST, NOV; SSC 30; WLC
See also CA 106; 132; CDALB 1865-1917; DA3; DLB 9, 12, 102, 137; DLBD 1; MTCW 1, 2
Drexler, Rosalyn 1926- .... CLC 2, 6
See also CA 81-84; CANR 68
Dreyer, Carl Theodor 1889-1968 ...... CLC 16
See also CA 116
Drieu la Rochelle, Pierre(-Eugene) 1893-1945 .... TCLC 21
See also CA 117; DLB 72
Drinkwater, John 1882-1937 .... TCLC 57
See also CA 109; 149; DLB 10, 19, 149

Drop Shot
See Cable, George Washington
Droste-Hulshoff, Annette Freiin von 1797-1848 .... NCLC 3
See also DLB 133
Drummond, Walter
See Silverberg, Robert
Drummond, William Henry 1854-1907 .... TCLC 25
See also CA 160; DLB 92
Drummond de Andrade, Carlos 1902-1987 .... CLC 18
See also Andrade, Carlos Drummond de
See also CA 132; 123
Drury, Allen (Stuart) 1918-1998 .... CLC 37
See also CA 57-60; 170; CANR 18, 52; INT CANR-18
Dryden, John 1631-1700 .... LC 3, 21; DA; DAB; DAC; DAM DRAM, MST, POET; DC 3; PC 25; WLC
See also CDBLB 1660-1789; DLB 80, 101, 131
Duberman, Martin (Bauml) 1930- ..... CLC 8
See also CA 1-4R; CANR 2, 63
Dubie, Norman (Evans) 1945- .... CLC 36
See also CA 69-72; CANR 12; DLB 120
Du Bois, W(illiam) E(dward) B(urghardt) 1868-1963 ... CLC 1, 2, 13, 64, 96; BLC 1; DA; DAC; DAM MST, MULT, NOV; WLC
See also BW 1, 3; CA 85-88; CANR 34, 82; CDALB 1865-1917; DA3; DLB 47, 50, 91; MTCW 1, 2; SATA 42
Dubus, Andre 1936-1999 ..... CLC 13, 36, 97; SSC 15
See also CA 21-24R; 177; CANR 17; DLB 130; INT CANR-17
Duca Minimo
See D'Annunzio, Gabriele
Ducharme, Rejean 1941- .... CLC 74
See also CA 165; DLB 60
Duclos, Charles Pinot 1704-1772 .... LC 1
Dudek, Louis 1918- .... CLC 11, 19
See also CA 45-48; CAAS 14; CANR 1; DLB 88
Duerrenmatt, Friedrich 1921-1990 ... CLC 1, 4, 8, 11, 15, 43, 102; DAM DRAM
See also CA 17-20R; CANR 33; DLB 69, 124; MTCW 1, 2
Duffy, Bruce 1953(?)- .... CLC 50
See also CA 172
Duffy, Maureen 1933- .... CLC 37
See also CA 25-28R; CANR 33, 68; DLB 14; MTCW 1
Dugan, Alan 1923- .... CLC 2, 6
See also CA 81-84; DLB 5
du Gard, Roger Martin
See Martin du Gard, Roger
Duhamel, Georges 1884-1966 .... CLC 8
See also CA 81-84; 25-28R; CANR 35; DLB 65; MTCW 1
Dujardin, Edouard (Emile Louis) 1861-1949 .... TCLC 13
See also CA 109; DLB 123
Dulles, John Foster 1888-1959 .... TCLC 72
See also CA 115; 149
Dumas, Alexandre (pere)
See Dumas, Alexandre (Davy de la Pailleterie)
Dumas, Alexandre (Davy de la Pailleterie) 1802-1870 ...... NCLC 11, 71; DA; DAB; DAC; DAM MST, NOV; WLC
See also DA3; DLB 119, 192; SATA 18
Dumas, Alexandre (fils) 1824-1895 .... NCLC 71; DC 1
See also AAYA 22; DLB 192
Dumas, Claudine
See Malzberg, Barry N(athaniel)

Dumas, Henry L. 1934-1968 .... CLC 6, 62
See also BW 1; CA 85-88; DLB 41
du Maurier, Daphne 1907-1989 .. CLC 6, 11, 59; DAB; DAC; DAM MST, POP; SSC 18
See also CA 5-8R; 128; CANR 6, 55; DA3; DLB 191; MTCW 1, 2; SATA 27; SATA-Obit 60
Du Maurier, George 1834-1896 ..... NCLC 86
See also DLB 153, 178
Dunbar, Paul Laurence 1872-1906 . TCLC 2, 12; BLC 1; DA; DAC; DAM MST, MULT, POET; PC 5; SSC 8; WLC
See also BW 1, 3; CA 104; 124; CANR 79; CDALB 1865-1917; DA3; DLB 50, 54, 78; SATA 34
Dunbar, William 1460(?)-1530(?) .... LC 20
See also DLB 132, 146
Duncan, Dora Angela
See Duncan, Isadora
Duncan, Isadora 1877(?)-1927 .... TCLC 68
See also CA 118; 149
Duncan, Lois 1934- .... CLC 26
See also AAYA 4, 34; CA 1-4R; CANR 2, 23, 36; CLR 29; JRDA; MAICYA; SAAS 2; SATA 1, 36, 75
Duncan, Robert (Edward) 1919-1988 .... CLC 1, 2, 4, 7, 15, 41, 55; DAM POET; PC 2
See also CA 9-12R; 124; CANR 28, 62; DLB 5, 16, 193; MTCW 1, 2
Duncan, Sara Jeannette 1861-1922 .... TCLC 60
See also CA 157; DLB 92
Dunlap, William 1766-1839 .... NCLC 2
See also DLB 30, 37, 59
Dunn, Douglas (Eaglesham) 1942- .... CLC 6, 40
See also CA 45-48; CANR 2, 33; DLB 40; MTCW 1
Dunn, Katherine (Karen) 1945- .... CLC 71
See also CA 33-36R; CANR 72; MTCW 1
Dunn, Stephen 1939- .... CLC 36
See also CA 33-36R; CANR 12, 48, 53; DLB 105
Dunne, Finley Peter 1867-1936 ...... TCLC 28
See also CA 108; 178; DLB 11, 23
Dunne, John Gregory 1932- .... CLC 28
See also CA 25-28R; CANR 14, 50; DLBY 80
Dunsany, Edward John Moreton Drax Plunkett 1878-1957
See Dunsany, Lord
See also CA 104; 148; DLB 10; MTCW 1
Dunsany, Lord TCLC 2, 59
See also Dunsany, Edward John Moreton Drax Plunkett
See also DLB 77, 153, 156
du Perry, Jean
See Simenon, Georges (Jacques Christian)
Durang, Christopher (Ferdinand) 1949- .... CLC 27, 38
See also CA 105; CANR 50, 76; MTCW 1
Duras, Marguerite 1914-1996 . CLC 3, 6, 11, 20, 34, 40, 68, 100; SSC 40
See also CA 25-28R; 151; CANR 50; DLB 83; MTCW 1, 2
Durban, (Rosa) Pam 1947- .... CLC 39
See also CA 123
Durcan, Paul 1944- .... CLC 43, 70; DAM POET
See also CA 134
Durkheim, Emile 1858-1917 .... TCLC 55
Durrell, Lawrence (George) 1912-1990 .... CLC 1, 4, 6, 8, 13, 27, 41; DAM NOV
See also CA 9-12R; 132; CANR 40, 77; CDBLB 1945-1960; DLB 15, 27, 204; DLBY 90; MTCW 1, 2

Durrenmatt, Friedrich
See Duerrenmatt, Friedrich
Dutt, Toru 1856-1877 .... **NCLC 29**
Dwight, Timothy 1752-1817 .... **NCLC 13**
See also DLB 37
Dworkin, Andrea 1946- .... **CLC 43**
See also CA 77-80; CAAS 21; CANR 16, 39, 76; INT CANR-16; MTCW 1, 2
Dwyer, Deanna
See Koontz, Dean R(ay)
Dwyer, K. R.
See Koontz, Dean R(ay)
Dwyer, Thomas A. 1923- .... **CLC 114**
See also CA 115
Dye, Richard
See De Voto, Bernard (Augustine)
Dylan, Bob 1941- .... **CLC 3, 4, 6, 12, 77**
See also CA 41-44R; DLB 16
E. V. L.
See Lucas, E(dward) V(errall)
Eagleton, Terence (Francis) 1943- .. **CLC 63, 132**
See also CA 57-60; CANR 7, 23, 68; MTCW 1, 2
Eagleton, Terry
See Eagleton, Terence (Francis)
Early, Jack
See Scoppettone, Sandra
East, Michael
See West, Morris L(anglo)
Eastaway, Edward
See Thomas, (Philip) Edward
Eastlake, William (Derry)
1917-1997 .... **CLC 8**
See also CA 5-8R; 158; CAAS 1; CANR 5, 63; DLB 6, 206; INT CANR-5
Eastman, Charles A(lexander)
1858-1939 .... **TCLC 55; DAM MULT**
See also CA 179; CANR 91; DLB 175; NNAL; YABC 1
Eberhart, Richard (Ghormley)
1904- .. **CLC 3, 11, 19, 56; DAM POET**
See also CA 1-4R; CANR 2; CDALB 1941-1968; DLB 48; MTCW 1
Eberstadt, Fernanda 1960- .... **CLC 39**
See also CA 136; CANR 69
Echegaray (y Eizaguirre), Jose (Maria Waldo) 1832-1916 .... **TCLC 4; HLCS 1**
See also CA 104; CANR 32; HW 1; MTCW 1
Echeverria, (Jose) Esteban (Antonino)
1805-1851 .... **NCLC 18**
Echo
See Proust, (Valentin-Louis-George-Eugene-) Marcel
Eckert, Allan W. 1931- .... **CLC 17**
See also AAYA 18; CA 13-16R; CANR 14, 45; INT CANR-14; SAAS 21; SATA 29, 91; SATA-Brief 27
Eckhart, Meister 1260(?)-1328(?) ... **CMLC 9**
See also DLB 115
Eckmar, F. R.
See de Hartog, Jan
Eco, Umberto 1932- .... **CLC 28, 60; DAM NOV, POP**
See also BEST 90:1; CA 77-80; CANR 12, 33, 55; DA3; DLB 196; MTCW 1, 2
Eddison, E(ric) R(ucker)
1882-1945 .... **TCLC 15**
See also CA 109; 156
Eddy, Mary (Ann Morse) Baker
1821-1910 .... **TCLC 71**
See also CA 113; 174
Edel, (Joseph) Leon 1907-1997 .. **CLC 29, 34**
See also CA 1-4R; 161; CANR 1, 22; DLB 103; INT CANR-22

Eden, Emily 1797-1869 .... **NCLC 10**
Edgar, David 1948- .. **CLC 42; DAM DRAM**
See also CA 57-60; CANR 12, 61; DLB 13; MTCW 1
Edgerton, Clyde (Carlyle) 1944- ...... **CLC 39**
See also AAYA 17; CA 118; 134; CANR 64; INT 134
Edgeworth, Maria 1768-1849 .... **NCLC 1, 51**
See also DLB 116, 159, 163; SATA 21
Edmonds, Paul
See Kuttner, Henry
Edmonds, Walter D(umaux)
1903-1998 .... **CLC 35**
See also CA 5-8R; CANR 2; DLB 9; MAI-CYA; SAAS 4; SATA 1, 27; SATA-Obit 99
Edmondson, Wallace
See Ellison, Harlan (Jay)
Edson, Russell CLC 13
See also CA 33-36R
Edwards, Bronwen Elizabeth
See Rose, Wendy
Edwards, G(erald) B(asil)
1899-1976 .... **CLC 25**
See also CA 110
Edwards, Gus 1939- .... **CLC 43**
See also CA 108; INT 108
Edwards, Jonathan 1703-1758 .... **LC 7, 54; DA; DAC; DAM MST**
See also DLB 24
Efron, Marina Ivanovna Tsvetaeva
See Tsvetaeva (Efron), Marina (Ivanovna)
Ehle, John (Marsden, Jr.) 1925- ...... **CLC 27**
See also CA 9-12R
Ehrenbourg, Ilya (Grigoryevich)
See Ehrenburg, Ilya (Grigoryevich)
Ehrenburg, Ilya (Grigoryevich)
1891-1967 .... **CLC 18, 34, 62**
See also CA 102; 25-28R
Ehrenburg, Ilyo (Grigoryevich)
See Ehrenburg, Ilya (Grigoryevich)
Ehrenreich, Barbara 1941- .... **CLC 110**
See also BEST 90:4; CA 73-76; CANR 16, 37, 62; MTCW 1, 2
Eich, Guenter 1907-1972 .... **CLC 15**
See also CA 111; 93-96; DLB 69, 124
Eichendorff, Joseph Freiherr von
1788-1857 .... **NCLC 8**
See also DLB 90
Eigner, Larry CLC 9
See also Eigner, Laurence (Joel)
See also CAAS 23; DLB 5
Eigner, Laurence (Joel) 1927-1996
See Eigner, Larry
See also CA 9-12R; 151; CANR 6, 84; DLB 193
Einstein, Albert 1879-1955 .... **TCLC 65**
See also CA 121; 133; MTCW 1, 2
Eiseley, Loren Corey 1907-1977 .... **CLC 7**
See also AAYA 5; CA 1-4R; 73-76; CANR 6; DLBD 17
Eisenstadt, Jill 1963- .... **CLC 50**
See also CA 140
Eisenstein, Sergei (Mikhailovich)
1898-1948 .... **TCLC 57**
See also CA 114; 149
Eisner, Simon
See Kornbluth, C(yril) M.
Ekeloef, (Bengt) Gunnar
1907-1968 ... **CLC 27; DAM POET; PC 23**
See also CA 123; 25-28R
Ekelof, (Bengt) Gunnar
See Ekeloef, (Bengt) Gunnar
Ekelund, Vilhelm 1880-1949 .... **TCLC 75**
Ekwensi, C. O. D.
See Ekwensi, Cyprian (Odiatu Duaka)

Ekwensi, Cyprian (Odiatu Duaka)
1921- ...... **CLC 4; BLC 1; DAM MULT**
See also BW 2, 3; CA 29-32R; CANR 18, 42, 74; DLB 117; MTCW 1, 2; SATA 66
Elaine TCLC 18
See also Leverson, Ada
El Crummo
See Crumb, R(obert)
Elder, Lonne III 1931-1996 .... **DC 8**
See also BLC 1; BW 1, 3; CA 81-84; 152; CANR 25; DAM MULT; DLB 7, 38, 44
Eleanor of Aquitaine 1122-1204 ... **CMLC 39**
Elia
See Lamb, Charles
Eliade, Mircea 1907-1986 .... **CLC 19**
See also CA 65-68; 119; CANR 30, 62; DLB 220; MTCW 1
Eliot, A. D.
See Jewett, (Theodora) Sarah Orne
Eliot, Alice
See Jewett, (Theodora) Sarah Orne
Eliot, Dan
See Silverberg, Robert
Eliot, George 1819-1880 ...... **NCLC 4, 13, 23, 41, 49, 89; DA; DAB; DAC; DAM MST, NOV; PC 20; WLC**
See also CDBLB 1832-1890; DA3; DLB 21, 35, 55
Eliot, John 1604-1690 .... **LC 5**
See also DLB 24
Eliot, T(homas) S(tearns)
1888-1965 ...... **CLC 1, 2, 3, 6, 9, 10, 13, 15, 24, 34, 41, 55, 57, 113; DA; DAB; DAC; DAM DRAM, MST, POET, PC 5; WLC**
See also AAYA 28; CA 5-8R; 25-28R; CANR 41; CDALB 1929-1941; DA3; DLB 7, 10, 45, 63; DLBY 88; MTCW 1, 2
Elizabeth 1866-1941 .... **TCLC 41**
Elkin, Stanley L(awrence)
1930-1995 .. **CLC 4, 6, 9, 14, 27, 51, 91; DAM NOV, POP; SSC 12**
See also CA 9-12R; 148; CANR 8, 46; DLB 2, 28; DLBY 80; INT CANR-8; MTCW 1, 2
Elledge, Scott CLC 34
Elliot, Don
See Silverberg, Robert
Elliott, Don
See Silverberg, Robert
Elliott, George P(aul) 1918-1980 .... **CLC 2**
See also CA 1-4R; 97-100; CANR 2
Elliott, Janice 1931- .... **CLC 47**
See also CA 13-16R; CANR 8, 29, 84; DLB 14
Elliott, Sumner Locke 1917-1991 ..... **CLC 38**
See also CA 5-8R; 134; CANR 2, 21
Elliott, William
See Bradbury, Ray (Douglas)
Ellis, A. E. CLC 7
Ellis, Alice Thomas CLC 40
See also Haycraft, Anna (Margaret)
See also DLB 194; MTCW 1
Ellis, Bret Easton 1964- ..... **CLC 39, 71, 117; DAM POP**
See also AAYA 2; CA 118; 123; CANR 51, 74; DA3; INT 123; MTCW 1
Ellis, (Henry) Havelock
1859-1939 .... **TCLC 14**
See also CA 109; 169; DLB 190
Ellis, Landon
See Ellison, Harlan (Jay)
Ellis, Trey 1962- .... **CLC 55**
See also CA 146
Ellison, Harlan (Jay) 1934- ... **CLC 1, 13, 42; DAM POP; SSC 14**
See also AAYA 29; CA 5-8R; CANR 5, 46; DLB 8; INT CANR-5; MTCW 1, 2

Ellison, Ralph (Waldo) 1914-1994 .... CLC 1, 3, 11, 54, 86, 114; BLC 1; DA; DAB; DAC; DAM MST, MULT, NOV; SSC 26; WLC
See also AAYA 19; BW 1, 3; CA 9-12R; 145; CANR 24, 53; CDALB 1941-1968; DA3; DLB 2, 76, 227; DLBY 94; MTCW 1, 2

Ellmann, Lucy (Elizabeth) 1956- ..... CLC 61
See also CA 128

Ellmann, Richard (David) 1918-1987 .... CLC 50
See also BEST 89:2; CA 1-4R; 122; CANR 2, 28, 61; DLB 103; DLBY 87; MTCW 1, 2

Elman, Richard (Martin) 1934-1997 .... CLC 19
See also CA 17-20R; 163; CAAS 3; CANR 47

Elron
See Hubbard, L(afayette) Ron(ald)

Eluard, Paul TCLC 7, 41
See also Grindel, Eugene

Elyot, Sir Thomas 1490(?)-1546 .... LC 11

Elytis, Odysseus 1911-1996 .... CLC 15, 49, 100; DAM POET; PC 21
See also CA 102; 151; MTCW 1, 2

Emecheta, (Florence Onye) Buchi 1944- .. CLC 14, 48, 128; BLC 2; DAM MULT
See also BW 2, 3; CA 81-84; CANR 27, 81; DA3; DLB 117; MTCW 1, 2; SATA 66

Emerson, Mary Moody 1774-1863 .... NCLC 66

Emerson, Ralph Waldo 1803-1882 . NCLC 1, 38; DA; DAB; DAC; DAM MST, POET; PC 18; WLC
See also CDALB 1640-1865; DA3; DLB 1, 59, 73, 223

Eminescu, Mihail 1850-1889 .... NCLC 33

Empson, William 1906-1984 ... CLC 3, 8, 19, 33, 34
See also CA 17-20R; 112; CANR 31, 61; DLB 20; MTCW 1, 2

Enchi, Fumiko (Ueda) 1905-1986 ..... CLC 31
See also CA 129; 121; DLB 182

Ende, Michael (Andreas Helmuth) 1929-1995 .... CLC 31
See also CA 118; 124; 149; CANR 36; CLR 14; DLB 75; MAICYA; SATA 61; SATA-Brief 42; SATA-Obit 86

Endo, Shusaku 1923-1996 ..... CLC 7, 14, 19, 54, 99; DAM NOV
See also CA 29-32R; 153; CANR 21, 54; DA3; DLB 182; MTCW 1, 2

Engel, Marian 1933-1985 .... CLC 36
See also CA 25-28R; CANR 12; DLB 53; INT CANR-12

Engelhardt, Frederick
See Hubbard, L(afayette) Ron(ald)

Engels, Friedrich 1820-1895 .... NCLC 85
See also DLB 129

Enright, D(ennis) J(oseph) 1920- .. CLC 4, 8, 31
See also CA 1-4R; CANR 1, 42, 83; DLB 27; SATA 25

Enzensberger, Hans Magnus 1929- .... CLC 43; PC 28
See also CA 116; 119

Ephron, Nora 1941- .... CLC 17, 31
See also AITN 2; CA 65-68; CANR 12, 39, 83

Epicurus 341B.C.-270B.C. .... CMLC 21
See also DLB 176

Epsilon
See Betjeman, John

Epstein, Daniel Mark 1948- .... CLC 7
See also CA 49-52; CANR 2, 53, 90

Epstein, Jacob 1956- .... CLC 19
See also CA 114

Epstein, Jean 1897-1953 .... TCLC 92

Epstein, Joseph 1937- .... CLC 39
See also CA 112; 119; CANR 50, 65

Epstein, Leslie 1938- .... CLC 27
See also CA 73-76; CAAS 12; CANR 23, 69

Equiano, Olaudah 1745(?)-1797 .... LC 16; BLC 2; DAM MULT
See also DLB 37, 50

ER TCLC 33
See also CA 160; DLB 85

Erasmus, Desiderius 1469(?)-1536 ...... LC 16

Erdman, Paul E(mil) 1932- .... CLC 25
See also AITN 1; CA 61-64; CANR 13, 43, 84

Erdrich, Louise 1954- .... CLC 39, 54, 120; DAM MULT, NOV, POP
See also AAYA 10; BEST 89:1; CA 114; CANR 41, 62; CDALBS; DA3; DLB 152, 175, 206; MTCW 1; NNAL; SATA 94

Erenburg, Ilya (Grigoryevich)
See Ehrenburg, Ilya (Grigoryevich)

Erickson, Stephen Michael 1950-
See Erickson, Steve
See also CA 129

Erickson, Steve 1950- .... CLC 64
See also Erickson, Stephen Michael
See also CANR 60, 68

Ericson, Walter
See Fast, Howard (Melvin)

Eriksson, Buntel
See Bergman, (Ernst) Ingmar

Ernaux, Annie 1940- .... CLC 88
See also CA 147

Erskine, John 1879-1951 .... TCLC 84
See also CA 112; 159; DLB 9, 102

Eschenbach, Wolfram von
See Wolfram von Eschenbach

Eseki, Bruno
See Mphahlele, Ezekiel

Esenin, Sergei (Alexandrovich) 1895-1925 .... TCLC 4
See also CA 104

Eshleman, Clayton 1935- .... CLC 7
See also CA 33-36R; CAAS 6; DLB 5

Espriella, Don Manuel Alvarez
See Southey, Robert

Espriu, Salvador 1913-1985 .... CLC 9
See also CA 154; 115; DLB 134

Espronceda, Jose de 1808-1842 ..... NCLC 39

Esquivel, Laura 1951(?)-
See also AAYA 29; CA 143; CANR 68; DA3; HLCS 1; MTCW 1

Esse, James
See Stephens, James

Esterbrook, Tom
See Hubbard, L(afayette) Ron(ald)

Estleman, Loren D. 1952- ..... CLC 48; DAM NOV, POP
See also AAYA 27; CA 85-88; CANR 27, 74; DA3; DLB 226; INT CANR-27; MTCW 1, 2

Euclid 306B.C.-283B.C. .... CMLC 25

Eugenides, Jeffrey 1960(?)- .... CLC 81
See also CA 144

Euripides c. 485B.C.-406B.C. .... CMLC 23; DA; DAB; DAC; DAM DRAM, MST; DC 4; WLCS
See also DA3; DLB 176

Evan, Evin
See Faust, Frederick (Schiller)

Evans, Caradoc 1878-1945 .... TCLC 85

Evans, Evan
See Faust, Frederick (Schiller)

Evans, Marian
See Eliot, George

Evans, Mary Ann
See Eliot, George

Evarts, Esther
See Benson, Sally

Everett, Percival L. 1956- .... CLC 57
See also BW 2; CA 129

Everson, R(onald) G(ilmour) 1903- . CLC 27
See also CA 17-20R; DLB 88

Everson, William (Oliver) 1912-1994 .... CLC 1, 5, 14
See also CA 9-12R; 145; CANR 20; DLB 212; MTCW 1

Evtushenko, Evgenii Aleksandrovich
See Yevtushenko, Yevgeny (Alexandrovich)

Ewart, Gavin (Buchanan) 1916-1995 .... CLC 13, 46
See also CA 89-92; 150; CANR 17, 46; DLB 40; MTCW 1

Ewers, Hanns Heinz 1871-1943 ..... TCLC 12
See also CA 109; 149

Ewing, Frederick R.
See Sturgeon, Theodore (Hamilton)

Exley, Frederick (Earl) 1929-1992 .... CLC 6, 11
See also AITN 2; CA 81-84; 138; DLB 143; DLBY 81

Eynhardt, Guillermo
See Quiroga, Horacio (Sylvestre)

Ezekiel, Nissim 1924- .... CLC 61
See also CA 61-64

Ezekiel, Tish O'Dowd 1943- .... CLC 34
See also CA 129

Fadeyev, A.
See Bulgya, Alexander Alexandrovich

Fadeyev, Alexander TCLC 53
See also Bulgya, Alexander Alexandrovich

Fagen, Donald 1948- .... CLC 26

Fainzilberg, Ilya Arnoldovich 1897-1937
See Ilf, Ilya
See also CA 120; 165

Fair, Ronald L. 1932- .... CLC 18
See also BW 1; CA 69-72; CANR 25; DLB 33

Fairbairn, Roger
See Carr, John Dickson

Fairbairns, Zoe (Ann) 1948- .... CLC 32
See also CA 103; CANR 21, 85

Falco, Gian
See Papini, Giovanni

Falconer, James
See Kirkup, James

Falconer, Kenneth
See Kornbluth, C(yril) M.

Falkland, Samuel
See Heijermans, Herman

Fallaci, Oriana 1930- .... CLC 11, 110
See also CA 77-80; CANR 15, 58; MTCW 1

Faludy, George 1913- .... CLC 42
See also CA 21-24R

Faludy, Gyoergy
See Faludy, George

Fanon, Frantz 1925-1961 ... CLC 74; BLC 2; DAM MULT
See also BW 1; CA 116; 89-92

Fanshawe, Ann 1625-1680 .... LC 11

Fante, John (Thomas) 1911-1983 ..... CLC 60
See also CA 69-72; 109; CANR 23; DLB 130; DLBY 83

Farah, Nuruddin 1945- ...... CLC 53; BLC 2; DAM MULT
See also BW 2, 3; CA 106; CANR 81; DLB 125

Fargue, Leon-Paul 1876(?)-1947 .... TCLC 11
See also CA 109

Farigoule, Louis
See Romains, Jules

Farina, Richard 1936(?)-1966 .... **CLC 9**
See also CA 81-84; 25-28R

Farley, Walter (Lorimer)
1915-1989 .... **CLC 17**
See also CA 17-20R; CANR 8, 29, 84; DLB
22; JRDA; MAICYA; SATA 2, 43

Farmer, Philip Jose 1918- .... **CLC 1, 19**
See also AAYA 28; CA 1-4R; CANR 4, 35;
DLB 8; MTCW 1; SATA 93

Farquhar, George 1677-1707 ... **LC 21; DAM
DRAM**
See also DLB 84

Farrell, J(ames) G(ordon)
1935-1979 .... **CLC 6**
See also CA 73-76; 89-92; CANR 36; DLB
14; MTCW 1

Farrell, James T(homas) 1904-1979 . **CLC 1,
4, 8, 11, 66; SSC 28**
See also CA 5-8R; 89-92; CANR 9, 61;
DLB 4, 9, 86; DLBD 2; MTCW 1, 2

Farren, Richard J.
See Betjeman, John

Farren, Richard M.
See Betjeman, John

Fassbinder, Rainer Werner
1946-1982 .... **CLC 20**
See also CA 93-96; 106; CANR 31

Fast, Howard (Melvin) 1914- .. **CLC 23, 131;
DAM NOV**
See also AAYA 16, CA 1-4R, 181; CAAE
181; CAAS 18; CANR 1, 33, 54, 75; DLB
9; INT CANR-33; MTCW 1; SATA 7;
SATA-Essay 107

Faulcon, Robert
See Holdstock, Robert P.

Faulkner, William (Cuthbert)
1897-1962 ...... **CLC 1, 3, 6, 8, 9, 11, 14,
18, 28, 52, 68; DA; DAB; DAC; DAM
MST, NOV; SSC 1, 35; WLC**
See also AAYA 7; CA 81-84; CANR 33;
CDALB 1929 1941; DA3; DLB 9, 11, 44,
102; DLBD 2; DLBY 86, 97; MTCW 1, 2

Fauset, Jessie Redmon
1884(?)-1961 .... **CLC 19, 54; BLC 2;
DAM MULT**
See also BW 1; CA 109; CANR 83; DLB
51

Faust, Frederick (Schiller)
1892-1944(?) .... **TCLC 49; DAM POP**
See also CA 108; 152

Faust, Irvin 1924- .... **CLC 8**
See also CA 33-36R; CANR 28, 67; DLB
2, 28; DLBY 80

Fawkes, Guy
See Benchley, Robert (Charles)

Fearing, Kenneth (Flexner)
1902-1961 .... **CLC 51**
See also CA 93-96; CANR 59; DLB 9

Fecamps, Elise
See Creasey, John

Federman, Raymond 1928- .... **CLC 6, 47**
See also CA 17-20R; CAAS 8; CANR 10,
43, 83; DLBY 80

Federspiel, J(uerg) F. 1931- .... **CLC 42**
See also CA 146

Feiffer, Jules (Ralph) 1929- ..... **CLC 2, 8, 64;
DAM DRAM**
See also AAYA 3; CA 17-20R; CANR 30,
59; DLB 7, 44; INT CANR-30; MTCW
1; SATA 8, 61, 111

Feige, Hermann Albert Otto Maximilian
See Traven, B.

Feinberg, David B. 1956-1994 .... **CLC 59**
See also CA 135; 147

Feinstein, Elaine 1930- .... **CLC 36**
See also CA 69-72; CAAS 1; CANR 31,
68; DLB 14, 40; MTCW 1

Feldman, Irving (Mordecai) 1928- ..... **CLC 7**
See also CA 1-4R; CANR 1; DLB 169

Felix-Tchicaya, Gerald
See Tchicaya, Gerald Felix

Fellini, Federico 1920-1993 .... **CLC 16, 85**
See also CA 65-68; 143; CANR 33

Felsen, Henry Gregor 1916-1995 ..... **CLC 17**
See also CA 1-4R; 180; CANR 1; SAAS 2;
SATA 1

Fenno, Jack
See Calisher, Hortense

Fenollosa, Ernest (Francisco)
1853-1908 .... **TCLC 91**

Fenton, James Martin 1949- .... **CLC 32**
See also CA 102; DLB 40

Ferber, Edna 1887-1968 .... **CLC 18, 93**
See also AITN 1; CA 5-8R; 25-28R; CANR
68; DLB 9, 28, 86; MTCW 1, 2; SATA 7

Ferguson, Helen
See Kavan, Anna

Ferguson, Samuel 1810-1886 .... **NCLC 33**
See also DLB 32

Fergusson, Robert 1750-1774 .... **LC 29**
See also DLB 109

Ferling, Lawrence
See Ferlinghetti, Lawrence (Monsanto)

Ferlinghetti, Lawrence (Monsanto)
1919(?)- .... **CLC 2, 6, 10, 27, 111; DAM
POET; PC 1**
See also CA 5 8R; CANR 3, 41, 73;
CDALB 1941-1968; DA3; DLB 5, 16;
MTCW 1, 2

Fern, Fanny 1811-1872
See Parton, Sara Payson Willis

Fernandez, Vicente Garcia Huidobro
See Huidobro Fernandez, Vicente Garcia

Ferre, Rosario 1942- .... **SSC 36; HLCS 1**
See also CA 131; CANR 55, 81; DLB 145;
HW 1, 2; MTCW 1

Ferrer, Gabriel (Francisco Victor) Miro
See Miro (Ferrer), Gabriel (Francisco
Victor)

Ferrier, Susan (Edmonstone)
1782-1854 .... **NCLC 8**
See also DLB 116

Ferrigno, Robert 1948(?)- .... **CLC 65**
See also CA 140

Ferron, Jacques 1921-1985 .... **CLC 94; DAC**
See also CA 117; 129; DLB 60

Feuchtwanger, Lion 1884-1958 .... **TCLC 3**
See also CA 104; DLB 66

Feuillet, Octave 1821-1890 .... **NCLC 45**
See also DLB 192

Feydeau, Georges (Leon Jules Marie)
1862-1921 .... **TCLC 22; DAM DRAM**
See also CA 113; 152; CANR 84; DLB 192

Fichte, Johann Gottlieb
1762-1814 .... **NCLC 62**
See also DLB 90

Ficino, Marsilio 1433-1499 .... **LC 12**

Fiedeler, Hans
See Doeblin, Alfred

Fiedler, Leslie A(aron) 1917- .. **CLC 4, 13, 24**
See also CA 9-12R; CANR 7, 63; DLB 28,
67; MTCW 1, 2

Field, Andrew 1938- .... **CLC 44**
See also CA 97-100; CANR 25

Field, Eugene 1850-1895 .... **NCLC 3**
See also DLB 23, 42, 140; DLBD 13; MAI-
CYA; SATA 16

Field, Gans T.
See Wellman, Manly Wade

Field, Michael 1915-1971 .... **TCLC 43**
See also CA 29-32R

Field, Peter
See Hobson, Laura Z(ametkin)

Fielding, Henry 1707-1754 ..... **LC 1, 46; DA;
DAB; DAC; DAM DRAM, MST, NOV;
WLC**
See also CDBLB 1660-1789; DA3; DLB
39, 84, 101

Fielding, Sarah 1710-1768 .... **LC 1, 44**
See also DLB 39

Fields, W. C. 1880-1946 .... **TCLC 80**
See also DLB 44

Fierstein, Harvey (Forbes) 1954- .... **CLC 33;
DAM DRAM, POP**
See also CA 123; 129; DA3

Figes, Eva 1932- .... **CLC 31**
See also CA 53-56; CANR 4, 44, 83; DLB
14

Finch, Anne 1661-1720 .... **LC 3; PC 21**
See also DLB 95

Finch, Robert (Duer Claydon)
1900- .... **CLC 18**
See also CA 57-60; CANR 9, 24, 49; DLB
88

Findley, Timothy 1930- . **CLC 27, 102; DAC;
DAM MST**
See also CA 25-28R; CANR 12, 42, 69;
DLB 53

Fink, William
See Mencken, H(enry) L(ouis)

Firbank, Louis 1942-
See Reed, Lou
See also CA 117

Firbank, (Arthur Annesley) Ronald
1886-1926 .... **TCLC 1**
See also CA 104; 177; DLB 36

Fisher, Dorothy (Frances) Canfield
1879 1958 .... **TCLC 87**
See also CA 114; 136; CANR 80; DLB 9,
102; MAICYA; YABC 1

Fisher, M(ary) F(rances) K(ennedy)
1908-1992 .... **CLC 76, 87**
See also CA 77-80; 138; CANR 44; MTCW
1

Fisher, Roy 1930- .... **CLC 25**
See also CA 81-84; CAAS 10; CANR 16;
DLB 40

Fisher, Rudolph 1897-1934 .. **TCLC 11; BLC
2; DAM MULT; SSC 25**
See also BW 1, 3; CA 107; 124; CANR 80;
DLB 51, 102

Fisher, Vardis (Alvero) 1895-1968 ...... **CLC 7**
See also CA 5-8R; 25-28R; CANR 68; DLB
9, 206

Fiske, Tarleton
See Bloch, Robert (Albert)

Fitch, Clarke
See Sinclair, Upton (Beall)

Fitch, John IV
See Cormier, Robert (Edmund)

Fitzgerald, Captain Hugh
See Baum, L(yman) Frank

FitzGerald, Edward 1809-1883 .... **NCLC 9**
See also DLB 32

Fitzgerald, F(rancis) Scott (Key)
1896-1940 .. **TCLC 1, 6, 14, 28, 55; DA;
DAB; DAC; DAM MST, NOV; SSC 6,
31; WLC**
See also AAYA 24; AITN 1; CA 110; 123;
CDALB 1917-1929; DA3; DLB 4, 9, 86;
DLBD 1, 15, 16; DLBY 81, 96; MTCW
1, 2

Fitzgerald, Penelope 1916-2000 . **CLC 19, 51,
61**
See also CA 85-88; CAAS 10; CANR 56,
86; DLB 14, 194; MTCW 2

Fitzgerald, Robert (Stuart)
1910-1985 .... **CLC 39**
See also CA 1-4R; 114; CANR 1; DLBY
80

FitzGerald, Robert D(avid)
1902-1987 .... CLC 19
See also CA 17-20R

Fitzgerald, Zelda (Sayre)
1900-1948 .... TCLC 52
See also CA 117; 126; DLBY 84

Flanagan, Thomas (James Bonner)
1923- .... CLC 25, 52
See also CA 108; CANR 55; DLBY 80; INT
108; MTCW 1

Flaubert, Gustave 1821-1880 .... NCLC 2, 10,
19, 62, 66; DA; DAB; DAC; DAM
MST, NOV; SSC 11; WLC
See also DA3; DLB 119

Flecker, Herman Elroy
See Flecker, (Herman) James Elroy

Flecker, (Herman) James Elroy
1884-1915 .... TCLC 43
See also CA 109; 150; DLB 10, 19

Fleming, Ian (Lancaster) 1908-1964 . CLC 3,
30; DAM POP
See also AAYA 26; CA 5-8R; CANR 59;
CDBLB 1945-1960; DA3; DLB 87, 201;
MTCW 1, 2; SATA 9

Fleming, Thomas (James) 1927- ...... CLC 37
See also CA 5-8R; CANR 10; INT CANR-
10; SATA 8

Fletcher, John 1579-1625 .... LC 33; DC 6
See also CDBLB Before 1660; DLB 58

Fletcher, John Gould 1886-1950 .... TCLC 35
See also CA 107; 167; DLB 4, 45

Fleur, Paul
See Pohl, Frederik

Flooglebuckle, Al
See Spiegelman, Art

Flying Officer X
See Bates, H(erbert) E(rnest)

Fo, Dario 1926- .... CLC 32, 109; DAM
DRAM; DC 10
See also CA 116; 128; CANR 68; DA3;
DLBY 97; MTCW 1, 2

Fogarty, Jonathan Titulescu Esq.
See Farrell, James T(homas)

Follett, Ken(neth Martin) 1949- ..... CLC 18;
DAM NOV, POP
See also AAYA 6; BEST 89:4; CA 81-84;
CANR 13, 33, 54; DA3; DLB 87; DLBY
81; INT CANR-33; MTCW 1

Fontane, Theodor 1819-1898 .... NCLC 26
See also DLB 129

Foote, Horton 1916- .... CLC 51, 91; DAM
DRAM
See also CA 73-76; CANR 34, 51; DA3;
DLB 26; INT CANR-34

Foote, Shelby 1916- ..... CLC 75; DAM NOV,
POP
See also CA 5-8R; CANR 3, 45, 74; DA3;
DLB 2, 17; MTCW 2

Forbes, Esther 1891-1967 .... CLC 12
See also AAYA 17; CA 13-14; 25-28R; CAP
1; CLR 27; DLB 22; JRDA; MAICYA;
SATA 2, 100

Forche, Carolyn (Louise) 1950- .... CLC 25,
83, 86; DAM POET; PC 10
See also CA 109; 117; CANR 50, 74; DA3;
DLB 5, 193; INT 117; MTCW 1

Ford, Elbur
See Hibbert, Eleanor Alice Burford

Ford, Ford Madox 1873-1939 ... TCLC 1, 15,
39, 57; DAM NOV
See also CA 104; 132; CANR 74; CDBLB
1914-1945; DA3; DLB 162; MTCW 1, 2

Ford, Henry 1863-1947 .... TCLC 73
See also CA 115; 148

Ford, John 1586-(?) .... DC 8
See also CDBLB Before 1660; DAM
DRAM; DA3; DLB 58

Ford, John 1895-1973 .... CLC 16
See also CA 45-48

Ford, Richard 1944- .... CLC 46, 99
See also CA 69-72; CANR 11, 47, 86; DLB
227; MTCW 1

Ford, Webster
See Masters, Edgar Lee

Foreman, Richard 1937- .... CLC 50
See also CA 65-68; CANR 32, 63

Forester, C(ecil) S(cott) 1899-1966 ... CLC 35
See also CA 73-76; 25-28R; CANR 83;
DLB 191; SATA 13

Forez
See Mauriac, Francois (Charles)

Forman, James Douglas 1932- .... CLC 21
See also AAYA 17; CA 9-12R; CANR 4,
19, 42; JRDA; MAICYA; SATA 8, 70

Fornes, Maria Irene 1930- . CLC 39, 61; DC
10; HLCS 1
See also CA 25-28R; CANR 28, 81; DLB
7; HW 1, 2; INT CANR-28; MTCW 1

Forrest, Leon (Richard) 1937-1997 .. CLC 4;
BLCS
See also BW 2; CA 89-92; 162; CAAS 7;
CANR 25, 52, 87; DLB 33

Forster, E(dward) M(organ)
1879-1970 ...... CLC 1, 2, 3, 4, 9, 10, 13,
15, 22, 45, 77; DA; DAB; DAC; DAM
MST, NOV; SSC 27; WLC
See also AAYA 2; CA 13-14; 25-28R;
CANR 45; CAP 1; CDBLB 1914-1945;
DA3; DLB 34, 98, 162, 178, 195; DLBD
10; MTCW 1, 2; SATA 57

Forster, John 1812-1876 .... NCLC 11
See also DLB 144, 184

Forsyth, Frederick 1938- .... CLC 2, 5, 36;
DAM NOV, POP
See also BEST 89:4; CA 85-88; CANR 38,
62; DLB 87; MTCW 1, 2

Forten, Charlotte L. TCLC 16; BLC 2
See also Grimke, Charlotte L(ottie) Forten
See also DLB 50

Foscolo, Ugo 1778-1827 .... NCLC 8

Fosse, Bob CLC 20
See also Fosse, Robert Louis

Fosse, Robert Louis 1927-1987
See Fosse, Bob
See also CA 110; 123

Foster, Stephen Collins
1826-1864 .... NCLC 26

Foucault, Michel 1926-1984 . CLC 31, 34, 69
See also CA 105; 113; CANR 34; MTCW
1, 2

Fouque, Friedrich (Heinrich Karl) de la
Motte 1777-1843 .... NCLC 2
See also DLB 90

Fourier, Charles 1772-1837 .... NCLC 51

Fournier, Pierre 1916- .... CLC 11
See also Gascar, Pierre
See also CA 89-92; CANR 16, 40

Fowles, John (Philip) 1926- .. CLC 1, 2, 3, 4,
6, 9, 10, 15, 33, 87; DAB; DAC; DAM
MST; SSC 33
See also CA 5-8R; CANR 25, 71; CDBLB
1960 to Present; DA3; DLB 14, 139, 207;
MTCW 1, 2; SATA 22

Fox, Paula 1923- .... CLC 2, 8, 121
See also AAYA 3; CA 73-76; CANR 20,
36, 62; CLR 1, 44; DLB 52; JRDA; MAI-
CYA; MTCW 1; SATA 17, 60

Fox, William Price (Jr.) 1926- .... CLC 22
See also CA 17-20R; CAAS 19; CANR 11;
DLB 2; DLBY 81

Foxe, John 1516(?)-1587 .... LC 14
See also DLB 132

Frame, Janet 1924- . CLC 2, 3, 6, 22, 66, 96;
SSC 29
See also Clutha, Janet Paterson Frame

France, Anatole TCLC 9
See also Thibault, Jacques Anatole Francois
See also DLB 123; MTCW 1

Francis, Claude 19(?)- .... CLC 50

Francis, Dick 1920- .... CLC 2, 22, 42, 102;
DAM POP
See also AAYA 5, 21; BEST 89:3; CA 5-8R;
CANR 9, 42, 68; CDBLB 1960 to Present;
DA3; DLB 87; INT CANR-9; MTCW 1,
2

Francis, Robert (Churchill)
1901-1987 .... CLC 15
See also CA 1-4R; 123; CANR 1

Frank, Anne(lies Marie)
1929-1945 . TCLC 17; DA; DAB; DAC;
DAM MST; WLC
See also AAYA 12; CA 113; 133; CANR
68; DA3; MTCW 1, 2; SATA 87; SATA-
Brief 42

Frank, Bruno 1887-1945 .... TCLC 81
See also DLB 118

Frank, Elizabeth 1945- .... CLC 39
See also CA 121; 126; CANR 78; INT 126

Frankl, Viktor E(mil) 1905-1997 ...... CLC 93
See also CA 65-68; 161

Franklin, Benjamin
See Hasek, Jaroslav (Matej Frantisek)

Franklin, Benjamin 1706-1790 .. LC 25; DA;
DAB; DAC; DAM MST; WLCS
See also CDALB 1640-1865; DA3; DLB
24, 43, 73

Franklin, (Stella Maria Sarah) Miles
(Lampe) 1879-1954 .... TCLC 7
See also CA 104; 164

Fraser, (Lady) Antonia (Pakenham)
1932- .... CLC 32, 107
See also CA 85-88; CANR 44, 65; MTCW
1, 2; SATA-Brief 32

Fraser, George MacDonald 1925- ...... CLC 7
See also CA 45-48, 180; CAAE 180; CANR
2, 48, 74; MTCW 1

Fraser, Sylvia 1935- .... CLC 64
See also CA 45-48; CANR 1, 16, 60

Frayn, Michael 1933- .... CLC 3, 7, 31, 47;
DAM DRAM, NOV
See also CA 5-8R; CANR 30, 69; DLB 13,
14, 194; MTCW 1, 2

Fraze, Candida (Merrill) 1945- .... CLC 50
See also CA 126

Frazer, J(ames) G(eorge)
1854-1941 .... TCLC 32
See also CA 118

Frazer, Robert Caine
See Creasey, John

Frazer, Sir James George
See Frazer, J(ames) G(eorge)

Frazier, Charles 1950- .... CLC 109
See also AAYA 34; CA 161

Frazier, Ian 1951- .... CLC 46
See also CA 130; CANR 54

Frederic, Harold 1856-1898 .... NCLC 10
See also DLB 12, 23; DLBD 13

Frederick, John
See Faust, Frederick (Schiller)

Frederick the Great 1712-1786 .... LC 14

Fredro, Aleksander 1793-1876 .... NCLC 8

Freeling, Nicolas 1927- .... CLC 38
See also CA 49-52; CAAS 12; CANR 1,
17, 50, 84; DLB 87

Freeman, Douglas Southall
1886-1953 .... TCLC 11
See also CA 109; DLB 17; DLBD 17

Freeman, Judith 1946- .... CLC 55
See also CA 148

Freeman, Mary E(leanor) Wilkins
1852-1930 .... TCLC 9; SSC 1
See also CA 106; 177; DLB 12, 78, 221

Freeman, R(ichard) Austin
1862-1943 .... TCLC 21
See also CA 113; CANR 84; DLB 70

French, Albert 1943- .... **CLC 86**
    See also BW 3; CA 167

French, Marilyn 1929- .... **CLC 10, 18, 60;**
    DAM DRAM, NOV, POP
    See also CA 69-72; CANR 3, 31; INT
    CANR-31; MTCW 1, 2

French, Paul
    See Asimov, Isaac

Freneau, Philip Morin 1752-1832 ... **NCLC 1**
    See also DLB 37, 43

Freud, Sigmund 1856-1939 .... **TCLC 52**
    See also CA 115; 133; CANR 69; MTCW
    1, 2

Friedan, Betty (Naomi) 1921- .... **CLC 74**
    See also CA 65-68; CANR 18, 45, 74;
    MTCW 1, 2

Friedlander, Saul 1932- .... **CLC 90**
    See also CA 117; 130; CANR 72

Friedman, B(ernard) H(arper)
    1926- .... **CLC 7**
    See also CA 1-4R; CANR 3, 48

Friedman, Bruce Jay 1930- ...... **CLC 3, 5, 56**
    See also CA 9-12R; CANR 25, 52; DLB 2,
    28; INT CANR-25

Friel, Brian 1929- .... **CLC 5, 42, 59, 115; DC**
    8
    See also CA 21-24R; CANR 33, 69; DLB
    13; MTCW 1

Friis-Baastad, Babbis Ellinor
    1921-1970 .... **CLC 12**
    See also CA 17-20R; 134; SATA 7

Frisch, Max (Rudolf) 1911-1991 ... **CLC 3, 9,**
    14, 18, 32, 44; DAM DRAM, NOV
    See also CA 85-88; 134, CANR 32, 74,
    DLB 69, 124; MTCW 1, 2

Fromentin, Eugene (Samuel Auguste)
    1820-1876 .... **NCLC 10**
    See also DLB 123

Frost, Frederick
    See Faust, Frederick (Schiller)

Frost, Robert (Lee) 1874-1963 .. **CLC 1, 3, 4,**
    9, 10, 13, 15, 26, 34, 44; DA; DAB;
    DAC; DAM MST, POET; PC 1; WLC
    See also AAYA 21; CA 89-92; CANR 33;
    CDALB 1917-1929; DA3; DLB 54;
    DLBD 7; MTCW 1, 2; SATA 14

Froude, James Anthony
    1818-1894 .... **NCLC 43**
    See also DLB 18, 57, 144

Froy, Herald
    See Waterhouse, Keith (Spencer)

Fry, Christopher 1907- .... **CLC 2, 10, 14;**
    DAM DRAM
    See also CA 17-20R; CAAS 23; CANR 9,
    30, 74; DLB 13; MTCW 1, 2; SATA 66

Frye, (Herman) Northrop
    1912-1991 .... **CLC 24, 70**
    See also CA 5-8R; 133; CANR 8, 37; DLB
    67, 68; MTCW 1, 2

Fuchs, Daniel 1909-1993 .... **CLC 8, 22**
    See also CA 81-84; 142; CAAS 5; CANR
    40; DLB 9, 26, 28; DLBY 93

Fuchs, Daniel 1934- .... **CLC 34**
    See also CA 37-40R; CANR 14, 48

Fuentes, Carlos 1928- .. **CLC 3, 8, 10, 13, 22,**
    41, 60, 113; DA; DAB; DAC; DAM
    MST, MULT, NOV; HLC 1; SSC 24;
    WLC
    See also AAYA 4; AITN 2; CA 69-72;
    CANR 10, 32, 68; DA3; DLB 113; HW
    1, 2; MTCW 1, 2

Fuentes, Gregorio Lopez y
    See Lopez y Fuentes, Gregorio

Fuertes, Gloria 1918- .... **PC 27**
    See also CA 178, 180; DLB 108; HW 2;
    SATA 115

Fugard, (Harold) Athol 1932- . **CLC 5, 9, 14,**
    25, 40, 80; DAM DRAM; DC 3
    See also AAYA 17; CA 85-88; CANR 32,
    54; DLB 225; MTCW 1

Fugard, Sheila 1932- .... **CLC 48**
    See also CA 125

Fukuyama, Francis 1952- .... **CLC 131**
    See also CA 140; CANR 72

Fuller, Charles (H., Jr.) 1939- .... **CLC 25;**
    BLC 2; DAM DRAM, MULT; DC 1
    See also BW 2; CA 108; 112; CANR 87;
    DLB 38; INT 112; MTCW 1

Fuller, John (Leopold) 1937- .... **CLC 62**
    See also CA 21-24R; CANR 9, 44; DLB 40

Fuller, Margaret NCLC 5, 50
    See also Fuller, Sarah Margaret

Fuller, Roy (Broadbent) 1912-1991 ... **CLC 4,**
    28
    See also CA 5-8R; 135; CAAS 10; CANR
    53, 83; DLB 15, 20; SATA 87

Fuller, Sarah Margaret 1810-1850
    See Fuller, Margaret
    See also CDALB 1640-1865; DLB 1, 59,
    73, 83, 223

Fulton, Alice 1952- .... **CLC 52**
    See also CA 116; CANR 57, 88; DLB 193

Furphy, Joseph 1843-1912 .... **TCLC 25**
    See also CA 163

Fussell, Paul 1924- .... **CLC 74**
    See also BEST 90:1; CA 17-20R; CANR 8,
    21, 35, 69; INT CANR-21; MTCW 1, 2

Futabatei, Shimei 1864-1909 .... **TCLC 44**
    See also CA 162; DLB 180

Futrelle, Jacques 1875-1912 .... **TCLC 19**
    See also CA 113; 155

Gaboriau, Emile 1835-1873 .... **NCLC 14**

Gadda, Carlo Emilio 1893-1973 .... **CLC 11**
    See also CA 89-92; DLB 177

Gaddis, William 1922-1998 ... **CLC 1, 3, 6, 8,**
    10, 19, 43, 86
    See also CA 17-20R; 172; CANR 21, 48;
    DLB 2; MTCW 1, 2

Gage, Walter
    See Inge, William (Motter)

Gaines, Ernest J(ames) 1933- ...... **CLC 3, 11,**
    18, 86; BLC 2; DAM MULT
    See also AAYA 18; AITN 1; BW 2, 3; CA
    9-12R; CANR 6, 24, 42, 75; CDALB
    1968-1988; CLR 62; DA3; DLB 2, 33,
    152; DLBY 80; MTCW 1, 2; SATA 86

Gaitskill, Mary 1954- .... **CLC 69**
    See also CA 128; CANR 61

Galdos, Benito Perez
    See Perez Galdos, Benito

Gale, Zona 1874-1938 .... **TCLC 7; DAM**
    DRAM
    See also CA 105; 153; CANR 84; DLB 9,
    78, 228

Galeano, Eduardo (Hughes) 1940- . **CLC 72;**
    HLCS 1
    See also CA 29-32R; CANR 13, 32; HW 1

Galiano, Juan Valera y Alcala
    See Valera y Alcala-Galiano, Juan

Galilei, Galileo 1546-1642 .... **LC 45**

Gallagher, Tess 1943- ...... **CLC 18, 63; DAM**
    POET; PC 9
    See also CA 106; DLB 212

Gallant, Mavis 1922- .. **CLC 7, 18, 38; DAC;**
    DAM MST; SSC 5
    See also CA 69-72; CANR 29, 69; DLB 53;
    MTCW 1, 2

Gallant, Roy A(rthur) 1924- .... **CLC 17**
    See also CA 5-8R; CANR 4, 29, 54; CLR
    30; MAICYA; SATA 4, 68, 110

Gallico, Paul (William) 1897-1976 ..... **CLC 2**
    See also AITN 1; CA 5-8R; 69-72; CANR
    23; DLB 9, 171; MAICYA; SATA 13

Gallo, Max Louis 1932- .... **CLC 95**
    See also CA 85-88

Gallois, Lucien
    See Desnos, Robert

Gallup, Ralph
    See Whitemore, Hugh (John)

Galsworthy, John 1867-1933 .... **TCLC 1, 45;**
    DA; DAB; DAC; DAM DRAM, MST,
    NOV; SSC 22; WLC
    See also CA 104; 141; CANR 75; CDBLB
    1890-1914; DA3; DLB 10, 34, 98, 162;
    DLBD 16; MTCW 1

Galt, John 1779-1839 .... **NCLC 1**
    See also DLB 99, 116, 159

Galvin, James 1951- .... **CLC 38**
    See also CA 108; CANR 26

Gamboa, Federico 1864-1939 .... **TCLC 36**
    See also CA 167; HW 2

Gandhi, M. K.
    See Gandhi, Mohandas Karamchand

Gandhi, Mahatma
    See Gandhi, Mohandas Karamchand

Gandhi, Mohandas Karamchand
    1869-1948 .... **TCLC 59; DAM MULT**
    See also CA 121; 132; DA3; MTCW 1, 2

Gann, Ernest Kellogg 1910-1991 ..... **CLC 23**
    See also AITN 1; CA 1-4R; 136; CANR 1,
    83

Garber, Eric 1943(?)-
    See Holleran, Andrew
    See also CANR 89

Garcia, Cristina 1958- .... **CLC 76**
    See also CA 141; CANR 73; HW 2

Garcia Lorca, Federico 1898-1936 . **TCLC 1,**
    7, 49; DA; DAB; DAC; DAM DRAM,
    MST, MULT, POET; DC 2; HLC 2;
    PC 3; WLC
    See also Lorca, Federico Garcia
    See also CA 104; 131; CANR 81; DA3;
    DLB 108; HW 1, 2; MTCW 1, 2

Garcia Marquez, Gabriel (Jose)
    1928- .... **CLC 2, 3, 8, 10, 15, 27, 47, 55,**
    68; DA; DAB; DAC; DAM MST,
    MULT, NOV, POP; HLC 1; SSC 8;
    WLC
    See also Marquez, Gabriel (Jose) Garcia
    See also AAYA 3, 33; BEST 89:1; 90:4; CA
    33-36R; CANR 10, 28, 50, 75, 82; DA3;
    DLB 113; HW 1, 2; MTCW 1, 2

Garcilaso de la Vega, El Inca 1503-1536
    See also HLCS 1

Gard, Janice
    See Latham, Jean Lee

Gard, Roger Martin du
    See Martin du Gard, Roger

Gardam, June 1928 .... **CLC 43**
    See also CA 49-52; CANR 2, 18, 33, 54;
    CLR 12; DLB 14, 161; MAICYA; MTCW
    1; SAAS 9; SATA 39, 76; SATA-Brief 28

Gardner, Herb(ert) 1934- .... **CLC 44**
    See also CA 149

Gardner, John (Champlin), Jr.
    1933-1982 ...... **CLC 2, 3, 5, 7, 8, 10, 18,**
    28, 34; DAM NOV, POP; SSC 7
    See also AITN 1; CA 65-68; 107; CANR
    33, 73; CDALBS; DA3; DLB 2; DLBY
    82; MTCW 1; SATA 40; SATA-Obit 31

Gardner, John (Edmund) 1926- ...... **CLC 30;**
    DAM POP
    See also CA 103; CANR 15, 69; MTCW 1

Gardner, Miriam
    See Bradley, Marion Zimmer

Gardner, Noel
    See Kuttner, Henry

Gardons, S. S.
    See Snodgrass, W(illiam) D(e Witt)

Garfield, Leon 1921-1996 .... **CLC 12**
    See also AAYA 8; CA 17-20R; 152; CANR
    38, 41, 78; CLR 21; DLB 161; JRDA;
    MAICYA; SATA 1, 32, 76; SATA-Obit 90

Garland, (Hannibal) Hamlin
1860-1940 .... **TCLC 3; SSC 18**
See also CA 104; DLB 12, 71, 78, 186
Garneau, (Hector de) Saint-Denys
1912-1943 .... **TCLC 13**
See also CA 111; DLB 88
Garner, Alan 1934- ..... **CLC 17; DAB; DAM POP**
See also AAYA 18; CA 73-76, 178; CAAE
178; CANR 15, 64; CLR 20; DLB 161;
MAICYA; MTCW 1, 2; SATA 18, 69;
SATA-Essay 108
Garner, Hugh 1913-1979 .... **CLC 13**
See also CA 69-72; CANR 31; DLB 68
Garnett, David 1892-1981 .... **CLC 3**
See also CA 5-8R; 103; CANR 17, 79; DLB
34; MTCW 2
Garos, Stephanie
See Katz, Steve
Garrett, George (Palmer) 1929- .. **CLC 3, 11, 51; SSC 30**
See also CA 1-4R; CAAS 5; CANR 1, 42,
67; DLB 2, 5, 130, 152; DLBY 83
Garrick, David 1717-1779 .... **LC 15; DAM DRAM**
See also DLB 84
Garrigue, Jean 1914-1972 .... **CLC 2, 8**
See also CA 5-8R; 37-40R; CANR 20
Garrison, Frederick
See Sinclair, Upton (Beall)
Garro, Elena 1920(?)-1998
See also CA 131; 169; DLB 145; HLCS 1;
HW 1
Garth, Will
See Hamilton, Edmond; Kuttner, Henry
Garvey, Marcus (Moziah, Jr.)
1887-1940 ...... **TCLC 41; BLC 2; DAM MULT**
See also BW 1; CA 120; 124; CANR 79
Gary, Romain CLC 25
See also Kacew, Romain
See also DLB 83
Gascar, Pierre CLC 11
See also Fournier, Pierre
Gascoyne, David (Emery) 1916- .... **CLC 45**
See also CA 65-68; CANR 10, 28, 54; DLB
20; MTCW 1
Gaskell, Elizabeth Cleghorn
1810-1865 .... **NCLC 70; DAB; DAM MST; SSC 25**
See also CDBLB 1832-1890; DLB 21, 144,
159
Gass, William H(oward) 1924- . **CLC 1, 2, 8, 11, 15, 39, 132; SSC 12**
See also CA 17-20R; CANR 30, 71; DLB
2, 227; MTCW 1, 2
Gassendi, Pierre 1592-1655 .... **LC 54**
Gasset, Jose Ortega y
See Ortega y Gasset, Jose
Gates, Henry Louis, Jr. 1950- .... **CLC 65; BLCS; DAM MULT**
See also BW 2, 3; CA 109; CANR 25, 53,
75; DA3; DLB 67; MTCW 1
Gautier, Theophile 1811-1872 .. **NCLC 1, 59; DAM POET; PC 18; SSC 20**
See also DLB 119
Gawsworth, John
See Bates, H(erbert) E(rnest)
Gay, John 1685-1732 .. **LC 49; DAM DRAM**
See also DLB 84, 95
Gay, Oliver
See Gogarty, Oliver St. John
Gaye, Marvin (Penze) 1939-1984 ..... **CLC 26**
See also CA 112
Gebler, Carlo (Ernest) 1954- .... **CLC 39**
See also CA 119; 133
Gee, Maggie (Mary) 1948- .... **CLC 57**
See also CA 130; DLB 207

Gee, Maurice (Gough) 1931- .... **CLC 29**
See also CA 97-100; CANR 67; CLR 56;
SATA 46, 101
Gelbart, Larry (Simon) 1923- .... **CLC 21, 61**
See also CA 73-76; CANR 45
Gelber, Jack 1932- .... **CLC 1, 6, 14, 79**
See also CA 1-4R; CANR 2; DLB 7, 228
Gellhorn, Martha (Ellis)
1908-1998 .... **CLC 14, 60**
See also CA 77-80; 164; CANR 44; DLBY
82, 98
Genet, Jean 1910-1986 .. **CLC 1, 2, 5, 10, 14, 44, 46; DAM DRAM**
See also CA 13-16R; CANR 18; DA3; DLB
72; DLBY 86; MTCW 1, 2
Gent, Peter 1942- .... **CLC 29**
See also AITN 1; CA 89-92; DLBY 82
Gentile, Giovanni 1875-1944 .... **TCLC 96**
See also CA 119
Gentlewoman in New England, A
See Bradstreet, Anne
Gentlewoman in Those Parts, A
See Bradstreet, Anne
George, Jean Craighead 1919- .... **CLC 35**
See also AAYA 8; CA 5-8R; CANR 25;
CLR 1; DLB 52; JRDA; MAICYA; SATA
2, 68
George, Stefan (Anton) 1868-1933 . **TCLC 2, 14**
See also CA 104
Georges, Georges Martin
See Simenon, Georges (Jacques Christian)
Gerhardi, William Alexander
See Gerhardie, William Alexander
Gerhardie, William Alexander
1895-1977 .... **CLC 5**
See also CA 25-28R; 73-76; CANR 18;
DLB 36
Gerstler, Amy 1956- .... **CLC 70**
See also CA 146
Gertler, T. CLC 34
See also CA 116; 121; INT 121
Ghalib NCLC 39, 78
See also Ghalib, Hsadullah Khan
Ghalib, Hsadullah Khan 1797-1869
See Ghalib
See also DAM POET
Ghelderode, Michel de 1898-1962 ..... **CLC 6, 11; DAM DRAM**
See also CA 85-88; CANR 40, 77
Ghiselin, Brewster 1903- .... **CLC 23**
See also CA 13-16R; CAAS 10; CANR 13
Ghose, Aurabinda 1872-1950 .... **TCLC 63**
See also CA 163
Ghose, Zulfikar 1935- .... **CLC 42**
See also CA 65-68; CANR 67
Ghosh, Amitav 1956- .... **CLC 44**
See also CA 147; CANR 80
Giacosa, Giuseppe 1847-1906 .... **TCLC 7**
See also CA 104
Gibb, Lee
See Waterhouse, Keith (Spencer)
Gibbon, Lewis Grassic TCLC 4
See also Mitchell, James Leslie
Gibbons, Kaye 1960- .... **CLC 50, 88; DAM POP**
See also AAYA 34; CA 151; CANR 75;
DA3; MTCW 1; SATA 117
Gibran, Kahlil 1883-1931 .... **TCLC 1, 9; DAM POET, POP; PC 9**
See also CA 104; 150; DA3; MTCW 2
Gibran, Khalil
See Gibran, Kahlil
Gibson, William 1914- .. **CLC 23; DA; DAB; DAC; DAM DRAM, MST**
See also CA 9-12R; CANR 9, 42, 75; DLB
7; MTCW 1; SATA 66

Gibson, William (Ford) 1948- ... **CLC 39, 63; DAM POP**
See also AAYA 12; CA 126; 133; CANR
52, 90; DA3; MTCW 1
Gide, Andre (Paul Guillaume)
1869-1951 . **TCLC 5, 12, 36; DA; DAB; DAC; DAM MST, NOV; SSC 13; WLC**
See also CA 104; 124; DA3; DLB 65;
MTCW 1, 2
Gifford, Barry (Colby) 1946- .... **CLC 34**
See also CA 65-68; CANR 9, 30, 40, 90
Gilbert, Frank
See De Voto, Bernard (Augustine)
Gilbert, W(illiam) S(chwenck)
1836-1911 .... **TCLC 3; DAM DRAM, POET**
See also CA 104; 173; SATA 36
Gilbreth, Frank B., Jr. 1911- .... **CLC 17**
See also CA 9-12R; SATA 2
Gilchrist, Ellen 1935- ...... **CLC 34, 48; DAM POP; SSC 14**
See also CA 113; 116; CANR 41, 61; DLB
130; MTCW 1, 2
Giles, Molly 1942- .... **CLC 39**
See also CA 126
Gill, Eric 1882-1940 .... **TCLC 85**
Gill, Patrick
See Creasey, John
Gilliam, Terry (Vance) 1940- .... **CLC 21**
See also Monty Python
See also AAYA 19; CA 108; 113; CANR
35; INT 113
Gillian, Jerry
See Gilliam, Terry (Vance)
Gilliatt, Penelope (Ann Douglass)
1932-1993 .... **CLC 2, 10, 13, 53**
See also AITN 2; CA 13-16R; 141; CANR
49; DLB 14
Gilman, Charlotte (Anna) Perkins (Stetson)
1860-1935 .... **TCLC 9, 37; SSC 13**
See also CA 106; 150; DLB 221; MTCW 1
Gilmour, David 1949- .... **CLC 35**
See also CA 138; 147
Gilpin, William 1724-1804 .... **NCLC 30**
Gilray, J. D.
See Mencken, H(enry) L(ouis)
Gilroy, Frank D(aniel) 1925- .... **CLC 2**
See also CA 81-84; CANR 32, 64, 86; DLB
7
Gilstrap, John 1957(?)- .... **CLC 99**
See also CA 160
Ginsberg, Allen 1926-1997 .... **CLC 1, 2, 3, 4, 6, 13, 36, 69, 109; DA; DAB; DAC; DAM MST, POET; PC 4; WLC**
See also AAYA 33; AITN 1; CA 1-4R; 157;
CANR 2, 41, 63; CDALB 1941-1968;
DA3; DLB 5, 16, 169; MTCW 1, 2
Ginzburg, Natalia 1916-1991 .... **CLC 5, 11, 54, 70**
See also CA 85-88; 135; CANR 33; DLB
177; MTCW 1, 2
Giono, Jean 1895-1970 .... **CLC 4, 11**
See also CA 45-48; 29-32R; CANR 2, 35;
DLB 72; MTCW 1
Giovanni, Nikki 1943- .... **CLC 2, 4, 19, 64, 117; BLC 2; DA; DAB; DAC; DAM MST, MULT, POET; PC 19; WLCS**
See also AAYA 22; AITN 1; BW 2, 3; CA
29-32R; CAAS 6; CANR 18, 41, 60, 91;
CDALBS; CLR 6; DA3; DLB 5, 41; INT
CANR-18; MAICYA; MTCW 1, 2; SATA
24, 107
Giovene, Andrea 1904- .... **CLC 7**
See also CA 85-88
Gippius, Zinaida (Nikolayevna) 1869-1945
See Hippius, Zinaida
See also CA 106

Giraudoux, (Hippolyte) Jean
1882-1944 .... TCLC 2, 7; DAM DRAM
See also CA 104; DLB 65
Gironella, Jose Maria 1917- .... CLC 11
See also CA 101
Gissing, George (Robert)
1857-1903 .... TCLC 3, 24, 47; SSC 37
See also CA 105; 167; DLB 18, 135, 184
Giurlani, Aldo
See Palazzeschi, Aldo
Gladkov, Fyodor (Vasilyevich)
1883-1958 .... TCLC 27
See also CA 170
Glanville, Brian (Lester) 1931- .... CLC 6
See also CA 5-8R; CAAS 9; CANR 3, 70;
DLB 15, 139; SATA 42
Glasgow, Ellen (Anderson Gholson)
1873-1945 .... TCLC 2, 7; SSC 34
See also CA 104; 164; DLB 9, 12; MTCW
2
Glaspell, Susan 1882(?)-1948 . TCLC 55; DC
10; SSC 41
See also CA 110; 154; DLB 7, 9, 78, 228;
YABC 2
Glassco, John 1909-1981 .... CLC 9
See also CA 13-16R; 102; CANR 15; DLB
68
Glasscock, Amnesia
See Steinbeck, John (Ernst)
Glasser, Ronald J. 1940(?)- .... CLC 37
Glassman, Joyce
See Johnson, Joyce
Glendinning, Victoria 1937 .... CLC 50
See also CA 120; 127; CANR 59, 89; DLB
155
Glissant, Edouard 1928- . CLC 10, 68; DAM
MULT
See also CA 153
Gloag, Julian 1930- .... CLC 40
See also AITN 1; CA 65-68; CANR 10, 70
Glowacki, Aleksander
See Prus, Boleslaw
Gluck, Louise (Elisabeth) 1943- .. CLC 7, 22,
44, 81; DAM POET; PC 16
See also CA 33-36R; CANR 40, 69; DA3;
DLB 5; MTCW 2
Glyn, Elinor 1864-1943 .... TCLC 72
See also DLB 153
Gobineau, Joseph Arthur (Comte) de
1816-1882 .... NCLC 17
See also DLB 123
Godard, Jean-Luc 1930- .... CLC 20
See also CA 93-96
Godden, (Margaret) Rumer
1907-1998 .... CLC 53
See also AAYA 6; CA 5-8R; 172; CANR 4,
27, 36, 55, 80; CLR 20; DLB 161; MAI-
CYA; SAAS 12; SATA 3, 36; SATA-Obit
109
Godoy Alcayaga, Lucila 1889-1957
See Mistral, Gabriela
See also BW 2; CA 104; 131; CANR 81;
DAM MULT; HW 1, 2; MTCW 1, 2
Godwin, Gail (Kathleen) 1937- ..... CLC 5, 8,
22, 31, 69, 125; DAM POP
See also CA 29-32R; CANR 15, 43, 69;
DA3; DLB 6; INT CANR-15; MTCW 1,
2
Godwin, William 1756-1836 .... NCLC 14
See also CDBLB 1789-1832; DLB 39, 104,
142, 158, 163
Goebbels, Josef
See Goebbels, (Paul) Joseph
Goebbels, (Paul) Joseph
1897-1945 .... TCLC 68
See also CA 115; 148
Goebbels, Joseph Paul
See Goebbels, (Paul) Joseph

Goethe, Johann Wolfgang von
1749-1832 . NCLC 4, 22, 34; DA; DAB;
DAC; DAM DRAM, MST, POET; PC
5; SSC 38; WLC
See also DA3; DLB 94
Gogarty, Oliver St. John
1878-1957 .... TCLC 15
See also CA 109; 150; DLB 15, 19
Gogol, Nikolai (Vasilyevich)
1809-1852 . NCLC 5, 15, 31; DA; DAB;
DAC; DAM DRAM, MST; DC 1; SSC
4, 29; WLC
See also DLB 198
Goines, Donald 1937(?)-1974 . CLC 80; BLC
2; DAM MULT, POP
See also AITN 1; BW 1, 3; CA 124; 114;
CANR 82; DA3; DLB 33
Gold, Herbert 1924- .... CLC 4, 7, 14, 42
See also CA 9-12R; CANR 17, 45; DLB 2;
DLBY 81
Goldbarth, Albert 1948- .... CLC 5, 38
See also CA 53-56; CANR 6, 40; DLB 120
Goldberg, Anatol 1910-1982 .... CLC 34
See also CA 131; 117
Goldemberg, Isaac 1945- .... CLC 52
See also CA 69-72; CAAS 12; CANR 11,
32; HW 1
Golding, William (Gerald)
1911-1993 ..... CLC 1, 2, 3, 8, 10, 17, 27,
58, 81; DA; DAB; DAC; DAM MST,
NOV; WLC
See also AAYA 5; CA 5-8R; 141; CANR
13, 33, 54; CDBLB 1945-1960; DA3;
DLB 15, 100; MTCW 1, 2
Goldman, Emma 1869-1940 .... TCLC 13
See also CA 110; 150; DLB 221
Goldman, Francisco 1954- .... CLC 76
See also CA 162
Goldman, William (W.) 1931- ...... CLC 1, 48
See also CA 9-12R; CANR 29, 69; DLB 44
Goldmann, Lucien 1913-1970 .... CLC 24
See also CA 25-28; CAP 2
Goldoni, Carlo 1707-1793 .... LC 4; DAM
DRAM
Goldsberry, Steven 1949- .... CLC 34
See also CA 131
Goldsmith, Oliver 1728-1774 . LC 2, 48; DA;
DAB; DAC; DAM DRAM, MST, NOV,
POET; DC 8; WLC
See also CDBLB 1660-1789; DLB 39, 89,
104, 109, 142; SATA 26
Goldsmith, Peter
See Priestley, J(ohn) B(oynton)
Gombrowicz, Witold 1904-1969 .... CLC 4, 7,
11, 49; DAM DRAM
See also CA 19-20; 25-28R; CAP 2
Gomez de la Serna, Ramon
1888-1963 .... CLC 9
See also CA 153; 116; CANR 79; HW 1, 2
Goncharov, Ivan Alexandrovich
1812-1891 .... NCLC 1, 63
Goncourt, Edmond (Louis Antoine Huot) de
1822-1896 .... NCLC 7
See also DLB 123
Goncourt, Jules (Alfred Huot) de
1830-1870 .... NCLC 7
See also DLB 123
Gontier, Fernande 19(?)- .... CLC 50
Gonzalez Martinez, Enrique
1871-1952 .... TCLC 72
See also CA 166; CANR 81; HW 1, 2
Goodman, Paul 1911-1972 .... CLC 1, 2, 4, 7
See also CA 19-20; 37-40R; CANR 34;
CAP 2; DLB 130; MTCW 1

Gordimer, Nadine 1923- ...... CLC 3, 5, 7, 10,
18, 33, 51, 70; DA; DAB; DAC; DAM
MST, NOV; SSC 17; WLCS
See also CA 5-8R; CANR 3, 28, 56, 88;
DA3; DLB 225; INT CANR-28; MTCW
1, 2
Gordon, Adam Lindsay
1833-1870 .... NCLC 21
Gordon, Caroline 1895-1981 . CLC 6, 13, 29,
83; SSC 15
See also CA 11-12; 103; CANR 36; CAP 1;
DLB 4, 9, 102; DLBD 17; DLBY 81;
MTCW 1, 2
Gordon, Charles William 1860-1937
See Connor, Ralph
See also CA 109
Gordon, Mary (Catherine) 1949- .... CLC 13,
22, 128
See also CA 102; CANR 44; DLB 6; DLBY
81; INT 102; MTCW 1
Gordon, N. J.
See Bosman, Herman Charles
Gordon, Sol 1923- .... CLC 26
See also CA 53-56; CANR 4; SATA 11
Gordone, Charles 1925-1995 .... CLC 1, 4;
DAM DRAM; DC 8
See also BW 1, 3; CA 93-96, 180; 150;
CAAE 180; CANR 55; DLB 7; INT 93-
96; MTCW 1
Gore, Catherine 1800-1861 .... NCLC 65
See also DLB 116
Gorenko, Anna Andreevna
See Akhmatova, Anna
Gorky, Maxim 1868-1936 .... TCLC 8; DAB;
SSC 28; WLC
See also Peshkov, Alexei Maximovich
See also MTCW 2
Goryan, Sirak
See Saroyan, William
Gosse, Edmund (William)
1849-1928 .... TCLC 28
See also CA 117; DLB 57, 144, 184
Gotlieb, Phyllis Fay (Bloom) 1926- .. CLC 18
See also CA 13-16R; CANR 7; DLB 88
Gottesman, S. D.
See Kornbluth, C(yril) M.; Pohl, Frederik
Gottfried von Strassburg fl. c.
1210- .... CMLC 10
See also DLB 138
Gould, Lois CLC 4, 10
See also CA 77-80; CANR 29; MTCW 1
Gourmont, Remy (-Marie-Charles) de
1858-1915 .... TCLC 17
See also CA 109; 150; MTCW 2
Govier, Katherine 1948- .... CLC 51
See also CA 101; CANR 18, 40
Goyen, (Charles) William
1915-1983 .... CLC 5, 8, 14, 40
See also AITN 2; CA 5-8R; 110; CANR 6,
71; DLB 2; DLBY 83; INT CANR-6
Goytisolo, Juan 1931- .... CLC 5, 10, 23, 133;
DAM MULT; HLC 1
See also CA 85-88; CANR 32, 61; HW 1,
2; MTCW 1, 2
Gozzano, Guido 1883-1916 .... PC 10
See also CA 154; DLB 114
Gozzi, (Conte) Carlo 1720-1806 .... NCLC 23
Grabbe, Christian Dietrich
1801-1836 .... NCLC 2
See also DLB 133
Grace, Patricia Frances 1937- .... CLC 56
See also CA 176
Gracian y Morales, Baltasar
1601-1658 .... LC 15
Gracq, Julien CLC 11, 48
See also Poirier, Louis
See also DLB 83
Grade, Chaim 1910-1982 .... CLC 10
See also CA 93-96; 107

Graduate of Oxford, A
See Ruskin, John
Grafton, Garth
See Duncan, Sara Jeannette
Graham, John
See Phillips, David Graham
Graham, Jorie 1951- .... **CLC 48, 118**
See also CA 111; CANR 63; DLB 120
Graham, R(obert) B(ontine) Cunninghame
See Cunninghame Graham, Robert
(Gallnigad) Bontine
See also DLB 98, 135, 174
Graham, Robert
See Haldeman, Joe (William)
Graham, Tom
See Lewis, (Harry) Sinclair
Graham, W(illiam) S(ydney)
1918-1986 .... **CLC 29**
See also CA 73-76; 118; DLB 20
Graham, Winston (Mawdsley)
1910- .... **CLC 23**
See also CA 49-52; CANR 2, 22, 45, 66;
DLB 77
Grahame, Kenneth 1859-1932 ...... **TCLC 64;**
DAB
See also CA 108; 136; CANR 80; CLR 5;
DA3; DLB 34, 141, 178; MAICYA;
MTCW 2; SATA 100; YABC 1
Granovsky, Timofei Nikolaevich
1813-1855 .... **NCLC 75**
See also DLB 198
Grant, Skeeter
See Spiegelman, Art
Granville-Barker, Harley
1877-1946 .... **TCLC 2; DAM DRAM**
See also Barker, Harley Granville
See also CA 104
Grass, Guenter (Wilhelm) 1927- ... **CLC 1, 2,**
4, 6, 11, 15, 22, 32, 49, 88; DA; DAB;
DAC; DAM MST, NOV; WLC
See also CA 13-16R; CANR 20, 75; DA3;
DLB 75, 124; MTCW 1, 2
Gratton, Thomas
See Hulme, T(homas) E(rnest)
Grau, Shirley Ann 1929- . **CLC 4, 9; SSC 15**
See also CA 89-92; CANR 22, 69; DLB 2;
INT CANR-22; MTCW 1
Gravel, Fern
See Hall, James Norman
Graver, Elizabeth 1964- .... **CLC 70**
See also CA 135; CANR 71
Graves, Richard Perceval 1945- .... **CLC 44**
See also CA 65-68; CANR 9, 26, 51
Graves, Robert (von Ranke)
1895-1985 .. **CLC 1, 2, 6, 11, 39, 44, 45;**
DAB; DAC; DAM MST, POET; PC 6
See also CA 5-8R; 117; CANR 5, 36; CD-
BLB 1914-1945; DA3; DLB 20, 100, 191;
DLBD 18; DLBY 85; MTCW 1, 2; SATA
45
Graves, Valerie
See Bradley, Marion Zimmer
Gray, Alasdair (James) 1934- .... **CLC 41**
See also CA 126; CANR 47, 69; DLB 194;
INT 126; MTCW 1, 2
Gray, Amlin 1946- .... **CLC 29**
See also CA 138
Gray, Francine du Plessix 1930- ..... **CLC 22;**
DAM NOV
See also BEST 90:3; CA 61-64; CAAS 2;
CANR 11, 33, 75, 81; INT CANR-11;
MTCW 1, 2
Gray, John (Henry) 1866-1934 ...... **TCLC 19**
See also CA 119; 162
Gray, Simon (James Holliday)
1936- .... **CLC 9, 14, 36**
See also AITN 1; CA 21-24R; CAAS 3;
CANR 32, 69; DLB 13; MTCW 1

Gray, Spalding 1941- ..... **CLC 49, 112; DAM**
POP; DC 7
See also CA 128; CANR 74; MTCW 2
Gray, Thomas 1716-1771 .... **LC 4, 40; DA;**
DAB; DAC; DAM MST; PC 2; WLC
See also CDBLB 1660-1789; DA3; DLB
109
Grayson, David
See Baker, Ray Stannard
Grayson, Richard (A.) 1951- .... **CLC 38**
See also CA 85-88; CANR 14, 31, 57
Greeley, Andrew M(oran) 1928- ..... **CLC 28;**
DAM POP
See also CA 5-8R; CAAS 7; CANR 7, 43,
69; DA3; MTCW 1, 2
Green, Anna Katharine
1846-1935 .... **TCLC 63**
See also CA 112; 159; DLB 202, 221
Green, Brian
See Card, Orson Scott
Green, Hannah
See Greenberg, Joanne (Goldenberg)
Green, Hannah 1927(?)-1996 .... **CLC 3**
See also CA 73-76; CANR 59
Green, Henry 1905-1973 .... **CLC 2, 13, 97**
See also Yorke, Henry Vincent
See also CA 175; DLB 15
Green, Julian (Hartridge) 1900-1998
See Green, Julien
See also CA 21-24R; 169; CANR 33, 87;
DLB 4, 72; MTCW 1
Green, Julien CLC 3, 11, 77
See also Green, Julian (Hartridge)
See also MTCW 2
Green, Paul (Eliot) 1894-1981 .... **CLC 25;**
DAM DRAM
See also AITN 1; CA 5-8R; 103; CANR 3;
DLB 7, 9; DLBY 81
Greenberg, Ivan 1908-1973
See Rahv, Philip
See also CA 85-88
Greenberg, Joanne (Goldenberg)
1932- .... **CLC 7, 30**
See also AAYA 12; CA 5-8R; CANR 14,
32, 69; SATA 25
Greenberg, Richard 1959(?)- .... **CLC 57**
See also CA 138
Greene, Bette 1934- .... **CLC 30**
See also AAYA 7; CA 53-56; CANR 4; CLR
2; JRDA; MAICYA; SAAS 16; SATA 8,
102
Greene, Gael CLC 8
See also CA 13-16R; CANR 10
Greene, Graham (Henry)
1904-1991 .... **CLC 1, 3, 6, 9, 14, 18, 27,**
37, 70, 72, 125; DA; DAB; DAC; DAM
MST, NOV; SSC 29; WLC
See also AITN 2; CA 13-16R; 133; CANR
35, 61; CDBLB 1945-1960; DA3; DLB
13, 15, 77, 100, 162, 201, 204; DLBY 91;
MTCW 1, 2; SATA 20
Greene, Robert 1558-1592 .... **LC 41**
See also DLB 62, 167
Greer, Germaine 1939- .... **CLC 131**
See also AITN 1; CA 81-84; CANR 33, 70;
MTCW 1, 2
Greer, Richard
See Silverberg, Robert
Gregor, Arthur 1923- .... **CLC 9**
See also CA 25-28R; CAAS 10; CANR 11;
SATA 36
Gregor, Lee
See Pohl, Frederik
Gregory, Isabella Augusta (Persse)
1852-1932 .... **TCLC 1**
See also CA 104; 184; DLB 10
Gregory, J. Dennis
See Williams, John A(lfred)

Grendon, Stephen
See Derleth, August (William)
Grenville, Kate 1950- .... **CLC 61**
See also CA 118; CANR 53
Grenville, Pelham
See Wodehouse, P(elham) G(renville)
Greve, Felix Paul (Berthold Friedrich)
1879-1948
See Grove, Frederick Philip
See also CA 104; 141, 175; CANR 79;
DAC; DAM MST
Grey, Zane 1872-1939 . **TCLC 6; DAM POP**
See also CA 104; 132; DA3; DLB 212;
MTCW 1, 2
Grieg, (Johan) Nordahl (Brun)
1902-1943 .... **TCLC 10**
See also CA 107
Grieve, C(hristopher) M(urray)
1892-1978 ..... **CLC 11, 19; DAM POET**
See also MacDiarmid, Hugh; Pteleon
See also CA 5-8R; 85-88; CANR 33;
MTCW 1
Griffin, Gerald 1803-1840 .... **NCLC 7**
See also DLB 159
Griffin, John Howard 1920-1980 ..... **CLC 68**
See also AITN 1; CA 1-4R; 101; CANR 2
Griffin, Peter 1942- .... **CLC 39**
See also CA 136
Griffith, D(avid Lewelyn) W(ark)
1875(?)-1948 .... **TCLC 68**
See also CA 119; 150; CANR 80
Griffith, Lawrence
See Griffith, D(avid Lewelyn) W(ark)
Griffiths, Trevor 1935- .... **CLC 13, 52**
See also CA 97-100; CANR 45; DLB 13
Griggs, Sutton (Elbert)
1872-1930 .... **TCLC 77**
See also CA 123; 186; DLB 50
Grigson, Geoffrey (Edward Harvey)
1905-1985 .... **CLC 7, 39**
See also CA 25-28R; 118; CANR 20, 33;
DLB 27; MTCW 1, 2
Grillparzer, Franz 1791-1872 .... **NCLC 1;**
SSC 37
See also DLB 133
Grimble, Reverend Charles James
See Eliot, T(homas) S(tearns)
Grimke, Charlotte L(ottie) Forten
1837(?)-1914
See Forten, Charlotte L.
See also BW 1; CA 117; 124; DAM MULT,
POET
Grimm, Jacob Ludwig Karl
1785-1863 .... **NCLC 3, 77; SSC 36**
See also DLB 90; MAICYA; SATA 22
Grimm, Wilhelm Karl 1786-1859 .. **NCLC 3,**
77; SSC 36
See also DLB 90; MAICYA; SATA 22
Grimmelshausen, Johann Jakob Christoffel
von 1621-1676 .... **LC 6**
See also DLB 168
Grindel, Eugene 1895-1952
See Eluard, Paul
See also CA 104
Grisham, John 1955- .... **CLC 84; DAM POP**
See also AAYA 14; CA 138; CANR 47, 69;
DA3; MTCW 2
Grossman, David 1954- .... **CLC 67**
See also CA 138
Grossman, Vasily (Semenovich)
1905-1964 .... **CLC 41**
See also CA 124; 130; MTCW 1
Grove, Frederick Philip TCLC 4
See also Greve, Felix Paul (Berthold
Friedrich)
See also DLB 92
Grubb
See Crumb, R(obert)

Grumbach, Doris (Isaac) 1918- . **CLC 13, 22, 64**
See also CA 5-8R; CAAS 2; CANR 9, 42, 70; INT CANR-9; MTCW 2
Grundtvig, Nicolai Frederik Severin 1783-1872 .... **NCLC 1**
Grunge
See Crumb, R(obert)
Grunwald, Lisa 1959- .... **CLC 44**
See also CA 120
Guare, John 1938- .... **CLC 8, 14, 29, 67; DAM DRAM**
See also CA 73-76; CANR 21, 69; DLB 7; MTCW 1, 2
Gudjonsson, Halldor Kiljan 1902-1998
See Laxness, Halldor
See also CA 103; 164
Guenter, Erich
See Eich, Guenter
Guest, Barbara 1920- .... **CLC 34**
See also CA 25-28R; CANR 11, 44, 84; DLB 5, 193
Guest, Edgar A(lbert) 1881-1959 ... **TCLC 95**
See also CA 112; 168
Guest, Judith (Ann) 1936- .... **CLC 8, 30; DAM NOV, POP**
See also AAYA 7; CA 77-80; CANR 15, 75; DA3; INT CANR-15; MTCW 1, 2
Guevara, Che CLC 87; HLC 1
See also Guevara (Serna), Ernesto
Guevara (Serna), Ernesto 1928-1967   **CLC 87; DAM MULT; HLC 1**
See also Guevara, Che
See also CA 127; 111; CANR 56; HW 1
Guicciardini, Francesco 1483-1540 ..... **LC 49**
Guild, Nicholas M. 1944- .... **CLC 33**
See also CA 93-96
Guillemin, Jacques
See Sartre, Jean-Paul
Guillen, Jorge 1893-1984 .... **CLC 11; DAM MULT, POET; HLCS 1**
See also CA 89-92; 112; DLB 108; HW 1
Guillen, Nicolas (Cristobal) 1902-1989 ... **CLC 48, 79; BLC 2; DAM MST, MULT, POET; HLC 1; PC 23**
See also BW 2; CA 116; 125; 129; CANR 84; HW 1
Guillevic, (Eugene) 1907- .... **CLC 33**
See also CA 93-96
Guillois
See Desnos, Robert
Guillois, Valentin
See Desnos, Robert
Guimaraes Rosa, Joao 1908-1967
See also CA 175; HLCS 2
Guiney, Louise Imogen 1861-1920 .... **TCLC 41**
See also CA 160; DLB 54
Guiraldes, Ricardo (Guillermo) 1886-1927 .... **TCLC 39**
See also CA 131; HW 1; MTCW 1
Gumilev, Nikolai (Stepanovich) 1886-1921 .... **TCLC 60**
See also CA 165
Gunesekera, Romesh 1954- .... **CLC 91**
See also CA 159
Gunn, Bill CLC 5
See also Gunn, William Harrison
See also DLB 38
Gunn, Thom(son William) 1929- .. **CLC 3, 6, 18, 32, 81; DAM POET; PC 26**
See also CA 17-20R; CANR 9, 33; CDBLB 1960 to Present; DLB 27; INT CANR-33; MTCW 1
Gunn, William Harrison 1934(?)-1989
See Gunn, Bill
See also AITN 1; BW 1, 3; CA 13-16R; 128; CANR 12, 25, 76

Gunnars, Kristjana 1948- .... **CLC 69**
See also CA 113; DLB 60
Gurdjieff, G(eorgei) I(vanovich) 1877(?)-1949 .... **TCLC 71**
See also CA 157
Gurganus, Allan 1947- . **CLC 70; DAM POP**
See also BEST 90:1; CA 135
Gurney, A(lbert) R(amsdell), Jr. 1930- ..... **CLC 32, 50, 54; DAM DRAM**
See also CA 77-80; CANR 32, 64
Gurney, Ivor (Bertie) 1890-1937 ... **TCLC 33**
See also CA 167
Gurney, Peter
See Gurney, A(lbert) R(amsdell), Jr.
Guro, Elena 1877-1913 .... **TCLC 56**
Gustafson, James M(oody) 1925- ... **CLC 100**
See also CA 25-28R; CANR 37
Gustafson, Ralph (Barker) 1909- ..... **CLC 36**
See also CA 21-24R; CANR 8, 45, 84; DLB 88
Gut, Gom
See Simenon, Georges (Jacques Christian)
Guterson, David 1956- .... **CLC 91**
See also CA 132; CANR 73; MTCW 2
Guthrie, A(lfred) B(ertram), Jr. 1901-1991 .... **CLC 23**
See also CA 57-60; 134; CANR 24; DLB 212; SATA 62; SATA-Obit 67
Guthrie, Isobel
See Grieve, C(hristopher) M(urray)
Guthrie, Woodrow Wilson 1912-1967
See Guthrie, Woody
See also CA 113; 93-96
Guthrie, Woody CLC 35
See also Guthrie, Woodrow Wilson
Gutierrez Najera, Manuel 1859-1895
See also HLCS 2
Guy, Rosa (Cuthbert) 1928- .... **CLC 26**
See also AAYA 4; BW 2; CA 17-20R; CANR 14, 34, 83; CLR 13; DLB 33; JRDA; MAICYA; SATA 14, 62
Gwendolyn
See Bennett, (Enoch) Arnold
H. D. CLC 3, 8, 14, 31, 34, 73; PC 5
See also Doolittle, Hilda
H. de V.
See Buchan, John
Haavikko, Paavo Juhani 1931- .. **CLC 18, 34**
See also CA 106
Habbema, Koos
See Heijermans, Herman
Habermas, Juergen 1929- .... **CLC 104**
See also CA 109; CANR 85
Habermas, Jurgen
See Habermas, Juergen
Hacker, Marilyn 1942- ...... **CLC 5, 9, 23, 72, 91; DAM POET**
See also CA 77-80; CANR 68; DLB 120
Haeckel, Ernst Heinrich (Philipp August) 1834-1919 .... **TCLC 83**
See also CA 157
Hafiz c. 1326-1389 .... **CMLC 34**
Hafiz c. 1326-1389(?) .... **CMLC 34**
Haggard, H(enry) Rider 1856-1925 .... **TCLC 11**
See also CA 108; 148; DLB 70, 156, 174, 178; MTCW 2; SATA 16
Hagiosy, L.
See Larbaud, Valery (Nicolas)
Hagiwara Sakutaro 1886-1942 ..... **TCLC 60; PC 18**
Haig, Fenil
See Ford, Ford Madox
Haig-Brown, Roderick (Langmere) 1908-1976 .... **CLC 21**
See also CA 5-8R; 69-72; CANR 4, 38, 83; CLR 31; DLB 88; MAICYA; SATA 12

Hailey, Arthur 1920- ..... **CLC 5; DAM NOV, POP**
See also AITN 2; BEST 90:3; CA 1-4R; CANR 2, 36, 75; DLB 88; DLBY 82; MTCW 1, 2
Hailey, Elizabeth Forsythe 1938- ..... **CLC 40**
See also CA 93-96; CAAS 1; CANR 15, 48; INT CANR-15
Haines, John (Meade) 1924- .... **CLC 58**
See also CA 17-20R; CANR 13, 34; DLB 212
Hakluyt, Richard 1552-1616 .... **LC 31**
Haldeman, Joe (William) 1943- .... **CLC 61**
See also Graham, Robert
See also CA 53-56, 179; CAAE 179; CAAS 25; CANR 6, 70, 72; DLB 8; INT CANR-6
Hale, Sarah Josepha (Buell) 1788-1879 .... **NCLC 75**
See also DLB 1, 42, 73
Haley, Alex(ander Murray Palmer) 1921-1992 . **CLC 8, 12, 76; BLC 2; DA; DAB; DAC; DAM MST, MULT, POP**
See also AAYA 26; BW 2, 3; CA 77-80; 136; CANR 61; CDALBS; DA3; DLB 38; MTCW 1, 2
Haliburton, Thomas Chandler 1796-1865 .... **NCLC 15**
See also DLB 11, 99
Hall, Donald (Andrew, Jr.) 1928- ...... **CLC 1, 13, 37, 59; DAM POET**
See also CA 5-8R; CAAS 7; CANR 2, 44, 64; DLB 5; MTCW 1; SATA 23, 97
Hall, Frederic Sauser
See Sauser-Hall, Frederic
Hall, James
See Kuttner, Henry
Hall, James Norman 1887-1951 ..... **TCLC 23**
See also CA 123; 173; SATA 21
Hall, Radclyffe
See Hall, (Marguerite) Radclyffe
See also MTCW 2
Hall, (Marguerite) Radclyffe 1886-1943 .... **TCLC 12**
See also CA 110; 150; CANR 83; DLB 191
Hall, Rodney 1935- .... **CLC 51**
See also CA 109; CANR 69
Halleck, Fitz-Greene 1790-1867 .... **NCLC 47**
See also DLB 3
Halliday, Michael
See Creasey, John
Halpern, Daniel 1945- .... **CLC 14**
See also CA 33-36R
Hamburger, Michael (Peter Leopold) 1924- .... **CLC 5, 14**
See also CA 5-8R; CAAS 4; CANR 2, 47; DLB 27
Hamill, Pete 1935- .... **CLC 10**
See also CA 25-28R; CANR 18, 71
Hamilton, Alexander 1755(?)-1804 .... **NCLC 49**
See also DLB 37
Hamilton, Clive
See Lewis, C(live) S(taples)
Hamilton, Edmond 1904-1977 .... **CLC 1**
See also CA 1-4R; CANR 3, 84; DLB 8
Hamilton, Eugene (Jacob) Lee
See Lee-Hamilton, Eugene (Jacob)
Hamilton, Franklin
See Silverberg, Robert
Hamilton, Gail
See Corcoran, Barbara
Hamilton, Mollie
See Kaye, M(ary) M(argaret)
Hamilton, (Anthony Walter) Patrick 1904-1962 .... **CLC 51**
See also CA 176; 113; DLB 191

Hamilton, Virginia 1936- ...... **CLC 26; DAM MULT**
See also AAYA 2, 21; BW 2, 3; CA 25-28R; CANR 20, 37, 73; CLR 1, 11, 40; DLB 33, 52; INT CANR-20; JRDA; MAICYA; MTCW 1, 2; SATA 4, 56, 79

Hammett, (Samuel) Dashiell 1894-1961 .... **CLC 3, 5, 10, 19, 47; SSC 17**
See also AITN 1; CA 81-84; CANR 42; CDALB 1929-1941; DA3; DLB 226; DLBD 6; DLBY 96; MTCW 1, 2

Hammon, Jupiter 1711(?)-1800(?) . **NCLC 5; BLC 2; DAM MULT, POET; PC 16**
See also DLB 31, 50

Hammond, Keith
See Kuttner, Henry

Hamner, Earl (Henry), Jr. 1923- ...... **CLC 12**
See also AITN 2; CA 73-76; DLB 6

Hampton, Christopher (James) 1946- .... **CLC 4**
See also CA 25-28R; DLB 13; MTCW 1

Hamsun, Knut TCLC **2, 14, 49**
See also Pedersen, Knut

Handke, Peter 1942- ... **CLC 5, 8, 10, 15, 38; DAM DRAM, NOV**
See also CA 77-80; CANR 33, 75; DLB 85, 124; MTCW 1, 2

Handy, W(illiam) C(hristopher) 1873-1958 .... **TCLC 97**
See also BW 3; CA 121; 167

Hanley, James 1901-1985 ..... **CLC 3, 5, 8, 13**
See also CA 73-76; 117; CANR 36; DLB 191; MTCW 1

Hannah, Barry 1942- .... **CLC 23, 38, 90**
See also CA 108; 110; CANR 43, 68; DLB 6; INT 110; MTCW 1

Hannon, Ezra
See Hunter, Evan

Hansberry, Lorraine (Vivian) 1930-1965 ..... **CLC 17, 62; BLC 2; DA; DAB; DAC; DAM DRAM, MST, MULT; DC 2**
See also AAYA 25; BW 1, 3; CA 109; 25-28R; CABS 3; CANR 58; CDALB 1941-1968; DA3; DLB 7, 38; MTCW 1, 2

Hansen, Joseph 1923- .... **CLC 38**
See also CA 29-32R; CAAS 17; CANR 16, 44, 66; DLB 226; INT CANR-16

Hansen, Martin A(lfred) 1909-1955 .... **TCLC 32**
See also CA 167

Hanson, Kenneth O(stlin) 1922- .... **CLC 13**
See also CA 53-56; CANR 7

Hardwick, Elizabeth (Bruce) 1916- .... **CLC 13; DAM NOV**
See also CA 5-8R; CANR 3, 32, 70; DA3; DLB 6; MTCW 1, 2

Hardy, Thomas 1840-1928 .. **TCLC 4, 10, 18, 32, 48, 53, 72; DA; DAB; DAC; DAM MST, NOV, POET; PC 8; SSC 2; WLC**
See also CA 104; 123; CDBLB 1890-1914; DA3; DLB 18, 19, 135; MTCW 1, 2

Hare, David 1947- .... **CLC 29, 58**
See also CA 97-100; CANR 39, 91; DLB 13; MTCW 1

Harewood, John
See Van Druten, John (William)

Harford, Henry
See Hudson, W(illiam) H(enry)

Hargrave, Leonie
See Disch, Thomas M(ichael)

Harjo, Joy 1951- ...... **CLC 83; DAM MULT; PC 27**
See also CA 114; CANR 35, 67, 91; DLB 120, 175; MTCW 2; NNAL

Harlan, Louis R(udolph) 1922- .... **CLC 34**
See also CA 21-24R; CANR 25, 55, 80

Harling, Robert 1951(?)- .... **CLC 53**
See also CA 147

Harmon, William (Ruth) 1938- .... **CLC 38**
See also CA 33-36R; CANR 14, 32, 35; SATA 65

Harper, F. E. W.
See Harper, Frances Ellen Watkins

Harper, Frances E. W.
See Harper, Frances Ellen Watkins

Harper, Frances E. Watkins
See Harper, Frances Ellen Watkins

Harper, Frances Ellen
See Harper, Frances Ellen Watkins

Harper, Frances Ellen Watkins 1825-1911 ...... **TCLC 14; BLC 2; DAM MULT, POET; PC 21**
See also BW 1, 3; CA 111; 125; CANR 79; DLB 50, 221

Harper, Michael S(teven) 1938- ... **CLC 7, 22**
See also BW 1; CA 33-36R; CANR 24; DLB 41

Harper, Mrs. F. E. W.
See Harper, Frances Ellen Watkins

Harris, Christie (Lucy) Irwin 1907- .... **CLC 12**
See also CA 5-8R; CANR 6, 83; CLR 47; DLB 88; JRDA; MAICYA; SAAS 10; SATA 6, 74; SATA-Essay 116

Harris, Frank 1856-1931 .... **TCLC 24**
See also CA 109; 150; CANR 80; DLB 156, 197

Harris, George Washington 1814-1869 .... **NCLC 23**
See also DLB 3, 11

Harris, Joel Chandler 1848-1908 ... **TCLC 2; SSC 19**
See also CA 104; 137; CANR 80; CLR 49; DLB 11, 23, 42, 78, 91; MAICYA; SATA 100; YABC 1

Harris, John (Wyndham Parkes Lucas) Beynon 1903-1969
See Wyndham, John
See also CA 102; 89-92; CANR 84

Harris, MacDonald **CLC 9**
See also Heiney, Donald (William)

Harris, Mark 1922- .... **CLC 19**
See also CA 5-8R; CAAS 3; CANR 2, 55, 83; DLB 2; DLBY 80

Harris, (Theodore) Wilson 1921- ..... **CLC 25**
See also BW 2, 3; CA 65-68; CAAS 16; CANR 11, 27, 69; DLB 117; MTCW 1

Harrison, Elizabeth Cavanna 1909-
See Cavanna, Betty
See also CA 9-12R; CANR 6, 27, 85

Harrison, Harry (Max) 1925- .... **CLC 42**
See also CA 1-4R; CANR 5, 21, 84; DLB 8; SATA 4

Harrison, James (Thomas) 1937- ...... **CLC 6, 14, 33, 66; SSC 19**
See also CA 13-16R; CANR 8, 51, 79; DLBY 82; INT CANR-8

Harrison, Jim
See Harrison, James (Thomas)

Harrison, Kathryn 1961- .... **CLC 70**
See also CA 144; CANR 68

Harrison, Tony 1937- .... **CLC 43, 129**
See also CA 65-68; CANR 44; DLB 40; MTCW 1

Harriss, Will(ard Irvin) 1922- .... **CLC 34**
See also CA 111

Harson, Sley
See Ellison, Harlan (Jay)

Hart, Ellis
See Ellison, Harlan (Jay)

Hart, Josephine 1942(?)- .... **CLC 70; DAM POP**
See also CA 138; CANR 70

Hart, Moss 1904-1961 .... **CLC 66; DAM DRAM**
See also CA 109; 89-92; CANR 84; DLB 7

Harte, (Francis) Bret(t) 1836(?)-1902 ... **TCLC 1, 25; DA; DAC; DAM MST; SSC 8; WLC**
See also CA 104; 140; CANR 80; CDALB 1865-1917; DA3; DLB 12, 64, 74, 79, 186; SATA 26

Hartley, L(eslie) P(oles) 1895-1972 ... **CLC 2, 22**
See also CA 45-48; 37-40R; CANR 33; DLB 15, 139; MTCW 1, 2

Hartman, Geoffrey H. 1929- .... **CLC 27**
See also CA 117; 125; CANR 79; DLB 67

Hartmann, Sadakichi 1867-1944 ... **TCLC 73**
See also CA 157; DLB 54

Hartmann von Aue c. 1160-c. 1205 .... **CMLC 15**
See also DLB 138

Hartmann von Aue 1170-1210 ...... **CMLC 15**

Haruf, Kent 1943- .... **CLC 34**
See also CA 149; CANR 91

Harwood, Ronald 1934- .... **CLC 32; DAM DRAM, MST**
See also CA 1-4R; CANR 4, 55; DLB 13

Hasegawa Tatsunosuke
See Futabatei, Shimei

Hasek, Jaroslav (Matej Frantisek) 1883-1923 .... **TCLC 4**
See also CA 104; 129; MTCW 1, 2

Hass, Robert 1941- ... **CLC 18, 39, 99; PC 16**
See also CA 111; CANR 30, 50, 71; DLB 105, 206; SATA 94

Hastings, Hudson
See Kuttner, Henry

Hastings, Selina **CLC 44**

Hathorne, John 1641-1717 .... **LC 38**

Hatteras, Amelia
See Mencken, H(enry) L(ouis)

Hatteras, Owen **TCLC 18**
See also Mencken, H(enry) L(ouis); Nathan, George Jean

Hauptmann, Gerhart (Johann Robert) 1862-1946 .... **TCLC 4; DAM DRAM; SSC 37**
See also CA 104; 153; DLB 66, 118

Havel, Vaclav 1936- ... **CLC 25, 58, 65; DAM DRAM; DC 6**
See also CA 104; CANR 36, 63; DA3; MTCW 1, 2

Haviaras, Stratis **CLC 33**
See also Chaviaras, Strates

Hawes, Stephen 1475(?)-1523(?) .... **LC 17**
See also DLB 132

Hawkes, John (Clendennin Burne, Jr.) 1925-1998 .. **CLC 1, 2, 3, 4, 7, 9, 14, 15, 27, 49**
See also CA 1-4R; 167; CANR 2, 47, 64; DLB 2, 7, 227; DLBY 80, 98; MTCW 1, 2

Hawking, S. W.
See Hawking, Stephen W(illiam)

Hawking, Stephen W(illiam) 1942- . **CLC 63, 105**
See also AAYA 13; BEST 89:1; CA 126; 129; CANR 48; DA3; MTCW 2

Hawkins, Anthony Hope
See Hope, Anthony

Hawthorne, Julian 1846-1934 .... **TCLC 25**
See also CA 165

Hawthorne, Nathaniel 1804-1864 . **NCLC 39; DA; DAB; DAC; DAM MST, NOV; SSC 3, 29, 39; WLC**
See also AAYA 18; CDALB 1640-1865; DA3; DLB 1, 74, 223; YABC 2

Haxton, Josephine Ayres 1921-
See Douglas, Ellen
See also CA 115; CANR 41, 83

Hayaseca y Eizaguirre, Jorge
See Echegaray (y Eizaguirre), Jose (Maria Waldo)
Hayashi, Fumiko 1904-1951 .... **TCLC 27**
See also CA 161; DLB 180
Haycraft, Anna (Margaret) 1932-
See Ellis, Alice Thomas
See also CA 122; CANR 85, 90; MTCW 2
Hayden, Robert E(arl) 1913-1980 .. **CLC 5, 9, 14, 37; BLC 2; DA; DAC; DAM MST, MULT, POET; PC 6**
See also BW 1, 3; CA 69-72; 97-100; CABS 2; CANR 24, 75, 82; CDALB 1941-1968; DLB 5, 76; MTCW 1, 2; SATA 19; SATA-Obit 26
Hayford, J(oseph) E(phraim) Casely
See Casely-Hayford, J(oseph) E(phraim)
Hayman, Ronald 1932- .... **CLC 44**
See also CA 25-28R; CANR 18, 50, 88; DLB 155
Haywood, Eliza (Fowler)
1693(?)-1756 .... **LC 1, 44**
See also DLB 39
Hazlitt, William 1778-1830 ...... **NCLC 29, 82**
See also DLB 110, 158
Hazzard, Shirley 1931- .... **CLC 18**
See also CA 9-12R; CANR 4, 70; DLBY 82; MTCW 1
Head, Bessie 1937-1986 .... **CLC 25, 67; BLC 2; DAM MULT**
See also BW 2, 3; CA 29-32R; 119; CANR 25, 82; DA3; DLB 117, 225; MTCW 1, 2
Headon, (Nicky) Topper 1956(?)- ..... **CLC 30**
Heaney, Seamus (Justin) 1939- ..... **CLC 5, 7, 14, 25, 37, 74, 91; DAB; DAM POET; PC 18; WLCS**
See also CA 85-88; CANR 25, 48, 75, 91; CDBLB 1960 to Present; DA3; DLB 40; DLBY 95; MTCW 1, 2
Hearn, (Patricio) Lafcadio (Tessima Carlos)
1850-1904 .... **TCLC 9**
See also CA 105; 166; DLB 12, 78, 189
Hearne, Vicki 1946- .... **CLC 56**
See also CA 139
Hearon, Shelby 1931- .... **CLC 63**
See also AITN 2; CA 25-28R; CANR 18, 48
Heat-Moon, William Least CLC 29
See also Trogdon, William (Lewis)
See also AAYA 9
Hebbel, Friedrich 1813-1863 .... **NCLC 43; DAM DRAM**
See also DLB 129
Hebert, Anne 1916-2000 .... **CLC 4, 13, 29; DAC; DAM MST, POET**
See also CA 85-88; CANR 69; DA3; DLB 68; MTCW 1, 2
Hecht, Anthony (Evan) 1923- ...... **CLC 8, 13, 19; DAM POET**
See also CA 9-12R; CANR 6; DLB 5, 169
Hecht, Ben 1894-1964 .... **CLC 8**
See also CA 85-88; DLB 7, 9, 25, 26, 28, 86
Hedayat, Sadeq 1903-1951 .... **TCLC 21**
See also CA 120
Hegel, Georg Wilhelm Friedrich
1770-1831 .... **NCLC 46**
See also DLB 90
Heidegger, Martin 1889-1976 .... **CLC 24**
See also CA 81-84; 65-68; CANR 34; MTCW 1, 2
Heidenstam, (Carl Gustaf) Verner von
1859-1940 .... **TCLC 5**
See also CA 104
Heifner, Jack 1946- .... **CLC 11**
See also CA 105; CANR 47
Heijermans, Herman 1864-1924 .... **TCLC 24**
See also CA 123

Heilbrun, Carolyn G(old) 1926- .... **CLC 25**
See also CA 45-48; CANR 1, 28, 58
Heine, Heinrich 1797-1856 .... **NCLC 4, 54; PC 25**
See also DLB 90
Heinemann, Larry (Curtiss) 1944- .. **CLC 50**
See also CA 110; CAAS 21; CANR 31, 81; DLBD 9; INT CANR-31
Heiney, Donald (William) 1921-1993
See Harris, MacDonald
See also CA 1-4R; 142; CANR 3, 58
Heinlein, Robert A(nson) 1907-1988 . **CLC 1, 3, 8, 14, 26, 55; DAM POP**
See also AAYA 17; CA 1-4R; 125; CANR 1, 20, 53; DA3; DLB 8; JRDA; MAICYA; MTCW 1, 2; SATA 9, 69; SATA-Obit 56
Helforth, John
See Doolittle, Hilda
Hellenhofferu, Vojtech Kapristian z
See Hasek, Jaroslav (Matej Frantisek)
Heller, Joseph 1923- .. **CLC 1, 3, 5, 8, 11, 36, 63; DA; DAB; DAC; DAM MST, NOV, POP; WLC**
See also AAYA 24; AITN 1; CA 5-8R; CABS 1; CANR 8, 42, 66; DA3; DLB 2, 28, 227; DLBY 80; INT CANR-8; MTCW 1, 2
Hellman, Lillian (Florence)
1906-1984 .. **CLC 2, 4, 8, 14, 18, 34, 44, 52; DAM DRAM; DC 1**
See also AITN 1, 2; CA 13-16R; 112; CANR 33; DA3; DLB 7, 228; DLBY 84; MTCW 1, 2
Helprin, Mark 1947- .... **CLC 7, 10, 22, 32; DAM NOV, POP**
See also CA 81-84; CANR 47, 64; CDALBS; DA3; DLBY 85; MTCW 1, 2
Helvetius, Claude-Adrien 1715-1771 .. **LC 26**
Helyar, Jane Penelope Josephine 1933-
See Poole, Josephine
See also CA 21-24R; CANR 10, 26; SATA 82
Hemans, Felicia 1793-1835 .... **NCLC 71**
See also DLB 96
Hemingway, Ernest (Miller)
1899-1961 .... **CLC 1, 3, 6, 8, 10, 13, 19, 30, 34, 39, 41, 44, 50, 61, 80; DA; DAB; DAC; DAM MST, NOV; SSC 1, 25, 36, 40; WLC**
See also AAYA 19; CA 77-80; CANR 34; CDALB 1917-1929; DA3; DLB 4, 9, 102, 210; DLBD 1, 15, 16; DLBY 81, 87, 96, 98; MTCW 1, 2
Hempel, Amy 1951- .... **CLC 39**
See also CA 118; 137; CANR 70; DA3; MTCW 2
Henderson, F. C.
See Mencken, H(enry) L(ouis)
Henderson, Sylvia
See Ashton-Warner, Sylvia (Constance)
Henderson, Zenna (Chlarson)
1917-1983 .... **SSC 29**
See also CA 1-4R; 133; CANR 1, 84; DLB 8; SATA 5
Henkin, Joshua CLC 119
See also CA 161
Henley, Beth CLC 23; DC 6
See also Henley, Elizabeth Becker
See also CABS 3; DLBY 86
Henley, Elizabeth Becker 1952-
See Henley, Beth
See also CA 107; CANR 32, 73; DAM DRAM, MST; DA3; MTCW 1, 2
Henley, William Ernest 1849-1903 .. **TCLC 8**
See also CA 105; DLB 19
Hennissart, Martha
See Lathen, Emma
See also CA 85-88; CANR 64

Henry, O. TCLC 1, 19; SSC 5; WLC
See also Porter, William Sydney
Henry, Patrick 1736-1799 .... **LC 25**
Henryson, Robert 1430(?)-1506(?) .... **LC 20**
See also DLB 146
Henry VIII 1491-1547 .... **LC 10**
See also DLB 132
Henschke, Alfred
See Klabund
Hentoff, Nat(han Irving) 1925- .... **CLC 26**
See also AAYA 4; CA 1-4R; CAAS 6; CANR 5, 25, 77; CLR 1, 52; INT CANR-25; JRDA; MAICYA; SATA 42, 69; SATA-Brief 27
Heppenstall, (John) Rayner
1911-1981 .... **CLC 10**
See also CA 1-4R; 103; CANR 29
Heraclitus c. 540B.C.-c. 450B.C. ... **CMLC 22**
See also DLB 176
Herbert, Frank (Patrick)
1920-1986 .... **CLC 12, 23, 35, 44, 85; DAM POP**
See also AAYA 21; CA 53-56; 118; CANR 5, 43; CDALBS; DLB 8; INT CANR-5; MTCW 1, 2; SATA 9, 37; SATA-Obit 47
Herbert, George 1593-1633 ..... **LC 24; DAB; DAM POET; PC 4**
See also CDBLB Before 1660; DLB 126
Herbert, Zbigniew 1924-1998 ..... **CLC 9, 43; DAM POET**
See also CA 89-92; 169; CANR 36, 74; MTCW 1
Herbst, Josephine (Frey)
1897-1969 .... **CLC 34**
See also CA 5-8R; 25-28R; DLB 9
Heredia, Jose Maria 1803-1839
See also HLCS 2
Hergesheimer, Joseph 1880-1954 ... **TCLC 11**
See also CA 109; DLB 102, 9
Herlihy, James Leo 1927-1993 .... **CLC 6**
See also CA 1-4R; 143; CANR 2
Hermogenes fl. c. 175- .... **CMLC 6**
Hernandez, Jose 1834-1886 .... **NCLC 17**
Herodotus c. 484B.C.-429B.C. .... **CMLC 17**
See also DLB 176
Herrick, Robert 1591-1674 .... **LC 13; DA; DAB; DAC; DAM MST, POP; PC 9**
See also DLB 126
Herring, Guilles
See Somerville, Edith
Herriot, James 1916-1995 ..... **CLC 12; DAM POP**
See also Wight, James Alfred
See also AAYA 1; CA 148; CANR 40; MTCW 2; SATA 86
Herris, Violet
See Hunt, Violet
Herrmann, Dorothy 1941- .... **CLC 44**
See also CA 107
Herrmann, Taffy
See Herrmann, Dorothy
Hersey, John (Richard) 1914-1993 .... **CLC 1, 2, 7, 9, 40, 81, 97; DAM POP**
See also AAYA 29; CA 17-20R; 140; CANR 33; CDALBS; DLB 6, 185; MTCW 1, 2; SATA 25; SATA-Obit 76
Herzen, Aleksandr Ivanovich
1812-1870 .... **NCLC 10, 61**
Herzl, Theodor 1860-1904 .... **TCLC 36**
See also CA 168
Herzog, Werner 1942- .... **CLC 16**
See also CA 89-92
Hesiod c. 8th cent. B.C.- .... **CMLC 5**
See also DLB 176

Hesse, Hermann 1877-1962 ... **CLC 1, 2, 3, 6, 11, 17, 25, 69; DA; DAB; DAC; DAM MST, NOV; SSC 9; WLC**
See also CA 17-18; CAP 2; DA3; DLB 66; MTCW 1, 2; SATA 50

Hewes, Cady
See De Voto, Bernard (Augustine)

Heyen, William 1940- .... **CLC 13, 18**
See also CA 33-36R; CAAS 9; DLB 5

Heyerdahl, Thor 1914- .... **CLC 26**
See also CA 5-8R; CANR 5, 22, 66, 73; MTCW 1, 2; SATA 2, 52

Heym, Georg (Theodor Franz Arthur)
1887-1912 .... **TCLC 9**
See also CA 106; 181

Heym, Stefan 1913- .... **CLC 41**
See also CA 9-12R; CANR 4; DLB 69

Heyse, Paul (Johann Ludwig von)
1830-1914 .... **TCLC 8**
See also CA 104; DLB 129

Heyward, (Edwin) DuBose
1885-1940 .... **TCLC 59**
See also CA 108; 157; DLB 7, 9, 45; SATA 21

Hibbert, Eleanor Alice Burford
1906-1993 .... **CLC 7; DAM POP**
See also BEST 90:4; CA 17-20R; 140; CANR 9, 28, 59; MTCW 2; SATA 2; SATA-Obit 74

Hichens, Robert (Smythe)
1864-1950 .... **TCLC 64**
See also CA 162; DLB 153

Higgins, George V(incent)
1939-1999 .... **CLC 4, 7, 10, 18**
See also CA 77-80; 186; CAAS 5; CANR 17, 51, 89; DLB 2; DLBY 81, 98; INT CANR-17; MTCW 1

Higginson, Thomas Wentworth
1823-1911 .... **TCLC 36**
See also CA 162; DLB 1, 64

Highet, Helen
See MacInnes, Helen (Clark)

Highsmith, (Mary) Patricia
1921-1995 .... **CLC 2, 4, 14, 42, 102; DAM NOV, POP**
See also CA 1-4R; 147; CANR 1, 20, 48, 62; DA3; MTCW 1, 2

Highwater, Jamake (Mamake)
1942(?)- .... **CLC 12**
See also AAYA 7; CA 65-68; CAAS 7; CANR 10, 34, 84; CLR 17; DLB 52; DLBY 85; JRDA; MAICYA; SATA 32, 69; SATA-Brief 30

Highway, Tomson 1951- .... **CLC 92; DAC; DAM MULT**
See also CA 151; CANR 75; MTCW 2; NNAL

Higuchi, Ichiyo 1872-1896 .... **NCLC 49**

Hijuelos, Oscar 1951- .... **CLC 65; DAM MULT, POP; HLC 1**
See also AAYA 25; BEST 90:1; CA 123; CANR 50, 75; DA3; DLB 145; HW 1, 2; MTCW 2

Hikmet, Nazim 1902(?)-1963 .... **CLC 40**
See also CA 141; 93-96

Hildegard von Bingen 1098-1179 . **CMLC 20**
See also DLB 148

Hildesheimer, Wolfgang 1916-1991 .. **CLC 49**
See also CA 101; 135; DLB 69, 124

Hill, Geoffrey (William) 1932- ...... **CLC 5, 8, 18, 45; DAM POET**
See also CA 81-84; CANR 21, 89; CDBLB 1960 to Present; DLB 40; MTCW 1

Hill, George Roy 1921- .... **CLC 26**
See also CA 110; 122

Hill, John
See Koontz, Dean R(ay)

Hill, Susan (Elizabeth) 1942- .... **CLC 4, 113; DAB; DAM MST, NOV**
See also CA 33-36R; CANR 29, 69; DLB 14, 139; MTCW 1

Hillerman, Tony 1925- . **CLC 62; DAM POP**
See also AAYA 6; BEST 89:1; CA 29-32R; CANR 21, 42, 65; DA3; DLB 206; SATA 6

Hillesum, Etty 1914-1943 .... **TCLC 49**
See also CA 137

Hilliard, Noel (Harvey) 1929- .... **CLC 15**
See also CA 9-12R; CANR 7, 69

Hillis, Rick 1956- .... **CLC 66**
See also CA 134

Hilton, James 1900-1954 .... **TCLC 21**
See also CA 108; 169; DLB 34, 77; SATA 34

Himes, Chester (Bomar) 1909-1984 .. **CLC 2, 4, 7, 18, 58, 108; BLC 2; DAM MULT**
See also BW 2; CA 25-28R; 114; CANR 22, 89; DLB 2, 76, 143, 226; MTCW 1, 2

Hinde, Thomas .... **CLC 6, 11**
See also Chitty, Thomas Willes

Hine, (William) Daryl 1936- .... **CLC 15**
See also CA 1-4R; CAAS 15; CANR 1, 20; DLB 60

Hinkson, Katharine Tynan
See Tynan, Katharine

Hinojosa(-Smith), Rolando (R.) 1929-
See Hinojosa-Smith, Rolando
See also CA 131; CAAS 16; CANR 62; DAM MULT; DLB 82; HLC 1; HW 1, 2; MTCW 2

Hinojosa-Smith, Rolando 1929-
See Hinojosa(-Smith), Rolando (R.)
See also CAAS 16; HLC 1; MTCW 2

Hinton, S(usan) E(loise) 1950- .... **CLC 30, 111; DA; DAB; DAC; DAM MST, NOV**
See also AAYA 2, 33; CA 81-84; CANR 32, 62; CDALBS; CLR 3, 23; DA3; JRDA; MAICYA; MTCW 1, 2; SATA 19, 58, 115

Hippius, Zinaida .... **TCLC 9**
See also Gippius, Zinaida (Nikolayevna)

Hiraoka, Kimitake 1925-1970
See Mishima, Yukio
See also CA 97-100; 29-32R; DAM DRAM; DA3; MTCW 1, 2

Hirsch, E(ric) D(onald), Jr. 1928- .... **CLC 79**
See also CA 25-28R; CANR 27, 51; DLB 67; INT CANR-27; MTCW 1

Hirsch, Edward 1950- .... **CLC 31, 50**
See also CA 104; CANR 20, 42; DLB 120

Hitchcock, Alfred (Joseph)
1899-1980 .... **CLC 16**
See also AAYA 22; CA 159; 97-100; SATA 27; SATA-Obit 24

Hitler, Adolf 1889-1945 .... **TCLC 53**
See also CA 117; 147

Hoagland, Edward 1932- .... **CLC 28**
See also CA 1-4R; CANR 2, 31, 57; DLB 6; SATA 51

Hoban, Russell (Conwell) 1925- . **CLC 7, 25; DAM NOV**
See also CA 5-8R; CANR 23, 37, 66; CLR 3; DLB 52; MAICYA; MTCW 1, 2; SATA 1, 40, 78

Hobbes, Thomas 1588-1679 .... **LC 36**
See also DLB 151

Hobbs, Perry
See Blackmur, R(ichard) P(almer)

Hobson, Laura Z(ametkin)
1900-1986 .... **CLC 7, 25**
See also CA 17-20R; 118; CANR 55; DLB 28; SATA 52

Hochhuth, Rolf 1931- .. **CLC 4, 11, 18; DAM DRAM**
See also CA 5-8R; CANR 33, 75; DLB 124; MTCW 1, 2

Hochman, Sandra 1936- .... **CLC 3, 8**
See also CA 5-8R; DLB 5

Hochwaelder, Fritz 1911-1986 .... **CLC 36; DAM DRAM**
See also CA 29-32R; 120; CANR 42; MTCW 1

Hochwalder, Fritz
See Hochwaelder, Fritz

Hocking, Mary (Eunice) 1921- .... **CLC 13**
See also CA 101; CANR 18, 40

Hodgins, Jack 1938- .... **CLC 23**
See also CA 93-96; DLB 60

Hodgson, William Hope
1877(?)-1918 .... **TCLC 13**
See also CA 111; 164; DLB 70, 153, 156, 178; MTCW 2

Hoeg, Peter 1957- .... **CLC 95**
See also CA 151; CANR 75; DA3; MTCW 2

Hoffman, Alice 1952- ... **CLC 51; DAM NOV**
See also CA 77-80; CANR 34, 66; MTCW 1, 2

Hoffman, Daniel (Gerard) 1923- . **CLC 6, 13, 23**
See also CA 1-4R; CANR 4; DLB 5

Hoffman, Stanley 1944- .... **CLC 5**
See also CA 77-80

Hoffman, William M(oses) 1939- ..... **CLC 40**
See also CA 57-60; CANR 11, 71

Hoffmann, E(rnst) T(heodor) A(madeus)
1776-1822 .... **NCLC 2; SSC 13**
See also DLB 90; SATA 27

Hofmann, Gert 1931- .... **CLC 54**
See also CA 128

Hofmannsthal, Hugo von
1874-1929 ...... **TCLC 11; DAM DRAM; DC 4**
See also CA 106; 153; DLB 81, 118

Hogan, Linda 1947- .. **CLC 73; DAM MULT**
See also CA 120; CANR 45, 73; DLB 175; NNAL

Hogarth, Charles
See Creasey, John

Hogarth, Emmett
See Polonsky, Abraham (Lincoln)

Hogg, James 1770-1835 .... **NCLC 4**
See also DLB 93, 116, 159

Holbach, Paul Henri Thiry Baron
1723-1789 .... **LC 14**

Holberg, Ludvig 1684-1754 .... **LC 6**

Holcroft, Thomas 1745-1809 .... **NCLC 85**
See also DLB 39, 89, 158

Holden, Ursula 1921- .... **CLC 18**
See also CA 101; CAAS 8; CANR 22

Holderlin, (Johann Christian) Friedrich
1770-1843 .... **NCLC 16; PC 4**

Holdstock, Robert
See Holdstock, Robert P.

Holdstock, Robert P. 1948- .... **CLC 39**
See also CA 131; CANR 81

Holland, Isabelle 1920- .... **CLC 21**
See also AAYA 11; CA 21-24R, 181; CAAE 181; CANR 10, 25, 47; CLR 57; JRDA; MAICYA; SATA 8, 70; SATA-Essay 103

Holland, Marcus
See Caldwell, (Janet Miriam) Taylor (Holland)

Hollander, John 1929- .... **CLC 2, 5, 8, 14**
See also CA 1-4R; CANR 1, 52; DLB 5; SATA 13

Hollander, Paul
See Silverberg, Robert

Holleran, Andrew 1943(?)- .... **CLC 38**
See also Garber, Eric
See also CA 144
Hollinghurst, Alan 1954- .... **CLC 55, 91**
See also CA 114; DLB 207
Hollis, Jim
See Summers, Hollis (Spurgeon, Jr.)
Holly, Buddy 1936-1959 .... **TCLC 65**
Holmes, Gordon
See Shiel, M(atthew) P(hipps)
Holmes, John
See Souster, (Holmes) Raymond
Holmes, John Clellon 1926-1988 ...... **CLC 56**
See also CA 9-12R; 125; CANR 4; DLB 16
Holmes, Oliver Wendell, Jr.
1841-1935 .... **TCLC 77**
See also CA 114; 186
Holmes, Oliver Wendell
1809-1894 .... **NCLC 14, 81**
See also CDALB 1640-1865; DLB 1, 189;
SATA 34
Holmes, Raymond
See Souster, (Holmes) Raymond
Holt, Victoria
See Hibbert, Eleanor Alice Burford
Holub, Miroslav 1923-1998 .... **CLC 4**
See also CA 21-24R; 169; CANR 10
Homer c. 8th cent. B.C.- .. **CMLC 1, 16; DA;
DAB; DAC; DAM MST, POET; PC
23; WLCS**
See also DA3; DLB 176
Hongo, Garrett Kaoru 1951- .... **PC 23**
See also CA 133; CAAS 22; DLB 120
Honig, Edwin 1919 .... **CLC 33**
See also CA 5-8R; CAAS 8; CANR 4, 45;
DLB 5
Hood, Hugh (John Blagdon) 1928- . **CLC 15,
28**
See also CA 49-52; CAAS 17; CANR 1,
33, 87; DLB 53
Hood, Thomas 1799-1845 .... **NCLC 16**
See also DLB 96
Hooker, (Peter) Jeremy 1941- .... **CLC 43**
See also CA 77-80; CANR 22; DLB 40
hooks, bell CLC 94; BLCS
See also Watkins, Gloria Jean
See also MTCW 2
Hope, A(lec) D(erwent) 1907- .... **CLC 3, 51**
See also CA 21-24R; CANR 33, 74; MTCW
1, 2
Hope, Anthony 1863-1933 .... **TCLC 83**
See also CA 157, DLB 153, 156
Hope, Brian
See Creasey, John
Hope, Christopher (David Tully)
1944- .... **CLC 52**
See also CA 106; CANR 47; DLB 225;
SATA 62
Hopkins, Gerard Manley
1844-1889 .... **NCLC 17; DA; DAB;
DAC; DAM MST, POET; PC 15; WLC**
See also CDBLB 1890-1914; DA3; DLB
35, 57
Hopkins, John (Richard) 1931-1998 .. **CLC 4**
See also CA 85-88; 169
Hopkins, Pauline Elizabeth
1859-1930 ...... **TCLC 28; BLC 2; DAM
MULT**
See also BW 2, 3; CA 141; CANR 82; DLB
50
Hopkinson, Francis 1737-1791 .... **LC 25**
See also DLB 31
Hopley-Woolrich, Cornell George 1903-1968
See Woolrich, Cornell
See also CA 13-14; CANR 58; CAP 1; DLB
226; MTCW 2
Horace 65B.C.-8B.C. .... **CMLC 39**
See also DLB 211

Horatio
See Proust, (Valentin-Louis-George-
Eugene-) Marcel
**Horgan, Paul (George Vincent
O'Shaughnessy)** 1903-1995 . **CLC 9, 53;
DAM NOV**
See also CA 13-16R; 147; CANR 9, 35;
DLB 212; DLBY 85; INT CANR-9;
MTCW 1, 2; SATA 13; SATA-Obit 84
Horn, Peter
See Kuttner, Henry
Hornem, Horace Esq.
See Byron, George Gordon (Noel)
**Horney, Karen (Clementine Theodore
Danielsen)** 1885-1952 .... **TCLC 71**
See also CA 114; 165
Hornung, E(rnest) W(illiam)
1866-1921 .... **TCLC 59**
See also CA 108; 160; DLB 70
Horovitz, Israel (Arthur) 1939- ...... **CLC 56;
DAM DRAM**
See also CA 33-36R; CANR 46, 59; DLB 7
Horton, George Moses
1797(?)-1883(?) .... **NCLC 87**
See also DLB 50
Horvath, Odon von
See Horvath, Oedoen von
See also DLB 85, 124
Horvath, Oedoen von 1901-1938 .., **TCLC 45**
See also Horvath, Odon von; von Horvath,
Oedoen
See also CA 118
Horwitz, Julius 1920-1986 .... **CLC 14**
See also CA 9-12R; 119; CANR 12
Hospital, Janette Turner 1942- .... **CLC 42**
See also CA 108; CANR 48
Hostos, E. M. de
See Hostos (y Bonilla), Eugenio Maria de
Hostos, Eugenio M. de
See Hostos (y Bonilla), Eugenio Maria de
Hostos, Eugenio Maria
See Hostos (y Bonilla), Eugenio Maria de
Hostos (y Bonilla), Eugenio Maria de
1839-1903 .... **TCLC 24**
See also CA 123; 131; HW 1
Houdini
See Lovecraft, H(oward) P(hillips)
Hougan, Carolyn 1943- .... **CLC 34**
See also CA 139
Household, Geoffrey (Edward West)
1900-1988 .... **CLC 11**
See also CA 77-80; 126; CANR 58; DLB
87; SATA 14; SATA-Obit 59
Housman, A(lfred) E(dward)
1859-1936 .... **TCLC 1, 10; DA; DAB;
DAC; DAM MST, POET; PC 2;
WLCS**
See also CA 104; 125; DA3; DLB 19;
MTCW 1, 2
Housman, Laurence 1865-1959 .... **TCLC 7**
See also CA 106; 155; DLB 10; SATA 25
Howard, Elizabeth Jane 1923- ..... **CLC 7, 29**
See also CA 5-8R; CANR 8, 62
Howard, Maureen 1930- .... **CLC 5, 14, 46**
See also CA 53-56; CANR 31, 75; DLBY
83; INT CANR-31; MTCW 1, 2
Howard, Richard 1929- .... **CLC 7, 10, 47**
See also AITN 1; CA 85-88; CANR 25, 80;
DLB 5; INT CANR-25
Howard, Robert E(rvin)
1906-1936 .... **TCLC 8**
See also CA 105; 157
Howard, Warren F.
See Pohl, Frederik
Howe, Fanny (Quincy) 1940- .... **CLC 47**
See also CA 117; CAAS 27; CANR 70;
SATA-Brief 52

Howe, Irving 1920-1993 .... **CLC 85**
See also CA 9-12R; 141; CANR 21, 50;
DLB 67; MTCW 1, 2
Howe, Julia Ward 1819-1910 .... **TCLC 21**
See also CA 117; DLB 1, 189
Howe, Susan 1937- .... **CLC 72**
See also CA 160; DLB 120
Howe, Tina 1937- .... **CLC 48**
See also CA 109
Howell, James 1594(?)-1666 .... **LC 13**
See also DLB 151
Howells, W. D.
See Howells, William Dean
Howells, William D.
See Howells, William Dean
Howells, William Dean 1837-1920 .. **TCLC 7,
17, 41; SSC 36**
See also CA 104; 134; CDALB 1865-1917;
DLB 12, 64, 74, 79, 189; MTCW 2
Howes, Barbara 1914-1996 .... **CLC 15**
See also CA 9-12R; 151; CAAS 3; CANR
53; SATA 5
Hrabal, Bohumil 1914-1997 .... **CLC 13, 67**
See also CA 106; 156; CAAS 12; CANR
57
Hroswitha of Gandersheim c. 935-c.
1002 .... **CMLC 29**
See also DLB 148
Hsun, Lu
See Lu Hsun
Hubbard, L(afayette) Ron(ald)
1911-1986 .... **CLC 43; DAM POP**
See also CA 77-80; 118; CANR 52; DA3;
MTCW 2
Huch, Ricarda (Octavia)
1864-1947 .... **TCLC 13**
See also CA 111; DLB 66
Huddle, David 1942- .... **CLC 49**
See also CA 57-60; CAAS 20; CANR 89;
DLB 130
Hudson, Jeffrey
See Crichton, (John) Michael
Hudson, W(illiam) H(enry)
1841-1922 .... **TCLC 29**
See also CA 115; DLB 98, 153, 174; SATA
35
Hueffer, Ford Madox
See Ford, Ford Madox
Hughart, Barry 1934- .... **CLC 39**
See also CA 137
Hughes, Colin
See Creasey, John
Hughes, David (John) 1930- .... **CLC 48**
See also CA 116; 129; DLB 14
Hughes, Edward James
See Hughes, Ted
See also DAM MST, POET; DA3
Hughes, (James) Langston
1902-1967 .... **CLC 1, 5, 10, 15, 35, 44,
108; BLC 2; DA; DAB; DAC; DAM
DRAM, MST, MULT, POET; DC 3;
PC 1; SSC 6; WLC**
See also AAYA 12; BW 1, 3; CA 1-4R; 25-
28R; CANR 1, 34, 82; CDALB 1929-
1941; CLR 17; DA3; DLB 4, 7, 48, 51,
86, 228; JRDA; MAICYA; MTCW 1, 2;
SATA 4, 33
Hughes, Richard (Arthur Warren)
1900-1976 .... **CLC 1, 11; DAM NOV**
See also CA 5-8R; 65-68; CANR 4; DLB
15, 161; MTCW 1; SATA 8; SATA-Obit
25
Hughes, Ted 1930-1998 . **CLC 2, 4, 9, 14, 37,
119; DAB; DAC; PC 7**
See also Hughes, Edward James
See also CA 1-4R; 171; CANR 1, 33, 66;
CLR 3; DLB 40, 161; MAICYA; MTCW
1, 2; SATA 49; SATA-Brief 27; SATA-
Obit 107

Hugo, Richard F(ranklin)
    1923-1982 .... **CLC 6, 18, 32; DAM POET**
    See also CA 49-52; 108; CANR 3; DLB 5, 206
Hugo, Victor (Marie) 1802-1885 .... **NCLC 3, 10, 21; DA; DAB; DAC; DAM DRAM, MST, NOV, POET; PC 17; WLC**
    See also AAYA 28; DA3; DLB 119, 192; SATA 47
Huidobro, Vicente
    See Huidobro Fernandez, Vicente Garcia
Huidobro Fernandez, Vicente Garcia
    1893-1948 .... **TCLC 31**
    See also CA 131; HW 1
Hulme, Keri 1947- .... **CLC 39, 130**
    See also CA 125; CANR 69; INT 125
Hulme, T(homas) E(rnest)
    1883-1917 .... **TCLC 21**
    See also CA 117; DLB 19
Hume, David 1711-1776 .... **LC 7, 56**
    See also DLB 104
Humphrey, William 1924-1997 .... **CLC 45**
    See also CA 77-80; 160; CANR 68; DLB 212
Humphreys, Emyr Owen 1919- .... **CLC 47**
    See also CA 5-8R; CANR 3, 24; DLB 15
Humphreys, Josephine 1945- ..... **CLC 34, 57**
    See also CA 121; 127; INT 127
Huneker, James Gibbons
    1857-1921 .... **TCLC 65**
    See also DLB 71
Hungerford, Pixie
    See Brinsmead, H(esba) F(ay)
Hunt, E(verette) Howard, (Jr.)
    1918- .... **CLC 3**
    See also AITN 1; CA 45-48; CANR 2, 47
Hunt, Francesca
    See Holland, Isabelle
Hunt, Kyle
    See Creasey, John
Hunt, (James Henry) Leigh
    1784-1859 .... **NCLC 1, 70; DAM POET**
    See also DLB 96, 110, 144
Hunt, Marsha 1946- .... **CLC 70**
    See also BW 2, 3; CA 143; CANR 79
Hunt, Violet 1866(?)-1942 .... **TCLC 53**
    See also CA 184; DLB 162, 197
Hunter, E. Waldo
    See Sturgeon, Theodore (Hamilton)
Hunter, Evan 1926- .... **CLC 11, 31; DAM POP**
    See also CA 5-8R; CANR 5, 38, 62; DLBY 82; INT CANR-5; MTCW 1; SATA 25
Hunter, Kristin (Eggleston) 1931- .... **CLC 35**
    See also AITN 1; BW 1; CA 13-16R; CANR 13; CLR 3; DLB 33; INT CANR-13; MAICYA; SAAS 10; SATA 12
Hunter, Mary
    See Austin, Mary (Hunter)
Hunter, Mollie 1922- .... **CLC 21**
    See also McIlwraith, Maureen Mollie Hunter
    See also AAYA 13; CANR 37, 78; CLR 25; DLB 161; JRDA; MAICYA; SAAS 7; SATA 54, 106
Hunter, Robert (?)-1734 .... **LC 7**
Hurston, Zora Neale 1903-1960 .. **CLC 7, 30, 61; BLC 2; DA; DAC; DAM MST, MULT, NOV; DC 12; SSC 4; WLCS**
    See also AAYA 15; BW 1, 3; CA 85-88; CANR 61; CDALBS; DA3; DLB 51, 86; MTCW 1, 2
Huston, John (Marcellus)
    1906-1987 .... **CLC 20**
    See also CA 73-76; 123; CANR 34; DLB 26
Hustvedt, Siri 1955- .... **CLC 76**
    See also CA 137

Hutten, Ulrich von 1488-1523 .... **LC 16**
    See also DLB 179
Huxley, Aldous (Leonard)
    1894-1963 .... **CLC 1, 3, 4, 5, 8, 11, 18, 35, 79; DA; DAB; DAC; DAM MST, NOV; SSC 39; WLC**
    See also AAYA 11; CA 85-88; CANR 44; CDBLB 1914-1945; DA3; DLB 36, 100, 162, 195; MTCW 1, 2; SATA 63
Huxley, T(homas) H(enry)
    1825-1895 .... **NCLC 67**
    See also DLB 57
Huysmans, Joris-Karl 1848-1907 ... **TCLC 7, 69**
    See also CA 104; 165; DLB 123
Hwang, David Henry 1957- .. **CLC 55; DAM DRAM; DC 4**
    See also CA 127; 132; CANR 76; DA3; DLB 212; INT 132; MTCW 2
Hyde, Anthony 1946- .... **CLC 42**
    See also CA 136
Hyde, Margaret O(ldroyd) 1917- ..... **CLC 21**
    See also CA 1-4R; CANR 1, 36; CLR 23; JRDA; MAICYA; SAAS 8; SATA 1, 42, 76
Hynes, James 1956(?)- .... **CLC 65**
    See also CA 164
Hypatia c. 370-415 .... **CMLC 35**
Ian, Janis 1951- .... **CLC 21**
    See also CA 105
Ibanez, Vicente Blasco
    See Blasco Ibanez, Vicente
Ibarbourou, Juana de 1895-1979
    See also HLCS 2; HW 1
Ibarguengoitia, Jorge 1928-1983 ...... **CLC 37**
    See also CA 124; 113; HW 1
Ibsen, Henrik (Johan) 1828-1906 ... **TCLC 2, 8, 16, 37, 52; DA; DAB; DAC; DAM DRAM, MST; DC 2; WLC**
    See also CA 104; 141; DA3
Ibuse, Masuji 1898-1993 .... **CLC 22**
    See also CA 127; 141; DLB 180
Ichikawa, Kon 1915- .... **CLC 20**
    See also CA 121
Idle, Eric 1943- .... **CLC 21**
    See also Monty Python
    See also CA 116; CANR 35, 91
Ignatow, David 1914-1997 .. **CLC 4, 7, 14, 40**
    See also CA 9-12R; 162; CAAS 3; CANR 31, 57; DLB 5
Ignotus
    See Strachey, (Giles) Lytton
Ihimaera, Witi 1944- .... **CLC 46**
    See also CA 77-80
Ilf, Ilya TCLC 21
    See also Fainzilberg, Ilya Arnoldovich
Illyes, Gyula 1902-1983 .... **PC 16**
    See also CA 114; 109
Immermann, Karl (Lebrecht)
    1796-1840 .... **NCLC 4, 49**
    See also DLB 133
Ince, Thomas H. 1882-1924 .... **TCLC 89**
Inchbald, Elizabeth 1753-1821 ...... **NCLC 62**
    See also DLB 39, 89
Inclan, Ramon (Maria) del Valle
    See Valle-Inclan, Ramon (Maria) del
Infante, G(uillermo) Cabrera
    See Cabrera Infante, G(uillermo)
Ingalls, Rachel (Holmes) 1940- .... **CLC 42**
    See also CA 123; 127
Ingamells, Reginald Charles
    See Ingamells, Rex
Ingamells, Rex 1913-1955 .... **TCLC 35**
    See also CA 167
Inge, William (Motter) 1913-1973 ..... **CLC 1, 8, 19; DAM DRAM**
    See also CA 9-12R; CDALB 1941-1968; DA3; DLB 7; MTCW 1, 2

Ingelow, Jean 1820-1897 .... **NCLC 39**
    See also DLB 35, 163; SATA 33
Ingram, Willis J.
    See Harris, Mark
Innaurato, Albert (F.) 1948(?)- ... **CLC 21, 60**
    See also CA 115; 122; CANR 78; INT 122
Innes, Michael
    See Stewart, J(ohn) I(nnes) M(ackintosh)
Innis, Harold Adams 1894-1952 .... **TCLC 77**
    See also CA 181; DLB 88
Ionesco, Eugene 1909-1994 ... **CLC 1, 4, 6, 9, 11, 15, 41, 86; DA; DAB; DAC; DAM DRAM, MST; DC 12; WLC**
    See also CA 9-12R; 144; CANR 55; DA3; MTCW 1, 2; SATA 7; SATA-Obit 79
Iqbal, Muhammad 1873-1938 .... **TCLC 28**
Ireland, Patrick
    See O'Doherty, Brian
Iron, Ralph
    See Schreiner, Olive (Emilie Albertina)
Irving, John (Winslow) 1942- ... **CLC 13, 23, 38, 112; DAM NOV, POP**
    See also AAYA 8; BEST 89:3; CA 25-28R; CANR 28, 73; DA3; DLB 6; DLBY 82; MTCW 1, 2
Irving, Washington 1783-1859 . **NCLC 2, 19; DA; DAB; DAC; DAM MST; SSC 2, 37; WLC**
    See also CDALB 1640-1865; DA3; DLB 3, 11, 30, 59, 73, 74, 186; YABC 2
Irwin, P. K.
    See Page, P(atricia) K(athleen)
Isaacs, Jorge Ricardo 1837-1895 ... **NCLC 70**
Isaacs, Susan 1943- .... **CLC 32; DAM POP**
    See also BEST 89:1; CA 89-92; CANR 20, 41, 65; DA3; INT CANR-20; MTCW 1, 2
Isherwood, Christopher (William Bradshaw)
    1904-1986 .. **CLC 1, 9, 11, 14, 44; DAM DRAM, NOV**
    See also CA 13-16R; 117; CANR 35; DA3; DLB 15, 195; DLBY 86; MTCW 1, 2
Ishiguro, Kazuo 1954- . **CLC 27, 56, 59, 110; DAM NOV**
    See also BEST 90:2; CA 120; CANR 49; DA3; DLB 194; MTCW 1, 2
Ishikawa, Hakuhin
    See Ishikawa, Takuboku
Ishikawa, Takuboku
    1886(?)-1912 ... **TCLC 15; DAM POET; PC 10**
    See also CA 113; 153
Iskander, Fazil 1929- .... **CLC 47**
    See also CA 102
Isler, Alan (David) 1934- .... **CLC 91**
    See also CA 156
Ivan IV 1530-1584 .... **LC 17**
Ivanov, Vyacheslav Ivanovich
    1866-1949 .... **TCLC 33**
    See also CA 122
Ivask, Ivar Vidrik 1927-1992 .... **CLC 14**
    See also CA 37-40R; 139; CANR 24
Ives, Morgan
    See Bradley, Marion Zimmer
Izumi Shikibu c. 973-c. 1034 .... **CMLC 33**
J. R. S.
    See Gogarty, Oliver St. John
Jabran, Kahlil
    See Gibran, Kahlil
Jabran, Khalil
    See Gibran, Kahlil
Jackson, Daniel
    See Wingrove, David (John)
Jackson, Jesse 1908-1983 .... **CLC 12**
    See also BW 1; CA 25-28R; 109; CANR 27; CLR 28; MAICYA; SATA 2, 29; SATA-Obit 48

Jackson, Laura (Riding) 1901-1991
See Riding, Laura
See also CA 65-68; 135; CANR 28, 89; DLB 48

Jackson, Sam
See Trumbo, Dalton

Jackson, Sara
See Wingrove, David (John)

Jackson, Shirley 1919-1965 . CLC 11, 60, 87; DA; DAC; DAM MST; SSC 9, 39; WLC
See also AAYA 9; CA 1-4R; 25-28R; CANR 4, 52; CDALB 1941-1968; DA3; DLB 6; MTCW 2; SATA 2

Jacob, (Cyprien-)Max 1876-1944 .... TCLC 6
See also CA 104

Jacobs, Harriet A(nn)
1813(?)-1897 .... NCLC 67

Jacobs, Jim 1942- .... CLC 12
See also CA 97-100; INT 97-100

Jacobs, W(illiam) W(ymark)
1863-1943 .... TCLC 22
See also CA 121; 167; DLB 135

Jacobsen, Jens Peter 1847-1885 .... NCLC 34

Jacobsen, Josephine 1908- .... CLC 48, 102
See also CA 33-36R; CAAS 18; CANR 23, 48

Jacobson, Dan 1929- .... CLC 4, 14
See also CA 1-4R; CANR 2, 25, 66; DLB 14, 207, 225; MTCW 1

Jacqueline
See Carpentier (y Valmont), Alejo

Jagger, Mick 1944- .... CLC 17

Jahiz, al- c. 780-c. 869 .... CMLC 25

Jakes, John (William) 1932- . CLC 29; DAM NOV, POP
See also AAYA 32; BEST 89:4; CA 57-60; CANR 10, 43, 66; DA3; DLBY 83; INT CANR-10; MTCW 1, 2; SATA 62

James, Andrew
See Kirkup, James

James, C(yril) L(ionel) R(obert)
1901-1989 .... CLC 33; BLCS
See also BW 2; CA 117; 125; 128; CANR 62; DLB 125; MTCW 1

James, Daniel (Lewis) 1911-1988
See Santiago, Danny
See also CA 174; 125

James, Dynely
See Mayne, William (James Carter)

James, Henry Sr. 1811-1882 .... NCLC 53

James, Henry 1843-1916 ..... TCLC 2, 11, 24, 40, 47, 64; DA; DAB; DAC; DAM MST, NOV; SSC 8, 32; WLC
See also CA 104; 132; CDALB 1865-1917; DA3; DLB 12, 71, 74, 189; DLBD 13; MTCW 1, 2

James, M. R.
See James, Montague (Rhodes)
See also DLB 156

James, Montague (Rhodes)
1862-1936 .... TCLC 6; SSC 16
See also CA 104; DLB 201

James, P. D. 1920- .... CLC 18, 46, 122
See also White, Phyllis Dorothy James
See also BEST 90:2; CDBLB 1960 to Present; DLB 87; DLBD 17

James, Philip
See Moorcock, Michael (John)

James, William 1842-1910 .... TCLC 15, 32
See also CA 109

James I 1394-1437 .... LC 20

Jameson, Anna 1794-1860 .... NCLC 43
See also DLB 99, 166

Jami, Nur al-Din 'Abd al-Rahman
1414-1492 .... LC 9

Jammes, Francis 1868-1938 .... TCLC 75

Jandl, Ernst 1925- .... CLC 34

Janowitz, Tama 1957- .. CLC 43; DAM POP
See also CA 106; CANR 52, 89

Japrisot, Sebastien 1931- .... CLC 90

Jarrell, Randall 1914-1965 .... CLC 1, 2, 6, 9, 13, 49; DAM POET
See also CA 5-8R; 25-28R; CABS 2; CANR 6, 34; CDALB 1941-1968; CLR 6; DLB 48, 52; MAICYA; MTCW 1, 2; SATA 7

Jarry, Alfred 1873-1907 . TCLC 2, 14; DAM DRAM; SSC 20
See also CA 104; 153; DA3; DLB 192

Jawien, Andrzej
See John Paul II, Pope

Jaynes, Roderick
See Coen, Ethan

Jeake, Samuel, Jr.
See Aiken, Conrad (Potter)

Jean Paul 1763-1825 .... NCLC 7

Jefferies, (John) Richard
1848-1887 .... NCLC 47
See also DLB 98, 141; SATA 16

Jeffers, (John) Robinson 1887-1962 .. CLC 2, 3, 11, 15, 54; DA; DAC; DAM MST, POET; PC 17; WLC
See also CA 85-88; CANR 35; CDALB 1917-1929; DLB 45, 212; MTCW 1, 2

Jefferson, Janet
See Mencken, H(enry) L(ouis)

Jefferson, Thomas 1743-1826 .... NCLC 11
See also CDALB 1640-1865; DA3; DLB 31

Jeffrey, Francis 1773-1850 .... NCLC 33
See also DLB 107

Jelakowitch, Ivan
See Heijermans, Herman

Jellicoe, (Patricia) Ann 1927- .... CLC 27
See also CA 85-88; DLB 13

Jen, Gish CLC 70
See also Jen, Lillian

Jen, Lillian 1956(?)-
See Jen, Gish
See also CA 135; CANR 89

Jenkins, (John) Robin 1912- .... CLC 52
See also CA 1-4R; CANR 1; DLB 14

Jennings, Elizabeth (Joan) 1926- ...... CLC 5, 14, 131
See also CA 61-64; CAAS 5; CANR 8, 39, 66; DLB 27; MTCW 1; SATA 66

Jennings, Waylon 1937- .... CLC 21

Jensen, Johannes V. 1873-1950 ...... TCLC 41
See also CA 170

Jensen, Laura (Linnea) 1948- .... CLC 37
See also CA 103

Jerome, Jerome K(lapka)
1859-1927 .... TCLC 23
See also CA 119; 177; DLB 10, 34, 135

Jerrold, Douglas William
1803-1857 .... NCLC 2
See also DLB 158, 159

Jewett, (Theodora) Sarah Orne
1849-1909 .... TCLC 1, 22; SSC 6
See also CA 108; 127; CANR 71; DLB 12, 74, 221; SATA 15

Jewsbury, Geraldine (Endsor)
1812-1880 .... NCLC 22
See also DLB 21

Jhabvala, Ruth Prawer 1927- . CLC 4, 8, 29, 94; DAB; DAM NOV
See also CA 1-4R; CANR 2, 29, 51, 74, 91; DLB 139, 194; INT CANR-29; MTCW 1, 2

Jibran, Kahlil
See Gibran, Kahlil

Jibran, Khalil
See Gibran, Kahlil

Jiles, Paulette 1943- .... CLC 13, 58
See also CA 101; CANR 70

Jimenez (Mantecon), Juan Ramon
1881-1958 .... TCLC 4; DAM MULT, POET; HLC 1; PC 7
See also CA 104; 131; CANR 74; DLB 134; HW 1; MTCW 1, 2

Jimenez, Ramon
See Jimenez (Mantecon), Juan Ramon

Jimenez Mantecon, Juan
See Jimenez (Mantecon), Juan Ramon

Jin, Ha
See Jin, Xuefei

Jin, Xuefei 1956- .... CLC 109
See also CA 152; CANR 91

Joel, Billy CLC 26
See also Joel, William Martin

Joel, William Martin 1949-
See Joel, Billy
See also CA 108

John, Saint 7th cent. - .... CMLC 27

John of the Cross, St. 1542-1591 .... LC 18

John Paul II, Pope 1920- .... CLC 128
See also CA 106; 133

Johnson, B(ryan) S(tanley William)
1933-1973 .... CLC 6, 9
See also CA 9-12R; 53-56; CANR 9; DLB 14, 40

Johnson, Benj. F. of Boo
See Riley, James Whitcomb

Johnson, Benjamin F. of Boo
See Riley, James Whitcomb

Johnson, Charles (Richard) 1948- .... CLC 7, 51, 65; BLC 2; DAM MULT
See also BW 2, 3; CA 116; CAAS 18; CANR 42, 66, 82; DLB 33; MTCW 2

Johnson, Denis 1949- .... CLC 52
See also CA 117; 121; CANR 71; DLB 120

Johnson, Diane 1934- .... CLC 5, 13, 48
See also CA 41-44R; CANR 17, 40, 62; DLBY 80; INT CANR-17; MTCW 1

Johnson, Eyvind (Olof Verner)
1900-1976 .... CLC 14
See also CA 73-76; 69-72; CANR 34

Johnson, J. R.
See James, C(yril) L(ionel) R(obert)

Johnson, James Weldon
1871-1938 .. TCLC 3, 19; BLC 2; DAM MULT, POET; PC 24
See also BW 1, 3; CA 104; 125; CANR 82; CDALB 1917-1929; CLR 32; DA3; DLB 51; MTCW 1, 2; SATA 31

Johnson, Joyce 1935- .... CLC 58
See also CA 125; 129

Johnson, Judith (Emlyn) 1936- .... CLC 7, 15
See also Sherwin, Judith Johnson
See also CA 25-28R, 153; CANR 34

Johnson, Lionel (Pigot)
1867-1902 .... TCLC 19
See also CA 117; DLB 19

Johnson, Marguerite (Annie)
See Angelou, Maya

Johnson, Mel
See Malzberg, Barry N(athaniel)

Johnson, Pamela Hansford
1912-1981 .... CLC 1, 7, 27
See also CA 1-4R; 104; CANR 2, 28; DLB 15; MTCW 1, 2

Johnson, Robert 1911(?)-1938 .... TCLC 69
See also BW 3; CA 174

Johnson, Samuel 1709-1784 . LC 15, 52; DA; DAB; DAC; DAM MST; WLC
See also CDBLB 1660-1789; DLB 39, 95, 104, 142

Johnson, Uwe 1934-1984 .. **CLC 5, 10, 15, 40**
See also CA 1-4R; 112; CANR 1, 39; DLB 75; MTCW 1

Johnston, George (Benson) 1913- .... **CLC 51**
See also CA 1-4R; CANR 5, 20; DLB 88

Johnston, Jennifer 1930- .... **CLC 7**
See also CA 85-88; DLB 14

Joinville, Jean de 1224(?)-1317 ..... **CMLC 38**

Jolley, (Monica) Elizabeth 1923- ..... **CLC 46; SSC 19**
See also CA 127; CAAS 13; CANR 59

Jones, Arthur Llewellyn 1863-1947
See Machen, Arthur
See also CA 104; 179

Jones, D(ouglas) G(ordon) 1929- ..... **CLC 10**
See also CA 29-32R; CANR 13, 90; DLB 53

Jones, David (Michael) 1895-1974 .... **CLC 2, 4, 7, 13, 42**
See also CA 9-12R; 53-56; CANR 28; CD-BLB 1945-1960; DLB 20, 100; MTCW 1

Jones, David Robert 1947-
See Bowie, David
See also CA 103

Jones, Diana Wynne 1934- .... **CLC 26**
See also AAYA 12; CA 49-52; CANR 4, 26, 56; CLR 23; DLB 161; JRDA; MAI-CYA; SAAS 7; SATA 9, 70, 108

Jones, Edward P. 1950- .... **CLC 76**
See also BW 2, 3; CA 142; CANR 79

Jones, Gayl 1949- ..... **CLC 6, 9, 131; BLC 2; DAM MULT**
See also BW 2, 3; CA 77-80; CANR 27, 66; DA3; DLB 33; MTCW 1, 2

Jones, James 1921-1977 ...... **CLC 1, 3, 10, 39**
See also AITN 1, 2; CA 1-4R; 69-72; CANR 6; DLB 2, 143; DLBD 17; DLBY 98; MTCW 1

Jones, John J.
See Lovecraft, H(oward) P(hillips)

Jones, LeRoi CLC 1, 2, 3, 5, 10, 14
See also Baraka, Amiri
See also MTCW 2

Jones, Louis B. 1953- .... **CLC 65**
See also CA 141; CANR 73

Jones, Madison (Percy, Jr.) 1925- ...... **CLC 4**
See also CA 13-16R; CAAS 11; CANR 7, 54, 83; DLB 152

Jones, Mervyn 1922- .... **CLC 10, 52**
See also CA 45-48; CAAS 5; CANR 1, 91; MTCW 1

Jones, Mick 1956(?)- .... **CLC 30**

Jones, Nettie (Pearl) 1941- .... **CLC 34**
See also BW 2; CA 137; CAAS 20; CANR 88

Jones, Preston 1936-1979 .... **CLC 10**
See also CA 73-76; 89-92; DLB 7

Jones, Robert F(rancis) 1934- .... **CLC 7**
See also CA 49-52; CANR 2, 61

Jones, Rod 1953- .... **CLC 50**
See also CA 128

Jones, Terence Graham Parry 1942- .... **CLC 21**
See also Jones, Terry; Monty Python
See also CA 112; 116; CANR 35; INT 116

Jones, Terry
See Jones, Terence Graham Parry
See also SATA 67; SATA-Brief 51

Jones, Thom (Douglas) 1945(?)- .... **CLC 81**
See also CA 157; CANR 88

Jong, Erica 1942- .... **CLC 4, 6, 8, 18, 83; DAM NOV, POP**
See also AITN 1; BEST 90:2; CA 73-76; CANR 26, 52, 75; DA3; DLB 2, 5, 28, 152; INT CANR-26; MTCW 1, 2

Jonson, Ben(jamin) 1572(?)-1637 .. **LC 6, 33; DA; DAB; DAC; DAM DRAM, MST, POET; DC 4; PC 17; WLC**
See also CDBLB Before 1660; DLB 62, 121

Jordan, June 1936- .... **CLC 5, 11, 23, 114; BLCS; DAM MULT, POET**
See also AAYA 2; BW 2, 3; CA 33-36R; CANR 25, 70; CLR 10; DLB 38; MAI-CYA; MTCW 1; SATA 4

Jordan, Neil (Patrick) 1950- .... **CLC 110**
See also CA 124; 130; CANR 54; INT 130

Jordan, Pat(rick M.) 1941- .... **CLC 37**
See also CA 33-36R

Jorgensen, Ivar
See Ellison, Harlan (Jay)

Jorgenson, Ivar
See Silverberg, Robert

Josephus, Flavius c. 37-100 .... **CMLC 13**

Josipovici, Gabriel (David) 1940- ...... **CLC 6, 43**
See also CA 37-40R; CAAS 8; CANR 47, 84; DLB 14

Joubert, Joseph 1754-1824 .... **NCLC 9**

Jouve, Pierre Jean 1887-1976 .... **CLC 47**
See also CA 65-68

Jovine, Francesco 1902-1950 .... **TCLC 79**

Joyce, James (Augustine Aloysius) 1882-1941 .. **TCLC 3, 8, 16, 35, 52; DA; DAB; DAC; DAM MST, NOV, POET; PC 22; SSC 3, 26; WLC**
See also CA 104; 126; CDBLB 1914-1945; DA3; DLB 10, 19, 36, 162; MTCW 1, 2

Jozsef, Attila 1905-1937 .... **TCLC 22**
See also CA 116

Juana Ines de la Cruz 1651(?)-1695 .... **LC 5; HLCS 1; PC 24**

Judd, Cyril
See Kornbluth, C(yril) M.; Pohl, Frederik

Juenger, Ernst 1895-1998 .... **CLC 125**
See also CA 101; 167; CANR 21, 47; DLB 56

Julian of Norwich 1342(?)-1416(?) . **LC 6, 52**
See also DLB 146

Junger, Ernst
See Juenger, Ernst

Junger, Sebastian 1962- .... **CLC 109**
See also AAYA 28; CA 165

Juniper, Alex
See Hospital, Janette Turner

Junius
See Luxemburg, Rosa

Just, Ward (Swift) 1935- .... **CLC 4, 27**
See also CA 25-28R; CANR 32, 87; INT CANR-32

Justice, Donald (Rodney) 1925- .. **CLC 6, 19, 102; DAM POET**
See also CA 5-8R; CANR 26, 54, 74; DLBY 83; INT CANR-26; MTCW 2

Juvenal c. 60-c. 13 .... **CMLC 8**
See also Juvenalis, Decimus Junius
See also DLB 211

Juvenalis, Decimus Junius 55(?)-c. 127(?)
See Juvenal

Juvenis
See Bourne, Randolph S(illiman)

Kacew, Romain 1914-1980
See Gary, Romain
See also CA 108; 102

Kadare, Ismail 1936- .... **CLC 52**
See also CA 161

Kadohata, Cynthia CLC 59, 122
See also CA 140

Kafka, Franz 1883-1924 . **TCLC 2, 6, 13, 29, 47, 53; DA; DAB; DAC; DAM MST, NOV; SSC 5, 29, 35; WLC**
See also AAYA 31; CA 105; 126; DA3; DLB 81; MTCW 1, 2

Kahanovitsch, Pinkhes
See Der Nister

Kahn, Roger 1927- .... **CLC 30**
See also CA 25-28R; CANR 44, 69; DLB 171; SATA 37

Kain, Saul
See Sassoon, Siegfried (Lorraine)

Kaiser, Georg 1878-1945 .... **TCLC 9**
See also CA 106; DLB 124

Kaletski, Alexander 1946- .... **CLC 39**
See also CA 118; 143

Kalidasa fl. c. 400- .... **CMLC 9; PC 22**

Kallman, Chester (Simon) 1921-1975 .... **CLC 2**
See also CA 45-48; 53-56; CANR 3

Kaminsky, Melvin 1926-
See Brooks, Mel
See also CA 65-68; CANR 16

Kaminsky, Stuart M(elvin) 1934- ..... **CLC 59**
See also CA 73-76; CANR 29, 53, 89

Kandinsky, Wassily 1866-1944 .... **TCLC 92**
See also CA 118; 155

Kane, Francis
See Robbins, Harold

Kane, Paul
See Simon, Paul (Frederick)

Kanin, Garson 1912-1999 .... **CLC 22**
See also AITN 1; CA 5-8R; 177; CANR 7, 78; DLB 7

Kaniuk, Yoram 1930- .... **CLC 19**
See also CA 134

Kant, Immanuel 1724-1804 ..... **NCLC 27, 67**
See also DLB 94

Kantor, MacKinlay 1904-1977 .... **CLC 7**
See also CA 61-64; 73-76; CANR 60, 63; DLB 9, 102; MTCW 2

Kaplan, David Michael 1946- .... **CLC 50**

Kaplan, James 1951- .... **CLC 59**
See also CA 135

Karageorge, Michael
See Anderson, Poul (William)

Karamzin, Nikolai Mikhailovich 1766-1826 .... **NCLC 3**
See also DLB 150

Karapanou, Margarita 1946- .... **CLC 13**
See also CA 101

Karinthy, Frigyes 1887-1938 .... **TCLC 47**
See also CA 170

Karl, Frederick R(obert) 1927- .... **CLC 34**
See also CA 5-8R; CANR 3, 44

Kastel, Warren
See Silverberg, Robert

Kataev, Evgeny Petrovich 1903-1942
See Petrov, Evgeny
See also CA 120

Kataphusin
See Ruskin, John

Katz, Steve 1935- .... **CLC 47**
See also CA 25-28R; CAAS 14, 64; CANR 12; DLBY 83

Kauffman, Janet 1945- .... **CLC 42**
See also CA 117; CANR 43, 84; DLBY 86

Kaufman, Bob (Garnell) 1925-1986 . **CLC 49**
See also BW 1; CA 41-44R; 118; CANR 22; DLB 16, 41

Kaufman, George S. 1889-1961 ...... **CLC 38; DAM DRAM**
See also CA 108; 93-96; DLB 7; INT 108; MTCW 2

Kaufman, Sue CLC 3, 8
See also Barondess, Sue K(aufman)

Kavafis, Konstantinos Petrou 1863-1933
See Cavafy, C(onstantine) P(eter)
See also CA 104

Kavan, Anna 1901-1968 .... **CLC 5, 13, 82**
See also CA 5-8R; CANR 6, 57; MTCW 1

Kavanagh, Dan
See Barnes, Julian (Patrick)

Kavanagh, Julie 1952- .... **CLC 119**
See also CA 163

Kavanagh, Patrick (Joseph)
1904-1967 .... **CLC 22**
See also CA 123; 25-28R; DLB 15, 20;
MTCW 1

Kawabata, Yasunari 1899-1972 ..... **CLC 2, 5,**
9, 18, 107; DAM MULT; SSC 17
See also CA 93-96; 33-36R; CANR 88;
DLB 180; MTCW 2

Kaye, M(ary) M(argaret) 1909- .... **CLC 28**
See also CA 89-92; CANR 24, 60; MTCW
1, 2; SATA 62

Kaye, Mollie
See Kaye, M(ary) M(argaret)

Kaye-Smith, Sheila 1887-1956 .... **TCLC 20**
See also CA 118; DLB 36

Kaymor, Patrice Maguilene
See Senghor, Leopold Sedar

Kazan, Elia 1909- .... **CLC 6, 16, 63**
See also CA 21-24R; CANR 32, 78

Kazantzakis, Nikos 1883(?)-1957 .... **TCLC 2,**
5, 33
See also CA 105; 132; DA3; MTCW 1, 2

Kazin, Alfred 1915-1998 .... **CLC 34, 38, 119**
See also CA 1-4R; CAAS 7; CANR 1, 45,
79; DLB 67

Keane, Mary Nesta (Skrine) 1904-1996
See Keane, Molly
See also CA 108; 114; 151

Keane, Molly CLC 31
See also Keane, Mary Nesta (Skrine)
See also INT 114

Keates, Jonathan 1946(?)- .... **CLC 34**
See also CA 163

Keaton, Buster 1895-1966 .... **CLC 20**

Keats, John 1795-1821 ...... **NCLC 8, 73; DA;**
DAB; DAC; DAM MST, POET; PC 1;
WLC
See also CDBLB 1789-1832; DA3; DLB
96, 110

Keble, John 1792-1866 .... **NCLC 87**
See also DLB 32, 55

Keene, Donald 1922- .... **CLC 34**
See also CA 1-4R; CANR 5

Keillor, Garrison CLC 40, 115
See also Keillor, Gary (Edward)
See also AAYA 2; BEST 89:3; DLBY 87;
SATA 58

Keillor, Gary (Edward) 1942-
See Keillor, Garrison
See also CA 111; 117; CANR 36, 59; DAM
POP; DA3; MTCW 1, 2

Keith, Michael
See Hubbard, L(afayette) Ron(ald)

Keller, Gottfried 1819-1890 .... **NCLC 2; SSC**
26
See also DLB 129

Keller, Nora Okja CLC 109

Kellerman, Jonathan 1949- .. **CLC 44; DAM**
POP
See also BEST 90:1; CA 106; CANR 29,
51; DA3; INT CANR-29

Kelley, William Melvin 1937- .... **CLC 22**
See also BW 1; CA 77-80; CANR 27, 83;
DLB 33

Kellogg, Marjorie 1922- .... **CLC 2**
See also CA 81-84

Kellow, Kathleen
See Hibbert, Eleanor Alice Burford

Kelly, M(ilton) T(errence) 1947- ...... **CLC 55**
See also CA 97-100; CAAS 22; CANR 19,
43, 84

Kelman, James 1946- .... **CLC 58, 86**
See also CA 148; CANR 85; DLB 194

Kemal, Yashar 1923- .... **CLC 14, 29**
See also CA 89-92; CANR 44

Kemble, Fanny 1809-1893 .... **NCLC 18**
See also DLB 32

Kemelman, Harry 1908-1996 .... **CLC 2**
See also AITN 1; CA 9-12R; 155; CANR 6,
71; DLB 28

Kempe, Margery 1373(?)-1440(?) ... **LC 6, 56**
See also DLB 146

Kempis, Thomas a 1380-1471 .... **LC 11**

Kendall, Henry 1839-1882 .... **NCLC 12**

Keneally, Thomas (Michael) 1935- ... **CLC 5,**
8, 10, 14, 19, 27, 43, 117; DAM NOV
See also CA 85-88; CANR 10, 50, 74; DA3;
MTCW 1, 2

Kennedy, Adrienne (Lita) 1931- ..... **CLC 66;**
BLC 2; DAM MULT; DC 5
See also BW 2, 3; CA 103; CAAS 20;
CABS 3; CANR 26, 53, 82; DLB 38

Kennedy, John Pendleton
1795-1870 .... **NCLC 2**
See also DLB 3

Kennedy, Joseph Charles 1929-
See Kennedy, X. J.
See also CA 1-4R; CANR 4, 30, 40; SATA
14, 86

Kennedy, William 1928- .. **CLC 6, 28, 34, 53;**
DAM NOV
See also AAYA 1; CA 85-88; CANR 14,
31, 76; DA3; DLB 143; DLBY 85; INT
CANR-31; MTCW 1, 2; SATA 57

Kennedy, X. J. CLC 8, 42
See also Kennedy, Joseph Charles
See also CAAS 9; CLR 27; DLB 5; SAAS
22

Kenny, Maurice (Francis) 1929- ..... **CLC 87;**
DAM MULT
See also CA 144; CAAS 22; DLB 175;
NNAL

Kent, Kelvin
See Kuttner, Henry

Kenton, Maxwell
See Southern, Terry

Kenyon, Robert O.
See Kuttner, Henry

Kepler, Johannes 1571-1630 .... **LC 45**

Kerouac, Jack CLC 1, 2, 3, 5, 14, 29, 61
See also Kerouac, Jean-Louis Lebris de
See also AAYA 25; CDALB 1941-1968;
DLB 2, 16; DLBD 3; DLBY 95; MTCW
2

Kerouac, Jean-Louis Lebris de 1922-1969
See Kerouac, Jack
See also AITN 1; CA 5-8R; 25-28R; CANR
26, 54; DA; DAB; DAC; DAM MST,
NOV, POET, POP; DA3; MTCW 1, 2;
WLC

Kerr, Jean 1923- .... **CLC 22**
See also CA 5-8R; CANR 7; INT CANR-7

Kerr, M. E. CLC 12, 35
See also Meaker, Marijane (Agnes)
See also AAYA 2, 23; CLR 29; SAAS 1

Kerr, Robert CLC 55

Kerrigan, (Thomas) Anthony 1918- .. **CLC 4,**
6
See also CA 49-52; CAAS 11; CANR 4

Kerry, Lois
See Duncan, Lois

Kesey, Ken (Elton) 1935- ..... **CLC 1, 3, 6, 11,**
46, 64; DA; DAB; DAC; DAM MST,
NOV, POP; WLC
See also AAYA 25; CA 1-4R; CANR 22,
38, 66; CDALB 1968-1988; DA3; DLB
2, 16, 206; MTCW 1, 2; SATA 66

Kesselring, Joseph (Otto)
1902-1967 .... **CLC 45; DAM DRAM,**
MST
See also CA 150

Kessler, Jascha (Frederick) 1929- ...... **CLC 4**
See also CA 17-20R; CANR 8, 48

Kettelkamp, Larry (Dale) 1933- .... **CLC 12**
See also CA 29-32R; CANR 16; SAAS 3;
SATA 2

Key, Ellen 1849-1926 .... **TCLC 65**

Keyber, Conny
See Fielding, Henry

Keyes, Daniel 1927- ...... **CLC 80; DA; DAC;**
DAM MST, NOV
See also AAYA 23; CA 17-20R, 181; CAAE
181; CANR 10, 26, 54, 74; DA3; MTCW
2; SATA 37

Keynes, John Maynard
1883-1946 .... **TCLC 64**
See also CA 114; 162, 163; DLBD 10;
MTCW 2

Khanshendel, Chiron
See Rose, Wendy

Khayyam, Omar 1048-1131 .... **CMLC 11;**
DAM POET; PC 8
See also DA3

Kherdian, David 1931- .... **CLC 6, 9**
See also CA 21-24R; CAAS 2; CANR 39,
78; CLR 24; JRDA; MAICYA; SATA 16,
74

Khlebnikov, Velimir TCLC 20
See also Khlebnikov, Viktor Vladimirovich

Khlebnikov, Viktor Vladimirovich 1885-1922
See Khlebnikov, Velimir
See also CA 117

Khodasevich, Vladislav (Felitsianovich)
1886-1939 .... **TCLC 15**
See also CA 115

Kielland, Alexander Lange
1849-1906 .... **TCLC 5**
See also CA 104

Kiely, Benedict 1919- .... **CLC 23, 43**
See also CA 1-4R; CANR 2, 84; DLB 15

Kienzle, William X(avier) 1928- ..... **CLC 25;**
DAM POP
See also CA 93-96; CAAS 1; CANR 9, 31,
59; DA3; INT CANR-31; MTCW 1, 2

Kierkegaard, Soren 1813-1855 ..... **NCLC 34,**
78

Kieslowski, Krzysztof 1941-1996 .... **CLC 120**
See also CA 147; 151

Killens, John Oliver 1916-1987 .... **CLC 10**
See also BW 2; CA 77-80; 123; CAAS 2;
CANR 26; DLB 33

Killigrew, Anne 1660-1685 .... **LC 4**
See also DLB 131

Killigrew, Thomas 1612-1683 .... **LC 57**
See also DLB 58

Kim
See Simenon, Georges (Jacques Christian)

Kincaid, Jamaica 1949- .... **CLC 43, 68; BLC**
2; DAM MULT, NOV
See also AAYA 13; BW 2, 3; CA 125;
CANR 47, 59; CDALBS; CLR 63; DA3;
DLB 157, 227; MTCW 2

King, Francis (Henry) 1923- .... **CLC 8, 53;**
DAM NOV
See also CA 1-4R; CANR 1, 33, 86; DLB
15, 139; MTCW 1

King, Kennedy
See Brown, George Douglas

King, Martin Luther, Jr.
1929-1968 .... **CLC 83; BLC 2; DA;**
DAB; DAC; DAM MST, MULT;
WLCS
See also BW 2, 3; CA 25-28; CANR 27,
44; CAP 2; DA3; MTCW 1, 2; SATA 14

King, Stephen (Edwin) 1947- ...... **CLC 12, 26,**
37, 61, 113; DAM NOV, POP; SSC 17
See also AAYA 1, 17; BEST 90:1; CA 61-
64; CANR 1, 30, 52, 76; DA3; DLB 143;
DLBY 80; JRDA; MTCW 1, 2; SATA 9,
55

King, Steve
See King, Stephen (Edwin)

King, Thomas 1943- ... **CLC 89; DAC; DAM MULT**
See also CA 144; DLB 175; NNAL; SATA 96

Kingman, Lee CLC 17
See also Natti, (Mary) Lee
See also SAAS 3; SATA 1, 67

Kingsley, Charles 1819-1875 .... **NCLC 35**
See also DLB 21, 32, 163, 190; YABC 2

Kingsley, Sidney 1906-1995 .... **CLC 44**
See also CA 85-88; 147; DLB 7

Kingsolver, Barbara 1955- .... **CLC 55, 81, 130; DAM POP**
See also AAYA 15; CA 129; 134; CANR 60; CDALBS; DA3; DLB 206; INT 134; MTCW 2

Kingston, Maxine (Ting Ting) Hong 1940- .... **CLC 12, 19, 58, 121; DAM MULT, NOV; WLCS**
See also AAYA 8; CA 69-72; CANR 13, 38, 74, 87; CDALBS; DA3; DLB 173, 212; DLBY 80; INT CANR-13; MTCW 1, 2; SATA 53

Kinnell, Galway 1927- ..... **CLC 1, 2, 3, 5, 13, 29, 129; PC 26**
See also CA 9-12R; CANR 10, 34, 66; DLB 5; DLBY 87; INT CANR-34; MTCW 1, 2

Kinsella, Thomas 1928- .... **CLC 4, 19**
See also CA 17-20R; CANR 15; DLB 27; MTCW 1, 2

Kinsella, W(illiam) P(atrick) 1935- . **CLC 27, 43; DAC; DAM NOV, POP**
See also AAYA 7; CA 97-100; CAAS 7; CANR 21, 35, 66, 75; INT CANR-21; MTCW 1, 2

Kinsey, Alfred C(harles) 1894-1956 .... **TCLC 91**
See also CA 115; 170; MTCW 2

Kipling, (Joseph) Rudyard 1865-1936 .... **TCLC 8, 17; DA; DAB; DAC; DAM MST, POET; PC 3; SSC 5; WLC**
See also AAYA 32; CA 105; 120; CANR 33; CDBLB 1890-1914; CLR 39, 65; DA3; DLB 19, 34, 141, 156; MAICYA; MTCW 1, 2; SATA 100; YABC 2

Kirkland, Caroline M. 1801-1864 . **NCLC 85**
See also DLB 3, 73, 74; DLBD 13

Kirkup, James 1918- .... **CLC 1**
See also CA 1-4R; CAAS 4; CANR 2; DLB 27; SATA 12

Kirkwood, James 1930(?)-1989 .... **CLC 9**
See also AITN 2; CA 1-4R; 128; CANR 6, 40

Kirshner, Sidney
See Kingsley, Sidney

Kis, Danilo 1935-1989 .... **CLC 57**
See also CA 109; 118; 129; CANR 61; DLB 181; MTCW 1

Kivi, Aleksis 1834-1872 .... **NCLC 30**

Kizer, Carolyn (Ashley) 1925- ... **CLC 15, 39, 80; DAM POET**
See also CA 65-68; CAAS 5; CANR 24, 70; DLB 5, 169; MTCW 2

Klabund 1890-1928 .... **TCLC 44**
See also CA 162; DLB 66

Klappert, Peter 1942- .... **CLC 57**
See also CA 33-36R; DLB 5

Klein, A(braham) M(oses) 1909-1972 . **CLC 19; DAB; DAC; DAM MST**
See also CA 101; 37-40R; DLB 68

Klein, Norma 1938-1989 .... **CLC 30**
See also AAYA 2; CA 41-44R; 128; CANR 15, 37; CLR 2, 19; INT CANR-15; JRDA; MAICYA; SAAS 1; SATA 7, 57

Klein, T(heodore) E(ibon) D(onald) 1947- .... **CLC 34**
See also CA 119; CANR 44, 75

Kleist, Heinrich von 1777-1811 ...... **NCLC 2, 37; DAM DRAM; SSC 22**
See also DLB 90

Klima, Ivan 1931- .... **CLC 56; DAM NOV**
See also CA 25-28R; CANR 17, 50, 91

Klimentov, Andrei Platonovich 1899-1951 .... **TCLC 14**
See also CA 108

Klinger, Friedrich Maximilian von 1752-1831 .... **NCLC 1**
See also DLB 94

Klingsor the Magician
See Hartmann, Sadakichi

Klopstock, Friedrich Gottlieb 1724-1803 .... **NCLC 11**
See also DLB 97

Knapp, Caroline 1959- .... **CLC 99**
See also CA 154

Knebel, Fletcher 1911-1993 .... **CLC 14**
See also AITN 1; CA 1-4R; 140; CAAS 3; CANR 1, 36; SATA 36; SATA-Obit 75

Knickerbocker, Diedrich
See Irving, Washington

Knight, Etheridge 1931-1991 . **CLC 40; BLC 2; DAM POET; PC 14**
See also BW 1, 3; CA 21-24R; 133; CANR 23, 82; DLB 41; MTCW 2

Knight, Sarah Kemble 1666-1727 .... **LC 7**
See also DLB 24, 200

Knister, Raymond 1899-1932 .... **TCLC 56**
See also CA 186; DLB 68

Knowles, John 1926- . **CLC 1, 4, 10, 26; DA; DAC; DAM MST, NOV**
See also AAYA 10; CA 17-20R; CANR 40, 74, 76; CDALB 1968-1988; DLB 6; MTCW 1, 2; SATA 8, 89

Knox, Calvin M.
See Silverberg, Robert

Knox, John c. 1505-1572 .... **LC 37**
See also DLB 132

Knye, Cassandra
See Disch, Thomas M(ichael)

Koch, C(hristopher) J(ohn) 1932- .... **CLC 42**
See also CA 127; CANR 84

Koch, Christopher
See Koch, C(hristopher) J(ohn)

Koch, Kenneth 1925- .... **CLC 5, 8, 44; DAM POET**
See also CA 1-4R; CANR 6, 36, 57; DLB 5; INT CANR-36; MTCW 2; SATA 65

Kochanowski, Jan 1530-1584 .... **LC 10**

Kock, Charles Paul de 1794-1871 . **NCLC 16**

Koda Rohan 1867-
See Koda Shigeyuki

Koda Shigeyuki 1867-1947 .... **TCLC 22**
See also CA 121; 183; DLB 180

Koestler, Arthur 1905-1983 ... **CLC 1, 3, 6, 8, 15, 33**
See also CA 1-4R; 109; CANR 1, 33; CDBLB 1945-1960; DLBY 83; MTCW 1, 2

Kogawa, Joy Nozomi 1935- ..... **CLC 78, 129; DAC; DAM MST, MULT**
See also CA 101; CANR 19, 62; MTCW 2; SATA 99

Kohout, Pavel 1928- .... **CLC 13**
See also CA 45-48; CANR 3

Koizumi, Yakumo
See Hearn, (Patricio) Lafcadio (Tessima Carlos)

Kolmar, Gertrud 1894-1943 .... **TCLC 40**
See also CA 167

Komunyakaa, Yusef 1947- .... **CLC 86, 94; BLCS**
See also CA 147; CANR 83; DLB 120

Konrad, George
See Konrad, Gyoergy

Konrad, Gyoergy 1933- .... **CLC 4, 10, 73**
See also CA 85-88

Konwicki, Tadeusz 1926- .... **CLC 8, 28, 54, 117**
See also CA 101; CAAS 9; CANR 39, 59; MTCW 1

Koontz, Dean R(ay) 1945- .... **CLC 78; DAM NOV, POP**
See also AAYA 9, 31; BEST 89:3, 90:2; CA 108; CANR 19, 36, 52; DA3; MTCW 1; SATA 92

Kopernik, Mikolaj
See Copernicus, Nicolaus

Kopit, Arthur (Lee) 1937- ..... **CLC 1, 18, 33; DAM DRAM**
See also AITN 1; CA 81-84; CABS 3; DLB 7; MTCW 1

Kops, Bernard 1926- .... **CLC 4**
See also CA 5-8R; CANR 84; DLB 13

Kornbluth, C(yril) M. 1923-1958 .... **TCLC 8**
See also CA 105; 160; DLB 8

Korolenko, V. G.
See Korolenko, Vladimir Galaktionovich

Korolenko, Vladimir
See Korolenko, Vladimir Galaktionovich

Korolenko, Vladimir G.
See Korolenko, Vladimir Galaktionovich

Korolenko, Vladimir Galaktionovich 1853-1921 .... **TCLC 22**
See also CA 121

Korzybski, Alfred (Habdank Skarbek) 1879-1950 .... **TCLC 61**
See also CA 123; 160

Kosinski, Jerzy (Nikodem) 1933-1991 .... **CLC 1, 2, 3, 6, 10, 15, 53, 70; DAM NOV**
See also CA 17-20R; 134; CANR 9, 46; DA3; DLB 2; DLBY 82; MTCW 1, 2

Kostelanetz, Richard (Cory) 1940- .. **CLC 28**
See also CA 13-16R; CAAS 8; CANR 38, 77

Kostrowitzki, Wilhelm Apollinaris de 1880-1918
See Apollinaire, Guillaume
See also CA 104

Kotlowitz, Robert 1924- .... **CLC 4**
See also CA 33-36R; CANR 36

Kotzebue, August (Friedrich Ferdinand) von 1761-1819 .... **NCLC 25**
See also DLB 94

Kotzwinkle, William 1938- ..... **CLC 5, 14, 35**
See also CA 45-48; CANR 3, 44, 84; CLR 6; DLB 173; MAICYA; SATA 24, 70

Kowna, Stancy
See Szymborska, Wislawa

Kozol, Jonathan 1936- .... **CLC 17**
See also CA 61-64; CANR 16, 45

Kozoll, Michael 1940(?)- .... **CLC 35**

Kramer, Kathryn 19(?)- .... **CLC 34**

Kramer, Larry 1935- .. **CLC 42; DAM POP; DC 8**
See also CA 124; 126; CANR 60

Krasicki, Ignacy 1735-1801 .... **NCLC 8**

Krasinski, Zygmunt 1812-1859 .... **NCLC 4**

Kraus, Karl 1874-1936 .... **TCLC 5**
See also CA 104; DLB 118

Kreve (Mickevicius), Vincas 1882-1954 .... **TCLC 27**
See also CA 170; DLB 220

Kristeva, Julia 1941- .... **CLC 77**
See also CA 154

Kristofferson, Kris 1936- .... **CLC 26**
See also CA 104

Krizanc, John 1956- .... **CLC 57**

Krleza, Miroslav 1893-1981 .... **CLC 8, 114**
See also CA 97-100; 105; CANR 50; DLB 147

Kroetsch, Robert 1927- . **CLC 5, 23, 57, 132; DAC; DAM POET**
See also CA 17-20R; CANR 8, 38; DLB 53; MTCW 1

Kroetz, Franz
See Kroetz, Franz Xaver

Kroetz, Franz Xaver 1946- .... **CLC 41**
See also CA 130

Kroker, Arthur (W.) 1945- .... **CLC 77**
See also CA 161

Kropotkin, Peter (Aleksieevich)
1842-1921 .... **TCLC 36**
See also CA 119

Krotkov, Yuri 1917- .... **CLC 19**
See also CA 102

Krumb
See Crumb, R(obert)

Krumgold, Joseph (Quincy)
1908-1980 .... **CLC 12**
See also CA 9-12R; 101; CANR 7; MAICYA; SATA 1, 48; SATA-Obit 23

Krumwitz
See Crumb, R(obert)

Krutch, Joseph Wood 1893-1970 ..... **CLC 24**
See also CA 1-4R; 25-28R; CANR 4; DLB 63, 206

Krutzch, Gus
See Eliot, T(homas) S(tearns)

Krylov, Ivan Andreevich
1768(?)-1844 .... **NCLC 1**
See also DLB 150

Kubin, Alfred (Leopold Isidor)
1877-1959 .... **TCLC 23**
See also CA 112; 149; DLB 81

Kubrick, Stanley 1928-1999 .... **CLC 16**
See also AAYA 30; CA 81-84; 177; CANR 33; DLB 26

Kueng, Hans 1928-
See Kung, Hans
See also CA 53-56; CANR 66; MTCW 1, 2

Kumin, Maxine (Winokur) 1925- ..... **CLC 5, 13, 28; DAM POET; PC 15**
See also AITN 2; CA 1-4R; CAAS 8; CANR 1, 21, 69; DLB 5; DA3; MTCW 1, 2; SATA 12

Kundera, Milan 1929- . **CLC 4, 9, 19, 32, 68, 115; DAM NOV; SSC 24**
See also AAYA 2; CA 85-88; CANR 19, 52, 74; DA3; MTCW 1, 2

Kunene, Mazisi (Raymond) 1930- ... **CLC 85**
See also BW 1, 3; CA 125; CANR 81; DLB 117

Kung, Hans 1928- .... **CLC 130**
See also Kueng, Hans

Kunitz, Stanley (Jasspon) 1905- ... **CLC 6, 11, 14; PC 19**
See also CA 41-44R; CANR 26, 57; DA3; DLB 48; INT CANR-26; MTCW 1, 2

Kunze, Reiner 1933- .... **CLC 10**
See also CA 93-96; DLB 75

Kuprin, Aleksander Ivanovich
1870-1938 .... **TCLC 5**
See also CA 104; 182

Kureishi, Hanif 1954(?)- .... **CLC 64**
See also CA 139; DLB 194

Kurosawa, Akira 1910-1998 .... **CLC 16, 119; DAM MULT**
See also AAYA 11; CA 101; 170; CANR 46

Kushner, Tony 1957(?)- .... **CLC 81; DAM DRAM; DC 10**
See also CA 144; CANR 74; DA3; DLB 228; MTCW 2

Kuttner, Henry 1915-1958 .... **TCLC 10**
See also CA 107; 157; DLB 8

Kuzma, Greg 1944- .... **CLC 7**
See also CA 33-36R; CANR 70

Kuzmin, Mikhail 1872(?)-1936 ...... **TCLC 40**
See also CA 170

Kyd, Thomas 1558-1594 .... **LC 22; DAM DRAM; DC 3**
See also DLB 62

Kyprianos, Iossif
See Samarakis, Antonis

La Bruyere, Jean de 1645-1696 .... **LC 17**

Lacan, Jacques (Marie Emile)
1901-1981 .... **CLC 75**
See also CA 121; 104

Laclos, Pierre Ambroise Francois Choderlos de 1741-1803 .... **NCLC 4, 87**

Lacolere, Francois
See Aragon, Louis

La Colere, Francois
See Aragon, Louis

La Deshabilleuse
See Simenon, Georges (Jacques Christian)

Lady Gregory
See Gregory, Isabella Augusta (Persse)

Lady of Quality, A
See Bagnold, Enid

La Fayette, Marie (Madelaine Pioche de la Vergne Comtes 1634-1693 .... **LC 2**

Lafayette, Rene
See Hubbard, L(afayette) Ron(ald)

La Fontaine, Jean de 1621-1695 .... **LC 50**
See also MAICYA; SATA 18

Laforgue, Jules 1860-1887 . **NCLC 5, 53; PC 14; SSC 20**

Lagerkvist, Paer (Fabian)
1891-1974 ...... **CLC 7, 10, 13, 54; DAM DRAM, NOV**
See also Lagerkvist, Par
See also CA 85-88; 49-52; DA3; MTCW 1, 2

Lagerkvist, Par SSC 12
See also Lagerkvist, Paer (Fabian)
See also MTCW 2

Lagerloef, Selma (Ottiliana Lovisa)
1858-1940 .... **TCLC 4, 36**
See also Lagerlof, Selma (Ottiliana Lovisa)
See also CA 108; MTCW 2; SATA 15

Lagerlof, Selma (Ottiliana Lovisa)
See Lagerloef, Selma (Ottiliana Lovisa)
See also CLR 7; SATA 15

La Guma, (Justin) Alex(ander)
1925-1985 .... **CLC 19; BLCS; DAM NOV**
See also BW 1, 3; CA 49-52; 118; CANR 25, 81; DLB 117, 225; MTCW 1, 2

Laidlaw, A. K.
See Grieve, C(hristopher) M(urray)

Lainez, Manuel Mujica
See Mujica Lainez, Manuel
See also HW 1

Laing, R(onald) D(avid) 1927-1989 . **CLC 95**
See also CA 107; 129; CANR 34; MTCW 1

Lamartine, Alphonse (Marie Louis Prat) de 1790-1869 . **NCLC 11; DAM POET; PC 16**

Lamb, Charles 1775-1834 ..... **NCLC 10; DA; DAB; DAC; DAM MST; WLC**
See also CDBLB 1789-1832; DLB 93, 107, 163; SATA 17

Lamb, Lady Caroline 1785-1828 ... **NCLC 38**
See also DLB 116

Lamming, George (William) 1927- ... **CLC 2, 4, 66; BLC 2; DAM MULT**
See also BW 2, 3; CA 85-88; CANR 26, 76; DLB 125; MTCW 1, 2

L'Amour, Louis (Dearborn)
1908-1988 ...... **CLC 25, 55; DAM NOV, POP**
See also AAYA 16; AITN 2; BEST 89:2; CA 1-4R; 125; CANR 3, 25, 40; DA3; DLB 206; DLBY 80; MTCW 1, 2

Lampedusa, Giuseppe (Tomasi) di
1896-1957 .... **TCLC 13**
See also Tomasi di Lampedusa, Giuseppe
See also CA 164; DLB 177; MTCW 2

Lampman, Archibald 1861-1899 ... **NCLC 25**
See also DLB 92

Lancaster, Bruce 1896-1963 .... **CLC 36**
See also CA 9-10; CANR 70; CAP 1; SATA 9

Lanchester, John CLC 99

Landau, Mark Alexandrovich
See Aldanov, Mark (Alexandrovich)

Landau-Aldanov, Mark Alexandrovich
See Aldanov, Mark (Alexandrovich)

Landis, Jerry
See Simon, Paul (Frederick)

Landis, John 1950- .... **CLC 26**
See also CA 112; 122

Landolfi, Tommaso 1908-1979 .... **CLC 11, 49**
See also CA 127; 117; DLB 177

Landon, Letitia Elizabeth
1802-1838 .... **NCLC 15**
See also DLB 96

Landor, Walter Savage
1775-1864 .... **NCLC 14**
See also DLB 93, 107

Landwirth, Heinz 1927-
See Lind, Jakov
See also CA 9-12R; CANR 7

Lane, Patrick 1939- ... **CLC 25; DAM POET**
See also CA 97-100; CANR 54; DLB 53; INT 97-100

Lang, Andrew 1844-1912 .... **TCLC 16**
See also CA 114; 137; CANR 85; DLB 98, 141, 184; MAICYA; SATA 16

Lang, Fritz 1890-1976 .... **CLC 20, 103**
See also CA 77-80; 69-72; CANR 30

Lange, John
See Crichton, (John) Michael

Langer, Elinor 1939- .... **CLC 34**
See also CA 121

Langland, William 1330(?)-1400(?) ... **LC 19; DA; DAB; DAC; DAM MST, POET**
See also DLB 146

Langstaff, Launcelot
See Irving, Washington

Lanier, Sidney 1842-1881 ..... **NCLC 6; DAM POET**
See also DLB 64; DLBD 13; MAICYA; SATA 18

Lanyer, Aemilia 1569-1645 .... **LC 10, 30**
See also DLB 121

Lao-Tzu
See Lao Tzu

Lao Tzu fl. 6th cent. B.C.- .... **CMLC 7**

Lapine, James (Elliot) 1949- .... **CLC 39**
See also CA 123; 130; CANR 54; INT 130

Larbaud, Valery (Nicolas)
1881-1957 .... **TCLC 9**
See also CA 106; 152

Lardner, Ring
See Lardner, Ring(gold) W(ilmer)

Lardner, Ring W., Jr.
See Lardner, Ring(gold) W(ilmer)

Lardner, Ring(gold) W(ilmer)
1885-1933 .... **TCLC 2, 14; SSC 32**
See also CA 104; 131; CDALB 1917-1929; DLB 11, 25, 86; DLBD 16; MTCW 1, 2

Laredo, Betty
See Codrescu, Andrei

Larkin, Maia
See Wojciechowska, Maia (Teresa)

Larkin, Philip (Arthur) 1922-1985 ... **CLC 3, 5, 8, 9, 13, 18, 33, 39, 64; DAB; DAM MST, POET; PC 21**
See also CA 5-8R; 117; CANR 24, 62; CDBLB 1960 to Present; DA3; DLB 27; MTCW 1, 2

Larra (y Sanchez de Castro), Mariano Jose de 1809-1837 .... **NCLC 17**

Larsen, Eric 1941- .... **CLC 55**
　See also CA 132

Larsen, Nella 1891-1964 .... **CLC 37; BLC 2; DAM MULT**
　See also BW 1; CA 125; CANR 83; DLB 51

Larson, Charles R(aymond) 1938- ... **CLC 31**
　See also CA 53-56; CANR 4

Larson, Jonathan 1961-1996 .... **CLC 99**
　See also AAYA 28; CA 156

Las Casas, Bartolome de 1474-1566 ... **LC 31**

Lasch, Christopher 1932-1994 .... **CLC 102**
　See also CA 73-76; 144; CANR 25; MTCW 1, 2

Lasker-Schueler, Else 1869-1945 ... **TCLC 57**
　See also CA 183; DLB 66, 124

Laski, Harold 1893-1950 .... **TCLC 79**

Latham, Jean Lee 1902-1995 .... **CLC 12**
　See also AITN 1; CA 5-8R; CANR 7, 84; CLR 50; MAICYA; SATA 2, 68

Latham, Mavis
　See Clark, Mavis Thorpe

Lathen, Emma CLC 2
　See also Hennissart, Martha; Latsis, Mary J(ane)

Lathrop, Francis
　See Leiber, Fritz (Reuter, Jr.)

Latsis, Mary J(ane) 1927(?)-1997
　See Lathen, Emma
　See also CA 85-88; 162

Lattimore, Richmond (Alexander) 1906-1984 .... **CLC 3**
　See also CA 1-4R; 112; CANR 1

Laughlin, James 1914-1997 .... **CLC 49**
　See also CA 21-24R; 162; CAAS 22; CANR 9, 47; DLB 48; DLBY 96, 97

Laurence, (Jean) Margaret (Wemyss) 1926-1987 . **CLC 3, 6, 13, 50, 62; DAC; DAM MST; SSC 7**
　See also CA 5-8R; 121; CANR 33; DLB 53; MTCW 1, 2; SATA-Obit 50

Laurent, Antoine 1952- .... **CLC 50**

Lauscher, Hermann
　See Hesse, Hermann

Lautreamont, Comte de 1846-1870 .... **NCLC 12; SSC 14**

Laverty, Donald
　See Blish, James (Benjamin)

Lavin, Mary 1912-1996 . **CLC 4, 18, 99; SSC 4**
　See also CA 9-12R; 151; CANR 33; DLB 15; MTCW 1

Lavond, Paul Dennis
　See Kornbluth, C(yril) M.; Pohl, Frederik

Lawler, Raymond Evenor 1922- .... **CLC 58**
　See also CA 103

Lawrence, D(avid) H(erbert Richards) 1885-1930 .... **TCLC 2, 9, 16, 33, 48, 61, 93; DA; DAB; DAC; DAM MST, NOV, POET; SSC 4, 19; WLC**
　See also CA 104; 121; CDBLB 1914-1945; DA3; DLB 10, 19, 36, 98, 162, 195; MTCW 1, 2

Lawrence, T(homas) E(dward) 1888-1935 .... **TCLC 18**
　See also Dale, Colin
　See also CA 115; 167; DLB 195

Lawrence of Arabia
　See Lawrence, T(homas) E(dward)

Lawson, Henry (Archibald Hertzberg) 1867-1922 .... **TCLC 27; SSC 18**
　See also CA 120; 181

Lawton, Dennis
　See Faust, Frederick (Schiller)

Laxness, Halldor CLC 25
　See also Gudjonsson, Halldor Kiljan

Layamon fl. c. 1200- .... **CMLC 10**
　See also DLB 146

Laye, Camara 1928-1980 ... **CLC 4, 38; BLC 2; DAM MULT**
　See also BW 1; CA 85-88; 97-100; CANR 25; MTCW 1, 2

Layton, Irving (Peter) 1912- .... **CLC 2, 15; DAC; DAM MST, POET**
　See also CA 1-4R; CANR 2, 33, 43, 66; DLB 88; MTCW 1, 2

Lazarus, Emma 1849-1887 .... **NCLC 8**

Lazarus, Felix
　See Cable, George Washington

Lazarus, Henry
　See Slavitt, David R(ytman)

Lea, Joan
　See Neufeld, John (Arthur)

Leacock, Stephen (Butler) 1869-1944 .... **TCLC 2; DAC; DAM MST; SSC 39**
　See also CA 104; 141; CANR 80; DLB 92; MTCW 2

Lear, Edward 1812-1888 .... **NCLC 3**
　See also CLR 1; DLB 32, 163, 166; MAICYA; SATA 18, 100

Lear, Norman (Milton) 1922- .... **CLC 12**
　See also CA 73-76

Leautaud, Paul 1872-1956 .... **TCLC 83**
　See also DLB 65

Leavis, F(rank) R(aymond) 1895-1978 .... **CLC 24**
　See also CA 21-24R; 77-80; CANR 44; MTCW 1, 2

Leavitt, David 1961- ..... **CLC 34; DAM POP**
　See also CA 116; 122; CANR 50, 62; DA3; DLB 130; INT 122; MTCW 2

Leblanc, Maurice (Marie Emile) 1864-1941 .... **TCLC 49**
　See also CA 110

Lebowitz, Fran(ces Ann) 1951(?)- ... **CLC 11, 36**
　See also CA 81-84; CANR 14, 60, 70; INT CANR-14; MTCW 1

Lebrecht, Peter
　See Tieck, (Johann) Ludwig

le Carre, John CLC 3, 5, 9, 15, 28
　See also Cornwell, David (John Moore)
　See also BEST 89:4; CDBLB 1960 to Present; DLB 87; MTCW 2

Le Clezio, J(ean) M(arie) G(ustave) 1940- .... **CLC 31**
　See also CA 116; 128; DLB 83

Leconte de Lisle, Charles-Marie-Rene 1818-1894 .... **NCLC 29**

Le Coq, Monsieur
　See Simenon, Georges (Jacques Christian)

Leduc, Violette 1907-1972 .... **CLC 22**
　See also CA 13-14; 33-36R; CANR 69; CAP 1

Ledwidge, Francis 1887(?)-1917 .... **TCLC 23**
　See also CA 123; DLB 20

Lee, Andrea 1953- ... **CLC 36; BLC 2; DAM MULT**
　See also BW 1, 3; CA 125; CANR 82

Lee, Andrew
　See Auchincloss, Louis (Stanton)

Lee, Chang-rae 1965- .... **CLC 91**
　See also CA 148; CANR 89

Lee, Don L. CLC 2
　See also Madhubuti, Haki R.

Lee, George W(ashington) 1894-1976 .... **CLC 52; BLC 2; DAM MULT**
　See also BW 1; CA 125; CANR 83; DLB 51

Lee, (Nelle) Harper 1926- . **CLC 12, 60; DA; DAB; DAC; DAM MST, NOV; WLC**
　See also AAYA 13; CA 13-16R; CANR 51; CDALB 1941-1968; DA3; DLB 6; MTCW 1, 2; SATA 11

Lee, Helen Elaine 1959(?)- .... **CLC 86**
　See also CA 148

Lee, Julian
　See Latham, Jean Lee

Lee, Larry
　See Lee, Lawrence

Lee, Laurie 1914-1997 .... **CLC 90; DAB; DAM POP**
　See also CA 77-80; 158; CANR 33, 73; DLB 27; MTCW 1

Lee, Lawrence 1941-1990 .... **CLC 34**
　See also CA 131; CANR 43

Lee, Li-Young 1957- .... **PC 24**
　See also CA 153; DLB 165

Lee, Manfred B(ennington) 1905-1971 .... **CLC 11**
　See also Queen, Ellery
　See also CA 1-4R; 29-32R; CANR 2; DLB 137

Lee, Shelton Jackson 1957(?)- .... **CLC 105; BLCS; DAM MULT**
　See also Lee, Spike
　See also BW 2, 3; CA 125; CANR 42

Lee, Spike
　See Lee, Shelton Jackson
　See also AAYA 4, 29

Lee, Stan 1922- .... **CLC 17**
　See also AAYA 5; CA 108; 111; INT 111

Lee, Tanith 1947- .... **CLC 46**
　See also AAYA 15; CA 37-40R; CANR 53; SATA 8, 88

Lee, Vernon TCLC 5; SSC 33
　See also Paget, Violet
　See also DLB 57, 153, 156, 174, 178

Lee, William
　See Burroughs, William S(eward)

Lee, Willy
　See Burroughs, William S(eward)

Lee-Hamilton, Eugene (Jacob) 1845-1907 .... **TCLC 22**
　See also CA 117

Leet, Judith 1935- .... **CLC 11**

Le Fanu, Joseph Sheridan 1814-1873 ..... **NCLC 9, 58; DAM POP; SSC 14**
　See also DA3; DLB 21, 70, 159, 178

Leffland, Ella 1931- .... **CLC 19**
　See also CA 29-32R; CANR 35, 78, 82; DLBY 84; INT CANR-35; SATA 65

Leger, Alexis
　See Leger, (Marie-Rene Auguste) Alexis Saint-Leger

Leger, (Marie-Rene Auguste) Alexis Saint-Leger 1887-1975 .. **CLC 4, 11, 46; DAM POET; PC 23**
　See also CA 13-16R; 61-64; CANR 43; MTCW 1

Leger, Saintleger
　See Leger, (Marie-Rene Auguste) Alexis Saint-Leger

Le Guin, Ursula K(roeber) 1929- ..... **CLC 8, 13, 22, 45, 71; DAB; DAC; DAM MST, POP; SSC 12**
　See also AAYA 9, 27; AITN 1; CA 21-24R; CANR 9, 32, 52, 74; CDALB 1968-1988; CLR 3, 28; DA3; DLB 8, 52; INT CANR-32; JRDA; MAICYA; MTCW 1, 2; SATA 4, 52, 99

Lehmann, Rosamond (Nina) 1901-1990 .... **CLC 5**
　See also CA 77-80; 131; CANR 8, 73; DLB 15; MTCW 2

Leiber, Fritz (Reuter, Jr.)
1910-1992 .... **CLC 25**
See also CA 45-48; 139; CANR 2, 40, 86;
DLB 8; MTCW 1, 2; SATA 45; SATA-
Obit 73

Leibniz, Gottfried Wilhelm von
1646-1716 .... **LC 35**
See also DLB 168

Leimbach, Martha 1963-
See Leimbach, Marti
See also CA 130

Leimbach, Marti CLC 65
See also Leimbach, Martha

Leino, Eino TCLC 24
See also Loennbohm, Armas Eino Leopold

Leiris, Michel (Julien) 1901-1990 ..... **CLC 61**
See also CA 119; 128; 132

Leithauser, Brad 1953- .... **CLC 27**
See also CA 107; CANR 27, 81; DLB 120

Lelchuk, Alan 1938- .... **CLC 5**
See also CA 45-48; CAAS 20; CANR 1, 70

Lem, Stanislaw 1921- .... **CLC 8, 15, 40**
See also CA 105; CAAS 1; CANR 32;
MTCW 1

Lemann, Nancy 1956- .... **CLC 39**
See also CA 118; 136

Lemonnier, (Antoine Louis) Camille
1844-1913 .... **TCLC 22**
See also CA 121

Lenau, Nikolaus 1802-1850 .... **NCLC 16**

L'Engle, Madeleine (Camp Franklin)
1918- .... **CLC 12; DAM POP**
See also AAYA 28; AITN 2; CA 1-4R;
CANR 3, 21, 39, 66; CLR 1, 14, 57; DA3;
DLB 52; JRDA; MAICYA; MTCW 1, 2;
SAAS 15; SATA 1, 27, 75

Lengyel, Jozsef 1896-1975 .... **CLC 7**
See also CA 85-88; 57-60; CANR 71

Lenin 1870-1924
See Lenin, V. I.
See also CA 121; 168

Lenin, V. I. TCLC 67
See also Lenin

Lennon, John (Ono) 1940-1980 .. **CLC 12, 35**
See also CA 102; SATA 114

Lennox, Charlotte Ramsay
1729(?)-1804 .... **NCLC 23**
See also DLB 39

Lentricchia, Frank (Jr.) 1940- .... **CLC 34**
See also CA 25-28R; CANR 19

Lenz, Siegfried 1926- .... **CLC 27; SSC 33**
See also CA 89-92; CANR 80; DLB 75

Leonard, Elmore (John, Jr.) 1925- . **CLC 28,
34, 71, 120; DAM POP**
See also AAYA 22; AITN 1; BEST 89:1,
90:4; CA 81-84; CANR 12, 28, 53, 76;
DA3; DLB 173, 226; INT CANR-28;
MTCW 1, 2

Leonard, Hugh CLC 19
See also Byrne, John Keyes
See also DLB 13

Leonov, Leonid (Maximovich)
1899-1994 .... **CLC 92; DAM NOV**
See also CA 129; CANR 74, 76; MTCW 1,
2

Leopardi, (Conte) Giacomo
1798-1837 .... **NCLC 22**

Le Reveler
See Artaud, Antonin (Marie Joseph)

Lerman, Eleanor 1952- .... **CLC 9**
See also CA 85-88; CANR 69

Lerman, Rhoda 1936- .... **CLC 56**
See also CA 49-52; CANR 70

Lermontov, Mikhail Yuryevich
1814-1841 .... **NCLC 47; PC 18**
See also DLB 205

Leroux, Gaston 1868-1927 .... **TCLC 25**
See also CA 108; 136; CANR 69; SATA 65

Lesage, Alain-Rene 1668-1747 .... **LC 2, 28**

Leskov, Nikolai (Semyonovich)
1831-1895 .... **NCLC 25; SSC 34**

Lessing, Doris (May) 1919- ... **CLC 1, 2, 3, 6,
10, 15, 22, 40, 94; DA; DAB; DAC;
DAM MST, NOV; SSC 6; WLCS**
See also CA 9-12R; CAAS 14; CANR 33,
54, 76; CDBLB 1960 to Present; DA3;
DLB 15, 139; DLBY 85; MTCW 1, 2

Lessing, Gotthold Ephraim 1729-1781 . **LC 8**
See also DLB 97

Lester, Richard 1932- .... **CLC 20**

Lever, Charles (James)
1806-1872 .... **NCLC 23**
See also DLB 21

Leverson, Ada 1865(?)-1936(?) .... **TCLC 18**
See also Elaine
See also CA 117; DLB 153

Levertov, Denise 1923-1997 .. **CLC 1, 2, 3, 5,
8, 15, 28, 66; DAM POET; PC 11**
See also CA 1-4R, 178; 163; CAAE 178;
CAAS 19; CANR 3, 29, 50; CDALBS;
DLB 5, 165; INT CANR-29; MTCW 1, 2

Levi, Jonathan CLC 76

Levi, Peter (Chad Tigar) 1931- .... **CLC 41**
See also CA 5-8R; CANR 34, 80; DLB 40

Levi, Primo 1919-1987 . **CLC 37, 50; SSC 12**
See also CA 13-16R; 122; CANR 12, 33,
61, 70; DLB 177; MTCW 1, 2

Levin, Ira 1929- .... **CLC 3, 6; DAM POP**
See also CA 21-24R; CANR 17, 44, 74;
DA3; MTCW 1, 2; SATA 66

Levin, Meyer 1905-1981 .... **CLC 7; DAM
POP**
See also AITN 1; CA 9-12R; 104; CANR
15; DLB 9, 28; DLBY 81; SATA 21;
SATA-Obit 27

Levine, Norman 1924- .... **CLC 54**
See also CA 73-76; CAAS 23; CANR 14,
70; DLB 88

Levine, Philip 1928- .. **CLC 2, 4, 5, 9, 14, 33,
118; DAM POET; PC 22**
See also CA 9-12R; CANR 9, 37, 52; DLB
5

Levinson, Deirdre 1931- .... **CLC 49**
See also CA 73-76; CANR 70

Levi-Strauss, Claude 1908- .... **CLC 38**
See also CA 1-4R; CANR 6, 32, 57; MTCW
1, 2

Levitin, Sonia (Wolff) 1934- .... **CLC 17**
See also AAYA 13; CA 29-32R; CANR 14,
32, 79; CLR 53; JRDA; MAICYA; SAAS
2; SATA 4, 68

Levon, O. U.
See Kesey, Ken (Elton)

Levy, Amy 1861-1889 .... **NCLC 59**
See also DLB 156

Lewes, George Henry 1817-1878 ... **NCLC 25**
See also DLB 55, 144

Lewis, Alun 1915-1944 .... **TCLC 3; SSC 40**
See also CA 104; DLB 20, 162

Lewis, C. Day
See Day Lewis, C(ecil)

Lewis, C(live) S(taples) 1898-1963 .... **CLC 1,
3, 6, 14, 27, 124; DA; DAB; DAC;
DAM MST, NOV, POP; WLC**
See also AAYA 3; CA 81-84; CANR 33,
71; CDBLB 1945-1960; CLR 3, 27; DA3;
DLB 15, 100, 160; JRDA; MAICYA;
MTCW 1, 2; SATA 13, 100

Lewis, Janet 1899-1998 .... **CLC 41**
See also Winters, Janet Lewis
See also CA 9-12R; 172; CANR 29, 63;
CAP 1; DLBY 87

Lewis, Matthew Gregory
1775-1818 .... **NCLC 11, 62**
See also DLB 39, 158, 178

Lewis, (Harry) Sinclair 1885-1951 . **TCLC 4,
13, 23, 39; DA; DAB; DAC; DAM
MST, NOV; WLC**
See also CA 104; 133; CDALB 1917-1929;
DA3; DLB 9, 102; DLBD 1; MTCW 1, 2

Lewis, (Percy) Wyndham
1882(?)-1957 .... **TCLC 2, 9; SSC 34**
See also CA 104; 157; DLB 15; MTCW 2

Lewisohn, Ludwig 1883-1955 .... **TCLC 19**
See also CA 107; DLB 4, 9, 28, 102

Lewton, Val 1904-1951 .... **TCLC 76**

Leyner, Mark 1956- .... **CLC 92**
See also CA 110; CANR 28, 53; DA3;
MTCW 2

Lezama Lima, Jose 1910-1976 .... **CLC 4, 10,
101; DAM MULT; HLCS 2**
See also CA 77-80; CANR 71; DLB 113;
HW 1, 2

L'Heureux, John (Clarke) 1934- ...... **CLC 52**
See also CA 13-16R; CANR 23, 45, 88

Liddell, C. H.
See Kuttner, Henry

Lie, Jonas (Lauritz Idemil)
1833-1908(?) .... **TCLC 5**
See also CA 115

Lieber, Joel 1937-1971 .... **CLC 6**
See also CA 73-76; 29-32R

Lieber, Stanley Martin
See Lee, Stan

Lieberman, Laurence (James)
1935- .... **CLC 4, 36**
See also CA 17-20R; CANR 8, 36, 89

Lieh Tzu fl. 7th cent. B.C.-5th cent.
B.C. .... **CMLC 27**

Lieksman, Anders
See Haavikko, Paavo Juhani

Li Fei-kan 1904-
See Pa Chin
See also CA 105

Lifton, Robert Jay 1926- .... **CLC 67**
See also CA 17-20R; CANR 27, 78; INT
CANR-27; SATA 66

Lightfoot, Gordon 1938- .... **CLC 26**
See also CA 109

Lightman, Alan P(aige) 1948- .... **CLC 81**
See also CA 141; CANR 63

Ligotti, Thomas (Robert) 1953- ...... **CLC 44;
SSC 16**
See also CA 123; CANR 49

Li Ho 791-817 .... **PC 13**

**Liliencron, (Friedrich Adolf Axel) Detlev
von** 1844-1909 .... **TCLC 18**
See also CA 117

Lilly, William 1602-1681 .... **LC 27**

Lima, Jose Lezama
See Lezama Lima, Jose

Lima Barreto, Afonso Henrique de
1881-1922 .... **TCLC 23**
See also CA 117; 181

Limonov, Edward 1944- .... **CLC 67**
See also CA 137

Lin, Frank
See Atherton, Gertrude (Franklin Horn)

Lincoln, Abraham 1809-1865 .... **NCLC 18**

Lind, Jakov CLC 1, 2, 4, 27, 82
See also Landwirth, Heinz
See also CAAS 4

Lindbergh, Anne (Spencer) Morrow
1906- .... **CLC 82; DAM NOV**
See also CA 17-20R; CANR 16, 73; MTCW
1, 2; SATA 33

Lindsay, David 1878-1945 .... **TCLC 15**
See also CA 113

Lindsay, (Nicholas) Vachel
1879-1931 . **TCLC 17; DA; DAC; DAM
MST, POET; PC 23; WLC**
See also CA 114; 135; CANR 79; CDALB
1865-1917; DA3; DLB 54; SATA 40

Linke-Poot
See Doeblin, Alfred
Linney, Romulus 1930- .... **CLC 51**
See also CA 1-4R; CANR 40, 44, 79
Linton, Eliza Lynn 1822-1898 .... **NCLC 41**
See also DLB 18
Li Po 701-763 .... **CMLC 2; PC 29**
Lipsius, Justus 1547-1606 .... **LC 16**
Lipsyte, Robert (Michael) 1938- ..... **CLC 21;**
DA; DAC; DAM MST, NOV
See also AAYA 7; CA 17-20R; CANR 8,
57; CLR 23; JRDA; MAICYA; SATA 5,
68, 113
Lish, Gordon (Jay) 1934- ... **CLC 45; SSC 18**
See also CA 113; 117; CANR 79; DLB 130;
INT 117
Lispector, Clarice 1925(?)-1977 .... **CLC 43;**
HLCS 2; SSC 34
See also CA 139; 116; CANR 71; DLB 113;
HW 2
Littell, Robert 1935(?)- .... **CLC 42**
See also CA 109; 112; CANR 64
Little, Malcolm 1925-1965
See Malcolm X
See also BW 1, 3; CA 125; 111; CANR 82;
DA; DAB; DAC; DAM MST, MULT;
DA3; MTCW 1, 2
Littlewit, Humphrey Gent.
See Lovecraft, H(oward) P(hillips)
Litwos
See Sienkiewicz, Henryk (Adam Alexander
Pius)
Liu, E 1857-1909 .... **TCLC 15**
See also CA 115
Lively, Penelope (Margaret) 1933- .. **CLC 32,**
50; DAM NOV
See also CA 41-44R; CANR 29, 67, 79;
CLR 7; DLB 14, 161, 207; JRDA; MAI-
CYA; MTCW 1, 2; SATA 7, 60, 101
Livesay, Dorothy (Kathleen) 1909- ... **CLC 4,**
15, 79; DAC; DAM MST, POET
See also AITN 2; CA 25-28R; CAAS 8;
CANR 36, 67; DLB 68; MTCW 1
Livy c. 59B.C.-c. 17 .... **CMLC 11**
See also DLB 211
Lizardi, Jose Joaquin Fernandez de
1776-1827 .... **NCLC 30**
Llewellyn, Richard
See Llewellyn Lloyd, Richard Dafydd Viv-
ian
See also DLB 15
Llewellyn Lloyd, Richard Dafydd Vivian
1906-1983 .... **CLC 7, 80**
See also Llewellyn, Richard
See also CA 53-56; 111; CANR 7, 71;
SATA 11; SATA-Obit 37
Llosa, (Jorge) Mario (Pedro) Vargas
See Vargas Llosa, (Jorge) Mario (Pedro)
Lloyd, Manda
See Mander, (Mary) Jane
Lloyd Webber, Andrew 1948-
See Webber, Andrew Lloyd
See also AAYA 1; CA 116; 149; DAM
DRAM; SATA 56
Llull, Ramon c. 1235-c. 1316 .... **CMLC 12**
Lobb, Ebenezer
See Upward, Allen
Locke, Alain (Le Roy) 1886-1954 . **TCLC 43;**
BLCS
See also BW 1, 3; CA 106; 124; CANR 79;
DLB 51
Locke, John 1632-1704 .... **LC 7, 35**
See also DLB 101
Locke-Elliott, Sumner
See Elliott, Sumner Locke
Lockhart, John Gibson 1794-1854 .. **NCLC 6**
See also DLB 110, 116, 144

Lodge, David (John) 1935- ... **CLC 36; DAM**
POP
See also BEST 90:1; CA 17-20R; CANR
19, 53; DLB 14, 194; INT CANR-19;
MTCW 1, 2
Lodge, Thomas 1558-1625 .... **LC 41**
Lodge, Thomas 1558-1625 .... **LC 41**
See also DLB 172
Loennbohm, Armas Eino Leopold 1878-1926
See Leino, Eino
See also CA 123
Loewinsohn, Ron(ald William)
1937- .... **CLC 52**
See also CA 25-28R; CANR 71
Logan, Jake
See Smith, Martin Cruz
Logan, John (Burton) 1923-1987 .... **CLC 5**
See also CA 77-80; 124; CANR 45; DLB 5
Lo Kuan-chung 1330(?)-1400(?) .... **LC 12**
Lombard, Nap
See Johnson, Pamela Hansford
London, Jack TCLC 9, 15, 39; SSC 4; WLC
See also London, John Griffith
See also AAYA 13; AITN 2; CDALB 1865-
1917; DLB 8, 12, 78, 212; SATA 18
London, John Griffith 1876-1916
See London, Jack
See also CA 110; 119; CANR 73; DA;
DAB; DAC; DAM MST, NOV; DA3;
JRDA; MAICYA; MTCW 1, 2
Long, Emmett
See Leonard, Elmore (John, Jr.)
Longbaugh, Harry
See Goldman, William (W.)
Longfellow, Henry Wadsworth
1807-1882 .... **NCLC 2, 45; DA; DAB;**
DAC; DAM MST, POET; PC 30;
WLCS
See also CDALB 1640-1865; DA3; DLB 1,
59; SATA 19
Longinus c. 1st cent. - .... **CMLC 27**
See also DLB 176
Longley, Michael 1939- .... **CLC 29**
See also CA 102; DLB 40
Longus fl. c. 2nd cent. - .... **CMLC 7**
Longway, A. Hugh
See Lang, Andrew
Lonnrot, Elias 1802-1884 .... **NCLC 53**
Lopate, Phillip 1943- .... **CLC 29**
See also CA 97-100; CANR 88; DLBY 80;
INT 97-100
Lopez Portillo (y Pacheco), Jose
1920- .... **CLC 46**
See also CA 129; HW 1
Lopez y Fuentes, Gregorio
1897(?)-1966 .... **CLC 32**
See also CA 131; HW 1
Lorca, Federico Garcia
See Garcia Lorca, Federico
Lord, Bette Bao 1938- .... **CLC 23**
See also BEST 90:3; CA 107; CANR 41,
79; INT 107; SATA 58
Lord Auch
See Bataille, Georges
Lord Byron
See Byron, George Gordon (Noel)
Lorde, Audre (Geraldine)
1934-1992 ... **CLC 18, 71; BLC 2; DAM**
MULT, POET; PC 12
See also BW 1, 3; CA 25-28R; 142; CANR
16, 26, 46, 82; DA3; DLB 41; MTCW 1,
2
Lord Houghton
See Milnes, Richard Monckton
Lord Jeffrey
See Jeffrey, Francis

Lorenzini, Carlo 1826-1890
See Collodi, Carlo
See also MAICYA; SATA 29, 100
Lorenzo, Heberto Padilla
See Padilla (Lorenzo), Heberto
Loris
See Hofmannsthal, Hugo von
Loti, Pierre TCLC 11
See also Viaud, (Louis Marie) Julien
See also DLB 123
Lou, Henri
See Andreas-Salome, Lou
Louie, David Wong 1954- .... **CLC 70**
See also CA 139
Louis, Father M.
See Merton, Thomas
Lovecraft, H(oward) P(hillips)
1890-1937 ...... **TCLC 4, 22; DAM POP;**
SSC 3
See also AAYA 14; CA 104; 133; DA3;
MTCW 1, 2
Lovelace, Earl 1935- .... **CLC 51**
See also BW 2; CA 77-80; CANR 41, 72;
DLB 125; MTCW 1
Lovelace, Richard 1618-1657 .... **LC 24**
See also DLB 131
Lowell, Amy 1874-1925 .... **TCLC 1, 8; DAM**
POET; PC 13
See also CA 104; 151; DLB 54, 140;
MTCW 2
Lowell, James Russell 1819-1891 .... **NCLC 2**
See also CDALB 1640-1865; DLB 1, 11,
64, 79, 189
Lowell, Robert (Traill Spence, Jr.)
1917-1977 .... **CLC 1, 2, 3, 4, 5, 8, 9, 11,**
15, 37, 124; DA; DAB; DAC; DAM
MST, NOV; PC 3; WLC
See also CA 9-12R; 73-76; CABS 2; CANR
26, 60; CDALBS; DA3; DLB 5, 169;
MTCW 1, 2
Lowenthal, Michael (Francis)
1969- .... **CLC 119**
See also CA 150
Lowndes, Marie Adelaide (Belloc)
1868-1947 .... **TCLC 12**
See also CA 107; DLB 70
Lowry, (Clarence) Malcolm
1909-1957 .... **TCLC 6, 40; SSC 31**
See also CA 105; 131; CANR 62; CDBLB
1945-1960; DLB 15; MTCW 1, 2
Lowry, Mina Gertrude 1882-1966
See Loy, Mina
See also CA 113
Loxsmith, John
See Brunner, John (Kilian Houston)
Loy, Mina CLC 28; DAM POET; PC 16
See also Lowry, Mina Gertrude
See also DLB 4, 54
Loyson-Bridet
See Schwob, Marcel (Mayer Andre)
Lucan 39-65 .... **CMLC 33**
See also DLB 211
Lucas, Craig 1951- .... **CLC 64**
See also CA 137; CANR 71
Lucas, E(dward) V(errall)
1868-1938 .... **TCLC 73**
See also CA 176; DLB 98, 149, 153; SATA
20
Lucas, George 1944- .... **CLC 16**
See also AAYA 1, 23; CA 77-80; CANR
30; SATA 56
Lucas, Hans
See Godard, Jean-Luc
Lucas, Victoria
See Plath, Sylvia
Lucian c. 120-c. 180 .... **CMLC 32**
See also DLB 176
Ludlam, Charles 1943-1987 .... **CLC 46, 50**
See also CA 85-88; 122; CANR 72, 86

Ludlum, Robert 1927- .... **CLC 22, 43; DAM NOV, POP**
See also AAYA 10; BEST 89:1, 90:3; CA 33-36R; CANR 25, 41, 68; DA3; DLBY 82; MTCW 1, 2

Ludwig, Ken CLC 60

Ludwig, Otto 1813-1865 .... **NCLC 4**
See also DLB 129

Lugones, Leopoldo 1874-1938 ...... **TCLC 15; HLCS 2**
See also CA 116; 131; HW 1

Lu Hsun 1881-1936 .... **TCLC 3; SSC 20**
See also Shu-Jen, Chou

Lukacs, George CLC 24
See also Lukacs, Gyorgy (Szegeny von)

Lukacs, Gyorgy (Szegeny von) 1885-1971
See Lukacs, George
See also CA 101; 29-32R; CANR 62; MTCW 2

Luke, Peter (Ambrose Cyprian) 1919-1995 .... **CLC 38**
See also CA 81-84; 147; CANR 72; DLB 13

Lunar, Dennis
See Mungo, Raymond

Lurie, Alison 1926- .... **CLC 4, 5, 18, 39**
See also CA 1-4R; CANR 2, 17, 50, 88; DLB 2; MTCW 1; SATA 46, 112

Lustig, Arnost 1926- .... **CLC 56**
See also AAYA 3; CA 69-72; CANR 47; SATA 56

Luther, Martin 1483-1546 .... **LC 9, 37**
See also DLB 179

Luxemburg, Rosa 1870(?)-1919 ..... **TCLC 63**
See also CA 118

Luzi, Mario 1914- .... **CLC 13**
See also CA 61-64; CANR 9, 70; DLB 128

Lyly, John 1554(?)-1606 .... **LC 41; DAM DRAM; DC 7**
See also DLB 62, 167

L'Ymagier
See Gourmont, Remy (-Marie-Charles) de

Lynch, B. Suarez
See Bioy Casares, Adolfo; Borges, Jorge Luis

Lynch, B. Suarez
See Bioy Casares, Adolfo

Lynch, David (K.) 1946- .... **CLC 66**
See also CA 124; 129

Lynch, James
See Andreyev, Leonid (Nikolaevich)

Lynch Davis, B.
See Bioy Casares, Adolfo; Borges, Jorge Luis

Lyndsay, Sir David 1490-1555 .... **LC 20**

Lynn, Kenneth S(chuyler) 1923- ...... **CLC 50**
See also CA 1-4R; CANR 3, 27, 65

Lynx
See West, Rebecca

Lyons, Marcus
See Blish, James (Benjamin)

Lyre, Pinchbeck
See Sassoon, Siegfried (Lorraine)

Lytle, Andrew (Nelson) 1902-1995 ... **CLC 22**
See also CA 9-12R; 150; CANR 70; DLB 6; DLBY 95

Lyttelton, George 1709-1773 .... **LC 10**

Maas, Peter 1929- .... **CLC 29**
See also CA 93-96; INT 93-96; MTCW 2

Macaulay, Rose 1881-1958 .... **TCLC 7, 44**
See also CA 104; DLB 36

Macaulay, Thomas Babington 1800-1859 .... **NCLC 42**
See also CDBLB 1832-1890; DLB 32, 55

MacBeth, George (Mann) 1932-1992 .... **CLC 2, 5, 9**
See also CA 25-28R; 136; CANR 61, 66; DLB 40; MTCW 1; SATA 4; SATA-Obit 70

MacCaig, Norman (Alexander) 1910- .... **CLC 36; DAB; DAM POET**
See also CA 9-12R; CANR 3, 34; DLB 27

MacCarthy, Sir(Charles Otto) Desmond 1877-1952 .... **TCLC 36**
See also CA 167

MacDiarmid, Hugh CLC 2, 4, 11, 19, 63; PC 9
See also Grieve, C(hristopher) M(urray)
See also CDBLB 1945-1960; DLB 20

MacDonald, Anson
See Heinlein, Robert A(nson)

Macdonald, Cynthia 1928- .... **CLC 13, 19**
See also CA 49-52; CANR 4, 44; DLB 105

MacDonald, George 1824-1905 .... **TCLC 9**
See also CA 106; 137; CANR 80; DLB 18, 163, 178; MAICYA; SATA 33, 100

Macdonald, John
See Millar, Kenneth

MacDonald, John D(ann) 1916-1986 .. **CLC 3, 27, 44; DAM NOV, POP**
See also CA 1-4R; 121; CANR 1, 19, 60; DLB 8; DLBY 86; MTCW 1, 2

Macdonald, John Ross
See Millar, Kenneth

Macdonald, Ross CLC 1, 2, 3, 14, 34, 41
See also Millar, Kenneth
See also DLBD 6

MacDougal, John
See Blish, James (Benjamin)

MacDougal, John
See Blish, James (Benjamin)

MacEwen, Gwendolyn (Margaret) 1941-1987 .... **CLC 13, 55**
See also CA 9-12R; 124; CANR 7, 22; DLB 53; SATA 50; SATA-Obit 55

Macha, Karel Hynek 1810-1846 .... **NCLC 46**

Machado (y Ruiz), Antonio 1875-1939 .... **TCLC 3**
See also CA 104; 174; DLB 108; HW 2

Machado de Assis, Joaquim Maria 1839-1908 ..... **TCLC 10; BLC 2; HLCS 2; SSC 24**
See also CA 107; 153; CANR 91

Machen, Arthur TCLC 4; SSC 20
See also Jones, Arthur Llewellyn
See also CA 179; DLB 36, 156, 178

Machiavelli, Niccolo 1469-1527 ..... **LC 8, 36; DA; DAB; DAC; DAM MST; WLCS**

MacInnes, Colin 1914-1976 .... **CLC 4, 23**
See also CA 69-72; 65-68; CANR 21; DLB 14; MTCW 1, 2

MacInnes, Helen (Clark) 1907-1985 .... **CLC 27, 39; DAM POP**
See also CA 1-4R; 117; CANR 1, 28, 58; DLB 87; MTCW 1, 2; SATA 22; SATA-Obit 44

Mackenzie, Compton (Edward Montague) 1883-1972 .... **CLC 18**
See also CA 21-22; 37-40R; CAP 2; DLB 34, 100

Mackenzie, Henry 1745-1831 .... **NCLC 41**
See also DLB 39

Mackintosh, Elizabeth 1896(?)-1952
See Tey, Josephine
See also CA 110

MacLaren, James
See Grieve, C(hristopher) M(urray)

Mac Laverty, Bernard 1942- .... **CLC 31**
See also CA 116; 118; CANR 43, 88; INT 118

MacLean, Alistair (Stuart) 1922(?)-1987 .. **CLC 3, 13, 50, 63; DAM POP**
See also CA 57-60; 121; CANR 28, 61; MTCW 1; SATA 23; SATA-Obit 50

Maclean, Norman (Fitzroy) 1902-1990 .... **CLC 78; DAM POP; SSC 13**
See also CA 102; 132; CANR 49; DLB 206

MacLeish, Archibald 1892-1982 ... **CLC 3, 8, 14, 68; DAM POET**
See also CA 9-12R; 106; CANR 33, 63; CDALBS; DLB 4, 7, 45; DLBY 82; MTCW 1, 2

MacLennan, (John) Hugh 1907-1990 . **CLC 2, 14, 92; DAC; DAM MST**
See also CA 5-8R; 142; CANR 33; DLB 68; MTCW 1, 2

MacLeod, Alistair 1936- .... **CLC 56; DAC; DAM MST**
See also CA 123; DLB 60; MTCW 2

Macleod, Fiona
See Sharp, William

MacNeice, (Frederick) Louis 1907-1963 .... **CLC 1, 4, 10, 53; DAB; DAM POET**
See also CA 85-88; CANR 61; DLB 10, 20; MTCW 1, 2

MacNeill, Dand
See Fraser, George MacDonald

Macpherson, James 1736-1796 .... **LC 29**
See also Ossian
See also DLB 109

Macpherson, (Jean) Jay 1931- .... **CLC 14**
See also CA 5-8R; CANR 90; DLB 53

MacShane, Frank 1927-1999 .... **CLC 39**
See also CA 9-12R; 186; CANR 3, 33, DLB 111

Macumber, Mari
See Sandoz, Mari(e Susette)

Madach, Imre 1823-1864 .... **NCLC 19**

Madden, (Jerry) David 1933- .... **CLC 5, 15**
See also CA 1-4R; CAAS 3; CANR 4, 45; DLB 6; MTCW 1

Maddern, Al(an)
See Ellison, Harlan (Jay)

Madhubuti, Haki R. 1942- . **CLC 6, 73; BLC 2; DAM MULT, POET; PC 5**
See also Lee, Don L.
See also BW 2, 3; CA 73-76; CANR 24, 51, 73; DLB 5, 41; DLBD 8; MTCW 2

Maepenn, Hugh
See Kuttner, Henry

Maepenn, K. H.
See Kuttner, Henry

Maeterlinck, Maurice 1862-1949 ... **TCLC 3; DAM DRAM**
See also CA 104; 136; CANR 80; DLB 192; SATA 66

Maginn, William 1794-1842 .... **NCLC 8**
See also DLB 110, 159

Mahapatra, Jayanta 1928- .... **CLC 33; DAM MULT**
See also CA 73-76; CAAS 9; CANR 15, 33, 66, 87

Mahfouz, Naguib (Abdel Aziz Al-Sabilgi) 1911(?)-
See Mahfuz, Najib
See also BEST 89:2; CA 128; CANR 55; DAM NOV; DA3; MTCW 1, 2

Mahfuz, Najib CLC 52, 55
See also Mahfouz, Naguib (Abdel Aziz Al-Sabilgi)
See also DLBY 88

Mahon, Derek 1941- .... **CLC 27**
See also CA 113; 128; CANR 88; DLB 40

Mailer, Norman 1923- ... **CLC 1, 2, 3, 4, 5, 8, 11, 14, 28, 39, 74, 111; DA; DAB; DAC; DAM MST, NOV, POP**
See also AAYA 31; AITN 2; CA 9-12R; CABS 1; CANR 28, 74, 77; CDALB 1968-1988; DA3; DLB 2, 16, 28, 185; DLBD 3; DLBY 80, 83; MTCW 1, 2

Maillet, Antonine 1929- .. **CLC 54, 118; DAC**
See also CA 115; 120; CANR 46, 74, 77; DLB 60; INT 120; MTCW 2

Mais, Roger 1905-1955 .... **TCLC 8**
See also BW 1, 3; CA 105; 124; CANR 82; DLB 125; MTCW 1

Maistre, Joseph de 1753-1821 .... **NCLC 37**

Maitland, Frederic 1850-1906 .... **TCLC 65**

Maitland, Sara (Louise) 1950- .... **CLC 49**
See also CA 69-72; CANR 13, 59

Major, Clarence 1936- . **CLC 3, 19, 48; BLC 2; DAM MULT**
See also BW 2, 3; CA 21-24R; CAAS 6; CANR 13, 25, 53, 82; DLB 33

Major, Kevin (Gerald) 1949- . **CLC 26; DAC**
See also AAYA 16; CA 97-100; CANR 21, 38; CLR 11; DLB 60; INT CANR-21; JRDA; MAICYA; SATA 32, 82

Maki, James
See Ozu, Yasujiro

Malabaila, Damiano
See Levi, Primo

Malamud, Bernard 1914-1986 .. **CLC 1, 2, 3, 5, 8, 9, 11, 18, 27, 44, 78, 85; DA; DAB; DAC; DAM MST, NOV, POP; SSC 15; WLC**
See also AAYA 16; CA 5-8R; 118; CABS 1; CANR 28, 62; CDALB 1941-1968; DA3; DLB 2, 28, 152; DLBY 80, 86; MTCW 1, 2

Malan, Herman
See Bosman, Herman Charles; Bosman, Herman Charles

Malaparte, Curzio 1898-1957 .... **TCLC 52**

Malcolm, Dan
See Silverberg, Robert

Malcolm X CLC 82, 117; BLC 2; WLCS
See also Little, Malcolm

Malherbe, Francois de 1555-1628 .... **LC 5**

Mallarme, Stephane 1842-1898 ...... **NCLC 4, 41; DAM POET; PC 4**

Mallet-Joris, Francoise 1930- .... **CLC 11**
See also CA 65-68; CANR 17; DLB 83

Malley, Ern
See McAuley, James Phillip

Mallowan, Agatha Christie
See Christie, Agatha (Mary Clarissa)

Maloff, Saul 1922- .... **CLC 5**
See also CA 33-36R

Malone, Louis
See MacNeice, (Frederick) Louis

Malone, Michael (Christopher)
1942- .... **CLC 43**
See also CA 77-80; CANR 14, 32, 57

Malory, (Sir) Thomas
1410(?)-1471(?) .... **LC 11; DA; DAB; DAC; DAM MST; WLCS**
See also CDBLB Before 1660; DLB 146; SATA 59; SATA-Brief 33

Malouf, (George Joseph) David
1934- .... **CLC 28, 86**
See also CA 124; CANR 50, 76; MTCW 2

Malraux, (Georges-)Andre
1901-1976 .... **CLC 1, 4, 9, 13, 15, 57; DAM NOV**
See also CA 21-22; 69-72; CANR 34, 58; CAP 2; DA3; DLB 72; MTCW 1, 2

Malzberg, Barry N(athaniel) 1939- ... **CLC 7**
See also CA 61-64; CAAS 4; CANR 16; DLB 8

Mamet, David (Alan) 1947- .. **CLC 9, 15, 34, 46, 91; DAM DRAM; DC 4**
See also AAYA 3; CA 81-84; CABS 3; CANR 15, 41, 67, 72; DA3; DLB 7; MTCW 1, 2

Mamoulian, Rouben (Zachary)
1897-1987 .... **CLC 16**
See also CA 25-28R; 124; CANR 85

Mandelstam, Osip (Emilievich)
1891(?)-1938(?) .... **TCLC 2, 6; PC 14**
See also CA 104; 150; MTCW 2

Mander, (Mary) Jane 1877-1949 ... **TCLC 31**
See also CA 162

Mandeville, John fl. 1350- .... **CMLC 19**
See also DLB 146

Mandiargues, Andre Pieyre de CLC 41
See also Pieyre de Mandiargues, Andre
See also DLB 83

Mandrake, Ethel Belle
See Thurman, Wallace (Henry)

Mangan, James Clarence
1803-1849 .... **NCLC 27**

Maniere, J.-E.
See Giraudoux, (Hippolyte) Jean

Mankiewicz, Herman (Jacob)
1897-1953 .... **TCLC 85**
See also CA 120; 169; DLB 26

Manley, (Mary) Delariviere
1672(?)-1724 .... **LC 1, 42**
See also DLB 39, 80

Mann, Abel
See Creasey, John

Mann, Emily 1952- .... **DC 7**
See also CA 130; CANR 55

Mann, (Luiz) Heinrich 1871-1950 ... **TCLC 9**
See also CA 106; 164; 181; DLB 66, 118

Mann, (Paul) Thomas 1875-1955 ... **TCLC 2, 8, 14, 21, 35, 44, 60; DA; DAB; DAC; DAM MST, NOV; SSC 5; WLC**
See also CA 104; 128; DA3; DLB 66; MTCW 1, 2

Mannheim, Karl 1893-1947 .... **TCLC 65**

Manning, David
See Faust, Frederick (Schiller)

Manning, Frederic 1887(?)-1935 ... **TCLC 25**
See also CA 124

Manning, Olivia 1915-1980 .... **CLC 5, 19**
See also CA 5-8R; 101; CANR 29; MTCW 1

Mano, D. Keith 1942- .... **CLC 2, 10**
See also CA 25-28R; CAAS 6; CANR 26, 57; DLB 6

Mansfield, Katherine TCLC 2, 8, 39; DAB; SSC 9, 23, 38; WLC
See also Beauchamp, Kathleen Mansfield
See also DLB 162

Manso, Peter 1940- .... **CLC 39**
See also CA 29-32R; CANR 44

Mantecon, Juan Jimenez
See Jimenez (Mantecon), Juan Ramon

Manton, Peter
See Creasey, John

Man Without a Spleen, A
See Chekhov, Anton (Pavlovich)

Manzoni, Alessandro 1785-1873 .... **NCLC 29**

Map, Walter 1140-1209 .... **CMLC 32**

Mapu, Abraham (ben Jekutiel)
1808-1867 .... **NCLC 18**

Mara, Sally
See Queneau, Raymond

Marat, Jean Paul 1743-1793 .... **LC 10**

Marcel, Gabriel Honore 1889-1973 . **CLC 15**
See also CA 102; 45-48; MTCW 1, 2

March, William 1893-1954 .... **TCLC 96**

Marchbanks, Samuel
See Davies, (William) Robertson

Marchi, Giacomo
See Bassani, Giorgio

Margulies, Donald CLC 76
See also DLB 228

Marie de France c. 12th cent. - ..... **CMLC 8; PC 22**
See also DLB 208

Marie de l'Incarnation 1599-1672 ...... **LC 10**

Marier, Captain Victor
See Griffith, D(avid Lewelyn) W(ark)

Mariner, Scott
See Pohl, Frederik

Marinetti, Filippo Tommaso
1876-1944 .... **TCLC 10**
See also CA 107; DLB 114

Marivaux, Pierre Carlet de Chamblain de
1688-1763 .... **LC 4; DC 7**

Markandaya, Kamala CLC 8, 38
See also Taylor, Kamala (Purnaiya)

Markfield, Wallace 1926- .... **CLC 8**
See also CA 69-72; CAAS 3; DLB 2, 28

Markham, Edwin 1852-1940 .... **TCLC 47**
See also CA 160; DLB 54, 186

Markham, Robert
See Amis, Kingsley (William)

Marks, J
See Highwater, Jamake (Mamake)

Marks-Highwater, J
See Highwater, Jamake (Mamake)

Markson, David M(errill) 1927- .... **CLC 67**
See also CA 49-52; CANR 1, 91

Marley, Bob CLC 17
See also Marley, Robert Nesta

Marley, Robert Nesta 1945-1981
See Marley, Bob
See also CA 107; 103

Marlowe, Christopher 1564-1593 ...... **LC 22, 47; DA; DAB; DAC; DAM DRAM, MST; DC 1; WLC**
See also CDBLB Before 1660; DA3; DLB 62

Marlowe, Stephen 1928-
See Queen, Ellery
See also CA 13-16R; CANR 6, 55

Marmontel, Jean-Francois 1723-1799 .. **LC 2**

Marquand, John P(hillips)
1893-1960 .... **CLC 2, 10**
See also CA 85-88; CANR 73; DLB 9, 102; MTCW 2

Marques, Rene 1919-1979 ..... **CLC 96; DAM MULT; HLC 2**
See also CA 97-100; 85-88; CANR 78; DLB 113; HW 1, 2

Marquez, Gabriel (Jose) Garcia
See Garcia Marquez, Gabriel (Jose)

Marquis, Don(ald Robert Perry)
1878-1937 .... **TCLC 7**
See also CA 104; 166; DLB 11, 25

Marric, J. J.
See Creasey, John

Marryat, Frederick 1792-1848 .... **NCLC 3**
See also DLB 21, 163

Marsden, James
See Creasey, John

Marsh, (Edith) Ngaio 1899-1982 .... **CLC 7, 53; DAM POP**
See also CA 9-12R; CANR 6, 58; DLB 77; MTCW 1, 2

Marshall, Garry 1934- .... **CLC 17**
See also AAYA 3; CA 111; SATA 60

Marshall, Paule 1929- .. **CLC 27, 72; BLC 3; DAM MULT; SSC 3**
See also BW 2, 3; CA 77-80; CANR 25, 73; DA3; DLB 33, 157, 227; MTCW 1, 2

Marshallik
See Zangwill, Israel

Marsten, Richard
See Hunter, Evan

Marston, John 1576-1634 .... **LC 33; DAM DRAM**
See also DLB 58, 172

Martha, Henry
See Harris, Mark

Marti (y Perez), Jose (Julian)
1853-1895 ...... **NCLC 63; DAM MULT; HLC 2**
See also HW 2

Martial c. 40-c. 104 .... **CMLC 35; PC 10**
See also DLB 211

Martin, Ken
See Hubbard, L(afayette) Ron(ald)

Martin, Richard
See Creasey, John

Martin, Steve 1945- .... **CLC 30**
See also CA 97-100; CANR 30; MTCW 1

Martin, Valerie 1948- .... **CLC 89**
See also BEST 90:2; CA 85-88; CANR 49, 89

Martin, Violet Florence
1862-1915 .... **TCLC 51**

Martin, Webber
See Silverberg, Robert

Martindale, Patrick Victor
See White, Patrick (Victor Martindale)

Martin du Gard, Roger
1881-1958 .... **TCLC 24**
See also CA 118; DLB 65

Martineau, Harriet 1802-1876 .... **NCLC 26**
See also DLB 21, 55, 159, 163, 166, 190; YABC 2

Martines, Julia
See O'Faolain, Julia

Martinez, Enrique Gonzalez
See Gonzalez Martinez, Enrique

Martinez, Jacinto Benavente y
See Benavente (y Martinez), Jacinto

Martinez Ruiz, Jose 1873-1967
See Azorin; Ruiz, Jose Martinez
See also CA 93-96; HW 1

Martinez Sierra, Gregorio
1881-1947 .... **TCLC 6**
See also CA 115

Martinez Sierra, Maria (de la O'LeJarraga)
1874-1974 .... **TCLC 6**
See also CA 115

Martinsen, Martin
See Follett, Ken(neth Martin)

Martinson, Harry (Edmund)
1904-1978 .... **CLC 14**
See also CA 77-80; CANR 34

Marut, Ret
See Traven, B.

Marut, Robert
See Traven, B.

Marvell, Andrew 1621-1678 .. **LC 4, 43; DA; DAB; DAC; DAM MST, POET; PC 10; WLC**
See also CDBLB 1660-1789; DLB 131

Marx, Karl (Heinrich) 1818-1883 . **NCLC 17**
See also DLB 129

Masaoka Shiki TCLC 18
See also Masaoka Tsunenori

Masaoka Tsunenori 1867-1902
See Masaoka Shiki
See also CA 117

Masefield, John (Edward)
1878-1967 ..... **CLC 11, 47; DAM POET**
See also CA 19-20; 25-28R; CANR 33; CAP 2; CDBLB 1890-1914; DLB 10, 19, 153, 160; MTCW 1, 2; SATA 19

Maso, Carole 19(?)- .... **CLC 44**
See also CA 170

Mason, Bobbie Ann 1940- ... **CLC 28, 43, 82; SSC 4**
See also AAYA 5; CA 53-56; CANR 11, 31, 58, 83; CDALBS; DA3; DLB 173; DLBY 87; INT CANR-31; MTCW 1, 2

Mason, Ernst
See Pohl, Frederik

Mason, Lee W.
See Malzberg, Barry N(athaniel)

Mason, Nick 1945- .... **CLC 35**

Mason, Tally
See Derleth, August (William)

Mass, William
See Gibson, William

Master Lao
See Lao Tzu

Masters, Edgar Lee 1868-1950 .... **TCLC 2, 25; DA; DAC; DAM MST, POET; PC 1; WLCS**
See also CA 104; 133; CDALB 1865-1917; DLB 54; MTCW 1, 2

Masters, Hilary 1928- .... **CLC 48**
See also CA 25-28R; CANR 13, 47

Mastrosimone, William 19(?)- .... **CLC 36**
See also CA 186

Mathe, Albert
See Camus, Albert

Mather, Cotton 1663-1728 .... **LC 38**
See also CDALB 1640-1865; DLB 24, 30, 140

Mather, Increase 1639-1723 .... **LC 38**
See also DLB 24

Matheson, Richard Burton 1926- .... **CLC 37**
See also AAYA 31; CA 97-100; CANR 88; DLB 8, 44; INT 97-100

Mathews, Harry 1930- .... **CLC 6, 52**
See also CA 21-24R; CAAS 6; CANR 18, 40

Mathews, John Joseph 1894-1979 .. **CLC 84; DAM MULT**
See also CA 19-20; 142; CANR 45; CAP 2; DLB 175; NNAL

Mathias, Roland (Glyn) 1915- .... **CLC 45**
See also CA 97-100; CANR 19, 41; DLB 27

Matsuo Basho 1644-1694 .... **PC 3**
See also DAM POET

Mattheson, Rodney
See Creasey, John

Matthews, (James) Brander
1852-1929 .... **TCLC 95**
See also DLB 71, 78; DLBD 13

Matthews, Greg 1949- .... **CLC 45**
See also CA 135

Matthews, William (Procter, III)
1942-1997 .... **CLC 40**
See also CA 29-32R; 162; CAAS 18; CANR 12, 57; DLB 5

Matthias, John (Edward) 1941- .... **CLC 9**
See also CA 33-36R; CANR 56

Matthiessen, Peter 1927- ... **CLC 5, 7, 11, 32, 64; DAM NOV**
See also AAYA 6; BEST 90:4; CA 9-12R; CANR 21, 50, 73; DA3; DLB 6, 173; MTCW 1, 2; SATA 27

Maturin, Charles Robert
1780(?)-1824 .... **NCLC 6**
See also DLB 178

Matute (Ausejo), Ana Maria 1925- .. **CLC 11**
See also CA 89-92; MTCW 1

Maugham, W. S.
See Maugham, W(illiam) Somerset

Maugham, W(illiam) Somerset
1874-1965 ... **CLC 1, 11, 15, 67, 93; DA; DAB; DAC; DAM DRAM, MST, NOV; SSC 8; WLC**
See also CA 5-8R; 25-28R; CANR 40; CD-BLB 1914-1945; DA3; DLB 10, 36, 77, 100, 162, 195; MTCW 1, 2; SATA 54

Maugham, William Somerset
See Maugham, W(illiam) Somerset

Maupassant, (Henri Rene Albert) Guy de
1850-1893 . **NCLC 1, 42, 83; DA; DAB; DAC; DAM MST; SSC 1; WLC**
See also DA3; DLB 123

Maupin, Armistead 1944- ..... **CLC 95; DAM POP**
See also CA 125; 130; CANR 58; DA3; INT 130; MTCW 2

Maurhut, Richard
See Traven, B.

Mauriac, Claude 1914-1996 .... **CLC 9**
See also CA 89-92; 152; DLB 83

Mauriac, Francois (Charles)
1885-1970 .... **CLC 4, 9, 56; SSC 24**
See also CA 25-28; CAP 2; DLB 65; MTCW 1, 2

Mavor, Osborne Henry 1888-1951
See Bridie, James
See also CA 104

Maxwell, William (Keepers, Jr.)
1908- .... **CLC 19**
See also CA 93-96; CANR 54; DLBY 80; INT 93-96

May, Elaine 1932- .... **CLC 16**
See also CA 124; 142; DLB 44

Mayakovski, Vladimir (Vladimirovich)
1893-1930 .... **TCLC 4, 18**
See also CA 104; 158; MTCW 2

Mayhew, Henry 1812-1887 .... **NCLC 31**
See also DLB 18, 55, 190

Mayle, Peter 1939(?)- .... **CLC 89**
See also CA 139; CANR 64

Maynard, Joyce 1953- .... **CLC 23**
See also CA 111; 129; CANR 64

Mayne, William (James Carter)
1928- .... **CLC 12**
See also AAYA 20; CA 9-12R; CANR 37, 80; CLR 25; JRDA; MAICYA; SAAS 11; SATA 6, 68

Mayo, Jim
See L'Amour, Louis (Dearborn)

Maysles, Albert 1926- .... **CLC 16**
See also CA 29-32R

Maysles, David 1932- .... **CLC 16**

Mazer, Norma Fox 1931- .... **CLC 26**
See also AAYA 5; CA 69-72; CANR 12, 32, 66; CLR 23; JRDA; MAICYA; SAAS 1; SATA 24, 67, 105

Mazzini, Guiseppe 1805-1872 .... **NCLC 34**

McAlmon, Robert (Menzies)
1895-1956 .... **TCLC 97**
See also CA 107; 168; DLB 4, 45; DLBD 15

McAuley, James Phillip 1917-1976 .. **CLC 45**
See also CA 97-100

McBain, Ed
See Hunter, Evan

McBrien, William (Augustine)
1930- .... **CLC 44**
See also CA 107; CANR 90

McCabe, Patrick 1955- .... **CLC 133**
See also CA 130; CANR 50, 90; DLB 194

McCaffrey, Anne (Inez) 1926- .... **CLC 17; DAM NOV, POP**
See also AAYA 6, 34; AITN 2; BEST 89:2; CA 25-28R; CANR 15, 35, 55; CLR 49; DA3; DLB 8; JRDA; MAICYA; MTCW 1, 2; SAAS 11; SATA 8, 70, 116

McCall, Nathan 1955(?)- .... **CLC 86**
See also BW 3; CA 146; CANR 88

McCann, Arthur
See Campbell, John W(ood, Jr.)

McCann, Edson
See Pohl, Frederik

McCarthy, Charles, Jr. 1933-
See McCarthy, Cormac
See also CANR 42, 69; DAM POP; DA3;
MTCW 2

McCarthy, Cormac 1933- ...... CLC 4, 57, 59,
101
See also McCarthy, Charles, Jr.
See also DLB 6, 143; MTCW 2

McCarthy, Mary (Therese)
1912-1989 .. CLC 1, 3, 5, 14, 24, 39, 59;
SSC 24
See also CA 5-8R; 129; CANR 16, 50, 64;
DA3; DLB 2; DLBY 81; INT CANR-16;
MTCW 1, 2

McCartney, (James) Paul 1942- . CLC 12, 35
See also CA 146

McCauley, Stephen (D.) 1955- .... CLC 50
See also CA 141

McClure, Michael (Thomas) 1932- ... CLC 6,
10
See also CA 21-24R; CANR 17, 46, 77;
DLB 16

McCorkle, Jill (Collins) 1958- .... CLC 51
See also CA 121; DLBY 87

McCourt, Frank 1930- .... CLC 109
See also CA 157

McCourt, James 1941- .... CLC 5
See also CA 57-60

McCourt, Malachy 1932- .... CLC 119

McCoy, Horace (Stanley)
1897-1955 .... TCLC 28
See also CA 108; 155; DLB 9

McCrae, John 1872-1918 .... TCLC 12
See also CA 109; DLB 92

McCreigh, James
See Pohl, Frederik

McCullers, (Lula) Carson (Smith)
1917-1967 .... CLC 1, 4, 10, 12, 48, 100;
DA; DAB; DAC; DAM MST, NOV;
SSC 9, 24; WLC
See also AAYA 21; CA 5-8R; 25-28R;
CABS 1, 3; CANR 18; CDALB 1941-
1968; DA3; DLB 2, 7, 173, 228; MTCW
1, 2; SATA 27

McCulloch, John Tyler
See Burroughs, Edgar Rice

McCullough, Colleen 1938(?)- .... CLC 27,
107; DAM NOV, POP
See also CA 81-84; CANR 17, 46, 67; DA3;
MTCW 1, 2

McDermott, Alice 1953- .... CLC 90
See also CA 109; CANR 40, 90

McElroy, Joseph 1930- .... CLC 5, 47
See also CA 17-20R

McEwan, Ian (Russell) 1948- .... CLC 13, 66;
DAM NOV
See also BEST 90:4; CA 61-64; CANR 14,
41, 69, 87; DLB 14, 194; MTCW 1, 2

McFadden, David 1940- .... CLC 48
See also CA 104; DLB 60; INT 104

McFarland, Dennis 1950- .... CLC 65
See also CA 165

McGahern, John 1934- ... CLC 5, 9, 48; SSC
17
See also CA 17-20R; CANR 29, 68; DLB
14; MTCW 1

McGinley, Patrick (Anthony) 1937- . CLC 41
See also CA 120; 127; CANR 56; INT 127

McGinley, Phyllis 1905-1978 .... CLC 14
See also CA 9-12R; 77-80; CANR 19; DLB
11, 48; SATA 2, 44; SATA-Obit 24

McGinniss, Joe 1942- .... CLC 32
See also AITN 2; BEST 89:2; CA 25-28R;
CANR 26, 70; DLB 185; INT CANR-26

McGivern, Maureen Daly
See Daly, Maureen

McGrath, Patrick 1950- .... CLC 55
See also CA 136; CANR 65

McGrath, Thomas (Matthew)
1916-1990 ..... CLC 28, 59; DAM POET
See also CA 9-12R; 132; CANR 6, 33;
MTCW 1; SATA 41; SATA-Obit 66

McGuane, Thomas (Francis III)
1939- .... CLC 3, 7, 18, 45, 127
See also AITN 2; CA 49-52; CANR 5, 24,
49; DLB 2, 212; DLBY 80; INT CANR-
24; MTCW 1

McGuckian, Medbh 1950- .... CLC 48; DAM
POET; PC 27
See also CA 143; DLB 40

McHale, Tom 1942(?)-1982 .... CLC 3, 5
See also AITN 1; CA 77-80; 106

McIlvanney, William 1936- .... CLC 42
See also CA 25-28R; CANR 61; DLB 14,
207

McIlwraith, Maureen Mollie Hunter
See Hunter, Mollie
See also SATA 2

McInerney, Jay 1955- .... CLC 34, 112; DAM
POP
See also AAYA 18; CA 116; 123; CANR
45, 68; DA3; INT 123; MTCW 2

McIntyre, Vonda N(eel) 1948- .... CLC 18
See also CA 81-84; CANR 17, 34, 69;
MTCW 1

McKay, Claude TCLC 7, 41; BLC 3; DAB;
PC 2
See also McKay, Festus Claudius
See also DLB 4, 45, 51, 117

McKay, Festus Claudius 1889-1948
See McKay, Claude
See also BW 1, 3; CA 104; 124; CANR 73;
DA; DAC; DAM MST, MULT, NOV,
POET; MTCW 1, 2; WLC

McKuen, Rod 1933- .... CLC 1, 3
See also AITN 1; CA 41-44R; CANR 40

McLoughlin, R. B.
See Mencken, H(enry) L(ouis)

McLuhan, (Herbert) Marshall
1911-1980 .... CLC 37, 83
See also CA 9-12R; 102; CANR 12, 34, 61;
DLB 88; INT CANR-12; MTCW 1, 2

McMillan, Terry (L.) 1951- .... CLC 50, 61,
112; BLCS; DAM MULT, NOV, POP
See also AAYA 21; BW 2, 3; CA 140;
CANR 60; DA3; MTCW 2

McMurtry, Larry (Jeff) 1936- .. CLC 2, 3, 7,
11, 27, 44, 127; DAM NOV, POP
See also AAYA 15; AITN 2; BEST 89:2;
CA 5-8R; CANR 19, 43, 64; CDALB
1968-1988; DA3; DLB 2, 143; DLBY 80,
87; MTCW 1, 2

McNally, T. M. 1961- .... CLC 82

McNally, Terrence 1939- ... CLC 4, 7, 41, 91;
DAM DRAM
See also CA 45-48; CANR 2, 56; DA3;
DLB 7; MTCW 2

McNamer, Deirdre 1950- .... CLC 70

McNeal, Tom CLC 119

McNeile, Herman Cyril 1888-1937
See Sapper
See also CA 184; DLB 77

McNickle, (William) D'Arcy
1904-1977 .... CLC 89; DAM MULT
See also CA 9-12R; 85-88; CANR 5, 45;
DLB 175, 212; NNAL; SATA-Obit 22

McPhee, John (Angus) 1931- .... CLC 36
See also BEST 90:1; CA 65-68; CANR 20,
46, 64, 69; DLB 185; MTCW 1, 2

McPherson, James Alan 1943- .. CLC 19, 77;
BLCS
See also BW 1, 3; CA 25-28R; CAAS 17;
CANR 24, 74; DLB 38; MTCW 1, 2

McPherson, William (Alexander)
1933- .... CLC 34
See also CA 69-72; CANR 28; INT
CANR-28

Mead, George Herbert 1873-1958 . TCLC 89

Mead, Margaret 1901-1978 .... CLC 37
See also AITN 1; CA 1-4R; 81-84; CANR
4; DA3; MTCW 1, 2; SATA-Obit 20

Meaker, Marijane (Agnes) 1927-
See Kerr, M. E.
See also CA 107; CANR 37, 63; INT 107;
JRDA; MAICYA; MTCW 1; SATA 20,
61, 99; SATA-Essay 111

Medoff, Mark (Howard) 1940- ... CLC 6, 23;
DAM DRAM
See also AITN 1; CA 53-56; CANR 5; DLB
7; INT CANR-5

Medvedev, P. N.
See Bakhtin, Mikhail Mikhailovich

Meged, Aharon
See Megged, Aharon

Meged, Aron
See Megged, Aharon

Megged, Aharon 1920- .... CLC 9
See also CA 49-52; CAAS 13; CANR 1

Mehta, Ved (Parkash) 1934- .... CLC 37
See also CA 1-4R; CANR 2, 23, 69; MTCW
1

Melanter
See Blackmore, R(ichard) D(oddridge)

Melies, Georges 1861-1938 .... TCLC 81

Melikow, Loris
See Hofmannsthal, Hugo von

Melmoth, Sebastian
See Wilde, Oscar (Fingal O'Flahertie Wills)

Meltzer, Milton 1915- .... CLC 26
See also AAYA 8; CA 13-16R; CANR 38;
CLR 13; DLB 61; JRDA; MAICYA;
SAAS 1; SATA 1, 50, 80

Melville, Herman 1819-1891 ..... NCLC 3, 12,
29, 45, 49; DA; DAB; DAC; DAM
MST, NOV; SSC 1, 17; WLC
See also AAYA 25; CDALB 1640-1865;
DA3; DLB 3, 74; SATA 59

Menander c. 342B.C.-c. 292B.C. ... CMLC 9;
DAM DRAM; DC 3
See also DLB 176

Menchu, Rigoberta 1959-
See also HLCS 2

Menchu, Rigoberta 1959-
See also CA 175; HLCS 2

Mencken, H(enry) L(ouis)
1880-1956 .... TCLC 13
See also CA 105; 125; CDALB 1917-1929;
DLB 11, 29, 63, 137; MTCW 1, 2

Mendelsohn, Jane 1965(?)- .... CLC 99
See also CA 154

Mercer, David 1928-1980 .... CLC 5; DAM
DRAM
See also CA 9-12R; 102; CANR 23; DLB
13; MTCW 1

Merchant, Paul
See Ellison, Harlan (Jay)

Meredith, George 1828-1909 .. TCLC 17, 43;
DAM POET
See also CA 117; 153; CANR 80; CDBLB
1832-1890; DLB 18, 35, 57, 159

Meredith, William (Morris) 1919- .... CLC 4,
13, 22, 55; DAM POET; PC 28
See also CA 9-12R; CAAS 14; CANR 6,
40; DLB 5

Merezhkovsky, Dmitry Sergeyevich
1865-1941 .... TCLC 29
See also CA 169

Merimee, Prosper 1803-1870 ... NCLC 6, 65;
SSC 7
See also DLB 119, 192

Merkin, Daphne 1954- .... CLC 44
See also CA 123

Merlin, Arthur
See Blish, James (Benjamin)

Merrill, James (Ingram) 1926-1995 .. **CLC 2, 3, 6, 8, 13, 18, 34, 91; DAM POET; PC 28**
See also CA 13-16R; 147; CANR 10, 49, 63; DA3; DLB 5, 165; DLBY 85; INT CANR-10; MTCW 1, 2

Merriman, Alex
See Silverberg, Robert

Merriman, Brian 1747-1805 .... **NCLC 70**

Merritt, E. B.
See Waddington, Miriam

Merton, Thomas 1915-1968 ..... **CLC 1, 3, 11, 34, 83; PC 10**
See also CA 5-8R; 25-28R; CANR 22, 53; DA3; DLB 48; DLBY 81; MTCW 1, 2

Merwin, W(illiam) S(tanley) 1927- ... **CLC 1, 2, 3, 5, 8, 13, 18, 45, 88; DAM POET**
See also CA 13-16R; CANR 15, 51; DA3; DLB 5, 169; INT CANR-15; MTCW 1, 2

Metcalf, John 1938- .... **CLC 37**
See also CA 113; DLB 60

Metcalf, Suzanne
See Baum, L(yman) Frank

Mew, Charlotte (Mary) 1870-1928 .. **TCLC 8**
See also CA 105; DLB 19, 135

Mewshaw, Michael 1943- .... **CLC 9**
See also CA 53-56; CANR 7, 47; DLBY 80

Meyer, Conrad Ferdinand
1825-1905 .... **NCLC 81**
See also DLB 129

Meyer, June
See Jordan, June

Meyer, Lynn
See Slavitt, David R(ytman)

Meyer-Meyrink, Gustav 1868-1932
See Meyrink, Gustav
See also CA 117

Meyers, Jeffrey 1939- .... **CLC 39**
See also CA 73-76; CAAE 186; CANR 54; DLB 111

Meynell, Alice (Christina Gertrude Thompson) 1847-1922 .... **TCLC 6**
See also CA 104; 177; DLB 19, 98

Meyrink, Gustav **TCLC 21**
See also Meyer-Meyrink, Gustav
See also DLB 81

Michaels, Leonard 1933- .... **CLC 6, 25; SSC 16**
See also CA 61-64; CANR 21, 62; DLB 130; MTCW 1

Michaux, Henri 1899-1984 .... **CLC 8, 19**
See also CA 85-88; 114

Micheaux, Oscar (Devereaux)
1884-1951 .... **TCLC 76**
See also BW 3; CA 174; DLB 50

Michelangelo 1475-1564 .... **LC 12**

Michelet, Jules 1798-1874 .... **NCLC 31**

Michels, Robert 1876-1936 .... **TCLC 88**

Michener, James A(lbert)
1907(?)-1997 ..... **CLC 1, 5, 11, 29, 60, 109; DAM NOV, POP**
See also AAYA 27; AITN 1; BEST 90:1; CA 5-8R; 161; CANR 21, 45, 68; DA3; DLB 6; MTCW 1, 2

Mickiewicz, Adam 1798-1855 .... **NCLC 3**

Middleton, Christopher 1926- .... **CLC 13**
See also CA 13-16R; CANR 29, 54; DLB 40

Middleton, Richard (Barham)
1882-1911 .... **TCLC 56**
See also DLB 156

Middleton, Stanley 1919- .... **CLC 7, 38**
See also CA 25-28R; CAAS 23; CANR 21, 46, 81; DLB 14

Middleton, Thomas 1580-1627 .... **LC 33; DAM DRAM, MST; DC 5**
See also DLB 58

Migueis, Jose Rodrigues 1901- .... **CLC 10**

Mikszath, Kalman 1847-1910 .... **TCLC 31**
See also CA 170

Miles, Jack **CLC 100**

Miles, Josephine (Louise)
1911-1985 .. **CLC 1, 2, 14, 34, 39; DAM POET**
See also CA 1-4R; 116; CANR 2, 55; DLB 48

Militant
See Sandburg, Carl (August)

Mill, John Stuart 1806-1873 .... **NCLC 11, 58**
See also CDBLB 1832-1890; DLB 55, 190

Millar, Kenneth 1915-1983 ... **CLC 14; DAM POP**
See also Macdonald, Ross
See also CA 9-12R; 110; CANR 16, 63; DA3; DLB 2, 226; DLBD 6; DLBY 83; MTCW 1, 2

Millay, E. Vincent
See Millay, Edna St. Vincent

Millay, Edna St. Vincent
1892-1950 .... **TCLC 4, 49; DA; DAB; DAC; DAM MST, POET; PC 6; WLCS**
See also CA 104; 130; CDALB 1917-1929; DA3; DLB 45; MTCW 1, 2

Miller, Arthur 1915- ...... **CLC 1, 2, 6, 10, 15, 26, 47, 78; DA; DAB; DAC; DAM DRAM, MST; DC 1; WLC**
See also AAYA 15; AITN 1; CA 1-4R; CABS 3; CANR 2, 30, 54, 76; CDALB 1941-1968; DA3; DLB 7; MTCW 1, 2

Miller, Henry (Valentine)
1891-1980 .... **CLC 1, 2, 4, 9, 14, 43, 84; DA; DAB; DAC; DAM MST, NOV; WLC**
See also CA 9-12R; 97-100; CANR 33, 64; CDALB 1929-1941; DA3; DLB 4, 9; DLBY 80; MTCW 1, 2

Miller, Jason 1939(?) .... **CLC 2**
See also AITN 1; CA 73-76; DLB 7

Miller, Sue 1943- .... **CLC 44; DAM POP**
See also BEST 90:3; CA 139; CANR 59, 91; DA3; DLB 143

Miller, Walter M(ichael, Jr.) 1923- ... **CLC 4, 30**
See also CA 85-88; DLB 8

Millett, Kate 1934- .... **CLC 67**
See also AITN 1; CA 73-76; CANR 32, 53, 76; DA3; MTCW 1, 2

Millhauser, Steven (Lewis) 1943- .... **CLC 21, 54, 109**
See also CA 110; 111; CANR 63; DA3; DLB 2; INT 111; MTCW 2

Millin, Sarah Gertrude 1889-1968 ... **CLC 49**
See also CA 102; 93-96; DLB 225

Milne, A(lan) A(lexander)
1882-1956 ..... **TCLC 6, 88; DAB; DAC; DAM MST**
See also CA 104; 133; CLR 1, 26; DA3; DLB 10, 77, 100, 160; MAICYA; MTCW 1, 2; SATA 100; YABC 1

Milner, Ron(ald) 1938- .... **CLC 56; BLC 3; DAM MULT**
See also AITN 1; BW 1; CA 73-76; CANR 24, 81; DLB 38; MTCW 1

Milnes, Richard Monckton
1809-1885 .... **NCLC 61**
See also DLB 32, 184

Milosz, Czeslaw 1911- ...... **CLC 5, 11, 22, 31, 56, 82; DAM MST, POET; PC 8; WLCS**
See also CA 81-84; CANR 23, 51, 91; DA3; MTCW 1, 2

Milton, John 1608-1674 .... **LC 9, 43; DA; DAB; DAC; DAM MST, POET; PC 19, 29; WLC**
See also CDBLB 1660-1789; DA3; DLB 131, 151

Min, Anchee 1957- .... **CLC 86**
See also CA 146

Minehaha, Cornelius
See Wedekind, (Benjamin) Frank(lin)

Miner, Valerie 1947- .... **CLC 40**
See also CA 97-100; CANR 59

Minimo, Duca
See D'Annunzio, Gabriele

Minot, Susan 1956- .... **CLC 44**
See also CA 134

Minus, Ed 1938- .... **CLC 39**
See also CA 185

Miranda, Javier
See Bioy Casares, Adolfo

Miranda, Javier
See Bioy Casares, Adolfo

Mirbeau, Octave 1848-1917 .... **TCLC 55**
See also DLB 123, 192

Miro (Ferrer), Gabriel (Francisco Victor)
1879-1930 .... **TCLC 5**
See also CA 104; 185

Mishima, Yukio 1925-1970 .... **CLC 2, 4, 6, 9, 27; DC 1; SSC 4**
See also Hiraoka, Kimitake
See also DLB 182; MTCW 2

Mistral, Frederic 1830-1914 .... **TCLC 51**
See also CA 122

Mistral, Gabriela **TCLC 2; HLC 2**
See also Godoy Alcayaga, Lucila
See also MTCW 2

Mistry, Rohinton 1952- .... **CLC 71; DAC**
See also CA 141; CANR 86

Mitchell, Clyde
See Ellison, Harlan (Jay); Silverberg, Robert

Mitchell, James Leslie 1901-1935
See Gibbon, Lewis Grassic
See also CA 104; DLB 15

Mitchell, Joni 1943- .... **CLC 12**
See also CA 112

Mitchell, Joseph (Quincy)
1908-1996 .... **CLC 98**
See also CA 77-80; 152; CANR 69; DLB 185; DLBY 96

Mitchell, Margaret (Munnerlyn)
1900-1949 . **TCLC 11; DAM NOV, POP**
See also AAYA 23; CA 109; 125; CANR 55; CDALBS; DA3; DLB 9; MTCW 1, 2

Mitchell, Peggy
See Mitchell, Margaret (Munnerlyn)

Mitchell, S(ilas) Weir 1829-1914 .... **TCLC 36**
See also CA 165; DLB 202

Mitchell, W(illiam) O(rmond)
1914-1998 .. **CLC 25; DAC; DAM MST**
See also CA 77-80; 165; CANR 15, 43; DLB 88

Mitchell, William 1879-1936 .... **TCLC 81**

Mitford, Mary Russell 1787-1855 ... **NCLC 4**
See also DLB 110, 116

Mitford, Nancy 1904-1973 .... **CLC 44**
See also CA 9-12R; DLB 191

Miyamoto, (Chujo) Yuriko
1899-1951 .... **TCLC 37**
See also CA 170, 174; DLB 180

Miyazawa, Kenji 1896-1933 .... **TCLC 76**
See also CA 157

Mizoguchi, Kenji 1898-1956 .... **TCLC 72**
See also CA 167

Mo, Timothy (Peter) 1950(?)- .... **CLC 46**
See also CA 117; DLB 194; MTCW 1

Modarressi, Taghi (M.) 1931- .... **CLC 44**
See also CA 121; 134; INT 134

Modiano, Patrick (Jean) 1945 .... **CLC 18**
See also CA 85-88; CANR 17, 40; DLB 83

Moerck, Paal
See Roelvaag, O(le) E(dvart)

Mofolo, Thomas (Mokopu)
1875(?)-1948 .. **TCLC 22; BLC 3; DAM MULT**
See also CA 121; 153; CANR 83; DLB 225; MTCW 2

Mohr, Nicholasa 1938- .... **CLC 12; DAM MULT; HLC 2**
See also AAYA 8; CA 49-52; CANR 1, 32, 64; CLR 22; DLB 145; HW 1, 2; JRDA; SAAS 8; SATA 8, 97; SATA-Essay 113

Mojtabai, A(nn) G(race) 1938- ..... **CLC 5, 9, 15, 29**
See also CA 85-88; CANR 88

Moliere 1622-1673 ..... **LC 10, 28; DA; DAB; DAC; DAM DRAM, MST; DC 13; WLC**
See also DA3

Molin, Charles
See Mayne, William (James Carter)

Molnar, Ferenc 1878-1952 .. **TCLC 20; DAM DRAM**
See also CA 109; 153; CANR 83

Momaday, N(avarre) Scott 1934- ...... **CLC 2, 19, 85, 95; DA; DAB; DAC; DAM MST, MULT, NOV, POP; PC 25; WLCS**
See also AAYA 11; CA 25-28R; CANR 14, 34, 68; CDALBS; DA3; DLB 143, 175; INT CANR-14; MTCW 1, 2; NNAL; SATA 48; SATA-Brief 30

Monette, Paul 1945-1995 .... **CLC 82**
See also CA 139; 147

Monroe, Harriet 1860-1936 .... **TCLC 12**
See also CA 109; DLB 54, 91

Monroe, Lyle
See Heinlein, Robert A(nson)

Montagu, Elizabeth 1720-1800 .... **NCLC 7**

Montagu, Elizabeth 1917- .... **NCLC 7**
See also CA 9-12R

Montagu, Mary (Pierrepont) Wortley
1689-1762 .... **LC 9, 57; PC 16**
See also DLB 95, 101

Montagu, W. H.
See Coleridge, Samuel Taylor

Montague, John (Patrick) 1929- ..... **CLC 13, 46**
See also CA 9-12R; CANR 9, 69; DLB 40; MTCW 1

Montaigne, Michel (Eyquem) de
1533-1592 .... **LC 8; DA; DAB; DAC; DAM MST; WLC**

Montale, Eugenio 1896-1981 ... **CLC 7, 9, 18; PC 13**
See also CA 17-20R; 104; CANR 30; DLB 114; MTCW 1

Montesquieu, Charles-Louis de Secondat
1689-1755 .... **LC 7**

Montgomery, (Robert) Bruce 1921(?)-1978
See Crispin, Edmund
See also CA 179; 104

Montgomery, L(ucy) M(aud)
1874-1942 .... **TCLC 51; DAC; DAM MST**
See also AAYA 12; CA 108; 137; CLR 8; DA3; DLB 92; DLBD 14; JRDA; MAICYA; MTCW 2; SATA 100; YABC 1

Montgomery, Marion H., Jr. 1925- .... **CLC 7**
See also AITN 1; CA 1-4R; CANR 3, 48; DLB 6

Montgomery, Max
See Davenport, Guy (Mattison, Jr.)

Montherlant, Henry (Milon) de
1896-1972 ..... **CLC 8, 19; DAM DRAM**
See also CA 85-88; 37-40R; DLB 72; MTCW 1

Monty Python
See Chapman, Graham; Cleese, John (Marwood); Gilliam, Terry (Vance); Idle, Eric; Jones, Terence Graham Parry; Palin, Michael (Edward)
See also AAYA 7

Moodie, Susanna (Strickland)
1803-1885 .... **NCLC 14**
See also DLB 99

Mooney, Edward 1951-
See Mooney, Ted
See also CA 130

Mooney, Ted CLC 25
See also Mooney, Edward

Moorcock, Michael (John) 1939- ...... **CLC 5, 27, 58**
See also Bradbury, Edward P.
See also AAYA 26; CA 45-48; CAAS 5; CANR 2, 17, 38, 64; DLB 14; MTCW 1, 2; SATA 93

Moore, Brian 1921-1999 ... **CLC 1, 3, 5, 7, 8, 19, 32, 90; DAB; DAC; DAM MST**
See also CA 1-4R; 174; CANR 1, 25, 42, 63; MTCW 1, 2

Moore, Edward
See Muir, Edwin

Moore, G. E. 1873-1958 .... **TCLC 89**

Moore, George Augustus
1852-1933 .... **TCLC 7; SSC 19**
See also CA 104; 177; DLB 10, 18, 57, 135

Moore, Lorrie CLC 39, 45, 68
See also Moore, Marie Lorena

Moore, Marianne (Craig)
1887-1972 .... **CLC 1, 2, 4, 8, 10, 13, 19, 47; DA; DAB; DAC; DAM MST, POET; PC 4; WLCS**
See also CA 1-4R; 33-36R; CANR 3, 61; CDALB 1929-1941; DA3; DLB 45; DLBD 7; MTCW 1, 2; SATA 20

Moore, Marie Lorena 1957-
See Moore, Lorrie
See also CA 116; CANR 39, 83

Moore, Thomas 1779-1852 .... **NCLC 6**
See also DLB 96, 144

Moorhouse, Frank 1938- .... **SSC 40**
See also CA 118

Mora, Pat(ricia) 1942-
See also CA 129; CANR 57, 81; CLR 58; DAM MULT; DLB 209; HLC 2; HW 1, 2; SATA 92

Moraga, Cherrie 1952- .... **CLC 126; DAM MULT**
See also CA 131; CANR 66; DLB 82; HW 1, 2

Morand, Paul 1888-1976 .... **CLC 41; SSC 22**
See also CA 184; 69-72; DLB 65

Morante, Elsa 1918-1985 .... **CLC 8, 47**
See also CA 85-88; 117; CANR 35; DLB 177; MTCW 1, 2

Moravia, Alberto 1907-1990 .... **CLC 2, 7, 11, 27, 46; SSC 26**
See also Pincherle, Alberto
See also DLB 177; MTCW 2

More, Hannah 1745-1833 .... **NCLC 27**
See also DLB 107, 109, 116, 158

More, Henry 1614-1687 .... **LC 9**
See also DLB 126

More, Sir Thomas 1478-1535 .... **LC 10, 32**

Moreas, Jean TCLC 18
See also Papadiamantopoulos, Johannes

Morgan, Berry 1919- .... **CLC 6**
See also CA 49-52; DLB 6

Morgan, Claire
See Highsmith, (Mary) Patricia

Morgan, Edwin (George) 1920- .... **CLC 31**
See also CA 5-8R; CANR 3, 43, 90; DLB 27

Morgan, (George) Frederick 1922- .. **CLC 23**
See also CA 17-20R; CANR 21

Morgan, Harriet
See Mencken, H(enry) L(ouis)

Morgan, Jane
See Cooper, James Fenimore

Morgan, Janet 1945- .... **CLC 39**
See also CA 65-68

Morgan, Lady 1776(?)-1859 .... **NCLC 29**
See also DLB 116, 158

Morgan, Robin (Evonne) 1941- .... **CLC 2**
See also CA 69-72; CANR 29, 68; MTCW 1; SATA 80

Morgan, Scott
See Kuttner, Henry

Morgan, Seth 1949(?)-1990 .... **CLC 65**
See also CA 185; 132

Morgenstern, Christian 1871-1914 .. **TCLC 8**
See also CA 105

Morgenstern, S.
See Goldman, William (W.)

Moricz, Zsigmond 1879-1942 .... **TCLC 33**
See also CA 165

Morike, Eduard (Friedrich)
1804-1875 .... **NCLC 10**
See also DLB 133

Moritz, Karl Philipp 1756-1793 .... **LC 2**
See also DLB 94

Morland, Peter Henry
See Faust, Frederick (Schiller)

Morley, Christopher (Darlington)
1890-1957 .... **TCLC 87**
See also CA 112; DLB 9

Morren, Theophil
See Hofmannsthal, Hugo von

Morris, Bill 1952- .... **CLC 76**

Morris, Julian
See West, Morris L(anglo)

Morris, Steveland Judkins 1950(?)-
See Wonder, Stevie
See also CA 111

Morris, William 1834-1896 .... **NCLC 4**
See also CDBLB 1832-1890; DLB 18, 35, 57, 156, 178, 184

Morris, Wright 1910-1998 .. **CLC 1, 3, 7, 18, 37**
See also CA 9-12R; 167; CANR 21, 81; DLB 2, 206; DLBY 81; MTCW 1, 2

Morrison, Arthur 1863-1945 .... **TCLC 72; SSC 40**
See also CA 120; 157; DLB 70, 135, 197

Morrison, Chloe Anthony Wofford
See Morrison, Toni

Morrison, James Douglas 1943-1971
See Morrison, Jim
See also CA 73-76; CANR 40

Morrison, Jim CLC 17
See also Morrison, James Douglas

Morrison, Toni 1931- . **CLC 4, 10, 22, 55, 81, 87; BLC 3; DA; DAB; DAC; DAM MST, MULT, NOV, POP**
See also AAYA 1, 22; BW 2, 3; CA 29-32R; CANR 27, 42, 67; CDALB 1968-1988; DA3; DLB 6, 33, 143; DLBY 81; MTCW 1, 2; SATA 57

Morrison, Van 1945- .... **CLC 21**
See also CA 116; 168

Morrissy, Mary 1958- .... **CLC 99**

Mortimer, John (Clifford) 1923- ..... **CLC 28, 43; DAM DRAM, POP**
See also CA 13-16R; CANR 21, 69; CDBLB 1960 to Present; DA3; DLB 13; INT CANR-21; MTCW 1, 2

Mortimer, Penelope (Ruth) 1918- ...... **CLC 5**
See also CA 57-60; CANR 45, 88

Morton, Anthony
See Creasey, John

Mosca, Gaetano 1858-1941 .... **TCLC 75**

Mosher, Howard Frank 1943- .... **CLC 62**
See also CA 139; CANR 65

Mosley, Nicholas 1923- .... **CLC 43, 70**
  See also CA 69-72; CANR 41, 60; DLB 14, 207
Mosley, Walter 1952- .... **CLC 97; BLCS; DAM MULT, POP**
  See also AAYA 17; BW 2; CA 142; CANR 57; DA3; MTCW 2
Moss, Howard 1922-1987 ...... **CLC 7, 14, 45, 50; DAM POET**
  See also CA 1-4R; 123; CANR 1, 44; DLB 5
Mossgiel, Rab
  See Burns, Robert
Motion, Andrew (Peter) 1952- .... **CLC 47**
  See also CA 146; CANR 90; DLB 40
Motley, Willard (Francis)
  1909-1965 .... **CLC 18**
  See also BW 1; CA 117; 106; CANR 88; DLB 76, 143
Motoori, Norinaga 1730-1801 .... **NCLC 45**
Mott, Michael (Charles Alston)
  1930- .... **CLC 15, 34**
  See also CA 5-8R; CAAS 7; CANR 7, 29
Mountain Wolf Woman 1884-1960 .. **CLC 92**
  See also CA 144; CANR 90; NNAL
Moure, Erin 1955- .... **CLC 88**
  See also CA 113; DLB 60
Mowat, Farley (McGill) 1921- .... **CLC 26; DAC; DAM MST**
  See also AAYA 1; CA 1-4R; CANR 4, 24, 42, 68; CLR 20; DLB 68; INT CANR-24, JRDA; MAICYA; MTCW 1, 2; SATA 3, 55
Mowatt, Anna Cora 1819-1870 ..... **NCLC 74**
Moyers, Bill 1934- .... **CLC 74**
  See also AITN 2; CA 61-64; CANR 31, 52
Mphahlele, Es'kia
  See Mphahlele, Ezekiel
  See also DLB 125
Mphahlele, Ezekiel 1919- .... **CLC 25, 133; BLC 3; DAM MULT**
  See also Mphahlele, Es'kia
  See also BW 2, 3; CA 81-84; CANR 26, 76; DA3; DLB 225; MTCW 2
Mqhayi, S(amuel) E(dward) K(rune Loliwe)
  1875-1945 ...... **TCLC 25; BLC 3; DAM MULT**
  See also CA 153; CANR 87
Mrozek, Slawomir 1930- .... **CLC 3, 13**
  See also CA 13-16R; CAAS 10; CANR 29; MTCW 1
Mrs. Belloc-Lowndes
  See Lowndes, Marie Adelaide (Belloc)
Mtwa, Percy (?)- .... **CLC 47**
Mueller, Lisel 1924- .... **CLC 13, 51**
  See also CA 93-96; DLB 105
Muir, Edwin 1887-1959 .... **TCLC 2, 87**
  See also CA 104; DLB 20, 100, 191
Muir, John 1838-1914 .... **TCLC 28**
  See also CA 165; DLB 186
Mujica Lainez, Manuel 1910-1984 ... **CLC 31**
  See also Lainez, Manuel Mujica
  See also CA 81-84; 112; CANR 32; HW 1
Mukherjee, Bharati 1940- .... **CLC 53, 115; DAM NOV; SSC 38**
  See also BEST 89:2; CA 107; CANR 45, 72; DLB 60; MTCW 1, 2
Muldoon, Paul 1951- .... **CLC 32, 72; DAM POET**
  See also CA 113; 129; CANR 52, 91; DLB 40; INT 129
Mulisch, Harry 1927- .... **CLC 42**
  See also CA 9-12R; CANR 6, 26, 56
Mull, Martin 1943- .... **CLC 17**
  See also CA 105
Muller, Wilhelm **NCLC 73**
Mulock, Dinah Maria
  See Craik, Dinah Maria (Mulock)

Munford, Robert 1737(?)-1783 .... **LC 5**
  See also DLB 31
Mungo, Raymond 1946- .... **CLC 72**
  See also CA 49-52; CANR 2
Munro, Alice 1931- .... **CLC 6, 10, 19, 50, 95; DAC; DAM MST, NOV; SSC 3; WLCS**
  See also AITN 2; CA 33-36R; CANR 33, 53, 75; DA3; DLB 53; MTCW 1, 2; SATA 29
Munro, H(ector) H(ugh) 1870-1916
  See Saki
  See also CA 104; 130; CDBLB 1890-1914; DA; DAB; DAC; DAM MST, NOV; DA3; DLB 34, 162; MTCW 1, 2; WLC
Murdoch, (Jean) Iris 1919-1999 ... **CLC 1, 2, 3, 4, 6, 8, 11, 15, 22, 31, 51; DAB; DAC; DAM MST, NOV**
  See also CA 13-16R; 179; CANR 8, 43, 68; CDBLB 1960 to Present; DA3; DLB 14, 194; INT CANR-8; MTCW 1, 2
Murfree, Mary Noailles 1850-1922 ... **SSC 22**
  See also CA 122; 176; DLB 12, 74
Murnau, Friedrich Wilhelm
  See Plumpe, Friedrich Wilhelm
Murphy, Richard 1927- .... **CLC 41**
  See also CA 29-32R; DLB 40
Murphy, Sylvia 1937- .... **CLC 34**
  See also CA 121
Murphy, Thomas (Bernard) 1935- ... **CLC 51**
  See also CA 101
Murray, Albert L. 1916- .... **CLC 73**
  See also BW 2; CA 49-52; CANR 26, 52, 78; DLB 38
Murray, Judith Sargent
  1751-1820 .... **NCLC 63**
  See also DLB 37, 200
Murray, Les(lie) A(llan) 1938- .... **CLC 40; DAM POET**
  See also CA 21-24R; CANR 11, 27, 56
Murry, J. Middleton
  See Murry, John Middleton
Murry, John Middleton
  1889-1957 .... **TCLC 16**
  See also CA 118; DLB 149
Musgrave, Susan 1951- .... **CLC 13, 54**
  See also CA 69-72; CANR 45, 84
Musil, Robert (Edler von)
  1880-1942 .... **TCLC 12, 68; SSC 18**
  See also CA 109; CANR 55, 84; DLB 81, 124; MTCW 2
Muske, Carol 1945- .... **CLC 90**
  See also Muske-Dukes, Carol (Anne)
Muske-Dukes, Carol (Anne) 1945-
  See Muske, Carol
  See also CA 65-68; CANR 32, 70
Musset, (Louis Charles) Alfred de
  1810-1857 .... **NCLC 7**
  See also DLB 192
Mussolini, Benito (Amilcare Andrea)
  1883-1945 .... **TCLC 96**
  See also CA 116
My Brother's Brother
  See Chekhov, Anton (Pavlovich)
Myers, L(eopold) H(amilton)
  1881-1944 .... **TCLC 59**
  See also CA 157; DLB 15
Myers, Walter Dean 1937- ..... **CLC 35; BLC 3; DAM MULT, NOV**
  See also AAYA 4, 23; BW 2; CA 33-36R; CANR 20, 42, 67; CLR 4, 16, 35; DLB 33; INT CANR-20; JRDA; MAICYA; MTCW 2; SAAS 2; SATA 41, 71, 109; SATA-Brief 27
Myers, Walter M.
  See Myers, Walter Dean
Myles, Symon
  See Follett, Ken(neth Martin)

Nabokov, Vladimir (Vladimirovich)
  1899-1977 .... **CLC 1, 2, 3, 6, 8, 11, 15, 23, 44, 46, 64; DA; DAB; DAC; DAM MST, NOV; SSC 11; WLC**
  See also CA 5-8R; 69-72; CANR 20; CDALB 1941-1968; DA3; DLB 2; DLBD 3; DLBY 80, 91; MTCW 1, 2
Naevius c. 265B.C.-201B.C. .... **CMLC 37**
  See also DLB 211
Nagai Kafu 1879-1959 .... **TCLC 51**
  See also Nagai Sokichi
  See also DLB 180
Nagai Sokichi 1879-1959
  See Nagai Kafu
  See also CA 117
Nagy, Laszlo 1925-1978 .... **CLC 7**
  See also CA 129; 112
Naidu, Sarojini 1879-1943 .... **TCLC 80**
Naipaul, Shiva(dhar Srinivasa)
  1945-1985 .... **CLC 32, 39; DAM NOV**
  See also CA 110; 112; 116; CANR 33; DA3; DLB 157; DLBY 85; MTCW 1, 2
Naipaul, V(idiadhar) S(urajprasad)
  1932- .... **CLC 4, 7, 9, 13, 18, 37, 105; DAB; DAC; DAM MST, NOV; SSC 38**
  See also CA 1-4R; CANR 1, 33, 51, 91; CDBLB 1960 to Present; DA3; DLB 125, 204, 206; DLBY 85; MTCW 1, 2
Nakos, Lilika 1899(?)- .... **CLC 29**
Narayan, R(asipuram) K(rishnaswami)
  1906- . **CLC 7, 28, 47, 121; DAM NOV; SSC 25**
  See also CA 81-84; CANR 33, 61; DA3; MTCW 1, 2; SATA 62
Nash, (Frediric) Ogden 1902-1971 . **CLC 23; DAM POET; PC 21**
  See also CA 13-14; 29-32R; CANR 34, 61; CAP 1; DLB 11; MAICYA; MTCW 1, 2; SATA 2, 46
Nashe, Thomas 1567-1601(?) .... **LC 41**
  See also DLB 167
Nashe, Thomas 1567-1601 .... **LC 41**
Nathan, Daniel
  See Dannay, Frederic
Nathan, George Jean 1882-1958 .... **TCLC 18**
  See also Hatteras, Owen
  See also CA 114; 169; DLB 137
Natsume, Kinnosuke 1867-1916
  See Natsume, Soseki
  See also CA 104
Natsume, Soseki 1867-1916 .... **TCLC 2, 10**
  See also Natsume, Kinnosuke
  See also DLB 180
Natti, (Mary) Lee 1919-
  See Kingman, Lee
  See also CA 5-8R; CANR 2
Naylor, Gloria 1950- .... **CLC 28, 52; BLC 3; DA; DAC; DAM MST, MULT, NOV, POP; WLCS**
  See also AAYA 6; BW 2, 3; CA 107; CANR 27, 51, 74; DA3; DLB 173; MTCW 1, 2
Neihardt, John Gneisenau
  1881-1973 .... **CLC 32**
  See also CA 13-14; CANR 65; CAP 1; DLB 9, 54
Nekrasov, Nikolai Alekseevich
  1821-1878 .... **NCLC 11**
Nelligan, Emile 1879-1941 .... **TCLC 14**
  See also CA 114; DLB 92
Nelson, Willie 1933- .... **CLC 17**
  See also CA 107
Nemerov, Howard (Stanley)
  1920-1991 .... **CLC 2, 6, 9, 36; DAM POET; PC 24**
  See also CA 1-4R; 134; CABS 2; CANR 1, 27, 53; DLB 5, 6; DLBY 83; INT CANR-27; MTCW 1, 2

Neruda, Pablo 1904-1973 .. **CLC 1, 2, 5, 7, 9, 28, 62; DA; DAB; DAC; DAM MST, MULT, POET; HLC 2; PC 4; WLC**
See also CA 19-20; 45-48; CAP 2; DA3; HW 1; MTCW 1, 2

Nerval, Gerard de 1808-1855 ... **NCLC 1, 67; PC 13; SSC 18**

Nervo, (Jose) Amado (Ruiz de)
1870-1919 .... **TCLC 11; HLCS 2**
See also CA 109; 131; HW 1

Nessi, Pio Baroja y
See Baroja (y Nessi), Pio

Nestroy, Johann 1801-1862 .... **NCLC 42**
See also DLB 133

Netterville, Luke
See O'Grady, Standish (James)

Neufeld, John (Arthur) 1938- .... **CLC 17**
See also AAYA 11; CA 25-28R; CANR 11, 37, 56; CLR 52; MAICYA; SAAS 3; SATA 6, 81

Neville, Emily Cheney 1919- .... **CLC 12**
See also CA 5-8R; CANR 3, 37, 85; JRDA; MAICYA; SAAS 2; SATA 1

Newbound, Bernard Slade 1930-
See Slade, Bernard
See also CA 81-84; CANR 49; DAM DRAM

Newby, P(ercy) H(oward)
1918-1997 .... **CLC 2, 13; DAM NOV**
See also CA 5-8R; 161; CANR 32, 67; DLB 15; MTCW 1

Newlove, Donald 1928- .... **CLC 6**
See also CA 29-32R; CANR 25

Newlove, John (Herbert) 1938- .... **CLC 14**
See also CA 21-24R; CANR 9, 25

Newman, Charles 1938- .... **CLC 2, 8**
See also CA 21-24R; CANR 84

Newman, Edwin (Harold) 1919- ...... **CLC 14**
See also AITN 1; CA 69-72; CANR 5

Newman, John Henry 1801-1890 .. **NCLC 38**
See also DLB 18, 32, 55

Newton, (Sir)Isaac 1642-1727 .... **LC 35, 52**

Newton, Suzanne 1936- .... **CLC 35**
See also CA 41-44R; CANR 14; JRDA; SATA 5, 77

Nexo, Martin Andersen
1869-1954 .... **TCLC 43**

Nezval, Vitezslav 1900-1958 .... **TCLC 44**
See also CA 123

Ng, Fae Myenne 1957(?)- .... **CLC 81**
See also CA 146

Ngema, Mbongeni 1955- .... **CLC 57**
See also BW 2; CA 143; CANR 84

Ngugi, James T(hiong'o) CLC 3, 7, 13
See also Ngugi wa Thiong'o

Ngugi wa Thiong'o 1938- .. **CLC 36; BLC 3; DAM MULT, NOV**
See also Ngugi, James T(hiong'o)
See also BW 2; CA 81-84; CANR 27, 58; DLB 125; MTCW 1, 2

Nichol, B(arrie) P(hillip) 1944-1988 . **CLC 18**
See also CA 53-56; DLB 53; SATA 66

Nichols, John (Treadwell) 1940- .... **CLC 38**
See also CA 9-12R; CAAS 2; CANR 6, 70; DLBY 82

Nichols, Leigh
See Koontz, Dean R(ay)

Nichols, Peter (Richard) 1927- .... **CLC 5, 36, 65**
See also CA 104; CANR 33, 86; DLB 13; MTCW 1

Nicolas, F. R. E.
See Freeling, Nicolas

Niedecker, Lorine 1903-1970 ..... **CLC 10, 42; DAM POET**
See also CA 25-28; CAP 2; DLB 48

Nietzsche, Friedrich (Wilhelm)
1844-1900 .... **TCLC 10, 18, 55**
See also CA 107; 121; DLB 129

Nievo, Ippolito 1831-1861 .... **NCLC 22**

Nightingale, Anne Redmon 1943-
See Redmon, Anne
See also CA 103

Nightingale, Florence 1820-1910 ... **TCLC 85**
See also DLB 166

Nik. T. O.
See Annensky, Innokenty (Fyodorovich)

Nin, Anais 1903-1977 ..... **CLC 1, 4, 8, 11, 14, 60, 127; DAM NOV, POP; SSC 10**
See also AITN 2; CA 13-16R; 69-72; CANR 22, 53; DLB 2, 4, 152; MTCW 1, 2

Nishida, Kitaro 1870-1945 .... **TCLC 83**

Nishiwaki, Junzaburo 1894-1982 .... **PC 15**
See also CA 107

Nissenson, Hugh 1933- .... **CLC 4, 9**
See also CA 17-20R; CANR 27; DLB 28

Niven, Larry CLC 8
See also Niven, Laurence Van Cott
See also AAYA 27; DLB 8

Niven, Laurence Van Cott 1938-
See Niven, Larry
See also CA 21-24R; CAAS 12; CANR 14, 44, 66; DAM POP; MTCW 1, 2; SATA 95

Nixon, Agnes Eckhardt 1927- .... **CLC 21**
See also CA 110

Nizan, Paul 1905-1940 .... **TCLC 40**
See also CA 161; DLB 72

Nkosi, Lewis 1936- ... **CLC 45; BLC 3; DAM MULT**
See also BW 1, 3; CA 65-68; CANR 27, 81; DLB 157, 225

Nodier, (Jean) Charles (Emmanuel)
1780-1844 .... **NCLC 19**
See also DLB 119

Noguchi, Yone 1875-1947 .... **TCLC 80**

Nolan, Christopher 1965- .... **CLC 58**
See also CA 111; CANR 88

Noon, Jeff 1957- .... **CLC 91**
See also CA 148; CANR 83

Norden, Charles
See Durrell, Lawrence (George)

Nordhoff, Charles (Bernard)
1887-1947 .... **TCLC 23**
See also CA 108; DLB 9; SATA 23

Norfolk, Lawrence 1963- .... **CLC 76**
See also CA 144; CANR 85

Norman, Marsha 1947- .... **CLC 28; DAM DRAM; DC 8**
See also CA 105; CABS 3; CANR 41; DLBY 84

Normyx
See Douglas, (George) Norman

Norris, Frank 1870-1902 .... **SSC 28**
See also Norris, (Benjamin) Frank(lin, Jr.)
See also CDALB 1865-1917; DLB 12, 71, 186

Norris, (Benjamin) Frank(lin, Jr.)
1870-1902 .... **TCLC 24**
See also Norris, Frank
See also CA 110; 160

Norris, Leslie 1921- .... **CLC 14**
See also CA 11-12; CANR 14; CAP 1; DLB 27

North, Andrew
See Norton, Andre

North, Anthony
See Koontz, Dean R(ay)

North, Captain George
See Stevenson, Robert Louis (Balfour)

North, Milou
See Erdrich, Louise

Northrup, B. A.
See Hubbard, L(afayette) Ron(ald)

North Staffs
See Hulme, T(homas) E(rnest)

Norton, Alice Mary
See Norton, Andre
See also MAICYA; SATA 1, 43

Norton, Andre 1912- .... **CLC 12**
See also Norton, Alice Mary
See also AAYA 14; CA 1-4R; CANR 68; CLR 50; DLB 8, 52; JRDA; MTCW 1; SATA 91

Norton, Caroline 1808-1877 .... **NCLC 47**
See also DLB 21, 159, 199

Norway, Nevil Shute 1899-1960
See Shute, Nevil
See also CA 102; 93-96; CANR 85; MTCW 2

Norwid, Cyprian Kamil
1821-1883 .... **NCLC 17**

Nosille, Nabrah
See Ellison, Harlan (Jay)

Nossack, Hans Erich 1901-1978 .... **CLC 6**
See also CA 93-96; 85-88; DLB 69

Nostradamus 1503-1566 .... **LC 27**

Nosu, Chuji
See Ozu, Yasujiro

Notenburg, Eleanora (Genrikhovna) von
See Guro, Elena

Nova, Craig 1945- .... **CLC 7, 31**
See also CA 45-48; CANR 2, 53

Novak, Joseph
See Kosinski, Jerzy (Nikodem)

Novalis 1772-1801 .... **NCLC 13**
See also DLB 90

Novis, Emile
See Weil, Simone (Adolphine)

Nowlan, Alden (Albert) 1933-1983 . **CLC 15; DAC; DAM MST**
See also CA 9-12R; CANR 5; DLB 53

Noyes, Alfred 1880-1958 ...... **TCLC 7; PC 27**
See also CA 104; DLB 20

Nunn, Kem CLC 34
See also CA 159

Nwapa, Flora 1931-1993 .... **CLC 133; BLCS**
See also BW 2; CA 143; CANR 83; DLB 125

Nye, Robert 1939- . **CLC 13, 42; DAM NOV**
See also CA 33-36R; CANR 29, 67; DLB 14; MTCW 1; SATA 6

Nyro, Laura 1947- .... **CLC 17**

Oates, Joyce Carol 1938- .. **CLC 1, 2, 3, 6, 9, 11, 15, 19, 33, 52, 108; DA; DAB; DAC; DAM MST, NOV, POP; SSC 6; WLC**
See also AAYA 15; AITN 1; BEST 89:2; CA 5-8R; CANR 25, 45, 74; CDALB 1968-1988; DA3; DLB 2, 5, 130; DLBY 81; INT CANR-25; MTCW 1, 2

O'Brien, Darcy 1939-1998 .... **CLC 11**
See also CA 21-24R; 167; CANR 8, 59

O'Brien, E. G.
See Clarke, Arthur C(harles)

O'Brien, Edna 1936- ..... **CLC 3, 5, 8, 13, 36, 65, 116; DAM NOV; SSC 10**
See also CA 1-4R; CANR 6, 41, 65; CDBLB 1960 to Present; DA3; DLB 14; MTCW 1, 2

O'Brien, Fitz-James 1828-1862 ..... **NCLC 21**
See also DLB 74

O'Brien, Flann CLC 1, 4, 5, 7, 10, 47
See also O Nuallain, Brian

O'Brien, Richard 1942- .... **CLC 17**
See also CA 124

O'Brien, (William) Tim(othy) 1946- . CLC 7,
   19, 40, 103; DAM POP
   See also AAYA 16; CA 85-88; CANR 40,
   58; CDALBS; DA3; DLB 152; DLBD 9;
   DLBY 80; MTCW 2
Obstfelder, Sigbjoern 1866-1900 .... TCLC 23
   See also CA 123
O'Casey, Sean 1880-1964 .... CLC 1, 5, 9, 11,
   15, 88; DAB; DAC; DAM DRAM,
   MST; DC 12; WLCS
   See also CA 89-92; CANR 62; CDBLB
   1914-1945; DA3; DLB 10; MTCW 1, 2
O'Cathasaigh, Sean
   See O'Casey, Sean
Ochs, Phil(ip David) 1940-1976 .... CLC 17
   See also CA 185; 65-68
O'Connor, Edwin (Greene)
   1918-1968 .... CLC 14
   See also CA 93-96; 25-28R
O'Connor, (Mary) Flannery
   1925-1964 .... CLC 1, 2, 3, 6, 10, 13, 15,
   21, 66, 104; DA; DAB; DAC; DAM
   MST, NOV; SSC 1, 23; WLC
   See also AAYA 7; CA 1-4R; CANR 3, 41;
   CDALB 1941-1968; DA3; DLB 2, 152;
   DLBD 12; DLBY 80; MTCW 1, 2
O'Connor, Frank CLC 23; SSC 5
   See also O'Donovan, Michael John
   See also DLB 162
O'Dell, Scott 1898-1989 .... CLC 30
   See also AAYA 3; CA 61-64; 129; CANR
   12, 30; CLR 1, 16; DLB 52; JRDA; MAI-
   CYA; SATA 12, 60
Odets, Clifford 1906-1963 ..... CLC 2, 28, 98;
   DAM DRAM; DC 6
   See also CA 85-88; CANR 62; DLB 7, 26;
   MTCW 1, 2
O'Doherty, Brian 1934- .... CLC 76
   See also CA 105
O'Donnell, K. M.
   See Malzberg, Barry N(athaniel)
O'Donnell, Lawrence
   See Kuttner, Henry
O'Donovan, Michael John
   1903-1966 .... CLC 14
   See also O'Connor, Frank
   See also CA 93-96; CANR 84
Oe, Kenzaburo 1935- .... CLC 10, 36, 86;
   DAM NOV; SSC 20
   See also CA 97-100; CANR 36, 50, 74;
   DA3; DLB 182; DLBY 94; MTCW 1, 2
O'Faolain, Julia 1932- .... CLC 6, 19, 47, 108
   See also CA 81-84; CAAS 2; CANR 12,
   61; DLB 14; MTCW 1
O'Faolain, Sean 1900-1991 ...... CLC 1, 7, 14,
   32, 70; SSC 13
   See also CA 61-64; 134; CANR 12, 66;
   DLB 15, 162; MTCW 1, 2
O'Flaherty, Liam 1896-1984 .... CLC 5, 34;
   SSC 6
   See also CA 101; 113; CANR 35; DLB 36,
   162; DLBY 84; MTCW 1, 2
Ogilvy, Gavin
   See Barrie, J(ames) M(atthew)
O'Grady, Standish (James)
   1846-1928 .... TCLC 5
   See also CA 104; 157
O'Grady, Timothy 1951- .... CLC 59
   See also CA 138
O'Hara, Frank 1926-1966 .... CLC 2, 5, 13,
   78; DAM POET
   See also CA 9-12R; 25-28R; CANR 33;
   DA3; DLB 5, 16, 193; MTCW 1, 2
O'Hara, John (Henry) 1905-1970 . CLC 1, 2,
   3, 6, 11, 42; DAM NOV; SSC 15
   See also CA 5-8R; 25-28R; CANR 31, 60;
   CDALB 1929-1941; DLB 9, 86; DLBD
   2; MTCW 1, 2

O Hehir, Diana 1922- .... CLC 41
   See also CA 93-96
Ohiyesa
   See Eastman, Charles A(lexander)
Okigbo, Christopher (Ifenayichukwu)
   1932-1967 ... CLC 25, 84; BLC 3; DAM
   MULT, POET; PC 7
   See also BW 1, 3; CA 77-80; CANR 74;
   DLB 125; MTCW 1, 2
Okri, Ben 1959- .... CLC 87
   See also BW 2, 3; CA 130; 138; CANR 65;
   DLB 157; INT 138; MTCW 2
Olds, Sharon 1942- ... CLC 32, 39, 85; DAM
   POET; PC 22
   See also CA 101; CANR 18, 41, 66; DLB
   120; MTCW 2
Oldstyle, Jonathan
   See Irving, Washington
Olesha, Yuri (Karlovich) 1899-1960 .. CLC 8
   See also CA 85-88
Oliphant, Laurence 1829(?)-1888 .. NCLC 47
   See also DLB 18, 166
Oliphant, Margaret (Oliphant Wilson)
   1828-1897 .... NCLC 11, 61; SSC 25
   See also DLB 18, 159, 190
Oliver, Mary 1935- .... CLC 19, 34, 98
   See also CA 21-24R; CANR 9, 43, 84; DLB
   5, 193
Olivier, Laurence (Kerr) 1907-1989 . CLC 20
   See also CA 111; 150; 129
Olsen, Tillie 1912- .... CLC 4, 13, 114; DA;
   DAB; DAC; DAM MST; SSC 11
   See also CA 1-4R; CANR 1, 43, 74;
   CDALBS; DA3; DLB 28, 206; DLBY 80;
   MTCW 1, 2
Olson, Charles (John) 1910-1970 .. CLC 1, 2,
   5, 6, 9, 11, 29; DAM POET; PC 19
   See also CA 13-16; 25-28R; CABS 2;
   CANR 35, 61; CAP 1; DLB 5, 16, 193;
   MTCW 1, 2
Olson, Toby 1937- .... CLC 28
   See also CA 65-68; CANR 9, 31, 84
Olyesha, Yuri
   See Olesha, Yuri (Karlovich)
Ondaatje, (Philip) Michael 1943- .... CLC 14,
   29, 51, 76; DAB; DAC; DAM MST; PC
   28
   See also CA 77-80; CANR 42, 74; DA3;
   DLB 60; MTCW 2
Oneal, Elizabeth 1934-
   See Oneal, Zibby
   See also CA 106; CANR 28, 84; MAICYA;
   SATA 30, 82
Oneal, Zibby CLC 30
   See also Oneal, Elizabeth
   See also AAYA 5; CLR 13; JRDA
O'Neill, Eugene (Gladstone)
   1888-1953 .... TCLC 1, 6, 27, 49; DA;
   DAB; DAC; DAM DRAM, MST; WLC
   See also AITN 1; CA 110; 132; CDALB
   1929-1941; DA3; DLB 7; MTCW 1, 2
Onetti, Juan Carlos 1909-1994 ... CLC 7, 10;
   DAM MULT, NOV; HLCS 2; SSC 23
   See also CA 85-88; 145; CANR 32, 63;
   DLB 113; HW 1, 2; MTCW 1, 2
O Nuallain, Brian 1911-1966
   See O'Brien, Flann
   See also CA 21-22; 25-28R; CAP 2
Ophuls, Max 1902-1957 .... TCLC 79
   See also CA 113
Opie, Amelia 1769-1853 .... NCLC 65
   See also DLB 116, 159
Oppen, George 1908-1984 ...... CLC 7, 13, 34
   See also CA 13-16R; 113; CANR 8, 82;
   DLB 5, 165
Oppenheim, E(dward) Phillips
   1866-1946 .... TCLC 45
   See also CA 111; DLB 70

Opuls, Max
   See Ophuls, Max
Origen c. 185-c. 254 .... CMLC 19
Orlovitz, Gil 1918-1973 .... CLC 22
   See also CA 77-80; 45-48; DLB 2, 5
Orris
   See Ingelow, Jean
Ortega y Gasset, Jose 1883-1955 ... TCLC 9;
   DAM MULT; HLC 2
   See also CA 106; 130; HW 1, 2; MTCW 1,
   2
Ortese, Anna Maria 1914- .... CLC 89
   See also DLB 177
Ortiz, Simon J(oseph) 1941- . CLC 45; DAM
   MULT, POET; PC 17
   See also CA 134; CANR 69; DLB 120, 175;
   NNAL
Orton, Joe CLC 4, 13, 43; DC 3
   See also Orton, John Kingsley
   See also CDBLB 1960 to Present; DLB 13;
   MTCW 2
Orton, John Kingsley 1933-1967
   See Orton, Joe
   See also CA 85-88; CANR 35, 66; DAM
   DRAM; MTCW 1, 2
Orwell, George TCLC 2, 6, 15, 31, 51; DAB;
   WLC
   See also Blair, Eric (Arthur)
   See also CDBLB 1945-1960; DLB 15, 98,
   195
Osborne, David
   See Silverberg, Robert
Osborne, George
   See Silverberg, Robert
Osborne, John (James) 1929-1994 .... CLC 1,
   2, 5, 11, 45; DA; DAB; DAC; DAM
   DRAM, MST; WLC
   See also CA 13-16R; 147; CANR 21, 56;
   CDBLB 1945-1960; DLB 13; MTCW 1,
   2
Osborne, Lawrence 1958- .... CLC 50
Osbourne, Lloyd 1868-1947 .... TCLC 93
Oshima, Nagisa 1932- .... CLC 20
   See also CA 116; 121; CANR 78
Oskison, John Milton 1874-1947 .. TCLC 35;
   DAM MULT
   See also CA 144; CANR 84; DLB 175;
   NNAL
Ossian c. 3rd cent. - .... CMLC 28
   See also Macpherson, James
Ostriker, Alicia (Suskin) 1937- .... CLC 132
   See also CA 25-28R; CAAS 24; CANR 10,
   30, 62; DLB 120
Ostrovsky, Alexander 1823-1886 .. NCLC 30,
   57
Otero, Blas de 1916-1979 .... CLC 11
   See also CA 89-92; DLB 134
Otto, Rudolf 1869-1937 .... TCLC 85
Otto, Whitney 1955- .... CLC 70
   See also CA 140
Ouida TCLC 43
   See also De La Ramee, (Marie) Louise
   See also DLB 18, 156
Ousmane, Sembene 1923- ... CLC 66; BLC 3
   See also BW 1, 3; CA 117; 125; CANR 81;
   MTCW 1
Ovid 43B.C.-17 . CMLC 7; DAM POET; PC
   2
   See also DA3; DLB 211
Owen, Hugh
   See Faust, Frederick (Schiller)
Owen, Wilfred (Edward Salter)
   1893-1918 .... TCLC 5, 27; DA; DAB;
   DAC; DAM MST, POET; PC 19; WLC
   See also CA 104; 141; CDBLB 1914-1945;
   DLB 20; MTCW 2
Owens, Rochelle 1936- .... CLC 8
   See also CA 17-20R; CAAS 2; CANR 39

Oz, Amos 1939- ...... **CLC 5, 8, 11, 27, 33, 54; DAM NOV**
See also CA 53-56; CANR 27, 47, 65; MTCW 1, 2

Ozick, Cynthia 1928- .... **CLC 3, 7, 28, 62; DAM NOV, POP; SSC 15**
See also BEST 90:1; CA 17-20R; CANR 23, 58; DA3; DLB 28, 152; DLBY 82; INT CANR-23; MTCW 1, 2

Ozu, Yasujiro 1903-1963 .... **CLC 16**
See also CA 112

Pacheco, C.
See Pessoa, Fernando (Antonio Nogueira)

Pacheco, Jose Emilio 1939-
See also CA 111; 131; CANR 65; DAM MULT; HLC 2; HW 1, 2

Pa Chin CLC 18
See also Li Fei-kan

Pack, Robert 1929- .... **CLC 13**
See also CA 1-4R; CANR 3, 44, 82; DLB 5

Padgett, Lewis
See Kuttner, Henry

Padilla (Lorenzo), Heberto 1932- ..... **CLC 38**
See also AITN 1; CA 123; 131; HW 1

Page, Jimmy 1944- .... **CLC 12**

Page, Louise 1955- .... **CLC 40**
See also CA 140; CANR 76

Page, P(atricia) K(athleen) 1916- ...... **CLC 7, 18; DAC; DAM MST; PC 12**
See also CA 53-56; CANR 4, 22, 65; DLB 68; MTCW 1

Page, Thomas Nelson 1853-1922 .... **SSC 23**
See also CA 118; 177; DLB 12, 78; DLBD 13

Pagels, Elaine Hiesey 1943- .... **CLC 104**
See also CA 45-48; CANR 2, 24, 51

Paget, Violet 1856-1935
See Lee, Vernon
See also CA 104; 166

Paget-Lowe, Henry
See Lovecraft, H(oward) P(hillips)

Paglia, Camille (Anna) 1947- .... **CLC 68**
See also CA 140; CANR 72; MTCW 2

Paige, Richard
See Koontz, Dean R(ay)

Paine, Thomas 1737-1809 .... **NCLC 62**
See also CDALB 1640-1865; DLB 31, 43, 73, 158

Pakenham, Antonia
See Fraser, (Lady) Antonia (Pakenham)

Palamas, Kostes 1859-1943 .... **TCLC 5**
See also CA 105

Palazzeschi, Aldo 1885-1974 .... **CLC 11**
See also CA 89-92; 53-56; DLB 114

Pales Matos, Luis 1898-1959
See also HLCS 2; HW 1

Paley, Grace 1922- .... **CLC 4, 6, 37; DAM POP; SSC 8**
See also CA 25-28R; CANR 13, 46, 74; DA3; DLB 28; INT CANR-13; MTCW 1, 2

Palin, Michael (Edward) 1943- .... **CLC 21**
See also Monty Python
See also CA 107; CANR 35; SATA 67

Palliser, Charles 1947- .... **CLC 65**
See also CA 136; CANR 76

Palma, Ricardo 1833-1919 .... **TCLC 29**
See also CA 168

Pancake, Breece Dexter 1952-1979
See Pancake, Breece D'J
See also CA 123; 109

Pancake, Breece D'J CLC 29
See also Pancake, Breece Dexter
See also DLB 130

Panko, Rudy
See Gogol, Nikolai (Vasilyevich)

Papadiamantis, Alexandros
1851-1911 .... **TCLC 29**
See also CA 168

Papadiamantopoulos, Johannes 1856-1910
See Moreas, Jean
See also CA 117

Papini, Giovanni 1881-1956 .... **TCLC 22**
See also CA 121; 180

Paracelsus 1493-1541 .... **LC 14**
See also DLB 179

Parasol, Peter
See Stevens, Wallace

Pardo Bazan, Emilia 1851-1921 .... **SSC 30**

Pareto, Vilfredo 1848-1923 .... **TCLC 69**
See also CA 175

Parfenie, Maria
See Codrescu, Andrei

Parini, Jay (Lee) 1948- .... **CLC 54, 133**
See also CA 97-100; CAAS 16; CANR 32, 87

Park, Jordan
See Kornbluth, C(yril) M.; Pohl, Frederik

Park, Robert E(zra) 1864-1944 ..... **TCLC 73**
See also CA 122; 165

Parker, Bert
See Ellison, Harlan (Jay)

Parker, Dorothy (Rothschild)
1893-1967 .... **CLC 15, 68; DAM POET; PC 28; SSC 2**
See also CA 19-20; 25-28R; CAP 2; DA3; DLB 11, 45, 86; MTCW 1, 2

Parker, Robert B(rown) 1932- .... **CLC 27; DAM NOV, POP**
See also AAYA 28; BEST 89:4; CA 49-52; CANR 1, 26, 52, 89; INT CANR-26; MTCW 1

Parkin, Frank 1940- .... **CLC 43**
See also CA 147

Parkman, Francis Jr., Jr.
1823-1893 .... **NCLC 12**
See also DLB 1, 30, 186

Parks, Gordon (Alexander Buchanan)
1912- .... **CLC 1, 16; BLC 3; DAM MULT**
See also AITN 2; BW 2, 3; CA 41-44R; CANR 26, 66; DA3; DLB 33; MTCW 2; SATA 8, 108

Parmenides c. 515B.C.-c.
450B.C. .... **CMLC 22**
See also DLB 176

Parnell, Thomas 1679-1718 .... **LC 3**
See also DLB 94

Parra, Nicanor 1914- ...... **CLC 2, 102; DAM MULT; HLC 2**
See also CA 85-88; CANR 32; HW 1; MTCW 1

Parra Sanojo, Ana Teresa de la 1890-1936
See also HLCS 2

Parrish, Mary Frances
See Fisher, M(ary) F(rances) K(ennedy)

Parson
See Coleridge, Samuel Taylor

Parson Lot
See Kingsley, Charles

Parton, Sara Payson Willis
1811-1872 .... **NCLC 86**
See also DLB 43, 74

Partridge, Anthony
See Oppenheim, E(dward) Phillips

Pascal, Blaise 1623-1662 .... **LC 35**

Pascoli, Giovanni 1855-1912 .... **TCLC 45**
See also CA 170

Pasolini, Pier Paolo 1922-1975 .. **CLC 20, 37, 106; PC 17**
See also CA 93-96; 61-64; CANR 63; DLB 128, 177; MTCW 1

Pasquini
See Silone, Ignazio

Pastan, Linda (Olenik) 1932- .... **CLC 27; DAM POET**
See also CA 61-64; CANR 18, 40, 61; DLB 5

Pasternak, Boris (Leonidovich)
1890-1960 .... **CLC 7, 10, 18, 63; DA; DAB; DAC; DAM MST, NOV, POET; PC 6; SSC 31; WLC**
See also CA 127; 116; DA3; MTCW 1, 2

Patchen, Kenneth 1911-1972 .. **CLC 1, 2, 18; DAM POET**
See also CA 1-4R; 33-36R; CANR 3, 35; DLB 16, 48; MTCW 1

Pater, Walter (Horatio) 1839-1894 .... **NCLC**
See also CDBLB 1832-1890; DLB 57, 156

Paterson, A(ndrew) B(arton)
1864-1941 .... **TCLC 32**
See also CA 155; SATA 97

Paterson, Katherine (Womeldorf)
1932- .... **CLC 12, 30**
See also AAYA 1, 31; CA 21-24R; CANR 28, 59; CLR 7, 50; DLB 52; JRDA; MAI-CYA; MTCW 1; SATA 13, 53, 92

Patmore, Coventry Kersey Dighton
1823-1896 .... **NCLC 9**
See also DLB 35, 98

Paton, Alan (Stewart) 1903-1988 ...... **CLC 4, 10, 25, 55, 106; DA; DAB; DAC; DAM MST, NOV; WLC**
See also AAYA 26; CA 13-16; 125; CANR 22; CAP 1; DA3; DLB 225; DLBD 17; MTCW 1, 2; SATA 11; SATA-Obit 56

Paton Walsh, Gillian 1937-
See Walsh, Jill Paton
See also AAYA 11; CANR 38, 83; DLB 161; JRDA; MAICYA; SAAS 3; SATA 4, 72, 109

Patton, George S. 1885-1945 .... **TCLC 79**

Paulding, James Kirke 1778-1860 ... **NCLC 2**
See also DLB 3, 59, 74

Paulin, Thomas Neilson 1949-
See Paulin, Tom
See also CA 123; 128

Paulin, Tom CLC 37
See also Paulin, Thomas Neilson
See also DLB 40

Pausanias c. 1st cent. - .... **CMLC 36**

Paustovsky, Konstantin (Georgievich)
1892-1968 .... **CLC 40**
See also CA 93-96; 25-28R

Pavese, Cesare 1908-1950 .. **TCLC 3; PC 13; SSC 19**
See also CA 104; 169; DLB 128, 177

Pavic, Milorad 1929- .... **CLC 60**
See also CA 136; DLB 181

Pavlov, Ivan Petrovich 1849-1936 . **TCLC 91**
See also CA 118; 180

Payne, Alan
See Jakes, John (William)

Paz, Gil
See Lugones, Leopoldo

Paz, Octavio 1914-1998 . **CLC 3, 4, 6, 10, 19, 51, 65, 119; DA; DAB; DAC; DAM MST, MULT, POET; HLC 2; PC 1; WLC**
See also CA 73-76; 165; CANR 32, 65; DA3; DLBY 90, 98; HW 1, 2; MTCW 1, 2

p'Bitek, Okot 1931-1982 .... **CLC 96; BLC 3; DAM MULT**
See also BW 2, 3; CA 124; 107; CANR 82; DLB 125; MTCW 1, 2

Peacock, Molly 1947- .... **CLC 60**
See also CA 103; CAAS 21; CANR 52, 84; DLB 120

Peacock, Thomas Love
1785-1866 .... **NCLC 22**
See also DLB 96, 116

Peake, Mervyn 1911-1968 .... **CLC 7, 54**
   See also CA 5-8R; 25-28R; CANR 3; DLB
   15, 160; MTCW 1; SATA 23

Pearce, Philippa CLC 21
   See also Christie, (Ann) Philippa
   See also CLR 9; DLB 161; MAICYA;
   SATA 1, 67

Pearl, Eric
   See Elman, Richard (Martin)

Pearson, T(homas) R(eid) 1956- .... **CLC 39**
   See also CA 120; 130; INT 130

Peck, Dale 1967- .... **CLC 81**
   See also CA 146; CANR 72

Peck, John 1941- .... **CLC 3**
   See also CA 49-52; CANR 3

Peck, Richard (Wayne) 1934- .... **CLC 21**
   See also AAYA 1, 24; CA 85-88; CANR
   19, 38; CLR 15; INT CANR-19; JRDA;
   MAICYA; SAAS 2; SATA 18, 55, 97;
   SATA-Essay 110

Peck, Robert Newton 1928- .... **CLC 17; DA;**
   DAC; DAM MST
   See also AAYA 3; CA 81-84, 182; CAAE
   182; CANR 31, 63; CLR 45; JRDA; MAI-
   CYA; SAAS 1; SATA 21, 62, 111; SATA-
   Essay 108

Peckinpah, (David) Sam(uel)
   1925-1984 .... **CLC 20**
   See also CA 109; 114; CANR 82

Pedersen, Knut 1859-1952
   See Hamsun, Knut
   See also CA 104; 119; CANR 63; MTCW
   1, 2

Peeslake, Gaffer
   See Durrell, Lawrence (George)

Peguy, Charles Pierre 1873-1914 ... **TCLC 10**
   See also CA 107

Peirce, Charles Sanders
   1839-1914 .... **TCLC 81**

Pellicer, Carlos 1900(?)-1977
   See also CA 153; 69-72; HLCS 2; HW 1

Pena, Ramon del Valle y
   See Valle-Inclan, Ramon (Maria) del

Pendennis, Arthur Esquir
   See Thackeray, William Makepeace

Penn, William 1644-1718 .... **LC 25**
   See also DLB 24

PEPECE
   See Prado (Calvo), Pedro

Pepys, Samuel 1633-1703 ..... **LC 11, 58; DA;**
   DAB; DAC; DAM MST; WLC
   See also CDBLB 1660-1789; DA3; DLB
   101

Percy, Walker 1916-1990 .... **CLC 2, 3, 6, 8,**
   14, 18, 47, 65; DAM NOV, POP
   See also CA 1-4R; 131; CANR 1, 23, 64;
   DA3; DLB 2; DLBY 80, 90; MTCW 1, 2

Percy, William Alexander
   1885-1942 .... **TCLC 84**
   See also CA 163; MTCW 2

Perec, Georges 1936-1982 .... **CLC 56, 116**
   See also CA 141; DLB 83

Pereda (y Sanchez de Porrua), Jose Maria
   de 1833-1906 .... **TCLC 16**
   See also CA 117

Pereda y Porrua, Jose Maria de
   See Pereda (y Sanchez de Porrua), Jose
   Maria de

Peregoy, George Weems
   See Mencken, H(enry) L(ouis)

Perelman, S(idney) J(oseph)
   1904-1979 .. **CLC 3, 5, 9, 15, 23, 44, 49;**
   DAM DRAM; SSC 32
   See also AITN 1, 2; CA 73-76; 89-92;
   CANR 18; DLB 11, 44; MTCW 1, 2

Peret, Benjamin 1899-1959 .... **TCLC 20**
   See also CA 117; 186

Peretz, Isaac Loeb 1851(?)-1915 ... **TCLC 16;**
   SSC 26
   See also CA 109

Peretz, Yitzhok Leibush
   See Peretz, Isaac Loeb

Perez Galdos, Benito 1843-1920 ... **TCLC 27;**
   HLCS 2
   See also CA 125; 153; HW 1

Peri Rossi, Cristina 1941-
   See also CA 131; CANR 59, 81; DLB 145;
   HLCS 2; HW 1, 2

Perlata
   See Peret, Benjamin

Perrault, Charles 1628-1703 ... **LC 3, 52; DC**
   12
   See also MAICYA; SATA 25

Perry, Anne 1938- .... **CLC 126**
   See also CA 101; CANR 22, 50, 84

Perry, Brighton
   See Sherwood, Robert E(mmet)

Perse, St.-John
   See Leger, (Marie-Rene Auguste) Alexis
   Saint-Leger

Perutz, Leo(pold) 1882-1957 .... **TCLC 60**
   See also CA 147; DLB 81

Peseenz, Tulio F.
   See Lopez y Fuentes, Gregorio

Pesetsky, Bette 1932- .... **CLC 28**
   See also CA 133; DLB 130

Peshkov, Alexei Maximovich 1868-1936
   See Gorky, Maxim
   See also CA 105; 141; CANR 83; DA;
   DAC; DAM DRAM, MST, NOV; MTCW
   2

Pessoa, Fernando (Antonio Nogueira)
   1888-1935 .... **TCLC 27; DAM MULT;**
   HLC 2; PC 20
   See also CA 125; 183

Peterkin, Julia Mood 1880-1961 ...... **CLC 31**
   See also CA 102; DLB 9

Peters, Joan K(aren) 1945- .... **CLC 39**
   See also CA 158

Peters, Robert L(ouis) 1924- .... **CLC 7**
   See also CA 13-16R; CAAS 8; DLB 105

Petofi, Sandor 1823-1849 .... **NCLC 21**

Petrakis, Harry Mark 1923- .... **CLC 3**
   See also CA 9-12R; CANR 4, 30, 85

Petrarch 1304-1374 .... **CMLC 20; DAM**
   POET; PC 8
   See also DA3

Petronius c. 20-66 .... **CMLC 34**
   See also DLB 211

Petrov, Evgeny TCLC 21
   See also Kataev, Evgeny Petrovich

Petry, Ann (Lane) 1908-1997 ... **CLC 1, 7, 18**
   See also BW 1, 3; CA 5-8R; 157; CAAS 6;
   CANR 4, 46; CLR 12; DLB 76; JRDA;
   MAICYA; MTCW 1; SATA 5; SATA-Obit
   94

Petursson, Halligrimur 1614-1674 .... **LC 8**

Peychinovich
   See Vazov, Ivan (Minchov)

Phaedrus c. 18B.C.-c. 50 .... **CMLC 25**
   See also DLB 211

Philips, Katherine 1632-1664 .... **LC 30**
   See also DLB 131

Philipson, Morris H. 1926- .... **CLC 53**
   See also CA 1-4R; CANR 4

Phillips, Caryl 1958- . **CLC 96; BLCS; DAM**
   MULT
   See also BW 2; CA 141; CANR 63; DA3;
   DLB 157; MTCW 2

Phillips, David Graham
   1867-1911 .... **TCLC 44**
   See also CA 108; 176; DLB 9, 12

Phillips, Jack
   See Sandburg, Carl (August)

Phillips, Jayne Anne 1952- .... **CLC 15, 33;**
   SSC 16
   See also CA 101; CANR 24, 50; DLBY 80;
   INT CANR-24; MTCW 1, 2

Phillips, Richard
   See Dick, Philip K(indred)

Phillips, Robert (Schaeffer) 1938- .... **CLC 28**
   See also CA 17-20R; CAAS 13; CANR 8;
   DLB 105

Phillips, Ward
   See Lovecraft, H(oward) P(hillips)

Piccolo, Lucio 1901-1969 .... **CLC 13**
   See also CA 97-100; DLB 114

Pickthall, Marjorie L(owry) C(hristie)
   1883-1922 .... **TCLC 21**
   See also CA 107; DLB 92

Pico della Mirandola, Giovanni
   1463-1494 .... **LC 15**

Piercy, Marge 1936- .... **CLC 3, 6, 14, 18, 27,**
   62, 128; PC 29
   See also CA 21-24R; CAAS 1; CANR 13,
   43, 66; DLB 120, 227; MTCW 1, 2

Piers, Robert
   See Anthony, Piers

Pieyre de Mandiargues, Andre 1909-1991
   See Mandiargues, Andre Pieyre de
   See also CA 103; 136; CANR 22, 82

Pilnyak, Boris TCLC 23
   See also Vogau, Boris Andreyevich

Pincherle, Alberto 1907-1990 .... **CLC 11, 18;**
   DAM NOV
   See also Moravia, Alberto
   See also CA 25-28R; 132; CANR 33, 63;
   MTCW 1

Pinckney, Darryl 1953- .... **CLC 76**
   See also BW 2, 3; CA 143; CANR 79

Pindar 518B.C.-446B.C. .... **CMLC 12; PC 19**
   See also DLB 176

Pineda, Cecile 1942- .... **CLC 39**
   See also CA 118

Pinero, Arthur Wing 1855-1934 ... **TCLC 32;**
   DAM DRAM
   See also CA 110; 153; DLB 10

Pinero, Miguel (Antonio Gomez)
   1946-1988 .... **CLC 4, 55**
   See also CA 61-64; 125; CANR 29, 90; HW
   1

Pinget, Robert 1919-1997 .... **CLC 7, 13, 37**
   See also CA 85-88; 160; DLB 83

Pink Floyd
   See Barrett, (Roger) Syd; Gilmour, David;
   Mason, Nick; Waters, Roger; Wright, Rick

Pinkney, Edward 1802-1828 .... **NCLC 31**

Pinkwater, Daniel Manus 1941- .... **CLC 35**
   See also Pinkwater, Manus
   See also AAYA 1; CA 29-32R; CANR 12,
   38, 89; CLR 4; JRDA; MAICYA; SAAS
   3; SATA 46, 76, 114

Pinkwater, Manus
   See Pinkwater, Daniel Manus
   See also SATA 8

Pinsky, Robert 1940- .... **CLC 9, 19, 38, 94,**
   121; DAM POET; PC 27
   See also CA 29-32R; CAAS 4; CANR 58;
   DA3; DLBY 82, 98; MTCW 2

Pinta, Harold
   See Pinter, Harold

Pinter, Harold 1930- .. **CLC 1, 3, 6, 9, 11, 15,**
   27, 58, 73; DA; DAB; DAC; DAM
   DRAM, MST; WLC
   See also CA 5-8R; CANR 33, 65; CDBLB
   1960 to Present; DA3; DLB 13; MTCW
   1, 2

Piozzi, Hester Lynch (Thrale)
   1741-1821 .... **NCLC 57**
   See also DLB 104, 142

Pirandello, Luigi 1867-1936 ...... **TCLC 4, 29; DA; DAB; DAC; DAM DRAM, MST; DC 5; SSC 22; WLC**
See also CA 104; 153; DA3; MTCW 2

Pirsig, Robert M(aynard) 1928- ... **CLC 4, 6, 73; DAM POP**
See also CA 53-56; CANR 42, 74; DA3; MTCW 1, 2; SATA 39

Pisarev, Dmitry Ivanovich 1840-1868 .... **NCLC 25**

Pix, Mary (Griffith) 1666-1709 .... **LC 8**
See also DLB 80

Pixerecourt, (Rene Charles) Guilbert de 1773-1844 .... **NCLC 39**
See also DLB 192

Plaatje, Sol(omon) T(shekisho) 1876-1932 .... **TCLC 73; BLCS**
See also BW 2, 3; CA 141; CANR 79; DLB 225

Plaidy, Jean
See Hibbert, Eleanor Alice Burford

Planche, James Robinson 1796-1880 .... **NCLC 42**

Plant, Robert 1948- .... **CLC 12**

Plante, David (Robert) 1940- ...... **CLC 7, 23, 38; DAM NOV**
See also CA 37-40R; CANR 12, 36, 58, 82; DLBY 83; INT CANR-12; MTCW 1

Plath, Sylvia 1932-1963 ..... **CLC 1, 2, 3, 5, 9, 11, 14, 17, 50, 51, 62, 111; DA; DAB; DAC; DAM MST, POET; PC 1; WLC**
See also AAYA 13; CA 19-20; CANR 34; CAP 2; CDALB 1941-1968; DA3; DLB 5, 6, 152; MTCW 1, 2; SATA 96

Plato 428(?)B.C.-348(?)B.C. ... **CMLC 8; DA; DAB; DAC; DAM MST; WLCS**
See also DA3; DLB 176

Platonov, Andrei
See Klimentov, Andrei Platonovich

Platt, Kin 1911- .... **CLC 26**
See also AAYA 11; CA 17-20R; CANR 11; JRDA; SAAS 17; SATA 21, 86

Plautus c. 251B.C.-184B.C. ... **CMLC 24; DC 6**
See also DLB 211

Plick et Plock
See Simenon, Georges (Jacques Christian)

Plimpton, George (Ames) 1927- .... **CLC 36**
See also AITN 1; CA 21-24R; CANR 32, 70; DLB 185; MTCW 1, 2; SATA 10

Pliny the Elder c. 23-79 .... **CMLC 23**
See also DLB 211

Plomer, William Charles Franklin 1903-1973 .... **CLC 4, 8**
See also CA 21-22; CANR 34; CAP 2; DLB 20, 162, 191, 225; MTCW 1; SATA 24

Plowman, Piers
See Kavanagh, Patrick (Joseph)

Plum, J.
See Wodehouse, P(elham) G(renville)

Plumly, Stanley (Ross) 1939- .... **CLC 33**
See also CA 108; 110; DLB 5, 193; INT 110

Plumpe, Friedrich Wilhelm 1888-1931 .... **TCLC 53**
See also CA 112

Po Chu-i 772-846 .... **CMLC 24**

Poe, Edgar Allan 1809-1849 ..... **NCLC 1, 16, 55, 78; DA; DAB; DAC; DAM MST, POET; PC 1; SSC 34; WLC**
See also AAYA 14; CDALB 1640-1865; DA3; DLB 3, 59, 73, 74; SATA 23

Poet of Titchfield Street, The
See Pound, Ezra (Weston Loomis)

Pohl, Frederik 1919- .... **CLC 18; SSC 25**
See also AAYA 24; CA 61-64; CAAS 1; CANR 11, 37, 81; DLB 8; INT CANR-11; MTCW 1, 2; SATA 24

Poirier, Louis 1910-
See Gracq, Julien
See also CA 122; 126

Poitier, Sidney 1927- .... **CLC 26**
See also BW 1; CA 117

Polanski, Roman 1933- .... **CLC 16**
See also CA 77-80

Poliakoff, Stephen 1952- .... **CLC 38**
See also CA 106; DLB 13

Police, The
See Copeland, Stewart (Armstrong); Summers, Andrew James; Sumner, Gordon Matthew

Polidori, John William 1795-1821 . **NCLC 51**
See also DLB 116

Pollitt, Katha 1949- .... **CLC 28, 122**
See also CA 120; 122; CANR 66; MTCW 1, 2

Pollock, (Mary) Sharon 1936- .... **CLC 50; DAC; DAM DRAM, MST**
See also CA 141; DLB 60

Polo, Marco 1254-1324 .... **CMLC 15**

Polonsky, Abraham (Lincoln) 1910- .... **CLC 92**
See also CA 104; DLB 26; INT 104

Polybius c. 200B.C.-c. 118B.C. ...... **CMLC 17**
See also DLB 176

Pomerance, Bernard 1940- ... **CLC 13; DAM DRAM**
See also CA 101; CANR 49

Ponge, Francis 1899-1988 . **CLC 6, 18; DAM POET**
See also CA 85-88; 126; CANR 40, 86

Poniatowska, Elena 1933-
See also CA 101; CANR 32, 66; DAM MULT; DLB 113; HLC 2; HW 1, 2

Pontoppidan, Henrik 1857-1943 .... **TCLC 29**
See also CA 170

Poole, Josephine .... **CLC 17**
See also Helyar, Jane Penelope Josephine
See also SAAS 2; SATA 5

Popa, Vasko 1922-1991 .... **CLC 19**
See also CA 112; 148; DLB 181

Pope, Alexander 1688-1744 .... **LC 3, 58; DA; DAB; DAC; DAM MST, POET; PC 26; WLC**
See also CDBLB 1660-1789; DA3; DLB 95, 101

Porter, Connie (Rose) 1959(?)- .... **CLC 70**
See also BW 2, 3; CA 142; CANR 90; SATA 81

Porter, Gene(va Grace) Stratton 1863(?)-1924 .... **TCLC 21**
See also CA 112

Porter, Katherine Anne 1890-1980 ... **CLC 1, 3, 7, 10, 13, 15, 27, 101; DA; DAB; DAC; DAM MST, NOV; SSC 4, 31**
See also AITN 2; CA 1-4R; 101; CANR 1, 65; CDALBS; DA3; DLB 4, 9, 102; DLBD 12; DLBY 80; MTCW 1, 2; SATA 39; SATA-Obit 23

Porter, Peter (Neville Frederick) 1929- .... **CLC 5, 13, 33**
See also CA 85-88; DLB 40

Porter, William Sydney 1862-1910
See Henry, O.
See also CA 104; 131; CDALB 1865-1917; DA; DAB; DAC; DAM MST; DA3; DLB 12, 78, 79; MTCW 1, 2; YABC 2

Portillo (y Pacheco), Jose Lopez
See Lopez Portillo (y Pacheco), Jose

Portillo Trambley, Estela 1927-1998
See also CANR 32; DAM MULT; DLB 209; HLC 2; HW 1

Post, Melville Davisson 1869-1930 .... **TCLC 39**
See also CA 110

Potok, Chaim 1929- ... **CLC 2, 7, 14, 26, 112; DAM NOV**
See also AAYA 15; AITN 1, 2; CA 17-20R; CANR 19, 35, 64; DA3; DLB 28, 152; INT CANR-19; MTCW 1, 2; SATA 33, 106

Potter, Dennis (Christopher George) 1935-1994 .... **CLC 58, 86**
See also CA 107; 145; CANR 33, 61; MTCW 1

Pound, Ezra (Weston Loomis) 1885-1972 .. **CLC 1, 2, 3, 4, 5, 7, 10, 13, 18, 34, 48, 50, 112; DA; DAB; DAC; DAM MST, POET; PC 4; WLC**
See also CA 5-8R; 37-40R; CANR 40; CDALB 1917-1929; DA3; DLB 4, 45, 63; DLBD 15; MTCW 1, 2

Povod, Reinaldo 1959-1994 .... **CLC 44**
See also CA 136; 146; CANR 83

Powell, Adam Clayton, Jr. 1908-1972 .... **CLC 89; BLC 3; DAM MULT**
See also BW 1, 3; CA 102; 33-36R; CANR 86

Powell, Anthony (Dymoke) 1905-2000 .... **CLC 1, 3, 7, 9, 10, 31**
See also CA 1-4R; CANR 1, 32, 62; CD-BLB 1945-1960; DLB 15; MTCW 1, 2

Powell, Dawn 1897-1965 .... **CLC 66**
See also CA 5-8R; DLBY 97

Powell, Padgett 1952- .... **CLC 34**
See also CA 126; CANR 63

Power, Susan 1961- .... **CLC 91**
See also CA 145

Powers, J(ames) F(arl) 1917-1999 ..... **CLC 1, 4, 8, 57; SSC 4**
See also CA 1-4R; 181; CANR 2, 61; DLB 130; MTCW 1

Powers, John J(ames) 1945-
See Powers, John R.
See also CA 69-72

Powers, John R. .... **CLC 66**
See also Powers, John J(ames)

Powers, Richard (S.) 1957- .... **CLC 93**
See also CA 148; CANR 80

Pownall, David 1938- .... **CLC 10**
See also CA 89-92, 180; CAAS 18; CANR 49; DLB 14

Powys, John Cowper 1872-1963 ... **CLC 7, 9, 15, 46, 125**
See also CA 85-88; DLB 15; MTCW 1, 2

Powys, T(heodore) F(rancis) 1875-1953 .... **TCLC 9**
See also CA 106; DLB 36, 162

Prado (Calvo), Pedro 1886-1952 ... **TCLC 75**
See also CA 131; HW 1

Prager, Emily 1952- .... **CLC 56**

Pratt, E(dwin) J(ohn) 1883(?)-1964 .... **CLC 19; DAC; DAM POET**
See also CA 141; 93-96; CANR 77; DLB 92

Premchand .... **TCLC 21**
See also Srivastava, Dhanpat Rai

Preussler, Otfried 1923- .... **CLC 17**
See also CA 77-80; SATA 24

Prevert, Jacques (Henri Marie) 1900-1977 .... **CLC 15**
See also CA 77-80; 69-72; CANR 29, 61; MTCW 1; SATA-Obit 30

Prevost, Abbe (Antoine Francois) 1697-1763 .... **LC 1**

Price, (Edward) Reynolds 1933- ... **CLC 3, 6, 13, 43, 50, 63; DAM NOV; SSC 22**
See also CA 1-4R; CANR 1, 37, 57, 87; DLB 2; INT CANR-37

Price, Richard 1949- .... **CLC 6, 12**
See also CA 49-52; CANR 3; DLBY 81

Prichard, Katharine Susannah
    1883-1969 .... **CLC 46**
    See also CA 11-12; CANR 33; CAP 1;
    MTCW 1; SATA 66
Priestley, J(ohn) B(oynton)
    1894-1984 .... **CLC 2, 5, 9, 34; DAM
    DRAM, NOV**
    See also CA 9-12R; 113; CANR 33; CD-
    BLB 1914-1945; DA3; DLB 10, 34, 77,
    100, 139; DLBY 84; MTCW 1, 2
Prince 1958(?)- .... **CLC 35**
Prince, F(rank) T(empleton) 1912- .. **CLC 22**
    See also CA 101; CANR 43, 79; DLB 20
Prince Kropotkin
    See Kropotkin, Peter (Aleksieevich)
Prior, Matthew 1664-1721 .... **LC 4**
    See also DLB 95
Prishvin, Mikhail 1873-1954 .... **TCLC 75**
Pritchard, William H(arrison)
    1932- .... **CLC 34**
    See also CA 65-68; CANR 23; DLB 111
Pritchett, V(ictor) S(awdon)
    1900-1997 ...... **CLC 5, 13, 15, 41; DAM
    NOV; SSC 14**
    See also CA 61-64; 157; CANR 31, 63;
    DA3; DLB 15, 139; MTCW 1, 2
Private 19022
    See Manning, Frederic
Probst, Mark 1925- .... **CLC 59**
    See also CA 130
Prokosch, Frederic 1908-1989 ...... **CLC 4, 48**
    See also CA 73-76; 128; CANR 82; DLB
    48; MTCW 2
Propertius, Sextus c. 50B.C.-c.
    16B.C. .... **CMLC 32**
    See also DLB 211
Prophet, The
    See Dreiser, Theodore (Herman Albert)
Prose, Francine 1947- .... **CLC 45**
    See also CA 109; 112; CANR 46; SATA
    101
Proudhon
    See Cunha, Euclides (Rodrigues Pimenta)
    da
Proulx, Annie
    See Proulx, E(dna) Annie
Proulx, E(dna) Annie 1935- .. **CLC 81; DAM
    POP**
    See also CA 145; CANR 65; DA3; MTCW
    2
**Proust, (Valentin-Louis-George-Eugene-)
    Marcel** 1871-1922 .... **TCLC 7, 13, 33;
    DA; DAB; DAC; DAM MST, NOV;
    WLC**
    See also CA 104; 120; DA3; DLB 65;
    MTCW 1, 2
Prowler, Harley
    See Masters, Edgar Lee
Prus, Boleslaw 1845-1912 .... **TCLC 48**
Pryor, Richard (Franklin Lenox Thomas)
    1940- .... **CLC 26**
    See also CA 122; 152
Przybyszewski, Stanislaw
    1868-1927 .... **TCLC 36**
    See also CA 160; DLB 66
Pteleon
    See Grieve, C(hristopher) M(urray)
    See also DAM POET
Puckett, Lute
    See Masters, Edgar Lee
Puig, Manuel 1932-1990 .... **CLC 3, 5, 10, 28,
    65, 133; DAM MULT; HLC 2**
    See also CA 45-48; CANR 2, 32, 63; DA3;
    DLB 113; HW 1, 2; MTCW 1, 2
Pulitzer, Joseph 1847-1911 .... **TCLC 76**
    See also CA 114; DLB 23

Purdy, A(lfred) W(ellington)
    1918-2000 .... **CLC 3, 6, 14, 50; DAC;
    DAM MST, POET**
    See also CA 81-84; CAAS 17; CANR 42,
    66; DLB 88
Purdy, James (Amos) 1923- .... **CLC 2, 4, 10,
    28, 52**
    See also CA 33-36R; CAAS 1; CANR 19,
    51; DLB 2; INT CANR-19; MTCW 1
Pure, Simon
    See Swinnerton, Frank Arthur
Pushkin, Alexander (Sergeyevich)
    1799-1837 . **NCLC 3, 27, 83; DA; DAB;
    DAC; DAM DRAM, MST, POET; PC
    10; SSC 27; WLC**
    See also DA3; DLB 205; SATA 61
P'u Sung-ling 1640-1715 .... **LC 49; SSC 31**
Putnam, Arthur Lee
    See Alger, Horatio Jr., Jr.
Puzo, Mario 1920-1999 .... **CLC 1, 2, 6, 36,
    107; DAM NOV, POP**
    See also CA 65-68; 185; CANR 4, 42, 65;
    DA3; DLB 6; MTCW 1, 2
Pygge, Edward
    See Barnes, Julian (Patrick)
Pyle, Ernest Taylor 1900-1945
    See Pyle, Ernie
    See also CA 115; 160
Pyle, Ernie 1900-1945 .... **TCLC 75**
    See also Pyle, Ernest Taylor
    See also DLB 29; MTCW 2
Pyle, Howard 1853-1911 .... **TCLC 81**
    See also CA 109; 137; CLR 22; DLB 42,
    188; DLBD 13; MAICYA; SATA 16, 100
Pym, Barbara (Mary Crampton)
    1913-1980 .... **CLC 13, 19, 37, 111**
    See also CA 13-14; 97-100; CANR 13, 34;
    CAP 1; DLB 14, 207; DLBY 87; MTCW
    1, 2
Pynchon, Thomas (Ruggles, Jr.)
    1937- ...... **CLC 2, 3, 6, 9, 11, 18, 33, 62,
    72; DA; DAB; DAC; DAM MST, NOV,
    POP; SSC 14; WLC**
    See also BEST 90:2; CA 17-20R; CANR
    22, 46, 73; DA3; DLB 2, 173; MTCW 1,
    2
Pythagoras c. 570B.C.-c. 500B.C. . **CMLC 22**
    See also DLB 176
Q
    See Quiller-Couch, SirArthur (Thomas)
Qian Zhongshu
    See Ch'ien Chung-shu
Qroll
    See Dagerman, Stig (Halvard)
Quarrington, Paul (Lewis) 1953- ..... **CLC 65**
    See also CA 129; CANR 62
Quasimodo, Salvatore 1901-1968 ..... **CLC 10**
    See also CA 13-16; 25-28R; CAP 1; DLB
    114; MTCW 1
Quay, Stephen 1947- .... **CLC 95**
Quay, Timothy 1947- .... **CLC 95**
Queen, Ellery CLC 3, 11
    See also Dannay, Frederic; Davidson,
    Avram (James); Lee, Manfred
    B(ennington); Marlowe, Stephen; Stur-
    geon, Theodore (Hamilton); Vance, John
    Holbrook
Queen, Ellery, Jr.
    See Dannay, Frederic; Lee, Manfred
    B(ennington)
Queneau, Raymond 1903-1976 ..... **CLC 2, 5,
    10, 42**
    See also CA 77-80; 69-72; CANR 32; DLB
    72; MTCW 1, 2
Quevedo, Francisco de 1580-1645 .... **LC 23**
Quiller-Couch, SirArthur (Thomas)
    1863-1944 .... **TCLC 53**
    See also CA 118; 166; DLB 135, 153, 190

Quin, Ann (Marie) 1936-1973 .... **CLC 6**
    See also CA 9-12R; 45-48; DLB 14
Quinn, Martin
    See Smith, Martin Cruz
Quinn, Peter 1947- .... **CLC 91**
Quinn, Simon
    See Smith, Martin Cruz
Quintana, Leroy V. 1944-
    See also CA 131; CANR 65; DAM MULT;
    DLB 82; HLC 2; HW 1, 2
Quiroga, Horacio (Sylvestre)
    1878-1937 .... **TCLC 20; DAM MULT;
    HLC 2**
    See also CA 117; 131; HW 1; MTCW 1
Quoirez, Francoise 1935- .... **CLC 9**
    See also Sagan, Francoise
    See also CA 49-52; CANR 6, 39, 73;
    MTCW 1, 2
Raabe, Wilhelm (Karl) 1831-1910 . **TCLC 45**
    See also CA 167; DLB 129
Rabe, David (William) 1940- .. **CLC 4, 8, 33;
    DAM DRAM**
    See also CA 85-88; CABS 3; CANR 59;
    DLB 7, 228
Rabelais, Francois 1483-1553 ...... **LC 5; DA;
    DAB; DAC; DAM MST; WLC**
Rabinovitch, Sholem 1859-1916
    See Aleichem, Sholom
    See also CA 104
Rablnyan, Dorit 1972- .... **CLC 119**
    See also CA 170
Rachilde
    See Vallette, Marguerite Eymery
Racine, Jean 1639-1699 . **LC 28; DAB; DAM
    MST**
    See also DA3
Radcliffe, Ann (Ward) 1764-1823 ... **NCLC 6,
    55**
    See also DLB 39, 178
Radiguet, Raymond 1903-1923 .... **TCLC 29**
    See also CA 162; DLB 65
Radnoti, Miklos 1909-1944 .... **TCLC 16**
    See also CA 118
Rado, James 1939- .... **CLC 17**
    See also CA 105
Radvanyi, Netty 1900-1983
    See Seghers, Anna
    See also CA 85-88; 110; CANR 82
Rae, Ben
    See Griffiths, Trevor
Raeburn, John (Hay) 1941- .... **CLC 34**
    See also CA 57-60
Ragni, Gerome 1942-1991 .... **CLC 17**
    See also CA 105; 134
Rahv, Philip 1908-1973 .... **CLC 24**
    See also Greenberg, Ivan
    See also DLB 137
Raimund, Ferdinand Jakob
    1790-1836 .... **NCLC 69**
    See also DLB 90
Raine, Craig 1944- .... **CLC 32, 103**
    See also CA 108; CANR 29, 51; DLB 40
Raine, Kathleen (Jessie) 1908- ..... **CLC 7, 45**
    See also CA 85-88; CANR 46; DLB 20;
    MTCW 1
Rainis, Janis 1865-1929 .... **TCLC 29**
    See also CA 170; DLB 220
Rakosi, Carl 1903- .... **CLC 47**
    See also Rawley, Callman
    See also CAAS 5; DLB 193
Raleigh, Richard
    See Lovecraft, H(oward) P(hillips)
Raleigh, Sir Walter 1554(?)-1618 .. **LC 31, 39**
    See also CDBLB Before 1660; DLB 172
Rallentando, H. P.
    See Sayers, Dorothy L(eigh)
Ramal, Walter
    See de la Mare, Walter (John)

Ramana Maharshi 1879-1950 .... **TCLC 84**

Ramoacn y Cajal, Santiago
1852-1934 .... **TCLC 93**

Ramon, Juan
See Jimenez (Mantecon), Juan Ramon

Ramos, Graciliano 1892-1953 .... **TCLC 32**
See also CA 167; HW 2

Rampersad, Arnold 1941- .... **CLC 44**
See also BW 2, 3; CA 127; 133; CANR 81;
DLB 111; INT 133

Rampling, Anne
See Rice, Anne

Ramsay, Allan 1684(?)-1758 .... **LC 29**
See also DLB 95

Ramuz, Charles-Ferdinand
1878-1947 .... **TCLC 33**
See also CA 165

Rand, Ayn 1905-1982 ...... **CLC 3, 30, 44, 79;**
DA; DAC; DAM MST, NOV, POP;
WLC
See also AAYA 10; CA 13-16R; 105; CANR
27, 73; CDALBS; DA3; DLB 227;
MTCW 1, 2

Randall, Dudley (Felker) 1914- .... **CLC 1;**
BLC 3; DAM MULT
See also BW 1, 3; CA 25-28R; CANR 23,
82; DLB 41

Randall, Robert
See Silverberg, Robert

Ranger, Ken
See Creasey, John

Ransom, John Crowe 1888-1974 .. **CLC 2, 4,**
5, 11, 24; DAM POET
See also CA 5-8R; 49-52; CANR 6, 34;
CDALBS; DA3; DLB 45, 63; MTCW 1,
2

Rao, Raja 1909- ..... **CLC 25, 56; DAM NOV**
See also CA 73-76; CANR 51; MTCW 1, 2

Raphael, Frederic (Michael) 1931- ... **CLC 2,**
14
See also CA 1-4R; CANR 1, 86; DLB 14

Ratcliffe, James P.
See Mencken, H(enry) L(ouis)

Rathbone, Julian 1935- .... **CLC 41**
See also CA 101; CANR 34, 73

Rattigan, Terence (Mervyn)
1911-1977 .... **CLC 7; DAM DRAM**
See also CA 85-88; 73-76; CDBLB 1945-
1960; DLB 13; MTCW 1, 2

Ratushinskaya, Irina 1954- .... **CLC 54**
See also CA 129; CANR 68

Raven, Simon (Arthur Noel) 1927- .. **CLC 14**
See also CA 81-84; CANR 86

Ravenna, Michael
See Welty, Eudora

Rawley, Callman 1903-
See Rakosi, Carl
See also CA 21-24R; CANR 12, 32, 91

Rawlings, Marjorie Kinnan
1896-1953 .... **TCLC 4**
See also AAYA 20; CA 104; 137; CANR
74; CLR 63; DLB 9, 22, 102; DLBD 17;
JRDA; MAICYA; MTCW 2; SATA 100;
YABC 1

Ray, Satyajit 1921-1992 .. **CLC 16, 76; DAM**
MULT
See also CA 114; 137

Read, Herbert Edward 1893-1968 ..... **CLC 4**
See also CA 85-88; 25-28R; DLB 20, 149

Read, Piers Paul 1941- .... **CLC 4, 10, 25**
See also CA 21-24R; CANR 38, 86; DLB
14; SATA 21

Reade, Charles 1814-1884 .... **NCLC 2, 74**
See also DLB 21

Reade, Hamish
See Gray, Simon (James Holliday)

Reading, Peter 1946- .... **CLC 47**
See also CA 103; CANR 46; DLB 40

Reaney, James 1926- .. **CLC 13; DAC; DAM**
MST
See also CA 41-44R; CAAS 15; CANR 42;
DLB 68; SATA 43

Rebreanu, Liviu 1885-1944 .... **TCLC 28**
See also CA 165; DLB 220

Rechy, John (Francisco) 1934- ...... **CLC 1, 7,**
14, 18, 107; DAM MULT; HLC 2
See also CA 5-8R; CAAS 4; CANR 6, 32,
64; DLB 122; DLBY 82; HW 1, 2; INT
CANR-6

Redcam, Tom 1870-1933 .... **TCLC 25**

Reddin, Keith CLC 67

Redgrove, Peter (William) 1932- . **CLC 6, 41**
See also CA 1-4R; CANR 3, 39, 77; DLB
40

Redmon, Anne CLC 22
See also Nightingale, Anne Redmon
See also DLBY 86

Reed, Eliot
See Ambler, Eric

Reed, Ishmael 1938- .. **CLC 2, 3, 5, 6, 13, 32,**
60; BLC 3; DAM MULT
See also BW 2, 3; CA 21-24R; CANR 25,
48, 74; DA3; DLB 2, 5, 33, 169, 227;
DLBD 8; MTCW 1, 2

Reed, John (Silas) 1887-1920 .... **TCLC 9**
See also CA 106

Reed, Lou CLC 21
See also Firbank, Louis

Reese, Lizette Woodworth 1856-1935 . **PC 29**
See also CA 180; DLB 54

Reeve, Clara 1729-1807 .... **NCLC 19**
See also DLB 39

Reich, Wilhelm 1897-1957 .... **TCLC 57**

Reid, Christopher (John) 1949- .... **CLC 33**
See also CA 140; CANR 89; DLB 40

Reid, Desmond
See Moorcock, Michael (John)

Reid Banks, Lynne 1929-
See Banks, Lynne Reid
See also CA 1-4R; CANR 6, 22, 38, 87;
CLR 24; JRDA; MAICYA; SATA 22, 75,
111

Reilly, William K.
See Creasey, John

Reiner, Max
See Caldwell, (Janet Miriam) Taylor
(Holland)

Reis, Ricardo
See Pessoa, Fernando (Antonio Nogueira)

Remarque, Erich Maria
1898-1970 ... **CLC 21; DA; DAB; DAC;**
DAM MST, NOV
See also AAYA 27; CA 77-80; 29-32R;
DA3; DLB 56; MTCW 1, 2

Remington, Frederic 1861-1909 ..... **TCLC 89**
See also CA 108; 169; DLB 12, 186, 188;
SATA 41

Remizov, A.
See Remizov, Aleksei (Mikhailovich)

Remizov, A. M.
See Remizov, Aleksei (Mikhailovich)

Remizov, Aleksei (Mikhailovich)
1877-1957 .... **TCLC 27**
See also CA 125; 133

Renan, Joseph Ernest 1823-1892 .. **NCLC 26**

Renard, Jules 1864-1910 .... **TCLC 17**
See also CA 117

Renault, Mary CLC 3, 11, 17
See also Challans, Mary
See also DLBY 83; MTCW 2

Rendell, Ruth (Barbara) 1930- . **CLC 28, 48;**
DAM POP
See also Vine, Barbara
See also CA 109; CANR 32, 52, 74; DLB
87; INT CANR-32; MTCW 1, 2

Renoir, Jean 1894-1979 .... **CLC 20**
See also CA 129; 85-88

Resnais, Alain 1922- .... **CLC 16**

Reverdy, Pierre 1889-1960 .... **CLC 53**
See also CA 97-100; 89-92

Rexroth, Kenneth 1905-1982 .... **CLC 1, 2, 6,**
11, 22, 49, 112; DAM POET; PC 20
See also CA 5-8R; 107; CANR 14, 34, 63;
CDALB 1941-1968; DLB 16, 48, 165,
212; DLBY 82; INT CANR-14; MTCW
1, 2

Reyes, Alfonso 1889-1959 .. **TCLC 33; HLCS**
2
See also CA 131; HW 1

Reyes y Basoalto, Ricardo Eliecer Neftali
See Neruda, Pablo

Reymont, Wladyslaw (Stanislaw)
1868(?)-1925 .... **TCLC 5**
See also CA 104

Reynolds, Jonathan 1942- .... **CLC 6, 38**
See also CA 65-68; CANR 28

Reynolds, Joshua 1723-1792 .... **LC 15**
See also DLB 104

Reynolds, Michael S(hane) 1937- ..... **CLC 44**
See also CA 65-68; CANR 9, 89

Reznikoff, Charles 1894-1976 .... **CLC 9**
See also CA 33-36; 61-64; CAP 2; DLB 28,
45

Rezzori (d'Arezzo), Gregor von
1914-1998 .... **CLC 25**
See also CA 122; 136; 167

Rhine, Richard
See Silverstein, Alvin

Rhodes, Eugene Manlove
1869-1934 .... **TCLC 53**

Rhodius, Apollonius c. 3rd cent.
B.C.- .... **CMLC 28**
See also DLB 176

R'hoone
See Balzac, Honore de

Rhys, Jean 1890(?)-1979 ...... **CLC 2, 4, 6, 14,**
19, 51, 124; DAM NOV; SSC 21
See also CA 25-28R; 85-88; CANR 35, 62;
CDBLB 1945-1960; DA3; DLB 36, 117,
162; MTCW 1, 2

Ribeiro, Darcy 1922-1997 .... **CLC 34**
See also CA 33-36R; 156

Ribeiro, Joao Ubaldo (Osorio Pimentel)
1941- .... **CLC 10, 67**
See also CA 81-84

Ribman, Ronald (Burt) 1932- .... **CLC 7**
See also CA 21-24R; CANR 46, 80

Ricci, Nino 1959- .... **CLC 70**
See also CA 137

Rice, Anne 1941- .. **CLC 41, 128; DAM POP**
See also AAYA 9; BEST 89:2; CA 65-68;
CANR 12, 36, 53, 74; DA3; MTCW 2

Rice, Elmer (Leopold) 1892-1967 ...... **CLC 7,**
49; DAM DRAM
See also CA 21-22; 25-28R; CAP 2; DLB
4, 7; MTCW 1, 2

Rice, Tim(othy Miles Bindon)
1944- .... **CLC 21**
See also CA 103; CANR 46

Rich, Adrienne (Cecile) 1929- ... **CLC 3, 6, 7,**
11, 18, 36, 73, 76, 125; DAM POET;
PC 5
See also CA 9-12R; CANR 20, 53, 74;
CDALBS; DA3; DLB 5, 67; MTCW 1, 2

Rich, Barbara
See Graves, Robert (von Ranke)

Rich, Robert
See Trumbo, Dalton

Richard, Keith CLC 17
See also Richards, Keith

Richards, David Adams 1950- .... **CLC 59;**
DAC
See also CA 93-96; CANR 60; DLB 53

Richards, I(vor) A(rmstrong)
1893-1979 .... **CLC 14, 24**
See also CA 41-44R; 89-92; CANR 34, 74;
DLB 27; MTCW 2
Richards, Keith 1943-
See Richard, Keith
See also CA 107; CANR 77
Richardson, Anne
See Roiphe, Anne (Richardson)
Richardson, Dorothy Miller
1873-1957 .... **TCLC 3**
See also CA 104; DLB 36
Richardson, Ethel Florence (Lindesay)
1870-1946
See Richardson, Henry Handel
See also CA 105
Richardson, Henry Handel TCLC 4
See also Richardson, Ethel Florence
(Lindesay)
See also DLB 197
Richardson, John 1796-1852 .... **NCLC 55;**
DAC
See also DLB 99
Richardson, Samuel 1689-1761 ...... **LC 1, 44;**
DA; DAB; DAC; DAM MST, NOV;
WLC
See also CDBLB 1660-1789; DLB 39
Richler, Mordecai 1931- ...... **CLC 3, 5, 9, 13,**
18, 46, 70; DAC; DAM MST, NOV
See also AITN 1; CA 65-68; CANR 31, 62;
CLR 17; DLB 53; MAICYA; MTCW 1,
2; SATA 44, 98; SATA-Brief 27
Richter, Conrad (Michael)
1890-1968 .... **CLC 30**
See also AAYA 21; CA 5-8R; 25-28R;
CANR 23; DLB 9, 212; MTCW 1, 2;
SATA 3
Ricostranza, Tom
See Ellis, Trey
Riddell, Charlotte 1832-1906 .... **TCLC 40**
See also CA 165; DLB 156
Ridge, John Rollin 1827-1867 ...... **NCLC 82;**
DAM MULT
See also CA 144; DLB 175; NNAL
Ridgway, Keith 1965- .... **CLC 119**
See also CA 172
Riding, Laura CLC 3, 7
See also Jackson, Laura (Riding)
Riefenstahl, Berta Helene Amalia 1902-
See Riefenstahl, Leni
See also CA 108
Riefenstahl, Leni CLC 16
See also Riefenstahl, Berta Helene Amalia
Riffe, Ernest
See Bergman, (Ernst) Ingmar
Riggs, (Rolla) Lynn 1899-1954 ..... **TCLC 56;**
DAM MULT
See also CA 144; DLB 175; NNAL
Riis, Jacob A(ugust) 1849-1914 ..... **TCLC 80**
See also CA 113; 168; DLB 23
Riley, James Whitcomb
1849-1916 .... **TCLC 51; DAM POET**
See also CA 118; 137; MAICYA; SATA 17
Riley, Tex
See Creasey, John
Rilke, Rainer Maria 1875-1926 .. **TCLC 1, 6,**
19; DAM POET; PC 2
See also CA 104; 132; CANR 62; DA3;
DLB 81; MTCW 1, 2
Rimbaud, (Jean Nicolas) Arthur
1854-1891 . **NCLC 4, 35, 82; DA; DAB;**
DAC; DAM MST, POET; PC 3; WLC
See also DA3
Rinehart, Mary Roberts
1876-1958 .... **TCLC 52**
See also CA 108; 166
Ringmaster, The
See Mencken, H(enry) L(ouis)

Ringwood, Gwen(dolyn Margaret) Pharis
1910-1984 .... **CLC 48**
See also CA 148; 112; DLB 88
Rio, Michel 19(?)- .... **CLC 43**
Ritsos, Giannes
See Ritsos, Yannis
Ritsos, Yannis 1909-1990 .... **CLC 6, 13, 31**
See also CA 77-80; 133; CANR 39, 61;
MTCW 1
Ritter, Erika 1948(?)- .... **CLC 52**
Rivera, Jose Eustasio 1889-1928 ... **TCLC 35**
See also CA 162; HW 1, 2
Rivera, Tomas 1935-1984
See also CA 49-52; CANR 32; DLB 82;
HLCS 2; HW 1
Rivers, Conrad Kent 1933-1968 .... **CLC 1**
See also BW 1; CA 85-88; DLB 41
Rivers, Elfrida
See Bradley, Marion Zimmer
Riverside, John
See Heinlein, Robert A(nson)
Rizal, Jose 1861-1896 .... **NCLC 27**
Roa Bastos, Augusto (Antonio)
1917- .... **CLC 45; DAM MULT; HLC 2**
See also CA 131; DLB 113; HW 1
Robbe-Grillet, Alain 1922- .... **CLC 1, 2, 4, 6,**
8, 10, 14, 43, 128
See also CA 9-12R; CANR 33, 65; DLB
83, MTCW 1, 2
Robbins, Harold 1916-1997 .... **CLC 5; DAM**
NOV
See also CA 73-76; 162; CANR 26, 54;
DA3; MTCW 1, 2
Robbins, Thomas Eugene 1936-
See Robbins, Tom
See also CA 81-84; CANR 29, 59; DAM
NOV, POP; DA3; MTCW 1, 2
Robbins, Tom CLC 9, 32, 64
See also Robbins, Thomas Eugene
See also AAYA 32; BEST 90:3; DLBY 80;
MTCW 2
Robbins, Trina 1938- .... **CLC 21**
See also CA 128
Roberts, Charles G(eorge) D(ouglas)
1860-1943 .... **TCLC 8**
See also CA 105; CLR 33; DLB 92; SATA
88; SATA-Brief 29
Roberts, Elizabeth Madox
1886-1941 .... **TCLC 68**
See also CA 111; 166; DLB 9, 54, 102;
SATA 33; SATA-Brief 27
Roberts, Kate 1891-1985 .... **CLC 15**
See also CA 107; 116
Roberts, Keith (John Kingston)
1935- .... **CLC 14**
See also CA 25-28R; CANR 46
Roberts, Kenneth (Lewis)
1885-1957 .... **TCLC 23**
See also CA 109; DLB 9
Roberts, Michele (B.) 1949- .... **CLC 48**
See also CA 115; CANR 58
Robertson, Ellis
See Ellison, Harlan (Jay); Silverberg, Robert
Robertson, Thomas William
1829-1871 .... **NCLC 35; DAM DRAM**
Robeson, Kenneth
See Dent, Lester
Robinson, Edwin Arlington
1869-1935 ... **TCLC 5; DA; DAC; DAM**
MST, POET; PC 1
See also CA 104; 133; CDALB 1865-1917;
DLB 54; MTCW 1, 2
Robinson, Henry Crabb
1775-1867 .... **NCLC 15**
See also DLB 107
Robinson, Jill 1936- .... **CLC 10**
See also CA 102; INT 102

Robinson, Kim Stanley 1952- .... **CLC 34**
See also AAYA 26; CA 126; SATA 109
Robinson, Lloyd
See Silverberg, Robert
Robinson, Marilynne 1944- .... **CLC 25**
See also CA 116; CANR 80; DLB 206
Robinson, Smokey CLC 21
See also Robinson, William, Jr.
Robinson, William, Jr. 1940-
See Robinson, Smokey
See also CA 116
Robison, Mary 1949- .... **CLC 42, 98**
See also CA 113; 116; CANR 87; DLB 130;
INT 116
Rod, Edouard 1857-1910 .... **TCLC 52**
Roddenberry, Eugene Wesley 1921-1991
See Roddenberry, Gene
See also CA 110; 135; CANR 37; SATA 45;
SATA-Obit 69
Roddenberry, Gene CLC 17
See also Roddenberry, Eugene Wesley
See also AAYA 5; SATA-Obit 69
Rodgers, Mary 1931- .... **CLC 12**
See also CA 49-52; CANR 8, 55, 90; CLR
20; INT CANR-8; JRDA; MAICYA;
SATA 8
Rodgers, W(illiam) R(obert)
1909-1969 .... **CLC 7**
See also CA 85-88; DLB 20
Rodman, Eric
See Silverberg, Robert
Rodman, Howard 1920(?)-1985 .... **CLC 65**
See also CA 118
Rodman, Maia
See Wojciechowska, Maia (Teresa)
Rodo, Jose Enrique 1872(?)-1917
See also CA 178; HLCS 2; HW 2
Rodriguez, Claudio 1934- .... **CLC 10**
See also DLB 134
Rodriguez, Richard 1944-
See also CA 110; CANR 66; DAM MULT;
DLB 82; HLC 2; HW 1, 2
Roelvaag, O(le) E(dvart)
1876-1931 .... **TCLC 17**
See also Rolvaag, O(le) E(dvart)
See also CA 117; 171; DLB 9
Roethke, Theodore (Huebner)
1908-1963 .... **CLC 1, 3, 8, 11, 19, 46,**
101; DAM POET; PC 15
See also CA 81-84; CABS 2; CDALB 1941-
1968; DA3; DLB 5, 206; MTCW 1, 2
Rogers, Samuel 1763-1855 .... **NCLC 69**
See also DLB 93
Rogers, Thomas Hunton 1927- .... **CLC 57**
See also CA 89-92; INT 89-92
Rogers, Will(iam Penn Adair)
1879-1935 ... **TCLC 8, 71; DAM MULT**
See also CA 105; 144; DA3; DLB 11;
MTCW 2; NNAL
Rogin, Gilbert 1929- .... **CLC 18**
See also CA 65-68; CANR 15
Rohan, Koda
See Koda Shigeyuki
Rohlfs, Anna Katharine Green
See Green, Anna Katharine
Rohmer, Eric CLC 16
See also Scherer, Jean-Marie Maurice
Rohmer, Sax TCLC 28
See also Ward, Arthur Henry Sarsfield
See also DLB 70
Roiphe, Anne (Richardson) 1935- .. **CLC 3, 9**
See also CA 89-92; CANR 45, 73; DLBY
80; INT 89-92
Rojas, Fernando de 1465-1541 .... **LC 23;**
HLCS 1
Rojas, Gonzalo 1917-
See also HLCS 2; HW 2

Rojas, Gonzalo 1917-
    See also CA 178; HLCS 2
**Rolfe, Frederick (William Serafino Austin
    Lewis Mary)** 1860-1913 .... **TCLC 12**
    See also CA 107; DLB 34, 156
Rolland, Romain 1866-1944 .... **TCLC 23**
    See also CA 118; DLB 65
Rolle, Richard c. 1300-c. 1349 ...... **CMLC 21**
    See also DLB 146
Rolvaag, O(le) E(dvart)
    See Roelvaag, O(le) E(dvart)
Romain Arnaud, Saint
    See Aragon, Louis
Romains, Jules 1885-1972 .... **CLC 7**
    See also CA 85-88; CANR 34; DLB 65;
    MTCW 1
Romero, Jose Ruben 1890-1952 .... **TCLC 14**
    See also CA 114; 131; HW 1
Ronsard, Pierre de 1524-1585 . **LC 6, 54; PC
    11**
Rooke, Leon 1934- . **CLC 25, 34; DAM POP**
    See also CA 25-28R; CANR 23, 53
Roosevelt, Franklin Delano
    1882-1945 .... **TCLC 93**
    See also CA 116; 173
Roosevelt, Theodore 1858-1919 ..... **TCLC 69**
    See also CA 115; 170; DLB 47, 186
Roper, William 1498-1578 .... **LC 10**
Roquelaure, A. N.
    See Rice, Anne
Rosa, Joao Guimaraes 1908-1967 ... **CLC 23;
    HLCS 1**
    See also CA 89-92; DLB 113
Rose, Wendy 1948- .. **CLC 85; DAM MULT;
    PC 13**
    See also CA 53-56; CANR 5, 51; DLB 175;
    NNAL; SATA 12
Rosen, R. D.
    See Rosen, Richard (Dean)
Rosen, Richard (Dean) 1949- .... **CLC 39**
    See also CA 77-80; CANR 62; INT
    CANR-30
Rosenberg, Isaac 1890-1918 .... **TCLC 12**
    See also CA 107; DLB 20
Rosenblatt, Joe CLC 15
    See also Rosenblatt, Joseph
Rosenblatt, Joseph 1933-
    See Rosenblatt, Joe
    See also CA 89-92; INT 89-92
Rosenfeld, Samuel
    See Tzara, Tristan
Rosenstock, Sami
    See Tzara, Tristan
Rosenstock, Samuel
    See Tzara, Tristan
Rosenthal, M(acha) L(ouis)
    1917-1996 .... **CLC 28**
    See also CA 1-4R; 152; CAAS 6; CANR 4,
    51; DLB 5; SATA 59
Ross, Barnaby
    See Dannay, Frederic
Ross, Bernard L.
    See Follett, Ken(neth Martin)
Ross, J. H.
    See Lawrence, T(homas) E(dward)
Ross, John Hume
    See Lawrence, T(homas) E(dward)
Ross, Martin
    See Martin, Violet Florence
    See also DLB 135
Ross, (James) Sinclair 1908-1996 ... **CLC 13;
    DAC; DAM MST; SSC 24**
    See also CA 73-76; CANR 81; DLB 88
Rossetti, Christina (Georgina)
    1830-1894 . **NCLC 2, 50, 66; DA; DAB;
    DAC; DAM MST, POET; PC 7; WLC**
    See also DA3; DLB 35, 163; MAICYA;
    SATA 20

Rossetti, Dante Gabriel 1828-1882 . **NCLC 4,
    77; DA; DAB; DAC; DAM MST,
    POET; WLC**
    See also CDBLB 1832-1890; DLB 35
Rossner, Judith (Perelman) 1935- . **CLC 6, 9,
    29**
    See also AITN 2; BEST 90:3; CA 17-20R;
    CANR 18, 51, 73; DLB 6; INT CANR-
    18; MTCW 1, 2
Rostand, Edmond (Eugene Alexis)
    1868-1918 .... **TCLC 6, 37; DA; DAB;
    DAC; DAM DRAM, MST; DC 10**
    See also CA 104; 126; DA3; DLB 192;
    MTCW 1
Roth, Henry 1906-1995 ..... **CLC 2, 6, 11, 104**
    See also CA 11-12; 149; CANR 38, 63;
    CAP 1; DA3; DLB 28; MTCW 1, 2
Roth, Philip (Milton) 1933- ... **CLC 1, 2, 3, 4,
    6, 9, 15, 22, 31, 47, 66, 86, 119; DA;
    DAB; DAC; DAM MST, NOV, POP;
    SSC 26; WLC**
    See also BEST 90:3; CA 1-4R; CANR 1,
    22, 36, 55, 89; CDALB 1968-1988; DA3;
    DLB 2, 28, 173; DLBY 82; MTCW 1, 2
Rothenberg, Jerome 1931- .... **CLC 6, 57**
    See also CA 45-48; CANR 1; DLB 5, 193
Roumain, Jacques (Jean Baptiste)
    1907-1944 ...... **TCLC 19; BLC 3; DAM
    MULT**
    See also BW 1; CA 117; 125
Rourke, Constance (Mayfield)
    1885-1941 .... **TCLC 12**
    See also CA 107; YABC 1
Rousseau, Jean-Baptiste 1671-1741 ...... **LC 9**
Rousseau, Jean-Jacques 1712-1778 .... **LC 14,
    36; DA; DAB; DAC; DAM MST; WLC**
    See also DA3
Roussel, Raymond 1877-1933 .... **TCLC 20**
    See also CA 117
Rovit, Earl (Herbert) 1927- .... **CLC 7**
    See also CA 5-8R; CANR 12
Rowe, Elizabeth Singer 1674-1737 ..... **LC 44**
    See also DLB 39, 95
Rowe, Nicholas 1674-1718 .... **LC 8**
    See also DLB 84
Rowley, Ames Dorrance
    See Lovecraft, H(oward) P(hillips)
Rowson, Susanna Haswell
    1762(?)-1824 .... **NCLC 5, 69**
    See also DLB 37, 200
Roy, Arundhati 1960(?)- .... **CLC 109**
    See also CA 163; CANR 90; DLBY 97
Roy, Gabrielle 1909-1983 .... **CLC 10, 14;
    DAB; DAC; DAM MST**
    See also CA 53-56; 110; CANR 5, 61; DLB
    68; MTCW 1; SATA 104
Royko, Mike 1932-1997 .... **CLC 109**
    See also CA 89-92; 157; CANR 26
Rozewicz, Tadeusz 1921- .. **CLC 9, 23; DAM
    POET**
    See also CA 108; CANR 36, 66; DA3;
    MTCW 1, 2
Ruark, Gibbons 1941- .... **CLC 3**
    See also CA 33-36R; CAAS 23; CANR 14,
    31, 57; DLB 120
Rubens, Bernice (Ruth) 1923- .... **CLC 19, 31**
    See also CA 25-28R; CANR 33, 65; DLB
    14, 207; MTCW 1
Rubin, Harold
    See Robbins, Harold
Rudkin, (James) David 1936- .... **CLC 14**
    See also CA 89-92; DLB 13
Rudnik, Raphael 1933- .... **CLC 7**
    See also CA 29-32R
Ruffian, M.
    See Hasek, Jaroslav (Matej Frantisek)
Ruiz, Jose Martinez CLC 11
    See also Martinez Ruiz, Jose

Rukeyser, Muriel 1913-1980 . **CLC 6, 10, 15,
    27; DAM POET; PC 12**
    See also CA 5-8R; 93-96; CANR 26, 60;
    DA3; DLB 48; MTCW 1, 2; SATA-Obit
    22
Rule, Jane (Vance) 1931- .... **CLC 27**
    See also CA 25-28R; CAAS 18; CANR 12,
    87; DLB 60
Rulfo, Juan 1918-1986 ...... **CLC 8, 80; DAM
    MULT; HLC 2; SSC 25**
    See also CA 85-88; 118; CANR 26; DLB
    113; HW 1, 2; MTCW 1, 2
Rumi, Jalal al-Din 1297-1373 .... **CMLC 20**
Runeberg, Johan 1804-1877 .... **NCLC 41**
Runyon, (Alfred) Damon
    1884(?)-1946 .... **TCLC 10**
    See also CA 107; 165; DLB 11, 86, 171;
    MTCW 2
Rush, Norman 1933- .... **CLC 44**
    See also CA 121; 126; INT 126
Rushdie, (Ahmed) Salman 1947- .... **CLC 23,
    31, 55, 100; DAB; DAC; DAM MST,
    NOV, POP; WLCS**
    See also BEST 89:3; CA 108; 111; CANR
    33, 56; DA3; DLB 194; INT 111; MTCW
    1, 2
Rushforth, Peter (Scott) 1945- .... **CLC 19**
    See also CA 101
Ruskin, John 1819-1900 .... **TCLC 63**
    See also CA 114; 129; CDBLB 1832-1890;
    DLB 55, 163, 190; SATA 24
Russ, Joanna 1937- .... **CLC 15**
    See also CA 5-28R; CANR 11, 31, 65; DLB
    8; MTCW 1
Russell, George William 1867-1935
    See Baker, Jean H.
    See also CA 104; 153; CDBLB 1890-1914;
    DAM POET
Russell, (Henry) Ken(neth Alfred)
    1927- .... **CLC 16**
    See also CA 105
Russell, William Martin 1947- .... **CLC 60**
    See also CA 164
Rutherford, Mark TCLC 25
    See also White, William Hale
    See also DLB 18
Ruyslinck, Ward 1929- .... **CLC 14**
    See also Belser, Reimond Karel Maria de
Ryan, Cornelius (John) 1920-1974 ..... **CLC 7**
    See also CA 69-72; 53-56; CANR 38
Ryan, Michael 1946- .... **CLC 65**
    See also CA 49-52; DLBY 82
Ryan, Tim
    See Dent, Lester
Rybakov, Anatoli (Naumovich)
    1911-1998 .... **CLC 23, 53**
    See also CA 126; 135; 172; SATA 79;
    SATA-Obit 108
Ryder, Jonathan
    See Ludlum, Robert
Ryga, George 1932-1987 .... **CLC 14; DAC;
    DAM MST**
    See also CA 101; 124; CANR 43, 90; DLB
    60
S. H.
    See Hartmann, Sadakichi
S. S.
    See Sassoon, Siegfried (Lorraine)
Saba, Umberto 1883-1957 .... **TCLC 33**
    See also CA 144; CANR 79; DLB 114
Sabatini, Rafael 1875-1950 .... **TCLC 47**
    See also CA 162
Sabato, Ernesto (R.) 1911- .... **CLC 10, 23;
    DAM MULT; HLC 2**
    See also CA 97-100; CANR 32, 65; DLB
    145; HW 1, 2; MTCW 1, 2
Sa-Carniero, Mario de 1890-1916 . **TCLC 83**
Sacastru, Martin
    See Bioy Casares, Adolfo

Sacastru, Martin
See Bioy Casares, Adolfo
Sacher-Masoch, Leopold von
1836(?)-1895 .... **NCLC 31**
Sachs, Marilyn (Stickle) 1927- .... **CLC 35**
See also AAYA 2; CA 17-20R; CANR 13,
47; CLR 2; JRDA; MAICYA; SAAS 2;
SATA 3, 68; SATA-Essay 110
Sachs, Nelly 1891-1970 .... **CLC 14, 98**
See also CA 17-18; 25-28R; CANR 87;
CAP 2; MTCW 2
Sackler, Howard (Oliver)
1929-1982 .... **CLC 14**
See also CA 61-64; 108; CANR 30; DLB 7
Sacks, Oliver (Wolf) 1933- .... **CLC 67**
See also CA 53-56; CANR 28, 50, 76; DA3;
INT CANR-28; MTCW 1, 2
Sadakichi
See Hartmann, Sadakichi
Sade, Donatien Alphonse Francois, Comte
de 1740-1814 .... **NCLC 47**
Sadoff, Ira 1945- .... **CLC 9**
See also CA 53-56; CANR 5, 21; DLB 120
Saetone
See Camus, Albert
Safire, William 1929- .... **CLC 10**
See also CA 17-20R; CANR 31, 54, 91
Sagan, Carl (Edward) 1934-1996 .... **CLC 30,**
112
See also AAYA 2; CA 25-28R; 155; CANR
11, 36, 74; DA3; MTCW 1, 2; SATA 58;
SATA-Obit 94
Sagan, Francoise CLC 3, 6, 9, 17, 36
See also Quoirez, Francoise
See also DLB 83; MTCW 2
Sahgal, Nayantara (Pandit) 1927- .... **CLC 41**
See also CA 9-12R; CANR 11, 88
Saint, H(arry) F. 1941- .... **CLC 50**
See also CA 127
St. Aubin de Teran, Lisa 1953-
See Teran, Lisa St. Aubin de
See also CA 118; 126; INT 126
Saint Birgitta of Sweden c.
1303-1373 .... **CMLC 24**
Sainte-Beuve, Charles Augustin
1804-1869 .... **NCLC 5**
Saint-Exupery, Antoine (Jean Baptiste
Marie Roger) de 1900-1944 .... **TCLC 2,**
56; DAM NOV; WLC
See also CA 108; 132; CLR 10; DA3; DLB
72; MAICYA; MTCW 1, 2; SATA 20
St. John, David
See Hunt, E(verette) Howard, (Jr.)
Saint-John Perse
See Leger, (Marie-Rene Auguste) Alexis
Saint-Leger
Saintsbury, George (Edward Bateman)
1845-1933 .... **TCLC 31**
See also CA 160; DLB 57, 149
Sait Faik TCLC 23
See also Abasiyanik, Sait Faik
Saki TCLC 3; SSC 12
See also Munro, H(ector) H(ugh)
See also MTCW 2
Sala, George Augustus NCLC 46
Saladin 1138-1193 .... **CMLC 38**
Salama, Hannu 1936- .... **CLC 18**
Salamanca, J(ack) R(ichard) 1922- .. **CLC 4,**
15
See also CA 25-28R
Salas, Floyd Francis 1931-
See also CA 119; CAAS 27; CANR 44, 75;
DAM MULT; DLB 82; HLC 2; HW 1, 2;
MTCW 2
Sale, J. Kirkpatrick
See Sale, Kirkpatrick
Sale, Kirkpatrick 1937- .... **CLC 68**
See also CA 13-16R; CANR 10

Salinas, Luis Omar 1937- ..... **CLC 90; DAM**
MULT; HLC 2
See also CA 131; CANR 81; DLB 82; HW
1, 2
Salinas (y Serrano), Pedro
1891(?)-1951 .... **TCLC 17**
See also CA 117; DLB 134
Salinger, J(erome) D(avid) 1919- .. **CLC 1, 3,**
8, 12, 55, 56; DA; DAB; DAC; DAM
MST, NOV, POP; SSC 2, 28; WLC
See also AAYA 2; CA 5-8R; CANR 39;
CDALB 1941-1968; CLR 18; DA3; DLB
2, 102, 173; MAICYA; MTCW 1, 2;
SATA 67
Salisbury, John
See Caute, (John) David
Salter, James 1925- .... **CLC 7, 52, 59**
See also CA 73-76; DLB 130
Saltus, Edgar (Everton) 1855-1921 . **TCLC 8**
See also CA 105; DLB 202
Saltykov, Mikhail Evgrafovich
1826-1889 .... **NCLC 16**
Samarakis, Antonis 1919- .... **CLC 5**
See also CA 25-28R; CAAS 16; CANR 36
Sanchez, Florencio 1875-1910 .... **TCLC 37**
See also CA 153; HW 1
Sanchez, Luis Rafael 1936- .... **CLC 23**
See also CA 128; DLB 145; HW 1
Sanchez, Sonia 1934- .... **CLC 5, 116; BLC 3;**
DAM MULT; PC 9
See also BW 2, 3; CA 33-36R; CANR 24,
49, 74; CLR 18; DA3; DLB 41; DLBD 8;
MAICYA; MTCW 1, 2; SATA 22
Sand, George 1804-1876 ..... **NCLC 2, 42, 57;**
DA; DAB; DAC; DAM MST, NOV;
WLC
See also DA3; DLB 119, 192
Sandburg, Carl (August) 1878-1967 . **CLC 1,**
4, 10, 15, 35; DA; DAB; DAC; DAM
MST, POET; PC 2; WLC
See also AAYA 24; CA 5-8R; 25-28R;
CANR 35; CDALB 1865-1917; DA3;
DLB 17, 54; MAICYA; MTCW 1, 2;
SATA 8
Sandburg, Charles
See Sandburg, Carl (August)
Sandburg, Charles A.
See Sandburg, Carl (August)
Sanders, (James) Ed(ward) 1939- ... **CLC 53;**
DAM POET
See also CA 13-16R; CAAS 21; CANR 13,
44, 78; DLB 16
Sanders, Lawrence 1920-1998 .... **CLC 41;**
DAM POP
See also BEST 89:4; CA 81-84; 165; CANR
33, 62; DA3; MTCW 1
Sanders, Noah
See Blount, Roy (Alton), Jr.
Sanders, Winston P.
See Anderson, Poul (William)
Sandoz, Mari(e Susette) 1896-1966 .. **CLC 28**
See also CA 1-4R; 25-28R; CANR 17, 64;
DLB 9, 212; MTCW 1, 2; SATA 5
Saner, Reg(inald Anthony) 1931- .... **CLC 9**
See also CA 65-68
Sankara 788-820 .... **CMLC 32**
Sannazaro, Jacopo 1456(?)-1530 .... **LC 8**
Sansom, William 1912-1976 .... **CLC 2, 6;**
DAM NOV; SSC 21
See also CA 5-8R; 65-68; CANR 42; DLB
139; MTCW 1
Santayana, George 1863-1952 .... **TCLC 40**
See also CA 115; DLB 54, 71; DLBD 13
Santiago, Danny CLC 33
See also James, Daniel (Lewis)
See also DLB 122
Santmyer, Helen Hoover 1895-1986 . **CLC 33**
See also CA 1-4R; 118; CANR 15, 33;
DLBY 84; MTCW 1

Santoka, Taneda 1882-1940 .... **TCLC 72**
Santos, Bienvenido N(uqui)
1911-1996 .... **CLC 22; DAM MULT**
See also CA 101; 151; CANR 19, 46
Sapper TCLC 44
See also McNeile, Herman Cyril
Sapphire
See Sapphire, Brenda
Sapphire, Brenda 1950- .... **CLC 99**
Sappho fl. 6th cent. B.C.- ..... **CMLC 3; DAM**
POET; PC 5
See also DA3; DLB 176
Saramago, Jose 1922- ..... **CLC 119; HLCS 1**
See also CA 153
Sarduy, Severo 1937-1993 .... **CLC 6, 97;**
HLCS 1
See also CA 89-92; 142; CANR 58, 81;
DLB 113; HW 1, 2
Sargeson, Frank 1903-1982 .... **CLC 31**
See also CA 25-28R; 106; CANR 38, 79
Sarmiento, Domingo Faustino 1811-1888
See also HLCS 2
Sarmiento, Felix Ruben Garcia
See Dario, Ruben
Saro-Wiwa, Ken(ule Beeson)
1941-1995 .... **CLC 114**
See also BW 2; CA 142; 150; CANR 60;
DLB 157
Saroyan, William 1908-1981 ... **CLC 1, 8, 10,**
29, 34, 56; DA; DAB; DAC; DAM
DRAM, MST, NOV; SSC 21; WLC
See also CA 5-8R; 103; CANR 30;
CDALBS; DA3; DLB 7, 9, 86; DLBY 81;
MTCW 1, 2; SATA 23; SATA-Obit 24
Sarraute, Nathalie 1900- . **CLC 1, 2, 4, 8, 10,**
31, 80
See also CA 9-12R; CANR 23, 66; DLB
83; MTCW 1, 2
Sarton, (Eleanor) May 1912-1995 ..... **CLC 4,**
14, 49, 91; DAM POET
See also CA 1-4R; 149; CANR 1, 34, 55;
DLB 48; DLBY 81; INT CANR-34;
MTCW 1, 2; SATA 36; SATA-Obit 86
Sartre, Jean-Paul 1905-1980 . **CLC 1, 4, 7, 9,**
13, 18, 24, 44, 50, 52; DA; DAB; DAC;
DAM DRAM, MST, NOV; DC 3; SSC
32; WLC
See also CA 9-12R; 97-100; CANR 21;
DA3; DLB 72; MTCW 1, 2
Sassoon, Siegfried (Lorraine)
1886-1967 .... **CLC 36, 130; DAB; DAM**
MST, NOV, POET; PC 12
See also CA 104; 25-28R; CANR 36; DLB
20, 191; DLBD 18; MTCW 1, 2
Satterfield, Charles
See Pohl, Frederik
Satyremont
See Peret, Benjamin
Saul, John (W. III) 1942- ...... **CLC 46; DAM**
NOV, POP
See also AAYA 10; BEST 90:4; CA 81-84;
CANR 16, 40, 81; SATA 98
Saunders, Caleb
See Heinlein, Robert A(nson)
Saura (Atares), Carlos 1932- .... **CLC 20**
See also CA 114; 131; CANR 79; HW 1
Sauser-Hall, Frederic 1887-1961 ...... **CLC 18**
See also Cendrars, Blaise
See also CA 102; 93-96; CANR 36, 62;
MTCW 1
Saussure, Ferdinand de
1857-1913 .... **TCLC 49**
Savage, Catharine
See Brosman, Catharine Savage
Savage, Thomas 1915- .... **CLC 40**
See also CA 126; 132; CAAS 15; INT 132

Savan, Glenn 19(?)- .... **CLC 50**

Sayers, Dorothy L(eigh)
1893-1957 .... **TCLC 2, 15; DAM POP**
See also CA 104; 119; CANR 60; CDBLB
1914-1945; DLB 10, 36, 77, 100; MTCW
1, 2

Sayers, Valerie 1952- .... **CLC 50, 122**
See also CA 134; CANR 61

Sayles, John (Thomas) 1950- . **CLC 7, 10, 14**
See also CA 57-60; CANR 41, 84; DLB 44

Scammell, Michael 1935- .... **CLC 34**
See also CA 156

Scannell, Vernon 1922- .... **CLC 49**
See also CA 5-8R; CANR 8, 24, 57; DLB
27; SATA 59

Scarlett, Susan
See Streatfeild, (Mary) Noel

Scarron
See Mikszath, Kalman

Schaeffer, Susan Fromberg 1941- ..... **CLC 6,
11, 22**
See also CA 49-52; CANR 18, 65; DLB 28;
MTCW 1, 2; SATA 22

Schary, Jill
See Robinson, Jill

Schell, Jonathan 1943- .... **CLC 35**
See also CA 73-76; CANR 12

Schelling, Friedrich Wilhelm Joseph von
1775-1854 .... **NCLC 30**
See also DLB 90

Schendel, Arthur van 1874-1946 ... **TCLC 56**

Scherer, Jean-Marie Maurice 1920-
See Rohmer, Eric
See also CA 110

Schevill, James (Erwin) 1920- .... **CLC 7**
See also CA 5-8R; CAAS 12

Schiller, Friedrich 1759-1805 . **NCLC 39, 69;
DAM DRAM; DC 12**
See also DLB 94

Schisgal, Murray (Joseph) 1926- .... **CLC 6**
See also CA 21-24R; CANR 48, 86

Schlee, Ann 1934- .... **CLC 35**
See also CA 101; CANR 29, 88; SATA 44;
SATA-Brief 36

Schlegel, August Wilhelm von
1767-1845 .... **NCLC 15**
See also DLB 94

Schlegel, Friedrich 1772-1829 .... **NCLC 45**
See also DLB 90

Schlegel, Johann Elias (von)
1719(?)-1749 .... **LC 5**

Schlesinger, Arthur M(eier), Jr.
1917- .... **CLC 84**
See also AITN 1; CA 1-4R; CANR 1, 28,
58; DLB 17; INT CANR-28; MTCW 1,
2; SATA 61

Schmidt, Arno (Otto) 1914-1979 ...... **CLC 56**
See also CA 128; 109; DLB 69

Schmitz, Aron Hector 1861-1928
See Svevo, Italo
See also CA 104; 122; MTCW 1

Schnackenberg, Gjertrud 1953- .... **CLC 40**
See also CA 116; DLB 120

Schneider, Leonard Alfred 1925-1966
See Bruce, Lenny
See also CA 89-92

Schnitzler, Arthur 1862-1931 . **TCLC 4; SSC
15**
See also CA 104; DLB 81, 118

Schoenberg, Arnold 1874-1951 ...... **TCLC 75**
See also CA 109

Schonberg, Arnold
See Schoenberg, Arnold

Schopenhauer, Arthur 1788-1860 .. **NCLC 51**
See also DLB 90

Schor, Sandra (M.) 1932(?)-1990 ..... **CLC 65**
See also CA 132

Schorer, Mark 1908-1977 .... **CLC 9**
See also CA 5-8R; 73-76; CANR 7; DLB
103

Schrader, Paul (Joseph) 1946- .... **CLC 26**
See also CA 37-40R; CANR 41; DLB 44

Schreiner, Olive (Emilie Albertina)
1855-1920 .... **TCLC 9**
See also CA 105; 154; DLB 18, 156, 190,
225

Schulberg, Budd (Wilson) 1914- .. **CLC 7, 48**
See also CA 25-28R; CANR 19, 87; DLB
6, 26, 28; DLBY 81

Schulz, Bruno 1892-1942 .. **TCLC 5, 51; SSC
13**
See also CA 115; 123; CANR 86; MTCW 2

Schulz, Charles M(onroe)
1922-2000 .... **CLC 12**
See also CA 9-12R; CANR 6; INT
CANR-6; SATA 10

Schumacher, E(rnst) F(riedrich)
1911-1977 .... **CLC 80**
See also CA 81-84; 73-76; CANR 34, 85

Schuyler, James Marcus 1923-1991 .. **CLC 5,
23; DAM POET**
See also CA 101; 134; DLB 5, 169; INT
101

Schwartz, Delmore (David)
1913-1966 ... **CLC 2, 4, 10, 45, 87; PC 8**
See also CA 17-18; 25-28R; CANR 35;
CAP 2; DLB 28, 48; MTCW 1, 2

Schwartz, Ernst
See Ozu, Yasujiro

Schwartz, John Burnham 1965- .... **CLC 59**
See also CA 132

Schwartz, Lynne Sharon 1939- .... **CLC 31**
See also CA 103; CANR 44, 89; MTCW 2

Schwartz, Muriel A.
See Eliot, T(homas) S(tearns)

Schwarz-Bart, Andre 1928- .... **CLC 2, 4**
See also CA 89-92

Schwarz-Bart, Simone 1938- . **CLC 7; BLCS**
See also BW 2; CA 97-100

**Schwitters, Kurt (Hermann Edward Karl
Julius)** 1887-1948 .... **TCLC 95**
See also CA 158

Schwob, Marcel (Mayer Andre)
1867-1905 .... **TCLC 20**
See also CA 117; 168; DLB 123

Sciascia, Leonardo 1921-1989 .. **CLC 8, 9, 41**
See also CA 85-88; 130; CANR 35; DLB
177; MTCW 1

Scoppettone, Sandra 1936- .... **CLC 26**
See also AAYA 11; CA 5-8R; CANR 41,
73; SATA 9, 92

Scorsese, Martin 1942- .... **CLC 20, 89**
See also CA 110; 114; CANR 46, 85

Scotland, Jay
See Jakes, John (William)

Scott, Duncan Campbell
1862-1947 .... **TCLC 6; DAC**
See also CA 104; 153; DLB 92

Scott, Evelyn 1893-1963 .... **CLC 43**
See also CA 104; 112; CANR 64; DLB 9,
48

Scott, F(rancis) R(eginald)
1899-1985 .... **CLC 22**
See also CA 101; 114; CANR 87; DLB 88;
INT 101

Scott, Frank
See Scott, F(rancis) R(eginald)

Scott, Joanna 1960- .... **CLC 50**
See also CA 126; CANR 53

Scott, Paul (Mark) 1920-1978 ...... **CLC 9, 60**
See also CA 81-84; 77-80; CANR 33; DLB
14, 207; MTCW 1

Scott, Sarah 1723-1795 .... **LC 44**
See also DLB 39

Scott, Walter 1771-1832 . **NCLC 15, 69; DA;
DAB; DAC; DAM MST, NOV, POET;
PC 13; SSC 32; WLC**
See also AAYA 22; CDBLB 1789-1832;
DLB 93, 107, 116, 144, 159; YABC 2

Scribe, (Augustin) Eugene
1791-1861 ..... **NCLC 16; DAM DRAM;
DC 5**
See also DLB 192

Scrum, R.
See Crumb, R(obert)

Scudery, Madeleine de 1607-1701 .. **LC 2, 58**

Scum
See Crumb, R(obert)

Scumbag, Little Bobby
See Crumb, R(obert)

Seabrook, John
See Hubbard, L(afayette) Ron(ald)

Sealy, I(rwin) Allan 1951- .... **CLC 55**
See also CA 136

Search, Alexander
See Pessoa, Fernando (Antonio Nogueira)

Sebastian, Lee
See Silverberg, Robert

Sebastian Owl
See Thompson, Hunter S(tockton)

Sebestyen, Ouida 1924- .... **CLC 30**
See also AAYA 8; CA 107; CANR 40; CLR
17; JRDA; MAICYA; SAAS 10; SATA
39

Secundus, H. Scriblerus
See Fielding, Henry

Sedges, John
See Buck, Pearl S(ydenstricker)

Sedgwick, Catharine Maria
1789-1867 .... **NCLC 19**
See also DLB 1, 74

Seelye, John (Douglas) 1931- .... **CLC 7**
See also CA 97-100; CANR 70; INT 97-
100

Seferiades, Giorgos Stylianou 1900-1971
See Seferis, George
See also CA 5-8R; 33-36R; CANR 5, 36;
MTCW 1

Seferis, George CLC 5, 11
See also Seferiades, Giorgos Stylianou

Segal, Erich (Wolf) 1937- . **CLC 3, 10; DAM
POP**
See also BEST 89:1; CA 25-28R; CANR
20, 36, 65; DLBY 86; INT CANR-20;
MTCW 1

Seger, Bob 1945- .... **CLC 35**

Seghers, Anna CLC 7
See also Radvanyi, Netty
See also DLB 69

Seidel, Frederick (Lewis) 1936- .... **CLC 18**
See also CA 13-16R; CANR 8; DLBY 84

Seifert, Jaroslav 1901-1986 .. **CLC 34, 44, 93**
See also CA 127; MTCW 1, 2

Sei Shonagon c. 966-1017(?) .... **CMLC 6**

Séjour, Victor 1817-1874 .... **DC 10**
See also DLB 50

Sejour Marcou et Ferrand, Juan Victor
See S

Selby, Hubert, Jr. 1928- .... **CLC 1, 2, 4, 8;
SSC 20**
See also CA 13-16R; CANR 33, 85; DLB
2, 227

Selzer, Richard 1928- .... **CLC 74**
See also CA 65-68; CANR 14

Sembene, Ousmane
See Ousmane, Sembene

Senancour, Etienne Pivert de
1770-1846 .... **NCLC 16**
See also DLB 119

Sender, Ramon (Jose) 1902-1982 ...... **CLC 8; DAM MULT; HLC 2**
See also CA 5-8R; 105; CANR 8; HW 1; MTCW 1

Seneca, Lucius Annaeus c. 1-c. 65 .... **CMLC 6; DAM DRAM; DC 5**
See also DLB 211

Senghor, Leopold Sedar 1906- .... **CLC 54, 130; BLC 3; DAM MULT, POET; PC 25**
See also BW 2; CA 116; 125; CANR 47, 74; MTCW 1, 2

Senna, Danzy 1970- .... **CLC 119**
See also CA 169

Serling, (Edward) Rod(man) 1924-1975 .... **CLC 30**
See also AAYA 14; AITN 1; CA 162; 57-60; DLB 26

Serna, Ramon Gomez de la
See Gomez de la Serna, Ramon

Serpieres
See Guillevic, (Eugene)

Service, Robert
See Service, Robert W(illiam)
See also DAB; DLB 92

Service, Robert W(illiam) 1874(?)-1958 .... **TCLC 15; DA; DAC; DAM MST, POET; WLC**
See also Service, Robert
See also CA 115; 140; CANR 84; SATA 20

Seth, Vikram 1952- .... **CLC 43, 90; DAM MULT**
See also CA 121; 127; CANR 50, 74; DA3; DLB 120; INT 127; MTCW 2

Seton, Cynthia Propper 1926-1982 .. **CLC 27**
See also CA 5-8R; 108; CANR 7

Seton, Ernest (Evan) Thompson 1860-1946 .... **TCLC 31**
See also CA 109; CLR 59; DLB 92; DLBD 13; JRDA; SATA 18

Seton-Thompson, Ernest
See Seton, Ernest (Evan) Thompson

Settle, Mary Lee 1918- .... **CLC 19, 61**
See also CA 89-92; CAAS 1; CANR 44, 87; DLB 6; INT 89-92

Seuphor, Michel
See Arp, Jean

Sevigne, Marie (de Rabutin-Chantal) Marquise de 1626-1696 .... **LC 11**

Sewall, Samuel 1652-1730 .... **LC 38**
See also DLB 24

Sexton, Anne (Harvey) 1928-1974 ..... **CLC 2, 4, 6, 8, 10, 15, 53; DA; DAB; DAC; DAM MST, POET; PC 2; WLC**
See also CA 1-4R; 53-56; CABS 2; CANR 3, 36; CDALB 1941-1968; DA3; DLB 5, 169; MTCW 1, 2; SATA 10

Shaara, Jeff 1952- .... **CLC 119**
See also CA 163

Shaara, Michael (Joseph, Jr.) 1929-1988 .... **CLC 15; DAM POP**
See also AITN 1; CA 102; 125; CANR 52, 85; DLBY 83

Shackleton, C. C.
See Aldiss, Brian W(ilson)

Shacochis, Bob CLC 39
See also Shacochis, Robert G.

Shacochis, Robert G. 1951-
See Shacochis, Bob
See also CA 119; 124; INT 124

Shaffer, Anthony (Joshua) 1926- ..... **CLC 19; DAM DRAM**
See also CA 110; 116; DLB 13

Shaffer, Peter (Levin) 1926- .. **CLC 5, 14, 18, 37, 60; DAB; DAM DRAM, MST; DC 7**
See also CA 25-28R; CANR 25, 47, 74; CDBLB 1960 to Present; DA3; DLB 13; MTCW 1, 2

Shakey, Bernard
See Young, Neil

Shalamov, Varlam (Tikhonovich) 1907(?)-1982 .... **CLC 18**
See also CA 129; 105

Shamlu, Ahmad 1925- .... **CLC 10**

Shammas, Anton 1951- .... **CLC 55**

Shandling, Arline
See Berriault, Gina

Shange, Ntozake 1948- .... **CLC 8, 25, 38, 74, 126; BLC 3; DAM DRAM, MULT; DC 3**
See also AAYA 9; BW 2; CA 85-88; CABS 3; CANR 27, 48, 74; DA3; DLB 38; MTCW 1, 2

Shanley, John Patrick 1950- .... **CLC 75**
See also CA 128; 133; CANR 83

Shapcott, Thomas W(illiam) 1935- .. **CLC 38**
See also CA 69-72; CANR 49, 83

Shapiro, Jane CLC 76

Shapiro, Karl (Jay) 1913- . **CLC 4, 8, 15, 53; PC 25**
See also CA 1-4R; CAAS 6; CANR 1, 36, 66; DLB 48; MTCW 1, 2

Sharp, William 1855-1905 .... **TCLC 39**
See also CA 160; DLB 156

Sharpe, Thomas Ridley 1928-
See Sharpe, Tom
See also CA 114; 122; CANR 85; INT 122

Sharpe, Tom CLC 36
See also Sharpe, Thomas Ridley
See also DLB 14

Shaw, Bernard
See Shaw, George Bernard
See also BW 1; MTCW 2

Shaw, G. Bernard
See Shaw, George Bernard

Shaw, George Bernard 1856-1950 .. **TCLC 3, 9, 21, 45; DA; DAB; DAC; DAM DRAM, MST; WLC**
See also Shaw, Bernard
See also CA 104; 128; CDBLB 1914-1945; DA3; DLB 10, 57, 190; MTCW 1, 2

Shaw, Henry Wheeler 1818-1885 .. **NCLC 15**
See also DLB 11

Shaw, Irwin 1913-1984 .... **CLC 7, 23, 34; DAM DRAM, POP**
See also AITN 1; CA 13-16R; 112; CANR 21; CDALB 1941-1968; DLB 6, 102; DLBY 84; MTCW 1, 21

Shaw, Robert 1927-1978 .... **CLC 5**
See also AITN 1; CA 1-4R; 81-84; CANR 4; DLB 13, 14

Shaw, T. E.
See Lawrence, T(homas) E(dward)

Shawn, Wallace 1943- .... **CLC 41**
See also CA 112

Shea, Lisa 1953- .... **CLC 86**
See also CA 147

Sheed, Wilfrid (John Joseph) 1930- . **CLC 2, 4, 10, 53**
See also CA 65-68; CANR 30, 66; DLB 6; MTCW 1, 2

Sheldon, Alice Hastings Bradley 1915(?)-1987
See Tiptree, James, Jr.
See also CA 108; 122; CANR 34; INT 108; MTCW 1

Sheldon, John
See Bloch, Robert (Albert)

Shelley, Mary Wollstonecraft (Godwin) 1797-1851 ..... **NCLC 14, 59; DA; DAB; DAC; DAM MST, NOV; WLC**
See also AAYA 20; CDBLB 1789-1832; DA3; DLB 110, 116, 159, 178; SATA 29

Shelley, Percy Bysshe 1792-1822 .. **NCLC 18; DA; DAB; DAC; DAM MST, POET; PC 14; WLC**
See also CDBLB 1789-1832; DA3; DLB 96, 110, 158

Shepard, Jim 1956- .... **CLC 36**
See also CA 137; CANR 59; SATA 90

Shepard, Lucius 1947- .... **CLC 34**
See also CA 128; 141; CANR 81

Shepard, Sam 1943- .... **CLC 4, 6, 17, 34, 41, 44; DAM DRAM; DC 5**
See also AAYA 1; CA 69-72; CABS 3; CANR 22; DA3; DLB 7, 212; MTCW 1, 2

Shepherd, Michael
See Ludlum, Robert

Sherburne, Zoa (Lillian Morin) 1912-1995 .... **CLC 30**
See also AAYA 13; CA 1-4R; 176; CANR 3, 37; MAICYA; SAAS 18; SATA 3

Sheridan, Frances 1724-1766 .... **LC 7**
See also DLB 39, 84

Sheridan, Richard Brinsley 1751-1816 .. **NCLC 5; DA; DAB; DAC; DAM DRAM, MST; DC 1; WLC**
See also CDBLB 1660-1789; DLB 89

Sherman, Jonathan Marc CLC 55

Sherman, Martin 1941(?)- .... **CLC 19**
See also CA 116; 123; CANR 86

Sherwin, Judith Johnson 1936-
See Johnson, Judith (Emlyn)
See also CANR 85

Sherwood, Frances 1940- .... **CLC 81**
See also CA 146

Sherwood, Robert E(mmet) 1896-1955 .... **TCLC 3; DAM DRAM**
See also CA 104; 153; CANR 86; DLB 7, 26

Shestov, Lev 1866-1938 .... **TCLC 56**

Shevchenko, Taras 1814-1861 .... **NCLC 54**

Shiel, M(atthew) P(hipps) 1865-1947 .... **TCLC 8**
See also Holmes, Gordon
See also CA 106; 160; DLB 153; MTCW 2

Shields, Carol 1935- .... **CLC 91, 113; DAC**
See also CA 81-84; CANR 51, 74; DA3; MTCW 2

Shields, David 1956- .... **CLC 97**
See also CA 124; CANR 48

Shiga, Naoya 1883-1971 ..... **CLC 33; SSC 23**
See also CA 101; 33-36R; DLB 180

Shikibu, Murasaki c. 978-c. 1014 ... **CMLC 1**

Shilts, Randy 1951-1994 .... **CLC 85**
See also AAYA 19; CA 115; 127; 144; CANR 45; DA3; INT 127; MTCW 2

Shimazaki, Haruki 1872-1943
See Shimazaki Toson
See also CA 105; 134; CANR 84

Shimazaki Toson 1872-1943 .... **TCLC 5**
See also Shimazaki, Haruki
See also DLB 180

Sholokhov, Mikhail (Aleksandrovich) 1905-1984 .... **CLC 7, 15**
See also CA 101; 112; MTCW 1, 2; SATA-Obit 36

Shone, Patric
See Hanley, James

Shreve, Susan Richards 1939- .... **CLC 23**
See also CA 49-52; CAAS 5; CANR 5, 38, 69; MAICYA; SATA 46, 95; SATA-Brief 41

Shue, Larry 1946-1985 .... **CLC 52; DAM DRAM**
See also CA 145; 117

Shu-Jen, Chou 1881-1936
See Lu Hsun
See also CA 104

Shulman, Alix Kates 1932- .... **CLC 2, 10**
See also CA 29-32R; CANR 43; SATA 7

Shuster, Joe 1914- .... **CLC 21**

Shute, Nevil CLC 30
See also Norway, Nevil Shute
See also MTCW 2

Shuttle, Penelope (Diane) 1947- .... **CLC 7**
See also CA 93-96; CANR 39, 84; DLB 14, 40

Sidney, Mary 1561-1621 .... **LC 19, 39**

Sidney, SirPhilip 1554-1586 . **LC 19, 39; DA; DAB; DAC; DAM MST, POET**
See also CDBLB Before 1660; DA3; DLB 167

Siegel, Jerome 1914-1996 .... **CLC 21**
See also CA 116; 169; 151

Siegel, Jerry
See Siegel, Jerome

Sienkiewicz, Henryk (Adam Alexander Pius) 1846-1916 .... **TCLC 3**
See also CA 104; 134; CANR 84

Sierra, Gregorio Martinez
See Martinez Sierra, Gregorio

Sierra, Maria (de la O'LeJarraga) Martinez
See Martinez Sierra, Maria (de la O'LeJarraga)

Sigal, Clancy 1926- .... **CLC 7**
See also CA 1-4R; CANR 85

Sigourney, Lydia Howard (Huntley) 1791-1865 .... **NCLC 21, 87**
See also DLB 1, 42, 73

Siguenza y Gongora, Carlos de 1645-1700 .... **LC 8; HLCS 2**

Sigurjonsson, Johann 1880-1919 ... **TCLC 27**
See also CA 170

Sikelianos, Angelos 1884-1951 ...... **TCLC 39; PC 29**

Silkin, Jon 1930-1997 .... **CLC 2, 6, 43**
See also CA 5-8R; CAAS 5; CANR 89; DLB 27

Silko, Leslie (Marmon) 1948- .... **CLC 23, 74, 114; DA; DAC; DAM MST, MULT, POP; SSC 37; WLCS**
See also AAYA 14; CA 115; 122; CANR 45, 65; DA3; DLB 143, 175; MTCW 2; NNAL

Sillanpaa, Frans Eemil 1888-1964 ... **CLC 19**
See also CA 129; 93-96; MTCW 1

Sillitoe, Alan 1928- ... **CLC 1, 3, 6, 10, 19, 57**
See also AITN 1; CA 9-12R; CAAS 2; CANR 8, 26, 55; CDBLB 1960 to Present; DLB 14, 139; MTCW 1, 2; SATA 61

Silone, Ignazio 1900-1978 .... **CLC 4**
See also CA 25-28; 81-84; CANR 34; CAP 2; MTCW 1

Silver, Joan Micklin 1935- .... **CLC 20**
See also CA 114; 121; INT 121

Silver, Nicholas
See Faust, Frederick (Schiller)

Silverberg, Robert 1935- .... **CLC 7; DAM POP**
See also AAYA 24; CA 1-4R, 186; CAAE 186; CAAS 3; CANR 1, 20, 36, 85; CLR 59; DLB 8; INT CANR-20; MAICYA; MTCW 1, 2; SATA 13, 91; SATA-Essay 104

Silverstein, Alvin 1933- .... **CLC 17**
See also CA 49-52; CANR 2; CLR 25; JRDA; MAICYA; SATA 8, 69

Silverstein, Virginia B(arbara Opshelor) 1937- .... **CLC 17**
See also CA 49-52; CANR 2; CLR 25; JRDA; MAICYA; SATA 8, 69

Sim, Georges
See Simenon, Georges (Jacques Christian)

Simak, Clifford D(onald) 1904-1988 . **CLC 1, 55**
See also CA 1-4R; 125; CANR 1, 35; DLB 8; MTCW 1; SATA-Obit 56

Simenon, Georges (Jacques Christian) 1903-1989 .... **CLC 1, 2, 3, 8, 18, 47; DAM POP**
See also CA 85-88; 129; CANR 35; DA3; DLB 72; DLBY 89; MTCW 1, 2

Simic, Charles 1938- .... **CLC 6, 9, 22, 49, 68, 130; DAM POET**
See also CA 29-32R; CAAS 4; CANR 12, 33, 52, 61; DA3; DLB 105; MTCW 2

Simmel, Georg 1858-1918 .... **TCLC 64**
See also CA 157

Simmons, Charles (Paul) 1924- .... **CLC 57**
See also CA 89-92; INT 89-92

Simmons, Dan 1948- .... **CLC 44; DAM POP**
See also AAYA 16; CA 138; CANR 53, 81

Simmons, James (Stewart Alexander) 1933- .... **CLC 43**
See also CA 105; CAAS 21; DLB 40

Simms, William Gilmore 1806-1870 .... **NCLC 3**
See also DLB 3, 30, 59, 73

Simon, Carly 1945- .... **CLC 26**
See also CA 105

Simon, Claude 1913- .... **CLC 4, 9, 15, 39; DAM NOV**
See also CA 89-92; CANR 33; DLB 83; MTCW 1

Simon, (Marvin) Neil 1927- ... **CLC 6, 11, 31, 39, 70; DAM DRAM**
See also AAYA 32; AITN 1; CA 21-24R; CANR 26, 54, 87; DA3; DLB 7; MTCW 1, 2

Simon, Paul (Frederick) 1941(?)- ..... **CLC 17**
See also CA 116; 153

Simonon, Paul 1956(?)- .... **CLC 30**

Simpson, Harriette
See Arnow, Harriette (Louisa) Simpson

Simpson, Louis (Aston Marantz) 1923- ...... **CLC 4, 7, 9, 32; DAM POET**
See also CA 1-4R; CAAS 4; CANR 1, 61; DLB 5; MTCW 1, 2

Simpson, Mona (Elizabeth) 1957- .... **CLC 44**
See also CA 122; 135; CANR 68

Simpson, N(orman) F(rederick) 1919- .... **CLC 29**
See also CA 13-16R; DLB 13

Sinclair, Andrew (Annandale) 1935- . **CLC 2, 14**
See also CA 9-12R; CAAS 5; CANR 14, 38, 91; DLB 14; MTCW 1

Sinclair, Emil
See Hesse, Hermann

Sinclair, Iain 1943- .... **CLC 76**
See also CA 132; CANR 81

Sinclair, Iain MacGregor
See Sinclair, Iain

Sinclair, Irene
See Griffith, D(avid Lewelyn) W(ark)

Sinclair, Mary Amelia St. Clair 1865(?)-1946
See Sinclair, May
See also CA 104

Sinclair, May 1863-1946 .... **TCLC 3, 11**
See also Sinclair, Mary Amelia St. Clair
See also CA 166; DLB 36, 135

Sinclair, Roy
See Griffith, D(avid Lewelyn) W(ark)

Sinclair, Upton (Beall) 1878-1968 ..... **CLC 1, 11, 15, 63; DA; DAB; DAC; DAM MST, NOV; WLC**
See also CA 5-8R; 25-28R; CANR 7; CDALB 1929-1941; DA3; DLB 9; INT CANR-7; MTCW 1, 2; SATA 9

Singer, Isaac
See Singer, Isaac Bashevis

Singer, Isaac Bashevis 1904-1991 .. **CLC 1, 3, 6, 9, 11, 15, 23, 38, 69, 111; DA; DAB; DAC; DAM MST, NOV; SSC 3; WLC**
See also AAYA 32; AITN 1, 2; CA 1-4R; 134; CANR 1, 39; CDALB 1941-1968;

CLR 1; DA3; DLB 6, 28, 52; DLBY 91; JRDA; MAICYA; MTCW 1, 2; SATA 3, 27; SATA-Obit 68

Singer, Israel Joshua 1893-1944 .... **TCLC 33**
See also CA 169

Singh, Khushwant 1915- .... **CLC 11**
See also CA 9-12R; CAAS 9; CANR 6, 84

Singleton, Ann
See Benedict, Ruth (Fulton)

Sinjohn, John
See Galsworthy, John

Sinyavsky, Andrei (Donatevich) 1925-1997 .... **CLC 8**
See also CA 85-88; 159

Sirin, V.
See Nabokov, Vladimir (Vladimirovich)

Sissman, L(ouis) E(dward) 1928-1976 .... **CLC 9, 18**
See also CA 21-24R; 65-68; CANR 13; DLB 5

Sisson, C(harles) H(ubert) 1914- .... **CLC 8**
See also CA 1-4R; CAAS 3; CANR 3, 48, 84; DLB 27

Sitwell, Dame Edith 1887-1964 ..... **CLC 2, 9, 67; DAM POET; PC 3**
See also CA 9-12R; CANR 35; CDBLB 1945-1960; DLB 20; MTCW 1, 2

Siwaarmill, H. P.
See Sharp, William

Sjoewall, Maj 1935- .... **CLC 7**
See also CA 65-68; CANR 73

Sjowall, Maj
See Sjoewall, Maj

Skelton, John 1463-1529 .... **PC 25**

Skelton, Robin 1925-1997 .... **CLC 13**
See also AITN 2; CA 5-8R; 160; CAAS 5; CANR 28, 89; DLB 27, 53

Skolimowski, Jerzy 1938- .... **CLC 20**
See also CA 128

Skram, Amalie (Bertha) 1847-1905 .... **TCLC 25**
See also CA 165

Skvorecky, Josef (Vaclav) 1924- ...... **CLC 15, 39, 69; DAC; DAM NOV**
See also CA 61-64; CAAS 1; CANR 10, 34, 63; DA3; MTCW 1, 2

Slade, Bernard CLC 11, 46
See also Newbound, Bernard Slade
See also CAAS 9; DLB 53

Slaughter, Carolyn 1946- .... **CLC 56**
See also CA 85-88; CANR 85

Slaughter, Frank G(ill) 1908- .... **CLC 29**
See also AITN 2; CA 5-8R; CANR 5, 85; INT CANR-5

Slavitt, David R(ytman) 1935- ..... **CLC 5, 14**
See also CA 21-24R; CAAS 3; CANR 41, 83; DLB 5, 6

Slesinger, Tess 1905-1945 .... **TCLC 10**
See also CA 107; DLB 102

Slessor, Kenneth 1901-1971 .... **CLC 14**
See also CA 102; 89-92

Slowacki, Juliusz 1809-1849 .... **NCLC 15**

Smart, Christopher 1722-1771 .. **LC 3; DAM POET; PC 13**
See also DLB 109

Smart, Elizabeth 1913-1986 .... **CLC 54**
See also CA 81-84; 118; DLB 88

Smiley, Jane (Graves) 1949- ...... **CLC 53, 76; DAM POP**
See also CA 104; CANR 30, 50, 74; DA3; DLB 227; INT CANR-30

Smith, A(rthur) J(ames) M(arshall) 1902-1980 .... **CLC 15; DAC**
See also CA 1-4R; 102; CANR 4; DLB 88

Smith, Adam 1723-1790 .... **LC 36**
See also DLB 104

Smith, Alexander 1829-1867 .... **NCLC 59**
See also DLB 32, 55

Smith, Anna Deavere 1950- .... **CLC 86**
  See also CA 133
Smith, Betty (Wehner) 1896-1972 .... **CLC 19**
  See also CA 5-8R; 33-36R; DLBY 82;
  SATA 6
Smith, Charlotte (Turner)
  1749-1806 .... **NCLC 23**
  See also DLB 39, 109
Smith, Clark Ashton 1893-1961 .... **CLC 43**
  See also CA 143; CANR 81; MTCW 2
Smith, Dave CLC 22, 42
  See also Smith, David (Jeddie)
  See also CAAS 7; DLB 5
Smith, David (Jeddie) 1942-
  See Smith, Dave
  See also CA 49-52; CANR 1, 59; DAM
  POET
Smith, Florence Margaret 1902-1971
  See Smith, Stevie
  See also CA 17-18; 29-32R; CANR 35;
  CAP 2; DAM POET; MTCW 1, 2
Smith, Iain Crichton 1928-1998 .... **CLC 64**
  See also CA 21-24R; 171; DLB 40, 139
Smith, John 1580(?)-1631 .... **LC 9**
  See also DLB 24, 30
Smith, Johnston
  See Crane, Stephen (Townley)
Smith, Joseph, Jr. 1805-1844 .... **NCLC 53**
Smith, Lee 1944- .... **CLC 25, 73**
  See also CA 114; 119; CANR 46; DLB 143;
  DLBY 83; INT 119
Smith, Martin
  See Smith, Martin Cruz
Smith, Martin Cruz 1942- .... **CLC 25; DAM**
  MULT, POP
  See also BEST 89:4; CA 85-88; CANR 6,
  23, 43, 65; INT CANR-23; MTCW 2;
  NNAL
Smith, Mary-Ann Tirone 1944- .... **CLC 39**
  See also CA 118; 136
Smith, Patti 1946- .... **CLC 12**
  See also CA 93-96; CANR 63
Smith, Pauline (Urmson)
  1882-1959 .... **TCLC 25**
  See also DLB 225
Smith, Rosamond
  See Oates, Joyce Carol
Smith, Sheila Kaye
  See Kaye-Smith, Sheila
Smith, Stevie CLC 3, 8, 25, 44; PC 12
  See also Smith, Florence Margaret
  See also DLB 20; MTCW 2
Smith, Wilbur (Addison) 1933- .... **CLC 33**
  See also CA 13-16R; CANR 7, 46, 66;
  MTCW 1, 2
Smith, William Jay 1918- .... **CLC 6**
  See also CA 5-8R; CANR 44; DLB 5; MAI-
  CYA; SAAS 22; SATA 2, 68
Smith, Woodrow Wilson
  See Kuttner, Henry
Smolenskin, Peretz 1842-1885 .... **NCLC 30**
Smollett, Tobias (George) 1721-1771 ... **LC 2,**
  46
  See also CDBLB 1660-1789, DLB 39, 104
Snodgrass, W(illiam) D(e Witt)
  1926- .... **CLC 2, 6, 10, 18, 68; DAM**
  POET
  See also CA 1-4R; CANR 6, 36, 65, 85;
  DLB 5; MTCW 1, 2
Snow, C(harles) P(ercy) 1905-1980 ... **CLC 1,**
  4, 6, 9, 13, 19; DAM NOV
  See also CA 5-8R; 101; CANR 28; CDBLB
  1945-1960; DLB 15, 77; DLBD 17;
  MTCW 1, 2
Snow, Frances Compton
  See Adams, Henry (Brooks)

Snyder, Gary (Sherman) 1930- . **CLC 1, 2, 5,**
  9, 32, 120; DAM POET; PC 21
  See also CA 17-20R; CANR 30, 60; DA3;
  DLB 5, 16, 165, 212; MTCW 2
Snyder, Zilpha Keatley 1927- .... **CLC 17**
  See also AAYA 15; CA 9-12R; CANR 38;
  CLR 31; JRDA; MAICYA; SAAS 2;
  SATA 1, 28, 75, 110; SATA-Essay 112
Soares, Bernardo
  See Pessoa, Fernando (Antonio Nogueira)
Sobh, A.
  See Shamlu, Ahmad
Sobol, Joshua CLC 60
Socrates 469B.C.-399B.C. .... **CMLC 27**
Soderberg, Hjalmar 1869-1941 ...... **TCLC 39**
Sodergran, Edith (Irene)
  See Soedergran, Edith (Irene)
Soedergran, Edith (Irene)
  1892-1923 .... **TCLC 31**
Softly, Edgar
  See Lovecraft, H(oward) P(hillips)
Softly, Edward
  See Lovecraft, H(oward) P(hillips)
Sokolov, Raymond 1941- .... **CLC 7**
  See also CA 85-88
Solo, Jay
  See Ellison, Harlan (Jay)
Sologub, Fyodor TCLC 9
  See also Teternikov, Fyodor Kuzmich
Solomons, Ikey Esquir
  See Thackeray, William Makepeace
Solomos, Dionysios 1798-1857 .... **NCLC 15**
Solwoska, Mara
  See French, Marilyn
Solzhenitsyn, Aleksandr I(sayevich)
  1918- .. **CLC 1, 2, 4, 7, 9, 10, 18, 26, 34,**
  78; DA; DAB; DAC; DAM MST, NOV;
  SSC 32; WLC
  See also AITN 1; CA 69-72; CANR 40, 65;
  DA3; MTCW 1, 2
Somers, Jane
  See Lessing, Doris (May)
Somerville, Edith 1858-1949 .... **TCLC 51**
  See also DLB 135
Somerville & Ross
  See Martin, Violet Florence; Somerville,
  Edith
Sommer, Scott 1951- .... **CLC 25**
  See also CA 106
Sondheim, Stephen (Joshua) 1930- . **CLC 30,**
  39; DAM DRAM
  See also AAYA 11; CA 103; CANR 47, 68
Song, Cathy 1955- .... **PC 21**
  See also CA 154; DLB 169
Sontag, Susan 1933- .... **CLC 1, 2, 10, 13, 31,**
  105; DAM POP
  See also CA 17-20R; CANR 25, 51, 74;
  DA3; DLB 2, 67; MTCW 1, 2
Sophocles 496(?)B.C.-406(?)B.C. .... **CMLC 2;**
  DA; DAB; DAC; DAM DRAM, MST;
  DC 1; WLCS
  See also DA3; DLB 176
Sordello 1189-1269 .... **CMLC 15**
Sorel, Georges 1847-1922 .... **TCLC 91**
  See also CA 118
Sorel, Julia
  See Drexler, Rosalyn
Sorrentino, Gilbert 1929- .. **CLC 3, 7, 14, 22,**
  40
  See also CA 77-80; CANR 14, 33; DLB 5,
  173; DLBY 80; INT CANR-14
Soto, Gary 1952- .... **CLC 32, 80; DAM**
  MULT; HLC 2; PC 28
  See also AAYA 10; CA 119; 125; CANR
  50, 74; CLR 38; DLB 82; HW 1, 2; INT
  125; JRDA; MTCW 2; SATA 80
Soupault, Philippe 1897-1990 .... **CLC 68**
  See also CA 116; 147; 131

Souster, (Holmes) Raymond 1921- .... **CLC 5,**
  14; DAC; DAM POET
  See also CA 13-16R; CAAS 14; CANR 13,
  29, 53; DA3; DLB 88; SATA 63
Southern, Terry 1924(?)-1995 .... **CLC 7**
  See also CA 1-4R; 150; CANR 1, 55; DLB
  2
Southey, Robert 1774-1843 .... **NCLC 8**
  See also DLB 93, 107, 142; SATA 54
Southworth, Emma Dorothy Eliza Nevitte
  1819-1899 .... **NCLC 26**
Souza, Ernest
  See Scott, Evelyn
Soyinka, Wole 1934- .... **CLC 3, 5, 14, 36, 44;**
  BLC 3; DA; DAB; DAC; DAM
  DRAM, MST, MULT; DC 2; WLC
  See also BW 2, 3; CA 13-16R; CANR 27,
  39, 82; DA3; DLB 125; MTCW 1, 2
Spackman, W(illiam) M(ode)
  1905-1990 .... **CLC 46**
  See also CA 81-84; 132
Spacks, Barry (Bernard) 1931- .... **CLC 14**
  See also CA 154; CANR 33; DLB 105
Spanidou, Irini 1946- .... **CLC 44**
  See also CA 185
Spark, Muriel (Sarah) 1918- ..... **CLC 2, 3, 5,**
  8, 13, 18, 40, 94; DAB; DAC; DAM
  MST, NOV; SSC 10
  See also CA 5-8R; CANR 12, 36, 76, 89;
  CDBLB 1945-1960; DA3; DLB 15, 139;
  INT CANR-12; MTCW 1, 2
Spaulding, Douglas
  See Bradbury, Ray (Douglas)
Spaulding, Leonard
  See Bradbury, Ray (Douglas)
Spence, J. A. D.
  See Eliot, T(homas) S(tearns)
Spencer, Elizabeth 1921- .... **CLC 22**
  See also CA 13-16R; CANR 32, 65, 87;
  DLB 6; MTCW 1; SATA 14
Spencer, Leonard G.
  See Silverberg, Robert
Spencer, Scott 1945- .... **CLC 30**
  See also CA 113; CANR 51; DLBY 86
Spender, Stephen (Harold)
  1909-1995 .... **CLC 1, 2, 5, 10, 41, 91;**
  DAM POET
  See also CA 9-12R; 149; CANR 31, 54;
  CDBLB 1945-1960; DA3; DLB 20;
  MTCW 1, 2
Spengler, Oswald (Arnold Gottfried)
  1880-1936 .... **TCLC 25**
  See also CA 118
Spenser, Edmund 1552(?)-1599 ...... **LC 5, 39;**
  DA; DAB; DAC; DAM MST, POET;
  PC 8; WLC
  See also CDBLB Before 1660; DA3; DLB
  167
Spicer, Jack 1925-1965 .... **CLC 8, 18, 72;**
  DAM POET
  See also CA 85-88; DLB 5, 16, 193
Spiegelman, Art 1948- .... **CLC 76**
  See also AAYA 10; CA 125; CANR 41, 55,
  74; MTCW 2; SATA 109
Spielberg, Peter 1929- .... **CLC 6**
  See also CA 5-8R; CANR 4, 48; DLBY 81
Spielberg, Steven 1947- .... **CLC 20**
  See also AAYA 8, 24; CA 77-80; CANR
  32; SATA 32
Spillane, Frank Morrison 1918-
  See Spillane, Mickey
  See also CA 25-28R; CANR 28, 63; DA3;
  DLB 226; MTCW 1, 2; SATA 66
Spillane, Mickey CLC 3, 13
  See also Spillane, Frank Morrison
  See also MTCW 2

Spinoza, Benedictus de 1632-1677 .. LC 9, 58
Spinrad, Norman (Richard) 1940- ... CLC 46
See also CA 37-40R; CAAS 19; CANR 20,
91; DLB 8; INT CANR-20
Spitteler, Carl (Friedrich Georg)
1845-1924 .... TCLC 12
See also CA 109; DLB 129
Spivack, Kathleen (Romola Drucker)
1938- .... CLC 6
See also CA 49-52
Spoto, Donald 1941- .... CLC 39
See also CA 65-68; CANR 11, 57
Springsteen, Bruce (F.) 1949- .... CLC 17
See also CA 111
Spurling, Hilary 1940- .... CLC 34
See also CA 104; CANR 25, 52
Spyker, John Howland
See Elman, Richard (Martin)
Squires, (James) Radcliffe
1917-1993 .... CLC 51
See also CA 1-4R; 140; CANR 6, 21
Srivastava, Dhanpat Rai 1880(?)-1936
See Premchand
See also CA 118
Stacy, Donald
See Pohl, Frederik
Stael, Germaine de 1766-1817
See Stael-Holstein, Anne Louise Germaine
Necker Baronn
See also DLB 119
Stael-Holstein, Anne Louise Germaine
Necker Baronn 1766-1817 .... NCLC 3
See also Stael, Germaine de
See also DLB 192
Stafford, Jean 1915-1979 .. CLC 4, 7, 19, 68;
SSC 26
See also CA 1-4R; 85-88; CANR 3, 65;
DLB 2, 173; MTCW 1, 2; SATA-Obit 22
Stafford, William (Edgar)
1914-1993 .. CLC 4, 7, 29; DAM POET
See also CA 5-8R; 142; CAAS 3; CANR 5,
22; DLB 5, 206; INT CANR-22
Stagnelius, Eric Johan 1793-1823 . NCLC 61
Staines, Trevor
See Brunner, John (Kilian Houston)
Stairs, Gordon
See Austin, Mary (Hunter)
Stairs, Gordon
See Austin, Mary (Hunter)
Stalin, Joseph 1879-1953 .... TCLC 92
Stannard, Martin 1947- .... CLC 44
See also CA 142; DLB 155
Stanton, Elizabeth Cady
1815-1902 .... TCLC 73
See also CA 171; DLB 79
Stanton, Maura 1946- .... CLC 9
See also CA 89-92; CANR 15; DLB 120
Stanton, Schuyler
See Baum, L(yman) Frank
Stapledon, (William) Olaf
1886-1950 .... TCLC 22
See also CA 111; 162; DLB 15
Starbuck, George (Edwin)
1931-1996 .... CLC 53; DAM POET
See also CA 21-24R; 153; CANR 23
Stark, Richard
See Westlake, Donald E(dwin)
Staunton, Schuyler
See Baum, L(yman) Frank
Stead, Christina (Ellen) 1902-1983 ... CLC 2,
5, 8, 32, 80
See also CA 13-16R; 109; CANR 33, 40;
MTCW 1, 2
Stead, William Thomas
1849-1912 .... TCLC 48
See also CA 167
Steele, Richard 1672-1729 .... LC 18
See also CDBLB 1660-1789; DLB 84, 101

Steele, Timothy (Reid) 1948- .... CLC 45
See also CA 93-96; CANR 16, 50; DLB
120
Steffens, (Joseph) Lincoln
1866-1936 .... TCLC 20
See also CA 117
Stegner, Wallace (Earle) 1909-1993 .. CLC 9,
49, 81; DAM NOV; SSC 27
See also AITN 1; BEST 90:3; CA 1-4R;
141; CAAS 9; CANR 1, 21, 46; DLB 9,
206; DLBY 93; MTCW 1, 2
Stein, Gertrude 1874-1946 .... TCLC 1, 6, 28,
48; DA; DAB; DAC; DAM MST, NOV,
POET; PC 18; WLC
See also CA 104; 132; CDALB 1917-1929;
DA3; DLB 4, 54, 86, 228; DLBD 15;
MTCW 1, 2
Steinbeck, John (Ernst) 1902-1968 ... CLC 1,
5, 9, 13, 21, 34, 45, 75, 124; DA; DAB;
DAC; DAM DRAM, MST, NOV; SSC
11, 37; WLC
See also AAYA 12; CA 1-4R; 25-28R;
CANR 1, 35; CDALB 1929-1941; DA3;
DLB 7, 9, 212; DLBD 2; MTCW 1, 2;
SATA 9
Steinem, Gloria 1934- .... CLC 63
See also CA 53-56; CANR 28, 51; MTCW
1, 2
Steiner, George 1929- .. CLC 24; DAM NOV
See also CA 73-76; CANR 31, 67; DLB 67;
MTCW 1, 2; SATA 62
Steiner, K. Leslie
See Delany, Samuel R(ay, Jr.)
Steiner, Rudolf 1861-1925 .... TCLC 13
See also CA 107
Stendhal 1783-1842 .... NCLC 23, 46; DA;
DAB; DAC; DAM MST, NOV; SSC
27; WLC
See also DA3; DLB 119
Stephen, Adeline Virginia
See Woolf, (Adeline) Virginia
Stephen, SirLeslie 1832-1904 .... TCLC 23
See also CA 123; DLB 57, 144, 190
Stephen, Sir Leslie
See Stephen, SirLeslie
Stephen, Virginia
See Woolf, (Adeline) Virginia
Stephens, James 1882(?)-1950 .... TCLC 4
See also CA 104; DLB 19, 153, 162
Stephens, Reed
See Donaldson, Stephen R.
Steptoe, Lydia
See Barnes, Djuna
Sterchi, Beat 1949- .... CLC 65
Sterling, Brett
See Bradbury, Ray (Douglas); Hamilton,
Edmond
Sterling, Bruce 1954- .... CLC 72
See also CA 119; CANR 44
Sterling, George 1869-1926 .... TCLC 20
See also CA 117; 165; DLB 54
Stern, Gerald 1925- .... CLC 40, 100
See also CA 81-84; CANR 28; DLB 105
Stern, Richard (Gustave) 1928- ... CLC 4, 39
See also CA 1-4R; CANR 1, 25, 52; DLBY
87; INT CANR-25
Sternberg, Josef von 1894-1969 .... CLC 20
See also CA 81-84
Sterne, Laurence 1713-1768 .. LC 2, 48; DA;
DAB; DAC; DAM MST, NOV; WLC
See also CDBLB 1660-1789; DLB 39
Sternheim, (William Adolf) Carl
1878-1942 .... TCLC 8
See also CA 105; DLB 56, 118
Stevens, Mark 1951- .... CLC 34
See also CA 122

Stevens, Wallace 1879-1955 ...... TCLC 3, 12,
45; DA; DAB; DAC; DAM MST,
POET; PC 6; WLC
See also CA 104; 124; CDALB 1929-1941;
DA3; DLB 54; MTCW 1, 2
Stevenson, Anne (Katharine) 1933- .. CLC 7,
33
See also CA 17-20R; CAAS 9; CANR 9,
33; DLB 40; MTCW 1
Stevenson, Robert Louis (Balfour)
1850-1894 . NCLC 5, 14, 63; DA; DAB;
DAC; DAM MST, NOV; SSC 11; WLC
See also AAYA 24; CDBLB 1890-1914;
CLR 10, 11; DA3; DLB 18, 57, 141, 156,
174; DLBD 13; JRDA; MAICYA; SATA
100; YABC 2
Stewart, J(ohn) I(nnes) M(ackintosh)
1906-1994 .... CLC 7, 14, 32
See also CA 85-88; 147; CAAS 3; CANR
47; MTCW 1, 2
Stewart, Mary (Florence Elinor)
1916- .... CLC 7, 35, 117; DAB
See also AAYA 29; CA 1-4R; CANR 1, 59;
SATA 12
Stewart, Mary Rainbow
See Stewart, Mary (Florence Elinor)
Stifle, June
See Campbell, Maria
Stifter, Adalbert 1805-1868 .. NCLC 41; SSC
28
See also DLB 133
Still, James 1906- .... CLC 49
See also CA 65-68; CAAS 17; CANR 10,
26; DLB 9; SATA 29
Sting 1951-
See Sumner, Gordon Matthew
See also CA 167
Stirling, Arthur
See Sinclair, Upton (Beall)
Stitt, Milan 1941- .... CLC 29
See also CA 69-72
Stockton, Francis Richard 1834-1902
See Stockton, Frank R.
See also CA 108; 137; MAICYA; SATA 44
Stockton, Frank R. TCLC 47
See also Stockton, Francis Richard
See also DLB 42, 74; DLBD 13; SATA-
Brief 32
Stoddard, Charles
See Kuttner, Henry
Stoker, Abraham 1847-1912
See Stoker, Bram
See also CA 105; 150; DA; DAC; DAM
MST, NOV; DA3; SATA 29
Stoker, Bram 1847-1912 .... TCLC 8; DAB;
WLC
See also Stoker, Abraham
See also AAYA 23; CDBLB 1890-1914;
DLB 36, 70, 178
Stolz, Mary (Slattery) 1920- .... CLC 12
See also AAYA 8; AITN 1; CA 5-8R;
CANR 13, 41; JRDA; MAICYA; SAAS
3; SATA 10, 71
Stone, Irving 1903-1989 . CLC 7; DAM POP
See also AITN 1; CA 1-4R; 129; CAAS 3;
CANR 1, 23; DA3; INT CANR-23;
MTCW 1, 2; SATA 3; SATA-Obit 64
Stone, Oliver (William) 1946- .... CLC 73
See also AAYA 15; CA 110; CANR 55
Stone, Robert (Anthony) 1937- ... CLC 5, 23,
42
See also CA 85-88; CANR 23, 66; DLB
152; INT CANR-23; MTCW 1
Stone, Zachary
See Follett, Ken(neth Martin)

Stoppard, Tom 1937- ... **CLC 1, 3, 4, 5, 8, 15, 29, 34, 63, 91; DA; DAB; DAC; DAM DRAM, MST; DC 6; WLC**
See also CA 81-84; CANR 39, 67; CDBLB 1960 to Present; DA3; DLB 13; DLBY 85; MTCW 1, 2

Storey, David (Malcolm) 1933- . **CLC 2, 4, 5, 8; DAM DRAM**
See also CA 81-84; CANR 36; DLB 13, 14, 207; MTCW 1

Storm, Hyemeyohsts 1935- ..... **CLC 3; DAM MULT**
See also CA 81-84; CANR 45; NNAL

Storm, Theodor 1817-1888 .... **SSC 27**

Storm, (Hans) Theodor (Woldsen)
1817-1888 .... **NCLC 1; SSC 27**
See also DLB 129

Storni, Alfonsina 1892-1938 . **TCLC 5; DAM MULT; HLC 2**
See also CA 104; 131; HW 1

Stoughton, William 1631-1701 .... **LC 38**
See also DLB 24

Stout, Rex (Todhunter) 1886-1975 ..... **CLC 3**
See also AITN 2; CA 61-64; CANR 71

Stow, (Julian) Randolph 1935- ... **CLC 23, 48**
See also CA 13-16R; CANR 33; MTCW 1

Stowe, Harriet (Elizabeth) Beecher
1811-1896 .... **NCLC 3, 50; DA; DAB; DAC; DAM MST, NOV; WLC**
See also CDALB 1865-1917; DA3; DLB 1, 12, 42, 74, 189; JRDA; MAICYA; YABC 1

Strabo c. 64B.C.-c. 25 .... **CMLC 37**
See also DLB 176

Strachey, (Giles) Lytton
1880-1932 .... **TCLC 12**
See also CA 110; 178; DLB 149; DLBD 10; MTCW 2

Strand, Mark 1934- .... **CLC 6, 18, 41, 71; DAM POET**
See also CA 21-24R; CANR 40, 65; DLB 5; SATA 41

Straub, Peter (Francis) 1943- . **CLC 28, 107; DAM POP**
See also BEST 89:1; CA 85-88; CANR 28, 65; DLBY 84; MTCW 1, 2

Strauss, Botho 1944- .... **CLC 22**
See also CA 157; DLB 124

Streatfeild, (Mary) Noel
1895(?)-1986 .... **CLC 21**
See also CA 81-84; 120; CANR 31; CLR 17; DLB 160; MAICYA; SATA 20; SATA-Obit 48

Stribling, T(homas) S(igismund)
1881-1965 .... **CLC 23**
See also CA 107; DLB 9

Strindberg, (Johan) August
1849-1912 .... **TCLC 1, 8, 21, 47; DA; DAB; DAC; DAM DRAM, MST; WLC**
See also CA 104; 135; DA3; MTCW 2

Stringer, Arthur 1874-1950 .... **TCLC 37**
See also CA 161; DLB 92

Stringer, David
See Roberts, Keith (John Kingston)

Stroheim, Erich von 1885-1957 ..... **TCLC 71**

Strugatskii, Arkadii (Natanovich)
1925-1991 .... **CLC 27**
See also CA 106; 135

Strugatskii, Boris (Natanovich)
1933- .... **CLC 27**
See also CA 106

Strummer, Joe 1953(?)- .... **CLC 30**

Strunk, William, Jr. 1869-1946 ...... **TCLC 92**
See also CA 118; 164

Stryk, Lucien 1924- .... **PC 27**
See also CA 13-16R; CANR 10, 28, 55

Stuart, Don A.
See Campbell, John W(ood, Jr.)

Stuart, Ian
See MacLean, Alistair (Stuart)

Stuart, Jesse (Hilton) 1906-1984 ... **CLC 1, 8, 11, 14, 34; SSC 31**
See also CA 5-8R; 112; CANR 31; DLB 9, 48, 102; DLBY 84; SATA 2; SATA-Obit 36

Sturgeon, Theodore (Hamilton)
1918-1985 .... **CLC 22, 39**
See also Queen, Ellery
See also CA 81-84; 116; CANR 32; DLB 8; DLBY 85; MTCW 1, 2

Sturges, Preston 1898-1959 .... **TCLC 48**
See also CA 114; 149; DLB 26

Styron, William 1925- .... **CLC 1, 3, 5, 11, 15, 60; DAM NOV, POP; SSC 25**
See also BEST 90:4; CA 5-8R; CANR 6, 33, 74; CDALB 1968-1988; DA3; DLB 2, 143; DLBY 80; INT CANR-6; MTCW 1, 2

Su, Chien 1884-1918
See Su Man-shu
See also CA 123

Suarez Lynch, B.
See Bioy Casares, Adolfo; Borges, Jorge Luis

Suassuna, Ariano Vilar 1927-
See also CA 178; HLCS 1; HW 2

Suckling, John 1609-1641 .... **PC 30**
See also DAM POET; DLB 58, 126

Suckow, Ruth 1892-1960 .... **SSC 18**
See also CA 113; DLB 9, 102

Sudermann, Hermann 1857-1928 .. **TCLC 15**
See also CA 107; DLB 118

Sue, Eugene 1804-1857 .... **NCLC 1**
See also DLB 119

Sueskind, Patrick 1949- .... **CLC 44**
See also Suskind, Patrick

Sukenick, Ronald 1932- .... **CLC 3, 4, 6, 48**
See also CA 25-28R; CAAS 8; CANR 32, 89; DLB 173; DLBY 81

Suknaski, Andrew 1942- .... **CLC 19**
See also CA 101; DLB 53

Sullivan, Vernon
See Vian, Boris

Sully Prudhomme 1839-1907 .... **TCLC 31**

Su Man-shu .... **TCLC 24**
See also Su, Chien

Summerforest, Ivy B.
See Kirkup, James

Summers, Andrew James 1942- .... **CLC 26**

Summers, Andy
See Summers, Andrew James

Summers, Hollis (Spurgeon, Jr.)
1916- .... **CLC 10**
See also CA 5-8R; CANR 3; DLB 6

Summers, (Alphonsus Joseph-Mary Augustus) Montague
1880-1948 .... **TCLC 16**
See also CA 118; 163

Sumner, Gordon Matthew .... **CLC 26**
See also Sting

Surtees, Robert Smith 1803-1864 .. **NCLC 14**
See also DLB 21

Susann, Jacqueline 1921-1974 .... **CLC 3**
See also AITN 1; CA 65-68; 53-56; MTCW 1, 2

Su Shih 1036-1101 .... **CMLC 15**

Suskind, Patrick
See Sueskind, Patrick
See also CA 145

Sutcliff, Rosemary 1920-1992 .... **CLC 26; DAB; DAC; DAM MST, POP**
See also AAYA 10; CA 5-8R; 139; CANR 37; CLR 1, 37; JRDA; MAICYA; SATA 6, 44, 78; SATA-Obit 73

Sutro, Alfred 1863-1933 .... **TCLC 6**
See also CA 105; 185; DLB 10

Sutton, Henry
See Slavitt, David R(ytman)

Svevo, Italo 1861-1928 ...... **TCLC 2, 35; SSC 25**
See also Schmitz, Aron Hector

Swados, Elizabeth (A.) 1951- .... **CLC 12**
See also CA 97-100; CANR 49; INT 97-100

Swados, Harvey 1920-1972 .... **CLC 5**
See also CA 5-8R; 37-40R; CANR 6; DLB 2

Swan, Gladys 1934- .... **CLC 69**
See also CA 101; CANR 17, 39

Swanson, Logan
See Matheson, Richard Burton

Swarthout, Glendon (Fred)
1918-1992 .... **CLC 35**
See also CA 1-4R; 139; CANR 1, 47; SATA 26

Sweet, Sarah C.
See Jewett, (Theodora) Sarah Orne

Swenson, May 1919-1989 ...... **CLC 4, 14, 61, 106; DA; DAB; DAC; DAM MST, POET; PC 14**
See also CA 5-8R; 130; CANR 36, 61; DLB 5; MTCW 1, 2; SATA 15

Swift, Augustus
See Lovecraft, H(oward) P(hillips)

Swift, Graham (Colin) 1949- ...... **CLC 41, 88**
See also CA 117; 122; CANR 46, 71; DLB 194; MTCW 2

Swift, Jonathan 1667-1745 ..... **LC 1, 42; DA; DAB; DAC; DAM MST, NOV, POET; PC 9; WLC**
See also CDBLB 1660-1789; CLR 53; DA3; DLB 39, 95, 101; SATA 19

Swinburne, Algernon Charles
1837-1909 .... **TCLC 8, 36; DA; DAB; DAC; DAM MST, POET; PC 24; WLC**
See also CA 105; 140; CDBLB 1832-1890; DA3; DLB 35, 57

Swinfen, Ann .... **CLC 34**

Swinnerton, Frank Arthur
1884-1982 .... **CLC 31**
See also CA 108; DLB 34

Swithen, John
See King, Stephen (Edwin)

Sylvia
See Ashton-Warner, Sylvia (Constance)

Symmes, Robert Edward
See Duncan, Robert (Edward)

Symonds, John Addington
1840-1893 .... **NCLC 34**
See also DLB 57, 144

Symons, Arthur 1865-1945 .... **TCLC 11**
See also CA 107; DLB 19, 57, 149

Symons, Julian (Gustave)
1912-1994 .... **CLC 2, 14, 32**
See also CA 49-52; 147; CAAS 3; CANR 3, 33, 59; DLB 87, 155; DLBY 92; MTCW 1

Synge, (Edmund) J(ohn) M(illington)
1871-1909 . **TCLC 6, 37; DAM DRAM; DC 2**
See also CA 104; 141; CDBLB 1890-1914; DLB 10, 19

Syruc, J.
See Milosz, Czeslaw

Szirtes, George 1948- .... **CLC 46**
See also CA 109; CANR 27, 61

Szymborska, Wislawa 1923- .... **CLC 99**
See also CA 154; CANR 91; DA3; DLBY 96; MTCW 2

T. O., Nik
See Annensky, Innokenty (Fyodorovich)

Tabori, George 1914- .... **CLC 19**
See also CA 49-52; CANR 4, 69

Tagore, Rabindranath 1861-1941 ... **TCLC 3, 53; DAM DRAM, POET; PC 8**
See also CA 104; 120; DA3; MTCW 1, 2

Taine, Hippolyte Adolphe
1828-1893 .... **NCLC 15**

Talese, Gay 1932- .... **CLC 37**
See also AITN 1; CA 1-4R; CANR 9, 58; DLB 185; INT CANR-9; MTCW 1, 2

Tallent, Elizabeth (Ann) 1954- .... **CLC 45**
See also CA 117; CANR 72; DLB 130

Tally, Ted 1952- .... **CLC 42**
See also CA 120; 124; INT 124

Talvik, Heiti 1904-1947 .... **TCLC 87**

Tamayo y Baus, Manuel
1829-1898 .... **NCLC 1**

Tammsaare, A(nton) H(ansen)
1878-1940 .... **TCLC 27**
See also CA 164; DLB 220

Tam'si, Tchicaya U
See Tchicaya, Gerald Felix

Tan, Amy (Ruth) 1952- . **CLC 59, 120; DAM MULT, NOV, POP**
See also AAYA 9; BEST 89:3; CA 136; CANR 54; CDALBS; DA3; DLB 173; MTCW 2; SATA 75

Tandem, Felix
See Spitteler, Carl (Friedrich Georg)

Tanizaki, Jun'ichiro 1886-1965 ... **CLC 8, 14, 28; SSC 21**
See also CA 93-96; 25-28R; DLB 180; MTCW 2

Tanner, William
See Amis, Kingsley (William)

Tao Lao
See Storni, Alfonsina

Tarantino, Quentin (Jerome)
1963- .... **CLC 125**
See also CA 171

Tarassoff, Lev
See Troyat, Henri

Tarbell, Ida M(inerva) 1857-1944 . **TCLC 40**
See also CA 122; 181; DLB 47

Tarkington, (Newton) Booth
1869-1946 .... **TCLC 9**
See also CA 110; 143; DLB 9, 102; MTCW 2; SATA 17

Tarkovsky, Andrei (Arsenyevich)
1932-1986 .... **CLC 75**
See also CA 127

Tartt, Donna 1964(?)- .... **CLC 76**
See also CA 142

Tasso, Torquato 1544-1595 .... **LC 5**

Tate, (John Orley) Allen 1899-1979 .. **CLC 2, 4, 6, 9, 11, 14, 24**
See also CA 5-8R; 85-88; CANR 32; DLB 4, 45, 63; DLBD 17; MTCW 1, 2

Tate, Ellalice
See Hibbert, Eleanor Alice Burford

Tate, James (Vincent) 1943- ..... **CLC 2, 6, 25**
See also CA 21-24R; CANR 29, 57; DLB 5, 169

Tauler, Johannes c. 1300-1361 ...... **CMLC 37**
See also DLB 179

Tavel, Ronald 1940- .... **CLC 6**
See also CA 21-24R; CANR 33

Taylor, Bayard 1825-1878 .... **NCLC 89**
See also DLB 3, 189

Taylor, C(ecil) P(hilip) 1929-1981 .... **CLC 27**
See also CA 25-28R; 105; CANR 47

Taylor, Edward 1642(?)-1729 ..... **LC 11; DA; DAB; DAC; DAM MST, POET**
See also DLB 24

Taylor, Eleanor Ross 1920- .... **CLC 5**
See also CA 81-84; CANR 70

Taylor, Elizabeth 1912-1975 ..... **CLC 2, 4, 29**
See also CA 13-16R; CANR 9, 70; DLB 139; MTCW 1; SATA 13

Taylor, Frederick Winslow
1856-1915 .... **TCLC 76**

Taylor, Henry (Splawn) 1942- .... **CLC 44**
See also CA 33-36R; CAAS 7; CANR 31; DLB 5

Taylor, Kamala (Purnaiya) 1924-
See Markandaya, Kamala
See also CA 77-80

Taylor, Mildred D. CLC 21
See also AAYA 10; BW 1; CA 85-88; CANR 25; CLR 9, 59; DLB 52; JRDA; MAICYA; SAAS 5; SATA 15, 70

Taylor, Peter (Hillsman) 1917-1994 .. **CLC 1, 4, 18, 37, 44, 50, 71; SSC 10**
See also CA 13-16R; 147; CANR 9, 50; DLBY 81, 94; INT CANR-9; MTCW 1, 2

Taylor, Robert Lewis 1912-1998 .... **CLC 14**
See also CA 1-4R; 170; CANR 3, 64; SATA 10

Tchekhov, Anton
See Chekhov, Anton (Pavlovich)

Tchicaya, Gerald Felix 1931-1988 .. **CLC 101**
See also CA 129; 125; CANR 81

Tchicaya U Tam'si
See Tchicaya, Gerald Felix

Teasdale, Sara 1884-1933 .... **TCLC 4**
See also CA 104; 163; DLB 45; SATA 32

Tegner, Esaias 1782-1846 .... **NCLC 2**

Teilhard de Chardin, (Marie Joseph) Pierre
1881-1955 .... **TCLC 9**
See also CA 105

Temple, Ann
See Mortimer, Penelope (Ruth)

Tennant, Emma (Christina) 1937- .. **CLC 13, 52**
See also CA 65-68; CAAS 9; CANR 10, 38, 59, 88; DLB 14

Tenneshaw, S. M.
See Silverberg, Robert

Tennyson, Alfred 1809-1892 ... **NCLC 30, 65; DA; DAB; DAC; DAM MST, POET; PC 6; WLC**
See also CDBLB 1832-1890; DA3; DLB 32

Teran, Lisa St. Aubin de CLC 36
See also St. Aubin de Teran, Lisa

Terence c. 184B.C.-c. 159B.C. ...... **CMLC 14; DC 7**
See also DLB 211

Teresa de Jesus, St. 1515-1582 .... **LC 18**

Terkel, Louis 1912-
See Terkel, Studs
See also CA 57-60; CANR 18, 45, 67; DA3; MTCW 1, 2

Terkel, Studs CLC 38
See also Terkel, Louis
See also AAYA 32; AITN 1; MTCW 2

Terry, C. V.
See Slaughter, Frank G(ill)

Terry, Megan 1932- .... **CLC 19; DC 13**
See also CA 77-80; CABS 3; CANR 43; DLB 7

Tertullian c. 155-c. 245 .... **CMLC 29**

Tertz, Abram
See Sinyavsky, Andrei (Donatevich)

Tesich, Steve 1943(?)-1996 .... **CLC 40, 69**
See also CA 105; 152; DLBY 83

Tesla, Nikola 1856-1943 .... **TCLC 88**

Teternikov, Fyodor Kuzmich 1863-1927
See Sologub, Fyodor
See also CA 104

Tevis, Walter 1928-1984 .... **CLC 42**
See also CA 113

Tey, Josephine TCLC 14
See also Mackintosh, Elizabeth
See also DLB 77

Thackeray, William Makepeace
1811-1863 ...... **NCLC 5, 14, 22, 43; DA; DAB; DAC; DAM MST, NOV; WLC**
See also CDBLB 1832-1890; DA3; DLB 21, 55, 159, 163; SATA 23

Thakura, Ravindranatha
See Tagore, Rabindranath

Tharoor, Shashi 1956- .... **CLC 70**
See also CA 141; CANR 91

Thelwell, Michael Miles 1939- .... **CLC 22**
See also BW 2; CA 101

Theobald, Lewis, Jr.
See Lovecraft, H(oward) P(hillips)

Theodorescu, Ion N. 1880-1967
See Arghezi, Tudor
See also CA 116; DLB 220

Theriault, Yves 1915-1983 .... **CLC 79; DAC; DAM MST**
See also CA 102; DLB 88

Theroux, Alexander (Louis) 1939- .... **CLC 2, 25**
See also CA 85-88; CANR 20, 63

Theroux, Paul (Edward) 1941- ..... **CLC 5, 8, 11, 15, 28, 46; DAM POP**
See also AAYA 28; BEST 89:4; CA 33-36R; CANR 20, 45, 74; CDALBS; DA3; DLB 2; MTCW 1, 2; SATA 44, 109

Thesen, Sharon 1946- .... **CLC 56**
See also CA 163

Thevenin, Denis
See Duhamel, Georges

Thibault, Jacques Anatole Francois
1844-1924
See France, Anatole
See also CA 106; 127; DAM NOV; DA3; MTCW 1, 2

Thiele, Colin (Milton) 1920- .... **CLC 17**
See also CA 29-32R; CANR 12, 28, 53; CLR 27; MAICYA; SAAS 2; SATA 14, 72

Thomas, Audrey (Callahan) 1935- .... **CLC 7, 13, 37, 107; SSC 20**
See also AITN 2; CA 21-24R; CAAS 19; CANR 36, 58; DLB 60; MTCW 1

Thomas, Augustus 1857-1934 .... **TCLC 97**

Thomas, D(onald) M(ichael) 1935- . **CLC 13, 22, 31, 132**
See also CA 61-64; CAAS 11; CANR 17, 45, 75; CDBLB 1960 to Present; DA3; DLB 40, 207; INT CANR-17; MTCW 1, 2

Thomas, Dylan (Marlais)
1914-1953 ... **TCLC 1, 8, 45; DA; DAB; DAC; DAM DRAM, MST, POET; PC 2; SSC 3; WLC**
See also CA 104; 120; CANR 65; CDBLB 1945-1960; DA3; DLB 13, 20, 139; MTCW 1, 2; SATA 60

Thomas, (Philip) Edward
1878-1917 .... **TCLC 10; DAM POET**
See also CA 106; 153; DLB 98

Thomas, Joyce Carol 1938- .... **CLC 35**
See also AAYA 12; BW 2, 3; CA 113; 116; CANR 48; CLR 19; DLB 33; INT 116; JRDA; MAICYA; MTCW 1, 2; SAAS 7; SATA 40, 78

Thomas, Lewis 1913-1993 .... **CLC 35**
See also CA 85-88; 143; CANR 38, 60; MTCW 1, 2

Thomas, M. Carey 1857-1935 .... **TCLC 89**

Thomas, Paul
See Mann, (Paul) Thomas

Thomas, Piri 1928- .... **CLC 17; HLCS 2**
See also CA 73-76; HW 1

Thomas, R(onald) S(tuart) 1913- ...... **CLC 6, 13, 48; DAB; DAM POET**
See also CA 89-92; CAAS 4; CANR 30; CDBLB 1960 to Present; DLB 27; MTCW 1

Thomas, Ross (Elmore) 1926-1995 .. **CLC 39**
See also CA 33-36R; 150; CANR 22, 63
Thompson, Francis Clegg
See Mencken, H(enry) L(ouis)
Thompson, Francis Joseph
1859-1907 .... **TCLC 4**
See also CA 104; CDBLB 1890-1914; DLB 19
Thompson, Hunter S(tockton)
1939- ... **CLC 9, 17, 40, 104; DAM POP**
See also BEST 89:1; CA 17-20R; CANR 23, 46, 74, 77; DA3; DLB 185; MTCW 1, 2
Thompson, James Myers
See Thompson, Jim (Myers)
Thompson, Jim (Myers)
1906-1977(?) .... **CLC 69**
See also CA 140; DLB 226
Thompson, Judith CLC 39
Thomson, James 1700-1748 ... **LC 16, 29, 40; DAM POET**
See also DLB 95
Thomson, James 1834-1882 .... **NCLC 18; DAM POET**
See also DLB 35
Thoreau, Henry David 1817-1862 .. **NCLC 7, 21, 61; DA; DAB; DAC; DAM MST; PC 30; WLC**
See also CDALB 1640-1865; DA3; DLB 1, 223
Thornton, Hall
See Silverberg, Robert
Thucydides c. 455B.C.-399B.C. ..... **CMLC 17**
See also DLB 176
Thumboo, Edwin 1933- .... **PC 30**
Thurber, James (Grover)
1894-1961 .... **CLC 5, 11, 25, 125; DA; DAB; DAC; DAM DRAM, MST, NOV; SSC 1**
See also CA 73-76; CANR 17, 39; CDALB 1929-1941; DA3; DLB 4, 11, 22, 102; MAICYA; MTCW 1, 2; SATA 13
Thurman, Wallace (Henry)
1902-1934 .... **TCLC 6; BLC 3; DAM MULT**
See also BW 1, 3; CA 104; 124; CANR 81; DLB 51
Tibullus, Albius c. 54B.C.-c. 19B.C. .... **CMLC 36**
See also DLB 211
Ticheburn, Cheviot
See Ainsworth, William Harrison
Tieck, (Johann) Ludwig
1773-1853 .... **NCLC 5, 46; SSC 31**
See also DLB 90
Tiger, Derry
See Ellison, Harlan (Jay)
Tilghman, Christopher 1948(?)- .... **CLC 65**
See also CA 159
Tillich, Paul (Johannes)
1886-1965 .... **CLC 131**
See also CA 5-8R; 25-28R; CANR 33; MTCW 1, 2
Tillinghast, Richard (Williford)
1940- .... **CLC 29**
See also CA 29-32R; CAAS 23; CANR 26, 51
Timrod, Henry 1828-1867 .... **NCLC 25**
See also DLB 3
Tindall, Gillian (Elizabeth) 1938- ...... **CLC 7**
See also CA 21-24R; CANR 11, 65
Tiptree, James, Jr. CLC 48, 50
See also Sheldon, Alice Hastings Bradley
See also DLB 8
Titmarsh, Michael Angelo
See Thackeray, William Makepeace

Tocqueville, Alexis (Charles Henri Maurice Clerel, Comte) de 1805-1859 . **NCLC 7, 63**
Tolkien, J(ohn) R(onald) R(euel)
1892-1973 .. **CLC 1, 2, 3, 8, 12, 38; DA; DAB; DAC; DAM MST, NOV, POP; WLC**
See also AAYA 10; AITN 1; CA 17-18; 45-48; CANR 36; CAP 2; CDBLB 1914-1945; CLR 56; DA3; DLB 15, 160; JRDA; MAICYA; MTCW 1, 2; SATA 2, 32, 100; SATA-Obit 24
Toller, Ernst 1893-1939 .... **TCLC 10**
See also CA 107; 186; DLB 124
Tolson, M. B.
See Tolson, Melvin B(eaunorus)
Tolson, Melvin B(eaunorus)
1898(?)-1966 .... **CLC 36, 105; BLC 3; DAM MULT, POET**
See also BW 1, 3; CA 124; 89-92; CANR 80; DLB 48, 76
Tolstoi, Aleksei Nikolaevich
See Tolstoy, Alexey Nikolaevich
Tolstoy, Alexey Nikolaevich
1882-1945 .... **TCLC 18**
See also CA 107; 158
Tolstoy, Count Leo
See Tolstoy, Leo (Nikolaevich)
Tolstoy, Leo (Nikolaevich)
1828-1910 .. **TCLC 4, 11, 17, 28, 44, 79; DA; DAB; DAC; DAM MST, NOV; SSC 9, 30; WLC**
See also CA 104; 123; DA3; SATA 26
Tomasi di Lampedusa, Giuseppe 1896-1957
See Lampedusa, Giuseppe (Tomasi) di
See also CA 111
Tomlin, Lily CLC 17
See also Tomlin, Mary Jean
Tomlin, Mary Jean 1939(?)-
See Tomlin, Lily
See also CA 117
Tomlinson, (Alfred) Charles 1927- .... **CLC 2, 4, 6, 13, 45; DAM POET; PC 17**
See also CA 5-8R; CANR 33; DLB 40
Tomlinson, H(enry) M(ajor)
1873-1958 .... **TCLC 71**
See also CA 118; 161; DLB 36, 100, 195
Tonson, Jacob
See Bennett, (Enoch) Arnold
Toole, John Kennedy 1937-1969 ..... **CLC 19, 64**
See also CA 104; DLBY 81; MTCW 2
Toomer, Jean 1894-1967 .... **CLC 1, 4, 13, 22; BLC 3; DAM MULT; PC 7; SSC 1; WLCS**
See also BW 1; CA 85-88; CDALB 1917-1929; DA3; DLB 45, 51; MTCW 1, 2
Torley, Luke
See Blish, James (Benjamin)
Tornimparte, Alessandra
See Ginzburg, Natalia
Torre, Raoul della
See Mencken, H(enry) L(ouis)
Torrence, Ridgely 1874-1950 .... **TCLC 97**
See also DLB 54
Torrey, E(dwin) Fuller 1937- .... **CLC 34**
See also CA 119; CANR 71
Torsvan, Ben Traven
See Traven, B.
Torsvan, Benno Traven
See Traven, B.
Torsvan, Berick Traven
See Traven, B.
Torsvan, Berwick Traven
See Traven, B.
Torsvan, Bruno Traven
See Traven, B.
Torsvan, Traven
See Traven, B.

Tournier, Michel (Edouard) 1924- .... **CLC 6, 23, 36, 95**
See also CA 49-52; CANR 3, 36, 74; DLB 83; MTCW 1, 2; SATA 23
Tournimparte, Alessandra
See Ginzburg, Natalia
Towers, Ivar
See Kornbluth, C(yril) M.
Towne, Robert (Burton) 1936(?)- ..... **CLC 87**
See also CA 108; DLB 44
Townsend, Sue CLC 61
See also Townsend, Susan Elaine
See also AAYA 28; SATA 55, 93; SATA-Brief 48
Townsend, Susan Elaine 1946-
See Townsend, Sue
See also CA 119; 127; CANR 65; DAB; DAC; DAM MST
Townshend, Peter (Dennis Blandford)
1945- .... **CLC 17, 42**
See also CA 107
Tozzi, Federigo 1883-1920 .... **TCLC 31**
See also CA 160
Traill, Catharine Parr 1802-1899 .. **NCLC 31**
See also DLB 99
Trakl, Georg 1887-1914 .... **TCLC 5; PC 20**
See also CA 104; 165; MTCW 2
Transtroemer, Tomas (Goesta)
1931- .... **CLC 52, 65; DAM POET**
See also CA 117; 129; CAAS 17
Transtromer, Tomas Gosta
See Transtroemer, Tomas (Goesta)
Traven, B. (?)-1969 .... **CLC 8, 11**
See also CA 19-20; 25-28R; CAP 2; DLB 9, 56; MTCW 1
Treitel, Jonathan 1959- .... **CLC 70**
Trelawny, Edward John
1792-1881 .... **NCLC 85**
See also DLB 110, 116, 144
Tremain, Rose 1943- .... **CLC 42**
See also CA 97-100; CANR 44; DLB 14
Tremblay, Michel 1942- .... **CLC 29, 102; DAC; DAM MST**
See also CA 116; 128; DLB 60; MTCW 1, 2
Trevanian CLC 29
See also Whitaker, Rod(ney)
Trevor, Glen
See Hilton, James
Trevor, William 1928- .. **CLC 7, 9, 14, 25, 71, 116; SSC 21**
See also Cox, William Trevor
See also DLB 14, 139; MTCW 2
Trifonov, Yuri (Valentinovich)
1925-1981 .... **CLC 45**
See also CA 126; 103; MTCW 1
Trilling, Diana (Rubin) 1905-1996 . **CLC 129**
See also CA 5-8R; 154; CANR 10, 46; INT CANR-10; MTCW 1, 2
Trilling, Lionel 1905-1975 .... **CLC 9, 11, 24**
See also CA 9-12R; 61-64; CANR 10; DLB 28, 63; INT CANR-10; MTCW 1, 2
Trimball, W. H.
See Mencken, H(enry) L(ouis)
Tristan
See Gomez de la Serna, Ramon
Tristram
See Housman, A(lfred) E(dward)
Trogdon, William (Lewis) 1939-
See Heat-Moon, William Least
See also CA 115; 119; CANR 47, 89; INT 119
Trollope, Anthony 1815-1882 ... **NCLC 6, 33; DA; DAB; DAC; DAM MST, NOV; SSC 28; WLC**
See also CDBLB 1832-1890; DA3; DLB 21, 57, 159; SATA 22
Trollope, Frances 1779-1863 .... **NCLC 30**
See also DLB 21, 166

Trotsky, Leon 1879-1940 .... **TCLC 22**
See also CA 118; 167

Trotter (Cockburn), Catharine
1679-1749 .... **LC 8**
See also DLB 84

Trotter, Wilfred 1872-1939 .... **TCLC 97**

Trout, Kilgore
See Farmer, Philip Jose

Trow, George W. S. 1943- .... **CLC 52**
See also CA 126; CANR 91

Troyat, Henri 1911- .... **CLC 23**
See also CA 45-48; CANR 2, 33, 67;
MTCW 1

Trudeau, G(arretson) B(eekman) 1948-
See Trudeau, Garry B.
See also CA 81-84; CANR 31; SATA 35

Trudeau, Garry B. CLC 12
See also Trudeau, G(arretson) B(eekman)
See also AAYA 10; AITN 2

Truffaut, Francois 1932-1984 ... **CLC 20, 101**
See also CA 81-84; 113; CANR 34

Trumbo, Dalton 1905-1976 .... **CLC 19**
See also CA 21-24R; 69-72; CANR 10;
DLB 26

Trumbull, John 1750-1831 .... **NCLC 30**
See also DLB 31

Trundlett, Helen B.
See Eliot, T(homas) S(tearns)

Tryon, Thomas 1926-1991 .... **CLC 3, 11;**
DAM POP
See also AITN 1; CA 29-32R; 135; CANR
32, 77; DA3; MTCW 1

Tryon, Tom
See Tryon, Thomas

Ts'ao Hsueh-ch'in 1715(?)-1763 .... **LC 1**

Tsushima, Shuji 1909-1948
See Dazai Osamu
See also CA 107

Tsvetaeva (Efron), Marina (Ivanovna)
1892-1941 .... **TCLC 7, 35; PC 14**
See also CA 104; 128; CANR 73; MTCW
1, 2

Tuck, Lily 1938- .... **CLC 70**
See also CA 139; CANR 90

Tu Fu 712-770 .... **PC 9**
See also DAM MULT

Tunis, John R(oberts) 1889-1975 ..... **CLC 12**
See also CA 61-64; CANR 62; DLB 22,
171; JRDA; MAICYA; SATA 37; SATA-
Brief 30

Tuohy, Frank CLC 37
See also Tuohy, John Francis
See also DLB 14, 139

Tuohy, John Francis 1925-1999
See Tuohy, Frank
See also CA 5-8R; 178; CANR 3, 47

Turco, Lewis (Putnam) 1934- ..... **CLC 11, 63**
See also CA 13-16R; CAAS 22; CANR 24,
51; DLBY 84

Turgenev, Ivan 1818-1883 .... **NCLC 21; DA;**
DAB; DAC; DAM MST, NOV; DC 7;
SSC 7; WLC

Turgot, Anne-Robert-Jacques
1727-1781 .... **LC 26**

Turner, Frederick 1943- .... **CLC 48**
See also CA 73-76; CAAS 10; CANR 12,
30, 56; DLB 40

Tutu, Desmond M(pilo) 1931- .... **CLC 80;**
BLC 3; DAM MULT
See also BW 1, 3; CA 125; CANR 67, 81

Tutuola, Amos 1920-1997 ...... **CLC 5, 14, 29;**
BLC 3; DAM MULT
See also BW 2, 3; CA 9-12R; 159; CANR
27, 66; DA3; DLB 125; MTCW 1, 2

Twain, Mark TCLC 6, 12, 19, 36, 48, 59; SSC
34; WLC
See also Clemens, Samuel Langhorne
See also AAYA 20; CLR 58, 60; DLB 11,
12, 23, 64, 74

Tyler, Anne 1941- . **CLC 7, 11, 18, 28, 44, 59,**
103; DAM NOV, POP
See also AAYA 18; BEST 89:1; CA 9-12R;
CANR 11, 33, 53; CDALBS; DLB 6, 143;
DLBY 82; MTCW 1, 2; SATA 7, 90

Tyler, Royall 1757-1826 .... **NCLC 3**
See also DLB 37

Tynan, Katharine 1861-1931 .... **TCLC 3**
See also CA 104; 167; DLB 153

Tyutchev, Fyodor 1803-1873 .... **NCLC 34**

Tzara, Tristan 1896-1963 ...... **CLC 47; DAM**
POET; PC 27
See also CA 153; 89-92; MTCW 2

Uhry, Alfred 1936- .. **CLC 55; DAM DRAM,**
POP
See also CA 127; 133; DA3; INT 133

Ulf, Haerved
See Strindberg, (Johan) August

Ulf, Harved
See Strindberg, (Johan) August

Ulibarri, Sabine R(eyes) 1919- .... **CLC 83;**
DAM MULT; HLCS 2
See also CA 131; CANR 81; DLB 82; HW
1, 2

Unamuno (y Jugo), Miguel de
1864-1936 ..... **TCLC 2, 9; DAM MULT,**
NOV; HLC 2; SSC 11
See also CA 104; 131; CANR 81; DLB 108;
HW 1, 2; MTCW 1, 2

Undercliffe, Errol
See Campbell, (John) Ramsey

Underwood, Miles
See Glassco, John

Undset, Sigrid 1882-1949 .... **TCLC 3; DA;**
DAB; DAC; DAM MST, NOV; WLC
See also CA 104; 129; DA3; MTCW 1, 2

Ungaretti, Giuseppe 1888-1970 ... **CLC 7, 11,**
15
See also CA 19-20; 25-28R; CAP 2; DLB
114

Unger, Douglas 1952- .... **CLC 34**
See also CA 130

Unsworth, Barry (Forster) 1930- .... **CLC 76,**
127
See also CA 25-28R; CANR 30, 54; DLB
194

Updike, John (Hoyer) 1932- . **CLC 1, 2, 3, 5,**
7, 9, 13, 15, 23, 34, 43, 70; DA; DAB;
DAC; DAM MST, NOV, POET, POP;
SSC 13, 27; WLC
See also CA 1-4R; CABS 1; CANR 4, 33,
51; CDALB 1968-1988; DA3; DLB 2, 5,
143, 227; DLBD 3; DLBY 80, 82, 97;
MTCW 1, 2

Upshaw, Margaret Mitchell
See Mitchell, Margaret (Munnerlyn)

Upton, Mark
See Sanders, Lawrence

Upward, Allen 1863-1926 .... **TCLC 85**
See also CA 117; DLB 36

Urdang, Constance (Henriette)
1922- .... **CLC 47**
See also CA 21-24R; CANR 9, 24

Uriel, Henry
See Faust, Frederick (Schiller)

Uris, Leon (Marcus) 1924- .... **CLC 7, 32;**
DAM NOV, POP
See also AITN 1, 2; BEST 89:2; CA 1-4R;
CANR 1, 40, 65; DA3; MTCW 1, 2;
SATA 49

Urista, Alberto H. 1947-
See Alurista
See also CA 45-48; 182; CANR 2, 32;
HLCS 1; HW 1

Urmuz
See Codrescu, Andrei

Urquhart, Guy
See McAlmon, Robert (Menzies)

Urquhart, Jane 1949- .... **CLC 90; DAC**
See also CA 113; CANR 32, 68

Usigli, Rodolfo 1905-1979
See also CA 131; HLCS 1; HW 1

Ustinov, Peter (Alexander) 1921- .... **CLC 1**
See also AITN 1; CA 13-16R; CANR 25,
51; DLB 13; MTCW 2

U Tam'si, Gerald Felix Tchicaya
See Tchicaya, Gerald Felix

U Tam'si, Tchicaya
See Tchicaya, Gerald Felix

Vachss, Andrew (Henry) 1942- .... **CLC 106**
See also CA 118; CANR 44

Vachss, Andrew H.
See Vachss, Andrew (Henry)

Vaculik, Ludvik 1926- .... **CLC 7**
See also CA 53-56; CANR 72

Vaihinger, Hans 1852-1933 .... **TCLC 71**
See also CA 116; 166

Valdez, Luis (Miguel) 1940- .. **CLC 84; DAM**
MULT; DC 10; HLC 2
See also CA 101; CANR 32, 81; DLB 122;
HW 1

Valenzuela, Luisa 1938- .... **CLC 31, 104;**
DAM MULT; HLCS 2; SSC 14
See also CA 101; CANR 32, 65; DLB 113;
HW 1, 2

Valera y Alcala-Galiano, Juan
1824-1905 .... **TCLC 10**
See also CA 106

Valery, (Ambroise) Paul (Toussaint Jules)
1871-1945 ... **TCLC 4, 15; DAM POET;**
PC 9
See also CA 104; 122; DA3; MTCW 1, 2

Valle-Inclan, Ramon (Maria) del
1866-1936 .... **TCLC 5; DAM MULT;**
HLC 2
See also CA 106; 153; CANR 80; DLB 134;
HW 2

Vallejo, Antonio Buero
See Buero Vallejo, Antonio

Vallejo, Cesar (Abraham)
1892-1938 .. **TCLC 3, 56; DAM MULT;**
HLC 2
See also CA 105; 153; HW 1

Valles, Jules 1832-1885 .... **NCLC 71**
See also DLB 123

Vallette, Marguerite Eymery
1860-1953 .... **TCLC 67**
See also CA 182; DLB 123, 192

Valle Y Pena, Ramon del
See Valle-Inclan, Ramon (Maria) del

Van Ash, Cay 1918- .... **CLC 34**

Vanbrugh, Sir John 1664-1726 .... **LC 21;**
DAM DRAM
See also DLB 80

Van Campen, Karl
See Campbell, John W(ood, Jr.)

Vance, Gerald
See Silverberg, Robert

Vance, Jack CLC 35
See also Vance, John Holbrook
See also DLB 8

Vance, John Holbrook 1916-
See Queen, Ellery; Vance, Jack
See also CA 29-32R; CANR 17, 65; MTCW
1

Van Den Bogarde, Derek Jules Gaspard
Ulric Niven 1921-1999 .... **CLC 14**
See also CA 77-80; 179; DLB 19

Vandenburgh, Jane CLC 59
See also CA 168

Vanderhaeghe, Guy 1951- .... **CLC 41**
See also CA 113; CANR 72

van der Post, Laurens (Jan)
1906-1996 .... **CLC 5**
See also CA 5-8R; 155; CANR 35; DLB
204

van de Wetering, Janwillem 1931- ... **CLC 47**
See also CA 49-52; CANR 4, 62, 90

Van Dine, S. S. **TCLC 23**
See also Wright, Willard Huntington

Van Doren, Carl (Clinton)
1885-1950 .... **TCLC 18**
See also CA 111; 168

Van Doren, Mark 1894-1972 .... **CLC 6, 10**
See also CA 1-4R; 37-40R; CANR 3; DLB
45; MTCW 1, 2

Van Druten, John (William)
1901-1957 .... **TCLC 2**
See also CA 104; 161; DLB 10

Van Duyn, Mona (Jane) 1921- ...... **CLC 3, 7,**
63, 116; DAM POET
See also CA 9-12R; CANR 7, 38, 60; DLB
5

Van Dyne, Edith
See Baum, L(yman) Frank

van Itallie, Jean-Claude 1936- .... **CLC 3**
See also CA 45-48; CAAS 2; CANR 1, 48;
DLB 7

van Ostaijen, Paul 1896-1928 .... **TCLC 33**
See also CA 163

Van Peebles, Melvin 1932- .... **CLC 2, 20;**
DAM MULT
See also BW 2, 3; CA 85-88; CANR 27,
67, 82

Vansittart, Peter 1920- .... **CLC 42**
See also CA 1-4R; CANR 3, 49, 90

Van Vechten, Carl 1880-1964 .... **CLC 33**
See also CA 183; 89-92; DLB 4, 9, 51

Van Vogt, A(lfred) E(lton) 1912- .... **CLC 1**
See also CA 21-24R; CANR 28; DLB 8;
SATA 14

Varda, Agnes 1928- .... **CLC 16**
See also CA 116; 122

Vargas Llosa, (Jorge) Mario (Pedro)
1936- .... **CLC 3, 6, 9, 10, 15, 31, 42, 85;**
DA; DAB; DAC; DAM MST, MULT,
NOV; HLC 2
See also CA 73-76; CANR 18, 32, 42, 67;
DA3; DLB 145; HW 1, 2; MTCW 1, 2

Vasiliu, Gheorghe 1881-1957
See Bacovia, George
See also CA 123; DLB 220

Vassa, Gustavus
See Equiano, Olaudah

Vassilikos, Vassilis 1933- .... **CLC 4, 8**
See also CA 81-84; CANR 75

Vaughan, Henry 1621-1695 .... **LC 27**
See also DLB 131

Vaughn, Stephanie **CLC 62**

Vazov, Ivan (Minchov) 1850-1921 . **TCLC 25**
See also CA 121; 167; DLB 147

Veblen, Thorstein B(unde)
1857-1929 .... **TCLC 31**
See also CA 115; 165

Vega, Lope de 1562-1635 .... **LC 23; HLCS 2**

Venison, Alfred
See Pound, Ezra (Weston Loomis)

Verdi, Marie de
See Mencken, H(enry) L(ouis)

Verdu, Matilde
See Cela, Camilo Jose

Verga, Giovanni (Carmelo)
1840-1922 .... **TCLC 3; SSC 21**
See also CA 104; 123

Vergil 70B.C.-19B.C. .... **CMLC 9, 40; DA;**
DAB; DAC; DAM MST, POET; PC
12; WLCS
See also Virgil
See also DA3; DLB 211

Verhaeren, Emile (Adolphe Gustave)
1855-1916 .... **TCLC 12**
See also CA 109

Verlaine, Paul (Marie) 1844-1896 .. **NCLC 2,**
51; DAM POET; PC 2

Verne, Jules (Gabriel) 1828-1905 ... **TCLC 6,**
52
See also AAYA 16; CA 110; 131; DA3;
DLB 123; JRDA; MAICYA; SATA 21

Very, Jones 1813-1880 .... **NCLC 9**
See also DLB 1

Vesaas, Tarjei 1897-1970 .... **CLC 48**
See also CA 29-32R

Vialis, Gaston
See Simenon, Georges (Jacques Christian)

Vian, Boris 1920-1959 .... **TCLC 9**
See also CA 106; 164; DLB 72; MTCW 2

Viaud, (Louis Marie) Julien 1850-1923
See Loti, Pierre
See also CA 107

Vicar, Henry
See Felsen, Henry Gregor

Vicker, Angus
See Felsen, Henry Gregor

Vidal, Gore 1925- ...... **CLC 2, 4, 6, 8, 10, 22,**
33, 72; DAM NOV, POP
See also AITN 1; BEST 90:2; CA 5-8R;
CANR 13, 45, 65; CDALBS; DA3; DLB
6, 152; INT CANR-13; MTCW 1, 2

Viereck, Peter (Robert Edwin)
1916- .... **CLC 4; PC 27**
See also CA 1-4R; CANR 1, 47; DLB 5

Vigny, Alfred (Victor) de
1797-1863 .. **NCLC 7; DAM POET; PC**
26
See also DLB 119, 192

Vilakazi, Benedict Wallet
1906-1947 .... **TCLC 37**
See also CA 168

Villa, Jose Garcia 1904-1997 .... **PC 22**
See also CA 25-28R; CANR 12

Villarreal, Jose Antonio 1924-
See also CA 133; DAM MULT; DLB 82;
HLC 2; HW 1

Villaurrutia, Xavier 1903-1950 ...... **TCLC 80**
See also HW 1

Villehardouin 1150(?)-1218(?) .... **CMLC 38**

Villiers de l'Isle Adam, Jean Marie Mathias
Philippe Auguste, Comte de
1838-1889 .... **NCLC 3; SSC 14**
See also DLB 123

Villon, Francois 1431-1463(?) .... **PC 13**
See also DLB 208

Vine, Barbara **CLC 50**
See also Rendell, Ruth (Barbara)
See also BEST 90:4

Vinge, Joan (Carol) D(ennison)
1948- .... **CLC 30; SSC 24**
See also AAYA 32; CA 93-96; CANR 72;
SATA 36, 113

Violis, G.
See Simenon, Georges (Jacques Christian)

Viramontes, Helena Maria 1954-
See also CA 159; DLB 122; HLCS 2; HW
2

Virgil 70B.C.-19B.C.
See Vergil

Visconti, Luchino 1906-1976 .... **CLC 16**
See also CA 81-84; 65-68; CANR 39

Vittorini, Elio 1908-1966 .... **CLC 6, 9, 14**
See also CA 133; 25-28R

Vivekananda, Swami 1863-1902 .... **TCLC 88**

Vizenor, Gerald Robert 1934- .... **CLC 103;**
DAM MULT
See also CA 13-16R; CAAS 22; CANR 5,
21, 44, 67; DLB 175, 227; MTCW 2;
NNAL

Vizinczey, Stephen 1933- .... **CLC 40**
See also CA 128; INT 128

Vliet, R(ussell) G(ordon)
1929-1984 .... **CLC 22**
See also CA 37-40R; 112; CANR 18

Vogau, Boris Andreyevich 1894-1937(?)
See Pilnyak, Boris
See also CA 123

Vogel, Paula A(nne) 1951- .... **CLC 76**
See also CA 108

Voigt, Cynthia 1942- .... **CLC 30**
See also AAYA 3, 30; CA 106; CANR 18,
37, 40; CLR 13, 48; INT CANR-18;
JRDA; MAICYA; SATA 48, 79, 116;
SATA-Brief 33

Voigt, Ellen Bryant 1943- .... **CLC 54**
See also CA 69-72; CANR 11, 29, 55; DLB
120

Voinovich, Vladimir (Nikolaevich)
1932- .... **CLC 10, 49**
See also CA 81-84; CAAS 12; CANR 33,
67; MTCW 1

Vollmann, William T. 1959- .. **CLC 89; DAM**
NOV, POP
See also CA 134; CANR 67; DA3; MTCW
2

Voloshinov, V. N.
See Bakhtin, Mikhail Mikhailovich

Voltaire 1694-1778 .... **LC 14; DA; DAB;**
DAC; DAM DRAM, MST; SSC 12;
WLC
See also DA3

von Aschendrof, BaronIgnatz
See Ford, Ford Madox

von Daeniken, Erich 1935- .... **CLC 30**
See also AITN 1; CA 37-40R; CANR 17,
44

von Daniken, Erich
See von Daeniken, Erich

von Hartmann, Eduard
1842-1906 .... **TCLC 96**

von Heidenstam, (Carl Gustaf) Verner
See Heidenstam, (Carl Gustaf) Verner von

von Heyse, Paul (Johann Ludwig)
See Heyse, Paul (Johann Ludwig von)

von Hofmannsthal, Hugo
See Hofmannsthal, Hugo von

von Horvath, Odon
See Horvath, Oedoen von

von Horvath, Oedoen -1938
See Horvath, Oedoen von
See also CA 184

von Liliencron, (Friedrich Adolf Axel)
Detlev
See Liliencron, (Friedrich Adolf Axel) De-
tlev von

Vonnegut, Kurt, Jr. 1922- . **CLC 1, 2, 3, 4, 5,**
8, 12, 22, 40, 60, 111; DA; DAB; DAC;
DAM MST, NOV, POP; SSC 8; WLC
See also AAYA 6; AITN 1; BEST 90:4; CA
1-4R; CANR 1, 25, 49, 75; CDALB 1968-
1988; DA3; DLB 2, 8, 152; DLBD 3;
DLBY 80; MTCW 1, 2

Von Rachen, Kurt
See Hubbard, L(afayette) Ron(ald)

von Rezzori (d'Arezzo), Gregor
See Rezzori (d'Arezzo), Gregor von

von Sternberg, Josef
See Sternberg, Josef von

Vorster, Gordon 1924- .... **CLC 34**
See also CA 133

Vosce, Trudie
See Ozick, Cynthia

Voznesensky, Andrei (Andreievich)
1933- .... **CLC 1, 15, 57; DAM POET**
See also CA 89-92; CANR 37; MTCW 1

Waddington, Miriam 1917- .... **CLC 28**
See also CA 21-24R; CANR 12, 30; DLB
68

Wagman, Fredrica 1937- .... **CLC 7**
See also CA 97-100; INT 97-100

Wagner, Linda W.
See Wagner-Martin, Linda (C.)

Wagner, Linda Welshimer
See Wagner-Martin, Linda (C.)

Wagner, Richard 1813-1883 .... **NCLC 9**
See also DLB 129

Wagner-Martin, Linda (C.) 1936- .... **CLC 50**
See also CA 159

Wagoner, David (Russell) 1926- .... **CLC 3, 5, 15**
See also CA 1-4R; CAAS 3; CANR 2, 71; DLB 5; SATA 14

Wah, Fred(erick James) 1939- .... **CLC 44**
See also CA 107; 141; DLB 60

Wahloo, Per 1926-1975 .... **CLC 7**
See also CA 61-64; CANR 73

Wahloo, Peter
See Wahloo, Per

Wain, John (Barrington) 1925-1994 . **CLC 2, 11, 15, 46**
See also CA 5-8R; 145; CAAS 4; CANR 23, 54; CDBLB 1960 to Present; DLB 15, 27, 139, 155; MTCW 1, 2

Wajda, Andrzej 1926- .... **CLC 16**
See also CA 102

Wakefield, Dan 1932- .... **CLC 7**
See also CA 21-24R; CAAS 7

Wakoski, Diane 1937- ...... **CLC 2, 4, 7, 9, 11, 40; DAM POET; PC 15**
See also CA 13-16R; CAAS 1; CANR 9, 60; DLB 5; INT CANR-9; MTCW 2

Wakoski-Sherbell, Diane
See Wakoski, Diane

Walcott, Derek (Alton) 1930- .... **CLC 2, 4, 9, 14, 25, 42, 67, 76; BLC 3; DAB; DAC; DAM MST, MULT, POET; DC 7**
See also BW 2; CA 89-92; CANR 26, 47, 75, 80; DA3; DLB 117; DLBY 81; MTCW 1, 2

Waldman, Anne (Lesley) 1945- .... **CLC 7**
See also CA 37-40R; CAAS 17; CANR 34, 69; DLB 16

Waldo, E. Hunter
See Sturgeon, Theodore (Hamilton)

Waldo, Edward Hamilton
See Sturgeon, Theodore (Hamilton)

Walker, Alice (Malsenior) 1944- ... **CLC 5, 6, 9, 19, 27, 46, 58, 103; BLC 3; DA; DAB; DAC; DAM MST, NOV, POET, POP; PC 30; SSC 5; WLCS**
See also AAYA 3, 33; BEST 89:4; BW 2, 3; CA 37-40R; CANR 9, 27, 49, 66, 82; CDALB 1968-1988; DA3; DLB 6, 33, 143; INT CANR-27; MTCW 1, 2; SATA 31

Walker, David Harry 1911-1992 ...... **CLC 14**
See also CA 1-4R; 137; CANR 1; SATA 8; SATA-Obit 71

Walker, Edward Joseph 1934-
See Walker, Ted
See also CA 21-24R; CANR 12, 28, 53

Walker, George F. 1947- . **CLC 44, 61; DAB; DAC; DAM MST**
See also CA 103; CANR 21, 43, 59; DLB 60

Walker, Joseph A. 1935- .... **CLC 19; DAM DRAM, MST**
See also BW 1, 3; CA 89-92; CANR 26; DLB 38

Walker, Margaret (Abigail) 1915-1998 .... **CLC 1, 6; BLC; DAM MULT; PC 20**
See also BW 2, 3; CA 73-76; 172; CANR 26, 54, 76; DLB 76, 152; MTCW 1, 2

Walker, Ted CLC 13
See also Walker, Edward Joseph
See also DLB 40

Wallace, David Foster 1962- ..... **CLC 50, 114**
See also CA 132; CANR 59; DA3; MTCW 2

Wallace, Dexter
See Masters, Edgar Lee

Wallace, (Richard Horatio) Edgar 1875-1932 .... **TCLC 57**
See also CA 115; DLB 70

Wallace, Irving 1916-1990 .... **CLC 7, 13; DAM NOV, POP**
See also AITN 1; CA 1-4R; 132; CAAS 1; CANR 1, 27; INT CANR-27; MTCW 1, 2

Wallant, Edward Lewis 1926-1962 ... **CLC 5, 10**
See also CA 1-4R; CANR 22; DLB 2, 28, 143; MTCW 1, 2

Wallas, Graham 1858-1932 .... **TCLC 91**

Walley, Byron
See Card, Orson Scott

Walpole, Horace 1717-1797 .... **LC 49**
See also DLB 39, 104

Walpole, Hugh (Seymour) 1884-1941 .... **TCLC 5**
See also CA 104; 165; DLB 34; MTCW 2

Walser, Martin 1927- .... **CLC 27**
See also CA 57-60; CANR 8, 46; DLB 75, 124

Walser, Robert 1878-1956 .... **TCLC 18; SSC 20**
See also CA 118; 165; DLB 66

Walsh, Jill Paton CLC 35
See also Paton Walsh, Gillian
See also CLR 2, 65

Walter, Villiam Christian
See Andersen, Hans Christian

Wambaugh, Joseph (Aloysius, Jr.) 1937- ...... **CLC 3, 18; DAM NOV, POP**
See also AITN 1; BEST 89:3; CA 33-36R; CANR 42, 65; DA3; DLB 6; DLBY 83; MTCW 1, 2

Wang Wei 699(?)-761(?) .... **PC 18**

Ward, Arthur Henry Sarsfield 1883-1959
See Rohmer, Sax
See also CA 108; 173

Ward, Douglas Turner 1930- .... **CLC 19**
See also BW 1; CA 81-84; CANR 27; DLB 7, 38

Ward, E. D.
See Lucas, E(dward) V(errall)

Ward, Mary Augusta
See Ward, Mrs. Humphry

Ward, Mrs. Humphry 1851-1920 .. **TCLC 55**
See also DLB 18

Ward, Peter
See Faust, Frederick (Schiller)

Warhol, Andy 1928(?)-1987 .... **CLC 20**
See also AAYA 12; BEST 89:4; CA 89-92; 121; CANR 34

Warner, Francis (Robert le Plastrier) 1937- .... **CLC 14**
See also CA 53-56; CANR 11

Warner, Marina 1946- .... **CLC 59**
See also CA 65-68; CANR 21, 55; DLB 194

Warner, Rex (Ernest) 1905-1986 ...... **CLC 45**
See also CA 89-92; 119; DLB 15

Warner, Susan (Bogert) 1819-1885 .... **NCLC 31**
See also DLB 3, 42

Warner, Sylvia (Constance) Ashton
See Ashton-Warner, Sylvia (Constance)

Warner, Sylvia Townsend 1893-1978 .... **CLC 7, 19; SSC 23**
See also CA 61-64; 77-80; CANR 16, 60; DLB 34, 139; MTCW 1, 2

Warren, Mercy Otis 1728-1814 ..... **NCLC 13**
See also DLB 31, 200

Warren, Robert Penn 1905-1989 .. **CLC 1, 4, 6, 8, 10, 13, 18, 39, 53, 59; DA; DAB; DAC; DAM MST, NOV, POET; SSC 4; WLC**
See also AITN 1; CA 13-16R; 129; CANR 10, 47; CDALB 1968-1988; DA3; DLB 2, 48, 152; DLBY 80, 89; INT CANR-10; MTCW 1, 2; SATA 46; SATA-Obit 63

Warshofsky, Isaac
See Singer, Isaac Bashevis

Warton, Thomas 1728-1790 ..... **LC 15; DAM POET**
See also DLB 104, 109

Waruk, Kona
See Harris, (Theodore) Wilson

Warung, Price 1855-1911 .... **TCLC 45**

Warwick, Jarvis
See Garner, Hugh

Washington, Alex
See Harris, Mark

Washington, Booker T(aliaferro) 1856-1915 ...... **TCLC 10; BLC 3; DAM MULT**
See also BW 1; CA 114; 125; DA3; SATA 28

Washington, George 1732-1799 .... **LC 25**
See also DLB 31

Wassermann, (Karl) Jakob 1873-1934 .... **TCLC 6**
See also CA 104; 163; DLB 66

Wasserstein, Wendy 1950- .. **CLC 32, 59, 90; DAM DRAM; DC 4**
See also CA 121; 129; CABS 3; CANR 53, 75; DA3; DLB 228; INT 129; MTCW 2; SATA 94

Waterhouse, Keith (Spencer) 1929- . **CLC 47**
See also CA 5-8R; CANR 38, 67; DLB 13, 15; MTCW 1, 2

Waters, Frank (Joseph) 1902-1995 .. **CLC 88**
See also CA 5-8R; 149; CAAS 13; CANR 3, 18, 63; DLB 212; DLBY 86

Waters, Roger 1944- .... **CLC 35**

Watkins, Frances Ellen
See Harper, Frances Ellen Watkins

Watkins, Gerrold
See Malzberg, Barry N(athaniel)

Watkins, Gloria Jean 1952(?)-
See hooks, bell
See also BW 2; CA 143; CANR 87; MTCW 2; SATA 115

Watkins, Paul 1964- .... **CLC 55**
See also CA 132; CANR 62

Watkins, Vernon Phillips 1906-1967 .... **CLC 43**
See also CA 9-10; 25-28R; CAP 1; DLB 20

Watson, Irving S.
See Mencken, H(enry) L(ouis)

Watson, John H.
See Farmer, Philip Jose

Watson, Richard F.
See Silverberg, Robert

Waugh, Auberon (Alexander) 1939- .. **CLC 7**
See also CA 45-48; CANR 6, 22; DLB 14, 194

Waugh, Evelyn (Arthur St. John) 1903-1966 .. **CLC 1, 3, 8, 13, 19, 27, 44, 107; DA; DAB; DAC; DAM MST, NOV, POP; SSC 41; WLC**
See also CA 85-88; 25-28R; CANR 22; CD-BLB 1914-1945; DA3; DLB 15, 162, 195; MTCW 1, 2

Waugh, Harriet 1944- .... **CLC 6**
See also CA 85-88; CANR 22

Ways, C. R.
See Blount, Roy (Alton), Jr.

Waystaff, Simon
See Swift, Jonathan

Webb, Beatrice (Martha Potter)
1858-1943 .... **TCLC 22**
See also CA 117; 162; DLB 190
Webb, Charles (Richard) 1939- .... **CLC 7**
See also CA 25-28R
Webb, James H(enry), Jr. 1946- ...... **CLC 22**
See also CA 81-84
Webb, Mary Gladys (Meredith)
1881-1927 .... **TCLC 24**
See also CA 182; 123; DLB 34
Webb, Mrs. Sidney
See Webb, Beatrice (Martha Potter)
Webb, Phyllis 1927- .... **CLC 18**
See also CA 104; CANR 23; DLB 53
Webb, Sidney (James) 1859-1947 .. **TCLC 22**
See also CA 117; 163; DLB 190
Webber, Andrew Lloyd CLC 21
See also Lloyd Webber, Andrew
Weber, Lenora Mattingly
1895-1971 .... **CLC 12**
See also CA 19-20; 29-32R; CAP 1; SATA
2; SATA-Obit 26
Weber, Max 1864-1920 .... **TCLC 69**
See also CA 109
Webster, John 1579(?)-1634(?) ... **LC 33; DA;
DAB; DAC; DAM DRAM, MST; DC
2; WLC**
See also CDBLB Before 1660; DLB 58
Webster, Noah 1758-1843 .... **NCLC 30**
See also DLB 1, 37, 42, 43, 73
Wedekind, (Benjamin) Frank(lin)
1864-1918 .... **TCLC 7; DAM DRAM**
See also CA 104; 153; DLB 118
Weidman, Jerome 1913-1998 .... **CLC 7**
See also AITN 2; CA 1-4R; 171; CANR 1;
DLB 28
Weil, Simone (Adolphine)
1909-1943 .... **TCLC 23**
See also CA 117; 159; MTCW 2
Weininger, Otto 1880-1903 .... **TCLC 84**
Weinstein, Nathan
See West, Nathanael
Weinstein, Nathan von Wallenstein
See West, Nathanael
Weir, Peter (Lindsay) 1944- .... **CLC 20**
See also CA 113; 123
Weiss, Peter (Ulrich) 1916-1982 .. **CLC 3, 15,
51; DAM DRAM**
See also CA 45-48; 106; CANR 3; DLB 69,
124
Weiss, Theodore (Russell) 1916- ... **CLC 3, 8,
14**
See also CA 9-12R; CAAS 2; CANR 46;
DLB 5
Welch, (Maurice) Denton
1915-1948 .... **TCLC 22**
See also CA 121; 148
Welch, James 1940- ..... **CLC 6, 14, 52; DAM
MULT, POP**
See also CA 85-88; CANR 42, 66; DLB
175; NNAL
Weldon, Fay 1931- . **CLC 6, 9, 11, 19, 36, 59,
122; DAM POP**
See also CA 21-24R; CANR 16, 46, 63;
CDBLB 1960 to Present; DLB 14, 194;
INT CANR-16, MTCW 1, 2
Wellek, Rene 1903-1995 .... **CLC 28**
See also CA 5-8R; 150; CAAS 7; CANR 8;
DLB 63; INT CANR-8
Weller, Michael 1942- .... **CLC 10, 53**
See also CA 85-88
Weller, Paul 1958- .... **CLC 26**
Wellershoff, Dieter 1925- .... **CLC 46**
See also CA 89-92; CANR 16, 37
Welles, (George) Orson 1915-1985 .. **CLC 20,
80**
See also CA 93-96; 117

Wellman, John McDowell 1945-
See Wellman, Mac
See also CA 166
Wellman, Mac 1945- .... **CLC 65**
See also Wellman, John McDowell; Well-
man, John McDowell
Wellman, Manly Wade 1903-1986 ... **CLC 49**
See also CA 1-4R; 118; CANR 6, 16, 44;
SATA 6; SATA-Obit 47
Wells, Carolyn 1869(?)-1942 .... **TCLC 35**
See also CA 113; 185; DLB 11
Wells, H(erbert) G(eorge)
1866-1946 . **TCLC 6, 12, 19; DA; DAB;
DAC; DAM MST, NOV; SSC 6; WLC**
See also AAYA 18; CA 110; 121; CDBLB
1914-1945; CLR 64; DA3; DLB 34, 70,
156, 178; MTCW 1, 2; SATA 20
Wells, Rosemary 1943- .... **CLC 12**
See also AAYA 13; CA 85-88; CANR 48;
CLR 16; MAICYA; SAAS 1; SATA 18,
69, 114
Welty, Eudora 1909- ...... **CLC 1, 2, 5, 14, 22,
33, 105; DA; DAB; DAC; DAM MST,
NOV; SSC 1, 27; WLC**
See also CA 9-12R; CABS 1; CANR 32,
65; CDALB 1941-1968; DA3; DLB 2,
102, 143; DLBD 12; DLBY 87; MTCW
1, 2
Wen I-to 1899-1946 .... **TCLC 28**
Wentworth, Robert
See Hamilton, Edmond
Werfel, Franz (Viktor) 1890-1945 ... **TCLC 8**
See also CA 104; 161; DLB 81, 124
Wergeland, Henrik Arnold
1808-1845 .... **NCLC 5**
Wersba, Barbara 1932 .... **CLC 30**
See also AAYA 2, 30; CA 29-32R, 182;
CAAE 182; CANR 16, 38; CLR 3; DLB
52; JRDA; MAICYA; SAAS 2; SATA 1,
58; SATA-Essay 103
Wertmueller, Lina 1928- .... **CLC 16**
See also CA 97-100; CANR 39, 78
Wescott, Glenway 1901-1987 .. **CLC 13; SSC
35**
See also CA 13-16R; 121; CANR 23, 70;
DLB 4, 9, 102
Wesker, Arnold 1932- ... **CLC 3, 5, 42; DAB;
DAM DRAM**
See also CA 1-4R; CAAS 7; CANR 1, 33;
CDBLB 1960 to Present; DLB 13, MTCW
1
Wesley, Richard (Errol) 1945- .... **CLC 7**
See also BW 1; CA 57-60; CANR 27; DLB
38
Wessel, Johan Herman 1742-1785 .... **LC 7**
West, Anthony (Panther)
1914-1987 .... **CLC 50**
See also CA 45-48; 124; CANR 3, 19; DLB
15
West, C. P.
See Wodehouse, P(elham) G(renville)
West, (Mary) Jessamyn 1902-1984 ... **CLC 7,
17**
See also CA 9-12R; 112; CANR 27; DLB
6; DLBY 84; MTCW 1, 2; SATA-Obit 37
West, Morris L(anglo) 1916- .... **CLC 6, 33**
See also CA 5-8R; CANR 24, 49, 64;
MTCW 1, 2
West, Nathanael 1903-1940 .... **TCLC 1, 14,
44; SSC 16**
See also CA 104; 125; CDALB 1929-1941;
DA3; DLB 4, 9, 28; MTCW 1, 2
West, Owen
See Koontz, Dean R(ay)
West, Paul 1930- .... **CLC 7, 14, 96**
See also CA 13-16R; CAAS 7; CANR 22,
53, 76, 89; DLB 14; INT CANR-22;
MTCW 2

West, Rebecca 1892-1983 ... **CLC 7, 9, 31, 50**
See also CA 5-8R; 109; CANR 19; DLB
36; DLBY 83; MTCW 1, 2
Westall, Robert (Atkinson)
1929-1993 .... **CLC 17**
See also AAYA 12; CA 69-72; 141; CANR
18, 68; CLR 13; JRDA; MAICYA; SAAS
2; SATA 23, 69; SATA-Obit 75
Westermarck, Edward 1862-1939 . **TCLC 87**
Westlake, Donald E(dwin) 1933- .... **CLC 7,
33; DAM POP**
See also CA 17-20R; CAAS 13; CANR 16,
44, 65; INT CANR-16; MTCW 2
Westmacott, Mary
See Christie, Agatha (Mary Clarissa)
Weston, Allen
See Norton, Andre
Wetcheek, J. L.
See Feuchtwanger, Lion
Wetering, Janwillem van de
See van de Wetering, Janwillem
Wetherald, Agnes Ethelwyn
1857-1940 .... **TCLC 81**
See also DLB 99
Wetherell, Elizabeth
See Warner, Susan (Bogert)
Whale, James 1889-1957 .... **TCLC 63**
Whalen, Philip 1923- .... **CLC 6, 29**
See also CA 9-12R; CANR 5, 39; DLB 16
Wharton, Edith (Newbold Jones)
1862-1937 .... **TCLC 3, 9, 27, 53; DA;
DAB; DAC; DAM MST, NOV; SSC 6;
WLC**
See also AAYA 25; CA 104; 132; CDALB
1865-1917; DA3; DLB 4, 9, 12, 78, 189;
DLBD 13; MTCW 1, 2
Wharton, James
See Mencken, H(enry) L(ouis)
**Wharton, William (a pseudonym) CLC 18,
37**
See also CA 93-96; DLBY 80; INT 93-96
Wheatley (Peters), Phillis
1754(?)-1784 ...... **LC 3, 50; BLC 3; DA;
DAC; DAM MST, MULT, POET; PC
3; WLC**
See also CDALB 1640-1865; DA3; DLB
31, 50
Wheelock, John Hall 1886-1978 .... **CLC 14**
See also CA 13-16R; 77-80; CANR 14;
DLB 45
White, E(lwyn) B(rooks)
1899-1985 . **CLC 10, 34, 39; DAM POP**
See also AITN 2; CA 13-16R; 116; CANR
16, 37; CDALBS; CLR 1, 21; DA3; DLB
11, 22; MAICYA; MTCW 1, 2; SATA 2,
29, 100; SATA-Obit 44
White, Edmund (Valentine III)
1940- .... **CLC 27, 110; DAM POP**
See also AAYA 7; CA 45-48; CANR 3, 19,
36, 62; DA3; DLB 227; MTCW 1, 2
White, Patrick (Victor Martindale)
1912-1990 ...... **CLC 3, 4, 5, 7, 9, 18, 65,
69; SSC 39**
See also CA 81-84; 132; CANR 43; MTCW
1
White, Phyllis Dorothy James 1920-
See James, P. D.
See also CA 21-24R; CANR 17, 43, 65;
DAM POP; DA3; MTCW 1, 2
White, T(erence) H(anbury)
1906-1964 .... **CLC 30**
See also AAYA 22; CA 73-76; CANR 37;
DLB 160; JRDA; MAICYA; SATA 12
White, Terence de Vere 1912-1994 ... **CLC 49**
See also CA 49-52; 145; CANR 3
White, Walter
See White, Walter F(rancis)
See also BLC; DAM MULT

White, Walter F(rancis)
1893-1955 .... **TCLC 15**
See also White, Walter
See also BW 1; CA 115; 124; DLB 51

White, William Hale 1831-1913
See Rutherford, Mark
See also CA 121

Whitehead, Alfred North
1861-1947 .... **TCLC 97**
See also CA 117; 165; DLB 100

Whitehead, E(dward) A(nthony)
1933- .... **CLC 5**
See also CA 65-68; CANR 58

Whitemore, Hugh (John) 1936- .... **CLC 37**
See also CA 132; CANR 77; INT 132

Whitman, Sarah Helen (Power)
1803-1878 .... **NCLC 19**
See also DLB 1

Whitman, Walt(er) 1819-1892 .. **NCLC 4, 31, 81; DA; DAB; DAC; DAM MST, POET; PC 3; WLC**
See also CDALB 1640-1865; DA3; DLB 3, 64; SATA 20

Whitney, Phyllis A(yame) 1903- ...... **CLC 42; DAM POP**
See also AITN 2; BEST 90:3; CA 1-4R; CANR 3, 25, 38, 60; CLR 59; DA3; JRDA; MAICYA; MTCW 2; SATA 1, 30

Whittemore, (Edward) Reed (Jr.)
1919- .... **CLC 4**
See also CA 9-12R; CAAS 8; CANR 4; DLB 5

Whittier, John Greenleaf
1807-1892 .... **NCLC 8, 59**
See also DLB 1

Whittlebot, Hernia
See Coward, Noel (Peirce)

Wicker, Thomas Grey 1926-
See Wicker, Tom
See also CA 65-68; CANR 21, 46

Wicker, Tom CLC 7
See also Wicker, Thomas Grey

Wideman, John Edgar 1941- ...... **CLC 5, 34, 36, 67, 122; BLC 3; DAM MULT**
See also BW 2, 3; CA 85-88; CANR 14, 42, 67; DLB 33, 143; MTCW 2

Wiebe, Rudy (Henry) 1934- .. **CLC 6, 11, 14; DAC; DAM MST**
See also CA 37-40R; CANR 42, 67; DLB 60

Wieland, Christoph Martin
1733-1813 .... **NCLC 17**
See also DLB 97

Wiene, Robert 1881-1938 .... **TCLC 56**

Wieners, John 1934- .... **CLC 7**
See also CA 13-16R; DLB 16

Wiesel, Elie(zer) 1928- .... **CLC 3, 5, 11, 37; DA; DAB; DAC; DAM MST, NOV; WLCS**
See also AAYA 7; AITN 1; CA 5-8R; CAAS 4; CANR 8, 40, 65; CDALBS; DA3; DLB 83; DLBY 87; INT CANR-8; MTCW 1, 2; SATA 56

Wiggins, Marianne 1947- .... **CLC 57**
See also BEST 89:3; CA 130; CANR 60

Wight, James Alfred 1916-1995
See Herriot, James
See also CA 77-80; SATA 55; SATA-Brief 44

Wilbur, Richard (Purdy) 1921- ..... **CLC 3, 6, 9, 14, 53, 110; DA; DAB; DAC; DAM MST, POET**
See also CA 1-4R; CABS 2; CANR 2, 29, 76; CDALBS; DLB 5, 169; INT CANR-29; MTCW 1, 2; SATA 9, 108

Wild, Peter 1940- .... **CLC 14**
See also CA 37-40R; DLB 5

Wilde, Oscar (Fingal O'Flahertie Wills)
1854(?)-1900 .... **TCLC 1, 8, 23, 41; DA; DAB; DAC; DAM DRAM, MST, NOV; SSC 11; WLC**
See also CA 104; 119; CDBLB 1890-1914; DA3; DLB 10, 19, 34, 57, 141, 156, 190; SATA 24

Wilder, Billy CLC 20
See also Wilder, Samuel
See also DLB 26

Wilder, Samuel 1906-
See Wilder, Billy
See also CA 89-92

Wilder, Thornton (Niven)
1897-1975 .. **CLC 1, 5, 6, 10, 15, 35, 82; DA; DAB; DAC; DAM DRAM, MST, NOV; DC 1; WLC**
See also AAYA 29; AITN 2; CA 13-16R; 61-64; CANR 40; CDALBS; DA3; DLB 4, 7, 9, 228; DLBY 97; MTCW 1, 2

Wilding, Michael 1942- .... **CLC 73**
See also CA 104; CANR 24, 49

Wiley, Richard 1944- .... **CLC 44**
See also CA 121; 129; CANR 71

Wilhelm, Kate CLC 7
See also Wilhelm, Katie Gertrude
See also AAYA 20; CAAS 5; DLB 8; INT CANR-17

Wilhelm, Katie Gertrude 1928-
See Wilhelm, Kate
See also CA 37-40R; CANR 17, 36, 60; MTCW 1

Wilkins, Mary
See Freeman, Mary E(leanor) Wilkins

Willard, Nancy 1936- .... **CLC 7, 37**
See also CA 89-92; CANR 10, 39, 68; CLR 5; DLB 5, 52; MAICYA; MTCW 1; SATA 37, 71; SATA-Brief 30

William of Ockham 1285-1347 ..... **CMLC 32**

Williams, Ben Ames 1889-1953 ..... **TCLC 89**
See also CA 183; DLB 102

Williams, C(harles) K(enneth)
1936- .... **CLC 33, 56; DAM POET**
See also CA 37-40R; CAAS 26; CANR 57; DLB 5

Williams, Charles
See Collier, James L(incoln)

Williams, Charles (Walter Stansby)
1886-1945 .... **TCLC 1, 11**
See also CA 104; 163; DLB 100, 153

Williams, (George) Emlyn
1905-1987 .... **CLC 15; DAM DRAM**
See also CA 104; 123; CANR 36; DLB 10, 77; MTCW 1

Williams, Hank 1923-1953 .... **TCLC 81**

Williams, Hugo 1942- .... **CLC 42**
See also CA 17-20R; CANR 45; DLB 40

Williams, J. Walker
See Wodehouse, P(elham) G(renville)

Williams, John A(lfred) 1925- ..... **CLC 5, 13; BLC 3; DAM MULT**
See also BW 2, 3; CA 53-56; CAAS 3; CANR 6, 26, 51; DLB 2, 33; INT CANR-6

Williams, Jonathan (Chamberlain)
1929- .... **CLC 13**
See also CA 9-12R; CAAS 12; CANR 8; DLB 5

Williams, Joy 1944- .... **CLC 31**
See also CA 41-44R; CANR 22, 48

Williams, Norman 1952- .... **CLC 39**
See also CA 118

Williams, Sherley Anne 1944-1999 . **CLC 89; BLC 3; DAM MULT, POET**
See also BW 2, 3; CA 73-76; 185; CANR 25, 82; DLB 41; INT CANR-25; SATA 78; SATA-Obit 116

Williams, Shirley
See Williams, Sherley Anne

Williams, Tennessee 1911-1983 . **CLC 1, 2, 5, 7, 8, 11, 15, 19, 30, 39, 45, 71, 111; DA; DAB; DAC; DAM DRAM, MST; DC 4; WLC**
See also AAYA 31; AITN 1, 2; CA 5-8R; 108; CABS 3; CANR 31; CDALB 1941-1968; DA3; DLB 7; DLBD 4; DLBY 83; MTCW 1, 2

Williams, Thomas (Alonzo)
1926-1990 .... **CLC 14**
See also CA 1-4R; 132; CANR 2

Williams, William C.
See Williams, William Carlos

Williams, William Carlos
1883-1963 .... **CLC 1, 2, 5, 9, 13, 22, 42, 67; DA; DAB; DAC; DAM MST, POET; PC 7; SSC 31**
See also CA 89-92; CANR 34; CDALB 1917-1929; DA3; DLB 4, 16, 54, 86; MTCW 1, 2

Williamson, David (Keith) 1942- ..... **CLC 56**
See also CA 103; CANR 41

Williamson, Ellen Douglas 1905-1984
See Douglas, Ellen
See also CA 17-20R; 114; CANR 39

Williamson, Jack CLC 29
See also Williamson, John Stewart
See also CAAS 8; DLB 8

Williamson, John Stewart 1908-
See Williamson, Jack
See also CA 17-20R; CANR 23, 70

Willie, Frederick
See Lovecraft, H(oward) P(hillips)

Willingham, Calder (Baynard, Jr.)
1922-1995 .... **CLC 5, 51**
See also CA 5-8R; 147; CANR 3; DLB 2, 44; MTCW 1

Willis, Charles
See Clarke, Arthur C(harles)

Willy
See Colette, (Sidonie-Gabrielle)

Willy, Colette
See Colette, (Sidonie-Gabrielle)

Wilson, A(ndrew) N(orman) 1950- .. **CLC 33**
See also CA 112; 122; DLB 14, 155, 194; MTCW 2

Wilson, Angus (Frank Johnstone)
1913-1991 . **CLC 2, 3, 5, 25, 34; SSC 21**
See also CA 5-8R; 134; CANR 21; DLB 15, 139, 155; MTCW 1, 2

Wilson, August 1945- ... **CLC 39, 50, 63, 118; BLC 3; DA; DAB; DAC; DAM DRAM, MST, MULT; DC 2; WLCS**
See also AAYA 16; BW 2, 3; CA 115; 122; CANR 42, 54, 76; DA3; DLB 228; MTCW 1, 2

Wilson, Brian 1942- .... **CLC 12**

Wilson, Colin 1931- .... **CLC 3, 14**
See also CA 1-4R; CAAS 5; CANR 1, 22, 33, 77; DLB 14, 194; MTCW 1

Wilson, Dirk
See Pohl, Frederik

Wilson, Edmund 1895-1972 .. **CLC 1, 2, 3, 8, 24**
See also CA 1-4R; 37-40R; CANR 1, 46; DLB 63; MTCW 1, 2

Wilson, Ethel Davis (Bryant)
1888(?)-1980 .... **CLC 13; DAC; DAM POET**
See also CA 102; DLB 68; MTCW 1

Wilson, John 1785-1854 .... **NCLC 5**

Wilson, John (Anthony) Burgess 1917-1993
See Burgess, Anthony
See also CA 1-4R; 143; CANR 2, 46; DAC; DAM NOV; DA3; MTCW 1, 2

Wilson, Lanford 1937- .... **CLC 7, 14, 36; DAM DRAM**
See also CA 17-20R; CABS 3; CANR 45; DLB 7

Wilson, Robert M. 1944- .... **CLC 7, 9**
See also CA 49-52; CANR 2, 41; MTCW 1

Wilson, Robert McLiam 1964- .... **CLC 59**
See also CA 132

Wilson, Sloan 1920- .... **CLC 32**
See also CA 1-4R; CANR 1, 44

Wilson, Snoo 1948- .... **CLC 33**
See also CA 69-72

Wilson, William S(mith) 1932- .... **CLC 49**
See also CA 81-84

Wilson, (Thomas) Woodrow
1856-1924 .... **TCLC 79**
See also CA 166; DLB 47

Winchilsea, Anne (Kingsmill) Finch Counte
1661-1720
See Finch, Anne

Windham, Basil
See Wodehouse, P(elham) G(renville)

Wingrove, David (John) 1954- .... **CLC 68**
See also CA 133

Winnemucca, Sarah 1844-1891 ..... **NCLC 79**

Winstanley, Gerrard 1609-1676 .... **LC 52**

Wintergreen, Jane
See Duncan, Sara Jeannette

Winters, Janet Lewis CLC 41
See also Lewis, Janet
See also DLBY 87

Winters, (Arthur) Yvor 1900-1968 .... **CLC 4, 8, 32**
See also CA 11-12; 25-28R; CAP 1; DLB 48; MTCW 1

Winterson, Jeanette 1959 .... **CLC 64; DAM POP**
See also CA 136; CANR 58; DA3; DLB 207; MTCW 2

Winthrop, John 1588-1649 .... **LC 31**
See also DLB 24, 30

Wirth, Louis 1897-1952 .... **TCLC 92**

Wiseman, Frederick 1930- .... **CLC 20**
See also CA 159

Wister, Owen 1860-1938 .... **TCLC 21**
See also CA 108; 162; DLB 9, 78, 186; SATA 62

Witkacy
See Witkiewicz, Stanislaw Ignacy

Witkiewicz, Stanislaw Ignacy
1885-1939 .... **TCLC 8**
See also CA 105; 162

Wittgenstein, Ludwig (Josef Johann)
1889-1951 .... **TCLC 59**
See also CA 113; 164; MTCW 2

Wittig, Monique 1935(?)- .... **CLC 22**
See also CA 116; 135; DLB 83

Wittlin, Jozef 1896-1976 .... **CLC 25**
See also CA 49-52; 65-68; CANR 3

Wodehouse, P(elham) G(renville)
1881-1975 .... **CLC 1, 2, 5, 10, 22; DAB; DAC; DAM NOV; SSC 2**
See also AITN 2; CA 45-48; 57-60; CANR 3, 33; CDBLB 1914-1945; DA3; DLB 34, 162; MTCW 1, 2; SATA 22

Woiwode, L.
See Woiwode, Larry (Alfred)

Woiwode, Larry (Alfred) 1941- ... **CLC 6, 10**
See also CA 73-76; CANR 16; DLB 6, INT CANR-16

Wojciechowska, Maia (Teresa)
1927- .... **CLC 26**
See also AAYA 8; CA 9-12R, 183; CAAE 183; CANR 4, 41; CLR 1; JRDA; MAICYA; SAAS 1; SATA 1, 28, 83; SATA-Essay 104

Wojtyla, Karol
See John Paul II, Pope

Wolf, Christa 1929- .... **CLC 14, 29, 58**
See also CA 85-88; CANR 45; DLB 75; MTCW 1

Wolfe, Gene (Rodman) 1931- .... **CLC 25; DAM POP**
See also CA 57-60; CAAS 9; CANR 6, 32, 60; DLB 8; MTCW 2

Wolfe, George C. 1954- .... **CLC 49; BLCS**
See also CA 149

Wolfe, Thomas (Clayton)
1900-1938 ...... **TCLC 4, 13, 29, 61; DA; DAB; DAC; DAM MST, NOV; SSC 33; WLC**
See also CA 104; 132; CDALB 1929-1941; DA3; DLB 9, 102; DLBD 2, 16; DLBY 85, 97; MTCW 1, 2

Wolfe, Thomas Kennerly, Jr. 1930-
See Wolfe, Tom
See also CA 13-16R; CANR 9, 33, 70; DAM POP; DA3; DLB 185; INT CANR-9; MTCW 1, 2

Wolfe, Tom CLC 1, 2, 9, 15, 35, 51
See also Wolfe, Thomas Kennerly, Jr.
See also AAYA 8; AITN 2; BEST 89:1; DLB 152

Wolff, Geoffrey (Ansell) 1937- .... **CLC 41**
See also CA 29-32R; CANR 29, 43, 78

Wolff, Sonia
See Levitin, Sonia (Wolff)

Wolff, Tobias (Jonathan Ansell)
1945- .... **CLC 39, 64**
See also AAYA 16; BEST 90:2; CA 114; 117; CAAS 22; CANR 54, 76; DA3; DLB 130; INT 117; MTCW 2

Wolfram von Eschenbach c. 1170 c. 1220   **CMLC 5**
See also DLB 138

Wolitzer, Hilma 1930- .... **CLC 17**
See also CA 65-68; CANR 18, 40; INT CANR-18; SATA 31

Wollstonecraft, Mary 1759-1797 ..... **LC 5, 50**
See also CDBLB 1789-1832; DLB 39, 104, 158

Wonder, Stevie CLC 12
See also Morris, Steveland Judkins

Wong, Jade Snow 1922- .... **CLC 17**
See also CA 109; CANR 91; SATA 112

Woodberry, George Edward
1855-1930 .... **TCLC 73**
See also CA 165; DLB 71, 103

Woodcott, Keith
See Brunner, John (Kilian Houston)

Woodruff, Robert W.
See Mencken, H(enry) L(ouis)

Woolf, (Adeline) Virginia
1882-1941 .. **TCLC 1, 5, 20, 43, 56; DA; DAB; DAC; DAM MST, NOV; SSC 7; WLC**
See also Woolf, Virginia Adeline
See also CA 104; 130; CANR 64; CDBLB 1914-1945; DA3; DLB 36, 100, 162; DLBD 10; MTCW 1

Woolf, Virginia Adeline
See Woolf, (Adeline) Virginia
See also MTCW 2

Woollcott, Alexander (Humphreys)
1887-1943 .... **TCLC 5**
See also CA 105; 161; DLB 29

Woolrich, Cornell 1903-1968 .... **CLC 77**
See also Hopley-Woolrich, Cornell George

Woolson, Constance Fenimore
1840-1894 .... **NCLC 82**
See also DLB 12, 74, 189, 221

Wordsworth, Dorothy 1771-1855 .. **NCLC 25**
See also DLB 107

Wordsworth, William 1770-1850 .. **NCLC 12, 38; DA; DAB; DAC; DAM MST, POET; PC 4; WLC**
See also CDBLB 1789-1832; DA3; DLB 93, 107

Wouk, Herman 1915- ... **CLC 1, 9, 38; DAM NOV, POP**
See also CA 5-8R; CANR 6, 33, 67; CDALBS; DA3; DLBY 82; INT CANR-6; MTCW 1, 2

Wright, Charles (Penzel, Jr.) 1935- .. **CLC 6, 13, 28, 119**
See also CA 29-32R; CAAS 7; CANR 23, 36, 62, 88; DLB 165; DLBY 82; MTCW 1, 2

Wright, Charles Stevenson 1932- ... **CLC 49; BLC 3; DAM MULT, POET**
See also BW 1; CA 9-12R; CANR 26; DLB 33

Wright, Frances 1795-1852 .... **NCLC 74**
See also DLB 73

Wright, Frank Lloyd 1867-1959 .... **TCLC 95**
See also AAYA 33; CA 174

Wright, Jack R.
See Harris, Mark

Wright, James (Arlington)
1927-1980 .... **CLC 3, 5, 10, 28; DAM POET**
See also AITN 2; CA 49-52; 97-100; CANR 4, 34, 64; CDALBS; DLB 5, 169; MTCW 1, 2

Wright, Judith (Arandell) 1915- ..... **CLC 11, 53; PC 14**
See also CA 13-16R; CANR 31, 76; MTCW 1, 2; SATA 14

Wright, L(auran) R. 1939- .... **CLC 44**
See also CA 138

Wright, Richard (Nathaniel)
1908-1960 .... **CLC 1, 3, 4, 9, 14, 21, 48, 74; BLC 3; DA; DAB; DAC; DAM MST, MULT, NOV; SSC 2; WLC**
See also AAYA 5; BW 1; CA 108; CANR 64; CDALB 1929-1941; DA3; DLB 76, 102; DLBD 2; MTCW 1, 2

Wright, Richard B(ruce) 1937- .... **CLC 6**
See also CA 85-88; DLB 53

Wright, Rick 1945- .... **CLC 35**

Wright, Rowland
See Wells, Carolyn

Wright, Stephen 1946- .... **CLC 33**

Wright, Willard Huntington 1888-1939
See Van Dine, S. S.
See also CA 115; DLBD 16

Wright, William 1930- .... **CLC 44**
See also CA 53-56; CANR 7, 23

Wroth, Lady Mary 1587-1653(?) .... **LC 30**
See also DLB 121

Wu Ch'eng-en 1500(?)-1582(?) .... **LC 7**

Wu Ching-tzu 1701-1754 .... **LC 2**

Wurlitzer, Rudolph 1938(?)- ... **CLC 2, 4, 15**
See also CA 85-88; DLB 173

Wyatt, Thomas c. 1503-1542 .... **PC 27**
See also DLB 132

Wycherley, William 1641-1715 ...... **LC 8, 21; DAM DRAM**
See also CDBLB 1660-1789; DLB 80

Wylie, Elinor (Morton Hoyt)
1885-1928 .... **TCLC 8; PC 23**
See also CA 105; 162; DLB 9, 45

Wylie, Philip (Gordon) 1902-1971 ... **CLC 43**
See also CA 21-22; 33-36R; CAP 2; DLB 9

Wyndham, John CLC 19
See also Harris, John (Wyndham Parkes Lucas) Beynon

Wyss, Johann David Von
1743-1818 .... **NCLC 10**
See also JRDA; MAICYA; SATA 29; SATA-Brief 27

Xenophon c. 430B.C.-c. 354B.C. ... **CMLC 17**
See also DLB 176

Yakumo Koizumi
See Hearn, (Patricio) Lafcadio (Tessima Carlos)

Yamamoto, Hisaye 1921- .... **SSC 34; DAM MULT**

Yanez, Jose Donoso
See Donoso (Yanez), Jose

Yanovsky, Basile S.
See Yanovsky, V(assily) S(emenovich)

Yanovsky, V(assily) S(emenovich)
1906-1989 .... **CLC 2, 18**
See also CA 97-100; 129

Yates, Richard 1926-1992 .... **CLC 7, 8, 23**
See also CA 5-8R; 139; CANR 10, 43; DLB 2; DLBY 81, 92; INT CANR-10

Yeats, W. B.
See Yeats, William Butler

Yeats, William Butler 1865-1939 .... **TCLC 1, 11, 18, 31, 93; DA; DAB; DAC; DAM DRAM, MST, POET; PC 20; WLC**
See also CA 104; 127; CANR 45; CDBLB 1890-1914; DA3; DLB 10, 19, 98, 156; MTCW 1, 2

Yehoshua, A(braham) B. 1936- .. **CLC 13, 31**
See also CA 33-36R; CANR 43, 90

Yellow Bird
See Ridge, John Rollin

Yep, Laurence Michael 1948- .... **CLC 35**
See also AAYA 5, 31; CA 49-52; CANR 1, 46; CLR 3, 17, 54; DLB 52; JRDA; MAICYA; SATA 7, 69

Yerby, Frank G(arvin) 1916-1991 . **CLC 1, 7, 22; BLC 3; DAM MULT**
See also BW 1, 3; CA 9-12R; 136; CANR 16, 52; DLB 76; INT CANR-16; MTCW 1

Yesenin, Sergei Alexandrovich
See Esenin, Sergei (Alexandrovich)

Yevtushenko, Yevgeny (Alexandrovich)
1933- .. **CLC 1, 3, 13, 26, 51, 126; DAM POET**
See also CA 81-84; CANR 33, 54; MTCW 1

Yezierska, Anzia 1885(?)-1970 .... **CLC 46**
See also CA 126; 89-92; DLB 28, 221; MTCW 1

Yglesias, Helen 1915- .... **CLC 7, 22**
See also CA 37-40R; CAAS 20; CANR 15, 65; INT CANR-15; MTCW 1

Yokomitsu, Riichi 1898-1947 .... **TCLC 47**
See also CA 170

Yonge, Charlotte (Mary)
1823-1901 .... **TCLC 48**
See also CA 109; 163; DLB 18, 163; SATA 17

York, Jeremy
See Creasey, John

York, Simon
See Heinlein, Robert A(nson)

Yorke, Henry Vincent 1905-1974 ..... **CLC 13**
See also Green, Henry
See also CA 85-88; 49-52

Yosano Akiko 1878-1942 .... **TCLC 59; PC 11**
See also CA 161

Yoshimoto, Banana CLC 84
See also Yoshimoto, Mahoko

Yoshimoto, Mahoko 1964-
See Yoshimoto, Banana
See also CA 144

Young, Al(bert James) 1939- . **CLC 19; BLC 3; DAM MULT**
See also BW 2, 3; CA 29-32R; CANR 26, 65; DLB 33

Young, Andrew (John) 1885-1971 ...... **CLC 5**
See also CA 5-8R; CANR 7, 29

Young, Collier
See Bloch, Robert (Albert)

Young, Edward 1683-1765 .... **LC 3, 40**
See also DLB 95

Young, Marguerite (Vivian)
1909-1995 .... **CLC 82**
See also CA 13-16; 150; CAP 1

Young, Neil 1945- .... **CLC 17**
See also CA 110

Young Bear, Ray A. 1950- ..... **CLC 94; DAM MULT**
See also CA 146; DLB 175; NNAL

Yourcenar, Marguerite 1903-1987 ... **CLC 19, 38, 50, 87; DAM NOV**
See also CA 69-72; CANR 23, 60; DLB 72; DLBY 88; MTCW 1, 2

Yuan, Chu 340(?)B.C.-278(?)B.C. . **CMLC 36**

Yurick, Sol 1925- .... **CLC 6**
See also CA 13-16R; CANR 25

Zabolotsky, Nikolai Alekseevich
1903-1958 .... **TCLC 52**
See also CA 116; 164

Zagajewski, Adam 1945- .... **PC 27**
See also CA 186

Zamiatin, Yevgenii
See Zamyatin, Evgeny Ivanovich

Zamora, Bernice (B. Ortiz) 1938- .. **CLC 89; DAM MULT; HLC 2**
See also CA 151; CANR 80; DLB 82; HW 1, 2

Zamyatin, Evgeny Ivanovich
1884-1937 .... **TCLC 8, 37**
See also CA 105; 166

Zangwill, Israel 1864-1926 .... **TCLC 16**
See also CA 109; 167; DLB 10, 135, 197

Zappa, Francis Vincent, Jr. 1940-1993
See Zappa, Frank
See also CA 108; 143; CANR 57

Zappa, Frank CLC 17
See also Zappa, Francis Vincent, Jr.

Zaturenska, Marya 1902-1982 ..... **CLC 6, 11**
See also CA 13-16R; 105; CANR 22

Zeami 1363-1443 .... **DC 7**

Zelazny, Roger (Joseph) 1937-1995 . **CLC 21**
See also AAYA 7; CA 21-24R; 148; CANR 26, 60; DLB 8; MTCW 1, 2; SATA 57; SATA-Brief 39

Zhdanov, Andrei Alexandrovich
1896-1948 .... **TCLC 18**
See also CA 117; 167

Zhukovsky, Vasily (Andreevich)
1783-1852 .... **NCLC 35**
See also DLB 205

Ziegenhagen, Eric CLC 55

Zimmer, Jill Schary
See Robinson, Jill

Zimmerman, Robert
See Dylan, Bob

Zindel, Paul 1936- ..... **CLC 6, 26; DA; DAB; DAC; DAM DRAM, MST, NOV; DC 5**
See also AAYA 2; CA 73-76; CANR 31, 65; CDALBS; CLR 3, 45; DA3; DLB 7, 52; JRDA; MAICYA; MTCW 1, 2; SATA 16, 58, 102

Zinov'Ev, A. A.
See Zinoviev, Alexander (Aleksandrovich)

Zinoviev, Alexander (Aleksandrovich)
1922- .... **CLC 19**
See also CA 116; 133; CAAS 10

Zoilus
See Lovecraft, H(oward) P(hillips)

Zola, Emile (Edouard Charles Antoine)
1840-1902 .... **TCLC 1, 6, 21, 41; DA; DAB; DAC; DAM MST, NOV; WLC**
See also CA 104; 138; DA3; DLB 123

Zoline, Pamela 1941- .... **CLC 62**
See also CA 161

Zoroaster 628(?)B.C.-551(?)B.C. ... **CMLC 40**

Zorrilla y Moral, Jose 1817-1893 .... **NCLC 6**

Zoshchenko, Mikhail (Mikhailovich)
1895-1958 .... **TCLC 15; SSC 15**
See also CA 115; 160

Zuckmayer, Carl 1896-1977 .... **CLC 18**
See also CA 69-72; DLB 56, 124

Zuk, Georges
See Skelton, Robin

Zukofsky, Louis 1904-1978 ... **CLC 1, 2, 4, 7, 11, 18; DAM POET; PC 11**
See also CA 9-12R; 77-80; CANR 39; DLB 5, 165; MTCW 1

Zweig, Paul 1935-1984 .... **CLC 34, 42**
See also CA 85-88; 113

Zweig, Stefan 1881-1942 .... **TCLC 17**
See also CA 112; 170; DLB 81, 118

Zwingli, Huldreich 1484-1531 .... **LC 37**
See also DLB 179

SSC Cumulative Nationality Index

ALGERIAN

Camus, Albert 9

AMERICAN

Adams, Alice (Boyd) 24
Aiken, Conrad (Potter) 9
Alcott, Louisa May 27
Algren, Nelson 33
Anderson, Sherwood 1
Auchincloss, Louis (Stanton) 22
Baldwin, James (Arthur) 10, 33
Bambara, Toni Cade 35
Barnes, Djuna 3
Barth, John (Simmons) 10
Barthelme, Donald 2
Beattie, Ann 11
Bellow, Saul 14
Benet, Stephen Vincent 10
Berriault, Gina 30
Bierce, Ambrose (Gwinett) 9
Bowles, Paul (Frederick) 3
Boyle, Kay 5
Boyle, T(homas) Coraghessan 16
Bradbury, Ray (Douglas) 29
Cable, George Washington 4
Caldwell, Erskine (Preston) 19
Calisher, Hortense 15
Capote, Truman 2
Carver, Raymond 8
Cather, Willa Sibert 2
Chandler, Raymond (Thornton) 23
Cheever, John 1, 38
Chesnutt, Charles W(addell) 7
Chopin, Kate 8
Cisneros, Sandra 32
Coover, Robert (Lowell) 15
Cowan, Peter (Walkinshaw) 28
Crane, Stephen (Townley) 7
Davenport, Guy (Mattison Jr.) 16
Davis, Rebecca (Blaine) Harding 38
Dixon, Stephen 16
Dreiser, Theodore (Herman Albert) 30
Dubus, Andre 15
Dunbar, Paul Laurence 8
Elkin, Stanley L(awrence) 12
Ellison, Harlan (Jay) 14
Ellison, Ralph (Waldo) 26
Farrell, James T(homas) 28
Faulkner, William (Cuthbert) 1, 35
Fisher, Rudolph 25
Fitzgerald, F(rancis) Scott (Key) 6, 31
Freeman, Mary E(leanor) Wilkins 1
Gardner, John (Champlin) Jr. 7
Garland, (Hannibal) Hamlin 18
Garrett, George (Palmer) 30
Gass, William H(oward) 12
Gilchrist, Ellen 14
Gilman, Charlotte (Anna) Perkins
    (Stetson) 13
Glasgow, Ellen (Anderson Gholson) 34
Glaspell, Susan 41
Gordon, Caroline 15

Grau, Shirley Ann 15
Hammett, (Samuel) Dashiell 17
Harris, Joel Chandler 19
Harrison, James (Thomas) 19
Harte, (Francis) Bret(t) 8
Hawthorne, Nathaniel 3, 29, 39
Hemingway, Ernest (Miller) 1, 25, 36, 40
Henderson, Zenna (Chlarson) 29
Henry, O. 5
Howells, William Dean 36
Hughes, (James) Langston 6
Hurston, Zora Neale 4
Huxley, Aldous (Leonard) 39
Irving, Washington 2, 37
Jackson, Shirley 9, 39
James, Henry 8, 32
Jewett, (Theodora) Sarah Orne 6
King, Stephen (Edwin) 17
Lardner, Ring(gold) W(ilmer) 32
Le Guin, Ursula K(roeber) 12
Ligotti, Thomas (Robert) 16
Lish, Gordon (Jay) 18
London, Jack 4
Lovecraft, H(oward) P(hillips) 3
Maclean, Norman (Fitzroy) 13
Malamud, Bernard 15
Marshall, Paule 3
Mason, Bobbie Ann 4
McCarthy, Mary (Therese) 24
McCullers, (Lula) Carson (Smith) 9, 24
Melville, Herman 1, 17
Michaels, Leonard 16
Mukherjee, Bharati 38
Murfree, Mary Noailles 22
Nabokov, Vladimir (Vladimirovich) 11
Nin, Anais 10
Norris, Frank 28
Oates, Joyce Carol 6
O'Connor, (Mary) Flannery 1, 23
O'Hara, John (Henry) 15
Olsen, Tillie 11
Ozick, Cynthia 15
Page, Thomas Nelson 23
Paley, Grace 8
Parker, Dorothy (Rothschild) 2
Perelman, S(idney) J(oseph) 32
Phillips, Jayne Anne 16
Poe, Edgar Allan 1, 22, 35
Pohl, Frederik 25
Porter, Katherine Anne 4, 31
Powers, J(ames) F(arl) 4
Price, (Edward) Reynolds 22
Pynchon, Thomas (Ruggles Jr.) 14
Roth, Philip (Milton) 26
Salinger, J(erome) D(avid) 2, 28
Saroyan, William 21
Selby, Hubert Jr. 20
Silko, Leslie (Marmon) 37
Singer, Isaac Bashevis 3
Stafford, Jean 26
Stegner, Wallace (Earle) 27
Steinbeck, John (Ernst) 11, 37
Stuart, Jesse (Hilton) 31

Styron, William 25
Suckow, Ruth 18
Taylor, Peter (Hillsman) 10
Thomas, Audrey (Callahan) 20
Thurber, James (Grover) 1
Toomer, Jean 1
Twain, Mark 6, 26
Updike, John (Hoyer) 13, 27
Vinge, Joan (Carol) D(ennison) 24
Vonnegut, Kurt Jr. 8
Walker, Alice (Malsenior) 5
Warren, Robert Penn 4
Welty, Eudora 1, 27
Wescott, Glenway 35
West, Nathanael 16
Wharton, Edith (Newbold Jones) 6
Williams, William Carlos 31
Wodehouse, P(elham) G(renville) 2
Wolfe, Thomas (Clayton) 33
Wright, Richard (Nathaniel) 2

ARGENTINIAN

Bioy Casares, Adolfo 17
Borges, Jorge Luis 4, 41
Cortazar, Julio 7
Valenzuela, Luisa 14

AUSTRALIAN

Jolley, (Monica) Elizabeth 19
Lawson, Henry (Archibald Hertzberg) 18
Moorhouse, Frank 40
White, Patrick (Victor Martindale) 39

AUSTRIAN

Grillparzer, Franz 37
Kafka, Franz 5, 29, 35
Musil, Robert (Edler von) 18
Schnitzler, Arthur 15
Stifter, Adalbert 28

BRAZILIAN

Lispector, Clarice 34
Machado de Assis, Joaquim Maria 24

CANADIAN

Atwood, Margaret (Eleanor) 2
Bellow, Saul 14
Gallant, Mavis 5
Laurence, (Jean) Margaret (Wemyss) 7
Leacock, Stephen (Butler) 39
Munro, Alice 3
Ross, (James) Sinclair 24
Thomas, Audrey (Callahan) 20

CHILEAN

Bombal, Maria Luisa 37
Donoso (Yanez), Jose 34

CHINESE

Chang, Eileen   28
Lu Hsun   20
P'u Sung-ling   31

COLOMBIAN

Garcia Marquez, Gabriel (Jose)   8

CUBAN

Cabrera Infante, G(uillermo)   39
Calvino, Italo   3
Carpentier (y Valmont), Alejo   35

CZECH

Capek, Karel   36
Kafka, Franz   5, 29, 35
Kundera, Milan   24

DANISH

Andersen, Hans Christian   6
Dinesen, Isak   7

ENGLISH

Aldiss, Brian W(ilson)   36
Ballard, J(ames) G(raham)   1
Bates, H(erbert) E(rnest)   10
Bowen, Elizabeth (Dorothea Cole)   3, 28
Campbell, (John) Ramsey   19
Carter, Angela (Olive)   13
Chesterton, G(ilbert) K(eith)   1
Clarke, Arthur C(harles)   3
Collier, John   19
Conrad, Joseph   9
Coppard, A(lfred) E(dgar)   21
de la Mare, Walter (John)   14
Dickens, Charles (John Huffam)   17
Doyle, Arthur Conan   12
du Maurier, Daphne   18
Forster, E(dward) M(organ)   27
Fowles, John (Philip)   33
Galsworthy, John   22
Gaskell, Elizabeth Cleghorn   25
Gissing, George (Robert)   37
Greene, Graham (Henry)   29
Hardy, Thomas   2
Huxley, Aldous (Leonard)   39
James, Montague (Rhodes)   16
Jolley, (Monica) Elizabeth   19
Kipling, (Joseph) Rudyard   5
Lawrence, D(avid) H(erbert Richards)   4, 19
Lee, Vernon   33
Lessing, Doris (May)   6
Lewis, (Percy) Wyndham   34
Lowry, (Clarence) Malcolm   31
Mansfield, Katherine   9, 23, 38
Maugham, W(illiam) Somerset   8
Morrison, Arthur   40
Naipaul, V(idiadhar) S(urajprasad)   38
Pritchett, V(ictor) S(awdon)   14
Rhys, Jean   21
Saki   12
Sansom, William   21
Trollope, Anthony   28
Warner, Sylvia Townsend   23
Waugh, Evelyn (Arthur St. John)   41
Wells, H(erbert) G(eorge)   6
White, Patrick (Victor Martindale)   39
Wilson, Angus (Frank Johnstone)   21
Wodehouse, P(elham) G(renville)   2
Woolf, (Adeline) Virginia   7

FRENCH

Ayme, Marcel (Andre)   41
Balzac, Honore de   5
Barbey d'Aurevilly, Jules Amedee   17
Baudelaire, Charles   18
Beauvoir, Simone (Lucie Ernestine Marie
  Bertrand) de   35

Beckett, Samuel (Barclay)   16
Camus, Albert   9
Colette, (Sidonie-Gabrielle)   10
Duras, Marguerite   40
Flaubert, Gustave   11
Gautier, Theophile   20
Gide, Andre (Paul Guillaume)   13
Jarry, Alfred   20
Laforgue, Jules   20
Lautreamont, Comte de   14
Maupassant, (Henri Rene Albert) Guy de   1
Mauriac, Francois (Charles)   24
Merimee, Prosper   7
Morand, Paul   22
Nerval, Gerard de   18
Nin, Anais   10
Sartre, Jean-Paul   32
Stendhal   27
Villiers de l'Isle Adam, Jean Marie Mathias
  Philippe Auguste, Comte de   14
Voltaire   12

GERMAN

Arnim, Achim von (Ludwig Joachim von
  Arnim)   29
Boell, Heinrich (Theodor)   23
Goethe, Johann Wolfgang von   38
Grimm, Jacob Ludwig Karl   36
Grimm, Wilhelm Karl   36
Hauptmann, Gerhart (Johann Robert)   37
Hesse, Hermann   9
Hoffmann, E(rnst) T(heodor) A(madeus)   13
Kleist, Heinrich von   22
Lenz, Siegfried   33
Mann, (Paul) Thomas   5
Storm, (Hans) Theodor (Woldsen)   27
Tieck, (Johann) Ludwig   31

INDIAN

Mukherjee, Bharati   38
Narayan, R(asipuram) K(rishnaswami)   25

IRISH

Beckett, Samuel (Barclay)   16
Bowen, Elizabeth (Dorothea Cole)   3, 28
Joyce, James (Augustine Aloysius)   3, 26
Lavin, Mary   4
Le Fanu, Joseph Sheridan   14
McGahern, John   17
Moore, George Augustus   19
O'Brien, Edna   10
O'Connor, Frank   5
O'Faolain, Sean   13
O'Flaherty, Liam   6
Trevor, William   21
Wilde, Oscar (Fingal O'Flahertie Wills)   11

ISRAELI

Agnon, S(hmuel) Y(osef Halevi)   30

ITALIAN

Boccaccio, Giovanni   10
Calvino, Italo   3
Levi, Primo   12
Moravia, Alberto   26
Pavese, Cesare   19
Pirandello, Luigi   22
Svevo, Italo   25
Verga, Giovanni (Carmelo)   21

JAPANESE

Dazai Osamu   41
Kawabata, Yasunari   17
Mishima, Yukio   4
Oe, Kenzaburo   20
Shiga, Naoya   23
Tanizaki, Jun'ichiro   21

MEXICAN

Arreola, Juan Jose   38
Castellanos, Rosario   39
Fuentes, Carlos   24
Rulfo, Juan   25

NEW ZEALANDER

Frame, Janet   29
Mansfield, Katherine   9, 23, 38

POLISH

Agnon, S(hmuel) Y(osef Halevi)   30
Conrad, Joseph   9
Peretz, Isaac Loeb   26
Schulz, Bruno   13
Singer, Isaac Bashevis   3

PUERTO RICAN

Ferre, Rosario   36

RUSSIAN

Babel, Isaak (Emmanuilovich)   16
Bulgakov, Mikhail (Afanas'evich)   18
Bunin, Ivan Alexeyevich   5
Chekhov, Anton (Pavlovich)   2, 28, 41
Dostoevsky, Fedor Mikhailovich   2, 33
Gogol, Nikolai (Vasilyevich)   4, 29
Gorky, Maxim   28
Leskov, Nikolai (Semyonovich)   34
Nabokov, Vladimir (Vladimirovich)   11
Pasternak, Boris (Leonidovich)   31
Platonov, Andrei   41
Pushkin, Alexander (Sergeyevich)   27
Solzhenitsyn, Aleksandr I(sayevich)   32
Tolstoy, Leo (Nikolaevich)   9, 30
Turgenev, Ivan   7
Zoshchenko, Mikhail (Mikhailovich)   15

SCOTTISH

Oliphant, Margaret (Oliphant Wilson)   25
Scott, Walter   32
Spark, Muriel (Sarah)   10
Stevenson, Robert Louis (Balfour)   11

SOUTH AFRICAN

Gordimer, Nadine   17

SPANISH

Cervantes (Saavedra), Miguel de   12
Pardo Bazan, Emilia   30
Unamuno (y Jugo), Miguel de   11

SWEDISH

Lagerkvist, Par   12

SWISS

Hesse, Hermann   9
Keller, Gottfried   26
Walser, Robert   20

TRINIDADIAN

Naipaul, V(idiadhar) S(urajprasad)   38

UKRAINIAN

Aleichem, Sholom   33

URUGUAYAN

Onetti, Juan Carlos   23

WELSH

Lewis, Alun   40
Machen, Arthur   20
Thomas, Dylan (Marlais)   3

YUGOSLAVIAN

Andric, Ivo   36

SSC Cumulative Title Index

"A & P" (Updike) **13**:372, 398-99; **27**:320-30
"A la Víbora de la mar" (Fuentes) **24**:29, 32, 57-8, 71-2
"A un dîner d' athées" (Barbey d'Aurevilly) **17**:6-8, 11-12, 17, 19-20, 33-4, 37, 43-4
"A une heure du matin" (Baudelaire) **18**:19, 41-2, 45-7, 49
"Aaron Trow" (Trollope) **28**:317, 319, 323-24, 330-33, 349, 357
"The Abandoned House" (Michaels) **16**:316
"L'abandonné" (Maupassant) **1**:259
"Abashiri made" (Shiga) **23**:352
"The Abbess of Castro" (Stendhal)
    See "L'Abbesse de Castro"
"L'Abbesse de Castro" (Stendhal) **27**:230-31, 247, 249-50, 262-63
"The Abbey Grange" (Doyle) **12**:60, 62
"The Abbot's Ghost; or, Maurice Treherne's Temptation" (Alcott) **27**:4, 57
ABC Book (Tolstoy) **9**:386-87
"Abdias" (Stifter) **28**:272-74, 276-81, 283, 290-91, 295-99
"The Abduction from the Seraglio" (Barthelme) **2**:46, 51-2
"Abdul Azziz Has His: An Adventure in the Yildiz Kiosk" (Leacock) **39**:267
"El abejorro" (Unamuno) **11**:312
Abel Sánchez (Unamuno)
    See *Abel Sánchez: Una historia de pasión*
Abel Sánchez: Una historia de pasión (Unamuno) **11**:314, 317, 325, 337-39, 345, 347, 349, 351
"Abel Staple Disapproves" (Coppard) **21**:27
"Abencaján el Bojarí, muerto en su laberinto" (Borges) **41**:72, 125
"Abenjacán the Bojarí, Dead in His Labyrinth" (Borges)
    See "Abencaján el Bojarí, muerto en su laberinto"
"Abenjacán the Buckharian, Dead in His Labyrinth" (Borges)
    See "Abencaján el Bojarí, muerto en su laberinto"
Die Abenteuer in der Sylvesternacht (Hoffmann) **13**:188-89, 210
"Abie's Irish Rose" (Lardner) **32**:134
"The Abortion" (Walker) **5**:412, 414
"About How Ivan Ivanovič Quarreled with Ivan Nikiforovič" (Gogol)
    See "The Tale of How Ivan Ivanovich Quarrelled with Ivan Nikiforovich"
"About the Devil" (Gorky)
    See "O cherte"
"About the Old and Young Pamukovices" (Andric)
    See "O starim i mladim Pamukovicima"
"About the Siskin Who Lied and the Woodpecker Who Loved the Truth" (Gorky)
    See "O chizhe, kotoryi lgal, i o diatle liubitele istiny"

"Above the River" (Williams) **31**:334
"Abril es el mes más cruel" (Cabrera Infante) **39**:18, 22
"Abroad" (Gordimer) **17**:157, 160
"Abrogast von Andelon und Elisa von Portugal, Albrecht von Werdenberg und Amisa von" (Arnim) **29**:10
"Absalom, My Son" (Warner) **23**:370-71
"The Absence of Mr. Glass" (Chesterton) **1**:131
"Absent without Leave" (Boell) **23**:2-3
"Absent-Mindedness in a Parish Choir" (Hardy) **2**:206, 215, 217
Absolute Love (Jarry)
    See *L'amour absolu*
"The Absolute Proof" (Capek)
    See "Naprostý důkaz"
"Absolution" (Fitzgerald) **6**:46, 77, 81, 83-4, 86, 100, 102-03
"Accents of Death" (Farrell) **28**:92
"An Acceptable Level of Pain" (Lenz) **33**:338
"Acceptance of Their Ways" (Gallant) **5**:139-40
"Access to the Children" (Trevor) **21**:231, 233, 260
"Accident" (Farrell) **28**:94
"An Accident" (Narayan) **25**:132, 154
"The Accident" (Williams) **31**:319, 329-30, 343, 345, 364
"Accident Zone" (Campbell) **19**:75
"Accidente" (Pardo Bazan) **30**:262
"The Accompanist" (Pritchett) **14**:263, 273
"According to His Lights" (Galsworthy) **22**:91
"An Account of Some Strange Disturbances in an Old House on Aungier Street" (Le Fanu)
    See "Some Strange Disturbances in an Old House on Augier Street"
"Account of Spring Breezes and Autumn Rain" (Tanizaki)
    See "Shumpū shūu roku"
"An Accursed Race" (Gaskell) **25**:55, 60, 66
"Ace in the Hole" (Updike) **13**:351-52; **27**:329
"Aceite guapo" (Castellanos) **39**:46, 57
"El acercamiento a Almotásim" (Borges) **4**:4, 16; **41**:53-55, 97, 163
"The Achievement of the Cat" (Saki) **12**:314, 327
"Achilles' Heel" (O'Connor) **5**:370, 372
Acia (Turgenev)
    See *Asya*
"Acme" (Galsworthy) **22**:79, 101
El acoso (Carpentier) **35**:91-2, 106, 114-15, 128
Acres and Pains (Perelman) **32**:211, 219, 224-25, 230
"Across Paris" (Ayme) **41**:4
Across Paris (Ayme)
    See *Across Paris and Other Stories*
Across Paris and Other Stories (Ayme) **41**:3-4
"Across the Airshaft" (Fisher) **25**:17, 19
"Across the Bay" (Bates) **10**:118, 134
"Across the Bridge" (Boell)
    See "An der Brücke"
"Across the Bridge" (Greene) **29**:212

"Across the Gulf" (Davis) **38**:110
"Across the Plains" (Moorhouse) **40**:309
Across the River and into the Trees (Hemingway) **25**:79
"Across the Straits" (Lawson) **18**:220
"An Act of Reparation" (Warner) **23**:373
"Acting Captain" (Lewis) **40**:271, 276
"Action Will Be Taken" (Boell) **23**:8, 10
Actions and Reactions (Kipling) **5**:272, 283-85
"The Actor and the Alibi" (Chesterton) **1**:138
"Acts of God" (Boyle) **16**:157
"Acuérdate" (Rulfo) **25**:245, 249, 265, 268
"Ad Astra" (Faulkner) **1**:147
Ad olam (Agnon) **30**:38, 40, 43, 46-7, 57-62, 71
"Ad porcos" (Biny Casares) **17**:56
"Adam and Eve" (Machado de Assis)
    See "Adão e Eva"
"Adam and Eve and Pinch Me" (Coppard) **21**:17
Adam and Eve and Pinch Me (Coppard) **21**:2, 4, 7, 15, 18, 20
"Adam, One Afternoon" (Calvino) **3**:112
Adam, One Afternoon, and Other Stories (Calvino)
    See *L'entrada en guerra*
Adam, Where Art Thou? (Boell)
    See *Wo warst du, Adam?*
"Adam's Bride" (Jolley) **19**:221, 233
"Adam's Death" (Boyle) **5**:57
"Adão e Eva" (Machado de Assis) **24**:127, 129, 153
"Adieu" (Balzac) **5**:17-18, 22, 24, 31, 33
"Adieu, New-York!" (Morand) **22**:174
Los adioses (Onetti) **23**:247, 253, 257-58, 260, 274, 276-79
"The Adjuster" (Fitzgerald) **6**:46
"Admiral's Night" (Machado de Assis) **24**:140, 152
"The Admiralty Spire" (Nabokov) **11**:124-25
"The Admirer" (Singer) **3**:378, 384
"Admiring the Scenery" (O'Faolain) **13**:284-86, 288, 297, 300, 302-05, 307, 309
"Admonition" (Dazai Osamu) **41**:232
"Adolescence" (Wescott) **35**:363-64, 368, 370, 372
"Adoration" (Gilchrist) **14**:157
"Adrift Just Off the Islets of Langerhans: Latitude 38 54'N, Longitude 00'13'"" (Ellison) **14**:109-11, 115, 118-21
"The Adulterous Woman" (Camus)
    See "La femme adultère"
"Adultery" (Dubus) **15**:74, 76, 87, 89-90, 92-4, 98, 100
Adultery, and Other Choices (Dubus) **15**:72-3, 75-6, 80-1, 92
"Advancing Luna—and Ida B. Wells" (Walker) **5**:412-13
"El Advenimiento del Aguila" (Castellanos) **39**:49, 73
"Adventure" (Anderson) **1**:18, 58
"The Adventure" (Boell) **23**:10

"The Adventure" (Lagerkvist)
See "Äventyret"
"An Adventure from a Work in Progress" (Thomas) 3:402, 407
"The Adventure of a Clerk" (Calvino) 3:116
"Adventure of a Photographer" (Calvino) 3:111
"The Adventure of a Poet" (Calvino) 3:111, 116
"The Adventure of a Reader" (Calvino) 3:112
"Adventure of a Traveller" (Calvino) 3:111
"The Adventure of Charles Augustus Milverton" (Doyle) 12:61
"The Adventure of Gloria Scott" (Doyle) 12:57
"The Adventure of Lieutenant Jergounoff" (Turgenev)
See "Istoriya leytenanta Ergunova"
"The Adventure of Peter Black" (Doyle) 12:50
"The Adventure of Shoscombe Old Place" (Doyle) 12:51-2, 63
"The Adventure of Six Napoleone" (Doyle) 12:55
"The Adventure of the Black Fisherman" (Irving) 2:241, 247
"The Adventure of the Blanched Soldier" (Doyle) 12:51-2
"The Adventure of the Blue Carbuncle" (Doyle) 12:55, 66, 68, 73-4
"The Adventure of the Cardboard Box" (Doyle) 12:62-4
"The Adventure of the Copper Beeches" (Doyle) 12:51, 55, 58-9, 68, 71-3
"The Adventure of the Creeping Man" (Doyle) 12:52, 63-4
"The Adventure of the Dancing Men" (Doyle) 12:49, 51
"Adventure of the Deserted Residence" (Machen) 20:206
"The Adventure of the Empty House" (Doyle) 12:61
"The Adventure of the Engineer's Thumb" (Doyle) 12:51, 58, 66, 68, 72-4
"The Adventure of the Englishman" (Irving) 2:262
"The Adventure of the German Student" (Irving) 2:241, 256-57, 261
"The Adventure of the Golden Pince-Nez" (Doyle) 12:62
"The Adventure of the Greek Interpreter" (Doyle) 12:51, 55
"The Adventure of the Illustrious Client" (Doyle) 12:54, 64
"The Adventure of the Mason" (Irving) 2:266
"The Adventure of the Missing Three-Quarter" (Doyle) 12:50-2
"Adventure of the Mysterious Picture" (Irving) 2:261, 265
"The Adventure of the Mysterious Stranger" (Irving) 2:261
"The Adventure of the Naval Treaty" (Doyle) 12:50-1, 58-60
"The Adventure of the Noble Bachelor" (Doyle) 12:53, 66, 71, 75
"The Adventure of the Norwood Builder" (Doyle) 12:51-2
"The Adventure of the Red-Headed League" (Doyle) 12:50, 54-5, 66, 70-1, 73
"The Adventure of the Reigate Puzzle" (Doyle) 12:58-9
"The Adventure of the Retired Colourman" (Doyle) 12:50
"The Adventure of the Second Stain" (Doyle) 12:51, 53, 62
"The Adventure of the Silver Blaze" (Doyle) 12:51
"The Adventure of the Speckled Band" (Doyle) 12:58-9, 66, 68, 71, 73-4
"The Adventure of the Stockbroker's Clerk" (Doyle) 12:50-1, 55
"The Adventure of the Sussex Vampire" (Doyle) 12:52, 63
"The Adventure of the Three Gables" (Doyle) 12:52, 64

"The Adventure of the Veiled Lodger" (Doyle) 12:52, 63
"The Adventure of the Yellow Face" (Doyle) 12:50-2, 58
"The Adventure of Wisteria Lodge" (Doyle) 12:62-3
Adventures du Baron de Gangan (Voltaire) 12:340
Adventures in the Skin Trade, and Other Stories (Thomas) 3:396, 403-04
"The Adventures of a Breach-of-Promise Swindler" (Capek)
See "Příběhy sňatkového podvodníka"
"Adventures of a Dead Man" (Bulgakov) 18:90
"The Adventures of a Melody" (Peretz) 26:206
"The Adventures of Chichikov" (Bulgakov) 18:73-4, 91, 98-9
"The Adventures of Françoise and Suzanne" (Cable) 4:49
"The Adventures of Frederick Pickering" (Trollope) 28:320, 323, 332-34, 348
Adventures of Gerard (Doyle) 12:81-2
Adventures of Martin Hewitt (Morrison) 40:332, 349
The Adventures of Menakhem-Mendl (Aleichem) 33:45, 47, 57
The Adventures of Sherlock Holmes (Doyle) 12:68, 72-4
"The Adventures of Simon and Susanna" (Harris) 19:196
"The Adventures of the Bruce-Partington Plans" (Doyle) 12:51-2, 55-6
"Advice to Young Men" (Chesnutt) 7:14
"Aepyornis Island" (Wells) 6:388, 399
"Aerial Ways" (Pasternak) 31:96-8, 113-14, 117, 120
"The Aeroplanes at Brescia" (Davenport) 16:161, 165, 167, 170, 176, 197
"Los afanes" (Bioy Casares) 17:87, 95
"Afar a Bird" (Beckett) 16:123, 125-26
"The Affair at 7, Rue de M----" (Steinbeck)
See "L'affaire du l'avenue de M----"
"The Affair at Coulter's Notch" (Bierce) 9:49
"The Affair at Grover Station" (Cather) 2:102
"An Affair of Honor" (Nabokov) 11:117
"An Affair of Outposts" (Bierce) 9:60, 96
"The Affair of the Clasps" (Gorky) 28:145, 149, 158
"The Affair with the Clasps" (Gorky)
See "The Affair of the Clasps"
"L'affaire du l'avenue de M----" (Steinbeck) 11:255-56, 258
"L'affichage céleste" (Villiers de l'Isle Adam) 14:377, 381-83, 390, 396
"The Aficionados" (Carver) 8:50
"Afloat" (Beattie) 11:10-11, 13, 29
Afloat (Maupassant)
See Sur l'eau
"Afonka Bida" (Babel) 16:52, 58
"Afra" (Pardo Bazan) 30:266, 280-81, 283-84
"Africa Emergent" (Gordimer) 17:57, 160, 174
"The African Magician" (Gordimer) 17:156, 162, 173-74
"African Morning" (Hughes) 6:116-17, 122
African Stories (Lessing) 6:189-91, 196, 212, 214-15, 217-18
"After Dark in the Playing Fields" (James) 16:251
"After Dinner" (Cortazar) 7:70
"After Fourteen Years" (O'Connor) 5:381, 387, 392
"After Holbein" (Wharton) 6:422-23
After Lazarus: A Filmscript (Coover) 15:58-9, 61
"After Lunch" (Cortazar) 7:70
"After Strange Gods" (Norris) 28:205, 207
After Such Pleasures (Parker) 2:273-74
"After the Ball" (Collier) 19:109, 112
"After the Ball" (Tolstoy) 9:367, 379, 388, 394-95
"After the Battle" (Babel) 16:12, 26-28, 30, 52, 54, 57-8

"After the Buffalo" (Algren) 33:114
"After the Denim" (Carver) 8:14
"After the Fair" (Thomas) 3:399
"After the Fireworks" (Huxley) 39:159, 173
"After the Game" (Dubus) 15:86, 100
"After the Race" (Joyce) 3:205, 208-09, 226, 231, 234, 247-48; 26:46-7
"After the Show" (Wilson) 21:320, 324, 337-39
"After the Storm" (Hemingway) 1:216, 234
"After the Sun Has Risen" (Farrell) 28:94
"After the Winter" (Chopin) 8:93
"After You, My Dear Alphonse" (Jackson) 39:210, 211, 219, 220, 224, 225, 229
"After You've Gone" (Adams) 24:18
After You've Gone (Adams) 24:16-19
After-Hours (Cortazar)
See Deshoras
"After-Image" (Caldwell) 19:5
"Afternoon" (Ellison) 26:8, 21, 28
"Afternoon" (Sansom) 21:86-7
"Afternoon in Linen" (Jackson) 39:211, 220, 222, 224
"An Afternoon Miracle" (Henry) 5:162, 181
"Afternoon of a Playwright" (Thurber) 1:424
"Afternoon of an Author" (Fitzgerald) 6:60
"Afternoon Waltz" (O'Hara) 15:277, 284
"An Afternoon with the Old Man" (Dubus) 15:74
"Afterward" (Wharton) 6:433
"Agafia" (Chekhov) 2:155
"Again" (Campbell) 19:71, 75
"Again the Antilles" (Rhys) 21:49, 61
"Agatha" (O'Hara) 15:282-83
"Agathon, or Concerning Wisdom" (Capek) 36:95
Age (Calisher) 15:12-14
L'âge de discrétion (Beauvoir) 35:46, 48-53, 72-3, 79, 81-3, 85
"The Age of a Wart" (White) 39:347-49
The Age of Discretion (Beauvoir)
See L'âge de discrétion
"The Age of Genius" (Schulz) 13:336, 344
"Agony" (Lish) 18:283
Agostino (Moravia) 26:131-33, 136, 140-41, 143, 146, 156, 180, 182-83
"Agunot: A Tale" (Agnon) 30:6-8, 10, 66, 69
"Aguri" (Tanizaki) 21:181
Ah King (Maugham) 8:374, 378
"Ah Life, Ah Death, Ah Music, Ah France" (Saroyan) 21:149
"Ah Q cheng-chuan" (Lu Hsun)
See "Ah Q zheng zhuan"
"Ah Q zheng zhuan" (Lu Hsun) 20:126, 129-30, 145, 150-51
"Ah Q—The Real Story" (Lu Hsun)
See "Ah Q zheng zhuan"
"Ah, the University!" (Collier) 19:101, 109
"Ah, Well" (Lawson) 18:243
"Ah, Woe Is Me" (Gordimer) 17:152, 160, 167
Ahasverus död (Lagerkvist) 12:184, 186-90, 192, 198
"Ahead" (Aldiss)
See "The Failed Men"
"Ah-Ha" (Saroyan) 21:165-66
"Ah-ha Ah-ha" (Saroyan) 21:166
"Ahí, pero dónde, cómo" (Cortazar) 7:61-2
Ahí y ahora (Cortazar) 7:91
Die Ahnenprobe (Tieck) 31:286
"El ahogado más hermoso del mundo" (Garcia Marquez) 8:160, 167-70, 183, 186
"Ahoy, Sailor Boy" (Coppard) 21:27
The Airs of Earth (Aldiss) 36:18
"Airwaves" (Mason) 4:1
"Akanishi Kakita" (Shiga) 23:345
Akëdysséril (Villiers de l'Isle Adam) 14:378-79, 383-84, 386, 388-90
"An Akoulina of the Irish Midlands" (Lavin) 4:182-83
"Akuma" (Tanizaki) 21:195, 208
"Alas, Poor Bollington" (Coppard) 21:11, 28
"Alas, Poor Maling" (Greene) 29:183-84
"Alaska" (Adams) 24:13

"Albatross" (Thomas) **20**:317
"Albergo Empedocle" (Forster) **27**:74, 83, 99, 102-03, 108, 119
"Albert" (Tolstoy) **9**:376, 389-90, 393; **30**:332
"Albert Nobbs" (Moore) **19**:298, 303, 310-11
"Albert Savarus" (Balzac) **5**:27
"Albert und Concordia" (Arnim) **29**:29-30
"Albertine" (Dreiser) **30**:142
Albertus, ou l'âme et le péché: légende théologique (Gautier) **20**:10, 24
"Album de familia" (Castellanos) **39**:30, 75, 76
Album de familia (Castellanos) **39**:30, 44, 46, 47, 51, 55, 60, 61, 72, 75, 80
Ale verk (Peretz) **26**:222
"Alec" (O'Connor) **5**:371, 390
"Alec's Cabin" (Stuart) **31**:227, 236
"Aleksandrit" (Leskov) **34**:110, 119
"The Aleph" (Borges)
   See "El aleph"
"El aleph" (Borges) **4**:25, 28, 31-2, 34; **41**:65-66, 134, 160-61, 164
El aleph (Borges) **4**:15, 18-20, 34, 36, 39-41; **41**:53, 60, 65, 115-17, 134, 157, 161-62
The Aleph, and Other Stories, 1933-1969 (Borges)
   See *El aleph*
"Alexander" (Bates) **10**:111-12, 124, 132
"Alexander the Great" (Capek) **36**:95, 130
"Alexandrian Tale" (Machado de Assis)
   See "Conto alexandrino"
"The Alexandrite" (Leskov)
   See "Aleksandrit"
"L'alfabeto" (Moravia) **26**:148
"Alguien desordena estas rosas" (Garcia Marquez) **8**:154, 158
"Alguien que anda por ahí" (Cortazar) **7**:83-7, 90-1
The Alhambra (Irving) **2**:242-46, 251, 254, 265, 268
"The Alibi" (du Maurier) **18**:127, 132
"Alibi Ike" (Lardner) **32**:114, 125, 145, 148, 155, 168
"Alice Doane's Appeal" (Hawthorne) **39**:121
"Alice Dugdale" (Trollope) **28**:311, 318, 322-23, 335, 356
"Alice Long's Dachsunds" (Spark) **10**:360, 362, 367, 371
"Alice Who Sees Mice" (Cisneros) **32**:8, 41
"Alicia and I Talking on Edna's Steps" (Cisneros) **32**:29
"Alicia's Diary" (Hardy) **2**:211, 214
"The Alien Corn" (Maugham) **8**:356-57, 366, 369, 378-79
"An Alien Flower" (Gallant) **5**:124, 132-33
"An Alien in the Pines" (Garland) **18**:154, 160
"The Alien Skull" (O'Flaherty) **6**:262, 280
"The Aliens" (McCullers) **9**:342-43, 347, 354, 356
"Los alimentos terrestres" (Arreola) **38**:7-8, 10, 22-23
"Alipaša" (Andric) **36**:65, 67, 78
"Alix de Morainville" (Cable) **4**:60
"Alix's Refusal" (Colette) **10**:292
"Alkmene" (Dinesen) **7**:165
"All, All Wasted" (Aiken) **9**:12, 14
"All at One Point" (Calvino) **3**:103, 108
"All Avoidable Talk" (Narayan) **25**:133, 156
"All Fires the Fire" (Cortazar)
   See "Todos los fuegos el fuego"
All Fires the Fire, and Other Stories (Cortazar)
   See *Todos los fuegos el fuego*
All Gone (Dixon) **16**:218
"All Hallows" (de la Mare) **14**:70, 71, 83, 92
"All Lovers Love the Spring" (Gordon) **15**:104-05
"All Saints" (Bowen) **3**:40, 42
"All Shook Up" (Boyle) **16**:144-45
"All Sorts of Impossible Things" (McGahern) **17**:299, 304, 309
"All Souls" (Wharton) **6**:423, 426-27
"All Strange Away" (Beckett) **16**:117
"All Summer in a Day" (Bradbury) **29**:80-1

"All That Glitters" (Clarke) **3**:134
"All That Messuage" (Morrison) **40**:337, 355, 367
All That Rises Must Converge (O'Connor)
   See *Everything That Rises Must Converge*
"All the Birds Come Home to Roost" (Ellison) **14**:124
"All the Dead Pilots" (Faulkner) **1**:147
"All the Girls He Wanted" (O'Hara) **15**:248, 255, 264, 266
"All the Good People I've Left Behind" (Oates) **6**:250, 252-53
All the Good People I've Left Behind (Oates) **6**:247-48, 250, 252-54
"All the King's Horses" (Vonnegut) **8**:434
"All the Other Stories" (Calvino) **3**:101
All the Sad Young Men (Fitzgerald) **6**:46, 94
"All the Sounds of Fear" (Ellison) **14**:105
"All the Time in the World" (Clarke) **3**:135
"All Things Are Nothing to Me" (Farrell) **28**:118, 120-21
"All Through the Night" (Algren) **33**:107
"All uscita" (Pirandello) **22**:234
"Allal" (Bowles) **3**:69
"Allan and Adelaide: An Arabesque" (Ligotti) **16**:286
"Allegiance" (Taylor) **10**:375-79
"Allende la verdad" (Pardo Bazan) **30**:262
"Aller et retour" (Barnes) **3**:7-8, 10, 14-17, 24
"The Alligators" (Updike) **13**:356
"All-seeing" (Moravia) **26**:160-61
"The All-Seeing" (Nin) **10**:303-04
"Alma Redeemed" (Malamud) **15**:235
"Al Mamon" (Gogol) **4**:83
"An Almanac of Pain" (Dazai Osamu) **41**:247-48, 250
"The Almighty Test" (Sansom) **21**:127
"The Almond Tree" (Grimm and Grimm) **36**:203
"The Almond Tree" (de la Mare) **14**:80
"Almost a Gentleman" (Lewis) **40**:271, 276
"Alms Giving" (Moore)
   See "An Déirc"
"The Aloe" (Mansfield) **9**:279, 282, 284, 301-03, 309; **23**:158; **38**:230
"Aloha Oe" (London) **4**:269
"Alone" (O'Hara) **15**:248, 265, 267, 274-76
"Alone" (Singer) **3**:360-61, 364
Alone Against Tomorrow: Stories of Alienation in Speculative Fiction (Ellison) **14**:143-47
Alone with the Horrors (Campbell) **19**:86 8
"Along Memory Lane" (Svevo)
   See "L'avvenire dei ricordi"
"Along the Edges" (McGahern) **17**:319
"The Alphabet" (Walser) **20**:355-56
"An Alpimalyan Dialogue" (Turgenev) **7**:335
"An Alpine Idyll" (Hemingway) **1**:210, 217; **36**:291
"Als der Krieg ausbrach" (Boell) **23**:2-4, 43-4, 46
"The Altar of the Dead" (James) **8**:269, 302, 304, 307-09
"Altdeutsche Landsleute" (Arnim) **29**:29-30
Das alte Buch und die Reise ins Blaue hinein (Tieck) **31**:284, 286
Der Alte vom Berge (Tieck) **31**:275
Alternating Currents (Pohl) **25**:227, 229-30, 232, 234
"Alternatives" (Adams) **24**:5, 13
Altogether: The Collected Stories of W. Somerset Maugham (Maugham) **8**:356, 358, 360, 370, 380, 382
Altogether: The Collected Stories of W. Somerset Maugham (Maugham)
   See *East and West: The Collected Short Stories of W. Somerset Maugham*
"Always Something to Do in Salinas" (Steinbeck) **11**:253
"Alyosha the Pot" (Tolstoy) **9**:379, 389
"Am I Not Your Rosalind?" (Thurber) **1**:420, 425

"Am I Spoiling You" (Bambara)
   See "The Apprentice"
"Am I Your World?" (Saroyan) **21**:162
"Amalia" (Ferre) **36**:159
L'amant (Duras) **40**:64-65, 72-74, 76-78, 96, 99-105, 107-23, 127-32, 134, 144-51
"L'amante di Gramigna" (Verga) **21**:283, 292, 298-99, 304, 308, 313
L'amante infelice (Moravia) **26**:143, 162
"El amante liberal" (Cervantes) **12**:3, 5, 7-8, 14-16, 18, 34, 44
"Les amants de Tolède" (Villiers de l'Isle Adam) **14**:390, 394, 397
"Amargura para tres sonámbulos" (Garcia Marquez) **8**:154-55, 157-58, 182
Amateurs (Barthelme) **2**:47
"The Amazon" (Leskov)
   See "Voitel' nica"
"The Ambassador from Wall Street" (Auchincloss) **22**:4
"The Ambassadress" (Auchincloss) **22**:3, 38
"The Ambitious Guest" (Hawthorne) **3**:182, 186-87
"The Ambitious Sophomore" (Vonnegut) **8**:431
"Ambrose His Mark" (Barth) **10**:41, 45-6, 53-4, 56, 60-1, 63, 89, 95, 97-8, 100
"Ambuscade" (Faulkner) **1**:170, 177
"An Ambuscade" (Harris) **19**:183
"L'ame de la maison ou la vie et la mort d'un grillon" (Gautier) **20**:15
"America First" (Auchincloss) **22**:43
An American Dream Girl (Farrell) **28**:98
American Earth (Caldwell) **19**:3-6, 9-13, 23, 25, 29-30, 34, 57
"American Honeymoon" (Benet) **10**:149
"The American Paul Johnson" (Moorhouse) **40**:301
"The American Poet's Visit" (Moorhouse) **40**:285, 290, 293, 302, 310
"The American Wife" (O'Connor) **5**:373
The Americans, Baby (Moorhouse) **40**:285-89, 291-92, 294, 297, 300-304, 308-11, 322-24
"The American's Tale" (Doyle) **12**:81, 84-5
"Les ames du purgatoire" (Merimee) **7**:283-4, 289-90, 292
"Les amies de pension" (Villiers de l'Isle Adam) **14**:378, 396
"Los amigos" (Cortazar) **7**:70, 88-9
"Las amistades efímeras" (Castellanos) **39**:35, 73, 75
"Amnesty" (Gordimer) **17**:182, 184, 187-88, 191
"Amo, amas, amat, amamus, amatis, Enough" (Perelman) **32**:222, 234
Among the Camps (Page) **23**:285
"Among the Corn Rows" (Garland) **18**:142, 144, 154, 159, 168-69, 172, 176, 180
"Among the Dahlias" (Sansom) **21**:90, 92, 95, 112-13
Among the Dahlias (Sansom) **21**:84, 112-14, 116, 126-27
Among the Lost People (Aiken) **9**:6, 28
"Among the Massagetae" (Hesse) **9**:244
"Among the Paths to Eden" (Capote) **2**:74-5
"Among the Pictures Are These" (Campbell) **19**:73
"Among Those Present" (Benet) **10**:154
"Amor" (Lispector) **34**:185, 188, 191, 193, 195-200, 202, 205, 214, 217-19, 221
"El amor ascsinado" (Pardo Bazan) **30**:264
"El amor que asalta" (Unamuno) **11**:312-13
L'amore coniugale, e altri racconti (Moravia) **26**:134-35, 138, 140, 150-51, 162
Gli amori difficili (Calvino) **3**:111-13, 116-18
Amori senza amore (Pirandello) **22**:275
La amortajada (Bombal) **37**:2-3, 9, 18-21, 23-24, 27, 29-30, 32, 36-39, 41, 47
"Amour" (Maupassant) **1**:278, 280
L'amour absolu (Jarry) **20**:50, 53, 61-2, 66
"L'amour du naturel" (Villiers de l'Isle Adam) **14**:396
"Amour dure" (Lee) **33**:302, 304-05, 309

L'amour en visites (Jarry) **20**:50
"L'amour suprême" (Villiers de l'Isle Adam) **14**:379, 384-85, 387, 390, 396
L'amour suprême (Villiers de l'Isle Adam) **14**:378, 396-97
The Amulet (Meyer)
    See *Das Amulett*
Das Amulett (Meyer) **30**:187, 209-12, 214-18
"Der Amüsierdoktor" (Lenz) **33**:327, 331-32
"An Amusing Adventure" (Zoshchenko) **15**:399
"Amy Foster" (Conrad) **9**:143
"An der Brücke" (Boell) **23**:5, 11, 34
"Ana María" (Donoso) **34**:4, 21, 25, 30, 32, 49
"Anabella's Hat" (Michaels) **16**:309
"Anacleto morones" (Rulfo) **25**:251, 262, 265, 270-71
Analytical Studies (Balzac)
    See *Etudes analytiques*
"Ananias" (Harris) **19**:149, 158, 180
"An Anarchist" (Conrad) **9**:157, 179, 181-83, 185
"Ancestors" (Woolf) **7**:381, 389
"Ancient Gentility" (Williams) **31**:333
"The Ancient Seal" (Stifter) **28**:281, 283
"& Answers" (Oates) **6**:232
"And Baby Makes Three" (Selby) **20**:278
"And Even Beyond" (Peretz) **26**:194
"And Man" (Saroyan) **21**:143, 151
And Other Stories (O'Hara) **15**:286
"And Some More" (Cisneros) **32**:5
"And the Crooked Shall Become Straight" (Agnon)
    See "Vehaya he'akov lemishor"
"And the Moon Be Still as Bright" (Bradbury) **29**:50
"And Then" (Barthelme) **2**:47
And Tomorrow, Monday (Pirandello)
    See *E domani lunedi*
And Where Were You, Adam? (Boell)
    See *Wo warst du, Adam?*
"Andare verso il popolo" (Moravia) **26**:163, 180
André Walter (Gide) **13**:59
"Andrea" (O'Hara) **15**:285
"Andreas Thameyer's Last Letter" (Schnitzler)
    See "Andreas Thameyers letzter brief"
"Andreas Thameyers letzter brief" (Schnitzler) **15**:377
"Andrei Kolosov" (Turgenev) **7**:313, 320, 323-24, 335, 339-40, 359
"Andrey Satchel and the Parson and Clerk" (Hardy) **2**:215
"Androcles and the Army" (O'Connor) **5**:369, 374
"Andromache" (Dubus) **15**:73-4, 81
"The Andventure of the Devil's Foot" (Doyle) **12**:63
"L'ane" (Maupassant) **1**:259
L'Ane d'or (Nerval) **18**:371
"L'Ane et le cheval" (Ayme) **41**:10, 15, 18
Anecdotes of Destiny (Dinesen) **7**:175
"Anedota pecuniária" (Machado de Assis) **24**:128
"Der Anfang von etwas" (Lenz) **33**:318-20, 327
L'angeau (Mauriac) **24**:164, 166-67, 174, 181-82
"The Angel" (Andersen) **6**:15
"The Angel and the Sweep" (Coppard) **21**:12
"The Angel at the Grave" (Wharton) **6**:414
"Angel in the Pasture" (Stuart) **31**:241-42
"Angel Levine" (Malamud) **15**:168, 170-71, 173, 203-04, 207-09, 214, 220
"The Angel of Mons" (Machen)
    See "The Bowmen"
"The Angel of the Bridge" (Cheever) **1**:96, 100, 110
"The Angel of the Lord" (Howells) **36**:387-90, 397
"The Angel of the Odd" (Poe) **1**:407-08
"An Angel on the Porch" (Wolfe) **33**:376, 383-84, 386, 399, 401

"Angel Pond Lure of the North" (Leacock) **39**:265
"The Angel Was a Yankee" (Benet) **10**:154, 160
"Angela" (Farrell) **28**:89, 92
"Angela" (Mukherjee) **38**:238-39, 252, 254, 265, 278
Angela Borgia (Meyer) **30**:187, 190, 195, 241, 244-45
"Angelic Butterfly" (Levi) **12**:278
Angelika, die Geueserin and Cosmusm, der Seilspringer (Arnim) **29**:5
Angélique (Nerval) **18**:362-65
"Angels at the Ritz" (Trevor) **21**:233, 262
Angels at the Ritz, and Other Stories (Trevor) **21**:233, 237, 260, 262
"Angels Unawares" (Henderson) **29**:327
"The Anglo-Saxons of Auxierville" (Stuart) **31**:244
"L'angoscia" (Moravia) **26**:182
Angry Candy (Ellison) **14**:141-42
"Angst" (Oates) **6**:241
"Anika's Times" (Andric)
    See "Anikina vremena"
"Anikina vremena" (Andric) **36**:33, 38, 43, 46, 48, 52, 66
"The Animal Game" (Machado de Assis) **24**:139, 155
"Animal Sketches" (Shiga) **23**:346
"Animals or Human Beings" (Wilson) **21**:358, 362
"Ann Lee's" (Bowen) **3**:54
Ann Lee's (Bowen) **3**:37, 39-40, 55
Ann Lee's and Other Stories (Bowen) **28**:4
"Ann Lisbeth" (Andersen) **6**:14-15
"Anna" (Dubus) **15**:96
"Anna Lisa's Nose" (Berriault) **30**:96-7
"Anna on the Neck" (Chekhov) **2**:131, 157
"Anna, Part I" (Gilchrist) **14**:157-60
"Anna Trivia Pluralized" (Perelman) **32**:229
"Annamalai" (Narayan) **25**:139, 145, 154-55, 164-65, 176
"Anne" (Beauvoir) **35**:60, 62-4, 66-71
"Anne" (Davis) **38**:122-23
"Anner Lizer's Stumblin' Block" (Dunbar) **8**:120-21, 129, 136
"Annette Delarbre" (Irving) **2**:241, 251, 259
"Anneve" (Caldwell) **19**:56
"Gli anni-lucci" (Calvino) **3**:92
"Anniversary" (Aiken) **9**:13, 31
"An Anniversary" (de la Mare) **14**:79, 84, 89
"Anniversary" (Lardner) **32**:133-34, 138, 140-41, 145, 149, 160, 162
"The Anniversary" (Price) **22**:367
"L'annonciateur" (Villiers de l'Isle Adam) **14**:381-87, 389-90, 395-96
"Announcement" (Arreola)
    See "Anuncio"
"The Annual Conference of 1930 and South Coast Dada" (Moorhouse) **40**:291
"The Annuity" (Pirandello) **22**:227-28
"An Anonym" (Capek) **36**:130
"Anonymiad" (Barth) **10**:40, 43-4, 46-8, 52, 54-6, 64, 74, 78-80, 83, 86-8, 90-1, 98-9, 100-02
"An Anonymous Story" (Chekhov) **2**:130-31, 157-58
"Another American Tragedy" (Collier) **19**:107-10, 112
"Another April" (Stuart) **31**:232-33, 266
"Another Christmas" (Trevor) **21**:262
"Another Community" (Narayan) **25**:134, 139, 141, 157
"Another Country" (Hemingway) **40**:215
"Another Day Another Dollar" (Selby) **20**:254-55, 258-59, 263, 267-69, 271-72
"Another face" (Agnon)
    See "Panim aherot"
"Another Hanging" (Stuart) **31**:234, 236, 267
"Another Man's Wife" (Anderson) **1**:39
"Another Pair of Hands" (Spark) **10**:370
"Another Part of the Sky" (Gordimer) **17**:151
"Another Story" (Cheever) **1**:112

"Another Time" (O'Brien) **10**:346-47
"Another Wife" (Anderson) **1**:31, 50-1
"Another World" (Campbell) **19**:77
"Ansell" (Forster) **27**:99, 103-04, 119
"The Answer" (Pirandello) **22**:254-55
"The Answer Depends" (O'Hara) **15**:262
"Answer to Prayer" (Wells) **6**:392
"The Antchar" (Turgenev) **7**:318-19
"Antes da ponte Rio-Niterói" (Lispector) **34**:209, 211
The Antheap (Lessing) **6**:189-91, 193-94, 196
"Anthony: Who Sought Things That Were Lost" (Waugh) **41**:325
"Anti-bureaucratisation and the Apparatchiki" (Moorhouse) **40**:322
"Antico furore" (Moravia) **26**:164
"The Antidote" (Narayan) **25**:140, 155
"Antigona" (Bunin) **5**:113
"Antigone" (Bunin)
    See "Antigona"
"The Antique Ring" (Hawthorne) **3**:189, 191
"The Antiquities of Elis" (Davenport) **16**:170, 176, 178, 195-96
"Antonie" (Villiers de l'Isle Adam) **14**:382
"Antónov Apples" (Bunin) **5**:81, 100
"Antonovskie jabloki" (Bunin) **5**:98-9
"Ants and the Fire" (Solzhenitsyn)
    See "Koster i murav'i"
"The Ant's Wedding" (Levi) **12**:275, 277
"Anuncio" (Arreola) **38**:12
"Anxiety" (Paley) **8**:411-12
"Any Purple Subjunctives Today?" (Perelman) **32**:213
"Any Reasonable Offer" (Vonnegut) **8**:433
Anya Kōro (Shiga) **23**:363
The Anything Box (Henderson) **29**:316
"Anywhere Out of the World" (Baudelaire)
    See "N'importe où hors du monde"
"Apacalipsis de Solentiname" (Cortazar) **7**:83, 86, 88, 90-1
"A-pao" (P'u Sung-ling) **31**:196-97
"Apartment" (Cowan) **28**:83
"The Ape" (Pritchett) **14**:271
"The Ape Lady in Retirement" (Boyle) **16**:148, 154
"Apellesova cherta" (Pasternak)
    See "Il tratto di Apelle"
"The Aperture Moment" (Aldiss) **36**:11-12, 25
"A-Playin' of Old Sledge at the Settlemint" (Murfree) **22**:188, 207-08
"Apocalypse at Solentiname" (Cortazar)
    See "Apacalipsis de Solentiname"
"An Apocryph" (Capek)
    See "Crucifixion"
Apocrypha (Capek) **36**:112, 129
Apocryphal Stories (Capek)
    See *Kniha apokryfů*
"Um apólogo" (Machado de Assis) **24**:128, 130
"An Apologue" (Hawthorne) **39**:126
"The Apostate" (London) **4**:263, 291-92
"An Apostle of the Tulles" (Harte) **8**:247-49
"The Apparatus for the Chemical Analysis of the Last Breath" (Villiers de l'Isle Adam)
    See "L'appareil pur l'analyse chimique du dernier soupir"
"L'appareil pur l'analyse chimique du dernier soupir" (Villiers de l'Isle Adam) **14**:379, 396
"Apparition" (Maupassant) **1**:265, 281
"An Apparition in the Engineers' Castle" (Leskov) **34**:127
"Appeal to the Authorities" (Dazai Osamu) **41**:238-39, 244-45
"Appearance and Reality" (Maugham) **8**:380
"An Appearance of Life" (Aldiss) **36**:11
"Appearances" (O'Hara) **15**:290
"The Apple" (Wells) **6**:359, 383
"The Apple Tree" (Bowen) **3**:33, 41
"The Apple Tree" (du Maurier) **18**:137-38
"The Apple Tree" (Galsworthy) **22**:61, 75-6, 80, 84, 86-8, 90, 94-7, 99-102

"The Apple Tree" (Mansfield) **9**:282, 284; **38**:204
The Apple Tree: A Short Novel and Some Stories (du Maurier) **18**:126, 130, 137
"Apples" (Campbell) **19**:71, 75
"Apples and Pears" (Davenport) **16**:185-89
Apples and Pears, and Other Stories (Davenport) **16**:183-89, 199-200
"The Apple-Tree Table" (Melville) **1**:294-95, 298
"An Application for a Film Grant" (Moorhouse) **40**:323
"An Appointment with the General" (Greene) **29**:216, 223, 226-27
"The Apprentice" (Bambara) **35**:15, 26, 28-9, 38-41
"Apprentice" (Warner) **23**:368
"The Approach to al Mu'tasim" (Borges)
    See "El acercamiento a Almotásim"
"The Approach to Almotasim" (Borges)
    See "El acercamiento a Almotásim"
"April 2000: The Third Expedition" (Bradbury) **29**:50, 68-75
"April 2026: The Long Years" (Bradbury) **29**:69
"April Fish" (Gallant) **5**:151
"April in Paris" (Le Guin) **12**:232
"April is the Cruelest Month" (Cabrera Infante)
    See "Abril es el mes más cruel"
"April, Late April" (Wolfe) **33**:401
"The April Witch" (Bradbury) **29**:47
"Àpropos of the Kreutzer Sonata" (Leskov) **34**:119
"Apropos of the Wet Snow" (Dostoevsky) **2**:169, 187
Apt Pupil (King) **17**:262-66, 271, 273
"Apuntes de un rencoroso" (Arreola) **38**:5
"Aquarius" (Thomas) **20**:287, 317-19
"The Aquatic Uncle" (Calvino)
    See "Lo zio acquatico"
Aquis Submersus (Storm) **27**:281, 284, 286-87, 289, 291-96, 302-03, 308-14
"Arabesque: The Mouse" (Coppard) **21**:15, 17, 26
Arabesques (Gogol) **4**:104; **29**:142
"Araby" (Joyce) **3**:202-03, 205, 208, 217-18, 225, 231, 234, 237, 242, 245-46, 249; **26**:46-7, 50, 73, 79, 83
Arap Petra Velikogo (Pushkin) **27**:129, 148, 162-63, 165, 178, 182, 186, 188
"Ararat" (Henderson) **29**:316, 326
"The Arbiter" (Auchincloss) **22**:35, 39, 45
"El árbol" (Bombal) **37**:9, 23, 26-27, 30, 33, 36-39, 44
Arcadian Adventures with the Idle Rich (Leacock) **39**:257, 262, 263, 265, 271, 273
"Arcadian London" (Dickens) **17**:123
"Archangel" (Updike) **13**:390, 397
"The Archduchess" (du Maurier) **18**:127
Arctic Summer, and Other Fiction (Forster) **27**:115
"Ardagh" (Le Fanu)
    See "The Fortunes of Sir Robert Ardagh"
"Ardessa" (Cather) **2**:99, 110-11
"Ardid de guerra" (Pardo Bazan) **30**:272
"Are These Actual Miles?" (Carver) **8**:47
"Are You a Doctor?" (Carver) **8**:9-10, 18, 32, 34, 47
"Arena" (Pardo Bazan) **30**:261
"Argamak" (Babel) **16**:27-8, 52, 56
"The Argentine Ant" (Calvino)
    See *La formica Argentina*
"Argo and his Master" (Svevo)
    See "Argo e il suo padrone"
"Argo e il suo padrone" (Svevo) **25**:329, 331-32, 336
"Argon" (Levi) **12**:255-57, 259, 264
"The Argonauts" (Pavese) **19**:369
"The Argonauts of North Liberty" (Harte) **8**:214, 216-17, 223
"The Argonauts of the Air" (Wells) **6**:359, 367, 374, 380, 383, 388, 403

"The Argument" (Dixon) **16**:211
"Aria Marcella, Souvenir de Pompei" (Gautier) **20**:3, 5-8, 16-20, 35
"Ariadna" (Chekhov)
    See "Ariadne"
"Ariadne" (Chekhov) **2**:131-32, 157; **28**:60
"Ariel. A Legend of the Lighthouse" (Alcott) **27**:58
"The Aristocrat" (Pritchett) **14**:270, 293, 296
Armance; ou, Quelques scènes d'un salon de Paris en 1827 (Stendhal) **27**:232, 252-55, 258, 264-71
"Armande" (Colette) **10**:274-75, 293
Die arme Baronin (Keller) **26**:92-3, 102-04, 110
Der Arme Spielmann (Grillparzer) **37**:84-191
"Der Arme Wohltäter" (Stifter) **28**:284, 288
"The Armenian & the Armenian" (Saroyan) **21**:133
"Army of Occupation" (Boyle) **5**:64, 74-5
"Around the Bend in Eighty Days" (Perelman) **32**:229
Around the Day in Eighty Worlds (Cortazar)
    See *La vuelta al día en ochenta mundos*
"Around the Dear Ruin" (Berriault) **30**:96-7
"Around the World Fliers" (Williams) **31**:334
"Arrangement in Black and White" (Parker) **2**:274-75, 278, 280, 283, 286
"Arrangements" (Dixon) **16**:216
"The Arrest of Lieutenant Golightly" (Kipling) **5**:288, 290
En arrière (Ayme) **41**:22
"The Arrow of Heaven" (Chesterton) **1**:128
Arrowroot (Tanizaki)
    See *Yoshinokuzu*
"Arrowroot Leaves in Yoshino" (Tanizaki) **21**:192
"Arsène Guillot" (Merimee) **7**:279, 290-2, 300
"Art and Mr. Mahoney" (McCullers) **9**:332, 343, 345-46, 354, 359
"Eine Art Erzahlung" (Walser) **20**:345
"The Art of Book-Making" (Irving) **2**:254
"The Art of Courtly Love" (Garrett) **30**:164
"The Art of Living" (Gardner) **7**:224-28, 235, 240
The Art of Living, and Other Stories (Gardner) **7**:223-28, 235
"Artemis, the Honest Well-Digger" (Cheever) **1**:107-08; **38**:46
"Arthur Jermyn" (Lovecraft) **3**:258, 264
"Arthur Smith salva sin alma" (Castellanos) **39**:49, 57
"Arthur Smith Saves His Soul" (Castellanos)
    See "Arthur Smith salva sin alma"
"Arthur Snatchfold" (Forster) **27**:90, 94, 96, 102-07, 123
"Artificial Flowers" (Capek)
    See "Falešné květiny"
"The Artificial Nigger" (O'Connor) **1**:343, 345, 347, 353; **23**:185, 206, 236-37
An Artificial Nigger (O'Connor)
    See *A Good Man Is Hard to Find and Other Stories*
"Artificial Roses" (Garcia Marquez) **8**:185
"The Artist" (Galsworthy) **22**:99
"The Artist at Work" (Camus)
    See "Jonas ou l'artiste au travail"
"The Artist of the Beautiful" (Hawthorne) **3**:169-71, 174, 183-84; **39**:121
"Un Artista" (Svevo) **25**:353
"The Artistic Career of Corky" (Wodehouse) **2**:342
"The Artistic Personality" (Auchincloss) **22**:40-1
"The Artist's Child" (Gissing) **37**:72, 75
"An Artist's Story" (Chekhov) **2**:131, 139, 157; **28**:62-3
"The Artist's Turn" (Narayan) **25**:140
"The Artless Age" (Glasgow) **34**:65-6, 71, 76, 78, 81, 102-03

"The Artus Exchange" (Hoffmann)
    See "Der Artushof"
"Der Artushof" (Hoffmann) **13**:183, 223
"Arvie Aspinall's Alarm Clock" (Lawson) **18**:201, 238, 241
"As academias de Sião" (Machado de Assis) **24**:128-30
"As águas do mundo" (Lispector) **34**:231, 233-34
"As Breathing and Consciousness Return" (Solzhenitsyn)
    See "Dykhanie"
"As Far as Abashiri" (Shiga)
    See "Abashiri made"
"As in the Good Old Days" (Capek) **36**:115
As Sad as She Is (Onetti)
    See *Tan triste como ella*
"As Strong as a Man" (Suckow)
    See "A Great Mollie"
"Ascension" (Thomas) **20**:324-25, 327-28
"El asesino" (Arreola) **38**:9, 21
"Ash" (Campbell) **19**:74
"Ash-Cake Hannah and Her Ben" (Dunbar) **8**:122
"The Ashen Moon" (Shiga)
    See "Hai-iro no tsuki"
Ashenden; or, The British Agent (Maugham) **8**:365, 367, 376-78, 380, 383
"Ashes of Descending Incense, First Brazier" (Chang) **28**:29, 32, 35-36
"Ashes of Descending Incense, Second Brazier" (Chang) **28**:32, 35
"Ashikari" (Tanizaki) **21**:182-83, 185, 188-89, 191, 195
"The Ash-Tree" (James) **16**:225, 229-30, 232, 234-36, 240-41, 251, 253, 256
Así en la paz como en la guerra (Cabrera Infante) **39**:7, 9, 10, 12, 17-19, 21-24
"Así y todo" (Pardo Bazan) **30**:264, 266
"Asigh" (Lavin) **4**:167-68, 181-83
"Aska and the Wolf" (Andric)
    See "Aska i vuk"
"Aska i vuk" (Andric) **36**:35, 38, 43, 73
"The Aspern Papers" (Bellow) **14**:25
The Aspern Papers (James) **8**:275, 300, 321-22, 324, 332, 335
"Asphodel" (Welty) **1**:467-69, 472
An Aspidistra in Babylon: Four Novellas (Bates) **10**:122
"Aspirin Is a Member of the NRA" (Saroyan) **21**:132, 136, 142, 166
"The Assassination of John Fitzgerald Kennedy Considered as a Downhill Motor Race" (Ballard) **1**:70-1, 75
L'assassinio di via Belpoggio (Svevo) **25**:357, 362
"Assault" (Oates) **6**:243
"The Assembly" (Borges)
    See *El congreso*
"The Assembly" (Gallant) **5**:147
Assembly (O'Hara) **15**:251, 252, 261, 279, 280-81, 287
"The Assessor of Success" (Henry) **5**:187
Assez (Beckett) **16**:71, 76-8, 83, 87, 95-9, 122, 135
"The Assignation" (Poe) **1**:394; **22**:304-07
"The Assistant" (O'Hara) **15**:279, 285
"The Assistant Producer" (Nabokov) **11**:113, 128
"The Associated Un-Charities" (Norris) **28**:214
"Assommons les pauvres" (Baudelaire) **18**:34, 47, 49-53
"Assumption" (Beckett) **16**:72
"The Assyrian" (Saroyan) **21**:155, 157
The Assyrian, and Other Stories (Saroyan) **21**:155
"Astley's" (Dickens) **17**:134
"An Astrologer's Day" (Narayan) **25**:132, 138, 140, 152-53, 155, 160-61, 169
An Astrologer's Day and Other Stories (Narayan) **25**:132-33, 135, 137, 139, 152, 154-55

"The Astronomer" (Updike) **13**:389

Asya (Turgenev) **7**:320, 323-24, 326-27, 334, 337, 339, 347-52, 360

"At a Dinner of Atheists" (Barbey d'Aurevilly)
See "A un dîner d' athées"

"At Age Forty-Seven" (Zoshchenko) **15**:407

"At Chênière Caminada" (Chopin) **8**:95, 99, 110

"At Christmas-Time" (Chekhov) **2**:130-31

"At Dawn" (Rulfo)
See "En la madrugada"

"At Daybreak" (Calvino) **3**:109

"At Daybreak" (Rulfo)
See "En la madrugada"

"At Evening, a Geranium" (Pirandello)
See "Di sera, un geranio"

"At First Sight" (Adams) **24**:10

"At First Sight" (Campbell) **19**:62, 73

"At First Sight" (de la Mare) **14**:71, 74, 89

"At Geisenheimer's" (Wodehouse) **2**:355

"At Hemdat's" (Agnon) **30**:68

"At Home" (Chekhov) **2**:139, 142, 155, 157-58

"At Kinosaki" (Shiga)
See "Kinosaki nite"

"At Laban's Well" (Coppard) **21**:19

"At Lehmann's" (Mansfield) **23**:137

"At One O'Clock in the Morning" (Baudelaire)
See "A une heure du matin"

"At Paso Rojo" (Bowles) **3**:59, 61-2, 66, 79

"At Sallygap" (Lavin) **4**:169, 171-72, 175, 178-79, 182

"At Shaft 11" (Dunbar) **8**:120-21, 127, 129, 131, 136, 139-40, 143

"At Sundown" (Saroyan) **21**:161

"At Teague Poteet's: A Sketch of the Hog Mountain Range" (Harris) **19**:131, 174-75, 179, 181

"At the Barber's" (Zoshchenko) **15**:407-08

"At the Bay" (Mansfield) **9**:278, 280, 282-83, 286, 288-92, 300, 302, 305-07, 309; **23**:139-41, 143, 153-54, 158-59; **38**:204, 229

"At the Beach" (Adams) **24**:11

"At the Bedside of a Dying Man" (Peretz)
See "At the Bedside of a Dying Man"

"At the 'Cadian Ball" (Chopin) **8**:72, 91, 95, 99, 106-07

"At the Castle" (Capek) **36**:82, 93, 124-25

"At the Doctors" (Andric)
See "Kod lekara"

"At the Drug Store" (Taylor) **10**:398-400, 418

"At the Edge of the World" (Leskov)
See "Na kraju sveta"

"At the End of the Mechanical Age" (Barthelme) **2**:47

"At the End of the Passage" (Kipling) **5**:264, 271-72, 274, 278, 280-81, 290-91

"At the Front" (Williams) **31**:305

"At the Gate" (Pirandello)
See "All uscita"

"At the Krungthep Plaza" (Bowles) **3**:80

"At the Landing" (Welty) **1**:468

"At the Mouse Circus" (Ellison) **14**:115

"At the Outset of the Day" (Agnon) **30**:4

"At the Portal" (Narayan) **25**:134-35, 154

"At the Prophet's" (Mann) **5**:323

"At the Rainbow's End" (London) **4**:286

"At the Rendezvous of Victory" (Gordimer) **17**:171

"At the Salt Marsh" (Gorky) **28**:158

"At the Seminary" (Oates) **6**:255-56

"At the Sign of the Savage" (Howells) **36**:397

"At the Start of the Day" (Solzhenitsyn) **32**:395

"At the Tolstoy Museum" (Barthelme) **2**:31, 35, 40, 48, 56

"At the Turn of the Road: An Irish Girl's Love Story" (Moore) **19**:345

At the University (Storm)
See *Auf der Universitat*

"At Third Hand: a Psychological Inquiry" (Howells) **36**:387

"Athénaïse" (Chopin) **8**:66, 72-3, 78, 86, 96, 99, 113-14

"Athene, Goddess of the Brave" (Auchincloss) **22**:52

"Atomo verde número cinco" (Donoso) **34**:8-11, 17, 33

"The Atrocity Exhibition" (Ballard) **1**:75

The Atrocity Exhibition (Ballard) **1**:70-1, 76-8, 80-3

"Atrophy" (Wharton) **6**:424

"Attack" (O'Connor) **5**:371, 391

"An Attack of Nerves" (Chekhov) **2**:153, 155-56; **41**:199

"An Attack on Lenin" (Zoshchenko) **15**:407

"Attalie Brouillard" (Cable) **4**:59

"The Attila" (Narayan) **25**:140-41, 154

"Attitude" (Lewis) **40**:281

"Attracta" (Trevor) **21**:235, 247, 262

"Attractive Modern Homes" (Bowen) **3**:54

"Au clair de la lune" (Ayme) **41**:10

"Au large" (Cable) **4**:58-9

"Au Seabhac" (O'Flaherty) **6**:286-89

"Au tombeau de Charles Fourier" (Davenport) **16**:168-69, 175, 177, 191, 193

"L'auberge" (Maupassant) **1**:265

L'auberge rouge (Balzac) **5**:18, 31, 33

"An Auction" (Crane) **7**:108, 110

Auf dem Staatshof (Storm) **27**:282, 286

"Auf der Galerie" (Kafka) **29**:343

Auf der Universitat (Storm) **27**:282, 286

Der Aufruhr in den Cevennen (Tieck) **31**:273, 275-76, 283, 287-88

"Auguiano Religious Articles Rosaries Statues" (Cisneros) **32**:38

"August" (Schulz) **13**:330-31, 339

"August Afternoon" (Caldwell) **19**:25-7, 32, 39, 46

August Holiday (Pavese)
See *Feria d'agosto*

"August Holiday Fun" (Moravia)
See "August Holiday Fun"

"Augustus" (Hesse) **9**:234

"Aunt Cora" (Wilson) **21**:358, 363

"Aunt Fountain's Prisoner" (Harris) **19**:124, 173, 178

"Aunt Gertrude" (Pritchett) **14**:263, 271

Aunt Jo's Scrap-Bag (Alcott) **27**:7-12, 22, 42-3, 50, 57

Aunt Jo's Scrap-Bag: My Boys (Alcott) **27**:42

"Aunt Juley's Courtship" (Galsworthy) **22**:70

"Aunt Lucy's Search" (Chesnutt) **7**:13

"Aunt Lympy's Interference" (Chopin) **8**:84

"Aunt Mandy's Investment" (Dunbar) **8**:121, 127, 137, 143, 147

"Aunt Mathilde's Drawings" (Wilson) **21**:358-59

"Aunt Mimy's Son" (Chesnutt) **7**:28

"Aunt Tempy's Revenge" (Dunbar) **8**:122

"Aunt Tempy's Triumph" (Dunbar) **8**:122

"Auntie Bissel" (Suckow) **18**:413, 422, 424

"The Aunt's Story" (White) **39**:288-89

"Auprès d'un mort" (Maupassant) **1**:281

Aura (Fuentes) **24**:29, 33-8, 43-51, 58-62

Aurélia (Nerval) **18**:334-37, 355, 361-62, 366-68, 373-81, 383-84

"The Aurelian" (Nabokov) **11**:130

"Aurora" (Morand) **22**:156-57, 165

Aus dem Leben eines bekannten Mannes (Hoffmann) **13**:187, 189

"The Author of Beltraffio" (James) **8**:300, 304-05, 345, 350

"The Author of the Acacia Seeds and Other Extracts from the 'Journal of the Association of Therolinguistics'" (Le Guin) **12**:230, 235

"The Author's Chamber" (Irving) **2**:265

"An Author's Confession" (Gogol) **4**:83

"Author's Outline of 'The Mute'" (McCullers) **9**:343

"Autobiografija" (Andric) **36**:50, 69-73

"The Autobiography" (Andric)
See "Autobiografija"

"Autobiography" (Atwood) **2**:15

"An Autobiography" (Gallant) **5**:133

"Autobiography: A Self-Recorded Fiction" (Barth) **10**:41-2, 46, 53-4, 60, 64, 72, 76-9, 80, 84, 91 97-8

"Autobiography of an Omnibus" (Alcott) **27**:43

"Ha'Autobus ha'Aharon" (Agnon) **30**:22, 37, 54

"L'automa" (Moravia) **26**:142, 146-47, 152, 155, 164-65, 182

L'automa (Moravia) **26**:141-42, 146, 148-49, 152-53, 155, 161-62, 164, 180, 182

"Die Automate" (Hoffmann) **13**:209, 213-14, 219

"The Automaton" (Moravia)
See "The Automaton"

"The Automobile That Wouldn't Run" (Caldwell) **19**:25, 39, 42, 47

"La autopista del sur" (Cortazar) **7**:54-5, 61

"Autre étude de femme" (Balzac) **5**:32-3, 35-6, 39

"Autres temps" (Wharton) **6**:424-26, 436

"Autrui" (Arreola) **38**:3, 7, 23, 25-28

"Autumn I" (Mansfield) **9**:284

"Autumn II" (Mansfield)
See "The Wind Blows"

"Autumn Loneliness" (Boell) **23**:38

"Autumn Sunshine" (Trevor) **21**:247, 262

"Gli avangnardisti a Mentone" (Calvino) **3**:97

"L'avaro" (Moravia) **26**:163

"Avec la bebe-sitter" (Updike) **13**:385

"L'aventure de Walter Schnafs" (Maupassant) **1**:263

"Äventyret" (Lagerkvist) **12**:181, 191

"Avenue Junot" (Ayme) **41**:17

"Averroes's Search" (Borges)
See "La busca de Averroes"

"L'aveu" (Maupassant) **1**:263, 274

"Avey" (Toomer) **1**:441, 443-45, 451, 453, 458-59

"The Aviator" (Walser) **20**:364

"Avremi Bass" (Peretz) **26**:202

"L'avvenire dei ricordi" (Svevo) **25**:360

"An Awakening" (Anderson) **1**:34, 44-5

"Awakening" (Babel) **16**:36, 41-2, 59

"The Awakening" (Clarke) **3**:143, 148

"Awakening" (Pavese) **19**:375

"The Awakening of Rollo Podmarsh" (Wodehouse) **2**:344

"The Awful Fate of Mr. Wolf" (Harris) **19**:172

"The Awful Gladness of the Mate" (Wodehouse) **2**:356

"Awful When You Think of it" (Greene) **29**:201

"The Awful Woman with the Spectacles" (Leacock) **39**:266

"The Axe" (Narayan) **25**:154

"Axolotl" (Cortazar) **7**:58, 63-4, 66-7, 70-5, 81

"Azalia" (Harris) **19**:124, 131, 149, 179

"Azathoth" (Lovecraft) **3**:273

"Azélie" (Chopin) **8**:110

"Azraël" (Villiers de l'Isle Adam)
See "L'annonciateur"

"Baa, Baa, Black Sheep" (Kipling) **5**:277-78, 283, 293

"Las babas del diablo" (Cortazar) **7**:54, 65-6, 68-9, 86

The Babe's Bed (Wescott) **35**:372-76

"Babes in the Woods" (Henry) **5**:193

"The Babes in the Woods" (O'Connor) **5**:380

"Babette's Feast" (Dinesen) **7**:166, 195

"The Babies in the Bush" (Lawson) **18**:220

"Baby" (Campbell) **19**:87

"The Baby" (Moravia) **26**:139, 150

"Baby" (Saroyan) **21**:159-60

"Baby H. P." (Arreola) **38**:5, 8, 12, 22, 30

"A Baby in the Siege" (Harris) **19**:182

Baby, It's Cold Inside (Perelman) **32**:212, 226-27, 229, 236, 245

"Baby Mike" (Farrell) **28**:96

"The Baby Party" (Fitzgerald) **6**:46, 94-5

"A Baby Tramp" (Bierce) **9**:87

"The Babylon Lottery" (Borges)
See "La lotería en Babilonia"

"The Babylon Lottery" (Borges)
   See "La lotería en Babilonia"
"The Babylon Night" (Morand)
   See "La nuit de Babylone"
"Babylon Revisited" (Fitzgerald) **6**:47, 51, 53,
   60, 63-4, 72, 74, 76, 81, 85-6, 99-100, 104;
   31:1-38
"Baby's Breath" (Bambara) **35**:42
"The Baby's Christmas" (Harris) **19**:182
"The Baby's Fortune" (Harris) **19**:182
"The Babysitter" (Coover) **15**:30, 38, 40, 48,
   50-1
"The Bachelor" (Stifter)
   See "Der Hagestolz"
"The Bachelor's Supper" (Aiken) **9**:6, 13
"Bachmann" (Nabokov) **11**:124
"Back before Day" (Price) **22**:379-81
"The Back Drawing-Room" (Bowen) **3**:40, 54
"Back for Christmas" (Collier) **19**:108-10, 112
"Back from Java" (Aldiss) **36**:14
"The Back of Beyond" (Maugham) **8**:375
"Back to the Bush" (Leacock) **39**:364
"Back to the Sea" (Moravia)
   See "Back to the Sea"
"The Background" (Saki) **12**:311
"The Backslider" (Fisher) **25**:17-20, 22, 25, 27
"Backwards" (Ayme) **41**:5
"Backwater" (Aldiss) **36**:26-7
"The Backwater" (Turgenev) **7**:320, 335
"Bad Characters" (Stafford) **26**:279, 281, 286,
   310
Bad Characters (Stafford) **26**:279-80
"Bad Company" (de la Mare) **14**:80, 88, 90
"A Bad Day" (Nabokov) **11**:132-33
"Bad Dreams" (Taylor) **10**:379-80, 384, 389,
   393
"The Bad Glazier" (Baudelaire)
   See "Le mauvais vitrier"
Bad Saint Vitalis (Keller)
   See *Bad Saint Vitalis*
"The Bag" (Saki) **12**:315
"The Bag of Gold" (Howells) **36**:399
"Bagombo Snuff Box" (Vonnegut) **8**:433, 437
"The Bagpipes of Spring" (Benet) **10**:150
"Der Bahnhof von Zimpren" (Boell) **23**:6
Bahnwärter Thiel (Hauptmann) **37**:196-201,
   207-8, 213-18, 220-24, 226-29, 231, 241-
   44, 252-53, 257-62
"Bai guang" (Lu Hsun) **20**:136
"The Bailbondsman" (Elkin) **12**:93, 95, 106-07,
   110, 112, 114, 116
Le baiser au lépreux (Mauriac) **24**:159-60, 162,
   179-80, 182, 206
"Bait" (Campbell) **19**:75
"Bajron u Sintri" (Andric) **36**:50
Bakante bilder (Peretz) **26**:218, 223
"The Baker's Dozen" (Saki) **12**:328
"The Baker's Story" (Naipaul) **38**:300, 323,
   328, 346-47
"Le bal de sceaux" (Balzac) **5**:4, 29
"Balaam" (Harris) **19**:131
Balaam and His Ass (Harris) **19**:49
"Balaam and His Master" (Harris) **19**:149, 182
*Balaam and His Master, and Other Sketches
   and Stories* (Harris) **19**:146-47, 149,
   180-82
"Balada o Juraji Čupovi" (Capek) **36**:99, 128
"The Balance" (Waugh) **41**:322, 326-28, 338-
   39, 352, 360
"Balance His, Swing Yours" (Stegner) **27**:197,
   202
"The Balcony" (Irving) **2**:266
"The Balek Scales" (Boell)
   See "Die Waage der Baleks"
"De balística" (Arreola) **38**:4, 8, 10, 12, 21, 23
"Ball der Wohltäter" (Lenz) **33**:317, 321-24,
   326-27
"Ball of Fat" (Pardo Bazan) **30**:291
"Ballad" (Arreola) **38**:13
"A Ballad" (Bunin)
   See "Ballada"
"A Ballad" (McGahern) **17**:315, 317

"The Ballad of Juraj Čup" (Capek)
   See "Balada o Juraji Čupovi"
The Ballad of the Sad Café (McCullers) **9**:322-
   26, 329, 331-32, 334-35, 338, 341-42, 344-
   46, 350, 353, 355, 358; **24**:231-86
*The Ballad of the Sad Cafe: The Novels and
   Stories of Carson McCullers* (McCullers)
   9:332; **24**:21
"Ballada" (Bunin) **5**:115
"Ballet for Opening Day" (Algren) **33**:96
"The Ballet Girl" (Coppard) **21**:11, 29
"The Ballet of Central Park" (Boyle) **5**:66
"The Ballet of the Nations" (Lee) **33**:307
"The Balloon" (Barthelme) **2**:31, 33, 36, 42
"The Balloon Hoax" (Poe) **1**:406
"The Ballroom" (Sansom) **21**:87, 126
"The Ballroom of Romance" (Trevor) **21**:253,
   260, 265, 270-71, 273
The Ballroom of Romance, and Other Stories
   (Trevor) **21**:232, 235-37, 261
"Baltasar Gérard" (1555-1582Arreola) **38**:9, 13
"Balthazar's Marvelous Afternoon" (Garcia
   Marquez)
   See "La prodigiosa tarde de Baltazar"
"The Baluchiterium" (Updike) **13**:348, 360
"Bananafish" (Salinger)
   See "Bananafish"
"Bandits" (Aleichem) **33**:51-2
"Bandy Callaghan's Girl" (Norris) **28**:201, 207
"Bang-Bang You're Dead" (Spark) **10**:353, 356-
   60, 364-65, 367, 370
"Bank Holiday" (McGahern) **17**:306, 311, 317-
   18, 321
"Bankruptcy" (Dazai Osamu) **41**:229, 233
"The Banks of the Jordan" (Trollope)
   See "A Ride across Palestine"
Bannen (Dazai Osamu) **41**:241, 246, 271
The Banner of the Upright Seven (Keller)
   See *The Banner of the Upright Seven*
"Banquet in Honor" (Hughes) **6**:122
"The Banquet of Crow" (Parker) **2**:280, 285
"Un baptême" (Maupassant) **1**:256, 259, 284
"Baptizing" (Munro) **3**:331, 339-40
"Bar Titanic" (Andric)
   See "Bife titanik"
"Bara no Yūrei" (Kawabata) **17**:242
Barabbas (Lagerkvist) **12**:178-8, 183, 185, 187,
   189, 193-4, 197-203
"Barbados" (Marshall) **3**:299-300, 302-04, 306-
   08, 316-17
"Barbara of the House of Grebe" (Hardy) **2**:204,
   209, 214-15, 221
"The Barbarian Woman" (Walser) **20**:348
"The Barbecue" (Dixon) **16**:206, 211
"The Barber" (Bates) **10**:112
"The Barber Whose Uncle Had His Head
   Bitten Off by a Circus Tiger" (Saroyan)
   21:133
"Barbie-Q" (Cisneros) **32**:8
"A Barefaced Lie" (West) **16**:402-03
"The Barefoot Saint" (Benet) **10**:145, 153
"Barker's Luck" (Harte) **8**:222, 244
"Barn Burning" (Faulkner) **1**:163, 165
"Barnby Robinson" (Warner) **23**:372
"Barney Take Me Home Again" (Lawson)
   18:211
"Baron Dorn" (Andric) **36**:65
The Baron in the Trees (Calvino)
   See *Il barone rampante*
Il barone rampante (Calvino) **3**:89-91, 93-5,
   99, 117-18
"Barrack Room Fiddle Tune" (Ross) **24**:307,
   311, 323-24
"The Barrel" (Maupassant) **1**:269
"The Barricade" (Hemingway) **1**:208
"The Barrow" (Le Guin) **12**:210, 213, 216, 218,
   247-48
"Bartleby, the Scrivener: A Story of
   Wall-Street" (Melville) **1**:293, 295, 297-
   98, 303-04, 311, 317, 322-23, 325, 328,
   331; **17**:326-92

"Baryshnia-krest'ianka" (Pushkin) **27**:129, 141-
   43, 166, 168, 171, 186
"Bás na Bó" (O'Flaherty) **6**:287-88
"Basement" (Bambara) **35**:22-3, 34
"The Basement" (Lagerkvist) **12**:179, 182,
   196-7
"The Basement Room" (Greene) **29**:182, 185-
   86, 192-93, 199, 213-14, 216-17, 220
The Basement Room and Other Stories
   (Greene) **29**:213
"Basil and Cleopatra" (Fitzgerald) **6**:50
"Basilisk" (Ellison) **14**:102-05
"Básník" (Capek) **36**:98, 102, 121, 127
"The Basque and Bijou" (Nin) **10**:326
"Bastille Day" (Berriault) **30**:98
"Batard" (London) **4**:288-89
"The Bath" (Carver) **8**:15, 19-24, 26-7, 30, 39,
   56-60
"The Bathroom Dance" (Jolley) **19**:234
"The Battle Ax" (Leskov)
   See "Voitel' nica"
"Battle Keaton Dies" (Stuart) **31**:225, 230-31,
   234, 251
"The Battle of Sempach" (Walser) **20**:356-59
"Battle with the Bees" (Stuart) **31**:265
"Battleground" (King) **17**:261
"The Battler" (Hemingway) **1**:242, 244-45, 247;
   40:166, 209, 221, 249, 251
"Der bau" (Kafka) **5**:206, 209, 241
"Baum Gabriel, 1935 -'" (Gallant) **5**:137-38
"Bavarian Gentians" (Lawrence) **4**:233
"Baxter's Procrustes" (Chesnutt) **7**:15
"Bay City Blues" (Chandler) **23**:59, 65, 67-8,
   72, 82-3, 88, 109
"HaBayit" (Agnon) **30**:22-3, 26, 34
Bayou Folk (Chopin) **8**:65-8, 72, 77, 84, 88-9,
   93, 97, 103-08, 110-11, 114
"The Beach" (Cowan) **28**:76; 80
"The Beach Murders" (Ballard) **1**:72-4
"The Beach of Falesá" (Stevenson) **11**:269, 279,
   283-84, 286-87, 296, 299
"The Beach Party" (Grau) **15**:148, 160
"The Beam" (Grimm and Grimm) **36**:200
"The Bear" (Faulkner) **1**:148, 152-58, 167, 172-
   74, 182; **35**:135-214
"A Bear Hunt" (Faulkner) **1**:177
"The Beard" (Singer) **3**:375
"The Bear-Hunt" (Tolstoy) **9**:387
"Bearskin" (Grimm and Grimm) **36**:228
*The Beast in Me, and Other Animals: A New
   Collection of Pieces and Drawings about
   Human Beings and Less Alarming
   Creatures* (Thurber) **1**:425
"The Beast in the Jungle" (James) **8**:302, 307-
   09, 320, 326, 338-40, 342, 347
"The Beast That Etcetera" (Ellison)
   See "The Beast That Shouted Love at the
   Heart of the World"
"The Beast That Shouted Love at the Heart of
   the World" (Ellison) **14**:106-07, 115, 117
Beasts and Super-Beasts (Saki) **12**:288, 291,
   294-96, 307-09, 313-14, 323, 329, 332
"Beat Me" (Perelman) **32**:202
Beatrice (Schnitzler)
   See *Frau Beate und ihr Sohn*
"Beatrice Trueblood's Story" (Stafford) **26**:284,
   299
"Beau Séjour" (Lewis) **34**:159, 167, 177
"The Beauties" (Chekhov) **2**:156
"Beautiful and Cruel" (Cisneros) **32**:6, 32
"A Beautiful Child" (Capote) **2**:81
"Beautiful Girl" (Adams) **24**:3-4, 6, 13
Beautiful Girl (Adams) **24**:2-3, 13, 15
"A Beautiful nature" (Frame) **29**:110
"The Beautiful Stranger" (Jackson) **9**:272
"The Beautiful Suit" (Wells) **6**:361-62, 376,
   391
"Beauty" (Greene) **29**:200-01, 230
"Beauty" (O'Flaherty) **6**:262, 285
"Beauty and Beast" (Sansom) **21**:86, 88
"Beauty Spots" (Kipling) **5**:280
"Beca" (Andric) **36**:32

"La beca" (Unamuno) **11**:312
"Because of the Dollars" (Conrad) **9**:152
Bech: A Book (Updike) **13**:356, 366-68, 379-82
"Bech Enters Heaven" (Updike) **13**:380, 383
"Bech in Rumania" (Updike) **13**:380
"Bech Panics" (Updike) **13**:380-81
"Bech Swings?" (Updike) **13**:380
"Bech Takes Pot Luck" (Updike) **13**:380
"Becker and the Boys from the Band" (Moorhouse) **40**:301
"Becker on the Moon" (Moorhouse) **40**:290, 301
"The Becker Wives" (Lavin) **4**:166-67, 184-90, 192
"The Beckoning Fair One" (Campbell) **19**:83
"Becky" (Toomer) **1**:445, 456-58
"The Bedfordshire Clanger" (Bates) **10**:117
"The Bedjacket" (Frame) **29**:108
Bedtime Stories (Dazai Osamu)
    See *Otogi zōshi*
"Bedtime Story" (Campbell) **19**:76, 78
Beer and Cold Cuts (Williams) **31**:333
"The Bees" (Zoshchenko) **15**:407-08
Beffe della morte e della vita (Pirandello) **22**:275
"Before Breakfast" (Cather) **2**:93-4
"Before Eden" (Clarke) **3**:127
"Before the Deluge" (Rhys) **21**:56
"Before the Grand Jury" (Stuart) **31**:226
"Before the Law" (Kafka)
    See "Vor dem gesetz"
"Before the Low Green Door" (Garland) **18**:148, 154, 160, 182-83, 185
"Before the Party" (Maugham) **8**:359, 362, 366-67, 372
"Before the Storm" (Campbell) **19**:72, 90
"Before the War" (Atwood) **2**:16
"The Beggar and the Diamond" (King) **17**:295
The Beggar Maid: Stories of Flo and Rose (Munro)
    See *Who Do You Think You Are?*
"The Beggars" (O'Flaherty) **6**:276-78
"The Beggars" (Pavese) **19**:386
"Beggar-Student" (Dazai Osamu) **41**:232
"Begger Woman of Locarno" (Kleist)
    See "Das Bettelweib von Locarno"
"The Beginning" (Grau) **15**:162
A Beginning, and Other Stories (de la Mare) **14**:79, 85, 89, 92
"The Beginning of an Idea" (McGahern) **17**:307, 323
"The Beginning of Something" (Dixon) **16**:207, 214
"Beginnings" (Coover) **15**:45-6
"Behind a Mask: Or, A Woman's Power" (Alcott) **27**:4-5, 12-17, 28, 31, 50, 57, 61-2
Behind a Mask: The Unknown Thrillers of Louisa May Alcott (Alcott) **27**:35, 61
Behind the Beyond (Leacock) **39**:262, 266
"Behind the Scenes at a Whist Game" (Barbey d'Aurevilly)
    See "Le dessous de cartes d'une partie de whist"
"Behind the Shade" (Morrison) **40**:328, 337, 367
"Behind the Singer Tower" (Cather) **2**:99, 103-04, 111
"Behind the Times" (Doyle) **12**:89
"Behold the Incredible Revenge of the Shifted P.O.V." (Lish) **18**:280
"Behold the Key" (Malamud) **15**:169, 181, 222
"The Beige Dolorosa" (Harrison) **19**:216-17
Beim Bau der Chinesischen Mauer (Kafka) **5**:206
Beim Vetter Christian (Storm) **27**:280, 282
"Being an Angel" (Campbell) **19**:77-8
"Being Kind to Titina" (White) **39**:280-281, 284, 286, 289, 291-93, 295, 317, 325, 344
"Being Moral" (Michaels) **16**:311
Ein Bekenntnis (Storm) **27**:279, 282, 307
"Bel Colore" (Galsworthy) **22**:58

"Un bel gioco dura poco" (Calvino) **3**:97
A bela e a fera (Lispector) **34**:229, 233, 235
"Belaja lošad'" (Bunin) **5**:98
"The Belated Travellers" (Irving) **2**:262
A Beleaguered City: Tale of the Seen and Unseen (Oliphant) **25**:179-82, 186, 193, 197, 199, 201-5, 207-08
"Belize" (Gilchrist) **14**:157-58
Belkin Tales (Pushkin)
    See *Povesti Belkina*
"The Bell" (Andersen) **6**:6-8, 15, 30, 33
"The Bell" (de la Mare)
    See "Out of the Deep"
"The Bell Remembered" (Wolfe) **33**:399
"La bella durmiente" (Ferre) **36**:135-37, 150, 156, 161-62, 169-70, 173
"Bella Fleace" (Waugh)
    See "Bella Fleace Gave a Party"
"Bella Fleace Gave a Party" (Waugh) **41**:311, 323, 325, 328, 330, 340
"The Bella Lingua" (Cheever) **1**:93, 106, 112; **38**:53
"Bella vista" (Colette) **10**:274
La bella vita (Moravia)
The Bellarosa Connection (Bellow) **14**:50, 56, 58-61
"La Belle Bayadère" (Alcott) **27**:44
"La belle Dorothée" (Baudelaire) **18**:3-7
"A Belle of St. Valerien" (Harris) **19**:183
"La Belle Zoraïde" (Chopin) **8**:71, 87, 90-1, 106
"Bellerophoniad" (Barth) **10**:44, 49-52, 54, 56, 61, 64-9, 91-3, 101-02
"Belles Demoiselles Plantation" (Cable) **4**:48, 53, 62-4, 66-7, 73-4
"The Bellin' of the Bride" (Stuart) **31**:231
"The Bell-Ringer of Angels" (Harte) **8**:214, 248-49
"The Bell-Tower" (Melville) **1**:298, 303
"The Belobrysov Story" (Bulgakov) **18**:91
"Below the Mill Dam" (Kipling) **5**:268, 283
"The Belt" (Moravia) **26**:172
"La belva" (Pavese) **19**:366, 388
"Ben sete 'arim" (Agnon) **30**:53-5, 66
"The Bench" (Dixon) **16**:207-08, 212-13
"The Bench" (Jolley) **19**:221
"The Bench of Desolation" (James) **8**:277, 304
"Beneath the Cards of a Game of Whist" (Barbey d'Aurevilly)
    See "Le dessous de cartes d'une partie de whist"
"Beneath the Willow-Tree" (Andersen) **6**:30
"Benediction" (Fitzgerald) **6**:45, 57-8
"Bénéfices de Guerre" (Morand) **22**:159
"The Benefit of the Doubt" (London) **4**:291
"Benefit Performance for Lord Cuzon" (Bulgakov)
    See "Lord Curzon's Benefit Day"
"The Benefits of American Life" (Farrell) **28**:100
"Benighted" (de la Mare) **14**:90
"Benito Cereno" (Melville) **1**:293, 295-300, 303-04, 310-12, 320-23, 328, 330; **17**:328, 338, 361
"The Bênitou's Slave" (Chopin) **8**:89
"Benjamin Button" (Fitzgerald)
    See "The Curious Case of Benjamin Button"
Benya Krik the Gangster, and Other Stories (Babel) **16**:14
"An Beo" (O'Flaherty) **6**:286-88
"Ber-Bulu" (Hammett) **17**:222
Berecche and the War (Pirandello)
    See *Berecche e la guerra*
Berecche e la guerra (Pirandello) **22**:231, 275
"Berenice" (Poe) **1**:396, 398; **22**:291, 329, 334
"Berestechko" (Babel) **16**:9, 27-8, 31, 52, 55-7
"Bergkristall" (Stifter) **28**:298
Bergkristall (Stifter) **28**:272
"Bergmilch" (Stifter)
"Die Bergwerke zu Falun" (Hoffmann) **13**:205, 209-11, 218, 220, 252, 255, 257

"Ein Beriht für eine Akademie" (Kafka) **5**:215-16, 220, 231; **29**:332, 345, 369-70; **35**:264
"Berkeley House" (Adams) **24**:15
Die Berlocken (Keller) **26**:103-04, 110
"Bernadette" (Gallant) **5**:122, 125, 139
"Bernice Bobs Her Hair" (Fitzgerald) **6**:58, 96
"Berry" (Hughes) **6**:121, 142
"The Berry Patch" (Stegner) **27**:197, 227
"Bertie Changes His Mind" (Wodehouse) **2**:356
"Bertram and Bini" (Kipling) **5**:274
"The Beryl Coronet" (Doyle) **12**:52, 58, 66, 71-3
"Der beschriebene Tännling" (Stifter) **28**:299
"Beside the River" (Boell) **23**:38
"Bess" (Phillips) **16**:336, 338-39
"Bess Waters" (Price) **22**:385
"Bessy's Troubles at Home" (Gaskell) **25**:58
"The Best and Worst People and Things of 1938" (Saroyan) **21**:163
"The Best China Saucer" (Jewett) **6**:166
Best Ghost Stories of J. S. Le Fanu (Le Fanu) **14**:237
Best of Aldiss (Aldiss) **36**:18
The Best of Arthur C. Clarke: 1937-1971 (Clarke) **3**:149
The Best of H. E. Bates (Bates)
    See *Seven by Five: Stories 1926-61*
The Best of John Collier (Collier) **19**:109
The Best of S. J. Perelman (Perelman) **32**:220
The Best of Saki (Saki) **12**:320
The Best of Simple (Hughes) **6**:137
The Best of the Lot (Suckow) **18**:400-01, 403
Best Science Fiction Stories of Brian W. Aldiss (Aldiss)
    See *But Who Can Replace a Man?*
The Best Short Stories of J. G. Ballard (Ballard) **1**:74
"The Best Years" (Cather) **2**:93-4, 105
"Bestiario" (Cortazar) **7**:57-8, 77-8
Bestiario (Arreola) **38**:36
Bestiario (Cortazar) **7**:50-1, 53-4, 69-70
"The Bestiary" (Arreola) **38**:12-13
Bestiary (Arreola)
    See *Bestiario*
Bestiary (Cortazar)
    See *Bestiario*
"Bestre" (Lewis) **34**:160, 167, 176, 178
"Best-Seller" (Henry) **5**:159
"The Bet" (Chekhov) **2**:130
"La bête à Maître Belhomme" (Maupassant) **1**:259, 273, 281
"The Betrayer of Israel" (Singer) **3**:383
Die Betrogene (Mann) **5**:313-16, 324-26, 340-42
"The Betrotal" (Ayme) **41**:26
"The Betrothed" (Chekhov) **2**:131, 139, 143, 149, 151
Betrothed (Agnon) **30**:5, 12-13, 15, 34, 37, 75-7, 79-80
"Das Bettelweib von Locarno" (Kleist) **22**:115, 117, 137, 142, 146
"Better Morphosis" (Aldiss) **36**:28
"Better Than to Burn" (Lispector)
    See "Melhor do que order"
"Better Think Twice about It, and Twelve Other Stories" (Pirandello) **22**:226, 228-29, 272
"Betty" (Atwood) **2**:14, 22
"Between Men" (Lessing) **6**:197, 200, 207
Between the Dark and the Daylight (Howells) **36**:357, 360-61, 365, 382, 400
"Between the Devil and the Deep Sea" (Kipling) **5**:268
"Between Two Cities" (Agnon)
    See "Ben sete 'arim"
"Between Two Cliffs" (Peretz)
    See "Between Two Cliffs"
"Between Two Kisses" (Capek) **36**:87
"Between Two Mountains" (Peretz)
    See "Between Two Mountains"
"Between Two Shores" (Glasgow) **34**:59, 64, 77, 80, 99

"Between Zero and One" (Gallant) **5**:134, 144
"Bewitched" (Wharton) **6**:422, 427
"A Bewitched Place" (Bulgakov) **18**:89
"A Bewitched Place" (Gogol)
　　See "Zakoldovannoe mesto"
"The Bewitched Spot" (Gogol)
　　See "Zakoldovannoe mesto"
"The Bewitched Tailor" (Aleichem)
　　See "Der farkishefter shnayder"
"Beyond" (Faulkner) **1**:162
"Beyond the Bayou" (Chopin) **8**:89, 104
"Beyond the End" (Barnes)
　　See "Spillway"
"Beyond the Glass Mountain" (Stegner) **27**:195, 197
"Beyond the Pale" (Kipling) **5**:261-62, 273
"Beyond the Pale" (Trevor) **21**:247-48, 262, 269
Beyond the Pale, and Other Stories (Trevor) **21**:262
"Beyond the Wall of Sleep" (Lovecraft) **3**:258, 268
"Beyond Words" (Campbell) **19**:77, 87
"Bezhin Meadow" (Turgenev)
　　See "Byezhin Prairie"
"Bezlyub'e" (Pasternak) **31**:117
Bianche e nere (Pirandello) **22**:231, 275
"La biblioteca de Babel" (Borges) **4**:6-7, 18, 29; **41**:61, 64, 69, 76-79, 137, 152, 158, 166
"La Bicha" (Pardo Bazan) **30**:266
"A Bicycle Gymkhana" (Norris) **28**:214
"Bicycles, Muscles, Cigarettes" (Carver) **8**:10, 20, 42
"Bidan" (Galsworthy) **22**:101
"Bien Pretty" (Cisneros) **32**:10, 16, 34, 38-9
"Los bienes ajenos" (Arreola) **38**:11
"Les bienfaits de la lune" (Baudelaire) **18**:4
"The Bienfilâtre Sisters" (Villiers de l'Isle Adam)
　　See "Les demoiselles de Bienfilâtre"
"Bienvenido, Bob" (Onetti) **23**:246, 249-50, 252
"Bife titanik" (Andric) **36**:37, 46, 74, 77
"Big Bertha Stories" (Mason) **4**:2
"The Big Black and White Game" (Bradbury) **29**:42
"Big Black Good Man" (Wright) **2**:364
"Big Blonde" (Parker) **2**:273-74, 276, 278-81, 284
"Big Boy Leaves Home" (Wright) **2**:360-61, 363, 365, 367-69, 371-76, 379-81, 386-90
"The Big Broadcast of 1938" (Barthelme) **2**:26
"Big Buck" (Caldwell) **19**:17
"Big Claus and Little Claus" (Andersen)
　　See "Little Claus and Big Claus"
"Big Fiddle" (Boyle) **5**:66-8
"Big Game" (Boyle) **16**:156-57
"The Big Game" (Coppard) **21**:11
"Big Game Hunt" (Clarke) **3**:133-34
"The Big Garage" (Boyle) **16**:140-42
"Big Kids and Little Kids" (Suckow) **18**:393
"The Big Knockover" (Hammett) **17**:200-1, 215, 219, 224, 230
The Big Knockover: Selected Stories and Short Novels (Hammett) **17**:201-4, 212
"Big Mama's Funeral" (Garcia Marquez)
　　See "Los funerales de la Mamá Grande"
Big Mama's Funeral (Garcia Marquez)
　　See *Los funerales de la Mamá Grande*
"Big Meeting" (Hughes) **6**:119, 122, 132-33
"The Big Outside World" (Beattie) **11**:25
"The Big Stick" (Sansom) **21**:84
"Big Swallow and Little Swallow" (Pirandello)
　　See "Rondone e rondinella"
"The Big Town" (Lardner) **32**:118, 131
The Big Town: How I and the Mrs. Go to New York to See Life and Get Katie a Husband (Lardner) **32**:127, 141, 148-49, 152-56

"Big Two-Hearted River" (Hemingway) **1**:208, 214, 220, 231, 234, 240, 243-48; **40**:155, 168, 209, 214, 250
"Big Wheels: A Tale of the Laundry Game" (King) **17**:275
"The Bigot" (Page) **23**:307
"Les bijoux" (Maupassant) **1**:273, 286, 288
"The Bill" (Malamud) **15**:169, 175, 202, 222-23
"The Bill" (Moravia) **26**:141
"Bill" (Powers) **4**:375, 381-82
"Bill Sprockett's Land" (Jolley) **19**:233
"Bill the Ventriloquial Rooster" (Lawson) **18**:206, 218, 263
"Billenium" (Ballard) **1**:68-9, 75
"Billy and the Gargoyles" (Auchincloss) **22**:3, 33, 48, 53
Billy Budd, Sailor: An Inside Narrative (Melville) **1**:294-303, 305-16, 318, 321, 329
Bing (Beckett) **16**:76-85, 122
"Biografía de Tadeo Isidoro Cruz" (Borges) **4**:9; **41**:59
"Biography of Tadeo Isidoro Cruz" (Borges)
　　See "Biografía de Tadeo Isidoro Cruz"
"Bird" (Hesse) **9**:244
A Bird in the House (Laurence) **7**:246-49, 251, 253-60, 262-64, 266-72
"A Bird of Bagdad" (Henry) **5**:196
"Bird of Prey" (Collier) **19**:109, 111
"The Bird of Travel" (de la Mare) **14**:66, 67, 80, 85, 90
"The Birds" (du Maurier) **18**:125-26, 130, 137-38
"Birds" (Schulz)
　　See "Ptaki"
"The Birds and the Foxes" (Thurber) **1**:426, 431
"The birds began to sing" (Frame) **29**:110
"Birds on the Western Front" (Saki) **12**:314
"Birth" (Nin) **10**:299-305
"Birth" (O'Flaherty) **6**:262
"The Birth of a Man" (Gorky) **28**:137, 139, 147
"A Birthday" (Mansfield) **9**:281, 284, 302-03; **23**:139
"The Birthday Gift" (Narayan) **25**:142
"The Birthday of the Infanta" (Wilde) **11**:364-65, 372, 374, 376, 382-83, 394-97, 399, 407-09
"The Birthmark" (Agnon) **30**:3
"The Birthmark" (Ellison) **26**:8, 21, 26-7, 29
"The Birthmark" (Hawthorne) **3**:159, 168-70, 178, 183-84, 189, 191-94; **39**:91
"The Bisara of Pooree" (Kipling) **5**:262, 265
"The Bishop" (Chekhov) **2**:131, 148-49, 157-58
"The Bishop of Borglum" (Andersen) **6**:18
"The Bishop's Beggar" (Benet) **10**:156
"The Bishop's Feast" (Rhys) **21**:55
"The Bishop's Fool" (Lewis) **34**:157
"The Bishop's Robe" (Singer) **3**:374
"A Bit of Advice" (Aleichem)
　　See "An eytse"
"A Bit of Shore Life" (Jewett) **6**:166
"A Bit of Young Life" (Gordimer) **17**:153, 168
"A Bit off the Map" (Wilson) **21**:321, 323, 339, 365
A Bit off the Map (Wilson) **21**:320, 328, 336-38, 357, 362
"The Biter Bit" (Sansom) **21**:116-17
"Bitter Honeymoon" (Moravia) **26**:138-39, 142
Bitter Honeymoon, and Other Stories (Moravia)
　　See *Bitter Honeymoon, and Other Stories*
"Bitter Sorrow for Three Sleepwalkers" (Garcia Marquez)
　　See "Amargura para tres sonámbulos"
"Bitterness for Three Sleepwalkers" (Garcia Marquez)
　　See "Amargura para tres sonámbulos"

"Blacamán el bueno vendedor de milagros" (Garcia Marquez)
　　See "Blacamán the Good, Vendor of Miracles"
"Blacamán the Good, Vendor of Miracles" (Garcia Marquez) **8**:167-69, 186
"The Black Bird's Mate" (O'Flaherty) **6**:280
"Black Boy" (Boyle) **5**:56
"Black Bread" (Verga) **21**:298
"The Black Cat" (Poe) **1**:389-90, 406, 408; **34**:241-42, 244, 274; **35**:298, 307-11, 313-15, 320, 343, 345-46
"Black Death" (Hurston) **4**:142
"The Black Dog" (Coppard) **21**:3
The Black Dog (Coppard) **21**:3, 8, 15, 19
"Black Ephram" (Garland) **18**:154
"The Black Ferris" (Bradbury) **29**:63
"The Black Friar" (Chekhov)
　　See "The Black Monk"
"The Black Godmother" (Galsworthy) **22**:75
"Black Horses" (Pirandello) **22**:229
"Black Is My Favorite Color" (Malamud) **15**:173-74, 207-09
"A Black Jack Bargainer" (Henry) **5**:162, 170
"Black Joe" (Lawson) **18**:202
"The Black Madonna" (Lessing) **6**:189, 193, 196-97, 212, 214
"The Black Madonna" (Spark) **10**:350-52, 355, 359, 361, 366, 368
Black Magic (Morand)
　　See *Magie noire*
"The Black Magic of Barney Haller" (Thurber) **1**:415
"The Black Mare" (O'Flaherty) **6**:264, 281
"The Black Mate" (Conrad) **9**:179
"The Black Monk" (Chekhov) **2**:126, 131-32, 143, 147-48; **28**:60; **41**:199-200
"The Black Prince" (Grau) **15**:147, 150, 156, 151, 164
The Black Prince, and Other Stories (Grau) **15**:148-52, 154, 156, 160, 164
"The Black Rabbit" (O'Flaherty) **6**:274, 281
"The Black Sheep" (Boell)
　　See "Die schwarzen schafe"
"Black Sheep No. Five: Clarence" (Dreiser) **30**:151
"Black Sheep No. Four: Ethelda" (Dreiser) **30**:151
"Black Sheep No. One: Johnny" (Dreiser) **30**:151
"Black Sheep No. Six: Harrison Barr" (Dreiser) **30**:151
"Black Sheep No. Three: Bill" (Dreiser) **30**:151
"Black Sheep No. Two: Otie" (Dreiser) **30**:151
"Black Shylock" (Auchincloss) **22**:13-14
"The Black Swan" (Mann)
　　See *Die Betrogene*
"Black Tickets" (Phillips) **16**:325, 327-28
Black Tickets (Phillips) **16**:325, 327-31, 333-34, 336-37, 339
"The Black Tsar" (Morand)
　　See "Le tsar noir"
"The Black Veil" (Dickens) **17**:117, 121, 125-26
"Black Venus" (Carter) **13**:17-20, 32-35
Black Venus (Carter) **13**:13-15, 17-18
"The Black Wedding" (Singer) **3**:359, 375-76
Black Wine (Campbell) **19**:83, 87
The Blackamoor of Peter the Great (Pushkin)
　　See *Povesti Belkina*
"Blackberry Winter" (Warren) **4**:387-94, 396-99, 401-04
"The Blackbird" (O'Flaherty) **6**:268, 280
"Blackbird Pie" (Carver) **8**:51
"Blacked Out" (Campbell) **19**:73
"Blackmail" (Galsworthy) **22**:79, 101
"Blackmailers Don't Shoot" (Chandler) **23**:56-8, 66, 68, 78, 80, 84-6, 91, 96, 102, 106
"Blades of Steel" (Fisher) **25**:5-6, 14-20, 22-3, 25-6
Blandings Castle (Wodehouse) **2**:346-47, 353
"The Blank Page" (Dinesen) **7**:200

"The Blast of the Book" (Chesterton) 1:131
"The Blazing Fire" (Capek)
    See "Živý plamen"
Le blé en herbe (Colette) 10:262
"The Bleeding Heart" (Stafford) 26:274, 276-77, 281, 283, 312
"Bless Me, Father" (Dubus) 15:83
"Bless Me, Father, For I Have Sinned" (Bradbury) 29:87
"Blessed Assurance" (Hughes) 6:123-24
"A Blessed Deceit" (Dunbar) 8:122
"The Blessed Man of Boston, My Grandmother's Thimble, and Fanning Island" (Updike) 13:400
"The Blessing" (Powers) 4:368-70, 373
"Blessings" (Dubus) 15:85
"Blessings of Railway" (Narayan) 25:137-38, 140
"The Blind" (Pavese) 19:365
"Blind Dog" (Narayan) 25:138, 140, 154, 169
"Blind Frank" (Steinbeck) 11:203
"Blind Geronimo and His Brother" (Schnitzler)
    See "Der blinde Geronimo und sein Bruder"
"Blind Girls" (Phillips) 16:328
"Blind Lightning" (Ellison) 14:113-15, 117
"Blind Love" (Pritchett) 14:259, 261, 266, 268, 280-81, 285-86, 289
Blind Love, and Other Stories (Pritchett) 14:255, 267
"The Blind Man" (Chopin) 8:100
"The Blind Man" (Lawrence) 4:231, 233-36, 242-46
"A Blind Man's Tale" (Tanizaki)
    See "Mōmoku monogatari"
"Blind Tom" (Davis) 38:117-19, 133-34, 137-39
"Der blinde Geronimo und sein Bruder" (Schnitzler) 15:343, 345, 377
"Blinder" (Gordimer) 17:171, 194
"Blindfold" (Oates) 6:231
"The Blinding of One-Eyed Bogan" (Lawson) 18:242
"Bliss" (Mansfield) 9:276, 279-80, 295, 297, 299, 301, 305-07, 309-11, 314; 23:164
Bliss, and Other Stories (Mansfield) 9:279, 281; 23:139; 38:203
"The Blizzard" (Pushkin)
    See "Metel"
"The Blizzard" (Singer) 3:374
"The Blockade" (Chang) 28:25; 28; 34
"The Blond Beast" (Wharton) 6:435
Der blonde Eckbert (Tieck) 31:271, 276-79, 281, 292-93, 296
"Blood" (Singer) 3:356, 358, 364, 375
"Blood Lust" (O'Flaherty) 6:261, 269, 277, 283
"The Blood of the Martyrs" (Benet) 10:142, 152, 154, 156
"Blood of the Walsungs" (Mann)
    See *Wälsungenblut*
"Blood, Sea" (Calvino)
    See "Il sangue, il mare"
"Blood-Burning Moon" (Toomer) 1:443, 445, 450, 452-53, 458
"Bloodfall" (Boyle) 16:141-42, 144, 151
"The Blood-Feud of Toad-Water" (Saki) 12:328
"Bloodshed" (Ozick) 15:302, 304, 306, 317
Bloodshed and Three Novellas (Ozick) 15:302, 304-06, 308-10, 315, 317-18, 323, 326, 333
"Bloodstain" (Stegner) 27:214
"Blood-Swollen Landscape" (Oates) 6:250
"The Bloody Chamber" (Carter) 13:5-9, 11-12, 17, 23, 26-28, 30
The Bloody Chamber, and Other Stories (Carter) 13:5-8, 17, 23, 27-8, 30
"The Bloomsbury Christening" (Dickens) 17:110-11, 116, 120, 136
"The Blow" (O'Flaherty) 6:260, 282, 287
"Blow-Up" (Cortazar)
    See "Las babas del diablo"
"Blue and Green" (Woolf) 7:374-75, 398
"The Blue Background" (Aldiss) 36:20, 22
"Blue Boy" (Caldwell) 19:9, 38

"The Blue Cart" (Naipaul) 38:318
"The Blue Chrysanthemum" (Capek)
    See "Modrá chryzantéma"
"The Blue Cross" (Chesterton) 1:119, 123, 133, 135, 138
"Blue Dave" (Harris) 19:131, 146-47, 151, 176
"The Blue Hotel" (Crane) 7:104-06, 108-16, 127, 129, 142-43, 145, 151-52, 154-55
"Blue Island" (Powers) 4:368, 372
"The Blue Lenses" (du Maurier) 18:127-28
"Blue Life" (Gorky)
    See "The Sky-blue Life"
"The Blue Light" (Grimm and Grimm) 36:228-29
"The Blue Moccasins" (Lawrence) 4:220
"Blue Moon" (Phillips) 16:335-36, 338
"The Blue Room" (Merimee)
    See "La chambre bleue"
"Blue Spanish Eyes" (Thomas) 20:323, 325, 328
"The Blue Woman" (Donoso) 34:21
"Bluebeard's Egg" (Atwood) 2:17, 21
Bluebeard's Egg (Atwood) 2:17-18, 20-2
"The Blue-Eyed Buddhist" (Gilchrist) 14:158
"Bluegill" (Phillips) 16:335-38
"Bluejay Yarn" (Twain) 6:310; 34:308
"The Blues I'm Playing" (Hughes) 6:121-22, 129, 134-36
"The Blue-Winged Teal" (Stegner) 27:195, 198, 201-04
"Blumfeld, an Elderly Bachelor" (Kafka) 5:243-44
"Bluzdajuscije ogon'ki" (Leskov) 34:108
"La boa" (Arreola) 38:11
"Le Boa" (Duras) 40:3, 6-7, 9, 65, 133-35
"The Boa" (Duras)
    See "Le Boa"
"The Boarding House" (Dickens) 17:110, 113, 117, 120
"The Boarding House" (Joyce) 3:201, 205-07, 234, 237, 247-48; 26:46-7, 50
"The Boar-Pig" (Saki) 12:295, 307, 320, 325
"Boat Animals" (Aldiss) 36:14, 20
"Boat Trip" (Walser) 20:354, 363-66
"Boaz the Teacher" (Aleichem) 33:19
"Bobbio's Ave Maria" (Pirandello) 22:255
Bödeln (Lagerkvist) 12:177, 180, 182, 185, 193, 197
"Bodies in the Moonlight" (Hughes) 6:117-18, 127
"Bodily Secrets" (Trevor) 21:246-47
"The body" (Lispector)
    See "O corpo"
The Body (King) 17:263-64, 267, 272, 276-78, 280, 284-85
"The Body Beautiful" (Perelman) 32:204
"The Body-Snatcher" (Stevenson) 11:269-70, 282, 296, 306
The Bodysnatcher (Onetti)
    See "Just a Little One"
"Le Boeufs" (Ayme) 41:6
"The Bog King's Daughter" (Andersen)
    See "The Marsh King's Daughter"
"The Bogey Man" (Coppard) 21:7, 9
"Bogg of Geebung" (Lawson) 18:248, 250
"The Bogus Policeman" (Ayme) 41:5
Boh (Moravia) 26:180
"The Bohemian Girl" (Cather) 2:96-7, 101, 103-05, 108
"Boiled Alive" (Campbell) 19:70-1
"The Boiler Room" (Sansom) 21:82, 86, 99
"Boitelle" (Maupassant) 1:263
"Les Boîtes de peinture" (Ayme) 41:8, 14-15
"Le Bol de punch" (Gautier) 20:5, 10-11, 22
"A Bold Deserter" (Harris) 19:182
"The Bold Dragoon" (Irving) 2:256
"Boles" (Gorky) 28:160, 190
"The Bomb Shop" (O'Faolain) 13:314
"Bombard" (Maupassant) 1:263
"Bombolo" (Pirandello) 22:241
"Bon Voyage" (Benet) 10:149

"Bona and Paul" (Toomer) 1:444, 446, 450, 452-54, 458-62
"Bonaventure" (Gallant) 5:144
Bonaventure: A Prose Pastoral of Acadian Louisiana (Cable) 4:48, 50-1, 53, 58-60, 62, 73, 75
"The Bond" (Singer) 3:385, 387
"Bone Bubbles" (Barthelme) 2:31
"The Bone Setter" (Le Fanu)
    See "The Ghost and the Bone Setter"
"The Bonefires" (Pavese) 19:369
"Bones of Contention" (O'Connor) 5:371, 377
Bones of Contention, and Other Stories (O'Connor) 5:364, 371, 377, 380, 382
"The Bonfire" (O'Hara) 15:283
"The Bonfire" (Sansom) 21:118-20
"Le bonheur dans le crime" (Barbey d'Aurevilly) 17:6-8, 11, 13-16, 19-20, 26, 44
"Bonn Diary" (Boell)
    See "Hauptstädtisches Journal"
"La Bonne Peinture" (Ayme) 41:5, 17-18, 32
"Les bons chiens" (Baudelaire) 18:39
"Bontche Schweig" (Peretz)
    See "Bontche Schweig"
"Bontsie Silent" (Peretz)
    See "Bontsie Silent"
"Bontsye Shvayg" (Peretz) 26:194, 197, 201-2, 207, 209, 220
"Bonvalpaša" (Andric) 36:65, 67
"The Bonzo's Secret" (Machado de Assis)
    See "O segrêdo do bonzo"
"The Book" (Schulz)
    See "Ksiega"
A Book (Barnes) 3:3-4, 14, 22, 26
The Book Class (Auchincloss) 22:29-30, 33, 47, 50-1
The Book of Brian Aldiss (Aldiss)
    See *The Comic Inferno*
The Book of Deeds (Agnon)
    See *Sefer ha-Maasim*
Book of Fables (Agnon)
    See *Sefer ha-Maasim*
"Book of Harlem" (Hurston) 4:155
The Book of Sand (Borges) 41:131, 133-34, 157, 160, 162, 167
The Book of the American Indian (Garland) 18:146, 177-79, 186-88
"The Book of the Dead" (Kawabata)
    See "Shisha no Sho"
"The Book of the Grotesque" (Anderson) 1:57
The Book of the State (Agnon) 30:68
Book That Doesn't Bite (Valenzuela)
    See *Libro que no muerde*
"The Book-Bag" (Maugham) 8:357, 360-61, 375, 378
"The Bookkeeper's Wife" (Cather) 2:99, 110
"The Bookshop" (Huxley) 39:153-54, 161
"Boom" (Norris) 28:213
Boom Town (Wolfe) 33:347, 375
"Boors Carousing" (Warner) 23:370
"The Boots of Buffalo Leather" (Grimm and Grimm) 36:228-29
"A Border Incident" (Cheever) 38:43
"The Border Line" (Lawrence) 4:219, 238
"A Border-Line Case" (du Maurier) 18:129, 135
"Borealis" (Morand) 22:181
"Boredom" (Gorky) 28:145-46, 160
"Borges and I" (Borges)
    See "Borges y yo"
"Borges y yo" (Borges) 41:46, 148, 151, 157, 164, 167
"Born Bad" (Cisneros) 32:6, 43
"A Born Farmer" (Jewett) 6:156, 158
"A Born Genius" (O'Faolain) 13:283-84, 309, 312, 314
"The Boscombe Valley Mystery" (Doyle) 12:66, 68-71, 73-4
"The Boss" (Gorky)
    See "Khoziain"
Bötjer Basch (Storm) 27:286

"Die Botschaft" (Boell) **23**:5
"Le Bottes de sept Lieues" (Ayme) **41**:10
"The Bottle" (Zoshchenko) **15**:404
"The Bottle Imp" (Stevenson) **11**:268-69, 283, 296, 298
"A Bottle of Milk for Mother" (Algren) **33**:87, 90-3, 100, 104-05, 109
"A Bottle of Perrier" (Wharton) **6**:423-24
"Bottle Party" (Collier) **19**:98, 103-04, 112
"Bottomless Hell" (Dazai Osamu) **41**:257
"The Bottomless Well" (Chesterton) **1**:122
Bought and Sold (Moravia)
    See *Bought and Sold*
"Boule de suif" (Maupassant) **1**:255-57, 259, 263, 266, 269, 271-76, 281-83, 286-88, 290
"Boulôt and Boulotte" (Chopin) **8**:88, 102-03
"The Bouquet" (Chesnutt) **7**:3, 16, 22-3, 29-30, 33, 36
"La bourse" (Balzac) **5**:29
"Bow Down, Isaac" (Aiken) **9**:7, 13, 42
"The Bowl" (de la Mare) **14**:87
"The Bowmen" (Machen) **20**:155, 157, 163, 166, 200
The Bowmen and Other Legends of the War (Machen) **20**:196
"The Bowmen of Shu" (Davenport) **16**:184-85, 187-88
"A Box of Ginger" (Calisher) **15**:5, 15, 17
"Box Seat" (Toomer) **1**:440, 443, 445-48, 450-53, 458
"A Box to Hide In" (Thurber) **1**:414, 417
"Los Boxers" (Cisneros) **32**:35
"Boxes" (Carver) **8**:43
A Boy and His Dog (Ellison) **14**:99-100, 115, 117, 124, 128-29, 138, 140-41
"The Boy and the Bayonet" (Dunbar) **8**:122, 147
"A Boy Asks a Question of a Lady" (Barnes) **3**:10-11
"Boy in Rome" (Cheever) **1**:100; **38**:53, 62
"The Boy Knows the Truth" (Singer) **3**:380
"The Boy Prodigy" (Tanizaki)
    See "Shindō"
A Boy Suffers (Meyer)
    See *Das Leiden eines Knaben*
"The Boy Who Hated Girls" (Vonnegut) **8**:431
"Boyhood" (Farrell) **28**:120
Boyhood (Tolstoy)
    See *Otrochestvo*
"Boys and Girls" (Farrell) **28**:110
"Boys and Girls" (Munro) **3**:321, 343-44
"Boys! Raise Giant Mushrooms in Your Cellar!" (Bradbury) **29**:58, 62
"A Boy's Town" (Howells) **36**:398
"A Boy's Will" (Frame) **29**:97-8
Boži muka (Capek) **36**:81, 88-9, 91-2, 96-7, 109-10, 121-26, 130
Bracebridge Hall (Irving) **2**:240, 244-46, 251, 254-55, 258-59, 265
"Braids" (Aquina) **37**:44
"Brain Damage" (Barthelme) **2**:32-3, 39-40, 42, 47, 55
"Brainsy" (O'Faolain) **13**:291, 312
"A Branch of the Service" (Greene) **29**:223, 230
"A Branch Road" (Garland) **18**:143, 150, 154-56, 159, 168-70, 172, 175-76, 192-93
"A Brand-New Approach" (Bioy Casares) **17**:75
"The Brandon House and the Lighthouse" (Jewett) **6**:154, 167
"Braska Comes Through" (Stuart) **31**:248
"Die Brautwahl" (Hoffmann) **13**:186
"The Brave Little Tailor" (Grimm and Grimm) **36**:229-30
"The Bravest Boat" (Lowry) **31**:43-4, 46, 48, 51-4, 59, 61-2, 71-5, 81, 84, 86-7
"Brazil" (Marshall) **3**:299, 300, 302-04, 306, 317
"A Breach of Promise" (Narayan) **25**:133, 135, 160, 162
"Bread" (Atwood) **2**:19-20
"Bread Alone" (O'Hara) **15**:248-49

"Bread Alone" (O'Hara) **15**:248-49
"Bread from Stones" (Garrett) **30**:166, 180
"Bread in Uzok" (Caldwell) **19**:41
"The Bread of Charity" (Turgenev) **7**:318
The Bread of Those Early Years (Boell)
    See *Das Brot der frühen Jahre*
"Bread, Sugar, and Milk" (Moorhouse) **40**:289, 292
The Break of Day (Colette)
    See *La naissance du jour*
"Breakfast" (Bowen) **3**:54; **28**:4
"Breakfast" (Cortazar)
    See "Desayuno"
"Breakfast" (Farrell) **28**:125
"Breakfast" (Steinbeck) **11**:225-26, 233-34, 238-39, 241
Breakfast at Tiffany's (Capote) **2**:67-76, 78-9, 81
"The Break-In" (Adams) **24**:11
The Breaking Point (du Maurier) **18**:127-28, 130, 132
"Breaking Strain" (Clarke) **3**:144, 150
"Breaking the Ice" (Thomas) **20**:320, 322, 325
"Breaking the News" (Boell)
    See "Die Botschaft"
"Breaking the News" (Nabokov) **11**:117
"The Breaking Up of the Winships" (Thurber) **1**:419, 435
"The Breakthrough" (du Maurier) **18**:129
"A Breath" (Pirandello)
    See "Soffio"
"Breath" (Price) **22**:386
"Breath from the Sky" (McCullers) **9**:342, 345, 354-55
"A Breath of Lucifer" (Narayan) **25**:139
"Breathing" (Solzhenitsyn)
    See "Dykhanie"
The Breathing Method (King) **17**:265-67, 272-73, 280
"Bred in the Bone" (Page) **23**:307
"The Breech" (Hammett) **17**:217
"Breeders" (Thomas) **20**:324, 327
"The Bremen Town Musicians" (Grimm and Grimm) **36**:208
"Brethren" (Bunin) **5**:80-2, 87-8, 93-7, 106, 115
"A Breton Innkeeper" (Lewis) **34**:164, 166, 177
"A Breton Journal" (Lewis) **34**:176-77
A Brian Aldiss Omnibus (Aldiss) **36**:18
"The Bridal Night" (O'Connor) **5**:363-64, 371, 377, 380, 383, 390, 395, 398
"The Bridal Party" (Fitzgerald) **6**:48, 61
"Bridal Sheets" (Lavin) **4**:165, 167, 180-81
"The Bride Comes to Yellow Sky" (Crane) **7**:104-05, 108-09, 116-17, 126-27, 149, 151
"The Bride of Christ" (Farrell) **28**:94, 118
"The Bride of Christ" (Gordimer) **17**:157
The Bride of Innisfallen (Welty) **1**:476, 479, 484, 495
"The Bridegroom" (Gordimer) **17**:154
"The Bridegroom's Body" (Boyle) **5**:58-63, 66, 68
"The Bridge" (Dixon) **16**:216
"The Bridge of Dreams" (Tanizaki)
    See "Yume no ukihashi"
"The Bridge on the Žepa" (Andric)
    See "Most na Žepi"
"The Bridge-Builders" (Kipling) **5**:267, 283, 294
"Bridges" (Andric)
    See "Mostovi"
Brief Candles (Huxley) **39**:171-74, 176
"The Brief Cure of Aunt Fanny" (Dunbar) **8**:122, 149
"The Brief Début of Tildy" (Henry) **5**:171
"The Brigade Commander" (Babel) **16**:26, 29, 50
"The Brigadier" (Turgenev)
    See "Brigadir"
"The Brigadier and the Golf Widow" (Cheever) **38**:50, 61, 68

The Brigadier and the Golf Widow (Cheever) **1**:94-5, 100; **38**:44, 63, 66
"Brigadir" (Turgenev) **7**:316, 320-21, 324, 337, 358
"The Brigands" (Villiers de l'Isle Adam)
    See "Les brigands"
"Les brigands" (Villiers de l'Isle Adam) **14**:381, 395-96
"Briggita" (Stifter) **28**:276, 290, 298-99, 301-03
"Bright and Morning Star" (Wright) **2**:363, 368, 373, 375, 377, 379-83, 387-88, 391-92
"The Bright Boy" (Machen) **20**:163, 198
"The Bright Day" (Grau) **15**:159
"The Bright Side" (Galsworthy) **22**:63, 78, 101
"The Bright Sun Will Bring It to Light" (Grimm and Grimm) **36**:229-30
"A Bright Sunday in Madison" (Narayan) **25**:135
"Brighten's Sister-in-Law" (Lawson) **18**:202-03, 229-30, 232, 241, 262
"Brigid" (Lavin) **4**:167
"The Brilliant Leaves" (Gordon) **15**:104, 108-09, 116, 139, 142
"Brillo" (Ellison) **14**:123
"Bring, Bring" (Aiken) **9**:12-13, 40
Bring! Bring! (Aiken) **9**:3, 5, 6, 28
"British Guiana" (Marshall) **3**:299-300, 302, 305, 317
"A briv tsu a gutn fraynd" (Aleichem) **33**:43
"Broadcast" (Campbell) **19**:87
"A Broadsheet Ballad" (Coppard) **21**:29
Brodie (Borges)
    See *El informe de Brodie*
Brodie's Report (Borges)
    See *El informe de Brodie*
"The Broken Boot" (Galsworthy) **22**:74, 78, 101
"Broken Field Running" (Bambara) **35**:15, 26, 28-30, 39-41
"The Broken Giraffe" (O'Hara) **15**:286
"The Broken Heart" (Irving) **2**:243, 245
"Broken Homes" (Trevor) **21**:234, 262
"The Broken Pot" (Narayan) **25**:137-38, 141
"Broken Sword" (Chesterton)
    See "The Sign of the Broken Sword"
"The Broken Wheel" (Saroyan) **21**:133-34
"Broken Wings" (James) **8**:304, 306
"A Broken World" (O'Faolain) **13**:283-84, 287, 293, 298, 300, 302, 306, 309, 316-17
"Brokers' and Marine-Store Shops" (Dickens) **17**:133
"The Bronze Door" (Chandler) **23**:64, 110-11
"Bronze Leaves and Red" (Davenport) **16**:198
"The Brooch" (Faulkner) **1**:165
"The Brood" (Campbell) **19**:71, 75
"Brooklyn" (Marshall) **3**:300, 302, 304-05, 307-08, 314-17
"Brooksmith" (James) **8**:304, 306
"Broomsticks" (de la Mare) **14**:68, 69, 87
Broomsticks, and Other Tales (de la Mare) **14**:82, 86
Das Brot der frühen Jahre (Boell) **23**:12
"Brotcotnaz" (Lewis) **34**:161-62
"The Brother" (Coover) **15**:33, 35, 48, 59
"Brother" (Greene) **29**:183, 212
"Brother" (O'Brien) **10**:345
"Brother and Sister" (Grimm and Grimm)
    See "Brüderchen und Schwesterchen"
"Brother Bear Learns to Comb His Head" (Harris) **19**:194
"Brother Boniface" (Lavin) **4**:183
"Brother Death" (Anderson) **1**:32, 37, 39, 50-1, 56-7
"Brother Earl" (Anderson) **1**:52
"Brother Francis" (Capek) **36**:129
"Brother Lustig" (Grimm and Grimm) **36**:196-99, 228
"Brother Rabbit and the Chickens" (Harris) **19**:197
Brother Rabbit and the Mosquitoes (Harris) **19**:189, 195
"Brother Rabbit Ties Mr. Lion" (Harris) **19**:197

Title Index

"Brother Rabbit's Courtship" (Harris) 19:195
"Brother Rabbit's Love-Charm" (Harris) 19:196
"Brother Tiger and Daddy Sheep" (Harris)
19:194
"A Brother to Diogenes" (Page) 23:288, 307,
312
"Brother Wolf Says Grace" (Harris) 19:150
"The Brotherhood Movement" (Bioy Casares)
17:75
"Brothers" (Anderson) 1:52
"Brothers" (Bunin)
See "Brethren"
"Brothers" (Lu Hsun)
See "Dixiong"
"Brothers and Sisters" (Le Guin) 12:210-11,
213-16, 249-50
"The Brother's House" (Algren) 33:88, 106
Brothers of the Head (Aldiss) 36:10, 15-18
"Brothpot" (Verga) 21:284
"Brown Dog" (Harrison) 19:211-15
"The Brown Grass" (Cowan) 28:78-80
"The Brown Hand" (Doyle) 12:62, 64
"The Brown House" (Yamamoto) 34:348-49,
352, 358, 364
"Brown of Calaveras" (Harte) 8:214, 236, 244,
246-48
"Brownie" (Gissing) 37:73, 79
Brownie (Gissing) 37:67, 79
"Brüderchen und Schwesterchen" (Grimm and
Grimm) 36:225-26
"Brugglesmith" (Kipling) 5:266
"Brummy Usen" (Lawson) 18:239
"Bruno" (Warner) 23:376
"The Brushwood Boy" (Kipling) 5:266-67, 273-
74, 283
"The Brute" (Capek) 36:93, 124
"The Brute" (Conrad) 9:152, 176, 183
"La bûche" (Maupassant) 1:274
"The Bucket of Blood" (O'Hara) 15:281
"Buckeye Hollow Inheritance" (Harte) 8:218
"The Buckles of Superior Dosset"
(Galsworthy) 22:71
"Buckthorne and His Friends" (Irving) 2:241,
251, 261-62
"The Buckwheat" (Andersen) 6:7, 12, 18, 34
"The Buddies" (Farrell) 28:91
"Buddy" (Dixon) 16:217
"Buenaventura Durruti's Funeral" (Moorhouse)
40:324
"Los buenos tiempos" (Pardo Bazan) 30:264
"O búfalo" (Lispector) 34:185, 189-90, 195-97,
201-02
"The Buffalos" (Williams) 31:303, 354, 359,
361
"Bugle Song" (Stegner) 27:195-97, 215, 222-23
"Building Alive" (Sansom) 21:81, 83, 90, 92,
124
"The Building Site" (Duras) 40:65
"Build-Up" (Ballard) 1:68, 76-7
"An Buille" (O'Flaherty) 6:286-89
"Buiyon no tsuma" (Dazai Osamu) 41:238-42,
244-45, 251, 253-54, 263
"Bukoemov" (Gorky) 28:146
Bulemanns Haus (Storm) 27:278
"Bulfinch" (Cheever) 38:44
"The Bulgarian Poetess" (Updike) 13:367, 374-
75, 378, 380-81
"The Bull" (Pavese) 19:369
"The Bull That Thought" (Kipling) 5:279, 286
"Bullring of the Summer Night" (Algren) 33:95
"The Bull-Run Style" (Lawson) 18:233
"The Bully" (Dubus) 15:74
"Bums at Sunset" (Wolfe) 33:369
"Bums in the Attic" (Cisneros) 32:31
"A Bundle of Letters" (James) 8:299
"Bunner Sisters" (Wharton) 6:418, 422, 433
Bunte Steine (Stifter) 28:272, 279, 283, 286,
288-89, 292, 300, 302-03
"La buonissima madre" (Svevo) 25:336, 360
"The Burden of Loveliness" (Williams) 31:327,
334

"The Bureau of Frauds" (P'u Sung-ling)
See "K'ao-pi ssu"
"The Burglar's Christmas" (Cather) 2:100
"The Burial of the Guns" (Page) 23:295-96,
298, 307
The Burial of the Guns (Page) 23:283, 285,
291, 326, 328
"Buried Lives" (Mukherjee) 38:245, 254, 267-
68, 282-83
"Una burla riuscita" (Svevo) 25:328-32, 335-
37, 340-50, 352-53, 357-58, 363-65
"The Burning" (Welty) 1:476, 479, 484; 27:332,
338
"The Burning Baby" (Thomas) 3:399, 407
"The Burning Eyes" (Gordon) 15:128-29, 142
The Burning Flames, and Other Stories
(Rulfo)
See El llano en llamas, y otros cuentos
"The Burning House" (Beattie) 11:10, 13, 22,
29
The Burning House (Beattie) 11:7, 9, 10-12, 19,
22-4, 26-7, 29, 32
"The Burning Plain" (Rulfo) 25:265, 268, 270
The Burning Plain, and Other Stories (Rulfo)
See El llano en llamas, y otros cuentos
"The Burning Shame" (Twain) 34:295
"The Burnt Ones" (White) 39:330
The Burnt Ones (White) 39:278-80, 282-83,
288, 292-94, 300, 303, 205-06, 309, 312,
316, 318, 320, 324, 335, 337, 343, 345
"The Burrow" (Kafka)
See "Der bau"
"Burutu Moon" (Hughes) 6:118
"The Bus" (Singer) 3:381-82
"The Bus to St. James's" (Cheever) 1:100, 106;
38:55
"La busca de Averroes" (Borges) 4:26, 37, 41
"La Buse et le cochon" (Ayme) 41:8, 15
"The Bush Undertaker" (Lawson) 18:201, 206-
07, 218, 221, 237-39, 241, 245, 259
"The Busher Comes Back" (Lardner) 32:143
"A Busher's Letters Home" (Lardner) 32:141-
43, 150, 152, 159
Bushūkō hiwa (Tanizaki) 21:182-86, 189-91,
195, 198, 219, 224, 226
The Bushwackers and Other Stories (Murfree)
22:187
"The Bushwhackers" (Murfree) 22:187
"Business Is Business" (Boell)
See "Geschäft ist Geschäft"
"The Business Man" (Poe) 1:407
"Busride" (Cortazar)
See "Omnibus"
"A Busy Day in a Lawyer's Office" (Chesnutt)
7:14
"A Busy Man" (Nabokov) 11:133
"But at the Stroke of Midnight" (Warner)
23:376
"But It's Going to Rain" (Lispector)
See "Mas vai chover"
But Who Can Replace a Man? (Aldiss) 36:18
"Butcher Bird" (Stegner) 27:196-97
"Butcher Rogaum's Door" (Dreiser) 30:1237,
127, 129-30, 132
"Butter Butter for a Boat" (Jolley) 19:245
"Butterball's Night" (Cortazar)
See "La noche de Mantequilla"
"Buttercup Night" (Galsworthy) 22:63, 101
"The Butterfly" (Chekhov) 2:126
"The Butterfly" (O'Hara) 15:282
"The Butterfly and the Traffic Light" (Ozick)
15:298, 313
"Buying a Horse" (Howells) 36:399
"By a Dying Man's Pillow" (Peretz) 26:204-05,
217
"By Himself" (Pirandello)
See "Da sé"
"By Moonlight" (Mansfield) 9:286; 23:146,
153-54
"By My Troth, Nerissa" (Aiken) 9:13
"By Oneself" (Pirandello)
See "Da sé"

"By Special Request" (Waugh) 41:330
"By the Brandy Still" (Andric) 36:45
"By the Gods' Mouth" (Fuentes)
See "Por boca de los dioses"
"By the Mouth of the Gods" (Fuentes)
See "Por boca de los dioses"
"By the People" (Faulkner) 1:178
"By the Road" (Bunin) 5:106
"By the Sea" (Adams) 24:9
"By the Water" (Bowles) 3:71-2
"By the Waters of Babylon" (Benet) 10:154,
157
"Byezhin Prairie" (Turgenev) 7:316, 345
"Byron in Sintra" (Andric)
See "Bajron u Sintri"
"The Bystander" (Berriault) 30:96-7
"Byvshii lyudi" (Gorky) 28:136-37, 146, 151,
157, 183, 185, 189, 191
Byways (Hesse) 9:230
"The Byzantine Omelet" (Saki) 12:295
"C. Musonius Rufus" (Davenport) 16:169, 171,
175, 177, 191
"The Cabalist of East Broadway" (Singer)
3:374, 383-84
"The Caballero's Way" (Henry) 5:167
"El caballo blanco" (Pardo Bazan) 30:290
Cabbages and Kings (Henry) 5:155, 160, 162-
63, 167-69, 172
"Cabecita blanca" (Castellanos) 39:75, 76
"The Cabin" (Carver) 8:50
"The Cabinet of Edgar Allan Poe" (Carter)
13:16-18, 20
"La cachet d'onyx" (Barbey d'Aurevilly) 17:9-
13, 17-18
"Cäcilie" (Kleist)
See Die heilige Cäcilie; oder, die Gewalt
der Musik
"A Caddy's Diary" (Lardner) 32:117, 123, 146,
149, 154-55
"Cadence" (Dubus) 15:73-4, 100
"The Cadjer" (Galsworthy) 22:58
"Cafard" (Galsworthy) 22:62-3, 101
"Café des exilés" (Cable) 4:58, 62, 68
"La Cafetière" (Gautier) 20:4, 9-10, 13, 16-17
"Caffs, Pools and Bikes" (Sansom) 21:106, 108,
126
"The Cage Birds" (Pritchett) 14:284, 298
"The Caged Lion" (Norris) 28:205, 207
"Cahoots" (Dunbar) 8:122, 132, 145
"Cain and Artyom" (Gorky)
See "Kain i Artem"
"Cain Rose Up" (King) 17:274
"A Cake of Soap" (Lu Hsun)
See "Feizao"
Cakes and Ale and Twelve Stories (Maugham)
8:384
"El calamar opta por su tinta" (Bioy Casares)
17:95
"Calico Shoes" (Farrell) 28:87, 112
Calico Shoes and Other Stories (Farrell) 28:86,
100, 118-22
"The Californian's Tale" (Twain) 26:331
"Caline" (Chopin) 8:94
"The Caliph and the Cad" (Henry) 5:158
"The Caliph, Cupid, and the Clock" (Henry)
5:158
"The Call" (Cowan) 28:82
"Call and I Follow, I Follow!" (Perelman)
32:243
"Call at Corazón" (Bowles) 3:59, 61-2, 66, 69,
77, 79
"Call Me, Call Me" (O'Hara) 15:252
"Call Me Knacknissel" (Aleichem) 33:74
"The Call of Blood" (Cervantes)
See "La fuerza de la sangre"
"The Call of Cthulhu" (Lovecraft) 3:258, 261,
263-64, 269-70, 274, 278, 280, 283, 290
"The Call of the Tame" (Henry) 5:191, 194
"A Call on Mrs. Forrester" (Thurber) 1:431
Call to Arms (Lu Hsun)
See Nahan
"The Call to Duty" (Pirandello) 22:226, 229

"Calling All Moths: Candle Dead Ahead"
  (Perelman) **32**:229
"Calling Card" (Campbell)
  See "First Foot"
"Calling Cards" (Bunin)
  See "Vizitnye kartochki"
"Calling Jesus" (Toomer) **1**:445, 447, 450
"The Calm" (Carver) **8**:14, 42
"Le Calmant" (Beckett) **16**:73-5, 87, 89-91
"The Calmative" (Beckett)
  See "Le Calmant"
Calvaries (Capek)
  See *Boži muka*
"La camara in attesa" (Pirandello) **22**:232-33,
  285-86
"The Camberwell Beauty" (Pritchett) **14**:262-
  63, 266, 272
The Camberwell Beauty, and Other Stories
  (Pritchett) **14**:267, 301, 305
Cambio de armas (Valenzuela) **14**:352, 355,
  359, 366-67, 372
"The Camel's Back" (Fitzgerald) **6**:45, 59, 96-7
"La camera e la strada" (Moravia) **26**:148
"El Camino de Santiago" (Carpentier) **35**:91,
  97, 99, 101-03, 105
"Il campo di granturco" (Pavese) **19**:385
"Can All This Grandeur Perish?" (Farrell)
  28:92, 130
*Can All This Grandeur Perish? and Other
  Stories* (Farrell) **28**:99, 122
"Can I Stay Here?" (O'Hara) **15**:262, 283
Can Such Things Be? (Bierce) **9**:59
"Can You Carry Me?" (O'Hara) **15**:270
"La caña" (Pardo Bazan) **30**:278-80
"The Canals of Mars" (Boyle) **5**:55
"The Canary" (Mansfield) **9**:282, 306, 310, 313;
  38:230
"A Canary for One" (Hemingway) **1**:209, 217,
  232, 237
Canary in a Cat House (Vonnegut) **8**:428
"Cancel All I Said" (Collier) **19**:103, 110
"La cancióndе Peronelle" (Arreola) **38**:6
Candide; or, Optimism (Voltaire)
  See *Candide; ou, L'optimisme*
Candide; ou, L'optimisme (Voltaire) **12**:338-44,
  347-55, 357-62, 364-65, 368-69, 372-74,
  376-78, 383-90, 393-6, 400
"The Candles" (Agnon)
  See "HaNerot"
"Candles for the Madonna" (Boell) **23**:11
"Candleshine" (Benet) **10**:149
"The Candy Country" (Alcott) **27**:44
"Candy-Man Beechum" (Caldwell) **19**:9, 16-
  17, 21-3, 28-9, 36-9
Cane (Toomer) **1**:439-55, 458-60, 462
"The Cane in the Corridor" (Thurber) **1**:420,
  422
"Canon Alberic's Scrap-Book" (James) **16**:232,
  234-36, 238, 242, 248, 250-52, 255-57
The Canopy of Time (Aldiss) **36**:18
"Canta l'epistola" (Pirandello) **22**:229, 233,
  248-50, 266-67
"Cantelman's Spring-Mate" (Lewis) **34**:254-56,
  165, 172, 175
"The Canterbury Pilgrims" (Hawthorne)
  3:185-86
"The Canterville Ghost: A Hylo-Idealistic
  Romance" (Wilde) **11**:372, 376, 399-401,
  407
"Cantiga de esponsais" (Machado de Assis)
  24:129
"Um cão de lata ão rabo" (Machado de Assis)
  24:130
The Cape Cod Lighter (O'Hara) **15**:281-82
"Cape Race" (de la Mare) **14**:82, 86, 89
"The Capital in My Notebook" (Bulgakov)
  18:90
"The Capital of the World" (Hemingway) **1**:217,
  232, 234, 245; **25**:113; **40**:209, 211
"A Capitalist" (Gissing) **37**:52
"La capitana" (Pardo Bazan) **30**:272

"The Capitulation of Jean Jacques"
  (Galsworthy) **22**:90
"Cap'n Jollyfax's Gun" (Morrison) **40**:329
"Caprice" (Verga)
  See "Fantasticheria"
"The Captain" (Dubus) **15**:93
"The Captain" (Michaels) **16**:305, 307-10
"Captain Boldheart" (Dickens) **17**:124
"Captain Candelario's Heroic Last Stand"
  (Ferre) **36**:152
"Captain d'Arce's Memoirs" (Verga)
  See "I Ricordi del Capitano d'Arce"
"The Captain Has Bad Dreams" (Algren) **33**:88,
  105, 110
"The Captain Is Impaled" (Algren) **33**:105
"The Captain of 'The Camel'" (Bierce) **9**:80
"Captain Sands" (Jewett) **6**:167
Captain Shigemoto's Mother (Tanizaki)
  See *Shōshō Shigemoto no haha*
"The Captains" (Jewett) **6**:154, 167
*The Captain's Daughter; or, the Generosity of
  the Russian Usurper Pugatscheff*
  (Pushkin)
  See *Kapitanskaya-dochka*
"The Captain's Doll" (Lawrence) **4**:197, 204,
  210-12, 223-26, 234-36, 239-40
"The Captain's Doll" (Wilson) **21**:364
"The Captain's Gift" (Stafford) **26**:278-79, 283,
  285, 301, 307
"The Captain's Son" (Taylor) **10**:396-97, 399,
  402
"The Captive" (Gordon) **15**:105-06, 110, 117,
  128, 133
"The Captive" (Kipling) **5**:283
"The Captive" (Pirandello) **22**:226, 229, 265
"The Captive" (Singer) **3**:374, 384
"The Captives" (Benet) **10**:154
"Captivity" (Henderson) **29**:328
"The Captured Shadow" (Fitzgerald) **6**:49
"The Captured Woman" (Barthelme) **2**:46
Captures (Galsworthy) **22**:65-6, 77, 97, 99,
  101-02
"The Car We Had to Push" (Thurber) **1**:431
La cara de la desgracia (Onetti) **23**:247, 250,
  252, 260-61, 279-80
"The Carafe" (Zoshchenko) **15**:407-08
"Carancro" (Cable) **4**:58
"Las caras de la verdad" (Bioy Casares) **17**:59
*Caravan: The Assembled Tales of John
  Galsworthy* (Galsworthy) **22**:67-9, 73-9
"Carbon" (Levi) **12**:257, 259, 262, 265, 268,
  280
"Carcassonne" (Faulkner) **1**:181
"The Cardinal's First Tale" (Dinesen) **7**:162-63,
  172, 186, 194, 198
"The Cardinal's Third Tale" (Dinesen) **7**:168,
  200
"Cards" (Beattie) **11**:26, 29
"A Career" (Narayan) **25**:141, 155
"The Career of Nightmares" (Ligotti) **16**:293
"Careful" (Carver) **8**:26, 31, 35, 51
"The Careful Man" (Galsworthy) **22**:98
"Careless Talk" (Bowen) **3**:31; **28**:7
"Careless Talk" (Gallant) **5**:151
"A Careless Widow" (Pritchett) **14**:300
A Careless Widow, and Other Stories
  (Pritchett) **14**:300
"The Caress" (O'Flaherty) **6**:267
"The Caretaker" (Moravia) **26**:139
"Caricature" (Singer) **3**:359, 375
"La caricia más profunda" (Cortazar) **7**:58, 61,
  94
"Carma" (Toomer) **1**:456-57
"Carmen" (Lardner) **32**:145
Carmen (Merimee) **7**:276, 280-2, 285-6, 290,
  294-6, 305-06, 308
"Carmilla" (Le Fanu) **14**:221, 223, 225, 233-
  38, 243-45, 251
Il carnevale de Morti (Pirandello) **22**:231, 275
"Carnival" (Caldwell) **19**:41
"Carnival" (Dinesen) **7**:190-91

The Carnival of the Dead (Pirandello)
  See *Il carnevale de Morti*
"A Carolina" (Machado de Assis) **24**:155
"Carpe Noctem, If You Can" (Thurber) **1**:424
"Carpenters" (Salinger)
  See "Raise   High   the   Roofbeam,
  Carpenters"
"The Carriage Lamps" (Crane) **7**:104
"La carriola" (Pirandello) **22**:270
Carry On, Jeeves (Wodehouse) **2**:337, 346
Carry-Over (Suckow) **18**:404
Carsten Curator (Storm) **27**:281, 284
"Carta a un senorita en París" (Cortazar) **7**:56-7,
  61, 70-1
"Carta a un srta. en París" (Cortazar)
  See "Carta a un senorita en París"
"Carta a un Zapatero" (Arreola) **38**:10
"La Carte" (Ayme) **41**:16-17, 19-21, 26-28
"A Cartomante" (Machado de Assis) **24**:128,
  134
"Cartoon" (Coover) **15**:60
"The Cartouche" (de la Mare) **14**:79
"The Caryatids" (Dinesen) **7**:167, 191-92,
  203-04
"Čas" (Capek) **36**:110
"Un cas de divorce" (Maupassant) **1**:286
"Le cas de Madame Luneau" (Maupassant)
  1:259, 286
"Cas voli Bozijej" (Leskov) **34**:108
"Caša" (Andric) **36**:33
"Casa Anna" (Taylor) **10**:379
"La casa de Asterión" (Borges) **4**:7, 10, 25
"La casa del Granella" (Pirandello) **22**:256, 259
"La casa en la arena" (Onetti) **23**:246, 251-52,
  279
"Casa tomada" (Cortazar) **7**:53, 81
"Casa velhas" (Machado de Assis) **24**:155
"Casada e viuva" (Machado de Assis) **24**:131
"El casamiento engañoso" (Cervantes) **12**:21,
  24, 33-4, 37-8, 40
Casanovas Heimfahrt (Schnitzler) **15**:352, 371,
  376
Casanova's Homecoming (Schnitzler)
  See *Casanovas Heimfahrt*
The Case Against Tomorrow (Pohl) **25**:212
"A Case for Kop" (Boell) **23**:8, 36
"A Case for Lombroso" (Norris) **28**:197, 206-
  07, 214
"A Case for Prosecution" (Capek) **36**:130
"A Case for the Oracle" (Lawson) **18**:250
"A Case from Practice" (Chekhov)
  See "Sluchai iz praktiki"
"A Case History" (O'Hara) **15**:252, 280
"A Case in a Thousand" (Beckett) **16**:72
"The Case of 'Ca'line': A Kitchen Monologue"
  (Dunbar) **8**:122, 127, 147
"A Case of Identity" (Doyle) **12**:49, 51, 59,
  66-8, 70-1, 73
"The Case of Lady Sannox" (Doyle) **12**:64
"The Case of Lieutenant Yelaghin" (Bunin)
  See "The Elaghin Affair"
"The Case of Lord Cornphillip" (Waugh)
  41:331
"A Case of Metaphantasmia" (Howells) **36**:360-
  61, 363-64, 397
"The Case of Smith vs. Jones" (Twain) **26**:326
"A Case That Was Dropped" (Leskov)
  See "Pogašsee delo"
"The Case with the Child" (Capek)
  See "Případ s dítětem"
The Case-Book of Sherlock Holmes (Doyle)
  12:62
"The Cask of Amontillado" (Poe) **1**:378, 394,
  407-08; **22**:293; **34**:264-65; **35**:297-354
"Cassandra" (Mansfield) **9**:282
"Cassation" (Barnes) **3**:6, 10, 16, 24-5
"The Cassowary" (Bowen) **3**:33
Cast a Cold Eye (McCarthy) **24**:215-18
"Castaway" (Clarke) **3**:125, 135-36, 149
"Casting the Runes" (James) **16**:227, 230, 233,
  236, 245, 248, 252-53, 255
"The Casting Vote" (Murfree) **22**:211

"The Castle of Crossed Destinies" (Calvino) 3:101-02

The Castle of Crossed Destinies (Calvino)
　See *Il castello dei destini incrociati*

"Castles in the Air" (Greene) 29:219

"Castor and Pollux" (Warner) 23:384

"A Casual Incident" (Farrell) 28:111

"The Casualty" (Boell) 23:38

The Casualty (Boell) 23:36

The Casuarina Tree (Maugham) 8:366-67, 371, 374

"The Cat" (Cheever) 38:43

"The Cat" (Saroyan) 21:135

The Cat (Colette)
　See *La chatte*

A Cat, a Man, and Two Women (Tanizaki)
　See *The Cat, Shōzō, and Two Women*

"The Cat in the Hat for President" (Coover) 15:45-6

"Cat in the Rain" (Hemingway) 1:244-45

"The Cat Jumps" (Bowen) 3:41, 53; 28:9, 12

The Cat Jumps and Other Stories (Bowen) 3:33, 41; 28:4

"A Cat Named Dempsey" (Benet) 10:154

The Cat, Shōzō, and Two Women (Tanizaki) 21:186, 192, 218

"The Cat That Walked by Himself" (Kipling) 5:284

"Cat up a Tree" (Sansom) 21:83, 92

"Cat Within" (Narayan) 25:157

"The Catalan Night" (Morand)
　See "La nuit Catalane"

"Catalina" (Villiers de l'Isle Adam) 14:397

"The Catalonian Night" (Morand)
　See "La nuit Catalane"

"A Catastrophe" (Wells) 6:389

"The Catbird Seat" (Thurber) 1:422, 425, 431-32, 435

"The Catch" (Gordimer) 17:151-52, 166

The Catch (Oe)
　See *Shiiku*

"The Catechist" (Barthelme) 2:37, 39, 55

"Caterina" (Moravia) 26:144, 165

"Cathedral" (Carver) 8:26, 30, 34-5, 40-1, 43-4, 48-9, 51

Cathedral (Carver) 8:17, 20, 23, 26-8, 30-2, 34, 39-40, 46, 49, 55-61

"The Cathedral Builder" (Auchincloss) 22:34, 50

"Catherine Carmichael" (Trollope) 28:317, 322, 327, 349, 356

"Catman" (Ellison) 14:109-10

"Cats" (Shiga) 23:346, 349

The Cat's Cradle Book (Warner) 23:367, 380

"The Cats of Ulthar" (Lovecraft) 3:262

"The Cat's Point of View" (Capek) 36:84

"The Cattle Dealers" (Chekhov) 2:128

"The Cattle Pen" (Leskov) 34:127

"A causa secreta" (Machado de Assis) 24:128, 133

"Cause of Death: Hooked Nose" (Boell) 23:36

"The Cause of the Difficulty" (Harris) 19:183

"Caution" (Naipaul) 38:306, 327

"Caution—Soft Prose Ahead" (Perelman) 32:202, 211

Il cavaliere inesistente (Calvino) 3:90-1, 99, 106-07, 117

"Cavalleria Rusticana" (Verga) 21:283-84, 286, 295, 298-301, 305

Cavalleria Rusticana, and Other Tales of Sicilian Peasant Life (Verga)
　See *Vita dei campi*

"Un cavallo nella luna" (Pirandello) 22:275

"Un cavallo sulla luna" (Pirandello) 22:279

"Cavanelle" (Chopin) 8:94, 108, 111

"Cavar un foso" (Bioy Casares) 17:95

"The Cave Man as He Is" (Leacock) 39:265

"Caveat Emptor" (Stafford) 26:279, 282

"La caverna" (Arreola) 38:4

"Caviar" (Boyle) 16:144

"C'è qualcuno che ride" (Pirandello) 22:261, 269

"Cefalea" (Cortazar) 7:58

"Čekárna" (Capek) 36:92, 110, 122-23

"The Celebrated Jumping Frog of Calaveras County" (Twain) 6:300, 309-12, 316-21; 26:357; 34:288-346

The Celebrated Jumping Frog of Calaveras County, and Other Sketches (Twain) 34:322, 336

"A Celebrity" (Machado de Assis) 24:153

"La céleste aventure" (Villiers de l'Isle Adam) 14:390

"The Celestial Omnibus" (Forster) 27:74-77, 81, 83, 85-6, 99, 102, 111, 114-15, 123

The Celestial Omnibus (Forster) 27:68-70, 74, 76, 89-90, 97, 108, 112, 124

"The Celestial Plot" (Bioy Casares) 17:85

The Celestial Plot (Bioy Casares)
　See *La trama celeste*

"Celestial Publicity" (Villiers de l'Isle Adam)
　See "L'affichage céleste"

"The Celestial Railroad" (Hawthorne) 3:178, 181, 183

Les célibataires (Balzac)
　See *Le curé de Tours*

Celibate Lives (Moore) 19:297-300, 302-04, 308, 310-11, 318

Celibates (Moore) 19:310, 341-43, 346

"The Cellars" (Campbell) 19:62, 74, 81, 86, 88, 90

"Celle-ci et Celle-là ou la Jeune-France passionnée" (Gautier) 20:10, 12, 14, 24

"El celoso extremeño" (Cervantes) 12:3-4, 8, 14, 16-17, 21, 23, 33-4, 37, 39

"Čelovek v futljare" (Chekhov) 2:139, 141, 143, 155, 157; 28:54-6, 63, 65-72

"The Cemetery at Kozin" (Babel) 16:27-8, 31, 55

"The Cemetery in the Demesne" (Lavin) 4:166, 176

"The Cenci" (Stendhal)
　See "Les Cenci"

"Les Cenci" (Stendhal) 27:231-39, 241-42, 244-47, 249, 261

"The Census Takers" (Pohl) 25:224

"Centaur in Brass" (Faulkner) 1:177

"Ceremonias de rechazo" (Valenzuela) 14:355, 358-59

"The Ceremony" (Machen) 20:200

"Le Cerf et le chien" (Ayme) 41:6

"Cerium" (Levi) 12:256, 258, 265, 280

"Certain Considerations" (Pirandello)
　See "Certi obblighi"

A Certain Lucas (Cortazar)
　See *Un tal Lucas*

"Certain Women" (Caldwell) 19:21-2, 42, 55-6

"Certi obblighi" (Pirandello) 22:253

"The Certificate" (Agnon)
　See "HaTe'udah"

"Čertogon" (Leskov) 34:114

"Červená povídka" (Capek) 36:96, 110

"Chac Mool" (Fuentes) 24:30, 38-41, 43-5, 52-5, 59, 62, 64-8, 82

"Chacun sa chimère" (Baudelaire) 18:4-5, 17-18, 35

"Chagrin d'Amour" (Hesse) 9:231, 235

"Chagrin in Three Parts" (Greene) 29:202

"A Chain of Love" (Price) 22:360, 363, 374, 384

"The Chain Smoker" (Pritchett) 14:286

"La chaîne d'or" (Gautier) 20:2, 15

"Chains" (Dreiser) 30:110, 122, 145

Chains (Dreiser) 30:110, 122, 152-53, 159

"Chai-p'ing kung-tzu" (P'u Sung-ling) 31:199

"The Chair" (Davenport) 16:185, 187

"Châli" (Maupassant) 1:259

"The Challenge" (O'Flaherty) 6:277-78

"Chambers" (Dickens) 17:123

"La Chambre" (Sartre) 32:255-59, 261, 263-64, 267-70

"La chambre 11" (Maupassant) 1:288

"La chambre bleue" (Merimee) 7:277, 296-7

Chambre d'hotel (Colette) 10:269-70

"La chambre double" (Baudelaire) 18:5, 8, 18

"The Champ" (Boyle) 16:140-41, 151-52

Le Champ d'Oliviers (Maupassant) 1:273, 283

"Champion" (Lardner) 32:117, 127, 129, 131-32, 136, 138, 143, 146, 148-49, 152, 154-55, 160-61, 163, 168-69

"The Champion" (Stuart) 31:234, 264-65

"The Champion of the Weather" (Henry) 5:159

"Chance" (Dazai Osamu) 41:251

Chance Aquaintances (Colette)
　See *Chambre d'hotel*

"A Chance for Mr. Lever" (Greene) 29:183, 186, 212, 217

"Chanclas" (Cisneros) 32:31

"A Change" (Narayan) 25:137, 141

"Ch'ang-ê" (P'u Sung-ling) 31:207, 209

"A Change of Circumstances" (Morrison) 40:366

"A Change of Heart" (Jewett) 6:156, 158

A Change of Light, and Other Stories (Cortazar) 7:62-3

"A Change of Office" (Sansom) 21:105, 110, 126

A Changed Man, The Waiting Supper, and Other Tales (Hardy) 2:210-11, 214-15, 220-21

"Chang-shih fu" (P'u Sung-ling) 31:200

"Chanson d'été" (Bulgakov) 18:90

"La chanson vitrier" (Baudelaire) 18:63

"Le chant du coq" (Villiers de l'Isle Adam) 14:396

"Chantal" (Beauvoir) 35:60, 62, 64-6, 68-70

"Les Chantiers" (Duras) 40:3, 9

Les chants de Maldoror: Chant premier (Lautreamont) 14:167-212

"Chants the Epistle" (Pirandello)
　See "Canta l'epistola"

"Le chapeau chinois" (Villiers de l'Isle Adam)
　See "Le secret de l'ancienne musique"

"The Chaplet" (Saki) 12:288

"A Chapter in the History of a Tyrone Family" (Le Fanu) 14:220, 237, 239, 247

"Charade" (Auchincloss) 22:51

"Charity" (O'Flaherty) 6:264

"Charles" (Jackson) 9:249; 39:211, 219, 220, 222, 225]

"Charles Ryder's Schooldays" (Waugh) 41:331, 346-49

Charles Ryder's Schooldays (Waugh)
　See *Charles Ryder's Schooldays and Other Stories*

Charles Ryder's Schooldays and Other Stories (Waugh) 41:329-31, 333-37

"El charlestón" (Donoso) 34:30, 32, 49

"Charleston" (Donoso)
　See "El charlestón"

El charlestón (Donoso) 34:24-5, 49-50

Charleston and Other Stories (Donoso)
　See *El charlestón*

"Charlie" (Chopin) 8:84, 86

Charlie in the House of Rue (Coover) 15:47, 59-60

"Charlie's Greek" (O'Faolain) 13:320

"Charlotte Esmond" (Bates) 10:112

"The Charlottenburg Night" (Morand)
　See "La nuit de Charlottenburg"

"A Charm" (Kipling) 5:283

"The Charmed Spot" (Gogol)
　See "Zakoldovannoe mesto"

"A Charming Family" (Gissing) 37:56

"Charnel House of the Moon" (Ligotti) 16:277

"An Charraig Dhubh" (O'Flaherty) 6:287

"The Chase" (Moravia) 26:159, 161

"The Chaser" (Collier) 19:98, 102, 105, 109, 111-12

"Chasy" (Turgenev) 7:324-25, 327, 358

"The Château of Prince Polignac" (Trollope) 28:317-18, 328, 330, 343, 347

"Le chat-qui-pelote" (Balzac)
　See "La maison du chat-qui-pelote"

"Chattanooga-Choo-Choo" (Donoso) 34:8-9, 13, 17, 32-3

La chatte (Colette) **10**:225-56, 262, 265, 269-71, 276-77
"Chattery Teeth" (King) **17**:295
"Chava" (Aleichem) **33**:29
"Chawdron" (Huxley) **39**:162, 173, 176-77
"Che ti dice la patria?" (Hemingway) **1**:232
"Che yü" (P'u Sung-ling) **31**:190
"Cheap in August" (Greene) **29**:200-02, 217
"The Cheapjack" (O'Connor) **5**:371, 389
"An Chearc Uisce" (O'Flaherty) **6**:287
Cheering from the Sidelines (Lu Hsun)
　　See *Nahan*
"The Cheery Soul" (Bowen) **3**:32, 54; **28**:3
"A Cheery Soul" (White) **39**:280, 282-83, 287, 291-94, 299-300, 316-17, 325, 327, 329, 344
"Cheese" (Coppard) **21**:16
"The Cheese Stands Alone" (Ellison) **14**:127
"Le chef d'oeuvre inconnu" (Balzac) **5**:12, 16, 23, 48-9
"Chefs Chafe as Steak Smugglers Flood Turkish Baths" (Perelman) **32**:240
"Chelkash" (Gorky) **28**:134, 136-37, 148, 154-56, 159, 178, 188-89
"Chelovék na chasákh" (Leskov) **34**:117
"Ch'eng hsien" (P'u Sung-ling) **31**:190, 192
"Ch'eng the Immortal" (P'u Sung-ling)
　　See "Ch'eng hsien"
Chéri (Colette) **10**:253-55, 257-58, 262, 267, 270, 277-78, 282, 285-86 288
"Cherries" (Dazai Osamu)
　　See "Ōto"
"The Cherry Tree" (Coppard) **21**:16, 28
"Chesniki" (Babel) **16**:26, 50, 58
"The Chest and the Ghost" (Stendhal)
　　See "Le coffre et le revenant"
"The Chestnut Tree" (Pritchett) **14**:271
"Chestnuts" (Lewis) **40**:281
"A cheval" (Maupassant) **1**:278, 280
"Un cheval de race" (Baudelaire) **18**:6, 20
"Le Chevalier double" (Gautier) **20**:8, 15, 31
"The Chevalier of the Place Blanche" (Rhys) **21**:56
"La chevelure" (Baudelaire) **18**:8
"Chi shêng" (P'u Sung-ling) **31**:204-05
"Chia êrh" (P'u Sung-ling) **31**:204
"Chia Feng-chih" (P'u Sung-ling) **31**:199
"Chiao Mi" (P'u Sung-ling) **31**:204
"Chiao-na" (P'u Sung-ling) **31**:205-06, 209
"Ch'iao-niang" (P'u Sung-ling) **31**:207, 209
"Chiao-nu" (P'u Sung-ling) **31**:196
"Chichi" (Dazai Osamu) **41**:249, 251
"Chichi Haha" (Kawabata) **17**:245-46
"Chichi yo, anata wa doko e ikuno ka?" (Oe) **20**:223-28
"Chickamauga" (Bierce) **9**:53-7, 64, 68, 70, 75, 77, 87
"Chickamauga" (Wolfe) **33**:354, 372-75
Chicken Inspector No. 23 (Perelman) **32**:225, 228, 242
"Chicken-Grethe" (Andersen) **6**:7
"Chief Justice Harbottle" (Le Fanu)
　　See "Mr. Justice Hartbottle"
"The Chief Mourner of Marne" (Chesterton) **1**:128, 138
"Le Chien" (Ayme) **41**:6
"Le chien" (Maupassant) **1**:259
"Le chien et le flacon" (Baudelaire) **18**:17, 33
"Chiisai arubamu" (Dazai Osamu) **41**:256
"Chijin no ai" (Tanizaki) **21**:183-84, 192-93, 195
"The Child" (Bates) **10**:112
"Child" (Frame) **29**:106
"Child" (Galsworthy) **22**:98
"The Child Born Out of the Fog" (Nin) **10**:301, 303
"Child by Tiger" (Wolfe) **33**:364, 377, 386-87, 389-91
The Child in Chains (Mauriac)
　　See *L'enfant chargé de chaînes*
"A Child in the Dark, and a Foreign Father" (Lawson) **18**:258, 263

"The Child in the Grave" (Andersen) **6**:15, 26
"A Child of Christmas: A Christmas Tale of North and South" (Harris) **19**:183
"The Child of God" (O'Flaherty) **6**:262, 269-70, 281
"The Child That Went with the Fairies" (Le Fanu) **14**:223
"The Child Who Favored Daughter" (Walker) **5**:403, 409-11
"The-Child-Who-Was-Tired" (Mansfield) **9**:286, 310, 316; **23**:130
"Childhood" (Hesse)
　　See "Kinderseele"
Childhood (Tolstoy)
　　See *Detstvo*
Childhood and Adolescence (Tolstoy)
　　See *Detstvo*
"Childhood: At Grandmother's" (Babel) **16**:36
"Childhood is Not Forever" (Farrell) **28**:122
Childhood Is Not Forever (Farrell) **28**:112, 116, 121
"The Childhood of a Leader" (Sartre)
　　See "L'Enfance d'un chef"
"The Childhood of Luvers" (Pasternak)
　　See "Detstvo Luvers"
"The Childhood of Zhenya Luvers" (Pasternak)
　　See "Detstvo Luvers"
"The Childish Fear" (Campbell) **19**:81
"The Children" (Algren) **33**:87-8, 106
"The Children" (Oates) **6**:225
"Children" (Tanizaki)
　　See "Shōnen"
Children and Older People (Suckow) **18**:391, 394, 405
"Children Are Bored on Sunday" (Stafford) **26**:276-77
Children Are Bored on Sunday (Stafford) **26**:274, 281, 285, 307
"Children Are Civilians Too" (Boell) **23**:11
Children Are Civilians, Too (Boell) **23**:11
Children of the Bush (Lawson) **18**:241, 257
Children of the Frost (London) **4**:258, 282, 285-88
"Children of the Great" (Lewis) **34**:163, 165
"The Children of the Night" (Pohl) **25**:224, 230
"The Children of the Pool" (Machen) **20**:177, 198
The Children of the Pool (Machen) **20**:166, 177-78, 194, 197
"The Children of the Zodiac" (Kipling) **5**:283, 286
"Children on Their Birthdays" (Capote) **2**:61, 63-6, 70, 72-3, 75-8
"The Children's Campaign" (Lagerkvist)
　　See "Det lilla fälttåget"
"The Children's Game" (Stafford)
"The Children's Grandmother" (Warner) **23**:370
"A Child's Dream of a Star" (Dickens) **17**:124, 131
"The Child's Evening Prayer" (Andersen) **6**:15
A Child's Garden of Curses (Perelman) **32**:245
"A Child's Heart" (Hesse) **9**:227
"Child's Play" (Adams) **24**:17-18
"Childybawn" (O'Faolain) **13**:288, 297, 301
"A Chilhowee Lily" (Murfree) **22**:212
"The Chimera" (Cheever) **1**:97, 105
"The Chimera" (Pavese) **19**:388
Chimera (Barth) **10**:44, 48-53, 55-7, 60-1, 64-5, 68-9, 70-2, 74, 81, 83-4, 91, 93-5 100-04
The Chimes (Dickens) **17**:99, 101, 103-09, 115, 127, 129-30, 132
"The Chimney" (Campbell) **19**:71
"Ch'in Kuei" (P'u Sung-ling) **31**:201
"Ch'in shêng" (P'u Sung-ling) **31**:205, 207
"China" (Donoso) **34**:13-14, 30, 32, 49
"The Chinago" (London) **4**:263
"The Chinaman's Ghost" (Lawson) **18**:245
"A chinela turca" (Machado de Assis) **24**:129
"A Chinese Perspective" (Aldiss) **36**:11
"A Chinese Tale" (Bulgakov) **18**:72-4, 99
"Ch'ing-mei" (P'u Sung-ling) **31**:207, 209-10

"The Chink" (Stegner) **27**:198-200, 202, 204-05, 224
"The Chink in Armor" (O'Hara) **15**:254-55
"Chin-ling Yi" (P'u Sung-ling) **31**:205
"Chintamans and Birds" (Capek)
　　See "Čintamani a ptáci"
"Il chiodo" (Pirandello) **22**:269
"A Chip of Glass Ruby" (Gordimer) **17**:155, 161, 173, 181
"Chip Off the Old Block" (Stegner) **27**:227
"Chippy" (Narayan) **25**:134, 138, 140, 155-56
"Chistyi ponedel'nik" (Bunin) **5**:114
"Chitatel" (Gorky) **28**:187
"Chiu yu" (P'u Sung-ling) **31**:205-06
"Chiu-shan wang" (P'u Sung-ling) **31**:208
"The Choice" (Galsworthy) **22**:74, 79
"The Choice" (Wharton) **6**:418
"Choice Grain" (Leskov)
　　See "Otbornoje zerno"
"A Choice of Profession" (Malamud) **15**:170, 173, 175, 220-21
"The Chords of Youth" (Bates) **10**:139
"The Chorus Girl" (Chekhov) **2**:130, 137, 139
"The Chosen" (Carpentier) **35**:106
"Ch'ou hu" (P'u Sung-ling) **31**:204, 206, 208
"Chou San" (P'u Sung-ling) **31**:204-05
"Chrisp Street, Poplar" (Morrison) **40**:354
"The Christening" (Lawrence) **4**:197, 202, 234
"A Christian Education" (Warren) **4**:390, 394, 396
"Christine's Letter" (Coppard) **21**:27
"Christmas" (McGahern) **17**:298, 302
"Christmas" (Nabokov) **11**:132-33
"The Christmas Banquet" (Hawthorne) **3**:181, 183
"Christmas by Injunction" (Henry) **5**:162
A Christmas Carol (Dickens) **17**:99, 101, 103-04, 108, 113-20, 124, 127, 129-30, 132, 139, 143, 145-48
"A Christmas Carol for Harold Ross" (Boyle) **5**:64
Christmas Chimes (Dickens)
　　See *The Chimes*
"Christmas Day at Kirby Cottage" (Trollope) **28**:317, 332, 341, 348, 355
"Christmas Day at Thompson Hall" (Trollope) **28**:322-23, 332, 335, 346, 348, 355
"Christmas Day in the Workhouse" (Wilson) **21**:321-22, 330, 332, 339, 355, 360
"A Christmas Dinner" (Dickens) **17**:110, 116
"A Christmas Dream, and How It Came True" (Alcott) **27**:44
"Christmas Eve" (Gogol)
　　See "Noč pered roždestvom"
"Christmas Eve at Johnson's Drugs N Goods" (Bambara) **35**:27, 29
"Christmas Eve in the Streets" (Morrison) **40**:365
"Christmas Every Day" (Boell)
　　See "Nicht nur zur Weihnachtzeit"
Christmas Every Day and Other Stories Told for Children" (Howells) **36**:400
"The Christmas Eves of Aunt Elise: A Tale of Possession in Old Grosse Pointe" (Ligotti) **16**:271, 278, 283
"Christmas Gift" (Warren) **4**:388-90, 394
"Christmas is a Sad Season for the Poor" (Cheever) **1**:107
"Christmas Jenny" (Freeman) **1**:191
"A Christmas Memory" (Capote) **2**:67, 72-3, 75-6
"Christmas Morning" (O'Connor) **5**:378
"A Christmas Party and a Wedding" (Dostoevsky)
　　See "A Christmas Tree and a Wedding"
"A Christmas Recollection" (Page)
　　See "Polly: A Christmas Recollection"
"A Christmas Song" (Bates) **10**:117
"Christmas Story" (Mauriac)
　　See "Conte de Noël"
"A Christmas Story" (Naipaul) **38**:321, 328, 346

"A Christmas Tale" (Oliphant) **25**:194-95, 204
"A Christmas Tree and a Wedding" (Dostoevsky) **2**:171, 190, 193-95, 197
"Christmas with Two Children's Stories" (Hesse) **9**:241, 244
"Christopherson" (Gissing) **37**:52-3, 64, 81
"Christos v gost'ax u muzika" (Leskov) **34**:108
"Chromium" (Levi) **12**:256, 268
"The Chronic Argonauts" (Wells) **6**:388
Chronicle of a Death Foretold (Garcia Marquez)
     See *Crónica de una muerte anunciada*
The Chronicles of Aunt Minervy Ann (Harris) **19**:147, 150-51, 155
Chronicles of Bustos Domecq (Bioy Casares)
     See *Crónicas de Bustos Domecq*
The Chronicles of Clovis (Saki) **12**:287-88, 293, 323, 330-35
Chronicles of Golden Friars (Le Fanu) **14**:220, 245
Chronicles of Martin Hewitt (Morrison) **40**:332, 349
Chronicles of the Canongate (Scott) **32**:285-86, 292, 298-302, 304-05, 317-19
Chroniques du XXme siècle (Morand) **22**:172
Chroniques italiennes (Stendhal) **27**:230-32, 247-50, 260-63
"Chronopolis" (Ballard) **1**:69, 84
Chronopolis, and Other Stories (Ballard) **1**:71
"Chrysalis" (Bradbury) **29**:82
"The Chrysanthemums" (Steinbeck) **11**:207, 210, 214, 221, 223-37, 240-41, 244; **37**:321-62
"Chu Chu, The Devotion of Enriquez" (Harte) **8**:228
Chuanqi (Chang) **28**:20; 26; 31; 38; 40
"An Chulaith Nua" (O'Flaherty) **6**:287
"Chums" (Gorky) **28**:137
"Chun Ah Chun" (London) **4**:269
"The Church at Novograd" (Babel) **16**:25, 28, 52, 56
"The Church in High Street" (Campbell) **19**:61, 66, 72, 90
"The Church That Was at Antioch" (Kipling) **5**:272
"The Church with an Overshot Wheel" (Henry) **5**:163, 180-81
"The Chymist" (Ligotti) **16**:266, 269, 271, 280-81, 283
"Ciaula Discovers the Moon" (Pirandello) **22**:250
"Cicadas" (Bunin) **5**:82
"Cicely's Dream" (Chesnutt) **7**:22-3, 33-4, 37
"The Cicerone" (McCarthy) **24**:215-16, 224, 226-27
"Ciclismo en Gringnan" (Cortazar) **7**:95
"The Cigarstore Robbery" (Hemingway) **1**:208
"Cimutti" (Svevo) **25**:329
"Cinci" (Pirandello) **22**:240, 244
"Cinderella" (Grimm and Grimm) **36**:190, 196, 208
"The Cinderella Waltz" (Beattie) **11**:8
Cinnamon Shops (Schulz) **13**:326-27, 332, 343-44
"Čintamani a ptáci" (Capek) **36**:97, 99, 127
"La ciociara" (Moravia) **26**:151
"A Circle in the Water" (Howells) **36**:397-98
"A Circle of Fire" (O'Connor) **1**:343-44, 347, 356; **23**:185, 235
"Circle of Prayer" (Munro) **3**:348
"The Circular Ruins" (Borges)
     See "Las ruinas circulares"
"The Circular Valley" (Bowles) **3**:66, 69-71, 79
"Circus" (Andric)
     See "Cirkus"
"The Circus" (Porter) **4**:331-34, 340, 353; **31**:175
"The Circus" (Saroyan) **21**:172
"Circus at Dawn" (Wolfe) **33**:369, 401
"The Circus at Denby" (Jewett) **6**:150, 155, 167
"The Circus at Luxor" (Naipaul) **38**:346

"The Circus Horse" (Colette) **10**:292
"The Circus in the Attic" (Warren) **4**:387-89, 391, 395-98, 404
The Circus in the Attic, and Other Stories (Warren) **4**:387-90, 393, 396-97
"Circus in Town" (Ross) **24**:305, 310-11, 315, 319, 323
"Cirkus" (Andric) **36**:66-7
"The Cistern" (Bradbury) **29**:66
"Citizen" (Pritchett) **14**:297
"Citizens of the Third Grade" (Saroyan) **21**:163
"La citta" (Pavese) **19**:378, 385
"The City" (Bradbury) **29**:81
"The City" (Hesse) **9**:230, 235
"The City" (Pavese)
     See "La citta"
"The City" (Updike) **13**:403, 409
"City Boy" (Michaels) **16**:301, 303, 312, 321
"The City Coat of Arms" (Kafka) **29**:371
"City Life" (Barthelme) **2**:40
City Life (Barthelme) **2**:30-5, 37-9
"A City of Churches" (Barthelme) **2**:37, 39, 41, 54
"The City of Dreadful Night" (Henry) **5**:188, 197
"City of London Churches" (Dickens) **17**:123
"The City of Refuge" (Fisher) **25**:4-5, 7-9, 13, 17-27
"A City of the Dead, a City of the Living" (Gordimer) **17**:171, 174, 191
"The City of the Living" (Stegner) **27**:195, 198, 219-20, 223-26
The City of the Living, and Other Stories (Stegner) **27**:193, 196-99, 207, 219
The City of the Yellow Devil (Gorky) **28**:135
"The City on the Neva" (Solzhenitsyn)
     See "Gorod na Neve"
Ciudad Real (Castellanos) **39**:29, 47, 49, 50, 55, 56, 73
"Civil War" (O'Flaherty) **6**:262, 274
Claire Lenoir (Villiers de l'Isle Adam) **14**:376
"The Clairvoyant" (Capek)
     See "Jasnovidec"
The Clairvoyant (Gass) **12**:148
"The Clam" (P'u Sung-ling)
     See "Ge"
"Clancy in the Tower of Babel" (Cheever) **1**:107; **38**:52
"Clara" (Meyer) **30**:249
"Clara" (O'Brien) **10**:333
"Clara Milich" (Turgenev)
     See "Klara Milich"
"Clarence" (Dreiser)
     See "Black Sheep No. Five: Clarence"
"Clarence" (Harte) **8**:222, 251-52
"Clarissa" (Morand) **22**:156-57, 165, 168
"The Classical Annex" (Forster) **27**:93, 96, 107
Claudine à l'école (Colette) **10**:269
Claudine at School (Colette)
     See *Claudine à l'école*
"Claudius' Diary" (Shiga)
     See "Kurōdiasu no nikki"
"Claudius' Journal" (Shiga)
     See "Kurōdiasu no nikki"
"Clave para un amor" (Bioy Casares) **17**:58
"The Claxtons" (Huxley) **39**:158-59, 173, 177
"Clay" (Joyce) **3**:205, 209, 211, 221-22, 226, 233-34, 237, 247; **26**:46-7, 50, 61, 79
"Clay" (White) **39**:280, 283, 286, 289-90, 292-93, 297, 312, 316-17, 323, 325, 328-29, 336, 344
"La Clé sous le paillasson" (Ayme) **41**:23
"A Clean, Well-Lighted Place" (Hemingway) **1**:216, 230, 232, 237-38; **36**:294, 298-99; **40**:154-269
"The Cleaner's Story" (Sansom) **21**:83
"The Clear Track" (O'Hara) **15**:289
"A Cleared Path" (Gilman) **13**:141-42
"A Clearing in the Sky" (Stuart) **31**:235, 264
Clearing in the Sky and Other Stories (Stuart) **31**:234-35, 243, 261, 264

"The Clemency of the Court" (Cather) **2**:96, 100, 103, 105
"Clement Moore's Vocation" (Davis) **38**:120-21
"Clementina" (Cheever) **1**:100, 107; **38**:53
"Clementine" (Caldwell) **19**:56
"Clerkenwell" (Morrison) **40**:353
"The Clerk's Quest" (Moore)
     See "Tóir Mhic Uí Dhíomasuigh"
"The Clerk's Tale" (Pritchett) **14**:271
"Clever Elsie" (Grimm and Grimm) **36**:188
"The Clever Little Tailor" (Grimm and Grimm) **36**:229-30
"The Clever Little Trick" (Zoshchenko) **15**:404
"A Clever-Kids Story" (Beattie) **11**:6, 15-16
The Clicking of Cuthbert (Wodehouse) **2**:344, 354
"The Climber" (Mason) **4**:3
"The Climbers" (Andric) **36**:78-9
"The Cloak" (Gogol)
     See "Shinel"
"The Clock" (Baudelaire)
     See "L'horloge"
"Clone" (Cortazar) **7**:69-71
"Clorinda Walks in Heaven" (Coppard) **21**:27
Clorinda Walks in Heaven (Coppard) **21**:7-8, 15
"A Close Shave" (Stuart) **31**:251
Closed All Night (Morand)
     See *Fermé la nuit*
"The Closed Door" (Andric)
     See "Zatvorena vrata"
"The Closed Door" (Donoso)
     See "La puerta cerrada"
"Closed Space" (Beckett) **16**:123, 126
"Clothe the Naked" (Parker) **2**:275, 280-81, 286
"The Cloud" (Fowles) **33**:233, 235-36, 240, 242-44, 246-49, 258, 260-61, 263-64, 266, 274-76, 278-80, 289-90
"Cloud, Castle, Lake" (Nabokov) **11**:108-09, 127
The Cloven Viscount (Calvino)
     See *Il visconte dimezzato*
"Clowns in Clover" (Gordimer) **17**:153
"The Club Bedroom" (Auchincloss) **22**:10
"Le club des hachichins" (Gautier) **20**:16, 23-5, 31
The Club of Queer Trades (Chesterton) **1**:120, 122, 139
"Clyde" (Farrell) **28**:100
"Clytie" (Welty) **1**:466, 468, 471, 481, 495
"The Coach House" (Chekhov) **2**:128
"The Coachman" (Gorky)
     See "Izvozchik"
"Cobardía" (Pardo Bazan) **30**:294
"The Cobweb" (Saki) **12**:296
"The Coca-Cola Kid" (Moorhouse) **40**:289
"Cock Crow" (Gordon) **15**:123-24, 126
"Cock-a-Doodle-Doo!" (Melville) **1**:295, 298, 303, 305, 322; **17**:363
"Cockadoodledoo" (Singer) **3**:358
"The Cockatoos" (White) **39**:302, 309-11, 319-20, 324-27, 329-31, 346
The Cockatoos (White) **39**:301, 303-04, 306, 308-10, 319-20, 337, 343, 345-46, 350, 352
"Cockney Corners" (Morrison) **40**:353
"Cockroaches" (Schulz) **13**:333-34
"Cocktail Party" (Arreola) **38**:21
"Cocky Olly" (Pritchett) **14**:300
"Coco" (Maupassant) **1**:275
"The Cocoons" (Ligotti) **16**:282-84
"Cocotte" (White) **39**:293
"Le Cocu nombreux" (Ayme) **41**:22-24
"Coda" (Selby) **20**:253, 255-57
"The Code of the Herdsman" (Lewis) **34**:165, 173, 177
"Un coeur simple" (Maupassant) **1**:286
Un coeur simple (Flaubert) **11**:37, 45-6, 54-6, 58-66, 70-1, 80-1, 84, 87, 91, 94, 96-9, 101, 103
"The Coffer and the Ghost" (Stendhal)
     See "Le coffre et le revenant"

The Coffin-Maker (Pushkin)
    See "Grobovshchik"
"Le coffre et le revenant" (Stendhal) **27**:247-49,
    259
"The Coice of a Bride" (Hoffmann)
    See "Die Brautwahl"
"A Coincidence" (Farrell) **28**:100
"The Cold" (Warner) **23**:370
"Cold Autumn" (Bunin) **5**:115-16
"A Cold, Calculating Thing" (O'Hara) **15**:252
"A Cold Day" (Saroyan) **21**:143
"Cold Ground Was My Bed Last Night"
    (Garrett) **30**:166
Cold Ground Was My Bed Last Night (Garrett)
    30:173-74
"The Cold House" (O'Hara) **15**:258, 265
"Cold Print" (Campbell) **19**:61-2, 64, 66, 71-3,
    81, 88, 90-1
Cold Print (Campbell) **19**:66, 70-2, 80, 87, 90
"Cold Spell" (Lewis) **40**:282
"Colic" (O'Flaherty) **6**:271
"Collaboration" (Collier) **19**:98, 114
Collages (Nin) **10**:305-06, 308
Collected Fictions (Borges) **41**:157, 159, 162-
    63, 166
Collected Ghost Stories (James) **16**:227, 230-
    32, 239, 241, 246, 249, 251, 255
Collected Short Stories (Forster) **27**:97-8, 103
Collected Short Stories (Huxley) **39**:161-62
The Collected Short Stories of Conrad Aiken
    (Aiken) **9**:9, 12, 28, 41
The Collected Stories (Babel) **16**:6, 8, 11, 14,
    17, 19, 21, 25, 35, 41, 59
The Collected Stories (Boyle) **16**:155
Collected Stories (Garcia Marquez) **8**:182-84
Collected Stories (Greene) **29**:200, 212, 216-17
Collected Stories (Lavin) **4**:174
Collected Stories (Lessing) **6**:196, 218-19
Collected Stories (Malamud)
    See *The Stories of Bernard Malamud*
Collected Stories (Mansfield) **9**:281
The Collected Stories (McGahern) **17**:318, 322
Collected Stories (O'Connor) **5**:398
The Collected Stories (Price) **22**:384-85, 388
The Collected Stories (Pritchett) **14**:301
The Collected Stories (Trevor) **21**:260-61, 264
Collected Stories I (Spark) **10**:359-60, 368
Collected Stories: 1939-1976 (Bowles) **3**:65,
    68-9
The Collected Stories of Caroline Gordon
    (Gordon) **15**:137-38, 141
The Collected Stories of Colette (Colette)
    10:280, 291
Collected Stories of Eileen Chang (Chang)
    28:30; 37
The Collected Stories of Ellen Glasgow
    (Glasgow) **34**:68
The Collected Stories of Hortense Calisher
    (Calisher) **15**:7-8, 15, 19, 21
The Collected Stories of Isaac Bashevis Singer
    (Singer) **3**:383-84
The Collected Stories of Jean Stafford
    (Stafford) **26**:281, 285-86, 289-91, 312
*The Collected Stories of Katherine Anne
    Porter* (Porter) **4**:347, 351, 358, 361;
    31:167
The Collected Stories of Louis Auchincloss
    (Auchincloss) **22**:52-3
The Collected Stories of Peter Taylor (Taylor)
    10:389
The Collected Stories Of Seán O'Faoláin
    (O'Faolain) **13**:313
Collected Stories of Wallace Stegner (Stegner)
    27:220, 222-23, 226-27
Collected Stories of William Faulkner
    (Faulkner) **1**:151, 161-62, 177, 181
Collected Stories to Collected Short Stories
    (Huxley)
    See *Collected Short Stories*
The Collected Tales of A. E. Coppard
    (Coppard) **21**:18

The Collected Tales of E. M. Forster (Forster)
    27:74
Collected Work (Andric) **36**:50-1
Collected Works (Bunin) **5**:99
Collected Works (Walser) **20**:339
Collected Works of Henry Lawson (Lawson)
    18:210
Collected Writings (Bierce) **9**:75
"The Collection" (Pritchett) **14**:296, 298
Collection of Fairy Tales (Dazai Osamu)
    See *Otogi zōshi*
"The Collector" (Auchincloss) **22**:13
"Collector" (Cowan) **28**:81
"Collector of Innocents" (Auchincloss) **22**:49
"Collectors" (Carver) **8**:11, 19
"Le collier" (Maupassant) **1**:259
"Colloquy" (Jackson) **9**:252; **39**:211, 223, 224,
    225, 228
"The Colloquy of Monos and Una" (Poe) **1**:401-
    02; **34**:250, 258; **35**:310
Colomba (Merimee) **7**:276-7, 280-3, 290,
    294-5, 300-05, 308
Le Colonel Chabert (Balzac) **5**:8, 18, 24-7
The Colonel Has No One to Write Him (Garcia
    Marquez)
    See *El colonel no tiene quien le escribe*
"Colonel Julian" (Bates) **10**:117
Colonel Julian, and Other Stories (Bates)
    10:115-17
El colonel no tiene quien le escribe (Garcia
    Marquez) **8**:162, 185, 192-97
"Colonel Starbottle for the Plaintiff" (Harte)
    8:229
"Colonel Starbottle's Client" (Harte) **8**:216, 245
"The Colonel's Awakening" (Dunbar) **8**:121,
    127, 131, 140
"The Colonel's Foundation" (Auchincloss)
    22:53
"The Colonel's Lady" (Maugham) **8**:366, 380
"The Colonel's 'Nigger Dog'" (Harris) **19**:182
"El coloquio de los perros" (Cervantes) **12**:4, 8,
    14-16, 21, 24, 26-8, 33-4, 37-8,
"Colorado" (Beattie) **11**:4-5, 7, 17
"The Colored Girls of Passenack—Old and
    New" (Williams) **31**:302, 332, 357, 359
Colored Stones (Stifter)
    See *Bunte Steine*
"Colour and Line" (Babel) **16**:22, 27, 59
"The Colour Out of Space" (Lovecraft) **3**:261,
    263, 267-69, 274, 281, 290-91
"The Colt" (Stegner) **27**:194, 196-97, 199
"Come Again Tomorrow" (Gordimer) **17**:165
"Come Along, Marjorie" (Spark) **10**:355-57,
    359, 365, 370
Come Along with Me (Jackson) **9**:254; **39**:210
Come Back, Dr. Caligari (Barthelme) **2**:26-9,
    31, 37-9, 46, 49, 51
"Come Dance with Me in Ireland" (Jackson)
    39:210, 211, 224, 225
"Come in if You Love Money" (Algren) **33**:96-7
"Come on a Coming" (Dixon) **16**:208
"Come On Back" (Gardner) **7**:224-25, 227-28,
    235, 240-41
"Come On, Wagon" (Henderson) **29**:317
"Come Out the Wilderness" (Baldwin) **10**:2-3,
    5, 7-9
"Começos de Uma Fortuna" (Lispector) **34**:194
"The Comedian" (Narayan) **25**:140-41
La Comédie humaine (Balzac) **5**:6-13, 16-17,
    19-20, 26-33, 43, 48
"Les comédiens sans le savoir" (Balzac) **5**:31
"Comedy Cop" (Farrell) **28**:90
"Comedy Entombed: 1930" (Williams) **31**:327,
    333, 345, 348-49
"Comedy Evening" (Walser) **20**:353
"A Comedy in Rubber" (Henry) **5**:158
"Comedy Is Where You Die and They Don't
    Bury You Because You Can Still Walk"
    (Saroyan) **21**:144
"The Comedy of War" (Harris) **19**:183
"The Comet" (Schulz)
    See "Kometa"

"The Comforts of Home" (O'Connor) **1**:343-
    44, 351, 353, 365
The Comic Inferno (Aldiss) **36**:18
"Comic Strip" (Garrett) **30**:165
"Coming Apart" (Walker) **5**:412-14
"Coming, Aphrodite!" (Cather) **2**:91-2, 95, 104,
    111-12
"Coming Down the Mountain" (Stuart) **31**:265
"Coming, Eden Bower!" (Cather) **2**:111-12, 114
"Coming Home" (Bowen) **3**:40
"Coming into His Kingdom" (McGahern)
    17:302, 322
"The Coming Out of Maggie" (Henry) **5**:171,
    197
Command, and I Will Obey You (Moravia)
    See *Command, and I Will Obey You*
A Commentary (Galsworthy) **22**:59-60, 97, 99
"Commerce and Sentiment" (Harris) **19**:183
"A Committee-Man of 'The Terror'" (Hardy)
    2:220
The Common Chord (O'Connor) **5**:364-65, 371,
    378, 380, 383-84
"A Common Confusion" (Kafka) **5**:207
"The Common Day" (Cheever) **38**:54
"Common Meter" (Fisher) **25**:14, 16-20, 22-3,
    25
"The Common Round" (Mansfield) **9**:304
"Common Sense Should Tell You" (O'Hara)
    15:250
"A Commonplace Story" (Gordimer) **17**:167
"Communion" (Coppard) **21**:11, 15
"Cómo perdí la vista" (Bioy Casares) **17**:83
"The Companion" (Campbell) **19**:65, 75
"The Companion" (Machado de Assis) **24**:153
Company (Beckett) **16**:100-02, 110-12, 115,
    129, 134, 137
"Company for Gertrude" (Wodehouse) **2**:346
"The Company Is Not Responsible"
    (McCarthy) **24**:221-22
"Company Manners" (Gaskell) **25**:65-6
"A Company of Laughing Faces" (Gordimer)
    17:155-56, 161
"The Company of the Dead" (Price) **22**:384,
    386
"The Company of Wolves" (Carter) **13**:5, 7, 9,
    13-14, 27, 28
The Company She Keeps (McCarthy) **24**:212-
    13, 215-19, 221, 228
"The Compartment" (Carver) **8**:26, 32, 35
The Compass Rose (Le Guin) **12**:235
"A Compatriot" (Bunin) **5**:81
"Compatriots from an Earlier Age" (Arnim)
    See "Altdeutsche Landsleute"
"Compensation" (Galsworthy) **22**:74, 79
"Competition at Slush Creek" (Stuart) **31**:252
"The Competitor" (Galsworthy) **22**:99
"The Complaint Ledger" (Chekhov) **2**:130
Complete Collected Stories (Pritchett) **14**:302-
    03, 305
The Complete Fiction of Bruno Schulz (Schulz)
    13:342
"The Complete Life of John Hopkins" (Henry)
    5:159, 188
The Complete Short Stories (Trollope) **28**:332-
    33, 343, 349-51
"The Complete Short Stories of Ernest
    Hemingway" (Hemingway) **40**:191-92
The Complete Short Stories of Thomas Wolfe
    (Wolfe) **33**:396-99
The Complete Stories of Erskine Caldwell
    (Caldwell) **19**:19-20, 25
Complete Tales of Uncle Remus (Harris)
    19:193-97
Complete Works (Borges)
    See *Obras completas*
Complete Works (Peretz)
    See *Complete Works*
The Complete Works of Nathanael West (West)
    16:367
The Completion of Love (Musil)
    See "Vollendung der Liebe"
"A Complicated Nature" (Trevor) **21**:262

Title Index

"Compression" (Thomas)
"Compulsory Figures" (Thomas) **20**:320, 322
"Comrade Stanley" (Farrell) **28**:98, 122, 125
"Comrades" (Gordimer) **17**:186, 188
"Comrades in Arms" (Gissing) **37**:64-5
Le Comte de Saint-Germain (Nerval) **18**:371
"Comte Hippolit" (Hoffmann)
    See "Der Vampyrismus"
"Con legítimo orgullo" (Cortazar) **7**:94
"Concerning the Bodyguard" (Barthelme) **2**:44
"Concerning Wet Snow" (Dostoevsky)
    See "Apropos of the Wet Snow"
Concierto barroco (Carpentier) **35**:130-34
"Conclusion" (Gorky) **28**:146
"The Concrete Mixer" (Bradbury) **29**:42, 62
"Concussion" (Campbell) **19**:63, 74, 78, 86, 92
"Condemned Door" (Cortazar) **7**:69
"El condenado" (Arreola) **38**:7, 9
Condensed Novels, and Other Papers (Harte)
    8:225, 230, 249
"The Condominium" (Elkin) **12**:93-5, 106-07,
    110
"Conducta en los velorios" (Cortazar) **7**:92
"The Conductor and a Member of the Imperial
    Family" (Bulgakov) **18**:90
"The Conductor Kalina's Story" (Capek)
    See "Historie dirigenta Kaliny"
"The Cone" (Wells) **6**:361, 383
"Coney Island" (Beattie) **11**:25-6, 29
Confabulario (Arreola) **38**:3-13, 18, 20-21, 23-
    26, 28-29
Confabulario Total, 1941-61 (Arreola) **38**:12-13
Confabulario y Varia invencion (Arreola) **38**:8
"The Conference" (Singer) **3**:385, 388
"A Conference of the Powers" (Kipling) **5**:259
Conference-ville (Moorhouse) **40**:294-97, 304-
    305, 307, 309, 323-24
"Confession" (Andric) **36**:45, 70
"Confession" (Gorky)
    See "Ispoved"
"The Confession of Brother Grimes" (Warren)
    4:390, 394, 396
"The Confessional" (O'Faolain) **13**:293
"Le confessioni del vegliardo" (Svevo) **25**:334,
    340, 350, 352-53, 360-61
"Confessions of a Baby Chick" (Perelman)
    32:240
"Confidencia" (Pardo Bazan) **30**:295
"Confidencias de un lobo" (Bioy Casares)
    17:53, 56
"Confissões de uma viúva moça" (Machado de
    Assis) **24**:131
"Le confitéor de l'artiste" (Baudelaire) **18**:4-5,
    8, 18
"A Conflict Ended" (Freeman) **1**:196-97, 199
"Confused" (Singer) **3**:384
"Confused Head" (Shiga) **23**:333
"The Conger Eel" (O'Flaherty) **6**:269, 274
El congreso (Borges) **4**:27-8
The Congress (Borges)
    See *El congreso*
Conjugal Love (Moravia)
    See *Conjugal Love*
The Conjure Woman (Chesnutt) **7**:2-5, 7-12, 14,
    26, 30, 33, 38-40, 43
"The Conjurer's Revenge" (Chesnutt) **7**:6-7,
    10, 18, 42
"The Conjuring Contest" (Dunbar) **8**:122, 149
"The Connoisseur" (de la Mare) **14**:70, 82
The Connoisseur, and Other Stories (de la
    Mare) **14**:70
"The Connoisseurs" (Stafford) **26**:298
"The Connor Girls" (O'Brien) **10**:334, 341
"A Conquest of Humility" (Freeman) **1**:198
"Conscience" (Galsworthy) **22**:74, 101
"The Conscript" (Balzac) **5**:12-13
"A Conscript's Christmas" (Harris) **19**:181-82
"Consequences" (Cather) **2**:110-11, 115
"Conservatory" (Barthelme) **2**:51
"Consolation" (Pardo Bazan) **30**:290
"Consolation" (Verga) **21**:298
"Consolations of Age" (Aldiss) **36**:20

"The Consolations of Horror" (Ligotti) **16**:261,
    271, 277-78, 283, 285, 288, 294
"A Consolatory Tale" (Dinesen) **7**:164, 186,
    193, 200
"The Constant Tin Soldier" (Andersen)
    See "The Steadfast Tin Soldier"
"A Constellation of Events" (Updike) **13**:402
"The Consummation" (Galsworthy) **22**:98
"Conte de fin d'été" (Villiers de l'Isle Adam)
    14:390
"Conte de Noël" (Ayme) **41**:13
"Conte de Noël" (Mauriac) **24**:185, 198-99, 208
"Conte du milieu" (Ayme) **41**:10
Contes cruels (Villiers de l'Isle Adam) **14**:377-
    78, 380-81, 391, 395-96, 403, 411
Contes cruels: Nouveaux contes cruels (Villiers
    de l'Isle Adam) **14**:404, 412
Contes de la bécasse (Maupassant) **1**:257
Contes drolatiques (Balzac) **5**:19-21
Les Contes du chat perché (Ayme) **41**:4-5, 7,
    10, 13-16, 18-19
Contes philosophiques (Balzac)
    See *Romans et contes philosophiques*
"The Contessina" (Bowen) **3**:40
"The Contest" (Paley) **8**:388, 394, 398
"A Contest" (Svevo)
    See "Una lotta"
"The Contest for Aaron Gold" (Roth) **26**:251-53
"A Contest of Ladies" (Sansom) **21**:84, 94, 111,
    126
A Contest of Ladies (Sansom) **21**:84, 90-1, 112,
    126
"The Contest of the Minstrels" (Hoffmann)
    See "Der Kampf der Sänger"
The Continental Op (Hammett) **17**:212-13, 217,
    227
"Continuation of the Yellow Millet" (P'u
    Sung-ling)
    See "Hsü huang-liang"
"Continuity of Parks" (Cortazar) **7**:54, 70, 83
"Conto alexandrino" (Machado de Assis)
    24:128-30, 133, 152-53
Contos flumineneses (Machado de Assis)
    24:131-32, 151
"The Contract" (Anderson) **1**:52
"Contract" (Lardner) **32**:128, 133, 135-36, 138,
    140, 145
"A Contract" (Svevo)
    See "Un contratto"
"Contratreta" (Pardo Bazan) **30**:272
"Un contratto" (Svevo) **25**:334, 360
"Contrition" (Dubus) **15**:74, 83
"The Convalescence of Jack Hamlin" (Harte)
    8:247, 249
"Convention" (Dreiser) **30**:112, 114, 122, 156
"The Conventional Wisdom" (Elkin) **12**:99
"A Conversation" (Aiken) **9**:14
"A Conversation" (Turgenev) **7**:335
"Conversation at Night" (Bunin)
    See "A Night Conversation"
"Conversation in the Atomic Age" (O'Hara)
    15:250, 258
"The Conversation of Eiros and Charmion"
    (Poe) **1**:402
"Conversation Piece, 1945" (Nabokov) **11**:109-
    10, 112-13, 127
"Conversation with Goya" (Andric)
    See "Razgovori sa Gojom"
"A Conversation with My Father" (Paley)
    8:390, 392, 395, 399-402, 405, 407, 415-16,
    418
"Conversations at Night" (Le Guin) **12**:211,
    213, 216
"Conversations in a Dead Language" (Ligotti)
    16:271, 275, 292, 294, 297
"Conversations with Goethe" (Barthelme) **2**:51
Conversations with Leukothea (Pavese)
    See *Dialoghi con Leucò*
"Converse at Night" (Dinesen) **7**:168, 171, 186
"A Conversion" (Morrison) **40**:328, 330, 354,
    366, 368

"The Conversion of Aurelian McGoggin"
    (Kipling) **5**:261, 274
"The Conversion of Sum Loo" (Cather) **2**:102
"The Conversion of the Jews" (Roth) **26**:229,
    234, 248, 257-60, 265-66
"The Conversion of William Kirkwood"
    (McGahern) **17**:305, 323
"El converso" (Arreola) **38**:8
"The Convert" (Lavin) **4**:165-68
"A Convert of the Mission" (Harte) **8**:216, 254
Los convidados de agosto (Castellanos) **39**:29,
    33, 34, 37, 38, 42, 43, 55, 59, 73
"Le convive des dernières fêtes" (Villiers de
    l'Isle Adam) **14**:378, 381-82, 384, 388-90,
    393-94
"Le convive inconnu" (Villiers de l'Isle Adam)
    See "Le convive des dernières fêtes"
"Cookie" (Taylor) **10**:382, 390
"The Cooking Lesson" (Castellanos)
    See "Lección de cocina"
"Cool Air" (Lovecraft) **3**:258, 262, 274
*A Cool Million: The Dismantling of Lemuel
    Pitkin* (West) **16**:343-48, 354-56, 362,
    366, 379-85, 387-94, 399-400, 402-03, 405-
    08, 411, 415, 418
"Coordination" (Forster) **27**:86, 103, 114
"The Cop and the Anthem" (Henry) **5**:173, 187
"Copenhagen Season" (Dinesen) **7**:166, 169-71,
    186, 190-91
"The Copper Charm" (Morrison) **40**:329
"Cops and Robbers" (Stafford) **26**:278, 283,
    285, 308
"Un coq chanta" (Maupassant) **1**:272
"Cora Unashamed" (Hughes) **6**:109-10, 118-19,
    121-23, 129
"El corazón perdido" (Pardo Bazan) **30**:264
"La corde" (Baudelaire) **18**:35, 39
"The Corduroy Pants" (Caldwell) **19**:36
"The Coreopsis Kid" (Calisher) **15**:5, 15-17
Corilla (Nerval) **18**:362, 367, 369
"Corkan and the German Woman" (Andric)
    See "Corkan i švabica"
"Corkan i švabica" (Andric) **36**:37-8, 42, 54,
    66
"Corkscrew" (Hammett) **17**:216, 222, 230
"The Corn Planting" (Anderson) **1**:37
"The Cornac and His Wife" (Lewis) **34**:147,
    161, 169
"The Corner" (Cowan) **28**:76; 81
Corner of the Woods (Storm)
    See *Waldwinkel*
"Cornet at Night" (Ross) **24**:290-92, 294-98,
    306, 310-11, 314-15, 319, 323-24
"The Cornet Yelagin Affair" (Bunin)
    See "The Elaghin Affair"
"La corpana" (Pardo Bazan) **30**:272
"O corpo" (Lispector) **34**:185, 189, 191, 195,
    197, 201-02
"Corporal of Artillery" (Dubus) **15**:73
"Correspondence" (McCullers) **9**:332-34, 343,
    345, 358
A Correspondence (Turgenev) **7**:317-18, 320,
    324-26, 328, 361
"A Correspondence Course" (Gordimer) **17**:171,
    173, 193
"Corrido" (Arreola) **38**:7, 10
"The Corsican Inn" (Pritchett) **14**:268, 298
"The Cortez Gang" (Algren) **33**:96
"Cortigiana stanca" (Moravia) **26**:138, 163,
    179, 182
"Cortísimo metraje" (Cortazar) **7**:95
"Corto Viaggio sentimentale" (Svevo) **25**:331-
    33, 336-38, 351-52, 354-57, 360, 363
*Corto viaggio sentimentale e altri racconti
    inediti* (Svevo) **25**:329-30, 332-33, 338
Una cosa è una cosa (Moravia) **26**:159-62, 165,
    173, 180
"Cosè il re" (Verga) **21**:292
"Cosmic Casanova" (Clarke) **3**:133
Le cosmicomiche (Calvino) **3**:92-6, 98-100,
    103-04, 106-07, 110, 112, 116-17

Cosmicomics (Calvino)
  See *Le cosmicomiche*
"A Cosmopolitan" (Galsworthy) **22**:93
Cosmopolitans (Maugham) **8**:366, 380
The Cossacks (Tolstoy) **30**:317, 331
"The Cost of Living" (Gallant) **5**:130, 140-41,
  149
"The Cost of Living" (Malamud) **15**:173-75
Costumes by Eros (Aiken) **9**:4, 28
"The Cosy Room" (Machen) **20**:163, 197
The Cosy Room (Machen) **20**:166, 177-78, 186,
  194, 197
"The Cottagette" (Gilman) **13**:126, 145
"The Cottonwood Part One: Story of Sun
  House" (Silko) **37**:303
"Cottonwood Part Two: Buffalo Story" (Silko)
  37:303
"Cottonwood Parts One and Two" (Silko)
  37:308
"A Council of State" (Dunbar) **8**:122, 124-25,
  128, 136, 141, 144, 150
"A Council of War" (Gilman) **13**:143
"Councillor Krespel" (Hoffmann)
  See "Rat Krespel"
"Counsel for Oedipus" (O'Connor) **5**:370
"Count Magnus" (James) **16**:228-30, 232, 237-
  38, 243, 245, 250-52, 256
"The Count of Crow's Nest" (Cather) **2**:100,
  102
"The Count of Monte Cristo" (Calvino) **3**:93,
  95-6
"The Counterfeit Coin" (Baudelaire)
  See "La fausse monnaie"
"Counterparts" (Joyce) **3**:200-01, 205, 209, 226,
  231, 234, 246, 249; **26**:46-7
"Countess" (Le Fanu)
  See "A Passage in the Secret History of an
  Irish Countess"
"Countess Varazoff" (Alcott) **27**:57
Counting (Phillips) **16**:332
"Counting the Waves" (Farrell) **28**:94
"The Counting-House" (Turgenev) **7**:313
"Country" (Phillips) **16**:327
"The Country Church" (Irving) **2**:244
"The Country Doctor" (Kafka)
  See "Ein landarzt"
"The Country Doctor" (Williams) **31**:354
A Country Doctor's Notebook (Bulgakov)
  See *Zapiski iunogo vracha*
"Country Full of Swedes" (Caldwell) **19**:4, 6,
  9, 12-13, 17, 19, 22-4, 27, 34, 39, 42, 47
"The Country Funeral" (McGahern) **17**:319-22,
  324
"The Country Husband" (Cheever) **1**:90, 100-
  02; **38**:50, 55-6, 61, 68, 71, 78, 80-4, 88-90
"The Country Inn" (Turgenev)
  See "The Inn"
"A Country Love Story" (Stafford) **26**:274, 277,
  283, 285, 307, 312
"The Country of the Blind" (Wells) **6**:361-62,
  368-73, 376-79, 383-84, 391-92, 399-400,
  405
The Country of the Blind, and Other Stories
  (Wells) **6**:359-61, 366, 380, 391-92
The Country of the Pointed Firs (Jewett) **6**:152,
  154-55, 157, 162-66, 168-69, 174-82
"Country Rain" (Williams) **31**:314, 327, 354
"Country Society" (Bates) **10**:118
"A Country Tale" (Dinesen) **7**:168-69
"A Country Walk" (Sansom) **21**:84, 91-2, 126
"The Count's Courtship" (de la Mare) **14**:66,
  81, 86
"The Coup de Grâce" (Bierce) **9**:55-6, 75-7
"Le coup de pistolet" (Merimee) **7**:277
"A Coupla Scalped Indians" (Ellison) **26**:11
"Le Couple" (Ayme) **41**:19
"A Couple of Fools" (Bates) **10**:131
"A Couple of Hamburgers" (Thurber) **1**:418-19
"Coupon" (Capek)
  See "Kupón"
"Coups de couteaux" (Mauriac) **24**:183, 185,
  196, 198-201, 204-07

"Courage" (Galsworthy) **22**:58, 74, 79
"The Courageous Tailor" (Grimm and Grimm)
  36:191
"Court in the West Eighties" (McCullers) **9**:342,
  345, 356
"The Courtesy Call" (Dazai Osamu)
  See "A Visitor"
"The Courting of Dinah Shadd" (Kipling)
  5:260, 263-64, 274
"The Courting of Sister Wisby" (Jewett) **6**:152,
  160, 162, 178
"Courtly Vision" (Mukherjee) **38**:264, 274, 277
"A Courtship" (Faulkner) **1**:151, 178
"Courtship" (O'Brien) **10**:334, 341
"The Courtship of Mr. Lyon" (Carter) **13**:6, 9,
  25, 30-31
"The Courtship of Susan Bell" (Trollope)
  28:318, 327-28, 333, 348
"Cousin Larry" (Parker) **2**:280, 283
Cousin Phyllis (Gaskell) **25**:32, 38, 40, 45-6,
  49-50, 54, 57-8, 61, 63-4, 74-7
"Cousin Poor Lesley and the Lousy People"
  (Elkin) **12**:117
"Cousin Teresa" (Saki) **12**:295, 302, 312
"Cousins" (Bellow) **14**:43, 46, 58
"The Covenant" (Auchincloss) **22**:44
"The Coverfield Sweepstakes" (Norris) **28**:203
Covering End (James) **8**:296
"The Covering of Blood" (Agnon) **30**:71-4
"Cow and Gate Baby Contest" (Naipaul) **38**:331
"The Coward" (Barnes) **3**:18-22
"A Coward" (Wharton) **6**:414
"The Cow's Death" (O'Flaherty) **6**:274
"The Cowslip Field" (Bates) **10**:120, 131-32,
  139
"The Coxon Fund" (James) **8**:317, 348
Crab Apple Jelly (O'Connor) **5**:362, 364, 371,
  377-78, 380, 383
"Crabforth" (Sansom) **21**:124
"The Cracked Looking-Glass" (Porter) **4**:327,
  329-30, 339-40, 342, 360
"Cracker Prayer" (Hughes) **6**:138
"The Crackling Mountain" (Dazai Osamu)
  41:234, 236, 264, 276
"Crackling Mountain" (Dazai Osamu)
  See "The Crackling Mountain"
Crackling Mountain (Dazai Osamu)
  See *Crackling Mountain and Other Stories*
Crackling Mountain and Other Stories (Dazai
  Osamu) **41**:263, 276
The Crapshooter (Steinbeck) **11**:248
"Craven Arms" (Coppard) **21**:8, 15
"Crawford's Consistency" (James) **32**:108
"The Crazy Batlen" (Peretz) **26**:201
"The Crazy Beggar-Student" (Peretz)
  See "The Crazy Beggar-Student"
"Crazy, Crazy, Now Showing Everywhere"
  (Gilchrist) **14**:154
"Crazy Crowd" (Wilson) **21**:319, 322, 325, 327,
  330, 336, 338, 342-44, 349, 352, 365
"The Crazy Hunter" (Boyle) **5**:58-9, 61-3, 65-6,
  68-9
The Crazy Hunter: Three Short Novels (Boyle)
  5:66
Crazy Like a Fox (Perelman) **32**:205, 213, 220,
  229, 237-39
"Crazy Sunday" (Fitzgerald) **6**:47, 52, 60-1,
  77-9
"The Creamery Man" (Garland) **18**:160
"The Creamery Manager" (McGahern) **17**:320,
  322
"Created He Them" (London) **4**:253
"Creation" (Tanizaki) **21**:190
"The Creation of Beauty: A Study in
  Sublimation" (Greene) **29**:219
"The Creative Impulse" (Maugham) **8**:369,
  378-79
"The Creative Instinct" (Maugham) **8**:358
"The Creature" (O'Brien) **10**:332-33
"The Creatures" (de la Mare) **14**:65, 80, 83, 85
"Creatures of Apogee" (Aldiss) **36**:19, 24, 27
Creatures of Circumstance (Maugham) **8**:380

"Creatures That Once Were Men" (Gorky)
  See "Byvshii lyudi"
"A Credibility Gap" (Gordimer) **17**:157
Credos and Curios (Thurber) **1**:424
"The Creeping Siamese" (Hammett) **17**:224
"Cremona Violin" (Hoffmann) **13**:225
"Le crépuscule du soir" (Baudelaire) **18**:5, 8,
  17, 33
"Cressy" (Harte) **8**:221
"Crevasse" (Faulkner) **1**:147
"Crewe" (de la Mare) **14**:73, 80, 84, 88-9, 90-1
"The Cricket" (P'u Sung-ling)
  See "Ts'u-chih"
"The Cricket on the Hearth" (Dickens) **17**:103,
  116, 127-28
"Criers and Kibitzers, Kibitzers and Criers"
  (Elkin) **12**:94-5, 116-18
"Crime and Punishment" (Narayan) **25**:133,
  139, 156
"The Crime at Pickett's Mill" (Bierce) **9**:98
"Crime at the Tennis Club" (Moravia)
  See "Crime at the Tennis Club"
"Le crime au père Boniface" (Maupassant)
  1:274
"Crime in the Cottage" (Capek)
  See "Zločin v chalupě"
"Crime in the Post-Office" (Capek)
  See "Zločin na poště"
"The Crime of Gabriel Gale" (Chesterton) **1**:124
"The Crime of Professor Sandwich" (Benet)
  10:149
"The Crime Wave at Blandings" (Wodehouse)
  2:344, 346, 349
"Crimen libre" (Pardo Bazan) **30**:279
"Crimes of Conscience" (Gordimer) **17**:171,
  174, 193
"The Criminal" (Dazai Osamu) **41**:240, 245
"The Criminal" (Tanizaki) **21**:194
"Criminal Courts" (Dickens) **17**:115
"The Crimson Curtain" (Barbey d'Aurevilly)
  See "Le rideau cramoisi"
"The Crimson Island" (Bulgakov) **18**:74, 91,
  110
"The Cripple" (Andersen) **6**:13
"The Crisis" (Zoshchenko) **15**:400
"The Critic" (Galsworthy) **22**:99
"Critical Mass" (Clarke) **3**:134
"Critique de la vie quotidienne" (Barthelme)
  2:39-40, 42, 55
"Croatoan" (Ellison) **14**:115-17, 128
Crónica de una muerte anunciada (Garcia
  Marquez) **8**:167, 173-82, 186, 190, 200-04
Crónicas de Bustos Domecq (Bioy Casares)
  17:48, 52, 74-5, 84, 86; **19**:48; **48**:36-7, 42
Cronopios and Famas (Cortazar)
  See *Historia de cronopios y de famas*
"The Crooked Branch" (Gaskell) **25**:37-8, 46-7,
  50-1, 60, 73
"The Crooked Made Straight" (Agnon)
  See "Vehaya he'akov lemishor"
The Croquet Player (Wells) **6**:400-02
"Crossbones" (Michals) **16**:302
"Cross-Country Snow" (Hemingway) **1**:217,
  244; **40**:209, 211
"Crossing into Poland" (Babel) **16**:25, 28-9, 31,
  33
"Crossing the Border" (Oates) **6**:248-49
Crossing the Border: Fifteen Tales (Oates)
  6:226-29, 231, 247-48, 250, 253-54
"Crossing the Line" (McGahern) **17**:315, 323
"Crossing the Rubicon" (Thomas) **20**:289, 296-
  98, 308, 317, 319
"Crossing the Zbruck" (Babel) **16**:51-4, 56, 58
"Crouch End" (King) **17**:295
"The Crow Catcher" (Arreola) **38**:12-13
"The Crow in the Woods" (Updike) **13**:400
"The Crowd" (Bradbury) **29**:65, 75, 88
"The Crowd Master" (Lewis) **34**:163-64
"Crowds" (Baudelaire)
  See "Les foules"
"Crown Fire" (Caldwell) **19**:5, 8
"A Crown of Feathers" (Singer) **3**:374

Title Index

A Crown of Feathers, and Other Stories (Singer) **3**:374-76, 380, 382, 384
"The Crowning Offer" (Auchincloss) **22**:33
"The Croxley Master" (Doyle) **12**:89
"Cruce de caminos" (Unamuno) **11**:312-13
Crucial Instances (Wharton) **6**:413
"Crucifixion" (Capek) **36**:114, 117
"Cruel and Barbarous Treatment" (McCarthy) **24**:213
"The Cruel Master" (Oates) **6**:237
"Cruise" (Letters from a Young Lady of LeisureWaugh) **41**:311, 323, 330-31, 340
The Cruise of "The Breadwinner" (Bates) **10**:129-30
"The Cruise of the 'Idlewild'" (Dreiser) **30**:107, 126
The Crusade of the Excelsior (Harte) **8**:245
"Cry of Peacock" (Galsworthy) **22**:70
"The Crying Organ" (Moorhouse) **40**:298
"Crystal Ball" (Grimm and Grimm) **36**:192
"The Crystal Egg" (Wells) **6**:383, 389-91, 393-94, 404-05
"The Crystal Fantasy" (Kawabata)
   See "Suishō Gensō"
"The Crystal Ship" (Vinge) **24**:328, 330, 332, 334-35, 339-40
"Crystals" (Calvino) **3**:108-09
"Cuando las mujeres quieren a los hombres" (Ferre) **36**:144, 146-47, 149, 157-59, 171
"Cuando se estudia gramática" (Cabrera Infante) **39**:22
"Cuarta versión" (Valenzuela) **14**:355, 367
"Cuarta vigilia" (Castellanos) **39**:49
"Cuatro socialistas" (Pardo Bazan) **30**:271
"The Cuckoo Clock" (Pritchett) **14**:269, 298
"The Cuckoo-Spit" (Lavin) **4**:172, 176, 183, 185
"Čudo u Olovu" (Andric) **36**:38, 52, 55
"Cuello de gatito negro" (Cortazar) **7**:61, 69
"Cuento primitivo" (Pardo Bazan) **30**:296
"Cuento soñado" (Pardo Bazan) **30**:265
Cuentos (Donoso) **34**:14-15, 20-3, 49-50
Cuentos completos (Onetti) **23**:258
Cuentos de amor (Pardo Bazan) **30**:264-65, 267, 269-70
Los cuentos de Juan Bobo (Ferre) **36**:146
Cuentos de la tierra (Pardo Bazan) **30**:263
Cuentos de Marineda (Pardo Bazan) **30**:270, 293-94
Cuentos nuevos (Pardo Bazan) **30**:262-63, 270-71
Cuentos sacroprofanos (Pardo Bazan) **30**:276
Cuentos trágicos (Pardo Bazan) **30**:278
"El cuervero" (Arreola) **38**:10
"La cuesta de las comadres" (Rulfo) **25**:245, 247, 249-50, 255, 258, 262, 264-65, 273, 280
"The Cuff Link" (Pardo Bazan) **30**:290
"La culpable" (Pardo Bazan) **30**:266-67
"Cunner-Fishing" (Jewett) **6**:155, 167
"The Cunning Snake" (Harris) **19**:162-63
"The Cup of Coffee" (Auchincloss) **22**:51
"A Cup of Cold Water" (Wharton) **6**:424
"Cup of Life" (Bulgakov) **18**:91
"The Cup of Life" (Bunin) **5**:90, 92, 109
The Cup of Life (Bunin) **5**:90
"A Cup of Tea" (Mansfield) **9**:310
"The Cupboard of the Yesterdays" (Saki) **12**:310, 328
"Cupid and Chow-Chow" (Alcott) **27**:17-22
Cupid and Chow-Chow (Alcott) **27**:43
"Cupid's Arrows" (Kipling) **5**:261
"Curado" (Pardo Bazan) **30**:272
"The Curate's Friend" (Forster) **27**:72-4, 86, 112-14, 119
Curator Carsten (Storm)
   See *Carsten Curator*
"The Curb in the Sky" (Thurber) **1**:418, 425
"The Cure" (Cheever) **1**:89; **38**:55
"The Cure" (Colette) **10**:280
Le curé de Tours (Balzac) **5**:5, 7-8, 18, 25-6

The Curé of Tours (Balzac)
   See *Le curé de Tours*
"The Curfew Tolls" (Benet) **10**:154
"El curioso impertinente" (Cervantes) **12**:3-4, 9-15
"A Curious Call" (Alcott) **27**:43
"The Curious Case of Benjamin Button" (Fitzgerald) **6**:59, 79-80, 92
"Curious if True" (Gaskell) **25**:37, 47, 55, 61-3, 73
"The Curse" (Clarke) **3**:124, 143-44
"The Cursed Play" (Tanizaki) **21**:194
"The Curtain" (Chandler) **23**:59, 65-7, 72-3, 80-3, 87, 92, 97-8, 106-07
"The Curtain Blown by the Breeze" (Spark) **10**:356, 359, 361, 370-71
"The Curtain Falls" (Harris) **19**:183
"A Curtain of Green" (Welty) **1**:465-67, 469, 471, 476, 481-82, 484, 487, 496
"A Curved Line" (Saroyan) **21**:132
"The Custard Heart" (Parker) **2**:275, 280-81, 286
"The Custody of the Pumpkin" (Wodehouse) **2**:346-47
"Custom House" (Hawthorne) **39**:129
"The Custom of the Country" (O'Connor) **5**:370-71, 384, 387, 389
"Custom-Made Bride" (Vonnegut) **8**:432, 436
"Customs" (Oates) **6**:227, 248-50
"Cut" (Dixon) **16**:204, 210
"Cut Glass Bowl" (Fitzgerald) **6**:57
"Cutta Cord-la" (Harris) **19**:162
"Cy" (Dixon) **16**:207, 211
"Cycling in Gringnan" (Cortazar)
   See "Ciclismo en Gringnan"
"The Cyclone" (Hesse) **9**:230-32, 235
Cyclone and Other Stories (Narayan) **25**:137-38, 152, 155
"C.Y.E." (McCarthy) **24**:215-16
"Les Cygnes" (Ayme) **41**:8
"Le Cygnes" (Ayme) **41**:15
"Cynthia" (Huxley) **39**:153-54, 167
"Cyprian's Narrative" (Hoffmann)
   See "Der Vampyrismus"
"Da sé" (Pirandello) **22**:255, 279
Da Vinci's Bicycle (Davenport) **16**:173-74, 176-77, 179-80, 182-83, 185, 187, 190, 193-98
"Dada" (Boyle) **16**:141, 143
"Daddy Deering" (Garland) **18**:160, 176, 194
"Daddy Jake the Runaway" (Harris) **19**:147, 151, 187
Daddy Jake the Runaway, and Short Stories Told after Dark by Uncle Remus (Harris) **19**:130, 147-48, 195-96
"The Daemon Lover" (Jackson) **9**:267, 272; **39**:209, 210, 211, 212, 213, 214, 216, 217, 218, 220, 223, 224, 225, 227, 228, 229
The Daffodil Sky (Bates) **10**:118-19
"The Dagger with Wings" (Chesterton) **1**:130-31
"Dagon" (Lovecraft) **3**:258, 262, 268, 272-73, 282, 285, 289
"The Daisy" (Andersen) **6**:3, 7
Daisy Miller: A Study (James) **8**:264, 274, 291, 298-99, 309-14, 334, 336-38; **32**:54-110
"Daisy Overend" (Spark) **10**:359-60
"Dalyrimple Goes Wrong" (Fitzgerald) **6**:45, 57
"Dama de pensamientos" (Arreola) **38**:11
"La dama joven" (Pardo Bazan) **30**:272-73
The Damned Yard (Andric)
   See *Prokleta avlija*
"Dan u Rimu" (Andric) **36**:46
"Danae" (Galsworthy) **22**:72-3
"The Dance" (Andric)
   See "Igra"
"The Dance" (Thomas) **20**:321
"The Dance at Chevalier's" (Cather) **2**:101, 105, 107
"The Dance of Death, or the Lovely and Pleasant" (Agnon) **30**:66, 81-6
"The Dance of the Chain" (Moorhouse) **40**:310

"Dance of the Happy Shades" (Munro) **3**:321, 328-30, 335, 346
Dance of the Happy Shades (Munro) **3**:320, 322, 328-29, 331, 335, 343-44, 347
"The Dancin' Party at Harrison's Cove" (Murfree) **22**:184, 186, 188, 196, 198, 203-04, 206-08, 217
"Dancing Girls" (Atwood) **2**:6-8, 10, 12
Dancing Girls, and Other Stories (Atwood) **2**:3-7, 10, 13-16, 20-2
"The Dancing Mistress" (Bowen) **3**:30, 43, 54
"Dancing with Both Feet on the Ground" (White) **39**:347, 349
Dandelion Wine (Bradbury) **29**:43, 45, 52, 86
"The Dandy Frightening the Squatter" (Twain) **6**:300; **59**:210; **34**:294, 297-98, 301
"Dandy Jim's Conjure Scare" (Dunbar) **8**:122, 149
"The Dane's Place" (Donoso)
   See "Dinamarquero"
"Danger!" (Doyle) **12**:80
"The Danger in the House" (Thurber) **1**:429
"The Danger of Shadows" (Benet) **10**:160
"The Dangerous Age" (Sansom) **21**:114
A Dangerous Perfume (Nin) **10**:306
"A Dangerous Woman" (Farrell) **28**:111
A Dangerous Woman and Other Stories (Farrell) **28**:110-11
"Les dangers de l'inconduite" (Balzac) **5**:4
"Daniel Jovard ou la Conversion d'un classique" (Gautier) **20**:5, 10, 12
"Daniel Webster and the Ides of March" (Benet) **10**:153, 158
"Daniel Webster and the Sea Serpent" (Benet) **10**:144, 153, 158
"Danny" (Jewett) **6**:150, 167
"Danny Sahib" (Mukherjee) **38**:240
"Danny's Girls" (Mukherjee) **38**:238, 254, 266, 273
"Danse Pseudomacabre" (Williams) **31**:305, 319-20, 325, 329, 364
"Dante and the Lobster" (Beckett) **16**:64, 69, 92-3
"Dante Street" (Babel) **16**:59
"Daoine Bochta" (O'Flaherty) **6**:287, 289
"Daphne's Lover" (Taylor) **10**:400, 416-17
"Daphnis and Chloe" (Moore) **19**:293
"Darby Dallow Tells His Tale" (Coppard) **21**:8
"Darcy in the Land of Youth" (O'Connor) **5**:371
"Dare's Gift" (Glasgow) **34**:57-8, 61-3, 66-7, 70, 73, 79-80, 82, 84-5, 87-8, 90, 92, 94-7, 100
"The Daring Young Man on the Flying Trapeze" (Saroyan) **21**:131-32, 135-36, 140, 142, 152, 157, 174-75
The Daring Young Man on the Flying Trapeze, and Other Stories (Saroyan) **21**:130-33, 136, 139, 141, 143, 145-46, 152, 154, 158-59, 165-67, 174
"Darius & the Clouds" (Cisneros) **32**:5
"The Dark" (Updike) **13**:348
Dark Alleys (Bunin)
   See *Dark Avenues*
"Dark Avenues" (Bunin) **5**:115
Dark Avenues (Bunin) **5**:82, 90, 113-16
"A Dark Brown Dog" (Crane) **7**:130
"Dark Came Early in That Country" (Algren) **33**:95, 98
Dark Carnival (Bradbury) **29**:39, 43, 59, 75, 86, 88-9
"The Dark Chamber" (Ligotti) **16**:296
"The Dark City" (Aiken) **9**:13-14, 31
Dark Companions (Campbell) **19**:65, 75-6, 78, 84, 87
Dark Feasts: The World of Ramsey Campbell (Campbell) **19**:70-1, 78, 86, 93
"The Dark Glasses" (Spark) **10**:356
"Dark in the Forest, Strange as Time" (Wolfe) **33**:369-70, 382
"The Dark Men" (Dubus) **15**:77-9
A Dark Night's Passing (Shiga)
   See *Anya Kōro*

"A Dark Night's Work" (Gaskell) **25**:46, 50-2, 58-60, 67

"The Dark Show" (Campbell) **19**:74

"Dark They Were, and Golden-Eyed" (Bradbury) **29**:61, 82

"The Dark Walk" (Taylor) **10**:392, 411

"The Darkening Moon" (Stafford) **26**:281, 289

The Dark-Eyed Lady (Coppard) **21**:19

Darkness (Mukherjee) **38**:238, 240, 247, 250, 254, 257, 263-65, 269-73, 277-79, 281, 291, 294

"Darkness Box" (Le Guin) **12**:232

"The Darling" (Chekhov) **2**:131-32, 135

"Darling" (Dixon) **16**:207, 211

"The Darling River" (Lawson) **18**:206

"The Darning Needle" (Andersen) **6**:20

"A Dashing Fellow" (Nabokov) **11**:117

"Dasi the Bridegroom" (Narayan) **25**:141, 154-55

"Datos para entender a los perqueos" (Cortazar) **7**:95

"Datura Fastuosa" (Hoffmann) **13**:221-23, 225-26

"Daughter" (Caldwell) **19**:9, 27-8, 33, 38

"The Daughter" (Suckow) **18**:389, 401, 409

"Daughter of Albion" (Chekhov) **2**:126

"A Daughter of the Aurora" (London) **4**:286

"A Daughter of the Lodge" (Gissing) **37**:56, 64, 81

"The Daughter of the Regiment" (Kipling) **5**:260

The Daughter of the Storage and Other Things in Prose and Verse (Howells) **36**:400

"The Daughter of the Yen Family" (P'u Sung-ling)
 See "Yen Shih"

"Daughters" (Anderson) **1**:52

Daughters of Fire (Nerval)
 See *Les filles du feu*

"The Daughters of the Late Colonel" (Mansfield) **9**:280-81, 300, 303-06, 310; **23**:154; **38**:229

"The Daughters of the Vicar" (Lawrence) **4**:197-98, 202, 204, 212, 233

Däumchen (Tieck) **31**:275

"Daumier" (Barthelme) **2**:39, 42, 49, 55

"De Daumier-Smith's Blue Period" (Salinger) **2**:293, 301, 315; **28**:262

"The Daunt Diana" (Wharton) **6**:421, 428

"Dave's Neckliss" (Chesnutt) **7**:18

"David Gaunt" (Davis) **38**:96, 134

"David Swan" (Hawthorne) **3**:160

"Dawn" (Powers) **4**:370

Dawn Ginsbergh's Revenge (Perelman) **32**:201, 214, 218-20, 226, 238

"The Dawn in Erewhon" (Davenport) **16**:162-67, 169-70, 176, 183, 185-86, 197

"The Dawn of Another Day" (Williams) **31**:306, 323-24

"Dawn of Remembered Spring" (Stuart) **31**:234

"A Day" (Pirandello)
 See "Una giornata"

"The Day after Christmas" (Andric)
 See "Na drugi dan Božica"

"Day after Day" (Lispector)
 See "Dia após dia"

"The Day before the Revolution" (Le Guin) **12**:231, 234, 241

"The Day He Himself Shall Wipe My Tears Away" (Oe)
 See "Mizu kara waga namida o nuguitamo hi"

"A Day in Coney Island" (Singer) **3**:374

"A Day in Rome" (Andric)
 See "Dan u Rimu"

"A Day in the Jungle" (Jackson) **9**:258

"A Day in the Life of a Galactic Empire" (Aldiss) **36**:28

"A Day in the Life of Able Charlie" (Pohl) **25**:236

"Day Million" (Pohl) **25**:214, 221, 225, 234-35

Day Million (Pohl) **25**:229, 232

"The Day My Days as a Child Ended" (Cabrera Infante)
 See "El día que terminó mi niñez"

"A Day of Grace" (Garland) **18**:154, 160, 181, 183

"A Day of Our Life" (Bulgakov) **18**:90

"The Day of Silence" (Gissing) **37**:55, 80-1

The Day of Silence and Other Stories (Gissing) **37**:80

"The Day of the Boomer Dukes" (Pohl) **25**:232

"Day of the Butterfly" (Munro) **3**:329-30, 337

"The Day of the Dying Rabbit" (Updike) **13**:359-61

"The Day of the Landslide" (Rulfo)
 See "El dia del derrumbe"

The Day of the Locust (West) **16**:345-49, 355-57, 359-62, 364, 366-67, 369-74, 379, 381, 383-85, 387-89, 394, 396, 399-402, 406-08, 411, 414-15, 418

"The Day of the Sheep" (Frame) **29**:109, 118

"A Day on a Selection" (Lawson) **18**:200, 237-38, 240-41

"A Day Out" (Sansom) **21**:118

"The Day Resurgent" (Henry) **5**:188

"A Day Saved" (Greene) **29**:184

"The Day the Dam Broke" (Thurber) **1**:426, 428, 432

"The Day the Icicle Works Closed" (Pohl) **25**:220, 230, 232

"The Day the Lift . . ." (Sansom) **21**:118, 127

"The Day the Martians Came" (Pohl) **25**:220

"The Day the Pig Fell into the Well" (Cheever) **1**:100; **38**:52, 55

"The Day They Burned the Books" (Rhys) **21**:49, 65, 69

The Day We Got Drunk on Cake, and Other Stories (Trevor) **21**:230, 232, 236, 254, 261

"A Day with Conrad Green" (Lardner) **32**:136, 138, 140, 146, 149, 152, 154-55, 163, 169

"A Day with Pegasus" (Ross) **24**:291, 296, 306-07, 310-12, 315-16, 323

Daybreak (Schnitzler)
 See *Spiel im Morgengrauen*

"Daydream of a Drunken Housewife" (Lispector)
 See "Devaneio e Embriaguez duma Rapariga"

"Daydreams" (Chekhov) **28**:56

"The Daydreams of a Drunken Woman" (Lispector)
 See "Devaneio e Embriaguez duma Rapariga"

Daylight and Nightmare (Chesterton) **1**:140

"Days" (O'Hara) **15**:253

Days and Nights: Journal of a Deserter (Jarry)
 See *Les jours et les nuits: Roman d'un déserter*

Day's End and Other Stories (Bates) **10**:111

"A Day's Lodging" (London) **4**:253

"Days of Sunshine" (Benet) **10**:149

"A Day's Pleasure" (Garland) **18**:154, 160

"A Day's Pleasure" (Howells) **36**:399

A Day's Pleasure and Other Sketches (Howells) **36**:399-400

"A Day's Work" (Capote) **2**:81

"A Day's Work" (Porter) **4**:339-40, 342, 360

The Day's Work (Kipling) **5**:266-68, 273-74, 283, 294-95

"Dayspring Mishandled" (Kipling) **5**:270, 278, 282-83, 299-303

"The Dazzling Light" (Machen) **20**:200

"De Mortuis" (Collier) **19**:102, 109-10, 112

"The De Wets Come to Kloof Grange" (Lessing) **6**:186, 189

"The Deacon" (Updike) **13**:361

"The Dead" (Joyce) **3**:202-06, 208, 210-11, 214-15, 217, 223-26, 228, 232-40, 242-45, 247, 249; **26**:32-86

"The Dead" (Oates) **6**:225, 234, 254

"The Dead Are Silent" (Schnitzler)
 See "Der toten schweigen"

"The Dead Child" (Andersen)
 See "The Child in the Grave"

"The Dead Fiddler" (Singer) **3**:369, 384

"The Dead Girl" (Agnon) **30**:66

Dead Leaves (Garcia Marquez)
 See *La hojarasca*

"The Dead Leman" (Gautier) **20**:3

"Dead Mabelle" (Bowen) **3**:30, 44, 54

"The Dead Man" (Borges)
 See "El muerto"

"The Dead Queen" (Coover) **15**:43-6

"Dead Roses" (White) **39**:279-82, 284, 290, 292-94, 297, 309, 312, 316-17, 336-37, 339, 344

"The Dead Season" (Schulz)
 See "Martwy sezon"

"The Dead Sexton" (Le Fanu) **14**:238

"The Dead Walk" (Bulgakov) **18**:90

"Dead Yellow Women" (Hammett) **17**:201, 222-24, 226, 230

"The Deadly Mission of P Snodgrass" (Pohl) **25**:234

"The Deal" (Michaels) **16**:301-03

"A Deal in Wheat" (Norris) **28**:198

A Deal in Wheat and Other Stories of the New and Old West (Norris) **28**:198-200

"Dean of Men" (Taylor) **10**:390, 399, 415, 418

Dear Baby (Saroyan) **21**:154-55

"Dear Greta Garbo" (Saroyan) **21**:132

"Dear John" (Updike) **13**:367

"Death" (Anderson) **1**:30, 42

"Death" (Calvino) **3**:110

"Death" (Svevo)
 See "La morte"

"Death and Decision" (Stuart) **31**:227, 236, 252

"Death and the Cherry Tree" (Bates) **10**:121

"Death and the Child" (Crane) **7**:100-01, 104-08

"Death and the Compass" (Borges)
 See "La muerte y la brújula"

"Death and the Senator" (Clarke) **3**:147

"Death Constant beyond Love" (Garcia Marquez)
 See "Muerte constante más allá der amor"

Death Dance: Twenty-Five Stories (Wilson) **21**:339

"The Death Disk" (Twain) **26**:331

"Death Has Two Good Eyes" (Stuart) **31**:266-67

"Death in Jerusalem" (Trevor) **21**:247, 262, 265

"Death in Midsummer" (Mishima) **4**:313-14, 318, 321-22

Death in Midsummer, and Other Stories (Mishima) **4**:313-18, 321-23

"Death in Sinan Monastery" (Andric) **36**:43, 55, 79

"A Death in the Country" (Benet) **10**:142, 149, 156-57

"A Death in the Desert" (Cather) **2**:90-1, 98, 103, 105, 113

"Death in the Sunday City" (Sansom) **21**:126

"Death in the Woods" (Anderson) **1**:31, 37-8, 40, 50-2, 56, 58-62

Death in the Woods (Anderson) **1**:31, 37, 50-1, 56

Death in Venice (Mann)
 See *Der Tod in Venedig*

"The Death of a Bachelor" (Schnitzler) **15**:343

Death of a Huntsman (Bates) **10**:119-20, 128-29

"The Death of a Kinsman" (Taylor) **10**:415

"Death of a Lesser Man" (Berriault) **30**:96-8

"The Death of a Political Boy" (Oe)
 See "Seiji shonen shisu"

"The Death of a Traveling Salesman" (Welty) **1**:466, 472, 481, 493, 497

The Death of Ahasuerus (Lagerkvist)
 See *Ahasverus död*

"The Death of Ankou" (Lewis) **34**:153, 161-62, 169

"The Death of Archimedes" (Capek) **36**:117, 129

"The Death of Baldy" (Sansom) **21**:88

Title Index

"The Death of Baron Gandara" (Capek)
See "Smrt barona Gandary"
"The Death of Children" (Saroyan) 21:133
"Death of Distant Friends" (Updike) 13:404
"The Death of Dolgushov" (Babel) 16:12, 24, 28-30, 41, 53, 58
"The Death of Edward Lear" (Barthelme) 2:49, 52
"The Death of Halpin Frayser" (Bierce) 9:70, 85-6
The Death of Ivan Ilych (Tolstoy)
See *Smert Ivana Ilyicha*
"The Death of Justina" (Cheever) 1:100; 38:50, 54, 61, 84, 88
"The Death of Ligoun" (London) 4:287
"The Death of Lully" (Huxley) 39:154
"The Death of Me" (Lish) 18:275, 281, 283
"The Death of Me" (Malamud) 15:174, 216, 227
The Death of Methusaleh, and Other Stories (Singer) 3:389
"The Death of Methusalah" (Singer) 3:389
"The Death of Monga" (Lewis) 40:280
"The Death of Mrs. Sheer" (Oates) 6:224
"The death of my mother and my new mother" (Shiga)
See "Haha no shi to atarishi haha"
"The Death of Peggy Meehan" (Trevor) 21:263
"The Death of Stevie Long" (O'Faolain) 13:315
"The Death of the Laird's Jock" (Scott) 32:319
"The Death of the Lion" (James) 8:281, 306, 317
The Death of the Poet (Tieck)
See *Der Tod des Dichters*
"The Death of the Prophet" (Baldwin) 10:17
"The Death of The Tiger" (Castellanos)
See "La muerte del tigre"
"Death Rides the Rails to Poston" (Yamamoto) 34:357
Death, the Proud Brother (Wolfe) 33:346-47, 349, 367, 371-72, 375, 380
"The Deathbird" (Ellison) 14:115, 118, 138, 140-41, 143, 145-46
Deathbird Stories: A Pantheon of Modern Gods (Ellison) 14:118, 121
"Deaths at Sea" (Dubus) 15:90
Debits and Credits (Kipling) 5:275, 279, 283, 296
"Debris" (Coover) 15:47
"The Debt" (Wharton) 6:421, 429
"A Debt of Honour" (Pritchett) 14:255, 298
"Debts" (Paley) 8:399, 403, 407
"Un début dans la vie" (Balzac) 5:8-9
Decameron (Boccaccio) 10:163-247
"The Deceitful Marriage" (Cervantes)
See "El casamiento engañoso"
"The Deceived" (Mann)
See *Die Betrogene*
"The Decision" (O'Hara) 15:250, 252, 254-55, 258
Decline and Fall (Waugh) 41:311, 318-22, 326, 328, 330, 336, 342-43, 345, 350-53, 355-66
"Decline & Fall of Dingdong-Daddyland" (Algren) 33:107
The Declining Years (Dazai Osamu)
See *Bannen*
"Décoré" (Maupassant) 1:256, 263
"Découverte" (Maupassant) 1:259
"A Decrepit Clan" (Leskov) 34:129
"Le Décret" (Ayme) 41:11, 16, 18-19, 21-24, 26-28
"DeDe's Talking, It's Her Turn" (Gilchrist) 14:154
"Dedication" (King) 17:295
"Deductible Yacht" (Auchincloss) 22:5
"Deeds of Light" (Price) 22:388
"Deep End" (Ballard) 1:69
Deep Sightings and Rescue Missions (Bambara) 35:42
Deephaven (Jewett) 6:150, 154-57, 165-69
"Deephaven Cronies" (Jewett) 6:150, 167
"Deephaven Excursions" (Jewett) 6:150, 168

"Deephaven Society" (Jewett) 6:154, 167
"Deer Dance/For Your Return" (Silko) 37:309
"Deer in the Works" (Vonnegut) 8:438
"Deer Season" (Beattie) 11:6
"Deer Song" (Silko) 37:309
"Defeat" (Boyle) 5:66
"Defeat" (Galsworthy) 22:63, 95, 101-02
"The Defeat of the City" (Henry) 5:184
"The Defeated" (Gordimer) 17:151
"The Defection of Mary Ann Gibbs" (Dunbar) 8:122
"A Defender of the Faith" (Dunbar) 8:122, 132
"Defender of the Faith" (Roth) 26:228, 231-32, 235-36, 239-42, 245, 249-50, 252, 257, 265-66, 268-70
"The Defenestration of Ermintrude Inch" (Clarke) 3:134
"A Defensive Diamond" (Saki) 12:296, 327
"An Déirc" (Moore) 19:319, 322, 324, 326, 328, 332, 334-35, 337
"The Deliberation of Mr. Dunkin" (Dunbar) 8:119, 121, 131, 136, 143
The Delicate Nature (Bates) 10:118
"The Delicate Prey" (Bowles) 3:59-63, 66, 72, 77
A Delicate Prey and Other Stories (Bowles) 3:58-65, 67, 70-2, 76-7, 79-80
"Delincuente honrado" (Pardo Bazan) 30:264-65
"Delitto al circolo di tennis" (Moravia) 26:163
"Delivering" (Dubus) 15:75, 81, 89, 96
"Dell Goes Into Politics" (Moorhouse) 40:286, 311
"Delphine" (Morand) 22:156-57, 165
"The Delta at Sunset" (Ballard) 1:69
"Delta Autumn" (Faulkner) 1:166; 35:140-41, 143, 145-48, 153-54, 157, 164-65, 167, 169, 173-74, 176, 178, 181, 190, 193-94, 198, 201-03
Delta of Venus (Nin) 10:305, 307, 324-25, 327
"The Deluge at Norderney" (Dinesen) 7:163, 170, 174, 176, 179-80, 182-83, 186, 190, 195-98, 200, 204
"Delusion for a Dragon Slayer" (Ellison) 14:108, 118, 120
"The Demi-Gods" (Galsworthy) 22:91
"Les demoiselles de Bienfilâtre" (Villiers de l'Isle Adam) 14:377-81, 383, 385-86, 393, 396, 411
"A Demon" (O'Brien) 10:347
"Le Démon de la connaissance" (Mauriac) 24:184, 197-98, 200, 203, 205-06
"The Demon Lover" (Bowen) 3:31-2, 41, 50-2, 54; 28:1-17
The Demon Lover and Other Stories (Bowen) 3:30-3, 41, 44, 48, 50-2; 28:2-7, 9-10, 14-17
"The Demon of Perversity" (Poe)
See "The Imp of the Perverse"
Demons and Darkness (Collier) 19:105
Demons by Daylight (Campbell) 19:60-3, 70, 73, 75, 78, 81-93
"The Demonstrators" (Welty) 1:488; 27:353
"Demos" (Galsworthy) 22:98
"The Dentist and the Gas" (Leacock) 39:262
"Dentistry and Doubt" (Updike) 13:351, 354, 395
"An Deóraidhe" (Moore) 19:319-21, 323, 330, 334-35
"Departure" (Anderson) 1:31, 42, 45-6
"Depend on Aunt Elly" (Algren) 33:88, 107, 110-11, 113
Le dépeupleur (Beckett) 16:71-2, 76-7, 88, 94, 98, 102, 105-07, 115, 123
"The Depths" (Campbell) 19:87
"El derecho de asilo" (Carpentier) 35:116-19
"Derletzebrief eines literaten" (Schnitzler) 15:355, 361-64
"Dermuche" (Ayme) 41:13, 17
Derrire chez Martin (Ayme) 41:20, 23
"Derring-Do" (Capote) 2:81
"Derzelez at the Inn" (Andric) 36:54

"Des Journées entières dans les arbres" (Duras) 40:3-6, 77
Des journées entières dans les arbres (Duras) 40:3, 9-10, 13-14, 65, 133-35
"Desayuno" (Cortazar) 7:95
"The Desborough Connections" (Harte) 8:220
"A Descendant of Kings" (Williams) 31:302, 324, 331, 359, 361
"A Descendant of the Cid" (Pardo Bazan)
See "El nieto del Cid"
"A Descent into the Maelström" (Poe) 1:385, 400, 402; 22:300; 34:249-50; 35:310, 321-22
"Descent of Man" (Boyle) 16:142, 148-49, 153
"The Descent of Man" (Wharton) 6:428-29
The Descent of Man (Wharton) 6:420-21
Descent of Man, and Other Stories (Boyle) 16:140-41, 143-44, 149-50, 154
"Description of a Fight" (Kafka) 29:349; 35:240
"Descriptions of a Battle" (Kafka)
See "Description of a Fight"
"A desejada des gentes" (Machado de Assis) 24:129
"The Deserter" (Babel) 16:35
"A Desertion" (Crane) 7:106
"Le désespoir de la vieille" (Baudelaire) 18:17, 32, 59, 64-5
Deshoras (Cortazar) 7:79
"Design for Departure" (Algren) 33:87-89, 102-03, 110
"Le désir de peindre" (Baudelaire) 18:6-7, 18
"Le désir d'être un homme" (Villiers de l'Isle Adam) 14:381, 384, 387, 389-90, 396
"Desire" (Beattie) 11:11, 20
Desire (O'Flaherty)
See *Dúil*
"Desire in November" (Calvino) 3:112
"The Desire to Be a Man" (Villiers de l'Isle Adam)
See "Le désir d'être un homme"
"The Desired Payment" (Bulgakov) 18:89
"Désirée's Baby" (Chopin) 8:66, 68, 74-6, 81-4, 91-2, 99, 103, 105-06
"Las desnudas" (Pardo Bazan) 30:272
"A Desperate Character" (Turgenev)
See "Otchayanny"
"Desquite" (Pardo Bazan) 30:268-69
"Le dessous de cartes d'une partie de whist" (Barbey d'Aurevilly) 17:7, 10-12, 15, 17-21, 27-8, 30-4, 38-9, 43-4
Destinies (Mauriac)
See *Destins*
"El destino" (Pardo Bazan) 30:272
Destins (Mauriac) 24:160, 165, 174, 201
El destripador (Pardo Bazan)
See *Un destripador de antaño*
"Un destripador de antaño" (Pardo Bazan) 30:262, 269, 272
Un destripador de antaño (Pardo Bazan) 30:270
"The Destruction of Kreshev" (Singer) 3:358-59, 368, 375, 383-84
"Destruction of the Man" (Pirandello)
See "La distruzione dell'uomo"
"Destructions" (Andric)
See "Razaranja"
"The Destructors" (Greene) 29:204-09, 212-15, 217, 222
"Details of a Sunset" (Nabokov) 11:131, 133
"Detroit Skyline, 1949" (Mason) 4:4
Detstvo (Tolstoy) 9:374-76, 380, 383, 399, 401-03; 30:331
"Detstvo Luvers" (Pasternak) 31:95-6, 98, 102, 107-08, 111-20
"Deutsches Requiem" (Borges) 4:9, 18, 24-6, 30, 37, 40-2
"Deux acteurs pour un rôle" (Gautier) 20:31
"Deux amis" (Maupassant) 1:275
"Deux augures" (Villiers de l'Isle Adam) 14:381, 395-96
"Les deux pigeons" (Laforgue) 20:101-2, 105
"Les deux rêves" (Balzac) 5:31

"Devaneio e Embriaguez duma Rapariga"
      (Lispector) **34**:187, 194-95, 197-98, 202,
      217, 221
"The Devil" (Tanizaki)
      See "Akuma"
"The Devil" (Tolstoy) **9**:377-78; **30**:312, 317,
      319, 328, 339-40, 342-43
"The Devil: A Sequel" (Tanizaki)
      See "Zoku Akuma"
The Devil and All (Collier) **19**:105
"The Devil and Daniel Webster" (Benet)
      10:143-44, 152-54, 156-58
"The Devil and his Grandmother" (Grimm and
      Grimm) **36**:228-29
"The Devil and Irv Cherniske" (Boyle) **16**:151,
      153
"The Devil and Television" (Stuart) **31**:227,
      236, 250
"The Devil and Tom Walker" (Irving) **2**:241,
      247-48, 250-51, 254, 262; **37**:267
"The Devil at Noon" (Tanizaki)
      See "Hakūchyukigo"
"The Devil, George and Rosie" (Collier)
      19:104-05
"The Devil Has Many Faces" (Stuart) **31**:250
"The Devil in the Belfry" (Poe) **1**:407
"The Devil with the Three Golden Hairs"
      (Grimm and Grimm) **36**:223
"The Devil-Drive" (Leskov)
      See "Čertogon"
"The Devil's Church" (Machado de Assis)
      See "A igreja do diabo"
"The Devil's Race-Track". Mark Twain's
      Great Dark Writings (Twain) **6**:336
"The Devil's Sooty Brother" (Grimm and
      Grimm) **36**:199, 228-29
"The Devil's Spittle" (Cortazar)
      See "Las babas del diablo"
The Devil's Yard (Andric)
      See *Prokleta avlija*
"The Devoted Friend" (Wilde) **11**:375-76, 380,
      386, 395, 398, 407, 409
"Devotion without End" (Peretz) **26**:211, 215
"Di grasso" (Babel) **16**:10-11, 16, 36, 41, 59
"Di sera, un geranio" (Pirandello) **22**:260
"Di shtot fun di kleyne mentshelek"
      (Aleichem) **33**:45
"Dia após dia" (Lispector) **34**:211
"El Dia de Muerte" (Bradbury) **29**:47
"El dia del derrumbe" (Rulfo) **25**:255, 265,
      271-74
"El día des las madres" (Fuentes)
      See "Mother's Day"
"El día que terminó mi niñez" (Cabrera
      Infante) **39**:23
"Le diable" (Maupassant) **1**:270, 284
"Diable—A Dog" (London)
      See "Batard"
"Diaboliad" (Bulgakov) **18**:72, 74, 93-5, 97,
      99, 104, 113
Diaboliad, and Other Stories (Bulgakov)
      See *D'iavoliada*
Les diaboliques (Barbey d'Aurevilly) **17**:2-4,
      7-8, 10-13, 15, 17-21, 24-5, 30, 33-4, 39-
      41, 43-4
"Diagnosis" (Wharton) **6**:424
"Dial F for Frankenstein" (Clarke) **3**:145
"The Dialectic" (Farrell) **28**:122, 125
Dialoghi con Leucò (Pavese) **19**:364-65, 371-
      72, 386, 388-89
"Diálogo del espejo" (Garcia Marquez) **8**:154-
      56, 182
"Dialogue" (Lessing) **6**:200-04
"Dialogue in a Mirror" (Garcia Marquez)
      See "Diálogo del espejo"
"The Dialogue of the Dogs" (Cervantes)
      See "El coloquio de los perros"
Dialogues de bêtes (Colette) **10**:261, 272
Dialogues with Leucò (Pavese)
      See *Dialoghi con Leucò*
"El diamante" (Arreola) **38**:22
"El diamante de Villasola" (Unamuno) **11**:312

"The Diamond as Big as the Ritz" (Fitzgerald)
      6:46-7, 58-60, 88, 92, 100-02
"A Diamond Guitar" (Capote) **2**:67
"The Diamond Maker" (Wells) **6**:383, 388, 408
"The Diamond Mine" (Cather) **2**:91-2
"The Diamond Necklace" (Maupassant)
      See "La parure"
"The Diamond of Kali" (Henry) **5**:184
"Diary, 1900" (Hesse) **9**:230
"The Diary of a Knight of King Arthur"
      (Lewis) **40**:280
"Diary of a Madman" (Gogol) **4**:82-3, 88, 91,
      98, 100-01, 105-07, 122, 124, 126, 128-29;
      29:127-28, 132, 135, 143, 148, 152, 163
"Diary of a Madman" (Lu Hsun)
      See *Kuangren riji*
"The Diary of a Madman" (Tolstoy)
      See *Zapiski sumasshedshego*
"Diary of a Sixteen-Year-Old" (Kawabata)
      See *Jūrokusai no Nikki*
"The Diary of a Superfluous Man" (Turgenev)
      See "Dnevnik lishnego cheloveka"
"The Diary of an African Nun" (Walker) **5**:402,
      404
"Diary of Hamlet" (Shiga) **23**:363
"The Diary of K. W." (Berriault) **30**:95-8, 104
"The Diary of Mr. Poynter" (James) **16**:223-24,
      229-30, 232-33, 235, 249, 255
"A Diary of Old New York" (Auchincloss)
      22:43
"A Diary of Sudden Death; By a
      Public Spirited Observer on the Inside"
      (Bierce) **9**:83
"The Diary of the Rose" (Le Guin) **12**:230,
      237-38
Los días enmascarados (Fuentes) **24**:30, 32,
      37-8, 40-1, 43-4, 46, 52-6, 58, 62
D'iavoliada (Bulgakov) **18**:72-3, 91-2, 97-100
"Dichter und Komponist" (Hoffmann) **13**:191
Dichterleben (Tieck) **31**:271-73, 276, 282-83,
      287, 289-90
"Dick Boyle's Business Card" (Harte) **8**:216,
      252
"Dick Denver's Idea" (Galsworthy) **22**:91
"Dickon the Devil" (Le Fanu) **14**:223
"Did I Invite You?" (Pritchett)
      See "Did You Invite Me?"
"Did You Ever Dream Lucky?" (Ellison) **26**:11
"Did You Invite Me?" (Pritchett) **14**:285, 298
"Diddling Considered as One of the Exact
      Sciences" (Poe) **1**:407
"An die Musik" (Le Guin) **12**:211-12, 214, 219-
      20, 222-23, 245, 250
"The Die-Hard" (Benet) **10**:154
Dietegen (Keller) **26**:91, 95, 107
"Dieu d'amour" (Wharton) **6**:428
"The Difference" (Glasgow) **34**:58, 64-7, 71,
      75, 78, 80-1, 94-5, 100-02
"Different Clowns for Different Towns"
      (Algren) **33**:96
"Different Faces" (Agnon)
      See "Panim aherot"
Different Seasons (King) **17**:262-67, 271-73,
      275, 282, 284
"A Difficult Case" (Howells) **36**:390-93, 396-98
Difficult Loves (Calvino)
      See *Gli amori difficili*
"Difficult People" (Chekhov) **2**:155
"Digging Our Own Graves" (Farrell) **28**:99,
      125
"Digroyse behole fun di kleyne mentshelekh"
      (Aleichem) **33**:7
"Díles que no me maten!" (Rulfo) **25**:246, 249,
      253-54, 261, 265, 272-73, 275, 278, 280
"The Dilettante" (Mann) **5**:320, 323, 330,
      335-37
"The Dilettante" (Wharton) **6**:424
"A Dill Pickle" (Mansfield) **9**:309-10
"Dinamarquero" (Donoso) **34**:30, 49
"The Diner Out" (Auchincloss) **22**:38
"Ding Dong" (Beckett) **16**:93
Ding Dong Bell (de la Mare) **14**:90, 92

"Dingle the Fool" (Jolley) **19**:223
"Dinner" (Lardner) **32**:133, 135, 138, 140-41,
      167-68
"A Dinner at Poplar Walk" (Dickens) **17**:120
"Dinol and Crede" (Moore) **19**:299, 311
"The Dinosaurs" (Calvino) **3**:103, 109
"Díoltas" (O'Flaherty) **6**:287-88
"Dionea" (Lee) **33**:302, 309
"El dios de los toros" (Bioy Casares) **17**:68, 70
"The Diploma" (Pirandello)
      See "La patente"
"The Diplomat" (Auchincloss) **22**:44
"The Diplomat" (Machado de Assis) **24**:153
"Direction of the Road" (Le Guin) **12**:234
"The Disappearance of Actor Benda" (Capek)
      36:105
"The Disappearance of an Actor" (Capek)
      36:127-28
"The Disappearing Duke" (Chandler) **23**:110
"The Dis-Associated Charities" (Norris)
      See "The Associated Un-Charities"
"The Discarded" (Ellison) **14**:103, 113-15, 117
"The Discarders" (Jolley) **19**:233
"The Discharged" (Capek) **36**:106
"The Disciple" (Aiken) **9**:4, 12-13
"El discípulo" (Arreola) **38**:6-7, 21
"El disco" (Borges) **41**:167
"Discord" (O'Faolain) **13**:284-286, 288, 293,
      309, 315
"The Discounters of Money" (Henry) **5**:159
"Discourse of a Lady Standing a Dinner to a
      Down-and-out Friend" (Rhys) **21**:62
"Discourse on the Tachanka" (Babel) **16**:27, 55
"A Discovery in the Woods" (Greene) **29**:187,
      189
"El disfraz" (Pardo Bazan) **30**:272
"A Disgrace to the Family" (Boyle) **5**:64
"Disillusioned" (de la Mare) **14**:83, 86
"Disillusionment" (Mann) **5**:321, 330
"The Disinherited" (Bowen) **3**:33, 41, 45, 48-9,
      51; **28**:9
"The Disintegration Machine" (Doyle) **12**:79
"The Dismissal" (Bowles) **3**:75, 80
"Disobedience" (Moravia) **26**:132-33, 136
Disobedience (Moravia)
      See *La disubbidienza*
Disorder and Early Sorrow (Mann) **5**:310-12,
      323, 350
"The Displaced Person" (O'Connor) **1**:335-36,
      338, 343-45, 347, 359; **23**:205, 235
"Displaced Persons" (Sansom) **21**:90, 94
"Distance" (Carver) **8**:4-5, 29, 42, 59
"Distance" (Oates) **6**:236-37
"Distance" (Paley) **8**:416-17
"The Distance of the Moon" (Calvino)
      See "La distanza della luna"
"The Distances" (Cortazar)
      See "Lejana"
"A Distant Episode" (Bowles) **3**:59, 61-2, 66-9,
      72, 78
"Distant Music" (Beattie) **11**:4, 6-7, 17
"The Distant Past" (Trevor) **21**:248, 260-62
The Distant Past, and Other Stories (Trevor)
      21:253
"La distanza della luna" (Calvino) **3**:92, 103,
      107, 109
Distortions (Beattie) **11**:2-5, 11-12, 15-16, 18-
      23, 26-8, 30-2
"The Distracted Preacher" (Hardy) **2**:203, 205,
      208, 213-15, 219-21
"Distraction" (Pirandello) **22**:249
"La distruzione dell'uomo" (Pirandello) **22**:280
"The Disturber" (Villiers de l'Isle Adam)
      See "L'inquiéteur"
"The Disturber of Traffic" (Kipling) **5**:283
La disubbidienza (Moravia) **26**:133, 140, 143,
      146, 156, 158, 165-66, 169-71, 182, 185-86
"The Ditch" (O'Flaherty) **6**:265
"The Diver" (Dinesen) **7**:163, 167-68, 171
"The Diver" (Pritchett) **14**:260-61, 288-89, 299
Divers Vanities (Morrison) **40**:329, 333, 349

A Diversity of Creatures (Kipling) **5**:275, 282-84
"Dividends" (O'Faolain) **13**:300
"The Division" (Turgenev) **7**:318
"A Division in the Coolly" (Garland) **18**:148, 160, 184
"Divorcing: A Fragment" (Updike) **13**:387
"Dixiong" (Lu Hsun) **20**:149
"Dizzy-Headed Dick" (Dunbar) **8**:122
"D'javoliada" (Bulgakov)
    See "Diaboliad"
"Djinn, No Chaser" (Ellison) **14**:127
"Djoûmane" (Merimee) **7**:285, 296-8
"Djuna" (Nin) **10**:300-01, 317
Dlia pol'zy dela (Solzhenitsyn) **32**:330, 333, 335-37, 340, 364, 390, 395, 397
"Dnevnik lishnego cheloveka" (Turgenev) **7**:314, 318-20, 339
"Do the Dead Sing?" (King)
    See "The Reach"
"Do You Know This Man?" (Auchincloss) **22**:51
"Do You Like It Here?" (O'Hara) **15**:266
"Do You Want to Make Something Out of It?" (Thurber) **1**:428
"Do Your Christmas Necking Now" (Perelman) **32**:240
"Doc Marlowe" (Thurber) **1**:414
"Doc Mellhorn and the Pearly Gates" (Benet) **10**:143, 154, 159-60
"Doc Rivers" (Williams)
    See "Old Doc Rivers"
"Las doce figuras del mundo" (Bioy Casares) **17**:70
"The Dock-Witch" (Ozick) **15**:297, 300, 312-13, 326
"The Doctor" (Dubus) **15**:70, 77-9
"The Doctor" (Gallant) **5**:135, 139
"The Doctor" (Williams) **31**:329
"The Doctor and His Divorced Wife" (Agnon)
    See "The Doctor's Divorce"
"The Doctor and His Divorcée" (Agnon)
    See "The Doctor's Divorce"
"The Doctor and the Doctor's Wife" (Hemingway) **1**:208, 217, 234, 241, 245
Doctor Brodie's Report (Borges)
    See *El informe de Brodie*
"Dr. Bullivant" (Hawthorne) **3**:164
"Doctor Chevalier's Lie" (Chopin) **8**:73
"Doctor Crombie" (Greene) **29**:200-01
"Doctor Havel after Ten Years" (Kundera) **24**:88-9, 91-2, 103
"Doctor Havel after Twenty Years" (Kundera) **24**:100, 104, 107-08, 118
"Doctor Havel Ten Years Later" (Kundera)
    See "Doctor Havel after Ten Years"
"Dr. Heidegger's Experiment" (Hawthorne) **3**:154, 178, 186-87
Doctor Jekyll and Mr. Hyde (Stevenson)
    See *The Strange Case of Dr. Jekyll and Mr. Hyde*
Doctor Martino, and Other Stories (Faulkner) **1**:180
"The Doctor of Hoyland" (Doyle) **12**:88
"A Doctor of Medicine" (Kipling) **5**:285
"Doctor or Patient?" (Peretz)
    See "Doctor or Patient?"
"Doctor Tristan's Treatment" (Villiers de l'Isle Adam)
    See "Le traitement du docteur Tristan"
"The Doctors" (Barnes) **3**:9-10
"The Doctor's Case" (King) **17**:295
"The Doctor's Divorce" (Agnon) **30**:3, 48, 54,63-6
"The Doctor's Son" (O'Hara) **15**:247, 252, 256-57, 265-66, 286
The Doctor's Son, and Other Stories (O'Hara) **15**:249, 263, 264-67, 273-74
"A Doctor's Visit" (Chekhov) **2**:127, 156-58
"The Doctor's Wife" (Ozick) **15**:297, 300, 313-14

"The Doctor's Word" (Narayan) **25**:138, 140, 153, 155-56
"Dodu" (Narayan) **25**:135, 137, 156, 160
Dodu and Other Stories (Narayan) **25**:137, 152
"Doe" (Coppard) **21**:29
"A Doer of the World" (Dreiser) **30**:112
"The Dog" (Shiga) **23**:346
"The Dog" (Turgenev) **7**:316, 321, 323-24, 326, 335-36, 338
"Dog Days" (Dixon) **16**:217
"The Dog Hervey" (Kipling) **5**:275, 284-85
"The Dog It Was That Died" (Galsworthy) **22**:63, 79, 101-02
"A Dog Named Trilby" (Hughes) **6**:122
"Dog of Timothy's" (Galsworthy) **22**:71
"Dog Scent" (Zoshchenko) **15**:406
"Doge und Dogressa" (Hoffmann) **13**:183-84
"A Dog's a Dog" (Collier) **19**:111
The Dogs' Colloquy (Cervantes)
    See "El coloquio de los perros"
"A Dog's Death" (Price) **22**:376
Doktor Murkes gesammeltes Schweigen, und andere Satiren (Boell) **23**:8, 36
"Dokutan" (Tanizaki) **21**:209-10
"Dolan's Cadillac" (King) **17**:294
"The Doldrums" (Galsworthy) **22**:72-3, 91
"The Doll" (Chesnutt) **7**:17
"The Doll" (Fuentes)
    See "El Muñeco"
"The Doll Queen" (Fuentes)
    See "La muñeca reina"
Dollari e vecchie mondane (Calvino) **3**:91
Dollars and the Demi-Mondaine (Calvino)
    See *Dollari e vecchie mondane*
"Dolls" (Campbell) **19**:76, 85
"The Doll's House" (Mansfield) **9**:280, 282, 286, 301-05, 308, 311, 313; **23**:153, 164, 169
"The Dolls' Journey" (Alcott) **27**:43
"Dolph Heyliger" (Irving) **2**:241, 247-48, 251, 254, 256, 259-60
"The Dolt" (Barthelme) **2**:38, 52
"The Domain of Arnheim" (Poe) **22**:303, 305
"Le domande" (Moravia) **26**:148
"A Domestic Dilemma" (McCullers) **9**:323, 331-32, 343, 353-54, 356, 359-60
Domestic Happiness (Tolstoy)
    See *Semeinoe schaste*
"Domestic Life in America" (Updike) **13**:385-86, 388-89
Domestic Relations: Short Stories (O'Connor) **5**:371, 375
"Domingo" (Castellanos) **39**:45, 75, 76
"El dominó verde" (Pardo Bazan) **30**:264-65
"Don" (Dixon) **16**:207, 212
Don Candelbro e Campagnin (Verga)
    See *Don Candelro*
Don Candeloro & Co. (Verga)
    See *Candeloro e Compagni*
Don Candelro (Verga) **21**:294-95
"Don Carmelo's Salvation" (Pardo Bazan)
    See "La salvación de don Carmelo"
Don Correa (Keller) **26**:103-04, 110
"Don Joaquin" (Cable) **4**:58
"Don Juan" (RetiredO'Connor) **5**:369, 371
"Don Juan's Temptation" (O'Connor) **5**:366, 371, 389
"El don rechazado" (Castellanos) **39**:39, 49
"El don supremo" (Bioy Casares) **17**:53
"Dona Benedita" (Machado de Assis) **24**:128
"Doña Faustina" (Bowles) **3**:64, 66, 80, 83
"Dona Paula" (Machado de Assis) **24**:153
Donde viven las águilas (Valenzuela) **14**:366
"Donnerhugel's Narrative" (Scott) **32**:288-89, 291, 300
"Le donneur d'eau bénite" (Maupassant) **1**:281
"Les dons des fées" (Baudelaire) **18**:17, 19, 43
"Don't Die" (Lish) **18**:283
"Don't Let Them" (Cortazar)
    See "No te dejes"
"Don't Let's Be Dramatic" (Moravia) **26**:160

"Don't Look Now" (du Maurier) **18**:129-30, 133, 137
Don't Look Now (du Maurier)
    See *Not after Midnight*
"Don't Smoke on the Apron" (Sansom) **21**:127
"Don't Take No for an Answer" (Garrett) **30**:163, 172, 180
"Don't You Hear the Dogs Barking?" (Rulfo)
    See "No oyes ladrar los perros"
"The Doom of the Darnaways" (Chesterton) **1**:131, 138
"The Doom of the Griffiths" (Gaskell) **25**:54-5
"The Door: A Prologue of Sorts" (Coover) **15**:33, 35, 51
"The Door in the Wall" (Wells) **6**:361-62, 368-70, 376, 381, 383-84, 391-92, 404, 406
"The Door of Opportunity" (Maugham) **8**:357, 374
"The Door of the Trap" (Anderson) **1**:27, 39, 52
"The Doorbell" (Nabokov) **11**:133
"The Doorkeeper" (Stifter)
    See "Tourmaline"
"The Doorkeeper at the Mansion" (Stifter)
    See "Tourmaline"
"Doorstep Acquaintance" (Howells) **36**:399
"Doorways" (McGahern) **17**:299, 308-09, 318-19, 321
"Doppelgänger" (Lewis) **34**:163, 165, 179-80
Ein Doppelgänger (Storm) **27**:306, 311
"Die Doppeltgänger" (Hoffmann) **13**:206
"El Dorado: A Kansas Recessional" (Cather) **2**:101, 105
"Dorfgeschichte" (Walser) **20**:333
"Doroga" (Babel) **16**:36, 59
Dorotheas Blumenkörbchen (Keller) **26**:100, 108
"Dorothée" (Baudelaire)
    See "La belle Dorothée"
"Dorothy" (Caldwell) **19**:34, 37, 41-2
"Dorothy and My Grandmother and the Sailors" (Jackson) **39**:210, 211, 222
The Dorrington Deed-box (Morrison) **40**:332, 349
"Dos cartas" (Donoso) **34**:30, 49
"Las dos doncellas" (Cervantes) **12**:4-5, 14, 17-18, 21, 26, 34, 37, 44
"Las dos Elenas" (Fuentes) **24**:29, 32, 51, 55-6, 58, 61-2, 70, 72
"Dos fantasías memorables" (Borges) **4**:16
Dos madres (Unamuno) **11**:313, 323-25, 327, 347, 356
"Dos meserl" (Aleichem) **33**:66, 71
"Dos Shtraiml" (Peretz) **26**:201-02, 220, 222-23
"Dos tepl" (Aleichem) **33**:19, 26-7, 35-9
Las dos Venecias (Ferre) **36**:146, 155
"'Dossing Out' and 'Camping'" (Lawson) **18**:215
"Dossy" (Frame) **29**:101, 105
"Double Birthday" (Cather) **2**:99, 113-15
"A Double Buggy at Lahey's Creek" (Lawson) **18**:201-06, 229, 262
"The Double Chamber" (Baudelaire)
    See "La chambre double"
"The Double Corner" (Stegner) **27**:197, 218
"Une double famille" (Balzac) **5**:22, 29-31
"Double Feature" (Selby) **20**:258
"The Double Gap" (Auchincloss) **22**:14, 21-2, 41-2
"The Double Happiness Bun" (Gilchrist) **14**:154
La double méprise (Merimee) **7**:276, 281, 283, 286, 290-2, 304
"The Double Mistake" (Merimee)
    See *La double méprise*
"Double Talk" (Nabokov)
    See "Conversation Piece, 1945"
"A Double Tragedy" (Alcott) **27**:34, 58
A Double-Barrelled Detective Story (Twain) **6**:295
"A Double-Dyed Deceiver" (Henry) **5**:182
".007" (Kipling) **5**:266, 268, 279

"The Dove Came Down" (Wescott) **35**:357, 363, 369-72, 374-75
"The Dove of Chapacalco" (Porter) **31**:162-63
"The Dover Road" (Machen) **20**:197
"The Doves Nest" (Mansfield) **9**:280;
The Doves' Nest, and Other Stories (Mansfield) **9**:281; **23**:137
"Down at the Dinghy" (Salinger) **2**:290-91, 295-96, 298-300, 314
"Down at the Dump" (White)
See "Down in the Dump"
"Down at the Hydro" (Sansom) **21**:117, 127
"Down by the Riverside" (Wright) **2**:360-61, 363, 365-69, 371, 374-75, 379-81, 387, 390-91
"Down in the Dump" (White) **39**:280-82, 287, 289, 291-94, 296, 299, 307, 312, 315-16, 318-19, 325, 327, 329, 336, 339-42, 344
"Down Pens" (Saki) **12**:306
"Down There" (Campbell) **19**:88
"Down with All Hands" (Algren) **33**:108
"Downers" (Michaels) **16**:308
"Downhill" (Beattie) **11**:17, 28
"The Downward Path to Wisdom" (Porter) **4**:339-40, 342, 359
"Downwind from Gettysbury" (Bradbury) **29**:56
"The Dowry of Angyar" (Le Guin) **12**:219, 224
Dr. Brodie's Report (Borges)
See *El informe de Brodie*
"Dr. Faustus" (Benet) **10**:145
"Dr. Locrian's Asylum" (Ligotti) **16**:269, 278-80, 283, 296
"Dr. Mejzlík's Case" (Capek)
See "Případ dra Mejzlíka"
Dr. Murke's Collected Silences (Boell)
See *Doktor Murkes gesammeltes Schweigen, und andere Satiren*
"Dr. Perelman, I Presume; or, Small Bore in Africa" (Perelman) **32**:213
"Dr. Tarr and Prof. Fether" (Poe) **34**:281
"Dr. Voke and Mr. Veech" (Ligotti) **16**:261, 265, 276, 284
"Dr. Woolacott" (Forster) **27**:90, 96, 102-07
"Draft" (Beckett) **16**:108
"The Dragon" (Spark) **10**:367, 370
"The Dragon at Hide and Seek" (Chesterton) **1**:140
"Dragonflies" (Shiga) **23**:346
La dragonne (Jarry) **20**:50
"The Dragon's Teeth" (Gordon)
See "One against Thebes"
"Dramas" (O'Brien) **10**:346
"Un drame au bord de la mer" (Balzac) **5**:11-13, 16, 26, 31
"The Draped Mirrors" (Borges) **41**:102
"Drawing In" (Campbell) **19**:75
"Drawing Names" (Mason) **4**:5
"Drawing Room B" (O'Hara) **15**:250
"Dreaded Hell" (Onetti)
See "El infierno tan temido"
"A Dream" (Howells) **36**:352-56, 396-97
"A Dream" (Peretz)
See "A Dream"
"The Dream" (Turgenev)
See "Son"
"A Dream Come True" (Onetti)
See "Un sueño realizado"
The Dream Department (Perelman) **32**:201, 205
A Dream Fulfilled, and Other Stories (Onetti)
See *Un sueño realizado y otros cuentos*
"Dream Journeys" (Hesse) **9**:230-32, 236
Dream Journeys (Hesse) **9**:230
The Dream Life of Balso Snell (West) **16**:345-47, 349-51, 354, 361-67, 369, 377, 379, 383-87, 389-90, 393-94, 396-98, 402-03, 406-11, 415, 417
"Dream of a Mannikin; or, The Third Person" (Ligotti) **16**:261, 263, 265, 271, 273, 275-78, 283, 288
"The Dream of a Queer Fellow" (Dostoevsky)
See "The Dream of a Ridiculous Man"

"The Dream of a Ridiculous Man" (Dostoevsky) **2**:166, 183, 185
"The Dream of an Hour" (Chopin)
See "The Story of an Hour"
"A Dream of Armageddon" (Wells) **6**:360, 383-84, 391, 404
"The Dream of Beg Karčic" (Andric)
See "San bega Karčica"
"A Dream of Butterflies" (Trevor) **21**:262
"A Dream of Oblómov's Grandson" (Bunin) **5**:81, 90
"The Dream of the Gods" (Hesse) **9**:243
"A Dream of Wolves" (P'u Sung-ling) **31**:198
"Dream Sequence" (Hesse) **9**:234-35
"Dreamer in a Dead Language" (Paley) **8**:410
"The Dreamers" (Dinesen) **7**:167, 170, 174, 191, 195, 197-98, 200, 209
"The Dreaming Child" (Dinesen) **7**:165, 171
"The Dreaming in Nortown" (Ligotti) **16**:284
"Dreams" (Chekhov) **2**:156
"The Dreams in the Witch-House" (Lovecraft) **3**:258, 260, 263, 268, 272, 274-76, 282
"The Dreams of Chang" (Bunin) **5**:80-1, 83-4, 93
Dreamtigers (Borges)
See *El hacedor*
"A Dreary Story" (Chekhov) **2**:126, 131, 143, 150, 156; **41**:199-201
"Die drei Erznarren" (Arnim) **29**:5, 29
Drei Frauen (Musil) **18**:292-93, 297, 322-23, 325
Die drei gerechten Kammacher (Keller) **26**:91, 107, 116, 125-26
Die drei liebreichen Schwestern und der glückliche Farber (Arnim) **29**:5-8
"Drei Matones" (Peretz) **26**:196, 202, 215
"Drei Schmiede ihres Schicksals" (Stifter) **28**:291
"Drenched in Light" (Hurston) **4**:136-38, 149-50
"A Dresden Lady in Dixie" (Chopin) **8**:94
"The Dress" (Thomas) **3**:399, 408
"Dressed Like Summer Leaves" (Dubus) **15**:87
"A Dressmaker" (Warner) **23**:373
"The Dreydl" (Aleichem) **33**:17-18
"Dreyfus in Kasrilevke" (Aleichem) **33**:47
"Dried Fruit" (Moore) **19**:340-41
"Drift" (Cowan) **28**:80
Drift (Cowan) **28**:76-80
"Drifted Back" (Lawson) **18**:248, 250
"Drifting Apart" (Lawson) **18**:229
"Drifting Crane" (Garland) **18**:147, 176, 187-88
"Drifting Down Lost Creek" (Murfree) **22**:188, 190, 196, 203, 206, 208, 215, 218
"Drink to Me Only with Labyrinthine Eyes" (Ligotti) **16**:265, 269, 271, 274, 276, 278, 294
"A Drive in the Country" (Greene) **29**:183, 186, 193, 212-13
Driving Blind (Bradbury) **29**:66
"Le droit du passé" (Villiers de l'Isle Adam) **14**:396
"Le drôle" (Mauriac) **24**:189-99, 206
Droll Stories (Balzac)
See *Contes drolatiques*
"Drømmerne" (Dinesen)
See "The Dreamers"
The Drop of Blood (Pardo Bazan)
See *La gota de sangre*
"Dropped Dead: A Ghost Story" (Howells) **36**:398
"The Drover's Wife" (Lawson) **18**:201-02, 206, 216-17, 219-23, 225-27, 248-51, 259, 263
"The Drowned Giant" (Ballard) **1**:68, 74
"The Drowned Girl" (Gogol)
See "Majskaja noč, ili Vtoplennica"
"Drowne's Wooden Image" (Hawthorne) **3**:185
"Drowning" (Boyle) **16**:142, 151, 156
"Drüben auf den Inseln" (Lenz) **33**:317, 319
"The Drum" (Coppard) **21**:16
"The Drummer of All the World" (Laurence) **7**:245, 248-50, 256, 260-61, 272

The Drummer of the Eleventh North Devonshire Fusiliers (Davenport) **16**:199-200
"The Drums of the Fore and Aft" (Kipling) **5**:264-65, 269, 273
"Drunk with Love" (Gilchrist) **14**:157
Drunk with Love (Gilchrist) **14**:156-59
"The Drunkard" (O'Connor) **5**:369, 371, 378
"Drunkard's Death" (Dickens) **17**:116, 125
"The Drunkard's Dream" (Le Fanu) **14**:220, 222-23
"A Drunken Steam-Engine" (Bulgakov) **18**:90
"Dry September" (Faulkner) **1**:148, 180-81
Dry Valley (Bunin)
See *Sukhodol*
"The Dryad" (Andersen) **6**:7
Dubliners (Joyce) **3**:201-03, 205-07, 210, 213-14, 216-18, 224-26, 228-30, 233-35, 237-39, 244-45, 247-49; **26**:32, 36, 39-40, 46-53, 67-70, 72, 76-77, 82, 84
Dubrovsky (Pushkin) **27**:164, 175-76, 185
"The Duc De L'Omellette" (Poe) **22**:305; **35**:336
"The Duchess" (Cheever) **1**:106
"The Duchess and the Bugs" (Thurber) **1**:430
"The Duchess and the Jeweller" (Woolf) **7**:377, 388
"The Duchess at Prayer" (Wharton) **6**:413, 415, 428
"The Duchess of Hamptonshire" (Hardy) **2**:204
"The Duchess of Palliano" (Stendhal)
See "La Duchesse de Palliano"
La Duchesse de Langeais (Balzac) **5**:43-5, 47
"La Duchesse de Palliano" (Stendhal) **27**:249-50, 261
"The Duckling" (Andersen)
See "The Ugly Duckling"
"The Duckling" (Solzhenitsyn)
See "Utenok"
"The Ducks" (Carver) **8**:10
"Dudley for the Dartmouth Cup" (Taylor) **10**:379
Due cortigiane e Serata di don Giovanni (Moravia) **26**:185
"Le due maschere" (Pirandello) **22**:275
"The Duel" (Borges)
See "El duelo"
"The Duel" (Chekhov) **2**:131, 143, 145, 150-51, 155, 157; **41**:189-224
"The Duel" (Conrad) **9**:163, 183
"The Duel" (Henry) **5**:191
"The Duel" (Kleist)
See *Der Zweikampf*
"The Duel of Dr. Hirsch" (Chesterton) **1**:138
"A Duel without Seconds" (Barnes) **3**:13
"El duelo" (Borges) **4**:20, 27
"Dúil" (O'Flaherty) **6**:286, 288-89
Dúil (O'Flaherty) **6**:285-89
"Duke of Portland" (Villiers de l'Isle Adam) **14**:381, 384, 388, 390-91, 393-96
"The Duke's Reappearance" (Hardy) **2**:210
Dulcima (Bates) **10**:117-18
"The Dulham Ladies" (Jewett) **6**:160
"A Dull Story" (Chekhov)
See "A Dreary Story"
"Dullborough Town" (Dickens) **17**:123
"Dulse" (Munro) **3**:346
"The Dumb Girl" (Peretz) **26**:205
"Dumb Show" (Aldiss) **36**:5
"Dumbledon Donkey" (Coppard) **21**:12
"Dumbrovic" (Farrell) **28**:126
"Dummy" (Carver) **8**:5, 29, 34
"The Dummy" (Jackson) **39**:211, 224, 227
"The Dunwich Horror" (Lovecraft) **3**:258-59, 263, 269-70, 274-76, 290-92, 294
"Dunyazadiad" (Barth) **10**:48-9, 51, 54, 56, 61, 66, 68-9, 71, 91, 93-7, 101-05
Duo (Colette) **10**:262-65, 269
"The Duplicity of Hargraves" (Henry) **5**:159, 171
"Duracok" (Leskov) **34**:111-12
"During a Winter Night" (Warner) **23**:380

"During the Encampment" (Andric)
    See "Za logorovanja"
"During the Jurassic" (Updike) **13**:360, 387
"Dusie" (Barnes) **3**:10, 16
"Dusk" (Saki) **12**:296, 305, 315
"Dusk before Fireworks" (Parker) **2**:273-74, 281, 284-85
"Dusky Ruth" (Coppard) **21**:2, 15-16, 18, 20, 25, 29
"Dust" (Fisher) **25**:6, 17, 20, 25-6
"The Dust Garden" (Ferre) **36**:157
"Dutch Courage" (Kipling) **5**:264
"The Dutch Letters" (Moorhouse) **40**:299, 307, 324
"Dux gospozi Zanlis" (Leskov) **34**:113
"Dvadtsat' shest' i odna" (Gorky) **28**:134, 136-37, 146, 160, 163-64, 167-68, 171, 176-77, 179, 189, 191
"The Dwarf" (Bradbury) **29**:67, 87, 89
"Dwarf House" (Beattie) **11**:15-16
"Dwellers in the Valley" (Lewis) **40**:280
"Dying" (Schnitzler)
    See "Sterben"
"Dying Fires" (Norris) **28**:210-11
"Dykhanie" (Solzhenitsyn) **32**:351
"The Dynamiter" (Stevenson)
    See *The New Arabian Nights*
"Dynd-Kongens Datter" (Andersen)
    See "The Marsh King's Daughter"
E domani lunedì (Pirandello) **22**:232, 234, 275
"E due" (Pirandello) **22**:234
"Each Other" (Lessing) **6**:197, 200, 214, 218
"The Ear of Grain" (Grimm and Grimm) **36**:199
"Early Afternoon" (O'Hara) **15**:248, 274
"An Early Christmas" (Price) **22**:384, 388
"Early Coaches" (Dickens) **17**:133
"An Early Evening Conversation" (Andric)
    See "Razgovor predveče"
"Early Sorrow" (Mann)
    See *Disorder and Early Sorrow*
Early Stories (Bowen) **3**:40; **28**:4
"The Ears of Johnny Bear" (Steinbeck) **11**:207-08, 225, 229-30, 233-34, 242-44; **37**:357
"Earth 18" (Pohl) **25**:225
"The Earth is a Syllable" (Lewis) **40**:278
"Earth, Moon" (Boyle) **16**:142
"Earthbound" (Oliphant) **25**:180, 184, 196-200, 203, 208-09
"Earthquake Almanac" (Twain) **34**:326
"The Earthquake in Chile" (Kleist)
    See "Das Erdbeben in Chili"
"Earth's Holocaust" (Hawthorne) **3**:162, 181-82, 189
East and West: The Collected Short Stories of W. Somerset Maugham (Maugham) **8**:356, 358, 360, 370, 382
East India and Company (Morand) **22**:167, 182
"The Easter Egg" (Saki) **12**:298, 306, 329
"The Easter Egg Party" (Bowen) **3**:43, 47
"Easter Eve" (Chekhov) **2**:130
"The Easter of the Soul" (Henry) **5**:188
"The Easter Procession" (Solzhenitsyn) **32**:365, 393, 395
"The Easter Wedding" (Dunbar) **8**:122, 136
Eastward Ha! (Perelman) **32**:230, 233-34
"Eating Out" (Michaels) **16**:308
"Eating the Placenta" (Dixon) **16**:208
The Ebony Tower (Fowles) **33**:233-69, 275-76, 283, 287-88, 291-95
"The Eccentric Seclusion of the Old Lady" (Chesterton) **1**:120
"Echo" (Barth) **10**:42, 47, 52-4, 59-61, 75-6, 80-1, 85, 89, 95, 99, 102
"The Echo" (Bowles) **3**:59, 61-2, 66, 72, 77, 79
"The Echo and the Nemesis" (Stafford) **26**:274, 277, 283-84, 312
"Echoes" (Dinesen) **7**:173-74
Echoes from the Macabre (du Maurier) **18**:130
"Echo's Bones" (Beckett) **16**:106-08
Eclogues (Davenport) **16**:183, 187-89
L'école des femmes (Gide) **13**:72, 95, 100-02, 104, 105

"Economic Conference, 1934" (Lowry) **31**:42
"The Ecstasy and Suffering of Toma Galus" (Andric)
    See "Zanos i stradanja Tome Galusa"
"Eddie" (Schulz) **13**:334
"Eddie Mac" (McGahern) **17**:305
"The Edge" (Narayan) **25**:159, 175
"The Edge of the Evening" (Kipling) **5**:269
"The Edge of the World" (Cheever) **1**:88; **38**:43
"Editha" (Howells) **36**:349, 351-52, 357, 371-74, 377, 379, 382-83, 385, 394, 397, 399
"The Editor Regrets..." (Pritchett) **14**:297
An Editor's Tales (Trollope) **28**:311, 313, 316, 320, 322-24, 332-33, 336, 339, 341-42, 353-54
"Edmund" (Hesse) **9**:230-31, 236
"Edna's Husband" (Farrell) **28**:122
"Edna's Ruthie" (Cisneros) **32**:32
Edo and Enam (Agnon) **30**:5, 15, 24, 26-8, 30, 32-4, 71, 75
"An Education" (Ozick) **15**:302, 305, 316-17
"Education of a Stuffed Shirt" (Machado de Assis) **24**:136, 138, 152
"The Education of Audrey" (Mansfield) **9**:301
"The Educational Experience" (Barthelme) **2**:53
"Edward" (Waugh)
    See "Edward of Unique Achievement"
"Edward and God" (Kundera) **24**:87-95, 102-03, 107, 111, 118-21, 124-25
"Edward and Pia" (Barthelme) **2**:30
"Edward of Unique Achievement" (Waugh) **41**:328
"Edward Randolph's Portrait" (Hawthorne) **3**:179, 182
Eekenhof (Storm) **27**:281, 286
"The Effective Remedy" (Bulgakov) **18**:89
"Effigy of War" (Boyle) **5**:63-4
Les égarements de Minne (Colette) **10**:257
"The Egg" (Anderson)
    See "The Triumph of the Egg"
"The Egg and the Hen" (Lispector)
    See "O ovo e a galinha"
"The Egg Race" (Updike) **13**:386
"El egía" (Arreola) **38**:6
"L'église" (Balzac) **5**:14, 23, 31
"The Egoist" (Collier) **19**:103
"Egotism; or, The Bosom Serpent" (Hawthorne) **3**:159, 178, 183, 189; **39**:91
"Egotists" (O'Faolain) **13**:309
"An Egyptian Cigarette" (Chopin) **8**:99
"Egyptian Darkness" (Bulgakov) **18**:86, 88
Die Ehenschmiede (Arnim) **29**:5
"Eidolons" (Ellison) **14**:142
Eigensinn und Laune (Tieck) **31**:275
Eight Men (Wright) **2**:364, 366, 370, 386, 388
"Eight O'Clock One Morning" (Grau) **15**:149, 160
"Eighteen Springs" (Chang) **28**:26
18 Stories (Boell) **23**:6, 8-9
"1830" (Davenport) **16**:161, 165-66, 170, 183
"Die Einfahrt" (Walser) **20**:341
Einsichten und Ausblicke (Hauptmann) **37**:246
"Einstein Crosses the Elbe Near Hamburg" (Lenz)
    See "Einstein überquert die Elbe bei Hamburg—Geschichte in drei Sätzen"
"Einstein überquert die Elbe bei Hamburg—Geschichte in drei Sätzen" (Lenz) **33**:330, 337
"Eiros and Charmion" (Poe)
    See "The Conversation of Eiros and Charmion"
"Either of One or of No One" (Pirandello)
    See "O di uno o di nessuno"
"The Elaghin Affair" (Bunin) **5**:82-3, 85, 87, 103, 108-09, 115, 119
The Elaghin Affair, and Other Stories (Bunin) **5**:82
"The Elaghin Case" (Bunin)
    See "The Elaghin Affair"
"The Elder Lady" (Borges) **4**:19

"The Elder Mother" (Andersen)
    See "The Elder-Tree Mother"
"Elder Pill, Preacher" (Garland) **18**:154, 160, 163, 176
"The Elder-Tree Mother" (Andersen) **6**:3-4, 14, 24
Eldorado (Lessing) **6**:191, 194-95
"Eleanor's House" (Cather) **2**:99, 103
"Electioneerin' on Big Injun Mounting" (Murfree) **22**:188, 207-09, 218
The Electrical Experience (Moorhouse) **40**:288, 290-92, 294-98, 303-305, 308-09, 321-22
"El Elefante X2dq2" (Arreola) **38**:36-39
"Elegies" (Price) **22**:370
"Elegy" (Capek) **36**:89, 107, 121-23
"Elegy for a Freelance" (Carter) **13**:4
"An Elegy for Alma's Aunt Amy" (Suckow) **18**:393, 395, 413, 422, 424
"The Element Follows You Around, Sir!" (Lowry) **31**:42-3
"Elementals" (Benet) **10**:145
"Der Elementargeist" (Hoffmann) **13**:215
"Elements of True Manhood" (Jewett) **6**:167
"Eleonora" (Poe) **22**:291
"Elephant" (Carver) **8**:43
"Elephant and Colosseum" (Lowry) **31**:40, 43-8, 51, 59-61, 63-4, 66, 71-5, 79, 82, 84-5
"An Elephant Never Forgets" (Wilson) **21**:358-59
"Les Eléphants" (Ayme) **41**:8
"Elephants to Ride Upon" (Thomas) **20**:317-18
"Elethia" (Walker) **5**:413
"The Elevator" (Coover) **15**:30-1,38-40,48, 50
"Eleven" (Cisneros) **32**:8, 52
"Eleven O'Clock" (Pritchett) **14**:270
"The Eleventh-Hour Guest" (Villiers de l'Isle Adam)
    See "Le convive des dernières fêtes"
"The Elfin Mound" (Andersen) **6**:7
"Eli the Fanatic" (Roth) **26**:229, 232, 234-35, 245-46, 249, 252, 257, 259, 265, 268
"Elias" (Tolstoy) **9**:388
"Elias Wildmanstadius ou l'Homme moyenage" (Gautier) **20**:10-11
Eligible Men (Elkin)
    See *Searches and Seizures*
"Die Elixiere des Teufels" (Hoffmann) **13**:188
"Elixirs of the Devil" (Hoffmann)
    See "Die Elixiere des Teufels"
"Elizabeth" (Adams) **24**:13
"Elizabeth" (Dreiser) **30**:148
"Elizabeth" (Jackson) **9**:252, 266, 270-71; **39**:211, 212, 223, 224
"Elizabeth Stock's One Story" (Chopin) **8**:100
"Ella and the Chinese" (O'Hara) **15**:263
"Ellen Adams Wrynn" (Dreiser) **30**:140-141
"The Elm Log" (Solzhenitsyn) **32**:395
"Elmer and Edna" (Suckow) **18**:390
"The Elm-Tree Mother" (Andersen)
    See "The Elder-Tree Mother"
"Elogio da vaidade" (Machado de Assis) **24**:128-29
Elogio de la sombra (Borges) **41**:157, 166
"An Eloquence of Grief" (Crane) **7**:130
"Elphenor and Weasel" (Warner) **23**:384
"Elsie in New York" (Henry) **5**:194
"Elsket" (Page) **23**:285, 297
Elsket, and Other Stories (Page) **23**:285
"Eltha" (Suckow) **18**:393, 414, 417-18, 422, 424-25
"L'elu des rêves" (Villiers de l'Isle Adam) **14**:390, 393
"Em" (Dixon) **16**:210
"The Emancipator" (Gilchrist) **14**:157-59
"Emanuela" (Dreiser) **30**:141-42
"The Embarkment for Cythera" (Cheever) **1**:93
"An Embarrassing Situation" (Chopin) **8**:72
"Emden" (Narayan) **25**:169
"Emelyan and the Empty Drum" (Tolstoy)
    See "The Empty Drum"
"Emelyan Pilyai" (Gorky) **28**:139, 145
"Emergency Exit" (Coppard) **21**:22

"Emeryt" (Schulz) **13**:328
Emilie (Nerval) **18**:362, 364
"Eminence" (Suckow) **18**:391-92, 411
"The Emissary" (Bradbury) **29**:86-7
"Emma Bovary" (Moore) **19**:344-45
"Emma Zunz" (Borges) **4**:16, 18-19, 23, 37, 39, 40; **41**:117, 124, 162, 164, 168-79
"Emmanuele! Emmanuele!" (Gordon) **15**:107-08, 121, 138, 142
"Emotional Bankruptcy" (Fitzgerald) **6**:50
"The Emperor's New Clothes" (Andersen) **6**:10-11, 13, 16, 18, 26, 30
"The Empire of the Ants" (Wells) **6**:361, 365, 382, 391-92, 403
"The Empty Amulet" (Bowles) **3**:76
"The Empty Drum" (Tolstoy) **9**:377, 380, 388
"An Empty Purse" (Jewett) **6**:156
"The Empty Room" (Caldwell) **19**:5-6
"The Empty Street" (Cowan) **28**:75, 77
The Empty Street (Cowan) **28**:74-6
"En defensa de la Trigolibia" (Fuentes) **24**:38, 53-5
"En el gran ecbó" (Cabrera Infante) **39**:18, 23
"En el presidio" (Pardo Bazán) **30**:279
"En famille" (Maupassant) **1**:259-60, 263, 272, 274, 278
"En la madrugada" (Rulfo) **25**:245, 249-50, 255, 257-58, 262-63, 265-66, 273-75
"En la Noche" (Bradbury) **29**:42
En tranvía (Pardo Bazán) **30**:270, 272
"En verdad os digo" (Arreola) **38**:4, 7-8, 22-23
"En voyage" (Maupassant) **1**:280
"En wagon" (Maupassant) **1**:263
"The Enamored Youth" (Hesse) **9**:243
"El encaje roto" (Pardo Bazán) **30**:264
"The Encantadas; or, The Enchanted Isles" (Melville) **1**:293, 297-99, 303-04, 308, 310-11, 321-22, 329
"The Enchanted Bluff" (Cather) **2**:97, 102, 104-05, 108
"The Enchanted Fruit" (Campbell) **19**:74, 84
"An Enchanted Garden" (Calvino)
    See "Un giardino incantato"
The Enchanted House (Musil)
    See *Die Versuchung der Stillen Veronika*
"The Enchanted Kiss" (Henry) **5**:159, 163
"The Enchanted Pilgrim" (Leskov)
    See "Očarovannyj strannik"
"The Enchanted Sea-Wilderness" (Twain) **6**:337
"The Enchanted Spot" (Gogol)
    See "Zakoldovannoe mesto"
"The Enchanted Wanderer" (Leskov)
    See "Očarovannyj strannik"
"The Enchantress" (Bates) **10**:123
The Enchantress, and Other Stories (Bates) **10**:123
"Encher Tempo" (Machado de Assis) **24**:145
"The Encounter" (Borges)
    See "El encuentro"
"An Encounter" (Coover) **15**:46
"An Encounter" (Joyce) **3**:201, 205, 208, 217-18, 225-26, 230, 232, 234, 237, 247; **26**:46-7, 50
"Encounter at Dawn" (Clarke) **3**:127, 135, 143
"Encounter with Evil" (Cortazar)
    See "Encuentro con el mal"
Encounters (Bowen) **3**:29, 40
"Encrucijada" (Bioy Casares) **17**:53, 56
"El encuentro" (Arreola) **38**:11
"El encuentro" (Borges) **41**:176
"Encuentro con el mal" (Cortazar) **7**:94
"The End" (Beckett)
    See "La Fin"
"The End" (Borges)
    See "El fin"
"The End of a Career" (Stafford) **26**:279, 283-84, 301, 316
"The End of a Good Man" (O'Faolain) **13**:288, 293
End of a Mission (Boell)
    See *Ende einer Dienstfahrt*

"End of a Summer's Day" (Campbell) **19**:63-4, 71, 73, 88, 92
"The End of a War" (Lenz) **33**:337-38
"End of August" (Pavese)
    See "Fine d'agosto"
"The End of Christy Tucker" (Caldwell) **19**:18, 38
"The End of Ice" (Moorhouse) **40**:290
"The End of Oplatka" (Capek)
    See "Oplatkuv konec"
"The End of Something" (Hemingway) **1**:208, 234, 244-45; **40**:209
"The End of the Beginning" (Bradbury) **29**:78
"The End of the Beginning" (Norris) **28**:201
"The End of the Duel" (Borges) **4**:20, 33-4
End of the Game (Cortazar)
    See *Final del juego*
"End of the Line" (Campbell) **19**:88
The End of the Night (Mauriac)
    See *La fin de la nuit*
"The End of the Old Folks' Home" (Babel) **16**:24
"The End of the Party" (Greene) **29**:184-85, 190, 193
"The End of the Passage" (Kipling)
    See "At the End of the Passage"
"The End of the Story" (London) **4**:256
"The End of the Tether" (Conrad) **9**:140-41, 143, 145
"The End of the Vendetta" (Davis) **38**:110
"The End of the World" (Adams) **24**:16-17
"The End of the World" (Turgenev) **7**:335
The End of the World, and Other Stories (Gallant) **5**:130
"An End of Troubles" (Narayan) **25**:138, 141
"The End of Wisdom" (Chesterton) **1**:140
"Das Ende der Welt" (Walser) **20**:334-35
Ende einer Dienstfahrt (Boell) **23**:9, 11, 19, 22-3, 33
"Endicott of the Red Cross" (Hawthorne) **3**:175-76
"Ending" (Grau) **15**:163
"Endless Mountains" (Price) **22**:384, 387
"L'endormeuse" (Maupassant) **1**:284
"The Enduring Chill" (O'Connor) **1**:342-43, 356, 365
"An Enduring Friendship" (O'Faolain) **13**:297
"Enemies" (Chekhov) **2**:158
"Enemies" (Gordimer) **17**:153, 187
"The Enemies" (Gordon) **15**:119
"The Enemies" (Thomas) **3**:407-09
Enemies of the System: A Tale of Homo Uniformis (Aldiss) **36**:10-12, 15, 17
"The Enemies to Each Other" (Kipling) **5**:283
"The Enemy" (Naipaul) **38**:300, 320, 322, 327, 345
The Enemy (Mauriac)
    See *Le mal*
"Energetic" (Walser) **20**:355
"L'Enfance d'un chef" (Sartre) **32**:254-55, 258-61, 270, 272
"L'enfant aux souliers de pain" (Gautier) **20**:16
L'enfant chargé de chaînes (Mauriac) **24**:172,176-79
"L'enfant malade" (Colette) **10**:274-76
Engine Trouble (Narayan) **25**:153, 156-57
"Engineer-Private Paul Klee Misplaces an Aircraft between Milbertschofen and Cambrai, March 1916" (Barthelme) **2**:49, 54
"Engladia's" (Narayan) **25**:156
"England, My England" (Lawrence) **4**:212-13, 229, 231-32, 235; **19**:280
England, My England, and Other Stories (Lawrence) **4**:202, 230-31, 233-37
"England versus England" (Lessing) **6**:199, 218
"An English Coast Picture" (Gissing) **37**:74
"The English Officer" (Moravia)
    See "The English Officer"
"The English Spanish Girl" (Cervantes)
    See "La española inglesa"

"English Summer: A Gothic Romance" (Chandler) **23**:110-11
"English Writers on America" (Irving) **2**:244, 254
"The Enigma" (Fowles) **33**:233-34, 236, 238, 244, 247-48, 257-61, 263-65, 268, 273-75, 283, 285-86, 289
"Enigmas" (Alcott) **27**:3
"Enjoy Enjoy" (Pohl) **25**:235
"L'enlèvement de la rédoute" (Merimee) **7**:278, 280-1, 283, 287-9
"The Enlightenments of Pagett, M. P." (Kipling) **5**:261
Enormous Changes at the Last Minute (Paley) **8**:391-92, 397, 407-08, 410-11, 415
"The Enormous Door" (Price) **22**:387
"The Enormous Radio" (Cheever) **1**:106, 109; **38**:52, 61, 66, 84
The Enormous Radio, and Other Stories (Cheever) **1**:89, 92, 95, 98-100;
"Enough" (Turgenev) **7**:323, 325, 336
Enough (Beckett)
    See *Assez*
"Enragée" (Maupassant) **1**:274
"Enter a Dragoon" (Hardy) **2**:215
Enter and Exit (Boell)
    See "Als der Krieg ausbrach"
"Enter Mitchell" (Lawson) **18**:215
"Enter the Fanatic" (Ellison) **14**:103
"Entered as Second-Class Matter" (Perelman) **32**:210
Entfernung von der Truppe (Boell) **23**:4, 11, 35
"The Entomologist" (Cable) **4**:50
L'entrada en guerra (Calvino) **3**:97, 116
"The Entrance" (Walser)
    See "Die Einfahrt"
"Entrance to an Unwritten Novel" (Forster) **27**:106, 120
L'entrave (Colette) **10**:257, 272
"Entrevue à Solesmes" (Villiers de l'Isle Adam) **14**:386, 396
"Entropy" (Pynchon) **14**:308, 312-13, 316-17, 319-22, 324, 330, 334, 339-44, 347-49
L'envers du music-hall (Colette) **10**:291
"L'Envoi: The Train to Mariposa" (Leacock) **39**:246, 253, 254, 257, 259, 260, 261, 270, 273, 275
"Envy: or, Yiddish in America" (Ozick) **15**:297-301, 304, 309, 312, 314, 316, 321
"Ephemeral Friendships" (Castellanos)
    See "Las amistades efímeras"
"EPICAC" (Vonnegut) **8**:429
L'epidemia: Racconti (Moravia) **26**:162-63, 180
The Epidemic (Moravia)
    See *The Epidemic*
The Epigram (Keller)
    See *The Epigram*
"Epilog to Stifters 'Nachsommer'" (Boell)
    See "Epilog zu Stifters 'Nachsommer'"
"Epilog zu Stifters 'Nachsommer'" (Boell) **23**:19
"Epilogue: The Photographer" (Munro) **3**:332, 338, 340, 343
"Les epingles" (Maupassant) **1**:263, 286
"Episcopal Justice" (Leskov)
    See "Vladyčnyj sud"
"Episode" (Maugham) **8**:380
"Episode at Gastein" (Sansom) **21**:91, 93, 95
"An Episode in Bachelor Life" (Moore) **19**:343
"An Episode in Married Life" (Moore) **19**:343-44
"Episode in the Life of an Ancestor" (Boyle) **5**:54, 70
"An Episode of Cathedral History" (James) **16**:226, 229-30, 232, 240, 244, 246, 248, 252, 255
"An Episode of War" (Crane) **7**:104, 109-10
"Episodes of a Return" (Farrell) **28**:125
"Epitafio" (Arreola) **38**:6-7, 12
"Epitalamio" (Arreola) **38**:5, 9
"Epitaph" (Arreola)
    See "Epitafio"

"Epitaph" (O'Brien) 10:345, 347
"Epithalamium" (Yamamoto) 34:348, 350, 358-59, 364
"Eppis Bars Boorish Bike Fans as Coaster Brakes Roar in Metropolitan Opera" (Perelman) 32:240
"Epstein" (Roth) 26:231, 238, 251, 257-60, 265-66
Equator (Aldiss) 36:18
The Equilibriad (Sansom) 21:83-4, 98, 127
"Equitable Awards" (Auchincloss) 22:51
"Erba del nosro orto" (Pirandello) 22:275
"Das Erdbeben in Chili" (Kleist) 22:106, 110-14, 116-19, 121, 124, 126, 128, 131-32, 135, 146-48, 150-53
"Eric Hermannson's Soul" (Cather) 2:96, 100-01, 105, 107
"The Erl-King" (Carter) 13:9, 27-28
Erma bifronte (Pirandello) 22:275
"Ermolai and the Miller's Wife" (Turgenev)
    See "Yermolai and the Miller's Wife"
"Ernestine" (Dreiser) 30:141-42
"Ernestine ou la Naissance de l'amour" (Stendhal) 27:247
"Ernesto de Tal" (Machado de Assis) 24:131, 151
"Ernst in Civilian Clothes" (Gallant) 5:133, 138
"Eros Rampant" (Updike) 13:387
"An Erotic Memoir in Six Parts" (Moorhouse) 40:310
Erotic Tales (Moravia) 26:171, 173-74
"Um erradio" (Machado de Assis) 24:128-29
"Errand" (Carver) 8:43
"Errant Wheat" (Fuentes)
    See "Trigo errante"
"Error" (Singer) 3:377
"An Error in Chemistry" (Faulkner) 1:179
"Der erste Schritt" (Walser) 20:338
"Erstes Leid" (Kafka) 5:239; 29:343, 358, 371
Erzählungen (Kleist) 22:114, 135, 142
Erzähungen 1949-1984 (Lenz) 33:338
"Es que somos muy pobres" (Rulfo) 25:245, 249-50, 263-65, 273, 279-80
"Esarhaddon, King of Assyria" (Tolstoy) 9:380, 388
"Esbjerg, en la costa" (Onetti) 23:246, 250, 252
"Esbjerg, on the Coast" (Onetti)
    See "Esbjerg, en la costa"
"Escape" (Galsworthy) 22:73
"The Escape" (Mansfield) 9:293
"The Escape" (Moravia) 26:142, 155
"Escape" (Pirandello) 22:231, 241, 244
The Escaped Cock (Lawrence)
    See *The Man Who Died*
"Escapement" (Ballard) 1:68
"La escritura del Dios" (Borges) 4:7, 23, 28-9
"La escuela de noche" (Cortazar) 7:91
"Eshche o cherte" (Gorky) 28:187
"Eskimo" (Munro) 3:347
"The Eskimo Connection" (Yamamoto) 34:359
"Eskimo Lamps, or The Trials and Tribulations of a Specialist" (Lenz) 33:337-38
"Esmé" (Saki) 12:305, 330-33
"Esmé" (Salinger)
    See "For Esmé—with Love and Squalor"
"La española inglesa" (Cervantes) 12:3-5, 7-8, 14-16, 18, 35, 44
El espejo de la muerte (Unamuno) 11:312
"La espera" (Borges) 4:5, 16, 37-9; 41:162
Essays and Fiction (Gissing) 37:79
"Esse est percipi" (Bioy Casares) 17:75
"Die Essenholer" (Boell) 23:4
The Essential Ellison: A 25-Year Retrospective (Ellison) 14:136, 143-47
"Estación de la mano" (Cortazar) 7:94
"La estéril" (Pardo Bazan) 30:262
"Esther" (Toomer) 1:445, 450-51, 457, 459
"Esther Kreindel the Second" (Singer) 3:363
"Esther Norn" (Dreiser) 30:134, 141
"Estos fueron los palacios" (Garvin)
    See "These Were Palaces"

"Et Dona Ferentes" (Wilson) 21:327, 331, 337, 342, 353, 357, 365
"Eterna" (Lavin) 4:184, 189
The Eternal Husband (Dostoevsky)
    See *Vechny muzh*
"Eternal Life" (Aleichem)
    See "Oylem-habe"
"The Eternal Moment" (Forster) 27:69-80, 87-8, 96-7, 100, 102-04, 121-23
The Eternal Moment and Other Stories (Forster) 27:68-70, 74, 76, 83, 89-90, 06, 114, 124
The Eternal Smile and Other Stories (Lagerkvist) 12:180-88, 192, 195, 197-98
"The Eternity of Forms" (London) 4:255-56, 295
"Ethan Brand" (Hawthorne) 3:159, 179-80, 182; 39:95, 136
Ethan Frome (Wharton) 6:415-17, 419, 422, 438-39
"The Ethics of Pig" (Henry) 5:166
"The Etiquette of Deception" (Moorhouse) 40:311
"El etnógrafo" (Borges) 41:152, 154-55
"L'etonnant couple moutonnet" (Villiers de l'Isle Adam) 14:384
"L'etranger" (Baudelaire) 18:4-5, 8, 59, 64
"Etude de femme" (Balzac) 5:31
Etudes analytiques (Balzac) 5:8-9, 31
Études de moeurs au XIXe siècle (Balzac) 5:3
Études philosophiques (Balzac) 5:8-9, 12, 31, 48
Eugenia (Keller) 26:97-8
"Eugénie Grandet" (Barthelme) 2:40
"Euphrasie" (Chopin) 8:69-70
"Eupompus Gave Splendour to Art by Numbers" (Huxley) 39:154, 165-66
Eureka: A Prose Poem (Poe) 22:308, 316
Europe at Love (Morand)
    See *L'Europe galante*
L'Europe galante (Morand) 22:167-69, 171-72, 182
"Eustacia" (Stuart) 31:263
"Eva" (Arreola) 38:9
"Eva está dentro de su gato" (Garcia Marquez) 8:154-55
"Eva Inside Her Cat" (Garcia Marquez)
    See "Eva está dentro de su gato"
"Evan" (Warner) 23:370
"Evangel in Cyrene" (Garland) 18:163
"Eva's Visit to Fairy Land" (Alcott) 27:39
"Eveline" (Joyce) 3:205, 226, 231, 234, 247-48; 26:46-7
"Evelyn and the Rest of Us" (Caldwell) 19:21, 33
"Even The Devil Can't Save the World" (Moravia) 26:173-74
"Evening" (Babel) 16:27-8, 50, 52-3, 54, 56
"Evening at Home" (Boyle) 5:63-4
"The Evening at Sissy Kamara's" (White) 39:280, 292-95, 317, 325, 335, 343
"The Evening Gift" (Narayan) 25:141
"An Evening Meal" (Price) 22:386, 388
"An Evening Performance" (Garrett) 30:173
An Evening Performance: New and Selected Short Stories (Garrett) 30:179-80
"Evening Primrose" (Collier) 19:99, 102-04, 110, 113-14
"Evening Twilight" (Baudelaire)
    See "Le crépuscule du soir"
"An Evening with Dr. Faust" (Hesse) 9:230, 236
"An Evening with John Joe Dempsey" (Trevor) 21:237, 265
"The Evening's at Seven" (Thurber) 1:417, 425
"An Evening's Entertainment" (James) 16:231, 234, 237
Evenings on a Farm near Dikanka (Gogol)
    See *Vechera ná khutore bliz Dikanki*
"L'eventail" (Capek) 36:109
"Eventide" (Sansom) 21:90, 96

"Events at Drimaghleen" (Trevor) 21:246-47, 249-50, 252-53, 260
"Events of That Easter" (Cheever) 1:93
Eventyr, fortalte for bøorn (Andersen) 6:8, 12, 15, 22, 30
"The Everlasting Secret Family" (Moorhouse) 40:297-300, 305, 307, 309-11, 320, 324
The Everlasting Secret Family and Other Secrets (Moorhouse) 40:323-24
"Everybody Was Very Nice" (Benet) 10:142, 144, 153
"An Every-Day Girl" (Jewett) 6:156-59
"Everyday Use" (Walker) 5:402-03, 406, 416-17
"Everything" (Saroyan) 21:163
"Everything I Know" (Lish) 18:284
"Everything in Its Right Place" (Andersen) 6:4, 22-3
"Everything Stuck to Him" (Carver)
    See "Distance"
"Everything That Rises Must Converge" (O'Connor) 1:341, 363; 23:227
Everything That Rises Must Converge (O'Connor) 1:341-43; 23:185, 193, 195, 209, 237
"Eve's Diary" (Twain) 6:295
"The Eviction" (O'Flaherty) 6:277, 280
"Evidence Is High Proof" (Stuart) 31:265
Det eviga leendet (Lagerkvist) 12:180-8, 192, 195, 197-8
"Evil Allures, but Good Endures" (Tolstoy) 9:388
"The Evil Angel" (Lagerkvist)
    See "Den onda ängeln"
"The Evil Eye" (Pavese) 19:375
"The Evil Eye" (Svevo)
    See "Il malocchio"
"The Evil Guest" (Le Fanu) 14:221, 247
Evil Sagas (Lagerkvist)
    See *Onda sagor*
"The Evil Spirit" (Pirandello) 22:254
Evil Tales (Lagerkvist)
    See *Onda sagor*
"Evil-Doers" (Gorky) 28:137
"The Evils of Spain" (Pritchett) 14:270, 285
"Evolution" (Machado de Assis) 24:155
"The Evolution of Lorna Treadway" (Auchincloss) 22:38
"Ex cathedra" (Machado de Assis) 24:129
"Ex Parte" (Lardner) 32:133-34, 139-41, 150
"The Exalted Omega" (Machen) 20:176
"Das Examen" (Lenz) 33:327, 337-38
"Examen de la obra de Herbert Quain" (Borges) 41:79
"The Examination" (Pirandello) 22:243
"Excellent People" (Chekhov) 2:155
"Excursion" (Andric) 36:43
"Excursion in Reality" (Waugh) 41:323
"The Executor" (Spark) 10:362, 366, 368, 370
Exemplary Novels (Cervantes)
    See *Novelas exemplares*
Exemplary Stories (Cervantes)
    See *Novelas exemplares*
Exemplary Tales (Cervantes)
    See *Novelas exemplares*
"Exercises in the Variable Foot" (Williams) 31:334
"Ex-Humans" (Gorky)
    See "Byvshii lyudi"
L'éxil et le royaume (Camus) 9:103-05, 108-11, 118, 122, 125-26, 131, 134
"The Exile" (Moore)
    See "An Deóraidhe"
Exile and the Kingdom (Camus)
    See *L'éxil et le royaume*
"Exile of Eons" (Clarke) 3:144
"The Exiles" (Bradbury) 29:47
"An Exorcism" (Malamud) 15:180, 183, 193-94
"The Expansion of the Universe" (Gilchrist) 14:157
"Expectations" (Galsworthy) 22:64, 74, 101
"Expedition to Earth" (Clarke) 3:150

Expedition to Earth (Clarke) **3**:124, 135, 149-50
"The Expelled" (Beckett)
See "L'Expulsé"
"Ex-People" (Gorky)
See "Byvshii lyudi"
"Experience" (Suckow) **18**:417
"Les expériences du Docteur Crookes" (Villiers de l'Isle Adam) **14**:396
"The Experiment" (James) **16**:251
"Experiment in Luxury" (Crane) **7**:136, 138
"An Experiment in Misery" (Crane) **7**:102, 108-09, 129, 136, 138, 145
"The Experiment of Professor Rous" (Capek) **36**:127
"The Experimental World" (Lagerkvist) **12**:195
"The Explanation" (Barthelme) **2**:35, 40-1, 55
"The Exploit of Choolah, the Chicksaw" (Murfree) **22**:187
Exploits and Opinions of Doctor Faustroll, Pataphysician (Jarry)
See *Gestes et opinions du Dr. Faustroll, pataphysicien, roman néo-scientifique*
The Exploits of Brigadier Gerard (Doyle) **12**:81-2
"Explosive Invention" (Fuentes)
See "El que inventó la pólvora"
"L'Expulsé" (Beckett) **16**:66, 71, 73-4, 87-8, 90-1
Extracts from Captain Stormfield's Visit to Heaven (Twain) **6**:295, 303, 339
"The Extraordinary Adventures of a Doctor" (Bulgakov) **18**:92
"Extraordinary Little Cough" (Thomas) **3**:394, 403, 406, 411-12
"The Extravagance of the Dead" (Oe)
See "Shisha no ogori"
"Extreme Magic" (Calisher) **15**:4-5
Extreme Magic (Calisher) **15**:4-5, 23-7
"Extricating Young Gussie" (Wodehouse) **2**:342
"The Eye" (Bowles) **3**:75, 80
"The Eye" (Powers) **4**:368
"The Eye Altering" (Le Guin) **12**:231, 238
"The Eye of Allah" (Kipling) **5**:283, 285
"The Eye of Apollo" (Chesterton) **1**:121, 136
"Eye of Childhood" (Campbell) **19**:76
The Eye of the Heron (Le Guin) **12**:231, 235
"Eye of the Lynx" (Ligotti) **16**:269-70
"The Eye of the Storm" (White) **39**:325
"The Eyes" (Wharton) **6**:424, 426, 428, 430, 433
"The Eye's Journey" (Nin) **10**:303, 305
Eyes of a Blue Dog (Garcia Marquez) **8**:182
Eyes of Amber (Vinge) **24**:328, 331, 333-35, 337-39, 346-49
"Eyes of Amber" and Other Stories (Vinge) **24**:338, 343, 345
"The Eyes of the Panther" (Bierce) **9**:87
"The Eyes of the Peacock" (Wilson) **21**:357, 359, 363-64
"The Eyes of the Poor" (Baudelaire)
See "Les yeux des pauvres"
"Eyes of Zapata" (Cisneros) **32**:7, 10, 37, 39, 48
"Eye-Witness" (Oates) **6**:251-52
"An eytse" (Aleichem) **33**:26-8, 35-9, 52
"Ezekiel" (Fisher) **25**:17, 20
"Ezekiel Learns" (Fisher) **25**:17, 20
"The Fabbri Tape" (Auchincloss) **22**:53
"A Fable" (Lavin) **4**:183
"The Fable of the Goat" (Agnon)
See "Ma'ase ha'Ez"
Fables and Would-be Tales (Capek) **36**:130
Fables for Our Time and Famous Poems Illustrated (Thurber) **1**:415, 417, 422, 424, 426-27
"La Fabrique" (Ayme) **41**:11, 18, 21
"La Fabulosa: A Texas Operetta" (Cisneros) **32**:35-6
"The Face" (de la Mare) **14**:79, 82, 84, 86, 89
"The Face and the Image" (Agnon)
See "Ha-panim la-panim"
"A Face from Atlantis" (Gordimer) **17**:152-53

"The Face in the Desert" (Campbell) **19**:81
"The Face in the Target" (Chesterton) **1**:122
"The Face of Helene Bournow" (Ellison) **14**:118
The Face of Misfortune (Onetti)
See *La cara de la desgracia*
"A Face of Stone" (Williams) **31**:304, 326, 332-33, 340, 344-45, 351
"The Face of the War" (Wolfe) **33**:370-71
"The Face on the Barroom Floor" (Algren) **33**:88, 108, 110
Face to Face (Gordimer) **17**:157, 165
Faces (Andric)
See *Lica*
"The Faces at Pine Dunes" (Campbell) **19**:66, 73, 92
"The Faces of the Medal" (Cortazar) **7**:63
Facino Cane (Balzac) **5**:26, 31, 33
"Facts" (Galsworthy) **22**:98
"The Facts" (Lardner) **32**:115, 195-96
"The Facts Concerning the Recent Carnival of Crime in Connecticut" (Twain) **26**:357
"The Facts in the Case of M. Valdemar" (Poe) **1**:379, 385, 400; **34**:250
"The Facts of Life" (Maugham) **8**:380
"The Fad of the Fisherman" (Chesterton) **1**:122
"A Faery Legend" (Hawthorne) **39**:126
Das Fähnlein der sieben Aufrechten (Keller) **26**:109, 114-15
"The Failed Men" (Aldiss) **36**:5
"The Failure of David Berry" (Jewett) **6**:151
"A Faint Heart" (Dostoevsky) **2**:170-72, 191-92, 195
"Faint Light" (Dazai Osamu)
See "Hakumei"
"The Fair at Sorotchintsy" (Gogol)
See "Sorocinskaja jamarka"
The Fair Egbert (Tieck)
See *Der blonde Eckbert*
"A Fair Exile" (Garland) **18**:182-83
"The Fair Young Willowy Tree" (Coppard) **21**:17, 27
"The Fairy Dell" (Alcott) **27**:38
"The Fairy Goose" (O'Flaherty) **6**:261-62, 269-70, 272, 275, 281, 285
"Fairy Pinafores" (Alcott) **27**:43
"The Fairy Spring" (Alcott) **27**:45
"Fairy Tale" (Chesterton) **1**:136
"Fairy Tale for Bored Bar-Flies" (Perelman) **32**:220
"The Fairy Tale of One Who Went Forth to Learn Fear" (Grimm and Grimm) **36**:191, 194
Fairy Tales (Andersen)
See *Eventyr, fortalte for børn*
Fairy Tales (Dazai Osamu)
See *Otogi zōshi*
"Fairy Tales for Tired Clubmen" (Perelman) **32**:241
"Fairy-Kist" (Kipling) **5**:284
"Fairyland" (Galsworthy) **22**:63, 101
"Faith" (Hammett) **17**:217
"Faith" (Pirandello) **22**:254
"The Faith Cure Man" (Dunbar) **8**:122, 128-29
"Faith, Hope, and Charity" (McGahern) **17**:299, 309, 317
"Faith in a Tree" (Paley) **8**:408
"Faith in the Afternoon" (Paley) **8**:392, 398, 406, 408
"The Faith of Men" (London) **4**:258-59, 282, 285, 287
"The Faithful Fiancée" (Pardo Bazan) **30**:290
"A Faithful Heart" (Moore) **19**:343
"Faithful John" (Grimm and Grimm) **36**:205
"Faithfulness" (Nin) **10**:306
"The Faithless Wife" (O'Faolain) **13**:296
"Faldum" (Hesse) **9**:235
"Falešné květiny" (Capek) **36**:110
"Falk" (Conrad) **9**:143, 147, 151-52
"The Fall" (Auchincloss) **22**:44
"The Fall" (Moravia) **26**:138, 141
"The Fall" (Pritchett) **14**:286, 298
"The Fall of a Sparrow" (Auchincloss) **22**:47

"The Fall of Edward Barnard" (Maugham) **8**:370
"The Fall of Joseph Timmins" (O'Flaherty) **6**:262
"The Fall of the House of Usher" (Poe) **1**:377, 379-80, 383, 385-86, 391, 398-99, 403-07; **22**:288-356; **34**:249, 258, 265, 274, 283; **35**:321, 331, 336
"The Fall of the House of Voticky" (Capek)
See "Pád rodu Votických"
"The Fall River Axe Murders" (Carter) **13**:14-18, 20
"Fallen" (Mann)
See "Gefallen"
"Fallen Star" (Collier) **19**:106, 110, 112
"The Fallguy's Faith" (Coover) **15**:47
"The Falling Dog" (Barthelme) **2**:55
"Falling in Love in Ashton, British Columbia" (Oates) **6**:230
"Falling Rocks, Narrowing Road, Cul-de-sac, Stop" (O'Faolain) **13**:296
"The Falling Sleet" (Dostoevsky) **2**:165; **33**:162
"The False Collar" (Andersen) **6**:7
"False Dawn" (Kipling) **5**:261
False Dawn (The 'Forties Wharton) **6**:439-40
"False Face" (Fisher)
See "The Man Who Passed"
False Gods (Auchincloss) **22**:51
"False-Dmitry Lunacharsky" (Bulgakov) **18**:89
"Fame" (Walker) **5**:412
"The Familiar" (Le Fanu) **14**:221, 223-26, 228, 233-36, 238-41, 247-48, 250
Familiar Scenes (Peretz)
See *Familiar Scenes*
"The Family" (Pavese) **19**:363, 377, 387
The Family (Mauriac) **24**:159-60, 179
"A Family Affair" (Chopin) **8**:84, 86
"Family Album" (Castellanos)
See "Album de familia"
Family Album (Castellanos)
See *Album de familia*
"The Family de Cats" (Dinesen) **7**:177
"Family Evening" (O'Hara) **15**:290
"A Family Feud" (Dunbar) **8**:120-21, 131, 140, 148
Family Happiness (Tolstoy)
See *Semeinoe schaste*
"Family in the Wind" (Fitzgerald) **6**:47, 60, 62
"A Family Man" (Pritchett) **14**:299
"The Family of Little Feet" (Cisneros) **32**:30-32, 46
A Family Party (O'Hara) **15**:292-93
"Family Portrait" (Andric)
See "Porodična slika"
"A Family Reunion" (Naipaul) **38**:333-35
"Family Sins" (Trevor) **21**:262
Family Sins, and Other Stories (Trevor) **21**:258, 262
Family Ties (Lispector)
See *Laços de família*
"Family Vitriol" (Zoshchenko) **15**:388
"Family-Peace" (Peretz) **26**:201
"The Famous Gilson Bequest" (Bierce) **9**:87-8
"The Fan" (Capek)
See "L'eventail"
"The Fanatic" (O'Flaherty) **6**:276, 288
A Fanatic Heart: Selected Stories of Edna O'Brien (O'Brien) **10**:340-41
Fancies and Goodnights (Collier) **19**:102-05
"Fancy Flights" (Beattie) **11**:21, 28
Fancy Goods (Morand)
See *Tendres stocks*
"The Fancy Woman" (Taylor) **10**:374-77, 386, 389, 398, 400, 406-07, 415
"Fancy's Friend" (Alcott) **27**:11, 42, 50-7
"Fancy's Show-Box" (Hawthorne) **3**:160, 190-91
La Fanfarlo (Baudelaire) **18**:9, 11-14, 19-27, 37, 54
"Fanny and Annie" (Lawrence) **4**:232, 234-35
"Fantaseando" (Pardo Bazan) **30**:294

"Fantasie printaniere" (Norris) **28**:201-03, 207, 213

The Fantasies of Harlan Ellison (Ellison) **14**:143-47

Fantasiestüeke in Callots Manier (Hoffmann) **13**:186, 203, 217

"El fantasma" (Pardo Bazan) **30**:265-66

Fantastic Fables (Bierce) **9**:59, 75

"Fantasticheria" (Verga) **21**:280-81, 285, 300-04

"A Fantasy" (Hawthorne) **39**:126

"Fantasy" (Lenz) **33**:338

Fantomas against the Multinational Vampires (Cortazar)
    See *Fantomas contra los vampiros multinacionales*

Fantomas contra los vampiros multinacionales (Cortazar) **7**:60

"The Far and the Near" (Wolfe) **33**:369, 386

Far Away from Anywhere Else (Le Guin)
    See *Very Far Away from Anywhere Else*

"The Far Distant Journey" (Bates) **10**:121

"Faraway Image" (Cortazar)
    See "Lejana"

"A Far-Away Melody" (Freeman) **1**:191

"Farce Normande" (Maupassant) **1**:272

"The Farcical History of Richard Greenow" (Huxley) **39**:153, 166-67, 172-73

"Fard" (Huxley) **39**:156

"The Fare to the Moon" (Price) **22**:380-81

"Farewell" (Barthelme) **2**:51

"Farewell" (Powers) **4**:381

"Farewell! Farewell! Farewell!" (Aiken) **9**:4, 12, 14

"The Farewell Murder" (Hammett) **17**:220, 230-31

"Farewell, My Lovely Appetizer" (Perelman) **32**:211, 214

"Farewell to Earth" (Clarke) **3**:128

"A Farewell to Omsk" (Perelman) **32**:222, 234

Farewells (Onetti)
    See *Los adioses*

"Der farkishefter shnayder" (Aleichem) **33**:41-2

"The Farm Murder" (Capek) **36**:105-06

"The Farmer in the Dell" (Garrett) **30**:174

"The Farmers' Daughters" (Williams) **31**:312, 314, 333-35

The Farmers' Daughters: The Collected Stories of William Carlos Williams (Williams) **31**:312, 327, 344

"El faro" (Arreola) **38**:9

Fasching (Hauptmann) **37**:241-42, 245

"The Fascination of the Pool" (Woolf) **7**:408, 410-12

"Fashion" (Galsworthy) **22**:98

"The Fast" (Singer) **3**:355, 361

"Fast and Firm--A Romance at Marseilles" (Howells) **36**:399

"Fast Lanes" (Phillips) **16**:335-37

Fast Lanes (Phillips) **16**:332-39

"The Fastest Runner on Sixty-First Street" (Farrell) **28**:99

"Fat" (Carver) **8**:3, 29, 42-3, 54

"The Fat Girl" (Dubus) **15**:74, 77, 80, 94

"The Fatal Eggs" (Bulgakov)
    See "Rokovye iaitsa"

"The Fate of Humphrey Snell" (Gissing) **37**:57, 80

"The Fate of the Forrests" (Alcott) **27**:57-8

"The Fate of the Freiherr von Leisenbohg" (Schnitzler)
    See "Das schicksal des Freiherr von Leisenbohg"

"The Father" (Babel) **16**:48-9

"The Father" (Carver) **8**:9, 18, 50-1, 55

"The Father" (Dazai Osamu)
    See "Chichi"

"A Father" (Mukherjee) **38**:238, 240, 242, 252-53, 257-59, 265, 270, 273, 279

"The Father" (O'Hara) **15**:290-91

"Father against Mother" (Machado de Assis)
    See "Pai contra mãe"

"Father Alexey's Story" (Turgenev)
    See "Rasskaz ottsa Aleksaya"

"Father and I" (Lagerkvist) **12**:179, 192, 196-97

"Father and Mother" (Howells) **36**:370

"Father and Mother" (Kawabata)
    See "Chichi Haha"

"Father and Son" (Hughes) **6**:109, 119, 121-22, 141-42

"The Father and Son Cigar" (Algren) **33**:108

"Father Giles of Ballymoy" (Trollope) **28**:320, 340, 348, 354

"Father of the Stars" (Pohl) **25**:220

"Father Raven" (Coppard) **21**:18, 27

"Father Scothine" (Moore) **19**:311

Father Sergius (Tolstoy)
    See *Otetz Sergii*

"Father Timothy Joyce" (Farrell) **28**:98, 118

"Father versus Mother" (Machado de Assis)
    See "Pai contra mãe"

"Father, Where Are You Going?" (Oe)
    See "Chichi yo, anata wa doko e ikuno ka?"

"Fathering" (Mukherjee) **38**:252, 254, 266-67, 271

"The Fatherland" (Walser) **20**:357

"Fathers" (Capek) **36**:124

"Fathers and Sons" (Hemingway) **1**:212, 216, 230, 240-42; **40**:251, 258, 260

"The Fathers and the Sons" (Agnon) **30**:11

"The Fathers' Daughters" (Spark) **10**:361, 366

"Father's Help" (Narayan) **25**:141, 153, 156, 160

"Father's Last Escape" (Schulz)
    See "Ostatnia ucieczka ojca"

"A Father's Story" (Dubus) **15**:76, 87, 93, 98-9

"A Father-to-Be" (Bellow) **14**:3, 22-3, 25, 27, 30-1

"Fatimas and Kisses" (O'Hara) **15**:279, 283

"La fausse monnaie" (Baudelaire) **18**:35, 39-40, 60

Faust (Turgenev) **7**:320, 323-25, 328, 334-35, 337

"Le faux policier" (Ayme) **41**:13

"Favors" (Adams) **24**:17-18

"The Favourite" (O'Brien) **10**:330, 332

"Fear" (Galsworthy) **22**:98

"The Fear" (Tanizaki)
    See "Kyofu"

"Fear: Four Examples" (Lish) **18**:266, 268

"Fear Here" (Thomas) **20**:287

"The Fear of Nice" (Nin) **10**:306

"The Fear That Walks by Noonday" (Cather) **2**:100

"A Fearful Responsibility" (Howells) **36**:399

A Fearful Responsibility, and Other Stories (Howells) **36**:400

"The Feast of Crispian" (Ballard) **1**:72

"The Feast of Nemesis" (Saki) **12**:296, 299

"A Feast of Reason" (Howells) **36**:397

"Feathers" (Carver) **8**:24, 31-2, 34-5, 44

"Feathertop" (Hawthorne) **3**:158, 179

"Federigo" (Merimee) **7**:283, 287, 289, 299-300

"Fedor Kuzmich" (Tolstoy) **9**:389

"Fedora" (Chopin) **8**:87, 100

"Feed My Lambs" (O'Faolain) **13**:291, 312

"Feizao" (Lu Hsun) **20**:129, 149

"Feldblumen" (Stifter) **28**:299

Felicidade clandestina (Lispector) **34**:231-33, 235

"Felicità" (Pirandello) **22**:275-76, 285-86

"Felis Catus" (Berriault) **30**:96-7

"Feliz aniversário" (Lispector) **34**:189, 194, 197, 200, 202

"Fellow-Feeling" (Narayan) **25**:138

"Fellow-Townsmen" (Hardy) **2**:202-03, 207, 215-16, 228-31

"Female Bandits" (Dazai Osamu) **41**:230, 232

La femme abandonnée (Balzac) **5**:8, 31

"La femme adultère" (Camus) **9**:103, 105, 108-110, 114-16, 119, 126-28

La femme cachée (Colette) **10**:274-76

"La femme de Paul" (Maupassant) **1**:259, 261

La femme rompue (Beauvoir) **35**:46, 48-50, 54, 57-8, 64, 67-8, 70-2, 75-9, 81-2, 85, 87

"La femme sauvage et la petite-maîtresse" (Baudelaire) **18**:33

"La femme vertueuse" (Balzac) **5**:4, 29

"The Fence" (Cowan) **28**:80

"Fên-chou hu" (P'u Sung-ling) **31**:207

"Fenella" (Warner) **23**:373

"Les fenêtres" (Baudelaire) **18**:6, 9

"Fêng hsien" (P'u Sung-ling) **31**:209

"Fêng San-niang" (P'u Sung-ling) **31**:209

"Feng-po" (Lu Hsun) **20**:136, 140

Feria d'agosto (Pavese) **19**:364-65, 380, 383-84, 386

"Die Fermate" (Hoffmann) **13**:183

Fermé la nuit (Morand) **22**:158, 160-61, 165-67, 171-73, 181

"Le fermier" (Maupassant) **1**:274, 285

"Fern" (Stuart) **31**:252

"Fern" (Toomer) **1**:441, 444, 457-58, 460

"Fernheim" (Agnon) **30**:3-4, 48, 66

"Ferragus" (Balzac) **5**:43-6

"The Ferry of Unfulfillment" (Henry) **5**:158, 186

"The Ferry; or, Another Trip to Venice" (Cortazar) **7**:63

Das Fest zu Kenilworth (Tieck) **31**:272

"Le feste" (Pavese) **19**:384

"The Festival" (Campbell) **19**:81

"The Festival" (Lovecraft) **3**:263, 269, 274, 292, 294-95

"Festival Nights" (Pavese) **19**:387

Festival Nights (Pavese) **19**:363

"Festival with Syphilis" (Bulgakov) **18**:90

"The Festivals" (Pavese)
    See "Le feste"

"Die Festung" (Lenz) **33**:316, 319-20, 328, 330

"The Fetish" (Moravia)
    See "The Fetish"

The Fetish, and Other Stories (Moravia)
    See *The Fetish, and Other Stories*

"A Feud" (Galsworthy) **22**:67, 82, 101

Das Feuerschiff (Lenz) **33**:316, 331

"Fever" (Carver) **8**:26-8, 30, 33-4, 40

"Fever Dream" (Bradbury) **29**:58-9, 62

"Fever Flower" (Grau) **15**:152, 156, 159

"A Few Crusted Characters" (Hardy) **2**:206, 209, 214-15, 217, 219-20

"A Few Trips and Some Poetry" (O'Hara) **15**:286

Fiabe Italiene (Calvino) **3**:105, 119

"An Fiach" (O'Flaherty) **6**:287

"Fiançailles" (Ayme) **41**:11, 19, 22, 26

Ficciones, 1935-1944 (Borges) **4**:15-16, 18-20, 41; **41**:44, 53, 56, 117, 135-41, 157, 159, 162

"La ficelle" (Maupassant) **1**:259, 262, 284, 286, 288

Fictions (Borges)
    See *Ficciones, 1935-1944*

"The Fiddler" (Melville) **1**:304; **17**:361, 363

"The Fiddler of the Reels" (Hardy) **2**:216-22, 224-25

"The Field Devil" (Hesse) **9**:231, 235

"Field Guide to the Western Birds" (Stegner) **27**:195, 198-99, 205-07, 220

"Field of Flowers" (Aiken) **9**:5, 12-13

"The Field of Maize" (Pavese)
    See "Il campo di granturco"

"The Field of Mustard" (Coppard) **21**:8, 16-17, 19, 25, 28

The Field of Mustard (Coppard) **21**:5-9, 21

"A Field of Snow on a Slope of the Rosenberg" (Davenport) **16**:174, 176, 180-82, 195, 198

"The Field of Vision" (Le Guin) **12**:233

"A Field of Wheat" (Ross) **24**:290, 292, 295, 297, 301-02, 319

"The Fiend" (Pohl) **25**:232

"La fiesta del Monstruo" (Bioy Casares) **17**:48, 50-2

"Fiesta en grande" (Donoso) **34**:3-4, 21, 23, 32, 49
"Fifteen Years" (Dazai Osamu) **41**:246-50
"The Fifth Quarter" (King) **17**:295
"Fifty Dollars" (Elkin) **12**:103
"Fifty Grand" (Hemingway) **1**:209, 211, 218, 232, 234-35, 248; **36**:270; **40**:191, 219
"Fifty Grand" (Lardner) **32**:117
"Fifty Pounds" (Coppard) **21**:11, 15, 18
Fifty Stories (Boyle) **5**:65
"Fifty-Seven Views of Fujiyama" (Davenport) **16**:184-85, 188
"The Fig Tree" (Porter) **4**:340, 352-53; **31**:175-76
"The Fig Tree" (Pritchett) **14**:263
"The Fight" (Anderson) **1**:31, 50
"The Fight" (O'Flaherty) **6**:269
"The Fight" (Thomas) **3**:402, 406, 411-12
"Fight Number Twenty-five" (Stuart) **31**:228, 265
"Fight Your Own War" (Saroyan) **21**:132
"Fighting for the Rebound" (Mukherjee) **38**:252, 254, 261, 266-67, 283
"Figura" (Leskov) **34**:110
"The Figure in the Carpet" (James) **8**:265, 280, 299, 301-02, 304, 306-07
"Filboid Studge, The Story of a Mouse that Helped" (Saki) **12**:288, 300
Files on Parade (O'Hara) **15**:264-65
La fille aux yeux d'ors (Balzac) **5**:44, 46-7
"La Fille du shérif" (Ayme) **41**:16-17, 24
"Les filles de Milton" (Villiers de l'Isle Adam) **14**:387, 390
Les filles du feu (Nerval) **18**:336, 362-64, 379
"Film Preview in the Morning" (Shiga) **23**:346, 348
"The Film Test" (Moravia) **26**:139
"Filmer" (Wells) **6**:403, 406
"Filming the Hatted Australian" (Moorhouse) **40**:290-91, 303
"Filosofia de um par de botas" (Machado de Assis) **24**:130
"Un fils" (Maupassant) **1**:275
"Filthy with Things" (Boyle) **16**:156-57
"La Fin" (Beckett) **16**:72-5, 87-91
"El fin" (Borges) **4**:10; **41**:47
La fin de Chéri (Colette) **10**:255, 257, 260-61, 264, 267-68, 270-71, 285-87
La fin de la nuit (Mauriac) **24**:168-69, 171, 180-81
"A Final Account" (Price) **22**:386
"Final Chapter" (Machado de Assis) **24**:152
Final del juego (Cortazar) **7**:50-1, 53, 62-3, 69-70, 79
"The Final Embarrassment" (Williams) **31**:334
The Final Mist (Bombal) **37**:41-42, 44
"A Final Note on Chanda Bell" (Thurber) **1**:421
"The Final Problem" (Doyle) **12**:57, 60
"Final Request" (Machado de Assis) **24**:140, 152
"Final Trophy" (Ellison) **14**:127
The Final Years (Dazai Osamu) **41**:249
"A Financial Failure" (Jewett) **6**:158
"A Find" (Gordimer) **17**:184, 187
"Find Me in Fire" (Bradbury) **29**:53
"Finding a Girl in America" (Dubus) **15**:76, 87, 93, 98-9
Finding a Girl in America (Dubus) **15**:74, 78, 81
"The Finding of Lieutenant Outhwaite" (Norris) **28**:203-04
"The Finding of Martha" (Dunbar) **8**:122
"The Finding of Zach" (Dunbar) **8**:122, 128, 147
"Der Findling" (Kleist) **22**:106, 114, 122, 124-28, 131
"Fine Accommodations" (Hughes) **6**:131, 133
"A Fine Beginning" (Thomas) **3**:403
"Fine d'agosto" (Pavese) **19**:375-76, 380
"Fine di una relazione" (Moravia) **26**:179
"Fine Feathers" (Coppard) **21**:8, 16-17, 30
"Fine Furniture" (Dreiser) **30**:152-53, 159

"A Fine Old Firm" (Jackson) **39**:211, 224, 225, 229
The Finer Grain (James) **8**:276, 302
"The Finest Diner in the World" (Villiers de l'Isle Adam)
     See "Le plus beau dîner du monde"
Finest Short Stories of Seán O'Faoláin (O'Faolain) **13**:292, 297, 308
"The Finest Story in the World" (Kipling) **5**:273, 280
"Fingal" (Beckett) **16**:93
"Finger Man" (Chandler) **23**:58, 65-7, 72, 102
"Fingers and Toes" (Michaels) **16**:302, 311
"Finis" (London) **4**:256
"Finish Good Lady" (Auchincloss) **22**:47
"The Finish of Patsy Barnes" (Dunbar) **8**:122, 125, 128, 137
"Finlandia" (Saroyan) **21**:158, 160
"Finn" (Michaels) **16**:302-03
"Fire and Cloud" (Wright) **2**:361, 363, 365, 368, 371, 373, 375, 379-81, 383-84, 387
"The Fire and the Hearth" (Faulkner) **1**:182; **35**:146, 157
"The Fire Balloons" (Bradbury) **29**:42-3, 46, 48, 53, 81
"Fire by Night" (Fisher) **25**:17-20, 23, 25
"Fire, Fire, Burn Books!" (Bradbury) **29**:53
"A Fire in Fontana" (Yamamoto) **34**:358-59, 381-83
"Fire of the Khans" (Bulgakov) **18**:92, 98
"The Fire Test" (Harris) **19**:162-63
"Fire Worship" (Hawthorne) **3**:182
"The Firebird" (Dazai Osamu) **41**:249
"The Fireman" (Bradbury) **29**:53
"Fireman Flower" (Sansom) **21**:82, 88, 96, 120, 122, 124
Fireman Flower and Other Stories (Sansom) **21**:82, 84, 92, 94, 97-8, 111, 122-24, 127
"The Fireman's Death" (O'Flaherty) **6**:284
"The Fires" (Shiga) **23**:346
Fires: Essays, Poems, Stories, 1966-1982 (Carver) **8**:18, 30, 32, 40-1, 45, 50, 57-60
"The Fires Within" (Clarke) **3**:125, 129, 135, 143, 149
Fireship (Vinge) **24**:327
Fireworks: Nine Profane Pieces (Carter) **13**:2-3, 8-9, 14
First and Last (Lardner) **32**:156
"The First and the Last" (Galsworthy) **22**:61, 75-6, 83, 94, 99, 100-02
"The First Autumn" (Caldwell) **19**:37
"First Blood" (Fitzgerald) **6**:50
"First Breech" (Bulgakov) **18**:86
"First Confession" (O'Connor) **5**:364, 366, 386, 389
"The First Countess of Wessex" (Hardy) **2**:204, 208-09
"The First Day in a Gay Town" (Andric)
     See "Prvi dan u radosnom gradu"
"The First Day of School" (Saroyan) **21**:135
"First Encounter" (Clarke) **3**:128
"A First Family of Tasajara" (Harte) **8**:216, 218
"First Foot" (Campbell) **19**:65
The First Forty-Nine Stories (Hemingway) **1**:230, 240
"First Love" (Babel) **16**:9, 17, 36, 41, 59
"First Love" (Gorky) **28**:153
"First Love" (Nabokov) **11**:108, 128
"First Love" (Pavese)
     See "Primo amore"
"First Love" (Welty) **1**:467-69, 482
First Love (Beckett)
     See *Premier amour*
First Love (Turgenev)
     See *Pervaya lyubov'*
"First Manhattans" (Gilchrist) **14**:157, 159
"The First Monday in Lent" (Bunin)
     See "Chistyi ponedel'nik"
"First Night" (Pirandello) **22**:250
"The First of April" (Barnes) **3**:13
"The First Poet" (London) **4**:256

"The First Report of the Shipwrecked Foreigner to the Kadanh of Derb" (Le Guin) **12**:231, 241
"The First Seven Years" (Malamud) **15**:168, 189, 212, 221
"First Sorrow" (Kafka)
     See "Erstes Leid"
"The First Step" (Walser)
     See "Der erste Schritt"
"The First Sunday in June" (Jewett) **6**:159
"First Wedding Night" (Pirandello)
     See "Prima notte"
"The First Year of My Life" (Spark) **10**:364, 366, 368
"The First-Class Passenger" (Chekhov) **2**:130
"The Fir-Tree" (Andersen) **6**:6, 14, 18, 30, 40
"Fish for Friday" (O'Connor) **5**:369
"Fish Story" (Lish) **18**:280-82
"The Fish Supper" (Aiken) **9**:14
"The Fish Trap" (Pirandello) **22**:249
"A Fisher of Men" (Galsworthy) **22**:58-9, 98
"The Fisherman and His Soul" (Wilde) **11**:365, 369, 371, 376, 383-84, 386-87, 394-99, 407-09
"Fishmonger's Fiddle" (Coppard) **21**:4, 9, 15, 27
Fishmonger's Fiddle (Coppard) **21**:4, 8-9, 15, 19-20
"Fishy" (Pritchett) **14**:269
"Fishy Waters" (Rhys) **21**:55-7, 66
"Fitcher's Bird" (Grimm and Grimm) **36**:198-99
"Fits" (Munro) **3**:347
"Five Acre Virgin" (Jolley) **19**:230, 245
Five Acre Virgin, and Other Stories (Jolley) **19**:221-22, 232, 244-45
"The Five Black Swans" (Warner) **23**:383
"Five Boons of Life" (Twain) **26**:331
"The Five Dollar Guy" (Williams) **31**:358
"The Five Hells of Orion" (Pohl) **25**:230
"Five Incidents Concerning the Flesh and the Blood" (Moorhouse) **40**:302
"Five Intimate Interviews" (Levi) **12**:275
"Five Loaves of Bread" (Capek) **36**:84, 130
"The Five Orange Pips" (Doyle) **12**:66, 68, 70, 72-4
"Five Peas from One Pod" (Andersen) **6**:35
"Five Ripe Pears" (Saroyan) **21**:133
Five Tales (Galsworthy) **22**:84, 94-7, 99-102
"The Five White Mice" (Crane) **7**:104, 106, 126, 150
"The Five-Forty-Eight" (Cheever) **1**:100; **38**:66, 84, 87
"Five Twenty" (White) **39**:301, 303, 306-07, 310-11, 319-20, 324, 326-28, 337, 346, 350-52
Fizzles (Beckett)
     See *Foirades*
"The Flag" (Aleichem) **33**:19
"The Flag" (Bates) **10**:116
The Flag of the Seven Upright Ones (Keller) **26**:115
"A Flag on the Island" (Naipaul) **38**:299, 302, 317, 323-24
A Flag on the Island: A Fantasy for a Small Screen (Naipaul) **38**:318-19, 328, 344, 347-49, 353
Flagman Thiel (Hauptmann)
     See *Bahnwärter Thiel*
"The Flame" (Bates) **10**:139
"Flanagan and His Short Filibustering Adventure" (Crane) **7**:100-01, 151
Flappers and Philosophers (Fitzgerald) **6**:45-6, 56-8
"Flash" (Arreola) **38**:11, 22-23
"A Flat Country Christmas" (Wilson) **21**:322-23, 333
"A Flat in London" (Waugh) **41**:328
"The Flats Road" (Munro) **3**:331-32
"A Flaubert Prose Piece" (Walser) **20**:354
"Flavia and Her Artists" (Cather) **2**:98, 103
"Flavour of Coconut" (Narayan) **25**:134, 140, 154

Title Index

"Flavours of Exile" (Lessing) **6**:191, 211
"The Flax" (Andersen) **6**:7
Flèche d'Orient (Morand) **22**:172, 181
"The Fleece of Gold" (Gautier)
  See "La chaîne d'or"
"Fleet-Footed Hester" (Gissing) **37**:80-1
"Flesh and the Mirror" (Carter) **13**:4
La fleur de l'age (Colette) **10**:274, 276
"Les fleurs" (Ligotti) **16**:269, 277, 288
"Fleurs de ténèbres" (Villiers de l'Isle Adam)
  14:395-96
"Flick" (Lewis) **40**:276
"Flight" (Grau) **15**:163
"Flight" (O'Hara) **15**:279, 285
"Flight" (Steinbeck) **11**:207-09, 225, 229, 231-
  34, 236-37, 244
"Flight" (Updike) **13**:367, 370, 384, 388,
  392-95
"Flight and Pursuit" (Fitzgerald) **6**:56
Flight into Darkness (Schnitzler)
  See *Flucht in die Finsternis*
"The Flight of Pigeons from the Palace"
  (Barthelme) **2**:37, 40, 55-6
"The Flight of Pony Baker" (Howells) **36**:398
"The Flight of the Israelites" (Ballard) **1**:72
"Flights" (Adams) **24**:3-4
"The Fling" (Carver) **8**:4, 34
"Flingin' Jim and His Fool-Killer" (Harris)
  19:183
"Flip, a California Romance" (Harte) **8**:253,
  255
"The Flip of a Coin" (Maugham) **8**:376-77
"Flirts and Their Ways" (Murfree) **22**:221
"The Floating Bridge of Dreams" (Tanizaki)
  See "Yume no ukihashi"
"The Floating Truth" (Paley) **8**:399
"The Flood" (Anderson) **1**:51
"A Flood" (Moore) **19**:345
"The Flood" (Pavese) **19**:370
"Una flor amarilla" (Cortazar) **7**:52
"Flor de retórica antigua" (Arreola) **38**:11
"Florence Green is 81" (Barthelme) **2**:27
"Flotsam and Jetsam" (Galsworthy) **22**:101
"The Flower" (Pavese) **19**:366
"Flower Days" (Walser) **20**:336
Flower Fables (Alcott) **27**:3, 33, 36, 38-41, 44,
  57
"The Flower Garden" (Jackson) **9**:249, 252;
  39:211, 220, 221, 222, 224, 225, 229
The Flower of Buffoonery (Dazai Osamu)
  See *Dōke no hana*
"Flowering Judas" (Porter) **4**:329, 339-40, 342,
  344, 346, 349-51, 356; **31**:123-81
Flowering Judas, and Other Stories (Porter)
  4:326-28, 347, 351, 354, 365; **31**:124, 127,
  134, 148, 172
"The Flowering of the Strange Orchid" (Wells)
  6:361, 365, 394-96, 404
"The Flowers" (Walker) **5**:402
"Flowers for Marjorie" (Welty) **1**:466, 487-88
"Flowers of a Clown" (Dazai Osamu) **41**:244
"Flowers of Darkness" (Villiers de l'Isle
  Adam)
  See "Fleurs de ténèbres"
"Flowers of the Abyss" (Ligotti) **16**:282, 284
"The Flower's Story" (Alcott) **27**:44-5
"The Flowers that Killed Him" (Ross) **24**:295,
  307, 311, 318-19
Flucht in die Finsternis (Schnitzler) **15**:344,
  368, 370, 378, 381, 383-84
"Die Flut ist pünktlich" (Lenz) **33**:317, 319
"Flute Dream" (Hesse) **9**:234
"The Flute Player" (O'Flaherty) **6**:281
"The Fly" (Dreiser) **30**:128
"The Fly" (Mansfield) **9**:282-84, 307, 312-13;
  23:158; **38**:201-32
"The Fly" (Pirandello) **22**:227-28
"Fly Away Ladybird" (Aiken) **9**:13-14
"A Fly in a Glass of Milk" (Cabrera Infante)
  See "La mosca en el vasode leche"
"The Fly in the Coffin" (Caldwell) **19**:14, 28-9

"The Fly in the Ointment" (Pritchett) **14**:271,
  298
"Fly Paper" (Hammett) **17**:202, 215-16, 220,
  222
"The Flying Dutchman" (Bulgakov) **18**:90
"Flying Home" (Ellison) **26**:4, 9-10, 13, 15, 21,
  24, 25
"The Flying Man" (Wells) **6**:397-98
"The Flying Stars" (Chesterton) **1**:119, 127,
  129
"A Flying Start" (Gallant) **5**:147
"The Flying Trunk" (Andersen) **6**:7, 30
"Den flyvende Kuffert" (Andersen)
  See "The Flying Trunk"
"FOAM" (Aldiss) **36**:28
"Fog" (Adams) **24**:16
"The Fog Horn" (Bradbury) **29**:59
"The Fog Man" (Boyle) **16**:157
Foirades (Beckett) **16**:100, 123-28
Folks from Dixie (Dunbar) **8**:118-21, 123, 127-
  29, 131, 140-41, 143, 145-46
"Foma, the Wolf" (Turgenev) **7**:316
"The Food of the Gods" (Clarke) **3**:133-34
"Fool about a Horse" (Faulkner) **1**:177
"The Foolish Butterfly" (O'Flaherty) **6**:264,
  278-79
"The Foolish Virgin" (Gissing) **37**:64, 81
"Fool's Education" (Price) **22**:365, 369-71,
  376-77
"A Fool's Love" (Tanizaki)
  See "Chijin no ai"
The Foot Journey to Amager (Andersen) **6**:4
"Foothold" (Bowen) **3**:40, 44
"The Footprint" (Capek)
  See "Šlépej"
"Footprint II" (Capek)
  See "Šlépeje"
"The Footprints" (Capek)
  · See "Šlépeje"
"Footprints in the Jungle" (Maugham) **8**:359,
  361, 374-75
"Footsteps in the Footprints" (Cortazar) **7**:63
"The Footwarmer" (Pirandello) **22**:241
"For a Good Purpose" (Levi) **12**:278
For a Nameless Tomb (Onetti)
  See *Para una tumba sin nombre*
"For a Place in the Sun" (Grau) **15**:155
"For Altar and Hearth" (Davis) **38**:104
"For Conscience' Sake" (Hardy) **2**:207, 212,
  214-15, 220
"For Dear Life" (Gordimer) **17**:192
"For Esmé—with Love and Squalor"
  (Salinger) **2**:289, 293-97, 299-300, 303-
  05, 314, 316-18; **28**:222, 229, 236, 244,
  248, 2 61
"For Good" (Adams) **24**:4
"For Grandmother" (Shiga) **23**:333
"For Jeromé—With Love and Kisses" (Lish)
  18:266-68, 284
"For Marse Chouchoute" (Chopin) **8**:89
For Maurice: Five Unlikely Stories (Lee)
  33:307-08, 311-12
"For Rupert—With No Promises" (Lish)
  18:267-68, 284
"For the Duration of the War" (Saki) **12**:285,
  326
For the Good of the Cause (Solzhenitsyn)
  See *Dlia pol'zy dela*
"For the Love of Brass" (Stuart) **31**:232
"For the Time Being" (Lispector) **34**:215
"For to end yet again" (Beckett) **16**:123, 127,
  129
For to end yet again and Other Fizzles
  (Beckett)
  See *Foirades*
"For White Men Only" (Farrell) **28**:121
"The Forbidden Buzzards" (Saki) **12**:315, 326
"The Forbidden Lighthouse" (Sansom) **21**:82,
  88-9
"Force Majeure" (Levi) **12**:274-75, 277
"The Force of Blood" (Cervantes)
  See "La fuerza de la sangre"

"The Force of Circumstance" (Maugham)
  8:372, 375
"Foreign Affairs" (O'Faolain) **13**:322
Foreign Affairs, and Other Stories (O'Faolain)
  13:296, 308, 313-14
Foreign Bodies (Aldiss) **36**:14, 18, 20
"The Foreign Policy of Company 99" (Henry)
  5:197
"The Foreigner" (Jewett) **6**:156, 174-76
"The Foreseeable Future" (Price) **22**:380-81
The Foreseeable Future (Price) **22**:379, 381,
  384
"The Forest" (Le Guin) **12**:213, 216, 247-48
"The Forest of the South" (Gordon) **15**:105,
  107, 118
The Forest of the South (Gordon) **15**:104, 108,
  116, 137
"The Forest Path to the Spring" (Lowry) **31**:41,
  44-53, 55-9, 61-3, 66-72, 75-6, 79-83, 86-7
"Forever and the Earth" (Bradbury) **29**:78
Forevermore (Agnon)
  See *Ad olam*
"The Forged Coupon" (Tolstoy) **9**:379
"Forgetting" (O'Brien) **10**:343
"Forging Ahead" (Fitzgerald) **6**:50
"Forgiveness in Families" (Munro) **3**:331
"The Forgotten Enemy" (Clarke) **3**:124
"A Forgotten Poet" (Nabokov) **11**:109-10, 112
"The Forks" (Powers) **4**:374, 382
"Form in Wood" (Cowan) **28**:80
"The Form of Space" (Calvino)
  See "La forma dello spazio"
"Forma" (Borges)
  See "La forma de la espada"
"La forma de la espada" (Borges) **4**:10, 25, 42;
  41:40, 42, 58, 123-30, 148, 180-85
"La forma dello spazio" (Calvino) **3**:92, 109
La formica Argentina (Calvino) **3**:91-2, 98, 117
"The Forsaken" (Turgenev) **7**:318-19
"Forschungen eines hundes" (Kafka) **5**:206,
  229, 238, 241; **29**:345-49, 351, 369, 371
"A Forsyte Encounters the People"
  (Galsworthy) **22**:71
The Forsyte Saga (Galsworthy) **22**:64-5, 69-71,
  81, 84
Forsytes, Pendyces and Others (Galsworthy)
  22:74, 84, 91, 97
"Forsythe and Forsythe" (Gilman) **13**:141
"Fortuna di essere un cavallo" (Pirandello)
  22:270
"Fortuna lo que ha querido" (Fuentes) **24**:32,
  56, 58, 74
"Fortune Always has Her Way" (Fuentes)
  See "Fortuna lo que ha querido"
"The Fortune of Arleus Kane" (Auchincloss)
  22:3, 48
"The Fortune Teller" (Spark) **10**:367, 370
"The Fortunes of Martin Waldock" (Scott)
  32:300
"The Fortunes of Sir Robert Ardagh" (Le
  Fanu) **14**:220-21, 223, 239, 247, 251
"The Fortune-Teller" (Capek)
  See "Věštkyně"
"The Fortune-Teller" (Machado de Assis)
  24:153
Fortunio (Gautier) **20**:3, 7, 14, 26
Forty Stories (Barthelme) **2**:56
"Forty Times Forty" (Bulgakov) **18**:90
"Forty-Five a Month" (Narayan) **25**:132, 137
Forty-Seventeen (Moorhouse) **40**:324
"The Forty-Seventh Saturday" (Trevor) **21**:233,
  262
"La Fosse aux péchés" (Ayme) **41**:11, 13, 17
"The Foster Portfolio" (Vonnegut) **8**:432, 435
"Le fou et la Vénus" (Baudelaire) **18**:3, 6, 8,
  15, 17
"Les foules" (Baudelaire) **18**:31, 38
"The Found Boat" (Munro) **3**:346
"Foundling" (Grimm and Grimm) **36**:223
"The Foundling" (Kleist)
  See "Der Findling"
"The Fountains" (Le Guin) **12**:211, 213, 247-48

"Four Bottles of Beer" (Williams) **31**:304-05, 333

Four Faultless Felons (Chesterton) **1**:126, 132

"The Four Fists" (Fitzgerald) **6**:58

"Four Generations" (Suckow) **18**:395-96, 405-07, 415

"The Four Lost Men" (Wolfe) **33**:401

"The Four Meetings" (James) **8**:334; **32**:106-09

The Four Million (Henry) **5**:155, 171-72, 192

Four Past Midnight (King) **17**:280-84

"Four Portraits" (Bulgakov) **18**:74, 92

"Four Rupees" (Narayan) **25**:141, 156

"The Four Seasons" (Gallant) **5**:130, 135, 137-38

"Four Stories About Lovers" (Beattie) **11**:17

"Four Women" (Garrett) **30**:165, 173

The Four-Dimensional Nightmare (Ballard) **1**:68

"14 Stories" (Dixon) **16**:208-09, 214

14 Stories (Dixon) **16**:204-05, 207-10, 214-15

"The Fourth Alarm" (Cheever) **1**:101, 110; **38**:53

"The Fourth Day Out from Santa Cruz" (Bowles) **3**:61-2, 72

"Fourth Version" (Valenzuela)
See "Cuarta versión"

"The Fox" (Lawrence) **4**:197, 203-04, 210-12, 223-26, 229, 231, 235-36

"The Fox" (Wilson) **21**:364

"The Fox and the Forest" (Bradbury) **29**:49

"The Fqih" (Bowles) **3**:68

"The Fragile Age" (Grau) **15**:156

A Fragment of Life (Machen) **20**:165-66, 168, 175, 177, 196, 199, 201

"A Fragment of Stained Glass" (Lawrence) **4**:202

"Fragments. They Dine with the Past" (Waugh) **41**:327

"Frail Vessel" (Lavin) **4**:165, 167, 183-84

"The Frame" (Dixon) **16**:205, 207, 211

"Frame-Tale" (Barth) **10**:40, 42, 48, 79, 81, 84-5, 89, 97

"Francie's Fourpenny Foreigner" (Galsworthy) **22**:71

"The Francis Spaight" (London) **4**:262, 291

"Franciscan Adventures" (Lewis) **34**:160, 170

Frank Norris of "The Wave": Stories and Sketches from the San Francisco Weekly, 1893 to 1897 (Norris) **28**:200-03, 206, 213-15

"Frank Sinatra or Carleton Carpenter" (Lish) **18**:267

"Frankie the Newspaperman" (Williams) **31**:321, 334

"The Franklin Stove" (Dixon) **16**:210, 214-15

"The Franklyn Paragraphs" (Campbell) **19**:86, 90-1

"Franny" (Salinger) **2**:291, 293, 297, 302-03, 305; **28**:221-24, 226-32, 234, 236, 238, 243-44, 246, 248-50, 253, 259, 262-63, 265-68

Franny and Zooey (Salinger) **2**:297, 304, 318; **28**:220-70

Frau Beate und ihr Sohn (Schnitzler) **15**:345-46

"Frau Brechenmacher Attends a Wedding" (Mansfield) **9**:301

"Die Frau des Richters" (Schnitzler) **15**:371

"Frau Holle" (Grimm and Grimm) **36**:214

Frau Regel Amrain und ihr Jüngster (Keller) **26**:107

"Frau Trude" (Grimm and Grimm) **36**:199

Frau von Savern (Arnim) **29**:5

"El fraude" (Arreola) **38**:8

Fräulein Else (Schnitzler) **15**:344-47, 367-69, 375

"Das Fräulein von Scudéri" (Hoffmann) **13**:181, 205-06, 209, 220, 225-26

"A Freak Melon" (P'u Sung-ling)
See "Gua yi"

"The Freak of a Genius" (Alcott) **27**:29-30, 33, 35 6, 58, 61

Freaks of Genius (Alcott) **27**:32, 34, 36

"Free" (Dreiser) **30**:107, 114-16, 122, 127, 144-45

"Free" (O'Hara) **15**:248, 270

Free, and Other Stories (Dreiser) **30**:107-09, 118, 120-27, 153

Free Joe, and Other Georgian Sketches (Harris) **19**:124, 134, 147, 151

"Free Joe and the Rest of the World" (Harris) **19**:124, 131, 147, 157-58, 173, 177-78, 184

"Free Will" (Pavese) **19**:387

"Free Will and the Commendatore" (Bioy Casares) **17**:73

"Freedom to Breathe" (Solzhenitsyn) **32**:394-95

"Freedom's a Hard-Bought Thing" (Benet) **10**:143, 154, 156

"The Freeholder Ovsyanikov" (Turgenev) **7**:313, 344

"Frei Simão" (Machado de Assis) **24**:131

"Das Fremde Kind" (Hoffmann) **13**:192, 194-95, 199-200

French Girls Are Vicious and Other Stories (Farrell) **28**:105

"French Harvest" (Boyle) **5**:64

"French Life" (Gaskell) **25**:59-60

"The French Poodle" (Lewis) **34**:164, 171

"The Frenchman Six Foot-Three" (Wescott) **35**:375

Frenzied Fiction (Leacock) **39**:265

"Fresh Air Fiend" (Wilson) **21**:319, 323-24, 327, 329-31, 333, 335, 342, 350-51

"The Freshest Boy" (Fitzgerald) **6**:49, 58, 80-1, 84-6

"Freud's Room" (Ozick) **15**:318-19

"Ein Freund der Regierung" (Lenz) **33**:318

"Die Freunde" (Tieck) **31**:281

"Freya of the Seven Isles" (Conrad) **9**:142-43, 149

"Friday's Footprint" (Gordimer) **17**:154

Friday's Footprint (Gordimer) **17**:153-54, 165, 168, 184

"The Friend" (Lish) **18**:282

"A Friend and Protector" (Taylor) **10**:382, 418

"A Friend of Kafka" (Singer) **3**:384

A Friend of Kafka, and Other Stories (Singer) **3**:370, 373, 375

"A Friend of the Earth" (Thurber) **1**:422, 427

"Friend of the Family" (Boyle) **5**:55

"The Friend of the Family" (McCarthy) **24**:215-16, 225

The Friend of the Family (Dostoevsky) **2**:164, 172, 175-76

"A Friend of the World" (Bowles) **3**:64, 83

"Friendly Brook" (Kipling) **5**:275, 279

"Friends" (Beattie) **11**:4-5, 7

"The Friends" (Cortazar)
See "Los amigos"

"Friends" (Paley) **8**:409-10

"Friends" (Pavese) **19**:368, 387

"Friends" (Sansom) **21**:110, 126

"A Friend's Death" (Dixon) **16**:217

"Friends from Philadelphia" (Updike) **13**:350-51, 354

"Friends of the Family" (O'Connor) **5**:371

"The Friends of the Friends" (James) **8**:270, 316

Fritz Kochers Aufsätze (Walser) **20**:332, 338-40, 357

"The Frog Prince" (Collier) **19**:104

"The Frog Prince" (Grimm and Grimm) **36**:204, 206, 208

"The Frog Song" (P'u Sung-ling)
See "Wa-ch'u"

"Frog Trouncin' Contest" (Stuart) **31**:234, 260-61

"The Frogs" (Agnon) **30**:68

"Froim grach" (Babel) **16**:27

"The Frolic" (Ligotti) **16**:261, 263, 269, 271, 276, 283, 286, 288

"From a French Prison" (Rhys) **21**:62

"From a Refugee's Notebook" (Ozick) **15**:306-07

"From a Window in Vartou" (Andersen) **6**:4

"From Bed and Board" (Auchincloss) **22**:48

From Death to Morning (Wolfe) **33**:346-47, 349, 351, 355, 369-72, 376, 382, 397

"From Each according to His Ability" (Henry) **5**:159

"From Lodging to Lodging" (Agnon) **30**:71

"From the Cabby's Seat" (Henry) **5**:158

"From the Childhood of Saint Francis of Assisi" (Hesse) **9**:231, 235

"From the Diary of a New York Lady" (Parker) **2**:278, 286

"From the Fifteenth District" (Gallant) **5**:136-37

From the Fifteenth District (Gallant) **5**:135-37

From the Four Winds (Galsworthy) **22**:57, 72, 80, 84, 90-1, 93, 97

"From the Water Junction" (Sansom) **21**:88

"From Your Side to Paradise" (Ferre) **36**:144

"A Front Page Story" (Farrell) **28**:91-2

"The Frontier" (Bates) **10**:116

"Frontiers" (Aldiss) **36**:14, 20

The Frontiersmen (Murfree) **22**:189

"The Frost Is on the Noggin" (Perelman) **32**:235

"The Frost King; or, The Power of Love" (Alcott) **27**:38-9

The Frost-King (Alcott) **27**:44

"A Froward Child" (de la Mare) **14**:82, 86, 89

"The Frozen Fields" (Bowles) **3**:65-6, 79, 84

"The Fruitful Sleeping of the Rev. Elisha Edwards" (Dunbar) **8**:122, 127

"Fruition at Forty" (Narayan) **25**:132, 155-56

"The Frying Pan" (O'Connor) **5**:371, 389

"Fu hu" (P'u Sung-ling) **31**:208

"El fuego" (Pardo Bazan) **30**:261

"La fuerza de la sangre" (Cervantes) **12**:3, 5, 14-16, 18-22, 33, 36-7, 39-40, 44

"Fuga" (Pirandello) **22**:278

"Fugaku hyakkei" (Dazai Osamu) **41**:240, 245

"Fugitives" (Moore) **19**:305, 312, 333, 336

"Fugue" (O'Faolain) **13**:302-03, 314

"Fulano" (Machado de Assis) **24**:128

"Fulfillment" (Dreiser) **30**:122

"The Fulfillment of the Pact" (Howells) **36**:397

"The Full Belly" (White) **39**:301, 303, 305, 308, 319-20, 324-25, 328, 337, 346, 350

"A Full Day" (Price) **22**:386

"Full Employment" (Levi) **12**:278-79

"Full Sun" (Aldiss) **36**:20

"The Fullness of Life" (Wharton) **6**:424

"Fumes" (Pirandello)
See "Il fumo"

"Fumiko no ashi" (Tanizaki) **21**:182, 210

"Fumiko's Feet" (Tanizaki)
See "Fumiko no ashi"

"Il fumo" (Pirandello) **22**:241, 244

"Funeral March" (Machado de Assis) **24**:155

The Funeral of Mama Grand (Garcia Marquez)
See *Los funerales de la Mamá Grande*

"Los funerales de la Mamá Grande" (Garcia Marquez) **8**:155, 162, 174, 185, 187, 191, 198

Los funerales de la Mamá Grande (Garcia Marquez) **8**:169-70, 183, 185, 187, 189

"Funes" (Borges)
See "Funes el memorioso"

"Funes el memorioso" (Borges) **4**:19-20, 30; **41**:60, 159, 162, 164

"Funes, His Memory" (Borges)
See "Funes el memorioso"

"Funes the Memorious" (Borges)
See "Funes el memorioso"

Der funfzehnte November (Tieck) **31**:274

"Funhouse" (Barth)
See "Lost in the Funhouse"

Funhouse (Barth)
See *Lost in the Funhouse: Fiction for Print, Tape, Live Voice*

Funny Pieces (Leacock) **39**:267

"Fur" (Saki) **12**:295

"The Fur Coat" (O'Faolain) **13**:288, 314

"The Fur Hat" (Peretz)
See "The Fur Hat"

"The Fur-Cap" (Peretz)
  See "The Fur-Cap"
"The Furious Seasons" (Carver) **8**:5, 50
Furious Seasons, and Other Stories (Carver)
  8:4, 30, 32, 34, 46, 50, 57-8
"The Furnished Room" (Henry) **5**:156, 171,
  174, 180-81, 184, 187-89
"Fürst Ganzgott und Sänger Halbogott"
  (Arnim) **29**:6-7
Further Confessions of Zeno (Svevo) **25**:334,
  338, 340, 342, 349
Further Fables for Our Time (Thurber)
  1:426-28
Futility and Other Animals (Moorhouse)
  40:286-89, 291-94, 297, 301-02, 307-11,
  321-25
"The Future, If Any, of Comedy; or, Where Do
  We Not-Go from Here?" (Thurber) **1**:424
"Fyrtøjet" (Andersen)
  See "The Tinder-Box"
G. K. Chesterton: Selected Short Stories
  (Chesterton) **1**:135
"Gabriel-Ernest" (Saki) **12**:316, 331
"'Gad, Lucy, You're Magnificent!' Breathed
  the Great Painter" (Perelman) **32**:212
The Gadsbys (Kipling)
  See *The Story of the Gadsbys*
"A Gala Dress" (Freeman) **1**:196, 201
"Le galant tireur" (Baudelaire) **18**:6, 18, 36-7
"Galar Dúithche" (Moore) **19**:303, 308, 319-20,
  322, 330-31, 333-35
"Galatea" (Thomas) **20**:289, 296, 318
Galaxies like Grains of Sand (Aldiss) **36**:4, 6,
  18-19
"Gale" (Schulz) **13**:335
"Galeria póstuma" (Machado de Assis) **24**:129,
  133
"A Galician Mother" (Pardo Bazan) **30**:290
Galigaï (Mauriac) **24**:163-64, 167-70, 206
"A Galinha" (Lispector) **34**:185, 189, 195
A Gallery of Women (Dreiser) **30**:110, 122, 133-
  42, 146-49, 151
"La gallina di reparto" (Calvino) **3**:98
"Galway Bay" (O'Flaherty) **6**:265, 269, 282
"Galya Ganskaya" (Bunin) **5**:114
"Gambara" (Balzac) **5**:16, 26
"The Gambler, the Nun, and the Radio"
  (Hemingway) **1**:218, 234; **25**:101; **40**:177,
  185, 209, 212, 215, 224, 245, 247, 249, 251
"Gambler's Luck" (Hoffmann)
  See "Spielerglück"
"The Game" (Barthelme) **2**:40
"A Game of Billiards" (Sansom) **21**:90, 92, 95
"A Game of Catch" (Garrett) **30**:173, 180
"A game of make-believe" (Kundera) **24**:89
"Games without End" (Calvino) **3**:109
"Gandhi's Appeal" (Narayan) **25**:137, 140, 153,
  156-57
"Ganymede" (du Maurier) **18**:127, 132, 137
"Gaol Birds" (Pavese) **19**:387
"The Garden" (Borges)
  See "El jardín de senderos que se bifurcan"
"The Garden" (Bowles) **3**:64, 68, 80
"The Garden" (Dazai Osamu)
  See "Niwa"
"The Garden at Mons" (Hemingway) **1**:208,
  236
"The Garden Lodge" (Cather) **2**:90, 98, 103
"The Garden of Eden" (Andersen) **6**:30, 37
"The Garden of Eden" (Moore) **19**:311
The Garden of Forking Paths (Borges)
  See *El jardín de senderos que se bifurcan*
The Garden of Krakonoš (Capek)
  See *Krakonošova zahrada*
"Garden of Paradise" (Andersen) **6**:7
"The Garden of the Forking Paths" (Borges)
  See "El jardín de senderos que se bifurcan"
"The Garden of Time" (Ballard) **1**:71, 74, 77
"The Garden Party" (Mansfield) **9**:276, 280,
  282, 284, 286, 309-11, 313; **23**:118-77;
  38:230

The Garden Party, and Other Stories
  (Mansfield) **9**:275-76, 281; **23**:139
"A Garden Story" (Jewett) **6**:156, 158-59
"The Gardener" (Kipling) **5**:276, 279, 282-83,
  296-97
"The Gardener" (Lavin) **4**:181
"The Gardener and the Family" (Andersen) **6**:15
"Gardens" (Narayan) **25**:138
"Gargantua" (Calisher) **15**:9, 15, 19, 21
Garland for Girls (Alcott) **27**:44
A Garland of Love (Bioy Casares)
  See *Guirnalda con amores*
A Garland of Straw, and Other Stories
  (Warner) **23**:367-68, 380, 387
"The Garment" (Agnon) **30**:38
"Gaspar Ruiz" (Conrad) **9**:151, 157, 179, 181
"Gaspard de la nuit" (Donoso) **34**:8, 12-13, 17,
  34
Gäst hos verkligheten (Lagerkvist) **12**:180-82,
  185, 197
"The Gate of the Hundred Sorrows" (Kipling)
  5:262, 265
"Le gâteau" (Baudelaire) **18**:8, 18
"Le gâteau" (Maupassant) **1**:274, 286
"The Gateman's Gift" (Narayan) **25**:133, 141,
  153, 155-56
"The Gatewood Caper" (Hammett) **17**:220, 222
"Gaudissart" (Balzac)
  See "L'illustre Gaudissart"
"The Gauzy Edge of Paradise" (Gilchrist)
  14:153-54
"Gavin O'Leary" (Collier) **19**:106, 110
"A Gay Adventure" (Zoshchenko)
  See "A Gay Little Episode"
"The Gay and Melancholy Flux" (Saroyan)
  21:137, 139
"A Gay Little Episode" (Zoshchenko) **15**:395
"Gazebo" (Carver) **8**:14-15, 19-20
"G.B.S. Interviews the Pope" (Farrell) **28**:94
"G.B.S., Mark V" (Bradbury) **29**:78
"Ge" (P'u Sung-ling) **31**:215
"Gedali" (Babel) **16**:8-10, 25, 27-30, 52-3, 55,
  57-8
"Geese" (Aleichem)
  See "Genz"
"Gefallen" (Mann) **5**:319, 323, 351-53
Der Geheimnisvolle (Tieck) **31**:270-71
"Gehenna" (Aiken) **9**:10, 12-13, 30
Die Geisterseher (Keller) **26**:110
Der Gelehrte (Tieck) **31**:274, 286
"Das Gelübde" (Hoffmann) **13**:209-11
Die Gemälde (Tieck) **31**:269-70, 286
"Gemcrack" (Phillips) **16**:328
"Das Gemeine" (Dazai Osamu) **41**:244
"The Gemlike Flame" (Auchincloss) **22**:3, 33,
  35-7, 53
"The General" (O'Hara) **15**:276-77, 285-86
"The General's Day" (Trevor) **21**:230, 236, 261
"The Generations of America" (Ballard) **1**:82
"The Generous Lover" (Cervantes)
  See "El amante liberal"
"Generous Pieces" (Gilchrist) **14**:150
"Generous Wine" (Svevo)
  See "Vino generoso"
"Genesis" (Stegner) **27**:199, 219, 221, 223
Geneviéve (Gide) **13**:72, 100-05
"The Genial Epoch" (Schulz)
  See "The Age of Genius"
"The Genial Host" (McCarthy) **24**:213, 225
"Das Genie" (Walser) **20**:334
Génitrix (Mauriac) **24**:160, 163, 179-80, 185-
  86, 188, 206, 208
"The Genius" (O'Connor) **5**:376
"Gentian" (Freeman) **1**:197
"The Gentle Art" (Gordimer) **17**:161, 184
"The Gentle Boy" (Hawthorne) **3**:164, 167,
  181, 185-87
"The Gentle Euphemia; or 'Love Shall Still Be
  Lord of All'" (Trollope) **28**:316, 347
The Gentle Grafter (Henry) **5**:155, 162, 172,
  182
"A Gentle Soul" (Lavin) **4**:165-66, 168

"The Gentleman from Cracow" (Singer) **3**:358,
  368, 383-84
"The Gentleman from New Orleans" (Chopin)
  8:99
"The Gentleman from San Francisco" (Bunin)
  5:80-3, 85, 87-90, 92, 94-7, 117
The Gentleman from San Francisco (Bunin)
  5:90
"A Gentleman of Bayou Têche" (Chopin) **8**:88,
  103
"A Gentleman's Agreement" (Jolley) **19**:233,
  245
"A Gentleman's Friend" (Chekhov) **2**:137-39
"Gentlemen of the Press" (Wolfe) **33**:374
"The Gentry" (O'Hara) **15**:286
"Genuflection in the Sun" (Perelman) **32**:211
"The Geological Spieler" (Lawson) **18**:206, 263
"Geometar i Julka" (Andric) **36**:66-7
"The Geometry of Love" (Cheever) **1**:97, 101;
  38:53
"George and the Pink House" (Naipaul) **38**:318
George Gissing: Lost Stories from America
  (Gissing) **37**:79
"George Silverman's Explanation" (Dickens)
  17:124
"George Thurston" (Bierce) **9**:67-9, 76-7
"George Walker at Suez" (Trollope) **28**:318,
  331, 335
Georgia Boy (Caldwell) **19**:15, 18, 25, 33, 35-7,
  41, 47-55, 57
"Georgia's Ruling" (Henry) **5**:162, 164, 170
"Geraldo" (Cisneros) **32**:4
"The Geranium" (O'Connor) **1**:364
Gerbersau (Hesse) **9**:231
"A Germ Destroyer" (Kipling) **5**:290
"A German Idyll" (Bates) **10**:113
"The German Refugee" (Malamud) **15**:171,
  173-74, 176, 213, 216, 221, 235-36
"The German Spy" (Tanizaki)
  See "Dokutan"
"A Geronimo Story" (Silko) **37**:295-96, 310-11
Gesammelte Erzählungen (Lenz) **33**:333
"Gesammelte Erzählungen und Märchen"
  (Hoffmann) **13**:217
"Geschäft ist Geschäft" (Boell) **23**:5
Geschichten (Walser) **20**:334
Geschichten aus der Tonne (Storm) **27**:278
Die Gesellschaft auf dem Lande (Tieck) **31**:271,
  275, 286
*Gestes et opinions du Dr. Faustroll,
  pataphysicien, roman néo-scientifique*
  (Jarry) **20**:45-7, 49-53, 55-6, 62, 67, 69-
  70, 77, 82
"Get a Seeing-Eyed Dog" (Hemingway) **40**:192
"Get Thee to a Monastery" (Thurber) **1**:429
"Getting Back on Dave Regan" (Lawson)
  18:233-35
"Getting into the Set" (Updike) **13**:402
"Getting Lucky" (Michaels) **16**:309, 316
"Getting off the Altitude" (Lessing) **6**:190, 214
Getting Through (McGahern) **17**:299, 303-04,
  306-09, 322-23
"Getzel the Monkey" (Singer) **3**:359
"The Ghost" (Andersen) **6**:30
"The Ghost and the Bone Setter" (Le Fanu)
  14:216, 219, 221, 239
"The Ghost in the Garden Room" (Gaskell)
  See "The Crooked Branch"
"The Ghost of the Crosstrees" (Norris) **28**:198
"The Ghost of the Rose" (Kawabata)
  See "Bara no Yūrei"
Ghost Stories and Mysteries (Le Fanu) **14**:237
Ghost Stories and Tales of Mystery (Le Fanu)
  14:217, 220-21
Ghost Stories of an Antiquary (James) **16**:222,
  226-27, 229-31, 237-39, 242, 245, 250-51,
  255, 258
"Ghostkeeper" (Lowry) **31**:72, 83
"A Ghostly Chess Game" (London) **4**:294
"The Ghostly Door" (Lawson) **18**:217
"Ghostly Father, I Confess" (McCarthy) **24**:214
Ghostly Tales (Campbell) **19**:63, 86-7, 89

"The Ghost-Maker" (Pohl) **25**:227-28, 230-32, 234-35

Ghosts (Wharton) **6**:426-27, 430

"La giachetta di cuoio" (Pavese) **19**:364, 378, 384, 387

"Giacomo" (Svevo) **25**:329

"The Giant and the Tailor" (Grimm and Grimm) **36**:229-30

"The Giant Mole" (Kafka) **5**:206

"The Giant Wistaria" (Gilman) **13**:128, 130-31, 138-140

"The Giant's House" (Benet) **10**:149

"La giara" (Pirandello) **22**:226, 229, 237-38, 256, 264, 281

"Un giardino incantato" (Calvino) **3**:90, 97, 112

"Gib'ath ha-hol" (Agnon) **30**:20, 54, 66

"The Gift" (Bradbury) **29**:80

"The Gift" (Ferre) **36**:147, 150

"The Gift" (Steinbeck) **11**:209-10, 212-13, 232-34, 237

"A Gift from the City" (Updike) **13**:353-54

"Gift from the Stars" (Clarke) **3**:128

"Gift of Grass" (Adams) **24**:2, 8

"The Gift of the Magi" (Henry) **5**:166, 171-72, 181-82, 184-85, 187-88

"The Gift of the Prodigal" (Taylor) **10**:407-08, 418

"Gifts" (Singer) **3**:389

"The Gifts of the Little Folk" (Grimm and Grimm) **36**:229-30

Gigi (Colette) **10**:269-70, 272-74, 293

"Gigolo and Gigolette" (Maugham) **8**:366, 379

"The Gilded Six-Bits" (Hurston) **4**:135-36, 138, 151-52

"Gilead" (Henderson) **29**:327

"Gimpel Tam" (Singer) **3**:352, 355, 363, 365 68, 375, 382-84, 389

Gimpel Tam und andere Dertseylungen (Singer) **3**:370

"Gimpel the Fool" (Singer)
See "Gimpel Tam"

Gimpel the Fool, and Other Stories (Singer)
See *Gimpel Tam und andere Dertseylungen*

"Gin and Goldenrod" (Lowry) **31**:44-6, 48, 51-4, 59, 62, 71-2, 74-5, 81, 86-7

"The Gingerbread House" (Coover) **15**:33, 38, 41, 48

"The Gioconda of the Twilight Noon" (Ballard) **1**:69

"The Gioconda Smile" (Huxley) **39**:155, 162-65, 167-70, 174-75

"Una giornata" (Pirandello) **22**:262, 270

"Girl" (Henry) **5**:163, 182

"The Girl" (Oates) **6**:232

"The Girl and the Habit" (Henry) **5**:158, 164

"The Girl from California" (O'Hara) **15**:281

"The Girl from Ciociaria" (Moravia) **26**:139

"The Girl from the Family of Man" (Moorhouse) **40**:286, 302

"The Girl I Left Behind Me" (Spark) **10**:356

"The Girl in the Bus" (Sansom) **21**:94, 96

"The Girl in the Pink Hat" (Gilman) **13**:126

"A Girl Named Peter" (Bates) **10**:115-16

"A Girl of Modern Tyre" (Garland)
See "A Stop-Over at Tyre"

"The Girl of My Dreams" (Malamud) **15**:217, 239, 240, 242-43

The Girl on the Baggage Truck (O'Hara) **15**:250-51, 271-72

"The Girl Who Had Been Presented" (O'Hara) **15**:263, 266

"The Girl Who Met Simone de Beauvoir in Paris" (Moorhouse) **40**:289, 302

"The Girl Who Sang" (Aldiss) **36**:20

"The Girl Who Trod on the Loaf" (Andersen) **6**:13

"The Girl with a Pimply Face" (Williams) **31**:304-05, 325, 332-33, 340-42, 345, 362

"Girl with Figurines" (Caldwell) **19**:54-5

"The Girl with the Cannon Dresses" (Jewett) **6**:157

"The Girl with the Flaxen Hair" (Grau) **15**:147, 150, 158, 165

"The Girl with the Silver Eyes" (Hammett) **17**:219, 221, 228, 230

"The Girl with the Stoop" (Bowen) **3**:54

"Girls and the Land" (Gilman) **13**:144

"A Girl's Story" (Bambara) **35**:28

"Gitanette" (Colette) **10**:292

"Gitl Purishkevitch" (Aleichem) **33**:19, 26, 38

"Giulia Lazzari" (Maugham) **8**:377

"Give Us a Prescription, Doctor" (Hemingway) **40**:245, 247, 251, 257

"The Given Case" (James) **8**:316

"Giving Birth" (Atwood) **2**:3-4, 6-10, 12, 14, 16

"Giving Blood" (Updike) **13**:373, 386

"Glad Ghosts" (Lawrence) **4**:220, 230

"Gladius Dei" (Mann) **5**:310, 323, 329, 331

"Glamour" (Benet) **10**:142, 144, 154

"The Glamour" (Ligotti) **16**:280

"The Glass Coffin" (Grimm and Grimm) **36**:223, 229-30

"The Glass Mountain" (Barthelme) **2**:34, 40

"A Glass of Tea" (White) **39**:280, 291-93, 296-97, 309, 317, 325, 329, 336, 344

"Glass Orchid" (Cowan) **28**:83

"The Glass Scholar" (Cervantes)
See "El licienciado Vidriera"

"Glazed Tiles" (Chang) **28**:25; 34

"The Glazier's Song" (Baudelaire)
See "La chanson vitrier"

"A Gleam" (Mann) **5**:322-23

"The Gleaner" (Bates) **10**:113, 128

"Gleanings from Snow Country" (Kawabata) **17**:251, 253, 255, 257

Glenda (Cortazar)
See *Queremos tanto a Glenda*

"The Glendale People" (O'Hara) **15**:282-83

"Gliding Gulls and Going People" (Sansom) **21**:91, 94, 122-23

"Gloire et malheur" (Balzac) **5**:4, 29

Gloomy People (Chekhov) **2**:146

"Glory in the Daytime" (Parker) **2**:273-74, 280, 283

"The Glory Machine" (Villiers de l'Isle Adam)
See "La machine à gloire"

"Glossolalia" (Barth) **10**:42-3, 45, 47, 54-5, 80, 90, 94-5, 97-8

"The Gloves" (Walser) **20**:364

"Gluck" (Hoffmann) **13**:225

Glück gibt Verstand (Tieck) **31**:274

"Die Glücksfamilie des Monats" (Lenz) **33**:318, 322-27

"The Gnats" (Pritchett) **14**:299

"Go Back to Your Precious Wife and Son" (Vonnegut) **8**:436

"Go Down, Moses" (Faulkner) **1**:148, 154, 165-67, 173, 180-83; **35**:146, 157, 160

Go Down, Moses and Other Stories (Faulkner) **35**:141, 146, 148-49, 157-58, 160, 164, 170, 173-76, 178, 184, 186-87, 197-98, 206, 210

"Go Forth" (Aleichem)
See "Lekh-lekh"

"A Goatherd at Luncheon" (Calvino) **3**:116

"The Go-Away Bird" (Spark) **10**:350-56, 358-59, 361, 366, 368, 370

The Go-Away Bird, and Other Stories (Spark) **10**:350-53

"Gobegger Foriu Tostay" (Cabrera Infante) **39**:22

"The Go-Between" (Moravia) **26**:139

"The Goblin at the Grocer's" (Andersen) **6**:30, 34, 41

"Gobseck" (Balzac) **5**:18, 22, 24, 28, 31, 33

"God and the Article Writer" (Berriault) **30**:101

"God and the Cobbler" (Narayan) **25**:152, 159

"God Bless the Lonesome Gas Man" (Algren) **33**:108

"The God of His Fathers" (London) **4**:258, 286-87

The God of His Fathers (London) **4**:264, 282, 285-87

"The God of the Gongs" (Chesterton) **1**:127

"God Rest You Merry, Gentlemen" (Hemingway) **1**:216

"God Sees the Truth but Waits" (Tolstoy) **9**:382, 386-87

"The Goddess" (Oates) **6**:231

The Goddess and Other Women (Oates) **6**:231, 243

"Godliness" (Anderson) **1**:18, 42, 57

"Godman's Master" (Laurence) **7**:245-46, 249-50, 252-53, 261, 263

"The Godmother" (Chopin) **8**:100

"The Gods" (Pavese) **19**:371

Gods, Demons, and Others (Narayan) **25**:135-36, 152, 166

"The Gods in Flight" (Aldiss) **36**:20, 22

"God's Little Traveling Salesman" (Lagerkvist) **12**:196

"God's Lonely Man" (Wolfe) **33**:374

"God's Ravens" (Garland) **18**:154, 160, 163

"The God's Script" (Borges)
See "La escritura del Dios"

"God's Wrath" (Malamud) **15**:217

"The Godson" (Tolstoy) **9**:388

"The Go-Getter" (Wodehouse) **2**:346

"A Goin' to the Buttin'" (Stuart) **31**:254

"Goin' to Town" (Storm)
See "Going to Town"

"The Going Away of Liza" (Chopin) **8**:71

"Going Blind" (Lawson) **18**:200, 202, 213

"Going Critical" (Bambara) **35**:42

"Going Home" (Trevor) **21**:244

"Going into Exile" (O'Flaherty) **6**:261, 269, 276-77, 281-82, 284

"Going Places" (Michaels) **16**:302-03, 311-13

Going Places (Michaels) **16**:301-03, 306-08, 310, 314-16, 322

"Going to Meet the Man" (Baldwin) **10**:3, 5, 7, 10, 17-18, 20

Going to Meet the Man (Baldwin) **10**:2, 4, 6, 8-9, 12, 17; **33**:116, 128, 143

"Going to Naples" (Welty) **1**:476, 484

"Going to the People" (Moravia)
See "Going to the People"

"Going to Town" (Stegner) **27**:196

"Going Under" (Dubus) **15**:82, 87, 89-90

"Gold" (Levi) **12**:256, 258

"Gold and Silver" (Tanizaki) **21**:190, 194

"The Gold at the Starbow's End" (Pohl) **25**:226

"The Gold Belt" (Narayan) **25**:138, 140-41

"The Gold Bug" (Poe) **1**:378, 390; **22**:293, 305

"The Gold Dress" (Benet) **10**:160

"Gold Is Not Always" (Faulkner) **1**:177

"A Gold Slipper" (Cather) **2**:91

"The Gold That Glittered" (Henry) **5**:188

"The Gold Watch" (Machado de Assis)
See "O relógio de ouro"

"The Gold Watch" (McGahern) **17**:304, 309-10, 315, 317, 320-21, 323-24

"The Gold-Children" (Grimm and Grimm) **36**:199, 201

"The Golden Age" (Cheever) **1**:106

"Golden Apple" (Kundera)
See "The Golden Apple of Eternal Desire"

"The Golden Apple" (Kundera)
See "The Golden Apple of Eternal Desire"

"The Golden Apple of Desire" (Kundera)
See "The Golden Apple of Eternal Desire"

"The Golden Apple of Eternal Desire" (Kundera) **24**:86, 88, 91-2, 97, 102-04, 106, 113-14

"The Golden Apples" (Welty) **1**:473-74, 479, 483-85, 492, 494, 497

"The Golden Apples of the Sun" (Bradbury) **29**:78, 84

The Golden Apples of the Sun (Bradbury) **29**:44, 48, 52, 78-9

"The Golden Bessie" (Benet) **10**:144, 146

"The Golden Bird" (Grimm and Grimm) **36**:199, 201, 206

The Golden Cangue (Chang)
See *The Golden Cangue*

Title Index

"The Golden Death" (Tanizaki)
See "Konjiki no shi"
"Golden Documents" (Bulgakov) **18**:91
"Golden Gate" (Hughes) **6**:138
"The Golden Goose" (Grimm and Grimm)
See "The Golden Bird"
"The Golden Graveyard" (Lawson) **18**:239
"The Golden Honeymoon" (Lardner) **32**:114-
17, 123, 125, 131-32, 139, 145, 149, 152,
154-55, 166, 195-96
"The Golden Horseshoe" (Hammett) **17**:200,
210, 219, 222-23, 225
"The Golden Kite, the Silver Wind"
(Bradbury) **29**:42
"Golden Land" (Faulkner) **1**:167
The Golden Oriole (Bates) **10**:123-24
The Golden Pot: Fairy Tale of Our Times
(Hoffmann)
See "Der goldene Topf"
"The Golden Town" (Bulgakov) **18**:90
"Golden Wedding" (Suckow) **18**:389, 396, 398-
99, 412
"Der goldene Topf" (Hoffmann) **13**:186, 189,
192-95, 197, 199-205, 208, 215, 218-19,
223, 226
"Goldfish" (Chandler) **23**:59, 63, 87, 107
"The Goldfish" (Pritchett) **14**:297
"Gollan" (Coppard) **21**:10
"Golubaia zhizn" (Gorky) **28**:179, 181-82
"Gone Away" (Bowen) **3**:53
"Goneril, Lear's Daughter" (Capek) **36**:84-5
"The Gonzaga Manuscripts" (Bellow) **14**:3,
22-3, 25
"Good and Bad Dreams" (Price) **22**:365, 367,
371-72
"Good Climate, Friendly Inhabitants"
(Gordimer) **17**:181
"The Good Corn" (Bates) **10**:118
"Good Country People" (O'Connor) **1**:335,
343-45, 350, 356, 359-60; **23**:185, 233
"Good Deeds" (Moore) **19**:330
"A 'Good Fellow's' Wife" (Garland) **18**:161
"The Good Girl" (Bowen) **3**:33
"Good Humor" (Andersen) **6**:7
"A Good Job Gone" (Hughes) **6**:109, 121-22,
128, 140, 142
"A Good Location" (O'Hara) **15**:278-79
"A Good Man Is Hard to Find" (O'Connor)
1:339, 344, 347-48, 356, 358, 360-63, 371;
23:178-241
*A Good Man Is Hard to Find and Other
Stories* (O'Connor) **23**:196, 202, 209, 213,
232-33, 236-37
"The Good Old Days" (Williams) **31**:334
"Good Pals" (Suckow) **18**:411, 417
"Good Samaritan" (O'Hara) **15**:286
Good Samaritan, and Other Stories (O'Hara)
15:273, 286
"The Good Soldier" (London) **4**:291
"A Good Temper" (Andersen) **6**:30, 36
"The Good Trip" (Le Guin) **12**:232
"Good-by, Jack" (London) **4**:269
"Goodbye and Good Luck" (Paley) **8**:388, 391,
394, 396, 398
Goodbye, Columbus (Roth) **26**:228, 230-34,
243, 245-49, 252, 254, 256-57, 260, 265-69
Goodbye, Columbus, and Five Short Stories
(Roth) **26**:228, 231, 233, 236, 238, 246-
48, 250, 257-60
"Goodbye, Goodbye, Be Always Kind and
True" (Garrett) **30**:173
Goodbye Harold, Good Luck (Thomas)
20:320-23
"Goodbye Marcus, Goodbye Rose" (Rhys)
21:39-40, 42-3, 51, 55-7, 66, 70
"Goodbye, My Brother" (Cheever) **1**:89, 99,
103-05, 108; **38**:52, 54-5, 66, 84
"Good-Bye, New York" (Morand)
See "Adieu, New-York!"
"Goodbye to Goodbye" (Dixon) **16**:207
Goodbye, Wisconsin (Wescott) **35**:356, 363-65,
367, 375, 377, 379

The Goodbyes (Onetti)
See *Los adioses*
"Good-for-Nothing" (Andersen) **6**:4, 14, 26, 30
"A Goodly Life" (Bunin) **5**:81, 90, 92
"Goodwood Comes Back" (Warren) **4**:387, 389-
90, 394, 396
"The Goophered Grapevine" (Chesnutt) **7**:4-6,
9-10, 41
"Goose Fair" (Lawrence) **4**:197
"The Goose Girl at the Spring" (Grimm and
Grimm) **36**:190, 208, 233
"Gooseberries" (Chekhov)
See "Kryžovnik"
"Gooseberry Winter" (Mason) **4**:6
"Gora" (Leskov) **34**:127
"Gorilla, My Love" (Bambara) **35**:4-5, 8, 32
Gorilla, My Love (Bambara) **35**:2-3, 10, 14-18,
20-5, 28-30, 36, 42
"Gorod na Neve" (Solzhenitsyn) **32**:352, 354,
394
"The Gospel according to Mark" (Borges) **4**:20,
28, 30; **41**:160
"Gospodjicd" (Andric) **36**:48
"Gossips' Slope" (Rulfo)
See "La cuesta de las comadres"
"Got a Letter from Jimmy" (Jackson) **39**:212,
228, 229
La gota de sangre (Pardo Bazan) **30**:277-79
"The Goth" (Page) **23**:288, 307-08
"Gothic Horror" (Ligotti) **16**:287
"A Gourdful of Glory" (Laurence) **7**:245-46,
248-50
"Governor of Kentucky" (Stuart) **31**:226, 231,
236
"Governor Warburton's Right-hand Man"
(Stuart) **31**:265
"The Go-wa-peu-zi Song" (Silko) **37**:309
"Grabež" (Leskov) **34**:127
"Gracchus the Huntsman" (Kafka)
See "Der jäger Gracchus"
"La Grâce" (Ayme) **41**:13, 16, 18
"Grace" (Joyce) **3**:202, 205-06, 208, 210-11,
214-15, 225-26, 232-235, 237, 247-48;
26:46-8, 50
"Grace Called" (Dixon) **16**:217
"Grace Calls" (Dixon) **16**:217
"Graduation" (Dubus) **15**:73-4
"Graffiti" (Cortazar) **7**:83, 85-6, 91
"Grail" (Ellison) **14**:127
"A Grain as Big as a Hen's Egg" (Tolstoy)
9:388
"Gramigna's Lover" (Verga)
See "L'amante di Gramigna"
"Gramigna's Mistress" (Verga)
See "L'amante di Gramigna"
"Grammar of Love" (Bunin) **5**:89-90, 93, 106
"Grammar's for the Birds" (Cabrera Infante)
See "Cuando se estudia gramática"
"El gran serafin" (Bioy Casares) **17**:53
El gran serafin (Bioy Casares) **17**:53, 56, 59
"The Grand Vizier's Daughter" (O'Connor)
5:381
"La grande bretèche" (Balzac) **5**:11-12, 14-15,
18-19, 31, 35-9
"The Grande Malade" (Barnes) **3**:5-6, 9-10, 16,
24-6
"Grandfather and Grandson" (Singer) **3**:374
The Grandmother's Tale (Narayan) **25**:169,
173, 175
The Grandmother's Tale: And Selected Stories
(Narayan) **25**:169
"Grandpa Birdwell's Last Battle" (Stuart)
31:247
"Grandy Devil" (Pohl) **25**:220, 228, 230, 232
"Granella's House" (Pirandello)
See "La casa del Granella"
"Granit" (Stifter) **28**:292-96
The Grapes of Paradise (Bates) **10**:121-22
The Grapes of Paradise: Four Short Novels
(Bates)
See *An Aspidistra in Babylon: Four
Novellas*

"The Grass Fire" (Caldwell) **19**:5-6, 14, 17
"Grass from Our Garden" (Pirandello)
See "Erba del nosro orto"
The Grass God (Bates) **10**:118
"The Grass Widows" (Trevor) **21**:233, 237, 260
"The Grasshopper" (Chekhov) **2**:155
"Grasshoppers" (Jolley) **19**:246
"Grateful to Life and Death" (Narayan) **25**:167
Grateful to Life and Death (Narayan)
See *The English Teacher*
"The Grave" (Porter) **4**:329-34, 340-42; 344,
352, 354, 365; **31**:160, 175-76
"The Grave by the Handpost" (Hardy) **2**:210
"The Grave Mound" (Grimm and Grimm)
36:228
"The Grave of the Famous Poet" (Atwood)
2:3-5, 7, 10-11, 16
"The Gravedigger" (Pardo Bazan) **30**:290
"The Gravedigger" (Singer) **3**:378
"Graven Image" (O'Hara) **15**:248-49, 270
"Graveyard Day" (Mason) **4**:7
"The Graveyard Shift" (King) **17**:262
"Gravity" (Beattie) **11**:10, 13
"The Gray Champion" (Hawthorne) **3**:164, 167,
171, 175-76, 178, 186-87
"Gray Days" (Colette) **10**:292
"The Gray Jacket of 'No. 4'" (Page) **23**:284,
292, 295, 328
"Gray Matter" (King) **17**:261-62
"The Gray Mills of Farley" (Jewett) **6**:156
"A Gray Moon" (Shiga)
See "Hai-iro no tsuki"
"The Gray Wolf's Ha'nt" (Chesnutt) **7**:7, 10-11,
40
"Greasy Lake" (Boyle) **16**:144-45, 151-52,
156-57
Greasy Lake, & Other Stories (Boyle) **16**:143-
46, 148, 153
Great Battles of the World (Crane) **7**:104
"The Great Brown-Pericord Motor" (Doyle)
12:65, 79
"The Great Carbuncle" (Hawthorne) **3**:157, 159,
181-82, 184-85, 188
"The Great Cat's Tale" (Capek) **36**:108
"The Great Dark" (Twain) **6**:331-42, 350-53;
26:324, 329, 332-33
"A Great Day for a Bananafish" (Salinger)
See "A Perfect Day for Bananafish"
"A Great Day for Bonzo" (Bates) **10**:120
Great Days (Barthelme) **2**:44, 46
"The Great Ekbo" (Cabrera Infante)
See "En el gran ecbó"
"The Great God Pan" (Machen) **20**:155, 158,
161-63, 165, 168, 171-73, 182, 185-86, 190-
93, 196-201, 204
The Great God Pan and the Inmost Light
(Machen)
"The Great Good Place" (James) **8**:269, 282,
302, 304, 306-07
"The Great Hulabaloo of the Small Folk"
(Aleichem)
See "Digroyse behole fun di kleyne
mentshelekh"
"The Great Interrogation" (London) **4**:265, 286
"The Great Keinplatz Experiment" (Doyle)
12:80
"A Great Mollie" (Suckow) **18**:391, 415
"The Great Mountains" (Steinbeck) **11**:209,
212-14, 232, 237
"The Great Mutation" (Levi) **12**:276
"The Great Panic of the Little People"
(Aleichem) **33**:47
"Great Possibilities" (Collier) **19**:110, 113
"The Great Red Drum" (Dazai Osamu) **41**:231
The Great Return (Machen) **20**:163, 166, 181-
84, 196, 200
"The Great Road" (Bunin) **5**:87
"A Great Sorrow" (Andersen) **6**:4, 7
"The Great Stone Face" (Hawthorne) **3**:159,
178, 182, 184
"Great Strength" (Dazai Osamu) **41**:228, 232
"The Great Swinglefield Derby" (Benet) **10**:155

"The Great Szarratar Opal" (Norris) **28**:203
"Great Uncle Crow" (Bates) **10**:132
"A Great Voice Stilled" (Jackson) **39**:224
"The Great Wall of China" (Kafka) **5**:206
The Great Wall of China, and Other Pieces
    (Kafka)
    See *Beim Bau der Chinesischen Mauer*
*The Great Wall of China: Stories and
    Reflections* (Kafka)
    See *Beim Bau der Chinesischen Mauer*
"The Great Wave" (Lavin) **4**:167-68, 174, 184
The Great Wave, and Other Stories (Lavin)
    4:166
"The Great Wildenberg" (Lenz) **33**:337
"The Great Winglebury Duel" (Dickens)
    17:110, 116-17
"The Great World and Timothy Colt"
    (Auchincloss) **22**:3, 33, 47
"The Greatcoat" (Gogol)
    See "Shinel"
"The Greater Festival of Masks" (Ligotti)
    16:261, 271, 273, 280, 283
The Greater Inclination (Wharton) **6**:413
"The Greatest Country in the World" (Saroyan)
    21:163
"The Greatest Love of Don Juan" (Barbey
    d'Aurevilly)
    See "Le plus bel amour de Don Juan"
"The Greatest Man in the World" (Thurber)
    1:420, 431
"The Greatest People in the World" (Bates)
    10:114
*The Greatest People in the World, and Other
    Stories* (Bates) **10**:138
"The Greatest Television Show on Earth"
    (Ballard) **1**:71
"Greatness" (Benet) **10**:154
"The Greek Dancing Girl" (Schnitzler) **15**:343
"The Green Banana" (Powers) **4**:379
"Green Christmas" (Benet) **10**:149
"The Green Door" (Henry) **5**:159, 190
"The Green Drake" (Coppard) **21**:17
Green Ginger (Morrison) **40**:329, 333, 349, 369
"The Green Grave and the Black Grave"
    (Lavin) **4**:166-67, 174, 180, 184
"Green Hell" (Boyle) **16**:140-42
"A Green Hill Far Away" (Galsworthy) **22**:62-3,
    101
"Green Holly" (Bowen) **3**:32, 54; **28**:3
"The Green Isle in the Sea" (Thurber) **1**:417
"The Green Man" (Chesterton) **1**:129
"The Green Room" (de la Mare) **14**:71-2, 83,
    86-7, 91
The Green Round (Machen) **20**:166, 177, 194,
    196-97
Green Shoots (Morand)
    See *Tendres stocks*
"The Green Spider" (Walser) **20**:348
"Green Tea" (Le Fanu) **14**:222-25, 227, 229,
    231-35, 237-38, 240, 242, 249-51
"A Green Thought" (Michaels) **16**:303
"Green Thoughts" (Collier) **19**:98-9, 103, 109
"Green Tunnels" (Huxley) **39**:155, 168, 171,
    177-78
Green Water, Green Sky (Gallant) **5**:123, 144,
    146
"The Green Wax" (Colette) **10**:292, 295
"Greenie and Yellow" (Naipaul) **38**:300, 318,
    322, 328, 345
"Greenleaf" (O'Connor) **1**:343, 358, 360;
    23:205
"Greenwich Fair" (Dickens) **17**:125, 134
"Greenwich Time" (Beattie) **11**:12
"Gregory's Island" (Cable)
    See "The Solitary"
"Greg's Peg" (Auchincloss) **22**:35-6, 47, 52
La grenadière (Balzac) **5**:8, 16
"Gretchen's Forty Winks" (Fitzgerald) **6**:46
"The Grey Angel" (Galsworthy) **22**:62-3, 74,
    100-02
"Grey Seagull" (O'Flaherty) **6**:262
"A Grey Sleeve" (Crane) **7**:103, 106

"The Grey Woman" (Gaskell) **25**:47-8, 50, 58,
    60
"Gribiche" (Colette) **10**:281
Der griechische Kaiser (Tieck) **31**:289
Griechischer Frühling (Hauptmann) **37**:220
"Grief" (Andersen) **6**:26
"Grigia" (Musil) **18**:289, 292-93, 297-99, 302-
    13, 322, 325
"Den grimme lling" (Andersen)
    See "The Ugly Duckling"
Grimm's Fairy Tales (Grimm and Grimm)
    See *Kinder-und Hausmärchen*
Grimscribe: His Lives and Works (Ligotti)
    16:279-80, 282-85, 293, 294, 296
"Grippes and Poche" (Gallant) **5**:147
"The Grisly Folk" (Wells) **6**:382
"The Grit of the Peagraves" (Perelman) **32**:240
"The Grit of Women" (London) **4**:286, 288
"Grjotgard Ålvesøon and Aud" (Dinesen)
    See "Grjotgard Ålvesøon og Aud"
"Grjotgard Ålvesøon og Aud" (Dinesen) **7**:177
"Grobovshchik" (Pushkin) **27**:129, 145-46, 163,
    166, 168-69, 175, 183, 186
"The Grocery Store" (Malamud) **15**:234-35
"La grosse fifi" (Rhys) **21**:62-3
"Der Grosse Wildenberg" (Lenz) **33**:317
A Group of Noble Dames (Hardy) **2**:203-07,
    209, 212-13, 220-21
"The Growing Season" (Caldwell) **19**:23-4
"The Growing Stone" (Camus)
    See "La pierre qui pousse"
"Growing Up in Edge City" (Pohl) **25**:236
"The Growtown 'Bugle'" (Jewett) **6**:156, 159
"Groza v gorakh" (Solzhenitsyn) **32**:352
Ein Grünes Blatt (Storm) **27**:278, 284
"Gua yi" (P'u Sung ling) **31**:215
"El guardaguias" (Arreola) **38**:4, 7-8, 12-20,
    23, 26-27, 29-31, 35
"The Guardian" (de la Mare) **14**:79, 85, 89, 91
"Guardian Angel" (Clarke) **3**:149
"Guardian of the Law" (Fisher) **25**:6, 10-12,
    16-17, 19-21, 25-6
"Guayaquil" (Borges) **4**:20, 27
"Gubin" (Gorky) **28**:150
"Guduzhe" (Lu Hsun) **20**:140-41, 149-50
"El güero" (Donoso) **34**:3, 21-3, 30-1, 49
"The Güero" (Donoso)
    See "El güero"
Guerra del tiempo (Carpentier) **35**:91, 102, 106,
    110, 125
"The Guest" (Aleichem) **33**:70
"The Guest" (Camus)
    See "L'hôte"
"The Guest" (Elkin) **12**:94, 117-18
"The Guest" (Pavese) **19**:368
"A Guest at Home" (Jewett) **6**:156, 158-59
Guest of Reality (Lagerkvist)
    See *Gäst hos verkligheten*
"Guests" (Dixon) **16**:217
"Guests" (Taylor) **10**:389-90, 394, 404, 415,
    417
"Guests from Gibbet Island" (Irving) **2**:241,
    247-48
The Guests of August (Castellanos)
    See *Los convidados de agosto*
"Guests of the Nation" (O'Connor) **5**:369, 375-
    76, 379-82, 384, 388-89, 393
Guests of the Nation (O'Connor) **5**:363, 370,
    375, 377-80, 382, 384, 387, 390-93
"The Guests Were Arriving at the Dacha"
    (Pushkin) **27**:163-64, 175
"The Guide" (Campbell) **19**:77-8
"A Guide to Berlin" (Nabokov) **11**:134
"Guide to Kasrilevke" (Aleichem) **33**:49
Guillotine Party and Other Stories (Farrell)
    28:100-1, 119, 121-2
"Guilt" (Lish) **18**:267-68
"The Guilty Party—An East Side Tragedy"
    (Henry) **5**:188, 198
Guilty Pleasures (Barthelme) **2**:39, 41
"The Guilty Woman" (Pardo Bazan) **30**:290

"A Guilty Woman" (Wescott) **35**:363, 365, 369,
    371-72
Guirnalda con amores (Bioy Casares) **17**:53,
    87, 95
"The Gulf Between" (Calisher) **15**:5, 7, 15, 18
Gulf Coast Stories (Caldwell) **19**:21, 42, 54-6
"Gullible's Travels" (Lardner) **32**:160-62
Gullible's Travels, Etc. (Lardner) **32**:127, 141,
    145, 148, 153, 155
"Gulliver" (Wolfe) **33**:369, 380
"The Gully" (Cowan) **28**:82
"The Gully of Bluemansdyke" (Doyle) **12**:84-5
The Gully of Bluemansdyke and Other Stories
    (Doyle)
    See *Mysteries and Adventures*
"Gumption" (Hughes) **6**:131, 133
"The Gun" (O'Hara) **15**:262
"The Gun and the Hat" (Garrett) **30**:173
"The Gunboat and Madge" (O'Hara) **15**:286
"An Gunna-Phósta" (Moore) **19**:308, 319-20,
    322, 324, 328-30, 332, 334
"Guns at Cyrano's" (Chandler) **23**:56, 59, 86,
    97, 105-06, 112
"Guo An" (P'u Sung-ling) **31**:214
"Guru" (Narayan) **25**:174
"Gusev" (Chekhov) **2**:128-29, 143, 147; **28**:58-9
Gushi xinbian (Lu Hsun) **20**:125, 129, 134,
    139-40
Gustav Adolfs Page (Meyer) **30**:186, 188, 213,
    249
"The Gutting of Couffignal" (Hammett) **17**:206,
    222, 224, 229-30
"Guxiang" (Lu Hsun) **20**:140-41, 150
"The Guy" (Campbell) **19**:74, 92-4
"Guy de Maupassant" (Babel) **16**:4, 5, 15, 20,
    36, 42, 59
"Gwilan's Harp" (Le Guin) **12**:231
"Gyotukuki" (Dazai Osamu) **41**:238, 240, 243,
    264-69, 271, 273-74
"The Gypsy Feeling" (Nin) **10**:306
"Ha" (Dazai Osamu) **41**:248, 270, 272
"Habakuk Jephson's Statement" (Doyle) **12**:85
"The Habit of Loving" (Lessing) **6**:218
"An Habitation Enforced" (Kipling) **5**:283
El hacedor (Borges) **41**:53, 148, 157, 159, 163
"La Hachich" (Gautier) **20**:23-4, 31
"Hacienda" (Porter) **4**:327, 329-30, 346, 351;
    31:160, 177
"Hackney Coach Stands" (Dickens) **17**:111
"Had a Horse" (Galsworthy) **22**:66-7, 69, 79,
    101
Hadji Murád (Tolstoy) **9**:376, 378, 394-97
"Hadjii murád" (Tolstoy)
    See "Khadzi murat"
Hadlaub (Keller) **26**:108, 111, 113
"The Hag" (Turgenev) **7**:335
"Der Hagestolz" (Stifter) **28**:281, 283, 286-88,
    290, 296, 298
"Haha no kouru ki" (Tanizaki) **21**:183, 192,
    210, 226
"Haha no shi to atarishi haha" (Shiga) **23**:334,
    346, 354
"Das Haidedorf" (Stifter) **28**:290
"Hai-iro no tsuki" (Shiga) **23**:352
"The Haile Selassie Funeral Train"
    (Davenport) **16**:173-74, 177, 183, 194
"Die Haimatochare" (Hoffmann) **13**:187
"The Hair" (Carver) **8**:50-1
"Hair" (Faulkner) **1**:147, 151
"Hair Jewellery" (Atwood) **2**:3, 5-7, 10-11, 14,
    16
Hair O' the Chine (Coover) **15**:47-8
"The Hair Shirt" (Powers) **4**:380
"Haircut" (Lardner) **32**:116-17, 119, 125, 131,
    135-36, 139-41, 146, 149, 152-56, 160-61,
    169, 1 6, 184-85, 193, 195
"The Hairless Mexican" (Maugham) **8**:369, 376
"Haïta the Shepherd" (Bierce) **9**:49, 87
"Hakūchyukigo" (Tanizaki) **21**:194
"Hakumei" (Dazai Osamu) **41**:249
"Hal Irwin's Magic Lamp" (Vonnegut) **8**:437

"Halberdier of the Little Rheinschloss" (Henry) **5**:181, 196
"Hale Hardy and the Amazing Animal Woman" (Beattie) **11**:11, 16, 28
"Half a Grapefruit" (Munro) **3**:334, 342
"Half a Lifetime Ago" (Gaskell) **25**:55, 58, 72
"Half a Rupee" (Narayan)
 See "Half-a-Rupee Worth"
"Half-a-Rupee Worth" (Narayan) **25**:135, 139, 157
"The Half-Brothers" (Gaskell) **25**:59
"Half-Holiday" (Huxley) **39**:157, 162
"The Half-Husky" (Laurence) **7**:253, 270
"Halfway to Hell" (Collier) **19**:104
"The Hall of Fantasy" (Hawthorne) **3**:181
Eine Halligfahrt (Storm) **27**:304
"The Hallucination" (Oates) **6**:250
"Hamlet; or, The Consequences of Filial Piety" (Laforgue)
 See "Hamlet; ou, les suites de piété filiale"
"Hamlet; or, The Results of Filial Devotion" (Laforgue)
 See "Hamlet; ou, les suites de piété filiale"
"Hamlet; ou, les suites de piété filiale" (Laforgue) **20**:86-7, 89, 91, 93-5, 100-4, 106, 114, 119
"Hamlet, Prince of Denmark" (Capek) **36**:114-15, 130
"The Hammer Man" (Bambara) **35**:2, 7, 24
"The Hammer of God" (Chesterton) **1**:124, 130, 136
"Hamrick's Polar Bear" (Caldwell) **19**:13, 39, 45-6
"Han Fang" (P'u Sung-ling) **31**:198
"Han no hanza" (Shiga) **23**:332, 341-42, 345-46, 348, 352, 359
"Hand" (Atwood) **2**:20
"Hand and Heart" (Gaskell) **25**:58-9
"Hand in Glove" (Bowen) **3**:54
"The Hand of Emmagene" (Taylor) **10**:397-98, 402, 404
"Hand upon the Waters" (Faulkner) **1**:179
"Handcarved Coffins: A Nonfiction Account of an American Crime" (Capote) **2**:80-2
"Hands" (Anderson) **1**:32-3, 42, 44, 57
"The Hands" (Campbell) **19**:71
"Hands across the Sea" (Williams) **31**:350, 358-60
"Handsome Brown" (Caldwell) **19**:17
"Handsome Brown and the Aggravating Goats" (Caldwell) **19**:50-1
"Handsome Brown and the Shirt-tail Woodpeckers" (Caldwell) **19**:51
"Handsome Is as Handsome Does" (Pritchett) **14**:268-69, 291, 298
"The Handsome Lady" (Coppard) **21**:3, 12
"The Handsomest Drowned Man in the World: A Tale for Children" (Garcia Marquez)
 See "El ahogado más hermoso del mundo"
"Hanka" (Singer) **3**:377
"Hannes" (Hesse) **9**:243
"Han's Crime" (Shiga)
 See "Han no hanza"
"Hans in Luck" (Grimm and Grimm) **36**:188, 193
"Hans My Hedgehog" (Grimm and Grimm) **36**:223
Hans und Heinz Kirch (Storm) **27**:279, 281, 284, 290, 305
"Hansel and Gretel" (Grimm and Grimm) **36**:196, 203-05, 208
"Hanz Kuechelgarten" (Gogol) **29**:149
"Ha-panim la-panim" (Agnon) **30**:21, 37-8
"The Happiest I've Been" (Updike) **13**:354
"Happily Ever After" (Huxley) **39**:153-54, 161-62
"Happiness" (Chekhov) **2**:130, 156
"Happiness" (Lavin) **4**:182, 185
"Happiness" (Pirandello)
 See "Felicità"
"Happiness" (Warner) **23**:373-74
"Happiness by Conquest" (Norris) **28**:213

"Happiness in Crime" (Barbey d'Aurevilly)
 See "Le bonheur dans le crime"
"The Happiness of Others" (Price) **22**:365, 369, 376-77
"Happy" (Beattie) **11**:14
"The Happy Autumn Fields" (Bowen) **3**:31-32, 50-51; **28**:3, 9-10
"Happy Birthday" (Bambara) **35**:4, 32
"Happy Birthday Dear Jesus" (Pohl) **25**:223, 230-31
"The Happy Children" (Machen) **20**:183
"The Happy Couple" (Maugham) **8**:380
"A Happy Death" (Lavin) **4**:165, 167
"Happy Endings" (Atwood) **2**:15, 19-20
"The Happy Failure" (Melville) **1**:303
"Happy Families" (Huxley) **39**:154, 166
Happy Families Are All Alike (Taylor) **10**:380, 389, 410
"The Happy Family" (Andersen) **6**:18
"The Happy Farmer" (Thomas) **20**:323-25, 327
"Happy Holiday Abroad" (Sansom) **21**:84
"Happy Matrimony" (Chang) **28**:25; 31; 34
"The Happy Prince" (Wilde) **11**:365, 372, 376-78, 380, 386, 389-90, 394-96, 402-03, 406-08
The Happy Prince, and Other Tales (Wilde) **11**:365-66, 375, 377, 381, 386, 390, 393, 402
"Happy Valley" (Taylor) **10**:394, 397
"Hapworth 16, 1924" (Salinger) **2**:308, 314; **28**:269
"A Harbinger" (Chopin) **8**:71
"The Harbinger" (Henry) **5**:158
"The Hard Passage" (Hesse) **9**:231-32, 234, 236, 243
"A Hard Row to Hoe" (Garrett) **30**:165, 172
"Hard Sell" (Boyle) **16**:150
"The Hard Sellers" (Levi) **12**:279
"The Hard-Headed Woman" (Harris) **19**:196
"The Hardy Tin Soldier" (Andersen)
 See "The Steadfast Tin Soldier"
"The Hare Chase" (Leskov)
 See "Zajačij remiz"
"The Hare Park" (Leskov)
 See "Zajačij remiz"
"Hari to Ciarasu to Kiri" (Kawabata) **17**:242, 254
"Harischandra" (Narayan) **25**:131
"A Harlequin" (Tanizaki)
 See "Hokan"
"Harmony" (Lardner) **32**:145
"The Harness" (Steinbeck) **11**:207, 225, 228, 230, 232-35, 240-41, 243-44; **37**:351-52
"The 'Harnt' That Walks Chilhowee" (Murfree) **22**:188, 200, 202-03, 205, 207-08, 222
"El haRofe" (Agnon) **30**:37-8
"Harper and Wilton" (Spark) **10**:356
"Harrison Barr" (Dreiser)
 See "Black Sheep No. Six: Harrison Barr"
"Harrison Bergeron" (Vonnegut) **8**:427, 434
"Harry" (Saroyan) **21**:132
"Harry and Violet" (Thomas) **20**:295, 298, 312
Harry Heathcote of Gangoil (Trollope) **28**:316, 322, 346
"The Hartleys" (Cheever) **38**:54
"Harv Is Plowing Now" (Updike) **13**:348-49, 375
"Harvest Bugs" (Shiga) **23**:345-46, 348
"Hashire Merosu" (Dazai Osamu) **41**:240, 260, 263, 276
Hasidism (Peretz) **26**:206
"The Hat" (Boyle) **16**:149, 154-55
"The Hat Act" (Coover) **15**:31, 33-4, 48, 59
The Hat on the Bed (O'Hara) **15**:259-60, 282-83
"Hat on the Bedpost" (Caldwell) **19**:55
"The Hated" (Pohl) **25**:220, 232
"The Haunted Baronet" (Le Fanu) **14**:220, 223-24, 237, 245
"The Haunted Boy" (McCullers) **9**:330, 332, 343, 345, 354, 356, 358

"The Haunted Dolls' House" (James) **16**:230, 237, 244, 256
"A Haunted House" (Woolf) **7**:369, 374-75, 389-90, 392, 399
A Haunted House, and Other Short Stories (Woolf) **7**:372, 374, 386, 388, 400
"The 'Haunted House' in Royal Street" (Cable) **4**:53, 59, 61, 75-6
The Haunted Man and the Ghost's Bargain (Dickens) **17**:127-32
"The Haunted Mind" (Hawthorne) **3**:181
"The Haunter of the Dark" (Lovecraft) **3**:259, 263, 273-75, 279, 284
"The Haunting of the Tiled House" (Le Fanu) **14**:224, 226
Hauntings (Lee) **33**:302, 304-09
"Hauptstädtisches Journal" (Boell) **23**:8, 10, 21
"Ein Haus aus lauter Liebe" (Lenz) **33**:316, 318-19, 333-36
"Hautot père et fils" (Maupassant) **1**:270, 280, 285, 288
"Have I Got Sun in My Eyes?" (Farrell) **28**:99
"De Havilland Hand" (Gilchrist) **14**:163-64
"Having a Wonderful Time" (Ballard) **1**:79
Häwelmann (Storm) **27**:284
"The Hawk" (O'Flaherty)
"The Haymaking" (Lavin) **4**:167
"He" (Lovecraft) **3**:259, 262, 283, 289
"He" (Porter) **4**:327-30, 339-40, 349-50, 354, 360
"He Couldn't Boogie-Woogie Worth a Damn" (Algren) **33**:108
"He Don't Plant Cotton" (Powers) **4**:368
"He Drank Me" (Lispector)
 See "El me bebeu"
"He is barehead" (Beckett) **16**:123-24, 126-27
"He of the Assembly" (Bowles) **3**:68, 83-4
"He Ran Off" (Gorky) **28**:160
"He Sings the Epistle" (Pirandello)
 See "Canta l'epistola"
"He Swung and He Missed" (Algren) **33**:88, 107
"He Thinks He's Wonderful" (Fitzgerald) **6**:47, 49
"He Who Spits at the Sky" (Stegner) **27**:224
"Head and Shoulders" (Fitzgerald) **6**:45, 57, 96-7
Head o' W-Hollow (Stuart) **31**:224, 230-31, 236, 256
"The Head of Babylon" (Barnes) **3**:19-20
"The Head of the Family" (Chekhov) **2**:127
"The Head-Hunter" (Henry) **5**:166
"Heading Home" (Campbell) **19**:75
"The Headless Hawk" (Capote) **2**:61-3, 66, 69, 72, 75-6
"Heads" (Dixon) **16**:219
"Heads of Houses" (Taylor) **10**:389-90, 404, 415-16
"Heady Wine" (Svevo)
 See "Vino generoso"
"The Healthiest Girl in Town" (Stafford) **26**:281, 286, 312
"Healthy Landscape with Dormouse" (Warner) **23**:373-74
"Hear O Israel" (Peretz) **26**:204-05
"Hear the Dogs Barking" (Rulfo)
 See "No oyes ladrar los perros"
"Hear the Nightingale Sing" (Gordon) **15**:107, 118
Hear Us O Lord from Heaven Thy Dwelling Place (Lowry) **31**:40-7, 50-5, 58-61, 63-4, 66-7, 70, 72, 74-6, 82-3, 86-7
"The Heart" (Naipaul) **38**:300, 320, 322, 328, 346
"Heart of a Champion" (Boyle) **16**:140-43, 157
"Heart of a Champion" (Lish) **18**:267
The Heart of a Dog (Bulgakov)
 See *Sobach'e serdtse*
The Heart of a Goof (Wodehouse) **2**:329, 350
Heart of Darkness (Conrad) **9**:140-41, 143-44, 148-56, 160, 168, 171, 173, 175-76, 178, 188-92, 196-207

"Heart of Elm" (Wilson) 21:329-31, 333, 355, 357, 365

The Heart of Happy Hollow (Dunbar) 8:120-22, 127-29, 131-32, 141, 145

"The Heart of John Middleton" (Gaskell) 25:60, 65, 71-3

The Heart of the West (Henry) 5:155, 172, 182

"The Heart Sutra" (Chang) 28:23; 35

"Heartbreak" (Andersen) 6:30, 32, 35

"Heartburn" (Calisher) 15:2, 6

"The Hearth and the Salamander" (Bradbury) 29:53

"Hearts and Crosses" (Henry) 5:155, 181

"Hearts of Oak and Bellies of Brass" (McGahern) 17:298, 302, 307-09

"Heat" (Dixon) 16:211

"Heat" (Rhys) 21:55, 65

"The Heat of the Sun" (O'Faolain) 13:283, 292, 311

The Heat of the Sun: Stories and Tales (O'Faolain) 13:290, 307, 313

"Heaven and Earth" (Galsworthy) 22:101

"Heaven on a Summer Night" (Beattie) 11:29

"The Heavenly Animal" (Phillips) 16:327-28, 330

"Hê-chien shêng" (P'u Sung-ling) 31:205

"The Hector Quesadilla Story" (Boyle) 16:145, 151

"He'd Come Back" (Lawson) 18:248

"A Hedge of Rosemary" (Jolley) 19:232, 235

"The Hedgehog" (Saki) 12:316

"A Hedonist" (Galsworthy) 22:66, 101

"Heed my Plea" (Dazai Osamu) 41:263

"Hee-Haw" (Warner) 23:370

"Heel Number One of the Year" (Saroyan) 21:163

"Hefker" (Agnon) 30:34, 69-70

"The Height of the Scream" (Campbell) 19:75, 84

The Height of the Scream (Campbell) 19:74, 78, 81, 83-4, 86, 89-90

Der Heilige (Meyer) 30:186-89, 192, 195, 204-11

Die heilige Cäcilie; oder, die Gewalt der Musik (Kleist) 22:109, 115-17, 137, 146

"Heilmann" (Lenz) 33:337

"Heimkehr" (Kafka) 5:254

"Heinrich" (Bunin) 5:114

"Heinrich von ofter dinger" (Hoffmann) 13:218

"The Heir of the McHulishes" (Harte) 8:217, 252

"An Heiress of Red Dog" (Harte) 8:248

An Heiress on Condition (Gissing) 37:79

The Heirs in Tail (Arnim)
    See *Die Majoratsherren*

"Hejda" (Nin) 10:300, 303

"Helbling's Story" (Walser) 20:336, 350

"Helen, I Love You" (Farrell) 28:90, 111, 118

"Helena" (Capek) 36:82, 93, 124

Det heliga landet (Lagerkvist) 12:198

"Hell" (Andric)
    See "Pakao"

"Hell Hath No Fury" (Collier) 19:106

"A Hell of a Good Time" (Farrell) 28:89

The Hell We Dread (Onetti)
    See *El infierno tan temido y otros cuentos*

Hellbox (O'Hara) 15:250, 255, 257-58, 264-65, 267

"Hello Fine Day Isn't It?" (Oates) 6:248-50

"Hello Jack" (Michaels) 16:309

"Hello, Tib" (Aiken) 9:13

"Hell's Acre" (Stuart) 31:261

"Héloïse" (Ayme) 41:23

"Help!" (Capek)
    See "Pomoc!"

"Un hemisphère dans une chevelure" (Baudelaire) 18:5-7, 17

"The Hen" (Saki) 12:296

"Hêng-niang" (P'u Sung-ling) 31:205

"Henne Fire" (Singer) 3:370, 383-84

"Henrietta Marr" (Moore) 19:296-97, 302, 310-11

"Henry and the Gold Mine" (Benet) 10:154

Henry Lawson, Fifteen Stories (Lawson) 18:221

"Henry the Ninth" (Bradbury) 29:47

"A Hepcat May Look at a King" (Perelman) 32:234

"Hephaestus God of Newfangled Things" (Auchincloss) 22:52

"Her Boss" (Cather) 2:111

"Her First Ball" (Mansfield) 9:282-83, 286, 304, 310-11; 23:137, 153-54, 158, 171-72

"Her Housekeeper" (Gilman) 13:142, 145

"Her Ladyship's Private Office" (Turgenev) 7:337

"Her Letters" (Chopin) 8:92, 98-9, 112-13

"Her Lover" (Gorky)
    See "Boles"

"Her Name Was Amelie" (Caldwell) 19:42, 54

"Her Need" (Taylor) 10:404

"Her Own People" (Warren) 4:389-90, 395, 399

"Her Quaint Honor" (Gordon) 15:104, 107, 119, 123

"Her Sense of Timing" (Elkin) 12:119

"Her Ship Came Home" (Wilson) 21:358, 361

"Her Son" (Wharton) 6:423-24

"Her Sweet Jerome" (Walker) 5:402, 405-06, 419

"Her Table Spread" (Bowen) 3:34-36, 38, 41, 51

"Her Virginia Mammy" (Chesnutt) 7:16, 23, 33-5, 37

"Herakleitos" (Davenport) 16:162-63, 166, 170

"The Herald" (Kundera) 24:103

"Herbert West—Reanimator" (Lovecraft) 3:282, 293-94

"The Herder of Storm Mountain" (Murfree) 22:213, 220

Here and Beyond (Wharton) 6:422

"Here and Today" (Caldwell) 19:21

"Here Come the Tigers" (Thurber) 1:429

"Here Comes the Maples" (Updike) 13:374, 386-87

Here Lies: The Collected Stories of Dorothy Parker (Parker) 2:274-76

"Here There Be Tygers" (Bradbury) 29:83

"Here to Learn" (Bowles) 3:75, 79-80

"Here We Are" (Parker) 2:273-74, 281, 283

"La Herencia de matilde Arcangel" (Rulfo) 25:257, 265, 272, 275

The Heretic of Soana (Hauptmann)
    See *Der Ketzer von Soana*

Los heréticos (Valenzuela) 14:366

The Heretics (Valenzuela)
    See *Los heréticos*

"Heritage" (Galsworthy) 22:101

"L'héritage" (Maupassant) 1:256, 259-60, 263, 270, 276, 283

"The Heritage of Dedlow Marsh" (Harte) 8:254

Hermann Lauscher (Hesse)
    See *Hinterlassene Schriften und Gedichte von Hermann Lauscher*

"Hermes, God of the Self-Made Man" (Auchincloss) 22:51

"The Hermit" (Gorky) 28:137

"The Hermit and the Wild Woman" (Wharton) 6:428

The Hermit and the Wild Woman (Wharton) 6:420, 435

"The Hermits" (Dinesen) 7:177

"A Hero" (Narayan) 25:141, 156

"A Hero in Dingo-Scrubs" (Lawson) 18:211, 220

"The Hero of Redclay" (Lawson) 18:234, 240, 250-51

Herod and Mariamne (Lagerkvist)
    See *Mariamne*

"Hérodias" (Flaubert) 11:37, 46, 50-3, 55-6, 61-5, 70-1, 81-2, 84-7, 91-3, 96-9, 101, 103

"The Heroes" (Algren) 33:87, 108

"A Heroic Death" (Baudelaire)
    See "Une mort héroïque"

"The Heroine" (Dinesen) 7:165, 168, 195

"The Heroine" (P'u Sung-ling)
    See "Hsieh-nü"

"L'héroïsme du docteur Hallidonhill" (Villiers de l'Isle Adam) 14:397

"A Hero's Death" (Lagerkvist) 12:182, 195

"Herostratus" (Sartre) 32:255, 257, 259, 261

Der Herr Etatsrat (Storm) 27:281

Hesitation (Lu Hsun)
    See *P'anghuang*

"Hester's Little Tour" (Galsworthy) 22:70-1

"He-Who-Intones-the-Epistle" (Pirandello)
    See "Canta l'epistola"

Der Hexensabbath (Tieck) 31:273, 289-90

"Hey Sailor, What Ship?" (Olsen) 11:164

"Hey! Taxi!" (Aiken) 9:4, 12-13

"Hickman Arrives" (Ellison) 26:11

"Hidden Art" (Maclean) 13:279

"Hidden Treasure" (Zoshchenko) 15:395

"Hide and Seek" (Clarke) 3:124-26, 133, 150

"Hiding Man" (Barthelme) 2:26, 41-2, 54

"Hier ist Tibten" (Boell) 23:7-8

"La hierba milagrosa" (Pardo Bazan) 30:270

"The Higgler" (Coppard) 21:8, 15-16, 18, 20, 24-5, 29

"High" (Oates) 6:252

"The High Constable's Wife" (Balzac) 5:19

"High Ground" (McGahern) 17:306, 311-12, 314-15, 324

High Ground (McGahern) 17:304-06, 309-12, 322-23

"The High Point" (O'Hara) 15:252

"The High Road of St. James" (Carpentier) 35:106, 126

"High School" (Beattie) 11:26, 29

"The High Test" (Pohl) 25:236

"High Yaller" (Fisher) 25:3-4, 7, 14, 17-18, 20-2, 24-5, 27

"The Higher Abdication" (Henry) 5:180-81

"The Higher Pragmatism" (Henry) 5:187

"Higher Standards" (Wilson) 21:323

"The High-heeled Shoes" (Yamamoto) 34:348-49

"The Highland Widow" (Scott) 32:286-87, 292, 297, 299-304, 306, 315, 317, 319

"High-Water Mark" (Harte) 8:210, 232

"The Highway" (Bradbury) 29:53

"El hijo de Andrés Aparicio" (Fuentes)
    See "The Son of Andrés Aparicio"

"El hijo de su amigo" (Bioy Casares) 17:48-52

"Hilda's Wedding" (Jolley) 19:222, 234, 248

"The Hill of Sand" (Agnon)
    See "Gib'ath ha-hol"

"The Hill of the Elves" (Andersen) 6:31

The Hills Beyond (Wolfe) 33:343, 355, 372-75, 380, 398-99

"Hills Like White Elephants" (Hemingway) 1:210, 217, 232, 234; 40:250

"The Hilton's Holiday" (Jewett) 6:152

"Him" (Atwood) 2:20

"Him with His Foot in His Mouth" (Bellow) 14:40, 42-6

Him with His Foot in His Mouth, and Other Stories (Bellow) 14:40, 42, 50, 56, 58

"Himitsu" (Tanizaki) 21:207-08

"Hindus" (Mukherjee) 38:252, 254, 264-65, 271-72, 277

"The Hint of an Explanation" (Greene) 29:184-85, 192, 202-04, 209-11, 213, 217

Hinterlassene Schriften und Gedichte von Hermann Lauscher (Hesse) 9:229-30, 235, 243

Hinzelmeier (Storm) 27:284

"Hips" (Cisneros) 32:14, 42, 44-45

"His Apparition" (Howells) 36:379-80, 382, 386-87, 397

"His Chest of Drawers" (Anderson) 1:52

"His Chosen Calling" (Naipaul) 38:327, 350

"His Christmas Miracle" (Murfree) 22:210

"His Country, After All" (Lawson) 18:201, 216

"His 'Day In Court'" (Murfree) 22:209

"His Dead Mother's Portrait" (Norris) 28:214

"His Excellency" (Maugham) 8:365, 377

"His Father" (Steinbeck) **11**:246, 252
"His Father's Mate" (Lawson) **18**:197-98, 201-02, 239, 257
"His Father's Son" (Wharton) **6**:421, 424, 435
"His Finest Hour" (Updike) **13**:355
"His General Line of Business" (Dickens) **17**:123
His Last Bow: Some Reminiscences of Sherlock Holmes (Doyle) **12**:50, 64
"His Last Bow: The War Service of Sherlock Holmes" (Doyle) **12**:62
"His Mother" (Gallant) **5**:135, 137
"His Single Blessedness" (Norris) **28**:206
"His Unquiet Ghost" (Murfree) **22**:211
"Hisbrien om en Moder" (Andersen)
    See "The Story of a Mother"
"Hissen som gick ner i helvete" (Lagerkvist) **12**:182, 196
L'histoire de Fenni (Voltaire) **12**:341, 343
"Histoire de lunes" (Carpentier) **35**:121-23
Histoire des treize (Balzac) **5**:5, 45-7
L'histoire du Calife Hakem (Nerval) **18**:364
"L'histoire d'une fille de ferme" (Maupassant) **1**:257, 259, 261, 272, 274-75
Histoires insolites (Villiers de l'Isle Adam) **14**:378, 384, 396-97
Historia de cronopios y de famas (Cortazar) **7**:50, 53, 60, 91-2, 94
"La historia de María Griseld" (Bombal) **37**:34, 37-38
"Historia del guerrero y de la cautiva" (Borges) **4**:29
"História interrompida" (Lispector) **34**:229-31, 233-34
"Historia prodigiosa" (Bioy Casares) **17**:59
Historia prodigiosa (Bioy Casares) **17**:58
Historia universal de la infamia (Borges) **4**:4, 17; **41**:39, 53-55, 63-65, 151, 162, 166
Histórias de meia-noite (Machado de Assis) **24**:131-32, 146, 151
Historias desaforados (Bioy Casares) **17**:86-7
Histórias sem data (Machado de Assis) **24**:152
"Historie dirigenta Kaliny" (Capek) **36**:83, 99, 127
"History Lesson" (Clarke) **3**:124, 133, 143-44
"The History of a Contraoctave" (Pasternak)
    See "The Story of Counter-Octave"
History of Infamy (Borges)
    See *Historia universal de la infamia*
"The History of Lieutenant Ergunov" (Turgenev)
    See "Istoriya leytenanta Ergunova"
"History of the Conductor Kalina" (Capek)
    See "Historie dirigenta Kaliny"
"The History of the Hardcomes" (Hardy) **2**:215
History of the Manor of Goryukhino (Pushkin) **27**:135
A History of the Village Goryukhino (Pushkin)
    See *Istoriia sela Goriukhino*
"History of the Warrior and the Captive" (Borges)
    See "Historia del guerrero y de la cautiva"
"History of the Young Man with Spectacles" (Machen) **20**:206
"History, or the Four Pictures of Vludka" (Lish) **18**:282
"The Hitch-Hikers" (Welty) **1**:466, 468, 481, 487-88, 494
"The Hitchhiking Game" (Kundera) **24**:86-8, 91-2, 94, 97, 103, 106-09, 114, 118, 121-25
"Hizo el bien mientras vivió" (Arreola) **38**:9
"The Hoax" (Svevo)
    See "Una burla riuscita"
"The Hobo and the Fairy" (London) **4**:255
"Hoboes That Pass in the Night" (London) **4**:291
"Der Hochwald" (Stifter) **28**:278, 298-99
Die Hochzeit des Mönchs (Meyer) **30**:186-89, 200, 203-04, 206-11
"Hochzeitsvorbereitungen auf dem Lande" (Kafka) **35**:242, 265
"Hog Pawn" (Faulkner) **1**:178

"Hoist High the Roof Beam, Carpenters" (Salinger)
    See "Raise High the Roofbeam, Carpenters"
La hojarasca (Garcia Marquez) **8**:154-55, 158, 160, 162, 171, 184, 193
"Hokan" (Tanizaki) **21**:194
"Hold That Christmas Tiger!" (Perelman) **32**:204
"Holding Her Down" (London) **4**:291
"The Hole" (Dixon) **16**:206, 208
"The Hole in the Wall" (Chesterton) **1**:122
"The Holiday" (Machado de Assis) **24**:140, 155
"Holiday" (Porter) **4**:347, 349-50, 355
"Holiday in Texas" (Algren) **33**:113
"A Holiday in the South" (Andric)
    See "Letovanje na jugu"
"Holiday Romance" (Dickens) **17**:124
"The Holiday Stew" (Aleichem)
    See "Der yontefdiker tsimes"
"The Hollow Boy" (Calisher) **15**:10, 14
"The Hollow of the Three Hills" (Hawthorne) **3**:154, 157, 180-81
"The Holy Door" (O'Connor) **5**:365, 367, 371, 384, 390
"The Holy Land" (Lagerkvist) **12**:198
"The Holy Night" (Capek) **36**:114, 129
"The Holy Six" (Thomas) **3**:399, 407-08
"Homage to Isaac Babel" (Lessing) **6**:196-99, 214
"Homage to Switzerland" (Hemingway) **1**:211; **40**:221, 231, 245, 256-57
"El hombre" (Rulfo) **25**:245, 249-50, 255, 258, 262, 264-66, 268, 275, 278, 280
"El Hombre de la esquina rosada" (Borges) **4**:10, 14-16; **41**:53-55, 162
"El hombre en el umbral" (Borges) **4**:4, 40-1; **41**:91, 95, 97
"El hombrecito" (Donoso) **34**:30, 32, 49
"Hombres de las orillas" (Borges)
    See "El Hombre de la esquina rosada"
"Home" (Boyle) **5**:57
"Home" (Gordimer) **17**:178, 180, 186, 188, 190-91
"Home" (Grau) **15**:163
"Home" (Hughes) **6**:109, 118-19, 121-22, 133
"Home" (Phillips) **16**:325, 327-28, 330
"Home" (Updike) **13**:397-98
"Home Delivery" (King) **17**:295
A Home for the Highland Cattle (Lessing) **6**:189-91, 195-96
"The Home Front" (Stafford) **26**:274, 276
"Home Is Where" (Adams) **24**:3-4, 13
"Home Life" (Price) **22**:370
"Home Sickness" (Moore)
    See "Galar Dúithche"
"Home to Marie" (Beattie) **11**:30-1, 34
"Home to Shawneetown" (Algren) **33**:107
Home Truths: Selected Canadian Stories (Gallant) **5**:138, 141, 143-44, 147
"The Homecoming" (Bradbury) **29**:47, 67, 88
"Homecoming" (Grau) **15**:148, 152
"The Homecoming" (Hesse) **9**:231, 235
"Homecoming" (Kafka)
    See "Heimkehr"
"A Homecoming" (Suckow) **18**:396-97, 401, 409
"The Home-Coming of 'Rastus Smith" (Dunbar) **8**:122, 135
"Um homem célebre" (Machado de Assis) **24**:129
"O homem que apareceu" (Lispector) **34**:209, 215
"Hometown" (Dazai Osamu) **41**:249, 252
"Hometown" (Lu Hsun)
    See "Guxiang"
L'homme aux quarante écus (Voltaire) **12**:342, 346
"Un homme d'affaires" (Balzac) **5**:32
"Un homme de lettres" (Mauriac) **24**:183, 196, 199, 203-05, 207
"The Honest Quack" (Chesterton) **1**:133

"An Honest Soul" (Freeman) **1**:198, 201
"An Honest Thief" (Dostoevsky) **2**:166, 171, 193
"An Honest Woman" (Gilman) **13**:126
"Honey" (Beattie) **11**:33-4
"The Honey Tree" (Jewett) **6**:156, 158
"Honey, We'll Be Brave" (Farrell) **28**:88, 92, 121
"Honeymoon" (Mansfield) **23**:137; **38**:230
"The Honeymoon" (Moravia)
    See "The Honeymoon"
"Honeymoon" (O'Brien) **10**:331, 333
"The Honeymoon" (Pritchett) **14**:298
"Honeymoon at Tramore" (Trevor) **21**:260, 262, 265
"Honolulu" (Maugham) **8**:359, 371-72
Honorine (Balzac) **5**:18, 31, 33
"The Honour of Israel Gow" (Chesterton) **1**:134, 137
"The Hook" (O'Flaherty) **6**:264, 269
"Hope" (Galsworthy) **22**:98
"The Hope Chest" (Stafford) **26**:301
"Hopeless" (Atwood) **2**:20
"Hopes Rise" (Boyle) **16**:156-57
"Hop-Frog" (Poe) **1**:408; **22**:305; **35**:306, 317, 344
"Hora" (Capek) **36**:82, 90-1, 110, 121-23, 126
"Horatio Sparkins" (Dickens) **17**:110, 120, 137
"Horatio's Trick" (Beattie) **11**:30-1, 34
"Horibata no sumai" (Shiga) **33**:359
"Horizon" (O'Hara) **15**:267-68
"Le horla" (Maupassant) **1**:259, 262, 265, 269, 273, 283-84, 286-88
"L'horloge" (Baudelaire) **18**:6
"Horn Came" (Beckett) **16**:123-24, 126
"Horn of Plenty" (Gordimer) **17**:152, 166
"The Horns of the Bull" (Hemingway) **25**:113
"The Horror at Red Hook" (Lovecraft) **3**:258, 262, 289
"The Horror from the Bridge" (Campbell) **19**:79-80, 89-90
"Horror House of Blood" (Campbell) **19**:86-7
"The Horror in the Museum" (Lovecraft) **3**:279
"The Horror of the Heights" (Doyle) **12**:62, 76-7, 79-80
"A Horse and Two Goats" (Narayan) **25**:145, 148, 155, 164, 169, 174-75
A Horse and Two Goats, and Other Stories (Narayan) **25**:135, 137, 139, 145, 152, 155
"A Horse in the Moon" (Pirandello)
    See "Un cavallo nella luna"
The Horse Knows the Way (O'Hara) **15**:262, 283
"Horse Thief" (Caldwell) **19**:19, 23
"The Horse-Dealer's Daughter" (Lawrence) **4**:202-03, 231-33, 235-36, 240
"A Horseman in the Sky" (Bierce) **9**:50, 55-6, 60, 68
Horses and Men (Anderson) **1**:23, 25, 27, 30, 46, 50
"The Horses and the Sea" (Saroyan) **21**:134
"The Horse's Ha" (Thomas) **3**:409
"A Horse's Name" (Chekhov) **2**:130
"Horses of the Night" (Laurence) **7**:255, 259, 262-63, 270
"A Horse's Tale" (Twain) **6**:303
"Horseshoes" (Lardner) **32**:145, 168
"Horses—One Dash" (Crane) **7**:104, 106, 108, 125-26, 149, 153-54
"The Horse-Stealers" (Chekhov) **2**:130
"Horse-trading Trembles" (Stuart) **31**:265
"Horsie" (Parker) **2**:273-75, 280, 283-84
"The Hoshane Rabe" (Aleichem) **33**:62
"The Hospital Patient" (Dickens) **17**:115
Hospital Sketches (Alcott) **27**:3, 40, 57, 62
"A Host of Furious Fancies" (Ballard) **1**:79
"Hostage" (Stegner) **27**:201, 220
"Hot and Cold" (Sansom) **21**:102
"Hot and Cold Blood" (Fitzgerald) **6**:46
"Hot-collared Mule" (Stuart) **31**:265
"L'hôte" (Camus) **9**:103, 105, 109-11, 113, 118-19, 120-26, 128, 135

"Hotel Behind the Lines" (Boyle) **5**:74
"Hotel Kid" (O'Hara) **15**:248, 265-66
"The Hotel of the Idle Moon" (Trevor) **21**:261
"Hotel Room in Chartres" (Lowry) **31**:41, 53
"Hot-Foot Hannibal" (Chesnutt) **7**:7, 10-11, 40
"The Hound" (Faulkner) **1**:177
"The Hound" (Lovecraft) **3**:258, 262, 274, 276, 282
"The Hounds of Fate" (Saki) **12**:288, 298, 306
"The Hour and the Years" (Gordimer) **17**:151
An Hour Beyond Midnight (Hesse)
    See *Eine Stunde hinter Mitternacht*
"The Hour That Stretches" (Ellison) **14**:128
"The Hours after Noon" (Bowles) **3**:64-6, 80, 82
"The House" (Agnon)
    See "HaBayit"
"The House" (Cowan) **28**:80
"The House" (Le Guin) **12**:213, 248-49
"The House" (de la Mare) **14**:86, 90, 92
"House by the Canal" (Shiga)
    See "Horibata no sumai"
The House in a Secluded Place (Andric)
    See *Kuca na osami*
"The House in Turk Street" (Hammett) **17**:218, 220-21
"The House of Asterión" (Borges) **41**:72
"The House of Asterión" (Borges)
    See "La casa de Asterión"
"The House of Cobwebs" (Gissing) **37**:60, 62-3, 66
The House of Cobwebs, and Other Stories (Gissing) **37**:51-2, 54-7, 79-80
"House of Flowers" (Capote) **2**:67, 69, 72, 75
"The House of Heine Brothers, in Munich" (Trollope) **28**:318, 331
"The House of My Dreams" (O'Brien) **10**:331, 333, 345
"A House of My Own" (Cisneros) **32**:2, 43
A House of Pomegranates (Wilde) **11**:362, 364-65, 375, 376-77, 381, 384, 394, 398, 407-08
The House of Pride, and Other Tales of Hawaii (London) **4**:268-69, 283
The House of Souls (Machen) **20**:155, 172, 185, 194, 198-99, 201
"The House of the Dead Hand" (Wharton) **6**:428
"The House of the Far and Lost" (Wolfe) **33**:347, 353, 376, 386
"The House of the Hundred Grassfires" (Algren) **33**:90, 98
"House of the Sleeping Beauties" (Kawabata)
    See "Nemureru bijo"
House of the Sleeping Beauties, and Other Stories (Kawabata)
    See *Nemureru bijo*
"The House on its Own" (Andric) **36**:70
The House on its Own (Andric) **36**:78-9
"The House on Mango Street" (Cisneros) **32**:4, 40
The House On Mango Street (Cisneros) **32**:2-4, 6-9, 11-12, 14-15, 27-30, 32-33, 36, 40, 42, 44-46, 51
"The House on Maple Street" (King) **17**:295
"The House on the Sand" (Onetti)
    See "La casa en la arena"
"The House Surgeon" (Kipling) **5**:272, 275, 284-85
"The House Taken Over" (Cortazar)
    See "Casa tomada"
"The House That Johnny Built" (O'Connor) **5**:363, 371
"The House That Was Never Built" (Lawson) **18**:252
"The House with a Mezzanine" (Chekhov)
    See "An Artist's Story"
"The House with an Attic" (Chekhov)
    See "An Artist's Story"
"The House with the Blinds" (Norris) **28**:197
"The House with the Lilacs" (Warner) **23**:369-70
"The House with the Loop-Holes" (Lee) **33**:307

"The House with the Maisonette" (Chekhov)
    See "An Artist's Story"
"Houseboat" (Nin) **10**:303-05
"The Housebreaker of Shady Hill" (Cheever) **1**:111; **38**:55, 66, 85-6, 90
The Housebreaker of Shady Hill (Cheever) **38**:84
The Housebreaker of Shady Hill, and Other Stories (Cheever) **1**:89-92, 95, 100; **38**:83-88, 90
"The Household" (Irving) **2**:265
"Household" (Narayan) **25**:141
Household Tales (Grimm and Grimm)
    See *Kinder-und Hausmärchen*
"Housekeeper" (Grau) **15**:163-64
"The Housekeeper" (Lewis) **40**:277
"The Housewife" (Galsworthy) **22**:60, 99
"How a Good Man Went Wrong" (Chesnutt) **7**:14
"How a Witch Was Caught" (Harris) **19**:196
"How about This?" (Carver) **8**:32
"How Andrew Carried the Precinct" (Page) **23**:289
"How Auntie Fedos'ja Chatted with Lenin" (Zoshchenko) **15**:407
"How Brother Fox Was Too Smart" (Harris) **19**:148
"How Brother Parker Fell from Grace" (Dunbar) **8**:122
"How Buton Got Married" (Bulgakov) **18**:90
"How Can I Tell You?" (O'Hara) **15**:260, 291
"How Claeys Died" (Sansom) **21**:90, 95
"How Dasdy Came Through" (Chesnutt) **7**:13
"How I Finally Lost My Heart" (Lessing) **6**:197, 200-01, 206, 220
"How I Left Miguel Street" (Naipaul) **38**:335, 343
"How I Write My Songs" (Barthelme) **2**:52
"How It Is to Be" (Saroyan) **21**:154
"How It Was Done in Odessa" (Babel)
    See "How Things Were Done in Odessa"
"How Lenin Bought a Boy a Toy" (Zoshchenko) **15**:407
"How Lenin Outsmarted the Police" (Zoshchenko) **15**:407
"How Lenin Quit Smoking" (Zoshchenko) **15**:407
"How Lenin Studied" (Zoshchenko) **15**:407
"How Lenin Was Given a Fish" (Zoshchenko) **15**:407
"How Many Midnights" (Bowles) **3**:60, 69, 72, 79
"How Mickey Made It" (Phillips) **16**:335-37, 339
"How Mr. Hogan Robbed a Bank" (Steinbeck) **11**:256-58
"How Mr. Rabbit Was Too Sharp for Mr. Fox" (Harris) **19**:140, 172
"How Much Land Does a Man Need?" (Tolstoy) **9**:377, 388
"How Much Shall We Bet?" (Calvino) **3**:104
"How Old Craney-Crow Lost His Head" (Harris) **19**:194
"How Pearl Button Was Kidnapped" (Mansfield) **9**:302; **23**:174-75
"How Santa Claus Came to Simpson's Bar" (Harte) **8**:223-24, 227, 236, 244
"How She Came By Her Name" (Bambara) **35**:42
"How Six Made Their Way in the World" (Grimm and Grimm) **36**:223, 228-29
"How Sleep the Brave" (Bates) **10**:139
How Sleep the Brave, and Other Stories (Bates) **10**:138
"How Sportsmanship Came to Carver College" (Stuart) **31**:227
"How the Birds Talk" (Harris) **19**:149
"How the Brigadier Bore Himself at Waterloo" (Doyle) **12**:82
"How the Brigadier Came to the Castle of Gloom" (Doyle) **12**:81

"How the Brigadier Held the King" (Doyle) **12**:82
"How the Brigadier Lost His Ear" (Doyle) **12**:82
"How the Brigadier Played for a Kingdom" (Doyle) **12**:82
"How the Brigadier Slew the Brothers of Ajaccio" (Doyle) **12**:81
"How the Brigadier Slew the Fox" (Doyle) **12**:82
"How the Brigadier Triumphed in England" (Doyle) **12**:82
"How the Brigadier Was Tempted by the Devil" (Doyle) **12**:82
"How the Brigadier Won His Medal" (Doyle) **12**:82
"How the Devil Came Down Division Street" (Algren) **33**:102-04, 109
"How the King Held the Brigadier" (Doyle) **12**:82
"How the Local Committee Bought a Present with an Old Woman's Money" (Bulgakov) **18**:89
"How Things Were Done in Odessa" (Babel) **16**:44-5, 48-9
"How to Become a Pillar of the Establishment" (Machado de Assis)
    See "Teoria do medalhão"
"How to Grow a Wisteria" (O'Brien) **10**:330
"How to Love America" (Updike) **13**:387
"How to Write a Blackwood Article" (Poe) **1**:405, **22**:330
"How to Write a Novel" (Lish) **18**:266, 268
"How to Write a Poem" (Lish) **18**:268
"How to Write a Short Story" (O'Faolain) **13**:296
How to Write Short Stories—With Samples (Lardner) **32**:114-15, 121, 124, 131-33, 150-51, 154
"How We Live Now" (Cheever) **38**:58, 61
"How Whalebone Caused a Wedding" (Harris) **19**:182
"The How, When and Wherefore" (Verga)
    See "Il Come, il Quando, et il Perche"
"Howard and the Spinach" (Steinbeck) **11**:203
"Howe's Masquerade" (Hawthorne) **3**:154, 187
"Hsiang-yü" (P'u Sung-ling) **31**:196
"Hsia-nü" (P'u Sung-ling) **31**:196, 204
"Hsiao Ts'ui" (P'u Sung-ling) **31**:207, 209
"Hsieh-nü" (P'u Sung-ling) **31**:192
"Hsien-jen tao" (P'u Sung-ling) **31**:196, 199
"Hsin Shih-ssu niang" (P'u Sung-ling) **31**:196, 206, 209
"Hsü huang-liang" (P'u Sung-ling) **31**:190, 199
"Hu ch'êng yü" (P'u Sung-ling) **31**:204
"Hu hsieh" (P'u Sung-ling) **31**:205
"Hu lien" (P'u Sung-ling) **31**:205
"Hu Ssu-chieh" (P'u Sung-ling) **31**:204
"Hu Ssu-hsiang-kung" (P'u Sung-ling) **31**:205
"Hua pi" (P'u Sung-ling) **31**:217
"Huai-chiu" (Lu Hsun)
    See "Huaijiu"
"Huaijiu" (Lu Hsun) **20**:135, 138, 147-48
"Huang Chiang-chün" (P'u Sung-ling) **31**:201
"Hubert and Minnie" (Huxley) **39**:156
"Huey, the Engineer" (Stuart) **31**:226, 239
"Hugh Monfert" (Moore) **19**:296, 298
"L'Huissier" (Ayme) **41**:12, 17, 22
"The Human Being and the Dinosaur" (Thurber) **1**:426, 430
The Human Comedy (Balzac)
    See *La Comédie humaine*
"The Human Element" (Maugham) **8**:357, 366, 378
"The Human Fly" (Boyle) **16**:154
"Human Habitation" (Bowen) **3**:55
"Human Lost" (Dazai Osamu) **41**:248
Human Odds and Ends (Gissing) **37**:54-6, 79-80
"The Human Thing" (O'Faolain) **13**:316
"A Humble Lover" (Leacock) **39**:265
"A Humble Romance" (Freeman) **1**:196

A Humble Romance, and Other Stories
(Freeman) **1**:191, 194-95, 197, 201
"The Hummingbird that Lived through the
Winter" (Saroyan) **21**:154
"A Humorous Southern Story" (Chesnutt) **7**:13
"Humplebee" (Gissing) **37**:55
"Hun duede ikke" (Andersen)
See "Good-for-Nothing"
"The Hunchback in the Park" (Thomas) **3**:400
A Hundred Camels in the Courtyard (Bowles)
3:68
"The Hungarian Night" (Morand)
See "La nuit Hongroise"
"Hunger" (Rhys) **21**:61-2
Hunger (Lessing) **6**:190, 192-93, 195-97
A Hunger Artist (Kafka)
See *Ein Hungerkünstler*
"The Hunger Wheel" (Castellanos)
See "La rueda del hambriento"
"A Hunger-Artist" (Kafka)
See "Ein Hungerkünstler"
"Hungerford" (Lawson) **18**:215, 261
"Ein Hungerkünstler" (Kafka) **5**:207-09, 220,
225, 237-40; **29**:331-79
Ein Hungerkünstler (Kafka) **29**:369, 371
"The Hungry" (Mann) **5**:319, 322-23, 330
The Hungry Ghosts (Oates) **6**:241, 243
"Hung-yü" (P'u Sung-ling) **31**:198, 209
"Hunktown" (Mason) **4**:8
"The Hunt of the Unicorn" (Vinge) **24**:345-46
"Hunted Down" (Dickens) **17**:124
"Hunter" (Grau) **15**:163
"The Hunter" (Hammett) **17**:217
"The Hunter Gracchus" (Kafka)
See "Der jäger Gracchus"
"A Hunter's Moon" (Thomas) **20**:323-25
"The Hunter's Waking Thoughts" (Gallant)
5:151
"Hunting" (Zoshchenko) **15**:407-08
"A Hunting Accident" (Gordimer) **17**:165, 193
"A Hunting Story" (Silko) **37**:309
"The Huntsman" (Chekhov) **2**:155
"The Hurly Burly" (Coppard) **21**:17, 26
"Hurricane Hazel" (Atwood) **2**:21-3
"Hurry Kane" (Lardner) **32**:125, 132, 135, 145,
163
"Hurt Feelings" (Wescott) **35**:375
"The Husband" (Bowles) **3**:80
"The Husband's Revenge" (Pirandello) **22**:265
"Hu-shih" (P'u Sung-ling) **31**:204
"Hyacinth" (Saki) **12**:302
"Die Hyänen" (Hoffmann)
See "Der Vampyrismus"
"The Hyannis Port Story" (Vonnegut) **8**:436
"Hydrogen" (Levi) **12**:259, 262, 264
"The Hyena" (Bowles) **3**:64-5, 68, 80
"The Hyena" (Hoffmann)
See "Der Vampyrismus"
"Hygeia at the Solito" (Henry) **5**:182
"The Hyland Family" (Farrell) **28**:118-9
"Hymeneal" (O'Faolain) **13**:291, 314
"Hyōfū" (Tanizaki) **21**:207
"The Hypnotist" (Bierce) **9**:75
"The Hypothesis of Failure" (Henry) **5**:184
"I a mournful God" (Kundera)
See "I Sad God"
"I Always Wanted You to Admire My Fasting;
or, Looking at Kafka" (Roth) **26**:251,
253-54
"I Am a Very Clean Person" (Moorhouse)
40:292, 309
"I Am Not Now, Nor Have I Ever Been, a
Matrix of Lean Meat" (Perelman) **32**:222
"I and My Chimney" (Melville) **1**:298, 304,
322, 326-27; **17**:359, 363
I Cannot Get You Close Enough (Gilchrist)
14:163-65
"I Can't Breathe" (Lardner) **32**:135, 139, 141,
154, 168
"I Can't Put Two and Two Together"
(Saroyan) **21**:134

"I Could See the Smallest Things" (Carver)
8:19, 34-5
I den tiden (Lagerkvist) **12**:179
"I Gave Up before Birth" (Beckett) **16**:123,
125-26
I Have a Thing to Tell You (Wolfe) **33**:347-49,
376, 392-93
"I Have No Mouth and I Must Scream"
(Ellison) **14**:97-9, 107, 110, 112-15, 117-
18, 124-25, 130-31, 138-39, 141, 143-47
I Have No Mouth and I Must Scream (Ellison)
14:143-47
"I Killed" (Bulgakov) **18**:86, 89
"I Know Who I Love" (Jackson) **9**:258, 270-71
The I. L. Peretz Reader (Peretz) **26**:212-13
"I Live on Your Visits" (Parker) **2**:283
"I Look Out for Ed Wolfe" (Elkin) **12**:94-5, 99,
102, 117-18
"I Love Someone" (Stafford) **26**:283, 285, 301
"I Love You Very Dearly" (Aiken) **9**:13-14, 29
"I Never Seen Anything Like It" (O'Hara)
15:265
"I Passed By Your Window" (Pritchett) **14**:299
"I Plinglot Who You?" (Pohl) **25**:230
I racconti (Moravia) **26**:138, 141, 143, 151,
162, 183, 185
"I Remember Babylon" (Clarke) **3**:131
"I Remember! I Remember!" (O'Faolain)
13:320-21
I Remember! I Remember! (O'Faolain) **13**:288-
89, 293, 311
"I Remember Mollie" (Stuart) **31**:252
"I Ricordi del Capitano d'Arce" (Verga) **21**:294
"I Sad God" (Kundera) **24**:89, 103
"I Sing the Body Electric!" (Bradbury) **29**:46,
56, 64
I Sing the Body Electric! (Bradbury) **29**:56, 81
"I sogni del pigro" (Moravia) **26**:164
I sogni del pigro: Racconti, miti e allegorie
(Moravia) **26**:162-63
"I Spend My Days in Longing" (O'Hara)
15:283
"I Spy" (Greene) **29**:183-84, 193
"I Spy a Stranger" (Rhys) **21**:35, 37-8, 48, 52-4,
73, 75-6
"I Stand Here Ironing" (Olsen) **11**:163-64, 166,
171, 177-80, 188, 190, 192-93, 195, 197
"I Used to Live Here Once" (Rhys) **21**:39, 42-3,
50-1, 55, 64
"I Want to Go Home" (Farrell) **28**:98
"I Want to Know Why" (Anderson) **1**:20, 23,
27, 35, 37-8, 40, 48-9, 62
"I Was a Teenage Grave Robber" (King) **17**:268
"I Will Not Let Thee Go, Except Thou Bless
Me" (Updike) **13**:358
"I Would Have Saved Them If I Could"
(Michaels) **16**:307-08, 313, 322
I Would Have Saved Them If I Could
(Michaels) **16**:305-06, 308, 310-11, 314,
316
"Ib and Christine" (Andersen) **6**:14
"Ibn Hakkan" (Borges)
See "Ibn Hakkan al-Bokhari, Dead in His
Labryinth"
"Ibn Hakkan al-Bokhari, Dead in His
Labryinth" (Borges) **4**:30, 35; **41**:81-82
"Icarus Montgolfier Wright" (Bradbury) **29**:79
"Ice" (Bambara) **35**:42
"The Ice House" (Gordon) **15**:104, 118, 139
"The Ice Maiden" (Andersen) **6**:12, 19, 26,
34-5, 37
"The Ice Palace" (Fitzgerald) **6**:57-8, 88, 96-7,
100, 103
"The Ice Wagon Going down the Street"
(Gallant) **5**:139, 144
"Icebreaker" (Gorky) **28**:150
"Icicles" (Gass) **12**:123, 133, 167, 168
"Iconography" (Atwood) **2**:15, 20
"Ida" (Bunin) **5**:106-07, 116-20
"Ida M'Toy" (Welty) **27**:338
"The Idea" (Carver) **8**:7
"An Ideal Craftsman" (de la Mare) **14**:88

"An Ideal Family" (Mansfield) **9**:282, 284;
23:158
"The Idealist" (Machen) **20**:199
"The Idealist" (Nin) **10**:306
"Idéis de canário" (Machado de Assis)
24:128-29
"Idenborough" (Warner) **23**:380
"The Idiots" (Conrad) **9**:179
"Idiots First" (Malamud) **15**:171-75, 195, 197,
204-05, 214, 216, 219-20, 225, 243
Idiots First (Malamud) **15**:170-72, 174, 188,
197, 213-14, 220, 225, 227, 235
"An Idiot's Love" (Tanizaki)
See "Chijin no ai"
"An Idle Fellow" (Chopin) **8**:73, 78, 98
"The Idol" (Pavese) **19**:364, 377, 387
"The Idol of the Cyclades" (Cortazar)
See "El ídolo de las cícladas"
"El ídolo" (Bioy Casares) **17**:87
"El ídolo de las cícladas" (Cortazar) **7**:57-8,
69-70, 76, 78
"The Idyl of Red Gulch" (Harte) **8**:210, 217,
236-37, 246
"An Idyll of North Carolina Sand-Hill Life"
(Chesnutt) **7**:14
"Une idylle" (Maupassant) **1**:256, 270
"'If I Forget Thee, O Earth'" (Clarke) **3**:124,
126, 143
"If I Should Open My Mouth" (Bowles) **3**:64,
68-9, 80, 83, 85
"If I Were a Man" (Gilman) **13**:126
"If Not Higher" (Peretz) **26**:201-02, 213-14
"If One Green Bottle. . ." (Thomas) **20**:293,
322
"If Such be Nature's Holy Plan..." (Lewis)
40:281
"If the River Was Whiskey" (Boyle) **16**:146-48,
150, 152, 154, 156
If the River Was Whiskey (Boyle) **16**:146, 148-
49, 153-54
"If They Knew Yvonne" (Dubus) **15**:69, 71, 90,
100
"If They Say He's Crazy—Believe It!"
(Peretz)
See "If They Say He's Crazy—Believe It!"
"If You Don't Want to Live I Can't Help You"
(Calisher) **15**:5
"If You Must Use Profanity" (Algren) **33**:113
"Ignat" (Bunin) **5**:100
"Ignaz Denner" (Hoffmann) **13**:183, 186, 209
"Igra" (Andric) **36**:49-50
"A igreja do diabo" (Machado de Assis) **24**:127-
30, 152
"Igur and the Mountain" (Aldiss) **36**:20
"Iisjomfruen" (Andersen)
See "Iisjomfruen"
"Ike and Nina" (Boyle) **16**:144-45, 151
Il castello dei destini incrociati (Calvino) **3**:99-
102, 106, 114, 116, 118
"Il coccodrillo" (Moravia) **26**:164
"Il Come, il Quando, et il Perche" (Verga)
21:280
"Il concorrenza" (Moravia) **26**:164
"Il Conde" (Conrad) **9**:151, 160, 179, 184
"Il malocchio" (Svevo) **25**:336, 360
"Il mare" (Moravia) **26**:164
"Il mio ozio" (Svevo) **25**:329-30, 360-61
"Il mostro" (Moravia) **26**:165
"Il naso" (Moravia) **26**:164
"Il negro e il vecchio dalla roncola" (Moravia)
26:151, 163
"Il Peccato di Donna Santa" (Verga) **21**:294-96,
298
"Il pensatore" (Moravia) **26**:174-76, 178
"Il reverendo" (Verga) **21**:292
"Il sangue, il mare" (Calvino) **3**:109-10
"Il Tramonto de Venere" (Verga) **21**:294
Il vecchione (Svevo) **25**:334, 350-53, 361
"Il viaggio di nozze" (Moravia) **26**:182
"Il viccolo di Madama Lucrezia" (Merimee)
7:283-4, 290, 295-6, 306-07
"I'll Be Waiting" (Chandler) **23**:89, 110

Ill Seen Ill Said (Beckett)
  See *Mal vu mal dit*
"The Illegality of the Imagination"
    (Moorhouse) **40**:299
The Ill-Tempered Clavichord (Perelman) **32**:245
"The Illuminated Man" (Ballard) **1**:69
"Les illuminés; ou, Les précurseurs de
    socialisme" (Nerval) **18**:328
"Illusion" (Rhys) **21**:54, 61
"An Illusion in Red and White" (Crane) **7**:104
The Illustrated Man (Bradbury) **29**:52, 57, 62,
    77, 79-82
"L'illustre Gaudissart" (Balzac) **5**:18, 26
"The Illustrious Gaudissart" (Balzac)
    See "L'illustre Gaudissart"
"The Illustrious Kitchen Maid" (Cervantes)
    See "La ilustre fregona"
"The Illustrious Serving Wench" (Cervantes)
    See "La ilustre fregona"
"La ilustre fregona" (Cervantes) **12**:4, 6-8, 15,
    17-18, 36-7, 40
"I'm a Fool" (Anderson) **1**:23, 25, 27, 30, 37-8,
    40, 48-50
"I'm Being Good" (Selby) **20**:275
"I'm Dancing Frences" (Farrell) **28**:111
"Im Lande der Rujuks" (Boell) **23**:6, 34
Im Schloss (Storm) **27**:279-81
"The Image" (Narayan) **25**:135
The Image, and Other Stories (Singer) **3**:384-86
The Image of Misfortune (Onetti)
    See *La cara de la desgracia*
"An Image of Success" (Gordimer) **17**:154
"The Image of the Lost Soul" (Saki) **12**:285,
    305
"The Image Trade" (Pritchett) **14**:300, 305
"Images" (Munro) **3**:326, 338, 343-44
"The Imaginary Assassin" (Mukherjee) **38**:255,
    271-72
"Imaginary Countries" (Le Guin) **12**:211-13,
    217-19, 248
"An Imaginative Woman" (Hardy) **2**:215, 220,
    223, 225
"Imagine a Day at the End of Your Life"
    (Beattie) **11**:30, 33-4
Imagine Kissing Pete (O'Hara) **15**:250, 272
"Imagined Scenes" (Beattie) **11**:2, 18, 21
"The Imbroglio" (Moravia) **26**:138
L'imbroglio: Cinque romanzi brevi (Moravia)
    26:162
"A imitação da rosa" (Lispector) **34**:185, 193,
    195, 197, 199, 201-02, 205
Immensee (Storm) **27**:282, 284, 286, 301-03,
    308
"The Immigrant Story" (Paley) **8**:406, 409
"The Immortal" (Borges)
    See "El inmortal"
"The Immortality Crew" (Aldiss) **36**:19
"The Immortals" (Bioy Casares) **17**:75
"Imogene" (Moorhouse) **40**:324
"Imogene Continued" (Moorhouse) **40**:299-300,
    307, 324
"Imp Among Aunts" (Lish) **18**:284
"The Imp and the Crust" (Tolstoy) **9**:377, 388
"The Imp of the Perverse" (Poe) **22**:348;
    34:241, 251, 281; **35**:307-11, 315, 343
"Impasse" (Stegner) **27**:197, 205, 220
"Impatience" (Sansom) **21**:93
"Impatience de la foule" (Villiers de l'Isle
    Adam) **14**:381, 388, 394
"The Impatient Mob" (Villiers de l'Isle Adam)
    See "Impatience de la foule"
"An Imperfect Conflagration" (Bierce) **9**:75
"The Impertinent Curiosity" (Cervantes)
    See "El curioso impertinente"
"Impertinent Daughters" (Lessing) **6**:215
"The Importance of Healing Ernest"
    (Perelman) **32**:213, 229
"The Impossible Man" (Ballard) **1**:75-7
"The Impossible Marriage" (O'Connor) **5**:372,
    374
"The Impresario" (Singer) **3**:389
"The Impressions of a Cousin" (James) **8**:316

"Impressions of a Journey Through the
    Tomaszow Region in the Year 1890"
    (Peretz) **26**:213
"The Improbable Tale of the Archibishop of
    Canterbridge" (Greene) **29**:221
"Impulse" (Aiken) **9**:6, 13, 24-5, 27, 32
"In a Café" (Lavin) **4**:183, 185, 189
"In a Café" (Rhys) **21**:39, 42-3, 62
"In a Dry Season" (Lawson) **18**:210, 261
"In a Far Country" (London) **4**:264, 267-68,
    279, 281-82, 284-86, 290
"In a Flemish Garden" (Fuentes) **24**:30, 37-8,
    41, 43-8, 53-5, 61-2, 69-70, 82
"In a Free State" (Naipaul) **38**:300, 305, 313,
    354
In a Free State (Naipaul) **38**:300-01, 303, 310-
    11, 314-15, 317-18, 323-24, 328, 353, 355
In a German Pension (Mansfield) **9**:284, 288,
    301; **23**:137, 139
In a Glass Darkly (Le Fanu) **14**:214, 225, 230,
    234-35, 239-41, 243-45, 248-49
"In a Grove" (O'Hara) **15**:251
"In a Public Place" (Oates) **6**:237
"In a Shaken House" (Warner) **23**:372
"In a Strange Country" (Ellison) **26**:10-12, 21
"In a Strange Town" (Anderson) **1**:50
"In a Thicket" (Wescott) **35**:363-64, 368, 370-
    72, 380, 382-83
"In a Thousand Years' Time" (Andersen) **6**:30
In a Vision (Peretz) **26**:205
"In a Wet Season" (Lawson) **18**:210
"In Amalfi" (Beattie) **11**:30-3
"In and Out of Old Natchitoches" (Chopin)
    8:103, 105, 113
"In Another Country" (Hemingway) **1**:209, 230-
    32, 234; **40**:177
"In at the Birth" (Trevor) **21**:230, 262
"In Autumn" (Bunin) **5**:114
"In Bed One Night" (Coover) **15**:47
In Bed One Night and Other Brief Encounters
    (Coover) **15**:46
"In Business" (Morrison) **40**:330, 337, 364, 367
"In Defense of Tigolobia" (Fuentes)
    See "En defensa de la Trigolibia"
"In der Finsternis" (Boell) **23**:5
"In der Strafkolonie" (Kafka) **5**:218, 223-24,
    229-30, 235-36, 240, 249-52; **29**:346, 372;
    35:217, 224, 239, 264
"Um in endio" (Machado de Assis) **24**:155
"In Exile" (Chekhov) **2**:157
"In Flight Sadism" (Moorhouse) **40**:304
"In Football Season" (Updike) **13**:367, 375, 404
"In Front of the Rio-Niterói Bridge" (Lispector)
    See "Antes da ponte Rio-Niterói"
"In Greenwich There Are Many Gravelled
    Walks" (Calisher) **15**:2, 10
"In High Places" (Aleichem) **33**:54
"In Honour Bound" (Gissing) **37**:54
"In Isfahan" (Trevor) **21**:233, 237
"In Kew Gardens" (Malamud) **15**:235
"In le Havre" (Lowry) **31**:41-2
"In Lilliput" (O'Faolain) **13**:308, 314
In Love and Trouble: Stories of Black Women
    (Walker) **5**:401-03, 405, 407, 411-12, 418-
    19, 422
"In Love with Ariadne" (Trevor) **21**:265
"In Memoriam" (Arreola) **38**:6, 21
"In Memory of Judith Cortright" (Caldwell)
    19:42, 54
"In Memory of L. I. Shigaev" (Nabokov)
    11:124, 126, 145
In Minor Keys (Moore) **19**:339, 341, 345
"In My Life" (Dubus) **15**:70, 77, 79, 81
"In No Man's Land" (Gissing)
"In Northern Waters" (Williams) **31**:334
In Old Plantation Days (Dunbar) **8**:120-22,
    127-29, 132, 134, 141, 145, 148
*In Ole Virginia, or Marse Chan and Other
    Stories* (Page) **23**:283-86, 289, 291-93,
    296-97, 299-300, 302-05, 314, 316-17, 319-
    23, 325-29

In Our Time (Hemingway) **1**:206-08, 212, 214-
    15, 234-36, 238, 243-45; **25**:85; **36**:251;
    40:156, 194, 209, 220-21, 230
"In paese straniero" (Moravia) **26**:147
"In Paris" (Bunin) **5**:114
In Peace as in War (Cabrera Infante)
    See *Así en la paz como en la guerra*
"In Praise of Darkness" (Borges)
    See *Elogio de la sombra*
In Praise of Darkness
    See *Elogio de la sombra*
In Praise of Darkness (Borges)
    See *Elogio de la sombra*
"In Sabine" (Chopin) **8**:90, 99, 103
"In Serenella" (Svevo) **25**:329
"In Shadow" (Jewett) **6**:150, 168
In Single Strictness (Moore) **19**:296-98, 310,
    344
In St. Jürgen (Storm) **27**:286, 307
"In St. Valentine's Church" (Babel) **16**:25, 53,
    55, 57-8
In That Time (Lagerkvist)
    See *I den tiden*
"In the Absence of Angels" (Calisher) **15**:5
In the Absence of Angels (Calisher) **15**:2, 4-5
"In the Abyss" (Wells) **6**:366, 389, 403, 408-09
"In the Alley" (Elkin) **12**:94
"In the Autumn of the Year" (Oates) **6**:247
"In the Avu Observatory" (Wells) **6**:361
"In the Bag" (Campbell) **19**:87
"In the Basement" (Babel) **16**:13, 15, 22, 36,
    41, 59
"In the Beauty of the Lillies" (Auchincloss)
    22:35, 45, 50
"In the Black Hills" (Lowry) **31**:71
"In the Bleak Mid-Winter" (Thomas) **20**:289,
    298, 303
"In the Bosom of the Country" (O'Faolain)
    13:283, 295, 322
"In the Briar Patch" (Garrett) **30**:165, 172
In the Briar Patch (Garrett) **30**:172
In the Cage (James) **8**:302-05, 329, 331
"In the Camp" (Andric) **36**:45
"In the Carquinez Woods" (Harte) **8**:216, 223,
    227, 233, 244, 251
"In the Cart" (Chekhov) **2**:156-58
"In the Clay" (Moore) **19**:312-14, 317, 319-20,
    322-23, 330-31, 333, 336
"In the Corner of a Small Sqauare" (Pushkin)
    27:163-64
*In the Days When the World Was Wide, and
    Other Verses* (Lawson) **18**:262
"In the Direction of the Beginning" (Thomas)
    3:396, 402, 407, 409
"In the Family" (Pavese) **19**:368
"In the Fifties" (Michaels) **16**:308
"In the Forest" (de la Mare) **14**:81-2, 87-8
"In the Forests of the North" (London) **4**:265,
    280
"In the Gallery" (Kafka)
    See "Auf der Galerie"
"In the Garrett" (Alcott) **27**:4
"In the Green Tree" (Lewis) **40**:272, 275-77
"In the Groove" (Thomas) **20**:324
"In the Guest House" (Andric) **36**:55, 78
"In the Heart of the Heart of the Country"
    (Gass) **12**:123-24, 128-29, 133-35, 141,
    152, 157-66, 171, 173
*In the Heart of the Heart of the Country, and
    Other Stories* (Gass) **12**:123
"In the Hour of Our Death" (Warner) **23**:368
"In the Hours of Darkness" (O'Brien) **10**:333
"In the House of Suddhu" (Kipling) **5**:265
In the Land of Dreamy Dreams (Gilchrist)
    14:150-55, 158-59, 161-62
"In the Land of the Rujuks" (Boell)
    See "Im Lande der Rujuks"
"In the Luxemburg Gardens" (Rhys) **21**:61
"In the Maelstrom" (Pirandello) **22**:255
"In the Mail Coach" (Peretz) **26**:212-13
"In the Market" (Davis) **38**:114-15
"In the Matter of a Private" (Kipling) **5**:260

"In the Maze" (Sansom) **21**:82, 86, 88
"In the Middle of the Fields" (Lavin) **4**:183, 185
In the Middle of the Fields, and Other Stories (Lavin) **4**:172
In the Midst of Life (Bierce)
   See *Tales of Soldiers and Civilians*
"In the Miro District" (Taylor) **10**:395, 397, 400-02, 408-09, 411
In the Miro District, and Other Stories (Taylor) **10**:397-99, 404
"In the Mist" (O'Hara) **15**:262
"In the Morning" (Sansom) **21**:82
"In the Morning Sun" (O'Hara) **15**:248, 265-66
"In the Orchard" (Woolf) **7**:411
"In The Park" (Wolfe) **33**:355
"In the Penal Colony" (Kafka)
   See "In der Strafkolonie"
"In the Picture" (Campbell) **19**:85
"In the Pride of His Youth" (Kipling) **5**:274
In the Prime of Her Life (Agnon) **30**:81-2, 87, 89-92
"In the Problem Pit" (Pohl) **25**:226
"In the River" (Chekhov)
   See "V ovrage"
"In the Rue de l'Arrivée" (Rhys) **21**:62
"In the Rukh" (Kipling) **5**:287
"In the Same Boat" (Kipling) **5**:284-85
"In the Shadow of Another World" (Ligotti) **16**:277-78, 284
"In the Square" (Bowen) **3**:31
"In the Stadium" (Andric)
   See "U Stadionu"
"In the Steppe" (Gorky)
   See "V Stepi"
In The Tennessee Mountains (Murfree) **22**:185, 188, 197-98, 200-01, 203-05, 207, 209, 213, 215-17
"In the Train" (O'Connor) **5**:364, 371, 376-77, 381-82, 388, 395
"In the Trees" (Campbell) **19**:75, 77, 87
"In the Tules" (Harte) **8**:244
"In the Tunnel" (Gallant) **5**:130-31, 144
"In the Twilight" (Stegner) **27**:194, 196-97
"In the Valley of the Thundering Hooves" (Boell) **23**:7, 10
"In the Vault" (Lovecraft) **3**:262
"In the Warehouse" (Oates) **6**:232
"In the White Night" (Beattie) **11**:25-6, 28
"In the Wineshop" (Lu Hsun)
   See "Zai jiulou shang"
"In the Zoo" (Stafford) **26**:278, 281, 283-88, 307
In This World (Hesse) **9**:230
"In Time" (Dixon) **16**:217-18
"In Time Which Made a Monkey of Us All" (Paley) **8**:403
"In Transit" (Gallant) **5**:150
In Transit: Twenty Stories (Gallant) **5**:150
"In Youth Is Pleasure" (Gallant) **5**:128-29, 134, 143, 148
"The Incarnation of Krishna Mulvaney" (Kipling) **5**:259, 262
"Incest" (Updike) **13**:355
"An Inch and a Half of Glory" (Hammett) **17**:217
"An Incident" (Shiga) **23**:336-37, 339, 345-46
"An Incident at Krechetovka Station" (Solzhenitsyn) **32**:330, 333, 335-37, 339, 357, 361, 364, 387, 395, 397
"An Incident at Yanagiyu" (Tanizaki) **21**:194
"Incident in a Far Country" (Aldiss) **36**:20, 22
"Incident in Azania" (Waugh) **41**:323, 340
"An Incident in the Park" (Oates) **6**:248-49
"An Incident on the Volga" (Zoshchenko) **15**:404
"Incipit vita nova" (Hesse) **9**:231
"El incivil Maestro de Ceremonias Kotsukéno Suké" (Borges) **41**:39
"L'inconnue" (Villiers de l'Isle Adam) **14**:379-81, 393
"The Inconsolable" (Pavese) **19**:368

"Incontro di vecchi amici" (Svevo) **25**:360
The Incredulity of Father Brown (Chesterton) **1**:128
"The Independence of Silas Bollender" (Dunbar) **8**:127, 134
"An Independent Thinker" (Freeman) **1**:196
"The Indian" (Updike) **13**:348, 387
"Indian Camp" (Hemingway) **1**:214, 219, 234, 240-41, 244-45; **25**:125; **36**:251, 291; **40**:209, 211, 249
"The Indian Sign" (Thurber) **1**:425
"Indian Summer" (Barnes) **3**:12, 22
"Indian Summer" (Caldwell) **19**:37
"Indian Summer: A Hsiao's Autumnal Lament" (Chang) **28**:26; 28; 31; 34-35
"The Indian Summer of a Forsyte" (Galsworthy) **22**:83-4, 95-6, 99-100
"The Indian Summer of Dry Valley Johnson" (Henry) **5**:162
"The Indian Uprising" (Barthelme) **2**:35-6, 38, 42, 46, 53
"Indifference" (Aldiss) **36**:14
"An Indiscreet Journey" (Mansfield) **9**:303, 317; **38**:230
The Indulgent Husband (Colette) **10**:261-62, 269-70
"El indulto" (Pardo Bazan) **30**:272, 295
"The Inevitable White Man" (London) **4**:266
"The Inexperienced Ghost" (Wells) **6**:400
Infamy (Borges)
   See *Historia universal de la infamia*
The Infant Prodigy (Mann)
   See *Das Wunderkind*
"Infatuation" (Shiga) **23**:352
"The Infernal Parliament" (Saki) **12**:322
"El infierno tan temido" (Onetti) **23**:250, 258, 260
El infierno tan temido y otros cuentos (Onetti) **23**:248, 258
"The Infinite Passion of Expectation" (Berriault) **30**:103
The Infinite Passion of Expectation (Berriault) **30**:98-100, 105
"Influenza" (Shiga) **23**:344, 346
"An Influx of Poets" (Stafford) **26**:298, 307, 312
El informe de Brodie (Borges) **4**:17-20, 26-7; **41**:117-18, 131, 157, 159, 161-62, 167
"The Informer" (Conrad) **9**:157, 179, 182-86
L'Ingénu (Voltaire) **12**:338-39, 341-43, 362, 364-68, 394
L'ingénue libertine (Colette) **10**:257, 262
"An Ingènue of the Sierra" (Harte) **8**:244, 252
"The Ingrate" (Dunbar) **8**:122-23, 128-29, 136, 142-43, 149
"The Inhabitant of the Lake" (Campbell) **19**:72, 90
The Inhabitant of the Lake and Less Welcome Tenants (Campbell) **19**:61-2, 66, 71-2, 81-6, 89-90, 92
Inhale and Exhale (Saroyan) **21**:132-33, 136-37, 143, 152-53, 161-62
"The Inherited Clock" (Bowen) **3**:31-2; **28**:3
The Injustice Collectors (Auchincloss) **22**:2-3, 9, 29, 33, 35-6, 38, 46-7, 50-1
"Inkalamu's Place" (Gordimer) **17**:157
"La inmiscusión terrupta" (Cortazar) **7**:95
"El inmortal" (Borges) **4**:7-8, 10-12, 14, 18-20, 26-7; **41**:59, 74, 88, 90
"The Inmost Light" (Machen) **20**:158, 165, 173, 182, 190-93, 196, 199, 201, 204-05
"The Inn" (Turgenev) **7**:315, 320, 323, 325, 337, 359
"Innocence" (Bates) **10**:113
"Innocence" (McGahern) **17**:321
The Innocence of Father Brown (Chesterton) **1**:119-21, 124-25
"The Innocence of Reginold" (Saki) **12**:321, 328
"The Innocent" (Greene) **29**:185, 193, 195, 198
The Innocent and the Guilty (Warner) **23**:375, 380

"Inochi no Ki" (Kawabata) **17**:246
"Inquest" (Williams) **31**:315, 334
"L'inquiéteur" (Villiers de l'Isle Adam) **14**:382
"The Inquisition" (O'Flaherty) **6**:264, 284
"The Inscription" (Capek)
   See "Nápis"
"The Insect World" (Rhys) **21**:56, 69-70
"Insectíada" (Arreola) **38**:7
"Insects and Birds" (Shiga) **23**:346
"The Insects from Shaggai" (Campbell) **19**:72, 90
"Inside and Outside" (Hesse) **9**:230-32, 236
Inside Kasrilevke (Aleichem) **33**:53
"An Inside Outside Complex" (O'Faolain) **13**:296, 309, 320
"The Insoluble Problem" (Chesterton) **1**:128
"Insomnia" (Lardner) **32**:156
"Insomnia" (Pavese) **19**:378
"Insomnie" (Mauriac) **24**:185, 196, 199-200, 204-06
"L'insonnia insieme" (Moravia) **26**:148
"The Inspector" (Sansom) **21**:92
"Inspector General with a Kicking Out" (Bulgakov) **18**:74, 90
"Inspector General with an Ejection" (Bulgakov)
   See "Inspector General with an Ejection"
"An Inspiration" (Gissing) **37**:54, 80
"Installation # 6" (Beattie) **11**:30-1
"Instant of the Hour After" (McCullers) **9**:342, 344-45, 354, 359-60
"Instrucciones para John Howell" (Cortazar) **7**:62
"Instructions for the Third Eye" (Atwood) **2**:16-17
"Instructions on How to Dissect a Ground Owl" (Cortazar) **7**:92
"The Insult" (Capek) **36**:124
Intangibles Inc., and Other Stories (Aldiss) **36**:18
"Intensive Care Unit" (Ballard) **1**:79
"Intercession" (Updike) **13**:355
"L'interdiction" (Balzac) **5**:8, 16, 26
"An Interest in Life" (Paley) **8**:389-90, 396-99, 415-18
"An Interesting Point" (Moorhouse) **40**:322
"The Interference of Patsy Ann" (Dunbar) **8**:122, 132
"The Interior Castle" (Stafford) **26**:274-75, 277, 283, 291-96, 312-13
The Interior Castle (Stafford) **26**:291
"The Interloper" (Borges) **41**:159, 162, 164
"The Interloper" (Campbell) **19**:90
"The Interlopers" (Saki) **12**:285, 317
"Interlopers at the Knap" (Hardy) **2**:203, 205, 207, 216, 229-31
"An Interlude" (Sansom) **21**:84, 89
"Interlude in a Book Shop" (Powers) **4**:368-69
"Interlude: Lea I" (Henderson) **29**:327
"Intermission" (Coover) **15**:60-1
"An International Episode" (James) **8**:299, 302; **32**:90
"Interpretation of a Dream" (Collier) **19**:110, 112
"The Interpreter" (Aldiss) **36**:5
"The Interrupted Class" (Hesse) **9**:229-30, 232-33, 235-36
"Interruption" (Lewis) **40**:271
"L'intersigne" (Villiers de l'Isle Adam) **14**:377, 379, 381-82, 394-96, 403-04, 407-11, 413, 415
"The Intervention of Peter" (Dunbar) **8**:121, 127, 140
"Interview" (Arreola) **38**:9, 25
"An Interview" (Capek) **36**:130
"An Interview" (Colette) **10**:292
"The Interview" (Singer) **3**:387
"The Interview" (Thurber) **1**:420
"Interview with a Lemming" (Thurber) **1**:417
"Intimacy" (Carver) **8**:43
"Intimacy" (Sartre)
   See "Intimité"

Intimacy, and Other Stories (Sartre)
  See *Le mur*
"The Intimate Disclosures of a Wronged
  Woman" (Leacock) **39**:266
"Intimations" (Michaels) **16**:302-03
"Intimité" (Sartre) **32**:250-53, 255, 258-59, 261,
  281
"Into Egypt" (Benet) **10**:154-56
"Into the Comet" (Clarke) **3**:147
"The Intoxicated" (Jackson) **39**:209, 210-214,
  227
The Intoxicated (Jackson) **39**:223
"Intoxication" (Oates) **6**:252
"Intracom" (Le Guin) **12**:235
"The Introducers" (Wharton) **6**:424, 437-38
"Introduction" (Andric)
  See "Uvod"
"The Introduction" (Woolf) **7**:381, 390-91, 393,
  395, 397, 399
"The Introspections of J. P. Powers" (Trevor)
  21:261
"The Intruder" (Borges)
  See "La intrusa"
"The Intruder" (Dixon) **16**:204, 214
"The Intruder" (Dixon) **16**:214
"An Intruder" (Gordimer) **17**:158, 181
"Intruder" (Pavese) **19**:387
"La intrusa" (Borges) **4**:14-15, 20, 37, 40-1;
  41:114-15, 117, 119, 162
"L'inutile beauté" (Maupassant) **1**:273, 275,
  286-87
La invención de Morel (Bioy Casares) **17**:53-
  61, 64-7, 75, 83-5, 90, 94-5
The Invention of Morel, and Other Stories
  (from "La trama celeste"Bioy Casares)
  See *La invención de Morel*
"The Invention of Photography in Toledo"
  (Davenport) **16**:169, 174, 179, 194
"The Invention of the Horse Collar" (Updike)
  13:360
"The Inventor" (Capek) **36**:130
"Inverno di malato" (Moravia) **26**:138, 163,
  182-83, 186
"Inverno di malato" (Moravia) **26**:179
"The Inverted Forest" (Salinger) **2**:309
"Investigations of a Dog" (Kafka)
  See "Forschungen eines hundes"
"The Invincible Slave-Owners" (Dinesen)
  7:177, 196
"Invisible Boy" (Bradbury) **29**:65
"The Invisible Dove Dancer of Strathpheen
  Island" (Collier) **19**:98, 110, 114
"The Invisible Japanese Gentlemen" (Greene)
  29:200-01, 229
The Invisible Knight (Calvino)
  See *Il cavaliere inesistente*
"The Invisible Man" (Chesterton) **1**:130, 134,
  136, 142
"L'invitation au voyage" (Baudelaire) **18**:5-6,
  8, 17, 35-6
"Invite" (O'Hara) **15**:253
"The Invited" (Sansom) **21**:83
"Invulnerable" (Ellison) **14**:127
"Ionitch" (Chekhov)
  See "Ionych"
"Ionych" (Chekhov) **2**:128, 131-32, 155
Iounn the Weeper (Bunin) **5**:90
Iowa Interiors (Suckow) **18**:389-90, 395, 405,
  418, 421-22
"Irina" (Gallant) **5**:128-32, 137
"Iris" (Hesse) **9**:234, 243
"Irish Revel" (O'Brien) **10**:341
"Iron" (Levi) **12**:256-57, 259, 262
"Iron Hans" (Grimm and Grimm) **36**:200-01
"The Iron Khiva" (Garland) **18**:147, 179
"The Iron Man and the Tin Woman" (Leacock)
  39:266
The Iron Man and the Tin Woman (Leacock)
  39:240
"Iron Mills" (Davis) **38**:118-19
"An Iron Will" (Leskov)
  See "Železnaja volja"

"The Ironbark Chip" (Lawson) **18**:217, 263
"The Iron-Man" (Grimm and Grimm) **36**:201
"An Irrevocable Diameter" (Paley) **8**:390
Irrlichter (Hauptmann) **37**:249, 251
"Is There a Writer in the House?" (Perelman)
  32:235
"Is There Nowhere Else Where We Can
  Meet?" (Gordimer) **17**:159, 168, 172
"Is Your Name Joe?" (Algren) **33**:88, 107
"Isaac" (Michaels) **16**:303
Isabella of Egypt (Arnim)
  See *Isabella von Ägypten, Kaiser Karl des
    Fünften erste Jugendliebe*
*Isabella von Ägypten, Kaiser Karl des Fünften
  erste Jugendliebe* (Arnim) **29**:10-11,
  15-25
Isabelle (Gide) **13**:42-3, 68-70, 72-3, 77-8, 94-9
"Ishui hsiu-ts'ai" (P'u Sung-ling) **31**:199
Isis (Nerval) **18**:338, 362
"La isla a mediodía" (Cortazar) **7**:55-6, 61
"The Island" (Capek)
  See "Ostrov"
"The Island" (Cheever) **38**:56
"The Island" (Cowan) **28**:76
"The Island" (Pavese) **19**:369
"The Island at Noon" (Cortazar)
  See "La isla a mediodía"
"The Island Dream" (Hesse) **9**:229-33, 235
"The Island of Fairies" (P'u Sung-ling)
  See "Hsien-jen tao"
"An Island Princess" (Bates) **10**:123
Island Tales (London)
  See *On the Makaloa Mat*
"The Island Ven" (Berriault) **30**:104
"Las islas nuevas" (Bombal) **37**:3, 9, 33, 38, 45
"The Isle of Voices" (Stevenson) **11**:269, 283
"Isolated Incidents" (Mukherjee) **38**:252-53,
  264-65, 272-73, 277
"Ispoved" (Andric) **36**:33, 37-8
"Ispoved" (Gorky) **28**:174
Istoriia moei golubiatni (Babel) **16**:9, 15, 17,
  20, 36, 41, 59
Istoriia sela Goriukhino (Pushkin) **27**:129-30,
  133, 162-63, 171-72, 183
"Istoriya leytenanta Ergunova" (Turgenev)
  7:316, 321, 326, 337, 358-59
"Iswaran" (Narayan) **25**:138, 153, 155
"It Always Breaks Out" (Ellison) **26**:11
"It Grows on You" (King) **17**:295
"It Happened Like This" (Caldwell) **19**:39
"It Helps If You Sing" (Campbell) **19**:77
"It Is Parallels That Are Deadly" (Dreiser)
  See "Tabloid Tragedy"
"It Isn't the Heat, It's the Cupidity"
  (Perelman) **32**:222, 231
"It May Never Happen" (Pritchett) **14**:263-65,
  286, 301, 305
It May Never Happen, and Other Stories
  (Pritchett) **14**:270
"It Must Have Been Spring" (O'Hara) **15**:266
"It Was the Devil's Work" (O'Flaherty) **6**:259
"It Wouldn't Break Your Arm" (O'Hara)
  15:248, 263, 266
"The Italian Banditti" (Irving) **2**:251, 261
Italian Chronicles (Stendhal)
  See *Chroniques italiennes*
Italian Folktales (Calvino)
  See *Fiabe Italiene*
"Italian Robber" (Irving) **2**:255
"Italian Sunshine" (Babel) **16**:27-8, 52-3, 55-7
"Itansha no kanashimi" (Tanizaki) **21**:193
"Itchy" (Hammett) **17**:218
"Ithaka" (Davenport) **16**:178-79, 185, 194-95
"It's a Young World" (Pohl) **25**:232
"It's about Your Daughter, Mrs. Page" (Jolley)
  19:233
"It's Cold in the Alps" (Farrell) **28**:111
Its Image on the Mirror (Gallant) **5**:122-23,
  135, 140, 148-49
"It's Just Another Day in Big Bear City,
  California" (Beattie) **11**:11, 15, 21

"It's Just the Way It Is" (Bates) **10**:114, 137,
  139
"It's Nothing Serious" (Pirandello) **22**:229, 264
"It's Perfectly True" (Andersen) **6**:30
"Ivan FederovičŠpon'ka and His Aunt"
  (Gogol)
  See "Ivan FederovičŠpon'ka i ego tetsuška"
"Ivan FederovičŠpon'ka i ego tetsuška"
  (Gogol) **4**:105, 117, 121; **29**:149
Ivan Ilyitch (Tolstoy) **30**:299
"Ivan the Fool" (Tolstoy) **9**:377, 380-81, 388
"Ivory, Apes, and People" (Thurber) **1**:426
"The Ivory Woman" (Andric)
  See "Žena iz slonove kosti"
"L'ivrogne" (Maupassant) **1**:274
"Ivy Day in the Committee Room" (Joyce)
  3:201, 205-06, 210-11, 214, 218-21, 225-
  26, 228, 231, 234, 237, 240, 242, 248;
  26:39-40, 46, 50, 79
"Ivy Gripped the Steps" (Bowen) **3**:31-2, 38,
  41, 48, 51; **28**:3-4
Ivy Gripped the Steps (Bowen)
  See *The Demon Lover and Other Stories*
"Izerghil the Crone" (Gorky)
  See "Starukha Izergil"
"The Izu Dancer" (Kawabata)
  See "Izu no Odoriko"
"Izu no Odoriko" (Kawabata) **17**:240-43, 249-
  50, 252
"Izvozchik" (Gorky) **28**:162
"Jachid and Jechidah" (Singer) **3**:357, 363, 375
"Jack and Gill of the Sierras" (Harte) **8**:214
"Jack in the Box" (Campbell) **19**:76
"The Jack Kerouac Wake" (Moorhouse) **40**:285
"Jack the Dullard" (Andersen) **6**:11
"Jack the Giant Killer" (Grimm and Grimm)
  36:194
"The Jackdaw" (Hesse) **9**:243-44
"Jack-in-the-Box" (Bradbury) **29**:42, 67, 88-9
Jackpot: The Short Stories of Erskine Caldwell
  (Caldwell) **19**:16, 25, 37-8, 50
"Jacob and the Indians" (Benet) **10**:143-44, 154
Jacob Pasinkov (Turgenev)
  See *Yakov Pasynkov*
"Jacob y el otro" (Onetti) **23**:258
"Die Jagd" (Goethe) **38**:189
"Jäger des Spotts" (Lenz) **33**:317-19, 327
Jäger des Spotts (Lenz) **33**:316, 318, 328-29,
  331
"Der jäger Gracchus" (Kafka) **5**:210; **29**:349
"Jakov, drug iz detinjstva" (Andric) **36**:66-7
"Jakov, the Childhood Friend" (Andric)
  See "Jakov, drug iz detinjstva"
"The Jama" (O'Hara) **15**:278, 285
"James Francis and the Star" (O'Hara) **15**:278,
  284-85
"Jamesie" (Powers) **4**:368, 371-72
"Jan Godfrey" (Frame) **29**:101, 115-16
"Jan the Unrepentant" (London) **4**:286
"Jane" (Maugham) **8**:356, 378-79
"Janice" (Jackson) **9**:266
"O Jantar" (Lispector) **34**:191, 193
"Janus" (Beattie) **11**:25-7
"The Japanese Quince" (Galsworthy) **22**:58, 77,
  85-6, 98
"The Jar" (Bradbury) **29**:67, 75, 86, 88
"The Jar" (Pirandello)
  See "La giara"
"El jardín" (Borges)
  See "El jardín de senderos que se bifurcan"
"El jardín de senderos que se bifurcan"
  (Borges) **4**:5, 8, 10-11, 13, 16, 18-19, 28;
  41:59, 91, 135-38, 140-41
El jardín de senderos que se bifurcan (Borges)
  4:4, 18; **41**:59, 79, 87, 157-59
"Jasmine" (Mukherjee) **38**:235-37, 245, 252,
  254, 267-68, 273, 279-80, 283, 286
Jasmine (Mukherjee) **38**:294
"Jasmine Tea" (Chang) **28**:23, 25, 35
"Jasnovidec" (Capek) **36**:96, 98, 102, 127
"The Jaunt" (King) **17**:276
"Jazz" (Cabrera Infante) **39**:22

"A Jazz Age Clerk" (Farrell) **28**:119
"Jazz, Jive and Jam" (Hughes) **6**:143-44, 146
"Je ne parle pas français" (Mansfield) **9**:280, 284, 295-96, 310
"Je Suis le Plus Malade des Surréalistes" (Nin) **10**:303-04, 306
"Je suis perdu" (Taylor) **10**:380-81, 416
"The Jealous Extremaduran" (Cervantes)
   See "El celoso extremeño"
"The Jealous Hens" (O'Flaherty) **6**:262, 280
"The Jealous Hidalgo" (Cervantes)
   See "El celoso extremeño"
"A Jealous Husband" (Adams) **24**:3-4
"Jealousy" (Dreiser)
   See "The Shadow"
"Jean Beicke" (Williams) **31**:305, 318, 325, 332-34, 346, 348, 351, 362
Jean Rhys: The Collected Short Stories (Rhys) **21**:67
"Jean-ah Poquelin" (Cable) **4**:67-70, 72-3
"Jeeves and the Dog MacIntosh" (Wodehouse) **2**:355-56
"Jeeves and the Greasy Bird" (Wodehouse) **2**:344
"Jeeves and the Yuletide Spirit" (Wodehouse) **2**:356
"Jeff Brigg's Love Story" (Harte) **8**:216
"Jeffty Is Five" (Ellison) **14**:124-25
"Jehla" (Capek) **36**:98-9, 127
"Jelena, the Woman Who Does not Exist" (Andric)
   See "Jelena, žena koje nema"
"Jelena, žena koje nema" (Andric) **36**:51
"Jeli il pastore" (Verga) **21**:283, 286, 295, 298-99, 301
"Jeli, the Shepard" (Verga)
   See "Jeli il pastore"
"The Jelly-Bean" (Fitzgerald) **6**:58-9
"Jemima, the Mountain Girl" (Fitzgerald) **6**:45, 58
Jemmy (Nerval) **18**:334, 362
"Jenny Garrow's Lovers" (Jewett) **6**:156-58, 166
"Jericho's Brick Battlements" (Laurence) **7**:252, 259, 267
"Jerry and Molly and Sam" (Carver) **8**:12
"Jesse and Meribeth" (Munro) **3**:347, 349
"The Jest of Jests" (Barnes) **3**:18
Jests of Death and Life (Pirandello)
   See *Beffe della morte e della vita*
"Die Jesuiterkirche in G." (Hoffmann) **13**:183
"Jesus Christ in Flanders" (Balzac)
   See "Jesus Christ in Flanders"
"Jesus Said to Watch for 28 Signs" (Moorhouse) **40**:289, 291
"Jesus upon Honshu" (Updike) **13**:360
"Jesusa" (Pardo Bazan) **30**:263, 269
"Jésus-Christ en Flandre" (Balzac) **5**:14, 16-17, 23
"The Jet Set" (O'Hara) **15**:283, 287-88
Jettatura (Gautier) **20**:6-8, 16-17, 19, 21, 31, 33
"Le jeu des grâces" (Villiers de l'Isle Adam) **14**:387
"La Jeune; or, Actress and Woman" (Alcott) **27**:31
Les jeunes-France, romans goguenards (Gautier) **20**:7, 9-11, 13, 22
"The Jew" (Turgenev) **7**:316, 320, 324, 359
"The Jew from Babylon" (Singer) **3**:389
"The Jew Who Became a Bird" (Aleichem) **33**:79
"The Jewbird" (Malamud) **15**:171, 173-75, 189, 195, 197-99, 200-02, 204, 220, 235, 240
"The Jewel of Jeopardy" (Coppard) **21**:10
"The Jewels of the Cabots" (Cheever) **1**:101; **38**:54
"The Jewess" (Babel) **16**:35
"The Jewish Refugee" (Malamud)
   See "The German Refugee"
"The Jilting of Granny Weatherall" (Porter) **4**:327-28, 340, 348, 356-58

"The Jilting of Jane" (Wells) **6**:360, 392
"Jim Blaine and His Grandfather's Old Ram" (Twain) **6**:310; **34**:308
"Jim O'Neill" (Farrell) **28**:118-9, 122
"Jim Pemberton and His Boy Trigger" (Saroyan) **21**:156
"Jim Smiley and His Jumping Frog" (Twain)
   See "The Celebrated Jumping Frog of Calaveras County"
"Jim Sullivan's Adventures in the Great Show" (Le Fanu) **14**:219
"Jimmy and the Desperate Woman" (Lawrence) **4**:219, 238
"Jimmy Goggles the God" (Wells) **6**:360
"Jimmy Rose" (Melville) **1**:303-04, 325-26; **17**:359, 363
"Jim's Big Brother from California" (Harte) **8**:254
"Jim's Probation" (Dunbar) **8**:122, 127
"Jimsella" (Dunbar) **8**:119, 121, 127, 129, 143, 146
Jin suoji (Chang) **28**:21; 23; 26-28; 31; 34-35; 41-42; 44-47
"Jo" (O'Connor) **5**:382
"The Job" (Saroyan) **21**:142
"The Job Appication" (Walser) **20**:336, 349
"The Jockey" (McCullers) **9**:322, 332, 347, 358; **24**:232
"Joe Craddock's Old Woman" (Caldwell) **19**:43
Joe Wilson and His Mates (Lawson) **18**:202-05, 208-09, 213, 221, 252, 261-62
"Joe Wilson's Courtship" (Lawson) **18**:202-03, 210, 228-29, 232, 252, 258, 262
"Johanna" (Walser) **20**:364
"Johannes-Wassersprung and Caspar-Wassersprung" (Grimm and Grimm) **36**:187
"John and I" (Leacock) **39**:265, 266
"John Archer's Nose" (Fisher) **25**:13, 20
"John Barleycorn Lives" (Boyle) **16**:142-43
"John Barrington Cowles" (Doyle) **12**:85-6
"John Bull" (Irving) **2**:244, 251, 253
"John Bull on the Guadalquivir" (Trollope) **28**:318, 328-29, 331, 340, 348, 354
"John Charles Tapner" (Davenport) **16**:180, 193
"John Hitchcock" (Farrell) **28**:96, 124, 127
"John Inglefield's Thanksgiving" (Hawthorne) **3**:189
"John Lamar" (Davis) **38**:133-37, 139
"John Napper Sailing through the Universe" (Gardner) **7**:214, 216-17, 222, 233, 235, 238
"John Nicholson's Predicament" (Stevenson)
   See "The Misadventures of John Nicholson"
"John Redding Goes to Sea" (Hurston) **4**:136-38, 149, 153
"Johnnie Brewer" (Warner) **23**:374
"Johnny" (Dreiser)
   See "Black Sheep No. One: Johnny"
"Johnny Bear" (Steinbeck)
   See "The Ears of Johnny Bear"
"Johnny Pye and the Fool-Killer" (Benet) **10**:142-44, 148, 154, 156-57, 159-60
"The Johnson Girls" (Bambara) **35**:3, 21, 23-4, 35
"Johnsonham, Jr." (Dunbar) **8**:135, 148
"Joining Charles" (Bowen) **3**:30, 47
Joining Charles and Other Stories (Bowen) **3**:30, 33, 40; **28**:4
"Jo-Jo" (Farrell) **28**:119, 122
"Joke" (Dixon) **16**:207
"The Joke on Eloise Morey" (Hammett) **17**:218, 222
"A Joker" (Baudelaire)
   See "Un plaisant"
"The Joker's Greatest Triumph" (Barthelme) **2**:28, 34
"The Jokers of New Gibbon" (London) **4**:266
"The Jolly Corner" (James) **8**:296, 304, 306, 308-09, 326-29

"Jonas ou l'artiste au travail" (Camus) **9**:103, 105, 108-09, 119, 129-35
"Jones's Alley" (Lawson) **18**:238
"Le Jongleur de Taillebois" (Norris) **28**:204, 212
"The Jongleur of Taillebois" (Norris)
   See "Le Jongleur de Taillebois"
"Jordan" (Henderson) **29**:326, 328-29
"Jordan's End" (Glasgow) **34**:57-8, 62-3, 66-7, 75-6, 78, 81, 92, 95-7, 103-04
"Jorinda and Jorindel" (Gallant) **5**:138, 141-44
"Josefina, Take Good Care of the Señores" (Cabrera Infante) **39**:18, 23
"Joseph and His Brother" (Thomas) **20**:290, 292, 319
"Joseph Yates' Temptation" (Gissing) **37**:67-8
"Josephine" (O'Flaherty) **6**:264
"Josephine de Montmorenci" (Trollope) **28**:321, 340
"Josephine, die Sängerin oder Das Volk der Mäuse" (Kafka) **5**:231, 240, 242; **29**:349-50
"Josephine the Chanteuse" (Kafka)
   See "Josephine, die Sängerin oder Das Volk der Mäuse"
"Josephine the Singer, or the Mouse Folk" (Kafka)
   See "Josephine, die Sängerin oder Das Volk der Mäuse"
"Josephine the Songstress" (Kafka)
   See "Josephine, die Sängerin oder Das Volk der Mäuse"
"Joshua" (Grau) **15**:156, 168, 164
"Le joueur généreux" (Baudelaire) **18**:19, 41
"Le joujou du pauvre" (Baudelaire) **18**:33-4, 47-51, 53
"Journal" (Michaels) **16**:314, 317
"The Journal of a Superfluous Man" (Turgenev)
   See "Dnevnik lishnego cheloveka"
"The Journal of J. P. Drapeau" (Ligotti) **16**:277, 283, 286
Journal of Katherine Mansfield (Mansfield) **9**:281, 294
"Journey" (Cowan) **28**:76
"A Journey" (Gordimer) **17**:177, 180, 183, 187-88, 190
"The Journey" (Irving) **2**:244, 265
"A Journey" (O'Brien) **10**:333
"The Journey" (Peretz) **26**:214
"The Journey" (Pirandello)
   See "Il viaggio"
"The Journey" (Porter) **4**:352, 358, 363
"A Journey" (Wharton) **6**:423
"The Journey and the Dream" (Saroyan) **21**:163
"Journey Back to the Source" (Carpentier)
   See "Viaje a la semilla"
"Journey into Smoke" (Sansom) **21**:124
"The Journey of Alija Djerzelez" (Andric)
   See "Put Alije Djerzeleza"
"The Journey to Hanford" (Saroyan) **21**:171
"The Journey to Panama" (Trollope) **28**:320, 323, 349-52
"Journey to Polessie" (Turgenev) **7**:335
Journey to the East (Hesse)
   See *Die Morgenlandfahrt*
"Journey to the Heartland" (Aldiss) **36**:10-11, 23, 26-7
"The Journeyman's Secret" (Howells) **36**:398
Les jours et les nuits: Roman d'un déserter (Jarry) **20**:46, 50-2, 58-9, 61, 67, 75, 77-9, 82
"Joy" (Singer) **3**:360, 363-64, 368
"Joy of Life" (Galsworthy) **22**:58
"The Joy of Mooching" (Perelman) **32**:235
"The Joy of Nelly Deane" (Cather) **2**:98, 104
"The Joy of the Just" (Gardner) **7**:226-28
"J's Marriage" (Coover) **15**:33, 35, 48, 59
"Juan Manso" (Unamuno) **11**:312
"Juan Muraña" (Borges) **4**:19-20
"Juanita" (Chopin) **8**:98, 110-11
"Judas" (O'Connor) **5**:368-69, 378, 381

"The Judas Tree" (Moravia) **26**:159, 161
"Judge Lu" (P'u Sung-ling)
    See "Lu p'an"
"Judgement Day" (O'Connor) **1**:343, 365
"The Judge's Wife" (Schnitzler)
    See "Die Frau des Richters"
"The Judgment" (Kafka)
    See "Das Urteil"
"A Judgment in the Mountains" (Benet) **10**:156
"The Judgment of Dungara" (Kipling) **5**:262
"A Judgment of Paris" (Dunbar) **8**:122, 128, 136
"Judith" (Coppard) **21**:12, 17, 29
Judith, and Other Stories (Farrell) **28**:112-3, 116
"Judy's Service of Gold Plate" (Norris) **28**:201-02, 207
"Jug and Bottle" (Ross) **24**:291, 293, 307, 311
"Jug of Silver" (Capote) **2**:63, 65-6, 70
"The Juggler Pamphalon" (Leskov)
    See "Skomorox Pamfalon"
The Jules Verne Steam Balloon (Davenport) **16**:198-200
Julia Bride (James) **8**:311-13, 343-45, 347-51
"Julia Cahill's Curse" (Moore) **19**:305, 317, 319, 322, 347-49
Julie de Carneilhan (Colette) **10**:269-70
"Julip" (Harrison) **19**:216-17
Julip (Harrison) **19**:215-17
"July the Fifteenth, 1988" (Lish) **18**:286
"Jumbo" (Saroyan) **21**:132
"Jumbo's Wife" (O'Connor) **5**:390
"Jump" (Gordimer) **17**:178, 181-82, 185, 187, 190-91
"A Jump Ahead" (Warner) **23**:375
Jump, and Other Stories (Gordimer) **17**:177-89, 191
"Jump to Chicago" (Farrell) **28**:112
"June Recital" (Welty) **1**:474, 480, 483, 485, 495, 497
"Juneteenth" (Ellison) **26**:11
Der Junge Tischlermeister (Tieck) **31**:269, 275, 282-83, 287, 290-91
Die Jungfrau als Ritter (Keller) **26**:92, 99, 108
Die Jungfrau und der Teufel (Keller) **26**:101
Die Jungfrau und die Nonne (Keller) **26**:99, 108
"The Jungle" (Bowen) **3**:30, 33, 49
The Jungle Books (Kipling) **5**:277, 279, 282, 285, 287-88, 292-94
"Junior" (Lewis) **34**:163, 165
"The Juniper-Tree" (Grimm and Grimm) **36**:233
"Jupiter Doke, Brigadier-General" (Bierce) **9**:96, 98-100
"Jupiter Five" (Clarke) **3**:124, 129, 134-35, 149
Jürg Jenatsch (Meyer) **30**:186-87, 200, 204, 249
"Jurge Dulrumple" (O'Hara) **15**:282
"Jūrokusai no Nikki" (Kawabata) **17**:248
"A Jury Case" (Anderson) **1**:50
"A Jury of Her Peers" (Glaspell) **41**:278-307
"The Juryman" (Capek)
    See "Porotce"
"The Juryman" (Galsworthy) **22**:61, 74, 78, 95, 99-100, 102
"Just a Little One" (Parker) **2**:281
"Just Before the War with the Eskimos" (Salinger) **2**:300; **28**:221
"Just Him and Her" (Suckow) **18**:409
"Just like Little Dogs" (Thomas) **3**:403, 406, 411-12
"Just Meat" (London) **4**:253-54, 262-63, 291
"Just One More Time" (Cheever) **1**:100; **38**:54
"The Just Ones" (Shiga) **23**:336
Just So Stories (Kipling) **5**:273, 279, 287, 293
"Just Tell Me Who It Was" (Cheever) **1**:90; **38**:87
"A Just Verdict" (P'u Sung-ling)
    See "Che yü"
"Just Waiting" (Campbell) **19**:92
"A Justice" (Faulkner) **1**:147, 177, 181
"Justice" (Galsworthy) **22**:98

"Justice" (O'Hara) **15**:287-88
"The Justice and the Vagabond" (Gissing) **37**:55
"Justicia?" (Pardo Bazan) **30**:264
Jyotaro (Tanizaki) **21**:195, 225
"The Kabbalists" (Peretz) **26**:206
"Kabnis" (Toomer) **1**:440, 442-44, 446-48, 451-54, 457, 459-60
"Kacheli" (Bunin) **5**:113
"Kain and Artyom" (Gorky)
    See "Kain i Artem"
"Kain i Artem" (Gorky) **28**:137, 159, 190
"Kaleidoscope" (Bradbury) **29**:42, 48, 79, 80
"Kalkstein" (Stifter) **28**:283-84, 286, 288-90, 298-99
"Der Kampf der Sänger" (Hoffmann) **13**:182,212
"The Kanaka Surf" (London) **4**:257, 266
"K'ao-pi ssu" (P'u Sung-ling) **31**:198
Kapitanskaya-dochka (Pushkin) **27**:130-33, 154-62, 164, 175-76, 178-81, 185-86, 188
"Karain" (Conrad) **9**:143
"Karamora" (Gorky) **28**:137, 161-62
"Karintha" (Toomer) **1**:441, 452, 455-56, 459
"Kärleken och döden" (Lagerkvist) **12**:195
"Karl-Yankel" (Babel) **16**:13, 16, 22
"Kartofel'nyy el'f" (Nabokov)
    See "The Potato Elf"
"Kashtánka" (Chekhov) **2**:130
"Kas'ian of the Beautiful Lands" (Turgenev) **7**:343-45
"Kata Ucle" (Kawabata) **17**:235, 240-41, 246-47
"Katastrofa" (Nabokov)
    See "Details of a Sunset"
"Katchen's Caprices" (Trollope) **28**:317, 333
"Kate Lancaster's Plan" (Jewett) **6**:167
"Kathleen's Field" (Trevor) **21**:246-47, 260, 262, 265, 270, 273-74
"Kathy" (Caldwell) **19**:54
"Katz" (Algren) **33**:106
"Katzenzilber" (Stifter) **28**:298-99, 303, 305-07
"Kazimír Stanislávovich" (Bunin) **5**:81
"Keel and Kool" (Frame)
    See "Keel, Kool"
"Keel, Kool" (Frame) **29**:100-01, 107
"Keela, the Outcast Indian Maiden" (Welty) **1**:468, 470, 497; **27**:338, 352-53
Keep It Crisp (Perelman) **32**:205-06
"Keep Your Pity" (Boyle) **5**:55
"Keeping Fit" (Gordimer) **17**:177, 185, 187-88, 190
"Keesh, the Son of Keesh" (London) **4**:287-88
"Keiserens nye Klæder" (Andersen)
    See "The Emperor's New Clothes"
The Képi (Colette)
    See *Le képi*
Le képi (Colette) **10**:274, 292-93, 295
"The Kerchief" (Agnon)
    See "HaMitpahat"
"Kerfol" (Wharton) **6**:426-28, 431-32
Der Ketzer von Soana (Hauptmann) **37**:195, 202, 204-7
"Kew Gardens" (Woolf) **7**:368, 370-71, 374-76, 378, 382-83, 385, 387-88, 392, 398-99, 404-07
Kew Gardens (Woolf) **7**:382
"Kewpie Doll" (Algren) **33**:113
"The Key" (Welty) **1**:468
"The Key to My Heart" (Pritchett) **14**:268
"The Keystone" (Powers) **4**:376, 381
"Kezia and Tui" (Mansfield) **9**:282
"Khadzi murat" (Tolstoy) **9**:376, 378, 394-97
"The Khan and His Son" (Gorky) **28**:144
"Khat" (Dreiser) **30**:113, 115
"A Kholem" (Peretz) **26**:222-23
"Khor and Kalinych" (Turgenev) **7**:313, 342, 362
"Khoziain" (Gorky) **28**:189
"Khozyaika" (Dostoevsky) **2**:163, 170-71, 173-74, 181, 191, 193
Khozyain i rabotnik (Tolstoy) **9**:368, 372, 377, 382-86

"The Kid Nobody Could Handle" (Vonnegut) **8**:432
"Kidnapped" (Kipling) **5**:274
"The Kidnapping of President Lincoln" (Harris) **19**:125, 133
"The Kid's Whistling" (Updike) **13**:355
"Kierkegaard Unfair to Schlegel" (Barthelme) **2**:31, 38-9, 54
"Kiev—a Town" (Bulgakov) **18**:91
"The Kill" (Boyle) **5**:64
"Killed at Resaca" (Bierce) **9**:67, 75-7
"Killer in the Rain" (Chandler) **23**:58, 65-8, 72, 80-2, 85, 87, 92, 98, 102, 104-07
Killer in the Rain (Chandler) **23**:67-8
"The Killers" (Hemingway) **1**:211, 218-19, 234-36, 242; **25**:84; **40**:166, 184, 191, 209, 211
"Killing" (Updike) **13**:402-03, 409
"The Killing Ground" (Ballard) **1**:76
"Killings" (Dubus) **15**:75, 88, 94, 96-7, 100-01
"Kimyōna shigoto" (Oe) **20**:214, 229
"Kin" (Welty) **1**:475-76, 487
Kindergeschichten (Stifter)
    See *Bunte Steine*
"Kinderseele" (Hesse) **9**:218
Kinder-und Hausmärchen (Grimm and Grimm) **36**:175-241
"The Kindest Thing to Do" (Gordimer) **17**:166-67
"The King" (Babel) **16**:17-18, 42-4, 48-9, 59
"King Bee" (Boyle) **16**:148, 155
"The King Business" (Hammett) **17**:222
"King Gregor and the Fool" (Gardner) **7**:234
"A King Lear of the Steppes" (Turgenev)
    See "Stepnoy Korol 'Lir"
King Leopold's Soliloquy (Twain) **26**:354
"A King Listens" (Calvino) **3**:119
"The King of Folly Island" (Jewett) **6**:154
The King of Folly Island and Other People (Jewett) **6**:154
"The King of Greece's Tea Party" (Hemingway) **1**:208
"King of the Bingo Game" (Ellison) **26**:3, 10, 13, 19-23, 25
"The King of the Cats" (Benet) **10**:143-44, 158
"The King of the Desert" (O'Hara) **15**:248-49, 270
"The King of the Foxes" (Doyle) **12**:64
"The King of the Golden Mountain" (Grimm and Grimm) **36**:189
"King of the Grey Spaces" (Bradbury)
    See "R Is for Rocket"
"King of the Mountain" (Garrett) **30**:163
King of the Mountain (Garrett) **30**:164-65, 172
"The King of the Trenches" (Lewis) **34**:164, 171
"King Pest" (Poe) **1**:406; **22**:300, 306; **35**:317
"The King Set Free" (Pirandello) **22**:229
"King Thrushbeard" (Grimm and Grimm) **36**:190
"The King Who Lived on Air" (Bates) **10**:112
"King Yu" (Hesse) **9**:244
"Kingdom City to Cairo" (Algren) **33**:107, 109
The Kingdoms of Elfin (Warner) **23**:378-80, 382-85
"King's Ankus" (Kipling) **5**:293
"The King's Bride" (Hoffmann)
    See "Königsbraut"
"The King's in Yellow" (Chandler) **23**:59, 65, 72, 88, 109-10
The King's Indian: Stories and Tales (Gardner) **7**:213-21, 226, 228-29, 235
"Kinjū" (Kawabata) **17**:235, 240-41
"Kinkies" (Trevor) **21**:233
"Kinosaki nite" (Shiga) **23**:344, 346, 348, 352, 359-60
"A Kinsman of His Blood" (Wolfe) **33**:374
Die Kirchenordnung (Arnim) **29**:6
"Kirilka" (Gorky) **28**:161
"Kirin" (Tanizaki) **21**:195, 206-08
"The Kiss" (Babel) **16**:16, 59
"The Kiss" (Carter) **13**:17
"The Kiss" (Chekhov) **2**:126, 156; **28**:56

"The Kiss" (Chopin) **8**:72, 111-12
"The Kiss" (Sansom) **21**:83
"Kiss Me Again, Stranger" (du Maurier) **18**:126, 138
Kiss Me Again, Stranger: A Collection of Eight Stories, Long and Short (du Maurier)
   See *The Apple Tree: A Short Novel and Some Stories*
"The Kiss of Moses" (Peretz) **26**:194
The Kiss to the Leper (Mauriac)
   See *Le baiser au lépreux*
"The Kitchen" (O'Faolain) **13**:311, 320
"The Kitchen Child" (Carter) **13**:17-18
"A Kitchen Knife" (Warner) **23**:370-71
"Kitchenware, Notions, Lights, Action, Camera!" (Perelman) **32**:211
"The Kite" (Maugham) **8**:380
"Kitty" (Bowles) **3**:76, 80
"Kitty the Wren" (O'Faolain) **13**:309
"Klara Milich" (Turgenev) **7**:321, 324, 326-28, 334, 338, 362
Die Klausenburg (Tieck) **31**:286
"Klee Dead" (Coover) **15**:33, 37, 41
Kleider machen Leute (Keller) **26**:96, 100, 107, 127
Klein und Wagner (Hesse) **9**:218, 227, 236-40
Klein Zaches gennant Zinnober (Hoffmann) **13**:192-93, 195, 197, 199, 200, 218-19
"Kleine Fabel" (Kafka) **5**:254; **29**:348
Der kleine Herr Friedemann (Mann) **5**:319, 323, 327, 332, 334, 336
"Die Kleine Komödie" (Schnitzler) **15**:377
"Eine Kleine Mothmusik" (Perelman) **32**:213
Kleine Prosa (Walser) **20**:334
"Kleist in Thun" (Walser) **20**:336-37
Kleyne mentshelekh mit kleyne hasoges (Aleichem) **33**:6
"Klingsor's Last Summer" (Hesse) **9**:218, 220, 227, 240-41
Klingsor's Last Summer (Hesse)
   See *Klingsors letzter Sommer*
Klingsors letzter Sommer (Hesse) **9**:219, 227, 238-39
"Klods-Hans" (Andersen)
   See "Jack the Dullard"
Das Kloster bei Sendomir (Grillparzer) **37**:160
"Kneel to the Rising Sun" (Caldwell) **19**:7, 9, 17-23, 33, 38, 43, 45-6
Kneel to the Rising Sun, and Other Stories (Caldwell) **19**:9, 12, 18-19, 21, 25, 35, 37-8, 57
"The Knife and the Naked Chalk" (Kipling) **5**:284, 292
"Knife Blows" (Mauriac)
   See "Coups de couteaux"
"The Knife of the Times" (Williams) **31**:302, 324, 334, 350-51, 357, 359-62
The Knife of the Times (Williams) **31**:302-03, 320, 324, 330-32, 357-59, 361-62, 365
"The Knife Thrower" (Boell)
   See "Der Mann mit den Messern"
"A Knife to Cut Corn Bread With" (Caldwell) **19**:13-14, 38-9
"A Knight" (Galsworthy) **22**:74, 79, 91-4, 97
"A Knight-Errant of the Foothills" (Harte) **8**:249
"Knight's Gambit" (Faulkner) **1**:178-81
Knight's Gambit (Faulkner) **1**:151, 178-79
Kniha apokryfů (Capek) **36**:94, 111-15, 117-18, 128, 130
"Der Knirps" (Walser) **20**:339
"Knjiga" (Andric) **36**:37
"The Knock at the Manor Gate" (Kafka) **5**:206
"Knock...Knock...Knock" (Turgenev)
   See "Stuk...stuk...stuk"
"Knots upon Knots" (Agnon) **30**:38
"Knowledge" (Lish) **18**:275, 283
"Knox" (Ellison) **14**:102, 104-05
"Kochergà" (Zoshchenko) **15**:398
"Kod kazana" (Andric) **36**:33, 38, 56
"Kod lekara" (Andric) **36**:51-2
Kohlhaas (Kleist)
   See *Michael Kohlhaas*

"The Kolkhoz Rucksack" (Solzhenitsyn) **32**:394
"The Komarov Case" (Bulgakov) **18**:91
"Kometa" (Schulz) **13**:330, 335
Konarmiia (Babel) **16**:2-7, 9-21, 23-7, 29-31, 35-36, 42, 49-54, 56-60
"Kong Yiji" (Lu Hsun) **20**:149
"Königsbraut" (Hoffmann) **13**:192, 195-96, 198-200, 223, 226
"Konjiki no shi" (Tanizaki) **21**:196, 209
"Konkin" (Babel) **16**:50
"Konkin's Prisoner" (Babel) **16**:26, 28
"Konovalov" (Gorky) **28**:156, 178, 189
"Koolau the Leper" (London) **4**:269
"Korea" (McGahern) **17**:298, 322
"Kosa" (Andric) **36**:45, 47
"Koster i murav'i" (Solzhenitsyn) **32**:354
"Kotin and Platonida" (Leskov)
   See "Kotin doilec"
"Kotin doilec" (Leskov) **34**:108, 118
"Ko-yi" (P'u Sung-ling) **31**:197
"Kozo no kamisama" (Shiga) **23**:352, 354, 360
Krakonošova zahrada (Capek) **36**:92, 109
"Krasavets" (Leskov) **34**:131
"Kreisler's Certificate" (Hoffmann) **13**:212
Kreitserova sonata (Tolstoy) **9**:363, 377-78, 396, 403-06; **30**:298-343
The Kreutzer Sonata (Tolstoy)
   See *Kreitserova sonata*
"Krøblingen" (Andersen)
   See "The Cripple"
"Kroy Wen" (Boyle) **5**:55
"Krushniker Delegation" (Aleichem) **33**:82
"Kryžovnik" (Chekhov) **2**:136-37, 139, 141-43, 155-57; **28**:48-72
"Ksiega" (Schulz) **13**:328, 334-36, 338
Ku shih hsin pien (Lu Hsun)
   See *Gushi xinbian*
"K'uang-jen jih-chi" (Lu Hsun)
   See *Kuangren riji*
Kuangren riji (Lu Hsun) **20**:125-26, 128, 141, 144, 148, 151
Kuca na osami (Andric) **36**:63-8
"Kuei-li" (P'u Sung-ling) **31**:200
"Kuma" (Shiga) **23**:346, 348
"Kung-sun Chiu-niang" (P'u Sung-ling) **31**:200
"Kung-sun Hsia" (P'u Sung-ling) **31**:192
"Kuniko" (Shiga) **23**:346-48, 352
"Der Kuntsenmakher" (Peretz) **26**:198, 217
"Kuo shêng" (P'u Sung-ling) **31**:205
"Kupón" (Capek) **36**:96, 128
"Kurōdiasu no nikki" (Shiga) **23**:339, 345-46, 348, 361-64
"Kusatsu Spa" (Shiga) **23**:349
"Der Kuss von Sentze" (Stifter) **28**:299
"The Kylin" (Tanizaki)
   See "Kirin"
"Kyofu" (Tanizaki) **21**:193
"De la grafología como ciencia aplicada" (Cortazar) **7**:95
"Labour Day Dinner" (Munro) **3**:346
"The Labyrinth" (Nin) **10**:317, 319
Labyrinths (Borges)
   See *Labyrinths: Selected Stories, and Other Writings*
Labyrinths: Selected Stories, and Other Writings (Borges) **41**:49-52, 56-64, 66, 77, 132, 135-37, 140, 148-49, 157, 162-63, 165, 168
"A Lack of Passion" (Hemingway) **40**:191
"Os Laços de família" (Lispector) **34**:194-95
Laços de família (Lispector) **34**:184-85, 187-97, 201-02, 211, 213-18
"The Ladder" (Pritchett) **14**:296
Ladies and Escorts (Thomas) **20**:287-90, 292, 317, 319-20
"Ladies and Gentleman" (Spark) **10**:356
"Ladies' Shoes" (Walser) **20**:356
"El lado de la sombra" (Bioy Casares) **17**:95
El lado de la sombra (Bioy Casares) **17**:87, 95
"The Lady" (Andric)
   See "Gospodjicd"

"A Lady" (Donoso)
   See "Una señora"
"The Lady and the Masters of History" (Farrell) **28**:126
"The Lady and the Pedlar" (Agnon) **30**:40
"The Lady Bandit" (Pardo Bazan) **30**:290
"The Lady Cornelia" (Cervantes)
   See "La Señora Cornelia"
"Lady Eleanore's Mantle" (Hawthorne) **3**:184
"The Lady from Guatemala" (Pritchett) **14**:268
"The Lady from Lucknow" (Mukherjee) **38**:238-41, 250, 252-55, 265, 271-73, 278
"The Lady from the Land" (Thurber) **1**:424
Lady Godiva and Other Stories (Moravia)
   See *Un'altra vita*
"The Lady Icenway" (Hardy) **2**:205
"The Lady in the Lake" (Chandler) **23**:65, 67, 72, 82-3, 88-9, 109-10
"The Lady in the Looking-Glass: A Reflection" (Woolf) **7**:375-76, 378-80, 388, 392, 399, 407-12
"The Lady Knight-Errant" (P'u Sung-ling)
   See "Hsia-nü"
"Lady Lucifer" (O'Faolain) **13**:300-02, 304-07
"A Lady Macbeth of the Mtsensk District" (Leskov)
   See "Ledi Makbet Mcenskogo uezda"
"Lady Mottisfont" (Hardy) **2**:208
"A Lady of Bayou St. John" (Chopin) **8**:72, 84, 87, 91, 106, 110
"The Lady of Beasts" (Pavese)
   See "La belva"
"The Lady of Launay" (Trollope) **28**:311, 322-23, 334, 344, 355, 357
"The Lady of Moge" (Le Guin) **12**:211, 213
"The Lady of the House of Love" (Carter) **13**:9, 28
"The Lady of the Lake" (Malamud) **15**:168, 178, 181, 217, 220
"The Lady of the Sagas" (O'Connor) **5**:371
"The Lady on the Gray" (Collier) **19**:104
"The Lady Penelope" (Hardy) **2**:209
"Lady Perkins" (Lardner) **32**:148
"A Lady Slipper" (Dunbar) **8**:122
"Lady Tal" (Lee) **33**:304
"The Lady Turned Peasant" (Pushkin)
   See "Baryshnia-krest'ianka"
"Lady with a Lamp" (Parker) **2**:273-74, 280, 285
"The Lady with the Dog" (Chekhov) **2**:127-28, 131-33, 135, 150, 155, 157; **28**:60, 62-3; **41**:194, 203
"Lady with a Little Dog" (Chekhov)
   See "The Lady with the Dog"
"The Lady with the Pet Dog" (Oates) **6**:234
"The Ladybird" (Lawrence) **4**:219, 231, 238-39
"The Lady-Peasant" (Pushkin)
   See "Baryshnia-krest'ianka"
"The Lady's Maid" (Mansfield) **9**:303, 311; **23**:139
"The Lady's Maid's Bell" (Wharton) **6**:427
"The Lady's Walk" (Oliphant) **25**:209
"The Lagoon" (Conrad) **9**:143-44, 152
"The Lagoon" (Frame) **29**:99-101, 105
The Lagoon and Other Stories (Frame) **29**:99-103, 105-08, 110, 111, 115
"Lágrimas de Xerxes" (Machado de Assis) **24**:128-29
"Laila min haLelot" (Agnon) **30**:38
"The Lake" (Bradbury) **29**:84-5, 88
"The Lake" (Cowan) **28**:78
"The Lake" (Pavese) **19**:369
The Lake (Moore) **19**:316, 318, 332, 334-39, 353-60
"Lake Greifen" (Walser) **20**:352, 364
"A Lake of Home-brew" (Bulgakov) **18**:92
"Lake Segden" (Solzhenitsyn)
   See "Ozero Segden"
The Lamb (Mauriac)
   See *L'angeau*
"The Lame Shall Enter First" (O'Connor) **1**:343-45, 356, 365

"The Lament" (O'Flaherty) 6:276
"The Lamentable Comedy of Willow Wood"
    (Kipling) 5:261
Laments for the Living (Parker) 2:272, 274
"The Lamias" (Wells) 6:380
"The Lamp" (Agnon)
    See "ha-Panas"
"The Lamp at Noon" (Ross) 24:289-93, 295,
    302, 309, 311, 319
The Lamp at Noon, and Other Stories (Ross)
    24:294, 300, 304, 306, 312, 319-20
"A Lamp in the Window" (Capote) 2:80
"The Lamp of Psyche" (Wharton) 6:424, 427
"The Lamplighter" (Dickens) 17:124
"Lance" (Nabokov) 11:108
"Lance Jack" (Lewis) 40:271, 276
"The Land and the Water" (Grau) 15:161
"A Land Beyond the River" (Stuart) 31:227,
    263
"The Land Ironclads" (Wells) 6:374, 380, 403
The Land of Darkness, along with Some
    Further Chapters in Experience of the
    Little Pilgrim (Oliphant) 25:185-86, 196
"Land of Exile" (Pavese)
    See "Terra d'esilio"
The Land of the Spirit (Page) 23:307-08, 312
"The Land They Gave Us" (Rulfo)
    See "Nos han dado la tierra"
"Land Where My Fathers Died" (Dubus) 15:81,
    86
"The Land Where There Is No Death" (Benet)
    10:160
"Ein landarzt" (Kafka) 5:213, 216, 230, 246;
    29:345, 349, 369
"The Landing" (O'Flaherty) 6:264, 269, 273,
    276-77
"Landing in Luck" (Faulkner) 1:177
"The Landlady" (Dostoevsky)
    See "Khozyaika"
"A Landlocked Sailor" (Jewett) 6:156
"The Landlord" (Pritchett) 14:255, 296
A Landlord's Morning (Tolstoy) 9:376, 399
"The Landmarker" (Auchincloss) 22:9, 12
"The Landowner" (Turgenev) 7:313
"The Landscape Chamber" (Jewett) 6:154
"Landsend" (Selby) 20:258, 261, 263, 265, 281
Der Landvogt von Greifensee (Keller) 26:94,
    109, 111, 113, 115
"Der Längere Arm" (Lenz) 33:317-18, 333-36
"The Langhe Hills" (Pavese) 19:377
The Langoliers (King) 17:280, 282-84
The Langston Hughes Reader (Hughes)
    6:122-23
"The Language of Flowers" (Warner) 23:368,
    387
Lantern Slides (O'Brien) 10:345-46
"Le lapin" (Maupassant) 1:263, 274
"Lappin and Lapinova" (Woolf) 7:376-77, 388,
    393-94, 398
"L'Lapse" (Barthelme) 2:40
"Laquelle des deux? Histoire perplexe"
    (Gautier) 20:13
"Laquelle est la vraie?" (Baudelaire) 18:6
"La larga historia" (Onetti) 23:247
"Las Vegas Charley" (Yamamoto) 34:348-49,
    352-53, 359-60
"The LaSalle Hotel in Chicago" (Saroyan)
    21:149
"The Last" (Dixon) 16:217
The Last Address (Lowry)
    See Lunar Caustic
"The Last Adventure of the Brigadier" (Doyle)
    12:83
"The Last Anniversary" (Caldwell) 19:54
"The Last Asset" (Wharton) 6:424-25
"The Last Austrian Who Left Venice"
    (Trollope) 28:319, 323
"The Last Bus" (Agnon)
    See "Ha'Autobus ha'Aharon"
"The Last Cab Driver, and the First Omnibus
    Cad" (Dickens) 17:121, 125
"The Last Carousel" (Algren) 33:98, 111, 114

The Last Carousel (Algren) 33:95-8
The Last Circle (Benet) 10:160
"The Last Crop" (Jolley) 19:245
"The Last Day" (Verga) 21:298, 300
"The Last Day in the Field" (Gordon) 15:120,
    128, 142
Last Days (Oates) 6:254
"Last Days in Deephaven" (Jewett) 6:167
"The Last Demon" (Singer) 3:383
"Last Descent to Earth" (Lish) 18:283
"The Last Dream of the Old Oak" (Andersen)
    6:18, 40
Last Exit to Brooklyn (Selby) 20:253-57, 264-
    65, 267-68, 273-75, 277-79
"The Last Feast of Harlequin" (Ligotti) 16:274,
    277-80, 282-83, 287, 289, 297
"The Last Fiddling of Mordaunts Jim"
    (Dunbar) 8:122, 149
"The Last Flight of Father" (Schulz)
    See "Ostatnia ucieczka ojca"
"The Last Galley" (Doyle) 12:80
"The Last Gas Station" (Grau) 15:148-49, 152,
    154, 160
The Last Inspection (Lewis) 40:271-72, 275-77,
    280-82
"The Last Judgment" (Capek)
    See "Poslední soud"
"The Last Kiss" (Gordimer) 17:154
"The Last Laugh" (Lawrence) 19:277-79
The Last Laugh (Perelman) 32:235-38
"The Last Leaf" (Henry) 5:185
"The Last Leaf" (Porter) 4:339, 352-53, 358,
    361
"The Last Letter of a Litterateur" (Schnitzler)
    See "Derletzebrief eines literaten"
"Last May" (Dixon) 16:203
"The Last Mohican" (Malamud) 15:169, 171,
    175, 179, 181-82, 187, 192-93, 195-96, 211-
    12, 219, 222
"The Last News" (Price) 22:386
"The Last Night in the Old Home" (Bowen)
    3:41
"The Last of a Long Correspondence" (Price)
    22:388
The Last of Chéri (Colette)
    See La fin de Chéri
"The Last of the Belles" (Fitzgerald) 6:46-8,
    100, 103, 31:33
"The Last of the Legions" (Benet) 10:143, 154
"The Last of the Spanish Blood" (Garrett)
    30:173, 180
"Last Orders" (Aldiss) 36:19, 24-5
Last Orders, and Other Stories (Aldiss) 36:18-
    20, 23-27
"The Last Pearl" (Andersen) 6:36
"The Last Resort" (Dixon) 16:215-16
"The Last Ride" (Sansom) 21:116
the Last Robin: Lyrics and Sonnets
    See "Eveline"
Last Round (Cortazar)
    See Ultimo round
The Last Summer (Pasternak)
    See Povest
Last Tales (Dinesen) 7:162, 166, 171, 175-76,
    180-81, 191, 198, 200
"The Last Tea" (Parker) 2:274, 285
"The Last Things of Man" (Capek)
    See "Poslední věci člověka"
"The Last Throw" (Pritchett) 14:273
"The Last Trolley Ride" (Calisher) 15:11
The Last Trolley Ride (Calisher) 15:5
"The Last Visit" (Aiken) 9:13, 29-30
"The Last Voyage of the Ghost Ship" (Garcia
    Marquez)
    See "El último viaje del buque fantasma"
"Last Wishes" (Trevor) 21:262
"The Last Word" (Greene) 29:217, 223, 229
"A Last Word" (Sansom) 21:93, 112
The Last Word and Other Stories (Greene)
    29:216-17, 223-30
Last Words (Crane) 7:103

The Last Worthless Evening (Dubus) 15:81,
    85-6, 96
"A Late Encounter with the Enemy"
    (O'Connor) 1:356; 23:192, 205, 237-38
"The Late Henry Conran" (O'Connor) 5:369,
    371, 398
"Late, Late Show" (O'Hara) 15:278-79
Late Prose (Hesse) 9:230
"The Late Sir Glamie" (Warner) 23:384
"A Late Supper" (Jewett) 6:166
"Late 299" (Galsworthy) 22:78, 101
"The Latehomecomer" (Gallant) 5:130, 133,
    136-37
Later the Same Day (Paley) 8:412, 419
"The Latin Scholar" (Hesse) 9:230-32, 235
"Das Läufer" (Lenz) 33:317-18, 329
"A Laugh and a Look" (Alcott) 27:31-2
Laughable Loves (Kundera)
    See Směsné lásky
"The Laughing Man" (Salinger) 2:293, 296,
    299, 313-14, 316
"Laughing Sam" (Saroyan) 21:135
Laughing to Keep from Crying (Hughes) 6:111-
    12, 116, 119, 121-22, 127, 131, 133
"Laughter" (O'Connor) 5:390-91
"Laughter and Grief" (Leskov) 34:127
"The Laughter of Gioia" (Moravia) 26:150-51
"Laura, Immortal" (Saroyan) 21:139, 143
"Lauth" (Norris) 28:204, 208-10, 212
"Lavana" (Narayan) 25:131
"Lavin" (McGahern) 17:302, 322
"Lavinia: An Old Story" (Paley) 8:412
"The Law Breaker" (O'Hara) 15:283
"The Law of Life" (London) 4:287-89, 292
"The Law of the Jungle" (Cheever) 1:99
"Lawley Road" (Narayan) 25:139, 157, 174
Lawley Road, and Other Stories (Narayan)
    25:132-35, 137, 139, 152, 155
"The Lawn Party" (Beattie) 11:6-7
"El lay de Aristotle" (Arreola) 38:6
"Layaways" (Dixon) 16:206, 208
A Lazy Man's Dreams (Moravia)
    See A Lazy Man's Dreams
"Lazy Sons" (Calvino) 3:112
"Léa" (Barbey d'Aurevilly) 17:9-11
"Lead" (Levi) 12:264, 268, 281
"The Leader of the People" (Steinbeck) 11:207-
    10, 212-13, 217-18, 220-21, 233, 236, 242;
    37:330, 333-34, 336, 340, 342, 351, 354,
    356-57, 359 60
"A Leaf From the Sky" (Andersen) 6:6
"Leaf Season" (Updike) 13:401
Leaf Storm (Garcia Marquez)
    See La hojarasca
"The Leaf Sweeper" (Spark) 10:356, 366
"The League of Old Men" (London) 4:265, 287
"Leander's Light" (Page) 23:307, 312
"The Leaning Tower" (Porter) 4:331, 339-40;
    31:124, 126-27, 161
The Leaning Tower, and Other Stories (Porter)
    4:331, 347, 352; 31:124
"The Leap" (Barthelme) 2:45, 55
"The Leap" (Oates) 6:250, 252
"The Leap Frog" (Andersen) 6:7, 10
"A Lear of the Steppes" (Turgenev)
    See "Stepnoy Korol 'Lir"
"Learnin'" (Fisher)
    See "The South Lingers On"
"Learning to Be Dead" (Calvino) 3:113
"Learning to Fall" (Beattie) 11:10, 13, 22-3, 29
"Learning's Little Tribute" (Wilson) 21:322,
    333, 346, 356-57
"The Leather Funnel" (Doyle) 12:65-6, 76
"The Leather Jacket" (Pavese)
    See "La giachetta di cuoio"
"Leaves" (Dazai Osamu)
    See "Ha"
"Leaves" (Updike) 13:375-77, 379
"Leaving School" (Gordimer) 17:166
"Leaving the Yellow House" (Bellow) 14:22-3,
    25-6, 32-3, 35, 37
Das Lebens Überfluss (Tieck) 31:286-87, 291

"Lección de cocina" (Castellanos) **39**:30, 45, 47, 51, 52, 53, 60, 62, 75, 76, 80, 82

"Lechery" (Phillips) **16**:325, 327-28, 337

"Lecturer in Morphology" (James) **16**:251

"Ledi Makbet Mcenskogo uezda" (Leskov) **34**:108, 116, 118, 128, 130-34

"Leela's Friend" (Narayan) **25**:138

"The Lees of Happiness" (Fitzgerald) **6**:45, 58-9

The Left Bank, and Other Stories (Rhys) **21**:33, 39, 44, 48, 58, 61-3, 65, 68-71

"The Left-handed Craftsman" (Leskov)
    See "Levša"

"The Left-Handed Smith and the Steel Flea" (Leskov)
    See "Levša"

"The Lefthander" (Leskov)
    See "Levša"

"Legacy" (Vinge) **24**:328-29, 332, 334-36, 338

"The Legacy" (Woolf) **7**:376-77, 388, 393-95

"The Legend" (Wharton) **6**:429, 437

"Legend of Khalif Hakem" (Nerval)
    See *L'histoire du Calife Hakem*

"The Legend of Lapwater Hall" (Morrison) **40**:365

"The Legend of Madame Krasinska" (Lee) **33**:310

"The Legend of Miss Sasagawara" (Yamamoto) **34**:348-49, 352, 355, 357-58, 360-62, 379

"Legend of Prince Ahmed Al Kemel, or The Pilgrim of Love" (Irving) **2**:267

"The Legend of Saamstadt" (Harte) **8**:250

The Legend of Saint Julien Hospitaller (Flaubert)
    See *La légende de Saint-Julien l'Hospitalier*

The Legend of Saint Julien the Hospitator (Flaubert)
    See *La légende de Saint-Julien l'Hospitalier*

"The Legend of Sleepy Hollow" (Irving) **2**:239, 241, 243-51, 253, 255, 259-60; **37**:265-84

"Legend of the Arabian Astrologer" (Irving) **2**:267

"The Legend of the Moor's Legacy" (Irving) **2**:246, 254, 268

"Legend of the Rose of Alhambra" (Irving) **2**:246, 268

"The Legend of the Scribe" (Agnon) **30**:8-9, 11, 66

"Legend of the Three Beautiful Princesses" (Irving) **2**:267

"La légende de l'éléphant blanc" (Villiers de l'Isle Adam) **14**:397

La légende de Saint-Julien l'Hospitalier (Flaubert) **11**:37-9, 42, 45, 53, 55, 61, 63, 65, 70, 78-9, 81, 84, 89-92

"La légende du Mont-Saint-Michel" (Maupassant) **1**:285, 288

"Légende poldève" (Ayme) **41**:11, 12-13, 17

"Legends" (Adams) **24**:9

"The Legends of Henry Everett" (Auchincloss) **22**:48

"Legends of the Fall" (Harrison) **19**:201-02, 204-06, 209

Legends of the Fall (Harrison) **19**:204-07, 209-11, 213-15

A legião estrangeira (Lispector) **34**:187-91, 231, 235

Das Leiden eines Knaben (Meyer) **30**:188-90, 204, 219-20

"Leil zeva'ah" (Peretz) **26**:223-24

"Lejana" (Cortazar) **7**:52, 56-7, 81

"Lekh-lekh" (Aleichem) **33**:8

"The Lemon" (Thomas) **3**:396, 399, 407-08

"Lemonade" (Lavin) **4**:166

"Lêng shêng" (P'u Sung-ling) **31**:205, 207

"Lenin and the Firewood" (Zoshchenko) **15**:407

"Lenin and the Sentry" (Zoshchenko) **15**:407, 409

"Lenin and the Stovemaker" (Zoshchenko) **15**:407

Lenin in Zurich (Solzhenitsyn) **32**:399-400, 403, 406

"The Lenton Croft Robberies" (Morrison) **40**:349

"Leon, dvoreckij syn" (Leskov) **34**:108, 112, 125

"Un león en el bosque de Palermo" (Bioy Casares) **17**:95

"Leon the Butler's Son" (Leskov)
    See "Leon, dvoreckij syn"

"Leonard" (O'Hara) **15**:278

"The Leonardo" (Nabokov) **11**:117

"Leopard George" (Lessing) **6**:186, 190

"Leopard in a Temple" (Lish) **18**:275

"The Leper's Helix" (Coover) **15**:59

Lessness (Beckett)
    See *Sans*

"The Lesson" (Bambara) **35**:2, 4-6, 32

"The Lesson" (O'Hara) **15**:290

"The Lesson of the Master" (James) **8**:279, 282, 302

"Lest the Traplock Click" (Algren) **33**:113

"Let the Ants Try" (Pohl) **25**:227, 230-32, 234-35

"Let the Old Dead Make Room for the Young Dead" (Kundera) **24**:86, 88-9, 91-2, 101, 103, 107-08, 116-18, 121

"Let Them Call It Jazz" (Rhys) **21**:49-50, 53, 65

"Let There Be Honour" (Boyle) **5**:56; **121**:33

"Let There Be Light" (Clarke) **3**:130

Let Your Mind Alone! and Other More or Less Inspirational Pieces (Thurber) **1**:414, 422-23, 426

"Letanía de la orquídea" (Fuentes) **24**:38, 54-5

"Letovanje na jugu" (Andric) **36**:51-2

"Let's Beat Down the Poor" (Baudelaire)
    See "Assommons les pauvres"

"Let's Get Organized" (Capek) **36**:130

"The Letter" (Agnon)
    See "HaMikhtav"

"A Letter" (Babel) **16**:27-8, 50

"A Letter" (Chekhov) **28**:62-3

"The Letter" (Maugham) **8**:359, 361, 367, 373-74, 382

"The Letter" (Oates) **6**:236

"The Letter" (O'Flaherty) **6**:262, 265, 276, 280

"A Letter from 1920" (Andric)
    See "Pismo iz 1920 godine"

"Letter from His Father" (Gordimer) **17**:169, 171

"A Letter from Home" (Lessing) **6**:199

"A Letter That Never Reached Russia" (Nabokov) **11**:132

"The Letter That Was Never Mailed" (Barnes) **3**:13

"Letter to a Young Lady in Paris" (Cortazar)
    See "Carta a un senorita en París"

"A Letter to Rome" (Moore) **19**:320, 332, 347, 350, 352

"The Letter Writer" (Singer) **3**:360, 384

"The Letters" (Wharton) **6**:424-25, 427, 436

"The Letters" (White) **39**:280-81, 286, 289, 292, 294, 299, 312, 316-17, 323, 325, 327-28, 344

"Letters from the Earth" (Twain) **26**:330

Letters from the Underworld (Dostoevsky)
    See *Zapiski iz podpol'ya*

"Letters from Tula" (Pasternak)
    See "Pis'ma iz Tuly"

"Letters in the Wind" (Dazai Osamu) **41**:239

"Letters to an Ex-wife Concerning a Reunion in Portugal" (Moorhouse) **40**:323

"Letters to the Editore" (Barthelme) **2**:40

"The Letters to Twiggy" (Moorhouse) **40**:290, 303, 322

"Letting Go" (Grau) **15**:161-62

Lettre d'un Ture (Voltaire) **12**:359

"Letty Coe" (Gissing) **37**:63, 79

Der letzte Betrug ist ärger als der erste (Tieck) **31**:274

Die Leute von Seldwyla (Keller) **26**:89, 102, 106, 108, 115, 117, 125, 127

Leutnant Gustl (Schnitzler) **15**:345, 351-53, 375

"The Level Crossing" (Warner) **23**:368

"The Level-Crossing" (Narayan) **25**:141, 154

"Levitation" (Ozick) **15**:307, 318

Levitation: Five Fictions (Ozick) **15**:306, 312, 318-19

"Levša" (Leskov) **34**:112, 116, 123-25

"Liadin and Curithir" (Moore) **19**:311

"Liaisons Dangereuses" (Zoshchenko) **15**:399

Liao-chai chih-i (P'u Sung-ling) **31**:183-88, 193-206, 211-21

Liaozhai zhiui (P'u Sung-ling)
    See *Liao-chai chih-i*

Liaozhai's Records of the Strange (P'u Sung-ling)
    See *Liao-chai chih-i*

"The Liar" (Faulkner) **1**:177

"The Liar" (James) **8**:275, 296, 318, 320-21

"Liars" (O'Faolain) **13**:312

"The Liars" (Pritchett) **14**:285-86, 296

"The Libation" (Jolley) **19**:223, 234, 242

"Libbie Marsh's Three Eras" (Gaskell) **25**:46, 54, 58

"The Liberal Lover" (Cervantes)
    See "El amante liberal"

"The Liberation" (Stafford) **26**:278, 283, 286-87, 312

"The Liberation of Jake Hanley" (Oates) **6**:230

"Libertà" (Verga) **21**:312

"Libertad" (Arreola) **38**:4

"The Libertine" (Bulgakov) **18**:89

"Liberty" (Arreola)
    See "Sinesio de Rodas"

"Liberty" (O'Faolain) **13**:296, 322-23

"Liberty Hall" (Lardner) **32**:117, 135-36, 139-40, 145, 159

"The Library Horror" (Gardner) **7**:226

"The Library of Babel" (Borges)
    See "La biblioteca de Babel"

"The Library of Byzantium" (Ligotti) **16**:278-80

The Library Policeman (King) **17**:282-84

"The Library Window" (Oliphant) **25**:186, 193, 196, 203

Libro que no muerde (Valenzuela) **14**:366, 368

"Lica" (Andric) **36**:63

Lica (Andric) **36**:46, 50, 63

"Licciu papa" (Verga) **21**:292

"The License" (Pirandello)
    See "La patente"

"Lichen" (Munro) **3**:347-49

"El licenciado Vidriera" (Cervantes) **12**:4, 8, 14-15, 17, 36, 38-40

"A Lickpenny Lover" (Henry) **5**:163, 171, 186

"Lída" (Capek) **36**:92, 121-24

"The Lie" (Carver) **8**:34

"Die Liebesgeschichte des Kanzlers Schlick und der schonen Sienerin" (Arnim) **29**:27

Liebeswerben (Tieck) **31**:286

"Lieblingsspeise der Hyänen" (Lenz) **33**:317

"Lien-hsiang" (P'u Sung-ling) **31**:209

"Lien-hua kung-chu" (P'u Sung-ling) **31**:190

"Lieutenant" (O'Hara) **15**:248-49

"The Lieutenant Died Last" (Greene) **29**:223, 225

Lieutenant Gustl (Schnitzler)
    See *Leutnant Gustl*

"Lieutenant Yergunov's Story" (Turgenev)
    See "Istoriya leytenanta Ergunova"

"Life" (Davis) **38**:106-07, 110, 113

"Life" (Machado de Assis) **24**:153

"Life" (O'Flaherty) **6**:260, 269, 271, 277-78, 280

The Life Adventurous and Other Stories (Farrell) **28**:119

"Life along the Passaic River" (Williams) **31**:304, 324, 332, 350, 362

Life along the Passaic River (Williams) **31**:300, 306, 318, 320, 324, 332, 340, 343, 345-46, 351, 357, 362-65
"Life among the Oilfields" (Yamamoto) **34**:351, 359
"The Life and Adventures of Matthew Pavlichenko" (Babel)
   See "The Life Story of Pavlichenko"
"Life and Letters" (Saroyan) **21**:160
"The Life and Work of Professor Roy Millen" (Warren) **4**:387, 389-90, 395, 400
"A Life at Angelo's" (Benet) **10**:144
"Life, Death" (Sansom) **21**:94, 103, 105, 108, 110-11, 118, 126
"Life Everlastin'" (Freeman) **1**:192, 195
"Life Hutch" (Ellison) **14**:112-15, 117
"Life in Its Nakedness" (Pirandello)
   See "La vita nuda"
"Life in the Iron Mills" (Davis) **38**:96, 98-106, 116-17, 123, 125, 127, 129, 131, 133-35, 142-45, 150
"Life Is Better than Death" (Malamud) **15**:173-75, 223
"Life Is No Abyss" (Stafford) **26**:302, 308
"Life Is Not to Be Taken too Seriously" (Rulfo)
   See "La vida no es muy seria en sus cosas"
"Life Isn't a Short Story" (Aiken) **9**:9, 13-14, 32, 40
"Life of a Peasant Woman" (Leskov)
   See "Zhitié odnói báby"
"The Life of Imagination" (Gordimer) **17**:158, 172
"Life of Ma Parker" (Mansfield) **9**:281, 310, 313-14
"A Life of Matter and Death" (Aldiss) **36**:28
"The Life of Nancy" (Jewett) **6**:152
"The Life of Pavlichenko" (Babel)
   See "The Life Story of Pavlichenko"
"The Life of Tadeo Isidoro Cruz" (Borges)
   See "Biografía de Tadeo Isidoro Cruz"
"Life on the Earth" (Gilchrist) **14**:162
"Life Story" (Barth) **10**:43, 47-8, 51-5, 73-4, 77-80, 83, 85-7, 91, 97-8, 100
"The Life Story of Pavlichenko" (Babel) **16**:28, 51-2
"The Life to Come" (Forster) **27**:92, 96, 103, 105, 106, 111, 123, 124
The Life to Come, and Other Stories (Forster) **27**:89-90, 102, 104, 106-09, 115, 117, 124
"Life Vanquished" (Lagerkvist) **12**:187
"Life with Freddie" (Wodehouse) **2**:344
"The Life You Save May Be Your Own" (O'Connor) **1**:343-44, 348-49, 356, 359-60; **23**:184, 210-11, 227, 237
"The Lifeguard" (Beattie) **11**:16
"Lifeguard" (Updike) **13**:348, 350, 398-99; **27**:323
"The Life-Ration" (Ayme) **41**:5
Life's Handicap (Kipling) **5**:274, 291
Life's Little Ironies (Hardy) **2**:205-08, 210, 212, 214-16, 220, 222-23
"The Lift" (Doyle) **12**:78, 80
"The Lift That Went Down into Hell" (Lagerkvist)
   See "Hissen som gick ner i helvete"
"Ligeia" (Poe) **1**:377, 379-80, 385, 393-97, 399; **22**:290, 299, 305-06, 308, 318, 325, 330, 351; **34**:274; **35**:321, 331
"Light" (O'Flaherty) **6**:265, 280
"The Light at Birth" (Berriault) **30**:105
"A Light Breath" (Bunin)
   See "Light Breathing"
"Light Breathing" (Bunin) **5**:81, 93, 104
"Light Can Be Both Wave and Particle" (Gilchrist) **14**:162
Light Can Be Both Wave and Particle (Gilchrist) **14**:161-62
"The Light of the World" (Hemingway) **1**:242, 245; **40**:257
"The Lighter When Needed" (O'Hara) **15**:252
"The Lighthouse" (Bates) **10**:115-17

"Lightning" (Barthelme) **2**:51
"The Lightning-Rod Man" (Melville) **1**:298, 303-04; **17**:361
"Lights" (Chekhov) **41**:190
"The Light-Years" (Calvino) **3**:104
"Den liile Idas Blomster" (Andersen)
   See "Little Ida's Flowers"
"Like a Bad Dream" (Boell) **23**:6
"Like a Lover" (Wescott) **35**:357, 363, 365, 368-72
"Like a Queen" (Anderson) **1**:31, 52-3
"Like All Other Men" (McGahern) **17**:321
"Like Glass" (Beattie) **11**:13
"Like Mother Used to Make" (Jackson) **9**:272; **39**:211, 214, 215, 217, 223, 227
"Like Old Times" (O'Hara) **15**:250
"Like That" (McCullers) **9**:342, 345, 354-55
"Like the Night" (Carpentier) **35**:106
"Like the Sad Heart of Ruth" (Taylor) **10**:376, 410
"Like the Sun" (Narayan) **25**:140
"Like Yesterday" (Sansom) **21**:127
"Liking Men" (Atwood) **2**:20
"Lilacs" (Chopin) **8**:72, 87, 108-10, 112
"Lilacs" (Lavin) **4**:171
"Liliana llorando" (Cortazar) **7**:62-3
"Liliana Weeping" (Cortazar)
   See "Liliana llorando"
"The Lilies" (Chopin) **8**:93
Lilít e altri racconti (Levi) **12**:260, 263, 272-73, 276, 280
"Lilith" (Nin) **10**:317, 319
"Lilith, and Other Stories" (Levi)
   See *Lilít e altri racconti*
"Lilith's" (Campbell) **19**:76
"Det lilla fälttåget" (Lagerkvist) **12**:179, 182, 195
"Lille Claus og Store Claus" (Andersen)
   See "Little Claus and Big Claus"
"Den Lille Havfrue" (Andersen)
   See "The Little Mermaid"
"Lily Bell and Thistledown" (Alcott) **27**:39
"Lily Daw and the Three Ladies" (Welty) **1**:470, 482, 497
"The Lily's Quest" (Hawthorne) **3**:181
"Limbo" (Huxley) **39**:161
"Limbo" (Lavin) **4**:167
Limbo (Huxley) **39**:153-54, 162, 166-67, 171-73
"Limestone" (Stifter)
   See "Kalkstein"
Limestone and Other Stories (Stifter) **28**:283, 285
Limits and Renewals (Kipling) **5**:278, 283
"The Limits of Fantasy" (Campbell) **19**:85
"The Limpet" (du Maurier) **18**:128
"The Limping Lady" (Coppard) **21**:10
"Linda" (Pardo Bazan) **30**:293
Linda Tressel (Trollope) **28**:317, 323
"The Lindy Hop" (Fisher) **25**:10-11, 16-19, 22
"Line and Colour" (Babel)
   See "Colour and Line"
"The Line of Apelles" (Pasternak)
   See "Il tratto di Apelle"
Lines of Life (Mauriac)
   See *Destins*
"The Linesman" (Frame) **29**:98
"Lingering Love" (Chang) **28**:26-27; **31**; 33-34
"A língua do 'p'" (Lispector) **34**:211
"The Linguister" (Murfree) **22**:189
"Linha reta e linha curva" (Machado de Assis) **24**:132, 151
"Linoleum Roses" (Cisneros) **32**:42
"Lion" (Faulkner) **1**:182; **35**:147-48, 161
"Lion" (Garrett) **30**:166
"The Lion at Morning" (Wolfe) **33**:374
"The Lion Hunter" (Garrett) **30**:165, 172
The Lion of Comarre (Clarke) **3**:145, 148
"A Lion on the Freeway" (Gordimer) **17**:164, 191-19
"Lionizing" (Poe) **35**:336
"The Lion's Den" (Pritchett) **14**:271

"Lions, Harts, Leaping Does" (Powers) **4**:371, 377-78, 380, 384
"The Lion's Skin" (Maugham) **8**:379
"The Lippia Lawn" (Stafford) **26**:284, 296
"Lips to Lips" (Nabokov) **11**:117
"Lisa" (Beauvoir) **35**:60, 62-4, 66, 68-71
"Lispet, Lispett & Vaine" (de la Mare) **14**:60, 80, 85
"Lispeth" (Kipling) **5**:262
"La Liste" (Ayme) **41**:16
Listen to the Mockingbird (Perelman) **32**:245
"Listening" (Paley) **8**:420
"Le lit 29" (Maupassant) **1**:274
Literary Lapses (Leacock) **39**:264, 266
"The Literary Life of Laban Goldman" (Malamud) **15**:235
"Literary Talk" (Michaels) **16**:316
"The Litigants" (Singer) **3**:385
"Litter" (Campbell) **19**:75
"A Little Album" (Dazai Osamu)
   See "Chiisai arubamu"
"Little Annie's Dream" (Alcott) **27**:39
"The Little Berliner" (Walser) **20**:336
"Little Bessie" (Twain) **6**:339
"The Little Black Goat" (Pirandello) **22**:252
"The Little Blond Fellow" (Farrell) **28**:92, 118
"The Little Boy and His Dogs" (Harris) **19**:196
"A Little Boy Lost" (Coppard) **21**:17
"Little Briar-Rose" (Grimm and Grimm) **36**:204-05, 208
"Little Bud" (Alcott) **27**:39
"Little Bull" (Cortazar)
   See "Torito"
"Little Caruso" (Saroyan) **21**:167
"A Little Child Shall Lead Them" (Harper) **15**:371
Little Children (Saroyan) **21**:134, 143, 153, 158, 175
"The Little Chill" (Boyle) **16**:148, 155
"Little Claus and Big Claus" (Andersen) **6**:4, 11, 13, 16, 18, 26, 30, 37
"A Little Cloud" (Joyce) **3**:205, 209-10, 226, 231, 234, 245, 248; **26**:46-7
"The Little Comedy" (Schnitzler)
   See "Die Kleine Komödie"
The Little Comedy, and Other Stories (Schnitzler) **15**:371
"A Little Companion" (Wilson) **21**:325, 329, 332, 337, 339, 346-47, 356-57
"Little Compton" (Harris) **19**:124, 131, 174, 178
"The Little Countess" (Capek) **36**:128
"The Little Cousins" (Taylor) **10**:383-84
"Little Curtis" (Parker) **2**:274, 280-81, 283
"Little Darby" (Page) **23**:284, 291, 296-98, 307, 328
"Little Did I Know" (Calisher) **15**:7
The Little Disturbances of Man (Paley) **8**:388, 391, 395, 407, 410, 414
"Little Dog" (Hughes) **6**:109, 121-23, 129-30, 142
"The Little Dog Laughed to See Such Sport" (Saroyan) **21**:162
"Little Dramas of the Curbstone" (Norris) **28**:199, 213-14
The Little Dream (Galsworthy) **22**:60
"Little Fable" (Kafka)
   See "Kleine Fabel"
"The Little Fan" (Pirandello)
   See "Il ventaglino"
"The Little Farm" (Bates) **10**:116
"The Little Fears" (Sansom) **21**:88
"The Little Fir Tree" (Andersen)
   See "The Fir-Tree"
"A Little Free Mulatto" (Chopin) **8**:105
"Little French Mary" (Jewett) **6**:155
"The Little Girl" (Mansfield) **9**:281, 284, 315-16; **38**:204
The Little Girl, and Other Stories (Mansfield) **9**:281, 301
"The Little Girl Continues" (Barnes)
   See "The Grande Malade"

"The Little Girl in Green" (Leacock) **39**:265
"A Little Girl Tells a Story to a Lady"
    (Barnes)
    See "Cassation"
"The Little Girl's Room" (Bowen) **3**:33, 43
"Little Girls Wiser than Men" (Tolstoy) **9**:388
"The Little Governess" (Mansfield) **9**:283
"The Little Gray Goat" (Zoshchenko) **15**:407-09
"Little Gulliver" (Alcott) **27**:41
"The Little Hero" (Dostoevsky) **2**:171, 189-90
Little Herr Friedemann (Mann)
    See *Der kleine Herr Friedemann*
"The Little Hours" (Parker) **2**:274, 281
"The Little House" (Bowles) **3**:76
"The Little House" (Jackson) **9**:270-71
"Little Ida's Flowers" (Andersen) **6**:3-4, 6, 23,
    30
"Little Imber" (Forster) **27**:115, 117-18
"The Little Kingdom" (Tanizaki) **21**:218
"Little Klaus and Big Criticism" (Andersen)
    See "Little Claus and Big Claus"
"Little Lizzy" (Mann) **5**:322-23, 327, 331,
    334-36
"A Little Local Color" (Henry) **5**:191
"The Little Madonna" (Pirandello) **22**:254
The Little Man, and Other Stories
    (Galsworthy) **22**:59-60, 97, 99
"The Little Man in Black" (Irving) **2**:242
"The Little Match Girl" (Andersen) **6**:18-9,
    25-6, 30, 41
"The Little Match Seller" (Andersen)
    See "The Little Match Girl"
"Little Memento" (Collier) **19**:109
"The Little Mermaid" (Andersen) **6**:6-7, 11-13,
    18, 26-30, 36-7, 40-1
"Little Mexican" (Huxley) **39**:156, 161-62
Little Mexican (Huxley) **39**:156, 168, 171, 173,
    175-76
"Little Miracles, Kept Promises" (Cisneros)
    32:16, 23, 25, 35-36, 38
The Little Misery (Mauriac)
    See *La sagouin*
"Little Miss Universe" (Saroyan) **21**:134
"The Little Mistress" (Coppard) **21**:21, 28
"The Little Mother" (O'Connor) **5**:371-72
Little Novels (Schnitzler) **15**:342-43
Little Novels of Sicily (Verga)
    See *Novelle rusticane*
"A Little of Chickamauga" (Bierce) **9**:99
"Little Old Spy" (Hughes) **6**:131
Little People with Little Minds (Aleichem)
    See *Kleyne mentshelekh mit kleyne hasoges*
"The Little Photographer" (du Maurier) **18**:127,
    138
"The Little Pilgrim Goes Up Higher"
    (Oliphant) **25**:185
A Little Pilgrim in the Unseen (Oliphant)
    25:180, 185
"A Little Place off the Edgware Road"
    (Greene) **29**:193, 217
Little Poems in Prose (Baudelaire)
    See *Petits poèmes en prose: Le spleen de
    Paris*
"The Little Pot" (Aleichem)
    See "Dos tepl"
"The Little Prince" (Lavin) **4**:165-67, 183
"A Little Ramble" (Walser) **20**:364
"The Little Red Book" (Pirandello) **22**:252
"Little Red Riding Hood" (Grimm and Grimm)
    36:184, 203, 208
"Little Red-Cap" (Grimm and Grimm)
    See "Little Red Riding Hood"
"The Little Regiment" (Crane) **7**:102, 106
*The Little Regiment, and Other Episodes of the
    American Civil War* (Crane) **7**:102
"A Little Respect" (Selby) **20**:275
"The Little Room" (Sansom) **21**:83, 89, 124
"The Little Sailor" (Sansom) **21**:102
"The Little Sea-Maid" (Andersen)
    See "The Little Mermaid"
"The Little Shoemakers" (Singer) **3**:356, 375,
    378, 383-84

The Little Stepmother (Storm)
    See *Viola tricolor*
"Little Tembi" (Lessing) **6**:191, 197
"Little Things in Bishops' Lives" (Leskov)
    34:127
"The Little Tree" (Walser) **20**:364
"Little Tuk" (Andersen) **6**:3-4
"The Little Virgin" (Hughes) **6**:127
"The Little Voice" (Campbell) **19**:87
"The Little White Dog" (O'Flaherty) **6**:280
"Little Willie" (Gordimer) **17**:154
"A Little Woman" (Kafka) **5**:239; **29**:358
Little Zack (Hoffmann)
    See *Klein Zaches gennant Zinnober*
"Liu Liang-ts'ai" (P'u Sung-ling) **31**:205
"Live? Our Computers Will Do That for Us"
    (Aldiss) **36**:19, 26
"Liver Pâté" (Capek) **36**:130
"Lives" (Andric)
    See *Života*
Lives of Girls and Women (Munro) **3**:323, 325-
    28, 330-33, 335-36, 338-46
"Lives of the Poets" (Atwood) **2**:3-4, 6, 10-11
"Lives of the Poets" (Stafford) **26**:285
"Lives of the Saints" (Berriault) **30**:103
"Living" (Cowan) **28**:80
"The Living" (Lavin) **4**:167
"Living" (Paley) **8**:391, 408-09, 416
"The Living and the Dead" (Saroyan) **21**:146,
    168
"The Living Flame" (Capek) **36**:82
"A Living Relic" (Turgenev) **7**:321-22, 326,
    337
"Livingstone's Companions" (Gordimer)
    17:157, 173
Livingstone's Companions (Gordimer) **17**:157-
    58, 168, 181, 186, 189
"Livvie" (Welty) **1**:467, 469, 471; **27**:338
"Lizards in Jamshyd's Courtyard" (Faulkner)
    1:177
"Lizer's First" (Morrison) **40**:366
"Lizerunt" (Morrison) **40**:328, 330, 335-36,
    338, 343, 355, 365-67, 370, 378
"Lizzie Leigh" (Gaskell) **25**:46, 54, 59, 65, 70-2
"Ljubav u kasabi" (Andric) **36**:34-5, 48
"Ljubka the Cossack" (Babel) **16**:48
"Ljuvabi" (Andric) **36**:67-8
"El llano en llamas" (Rulfo) **25**:250, 262, 264-
    65, 267-68
El llano en llamas, y otros cuentos (Rulfo)
    25:244, 247-49, 251, 253, 256, 265, 270-73,
    277-80
"Lo" (Faulkner) **35**:159
"The Loaded Dog" (Lawson) **18**:201, 206, 217,
    242, 244-45, 248, 262-63
"The Loan" (Malamud) **15**:169, 212, 216, 220,
    234
"Local Customs" (Thomas) **20**:320-21
"Lo-ch'a hai-shih" (P'u Sung-ling) **31**:200
"Loco de amor" (Arreola) **38**:6
"Locomotive 38, the Ojibway" (Saroyan)
    21:169
"The Locum Tenens" (Warner) **23**:372
"The Lodger in Maze Pond" (Gissing) **37**:52,
    65
"A Lodging for the Night: A Story of François
    Villon" (Stevenson) **11**:269, 279, 284-86
"Lofty" (Beattie) **11**:29
"Lofty" (O'Connor) **5**:382
"Logarithms" (Singer) **3**:388
"Logging and Pimping and 'Your Pal, Jim'"
    (Maclean) **13**:260, 270-71
"Lohengrin, fils de Parsifal" (Laforgue) **20**:86,
    89, 91-2, 101, 105, 114-6
"Lohengrin, Son of Parsifal" (Laforgue)
    See "Lohengrin, fils de Parsifal"
"Lohengrin's Tod" (Boell) **23**:5
"Lois the Witch" (Gaskell) **25**:37-8, 47, 55-7,
    60, 72-3
"Lokis" (Merimee) **7**:276-7, 283, 285-6, 296-9
"London Hospital" (Morrison) **40**:354, 365
"The London Times of 1904" (Twain) **26**:331

"The Lone Charge of Francis B. Perkins"
    (Crane) **7**:108
"Lone Wolf's Old Guard" (Garland) **18**:147
"The Loneliest Man in the U.S. Army" (Boyle)
    5:55
"Loneliness" (Anderson) **1**:30, 44
"Loneliness" (Schulz) **13**:330
"The Lonely Day" (Caldwell) **19**:20
"The Lonely One" (Grau) **15**:155
"A Lonely Ride" (Harte) **8**:210
"Lonely Rock" (O'Connor) **5**:371-72
"The Lonely Track" (Lawson) **18**:225
"The Loner" (Lu Hsun)
    See "Guduzhe"
"Lonesome Road" (Berriault) **30**:97
"The Long Affair" (Onetti)
    See "La larga historia"
"Long After Bedtime" (Leacock) **39**:240
Long after Midnight (Bradbury) **29**:78, 81-2
"Long Black Song" (Wright) **2**:360-63, 365,
    367, 369, 371, 374, 376, 379-81, 387
"The Long Day" (Gordon) **15**:104, 106, 119,
    139-40
"The Long Distance Runner" (Paley) **8**:397-98,
    408-09, 415
"The Long Dress" (Pirandello)
    See "La veste lunga"
"The Long Exile" (Tolstoy)
    See "God Sees the Truth but Waits"
"A Long Fourth" (Taylor) **10**:374-77, 379, 387-
    88, 397-400, 402
A Long Fourth, and Other Stories (Taylor)
    10:375-76, 381, 384-86, 395
"Long, Long Ago" (Bunin) **5**:82
The Long March (Styron) **25**:283, 285-88, 291-
    94, 296, 300, 305-6, 308-12, 316, 319-21,
    323, 325
"The Long Night" (Bambara) **35**:27-8, 40-1
"Long Night" (Price) **22**:384
"A Long Night" (Warner) **23**:375
"The Long Rain" (Bradbury) **29**:80
"The Long Road to Ummera" (O'Connor)
    5:362-65, 378, 380, 383, 388-89, 397-98
"The Long Run" (Wharton) **6**:418, 424-25, 436
"The Long Sheet" (Sansom) **21**:82-3, 88, 92,
    100
The Long Valley (Steinbeck) **11**:207-08, 210,
    221, 225-27, 229-34, 236, 239-40, 244-45,
    249
"The Long Walk to Forever" (Vonnegut) **8**:424
"A Long-ago Affair" (Galsworthy) **22**:101
"The Longest Day of the Year" (Beattie) **11**:30,
    34
"The Longest Science Fiction Story Ever Told"
    (Clarke) **3**:133
"Longing for Mother" (Tanizaki)
    See "Haha no kouru ki"
"Look at All Those Roses" (Bowen) **3**:55; **28**:4
Look at All Those Roses (Bowen) **3**:33, 39, 41,
    28
"Look How the Fish Live" (Powers) **4**:368,
    373-74, 376-77
Look How the Fish Live (Powers) **4**:375-76,
    380-82
Look Who's Talking! (Perelman) **32**:202, 205
Looking Backwards (Colette) **10**:293
"Looking 'Em Over" (Farrell) **28**:90, 92, 119,
    121
"Looking for Mr. Green" (Bellow) **14**:3, 22-3,
    25, 27-8, 30-2
"The Looking Glass" (de la Mare) **14**:66, 84,
    87, 90
"The Looking Glass" (Machado de Assis)
    See "O espelho"
"Looking Out" (Campbell) **19**:75
"A Looking-Glass for Saint Luke" (Coppard)
    21:8
"The Loons" (Laurence) **7**:255, 259, 270
"Loophole" (Clarke) **3**:125, 148-50
"Loopy Ears" (Bunin)
    See "Petlistye ushi"

"Loose Ends" (Mukherjee) **38**:252-53, 261-62, 266, 273, 283, 285

"Lord Arthur Savile's Crime: A Study of Duty" (Wilde) **11**:362, 366-69, 371, 373, 375-77, 394, 399-402

Lord Arthur Savile's Crime, and Other Stories (Wilde) **11**:407

"Lord Curzon's Benefit Day" (Bulgakov) **18**:90, 110

"Lord Douglas" (Lawson) **18**:243

"Lord Emsworth Acts for the Best" (Wodehouse) **2**:346, 348

"Lord Emsworth and the Girl Friend" (Wodehouse) **2**:346-49

"The Lord Knows" (Greene) **29**:222

Lord Love Us (Sansom) **21**:84, 102, 111, 118, 125

"Lord Mountdrago" (Maugham) **8**:369, 380

"The Lord of the Dynamos" (Wells) **6**:361, 365-67, 375-76, 381-82, 396-97

"The Lord's Day" (Powers) **4**:380-81

"Lorelei of the Roads" (Sansom) **21**:94, 102

"The Los Amigos Fiasco" (Doyle) **12**:81

"De los reyes futuros" (Bioy Casares) **17**:54

"Lose With a Smile" (Lardner) **32**:120

Lose with a Smile (Lardner) **32**:116-17, 129

"A Losing Game" (Powers) **4**:370

"Loss" (Oates) **6**:236

"The Loss of a Friend by Cablegram" (Moorhouse) **40**:306

"Loss of Breath" (Poe) **1**:407; **22**:334

"The Lost" (Boyle) **5**:57, 74-6

"The Lost" (Campbell) **19**:62-3, 74, 83

"The Lost" (Dazai Osamu) **41**:240, 245

"The Lost Art of Twilight" (Ligotti) **16**:269, 271, 273

"Lost Ball" (Bates) **10**:123

"The Lost Blend" (Henry) **5**:163

"The Lost Boy" (Wolfe) **33**:340, 342-45, 355-57, 360-64, 372-75, 386, 399, 401

"Lost Cat" (Adams) **24**:18

"Lost City of Mars" (Bradbury) **29**:81

"A Lost Dog" (Galsworthy) **22**:98

"Lost Face" (London) **4**:265, 289

Lost Face (London) **4**:265, 283, 288

"A Lost Halo" (Baudelaire)
   See "Perte d'auréole"

"Lost Hearts" (James) **16**:230, 232-33, 236-39, 241-42, 245, 250-51, 255-56

The Lost Honor of Katharina Blum: How Violence Develops and Where It Can Lead (Boell)
   See *Die verlorene Ehre der Katharina Blum: oder, Wie Gewalt entstehen und wohin sie führen kann*

"Lost in the Funhouse" (Barth) **10**:35, 37, 39, 41-3, 46-8, 52-4, 57, 61, 63, 65, 67, 80, 84-5, 88-9, 95, 97-100

Lost in the Funhouse: Fiction for Print, Tape, Live Voice (Barth) **10**:38-43, 45, 48-50, 52-60, 63-5, 67, 73-85, 87-91, 94-5, 97-9, 100-03

"The Lost Leg" (Capek) **36**:128

"The Lost Legion" (Kipling) **5**:272-75, 285

"The Lost Letter" (Gogol)
   See "Propavšaja gramotax"

"The Lost Love Blues" (Fisher) **25**:17-19

"A Lost Lover" (Jewett) **6**:156, 159, 166

"Lost Luggage" (Adams) **24**:13, 15, 19, 21, 23

"A Lost Masterpiece" (Moore) **19**:341

"The Lost Novel" (Anderson) **1**:31

"Lost on Dress Parade" (Henry) **5**:158, 189

The Lost Ones (Beckett)
   See *Le dépeupleur*

"The Lost Phoebe" (Dreiser) **30**:107, 112, 114-16, 122, 145

"The Lost Reflection" (Hoffmann)
   See "Das Verlorene Spiegelbild"

The Lost Smile (Keller)
   See *The Lost Smile*

Lost Stories from America (Gissing)
   See *Lost Stories from America*

"The Lost Track" (de la Mare) **14**:80, 84

"The Lost Turkey" (Jewett) **6**:156

"The Lost Way" (Capek) **36**:89-90, 122

"A Lot You Got to Holler" (Algren) **33**:106

"La lotería en Babilonia" (Borges) **4**:5-7, 11-12, 14; **41**:61-62, 137, 147, 166

"Una lotta" (Svevo) **25**:357, 362

"Lotta Schmidt" (Trollope) **28**:319, 323

Lotta Schmidt and Other Stories (Trollope) **28**:319, 322-23, 332, 339, 342, 350

"The Lottery" (Jackson) **9**:249-52, 254-55, 258, 261, 264-70; **39**:182-235

"The Lottery in Babylon" (Borges)
   See "La lotería en Babilonia"

"The Lottery in Babylon" (Borges)
   See "La lotería en Babilonia"

"The Lottery of Babylon" (Borges)
   See "La lotería en Babilonia"

The Lottery; or, The Adventures of James Harris (Jackson) **9**:249; **39**:209, 210, 212, 213, 214, 216, 217, 219, 220, 222, 223, 224, 225, 226, 227, 228, 230, 231

"The Lottery Ticket" (Greene) **29**:223, 224

"The Lotus" (Rhys) **21**:52, 64, 69

"The Lotus-Eater" (Maugham) **8**:379

"Lou and Liz" (Gissing) **37**:63, 80

"Lou, the Prophet" (Cather) **2**:96, 100, 105

"The Loudest Voice" (Paley) **8**:388

"Louisa" (Freeman) **1**:196

"Louisa, Please Come Home" (Jackson) **9**:267, 272

"Louise" (Saki) **12**:322

"Loulou, or, The Domestic Life of the Language" (Atwood) **2**:18, 21, 23

"Le Loup" (Ayme) **41**:15

"Love" (Bowen) **3**:33, 41

"Love" (Cowan) **28**:75

"Love" (Dreiser)
   See *Chains*

"Love" (Paley) **8**:419

"Love" (Zoshchenko) **15**:399

Love (Saroyan) **21**:156

"Love seventy-seven" (Cortazar) **7**:93

"Love among the Haystacks" (Lawrence) **4**:197

"Love Among the Ruins" (Waugh) **41**:311

Love Among the Ruins (Waugh) **41**:313-17

"Love and Death" (Lagerkvist)
   See "Kärleken och döden"

"Love and Death" (Oates) **6**:225, 254

"Love and Lethe" (Beckett) **16**:68, 72, 93

Love and Napalm: Export U.S.A. (Ballard)
   See *The Atrocity Exhibition*

"Love and Russian Literature" (Maugham) **8**:378

Love and Will (Dixon) **16**:211, 216-19

"Love at First Sight" (Sansom) **21**:115

"Love Day" (Styron) **25**:312-15, 317-18

"Love, Death, Sacrifice, and So Forth" (Saroyan) **21**:132

"Love. Friendship." (Oates) **6**:227-28

Love Goes Visiting (Jarry)
   See *L'amour en visites*

"Love Has Its Own Action" (Dixon) **16**:204, 210, 214

Love, Here Is My Hat (Saroyan) **21**:153, 155, 158, 161, 167

"Love in a Wych Elm" (Bates) **10**:133

"Love in the Fallen City" (Chang) **28**:25; 27; 31-32; 35-36

"Love in the Kasaba" (Andric)
   See "Ljubav u kasabi"

"Love in the Slump" (Waugh) **41**:323, 328-29

"Love in the Spring" (Stuart) **31**:227-28, 244, 249

"Love is for Lovers" (Lavin) **4**:166

"Love Life" (Mason) **4**:9

Love Life (Mason) **4**:28

"Love Love Love Alone" (Naipaul) **38**:341

"A Love Match" (Warner) **23**:375

"The Love Nest" (Lardner) **32**:116, 124-25, 127, 133-34, 137-38, 140, 147, 149, 152-56, 160, 162, 168, 182-83, 195

The Love Nest, and Other Stories (Lardner) **32**:119, 131-33, 139, 149, 151, 190

The Love Object (O'Brien) **10**:330, 341

"The Love of Elsie Barton: A Chronicle" (Warren) **4**:389-91, 394

"Love of Life" (London) **4**:253, 265, 272-73, 278, 288-89, 291-92

Love of Life, and Other Stories (London) **4**:252, 264-65, 282, 285, 288-89

"Love on the Bon-Dieu" (Chopin) **8**:89

"The Love Song of the Conquering Lovers" (Turgenev)
   See "Pesn' torzhestruyushchey lyubvi"

"The Love Song--Lída II" (Capek) **36**:92, 121-22

"A Love Story" (Bowen) **3**:41, 54

"A Love Story" (Lawson) **18**:239

"The Love Story of Chancellor Schlick and the Beautiful Sienese" (Arnim)
   See "Die Liebesgeschichte des Kanzlers Schlick und der schonen Sienerin"

"A Love Story of Our Time" (Farrell) **28**:125

"Love Suicides" (Kawabata) **17**:258

Love without Love (Pirandello)
   See *Amori senza amore*

The Loved and the Unloved (Mauriac)
   See *Galigaï*

"Lovelessness" (Pasternak)
   See "Bezlyub'e"

"The Lovely April" (Grau) **15**:153

"The Lovely Lady" (Lawrence) **4**:220

The Lovely Lady, and Other Stories (Lawrence) **4**:230, 238

"The Lovely Leave" (Parker) **2**:277, 280, 285 86

"The Lovely Myfwanwy" (de la Mare) **14**:69

"The Lovely Troubled Daughters of Our Old Crowd" (Updike) **13**:403

"Loveman's Comeback" (Campbell) **19**:88

"Love-o'-Women" (Kipling) **5**:266, 276, 279

"The Love-Philtre of Ikey Schoenstein" (Henry) **5**:182

"The Lover" (Bowen) **3**:40

"The Lover" (Walker) **5**:413-14

The Lover (Duras)
   See *L'amant*

"The Lovers" (Andersen) **6**:7

"Lovers" (O'Flaherty) **6**:282

"Lovers of the Lake" (O'Faolain) **13**:288, 295, 297

"Lovers of Their Time" (Trevor) **21**:258, 262

Lovers of Their Time, and Other Stories (Trevor) **21**:262

"Loves" (Andric)
   See "Ljuvabi"

"The Loves of Lady Purple" (Carter) **13**:3-5

"Love's Young Dream" (O'Faolain) **13**:315, 319-20

"Loving Memory" (Lavin) **4**:166, 168

"The Lowboy" (Cheever) **1**:112; **38**:55

"Low-Flying Aircraft" (Ballard) **1**:73-4, 83

Low-Flying Aircraft, and Other Stories (Ballard) **1**:71-3

"Low-Lands" (Pynchon) **14**:308, 310, 312, 321-22, 324, 329, 334-35, 340-42, 344, 347-48

"Lu p'an" (P'u Sung-ling) **31**:190

"Luani of the Jungle" (Hughes) **6**:127

"Luc and His Father" (Gallant) **5**:147

Luca (Moravia)
   See *Luca*

"Lucas, His Modesty" (Cortazar)
   See "Lucas, sus pudores"

"Lucas, His Partisan Arguments" (Cortazar)
   See "Lucas, sus discusiones partidarias"

"Lucas, sus discusiones partidarias" (Cortazar) **7**:94

"Lucas, sus pudores" (Cortazar) **7**:94

"Lucerne" (Tolstoy) **9**:376, 389-91, 393; **30**:332

"The Luceys" (O'Connor) **5**:371, 378, 381-83, 389

"An Luchóg" (O'Flaherty) **6**:287

"Lucilla" (Pirandello) **22**:286

Title Index

"The Luck of Roaring Camp" (Harte) **8**:208, 210, 219, 225-26, 228, 231-32, 237-39, 241, 243-44, 245, 249, 251-52, 255, 257

The Luck of Roaring Camp, and Other Sketches (Harte) **8**:219, 229, 236, 238, 255-56

"The Luckiest Man in Kodny" (Aleichem) **33**:62

"The Lucksmith" (Benet) **10**:148

"The Lucky Fist" (Benet) **10**:147-48

"The Lucky Pair" (Lavin) **4**:173, 183

"Lucretia Burns" (Garland) **18**:173, 182

"Lucy" (de la Mare) **14**:69, 87

"Lucy Friend" (Cisneros) **32**:8

"Lucy Grange" (Lessing) **6**:191

Ludwig Tieck's Schriften (Tieck) **31**:282-84

"The Luftbad" (Mansfield) **9**:307

"Lui?" (Maupassant) **1**:265-66, 281

"Luís Soares" (Machado de Assis) **24**:131

"Lukas, Sanftmütiger Knecht" (Lenz) **33**:317-18, 331

"The Lull" (Saki) **12**:295-96, 299, 306, 324

"Lullaby" (Gorky) **28**:137

"Lullaby" (Silko) **37**:294, 303, 307

"Lulu" (Hesse) **9**:243

Lulu's Library (Alcott) **27**:44

"The Lumber Room" (Saki) **12**:293, 297, 308-09, 320

"Il lume dell'altra casa" (Pirandello) **22**:231, 233

"Lumìe di Sicilia" (Pirandello) **22**:269

"The Luminous Depths" (Capek) **36**:87-8

Luminous Depths (Capek)
    See *Zářivé hlubiny*

"A Lump of Sugar" (Walser) **20**:335-56

"Luna de miel" (Arreola) **38**:11, 25

"Luna e G N A C" (Calvino) **3**:97

Lunar Caustic (Lowry) **31**:41, 43-4, 50, 66-70, 73, 83, 86-7

"Lunch" (Bowen) **3**:40

"La lune de pluie" (Colette) **10**:281

"Lung-fei hsiang kung" (P'u Sung-ling) **31**:191

"Luosha haishi" (P'u Sung-ling) **31**:213

"La Lupa" (Verga) **21**:283-84, 286, 301, 305

"The Lurking Fear" (Lovecraft) **3**:258, 260, 281

"Luther on Sweet Auburn" (Bambara) **35**:42

"Luvina" (Rulfo) **25**:247, 249-50, 255-56, 258, 262, 265, 267, 277-79

"Luxury" (Coppard) **21**:11-12, 19, 28

"The Lynching of Jube Benson" (Dunbar) **8**:121-22, 126, 128-30, 132, 136

"The Lynching of Nigger Jeff" (Dreiser)
    See "Nigger Jeff"

"Lynx Hunting" (Crane) **7**:104

"The Lyrical Thief" (Capek)
    See "O lyrickém zloději"

"Ma Chieh-fu" (P'u Sung-ling) **31**:205, 207

"Ma femme" (Maupassant) **1**:280

"Ma'ame Pélagie" (Chopin) **8**:87, 105

"Ma'ase ha'Ez" (Agnon) **30**:4, 39

"Maata" (Mansfield) **23**:153

"Mac in Love" (Dixon) **16**:203, 209-10, 213

"Macacos" (Lispector) **34**:189

"Macario" (Rulfo) **25**:245, 249, 263-65, 267, 273, 275-76, 279

"The Macbeth Murder Mystery" (Thurber) **1**:426

"La machine à gloire" (Villiers de l'Isle Adam) **14**:377, 379, 383, 396

"The Machine Stops" (Forster) **27**:68-9, 72, 74-5, 81, 83, 87, 101, 103-04, 114-15, 122-23

"The Machine-Gun Corps in Action" (O'Connor) **5**:369, 371, 390-91

"The Machineries of Joy" (Bradbury) **29**:82

The Machineries of Joy (Bradbury) **29**:48, 58-60, 82

"Mackintosh" (Maugham) **8**:359, 370, 372

"Mackintosh Willy" (Campbell) **19**:75, 88

"The Mad Convalescent at Fort Rattonneau" (Arnim)
    See "Der Tolle Invalide auf dem Fort Ratonneau"

"The Mad Idler" (Peretz)
    See "The Mad Idler"

"The Mad Laundress of Ding Dong Daddyland" (Algren) **33**:96, 98

"The Mad Lomasneys" (O'Connor) **5**:363, 370-71, 378, 383, 389

"Mad Night of Atonement" (Ligotti) **16**:276-77, 288, 292, 295, 297

"The Mad Talmudist" (Peretz)
    See "The Mad Talmudist"

"Madam Cluck, and Her Family" (Alcott) **27**:42

"Madame Celestine's Divorce" (Chopin) **8**:72-3, 84, 91

"Madame de Mauves" (James) **32**:108

"Madame Délicieuse" (Cable) **4**:48, 56, 67, 69-71

Madame Delphine (Cable) **4**:48, 51-2, 56-7, 67, 75-8

"Madame Dodin" (Duras) **40**:3, 8-9, 65

"Madame Zilensky and the King of Finland" (McCullers) **9**:322, 330, 332, 347, 357-58; **24**:232

"Made in Goatswood" (Campbell) **19**:63, 74

"Made in Heaven" (Updike) **13**:404

"The Madeline Wherry Case" (O'Hara) **15**:262, 283, 287-88, 290

"Mademoiselle Bistouri" (Baudelaire) **18**:15-16, 19, 36, 38, 42

Mademoiselle Coeur-Briée (West)
    See *Miss Lonelyhearts*

"Mademoiselle O" (Nabokov) **11**:108, 113, 128

"Mademoisselle Fifi" (Maupassant) **1**:256, 259, 274, 287

"A Madman's Diary" (Gogol)
    See "Diary of a Madman"

"The Madness of Ortheris" (Kipling) **5**:260

"A Madonna of the Trenches" (Kipling) **5**:271

"Le madre" (Svevo) **25**:328, 335-36, 352-53, 357-58

"Una Madre" (Svevo) **25**:352

"Madre gallega" (Pardo Bazan) **30**:272

"Maelstrom II" (Clarke) **3**:129, 147

"The Maenads" (Cortazar) **7**:69-70

"The Magazine" (Singer) **3**:374

"Maggie Meriwether's Rich Experience" (Stafford) **26**:312

"Maggie of the Green Bottles" (Bambara) **35**:7-8, 23, 33

"Magic" (Greene) **29**:219-20

"Magic" (Porter) **4**:327-30, 339-40, 360

"The Magic Barrel" (Malamud) **15**:168, 170, 172, 176, 186, 188, 192, 195-96, 211, 213, 217, 221, 227-34, 239, 241-43

"Magic Fishbone" (Dickens) **17**:124

The Magic of Shirley Jackson (Jackson) **9**:252

"The Magic Poker" (Coover) **15**:31, 38, 41-2, 48, 50, 53-6

The Magic Striptease (Garrett) **30**:167-69

"The Magic Table, the Gold Donkey, and the Club in the Sack" (Grimm and Grimm) **36**:206, 229-30

"The Magician" (Peretz)
    See "The Magician"

"The Magician" (Singer) **3**:375

Magie noire (Morand) **22**:169, 172, 174-75, 182

"Magna Mater" (Oates) **6**:232

"Magna . . . Reading" (Dixon) **16**:217

"Magna Takes the Calls" (Dixon) **16**:207

"Magnetism" (Fitzgerald) **6**:61

"Magnolia Flower" (Hurston) **4**:136

"Mags" (Trevor) **21**:263

"The Mahatma's Little Joke" (London) **4**:294

"The Maid of Saint Phillippe" (Chopin) **8**:71

"The Maiden" (Stafford) **26**:274, 276, 285

"The Maiden and Death" (Gorky) **28**:144

"Maiden in a Tower" (Stegner) **27**:197, 207, 220

"Maiden, Maiden" (Boyle) **5**:56, 65

"The Maid's Shoes" (Malamud) **15**:173, 175

"Maidstone Comfort" (Gilman) **13**:144

"La main" (Maupassant) **1**:281

"The Main Death" (Hammett) **17**:213

"La main d'ecorché" (Maupassant) **1**:281

"Main Road" (Pritchett) **14**:269, 286, 298

"Main Street" (Hawthorne) **39**:120-22

Main-Travelled Roads (Garland) **18**:142-46, 148, 150, 155-56, 158-75, 177, 180-81, 183, 186, 191-94

"Mais dois bêbedos" (Lispector) **34**:230, 233, 236

La maison de Claudine (Colette) **10**:278-79

"La maison du bonheur" (Villiers de l'Isle Adam) **14**:384, 387, 390, 396

"La maison du chat-qui-pelote" (Balzac) **5**:21-2, 29, 31-3

La maison nucingen (Balzac) **5**:31

"La maison Tellier" (Maupassant) **1**:256-57, 259-60, 263, 266, 271-72, 274, 276, 282-83, 287

"The Maja" (Nin) **10**:326

"Majesty" (Fitzgerald) **6**:47

"The Majesty of the Law" (O'Connor) **5**:364-66, 369, 371, 377, 381, 389, 395, 398

"Major Bruce and Mrs. Conway" (Warner) **23**:369

"The Major of Hussars" (Bates) **10**:117

Die Majoratsherren (Arnim) **29**:5, 11-15

"Majskaja noč, ili Vtoplennica" (Gogol) **4**:118-19; **29**:132, 171

"Majutah" (Fisher)
    See "The South Lingers On"

"Makar Chudra" (Gorky) **28**:134, 136, 144, 148, 152-53, 178, 183-84, 186-88

Make Light of It (Williams) **31**:326, 333, 347-48

The Maker (Borges)
    See *El hacedor*

The Maker of His Fortune (Keller)
    See *The Maker of His Fortune*

"The Make-Up Artist" (Leskov)
    See "Tupejnyi xudožnik"

"Making a Change" (Gilman) **13**:126, 141-42

"Making a Night of It" (Dickens) **17**:116, 122

"Making Arrangements" (Bowen) **3**:54

"Making Changes" (Michaels) **16**:301-02, 311-12

"Making Love" (Pohl) **25**:229

"The Making of a New Yorker" (Henry) **5**:194

"The Making of a Statesman" (Harris) **19**:184

The Making of a Statesman (Harris) **19**:183

The Making of Ashenden (Elkin) **12**:93, 95, 106-07, 110, 114-16; **91**:97

"Making Poison" (Atwood) **2**:17

"Making Westing" (London) **4**:263

Le mal (Mauriac) **24**:160-62, 171, 174, 180, 206-08

"Mal di mestiere" (Pavese) **19**:384

Mal vu mal dit (Beckett) **16**:129-30, 132, 134-37

"Malachi" (Lawson) **18**:200

"Malachi's Cove" (Trollope) **28**:316-17, 319, 322, 324, 334, 349, 357

"Malan'ja--golova baran'ja" (Leskov) **34**:108

"Malaria" (Verga) **21**:292, 298, 300

"Maldito amor" (Ferre) **36**:159

Eine Malerarbeit (Storm) **27**:282-83, 305, 307, 314

Malgudi Days (Narayan) **25**:137-38, 152, 157, 159, 165, 170

"The Malice of Inanimate Objects" (James) **16**:251

"The Maltese Cat" (Kipling) **5**:279

"Malva" (Gorky) **28**:136, 148, 178, 184-85, 190

"Mam Lyddy's Recognition" (Page) **23**:311

Mama Grande's Funeral (Garcia Marquez)
    See *Los funerales de la Mamá Grande*

"Mama's Little Girl" (Caldwell) **19**:6

"Mame" (Suckow) **18**:389, 396, 398, 405, 407

"Mamma" (Lardner) **32**:129

"Mamma Mia" (Sansom) **21**:117

"Mamma's Plot" (Alcott) 27:22
"Mammon and the Archer" (Henry) 5:195
"Mammy Peggy's Pride" (Dunbar) 8:121, 128, 131
"Mamouche" (Chopin) 8:93
"The Man" (Bradbury) 29:46, 48, 53, 81
"The Man" (Rulfo)
  See "El hombre"
"A Man Alone at Lunch" (Aiken) 9:14
"A Man and a Woman" (Caldwell) 19:13, 17-18, 33
"Man and Daughter in the Cold" (Updike) 13:361
"A Man and His Dog" (Mann) 5:312
"The Man and the Darwinian Theory" (Svevo)
  See "L'uomo e la teoria darwiniana"
"The Man and the Snake" (Bierce) 9:53, 88
"A Man and Two Women" (Lessing) 6:198, 200-01, 203, 208
"A Man by the Name of Ziegler" (Hesse) 9:230, 235
"The Man Child" (Baldwin) 10:4, 7-8, 10, 17
"The Man from Archangel" (Doyle) 12:85-8
"A Man from Fort Necessity" (Benet) 10:151, 154
"A Man from Glasgow" (Maugham) 8:380
"The Man from Kilsheelan" (Coppard) 21:3, 17-18
"The Man from Mars" (Atwood) 2:3, 5-7, 10-11, 14, 21
"The Man Higher Up" (Henry) 5:166, 193
"The Man in a Case" (Chekhov)
  See "Čelovek v futljare"
"The Man in a Shell" (Chekhov)
  See "Čelovek v futljare"
"The Man in the Brooks Brothers Shirt" (McCarthy) 24:213, 215, 218
"The Man in the Brown Coat" (Anderson) 1:21, 27
"Man in the Drawer" (Malamud) 15:189, 191, 216
"The Man in the Passage" (Chesterton) 1:136
"The Man in the Rorschach Shirt" (Bradbury) 29:47
"The Man in the Underpass" (Campbell) 19:88
"A Man is Born" (Gorky)
  See "The Birth of a Man"
"Man Not Overboard" (Lardner) 32:135, 138, 140-41
"The Man of Adamant" (Hawthorne) 3:171, 185; 39:114
"Man of All Work" (Wright) 2:388
"A Man of Devon" (Galsworthy) 22:58, 74-5, 82, 89-90, 93, 97
A Man of Devon (Galsworthy) 22:57-8, 88-9, 91-4, 97, 99, 102
"Man of Letters" (Dixon) 16:210, 215
"The Man of No Account" (Harte) 8:236
"The Man of the Crowd" (Poe) 1:379; 34:243, 246-7
"The Man of the Family" (Bowen) 3:45
"The Man of the Family" (Suckow) 18:395, 410
"The Man of the Forests" (Hesse) 9:243
"The Man of the House" (O'Connor) 5:371
"A Man of the World" (Hemingway) 40:191-96
"The Man of the World" (O'Connor) 5:386
"Man on an Island of History" (Farrell) 28:126
"Man on the Pink Corner" (Borges)
  See "El Hombre de la esquina rosada"
"The Man on the Threshold" (Borges)
  See "El hombre en el umbral"
"The Man on the Tractor" (O'Hara) 15:259, 283
"Man Orchid" (Williams) 31:356
"The Man That Corrupted Hadleyburg" (Twain) 6:293-95, 301-03, 305-09, 325, 334-35, 345; 26:351; 34:340
"The Man That Stopped" (O'Connor) 5:371
"The Man That Was Used Up" (Poe) 1:407-08; 22:330; 34:245; 35:336
"A Man to Be Trusted" (O'Hara) 15:286

"The Man to Send Rainclouds" (Silko) 37:309
"The Man Upstairs" (Bradbury) 29:67, 88
The Man Upstairs, and Other Stories (Wodehouse) 2:347
"The Man Who Appeared" (Lispector)
  See "O homem que apareceu"
"The Man Who Ate the World" (Pohl) 25:223, 232
"The Man Who Became a Woman" (Anderson) 1:30, 37, 48-50
"The Man Who Could Not Shake Hands" (King) 17:266
"The Man Who Could Work Miracles: A Pantoum in Prose" (Wells) 6:367, 375, 383, 389, 404-06
"The Man Who Couldn't Sleep" (Capek)
  See "Muž, který nemohl spát"
"The Man Who Died" (Lawson) 18:215
The Man Who Died (Lawrence) 4:212, 220-21, 226, 238
"The Man Who Gave Up His Name" (Harrison) 19:201-06, 209
"The Man Who Got Fat" (Saroyan) 21:135
"The Man Who Had to Talk to Somebody" (O'Hara) 15:265-66
"The Man Who Invented Sin" (O'Faolain) 13:293, 301, 306, 314, 318
"The Man Who Kept His Form" (Galsworthy) 22:67, 79, 101
"The Man Who Kept His Money in a Box" (Trollope) 28:318, 330-32, 335, 347
"The Man Who Kicked Cancer's Ass" (Gilchrist) 14:163
"The Man Who Killed a Shadow" (Wright) 2:366, 385-86
The Man Who Knew Too Much (Chesterton) 1:121-22, 125-26
"The Man Who Liked Dickens" (Waugh) 41:328-29, 334, 340
"The Man Who Liked Dogs" (Chandler) 23:65, 67, 72, 82, 86, 106-07, 109
"The Man Who Lived Underground" (Wright) 2:364, 366, 370, 373-74, 377, 379, 387-88
"The Man Who Loved His Kind" (Woolf) 7:373, 376, 381, 388
"The Man Who Loved Islands" (Lawrence) 4:197, 212-17, 221, 230, 233, 238
"The Man Who Passed" (Fisher) 25:17-19, 21
"The Man Who Ploughed the Sea" (Clarke) 3:134
"The Man Who Saw the Flood" (Wright) 2:366
"The Man Who Stole the Eiffel Tower" (Greene) 29:223, 226-27
"The Man Who Turned into a Statue" (Oates) 6:224
"The Man Who Was" (Kipling) 5:293
"The Man Who Was Almost a Man" (Wright) 2:366, 376, 388
"The Man Who was Drowned" (Lawson) 18:242, 255
"The Man Who Was Unlucky With Women" (Lewis) 34:163, 165
"The Man Who Was Very Homesick for New York" (Cheever) 38:43
"The Man Who Watched" (Moravia)
  See "The Man Who Watched"
"The Man Who Would Be King" (Kipling) 5:262, 264, 273, 278, 282, 291, 299
"The Man Whom Women Adored" (Oates) 6:255
"A Man with a Conscience" (Maugham) 8:379
"Man with a Thermometer" (Bulgakov) 18:90
"The Man with Clam Eyes" (Thomas) 20:320, 322
The Man with Forty Ecus (Voltaire)
  See *L'homme aux quarante écus*
"The Man with His Heart in the Highlands" (Saroyan) 21:143, 168, 175
"The Man with the Broken Arm" (O'Hara) 15:252
"The Man with the French Postcards" (Saroyan) 21:132

"The Man with the Knives" (Boell)
  See "Der Mann mit den Messern"
"The Man with the Moon in Him" (Sansom) 21:113
"The Man with the Twisted Lip" (Doyle) 12:51, 59, 68, 70, 74-5
The Man with Two Left Feet (Wodehouse) 2:327
"The Man Within" (Greene) 29:184
"Man without a Fig Leaf" (Garrett) 30:166, 174
"The Man without a Temperament" (Mansfield) 9:284, 314
"The Management of Grief" (Mukherjee) 38:238, 242, 252-53, 266, 271, 287, 290, 292
"The Manager" (O'Hara) 15:283
"The Manchester Marriage" (Gaskell) 25:55, 58
"The Mandarin" (Fuentes) 24:61-2
"Mandarin's Jade" (Chandler) 23:59, 65, 67-8, 72, 80, 82, 87, 98, 108, 110
"The Mangler" (King) 17:262
"Mango Says Goodbye Sometimes" (Cisneros) 32:43
Mango Street (Cisneros)
  See *The House On Mango Street*
"Manhole 69" (Ballard) 1:68
"Man-hunt" (Narayan) 25:156
Manhunt (Carpentier)
  See *El acoso*
"The Maniac" (Oates) 6:243
"Manikin" (Michaels) 16:301, 303, 311-12
"Mankind" (Pavese) 19:370, 389
"Der Mann mit den Messern" (Boell) 23:12
"Manna" (Galsworthy) 22:63, 78, 101
"Mannequin" (Rhys) 21:62
"Man's Fate" (Dubus) 15:88
"The Man's Story" (Anderson) 1:39, 52
"The Mantle of Whistler" (Parker) 2:273, 283
"Manuel" (Lewis) 40:275
"Manuscript Found in a Pocket" (Cortazar)
  See "Manuscrito hallado en un bolsillo"
"Manuscrito de um sacristão" (Machado de Assis) 24:129-30
"Manuscrito hallado en un bolsillo" (Cortazar) 7:61-2, 69
"Many Are Disappointed" (Pritchett) 14:255, 259, 269, 271, 282, 284, 297
Many Inventions (Kipling) 5:266, 273, 283, 287
"The Map of Love" (Thomas) 3:399, 402, 407
The Map of Love (Thomas) 3:410
"El mapa de objetos perdidos" (Arreola) 38:11, 26-28
"The Mapmakers" (Pohl) 25:224, 227, 229-31, 234-35
"Die Mappe meines Urgrossvaters" (Stifter) 28:285, 298-99
"The Mappined Life" (Saki) 12:290, 297, 305, 310, 313, 321, 323
"El mar del tiempo perdido" (Garcia Marquez) 8:155, 167-68, 172
"Mar, mar, enemigo" (Cabrera Infante) 39:22
"Mara milosnica" (Andric) 36:30, 34-5, 37-8, 45, 48, 59-62, 65, 67
"Mara the Concubine" (Andric)
  See "Mara milosnica"
Les marana (Balzac) 5:8, 26, 31
"Maravillosas ocupaciones" (Cortazar) 7:92
"A Marble Woman; or, The Mysterious Model" (Alcott) 27:4, 45-50, 58-60
"The Marble Works" (Hesse) 9:230-31, 234-35
"Marcelle" (Beauvoir) 35:60, 62-65, 67-9, 71
"The March" (McCullers) 9:332, 354, 360
"The March Hare" (Leskov)
  See "Zajačij remiz"
"The March of Progress" (Chesnutt) 7:27-8, 37
"Das Märchen" (Hauptmann) 37:246-47
Märchen (Hesse) 9:244
"Ein Märchen aus der neuen Zeit" (Hoffmann) 13:218-19
Das Märchen von blonden Eckbert (Tieck)
  See *Der blonde Eckbert*
"Marching through Boston" (Updike) 13:386

"The Marchioness of Stonehenge" (Hardy)
2:204, 217
"Marcia" (Davis) 38:104-05, 119-20
Marcovaldo: or, The Seasons in the City
(Calvino)
See *Marcovaldo ouvero le stagioni in citta*
Marcovaldo ouvero le stagioni in citta
(Calvino) 3:106-07
"Il mare" (Pavese) 19:365, 384
"The Mares" (Pavese) 19:365-66
Marginalia (Poe) 22:304, 312, 325
"Marguerite" (Beauvoir) 35:60, 62-4, 66, 68, 71
"María Concepción" (Porter) 4:326, 328, 330, 339-40, 346, 349
"Maria Cora" (Machado de Assis) 24:134
"Maria-Fly" (de la Mare) 14:86-7
Mariamne (Lagerkvist) 12:198-99, 201-03
"Mariana" (Machado de Assis) 24:128, 134, 145, 153, 155
"Marianno" (Svevo) 25:329
"Marie, Marie, Hold On Tight" (Barthelme) 2:34, 40
"Marina and the Lion" (Ferre)
See "Marina y el leon"
"Marina y el leon" (Ferre) 36:157, 160
"The Marine Excursion of the Knights of Pythias" (Leacock) 39:269
"A Marine Merry-Making" (Alcott) 27:43
Mario and the Magician (Mann)
See *Mario und der Zauberer*
Mario und der Zauberer (Mann) 5:310-12, 337, 340-41, 353-59
"The Mariposa Bank Mystery" (Leacock) 39:270
"The Mark of Apelles" (Pasternak)
See "Il tratto di Apelle"
"The Mark of the Beast" (Kipling) 5:271, 273-74, 280, 299
"The Mark on the Wall" (Woolf) 7:368, 370-71, 378, 382-83, 385-88, 392, 397-98, 405, 409
The Mark on the Wall (Woolf) 7:382
Mark Twain"s Skethces, New and Old (Twain) 34:336
Mark Twain's "Which Was the Dream?" and Other Symbolic Writings of the Later Years (Twain) 6:331
"The Marker" (Coover) 15:37
"Market" (Walser) 20:355
"Markheim" (Stevenson) 11:266, 268-69, 276, 278-79, 281-82, 292, 297
"Marklake Witches" (Kipling) 5:285
"Marley's Chain" (Auchincloss) 22:51
"Marlowe Takes on the Syndicate" (Chandler) 23:110
"Marmalade" (O'Faolain) 13:322
The Marmalade Bird (Sansom) 21:115-19, 127
El marqués de Lumbría (Unamuno) 11:313, 323-24
"Die Marquise de la Pivadière" (Hoffmann) 13:188
The Marquise of —— and Other Stories (Kleist) 22:136
"Die Marquise von O..." (Kleist) 22:105-08, 110, 116, 125-26, 128, 130-32, 134-35, 142
"Marrakesh" (Munro) 3:346
"Marriage à la mode" (Mansfield) 9:279, 310
"The Marriage Contract" (Auchincloss) 22:41-2
"The Marriage Feast" (Lagerkvist) 12:179, 196
"The Marriage of Phaedra" (Cather) 2:98, 103
The Marriage of the Monk (Meyer)
See *Die Hochzeit des Mönchs*
"Marriage—For One" (Dreiser) 30:112, 114, 122, 145-46, 156
Marriages and Infidelities (Oates) 6:224, 234, 254
"Married" (Dreiser) 30:122, 142-43
"The Married Couple" (Kafka) 5:206-07
"Married Life" (Leacock) 39:266
The Married Lover (Colette)
See *Duo*

"A Married Man's Story" (Mansfield) 9:282, 311
"Marroca" (Maupassant) 1:257
"The Marry Month of May" (Henry) 5:163
"Mars by Moonlight" (Pohl) 25:232
"Mars Is Heaven" (Bradbury) 29:55
"Mars Jeems's Nightmare" (Chesnutt) 7:7-8, 10, 40
"Marse Chan" (Page) 23:284, 287-93, 295-98, 300-02, 305-06, 308, 311-12, 314, 316-17, 320-21, 323, 325-26, 328
"The Marsh King's Daughter" (Andersen) 6:13-15, 35-7
"Marsh Rosemary" (Jewett) 6:150
"Marshall's Capture" (Garland) 18:167
"Marshall's Dog" (Beattie) 11:18, 20-3
Marshlands (Gide)
See *Paludes*
"Martha and Mary" (Capek) 36:85, 117, 129
"Martha Jean" (Caldwell) 19:18, 38, 42, 46
"Martha Preston" (Gaskell) 25:72
Marthe und ihre Uhr (Storm) 27:283
The Martian Chronicles (Bradbury) 29:38-40, 46, 49-52, 55, 60-1, 64, 75, 79, 87
"The Martian Stargazers" (Pohl) 25:225
Martin Hewitt, Investigator (Morrison) 40:332, 349
"Martin Martir" (Arnim) 29:6, 7
"Martina" (Pardo Bazan) 30:264
"Martin's Close" (James) 16:232, 237, 252, 256
"El martirio de Sor Bibiana" (Pardo Bazan) 30:262
"Martwy sezon" (Schulz) 13:326-27, 334
"The Martydom of Solomon" (Coppard) 21:8
"The Martyr" (Auchincloss) 22:44
"The Martyr" (Farrell) 28:98-9, 122, 125
"The Martyr" (Peretz) 26:215-16
"The Martyr" (Porter) 31:178
"The Martyr's Corner" (Narayan) 25:134, 139-41
"Maruja" (Harte) 8:216, 244, 251
"The Marvelous Girl" (Pritchett) 14:261
"Marvelous Pursuits" (Cortazar)
See "Maravillosas ocupaciones"
"Marvels and Miracles-Pass It On!" (Bradbury) 29:76
"Mary" (Collier) 19:104, 109
"Mary" (Mansfield) 9:284
"Mary" (O'Hara) 15:266
"Mary and Norma" (O'Hara) 15:252, 281
"Mary Button's Principles" (Gilman) 13:141
"Mary Gresley" (Trollope) 28:321, 324, 335, 340, 348
"Mary O'Reilley" (Farrell) 28:118, 122
"Mary Postgate" (Kipling) 5:279, 281-83
"Mary Winosky" (Hughes) 6:117-19
"Maryelle" (Villiers de l'Isle Adam) 14:378, 381-82, 384, 393, 396
"Mary's Piece" (Dixon) 16:210
"Más allá" (Pardo Bazan) 30:264
"Mas vai chover" (Lispector) 34:211
"Mascarada" (Onetti) 23:249, 252
"The Masculine Principle" (O'Connor) 5:366, 371-72, 381, 388-89
"Masculine Protest" (O'Connor) 5:387
"The Mask of the Bear" (Laurence) 7:254, 259, 263
The Masked Days (Fuentes)
See *Los días enmascarados*
"Le masque" (Maupassant) 1:274, 286
"The Masque of the Red Death" (Poe) 1:379, 389-90, 398, 406; 22:305, 307; 35:322
"Masquerade" (Onetti)
See "Mascarada"
Masquerade, and Other Stories (Walser) 20:354-56, 363, 365-66
"Masquerade of a Dead Sword" (Ligotti) 16:269, 273, 277-78
"The Mass Island" (O'Connor) 5:372
"Masses of Men" (Caldwell) 19:9, 38-9
"Massimilla doni" (Balzac) 5:16
"Master" (Carter) 13:4

Master and Man (Tolstoy)
See *Khozyain i rabotnik*
Master Flea (Hoffmann)
See *Meister Floh: Ein Märchen in seiben Abenteuern zweier Freunde*
"Master Glass" (Cervantes)
See "El licienciado Vidriera"
"Master Hynek Ráb of Kufštejn" (Capek) 36:95, 117
"Master John Horseleigh, Knight" (Hardy) 2:210
"Master Misery" (Capote) 2:63-5, 72-3, 75, 78
"The Master Thief" (Grimm and Grimm) 36:199, 235
"The Masters" (Le Guin) 12:223, 232-33, 241
"The Maternal Instinct" (Naipaul) 38:326, 341, 350
"Mathewson" (Dreiser) 30:149-51
Matilda's England (Trevor) 21:235, 260
"The Mating of Marjorie" (Caldwell) 19:34, 46
"Matryona's Home" (Solzhenitsyn)
See "Matryonin Dvor"
"Matryona's House" (Solzhenitsyn)
See "Matryonin Dvor"
"Matryonin Dvor" (Solzhenitsyn) 32:330-33, 337-39, 342, 359, 361-65, 370-75, 377, 379-86, 394-95, 397, 409
Matteo Falcone (Merimee) 7:278, 280-1, 283, 285, 287-9, 300-01
"A Matter of Chance" (Nabokov) 11:123-24, 126
"A Matter of Doctrine" (Dunbar) 8:122
"A Matter of Prejudice" (Chopin) 8:93
"A Matter of Principle" (Chesnutt) 7:16, 23, 33-6
"A Matter of Taste" (Collier) 19:108
"Mauá Square" (Lispector)
See "Praça Mauá"
"Maud Island" (Caldwell) 19:17
"Maude" (Auchincloss) 22:3, 30, 47
"Maupassant" (Babel)
See "Guy de Maupassant"
"Le Mauvais Jars" (Ayme) 41:6, 14-15
"Le mauvais vitrier" (Baudelaire) 18:6, 16, 18, 34, 45, 60-1, 63
"Le Mauvaises fivres" (Ayme) 41:11
"The Mavericks" (Auchincloss) 22:5, 53
"May Day" (Fitzgerald) 6:45, 57-9, 74-6, 96-101
"A May Night; or, The Drowned Maiden" (Gogol)
See "Majskaja noč, ili Vtoplennica"
"May We Borrow Your Husband" (Greene) 29:201, 213
May We Borrow Your Husband? and Other Comedies of the Sexual Life (Greene) 29:200-02, 212-13, 217, 221, 223, 228, 230
"May you learn to open the door to go out to play" (Cortazar)
See "que sepa abrir la puerta para ir a jugar"
"The Mayor" (O'Hara) 15:260
"La mayorazga de Bouzas" (Pardo Bazan) 30:272
"The Mayor's Committee" (Farrell) 28:125
"The Maypole of Merry Mount" (Hawthorne) 3:164-67, 180-81, 183-84, 187, 188
"May-Ry" (Calisher) 15:15-16
Mayses far yidishe kinder (Aleichem) 33:5, 16
"The Maysville Minstrel" (Lardner) 32:117, 128, 135-36, 138, 174-76
"Mazes" (Le Guin) 12:230, 235
"A Mæcenas of the Pacific Slope" (Harte) 8:216, 255
"McEwen of the Shining Slave Makers" (Dreiser) 30:115, 122-23, 127-30, 132
"Me and Miss Mandible" (Barthelme) 2:26-7, 35, 47, 49, 53
"El me bebeu" (Lispector) 34:215
"Me Cago en la Leche" (Robert Jordan in NicaraguaBoyle) 16:151
"Mearbhall" (O'Flaherty) 6:287-89

"The Measurements" (Moravia) **26**:142,155
"Meccana d'amore" (Levi) **12**:276
"Un mécène" (Villiers de l'Isle Adam)
    See "Le tueur de cygnes"
"El mechón blanco" (Pardo Bazan) **30**:294
"Le médaillon" (Villiers de l'Isle Adam)
    See "Antonie"
"The Medals" (Pirandello) **22**:235
"The Medals, and Other Stories" (Pirandello)
    22:234, 236
"Meddlance Tersplat" (Cortazar)
    See "La inmiscusión terrupta"
"Meddlesome Curiosity" (Cervantes)
    See "El curioso impertinente"
"Meddlesome Jack" (Caldwell) **19**:6, 23, 39, 44
"Media Man" (Vinge)
    See "Mediaman"
"Mediaman" (Vinge) **24**:338
"Las medias rojas" (Pardo Bazan) **30**:272
"Medicine" (Lu Hsun)
    See "Yao"
A Medicine for Melancholy (Bradbury) **29**:58,
    61, 78, 80-1, 83
"The Medicine Man" (Caldwell) **19**:6, 21, 25-6
"Medicine Men of Civilisation" (Dickens)
    17:123
"A Medieval Romance" (Twain) **34**:343
El medio pollito (Ferre) **36**:146, 149
"Meditations in Monmouth Street" (Dickens)
    17:115, 117, 121
"Medley" (Bambara) **35**:11, 18, 27
"Medusa" (Campbell) **19**:85
"The Medusa" (Ligotti) **16**:274, 294, 297
Meet Mr. Mulliner (Wodehouse) **2**:325, 338
"Meet the Girls" (Farrell) **28**:121
"The Meeting" (Borges) **4**:20
"The Meeting" (Cortazar)
    See "Reunión"
"The Meeting" (Dixon) **16**:210
"The Meeting" (Galsworthy) **22**:58, 98
"A Meeting" (O'Faolain) **13**:293-95, 309, 316
"Meeting a Moscow Acquaintance in the
    Detachment" (Tolstoy) **9**:389-90
"Meeting Aline" (Dixon) **16**:212-13
"A Meeting in Middle Age" (Trevor) **21**:254,
    260
"A Meeting in Rauch" (Bioy Casares) **17**:95-6
"A Meeting in Space" (Gordimer) **17**:158
"A Meeting South" (Anderson) **1**:37, 52-3
"Meeting the Author" (Campbell) **19**:77-8
"A Meeting with Medusa" (Clarke) **3**:128, 130,
    132, 135-36, 138-40, 146
"The Megalopolis Millennia" (Aldiss) **36**:19
"Meh Lady: A Story of the War" (Page) **23**:284,
    286-87, 289, 291-93, 297, 302-03, 307-08,
    311, 314, 316-18, 320, 322-23, 325, 327-28
"Mein Onkel Fred" (Boell) **23**:5
"Mein teures Bein" (Boell) **23**:34
"Mein verdrossenes Gesicht" (Lenz) **33**:316-18,
    320, 331
"Meine Bemühungen" (Walser) **20**:332
"Mei-nü" (P'u Sung-ling) **31**:198
"Meiosis" (Calvino) **3**:109
*Meister Floh: Ein Märchen in seiben
    Abenteuern zweier Freunde* (Hoffmann)
    13:186, 192, 195, 197-200, 218-19, 225
Meister Martin (Hoffmann) **13**:182
"Mejdoub" (Bowles) **3**:68
Los Mejores cuentos de Donoso (Donoso)
    See *Cuentos*
"The Melancholy Hussar of the German
    Legion" (Hardy) **2**:214-15, 220
"Melhor do que order" (Lispector) **34**:215
"Mellonta Tauta" (Poe) **1**:401, 406
"Melmoth Converted" (Balzac)
    See "Melmoth réconcilié"
"Melmoth réconcilié" (Balzac) **5**:12, 31
"Melos, Run!" (Dazai Osamu)
    See "Hashire Merosu"
"A Member of the Family" (Spark) **10**:364, 367
"The Memento" (Henry) **5**:185
"Memento Mori" (Farrell) **28**:110-11

Memnon; ou, La sagesse humaine (Voltaire)
    12:340-42, 357, 379-81, 383, 392-94, 396-
    97, 399-401
"A Memoir" (Suckow) **18**:396
Memoires (Flaubert)
    See *Les mémoires d'un fou*
Les mémoires d'un fou (Flaubert) **11**:71
"Memoirs" (Balzac) **5**:11
Memoirs from Underground (Dostoevsky)
    See *Zapiski iz podpol'ya*
The Memoirs of a Billiard-Marker (Tolstoy)
    9:375
Memoirs of a Madman (Tolstoy)
    See *Zapiski sumasshedshego*
The Memoirs of Sherlock Holmes (Doyle)
    12:49-51, 59
"Memorandum of Sudden Death" (Norris)
    28:198-99
"Memorial" (Munro) **3**:331
"Memorial Eve" (Suckow) **18**:414, 422, 424
"Memories" (Dazai Osamu)
    See "Omoide"
"Memories of D. H. Lawrence" (Thurber) **1**:414
"Memories of Youghal" (Trevor) **21**:262
"Memories of Yugashima" (Kawabata)
    See "Yugashima no Omoide"
"A Memory" (Lavin) **4**:178-79, 182-83
"A Memory" (Welty) **1**:466, 469-70, 472
"The Memory of Martha" (Dunbar) **8**:122
"A Memory of Yamashina" (Shiga) **23**:352
"Memphis" (Gilchrist) **14**:159
"Memphis" (Mason) **4**:10
"Men in the Storm" (Crane) **7**:108, 110, 136-
    37, 145
"The Men of Forty Mile" (London) **4**:267, 282,
    284, 286
"Men of the Mountains" (Stuart) **31**:252
Men of the Mountains (Stuart) **31**:231-32
"The Men with Bowler Hats" (Wilson) **21**:358,
    360-63
"Men with Their Big Shoes" (Jackson) **9**:270;
    39:212, 227, 229, 231
Men without Women (Hemingway) **1**:209-12,
    214, 216-17
"Az men zogt meshuge—gleyb!" (Peretz)
    26:224
"The Menace" (du Maurier) **18**:127-28
"Mendel and His Wife" (Farrell) **28**:89, 122
"Mendel Breines" (Peretz) **26**:201
"Le Mendiant" (Ayme) **41**:13
"Menelaiad" (Barth) **10**:39, 43, 47-51, 54, 58,
    60-1, 75-6, 80, 90, 97-8, 100-02
"Meng-lang" (P'u Sung-ling) **31**:197
"A Menor Mulher do Mundo" (Lispector)
    34:194-96, 200
"A mensagem" (Lispector) **34**:188, 229, 231-34
"A Mental Suggestion" (Chopin) **8**:72, 100
"Menudo" (Carver) **8**:43
"Menuet" (Maupassant) **1**:278
"Meola's Defence" (Pirandello) **22**:254
"A Mercenary" (Ozick) **15**:302, 304, 316-17,
    333-35
"The Merchant of Heaven" (Laurence) **7**:245-
    46, 249-50, 255, 260
"The Merchants of Venus" (Pohl) **25**:226, 230
"Mercury" (Levi) **12**:264, 268, 281
"A Mercury of the Foothills" (Harte) **8**:214,
    249
"The 'Mercy' of God" (Dreiser) **30**:158-59
"La Mère Bauche" (Trollope) **28**:316-18, 323,
    327-28, 330, 333, 343, 349, 357
"A Mere Formality" (Pirandello) **22**:241, 245
"A Mere Interlude" (Hardy) **2**:211, 215
"Mère Pochette" (Jewett) **6**:156
"La mère sauvage" (Maupassant) **1**:277-78
"Merle" (Marshall) **3**:317
Merle: A Novella, and Other Stories (Marshall)
    See *Reena, and Other Stories*
"Mermaid Sea" (Dazai Osamu) **41**:229
"The Merman" (Hesse) **9**:242-43
"Merrittsville" (Suckow) **18**:393, 413, 422, 424
"The Merry Chase" (Lish) **18**:278

"Merry May" (Campbell) **19**:76
"The Merry Men" (Stevenson) **11**:268, 281-82,
    303, 306
"Mes vingt-cinq jours" (Maupassant) **1**:274
"Der meshugener batlen" (Peretz) **26**:218-20,
    223-24
"Der meshulekh" (Peretz) **26**:218, 223-24
"Mesiras Nefesh" (Peretz) **26**:197
"Mesmeric Revelation" (Poe) **1**:401; **34**:250
"A Mess of Pottage" (Dunbar) **8**:122, 124, 128
"Le message" (Balzac) **5**:8, 31, 40-1, 43
"The Message" (Boell)
    See "Die Botschaft"
"Message in a Bottle" (Gordimer) **17**:156
Messaline, roman de l'acienne Rome (Jarry)
    20:50, 63-8
"La messe de l'athée" (Balzac) **5**:16, 26, 31
"The Messenger" (Peretz)
    See "The Messenger"
"The Messiah" (Bradbury) **29**:82
"Metamorphoses" (Cheever) **1**:94, 100
"Metamorphosis" (Agnon)
    See "Panim aherot"
"Metamorphosis" (Dazai Osamu)
    See "Gyofukuki"
"Metamorphosis" (Moravia) **26**:136
"The Metamorphosis" (Oates) **6**:225, 234
The Metamorphosis (Kafka)
    See *Die verwandlung*
"Metel" (Pushkin) **27**:129, 141-45, 163, 166,
    168, 171, 183, 186-87
"Methinks the Lady Doth Propel too Much"
    (Perelman) **32**:235
"Methuseleh, a Jewish Horse" (Aleichem) **33**:20
"Metropolitan Journal" (Doell) **23**:34
"Metzengerstein" (Poe) **1**:379; **22**:300, 331, 334
"The Mex Would Arrive at Gentry's Junction
    at 12:10" (Coover) **15**:43-6
"The Mexican" (London) **4**:291
"The Mexican" (Moravia) **26**:151
"The Mexican General" (Bellow) **14**:37-8, 40
"Mexican Movies" (Cisneros) **32**:8
"Mexico" (Gilchrist) **14**:161-63
"The Mezzotint" (James) **16**:232, 237, 240,
    243-44, 251-52, 255, 257
"Mi suicidio" (Pardo Bazan) **30**:264
"Michael Egerton" (Price) **22**:363, 384, 388
Michael Kohlhaas (Kleist) **22**:106, 109-10, 117,
    119-21, 125-26, 128-29, 132-37, 139,
    141-42
"Michael's Wife" (O'Connor) **5**:377
"Michel Siniagin" (Zoshchenko) **15**:399
Micromégas (Voltaire) **12**:341, 343, 390-94
"The Midas Plague" (Pohl) **25**:212-13, 220, 223
"The Middle Drawer" (Calisher) **15**:7, 15,
    19-21
"The Middle of Nowhere" (Pohl) **25**:232
The Middle Years (James) **8**:291, 299-300
*The Middle-Aged Man on the Flying Trapeze:
    A Collection of Short Pieces* (Thurber)
    1:413, 420, 423
"A Middle-Class Education" (Oates) **6**:246
"The Middleman" (Mukherjee) **38**:245, 254,
    260, 265-66, 272, 279, 283, 285, 292
The Middleman, and Other Stories
    (Mukherjee) **38**:235, 238-39, 241-45, 247,
    250, 255, 257, 260, 262-63, 269-70, 273,
    278-79, 281, 287, 291-92, 294
"A Middling Type" (Moravia) **26**:159-60
"The Midget" (Walser)
    See "Der Knirps"
"Midnight at Tim's Place" (Thurber) **1**:429
"Midnight Blue" (Collier) **19**:109-11
"Midnight Magic" (Mason) **4**:11
"Midnight Mass" (Bowles) **3**:75, 80
"Midnight Mass" (Machado de Assis) **24**:139,
    154-55
Midnight Mass (Bowles) **3**:75-6, 79-80
"Midsummer" (Machen) **20**:200
"A Midsummer Knight's Dream" (Henry) **5**:184
"Midsummer Madness" (Galsworthy) **22**:70

Title Index

"Midsummer Night Madness" (O'Faolain) **13**:295, 301-02, 304, 309, 314-15

Midsummer Night Madness, and Other Stories (O'Faolain) **13**:284, 292, 308, 312-13, 316-17

"Midsummer Passion" (Caldwell) **19**:34, 39, 46

"Mid-western Primitive" (Suckow) **18**:391, 412, 416

"The Midwinter Guest" (Caldwell) **19**:17

"La migala" (Arreola) **38**:9, 25

"Miggles" (Harte) **8**:209-10, 236, 254

Miguel Street (Naipaul) **38**:305-06, 311, 315-20, 322-28, 330, 335-37, 339-45, 347-50, 352

"HaMikhtav" (Agnon) **30**:22, 37

"Mila and Prelac" (Andric) **36**:43

"El milagro secreto" (Borges) **4**:29-30, 37; **41**:52, 57-58, 91, 164

"A Mild Attack of Locusts" (Lessing) **6**:191

"Mildred Lawson" (Moore) **19**:341

"Miles City, Montana" (Munro) **3**:347-48

"Milford Junction, 1939: A Brief Encounter" (Coover) **15**:61

"Militona" (Gautier) **20**:3, 7

"Milk Is Very Good for You" (Dixon) **16**:204, 210, 214

"Milking Time" (O'Flaherty) **6**:262, 277

"The Milkmaid of Samaniago" (Coover) **15**:36

"Milkman 2" (King)
See "Big Wheels: A Tale of the Laundry Game"

"The Mill" (Bates) **10**:126, 130-31, 133

"La Mille et deuxieme nuit" (Gautier) **20**:15

"The Millennium, and What They Can Do With It" (Perelman) **32**:230

"A Miller of Dee" (Galsworthy) **22**:58, 93

"Millie" (Mansfield) **9**:302

"A Millionaire of Rough and Ready" (Harte) **8**:254

"Million-Dollar Brainstorm" (Algren) **33**:107

"The Million-Year Picnic" (Bradbury) **29**:50, 61

"Mina de Vanghel" (Stendhal) **27**:251-53, 259

"Mind and Body" (Williams) **31**:303, 312, 324, 331, 352-53, 359-60

"Mine" (Carver) **8**:30, 34

"Mingo: A Sketch of Life in Middle Georgia" (Harris) **19**:131, 149, 174-75, 178, 184

Mingo, and Other Sketches in Black and White (Harris) **19**:134, 146-47, 151, 173, 176, 181

"Mingtian" (Lu Hsun) **20**:128, 141

"Minister Dragon's Flight" (P'u Sung-ling)
See "Lung-fei hsiang kung"

"The Minister's Black Veil" (Hawthorne) **3**:154, 159-60, 164, 171, 177-78, 184, 186-87; **39**:86-150

"The Minister's Books" (Benet) **10**:154, 160

"Ministers of Grace" (Saki) **12**:334

Minne (Colette) **10**:257

"The Minority Committee" (Dunbar) **8**:127

"Minotaur" (Walser) **20**:356

"The Miracle" (Auchincloss) **22**:47

"The Miracle" (O'Connor) **5**:388

"The Miracle at Ballinspittle" (Boyle) **16**:148, 151-2, 154-55

"Le Miracle des roses" (Laforgue) **20**:86, 88-9, 91, 100-2, 114

"The Miracle in Olovo" (Andric)
See "Čudo u Olovu"

"Miracle Joyeaux" (Norris) **28**:200

"The Miracle of Purun Bhagat" (Kipling) **5**:295

"The Miracle of Tepayac" (Steinbeck) **11**:249-51

"The Miracle of the Roses" (Laforgue)
See "Le Miracle des roses"

"Miracles" (Singer) **3**:385-86

"The Miracles of Jamie" (Bradbury) **29**:47

"La mirada" (Pardo Bazan) **30**:284-86, 289-90

"Miranda over the Valley" (Dubus) **15**:69-70, 85, 87

Mirgorod (Gogol) **4**:86-7, 117; **29**:142

"Miriam" (Capote) **2**:61-2, 64, 66, 69, 73-5, 78-9, 83

"Le miroir" (Baudelaire) **18**:16, 49

"The Mirror" (Machado de Assis)
See "O espelho"

"The Mirror" (O'Flaherty) **6**:260, 265, 276-77, 279

"The Mirror" (Singer) **3**:364, 368, 375

The Mirror Maker (Levi)
See *Racconti e Saggi*

"The Mirror of Ink" (Borges) **41**:65

"The Misadventures of a Matrimonial Swindler" (Capek) **36**:128

"The Misadventures of John Nicholson" (Stevenson) **11**:269, 282, 303, 305-06

"The Misanthrope" (Lu Hsun)
See "Guduzhe"

Miscellaneous Papers (Machado de Assis)
See *Papéis avulsos*

"A Miscellany of Characters That Will Not Appear" (Cheever) **1**:93, 100; **38**:61

"The Miser" (O'Connor) **5**:371

"Misery" (Chekhov) **2**:128, 130, 155

"A Misfortunate Girl" (Turgenev)
See "Neschastnaya"

"The Misfortunes of Frederick Pickering" (Trollope)
See "The Adventures of Frederick Pickering"

"The Misogamist" (Dubus) **15**:75

"Miss Algrave" (Lispector) **34**:205, 212-14

"Miss Baker" (Pritchett) **14**:269

"Miss Brill" (Mansfield) **9**:287, 299, 307, 309, 312-13

"Miss Chauncey" (Jewett) **6**:168

"Miss Chia-no" (P'u Sung-ling)
See "Ying-ning"

"Miss Cynthie" (Fisher) **25**:5, 7, 11, 16-17, 19-21, 24-6

"Miss Dangerlie's Roses" (Page) **23**:328

"Miss Dollar" (Machado de Assis) **24**:151

"Miss Duveen" (de la Mare) **14**:68, 83-4, 87

"Miss Gibson" (Frame) **29**:104

"Miss Godwin's Inheritance" (Page) **23**:288, 307

"Miss Harriet" (Maupassant) **1**:259, 271, 274, 280, 285-87

"Miss Huan-niang" (P'u Sung-ling) **31**:192

"Miss Jemima" (de la Mare) **14**:69

"Miss Leonora When Last Seen" (Taylor) **10**:390, 401, 406, 407, 409, 415

Miss Lonelyhearts (West) **16**:345-49, 351-52, 354, 356-57, 359-60, 362, 364, 366-67, 369, 375-81, 383-86, 389-90, 394-402, 404, 407-08, 411, 415, 417

"Miss Manning's Minister" (Jewett) **6**:156, 159

"Miss Mary Pask" (Wharton) **6**:431

"Miss Miller" (de la Mare) **14**:87

"Miss Ophelia Gledd" (Trollope) **28**:319, 323, 348

"Miss Pinkerton's Apocalypse" (Spark) **10**:350, 355, 359, 366

"Miss Plarr" (Ligotti) **16**:280

"Miss Puss's Parasol" (Harris) **19**:183

"Miss Rodney's Leisure" (Gissing) **37**:56

"Miss Sarah Jack, of Spanish Town, Jamaica" (Trollope) **28**:318, 329

"Miss Slattery and her Demon Lover" (White) **39**:280, 283, 286-87, 291-92, 298-99, 312, 316, 328, 335, 344

"Miss Smith" (Trevor) **21**:246-47, 262

"Miss Sydney's Flowers" (Jewett) **6**:157, 166, 168

"Miss Tempy's Watcher's" (Jewett) **6**:151, 156

"Miss W." (O'Hara) **15**:258

"Miss Willie Lou and the Swan" (Benet) **10**:148

"Miss Winchelsea's Heart" (Wells) **6**:391

"Miss Witherwell's Mistake" (Chopin) **8**:84, 86

"Miss Yellow Eyes" (Grau) **15**:158, 164

Die Missbrauchten Liebesbriefe (Keller) **26**:107

"Missed Connection" (Campbell) **19**:75

"Missed Vocation" (Pavese)
See "Mal di mestiere"

"Missing" (Campbell) **19**:74

"Missing" (de la Mare) **14**:70, 80, 83, 87-8, 92

"The Missing Eye" (Bulgakov) **18**:86-7

"The Missing Line" (Singer) **3**:389

"Missing Mail" (Narayan) **25**:138, 140, 153, 155

"The Mission of Jane" (Wharton) **6**:424-25

"The Mission of Mr. Scatters" (Dunbar) **8**:122, 132, 137, 147

"Mississippi, Ham Rider" (Bambara) **35**:24

"Mrs. Bullfrog" (Hawthorne) **3**:180

"Mrs. Moysey" (Bowen) **3**:30, 33, 40, 42

"Mrs. Windermere" (Bowen) **3**:40, 54

The Mist (Bombal) **37**:43

The Mist (King) **17**:265, 268-71, 273-76, 283

"The Mistake" (Gorky) **28**:159

"A Mistake" (Zoshchenko)
See "A Slight Mistake"

"The Mistake of the Machine" (Chesterton) **1**:131

"The Mistaken Milliner" (Dickens) **17**:135

"Mr. Andrews" (Forster) **27**:69, 75-6, 86, 97, 100, 114, 122, 123

"Mr. Higginbotham's Catastrophe" (Hawthorne) **3**:154

"Mr. Kempe" (de la Mare) **14**:70, 80, 85, 90

"Mr. Lyon" (Carter)
See "The Courtship of Mr. Lyon"

Mr. (Calvino)
See *Palomar*

"Mister Palomar in the City" (Calvino) **3**:113, 115

"Mister Palomar's Vacation" (Calvino) **3**:113

"Mister Toussan" (Ellison) **26**:7-9, 11, 21, 28-9

"Mistério em São Cristóvão" (Lispector) **34**:194-96

"The Mistletoe Bough" (Sansom) **21**:110, 126

"The Mistletoe Bough" (Trollope) **28**:318, 326, 331, 333, 340, 346, 349, 355

"The Mistress" (Berriault) **30**:95, 97-8

The Mistress and Other Stories (Berriault) **30**:95-8

"Mistress into Maid" (Pushkin)
See "Baryshnia-krest'ianka"

"Mistris Lee" (Arnim) **29**:29-30

"A Misunderstanding (Farrell) **28**:99

"Mitchell on Matrimony" (Lawson) **18**:250-51

"Mitchell on the 'Sex,' and Other 'Problems'" (Lawson) **18**:250

"Mitchell on Women" (Lawson) **18**:250

"Mitosis" (Calvino) **3**:109-10

"HaMitpahat" (Agnon) **30**:4, 35-6

Mitsou (Colette) **10**:257, 271-74

"A Mixed Bag" (Sansom) **21**:102, 127

"Mixing Cocktails" (Rhys) **21**:68-9

The Mixture as Before (Maugham) **8**:379

"Mizu kara waga namida o nuguitamo hi" (Oe) **20**:220-21, 223, 225, 227-32, 234, 237-44, 246-47, 249-50

"M'liss" (Harte) **8**:210, 219, 222, 224-25, 231-32, 234

"Mlle de Scudèry" (Hoffmann) **13**:202

"The Mnemogogues" (Levi) **12**:279

"Mobile" (Ballard) **1**:68

"Mobiles" (Cowan) **28**:78; 80

Mobiles (Cowan) **28**:80; 83

The Mocassin Ranch (Garland) **18**:182

"The Mock Auction" (Lavin) **4**:183

"The Mocking-Bird" (Bierce) **9**:64, 67-8, 96

"The Model" (Nin) **10**:326

A Model for Death (Bioy Casares)
See *Un modelo para la muerte*

"A Model Millionaire: A Note of Admiration" (Wilde) **11**:362, 399, 401, 407

Un modelo para la muerte (Bioy Casares) **17**:48, 74; **48**:42

"The Moderate Murderer" (Chesterton) **1**:132

Moderato cantabile (Duras) **40**:2-3, 10-17, 21, 25, 31, 33-34, 36-38, 40-50, 53-54, 58-61, 66-68, 75, 77-79, 82, 84-95, 106, 114, 136-40, 142
"A Modern Brutus" (Page)
   See "The Outcast"
"Modern Children" (Aleichem) **33**:8
A Modern Comedy (Galsworthy) **22**:70-1
"Modern Love" (Boyle) **16**:148, 154-56
A Modern Lover (Lawrence) **4**:230
"A Modest Proposal" (Stafford) **26**:274-76, 285, 299, 307, 312
"Modesta Gómez" (Castellanos) **39**:58, 73
"Modrá chryzantéma" (Capek) **36**:99, 102, 128
"Moebius Strip" (Cortazar) **7**:69
"Mohammed Fripouille" (Maupassant) **1**:275
"The Mohican" (Nin) **10**:303
"Mojave" (Capote) **2**:79-80
"Molly" (Dubus) **15**:86, 90-1
"Molly Cottontail" (Caldwell) **19**:46
"Molly's Dog" (Adams) **24**:11, 14
"Mom Bi: Her Friends and Enemies" (Harris) **19**:146, 157, 180
"The Moment" (Aiken) **9**:5, 13-14, 41
"The Moment before the Gun Went Off" (Gordimer) **17**:178, 187, 189-90
The Moment of Eclipse (Aldiss) **36**:18, 25
"The Moment of Truth" (Greene) **29**:223, 228
"Moments of Being: 'Slater's Pins Have No Points'" (Woolf) **7**:375, 388-89, 391-92, 398, 408-10
Moments of Reprieve (Levi)
   See *Lilít e altri racconti*
"Mōmoku monogatari" (Tanizaki) **21**:181, 188-89, 191, 198, 210-11, 224
"Mon oncle Jules" (Maupassant) **1**:277
"Mon oncle Sosthène" (Maupassant) **1**:263, 272
The Monastery of Sendomir (Grillparzer)
   See *The Monastery of Sendomir*
"A Monday Dream at Alameda Park" (Thomas) **20**:317
"Monday Is Another Day" (Farrell) **28**:120-1
"Monday or Tuesday" (Woolf) **7**:371, 374-75, 390, 392, 397-98, 402
Monday or Tuesday (Woolf) **7**:367-69, 371, 374, 392, 398-401, 404
Monde Comme il va (Voltaire) **12**:340, 393-94
"Money" (Capek) **36**:92-3, 124
"Money" (Galsworthy) **22**:98
Money and Other Stories (Capek)
   See *Trapné providky*
"The Money Diggers" (Irving) **2**:251, 261-62
"The Money Juggler" (Auchincloss) **22**:9, 34, 49-50
"The Mongoose" (Grimm and Grimm) **36**:190
"Monk" (Faulkner) **1**:165, 179
"Monk Eastman" (Borges) **41**:164
"The Monkey" (Dinesen) **7**:163, 167, 170, 173, 200-01, 203
"The Monkey" (King) **17**:274-75, 290-91, 293
"The Monkey Garden" (Cisneros) **32**:31-32
"The Monkey Island" (Dazai Osamu)
   See "Sarugashima"
"Monkey Nuts" (Lawrence) **4**:231, 234-35
"Monkey-Faced Youngster" (Dazai Osamu) **41**:244
"The Monkey's Grave" (Dazai Osamu) **41**:228, 232, 234
"The Monkey's Mound" (Dazai Osamu) **41**:276
"Monólogo del insumiso" (Arreola) **38**:9
Monologue (Beauvoir) **35**:46-50, 53-4, 74-5, 79, 81-6
"Monologue of an Old Pitcher" (Farrell) **28**:112
"Monologue of Isabel Watching It Rain in Macondo" (Garcia Marquez) **8**:194
"Monsieur les deux chapeaux" (Munro) **3**:348
"Monsieur Parent" (Maupassant) **1**:259-60, 283
"The Monster" (Moravia)
   See "The Monster"
The Monster (Crane) **7**:103-05, 107, 114, 116, 131, 134, 138, 146-48
The Monster, and Other Stories (Crane) **7**:104

Monte Verità (du Maurier) **18**:126, 137
A Month by the Lake, and Other Stories (Bates) **10**:122, 139-40
"Le Monument" (Ayme) **41**:24
"A Monument of French Folly" (Dickens) **17**:124
"The Monumental Arena" (Saroyan) **21**:163
"The Moon and GNAC" (Calvino)
   See "Luna e G N A C"
"The Moon and Six Guineas" (Auchincloss) **22**:49
"The Moon in Letters" (Bierce) **9**:78
"The Moon in the Mill-Pond" (Harris) **19**:173
"The Moon in the Orange Street Skating Rink" (Munro) **3**:348-49
"Moon Lake" (Welty) **1**:474, 486
"The Moon Lens" (Campbell) **19**:72, 81
"The Moon of the Arfy Darfy" (Algren) **33**:95, 97, 108
"Moon-Face" (London) **4**:252, 258-59
Moon-Face, and Other Stories (London) **4**:252
"A Moonlight Fable" (Wells) **6**:376
"Moonlight on the Snow" (Crane) **7**:108
The Moons of Jupiter (Munro) **3**:346-47
"Moonshine Lake" (Bulgakov) **18**:74
"The Moonshiners of Hoho-Hehee Falls" (Murfree) **22**:211
"Moon-Watcher" (Clarke) **3**:127-28
The Moor of Peter the Great (Pushkin)
   See *Arap Petra Velikogo*
Moorland Cottage (Gaskell) **25**:31, 47, 58, 60, 65, 71-2
Moral Tales (Laforgue)
   See *Moralités légendaires*
Moralités légendaires (Laforgue) **20**:85-6, 88-91, 93-5, 97-100, 102, 104-6, 108, 114, 122-3
"A Morality" (Forster)
   See "What Does It Matter? A Morality"
"A Morality" (Hawthorne) **39**:126
"Mordecai and Cocking" (Coppard) **21**:3
"The Mordivinian Sarafin" (Bunin)
   See "Mordovskiy sarafan"
"Mordovskiy sarafan" (Bunin) **5**:82, 106-08
"More about the Devil" (Gorky)
   See "Eshche o cherte"
"More Alarms at Night" (Thurber) **1**:428
"More Friend Than Lodger" (Wilson) **21**:320-21, 337, 339
"More Geese than Swans" (Garrett) **30**:166, 174
More Ghost Stories of an Antiquary (James) **16**:231, 238, 251-52, 255, 258
"More Joy in Heaven" (Warner) **23**:380
"The More Little Mummy in the World" (Thomas) **20**:287, 308, 317
More Pricks than Kicks (Beckett) **16**:64-8, 70-2, 76, 78, 87, 92-4, 106, 108
More Roman Tales (Moravia)
   See *More Roman Tales*
"More Stately Mansions" (Updike) **13**:402, 409
"More Stately Mansions" (Vonnegut) **8**:433
More Stories by Frank O'Connor (O'Connor) **5**:371
"Morella" (Poe) **22**:299, 329; **35**:336
Die Morgenlandfahrt (Hesse) **9**:227-29, 240-41, 244-45
"Morning" (Barthelme) **2**:45, 55
"Morning" (Dazai Osamu) **41**:238, 240, 242
"The Morning" (Updike) **13**:375
"The Morning after the Ball" (Tolstoy)
   See "After the Ball"
"Morning, Noon, Evening" (Shiga) **23**:344, 346, 348
"The Morning of a Landed Proprietor" (Tolstoy)
   See *A Landlord's Morning*
"A Morning Walk" (Chopin) **8**:98
Morning-Glories and Other Stories (Alcott) **27**:11, 41-3
"Morphine" (Bulgakov) **18**:86, 89
"Morris in Chains" (Coover) **15**:31, 50-1

"Mort and Mary" (O'Hara) **15**:248
"Une mort héroïque" (Baudelaire) **18**:15-16, 18, 27, 29-30, 34, 60
"The Mortal Coil" (Lawrence) **4**:235
Mortal Coils (Huxley) **39**:155-56, 163, 165, 167, 171, 174-75, 177
"Mortality and Mercy in Vienna" (Pynchon) **14**:308, 310, 312, 320, 322-25, 328, 342-43, 347-49
"La morte" (Svevo) **25**:330-32, 336-37, 351, 360
"Una morte" (Svevo)
   See "La morte"
"La morte addosso" (Pirandello) **22**:281, 283
"La morte amoureuse" (Gautier) **20**:3-4, 6-8, 13, 17-20, 31-2, 38, 41
The Mortgaged Heart (McCullers) **9**:341-44, 355-57, 359
"The Mortification of the Flesh" (Dunbar) **8**:127
"Mortmain" (Greene) **29**:200, 202
"Morton Hall" (Gaskell) **25**:48-9, 59-60, 73
Mosaïque (Merimee) **7**:287-8, 290, 300
"Mosby's Memoirs" (Bellow) **14**:22, 24-5
Mosby's Memoirs, and Other Stories (Bellow) **14**:22-3, 25, 56
"La mosca en el vasode leche" (Cabrera Infante) **39**:23
"Moscas y arañas" (Bioy Casares) **17**:87-9
"Moscow of the Twenties" (Bulgakov) **18**:92
"The Moslem Wife" (Gallant) **5**:135-38
"The Moss People" (Alcott) **27**:43
Mosses from an Old Manse (Hawthorne) **3**:155, 160, 174, 180, 185
"The Most Extraordinary Thing" (Andersen) **6**:11
"Most na Žepi" (Andric) **36**:30, 35, 37, 40, 43, 45-7, 52, 78-9
"The Most Noble Conquest of Man" (Norris) **28**:205
The Most of S. J. Perelman (Perelman) **32**:209, 215, 219, 227-28, 234
"The Most Profound Caress" (Cortazar)
   See "La caricia más profunda"
"Mostovi" (Andric) **36**:50
"Motel Architecture" (Ballard) **1**:79
"The Moth" (Wells) **6**:383
"Mother" (Anderson) **1**:33, 44
"Mother" (Barnes) **3**:22, 26
"A Mother" (Galsworthy) **22**:59, 98
"A Mother" (Joyce) **3**:205, 210-11, 234, 237, 245, 247, 249; **26**:46, 50
"The Mother" (Pavese) **19**:366, 368, 389
"The Mother" (Saroyan) **21**:134
"The Mother" (Svevo)
   See "Le madre"
"Mother and Child" (Hughes) **6**:119, 142
Mother and Child (Vinge) **24**:327-28, 331, 333-35, 337, 345
"Mother and Daughter" (Lawrence) **4**:205, 220; **19**:267
"Mother and Son" (Narayan) **25**:135, 137, 153, 156, 159
"Mother and Son" (O'Flaherty) **6**:262
"The Mother Bit Him" (Narayan) **25**:135
"The Mother Hive" (Kipling) **5**:279
"Mother Matilda's Book" (O'Faolain) **13**:293, 297
"The Mother of a Queen" (Hemingway) **1**:211
The Mother of Captain Shigemoto (Tanizaki)
   See *Shōshō Shigemoto no haha*
"The Mother Stone" (Galsworthy) **22**:101
"The Mother Trip" (Pohl) **25**:236
"Motherhood" (Anderson) **1**:27
"Mothering Sunday" (Thomas) **20**:321-22
"A Mother-in-Law" (Pirandello) **22**:236
"Mother's Day" (Fuentes) **24**:61, 75-8
"Mother's Death and the New Mother" (Shiga)
   See "Haha no shi to atarishi haha"
"Mother's Sense of Fun" (Wilson) **21**:319, 321, 323, 330-31, 333, 337-38, 342-43, 351, 364
"A Mother's Vision" (Peretz) **26**:205
"The Motive" (Cortazar) **7**:69-70

"The Motive" (du Maurier) **18**:125, 138

A Motley (Galsworthy) **22**:58-60, 97-100

Mottel, the Cantor's Son (Aleichem) **33**:7, 57, 83

"The Motto" (Capek) **36**:89-90

"Mouche" (Maupassant) **1**:273, 284

"The Mound" (Lovecraft) **3**:270-71, 274, 279

"Mount Yoshino" (Dazai Osamu) **41**:232, 236

"The Mountain" (Capek)
See "Hora"

"The Mountain" (Leskov)
See "Gora"

"The Mountain" (Pavese) **19**:368, 390

"The Mountain Day" (Stafford) **26**:289

"The Mountain Tavern" (O'Flaherty) **6**:277-78, 281, 284

The Mountain Tavern, and Other Stories (O'Flaherty) **6**:262-65, 278, 283

"Mountjoy" (Irving) **2**:242

Mourner at the Door (Lish) **18**:275, 277-78, 280-83

"The Mourners" (Malamud) **15**:203, 205, 214, 217-18, 222-23, 225, 227

"The Mourners" (Naipaul) **38**:317, 321, 328, 331, 334, 344

"The Mouse" (Lavin) **4**:167, 182

"The Mouse" (Nin) **10**:299-303, 319

"The Mouse and the Woman" (Thomas) **3**:399-402, 408

"Mouse Performance" (P'u Sung-ling)
See "Shu'hsi"

"La moustache" (Maupassant) **1**:274

"Le Mouton" (Ayme) **41**:15

"The Moviemaker" (Dixon) **16**:211

"Movies" (Dixon) **16**:206, 208, 214

Movies (Dixon) **16**:205-08, 211, 214-15

"The Moving Finger" (King) **17**:294

"The Moving Finger" (Wharton) **6**:414

"Moving Spirit" (Clarke) **3**:134

"The Mower" (Bates) **10**:124, 131-32

"Mowgli's Brothers" (Kipling) **5**:293

"Moxon's Master" (Bierce) **9**:72, 88

"Mr and Mrs Dove" (Mansfield) **9**:305

"Mr. and Mrs. Elliot" (Hemingway) **1**:208

"Mr. and Mrs. Fix-It" (Lardner) **32**:117, 134-36, 139, 141, 145, 158-59

"Mr. Arcularis" (Aiken) **9**:5-6, 9, 12-13, 15, 18-19, 33-41

"Mr. Auerbach in Paris" (Wescott) **35**:375-76

"Mr. Austin" (Farrell) **28**:114, 116

"Mr. Bruce" (Jewett) **6**:157, 166

"Mr. Cass and the Ten Thousand Dollars" (O'Hara) **15**:248

"Mr. Coffee and Mr. Fixit" (Carver) **8**:18-19, 32-3, 59-60

"Mr. Cornelius Johnson, Office Seeker" (Dunbar) **8**:122, 125, 128, 131, 141, 144

"Mr. Durant" (Parker) **2**:274

Mr. Featherstone Takes a Ride (Bates) **10**:124

"Mr. Foolfarm's Journal" (Barthelme) **2**:40

"Mr. Fox Gets into Serious Business" (Harris) **19**:171

"Mr. Frisbie" (Lardner) **32**:117, 146

"Mr. Groby's Slippery Gift" (Dunbar) **8**:122

"Mr. Harrington's Washing" (Maugham) **8**:369, 377, 383

"Mr. Harrison's Confessions" (Gaskell) **25**:32-3, 55, 66-7, 73

"Mr. Havlena's Verdict" (Capek) **36**:127

"Mr. Humphreys and His Inheritance" (James) **16**:230-32, 234, 245, 252-53, 258

"Mr. Icky" (Fitzgerald) **6**:58

"Mr. Jack Hamlin's Mediation" (Harte) **8**:248-49

"Mr. Janík's Cases" (Capek)
See "Případy pana Janíka"

"Mr. Jones" (Wharton) **6**:426-27

"Mr. Justice Harbottle" (James) **16**:238

"Mr. Justice Hartbottle" (Le Fanu) **14**:223-25, 232-34, 236-38, 240-41, 248

"Mr. Know-All" (Maugham) **8**:366

"Mr. Lightfoot in the Green Isle" (Coppard) **21**:19

"Mr. Loveday's Little Outing" (Waugh) **41**:311, 323, 330

Mr Loveday's Little Outing and Other Sad Stories (Waugh) **41**:322, 328, 330-31

"Mr. McNamara" (Trevor) **21**:247

"Mr. Minns and His Cousin" (Dickens) **17**:121, 125

Mr. Mulliner Speaking (Wodehouse) **2**:338

"Mr. Pale" (Bradbury) **29**:66

"Mr. Peebles' Heart" (Gilman) **13**:126

"Mr. Pietro" (Pavese) **19**:378

"Mr. Potter Takes a Rest Cure" (Wodehouse) **2**:355-56

"Mr. Powers" (Gordon) **15**:143

"Mr. Preble Gets Rid of His Wife" (Thurber) **1**:418

"Mr. Prokharchin" (Dostoevsky) **2**:170, 191-94

"Mr. Rabbit Grossly Deceives Mr. Fox" (Harris) **19**:172, 194

"Mr. Rabbit Nibbles Up the Butter " (Harris) **19**:195

"Mr. Skelmersdale in Fairyland" (Wells) **6**:391-92

"Mr. Smellingscheck" (Lawson) **18**:215

"Mr. Taylor's Funeral" (Chesnutt) **7**:18

"Mr. U" (Morand) **22**:178-80

"Mr. Wolf Makes a Failure" (Harris) **19**:171

"Mrs. Acland's Ghosts" (Trevor) **21**:262

"Mrs. Bathurst" (Kipling) **5**:266, 278-79, 281

"Mrs. Billingsby's Wine" (Taylor) **10**:392, 401-02

"Mrs. Bonny" (Jewett) **6**:150, 168

"Mrs. Brown" (O'Hara) **15**:248

"Mrs. Brumby" (Trollope) **28**:321, 335, 348, 353

"Mrs. Dalloway in Bond Street" (Woolf) **7**:381-82

Mrs. Dalloway's Party (Woolf) **7**:381-82, 388, 392

"Mrs. Fay Dines on Zebra" (Calisher) **15**:3, 7

"Mrs. Frola and Her Son-in-Law, Mr. Ponza" (Pirandello)
See "La Signora Frola e il signor Ponza, suo genero"

"Mrs. Galt and Edwin" (O'Hara) **15**:248, 266

Mrs. Gaskell's Tales of Mystery and Horror (Gaskell) **25**:37

"Mrs. General Talboys" (Trollope) **28**:317-18, 330, 332, 336, 347, 357

"Mrs. Gunton of Poughkeepsie" (James) **8**:311

"Mrs. Hofstadter on Josephine Street" (Parker) **2**:283

"Mrs. Hospitality" (Dazai Osamu) **41**:240, 242

"Mrs. Johnson" (Howells) **36**:399

"Mrs. Kemper" (Suckow) **18**:393, 409

"Mrs. M" (Williams) **31**:329

"Mrs. Mean" (Gass) **12**:123, 134,138-9

"Mrs. Merrill's Duties" (Gilman) **13**:141

"Mrs. Mobry's Reason" (Chopin) **8**:71

"Mrs. Parkins's Christmas Eve" (Jewett) **6**:156, 159

"Mrs. Partridge Has a Fit" (Harris) **19**:195

"Mrs. Peckover's Sky . . ." (Wilson) **21**:358, 362

"Mrs. Powers' Duty" (Gilman) **13**:141

"Mrs. Reinhardt" (O'Brien) **10**:333

Mrs. Reinhardt, and Other Stories (O'Brien) **10**:333

"Mrs. Rinaldi's Angel" (Ligotti) **16**:280, 292, 294-95, 297

"Mrs. Ripley's Trip" (Garland) **18**:143, 159, 162-63, 165-67, 172, 192

"Mrs. Silly" (Trevor) **21**:233

"Mrs. Skagg's Husbands" (Harte) **8**:234, 244

"Mrs. Stratton of Oak Knoll" (O'Hara) **15**:252, 280

"Mrs. Todd's Shortcut" (King) **17**:275

"Mrs. Vane's Charade" (Alcott) **27**:32, 60

"Mrs. Vincent" (Bates) **10**:117

"Mrs. Vogel and Ollie" (Suckow) **18**:394-95, 413, 416, 422-23

"Mrs. Whitman" (O'Hara) **15**:264

"MS. Found in a Bottle" (Poe) **1**:379, 391-92, 398; **35**:310

"Mt. Pisgah's Christmas Possum" (Dunbar) **8**:121, 127, 131, 136

"Muddler on the Roof" (Perelman) **32**:231

"The Mudfog Association" (Dickens) **17**:121

"Muerte constante más allá der amor" (Garcia Marquez) **8**:167, 169-72, 186

"La muerte del tigre" (Castellanos) **39**:47, 48, 56

"La muerte y la brújula" (Borges) **4**:4, 10, 16, 19-24, 28-30, 35-6; **41**:64-65, 69-72, 75-76, 152, 164, 166

"El muerto" (Borges) **4**:4-5, 8-9, 23, 37-9; **41**:114-17, 119

"Les muets" (Camus) **9**:103, 105, 108, 110, 116, 119, 121-22, 125

"The Muffled Ship" (Galsworthy) **22**:62, 101

"Una mujer amaestrada" (Arreola) **38**:10-11

"Mule in the Yard" (Faulkner) **1**:177

Mules and Men (Hurston) **4**:133-36, 139-49, 153, 155-56, 158-59

"A mulher de preto" (Machado de Assis) **24**:132

Mulliner Nights (Wodehouse) **2**:338

"Mulvihill's Memorial" (Trevor) **21**:262

"Mummy to the Rescue" (Wilson) **21**:337, 346, 348, 354-55

The Mummy's Tale (Gautier)
See *Le Roman de la momie*

"Mumu" (Turgenev) **7**:315, 320, 323, 326, 352-57, 363

Munchmeyer (Thomas) **20**:286-87, 313-16, 320

"El mundo" (Pardo Bazan) **30**:272

"La muñeca menor" (Ferre) **36**:142-43, 148, 150-51, 156, 159-60, 163-67

"La muñeca reina" (Fuentes) **24**:29, 31, 44, 51, 56, 58, 61-3, 70, 73, 82

Una muñeca rusa (Bioy Casares) **17**:94, 96

"El Muñeco" (Fuentes) **24**:37

"A Municipal Report" (Henry) **5**:156, 165, 171-72, 179, 182, 192

"Munitions of War" (Machen) **20**:200

"Le Mur" (Sartre) **32**:255, 261, 264-67, 273-74, 276, 278-82

Le mur (Sartre) **32**:254-55, 265, 267-68, 270, 272

"The Murder" (Boell) **23**:38

"The Murder" (Chekhov) **2**:150

"Murder" (Sansom) **21**:94, 125

"The Murder" (Steinbeck) **11**:207, 210, 225, 229-33, 235, 244, 247, 254; **37**:330, 357

"Murder at Cobbler's Hulk" (O'Faolain) **13**:296

"Murder at Full Moon by Peter Pym" (Steinbeck) **11**:254-55

"Murder for the Wrong Reason" (Greene) **29**:216-17, 223

Murder in the Dark (Atwood) **2**:15, 17-20

"Murder on Belpoggio Street" (Svevo)
See *L'assassinio di via Belpoggio*

"The Murdered Cousin" (Le Fanu)
See "A Passage in the Secret History of an Irish Countess"

"The Murderer" (Bulgakov) **18**:101

"Murderers" (Michaels) **16**:306, 308-11, 316, 321

"The Murders in the Rue Morgue" (Poe) **1**:378, 387, 389, 395, 406; **22**:293, 303, 306; **35**:307-08

"Muriel" (Gardner) **7**:234

Murke's Collected Silences (Boell)
See *Doktor Murkes gesammeltes Schweigen, und andere Satiren*

"The Muse of the Coming Age" (Andersen) **6**:7

"The Muses" (Pavese) **19**:370-71, 390

"The Muse's Tragedy" (Wharton) **6**:414, 428

"Museum of Cheats" (Warner) **23**:370

The Museum of Cheats (Warner) **23**:369, 380

"Museums and Women" (Updike) **13**:348, 375

Museums and Women, and Other Stories
　(Updike) **13**:356-61, 366-68
"Mushrooms" (Bradbury) **29**:58-9
"Music" (Gilchrist) **14**:154
"Music" (de la Mare) **14**:92
"Music" (Nabokov) **11**:122, 125
"Music" (Trevor) **21**:246, 248
"Music for Chameleons" (Capote) **2**:80
Music for Chameleons (Capote) **2**:79-81
"Music from Spain" (Welty) **1**:474, 495
"The Music Lesson" (Cheever) **1**:100
"The Music Lover" (Gardner) **7**:223, 225-26,
　238
"The Music of Erich Zann" (Lovecraft) **3**:269
"The Music of the Moon" (Ligotti) **16**:278
"The Music on the Hill" (Saki) **12**:288, 315,
　331, 334
"The Music School" (Updike) **13**:348, 375
The Music School (Updike) **13**:352, 354, 356,
　366-67, 374-76, 378, 380
"The Music Teacher" (Cheever) **1**:106; **38**:47
"The Musician" (Selby) **20**:275
Musikalische Leiden und Freuden (Tieck)
　31:271, 286
"The Musk Ox" (Leskov)
　See "Ovcebyk"
"Mustafa Madjar" (Andric) **36**:30, 33, 38, 52
"The Mutability of Literature" (Irving) **2**:251,
　254
"Mute" (Atwood) **2**:16
"The Mute Companions" (Narayan) **25**:134,
　138, 140, 154
"Mutimer's Choice" (Gissing) **37**:63
"Muttsy" (Hurston) **4**:136, 138, 151
"Muž, který nemohl spát" (Capek) **36**:98
"Muž, který se nelíbil" (Capek) **36**:97, 101-02,
　105, 128
"Muza" (Bunin) **5**:114
"My Aunt" (Irving) **2**:242
"My Aunt Gold Teeth" (Naipaul) **38**:300, 318,
　320, 328, 334, 344
"My Aunt Margaret's Mirror" (Scott) **32**:319
My Boys (Alcott)
　See *Aunt Jo's Scrap-Bag: My Boys*
"My Brother Elye's Drink" (Aleichem) **33**:83
"My Brother Paul" (Dreiser) **30**:112, 114
"My Clerical Rival" (Gissing) **37**:79
"My Cousin Dickran, The Orator" (Saroyan)
　21:172
"My Cousin Fanny" (Page) **23**:284, 326, 328
"My Cousins who could eat cooked turnips"
　(Frame) **29**:106
"My Da" (O'Connor) **5**:388
"My Daily Horse" (Valenzuela) **14**:366
"My Daughter's Admirers" (Murfree) **22**:221
My Day (Rhys) **21**:48
"My Disciple" (Lewis) **34**:157
"My Expensive Leg" (Boell)
　See "Mein teures Bein"
"My Father" (Michaels) **16**:321
"My Father Is an Educated Man" (Stuart)
　31:232-33, 266
"My Father Joins the Fire Brigade" (Schulz)
　13:335
"My Father Leaves Home" (Gordimer) **17**:177,
　182-85
"My Father's Best Suit" (Frame) **29**:106
"My Father's Cough" (Boell) **23**:34
"My Fellow-Traveler to Oxford" (Lewis)
　34:157
"My Fellow-Traveller" (Gorky) **28**:136, 148,
　158
"My Financial Career" (Leacock) **39**:261
"My First and Only House" (Adams) **24**:15
"My First Goose" (Babel) **16**:9, 10, 16, 28, 30,
　53-4, 57-8
"My First Protestant" (O'Connor) **5**:386-87
"My First Rehearsal" (Gissing) **37**:79
My First Rehearsal and My Clerical Rival
　(Gissing) **37**:79
"My First Two Women" (Gordimer) **17**:152
"My French Master" (Gaskell) **25**:67

"My Friend Naboth" (Page) **23**:311-12
"My Friend the Doctor" (Page) **23**:288, 307
"My Girls" (Alcott) **27**:9
My Girls (Alcott) **27**:43
"My Great-Grandfather's Papers" (Stifter)
　See "Die Mappe meines Urgrossvaters"
"My Heart Is Broken" (Gallant) **5**:141
My Heart Is Broken (Gallant) **5**:122-23, 130,
　139-41
My House in Umbria (Trevor)
　See *Two Lives: Reading Turgenev; My
　House in Umbria*
"My Hundredth Tale" (Coppard) **21**:10, 12, 17,
　28
"My Husband Is Right" (Wilson) **21**:357, 363
"My Kinsman, Major Molineux" (Hawthorne)
　3:164-65, 167, 171, 175-76, 179-80, 182-
　83, 186-87, 189; **39**:100, 128, 135
"My Lady Brandon and the Widow Jim"
　(Jewett) **6**:154
"My Lady Greensleeves" (Pohl) **25**:223-24
My Lady Ludlow (Gaskell) **25**:34-6, 41, 54-5,
　57-9, 66, 73
"My Last Duchess" (Lardner) **32**:133
"My Last Journey" (Pirandello) **22**:236
"My Last Story" (Frame) **29**:103, 110, 115
"My Life" (Chekhov) **2**:128, 130-32, 135-36,
　145, 155, 157; **28**:60; **41**:202
My Life and Hard Times (Thurber) **1**:413-14,
　419, 421-24, 426-28, 435
"My Life with R. H. Macy" (Jackson) **9**:252,
　267; **39**:211, 216, 217, 222
"My Little Robins" (Sansom) **21**:91, 93
"My Lost Opportunities" (Leacock) **39**:262
"My Love, My Umbrella" (McGahern) **17**:302,
　308-09, 318, 323
"My Lucy Friend Who Smells Like Corn"
　(Cisneros) **32**:4
"My Man Bovanne" (Bambara) **35**:18, 24, 33
"My Metamorphosis" (Harte) **8**:254
"My Molly" (Lavin) **4**:167
"My Mother's Death and the Coming of My
　New Mother" (Shiga)
　See "Haha no shi to atarishi haha"
My Mother's House (Colette)
　See *La maison de Claudine*
"My Mother's Life" (Lessing) **6**:216
"My Mother's Mother" (O'Brien) **10**:334
"My Name" (Cisneros) **32**:32, 41, 46
My Name is Aram (Saroyan) **21**:146-47, 153,
　156, 169, 173-75
"My Name is Everyone" (Vonnegut) **8**:433, 437
"My Neighbor" (Kafka) **5**:206
"My Nurse Above All Others" (Kundera)
　24:103
"My Oedipus Complex" (O'Connor) **5**:368-69,
　378, 386-87
"My Old Home" (Lu Hsun)
　See "Guxiang"
"My Old Man" (Caldwell) **19**:17-18, 41, 47, 50
"My Old Man" (Hemingway) **1**:208, 219, 234,
　245; **36**:280
"My Old Man" (Lardner) **32**:117
"My Old Man and Pretty Sooky" (Caldwell)
　19:50-1
"My Old Man and the Gypsy Queen"
　(Caldwell) **19**:51
"My Old Man Hasn't Been the Same Since"
　(Caldwell) **19**:50-2
"My Old Man's Baling Machine" (Caldwell)
　19:51
"My Old Man's Political Appointment"
　(Caldwell) **19**:50-1
"My Own True Ghost-Story" (Kipling)
　5:272-73
"My Pal with the Long Hair" (Boell) **23**:11
"My Picture in the Paper" (Saroyan) **21**:137
"My Picture Left in Scotland" (Garrett) **30**:166,
　174
"My Platonic Sweetheart" (Twain) **26**:330
"My Pretty Birdie, Birdie in My Cage"
　(Garrett) **30**:174

"My Pretty Pony" (King) **17**:294
"My Professions" (Zoshchenko) **15**:400
"My Roomy" (Lardner) **32**:115-16, 128-29,
　131, 142-43, 145, 148, 154-55, 164-65
"My Sad Face" (Boell) **23**:11-12
"My Side of the Matter" (Capote) **2**:61-2, 65,
　70, 83-5
"My Son Austin" (O'Faolain) **13**:284
"My Tears" (Oe)
　See "Mizu kara waga namida o nuguitamo
　hi"
"My Tocaya" (Cisneros) **32**:9, 35-36
"My Travelling Companion" (Gorky)
　See "My Fellow-Traveller"
"My Tree" (Sansom) **21**:85
"My Uncle John" (Irving) **2**:242
My Uncle Silas (Bates) **10**:117, 130-31
"My Unforgettable Character" (Cabrera
　Infante) **39**:24
"My Vocation" (Lavin) **4**:167
"My Warszawa: 1980" (Oates) **6**:255
My World—And Welcome to It (Thurber) **1**:420
"My Youngest Child" (Shiga) **23**:349
"Myra" (Berriault) **30**:97-8
"Myra Meets His Family" (Fitzgerald) **6**:56, 96
"Myself upon the Earth" (Saroyan) **21**:132, 135,
　141, 143
Mysteries and Adventures (Doyle) **12**:58-9
"The Mysterious Key" (Alcott) **27**:57
"Mysterious Kôr" (Bowen) **3**:31-32, 39, 41-42,
　44, 53; **28**:3-4, 9
"The Mysterious Lodger" (Le Fanu) **14**:238
"The Mysterious Stranger" (Twain) **6**:331
The Mysterious Stranger (Twain) **6**:294-99,
　301-02, 305-06, 312-16, 322-25, 331, 334,
　345-50, 353; **26**:318-64
"The Mystery" (Pavese) **19**:365, 370
"The Mystery of Dave Regan" (Lawson)
　18:217, 238-39
"A Mystery of Heroism" (Crane) **7**:102, 106,
　109
"The Mystery of Marie Rogêt" (Poe) **1**:386,
　388, 400, 406; **35**:306
"The Mystery of Sasassa Valley, a South
　African Story" (Doyle) **12**:84
"The Mystery of the Time Piece" (Moorhouse)
　40:324
"The Mystery of Witch-Face Mountain"
　(Murfree) **22**:196, 212
"The Mystic Journal" (Auchincloss) **22**:45, 50
"The Mystics of Muelenburg" (Ligotti) **16**:263,
　267, 276, 278, 283-84, 286-87, 295
"Mystification" (Poe) **22**:300
"Myten om människorna" (Lagerkvist) **12**:181
"The Myth of Mankind" (Lagerkvist)
　See "Myten om människorna"
"Myths of the Near Future" (Ballard) **1**:78-9
Myths of the Near Future (Ballard) **1**:78-9, 82
"My-to ne umrem" (Solzhenitsyn) **32**:353, 395
"N" (Machen) **20**:177, 186-87, 196
"Na arca" (Machado de Assis) **24**:128-29, 132
"N.A. Bugrov" (Gorky) **28**:182
"Na drugi dan Božica" (Andric) **36**:47, 52
"Na kamenu u Počitelju" (Andric) **36**:50
"Na kraj sveta" (Bunin) **5**:98
"Na kraju sveta" (Leskov) **34**:108, 114, 129
"Na obali" (Andric) **36**:47
"Na plotakh" (Gorky) **28**:144, 159, 178, 190
"Na xutore" (Bunin) **5**:98
"Nabo: The Black Man Who Made the Angels
　Wait" (Garcia Marquez) **8**:154-55, 157-
　58, 183, 185
Nabokov's Dozen (Nabokov) **11**:108, 110, 126-
　28, 130
"Nabonides" (Arreola) **38**:13
"Nachkommenschaften" (Stifter) **28**:299
Nachstücke (Hoffmann) **13**:180, 182, 186-88,
　234
"Die Nacht im Hotel" (Lenz) **33**:318
"Der Nachtzug" (Hauptmann) **37**:258

Nada menos que todo un hombre (Unamuno) **11**:313-14, 320-22, 324-25, 327, 345, 351-52
"Naga" (Narayan) **25**:170
Nahan (Lu Hsun) **20**:125-26, 136, 138-39, 141-42, 144, 146, 148
"The Nails in Mr. Caterer" (Hammett) **17**:224
"Le Nain" (Ayme) **41**:18-19, 22
"Los naipes del Tahur" (Borges) **41**:65
La naissance du jour (Colette) **10**:262, 274, 278-79, 285
"Naked" (Michaels) **16**:311
"Naked in the River" (Dazai Osamu) **41**:229
Naked Life (Pirandello)
    See *La vita nuda*
"Naked Nude" (Malamud) **15**:171, 173-75, 183, 192-94, 222
"The Naked Truth" (Pirandello) **22**:227
The Naked Truth (Pirandello) **22**:226, 228
"Nakedness" (Pavese)
    See "Nudismo"
"Nakedness" (Updike) **13**:387
"Nala" (Narayan) **25**:131
"The Name" (Pavese) **19**:376, 387
"The Name, the Nose" (Calvino) **3**:119
"The Name-Day" (Saki) **12**:317
"The Name-Day Party" (Chekhov) **2**:128, 130-31, 133, 149, 155-56
"The Nameless City" (Lovecraft) **3**:262-63, 269, 274, 276
"Names" (Dixon) **16**:204
"The Names and Faces of Heroes" (Price) **22**:361, 375, 382-84, 387
The Names and Faces of Heroes (Price) **22**:359-60, 363-64, 367, 374, 384-85
"The Namesake" (Cather) **2**:97, 103-04, 113
"Namgay Doola" (Kipling) **5**:262
"The Naming of Names" (Bradbury)
    See "Dark They Were, and Golden-Eyed"
"Nancy Culpepper" (Mason) **4**:13
"Nanette: An Aside" (Cather) **2**:101
"Nanni Volpe" (Verga) **21**:298
"The Nap" (de la Mare) **14**:70, 79, 83, 86, 88
"Napier Court" (Campbell) **19**:62, 87
"Nápis" (Capek) **36**:111, 122
"Naprostý dukaz" (Capek) **36**:96, 102
Narcissa, and Other Fables (Auchincloss) **22**:35, 47, 51
"Narcissus" (Dazai Osamu)
    See "Suisen"
Der Narr auf Manegg (Keller) **26**:92, 108, 113
The Narrative (Pasternak)
    See *Povest*
"Die Narrenburg" (Stifter) **28**:290, 299
"A Narrow Heart: The Portrait of a Woman" (Gordon) **15**:122-23, 126
"A Nasty Type" (Bulgakov) **18**:89
Natasqua (Davis) **38**:96
"Nathalie" (Bunin) **5**:87, 113, 115
Natica Jackson (O'Hara) **15**:278, 284-85
"A Nation of Wheels" (Barthelme) **2**:40
"The National Pastime" (Cheever) **1**:100
"Native of Winby" (Jewett) **6**:155
"Native's Return" (Farrell) **28**:112
"Nattergalen" (Andersen)
    See "The Nightingale"
"Natural Boundaries" (Oates) **6**:248-50
"A Natural History of the Dead" (Hemingway) **1**:211
Natural Stories (Levi)
    See *Storie naturali*
Natural Supernaturalism (Abrams) **20**:289, 295-96, 298, 317, 319
"Nature" (Machen) **20**:159
"Nature" (Turgenev) **7**:335
The Nature of Love (Bates) **10**:117-21
"Las náufragas" (Pardo Bazan) **30**:271-72
"The Naughty Boy" (Andersen) **6**:30, 32
"The Navigator Returns to His Country" (Bioy Casares) **17**:94
Neanderthal Planet (Aldiss) **36**:18

"Necessity's Child" (Wilson) **21**:333, 346, 348, 354, 359
"The Necklace" (Maupassant)
    See "La parure"
"The Necklace" (Pritchett) **14**:280, 299, 305
"The Necktie" (Aiken) **9**:5, 9, 13-14
"Nedda" (Verga) **21**:284-86, 301-04, 308
"A Need for Something Sweet" (Gordimer) **17**:193-94
"The Needle" (Capek)
    See "Jehla"
"Needle and Glass and Fog" (Kawabata)
    See "Hari to Ciarasu to Kiri"
"The Needlecase" (Bowen) **3**:41
"Der Neger" (Walser) **20**:341
"A Neglected Class" (Page) **23**:311
"Negriero" (Moravia) **26**:144
"The Negro" (Walser)
    See "Der Neger"
"The Negro and the Old Man with the Knife" (Moravia)
    See "The Negro and the Old Man with the Knife"
"The Negro in the Drawing Room" (Hughes) **6**:121-22
"The Negro in the Well" (Caldwell) **19**:14
The Negro of Peter the Great (Pushkin)
    See *Arap Petra Velikogo*
"The Neighborhood" (O'Hara) **15**:279
"The Neighboring Families" (Andersen) **6**:7
"Neighbors" (Carver) **8**:4-6, 9-10, 34, 42, 47, 54
"Neighbors" (Singer) **3**:384
Neighbors (Hesse) **9**:230
"A Neighbor's Landmark" (James) **16**:236, 252, 254
"Neighbour Rosicky" (Cather) **2**:105, 115-17
"Neighbours" (Andric)
    See "Susedi"
"The Neighbours" (Galsworthy) **22**:58, 80, 82
"Neighbours" (de la Mare) **14**:87
"Neighbours" (Pritchett) **14**:277
"Neighbour's Help" (Narayan) **25**:138
"Neil MacAdam" (Maugham) **8**:376
"Neither the Most Terrifying nor the Least Memorable" (Valenzuela) **14**:367
"Nell" (Ross) **24**:297, 306, 310
"Nelse Hatton's Revenge" (Dunbar) **8**:119, 121, 127, 140, 143
"Nelse Hatton's Vengeance" (Dunbar)
    See "Nelse Hatton's Revenge"
Nelson Algren's Own Book of Lonesome Monsters (Algren) **33**:89
"Nelson Redline" (Hammett) **17**:217
"Nemirna godina" (Andric) **36**:34
"Nemureru bijo" (Kawabata) **17**:235-41, 243-45
Nemureru bijo (Kawabata) **17**:234, 240, 246
"Neo-Einstein Stirs Savants!" (Perelman) **32**:240
The Neon Wilderness (Algren) **33**:87-9, 99, 101-02, 107-11, 113
"Neron tiple o el calvario de un inglé" (Unamuno) **11**:312
"HaNerot" (Agnon) **30**:37
"Nervous" (Walser) **20**:349
"A Nervous Breakdown" (Chekhov)
    See "An Attack of Nerves"
Nervous People, and Other Stories (Zoshchenko) **15**:405-07
"Neschastnaya" (Turgenev) **7**:321, 324, 326, 336-38, 358-59
"Nesselrode to Jeopardy" (Perelman) **32**:211
"Nest, Door, Neighbours" (Cabrera Infante) **39**:24
"Nest Egg" (Stuart) **31**:233, 263
"The Nest of Nightingales" (Gautier) **20**:3
"Nethescurial" (Ligotti) **16**:284, 293
"Neutron Tide" (Clarke) **3**:133
"Nevada Gas" (Chandler) **23**:56, 59, 85, 104, 106-07, 109
"Never Bet the Devil Your Head" (Poe) **1**:407

"Never Marry a Mexican" (Cisneros) **32**:10, 15-17, 20-21, 23, 25, 34, 36-37, 39
"Never, Never—Never, Never" (Trollope) **28**:317, 333
"Nevermore Without End" (Sansom) **21**:122
"Nevskij Avenue" (Gogol)
    See "Nevsky Prospect"
"Nevsky Prospect" (Gogol) **4**:95, 122, 124-25, 128; **29**:135, 152
"The New Accelerator" (Wells) **6**:367, 391, 393, 404, 406
The New Arabian Nights (Stevenson) **11**:268-70, 280
New Arrivals, Old Encounters (Aldiss) **36**:13-14, 18
"The New Atlantis" (Le Guin) **12**:220
"The New Catacomb" (Doyle) **12**:49
"The New Country House" (Chekhov)
    See "The New Villa"
"New Day" (O'Hara) **15**:248
"The New Dress" (Woolf) **7**:373, 376, 381-82, 387, 393, 395
"New Dresses" (Mansfield) **9**:281; **38**:204
"A New England Nun" (Freeman) **1**:192, 197, 199
A New England Nun, and Other Stories (Freeman) **1**:191, 194-95, 197
"A New England Prophet" (Freeman) **1**:197
"The New Englander" (Anderson) **1**:27, 30, 39, 46-7, 53, 55
"New Eve and Old Adam" (Lawrence) **4**:220
"The New Father Christmas" (Aldiss) **36**:20
"The New House" (Bowen) **3**:40, 54
"The New House" (Greene) **29**:222-23
New Islands and Other Stories (Bombal) **37**:41
"The New Lebanon Agent" (Page) **23**:307, 311-12
"The New Man" (Lessing) **6**:191, 198
"A New Melody" (Peretz) **26**:206
"A New Method of Book Distribution" (Bulgakov) **18**:90
"The New Moon Party" (Boyle) **16**:143-44, 146
"The New Music" (Barthelme) **2**:55
"A New Refutation of Time" (Borges) **4**:5
New Stories (Andersen)
    See *Eventyr, fortalte for bøorn*
"A New Stretch of Woods" (Price) **22**:387
"The New Suit" (O'Flaherty) **6**:287
New Tales of the Provinces (Dazai Osamu) **41**:247
"The New Teacher" (O'Connor)
    See "The Cheapjack"
"The New Villa" (Chekhov) **2**:131, 156
"A New World" (Jolley) **19**:234
"The New Year" (Dickens) **17**:116
"New Year's Bells" (Dreiser)
    See "When the Old Century Was New"
New Year's Eve (The 'SeventiesWharton) **6**:439-40, 442
"The New Year's Sacrifice" (Lu Hsin)
    See "Zhufu"
"New York by Campfire Light" (Henry) **5**:159
"New York Lady" (Parker)
    See "From the Diary of a New York Lady"
New York Quartet (Wharton)
    See *Old New York*
"New York to Detroit" (Parker) **2**:274, 280, 285
"News for the Church" (O'Connor) **5**:371, 383, 385, 389
"News from Chelsea" (Sansom) **21**:102
"The News from Ireland" (Trevor) **21**:247-48, 250, 252-53, 262, 267-68
The News from Ireland, and Other Stories (Trevor) **21**:246, 262
"News from the Sun" (Ballard) **1**:78-9
"The News in English" (Greene) **29**:217, 223, 225-26
"The Newspaper" (Wolfe) **33**:401
The Newspaper of Claremont Street (Jolley) **19**:221, 229, 233, 237, 242, 244-46
"A New-Wave Format" (Mason) **4**:14
"The Next in Line" (Bradbury) **29**:41, 66, 88

"The Next Tenants" (Clarke) **3**:135
"The Next Time" (James) **8**:281, 317
"Next Time You'll Know Me" (Campbell) **19**:77-8
"Nice Day at School" (Trevor) **21**:231, 233
"Nice Girl" (Anderson) **1**:52
"The Nice Old Man and the Pretty Girl" (Svevo)
    See "La novella del buon vecchio e della bella fanciulla"
The Nice Old Man and the Pretty Girl, and Other Stories (Svevo)
    See *La novella del buon vecchio e della bella fanciulla*
"A Nice Old-Fashioned Romance with Love Lyrics and Everything" (Saroyan) **21**:172
"A Nice Quiet Place" (Fitzgerald) **6**:80
"Nicht nur zur Weihnachtzeit" (Boell) **23**:38
The Nick Adams Stories (Hemingway) **1**:240
"Nickel" (Levi) **12**:268, 280
"Un nido de gorrionesen un toldo" (Cabrera Infante) **39**:24
"Nieh Hsiao-ch'ien" (P'u Sung-ling) **31**:192
"Nien yang" (P'u Sung-ling) **31**:205
"Niente" (Moravia) **26**:148
"El nieto del Cid" (Pardo Bazan) **30**:272, 290
"The Nigger" (Barnes) **3**:5, 10-11, 14, 22
"Nigger Jeff" (Dreiser) **30**:114-22, 126-27, 129, 131-33
The Nigger of Peter the Great (Pushkin)
    See *Arap Petra Velikogo*
"The Night" (Agnon)
    See "Laila min haLelot"
"The Night" (Bradbury) **29**:63, 65
"Night" (Bunin) **5**:100, 108, 114
"Night" (O'Brien) **10**:345
"Night" (Pirandello)
    See "Notte"
"A Night among the Horses" (Barnes) **3**:5-7, 10, 14, 16, 22-4
"Night and Silence" (Price) **22**:384
"A Night at Greenway Court" (Cather) **2**:100
"A Night at the Fair" (Fitzgerald) **6**:49
A Night at the Movies, or You Must Remember This (Coover) **15**:57, 61, 63
"The Night before Prohibition" (Aiken) **9**:12, 14
"Night Call, Collect" (Bradbury) **29**:56
"The Night Came Slowly" (Chopin) **8**:98, 110-11
"The Night Club in the Woods" (Calisher) **15**:5, 8
"A Night Conversation" (Bunin) **5**:81, 90-1
"The Night Driver" (Calvino) **3**:109
"The Night Face Up" (Cortazar)
    See "La noche boca arriba"
"The Night Flier" (King) **17**:295
"A Night for Love" (Vonnegut) **8**:433
"The Night He Was Left Alone" (Rulfo)
    See "La noche que lo dejaron solo"
A Night in Acadie (Chopin) **8**:66-8, 77, 84, 93-4, 97, 110-14
"A Night in June" (Williams) **31**:304-05, 325, 332-33, 340, 342, 344-45, 347-48
"A Night in New Arabia" (Henry) **5**:184
"A Night in the Alhambra" (Andric)
    See "Noc u Alhambri"
"A Night in the Woods" (Barnes) **3**:18
"Night Journey" (Lewis) **40**:278-79
"The Night My Old Man Came Home" (Caldwell) **19**:14, 49-50, 52
"A Night of Cyclone" (Narayan) **25**:138, 155-56
"The Night of Denial" (Bunin) **5**:82
"A Night of Horror" (Peretz)
    See "A Night of Horror"
"A Night of Nothing" (Saroyan) **21**:134
"Night of Six Days" (Morand)
    See "La nuit de seis jours"
"The Night of the Curlews" (Garcia Marquez)
    See "La noche de los alcaravanes"

"Night of the Great Season" (Schulz)
    See "Noc wielkiego sezonu"
"A Night on the Divide" (Harte) **8**:216, 253
"Night Out, 1925" (Rhys) **21**:55-6
"Night Owls" (Leskov)
    See "Polunoščniki"
Night Pieces after the Manner of Callot (Hoffmann)
    See *Phantasiestüeke in Callots Manier*
"Night Report" (Jolley) **19**:234
Night Run to the West (Bates) **10**:119
Night Shift (King) **17**:261-62, 273-76, 294
"Night Sketches" (Hawthorne) **3**:189, 191; **39**:111
"Night Surf" (King) **17**:269
"The Night the Bed Fell" (Thurber) **1**:428
"The Night the Favorite Came Home" (Gordimer) **17**:161
"The Night the Ghost Got In" (Thurber) **1**:428, 432
"The Night the Prowler" (White) **39**:301, 303, 306, 309-11, 319, 324, 327, 329, 337, 345
"The Night They Left Him Alone" (Rulfo)
    See "La noche que lo dejaron solo"
Night Visions 3 (Campbell) **19**:87
"The Night Watchman's Occurrence Book" (Naipaul) **38**:321, 328, 346-47
"Night! Youth! Paris! and the Moon!" (Collier) **19**:101-02, 110, 114-15
"The Night-Born" (London) **4**:266, 291
"The Nightingale" (Andersen) **6**:7, 16, 27, 30, 32-4, 37, 40
"The Nightingale and the Rose" (Wilde) **11**:372, 375-76, 378-79, 386-87, 389, 393, 395, 402-04, 406-09
Nightlines (McGahern) **17**:298, 301-03, 306-09, 320, 322
"The Nightmare Child" (Galsworthy) **22**:63, 74, 79, 101
"Nightmares" (Cortazar)
    See "Pesadillas"
Nightmares and Dreamscapes (King) **17**:293-96
"Nightpiece with Figures" (O'Connor) **5**:382, 385, 391-92
"Nights in Europe's Ministeries" (Cortazar)
    See "Noches en los ministerios de Europa"
"Nights in the Gardens of Spain" (Berriault) **30**:96-8, 104
"The Nights of Goliadkin" (Bioy Casares)
    See "Las noches de Goliadkin"
Nights with Uncle Remus: Myths and Legends of the Old Plantation (Harris) **19**:130, 133-34, 144, 146, 148, 151, 156, 160-64, 166, 169, 187, 189, 193-96
"A Night's Work" (Gaskell)
    See "A Dark Night's Work"
"Night-Sea Journey" (Barth) **10**:41-3, 45-8, 53-4, 56-7, 60-1, 75-6, 80, 90, 97-8, 80, 84, 87, 89, 91, 97-100
"The Night-Worker" (Pritchett) **14**:297
"Nilushka" (Gorky) **28**:150
"N'importe où hors du monde" (Baudelaire) **18**:5, 40
"Nimram" (Gardner) **7**:223-27, 235, 238, 241
Nina Balatka (Trollope) **28**:317
"La niña mártir" (Pardo Bazan) **30**:263, 271
"The Nine Billion Names of God" (Clarke) **3**:134-35, 137, 145
"Nine Dollars Worth of Mumble" (Caldwell) **19**:44
Nine Fairy Tales (Capek) **36**:84, 108
"Nine Hours Alone" (Price) **22**:386
"Nine Lives" (Le Guin) **12**:231-33
Nine Stories (Salinger) **2**:289-91, 299, 312-13, 316, 318-19; **28**:261
Nine Women (Grau) **15**:161-64
"Ninepenny Flute" (Coppard) **21**:17, 29
"Nineteen Fifty-Five" (Walker) **5**:412, 414
Nineteen Stories (Greene) **29**:182-86, 190, 213, 224-25
"1957, a Romance" (Gilchrist) **14**:150
"1940: FALL" (Adams) **24**:16

"1944" (Gilchrist) **14**:150
"1934" (Phillips) **16**:326, 328, 337
"1939" (Taylor) **10**:381-82, 385, 416
"Ninety Minutes Away" (O'Hara) **15**:259
"Ningyo no nageki" (Tanizaki) **21**:197
"El niño de San Antonio" (Pardo Bazan) **30**:262
"Nirvana Small by a Waterfall" (Perelman) **32**:211
"Nitrogen" (Levi) **12**:255, 265, 268
"Niwa" (Dazai Osamu) **41**:247-48
"Nixey's Harlequin" (Coppard) **21**:28
Nixey's Harlequin (Coppard) **21**:10, 12
"No Country for Old Men" (O'Faolain) **13**:314
"No Crime in the Mountains" (Chandler) **23**:65, 67-8, 72, 82, 89, 110
"No Cure for It" (Wolfe) **33**:374, 398-99, 401
"No Different Flesh" (Henderson) **29**:327
"No Dogs Bark" (Rulfo) **25**:269-70
No Door (Wolfe) **33**:347-49, 351-54, 367, 369-70, 376
"No Friend Like a New Friend" (Auchincloss) **22**:43
"No Haid Pawn" (Page) **23**:283, 292, 300, 303, 314-16, 320, 325
"No Harm Trying" (Fitzgerald) **6**:69-70
"No Hero" (Stuart) **31**:228, 265
"No Man's Laughter" (Algren) **33**:108
"No More Rivers" (Wolfe) **33**:401
"No More the Nightingales" (Bates) **10**:116-17
"No Morning After" (Clarke) **3**:149
"No Motive" (du Maurier)
    See "The Motive"
"No, No, Go Not to Lethe" (Aiken) **9**:6, 9, 14, 41
No One Writes to the Colonel (Garcia Marquez)
    See *El colonel no tiene quien le escribe*
"No Other Way" (Ross) **24**:291-92, 306, 309-10
"No oyes ladrar los perros" (Rulfo) **25**:246, 249-50, 263, 265, 269, 274, 276, 278
"No Particular Night or Morning" (Bradbury) **29**:42, 80
"No Petty Thief" (Stuart) **31**:229
"No Place for a Woman" (Lawson) **18**:252
"No Place for You, My Love" (Welty) **1**:476, 479, 484, 493
"No Place Like" (Gordimer) **17**:158
No Relief (Dixon) **16**:203, 209-10, 213, 215
"No Starch in the Dhoti, s'il vous plaît" (Perelman) **32**:222
"No te dejes" (Cortazar) **7**:95
No Time like Tomorrow (Aldiss) **36**:6, 18
"No Use to Talk to Me" (Le Guin) **12**:231
"No Witchcraft for Sale" (Lessing) **6**:186, 190-91
"A No-Account Creole" (Chopin) **8**:90, 103
"Nobody Knows" (Anderson) **1**:34, 45
"Nobody Knows the Rubble I've Seen/Nobody Knows but Croesus" (Perelman) **32**:225, 231
"Nobody Said Anything" (Carver) **8**:54
"Noč pered roždestvom" (Gogol) **4**:86, 118; **29**:135
"Noc u Alhambri" (Andric) **36**:46
"Noc wielkiego sezonu" (Schulz) **13**:327, 334, 344
"La noche boca arriba" (Cortazar) **7**:52, 54, 57, 64, 69-71, 81
"La Noche Buena en el Limbo" (Pardo Bazan) **30**:263
"La noche de los alcaravanes" (Garcia Marquez) **8**:154-55, 159, 183
"La noche de Mantequilla" (Cortazar) **7**:89, 91
"La noche que lo dejaron solo" (Rulfo) **25**:245, 249-50, 258-59, 265, 268
"Las noches de Goliadkin" (Bioy Casares) **17**:70, 74
"Noches en los ministerios de Europa" (Cortazar) **7**:94
Noctuary (Ligotti) **16**:291, 292, 294, 296-97
"Nocturnal Games" (Hesse) **9**:244

"Noise of Footsteps" (Lispector)
 See "Ruído de passos"
"Noise of Strangers" (Garrett) **30**:168, 179
"Noisy Flushes the Birds" (Pritchett) **14**:305
"Noite de almirante" (Machado de Assis)
 24:129
"No-Man's-Mare" (Barnes) **3**:11-12, 22
"Non approfondire" (Moravia) **26**:144
"Non sanno parlare" (Moravia) **26**:144
"Non ti senti meglio?" (Moravia) **26**:148
"Nona" (King) **17**:274
None but the Brave (Schnitzler)
 See *Leutnant Gustl*
"None of That" (Lawrence) **4**:219, 230
The Nonexistent Knight (Calvino)
 See *Il cavaliere inesistente*
*The Nonexistent Knight and the Cloven
 Viscount* (Calvino)
 See *Il visconte dimezzato*
"Nonsense Novels" (Leacock) **39**:240
"Noon Street Nemesis" (Chandler) **23**:106
"Noon Wine" (Porter) **31**:147
Noon Wine (Porter) **4**:327-30, 339-40, 347, 349-
 52, 355-56, 359-60
"Noonday Dark Enfolding Texas" (Saroyan)
 21:162
"Nora" (Lardner) **32**:140-41
"The Nordic Night" (Morand)
 See "La nuit Nordique"
"Norman Allen" (Farrell) **28**:110
"Norman and the Killer" (Oates) **6**:224, 226
"Un normand" (Maupassant) **1**:288
"North of the Abyss" (Aldiss) **36**:28
"Northern Pass" (Rulfo)
 See "El paso del norte"
"Nos Anglais" (Maupassant) **1**:263
"Nos han dado la tierra" (Rulfo) **25**:244, 246,
 249-50, 255, 258, 262, 264-65, 273, 278-79
"The Nose" (Gogol) **4**:82-4, 91-5, 97, 124-25,
 127-29; **29**:120, 149, 152, 167, 172, 175,
 177
"A Nose" (de la Mare) **14**:69
"The Nose" (Moravia)
 See "The Nose"
"Nostalgia" (Mukherjee) **38**:238-39, 252-55,
 270-71
I nostri antenati (Calvino) **3**:91-2, 106, 117
"Not a Leg to Stand On" (Boyle) **16**:144-45
"Not a Love Story" (Howells) **36**:396
"Not a Very Nice Story" (Lessing) **6**:188, 197,
 220
"Not After Midnight" (du Maurier) **18**:129
Not after Midnight (du Maurier) **18**:128, 130,
 133
"Not by Rain Alone" (Ross) **24**:289, 292-93,
 295, 297, 300, 302, 319-20
"Not Charles" (Dixon) **16**:206, 208, 214
"Not for Publication" (Gordimer) **17**:155
Not for Publication, and Other Stories
 (Gordimer) **17**:154, 168, 181, 183
"Not for the Sabbath" (Singer) **3**:381
"Not If I Know It" (Trollope) **28**:317, 322, 325,
 339, 345, 348, 356
"Not Sixteen" (Anderson) **1**:52
"The No-Talent Kid" (Vonnegut) **8**:431
"Notch" (Gorky)
 See "Zazubrina"
"A Note on the Russian War" (Frame) **29**:104
"Notes by Flood and Field" (Harte) **8**:210
"Notes for a Case History" (Lessing) **6**:198,
 200, 208, 218
Notes from the Underground (Dostoevsky)
 See *Zapiski iz podpol'ya*
"Notes of a Madman" (Gogol)
 See "Diary of a Madman"
Notes of a Madman (Tolstoy)
 See *Zapiski sumasshedshego*
The Notes of a Young Doctor (Bulgakov)
 See *Zapiski iunogo vracha*
"Notes on the Cuffs" (Bulgakov) **18**:75, 92, 100

"Notes on the Writing of Horror: A Story"
 (Ligotti) **16**:269, 271, 277-78, 284, 286-
 87, 293, 295
"Nothing at All" (Walser) **20**:336
"Nothing But the Tooth" (Perelman) **32**:231,
 234
"Nothing Could Be Finer Than To Dine From
 Manny's China in the Mornin"
 (Perelman) **32**:234
Nothing Ever Breaks Except the Heart (Boyle)
 5:63
"The Nothing Machine" (O'Hara) **15**:282
"Nothing Missing" (O'Hara) **15**:248, 270
Nothing Serious (Wodehouse) **2**:345
Nothing So Monstrous (Steinbeck) **11**:206
"Notizbuchauszug" (Walser) **20**:334
"Notte" (Pirandello) **22**:249-50, 282
Nouveaux contes cruels (Villiers de l'Isle
 Adam) **14**:378, 396, 398
Nouvelles (Beckett) **16**:72-5, 87
Nouvelles complètes (Morand) **22**:181
"A Novel in Nine Letters" (Dostoevsky) **2**:170
"A Novel in One Chapter" (Aldiss) **36**:28
"The Novel of the Black Seal" (Machen)
 20:156, 162-63, 165, 174, 182-83, 186, 198-
 99, 203-04
"Novel of the Dark Valley" (Machen) **20**:173,
 199
"The Novel of the Iron Maid" (Machen) **20**:199
"The Novel of the White Powder" (Machen)
 20:156, 162, 165, 168, 172, 182-83, 190-92,
 199, 201, 203-04
Novelas exemplares (Cervantes) **12**:2-3, 5, 16,
 29-34, 36-40, 44
"The Novelist of Manners" (Auchincloss)
 22:39-40, 48-9, 53
"La novella del buon vecchio e della bella
 fanciulla" (Svevo) **25**:329-31, 333, 335-
 37, 351-52, 357, 359-60, 362-63
*La novella del buon vecchio e della bella
 fanciulla* (Svevo) **25**:328
Novelle (Goethe) **38**:156-98
Novelle per un anno (Pirandello) **22**:226, 231-
 34, 256, 270, 274-75, 277-78
Novelle rusticane (Verga)
Novels and Stories (Stevenson) **11**:287
"November Night" (Hesse) **9**:230-31, 234
Novembre: Fragments de style quelconque
 (Flaubert) **11**:71
"La novia fiel" (Pardo Bazan) **30**:266
"La novia robada" (Onetti) **23**:252, 275, 280
"Now and Then" (Lardner) **32**:128, 133-34,
 139-41, 145, 149
"Now I Lay Me" (Hemingway) **1**:220, 241,
 247; **40**:155, 166, 184, 209. 212, 214
"Now Sleeps the Crimson Petal" (Bates) **10**:123
"Now We Know" (O'Hara) **15**:248, 265, 270
"Now: Zero" (Ballard) **1**:68
"Nube de paso" (Pardo Bazan) **30**:280
"Nudismo" (Pavese) **19**:385-86
"The Nuisance" (Lessing) **6**:186, 217
"La nuit Catalane" (Morand) **22**:160, 166, 172,
 176, 178
"La nuit de Babylone" (Morand) **22**:160, 166,
 173
"La nuit de Charlottenburg" (Morand) **22**:158,
 160, 166
"Une nuit de Clèopâtre" (Gautier) **20**:5-6, 8,
 14, 17, 22, 24, 28-9
"La nuit de Portofine Kulm" (Morand) **22**:159-
 60, 166, 173
"La nuit de Putney" (Morand) **22**:167, 176
"La nuit de seis jours" (Morand) **22**:160, 163,
 166, 173, 178
"La nuit des Six Hours" (Morand) **22**:160
"La nuit du borreau de soi-même" (Mauriac)
 24:205
"La nuit Hongroise" (Morand) **22**:160, 166, 173
"La nuit Nordique" (Morand) **22**:160, 166, 173
"La nuit Romaine" (Morand) **22**:166, 173, 176
"La nuit Turque" (Morand) **22**:159-60, 166

Les nuits d'Octobre (Nerval) **18**:334-35, 350,
 373
"Numancia" (Arreola) **38**:10
"Number 13" (James) **16**:230, 232, 248, 250-52
"No. 13: The Elpit-Rabkommun Building"
 (Bulgakov) **18**:72, 74, 92, 98-9
"No. 16" (Bowen) **3**:41
"Nung-jên" (P'u Sung-ling) **31**:204
"Nuns at Luncheon" (Huxley) **39**:155, 159, 161,
 168-69, 171, 174-76
"The Nuns of Crith Gaille" (Moore) **19**:293,
 311
Nuovi racconti romani (Moravia) **26**:144, 149-
 50, 152-53, 164, 175, 180
"Nur auf Sardinien" (Lenz) **33**:317-18
"The Nurse" (Pardo Bazan) **30**:290
Nursery and Household Tales (Grimm and
 Grimm)
 See *Kinder-und Hausmärchen*
"A Nursery Tale" (Nabokov) **11**:123, 125
Nursery Tales (Dazai Osamu) **41**:238, 244
"Nurse's Stories" (Dickens) **17**:123
"A Nurse's Story" (Alcott) **27**:28-30, 33-6, 57,
 59, 61
"Nutcracker" (Hoffmann) **13**:192, 194-95, 197,
 199-200, 213
La nuvola di smog (Calvino) **3**:98, 111-12, 117
"Nyarlathotep" (Lovecraft) **3**:269, 273
"O alienista" (Machado de Assis) **24**:128-30,
 132
"O caso de vara" (Machado de Assis) **24**:128,
 133, 139, 145
"O cherte" (Gorky) **28**:187
"O chizhe, kotoryi lgal, i o diatle liubitele
 istiny" (Gorky) **28**:136, 187
"O City of Broken Dreams" (Cheever) **1**:89,
 107; **38**:53
"O cônego" (Machado de Assis) **24**:129
"The O. D. and Hepatitis Railroad or Bust"
 (Boyle) **16**:151
"O di uno o di nessuno" (Pirandello) **22**:245-46
"O dicionário" (Machado de Assis) **24**:129
"O enfermeiro" (Machado de Assis) **24**:129
"O espelho" (Machado de Assis) **24**:128, 135,
 138, 152
"O Fat White Woman" (Trevor) **21**:231, 262,
 265
"O How She Laughed!" (Aiken) **9**:6, 9, 14
"The O in Jose" (Aldiss) **36**:20
"O lapso" (Machado de Assis) **24**:128, 133
"O Lasting Peace" (Gallant) **5**:124, 133
"O ljubvi" (Chekhov) **2**:139, 141, 143, 157;
 28:54-6, 65-6, 68-72
"O lyrickém zloději" (Capek) **36**:101-02, 127
"O machete" (Machado de Assis) **24**:134
"O relógio de ouro" (Machado de Assis) **24**:131,
 151
"O Russet Witch!" (Fitzgerald) **6**:45, 59, 91-3
"O segrêdo de Augusta" (Machado de Assis)
 24:131
"O segrêdo do bonzo" (Machado de Assis)
 24:128-29, 152
"O starim i mladim Pamukovicima" (Andric)
 36:59-60, 62
"O vrede filosofii" (Gorky) **28**:181-82
"O Yes" (Olsen) **11**:164-66
"O Youth and Beauty!" (Cheever) **1**:90, 110;
 38:47, 51, 54, 60, 84-6
"The Oar" (O'Flaherty) **6**:262, 265, 274, 276-77
The Oasis (McCarthy) **24**:214-15, 217, 219,
 221-22, 227, 28
"The Obelisk" (Forster) **27**:94, 06, 104-05, 107,
 119
Obituaries (Saroyan) **21**:173
"Obligation" (Dazai Osamu) **41**:229-30, 233
"La obra" (Bioy Casares) **17**:95
Obras (Borges)
 See *Obras completas, 1923-1972*
Obras completas, 1923-1972 (Borges) **41**:39-
 42, 137-38, 144, 149, 157, 163, 180, 184
Obscure Destinies (Cather) **2**:92, 115, 117-18
"Obyčejná vražda" (Capek) **36**:98

"Očarovannyj strannik" (Leskov) **34**:109-10, 113-16, 118, 120-21, 123, 129-30, 135-36, 138, 141
"The Occasional Garden" (Saki) **12**:311-12, 325
"L'occhio del padrone" (Calvino) **3**:97
"Occult Memories" (Villiers de l'Isle Adam) See "Souvenirs occulte"
"An Occurrence at Owl Creek Bridge" (Bierce) **9**:49-50, 53-6, 60-1, 75, 77-82, 85-6, 89, 92, 95
"The Ocean" (Cheever) **1**:94, 111; **38**:47, 50, 52-3
"The Ocean" (Mason) **4**:15
"The O'Conors of Castle Conor, Conty Mayo (Trollope) **28**:318, 328, 340, 348
"Ocracoke Island" (Adams) **24**:16
Octaedro (Cortazar) **7**:60
"The Octascope" (Beattie) **11**:6, 14
Octavie: L'illusion (Nerval) **18**:362, 369-70
"October and June" (Henry) **5**:182
The October Country (Bradbury) **29**:65-8, 75, 88-92
October Nights (Nerval) See *Les nuits d'Octobre*
"Odalie Misses Mass" (Chopin) **8**:93
"Das öde Haus" (Hoffmann) **13**:185
An Ode to Truth (Gissing) **37**:81
"Odessa" (Babel) **16**:35, 59
The Odessa Stories (Babel) See *The Odessa Tales*
The Odessa Tales (Babel) **16**:5, 9, 13, 17-18, 20-2, 35, 42, 44, 49
Odin den' Ivana Denisovicha (Solzhenitsyn) **32**:330-34, 337-41, 344-50, 355-56, 361, 367-70, 372-74, 376, 387, 395, 402
"Odnazhdy osen'iu" (Gorky) **28**:137, 145, 161, 190
"The Odor of Sanctity" (Benet) **10**:146-47
"An Odor of Verbena" (Faulkner) **1**:171; **35**:159
"The Odour of Chrysanthemums" (Lawrence) **4**:197-98, 202, 220, 230
"Odrazy" (Capek) **36**:89, 111, 122
"An Odyssey of the North" (London) **4**:251, 258, 278, 282-84, 289, 291
"Oedipus at Colonus" (Forster) **27**:96
"The Oedipus Complex" (Pritchett) **14**:271, 285
Oeuvres (Nerval) **18**:379
Oeuvres complètes (Baudelaire) **18**:9, 20, 32, 35, 37-8, 52, 63-4
"Of Birds and Beasts" (Kawabata) See "Kinjū"
"Of Course" (Jackson) **39**:212, 226
"Of Emelya, the Fool" (Bunin) **5**:82
Of Intimate Things (Capek) **36**:84
"Of Love: A Testimony" (Cheever) **1**:88, 99
"Of Our Young People and Our Elders" (Agnon) **30**:68
"Of Sanctity and Whiskey" (O'Faolain) **13**:291
"Una of the Hill Country" (Murfree) **22**:213
"The Off Season" (Bradbury) **29**:50, 61
"The Offended Man" (Capek) **36**:93
"An Offering to the Dead" (Campbell) **19**:81
"Offerings" (Mason) **4**:16
"Offerings" (O'Flaherty) **6**:262, 264, 281
Off-Hours (Cortazar) See *Deshoras*
"The Office" (Munro) **3**:322, 325, 340, 343
"Office Romances" (Trevor) **21**:233, 237
"An Official Position" (Maugham) **8**:379
"The Offshore Pirate" (Fitzgerald) **6**:45, 56, 58-9, 96-7
"Oft in a Stilly Night" (O'Brien) **10**:345-46
"Gli oggetti" (Moravia) **26**:148
"Oh, My Name Is William Kidd" (Benet) **10**:154
Oh What a Paradise It Seems (Cheever) **1**:108, 113-15;
"Oh Whistle and I'll Come to You, My Lad" (James) **16**:225, 228, 230, 232-33, 235-37, 240, 251-54, 256-57
"O'Halloran's Luck" (Benet) **10**:154, 158-59
"An Ohio Pagan" (Anderson) **1**:27, 30, 39

Ohio Pastorals (Dunbar) **8**:127, 134
"Oifig an Phoist" (O'Flaherty) **6**:280, 287, 289
"O.K. Baby, This Is the World" (Saroyan) **21**:143, 163
"Oke of Okehurst" (Lee) **33**:302, 305, 308
"Ol' Bennet and the Indians" (Crane) **7**:103
"Ol' Pap's Flaxen" (Garland) **18**:163
"Olalla" (Stevenson) **11**:269, 282, 296, 298
"Old Abe's Conversion" (Dunbar) **8**:122, 146
"The Old Adam" (Lawrence) **4**:220
"Old Age" (Galsworthy) **22**:98
"The Old Age Pensioner" (Schulz) See "Emeryt"
"The Old Apple Dealer" (Hawthorne) **3**:189
"The Old Army Game" (Garrett) **30**:166, 174
"Old Aunt Peggy" (Chopin) **8**:89
"The Old Bachelor's Nightcap" (Andersen) **6**:12
"The Old Bascom Place" (Harris) **19**:147, 149, 180
"The Old Beauty" (Cather) **2**:93-4
The Old Beauty and Others (Cather) **2**:93
"The Old Bird, a Love Story" (Powers) **4**:368, 371, 373
"Old Bones" (Narayan) **25**:132, 138, 141, 154
"An Old Boot" (Lavin) **4**:165, 168
"The Old Bucket" (Solzhenitsyn) See "Staroe vedro"
"The Old Chevalier" (Dinesen) **7**:163, 165-66, 169, 175
"The Old Chief Mshlanga" (Lessing) **6**:186, 189, 196-97, 213
"Old Clothes" (Campbell) **19**:77, 87
"Old Country Advice to the American Traveler" (Saroyan) **21**:170
Old Creole Days (Cable) **4**:47, 49-58, 60-2, 64-8, 75-6, 78
"Old Daddy Deering" (Garland) See "Daddy Deering"
"Old Dick" (Stuart) **31**:227
"Old Doc Rivers" (Williams) **31**:303-04, 312-13, 324, 331, 357, 359-60
"Old Earth" (Beckett) **16**:123, 126
"Old Esther Dudley" (Hawthorne) **3**:186
"The Old Faith" (O'Connor) **5**:369, 372, 385, 398
"Old Fellows" (O'Connor) **5**:366, 389
"Old Folks Christmas" (Lardner) **32**:134-37, 141, 163
"The Old Forest" (Taylor) **10**:403, 409-10, 416, 418-20, 424
The Old Forest (Taylor) **10**:410
"The Old Friends" (Gallant) **5**:124, 133
Old Friends and New (Jewett) **6**:165-66, 168
"Old Friends Meet" (Svevo) See "Incontro di vecchi amici"
"Old Garbo" (Thomas) **3**:403-06, 410-12
"The Old Gentleman of the Black Stock" (Page) **23**:284, 298, 307, 313
"The Old Horns" (Campbell) **19**:63-4, 74
"The Old House" (Andersen) **6**:4, 25
"The Old Hunter" (O'Flaherty) **6**:264, 280
"Old Izergil" (Gorky) See "Starukha Izergil"
"Old John's Place" (Lessing) **6**:186, 190, 211, 213-14, 217
Old Lady Mary (Oliphant) **25**:180, 182, 184-86, 196, 204, 209
"Old Love" (Singer) **3**:376, 384
Old Love (Singer) **3**:380-82
The Old Maid (The 'Fifties (Wharton) **6**:439-41
"An Old Maid's Triumph" (Gissing) **37**:64
"The Old Man" (Coover) **15**:46
"The Old Man" (du Maurier) **18**:138
"Old Man" (Faulkner) **1**:159-61, 167-68
"The Old Man" (Naipaul) **38**:332, 334-35
"The Old Man" (Shiga) **23**:332-33
"The Old Man" (Singer) **3**:355-56
"Old Man Alone" (Sansom) **21**:102, 127
The Old Man and the Sea (Hemingway) **1**:222-24, 226-28, 238-39, 247-50; **36**:242-347; **40**:156-57
"Old Man at the Bridge" (Hemingway) **1**:234

"Old Man of the Temple" (Narayan) **25**:132, 154
"The Old Man with a Wen" (Dazai Osamu) **41**:238
"An Old Man's Confessions" (Svevo) See "Le confessioni del vegliardo"
"An Old Man's Memory" (Greene) **29**:223, 229-30
"The Old Manse" (Hawthorne) **3**:159, 174, 184; **39**:105
"The Old Master" (O'Faolain) **13**:284, 287, 300, 309
"An Old Mate of Your Father's" (Lawson) **18**:200, 215, 262
"The Old Men" (McCarthy) **24**:216
"The Old Morality" (Fuentes) See "Vieja moralidad"
"Old Mortality" (Gilchrist) **14**:151
"Old Mortality" (Porter) **31**:161
Old Mortality (Porter) **4**:327, 329-34, 338, 340-42, 346-52, 361-65
"Old Mr. Marblehall" (Welty) **1**:466, 471, 498
"Old Mrs. Crosley" (Gilman) **13**:143
"Old Mrs. Harris" (Cather) **2**:97, 102, 115-17
"The Old Neighborhood" (Dreiser) **30**:122
Old New York (Wharton) **6**:439-40, 442
"Old News" (Hawthorne) **3**:174
"The Old Nun" (Warner) **23**:372
"The Old Nurse's Story" (Gaskell) **25**:37-8, 41, 47, 55, 72
"Old Oak Tree's Last Dream" (Andersen) See "The Last Dream of the Old Oak"
The Old, Old Man (Svevo) See *Il vecchione*
"Old, Old Message" (Wilson) **21**:333
"The Old Order" (Porter) **4**:339-40, 348, 350-54, 358, 361-62, 365; **31**:178
"The Old People" (Faulkner) **35**:141, 145-46, 157, 164-65, 178, 181-82, 197, 200-02, 210
"The Old Planters" (Page) **23**:309, 312
"Old Portraits" (Turgenev) See "Starye portrety"
"Old Red" (Gordon) **15**:106, 119-21, 129-30, 141, 143
Old Red, and Other Stories (Gordon) **15**:116, 131, 137
"Old Rogaum and His Theresa" (Dreiser) **30**:107, 122, 152-53
"The Old School" (Campbell) **19**:77-8
"Old Sid's Christmas" (Garland) **18**:167
"The Old Stock" (Calisher) **15**:14-15, 18-19
"The Old Street Lamp" (Andersen) **6**:4, 7
"The Old System" (Bellow) **14**:22, 24-5, 27
Old Tales Newly Collected (Lu Hsun) See *Gushi xinbian*
Old Tales Retold (Lu Hsun) See *Gushi xinbian*
"Old Tar" (Mansfield) **9**:301
"Old Things" (Mason) **4**:17
"Old Ticonderoga" (Hawthorne) **3**:174
"An Old Time Christmas" (Dunbar) **8**:122, 125, 128, 133, 144
"An Old Time Raid" (Williams) **31**:302-03, 324, 359, 361
"Old Unhappy Faroff Things..." (Lewis) **40**:280
"The Old Venerable" (Coppard) **21**:5, 7, 9, 12, 17
"The Old Woman" (O'Flaherty) **6**:277-78, 280
"An Old Woman and Her Cat" (Lessing) **6**:188
"The Old Woman in the Forest" (Grimm and Grimm) **36**:223
"The Old Woman Izergil" (Gorky) See "Starukha Izergil"
"The Old Woman's Despair" (Baudelaire) See "Le désespoir de la vieille"
"Old-Age Pensioners" (O'Connor) **5**:369
"Oldfashioned" (McGahern) **17**:304-05, 308, 311, 317-18, 320, 323
"Old-Fashioned Landowners" (Gogol) See "Starosvetskie Pomeščiki"
An Old-Fashioned Thanksgiving (Alcott) **27**:43

The Oldster (Svevo)
  See *Il vecchione*
"An Old-Time Indian Attack" (Silko) **37**:292
"Old-World Landowners" (Gogol)
  See "Starosvetskie Pomeščiki"
"Ole Luköie" (Andersen) **6**:12
"Ole 'Stracted" (Page) **23**:284, 297, 303, 307, 322-23, 325
"Ole Underwood" (Mansfield) **9**:278, 302
Olinger Stories: A Selection (Updike) **13**:350, 354, 366, 368-69, 404
"Olive" (O'Hara) **15**:264
"Olive and Camilla" (Coppard) **21**:21-2, 28
"Olive Brand" (Dreiser) **30**:139, 142
"The Olive Garden" (Gordon) **15**:118, 138, 142-43
"Olujaci" (Andric) **36**:34, 38, 48, 66
"Omar James" (Farrell) **28**:96
"Omnibus" (Cortazar) **7**:50, 54, 56
"Omnibuses" (Dickens) **17**:112, 137
"Omo" (Thomas) **20**:290-92, 317
"Omoide" (Dazai Osamu) **41**:238, 240, 247, 256-57, 259, 263, 266, 268, 271-76
"Omphale ou la Tapisserie amoureuse, histoire rococo" (Gautier) **20**:5, 13, 16, 33
"On a Field, Rampant" (Elkin) **12**:94-6, 99, 101, 118
"On a Mountain" (Bierce) **9**:61
"On A Wagon" (Singer) **3**:375
"On Account of a Hat" (Aleichem) **33**:22
"On an Amateur Beat" (Dickens) **17**:124
"On Angels" (Barthelme) **2**:32, 38
"On Approval" (Saki) **12**:314
"On Ballistics" (Arreola)
  See "De balística"
"On Being Courteous when Compelled to Break the Law" (Boell) **23**:36
"On Blackwell Pier" (Morrison) **40**:335, 352
"On Clothes" (Dazai Osamu) **41**:238, 240, 242
"On for the Long Haul" (Boyle) **16**:146
On Forsyte 'Change (Galsworthy) **22**:69-70, 74, 84, 92, 97
"On Graphology As an Applied Science" (Cortazar)
  See "De la grafología como ciencia aplicada"
"On Greenhow Hill" (Kipling) **5**:260
"On Guard" (Waugh) **41**:323, 329-31
"On His Back under the Night" (Cortazar)
  See "La noche boca arriba"
"On Keeping a Dog" (Dazai Osamu) **41**:244
"On Leprechauns" (Wolfe) **33**:374
"On Living for Others" (Warner) **23**:272
"On Neutral Ground" (Harris) **19**:183
"On Not Shooting Sitting Birds" (Rhys) **21**:55-6
"On Official Duty" (Chekhov) **2**:128
"On Parables" (Kafka) **35**:241
"On Sparrows" (Shiga) **23**:346
"On Stony Ground" (Sansom) **21**:93-4
"On Taxes" (Agnon) **30**:68
"On the car" (Frame) **29**:110
"On the City Wall" (Kipling) **5**:265
"On the Confederate Side" (Harris) **19**:183
"On the Dark Mountains" (Oliphant) **25**:185-86
"On the Divide" (Cather) **2**:96-7, 100-01, 105-07
"On the Downhill Side" (Ellison) **14**:115
On the Edge (de la Mare) **14**:70-2, 74, 83, 89
"On the Edge of the Cliff" (Pritchett) **14**:263, 267, 272-73, 291
On the Edge of the Cliff, and Other Stories (Pritchett) **14**:263, 290, 292, 299
"On the Edge of the Plain" (Lawson) **18**:211, 213, 239, 261
"On the Gate" (Kipling) **5**:271, 283
"On the Great Wall" (Kipling) **5**:292
"On the Gulls' Road" (Cather) **2**:99, 104
"On the Makaloa Mat" (London) **4**:266
On the Makaloa Mat (London) **4**:256-57, 266, 270
"On the Quai at Smyrna" (Hemingway) **1**:244

"On the Question of Apparel" (Dazai Osamu) **41**:276
"On the Rafts" (Gorky)
  See "Na plotakh"
"On the Road" (Adams) **24**:18
"On the Road" (Agnon) **30**:4
"On the Road" (Hughes) **6**:122, 131-32
"On the Rock in Počitelj" (Andric)
  See "Na kamenu u Počitelju"
"On the Run" (Boyle) **5**:70, 72
"On the Shore" (Andric)
  See "Na obali"
"On the Slab" (Ellison) **14**:138
"On the Stairs" (Morrison) **40**:328, 337, 355, 367
"On the Telephone" (Bulgakov) **18**:89
On the Track and Over the Sliprails (Lawson) **18**:208, 250, 252
"On the Union Side" (Harris) **19**:183
"On the Usefulness of Alcoholism" (Bulgakov) **18**:90
"On the Veldt" (Galsworthy) **22**:90
"On the Walpole Road" (Freeman) **1**:201
"On the Way Back: A Work Not in Progress" (Greene)
  See "An Appointment with the General"
"On the Way Home" (Hughes) **6**:119, 121-23, 132-33
"On the Western Circuit" (Hardy) **2**:206-07, 214, 220, 222-23
On the Wing of Occasions (Harris) **19**:125
"On Time" (O'Hara) **15**:265, 270
"On Writing" (Hemingway) **1**:240, 243
"Once in Autumn" (Gorky)
  See "Odnazhdy osen'iu"
"Once More" (Galsworthy) **22**:59, 74, 78, 99
"Once Upon a Time" (Gordimer) **17**:177, 183, 185, 187, 190-91
"Den onda ängeln" (Lagerkvist) **12**:179, 195
Onda sagor (Lagerkvist) **12**:179
"Onde estivestes de noite" (Lispector) **34**:233, 235
Onde estivestes de noite? (Lispector) **34**:203, 233, 235
"One against Thebes" (Gordon) **15**:119, 123, 126, 138-39
"The One and the Other" (Warner) **23**:384
"One Arm" (Kawabata)
  See "Kata Ucle"
"One Autumn Evening" (Gorky)
  See "Odnazhdy osen'iu"
"One Christmas at Shiloh" (Dunbar) **8**:122, 138, 146
"One Christmas Eve" (Hughes) **6**:109
"One Dash—Horses" (Crane)
  See "Horses—One Dash"
"One Day After Saturday" (Garcia Marquez) **8**:185
One Day in the Life of Ivan Denisovich (Solzhenitsyn)
  See *Odin den' Ivana Denisovicha*
"One Day of Happiness" (Singer) **3**:385-86
"One Friday Morning" (Hughes) **6**:111-12, 119, 121
"One Good Time" (Freeman) **1**:198
"One Holy Night" (Cisneros) **32**:34, 38
"$106,000 Blood Money" (Hammett) **17**:200, 202, 215, 219-220, 222, 224, 230
"One Hundred Views of Mount Fuji" (Dazai Osamu)
  See "Fugaku hyakkei"
"One Interne" (Fitzgerald) **6**:47-8
"One is a Wanderer" (Thurber) **1**:417, 420, 425, 427, 435
"One Is One and All Alone" (Thomas) **20**:290, 292, 317
"One Kind of Officer" (Bierce) **9**:52, 61
"One Life Furnished in Early Poverty" (Ellison) **14**:109-10, 115
"One Man, One Boat, One Girl" (O'Faolain) **13**:322

"One Man's Fortune" (Dunbar) **8**:120, 122, 125, 128, 131, 136, 145, 150
"One More Thing" (Carver) **8**:17, 19, 38, 53
"One More Time" (Gordon) **15**:106, 120, 130
"One Night in Bed" (Moorhouse) **40**:293
"One Night in Turin" (O'Faolain) **13**:288, 320, 322
"One of Cleopatra's Nights" (Gautier)
  See "Une nuit de Clèopâtre"
"One of the Chosen" (Calisher) **15**:14
"One of the Family" (Spark) **10**:369
"One of the Girls in Our Party" (Wolfe) **33**:380
"One of the Lost Tribe" (Stuart) **31**:224
"One of the Missing" (Bierce) **9**:53, 55-6, 61-2, 65-8, 76-7, 87
"One of Them" (Powers) **4**:375-76
"One of Three Others" (Suckow) **18**:394-95, 413-14, 416, 422-23
"One Off the Short List" (Lessing) **6**:197, 199, 200, 203-08, 214, 218
"One Officer, One Man" (Bierce) **9**:53, 55, 57, 64, 67-8
"One Ordinary Day, with Peanuts" (Jackson) **9**:267
"One Out of Many" (Naipaul) **38**:301, 303-04, 309, 311, 323, 353-54
"One Reader Writes" (Hemingway) **1**:211
"One Size Fits All" (Thomas) **20**:320, 322
"One Summer" (Grau) **15**:159, 165
"One Summer" (Lavin) **4**:173, 183
"One Sunday Morning" (Boyle) **5**:64
"One Sunny Afternoon" (Sansom) **21**:85
One Thing Leading to Another, and Other Stories (Warner) **23**:381
"One Thousand Dollars" (Henry) **5**:184
"$1,000 a Week" (Farrell) **28**:94-5, 119
$1,000 a Week, and Other Stories (Farrell) **28**:121
"£1000 for Rosebud" (O'Faolain) **13**:295, 318, 320, 322
"One Trip Abroad" (Fitzgerald) **6**:61, 100, 104
"One Trip Across" (Hemingway) **25**:113
"One True Friend" (O'Faolain) **13**:288
"1,2,3,4,5,6,7,8" (Saroyan) **21**:136, 140, 142, 148, 164
"One Warm Saturday" (Thomas) **3**:394-95, 398, 403, 410-12
"One Way of Happiness" (Gissing) **37**:80
"The One Who Waits" (Bradbury) **29**:60, 81
"The One-Armed Giant" (Narayan) **25**:137
"One-Eyed Dogs" (Lawson) **18**:233
"Oneiric Horror" (Ligotti) **16**:288
"The £1,000,000 Bank-Note" (Twain) **6**:303, 328-30
"One's a Heifer" (Ross) **24**:290, 292, 295, 307-08, 310-11, 317-19
"The Ones Who Walk Away From Omelas" (Le Guin) **12**:234, 239-41
"Only a Daisy" (Glasgow) **34**:61, 65
"Only a Subaltern" (Kipling) **5**:272
"The Only Rose" (Jewett) **6**:169
"The Only Son" (Farrell) **28**:118, 120-1
"An Only Son" (Jewett) **6**:152-53
"Only the Dead Know Brooklyn" (Wolfe) **33**:350, 367, 369-70, 380, 382, 386
"Onnagata" (Mishima) **4**:313, 315, 318, 322-23
"Onuphrius ou les Vexations fantastiques d'un admirateur d'Hoffmann" (Gautier) **20**:4, 10, 31
Open All Night (Morand)
  See *Ouvert la nuit*
"The Open Boat" (Crane) **7**:100-01, 103-04, 107-13, 116-18, 120, 140, 142-43, 145, 148-49, 151-53
The Open Boat, and Other Tales of Adventure (Crane) **7**:102, 104
The Open Door (Oliphant) **25**:180, 182, 193, 208-09
Open Door (Valenzuela) **14**:365-66
"Open House" (Gordimer) **17**:157, 160, 186
"The Open Window" (Saki) **12**:315, 318-19, 321, 324

"L'Opera del Divino Amore" (Verga) 21:294-95
"The Opinions of Leander" (Norris) 28:202
"Oplatka's End" (Capek)
    See "Oplatkuv konec"
"Oplatkuv konec" (Capek) 36:97-8, 105, 128
"An Optimistic Story" (Boell) 23:38
"Orache" (Nabokov) 11:133
"The Oracle of the Dog" (Chesterton) 1:133-34, 136
"Oral Confession" (Capek) 36:83
"Oral History" (Gordimer) 17:163, 191-92
"The Orange Grove" (Lewis) 40:272, 274, 278-79
"The Orange Moth" (Aiken) 9:3-4, 13-14
The Orange Tree (Fuentes) 24:78-80
"The Oranges" (Saroyan) 21:134, 143
"The Oratory Contest" (Farrell) 28:89, 118, 122
"Orazio Cima" (Svevo) 25:360
"Orbiting" (Mukherjee) 38:244-47, 250, 252-54, 261, 266-67, 282-83, 286
"The Orchards" (Thomas) 3:396, 399-402, 407-08
"The Orchestra" (Agnon)
    See "HaTizmoret"
"Orchid Litany" (Fuentes)
    See "Letanía de la orquídea"
"The Ordeal" (Fitzgerald) 6:58
"The Ordeal at Mt. Hope" (Dunbar) 8:118, 120-21, 127, 131, 146
"Order of Illusion" (Ligotti) 16:276
"Order of Insects" (Gass) 12:123-4, 133, 139, 152, 156-7
"An Ordinary Murder" (Capek)
    See "Obyčejná vražda"
Les oreilles du comte de Chesterfield (Voltaire) 12:341-43
"The Organizer's Wife" (Bambara) 35:17-18, 26, 28-9, 34, 39-40
"The Orgy: An Idyll" (de la Mare) 14:72, 74, 87-8
"Orientation of Cats" (Cortazar) 7:69, 71
"The Origin of the Birds" (Calvino) 3:108-10
"The Origin of the Hatchet Story" (Chesnutt) 7:14-15
"The Origin of the Ocean" (Harris) 19:195
"The Original Sins of Edward Tripp" (Trevor) 21:269
"The Orlov Couple" (Gorky) 28:149, 151, 157
"Orlov Married Couple" (Gorky)
    See "The Orlov Couple"
"The Orlovs" (Gorky)
    See "The Orlov Couple"
"The Ormolu Clock" (Spark) 10:353, 361-63
Ornaments in Jade (Machen) 20:159-60, 177, 196, 199-200
"The Orphanage" (McCullers) 9:342, 345, 354-55
"The Orphaned Swimming Pool" (Updike) 13:367
"The Orphans" (Verga) 21:298
"Orphan's Progress" (Gallant) 5:138
"Orpheus and His Lute" (O'Connor) 5:377, 382
Orsinian Tales (Le Guin) 12:212-19, 222-23, 231, 234, 245-48, 250
"Osan" (Dazai Osamu) 41:240-41, 249, 251-52, 254-56
"Osatičani" (Andric) 36:47-9, 72
"Oscar" (Barnes) 3:2-4
"Oscar et Erick" (Ayme) 41:24
"Ostatnia ucieczka ojca" (Schulz) 13:328-29, 334
"Ostras interrogadas" (Cabrera Infante) 39:24
"Ostrov" (Capek) 36:82, 87, 110
"Otbornoje zerno" (Leskov) 34:112, 114, 141
"Otchayanny" (Turgenev) 7:324, 337, 362-63
Otetz Sergii (Tolstoy) 9:377-78, 397; 30:317, 320-22, 339-40, 342-43
"The Other" (Updike) 13:402
"The Other Boat" (Forster) 27:90-1, 95-6, 102-07, 110-11, 119-21, 124-25
"The Other Death" (Borges)
    See "La otra muerte"

"The Other Gods" (Lovecraft) 3:274
"Other Kingdom" (Forster) 27:72, 74, 76, 81-83, 85-6, 99, 102-03, 112-13, 122
"The Other Labrynth" (Bioy Casares)
    See "El otro labertino"
Other Main-Travelled Roads (Garland) 18:148, 180, 182
"The Other Man" (Kipling) 5:274
The Other One (Colette)
    See *La seconde*
"The Other Paris" (Gallant) 5:125-26, 148
Other People's Ambitions (Suckow) 18:400-03
"Other People's Stories" (Ozick)
    See "Usurpation (Other People's Stories)"
"The Other Rib of Death" (Garcia Marquez)
    See "La otra costilla de la muerte"
"The Other Side" (Campbell) 19:77
"The Other Side" (Lardner) 32:118
"The Other Side of Death" (Garcia Marquez)
    See "La otra costilla de la muerte"
"The Other Side of the Border" (Greene) 29:183
"The Other Side of the Hedge" (Forster) 27:74, 76-7, 86-87, 97, 114-15, 122-23
"The Other Side of the Lake" (Aldiss) 36:20
The Other Side of the Sky (Clarke) 3:125, 131-32
"The Other Son" (Pirandello) 22:226, 229, 272
"The Other Two" (Wharton) 6:421, 424-26
"The Other Way" (Grau) 15:149, 160
Other Weapons (Valenzuela)
    See *Cambio de armas*
"The Other Woman" (Anderson) 1:42
"The Other Woman" (Campbell) 19:84
"Other Women's Households" (O'Hara) 15:255
"Others' Dreams" (Oates) 6:234
"Ōtō" (Dazai Osamu) 41:240, 249, 256
Otogi zōshi (Dazai Osamu) 41:226, 247, 260, 276
"La otra costilla de la muerte" (Garcia Marquez) 8:154-56, 182
"La otra muerte" (Borges) 4:35, 37, 42-4; 41:46-47
"Otrazhenie v vode" (Solzhenitsyn) 32:351
"El otro cielo" (Cortazar) 7:55, 57, 59, 61-2
"El otro labertino" (Bioy Casares) 17:75-9, 81-2
Otrochestvo (Tolstoy) 9:375; 30:331
Ōtsu junkichi (Shiga) 23:339, 344, 352-54, 362-63
"The Ottawa Valley" (Munro) 3:337
Ottilie (Lee) 33:301, 306
Our Ancestors (Calvino)
    See *I nostri antenati*
"Our Bovary" (Gordimer) 17:154
"Our Demeanor at Wakes" (Cortazar)
    See "Conducta en los velorios"
"Our English Watering-Place" (Dickens) 17:124
"Our Exploits at West Poley" (Hardy) 2:214, 216, 221
"Our Fearful Innocence" (O'Faolain) 13:292, 312, 322
"Our French Watering-Place" (Dickens) 17:124
"Our Friend Judith" (Lessing) 6:201-02, 218-20
"Our Humble Notice" (Oe) 20:231
"Our Lady of the Easy Death of Alferce" (Oates) 6:237
"Our Lady of the Massacre" (Carter) 13:16-19
"Our Lady's Child" (Grimm and Grimm) 36:196-98, 200
"Our Little Brown Brothers the Filipinos" (Saroyan) 21:133-34, 137
"Our Oldest Friend" (Pritchett) 14:255, 298
"Our Pipes" (Lawson) 18:261
"Our School" (Dickens) 17:124
"Our Story of Ah Q" (Lu Hsun)
    See "Ah Q zheng zhuan"
"Our Trip" (A Diary)(Bioy Casares) 17:95
"Our Wall" (Oates) 6:255
"Our Wife" (Pritchett) 14:273
"Out in the Midday Sun" (Thomas) 20:288, 290, 294, 296-97, 318
"Out of Boredom" (Gorky)
    See "Boredom"

"Out of Business" (Narayan) 25:132, 153
"Out of Copyright" (Campbell) 19:70
"Out of Depth" (Waugh) 41:323, 329, 340
"Out of My Generation" (Updike) 13:387
"Out of Nowhere into Nothing" (Anderson) 1:21, 27, 30, 39, 46-7, 53
"Out of Season" (Gordimer) 17:187
"Out of Season" (Hemingway) 1:245; 36:334
"Out of the Deep" (de la Mare) 14:65, 68, 80, 86-7, 92
"Out of the Earth" (Machen) 20:158, 183, 198, 200
"Out of the Eons" (Lovecraft) 3:279
"Out of the Sun" (Clarke) 3:132, 135-36
"The Outcast" (Agnon) 30:9-11
"The Outcast" (Page) 23:307-09, 312
"The Outcasts" (O'Flaherty) 6:262, 264, 284
"The Outcasts of Poker Flat" (Harte) 8:209-10, 219, 223, 226-27, 232-33, 236, 244, 250-51, 254-55, 257
The Outcry (Lu Hsun)
    See *Nahan*
"The Outing" (Baldwin) 10:2-4, 6-9
"The Outlaw" (Ross) 24:290, 295-96, 304, 310-11, 316-19, 323-24
"Outlink to Uncle's Place" (Jolley) 19:230
The Outpost of Progress (Conrad) 9:143-44, 163
Outros contos (Machado de Assis) 24:151, 155
Outros relíquias (Machado de Assis) 24:151
"Outside the Cabinet-Maker's" (Fitzgerald) 6:51
"Outside the Machine" (Rhys) 21:50, 65
"Outside the Ministry" (Lessing) 6:199
"Outside the Zenana" (Norris) 28:205
"The Outsider" (Lovecraft) 3:258, 260, 262, 264, 274
"The Outstation" (Maugham) 8:357, 359, 361, 366-67, 372
"Outward and Visible Signs" (Norris) 28:212
Ouvert la nuit (Morand) 22:158-67, 171-73, 178, 180-82
"Ovadia the Cripple" (Agnon) 30:66-7, 71
"The Oval Portrait" (Poe) 1:392; 22:305
"Ovcebyk" (Leskov) 34:128
"Over" (O'Brien) 10:330-31, 333
"Over Insurance" (Collier) 19:107, 109
"Over on the T'other Mounting" (Murfree) 22:188, 202, 207-09, 213, 222
"Over the Brandy-Still" (Andric) 36:56
"Over the Green Mountains" (Caldwell) 19:5, 37, 44
"Over the River and through the Wood" (O'Hara) 15:252-54, 264-65
"The Overcoat" (Agnon) 30:71
"The Overcoat" (Gogol)
    See "Shinel"
"The Overcoat II" (Boyle) 16:143, 145, 151
Overhead in a Balloon: Stories of Paris (Gallant) 5:147
The Overloaded Man (Ballard) 1:73-7
"The Over-Night Bag" (Greene) 29:200-01
Overnight to Many Distant Cities (Barthelme) 2:50-1, 56
"An Oversight" (Pirandello) 22:236
"The Overtone" (Lawrence) 4:238-39
"Overture and Beginners Please" (Rhys) 21:55-6
"Overture and Incidental Music for A Midsummer Night's Dream" (Carter) 13:17-18
"O ovo e a galinha" (Lispector) 34:189
"Ovsianko the Freeholder" (Turgenev)
    See "The Freeholder Ovsyanikov"
Owen Tudor (Arnim) 29:5-7
"Owen Wingrave" (James) 8:270
"An Owl's Letter" (Dazai Osamu) 41:246
Own Your Own Home (Lardner) 32:127
The Owners of the Entail (Arnim)
    See *Die Majoratsherren*
"The Ox" (Bates) 10:131, 133
"Oyb Nish Noch Hecher" (Peretz) 26:191
"Oylem ha-be" (Peretz) 26:222

"Oylem-habe" (Aleichem) 33:68, 82-3
"Oysgetreyslt" (Aleichem) 33:41
"Oysters Helping with Their Inquiry" (Cabrera Infante)
    See "Ostras interrogadas"
"Ozème's Holiday" (Chopin) 8:94, 113
"Ozero Segden" (Solzhenitsyn) 32:352
"P. & O." (Maugham) 8:359, 366, 372, 375
"P. S. What's Octagon Soap?" (Garrett) 30:174
"Pablo" (Arreola) 38:8
"The Pace of Youth" (Crane) 7:149
"The Pack" (Galsworthy) 22:58, 75
"The Package" (Vonnegut) 8:437
"The Package Store" (Dixon) 16:207
"Packed Dirt, Churchgoing, A Dying Cat, A Traded Car" (Updike) 13:370, 388, 397
"Un pacto con el diablo" (Arreola) 38:8
"Pád rodu Votických" (Capek) 36:102, 121, 127
"Los padres de un santo" (Pardo Bazan) 30:272
"The Pagan Rabbi" (Ozick) 15:297-98, 300-01, 311-13, 315, 335, 337-39
The Pagan Rabbi, and Other Stories (Ozick) 15:297-98, 304, 306, 311-12, 314, 328, 331
"The Page" (Atwood) 2:15, 17
"Page and Monarch" (Pritchett) 14:296
The Page of Gustavus Adolphus (Meyer)
    See Gustav Adolfs Page
"A Pageant of Birds" (Welty) 27:338, 353
"Pages from Cold Point" (Bowles) 3:59, 61-2, 66, 69, 73, 76-7, 85
Páginas recolhidas (Machado de Assis) 24:154
"Pai contra mãe" (Machado de Assis) 24:133, 139, 145, 155
"Pai kuang" (Lu Hsun)
    See "Bai guang"
"Pain maudit" (Maupassant) 1:263
"A Painful Case" (Joyce) 3:203, 205, 209-11, 234-35, 246, 249; 26:40, 46-7
Painful Stories (Capek)
    See Trapné providky
"Paingod" (Ellison) 14:106-07, 118
"Paint Me a Pinion Immortal, Limner Dear" (Perelman) 32:229
"The Painted Door" (Ross) 24:289-93, 295, 297, 299, 303, 319-20
"The Painted Skin" (P'u Sung-ling)
    See "Hua pi"
"The Painted Woman" (O'Flaherty) 6:262, 264
"The Painter" (Hesse) 9:243
"The Painter's Adventure" (Irving) 2:262
A Painter's Work (Storm)
    See Eine Malerarbeit
"A Pair" (Singer) 3:377, 384
"A Pair of Eyes" (Alcott) 27:33, 58, 60
"A Pair of Patient Lovers" (Howells) 36:394-95, 397-98
A Pair of Patient Lovers (Howells) 36:394, 400
"A Pair of Silk Stockings" (Chopin) 8:72
"A Pair of Vikings" (Aiken) 9:7, 13
"Pairen" (Vinge) 24:338
"La paix du ménage" (Balzac) 5:5, 29, 31
"Pakao" (Andric) 36:47, 55
Pal Joey (O'Hara) 15:263
"La palabra asesino" (Valenzuela) 14:361-62, 364-65
"A Pale and Perfectly Oval Moon" (Adams) 24:2, 4-5, 8
"Pale Hands I Loathe" (Perelman) 32:222
"Pale Horse, Pale Rider" (Porter) 31:160, 179
Pale Horse, Pale Rider (Porter) 4:327, 329, 331-35, 339-41, 347, 349, 361, 364-65
Pale Horse, Pale Rider: Three Short Novels (Porter) 4:327-28, 331, 339
"The Pale Pink Roast" (Paley) 8:389, 397, 414-16
Palm-of-the-Hand Stories (Kawabata)
    See Tanagokoro no Shōsetsu
The Palm-Sized Stories (Kawabata)
    See Tanagokoro no Shōsetsu
"La paloma negra" (Pardo Bazan) 30:271
Palomar (Calvino) 3:113-18

Paludes (Gide) 13:52-3, 56-7, 59, 61-5, 70, 72, 80, 86-9, 91-5, 99, 101
"Pamfalon the Clown" (Leskov)
    See "Skomorox Pamfalon"
"Pan and the Syrinx" (Laforgue)
    See "Pan et la Syrinx"
"Pan Apolek" (Babel) 16:6-7, 26, 28, 30-1, 50, 53, 55, 58-9
"Pan et la Syrinx" (Laforgue) 20:86, 89, 91, 93-4, 101-2, 105
"ha-Panas" (Agnon) 30:85
"La panchina" (Calvino) 3:97
"Pandora" (James) 8:310-12
Pandora (Nerval) 18:346-48, 350-52, 354, 362, 369-72
"Panel Game" (Coover) 15:32, 37
P'anghuang (Lu Hsun) 20:125-26, 138-44, 146, 148
"Panim aherot" (Agnon) 30:3-4, 16-18, 20, 47-9, 52, 54, 66
"The Panjandrum" (Trollope) 28:320, 335-37, 340, 348, 354
Pankraz, der Schmoller (Keller) 26:106, 108, 125, 127
"Pantaloon in Black" (Faulkner) 1:148, 174, 183; 35:157, 192
"Pantera en jazz" (Fuentes) 24:31, 37
"Panther in Jazz" (Fuentes)
    See "Pantera en jazz"
"The Panther of Jolton's Ridge" (Murfree) 22:187, 203
"Pao Chu" (P'u Sung-ling) 31:188
"Le Paon" (Ayme) 41:8, 15
"Le papa de Simon" (Maupassant) 1:261, 271
"Papa Sisto" (Verga) 21:294-95
Papéis avulsos (Machado de Assis) 24:132, 144, 152
Papeles de Pandora (Ferre) 36:135, 137, 146-47, 153-54, 156, 159, 162-63, 169
"Paper Children" (Jolley) 19:240
The Paper Door and Other Stories (Shiga) 23:352, 360
"The Papers" (James) 8:321
Para una tumba sin nombre (Onetti) 23:247, 252, 260-61, 272-73
"Parábola del trueque" (Arreola) 38:10-11
"Parachutes" (McGahern) 17:308, 310-15, 318-19, 323
"Paradise" (Lagerkvist) 12:179, 195
"Paradise" (O'Brien) 10:330, 341, 343
Paradise, and Other Stories (Moravia)
    See Il paradiso
"The Paradise Lounge" (Trevor) 21:262, 265
"The Paradise of Bachelors" (Melville) 17:359
"The Paradise of Bachelors and the Tartarus of Maids" (Melville) 1:298, 303-05, 323; 49:393-94
Il paradiso (Moravia) 26:161-63, 165
The Paradoxes of Mr. Pond (Chesterton) 1:125, 139
"The Paragon" (O'Connor) 5:371-72
"Paragraph" (Lish) 18:286
"Paraguay" (Barthelme) 2:35, 38, 41
"Le parapluie" (Maupassant) 1:286
"A Parasita Azul" (Machado de Assis) 24:146-51
"Pardner" (O'Hara) 15:250
"The Pardon" (Pardo Bazan) 30:290
"Un parecido" (Pardo Bazan) 30:265
"Paris at Nightfall" (Baudelaire)
    See "Le crépuscule du soir"
Paris Spleen (Baudelaire)
    See Petits poèmes en prose: Le spleen de Paris
The Parisian Prowler (Baudelaire)
    See Petits poèmes en prose: Le spleen de Paris
"The Park" (Frame) 29:108-09, 118
"Parker Adderson, Philosopher" (Bierce) 9:60, 68, 84-5
"Parker's Back" (O'Connor) 1:344-45, 357, 359, 368-70

"The Parking Lot" (Beattie) 11:17-18, 20, 22
Parlor, Bedlam, and Bath (Perelman) 32:206, 219
"La Parola Mamma" (Moravia) 26:144
"Le parole e la notte" (Moravia) 26:148
"The Parrot" (Bowen) 3:37, 55
"The Parrot" (Singer) 3:358
"A Parrot Story" (Narayan) 25:138
"The Parshley Celebration" (Jewett) 6:156
"The Parsley Garden" (Saroyan) 21:155
"The Parson's Daughter of Oxney Colne" (Trollope) 28:318, 331-33, 349
A Part of the Institution (Suckow) 18:400, 403
"Parted" (Moore) 19:343
Parti-colored Stories (Chekhov) 2:130
"Une partie de campagne" (Maupassant) 1:260-61
"A Parting" (Galsworthy) 22:58, 98
"The Parting" (O'Flaherty) 6:265, 281, 286, 288
"A Parting and a Meeting" (Howells) 36:398
The Partners (Auchincloss) 22:22, 26, 28, 33-4, 38, 40-1, 46-50
"The Partridge Festival" (O'Connor) 1:356
"Parturient montes" (Arreola) 38:10-11
"The Party" (Barthelme) 2:39, 55
"The Party" (Chekhov)
    See "The Name-Day Party"
"Party" (Cowan) 28:74
The Party at Jack's (Wolfe) 33:348-49, 368, 376
"A Party for the Girls" (Bates) 10:131
"La parure" (Maupassant) 1:273, 278, 280, 284, 286, 288
"Pas de Deux" (Sansom) 21:89, 126
"El pasa del norte" (Rulfo) 25:246, 249, 265, 270
"Paseo" (Donoso) 34:4-6, 22, 25, 29-31, 34-9, 41-2, 49, 50-1
"The Pasha's Concubine" (Andric)
    See "Mara milosnica"
The Pasha's Concubine, and Other Stories (Andric) 36:44-5
"El Paso" (Phillips) 16:326-28, 330, 337
"Los paso en las huellas" (Cortazar) 7:62
"A Passage in the Life of Mr. John Oakhurst" (Harte) 8:233
"Passage in the Life of Mr. Watkins Tottle" (Dickens) 17:110, 138
"A Passage in the Secret History of an Irish Countess" (Le Fanu) 14:220, 221, 237
Passaic (Williams)
    See Life along the Passaic River
"Le passe muraille" (Ayme) 41:10-13, 18, 21-25
    See
"The Passenger" (Calisher) 15:9
"The Passenger" (Nabokov) 11:134
"The Passenger's Story" (Twain) 6:337
"Passer-By" (Clarke) 3:134
"Passing" (Galsworthy) 22:91
"Passing" (Hughes)
    See "Who's Passing for Who?"
"The Passing of Ambrose" (Wodehouse) 2:356
"The Passing of Black Eagle" (Henry) 5:158
"The Passing of Enriquez" (Harte) 8:228
"The Passing of Grandison" (Chesnutt) 7:16, 19, 22-3, 25-6
"A Passing Storm" (Lu Hsun) 20:148
"The Passion" (Barnes) 3:5, 24-7
"Une passion" (Maupassant) 1:274
"Passion" (O'Faolain) 13:294-95
"Une passion dans le désert" (Balzac) 5:12-14, 31
"A Passion for Snakes" (P'u Sung-ling)
    See "She pi"
"A Passion in the Desert" (Balzac)
    See "Une passion dans le désert"
The Passionate North (Sansom) 21:84, 114
"A Passionate Pilgrim" (James) 8:302
"Passions" (Singer) 3:378
Passions, and Other Stories (Singer) 3:376-77, 381, 384

"The Past" (Glasgow) **34**:56, 61-2, 68, 74, 79-80, 82, 88-90, 95, 101
"The Past" (Lu Hsun)
   See "Huaijiu"
"Past Carin'" (Lawson) **18**:210, 225
"Past One at Rooney's" (Henry) **5**:198
"Pastel rancio" (Fuentes) **24**:31, 37
Pastime Stories (Page) **23**:289, 292
"Pastor Dowe at Tacaté" (Bowles) **3**:59, 61-3, 66-7, 69, 79
"The Pastor of Six Mile Bush" (Lavin) **4**:169
"Pastoral" (Anderson) **1**:52
"Pastoral" (Carver) **8**:5, 30, 50
"Pastoral Care" (Gardner) **7**:217, 219-22, 229, 232
The Pastoral Symphony (Gide)
   See *La Symphonie pastorale*
"Pastorale" (Ayme) **41**:16-17, 20
"Pastorale" (Sansom) **21**:91, 94-6
The Pastures of Heaven (Steinbeck) **11**:202-03, 206-07, 225, 233, 242, 244, 246; **37**:354
"Pat Collins" (O'Hara) **15**:282
"Pat Hobby's Christmas Wish" (Fitzgerald) **6**:69-70
"Pat Shlema" (Agnon) **30**:4, 22, 24, 26, 37-9, 71
"The Patagonia" (James) **8**:299, 311
"Patchwork" (Moore) **19**:304
"Patent Pending" (Clarke) **3**:133-34
"La patente" (Pirandello) **22**:254, 257
"The Patented Gate and the Mean Hamburger" (Warren) **4**:387, 390, 394, 396, 399
"The Path of the Moon's Dark Fortnight" (Gordimer) **17**:154
"The Path through the Wood" (Stifter)
   See "Der Waldsteig"
"Paths" (Andric)
   See "Staze"
"The Pathways of Desire" (Le Guin) **12**:235
"A Patient Waiter" (Freeman) **1**:201
"The Patriarch" (Grau) **15**:149, 152, 160-61
"The Patriarch" (O'Connor) **5**:393-94
"Patricia, Edith, and Arnold" (Thomas) **3**:402, 405, 410, 412
"Patricide" (Oates) **6**:237
"The Patriot" (Galsworthy) **22**:79
"The Patriot" (O'Faolain) **13**:286, 314, 316
"The Patriot Son" (Lavin) **4**:167, 172, 183
The Patriot Son, and Other Stories (Lavin) **4**:165
"The Patriotic Honeymoon" (Waugh) **41**:328, 340
"A Patriotic Short" (Fitzgerald) **6**:70-1
"Patriotism" (Mishima) **4**:313-15, 317-23
"The Patron" (Phillips) **16**:330
"La patronne" (Maupassant) **1**:256
"La Patte du chat" (Ayme) **41**:7, 15
"The Pattern" (Campbell) **19**:84, 87
"Paul Blecker" (Davis) **38**:96
"Pauline's Passion and Punishment" (Alcott) **27**:3, 12, 23, 33, 57, 60, 62
"Paul's Case" (Cather) **2**:90-1, 94, 103, 113, 118, 121-22
"The Pavilion on the Links" (Stevenson) **11**:265, 268-69, 280, 296-97, 303, 306
"Le Pavillon sur l'eau" (Gautier) **20**:16
"The Pawnbroker's Shop" (Dickens) **17**:115
"The Pawnbroker's Wife" (Spark) **10**:350, 354, 359, 363
"Payable Gold" (Lawson) **18**:220
The Paying Guest (Gissing)
Peace, It's Wonderful (Saroyan) **21**:144, 153, 158, 160, 162-63
"The Peace Meeting" (Galsworthy) **22**:62, 101
"Peace of Mind" (Boyle) **16**:148, 153, 155
"The Peace of Mowsle Barton" (Saki) **12**:288
"The Peace of Utrecht" (Munro) **3**:321, 326
"The Peacelike Mongoose" (Thurber) **1**:426
"Peaches" (McGahern) **17**:298, 303, 309, 319
"The Peaches" (Thomas) **3**:394, 396, 402, 404-05, 410-12

"The Peach-house Potting Shed" (Sansom) **21**:88, 100
"The Peach-Tree" (Bates) **10**:112
"Peacock" (Carver) **8**:39
"The Peacock Cry" (Galsworthy) **22**:71
"Pear Tree Dance" (Jolley) **19**:233
"The Pearl" (Dinesen) **7**:165, 167-68, 198
"The Pearl" (Mishima) **4**:313, 317-18, 322
"The Pearl of Love" (Wells) **6**:376
"Pearls Are a Nuisance" (Chandler) **23**:72, 88-9, 97, 110
"The Peasant Marey" (Dostoevsky) **2**:166
"Peasant Women" (Chekhov) **2**:155
"Peasants" (Chekhov) **2**:126, 131, 156
"Peasants" (O'Connor) **5**:371, 377-78, 389, 394-95, 398
"Pecheneg" (Chekhov) **2**:155; **28**:60
"Peddler's Apprentice" (Vinge) **24**:337, 344
"The Pedersen Kid" (Gass) **12**:123-24, 126, 129, 131-32, 137, 139, 152-53, 156, 166, 168-73
"A Pedestrian Accident" (Coover) **15**:32
"Pedro Salvadores" (Borges) **4**:14-17
"The Pegnitz Junction" (Gallant) **5**:124, 127, 132-34, 143
The Pegnitz Junction (Gallant) **5**:124, 127, 130-32
"Le Pelerin enchante" (Leskov) **34**:114
"The Pelican" (Wharton) **6**:413, 423, 428-29
"The Pemberton Thrush" (Bates) **10**:121
"Pen and Inkstand" (Andersen) **6**:7
"The Penance" (Saki) **12**:302
"The Pencil" (Chandler) **23**:89, 110
"Los pendientes" (Pardo Bazan) **30**:274-77
"The Pendulum" (Henry) **5**:158-59, 163, 188
"La penitencia de Dora" (Pardo Bazan) **30**:262
"The Penknife" (Aleichem)
   See "Dos meserl"
"A Penny for Your Thoughts" (Selby) **20**:282
"The Pension Beaurepas" (James) **8**:299
"I pensionati della memoria" (Pirandello) **22**:232
"The Pensioners of Memory" (Pirandello)
   See "I pensionati della memoria"
"The Penthouse Apartment" (Trevor) **21**:261
"Pentolaccia" (Verga) **21**:286
"The Penultimate Puritan" (Auchincloss) **22**:46, 50
The People, and Uncollected Short Stories (Malamud) **15**:234-35
The People: No Different Flesh (Henderson) **29**:319-20
"The People of Osatica" (Andric)
   See "Osaticani"
The People of Seldwyla (Keller)
   See *The People of Seldwyla*
"People That Once Were Men" (Gorky)
   See "Byvshii lyudi"
"The People v. Abe Lathan, Colored" (Caldwell) **19**:38
"The People, Yes and Then Again No" (Saroyan) **21**:163
"The People's Choice" (Caldwell) **19**:6, 11-12
"Un pequeño paraíso" (Cortazar) **7**:93
Per le vie (Verga) **21**:291, 297
"Percy" (Cheever) **38**:50, 52
"Le père" (Maupassant) **1**:275
"Le père amable" (Maupassant) **1**:259, 284
"Père Raphaël" (Cable) **4**:51, 77-9
Perelman's Home Companion: A Collector's Item of Thirty-Six Otherwise Unavailable Pieces by Himself (The Collector Being S. J. Perelman—Perelman) **32**:208
"Pereval" (Bunin) **5**:98
"A Perfect Day for Bananafish" (Salinger) **2**:290-93, 295, 297-99, 303, 305, 308, 312, 314, 318; **28**:229, 236-38, 243, 263, 265-66
"The Perfect Life" (Fitzgerald) **6**:47, 49
"The Perfect Murder" (Barnes) **3**:13
"The Perfect Setting" (Warner) **23**:376
"The Perfect Tenants" (Naipaul) **38**:322, 328, 336, 345

The Perfecting of a Love (Musil)
   See "Vollendung der Liebe"
"Perfection" (Nabokov) **11**:123
"The Performance" (Jolley) **19**:220, 234, 243-44
"The Performing Child" (Narayan) **25**:135, 140, 156
"The Perfume Sea" (Laurence) **7**:245, 248-50, 256
"Perhaps We Are Going Away" (Bradbury) **29**:59
"The Peril in the Streets" (Cheever) **1**:99
"Perilous Play" (Alcott) **27**:59-60
"Period Piece" (Waugh) **41**:323, 328-29, 331-32
The Periodic Table (Levi)
   See *Il sistema periodico*
"The Perishing of the Pendragons" (Chesterton) **1**:131, 138
"El perjurio de la nieve" (Bioy Casares) **17**:59, 85
"The Perjury of the Snow" (Bioy Casares)
   See "El perjurio de la nieve"
"La perla rosa" (Pardo Bazan) **30**:264-65
"Perlmutter at the East Pole" (Elkin) **12**:94-5, 117-18
Permanent Errors (Price) **22**:366-70, 372, 376, 384-85
"Permutations Among the Nightingales" (Huxley) **39**:155
"Pero Venceremos" (Algren) **33**:88, 108
"Perpetua" (Barthelme) **2**:55
Perronik the Fool (Moore) **19**:309
"Persecution" (Andric) **36**:71 2
"Persecution Mania" (O'Faolain) **13**:297
"Persée et Andromède" (Laforgue) **20**:86, 90-4, 99-103, 122-3
"El Perseguidor" (Cortazar) **7**:50-1, 58, 61, 67-8, 70
"Perseid" (Barth) **10**:44, 51, 55-6, 66-9, 71, 91, 93, 101-02, 104
"Pershing or Ten Eyck, Ten Eyck or Pershing" (O'Hara) **15**:253
"The Persistence of Desire" (Updike) **13**:391-92
"Perte d'auréole" (Baudelaire) **18**:35, 49
Pervaya lyubov' (Turgenev) **7**:321, 323-24, 327-29, 332-34, 337-39, 341, 352
"Pesadillas" (Cortazar) **7**:91
Pescara'a Temptation (Meyer)
   See *Die Versuchung des Pescara*
"Pesci grossi, pesci piccoli" (Calvino) **3**:96
"The Peseta with the Hole in the Middle" (Algren) **33**:109
"Pesn' torzhestruyushchey lyubvi" (Turgenev) **7**:321, 323, 337-38, 362
"Pesnia o burevestnike" (Gorky) **28**:178
"Pesnia o sokole" (Gorky) **28**:144, 178, 187-88
"Pete and Emil" (Stegner) **27**:214
"Peter" (Cather) **2**:96-7, 100, 105
"Peter and the Wolf" (Carter) **13**:14, 17-18
"Peter Atherley's Ancestors" (Harte) **8**:215
"Peter Goldthwaite's Treasure" (Hawthorne) **3**:183, 185
"Le petit coq noir" (Ayme) **41**:15
"Le petit fût" (Maupassant) **1**:259, 284
"Petit soldat" (Maupassant) **1**:259
"La petite danceuse de quatorze ans" (Beattie) **11**:6, 17
"La petite rogue" (Maupassant) **1**:275, 283, 288
"Petition" (Barth) **10**:38, 41-3, 46, 52, 54, 56-7, 59-60, 76, 79, 84, 91, 95, 97
Petits poèmes en prose: Le spleen de Paris (Baudelaire) **18**:3, 6-8, 14-16, 19, 22-5, 27-9, 31-4, 38, 44-8, 50, 52-4, 59, 61-5
"Petlistye ushi" (Bunin) **5**:81, 101-04, 110-13
Petlistye ushi i drugie rasskazy (Bunin) **5**:101
"The Petrified Man" (Welty) **1**:465, 467, 469, 471, 482, 490, 493-95, 497; **27**:332, 340
"The Petrified Woman" (Gordon) **15**:119-20, 123, 139
"The Petrol Dump" (Pritchett) **14**:296
"Petunias" (Walker) **5**:413

Title Index

"Le peuple des etoiles filantes" (Morand)
22:175
"La peur" (Maupassant) **1**:265, 288
"Der Pförtner im Herrenhause" (Stifter)
See "Tourmaline"
Phantasiestüeke in Callots Manier (Hoffmann)
13:179, 188-90
"Les Phantasmes de M. Redoux" (Villiers de
l'Isle Adam) **14**:397
Phantasus (Tieck) **31**:282, 286, 289
"Phantom Gold" (Dreiser) **30**:112
"The Phantom Lover" (Jackson) **39**:212, 213
"A Phantom Lover" (Lee) **33**:308
"The Phantom of the Movie Palace" (Coover)
15:57, 59, 63, 65
"The Phantom of the Opera's Friend"
(Barthelme) **2**:31, 35, 52, 54
"The Phantom 'Rickshaw" (Kipling) **5**:261,
265, 271-75, 297-99
The Phantom 'Rickshaw (Kipling) **5**:272-73
"Phantoms" (Turgenev) **7**:321, 323, 325, 334-
35, 338
"The Phantoms of the Foot-Bridge" (Murfree)
22:212
"The Pheasant" (Carver) **8**:53
"Philander unter den streifenden Soldaten und
Zigeunern im Dreissigjahrigen Kreige"
(Arnim) **29**:9
"Philanthropy" (Galsworthy) **22**:101
"Philip and Margie" (Jewett) **6**:156
"Philip Marlowe's Last Case" (Chandler)
23:110
"A Philistine in Bohemia" (Henry) **5**:190, 196
"The Philosopher's Stone" (Andersen) **6**:26, 34
Philosophic Studies (Balzac)
See *Etudes philosophiques*
Philosophie's (Voltaire) **12**:364
"The Philosophy Lesson" (Stafford) **26**:286-87,
289, 307
"The Philter" (Stendhal)
See "Le Phitre"
"Le Phitre" (Stendhal) **27**:247-48, 259
"Phoebe" (Gissing) **37**:63, 75, 79
"Phoenix in the Ashes" (Vinge) **24**:328, 330,
332, 334-35, 337-38, 343, 345
Phoenix in the Ashes (Vinge) **24**:343, 345
"Phosphorus" (Levi) **12**:256
"The Photograph Album" (Onetti) **23**:280
"Physic" (de la Mare) **14**:80, 83
"Piano" (Saroyan) **21**:144
"Piano Fingers" (Mason) **4**:18
"The Piazza" (Melville) **1**:303
The Piazza Tales (Melville) **1**:295-97
"El pichon" (Rulfo) **25**:268
"Picking Cotton" (Caldwell) **19**:6
"Pickman's Model" (Lovecraft) **3**:261-62
"Pick-Up on Noon Street" (Chandler) **23**:80,
86, 106
"The Picnic" (de la Mare) **14**:83-4
"Picnic" (Lewis) **40**:277
"Pico Rico Mandorico" (Ferre) **36**:147, 151
"Pictor's Metamorphoses" (Hesse) **9**:221, 242,
244-45
Pictor's Metamorphoses, and Other Fantasies
(Hesse) **9**:244
"The Picture" (de la Mare) **14**:83-4
"The Picture in the House" (Lovecraft) **3**:262,
275-76, 292-95
A Picture-Book without Pictures (Andersen)
6:4, 15, 30
"The Pictures" (Frame) **29**:109
"Pictures" (Mansfield) **9**:304, 307, 311
"Pictures in the Fire" (Collier) **19**:106, 110
Pictures in the Fire (Collier) **19**:105
"Pictures of Corruption" (Moorhouse) **40**:323
"Pictures of Fidelman" (Malamud) **15**:186-87
Pictures of Fidelman: An Exhibition
(Malamud) **15**:178, 181, 184, 190, 192-
93, 195, 211, 218, 220, 236, 240-41
"Pictures of the Artist" (Malamud) **15**:185,
193-94
"The Picture-Well" (Ayme) **41**:3-4

"A Piece of Advice" (Aleichem)
See "An eytse"
"A Piece of Advice" (Singer) **3**:368
"The Piece of Glass" (Peretz) **26**:216
"A Piece of Land" (Harris) **19**:177, 181
"A Piece of News" (Welty) **1**:468, 478, 487,
496
"A Piece of Steak" (London) **4**:253, 262-63,
291
"A Piece of String" (Maupassant)
See "La ficelle"
"Le Pied de la momie" (Gautier) **20**:15
"Pierre Grassou" (Balzac) **5**:18
"Pierre Menard, Author of the Quixote"
(Borges)
See "Pierre Menard, autor del Quixote"
"Pierre Menard, autor del Quixote" (Borges)
4:15, 26, 30, 34-5; **41**:55, 66, 103-13, 158,
163, 165-66
"La pierre qui pousse" (Camus) **9**:103, 106,
108-110, 118-19, 131-34
"Pierrette" (Balzac) **5**:9
"Pierrot" (Maupassant) **1**:277-78
*Pietro von Abano oder Petrus Apone,
Zaubergeschichte* (Tieck) **31**:271-72, 286
"The Pig" (Lessing) **6**:196-97, 212-17
"The Pig" (O'Hara) **15**:291
"Pig Hoo-o-o-o-ey!" (Wodehouse) **2**:346, 348
"Pig Latin" (Lispector)
See "A língua do 'p'"
"The Pigeon" (Oe) **20**:219
"Pigeon Feathers" (Updike) **13**:370-71, 388,
395, 397, 404, 407
Pigeon Feathers, and Other Stories (Updike)
13:356, 366, 389-90, 392, 400, 404; **27**:321,
323-24
"Pigtails, Ltd." (de la Mare) **14**:68, 85, 87
Pikovaya dama (Pushkin) **27**:130, 133-34, 146-
54, 164-65, 172-75, 176-78, 184-88
"Pilate's Creed" (Capek) **36**:113, 117
"A Pilgrim and a Stranger" (Suckow) **18**:409,
414
Pilgrim at Sea (Lagerkvist) **12**:188, 191, 194,
198
The Pilgrim Hawk: A Love Story (Wescott)
35:357-65, 372, 376, 378-79
"A Pilgrimage" (Galsworthy) **22**:58
Pilgrimage: The Book of the People
(Henderson) **29**:320
"Pillar of Fire" (Bradbury) **29**:90-1
"Pillar of Salt" (Jackson) **9**:252, 258; **39**:210,
212, 227
"Pillow of Stone" (Grau) **15**:148, 160
"A Pimp's Revenge" (Malamud) **15**:183-84,
192, 194
"Piña" (Pardo Bazan) **30**:295
"A Pinch of Salt" (Jewett) **6**:158
"The Pine Tree" (Andersen) **6**:12, 40-1
"The Pines" (Bunin) **5**:100
Ping (Beckett)
See *Bing*
"Pink and Blue" (Williams) **31**:303, 324, 331,
333, 359, 361
The Pink and the Green (Stendhal)
See *Le rose et le vert*
"The Pink Corner Man" (Borges)
See "El Hombre de la esquina rosada"
"Pink May" (Bowen) **3**:31-2, 41; **28**:3-4
"The Pioneer Hep-Cat" (O'Hara) **15**:280
"Pioneers, Oh, Pioneers" (Rhys) **21**:50, 55-6,
65
"The Pious Cat" (Peretz) **26**:201
"La Pipe d'opium" (Gautier) **20**:23-5
Pipe Night (O'Hara) **15**:248-50, 262, 264-65,
267, 269
"Pisces" (Agnon) **30**:68
"Pish-Tush" (Lewis) **34**:165
"Pis'ma iz Tuly" (Pasternak) **31**:98, 105, 108,
111, 116-18
"Pismo iz 1920 godine" (Andric) **36**:35, 43, 47,
79

The Pit (Onetti)
See *El pozo*
"The Pit and the Pendulum" (Poe) **1**:405-06;
22:305; **34**:249-50, 259, 263; **35**:310, 320,
345
"The Pitcher" (Dubus) **15**:83, 100
"Pity for Living Creatures" (Aleichem) **33**:18
"The Pixy and the Grocer" (Andersen)
See "The Goblin at the Grocer's"
"A Place in the Heart" (Bates) **10**:119
"The Place of the Gods" (Benet)
See "By the Waters of Babylon"
"A Place to Lie Down" (Algren) **33**:113
"The Place with No Name" (Ellison) **14**:109,
118, 120, 138
"Les plagiaires de la foudre" (Villiers de l'Isle
Adam) **14**:397
"Plagiarized Material" (Oates) **6**:237, 242
"The Plague-Cellar" (Stevenson) **11**:304
"The Plain in Flames" (Rulfo)
See "El llano en llamas"
The Plain in Flames (Rulfo)
See *El llano en llamas, y otros cuentos*
"The Plain Man" (Galsworthy) **22**:60, 99
Plain of Fire (Rulfo)
See *El llano en llamas, y otros cuentos*
Plain Tales (Kipling)
See *Plain Tales from the Hills*
Plain Tales from the Hills (Kipling) **5**:273-74,
278, 288
"The Plain, the Endless Plain" (Aldiss) **36**:20,
22
"Un plaisant" (Baudelaire) **18**:17-18, 32, 60
Plan de evasión (Bioy Casares) **17**:53-5, 61,
63-4, 94
A Plan for Escape (Bioy Casares)
See *Plan de evasión*
"Planchette" (London) **4**:265, 294-95
Planet Stories (Bradbury) **29**:90
"The Planets of the Years" (O'Faolain) **13**:291,
318-19
"A Plantation Witch" (Harris) **19**:140, 195
"The Planter of Malata" (Conrad) **9**:147
"Plants and Girls" (Lessing) **6**:217
"The Plattner Story" (Wells) **6**:359, 364-66,
394, 405
The Plattner Story, and Others (Wells) **6**:366-
67, 380, 388
The Play, and Other Stories (Dixon) **16**:215
Play Days (Jewett) **6**:165-66
"Playback" (Beattie) **11**:11, 22
"The Playhouse Called Remarkable" (Spark)
10:359, 361, 370
"A Play-House in the Waste" (Moore)
See "San n-Diothramh Dubh"
"Playing the Game" (Campbell) **19**:76, 78, 90
"Playing With Fire" (Doyle) **12**:64
"Playing with Punjab" (Bambara) **35**:24-5
"Please Don't Talk About Me When I'm
Gone" (Algren) **33**:106
"Pleasure" (Lessing) **6**:197
"Pleasure" (O'Hara) **15**:248, 265
"The Pleasure of Plain Rice" (Yamamoto) **34**:58
"The Pleasure-Cruise" (Kipling) **5**:284
"The Pleasures of Solitude" (Cheever) **1**:88
"The Pleasure-Seeker" (Capek) **36**:130
"Pledges, Vows and Pass this Note"
(Moorhouse) **40**:312-18
Plongées (Mauriac) **24**:183-84, 196, 203, 206,
208
"The Plot" (Borges) **41**:176
"Plots and Counterplots" (Alcott)
See "V.V.: or Plots and Counterplots"
"The Ploughman" (Dinesen) **7**:177
"Plowshare in Heaven" (Stuart) **31**:245, 251-52
Plowshare in Heaven (Stuart) **31**:226-27, 235-
36, 245, 255
"Plumbing" (Updike) **13**:348
"A Plunge into Real Estate" (Calvino)
See "La speculazionc ediliziа"
"Le plus beau dîner du monde" (Villiers de
l'Isle Adam) **14**:377

"Le plus bel amour de Don Juan" (Barbey
    d'Aurevilly) **17**:7, 11-14, 19-20, 42-4
"Plus Ultra!" (Machado de Assis) **24**:152
"Plutarco Roo" (Warner) **23**:368
"Po povodu Krejcerovoj sonaty" (Leskov)
    34:108
"Po' Sandy" (Chesnutt) **7**:5-7, 10, 13, 42
Pocket Stories (Capek)
    See *Tales from Two Pockets*
"Pocock Passes" (Pritchett) **14**:271, 285-86, 297
"Pod prazdnik obideli" (Leskov) **34**:108
"A Poem as the Corpus Delicti" (P'u
    Sung-ling)
    See "Shih-yen"
Poems in Prose from Charles Baudelaire
    (Baudelaire)
    See *Petits poèmes en prose: Le spleen de
    Paris*
"The Poet" (Capek)
    See "Básník"
"The Poet" (Dinesen) **7**:167-68, 180, 203, 209
"The Poet" (Hesse) **9**:234
The Poet and the Lunatics (Chesterton) **1**:124-
    26, 132
"The Poet and the Peasant" (Henry) **5**:194
"The Poet at Home" (Saroyan) **21**:155
"The Poetess of Clap City" (Davis) **38**:120-21,
    123
"A Poetics for Bullies" (Elkin) **12**:94-7, 99,
    117-18
"A Poetizing Thief" (Capek)
    See "O lyrickém zloději"
"The Poetry of Modern Life" (Greene) **29**:218
"Poet's Ashes" (Solzhenitsyn)
    See "Prakh poeta"
"The Poet's Portmanteau" (Gissing) **37**:64
"Pogasšce delo" (Leskov) **34**:109
Polilstars (Pohl) **25**:235
"A Point at Issue" (Chopin) **8**:70, 73
"A Point in Morals" (Glasgow) **34**:57-9, 65, 67,
    77-8, 97, 99
"The Point of It" (Forster) **27**:69, 71, 74, 76-7,
    83, 86, 96, 100, 114-15
"A Point of Law" (Faulkner) **1**:177
"Poison" (Mansfield) **9**:310-11
The Poisoned Kiss (Oates) **6**:236, 241-43
"The Poisoned Pastries" (Donoso) **34**:21
"The Poisoned Story" (Ferre) **36**:151, 156
"Poker Night" (Updike) **13**:409
"Polar Bears and Others" (Boyle) **5**:54
"Polaris" (Lovecraft) **3**:288
"Polarities" (Atwood) **2**:2-5, 7-8, 10, 13-14
"Poldi" (McCullers) **9**:342, 345, 357
"The Pole" (Lewis) **34**:166-67, 177,179
Pole Poppenspäler (Storm) **27**:279, 282, 284
"The Policeman's Ball" (Barthelme) **2**:31, 45
Polikushka (Tolstoy) **9**:376, 389, 393-94, 399,
    403
"Polite Conversation" (Stafford) **26**:297, 312
"A Political Boy Is Now Dead" (Oe)
    See "Seiji shonen shisu"
"Political Director of Divine Worship"
    (Bulgakov) **18**:90
"Pollock and the Porroh Man" (Wells) **6**:388
"Polly: A Christmas Recollection" (Page)
    23:283-84, 297, 303-04
"Polunoščniki" (Leskov) **34**:109, 112, 125, 127
"Polydore" (Chopin) **8**:93
"Polyhymnia Muse of Sacred Song"
    (Auchincloss) **22**:51
"Polzunkov" (Dostoevsky) **2**:170, 192-93
"Pomegranate Seed" (Wharton) **6**:426-27,
    431-32
"The Pomegranate Trees" (Saroyan) **21**:150,
    168, 172, 174
"Un pomeriggio Adamo" (Calvino) **3**:97
"Pomoc!" (Capek) **36**:91-2, 110, 122, 125
"Pompeii" (Lowry)
    See "Present Estate of Pompeii"
The Ponder Heart (Welty) **1**:474, 477, 483,
    494-95, 497
"Ponto de vista" (Machado de Assis) **24**:151

"Poodle" (Lardner) **32**:129
The Poodle Springs Story (Chandler) **23**:111
"The Pool" (du Maurier) **18**:127-28
"The Pool" (Maugham) **8**:369-71
"The Pool of Narcissus" (Calisher) **15**:15, 17
"The Poor and the Rich" (Saroyan) **21**:166
"The Poor Benefactor" (Stifter)
    See "Der Arme Wohltäter"
"The Poor Bird" (Andersen) **6**:4
"The Poor Boy" (Peretz) **26**:201
"The Poor Child's Toy" (Baudelaire)
    See "Le joujou du pauvre"
"The Poor Clare" (Gaskell) **25**:41, 54-5, 60
"The Poor Fiddler" (Grillparzer)
    See *Der Arme Spielmann*
"A Poor Gentleman" (Gissing) **37**:53, 56
"A Poor Girl" (Chopin) **8**:69
"The Poor Heart" (Saroyan) **21**:162
"Poor John" (Andersen) **6**:4
"Poor Koko" (Fowles) **33**:233, 235-36, 244,
    246-48, 257-61, 263-65, 272, 275, 288-89
"Poor Little Black Fellow" (Hughes) **6**:118,
    121-22, 134
"Poor Little Rich Town" (Vonnegut) **8**:436
"The Poor Man" (Coppard) **21**:3, 15, 17, 27
"A Poor Man's Got His Pride" (Dazai Osamu)
    41:264, 276
"Poor Man's Pennies" (Algren) **33**:105, 109
"Poor Man's Pudding and Rich Man's
    Crumbs" (Melville) **1**:303, 323
"Poor Mary" (Warner) **23**:370
The Poor Musician (Grillparzer)
    See *Der Arme Spielmann*
"Poor People" (O'Flaherty) **6**:262, 264, 280,
    283
"A Poor Stick" (Morrison) **40**:368
"The Poor Thing" (Powers) **4**:368, 372-73
"Poor Thumbling" (Andersen) **6**:4, 7
"Pop Goes the Alley Cat" (Stegner) **27**:218,
    220
"Pope Jacynth" (Lee) **33**:310
Pope Jacynth, and Other Fantastic Tales (Lee)
    33:303, 307, 309
"Pope Zeidlus" (Singer) **3**:364
"Poppy Seed and Sesame Rings" (Jolley)
    19:241
"Popsy" (King) **17**:295
"Popular Mechanics" (Carver) **8**:14, 18, 26, 30,
    44-5
Popular Stories (Grimm and Grimm)
    See *Kinder-und Hausmärchen*
"Por boca de los dioses" (Fuentes) **24**:30, 38,
    40, 43-4, 54-5
"Por enquanto" (Lispector) **34**:208, 215
"Por qué ser así?" (Unamuno) **11**:312
"Porcelain and Pink" (Fitzgerald) **6**:59
"Porcupines at the University" (Barthelme) **2**:56
"Porn" (Walker) **5**:412-14
"Porodična slika" (Andric) **36**:48
"Porotce" (Capek) **36**:102
"Le port" (Baudelaire) **18**:6
"Le port" (Maupassant) **1**:264
"Port Swettenham" (Lowry) **31**:41
The Portable Ring Lardner (Lardner) **32**:131,
    156
"Porte cochère" (Taylor) **10**:379, 407
"The Porter's Son" (Andersen) **6**:11-12
"The Portly Gentleman" (O'Hara) **15**:284
"The Portobello Road" (Spark) **10**:350-53, 355,
    357-58, 360, 365-66, 368, 370-71
"Portrait" (Boyle) **5**:54
"A Portrait" (Galsworthy) **22**:58, 74-5, 98, 100
"The Portrait" (Gogol)
    See "Portret"
"The Portrait" (Huxley) **39**:156, 175
"The Portrait" (Oliphant) **25**:196, 209
"The Portrait" (Wharton) **6**:414
"Portrait of a Literary Critic" (Wolfe) **33**:401
A Portrait of Bascom Hawke (Wolfe) **33**:345-
    49, 357, 359-60, 375
"A Portrait of Shunkin" (Tanizaki)
    See "Shunkin shō"

Portrait of the Artist as a Young Dog
    (Thomas) **3**:394-97, 399, 402-04, 410-13
"Portrait of the Intellectual as a Yale Man"
    (McCarthy) **24**:213
"Portraits de maîtresses" (Baudelaire) **18**:18,
    25, 37
"Portret" (Gogol) **9**:102-03, 116, 122, 125;
    29:128, 135, 172
Die Portugiesin (Musil) **18**:292-93, 297-303,
    322
The Portuguese Lady (Musil)
    See *Die Portugiesin*
"The Porush and the Bear" (Peretz) **26**:216
"Poseidon and Company" (Carver) **8**:50-1
"Poseidon's Daughter" (Sansom) **21**:86-7, 124
"Poseshchenie muzeia" (Nabokov)
    See "The Visit to the Museum"
"Posesión" (Pardo Bazan) **30**:274-76
"Poslední soud" (Capek) **36**:83, 98, 106, 128
"Poslední věci člověka" (Capek) **36**:98
"The Possessed" (Clarke) **3**:132, 135, 143-44,
    148
"Possession of Angela Bradshaw" (Collier)
    19:98, 101, 110, 114
"The Possibility of Evil" (Jackson) **9**:256
"Posson Jone" (Cable) **4**:48, 56, 58, 62, 64-5,
    67, 77-80
"The Post" (Chekhov) **2**:130, 156
"The Post Card" (Boell)
    See "Die Postkarte"
"The Post Office" (O'Flaherty)
    See "Oifig an Phoist"
"The Post Office Crime" (Capek)
    See "Zločin na poště"
"The Postcard" (Dixon) **16**:217
"Postcard" (Munro) **3**:322
*The Posthumous Writings and Poems of
    Hermann Lauscher* (Hesse)
    See *Hinterlassene Schriften und Gedichte
    von Hermann Lauscher*
"Post-Impressionist Daddy" (Perelman) **32**:202
"Die Postkarte" (Boell) **23**:8
"The Postmaster" (Pushkin)
    See "Stantsionnyi smotritel"
"The Postoffice and the Serpent" (Coppard)
    21:10
"Posy" (Lavin) **4**:166
"The Pot" (Aleichem)
    See "Dos tepl"
"The Pot of Gold" (Cheever) **1**:89, 99; **38**:55
"The Pot of Gold" (O'Flaherty) **6**:271
"Potassium" (Levi) **12**:257
"The Potato Elf" (Nabokov) **11**:117, 137,
    139-40
"Potatoes" (Naipaul) **38**:331-34
"The Pot-Boiler" (Wharton) **6**:435
"Potential" (Campbell) **19**:73, 84, 92-3
"Pottage" (Henderson) **29**:326-27
"Potter" (Gallant) **5**:136-37
The Potter's House (Stegner) **27**:194, 216-17
Pour finir encour et Autres Foirades (Beckett)
    See *Foirades*
"Poverty" (Zoshchenko) **15**:404
Povest (Pasternak) **31**:98, 105-06, 110, 114-17,
    120-21
Povesti Belkina (Pushkin) **27**:129, 134-35, 141-
    46, 148-49, 163-67, 176, 181-83, 185-87
Povídky z druhé kapsy (Capek) **36**:83, 96, 98,
    100, 103, 105, 120-21, 126
Povídky z jedné kapsy (Capek) **36**:83, 96, 98,
    100, 104, 120-21, 126
"The Powder Blue Dragon" (Vonnegut)
    8:432-33
"The Powder of the Angels and I'm Yours"
    (Phillips) **16**:325, 328
"Powder-White Faces" (Hughes) **6**:118, 122
"Power in Trust" (Auchincloss) **22**:4
"The Power of Appointment" (Auchincloss)
    22:4
"The Power of Literature" (Farrell) **28**:127
"The Power of Words" (Poe) **22**:320
"Powerhouse" (Bradbury) **29**:42, 48

Title Index

"Powerhouse" (Welty) 1:466, 488, 494; 27:338
"Powers" (Singer) 3:360
Powers of Attorney (Auchincloss) 22:4-7, 9, 17-19, 33-4, 37, 46-50
"A Pox on You, Mine Goodly Host" (Perelman) 32:201-02
El pozo (Onetti) 23:244, 246, 248-49, 251-52, 258-61, 264, 273-74
"El pozo de la vida" (Pardo Bazan) 30:261
"Praça Mauá" (Lispector) 34:207, 215
Prairie Folks (Garland) 18:144-45, 148, 150, 160, 174-77, 182, 194
"A Prairie Heroine" (Garland) 18:163, 166, 173
"Prakh poeta" (Solzhenitsyn) 32:352-53
"Pranzo con un pastore" (Calvino) 3:97
"Pravaya kist" (Solzhenitsyn) 32:386, 392
"Prayer to the Pacific" (Silko) 37:309
"A Preacher's Love Story" (Garland) 18:148, 160
"Precinct Captain" (Farrell) 28:90
"Preciosidade" (Lispector) 34:194-97, 200-02, 217, 224-25
"The Precipice" (Oates) 6:247
"A Predestined Disaster" (Aleichem) 33:26, 48
"A Predicament" (Poe) 1:405-06; 22:330
"Prelude" (Mansfield) 9:279-80, 282-84, 286, 288-91, 298, 300-01, 303, 305, 307, 309, 311, 313, 316; 23:139, 153, 158
"Prelude to an American Symphony" (Saroyan) 21:134
"A Premature Autobiography" (Oates) 6:232
"The Premature Burial" (Poe) 1:407; 22:330, 334
Premier amour (Beckett) 16:73-4, 87-8, 90-1, 97
"Premier prix decomédie" (Ayme) 41:24
"The Presence" (Gordon) 15:116, 121, 131
"The Presence of Grace" (Powers) 4:370, 381
The Presence of Grace (Powers) 4:372-73
"Present Estate of Pompeii" (Lowry) 31:44-5, 47-8, 51, 59-60, 62, 72-4, 81, 86
"A Present for a Good Girl" (Gordimer) 17:167
Presenting Moonshine (Collier) 19:98, 103, 105
"Preservation" (Carver) 8:26, 32
"The President" (Barthelme) 2:31
"The President of the Louisiana Live Oak Society" (Gilchrist) 14:151-52, 155
"El Presidente de Méjico" (Algren) 33:106, 113
"Press Clippings" (Cortazar)
   See "Recortes de prensa"
"The Presser" (Coppard) 21:9, 28
"The Pretender" (Gordimer)
   See "My First Two Women"
"The Pretender" (O'Connor) 5:386, 390
"The Pretty Girl" (Dubus) 15:76, 87-9, 91, 93-4, 96, 101
"Pretty Maggie Moneyeyes" (Ellison) 14:107-08, 115
"Pretty Mouth and Green My Eyes" (Salinger) 2:290, 293, 298, 300
"Pretty Poll" (de la Mare) 14:85
"Previous Condition" (Baldwin) 10:3, 5, 7, 9-10, 17
"Previous Days" (Algren) 33:96
"The Previous Tenant" (Campbell) 19:83, 87
"Las previsiones de Sangiácomo" (Bioy Casares) 17:68-70
"Prey" (O'Flaherty) 6:281
"Příběh o kasaři a žháři" (Capek) 36:101
"Příběhy sňatkového podvodníka" (Capek) 36:97, 101
"Priča" (Andric) 36:65-6, 78
"Priča iz Japana" (Andric) 36:32
"Priča o soli" (Andric) 36:38
"Priča o vezirovom slonu" (Andric) 36:33-6, 37-8, 46-7, 78
"The Price of the Harness" (Crane) 7:104
"Price's Always Open" (O'Hara) 15:255-56
Pricksongs and Descants (Coover) 15:34-5, 37-41,43, 45, 47, 49-50, 53, 56, 58, 63
"The Pride of the Cities" (Henry) 5:159, 194

"The Pride of the Village" (Irving) 2:240-41, 245, 251
"The Priest of Shiga Temple and His Love" (Mishima) 4:313, 315-17, 322-23
"Priestly Fellowship" (Powers) 4:376, 381-82
"The Priestly Prerogative" (London) 4:282
"Prima Belladonna" (Ballard) 1:68
"Prima notte" (Pirandello) 22:231
"Prime Leaf" (Warren) 4:387-90, 393, 395, 400
"O primeiro beijo" (Lispector) 34:231, 233-34
"Primer amor" (Pardo Bazan) 30:265
"Primo amore" (Pavese) 19:375, 378, 384, 387
"Primo rapporto sulla terra dell' Inviato speciale dalla luna" (Moravia) 26:164
"The Primrose Path" (Lawrence) 4:234-37
"Prince Alberic and the Snake Lady" (Lee) 33:302, 309
"The Prince and the Pauper" (Auchincloss) 22:14, 50, 53
"Un Prince de la Bohème" (Balzac) 5:31-3
"Prince Hamlet of Shehrigov Province" (Turgenev)
   See "A Russian Hamlet"
"The Prince of a 100 Soups" (Lee) 33:300
"Prince of Darkness" (Powers) 4:370, 383
Prince of Darkness and Other Stories (Powers) 4:369-71
"The Prince Who Was a Thief" (Dreiser) 30:113, 115
"The Princess" (Chekhov) 2:130, 144
"The Princess" (de la Mare) 14:80
The Princess (Lawrence) 4:238-40, 242; 19:251
"The Princess and All the Kingdom" (Lagerkvist) 12:195
"The Princess and the Pea" (Andersen) 6:7, 13, 18, 26, 30
"The Princess and the Zucchini" (Thomas) 20:320, 322
"The Princess Baladina—Her Adventure" (Cather) 2:100
"The Princess Bob and Her Friends" (Harte) 8:216
Princess Brambilla (Hoffmann)
   See Prinzessin Brambilla: Ein Capriccio nach Jakob Callot
"Princess Lotus Bloom" (P'u Sung-ling)
   See "Lien-hua kung-chu"
"The Princess on the Pea" (Andersen)
   See "The Princess and the Pea"
La princesse de Babylon (Voltaire) 12:341-42
"Prinzessin Brambilla" (Hoffmann) 13:192, 198, 218-19
Prinzessin Brambilla: Ein Capriccio nach Jakob Callot (Hoffmann) 13:183-84
"Případ dra Mejzlíka" (Capek) 36:96, 102, 121
"Případ s dítětem" (Capek) 36:83, 127
"Případ Selvinuv" (Capek) 36:96, 99, 128
"Případy pana Janíka" (Capek) 36:96, 98, 102, 128
"Prischepa's Revenge" (Babel) 16:7, 24-5
"Priscilla" (Calvino) 3:95-6
"Priscilla and Emily Lofft" (Moore) 19:301, 310-11, 344-45
"Prishchepa" (Babel) 16:50
"The Prison" (Malamud) 15:175
"The Prison Window" (Auchincloss) 22:13, 53
"The Prisoner" (Galsworthy) 22:58, 82, 98
"The Prisoner of the Caucasus" (Tolstoy) 9:382, 386-87
"The Prisoners" (Lewis) 40:272
"Pristupaia ko dniu" (Solzhenitsyn) 32:353
"Private Jones" (Lewis) 40:271, 277
"Private Lies" (Mason) 4:19
"Private Life" (Arreola)
   See "La vida privada"
"The Private Life" (James) 8:280-81
"The Private Life of Mr. Bidwell" (Thurber) 1:419
"Private Property" (Sill) 37:37, 315
"Private Theatres" (Dickens) 17:117, 122
"Privilege" (Munro) 3:334
"The Privy Councilor" (Chekhov) 2:130

"The Prize Lodger" (Gissing) 37:56, 64
Prize Stock (Oe)
   See Shiiku
"Prizes" (Frame) 29:97
"Pro Aris et Focis" (Davis) 38:104
"The Problem of Art" (Gardner) 7:226
"The Problem of Thor Bridge" (Doyle) 12:52, 63-4
"Le Problème" (Ayme) 41:8
Problems, and Other Stories (Updike) 13:383, 385-86, 388
"Problems of Adjustment in Survivors of Natural/Unnatural Disasters" (Oates) 6:225
"The Procession of Life" (Hawthorne) 3:181, 190
"The Procession of Life" (O'Connor) 5:381, 393
"A procura de uma dignidade" (Lispector) 34:233
"The Prodigal Children" (Benet) 10:156
"Prodigal Father" (Gallant) 5:138
"The Prodigal Father" (London) 4:256
"La prodigiosa tarde de Baltazar" (Garcia Marquez) 8:185, 187-91
"El prodigioso miligramo" (Arreola) 38:7
"The Prodigy" (Singer) 3:374
"The Prodigy of Dreams" (Ligotti) 16:277-79, 295, 297
"Proditoriamente" (Svevo) 25:329-30, 336, 360
"The Professional Instinct" (Glasgow) 34:62, 65-6, 69-71, 78, 81
"The Professor" (Farrell) 28:89, 92
"Professor" (Hughes) 6:112, 118, 122, 131-32
"Professor Bingo's Snuff" (Chandler) 23:64, 111
"Professor Nobody's Little Lectures on Supernatural Horror" (Ligotti) 16:261, 269, 284-85, 293
"Professor Rado" (Tanizaki) 21:218
"Il Professor Terremoto" (Pirandello) 22:278
"The Professor's Commencement" (Cather) 2:99, 103, 113
"The Professor's Escape" (Aiken) 9:14
"The Profile" (Cather) 2:98, 103-04
"Progress" (Galsworthy) 22:98
"The Progress of Love" (Munro) 3:347, 349
The Progress of Love (Munro) 3:346-48
"Prohibition" (Wescott) 35:357, 364, 366-67, 369-72
"Les projets" (Baudelaire) 18:6-7
"Prokhodimets" (Gorky) 28:156, 189
Prokleta avlija (Andric) 36:31, 33, 36, 38, 43, 46-8, 57, 77-8
"A Prologue to America" (Wolfe) 33:401
"Prologue to an Adventure" (Thomas) 3:399, 401
"La prolongada busca de Tai An" (Bioy Casares) 17:70
"Promenade" (Maupassant) 1:260, 274
Prométhée (Gide) 13:52-57, 67
Le Prométhée mal enchaîné (Gide) 13:59, 61, 65, 72, 79-81, 86
Prometheus Illbound (Gide)
   See Le Prométhée mal enchaîné
Prometheus Misbound (Gide)
   See Le Prométhée mal enchaîné
"Prometheus' Punishment" (Capek) 36:85, 113, 129
"The Promise" (Steinbeck) 11:209-10, 212-13, 232
"The Promise of America" (Wolfe) 33:401
"Promise of Rain" (Taylor) 10:417
"The Promised Land" (Fisher) 25:5, 9-10, 14, 16, 19-21, 25, 27
"The Promoter" (Dunbar) 8:122, 147
"Proof of the Pudding" (Henry) 5:165
"Proof Positive" (Capek) 36:128
"Proof Positive" (Greene) 29:184, 193
"Propavšaja gramotax" (Gogol) 4:117, 121
"The Properties of Love" (O'Hara) 15:252

"Property" (Singer) **3**:374

"Property" (Verga) **21**:298, 300

"The Property of Colette Nervi" (Trevor) **21**:246-47, 262, 270

"The Prophecy" (Schnitzler) **15**:343

"The Prophet Peter" (Chesnutt) **7**:17

"The Prophetic Pictures" (Hawthorne) **3**:158, 181, 185-86, 190-91

"Proprietors of the Olden Time" (Gogol)
See "Starosvetskie Pomeščiki"

"Prose Piece" (Walser) **20**:364-65

Prose Poems (Baudelaire)
See *Petits poèmes en prose: Le spleen de Paris*

Prose Works of Henry Lawson (Lawson) **18**:202

"Prosody" (Arreola) **38**:13

A Prospect of the Orchards (Bates) **10**:121-22

"A Prospect of the Sea" (Thomas) **3**:394, 399, 401, 407-09

Prospero on the Island (Thomas) **20**:286-87, 313, 315-17

"Le protecteur" (Maupassant) **1**:280

"A Protégée of Jack Hamlin's" (Harte) **8**:249

The Proverb, and Other Stories (Ayme) **41**:5

"Providence and the Guitar" (Stevenson) **11**:280

"La provinciale" (Moravia) **26**:163

Provintzreise (Peretz) **26**:191

"The Prowler in the City at the End of the War" (Ellison) **14**:115

"The Prussian Officer" (Lawrence) **4**:197-99, 210, 212, 214-18, 235; **19**:268

The Prussian Officer, and Other Stories (Lawrence) **4**:196-98, 202, 230, 235 36

"Prvi dan u radosnom gradu" (Andric) **36**:50

"A Psalm" (Bulgakov) **18**:74, 92

"Psiren" (Vinge) **24**:337, 344

"The Psoriasis Dict" (Lish) **18**:284

"P-s s t, Partner, Your Peristalsis Is Showing" (Perelman) **32**:201-02

"Psyche" (Andersen) **6**:36, 38

Psyche (Storm) **27**:314

"Psyche and the Pskyscraper" (Henry) **5**:162

"Psychiatric Services" (Oates) **6**:232

"The Psychiatrist" (Machado de Assis) **24**:136-38, 140, 152

The Psychiatrist and Other Stories (Machado de Assis) **24**:135

"Psychology" (Machen) **20**:200

"Psychology" (Mansfield) **9**:280, 284, 310

"The Psychophant" (Levi) **12**:279

"Ptaki" (Schulz) **13**:327, 333-34

"The Public Career of Mr. Seymour Harrisburg" (O'Hara) **15**:248

"A Public Example" (Lu Hsun)
See "Shizhong"

"Public Opinion" (O'Connor) **5**:374

"Public Speech" (Saroyan) **21**:163

"Publicity Campaign" (Clarke) **3**:134, 150

"Puck of Pook's Hill" (Kipling) **5**:271-73, 292

"Pueblerina" (Arreola) **38**:5, 7, 9, 13, 23

"La puerta cerrada" (Donoso) **34**:143, 23, 25, 31, 49

Le Puits aux images (Ayme) **41**:10

"Punctum Indifferens Skibet Gaar Videre" (Lowry) **31**:41

"Punin and Barbarin" (Turgenev) **7**:321, 323-24, 326, 337, 358, 360

"The Punishment" (Lenz) **33**:337

"The Punishment of Prometheus" (Capek)
See "Prometheus' Punishment"

Punta de Plata (Arreola) **38**:12, 30

"The Pupil" (James) **8**:291, 316

"The Puppets and the Puppy" (Norris) **28**:202, 214-18

"The Puppy" (Solzhenitsyn) **32**:395

Le pur et l'impur (Colette) **10**:262

The Purcell Papers (Le Fanu) **14**:217, 221, 245

"A Purchase of Some Golf Clubs" (O'Hara) **15**:270

The Pure and Impure (Colette)
See *Le pur et l'impur*

"Pure as the Driven Snow" (Aiken) **9**:6, 14

"The Pure Diamond Man" (Laurence) **7**:245

"The Purim Feast" (Aleichem) **33**:16

"Purl and Plain" (Coppard) **21**:27

"The Purloined Letter" (Poe) **1**:387-88; **35**:306, 308-10, 322

"The Purple Envelope" (Forster) **27**:97, 103

"The Purple Hat" (Welty) **1**:468-69, 471, 479

"The Purple of the Balkan Kings" (Saki) **12**:322

"The Purple Pileus" (Wells) **6**:360, 383, 389, 404

"The Purple Wig" (Chesterton) **1**:131

A Purse of Coppers (O'Faolain) **13**:284, 286, 293, 301-02, 309, 312-13, 316

"The Pursuer" (Cortazar)
See "El Perseguidor"

"A Pursuit Race" (Hemingway) **1**:216, 219; **40**:166

"Purun Bhagat" (Kipling)
See "The Miracle of Purun Bhagat"

"Put Alije Djerzeleza" (Andric) **36**:30, 32, 43, 45-7, 54, 56, 65-6

"Put Yourself in My Shoes" (Carver) **8**:9, 13, 20, 46, 49

"Puteshestvuia vdol' Oki" (Solzhenitsyn) **32**:352-53

"The Putney Night" (Morand)
See "La nuit de Putney"

"Puttermesser and Xanthippe" (Ozick) **15**:307-08, 319-23, 325, 327

"Puttermesser: Her Work History, Her Ancestry, Her Afterlife" (Ozick) **15**:307, 320, 322, 326

"Pyetushkov" (Turgenev) **7**:320

"Pylades and Orestes" (Machado de Assis) **24**:155

"The Pyrotechnicist" (Naipaul) **38**:349

"The Pyrrhon of Elis" (Davenport) **16**:198-99

"Pythias" (Pohl) **25**:227, 229-31

"Pytor Petrovich Karataev" (Turgenev) **7**:313

"Quality" (Galsworthy) **22**:74, 79

"The Quality of Mercy" (Warner) **23**:376

Quand prime le spirituel (Beauvoir) **35**:61-2, 64-5, 67-8, 71-3, 76, 78

"Quand'ero matto" (Pirandello) **22**:231, 259, 275

"Quant'è caro" (Moravia) **26**:145

"Quanto scommettiamo" (Calvino) **3**:92

"The Quare Gander" (Le Fanu) **14**:219-20

"The Quarrel of Two Ivans" (Gogol)
See "The Tale of How Ivan Ivanovich Quarrelled with Ivan Nikiforovich"

"Quarter, Half, Three-Quarter, and Whole Notes" (Saroyan) **21**:160

"The Quartette" (Gautier) **20**:3

"El que inventó la pólvora" (Fuentes) **24**:38, 54-5

"que sepa abrir la puerta para ir a jugar" (Cortazar) **7**:95

"The Queen Bee" (Grimm and Grimm) **36**:188-89, 206, 208

"The Queen Doll" (Fuentes)
See "La muñeca reina"

"The Queen Is Dead" (Selby) **20**:253, 260, 262-67, 273, 278

"Queen Louisa" (Gardner) **7**:233

The Queen of Spades (Pushkin)
See *Pikovaya dama*

The Queen of Spain Fritillary (Bates) **10**:119

"Queen of the Night" (Oates) **6**:246

"Queen Ysabeau" (Villiers de l'Isle Adam)
See "La reine Ysabeau"

"The Queen's Twin" (Jewett) **6**:152

"The Queer Feet" (Chesterton) **1**:119, 125, 127, 130

"A Queer Heart" (Bowen) **3**:33, 41, 43, 49-50

"A Queer Job" (Oe)
See "Kimyōna shigoto"

"A Queer Streak" (Munro) **3**:347

"Quenby and Ola, Swede and Carl" (Coover) **15**:38, 48, 51

Queremos tanto a Glenda (Cortazar) **7**:64, 68, 71-2, 79, 90

"The Quest" (Saki) **12**:299

"A Quest for the Night" (Agnon) **30**:48

"The Quest of Iranon" (Lovecraft) **3**:274

"Question and Answer" (Sansom) **21**:90-1

"A Question of Re-Entry" (Ballard) **1**:68

"The Question of the Existence of Waring Stohl" (Auchincloss) **22**:39, 49

Questionable Shapes (Howells) **36**:360-61, 365, 386-89, 400

"Quetzalcoatl Lite" (Boyle) **16**:143

"Qui sait?" (Maupassant) **1**:273

"The Quick and the Dead" (Pirandello) **22**:226, 229

"Quick Returns" (Lardner) **32**:148

"The Quicksand" (Wharton) **6**:424

"Quidquid volueris" (Flaubert) **11**:71-3, 75-6

"The Quiet City" (Levi) **12**:273

The Quiet One (Bates) **10**:124

"A Quiet Spot" (Turgenev) **7**:328

"The Quiet Woman" (Coppard) **21**:15

"The Quince Tree" (Saki) **12**:295

"The Quincunx" (de la Mare) **14**:84, 91

"A Quinta História" (Lispector) **34**:189

"Quitclaim" (Agnon)
See "Hefker"

Quite Contrary: The Mary and Newt Story (Dixon) **16**:204-05, 210, 214-15

Quite Early One Morning (Thomas) **3**:392

"Quitters, Inc" (King) **17**:262

"R Is for Rocket" (Bradbury) **29**:77, 85

R Is for Rocket (Bradbury) **29**:75, 83

"The R. K. K." (Bulgakov) **18**:89

"The Rabbi" (Babel) **16**:9, 25-6, 28-30

"The Rabbi's Daughter" (Calisher) **15**:4, 7, 12, 15, 19

"The Rabbi's Son" (Babel) **16**:16, 26, 28, 30-1, 52, 55-6

"The Rabbit" (Barnes) **3**:6-7, 22-4

"Rabbit" (Shiga) **23**:348

"The Rabbit-Pen" (Anderson) **1**:52

"The Rabbits Who Caused All the Trouble" (Thurber) **1**:431

I racconti (Calvino) **3**:96-7, 116

Racconti e Saggi (Levi) **12**:273-78, 280-82

I racconti Romani (Moravia) **26**:139, 143-46, 150, 152-53, 155, 156, 160, 162, 164, 174-75, 180

Racconti surrealistici e satirici (Moravia) **26**:179

"The Race" (Ross) **24**:309-11, 323

The Race and Other Stories (Ross) **24**:309, 319

"The Race Question" (Dunbar) **8**:122, 147

"Rachel" (Caldwell) **19**:5

"Radio" (O'Hara) **15**:265, 267-68, 270

"Rafaela Who Drinks Coconut and Papaya Juice on Tuesdays" (Cisneros) **32**:41

"Rafferty's Reasons" (Pohl) **25**:223-24, 227-28, 230-32, 234

"The Raffle" (Naipaul) **38**:300, 320, 328, 345

"The Raft" (King) **17**:274-75

"Rags and Bones" (Gordimer) **17**:169, 171

"Rags Martin-Jones and the Pr-nce of W-les" (Fitzgerald) **6**:46, 56

"Ragtime" (Nin) **10**:299, 301, 303, 305

"Rahamim" (Agnon) **30**:18

"The Raid" (Bulgakov) **18**:74, 90

"Raid" (Faulkner) **1**:170

"The Raid" (Lewis) **40**:276, 278

"The Raid" (Steinbeck) **11**:207-08, 225, 232-33, 239-40

"The Raid" (Tolstoy) **9**:375

Railroad Stories (Aleichem) **33**:25, 29, 61-4, 74

"Railway Accident" (Mann) **5**:323-24, 330, 348-50

"The Railway Police" (Calisher) **15**:5, 11

The Railway Police (Calisher) **15**:5-6, 21-3

"Rain" (Maugham) **8**:356-61, 371, 373, 375, 377, 381-84

"The Rain Child" (Laurence) **7**:246, 248, 250, 253, 272

"The Rain Gutter" (Boell) **23**:38

"Rain in May" (Moravia) **26**:139

Title Index

"Rain in the Heart" (Taylor) **10**:374-76, 385, 387

"Rain in the Sierra" (Pritchett) **14**:268, 273, 285

"Rain on Tanyard Hollow" (Stuart) **31**:228, 260-61

"Rainbow Villa" (Warner) **23**:369

"Rain-Queen" (Gordimer) **17**:158

"The Rainy Moon" (Colette)
See "La lune de pluie"

"Rainy Season" (King) **17**:295

"The Rainy Station" (Kawabata) **17**:251

"Raise High the Roofbeam, Carpenters" (Salinger) **2**:291-93, 298, 307, 314; **28**:221-24, 243, 245, 248, 262, 265, 269

Raise High the Roofbeam, Carpenters and Seymour: An Introduction (Salinger) **2**:318; **28**:265, 269

"The Raising of Elvira Tremlett" (Trevor) **21**:247, 259

"Raisins" (Saroyan) **21**:134

"The Rakshas and the Sea Market" (P'u Sung-ling)
See "Luosha haishi"

Ralph and Tony (Forster) **27**:115-117

"Ralph Ringwood" (Irving) **2**:241

"A Ramble among the Hills" (Irving) **2**:266

"Rambling Boy" (Moorhouse) **40**:325

"Rancid Pastry" (Fuentes)
See "Pastel rancio"

"Rancors Aweigh" (Perelman) **32**:231

"Le rang" (Mauriac) **24**:185, 196-98, 203, 205, 208

"Rangta" (Narayan) **25**:137

"Rank" (Mauriac)
See "Le rang"

"Ranocchi Sulla Luna" (Levi) **12**:276

"The Ransom of Red Chief" (Henry) **5**:193

"Rape Fantasies" (Atwood) **2**:3-4, 6-8, 10-12

"The Rape of the Drape" (Perelman) **32**:247

"Rappaccini's Daughter" (Hawthorne) **3**:159, 171, 173-74, 179-80, 189, 191-92; **39**:91, 100, 125

"Rapunzel" (Grimm and Grimm) **36**:204, 208

"Rapunzel" (Thomas) **20**:287, 290, 292, 294, 317

"Rapunzel, Rapunzel" (Rhys) **21**:51, 56, 59, 65

"Rara Avis" (Boyle) **16**:146

"Rare Bit of Coolidgeana Bobs Up; Quickly Bobs Down Again" (Perelman) **32**:240

"Raspberry Jam" (Wilson) **21**:318, 322-27, 332, 336, 343, 346, 348-49, 352-54, 359, 361, 363, 365

"Raspberry Spring" (Turgenev) **7**:341

"Rasskaz o geroe" (Gorky) **28**:184

"Rasskaz ottsa Aleksaya" (Turgenev) **7**:324, 338, 361-62

"Rasskazy kstati" (Leskov) **34**:109

"Rat Krespel" (Hoffmann) **13**:200, 202, 205-06

"Ratbird" (Aldiss) **36**:28

"Un rato de tenmeallá" (Cabrera Infante) **39**:18, 22

"Rats" (James) **16**:236, 245, 251, 254, 256

"Rats" (Lawson) **18**:218, 240-41, 245

The Rats (Hauptmann)
See *Die Ratten*

"The Rats in the Walls" (Lovecraft) **3**:258, 262, 267, 269, 275, 277

Die Ratten (Hauptmann) **37**:258

"Rattlesnake Creek" (Cather) **2**:106

"The Ravages of Spring" (Gardner) **7**:214-15, 218, 222, 228-29, 232-33

"The Raven" (Bunin)
See "Voron"

"Raw Materials" (Atwood) **2**:17-19

"Rawdon's Roof" (Lawrence) **4**:220

"Ray Taite" (Farrell) **28**:112

"Rayme" (Phillips) **16**:336-37, 339

"Raymond Bamber and Mrs. Fitch" (Trevor) **21**:262, 265, 270

"Raymond's Run" (Bambara) **35**:7, 9-10, 18, 22, 33, 36-7

"Razaranja" (Andric) **36**:48

"Razbojnik" (Leskov) **34**:109

"Razgovor predveče" (Andric) **36**:65

"Razgovori sa Gojom" (Andric) **36**:50, 56

"The Razor" (Shiga) **23**:333-34, 345-46, 351

"Razzle-dazzle in the Rib Room" (Perelman) **32**:229

"The Reach" (King) **17**:275

Reach for Tomorrow (Clarke) **3**:124, 129

"The Reader" (Gorky)
See "Chitatel"

"Reading a Wave" (Calvino) **3**:113

"A Reading Problem" (Stafford) **26**:279, 286, 309-10

"The Reading Public: A Book Store Study" (Leacock) **39**:263

Reading Turgenev (Trevor)
See *Two Lives: Reading Turgenev; My House in Umbria*

"A Real Discovery" (Chesterton) **1**:140

The Real Dope (Lardner) **32**:144

"Real Impudence" (Calisher) **15**:9

"Real Mothers" (Thomas) **20**:295-96, 298, 312, 319

Real Mothers (Thomas) **20**:288-90, 295, 305, 307, 309-10, 318-20

"The Real Thing" (James) **8**:296-98, 302

"The Reality of Dream" (Pirandello)
See "La realtà del sogno"

"Really, Doesn't Crime Pay?" (Walker) **5**:401, 405, 408-09, 419

"Realpoltik" (Wilson) **21**:319, 324, 330, 332-33, 344, 350, 364

"La realtà del sogno" (Pirandello) **22**:285

"The Reaping Race" (O'Flaherty) **6**:264, 281

"A Reasonable Facsimile" (Stafford) **26**:278-280

"A Reasonable Man" (Beattie) **11**:12, 15-17, 29

"Reassurance" (O'Hara) **15**:281

The Rebecca Notebook and Other Memories (du Maurier) **18**:130

"Rebel Families" (P'u Sung-ling)
See "Tao-hu"

The Rebellion in the Cévennes (Tieck)
See *Der Aufruhr in den Cevennen*

"Recent Photograph" (Bowen) **3**:40

"Rechute" (Ayme) **41**:22, 26-28

"Reci" (Andric) **36**:47, 71-2

"The Reckoning" (Wharton) **6**:425-26

"A Recluse" (de la Mare) **14**:72-3, 80-1, 83, 85, 88, 90

"The Recluse" (Stifter)
See "Der Hagestolz"

"Recollection of a Young King" (Boell) **23**:35

"A Recollection of Childhood" (Mansfield) **9**:282

"Recollections" (Dazai Osamu)
See "Omoide"

"Recollections of a Billiard Marker" (Tolstoy) **9**:375

"The Recollections of Captain Wilkie" (Doyle) **12**:88

"Recollections of Mortality" (Dickens) **17**:123

"Recollections of My Mother's Death and of Her Tabi" (Shiga) **23**:336

"Recollections of the Gas Buggy" (Thurber) **1**:431

Reconciliation (Shiga)
See *Wakai*

"Record" (Capek)
See "Rekord"

"A Record As Long As Your Arm" (Garrett) **30**:172, 174

"The Record of Badalia Herodsfoot" (Kipling) **5**:261

"A Record of Longing for Mother" (Tanizaki)
See "Haha no kouru ki"

"Recorded" (Galsworthy) **22**:101

Records of the Strange (P'u Sung-ling)
See *Liao-chai chih-i*

"Recortes de prensa" (Cortazar) **7**:69, 71, 83, 87, 91

"The Recovery" (Chopin) **8**:99

"The Recovery" (Wharton) **6**:414, 420, 423, 428-29

"The Recrudescence of Imray" (Kipling)
See "The Return of Imray"

"The Recruit" (Galsworthy) **22**:82, 101-02

"The Recruiting Officer" (McGahern) **17**:302, 307, 309, 323

"Red" (Gorky) **28**:137

"Red" (Maugham) **8**:370

"Red Barbara" (O'Flaherty) **6**:260, 262, 271, 277-78, 285

"A Red Carnation" (Warner) **23**:368, 387

Red Cavalry (Babel)
See *Konarmiia*

"Red Clowns" (Cisneros) **32**:32

"The Red Cow Group" (Morrison) **40**:328, 338, 366-67

"Red Crown" (Bulgakov) **18**:91

"The Red Devil" (Gorky) **28**:146

"The Red Hand" (Machen) **20**:165, 186, 197-99, 201

"The Red Head" (Williams) **31**:334

"The Red Inn" (Balzac)
See *L'auberge rouge*

"Red Jacket: The Knocking Spirit" (Stuart) **31**:226, 245, 256

"Red Leaves" (Faulkner) **1**:147, 162, 168-70, 180

"The Red Moon of Meru" (Chesterton) **1**:129

"The Red Petticoat" (O'Flaherty) **6**:271

The Red Pony (Steinbeck) **11**:204, 207, 209-10, 212-14, 217, 220, 225, 232-33; 359

"The Red Room" (Wells) **6**:366, 383, 388

"Red Roses and White Roses" (Chang) **28**:28; 35

"The Red Shoes" (Andersen) **6**:4, 7, 34, 37-8

"Red Story" (Capek)
See "Červená povídka"

The Red Triangle (Morrison) **40**:332, 349

"Red Wind" (Chandler) **23**:59, 88, 108, 110, 112

"The Red-Backed Spiders" (Cowan) **28**:80

"Redemption" (Gardner) **7**:224-27, 235-36, 238, 240-41

"Red-Headed Baby" (Hughes) **6**:109, 118-19, 121, 123-25, 129-30, 141

"Red-Herring Theory" (Updike) **13**:387

"Red-Stoned Moscow" (Bulgakov) **18**:90

"Reduced" (Bowen) **3**:33

The Reed Cutter (Tanizaki) **21**:224-27

"The Reed Flute" (Chekhov)
See "Svirel'"

"The Reed Pipe" (Chekhov)
See "Svirel'"

"Reena" (Marshall) **3**:300, 303, 308, 310, 313, 315, 317

Reena, and Other Stories (Marshall) **3**:313, 315-17

"The Reference" (Barthelme) **2**:55

"The Refined Man" (Dazai Osamu) **41**:231

"Reflection in the Water" (Solzhenitsyn)
See "Otrazhenie v vode"

"Reflections" (Capek)
See "Odrazy"

"Reflections" (Carter) **13**:2, 4

"Reflections" (Solzhenitsyn) **32**:395

"The Refuge of the Derelicts" (Twain) **6**:339

"The Regal" (Narayan) **25**:135, 156

Die Regentrude (Storm) **27**:278, 284

Regina (Keller) **26**:102-03, 110

Reginald (Saki) **12**:286-87, 322, 327-28, 332

Reginald in Russia, and Other Stories (Saki) **12**:287, 322, 328, 331

"Reginald on Besetting Sins" (Saki) **12**:322, 328

"Reginald on House Parties" (Saki) **12**:325, 327, 329

"Reginald on Tariffs" (Saki) **12**:328

"Reginald's Choir Treat" (Saki) **12**:329

"Reginald's Christmas Revel" (Saki) **12**:303, 324

"The Region Between" (Ellison) **14**:146
"Regret" (Chopin) **8**:72-3, 84, 93, 111
"Regret for the Past" (Lu Hsun)
  See "Shang shi"
Regretful Parting (Dazai Osamu) **41**:247
"The Rehearsal" (Dixon) **16**:211
"Reina" (Dreiser) **30**:146
"The Reincarnation of Smith" (Harte) **8**:254
"La reine Ysabeau" (Villiers de l'Isle Adam) **14**:378, 382, 396
Die Reisenden (Tieck) **31**:270
"The Rejected Gift" (Castellanos)
  See "El don rechazado"
"Rejuvenation through Joy" (Hughes) **6**:109, 128
"Rekord" (Capek) **36**:102, 127
"Relato con un fondo de agua" (Cortazar) **7**:58
Los Relatos (Cortazar) **7**:91
"Relics" (Thomas) **20**:321-22
"Relics of General Chassé" (Trollope) **28**:318, 323, 328, 335, 348
Réliquas de casa velha (Machado de Assis) **24**:155
"Rella" (Dreiser) **30**:141
"The Reluctant Orchid" (Clarke) **3**:133-34
"Rem the Rememberer" (Pohl) **25**:235
"The Remarkable Case of Davidson's Eyes" (Wells) **6**:364-66, 376, 393-95, 405
"The Remarkable Rocket" (Wilde) **11**:365, 375-76, 380, 386, 395, 407-09
"The Rembrandt" (Wharton) **6**:414
"Rembrandt's Hat" (Malamud) **15**:187-88, 190, 221
Rembrandt's Hat (Malamud) **15**·188, 190, 197 98, 220
"The Remedy: Geography" (Pirandello)
  See "Rimedio: La geografia"
"Remember" (Rulfo)
  See "Acuérdate"
"Remember the Alamo" (Cisneros) **32**:35
Remembering Laughter (Stegner) **27**:194-95, 215-17, 219-21
"Remembrances of the Past" (Lu Hsun)
  See "Huaijiu"
"Reminders of Bousclham" (Bowles) **3**:66
"Reminiscence of My Beloved Mother" (Tanizaki)
  See "Haha no kouru ki"
"Reminiscences" (Dazai Osamu)
  See "Omoide"
"The Remission" (Gallant) **5**:135-38
"Remnants" (Singer) **3**:385, 387
"Remordimiento" (Pardo Bazan) **30**:268-69
"The Remount Officer" (Babel) **16**:7, 27, 50, 53
"Le remplacant" (Maupassant) **1**:256
"Rena Walden" (Chesnutt) **7**:19, 21, 33, 35
Renate (Storm) **27**:283, 286, 307
"Le rendez-vous" (Colette) **10**:274-75
"The Rendezvous" (du Maurier) **18**:136
The Rendezvous and Other Stories (du Maurier) **18**:130, 136
"The Renegade" (Camus)
  See "Le renégat"
"The Renegade" (Farrell) **28**:122, 126
"Renegade" (Jackson) **9**:252, 266; **39**:209, 211, 217, 219, 220, 221, 226, 229, 231
"Le renégat" (Camus) **9**:106-07, 109, 116-17, 119, 130-31
"Renner" (Powers) **4**:368, 370, 372-73
"Renters" (Suckow) **18**:396, 398
"Renunciation" (Barnes) **3**:16
"A Repartição dos Pães" (Lispector) **34**:191
"'Repent, Harlequin!' Said the Ticktockman" (Ellison) **14**:105, 112-15, 117, 124, 134-36
"The Repentant Sinner" (Tolstoy) **9**:387
"Repitition" (Moravia)
  See "Repitition"
"A Report" (Gallant) **5**:138
"Report from Normalia" (Hesse) **9**:244
"Report on the Barnhouse Effect" (Vonnegut) **8**:428-29

"Report on the Threatened City" (Lessing) **6**:188
"A Report to an Academy" (Kafka)
  See "Ein Beriht für eine Akademie"
Reprinted Pieces (Dickens) **17**:124
"The Reptile Enclosure" (Ballard) **1**:68-9
"Una reputación" (Arreola) **38**:7, 10, 21-23
"Repy Guaranteed" (Campbell) **19**:83
"Requa" (Olsen) **11**:187-89, 191, 193-97
"The Requiem" (Chekhov) **2**:155
"Requiem" (Cowan) **28**:80
"Requiescat" (Bowen) **3**:40
"Le réquisitionnaire" (Balzac) **5**:16
"De rerum natura" (Boyle) **16**:143
"Resaca" (Cabrera Infante) **39**:18
"Rescue" (Pardo Bazan) **30**:290
"The Rescue" (Pritchett) **14**:272, 288-89
"Rescue Party" (Clarke) **3**:124-26, 135-36, 148-49
"The Rescuer" (Conrad) **9**:206
"The Rescuer" (Dixon) **16**:216
"The Rescuer" (Wescott) **35**:375
"Reservations: A Love Story" (Taylor) **10**:417
"The Reservoir" (Frame) **29**:96, 100
The Reservoir: Stories and Sketches (Frame) **29**:95-7, 103, 112-13, 115
"The Reshaping of Rossiter" (Campbell) **19**:82
"The Residence at Whitminster" (James) **16**:230, 232, 234, 237, 246, 255-56
"Residents and Transients" (Mason) **4**:20
Residua (Beckett) **16**:135
"Respectability" (Anderson) **1**:18, 53, 58
"A Respectable Place" (O'Hara) **15**:248, 270
"A Respectable Woman" (Chopin) **8**:72, 96-7, 110, 113
"The Resplendent Quetzal" (Atwood) **2**:3, 5, 7, 10-11, 15-16, 19, 22
"Responsable" (Pardo Bazan) **30**:263
"Rest Cure" (Boyle) **5**:55
"The Rest Cure" (Huxley) **39**:159, 162, 172-74, 176
"The Restoration of Whiskers: A Neglected Factor in the Decline of Knowledge" (Leacock) **39**:262
"Resurrection" (Lish) **18**:280
"The Resurrection" (Suckow) **18**:396, 405, 408, 415
"Resurrection of a Life" (Saroyan) **21**:143
"The Resurrection of Father Brown" (Chesterton) **1**:129, 137-38
A Retelling of the Tales from the Provinces (Dazai Osamu) **41**:226, 228-30, 232-33
"The Reticence of Lady Anne" (Saki) **12**:296, 315
"Retired" (Suckow) **18**:395-97, 409, 414
"The Retired Man" (Schulz)
  See "Emeryt"
"Le retour" (Maupassant) **1**.285
"Retreat" (Faulkner) **1**:170-71; **35**:159
"The Retreat" (Mason) **4**:21
"Retreat from Earth" (Clarke) **3**:148
"A Retrieved Reformation" (Henry) **5**:158, 170, 193
"The Return" (Anderson) **1**:31, 39, 50
"The Return" (Bowen) **3**:40, 53
"The Return" (Conrad) **9**:151-52
"Return" (Henderson) **29**:328
"The Return of a Private" (Garland) **18**:142, 144, 150, 154, 159, 168, 170, 172, 176, 192
"The Return of Chorb" (Nabokov) **11**:131, 133
"The Return of Imray" (Kipling) **5**:262, 273-75, 285
The Return of Sherlock Holmes (Doyle) **12**:51, 60, 62-3
"Return of the Native" (Thurber) **1**:424
"The Return of the Prodigal" (Wolfe) **33**:374
"Return to Lavinia" (Caldwell) **19**:14
"Return Trip Tango" (Cortazar) **7**:69
"Return Trips" (Adams) **24**:14
Return Trips (Adams) **24**:11-15
Returning (O'Brien) **10**:334

"Returning Home" (Trollope) **28**:318, 323, 331, 349, 357
"Reunion" (Cheever) **1**:100
"Reunion" (Clarke) **3**:133
"The Reunion" (Coover) **15**:35, 43, 45-6
"Reunión" (Cortazar) **7**:83, 89-90
"Reunion" (Lardner) **32**:134-35, 138, 145
"The Reunion" (Lewis) **40**:278
"The Reunion" (Nabokov) **11**:133
"Reunion Abroad" (Farrell) **28**:112, 126
"Reunión con un círculo rojo" (Cortazar) **7**:85
"Reunion in the Avenue" (Boell)
  See "Wiedersehen in der Allee"
"Rêve d'enfer" (Flaubert) **11**:71
Le rêve et la vie (Nerval) **18**:328, 330, 337
"Rêveil" (Maupassant) **1**:274
"Revelation" (O'Connor) **1**:341-42, 344
"Revelations" (Mansfield) **9**:313
"A Revenant" (de la Mare) **14**:80, 83, 86-7, 90, 93
"Revenge" (Balzac)
  See "La vendetta revenge"
"Revenge" (Gilchrist) **14**:150-51, 159
"The Revenge" (Gogol) **4**:85
"Revenge" (Harrison) **19**:201-06, 209, 214
"Revenge" (O'Hara) **15**:248
"Revenge for the Dog" (Pirandello) **22**:251
"The Revenge of Lard Ass Hogan" (King) **17**:272, 279, 285, 290
"Revenge of Truth" (Dinesen) **7**:177, 180
"The Revenges of Mrs Abercrombie" (Auchincloss) **22**:4
"Reverend Father Gilhooley" (Farrell) **28**:92, 118-9
"Reversal" (Dixon) **16**.208
"The Reversed Man" (Clarke)
  See "Technical Error"
"A Reversion to a Type" (Galsworthy) **22**:82
"A Reversion to Type" (Norris) **28**:197, 199, 207, 214
"Revival" (Fisher)
  See "The South Lingers On"
"The Revolt at Brocéliande" (Warner) **23**:379
"Revolt at Roger's" (Galsworthy) **22**:71
"The Revolt of 'Mother'" (Freeman) **1**:192, 196-97, 200
"The Revolutionist" (Hemingway) **1**:244
"Revolving Lantern of Romance" (Dazai Osamu) **41**:244
Rewards and Fairies (Kipling) **5**:273, 283, 285, 292
"Rex Imperator" (Wilson) **21**:330-32, 354
"El rey negro" (Arreola) **38**:25
"Rhapsody: A Dream Novel" (Schnitzler)
  See *Traumnovelle*
"Rhobert" (Toomer) **1**:445, 450, 458-59
"Rhythm" (Lardner) **32**:136-38, 149, 151
"Rich" (Gilchrist) **14**:151
"The Rich Boy" (Fitzgerald) **6**:46-7, 76, 86-9, 95, 100-03
"Rich in Russia" (Updike) **13**:380
"Rich Man's Crumbs" (Melville)
  See "Poor Man's Pudding and Rich Man's Crumbs"
"Richard Greenow" (Huxley)
  See "The Farcical History of Richard Greenow"
"The Richard Nixon Freischütz Rag" (Davenport) **16**:168, 173-74, 177, 191
Die Richterin (Meyer) **30**:187-90, 195, 199, 223, 227
"The Riddle" (Grimm and Grimm) **36**:223
"The Riddle" (de la Mare) **14**:67, 74, 76-9, 80, 82, 90
The Riddle, and Other Stories (de la Mare) **14**:65-7, 90, 92
"The Riddle of the Rocks" (Murfree) **22**:210
"The Ride" (Ross) **24**:324
"A Ride across Palestine" (Trollope) **28**:318, 330, 333, 335, 340, 347-48
"A Ride with Olympy" (Thurber) **1**:431

"Le rideau cramoisi" (Barbey d'Aurevilly) **17**:7-8, 10-14, 19, 21, 24-6, 40-1, 43-4
"Riders in the Chariot" (White) **39**:288-89
Ridiculous Loves (Kundera)
    See *Směsné lásky*
"The Riding of Felipe" (Norris) **28**:198, 207
"Riding Pants" (Malamud) **15**:235
"The Right Eye of the Commander" (Harte) **8**:245-46
"The Right Hand" (Solzhenitsyn)
    See "Pravaya kist"
"Right of Sanctuary" (Carpentier) **35**:106, 125-30
"The Right Side" (Collier) **19**:101
"The Righteous" (Shiga) **23**:347
"Rikki-Tikki-Tavi" (Kipling) **5**:293
"Rimedio: La geografia" (Pirandello) **22**:281
"Rinconete y Cortadillo" (Cervantes) **12**:3-4, 6-8, 14, 16, 23, 26-7, 35
"The Ring" (Kawabata) **17**:256-57
The Ring Lardner Reader (Lardner) **32**:156
"The Ring of Thoth" (Doyle) **12**:85-6
The Ring of Truth (Bates) **10**:124
"Ring the Bells of Heaven" (Coppard) **21**:27
"Ringtail" (Fisher) **25**:4, 8-9, 17-18, 20-1, 25, 27
"El rinoceronte" (Arreola) **38**:5, 7, 9
"El río" (Cortazar) **7**:59, 70, 79, 81-3
"Rip Van Winkle" (Irving) **2**:239-51, 253, 256-60, 262-64; **37**:273-74, 276, 280
"Ripe Figs" (Chopin) **8**:93
The Ripening Seed (Colette) **10**:276-77
"La ripetizione" (Moravia) **26**:142, 149, 155
"Ripped Off" (Adams) **24**:3
"Ripple the Water Spirit" (Alcott) **27**:40
"The Rise of Capitalism" (Barthelme) **2**:37, 39, 47
Risibles Amours (Kundera)
    See *Směsné lásky*
"Risiko für Weihnachtsmänner" (Lenz) **33**:316, 318, 321-26
The Rising Gorge (Perelman) **32**:212-13, 230, 236
"Rising Wolf—Ghost Dancer" (Garland) **18**:178
Rita Hayworth and Shawshank Redemption (King) **17**:262-65, 271
"Ritorno al mare" (Moravia) **26**:138, 163
"Ritter Glück" (Hoffmann) **13**:203, 217-18
"Rituals of Rejection" (Valenzuela)
    See "Ceremonias de rechazo"
"The Rivals" (Garrett) **30**:163, 172
"The River" (Cortazar)
    See "El río"
"The River" (O'Connor) **1**:344-45, 356; **23**:237
"River of the Naked" (Dazai Osamu) **41**:230, 233
"River Rising" (Oates) **6**:227-28, 230, 249-50
A River Runs Through It (Maclean) **13**:260-63, 265-67, 270-72, 274-76, 278-80
"The Road" (Babel)
    See "Doroga"
"The Road" (Pavese) **19**:368
"The Road East" (Le Guin) **12**:213, 249-50
"The Road from Colonus" (Forster) **27**:70-72, 74-8, 80-1, 87-88, 91, 98-99, 103-04, 112, 114-15, 118, 121-22
"Road Number One" (Stuart) **31**:265
"The Road to Brody" (Babel) **16**:25, 27, 29, 31, 54-8
The Road to Miltown; or, Under the Spreading Atrophy (Perelman) **32**:209, 229
"The Road to the Sea" (Clarke) **3**:135-36
Road to Within (Hesse)
    See *Weg nach Innen*
"Roads of Destiny" (Henry) **5**:163
"The Roads Round Pisa" (Dinesen) **7**:164, 167-68, 171, 175, 179-80, 182, 187, 198, 208
"The Robber Bridegroom" (Grimm and Grimm) **36**:199, 203, 206, 208
The Robber Bridegroom (Welty) **1**:471-72, 483, 489-90, 496
"Robbers!" (Aleichem) **33**:20

"A Robbery" (Leskov)
    See "Grabež"
Robert (Gide) **13**:72, 100, 104-05
"Robert Aghion" (Hesse) **9**:231-32, 235
"Robert Kennedy Saved from Drowning" (Barthelme) **2**:31, 36, 42, 46-7
"Robinja" (Andric) **36**:66-7
"The Robin's House" (Barnes) **3**:12
"Robot" (Davenport) **16**:162, 165-66, 170
"The Robot Millennia" (Aldiss) **36**:19
"The Rock" (Cowan) **28**:76
"The Rock" (Forster) **27**:98-99, 103
"The Rock" (Jackson) **9**:254
"Rock, Church" (Hughes) **6**:133
"Rock Crystal" (Stifter)
    See "Bergkristall"
Rock Crystal (Stifter)
    See *Bergkristall*
"Rock God" (Ellison) **14**:118
"The Rocket" (Bradbury) **29**:47
"The Rocket Man" (Bradbury) **29**:77-8
"The Rockfish" (O'Flaherty) **6**:260-61, 267-69, 280
"The Rocking Chair" (Gilman) **13**:128-30
"The Rocking-Horse Winner" (Lawrence) **4**:200-01, 206, 212, 221, 229-30, 233, 238; **19**:250-91
"The Rockpile" (Baldwin) **10**:4, 7-9, 17
Rococo (Morand) **22**:169
"The Rod of Justice" (Machado de Assis)
    See "O caso de vara"
"Rofe' 'o chole?" (Peretz) **26**:224
"Roger Malvin's Burial" (Hawthorne) **3**:157, 164, 166-67, 171, 185-86, 189; **39**:105
"Rogue's Gallery" (McCarthy) **24**:213
"Le Roi candaule" (Gautier) **20**:5-6, 8, 15, 17, 26, 28-9
"Rokovye iaitsa" (Bulgakov) **18**:69, 72-6, 78, 81-2, 93-9, 105, 108-13
Rolling All the Time (Ballard) **1**:72
"A Rolling Stone" (Gorky)
    See "Prokhodimets"
Le Roman de la momie (Gautier) **20**:3, 7, 20-1, 29
"Roman Fever" (Wharton) **6**:423-24
"Roman Figures" (Bates) **10**:119
"A Roman Holiday" (Sansom) **21**:84
"The Roman Image" (Narayan) **25**:138, 155, 160
"The Roman Legions" (Capek) **36**:129
"The Roman Night" (Morand)
    See "La nuit Romaine"
Roman Tales (Moravia)
    See *I racconti Romani*
"Romance and Sally Byrd" (Glasgow) **34**:65-67, 72, 76, 78, 81, 103-04
"Romance Lingers, Adventure Lives" (Collier) **19**:110, 115
"The Romance of a Bouquet" (Alcott) **27**:32
"The Romance of a Busy Broker" (Henry) **5**:158, 181-82, 194
The Romance of a Mummy (Gautier)
    See *Le Roman de la momie*
"The Romance of Madrono Hollow" (Harte) **8**:225
"A Romance of Real Life" (Howells) **36**:397
"The Romance of Sunrise Rock" (Murfree) **22**:188, 203, 206-08, 218
"Romance of the Crossing" (Howells) **36**:398-99
"A Romance of the Equator" (Aldiss) **36**:14, 20
The Romance of the Swag (Lawson) **18**:208, 217, 233, 235
"Romance of the Thin Man and the Fat Lady" (Coover) **15**:32-4, 51
"The Romancers" (Saki) **12**:296
Romances (Chang)
    See *Romances*
"Le Romancier Martin" (Ayme) **41**:18, 20, 23
"Romanesque" (Dazai Osamu)
    See "Romanesuku"
"Romanesuku" (Dazai Osamu) **41**:240

Romans et Contes (Gautier) **20**:7, 23
Romans et contes philosophiques (Balzac) **5**:22-3, 31
"The Romantic Adventures of a Milkmaid" (Hardy) **2**:211, 215-18, 221, 224
"The Romantic Egoists" (Auchincloss) **22**:38
The Romantic Egoists (Auchincloss) **22**:3-4, 7-9, 17, 33, 36-7, 46-8, 50, 53
"A Romantic Interlude in the Life of Willie Collins" (Farrell) **28**:99
"A Romantic Young Lady" (Maugham) **8**:380
Romantische Dichtungen (Tieck) **31**:282
"Rome" (Gogol) **4**:83
"Romeo and Juliet" (Capek) **36**:85
Romeo und Julia auf dem Dorfe (Keller) **26**:89, 90-1, 106, 116-19, 121-23, 125
"Romolo e Remo" (Moravia) **26**:180
"Rondone e rondinella" (Pirandello) **22**:253, 269
"Roof Beam" (Salinger)
    See "Raise High the Roofbeam, Carpenters"
"The Roof, the Steeple and the People" (Ellison) **26**:11
"The Rookers" (Mason) **4**:22
"A Room" (Lessing) **6**:200-01
"The Room" (Sartre)
    See "La Chambre"
"The Room in the Castle" (Campbell) **19**:70, 72, 86, 90
"The Room in the Dragon Volant" (Le Fanu) **14**:214, 216, 225, 237-39, 243
Room Service (Moorhouse) **40**:324
"Root Cause" (Campbell) **19**:75
"The Root of All Evil" (Greene) **29**:201
"Roots" (Thomas) **20**:325, 328
"The Rope" (Baudelaire)
    See "La corde"
"Rope" (Porter) **4**:327-28, 339-40, 342
"Rope Enough" (Collier) **19**:98, 104, 109, 112
"Rosa" (Ozick) **15**:327
"La rosa" (Pirandello) **22**:240-41, 245, 271-72
"Rosalie" (Harris) **19**:178, 181
"Rosalie Prudent" (Maupassant) **1**:286
"Rosa's Tale" (Alcott) **27**:43
"Rose" (Dubus) **15**:86, 89, 91, 95-6, 101
"The Rose" (Pirandello)
    See "La rosa"
Die Rose (Walser) **20**:333, 335, 344
"The Rose Elf" (Andersen) **6**:12, 30
Le rose et le vert (Stendhal) **27**:251-53, 259
"A Rose for Emily" (Faulkner) **1**:147-52, 158, 162, 165, 180-81; **35**:172
"The Rose Garden" (James) **16**:229-30, 240, 244, 249, 252-53, 256
"The Rose Garden" (Machen) **20**:180
A Rose in the Heart (O'Brien) **10**:333, 342, 344
"The Rose of Dixie" (Henry) **5**:159, 171
"A Rose of Glenbogie" (Harte) **8**:217, 222, 252
"The Rose of Jutland" (Dinesen) **7**:169
"The Rose of New York" (O'Brien) **10**:340
"The Rose of Tuolumne" (Harte) **8**:223, 233
"Roselily" (Walker) **5**:401-02, 405, 408-09
"Rosendo Juarez" (Borges) **41**:46
"Rosendo's Tale" (Borges) **4**:18, 20
"Roses, Rhododendron" (Adams) **24**:2-3, 5-6, 13, 16
"Le rosier de Madame Husson" (Maupassant) **1**:280
"Rosso malpelo" (Verga) **21**:283-84, 300-01, 313
"Rosy's Journey" (Alcott) **27**:44
"The Rot" (Lewis) **34**:153, 163
"The Rot-Camp" (Lewis) **34**:158
"Rothschild's Fiddle" (Chekhov)
    See "Rothschild's Violin"
"Rothschild's Violin" (Chekhov) **2**:157-58; **28**:61-3
"Rotkäppchen" (Grimm and Grimm) **36**:184-85
Rotting Hill (Lewis) **34**:148-49, 151-53, 157-58, 163-64, 180
"Rouge High" (Hughes) **6**:112, 118

"The Rough Crossing" (Fitzgerald) **6**:61, 100, 103-04

"A Rough Shed" (Lawson) **18**:215

"La rouille" (Maupassant) **1**:256, 272, 274

"Round by Round" (Aiken) **9**:13, 40

"The Round Dozen" (Maugham) **8**:364, 378-79

Round the Red Lamp: Being Facts and Fancies of Medical Life (Doyle) **12**:88-9

Round Up (Lardner) **32**:122-23, 132-33, 149, 194-95, 197

"The Rout of the White Hussars" (Kipling) **5**:260

"The Royal Man" (P'u Sung-ling)
    See "Wang-che"

"A Rude Awakening" (Chopin) **8**:88, 103

"Rue de l'Évangile" (Ayme) **41**:4

"La rueda del hambriento" (Castellanos) **39**:29, 49, 57

"The Ruffian" (Dickens) **17**:124

"The Rug" (Andric) **36**:43

"Ruído de passos" (Lispector) **34**:213

"Las ruinas circulares" (Borges) **4**:5, 10, 18-19, 28-9, 33, 35-6; **41**:49-50, 56, 58, 64, 87, 152, 161, 166

"The Rule of Names" (Le Guin) **12**:225, 231-32

"Rules and Practices for Overcoming Shyness" (Moorhouse) **40**:322

"Rummy" (Coppard) **21**:19

"The Rumor" (Caldwell) **19**:44

"Rumpelstiltskin" (Grimm and Grimm) **36**:204, 208

"Run of Luck" (Harris) **19**:182

"Run to Seed" (Page) **23**:297-98

"The Runaway" (Caldwell) **19**:38

"The Runaway" (Ross) **24**:293, 295, 305, 319-23

"Runaways" (Vonnegut) **8**:433

"The Runaways" (Wescott) **35**:363, 366-67, 370-72

The Runenberg (Tieck) **31**:276

"The Running Amok of Synge Sahib" (Galsworthy) **22**:90

"Running Dreams" (Beattie) **11**:10, 23

"Rupert Beersley and the Beggar Master of Sivani-Hotta" (Boyle) **16**:143, 145

"A Rural Community" (Suckow) **18**:395-97, 405, 408

"Rural Life in England" (Irving) **2**:244

"Rus in Urbe" (Henry) **5**:191

"Rusia" (Bunin) **5**:113

Russia Laughs (Zoshchenko) **15**:387-88

"A Russian Beauty" (Nabokov) **11**:116

A Russian Beauty, and Other Stories (Nabokov) **11**:116

"A Russian Doll" (Bioy Casares) **17**:94, 96

A Russian Doll, and Other Stories (Bioy Casares)
    See *Una muñeca rusa*

"A Russian Hamlet" (Turgenev) **7**:316, 344

"A Russian Husband" (Moore) **19**:340

"The Russian Who Did Not Believe in Miracles and Why" (Nin) **10**:306

"Rusya" (Bunin)
    See "Rusia"

"Ruth and Bertram" (Farrell) **28**:106

"Ruthie and Edie" (Paley) **8**:411

"Ryder by Gaslight" (Waugh) **41**:333-35, 337

"Rzavski bregovi" (Andric) **36**:34-5

"Rzavski bregovi" (Andric) **36**:33

S Is for Space (Bradbury) **29**:75, 82, 90

"Sabbath in Gehenna" (Singer) **3**:389

"Sabbath in Portugal" (Singer) **3**:376

"Les sabines" (Ayme) **41**:23

"The Sack of Lights" (Pritchett) **14**:269, 297

"The Sack Race" (Sansom) **21**:126

"Sacks" (Carver) **8**:14-15, 18, 20-1, 37-8

Sacred Families; Three Novellas (Donoso)
    See *Tres novelitas burguesas*

"The Sacred Marriage" (Oates) **6**:254

Sacred Water (Silko) **37**:314

"The Sacrifice" (Auchincloss) **22**:13-14, 50

"A Sacrifice Hit" (Henry) **5**:184

The Sacrilege of Alan Kent (Caldwell) **19**:6, 8, 11-13, 23-4, 29-33, 40-1, 50

Sad as She Is (Onetti)
    See *Tan triste como ella*

"A Sad Fall" (Wilson) **21**:323-24

"The Sad Fate of Mr. Fox" (Harris) **19**:195

"The Sad Horn Blowers" (Anderson) **1**:23, 27, 30

"A Sad Tale's Best for Winter" (Spark) **10**:359, 362

Sadness (Barthelme) **2**:37-40, 46-7, 49

"Safe Houses" (Gordimer) **17**:178, 182, 184, 186-87

"Saffercisco" (O'Hara) **15**:253

"Saga y Agar" (Pardo Bazan) **30**:266

La sagouin (Mauriac) **24**:173, 181, 206

"Said" (Dixon) **16**:216-17

"Sailing down the Chesapeake" (Saroyan) **21**:154

"The Sailor" (Pritchett) **14**:263, 269, 271, 281, 286, 299, 304-05

"The Sailor" (Wescott) **35**:357, 363-64, 366-67, 371-73

"The Sailor and the Steward" (Hughes) **6**:131

"Sailor Ashore" (Hughes) **6**:122, 132

"The Sailor Boy's Tale" (Dinesen) **7**:199

The Sailor, Sense of Humour, and Other Stories (Pritchett) **14**:256, 267, 271

"The Sailor's Son" (Williams) **31**:302, 324, 331, 351, 360-61

"The Saint" (Pritchett) **14**:256, 263-64, 267, 269, 271, 292, 298, 305

The Saint (Meyer)
    See *Der Heilige*

"The Saint and the Goblin" (Saki) **12**:305

"Saint Cecilia" (Kleist)
    See *Die heilige Cäcilie, oder, die Gewalt der Musik*

Saint Emmanuel the Good, Martyr (Unamuno)
    See *San Manuel Bueno, mártir*

"St. John's Eve" (Gogol)
    See "Večer nakanune Ivana Kupala"

"Saint Joseph in the Forest" (Grimm and Grimm) **36**:224

"Saint Julien" (Flaubert)
    See *La légende de Saint-Julien l'Hospitalier*

"Saint Katy the Virgin" (Steinbeck) **11**:225-26, 232-33, 245-46

Saint Katy the Virgin (Steinbeck) **11**:207

St. Mawr (Lawrence) **4**:205, 211-12, 238-29, 241-42

"Saints" (Mukherjee) **38**:252-54, 271

"Saints" (Trevor) **21**:247

Saints and Strangers (Carter)
    See *Black Venus*

"Lo Sakhmud" (Peretz) **26**:196

"The Salad of Colonel Cray" (Chesterton) **1**:131

"A Sale" (Maupassant) **1**:262

"The Saliva Tree" (Aldiss) **36**:20

The Saliva Tree and Other Strange Growths (Aldiss) **36**:18

"Sally" (Cisneros) **32**:32

Salmagundi (Irving) **2**:241, 250-53

"Salomé" (Laforgue) **20**:85-6, 89, 91-2, 100-2, 104-7, 111, 119

Salome (Keller) **26**:104

"Salome Müller, the White Slave" (Cable) **4**:49, 59

"Salon des refusés" (Thomas) **20**:310, 318

"Salon Episode" (Walser) **20**:354

"Salt" (Babel) **16**:27-8, 51, 53

"Salt and Sawdust" (Narayan) **25**:175

"The Salt Garden" (Atwood) **2**:21

"Salta pro Nobis" (A Variation Galsworthy) **22**:101

"Les Saltimbanques" (Lewis) **34**:177

"The Saltmine" (Gorky) **28**:150

"La salud de los enfermos" (Cortazar) **7**:61

The Salutation (Warner) **23**:380

"La salvación de don Carmelo" (Pardo Bazan) **30**:262, 290

"Salvador, Late or Early" (Cisneros) **32**:8

"The Salvation of a Forsyte" (Galsworthy) **22**:59, 69, 74, 89, 91-4

"The Salvation of Swithin Forsyte" (Galsworthy) **22**:88-90, 97

"Salvatore" (Maugham) **8**:366

"The Same as Twenty Years Ago" (Saroyan) **21**:144

The Same Door (Updike) **13**:350-52, 354, 356, 366, 395, 404

Sämmtliche Werke (Tieck) **31**:282

"Samson" (Ayme) **41**:13, 22

"Samson and Delilah" (Lawrence) **4**:202, 232-36

"Samuel" (London) **4**:254-55

"San bega Karčica" (Andric) **36**:52

San Manuel Bueno, mártir (Unamuno) **11**:320, 322, 327, 329-30, 339-44, 351-56, 58

"San n-Diothramh Dubh" (Moore) **19**:310, 319, 322, 330, 347-50, 352

"Sanatorium" (Maugham) **8**:369, 380

Sanatorium pod klepsydra (Schulz) **13**:330, 333-38, 343, 344

Sanatorium under the Sign of the Hourglass (Schulz)
    See *Sanatorium pod klepsydra*

Sanatorium under the Water Clock (Schulz)
    See *Sanatorium pod klepsydra*

"San-ch'ao Yüan-lao" (P'u Sung-ling) **31**:201

"Sanctuary" (Dreiser) **30**:110, 122, 153

"The Sand Castle" (Lavin) **4**:178-81

"The Sand Hill" (Agnon)
    See "Gib'ath ha-hol"

"The Sandman" (Andersen)
    See "Ole Lukòie"

"The Sandman" (Barthelme) **2**:52

"The Sandman" (Hoffmann)
    See "Der Sandmann"

"Der Sandmann" (Hoffmann) **13**:179-181, 190, 200, 204-05, 214-15, 219-20, 223-25, 234-39, 242-47, 250-52

"Sandy the Christ" (Babel) **16**:25, 29-31, 50, 53, 55

"The Sanitary Fair" (Alcott) **27**:4

Sans (Beckett) **16**:76-9, 83-6, 88, 94, 100, 123

"Santa Claus vs. S.P.I.D.E.R." (Ellison) **14**:104, 133

"Santa Claus's Partner" (Page) **23**:285

"Santa Lucia" (Galsworthy) **22**:101

"Santelices" (Donoso) **34**:4-7, 14-15, 22-3, 25, 31, 35-6, 39-40, 42, 49, 50-1

"El sapo" (Arreola) **38**:7

"A Sappho of Green Springs" (Harte) **8**:247-48, 255

"Sarah" (Lavin) **4**:167, 184

"Sarah Bas Tovim" (Peretz) **26**:198, 215-16

"Sarah Gwynn" (Moore) **19**:296, 303, 311

"Saratoga, Hot" (Calisher) **15**:9

Saratoga, Hot (Calisher) **15**:9, 23-5, 27

"Saratoga Rain" (Hughes) **6**:112

"The Sardonic Star of Tom Dooley" (Hammett) **17**:218

Sardonic Tales (Villiers de l'Isle Adam)
    See *Contes cruels*

Sarrasine (Balzac) **5**:33-4

"The Sartorial Revolution" (I Bioy Casares) **17**:74, 86

"Sarugashima" (Dazai Osamu) **41**:240, 245

"Sasaki's Case" (Shiga) **23**:347

"Sashka the Christ" (Babel)
    See "Sandy the Christ"

"Satan" (Tanizaki)
    See "Akuma"

"Satarsa" (Cortazar) **7**:91

"Satisfaction" (Phillips) **16**:328

"The Satisfactory" (Pritchett) **14**:281, 285, 297

"Saturation Point" (Sansom) **21**:124

"Saturday" (Gallant) **5**:141

"Saturday Afternoon" (Caldwell) **19**:16-17, 25, 38, 43

"Saturday Lunch" (O'Hara) **15**:288-89

"Saturday Night" (Calisher) **15**:5

"Saturday Night" (Farrell) **28**:118-9
"Saturday Night" (Ross) **24**:307, 311
"A Saturday Night in America" (Farrell) **28**:111
"Saturday Night on the Farm" (Garland) **18**:160, 177
"Saturn, November 11th" (Ellison) **14**:127
"Saturn Rising" (Clarke) **3**:132
"Saturnalia" (Wilson) **21**:319, 322, 326, 330, 332-33, 338-39, 342, 344, 349-50
"The Satyr Shall Cry" (Garrett) **30**:168
"Sauce for the Gander" (Perelman) **32**:204
"Savages" (O'Brien) **10**:341
"Savannah River Payday" (Caldwell) **19**:38, 46
"Saved from the Dogs" (Hughes) **6**:121
"A Saving Grace" (Sansom) **21**:86, 91, 95, 124
"Saviour John" (Lagerkvist) **12**:179, 196
"Savitri" (Narayan) **25**:131
"Saw Gang" (Stegner) **27**:200-02, 204, 206, 220
"Sbírka známek" (Capek) **36**:98-9, 127
"A Scandal and the Press" (Capek) **36**:87
"The Scandal Detectives" (Fitzgerald) **6**:49
"A Scandal in Bohemia" (Doyle) **12**:49, 51-3, 57-8, 66, 68, 70, 72-3
The Scandal of Father Brown (Chesterton) **1**:128, 139
"A Scandalous Woman" (O'Brien) **10**:332, 340-41, 344
A Scandalous Woman, and Other Stories (O'Brien) **10**:330, 332
"The Scapegoat" (Dunbar) **8**:122, 129, 132, 137, 141-43
"The Scapegoat" (Pritchett) **14**:286, 299
"The Scar" (Campbell) **19**:62, 71, 74, 82, 87-8
"The Scarecrow" (Farrell) **28**:87, 112, 118
Scared Stiff (Campbell) **19**:69-70, 74, 76, 84-5, 87-8
"Scarlet Ibis" (Atwood) **2**:18, 22
"The Scarlet Letter" (Stafford) **26**:310
"The Scarlet Moving Van" (Cheever) **38**:47-8, 53
Scarmentado (Voltaire) **12**:340, 342, 357
"Scars" (Price) **22**:376
"An Scáthán" (O'Flaherty) **6**:289
"Scatter-Brains" (Moravia) **26**:142
"Scenario" (Perelman) **32**:204, 209, 222
"A Scenario for Karl Marx" (Saroyan) **21**:143
"Scene" (Howells) **36**:399
"Scene for Winter" (Coover) **15**:36, 58
Scènes de la vie de campagne (Balzac) **5**:9
Scènes de la vie de province (Balzac) **5**:3, 5, 7-9, 13
Scènes de la vie militaire (Balzac) **5**:7-9
Scènes de la vie orientale (Nerval)
    See *Voyage en Orient*
Scènes de la vie Parisienne (Balzac) **5**:3, 5, 7-9
Scènes de la vie politique (Balzac) **5**:7-9, 13
Scènes de la vie privée (Balzac) **5**:3-4, 7, 9, 21-2, 25, 28-31
"Scenes from the Life of a Double Monster" (Nabokov) **11**:110, 113, 128
Scenes of Country Life (Balzac)
    See *Scènes de la vie de campagne*
Scenes of Parisian Life (Balzac)
    See *Scènes de la vie Parisienne*
Scenes of Political Life (Balzac)
    See *Scènes de la vie politique*
Scenes of Private Life (Balzac)
    See *Scènes de la vie privée*
Scenes of Provincial Life (Balzac)
    See *Scènes de la vie de province*
"A Scent of Sarsaparilla" (Bradbury) **29**:63
"The Schartz-Metterklume Method" (Saki) **12**:296, 311, 324, 329-30
"Scherzi di Ferragosto" (Moravia) **26**:150
"Scherzo e gelosia" (Moravia) **26**:149
"Das schicksal des Freiherr von Leisenbohg" (Schnitzler) **15**:346
Der Schimmelreiter (Storm) **27**:274, 284-91, 293, 296, 304-07
Der Schlimm-heilige Vitalis (Keller) **26**:99-100, 108

Der Schmied seines Glückes (Keller) **26**:107, 121
"Schneeweisschen und Rosenrot" (Grimm and Grimm) **36**:208, 212
"Scholar with a Hole in his Memory" (Cortazar) **7**:59
"The Scholarship" (Mansfield) **9**:282
"The School" (Barthelme) **2**:53
"School" (O'Hara) **15**:262
"The School by Night" (Cortazar)
    See "La escuela de noche"
"The School for Witches" (Thomas) **3**:399, 408-09
The School for Wives (Gide)
    See *L'école des femmes*
"A School Story" (James) **16**:233, 245-46, 256
"A School Story" (Trevor) **21**:230, 262
"Schoolgirl" (Dazai Osamu) **41**:244-45
"The Schoolmaster's Vision" (Gissing) **37**:65
"The Schoolmistress" (Chekhov) **2**:128
"Schooner Fairchild's Class" (Benet) **10**:144, 152, 154
Schriften (Tieck)
    See *Ludwig Tieck's Schriften*
"Schrödinger's Cat" (Le Guin) **12**:227-30, 236, 241
Der Schu von der Kanzel" (Meyer) **30**:187-88, 195-96, 199-200, 207-11, 213
Der Schutzgeist (Tieck) **31**:272
"Schwallinger's Philanthropy" (Dunbar) **8**:122, 132, 137, 147
"Die schwarzen schafe" (Boell) **23**:6, 11
"Schwierige Trauer" (Lenz) **33**:317-18, 320, 330
"Scialle nero" (Pirandello) **22**:233
"The Science Club Meets" (Moorhouse) **40**:298
"Scissors" (Pardo Bazan) **30**:290
"The Scorched Face" (Hammett) **17**:203, 219, 222-23, 225
"The Scorn of Women" (London) **4**:286
"The Scorpion" (Bowles) **3**:59, 61, 68, 70-2, 79
Scott-King (Waugh)
    See *Scott-King's Modern Europe*
Scott-King's Modern Europe (Waugh) **41**:309, 311, 314-16
"The Scoutmaster" (Taylor) **10**:374-76
"Scram You Made the Pants Too Short" (Perelman) **32**:238
"A Scrap and a Sketch" (Chopin) **8**:98
Scrap-Bag (Alcott)
    See *Aunt Jo's Scrap-Bag*
The Scrapbook of Katherine Mansfield (Mansfield) **9**:281, 309
"The Scream" (Oates) **6**:248-49
"The Scream on Fifty-Seventh Street" (Calisher) **15**:3
"The Screaming Potato" (White) **39**:347-49
"The Scrupulous Father" (Gissing) **37**:53
"The Sculptor's Funeral" (Cather) **2**:90, 94-5, 98, 100, 103, 105
"Scylla and Charybdis" (Lavin) **4**:183
"The Scythe" (Andric)
    See "Kosa"
"The Sea" (Dazai Osamu) **41**:244
"The Sea" (Pavese)
    See "Il mare"
"The Sea Birds Are Still Alive" (Bambara) **35**:17, 40-1
The Sea Birds Are Still Alive: Collected Stories (Bambara) **35**:15-18, 20, 25, 28-30, 38, 40-2
"The Sea Change" (Hemingway) **40**:166
"The Sea Changes" (Cabrera Infante)
    See "Mar, mar, enemigo"
"Sea Constables" (Kipling) **5**:270
"Sea Foam" (Pavese) **19**:368
The Sea in Being (Hemingway)
    See *The Old Man and the Sea*
"The Sea of Hesitation" (Barthelme) **2**:51
"The Sea of Lost Time" (Garcia Marquez)
    See "El mar del tiempo perdido"

"The Sea Raiders" (Wells) **6**:361, 365, 367, 389, 393, 406
"The Seacoast of Bohemia" (Garrett) **30**:163-65, 172
"The Sea-Farmer" (London) **4**:254
"The Seagull" (Auchincloss) **22**:51
"Seagulls" (Dazai Osamu) **41**:238
"The Seal" (O'Flaherty) **6**:282
"The Sealed Angel" (Leskov)
    See "Zapečatlennyj angel"
"The Sealed Room" (Doyle) **12**:65
"The Séance" (Singer) **3**:369
The Séance, and Other Stories (Singer) **3**:362, 369-70, 373
"The Search for J. Kruper" (Berriault) **30**:99, 103
Searches and Seizures (Elkin) **12**:92-3, 95, 106-07, 110, 114
"The Searchlight" (Woolf) **7**:377, 390, 392, 396
"The Sea's Green Sameness" (Updike) **13**:359-61, 376
"A Seashore Drama" (Balzac)
    See "Un drame au bord de la mer"
"The Seaside Houses" (Cheever) **1**:100, 105; **38**:51, 60
"Season of Disbelief" (Bradbury) **29**:86
"The Season of Divorce" (Cheever) **1**:99; **38**:53-4
"Season of Mists" (Collier) **19**:104
"Season of the Hand" (Cortazar)
    See "Estación de la mano"
Seasons in Flight (Aldiss) **36**:18, 20-22
"Seaton's Aunt" (de la Mare) **14**:65-6, 68, 71, 80-1, 84-5, 87, 89-91
"Sebunchin" (Oe)
    See "Sevuntiin"
"The Secession" (Bowen) **3**:40
"Der sechste Geburtstag" (Lenz) **33**:320-26, 333, 335-36
"The Second" (Schnitzler)
    See "Der sekundant"
"Second Best" (Lawrence) **4**:197
Second Book of Laughable Loves (Kundera) **24**:103
"Second Chance" (Auchincloss) **22**:14, 42, 49
"Second Chance" (Campbell) **19**:75
Second Chance: Tales of Two Generations (Auchincloss) **22**:12-14, 17, 21, 28, 34, 42, 50
"The Second Choice" (Dreiser) **30**:107, 122, 134, 143-44, 153
"Second Coming" (Pohl) **25**:236
"Second Dawn" (Clarke) **3**:131, 135, 144, 150
"The Second Death" (Greene) **29**:184
"Second Hand" (Lavin) **4**:167, 183
"The Second Hut" (Lessing) **6**:186, 189, 191
The Second Jungle Book (Kipling) **5**:287, 295
"A Second Life" (Machado de Assis) **24**:152
"Second Opinion" (Narayan) **25**:159, 174
"Second Sight" (Campbell) **19**:77
"The Second Swimming" (Boyle) **16**:143
"Second Time Around" (Cortazar)
    See "Segunda vez"
"Second Trip" (Cortazar)
    See "Segundo viaje"
"Second-Class Matter" (Perelman) **32**:204, 229
La seconde (Colette) **10**:254, 261-62, 267-69, 272
"The Second-Story Angel" (Hammett) **17**:218
"The Secret" (Frame) **29**:99, 107
"The Secret" (Singer) **3**:385-86
"Secret" (Tanizaki)
    See "Himitsu"
"The Secret Cause" (Machado de Assis)
    See "A causa secreta"
"The Secret Chamber" (Oliphant) **25**:193-96, 204-05
"Le secret de la belle Ardiane" (Villiers de l'Isle Adam) **14**:386
"Le secret de l'ancienne musique" (Villiers de l'Isle Adam) **14**:395

"Le secret de l'échafaud" (Villiers de l'Isle Adam) **14**:389, 397
"The Secret Garden" (Chesterton) **1**:119, 134, 137
"The Secret Heart" (Machado de Assis) **24**:139, 153
The Secret History of the Lord of Musashi (Tanizaki)
   See *Bushūkō hiwa*
"The Secret Integration" (Pynchon) **14**:308, 315, 320, 322, 332, 335, 340-42, 344-48
The Secret Life of the Lord of Musashi (Tanizaki)
   See *Bushūkō hiwa*
"The Secret Life of Walter Mitty" (Thurber) **1**:420, 422, 424, 427, 431-32, 435
"The Secret Miracle" (Borges)
   See "El milagro secreto"
"The Secret Mirror" (Oates) **6**:237
"The Secret of Father Brown" (Chesterton) **1**:128, 131
"The Secret of Flambeau" (Chesterton) **1**:126
"A Secret of Telegraph Hill" (Harte) **8**:233
"The Secret of the Old Music" (Villiers de l'Isle Adam)
   See "Le secret de l'ancienne musique"
"The Secret of the Pyramids" (Mason) **4**:23
"The Secret Sharer" (Conrad) **9**:141-45, 147-51, 156-61, 166, 171-74, 191, 205
"The Secret Sin of Septimus Brope" (Saki) **12**:335
Secret Stories of the Lord of Musashi (Tanizaki)
   See *Bushūkō hiwa*
The Secret Tales of the Lord of Musashi (Tanizaki)
   See *Bushūkō hiwa*
"Secret Weapons" (Cortazar)
   See "Las armas secretas"
Secret Window, Secret Garden (King) **17**:281-83
"A secreto agravio" (Pardo Bazan) **30**:264-65
Secrets and Surprises (Beattie) **11**:4-6, 8, 12-13, 15-16, 22, 27, 29, 32
"Les secrets de la Princesse de Cadignan" (Balzac) **5**:31
"Secrets of Alexandria" (Saroyan) **21**:134, 140
"Secrets of Lord Bushu" (Tanizaki)
   See *Bushūkō hiwa*
"The Sect of the Idiot" (Ligotti) **16**:264-65, 267, 276, 282-83, 286-87
"The Sect of the Phoenix" (Borges)
   See "La secta del Fénix"
"La secta del fénix" (Borges) **41**:85, 124, 133
"The Security Guard" (Dixon) **16**:204
"Sedile sotto il vecchio cipresso" (Pirandello) **22**:270
"The Seductress" (Campbell) **19**:76
"Seduta spiritica" (Moravia) **26**:180-82
"See the Moon?" (Barthelme) **2**:35, 42-3, 53
"The Seed of Faith" (Wharton) **6**:422
"Seeds" (Anderson) **1**:20, 27, 46
"Seeing the World" (Campbell) **19**:70-1, 88
"Der seelische Ratgeber" (Lenz) **33**:317-18
"Seen from Afar" (Levi) **12**:279
Sefer ha-Maasim (Agnon) **30**:3, 21-2, 36-40, 58, 69
"Un segno" (Calvino) **3**:92
"Segunda vez" (Cortazar) **7**:83-5, 90-1
"Segundo viaje" (Cortazar) **7**:89
"Seibei's Gourds" (Shiga) **23**:332, 340, 342, 346
"Seiji shonen shisu" (Oe) **20**:215, 231-32, 234
Seis problemas para Don Isidro Parodi (Bioy Casares) **4**:25; **17**:48, 60, 67-8, 71-2, 74
Seize the Day (Bellow) **14**:3-7, 11, 13-18, 21-3, 26, 32, 34, 46, 49-56, 59
"Der sekundant" (Schnitzler) **15**:377
"A Select Party" (Hawthorne) **3**:181
Selected Prose (Bulgakov) **18**:86
The Selected Short Stories of John O'Hara (O'Hara) **15**:252
Selected Stories (Coppard) **21**:23

Selected Stories (Debus) **15**:94-5, 100-01
Selected Stories (Gordimer) **17**:158, 160, 162, 165, 169, 172, 181, 184, 189, 191
Selected Stories (Lavin) **4**:163, 186
Selected Stories (Peretz) **26**:209
Selected Stories (Pritchett) **14**:260, 272
Selected Stories (Walser) **20**:349, 356, 360, 364
The Selected Stories of Siegfried Lenz (Lenz) **33**:337-38
Selected Works of Djuna Barnes (Barnes) **3**:5, 7, 13, 20, 22
The Selected Works of Henry Lawson (Lawson) **18**:201
Selected Works of Stephen Vincent Benét (Benet) **10**:143, 156
Selected Writings of Truman Capote (Capote) **2**:72, 74
"Selection" (Le Guin) **12**:237
"Selections of Lovecraft" (Ligotti) **16**:287
"Selections of Poe" (Ligotti) **16**:287
"The Selector's Daughter" (Lawson) **18**:250
"The Selfish Giant" (Wilde) **11**:365, 372, 375-76, 379, 386, 388, 390-93, 396, 401-02, 408
"A Self-Made Man" (Crane) **7**:108-09
"Self-Portrait" (Dixon) **16**:207, 215
"Self-Sacrifice" (Peretz)
   See "Self-Sacrifice"
"Selina's Parable" (de la Mare) **14**:83
"Selma" (Caldwell) **19**:56
"Das seltsame Mädchen" (Walser) **20**:333
"The Selvin Case" (Capek)
   See "Případ Selvinuv"
Semeinoe schaste (Tolstoy) **9**:376, 389, 391-92, 403
"Semejante a la noche" (Carpentier) **35**:91
"Seminar" (Cowan) **28**:80
"Semley's Necklace" (Le Guin) **12**:219, 224-28, 231-32
"Semper Idem" (London) **4**:263
"El sencillo don Rafael, cazador y tresillista" (Unamuno) **11**:312-13
"Send Round the Hat" (Lawson) **18**:206, 218, 245, 257
"Uma senhora" (Machado de Assis) **24**:128
"A senhora do Galvão" (Machado de Assis) **24**:128
"Senility" (Lavin) **4**:182
"The Senior Partner's Ghosts" (Auchincloss) **22**:9, 37
"Senior Prom" (Farrell) **28**:111
"Señor Ong and Señor Ha" (Bowles) **3**:59, 61, 69, 79
"Una señora" (Donoso) **34**:3, 21, 25-28, 30, 49
"La Señora Cornelia" (Cervantes) **12**:4-5, 8, 34, 36-7
"Sense of Humour" (Pritchett) **14**:259, 269, 271, 276, 281, 301-02, 305
"A Sense of Proportion" (Frame) **29**:103, 115, 117
A Sense of Reality (Greene) **29**:187-90, 195, 211, 213, 215
"A Sense of Responsibility" (O'Connor) **5**:372
"A Sense of Shelter" (Updike) **13**:388, 392-94
"The Sensible Thing" (Fitzgerald) **6**:46
"The Sentence" (Barthelme) **2**:38, 41, 44
"Sentences" (Lish) **18**:286
"Sentiment" (Parker) **2**:273-74, 280, 285
A Sentimental Education (Oates) **6**:246-47
"Sentimental Journey" (Oates) **6**:251-52
"A Sentimental Soul" (Chopin) **8**:72, 95, 108, 110, 112
Sentimental Tales (Zoshchenko) **15**:395, 403
"Sentimentalisme" (Villiers de l'Isle Adam) **14**:378, 381, 384, 396
"Sentimentality" (Villiers de l'Isle Adam)
   See "Sentimentalisme"
"The Sentimentality of William Tavener" (Cather) **2**:101
"The Sentinel" (Clarke) **3**:124, 127, 135, 145-46, 149-50
"The Sentinels" (Campbell) **19**:92

"The Sentry" (Leskov)
   See "Chelovék na chasákh"
"The Sentry" (O'Connor) **5**:369, 372
"Senza colori" (Calvino) **3**:92
"Separate Flights" (Dubus) **15**:71, 77, 80, 82, 87, 90
Separate Flights (Dubus) **15**:69-70, 72, 75-7, 81, 91
"Separating" (Updike) **13**:374, 387
"September Dawn" (O'Connor) **5**:385, 391-92
"September Snow" (Ross) **24**:290, 295, 302-03, 320
"The Seraph and the Zambesi" (Spark) **10**:354, 356, 358-359, 361, 366, 370
"The Serapion Brothers" (Hoffmann)
   See *Die Serapions Brüder*
Die Serapions Brüder (Hoffmann) **13**:191-92, 195, 202, 217, 228
"La Serata della Diva" (Verga) **21**:294
"Serenade" (Benet) **10**:150
"A screníssima República" (Machado de Assis) **24**:128-30
"The Sergeant" (Barthelme) **2**:53
"Sergeant Carmichael" (Bates) **10**:114
"Sergeant Prishibeev" (Chekhov) **2**:155
"Serious Need" (Price) **22**:387
"A Serious Question" (Pritchett) **14**:297
"A Serious Talk" (Carver) **8**:14, 18-19, 53
Sermons and Soda Water (O'Hara) **15**:251, 271
"The Serpent of Fire" (Bunin) **5**:87
"The Servant" (Levi) **12**:278-79
"A Service of Love" (Henry) **5**:171, 185
A Set of Six (Conrad) **9**:147, 151, 157, 179
A Set of Variations (O'Connor) **5**:373-74, 378
"A Set of Variations on a Borrowed Theme" (O'Connor) **5**:373
"Šetnja" (Andric) **36**:47
"Setteragic On" (Warner) **23**:369
"The Setting of Venus" (Verga)
   See "Il Tramonto de Venere"
"Settling on the Land" (Lawson) **18**:201, 215
Sevastopol (Tolstoy)
   See *Tales of Sevastopol*
"Sevastopol in August, 1855" (Tolstoy) **9**:375; **30**:311, 317-19, 323-24
"Sevastopol in December 1854" (Tolstoy) **9**:375
"Sevastopol in May, 1855" (Tolstoy) **9**:374-75, 389; **30**:332
"The Seven Bridges" (Mishima) **4**:313, 315, 317, 322
Seven by Five: Stories 1926-61 (Bates) **10**:125
"The Seven Deadly Sins of Today" (Waugh) **41**:339
"The Seven Deadly Virtues" (Pohl) **25**:232
Seven Gothic Tales (Dinesen) **7**:161, 166, 170, 172, 175, 180, 191, 196-98, 200-03, 208-09
Seven Japanese Tales (Tanizaki) **21**:180
"The Seven League Boots" (Ayme) **41**:4
Seven Legends (Keller)
   See *Sieben Legenden*
"The Seven Ravens" (Grimm and Grimm) **36**:225-26, 233
Seven Tales and Alexander (Bates) **10**:111
"Seven Types of Ambiguity" (Jackson) **39**:210, 211, 212, 225, 227
"Seven Years of Plenty" (Peretz)
   See "Seven Years of Plenty"
"The Seven-Ounce Man" (Harrison) **19**:215-18
"Seventeen" (Farrell) **28**:92
"Seventeen" (Oe)
   See "Sevuntiin"
"Seventeen" (Saroyan) **21**:161
"Seventeen Syllables" (Yamamoto) **34**:348, 350, 352, 355, 357-61, 365-67, 369, 371-79, 387, 389-90
Seventeen Syllables and Other Stories (Yamamoto) **34**:356, 364, 374, 381
Seventeen Syllables: Five Stories of Janpanese American Life (Yamamoto) **34**:352
"The Seventh House" (Narayan) **25**:139-40, 153, 156, 160
"The Seventh Pullet" (Saki) **12**:301

"Seventh Street" (Toomer) **1**:443, 450, 458
"Seventy Thousand Assyrians" (Saroyan) **21**:132, 146, 156-57, 165, 174
76 Short Stories (Saki) **12**:314
"Sevuntiin" (Oe) **20**:215-16, 231, 234-38, 240-42
"Sex Ex Machina" (Thurber) **1**:431
"The Sexes" (Parker) **2**:273, 281, 283
"Seymour: An Introduction" (Salinger) **2**:296, 307-09
Seymour: An Introduction (Salinger)
   See *Raise High the Roofbeam, Carpenters and Seymour: An Introduction*
"Shabbes nakhamu" (Babel) **16**:34
"Shabby-Genteel People" (Dickens) **17**:111, 116, 133
"Shabos nahamu" (Babel)
   See "Shabbes nakhamu"
The Shackle (Colette)
   See *L'entrave*
"The Shades of Spring" (Lawrence) **4**:197-98, 219
"The Shadow" (Andersen) **6**:7, 24, 30, 35, 41
"The Shadow" (Dreiser) **30**:114, 146
"A Shadow" (Narayan) **25**:135
"Shadow, a Parable" (Poe) **1**:379
"The Shadow at the Bottom of the World" (Ligotti) **16**:280, 289
"The Shadow Line" (Conrad) **9**:151
"The Shadow of a Crib" (Singer) **3**:361
"The Shadow of the Glen" (Le Fanu) **14**:219-20
"The Shadow of the Shark" (Chesterton) **1**:124
"The Shadow out of Time" (Lovecraft) **3**:258-61, 263, 266, 268, 271-72, 274-75, 279, 290
"The Shadow over Innsmouth" (Lovecraft) **3**:259. 263, 271-77, 291
"The Shadow-Children" (Alcott) **27**:41
"The Shadow Crown" (Benet) **10**:147
"The Shadowy Land" (Grau) **15**:155
"The Shadowy Third" (Bowen) **3**:54
"The Shadowy Third" (Glasgow) **34**:56, 58-9, 62, 70, 73, 79, 82, 87-90, 93-97, 100
The Shadowy Third, and Other Stories (Glasgow) **34**:56-64, 70- 78, 82, 85, 88, 92, 97, 103-04
"Shadrach" (Styron) **25**:312-13, 315, 317
"The Shaker Bridal" (Hawthorne) **3**:185-86
Shakespeare's Memory (Borges) **41**:157, 160
"Shakuntala" (Narayan) **25**:131
"Shame" (Crane) **7**:104
"A Shameful Affair" (Chopin) **8**:71, 86
"Shang shi" (Lu Hsun) **20**:140
"Shao nü" (P'u Sung-ling) **31**:207
"The Shape of the Sword" (Borges)
   See "La forma de la espada"
"The Shape of Things" (Capote) **2**:65
"Sharing Joys and Sorrows" (Grimm and Grimm) **36**:229-30
"The Sharks" (O'Hara) **15**:280
"Shatterday" (Ellison) **14**:124
Shatterday (Ellison) **18**:125-26
"Shattered Like a Glass Goblin" (Ellison) **14**:115
"The Shawl" (Ozick) **15**:327
The Shawl (Ozick) **15**:327-28
She (Peretz) **26**:205
"She and the Other Fellow" (Norris) **28**:205
"She Chiang-chün" (P'u Sung-ling) **31**:201
"The She Devil" (Lawson) **18**:255
"She Kept Her Distance" (Stuart) **31**:251
"She Married Her Double, He Married Himself" (Perelman) **32**:202
"She pi" (P'u Sung-ling) **31**:215
"She Walks in Beauty—Single File, Eyes Front and No Hanky-Panky" (Perelman) **32**:229
"She Was Good for Nothing" (Andersen)
   See "Good-for-Nothing"
"She Was No Good" (Andersen)
   See "Good-for-Nothing"
"The Shearing of the Cook's Dog" (Lawson) **18**:201, 244
"The Shed" (Jolley) **19**:243-44

The She-Dragoon (Jarry)
   See *La dragonne*
"Sheep" (Oe) **20**:210-11, 213
"The Sheep" (Saki) **12**:316
"The Shelter" (Narayan) **25**:140, 156
"The Shepard on the Roof" (Jolley) **19**:222, 245
"Shepherd, Lead Us" (Fisher)
   See "The South Lingers On"
"The Shepherd Who Watched by Night" (Page) **23**:308
"The Shepherdess and the Chimney Sweep" (Andersen) **6**:6, 18, 36
"The Shepherd's Pipe" (Chekhov) **2**:130, 156
"The Sheridans" (Mansfield) **9**:286-87; **38**:205
"The Sheriff of Kona" (London) **4**:269
"The Sheriff's Children" (Chesnutt) **7**:13, 16, 18-19, 21-6, 29, 32-5, 37
"The She-Wolf" (Saki) **12**:307, 323
"The She-Wolf" (Verga) **21**:298, 305-07
"Shifting" (Beattie) **11**:4, 7-8, 15, 17
"Shih Ch'ing-hsü" (P'u Sung-ling) **31**:191, 197
"Shih-chung" (Lu Hsun)
   See "Shizhong"
"Shih-yen" (P'u Sung-ling) **31**:190
Shiiku (Oe) **20**:214-16
"The Shilling" (O'Flaherty) **6**:271
"Shiloh" (Mason) **4**:299-03, 307, 309
Shiloh, and Other Stories (Mason) **4**:299-03, 306-07, 309
"Shin Bones" (London) **4**:256, 270
"Shindō" (Tanizaki) **21**:205
"Shinel" (Gogol) **4**:82-3, 87-91, 93, 106-08, 110-11, 113-17, 127, 129-30; **29**:119-79
"Shingles for the Lord" (Faulkner) **1**:178
Shining Deeps (Capek)
   See *Zářivé hlubiny*
"The Shining Houses" (Munro) **3**:321, 336, 343
"The Shining Ones" (Clarke) **3**:132
"The Shining Pyramid" (Machen) **20**:158, 169, 182-83, 197-98
The Shining Pyramid: Tales and Essays (Machen) **20**:166, 194
"The Shining Slave Makers" (Dreiser)
   See "McEwen of the Shining Slave Makers"
"The Ship That Found Herself" (Kipling) **5**:279
"Ship that Saw a Ghost" (Norris) **28**:198
"A Ship-Load of Crabs" (Calvino) **3**:116
"The Shipwreck" (Dickens) **17**:123
"The Shipwrecked Buttons" (Jewett) **6**:157
"Shir-hashirim: a yugnt-roman in fir teyl" (Aleichem) **33**:41-2
"The Shirt" (Dixon) **16**:211
"The Shirt Collar" (Andersen) **6**:30, 32, 35
"The Shirts" (Capek) **36**:92-3, 124-25
"Shisei" (Tanizaki) **21**:181-82, 190-92, 195-96, 200, 206-08
"Shisha no ogori" (Oe) **20**:214
"Shisha no Sho" (Kawabata) **17**:247
"Shit" (Lish) **18**:275, 282
"Shizhong" (Lu Hsun) **20**:137, 147
"Shock Tactics" (Saki) **12**:303-04, 323, 325
"A Shocking Accident" (Greene) **29**:201
"The Shocks of Doom" (Henry) **5**:182, 184
"Shoes: An International Episode" (Bowen) **3**:30, 49
"Shōkonsai Ikkei" (Kawabata) **17**:248-49
"Shōnen" (Tanizaki) **21**:206-08
"The Shooting" (Caldwell) **19**:39
"The Shooting" (Dubus) **15**:73, 88
"The Shooting of Judge Price" (Caldwell) **19**:42
"The Shooting of the Cabinet Ministers" (Hemingway) **1**:208, 238
"The Shooting Party" (Woolf) **7**:375, 390, 392
"The Shopboy's God" (Shiga)
   See "Kozo no kamisama"
"Shoppe Keeper" (Ellison) **14**:126
"Shops and Their Tenants" (Dickens) **17**:117
"The Shore and the Sea" (Thurber) **1**:430
"The Shore House" (Jewett) **6**:150, 157, 167, 170

"Short Easterly Squall, With Low Visibility and Rising Gorge" (Perelman) **32**:222
"Short Feature" (Cortazar)
   See "Cortísimo metraje"
"Short Friday" (Singer) **3**:355, 360, 363-64, 383
Short Friday, and Other Stories (Singer) **3**:357, 370, 373, 376
"The Short Happy Life of Cash Bentley" (Cheever) **38**:47
"The Short Happy Life of Francis Macomber" (Hemingway) **1**:217, 230, 232, 234; **25**:79-80, 87, 89, 92, 97, 99-100, 102; **36**:251; **40**:155, 191, 208-09, 214-15
Short Novels of Colette (Colette) **10**:266-67, 269
The Short Novels of Thomas Wolfe (Wolfe) **33**:375-76
Short Prose Poems (Baudelaire)
   See *Petits poèmes en prose: Le spleen de Paris*
"Short Sentimental Journey" (Svevo)
   See "Short Sentimental Journey"
"A Short Sentimental Journey" (Svevo)
   See *Corto viaggio sentimentale e altri racconti inediti*
"A Short Sleep in Louisiana" (Caldwell) **19**:23
Short Stories (Pirandello) **22**:242, 244
Short Stories in Prose and Verse (Lawson) **18**:220, 240, 256, 258
The Short Stories of Conrad Aiken (Aiken) **9**:151
The Short Stories of Ernest Hemingway (Hemingway) **40**:166, 173, 181, 184, 204, 245, 247
The Short Stories of James T. Farrell (Farrell) **28**:90
The Short Stories of Saki (Saki) **12**:296, 307, 309
The Short Stories of Thomas Hardy (Hardy) **2**:212
"A Short Trip Home" (Fitzgerald) **6**:47-8, 60, 62
"The Short-Short Story of Mankind: An Improbable Allegory of Human History Compressed for a Very Small Time Capsule" (Steinbeck) **11**:257-58
"Shorty Stack, Pugilist" (Norris) **28**:199, 207, 213
Shōshō Shigemoto no haha (Tanizaki) **21**:182, 186, 188-89, 191, 198, 223-25
"The Shot" (Pushkin)
   See "Vystrel"
The Shot from the Pulpit (Meyer)
   See *Der Schu von der Kanzel"*
"Shots" (Ozick) **15**:307, 318-19
"Should Wizard Hit Mommy?" (Updike) **13**:400
"A Shower of Gold" (Barthelme) **2**:27-8, 38, 42, 52, 55
"Shower of Gold" (Welty) **1**:483, 485, 493; **27**:332
"Shprintse" (Aleichem) **33**:7
"The Shrine" (Lavin) **4**:183
The Shrine, and Other Stories (Lavin) **4**:181
"The Shrink Flips" (Pynchon) **14**:308
The Shrouded Woman (Bombal)
   See *La amortajada*
"Shuang teng" (P'u Sung-ling) **31**:207
"Shu-chih" (P'u Sung-ling) **31**:196-97
Shuffle (Michaels) **16**:314, 316-21
"Shu'hsi" (P'u Sung-ling) **31**:192
"Shumpū shūu roku" (Tanizaki) **21**:205
"Shunkin shō" (Tanizaki) **21**:180, 182-83, 185, 188-91, 195, 198, 200-04, 219, 224, 227
"The Shunned House" (Lovecraft) **3**:262, 276, 282
Shut Up, He Explained (Lardner) **32**:156
"Shy Neighbourhoods" (Dickens) **17**:123
"Sibi" (Narayan) **25**:131
The Sibyl (Lagerkvist) **12**:185-92, 194, 198
"Sicilian Honor" (Pirandello) **22**:235-36, 265-66

"Sicilian Tangerines" (Pirandello) **22**:236
"Sicilian Vespers" (White) **39**:302-03, 307, 310, 319-20, 324-25, 329, 337, 345
"A Sick Boy's Winter" (Moravia)
   See "A Sick Boy's Winter"
"A Sick Collier" (Lawrence) **4**:202
"The Sickness of Lone Chief" (London) **4**:287
"Sictransit" (Auchincloss) **22**:51
Siddhartha (Hesse) **9**:211-15, 217, 221-26, 231, 234, 240, 246
"The Sidi" (Rhys) **21**:62
Sido (Colette) **10**:278-79, 285
"Sidonie" (Dreiser) **30**:148
Sieben Legenden (Keller) **26**:97, 100, 102, 106-07, 115
"Siegfried et la Limousin" (Morand) **22**:158
"Sierra Leone" (McGahern) **17**:307, 309, 316-17, 321, 323
"La sierva ajena" (Bioy Casares) **17**:83
"Siestas" (Cortazar) **7**:57
"Sieur George" (Cable) **4**:50, 52, 65-7
"The Sight of a Dead Body" (Wescott) **35**:375-76
"Sigismund" (Lewis) **34**:170, 178-79
"The Sign" (Villiers de l'Isle Adam)
   See "L'intersigne"
"A Sign in Space" (Calvino)
   See "Sign of Space"
"The Sign of Apelles" (Pasternak)
   See "Il tratto di Apelle"
"A Sign of Blood" (Price) **22**:367-68
"Sign of Space" (Calvino) **3**:104, 109
"The Sign of the Broken Sword" (Chesterton) **1**:127, 136-37, 142
"The Sign of the Potent Pills" (Hammett) **17**:226
"Signatures" (Dixon) **16**:207
"Significant Experience" (Wilson) **21**:322, 331, 351, 365
"Significant Moments in the Life of My Mother" (Atwood) **2**:17, 21-3
"Signor Formica" (Hoffmann) **13**:183
"La Signora Frola e il signor Ponza, suo genero" (Pirandello) **22**:245, 247, 270
"Signs" (Moravia) **26**:161
"Signs along the Road" (Andric)
   See "Znakovi pored puta"
"Signs and Symbols" (Nabokov) **11**:109, 117-18, 120-22, 129, 135-36, 140, 144, 147-48, 150-51, 153, 157-60
"Silas Jackson" (Dunbar) **8**:122, 128, 133, 135, 147
"The Silence" (Galsworthy) **22**:92, 97
"Silence, a Fable" (Poe) **1**:379; **22**:330
"The Silence of the Valley" (O'Faolain) **13**:288, 293, 297-98, 302, 305, 312, 314, 318
"Silence Please" (Clarke) **3**:133
"The Silences of Mr. Palomar" (Calvino) **3**:113
"El silencio de Dios" (Arreola) **38**:8
"Silent Bontche" (Peretz)
   See "Silent Bontche"
"The Silent Eaters" (Garland) **18**:147, 177-79, 186, 188-89
"Silent in Gehenna" (Ellison) **14**:102-03
"The Silent Men" (Camus)
   See "Les muets"
The Silent Mr. Palomar (Calvino)
   See *Palomar*
"Silent Pianist" (Wilson) **21**:359
"Silent Samuel" (Dunbar) **8**:122, 128
"Silent Snow, Secret Snow" (Aiken) **9**:5-7, 9, 12, 20, 22, 30-40, 42-4
Silhouettes of American Life (Davis) **38**:95
"Silver" (Levi) **12**:268
"Silver Circus" (Coppard) **21**:29
Silver Circus (Coppard) **21**:7, 9, 15
"The Silver Crown" (Malamud) **15**:190, 195, 197-99, 220
"A Silver Dish" (Bellow) **14**:43
"Silver Jemmy" (Benet) **10**:151-52
"The Silver Key" (Lovecraft) **3**:258, 262, 276, 286

"Silver Throat" (Bulgakov)
   See "Steel Throat"
"Silver Wig" (Chandler) **23**:107
"Silvester-Unfall" (Lenz) **33**:317-26
"Silvia" (Cortazar) **7**:57
"Sim Burns's Wife" (Garland) **18**:154-55, 160, 176, 184
"A Similarity" (Pardo Bazan)
   See "Un parecido"
"Simmering" (Atwood) **2**:19-20
The Simple Art of Murder (Chandler) **23**:67
"A Simple Enquiry" (Hemingway) **1**:216
A Simple Heart (Flaubert)
   See *Un coeur simple*
"Simple Simon" (Andersen) **6**:30
"Simple Simon" (Coppard) **21**:3
Simple Speaks His Mind (Hughes) **6**:110-11, 113, 137
Simple Stakes a Claim (Hughes) **6**:143
Simple Takes a Wife (Hughes) **6**:113
"A Simple Tale" (Galsworthy) **22**:99
"Simulacra" (Cortazar)
   See "Simulacros"
"Simulacros" (Cortazar) **7**:92
"The Sin Eater" (Atwood) **2**:15, 18, 22
"Since It's Not Raining" (Pirandello) **22**:253-54
"Sinesio de Rodas" (Arreola) **38**:12-13, 22
"Sinesius of Rhodes" (Arreola)
   See "Sinesio de Rodas"
"Sing a Song of Sixpence" (Gissing) **37**:55
"Sing the Epistle" (Pirandello)
   See "Canta l'epistola"
"The Singers" (Turgenev) **7**:316
"A Singer's Romance" (Cather) **2**:101
"The Singing Lesson" (Mansfield) **9**:280
"A Single Lady" (Lavin) **4**:166
A Single Lady, and Other Stories (Lavin) **4**:164
"The Single Reader" (Auchincloss) **22**:4, 37, 48, 52
"The Sing-Song of Old Man Kangaroo" (Kipling) **5**:287
"Singular ocorrência" (Machado de Assis) **24**:129, 152
"The Sinking House" (Boyle) **16**:153, 155
"The Sinner" (O'Flaherty) **6**:277, 280
"Sinners" (O'Faolain) **13**:284, 287-88, 302
Das Sinngedicht (Keller) **26**:95, 102-06, 109-10, 121
"El sino" (Pardo Bazan) **30**:261
"The Sins of the Fathers" (Gissing) **37**:79
The Sins of the Fathers (Gissing) **37**:67, 72, 79
"Sins of the Third Age" (Gordimer) **17**:169, 171, 193
"Sir Dominick's Bargain" (Le Fanu) **14**:223, 228
"Sir Hercules" (Huxley) **39**:162
"Sir Rabbit" (Welty) **1**:474, 480, 486, 495
"The Sire de Malétroit's Door" (Stevenson) **11**:269-72, 279, 281, 296-97
La sirena negra (Pardo Bazan) **30**:262-63, 267, 270
"The Siren's Story" (Forster)
   See "The Story of the Siren"
"Sis' Becky's Pickaninny" (Chesnutt) **7**:7, 10, 40, 42
"The Siskin Who Lied and the Truth-Loving Woodpecker" (Gorky)
   See "O chizhe, kotoryi lgal, i o diatle liubitele istiny"
Il sistema periodico (Levi) **12**:255-57, 259-61, 263-69, 274-76, 279-81
"Sister" (Farrell) **28**:113
Sister Benvenuta and the Christ Child (Lee) **33**:307, 310
"Sister Imelda" (O'Brien) **10**:334, 341, 345
"Sister Liddy" (Freeman) **1**:199-200
"Sister Peacham's Turn" (Jewett) **6**:156
"Sister Superior" (Wilson) **21**:330, 332, 354, 360
"The Sisters" (Joyce) **3**:201, 205-06, 208, 211-12, 216-17, 225, 230, 232, 234-35, 237, 244-47, 249; **26**:46 8, 50

"The Sisters" (O'Connor) **5**:392
"Sittin' up with Grandma" (Stuart) **31**:251
"Siwash" (London) **4**:286
Six Feet of the Country (Gordimer) **17**:152-3, 187
Six Moral Tales from Jules Laforgue (Laforgue)
   See *Moralités légendaires*
Six Problems for Don Isidro Parodi (Bioy Casares)
   See *Seis problemas para Don Isidro Parodi*
"The Six Servants" (Grimm and Grimm) **36**:190
Six Stories Written in the First Person Singular (Maugham) **8**:356, 364, 378
"The Six Swans" (Grimm and Grimm) **36**:225-26
Six Trees (Freeman) **1**:194
"Six Weeks at Heppenheim" (Gaskell) **25**:49-50, 59
"Six Years After" (Mansfield) **9**:282; **38**:228
"The Six-Day Night" (Morand)
   See "La nuit de seis jours"
"Sixpence" (Mansfield) **9**:282, 310-11
"The Sixth Day" (Levi) **12**:279
The Sixth Day, and Other Stories (Levi) **12**:278-81
"A Sixties Romance" (Adams) **24**:16, 19
"Sixty Acres" (Carver) **8**:3, 10, 34
Sixty Stories (Barthelme) **2**:46, 51, 56
"Sixty-six" (Aleichem) **33**:26, 29
"The Skeleton" (Aldiss) **36**:14
"Skeleton" (Bradbury) **29**:43, 68, 88
"The Skeleton" (Pritchett) **14**:268, 285, 297, 299, 305
"Skeleton Crew" (Aldiss) **36**:7, 20
Skeleton Crew (King) **17**:273-76, 290, 294
"Skeleton Fixer" (Silko) **37**:288, 293
"The Skeleton in the Closet" (Alcott) **27**:59
"Skeletons" (Beattie) **11**:29
"The Skeletons" (O'Hara) **15**:279, 283
"Sketch" (Walser)
   See "Skizze"
The Sketch Book (Irving)
   See *The Sketch Book of Geoffrey Crayon, Gent.*
The Sketch Book of Geoffrey Crayon, Gent. (Irving) **2**:238-46, 250-55, 257-59, 262, 265, 267; **37**:265-66, 269, 271, 274
Sketches and Stories (Gorky) **28**:186, 188
Sketches by Boz of Every-Day Life and Every-Day People (Dickens) **17**:109, 111, 113, 115-17, 120-22, 124-26, 132-34, 139
"Sketches from Memory" (Hawthorne) **3**:157
"Sketches of Life in an English Manufacturing Town" (Gissing) **37**:70-2
"Sketches of the Nineteen Seventies" (Auchincloss) **22**:35, 51
"A Sketching Trip" (Welty) **1**:480
Skinny Island (Auchincloss) **22**:30, 42-3
"The Skipping Shoes" (Alcott) **27**:44
"Skirmish at Sartoris" (Faulkner) **1**:170-71
"Skizze" (Walser) **20**:343, 364
"Skoler Rebbetzin" (Peretz) **26**:191
"Skomorox Pamfalon" (Leskov) **34**:130
"Skull Hunters" (Bulgakov) **18**:89
"The Sky" (Cowan) **28**:83
The Sky Blue Life and Selected Stories (Gorky) **28**:179
"Sky Line" (Taylor) **10**:375-76, 385-87
"The Sky-blue Life" (Gorky) **28**:139, 180-81
"Skyggen" (Andersen)
   See "The Shadow"
"The Slashers" (Kipling) **5**:277-78
"Slater's Pins Have No Points" (Woolf)
   See "Moments of Being: 'Slater's Pins Have No Points'"
"The Slaughterer" (Singer) **3**:358, 384
"Slave" (Phillips) **16**:327-28
"The Slave Girl" (Andric)
   See "Robinja"
"Slave on the Block" (Hughes) **6**:119, 121-22, 128, 134

"A Sleep and a Forgetting" (Howells) **36**:365-66, 368-70, 396-97, 399
"Sleep in Unheavenly Peace" (Saroyan) **21**:166
"Sleep it Off, Lady" (Rhys) **21**:51, 53-5, 58, 63-4, 69
Sleep It Off, Lady (Rhys) **21**:39-40, 42, 48, 50-2, 54, 56, 58, 61, 63-7, 69-71
"Sleeping Beauty" (Clarke) **3**:134
"Sleeping Beauty" (Collier) **19**:99, 107-09, 115
"Sleeping Beauty" (Ferre)
  See "La bella durmiente"
"Sleeping Beauty" (Grimm and Grimm) **36**:177-79
"The Sleeping Beauty" (Perelman) **32**:241
"The Sleeping Beauty in the Fridge" (Levi) **12**:278
"Sleeping like Dogs" (Calvino) **3**:112
"Sleepy" (Chekhov) **2**:130, 146-49
"Šlépej" (Capek) **36**:89, 97, 110-11, 121-24
"Šlépeje" (Capek) **36**:97, 104-06, 121, 126, 128
"Slice Him Down" (Hughes) **6**:118, 132
"A Slice of Life" (Wodehouse) **2**:347
"Slick Gonna Learn" (Ellison) **26**:7-8, 21-2, 29
"A Slight Maneuver" (Stafford) **26**:303-04, 306
"A Slight Mistake" (Zoshchenko) **15**:388-89, 407-08
"A Slip under the Microscope" (Wells) **6**:360, 381, 384, 393
"The Slipover Sweater" (Stuart) **31**:234
"A Slippery Floor" (Nin) **10**:306
"A Slip-Up" (McGahern) **17**:309, 317
"Slooter's Vengeance" (Pritchett) **14**:298
"A Sloppy Story" (Dixon) **16**:217
"Slouch" (Farrell) **28**:99
"Slow Death" (Caldwell) **19**:37-8
Slow Learner: Early Stories (Pynchon) **14**:333-34, 340-42, 346-49
"The Slow of Despond" (Thomas) **20**:325-27
"Sluchai iz praktiki" (Chekhov) **28**:59
"The Small Assassin" (Bradbury) **29**:65, 75, 87-9
"Small Avalanches" (Oates) **6**:231
"Small Bear" (Dixon) **16**:206, 211
"A Small Bequest" (Lavin) **4**:167
"A Small Day" (Caldwell) **19**:13, 23
"A Small, Good Thing" (Carver) **8**:19-26, 30, 39, 56-9
"A Small Incident" (Lu Hsun)
  See "Yijian xiaoshi"
"The Small Lady" (O'Faolain) **13**:314
"A Small Paradise" (Cortazar)
  See "Un pequeño paraíso"
"A Small Piece of Spite" (Twain) **34**:327
"The Small Rain" (Pynchon) **14**:327, 334, 340, 342-43, 347-49
"A Small Star in the East" (Dickens) **17**:123-24
"The Small Stones of Tu Fu" (Aldiss) **36**:14, 20
"Small Town Affair" (Arreola) **38**:13
"The Small Town Lovers" (O'Brien) **10**:333
"A Small World" (Sansom) **21**:88
"Small-Bore in Africa" (Perelman) **32**:229
"Small-Town Taxi Cab Driver" (Farrell) **28**:112
"A Smart Cookie" (Cisneros) **32**:46
"Smart-Aleck Kill" (Chandler) **23**:58, 80, 102, 106
"The Smell of Death and Flowers" (Gordimer) **17**:153, 160
Smert Ivana Ilyicha (Tolstoy) **9**:368-69, 373-74, 377, 382-83, 394, 396-97
Směsné lásky (Kundera) **24**:86-8, 90-2, 94-6, 98-9, 101, 103-06, 108-11, 113, 116, 118, 121-22, 125
"The Smile" (Ballard) **1**:79
"Smile" (Lawrence) **4**:219
"The Smile" (Sansom) **21**:125
"A Smile of Fortune" (Conrad) **9**:142-43
"The Smile of Winter" (Carter) **13**:2, 4
"The Smilers" (Fitzgerald) **6**:56-7
The Smiles Gone (Keller)
  See *Das Verlorene Lachen*
"Smith and Jones" (Aiken) **9**:4, 12-13

"Smith vs. Jones" (Twain) **34**:297
Smog (Calvino)
  See *La nuvola di smog*
"Smoke" (Barnes) **3**:18
"Smoke" (Faulkner) **1**:178-80
Smoke, and Other Early Stories (Barnes) **3**:17, 19
Smoke Bellew Tales (London) **4**:289
"The Smoke Trees of San Pietro" (Trevor) **21**:263
The Smoking Mountain: Stories of Postwar Germany (Boyle) **5**:56
"Smrt barona Gandary" (Capek) **36**:97, 102, 104
"Smrt u sinanovoj tekiji" (Andric) **36**:38
"The Smuggler" (Singer) **3**:389
"Snacker" (Caldwell) **19**:14
"The Snag" (Pritchett) **14**:285
"The Snail and the Rose-Tree" (Andersen) **6**:7
"The Snake" (Andric)
  See "Zmija"
"The Snake" (Steinbeck) **11**:207-08, 225, 233, 237-38
"Snake and Hawk" (Benet) **10**:145-46
The Snake Lady, and Other Stories (Lee) **33**:302
"Snake Teeth" (Stuart) **31**:226, 231, 245
"The Snake-Song" (Narayan) **25**:141, 154
"Snapdragons" (Frame) **29**:108, 112
"Sne talmide hakamim sehayu be'irenu" (Agnon) **30**:53, 55
"Sneakers" (King) **17**:295
"Sneewittchen" (Grimm and Grimm) **36**:196, 204-05, 207-08, 223
"The Sniff" (Pritchett) **14**:297
"The Sniper" (O'Flaherty) **6**:261, 280
"A Snobbish Story" (Fitzgerald) **6**:50
"Snopici" (Andric) **36**:38
"Snow" (Adams) **24**:11
"Snow" (Beattie) **11**:25-6, 29
"Snow" (Phillips) **16**:330
"Snow Bound at the Eagle's" (Harte) **8**:254
"The Snow Child" (Carter) **13**:9-10, 28
"The Snow Guest" (Warner) **23**:373
"The Snow Image: A Childish Miracle" (Hawthorne) **3**:159, 177, 183
The Snow Image, and Other Twice-Told Tales (Hawthorne) **3**:184
"The Snow Queen, a Folk Tale in Seven Parts" (Andersen) **6**:4, 6-8, 13, 18-20, 24-8, 30, 36-7, 40
"Snowdrops" (Walser) **20**:364
"Snowing in Greenwich Village" (Updike) **13**:352
"Snowman, Snowman" (Frame) **29**:97, 101, 112-15
Snowman, Snowman: Fables and Fantasies (Frame) **29**:95-7, 113, 115
"The Snowmen" (Pohl) **25**:224; 229
"The Snows of Kilimanjaro" (Hemingway) **1**:214-15, 217-18, 229, 234; **25**:79-81, 84-97, 99, 102-3, 105-7, 120-21, 125-28; **36**:251, 273, 281, 289; **40**:156, 208-09, 214-15, 250
The Snows of Kilimanjaro and Other Stories (Hemingway) **40**:173
"Snowstorm" (Bulgakov) **18**:86, 88
"The Snowstorm" (Pushkin)
  See "Metel"
The Snowstorm (Tolstoy) **9**:382, 389
"Snow-White" (Grimm and Grimm)
  See "Sneewittchen"
"Snow-White and Rose-Red" (Grimm and Grimm)
  See "Schneeweisschen und Rosenrot"
"A Snowy Day" (Shiga) **23**:346
"So Help Me" (Algren) **33**:88, 101-02, 104, 111-14
"So Many Worlds" (Grau) **15**:155
"So Much Water So Close to Home" (Carver) **8**:5, 14-15, 19, 21, 29, 42, 53, 57-60
"So On He Fares" (Moore) **19**:308, 319-21, 324, 327-38

So zärtlich war Suleyken (Lenz) **33**:315, 318
"Soames and the Flag" (Galsworthy) **22**:71
"Soap" (Farrell) **28**:92
"Soap" (Lu Hsun)
  See "Feizao"
Sobach'e serdtse (Bulgakov) **18**:69-71, 73, 75, 82, 86, 93, 96-7, 103-08, 113-22
"The Sobbin' Women" (Benet) **10**:144, 146, 148
"Sobremesa" (Pardo Bazan) **30**:262, 295
"The Sociable at Dudley's" (Garland) **18**:154-55, 160
"Social Cares" (Zoshchenko) **15**:388
"The Social Triangle" (Henry) **5**:198
"A Society" (Woolf) **7**:368, 371, 374, 377, 392-93, 396, 400-02, 404
"Society Chit-Chat" (Leacock) **39**:266
"Sodom in the Suburbs" (Perelman) **32**:220
"Les soeurs Rondoli" (Maupassant) **1**:256, 259, 270, 274, 283, 288
"Soffio" (Pirandello) **22**:260
"The Soft Moon" (Calvino) **3**:94, 108-09
"The Soft Touch of Grass" (Pirandello) **22**:240, 243
"The Soft Voice of the Serpent" (Gordimer) **17**:166-67
The Soft Voice of the Serpent (Gordimer) **17**:151-52, 157, 166, 186
"Soft-Boiled Eggs" (Pardo Bazan) **30**:291
"Der Sohn" (Schnitzler) **15**:351, 371
Die Söhne des Senators (Storm) **27**:286
"Un soir" (Maupassant) **1**:274, 280
"The Sojourner" (McCullers) **9**:323, 332, 341, 345-46, 358; **24**:232
"A Soldier of Humour" (Lewis) **34**:151, 158-60, 169, 176, 178
"A Soldier of the Empire" (Page) **23**:2902
"A Soldier's Embrace" (Gordimer) **17**:163-64
A Soldier's Embrace (Gordimer) **17**:162, 164-65, 181, 191
"Soldier's Home" (Hemingway) **1**:244; **40**:155, 224, 251
"A Soldier's Legacy" (Boell) **23**:34
"Soldiers of the Republic" (Parker) **2**:276, 281-82
"Soldiers Three" (Kipling) **5**:269
Soldiers Three (Kipling) **5**:259
"Solemn Advice to a Young Man about to Accept Undertaking as a Profession" (Saroyan) **21**:137, 156
"A Solid House" (Rhys) **21**:50-1, 53, 64-5, 69
"Solid Objects" (Woolf) **7**:373, 377, 387, 397
"Solitaire" (Updike) **13**:385
"The Solitary" (Cable) **4**:50, 72-4
"A Solitary" (Freeman) **1**:197
"La solitude" (Baudelaire) **18**:39
"Solitude" (Maupassant) **1**:262
"Solnechnyy udar" (Bunin) **5**:91, 93, 104-06, 114, 119
"Un solo cabello" (Pardo Bazan) **30**:261
"Solo Dance" (Phillips) **16**:330
"Solus Rex" (Nabokov) **11**:117
"Solution" (Dreiser) **30**:153-55, 159
"Solution of a Forsyte" (Galsworthy) **22**:75
"Sombre récit, conteur plus sombre" (Villiers de l'Isle Adam) **14**:381
"Sombre Tale, Sombre Teller" (Villiers de l'Isle Adam)
  See "Sombre récit, conteur plus sombre"
"Some Account of the Latter Days of the Hon. Richard Marston of Dunoran" (Le Fanu) **14**:247
"Some Approaches to the Problem of the Shortage of Time" (Le Guin) **12**:235
"Some Are Born to Sweet Delight" (Gordimer) **17**:178-79, 186, 188, 190-91
"Some Blue Hills at Sundown" (Gilchrist) **14**:161
Some Champions (Lardner) **32**:156
"Some Day" (Lawson) **18**:239, 248, 250-51, 261
"Some Effects of a Hat" (Warner) **23**:381

"Some Effects of the Mimer" (Levi) **12**:278
"Some Facts for Understanding the Perkians" (Cortazar)
　See "Datos para entender a los perqueos"
"Some Get Wasted" (Marshall) **3**:303
"Some Innkeepers and Bestre" (Lewis) **34**:166-67
"Some Like Them Cold" (Lardner) **32**:114, 117, 124, 131-32, 135, 141, 146, 150-52, 154-56, 160
"Some Monday for Sure" (Gordimer) **17**:155, 160, 183
"Some Notes on River Country" (Welty) **27**:340
Some Others and Myself (Suckow) **18**:393-95, 413, 422-26
"Some Parishioners" (Moore) **19**:330, 332, 334
"Some Passages in the Life of a Lion" (Poe) **35**:339
Some People, Places, and Things That Will Not Appear in My Next Novel (Cheever) **1**:92, 100; **38**:61-2
"Some Strange Disturbances in an Old House on Augier Street" (Le Fanu) **14**:223-24, 238, 251
"Some Village Cronies" (Garland) **18**:161
"Some Words with a Mummy" (Poe) **1**:402
"Someone Has Disturbed the Roses" (Garcia Marquez)
　See "Alguien desordena estas rosas"
"Someone to Trust" (O'Hara) **15**:255, 264
"Someone Walking Around" (Cortazar)
　See "Alguien que anda por ahí"
"Something" (Williams) **31**:329, 332
Something Childish, and Other Stories (Mansfield)
　See *The Little Girl, and Other Stories*
"Something Entirely Different" (Warner) **23**:377
"Something for the Time Being" (Gordimer) **17**:173
Something In Common, and Other Stories (Hughes) **6**:122-23, 127, 133
"Something in His Nature" (Berriault) **30**:96
Something I've Been Meaning to Tell You (Munro) **3**:328, 331, 335, 339, 346
"Something Out There" (Gordimer) **17**:169, 172, 174-76, 185-86, 192
Something Out There (Gordimer) **17**:170, 173, 191
"Something Spurious From the Mindanao Deep" (Stegner) **27**:220, 223-26
"Something Squishy" (Wodehouse) **2**:355-56
"Something Terrible, Something Lovely" (Sansom) **21**:84, 91, 124
Something Terrible, Something Lovely (Sansom) **21**:112, 124
"Something That Happened" (Phillips) **16**:335
Something to Remember Me By (Bellow) **14**:60 1
"Something to Write About" (Andersen) **6**:36
"Sometimes It's OK to Eat Inkwells" (Zoshchenko) **15**:407
"Sometimes They Come Back" (King) **17**:262
"Somewhere a Roscoe ..." (Perelman) **32**:204
"Somewhere Else" (Paley) **8**:420
Die Sommernacht (Tieck) **31**:282
Eine Sommerreise (Tieck) **31**:290
"The Son" (Bunin) **5**:81, 103-04, 106, 108-10
"The Son" (Schnitzler)
　See "Der Sohn"
"Son" (Turgenev) **7**:321, 325-28, 338, 361
"Son" (Updike) **13**:387
"The Son From America" (Singer) **3**:374
"The Son of Andrés Aparicio" (Fuentes) **24**:44, 63
"The Son of God and His Sorrow" (Oates) **6**:237
"The Son of Icarus" (Bradbury) **29**:53
"A Son of the Celestial" (Cather) **2**:100, 102
"A Son of the Gods" (Bierce) **9**:55-6, 60, 63-4
"The Son of the Sheik" (Norris) **28**:204, 212, 214
A Son of the Sun (London) **4**:266

"The Son of the Wolf" (London) **4**:267
The Son of the Wolf: Tales of the Far North (London) **4**:250-52, 258, 264, 278-79, 281-82, 284-87, 290
"El soñado" (Arreola) **38**:9, 23
Sonatinas (Ferre) **36**:146, 151
"The Song" (Babel) **16**:27, 31, 52, 54-8
"The Song in the Garden" (Nin) **10**:306
"A Song of Innocence" (Ellison) **26**:11
"The Song of Peronelle" (Arreola) **38**:12
"The Song of Songs" (Gilchrist) **14**:162-63
"The Song of Songs" (Warner) **23**:368
"The Song of the Falcon" (Gorky)
　See "Pesnia o sokole"
"The Song of the Flying Fish" (Chesterton) **1**:129, 138
"Song of the Shirt, 1941" (Parker) **2**:277, 280-81, 285-86
"Song of the Silencer" (Aldiss) **36**:13-14
Song of the Silent Snow (Selby) **20**:275, 280, 282
"The Song of the Siren" (Forster) **27**:68
"The Song of the Stormy Petrel" (Gorky)
　See "Pesnia o burevestnike"
"The Song of the Triumphant Love" (Turgenev)
　See "Pesn' torzhestruyushchey lyubvi"
"The Song of the Wren" (Bates) **10**:139
"Song without Words" (O'Connor) **5**:365, 371, 383, 398
"Songs My Father Sang Me" (Bowen) **3**:41; **28**:4, 7, 9
"Songs My Mother Taught Me" (Calisher) **15**:8
Songs of a Dead Dreamer (Ligotti) **16**:261, 269-70, 279, 282-85, 287, 293, 296
"The Songs of Distant Earth" (Clarke) **3**:135-36
"Sonny's Blues" (Baldwin) **10**:2-3, 5-7, 9, 12, 14-17, 21 5; **33**.113-51
"The Son's Veto" (Hardy) **2**:215-16, 223
"Sophistication" (Anderson) **1**:30, 42, 44-5
"Soquots" (Caldwell) **19**:23
"Sor Aparición" (Pardo Bazan) **30**:264-66
"The Sorcerer's Apprentice" (O'Connor) **5**:371-72
"Sorcières espagnoles" (Merimee) **7**:283
"Sorel" (Farrell) **28**:94
"Sorghum" (Mason) **4**:25
"Soročinskaja jamarka" (Gogol) **4**:85, 118, 121; **29**:149, 171
Sorok Sorokov (Bulgakov) **18**:106-07
"Sorrow" (Chekhov) **2**:128
"The Sorrow of the Mermaid" (Tanizaki)
　See "Ningyo no nageki"
"The Sorrow of the Pagan Outcast" (Tanizaki)
　See "Itansha no kanashimi"
"Sorrow-Acre" (Dinesen) **7**:164, 167, 170-71, 174, 177, 185-86, 188-90, 196, 205-08
"Sorrowful Mysteries" (Dubus) **15**:83
"The Sorrows of a Summer Guest" (Leacock) **39**:265
"The Sorrows of Gin" (Cheever) **1**:100; **38**:55, 87
"Sorry Fugu" (Boyle) **16**:146, 148-49, 155
"Sorry, Right Number" (King) **17**:295
"Sosny" (Bunin) **5**:98-9
Sotto il sole giaguro (Calvino) **3**:119
"Soul and Money" (Berriault) **30**:103
Soul Clap Hands and Sing (Marshall) **3**:299-304, 307-08, 316-17
"The Soul of Laploshka" (Saki) **12**:316
"A Soulless Corporation" (Chesnutt) **7**:14
"Souls Belated" (Wharton) **6**:423-23
"The Sound" (Selby) **20**:275, 280
"The Sound of Hammering" (Dazai Osamu) **41**:263, 276
"The Sound of the River" (Rhys) **21**:50, 59, 64
"The Sound of the Singing" (Laurence) **7**:254, 259-60, 268
"A Sound of Thunder" (Bradbury) **29**:51
"The Sound of Waiting" (Calisher) **15**:7, 15, 19
"Sound Sweep" (Ballard) **1**:68
"Sound Track" (Calisher) **15**:9

"Soup on a Sausage Peg" (Andersen) **6**:13-4
"The Source" (Porter) **4**:339, 352, 363
A Source of Embarrassment (McCarthy)
　See *The Oasis*
"Source of the World" (Bates) **10**:121
"Sous la table, dialogue bachique sur plusieurs questions de haute morale" (Gautier) **20**:5, 10-11, 22
"The South" (Borges)
　See "Le sud"
South: Aspects and Images from Corsica, Italy, and Southern France (Sansom) **21**:84, 93, 124-25
"The South Lingers On" (Fisher) **25**:9-10, 17-21, 25
"South of the Slot" (London) **4**:254
South Sea Tales (London) **4**:266, 283
"The Southern Thruway" (Cortazar)
　See "La autopista del sur"
Southways (Caldwell) **19**:14, 25, 38, 54, 57
"Souvenir" (Phillips) **16**:326-30
"A Souvenir of Japan" (Carter) **13**:4
"Souvenirs d'un gentilhomme italien" (Stendhal) **27**:247, 249
"Souvenirs occulte" (Villiers de l'Isle Adam) **14**:381-82, 389, 393
"Space for Reflection" (Aldiss) **36**:13
Space, Time, and Nathaniel (Aldiss) **36**:5, 18
"The Spanish Bed" (Pritchett) **14**:263
"Spanish Blood" (Chandler) **23**:59, 80, 86, 97, 105-07, 109
"Spanish Blood" (Hughes) **6**:118, 132
"A Spanish Household" (Lewis) **34**:177
"The Spanish Lady" (Munro) **3**:339
"A Spanish Priest" (Maugham) **8**:380
The Spanish Virgin, and Other Stories (Pritchett) **14**:268-69, 271
Spanking the Maid (Coover) **15**:47, 52 3
"A Spark Neglected Burns the House" (Tolstoy) **9**:388
The Spark (The 'Sixties Wharton) **6**:439-40
"Sparkling Life" (Bulgakov) **18**:91
"Der Spaziergang" (Walser) **20**:333, 335
"Lo specchio a tre luci" (Moravia) **26**:149
"Special Delivery" (Collier) **19**:104, 115
"The Specific of Doctor Menghi" (Svevo)
　See "Lo specifico del dottor Menghi"
"Lo specifico del dottor Menghi" (Svevo) **25**:350, 357, 359
"Speck's Idea" (Gallant) **5**:147
"The Spectacles" (Poe) **1**:407-08
"The Spectacles in the Drawer" (Ligotti) **16**:278-79, 284, 294
"The Spectral Estate" (Ligotti) **16**:297
"Spectral Horror" (Ligotti) **16**:287
"The Spectre Bridegroom" (Irving) **2**:240-41, 246, 251, 255-56; **37**:266
"The Speculation of the Building Constructors" (Calvino)
　See "La speculazione edilizia"
"La speculazione edilizia" (Calvino) **3**:91, 111-12, 117-18
"The Speech" (Pritchett) **14**:296-98
"Speed Trap" (Pohl) **25**:220, 225
"Spell Bereavement" (Lish) **18**:278, 283
"Spelling" (Munro) **3**:339
"Spending a Day at the Lottery Fair" (Pohl) **25**:236
"The Sphinx" (Poe) **22**:330
"The Sphinx without a Secret: An Etching" (Wilde) **11**:386, 399, 407
"The Sphynx Apple" (Henry) **5**:162
"Spider, Spider" (Aiken) **9**:5, 12, 14, 32-3, 42
"Spider Town" (Moorhouse) **40**:293
Spiegel das Kätzchen (Keller) **26**:107, 125-27
Der Spiegel des Cyprianus (Storm) **27**:278
Spiel im Morgengrauen (Schnitzler) **15**:345, 367
"Spielerglück" (Hoffmann) **13**:188
"Der Spielverderber" (Lenz) **33**:327
Der Spielverderber (Lenz) **33**:316
"Spike" (Ross) **24**:311, 323

Title Index

"Spillway" (Barnes) **3**:8-10, 24
Spillway (Barnes) **3**:4-5, 12-14, 16, 22
"Spindleberries" (Galsworthy) **22**:63-4, 75-6, 101
"The Spinoza of Market Street" (Singer) **3**:361, 368, 375, 384
The Spinoza of Market Street, and Other Stories (Singer) **3**:370
"The Spinster and the Cat" (Suckow) **18**:393
"A Spinster's Tale" (Taylor) **10**:374-75, 386, 390, 397-98, 406, 409, 412-15, 417
"The Spiral" (Calvino)
    See "La spirale"
"La spirale" (Calvino) **3**:92, 103-04, 108-09
"Spirit" (Frame) **29**:109, 118
"The Spirit of the Karroo" (Galsworthy) **22**:90
A Spirit Rises (Warner) **23**:372, 380
Spirite (Gautier) **20**:7-8, 20-1, 25, 30
"Spiritual Séance" (Bulgakov) **18**:92
"Spiritus" (Beattie) **11**:25, 29
Le spleen de Paris (Baudelaire)
    See *Petits poèmes en prose: Le spleen de Paris*
"The Split Second" (du Maurier) **18**:126, 138
"The Split-Tongue Sparrow" (Dazai Osamu) **41**:235-36
"Spoils" (Gordimer) **17**:177, 183-84, 187
"The Spooks of Long Gully" (Lawson) **18**:232, 234-36
"Sport" (Galsworthy) **22**:98
"The Sport of Kings" (Farrell) **28**:94
"Sport: The Kill" (O'Flaherty) **6**:261
"Sportsmanship" (O'Hara) **15**:248, 264-65
"A Spot of Konfrontation" (Aldiss) **36**:14
"The Spotted Dog" (Trollope) **28**:316-17, 321-22, 335, 339-40, 342-43, 349, 353-54, 357
"Spotted Horses" (Faulkner) **1**:167, 177
"The Spree" (Pritchett) **14**:260, 273, 285
"Spring" (Schulz)
    See "Wiosna"
"Spring Bandit" (Dazai Osamu) **41**:240, 244
"A Spring Evening" (Bunin) **5**:90, 92, 102
"Spring Fever" (Collier) **19**:110, 114
Spring Freshets (Turgenev)
    See *Veshnie vody*
"The Spring Hat" (Bates) **10**:123
"Spring in Fialta" (Nabokov) **11**:112, 114, 128-29
"A Spring Morning" (Pritchett) **14**:270, 298
"Spring Rain" (Malamud) **15**:235
"A Spring Romance" (Garland) **18**:163
"The Spring Running" (Kipling) **5**:287
"Spring Song of the Frogs" (Atwood) **2**:22
"Spring Sowing" (O'Flaherty) **6**:260-62, 264, 269, 271, 273, 281, 283
Spring Sowing (O'Flaherty) **6**:261-65, 278, 281, 283
"A Spring Sunday" (Jewett) **6**:156-57
"A Spring Time Case" (Tanizaki) **21**:192
Spring-Torrents (Turgenev)
    See *Veshnie vody*
"A Sprinkle of Comedy" (Barnes) **3**:18
"Spunk" (Hurston) **4**:135-37, 150, 152
Spunk: The Selected Stories of Zora Neale Hurston (Hurston) **4**:155
"SQ" (Le Guin) **12**:230-31, 241
"Squadron Commander Trunov" (Babel) **16**:24, 26, 28-30, 52, 57-8
The Square Egg, and Other Sketches, with Three Plays (Saki) **12**:322
"Squibs for the Guy" (Lewis) **40**:281
"Squire Napper" (Morrison) **40**:337, 367
"Squire Toby's Will" (Le Fanu) **14**:223-24
"The Squire's Daughter" (Pushkin) **27**:163
"The Squire's Story" (Gaskell) **25**:55, 60
"Squirrles Have Bright Eyes" (Collier) **19**:98
"Sredni Vashtar" (Saki) **12**:287, 293-94, 297, 316-17, 320, 331, 333
"La srta. Cora" (Cortazar) **7**:62
"The S.S. Cow Wheat" (Babel) **16**:22
"Ssu-hsün" (P'u Sung-ling) **31**:205
"Ssu-wen lang" (P'u Sung-ling) **31**:199

"St. Anthony's Child" (Pardo Bazan)
    See "El niño de San Antonio"
St. Cecilia, or the Power of Music (Kleist)
    See *Die heilige Cäcilie; oder, die Gewalt der Musik*
"The St Louis Rotary Convention 1923, Recalled" (Moorhouse) **40**:289, 322
"The Stable of the Inn" (Page) **23**:308
"The Staech Affair" (Boell)
    See "Veränderungen in Staech"
"The Stage Coach" (Irving) **2**:245
"The Stage Tavern" (Jewett) **6**:159
"Stages" (Campbell) **19**:76
"The Stairs" (Bradbury) **29**:88
"Stalking the Nightmare" (Ellison) **14**:126-27
Stalky and Co. (Kipling) **5**:277-78, 282
"The Stalled Ox" (Saki) **12**:296
"The Stalls of Barchester Cathedral" (James) **16**:228-30, 232, 237, 245, 253, 256-57
"The Stammerer" (Moravia) **26**:160
"Stamp Collection" (Capek)
    See "Sbírka známek"
"The Stampeding of Lady Bastable" (Saki) **12**:313, 324
"The Standard of Living" (Parker) **2**:278, 281, 283
"Den standhaftige Tinsoldat" (Andersen)
    See "The Steadfast Tin Soldier"
"The Standstill of Time" (Capek) **36**:82
"Stanley" (Grau) **15**:148, 152, 160-61
"The Stanton Coachman" (Dunbar) **8**:122
"Stantsionnyi smotritel'" (Pushkin) **27**:129, 141-45, 149, 163, 166, 168-71, 175, 182, 186-87
"Stantsye Baranovitsh" (Aleichem) **33**:25-6, 29, 61-5, 82-3
"The Star" (Clarke) **3**:125-27, 130, 136-38, 141-42
"The Star" (Wells) **6**:360-61, 365, 367, 382, 385-89, 393, 403, 406
"The Star in the Valley" (Murfree) **22**:188, 203, 206-08, 218
"The Star That Bids the Shepherd Fold" (O'Connor) **5**:383
"The Star-Child" (Wilde) **11**:364, 374, 376, 384, 386, 394-95, 408
"The Stare" (Updike) **13**:375
"Starley" (Beattie) **11**:15, 17
"The Starlight Express" (Gilchrist) **14**:161-62
"Staroe vedro" (Solzhenitsyn) **32**:352
"Starosvetskie Pomeščiki" (Gogol) **4**:86, 119-20; **29**:124, 126, 132, 149, 152
"Starry Rash" (Bulgakov) **18**:86, 89
"The Stars Below" (Le Guin) **12**:223
"The Star's Great Night" (Verga)
    See "La Serata della Diva"
Starswarm (Aldiss) **36**:6, 18
"A Start in Life" (Dreiser) **30**:156-57, 159
"A Start in Life" (Suckow) **18**:389-91, 396, 398, 410, 418-19, 421
"Starting the Day" (Solzhenitsyn)
    See "Pristupaia ko dniu"
"Starukha Izergil" (Gorky) **28**:136, 144, 148, 152-54, 178, 183, 186-88
"The Starveling" (Colette) **10**:281
"Starye portrety" (Turgenev) **7**:327, 362-63
"Staryj genij" (Leskov) **34**:108
"State Champions" (Mason) **4**:26
"The State of Grace" (Ayme) **41**:3
"State of Mind" (Aiken) **9**:5, 13-14, 19
"The Statement of Randolph Carter" (Lovecraft) **3**:258-60, 262, 282
"The Station" (Bates) **10**:132
"The Station at Baranovitch" (Aleichem)
    See "Stantsye Baranovitsh"
"The Stationmaster" (Pushkin)
    See "Stantsionnyi smotritel'"
"The Station-Master's Cradle" (Bulgakov) **18**:89-90
The Stations of the Body (Lispector)
    See *A via crucis do corpo*
"Staze" (Andric) **36**:50

"The Steadfast Tin Soldier" (Andersen) **6**:7, 16, 18-19, 36, 40-1
"Stealthily" (Svevo)
    See "Proditoriamente"
"The Steam Excursion" (Dickens) **17**:116-17
"Steam Tugs and Gray Tape" (Sansom) **21**:81, 99
"The Steel Cat" (Collier) **19**:110, 114
"Steel Throat" (Bulgakov) **18**:86, 88
"Steelman's Pupil" (Lawson) **18**:249
"Stefano Giogli, One and Two" (Pirandello) **22**:254
"Das Steinerne Herz" (Hoffmann) **13**:187
"Stella" (Nin) **10**:317, 320
"Step'" (Chekhov) **2**:129-30, 143, 146, 151, 156; **28**:58
"Stepnoy Korol 'Lir" (Turgenev) **7**:318-23, 336, 338, 358, 360-61
"The Steppe" (Chekhov)
    See "Step'"
"Sterben" (Schnitzler) **15**:371
"Sterben" (Schnitzler) **15**:371
"The Sterile Millennia" (Aldiss) **36**:19
"Sterling Silver" (O'Hara) **15**:280
"The Steward" (Turgenev) **7**:313, 342
"Stickman's Laughter" (Algren) **33**:88, 106
"Sticks and Stones" (Michaels) **16**:302-03, 311-12, 321
"Stigmata" (Oates) **6**:224, 226
"Still" (Beckett) **16**:123, 126-27
"Still Life" (Malamud) **15**:171, 174-75, 182-84, 192-94, 222
"Still Life" (Updike) **13**:392
"Still Life with Watermelon" (Mason) **4**:27
"A Still Moment" (Welty) **1**:467-69, 482; **27**:340
"Still of Some Use" (Updike) **13**:403, 409
Ein Stiller Musikant (Storm) **27**:283
"Stillness" (Gardner) **7**:223, 226, 235, 237, 240
"Stimmungen der See" (Lenz) **33**:316-19, 331
"Stinkpot" (Verga) **21**:298-99
"Stirling's Folly" (Auchincloss) **22**:49
"Stoat" (McGahern) **17**:299, 309
"The Stocking" (Campbell) **19**:74, 83, 91
"A Stoic" (Galsworthy) **22**:61, 69, 74, 76, 82, 94, 96, 99-100, 102
"The Stolen Bacillus" (Wells) **6**:360, 374-75, 381-83, 395-99, 403
The Stolen Bacillus and Other Incidents (Wells) **6**:364-66, 380, 388, 403
"The Stolen Body" (Wells) **6**:381, 404
"The Stolen Bride" (Onetti)
    See "La novia robada"
"The Stolen Cactus" (Capek)
    See "Ukradený kaktus"
"The Stolen Cactus" (Capek)
    See "Ukradený kaktus"
"The Stolen Murder" (Capek)
    See "UkradenaÁ vražda"
"The Stolen Papers 139/VII Dep. C." (Capek)
    See "Ukradený spis 139/VII odd. C."
"Stolen Pleasures" (Berriault) **30**:104
"Stolen Pleasures" (Jewett) **6**:156-58
"The Stone" (O'Flaherty) **6**:281
"The Stone Boy" (Berriault) **30**:95-8
"Stone from Heaven" (P'u Sung-ling)
    See "Shih Ch'ing-hsü"
"The Stone on the Island" (Campbell) **19**:62, 72
"Stones in My Passway, Hellhound on My Trail" (Boyle) **16**:144
Stones of Many Colors (Stifter)
    See *Bunte Steine*
"Stoney Batter" (O'Flaherty) **6**:280-81
"Stop" (Dixon) **16**:207
"Stopal'scik" (Leskov) **34**:108
"A Stop-Over at Tyre" (Garland) **18**:148, 154-55, 161, 163, 166
Storie naturali (Levi) **12**:274-76, 278-79
"Stories" (Peretz) **26**:193, 213
Stories (Andersen)
    See *Eventyr, fortalte for bøorn*

Stories (Bowen) **3**:39; **28**:10
Stories (Bulgakov) **18**:89, 91
Stories (Jolley) **19**:233, 243, 245-46
Stories (Pavese) **19**:386, 388
Stories about Lenin (Zoshchenko)
  See *Tales of Lenin*
Stories and Prose Poems: by Aleksandr
  Solzhenitsyn (Solzhenitsyn) **32**:394, 398
Stories and Sketches (Gissing) **37**:79-80
Stories by Erskine Caldwell (Caldwell) **19**:35
Stories for a Year (Pirandello)
  See *Novelle per un anno*
Stories for Every Day in the Year (Pirandello)
  See *Novelle per un anno*
Stories for Jewish Children (Aleichem)
  See *Mayses far yidishe kinder*
Stories from One Pocket (Capek)
  See *Tales from Two Pockets*
Stories from the Other Pocket (Capek)
  See *Tales from Two Pockets*
"Stories I Tell Myself" (Cortazar) **7**:69
The Stories of Bernard Malamud (Malamud)
  15:216, 218
"Stories of Death and Society" (Auchincloss)
  22:51
The Stories of F. Scott Fitzgerald (Fitzgerald)
  6:60
Stories of Five Decades (Hesse) **9**:232-33,
  235-36
The Stories of Frank O'Connor (O'Connor)
  5:365
The Stories of Heinrich Böll (Boell) **23**:33, 35
The Stories of Henry Lawson (Lawson) **18**:206
The Stories of John Cheever (Cheever) **1**:105-
  06, 108-09; **38**:49, 52, 63, 83
The Stories of Liam O'Flaherty (O'Flaherty)
  6:260, 265
"Stories of Lough Guir" (Le Fanu) **14**:223
The Stories of Muriel Spark (Spark) **10**:365-66,
  368, 370-71
The Stories of Ray Bradbury (Bradbury) **29**:62-5
The Stories of Seán O'Faoláin (O'Faolain)
  See *Finest Short Stories of Seán O'Faoláin*
Stories of Sinebriukhov (Zoshchenko)
  See *The Tales by Nazar Ilyich Sinebriukhov*
Stories of Three Decades (Mann) **5**:308-09, 311
The Stories of William Sansom (Sansom) **21**:92,
  96, 112, 114, 118
Stories Told for Children (Andersen)
  See *Eventyr, fortalte for bøorn*
"The Storm" (Bowen) **3**:38-9
"The Storm" (Chopin) **8**:80, 84, 86, 91, 95
"Storm" (O'Brien) **10**:345-46
"The Storm" (Stuart) **31**:233, 263
"Storm Child" (Garland) **18**:147
"Storm in a Teacup" (Lu Hsun)
  See "Feng-po"
"A Storm in the Mountains" (Solzhenitsyn)
  See "Groza v gorakh"
"The Storm King" (Vinge) **24**:337, 344
"The Storm Ship" (Irving) **2**:254
"A Story" (Andric)
  See "Priča"
The Story (Pasternak)
  See *Povest*
"A Story about Money" (Farrell) **28**:125
"The Story about the Anteater" (Benet) **10**:149
"A Story about the Little Rabbits" (Harris)
  19:170, 186, 195
Story Book (Hesse) **9**:230-31
"A Story by Angela Poe" (Benet) **10**:142, 144
"The Story fo the Beetle Hunter" (Doyle) **12**:64
"Story from Bear Country" (Silko) **37**:310, 314
"A Story from the Dunes" (Andersen) **6**:18-9,
  34
"The Story Hearer" (Paley) **8**:420
"Story in Harlem Slang" (Hurston) **4**:139
"The Story Not Shown" (Moorhouse) **40**:325
"The Story of a Blind Man" (Tanizaki)
  See "Mōmoku monogatari"
"The Story of a Conscience" (Bierce) **9**:64, 67

"The Story of a Disappearance and an
  Appearance" (James) **16**:230, 232, 237,
  245
"The Story of a Horse" (Babel) **16**:25, 28, 50-3
"The Story of a Horse, Continued" (Babel)
  16:27
"The Story of a Lie" (Stevenson) **11**:269, 281
"The Story of a Mine" (Harte) **8**:216
"The Story of a Mother" (Andersen) **6**:6-7,
  18-9, 30, 35
"The Story of a Mouse" (Babel)
  See "Istoriia moei golubiatni"
"The Story of a Non-Marrying Man" (Lessing)
  6:188, 211
"The Story of a Panic" (Forster) **27**:72-5, 81,
  85-7, 97-8, 102-03, 111-13, 115, 119,
  121-23
"Story of a Patron" (Warner) **23**:369-70
"The Story of an Hour" (Chopin) **8**:72-3, 79-
  80, 84, 87, 99, 102, 108
"A Story of Beer" (Bulgakov) **18**:90
"The Story of Bras-Coupé" (Cable) **4**:61
"The Story of Counter-Octave" (Pasternak)
  31:108-10, 115
"The Story of Father Alexis" (Turgenev)
  See "Rasskaz ottsa Aleksaya"
"A Story of Historical Interest" (Wilson)
  21:329, 331, 333, 336, 342, 351
"The Story of Howling Wolf" (Garland) **18**:147,
  167, 179-80, 188
"The Story of Jees Uck" (London) **4**:271
"The Story of Keesh" (London) **4**:253
"The Story of Lahcen and Idir" (Bowles) **3**:80
"The Story of Lieutenant Ergunov" (Turgenev)
  See "Istoriya leytenanta Ergunova"
"The Story of Mahlon" (Caldwell) **19**:41
"The Story of María Griselda" (Bombal)
  See "The Story of Marfa Griselda"
"The Story of Mr. Rabbit and Mr. Fox"
  (Harris) **19**:185
"The Story of Muhammad Din" (Kipling) **5**:296
"The Story of My Dovecot" (Babel)
  See "Istoriia moei golubiatni"
"The Story of Nature" (Moorhouse) **40**:302,
  322
"Story of Saint Joseph's Ass" (Verga) **21**:293,
  298-99
"The Story of St. Vespaluus" (Saki) **12**:306
"A Story of Stories" (Dreiser) **30**:107, 122, 155,
  157
"The Story of Teenchy-Tiny Duck" (Harris)
  19:196
"The Story of the Brazilian Cat" (Doyle) **12**:64
"A Story of the Days to Come" (Wells) **6**:389,
  390, 403-04, 406-08
"The Story of the Deluge, and How It Came
  About" (Harris) **19**:195
The Story of the Gadsbys (Kipling) **5**:260, 264-
  65, 274
"A Story of the Head Gardener" (Chekhov)
  28:60
"The Story of the Japanned Box" (Doyle) **12**:64
"The Story of the Knife" (Moorhouse) **40**:309
"The Story of the Late Mr. Elvesham" (Wells)
  6:361, 363, 366, 383, 388, 405
"The Story of the Nice Old Man" (Svevo)
  See "La novella del buon vecchio e della
  bella fanciulla"
"The Story of the Oracle" (Lawson) **18**:250
"The Story of the Siren" (Forster) **27**:67, 69-71,
  73-5, 83-5, 87, 99-100, 102-03, 112, 114
The Story of the Siren (Forster) **27**:75, 83-85,
  87, 99-100, 102-03, 112, 114
"A Story of the Stone Age" (Wells) **6**:389-90,
  403-04
"Story of the Vizier's Elephant" (Andric)
  See "Priča o vezirovom slonu"
"A Story of the War" (Harris) **19**:121, 179
"Story of the Warrior and the Captive"
  (Borges)
  See "Historia del guerrero y de la cautiva"
"The Story of the Year" (Andersen) **6**:30

"The Story of the Young Italian" (Irving) **2**:260-
  61, 268
"Story of the Young Man with the Cream
  Tarts" (Stevenson) **11**:265
"The Story of the Young Robber" (Irving)
  2:255, 257, 262
"A Story of Tomoda and Matsunaga"
  (Tanizaki)
  See "Tomoda to Matsunaga no hanashi"
"The Story of Two Dogs" (Lessing) **6**:198, 200,
  203-04, 206, 208
"A Story of Yesterday" (Tolstoy) **9**:374
"A Story with a Pattern" (Lavin) **4**:163, 167-69,
  184-85
"Story with Spiders" (Cortazar) **7**:69
"A Story without a Title" (Chekhov)
  See "An Anonymous Story"
"Story without Words" (Capek) **36**:121-22, 125
"The Story-Teller" (Saki) **12**:289, 291, 293,
  295, 302
"Storyteller" (Silko) **37**:289, 295, 307, 315
Storyteller (Silko) **37**:287-90, 292-96, 298-99,
  301, 303-12, 314-15
"Storyteller's Escape" (Silko) **37**:296
A Story-Teller's Holiday (Moore) **19**:293-96,
  298-300, 305-09, 311-12, 345-46
"Storytellers, Liars, and Bores" (Michaels)
  16:306, 309, 311
"Storytelling" (Silko) **37**:289, 308
"The Stout Gentleman" (Irving) **2**:250-51, 254,
  259; **37**:274
"La strada di San Giovanni" (Calvino) **3**:97
"Straight Pool" (O'Hara) **15**:248, 264
"Strandhill, the Sea" (McGahern) **17**:302, 308,
  318, 320
The Strange Case of Dr. Jekyll and Mr. Hyde
  (Stevenson) **11**:262, 264, 276, 279, 290-
  92, 301-02
"The Strange Child" (Kuhatschek)
  See "Das Fremde Kind"
"Strange Comfort Afforded by the Profession"
  (Lowry) **31**:44-5, 47-8, 51-2, 54, 59-61,
  64-5, 71, 73-4, 82, 84, 86
"The Strange Crime of John Boulais"
  (Chesterton) **1**:138
"A Strange Death" (Moore) **19**:342
"The Strange Design of Master Rignolo"
  (Ligotti) **16**:271, 277, 292, 296
"The Strange Disease" (O'Flaherty) **6**:262
"Strange Disturbances on Aungier Street" (Le
  Fanu)
  See "Some Strange Disturbances in an Old
  House on Augier Street"
"A Strange Event in the Life of Schalken the
  Painter" (Le Fanu)
  See "A Strange Event in the Life of
  Schalken the Painter"
"A Strange Event in the Life of Schalken the
  Painter" (Le Fanu) **14**:220-21, 224-25,
  232-36, 238-39, 252
"The Strange Experiences of Mr.Janík"
  (Capek)
  See "Případy pana Janíka"
"The Strange Girls" (Walser) **20**:355-56
"The Strange High House in the Mist"
  (Lovecraft) **3**:262, 277
"A Strange Island" (Alcott) **27**:42
"Strange Meeting" (Sansom) **21**:127
"Strange Moonlight" (Aiken) **9**:4, 7-8, 13-14,
  32-3, 35, 38, 40
"Strange News from Another Star" (Hesse)
  9:235
*Strange News from Another Star, and Other
  Tales* (Hesse) **9**:234-35, 244
"The Strange Ride of Morrowbie Jukes"
  (Kipling) **5**:262, 265, 273, 278, 299
"Strange Stories by a Nervous Gentleman"
  (Irving) **2**:251, 261
Strange Stories from a Chinese Studio (P'u
  Sung-ling)
  See *Liao-chai chih-i*

Strange stories from the Refuge of My Study
    (P'u Sung-ling)
    See *Liao-chai chih-i*
"A Strange Story" (Turgenev)
    See "Strannaya istoriya"
"The Strange Story of the Three Golden
    Fishes: A Comedy of a Man Who Always
    Was Lucky—Especially in Marriage"
    (Moore) **19**:346
The Strange Tales of Liao-chai (P'u Sung-ling)
    See *Liao-chai chih-i*
"A Strange Thing" (Galsworthy) **22**:63, 74, 79,
    101
"A Strange Thing" (Machado de Assis)
    See "Singular ocorrência"
Strange Things Happen Here (Valenzuela)
    14:366-67, 369-70
Strange True Stories of Louisiana (Cable) **4**:49,
    51, 53, 58-62, 75
"The Stranger" (Baudelaire)
    See "L'etranger"
"A Stranger" (de la Mare) **14**:80
"The Stranger" (Mansfield) **9**:280, 282-83
"The Stranger" (Schnitzler) **15**:342
"Stranger, Bear Words to the Spartans We..."
    (Boell)
    See "Wanderer, kommst du nach Spa..."
"A Stranger with a Bag" (Warner) **23**:374
A Stranger with a Bag, and Other Stories
    (Warner) **23**:380
"Strangers and Pilgrims" (de la Mare) **14**:80,
    83, 86, 92
"Strangers in the Night" (Phillips) **16**:325
"The Stranger's Pew" (Page) **23**:308, 312
"The Strangest Thing" (Norris) **28**:213
"Strannaya istoriya" (Turgenev) **7**:315, 321,
    324, 337, 358-59
"Strašnaja mest'" (Gogol) **4**:103-04, 118-19;
    29:132, 149
"Die Strasse" (Walser) **20**:341
"The Strategy of the Were-Wolf Dog" (Cather)
    2:100
"Stratford-on-Avon" (Irving) **2**:245
"The Strawberry Season" (Caldwell) **19**:37
"Strawberry Spring" (King) **17**:265
"The Stream" (O'Flaherty) **6**:265, 277-78
"The Street" (Lovecraft) **3**:292
"A Street" (Morrison) **40**:330, 335, 352, 354-
    55, 365-67, 370
"The Street" (Morrison) **40**:348
"The Street" (Walser)
    See "Die Strasse"
"Streetcorner Man" (Borges)
    See "El Hombre de la esquina rosada"
"Streets" (Dixon) **16**:205
"The Streets—Morning" (Dickens) **17**:116, 134
"The Strength of Gideon" (Dunbar) **8**:128, 136,
    141, 144
The Strength of Gideon and Other Stories
    (Dunbar) **8**:120-21, 124-25, 127, 131,
    144-45
"The Strength of God" (Anderson) **1**:18
"The Strength of the Strong" (London) **4**:255
The Strength of the Strong (London) **4**:254-55,
    283
Strictly Business (Henry) **5**:171
"Strictly from Hunger" (Perelman) **32**:211, 237
Strictly from Hunger (Perelman) **32**:205, 219
Strider (Tolstoy) **9**:393
"Strike" (Selby) **20**:253, 255, 258, 260, 262,
    264-65, 267-69, 271-73, 279, 281
"The String Quartet" (Woolf) **7**:368-69, 374-75,
    390, 392, 399
"The Stroke of Apelles" (Pasternak)
    See "Il tratto di Apelle"
"A Stroke of Good Fortune" (O'Connor) **23**:237
"Stroke of Lightning" (Galsworthy) **22**:75, 101
"The Stroll" (Andric)
    See "Šetnja"
"Strong as Death is Love" (Singer) **3**:386
Strong Hearts (Cable) **4**:50, 62, 75
"Strong Horse Tea" (Walker) **5**:401, 403

"The Struggle" (O'Flaherty) **6**:264, 269
"A Struggle" (Svevo)
    See "Una lotta"
"Stubborn in Poverty" (Dazai Osamu) **41**:226-
    28, 232
"Stud City" (King) **17**:272, 278-79, 285, 289-90
"The Student" (Chekhov) **2**:158
"The Student of Salamanca" (Irving) **2**:251,
    254, 259
"The Student's Wife" (Carver) **8**:11, 46, 50-1,
    53
Studien (Stifter) **28**:272, 286, 290-92, 298,
    300-01
Studies (Stifter)
    Sec *Studien*
"Studies in Extravagance" (Galsworthy) **22**:60
"Studies in Horror" (Ligotti) **16**:287
"Studs" (Farrell) **28**:90, 97, 122
"The Study of History" (O'Connor) **5**:376
"Stuk...stuk...stuk" (Turgenev) **7**:319, 321, 324-
    25, 338, 358-59
Eine Stunde hinter Mitternacht (Hesse)
    9:229-31
"The Stylish Child" (Dazai Osamu) **41**:255
"The Sub" (Dixon) **16**:207
"Subcommittee" (Henderson) **29**:321, 323-25
"A Subject of Childhood" (Paley) **8**:396, 398,
    407
"Sublimating" (Updike) **13**:387
"The Subliminal Man" (Ballard) **1**:68-9, 77-8
"Subpoena" (Barthelme) **2**:37, 39
"The Substitute" (Pardo Bazan) **30**:290
"A Suburban Fairy Tale" (Mansfield) **9**:311
Suburban Sketches (Howells) **36**:399-400
"Success Story" (Farrell) **28**:110
"The Successor" (Bowles) **3**:64-5, 80, 83
"Such Darling Dodos" (Wilson) **21**:324, 337,
    345, 355, 357
Such Darling Dodos (Wilson) **21**:320, 328-29,
    331, 336, 338, 345-46, 348-49, 354-55, 357-
    58, 364-65
"Such Is Life" (Pirandello) **22**:242-43
"Such Perfection" (Narayan) **25**:135, 138, 140,
    156
"Sucker" (McCullers) **9**:332, 341-42, 344-45,
    354-55
"Le Sud" (Borges) **41**:43-44, 46-47, 55, 58,
    160
"A Sudden Trip Home in the Spring" (Walker)
    5:414
"Le Sue giornate" (Moravia) **26**:174, 178
"Un sueño realizado" (Onetti) **23**:246, 249, 252,
    279-80
Un sueño realizado y otros cuentos (Onetti)
    23:245-46, 251, 258
"La suerte de Teodoro Méndez Acubal"
    (Castellanos) **39**:48, 57
"Suffer the Little Children" (King) **17**:295
The Sugar Crock (Gass) **12**:148
"Sugar for the Horse" (Bates) **10**:117, 131
Sugar for the Horse (Bates) **10**:131
"The Sugawn Chair" (O'Faolain) **13**:314, 320
"Suicide Club" (Doyle) **12**:58
The Suicide Club (Stevenson) **11**:280
"Suicides" (Gilchrist) **14**:150-51
"Suicides" (Pavese) **19**:374-75, 377-78, 387
"Suisen" (Dazai Osamu) **41**:254
"Suishō Gensō" (Kawabata) **17**:242
"The Suitcase" (Ozick) **15**:298-300, 311, 314-
    15, 319, 328-35
Sukhodol (Bunin) **5**:81-3, 87, 90, 100-01
"Sulfur" (Levi) **12**:264, 268
"Sullivan's Trousers" (O'Faolain) **13**:309, 316
"Summer" (Boyle) **5**:54
"Summer" (Cortazar)
    See "Verano"
"Summer" (Frame) **29**:106
"The Summer Before" (Steinbeck) **11**:253-54
"A Summer Day" (Stafford) **26**:275-76, 281,
    289, 308
"Summer Dust" (Gordon) **15**:116, 119, 123,
    126, 137, 139

"The Summer Farmer" (Cheever) **1**:99, 106;
    38:53, 66
"A Summer in Maine" (Gilchrist) **14**:163-64
"A Summer in the South" (Andric) **36**:46
"Summer Morning in Dublin" (Farrell) **28**:126
"Summer Night" (Bowen) **3**:39, 41, 46, 51
"The Summer Night" (Bradbury) **29**:60
"The Summer of the Beautiful White Horse"
    (Saroyan) **21**:169-71
"Summer People" (Beattie) **11**:25-6, 29
"The Summer People" (Jackson) **9**:258
"Summer Remembered" (Cheever) **38**:43
"Summer Shore" (Grau) **15**:161, 163-64
"Summer Storm" (Pavese) **19**:364, 373
Summer Storm, and Other Stories (Pavese)
    19:363
"Summer Swimmingpool" (Pavese) **19**:375
"Summer Theatre" (Cheever) **1**:99; **38**:63-6
"Summer Thunder" (Ross) **24**:302
"Summer Tryout" (Farrell) **28**:99, 122
"Summer's Day" (O'Hara) **15**:248-49, 252-53,
    258, 270
"A Summer's Reading" (Malamud) **15**:168, 221
Summertime and Other Stories (Donoso)
    See *Veraneo y otros cuentos*
"Summertime on Icarus" (Clarke) **3**:130, 138,
    147
"Summertime Was Nearly Over" (Aldiss) **36**:28
"The Summing Up" (Woolf) **7**:376, 381, 390,
    392, 411
"The Sun" (Andric)
    See "Sunce"
"Sun" (Lawrence) **4**:238, 240-42
"Sun and Moon" (Mansfield) **9**:282
"The Sun between Their Feet" (Lessing) **6**:198-
    99, 203, 212
"Sun Cured" (Lardner) **32**:117, 136-38, 140,
    149
The Sun Dog (King) **17**:282, 284
"The Sun Rises Twice" (Bates) **10**:113
"Sunce" (Andric) **36**:50
"Sunday" (Shiga) **23**:348
"Sunday Afternoon" (Bowen) **3**:41, 53
"Sunday Afternoon" (Gallant) **5**:141
"Sunday Afternoon" (Munro) **3**:343
"Sunday Afternoon Hanging" (Stuart) **31**:236,
    262-63
"Sunday at Home" (Hawthorne) **3**:189; **39**:120,
    122
"Sunday Brings Sunday" (Lavin) **4**:176
"Sunday Evening" (Bowen) **3**:53
"Sunday Evening" (Farrell) **28**:112
"Sunday Morning" (O'Hara) **15**:282, 289
"Sunday Morning, June 4, 1989" (Thomas)
    20:324-25, 328
"A Sunday Out of Town" (Dickens) **17**:120-21
"Sunday Teasing" (Updike) **13**:355
"Sunday under Three Heads" (Dickens) **17**:124
"The Sun-Dodgers" (O'Hara) **15**:282
"The Sun-Dog Trail" (London) **4**:253, 290
"Sunjammer" (Clarke) **3**:132
"Sunlight/Twilight" (Oates) **6**:236-37
"A Sunny Place" (Kawabata) **17**:252
"The Sunrise" (Atwood) **2**:17-18, 21-2
"A Sunrise on the Veld" (Lessing) **6**:186
"Sunset" (Faulkner) **1**:177
Sunset (Babel)
    See *Zakat*
"Sunset Limited" (Harrison) **19**:211-14
"Sunshine and Shadow" (Beattie) **11**:10
"The Sunshine Club" (Campbell) **19**:82
Sunshine Sketches of a Little Town (Leacock)
    39:241, 242, 243, 245, 246, 247, 249, 250,
    251, 252, 253, 254, 255, 256, 257, 258, 259,
    260, 261, 269, 273, 274, 275
"Sunstroke" (Bunin)
    See "Solnechnyy udar"
A Sunstroke (Bunin) **5**:90
"Suora Scolastica" (Stendhal) **27**:249, 251, 263
"The Superintendent" (Cheever) **1**:99, 107;
    38:53
"Superiority" (Clarke) **3**:126, 150

The Supermale (Jarry)
    See *Le surmâle, roman moderne*
Supernatural Tales: Excursions into Fantasy
    (Lee) **33**:310
"The Superstitious Man's Story" (Hardy) **2**:217
"Super-Toys Last All Summer Long" (Aldiss)
    36:20
"The Supper at Elsinore" (Dinesen) **7**:168, 177,
    186, 190, 203-04
"A Supper by Proxy" (Dunbar) **8**:122, 135, 139
"Suppose a Wedding" (Malamud) **15**:173-75
"El Sur" (Borges) **41**:41, 152
Sur l'eau (Maupassant) **1**:261-62, 265, 278
"The Surgeon's Daughter" (Scott) **32**:287, 299,
    319
"Surgery" (Chekhov) **2**:130
Le surmâle, roman moderne (Jarry) **20**:44, 50-2,
    54, 59, 62, 67, 70-2, 76
"A Surplus Woman" (Gilman) **13**:143
"'Surprise, Surprise!' from Matron" (Jolley)
    19:234, 245
"The Surveyor and Julka" (Andric)
    See "Geometar i Julka"
"The Survival of Childhood" (Oates) **6**:224
"The Survival of the Fittest" (Thomas) **20**:324-
    25, 327
Survival Techniques (Calisher) **15**:21, 23
"The Survivor" (Bambara) **35**:17
"Survivor Type" (King) **17**:274-75
"Susan and the Doctor" (Suckow) **18**:393-94,
    409, 416-17
"Susedi" (Andric) **36**:47
"Susy" (Harte) **8**:222, 251-52
"Suterareru made" (Tanizaki) **21**:195
"Suttee" (Auchincloss) **22**:14
"Suzette" (Chopin) **8**:100
"Svajatye gory" (Bunin) **5**:98
"Svinedrengen" (Andersen)
    See "The Swineherd"
"Svirel" (Chekhov) **28**:58, 60-1
"Swaddling Clothes" (Mishima) **4**:313, 317,
    322-23
"Swallows" (McGahern) **17**:299, 304, 308
"Swans" (Frame) **29**:100, 106, 108-09
"The Swan's Nest" (Andersen) **6**:4
"Swans on an Autumn River" (Warner) **23**:374
"The Swastika on Our Door" (Adams) **24**:2-3,
    6
"The Sway-Backed House" (Chesnutt) **7**:33
"Sweat" (Hurston) **4**:136-38, 151, 155
"Sweet and Hot" (Perelman) **32**:204
"A Sweet Colleen" (O'Faolain) **13**:305
Sweet Diamond Dust and Other Stories (Ferre)
    36:146-47, 149-50
"The Sweet Sad Queen of the Grazing Isles"
    (Pohl) **25**:236
"The Sweet Singer of Omsk" (Saroyan) **21**:160
"Sweet Town" (Bambara) **35**:4, 6, 22, 32
"The Sweethearts" (Andersen) **6**:28, 30, 36
"Sweethearts" (Phillips) **16**:326, 328
Sweethearts (Phillips) **16**:332
"The Sweetness of Twisted Apples" (Stegner)
    27:195, 197, 201, 204, 220
"Sweets for Angels" (Narayan) **25**:135, 141,
    156
"A Swell-Looking Girl" (Caldwell) **19**:25, 46
"Swept and Garnished" (Kipling) **5**:275, 282
"The Swiftest Runners" (Andersen) **6**:10
"The Swimmer" (Cheever) **1**:94, 100, 102, 106,
    108; **38**:44, 47-8, 51, 54, 57-61, 63-6, 72,
    74, 76
"The Swineherd" (Andersen) **6**:7, 18, 24, 26,
    30-1, 34
"The Swing" (Bunin)
    See "Kacheli"
"Swing Out, Sweet Chariot" (Perelman) **32**:201
"Swinging the Maelstrom" (Lowry) **31**:67
The Swiss Family Perelman (Perelman) **32**:219,
    224, 233
"The Switchman" (Arreola)
    See "El guardagujas"

"A s'y méprendre" (Villiers de l'Isle Adam)
    14:381, 388, 391
"Sylvania is Dead" (Stuart) **31**:227, 236-38,
    255
"Sylvesternacht" (Hoffmann) **13**:189
"Sylvia" (Michaels) **16**:314, 317, 320
Sylvia: A Fictional Memoir (Michaels)
    16:317-18
Sylvie: Recollections of Valois (Nerval) **18**:328,
    332-35, 337, 343-46, 355, 357, 359-62, 365,
    367, 369-70, 376-77, 380, 383
"Sympathy" (Woolf) **7**:409
La Symphonie pastorale (Gide) **13**:43, 48-52,
    62, 72, 77, 98-9
Symphonies (Gide)
    See *Two Symphonies*
"A Symphony in Lavender" (Freeman) **1**:199
"A Symposium" (Kundera) **24**:88-94, 97, 99-
    100, 103-04, 107, 114-16, 118, 122
"Syracuse; or, The Panther Man" (Morand)
    22:169
"The System" (Capek) **36**:88, 109
"The System of Doctor Tarr and Professor
    Fether" (Poe) **1**:407; **22**:307-08, 330-31,
    333; **35**:350
"T" (Aldiss) **36**:19
"t zero" (Calvino) **3**:93
t zero (Calvino)
    See *Ti con zero*
"The Tabernacle" (Pirandello) **22**:254
"The Table, the Ass and the Stick" (Grimm
    and Grimm)
    See "The Magic Table, the Gold Donkey,
    and the Club in the Sack"
"Tabloid Tragedy" (Dreiser) **30**:155-56, 159
"Tactical Exercise" (Waugh) **41**:311
Tactical Exercise (Waugh) **41**:328
"Tadeo Limardo's Victim" (Bioy Casares)
    See "La victima de Tadeo Limardo"
"Das Tagebuch der Redegonda" (Schnitzler)
    15:346
"The Tailor in Heaven" (Grimm and Grimm)
    36:229-30
"Tailors' Dummies" (Schulz)
    See "Traktat o manekinach"
"Tails" (Dixon) **16**:211
"Taily-po" (Harris) **19**:196
"Tain't So" (Hughes) **6**:121, 131
"Take a Deep Breath" (Pohl) **25**:213
"Take Pity" (Malamud) **15**:169, 175, 212, 216-
    17, 219, 221, 223, 243
"Takes" (Dixon) **16**:218
"The Taking of Lungtungpen" (Kipling) **5**:260,
    265
"The Taking of the Redoubt" (Merimee)
    See "L'enlèvement de la rédoute"
"Taking The Blue Ribbon at the Fair"
    (Murfree) **22**:184, 203, 211
"Taking the Veil" (Mansfield) **9**:282, 310;
    38:230
"Taking the Wen" (Dazai Osamu)
    See "Taking the Wen Away"
"Taking the Wen Away" (Dazai Osamu) **41**:233,
    235-36, 276
Un tal Lucas (Cortazar) **7**:91-4
A Tale (Pasternak)
    See *Povest*
"A Tale about the Safe-Breaker and the
    Fire-Raiser" (Capek)
    See "Příběh o kasaři a žháři"
"Tale for the Mirror" (Calisher) **15**:3
*Tale for the Mirror: A Novella and Other
    Stories* (Calisher) **15**:3-5, 7
"The Tale of a Dwarf" (Lewis) **40**:279
"Tale of a Vampire" (Hoffmann)
    See "Der Vampyrismus"
"The Tale of Astolpho on the Moon" (Calvino)
    3:101
"The Tale of How Ivan Ivanovich Quarrelled
    with Ivan Nikiforovich" (Gogol) **4**:82, 84,
    86, 105; **29**:124-26
"A Tale of Jerusalem" (Poe) **1**:407

"A Tale of Love and Politics" (Howells) **36**:398
"Tale of Moons" (Carpentier)
    See "Histoire de lunes"
"The Tale of Rabbi Gadiel, the Infant"
    (Agnon) **30**:66
"The Tale of the Good Old Man and the
    Beautiful Girl" (Svevo)
    See "La novella del buon vecchio e della
    bella fanciulla"
"The Tale of the Ingrate and His Punishment"
    (Calvino) **3**:101-02
"A Tale of the Ragged Mountains" (Poe) **1**:400,
    402
"The Tale of the Scribe" (Agnon)
    See "The Legend of the Scribe"
"The Tale of the Squint-Eyed Left-Handed
    Smith from Tula and the Steel Flea"
    (Leskov)
    See "Levša"
"A Tale of the White Pyramid" (Cather) **2**:100
"Tale of the Wicker Chair" (Hesse) **9**:242, 244
"The Tale of Tod Lapraik" (Stevenson)
    11:303-06
"The Tale of Two Ivans" (Gogol)
    See "The Tale of How Ivan Ivanovich
    Quarrelled with Ivan Nikiforovich"
"A Tale of Two Liars" (Singer) **3**:375
"A Tale of Two Sisters" (Singer) **3**:377
"A Tale of Unrequited Love" (Gorky) **28**:162
"The Tale of Urashima" (Dazai Osamu) **41**:234
"A Tale Without an End" (Aleichem) **33**:68, 71
Tales before Midnight (Benet) **10**:154, 158-59
Tales by Belkin (Pushkin)
    See *Povesti Belkina*
Tales by Edgar A. Poe (Poe) **1**:388
The Tales by Nazar Ilyich Sinebriukhov
    (Zoshchenko) **15**:395
Tales for Children (Tolstoy) **9**:382
Tales from Bective Bridge (Lavin) **4**:170-72,
    185
Tales from Olden Times (Leskov) **34**:119
Tales from One Pocket (Capek)
    See *Povídky z druhé kapsy*
Tales from the Other Pocket (Capek)
    See *Povídky z jedné kapsy*
Tales from the Plum Grove Hills (Stuart)
    31:232-34, 260, 266
Tales from the White Hart (Clarke) **3**:131, 133
Tales from Two Pockets (Capek) **36**:84, 93, 109,
    120-21, 125-26, 128, 130
Tales of a Traveller (Irving) **2**:241, 244, 246,
    250-51, 254-55, 258-62, 268
Tales of All Countries (Trollope) **28**:328, 332,
    340, 342, 347
Tales of All Countries: First Series (Trollope)
    28:317, 323, 326, 332, 339
Tales of All Countries: Second Series
    (Trollope) **28**:318, 323, 326-27, 330-32
Tales of Horror and the Supernatural
    (Machen) **20**:163, 186, 201
The Tales of Ivan Belkin (Pushkin)
    See *Povesti Belkina*
Tales of Lenin (Zoshchenko) **15**:404, 407, 409
Tales of Manhattan (Auchincloss) **22**:9-10, 12,
    17, 19, 20, 29, 34, 37, 39, 46, 49-51
Tales of Mean Streets (Morrison) **40**:328-332,
    334-41, 343-45, 347-48, 350-51, 354-56,
    364-68, 370-71, 375-75
Tales of Men and Ghosts (Wharton) **6**:421, 435
Tales of Mystery and Romance (Moorhouse)
    40:292-93, 297, 305-07, 309, 323-24
Tales of Odessa (Babel)
    See *The Odessa Tales*
Tales of Poland (Agnon) **30**:81-2
Tales of Sevastopol (Tolstoy) **9**:380
Tales of Soldiers and Civilians (Bierce) **9**:49-
    50, 55, 59, 65, 75
Tales of Space and Time (Wells) **6**:366-67, 380,
    389
Tales of Terror and Mystery (Doyle) **12**:60, 64
Tales of the Grotesque and Arabesque (Poe)
    1:389-90; **22**:329, 333-34, 349; **35**:335-36

Title Index

Tales of the Home Folks in Peace and War (Harris) **19**:182-83
Tales of the Jazz Age (Fitzgerald) **6**:45-6, 56, 58-9, 74, 101
Tales of the Long Bow (Chesterton) **1**:133
"Tales of the Moon" (Peretz) **26**:205
Tales of Twilight and the Unseen (Doyle) **12**:60
"Tales of Two Old Gentlemen" (Dinesen) **7**:173
Tales of Unrest (Conrad) **9**:151-52
"The Talisman" (de la Mare) **14**:83
"A Talk among Leisured People" (Tolstoy) **9**:396
"Talk by the River" (Pavese) **19**:376
"The Talkative Man" (Narayan) **25**:136
"Talkin 'Bout Sonny" (Bambara) **35**:24
"Talking Horse" (Malamud) **15**:189, 190, 198, 220, 222
The Talking Trees (O'Faolain) **13**:291, 313-14
"The Tall Men" (Faulkner) **1**:151, 162
"Tally Ho Budmâsh" (Galsworthy) **22**:90
"Talpa" (Rulfo) **25**:245, 249-53, 257-58, 262, 265, 274-75
"Tamango" (Merimee) **7**:280-1, 283, 287-9, 300
"Taming a Tartar" (Alcott) **27**:29, 57-8, 61
"The Taming of the Nightmare" (Chesterton) **1**:140
"Tamurlane" (Mukherjee) **38**:252, 254, 265
Tan triste como ella (Onetti) **23**:248, 260, 264-71, 275, 280
Tanagokoro no Shōsetsu (Kawabata) **17**:242, 251-58
"Tanhum" (Singer) **3**:380
"Tania" (Bunin) **5**:113
"Tanil" (Coppard) **21**:3
"Tante Cat'rinette" (Chopin) **8**:94
"Ho tante cose da dirvi . . ." (Pirandello) **22**:285
"Tanya" (Bunin)
    See "Tania"
Das Tanzlegendchen (Keller) **26**:101, 108
"Tao-hu" (P'u Sung-ling) **31**:191, 204
"An tAonach" (O'Flaherty) **6**:287-88
"The Tapestried Chamber" (Scott) **32**:319
"Tapiama" (Bowles) **3**:64-5, 80, 83
Taps at Reveille (Fitzgerald) **6**:46-7, 56, 60; **31**:15, 18-19, 21, 25-6, 29
"The Tar Baby" (Harris)
    See "The Wonderful Tar-Baby Story"
"Taras Bulba" (Gogol) **4**:83, 85-6, 117-19; **29**:128, 130, 132, 135, 149
Taratuta (Donoso) **34**:42-3, 45-8
"Target One" (Pohl) **25**:227, 229-32, 234-35
"Tarquin of Cheapside" (Fitzgerald) **6**:58, 60
"Tarr and Fether" (Poe)
    See "The System of Doctor Tarr and Professor Fether"
"La tartaruga" (Pirandello) **22**:269
"A Taste of Honey" (Freeman) **1**:196
"Tatlin!" (Davenport) **16**:161-62, 165, 167-69, 171, 197
Tatlin! (Davenport) **16**:160-61, 163-68, 170-71, 173-77, 183, 185, 187, 195, 197
Tatterdemalion (Galsworthy) **22**:63, 97, 100-01
"Tattooer" (Tanizaki)
    See "Shisei"
Le taureau blanc (Voltaire) **12**:342
"The Taxidermist" (Cable) **4**:50
"Tea" (Gallant)
    See "Thank You for the Lovely Tea"
"Tea" (Saki) **12**:313
"Tea on the Mountain" (Bowles) **3**:61, 72, 79
"The Tea Time of Stouthearted Ladies" (Stafford) **26**:286
"Tea with an Artist" (Rhys) **21**:58, 62
"Tea with Mrs. Bittell" (Pritchett) **14**:272
"Teach Us to Outgrow Our Madness" (Oe)
    See "Warera no Kyoki o ikinobiru michi o oshieyo"
"The Teacher" (Anderson) **1**:18, 45, 52
"The Teacher of Literature" (Chekhov) **2**:128, 131-32, 155; **28**:59
"Teacher's Pet" (Thurber) **1**:422-23

"Teaching and Story Telling" (Maclean) **13**:278-79
"The Teachings of Don B.: A Yankee Way of Knowledge" (Barthelme) **2**:40
"A Teamster's Payday" (Farrell) **28**:118
"Teangabháil" (O'Flaherty) **6**:286-89
"Tears, Idle Tears" (Bowen) **3**:33, 41, 47
"The Tears of Ah Kim" (London) **4**:257, 270
"Tears—Idle Tears" (O'Connor) **5**:371, 395
"Technical Error" (Clarke) **3**:124-25, 129
"A Technical Error" (Henry) **5**:165
"Teddy" (Salinger) **2**:293, 295, 300-01, 307, 309, 311-12, 316; **28**:262, 265
"The Teddy-Bears' Picnic" (Trevor) **21**:262, 265
"Ted's Wife" (Thomas) **20**:297, 305, 311
"Teibele and Her Demon" (Singer) **3**:375, 384
"The Telegram" (Capek) **36**:98, 127
"The Telegraph Girl" (Trollope) **28**:311, 322, 327, 333-34, 348, 355-56
"Telemachus, Friend" (Henry) **5**:179
"A Telephone Call" (Parker) **2**:274, 278, 280, 285
"A Telephone Call on Yom Kippur" (Singer) **3**:385-86
"Television" (Beattie) **11**:31
"Tell Churchill that T. George McDowell is on His Feet" (Moorhouse) **40**:291
"Tell It Like It Is" (Ellison) **26**:11
"Tell Me a Riddle" (Olsen) **11**:164-68, 171, 174, 176, 178-79, 181, 185, 187, 195, 197
Tell Me a Riddle (Olsen) **11**:163, 169, 171, 174, 187-88, 193, 197-98
"Tell Me Who to Kill" (Naipaul) **38**:301, 303-04, 309, 312-13, 353-54
"Tell Me Yes or No" (Munro) **3**:335
"Tell the Women We're Going" (Carver) **8**:14, 30
"Tell Them Not to Kill Me" (Rulfo)
    See "Díles que no me maten!"
"Telling" (Bowen) **3**:30, 33, 40
"Telling Mrs. Baker" (Lawson) **18**:213, 243, 252, 262
"The Tell-Tale Heart" (Poe) **1**:384, 393-94, 408; **34**:239-87; **35**:307-11, 314, 343, 345-46
"El Tema del traidor y del héroe" (Borges) **4**:10, 23, 30, 39; **41**:40, 58, 147-48
"El tema del traidor y el héroe" (Borges)
    See "El Tema del traidor y del héroe"
"The Temperate Zone" (Wharton) **6**:428
"Tempests" (Dinesen) **7**:171, 197
"The Temple" (Lovecraft) **3**:282, 289
"The Temple at Thatch" (Waugh) **41**:350
"A Temple of the Holy Ghost" (O'Connor) **1**:343
"Le Temps mort" (Ayme) **41**:19-20
"Temps Perdi" (Rhys) **21**:35, 37-8, 53, 55, 67, 75-7
"Temptation" (Capek) **36**:125
"The Temptation of Jack Orkney" (Lessing) **6**:188
The Temptation of Jack Orkney, and Other Stories (Lessing) **6**:188
The Temptation of Quiet Veronica (Musil)
    See *Die Versuchung der Stillen Veronika*
"The Temptation of St. Anthony" (Barthelme) **2**:37, 54
"The Temptation of St. Ivo" (Gardner) **7**:214, 222, 229-30, 232
The Temptation of the Silent Veronika (Musil)
    See *Die Versuchung der Stillen Veronika*
"The Tempter" (Oates) **6**:227
"Ten Centavos" (Capek) **36**:130
Ten Green Bottles (Thomas) **20**:285, 287-90, 292, 317, 320
"Ten Minutes to Twelve" (Wilson) **21**:324, 363
"The Ten O'Clock People" (King) **17**:294-95
"The Ten Righteous" (Capek) **36**:117, 129
"Ten Years Dead" (Garland) **18**:165
"The Tenant" (Mukherjee) **38**:235, 237-41, 245, 252-55, 261, 267, 271, 273, 275-76, 279-80, 282-84, 286

"Tenants of the Last Tree-House" (Gordimer) **17**:155-56
"The Tender Age" (Collier) **19**:113
"A Tender Man" (Bambara) **35**:11, 13, 27-9
"The Tender Shoot" (Colette)
    See "Le tendron"
Tendres stocks (Morand) **22**:156-59, 161, 164-65, 167-71, 178, 181
"The Tendrils of the Vine" (Colette) **10**:291
"Le tendron" (Colette) **10**:293-94
"Tennessee's Partner" (Harte) **8**:210, 219, 221, 226, 230, 232-33, 236, 244, 255-56, 258-59
"The Tennis Court" (Trevor) **21**:233
"The Tent" (O'Flaherty) **6**:262, 282
The Tent (O'Flaherty) **6**:262-65, 278-79, 283
"Les Tentations" (Baudelaire) **18**:15, 17, 19, 36, 38, 41
"The Tenth Clew" (Hammett) **17**:218, 220, 226
"The Tenth Man" (Aleichem) **33**:25
"The Tents of Kedar" (Kipling) **5**:261
"Teodoro Méndez's Luck" (Castellanos)
    See "La suerte de Teodoro Méndez Acubal"
"Los téologos" (Borges) **41**:40
"Teoría de Dulcinea" (Arreola) **38**:7, 9
"Teoria do medalhão" (Machado de Assis) **24**:128-29, 132
"Tepeyac" (Cisneros) **32**:51
"Teraloyna" (Gordimer) **17**:177, 183, 185, 189-90
"La tercera resignación" (Garcia Marquez) **8**:154-55, 169, 182
Tercets (Pirandello)
    See *Terzetti*
"Teresa" (O'Faolain) **13**:286, 288, 293, 297, 312, 314
"Teresa's Wedding" (Trevor) **21**:247, 270, 277
"Terminal" (Gordimer) **17**:171
"The Terminal Beach" (Ballard) **1**:69, 76, 80
The Terminal Beach, and Other Stories (Ballard) **1**:68-70, 73
"The Termitary" (Gordimer) **17**:181
"Terra d'esilio" (Pavese) **19**:375, 377, 380, 387
"Terra incognita" (Nabokov) **11**:117, 154
"The Terrible Conflagration up at the Place" (Bradbury) **29**:65
"A Terrible Mistake" (Gissing) **37**:74
"The Terrible Old Man" (Lovecraft) **3**:292
"A Terrible Vengeance" (Gogol)
    See "Strašnaja mest"
"Terror" (Anderson) **1**:30
"Terror" (Nabokov) **11**:124-25
"Terror" (Tanizaki) **21**:181
The Terror (Machen) **20**:155, 157, 163, 166, 182-83, 196, 200-01
"The Terror of Blue John Gap" (Doyle) **12**:61, 80
"The Terrorist" (O'Flaherty) **6**:262, 284
"The Terrorists" (Barnes) **3**:19
Terzetti (Pirandello) **22**:231, 275
"El tesoro" (Pardo Bazan) **30**:270
"El tesoro de la juventud" (Cortazar) **7**:95
"The Test" (Garrett) **30**:172
"The Test of Courage" (O'Flaherty) **6**:281
"The Test of Elder Pill" (Garland)
    See "Elder Pill, Preacher"
"La testa contro il muro" (Moravia) **26**:182
"Testament of Flood" (Warren) **4**:389, 394
"Los testigos" (Cortazar) **7**:95
"Testimony of Trees" (Stuart) **31**:261, 264
"HaTe'udah" (Agnon) **30**:34, 38
"Tevye and Seri" (Peretz) **26**:201
"Tevye Goes to Palestine" (Aleichem) **33**:29
Tevye the Dairyman (Aleichem) **33**:7-8, 57
"Texarcana Was a Crazy Town" (Garrett) **30**:166, 180
The Texas Stories of Nelson Algren (Algren) **33**:111-14
"Text in a Notebook" (Cortazar) **7**:69
Textes pour rien (Beckett) **16**:71, 75-7, 110-14, 117-23, 130
Texts for Nothing (Beckett)
    See *Textes pour rien*

"Texturologías" (Cortazar) 7:93
"Texturologies" (Cortazar)
    See "Texturologías"
"Thanasphere" (Vonnegut) 8:428
"Thank You" (Kawabata) 17:252-53
"Thank You for the Lovely Tea" (Gallant)
    5:138, 142
"Thanks for the Ride" (Munro) 3:322, 329, 331,
    336, 343
"Thanksgiving Hunter" (Stuart) 31:266
"Thanksgiving Spirit" (Farrell) 28:89
"That Brute Simmons" (Morrison) 40:329-30,
    337, 366-67
"That Evening Sun" (Faulkner) 1:147, 162, 181,
    183
"That Fellow Tolstoy" (Coppard) 21:8
"That Good May Come" (Wharton) 6:424
"That I Had the Wings" (Ellison) 26:8-9, 12,
    21, 29
"That in Aleppo Once..." (Nabokov) 11:108-09,
    111, 113, 129
*That Old Gang O' Mine: The Early and
    Essential S. J. Perelman* (Perelman)
    32:239-42
"That Pretty Girl in the Army" (Lawson)
    18:217, 220, 241, 243-44
"That Sophistication" (Anderson) 1:50
"That There Dog o' Mine" (Lawson) 18:244
"That Tree" (Porter) 4:327-28, 330, 339-40,
    349
"That's the Way It's Always Been" (Algren)
    33:108
"Thawing Out" (Boyle) 16:146-48, 154
"Theater" (Toomer) 1:441, 443-45, 450, 452,
    458, 460-61
"Theatre of War" (Ballard) 1:79, 82
"The Theatrical Young Gentleman" (Dickens)
    17:122
"Theft" (Porter) 4:327, 329, 337-40, 342, 349,
    360; 31:154
A Theft (Bellow) 14:48-50, 56, 59-61
"Their Losses" (Taylor) 10:391
"Their Pretty Ways" (Gissing) 37:81
"Their Quiet Lives" (Warner) 23:374
"Them Old Moth-Eaten Lovyers" (Murfree)
    22:213
"Theme of the Traitor and the Hero" (Borges)
    See "El Tema del traidor y el héroe"
"The Theme of the Traitor and the Hero"
    (Borges)
    See "El Tema del traidor y el héroe"
"Then It All Came Down" (Capote) 2:81
"The Theologians" (Borges) 4:5-6, 25, 28, 30;
    41:148
"The Theological Student" (Saroyan) 21:155
"There" (Taylor) 10:397
There and Now (Cortazar)
    See *Ahí y ahora*
"There Are More Things" (Borges) 41:120
"There Are No Thieves in This Town" (Garcia
    Marquez) 8:185
"There Are Smiles" (Lardner) 32:135, 138, 140-
    41, 147
"There Is No Hope for That" (Cortazar)
    See "Ya no quedan esperanzas de"
"There She Is—She Is Taking Her Bath"
    (Anderson) 1:50
"There Was a Man Dwelt by a Churchyard"
    (James) 16:249, 251
"There Was an Old Woman" (Bradbury) 29:65,
    68, 86
"There Was Something Shady about the Man"
    (Capek)
    See "Muž, který se nelíbil"
"There Will Come Soft Rains" (Bradbury) 29:51
"There's a Garden of Eden" (Gilchrist) 14:152
"There's No Future in It" (Bates) 10:139
"There's Someone Who Is Laughing"
    (Pirandello)
    See "C'è qualcuno che ride"
There's Something in the Air (Bates) 10:113-15

"Thérése á the Hotel" (Mauriac) 24:184-85,
    196, 202-03, 208
"Thérése and the Doctor" (Mauriac)
    See "Thérése chez le docteur"
"Thérése chez le docteur" (Mauriac) 24:184-85,
    196, 202-03, 206-08
Thérèse Desqueyrous (Mauriac) 24:167-69,
    173, 180-82, 184, 188-95, 199, 201-03,
    206-07
"Thermos Bottles" (Mishima) 4:313-14, 316-
    18, 322
"Thermos Flasks" (Mishima)
    See "Thermos Bottles"
"Thersites" (Capek) 36:116, 129
These Thirteen (Faulkner) 1:180-81, 184
"These Walls Are Cold" (Capote) 2:65
"These Were Palaces" (Fuentes) 24:61-4
Thésée (Gide) 13:43, 48, 52, 54-57, 71, 72, 105-
    110, 112
Thésée (Gide) 13:43, 48, 52, 54-7, 62, 71-2,
    105-10, 112
Theseus (Gide)
    See *Thésée*
"!!!The!!!Teddy!Crazy!!Show!!!" (Ellison)
    14:128
"They" (Kipling) 5:266, 271-72, 275, 279-82,
    284
"They Ain't the Men They Used to Be"
    (Farrell) 28:105
"They Called for More Structure..."
    (Barthelme) 2:50
"They Called Him 'Ally' for Short" (Lawson)
    18:218
"They Came" (Lewis) 40:271-72, 277
They of the High Trails (Garland) 18:164
"They say there's a Boat on the River"
    (Lewis) 40:279
"They Wait on the Wharf in Black" (Lawson)
    18:210, 215, 234
"They Way of a Man" (Grau) 15:158, 165
"They Weren't Going to Die" (Boyle) 5:63
"They're Hiding the Ham on the Pinball King,
    or, Some Came Stumbling" (Algren)
    33:109
"They're Not Your Husband" (Carver) 8:9, 34
"They've Given Us the Land" (Rulfo)
    See "Nos han dado la tierra"
"The Thief" (O'Connor) 5:371
"The Thief" (Tanizaki) 21:181
"The Thief and His Master" (Grimm and
    Grimm) 36:199
"The Thieves" (Grau) 15:147
"Thieves" (O'Faolain) 13:292, 316
"Thieves' Ears" (Bunin)
    See "Petlistye ushi"
"The Thimble" (Lawrence) 4:235, 237
"Thimble, Thimble" (Henry) 5:159, 171
A Thin Ghost and Others (James) 16:238, 251,
    255
"Thin Lips and False Teeth" (Lawson) 18:249
"The Thing" (Moravia) 26:171-73
"A Thing for Nothing" (O'Connor) 5:365
"A Thing is a Thing" (Moravia) 26:159, 165
"A Thing of the Past" (Gordimer) 17:154
"The Thing on the Doorstep" (Lovecraft) 3:259,
    263, 272, 274-75, 283
"Things" (Le Guin) 12:232
"Things" (Lawrence) 4:219
"Things as They Are" (Pritchett) 14:255, 285
The Things That I Know (Hemingway)
    See *Across the River and into the Trees*
"The Things You Keep" (Grau) 15:156
"The Thinker" (Anderson) 1:43-5
"Thinking Makes It So" (Glasgow) 34:65, 67,
    70-2, 77, 80, 100-02
Third Book of Laughable Loves (Kundera)
    24:103
"The Third Circle" (Norris) 28:197, 199-200,
    207, 213
The Third Circle (Norris) 28:199-200, 202, 208
"The Third Cock-Crow" (Bunin) 5:82-3

"The Third Day after Christmas" (Saroyan)
    21:155
"The Third Expedition" (Bradbury)
    See "April 2000: The Third Expedition"
"The Third Ingredient" (Henry) 5:181-82
"The Third Murder" (Lawson) 18:217
"The Third Party" (Trevor) 21:246, 248, 262
"The Third Person" (James) 8:325
"A Third Presence" (Gordimer) 17:158
"The Third Prize" (Coppard) 21:29
"The Third Resignation" (Garcia Marquez)
    See "La tercera resignación"
"The Third Thing that Killed My Father Off"
    (Carver) 8:14
"Thirst" (Andric)
    See "Zedj"
The Thirteen (Balzac)
    See *Histoire des treize*
Thirteen Ghost-stories by Mr. James (James)
    16:223
Thirteen O'Clock: Stories of Several Worlds
    (Benet) 10:142, 154, 158
Thirty Stories (Boyle) 5:56, 63
"The $30,000 Bequest" (Twain) 6:303, 328-30,
    343-45
"Thirty-two Votes before Breakfast" (Stuart)
    31:265
"This Indolence of Mine" (Svevo)
    See "Il mio ozio"
"This International Stuff" (Leacock) 39:267
"This is Home" (Naipaul) 38:331, 334
"This Is the Place" (Stuart) 31:246, 263
"This Is Tibet!" (Boell)
    See "Hier ist Tibten"
"This Madness" (Dreiser)
    See "This Madness—An Honest Novel
    About Love"
"This Madness—An Honest Novel About
    Love" (Dreiser) 30:147-49
"This Morning, This Evening, So Soon"
    (Baldwin) 10:5-7, 9
"This Mortal Coil" (O'Connor) 5:386, 389
"This Son of Mine" (Vonnegut) 8:432, 438
"This Time" (Campbell) 19:75
"This Wait" (Price) 22:384
This Was the Old Chief's Country (Lessing)
    6:186, 196
"Thistledown" (Aiken) 9:12, 14, 30, 42
"The Thorn in the Flesh" (Lawrence) 4:197,
    202
"The Thorny Path of Honor" (Andersen) 6:4,
    34
"Thoroughbred" (Norris) 28:205, 207
"Those Cousins from Sapucaia" (Machado de
    Assis) 24:152
Those Days (Carver) 8:51
"Those Who Don't" (Cisneros) 32:5
"Thou Art the Man" (Poe) 1:406; 35:309
"Thou Shall Not Covet" (Peretz)
    See "Thou Shall Not Covet"
"Though One Rose from the Dead" (Howells)
    36:389, 397
"Thought and the Violin" (Peretz) 26:205
"Thoughts about People" (Dickens) 17:116,
    132, 136
The Thousand and One Nights (Andric) 36:74
"A Thousand Deaths" (London) 4:277
"Thrawn Janet" (Stevenson) 11:268-69, 279,
    281-82, 304-06
"Three" (Capek) 36:92-3, 124
"Three" (Grau) 15:149, 160
Three (Sansom) 21:81, 83-4, 124
"Three Bears Cottage" (Collier) 19:104, 109,
    112
"Three Calls" (Peretz) 26:205
"Three Chapters from a Tale" (Pasternak)
    31:108
"Three Courses and a Dessert: Being a New
    and Gastronomic Version of the Game of
    Consequences" (Forster) 27:90
Three Deaths (Tolstoy)
    See *Tri smerti*

Title Index

"Three Degrees Over" (Aldiss) **36**:28
"Three Dogs of Siena" (Sansom) **21**:86, 90, 95, 97
"The Three Eras of Libbie Marsh" (Gaskell)
    See "Libbie Marsh's Three Eras"
Three Exemplary Novels and a Prologue (Unamuno)
    See *Tres novelas ejemplares y un prólogo*
"Three Fantasies in Minor Key" (Bioy Casares) **17**:95
"Three Fat Women of Antibes" (Maugham) **8**:379
"The Three Feathers" (Grimm and Grimm) **36**:188
"The Three Friends" (de la Mare) **14**:68, 83, 90
"Three Gifts" (Peretz)
    See "Three Gifts"
"The Three Girls" (Pavese) **19**:377, 387
"The Three Golden Apples" (Lee) **33**:307, 310
"The Three Hermits" (Tolstoy) **9**:373-74, 388
"Three Heroines" (Taylor) **10**:408
"Three Hundred Acres of Elbow Room" (Stuart) **31**:244, 251
The Three Impostors (Machen) **20**:156-57, 159, 162-63, 165, 173-74, 176, 186, 190, 196-97, 199, 201, 205-07
"Three Knots in the Net" (Castellanos)
    See "Tres nudos en la red"
"Three Kopeks" (Bulgakov) **18**:89
"Three Lambs" (O'Flaherty) **6**:264, 274
"Three Letters" (Williams) **31**:329
"Three Lindens" (Hesse) **9**:242-43
"The Three Little Men in the Wood" (Grimm and Grimm) **36**:205
"Three Meetings" (Turgenev) **7**:314-15, 324-25, 328, 335
"The Three Million Yen" (Mishima) **4**:313-14, 316-18, 322
"Three Miraculous Soldiers" (Crane) **7**:103, 106
"The Three Notorious Fools" (Arnim)
    See "Die drei Erznarren"
"Three Partners" (Harte) **8**:216, 222, 248
"Three Pictures" (Woolf) **7**:408, 410-12
"Three Portraits" (Turgenev) **7**:313, 318, 320, 323
"Three Portraits and a Prayer" (Pohl) **25**:220
Three Professional Studies (Williams) **31**:329
"Three Questions" (Tolstoy) **9**:388
The Three Righteous Combmakers (Keller)
    See *The Three Righteous Combmakers*
"Three Rounds" (Morrison) **40**:328, 361
"Three Shots" (Hemingway) **40**:250
"Three Sisters" (Agnon) **30**:65-7, 71
"The Three Sisters" (Cisneros) **32**:6, 28-29, 32, 43
"The Three Snake Leaves" (Grimm and Grimm) **36**:228-29
"Three Stories" (Saroyan) **21**:132
Three Stories (Gogol) **29**:142
Three Stories and Ten Poems (Hemingway) **1**:206
"The Three Strangers" (Hardy) **2**:202-03, 205, 208, 212-15, 218, 220, 223, 226-27
Three Tales (Flaubert)
    See *Trois contes: Un coeur simple; La légende de Saint-Julien l'hospitalier; Hérodias*
Three Tales (Mauriac)
    See *Trois Récits*
"Three Thousand Years among the Microbes" (Twain) **6**:333, 336, 338, 350-53; **26**:325, 330, 333, 358-64
Three Times Three (Saroyan) **21**:141, 143, 146, 153, 158-60, 163, 168
"Three Tools" (Chesterton) **1**:136
Three Uneasy Pieces (White) **39**:347-48
"Three Vagabonds of Trinidad" (Harte) **8**:245, 251
"Three Without, Doubled" (Lardner) **32**:145, 148
Three Women (Musil)
    See *Drei Frauen*

"Three Women and Two Men" (Thomas) **20**:317
"Three Years" (Chekhov) **2**:131, 155-57; **28**:59
"The Three-Day Blow" (Hemingway) **1**:208, 219, 244; **36**:291, 310; **40**:185, 209, 219-22, 229-30, 233
"The Threefold Destiny" (Hawthorne) **3**:160, 177-78, 182-83, 189
"Throat of a Black Cat" (Cortazar)
    See "Cuello de gatito negro"
"Through the Gates of the Silver Key" (Lovecraft) **3**:262, 267, 272-73, 286, 294
"Through the Looking Glass" (Oates) **6**:228
"Through the Panama" (Lowry) **31**:40-1, 43-5, 47-50, 52-5, 59-63, 71-5, 82, 84, 86-7
"Through the Quinquina Glass" (Sansom) **21**:87, 92
"Through the Streets of My Own Labyrinth" (Nin) **10**:303
"Through the Veil" (Doyle) **12**:80
"Through the Walls" (Levi) **12**:277
"The Thrower-Away" (Boell)
    See "Der Wegwerfer"
"Thrown Away" (Kipling) **5**:261
"Thumbelina" (Andersen) **6**:27-8, 36
"Thumbling" (Andersen)
    See "Poor Thumbling"
"Thumbling's Travels" (Grimm and Grimm) **36**:199, 223, 229-30
"Thundermug" (Algren) **33**:111, 113
The Thurber Carnival (Thurber) **1**:416, 426
"Thus I Refute Beelzy" (Collier) **19**:98, 101, 103, 105, 107
"Le Thyrse" (Baudelaire) **18**:59, 63
"The Thyrsus" (Baudelaire)
    See "Le Thyrse"
Ti con zero (Calvino) **3**:92, 94-6, 98-9, 107, 117
"Ti Démon" (Chopin) **8**:100
"Ti Frére" (Chopin) **8**:72
La tía Tula (Unamuno) **11**:313-14, 317, 324-25, 327, 330, 335, 344-45, 347-48
"The Tick of the Clock" (Greene) **29**:218
"A Ticket on Skoronski" (Algren) **33**:96, 108
"Tickets, Please" (Lawrence) **4**:222-23, 226, 228, 231, 233-35, 242-46
"The Tide" (O'Flaherty) **6**:262, 279, 285
"Tide Pools" (Adams) **24**:17-18
"A Tidewater Morning" (Styron) **25**:312-13, 317-18
"The Tie" (Kipling) **5**:278
"La tierra que nos han dado" (Rulfo)
    See "Nos han dado la tierra"
"The Tiger" (Saroyan) **21**:143-44, 163
"Tiger, Tiger" (Frame) **29**:105, 106
"Tigers Are Better-Looking" (Rhys) **21**:57, 69
Tigers Are Better-Looking (Rhys) **21**:33, 39, 41, 48, 57, 60-1, 63-7, 69-71
"The Tiger's Bride" (Carter) **13**:6, 9, 23, 25, 27, 30-32
"The Tiger's Claw" (Narayan) **25**:139
The Tiger's Daughter (Mukherjee) **38**:243
"A Tight Boat" (Chesnutt) **7**:13
"Till September Petronella" (Rhys) **21**:39, 41-3, 48-9, 54, 60, 65, 67, 70
"The Tillotson Banquet" (Huxley) **39**:155, 168, 171, 174-75, 177
"Tim" (Stuart) **31**:239-40
"Timber" (Galsworthy) **22**:67, 101
"Timbuktu" (Thomas) **20**:290, 294-95, 298, 318
"Time" (Capek)
    See "Čas"
"Time" (Pavese) **19**:375
"Time and Ebb" (Nabokov) **11**:108, 127, 130
"Time and Place" (Sansom) **21**:89, 91, 95
Time and the Hunter (Calvino)
    See *Ti con zero*
"The Time Capsule" (Gilchrist) **14**:161-62
"Time Checkmated" (Levi) **12**:280
"Time Did" (Gordimer) **17**:164, 193
The Time Element, and Other Stories (O'Hara) **15**:286
"Time Expired" (Bates) **10**:117

"Time, Gentlemen!" (Calisher) **15**:8, 15-17, 19
"Time Gents, Please" (Sansom) **21**:108, 110-11, 126
"The Time Handsome Brown Ran Away" (Caldwell) **19**:48, 51-2
"The Time Ma Spent the Day at Aunt Bessie's" (Caldwell) **19**:51
"Time of Bitter Children" (Garrett) **30**:173
"The Time of Death" (Munro) **3**:329-30
"The Time of Friendship" (Bowles) **3**:63-7, 81-2
The Time of Friendship (Bowles) **3**:63-5, 70, 79-81, 84
"The Time of Their Lives" (O'Faolain) **13**:320
"The Time of Year" (Trevor) **21**:247
"Time Stands Still" (Capek) **36**:92
"Time the Tiger" (Lewis) **34**:157
"The Time the Wolves Ate the Vice-Principal" (Steinbeck) **11**:248
"Time to Go" (Dixon) **16**:207-08, 212
Time to Go (Dixon) **16**:206-08, 212-15
"Times" (Beattie) **11**:29
The Times Are Never So Bad: A Novella and Eight Short Stories (Dubus) **15**:76, 81, 83, 88, 97
"Time's Arrow" (Clarke) **3**:133-34, 142
"Timothy's Narrow Squeak" (Galsworthy) **22**:71
"A Tin Can" (O'Flaherty) **6**:276
"Tin Soldier" (Vinge) **24**:340-41, 351
"Tin Tan Tann" (Cisneros) **32**:35, 38
"The Tinder-Box" (Andersen) **6**:4, 18, 23, 26-7, 30-2, 36-7
"The Tinkerer" (Coover) **15**:47
"The Tins" (Cowan) **28**:77; 80
The Tins and Other Stories (Cowan) **28**:77-78
"Le tir et le cimetière" (Baudelaire) **18**:3, 18, 35
"Tired Courtesan" (Moravia)
    See "Tired Courtesan"
"Tišina" (Bunin) **5**:98
"Titanium" (Levi) **12**:264, 268
"Titbull's Alms-houses" (Dickens) **17**:123
"Tite Poulette" (Cable) **4**:52, 62, 67-8, 76-7
"The Tithe of the Lord" (Dreiser) **30**:157-59
"Title" (Barth) **10**:42-3, 46-8, 54-5, 61, 63-4, 73-4, 76, 79-81, 85-8, 91, 97-100
"HaTizmoret" (Agnon) **30**:38
"Tlactocatzine del jardin de Flandes" (Fuentes)
    See "In a Flemish Garden"
"Tlactocatzine in the Garden of Flanders" (Fuentes)
    See "In a Flemish Garden"
"Tlactocatzine, of the Flemish Garden" (Fuentes)
    See "In a Flemish Garden"
"Tlön, Uqbar, Orbis Tertius" (Borges) **4**:6-7, 10-12, 15, 18, 25, 29, 33, 35, 43; **41**:55, 62-64, 79, 83-86, 138, 144-47, 158
"To a Person Sitting in Darkness" (Twain) **26**:354
"To Be Read at Dusk" (Dickens) **17**:124
"To Bell the Cat" (Vinge) **24**:341
"To Bow Bridge" (Morrison) **40**:338, 368
"To Build a Fire" (1902London) **4**:272-74
"To Build a Fire" (1908London) **4**:265, 267, 272-76, 278, 280-82, 289-93
"To Come So Far" (Warner) **23**:369
"To Cool the Air" (Warner) **23**:369
"To Da-duh, In Memoriam" (Marshall) **3**:301, 303, 307, 313-15, 317
"To Father's House" (Agnon) **30**:4
"To Hell with Dying" (Walker) **5**:403, 406, 419, 422
"To Market, to Market" (Stuart) **31**:265
"To Nature and Back Again" (Leacock) **39**:264
"To Room Nineteen" (Lessing) **6**:198, 201-02, 208, 214, 218, 220
"To See You Again" (Adams) **24**:19, 23, 25
To See You Again (Adams) **24**:9-11, 15
"To Set Our House in Order" (Laurence) **7**:252, 262, 264-65, 269

"To Sleep, Perchance to Steam" (Perelman) **32**:204, 222, 231

"To the Chicago Abyss" (Bradbury) **29**:46

"To the Doctor" (Agnon)
See "El haRofe"

"To the Man on Trail" (London) **4**:250, 267, 277, 279

"To the Rescue!" (Sansom) **21**:92

"To the Sea Serpent" (Fuentes)
See "A la Víbora de la mar"

"To the Snake of the Sea" (Fuentes)
See "A la Víbora de la mar"

"To the Unknown God" (Moravia) **26**:173

"To Thy Chamber Window, Sweet" (Gordon) **15**:106, 120, 129

"To Whom It May Concern" (Farrell) **28**:96

"To Yearn Is Subhuman, to Forestall Divine" (Perelman) **32**:235-36

"Tobermory" (Saki) **12**:287, 302, 304, 312, 333

"Tobias Mindernickel" (Mann) **5**:322, 334, 336

"Tobold" (Walser) **20**:353

"Tocayos" (Donoso) **34**:21, 25, 29-30, 35-36, 41-42, 49

"Toc...toc...toc" (Turgenev)
See "Stuk...stuk...stuk"

Der Tod des Dichters (Tieck) **31**:289-90

Der Tod in Venedig (Mann) **5**:307, 309-11, 313-14, 319, 322-27, 331, 338-40, 342-45, 348, 355-56

"Today Is Friday" (Hemingway) **1**:228-29

"Todos los fuegos el fuego" (Cortazar) **7**:61, 69

Todos los fuegos el fuego (Cortazar) **7**:52-4, 60, 62, 64

"Together and Apart" (Woolf) **7**:376, 381, 388

"Tóir Mhic Uí Dhíomasuigh" (Moore) **19**:307, 319-26, 328-32, 334, 341

"La toison d'or" (Gautier) **20**:8, 14-15

"Tōkyō Hakkei" (Dazai Osamu) **41**:247 50, 256 59

"Told by the Schoolmaster" (Galsworthy) **22**:73

Told by Uncle Remus: New Stories of the Old Plantation (Harris) **19**:149, 164, 187, 191, 197

"Told in the Drooling Ward" (London) **4**:255-56, 266

"Told in the Tavern" (Jewett) **6**:159

"Der Tolle Invalide auf dem Fort Ratonneau" (Arnim) **29**:2-6, 30-5

"The Toll-Gatherer's Day" (Hawthorne) **3**:158

"Tom Carroll" (Farrell) **28**:114, 125-6

"Tom Rivers" (Gordon) **15**:106-07

"The Tomb of His Ancestors" (Kipling) **5**:266

"The Tomb of Pletone" (Forster) **27**:115, 117

"Les tombales" (Maupassant) **1**:263

"The Tomb-Herd" (Campbell) **19**:66, 89

The Tomb-Herd and Others (Campbell) **19**:87

"The Tombling Day" (Bradbury) **29**:65

"Tomelen'je duxa" (Leskov) **34**:108, 111

"Tommelise" (Andersen)
See "Thumbelina"

"The Tommy Crans" (Bowen) **3**:33, 41

Tommy Gallagher's Crusade (Farrell) **28**:93-4, 96-7, 120, 126

"Tommy, the Unsentimental" (Cather) **2**:100, 105

"Tomoda to Matsunaga no hanashi" (Tanizaki) **21**:194

"Tomorrow" (Conrad) **9**:143

"Tomorrow" (Faulkner) **1**:165, 179, 181

"Tomorrow" (Lu Hsun)
See "Mingtian"

"Tomorrow and Tomorrow" (Farrell) **28**:114, 116

"Tomorrow and Tomorrow and So Forth" (Updike) **13**:352

"Tomorrow and Tomorrow and Tomorrow" (Vonnegut) **8**:425, 429-31

Tomorrow Times Seven (Pohl) **25**:232

"Tomorrow's Child" (Bradbury) **29**:49, 65

"The Tomorrow-Tamer" (Laurence) **7**:249, 261

The Tomorrow-Tamer (Laurence) **7**:245-50, 260-61, 272

"Tom's Warm Welcome" (Chesnutt) **7**:14

"Tonelli's Marriage" (Howells) **36**:396-97

"The Tongue-Cut Sparrow" (Dazai Osamu) **41**:238

Tonio Kröger (Mann) **5**:307, 310-11, 316, 318, 324, 331, 342-44, 355

Tonka (Musil) **18**:292-97, 305, 313-17, 322-25

"Tony" (Capek) **36**:130

"Tony Kytes, the Arch Deceiver" (Hardy) **2**:206-07

"Tony's Story" (Silko) **37**:295, 308-9

"Too Bad" (Parker) **2**:274, 280, 285

"Too Dearly Bought" (Gissing) **37**:70

"Too Early Spring" (Benet) **10**:144

Too Far to Go: The Maples Stories (Updike) **13**:373, 383, 387-88

"Too Much Tolerance" (Waugh) **41**:339

"Too Rich" (Moravia) **26**:142, 155

"Too Young" (O'Hara) **15**:248, 265, 270

"The Tooth" (Jackson) **9**:249, 258-60, 266; **39**:210, 211, 212, 224, 227, 229, 231

"A Tooth for Paul Revere" (Benet) **10**:143, 154, 159

"The Top and the Ball" (Andersen) **6**:18, 32

"Topham's Chance" (Gissing) **37**:51-2, 80

"Topos" (Arreola) **38**:4, 7, 11

"Toppan" (Norris) **28**:207

"Torch Song" (Cheever) **1**:89, 99, 106, 109-10; **38**:53, 84

"Torito" (Cortazar) **7**:54, 88-9

"The Torn Lace" (Pardo Bazan) **30**:290

"Torpid Smoke" (Nabokov) **11**:117, 154-6

"The Torque" (Forster) **27**:90, 96, 105, 107, 117

"A Torrent Dammed" (O'Connor) **5**:387

The Torrents of Spring (Turgenev)
See *Veshnie vody*

"Torridge" (Trevor) **21**:262

"The Torture" (Andric)
See "Zlostavljanje"

"La torture par l'espérance" (Villiers de l'Isle Adam) **14**:378, 398

"Total Environment" (Aldiss) **36**:20

"Total Loss" (Warner) **23**:373

"Der toten schweigen" (Schnitzler) **15**:345, 376

"Totentanz" (Wilson) **21**:319, 322, 332-33, 337-39, 346-47, 355-57

"The Touch" (O'Flaherty) **6**:265, 285

"A Touch of Autumn in the Air" (O'Faolain) **13**:289, 293-95, 314, 320

The Touch of Nutmeg (Collier) **19**:103, 105, 115

"The Touch of Nutmeg Makes It" (Collier) **19**:103, 109, 113

"A Touch of Realism" (Saki) **12**:294, 306

A Touch of the Sun (Sansom) **21**:84

"Touched with Fire" (Bradbury) **29**:67, 88

"A Touching Story of George Washington's Boyhood" (Twain) **34**:343

The Touchstone (Wharton) **6**:413

"A Tough Tussle" (Bierce) **9**:49, 67

"A Tour of the Forest" (Turgenev) **7**:320, 337-38

A Tour on the Prairies (Irving) **2**:244

"The Tourist City in the South" (Hesse) **9**:244

"Tourmaline" (Stifter) **28**:284, 286-88, 290

"The Tout of Yarmouth Bridge" (Gissing) **37**:55

Le toutounier (Colette) **10**:263

"Toward Evening" (Updike) **13**:355

"Towel with a Rooster" (Bulgakov) **18**:86

"Tower from Yuggoth" (Campbell) **19**:72, 89

"Town and Country Lovers" (Gordimer) **17**:164-65, 193-94

"Town Crier Exclusive, Confessions of a Princess Manque: How Royals Found Me Unsuitable to Marry Their Larry" (Elkin) **12**:119-20

"The Town of the Little People" (Aleichem)
See "Di shtot fun di kleyne mentshelek"

"The Town Philosopher's Banquet" (Moorhouse) **40**:298, 311

"The Town Poor" (Jewett) **6**:151

"Townies" (Dubus) **15**:77, 79-81, 88, 96

"Townsend" (Dreiser) **30**:149

"The Toys of Peace" (Saki) **12**:285

The Toys of Peace, and Other Papers (Saki) **12**:285, 289, 322, 328-29

"Traceleen Turns East" (Gilchrist) **14**:162-63

"Track 12" (Ballard) **1**:68

"A Tractate Middoth" (James) **16**:232, 234, 240, 245, 252, 255, 257

"The Tractor" (Cowan) **28**:75; 79-80; 82

"The Tradesman's Return" (Hemingway) **25**:113

"A Tradition of 1804" (Hardy) **2**:215, 220-21

Traffics and Discoveries (Kipling) **5**:266, 272, 283

"A Tragedy" (Lavin) **4**:165, 176, 183

"The Tragedy at Three Corners" (Dunbar)
See "The Tragedy at Three Forks"

"The Tragedy at Three Forks" (Dunbar) **8**:121-22, 125, 136

"Tragedy in a Greek Theatre" (Pritchett) **14**:268-69, 273

"A Tragedy of Error" (James) **8**:302

"A Tragedy of Two Ambitions" (Hardy) **2**:205-06, 214-17, 223

"Tragic" (Hesse) **9**:232, 236

"The Trail of the Green Blazer" (Narayan) **25**:135, 140, 153

"The Train" (Carver) **8**:25-6, 34

"The Train and the City" (Wolfe) **33**:346, 348, 366, 375, 380, 401

"Train from Rhodesia" (Gordimer) **17**:167, 173, 186

"The Train Station" (Coover) **15**:48

"The Train Was on Time" (Boell)
See "Der Zug war pünktlich"

"The Train Whistled" (Pirandello)
See "Il treno ha fischiato"

"Training" (Atwood) **2**:3-4, 7-8, 10, 12-13, 16

"The Trains" (Saroyan) **21**:161

"Le traitement du docteur Tristan" (Villiers de l'Isle Adam) **14**:381-82

"The Traitor" (Maugham) **8**:368, 377

"Traitorously" (Svevo)
See "Proditoriamente"

"Traitors" (Lessing) **6**:217

"Traktat o manekinach" (Schulz) **13**:328-30, 333, 335, 338

"Tralala" (Selby) **20**:253-54, 256, 259, 261-63, 265-69, 272, 277, 279

La trama celeste (Bioy Casares) **17**:54, 59, 61, 75, 85, 87

"The Tramp" (O'Flaherty) **6**:275, 285

"La trampa" (Arreola) **38**:25

"The Tramp's Tale" (Capek) **36**:108

"La transaction" (Balzac) **5**:24

"Transaction" (O'Hara) **15**:257-58

"Transcendent Horror" (Ligotti) **16**:287

"The Transformation of Martin Burney" (Henry) **5**:197

"The Transformation of Vincent Scoville" (Oates) **6**:230

"Transience" (Clarke) **3**:127, 135, 142

"Transients in Arcadia" (Henry) **5**:158, 189

"Transit Bed" (Calvino) **3**:112

"Transit of Earth" (Clarke) **3**:147

"A Transit of Venus" (Leacock) **39**:265

"Transmigrations of a Melody" (Peretz) **26**:202

The Transposed Heads (Mann)
See *Die vertauschten Köpfe*

"The Trap" (Pirandello)
See "La trappola"

Trapné providky (Capek) **36**:81-3, 92-3, 96-7, 124-26

"Trapped" (O'Flaherty) **6**:273, 276, 279, 283

"La trappola" (Pirandello) **22**:275

"Trash" (Thomas) **20**:324, 326

"Trastevere" (Lavin) **4**:183, 185

"Il tratto di Apelle" (Pasternak) **31**:98, 104-06, 108, 110, 116-18

Traumnovelle (Schnitzler) **15**:344, 353-54, 366, 372, 374

"Travel Notes" (Bulgakov) **18**:90
"A Travel Piece" (Atwood) **2**:3-4, 6-7, 10, 12, 15-16
"The Traveler" (Stegner) **27**:205, 219-20, 223, 225
"Traveling Together" (Adams) **24**:16
"Traveller" (Gilchrist) **14**:150-51
"Traveller, If You Come to the Spa" (Boell)
   See "Wanderer, kommst du nach Spa..."
"Traveller, If You Go to Spa" (Boell)
   See "Wanderer, kommst du nach Spa..."
Traveller's Samples (O'Connor) **5**:371
"Travelling Abroad" (Dickens) **17**:123
"Travelling along the Oka" (Solzhenitsyn)
   See "Puteshestvuia vdol' Oki"
"The Travelling Companion" (Andersen) **6**:18-19, 30-1, 35
"Travelling Companions" (James) **32**:106
"The Travelling Entertainer" (Jolley) **19**:220, 230, 243
The Travelling Entertainer (Jolley) **19**:220-21, 233
"Travelogue" (Lardner) **32**:135, 140, 146, 149, 167
"La Traversée de Paris" (Ayme) **41**:30-35
"Travis Hallett's Half-Back" (Norris) **28**:205
"Treacherously" (Svevo)
   See "Proditoriamente"
"Treason" (Babel) **16**:27-8, 51
"Treasure" (Frame) **29**:104
"The Treasure" (Maugham) **8**:380
"Treasure of Abbot Thomas" (James) **16**:225, 228-29, 232-34, 236, 244, 251-53, 255-57
"The Treasure of Franchard" (Stevenson) **11**:268-69, 281, 284
"The Treasure of Youth" (Cortazar)
   See "El tesoro de la juventud"
"The Treasure Ship" (Saki) **12**:295, 308, 312
Treat 'Em Rough: Letters from Jack the Kaiser Killer (Lardner) **32**:144
"A Treatise on Housing" (Bulgakov) **18**:92
"Treatise on Tailors' Dummies" (Schulz)
   See "Traktat o manekinach"
"The Tree" (de la Mare) **14**:66, 85-6
"The Tree" (Thomas) **3**:399, 402, 408-09
"A Tree. A Rock. A Cloud." (McCullers) **9**:322-23, 327, 329-30, 332, 341, 345-46, 353-54; **24**:232
"The Tree Fort" (Gilchrist) **14**:161-62
"Tree Frogs" (Shiga) **23**:346
"The Tree of Justice" (Kipling) **5**:292
"The Tree of Knowledge" (James) **8**:301
"The Tree of Life" (Kawabata)
   See "Inochi no Ki"
"The Tree of Life" (Machen) **20**:178
"A Tree of Night" (Capote) **2**:61-3, 66, 69, 72-5
A Tree of Night, and Other Stories (Capote) **2**:61-4, 72, 74, 83
"The Trees of Pride" (Chesterton) **1**:122
"La tregua" (Castellanos) **39**:48, 57, 66, 67, 70
The Trembling of a Leaf (Maugham) **8**:370-72
"Il treno ha fischiato" (Pirandello) **22**:255, 270
"Trenzas" (Bombal) **37**:38
Tres novelas ejemplares y un prólogo (Unamuno) **11**:313, 317, 323, 331, 345, 348
Tres novelitas burguesas (Donoso) **34**:8, 12-13, 17, 32, 34
"Tres nudos en la red" (Castellanos) **39**:74
"Três tesouros perdidos" (Machado de Assis) **24**:128, 151
Tri smerti (Tolstoy) **9**:382-83, 389-90
"Trial by Combat" (Jackson) **9**:250; **39**:211, 215, 219, 224, 227
"The Trial of Pan" (Greene) **29**:221
"The Trial of the Old Watchdog" (Thurber) **1**:426
"The Trial Sermon on Bull-Skin" (Dunbar) **8**:118, 121, 127, 136
"The Tribe" (Svevo)
   See "La tribù"
"La tribù" (Svevo) **25**:357-58

Tribulat Bonhomet (Villiers de l'Isle Adam) **14**:378-79
"The Tribunal" (Capek) **36**:82, 93, 124-25
"Tribuneaux rustiques" (Maupassant) **1**:259, 286
"The Trick" (Campbell) **19**:76, 78
"Trick of Nature" (Bulgakov) **18**:90
"Trigo errante" (Fuentes) **24**:31, 37-8, 43
"A Trillion Feet of Gas" (Updike) **13**:355
"The Trimmed Lamp" (Henry) **5**:171, 185, 198
The Trimmed Lamp (Henry) **5**:155, 192
"The Trinket Box" (Lessing) **6**:196-97, 212-20
"Trio" (Rhys) **21**:61, 70
"Trio em lá menor" (Machado de Assis) **24**:128
"The Trip" (O'Hara) **15**:252, 261, 280-81
"A Trip to Chancellorsville" (Fitzgerald) **6**:47
"A Trip to the Head" (Le Guin) **12**:232-33
Trip to the Orient (Nerval)
   See *Voyage en Orient*
"The Triplets" (Auchincloss) **22**:45
Tristan (Mann) **5**:307-11, 321, 323-24
"The Triumph of Night" (Wharton) **6**:418, 428, 431-32
"The Triumph of the Egg" (Anderson) **1**:20, 23, 27, 30, 34, 37-8, 40, 47, 52, 54-5
"The Triumphs of a Taxidermist" (Wells) **6**:380, 384, 388
Trois contes: Un coeur simple; La légende de Saint-Julien l'hospitalier; Hérodias (Flaubert) **11**:37, 52-3, 56-7, 62-6, 70-1, 76-84, 87, 96-9, 101
"Les trois filles de Milton" (Villiers de l'Isle Adam)
   See "Les filles de Milton"
Trois Récits (Mauriac) **24**:183, 196, 203-05
The Troll Garden (Cather) **2**:90, 93, 96, 103, 113
"Trop de faveur tue" (Stendhal) **27**:249, 263
"Trotsky's Garden" (Michaels) **16**:307, 309
"The Trouble" (Powers) **4**:368-69, 372
"The Trouble about Sophiny" (Dunbar) **8**:122
"Trouble in Wilton Road Victoria" (Sansom) **21**:105, 108
"Trouble Is My Business" (Chandler) **23**:65-6, 72, 89, 110
"The Trouble of Marcie Flint" (Cheever) **1**:90; **38**:53, 55, 85, 87-8
"Trouble on Lost Mountain" (Harris) **19**:124, 131, 179, 181
"The Trouble with Stamps" (Bulgakov) **18**:89
"Trouble with the Angels" (Hughes) **6**:112, 118-19, 122, 131
"Trouble with the Natives" (Clarke) **3**:124, 149
The Trouble with Tigers (Saroyan) **21**:142-46, 153, 158, 163
"Troubled Sleep" (Price) **22**:387-88
"The Troubles of Dr. Thoss" (Ligotti) **16**:261, 263, 271, 274, 278, 283, 289
"The Troublesome Grandfathers" (Zoshchenko) **15**:388
"Troubling of the Water" (Henderson) **29**:326, 328
"The Trousers" (Dunbar) **8**:122
"The Trout" (O'Faolain) **13**:297
"The Truant" (Irving) **2**:265
"Trucks" (King) **17**:261-62
The True Story of Ah Q (Lu Hsun)
   See "Ah Q zheng zhuan"
"The True Story of Lavinia Todd" (Auchincloss) **22**:5, 38
"True Thomas" (Benet) **10**:148
"The Trumpet" (de la Mare) **14**:88-90, 93
"The Trumpet Shall Sound" (Warner) **23**:369
"Trumpeter" (Gardner) **7**:225-26, 233, 235
"Trup" (Andric) **36**:33
"Trust" (London) **4**:265
Trust Me (Updike) **13**:401-02, 409
"The Trustfulness of Polly" (Dunbar) **8**:122, 128, 147
"Trut" (Andric) **36**:38
"The Truth" (Pirandello) **22**:252-53

"The Truth About Pyecraft" (Wells) **6**:360, 392, 404
"Truth and Lies" (Price) **22**:370, 386
"Truth or Consequences" (Adams) **24**:11
"Try the Girl" (Chandler) **23**:59, 65, 67-8, 72, 80, 82, 87, 96, 98-9, 107-10
"The Tryst" (Oates) **6**:251-52
"The Tryst" (Turgenev) **7**:342-43
"A Tryst at an Ancient Earthwork" (Hardy) **2**:210, 214-15
"The Tsalal" (Ligotti) **16**:292, 295, 297
"Le tsar noir" (Morand) **22**:169, 174
"Ts'u-chih" (P'u Sung-ling) **31**:191, 198
"Tu más profunda piel" (Cortazar) **7**:95
"Tubal-Cain Forges A Star" (Garcia Marquez)
   See "Tubal-Caín forja una estrella"
"Tubal-Caín forja una estrella" (Garcia Marquez) **8**:154, 156
"Tudor Witch" (Lewis) **40**:280
"The Tuesday Afternoon Siesta" (Garcia Marquez)
   See "Tuesday Siesta"
"Tuesday Night" (Beattie) **11**:14, 16
"Tuesday Siesta" (Garcia Marquez) **8**:183, 185
"Le tueur de cygnes" (Villiers de l'Isle Adam) **14**:397
"The Tugging" (Campbell) **19**:66, 73, 90
"The Tuggses at Ramsgate" (Dickens) **17**:117, 138
"Tulip" (Hammett) **17**:201, 203, 206, 227, 229
"Tuman" (Bunin) **5**:98
Una tumba sin nombre (Onetti)
   See *Para una tumba sin nombre*
"Tung shêng" (P'u Sung-ling) **31**:204
"The Tunnel Under the World" (Pohl) **25**:213, 220, 222, 224-27, 229-32, 234, 237
"Tupejnyi xudožnik" (Leskov) **34**:110-11
A Tupolev Too Far (Aldiss) **36**:27
An T-úr-Ghort (Moore) **19**:300, 303-10, 312, 314, 316-25, 328-39, 341, 344-47, 352
"A Turkey Hunt" (Chopin) **8**:88
"The Turkey Season" (Munro) **3**:346
"The Turkish Bath" (Trollope) **28**:321, 335, 340, 348
"The Turkish Night" (Morand)
   See "La nuit Turque"
"Turmalin" (Stifter)
   See "Tourmaline"
Turn Left at Thursday (Pohl) **25**:232
"The Turn of the Screw" (Oates) **6**:225
The Turn of the Screw (James) **8**:271-76, 283, 291-96, 298, 316, 318, 320, 325-26
"Turn the Page" (Henderson) **29**:316
"Turned" (Gilman) **13**:126, 141
"The Turtles of Tasman" (London) **4**:255-56, 266
Tuscan Fairy Tales (Lee) **33**:307, 310
"The Tutor's Tale" (Waugh) **41**:327
"Tutti Frutti" (Sansom) **21**:87, 105
"Tutto in un punto" (Calvino) **3**:92
"The Twelve Brothers" (Grimm and Grimm) **36**:225-26
Twelve Men (Dreiser) **30**:110-11, 122, 133-34, 147-51
"The Twelve Months" (Grimm and Grimm) **36**:237
"The Twelve Mortal Men" (McCullers) **9**:322, 338
"Twelve O'Clock" (Crane) **7**:108
Twelve Stories and a Dream (Wells) **6**:366-67, 380, 391, 400
"Twenty-Five Bucks" (Farrell) **28**:87
Twenty-Five Short Stories by Stephen Vincent Benét (Benet) **10**:143, 156
"Twenty-Four Hours in a Strange Diocese" (Powers) **4**:380
"Twenty-Nine Inventions" (Oates) **6**:225
Twenty-one Stories (Agnon) **30**:3-4, 21
Twenty-One Stories (Greene) **29**:186, 213-14
"Twenty-Six and One" (Gorky)
   See "Dvadtsat' shest' i odna"

"Twenty-Six Men and a Girl" (Gorky)
　　See "Dvadtsat' shest' i odna"
Twice-Told Tales (Hawthorne) **3**:154-55, 157-61, 180, 184-85, 190; **39**:126
"Twin Beds in Rome" (Updike) **13**:386
"The Twinkle in His Eye" (O'Hara) **15**:287, 291
"The Twins" (Spark) **10**:350, 352, 354, 356, 366
"The Twitching Colonel" (White) **39**:284, 293, 333-35
Twixt Land and Sea: Tales (Conrad) **9**:141, 148
"Two" (Singer) **3**:381
Two Adolescents (Moravia) **26**:132-34, 136, 140-41, 156
"Two Augurs" (Villiers de l'Isle Adam)
　　See "Deux augures"
"Two Blue Birds" (Lawrence) **4**:220
"Two Boys at Grinder Brothers" (Lawson) **18**:202
"The Two Brothers" (Hesse) **9**:241-43
"The Two Brothers" (Pritchett) **14**:280, 285-86, 298, 305
"The Two Captains" (Lewis) **34**:163, 165
"Two Colonials" (Calisher) **15**:4, 14
"Two Corpses Go Dancing" (Singer) **3**:370
"Two Days Wasted in Kansas City" (Saroyan) **21**:134
"Two Doctors" (James) **16**:245, 256
"Two Dogs and a Fence" (Lawson) **18**:233, 244
"The Two Drovers" (Scott) **32**:287, 292-93, 297-305, 310-12, 314-22, 324, 326
"The Two Elenas" (Fuentes)
　　See "Las dos Elenas"
"Two Families" (Lish) **18**:268
"The Two Flags" (Levi) **12**:276
Two Forsyte Interludes (Galsworthy) **22**:97
"Two Friends" (Cather) **2**:100, 109, 115, 117-18
Two Friends (Turgenev) **7**:327
"Two Gallants" (Joyce) **3**:200-01, 205-06, 209, 214, 220-21, 225, 231-34, 237, 246; **26**:39, 46-7, 50
"The Two Generals" (Trollope) **28**:319, 323, 326, 341, 346, 348
"Two Gentle People" (Greene) **29**:202, 212
"The Two Heroines of Plumplington" (Trollope) **28**:314-15, 321, 325, 327, 339, 342-43, 348, 355-57
Two Hussars (Tolstoy) **9**:376, 389
"Two in the Bush" (Thomas) **20**:290, 292, 294, 319
"Two in the Bush, and Other Stories" (Thomas) **20**:289, 290
"Two Ivans" (Babel) **16**:50, 56, 58
"The Two Ivans" (Gogol)
　　See "The Tale of How Ivan Ivanovich Quarrelled with Ivan Nikiforovich"
"The Two Kings and Their Two Labyrinths" (Borges) **4**:28, 30-1, 35
"Two Ladies in Retirement" (Taylor) **10**:379-80, 382, 384, 392, 418
"Two Little Confederates" (Page) **23**:295
Two Little Confederates (Page) **23**:285, 291-92, 308, 319
Two Lives: Reading Turgenev; My House in Umbria (Trevor) **21**:258-59, 261, 263, 265
"Two Looks" (Galsworthy) **22**:63, 101
"Two Lovely Beasts" (O'Flaherty) **6**:269-70, 274, 281-82, 285
Two Lovely Beasts, and Other Stories (O'Flaherty) **6**:262-63, 265, 276, 278, 281-83, 285
The Two Magics (James) **8**:296
"The Two Maidens" (Cervantes)
　　See "Las dos doncellas"
"Two Markets" (Singer) **3**:377
"The Two Masks" (Pirandello)
　　See "Le due maschere"
"Two Meditations" (Barth) **10**:42, 54-5, 75, 89-90, 98, 100
Two Memorable Fantasies (Bioy Casares) **17**:48

"Two Men Running" (Jolley) **19**:223, 236-37, 244
"Two More Gallants" (Trevor) **21**:246-47
Two Mothers (Unamuno)
　　See *Dos madres*
"The Two Numantias" (Fuentes) **24**:79
"Two of a Trade" (Morrison) **40**:365
"Two Old Lovers" (Freeman) **1**:197, 200-01
"Two Old Men" (Tolstoy) **9**:377, 387
"Two Old-Timers" (Fitzgerald) **6**:71
"Two or Three Graces" (Huxley) **39**:158, 173-74
Two or Three Graces (Huxley) **39**:157, 171
"Two Portraits" (Chopin) **8**:72, 87, 98, 110
"Two Potters" (Lessing) **6**:200
"Two Rivers" (Stegner) **27**:196-97, 199
"Two Scholars Who Lived in Our Town" (Agnon)
　　See "Sne talmide hakamim sehayu be'irenu"
"Two Sheep" (Frame) **29**:97-8, 115
"Two Ships" (Boyle) **16**:145-46
"Two Sisters" (Farrell) **28**:101
"Two Sisters" (Stifter)
　　See "Zwei Schwestern"
"Two Soldiers" (Faulkner) **1**:151
Two Stories of the Seen and Unseen (Oliphant) **25**:182, 184, 203
"Two Summers and Two Souls" (Chopin) **8**:99
Two Symphonies (Gide) **13**:42-3
"The Two Temples" (Melville) **1**:303, 323
"Two Thanksgiving Day Gentlemen" (Henry) **5**:187
"Two Thousand and Some Odd Dollars" (Saroyan) **21**:134
"The Two Travelers" (Grimm and Grimm) **36**:229-30
"Two Useful Visits" (Price) **22**:385, 388
"Two Views of a Cheap Theatre" (Dickens) **17**:123
"Two White Beans" (Benet) **10**:149
"Two Worlds" (Maclean) **13**:278
"Two Wrongs" (Fitzgerald) **6**:51, 60, 61
Two-faced Herma (Pirandello)
　　See *Erma bifronte*
"Typhoon" (Dreiser) **30**:122, 153
"Typhoon" (Shiga) **23**:348
Typhoon (Conrad) **9**:141, 143-45, 147, 151-52, 157, 160, 163, 166, 186-88
"Tyrannosaurus Rex" (Bradbury) **29**:47
"The Tyranny of Realism" (Greene) **29**:219-20
"The Tyrant" (O'Flaherty) **6**:264
"Tyrants Destroyed" (Nabokov) **11**:126
Tyrants Destroyed, and Other Stories (Nabokov) **11**:122-24
"Tyrant's Territory" (Aldiss) **36**:20
"Le tzar et les grands-ducs" (Villiers de l'Isle Adam) **14**:396
"Tzvishen Zwee Berg" (Peretz) **26**:196, 202, 220
"U istoka dnej" (Bunin) **5**:98-9
"U musafirhani" (Andric) **36**:33
"U Stadionu" (Andric) **36**:51
"U vodenici" (Andric) **36**:33
"U zindanu" (Andric) **36**:33, 38
"L'ufficiale inglese" (Moravia) **26**:138, 151, 163
Ugly Anna (Coppard) **21**:16
"The Ugly Duckling" (Andersen) **6**:5, 7, 10-11, 18, 30-1, 35, 40
"Uglypuss" (Atwood) **2**:18, 22
"Uisce faoi Dhraíocht" (O'Flaherty) **6**:287-88
"UkradenáÁ vražda" (Capek) **36**:97
"Ukradený kaktus" (Capek) **36**:99, 102, 127
"Ukradený spis 139/VII odd. C." (Capek) **36**:96, 102, 105, 126
"Ukridge Sees Her Through" (Wodehouse) **2**:354
"The Ulcerated Milkman" (Sansom) **21**:115
The Ulcerated Milkman (Sansom) **21**:101, 115, 127
Ulick and Soracha (Moore) **19**:299

"Ulrike" (Borges) **41**:131-34
"Ultima ilusión" (Pardo Bazan)
　　See *La última ilusión de don Juan"*
La última ilusión de don Juan" (Pardo Bazan) **30**:265, 267-69
La última niebla (Bombal) **37**:2-3, 9, 12-17, 19-21, 23-30, 32-33, 36, 38, 40-41, 46-47
"Ultima Thule" (Galsworthy) **22**:60, 74, 79, 99
"Ultima Thule" (Nabokov) **11**:117
"The Ultimate City" (Ballard) **1**:72, 74, 83-4
"The Ultimate Melody" (Clarke) **3**:133-34
"The Ultimate Millennia" (Aldiss) **36**:19
"The Ultimate Safari" (Gordimer) **17**:178, 180, 184-85, 188, 191
"Último capítulo" (Machado de Assis) **24**:128-29
Ultimo round (Cortazar) **7**:53, 70-1, 80, 91, 94-5
"El último viaje del buque fantasma" (Garcia Marquez) **8**:154, 160, 167-68, 170-72, 186
Ultimo viene il corvo (Calvino) **3**:106, 116
"Ultor de Lacy" (Le Fanu) **14**:252
"Umbertino" (Svevo) **25**:334, 351, 361
"The Umbrella" (Pirandello) **22**:241
"Umney's Last Case" (King) **17**:295
"The Unacknowledged Champion of Everything" (Algren) **33**:108
Un'altra vita (Moravia) **26**:180
"Unapproved Route" (O'Connor) **5**:371
"An Unbiased Criticism" (Twain) **34**:324
"Unbreakable Doll" (Narayan) **25**:142
"Unc' Edinburg's Drowndin'" (Page) **23**:284-85, 291, 293, 297, 301-02, 316-17, 325-26
"Uncertain Flowering" (Laurence) **7**:271-72
"Uncle" (Narayan) **25**:139, 155, 167
"Uncle Anne" (Boyle) **5**:54
"Uncle Casper" (Stuart) **31**:261
"Uncle Fonse Laughed" (Stuart) **31**:263
"Uncle Gabe's White Folks" (Page) **23**:290
"Uncle Grant" (Price) **22**:361, 388
"Uncle Henry's Love Nest" (Caldwell) **19**:14
"Uncle Jeff" (Stuart) **31**:231, 239-41
"Uncle Jim and Uncle Billy" (Harte) **8**:227, 244
"Uncle John, The Baptist" (Stuart) **31**:249
"Uncle Ned's Short Stay" (Caldwell) **19**:41, 51
"Uncle Otto's Truck" (King) **17**:274
"Uncle Peter's House" (Chesnutt) **7**:12, 27
"Uncle Remus" (Harris) **19**:131
Uncle Remus and Brer Rabbit (Harris) **19**:196
Uncle Remus and His Friends: Old Plantation Stories, Songs and Ballads (Harris) **19**:130, 133, 163-64, 187
Uncle Remus and His Legends of the Old Plantation (Harris) **19**:121
Uncle Remus and the Little Boy (Harris) **19**:196
Uncle Remus, His Songs and His Sayings: Folklore of the Old Plantation (Harris) **19**:133, 136, 139, 144, 148, 160-62, 166-67, 169, 185, 187, 189, 193, 195-96
"Uncle Remus Initiates the Little Boy" (Harris) **19**:185, 189, 197
"Uncle Simon's Sunday Out" (Dunbar) **8**:122, 127, 144
"Uncle Spencer" (Huxley) **39**:156, 173, 176
Uncle Tom's Children (Wright) **2**:360-61, 363, 365-68, 370-71, 373-75, 379, 381-84, 386-88
"Uncle Valentine" (Cather) **2**:98, 113-15
"Uncle Wellington's Wives" (Chesnutt) **7**:3, 16, 23, 28-9, 33, 37
"Uncle Wiggily in Connecticut" (Salinger) **2**:290, 292, 295, 299, 305-06, 313-14
"Uncle Willy" (Faulkner) **1**:151
"Unclean" (O'Flaherty) **6**:259
"Uncles" (Taylor) **10**:379
"Uncle's Dream" (Dostoevsky) **2**:164, 172, 184
"Uncle's Letters" (Narayan) **25**:139, 155
The Uncollected Short Stories (Jewett) **6**:156, 166
The Uncollected Wodehouse (Wodehouse) **2**:343

"The Uncomfortable Pause Between Life and Art" (Aldiss) **36**:20, 25-6

The Uncommercial Traveller (Dickens) **17**:123

"The Uncommon Prayer-Book" (James) **16**:229-32, 239, 241, 244-45

"The Unconquered" (Maugham) **8**:380

"Uncovenanted Mercies" (Kipling) **5**:271, 283

"The Undefeated" (Hemingway) **1**:209, 216, 218-19, 224, 230, 234; **36**:252, 270, 325; **40**:191, 209, 212, 215, 219

"Under a Glass Bell" (Nin) **10**:299, 303-04

Under a Glass Bell (Nin) **10**:299-300, 302-06

"Under a Glass Sky" (Bulgakov) **18**:90

"Under Glass" (Atwood) **2**:3, 6, 10, 13, 16

"Under New Management" (Warner) **23**:370-71

"Under the Banyan Tree" (Narayan) **25**:135, 138

"Under the Boardwalk" (Phillips) **16**:328-29

Under the Crust (Page) **23**:287, 307

"Under the Deck Awnings" (London) **4**:291

Under the Deodars (Kipling) **5**:265

"Under the Fan" (Moore) **19**:339-40, 342

"Under the Garden" (Greene) **29**:187-88, 190, 195-200, 212-13, 215, 217, 226, 229-30

"Under the Greenwood Tree" (Williams) **31**:325, 333

"Under the Jaguar Sun" (Calvino) **3**:118-19

Under the Jaguar Sun (Calvino)
    See *Sotto il sole giaguro*

"Under the Knife" (Singer) **3**:362

"Under the Knife" (Wells) **6**:360, 389, 393-94, 405

"Under the Lion's Paw" (Garland) **18**:142, 148, 150, 154-55, 159, 163, 167-69, 172, 176, 182-83

"Under the Microscope" (Updike) **13**:360, 387

"Under the Rose" (Pynchon) **14**:308, 331, 334-38, 341-42, 344, 347-48

"Under the Shrinking Royalty the Village Smithy Stands" (Perelman) **32**:235

"Under the Sky" (Bowles) **3**:59, 61-2, 67, 79

"Under the Spreading Atrophy" (Perelman) **32**:231

"Under the Volcano" (Lowry) **31**:42

"Under the Willow-Tree" (Andersen) **6**:4

"The Underground" (Dostoevsky) **2**:187

"Underground Lady" (Yamamoto) **34**:359

"The Undertaker" (Pushkin)
    See "Grobovshchik"

"Undertakers" (Kipling) **5**:293

"Underwater" (Bioy Casares) **17**:94, 96

"Undine" (Dazai Osamu) **41**:276

Undiscovered Country: The New Zealand Stories of Katherine Mansfield (Mansfield) **9**:281

"The Undismayed Operator" (Bulgakov) **18**:89

"Unearthing Suite" (Atwood) **2**:17, 22

"Unequally Yoked" (Norris) **28**:205

"The Unexpected" (Chopin) **8**:72, 100

"The Unexpected" (London) **4**:253, 260-62

"Unexpected Guests" (Boell) **23**:7

"An Unfinished Collection" (Wodehouse) **2**:343

"An Unfinished Love Story" (Lawson) **18**:201, 248, 250-51

"Unfinished Short Story" (Forster) **27**:117

"An Unfinished Story" (Henry) **5**:163, 171, 178-79, 182, 185

"The Unfortunate" (Turgenev)
    See "Neschastnaya"

"The Unfortunate Lover" (Moravia) **26**:138

The Unfortunate Lover (Moravia)
    See *The Unfortunate Lover*

The Unfortunate Ones (White) **39**:292

"An Unhappy Girl" (Turgenev)
    See "Neschastnaya"

"Unholy Living and Half Dying" (O'Faolain) **13**:301, 305

"The Unholy Three" (Auchincloss) **22**:29

"Unicorn" (Tanizaki)
    See "Kirin"

"The Unicorn in the Garden" (Thurber) **1**:427-28, 431

"The Uniformed Stray" (Moorhouse) **40**:293

"Uninhabitedness" (Pasternak) **31**:108

"The Union Buries Its Dead" (Lawson) **18**:201-02, 206, 211, 213, 218, 220-21, 233-35, 237-38, 241, 243, 259, 261

"Union Reunion" (Wilson) **21**:318, 321, 332, 344, 351, 357

Unions (Musil)
    See *Vereinigungen*

"The Unit" (Capek) **36**:92

A Universal History of Infamy (Borges)
    See *Historia universal de la infamia*

A Universal History of Iniquity (Borges) **41**:157

"The Unkindest Blow" (Saki) **12**:295-96

"The Unknown" (Bombal) **37**:45

"The Unknown Masterpiece" (Balzac)
    See "Le chef d'oeuvre inconnu"

"The Unknown Quantity" (Henry) **5**:197

"The Unknown Woman" (Villiers de l'Isle Adam)
    See "L'inconnue"

"The Unknown Woman of the Seine" (Nin) **10**:304

"Unlighted Lamps" (Anderson) **1**:27, 30, 39, 46-7, 53, 55

Unlucky for Pringle (Lewis) **34**:163-64, 170, 178

"An Unmarried Man's Summer" (Gallant) **5**:122, 130-31

"The Unnameable" (Lovecraft) **3**:262, 276, 293-94

"The Unnatural Mother" (Gilman) **13**:126

"Uno de dos" (Arreola) **38**:25

"Unpaid Consultant" (Vonnegut) **8**:436

"The Unparalleled Adventure of One Hans Pfaall" (Poe) **1**:400, 402, 406

"The Unparalleled Invasion" (London) **4**:255

"An Unpleasant Predicament" (Dostoevsky) **2**:166, 184

"An Unpleasantness" (Chekhov) **28**:58

The Unploughed Land (Cowan) **28**:76

"Unprofessional" (Kipling) **5**:285

"An Unprotected Female at the Pyramids" (Trollope) **28**:318, 323, 328-29, 332, 347

"Unready to Wear" (Vonnegut) **8**:434

"The Unrest Cure" (Saki) **12**:287, 300, 324, 326

"The Unseen" (Singer) **3**:358, 362, 383-84

"Unser Karl" (Harte) **8**:220

"Unshorn Locks and Bogus Bagels" (Perelman) **32**:230

Unspeakable Practices, Unnatural Acts (Barthelme) **2**:29-31, 35, 37-8, 51

"The Unspoiled Reaction" (McCarthy) **24**:221-24

"Unstuck" (Updike) **13**:404, 409

Unterhaltungen deutscher Ausgewanderten (Goethe) **38**:161-62, 166, 187

"Until Forsaken" (Tanizaki)
    See "Suterareru made"

"Until One Is Deserted" (Tanizaki) **21**:208

The Untilled Field (Moore)
    See *An T-úr-Ghort*

"Untitled Piece" (McCullers) **9**:343, 345, 356-57

"The Untold Lie" (Anderson) **1**:21, 34, 39, 41-2, 44, 52

"'Unused'" (Anderson) **1**:23, 27, 30, 39-40, 46-7, 53, 55

The Unvanquished (Faulkner) **1**:151, 170, 177, 180; **35**:176

Unveröffentlichte Prosadichtungen (Walser) **20**:333, 335

"The Unvexed Isles" (Warren) **4**:387, 389-90, 395, 400

"Unwanted Heroine" (Wilson) **21**:358, 361

"Unwelcome Words" (Bowles) **3**:85-6

Unwelcome Words: Seven Stories (Bowles) **3**:85

"The Unworthy Friend" (Borges) **4**:18

"An Unwritten Novel" (Woolf) **7**:368, 371-72, 375-76, 378, 382, 388, 392, 397-99, 405, 408-09

"L'uomo che guarda" (Moravia) **26**:142, 149

"L'uomo e la teoria darwiniana" (Svevo) **25**:360

"Uomo nei gerbidi" (Calvino) **3**:96

"Up, Aloft in the Air" (Barthelme) **2**:38

"Up Among the Eagles" (Valenzuela) **14**:359, 361, 366

Up Among the Eagles (Valenzuela)
    See *Donde viven las águilas*

"Up in Michigan" (Hemingway) **1**:207, 219; **40**:221

"Up North" (Cowan) **28**:78

"Up the Bare Stairs" (O'Faolain) **13**:300, 302, 304, 306-07

"Up the Coulée" (Garland) **18**:142, 144, 148, 150, 154-56, 158-59, 161, 163, 168-70, 172, 175-76, 182, 193

"Upon the Dull Earth" (Campbell) **19**:81

"Upon the Sweeping Flood" (Oates) **6**:224-25

Upon the Sweeping Flood, and Other Stories (Oates) **6**:224-25

The Uprising in the Cévennes (Tieck)
    See *Der Aufruhr in den Cevennen*

"Uprooted" (Chekhov) **2**:130

"Uprooted" (O'Connor) **5**:369, 371, 375-77, 383, 397

"Uprooted" (Suckow) **18**:394, 399-400, 405, 407-08, 415

"Upstairs in the Wineshop" (Lu Hsun)
    See "Zai jiulou shang"

"The Upturned Face" (Crane) **7**:109, 143-45

"Uriah's Son" (Benet) **10**:146

Urien's Voyage (Gide)
    See *Le voyage d'Urien*

Ursula (Keller) **26**:91, 107-08, 111, 113

"Das Urteil" (Kafka) **5**:225-26, 228-29, 232, 240, 243-45, 252-55; **35**:227-28, 243, 262-63, 290

"The Use of Force" (Williams) **31**:304-05, 312, 315, 317-23, 325, 333, 335-36, 338-39, 344-46, 351, 363-64

"The Used-Boy Raisers" (Paley) **8**:399, 406-07

USFS 1919: The Ranger, The Cook and a Hole in the Sky (Maclean) **13**:260, 270-71

"Usher II" (Bradbury) **29**:50-1

"Usurpation" (Other People's StoriesOzick) **15**:302, 305, 311, 315-17, 326

"Utenok" (Solzhenitsyn) **32**:352, 395

"Uvod" (Andric) **36**:63-4, 68

"V ovrage" (Chekhov) **2**:128, 131-32, 145, 156-57; **28**:59, 61

"V Stepi" (Gorky) **28**:150, 190

"Va bene" (Pirandello) **22**:228

"Vacation Time" (Boyle) **5**:54

"Le Vaches" (Ayme) **41**:14

The Vagabond (Colette)
    See *La vagabonde*

Vagabondaggio (Verga) **21**:291, 297

La vagabonde (Colette) **10**:257, 272-73, 291

"The Valentine" (Howells) **36**:399

"The Valet" (Barnes) **3**:22-4

"The Valiant Woman" (Powers) **4**:380-81, 383

"The Valley Between" (Marshall) **3**:303, 308-09, 312, 315, 317

"The Valley of Childish Things" (Wharton) **6**:427

The Valley of the Moon (London) **4**:254

"The Valley of the Shadow" (Kipling) **5**:261

"The Valley of the Spiders" (Wells) **6**:361

"Vals capricho" (Castellanos) **39**:36, 42

"Vampirism" (Hoffmann)
    See "Der Vampyrismus"

"Eine Vampyrgeschichte" (Hoffmann)
    See "Der Vampyrismus"

"Der Vampyrismus" (Hoffmann) **13**:186, 215, 228, 230

"Van Gogh's Room at Arles" (Elkin) **12**:119-20

"Vanadium" (Levi) **12**:256, 258, 265-67

"The Vane Sisters" (Nabokov) **11**:116, 122-23, 125, 144

"Vanina Vanini" (Stendhal) **27**:231, 248-49, 260

"The Vanishing of Vaudrey" (Chesterton) **1**:131

"The Vanishing Prince" (Chesterton) **1**:122

"Vanity and Some Sables" (Henry) **5**:187
"Vánka" (Chekhov) **2**:130
"Vanka Mazin" (Gorky) **28**:161
"Vanvild Kava" (Singer) **3**:383
"Varenka Olesova" (Gorky) **28**:151
Varia Invención (Arreola) **38**:3, 8-12, 30
Várias histórias (Machado de Assis) **24**:153
"Variation on a Theme" (Collier) **19**:98, 110, 114
"Varieties of Exile" (Gallant) **5**:134-35, 143
Various Inventions (Arreola)
    See *Varia Invención*
"Various Temptations" (Sansom) **21**:90, 92-5, 112-13, 124
"Le vase étrusque" (Merimee) **7**:278, 280-1, 283, 286-91, 300, 304
"Vastarien" (Ligotti) **16**:263-64, 267, 269, 274, 276-80, 283, 285-89, 294
"Vaster than Empires and More Slow" (Le Guin) **12**:208-10, 216, 231-33
"The Vats" (de la Mare) **14**:66, 82, 90
"A vayse kapore" (Aleichem) **33**:38-9
"Večer nakanune Ivana Kupala" (Gogol) **4**:88, 119-21; **29**:132, 135
Vechera ná khutore bliz Dikanki (Gogol) **4**:85-7, 98, 117
Vechny muzh (Dostoevsky) **2**:166-67, 175-77, 184-85
"Vehaya he'akov lemishor" (Agnon) **30**:7 8
"The Veldt" (Bradbury) **29**:42, 51
"Velga" (Bunin) **5**:98
"Vendée" (Faulkner) **1**:171
"Une vendetta" (Maupassant) **1**:277
"La vendetta revenge" (Balzac) **5**:4, 22, 29, 31
"The Venerated Bones" (Lagerkvist) **12**:195
"La vengeance d'une femme" (Barbey d'Aurevilly) **17**:11, 15, 18-21, 33-4, 36-7, 44
"The Vengeance of 3902090" (Thurber) **1**:419
"Venice" (Sansom) **21**:86
"The Venomous Viper of the Volga" (Lardner) **32**:132
"Il ventaglino" (Pirandello) **22**:233, 284-86
"The Venturers" (Henry) **5**:159, 190-91
"The Venus" (Williams) **30**:301, 343, 345, 360
"Venus, Cupid, Folly, and Time" (Taylor) **10**:391, 407, 409, 419
"La Vénus d'Ille" (Merimee) **7**:276, 279-80, 283-6, 288, 290, 293-5, 297, 301, 306
"The Venus of Ille" (Merimee)
    See "La Vénus d'Ille"
"Véra" (Villiers de l'Isle Adam) **14**:377, 379, 381-82, 384, 387, 390, 396, 398, 403, 408
"Veränderungen in Staech" (Boell) **23**:35
"Veraneo" (Donoso) **34**:5-6, 21-23, 29-31, 35, 49
Veraneo y otros cuentos (Donoso) **34**:3, 24, 29,49
"Verano" (Cortazar) **7**:61-3
"Verba testamentária" (Machado de Assis) **24**:128-29, 132
"Verbal Transcription—6 AM" (Williams) **31**:322, 334
"The Verdict" (Wharton) **6**:435
El verdugo (Balzac) **5**:21, 31
Vereinigungen (Musil) **18**:288, 290-93, 317
"Verlie I Say unto You" (Adams) **24**:5
Die Verlobung (Tieck) **31**:270-71, 286
Die Verlobung in St. Domingo (Kleist) **22**:122-24, 146, 151-52
Die verlorene Ehre der Katharina Blum: oder, Wie Gewalt entstehen und wohin sie führen kann (Boell) **23**:13-15, 19, 25-6, 28-30, 33, 36, 39
Das Verlorene Lachen (Keller) **26**:91, 107, 121
"Das Verlorene Spiegelbild" (Hoffmann) **13**:183, 200
Vermilion Sands (Ballard) **1**:78
Veronika (Storm) **27**:281
"Versamina" (Levi) **12**:278-79
Die Versuchung der Stillen Veronika (Musil) **18**:288-89, 291-93, 302, 317, 320-22

Die Versuchung des Pescara (Meyer) **30**:187-88, 204-05, 236-38, 240-42
Die vertauschten Köpfe (Mann) **5**:312-13, 315, 323, 326
"The Vertical Ladder" (Sansom) **21**:90-92
"Vertigo" (Capek) **36**:128
Die verwandlung (Kafka) **5**:210-13, 215, 217-20, 224-25, 231, 234, 239-40, 245, 252; **29**:340-42, 346, 349, 355, 365, 369-70; **35**:215-96
Very Far Away from Anywhere Else (Le Guin) **12**:231, 241
"A Very Fine Fiddle" (Chopin) **8**:88, 103
Very Good, Jeeves (Wodehouse) **2**:346
"The Very Good Mother" (Svevo)
    See "La buonissima madre"
"The Very Image" (Villiers de l'Isle Adam)
    See "A s'y méprendre"
"A Very Late Spring" (Caldwell) **19**:34
A Very Long Way from Anywhere Else (Le Guin)
    See *Very Far Away from Anywhere Else*
"The Very Proper Gander" (Thurber) **1**:431
Das verzauberte Haus (Musil)
    See *Die Versuchung der Stillen Veronika*
"Der Verzicht" (Lenz) **33**:318, 320
"Veselyi dvor" (Bunin) **5**:87
Veshnie vody (Turgenev) **7**:316-17, 320-21, 324-25, 327-29, 334, 336-38, 357-58, 361-62
"The Vessel of Wrath" (Maugham) **8**:375, 378
"La veste lunga" (Pirandello) **22**:250, 283-85
"Vesti iz rodiny" (Bunin) **5**:98
"Vestiges: Harlem Sketches" (Fisher)
    See "Vestiges: Harlem Sketches"
"Věštkyně" (Capek) **36**:96, 98-9, 127
"A Veteran Falls" (Hughes) **6**:122
"Veteran of the Private Evacuations" (Ballard) **1**:70
"Les veuves" (Baudelaire) **18**:4, 9, 17, 32, 39, 60
"Via Crucis" (Lispector) **34**:207, 213
A via crucis do corpo (Lispector) **34**:203-05, 209-15
The Via Crucis of the Body (Lispector)
    See *A via crucis do corpo*
"Il viaggio" (Pirandello) **22**:255, 275, 277, 283-84, 286
"Viaje a la semilla" (Carpentier) **35**:91, 95, 106, 110, 113, 126
"Viaje de novios" (Pardo Bazan) **30**:272
"El viajero" (Pardo Bazan) **30**:264
"The Vice-Consul" (Pritchett) **14**:273
"A Victim of Circumstances" (Gissing) **37**:64
A Victim of Circumstances (Gissing) **37**:80
"Victim of Justice" (Dreiser)
    See "Nigger Jeff"
"Victim or Hero?" (Farrell) **28**:125
"La víctima de Tadeo Limardo" (Bioy Casares) **17**:70, 73
"The Victor" (Dreiser) **30**:122
"Victor Blue" (Beattie) **11**:15, 18, 21
"Victoria Kazimirovna" (Zoshchenko) **15**:400-01
"Victory" (Faulkner) **1**:148
"The Victory Burlesk" (Atwood) **2**:19
Victory over Japan (Gilchrist) **14**:152-55, 157-59, 162-63
"La vida no es muy seria en sus cosas" (Rulfo) **25**:244
"Vida nueva" (Pardo Bazan) **30**:262
"La vida privada" (Arreola) **38**:9, 12-13
"El vidrio roto" (Pardo Bazan) **30**:272
"La vie boheme" (Gordimer) **17**:167
"Vieja moralidad" (Fuentes) **24**:29, 32, 45, 56, 58, 62, 71, 73
"Vienne" (Rhys) **21**:53, 61-2, 67, 74-5
"The Viennese Opera Ball" (Barthelme) **2**:28
"Le vieux saltimbanque" (Baudelaire) **18**:4-5, 15, 17-18, 27-32
"View from a Height" (Vinge) **24**:336, 342-43
"A View from a Hill" (James) **16**:231, 233, 237, 240, 244

"The View from the Balcony" (Stegner) **27**:195, 197, 202, 224
A View of Dawn in the Tropics (Cabrera Infante)
    See *Vista del amanecer en el trópico*
"The View of Rome" (Warner) **23**:373-74
"A View of the Woods" (O'Connor) **1**:342-45, 356
"A View of the Yasukuni Festival" (Kawabata)
    See "Shōkonsai Ikkei"
"Views of My Father Weeping" (Barthelme) **2**:31, 42, 46, 48, 55
"Vigilante" (Steinbeck) **11**:208, 225, 232-33, 241-42, 244
"La vigna" (Pavese) **19**:369, 376, 385
"A Vignette" (James) **16**:251, 254
The Viking Portable Library Dorothy Parker (Parker) **2**:276, 278
"De vilde Svaner" (Andersen)
    See "The Wild Swans"
"Villa on the Hill" (Pavese) **19**:387
"Villa Violetta" (Lavin) **4**:183, 185
"The Village" (Dixon) **16**:217
"The Village Angler" (Irving) **37**:266
"A Village Lear" (Turgenev)
    See "Stepnoy Korol 'Lir"
"Village of Goryukhino" (Pushkin)
    See *Istoriia sela Goriukhino*
The Village of Stepanchikovo (Dostoevsky)
    See *The Friend of the Family*
A Village Romeo and Juliet (Keller)
    See *Romeo und Julia auf dem Dorfe*
"A Village Singer" (Freeman) **1**:197, 200
"The Village That Voted the Earth Was Flat" (Kipling) **5**:277, 280, 282
"The Villager" (Jackson) **39**:210, 215, 216, 217, 223, 225
"Villon's Wife" (Dazai Osamu)
    See "Buiyon no tsuma"
"The Vindication of Jared Hargot" (Dunbar) **8**:138
"Le Vin de Paris" (Ayme) **41**:3, 11, 17, 32-33
Vinegar Puss (Perelman) **32**:229, 236
"The Vineyard" (Pavese)
    See "La vigna"
"Viney's Free Papers" (Dunbar) **8**:122, 127, 131, 133, 144
"Vino" (Andric) **36**:50
"Vino generoso" (Svevo) **25**:329, 331, 335-36, 351, 354, 357, 359-60
"A Vintage Thunderbird" (Beattie) **11**:4-5, 17, 29
Vinter-Eventyr (Dinesen)
    See *Winter's Tales*
Viola tricolor (Storm) **27**:282
"Violet" (Mansfield) **38**:203, 231
"The Virgin and the Gipsy" (Lawrence) **4**:205-06
The Virgin and the Nun (Keller)
    See *The Virgin and the Nun*
The Virgin as Knight (Keller)
    See *The Virgin as Knight*
"The Virgin of Seven Daggers" (Lee) **33**:302, 308, 310-11
"Virgin Violeta" (Porter) **4**:341, 350; **31**:163, 178
"Virginia and Paul" (Villiers de l'Isle Adam)
    See "Virginie et Paul"
"The Virginians Are Coming" (Farrell) **28**:127
"Virginie et Paul" (Villiers de l'Isle Adam) **14**:379, 381, 384, 386-87, 390, 394, 396
"Virgínius: narrativa de um advogado" (Machado de Assis) **24**:155
"Virgins" (Trevor) **21**:246, 248
"Virility" (Ozick) **15**:298, 300, 313
"Virtue" (Galsworthy) **22**:101
"Virtue" (Maugham) **8**:378
"A Virtuoso's Collection" (Hawthorne) **3**:171
"Virus X" (Gallant) **5**:139
Il visconte dimezzato (Calvino) **3**:90-1, 94, 99, 106, 117
Vision de Babouc (Voltaire) **12**:340-1

La vision de Babouc (Voltaire) **12**:342

"La vision de Charles XI" (Merimee) **7**:287, 289

"A Vision of Judgment" (Wells) **6**:360, 391

"The Vision of the Fountain" (Hawthorne) **3**:178, 182

"A Vision of the World" (Cheever) **1**:93-6, 105; **38**:54-5, 61, 66

"The Vision of Tom Chuff" (Le Fanu) **14**:220, 223

"Visions" (Turgenev) **7**:315

"A Visit in Bad Taste" (Wilson) **21**:322, 327, 332, 339, 344, 352-53

"A Visit Next Door" (Jewett) **6**:158

"A Visit of Charity" (Welty) **1**:470

"A Visit of Condolence" (Lawson) **18**:201

"A Visit to America" (Thomas) **3**:393

"A Visit to Avoyelles" (Chopin) **8**:72, 84

"A Visit to Grandpa's" (Thomas) **3**:397, 402, 405, 410, 412

"A Visit to Mingus County" (Caldwell) **19**:41

"A Visit to Morin" (Greene) **29**:187, 189, 198, 211

"A Visit to Newgate" (Dickens) **17**:110, 116-17, 121

"A Visit to the Cemetery" (Lavin) **4**:164-66, 168-69

"A Visit to the Dentist" (Sansom) **21**:99, 116, 126

"Visit to the Fair" (Williams) **31**:331, 350, 359, 361

"The Visit to the Museum" (Nabokov) **11**:117, 145, 147, 152

"La visita" (Pirandello) **22**:261, 269

"Una visita al viejo poeta" (Unamuno) **11**:312

"The Visitants from Yesterday" (Murfree) **22**:220-22

"Visitation" (Schulz) **13**:333, 339

"Le visiteur nocturne" (Mauriac) **24**:197, 203-05

"The Visiting of Mother Danbury" (Dunbar) **8**:127

"Visiting with King Ahasuerus" (Aleichem) **33**:20

"The Visitor" (Bowen) **3**:40

"A Visitor" (Dazai Osamu) **41**:238, 240, 242

"The Visitor" (Thomas) **3**:400, 407, 409

"A Visitor and His Opinions" (Oliphant) **25**:204

"Visitors" (Barthelme) **2**:56

"Visitors" (Mukherjee) **38**:238-41, 252, 255, 265, 271

"Uma vista de Alcebíades" (Machado de Assis) **24**:129

Vista del amanecer en el trópico (Cabrera Infante) **39**:2-19, 21

Vita dei campi (Verga) **21**:280-81, 285-86, 291, 294, 298-99, 301-02, 305, 308, 313

"La vita nuda" (Pirandello) **22**:231

La vita nuda (Pirandello) **22**:231, 275

"Vitamins" (Carver) **8**:26, 32

"Vittoria Accoramboni, duchesse de Bracciano" (Stendhal) **27**:231, 249, 260-61

"Vittoria delle formiche" (Pirandello) **22**:270

"La viuda de Montiel" (Garcia Marquez) **8**:187-90

"El viudo Román" (Castellanos) **39**:30, 34, 37, 38, 73

"Viva la introyección!" (Unamuno) **11**:312

"Vive la France" (Boell) **23**:38

"Viver!" (Machado de Assis) **24**:127-29

"Vivian Thanks God" (Farrell) **28**:112

"Viy" (Gogol) **4**:82, 86, 102-03; **29**:149

"Vizitnye kartochki" (Bunin) **5**:114

"Vladyčnyj sud" (Leskov) **34**:111

"Vlemk the Box-Painter" (Gardner) **7**:223-26, 238-41

"A Vocation and a Voice" (Chopin) **8**:93, 97, 99

"Les vocations" (Baudelaire) **18**:5

"La Vocazione de Suora Agnese" (Verga) **21**:294

Die Vogelscheuche (Tieck) **31**:275, 286-87

"The Voice" (Cowan) **28**:75

"The Voice" (Nin) **10**:300-01, 307-11, 314-15, 317, 322-23

"The Voice" (Pritchett) **14**:271, 286

"The Voice in the Bones" (Ligotti) **16**:271, 274, 280, 288, 296, 297

"The Voice of . . ." (Galsworthy) **22**:99

"The Voice of the Beach" (Campbell) **19**:66, 70-1, 73, 80, 84, 88, 90

"The Voice of the City" (Henry) **5**:171, 191, 194

The Voice of the City (Henry) **5**:155, 192

"The Voice of the Mountain" (Moore) **19**:345

The Voice of the People (Peretz) **26**:204-05

"The Voice of the Turtle" (Maugham) **8**:379

Voices (Cowan) **28**:81-83

Voices at Play (Spark) **10**:353, 355, 359

"Voices from the Dust" (Vinge) **24**:337, 343

"Voices from the Moon" (Dubus) **15**:94, 96, 100-01

Voices From the Moon (Dubus) **15**:81-3, 85-6, 89-96, 98

"Voices Lost in the Snow" (Gallant) **5**:135, 139

"The Voices of Adamo" (Laurence) **7**:245, 249-50

"The Voices of Time" (Ballard) **1**:71, 80

"Voitel' nica" (Leskov) **34**:111-12, 117, 125

"The Volcano" (Stegner) **27**:195, 220, 224

"Vollendung der Liebe" (Musil) **18**:288-93, 317-20

"The Volunteer" (Stegner) **27**:198

Von Jenseit des Meeres (Storm) **27**:278, 283-84

"Von Kempelen and His Discovery" (Poe) **1**:402

"Vor dem gesetz" (Kafka) **5**:254; **29**:339, 351

"Vorgeschichte" (Lenz) **33**:321-23, 325-27

"Voron" (Bunin) **5**:113

"Vos heyst 'neshome'" (Peretz) **26**:218

"Vox populi" (Villiers de l'Isle Adam) **14**:381-82, 386, 394-96

"The Voyage" (Mansfield) **9**:278, 282, 303-04; **38**:203

Le voyage d'Urien (Gide) **13**:57-61, 63, 72

Voyage en Orient (Nerval) **18**:328, 334, 336, 346-47, 366

"The Voyage to Rosewood" (Oates) **6**:231

"Vozdushnye puti" (Pasternak)
See "Aerial Ways"

Les vrilles de la vigne (Colette) **10**:261, 263

La vuelta al día en ochenta mundos (Cortazar) **7**:53, 61, 91, 94

"V.V.: or Plots and Counterplots" (Alcott) **27**:3-5, 32

"Vystrel" (Pushkin) **27**:129, 134-44, 163, 166-68, 182-83, 186-87

"Die Waage der Baleks" (Boell) **23**:6-8, 22

"Wa-ch'u" (P'u Sung-ling) **31**:192

"Waga namida o nuguitamo, hi" (Oe)
See "Mizu kara waga namida o nuguitamo hi"

"The Wages of Sin" (Dreiser) **30**:155

"The Waging of the Peace" (Pohl) **25**:223, 237

"A Wagner Matinée" (Cather) **2**:90-1, 96, 103, 105, 108

"The Wagnerians" (Auchincloss) **22**:29

"Wahiah—A Spartan Mother" (Garland) **18**:147, 178

"A Waif of the Plains" (Harte) **8**:222, 251

"Wailing Well" (James) **16**:242, 244, 251

"Waiting" (Beattie) **11**:13, 22

"The Wait" (Borges)
See "La espera"

"Waiting" (Chang) **28**:26; 31; 34

"Waiting" (Dubus) **15**:89

"Waiting" (Oates) **6**:232

"Waiting at Dachau" (Price) **22**:366, 369, 376, 378-79, 384, 388

"Waiting for Santy" (Perelman) **32**:211

"Waiting for Stella" (Adams) **24**:12

"Waiting for the Moving of the Water" (Leskov) **34**:128

"Waiting for the Universe to Begin" (Aldiss) **36**:19

Waiting for Winter (O'Hara) **15**:276-79, 283-86

"The Waiting Grounds" (Ballard) **1**:68, 76

"The Waiting Room" (Boell) **23**:38

"The Waiting Room" (Capek)
See "Čekárna"

"The Waiting Supper" (Hardy) **2**:211, 215-16, 219, 223

"Waiting Up" (Updike) **13**:387

Wakai (Shiga) **23**:339, 344, 346, 350-58, 363

"Wake for the Living" (Bradbury) **29**:51

"The Wake of Patsy McLaughlin" (Farrell) **28**:100

"Wakefield" (Hawthorne) **3**:154, 159, 161-62, 178, 189, 191

Waking Nightmares (Campbell) **19**:76-8, 87

Waldeinsamkeit (Tieck) **31**:286

"Waldemar Daa and His Daughters" (Andersen)
See "The Wind Tells of Valdemar Daae and His Daughters"

"Der Waldgänger" (Stifter) **28**:273, 297

"Der Waldsteig" (Stifter) **28**:287, 290, 299

Waldwinkel (Storm) **27**:286, 314

"The Walk" (Donoso)
See "Paseo"

"The Walk" (Walser) **20**:336-37, 349, 360-61

The Walk, and Other Stories (Walser) **20**:337

"A Walk in the Dark" (Clarke) **3**:124, 147-49

"Walk in the Moon Shadows" (Stuart) **31**:226-27, 236

"A Walk in the Woods" (Bowen) **3**:54

"Walker Brothers Cowboy" (Munro) **3**:321, 329, 343, 347

"A Walking Delegate" (Kipling) **5**:279

"Walking Lessons" (Price) **22**:365-66, 368, 372-73, 385, 387

"Walking on Water" (Munro) **3**:331, 346

"Walking Out" (Beckett) **16**:100

"Die Walkuere" (Mann) **5**:310

"The Wall" (Sansom) **21**:81-2, 90-2, 95, 122-24

"The Wall" (Sartre)
See "Le Mur"

The Wall, and Other Stories (Sartre)
See *Le mur*

"The Wall of Darkness" (Clarke) **3**:125, 129, 147

"Walled City" (Oates) **6**:251-52

"A Walled Garden" (Taylor) **10**:382, 410

"The Wallet" (Updike) **13**:402

"The Walls of Jericho" (Dunbar) **8**:122, 136, 149

"Wally" (Auchincloss) **22**:48

"Wally Whistles Dixie" (Beattie) **11**:16, 23, 28

"The Walnut Hunt" (Caldwell) **19**:9

Wälsungenblut (Mann) **5**:310-11, 321, 323, 344

"Walter Briggs" (Updike) **13**:390, 400

"Walter Kömpff" (Hesse) **9**:235

"Walter T. Carriman" (O'Hara) **15**:264, 269

"The Waltz" (Parker) **2**:274, 281, 283, 285-86

"Waltz Caprice" (Castellanos)
See "Vals capricho"

"Wan Lee, the Pagan" (Harte) **8**:249

"Wanda's" (Beattie) **11**:16

"Wanderer, kommst du nach Spa..." (Boell) **23**:37

"The Wanderers" (Lewis) **40**:272, 276-77, 280-82

"Wanderers" (Suckow) **18**:389, 415

"The Wanderers" (Welty) **1**:479, 493

Wandering (Lu Hsun)
See *P'anghuang*

"Wandering Willie's Tale" (Scott) **32**:288-89, 291, 299-300, 303, 306, 308-10, 314, 320

"A Wand'ring Minstrel, I" (Gordimer) **17**:153

"Wang Ch'eng" (P'u Sung-ling) **31**:191, 206

"Wang Tzu-an" (P'u Sung-ling) **31**:199

"Wang-che" (P'u Sung-ling) **31**:192

"A Waning Moon" (Sansom) **21**:89-92, 95, 114

"Wants" (Paley) **8**:397, 399, 416

"Wapping Workhouse" (Dickens) **17**:123

"The War" (Saroyan) **21**:133, 136

"War and Peace" (Saroyan) **21**:161

"The War Baby" (Lewis) **34**:153, 165, 172, 175
"War Between Saints" (Verga) **21**:300
"The War in Spain" (Saroyan) **21**:163
"The War in the Bathroom" (Atwood) **2**:4, 6-8, 10
"The War Millennia" (Aldiss) **36**:19
"The War of the Wall" (Bambara) **35**:42
The War of Time (Carpentier)
　　See *Guerra del tiempo*
"Ward No. Six" (Chekhov) **2**:126, 131-32, 143, 152, 157
"Ward O 3 b" (Lewis) **40**:272-73, 277, 279, 283
"A Ward of Colonel Starbottle's" (Harte) **8**:249
"The Warden" (Gardner) **7**:213-14, 218, 222, 231
"The Wardrobe" (Mann) **5**:330
"The Warehouse" (Singer) **3**:358, 360
"Warera no Kyoki o ikinobiru michi o oshieyo" (Oe) **20**:223-28
"The Wares in Rio" (Ellison) **14**:146
"The Warlock" (Stafford) **26**:300
"The Warm, Quiet Valley of Home" (Saroyan) **21**:144, 150
"Warm River" (Caldwell) **19**:4, 6
"A Warning to the Curious" (James) **16**:232-33, 236-37, 252, 256
A Warning to the Curious (James) **16**:238, 251, 255
"The Warrior Princess Ozimbu" (Price) **22**:361, 384-85
"Der Wärter" (Hauptmann) **37**:258
"Was" (Faulkner) **1**:148, 173-74, 182; **35**:146-47, 157, 186, 195
"Wash" (Faulkner) **1**:166, 180
Waste of Timelessness, and Other Early Stories (Nin) **10**:305-06
"The Watch" (Dixon) **16**:200, 211
"The Watch" (Turgenev)
　　See "Chasy"
"Watch and Ward" (Pirandello) **22**:244
"Watch Out for Daddy" (Algren) **33**:96, 98
"Watch the Birdie" (Campbell) **19**:77
"Watch This Space" (Clarke) **3**:133
"Watch Town" (Moorhouse) **40**:291
"The Watcher" (Le Fanu)
　　See "The Familiar"
"A Watcher by the Dead" (Bierce) **9**:49
"A Watcher of the Dead" (Gordimer) **17**:151-52
"The Watchers" (Calisher) **15**:5, 17-18
"The Watchful Poker Chip of Henri Matisse" (Bradbury) **29**:88
"The Watchman" (Narayan) **25**:133, 139, 141, 156
"Water" (Galsworthy) **22**:73
"The Water Baby" (London) **4**:270
"The Water Hen" (O'Flaherty) **6**:268
The Water Is Wide (Le Guin) **12**:231
"The Water of Izli" (Bowles) **3**:68
"Water Them Geraniums" (Lawson) **18**:202, 204, 220-23, 226-27, 229-30, 232, 234, 262
"The Watercress Girl" (Bates) **10**:120, 131-33
"The Watercress Girl" (Coppard) **21**:4, 10, 20, 26
The Watercress Girl, And Other Stories (Bates) **10**:120-21
"The Waterfall" (Gordon) **15**:142
"Water-Message" (Barth) **10**:41-3, 46-8, 54, 56, 60, 63, 67, 79, 84, 87, 89, 91, 95, 97-101
"The Wave" (O'Flaherty) **6**:261, 264, 268, 285
"The Wave of Osiris" (Lagerkvist) **12**:181
"The Waves of Lake Balaton" (Lenz) **33**:337
"The Wax Madonna" (Pirandello) **22**:228
"The Way Back" (Grau) **15**:148
"The Way Back" (Moore) **19**:312-17, 319-22, 330-31, 333, 336
"Way Down on Lonesome Cove" (Murfree) **22**:196-97, 209
"Way in the Middle of the Air" (Bradbury) **29**:42
"The Way It Was" (Pohl) **25**:235

"The Way of a Woman" (Dunbar) **8**:122, 128, 136
"The Way of the Cross" (du Maurier) **18**:129, 137
"The Way of the World" (Cather) **2**:102-03
"The Way of the World" (Norris) **28**:204
"The Way Some People Live" (Cheever) **38**:43
The Way Some People Live (Cheever) **1**:87-8, 92, 98-100; **38**:61, 63
"The Way to Majorca" (O'Hara) **15**:277, 284
"The Way to the Churchyard" (Mann) **5**:322, 328-29, 334-37
"The Way to the Dairy" (Saki) **12**:314
"A Way You'll Never Be" (Hemingway) **1**:218, 245, 247; **40**:155, 209, 212, 214
The Ways of White Folks (Hughes) **6**:109-10, 121-23, 126-29, 131-34, 136-38, 140-42
Wayside Courtships (Garland) **18**:160
Wayside Crosses (Capek)
　　See *Boží muka*
"A Wayside Episode" (Davis) **38**:95, 110
"The Wayside Inn" (Turgenev)
　　See "The Inn"
The Wayward Wife, and Other Stories (Moravia)
　　See *The Wayward Wife, and Other Stories*
"We Are Looking at You, Agnes" (Caldwell) **19**:27
"We Are Norsemen" (Boyle) **16**:142-43, 151
We Are the Living (Caldwell) **19**:4-6, 9, 11-12, 25, 34-5, 54, 57
"We Are Very Poor" (Rulfo)
　　See "Es que somos muy pobres"
"We Don't Live Here Anymore" (Dubus) **15**:69-71, 73, 76, 82, 87, 91, 98
We Don't Live Here Anymore (Dubus) **15**:81, 91-3
"We Drink the Wine in France" (Walker) **5**:401
"We Love Glenda So Much" (Cortazar) **7**:69
We Love Glenda So Much, and Other Tales (Cortazar)
　　See *Queremos tanto a Glenda*
"We Often Think of Lenin in The Clothespin Factory" (Davenport) **16**:198
"We Purchased People" (Pohl) **25**:226
"We Shall Never Die" (Solzhenitsyn)
　　See "My-to ne umrem"
"We Want a Touchdown" (Saroyan) **21**:143
"We Were Spending an Envening at Princess D.'s Dacha" (Pushkin) **27**:164
"A Weak Heart" (Dostoevsky)
　　See "A Faint Heart"
"Weak Heart" (Mansfield) **9**:282
"The Weaker Sex" (Kawabata)
　　See "Yowaki Utsuwa"
The Weaker Vessel (Kawabata)
　　See *The Weaker Vessel*
The Weakling (Mauriac) **24**:160-62
The Weakling and the Enemy (Mauriac) **24**:160
"A Weary Hour" (Mann) **5**:330
"The Weaver and the Worm" (Thurber) **1**:428
"The Web of Circumstance" (Chesnutt) **7**:3, 16, 19, 22-3, 29-33, 37
The Web of Earth (Wolfe) **33**:346-49, 351, 354, 369, 372, 374-76, 380
"The Wedding" (Bates) **10**:113
"The Wedding" (Gogol) **29**:120-21
"The Wedding" (O'Flaherty) **6**:260, 265, 277-78, 285
"The Wedding" (Pritchett) **14**:281, 299
"A Wedding Chest" (Lee) **33**:302, 307
"Wedding Day" (Boyle) **5**:54-5, 65, 70-2
Wedding Day, and Other Stories (Boyle) **5**:54
"The Wedding Dress" (Moore)
　　See "An Gúnna-Phósta"
"The Wedding Feast" (Moore) **19**:310, 335
"The Wedding Gown" (Moore)
　　See "An Gúnna-Phósta"
"The Wedding Guest" (Auchincloss) **22**:43
"A Wedding in Brownsville" (Singer) **3**:360, 363, 376

"The Wedding in the Garden" (Trevor) **21**:246-47, 260, 262, 270, 274
"The Wedding Knell" (Hawthorne) **3**:154
"The Wedding March" (Wescott) **35**:364, 369-72, 374-75, 379
"The Wedding of the Painted Doll" (Jolley) **19**:233
"Wedding Pictures" (Phillips) **16**:325, 328
"Wedding Preparations in the Country" (Kafka)
　　See "Hochzeitsvorbereitungen auf dem Lande"
"Wedding Trip" (Pavese) **19**:374-75, 387
"Wednesdays and Fridays" (Jolley) **19**:245
"Wednesday's Child" (Oates) **6**:225
"Wee Willie Winkie" (Kipling) **5**:269
"The Weeds" (McCarthy) **24**:215-16, 225
"A Week in the Country" (Le Guin) **12**:210, 213, 215-16, 245, 249
"Weekend" (Beattie) **11**:6-7, 14, 17, 29
"Weekly Serial" (Coover) **15**:39
"Weep No More, My Lady" (Stuart) **31**:233-34, 244, 250, 252-53
"Weep Not My Wanton" (Coppard) **21**:11
"The Weeping Man" (Lewis) **34**:163-64
Weg nach Innen (Hesse) **9**:211
"Der Wegwerfer" (Boell) **23**:6-8, 10
"Weir of Hermiston" (Stevenson) **11**:296, 299-300
Weir of Hermiston (Stevenson) **11**:268-69, 282, 286
Weird Women (Barbey d'Aurevilly)
　　See *Les diaboliques*
"Welcome, Bob" (Onetti)
　　See "Bienvenido, Bob"
"The Welcome Table" (Walker) **5**:401, 403, 406, 410-11
Welcome to the Monkey House: A Collection of Short Works (Vonnegut) **8**:424-30, 435-36
The Well (Onetti)
　　See *El pozo*
"We'll Have Fun" (O'Hara) **15**:286
"The Well of Days" (Bunin) **5**:100
"The Well of Miriam" (Agnon) **30**:34
"The Well of Pen-Morfa" (Gaskell) **25**:58, 65, 71
"Well, That's That" (Farrell) **28**:87
"Welt" (Walser)
We're Friends Again (O'Hara) **15**:250-51, 272
"We're Very Poor" (Rulfo)
　　See "Es que somos muy pobres"
"The Werewolf" (Carter) **13**:5, 7, 27
"The Werewolf" (Pavese) **19**:368
Wessex Tales (Hardy) **2**:202-03, 205, 212, 214-15, 220, 223, 225-26, 229
"West End" (Aiken) **9**:9, 12, 14
"A West Indian Slave Insurrection" (Cable) **4**:59, 75
"The Westbound Train" (Cather) **2**:102
The Western Stories of Stephen Crane (Crane) **7**:153
"Westminster Abbey" (Irving) **2**:244-45, 250-51
"Westward" (Levi) **12**:278-79
Westward Ha!; or, Around the World in Eighty Clichés (Perelman) **32**:211, 219, 230, 233
"A Wet Night" (Beckett) **16**:65, 92-3
"The Wet Nurse" (Pirandello) **22**:229
"Wet Saturday" (Collier) **19**:103, 109, 111
"Whacky" (Clarke) **3**:134
"The Whale Tooth" (London) **4**:266
"The Whale's Story" (Alcott) **27**:42
"Whales Weep" (Boyle) **16**:146
"The Wharf" (de la Mare) **14**:80, 82, 88, 90
"What a Misfortune" (Beckett) **16**:69, 92
"What a Thing, to Keep a Wolf in a Cage!" (Calisher) **15**:3
"What Becomes of the Pins" (Alcott) **27**:43
"What Death with Love Should Have to Do" (Oates) **6**:224, 226
"What Destiny Wanted" (Fuentes)
　　See "Fortuna lo que ha querido"

Title Index

"What Do Hippos Eat?" (Wilson) **21**:322-23, 332-33, 345, 354

"What Do You Do in San Francisco?" (Carver) **8**:32, 34

"What Do You Mean It Was Brillig?" (Thurber) **1**:428

"What Do You See, Madam?" (Barnes) **3**:18

"What Does It Matter? A Morality" (Forster) **27**:91, 104, 107-08

"What Dreams May Come" (de la Mare) **14**:80, 83, 84

"What Fanny Heard" (Alcott) **27**:43

"What Father Does is Always Right" (Andersen) **6**:18, 26, 30

"What Goes Up" (Clarke) **3**:134

What I Know So Far (Lish) **18**:266-68, 270, 274, 278, 280, 284

"What I Saw of Shiloh" (Bierce) **9**:98-9

"What Is It?" (Carver) **8**:4, 10, 32

"What Is Left to Link Us" (Lish) **18**:284

"What Is Soul?" (Peretz)
    See "What Is Soul?"

"What Kind of Day Did You Have?" (Bellow) **14**:41-2, 50-1, 53-6, 58

"What Men Live By" (Tolstoy) **9**:387

"What the Nightingale Sang" (Zoshchenko) **15**:387, 395

"What the Shepherd Saw" (Hardy) **2**:210

"What the Swallows Did" (Alcott) **27**:41

"What to Do Till the Analyst Comes" (Pohl) **25**:224, 228-29, 230-31, 235

"What to Wear" (Adams) **24**:16-17

"What Was Mine" (Beattie) **11**:30-1

What Was Mine, and Other Stories (Beattie) **11**:30-2,

"What We Talk about When We Talk about Love" (Carver) **8**:15, 17-23, 26, 30, 32, 34, 37-44, 46-8, 51, 56-9

What We Talk about When We Talk about Love (Carver) **8**:13, 15, 17-23, 26, 30, 32, 37-40, 43-4, 46, 48, 56-9

"What Were You Dreaming?" (Gordimer) **17**:183, 188-89

"What You Hear from 'Em?" (Taylor) **10**:379, 396, 399, 401, 407, 411, 415

"What You Want" (Henry) **5**:187

"What's in Alaska?" (Carver) **8**:7, 10-11, 32, 34, 53

"What's the Purpose of the Bayonet?" (Garrett) **30**:164-65, 179-80

The Wheel of Love, and Other Stories (Oates) **6**:247

"The Wheelbarrow" (Pritchett) **14**:268, 280, 287

"Wheels" (Dixon) **16**:208

"Wheels" (McGahern) **17**:301-02, 307-09, 318, 323-24

"When Alice Told Her Soul" (London) **4**:257, 270

"When Boyhood Dreams Come True" (Farrell) **28**:96, 127-8

When Boyhood Dreams Come True (Farrell) **28**:126

"When Everyone Was Pregnant" (Updike) **13**:358, 387

"When God Laughs" (London) **4**:253

When God Laughs, and Other Stories (London) **4**:253-54

"When Greek Meets Greek" (Greene) **29**:183-84, 217

"When I Was a Witch" (Gilman) **13**:125

When I Was Mad (Pirandello)
    See *Quand'ero matto*

"When It Happens" (Atwood) **2**:4, 6-7, 10, 13, 16

"When My Girl Comes Home" (Pritchett) **14**:261, 266-67, 301

When My Girl Comes Home (Pritchett) **14**:267, 286

"When Old Baldy Spoke" (Murfree) **22**:201

"When the Dead Rise from Their Graves" (Bulgakov) **18**:90

"When the Light Gets Green" (Warren) **4**:389-90, 394, 396, 399, 401

"When the Old Century Was New" (Dreiser) **30**:122, 127, 129, 132

"When the Sun Went Down" (Lawson) **18**:198, 239

When the War Began (Boell)
    See "Als der Krieg ausbrach"

When the War Started (Boell)
    See "Als der Krieg ausbrach"

"When the Waters Were Up at Jules" (Harte) **8**:214

When the World Screamed (Doyle) **12**:81

When Things of the Spirit Come First: Five Early Tales (Beauvoir)
    See *Quand prime le spirituel*

"When We Were Nearly Young" (Gallant) **5**:148

"When Women Love Men" (Ferre)
    See "Cuando las mujeres quieren a los hombres"

"When You Think of Me" (Caldwell) **19**:42

When You Think of Me (Caldwell) **19**:41

"Where Are You Going, Where Have You Been?" (Oates) **6**:238, 244-46

"Where I Lived, and What I Lived For" (Oates) **6**:225, 234-35

"Where I'm Calling From" (Carver) **8**:17, 26-8, 32, 51

Where I'm Calling From: New and Selected Stories (Carver) **8**:41, 45-6, 48-50, 55, 57, 59-61

"Where Is Everyone?" (Carver) **8**:18, 32, 59-60

"Where is the Voice Coming From" (Welty) **27**:353-54

"Where It Was, There I Must Begin to Be" (Davenport)
    See "Wo es war, soll ich werden"

"Where Love Is, God Is" (Tolstoy) **9**:387

"Where Mountain Lion Lay Down with Deer" (Silko) **37**:309

"Where Tawe Flows" (Thomas) **3**:397, 406, 411-12

"Where the Cloud Breaks" (Bates) **10**:139

"Where the Eagles Dwell" (Valenzuela)
    See "Up Among the Eagles"

"Where the Girls Were Different" (Caldwell) **19**:25-6

"Where the Harrycans Comes From" (Harris) **19**:196

"Where the Heart Is" (Campbell) **19**:77-8

"Where the Trail Forks" (London) **4**:258, 286

Where You'll Find Me, and Other Stories (Beattie) **11**:25, 28-9, 32

"Where's Duncan?" (Harris) **19**:147, 173, 181

"Which Is the True One?" (Baudelaire)
    See "Laquelle est la vraie?"

"Which New Era Would That Be?" (Gordimer) **17**:153, 161

"Which Was It?" (Twain) **6**:331-34, 337, 350

"Which Was the Dream?" (Twain) **6**:331-34, 337, 340, 350

"While the Auto Waits" (Henry) **5**:158, 189

While the Billy Boils (Lawson) **18**:198, 200, 208, 215, 248-50, 254, 257, 259, 261-62

Whilomville Stories (Crane) **7**:104

"The Whimper of Whipped Dogs" (Ellison) **14**:105, 118

"The Whining" (Campbell) **19**:74, 86

"The Whip-Poor-Will" (Thurber) **1**:422

The Whir of Gold (Ross) **24**:323

Whirligigs (Henry) **5**:182

"Whirlwind" (Tanizaki)
    See "Hyōfū"

"Whirlwind" (Tanizaki)
    See "Hyōfū"

"A Whisper in the Dark" (Alcott) **27**:22-8, 45-50, 59

"The Whisperer in Darkness" (Lovecraft) **3**:258-60, 263, 269-71, 274-75, 278-80, 284, 291, 294

"Whispering Leaves" (Glasgow) **34**:56, 61-3, 74-6, 80, 89-90, 95-6, 102

"The Whistle" (Welty) **1**:468

"Whistling Dick's Christmas Stocking" (Henry) **5**:161, 170

Whistling in the Dark (Garrett) **30**:184

"The Whistling Swan" (Wescott) **35**:363-64, 366-67, 371-73, 379

"Whit Monday" (Lewis) **40**:281

White and Black (Pirandello)
    See *Bianche e nere*

"The White Cat of Drumgunniol" (Le Fanu) **14**:223

"The White Counterpane" (Dunbar) **8**:127, 134

"White Dump" (Munro) **3**:347-49

"The White Eagle" (Chopin) **8**:99

"The White Flower" (Kawabata) **17**:251

"The White Flower" (Narayan) **25**:138-40, 156, 160

"White Girl, Fine Girl" (Grau) **15**:149, 156

"White Glow" (Lu Hsun)
    See "Bai guang"

"The White Goddess and the Mealie Question" (Gordimer) **17**:153

"The White Hair" (Pardo Bazan) **30**:290

"A White Heron" (Jewett) **6**:157, 160, 170-73

A White Heron, and Other Stories (Jewett) **6**:171

"The White Horse" (Pardo Bazan)
    See "El caballo blanco"

"The White Horses of Vienna" (Boyle) **5**:63-4

"The White Knight" (Moorhouse) **40**:325

"A White Lie" (Sansom) **21**:87

"The White Man's Way" (London) **4**:253

"White Nights" (Dostoevsky) **2**:171-72

"The White Old Maid" (Hawthorne) **3**:154, 159, 180-81

The White People (Machen) **20**:161, 165, 175-77, 183, 186, 194, 196-201

"The White Pony" (Bates) **10**:132

"The White Quail" (Steinbeck) **11**:207-08, 221, 225, 227-28, 230, 233-36; **37**:334, 339, 351, 354-55, 357, 359, 361

"The White Rabbit" (Pritchett) **14**:269

"The White Rabbit Caper" (Thurber) **1**:431

"The White Scapegoat" (Aleichem)
    See "A vayse kapore"

"The White Sea" (Kipling) **5**:293

"The White Silence" (London) **4**:250-51, 258, 267, 277, 281-84, 287-88

"The White Snake" (Grimm and Grimm) **36**:189

"White Spot" (Anderson) **1**:52

"The White Stocking" (Lawrence) **4**:198, 202, 230

"Whitechapel" (Morrison) **40**:334, 365

"White-Eyes, Bulbuls, and a Bat" (Shiga) **23**:346

"Who Am I This Time?" (Vonnegut)
    See "My Name is Everyone"

Who Can Replace a Man? (Aldiss) **36**:6

"Who Crosses Storm Mountain?" (Murfree) **22**:210

"Who Dealt?" (Lardner) **32**:117, 127, 139-41, 145

"Who Do You Think You Are?" (Munro) **3**:343

Who Do You Think You Are? (Munro) **3**:333, 335-40, 342-43, 345-47

"Who Do You Wish Was with Us" (Thomas) **3**:395, 398, 403, 406, 411-12

"Who for Such Dainties?" (Wilson) **21**:360

"Who Has Seen the Wind" (McCullers)

"Who Is It Can Tell Me Who I Am?" (Berriault) **30**:103-04

"Who Is This Tom Scarlett?" (Barnes) **3**:18

"Who Knows What's Up in the Attic?" (Rhys) **21**:56

"Who Made Yellow Roses Yellow?" (Updike) **13**:355

"Who Pays the Piper . . ." (Pirandello) **22**:244

"Who Stand for the Gods" (Dunbar) **8**:122

"Whoever Was Using This Bed" (Carver) **8**:43

"Whole Days in the Trees" (Duras)
    See "Des Journées entières dans les arbres"

Whole Days in the Trees (Duras)
   See *Des journées entières dans les arbres*
"A Whole Loaf" (Agnon)
   See "Pat Shlema"
"The Whole World Knows" (Welty) **1**:474, 479-80, 483
"A Whole Year Drunk and Purim Sober" (Peretz) **26**:216
"Whoopee for the New Deal!" (Farrell) **28**:94-5
"Who's Passing for Who?" (Hughes) **6**:132, 141
"Who's There" (Clarke) **3**:134
"The Whosis Kid" (Hammett) **17**:219, 221
"Why Brer Possum Loves Peace" (Harris) **19**:130, 171
"Why Brother Bear Has No Tail" (Harris) **19**:196
"Why Brother Fox's Legs Are Black" (Harris) **19**:196
"Why Brother Wolf Didn't Eat the Little Rabbits" (Harris) **19**:195
"Why Don't You Dance" (Carver) **8**:32, 37, 42-3, 47-8, 51
"Why Frau Frohmann Raised Her Prices" (Trollope) **28**:311, 322-23, 355
Why Frau Frohmann Raised Her Prices and Other Stories (Trollope) **28**:311, 322-23, 332-33, 339, 350, 354
"Why Heisherik Was Born" (Singer) **3**:385, 387
"Why Honey?" (Carver) **8**:32
"Why I Live at the P. O." (Welty) **1**:465, 468-69, 471, 476-79, 482, 489, 494, 497
"Why I Want to Fuck Ronald Reagan" (Ballard) **1**:70, 75, 82
"Why Mr. Cricket Has Elbows on His Tail" (Harris) **19**:196
"Why Mr. Possum Has No Hair on His Tail" (Harris) **19**:157
"Why Mr. Possum Loves Peace" (Harris)
   See "Why Brer Possum Loves Peace"
"Why the Alligator's Back Is Rough" (Harris) **19**:196
"Why the Confederacy Failed" (Harris) **19**:125
"Why the Guinea-Fowls Are Speckled" (Harris) **19**:196
"Why the Little Frenchman Wears His Arm in a Sling" (Poe) **1**:407; **35**:316
"Why the Negro Is Black" (Harris) **19**:140, 195
"Why the Waves Have Whitecaps" (Hurston) **4**:140
"Why, Who Said So?" (Moravia) **26**:161
"Why, You Reckon?" (Hughes) **6**:118, 132
"A Wicked Voice" (Lee) **33**:302, 305, 309, 311-12
"The Widder Tree Shadder Murder" (Jolley) **19**:248
"The Wide Net" (Welty) **1**:467, 469, 471, 494
The Wide Net, and Other Stories (Welty) **1**:466-68, 471, 482, 496
"The Widow" (Babel) **16**:26, 50, 53-4, 58
"The Widow and Her Son" (Irving) **2**:240-41, 251
"The Widower" (Schnitzler)
   See "Der wittwer"
"The Widower Roman" (Castellanos)
   See "El viudo Román"
"Widows" (Baudelaire)
   See "Les veuves"
"A Widow's Dilemma" (Pirandello) **22**:236
"The Widow's Might" (Gilman) **13**:126
"The Widow's Mite" (Trollope) **28**:317, 320, 326, 341, 348
The Widows of Thornton (Taylor) **10**:388-89, 411, 415
"The Widow's Ordeal" (Irving) **2**:241
"Widow's Walk" (Grau) **15**:163
"Das Wiedergefundene Paradies" (Arnim) **29**:9-10
Der wiederkehrende griechische Kaiser (Tieck) **31**:276
"Wiedersehen in der Allee" (Boell) **23**:4
"Wiedersehen mit Drüng" (Boell) **23**:4

"The Wife" (Irving) **2**:240-41, 243, 245, 251
Wife (Mukherjee) **38**:243
"The Wife of a King" (London) **4**:258, 282, 284, 286
"The Wife of Another and the Husband under the Bed" (Dostoevsky) **2**:171, 193
"The Wife of his Youth" (Chesnutt) **7**:2, 15-16, 23, 33-7
The Wife of his Youth, and Other Stories of the Color Line (Chesnutt) **7**:2-3, 15, 19, 21-3, 26, 30, 33, 37-8
"A Wife of Nashville" (Taylor) **10**:415-16
"The Wife of the Autumn Wind" (Kawabata) **17**:252
"The Wife of Usher's Well" (James) **16**:234
"The Wife-Killer" (Singer) **3**:358
"Wife's Holiday" (Narayan) **25**:139-40, 155
"The Wife's Story" (Davis) **38**:110, 114, 119-20
"The Wife's Story" (Le Guin) **12**:235
"A Wife's Story" (Mukherjee) **38**:235, 237-38, 240-41, 244, 250, 252-54, 257-59, 261, 266, 279-80, 282-84, 286
"Wife-Wooing" (Updike) **13**:348-50, 373, 384, 395
"The Wild Blue Yonder" (Thomas) **20**:323, 327
The Wild Blue Yonder (Thomas) **20**:323-28
The Wild Body (Lewis) **34**:146-47, 149-54, 156, 158-60, 162-67, 169-75, 179
"Wild Flowers" (Caldwell) **19**:13-14, 38
"The Wild Goat's Kid" (O'Flaherty) **6**:260, 262, 264, 268-69
"The Wild Goose" (Moore) **19**:303, 305, 308, 312, 330, 333
"A Wild Irishman" (Lawson) **18**:206
The Wild Palms (Faulkner) **1**:159-61, 167-68; **35**:157
"The Wild Swan" (O'Flaherty) **6**:268
The Wild Swan, and Other Stories (O'Flaherty) **6**:259, 271
"The Wild Swans" (Andersen) **6**:13, 19, 30, 35, 40
Die wilde Engländerin (Tieck) **31**:287
"The Wilderness" (Bradbury) **29**:78
"Wilderness" (Henderson) **29**:327
"The Wildgoose Chase" (Coppard) **21**:19-21
"Wilfrid Holmes" (Moore) **19**:296, 298, 300, 310
"The Will" (Lavin) **4**:165-66
"Will as a Boy" (Dixon) **16**:215
"Will o' the Mill" (Stevenson) **11**:268-69, 281
"A Will of Iron" (Leskov) **34**:127
"The Will of Stanley Brooke" (Campbell) **19**:61-2, 72, 81
"The Will to Happiness" (Mann) **5**:322-23
"Will You Please Be Quiet, Please?" (Carver) **8**:3-4, 7, 10-11, 18-19, 22, 32
Will You Please Be Quiet, Please? (Carver) **8**:3-6, 17-18, 26, 29, 32, 34, 45, 50, 54
"Will You Tell Me" (Barthelme) **2**:27
"Will You Walk into My Parlor?" (Dreiser) **30**:107
Willa Cather's Collected Short Fiction (Cather) **2**:103, 105
"The Willful Child" (Grimm and Grimm) **36**:199
"Willi" (Gallant) **5**:138
"William Bacon's Man" (Garland) **18**:148
"William Reilly and the Fates" (Benet) **10**:160
"William the Conqueror" (Kipling) **5**:283
"William Wilson" (Poe) **1**:378, 385-86, 394-97, 407; **22**:293, 351; **34**:251, 274; **35**:309, 331, 333-36
"William's Wedding" (Jewett) **6**:180
Willie Masters' Lonesome Wife (Gass) **12**:125, 128, 141-46, 148-50, 152-53
"Willie Waugh" (Coppard) **21**:11
"Willie Winkie" (Andersen) **6**:24
"The Willing Muse" (Cather) **2**:98, 103
"A Willing Slave" (Narayan) **25**:135, 154, 156, 158
"Willows" (de la Mare) **14**:71

"Willy-Wagtails by Moonlight" (White) **39**:279-80, 285-86, 290, 292-93, 298, 312-16, 325, 328-29, 335, 345
"The Wilshire Bus" (Yamamoto) **34**:349, 359
"Wilt Thou Leave Me Thus" (Coppard) **21**:10
"The Wind" (Bradbury) **29**:67
"The Wind at Beni Midar" (Bowles) **3**:64, 85
"The Wind Blows" (Mansfield) **9**:282, 284, 302, 305; **23**:139, 153; **38**:230
The Wind Blows Over (de la Mare) **14**:89, 92
"The Wind Shifting West" (Grau) **15**:148, 152, 150, 164
The Wind Shifting West (Grau) **15**:147-48, 152, 154, 160-61
"The Wind Tells of Valdemar Daae and His Daughters" (Andersen) **6**:12, 15, 18, 24
"The Wind Tells the Story of Valdemar Daa and his Daughters" (Andersen)
   See "The Wind Tells of Valdemar Daae and His Daughters"
"The Windfall" (Caldwell) **19**:19, 41
"The Window" (Andric) **36**:43
"The Window" (Moore) **19**:308, 345
A Window in Mrs. X's Place (Cowan) **28**:79
"The Windowpane Check" (O'Hara) **15**:283
"The Windows" (Sansom) **21**:86
"The Winds" (Welty) **1**:472
"The Wind's Tale" (Andersen)
   See "The Wind Tells of Valdemar Daae and His Daughters"
The Wind's Twelve Quarters (Le Guin) **12**:209, 212, 219, 224, 231, 234, 245
"Windy Day at the Reservoir" (Beattie) **11**:30-1, 34
"Wine" (Andric)
   See "Vino"
"The Wine Breath" (McGahern) **17**:304, 309, 319, 322
"The Wine of Paris" (Ayme)
   See "Le Vin de Paris"
"Wine of Surany" (Caldwell) **19**:41
"Wine of Wyoming" (Hemingway) **40**:251
Winesburg, Ohio (Anderson) **1**:17-19, 22, 24-35, 38-46, 48, 51-2, 55, 57-8
"Winged Creatures" (Warner) **23**:383, 385
Winner Take Nothing (Hemingway) **1**:211, 216-17; **25**:113; **40**:172, 210, 237, 245, 247, 249-50, 256-60, 263
"Winner Takes All" (Waugh) **41**:323, 331
Winsome Winnie (Leacock) **39**:265
"Winter" (Dubus) **15**:96
"Winter" (Gilchrist) **14**:163-64
"Winter: 1978" (Beattie) **11**:9, 23-4
"Winter Cruise" (Maugham) **8**:380
"Winter Dreams" (Fitzgerald) **6**:46, 59, 66, 69, 76, 88, 90-1, 100, 102, 104
"The Winter Father" (Dubus) **15**:75, 82
"Winter in July" (Lessing) **6**:186, 191, 213-14, 217-18
Winter in the Air, and Other Stories (Warner) **23**:370-71, 380
"Winter Nelis" (Jolley) **19**:234, 246
"Winter Night" (Boyle) **5**:55
"The Winter of Artifice" (Nin) **10**:309-12, 314-17, 319-20, 323
The Winter of Artifice (Nin) **10**:300-02, 305-06, 317, 319, 322, 324
"Winter Rain" (Adams) **24**:4, 7
"Winter Wind" (Munro) **3**:331
Der Wintergarten (Arnim) **29**:5, 9-10, 17, 25-30
"The Winters and the Palmeys" (Hardy) **2**:207, 209
"A Winter's Day" (Leskov)
   See "Zimnij den'"
"Winter's King" (Le Guin) **12**:231-32
"A Winter's Tale" (Stafford) **26**:276, 278-80, 307
"A Winter's Tale" (Thomas) **20**:317-18
Winter's Tales (Dinesen) **7**:164, 166, 170-71, 175, 180, 193, 195-96, 199-200, 205, 208
"Winterton" (Dreiser) **30**:149-50

Title Index

The Winthrop Covenant (Auchincloss) **22**:27, 29, 33, 35, 39, 43-4, 47, 50-1
"Winthrop's Adventure" (Lee) **33**:312
"Wintry Peacock" (Lawrence) **4**:231, 234-35
"Wiosna" (Schulz) **13**:327
"Wir Besenbinder" (Boell) **23**:5
"Wireless" (Kipling) **5**:266, 275, 280
The Wisdom of Father Brown (Chesterton) **1**:120-21, 124
"The Wisdom of Silence" (Dunbar) **8**:122, 126, 132, 135, 146
"The Wisdom of the Trail" (London) **4**:282-85, 288
"Wise Guy" (O'Hara) **15**:264
"The Wise Men" (Crane) **7**:101, 126
"The Wise She-Frog" (Ferre) **36**:149
"Wiser than a God" (Chopin) **8**:69-70, 73, 84, 99
"The Wish House" (Kipling) **5**:275, 280-81
"The Witch" (Jackson) **9**:255-56; **39**:211, 217, 218, 219, 220, 227
"The Witch" (Singer) **3**:377
"The Witch à La Mode" (Lawrence) **4**:220
"Witchbird" (Bambara) **35**:15, 27, 29-30
"Witchcraft" (Machen) **20**:160
"Witcherley Ways: A Christmas Tale" (Oliphant) **25**:204
"The Witches" (Pavese) **19**:369
"Witches Loaves" (Henry) **5**:184
"Witch's Money" (Collier) **19**:98-9, 104, 110, 113-14
"With Justifiable Pride" (Cortazar)
See "Con legítimo orgullo"
"With Old Man Makhno" (Babel) **16**:22
"With the Death of the Saint" (Agnon) **30**:68
"With the Nameless Dead" (Dreiser) **30**:118
"With the Nationalists" (Warner) **23**:386-87
"With the Night Mail" (Kipling) **5**:268
"The Withered Arm" (Hardy) **2**:202-03, 205, 208, 213-14, 217-20, 227-28, 231-34
"The Withered Flowers" (Chang) **28**:34
Within the Wall (Agnon) **30**:71
"Without a Hero" (Boyle) **16**:156-57
Without a Hero, and Other Stories (Boyle) **16**:156-57
"Without Benefit of Clergy" (Kipling) **5**:262, 291, 295-97, 299
"Without Benefit of Galsworthy" (Collier) **19**:108-09
"Without Colors" (Calvino) **3**:104, 108-09
"Without Visible Means" (Morrison) **40**:328, 367
"The Witness" (Porter) **4**:339-40, 358
"The Witnesses" (Cortazar)
See "Los testigos"
"The Witnesses" (Sansom) **21**:86-7
"The Witnesses" (Updike) **13**:358
"Der wittwer" (Schnitzler) **15**:345, 376-77
"The Wives of the Dead" (Hawthorne) **3**:159, 164, 186
"The Wizards of Pung's Corners" (Pohl) **25**:213, 222-23, 237
"Wo es war, soll ich werden" (Davenport) **16**:199-200
Wo warst du, Adam? (Boell) **23**:36
Wodehouse on Crime (Wodehouse) **2**:352
"The Wolf" (Hesse) **9**:230, 235
"Wolf Alice" (Carter) **13**:7, 9, 27-8
"Wolf Dreams" (Beattie) **11**:11, 19-20
"Wolf Lonigan's Death" (O'Flaherty) **6**:261, 276, 280
"Wolfert Webber" (Irving) **2**:241, 247, 249, 251-52, 262, 266, 268
"Wolfert's Roost" (Irving) **2**:246
"Wolf's Head" (Murfree) **22**:212
"The Wolves of Cernogratz" (Saki) **12**:306, 317, 329
"A Woman" (Galsworthy) **22**:74, 93
"The Woman at the Store" (Mansfield) **9**:281, 284, 302, 305
The Woman Destroyed (Beauvoir)
See *La femme rompue*

"Woman Hollering Creek" (Cisneros) **32**:15-17, 21, 24-25, 37
Woman Hollering Creek and Other Stories (Cisneros) **32**:7-8, 11, 15, 17, 25, 34, 36, 38, 51-52
Woman in a Lampshade (Jolley) **19**:221-23, 233-34, 240, 242, 244-45, 248
"The Woman in Black" (Moravia) **26**:173
"A Woman in the House" (Caldwell) **19**:5, 23
"The Woman Lit by Fireflies" (Harrison) **19**:212-14, 218
The Woman Lit by Fireflies (Harrison) **19**:207, 210-15
"A Woman of Fifty" (Maugham) **8**:380
A Woman of Means (Taylor) **10**:379, 388
Woman of the River (Alegria)
See "A Temple of the Holy Ghost"
"A Woman of Tomorrow" (Glasgow) **34**:77
"A Woman on a Roof" (Lessing) **6**:199, 206
"The Woman on the Rock" (Andric)
See "Žena na kamenu"
"A Woman Seldom Found" (Sansom) **21**:89, 126
"The Woman Who Came at Six O'Clock" (Garcia Marquez) **8**:172, 183, 185
The Woman Who Could Not Read, and Other Tales (Zoshchenko) **15**:388, 390
"The Woman Who Had Imagination" (Bates) **10**:130
The Woman Who Had Imagination, and Other Stories (Bates) **10**:112
"The Woman Who Married Clark Gable" (O'Faolain) **13**:293, 322
"The Woman Who Rode Away" (Lawrence) **4**:219, 226, 239
The Woman Who Rode Away, and Other Stories (Lawrence) **4**:230
"The Woman Who Was Everybody" (Calisher) **15**:2, 5
"The Woman Who Was Not Allowed to Keep Cats" (White) **39**:280, 282, 284, 286, 289, 291-95, 312, 316-18, 325, 327, 343
"A Woman with a Past" (Fitzgerald) **6**:50
"The Woman with Blue Eyes" (Gorky)
See "Zhenshchina s golubymi glazami"
"A Woman without a Country" (Cheever) **1**:95, 100
"A Woman, Young and Old" (Paley) **8**:388, 390, 396, 398
"The Woman-Hater" (Aiken) **9**:5, 14
"A Woman's Arms" (Machado de Assis) **24**:138, 153
"A Woman's Hand" (White) **39**:301, 303-04, 306, 308-09, 311, 319, 324-25, 329, 337, 345
"A Woman's Kingdom" (Chekhov) **2**:156-57
"A Woman's Revenge" (Barbey d'Aurevilly)
See "La vengeance d'une femme"
"Women" (Lardner) **32**:132, 135, 140, 145
"Women" (Singer) **3**:358
Women in Their Beds: New and Selected Stories (Berriault) **30**:103, 105
"The Women of Madison Avenue" (O'Hara) **15**:282
"The Women on the Wall" (Stegner) **27**:191, 195, 197, 203-05, 220, 227
The Women on the Wall (Stegner) **27**:194, 196-97, 199, 219
"Women, Politics and Murder" (Hammett) **17**:200
"A Women's Restaurant" (Boyle) **16**:140-42
Wonder Stories Told for Children (Andersen)
See *Eventyr, fortalte for børn*
"The Wonderful Death of Dudley Stone" (Bradbury) **29**:89
"The Wonderful Old Gentleman" (Parker) **2**:274, 281, 283
Wonderful Tales (Andersen)
See *Eventyr, fortalte for børn*
Wonderful Tales for Children (Andersen)
See *Eventyr, fortalte for børn*

"The Wonderful Tar-Baby Story" (Harris) **19**:140, 173, 195
"A Wonderful Woman" (Adams) **24**:9, 19
Wondering Where to Turn (Lu Hsun)
See *P'anghuang*
"The Wonder-Worker" (Peretz)
See "The Wonder-Worker"
"The Wood Duck" (Thurber) **1**:414, 422
"The Wooden Dove of Archytas" (Davenport) **16**:178, 192
"The Woodfelling" (Tolstoy) **9**:375
"Woof Woof" (Saroyan) **21**:144
"Word and the Flesh" (Stuart) **31**:263
The Word for World Is Forest (Le Guin) **12**:207-10, 216, 219, 223, 234, 242-43
"The Word of Unbinding" (Le Guin) **12**:231-32
"The Word Processor of the Gods" (King) **17**:276
"Words" (Andric)
See "Reci"
The Words that Count (Campbell) **19**:70, 86
"Work, Death, and Sickness" (Tolstoy) **9**:388
"Work Not in Progress" (Greene) **29**:223, 226
"The Work on Red Mountain" (Harte) **8**:231, 254
"Work Suspended" (Waugh) **41**:311
Work Suspended (Waugh) **41**:330
"The Workers" (Galsworthy) **22**:82
"The Working Girl" (Beattie) **11**:33
"Working on the Spaceship Yards" (Aldiss) **36**:11
"The Working Party" (Bowen) **3**:30, 40, 49
"The World according to Hsü" (Mukherjee) **38**:252, 254-55, 264, 272, 277-78
"The World and the Bubble" (Dreiser) **30**:129
"The World and the Door" (Henry) **5**:182
"The World & the Theatre" (Saroyan) **21**:139, 142, 159
The World Is Too Much With Us (Bates) **10**:124
"The World of Apples" (Cheever) **1**:112; **38**:45, 47, 49, 56, 63, 66
The World of Apples (Cheever) **1**:97-8, 101; **38**:45, 65
"A World of Glass" (Sansom) **21**:95
"The World, the Flesh, and the Testament of Pierce Inverarity" (This OneMrs. Oedipa MaasPynchon) **14**:308
"The World to Come" (Peretz)
See "The World to Come"
"World's End" (Williams) **31**:305, 323-24, 332, 339-40, 344
"The Worm in The Apple" (Cheever) **38**:56, 85-6
"A Worn Path" (Welty) **1**:466, 470, 491-92, 494; **27**:332-66
"The Worn-Out Dancing Shoes" (Grimm and Grimm) **36**:228
"The Worn-Out Man" (Walser) **20**:355-56
"Worship" (Atwood) **2**:20
"The Worst Crime in the World" (Chesterton) **1**:129, 138
"The Worst Thing of All" (Gordimer) **17**:155
Worstward Ho (Beckett) **16**:109, 129-34
"Would You Do It for a Penny?" (Ellison) **14**:126
"The Wounded Cormorant" (O'Flaherty) **6**:260, 262, 268, 282-83
"The Wounded Soldier" (Garrett) **30**:166, 173, 180
Wounds in the Rain: A Collection of Stories Relating to the Spanish-American War of 1898 (Crane) **7**:104, 108
"Das Wrack" (Lenz) **33**:317, 329, 331-32
"Wratislaw" (Saki) **12**:317
"The Wreath" (O'Connor) **5**:372, 389
"The Wreath" (Pirandello) **22**:242
A Wreath for Garibaldi (Garrett) **30**:174
"Wrens and Starlings" (Powers) **4**:380
"The Wren's Nest" (O'Flaherty) **6**:274, 279
"Wressley of the Foreign Office" (Kipling) **5**:279
"The Writer" (Galsworthy) **22**:60, 99

Writes of Passage (Cabrera Infante) **39**:21
"Writing Yourself a Proper Narrative" (Moorhouse) **40**:308
"The Wrong House" (Mansfield) **9**:279
"Wrong Pigeon" (Chandler) **23**:110
"The Wrong Set" (Wilson) **21**:321, 323, 325, 327, 330-32, 336, 338-39, 342-44, 350, 352, 354
The Wrong Set, and Other Stories (Wilson) **21**:318-22, 326, 331, 335-36, 338, 341, 344, 348-49, 351, 353-54, 357-58, 364-65
"The Wrong Shape" (Chesterton) **1**:121, 129-30, 136
"The Wrong Trousers" (Bulgakov) **18**:90
"A Wronged Husband" (Pirandello) **22**:236
"Wu hsiao-lien" (P'u Sung-ling) **31**:206, 208-09
"Wunderkind" (McCullers) **9**:322, 332, 342-43, 345, 347-48, 350, 354-55; **24**:232
Das Wunderkind (Mann) **5**:324, 330-31
Die Wundersüchtigen (Tieck) **31**:275, 286
"Xanadu" (Thomas) **20**:290-93, 317
"Xingu" (Wharton) **6**:418, 422, 428-29, 437
Xingu, and Other Stories (Wharton) **6**:417-19, 421, 435
"Ya no quedan esperanzas de" (Cortazar) **7**:95
"The Yachting Cap" (Lewis) **34**:163-65
"Yah! Yah! Yah!" (London) **4**:266
"Yajima Ryūdō" (Shiga) **23**:346
Yakov Pasynkov (Turgenev) **7**:314, 320, 324
"The Yankee Fox" (Benet) **10**:150
"The Yanks Are Coming, in Five Breathless Colors" (Perelman) **32**:222
"Yao" (Lu Hsun) **20**:128, 140-41
"A Yard of String" (Stuart) **31**:249
"Ya-t'ou" (P'u Sung-ling) **31**:196-97, 207, 209
"Year by Year the Evil Gains" (Aldiss) **36**:17
"The Year of Heaven" (Saroyan) **21**:144
"Yearning for My Mother" (Tanizaki) See "Haha no kouru ki"
"Yeh-ch'a kuo" (P'u Sung-ling) **31**:200
"Yeh-kou" (P'u Sung-ling) **31**:200
"The Yelagin Affair" (Bunin) See "The Elaghin Affair"
"Yellow" (Beckett) **16**:70
"The Yellow Beret" (Lavin) **4**:167
"The Yellow Bird" (Chesterton) **1**:124-25, 133
"A Yellow Flower" (Cortazar) See "Una flor amarilla"
"Yellow Girl" (Caldwell) **19**:19
"The Yellow Gown" (Anderson) **1**:52
"Yellow Streak" (Farrell) **28**:99
"The Yellow Streak" (Maugham) **8**:367, 372
"The Yellow Wallpaper" (Gilman) **13**:118-19, 121-25, 128-41, 145, 147-62, 166, 168, 170-71, 175
"Yellow Woman" (Silko) **37**:295, 302-3, 308
"Yemelyan Pilyai" (Gorky) See "Emelyan Pilyai"
"Yen Shih" (P'u Sung-ling) **31**:196
"Yentl the Yeshiva Boy" (Singer) **3**:359, 384
"Yermolai and the Miller's Wife" (Turgenev) **7**:342
"Les yeux des pauvres" (Baudelaire) **18**:4, 6, 33, 47-51, 53
"Yi yüan kuan" (P'u Sung-ling) **31**:204-05
"Yid Somersault" (Leskov) See "Židovskaja kuvyrkalegija"
"Yijian xiaoshi" (Lu Hsun) **20**:146-47
"Ying-ning" (P'u Sung-ling) **31**:192, 196-97
"Ylla" (Bradbury) **29**:50
"A Yom Kippur Scandal" (Aleichem) **33**:82
"Yonder Peasant, Who Is He?" (McCarthy) **24**:215-16
"Yoneko's Earthquake" (Yamamoto) **34**:348, 350, 352, 354-55, 358, 360-62, 364-65, 367, 369, 379, 387-90
"Der yontefdiker tsimes" (Aleichem) **33**:38
Yoshinokuzu (Tanizaki) **21**:219-22, 224, 226
"Yostie" (O'Hara) **15**:278, 283
"You Are Not I" (Bowles) **3**:59-61, 66, 68-9, 72, 76-7

"You Are Now Entering the Human Heart" (Frame) **29**:112-13
"You Broke My Dream" (Lewis) **34**:178-79
"You Can Always Tell Newark" (O'Hara) **15**:251
You Can't Keep a Good Woman Down (Walker) **5**:412-14
"You Can't Tell a Man by the Song He Sings" (Roth) **26**:257, 265, 268
"You Have Left Your Lotus Pods on the Bus" (Bowles) **3**:69
You Know Me Al: A Busher's Letters (Lardner) **32**:113-14, 117, 121-22, 127, 131, 141-45, 148-50, 152, 155-56, 159, 165, 170-71, 180
"You Know Me, Carlo" (Moravia) **26**:160
"You Know They Got a Hell of a Band" (King) **17**:294-95
"You Know What" (Beattie) **11**:30, 33-4
"You Make Your Own Life" (Pritchett) **14**:269, 271, 297
You Make Your Own Life (Pritchett) **14**:269, 293
"You Must Know Everything" (Babel) **16**:34
You Must Know Everything: Stories, 1915-1937 (Babel) **16**:34
"You Must Remember This" (Coover) **15**:61-2
"You Name It" (Gordimer) **17**:194
"You Should Have Seen the Mess" (Spark) **10**:350, 355, 359, 363, 369
"You Were Perfectly Fine" (Parker) **2**:272, 278, 281
"You Were Too Trusting, Captain" (Babel) **16**:22
"You'll Never Know, Dear, How Much I Love You" (Updike) **27**:327-28
"Young Archimedes" (Huxley) **39**:162, 168-70
"The Young Aunt with the White Hair" (Cable) **4**:49
"The Young Girl" (Mansfield) **9**:279, 310
"The Young Girl and the American Sailor" (Moorhouse) **40**:293
"The Young Glory of Him" (Hughes) **6**:127
"Young Goodman Brown" (Hawthorne) **3**:164-68, 171-74, 177-78, 180, 182-83, 185-87, 189, 191-93; **29**:233-313; **39**:91, 105, 115, 128
"The Young Italian" (Irving) See "The Story of the Young Italian"
"The Young King" (Wilde) **11**:364, 373, 375-76, 381-82, 384-86, 394-97, 407-09
"The Young Lady-Peasant Girl" (Pushkin) See "Baryshnia-krest'ianka"
"Young Lochinvar" (Benet) **10**:150
"The Young Man from Kalgoorlie" (Bates) **10**:113, 139
Young Man in Chains (Mauriac) See *L'enfant chargé de chaînes*
"The Young Man with the Carnation" (Dinesen) **7**:164, 191-92, 194, 198
The Young Master Carpenter (Tieck) See *Der junge Tischlermeister*
Young Men in Spats (Wodehouse) **2**:325, 328
"The Young Robber" (Irving) See "The Story of the Young Robber"
"Young Robin Gray" (Harte) **8**:223
"A Young Woman in Green Lace" (Parker) **2**:273, 283
"The Youngest Doll" (Ferre) See "La muñeca menor"
The Youngest Doll (Ferre) See *Papeles de Pandora*
"Your Doctor Loves You" (Adams) **24**:16
"Your Lover Just Called" (Updike) **13**:387
Your Lover Just Called: Stories of Joan and Richard Maple (Updike) See *Too Far to Go: The Maples Stories*
"Your Most Profound Skin" (Cortazar) See "Tu más profunda piel"
"Your Obituary, Well Written" (Aiken) **9**:4-5, 7, 12, 14, 30, 34
"Youth" (Conrad) **9**:140, 143-44, 146-47, 152, 157, 160-66, 171, 175-78

Youth (Tolstoy) See *Yunost*
Youth: A Narrative, and Two Other Stories (Conrad) **9**:151
Youth and the Bright Medusa (Cather) **2**:91-2, 94, 98, 103, 111-13
"Youth and the Lady" (Warner) **23**:372
"Youth from Vienna" (Collier) **19**:110, 112
"The Youthful Years" (Chang) **28**:28; 35
"Yowaki Utsuwa" (Kawabata) **17**:247
"Yoysef" (Aleichem) **33**:39
"Yü Ch'ü-wo" (P'u Sung-ling) **31**:199
"Yucca Knolls" (O'Hara) **15**:259
"Yü-ch'ien" (P'u Sung-ling) **31**:199
"Yugashima no Omoide" (Kawabata) **17**:249-50
"Yume no ukihashi" (Tanizaki) **21**:180-81, 183, 198, 203-04, 210-11, 217, 225-27
Yunost (Tolstoy) **9**:375
"Yveline Samoris" (Maupassant) **1**:283
"Yvette" (Maupassant) **1**:263, 275, 283
"Z. Marcas" (Balzac) **5**:27, 31, 33
"Za logorovanja" (Andric) **36**:66-7
"Zagrowsky Tells" (Paley) **8**:412
"El Zahir" (Borges) **4**:10, 25; **41**:51
"The Zahir" (Borges) See "El Zahir"
"Zai jiulou shang" (Lu Hsun) **20**:140-42, 149-50
"Zajačij remiz" (Leskov) **34**:108-10, 117
Zakat (Babel) **16**:35
"Zakhar-Kalita" (Solzhenitsyn) **32**:341, 361-62, 364-65, 392, 394
"Zakhar-the-Pouch" (Solzhenitsyn) See "Zakhar Kalita"
"Zakoldovannoe mesto" (Gogol) **4**:117, 121; **29**:135
"Zametki neizvestnogo" (Leskov) **34**:108
"Zamostye" (Babel) **16**:27, 54, 57-8
"Zanos i stradanja Tome Galusa" (Andric) **36**:47, 52
"Zapečatlennyj angel" (Leskov) **34**:109-10, 113-15, 127-30
Zapiski iunogo vracha (Bulgakov) **18**:75, 86, 88-9
Zapiski iz podpol'ya (Dostoevsky) **2**:164-65, 168, 172-73, 178-83, 186, 188-89; **33**:158-30
Zapiski sumasshedshego (Tolstoy) **9**:366-68, 377, 388
Zářivé hlubiny (Capek) **36**:81-2, 87, 96, 109
"Zatvorena vrata" (Andric) **36**:48
Das Zauberschloss (Tieck) **31**:275, 285-87
"Zazubrina" (Gorky) **28**:137, 192
"Zeal" (Powers) **4**:370
"Zedj" (Andric) **36**:46, 70-1
"Zeitl and Rickel" (Singer) **3**:359
"Zeke Hammertight" (Stuart) **31**:226, 238-39
"Zeko" (Andric) **36**:36, 46-9
"Žcleznaja volja" (Leskov) **34**:108, 110, 112, 114
"Zena iz slonove kosti" (Andric) **36**:50-1
"Žena na kamenu" (Andric) **36**:46-7, 49
"Zero Hour" (Bradbury) **29**:57-8
"Zetland: By a Character Witness" (Bellow) **14**:41-2
"Zhenia's Childhood" (Pasternak) See "Detstvo Luvers"
"Zhenshchina s golubymi glazami" (Gorky) **28**:190
"Zhitié odnói báby" (Leskov) **34**:131
"Zhufu" (Lu Hsun) **20**:140-42
"Zibn Gite Yor" (Peretz) **26**:197, 217
"Židovskaja kuvyrkalegija" (Leskov) **34**:112
Zig-Zags at the Zoo (Morrison) **40**:349
"Zigzags of Treachery" (Hammett) **17**:200
"Zimnij den'" (Leskov) **34**:108, 127, 130
Zimzum (Lish) **18**:285-86
"Zinc" (Levi) **12**:256-57, 259, 262
"Lo zio acquatico" (Calvino) **3**:92-3, 109
"Životi" (Andric) **36**:66, 68
"Živý plamen" (Capek) **36**:96
"Zločin na poště" (Capek) **36**:98-9, 105-06, 127

"Zločin v chalupě" (Capek) **36**:102, 128

"Zlostavljanje" (Andric) **36**:47-8, 50

"Zmija" (Andric) **36**:35-6, 46-7

"Znakovi pored puta" (Andric) **36**:35, 38, 50

"Zodiac 2000" (Ballard) **1**:79

"Zoku Akuma" (Tanizaki) **21**:195

"Zone of Quiet" (Lardner) **32**:131, 133, 135, 138, 140-41, 146, 149, 152-55, 159, 166-67, 174-75, 193-95

"Zone of Terror" (Ballard) **1**:68

"Zooey" (Salinger) **2**:291, 293-94, 296-97, 302-05, 308; **28**:221-29, 231-34, 236-40, 244-45, 248-50, 253-55, 259, 262, 266, 268-69

"Der Zug war pünktlich" (Boell) **23**:34, 36

"Zuja" (Andric) **36**:65, 67

Die Zürcher Novellen (Keller) **26**:106, 108-09, 111, 113, 115

"Zwei Herzen in die Drygoods Schlock" (Perelman) **32**:235

"Zwei Schwestern" (Stifter) **28**:291, 298-99

Der Zweikampf (Kleist) **22**:105-10, 113, 116-17, 123-24, 128, 131